# ATHLET

## THE INTERNATIONAL TRACK AND FIELD ANNUAL 1987

## ASSOCIATION OF TRACK & FIELD STATISTICIANS

### EDITED BY PETER MATTHEWS

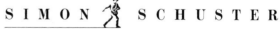

London　　　Sydney　　　New York

Published by Sports World Ltd, a division of London and International Publishers in association with Simon and Schuster Ltd 1987

© Copyright for world lists and index:
Association of Track and Field Statisticians 1987

© Copyright for all other material:
Peter Matthews and London & International Publishers Ltd, 1987

London & International Publishers Ltd, 49 St James's Street, London SW1A 1JT

Simon & Schuster Ltd, West Garden Place, Kendal Street, London W2 2AQ

Simon & Schuster (Australia) Pty Ltd, PO Box 151, 7 Grosvenor Place, Brookvale, N.S.W. 2100, Australia

Prentice Hall Press, 1 Gulf and Western Plaza, New York, NY 10023, USA

This publication incorporates the ATFS Annual.

Photographs provided by Mark Shearman, Associated Sports Photography (George Herringshaw) and Mobil Oil Inc.

**British Library Cataloguing in Publication Data**

International athletics annual: current world lists, world
records, athletics' profiles, major events—1987–
    1. Track–athletics—periodicals
    I. ATFS annual
    796.4'2'05   GV1060.5

ISBN 0-948208-04-X (London & International Publishers Ltd)
ISBN 0-671-65456-X (Simon & Schuster Ltd)

Typesetting by Florencetype Ltd, Kewstoke, Avon
Printed and bound in Great Britain by
Butler & Tanner Ltd, Frome

Design by Sandie Boccacci
Cover Design by The Beaver Design Company
Cover Illustration by Ray Winder

# CONTENTS

Introduction including tribute to
Marita Koch 1
 *by Peter Matthews*
Metric–Imperial conversion table 4
Acknowledgements, abbreviations and notes 5
List of ATFS members 6
In memory of Jan Popper 10
 *by Ladislav Krnáč*

**Review of 1986**

Athletes of the year

MEN 11
 – Said Aouita, Daley Thompson,
 event by event review
WOMEN 18
 – Ingrid Kristiansen, Jackie Joyner,
 Heike Drechsler, event by event review
JUNIOR athletes of 1986 25

Diary of the year 28

 – the track and field highlights
 of 1986 chronologically

Major championships 1986

 World cross-country championships 36
 Cross-country 1986 37
 Commonwealth Games 39
 European championships 42
 World junior championships 54
 Pan-American junior championships 55
 East & Central African championships 56
 Balkan Games 57
 Ibero-American championships 57
 Asian Games 57
 IAAF women's world road race
  championships 60
 IAAF world challenge road relay 60
 IAAF/Mobil Grand Prix 1986 61

Road race review 1986 (10 km to marathon) 64
 *by Roger Gynn*
1986 marathon review 70
 *by Roger Gynn*
Ultra-distance review 1986 73
 *by Andy Milroy*
Obituaries 1986 78
Athletics books 1986 81

**1987 preview**

World championships 84
IAAF/Mobil Grand Prix 86
Programme of future events 1987–90 87
1988 Olympic qualifying standards 87

**Special features**

The pace of record breaking 88
 *by Peter Matthews*
Great world records – and criteria for
 their assessment 91
 *by Richard Szreter*
The end of an era 95
 *by Tony Isaacs*
Jarmila Kratochvílová 97
 *by Ladislav Krnáč*
Sara Simeoni 100
 *by Roberto Quercetani*
The 85 metre hammer throwers 103
 *by Peter Matthews*
Progress, and a look back at times past
 – 75, 50 and 25 years ago, the bests in
 1912, 1937 and 1962 106
 *by Peter Matthews*
Blood oxygen and distance-running
 performance 109
 *by David E. Martin*
The truth . . . a final think piece 112
 *by A. Lennart Julin*

Drug test suspensions 114

Corrections to the 1986 annual 115

**National champions 1986 and
biographies of leading athletes** 118


**WORLD AND CONTINENTAL
RECORDS** 225

**MEN'S LISTS**
All-time world lists 239
1986 world lists 299
1986 world junior lists 399
Index of 1986 world lists 411

**WOMEN'S LISTS**
All-time world lists 455
1986 world lists 489
1986 world junior lists 569
Index of 1986 world lists 579

**1987 indoor results** 615

**Late additions and amendments** 618

# INTRODUCTION

This year the International Athletics Annual is distributed for the first time by Simon & Schuster. This will ensure much greater availability of the Annual worldwide.

To bring together the facts and figures of a season's athletics is a formidable task, made possible only by the dedicated efforts of many ATFS members throughout the world. Athletics is such a diverse sport and the details we require often so difficult to gather and to check, that the production of such a compendium within a few months of the end of a year involves a series of very tight deadlines.

Once again the authoritative all-time and year lists compiled by the ATFS form the core of this book. These are complemented by a review and results of the past, memorable year, with biographical details on more than 630 of the world's most notable athletes. There is, of course, considerable pressure of space in catering so comprehensively for such a multi-faceted sport, so it is not possible, every year, to include all those items that readers have requested. One example, however, of our aim to cater for this over a period of time, is that this year we have extended the men's all-time lists, previously 50 deep, to 100 per event. Next year the women's list will be 100 deep. Such historical perspective is, I hope, helped by the feature which takes a quick look back at the year's best performances and highlights of 25, 50 and 75 years ago. The tremendous progress that has been made is readily shown.

Amongst the features this year I am particularly pleased to be able to include an article on one of the most pernicious of practices that threaten the integrity of our sport, namely that of blood doping or packing, about which there has been much conjecture. The author, David Martin, is particularly qualified to examine the subject from an authoritative medical perspective for he is both a distinguished practitioner and a notable athletics enthusiast, particulary known for his work on the marathon and high jump, and with various leading athletes.

ATFS members have been greatly saddened by the deaths in 1986 of some doyens of their organisation, notably Bernie Cecins, Arrie Joubert and especially Jan Popper, to whom Ladislav Krnac pays tribute.

One of the great fascinations of our sport is the constant arrival of exciting new talent, but also one of the benefits of the upsurge of interest in and commercial support for athletics is that top athletes stay in the sport for longer. There comes a time, however, when those who have reached the highest peaks of endeavour must call it a day. We look back at the careers of two great women athletes who have decided to retire – Jarmila Kratochvilova and Sara Simeoni. The term great is not one that we should cast around too easily, but these two women certainly deserve such acclaim.

Just as we were going to press came news of the retirement of another – Marita Koch. She succeeded Irena Szewinska as the 'Queen' of track and field athletics, taking over her mantle of the world's best 400m runner. Szewinska held on to that in their epic duel at the 1977 World Cup, but in the decade since then Koch has been supreme. She was challenged by Kratochvilova in 1981-3, but, as I wrote in the 1985 Annual, Koch's aim was to seal her career with a world record for 400m in the 1985 World Cup. She did just that, gloriously regaining the record and setting a time (47.60) that may well last for many years. She gave it one more year however, but has now decided that her Achilles tendon problems are too much to overcome. Her last race was thus the Grand Prix Final 400m in Rome to complete yet another unbeaten year at her best event, a year in which she added a fourth European indoor title and third successive gold medals at both 400m and 4x400m relay at the outdoor European championships. In the following table, updated from my Guinness book *Track & Field Athletics – The Records* I have listed her staggering collection of titles and records. To the more than adequate testimony there shown, one can but add that she always displayed great style and charm.

It is not a title lightly bestowed, but for me she is simply the greatest woman athlete of all time. The world of athletics will miss her, but will wish her well on her concentration on her medical studies and, one assumes, her marriage to her long-time coach, Wolfgang Meier.

We now anticipate another fascinating year of competition, looking ahead especially to Rome 1987 and Seoul 1988.

*Peter Matthews*
February 1987

# Marita Koch – career record

| Date | Venue | Event | Place | Time |
|------|-------|-------|-------|------|
| **1. World records and major championship appearances – outdoors** | | | | |
| 23 Aug 75 | Athens – European Junior | 400m | 2 | 51.60 (1. Brehmer) |
| 24 Aug 75 | | 4x400mR | 1 | 3:33.7 |
| 28 Jul 76 | Montreal – Olympics | 400m | – | scratched from semis |
| 2 Jul 77 | Dresden – GDR Ch. | 400m | 1 | 51.47 |
| 13 Aug 77 | Helsinki – European Cup | 400m | 1 | 49.53 |
| 14 Aug 77 | | 4x400mR | 1 | 3:23.70 |
| 2 Sep 77 | Düsseldorf – World Cup | 4x400mR | 1 | 3:24.04 |
| | | 400m | 2 | 49.76 (1. Szewinska) |
| 28 May 78 | Erfurt | 200m | 1 | 22.06   WR |
| 2 Jul 78 | Leipzig – GDR Ch. | 400m | 1 | 49.19   WR |
| 19 Aug 78 | Potsdam | 400m | 1 | 49.03   WR |
| 31 Aug 78 | Prague – European Ch. | 400m | 1 | 48.94   WR |
| 3 Sep 78 | | 4x400mR | 1 | 3:21.20 |
| 3 Jun 79 | Leipzig | 200m | 1 | 22.02   WR |
| 10 Jun 79 | Karl-Marx-Stadt | 200m | 1 | 21.71   WR |
| | | 4x100mR | 1 | 42.10   WR |
| 29 Jul 79 | Potsdam | 400m | 1 | 48.89   WR |
| 4 Aug 79 | Turin – European Cup | 400m | 1 | 48.60   WR |
| 5 Aug 79 | | 4x400mR | 1 | 3:19.62 |
| 11 Aug 79 | Karl-Marx-Stadt – GDR Ch. | 200m | 1 | 22.05 |
| 24 Aug 79 | Montreal – World Cup | 200m | 2 | 22.02 (1. Ashford) |
| 24 Aug 79 | | 4x400mR | 1 | 3:20.37 |
| 26 Aug 79 | | 400m | 1 | 48.97 |
| 12 Sep 79 | Mexico C. – World Student G | 200m | 1 | 21.91 |
| 17 Jul 80 | Cottbus – GDR Ch. | 400m | 1 | 49.55 |
| 28 Jul 80 | Moscow – Olympics | 400m | 1 | 48.88 |
| 1 Aug 80 | | 4x400mR | 2 | 3:20.35 (1. USSR) |
| 9 Aug 80 | Jena | 4x200mR | 1 | 1:28.15   WR |
| 8 Aug 81 | Jena – GDR Ch. | 400m | 1 | 49.64 |
| 15 Aug 81 | Zagreb – European Cup | 400m | 1 | 49.43 |
| 16 Aug 81 | | 4x400mR | 1 | 3:19.83 |
| 4 Sep 81 | Rome – World Cup | 4x400mR | 1 | 3:20.62 |
| | | 400m | 2 | 49.27 |
| | | | | (1. Kratochvilova) |
| 1 Jul 82 | Dresden – GDR Ch. | 100m | 3 | 11.01 |
| 3 Jul 82 | | 200m | 1 | 21.76 |
| 8 Sep 82 | Athens – European Ch. | 400m | 1 | 48.16   WR |
| 11 Sep 82 | | 4x400mR | 1 | 3:19.04   WR |
| 31 Jul 83 | Berlin | 4x100mR | 1 | 41.53   WR |
| 16 Jun 83 | Karl-Marx-Stadt –GDR Ch. | 100m | 2 | 10.99 |
| 18 Jun 83 | | 200m | 1 | 21.82 |
| 8 Aug 83 | Helsinki – World Ch. | 100m | 2 | 11.02 |
| 10 Aug 83 | | 4x100mR | 1 | 41.76 |
| 14 Aug 83 | | 200m | 1 | 22.13 |
| 14 Aug 83 | | 4x400mR | 1 | 3:19.73 |
| 20 Aug 83 | London – European Cup | 4x100mR | 1 | 42.63 |
| 21 Aug 83 | | 200m | 2 | 22.40 |
| | | | | (1. Kratochvilova) |
| 2 Jun 84 | Erfurt – GDR Ch. | 400m | 1 | 48.86 |
| 3 Jun 84 | | 4x400mR | 1 | 3:15.92   WR |
| 21 Jul 84 | Potsdam | 200m | 1 | 21.71   (WR=) |

| Date | Venue | Event | Place | Time |
|------|-------|-------|-------|------|
| 16 Aug 84 | Prague – Friendship G | 400m | 1 | 48.16 NR |
| 9 Aug 85 | Leipzig – GDR Ch. | 100m | 2 | 10.97 |
| 11 Aug 85 | | 200m | 1 | 21.78 |
| 17 Aug 85 | Moscow – European Cup | 4x100mR | 1 | 41.65 |
| 18 Aug 85 | | 200m | 1 | 22.02 |
| 4 Oct 85 | Canberra – World Cup | 200m | 1 | 21.90 |
| 4 Oct 85 | | 4x400mR | 1 | 3:18.49 |
| 6 Oct 85 | | 400m | 1 | 47.60 WR |
| 28 Aug 86 | Stuttgart – European Ch. | 400m | 1 | 48.22 |
| 31 Aug 86 | | 4x400mR | 1 | 3:16.87 |
| 10 Sep 86 | Rome – Grand Prix Final | 400m | 1 | 49.17 |

## 2. Indoor world bests and major championships

| Date | Venue | Event | Place | Time |
|------|-------|-------|-------|------|
| 24 Feb 77 | Milan | 400m | 1ht | 51.80 WB |
| | | 400m | 1 | 51.57 WB |
| 13 Mar 77 | San Sebastian – Euro. Ch. | 400m | 1 | 51.14 WB |
| 10 Feb 78 | Senftenberg | 100y | 1 | 10.47 WB |
| 18 Feb 79 | Senftenberg | 100y | 1 | 10.33 WB |
| 25 Feb 79 | Vienna – European Ch. | 60m | 2 | 7.19 (1. Göhr) |
| 12 Jan 80 | Berlin | 100m | 1 | 11.15 WB |
| 2 Feb 80 | Grenoble | 50m | 1 | 6.16 WB |
| | | 50m | 1 | 6.11 WB |
| 14 Feb 81 | Senftenberg | 60m | 1 | 7.10 WB (=) |
| 22 Feb 81 | Grenoble – European Ch. | 50m | 3 | 6.19 (1. Popova) |
| 29 Jan 83 | Senftenberg | 60m | 1 | 7.08 WB |
| | | 200m | 1 | 22.63 WB |
| 3 Mar 83 | Budapest – European Ch. | 200m | 1 | 22.39 WB |
| 18 Jan 85 | Paris – World Indoor Games | 200m | 1 | 23.09 |
| 16 Feb 85 | Senftenberg | 60m | 1 | 7.04 WB |
| | | 100y | 1 | 10.25 WB |
| 3 Mar 85 | Athens – European Ch. | 200m | 1 | 22.82 |
| 6 Feb 86 | Senftenberg | 200m | 1 | 22.33 WB |
| 23 Feb 86 | Madrid – European Ch. | 200m | 1 | 22.58 |
| 28 Feb 86 | New York – TAC | 220y | 1 | 22.89 WB |

WR = World record, WB = World best (indoors), NR = GDR record
R – relay legs, all for GDR national team

Marita Koch wins the European title in Stuttgart, her last major title. *Mark Shearman*

# METRIC–IMPERIAL CONVERSION TABLES

Throughout this book measurements are given in the metric system. For those readers who are more familiar with imperial units we give a basic conversion table which specifically covers those distances achieved by top class athletes in the field events. This will be hope provide a useful cross check for those wishing to convert.

| | | | | | | | |
|---|---|---|---|---|---|---|---|
| 1.70m – | 5ft 7in | 17.50m – | 57ft 5in | 5.60 | 18ft 4½in | 66.00 | 216ft 6in |
| 1.75 | 5ft 8¾in | 18.00 | 59ft 0¾in | 5.80 | 18ft 0¼in | 68.00 | 223ft 1in |
| 1.80 | 5ft 10¾in | 18.50 | 60ft 8½in | 6.00 | 19ft 8¼in | 70.00 | 229ft 8in |
| 1.85 | 6ft 0¾in | 19.00 | 62ft 4in | 6.25 | 20ft 6¼in | 72.00 | 236ft 3in |
| 1.90 | 6ft 2¾in | 19.50 | 63ft 11¾in | 6.50 | 21ft 4in | 74.00 | 242ft 9in |
| 1.95 | 6ft 4¾in | 20.00 | 65ft 7½in | 6.75 | 22ft 1¾in | 76.00 | 249ft 4in |
| 2.00 | 6ft 6¾in | 20.50 | 67ft 3¼in | 7.00 | 22ft 11¾in | 78.00 | 255ft 11in |
| 2.05 | 6ft 8¾in | 21.00 | 68ft 10¾in | 7.25 | 23ft 9½in | 80.00 | 262ft 5in |
| 2.10 | 6ft 10¾in | 21.50 | 70ft 6½in | 7.50 | 24ft 7¼in | 82.00 | 269ft 0in |
| 2.15 | 7ft 0½in | 22.00 | 72ft 2¼in | 7.75 | 25ft 5¼in | 84.00 | 275ft 7in |
| 2.20 | 7ft 2½in | 22.50 | 73ft 10in | 8.00 | 26ft 3in | 86.00 | 282ft 2in |
| 2.25 | 7ft 4½in | 23.00 | 75ft 5½in | 8.25 | 27ft 0¾in | 88.00 | 288ft 8in |
| 2.30 | 7ft 6½in | 50.00 | 164ft 0in | 8.50 | 27ft 10¾in | 90.00 | 295ft 3in |
| 2.35 | 7ft 8½in | 52.00 | 170ft 7in | 8.75 | 28ft 8½in | 92.00 | 301ft 10in |
| 2.40 | 7ft 10½in | 54.00 | 177ft 2in | 9.00 | 29ft 6½in | 94.00 | 308ft 5in |
| 4.60 | 15ft 1in | 56.00 | 183ft 9in | 15.00 | 49ft 2½in | 96.00 | 314ft 11in |
| 4.80 | 15ft 9in | 58.00 | 190ft 3in | 15.50 | 50ft 10¼in | 98.00 | 321ft 6in |
| 5.00 | 16ft 4¾in | 60.00 | 196ft 10in | 16.00 | 52ft 6in | 100.00 | 328ft 1in |
| 5.20 | 17ft 0¾in | 62.00 | 203ft 5in | 16.50 | 54ft 1¾in | 102.00 | 334ft 8in |
| 5.40 | 17ft 8½in | 64.00 | 210ft 0in | 17.00 | 55ft 9¼in | 104.00 | 341ft 2in |

In the biographies section athletes' weights are given in kilograms, the following guide will help those who are more familiar with weights in pounds:

| | | | |
|---|---|---|---|
| 50kg – | 110lbs | 100kg – | 220lbs |
| 60 | 132 | 110 | 243 |
| 70 | 154 | 120 | 265 |
| 80 | 176 | 130 | 287 |
| 90 | 198 | 140 | 309 |

# ACKNOWLEDGEMENTS

Once again the compilation of the statistics for the Annual has been very much as a team effort by ATFS members, with a large number of experts contributing valuable assistance.

The principal lists compilers were Nejat Kök, Richard Hymans and Jiří Havlín with the CS group. The world year lists (men and women) were prepared by Nejat Kök. Richard Hymans produced the men's all-time lists and index, and Jiří Havlín the women's all-time lists and index. Roberto Quercetani gave his usual great assistance.

Milan Skočovský and Ian Hodge prepared the junior lists, and the records section was prepared by ATFS president Bob Sparks.

The ATFS are indebted to the following experts for vital assistance on specific sections:

*Indoor marks:* Ed Gordon (USA). *Decathlon and Heptathlon:* Václav Klvaňa (Cs), Leo Heinla (SU) and Frank Zarnowski (USA); *Heptathlon:* Milan Urban (Cs). *Marathon:* Roger Gynn (UK) and Antonin Hejda (Swz). *Walks:* Palle Lassen and Egon Rasmussen (Den). *Middle and Long distance events:* Ian Smith (UK). *Women's marks:* Luigi Mengoni (Ita). *Relays:* Emmerich Götze (GDR).

The following specialists supplied information for their respective areas and countries:

*Africa:* Yves Pinaud (Fra) and Walter Abmayr (FRG); *Asia:* Balwant Singh Kler (Mal); *Australia:* Paul Jenes; *Austria:* Erich Kamper and Otto Baumgarten; *Belgium:* André de Hooghe; *Brazil:* José Goncalves; *Bulgaria:* Grigor Khristov and Alexander Vangelov; *Canada:* Cecil Smith; *Central America:* Bernard Linley (Tri); *China:* Chinese Athletic Association; *Czechoslovakia:* Milan Skočovský; *Cuba:* Basilio Fuentes; *Finland:* Juhani Jalava and Matti Hannus; *France:*

Jacques Carmelli and Jean Gilbert-Touzeau; *GDR:* Dieter Huhn, Werner Kunze and *Der Leichtathlet*; *FRG:* Heinz Vogel and Sven Kuus; *Greece:* Georgios Constantopoulos and John Theodorakopoulos; *Hungary:* Gabriel Szabó, Zoltán Subert and Gábor Kobzos (Swz); *Israel:* David Eiger; *Italy:* Raul Leoni; *India:* R.Murali Krishnan; *Japan:* Atsushi Hoshino and Tatsumi Senda; *Netherlands:* Jacobus Koumans; *New Zealand:* Barry Hunt; *Norway:* Tore Johansen, Hans Halvorsen, Jo Nesse, Ole Petter Sandvig, Jan Jorgen Møe and Bernd Solaas; *Poland:* Tadeusz Wołejko, Wojciech Gaczkowski, Tadeusz Dziekonski and Edward Szatkowski; *Portugal:* Luis Lopes; *Romania:* National Federation; *South Africa:* Gert Le Roux and Harry Beinart; *South America:* Luis Vinker (Arg); *Soviet Union:* Ants Teder, Anatoliy Kashcheyev, Nikolay Ivanov and Andris Stagis; *Spain:* José Maria Garcia, Ignacio Romo, Manuel Villuendas, Andres de Acuña Lopez and Josep Corominas; *Sweden:* Lennart Julin and Owe Fröberg; *Switzerland:* Fulvio Regli and Alberto Bordoli; *UK:* Peter Matthews and Ian Hodge; *USA:* Scott Davis, Dave Johnson, Howard Willman, Pete Cava, Tom Feuer and Mike Renfro; *Yugoslavia:* Ozren Karamata.

Special features were written and compiled by Roger Gynn, Tony Isaacs, Lennart Julin, Ladislav Krnáč, David Martin, Andy Milroy, Roberto Quercetani and Richard Szreter.

The compilers wish to thank all the above and others that they have contacted during the past year, also many national federations and athletics magazines.

Finally we would like to thank the IAAF for its continuing cooperation and assistance.

# ABBREVIATIONS

In order to save space, particularly in the section giving biographical details on leading athletes the following abbreviations have been used for athletics events and meetings etc.

## Championships and governing bodies

| | |
|---|---|
| AAA | Amateur Athletic Association (UK) |
| AfCh | African Championships |
| AfG | African Games |
| AsCh | Asian Championships |
| AsG | Asian Games |
| CAmG | Central American and Caribbean Games |
| CG | Commonwealth Games |
| ECh | European Championships |
| ECp | European Cup |
| EI | European Indoor Championships |
| EJ | European Junior Championships |
| IAAF | International Amateur Athletic Federation |
| LT | Lugano Trophy / World Race Walking Cup |
| NCAA | National Collegiate Athletic Association (USA) |
| OG | Olympic Games |
| PAm | Pan American Games |
| SACh | South American Championships |
| TAC | The Athletics Congress (USA) |
| WAAA | Women's Amateur Athletic Association (UK) |
| WCh | World Championships |
| WCp | World Cup |
| WICh | World Indoor Championships |
| WIG | World Indoor Games |
| WJ | World Junior Championships |
| WSG | World Student Games |

## Events

| | |
|---|---|
| CC | Cross-country |
| Dec | Decathlon |
| DT | Discus |
| h | Hurdles |
| Hep | Heptathlon |
| HJ | High jump |
| HT | Hammer |
| JT | Javelin |
| LJ | Long jump |
| Mar | Marathon |
| PV | Pole vault |

| | |
|---|---|
| R | Relay |
| SP | Shot |
| St | Steeplechase |
| TJ | Triple Jump |
| W | Walk |

## Miscellaneous

| | |
|---|---|
| b. | date of birth |
| dnf | did not finish |
| dnq | did not qualify |
| exh | exhibition |
| h | heat |
| i | indoor |
| kg | kilograms |
| km | kilometres |
| m | metres |
| M | miles |
| pb | personal best |
| sf | semi final |
| w | wind assisted |
| y | yards |

# Nations abbreviations used in this book

| | |
|---|---|
| ALB | Albania |
| ALG | Algeria |
| ARG | Argentina |
| AUS | Australia |
| AUT | Austria |
| BAH | Bahamas |
| BAR | Barbados |
| BEL | Belgium |
| BER | Bermuda |
| BHN | Bahrain * (BHR) |
| BRA | Brazil |
| BUL | Bulgaria |
| CAM | Cameroon * (CMR) |
| CAN | Canada |
| CHL | Chile * (CHI) |
| CHN | P.R. China * (PRC) |
| COL | Colombia |
| CON | Congo * (CGO) |
| CS | Czechoslovakia * (TCH) |
| CUB | Cuba |
| CYP | Cyprus |

| | | | | |
|---|---|---|---|---|
| DEN | Denmark | | PER | Peru |
| DJI | Djibouti | | PHI | Philippines |
| DOM | Dominican Republic | | POL | Poland |
| ECU | Ecuador | | POR | Portugal |
| EGY | Egypt | | PR | Puerto Rico * (PUR) |
| ENG | England | | QAT | Qatar |
| ETH | Ethiopia | | RSA | South Africa |
| FIN | Finland | | RUM | Romania * (ROM) |
| FRA | France | | SCO | Scotland |
| FRG | Federal Republic of Germany | | SEN | Senegal |
| GAB | Gabon | | SKO | South Korea * (KOR) |
| GAM | The Gambia | | SOM | Somalia |
| GDR | German Democratic Republic | | SPA | Spain * (ESP) |
| GHA | Ghana | | SU | Soviet Union * (URS) |
| GRE | Greece | | SUD | Sudan |
| GUA | Guatemala | | SWE | Sweden |
| GUY | Guyana | | SWZ | Switzerland * (SUI) |
| HOL | Holland (Netherlands) | | TAI | Taiwan * (TPE) |
| HUN | Hungary | | TAN | Tanzania |
| ICE | Iceland * (ISL) | | THA | Thailand |
| INA | Indonesia | | TRI | Trinidad & Tobago |
| IND | India | | TUN | Tunisia |
| IRL | Ireland * (IRE) | | TUR | Turkey |
| IRN | Iran | | UGA | Uganda |
| IRQ | Iraq | | UK | United Kingdom * (GBR) |
| ISR | Israel | | URU | Uruguay |
| ITA | Italy | | USA | United States of America |
| IVC | Ivory Coast * (CIV) | | UVI | US Virgin Islands * (ISV) |
| JAM | Jamaica | | VEN | Venezuela |
| JAP | Japan | | WAL | Wales |
| KEN | Kenya | | YUG | Yugoslavia |
| KUW | Kuwait | | ZAM | Zambia |
| LUX | Luxembourg | | ZIM | Zimbabwe |
| MAL | Malaysia | | | |
| MEX | Mexico | | | |
| MOR | Morocco * (MAR) | | | |
| NIG | Nigeria * (NGR) | | | |
| NKO | Korean PDR* (PRK) | | | |
| NOR | Norway | | | |
| NZ | New Zealand * (NZL) | | | |
| PAK | Pakistan | | | |
| PAN | Panama | | | |

* These ATFS abbreviations differ from those used by the IAAF (which are shown in brackets). In the case of Taiwan, the IAAF call the country Chinese–Taipeh (its official name is the Republic of China).

# ASSOCIATION OF TRACK & FIELD STATISTICIANS (ATFS) MEMBERS

## Executive Committee (1984–88)

*President:* R. Sparks (UK)
*Secretary General:*
A. Huxtable (UK)
*Treasurer:* P. Lassen (DEN)

R.G. Ashenheim (JAM)
S.S. Davis (USA)
R. Hymans (UK)
N. Kök (TUR)
R. Magnusson (SWE)
V.A. Otkalenko (USSR)
Y. Pinaud (FRA)
D.H. Potts (USA)
R.L. Quercetani (ITA)
H. Vogel (FRG)
B.S. Kler (MAL) co-opted

## Members

*As at 1 January 1987*

ALGERIA
  Kamel Bensemmane
ARGENTINA
  Gerardo Bönnhoff
  Luis R. Vinker
AUSTRALIA
  Paul Jenes
  Fletcher McEwen
  Michael J. McLaughlin
AUSTRIA
  Karl Graf
  Erich Kamper (HM)
BAHAMAS
  Gerald L. Wisdom
BELGIUM
  Willy Bouvier
  André de Hooghe
  Bienvenu Lams
BOLIVIA
  Juan Coronel Quiroga
BRAZIL
  José C. Gonçalves

BRITISH VIRGIN IS
  Reynold O'Neal
BULGARIA
  Grigor Christov
  Georgi Kaburov
  Alexander Vangelov
CANADA
  Doug Clement
  Paul F. Houde
  Dave Lach
  Tom MacWilliam
  Cecil Smith
  Ted Radcliffe
CHILE
  J. Francisco Baraona Urzua
COLOMBIA
  Jaime Ortiz Alvear
CUBA
  Prof Jesus Arguëlles
  Basilio Fuentes
CYPRUS
  Antonios Dracos
CZECHOSLOVAKIA
  Miloš Alter
  Svatopluk Dubský
  Luděk Follprecht
  Přemysl Hartman
  Jiri Havlín
  Jiri Hetfleiš
  Milan Hlavaček
  Peter Horváth
  Stanislav Hrnčíř
  Zdeněk Jebavý
  Alfons Juck
  Zdeněk Kašlík
  Václav Klvaňa
  Ceněk Kohlmann
  Ladislav Krnáč
  Otto Kudelka
  Marián Malek
  Karel Míšek
  Miroslav Ondruška
  Milan Skočovský
  Milan Urban
  Vladimír Višek
  Josef Zdychynec
DENMARK
  Hans A. Larsen
  Palle Lassen

  Valborg Lassen
  Egon Rasmussen
  Emanuel Rose
ECUADOR
  Ramiro Almeida Rothenbach
FINLAND
  Kaj Böstrom
  Matti Hannus
  Juhani Jalava
  Erkki Kiilunen
  Esa Laitinen
  Torsten Lindqvist
  Kauko Niemela
  Björn-Johan Weckman (HM)
FRANCE
  André Alberty
  Alain Bouillé
  Jacques Carmelli
  Jean-Louis Absin de Cassière
  Jean Creuzé
  Jean Gilbert-Touzeau
  Vincenzo Guglielmelli
  André Halphen
  Guy Kerfant
  Michel Nazé
  Robert Parienté
  Jean Claude Patinaud
  Yves Pinaud
  Daniel Urien
GERMAN DEM. REP.
  Werner Gessner
  Dieter Huhn
  Werner Kurtze
FEDERAL REP. GERMANY
  Walter Abmayr
  Klaus Amrhein
  Hans-Peter Car
  Max Heilrath
  Raymund Herdt
  Heinrich Hubbeling
  Heinz Klatt
  Winfried Kramer
  Rolf von der Laage
  Ekkehard zur Megede
  Reinhard Müller
  Fritz Steinmetz (HM)
  Otto Verhoeven
  Heinz Vogel

GIBRALTAR
  Mark Sanchez
GREECE
  Akis Andrikopulos
  Angelos Cocconis
  Yorgos Konstantopoulos
  John A. Kyriacos
  Karolos Sargologos
  Leandros J. Slavis
  John Theodorakopoulos
HONG KONG
  Ian Buchanan
HUNGARY
  Endre Kahlich
  György Lévai
  Zoltán Subert
  Gabriel Szabó
  Dr István Zahumenszky
ICELAND
  Ørn Eidsson
  Brynjolfur Ingolfsson
INDIA
  Ranjit Bhatia
  Inder Khanna
  Rameshchandra G. Kharkar
  R. Murali Krishnan
  Norris Pritam Marquis
  Jal D. Pardivala
  Lokesh Sharma
IRAN
  Fred Sahebjam
IRELAND
  Fionnbar Callanan
  Liam Hennessy
  John Murray
  Tony O'Donoghue
ISRAEL
  Elchanan Bar-Lev
  Arieh Cooks
  David Eiger
  Uri Goldbourt
ITALY
  Ottavio Castellini
  Gastone Dannecker
  Gianni Galeotti
  Tiziano Gambalonga
  Silvio Garavaglia
  Michelangelo Granata
  Raul Leoni
  Giorgio Malisani
  Gabriele Manfredini
  Giuseppe Mappa
  Salvatore Massara
  Luigi Mengoni (HM)
  Pino Montagna
  Matteo Piombo
  Dr Roberto L. Quercetani
    (HM)
  Carlo Santi

Raffaele Tummolo
JAMAICA
  Richard G. Ashenheim
JAPAN
  Atsushi Hoshino
  Wakaki Maeda
  Tatsumi Senda
LIECHTENSTEN
  Robert Schumacher
LUXEMBOURG
  Gérard Rasquin
MALAYSIA
  Balwant Singh Kler
  Gurbaksh Singh Kler
  Loong Teck Chew
MEXICO
  Jorge Molina Celis
NETHERLANDS
  Jacobus Koumans
  Nic Lemmens
NEW ZEALAND
  Barry S. Hunt
NORWAY
  Hans T. Halvorsen
  Tore Johansen
  Jan-Jørgen Moe
  Ingmund Ofstad
  Einar Otto Øren
  Ole Petter Sandvig
  Bernt A. Solaas
  Magne Teigen
PANAMA
  Luis Rossi
PHILIPPINES
  Col Romulo A. Constantino
  Sy Yinchow
POLAND
  Zbigniew Dobrowolny
  Marek Drzewowski
  Wojciech Gaczkowski
  Zygmunt Gluszek
  Daniel Grinberg
  Zbigniew Lojewski
  Stefan J.K. Pietkiewicz
  Jozsef Pliszkiewicz
  Janusz Rozum
  Leslaw Skinder
  Edward Szatkowski
  Jerzy Szymonek
  Tadeusz Wolejko
PORTUGAL
  Luis O.H. Lopes
PUERTO RICO
  Fernando Rodil-Vivas
ROMANIA
  Adrian Ionescu
  Nicolae Marasescu
  Romeo Vilara
  Tudor Vornicu

SINGAPORE
  Teong Cheng Ong
SOUTH AFRICA
  Harry N. Beinart (HM)
  Mrs Naomi Beinart
  Hennie A.J. Ferreira
  Colin E. Hasses
  Riel Hauman
  Harry Lombaard
  Hans Prinsloo
  Quintus van Rooyen
  Gert J.J. le Roux
  Joe Stutzen
SPAIN
  Andres de Acuña
  José Corominas
  Pedro Escamilla
  José Maria Garcia
  Ignacio Romo
  Alberto Sanchez
  Manuel Villuendas
SWEDEN
  Mats Åkesson
  Owe Fröberg
  A. Lennart Julin
  Ove Karlsson
  Rooney Magnusson (HM)
  Stig L. Nilsson (HM)
  Reino Sepp
  Nils Tangen
  Ture Widlund
SWITZERLAND
  Alberto Bordoli
  Antonin Heyda
  Gabor Kobzos
  Fulvio Regli (HM)
SYRIA
  Fouad Habash
TAIWAN
  Liao Han-shui
TRINIDAD & TOBAGO
  Bernard A. Linley
TURKEY
  Turhan Göker
  Nejat Kök
  Cüneyt E. Koryüek
  I. Süreyya Yigit
USSR
  Leo Heinla
  Nikolay Ivanov
  Anatoliy K. Kashcheyev
  Boris Y. Kozvintsev
  Ilya M. Lokshin
  Boris N. Lvov
  Andrey B. Mikhailov
  Rostislav V. Orlov
  Vladimir A. Otkalenko
  Jaan Otsason
  Eugen Piisang

Andris Stagis
Ants Teder
Erlend Teemagi
UNITED KINGDOM
John W. Brant
Eric L. Cowe
Leslie J. Crouch
Dr David P. Dallman
Peter Graham
Stan Greenberg
Roger W.H. Gynn
Ian M.M. Hodge
John B. Holt (HM)
Andrew Huxtable
Richard Hymans
Tony Isaacs
Alan Lindop
Peter H. Lovesey
Tim Lynch-Staunton
Norris D. McWhirter (HM)
David Martin
Peter V. Martin
Peter J. Matthews
Lionel Peters
Ian R. Smith
Bob Sparks
Richard Szreter

M. David Terry
Melvyn F. Watman
Mark A.A. Woodlands
USA
Jon W. Alquist
David A. Batchelor
Hal Bateman
Kirk Blackerby
Jed Brickner
Frank Candida
Dave Carey
Pete Cava
Scott S. Davis
Wally Donovan
James O. Dunaway
Tom Feuer
Edward C. Gordon
Bob Hersh
Istvan Hidvegi
Garry Hill
David Johnson
Michael Kennedy
Frank Litsky
Steven McPeek
Dr Bill Mallon
Dr David E. Martin
Jeff Matlock

Alan Mazursky
Walt Murphy
Albert D. Nelson
Cordner B. Nelson
Rich Perelman
Jack Pfeifer
Martin A. Post
Dr Donald H. Potts
Dr J. Gerry Purdy
S.F. Vince Reel
Mike Renfro
Stan Saplin
James L. Spier
J. Larry Story
Carol R. Swenson
Michael Takaha
Bruce Tenen
H.D. Thoreau
Howard Willman
Frank Zarnowski
YUGOSLAVIA
Olga Acic
Mladen Delic
Ozren Karamata
ZAMBIA
Matthew Mulwanda

# JAN—IN MEMORY OF JAN POPPER

## BY LADISLAV KRNÁČ

The first time I met Jan was 33 years ago during the Czechoslovakia–Sweden international in Prague. What struck me immediately was his charm, knowledge of languages and easy art of making contacts; but the most interesting quality was the respect of our athletes to this young reporter, a characteristic lasting until he left us so prematurely. They knew he was not chasing sensations, it was clear to them that he always tried to inform the readers about the backstage of the wonderful sport called track and field with the help of exact, true, unknown details from the happy and sad days of his cinder heroes. For many years he was one of the most active and dynamic members of the ATFS and the one possibly responsible for making women's statistics 'salon-fähig' on a world scale.

I am not overplaying it to mention that he was a fanatic of 24 hours working days, always making notes, conferring with friends and foes, sipping coffee and caressing one of those cigarettes . . . The lucky man to whom his hobby was his job and his job his hobby. The insiders knew that he was the man responsible for the excellent press services during the 1978 European championships. Pushing his aims over the last years very hard, one had the bad feeling that sooner or later the 'bill' will come. Two years ago, jokingly, I asked him if he was campaigning to be the next secretary general of UN? 'Don't speak with me like this anymore. I will follow this tempo until I am 55 and then I will see . . . ,' was his answer. He died a few days before achieving this limit.

Jan set a standard for everybody trying to be his successor—in his paper, in the family of Czechoslovak nuts, in the world of women's statistics. Few may be lucky enough to match it.

**Laco Krnac**

# THE ATHLETES OF 1986—MEN

## BY PETER MATTHEWS

The criteria by which one may judge candidates for such an accolade as athlete of the year include major championships success, records set and superiority over one's rivals.

In 1986 it was perhaps easier to select women who satisfied such criteria. Heike Drechsler, Jackie Joyner, Stefka Kostadinova and Ingrid Kristiansen lead the list of those who dominated their events and set world records. None of the four (or five if we include the new javelin) men's field events record breakers were undefeated.

Although Saïd Aouita came very close on several occasions, amazingly no men's track records were set during the year. That may or may not be significant, perhaps mostly it was because it was a big championships year for many, but nonetheless it is remarkable, because since world records were first officially recognised in 1913 that has *never* happened before!

## Outstanding male athletes 1986

The world record setters in 1986 were Sergey Bubka at pole vault, Udo Beyer, shot, Jürgen Schult, discus, Yuriy Sedykh, hammer, and Josef Priblinec at 1 hour walk. Of these Schult performed poorly in major events and Beyer was third ranked at his event. Rather surprisingly very few athletes who competed at the highest levels went through the year undefeated, just Saïd Aouita at all distances; Steve Cram, 1500m or 1 mile; Ed Moses, 400mh; Carl Lewis, long jump; and Daley Thompson, decathlon; come into contention in this category. Of those Aouita, Moses and Lewis did not have major championships to contest, but neither Lewis (at long jump) nor Moses met all their leading rivals.

Consideration of all factors leaves me with a short list from which I select as my top two Saïd Aouita and Daley Thompson, followed by Bubka, Cram and Sedykh.

## Saïd AOUITA

In 1985, Saïd Aouita had set world records at 1500m and 5000m. In 1986 his record attempts 'failed', yet whereas he had lost to Steve Cram at

1500m the previous year, in 1986 he won everything and never looked like being beaten. True, he did not meet Cram or Coe at 1500m, but he extended his range upwards to 10000m. On that occasion, at Oslo's Bislett Games, he was severely spiked early in the race, but nonetheless beat most of the world's best at his debut at the distance. Once again he showed his ability to run smoothly at speed with great finishing pace, and yet perhaps this seemingly tremendously confident man has a very slight failing, for he kept just missing world records. That showed just how hard they are to break, but on several occasions one was left with the thought that just a little more commitment on the penultimate laps might have seen the gain of the precious second needed, as four times within a month he missed the record by less than that margin. Despite the pace-setting organised for him, he ran best once he was out on his own. Perhaps he relaxed a little too much behind the pacemaker. Nonetheless those records will surely come and he is establishing a place as the greatest distance runner of our time, needing only some more World or Olympic titles to rank with Nurmi and Zatopek.

## Daley THOMPSON

We almost take it for granted that Daley Thompson will win every major event that he contests. Yet the decathlon is the greatest of all athletic challenges, one serious mistake or mishap can cost the athlete the chance of winning, and Thompson has won all his major decathlons since his European silver medal in 1978. Then he had already won the European Junior title in 1977 and the Commonwealth in 1978, and he went on to win successively Olympic, European, Commonwealth and World titles in 1980–3. Now he is three-quarters through another complete set.

In 1986 he won his three decathlons: 8667 at Arles for the UK against France and Canada, 8663 at Edinburgh for the Commonwealth title, and 8811 at Stuttgart for the European. In the latter he was given a tremendous battle by the West Germans Jürgen Hingsen and Siggy Wentz, but his talent and determination left him supreme once more; his poor showing at high jump and

Daley Thompson's decisive hurdles triumph in Stuttgart. *ASP*

discus compensated by the world's fastest ever decathlon 100m, 10.26, and a pb 110m hurdles of 14.04, the latter particularly vital as he beat the Germans, both of whom had much faster personal bests. His score could also be regarded as a 'world record', for although 36 points short of his Los Angeles total, it was the best ever with the new javelin, which might cost him 60–70 points.

During the year he showed fine speed, not only running that 10.26 but also placing third in the AAA 100 metres and, to his great delight, gaining sprint relay medals: silver at the Commonwealth and bronze at the European, running the second leg. He also set personal bests at discus, 49.10m, and 400m hurdles, 52.14, in his first attempt at the event for nine years. Indisputably the world's greatest ever decathlete.

## EVENT BY EVENT SURVEY

Particular emphasis thoughout this section is placed on the major championships, especially the Europeans at Stuttgart, and on those events at which many of the world's best met, such as the Weltklasse at Zürich, the Goodwill Games in Moscow, the Van Damme Memorial at Brussels, the Bislett Games at Oslo and the Grand Prix Final in Rome. Also note the Commonwealth Games in Edinburgh and the US Olympic Sports Festival in Houston.

## 100 metres

**Ben Johnson**, who had rivalled Carl Lewis for the title in 1985, laid undoubted claim to be the world's fastest man. He started indoors with two world records at 60m, and won eight major races, although second three times, to Lee McRae at the TAC and twice to Emmit King in Japan. Outdoors he was superb at 100m, losing just one minor race at Gateshead. He beat Carl Lewis 3–0 and Chidi Imo 4–0, and bettered 10.10 in 10 races to 4 for Lewis and 3 for Imo. His 12 major victories included the Commonwealth Games, Weltklasse, Van Damme and Grand Prix Final, as well as the Goodwill Games, which saw the world's best at their peak: Johnson 9.95, Imo 10.04, Lewis 10.06, McRae 10.12.

**Chidi Imo** was runner-up to Johnson five times and was beaten by McRae at the NCAA, but was a clear choice for second. **Carl Lewis** won the TAC title in 9.91w from McRae 10.02w and Harvey Glance 10.04w, and ran just twice in Europe, in Moscow and Zürich, each time third behind Johnson and Imo. He had also lost once to

Saïd Aouita (300) with Mark Nenow (308) in the Bislett Games 10 000 metres, *ASP*

### Saïd Aouita's races in 1986

| Date | Venue/meeting | Event | Place | Mark |
|------|---------------|-------|-------|------|
| 27 Apr | Shizuoka | 5000m | 1 | 13:45.82 |
| 17 May | Milan | 2000m | 1 | 5:04.95 |
| 20 Jun | Madrid | 1500m | 1 | 3:38.05 |
| 1 Jul | Stockholm – DN Galan | 5000m | 1 | 13:19.43 |
| 5 Jul | Oslo – Bislett Games | 10000m | 1 | 27:26.11 NR |
| 22 Jul | Paris | 3000m | 1 | 7:43.32 |
| 30 Jul | Rovereto | 5000m | 1 | 13:19.64 |
| 6 Aug | La Coruna | 5000m | 1 | 13:00.86 |
| 13 Aug | Zürich – Weltklasse | 3000m | 1 | 7:32.54 NR |
| 15 Aug | W.Berlin – ISTAF | 1 mile | 1 | 3:50.33 |
| 17 Aug | Köln | 3000m | 1 | 7:32.23 NR |
| 2 Sep | Lausanne | 1 mile | 1 | 3:51.86 |
| 5 Sep | Brussels – van Damme | 2000m | 1 | 4:51.98 AR |
| 10 Sep | Rome – Grand Prix Final | 5000m | 1 | 13:13.13 |
| 12 Sep | London | 2 miles | 1 | 8:14.81 NR |
| 14 Sep | Cagliari | 1500m | 1 | 3:36.75 |

AR African record, NR national record

Glance in the USA. Linford Christie was clearly Europe's best, with a Commonwealth silver as well as his European gold and ended the year ahead of all but the big three.

# 200 metres

There was rather less classy running at 200 metres than at 100 metres. New star **Floyd Heard** was probably the best; he won NCAA, TAC and Goodwill Games, but lost 2–1 to Kirk Baptiste, at Houston and at Zürich, when both were also beaten by Calvin Smith. Smith ran only seven major 200m races, not finishing in Lausanne and otherwise losing only to Commonwealth champion Atlee Mahorn at Nice. Carl Lewis ran only four meetings, but beat Baptiste twice in the USA, before disappointing with a TAC fourth place.

# 400 metres

**Gabriel Tiacoh** had a brilliant season, running nine sub-45 sec. times to six by Darrell Robinson and five by Antonio McKay. He beat Robinson 3–1, the one loss coming at the ISTAF meeting, 44.87 to 44.86. Tiacoh twice improved the African record: winning at the Pepsi Invitational in 44.32 from Robinson 44.45, Andre Phillips 44.71 and Innocent Egbunike 44.82; and then when he won the NCAA title in 44.30 from Roddie Haley 45.01. The year's key race was in Zürich: 1. Tiacoh 44.46, 2. Egbunike 44.50, 3. Bert Cameron 44.44, 4= McKay and Robinson 44.69, 6. Darren Clark 44.72, 7. Roger Black 45.00. Black had earlier beaten Clark in Edinburgh and went on to triumph in Stuttgart, when he added a 43.95 relay leg to his 44.59 national record.

# 800 metres

Three men stood out, but none had perfect records. **Steve Cram** ran the year's two fastest times, 1:43.19 in Rieti, after his 1:43.22 to win in Edinburgh from Tom McKean. He won 6/7 finals, but lost to **Seb Coe** and McKean in a British medal sweep at Stuttgart. Coe had had to miss the Commonwealth final through illness, but finally won a major 800m gold medal at the Europeans, after trading wins with Johnny Gray, for a 5/6 record. Johnny Gray was again consistently fast and won 10 out of 14 800m races, including three indoors. His fastest came at Zürich, 1:43.46 from Earl Jones and William Wuyke.

# 1500 metres / 1 mile

**Steve Cram** was supreme, winning all seven races, retaining both his Commonwealth and European titles. He ran the year's fastest mile, 3:48.31 in Oslo, while still building up to the peak form, which he showed so brilliantly in Edinburgh. **Seb Coe** was second to Steve Scott in Zürich and to Cram at the Europeans, but showed that like Cram he could challenge world records when his last race of the year, in Rieti, resulted in the year's fastest 1500m, 3:29.77. Add their 800m form and the year's three fastest times at 1000m, one by Coe and two by Cram, and the two Englishman are still the world's top middle distance runners. Steve Scott, like Seb Coe in his tenth season in the world's top ten, was only fifth in Rieti at the end of a long, hard season, but was the next best with seven wins, including the Grand Prix final, five seconds and two thirds in major 1500m or mile races.

# Distances

**Said Aouita**, profiled earlier, was out on his own. **Stefano Mei** had the next best overall record. Having but recently stepped up from the 1500m, he overtook countryman Alberto Cova to win the European 10000m title and place second to Jack Buckner at 5000m, with Tim Hutchings third. At 5000m Mei was Italian champion, but won only one other race, as he was second to Aouita in Rome, and third in Stockholm (to Aouita and Vincent Rousseau) and Zürich (to Cova and Pierre Délèze, but ahead of Buckner 5th and Tim Hutchings 7th). At 10000m Mei won at Florence and was fourth in the Bislett Games, won by Aouita from Mark Nenow, who went on to break the US record in Brussels, and Salvatore Antibo. Steve Ovett beat Buckner and Hutchings to take Commonwealth 5000m gold but was forced to drop out of the European 5000m through illness,

# Marathon

The leading men each won two major races: Rob de Castella, Boston 2:07:51 and Commonwealth 2:10:15, but he was third at New York; Toshihiko Seko, London 2:10:02 and Chicago 2:08:27; Taisuke Kodama, Beppu 2:10:34 and Beijing 2:07:35. The latter was the year's fastest, with second in 2:07:57, Kunimitsu Ito, and third in 2:08:39, Juma Ikangaa, who had earlier won the Tokyo marathon in 2:08:10 from Belayneh Densimo 2:08:29 and Abebe Mekonen 2:08:39. Mekonen went on to beat Densimo in Rotterdam, and also won at Addis Abada and Montreal; and Ikangaa won at Fukuoka in 2:10:06.

Steve Cram. *Mark Shearman*

Josef Pribilinec. *Mark Shearman*

## Steeplechase

Although he was only fifth in Stuttgart and seventh in Stockholm the best overall record was that of **William van Dijck**, who ran the year's two fastest times when beating talented fields: 8:10.01 at Brussels and 8:11.52 at Nice. Although the times were slow, the Grand Prix Final showed the relative merits fairly clearly as the order was 1. Van Dijck, 2. Hagen Melzer, the European champion, 3. Henry Marsh, 4. Graeme Fell, the Commonwealth champion, 5. Colin Reitz, the year's second fastest, 6. Julius Kariuki. Four more Kenyans: Julius Korir, Peter Koech, Joshua

Kipkemboi and Samson Obwocha produced the year's third to sixth fastest times.

## 110m hurdles

For the first time since Guy Drut in 1975/6 the year's fastest time was run by a European, **Stéphane Caristan**, to beat Drut's French and European records to win in Stuttgart with 13.20. Caristan also had a hand-timed 13.0. He lost just two races: at Zürich to Greg Foster and the World Junior champion, Colin Jackson, who had to miss the Europeans through injury; and at Berlin to Roger Kingdom and Greg Foster, who both ran

13.43. That was the one defeat, apart from not finishing in Houston, and indeed the slowest final for **Greg Foster**, who surely must again be counted the world's best, as he ran eight sub-13.40 times to four by Caristan and three by Mark McKoy. McKoy, who won Commonwealth gold from Jackson, had been fourth in Zürich with Kingdom fifth.

## 400m hurdles

**Ed Moses** returned to win all his ten races, including the year's best 47.38, but he did not meet his leading rivals, Andre Phillips, Danny Harris or Harald Schmid. **Andre Phillips** ran seven races, all between 47.51 and 48.15, the latter his one loss, to Danny Harris at the Bislett Games. But he beat Harris at the Jenner Classic, Brussels and Rome. **Danny Harris** was the busiest of the big three, winning 12/15 finals, including the NCAA/TAC double. The tally of sub-49 second times for the leaders reads: 12 Harris, 10 Moses, 9 Amadou Dia Ba, who was second ahead of Harris in Rome, 7 Phillips and Aleksandr Vasilyev, 5 Harald Schmid, who won his third successive European title from Vasilyev.

## High jump

**Jimmy Howard** had 12 indoor and 11 competitions at 2.30m or higher, was first 20 times, 2nd eight times and 3rd twice in a hectic season, but he must yield top ranking to the European champion **Igor Paklin**. Paklin had the year's two best jumps: 2.38m at Rieti and 2.37 at Köln and also won the Grand Prix Final, although he did lose three outdoors, including to Doug Nordquist at the Goodwill Games.

## Pole vault

**Sergey Bubka** no heighted in three competitions: indoors at the Millrose Games, and outdoors at St. Denis and Köln, but was otherwise clearly supreme once again. He won five indoor competitions with four world bests, and outdoors won four times, including a 6.01m world record in Moscow, and the European title.

The other world indoor record breakers Joe Dial (5.91m) and Billy Olson (5.93m) featured less outdoors. Dial set three US records in April, 5.86–5.88–5.90m, but thereafter only competed twice, jumping 5.70m on each occasion, for third at the TAC and in Sao Paulo in September. Olson, brilliant indoors, but no-heighted at the TAC, and managed only 5.50m outdoors. So behind Bubka

the best were his compatriots Rodion Gataullin, with six competitions at 5.80–5.85, but a no-height in Stuttgart, and his brother Vasiliy, the European silver medallist. Of the next group Philippe Collet and Earl Bell were the most consistent with respectively 11 and 9 competiions at 5.70m or better. Collet won the bronze in Stuttgart, when Thierry Vigneron, who had jumped 5.90m in Paris, was another to fail to clear a height.

## Long jump

**Carl Lewis** again competed rarely, once indoors and three times outdoors, but he extended his win streak to 48 successive competitions from 1981. His season was capped by TAC victory with 8.67w over Mike Conley 8.63w and Larry Myricks 8.47w. He must, however, be challenged for top ranking by **Robert Emmiyan**, who won 11/12, including European titles indoors and out, and a season's best 8.61m at the Goodwill Games from the 8.41m of Myricks, who had 14 competitions at 8.20m or better. Emmiyan's one loss was to Sergey Layevskiy at the Znamenksiy Memorial. Layevskiy also won the Soviet title, but a measure of Emmiyan's superiority was shown in Stuttgart when his 8.41m in poor conditions was 40cm better than runner-up Layevskiy.

## Triple jump

**Mike Conley**'s longest jump of the year, 17.84w, was in second place to Charlie Simpkins in a great TAC competion, with Willie Banks third at 17.52w. However Conley beat Simpkins 3–1 indoors and 4–1 out; overall he had ten wins and five second places, including winning the Goodwill Games at 17.69m to 17.35m for **Khristo Markov**, and that makes him the number one in 1986. Markov had a great August, winning the European title and jumping 17.80m in Budapest, but his record was otherwise somewhat patchy, as was that of Maris Bruzhiks, European champion indoors and silver medallist out.

## Shot

**Werner Günthör** won the European indoor title and improved further to take the gold medal in Stuttgart with 22.22m. He was, however second four times, once to Udo Beyer, who recaptured the world record with 22.64m in East Berlin, and three times to **Ulf Timmermann**. In Stuttgart Timmermann was second at 21.84m followed by Beyer 20.74m and Alessandro Andrei 20.73m, as Sergey Smirnov, indoor silver medallist, did not contest the final. These five all exceeded 22m during the year. Timmermann beat Günthör 3–1 and Beyer 4–1, winning 11/13 competitions, as Beyer took the GDR title, 22.14m to Timmermann's 22.00m, only the second time that such a distance had not been a winning one. The first occasion was just six days earlier at a titanic tussle at the GDR v USSR match in Tallinn when the order was 1. Timmermann 22.60, 2. Smirnov 22.24, 3. Beyer 22.05. Timmermann's wins over Günthör were all very close: 21.38m to 21.36m at Dresden, both putting 21.51m at Brussels, and 21.67m to 21.61m in Rome, when Andrei waa third at 21.20m.

## Discus

**Romas Ubartas** had never previously ranked in the world's top ten, and his season's best of 67.88m was a long way behind Jürgen Schult's new world record of 74.08m, but he had the best competitive record, winning the European and Soviet titles, at the Goodwill Games and against the GDR. Schult could not match his long throw elsewhere and was only seventh in Stuttgart, when Vaclavas Kidikas and Georgiy Kolnootchenko completed a Soviet 1–2–3.

## Hammer

**Yuriy Sedykh** has long since established his place in history as the greatest ever hammer thrower. He added two more world records, 86.66m against the GDR and 86.74m to win his third European gold medal. He won 9/11 competitions, both defeats being at the hands of European silver medallist **Sergey Litvinov**, in Dresden, 84.92m to 86.04m, and at the Grand Prix Final when he was unwell. Litvinov's 85.74m in Stuttgart was the best ever non-winning mark. These two great throwers were followed in 1986 by the Soviet trio of Igor Nikulin, Juri Tamm and Benjaminas Viluckis; Nikulin leading them with a best of 82.34m. Over 85m Sedykh had 12 throws, Litvinov 4 both in 3 competitions; over 84m Sedykh 23 in 8, Litvinov 10 in 7; a clear measure of their superiority.

## Javelin

The new javelin was introduced for competition in 1986, and by the season's end two men had thrown it over 85 metres: **Klaus Tafelmeier** 85.74m and **Tom Petranoff** 85.38m. Tafelmeier at last came good in a major event as he won in

Stuttgart with 84.76m, and had only two poor competitions, eighth in Dresden and fourth in Koblenz, although he was also second at his national championships. He did not meet Petranoff, who won 10/15, including fifth at Eugene and second to Seppo Räty at the Finnish Championships. European silver medallist Detlef Michel was as always consistently strong, winning 5/7.

## Decathlon

**Daley Thompson** (see earlier) won the European title from Jürgen Hingsen 8730, Siggy Wentz 8676 and Torsten Voss 8450. Earlier at Bernhausen, Wentz had beaten Hingsen 8590 to 8418, and the only other score over 8500 was by Guido Kratschmer, who had had to drop out in Stuttgart, 8519 at Götzis.

## Walks

**Josef Pribilinec** is my selection as walker of the year. He won six of his seven 20km races, including the European title, and also set world bests indoors at 10km, 38:49, and outdoors at 15km, 58:22.4, and 1 hour, 15547m. **Hartwig Gauder** won his three 20km races and 2/3 at 50km. He lost to Ronald Weigel's world best 3:38:17 at Potsdam, but won at Naumberg and Stuttgart, when Weigel respectively failed to finish and was disqualified.

Robert Emmiyan. *Mark Shearman*

# THE ATHLETES OF 1986—WOMEN

## BY PETER MATTHEWS

At the start of the men's review I pointed out that there were outstanding candidates for the title of Woman Athlete of the Year. The four I mentioned all set at least two world records and compiled brilliant competitive results. While it is difficult to choose between athletes competing in very different events, my choice for the title is Ingrid Kristiansen, ahead of Heike Drechsler and Jackie Joyner.

## Ingrid KRISTIANSEN

Undefeated in 1986, Ingrid Kristiansen truly dominated the world of women's distance running. In her two marathon victories she did not threaten the world best that she had set in 1985, but late in the year she improved the road best for the half-marathon, after a track season in which she smashed the records for 5000m and 10000m. With her 14:37.33 for 5000 metres in Stockholm she regained not only the world record from Zola Budd, but also the distinction that she had had for a month in 1985 of being the only athlete, man or woman, to be simultaneously the world's fastest at 5000m, 10000m and marathon. A month earlier, at the Bislett Games, she had run 10000 metres in 30:13.74, taking an amazing 45.68 seconds off her own world record. She won her first gold medal, winning the European 10000m by about half a lap, and, stepping down in distance set personal bests at 1500m and 3000m, at which distance she beat Maricica Puica and Olga Bondarenko comprehensively.

Ingrid Kristiansen can be likened to Emil Zatopek, not only for the margin of superiority over her rivals, just as he had in the early 1950s, but also for her seemingly anguished style, and not least for the enjoyment which, the race won, she so obviously gains from her superb running exploits.

## Jackie JOYNER

Jackie Joyner competed in four heptathlons in 1986, all greatly superior to the world's second ranked all-rounder Anke Behmer. Joyner started with 6910 at Walnut in April, which would have added 107 points to the US record, but for the fact that the 100m hurdles was hand-timed. That record came her way however with 6841 at Götzis a month later. Then she realised the potential, which had been apparent for this multi-talented athlete for several years, with two great world records. First she added 202 points to the world mark that Sabine Paetz had set in 1984, with 7148 at Moscow's Goodwill Games and then to 7158 at Houston.

At individual events she ranked in the world's top ten at long jump, with season's bests of 7.12m and 7.15w, and at 100m hurdles, at which she ran a pb 12.84 for fifth in the Grand Prix final. In both her world records she high jumped 1.88m, and improved her 200m best to 23.00 and 22.85, and at her weaker events improved significantly: shot to 15.20m, javelin to 50.12m. Her margin of superiority over other all-rounders is now even greater than that of Daley Thompson.

## Heike DRECHSLER

Ever since she won the world title as an 18-year-old in 1983 she has been the world's best long jumper, but in 1986 Heike Drechsler added even greater lustre to her career as she showed herself at least the equal of the world's best sprinters. At the start of the year her personal bests were but 11.71 for 100m and 23.19 for 200m; by the end she had run 100m in 10.91 and 10.80w, and had twice equalled Marita Koch's world record for 200m of 21.71. She lost just twice, both times to Evelyn Ashford, at the Goodwill Games when both were timed in 10.91 for 100m, and in her final competition of the year, in Brussels, 22.10 to Ashford's 22.06 for 200m. Over the shorter distance she beat the GDR stars Marlies Göhr and Silke Gladisch and at the longer won the European title in brilliant style. But all this did not stop her remaining at the top of world long jumpers, as she twice set a world record of 7.45m and won all her 13 competitions, every one of them at more than 7 metres, which is superior to the world record prior to 1978.

**Ingrid Kristiansen's races in 1986**

| Date | Venue/meeting | Event | Place | Mark |
|---|---|---|---|---|
| 18 Jan | Oslo | 1500m | 1 | 4:16.6 |
| 25 Jan | Alesund | 6km CC | 1 | 18:54 |
| 1 Feb | Miami – Orange Bowl | 10km road | 1 | 31:31 |
| 8 Feb | Tampa – Gasparilla | 15km road | 1 | 48:01 |
| 22 Feb | Yokohama – Ekiden Relay (leg) | 10km road | – | 30:39 (WB) |
| 16 Mar | Bergen – Norwegian Champs | 6km CC | 1 | 19:45 |
|  |  | 2 km CC | 1 | 6:20 |
| 2 Apr | Stavanger | 8.2km CC | 1 | 25:55 |
| 5 Apr | Vikersund | 7.7km CC | 1 | 22:13 |
| 21 Apr | Boston | Marathon | 1 | 2:24:55 |
| 20 May | Oslo | 1500m | 1 | 4:12.42 |
| 25 May | Bergen | 10km road | 1 | 30:47 WB |
| 31 May | New York – L'Eggs | 10km road | 1 | 31:45 |
| 10 Jun | Fana | 3000m | 1 | 8:48.85 |
| 21 Jun | Lucerne – v.SWE, SWI | 3000m | 1 | 8:47.03 |
| 27 Jun | Hengelo | 5000m | 1 | 14:58.70 |
| 5 Jul | Oslo – Bislett Games | 10000m | 1 | 30:13.74 WR |
| 15 Jul | Nice – Nikaia | 3000m | 1 | 8:35.88 PB |
| 5 Aug | Stockholm Games | 5000m | 1 | 14:37.33 WR |
| 10 Aug | Sandnes – Norwegian Champs |  | 1 | 4:05.97 PB |
| 13 Aug | Zürich – Weltklasse | 3000m | 1 | 8:34.10 PB |
| 30 Aug | Stuttgart – European Champs | 10000m | 1 | 30:23.25 |
| 13 Sep | Oslo | Half marathon | 1 | 1:07:59 WB |
| 21 Sep | Copenhagen | 10km road | 1 | 30:45.7 WB |
| 5 Oct | Drammen | Half marathon | 1 | 1:09:03 |
| 11 Oct | Boston | 10km road | 1 | 31:40 |
| 26 Oct | Chicago | Marathon | 1 | 2:27:08 |

WR world record, WB world road best, PB personal best

Ingrid Kristiansen. *Mark Shearman*

**Jackie Joyner in 1986**

| Date | Venue/meeting | Event | Place | Mark |
|------|---------------|-------|-------|------|
| INDOORS | | | | |
| 1 Feb | Dallas | LJ | 2 | 6.43 |
| 8 Feb | East Rutherford | LJ | 1 | 6.60 indoor PR |
| 14 Feb | New York – Millrose Games | LJ | 1 | 6.69 indoor PR |
| 16 Feb | Rosemont | LJ | 1 | 6.66 |
| 21 Feb | Inglewood – LA Times Games | LJ | 1 | 6.83 AIR |
| 28 Feb | New York – TAC Championship | LJ | 2 | 6.97 AIR |
| | | | | (also 6.96 AIR) |
| | | | | |
| OUTDOORS | | | | |
| 2 Mar | Long Beach | SP | 1 | 14.43 |
| | | 400mH | 1 | 56.27 |
| 29 Mar | Santa Monica | JT | 2 | 44.52 |
| | | HJ | 1 | 1.85 |
| | | SP | 1 | 14.78 PR |
| 5 Apr | Fresno – Fresno Bee Games | SP | 3 | 14.81 PR |
| | | HJ | 6 | 1.78 |
| 14 Apr | Westwood | JT | 2 | 46.52 |
| 24–25 Apr | Walnut – Mt. SAC Relays | Hept | 1 | 6910 AB |
| | (12.9, 1.86, 14.75, 23.24w pb, 6.85w, 48.30 PR, 2:14.11) | | | |
| 24–25 May | Götzis | Hept | | 6841 AR |
| | (13.09, 1.87 =PR, 14.34, 23.63, 6.76, 48.88 PR, 2:14.58) | | | |
| 1 Jul | Stockholm – DN Galan | 100mH | 5 | 13.16 |
| 6–7 Jul | Moscow – Goodwill Games | Hept | 1 | 7148 WR |
| | (12.85 PR, 1.88 PR, 14.76, 23.00 PR, 7.01 Hept WR, | | | |
| | 49.86 PR, 2:10.02) | | | |
| 1–2 Aug | Houston – US Olympic Fest | Hept | 1 | 7158 WR |
| | (13.18, 1.88 =PR, 15.20 PR, 22.85 PR, Hept WR, 7.03w | | | |
| | Hept WR, 50.12 PR, 2:09.69) | | | |
| 13 Aug | Zürich – Weltklasse | 100mH | 3 | 13.22 |
| 15 Aug | Berlin – ISTAF | 100mH | 4 | 12.96 |
| 17 Aug | Köln – Weltklasse | 100mH | 5 (h2) | 13.36 |
| 19 Aug | Malmo – MAI Games | 100m | 3 | 11.71 PR |
| | | 200m | 2 | 23.57 |
| 20 Aug | Bern | 100mH | 2 | 13.57 |
| 5 Sep | Brussels – Van Damme Mem | LJ | 2 | 7.12 |
| 7 Sep | Rieti | LJ | 2 | 7.15w (7.03) |
| 10 Sep | Rome – GP Final | 100mH | 2 (hl) | 12.85 =PR |
| | | 100mH | 5 | 12.84 PR |

WR = world record, AR = American record, AB = American best,
AIR = American indoor record, PR = personal record, PB = personal best,
Hept WR = best mark ever recorded in a multiple event.

**Heike Drechsler's 1986 season**

| Date | Venue/meeting | Place | Mark | Heat |
|------|---------------|-------|------|------|
| **100 YARDS INDOORS** | | | | |
| 15 Feb | Senftenberg – GDR Champs | 1 | 10.24 WIB | (10.39 ht) |
| **100 METRES** | | | | |
| 6 Jun | Neubrandenburg | 1 | 11.02 | |
| 11 Jun | Potsdam | 1 | 10.97 | (11.06 ht) |
| 5 Jul | Oslo – Bislett Games | 1 | 10.80w | |
| 6 Jul | Moscow – Goodwill Games | 2 | 10.91 | |
| 16 Aug | Dresden | 1 | 10.94 | (10.96 ht) |
| **200 METRES** | | | | |
| 12 Jun | Potsdam | 1 | 22.45 | |
| 22 Jun | Tallinn – v USSR | 1 | 22.13 | |
| 29 Jun | Jena – GDR Champs | 1 | 21.71 WR | (22.60 ht) |
| 29 Aug | Stuttgart – European Ch. | 1 | 21.71 WR | (22.52, 22.33 hts) |
| **LONG JUMP** | | | | |
| 25 Jan | East Berlin | 1 | 7.29 WB | (also 7.25 WB) |
| 1 Feb | Lievin – v France | 1 | 7.08 | |
| 15 Feb | Senftenberg – GDR Champs | 1 | 7.17 | |
| 22 Feb | Madrid – European Indoors | 1 | 7.18 | |
| 31 May | Erfurt | 1 | 7.31 | |
| 7 Jun | Neubrandenburg | 1 | 7.10 | |
| 21 Jun | Tallinn – v USSR | 1 | 7.45 WR | |
| 28 Jun | Jena – GDR Champs | 1 | 7.35w/7.29 | |
| 3 Jul | Dresden – Olympischer Tag | 1 | 7.45 WR | |
| 20 Aug | East Berlin | 1 | 7.23 | |
| 27 Aug | Stuttgart | 1 | 7.27 | (6.85 qual) |
| 5 Sep | Brussels – van Damme | 1 | 7.23 | |

WR world record, WIB world indoor best

Heike Drechsler. *ASP*

## Sprints

**Evelyn Ashford** returned to competition after the birth of her baby in 1985 to be the world's number one sprinter. At 100m she ran six sub-11 second times, and although only third in the TAC to Pam Marshall and Alice Brown, won 14 other finals. At 200m Ashford won eight races, before losing her last race to **Valerie Brisco-Hooks**, 22.31 to 22.30 in Rome. She beat Drechsler at both distances and handed Brisco-Hooks her only defeat of the year in six 200m finals, 21.97 to 22.26 at Zürich. **Marlies Göhr** did not start her outdoor season until August, but lost only to Drechsler amd Ashford at 100m, as she ran her four finals in 11.02, 11.01, 10.91 to win her third European title, and 11.01. **Pam Marshall** won the TAC 100m/200m double and the Goodwill Games 200m, but a groin injury restricted her, particularly at 100m, thereafter.

## 400 metres

**Marita Koch** ran just two outdoor 200m races, second at Jena to Silke Gladisch in June and a

22.20 win in August, after an unbeaten indoor season in which she had set an indoor world best of 22.33 and won the European title. Like Göhr, injury delayed her outdoor season at her prime event the 400m, but once again she was unapproachable. Her four finals with the runners-up were:

16 Aug Dresden 49.24 from Petra Müller 49.79; 28 Aug Stuttgart 48.22 from Olga Vladykina 49.67; 5 Sep Brussels 49.28 from Valerie Brisco-Hooks 50.29; 10 Sep Rome 49.17 from Valerie Brisco-Hooks, 50.21.

Truly an athlete apart, consolidating her position as the greatest woman athlete of all-time. The European silver medallist Olga Vladykina won all her other races to rank second.

## 800 metres

Form in this event was rather mixed. Nadezhda Olizarenko won the European title, but she had been only sixth at the Goodwill Games and third in the Soviet championships. Stuttgart silver medallist Sigrun Wodars had perhaps the best overall record, winning against the USSR and otherwise losing only once each to Milena Strnadova and Christine Wachtel, respectively fifth and eighth at Stuttgart, and to Heike Oehme. The big Moscow races were won by Lyubov Kiryukhina and Lyubov Gurina, European seventh and third places.

## 1500 metres

Four women broke four minutes; the two Romanians Doina Melinte and Maricica Puica and the Soviets Tatyana Samolenko and Ravilya Agletdinova. The European result was 1. Agletdinova, 2. Samolenko, 3. Melinte, 4. Ivana Walterova, 5. Puica. The latter was supreme early on, but overraced and ended with third at the Van Damme and second in the Grand Prix Final, in which races Melinte was second and fourth. **Tatyana Samolenko** won the Goodwill Games, Soviet titles indoors and out, and in Rome, and beat Agletdinova, fifth in Rome, 3–1.

## 3000 to 10000 metres

**Ingrid Kristiansen** (see earlier) won every time out; four times at 3000m including clear victories over Bondarenko and Puica; and two each at 5000m and 10000m. **Olga Bondarenko**, was European champion at 3000m and silver medallist at 10000m. Outdoors she lost only to Kristiansen, and to Svetlana Guskova at 5000m against the

GDR, a result she reversed in Rome. **Maricica Puica** had a busy season at 3000m as well as at shorter distances, and ran consistently well, winning three and second three times – to Doina Melinte, when the latter ran 8:37.11 in her only 3000m race apart from dropping out in her European heat, to Kristiansen in Zürich, and to Bondarenko in Stuttgart.

Third and fourth in the European 10000m were Ulrike Bruns, with a GDR record, and Aurora Cunha, later to win her third successive world road race championship.

## Marathon

The top three did not meet, but each won two of the major races: Ingrid Kristiansen, Boston 2:24:55 and Chicago 2:27:08; Grete Waitz, London 2:24:54 and New York 2:28:06; Rosa Mota, European 2:28:38 and Tokyo 2:27:15. The depth of competition was strongest in New York as behind Waitz were Lisa Martin, Commonwealth champion, and Laura Fogli, European silver medallist.

## 100 metres hurdles

**Yordanka Donkova** ran eleven sub-12.50 times, including four world records as well as the best-ever time, a hand-timed 12.0w. She was beaten twice, but ended the year with a clear margin of superiority, 4–1 over **Cornelia Oschkenat** and 10–1 over Ginka Zagorcheva, second and third at Stuttgart and 2–2 against each other. Oschkenat also had a splendid unbeaten indoor season, with three world bests at 50mh and the European title.

## 400 metres hurdles

**Marina Stepanova** lost to Sabine Busch in the USSR–GDR match, but won in a world record 53.32 to 53.60 for Busch in Stuttgart, and further improved that record to 52.94 in Tashkent; at 36 she is the oldest ever women's world record setter. Her Tashkent win completed a clean sweep of the major Soviet races. Sabine Busch, still to be completely confident over the hurdles, won 8/10, her only other loss being to **Debbie Flintoff** at the Bislett Games, when the Australian improved her Commonwealth record to 53.76. Flintoff added the Commonwealth titles at 400m and 400mh and was undefeated over the hurdles.

## High jump

**Stefka Kostadinova** was again in a class of her own. Her 34 consecutive winning high jump competitions were ended when she only cleared 1.85m behind Heike Redetzky's 1.88m in Munich on 17 June, but she added a further 11 wins after that. She set world records at 2.08m and 2.07m, and was over 2.03m in eight competitions. Olga Turchak, 2.01m for second at the Goodwill Games and 2.00m in Tashkent, and Desiré du Plessis, with jumps of 2.01m and 2.00m in South Africa, were the only other woman to clear 2 metres.

## Long jump

**Heike Drechsler** (see earlier) was undefeated. **Galina Chistyakova** was runner-up in Stuttgart and set a Soviet record of 7.34m, but she was also beaten by Jackie Joyner indoors, and at the Znamenskiy meeting by Yelena Byelevskaya, who won the Soviet title at 7.31m. Helga Radtke was the European bronze medallist and a most consistent jumoer as can be seen by the list of those with most competitions over 7 metres: Drechsler 13; Radtke and Chistyakova 6; Byelevskaya, Vali Ionescu and Joyner 4 each.

## Shot

One of the biggest upsets at Stuttgart was that Natalya Lisovskaya could manage only ninth place, after nine wins in 1986 and the season's best 21.70m against the GDR. Behind her then were Natalya Akhrimenko 21.39m, Ines Müller 21.34m and Heide Krieger 20.29m. Those three reversed the placings in Stuttgart, but Ines Müller was the top East German as she beat Krieger 9–1 and lost on only one other occasion, to European fifth-placer Heike Hartwig.

## Discus

**Tsvetanka Khristova** won 18/20, her worst at 65.84m. So she must be top ranked, even though she lost in Stuttgart to Diana Sachse, who she otherwise beat three times. Her other loss was to Irina Meszynski in May. GDR champion and European bronze medallist Martina Hellmann traded wins 2-2 with Sachse. These three had bests at over 72m, with the world's fourth spot at 69.66m.

Yordanka Donkova. *Mark Shearman*

## Javelin

**Fatima Whitbread** won all her ten competitions prior to the Commonwealth Games, when Tessa Sanderson upset her considerably by winning, 69.80m to 68.54m. However Whitbread picked herself up with a season's best of 72.26m at Gateshead and a further three wins at over 71.50m before Stuttgart. She was obviously ready, but her 77.44m qualifying throw at 9.18am was truly amazing. One could, however, recall that Yelena Gorchakova had set a world record (62.40m) in the qualifying round at the 1964 Olympics but had had to settle for the bronze in the final, some five metres down. **Petra Felke** was yet again in the midst of an oustanding season, coming to the Europeans unbeaten in ten competitions, with a best of 75.04m the previous week. She responded with 72.62m in the qualifying and led in the final with 72.00m before Whitbread's fourth round 72.68m. Felke improved to 72.52m, but Whitbread had won and sealed the day with the second longest throw ever of 76.32m. Felke gained revenge with victory in the Grand Prix final, so that Whitbread's overall record was 18 wins out of 20, and 23 70-metre throws in 12 competitions. Felke won 12/13, all but two over 70m.

## Heptathlon

**Jackie Joyner** (see earlier) was the world's number one by a long way. Then came **Anke Behmer**, who returned from maternity leave in 1985 to win an exciting contest for the European title. Her one loss, apart from failing to finish at the Goodwill Games, was to Joyner, by 289 points at Götzis.

## Walks

While the Chinese girls set world records, **Kerry Saxby** of Australia has perhaps the best claim to be walker of the year for she defeated Guan Ping, who went on to win the Asian Games title, in the Goodwill Games 10km. Saxby, who had set the world best for 20km in 1985, speeded in 1986 to Commonwealth bests at 5km and 10km.

Jackie Joyner. *Mark Shearman*

# JUNIOR ATHLETES OF 1986

## BY PETER MATTHEWS

The advent of the World Junior Championships made 1986 a highly significant one in the annals of junior athletics. A total of 1188 athletes from 143 nations took part in Athens at a highly successful inaugural championships.

It is not particularly easy to select the world junior athlete of the year, perhaps surprisingly, given that so many of the world's best juniors competed in Athens. Winning performances there included two world junior records: the US team of Clifton Campbell, Chip Rish, Percy Waddle and William Reed ran the 4x400m relay in 3:01.90 and Vladimir Sosimovich (USSR) threw the new javelin 78.86m. Indeed it was not a vintage year for records as the only other world junior records during 1986 came from Javier Sotomayor (Cub), 2.36m high jump, a further improvement in the javelin from Gavin Lovegrove (NZ) to 79.58m and in the women's events by the walker Wang Yan.

In Athens, Peter Chumba of Kenya won a notable double at 5000m and 10000m, but in looking for the athlete of the year, one can perhaps best judge the outstanding candidates against senior form. Fewer than usual juniors made the world top ten rankings, indeed only one man and one or two women walkers certainly qualify on that basis, as can be seen as we look briefly through the outstanding candidates.

## Men

The two Americans Derrick Florence and Stanley Kerr won world junior gold and silver medals at 100m and 200m. After Kerr had won both events at the US junior championships, he was beaten by Florence in Athens, but gained his revenge at 200m. Kerr went on to win the Pan-American Junior 100m and had season's bests of 10.10 and 20.39/20.10w; Florence ran 10.13 and 20.63/20.5. At 400m Roberto Hernandez (Cub) was the fastest junior of the year at 45.05, but was surprisingly pipped by Australian Miles Murphy in Athens, when both ran 45.64.

David Sharpe was the top middle-distance runner. He won the world junior 800m, but the attempt to double was too much for him as he faded to fifth in the 1500m. Other highlights of his highly successful season included UK junior records at 800m and 1000m. His 1:45.64 for 800m, when fifth at the van Damme meeting in Brussels, bettered Steve Ovett's 11-year-old record.

**Javier Sotomayor** (Cub) had ranked fifth in the world as a 17-year-old in 1985, but in 1986 he just missed the top ten overall. In the Grand Prix events he disappointed somewhat, as he was consistent in the 2.25–2.28m area. Nonetheless his 2.36m junior record was the best men's mark of the year; the previous record of 2.35m was set

| Colin Jackson – 110mh competitions in 1986 | | | |
|---|---|---|---|
| Date | Venue/Meeting | Place | Time |
| 10 May | West London – League | 1 | 14.3 |
| 17 May | Vic – Wales v Catalonia | 1 | 14.02 |
| 25 May | Cwmbran – UK Champs | 1 | 13.73 (13.97ht) |
| 31 May | Cwmbran – League | 1 | 13.85 |
| 8 Jun | Wrexham | 1 | 13.62 |
| 14 Jun | Cwmbran – Welsh Champs | 1 | 13.51 (13.73ht) |
| 21 Jun | London – AAA | 1 | 13.51 (13.74wht) |
| 30 Jun | Belfast – Ulster Games | 3 | 13.60 |
| 11 Jul | London – PTG | 4 | 13.76 |
| 19 Jul | Athens – World Junior | 1 | 13.44 (14.25ht, 13.72sf) |
| 27 Jul | Edinburgh – Commonwealth | 2 | 13.42w (13.69ht) |
| 13 Aug | Zürich – Weltklasse | 2 | 13.47 |

**Ilke Wyludda – competitions in 1986**

| Date | Venue/Meeting | Place | Mark |
|------|---------------|-------|------|
| **SHOT** | | | |
| 29 Jun | Jena – GDR Champs | 8 | 18.39 |
| 4 Jul | Berlin | 3 | 18.15 |
| 10 Jul | Berlin | 2 | 18.40 |
| 9 Aug | Karl-Marx-Stadt v USSR Jnr | 1 | 19.08 |
| **DISCUS** | | | |
| 22 Jun | Cottbus | 1 | 64.42 |
| 28 Jun | Jena – GDR Champs | 5 | 61.70 |
| 20 Jul | Athens – World Jnr | 1 | 64.02 |
| 26 Jul | Cottbus – GDR Jnr | 1 | 63.80 |
| 2 Aug | Neubrandenburg | 1 | 65.86 |
| 10 Aug | Karl-Marx-Stadt v USSR Jnr | 1 | 63.74 |

by Vladimir Yashchenko (USSR) indoors in 1978 and Dietmar Mögenburg (FRG) in 1980, both former senior world bests. Sotomayor also won the Pan-American junior title and the Ibero-American title.

David Sharpe. *ASP*

The US long jumper Eric Metcalf would perhaps have been a strong candidate for top junior, but he did not compete in Athens and this may also have cost him a top ten world ranking at senior level. He showed immense promise, with an NCAA victory at 8.24m and the US Junior with a windy 8.15m.

Other notable juniors included the champions at triple jump, Igor Parigin (USSR), who won in Athens with the best junior jump of the year, 16.97m, and the Cuban hurdler Emilio Valle, winner at 400mh and also third at 110mh behind the British duo of Colin Jackson and Jonathan Ridgeon. The former is my selection for world junior male athlete of the year.

It was a long season for **Colin Jackson**, for following Athens he had two more major championships to aim for, Commonwealth and European. In the first he gained the silver medal behind Mark McKoy, but sadly had to miss the chance of challenging Stéphane Caristan for the European title through a hamstring injury. Just before then, however, in what turned out to be his last race of the year, he had run splendidly in Zürich at the Weltklasse to place runner-up to Greg Foster and ahead of Caristan, McKoy and Roger Kingdom, the European, Commonwealth and Olympic champions.

Jackson started 1987 in brilliant style with a UK indoor 60mh record of 7.60, and looks set to challenge the world's best.

## Women

The sprints in Athens were Nigerian dominated. Mary Onyali was the best known and indeed topped the year's rankings with 11.28 and 22.90, but was beaten into second place in both events, to

Falilat Ogunkoya at 200m, and was disqualified at 100m, won by Tina Iheagwan. Despite this individual domination the Nigerian sprint relay team displayed poor baton changing to place third behind the USA and GDR.

In the middle distances Sabina Chirchir (Ken) won the 800m and was second at 1500m to Ana Padurean (Rom), who also topped the world list with a fine 4:06.02. The GDR junior women were, as usual, exemplary, and two who set year's junior bests to win in Athens were long jumper Patricia Bille at 6.70m and Heike Tillack who won the 100mh in 13.10 to equal the European Junior record. Another champion is my selection as the best junior woman at track and field events – **Ilke Wyludda**. While such is the strength of GDR discus throwers that she ranked but fifth amongst the seniors, her year's best of 65.86m was just 10cm short of the world junior record that her compatriot Grit Haupt had set in 1984. In 1985 Wyludda had won gold at discus and silver at shot in the European Juniors. In Athens she left the shot to Heike Rohrmann, but with a best of 19.08m to Rohrmann's winning 18.39m might well have won that event as well. Ilke Wyludda,

born in Leipzig on 28 Mar 1969, a member of the SC Chemie Halle, and at 1.83m and 90kg the ideal build for a discus thrower, remains a junior in 1987, with the European Juniors once again in her sights and surely too the world junior records.

However, despite Wyludda's claims the palm of junior woman athlete of the year must surely go to the amazing Chinese walker **Wang Yan**. She turned 16 on 9 April, yet in the month before then had set a world record, 21:33.8 for 5000m in Jian and a world best 12:39.1 for 3000m in Beijing. Her 44:59.3 for 10000m in Beijing was just one tenth of a second behind the new world record set by Xu Yongjiu. At 15 she is the youngest world record holder in the history of athletics. She went on to win the 5000m walk in Athens, well clear in 22:03.65 ahead of Natalya Zykova (USSR), who set a European Junior record of 22:17.76, 0.07 ahead of another 16-year-old Chinese girl, Jin Bingjie. Surprisingly only fourth was the 1985 European junior champion Maria Cruz Diaz (Spa). However she made up for that disappointment with the senior European title, while still two months short of her 17th birthday – the youngest ever champion.

Colin Jackson (l) won the silver behind Canada's Mark McKoy at the Commonwealth Games. *Mark Shearman*

Maria Cruz Diaz wins the first ever women's European walking title. *ASP*

# REVIEW OF 1986

## BY PETER MATTHEWS

Chronological survey of major events in the world of track and field athletics during the year.

## JANUARY

**8–12 3rd Central American Games** held at Guatemala City.

**15 Yomiuri International** at Osaka, Japan. World indoor bests were set by Ben Johnson, 6.50 for 60m (4/100ths off Houston McTear's 1978 mark), and by Sergey Bubka with a 5.87m pole vault.

**17 Sunkist Invitational** at Los Angeles. World indoor bests were set by Greg Foster, 5.88 for 50y hurdles, Charlie Simpkins, 17.50m triple jump, and Billy Olson, with a 5.88m pole vault. Olson had increased his hold on the pole by 18cm to 5 metres. Marcus O'Sullivan won the mile (3:58.37), beating Eamonn Coghlan, whose loss was his first indoors at the distance for five years.

**18 Johnson City**, Tennessee, USA. World indoor bests are generally recognised as those set on tracks of 220y or less circumference, but Antonio McKay's 45.45 for 440 yards on this 293.3y track is the fastest ever for 400m or 440y indoors.

**24/25 AAA/WAAA Indoor Championships** at Cosford. Zola Budd set a Commonwealth best of 4:06.87 for 1500m. After clearing a national high jump best of 2.30m, Geoff Parsons had the audacity to try a world best of 2.40m. Seb Coe was third at 3000m, his first indoor loss for ten years; the title was won in 7:49.61 by David Lewis. Judy Oakes won her eighth indoor title at shot, to equal the record for one event.

**25 Albuquerque**, USA. Billy Olson added a further centimetre to the pole vault best and Jimmy Howard jumped an American indoor high jump best of 2.36m.

**25/26 East Berlin**, GDR. With fourth and fifth round jumps of 7.25m and 7.29m, Heike Drechsler twice improved the world indoor long jump best and Cornelia Oschkenat, with 6.73, took a tenth off the world 50m hurdles best.

**28 Volgograd**, USSR. Olga Bondarenko took five seconds off Mary Slaney's world indoor best for 3000m with 8:42.30.

## FEBRUARY

**1 Columbia**, Missouri, USA. Joe Dial interrupted the Bubka–Olson battle for the world indoor pole vault best with 5.91m in a college open meeting.

**8 East Berlin**, GDR. Cornelia Oschkenat twice set world bests for 50m hurdles, at 6.73 and 6.71.

**6–8 USSR Indoor Championships** at Moscow. Bubka's turn again with a 5.92m vault. Robert Emmiyan set European long jump bests with third and fifth round jumps of 8.29m and 8.34m to, at last, beat Igor Ter-Ovanesyan's 8.23m when he won the first European Indoor title at Dortmund in 1966.

**8 Vitalis/Olympic Invitational**, East Rutherford, New Jersey. Billy Olson was back with 5.93m, his eleventh indoor vault best, following Bubka's 5.92m earlier the same day.

**8 United Kingdom v Hungary** at Cosford. The UK won both matches, men 83–54 and women 69–34. Zola Budd ran 3000m in 8:39.79 to improve the world best from Bondarenko's 8:42.30.

**9 Vienna**, Austria. Thomas Schönlebe regained the world indoor 400m best with 45.41.

**9 Tokyo Marathon**. For the first time four men ran under 2:09, as Juma Ikangaa's 2:08:10 headed 2:08:29 by Belaine Dinsamo in only his second marathon. They were followed by Abebe Mekonnen and Takeyuki Nakayama. Carlos Lopes dropped out at 18km.

**14 Millrose Games**, New York. The US season's biggest crowd of 18,325 packed Madison Square Garden for this traditional fiesta of top-class action. The all-star pole vault was won by Billy Olson from Dave Volz, but Olson's clearance was re-measured at 5.79m and Volz's at 5.80m! Both Joe Dial and Sergey Bubka no-heighted as the vaulters encountered considerable problems from people obstructing the runway.

15/16 **GDR Indoor Championships** at Senftenberg. The 23rd edition of this meeting featured a world best, on the oversized 250m track, from Marita Koch, the fifteenth in her career, this time 22.33 for 200m. Steffen Bringmann ran European indoor bests for 100y, 9.50, and 60m, 6.54 in his heat before winning the final in 6.62. Heike Drechsler won the long jump at 7.17m and demonstrated her sprinting with a world best for 100y of 10.24.

21 **Los Angeles Times**, Inglewood, California, USA. Sergey Bubka beat Billy Olson 5.94m to 5.75m to regain the world best, and Jeanette Bolden equalled Evelyn Ashford's four-year-old 60y mark of 6.54.

22/23 **Canadian Championships** at Edmonton. Ben Johnson equalled his 60m world best of 6.50 for 60m.

22/23 **European Indoor Championships** at Madrid, Spain. A highly enthusiastic crowd enjoyed fine competition. Fast sprinting was helped by the 640m altitude and there were world bests by Nellie Cooman, 7.00 for 60m in an upset win over Marlies Göhr 7.08, and by Maris Bruzhiks, 17.54m triple jump. The small (164m) track caused problems, for athletes drawn on the inside had no chance, as they fought to cope with the tight bends. Despite the track size Marita Koch's 200m time of 22.58 was the second fastest ever. Dietmar Mögenburg won his fourth high jump title with 2.34m. *Medallists were listed in the 1986 Annual.*

23 **Michelob**, San Diego, California, USA. World indoor bests came from Johnny Gray, 1000 yards in 2:04.39, and Galina Chistyakova, 13.58m at the, as yet, rarely contested triple jump for women.

23 **Women's Ekiden Relay**, Yokohama, Japan. The women's international road relay race over the marathon distance was won by the Norwegian team of Anne Marie Kirkeberg, Bente Moe, Anita Håkenstad, Ingrid Kristiansen, Grete Kirkeberg and Christin Sørum. They clocked a course record 2:16:42 ahead of the USA 2:18:51 and Portugal 2:19:22. Kristiansen ran her 10km stage in 30:39, the fastest ever by a woman.

25 **UK v USSR** at Cosford. The Soviet men won both matches comfortably, men 80–58 and women 77–40. All four runners were disqualified in the 400m!

28 **TAC Indoor Championships** at New York. Sergey Bubka sealed the battle of the pole vault with 5.95m, the ninth improvement of the world best in the 1985/6 indoor season. Olson failed to clear his opening height of 5.60m, and Joe Dial was seventh at 5.50m, as the Americans had to give best to the Europeans;

Sergey's brother Vasiliy was second at 5.75m, followed by the Frenchmen Philippe Collet 5.70m and Pierre Quinon 5.60m. This meeting was the climax of the 14-event Mobil Indoor Grand Prix series. By winning the high jump at 2.34m Jimmy Howard retained his men's overall title and added $10,000 to the $3,000 for his event win. The women's overall winner was Diane Dixon, the 440y champion. World bests were set at Imperial distances by Marita Koch, 220y 22.89, Lynn Jennings, 2 miles 9:28.15, and for the third successive year in the 2 miles walk by Jim Heiring, 12:05.94. *See the 1986 Annual for Mobil and TAC winners.*

# MARCH

5 **Kobe**, Japan. Mark McKoy ran a world 50m hurdles best of 6.25.

8 **Tokyo**, Japan. McKoy was again in form, a world indoor best 60m hurdles of 7.47.

14/15 **NCAA Indoor Championships**, Oklahoma City, USA. There was a world best for 55m of 6.00 but the track was incorrectly measured (64cm short per lap) so Roddie Haley's times of 1:00.69 and 59.82 for 500m could not count, although the latter equates to 59.94, compared to Clarence Daniel's world best of 1:00.85. Leading team results: MEN: 1. Arkansas 49, 2. Villanova 22, 3= Boston U & Georgetown 20. WOMEN: 1. Alabama 41, 2. Texas 31, 3= Tennessee & USC 26.

15 **Virginia Beach**, USA. Grete Waitz ran a women's world road best at 8km of 25:03, winning the race by two minutes.

23 **World Cross-country Championships**, Neuchatel, Switzerland. The men's races were dominated by the Africans. Ethiopia had won the men's team title on all five previous occasions on which they had competed, but this sequence was ended by Kenya, with five men in the first eight, including the surprise winner John Ngugi. The Ethiopians were second but made it five successive junior wins; their Melese Feyisa was the individual champion and there were ten Africans in the first eleven. Zola Budd retained her title and led England to the women's team victory by just two points from New Zealand, but only after protests following the original missing of an English athlete, as there was chaos at the finish with runners piling up before the line. There were record numbers of competitors and teams in all three races. *See the cross-country section for further details.*

29–31 **CARIFTA Games**, Guadeloupe. The 15th Caribbean Junior Championships. Highlights included a women's 100m/200m double by Jillian Forde (Tri) 11.45/23.14.

# APRIL

6 **Cherry Blossom**, Washington, USA. Rosa Mota broke Joan Benoit's world road best for 10 miles, running 53:09 to win from Lorraine Moller 53:48.

20 **London Marathon**. There was a world record 19,261 starters, of whom 18,175 finished. 200 broke 2 hrs 30 mins, and there were 2317, including 56 women, inside 3 hours. Toshihiko Seko won in 2:10:02, slowed by running into a fierce wind over the final miles. He had passed half-way in 1:03:30 and 20 miles in 1:37:16. Hugh Jones was 1:40 behind. Grete Waitz won the women's race by nearly 6 minutes in 2:24:54.

21 **Boston Marathon**. The 90th Boston was back to its traditional world-class standard as prize money was paid for the first time, with the race sponsored by the John Hancock Insurance Company. Rob de Castella earned $30,000 for winning, $25,000 for setting a course record 2:07:51, $5,000 for sub 2:10 and a new Mercedes-Benz; all that and appearance money too! His time was the third fastest ever. The women's winner was Ingrid Kristiansen in 2:24:55 for $35,000 and a Mercedes-Benz.

24–26 **Penn Relays**, Philadelphia, USA. Texas Christian University's 4 x 200m relay time of 1:20.20 was the fastest ever run, but cannot count as a world record as the runners, Roscoe Tatum and Greg Sholars (USA), Andrew Smith and Leroy Reid (Jam). were not all from the same country. Villanova's multi-national squad ran the fastest ever distance medley: Gary Taylor (UK) 3/4 mile 2:51.2, Rodie Haley (USA) 43.5 440y, Espen Borge (Nor) 1:48.9 880y, Doug Consiglio (Can) 3:59.0 mile for 9:22.6.

26/27 **Mt.SAC Relays**, Walnut, California, USA. Evelyn Ashford won the 100m in 11.11 in her first major race since 1984, Carl Lewis won a 100m/LJ double with 10.14/8.33w and Jackie Joyner's 6910 hepathlon was just 36 points off the world record, although her 100m hurdles was hand-timed.

# MAY

1 **Naumberg**, GDR. Winners at this 17th international walks event: 20km: Ralf Kowalsky 1:22:08, 50km: Hartwig Gauder 3:43:51,

women's 10km: Dana Vavracova 47:54.

17 **Pepsi Invitational** at Los Angeles. Four men broke 45 secs in the 400m won by Gabriel Tiacoh in 44.32, an African record and just 0.17 off the low-altitude best ever. Valerie Brisco-Hooks won the 100m in a pb 10.99.

18 **Bay-to-Breakers**, San Francisco, USA. The world's largest mass-participation race, with over 85,000 runners, and a reputed further 15,000 or more joining in, is run over 12km. The winner was Ed Eyestone in 34:33 and first woman was Grete Waitz 38:45, both course records.

24 **Santa Monica**, USA. Johnny Gray ran 600m in 1:12.81, 1.35 sec. inside the previous world best for this rarely run distance. Second was Earl Jones 1:13.80 and third David Mack 1:14.15.

24/25 **Potsdam**, GDR. The individual winners at this 6-nation international: 20km: Ralf Kowalsky 1:20:31; 50km: Ronald Weigel 3:38:17, a world road best; junior 10km: Giovanni De Benedictis 41:08; women's 10km: Monica Gunnarsson 46:05. Team result: 1. GDR 177, 2. ITA 154, 3. SWE 105, 4. SPA 87, 5. FRA 79, 6. UK 79.

24-25 **Götzis**, Austria. Winners in this major annual multi-events competition: Decathlon: Guido Kratschmer 8519, Heptathlon: Jackie Joyner 6841.

25 **Sport Aid**. The world's greatest mass participation sporting event. On this day, the climax of the event, at least 15 million runners took part in the 'Race Against Time' in 277 cities in 78 countries. The Sudanese runner Omer Khalifa had set out from a relief camp in Khartoum eight days earlier and by air and foot carried his 'Torch of Hope' through twelve European cities to reach the United Nations in New York. Huge sums were raised to combat famine in Africa.

25 **Sofia**, Bulgaria. Stefka Kostadinova equalled the world high jump record of 2.07m, set by her now-banned countrywomen Lyudmila Andonova.

31 **Narodna Mladeje**, Sofia, Bulgaria. Kostadinova made the women's high jump record her own with a second attempt clearance at 2.08m.

31 **Jenner Bud Light Classic** at San Jose, USA. This was the first of the IAAF/Mobil Grand Prix series. Ben Johnson beat Carl Lewis at 100m 10.01 to 10.18, but Lewis beat Kirk Baptiste at 200m 20.1 to 20.2. Evelyn Ashford returned to international competition with a 200m win in 22.30.

31 May – 1 June **European Men's Club Cup** at Lisbon. First three teams: 1. Racing Club de France 290, 2. Pro Patria Freedent Milano (Ita) 288, 3. FC Barcelona (Spa) 275.

# JUNE

1 **European Women's Club Cup** at Amsterdam. Bayer Leverkusen (FRG) won, as they had every year since this competition started in 1981 with 197 points. 2. Snia Milano (Ita) 82.5, 3. Osijek Slovenia (Yug) 159.5.

4–7 **NCAA Championships** at Indianapolis, USA. Leading team results: MEN: 1. Southern Methodist 53, 2. Washington State 52, 3. Texas 47; WOMEN: 1. Texas 65, 2. Alabama 55, 3. Texas Southern 47. Non-Americans won a record 38.7% of the men's points and 28.5% of the women's; most notably Texas Southern's winning women's sprint relay team was all Nigerian; their 43.71 was an African record. Gabriel Tiacoh improved the African 400m record to 44.30, and with 48.33 Danny Harris won his third 400mh title. Doubles were won by Stephanie Herbst, at 5000m and 10000m, and Juliet Cuthbert, who defended her 200m title and also won the 100m. In a tragic incident Kathy Ormsby, a former Collegiate record holder, ran off the track during the 10000m, out of the stadium and jumped off a bridge. The 30ft fall resulted in a collapsed lung and spinal cord injuries, leaving her paralysed from the waist down.

6 **Neubrandenburg**, GDR. Jürgen Schult set a world discus record of 74.08m, 4.34m ahead of his previous best, and (at 2.22m) the biggest ever improvement on the official world record.

7/8 **Znamenskiy Memorial**, Moscow, USSR. Nikolay Musiyenko set a European triple jump record of 17.78m, and Viktor Yevsyukov threw a best with the new javelin of 83.68m.

8 **Great North Run**, Tyneside, UK. Mike Musyoki ran a world best 60:43 for the half marathon. Second was Steve Jones, whose 60:59 was a British best. The women's winner Lisa Martin set a Commonwealth best 69:45. About 25,000 runners took part.

13/14 **Pravda-Televizia-Slovnaft**, Bratislava, Czechoslovakia. The first IAAF/Mobil Grand Prix meeting of the year in Europe. Cornelia Oschkenat just beat Yordanka Donkova 12.50 to 12.51 to launch a great year at the event.

18–21 **TAC Championships** at Eugene, Oregon. Carl Lewis won the 100m in 9.91w and the long jump with 8.67w, his eighth and ninth outdoor TAC titles, but was only fourth at 200m in which Floyd Heard (20.03w) completed the NCAA/TAC double, a feat matched by Danny Harris at 400mh and Helena Uusitalo at women's javelin. Mike Conley's 8.63w long jump was much the best non-winning performance, and he repeated that feat with 17.84w in the triple jump, at which the winner was Charlie Simpkins 17.91w; last year's world record setter Willie Banks was third with 17.52w. Pam Marshall won the women's sprint double in 10.80w and 22.24w; in the former there was the best ever standard in depth, as there followed Alice Brown 10.84, Evelyn Ashford 10.85 and Diane Williams 10.92. With wind assistance Wendy Brown's 13.78m was the best ever triple jump. Jane Frederick's heptathlon win was her ninth TAC multi-events title, Henry Marsh won his eighth steeplechase title in nine years, and there were sixth titles for Steve Scott at 1500m and John Powell discus. *See US section for winners.*

20/21 **USSR v GDR** at Tallinn. The USSR won both matches, the men's 122–90, and the women's 88–78. There were two world records: Yuriy Sedykh 86.66m hammer and Heike Drechsler 7.45m long jump. Sedykh's series: 86,00, 86.66, N, 84.12, 85.82, P; Drechsler's series was 6.72, 7.13, 7.35, 7.27, 6.94, 7.45 and she also won the 200m in 22.13. Behind her Galina Chistyakova had the best ever non-winning mark of 7.34m and Helga Radtke was fifth and last with 7.07m, a world record distance only eight years ago! For the first time three men put the shot beyond 22m, Uwe Timmermann 22.60m, Sergey Smirnov 22.24m and Udo Beyer 22.05m.

20/21 **AAA Championships**, Crystal Palace. Darren Clark (Aus) won his fourth successive AAA title, and Steve Cram's 800m win made it five successive years as AAA champion, three at 1500m and two at 800m.

26 **Lappeenranta**, Finland. Ed Moses ran his first 400mh since 31 Aug 1984, and clocked up win number 95 in finals (110 including heats).

27–29 **GDR Championships**, Jena. Heike Drechsler won both 200m and long jump. She equalled the world record with 21.71 at 200m, and jumped 7.35w and 7.29m. Udo Beyer beat Uwe Timmermann 22.14m to 22.00m and won his tenth successive shot title, a GDR record for any event.

29 June–4 July **Central American and Caribbean Championships**, Santiago, Dominican Republic. Dominated by the Cubans, who won 17/24 men's events and 12/19 women's, including all the field events.

# JULY

1 **DN Galan**, Stockholm. Said Aouita started his Grand Prix campaign with a win at 5000m in 13:19.43, and Johnny Gray beat Seb Coe at 800m, 1:43.85 to 1:44.17.

3 **Olympischer Tag**, Dresden, GDR. Heike Drechsler continued to star as she equalled her long jump world record; her series was the best ever: 7.20, 7.28, 7.30, 7.29, 7.24 and finally the record 7.45m. Sergey Litvinov beat Yuriy Sedykh 86.04m to 84.92m in the hammer, and behind them were the best ever marks for third and fourth, Igor Nikulin 82.34m and Juri Tamm 79.62m.

4–5 **East and Central African Championships**, Nairobi, Kenya. Joyce Odhiambo (Ken) won a treble at 100m, 200m and long jump. Kenyans won all but two events.*

4–6 **Pan-American Junior Championships**, Winter Park, Florida, USA. The USA took 15 golds and the Cubans 12. Double individual gold medallists were the Cubans Roberto Hernandez, 200m and 400m, and Emilio Valle 110mh and 400mh, and the American Carlette Guidry 200m and LJ. Hernandez and Guidry won third golds on their relay teams.*

5 **Bislett Games**, Oslo. Ingrid Kristiansen ran 10,000 metres in 30:13.74, to take 45.68 secs off her 1985 world record. It was the 46th, and one of the greatest, world record to be set at this historic stadium. She took the lead after reaching 3000m in 9:10.01, passed 5000m in 15:11.33 and just got faster as she added a second 5000m of 15:02.41. Aurora Cunha's second place time of 31:29.41 was one of five more national records. Steve Cram led Steve Scott and Jim Spivey under 3:50 in the mile, and Said Aouita made his debut at 10000m a winning one despite a bad spiking of his left ankle, which necessitated three stitches. His 27:26.11 headed 27:28.80 for Mark Nenow as twelve men bettered 28 minutes. Other top marks came in the 400mh men's 47.82 by Danny Harris, who beat Andre Phillips and Harald Schmid, and women's, a Commonwealth record 53.76 by Debbie Flintoff, who beat Sabine Busch.

7 **World Games**, Helsinki. Tom Petranoff became the first man to throw the javelin beyond 85m or 280ft with 85.38m in the second round. Rather surprisingly it was the first men's javelin 'world record' to be set in this historic Olympic stadium in the land of javelin throwing.

5–8 **Goodwill Games**, Moscow. Financed by Ted Turner's cable TV, the meeting was predominantly a USA–USSR duel. Jackie Joyner smashed the world record for the heptathlon with 7148 points, including four personal bests. Sergey Bubka added a centimetre to take his pole vault world record to 6.01m; this was just his third jump of the competition, after first-time successes at 5.70m and 5.85m. Ben Johnson ran a Commonwealth 100m record of

9.95 to again beat Carl Lewis 10.06, with Chidi Imo between them in an African record 10.04. Lewis, however anchored the US sprint relay team to victory in 37.98, the third fastest ever from the USSR's 38.19, a European record, as was Robert Emmiyan's long jump of 8.61m. Evelyn Ashford just beat Heike Drechsler, with both timed in 10.91 for 100m.

11 **Peugeot-Talbot Games** at Crystal Palace, London. Maricica Puica set a world record for the rarely run 2000m of 5:28.69. Zola Budd led for all but the last 200m, but had to settle for third in 5:30.19, as she was also overtaken by Yvonne Murray, who set a Commonwealth record 5:29.58. Seb Coe beat Johnny Gray 1:44.10 to 1:44.72 at 800m.

14–17 **USSR Championships**, Kiev. Top marks included Rodion Gataullin 5.85m PV, Marina Stepanova 53.84 400mh and Yelena Byelevskaya 7.31 LJ.

15 **Nikaia** at Nice, France. Steve Cram, who had set his first world record at the 1500m in this meeting the previous year, turned to 800m and won with 1:43.62. A high standard steeplechase was won by William van Dijck in a Belgian record 8:11.52 from the Kenyans Julius Korir and Peter Koech, as tenth was 8:21.01.

16–20 **World Junior Championships**, Athens. These inaugural championships were a great success, contested by 1188 athletes from 143 nations. Medals often followed national traditions, as the GDR dominated the women's events, with eight gold, four silver and four bronze, yet only three bronze medals went to their men; and Kenyans and Ethiopians took 11 of the 15 medals in the men's events from 1500m upwards. Surprisingly the USSR took no women's gold medals, but six men's. The USA fared less well than might have been expected, but were not at full strength. Two world junior records were set, by Vladimir Zasimovich in the javelin and the USA men's 4 x 400m team. Peter Chumba of Kenya was the one double individual gold medallist, winning at 5000m and 10000m.*

18/19 **Pearl Assurance**, Birmingham, UK. Samson Obwocha set a world best for the 2000m steeplechase of 5:19.68 as he outsprinted Julius Korir 5:20.25.

26 July–2 August **Commonwealth Games**, Edinburgh. Sadly marred by the boycott by 32 nations and indeed the weather, there was nonetheless much good athletics. Steve Cram's majestic form in winning the 800m/1500m double was perhaps the highlight. *See results section for report and medallists.*

28 July–2 August **European Veterans Championships**, Malmö, Sweden. This was the fifth of these biennial events for the over-40s (men)

and over-35s (women). World age bests included 22.91 over-50 200m by Ron Taylor (UK).

# AUGUST

1-3 **US Olympic Festival**, Houston. In humid, 100-degree (38 degrees C) weather Jackie Joyner further improved the world heptathlon record to 7161, with pbs at shot, 200m, javelin and equalled at high jump.

3 **Sofia**, Bulgaria. Hand-timing does not count for sprint world records, but Yordanka Donkova and Ginka Zagorcheva ran 12.0 and 12.1 for 100m hurdles, compared to the world record of 12.36, but it was just too windy.

5 **UK v Commonwealth**, Gateshead, UK. Several athletes who had had to obey the boycott competed at this post-Games celebration, with wins by the Jamaicans Bert Cameron, Merlene Ottey-Page and Grace Jackson. But the most notable occurence was the astonishing return of Allan Wells, winning both 100m and 200m after two years out of top-class athletics; Ben Johnson was only fourth at 100m. Two more long-established stars also won their events, John Walker the 1 mile and David Moorcroft the 3000m. The Commonwealth, aided by some UK athletes, beat the UK 285.5 to 252.5.

5 **Stockholm**, Sweden. Ingrid Kristiansen regained the 5000m world record that she had lost to Zola Budd in 1985, taking 10.74 seconds off that time with 14:37.33. Following Elly van Hulst for the first 2200m, her kilometre splits were: 1000m 2:52.90, 2000m 5:48.0, 3000m 8:45.44, 4000m 11:43.9.

6 **Viareggio**, Italy. The world record holder Renaldo Nehemiah returned to win the 110m hurdles in 13.48, his first race for nearly five years. He had been reinstated by the IAAF following receipt of a declaration from Nehemiah that he would no longer compete for pecuniary reward or compensation at American Football. Alessandro Andrei, with a national record 22.06m moved to sixth best ever in the shot.

6 **Koblenz**, FRG. Steve Ovett ran his fastest 1500m, 3:33.78, since his then world record 3:30.77 in 1983. The Kenyans Joshua Kipkemboi, 8:14.13, and Samson Obwocha, 8:14.17, beat Henry Marsh, 8:14.61, in the steeplechase.

6 **La Coruna**, Spain. Said Aouita ran the third fastest 5000m of all-time, 13:00.86, just 0.46 off his world record. Gabriel Tiacoh ran 300m in 31.74, the second fastest ever.

8 **IAC**, Crystal Palace, London. Ed Moses extended his 400mh win-streak to 99 finals with a 48.21.

9/10 **Finland v Sweden**, Helsinki. Sweden repeated last year's victories, men 210.5–198.5, women 184–138.

11 **Budapest Grand Prix**. Khristo Markov triple jumped a European record 17.80m, backed by other jumps at 17.74m and 17.64m and three massive fouls, one of which might have been over 18m. Yordanka Donkova started a great week with a national record 12.38 for 100mh, Ed Moses won his 100th successive 400mh final in 47.76 and Yuriy Sedykh had the best-ever 6-throw series in the hammer: 83.90, 85.68, 85.42, 85.26, 85.24, 84.64.

13 **Weltklasse, Zürich**, Switzerland. As usual this meeting was of the very highest quality. Said Aouita's 7:32.54 for 3000m was the second fastest ever, Evelyn Ashford won the 100m/200m double in 10.95 and 21.97, and Gabriel Tiacoh won from a great 400m field in 44.46 as for the first time there were seven men at 45.00 or better. Ingrid Kristiansen moved down to 3000m and triumphed there too, beating Maricica Puica and Zola Budd in a world-leading 8:34.10. Ben Johnson underlined his supremacy at 100m; his 10.03 left him well clear of his leading rivals Chidi Imo 10.22 and Carl Lewis 10.25.

13 **Bulgarian Championships**, Sofia. Yordanka Donkova equalled Grazyna Rabsztyn's 100mh record of 12.36.

15 **ISTAF**, West Berlin, FRG. Continued fine form was shown by Donkova, 12.37, Moses 47.53, Said Aouita 1M 3:50.33 and Evelyn Ashford 100m 10.93. Chidi Imo won the 100m in an African record 10.00 on the 50th anniversary of Jesse Owens's Olympic triumphs in the same stadium.

17 **Weltklasse, Köln**, FRG. Yordanka Donkova twice improved the world 100mh record, to 12.35 in her heat and 12.29 in the final, the latter despite a 0.4 head-wind. Said Aouita's series of near misses continued as he ran 3000m in 7:32.23, just 0.13 off Henry Rono's world record.

20 **East Berlin**, GDR. Udo Beyer regained the world record, that he had set in 1978 and 1983, with 22.64m. His series: 22.24, 22.58, 22.64, 22.15, N, P.

23/24 **IAAF Congress**, Stuttgart, FRG. Five new members were elected: American Samoa, Aruba, Dominica, Equatorial Guinea and Guam, bringing the total membership to 179. It was agreed to establish official world junior and world indoor records. Amendments were agreed to eligibility rules, and to the sizing and placement of advertising within the arena and on clothing.

24 **Stockholm**, Sweden. There was the largest ever entry for a women's only race, about 16,000 started from an entry of c.22,000 over 10km.

26–31 **European Championships**, Stuttgart. One of the greatest meetings in athletics history included four world records, from Heike Drechsler at 200m, Yuriy Sedykh, hammer, Marina Stepanova, 400mh and Fatima Whitbread, JT. *See results section for report and first eight at each event.*

# SEPTEMBER

2 **Lausanne**, Switzerland. Ed Moses made it 103 final wins in a row and continued to get faster, this time to 47.38.

5 **Van Damme Memorial** in Brussels. Said Aouita's 4:51.98 missed the world record for 2000m by 0.59. Other world-leading times came from Steve Cram, 3:30.15 for 1500m, and William van Dijck, 8:10.01 for 3000m steeplechase, the latter an ecstatically received Belgian record. Mark Nenow won the 10000m by more than half a lap as he set an American record 27:20.56. Heike Drechsler won the long jump with 7.23m, but lost to Evelyn Ashford at 200m, 22.06 to 22.10. Andre Phillips ran a pb 47.51 400mh to beat Danny Harris 48.42, and Ulf Timmermann revenged his European defeat by Werner Günthör, but only on his second best put, as both men reached 21.51m.

6/7 **Balkan Games**, Ljubljana, Yugoslavia. Yordanka Donkova set her fourth world record within a month with 12.26 for 100mh, from Ginka Zagorcheva, whose 12.39 moved her to third equal on the all-time list.*

7 **Rieti**, Italy. Steve Cram and Seb Coe celebrated their European gold medals with world-leading times at their 'other' distances, Cram 1:43.19 for 800m, and Coe 3:29.77 for 1500m to make him the fourth man under 3:30 and his first pb at the distance for five years. Evelyn Ashford met Marlies Göhr at 100m for the first time since Zürich in 1984, when Ashford set the world record; she won again, 10.88 to Göhr's 11.01. The high jumpers Igor Paklin and Stefka Kostadinova won at 2.38m and 2.05m, before trying world record heights.

10 **IAAF/Mobil Grand Prix Final**, Rome. As in 1985 the Grand Prix final was perhaps not as exciting as some of the preceding meetings, but there was nonetheless an improvement in overall standard. Said Aouita ensured his overall success by winning the 5000m in 13:13.13, as did Yordanka Donkova in the women's

100m hurdles, 12.47. Previous maximum points winners Jimmy Howard, second to Igor Paklin in the high jump, and Danny Harris, third in the 400mh won by Andre Phillips, thus lost their chances at the title. Similarly Maricica Puica needed a win to match Donkova, but lost to Tatyana Samolenko at 1500m.*

12 **McVitie's Challenge**, Crystal Palace, London. Ed Moses completed another unbeaten season at 400mh in 48.53. Seb Coe, 1:44.28 800m, Steve Cram, 3:49.49 mile, and Said Aouita, 8:14.81 2 miles, all scored easy victories, but Yordanka Donkova lost to her compatriot Ginka Zagorcheva, 12.51 to 12.55 at 100mh.

13 **Mercedes Mile**, Fifth Avenue, New York. Men's and women's winners were respectively José-Luis Gonzalez, 3:53.52 from John Walker 3:54.13 and José-Manuel Abascal 3:54.49; and Maricica Puica, a course record 4:19.48 from Lynn Williams 4:22.31 and Yvonne Murray 4:22.79. Mary Slaney returned to competition with sixth place at 4:32.01.

13–16 **South American Junior Championships**, Quito, Ecuador. The 2700m altitude was conducive to fast sprinting, with Luis Smith (Por) winning the 100m in 10.31w, after a 10.1 heat. Best mark was 2.20m HJ by José Mendez (Bra).

16–20 **9th Soviet Spartakiade**, Tashkent. Marina Stepanova further improved her world record for 400m hurdles to 52.94. At 36 years 139 days she is the oldest ever women's world record holder.

21 **Como**, Italy. Klaus Tafelmeier followed his European gold medal with a further improvement on the best throw with the new javelin, 85.74m.

27/28 **Ibero-American Championships**, Havana, Cuba. Robson Caetano da Silva smashed the South American 100m record with 10.02.*

28 **Berlin Marathon**. 12,280 started and 11,461 finished the race won by Boguslaw Psujek with 2:11:03 in his first marathon.

29 Sep–5 Oct **Asian Games**, Seoul. The best ever standard was reflected by a host of new Games records. *See results section for report and medallists.*

# OCTOBER

4/5 **Pan-American Racewalking Championships**, Saint-Leonard, Quebec, Canada. The men's 20km was won by Guillaume Leblanc in 1:21:13 (Canadian record) from Carlos Mercenario 1:21:33 (world junior best) and

Tim Lewis 1:21:48 (US record). Martin Bermudez won the 50km in 3:56:21 and Graciela Mendoza the women's 10km in a Mexican record 45:23.

5 **Lidingöloppet**, Stockholm, Sweden. There were 13,732 finishers in the annual cross-country race. Suleiman Nyambui won over 30km in 1:36:38. Grete Waitz won the women's race over 15km for the eleventh successive year in 53:12.

12–18 **91st Session of the IOC**, Lausanne, Switzerland. Barcelona, the favourite, was selected to host the 1992 Summer Olympic Games, from Paris, Brisbane, Belgrade, Birmingham and Amsterdam.

19 **Beijing Marathon**, China. Taisuke Kodama set an Asian record 2:07:35 to win from Kunimitsu Ito 2:07:57 and Juma Ikangaa 2:08:39, with 21 men under 2:15 and 46 under 2:20.

26 **Chicago marathon**, USA. Men's and women's winners were Toshihiko Seko, 2:08:27, and Ingrid Kristiansen, 2:27:08.

# NOVEMBER

2 **New York marathon**, USA. Gianni Poli won in 2:11:06 as Rob de Castella was surprisingly only third. The second placer, Antoni Niemczak was later disqualified for drugs abuse.

Grete Waitz won the women's race for the eighth time from Lisa Martin, with Laura Fogli third for the fourth year in succession. There were a record 20,502 runners with 19,689 finishers.

9 **IAAF World 15km Road Race Championships for Women**, Lisbon, Portugal. Aurora Cunha won her third successive world road race from her compatriot Rosa Mota, but the USSR won the team title.\*

30 **IAAF World Challenge Road Relay**, Hiroshima, Japan. Road relays for men and women over the marathon distance for national and continental teams. Both winning teams had been runners-up in the 1986 world cross-country championships. The men's five-stage race was won by Ethiopia from the United Kingdom, and the women's six-stage by New Zealand from the USSR. \*

# DECEMBER

31 **St. Silvestre Midnight Races**. Rolando Vera (Ecu) won the annual Round-the-Houses race in Sao Paulo, and Rosa Mota was first woman. In Madrid Antonio Leitao (Por) beat a classy field.

\* See Championships section for leading results of meetings so marked.

Ed Moses. *Mark Shearman*

# World cross-country championships 1986
*at Neuchatel, Switzerland 23 March*

MEN (12000m)
1. John Ngugi (Ken) 35:33
2. Abebe Mekonnen (Eth) 35:35
3. Joseph Kiptum (Ken) 35:40
4. Bekele Debele (Eth) 35:43
5. Paul Kipkoech (Ken) 35:48
6. Pat Porter (USA) 35:49
7. Kipsubai Koskei (Ken) 35:55
8. Some Muge (Ken) 35:56
9. Alberto Cova (Ita) 35:59
10. John Easker (USA) 36:00
11. Ezequiel Canario (Por) 36:04
12. Thierry Watrice (Fra) 36:05
13. Ed Eyestone (USA) 36:06
14. Rob de Castella (Aus) 36:11
15. Bruce Bickford (USA) 36:13
16. Dave Clarke (Eng) 36:15
17. Paul McCloy (Can) 36:17
18. Dionisio Castro (Por) 36:18
19. John Woods (Ire) 36:20
20. Santiago Llorente (Spa) 36:23
328 men finished

WOMEN (4650m)
1. Zola Budd (Eng) 14:50
2. Lynn Jennings (USA) 15:08
3. Annette Sergent (Fra) 15:13
4. Martine Fays (Fra) 15:15
5. Rosa Mota (Por) 15:19
6. Nanette Doak (USA) 15:24
7. Christine McMiken (NZ) 15:24
8. Albertina Machado (Por) 15:25
9. Elena Fidatov (Rom) 15:26
10. Carole Bradford (Eng) 15:28
11. Lieve Slegers (Bel) 15:29
12. Lyudmila Matveyeva (SU) 15:29
13. Renata Kokowska (Pol) 15:31
14. Cornelia Bürki (Swi) 15:32
15. Grete Kirkeberg (Nor) 15:33
16. Marina Rodchenkova (SU) 15:33
17. Elisabeth Franzis (FRG) 15:34
18. Gail Rear (NZ) 15:34
19. Mary O'Connor (NZ) 15:34
20. Ruth Partridge (Eng) 15:34
161 women finished

MEN'S TEAM
1. Kenya 45
2. Ethiopia 119
3. USA 204
4. France 255
5. Italy 256
6. Portugal 263
7. Spain 297
8. England 360
9. Australia 412
10. Belgium 534

39 nations completed teams, and a further 11 nations took part.

WOMEN'S TEAM
1. England 65
2. New Zealand 67
3. France 76
4. USA 82
5. Portugal 118
6. FR Germany 129
7. USSR 140
8. Romania 140
9. Norway 141
10. Belgium 182

28 nations completed teams and a further 8 nations took part.

JUNIOR MEN (7750m)
1. Melese Feyisa (Eth) 22:48
2. Sammy Kibiwot (Ken) 22:53
3. Demeke Bekele (Eth) 22:56
4. Workneh Rafera (Eth) 22:58
5. Ararso Fufa (Eth) 23:07
6. Negash Habte (Eth) 23:08
7. Moulay Brahim Boutayeb (Mor) 23:10
8. Alejandro Gomez (Spa) 23:18
9. William Mutwol (Ken) 23:22
10. Peter Rono (Ken) 23:34
171 juniors finished

JUNIOR MEN'S TEAM
1. Ethiopia 13
2. Kenya 32
3. Spain 52
4. Australia 91
5. USA 94
6. Morocco 137
7. Japan 152
8. Belgium 159
9. England 218
10. Sweden 230

29 nations completed teams and a further 5 nations took part.

# Cross-country – National champions 1986

| Country | Men | Women |
|---|---|---|
| Australia | Adam Hoyle | Krishna Wood |
| Austria | Gerhard Hartmann | Anni Müller |
| Belgium | Eddy de Pauw | Corinne Debaets |
| Canada | Paul McCloy | Debbie Bowker |
| Czechoslovakia | Ivan Uvizl | Jana Kucerikova |
| Denmark | Niels Kim Hjort | Dorthe Rasmussen |
| England | Tim Hutchings | Carole Bradford |
| Finland | Martti Vainio | Päivi Tikkanen |
| France | Pierre Levisse | Annette Sergent |
| GDR | Frank Heine | Gabriele Veith |
| F.R. Germany | Werner Grommisch | Charlotte Teske |
| Ireland | Noel Harvey | Mary Donoghue |
| Italy | Alberto Cova | Agnese Possamai |
| Kenya | John Ngugi | |
| Netherlands | Tonny Dirks | Carla Beurskens |
| New Zealand | Ken Maloney | Gail Rear |
| Northern Ireland | Deon McNeilly | Rosemary Bogle |
| Norway | Roy Andersen | Ingrid Kristiansen |
| Poland | Boguslaw Psujek | Renata Kokowska |
| Portugal | Fernando Mamede | Aurora Cunha |
| Romania | Gheorghe Sandu | Mariana Stanescu |
| Scotland | Nat Muir | Jean Lorden |
| South Africa | Matthews Temane | Marjorie van der Merwe |
| Spain | Vincente Polo | Carmen Valero |
| Sweden | Lars-Erik Nilsson | Eve Ernström |
| Switzerland | Markus Ryffel | Cornelia Bürki |
| USA (Nov) | Pat Porter | Lesley Welch |
| USSR | Sergey Skorikov | Natalya Sorokivskaya |
| Wales | Steve Jones | Angela Tooby |
| Yugoslavia | Stanislav Rozman | Tatyana Smolnikar |
| | | |
| Arab Champs | Abdellah Boubya (Mor) | Hassania Darami (Mor) |
| Balkans | Evgeni Ignatov (Bul) | Elena Fidatov (Rom) |
| European Clubs Cup | Alberto Cova (Ita) | Angela Tooby (Wal) |
| European Team | Sporting Club Lisbon (Por) | Dublin City (Ire) |
| South American Confederation | | |
| Cup | Omar Aguilar (Chl) | Olga Cacaviello (Arg) |
| World Students | Stephen Moneghetti (Aus) | Anne Viallix (Fra) |

Where countries have national championships over more than one distance the winners of the event over c.10–12 km for men, or 5–8km for women are listed.

**Classic races**

| | | |
|---|---|---|
| Five Mills, Milan | Alberto Cova (Ita) | Lynn Jennings (USA) |
| Hannut | Vincent Rousseau (Bel) | Betty van Steenbroeck (Bel) |
| L'Equipe, Paris | Vincent Rousseau (Bel) | Annette Sergent (Fra) |
| Lidingo Loppet | Suleiman Nyambui (Tan) | Grete Waitz (Nor) |
| San Sebastian | Constantino Esparcia (Spa) | Jane Shields (UK) |
| Gateshead (Nov) | Tim Hutchings (UK) | Elizabeth Lynch (UK) |
| IAC, Cardiff (Dec) | Tim Hutchings (UK) | Kirsty Wade (UK) |

The World Cross-Country champions of 1986.
John Ngugi (top left), Zola Budd (top right),
Melese Feyisa. *All Mark Shearman*

# COMMONWEALTH GAMES
## Edinburgh, 26 July – 2 August

BY PETER MATTHEWS

The XIII Commonwealth Games were marred by a boycott by 32 Commonwealth nations, as 26 took part. The pretext for this boycott was the failure of the British government to impose economic sanctions on South Africa. This was an issue far removed from the Scottish capital, and once again competitors from the boycotting countries were the ones to suffer, just as they had been in the Olympic boycotts of recent years. Edinburgh again staged a fine Games, as it had in 1970. As then, however, the weather was pretty awful, with strong winds and rain on many of the days.

While there was much outstanding action, the effect of the boycott was the severe lack of depth. Steve Cram swept majestically to victory twice, with a fast time in the 800 metres, and in a very slow overall time, but with a 51.3 last lap, in the 1500 metres. In the latter John Gladwin led Cram by at least 20 metres just prior to the bell, but few who had followed Cram throughout the Games believed anything other than that victory was inevitable, as indeed it proved. Sadly Cram's expected clashes with Seb Coe did not occur, as Coe had to withdraw after the 800m semi-finals due to a throat infection.

Daley Thompson was again too good for the rest as he won his third Commonwealth decathlon title, and Ben Johnson displayed his form as the world's fastest man. Two Commonwealth records were set, both in the women's distance races, from Liz Lynch, who won Scotland's one gold medal, in the 10000 metres, and from Lisa Martin, who led from start to finish in the marathon. Emulating Cram in winning twice were Kirsty Wade, with the first ever women's 800m/1500m double, Gael

Mulhall at shot and discus, and Debbie Flintoff at 400m and 400mh. The latter won a third medal at 4x400m relay. Although below form Kathy Cook gained the most medals, with a gold (her third at 4x100m) and a silver from the relays, and individual silver and bronze. That took her overall Commonwealth medal haul (1978–86) to seven, third equal best ever, a feat matched by 100m champion Angella Issajenko, who added three medals to the four she had won in 1982. Issajenko had won at 100m in Brisbane, from where there were eight repeat winners. Steve Ovett returned from his illness problems to lead an English 1–2–3 at 5000m and become the first man to win major titles at 800m, 1500m and 5000m.

The effect of the wind was shown by the times in the men's 400 metres, won brilliantly by Roger Black. At the time I estimated his 45.57 to be worth a second faster in good conditions, and indeed he demonstrated that speed a month later in Stuttgart. Fortunately the weather was kind for the marathons, with a gentle breeze, very atypical for Edinburgh. In the field the best competitions were the two high jumps, and notable duels in the women's shot and javelin, at which the 1978 champions, Gael Martin and Tessa Sanderson, regained their titles. In the latter Fatima Whitbread was distraught at her loss to her arch-rival. The narrowest victory margin must be the four points by which Judy Simpson won the heptathlon. She trailed Jane Flemming by 23 points before the final event, but bravely struck out to win, running 2:13.72 (after a 64.81 first lap) for 800 metres to 2:15.63 for Flemming, who would have needed 2:15.3 to win.

| Medal table | | | | | | | |
| --- | --- | --- | --- | --- | --- | --- | --- |
| Nation | 1st | 2nd | 3rd | Nation | 1st | 2nd | 3rd |
| England | 18 | 18 | 11 | Scotland | 1 | 2 | 3 |
| Canada | 10 | 9 | 9 | Northern Ireland | 1 | 2 | 1 |
| Australia | 9 | 5 | 12 | New Zealand | 0 | 2 | 2 |
| Wales | 2 | 3 | 3 | | | | |

## Medal winners

MEN
100m: (+1.6)
   1. Ben Johnson (Can) 10.07 GBP (legal)
   2. Linford Christie (Eng) 10.28
   3. Mike McFarlane (Eng) 10.35
200m: (+2.2)
   1. Atlee Mahorn (Can) 20.31w
2. Todd Bennett (Eng) 20.54w
   3. Ben Johnson (Can) 20.64w
400m:
   1. Roger Black (Eng) 45.57
   2. Darren Clark (Aus) 45.57
   3. Phil Brown (Eng) 46.80
800m:
   1. Steve Cram (Eng) 1:43.22 GBP
   2. Tom McKean (Sco) 1:44.80
   3. Peter Elliott (Eng) 1:45.42
1500m:
   1. Steve Cram (Eng) 3:50.87
   2. John Gladwin (Eng) 3:52.17
   3. Dave Campbell (Can) 3:54.06
5000m:
   1. Steve Ovett (Eng) 13:24.11
   2. Jack Buckner (Eng) 13:25.87
   3. Tim Hutchings (Eng) 13:26.84
10000m:
   1. Jonathan Solly (Eng) 27:57.42
   2. Steve Binns (Eng) 27:58.01
   3. Steve Jones (Wal) 28:02.48
Marathon:
   1. Rob de Castella (Aus) 2:10:15
   2. Dave Edge (Can) 2:11:08
   3. Steve Moneghetti (Aus) 2:11:18
3000mSt:
   1. Graeme Fell (Can) 8:24.49
   2. Roger Hackney (Wal) 8:25.15
   3. Colin Reitz (Eng) 8:26.14
110mh:
   1. Mark McKoy (Can) 13.31w GBP
   2. Colin Jackson (Wal) 13.42
   3. Don Wright (Aus) 13.64
400mh:
   1. Phil Beattie (NI) 49.60
   2. Max Robertson (Eng) 49.77
   3. John Graham (Can) 50.25
HJ:
   1. Milt Ottey (Can) 2.30
   2. Geoff Parsons (Sco) 2.28

   3= Alain Metellus (Can) 2.14
   3= Henderson Pierre (Eng) 2.14
PV:
   1. Andrew Ashurst (Eng) 5.30 GBP
   2. Bob Ferguson (Can) 5.20
   3. Neil Honey (Aus) 5.20
LJ:
   1. Gary Honey (Aus) 8.08
   2. Fred Salle (Eng) 7.83
   3. Kyle McDuffie (Can) 7.79w
TJ:
   1. John Herbert (Eng) 17.27w
   2. Michael Makin (Eng) 16.87 GBP (legal)
   3. Peter Beames (Aus) 16.42
SP:
   1. Billy Cole (Eng) 18.16
   2. Joe Quigley (Aus) 17.97
   3. Stuart Gyngell (Aus) 17.70
DT:
   1. Ray Lazdins (Can) 58.86
   2. Paul Nandapi (Aus) 57.74
   3. Werner Reiterer (Aus) 57.34
HT:
   1. David Smith (Eng) 74.06
   2. Martin Girvan (NI) 70.48
   3. Phil Spivey (Aus) 70.30
JT:
   1. David Ottley (Eng) 80.62 GBP (new
javelin)
   2. Michael Hill (Eng) 78.56
   3. Gavin Lovegrove (NZ) 76.22
Dec:
   1. Daley Thompson 8663 GBP
   2. Dave Steen (Can) 8173
   3. Simon Poelman (NZ) 8015
4x100mR:
   1. Canada 39.15 =GBP
   2. England 39.19
   3. Scotland 40.41
4x400mR:
   1. England 3:07.19
   2. Australia 3:07.81
   3. Canada 3:08.69
30km walk:
   1. Simon Baker (Aus) 2:07:47 GBP
   2. Guillaume Leblanc (Can) 2:08:38
   3. Ian McCombie (Eng) 2:10:36

WOMEN

100m: (+2.3)
1. Heather Oakes (Eng) 11.20w
2. Paula Dunn (Eng) 11.21
3. Angella Issajenko (Can) 11.21

200m: (+2.1)
1. Angella Issajenko (Can) 22.91w
2. Kathy Cook (Eng) 23.18w
3. Sandra Whittaker (Sco) 23.46w

400m:
1. Debbie Flintoff (Aus) 51.29
2. Jillian Richardson (Can) 51.62
3. Kathy Cook (Eng) 51.88

800m:
1. Kirsty Wade (Wal) 2:00.94 GBP
2. Diane Edwards (Eng) 2:01.12
3. Lorraine Baker (Eng) 2:01.79

1500m:
1. Kirsty Wade (Wal) 4:10.91
2. Debbie Bowker (Can) 4:11.94
3. Lynn Williams (Can) 4:12.66

3000m:
1. Lynn Williams (Can) 8:54.29
2. Debbie Bowker (Can) 8:54.83
3. Yvonne Murray (Sco) 8:55.32

10000m:
1. Elizabeth Lynch (Sco) 31:41.42 CR
2. Anne Audain (NZ) 31:53.31
3. Angela Tooby (Wal) 32:25.38

Marathon:
1. Lisa Martin (Aus) 2:26:07 CR
2. Lorraine Moller (NZ) 2:28:17
3. Odette Lapierre (Can) 2:31:48

100mh: (−1.2)
1. Sally Gunnell (Eng) 13.29
2. Wendy Jeal (Eng) 13.41
3. Glynis Nunn (Aus) 13.44

400mh:
1. Debbie Flintoff (Aus) 54.94 GBP
2. Donalda Duprey (Can) 56.55
3. Jenny Laurendet (Aus) 56.57

HJ:
1. Christine Stanton (Aus) 1.92
2. Sharon McPeake (NI) 1.90
3. Janet Boyle (NI) 1.90

LJ:
1. Joyce Oladapo (Eng) 6.43
2. Mary Berkeley (Eng) 6.40
3. Robyn Lorraway (Aus) 6.35

SP:
1. Gael Martin (Aus) 19.00 GBP
2. Judy Oakes (Eng) 18.75
3. Myrtle Augee (Eng) 17.52

DT:
1. Gael Martin (Aus) 56.42
2. Venissa Head (Wal) 56.20
3. Karen Pugh (Eng) 54.72

JT:
1. Tessa Sanderson (Eng) 69.80 GBP
2. Fatima Whitbread (Eng) 68.54
3. Sue Howland (Aus) 64.74

Hep:
1. Judy Simpson (Eng) 6282w GBP
2. Jane Flemming (Aus) 6278w
3. Kim Hagger (Eng) 5823w

4x100mR:
1. England 43.39
2. Canada 43.83
3. Wales 45.37

4x400mR:
1. Canada 3:28.92
2. England 3:32.82
3. Australia 3:32.86

CR – Commonwealth record; GBP – Games best performance

Commonwealth Games, women's 200 metres. Angella Issajenko (214) wins from Kathy Cook (278) and Sandra Whittaker (707). *Mark Shearman*

# EUROPEAN CHAMPIONSHIPS 1986

## Stuttgart 26–31 August

### BY PETER MATTHEWS

Keenly anticipated, these were splendid championships, fully living up to such anticipation. Indeed, seasoned track fans were so enthused by the standard of competition that there was much conjecture about how they fared with great meetings of the past. Certainly, free of the political pressures that have so beset recent Olympic Games, it was the best meeting since the 1983 World Championships in Helsinki.

The weather was the one really disappointing feature, cool and wet throughout, most untypical for the area at this time of year. Yet despite that four world records were set, two in the women's track events, from Heike Drechsler at 200 metres and Marina Stepanova at 400m hurdles, and two in the field, men's hammer from Yuriy Sedykh and women's javelin by Fatima Whitbread. Drechsler was the one double winner at individual events, as she won the long jump as decisively as she had the 200m. Including relays, other double gold medallists were the GDR super-stars Marlies Göhr and Marita Koch, who took their tallies of European gold medals to seven and six respectively. They both completed a hat-trick of titles at one event, Göhr at 100m and Koch at 400m, a feat emulated by Harald Schmid at 400m hurdles. With 4 x 400m relay golds in 1978 and 1982 as well, Schmid now has the men's record total of five European gold medals.

There was, above all, great competition. Never before has there been such a standard of hammer throwing as in the duel between Sedykh and Sergey Litvinov; there were the Seb Coe and Steve Cram battles at the middle distances, with each winning once, and Tom McKean stepping between them at 800 metres to ensure a unique British 1–2–3; and the decathlon and heptathlon competions, which kept spectators enthused through long days of intense excitement. Then there were supreme champions at events where the thrill came not from close rivalry, but in seeing a very great athlete show their skill and authority; athletes like Ingrid Kristiansen, Marita Koch, Yordanka Donkova, Stefka Kostadinova, Robert Emmiyan and Sergey Bubka. The latter had a scare, needing three attempts at his opening

height, but came through supreme once again, just as Daley Thompson did at the decathlon. And there were exciting new talents like the youngest ever champion Maria Cruz Diaz, French hurdler Stèphan Caristan, who first equalled then broke Guy Drut's European record, and Roger Black, who had only been running the 400 metres for 18 months, but who now has six gold medals at major events.

A wonderful meeting to look back on, for both the exceptionally knowledgable and enthusiastic supporters in the Neckarstadion or the millions of television viewers who saw much of what is best about our sport.

## Events survey – Men

Listed are the first eight in each event together with brief comments.

## 100 metres

Christie was Britain's first European 100m champion since Jack Archer in 1946. European record holder Marian Woronin (Pol) pulled a leg muscle in his heat. Championship bests were set by Bringmann, 10.16 (+1.5 m/s) in the semis, and by Christie in the final. At 34 years 114 days Wells was the oldest ever finallist at the event (as he was two days later at 200m). (wind –0.1m/s)

1. Linford Christie (UK) 10.15 CBP
2. Steffen Bringmann (GDR) 10.20
3. Bruno Marie-Rose (Fra) 10.21
4. Thomas Schröder (GDR) 10.24
5. Allan Wells (UK) 10.24
6. Mike McFarlane (UK) 10.29
7. Attila Kovacs (Hun) 10.34
8. Viktor Bryzgin (SU) 10.38

## Analysis of places 1–8 by nation

| Nation | 1st | 2nd | 3rd | 4th | 5th | 6th | 7th | 8th |
|---|---|---|---|---|---|---|---|---|
| USSR | 11 | 13 | 12 | 4 | 6 | 11 | 6 | 5 |
| GDR | 11 | 10 | 8 | 9 | 6 | 5 | 6 | 2 |
| United Kingdom | 8 | 2 | 5 | 4 | 5 | 2 | 3 | 3 |
| Bulgaria | 3 | 4 | 1 | 5 | 2 | 1 | 2 | – |
| Italy | 2 | 6 | 2 | 2 | 3 | – | – | 2 |
| F.R. Germany | 2 | 4 | 5 | 5 | 3 | 4 | 3 | 5 |
| France | 1 | 1 | 2 | 2 | 1 | 3 | 5 | 8 |
| Spain | 1 | – | 2 | 1 | 2 | 3 | – | – |
| Portugal | 1 | – | – | 1 | 2 | – | – | 1 |
| Czechoslovakia | 1 | – | – | 1 | 2 | 3 | 1 | 3 |
| Norway | 1 | – | – | 1 | 1 | 1 | – | – |
| Switzerland | 1 | – | – | – | – | – | 2 | 1 |
| Sweden | – | 1 | 2 | 2 | – | 1 | 2 | 1 |
| Romania | – | 1 | 1 | 1 | 1 | 1 | 4 | 2 |
| Finland | – | 1 | – | 3 | 2 | 1 | 1 | – |
| Netherlands | – | – | 2 | 2 | – | 2 | 2 | – |
| Poland | – | – | 1 | – | 6 | 2 | 1 | 2 |
| Ireland | – | – | – | – | – | 2 | – | 1 |
| Belgium | – | – | – | – | 1 | – | 1 | 1 |
| Hungary | – | – | – | – | – | 1 | 1 | 2 |
| Yugoslavia | – | – | – | – | – | – | 3 | – |
| Greece | – | – | – | – | – | – | – | 1 |

Just three nations provided nearly three-quarters of the gold medallists, the usual top two of the USSR and GDR, being pressed by Britain, which had its best ever European Championships, displaying especially strength in men's track events. Bulgaria also had its best ever showing, and Italy, thanks to its distance runners, again fared well; but the FRG fell back and Poland, once a major European force, had its worst championships since 1950. Finland's medal count was its worst since 1966.

## 200 metres

Krylov, best known as a 400m runner, was perhaps the most surprising European champion of 1986. Todd Bennett (UK) pulled a muscle in his heat and Linford Christie was only fifth in his semi-final. (wind nil)

1. Vladimir Krylov (SU) 20.52
2. Jürgen Evers (FRG) 20.75
3. Andrey Fedoriv (SU) 20.84
4. Thomas Schröder (GDR) 20.89
5. Allan Wells (GB) 20.89
6. Aleksandr Yevgenyev (SU) 20.91
7. Olaf Prenzler (GDR) 21.00
8. Frank Emmelmann (GDR) 21.03

## 400 metres

Roger Black, the sixth UK European 400m champion, set a national record to add another gold to his European Junior and Commonwealth titles,
won within two years of starting running seriously.

1. Roger Black (UK) 44.59 CBP
2. Thomas Schönlebe (GDR) 44.63
3. Mathias Schersing (GDR) 44.85
4. Derek Redmond (UK) 45.25
5. Ralf Lübke (FRG) 45.35
6. Antonio Sanchez (Spa) 45.41
7. Aldo Canti (Fra) 45.93
8. Erwin Skamrahl (FRG) 46.38

## 800 metres

Seb Coe at last won a major 800m title as he led the first European medal sweep ever by British athletes, and only the second ever at a men's track event. Coe had previously won bronze (1978) and silver (1982) in the European 800m. Braun led at 400m in 51.98, with Coe (52.7) following Cram at the back. Coe's last 200m took just 24.9 secs.

1. Sebastian Coe (UK) 1:44.50
2. Tom McKean (UK) 1:44.61

3. Steve Cram (UK) 1:44.88
4. Rob Druppers (Hol) 1:45.53
5. Ryszard Ostrowski (Pol) 1:45.54
6. Peter Braun (FRG) 1:45.83
7. Philippe Collard (Fra) 1:45.96
8. Viktor Kalinkin (SU) 1:47.36

## 1500 metres

In a slowly run final (1:03.85, 2:07.59, 3:03.21), Steve Cram retained his title and won his seventh major championships gold medal. Cram's last 400m was 50.9 and 800m 1:49.0. The British 1–2 was the first at the event since the Swedes in 1946. José Abascal (Spa) was a surprise casualty in the heats, when the fastest was Gladwin, whose 3:36.85 led six men under 3:38 in the third heat.

1. Steve Cram (UK) 3:41.09
2. Sebastian Coe (UK) 3:41.67
3. Han Kulker (Hol) 3:42.11
4. José Luis Gonzalez (Spa) 3:42.54
5. John Gladwin (UK) 3:42.57
6. Marcus O'Sullivan (Ire) 3:42.60
7. Johnny Kroon (Swe) 3:42.61
8. Frank O'Mara (Ire) 3:42.90

## 5000 metres

The first four were well inside the championship best. Leaders: 1000m Cova 2:39.04, 2000m Fernando Couto (Por) 5:19.72, 3000m: Leitao 7:58.97, 4000m: Hutchings 10:42.20. Buckner's last 400m was 56.22 and last 800m 1:56.7. Steve Ovett (UK), ill, dropped out before 3000m.

1. Jack Buckner (UK) 13:10.15 CBP
2. Stefano Mei (Ita) 13:11.57
3. Tim Hutchings (UK) 13:12.88
4. Evgeni Ignatov (Bul) 13:13.15
5. Antonio Leitao (Por) 13:17.67
6. Martti Vainio (Fin) 13:22.67
7. Pierre Délèze (Swi) 13:28.80
8. Alberto Cova (Ita) 13:35.86

## 10,000 metres

The Italian 1–2–3 was the first ever European clean sweep at a men's track event. The arch-kicker Cova, for once was beaten at his own game, as Mei ran the last 400m in 55.3 (26.3 last 200m) to Cova's 56.8. A straight final, the early pace was slow, as Vainio led at 5000m in 14:13.74. Vainio made the first major move at 8000m, and Mei's time for the last 2000m was 5:16.10. Hansjörg Kunze (GDR), fastest European of the year, dropped out after 6000m.

1. Stefano Mei (Ita) 27:56.79
2. Alberto Cova (Ita) 27:57.93
3. Salvatore Antibo (Ita) 28:00.25
4. Mats Erixon (Swe) 28:01.50
5. Domingos Castro (Por) 28:01.62
6. John Treacy (Ire) 28:04.10
7. Martti Vainio (Fin) 28:08.72
8. Jean-Louis Prianon (Fra) 28:12.29

The European 110m hurdles final: (l-r:) Nigel Walker, Carlos Sala, Stéphane Caristan, Andreas Oschkenat, Liviu Giurgean. *ASP*

6. Gerard Nijboer (Hol) 2:12:46
7. Jacques Lefrand (Fra) 2:12:53
8. Antoni Niemczak (Pol) 2:13:04

## 3000m steeplechase

Panetta made a brave bid to run away from the field. Only Nikolay Matyuschenko (SU) went with him as he passed 1000m in 2:43.42; the Soviet fell and Panetta was 40m up at 2000m (5:30.54). He was caught by Melzer and Ilg at the last barrier, but rallied to pass Ilg, who added a bronze to his gold (1982) and silver (1978) medals. Boguslaw Maminski (Pol), the 1982 silver medallist, dropped out at the bell.

1. Hagen Melzer (GDR) 8:16.65
2. Francesco Panetta (Ita) 8:16.85
3. Patriz Ilg (FRG) 8:16.92
4. Colin Reitz (UK) 8:18.12
5. William van Dijck (Bel) 8:20.19
6. Joseph Mahmoud (Fra) 8:20.25
7. Rainer Schwarz (FRG) 8:20.90
8. Roger Hackney (UK) 8:20.97

## 110 metres hurdles

In his semi-final (wind +0.9) Caristan equalled the European record of 13.28 that his countryman Guy Drut had set in 1975. He improved further with another fluent run in the final. Bryggare added a silver to his previous two bronze medals. Andrey Prokofyev (SU), who had equalled the European record of 13.28 earlier in the year, was sixth in his heat in 14.06. (wind +2.0m/s)

1. Stéphane Caristan (Fra) 13.20 ER
2. Arto Bryggare (Fin) 13.42
3. Carlos Sala (Spa) 13.50
4. Nigel Walker (UK) 13.52
5. Andreas Oschkenat (GDR) 13.55
6. Jonathan Ridgeon (UK) 13.70
7. Liviu Giurgean (Rom) 13.71
8. György Bakos (Hun) 13.84

Stefano Mei beats Alberto Cova at 10 000 metres. *ASP*

## Marathon

Italian distance success continued with a marathon 1–2. Steve Jones (UK) led by nearly a minute at 10km (30:11) and two minutes at 20km (1:00:00), but was back to a minute up at 30km (1:31:49) and, slowing drastically, suffering from dehydration, was passed soon afterwards; he struggled on to finish 20th in 2:22:12.

1. Gelindo Bordin (Ita) 2:10:54 CBP
2. Orlando Pizzolato (Ita) 2:10:57
3. Herbert Steffny (FRG) 2:11:30
4. Ralf Salzmann (FRG) 2:11:41
5. Hugh Jones (UK) 2:11:49

## 400 metres hurdles

Harald Schmid completed a hat-trick of titles, a record for the event. With two relay golds he also has a men's record five gold medals.

1. Harald Schmid (FRG) 48.65
2. Aleksandr Vasilyev (SU) 48.76
3. Sven Nylander (Swe) 49.38
4. Toma Tomov (Bul) 49.62
5. Tagir Zemskov (SU) 50.02

6. José Alonso (Spa) 50.30
7. Rik Tommelein (Bel) 50.45
8. Thanassis Kalogiannis (Gre) 51.83

## High jump

The world record holder, Paklin, jumped clear at 2.21, 2.25 and 2.31 before sealing victory with 2.34 on the third attempt. The others needed three attempts at 2.31, and Thränhardt won his first outdoor championships medal in a ten-year career amongst Europe's best.

1. Igor Paklin (SU) 2.34 CBP
2. Sergey Malchenko (SU) 2.31
3. Carlo Thränhardt (FRG) 2.31
4. Dietmar Mögenburg (FRG) 2.28
5. Krzysztof Krawczyk (Pol) 2.28
6. Patrik Sjöberg (Swe) 2.25
7= Gerd Wessig (GDR) 2.25
7= Eugen Popescu (Rom) 2.25

## Pole vault

Sergey Bubka had an alarm, when he only cleared his opening height of 5.70 on his third attempt, but then went over 5.85 first time before attempting a world record 6.05m. Vasiliy's silver medal gave the Bubka brothers a unique European 1–2. Pouring rain held up the event for 20 minutes when the bar was at 5.65m. Thierry Vigneron (Fra) failed to clear a height in the final, jumping twice at 5.65 and once at 5.70, as did Rodion Gataullin (USSR) in the qualifying round (at 5.50).

1. Sergey Bubka (SU) 5.85 CBP
2. Vasiliy Bubka (SU) 5.75
3. Philippe Collet (Fra) 5.75
4. Atanas Tarev (Bul) 5.70
5. Kimmo Kuusela (Fin) 5.55
6. Zdenek Lubensky (Cs) 5.55
7. Stanimir Penchev (Bul) 5.55
8. Serge Ferreira (Fra) 5.35

## Long jump

Emmiyan was in a class of his own: 8.24 in qualifying, and a final series of 8.29, 8.41, N, N, N, 8.04. His 40cm margin over Layevskiy was the greatest ever for the event at European Championships.

1. Robert Emmiyan (SU) 8.41 CBP
2. Sergey Layevskiy (SU) 8.01
3. Giovanni Evangelisti (Ita) 7.92
4. Emiel Mellaard (Hol) 7.91

5. Stanislaw Jaskulka (Pol) 7.85
6. Norbert Brige (Fra) 7.72
7. Ivo Krsek (Cs) 7.69
8. Zdenek Hanacek (Cs) 7.59.

## Triple jump

Markov's winning jump (+1.9 m/s) came in the first round; he followed it with 17.30, 17.35, 15.80, 17.34, 17.47. The 1985 European Cup winner, John Herbert (UK), failed to qualify with 16.32m.

1. Khristo Markov (Bul) 17.66 CBP
2. Maris Bruzhiks (SU) 17.33
3. Oleg Protsenko (SU) 17.28w
4. Georgi Pomashki (Bul) 16.99
5. Dirk Gamlin (GDR) 16.89
6. Nikolay Musiyenko (SU) 16.86
7. Volker Mai (GDR) 16.74
8. Didier Falise (Bel) 16.74

## Shot

Günthör became the first Swiss to win a medal in a throwing event at the European Championships. His 22.22 came in the second round and added 56cm to his national record. His series: 21.58, 22.22, 21.62, N, 21.24, N; Timmermann's 20.89, 20.02, 21.84, 21.45, 20.57, 21.43. Beyer is the first triple medallist in the event; he had won in 1978 and 1982, and was eighth in 1974. Sergey Smirnov (SU) qualified but did not contest the final.

1. Werner Günthör (Swi) 22.22 CBP
2. Ulf Timmermann (GDR) 21.84
3. Udo Beyer (GDR) 20.74
4. Alessandro Andrei (Ita) 20.73
5. Lars Arvid Nilsen (Nor) 20.52
6. Karsten Stolz (FRG) 19.89
7. Vladimir Milic (Yug) 19.85
8. Udo Gelhausen (FRG) 19.76

## Discus

The Soviet 1–2–3 was the ninth in European Championships history; GDR did it in the discus in 1966. Ubartas and Kidikas were competing in their first major championships. Ubartas's series: 65.14, 65.38, 66.12, N, 67.08, N; each of his valid throws took the lead, also held at various times by the next three men.

1. Romas Ubartas (SU) 67.08
2. Georgiy Kolnootchenko (SU) 67.02
3. Vaclavas Kidikas (SU) 66.32
4. Knut Hjeltnes (Nor) 65.60
5. Gejza Valent (Cs) 65.00

6. Erik De Bruin (Hol) 64.52
7. Jürgen Schult (GDR) 64.38
8. Imrich Bugar (Cs) 63.56

## Hammer

Sedykh improved the championship best to 82.90 in the qualifying round, then to 83.94 in the first round, only for Litvinov to respond with 85.74. Sedykh then produced the finest series ever: 85.28, 85.46, 86.74, 86.68, 86.62. His fourth throw was his sixth world record. It won him his third successive European title. The first nine neatly comprised three each from USSR (the same trio as in 1982, with Litvinov and Nikulin swapping places), GDR and FRG. Litvinov's effort was the best ever non-winning throw, and there were also best evers for places 4, 5, 7 and 8.

1. Yuriy Sedykh (SU) 86.74 WR
2. Sergey Litvinov (SU) 85.74
3. Igor Nikulin (SU) 82.00
4. Gunther Rodehau (GDR) 79.84
5. Jörg Schaefer (FRG) 79.68
6. Ralf Haber (GDR) 78.74
7. Mathias Moder (GDR) 78.70
8. Christoph Sahner (FRG) 77.12

## Javelin

Tafelmeier's third round throw was a European best with the new javelin. He had also led the qualifiers with 82.68, but Gerald Weiss (GDR) 81.40 and Marek Kaleta (SU) 81.32 were unable to reproduce their qualifying throws.

1. Klaus Tafelmeier (FRG) 84.76 ER
2. Detlef Michel (GDR) 81.90
3. Viktor Yevsyukov (SU) 81.80
4. Jyrki Blom (Fin) 80.48
5. Heino Puuste (SU) 80.34
6. Wolfram Gambke (FRG) 79.88
7. Sejad Krdzalic (Yug) 79.50
8. Michael Hill (UK) 77.34

## Decathlon

The 1–2–3 was the same as in the 1983 World Championships and 1984 Olympics, but both the Germans fought brilliantly against Thompson, who once again proved invincible, beating Hingsen for the eighth time in eight encounters and winning his ninth championship gold medal. Thompson started with a world decathlon best of 10.26 for 100m. Hingsen led after four events and after seven, the rest was Thompson. Guido

Kratschmer (FRG) had to withdraw after pulling a muscle in the long jump.

1. Daley Thompson (UK) 8811 CBP
2. Jürgen Hingsen (FRG) 8730
3. Siegfried Wentz (FRG) 8676
4. Torsten Voss (GDR) 8450
5. Aleksandr Apaychev (SU) 8199
6. Uwe Freimuth (GDR) 8197
7. Christian Plaziat (Fra) 8196
8. Alain Blondel (Fra) 8185

## 20km walk

The 5km splits for the leaders were: 21:25 Damilano, 41:37 Mostovik, 1:01:50 Pribilinec. After silver medals at the 1982 European and 1983 World, Pribilinec just held off the 1980 Olympic champion for his first gold medal.

1. Jozef Pribilinec (Cs) 1:21:15 CBP
2. Maurizio Damilano (Ita) 1:21:17
3. Miguel Prieto (Spa) 1:21:36
4. Viktor Mostovik (SU) 1:21:52
5. Walter Arena (Ita) 1:22:42
6. Pavol Blazek (Cs) 1:23:26
7. Aleksey Pershin (SU) 1:24:11
8. Aleksandr Bolarschinov (SU) 1:24:16

## 50km walk

In ninth place at 3:52:12 Jorge Llopart (Spa) was inside the championship best that he had set in 1978. 10km splits were: 45:53, 1:29:44, 2:13:43, 2:57:21. The leading four were together for the first 30km, but at 40km Ivanchenko had a 20 second lead over Gauder, who finished strongly. The world's fastest, Ronald Weigel (GDR), was disqualified.

1. Hartwig Gauder (GDR) 3:40:55 CBP
2. Vyacheslav Ivanchenko (SU) 3:41:54
3. Valeriy Suntsov (SU) 3:42:38
4. Sergey Protsishin (SU) 3:45:51
5. Reima Salonen (Fin) 3:46:14
6. Dietmar Meisch (GDR) 3:48:01
7. Bo Gustafsson (Swe) 3:50:13
8. Pavol Szikora (Cs) 3:51:35

## 4 x 100 metres relay

Just one team was eliminated from the heats: the West Germans who were disqualified. The well-drilled Soviet team of Aleksandr Yevgenyev, Nikolay Yushmanov, Vladimir Muravyov and Viktor Bryzgin won clearly, as Linford Christie (UK) ran the fastest final 100m, 9.14.

l-r: Derek Redmond, Brian Whittle, Roger Black and Kriss Akabusi. *Mark Shearman*

1. USSR 38.29 CBP
2. GDR 38.64
3. UK 38.71
4. France 38.81
5. Italy 38.86
6. Hungary 39.15
7. Bulgaria 39.33
8. Portugal 39.74

## 4 x 400 metres relay

Having lost two of their stalwarts, Todd Bennett and Phil Brown through injury, the British team ran brilliantly: Derek Redmond 45.45, Kriss Akabusi 45.35, Brian Whittle (on one shoe!) 45.09 and Roger Black 43.95. The latter made it six gold medals out of six in the three major championships he has contested in just a week over one year. Harald Schmid (FRG) took the lead with a 44.5 third leg and gained his record-equalling sixth European medal.

1. UK 2:59.84 CBP
2. FRG 3:00.17
3. USSR 3:00.47
4. Italy 3:01.37
5. Spain 3:04.12
6. GDR 3:04.87
7. Yugoslavia 3:05.27
8. France 3:10.17

## Events survey – Women

## 100 metres

Göhr won her third successive European 100m title, improving her championship best twice, first with a 10.98 semi. Behind her Nuneva and Cooman both set national records. (wind +0.8m/s)

1. Marlies Göhr (GDR) 10.91 CBP
2. Anelia Nuneva (Bul) 11.04
3. Nelli Cooman (Hol) 11.08
4. Silke Gladisch (GDR) 11.09
5. Ingrid Auerswald (GDR) 11.11
6. Olga Zolotaryeva (SU) 11.23
7. Paula Dunn (UK) 11.25
8. Heide-Elke Gaugel (FRG) 11.26

## 200 metres

Heike Drechsler won her second gold medal of the championships, and ran the fourth 21.71 WR, following her own two months earlier and the two by Koch. This must be rated the best, into the wind, and on a cold, wet day. Cazier set French records in both semi (22.45 behind Gladisch 22.29) and final. (wind –0.8m/s)

1. Heike Drechsler (GDR) 21.71 WR
2. Marie-Christine Cazier (Fra) 22.32
3. Silke Gladisch (GDR) 22.49
4. Marina Molokova (SU) 22.71
5. Ewa Kasprzyk (Pol) 22.73
6. Natalya Bochina (SU) 22.87
7. Sabine Günther (GDR) 22.98
8. Marina Zhirova (SU) 23.18

Annette Sergent (216) is the early leader in the European 3000m, from Zola Budd (283) and Olga Bondarenko, with Yvonne Murray (301) and Maricica Puica (644) following. *ASP*

## 400 metres

The incomparable Marita Koch won her third successive title, and (just) by her biggest margin. In just her second 400m final of the year she smashed the field with a 22.8 first 200m and ended with the fifth fastest ever, a fantastic run in pouring rain.

1. Marita Koch (GDR) 48.22
2. Olga Vladykina (SU) 49.67
3. Petra Müller (GDR) 49.88
4. Kirsten Emmelmann (GDR) 50.43
5. Ute Thimm (FRG) 51.15
6. Tatana Kocembova (Cs) 51.50
7. Fabienne Ficher (Fra) 51.91
8. Karin Lix (FRG) 52.89

## 800 metres

The 1980 Olympic champion returned to add a European title. Kiryukhina led at 400m in 56.17.

1. Nadezhda Olizarenko (SU) 1:57.15
2. Sigrun Wodars (GDR) 1:57.42
3. Lyubov Gurina (SU) 1:57.73
4. Gaby Bussmann (FRG) 1:58.57
5. Milena Strnadova (Cs) 1:58.89
6. Mitica Junghiatu (Rom) 1:59.22
7. Lyubov Kiryukhina (SU) 1:59.67
8. Christine Wachtel (GDR) 2:00.02

## 1500 metres

At 400m Heike Oehme (GDR) led in 1:07.43, then Zola Budd (UK) (9th 4:05.32) led though 800m in 2:15.80, the bell 3:02.3 and 1200m 3:17.92, but Agletdinova kicked away and ran a 58.9 last lap to Samolenko's 60.1.

1. Ravilya Agletdinova (SU) 4:01.19
2. Tatyana Samolenko (SU) 4:02.36
3. Doina Melinte (Rom) 4:02.44
4. Ivana Walterova (Cs) 4:03.09
5. Maricica Puica (Rom) 4:03.90
6. Svetlana Kitova (SU) 4:04.74
7. Kirsty Wade (UK) 4:04.99
8. Cornelia Bürki (Swi) 4:05.31

## 3000 metres

As in the 1500m Zola Budd (running in shoes this time) led, passing 1000m in 2:48.78 and 2000m in

The finish of the women's 800 metres: 1st Olizarenko (846), 2nd Wodars (116), 3rd Gurina (831). *ASP*

5:45.09, until the bell, then Bondarenko pounced to run 64.1 for the last lap and ended with a pb. Puica ran just 0.04 faster than when she had won Olympic gold, and Yvonne Murray improved her pre-meeting pb of 8:55.32, first to 8:49.56 in the semi and then by a further 12 seconds.

1. Olga Bondarenko (SU) 8:33.99
2. Maricica Puica (Rom) 8:35.92
3. Yvonne Murray (UK) 8:37.15
4. Zola Budd (UK) 8:38.20
5. Tatyana Samolenko (SU) 8:40.35
6. Yelena Zhupiyeva (SU) 8:40.74
7. Cornelia Bürki (Swi) 8:44.44
8. Annette Sergent (Fra) 8:47.52

## 10000 metres

In this new event, Kristiansen ran away from the field from the second lap. She ran with metronomic brilliance, passing 3000m in 9:02.93 and 5000m in 15:07.76 (when she led by 33.12 sec). Behind her were the best ever marks for each place and eight national records from the 27 finishers. One of those records was by Bruns, who won her first European medal in her fourth championships.

1. Ingrid Kristiansen (Nor) 30:23.25 CBP
2. Olga Bondarenko (SU) 30:57.21
3. Ulrike Bruns (GDR) 31:19.76
4. Aurora Cunha (Por) 31:39.35
5. Svetlana Guskova (SU) 31:42.43
6. Yelena Zhupiyeva (SU) 31:42.99
7. Elizabeth Lynch (UK) 31:49.46
8. Karolina Szabo (Hun) 31:55.93

## Marathon

The first two were the same as in 1982, Mota leading from 10km. Beurskens was in the first three most of the way, but had to make three stops. 23 finished, one who did not was Katrin Dörre (GDR).

1. Rosa Mota (Por) 2:28:38
2. Laura Fogli (Ita) 2:32:52
3. Yekaterina Khramenkova (SU) 2:34:18
4. Sinikka Keskitalo (Fin) 2:34:31
5. Jocelyne Villeton (Fra) 2:35:17
6. Bente Moe (Nor) 2:35:34
7. Carla Beurskens (Hol) 2:39:05
8. Paola Moro (Ita) 2:39:19

Marina Stepanova (l) leads Sabine Busch (r) in the European 400m hurdles. *Mark Shearman*

## 100 metres hurdles

Despite the wet track and a headwind, Donkova's winning time has only been bettered five times (four by herself). This was the sixth successive Eastern European medal sweep at the event. (wind −0.7m/s)

1. Yordanka Donkova (Bul) 12.38 CBP
2. Cornelia Oschkenat (GDR) 12.55
3. Ginka Zagorcheva (Bul) 12.70
4. Heike Theele (GDR) 12.82
5. Kerstin Knabe (GDR) 12.82
6. Laurence Elloy (Fra) 12.93
7. Natalya Grigoryeva (SU) 12.96
8. Mihaela Pogacian (Rom) 13.17

## 400 metres hurdles

At 36 years 121 days Stepanova became the oldest ever women's world record breaker, as she regained the record she had held at 54.78 in 1979. Stepanova also set a championship best in her semi to beat Busch 53.83 to 53.97. Defending champion Skoglund improved her national record. It was the highest standard ever, with bests for each position except sixth.

1. Marina Stepanova (SU) 53.32 WR
2. Sabine Busch (GDR) 53.60
3. Cornelia Feuerbach (GDR) 54.13
4. Ann-Louise Skoglund (Swe) 54.15
5. Genowefa Blaszak (Pol) 54.74
6. Ellen Fiedler (GDR) 54.90
7. Christeana Matei (Rom) 55.23
8. Margarita Khromova (SU) 55.56

## High jump

Kostadinova cleared 1.96 on her second attempt and 2.00 on her third, before going out at 2.04, fine jumping in the rain. Former world record holders Sara Simeoni (Ita) and Tamara Bykova (SU) managed only 1.86 and did not qualify for the final.

1. Stefka Kostadinova (Bul) 2.00
2. Svetlana Issaeva (Bul) 1.93
3. Olga Turchak (SU) 1.93
4= Andrea Bienias (GDR) 1.90
4= Susanne Helm (GDR) 1.90
6. Heike Redetzky (FRG) 1.90
7. Danuta Bulkowska (Pol) 1.90
8. Diana Davies (UK) 1.87

## Long jump

Drechsler had four jumps better than the runner-up; her series 6.97, 7.27, 7.17, 7.05, 7.25, 7.14.

1. Heike Drechsler (GDR) 7.27 CBP
2. Galina Chistyakova (SU) 7.09
3. Helga Radtke (GDR) 6.89
4. Vali Ionescu (Rom) 6.81
5. Lyudmila Ninova (Bul) 6.65
6. Silvia Khristova (Bul) 6.61
7. Yelena Byelevskaya (SU) 6.58
8. Nadine Fourcade (Fra) 6.52

Heidi Krieger. *Mark Shearman*

## Shot

Krieger, the 1983 European Junior champion, improved her pb by 39cm in the first round, and also had a 21.03 in the fifth. Losch just missed being the first Western medallist since 1958. Way below form in the rainy conditions at ninth (18.95) and tenth (18.48) were the world record setters Natalya Lisovskaya (SU) and Helena Fibingerova (Cs), who equalled the record by competing at her sixth European championships.

1. Heidi Krieger (GDR) 21.10
2. Ines Müller (GDR) 20.81
3. Natalya Akhrimenko (SU) 20.54
4. Claudia Losch (FRG) 20.54
5. Heike Hartwig (GDR) 20.14
6. Nunu Abashidze (SU) 19.99
7. Iris Plotzitzka (FRG) 19.26
8. Mihaela Loghin (Rom) 19.15

## Discus

The first eight were all from Eastern Europe, as they had been in 1978 and 1982. Sachse's series: 59.84, 68.34, 67.60, 67.00, 70.54, 71.36. Khristova led after three rounds.

1. Diana Sachse (GDR) 71.36 CBP
2. Tsvetanka Khristova (Bul) 69.52
3. Martina Hellmann (GDR) 68.26
4. Irina Meszynski (GDR) 65.20
5. Svetla Mitkova (Bul) 63.98
6. Galina Yermakova (SU) 63.20
7. Daniela Costian (Rom) 61.42
8. Renata Katewicz (Pol) 58.36

## Javelin

At 9.18am, in the qualifying round Fatima Whitbread smashed the world record with 77.44. Felke qualified with 72.62 and led the final for three rounds. With the competition won, Whitbread's last throw was the second best ever, and was Britain's first European gold medal at a women's throwing event. Series for Whitbread: 66.66, N, 71.94, 72.68, N, 76.32; Felke: 68.54, 72.00, 69.60, 62.00, 70.34, 72.52, the last was the best ever non-winning mark.

1. Fatima Whitbread (UK) 76.32
2. Petra Felke (GDR) 72.52
3. Beate Peters (FRG) 68.04
4. Tiina Lillak (Fin) 66.66
5. Genowefa Olejarz (Pol) 63.34
6. Natalya Yermolovich (SU) 62.84
7. Ingrid Thyssen (FRG) 62.42
8. Irina Kostyuchenkova (SU) 61.40

## Heptathlon

Simpson set five pbs and added 276 points to her British record. She led after each of the first six events, but Behmer, a much stronger second day athlete, whittled back her lead, setting pbs at 100mh and JT, and ran 800m in 2:03.96 to 2:04.40 for Shubenkova and 2:11.70 for Simpson.

1. Anke Behmer (GDR) 6717 CBP
2. Natalya Shubenkova (SU) 6645
3. Judy Simpson (UK) 6623
4. Birgit Dressel (FRG) 6487
5. Marianna Maslennikova (SU) 6396
6. Malgorzata Nowak (Pol) 6352
7. Valda Ruskite (SU) 6331
8. Chantal Beaugeant (Fra) 6221

## 4 x 100 metres relay

The GDR team of Silke Gladisch, Sabine Günther, Ingrid Auerswald and Marlies Göhr, the same as had set the world record in 1985, won easily. Günther and Göhr gaining their second gold at the event. That brought Göhr's overall tally at European Championships to seven (five gold, a silver and a bronze).

1. GDR 41.84 CBP
2. Bulgaria 42.68
3. USSR 42.74
4. France 43.11
5. UK 43.44
6. Poland 43.54
7. Netherlands 44.38
dq FRG

## 4 x 400 metres relay

The splits for the team that brought the GDR its fifth successive European title were: Kirsten Emmelmann 50.9, Sabine Busch 48.8, Petra Müller 49.0, Marita Koch 48.21. That was Koch's record sixth gold medal. The USSR crossed the line second in 3:22.71 but were disqualified.

1. GDR 3:16.87 CBP
2. GFR 3:22.80
3. Poland 3:24.65
4. Bulgaria 3:26.26
5. Italy 3:32.30
6. Spain 3:32.51
dq USSR

## 10,000 metres walk

The joint European Junior champion of 1985, Maria Cruz Diaz, was only fourth in the World Junior 5km, but made up for that disappointment. At 16 years 306 days she became the youngest ever European winner of an individual event. New event this year.

1. Maria Cruz Diaz (Spa) 46:09 CBP
2. Ann Jansson (Swe) 46:14
3. Siw Ybanez (Swe) 46:19
4. Yelena Rodionova (SU) 46:28
5. M.Reyes Sobrino (Spa) 46:35
6. Lidia Levandovskaya (SU) 46:36
7. Aleksandra Grigoryeva (USSR) 47:16
8. Monica Gunnarsson (Swe) 47:24

WR – world record,
ER – European record,
CBP – championship best

# WORLD JUNIOR CHAMPIONSHIPS 1986, *Athens, Greece 16–20 July*

**Medal table for leading nations**

| Nation | 1st | 2nd | 3rd |
|---|---|---|---|
| GDR | 8 | 4 | 7 |
| USSR | 6 | 6 | 7 |
| USA | 5 | 4 | 2 |
| Kenya | 4 | 4 | – |
| United Kingdom | 3 | 3 | 2 |

| Nation | 1st | 2nd | 3rd |
|---|---|---|---|
| Cuba | 3 | 3 | 1 |
| Nigeria | 2 | 2 | 1 |
| Bulgaria | 2 | 2 | 2 |
| Romania | 2 | 1 | 2 |

## MEN

100m: (+0.89)
1. Derrick Florence (USA) 10.17
2. Stanley Kerr (USA) 10.23
3. Jamie Henderson (UK) 10.34

200m: (+0.19)
1. Stanley Kerr (USA) 20.74
2. Derrick Florence (USA) 21.12
3. Steven McBain (Aus) 21.21

400m:
1. Miles Murphy (Aus) 45.64
2. Roberto Hernandez (Cub) 45.64
3. Edgar Itt (FRG) 45.72

800m:
1. David Sharpe (UK) 1:48.32
2. Manuel Balmaceda (Chl) 1:48.91
3. Andrey Sudnik (SU) 1:48.93

1500m:
1. Oanda Kirochi (Ken) 3:44.62
2. Peter Rono (Ken) 3:45.52
3. Johan Boakes (UK) 3:45.80

5000m:
1. Peter Chumba (Ken) 13:55.25
2. Alejandro Gomez (Spa) 13:55.94
3. Melese Feyisa (Eth) 13:56.45

10000m:
1. Peter Chumba (Ken) 28:44.00
2. Juma Munyampanda (Ken) 28:45.14
3. Debede Demisse (Eth) 28:49.09

20km Road:
1. Tadesse Gebre (Eth) 1:01.32
2. Juma Munyampanda (Ken) 1:01:45
3. Negash Dube (Eth) 1:04:23

2000mSt:
1. Juan Azkueta (Spa) 5:28.56
2. Johnstone Kipkoech (Ken) 5:29.56
3. Jens Volkmann (FRG) 5:29.60

110mh: (−0.80)
1. Colin Jackson (UK) 13.44
2. Jon Ridgeon (UK) 13.91
3. Emilio Valle (Cub) 14.00

400mh:
1. Emilio Valle (Cub) 50.02
2. Hiroshi Kakimori (Jap) 50.09
3. Pascal Maran (Fra) 50.39

HJ:
1. Javier Sotomayor (Cub) 2.25
2. Hollis Conway (USA) 2.22
3. Thomas Müller (GDR) 2.22

PV:
1. Igor Potapovich (SU) 5.50
2. Delko Lessev (Bul) 5.40
3. Mike Thiede (GDR) 5.30

LJ:
1. Dietmar Haaf (FRG) 7.93
2. Ivo Krsek (Cs) 7.87
3. Thomas Wolf (GDR) 7.77

TJ:
1. Igor Parigin (USSR) 16.97
2. Zdravko Dimitrov (Bul) 16.13
3. Du Benzhong (Chn) 16.00

SP:
1. Aleksey Lukashenko (SU) 18.90
2. Vyacheslav Lykho (SU) 18.71
3. Radoslav Despotov (Bul) 18.17

DT:
1. Vasil Baklarov (Bul) 60.60
2. Werner Reiterer (Aus) 58.64
3. Vasiliy Kaptyukh (SU) 58.22

HT:
1. Vitaliy Alissevich (SU) 72.00
2. Valeriy Gubkin (SU) 71.78
3. Sabin Khristov (Bul) 68.96

JT:
1. Vladimir Zasimovich (SU) 78.84
2. Mark Roberson (UK) 74.24
3. Gavin Lovegrove (NZ) 74.22

Dec:
1. Petri Keskitalo (Fin) 7623
2. Mike Smith (Can) 7523
3. Nikolay Zaiyats (SU) 7509

4x100mR:
1. United Kingdom 39.80
2. FR Germany 39.81
3. Poland 39.98

4x400mR:
1. USA 3:01.90
2. Cuba 3:04.22
3. Jamaica 3:05.16

10kmW:
1. Mikhail Shchennikov (SU) 40:38.01
2. Salvatore Cacia (Ita) 40:40.73
3. Ricardo Pueyo (Spa) 40:41.05

## WOMEN

**100m:** (+0.87)
1. Tina Iheagwan (Nig) 11.34
2. Caryl Smith (USA) 11.46
3. Maicel Malone (USA) 11.49

**200m:** (+0.58)
1. Falilat Ogunkoya (Nig) 23.11
2. Mary Onyali (Nig) 23.30
3. Katrin Krabbe (GDR) 23.31

**400m:**
1. Susanne Sieger (GDR) 52.02
2. Olga Pesnopevtseva (USSR) 52.17
3. Sandie Richards (Jam) 52.23

**800m:**
1. Selina Chirchir (Ken) 2:01.40
2. Gabriela Sedlakova (Cs) 2:01.49
3. Adriana Dumitru (Rom) 2:01.93

**1500m:**
1. Ana Padurean (Rom) 4:14.63
2. Selina Chirchir (Ken) 4:15.59
3. Snezana Pajkic (Yug) 4:16.03

**3000m:**
1. Cleopatra Palacian (Rom) 9:02.91
2. Philippa Mason (UK) 9:03.35
3. Dorina Calenic (Rom) 9:06.94

**10000m:**
1. Katrin Kley (GDR) 33:19.67
2. Norah Maraga (Ken) 33:57.99
3. Marleen Renders (Bel) 33:59.36

**100mh:** (−0.77)
1. Heike Tillack (GDR) 13.10
2. Aliuska Lopez (Cub) 13.14
3. Tanya Davis (USA) 13.46

**400mh:**
1. Claudia Bartl (GDR) 56.76
2. Kellie Roberts (USA) 56.80
3. Svetlana Lukashevich (SU) 57.92

**HJ:**
1. Karen Scholz (GDR) 1.92
2. Galina Astafei (Rom) 1.90
3. Yelena Obukhova (SU) 1.88

**LJ:**
1. Patricia Bille (GDR) 6.70
2. Anu Kaljurand (SU) 6.46
3. Tatyana Ter-Mesrobian (SU) 6.39

**SP:**
1. Heike Rohrmann (GDR) 18.39
2. Stephanie Storp (FRG) 18.20
3. Ines Wittich (GDR) 18.19

**DT:**
1. Ilke Wyludda (GDR) 64.02
2. Franka Dietzsch (GDR) 60.26
3. Min Chunfeng (Chn) 54.00

**JT:**
1. Xiomara Rivero (Cub) 62.86
2. Anja Reiter (GDR) 60.24
3. Alexandra Beck (GDR) 59.92

**Hep:**
1. Svetla Dimitrova (Bul) 6041
2. Marina Shcherbina (USSR) 5953
3. Anke Schmidt (GDR) 5900

**4x100mR:**
1. USA 43.78
2. GDR 43.97
3. Nigeria 44.13

**4x400mR:**
1. USA 3:30.45
2. GDR 3:30.90
3. USSR 3:32.35

**5kmW:**
1. Wang Yan (Chn) 22:03.65
2. Natalya Zykova (SU) 22:17.76
3. Jin Bingjie (Chn) 22:17.83

Juan Lopez (Cub) was found to have contravened IAAF doping regulations and thus lost his TJ second place (16.94w).

## Pan-American Junior Championships 1986

*Winter Park, Florida 4–6 July*

Winners: MEN    100m: Stanley Kerr (USA) 10.20, 200m/400m: Roberto Hernandez (Cub) 20.83/45.64, 800m: Manuel Balmaceda (Chl) 1:50.41, 1500m: Carson Hoeft (USA) 3:51.10, 5000m: Greg Anderson (Can) 14:12.54, 2000mSt: Angel Rodriguez (Cub) 5:41.64, 110mh/400mh: Emilio Valle (Cub) 14.16/51.33, HJ: Javier Sotomayor (Cub) 2.27, PV: Timothy McMichael (USA) 5.30, LJ: Scott Sanders (USA) 7.74, TJ: Juan Lopez (Cub) 16.49, SP: Tony Sylvester (USA) 16.94, DT: Brent Patera (USA) 51.78, HT: Eldon Pfeiffer (Can) 61.24, JT: Juan Oxamendi (Cub) 70.84, Dec: Miguel Valle (Cub) 6900, 4x100mR: USA 39.76, 4x400mR: Cuba 3:04.30, 10kmW: Carlos Mercenario (Mex) 43:06.80.

Winners: WOMEN    100m: Caryl Smith (USA) 11.56w, 200m/LJ: Carlette Guidry (USA) 23.73/6.42, 400m: Sandie Richards (Jam) 52.48, 800m: Andrea Thomas (Jam) 2:07.33, 1500m: Suzy Favor (USA) 4:26.84, 3000m: Maricarmen Diaz (Mex) 9:42.49, 100mh: Yolanda Johnson (USA) 13.38, 400mh: Jill McDermid (Can) 59.62, HJ: Fernanda Mosquera (Col) 1.80, SP: Brandi Gail (USA) 14.10, DT: Idalmis Leyva (Cub) 51.98, JT: Xiomara Rivero (Cub) 60.86, Hep: Kelly-Anne Kempf (Can) 50.45, 4x100mR/4x400mR: USA 44.62/3:35.81, 3kmW: Laura Rigutto (Can) 15:16.83.

# Central American and Caribbean Championships

*Santiago, Dominican Republic*
*29 June – 4 July 1986*

Winners: MEN
100m: Andres Simon (Cub) 10.29, 200m: Leandro Penalver (Cub) 20.70, 400m: Felix Stevens (Cub) 44.98, 800m: Oslen Barr (Guy) 1:49.42, 1500m: Jacinto Navarette (Col) 3:43.72, 5000m: Mauricio Gonzalez (Mex) 14:11.73, 10000m: Francisco Pacheco (Mex) 29:39.56, Mar: Francisco Amariles (Col) 2:23:00, 3kmSt: Juan Conde (Cub) 8:42.38, 110mh: Angel Bueno (Cub) 13.86, 400mh: Winthrop Graham (Jam) 50.03, HJ: Francisco Centelles (Cub) 2.22, PV: Ruben Camino (Cub) 5.20, LJ: Jaime Jefferson (Cub) 8.34, TJ: Lazaro Betancourt (Cub) 16.83, SP: Paul Ruiz (Cub) 19.01, DT: Luis Delis (Cub) 63.16, HT: Vicente Sanchez (Cub) 68.04, JT: Ramon Gonzalez (Cub) 77.32, Dec: Ernesto Betancourt (Cub) 7333, 20kmW: Ernesto Canto (Mex) 1:26:25, 50kmW: Martin Bermudez (Mex) 4:04:47, 4x100mR/ 4x400mR: Cuba 38.74/3:02.41.

Winners: WOMEN
100m/200m: Pauline Davis (Bah) 11.51/23.06, 400m/800m: Ana Quirot (Cub) 51.01/1:59.00, 1500m: Angelita Lind (PR) 4:18.67, 3000m: Rueda Garcia (Col) 9:30.25, 10000m: Genoveva Dominguez (Mex) 36:24.39, Mar: Naydi Nazario Muniz (PR) 2:55:44, 100mh: Odalys Adams (Cub) 13.50, 400mh: Flora Hyacinth (UVI) 57.55, HJ: Silvia Costa (Cub) 1.96, LJ: Eloina Echevarria (Cub) 6.61, SP: Marcelina Rodriguez (Cub) 17.22, DT: Hilda Ramos (Cub) 63.44, JT: Maria Colon (Cub) 67.00, Hep: Caridad Balcindes (Cub) 5313, 10kmW: Maria Colin (Mex) 50:43.62, 4x100mR/ 4x400mR: Cuba 44.35/3:33.60.

# East and Central African Championships

*Nairobi, Kenya 4/5 July 1986*

Winners: MEN:
100m: Peter Wekesa (Ken) 10.4, 200m: Simon Kipkemboi (Ken) 20.8, 400m: Alfred Nyambane (Ken) 46.2, 800m: Edwin Koech (Ken) 1:48.2, 1500m: Getahun Ayana (Eth) 3:40.6, 5000m: John Ngugi (Ken) 13:59.6, 10000m: Kipsubai Koskei (Ken) 28:59.1, 3000mSt: Joshua Kipkemboi (Ken) 8:28.1, 110mh: Charles Kokoyo (Ken) 14.0, 400mh: Simon Kitur (Ken) 50.2, HJ: Nathan Rotich (Ken) 2.07, PV: S.C.Maina (Ken) 3.80, LJ:

Ben K.Mugun (Ken) 7.12, TJ: James Kipngetich (Ken) 15.71, SP: Simon Murei (Ken) 15.33, DT: John Pondo (Ken) 48.76, HT: Peter Monyancha (Ken) 47.20, JT (old): George Odera (Ken) 76.00, 4x100mR/4x400mR: Kenya 39.9/3:04.4.

Winners: WOMEN
100m/200m/LJ: Joyce Odhiambo (Ken) 11.3/ 23.9/6.18, 400m: Geraldine Shitandayi (Ken) 53.4, 800m/1500m: Selina Chirchir (Ken) 2:04.3/4:18.7, 5000m: Susan Sirma (Ken) 16:16.4, HJ: Leah Serem (Ken) 1.60, SP: Herina Malit (Ken) 12.10, DT: Helen Alyek (Uga) 40.76, JT: Martha Johnson (Ken) 44.06, 4x400mR: Kenya.

# 10th Maghreb Games

*Tunis, Tunisia 7–9 August 1986*

Winners: MEN
100m/200m: Mohamed Kamel Selmi (Alg) 10.41w/21.09, 400m: Mohamed Filali (Alg) 48.11, 800m/1500m: Faouzi Lahbi (Mor) 1:52.16/ 4:00.05, 5000m/10000m: Habib Romdhani (Tun) 14:22.14/28:06 (one lap short), Mar: Mohamed Abaidia (Alg) 2:29:13, 3000mSt: Féthi Baccouche (Tun) 8:36.49, 110mh: Nordine Tadjine (Alg) 13.9w, 400mh: Fadhel Khayatti (Tun) 52.11, HJ: Nabil Berbiche (Alg) 2.08, PV: Chokri Abahnini (Tun) 4.83, LJ: Mustapha Benmrah (Mor) 7.55w, TJ: Abdelhamid Sekai (Alg) 15.74w, SP: Mohamed Fatihi (Mor) 15.90, DT: Abderrazak Ben Hassine (Tun) 49.06, HT: Hakim Toumi (Alg) 66.82, JT: Tarek Chaabani (Tun) 72.52, Dec: Hatem Bachar (Tun) 6802, 20kmW: Abdelwahab Ferguène (Alg) 1:36:19, 4x100mR/4x400mR: Algeria 41.10/3:09.8.

Winners: WOMEN
100m: Mahdjouba Bouhdiba (Alg) 11.93w, 200m: Lamia Makni (Tun) 24.72, 400m: Hassiba Allilou (Alg) 57.68, 800m: Hassiba Boulmerka (Alg) 2:13.91, 1500m/3000m: El Hadj Mébarka Abdellah (Alg) 4:38.58/9:43.26, 100mh/Hep: Yasmina Azzizi (Alg) 13.90w/5483, 400mh: Rachida Ferdjaoui (Alg) 62.28, HJ: Nacèra Achir (Alg) 1.74, LJ: Kawther Akrémi (Tun) 5.79, SP: Aicha Dahmous (Alg) 13.78, DT: Nabila Mouelhi (Tun) 49.96, JT: Samia Djémaa (Alg) 53.04, 4x100mR: Morocco 48.21, 4x400mR: Algeria 3:47.7.

## 44th Balkan Games

*Ljubljana, Yugoslavia 6–7 September 1986*

Winners: MEN:
100m: Valentin Atanasov (Bul) 10.32, 200m: Nikolay Markov (Bul) 21.17, 400m: Zelicko Knapic (Yug) 46.41, 800m: Slobodan Popovic (Yug) 1:48.19, 1500m: Petru Dragoescu (Rom) 3:40.74, 5000m: Romeo Zivko (Yug) 13:57.48, 10000m: Necdet Ayaz (Tur) 29:24.41, Mar: Mehmet Terzi (Tur) 2:22:11, 3000mSt: Kiriakis Moutesidis (Gre) 8:41.54, 110mh: Liviu Giurgean (Rom) 13.73, 400mh: Toma Tomov (Bul) 49.40, HJ: Eugen Popescu (Rom) 2.30, PV: Nikolay Nikolov (Bul) 5.60, LJ: Atanas Chochev (Bul) 7.87, TJ: Haralambis Giannoulis (Gre) 16.36, SP: Vladimir Milic (Yug) 19.81, DT: Kamen Dimitrov (Bul) 63.44, HT: Ivan Tanev (Bul) 77.74, JT: Sead Krzalic (Yug) 79.04, Dec: Tsetsko Mitrakyev (Bul) 7454, 20kmW: Alik Basriev (Bul) 1:26:09, 4x100mR: Bulgaria 39.70, 4x400mR: Yugoslavia 3:04.53.
Team: 1. Bulgaria 234, 2. Yugoslavia 228, 3. Greece 212.5, 4. Romania 93, 5. Turkey 76.5, 6. Albania 6.

Winners: WOMEN
100m/200m: Anelia Nuneva (Bul) 11.17/22.58, 400m: Rositsa Stamenova (Bul) 51.45, 800m: Svobodka Colovic (Yug) 1:59.94, 1500m/3000m: Nikolina Shtereva (Bul) 4:13.80/9:24.11, 100mh: Yordanka Donkova (Bul) 12.26, 400mh: Nicolata Carutasu (Rom) 55.72, HJ: Stefka Kostadinova (Bul) 2.01, LJ: Lyudmila Ninova (Bul) 6.72, SP: Mihaela Loghin (Rom) 19.81, DT: Tsvetanka Khristova (Bul) 69.58, JT: Sofia Sakorafa (Gre) 61.00, Hep: Emilia Dimitrova (Bul) 6304, 4x100mR/4x400mR: Bulgaria 44.83/3:31.36.
Team: 1. Bulgaria 213, 2. Romania 170.5, 3. Yugoslavia 138.5, 4. Greece 73.5, 5. Turkey 24.5.

## Ibero-American Championships

*Havana, Cuba 27/28 September 1986*

Winners: MEN
100m/200m: Robson Caetano da Silva (Bra) 10.02/20.43, 400m: Felix Stevens (Cub) 45.83, 800m: Mauricio Hernandez (Mex) 1:48.05, 1500m: José-Luis Carreira (Spa) 3:44.93, 5000m: Abel Anton (Spa) 13:49.76, 3000mSt: Adauto Domingues (Bra) 8:31.91, 110mh: Carlos Sala (Spa) 13.89, 400mh: José Alonso (Spa) 49.96, HJ: Javier Sotomayor (Cub) 2.30, PV: Alberto Ruiz (Spa) 5.20, LJ: Luis Bueno (Cub) 8.25, TJ: Hector Marquetti (Cub) 16.26, SP: Gert Weil (Chl) 19.82, DT: Roberto Moya (Cub) 59.04, HT: Raul Jimeno (Spa) 66.90, JT: Ramon Gonzalez (Cub) 76.38, 20kmW: Marcelino Colin (Mex) 1:33:04, 4x100mR: Brazil 39.30, 4x400mR: Spain 3:08.54.

Winners: WOMEN
100m: Alma Vazquez (Mex) 11.76, 200m: Ximena Restrepo (Col) 23.76, 400m/800m: Ana Quirot (Cub) 50.78/2:00.23, 1500m: Alejandra Ramos (Chl) 4:22.34, 3000m: Asuncion Sinovas (Spa) 9:36.92, 100mh: Odalys Adams (Cub) 13.49, 400mh: Cristina Perez (Spa) 58.51, HJ: Silvia Costa (Cub) 1.84, LJ: Eloina Echevarria (Cub) 6.29, SP: Belsis Laza (Cub) 15.93, DT: Rita Alvarez (Cub) 58.90, JT: Maria Colon (Cub) 61.80, 4x100mR: Mexico 45.95, 4x400mR: Cuba 3:33.70.

---

## ASIAN GAMES 1986    *Seoul 29 September – 5 October*

These most successful Games, using the facilities ready for the 1988 Olympics, were contested by athletes from 24 nations. P.T.Usha, the Indian woman sprinter, won an Asian Games record four gold (200m, 400m, 400mh, 4x400mR) and five medals overall with the addition of silver at 100m. The previous record of three golds at one celebration was equalled by Lim Chun-Ae, who won at 800m, 1500m and 3000m. Shigenobu Murofushi won the hammer, a record five gold medals at the event from his first win in 1970.

**Medal table**

| Nation | 1st | 2nd | 3rd | Nation | 1st | 2nd | 3rd |
|--------|-----|-----|-----|--------|-----|-----|-----|
| China | 17 | 18 | 8 | Qatar | 1 | – | 1 |
| Japan | 11 | 13 | 11 | Philippines | 1 | 2 | 1 |
| South Korea | 7 | 5 | 13 | India | 4 | 2 | 3 |

One gold: Bahrain; silver and bronze: Thailand; one silver: Iraq; two bronze: Kuwait; one bronze: Malaysia, Oman.

**Asian Games 1986 – Men**

MEN

100m:
1. Talal Mansoor (Qat) 10.30
2. Hiroki Fuwa (Jap) 10.44
3. Zheng Chen (Chn) 10.47
200m:
1. Chang Jae-Keun (SKO) 20.71 GBP
2. Li Feng (Chn) 20.97
3. Masahiro Nagura (Jap) 21.10
400m:
1. Susumu Takano (Jap) 45.00 AR
2. Isidro Del Prado (Phi) 45.96
3. Mohamed Amur Al Malky (Oman) 46.42
800m:
1. Kim Bok-Joo (SKO) 1:49.15
2. Ryu Tae-Kyung (SKO) 1:49.89
3. Najem Al Sowailem (Kuw) 1:50.31
1500m:
1. Shuji Oshida (Jap) 3:43.88
2. Ryu Tae-Kyung (SK0) 3:44.51
3. Mohamed Sulaiman (Qat) 3:44.68
5000m:
1. Kim Jong-Yoon (SKO) 13:50.63 GBP
2. Masanari Shintaku (Jap) 13:52.65
3. Yutaka Kanai (Jap) 13:53.73
10000m:
1. Masanari Shintaku (Jap) 28:26.74 GBP
2. Kim Jong-Yoon (SKO) 28:30.54
3. Toshihiko Seko (Jap) 29:31.90
Mar:
1. Takeyuki Nakayama (Jap) 2:08:21
2. Hiromi Taniguchi (Jap) 2:10:08
3. Ryu Jae-Sung (SKO) 2:16:55
3000mSt:
1. Shigeyuki Aikyo (Jap) 8:36.98
2. Cheng Shouguo (Chn) 8:37.33
3. Hajime Nagasato (Jap) 8:42.30
110mh:
1. Yu Zhicheng (Chn) 14.07 GBP
2. Lu Quanbin (Chn) 14.34
3. Kim Jin-Tae (SKO) 14.37
400mh:
1. Ahmad Hamada (BHN) 49.31 AR
2. Ryoichi Yoshida (Jap) 49.40
3. Jasem Al Douwaila (Kuw) 50.22
HJ:
1. Zhu Jianhua (Chn) 2.31

2. Liu Yunpeng (Chn) 2.27
3. Shuji Ujino (Jap) 2.21
PV:
1. Jie Zebiao (Chn) 5.40 GBP
2. Liang Xueren (Chn) 5.30
3. Lee Jae-Bok (SKO) 5.00
LJ:
1. Kim Jong-Il (SKO) 7.94
2. Junichi Usui (Jap) 7.92
3. Chen Zunrong (Chn) 7.80
TJ:
1. Norifumi Yamashita (Jap) 17.01 GBP
2. Park Young-Jun (SK0) 15.97
3. Zhou Zhenxian (Chn) 15.76
SP:
1. Ma Yongfeng (Chn) 18.30
2. Gong Yitian (Chn) 17.82
3. Yoshihisa Urita (Jap) 17.51
DT:
1. Li Weinan (Chn) 58.28
2. Yuko Maeda (Jap) 54.14
3. Manjit Singh (Ind) 52.80
HT:
1. Shigenobu Murofushi (Jap) 69.20
2. Luo Jun (Chn) 66.34
3. Lu Dongping (Chn) 66.28
JT:
1. Kazuhiro Mizoguchi (Jap) 76.60
2. Kim Jae-Sang (SKO) 74.44
3. Park Jong-Sam (SKO) 74.12
Dec:
1. Chen Zebin (Chn) 7255
2. Takeshi Kojo (Jap) 7171
3. Park Young-Jun (SKO) 7163
4x100mR:
1. China 39.17 AR
2. Japan 39.31
3. South Korea 39.66
4x400mR:
1. Japan 3:02.33 AR
2. Iraq 3:07.28
3. Philippines 3:09.26
20kmW:
1. Sun Xiaoguang (Chn) 1:25:46 GBP
2. Jiang Shaohong (Chn) 1:26:57
3. Chand Ram (Ind) 1:28:03

**Asian Games 1986 – Women**

WOMEN

100m:
1. Lydia De Vega (Phi) 11.53 GBP
2. P.T.Usha (Ind) 11.67
3. Ratjai Sripet (Tha) 11.75
200m:
1. P.T.Usha (Ind) 23.44 GBP
2. Lydia De Vega (Phi) 23.47
3. Park Mi-Sun (SKO) 23.80
400m:
1. P.T.Usha (Ind) 52.16 GBP
2. Shiny Abraham (Ind) 53.32
3. Hiromi Isozaki (Jap) 53.76
800m:
1. Lim Chun-Ae (SKO) 2:05.72
2. Yang Liuxia (Chn) 2:06.04
3. Josephine Mary Singarayar (Mal)
   2:07.44
1500m:
1. Lim Chun-Ae (SKO) 4:21.38
2. Yang Liuxia (Chn) 4:22.07
3. Kim Wel-Ja (SKO) 4:23.47
3000m:
1. Lim Chun-Ae (SKO) 9:11.92 GBP
2. Zhang Xiuyun (Chn) 9:12.64
3. Suman Rawat (Ind) 9:14.70
10000m:
1. Wang Xiuting (Chn) 32:47.77 AR
2. Kumi Araki (Jap) 33:20.75
3. Xiao Hongyan (Chn) 33:47.22
Mar:
1. Eriko Asai (Jap) 2:41:03
2. Misako Miyahara (Jap) 2:41:36
3. Weng Yanmin (Chn) 2:42:21
100mh:
1. Chen Kemei (Chn) 13.78
2. Chizuko Akimoto (Jap) 13.88
3. Naomi Jojima (Jap) 14.07
400mh:
1. P.T.Usha (Ind) 56.08 GBP

2. Zhao Qianqian (Chn) 59.37
3. Chen Juying (Chn) 59.37
HJ:
1. Megumi Sato (Jap) 1.89 =GBP
2. Zheng Dazhen (Chn) 1.89 =GBP
3. Kim Hee-Sun (SKO) 1.89 =GBP
LJ:
1. Liao Wenfen (Chn) 6.37
2. Huang Donghuo (Chn) 6.19
3. Minako Isogai (Jap) 6.14
SP:
1. Huang Zhihong (Chn) 17.51
2. Cong Yuzhen (Chn) 17.44
3. Aya Suzuki (Jap) 15.06
DT:
1. Hou Xuemei (Chn) 59.28 GBP
2. Li Xiaohui (Chn) 58.94
3. Lee Sang-Yuk (SKO) 50.26
JT:
1. Li Baolian (Chn) 59.42
2. Emi Matsui (Jap) 55.00
3. Jang Sun-Hee (SKO) 52.78
Hep:
1. Zhu Yuqing (Chn) 5580
2. Ye Lianying (Chn) 5413
3. Ji Jung-Mi (SKO) 5067
4x100mR:
1. China 44.78 AR
2. Thailand 45.14
3. South Korea 45.59
4x400mR:
1. India 3:34.58 GBP
2. Japan 3:39.77
3. China 3:41.59
10kmW:
1. Guan Ping (Chn) 48:40
2. Xu Yongjiu (Chn) 49:50
3. Hideko Hirayama (Jap) 51:12

AR – Asian record, GBP – Asian Games best performance

## Women's World 15km Road Race Championship

*Lisbon, 9 November 1986*

INDIVIDUAL
1. Aurora Cunha (Por) 48:31
2. Rosa Mota (Por) 48:35
3. Carla Beurskens (Hol) 48:36
4. Marty Cooksey (USA) 48:41
5. Tatyana Kazankina (USSR) 49:12
6. Lyudmila Matveyeva (USSR) 49:13
7. Maria Curatolo (Ita) 49:14
8. Nancy Rooks (Can) 49:22
9. Marina Rodchenkova (USSR) 49:26
10. Kellie Cathey (USA) 49:42
11. Agnes Pardaens (Bel) 49:49
12. Suzanne Girard (USA) 50:12
13. Christine Loiseau (Fra) 50:20
14. Kerstin Pressler (FRG) 50:23
15. Jocelyn Villeton (Fra) 50:30

TEAM
1. USSR 20, 2. Portugal 24, 3. USA 26, 4. France 47, 5. Italy 58, 6. United Kingdom 60, 7. FR Germany 69, 8. Ireland 104, 9. Netherlands 106, 10. Spain 110.
14 nations completed.

## IAAF World Challenge Road Relay

*Hiroshima, Japan 30 November 1986*

The men's race was contested by the first eight teams from the IAAF World Cross-Country Championships 1986 with Japan and continental teams. Each team had five members, running stages of 10km, 7km, 8km, 5km, and 12.195km to make up the marathon distance.

1. Ethiopia (Wodajo Bulti, Debede Demissie, Bekele Debele, Melese Feyisa, Abebe Mekonnen) 1:59:11
2. UK (Carl Thackery, Jonathan Solly, Mark Scrutton, David Clarke, Karl Harrison) 1:59:14
3. Oceania 2:00:12
4. Japan 2:00:43
5. Americas 2:00:49
6. Kenya 2:01:01
7. Portugal 2:03:23
8. Italy 2:03:39
9. USA 2:03:39
10. France 2:05:07
11. Spain 2:05:54
12. Asia 2:09:44

The women's race was contested by the first six teams from the IAAF World Cross-Country Championships 1986 with others from Japan, Asia, the Americas and the USSR. Each team had six members, running stages of 10km, 7km, 8km, 5km, 8km and 4.195km to make up the marathon distance.

1. New Zealand (Lorraine Moller, Hazel Stewart, Mary O'Connor, Sue Bruce, Anne Audain, Anne Hare) 2:18:18
2. USSR (Tatyana Kazankina, Marina Rodchenkova, Lyudmila Matveyeva, Svetlana Guskova, Olga Bondarenko, Tatyana Samolenko) 2:18:33
3. USA 2:19:11
4. UK 2:20:31
5. Americas 2:21:20
6. FR Germany 2:21:45
7. France 2:21:57
8. Japan 2:22:39
9. Portugal 2:26:52
10. Asia 2:30:03

Aurora Cunha – world champion again. *Mark Shearman*

# IAAF/MOBIL GRAND PRIX 1986

Sixteen meetings comprised the 1986 Grand Prix, from the Jenner Classic on May 31st, the one meeting outside Europe, to the Final in Rome on September 10th. A total of 792 athletes scored Grand Prix points; 468 men and 324 women. The awards were: overall 1st $25,000, 2nd $15,000, 3rd $10,000; for each event 1st $10,000, 2nd $8,000, 3rd $6,000, 4th $5,000, 5th $4,000, 6th $3,000, 7th $2,000, 8th $1,000.

## Leading Scorers – Men

OVERALL
63 Saïd Aouita (Mor)
61 Andre Phillips (USA)
61 Steve Scott (USA)
61 Mike Conley (USA)
59 Jimmy Howard (USA)
57 Yuriy Sedykh (SU)
57 Chidi Imo (Nig)
57 Danny Harris (USA)

100 METRES
57 Chidi Imo (Nig)
54 Ben Johnson (Can)
41 Harvey Glance (USA)
34 Calvin Smith (USA)
33 Bruno Marie-Rose (Fra)
32 Linford Christie (UK)
31 Desai Williams (Can)
26 Marian Woronin (Pol)

800 METRES
50 José-Luis Barbosa (Bra)
49 Earl Jones (USA)
49 William Wuyke (Ven)
44 Peter Elliott (UK)
43 Johnny Gray (USA)
39 Moussa Fall (Sen)
33 Ryszard Ostrowski (Pol)
23 Babacar Niang (Sen)

1 MILE
61 Steve Scott (USA)
42 José-Luis Gonzalez (Spa)
37 Jim Spivey (USA)
34 Frank O'Mara (Ire)
32 John Walker (NZ)
27 José-Manuel Abascal (Spa)
21 Robert Harrison (UK)

18 Saïd Aouita (Mor)

5000 METRES
54 Saïd Aouita (Mor)
47 Vincent Rousseau (Bel)
38 Stefano Mei (Ita)
30 Sydney Maree (USA)
28 Pierre Délèze (Swi)
25 Mark Nenow (USA)
19 Antonio Leitao (Por)
19 Markus Ryffel (Swi)

3000m STEEPLECHASE
54 William van Dijck (Bel)
52 Henry Marsh (USA)
39 Graeme Fell (Can)
35 Hagen Melzer (GDR)
28 Ivan Huff (USA)
26 Pascal Debacker (Fra)
25 Julius Kariuki (Ken)
21 Julius Korir (Ken)

400 METRES HURDLES
61 Andre Phillips (USA)
57 Danny Harris (USA)
46 Amadou Dia Ba (Sen)
39 Dave Patrick (USA)
36 Ed Moses (USA)
35 René Djédjémel (IvC)
28 Toma Tomov (Bul)
25 Harald Schmid (FRG)

HIGH JUMP
59 Jimmy Howard (USA)
52.5 Doug Nordquist (USA)

50.75 Igor Paklin (SU)
37 Carlo Thränhardt (FRG)
33.5 Sorin Matei (Rom)
32.5 Jake Jacoby (USA)
32 Jan Zvara (Cs)
31 Geoff Parsons (UK) &
31 Milt Ottey (Can)

TRIPLE JUMP
61 Mike Conley (USA)
46 Khristo Markov (Bul)
44 Joseph Taiwo (Nig)
34 Nikolay Musiyenko (SU)
30 Willie Banks (USA)
29 Charlie Simpkins (USA)
29 Ajayi Agbebaku (Nig)
28 Maris Bruzhiks (SU)

SHOT
44 Werner Günthör (Swi)
40 Ron Backes (USA)
38 John Brenner (USA)
36 Ulf Timmermann (GDR)
24 Brian Oldfield (USA)
21 Udo Beyer (GDR)
18 Gregg Tafralis (USA)
14 Josef Kubes (Cs)

HAMMER
57 Yuriy Sedykh (SU)
50 Sergey Litvinov (SU)
31 Juri Tamm (SU)
23 Ivan Tanev (Bul)
22 Igor Nikulin (SU)
19 Klaus Ploghaus (FRG)
19 Harri Huhtala (Fin)
17 Juha Tiainen (Fin)

# Leading Scorers – Women

OVERALL
69 Yordanka Donkova (Bul)
65 Maricica Puica (Rom)
63 Tsvetanka Khristova (Bul)
63 Petra Felke (GDR)
59 Evelyn Ashford (USA)
59 Fatima Whitbread (UK)
59 Valerie Brisco-Hooks (USA)
53 Diane Dixon (USA)

200 METRES
59 Evelyn Ashford (USA)
49 Ewa Kasprzyk (Pol)
43 Valerie Brisco-Hooks (USA)
39 Grace Jackson (Jam)
21 Pam Marshall (USA)
24 Merlene Ottey-Page (Jam)
22 Marie-Christine Cazier (Fra)
21 Kathy Cook (UK)

400 METRES
53 Diane Dixon (USA)
51 Valerie Brisco-Hooks (USA)
45 Lillie Leatherwood (USA)
40 Genowefa Blaszak (Pol)
30 Tatana Kocembova (Cs)
30 Petra Müller (GDR)

27 Marita Koch (GDR)
27 Ana Quirot (Cub)


1500 METRES
62 Maricica Puica (Rom)
51 Doina Melinte (Rom)
33 Cornelia Bürki (Swi)
33 Kirsty Wade (UK)
30 Sue Addison (USA)
29 Elly Van Hulst (Hol)
29 Claudette Groenendaal (USA)
27 Tatyana Samolenko (SU)

5000 METRES
41 Svetlana Guskova (SU)
41 PattiSue Plumer (USA)
39 Mary Knisely (USA)
34 Olga Bondarenko (SU)
33 Ingrid Kristiansen (Nor)
25 Maricica Puica (Rom)
23 Erika Vereb (Hun)
16 Gabriele Veith (GDR)

100 METRES HURDLES
69 Yordanka Donkova (Bul)
52 Cornelia Oschkenat (GDR)

47 Ginka Zagorcheva (Bul)
40 Laurence Elloy (Fra)
39 Benita Fitzgerald-Brown (USA)
31 Xenia Siska (Hun)
24 Stephanie Hightower (USA)
23 Jackie Joyner (USA)


DISCUS
63 Tsvetanka Khristova (Bul)
39 Svetla Mitkova (Bul)
28 Marta Kripli (Hun)
20 Diane Sachse (GDR)
19 Martina Hellmann (GDR)
14 Silvia Madetzky (GDR)
14 Penny Neer (USA)
11 Irina Meszynski (GDR)


JAVELIN
63 Petra Felke (GDR)
59 Fatima Whitbread (UK)
43 Trine Solberg (Nor)
33 Maria Colon (Cub)
32 Zsuzsa Malovecz (Hun)
29 Tiina Lillak (Fin)
29 Natalya Yermolovich (SU)
26 Ingrid Thyssen (FRG)

Zola Budd (19) leads Maricica Puica (16), who went on to win the 2000 metres race at the IAC meeting in a new world record of 5:28.69. *ASP*

# First three in the Final at Rome – Men

100m:
1. Ben Johnson (Can) 10.02
2. Chidi Imo (Nig) 10.08
3. Linford Christie (UK) 10.15

800m:
1. Peter Elliott (UK) 1:46.91
2. William Wuyke (Ven) 1:47.03
3. Earl Jones (USA) 1:47.16

1 mile
1. Steve Scott (USA) 3:50.28
2. José-Manuel Abascal (Spa) 3:50.54
3. John Walker (NZ) 3:50.93

5000m:
1. Said Aouita (Mor) 13:13.13
2. Stefano Mei (Ita) 13:14.29
3. Sydney Maree (USA) 13:14.62

3000mSt
1. William van Dijck (Bel) 8:25.34
2. Hagen Melzer (GDR) 8:25.65
3. Henry Marsh (USA) 8:25.85

400mh:
1. Andre Phillips (USA) 48.14
2. Amadou Dia Ba (Sen) 48.47
3. Danny Harris (USA) 49.28

HJ:
1. Igor Paklin (SU) 2.34
2. Jim Howard (USA) 2.31
3. Doug Nordquist (USA) 2.28

TJ:
1. Mike Conley (USA) 17.16
2. Dario Badenelli (Ita) 16.82
3. Joseph Taiwo (Nig) 16.79

SP:
1. Ulf Timmermann (GDR) 21.67
2. Werner Günthör (Swi) 21.61
3. Alessandro Andrei (Ita) 21.20

HT:
1. Sergey Litvinov (SU) 84.88
2. Yuriy Sedykh (SU) 81.98
3. Igor Nikulin (SU) 79.84

# Women

200m:
1. Valerie Brisco-Hooks (USA) 22.30
2. Evelyn Ashford (USA) 22.31
3. Ewa Kasprzyk (Pol) 22.58

400m:
1. Marita Koch (GDR) 49.17
2. Valerie Brisco-Hooks (USA) 50.21
3. Diane Dixon (USA) 50.64

1500m:
1. Tatyana Samolenko (SU) 4:02.71
2. Maricica Puica (Rom) 4:03.55
3. Kirsty Wade (UK) 4:03.74

5000m:
1. Olga Bondarenko (SU) 15:16.84
2. Svetlana Guskova (SU) 15:17.95
3. Mary Knisely (USA) 15:22.33

100mh:
1. Yordanka Donkova (Bul) 12.47
2. Ginka Zagorcheva (Bul) 12.49
3. Cornelia Oschkenat (Bul) 12.71

DT:
1. Tsvetanka Khristova (Bul) 68.90
2. Svetlana Mitkova (Bul) 58.98
3. Marta Kripli (Hun) 58.52

JT:
1. Petra Felke (GDR) 70.64
2. Fatima Whitbread (UK) 69.40
3. Tiina Lillak (Fin) 65.46

Jimmy Howard. *duomo*

# ROAD RACE REVIEW

## BY ROGER GYNN

## 10km to half marathon 1986 highlights

Not since 1982, when Kenyan Mike Musyoki won five of the major classics, has there been such a dominant figure on the American road race circuit as was Arturo Barrios in 1986. The Mexican ran nine races over distances of between 4 miles and 15km, bettering two world bests and two course records in the process, and was in a class of his own among the male elite.

Most prolific of the 'also rans' was American Ed Eyestone, who had five wins including the Boston Milk run, the Bobby Crim 10M and a course record in the Bay to Breakers, as well as a winning 27:40 performance in the downhill Deseret News 10km. Newcomer John Doherty (UK) scored four notable victories, his two best being the Peachtree 10km when he beat Musyoki and Eyestone among others in a course record 27:56, and the Rainbow Classic 10km, ahead of Rob de Castella and Jon Sinclair. The evergreen Musyoki was never outside the first four, winning three races to add to his Great North Run victory in world record time over the half-marathon distance. Commonwealth stars Peter Koech (Kenya) and Paul McCloy (Canada) also ran well, at the start and end of the season respectively, each scoring two wins, as did Mark Curp, Jon Sinclair and Geoff Smith, among others.

Equally dominant was Ingrid Kristiansen among the female road runners. Unbeaten on the track in 1986 with world records over 5,000m and 10,000m as well as a European gold medal in the latter, the Norwegian was no less impressive on

the road setting an undisputed world record over the half-marathon (see the athlete of the year section for her complete race record).

Grete Waitz showed that she is still a force to be reckoned with, setting course records in the River Run 15km and San Francisco 12km, beating Joan Samuelson, Lisa Martin and Lorraine Moller in the latter. Following a world record in the Shamrock 8km and a victory in the Peachtree 10km, a perfect American season was upset by Moller in the Cascade 15km. The latter scored five good wins in the second half of the season taking the scalps of Joan Samuelson and Anne Audain among others. Samuelson herself suffered three early season losses (Milk Run, Bay to Breakers and L'Eggs) but then set a course record in the Trevira 10M and an American record of 1:24:43 in the Old Kent 25km on 10 May. Waitz had also run this distance, at Paderborn (FRG) on 29 March where she recorded 1:22:28 over an uncertified course. Portuguese stars Aurora Cunha and Rosa Mota (1–2 in the IAAF World 15km Championship) made brief incursions into the American scene, the highlight being Mota's 10M world record at Washington, DC.

## All-time top ten lists

With the verification of the Oslo half-marathon distance (correct since 1983) and the knowledge that the race at Milano has used a 'rolling start' plus that at the Hague remaining very doubtful, the following inaugural all-time lists have been compiled for the half-marathon.

---

**Arturio Barrios – road races in 1986**

| 1 Mar | Phoenix 10km | (1) | 27:41* |
|---|---|---|---|
| 8 Mar | Jacksonville 15km | (1) | 43:18 |
| 29 Mar | Mexico City 15km | (1) | 48:19A |
| 5 Apr | New Orleans 10km | (1) | 28:16 |
| 26 May | Boulder 10km | (1) | 28:46A# |

| 14 Jun | Peoria 4M | (1) | 17:34* |
|---|---|---|---|
| 29 Jun | Portland 15km | (1) | 42:36 |
| 17 Aug | Falmouth 7.1M | (1) | 32:17 |
| 26 Oct | Denver 10km | (1) | 29:32A# |

* world loop best.   # course record.

## All-time half marathon list

| Hr:min:sec | Name | Place | Venue | Date |
|---|---|---|---|---|
| **MEN** | | | | |
| 1:00:43 | Mike Musyoki (Ken) | (1) | Newcastle | 8 Jun 86 |
| 1:00:55 | Mark Curp (USA) | (1) | Philadelphia | 18 Sep 85 |
| 1:00:59 | Steve Jones (UK) | (2) | Newcastle | 8 Jun 86 |
| 1:01:03 | Nick Rose (UK) | (3) | Philadelphia | 18 Sep 85 |
| 1:01:31 | Steve Kenyon (UK) | (3) | Newcastle | 8 Jun 86 |
| 1:01:32 | Paul Cummings (USA) | (1) | Dayton | 25 Sep 83 |
| 1:01:39 | Geoff Smith (UK) | (2) | Dayton | 25 Sep 83 |
| 1:01:43 | George Malley (USA) | (2) | Philadelphia | 19 Sep 82 |
| 1:01:47 | Herb Lindsay (USA) | (1) | Manchester | 20 Sep 81 |
| 1:01:47 | Bill Reifsnyder (USA) | (4) | Philadelphia | 18 Sep 85 |
| 1:01:47 | Jon Sinclair (USA) | (5) | Philadelphia | 18 Sep 85 |
| | | | | |
| **WOMEN** | | | | |
| 1:07:59 | Ingrid Kristiansen (Nor) | (1) | Oslo | 13 Sep 86 |
| 1:08:34 | Joan Samuelson (USA) | (1) | Philadelphia | 16 Sep 84 |
| 1:09:39 | Lisa Martin (Aus) | (1) | Newcastle | 8 Jun 86 |
| 1:09:54 | Rosa Mota (Por) | (1) | Newcastle | 30 Jun 85 |
| 1:10:23 | Veronique Marot (UK) | (1) | Bath | 16 Mar 86 |
| 1:10:27 | Grete Waitz (Nor) | (1) | Newcastle | 17 Jun 84 |
| 1:10:34 | Grete Kirkeberg (Nor) | (2) | Oslo | 13 Sep 86 |
| 1:10:55 | Judi St Hilaire (USA) | (2) | Philadelphia | 16 Sep 84 |
| 1:11:04 | Priscilla Welch (UK) | (3) | Oslo | 1 Sep 84 |
| 1:11:28 | Anne Audain (NZ) | (1) | Manchester | 17 Sep 83 |
| 1:11:28 | Kellie Cathey (USA) | (2) | Philadelphia | 18 Sep 83 |
| 1:11:28 | Aurora Cunha (Por) | (1) | Oslo | 1 Sep 85 |

Mike Musyoki and Steve Jones on their way to records in the Great North Run 1986. *Mark Shearman*

## World top ten performers 1986 – MEN

| Hr:min:sec | Name | Place | Venue | Date |
|---|---|---|---|---|

**10km** (World best: 27.22 Mark Nenow (USA) New Orleans 1 Apr 84)

| | | | | |
|---|---|---|---|---|
| 27:41 | Arturo Barrios (Mex) | (1) | Phoenix | 1 Mar |
| 27:47 | Peter Koech (Ken) | (2) | Phoenix | 1 Mar |
| 27:48 | Mike Musyoki (Ken) | (3) | Phoenix | 1 Mar |
| 27:48 | Paul McCloy (Can) | (1) | Ukiah | 19 Oct |
| 27:48 | Gerardo Alcala (Mex) | (2) | Ukiah | 19 Oct |
| 27:49 | Dirk Lakeman (USA) | (3) | Ukiah | 19 Oct |
| 27:49 | Bruce Bickford (USA) | (4) | Ukiah | 19 Oct |
| 27:50 | Joseph Kipsang (Ken) | (5) | Ukiah | 19 Oct |
| 27:50 | Gabriel Kamau (Ken) | (6) | Ukiah | 19 Oct |
| 27:53 | Mike O'Reilly (UK) | (7) | Ukiah | 19 Oct |

**15km** (World best: 42:27 Mike Musyoki (Ken) Portland 26 Jun 83)

| | | | | |
|---|---|---|---|---|
| 42:36 | Arturo Barrios (Mex) | (1) | Portland | 29 Jun |
| 42.44 | Ibrahim Hussein (Ken) | (2) | Portland | 29 Jun |
| 43:00 | John Treacy (Ire) | (1) | Tampa | 8 Feb |
| 43:13 | Jose Gomez (Mex) | (2) | Tampa | 8 Feb |
| 43:27 | Peter Koech (Ken) | (3) | Tampa | 8 Feb |
| 43:30 | Mike Musyoki (Ken) | (3) | Portland | 29 Jun |
| 43:31 | Bruce Bickford (USA) | (2) | Jacksonville | 8 Mar |
| 43:32 | Steve Harris (UK) | (4) | Tampa | 8 Feb |
| 43:34 | Hans Koeleman (USA) | (5) | Tampa | 8 Feb |
| 43:39 | Jon Sinclair (USA) | (4) | Portland | 29 Jun |

**10 miles** (World best: 46:00 Herb Lindsay (USA) New York 27 Apr 80)

| | | | | |
|---|---|---|---|---|
| 46:15 | Thom Hunt (USA) | (1) | Washington, DC | 6 Apr |
| 46:41 | Roger Hackney (UK) | (2) | Washington, DC | 6 Apr |
| 47:00 | Jim Cooper (USA) | (3) | Washington, DC | 6 Apr |
| 47:01 | Joseph Kipsang (Ken) | (4) | Washington, DC | 6 Apr |
| 47:02 | Bill Reifsnyder (USA) | (5) | Washington, DC | 6 Apr |
| 47:03 | Jon Sinclair (USA) | (6) | Washington, DC | 6 Apr |
| 47:12 | Greg Meyer (USA) | (7) | Washington, DC | 6 Apr |
| 47:12 | Ashley Johnson (USA) | (1) | Cherry Hill | 23 Mar |
| 47:16 | Brian Sheriff (Zim) | (2) | Cherry Hill | 23 Mar |
| 47:20 | Marcos Barreto (Mex) | (3) | Cherry Hill | 23 Mar |

*uncertified course:* Amsterdam 12 Oct:
1. Fernando Mamede (Por) 45:14; 2. Vincent Rousseau (Bel) 46:08;
3. Charlie Spedding (UK) 46:14; 4. Alex Hagelsteens (Bel) 46:39

**Half marathon** (World best: 1:00:43 Mike Musyoki (Ken) Newcastle 8 Jun 86)

| | | | | |
|---|---|---|---|---|
| 1:00:43 | Mike Musyoki (Ken) | (1) | Newcastle | 8 Jun |
| 1:00:59 | Steve Jones (UK) | (2) | Newcastle | 8 Jun |
| 1:01:31 | Steve Kenyon (UK) | (3) | Newcastle | 8 Jun |
| 1:01:43 | Mark Curp (USA) | (1) | Philadelphia | 14 Sep |
| 1:01:57 | Bruce Bickford (USA) | (2) | Philadelphia | 14 Sep |
| 1:02:06 | Geoff Smith (UK) | (1) | New Bedford | 16 Mar |
| 1:02:08 | Bill Reifsnyder (USA) | (3) | Philadelphia | 14 Sep |
| 1:02:15 | Bill Donakowski (USA) | (4) | Philadelphia | 14 Sep |
| 1:02:19 | Mark Stickley (USA) | (5) | Philadelphia | 14 Sep |
| 1:02:24 | Jimmy Ashworth (UK) | (4) | Newcastle | 8 Jun |

**World top ten performers 1986 – WOMEN**

| Hr:min:sec | Name | Place | Venue | Date |
|---|---|---|---|---|
| **10km** (World best: 31:29 Wendy Sly (UK) New Orleans 27 Mar 83 – but see below) | | | | |
| 31:32 | Ingrid Kristiansen (Nor) | (1) | Miami | 1 Feb |
| 31:38 | Brenda Webb (USA) | (1) | Ukiah | 19 Oct |
| 31:47 | Lisa Martin (Aus) | (2) | Ukiah | 19 Oct |
| 32:07 | Lynn Jennings (USA) | (1) | Boston | 13 Apr |
| 32:10 | Grete Waitz (Nor) | (1) | Atlanta | 4 Jul |
| 32:13 | Betty Springs (USA) | (1) | Albany, NY | 17 May |
| 32:14 | Lynn Williams (Can) | (1) | San Diego | 23 Mar |
| 32:18 | Leslie Welch (USA) | (2) | Boston | 13 Apr |
| 32:18 | Marty Cooksey (USA) | (2) | Atlanta | 4 Jul |
| 32:24 | Liz Lynch (UK) | (1) | Mobile | 8 Mar |
| *uncertified course:* | | | | |
| 30:46 | Ingrid Kristiansen (Nor) | (1) | Kobenhavn | 21 Sep |
| 30:47 | Ingrid Kristiansen (Nor) | (1) | Bergen | 25 May |
| 32:49 | Grete Kirkeberg (Nor) | (2) | Kobenhavn | 21 Sep |
| **15km** (World best: 47:53 Grete Waitz (Nor) Tampa 11 Mar 84) | | | | |
| 48:00 | Ingrid Kristiansen (Nor) | (1) | Tampa | 8 Feb |
| 48:31 | Aurora Cunha (Por) | (1) | Lisbon | 9 Nov |
| 48:35 | Rosa Mota (Por) | (2) | Lisbon | 9 Nov |
| 48:36 | Carla Beurskens (Bel) | (3) | Lisbon | 9 Nov |
| 48:41 | Martha Cooksey (USA) | (4) | Lisbon | 9 Nov |
| 48:53 | Grete Waitz (NZ) | (1) | Jacksonville | 8 Mar |
| 49:09 | Lorraine Moller (NZ) | (1) | Portland | 29 Jun |
| 49:12 | Tatyana Kazankina :SU) | (5) | Lisbon | 9 Nov |
| 49:13 | Ludmila Matveyeva (SU) | (6) | Lisbon | 9 Nov |
| 49:14 | Maria Curatalo (Ita) | (7) | Lisbon | 9 Nov |
| **10 miles** (World best: 53:09 Rosa Mota (Por) Washington, DC 6 Apr 86) | | | | |
| 53:09 | Rosa Mota (Por) | (1) | Washington, DC | 6 Apr |
| 53:18 | Joan Samuelson (USA) | (1) | New York | 26 Apr |
| 53:48 | Lorraine Moller (NZ) | (2) | Washington, DC | 6 Apr |
| 54:41 | Joan Nesbit (USA) | (3) | Washington, DC | 6 Apr |
| 54:47 | Lisa Weidenbach (USA) | (1) | Flint | 23 Aug |
| 54:59 | Lisa Welch (USA) | (2) | Flint | 23 Aug |
| 55:02 | Anne Audain (NZ) | (1) | Lynchburg | 27 Sep |
| 55:10 | Kim Rosenquist (USA) | (4) | Washington, DC | 6 Apr |
| 55:19 | Paolo Mora (Ita) | (5) | Washington, DC | 6 Apr |
| 55:30 | Michele Bush (USA) | (6) | Washington, DC | 6 Apr |
| *uncertified course:* | | | | |
| 53:04 | Carla Beurskens (Hol) | (1) | Amsterdam | 12 Oct |
| 53:27 | Carla Beurskens (Hol) | (1) | The Hague | 2 Nov |
| **Half marathon** (World best: 1:07:58 Ingrid Kristiansen (Nor) Oslo 13 Sep 86) | | | | |
| 1:07:59 | Ingrid Kristiansen (Nor) | (1) | Oslo | 13 Sep |
| 1:09:39 | Lisa Martin (Aus) | (1) | Newcastle | 8 Jun |
| 1:10:23 | Veronique Marot (UK) | (1) | Bath | 16 Mar |
| 1:10:34 | Grete Kirkeberg (Nor) | (2) | Oslo | 13 Sep |
| 1:10:59 | Liz Lynch (UK) | (1) | Dundee | 12 Oct |
| 1:11:41 | Midde Hamrin (Swe) | (1) | Philadelphia | 14 Sep |

| Hr:min:sec | Name | Place | Venue | Date |
|---|---|---|---|---|
| 1:12:09 | Ann Ford (UK) | (1) | Reading | 6 Apr |
| 1:12:46 | Nancy Ditz (USA) | (2) | Philadelphia | 14 Sep |
| 1:12:47 | Glynis Penny (UK) | (1) | Swanley | 16 Mar |
| 1:12:47 | Paula Fudge (UK) | (1) | Fleet | 23 Mar |
| *uncertified course:* | | | | |
| 1:09:28 | Carla Beurskens (Hol) | (1) | The Hague | 5 Apr |
| 1:11:45 | Sinikka Keskitalo (Fin) | (2) | The Hague | 5 Apr |

## United States road race circuit – Major results diary, 1986

| Date | Venue | Event | Winners | Time | Time |
|---|---|---|---|---|---|
| Men's winner shown on first line, women's on second | | | | | |
| 26 Jan | Phoenix | Runners Den, 10km | Dietmar Millonig (Aut) | 28.32 | |
| | | | Lisa Martin (Aus) | | 32:24 |
| 1 Feb | Miami | Orange Bowl, 10km | Peter Koech (Ken) | 28:20 | |
| | | | Ingrid Kristiansen (Nor) | | 31:31 |
| 8 Feb | Tampa | Gasparilla, 15km | John Treacy (Ire) | 43:00 | |
| | | | Ingrid Kristiansen (Nor) | | 48:00 |
| 1 Mar | Phoenix | Cont. Homes, 10km | Arturo Barrios (Mex) | 27:41 | |
| | | | Brenda Webb (USA) | | 32:20 |
| 8 Mar | Jacksonville | River Run, 15km | Arturo Barrios (Mex) | 43:18 | |
| | | | Grete Waitz (Nor) | | 48:53 |
| 8 Mar | Mobile | Azalea, 10km | Peter Koech (Ken) | 28:03 | |
| | | | Liz Lynch (UK) | | 32:24 |
| 16 Mar | New Bedford | NB half-marathon | Geoff Smith (UK) | 1:02:06 | |
| | | | Charlotte Teske (FRG) | | 1:13:23 |
| 23 Mar | Cherry Hill | New Jersey, 10M | Ashley Johnson (USA) | 47:12 | |
| | | | Michele Bush (USA) | | 55:42 |
| 23 Mar | San Diego | Buick, 10km | Mike Musyoki (Ken) | 28.17 | |
| | | | Lyn Williams (Can) | | 32:14 |
| 5 Apr | New Orleans | Crescent City, 10km | Arturo Barrios (Mex) | 28:16 | |
| | | | Lisa Martin (Aus) | | 32:18 |
| 6 Apr | Washington, DC | Cherry Blossom, 10M | Thom Hunt (USA) | 46:15 | |
| | | | Rosa Mota (Por) | | 53:09 |
| 13 Apr | Boston | Milk Run, 10km | Ed Eyestone (USA) | 28:21 | |
| | | | Lynn Jennings (USA) | | 32:07 |
| 26 Apr | New York | Trevira, 10M | Ibrahim Hussein (Ken) | 47:29 | |
| | | | Joan Samuelson (USA) | | 53:18 |
| 4 May | Spokane | Lilac Bloomsday, 12km | Jon Sinclair (USA) | 34:25 | |
| | | | Anne Audain (NZ) | | 38:48 |
| 17 May | Albany, NY | Freihofer's, 10km | *women only* | | |
| | | | Betty-Jo Springs (USA) | | 32:13 |
| 18 May | Cleveland | Revco, 10km | Mike Musyoki (Ken) | 28:31 | |
| | | | Anne Audain (NZ) | | 32:45 |
| 18 May | San Francisco | Bay to Breakers, 12km | Ed Eyestone (USA) | 34:33 | |
| | | | Grete Waitz (Nor) | | 38:45 |
| 24 May | Wheeling | Elbys, 20km | Ron Lanzoni (CRC) | 1:01:16 | |
| | | | Aurora Cunha (Por) | | 1:11:24 |
| 26 May | Boulder | Bolder, 10km | Arturo Barrios (Mex) | 28:46 | |
| | | | Rosa Mota (Por) | | 33:54 |

| Date | Venue | Event | Winners | Time | Time |
|------|-------|-------|---------|------|------|
| Men's winner shown on first line, women's on second | | | | | |
| 31 May | New York | L'Eggs, 10km | *women only* | | |
| | | | Ingrid Kristiansen (Nor) | | 31:45 |
| 29 Jun | Portland | Cascade, 15km | Arturo Barrios (Mex) | 42:36 | |
| | | | Lorraine Moller (NZ) | | 49:09 |
| 4 Jul | Atlanta | Peachtree, 10km | John Doherty (UK) | 27:56 | |
| | | | Grete Waitz (Nor) | | 32:10 |
| 13 Jul | Ames | Midnight, 20km | Phil Coppes (USA) | 1:02:18 | |
| | | | *men only* | | |
| 26 Jul | Davenport | Bix, 7M | Geoff Smith (UK) | 33:16 | |
| | | | Joan Samuelson (USA) | | 37:56 |
| 9 Aug | Asbury Park | Asbury, 10km | Keith Brantly (USA) | 28:57 | |
| | | | Lesley Welch (USA) | | 32:37 |
| 17 Aug | Falmouth | Falmouth, 7.1M | Arturo Barrios (Mex) | 32:17 | |
| | | | Lorraine Moller (NZ) | | 36:54 |
| 23 Aug | Waynesville | Maggie Valley, 8km | Mike Musyoki (Ken) | 22:41 | |
| | | | Lynn Jennings (USA) | | 26:27 |
| 23 Aug | Flint | Bobby Crim, 10M | Ed Eyestone (USA) | 47:36 | |
| | | | Lisa Weidenbach (USA) | | 54:47 |
| 1 Sep | New Haven | NH, 20km | Bill Reifsnyder (USA) | 59:53 | |
| | | | Nancy Conz (USA) | | 1:10:35 |
| 14 Sep | Philadelphia | Philly half-marathon | Mark Curp (USA) | 1:01:43 | |
| | | | Midde Hamrin (Swe) | | 1:11:41 |
| 20 Sep | Dallas | Southfork, 10km | John Doherty (UK) | 29:02 | |
| | | | Lorraine Moller (NZ) | | 33:36 |
| 27 Sep | Lynchburg | Virginia, 10M | Rob de Castella (Aus) | 47:49 | |
| | | | Anne Audain (NZ) | | 55:02 |
| 5 Oct | Itasca | Oktoberfest, 12km | Paul McCloy (Can) | 34:23 | |
| | | | Anne Audain (NZ) | | 39:36 |
| 11 Oct | Boston | Tufts, 10km | *women only* | | |
| | | | Ingrid Kristiansen (Nor) | | 31:40 |
| 19 Oct | Ukiah | Penofin, 10km | Paul McCloy (Can) | 27:48 | |
| | | | Brenda Webb (USA) | | 31:38 |
| 26 Oct | Tulsa | Tulsa Run, 15km | Paul Donovan (USA) | 44:06 | |
| | | | Midde Hamrin (Swe) | | 50:41 |
| 16 Nov | Raleigh | Old Reliable, 10km | John Gregorek (USA) | 28:07 | |
| | | | Sabrina Dornhoefer (US) | | 32:35 |
| 6 Dec | Orlando | Citrus Bowl, half-mar. | Art Boileau (Can) | 1:03:43 | |
| | | | Brenda Webb (USA) | | 1:16:36 |

# 1986 MARATHON REVIEW

## BY ROGER GYNN

A lack of direct head to head clashes among the élite in both men's and women's divisions meant that 1986 was a relatively uninspired year.

In only one race (Tokyo) did more than two of those eventually ranked at the top meet, the winner Juma Ikangua proving to be the season's best on merit, albeit by a narrow margin. For the first time three sub 2:08 times were recorded in a year, two in one race (Beijing), and yet three of the top runners: Rob de Castella, Toshihiko Seko and Ikangaa each won two big races but never met each other. It is not surprising therefore that there were no nail biting finishes in any of the so called 'classics' – Seko winning at both London and Chicago with a minute and a half to spare; de Castella a big 3:24 margin at Boston; Abebe Mekonnen an even bigger 4:30 at Montreal; Ikangaa 1:03 at Fukuoka; the list is endless. The prime cause could only have been money, and the wheeling and dealing of the entrepreneurs in their greedy attempts to buy the biggest names for their particular races, to which Boston succumbed in 1986. Now only Fukuoka remains out in the cold, and one wonders for how much longer that classic of classics can afford to stay aloof from the rabble.

1986 was also a year of some controversy. Besides the heavy cash involvement there were rumours of blood doping, and of a short course in the year's fastest race, plus a disqualification. The route at Beijing had been accurately measured but when the results were published it appeared that the markers at 20km and 40km were, in all likelihood, wrongly placed. The very fast times by Kodama (2:07:35) and Kunimitsu Itoh (2:07:57) were attributed to exceptional weather conditions and the ultra fast course, little concern being apparent over the fact that Kodama had improved by a startling 2:59 and Itoh, a veteran of some 20 marathons in nine years, by 1:38 from his best which dated back to 1981!

It is unfortunate that, as yet, allegations of blood doping cannot be proved. Such allegations, levelled (for the first time against the marathon runners) at the Italian long distance stars after a highly successful European Championships, followed Gianni Poli and Orlando Pizzolato to New York, where the former upset favoured de Castella.

The use of steroids has been proven, particularly among the throwers. However the disqualification of second placed Antoni Niemczak at New York was the first time that the marathon has been so tainted, and one hopes the last. There were reports that some form of anabolic steroid was administered to Niemczak following a tooth extraction. If so, any such prescribed drug should be carefully monitored as to its legality, so that such 'accidents' never happen again.

As stated earlier there was nothing spectacular about many of the year's races. Even the major Games (Commonwealth, European and Asian) marathons were uncomplicated affairs and devoid of excitement, including Stuttgart where a competent team effort resulted in an Italian 1–2, led by the relatively unknown Gelindo Bordin.

None of the aforesaid should detract from the excellent performances witnessed at Tokyo and Beijing. In the former for the first time four runners were timed in under 2:09 in a single race, led by Ikangaa (2:08:10), newcomer Belaine Dinsamo (2:08:29), Mekonnen (2:08:39) and Takeyuki Nakayama (2:08(43). The latter, recovering from injury, was destined to record the fastest ever time in a major Games marathon when he won the Asian title with 2:08:21. At Beijing Kodama and Itoh finished ahead of Ikangaa (2:08:39) and the 1978 Commonwealth Champion Gidamis Shahanga (2:09:39), whose time was a personal best by half a minute in something like his 24th marathon!

A similar state of affairs prevailed among the women. Grete Waitz (London and New York), Ingrid Kristiansen (Boston and Chicago) and Rosa Mota (European and Tokyo) each won two marathons decisively and were clearly superior to the rest, yet they did not meet each other. The inaugural Commonwealth Champion, Lisa Martin, finished a good second to Waitz at New York, ahead of consistent Laura Fogli, silver medallist at Stuttgart. Surprise of the women's season was without doubt the drop-out of Katrin Dörre at the European, although she partially redeemed herself when second at Tokyo.

Nevertheless 1986 was a year when the dollar appeared to be the over-riding factor, and whilst rightly beneficial to the runners, was possibly detrimental to marathon running as a whole.

**International marathons – major results diary 1986**

| Date | Venue | Men's winner | Time | Women's winner | Time |
|---|---|---|---|---|---|
| 19 Jan | Houston | Paul Cummings (USA) | 2:11:31 | Veronique Marot (UK) | 2:31:33 |
| 19 Jan | Manila | Eddy Hellebuyck (Bel) | 2:19:00 | Tani Ruckle (Can) | 2:46:58 |
| 26 Jan | Hong Kong | Zhu Shuchun (Chn) | 2:15:08 | Weng Yanmin (Chn) | 2:36:55 |
| 26 Jan | Osaka | *women only* | | Lorraine Moller (NZ) | 2:30:24 |
| 1 Feb | Auckland | Allan Zachariassen (Den) | 2:12:36 | Kersti Jakobsen (Den) | 2:36:58 |
| 2 Feb | Beppu | Taisuke Kodama (Jap) | 2:10:34 | *men only* | |
| 2 Feb | Sevilla | Vicente Anton (Spa) | 2:14:40 | *men only (Ibero-American)* | |
| 9 Feb | Tokyo | Juma Ikangaa (Tan) | 2:08:10 | *men only* | |
| 16 Feb | Manila | Jose Reveyn (Bel) | 2:18:58 | Denise Verhaert (Bel) | 2:49:39 |
| 16 Feb | Valencia | Pawel Lorens (Pol) | 2:16:43 | Malgorzata Szuminska (Pol) | 2:36:31 |
| 2 Mar | Nagoya | *women only* | | Katrin Dörre (GDR) | 2:29:33 |
| 9 Mar | Los Angeles | Richard Sayre (USA) | 2:12:59 | Nancy Ditz (USA) | 2:36:27 |
| 9 Mar | Otsu | Toshihiro Shibutani (Jap) | 2:14:55 | *men only* | |
| 9 Mar | Taipei | Akio Tokoro (Jap) | 2:18:51 | Winnie lai-Chu Ng (HK) | 2:53:53 |
| 16 Mar | Barcelona | Fredrik Vandervennet (Bel) | 2:15:45 | Debbie Heath (UK) | 2:48:22 |
| 22 Mar | Szeged | Istvan Kerekjarto (Hun) | 2:13:35 | Karolina Szabo (Hun) | 2:30:31 |
| 23 Mar | Shanghai | *women only* | | Carey Edge (Ire/Can) | 2:41:46 |
| 6 Apr | Debno | Antoni Niemczak (Pol) | 2:10:34 | Renata Walendziak (Pol) | 2:32:30 |
| 12 Apr | Maassluis | Alex Hagelsteens (Bel) | 2:14:45 | Eefje Pinkster (Hol) | 2:40:07 |
| 13 Apr | Stamford | Gerry Kiernan (Ire) | 2:12:47 | Kellie Cathey (USA) | 2:38:50 |
| 13 Apr | Vienna | Gerhard Hartmann (Aut) | 2:12:22 | Birgit Lennartz (FRG) | 2:38:31 |
| 19 Apr | Rotterdam | Abebe Mekonnen (Eth) | 2:09:08 | Ellinor Ljungros (Swe) | 2:41:06 |
| 20 Apr | London | Toshihiko Seko (Jap) | 2:10:02 | Grete Waitz (Nor) | 2:24:54 |
| 21 Apr | Boston | Rob de Castella (Aus) | 2:07:51 | Ingrid Kristiansen (Nor) | 2:24:55 |
| 26 Apr | Karl Marx St | Michael Heilmann (GDR) | 2:15:11 | Katrin Dörre (GDR) | 2:38:03 |
| 4 May | Jersey City | Bill Donakowski (USA) | 2:11:41 | Rita Borralho (Por) | 2:35:37 |
| 4 May | Munich | Istvan Kerekjarto (Hun) | 2:17:46 | Olivia Grüner (FRG) | 2:38:51 |
| 4 May | Paris | Ahmed Salah (Dji) | 2:12:44 | Maria Lelut (Fra) | 2:32:16 |
| 11 May | Amsterdam | Willy v. Huylenbroeck (Bel) | 2:14:46 | Theresa Kidd (Ire) | 2:46:20 |
| 11 May | Geneva | Bernard Bobes (Fra) | 2:18:11 | Nadezhda Gumerova (SU) | 2:38:33 |
| 18 May | Pittsburgh | Dean Matthews (USA) | 2:18:17 | Laura Fogli (Ita) | 2:37:04 |
| 25 May | Hamburg | Karel Lismont (Bel) | 2:12:12 | Magda Ilands (Bel) | 2:35:17 |
| 7 Jun | Stockholm | Kjell-Erik Stahl (Swe) | 2:12:33 | Evy Palm (Swe) | 2:34:42 |
| 8 Jun | Sydney | Eloi Schleder (Bra) | 2:12:54 | Ngaire Drake (NZ) | 2:38:52 |
| 14 Jun | Addis Ababa | Abebe Mekonnen (Eth) | 2:16:07 | | |
| 21 Jun | Duluth | Joseph Kipsang (Ken) | 2:12:53 | Karlene Erickson (USA) | 2:38:45 |
| 5/6 Jul | Moscow (GG) | Belaine Dinsamo (Eth) | 2:14:42 | Nadezhda Gumerova (SU) | 2:33:35 |
| 20 Jul | San Francisco | Pete Pfitzinger (USA) | 2:13:29 | Maria Trujillo (Mex) | 2:37:58 |
| 2 Aug | Helsinki | Tommy Persson (Swe) | 2:17:11 | Sinikka Kiipa (Fin) | 2:49:29 |
| 23 Aug | Rio | Eloi Schleder (Bra) | 2:22:02 | Liz McElhinny (USA) | 2:46:54 |
| 13 Sep | Oslo | Kjell-Erik Stahl (Swe) | 2:14:59 | Sissel Grottenberg (Nor) | 2:40:01 |
| 21 Sep | Glasgow | Kenny Stuart (UK) | 2:14:04 | Sandra Branney (UK) | 2:37:29 |
| 28 Sep | W Berlin | Boguslaw Psujek (Pol) | 2:11:03 | Charlotte Teske (FRG) | 2:32:10 |
| 28 Sep | Milan | Jeff Martin (Can) | 2:17:04 | Mary Marsiletti (Ita) | 2:47:11 |
| 28 Sep | Montreal | Abebe Mekonnen (Eth) | 2:10:31 | Ellen Rochefort (Can) | 2:35:51 |
| 5 Oct | Kosice | Frantisek Visnicky (Cs) | 2:18:43 | Christa Vahlensieck (FRG) | 2:41:08 |

| Date | Venue | Men's winner | Time | Women's winner | Time |
|------|-------|--------------|------|----------------|------|
| 12 Oct | Melbourne | Richard Umberg (Swz) | 2:17:21 | Tani Ruckle (Can) | 2:36:06 |
| 19 Oct | Beijing | Taisuke Kodama (Jap) | 2:07:35 | *women only* | |
| 26 Oct | Chicago | Toshihiko Seko (Jap) | 2:08:27 | Ingrid Kristiansen (Nor) | 2:27:08 |
| 27 Oct | Dublin | Dick Hooper (Ire) | 2:18:10 | Maureen Hurst (UK) | 2:46:29 |
| 27 Oct | Budapest | Peter Antal (Hun) | 2:14:48 | Agnes Sipka (Hun) | 2:28:51 |
| 2 Nov | New York | Gianni Poli (Ita) | 2:11:06 | Grete Waitz (Nor) | 2:28:06 |
| 16 Nov | Columbus | Mike O'Reilly (Ire) | 2:13:19 | Midde Hamrin (Swe) | 2:33:49 |
| 16 Nov | Tokyo | *women only* | | Rosa Mota (Por) | 2:27:15 |
| 7 Dec | Honolulu | Ibrahim Hussein (Ken) | 2:11:44 | Carla Beurskens (Hol) | 2:31:02 |
| 7 Dec | Florence | Andy Girling (UK) | 2:15:57 | | |
| 7 Dec | Singapore | Alain Lazare (Fra) | 2:19:04 | Kersti Jakobsen (Den) | 2:39:03 |
| 7 Dec | Sacramento | Daniel Gonzalez (USA) | 2:13:20 | Christa Vahlensieck (FRG) | 2:39:31 |
| 7 Dec | Fukuoka | Juma Ikangaa (Tan) | 2:10:06 | *men only* | |
| 14 Dec | San Diego | Thom Hunt (USA) | 2:12:26 | Janine Aiello (USA) | 2:34:34 |

*see also the major championships section and national championships*

London marathon winners Toshihiko Seko and Grete Waitz. *Mark Shearman*

# 1986 ULTRAMARATHON REVIEW

## BY ANDY MILROY

1986 was the year that Ultrarunning became a world sport. Previously the province of the developed nations, ultramarathons this year featured runners from such diverse countries as Iran, Botswana, Kuwait, Brazil, Morocco and Mexico. It was not just from the Third World that ultrarunners emerged. Countries without ultrarunning traditions like Japan, Sweden and Hungary produced performers of note.

The Spartathlon, a 250km race from Athens to Sparta commemorating the historic run of Pheidippides in 490BC, was a microcosm of this world wide development. The race was won by a Greek; the next four places were filled by an Hungarian, a Swede, an Iranian and a Briton. Other finishers came from Finland, the FRG, USA, France and Japan.

Rab'ali James Zarei of Iran led this widening interest in ultra running. The seemingly tireless Zarei ran twelve ultras, winning four. He posted the best road 24 hour mark of the year, as well as setting new Asian bests with virtually every race. However late in the year he lost his Asian 100km road best to Saleh Ali (Kuw), competing in the USA. Elsewhere at 100km Mohammed Lahouari broke seven hours to set a new African mark, and Brazilian Celso da Silva set a continental best of 7:19:26.

The continuing development of the 100km road race was another major feature. In 1985 there were several top class, highly competitive races. In 1986 standards were even higher, with three sub 6:20 performances. Jean-Paul Praet's mark of 6:03:51, set at Torhout in Belgium, is still under investigation, but should this mark prove correct it will be a major step forward for the event. Domingo Catalan's 6.15.17 or Jan Szumiec's 6.17.57 are possible candidates to supplant Praet's mark if the Torhout course proves short.

Yiannis Kouros of Greece, so dominant at 24 hours and beyond in 1985, missed the early season through a broken toe and this was to hamper him throughout much of the year. Standards at 24 hours remained high with four men over 255km. Peter Mann and Hans Erdmann (FRG) contested the Apeldoorn road 24 hours in Holland, the former setting a world over 45 best, Rune Larsson

(Swe) won the Honefoss 24 hour track in July, and Rab'ali James Zarei the Chorley road event in August. Jean-Gilles Boussiquet (Fra) won the French 48 Hours Championship at Montauban with a new over-40 best of 410.550km.

Six Day action was limited to a handful of races. Indoors at La Rochelle in October, 51 year old Gilbert Mainix went over 600 miles (980km) to set the second best mark of modern times. He finished in front of Patrick Macke (UK) (931km). Macke had finished fifth in the Spartathlon only two days before the start of the 6 Day event! Eleven different nationalities contested this race, and seven national bests were set. In part the place of the 6 Day has been taken by the 1000 miler. In New York in early May Stu Mittleman (USA) ran a yet unverified world best of 11:20:36:50 ahead of the previous holder of the world best Siegfried Bauer (NZ).

Apart from perhaps the La Rochelle race, the best indoor event of the year took place in Chicago in February, when at 24 hours Yiannis Kouros surpassed the long standing professional indoor performance of Arthur Newton, set in 1934, with 251.064km. Patrick Macke (UK) also surpassed the previous world amateur best with 239.197km in second place, as well as breaking Charles Rowell's 104 year old 100 mile best with 13:00:49.

The fair sex were equally busy. On the track Ann Franklin (UK) set new world bests for 30 miles, 50km and 40 miles at Barry, Wales, and Arlette Touchard (Fra) 347.420km for 48 hours at Montauban. On the road, first Waltraud Reisert (FRG), then Hilary Walker (UK) set new 24 hour world marks. Pre-eminent was Eleanor Adams (UK), who set a new 6 Day best at Colac, followed by 100 miles and 200km bests at Honefoss. She also won the Sydney to Melbourne race. At 100km Sandra Kiddy (USA) ran 7.56 in America, and 8.01 in Europe, but was almost matched in the rankings by Agnes Eberle (SWZ), who ran four sub 9 hour performances. Angela Mertens ran the second fastest track 100km of all-time at Arcueil in November.

Not all ultras are subject to the demands of comparability. In April the Sydney—Melbourne

## 1986 Ultra Marathon Lists—Men

| hr:min:sec | Name | Nation | Born | Place | Venue | Date |
|---|---|---|---|---|---|---|
| **100 KM ROAD** | | | | | | |
| 6:03:51 | Jean-Paul Praet | (BEL) | (56) | (1) | Torhout | 20/21 Jun |
| 6:15:17 | Domingo Catalan | (SPA) | (48) | (1) | Auron—Nice | 16 Nov |
| 6:17:56 | Jan Szumiec | (POL) | (54) | (1) | Winschoten | 13 Sep |
| 6:27:08 | Bruno Scelsi | (FRA) | (54) | (1) | Vogelgrun | 13 Sep |
| 6:28:22 | Scelsi | | | (2) | Torhout | 20/21 Jun |
| 6:29:33 | Szumiec | | | (1) | Kalisz | 25 Oct |
| 6:30:36 | Risto Laitinen | (FIN) | (48) | (1) | Hartola | 27 Jun |
| 6:30:37 | Vaclav Kamenik | (CS) | (51) | (3) | Torhout | 20/21 Jun |
| 6:32:09 | Catalan | | | (1) | Santander | 4 Oct |
| 6:35:47 | Johannes Knupfer | (SWZ) | (60) | (4) | Torhout | 20/21 Jun |
| 6:36:02 | Don Ritchie | (UK) | (44) | (1) | Torino—St. V. | 4 May |
| 6:36:05 | Roger Julien | (FRA) | (52) | (1) | La Ferte | 24 May |
| 6:37:10 | Kamenik | (CS) | (51) | (1) | Rodenbach | 19 Apr |
| 6:37:17 | Kamenik | (CS) | (51) | (2) | Winschoten | 13 Sep |
| 6:38:29 | Robert Schlapfer | (SWZ) | (54) | (1) | Biel | 6 Jun |
| 6:39:28 | Peter Rupp | (SWZ) | (46) | (5) | Torhout | 20/21 Jun |
| 6:41:00 | Christian Roig | (FRA) | (52) | (6) | Torhout | 20/21 Jun |
| 6:42:29 | Mohammed Lahouari | (FRA) | (49) | (1) | Amiens | 27 Sep |
| 6:42:38 | Jean-Marc Bellocq | (FRA) | (57) | (2) | Vogelgrun | 13 Sep |
| 6:43:16 | Bellocq | | | (1) | Belves | 26 Apr |
| 6:43:49 | Roig | | | (3) | Vogelgrun | 13 Sep |
| 6:45:46 | Tom Zimmerman | (USA) | (57) | (1) | Dallas | 18 Jan |
| 6:46:37 | Robert Buzon | (FRA) | (55) | (4) | Vogelgrun | 13 Sep |
| 6:47:15 | Claud Ansard | (FRA) | (54) | (2) | Amiens | 27 Sep |
| 6:47:20 | Stefan Fekner | (CAN) | (52) | (2) | Dallas | 18 Jan |
| 6:47:49 | Don Ritchie | (UK) | (44) | (2) | Santander | 4 Oct |
| 6:49:07 | Roland Villemont | (FRA) | (46) | (5) | Vogelgrun | 13 Sep |
| 6:51:06 | Charlie Trayer | (USA) | (54) | (1) | Philadelphia | 16 Nov |
| 6:51:31 | Rune Larsson | (SWE) | (56) | (1) | Lund | 17 Aug |
| 6:51:59 | Hanspeter Roos | (SWZ) | (58) | (7) | Torhout | 20/21 jun |
| **100KM TRACK** | | | | | | |
| 6:54:23 | Bruno Scelsi | (FRA) | (54) | (1) | Carmaux | 18 May |
| 7:04:40 | Wolfgang Schwerk | (FRG) | (55) | (1) | Rodenbach | 29 Nov |

race stretched to 1005km, and was won by Dusan Mravlje (Yug) with 6:12:38:30. Another point to point event, the Comrades in South Africa, run this year from Pietermaritzburg to Durban (88.7km) was won for a record sixth time by Bruce Fordyce. (This race incidentally was the largest ultra ever with 9653 finishers.) In June in the Western States, the most famous of the American trail races, Chuck Jones finished first in 16:37:47, before establishing himself as the dominant figure over the trail 100 miles. The classic London to Brighton race (85.7km) was won by Terry Tullett (5:53), and the Spartathlon by Yiannis Kouros for the third time in 21:57.

Ultramarathon running's steady growth, numerically, geographically and organisationally, continued in 1986. The future looks full of promise. As interest in ultras in Third World countries and elsewhere grows and competition between top runners becomes common, standard will continue to rise. The sheer variety of the sport will ensure, that along with the development of the 24 hours and 100km, there will be a constant stream of new challenges and events to test ultra-runners in the coming year.

## 1986 Ultra Marathon Lists – Men

| hr:min:sec | Name | Nation | Born | Place | Venue | Date |
|---|---|---|---|---|---|---|
| **24 HOUR – ROAD** | | | | | | |
| 261.128 | Rab'ali James Zarei | (IRN) | (44) | (1) | Chorley | 23/24 Aug |
| 258.108 | Peter Mann | (FRG) | (39) | (1) | Apeldoorn | 9/10 May |
| 256.138 | Hans Erdmann | (FRG) | (39) | (2) | Apeldoorn | 9/10 May |
| 247.330 | Bernhard Schoneck | (FRG) | (43) | (1) | Gent | 18/19 Oct |
| 245.712 | Joseph Tudo | (FRA) | (35) | (1) | d'Eppeville | 31 May–1 Jun |
| 245.306 | Terry Edmondson | (UK) | (45) | (1) | Cranwell | 7/8 Jun |
| 239.016 | Paul Bream | (UK) | (44) | (1) | Niort | 10/11 Nov |
| 237.757 | Ronald Teuniss | (HOL) | ( ) | (3) | Apeldoorn | 9/10 May |
| 237.107 | Bob Meadowcroft | (UK) | (37) | (2) | Cranwell | 7/8 Jun |
| 236.366 | Clemens Schewe | (FRG) | ( ) | (1) | Morlenbach | 13/14 Sep |
| 234.312 | Marcel Giraud | (FRA) | ( ) | (2) | Niort | 10/11 Nov |
| 233.705 | Edmondson | | | (2) | Chorley | 23/24 Aug |
| 233.253 | Zarei | | | (3) | Cranwell | 7/8 Jun |
| **24 HOUR – TRACK** | | | | | | |
| 262.640 | Rune Larsson | (SWE) | (56) | (1) | Honefoss | 12/13 Jul |
| 247.216 | Richard Tout | (NZ) | ( ) | (1) | Auckland | 27/28 Sep |
| 247.200 | Jean-Gilles Boussiquet | (FRA) | (44) | (1) | Montauban | 14/15 Mar |
| 245.026 | Rae Clark | (USA) | ( ) | (1) | Santa Rosa | 22/23 Mar |
| 243.600 | Dusan Mravlje | (YUG) | (53) | (2) | Honefoss | 12/13 Jul |
| 242.598 | Brian Bloomer | (AUS) | ( ) | (1) | Melbourne | 15/16 Feb |
| 240.453 | Don Michell | (NZ) | (46) | (2) | Auckland | 27/28 Sep |
| 236.539 | Rab'ali James Zarei | (IRN) | (44) | (1) | Gateshead | 28/29 Jun |
| 236.204 | Gilbert Gevaert | (BEL) | (48) | (1) | Haren | 17/18 May |
| 235.600 | Gilbert Mainix | (FRA) | (35) | (2) | Montauban | 14/15 Mar |
| 229.250 | Rene Mimeur | (BEL) | ( ) | (2) | Haren | 17/18 May |
| 229.188 | Peter King | (UK) | (43) | (1) | Solihull | 12/13 Jul |
| 228.556 | David Standeven | (AUS) | ( ) | (1) | Adelaide | 1/2 Nov |
| **INDOORS** | | | | | | |
| 251.064 | Yiannis Kouros | (GRE) | (56) | (1) | Chicago | 14/15 Feb |
| 239.197 | Patrick Macke | (UK) | (55) | (2) | Chicago | 14/15 Feb |
| 227.599 | Jean-Gilles Boussiquet | (FRA) | (44) | (3) | Chicago | 14/15 Feb |

## 1986 Ultra Marathon Lists – Women

| hr:min:sec | Name | Nation | Born | Place | Venue | Date |
|---|---|---|---|---|---|---|
| **100 KM ROAD** | | | | | | |
| 7:56:21 | Sandra Kiddy | (USA) | (36) | (1) | Philadelphia | 16 Nov |
| 7:58:22 | Agnes Eberle | (SWZ) | (50) | (1) | Rodenbach | 19 Apr |
| 8:01:16 | Kiddy | | | (1) | Torhout | 20/21 Jun |
| 8:06:32 | Monique Exbrayat | (FRA) | (45) | (1) | Auron-Nice | 16 Nov |
| 8:07:46 | Eberle | | | (1) | Vogelgrun | 13 Sep |
| 8:22:31 | Exbrayat | | | (2) | Vogelgrun | 13 Sep |
| 8:25:00 | Eberle | | | (1) | Biel | 6 Jun |
| 8:32:30 | Martine Blandin | (FRA) | (49) | (3) | Vogelgrun | 13 Sep |
| 8:33:40 | Angela Mertens | (BEL) | (41) | (1) | Santander | 4 Oct |
| 8:34:40 | Riet Horber | (SWZ) | (38) | (1) | Winschoten | 13 Sep |
| 8:35:50 | Eberle | | | (1) | Hirtenberg | 27 Jun |

## 100 KM ROAD (WOMEN)–*cont*

| hr:min:sec | Name | Nation | Born | Place | Venue | Date |
|---|---|---|---|---|---|---|
| 8:36:36 | Ginette Baudrand | (FRA) | (47) | (4) | Vogelgrun | 13 Sep |
| 8:37:21 | Blandin | | | (2) | Auron-Nice | 16 Nov |
| 8:37:46 | Erika Hahn | (FRG) | (50) | (2) | Rodenbach | 19 Apr |
| 8:47:58 | Mertens | | | (2) | Torhout | 20 Jun |
| 8:49:35 | Katharina Janicke | (FRG) | (53) | (1) | Unna | 6 Sep |

### 100KM TRACK

| hr:min:sec | Name | Nation | Born | Place | Venue | Date |
|---|---|---|---|---|---|---|
| 8:28:20 | Angela Mertens | (BEL) | (41) | (1) | Arcueil | 15 Nov |
| 8:38:21 | Eleanor Adams | (UK) | (47) | (1) | Honefoss | 12/13 Jul |

| km | Name | Nation | Born | Place | Venue | Date |
|---|---|---|---|---|---|---|
| **24 HOUR – ROAD** | | | | | | |
| 220.568 | Hilary Walker | (UK) | (53) | (4) | Cranwell | 7/8 Jun |
| 215.402 | Waltraud Reisert | (FRG) | (39) | (5) | Apeldoorn | 9/10 May |
| 208.606 | Mareike Bestenbreur | (HOL) | (48) | (7) | Apeldoorn | 9/10 May |
| 203.411 | Renate Nierkens | (FRG) | (44) | (6) | Morlenbach | 13/14 Sep |
| **24 HOUR – TRACK** | | | | | | |
| 221.200 | Eleanor Adams | (UK) | (47) | (3) | Honefoss | 12/13 Jul |
| 213.622 | Mary Hanudel | (USA) | ( ) | (4) | Honefoss | 12/13 Jul |
| 201.383 | Angela Mertens | (BEL) | (41) | (3) | Haren | 17/18 May |
| 200.615 | Cynthia Cameron | (AUS) | ( ) | (4) | Adelaide | 1/2 Nov |
| 200.400 | Arlette Touchard | (FRA) | (41) | (4) | Montauban | 14/15 Mar |

## Men's World Bests – Track

| Event | hr:min:sec | Name | Place | Date | |
|---|---|---|---|---|---|
| 30 miles | 2:42:00 | Jeff Norman (UK) | Timperley | 7 Jun | 1980 |
| 50 km | 2:48:06 | Jeff Norman (UK) | Timperley | 7 Jun | 1980 |
| 40 miles | 3:48:35 | Don Ritchie (UK) | Hendon, London | 16 Oct | 1980 |
| 50 miles | 4:51:49 | Don Ritchie (UK) | Hendon, London | 12 Mar | 1983 |
| 100km | 6:10:20 | Don Ritchie (UK) | Crystal Palace | 28 Oct | 1978 |
| 150km | 10:36:42 | Don Ritchie (UK) | Crystal Palace | 15 Oct | 1977 |
| 100 miles | 11:30:51 | Don Ritchie (UK) | Crystal Palace | 15 Oct | 1977 |
| 200km | 16:32:30 | Don Ritchie (UK) | Coatbridge | 29/30 Oct | 1983 |
| | 15:11:10† | Yiannis Kouros (Gre) | Montauban (Fra) | 15/16 Mar | 1985 |
| 500km | 60:23:00 | Yiannis Kouros (Gre) | Colac (Aus) | 26/29 Nov | 1984 |
| 500 miles | 105:42:09 | Yiannis Kouros (Gre) | Colac (Aus) | 26/30 Nov | 1984 |
| 1000km | 136:17:00 | Yiannis Kouros (Gre) | Colac (Aus) | 26/31 Nov | 1984 |
| 1500km | 14d 20:10:13 | Malcolm Campbell (UK) | Gateshead | 11/26 Nov | 1985 |
| 1000 miles | 15d 21:07:43 | Malcolm Campbell (UK) | Gateshead | 11/27 Nov | 1985 |
| 24 hours | 283.600km | Yiannis Kouros (Gre) | Montauban | 15/16 Mar | 1985 |
| 48 hours | 452.270km | Yiannis Kouros (Gre) | Montauban | 15/16 Mar | 1985 |
| 6 days | 1023.200km | Yiannis Kouros (Gre) | Colac | 26 Nov/1 Dec | 1984 |

† Running watch time, stopped times not known.

## Men's Best Performances – Road

where superior to track bests and run on properly measured road courses

| Event | Time | Name | Place | Date | |
|---|---|---|---|---|---|
| 40 miles | 3:46:31 | Barney Klecker (USA) | Chicago | 5 Oct | 1980 |
| 50 miles | 4:50:21 | Bruce Fordyce (SAf) | London–Brighton | 25 Sep | 1983 |
| 1000 miles | 12d 12:36:20 | Siegfried Bauer (NZ) | Melbourne–Colac | 15/28 Nov | 1983 |
| | 11d 20:36† | Stu Mittleman (USA) | Queens, New York | 26 Apr–8 May | 1986 |
| 24 hours | 286.463km | Yiannis Kouros (Gre) | New York | 27/28 Sep | 1985 |

† Verification pending (may be a lap short)

## Women's World Bests – Track

| Event | hr:min:sec | Name | Place | Date | |
|---|---|---|---|---|---|
| 30 miles | 3:28:12 | Ann Franklin (UK) | Barry, Wales | 9 Mar | 1986 |
| 50 km | 3:36:58 | Ann Franklin (UK) | Barry, Wales | 9 Mar | 1986 |
| 40 miles | 4:47:27 | Ann Franklin (UK) | Barry, Wales | 9 Mar | 1986 |
| 50 miles | 6:17:30* | Monika Kuno (FRG) | Vogt | 8–9 Jul | 1983 |
| 100 km | 8:01:01 | Monika Kuno (FRG) | Vogt | 8–9 Jul | 1983 |
| 150 km | 14:20:32* | Eleanor Adams (UK) | Honefoss, Norway | 12–13 Jul | 1986 |
| 100 miles | 15:25:46 | Eleanor Adams (UK) | Honefoss, Norway | 12–13 Jul | 1986 |
| 200 km | 20:09:28* | Eleanor Adams (UK) | Honefoss, Norway | 12–13 Jul | 1986 |
| 200 miles | 44:44:08 | Eleanor Adams (UK) | Montauban, France | 15–17 Mar | 1985 |
| 500 km | 86:31:21 | Eleanor Adams (UK) | Colac, Australia | 24–28 Feb | 1986 |
| 500 miles | 143:38:55 | Eleanor Adams (UK) | Colac, Australia | 24 Feb–2 Mar | 1986 |

| Event | kilometres | Name | Place | Date | |
|---|---|---|---|---|---|
| 24 hrs | 222.8 | Eleanor Adams (UK) | Nottingham | 4–5 Aug | 1985 |
| 48 hrs | 347.420 | Arlette Touchard (FRA) | Montauban, France | 14–16 Mar | 1986 |
| 6 days | 808.0 | Eleanor Adams (UK) | Colac, Australia | 24 Feb–2 Mar | 1986 |

* Timed on one running watch only

## Women's Best Performances – Road

Where superior to track tests and run on properly measured courses.

| Event | hr:min:sec | Name | Place | Date | |
|---|---|---|---|---|---|
| 50 km | 3:13:51 | Janis Klecker (USA) | Tallahassee | 17 Dec | 1983 |
| 40 miles | 4:43:22 | Marcy Schwam (USA) | Chicago | 3 Oct | 1982 |
| 50 miles | 5:59:26 | Marcy Schwam (USA) | Chicago | 3 Oct | 1982 |
| 100 km | 7:26:01 | Chantal Langlacé (FRA) | Migennes, France | 17 Jun | 1984 |
| 100 miles | 15:07:45 | Christine Barrett (UK) | Forthampton | 14 Apr | 1984 |
| 500 km | 82:10† | Annie van der Meer (HOL) | Paris–Colmar | 8–11 Jun | 1983 |

† for 518 km.

# OBITUARIES 1986

## BY PETER MATTHEWS

Deaths were reported of the following notable athletes and offficials in 1986:

**Eddie BANNON** (UK) aged 56 on 16 July. Scottish cross-country champion 1952–4 and 1956. Father of Paul Bannon, 1978 Commonmwealth marathon bronze medallist.

**Sulo BÄRLUND** (FIN) (b.15 Apr 1910) on 13 April. Olympic silver medallist in 1936 at the shot, at which his Finnish record that year of 16.23m stood for 19 years. In the European Championships he was fourth in 1938 and sixth in 1946. He won seven Finnish shot titles between 1935 and 1948.

**Bruno BETTI** (ITA) (b. 31 May 1911). Sixth at 10000m in the 1934 European Championships. Italian champion at 5000m 1933, with personal bests: 3000m: 8.36.6 '36, 5000m: 15:07.8 '34, 10000m: 32:54.0 '34.

**Sidney BOWMAN** (USA) (b.8 Jun 1907) on 29 April. At the triple jump he was AAU champion in 1932 and at the Olympics was equal ninth in 1928 and seventh in 1932; pb 15.19m in 1934.

**Erik BYLÉHN** (SWE) (b. 15 Jan 1898) in November. Won two Olympic silver medals, at 4 x 400m relay in 1924 and at 800m in 1928. He was Swedish champion at 400m in 1925 and at 800m in 1925 and 1928 and set a Swedish 800m record of 1:52.8 in 1928.

**Nils CARLIUS** (SWE) (b.1911) on 6 Sep. President of the Swedish Athletic Association 1959–64 and a member of the IAAF Women's Committee 1956–81.

**Bernie CECINS** (AUS) on 3 Jan at the age of 59. Born in Latvia he emigrated to Australia in 1950 where he speedily gained respect as a leading statistician and journalist.

**Kathleen DALE** (UK) née Tiffen (b.15 Jul 1912) in May. Three times second at the WAAA 80mh in the 1930s, she was a semi-finalist at the World Games 1930, Empire Games 1934 and Olympics

1936, and sixth in the 1938 Empire Games at 80mh (pb 11.6 in 1936).

**Jeff DRENTH** (USA) (b.30 Jun 1961) on 2 June of heart failure. He had run three times for the USA in the world cross-country championships and had pbs of 13:44.4 '85 for 5000m and 28:41.11 '84 for 10000m.

**Henry DREYER** (USA) (b.2 Feb 1911) on 27 May. He was ninth in the Olympic hammer in both 1936 and 1948. In AAU competition at the hammer he placed in the top six 16 times from 1934 to 1952, winning in 1935 and 1943–5; he also won at 56lb weight in 1940, 1945, 1948–9 and 1951–2. He was NCAA hammer champion in 1934 and had a pb of 55.88m in 1949.

**Len EYRE** (UK) (b.27.11.25). At the 1950 Empire Games he won gold at 3 miles and silver at 1 mile. At 1500m he was fifth in the 1950 Europeans and eliminated in a heat at the 1952 Olympics. His pbs: 1500m: 3:50.0 '51, 1M: 4:10.6 '51, 2M: 8:54.7 '53, 3M: 13:57.9 '54, 5000m: 14:31.4 '53.

**Crawford FAIRBROTHER** (UK) (b.1 Dec 1936). At high jump set five UK records 1959–62, with a pb of 2.07m in 1964; AAA champion outdoors 1961 and 1964, and indoors 1963 and 1966, and Scottish champion for a record 13 successive years 1957–69. He competed in 53 internationals for the UK 1957–69, then a record. Competed at four Commonwealth Games, with a best placing of fourth in 1966.

**Rich FERGUSON** (CAN) (b.3 Aug 1931) on 26 May. Bronze medallist in the classic 1954 Empire Games mile in his pb 4:04.6. He had set Canadian records for 3 miles, 14:57.4 in 1950, and 2 miles, 9:31.6 in 1950 and 9:22.8 in 1951.

**Howard FORD** (UK) (b.18 Dec 1905) in April. At the 1930 Empire Games he won a silver medal at the pole vault, was fifth at shot and sixth at discus. He had failed to finish the 1928 Olympic decathlon. At the pole vault he was AAA champion in 1929 and his pb was 3.73m in 1931. He had a distinguished career in the RAF, retiring as an Air Vice Marshal.

**Edward GENUNG** (USA) (b.15 Feb 1908) on 2 May. Fourth in the 1932 Olympic 800m in a pb 1:51.7, he was NCAA champion in 1929 and AAU champion each year from 1930 to 1932.

**Robert 'Bonzo' HOWLAND** (UK) (b.25 Mar 1905) on 7 Mar. A Cambridge don, who had been the UK's best shot-putter in pre-war days. He never won an outdoor AAA title, but was second nine times and third once between 1929 and 1939, on each occasion the leading British thrower. He was also Empire Games silver medallist in 1930 and 1934 and set many English native records, with a best of 14.86m in 1935.

**Stanislav JUNGWIRTH** (CS) (b.15 Aug 1930) on 11 April. He set three world records: 2:21.2 for 1000m in 1952, a relay leg on the 4 x 800m relay record in 1953, and 3:38.1 for 1500m in 1957, when he took 2.1 secs off the record. World ranked throughout the 1950s, his other pbs included: 800m: 1:47.5 '57, 1000m: 2:19.1 '56, 1M: 3:59.1 '57, 2000m: 5:10.8 '55, 3000m: 8:02.8 '59. At 1500m he was European bronze medallist in 1954, and eighth in 1958, and sixth at the 1956 Olympics.

**Urho KEKKONEN** (FIN) (b.3 Sep 1900) on 30 August. President of Finland 1956–81, and Prime Minister 1950–3 and 1954–6. He was Finnish champion in 1924 at high jump (1.85m) and standing triple jump and second at 100m (11.0). pb TJ: 14.06m '27. President of the Finnish Athletic Association 1932–48, and Finnish Olympic Committee 1937–46.

**Sulo KOLKKA** (FIN) (b.30 May 1902) on 7 February. He had been press chief at the 1952 Olympic Games.

**Erkki KOUTONEN** (USA) (b. 25 Mar 1926) on 15 December. He competed in the 1948 Olympics at triple jump and was second in the 1949 AAU.

**Vladimir KUZNETSOV** (USSR) (b.2 Apr 1931) on 29 August. At the javelin he competed in three Olympic Games: '52– 10, '56– 12, '64– 8, and three European Championships: '54– 2, '58– 6, '62– dnq. He set nine Soviet records with a best of 85.64m in 1962 and was Soviet champion in 1953–4, 1958 and 1961. He became a distinguished coach and was Vice-President of the International Track & Field Coaches Association.

**Leslie LEWIS** (UK) (b.26.12.24) on 7 April. At the 1950 Empire Games he won silver medals at

both 440y (in a pb 48.0) and 4x440y relay. He was also AAA champion and fifth in the Europeans in 1950, and an Olympic quarter-finalist in 1952.

**Clive LONGE** (UK/Guy) (b.23 Feb 1939) in December in his native Guyana. Set seven UK, including two Commonwealth decathlon records 1966–69, with a best (1984 tables) of 7308. Commonwealth silver medallist in 1966 and 13th Olympics 1968.

**Max MAYR** (GER) on 1 January. He was, at 400mh, World Student Games champion in 1939 and German champion in 1940, with a pb of 53.9 in 1939.

**Christa MERTEN** (FRG) née Basche (b.14 Oct 1944) from head injuries after a fall at her house in Spain. Eliminated in heats at the 1971 Europeans and 1972 Olympics at 1500m; FRG champion at 3000m in 1973. pbs: 800m: 2:02.7 '72, 1500m: 4:12.6 '72, 3000m: 9:20.6 '73.

**Dr.Harold MOODY** (UK) (b.1 Nov 1915) on 12 September in New Zealand, whence he emigrated after winning the shot put silver medal in the 1950 Empire Games in Auckland. New Zealand champion at shot 1952–3 and discus 1953. In the AAA shot he was 3rd in 1946–7, 2nd 1948–9. Shot pb 14.32m '50.

**Hew NEILSON** (UK) on 9 January. He set world track walking bests for 100 miles: 17hr 18:51 and 24 hours: 214.062km in 1960.

**Ernst PAULUS** (GER) (b.3 Jan 1897). At the discus in 1928 he was seventh in the Olympics, was German champion and set a German record 47.52m.

**Jan POPPER** (CS) (b.26 Jun 1931) on 29 May. The highly respected journalist and statistician, editor of the sports daily 'Ceskoslovensky Sport'. *See tribute.*

**Eugen RAY** (GDR) (b.26 Jul 1957) on 18 January in a car accident while on police duty in Leipzig. He sprung to fame in 1977 with a sprint treble at the European Cup Final followed by 2nd at 100m and 4th 200m at the World Cup. He went on to win silver medals at 100m and sprint relay at the 1978 Europeans and was GDR 100m champion in 1977–8 and 1980, but did not improve his pbs from his 1977 times of 10.12 (10.01w) and 20.37. His 100m times of 10.21 and 10.16 indoors in 1976 were European Junior and world indoor bests.

**Bob ROGGY** (USA) (b.6 Aug 1956) on 3 August of a broken neck sustained in a fall from the back of a pick-up truck. At the javelin he was NCAA champion in 1978 and TAC champion in 1982 (2nd 1986), with a pb in 1982 of 95.80m, the last of three US records.

**Ilmari SALMINEN** (FIN) (b.21 Sep 1902) on 6 January. At 10000m he broke Paavo Nurmi's 13-year-old world record with 30:05.5 in 1937 at the age of 34, was Olympic champion in 1936 and European Champion in 1934 and 1938. He won four Finnish titles at 10000m and one at 5000m, at which his pb was 14:22.0 in 1939.

**Jackson SCHOLZ** (USA) (b.15 Mar 1897) on 26 October. Won Olympic gold medals at 4x100m relay in 1920 and 200m in 1924, when he also won a silver at 100m. At his third Olympics in 1928 he was fourth at 200m, having declined the offer of a run–off for the bronze medal. He set a world record for 100m at 10.6 in 1920, but his 100y best of 9.5 in 1925 was not ratified. At 220y he was AAU champion in 1925 with his pb of 20.8w. He became a well–known author of pulp fiction.

**Eric SVENSSON** (SWE) (b.10 Sep 1903) on 22 September. Triple jump silver medallist at 1932 Olympics and 1934 Europeans (4th and 10th LJ respectively). Swedish LJ and TJ champion 1933 and national records: LJ 7.53 '34, TJ 15.32 '32.

**Bela SZEPES** (HUN) (b.5 Sep 1903). Olympic javelin silver medallist in 1928. pb 66.70m 1929.

**Dr.Harry VOIGT** (FRG) (b.15 Jun 1913) on 29 October. At 4x400m relay he won European gold in 1934 and Olympic silver in 1936. He was German 400m champion in 1933, with a pb of 48.0, the European best for 1933.

**Rex Salisbury WOODS** (UK) (b.15 Oct 1891). Competed in the shot at the 1924 and 1928 Olympic Games, without qualifying for the finals. He was AAA champion in 1924 and 1926 and had a pb of 13.75m in 1927. He practised as a doctor in Cambridge until the age of 90.

The following deaths in 1985 are in addition to those included in the 1986 Annual:

**Charles HOFF** (NOR) (b.9 May 1902) set 12 indoor world bests in the pole vault, all on a tour of the USA in 1926, topped by 4.17m in Chicago on 9 April. Later that year he was barred by the AAU on a charge of professionalism and his records removed from official lists. Outdoors he set four world records from 4.12m in 1922 to 4.25m in 1925. Prevented from competing in the pole vault at the 1924 Olympics, he placed eighth in the 800m and fourth in a semi-final at 400m. He set Norwegian records at 200m, 400m, 800m, pole vault and long jump. His best vault came as a professional, 4.32m in 1931. He was reinstated as an amateur and won the Norwegian title in 1933.

**Sverre STRANDLI** (NOR) (b.30 Sep 1925) was the first to throw the hammer over 200ft, with the first of his two world records, 61.25m 1952 and 62.36m 1953. In all he set 21 Norwegian records from 50.82m in 1949 to 63.88m in 1962. He was European champion in 1950 and won the silver medal in 1954, and at the Olympics, 7th 1952, 8th 1956 and 11th 1960.

# ATHLETICS REFERENCE BOOKS 1986

## BY PETER MATTHEWS

Track and Field Performances through the years, Volume I 1929–36 by Dr. Roberto Quercetani and Rooney Magnusson with the assistance of many other members of the ATFS, the book's publishers. 350 pages. This most valuable work features deep world lists for each of these years, the product of thousands of hours of diligent research. Further volumes, reconstructing world lists prior to the formation of the ATFS will be keenly awaited. Obtainable from Palle Lassen, Bülowsvej 40/3, 1870 Fredriksberg C, Denmark at $13.

Guinness Track & Field Athletics – The Records by Peter Matthews. Published by Guinness Books, 33 London Road, Enfield, Middlesex EN2 6DJ, England. Price £7.95 (plus postage: £1.00 UK, £1.50 overseas). 176 pages plus 8 of colour illustrations. Event by event reviews of records and record-breakers; summaries of major championships, national championships and records; features on leading athletes etc.

El Libro de la Piste Cubierta (The Indoor Athletics Book) by Miguel Villuendas, Alberto Sanchez Traver and José Maria Garcia for the Spanish Athletics Federation. A5 300pp. Produced for the European Indoor Championships in Madrid. Text in Spanish and English, a most comprehensive survey of the history of indoor athletics, with progressive world and European records and all-time lists. European Indoor medallists and much detail on Spanish indoor athletics.

Coqs et Centurions edited by Jean-Gilbert Touzeau. A5, 400pp. 100 FF in Europe, 120 FF elsewhere from the Fédération Française d'Athlétisme, 10 rue du Faubourg-Poissonnière, 75010 Paris, France. A magnificent compendium of statistical information on French athletics, indeed a model for all nations. Included are 100-deep all-time lists, indexes of all athletes in these lists and all internationals, medallists in major meetings, all-time lists as at 1940, age records etc.

Österreichs Leichtathletik in Namen und Zahlen by Erich Kamper, with Karl Graf. A5 288pp. DM 40 from Erich Kamper, Postfach 328,

8010 Graz, Austria. As with the French publication, this is a definitive national collection of statistics, with progressive Austrian records, lists of Austrian champions, 50-deep all-time lists etc.

The United States' National Championships in Track and Field Athletics 1876–1985 by Bill Mallon, MD, and Ian Buchanan. $12 in the USA and Canada, $20 elsewhere from the Press Information Department, TAC, PO Box 120, Indianapolis, Indiana 46206, USA. 313 pages, A4. There are most comprehensive surveys of the US championships and complete details of the first six for each men's event, as well as an index for all finishing in the first three.

Commonwealth Athletics Statistics by Stan Greenberg, Paul Jenes, Peter Matthews and Lionel Peters. A5, 160pp. Published as a Track Stats special, £5 from Tim Lynch-Staunton, 17 St Martin's Drive, Walton-on-Thames, Surrey KT12 3BW, England. 100-deep Commonwealth all-time lists, progressive Commonwealth records, and results of Commonwealth Games finals 1930–82.

Laursens Lille Lommebog For Stati-Stiknar-komaner by Erik Laursen. A6 148pp. Small but splendid, packed with Danish all–time lists, 100 deep for most events. 26 kroner from Erik Laursen, Risdalsvej 46, vaer.117, 8260 Viby J, Denmark.

European Championships Statistics by Mark Butler. A5, 96pp. This was a special issue of Track Stats, containing detailed statistical summaries of the European Championships. Out of print.

EM Statistik 1934–1982 A5, 148pp. Produced by the organising commmittee of the European Championships in Stuttgart, contains details of all European finals.

Statistics Handbook for the World Junior Athletics Championships 1986 published by the IAAF and compiled by ATFS members for the inaugural championships in Athens. Included are national junior records, all-time top 50s, and progressive world junior records. Obtainable from the IAAF.

**European Junior Athletics Part 2 (Women)** by Raul Leoni. A5. 108 pp. Follows his men's volume published in 1985, with complete women's results from the European Junior Championships 1964–85, European all-time junior lists, and national records. Lira 12,000 from Raul Leoni, Via Paolo Maria Martinez n.11, 00151 Roma, Italy.

**TAFWA All-Time Indoor List 1987** by Ed Gordon. This most useful A5 102-page booklet is produced annually by the compiler for the Track and Field Writers of America. It contains indoor world bests and all-time lists of performers and performances for all events, men and women. From Ed Gordon, 180 Ardmore Road, Berkeley, CA 94707, USA.

**Osiagnecia Polskiej Lekkiej Atletyki W 40 Leciu PRL**. A5, 212 pp. Volume two of the ambitious project to fully document the statistics of Polish athletics. This book details the triple jump, with year lists, championship and international match results, progressive records of athletes etc., 1945–84. Available from Wojciech Gaczkowski, Nowogrodzka, 78m 26, 02018, Warszawa, Poland.

**KNAU Ranglijsten Aller Tijden** A5, 216pp. 18 florins. Comprehensive senior and junior all-time lists for all events for the Netherlands.

**25 Jaar Indoor Atletiek in Nederland 1961–86** A5, 116pp. 18 florins. 30 deep all-time indoor lists for seniors and juniors and details of Dutch participation in the European Indoor Championships.

Both books compiled by and available from Jacobus Koumans, Postbus 19127, 2500 CC Den Haag, Netherlands.

**TV Viewers' Guide to Athletics 1986/87**, by Steven Downes and Peter Matthews, published in England by Aurum Press, 33 Museum Street, London WC1A 1LD, £7.95. A4 128pp. Profusely illustrated guide to the major televised events, with background information to help TV viewers.

**Running: The Power and the Glory**, edited by Norman Harris, published in England by Partridge Press, Maxwelton House, Boltro Road, Haywards Heath, W. Sussex, £12.95. A4 144pp. An attractively illustrated collection of writings by distinguished authors on some of the great races in athletics history.

# Annuals

Annuals in varying sizes are produced for most major athletics nations. The following, containing year lists for 1985, records and in some cases results for the previous season, are amongst the most notable ones seen by this reviewer, and all give comprehensive details for their respective countries. Most should be obtainable from their national federations, whose addresses are given elsewhere in this Annual. The editions to be published during 1987 will cover the 1986 season.

**Svetove Tabulky 1985**. Edited by Jiri Havlin, Jan Popper and Milan Urban and the Czechoslovak statistical group. A4, 142pp. This booklet is complementray to the *International Athletics Annual*, with 200 deep performance lists for 1985. There are also national bests for each event and the best marks by the 15 top athletes at each event.

**The Race Walking World Statistics 1985** by Egon Rasmussen and Palle Lassen. Year and all-time lists for the walks. Two volumes, A5 size – men's 76pp US $4, and women's 40pp US $3 from Palle Lassen, Bülowsvej 40/3, 1870 Fredriksberg C, Denmark. Egon Rasmussen also produced a 24 page Danish walking annual, Dansk Gangforbunds Ranglister 1986.

**L'Athlétisme Africain/African Athletics 1986** by Yves Pinaud and Walter Abmayr A5, 144p. 100 deep men's and women's lists for Africa for 1985, with 10 deep junior and all-time lists, and national championships results. FF 60 from Yves Pinaud, 66 rue Labrouste, 75015 Paris, France.

**Athléterama 85–86**. This French Annual, edited by Jean Gilbert-Touzeau, must take the prize for the best of all the national athletics annuals. In addition to the most comprehensive lists covering all age groups of French athletes, there are records, championships and internationals results, profiles of leading French athletes, all-time lists etc. And world top 20 lists and profiles of a selection of the best athletes in the world. A5, 382p. Magnificent value at FF 90 from the Fédération Francaise d'Athlétisme.

**Atletica – Annuario 1985/6** published by FIDAL, Viale Tiziano, 70 00196 Roma, Italy. 544pp. The Italian annual changed shape this year to a square size. Once again it offered encyclopaedic coverage of Italian athletics. There were 30 deep Italian year lists, and masses of results, records, complete lists of all Italian internationals, athlete profiles, records, all-time lists, Italian champions, progressive records and so on.

**Atletismo 86** by Luis R. Vinker. For the Confederacion Argentinade Atletismo. 3260. A5, 252p. Covers results, records, 1985 and year lists for the whole of South America as well as for Argentina.

From the compiler, Corrientes 4258–130A, 1195 Buenos Aires, Argentina.

**British Athletics 1986**, compiled by the National Union of Track Statisticians, general editor Ian Hodge. A5, 336p. Detailed results and statistics on 1985 for the UK. £5.95 plus postage from BAAB Sales Office, 5 Church Road, Great Bookham, Surrey, KT23 3PW, England.

**Canadian Athletics Annual 1985**. A5, 224p. Covering the 1985 season, compiled for the Canadian Track and Field Association. 4 Canadian dollars in Canada, $5 USA, $6 elsewhere from Canadian T&F Association, 333 River Road, Ottawa, Ontario, K1L 8H9.

**Canadian Indoor Athletics Annual 1986**, A5 68pp. Covering the 1986 indoor season, with indoor best performances and 1986 lists. Canada and the USA are, I think, the only nations for which indoor annuals are produced. A fine job, as with the outdoor annual by the Canadian Association of Athletics Statisticians (CATS). Price $2, available as above.

**Friidretts-kalenderen 1986**, editor Jo Nesse. 50 kroner from Norges Fri-idrettsforbund. A5, 304p. Meticulously compiled year lists for Norway. NKr 50 from Ole Petter Sandvig, Uranienborgveien 9c, 0351 Oslo 3, Norway. Usually the first national annual to appear, in February each year.

**De Beste Nederlandse Atlekiekprestaties 1985**, edited by Jacobus Koumans. A5, 156pp. 17 florins from the editor, address as above. Always one of the earliest, this is the 42nd annual for the Netherlands.

**Pacific Islands Athletics Annual 1986** by Tony Isaacs. A5, 100pp. £4 or $6 from Tony Isaacs, 11 Manton Close, Trowbridge, Wiltshire BA14 0RZ, England. Top 20 lists for 1985, results of international meetings and national championships, all-time top 50s for the Pacific Islands.

**SA Athletics Annual 1985**. A5, 168p. The 34th edition of the South African Annual. Rand 4.48 from Harry Beinart, PO Box 1566, Cape Town 8000, Republic of South Africa.

**United States Annual 1986**, general editor Scott Davis of FAST, Federation of American Statisticians of Track. A5 size, 332p. £13 from Scott Davis, 4432 Snowbird Circle, Cerritos, CA 90701, USA. In addition to US records, year and all-time lists there is a most useful nearly 200 pages of index. Basic details are given for all athletes in the year lists and then progressions and championships records for scores of leading US athletes.

**American Athletics Annual 1986**, general editor Hal Bateman. A5 302pp. Published by the Press Information Department, TAC, PO Box 120, Indianapolis, IN 46206, USA. $10 in US and Canada, $15 elsewhere. Whereas the US Annual concentrates on all-time and year lists, this annual has detailed results of US and international meetings for the past year and lists of winners of AAU/TAC and NCAA championships, although there is some duplication, with the index of athletes.

**Indoor Track '87**, by Hal Bateman and Ed Gordon. A4 249pp. Published by TAC at $8 in US; $10 elsewhere – the official stats book for the World Indoor Championships.

**Amateur Athletic Union of Australia** Handbook of Records and Results 1986. Covering the Australian season to the end of April 1986. A5 88p.

**International Athletics Guide 1986–87**, edited by Mel Watman. A5 256pp. Published by Tantivy Press, 136–148 Tooley Street, London SE1 2TT at £7.95 or $12.95. An attractively produced survey of athletics around the world for 1985 and 1986 to September. There are feature articles on athletes of the year and basic top 20 lists.

# General

**Idrottsboken 1986**. 632 pp, A4. 569 Swedish kroner from Idrottsföretaget Förlags AB, Box 65, 162 11 Vällingby, Sweden. The 42nd edition of this magnificently produced and illustrated compendium gives results for 1985 on a very large number of sports. Coverage is both international as well as Swedish and there are an increased number of feature articles this year.

**The Official Commonwealth Games Book 1986**, edited by Peter Matthews. A4, 236pp. The official guide to the Games in Edinburgh 1986, including historical surveys of all sports and complete lists of medallists. Extensively illustrated in colour throughout. £5.50 from the Commonwealth Games Consortium, 17 Abercromby Place, Edinburgh EH3 6LT, Scotland.

Books for review would be welcomed by the editor: Peter Matthews, 10 Madgeways Close, Great Amwell, Ware, Herts SG12 9RU, England.

**The International Athletics Annual** can be obtained from the publishers: London & International Publishers, 49 St James St, London SW1A 1JT, England. Price £9.95 plus £1.00 postage.

# PREVIEW 1987 – WORLD CHAMPIONSHIPS

## BY PETER MATTHEWS

World Championships year is here again. The first World Championships in athletics, separate from the Olympic Games, held four years ago in Helsinki, are fondly remembered by enthusiasts. Keenly anticipated, they even exceeded our expectations, providing a feast of athletics, untarnished by political activity. Held in a land with a great athletics tradition, they were followed by an enthusiastic and knowledgeable crowd. Even the great tradition of Olympic competition was surpassed for there were no boycotts, no excess commercialism, just supreme quality athletics.

Who, present in the stadium that day, will ever forget the great roar that followed Tiina Lillak's javelin as it soared out to bring her the gold medal; the first Finnish woman to win a major javelin title. A triumph of character and skill, and where better to produce it than in the heartland of javelin throwing. The major stars included Jarmila Kratochvilova, who won an unprecedented 400m/800m double, Mary Decker, double winner, and Carl Lewis, triple gold medallist. Decker started with the 3000 metres, in which she led throughout and still moved smoothly away from her challengers at the end; and she returned four days later to win a second gold at 1500 metres. Again she made a determined front-running effort and again she had the strength at the finish to hold off her challengers, Zamira Zaytseva making a despairing lunge for the line to crash unavailingly to the track.

Winner of the most medals was Marita Koch with golds at the women's 200m and both relays, and silver at 100m behind Marlies Göhr. Carl Lewis's triple was at 100m, long jump and 4x100mR. His individual victories were by big margins, 10.07 at 100m to 10.21 for Calvin Smith, who went on to win the 200m, and 8.55m on his first long jump to 8.29m for Jason Grimes. In the sprint relay the US team's 37.86 by Emmit King, Willie Gault, Calvin Smith and Lewis was one of two world records set at the Championships. The other was 47.99 for 400m by Jarmila Kratochvilova, who also won the 800m on the previous day, just 36 minutes after her 400m semi final, giving an awe-inspiring display of strength and speed. A total of 1572 competitors took part from a record 157 nations.

For me one of the great moments came in the triple jump. The competition had been magnificent. After Ajayi Agbebaku had been the first to exceed 17 metres with his 17.01m opener, the lead changed several times; in the first round to Willie Banks 17.08m, in the third round to Mike Conley 17.13m and then Banks again 17.18m. With the final jump of the fourth round Zdzislaw Hoffmann matched that 17.18m and then took the lead with 17.35m in the fifth. In the final round Agbebaku also reached out to 17.18m, although still third on second best jumps. The charismatic Banks was getting tremendous support from the crowd, clapping him down the runway. Such support, by no means exclusively for him, reached a frenzy on his last attempt, but, though a massive effort, it was a no jump and Hoffmann was left as the winner. The silver medal may have been a disappointment for Banks, but this great man showed no sign of that. Willie Banks, his competition over, went out into the centre of the arena and personally conducted the crowd to clap Hoffmann on his last effort – to great success as he improved further to 17.42m to seal a competition which had brought so much enjoyment to everybody and which, with Banks's gesture of joy and sportsmanship, epitomised all that was best about these championships.

The second World Championships of Athletics will be staged in Rome's Stadio Olympico from 29 August to 6 September 1987. Helsinki provided quite an act to follow, and it will be hard to match the knowledge of Finnish fans, but Rome's magnificent stadium can house a much bigger crowd, and has staged many superb events since it was built for the 1960 Olympic Games. Other major meetings there have included the 1974 European Championships, 1981 World Cup and the 1985 and 1986 IAAF/Mobil Grand Prix finals, following the annual Golden Gala meetings.

**1983 Champions**

| MEN | | | WOMEN | | |
|---|---|---|---|---|---|
| 100m: | Carl Lewis (USA) | 10.07 | 100m: | Marlies Göhr (GDR) | 10.97 |
| 200m: | Calvin Smith (USA) | 20.14 | 200m: | Marita Koch (GDR) | 22.13 |
| 400m: | Bert Cameron (Jam) | 45.05 | 400m: | Jarmila Kratochvilova (Cs) | 47.99 |
| 800m: | Willi Wülbeck (FRG) | 1:43.65 | 800m: | Jarmila Kratochvilova (Cs) | 1:54.68 |
| 1500m: | Steve Cram (UK) | 3:41.59 | 1500m: | Mary Decker (USA) | 4:00.90 |
| 5000m: | Eamonn Coghlan (Ire) | 13:28.53 | 3000m: | Mary Decker (USA) | 8:34.62 |
| 10000m: | Alberto Cova (Ita) | 28:01.04 | Mar: | Grete Waitz (Nor) | 2:28:09 |
| Mar: | Rob de Castella (Aus) | 2:10:03 | 100mh: | Bettina Jahn (GDR) | 12.35 |
| 3000mSt: | Patriz Ilg (FRG) | 8:15.06 | 400mh: | Yekaterina Fesenko | |
| 110mh: | Greg Foster (USA) | 13.42 | | (USSR) | 54.14 |
| 400mh: | Edwin Moses (USA) | 47.50 | HJ: | Tamara Bykova (USSR) | 2.01 |
| HJ: | Gennadiy Avdeyenko | | LJ: | Heike Daute (GDR) | 7.27w |
| | (USSR) | 2.32 | Shot: | Helena Fibingerova (Cs) | 21.05 |
| PV: | Sergey Bubka (USSR) | 5.70 | Discus: | Martina Opitz (GDR) | 68.94 |
| LJ: | Carl Lewis (USA) | 8.55 | Javelin: | Tiina Lillak (Fin) | 70.82 |
| TJ: | Zdzislaw Hoffmann (Pol) | 17.42 | Hep: | Ramona Neubert (GDR) | 6770 |
| Shot: | Edward Sarul (Pol) | 21.39 | 4x100R: | GDR 41.76 | |
| Discus: | Imrich Bugar (Cs) | 67.72 | 4x400R: | GDR 3:19.73 | |
| Hammer: | Sergey Litvinov (USSR) | 82.68 | | | |
| Javelin: | Detlef Michel (GDR) | 89.48 | | | |
| Dec: | Daley Thompson (UK) | 8714 | | | |
| 4x100R: | USA 37.86 | | | | |
| 4x400R: | USSR 3:00.79 | | | | |
| 20kmW: | Ernesto Canto (Mex) | 1:20:49 | | | |
| 50kmW: | Ronald Weigel (GDR) | 3:43:08 | | | |

The championships bests are as for the winner's performances above except for:

| MEN | | | | |
|---|---|---|---|---|
| 1500m: | 3:35.77 | Steve Cram (UK) | sf |
| 10000m: | 27:45.54 | Fernando Mamede (Por) | sf |
| 110mh: | 13.22 | Greg Foster (USA) | sf |
| Javelin: | 90.40 | Detlef Michel (GDR) | qual |

One new event is being added in 1987, the 10 kilometres walk for women.

### Qualifying standards

Each IAAF member federation can send one male and one female competitor to the Championships; apart from that 'B' standards must be met for nations to enter one per event, or 'A' standards by each of up to three competitors per nation per event (between 1 Jan 1986 and 16 Aug 1987).

| Men's standards | A | B | Women's standards | A | B |
|---|---|---|---|---|---|
| 100m: | 10.30 | 10.45 | 100m: | 11.40 | 11.65 |
| 200m: | 20.70 | 20.95 | 200m: | 23.10 | 23.60 |
| 400m: | 45.70 | 46.50 | 400m: | 52.00 | 53.00 |
| 800m: | 1:46.00 | 1:47.50 | 800m: | 1:59.50 | 2:03.00 |
| 1500m: | 3:37.50 | 3:40.50 | 1500m: | 4:06.00 | 4:14.00 |
| 5000m: | 13:25.00 | 13:38.00 | 3000m: | 8:55.00 | 9:10.00 |
| 10000m: | 28:00.00 | 28:30.00 | 10000m: | 33:00.00 | 34:00.00 |
| Mar: | 2:15:00 | 2:25:00 | Mar: | 2:40:00 | 2:55:00 |
| 3kmSt: | 8:25.00 | 8:35.00 | 100mh: | 13.30 | 13.70 |
| 110mh: | 13.85 | 14.10 | 400mh: | 56.50 | 58.50 |
| 400mh: | 50.00 | 50.80 | HJ: | 1.93 | 1.86 |
| HJ: | 2.28 | 2.22 | LJ: | 6.65 | 6.40 |
| PV: | 5.55 | 5.40 | SP: | 18.30 | 16.50 |
| LJ: | 8.00 | 7.85 | DT: | 62.50 | 56.00 |
| TJ: | 17.00 | 16.50 | JT: | 62.50 | 56.00 |
| SP: | 20.30 | 19.00 | Hep: | 6000 | 5600 |
| DT: | 65.00 | 60.00 | 4x100mR: | – | 45.40 |
| HT: | 76.00 | 70.00 | 4x400mR: | – | 3:38.00 |
| JT: | * | * | | | |
| Dec: | 7900 | 7600 | * to be announced. | | |
| 4x100mR: | – | 40.30 | | | |
| 4x400mR: | – | 3:10.00 | | | |

## IAAF/MOBIL GRAND PRIX 1987
## Schedule of events

MAY
30 Bruce Jenner's Bud Lite Classic, San Jose (USA)

JUNE
7 Znamenskiy Memorial, Moscow (SU)
23 Rosicky Memorial, Prague (Cs)
30 DN Galan, Stockholm (Swe)

JULY
2 Maailmankisat (World Games), Helsinki (Fin)
4 Bislett Games, Oslo (Nor)
6 Grand Prix, Budapest (Hun)
8 Olympischer Tag, East Berlin (GDR)
10 Peugeot Talbot Games, London (UK)
13 Nikaia, Nice (Fra)
22 Golden Gala, Rome (Ita)

AUGUST
14 Miller Lite IAC International, London (UK)
16 ASV Sportfest der Weltklasse, Köln (FRG)
19 Weltklasse, Zürich (Swi)
21 ISTAF, West Berlin (FRG)

SEPTEMBER
IAC/Mobil Grand Prix Final:
11 Ivo van Damme Memorial, Brussels (Bel)

In addition the Grand Prix events will be divided, as an experiment, between four meetings in North America:

April 23–25 Penn Relays, Philadelphia (USA)
May 9 S&W Modesto Invitational, Modesto, Cal (USA)
June 6 Prefontaine Classic, Eugene, Oregon (USA)
June 9 Harry Jerome Classic, Vancouver (Can)

Grand Prix events in 1987 are:
MEN: 200m, 400m, 1500m, 5000m, 110mh, PV, LJ, DT, JT
WOMEN: 100m, 800m, 1 mile, 3000m, 400mh, HJ, LJ, SP

The Mobil grant to the IAAF has been increased by $250,000, to $1,250,000 for 1987.

# MAJOR INTERNATIONAL EVENTS 1987–90

## 1987
European Indoor Championships – Lievin, France (21–22 Feb)
World Indoor Championships – Indianapolis, USA (6–8 Mar)
World Cross-Country Championships – Warsaw, Poland (22 March)
World Marathon Cup – Seoul, Korea (11–12 Apr)
World Race Walking Cup – New York, USA (2–3 May)
GDR v USSR – Dresden, GDR (20–21 June)
European Cup Bruno Zauli: (27–28 June)
    A – Prague, Czechoslovakia
    B – Göteborg, Sweden
    C1 – Athens, Greece
    C2 – Porto, Portugal
European Cup for Multi-events: (4–5 July)
    Basel, Switzerland: A Dec, B Hep
    Arles, France: A Hep, B Dec
    Madrid, Spain: C Dec, C Hep
Arab Athletic Championships – Algiers (5–9 July)
World University Games – Zagreb, Yugoslavia (13–19 July)
Asian Track and Field Meeting – Singapore (22–26 July)
East & Central African Championships – Arusha, Tanzania (31 July – 2 Aug)
European Junior Championships – Birmingham, UK (6–9 Aug)
Pan-American Games – Indianapolis, USA (8–16 August)
African Games – Nairobi, Kenya (8–12 Aug)
World Championships – Rome, Italy (29 Aug – 6 Sep)

South East Asia Games – Jakarta, Indonesia (9–20 Sep)
IAAF/Mobil Grand Prix Final – Brussels, Belgium (11 Sep)
Mediterranean Games – Latakia, Syria (21–25 Sep)
South American Championships – San Pablo, Brazil (12 Oct)
Women's World 15km Road Race Championship – Monte Carlo, Monaco (21 Nov)
World Veterans Championships – Melbourne, Australia (28 Nov – 6 Dec)

## 1988
European Indoor Championships – Bucharest, Romania (27–28 Feb)
World Cross-Country Championships – Auckland, New Zealand (26 Mar)
European Marathon Cup
World Junior Championships – Sudbury, Canada (27–31 Jul)
African Championships – Algiers (Aug)
Olympic Games – Seoul, Korea (23 Sep – 2 Oct)
Women's World Road Race Championship – Australia

## 1989
World Cross-Country Championships – Stavanger, Norway (19 Mar)
World Indoor Championships – Budapest, Hungary
World Marathon Cup
World Cup – Barcelona, Spain
World Race Walking Cup

## 1990
Commonwealth Games – Auckland, New Zealand
World Junior Championships
European Championships – Split, Yugoslavia
Asian Games

# Qualifying standards for the 1988 Olympic Games

To be achieved between 29 August 1987 and 7 September 1988

\* To be announced.
No standards for marathon, walks and relays.

### Men's standards

| | | | |
|---|---|---|---|
| 100m: | 10.44/10.2h | HJ: | 2.25 |
| 200m: | 20.84/20.6h | PV: | 5.45 |
| 400m: | 46.14/46.0h | LJ: | 7.85 |
| 800m: | 1:46.8 | TJ: | 16.60 |
| 1500m: | 3:38.5 | SP: | 19.50 |
| 5000m: | 13:33.0 | DT: | 61.50 |
| 10000m: | 28:20.0 | HT: | 72.00 |
| 3000mSt: | 8:28.0 | JT: | * |
| 110mh: | 13.94/13.7h | Dec: | 7600/7700h |
| 400mh: | 50.24/50.1h | | |

### Women's standards

| | | | |
|---|---|---|---|
| 100m: | 11.54/11.3h | LJ: | 6.50 |
| 200m: | 23.64/23.4h | SP: | 16.90 |
| 400m: | 52.74/52.6h | DT: | 57.50 |
| 800m: | 2.01.5 | JT: | 56.50 |
| 1500m: | 4:09.0 | Hep: | 5700/5750h |
| 3000m: | 9:03.0 | | |
| 10000m: | * | | |
| 100mh: | 13.44/13.2h | | |
| 400mh: | 58.04/57.9h | | |
| HJ: | 1.88 | | |

# THE PACE OF RECORD BREAKING

## BY PETER MATTHEWS

Pacemaking is provided for scores of middle distance races, especially those that are featured at many of the European circuit meetings. Regularly, if one of the top men or women runners are taking part, such races are billed as world record attempts. Promoters have for long used such 'hype' to attract attention to their meetings, building up interest in the media and trying to fill their stadia. But, as we will see, world records are scarce commodities, and most such attempts are doomed to 'failure'.

There is growing disillusion with the current practice of pacemaking. Such overt assistance as is now widespread, with runners put into races for no other reason than to assist the big name around the opening laps, was once specifically disallowed for records; perhaps it still is, but blind eyes have nearly always been turned to it. How, however, is it possible to judge between what is and what is not permissible? Is there any effective difference between the help that may be given by a genuine front-runner, who 'dies' over the last couple of laps, to that given by one who steps off the track at the bell, never intending to go further? In either case those following may have had the benefit of a fast pace, one of the requisites for records.

For a record to be set on any particular occasion a high proportion of such factors must be favourable. The weather should be perfect, the track in good condition, the athletes properly prepared. Then there is the need for incentive, whether that be the stimulus of competition, the prestige of winning or financial advantage. Pacemaking may help, although athletes such as Filbert Bayi, Dave Bedford, Mary Slaney or Ingrid Kristiansen have shown the ability to run world records without such help.

The provision of fast pace does ensure truly run races, rather than a preponderance of last lap charges. Back in the 1960s British miling was going through a bad patch, and most domestic races were settled by sprint finishes after a dawdling pace, but the top men were not able to shine at the major championships. The British Milers Club was formed to improve standards, and one of the things that it has done ever since is to organise races all over Britain, particularly for improving talent. In these races efforts are made to ensure appropriate fast pace, so that athletes have

the opportunity to run faster and explore the unknown by pushing themselves hard. Lessons learnt, such athletes are then better able to cope with any conditions that they might find in championship tests. Partly through such efforts British miling has stood supreme for the past decade, with Ovett, Coe and Cram leading the pack.

So there is something to be said for pacemaking, but the sport is in danger of being dragged into disrepute when promoters put in a rabbit who sets off at world record pace, only to be ignored by the rest of the field. Records are a vital aspect of the sport, as men and women strive for their ultimate performances, but they should not detract from the pleasure that spectators and athletes alike can gain from real racing, where maximum overall speed may not come from the mix of tactics that are indulged in by a group of runners each concerned with winning. To put record breaking into perspective I have updated the analysis that I did for *Running Magazine* a couple of years ago. I looked at world records each year from 1975 to determine at what kind of meeting they were set. These are the number of world records, year by year, divided into seven categories of meeting (see table below).

I excluded long distance races (greater than 10km) and walks from the above lists. Occasionally I had some difficulty in determining the category, for instance for several records set in East German pre-championship meetings; these I have included under 'Other', rather than under 'Major E.European meetings', which I have restricted to international gatherings.

No world records were set in men's track events in 1986, despite several specific attempts, most notably by Saïd Aouita, and indeed there were only four world records in field events, the least overall for a very long time. There were 18 women's world records, but it looks as if there may be a general decline in record breaking. Perhaps we are getting closer to peak performances.

There were four world records at the great European Championships. There were two at the 1983 World Championships and one at the 1984 Olympics. Records do continue to be set on such occasions but much less than in the past. The

## The 'spectaculars' – and their world records

World records 1975–86 at standard events set at the established major invitational meetings (see below).

| Meeting | No. recs | Meeting | No. recs |
|---|---|---|---|
| **WESTERN EUROPE** | | **EASTERN EUROPE** | |
| Bislett Games, Oslo (Nor) | 10 | Olympischer Tag, Berlin (GDR) | 6 |
| Weltklasse, Zürich (Swi) | 8 | Znamenskiy Memorial (SU) | 3 |
| ISTAF, W. Berlin (FRG) | 6 | Kusocinski Memorial (Pol) | 2 |
| DN Galan, Stockholm (Swe) | 4 | Budapest Grand Prix (Hun) | 1 |
| Oslo Games (Nor) | 4 | PTS Bratislava (Cs) | 1 |
| Weltklasse, Köln (FRG) | 4 | Rosicky Memorial, Prague (Cs) | 0 |
| Golden Gala, Rome (Ita) | 3 | | |
| Koblenz (FRG) | 3 | **USA** | |
| Peugeot Talbot Games (UK) | 2 | Prefontaine Classic, Eugene | 3 |
| Citta de Rieti (Ita) | 2 | Jenner Classic, San Jose | 1 |
| Van Damme Memorial (Bel) | 2 | | |
| World Games, Helsinki (Fin) | 2 | | |
| Nikaia, Nice (Fra) | 1 | | |
| IAC Meeting (UK) | 0 | | |

All this helps to show that we should watch top athletics meetings for the competitions provided and not get obsessed with the anticipation of records. If and when a world record does come along, then we can savour the brilliance of the deed all the more.

**World records 1975–86**

| Category | 1986 | '85 | '84 | '83 | '82 | '81 | '80 | '79 | '78 | '77 | '76 | '75 |
|---|---|---|---|---|---|---|---|---|---|---|---|---|
| **MEN** | | | | | | | | | | | | |
| Major international championships | 1 | 1 | 1 | 1 | 1 | – | 3 | 1 | – | 2 | 5 | 1 |
| International matches | 2 | – | – | 2 | – | 2 | – | – | – | 2 | 1 | 2 |
| National championships | – | 1 | 1 | 2 | 1 | – | 2 | – | – | 1 | 2 | – |
| Major W. European | – | 5 | 5 | 5 | 2 | 7 | 6 | 3 | 2 | 2 | 1 | 5 |
| Major E. European | – | 2 | 2 | – | – | – | – | – | 2 | – | – | 1 |
| Major US meetings | – | – | – | 2 | – | 1 | – | 2 | 1 | 1 | 10 | 5 |
| Other | 1 | 1 | 2 | 3 | 1 | 2 | 10 | – | 7 | 1 | 3 | 7 |
| **WOMEN** | | | | | | | | | | | | |
| Major international championships | 3 | – | – | 1 | 3 | – | 5 | – | 4 | – | 4 | – |
| International matches | 3 | 1 | 1 | 4 | 1 | 2 | – | 5 | 1 | 4 | 2 | 1 |
| National championships | 2 | – | 1 | 1 | 4 | 2 | 4 | – | 1 | 3 | 2 | – |
| Major W. European | 5 | 3 | 2 | 1 | 3 | 2 | 1 | – | 2 | 3 | 1 | 1 |
| Major E. European | 3 | – | 5 | 4 | 1 | – | 2 | 4 | 1 | – | 5 | – |
| Major US meetings | 1 | – | – | 1 | 1 | – | – | – | – | – | – | – |
| Other | 1 | 4 | 5 | 5 | 3 | 3 | 9 | 2 | 7 | 4 | 11 | 2 |
| **TOTAL** | 22 | 18 | 25 | 32 | 21 | 21 | 42 | 17 | 28 | 23 | 47 | 25 |

Olympic Games used to be the one occasion at which the world's best athletes met under good conditions. These days they can meet regularly during the season, an indication of how the sport is now so much more broadly based.

## World records set at Olympic Games

Totals for men and women each year since women's events introduced in 1928:

1928 – 11, 1932 – 18, 1936 – 7, 1948 – 0, 1952 – 11, 1956 – 7, 1960 – 11, 1964 – 9, 1968 – 23, 1972 – 17, 1976 – 9, 1980 – 8, 1984 – 1.

Standing out from the overall trends are perhaps the zero at the 1948 Games in London, when the world was recovering from the effects of war and conditions were poor; and the 1968 Games, when the opportunity of competing at high altitude saw an extraordinary number of records, five in the triple jump alone. The Eastern bloc boycott in 1984 may also have had its effect.

Records are rarely set now in international matches, although in 1986 the USSR v GDR clash had two, by Yuriy Sedykh and Heike Drechsler; or in national championships. In 1986 Drechsler in the GDR 200m and Yordanka Donkova in the Bulgarian 100mh did so, but note that there have been none in the US championships since Ed Moses at 400mh in 1977.

Quite a high proportion of world records are now set in the major invitational meetings on the circuit. Even so one should consider that there are 16 Grand Prix meetings each year and the chances are quite heavily against a new world record at any one meeting, as can be seen by my table covering the last 12 years. Even the 'world record champions' The Bislett Games and the Weltklasse average less than one a year.

Zola Budd set a world indoor record for 3000 metres in an indoor international match at Cosford in 1986. *Mark Shearman*

# GREAT WORLD RECORDS—AND CRITERIA FOR THEIR ASSESSMENT

## BY RICHARD SZRETER

The twin peaks of achievement in athletics are the competitive one of an Olympic gold medal and the statistical one of a world record. After the last decade of misguided political boycotts, Olympic gold medals can, arguably, no longer be said to be of equal merit, but world records may also vary in merit. For example when Said Aouita broke David Moorcroft's 5000m WR he did so by the absurdly small margin of 1/100th of a second, in a meeting that was not a major championship (13:00.40 Oslo 27 Jul 1985); a world record indeed, but could it be called a great one, especially with the oh-so-near 'barrier' of 13 minutes remaining intact? On the other hand when Jozsef Csermak (Hun) hurled the hammer 60.34m in Helsinki on 24 Jul 1952, the excitement was boundless, for it was not just a world record, but one that won an Olympic gold medal and broke a 'magic barrier', 60 metres; even if it did not improve the previous world record (59.88m in 1950 by another Magyar, Imre Nemeth, father of the javelin expert) by a large margin.

And yet Csermak's mark did not 'live' even a couple of months; for on 14 Sep 1952 Sverre Strandli (Nor) bettered it by almost a metre with 61.25m. Not many people now remember Csermak's mark. And as for Aouita's 13:00.40 . . . well, who is to say that it might not stand for maybe a couple of decades? And if it should do, would it not then wax and wax in fame and become a very great world record in the historical perspective?

For, 'at the end of the day', it is durability that above all can ensure immortality for a world record, far beyond its own span, and which must be rated the chief criterion of its greatness. Olympics come but every four years; margins of improvement are relative, and 'psycho-barriers' artificial; but every time a bunch of leading athletes come together in competition the existing world record is on trial, and one that can resist and challenge them for several years is a mark of true distinction.

The choice of Csermak's and Aouita's records was dictated not only by the fact that they exemplified my point well, but also because they spanned virtually the whole post-war period

under consideration in this article. Initially, the modest germ of it was to tabulate all world records in the standard men's events that managed to survive at least ten years, starting with those at 1945. However, nearly all of those were set in the 1930s, such as Glenn Hardin's 400mh of 50.6 (26 Jul 1934 to 20 Sep 1953) or Naoto Tajima's 16.00m triple jump (6 Aug 1936 to 30 Sep 1951). Their longevity was 'unfairly' aided by the quiescence of international athletics caused by World War II and its aftermath, adding up to something like ten years. For this reason this exercise has been limited to world records actually established after 1945. Of course this does mean that a great world record like the 8.13m long jump by Jesse Owens (25 May 1935 to 12 Aug 1960) is not included in the survey.[1]

The idea of this article goes beyond the simple task, of listing long-lived WRs. The following may be suggested as other criteria for evaluating their comparative greatness:

(a) The importance and prestige of the meeting at which a mark was made. Given that we are dealing with world records, the Olympic Games stands out, followed at a respectful distance by the European Championships, and clearly also the infant World Championships.

(b) The margin by which the new WR exceeded the previous one. The obvious method is the percentage improvement, but it is patently easier to improve a record percentage-wise at 5000m than at 200m, or in the hammer rather than the high jump. So let us consider also (c) a less objective and more impressionistic approach, call it 'comparative' (or 'historical'), whereby a careful scrutiny of the WR progression in particular events enables improvements to be labelled from 'very large', like Beamon's, down to 'very small'.

(d) Breaching some round figure 'barrier'. Insofar as time and distance are continuous this is scarcely a valid criterion, but it certainly endows a record with extra publicity and renown, and, more relevantly, often implies a prolonged prior hunt.[2]

The table incorporates these criteria, although the records are listed by their durability. Even this criterion is not quite unequivocal. It has been said rightly but rather optimistically that: 'Implied in the recognised sports records of our time are, of course, the perfect standardisation of conditions . . . [witness] the tail-wind rule in foot-race sprints.'[3] In fact, however, we face a problem with the two oldest records in existence today. Both Lee Evans, 400m in 43.86, and Bob Beamon, long jump of 8.90m, set their records aided by being performed at the height of 2240m in the rarefied air of the Mexico Olympics, but the IAAF takes no cognisance of altitude, so they are included. The best long-lived non-altitude marks for their and other events are listed separately. The IAAF's decision also means that some great records set at sea level but broken at altitude show up less well than they might have done: e.g. the 17.03m triple jump by Jozef Schmidt had a 'life' of over eight years officially (5 Aug 1960 to 16 Oct 1968) but a further year (to 18 Oct 1969) at sea level.

Precluded are not only wind-aided marks but also those not recognised by the IAAF, such as Brian Oldfield's professional 22.86m shot put, not beaten since 1975. For 200 metres only the 'turn' version is included, with apologies to Mel Patton and Dave Sime, whose long-lived straight course times of 20.2 and 20.0 in 1949 and 1956 respectively were ratified by the IAAF before 1970. The 'length of life' of a record was counted until it was beaten rather than equalled. If the same athlete broke the WR consecutively several times, then, consistently, if ungenerously, what counted was the longest interval between his own consecutive WRs, or his last one and his successor's, rather than the total period of his monopoly. For example Parry O'Brien set nine consecutive shot records from 9 May 1953 to 1 Nov 1956, the last of which was only equalled by Dallas Long on 28 Mar 1959 before O'Brien regained it. Randy Matson does qualify, as his 21.78m on 22 Apr 1967 stood as a WR for just over six years, but he actually held the WR for much longer, as the previous improvement, by a much larger margin incidentally, was also made by him, on 8 May 1965. Yet since this article is concerned with records and not record breakers, it is not surprising that some undeniably all-time greats are absent from the table, while it features some lesser-known names whose fine WR was in the nature of a 'fluke' insofar as they never closely approached it before or after.

Even including the altitude-aided results fewer than 30 world records qualify as having survived for five years or more. The simple criterion of longevity is, however far from simple, for of the top nine WRs in the table there are reservations, altitude or as explained in footnotes, attaching to eight. The exception is Snell's great 800m mark, yet as an unrivalled WR it stood for only half the time shown, for it was equalled first by Ralph

Doubell (Aus) on 15 Oct 1968 and then by Dave Wottle (USA) on 1 Jul 1972 before Marcello Fiasconaro (Ita) reduced it to 1:43.7 on 27 Jun 1973. There is, thus, no world record in modern athletics that can satisfy all purists whose 'life' stretched into double figures, although Rono's steeplechase mark has yet to be broken!

The idea of this article was to go beyond that, in seeking a comparative evaluation of WRs. How can the other suggested criteria be assimilated to, or combined and integrated with that of longevity? Perhaps they cannot, perhaps by weighting them, and then translating into comparable figures (years or points). This author does not feel competent to, let alone bold enough, so it's every reader to himself or herself one hopes. Serious students of athletics may prefer to consider such deeper questions as: why do some events, some periods, show up better in terms of the excellence of their WRs than others? Or of the comparative contribution to their ceaseless improvement by differential growth of popularity and competition, superior technology, better training methods and sheer individual talent and application – let alone luck?

Meanwhile, on any reckoning, the 'heavenly twins' of Ciudad Mexico, both set on 18 Oct 1968 are likely to come out on top. Unless . . . a reliable method of assessing altitude advantage is found and this detracts much from their marks or, indeed (more fanciful still) it should be accepted that to set WRs in Olympic Games is relatively 'easy' – for if the stress is tremendous, there is also the supreme incentive to make the adrenaline flow and the superb competion to assist achievement. Bob Beamon and Lee Evans are to be counted among track and field immortals, but will their world records stand forever? This is unlikely. When Beamon long jumped 8.90m it was promptly dubbed a 21st century record, but Carl Lewis has already repeatedly come within inches of that mark, and at sea level at that, and we are still a long way from AD 2000. Uwe Hohn's astonishing javelin mark of 104.80m may be looked at as a record that will stand forever, because it forced the authorities to alter the rules, but I would venture to say that it will not, unless they change them again! Meanwhile should historically-minded fellow-statisticians wish to put forward and argue schemes of evaluation of records that will supersede mine, it is to be hoped that they will apply them also to categories of records other than just the simplest and most obvious one of senior men in standard events. World records will meanwhile continue to fall, for it is as difficult to see an end to the resourcefulness of athletics promoters as it is to envisage a limit to man's physical prowess.

**Durability of world records**

| Yrs | Days | Name | | Event | Mark | Date | %[4] | Comp.[5] | Meet.[7] |
|---|---|---|---|---|---|---|---|---|---|
| 18 | 74* | Bob Beamon (USA) | [1] | LJ | 8.90 | 18.10.68 | 6.6 | VL | OG[6] |
| 18 | 74* | Lee Evans (USA) | [1] | 400m | 43.86 | 18.10.68 | 0.75 | L | OG[6] |
| 14 | 262 | Jim Hines (USA) | [1] | 100m | 9.95 | 14.10.68 | 0.05 | S | OG[6] |
| 13 | 364 | Martin Lauer (FRG) | | 110mh | 13.2 | 7.7.59[2] | 1.5 | Av | – |
| 11 | 145 | Peter Snell (NZ) | | 800m | 1:44.3 | 3.2.62 | 1.3 | VL | –[6] |
| 10 | 331 | Tommie Smith (USA) | [1] | 200m | 19.83 | 16.10.68 | 0.9 | L | OG[6] |
| 9 | 257 | Lloyd La Beach (Pan) | | 100m | 10.1 | 7.10.50 | 1.0 | Av | – |
| 9 | 244 | Joao de Oliveira (Bra) | [1] | TJ | 17.89 | 15.10.75 | 2.6 | VL | PAm[6] |
| 9 | 2 | Andy Stanfield (USA) | | 200m | 20.6 | 26.5.51[3] | 0.5 | S | – |
| 8 | 232* | Henry Rono (Ken) | | 3kmSt | 8:05.4 | 13.5.78 | 0.5 | Av | – |
| 8 | 42 | Jozef Schmidt (Pol) | | TJ | 17.03 | 5.8.60 | 2.0 | VL | –[6] |
| 7 | 364 | Armin Hary (FRG) | | 100m | 10.0 | 21.6.60[2] | 1.0 | Av | – |
| 7 | 347 | Valeriy Brumel (SU) | | HJ | 2.28 | 21.7.63 | 0.4 | Av | – |
| 7 | 110 | Pietro Mennea (Ita) | [1] | 200m | 19.72 | 12.9.69 | 0.6 | Av | WSG |
| 7 | 95 | Vladimir Kuts (SU) | | 5km | 13:35.0 | 13.10.57 | 0.2 | S | – |
| 7 | 49 | Ron Clarke (Aus) | | 10km | 27:39.4 | 14.7.65 | 2.1 | VL | – |
| 6 | 304 | Herb Elliott (Aus) | | 1500m | 3:35.6 | 6.9.60 | 0.2 | VS | OG |
| 6 | 209 | Jim Ryun (USA) | | 1500m | 3:33.1 | 8.7.67 | 2.2 | VL | – |
| 6 | 194 | Filbert Bayi (Tan) | | 1500m | 3:32.16 | 2.2.74 | 0.4 | Av | CG |
| 6 | 184 | Roger Moens (Bel) | | 800m | 1:45.7 | 3.8.55 | 0.85 | Av | – |
| 6 | 71 | Ron Clarke (Aus) | | 5km | 13:16.6 | 5.7.66 | 1.0 | L | – |
| 6 | 21 | Henry Rono (Ken) | | 10km | 27:22.5 | 11.6.78 | 0.5 | Av | – |
| 6 | 13 | Randy Matson (USA) | | SP | 21.78 | 22.4.67 | 1.2 | Av | – |
| 5 | 347 | Dick Attlesey (USA) | | 110mh | 13.5 | 10.7.50 | 0.7 | Av | – |
| 5 | 296 | Fortune Gordien (USA) | | DT | 59.28 | 22.8.53 | 2.0 | VL | – |
| 5 | 204* | Sebastian Coe (UK) | | 800m | 1:41.73 | 10.6.81 | 0.6 | Av | – |
| 5 | 134* | Renaldo Nehemiah (USA) | [1] | 110mh | 12.93 | 19.8.81 | 0.5 | Av | –[6] |

**Note:** Udo Beyer (GDR) SP, 22.15 on 6.7.78 was just 11 days short of five years when broken by himself (22.22m, 25.6.83 to 22.9.85).

*Sea level records/bests excluded from main table by altitude WRs*

| Yrs | Days | Name | Event | Mark | Date | % | Comp. | Meet. |
|---|---|---|---|---|---|---|---|---|
| 10 | 155* | Alberto Juantorena (Cub) | 400m | 44.26 | 29.7.76 | – | – | OG |
| 10 | 53 | Ralph Boston (USA) | LJ | 8.35 | 29.5.65 | 0.1 | VS | – |
| 8 | 277 | Viktor Saneyev (USSR) | TJ | 17.44 | 17.10.72 | 0.2 | VS | – |

* At 31 Dec 1986

---

1. Altitude over 1000m.
2. These sprint times are difficult to judge; Hary's 10.0 was 10.25 on auto-timing, Lauer's 13.2 was 13.56.
3. James Carlton (Aus) ran 200m in 20.6 on 16.1.32, but this was not ratified by the IAAF. However La Beach's 10.1 has been included even though it was not ratified.
4. Percentage improvement.
5. Comparative improvement: VL very large, L large, Av average, S small, VS very small.
6. Breaking a barrier.
7. Major Championships: OG Olympic Games, CG Commonwealth Games, WSG World Student Games. No qualifying marks were set at World Championships or European Championships.

Renaldo Nehemiah – how long will his 1981 hurdles record last? *Sutton/duomo*

Ralph Boston – broke Owens' 25-year-old record. *Mark Shearman*

1. Apart from the three mentioned above, the other long-lasting world records from that era in order of longevity were: Rudolf Harbig (Ger) 800, 1:46.6, 15.7.39 to 3.8.55; Cornelius Warmerdam (USA), PV 4.77, 23.5.42 to 27.4.57; Yrjö Nikkanen (Fin), JT 78.70, 16.10.38 to 8.8.53; Glenn Morris (USA), Dec 7900, 8.8.36 to 30.6.50; Jack Torrance (USA), SP 17.40, 5.8.34 to 17.4.48; Gunder Hägg (Swe), 5000m, 13:58.2, 20.9.42 to 30.5.54; Les Steers (USA), HJ 2.11, 17.6.41 to 27.6,53; Forrest Towns (USA), 110mh, 13.7, 27.8.36 to 17.4.48. Erwin Blask (Ger), HT 59.00, 27.8.38 lasted a few weeks short of ten years, as did Hägg's 1500m of 3:43.0, 7.7.44, although equalled in 1947 and 1952.

2. A world record, however, that is particularly famous as a 'barrier-breaker', Roger Bannister's first sub-4 minute mile, 3:59.4 on 6 May 1954, shows why only the universally competed in Olympic events have been adhered to in this article. For the 3:43.0 WR for the equivalent 1500m was equally good for most afficionados and this was first set ten years earlier by Gunder Hägg.

3. R.D. Mandell, 'The Invention of the Sports Record', *Stadion*, vol. II/2, 1976. Mandell's treatment is mainly historical; for a larger and mainly sociological scholarly work, see A. Guttman, *From Ritual to Record*, N.Y., 1978.

# THE END OF AN ERA

## BY TONY ISAACS

An era in the history of throwing ended on 1st April 1986 when, quite uniquely in terms of athletics progress, the IAAF imposed a change to the design of the men's javelin with the deliberate intention of reducing the distances achieved at the top level of the event. As a result, the record and ranking lists for the men's javelin have been thrown into a state of some confusion and, throughout 1986, throwers around the world have been struggling to match distances already surpassed years ago whereas, in other events, athletes are still striving to register times and distances not yet achieved by anyone.

As an ancient implement of war, the javelin has a long history and, linked to the widespread use of the spear in warfare and hunting, many of the world's peoples have a traditional ability for this most natural of all the field events. There are even early references to the javelin in the Bible, notably the occasion when Saul cast one in anger at David (see 1 Samuel 18 v. 10 and 11). Javelin throwing was included in the ancient Olympic pentathlon, the Greeks using a thong looped over a finger of the throwing hand to improve the impetus of release. It is therefore surprising that the javelin event did not appear in the modern Olympics until the fourth Games in 1908. Since then, improvements in throwing techniques and changes in specification have all conspired to produce the relentless progress past the metric barriers—60m in 1912, 80m in 1953 and 100m in 1984. The most significant changes in the event have been the abolition of the favoured tail-end (so called 'freestyle') grip after 1910, the switch from wood to metal implements in the 1940s and the introduction of aerodynamic models (pioneered by Franklin 'Bud' Held) in the 1950s.

Now, with the 1986 specification change, progress stands still at 1st April 1986 and it is therefore timely to 'stop the clock' at that date and place on record the ahievements of past champions and barrier-breakers.

## The barrier breakers

| | Date | Name | Record |
|---|---|---|---|
| 50m | 1902 | Eric Lemming (SWE) | 50.44 |
| 55m | 1908 | Eric Lemming (SWE) | 57.33 |
| 55m | 1901 | Jacoslav Merteczy (CS) (with freestyle grip) | 55.20 |
| 60m | 1911 | Mor Koczan (HUN) (with freestyle grip) | 60.64 |
| | 1912 | Julius Saaristo (FIN) | 61.45 |
| 65m | 1919 | Jonni Myrrä (FIN) | 66.10 |
| 70m | 1928 | Erik Lundquist (SWE) | 71.01 |
| 75m | 1933 | Matti Järvinen (FIN) | 76.10 |
| 80m | 1953 | Franklin 'Bud' Held (USA) | 80.41 |
| 85m | 1956 | Egil Danielsen (NOR) | 85.71 |
| 90m | 1964 | Terje Pedersen (NOR) | 91.72 |
| 95m | 1980 | Ferenc Paragi (HUN) | 96.72 |
| 100m | 1984 | Uwe Hohn (GDR) | 104.80 |

## The world winners:
### Olympic Champions

| Date | Name | Record |
|---|---|---|
| 1908 | Eric Lemming (SWE) | 54.82 |
| 1908 | Eric Lemming (SWE) (freestyle) | 54.45 |
| 1912 | Eric Lemming (SWE) | 60.64 |
| 1912 | Julius Saaristo (FIN) (both hands) (61.00 (WR), 48.42) | 109.42 |
| 1920 | Jonni Myrrä (FIN) | 65.78 |
| 1924 | Jonni Myrrä (FIN) | 62.96 |
| 1928 | Erik Lundquist (SWE) | 66.60 |
| 1932 | Matti Järvinen (FIN) | 72.70 |
| 1936 | Gerhard Stock (GER) | 71.84 |
| 1948 | Tapio Rautavaara (FIN) | 69.76 |
| 1952 | Cyrus Young (USA) | 73.78 |
| 1956 | Egil Danielsen (NOR) | 85.70 |
| 1960 | Victor Tsibulenko (USSR) | 84.64 |
| 1964 | Pauli Nevala (FIN) | 82.66 |
| 1968 | Janis Lusis (USSR) | 90.10 |
| 1972 | Klaus Wolfermann (FRG) | 90.48 |
| 1976 | Miklos Nemeth (HUN) | 94.58 |
| 1980 | Dainis Kula (USSR) | 91.20 |
| 1984 | Arto Härkönen (FIN) | 86.76 |

### World Champion
| | | |
|---|---|---|
| 1983 | Detlef Michel (GDR) | 89.48 |

# The continental champions
## European Championships

| Date | Name | Record |
|------|------|--------|
| 1934 | Matti Järvinen (FIN) | 76.66 |
| 1938 | Matti Järvinen (FIN) | 76.87 |
| 1946 | Lennart Atterwall (SWE) | 68.74 |
| 1950 | Toivo Hyytiäinen (FIN) | 71.26 |
| 1954 | Janusz Sidlo (POL) | 76.35 |
| 1958 | Janusz Sidlo (POL) | 80.18 |
| 1962 | Janis Lusis (USSR) | 82.04 |
| 1966 | Janis Lusis (USSR) | 84.48 |
| 1969 | Janis Lusis (USSR) | 91.52 |
| 1971 | Janis Lusis (USSR) | 90.68 |
| 1974 | Hannu Siitonen (FIN) | 89.58 |
| 1978 | Michael Wessing (FRG) | 89.12 |
| 1982 | Uwe Hohn (GDR) | 91.34 |
| 1986 | Klaus Tafelmeier (FRG) (new model) | 84.76 |

## Asian Games

| Date | Name | Record |
|------|------|--------|
| 1951 | Haruo Nagayasu (JAP) | 63.97 |
| 1954 | Mohammad Nawaz (PAK) | 64.26 |
| 1958 | Mohammad Nawaz (PAK) | 69.41 |
| 1962 | Takachi Miki (JAP) | 74.56 |
| 1966 | Nashatar Singh (MAL) | 72.92 |
| 1970 | Hisao Yamamoto (JAP) | 71.24 |
| 1974 | Toshihiro Yamada (JAP) | 76.12 |
| 1978 | Shen Mao-Mao (CHN) | 79.24 |
| 1982 | Toshihiko Takeda (JAP) | 75.04 |
| 1986 | Kazuhiro Mizoguchi (JAP) (new model) | 74.12 |

## Asian Championships

| Date | Name | Record |
|------|------|--------|
| 1973 | Allah Dad (PAK) | 63.58 |
| 1975 | Toshihiro Yamada (JAP) | 74.92 |
| 1979 | Shen Mao-Mao (CHN) | 86.50 |
| 1981 | Shen Mao-Mao (CHN) | 85.40 |
| 1983 | Masami Yoshida (JAP) | 79.50 |
| 1985 | Pubuciren (CHN) | 76.56 |

## Pan American Games

| Date | Name | Record |
|------|------|--------|
| 1951 | Ricardo Heber (ARG) | 68.08 |
| 1955 | Franklin 'Bud' Held (USA) | 69.77 |
| 1959 | Buster Quist (USA) | 70.50 |
| 1963 | Dan Studney (USA) | 75.60 |
| 1967 | Frank Covelli (USA) | 74.28 |
| 1971 | Cary Feldman (USA) | 81.52 |
| 1975 | Sam Colson (USA) | 83.82 |
| 1979 | Duncan Atwood (USA) | 84.16 |
| 1983 | Laslo Babits (CAN) | 81.40 |

## African Games

| Date | Name | Record |
|------|------|--------|
| 1965 | Anthony Okayhire (NIG) | 71.52 |
| 1973 | Jacques Aye (IVC) | 77.22 |
| 1978 | Justin Arop (UGA) | 76.94 |

## African Championships

| Date | Name | Record |
|------|------|--------|
| 1979 | Jacques Aye (IVC) | 76.74 |
| 1982 | Zakayo Malekwa (TAN) | 76.18 |
| 1984 | Tarek Chaabani (TUN) | 77.40 |
| 1985 | Mahour Bacha (ALG) | 80.04 |

Janis Lusis. *ASP*

# JARMILA KRATOCHVÍLOVÁ

## BY LADISLAV KRNÁČ

Her own willpower, the knowledge and dedication of her coach Miroslav Kváč (from 1967), and their desire to prove something are the background of this country girl who made her way from Golčuv Jenikov, the birthplace she never left, a rather sleepy village of 5000, to the top of the athletics world in the first half of the eighties. Experts say that her biggest achievements are those three medals from the 1983 World Championships. Remember there was only 35 minutes between the 400m semi-finals and the 800m final. Nine competitions, never tried by anybody before, in seven days with two days rest after the 400m final. Insiders would like to prove that her day of days was the 2nd August 1981. In Pescara, during one afternoon of the European Cup B final she ran: 11.38 (3rd)—52.10 (1st)—44.60 (1st)—22.40 (1st) and a 49.2 anchor with the winning relay team of CSSR (3:28.90).

On the last day of 1986 she told me that her greatest satisfaction came from the silver medal of the 1980 Olympics. Why? 'They told me, more than one so-called expert, that I am without perspectives. Only with a big portion of luck will I make the final of 400 metres . . .' That medal gave her the strength to continue for another six years. Do not forget she was almost thirty at Luzhniki . . . The worst season? The Olympic year of 1984, when she was not very far away from retiring. The reasons are obvious.

No other woman can match her personal bests: 11.09–21.97–47.99–1:53.28. Beside that (indoors and out) she has 20 CS titles, 43 records, six indoor world bests, four European indoor titles, two silver medals from the 1982 European Championships. Until January 1st, 1987 she produced 37 under 50 second lap times. 'You know, it hurts whether you run a 51 or a 48 lap . . .'

At the Millrose Games in 1986, Kratochvílová left the track after 620 metres. On March 25th she had surgery on the tendon of her left foot, but from 1st May she was training again. Her goal? 'To say a nice farewell to athletics in Rome '87 . . .' The day after? Coaching children and learn to love them running.

Her bad luck? She was competing in the era of Marita Koch.

Jarmila Kratochvilova. ASP

# JARMILA KRATOCHVILOVA – Career highlights

b.26 Jan 1951 Golcuv Jenikov 1.70m 64kg. Club: VS Praha.

Summary of career at each race distance. For 200m, 400m and 800m the tables show each year from 1978–85 her number of competitions, year's best, CS and world list positions, world ranking (as published in *Track & Field News*), and number of races under 23 sec., 50 sec. and 2 mins. respectively.

## 60 metres
1976: 7.4
1981: 7.30 CS indoor record (7 Feb)

## 100 metres
Early progression: 1972– 12.1, 1976– 11.5, 1977– 11.6

| Year | Comps | Best | CS | World | W. rank |
|------|-------|------|-----|-------|---------|
| 1978 | 10 | 11.4 | 1st | 88th | |
| 1979 | 15 | 11.57 | 1st | 59th | |
| 1980 | 14 | 11.43 | 1st | 50th | |
| 1981 | 16 | 11.09 | 1st | 3rd | 6th |
| 1982 | 8 | 11.10 | 1st | 7th | 8th |
| 1983 | 4 | 11.37 | 2nd | 40th | |
| 1984 | 4 | 11.50 | 3rd | 89th | |

CS records: 11.43 (17.8.80), 11.22 (23.5.81), 11.09 (6.6.81)
Major events: 1981 3rd European Cup B 11.38
CS champion 1979–80

## 200 metres
Early progression: 1972– 24.8, 1973– 25.3, 1974– 24.7, 1976– 23.6, 1977– 24.35/24.24w.

| Year | Comps | Best | CS | World | W. rank | Sub 23 sec times |
|------|-------|------|-----|-------|---------|------------------|
| 1978 | 18 | 23.50 | 1st | 54th | | |
| 1979 | 14 | 23.46* | 1st | 58th | | |
| 1980 | 12 | 22.53 | 1st | 11th | 5th | |
| 1981 | 14 | 21.97 | 1st | 2nd | 2nd | 11 |
| 1982 | 10 | 22.36 | 1st | 8th | 10th | 6 |
| 1983 | 4 | 22.40 | 1st | 8th | 3rd | 3 |
| 1984 | 10 | 22.57 | 2nd | 17th | 9th | 7 |
| 1985 | 2 | 22.73 | 2nd | 18th | 2th | |

* also 23.19 indoors

CS records: 23.3h (28.5.78), 23.50 (10.6.78), 23.48 (6.6.79), 23.47 (16.6.79), 23.46 (24.6.79), 23.14 (17.5.80), 22.91 (24.5.80), 22.80 (5.7.80), 22.53 (16.8.80), 22.50 (23.5.81), 22.07 (3.6.81), 21.97 (6.6.81)
World indoor bests: 23.19 (4.2.79), 22.76 (28.1.81)
CS champion 1976, 1978–80

## Major events:
| | | | | | | | |
|------|------|------|------|------|------|------|------|
| 1981 | 1st | European Cup B | 22.40 | 1983 | 1st | European Cup | 22.40 |
| | 2nd | World Cup | 22.31 | 1984 | 1st | European Indoors | 23.02 |
| | | | | 1985 | 6th | European Cup | 22.96 |

In 1980–5 lost only twice in 52 comptitions, to Natalya Bochina at the 1980 Znamenskiy Memorial and to Evelyn Ashford at the 1981 World Cup.

## 300 metres
Indoor world bests: 37.4 (24.1.79), 35.9 (28.1.81), 35.6 (7.3.82)

## 400 metres
Early progression: 1971– 60.2, 1972– 55.0, 1973– 56.0, 1974– 55.5, 1975– 57.4, 1976–
53.1, 1977– 53.3.

| Year | Comps | Best | CS | World | W. rank | Sub 50 sec times |
|------|-------|------|-----|-------|---------|-------------------|
| 1978 | 15 | 51.09 | 1st | 9th | 14th | – |
| 1979 | 17 | 51.47 | 1st | 17th | 13th | – |
| 1980 | 8 | 49.46 | 1st | 2nd | 2nd | 2 |
| 1981 | 11 | 48.61 | 1st | 1st | 1st | 6 |
| 1982 | 10 | 48.85 | 1st | 2nd | 2nd | 6 |
| 1983 | 11 | 47.99 | 1st | 1st | 1st | 5 |
| 1984 | 15 | 49.02 | 2nd | 5th | 3rd | 11 |
| 1985 | 7 | 49.89 | 1st | 5th | 10th | 1 |

World record: 47.99 (10.8.83)
CS records: 51.09 (9.6.78), 50.51 (8.7.80), 49.46 (28.7.80), 49.23 (19.6.81), 49.17 (5.7.81),
49.01 (23.8.81), 48.61 (6.9.81), 48.45 (23.7.83), 47.99 (10.8.83)
World indoor bests: 51.02 oversized track (24.1.81), 49.64 (28.1.81), 49.59 (7.3.82)
Other CS indoor bests: 51.99 (3.2.79), 51.81 (25.2.79)
CS champion 1976, 1982–4

**Major events:**

| | | | | | | | |
|------|-----|------------------|--------|------|-----|-------------------|--------|
| 1978 | 7th | European Champs | 53.93 | 1982 | 1st | European Indoors | 49.59 |
| 1979 | 2nd | European Indoors | 51.81 | | 2nd | European Champs | 48.85 |
| 1980 | 2nd | Olympics | 49.46 | 1983 | 1st | European Indoors | 49.69 |
| 1981 | 1st | European Indoors | 50.07 | | 1st | World Champs | 47.99 |
| | 1st | European Cup B | 52.10 | 1984 | 5th | CS Spartakiad | 49.94 |
| | 1st | World Cup | 48.61 | 1985 | 5th | World Cup | 50.95 |

In 40 competitions in 1980–3 lost only to Marita Koch at 1980 Olympics, 1982 Europeans. She
beat Koch at 1981 World Cup.

## 800 metres
Early progression: 1973– 2:13.8, 1974– 2:13.7, 1975– 2:11.4. No races 1976–81.

| Year | Comps | Best | CS | World | W. rank | Sub 2 min times |
|------|-------|------|-----|-------|---------|------------------|
| 1982 | 1 | 1:56.59 | 1st | 6th | 1 | – |
| 1983 | 8 | 1:53.28 | 1st | 1st | 1st | 6 |
| 1984 | 5 | 1:57.68 | 1st | 12th | 1st | 4 |
| 1985 | 20 | 1:55.91 | 1st | 2nd | 1st | 13 |
| 1986 | 4 | 2:04.02i | (all indoors) | | | |

World record: 1:53.28 (26.7.83)
CS records: 1:56.59 (18.9.82), 1:53.28 (26.7.83)
World indoor bests: 1:58.33 (oversized track) (12.2.83)
CS champion 1985

**Major events:**

| | | | | | | | |
|------|-----|--------------|---------|------|-----|------------------|---------|
| 1983 | 1st | World Champs | 1:54.68 | 1985 | 1st | European Cup | 1:55.91 |
| | 1st | European Cup | 1:58.79 | | 1st | Grand Prix Final | 1:59.0 |
| Unbeaten in 14 competitions 1982–4. | | | | | 2nd | World Cup | 2:01.99 |

## 4 x 400 metres relay

**Major events:**

| | | | | |
|------|----------------------------------------|------|----------------------------------|
| 1973 | CS 5th European Cup sf (first int.) | 1982 | CS 2nd European Chs – 47.6 anch. |
| 1979 | Europe 4th World Cup – 52.5 leg | 1983 | CS 2nd World Champs – 47.75 anchor |
| 1981 | CS 2nd European Cup sf – 47.9 anchor | | CS 1st European Cup – 47.9 anchor |
| | CS 1st European Cup B – 49.2 anchor | 1984 | CS 2nd CS Spartakiad – 49.39 anchor |
| | Europe 2nd World Cup – 48.12 anchor | 1985 | Europe 3rd World Cup – anchor |

# SARA SIMEONI, COMETHROUGH PERFORMER EXEMPLIFIED

## BY R.L. QUERCETANI

Comethrough performers are the delight of track lovers. Statisticians in particular are apt to identify them as the characters who supply the 'noblest' figures. The art of surpassing oneself in a major meet, exemplified by the ancient motto: 'Hic Rhodos, hic salta!', is the trademark of true champions. Sara Simeoni, Italy's sterling high jumper, surely belongs to that rare breed. In the twenty years during which she graced the runways of so many fields at home and abroad, her production of comethrough performances has been simply amazing.

It all began on 3 May 1966, a few days after turning 13, when she made her official debut in a high jump competition at Verona, very much her own backyard as she was born at Rivoli Veronese, in the countryside close to the town of Romeo and Juliet. She won with a jump of 1.35m, good enough to rank as an Italian age best! That was the first step of a wondrous journey which came to an end, alas not so happy, on 14 September 1986, when she bowed to Stefka Kostadinova in her farewell competition at Cagliari.

As it happens, the tale wouldn't have begun at all but for a 'mishap' which befell Sara, the daughter of a middle class family, when she was 12. That was when she applied for the 'corps de ballet' in 'Aida' at the Arena, Verona's famous open air theatre. The recruiter, a woman, turned her down on the grounds that she had big feet and was a bit too tall for her age. (In her prime Sara stood 1.78, slightly above the average of female jumpers in the leading ranks.) She sometimes regrets having lost that opportunity: an artist's life certainly appealed to her. As we all know, however, she used her big feet to good advantage in another walk of life.

In 1969 she turned from the 'scissors' to the Fosbury Flop. The following year she went to Paris for the inaugural European Junior Championships. She finished no higher than fifth with a 1.70, but she was one of the 'greenest' jumpers in the field. Then it's not always true, as the Italian saying goes, that 'Il buon dì si vede dal mattino' (literally 'you can tell a good day from the morning'). Another young Italian who also finished fifth in his event, the 200m, was Pietro Mennea. Both he and Sara were beaten by people very few

of us would now remember, the bright exception being Franz-Peter Hofmeister of West Germany, who won the 200m in Paris and came back to annex the European senior title over 400m eight years later in Prague.

Sara's portent as a comethrough performer is enshrined in the period 1971–78, the years of her ascent. See what she managed to do in the five major meetings of that period: (A = personal best going in the meet; B = result and placing; C = gain).

Sara Simeoni. *George Herringshaw*

| Date | | A | B | C |
|------|--|---|---|---|
| 1971 | European Championships | 1.76 | 1.78 (9th) | + 2cms |
| 1972 | Olympic Games | 1.80 | 1.85 (6th) | + 5cms |
| 1974 | European Championships | 1.86 | 1.89 (3rd) | + 3cms |
| 1976 | Olympic Games | 1.90 | 1.91 (2nd) | + 1cm |
| 1978 | European Championships | 2.01 | 2.01 (1st) | = |

But for 1978, those were the years when she normally played second fiddle to the great Rosi Witschas-Ackermann (GDR), who on 26 August 1977 at West Berlin became the first woman to clear a high jump bar set at exactly 2 meters. Although only one year older than her Italian rival, Rosi had been considerably quicker in reaching the top. It was only in the winter 1977/78 that the Veronese and her coach—fiancé Erminio Azzaro (himself an Italian record holder in the high jump: 2.18 in 1971) began to give serious thought to the possibility of finally turning the tables on Rosi. Sara's training during those months was described by an insider as 'unbelievably hard and boring'. But results were rewarding: in 1978 she added 8 centimeters to her personal best of the year before (1.93) and thus succeeded Rosi as world record holder. Her 2.01 clearance came during an international match at Brescia on 4 August. That was a fitting prelude to one of the greatest battles in the history of women athletics: the Simeoni v. Ackermann duel at the European Championships in Prague. The German, herself a supreme competitor, was ready for the challenge, less than a year after an operation on her Achilles tendon. A tremendous ding-dong battle unfolded before a large crowd, in the rainy atmosphere of Rošický Stadium. The connoisseurs were offered a series of confrontations between two schools of jumping: the Straddle (Ackermann) and the Flop (Simeoni). Rosi was in the lead at 1.97, but Sara wrested it from her by going over 1.99 first time, while the German needed two tries. This put Sara in lane 1 by the time the bar was raised to 2.01, equal to her world record of four weeks ago. On her second attempt she mastered the height once more and brought the crowd to its feet. The indomitable Rosi finally had to bow—but her last try was tantalizingly close, a reminder of how infinitesimal can be the difference between success and failure in human endeavours.

That marked the apex of Sara's career. What came after Prague, the years between 1979 and 1986, was a mixture of joys and woes. She began to suffer from a persistent form of tendinitis from which she would never fully recover. Often unable to train adequately, she was forced to ration her appearances and in some competitions even

her jumps. Occasionally she would have a breathing spell—as in the summer of 1980, when she managed to win the most coveted of medals, Olympic gold. In the Moscow Games she jumped 1.97 (one centimeter *below* her seasonal best!) and thus became Italy's second Olympic champion on the distaff side (first was Trebisonda 'Ondina' Valla, who won the 80m hurdles in 1936).

In the second part of her international career, Sara often had thoughts of retiring. On occasion she felt she would never regain her onetime form. Early in 1984 prospects were dimmer than ever in view of her fourth Olympic adventure. Just a few weeks before the Los Angeles Games, she was in great pain, and in a terrible quandary: give it one more try in far from perfect physical condition or quit. She chose 'self-punishment' and went to Los Angeles with a seasonal best of 'only' 1.95. In the Coliseum, stirred to action by the 'Bombenform' of her old rival Ulrike Meyfarth of West Germany, Sara surprised many people, including herself, by going over a bar set at 2.00, a height she had last mastered *six years ago*. She was second to Meyfarth (2.02), yet I rank that comethrough achievement as her greatest ever.

Sara's Olympic tally—one gold, two silver and a sixth place—classifies her as one of the all time Greats of the event, along with Iolanda Balas and Ulrike Meyfarth, both of whom won twice but had no other medals. Sara can point to a set of three medals in the European outdoor Championships as well (one gold and two bronze) plus one of four golds in the European indoor Championships. ATFS member Silvio Garavaglia has collected all of her marks ever since she mastered 1.60 for the first time, in 1969. His list includes 329 performances, 101 of which at 1.90 or higher! He also reckoned that during the same period she won 76.6% of her competitions and placed lower than third in only 3.1%!

Even outside the fields of friendly strife, Sara has been a great asset to Italian athletics. She is the kind of woman whose behaviour calls for admiration and respect at the same time. It is safe to assume that no other Italian sportswoman has ever attracted so much attention. Her smile, same as her flowing style of jumping, will be remembered well beyond the boundaries of her track career.

**Sara SIMEONI** b.19.4.53 Verona 1.78m 60kg. Physical education instructor.

At HJ: OG: '72– 6, '76– 2, '80– 1, '84– 2; WCh: '83– dnq; ECh: '71– 9, '74– 3, '78– 1, '82– 3, '86– dnq; EI: '77– 1, '78– 1, '80– 1, '81– 1; EJ: '70– 5; WSG: '73– 3, '75– 2, '77– 1, '79– 3, '81– 1; WCp: '77– 2, '79– 2; ECp: '79– 2, '85– 5. Italian titles: 14 HJ 1970–80, 1982–3, 1985; 1 Pen 1972.

Two world high jump records at 2.01m in 1978. 21 Italian records, the most for any event, from 1.71m 1970. 67 internationals.

Progression at HJ: 1966– 1.45, 1967– 1.48, 1968– 1.55, 1969– 1.65, 1970– 1.75, 1971– 1.80, 1972– 1.85, 1973– 1.86, 1974– 1.90, 1975– 1.89, 1976– 1.91, 1977– 1.93, 1978– 2.01, 1979– 1.98, 1980– 1.98, 1981– 1.97i, 1982– 1.98, 1983– 1.93, 1984– 2.00, 1985– 1.94, 1986– 1.94.

Sara Simeoni (Italy), gold medallist for the high jump at the Moscow Olympic Games 1980. *Mark Shearman*

# THE 85 METRE HAMMER THROWERS

## BY PETER MATTHEWS

Sergey Litvinov's opening throw in the 1986 European Championships was 85.74m. That smashed the championship best and was a distance that had only ever been bettered by himself and by Yuriy Sedykh. Yet it was not enough to win, as Sedykh gained steadily with throws of 83.94m, 85.28m and 85.46m before setting his sixth world record at 86.74m and following that with 86.68m and 86.62m. Setting a world best non-winning performance was no new experience for Litvinov, for he had done the same back in 1980 at the Olympic Games and in Cork in 1985, on all three occasions behind world records set by Sedykh.

Writing in the 1985 *Annual* I said that even before the 1984 season started there could be little doubt as to Yuriy Sedykh's status as the greatest hammer thrower of all time. In 1984, despite not being able to win his third Olympic gold medal, as

he surely would have but for the Soviet boycott, his performances reached new heights, as exemplified by the fact that he beat the pre-season world record, Litvinov's 84.14m, 13 times in his final six competitions of the year. Sedykh has made a habit of peaking in even numbered years, the major championships years, so 1985 was a relatively quiet season for him, as another of the talented Soviet throwers, Juri Tamm, ranked number one. But in 1986 Sedykh once again was supreme, adding yet more lustre to his brilliant career. Litvinov, too, improved, and of course these great throwers are but the top of the tremendous depth of hammer talent in the Soviet Union.

Yuriy Sedykh first reached the top of world hammer throwing in 1976 and Sergey Litvinov in 1979. The first 80-metre throw was by Boris

---

**80 metre competitions**
(not including supplementary marks in a series)

(a) Number each year:
1978 – 2, 1980 – 19, 1981 – 2, 1982 – 10, 1983 – 22, 1984 – 48, 1985 – 35, 1986 – 46.
Total 184.

(b) By thrower—ranked by average of ten best competitions:

| Name | Best ever | Average | Over 84m | Over 82m | Over 80m | Years 80m+ |
|------|-----------|---------|----------|----------|----------|------------|
| Yuriy Sedykh | 86.74 | 85.59 | 13 | 20 | 35 | 1980–6 |
| Sergey Litvinov | 86.04 | 84.81 | 9 | 15 | 30 | 1980–6 |
| Juri Tamm | 84.40 | 82.97 | 2 | 8 | 25 | 1980–6 |
| Igor Nikulin | 83.54 | 82.14 | – | 7 | 23 | 1980–6 |
| Juha Tiainen | 81.52 | 80.71 | – | – | 8 | 1983–4 |
| Gunther Rodehau | 82.64 | 80.45 | – | 1 | 6 | 1984–6 |
| Yuriy Tarasyuk | 81.44 | 80.36 | – | – | 7 | 1982–5 |
| Benjaminas Viluckis | 82.24 | 80.28 | – | 1 | 7 | 1985–6 |
| Karl-Hans Riehm | 80.80 | 80.20 | – | – | 8 | 1978–83 |
| Klaus Ploghaus | 81.32 | 80.07 | – | – | 5 | 1981–6 |
| Matthias Moder | 80.92 | 79.84 | – | – | 6 | 1985–6 |
| Christoph Sahner | 81.56 | 79.74 | – | – | 3 | 1985–6 |
| Igor Astapkovich | 80.68 | 79.28 | – | – | 2 | 1985–6 |
| 13 Others |  |  |  |  | 19 |  |
| TOTALS |  |  | 24 | 52 | 184 |  |

Zaichuk in 1978, followed that year by Karl-Hans Riehm, but Sedykh and Litvinov set their first world records in 1980, when six men broke through that barrier. Indeed at Leselidze on 16 May 1980, after Sedykh's first record of 80.38m, Juri Tamm broke that with 80.46m, but Sedykh came straight back with 80.64m, three world records at one event. Since then the record has stayed with Sedykh and Litvinov, and now they are the only two men ever to have thrown 85 metres. In 1984 and 1986 the super-consistent Sedykh had 20 throws in 7 competitions over that line and Litvinov 5 in 4.

### Yearly analysis

A table which shows the progress of the top Soviet throwers over the past decade and their current dominance. Season's bests and number of performances in the world's top 20:

| Year | Sedykh | | Litvinov | | Nikulin | | Tamm | |
|------|--------|---|----------|---|---------|---|------|---|
| 1976 | 78.86 | 6 | 72.38 | – | 58.14 | – | 66.86 | – |
| 1977 | 76.60 | 1 | 74.32 | – | 71.22 | – | 72.44 | – |
| 1978 | 79.76 | 2 | 76.22 | – | 71.60 | – | 74.58 | – |
| 1979 | 79.58 | 2 | 79.82 | 7 | 75.20 | – | 75.18 | – |
| 1980 | 81.80 | 5 | 81.66 | 4 | 80.34 | 3 | 80.46 | 2 |
| 1981 | 80.18 | 5 | 79.60 | 1 | 77.50 | 1 | 77.26 | – |
| 1982 | 81.66 | 5 | 83.98 | 4 | 83.54 | 8 | 74.82 | – |
| 1983 | 80.94 | 3 | 84.14 | 6 | 82.92 | 3 | 79.18 | – |
| 1984 | 86.34 | 8 | 85.20 | 3 | 82.56 | 2 | 84.40 | 4 |
| 1985 | 82.70 | 5 | 76.94 | – | 78.88 | – | 84.08 | 11 |
| 1986 | 86.74 | 10 | 86.04 | 8 | 82.34 | 1 | 80.88 | – |

And their championships performances:

| | |
|---|---|
| Olympics 1976: | 1. Sedykh 77.52 |
| European 1978: | 1. Sedykh 77.28 |
| Olympics 1980: | 1. Sedykh 81.80, 2. Litvinov 80.64, 3. Tamm 78.96 |
| European 1982: | 1. Sedykh 81.66, 2. Nikulin 79.44, 3. Litvinov 78.66 |
| World 1983: | 1. Litvinov 82.68, 2. Sedykh 80.94, 4. Nikulin 79.34 |
| European 1986: | 1. Sedykh 86.74, 2. Litvinov 85.74, 3. Nikulin 82.00. |

Yuriy Sedykh. *Mark Shearman*

Sergey Litvinov. *ASP*

**The Sedykh–Litvinov duels**

All their meetings from 1978:

| Date | Venue meeting | | Sedykh | | Litvinov |
|------|---------------|---|--------|---|----------|
| 28 Feb 78 | Dushanbe | 1 | 74.40 | 3 | 73.24 |
| 16 Jun 78 | Tbilisi | 5 | 74.48 | 4 | 75.20 |
| 22 Jul 78 | Vilnius – Znamenskiy | 1 | 77.44 | 7 | 72.46 |
| 19 Aug 78 | Podolsk | 3 | 74.24 | 5 | 74.00 |
| 10 Sep 78 | Bydgoszcz | 2 | 75.98 | 3 | 73.62 |
| 24 Feb 79 | Dushanbe | 2 | 75.14 | 1 | 75.94 |
| 29 May 79 | Sochi | 2 | 75.14 | 4 | 74.10 |
| 28 Jul 79 | Moscow – Spartakiad | 4 | 74.76 | 1 | 77.08 |
| 24 Feb 80 | Sochi | 3 | 76.76 | 1 | 78.32 |
| 16 May 80 | Leselidze | 1 | 80.64* | 3 | 78.94 |
| 24 May 80 | Sochi | 3 | 79.98 | 1 | 81.66* |
| 5 Jul 80 | Moscow – Znamenskiy | 3 | 78.96 | 2 | 79.86 |
| 31 Jul 80 | Moscow – Olympics | 1 | 81.80* | 2 | 80.64 |
| 8 Sep 80 | Donetsk – SU Champs | 1 | 80.84 | 3 | 77.14 |
| 24 May 81 | Rome v It,Sp,Gr | 1 | 78.40 | 2 | 76.66 |
| 31 May 81 | Sochi | 1 | 76.82 | 3 | 75.04 |
| 27 Jun 81 | Tbilisi – v GDR | 1 | 80.18 | 2 | 76.88 |
| 11 Jul 81 | Leningrad v USA | 1 | 77.20 | 2 | 77.08 |
| 25 Jul 81 | Leningrad | 1 | 79.68 | 2 | 76.86 |
| 26 Feb 82 | Leselidze | 1 | 77.32 | 3 | 75.28 |
| 30 May 82 | Sochi | 1 | 79.38 | 2 | 78.72 |
| 25 Jun 82 | Cottbus – v GDR | 1 | 79.60 | 2 | 78.64 |
| 3 Jul 82 | Indianapolis v USA | 1 | 80.46 | 2 | 79.32 |
| 10 Sep 82 | Athens – European | 1 | 81.66 | 3 | 78.66 |
| 12 Feb 83 | Adler | 6 | 74.24 | 1 | 79.44 |
| 21 Jun 83 | Moscow – Spartakiad | 4 | 78.68 | 1 | 84.14* |
| 9 Aug 83 | Helsinki – World Champs | 2 | 80.94 | 1 | 82.68 |
| 2 Jun 84 | Turin – v Italy | 1 | 81.52 | 2 | 80.60 |
| 21 Jun 84 | Kiev | 1 | 82.60 | 2 | 82.60 |
| 3 Jul 84 | Cork | 1 | 86.34* | 2 | 85.20 |
| 17 Aug 84 | Moscow – Druzhba | 1 | 85.60 | 3 | 81.30 |
| 31 Aug 84 | Rome – Golden Gate | 1 | 83.90 | 2 | 80.58 |
| 2 Jun 85 | Rome – v Italy | 1 | 81.80 | 2 | 76.94 |
| 24 May 86 | Sochi | 1 | 83.02 | 3 | 80.66 |
| 8 Jun 86 | Moscow – Znamenskiy | 1 | 84.58 | 2 | 82.10 |
| 22 Jun 86 | Tallinn – v GDR | 1 | 86.66* | 2 | 84.36 |
| 3 Jul 86 | Dresden – OT | 2 | 84.92 | 1 | 86.04 |
| 7 Jul 86 | Helsinki | 1 | 84.14 | 2 | 84.02 |
| 9 Jul 86 | Moscow – Goodwill Games | 1 | 84.72 | 2 | 84.64 |
| 30 Aug 86 | Helsinki – European | 1 | 86.74* | 2 | 85.74 |
| 10 Sep 86 | Rome – Grand Prix Final | 2 | 81.98 | 1 | 84.88 |

So the score from 1978 is 30–11 in Sedykh's favour.

* World record.

# PROGRESS – AND A LOOK BACK AT TIMES PAST

## BY PETER MATTHEWS

An indication of just how standards have improved at the top in world track and field athletics can be gained by looking back at the world bests in the seasons of 1952, 1937 and 1912, respectively 25, 50 and 75 years ago.

## 1912

This was an Olympic year, and new peaks were reached in overall athletic attainment. The Games were held in Stockholm, men's events only in those days, when women were not expected to take part in such strenuous activity. World records were set at seven events. Hannes Kolehmainen (Fin) won three gold medals. His time of 14:36.6 for 5000m was the first ever sub-15 minute time, but he only beat Jean Bouin (Fra) 14:36.7 by inches. Two days earlier he had won the 10000m in 31:20.8 by 45.8 seconds and he later won the 12km cross–country race by another big margin, 33.2 seconds.

Another great champion was Ted Meredith (USA), who won gold medals and set world records at 800m and 4x400m relay. Before the Games the world record for 800m was the 1:52.8 run by Mel Sheppard at the 1908 Games. Sheppard set a very fast pace at Stockholm, passing 400m in 52.5, but the 19-year-old Meredith edged ahead, winning with 1:51.9 to 1:52.0 for both Sheppard and Ira Davenport (USA).

Jim Thorpe (USA) won both pentathlon and decathlon by huge margins, the former at 4041.53 points to 3623.84 by Ferdinand Bie (Nor), and the latter with 8412.955 to 7724.495 by Hugo Wieslander (Swe); his performances score 3367 and 6564 respectively on the current (1984) scoring tables. Sadly he was disqualified following an admission by him that he had earned $25 a week playing minor league baseball in 1909–10. That injustice was eventually put right, when in 1984 the IAAF posthumously restored him as gold medallist.

## 1937

The post-Olympic season of 1937 was rather quieter, as in those days each Olympiad saw the

retirement of many athletes after their attempts at ultimate success at the Games. American college athletes, for instance, and certainly the USA was the dominant power in sport at the time, rarely pursued athletics careers on leaving college. All very different from today, when there are major international fixtures every year and rewards sufficient to keep athletes in the sport for much longer.

Once such collegian was Bill Sefton, who retired, aged 22, at the end of the 1937 season, surely before he had reached his potential. Nonetheless his pole vault duels with his University of Southern California teammate Earle Meadows brought three new world records in April-May 1937. First Sefton added 2cm with 4.45m at Los Angeles with Meadows second (4.38m). Then both cleared 4.48m at Palo Alto for first equal, and then both did 4.54m at Los Angeles on 29 May, this time Sefton winning.

Another highlight was the first world record by Sydney Wooderson, who took 0.4sec off Glenn Cunningham's three-year-old mile record. Wooderson had set British mile records in 1934, an estimated 4:13.4 when runner-up to Jack Lovelock at the Empire Games, in 1935, 4:13.7, and in 1936, 4:10.8 to win the Southern title at Chelmsford. He had been one of the favourites for the 1936 Olympic 1500m title, but a broken bone in his ankle had put paid to his chances as Lovelock won in a world record time. In 1937 Wooderson was back, and his record came in a specially staged handicap race at Motspur Park on 28 August. He followed the former British record holder Reggie Thomas, who started ten yards ahead through a fast first half, Wooderson's times, 440y in 58.6 and 880y 2:02.6, but slowed to 3:07.2 at three-quarters. However he managed to pick up the pace for the record, Britain's first mile record of the century. Since then Roger Bannister, Derek Ibbotson, Seb Coe, Steve Ovett and Steve Cram have followed his example.

## 1962

By 1962 we were into the middle of a couple of decades of huge improvements in athletics standards, and although not an Olympic Year, it was one in which European Championships and Commonwealth Games were contested.

Many great names in athletics history set world records during the year. In addition to those in the table of year's bests, note Harry Jerome and Bob Hayes with 9.2 for 100 yards, and Michel Jazy, 5:01.6 for 2000m and 7:49.2 for 3000m. The two athletes who most stood out from their contemporaries were the high jumpers Valeriy Brumel and Iolanda Balas. Brumel added two more world records, 2.26m when he won in the great USSR v USA match at Palo Alto, and 2.27m in Moscow; the world's second best was 2.17m. The superpower duel at Stanford was watched by the largest crowd ever for a track meeting in the USA, 81,000 on the second day, following 72,000 on the first. The USA won the men's match 128–107, but the Soviets won their usual women's victory 66–41. Balas did not beat her world record 1.91m of the previous year, but her 1.87m best was way ahead of the second best 1.78m.

Both Brumel and Balas won European titles at Belgrade. Other notable men's gold medallists included Michel Jazy (Fra), 1500m, Igor Ter-Ovanesyan (USSR), LJ, Jozef Schmidt (Pol), TJ, Janis Lusis (USSR), JT, and Pyotr Bolotnikov

(USSR) at 10000m, but the latter had to give best in the 5000m to an inspired barefooted Bruce Tulloh (UK), who streaked away on the penultimate lap to win from Kazimierz Zimny (Pol), with Bolotnikov third. Salvatore Morale (Ita) equalled the world record of 49.2 at 400m hurdles. In the women's events Tamara Press (USSR) won the shot/discus double, equalling her world record of 18.55m in the shot, and other winners included the Soviet athletes Tatyana Shchelkanova, LJ, Galina Bystrova, pentathlon, and Maria Itkina, 400m. The closest final was the women's 80m hurdles, with the first four timed at 10.6, the gold medal going to Tereza Ciepla (Pol) from Karin Balzer, who thus missed the opportunity to be the first European women's champion from the GDR, an honour gained on the men's side the previous day by Manfred Matuschewski at 800m.

At the Commonwealth Games held in very hot weather in'Perth at the end of November, double winners were two men, Seraphino Antao (Ken) 100y/220y and Peter Snell (NZ) 880y/1 mile; and three women, Dorothy Hyman (Eng) 100y/220y, Val Young (NZ) SP/DT, and Pam Kilborn (Aus) 80mh/LJ.

## Best times set during the year – 1962

| MEN | | | WOMEN | | |
|---|---|---|---|---|---|
| 100m | 10.1 | Bob Hayes (USA) | 100m | 11.4 | Jutta Heine (FRG) |
| 200m | 20.55† | Paul Drayton (USA) | | 11.4 | Wilma Rudolph (USA) |
| 400m | 45.5† | Ulis Williams (USA) | 200m | 23.3 | Jutta Heine (FRG) |
| 800m | 1:44.3 | Peter Snell (NZ)* | 400m | 51.9 | Shin Keum Dan (NKo)* |
| 1500m | 3:38.3 | Michel Jazy (Fra) | 800m | 2:01.2 | Dixie Willis (Aus)* |
| 1 mile | 3:54.4 | Peter Snell (NZ)* | 1500m | 4:19.0 | Marise Chamberlain (NZ)* |
| 5000m | 13:38.4 | Murray Halberg (NZ) | 1 mile | 4:41.4 | Marise Chamberlain (NZ)* |
| 10000m | 28:18.2 | Pyotr Bolotnikov (USSR)* | 80mh | 10.5 | Betty Moore (UK/Aus)* |
| Mar | 2:16:09.6 | Yu Mang Hyang (NKo) | HJ | 1.87 | Iolanda Balas (Rom) |
| 3000mSt | 8:32.6 | Gaston Roelants (Bel) | LJ | 6.62 | Tatyana Shchelkanova |
| 110mh | 13.3y | Jerry Tarr (USA) | | | (USSR)* |
| 400mh | 49.2 | Salvatore Morale (Ita)* | SP | 18.55 | Tamara Press (USSR)* |
| HJ | 2.27 | Valeriy Brumel (USSR)* | DT | 58.17 | Tamara Press (USSR) |
| PV | 4.94 | Pentti Nikula (Fin)* | JT | 58.33 | Elvira Ozolina (USSR) |
| LJ | 8.31 | Igor Ter-Ovanesyan | Pen | 4975 | Irina Press (USSR) |
| | | (USSR)* | 4x100mR | 44.5 | Poland |
| TJ | 16.65 | Vladimir Goryayev (USSR) | | | |
| SP | 20.08 | Dallas Long (USA)* | | | |
| DT | 62.45 | Al Oerter (USA)* | | | |
| HT | 70.66 | Hal Connolly (USA)* | | | |
| JT | 86.04 | Janis Lusis (USSR) | | | |
| Dec | 7694 | Yang Chuan-Kwang (Tai) | | | |
| 4x100mR | 39.5 | FR Germany, Poland | | | |
| 4x400mR | 3:03.7 | USA | | | |

* world record.   † time converted from Imperial distance equivalent.

## Olympic medal table of leading nations 1912

| Nation | Gold | Silver | Bronze | | Nation | Gold | Silver | Bronze |
|--------|------|--------|--------|---|--------|------|--------|--------|
| USA | 14 | 14 | 11 | | United Kingdom | 2 | 1 | 5 |
| Finland | 6 | 4 | 3 | | Canada | 1 | 1 | 2 |
| Sweden | 4 | 5 | 5 | | | | | |

### Best times set during the year – 1912

| | | | | | | |
|---|---|---|---|---|---|---|
| 100m | 10.6 | Donald Lippincott (USA)* | HJ | 2.007 | George Horine (USA)* |
| | 10.6 | William Applegarth (UK)* | PV | 4.02 | Marc Wright (USA)* |
| 200m | 21.7 | Ralph Craig (USA) | LJ | 7.60 | Albert Gutterson (USA) |
| 400m | 47.7* | Charles Reidpath (USA) | TJ | 14.87 | Karl Baaske (Ger) |
| 800m | 1:51.9 | Ted Meredith (USA)* | SP | 15.54 | Ralph Rose (USA) |
| 1500m | 3:55.8 | Abel Kiviat (USA)* | DT | 47.58 | James Duncan (USA)* |
| 1 mile | 4:15.6 | Abel Kiviat (USA) | HT | 55.77 | Patrick Ryan (USA) |
| 5000m | 14:36.6 | Hannes Kolehmainen (Fin)* | JT | 62.32 | Eric Leeming (Swe)* |
| | | | Dec | 6564 | Jim Thorpe (USA)* |
| 10000m | 31:20.8 | Hannes Kolehmainen (Fin) | 4x100mR | 42.3 | Germany* |
| | | | 4x400mR | 3:16.6 | USA* |
| 3000mSt | 10:15.7 | Paul Seyffert (Ger) | | | |
| 110mh | 15.1 | Frederick Kelly (USA) | | | |
| 400mh | 58.0 | Charles Poulenard (Fra) | * world record | | |

### Best times set during the year – 1937

**MEN**

| | | | |
|---|---|---|---|
| 100m | 10.4 | several men |
| 200m | 20.9 | Jack Weiershauser (USA) |
| 400m | 46.6* | Loren Benke (USA) |
| 800m | 1:49.0* | Elroy Robinson (USA)* |
| 1500m | 3:48.6 | Miklos Szabo (Hun) |
| 1 mile | 4:06.4 | Sydney Wooderson (UK)* |
| 5000m | 14:28.8 | Taisto Mäki (Fin) |
| 10000m | 30:05.5 | Ilmari Salminen (Fin)* |
| Mar | 2:30:38 | Manuel Dias (Por) |
| 3000mSt | 9:16.6 | Kaarlo Tuominen (Fin) |
| 110mh | 14.0y | Robert Osgood (USA) |
| 400mh | 52.3 | Jack Patterson (USA) |
| HJ | 2.09 | Melvin Walker (USA) |
| PV | 4.54 | Bill Sefton (USA)* |
| | 4.54 | Earle Meadows (USA)* |
| LJ | 7.90 | Luz Long (Ger) |
| TJ | 15.86 | Kaneyuki Togami (Jap) |
| SP | 16.30 | Samuel Francis (USA) |
| DT | 51.67 | Kenneth Carpenter (USA) |
| HT | 59.55 | Pat O'Callaghan (Ire)*(u) |
| JT | 76.47 | Matti Järvinen (Fin) |
| Dec | 6780 | Olle Bexell (Swe) |

**WOMEN**

| | | | |
|---|---|---|---|
| 100m | 11.6 | Stanislawa Walasiewicz (Pol)‡ |
| | 11.9 | Käthe Krauss (Ger) |
| 200m | 24.5 | Stanislawa Walasiewicz (Pol)‡ |
| | 24.8* | Aileen Meagher (Can) |
| | 24.8 | Dorothy Saunders (UK) |
| 800m | 2:16.5 | Yevdokiya Vasilyeva (USSR) |
| 1500m | 4:45.2 | Yevdokiya Vasilyeva (USSR)* |
| 80mh | 11.6 | Barbara Burke (SAf)* |
| HJ | 1.63 | Dorothy Odam (UK) |
| LJ | 6.09 | Stanislawa Walasiewicz (Pol)‡ |
| | 5.95 | Käthe Krauss (Ger) |
| SP | 13.29 | Hermine Schröder (Ger) |
| DT | 45.78 | Nina Dumbadze (USSR) |
| JT | 43.77 | Hildegard Döge (Ger) |

‡ Now considered to have been of doubtful feminine gender
* world record

# BLOOD OXYGEN AND DISTANCE-RUNNING PERFORMANCE

BY DAVID E. MARTIN Ph.D.

Professor of Physiology at Georgia State University, Atlanta, USA

Chairman of Sports Sciences, TAC

Statisticians and other devotees of athletics who peruse handbooks that document details of competitive performances generally develop an ability to discern and appreciate individual excellence. However, unless one is a sport scientist it may be difficult to appreciate in equally precise terms the marvellous adaptations that the human body makes as it absorbs the effects of arduous training in order to deliver these excellent performances. In fact, even the sport scientists are often amazed. Resting physiological variables in a competitive distance runner, for example—a heart rate of 40 beats per minutes, oxygen consumption of 250 millilitres per minute, ventilation rate of 6 litres of air per minute—are no more indicative of this person's performance potential than is the observation of an idling diesel locomotive in exemplifying the enormous loads it can pull once it leaves the station.

By comparison, think of Carlos Lopes running his current world fastest 2:07:12 marathon—with a heart rate averaging 167 beats per minute, an oxygen uptake of around 4,000 ml/min, and a ventilatory rate of 110 litres per minute. He ran the equivalent of very nearly 105.5 laps nonstop around a 400 metre track at an average pace of 72.3 sec/lap. One need only try matching that performance if one is in doubt as to its quality!

But athletes want to run faster (and jump higher and throw farther). Track and field as a sport thus becomes a game for athlete and coach: what can be done to improve upon what has been done before? Sports science has gone far in its delineation of adaptive changes that occur in the human body with training, thereby identifying for coaches various strategies for optimizing performance. Aerobic distance running, for example, increases the size of the heart's ventricular chambers, permitting an increased output per beat (this is called stroke volume), whereas strength training thickens the heart walls with no change in chamber size. Thus, while both types of training would be useful, the former ought to be emphasized in those athletes aspiring excellence in distance running. Endurance training also increases the

circulating blood volume, both the plasma and red blood cell fractions, the former more so than the latter. This ensures better perfusion—more blood to working muscles for provision of oxygen and fuels, and more blood to the skin for heat dissipation. This transport also occurs at minimum energy cost—thinner blood is less viscous, putting less strain on the heart in pumping it.

For distance runners to be competitive, they require sufficient oxygen to permit nearly complete metabolism of all their needed fuels as they are racing. Beyond a certain running pace—which varies with the distance contended, athlete condition, and genetic factors—metabolic acids begin to accumulate if sufficient oxygen is unavailable. The effects of these acids can be so debilitating as to stop fuel metabolism completely, although before this happens runners generally incur sufficient discomfort that they slow their running to a more tolerable pace. But then they may not be in a position to place well in their race. Thus, adequate oxygen circulating in the bloodstream, for diffusion into the working muscles, is crucial.

How does one increase oxygen supplies? By increasing the content of haemoglobin circulating in the blood. Haemoglobin molecules transport 98.5% of the blood's oxygen; the remainder is dissolved in the plasma. Haemoglobin is carried in the red blood cells. In the lungs at rest, red blood cells are in contact with the tiny air-containing alveoli for only 0.75 second. Yet this is far more than enough time to virtually saturate the haemoglobin molecules with oxygen. They then will travel back to the heart and out to the working tissues, returning to the lungs with about 25% of their oxygen content removed. (During exercise, of course, this oxygen extraction increases.) Reoxygenation occurs again when the blood recirculates through the lungs.

This reoxygenation process is so wonderfully efficient that the red blood cell transit time across the lung oxygenating surfaces could be cut in half, and still the haemoglobin molecules would be oxygenated almost completely. Given the quantity of haemoglobin moving through the lung blood vessels, and the number of oxygen molecules in alveoli that can combine with haemoglobin, there is thus a sizable margin of safety. Or, to put it another way, a considerably higher haemoglobin (or red blood cell) content could be presented to the lungs during vigorous exercise and complete blood oxygenation would still occur. One only needs more red blood cells. How to achieve this has been on the minds of athletes, coaches, and sport scientists for decades.

One method would be to go to altitude and train. As one ascends to higher elevations, the lower atmospheric oxygen results in decreased blood oxygen levels. This is detected by the kidney, which initiates a compensatory mechanism to (hopefully) restore original blood oxygen content. Circulating levels of a protein called erythropoietin are raised, and this protein increases the activity of the bone marrow to release more red blood cells into the circulation. The response begins to be significant above about 6,000 feet (1,828 metres). When adaptation is complete, which takes several weeks, the blood will have a concentration of red blood cells greater than that found at sea level and, hopefully, a blood oxygen concentration comparable to that at sea level. Aerobic training done earlier at a given velocity and intensity at sea level (before travel to altitude) should now be tolerated comparably well at that altitude. Oxygen transport abilities for this altitude-trained athlete who now returns to sea-level to compete in longer distance events should be improved. Several details regarding the timing of return to sea level are crucial for optimum performance benefits. These relate to acid-base changes in the runner's tissues, and a gradual return of sea-level red blood cell concentrations over time. There is considerable individual athlete variation regarding these details. For several years, we have been working with and assisting such athletes as Pat Porter and Jon Sinclair, who live and train at altitude but who race at sea level, in identifying these variations, thereby enabling them to improve their athletic performances.

A second method would be to submit to the administration of certain kinds of anabolic steroids (the synthetic substance Nandrolone is one such example). 'Anabolic' refers to the ability of such substances to increase protein synthesis. The globin portion of haemoglobin is a protein. So also is erythropoietin. Thus, anabolic steroids in higher concentration than normally found in the body should be beneficial for increasing oxygen-carrying potential. Incidentally, it is the higher levels of circulating testosterone in men, compared to women, that account for the higher concentrations of erythropoietin, haemoglobin and red blood cells in men. Testosterone is a naturally-occurring anabolic steroid. Prepubertal boys and girls have haemoglobin and red blood cell concentrations similar to those found in adult women.

A third method would be to be 'blood-doped,' or 'blood-boosted,' or 'blood-packed,' all terms essentially synonymous with 'induced erythrocythemia.' In short, the circulating red blood cell concentration (and thus, haemoglobin) is elevated significantly. There are several techniques for doing this. The safest and most effective involves removal of about 900 ml of the athlete's own blood, freezing this blood at −80 C, waiting for about 5 weeks to permit return of red blood cell and haemoglobin concentrations to normal levels, and then infusing the thawed red blood cells, which have been washed free of plasma. Since the average life of a red blood cell is 120 days, some of the infused cells will be nonfunctional, and duly metabolized by the body's blood purification mechanisms. Even so, for about three weeks after this infusion, red blood cell and hemoglobin levels will be 8 to 12% higher than previously. This should raise the maximum oxygen carrying capacity of the blood, in turn improving aerobic capabilities. An analogy might be made to a hot-meal line serving food to the homeless in a large city. With more food available, more people can be served, and each can eat more.

Is the maximum oxygen carrying capacity in fact improved with blood re-infusion? What are the facts of oxygen transport? Let us assume an average male haemoglobin value of 15.8 gm/100 ml of blood, and for a female 13.9 gm/100 ml. (The normal range for men is 14.0 to 18.0, that for women 11.5 to 16.0). Each gram of haemoglobin can carry 1.31 ml of oxygen. Typically, when each haemoglobin molecule leaves the lungs, after equilibration with environmental air, it is about 97% saturated with oxygen. Thus, the male haemoglobin oxygen content in arterial blood will average $15.8 \times 1.31 \times 0.97 = 20.1$ ml/100 ml blood; that of the female will be $13.9 \times 1.31 \times 0.97 = 17.7$ ml/100 ml. Induced erythrocythemia can raise haemoglobin levels by 10%. Thus, the male cited above could now carry $20.1 + 2.1 = 22.1$ ml oxygen/100 ml blood, the female $17.7 + 1.7 = 19.4$ ml/100 ml.

Can this improve aerobic performance? One standard indicator of aerobic capabilities is determination of the maximum (max) volume (V) of oxygen ($O_2$) utilizable per minute by the entire body during exercise. For a runner, this is best measured using a treadmill run to voluntary exhaustion, with analysis of expired ventilatory gases. Whereas a resting $VO_2$ value might be 3.5 ml/min/kg [0.2 L/min for a 132lb (60kg) runner], if he were elite he might have a max-$VO_2$ of 80 ml/min/kg [4.8 L/min]. A 110lb [56kg] female elite runner might have a max-$VO_2$ of 70 ml/min/kg

[3.5 L/min]. The most reputable studies of red blood cell infusion report a 5% improvement in max-$VO_2$, and as much as a 25% increase in treadmill running time to voluntary exhaustion.

Which running events depend primarily on max-$VO_2$ for their competitive completion? The shorter, sprint-type events are performed primarily anaerobically. That is, insufficient oxygen can be provided by the body to the working muscles during the actual race effort to metabolize completely the fuels required. Metabolites such as lactic acid accumulate rapidly at those race velocities, decreasing profoundly the time that such effort intensity can be maintained. Over time, continued elevated breathing post-exercise provides the required oxygen to complete the metabolic task.

An 800 metre race is completed at about 135% of max-$VO_2$, and thus there is still an enormous anaerobic component. The 1,500 metres run is completed at about 112% of max-$VO_2$. The 5,000 and 10,000 metres events, being run at 97% and 92% of max-$VO_2$, respectively, are thus most closely matched to a max-$VO_2$ energy utilization requirement, and should most likely benefit by an elevated max-$VO_2$. The marathon is run at 80 to 85% of max-$VO_2$, and is primarily an event dependent on a runner's ability to select a pace that permits an optimum balance between free fatty acid and carbohydrate use. Insufficient carbohydrates exist to permit their use for the entire race, but free fatty acids cannot be metabolized quickly enough to serve as the sole fuel source.

Specifically, how would an increased max-$VO_2$ improve performance for 5,000 and 10,000 metres? Let's take an example. A runner must race at a pace of 4:29 per mile (66.9 sec/400 metres) to achieve 27:52 in a 10,000 metre race and be victo-

rious. At this intensity he is racing at a pace which is 95% of his max-$VO_2$ pace. But he can only manage to race at 92% of his max-$VO_2$ pace without debilitating lactic acid accumulation. Thus, for him such a pace (66.9 sec laps) is too difficult. If he could raise his max-$VO_2$, and still keep his ability to race at 92% of his max-$VO_2$ pace, then 66.9 sec laps may indeed become possible. If his max-$VO_2$ is raised even further, he may be able to beat the entire field with ease, or run even faster. Induced erythrocythemia is one method, in addition to training, for raising one's max-$VO_2$ quickly, and without the injury risks associated with additional training stress.

Should blood infusion be condoned as acceptable? The view of this writer is that it is little different from the use of anabolic steroids. Both are medical pharmacologic regimens specifically intended, in premeditated fashion, to provide an unnatural competitive advantage. The risks of successfully collecting, storing and infusing an individual's own blood, even using well-supervised medical healthcare standards, with no transfusion reactions, are not small enough. Added to this is the still-not-completely-understood effect of higher viscosity blood on cardiac strain during the prolonged near-maximum work intensities associated with competitive racing in highly trained runners.

Sports medicine personnel should not accept either the challenge or the liability of tampering with the preciousness of an athlete's chosen goal to achieve the best performance possible within natural limitations. Those who appreciate fine athletics performances should work diligently to suggest that their surpassing is not worth the giving-up of the sole use of natural abilities in favour of a new set of values based upon unnatural ergogenics.

Kaarlo Maaninka (208), who was reported to have said that he had been 'blood doped' when he won two medals at the 1980 Olympic Games. *Mark Shearman*

# THE TRUTH, THE WHOLE TRUTH AND NOTHING BUT THE TRUTH?

BY A. LENNART JULIN

Track and field athletics is a sport characterised by its ambition to be objective and accurate when judging and measuring the performances of the competitors. Due to this ambition we have very detailed rules that are continuously revised to keep up with the development in equipment and techniques. But 'objective and accurate' is not enough for us, although those criteria are sufficient for fair head-to-head competitions!

No, we also strive for absolute results, i.e. performances from different meets in different places on different occasions which it should be possible to compare strictly mathematically. That is the basic requirement to make record-lists and other kinds of statistical compilations (like this voluminous publication!) meaningful.

There is however a great risk for everyone who has been infected by the 'statistical disease' to be carried away by the magic of figures and start viewing them as 'the undisputed truth'. A world record *is* the greatest performance ever! It *must* be, because athletic results are *exact* – the timing or measuring equipment *never* lies!

To achieve the objective 'absolute results' that could be compared strictly mathematically like that we need rules that create competitive conditions that are similar in all relevant aspects. But do we have such rules? If not – could such rules be written?

Those of you who would not like to have your illusions destroyed should stop reading now, before the serious differences between the real world and our statistical dreams of the divine nature of athletic results are disclosed:

**SPRINT** results are significantly affected at least by the timing equipment, by how that is handled, by the wind, the temperature and other weather factors, by the altitude, by the 'quality' of the starter, by the condition of the track, by the lane, by the type of stands surrounding the track:

\* The timing is not absolutely automatic as the camera is positioned and the photo-finish picture evaluated by human judges.

\* The wind measurement is a procedure with so many short-comings that the value registered is not reliable even to tenths of metres per second, despite the fact that modern wind-gauges give values in hundredths! Also it is highly question-

able if the values (average wind at mid-point of the straight) reflects the wind effect on the runners in an absolutely fair way.

\* The wind could be significantly different in lane 8 compared to lane 1 even during a given race.

\* At 200m runners in the inner lanes are – due to the much tighter turns – at an indisputable disadvantage to those in the outer lanes.

\* A 'fertig-bang'-starter eliminates the reaction delay for runners who 'know' the starter. This could improve times by 1-2 tenths compared to the situation with a skilful starter.

**LONG DISTANCE** results are also significantly affected by the weather, by the condition of the track and by the altitude! It is in fact 'more impossible' to run a long distance WR at high altitude than to run a sprint WR at low altitude. So low altitude distance marks could be viewed as 'aided' in the same way as high altitude sprint marks are 'aided'!

**HIGH JUMP AND POLE VAULT** performances depend quite a lot on the type of cross-bar used. A highly flexible fibre-glass bar (fully legal) can stay on the supports when a stiff metal bar would have been knocked off. High-friction ends (definitely illegal but still used every now and then) makes the flexible bar even more advantageous.

In the **POLE VAULT** an aiding wind during the run-up can be just as helpful as a tail-wind in the sprints and the horizontal jumps but there is no wind-limit for pole vault.

In the **LONG JUMP** and the **TRIPLE JUMP** the pit is quite often not absolutely level with the runway as it should be. The measured length is also affected by the type of sand and the dampness of the sand because that decides how far behind the actual landing point that the 'nearest break' in the sand surface will be.

More than in the sprints where a number of athletes run at the same time the **HORIZONTAL JUMPERS** who compete one at a time will experience dissimilar wind conditions even within the same competition!

In the **THROWING EVENTS** electronic distance measuring has been used with increasing intensity. This development is probably viewed by many observers as parallel in quality to the introduction of electronic timing in the running events. But this is not so!

It is true that the errors caused by twisted measuring tapes and reading errors are eliminated but these are not the major problems when results should be determined. No, the problem in the throwing events is to define the two points between which we shall measure with high accuracy and here the sophisticated electronical equipment is not capable of helping us.

In the **SHOT PUT** and the **HAMMER THROW** we get a fairly distinct landing mark but the size of that (which determines the position of the measuring point) depends on the softness of the landing surface. Dry cinders could mean a couple of centimeters advantage compared to damp grass. In the **MEN'S JAVELIN THROW** we now have got an implement that lands with the metal head first creating a quite well-defined (plus/minus a couple of centremetres) measuring point.

But in the **WOMEN'S JAVELIN THROW** as well as in the **DISCUS THROW** perhaps some 50% of the throws land in such a way that no distinct mark is made on the ground, especially not on a dry and firm grass surface. Unless the judge is quite close (a couple of metres) to where the implement is touching down mis-markings of 10–50 cm are not at all uncommon. If the measuring point is so inadequately fixed what is then the importance of using a high-precision electronic equipment with an uncertainty of perhaps less than 0.1 cm? It could be compared to hand-times in hundredths achieved through handling an electronical digital stopwatch with woollen mittens on the hands!

One other little known factor that strongly influences the performances in the **THROWING EVENTS** is that the grass-surface used as landing area normally isn't flat! The mid-point of the field could lie as much as 30 cm higher than the outer limits. This means that a throw in the middle of the sector will hit the ground earlier than a similar throw close to the border of the sector. For a landing angle of 45 degrees you will lose as much in length of the throw as the difference in height, i.e. you could be robbed of 30 cm! It will be even more if the landing angle is considerably smaller than 45 degrees, as it usually is with the discus and the women's javelin.

This catalogue of more or less well-known factors that influence the 'truthfulness' of athletic results does definitely not claim to be complete! The ambition has only been to give some concrete examples of how all these figures that are the bricks our compilations buildings are built with are affected in a significant way. The rules neither currently nor in future specified will be able to eliminate all those cracks and other defects to the bricks.

So we have to realise that perfectly 'absolute' athletic results are impossible as long as we want our sport to be something that could be carried out in open air anywhere in the world. The world record is not necessarily synonymous with 'the greatest performance ever' but is just the best mark achieved in a legitimate competition.

But this is not the same as saying that it is meaningless to spend time, money and energy on athletics statistics. It is fun and although it is impossible to say that a 10.02 here is 'undoubtedly better' than a 10.05 there lots of interesting observations concerning trends and similar things could be deduced from a statistical compilation as long as we don't view and treat individual marks as pieces of divine truth.

# SUSPENDED AFTER FAILING DRUG TEST

MEN
Gary Armstrong (USA), 1986
Duncan Attwood (USA), 1985
Wayne Barber (Aus), 1986
Lázaro Betancourt (Cub), 1986
Darren Crawford (USA), 1986
Peter Dajia (Can(, 1986
Juan de la Cruz (Dom), 1983
Dimitrios Delifotis (Gre), 1984
Ronald Desruelles (Bel), 1980
Naser Fahemy (Irn), 1983
Bob Gray (Can), 1986
Knut Hjeltnes (Nor), 1977
Seppo Hovinen (Fin), 1977
Kleanthis Ierisotis (Gre), 1984
Tom Jadwin (USA), 1986
Dariusz Juzyszyn (Pol), 1963
Jerzy Kaduskiewicz (Pol), 1982
Lars-Erik Källström (Swe), 1983
Markus Kessler (FRG), 1986
Hans-Joachim Krug (FRG), 1978
Juan-Miguel López (Cub), 1986
Greg McSeveney (USA), 1986
Remigius Machura (CS), 1985
Mike Mahovlich (Can), 1986
Yevgeniy Mironov (SU), 1978
Hein-Direck Neu (FRG), 1978
Antoni Niemczak (Pol), 1986
Juan Núñez (Dom), 1983
Arne Pedersen (Nor), 1982
Asko Pesonen (Fin), 1977
Ben Plucknett (USA), 1981
Elisio Rios (Por), 1983
Walter Schmidt (FRG), 1977
Al Schoterman (USA), 1984
Vladimir Shaloshik (SU), 1974
Ahmed Kamel Shatta (Egy), 1985
Mike Spiritoso (Can), 1986
Lars Sundin (Swe), 1985
Göran Svensson (Swe), 1985
Art Swarts (USA), 1986
László Szabó (Hun), 1981
Markku Tuokko (Fin), 1977
Martti Vainio (Fin), 1984
Velko Velev (Bul), 1975
Gary Williky (USA), 1985
Nikolaos Yendenkos (Gre), 1985
Vasiliy Yershov (SU), 1978
Joe Zelezniak (USA), 1986

WOMEN
Nunu Abashidze (SU), 1981
Lyudmila Andonova (Bul), 1985
Maria-Cristina Betancourt (Cub), 1983
Ilona Briesenick – see Slupianek
Valentina Cioltan (Rum), 1975
Rosa Colorado (Spa), 1980
Rosa Fernández (Cub), 1983
Yekaterina Gordienko (SU), 1978
Linda Haglund (Swe), 1981
Ágnes Herczeg (Hun), 1983
Karoline Käfer (Aut), 1981
Yelena Kovalyova (SU), 1979
Nadya Kudryavtseva (SU), 1979
Evelyn Lendl (Aut), 1981
Natalia Maraşescu/Betini (Rum), 1979
Alice Matejková (CS), 1986
Gael Mulhall/Martin (Aus), 1981
Alexis Paul-MacDonald (Can), 1981
Totka Petrova (Bul), 1979
Danuta Rosani (Pol), 1976
Ileana Silai (Rum), 1979
Zděnka Šilhavá (CS), 1985
Ilona Slupianek/Briesenik (GDR), 1977
Elena Stoyanova (Bul), 1978 & 1982
Daniela Teneva (Bul), 1979
Nadyezhda Tkachenko (SU), 1978
Vera Tsapkalenko (SU), 1977
Anna Verouli (Gre), 1984
Mayra Vila (Cub), 1985
Sanda Vlad (Rum), 1979
Joan Wenzel (Can), 1975
Anna Włodarczyk (Pol), 1982

**Suspended for refusing drug test**
MEN
Colin Sutherland (UK), 1978
Dave Voorhees (USA), 1978
August Wolf (USA), 1985

WOMEN
Tatyana Kazankina (SU), 1984
Maria Lambrou (Gre/Cyp), 1982

# CORRECTIONS TO INTERNATIONAL ATHLETICS ANNUAL 1986

In addition to those shown on pages 588 and 589 of the 1986 Annual. Note that lists amendments will also affect the indexes.

## 1985 World Lists – Men

*Page*
279 **100m:** add 10.2A M. Elizondo MEX
284 **200m:** add 20.6A Jesus Aguilasocho MEX 60
288 **400m:** add 45.9A Jesus Aguilasocho MEX 60
290 **800m:** Antonio Paez 1:46.88 (4) Bern 16 Aug (not 1:47.26)
302 **5000m:** Toshihiko Seko 13:35.4 (1) Tokyo 22 Jun (from 13:36.28)
304 **10000m:** Shuichi Yoneshige 28:26.8 (1) Ageo 20 Oct (from 28:39.04)
    add: Takeyuki Nakayama JAP 60 28:26.9 (1) Uji 16 Nov
305 Jose Zapata VEN 28:47.5. add Takao Nakamura JAP 58 28:31.91 (2) Kobe 29 Apr, Kazuyoshi
    Kudo JAP 61 28:37.7 (1) Yokohama 4 Nov, Shozo Shimojo JAP 57 28:42.2 12 May, Satoshi Kato
    JAP 61 28:47.5 4 Nov
310 **Mar:** add Yoshiharu Nakai JAP 60 2:13:24 (1) Hofu 22 Dec
311 add Yasuro Hiraoka JAP 61 2:13:53 22 Dec, Takaski Kaneda JAP 60 2:13:59 22 Dec, Masayuki
    Nishi JAP 2:14:31 22 Dec
314 **110mh:** add Hiroshi Kakimori JAP 68 14.13 –0.1 21 Oct
316 add Masahiro Sugii JAP 63 14.05 3.2 24 Oct
318 **400mh:** add Hiroshi Kakimori JAP 68 50.03 (1) Ise 31 Aug
319 add Yao Yongzhi CHN 50.62 (1) Nanjing 23 Oct
322 **HJ:** add Satoru Nonaka JAP 63 2.27 (1) Tottori 24 Oct
323 Takao Sakamoto 2.24 (2) 2 Jun Tokyo (from 2.23); delete 2.23 Inaoka; add Liu Yunping CHN
    2.24 Guangzhou 4 Mar, Cai Shu CHN 62 2.21 4 Mar, Motochika Inoue JAP 66 2.21i 10 Mar,
    Takashi Katamine JAP 2.21 2 Jun, Eiji Kito JAP 60 2.21 24 Oct
327 **PV:** Liang Xuereng CHN 5.50 (1) Beijing 27 Jul (from 5.48), Ji Zebao 5.40 Shanghai 8 Jun (from
    5.35), Tomomi Takahashi 5.35 11 Apr (from 5.30); add Huang Enfu CHN 5.40 Nanjing 10 Apr
328 add Toshiyuki JAP 64 5.30 2 Jun, Yang Weimin CHN 5.30 8 Jun
331 **LJ:** add Li Guoxiong CHN 64 7.89 Nanjing 23 Oct, Noboru Sasano JAP 59 7.87 20 Jul, Nobuyuki
    Ito JAP 64 7.87 18 Aug, Wang Wenhao CHN 7.86 20 Apr, Hiroyuki Shibata JAP 63 7.81 23 Oct,
    Alberto Solanas SPA 55 7.78i 15 Feb
332 add Hiroyuki Shibata JAP 63 7.97 2.5 1 Hiroshima 3 May
335 **TJ:** add Yasushi Ueta JAP 55 16.60 (1) Hiroshima 3 May
336 add Chen Yanping CHN 66 16.40 14 Oct, Mai Guoqiang CHN 62 16.22 6 Jun, 16.17 Masanobu
    Tsudo JAP 56 16.17 21 Jul.
337 Masami Nakanishi 16.18 4.2 (from p. 336); add Yasushi Ueta JAP 55 16.63 2.4 1 Tokyo 2 Jun
346 **HT:** Vladimir Gudilin 72.38
349 **JT:** add Pei Xueliang CHN 64 82.22 Taiyuan 2 May, Pubu Ciren CHN 56 80.82 17 Apr, Ji
    Zhanzheng CHN 63 80.52 2 May
350 add Ken Asakura JAP 61 79.10 24 Oct, Masaki Kawaga JAP 64 78.76 3 Nov, Masato Inada JAP
    63 78.36 4 Oct, Masahiko Kakita JAP 55 78.26 18 Aug, Zhu Hua CHN 64 78.22 13 Apr, Zhao Ming
    CHN 63 78.16 23 Mar
352 **Dec:** Ahmed Mahour Bacha 7934M
361 **20kmW:** Jianli Liu CHN 66 1:21:39, Yang Zheng CHN 63 1:22:23
362 Zhimin Hang CHN 64 1:25:06, Lizheng Wang CHN 64 1:26:00, Jianping Zhao CHN 65 1:26:17

## Junior All-time Lists

368 **2000St:** Arsenios Tsiminos 5:25.01
371 **400mh:** add Hiroshi Kakimori JAP 68 50.03 (1) Ise 31 Aug 85


## 1985 Junior Lists – Men

383 **110mh:** add Hiroshi Kakimori JAP 68 14.13 –0.1 (1) Tottori 21 Oct
384 **400mh:** add Hiroshi Kakimori JAP 68 50.03 (1) Ise 31 Aug
386 **TJ:** add Chen Yanping CHN 66 16.40 Zhengzhou 14 Oct
387 **JT:** add Chen Zeshen CHN 66 76.92 Zhengzhou 14 Oct
388 **Dec:** Pedro Silva 7422 (10.9 7.25 13.85 2.05 50.9 14.5 38.24 4.50 54.26 5:18.1)


## 1985 World Lists – Women

429 **400m:** Madele Naude A51.65 1 Johannesburg 3 Apr (from 51.78)
444 **5000m:** add Li Xiuxia CHN 67 16:07.25 Shanghai 5 Jun (not 16:03.36)
446 **10000m:** add Luo Yuxiu CHN 33:52.84 8 Sep (not 33:53.84)
447 add Yoshiko Hidaka JAP 65 33:57.7 (2) Tokyo 10 Oct, Kumi Araki JAP 65 33:58.2 (3) Tokyo 10 Oct
452 **100mh:** add Feng Yinghua CHN 66 13.51 24 Oct, Naomi Jojima JAP 68 13.69 0.2 14 Sep, Cheng Hongwei CHN 66 13.76 11 Jun
455 **400mh:** add Chen Juying CHN 63 56.86 Nanjing 23 Oct
457 add Chen Dongmei CHN 60 59.06 7 Jun; hand timing: 55.5 Charmaine Fick RSA 59 A55.5 (1) Pretoria 23 Mar
460 **HJ:** Ni Xiuling 1.90 Beijing 18 May, 1.89 Hisayo Fukumitsu 1.89 (1) Saga 25 May (from 1.87), add Zheng Dazhen CHN 59 1.86 5 Jun
461 add Cao Zhongping CHN 66 1.85 20 Jul
464 **LJ:** add Minako Isogai JAP 67 6.40 1.2 2 Jun
467 **SP:** 18.10 Yang Yanqin 18.10 Shijiazhuang 29 Mar (from 17.99), Li Meisu 18.07 Taiyuan 1 May (from 17.99), Huang Zhiyong 18.01 Shanghai 9 Jun (from 17.51)
468 Peng Qinyun 17.69 Shanghai 9 Jun (from 16.93), add Kuang Cuiyun CHN 63 16.98 Beijing 25 Oct
471 **DT:** Yu Hourun CHN 63 57.14; add Xing Ailan CHN 65 57.46 Beijing 27 Jul, Hou Xuemei CHN 62 56.70 10 May, Wang Dan CHN 55 56.66 10 May
473 **JT:** Wang Jin 64.18 Beijing 17 Aug (from 60.22), Zhu Hongyang CHN 63.08 9 Jun, Li Baolian 60.50 Beijing 10 May (from 58.12), Gao Zhiying 59.36 Shanghai 9 Jun (from 58.58), Yu Xueqing CHN 63 59.02 Xuzhou 13 Apr; add Han Jinli CHN 66 61.24 Nanjing 12 Jun
474 add Xu Demei CHN 67 58.82 Xuzhou 17 Apr, Zhou Yuanxiang CHN 64 58.70 Qingdao 14 Jun, Tang Guoli CHN 61 57.76 Shanghai 9 Jun, Zheng Wei CHN 67 57.54 Zhengzhou 15 Oct, Xin Xiaoli CHN 67 57.44 Zhengzhou 15 Oct, Song Ruiling CHN 66 57.26 Xuzhou 21 Apr, An Xuehong CHN 62 57.14 Beijing 21 Sep
484 **4 x 400m:** add China 3:37.60 Nanjing 25 Oct (Chen, Sun, Li, Lu)


## Junior All-time Lists

494 **100mh:** Gloria Kovarik 13.26
498 **JT:** Regine Kempter 63.06. Hep Thiele 6309 (not 6308)

## Junior Lists – Women

502 **400m:** add Kasumi Yamaji JAP 68 53.74 (1) Tottori 23 Oct
503 **800m:** add Ayako Arai JAP 67 2:04.82 (1) Tottori 23 Oct
504 **3000m:** add Li Xiuxia CHN 67 9:16.43 Nanjing 12 Jun
    **100mh:** add Naomi Jajima JAP 68 13.69 0.2 Seoul 14 Sep
505 **LJ:** add Minako Isogai JAP 67 6.40 1.1 (1) Tokyo 2 Jun
506 **DT:** add Min Chuenfeng CHN 69 54.70 Shanghai 8 Jun
507 **JT:** add Xu Demei CHN 67 58.82 Xuzhou 17 Apr, Zheng Wei CHN 57.54 Zhengzhou 15 Oct, Aiko
    Miyajima JAP 67 55.94 Tokyo 31 May

# CORRECTIONS TO INTERNATIONAL ATHLETICS ANNUAL 1985

*PAGE*
83 Delete reference to Italy in seventh line from bottom.
223 delete 10.43 Fernando Arroyo.

# NATIONAL CHAMPIONS 1986
# AND BIOGRAPHIES OF LEADING ATHLETES

## COMPILED BY PETER MATTHEWS

This section incorporates biographies of 632 (396 men and 236 women) of the world's top athletes, listed by nation, with national champions at standard events for the leading countries prominent in athletics.

Once again the biographies have changed materially from the previous year's Annual, not only that all entries have been updated, but also that many newcomers have been introduced to replace those who have retired or faded a little from the spotlight.

When this section was introduced in the 1985 Annual, biographies were given for 569 athletes, in 1986 there were 632, including 163 newcomers. This year there are 632, including 159 newcomers (including a few reinstated from the 1985 Annual), again a measure of the rate of change at the top in track and field athletics.

Some athletes who did not compete in 1986 have been retained in anticipation of their return in 1987, after injury, or pregnancy or simply a rest from competition. No doubt too, some of those dropped from this compilation will also again make their presence felt; the keen reader can look up their credentials in the 1985 or 1986 Annuals, and, of course, basic details may be in the athletes' index at the end of this book.

The biographical information includes:
a) Name; date and place of birth; height (in metres); weight (in kilograms).
b) Previous name(s) for married women; club or university; occupation.
c) Major championships record – all placings in such events as the Olympic Games, World Championships, European Championships, Commonwealth Games, World Cup and European Cup Final; leading placings in the European or World Junior Championships, and other Continental Championships; and first three in European Indoors or World Student Games.

Abbreviations used for these events are:
AfCh    African Championships
AfG     African Games

AsCh    Asian Championships
AsG     Asian Games
CAmG    Central American and Caribbean Games
CG      Commonwealth Games
ECh     European Championships
ECp     European Cup
EI      European Indoor Championships
EJ      European Junior Championships
LT      Lugano Trophy/World Race Walking Cup
OG      Olympic Games
PAm     Pan American Games
SACh    South American Championships
WCh     World Championships
WCp     World Cup
WIG     World Indoor Games
WJ      World Junior Championships
WSG     World Student Games

d) National titles won or successes in other major events.
e) Records set - world, continental and national; indoor world bests.
f) Progression of best marks over the years at major event(s).
g) Personal best performances at other events.
h) Other comments.

Note that for comparison purposes decathlons and heptathlons have been rescored using the 1984 IAAF Tables, except those marked *, for which event breakdowns were unavailable. Women's pentathlons (p) have not been rescored.

Details are to the end of 1986, with the addition of some performances made in January 1987.

I am most grateful to various ATFS members who have helped check these details. Additional information or corrections would be welcomed for next year's Annual.

**Peter Matthews,**
**10 Madgeways Close, Great Amwell,**
**Ware, Herts SG12 9RU, England**

# ARGENTINA

**Governing body**: Confederacion Argentina de Atletismo, Bvd.Irigoyen 396, (3260) Concepcion del Uruguay, Entre Rios.

**National Championships** first held in 1920 (men), 1939 (women)
**1986 Champions: MEN**
100m/200m: Gerardo Meinardi 11.06/21.42, 400m: José Beduino 47.88, 800m: Luis Migueles 1:51.45, 1500m/3000mSt: Marcelo Cascabelo 3:49.45/8:43.7, 5000m/10000m: Juan Pablo Juarez 14:12.7/29:52.1, Mar: Juan Rios 2:20:49, 110mh: Carlos Varas 14.7, 400mh: Dardo Angerami 52.64, HJ: Fernando Pastoriza 2.12, PV: Oscar Veit 4.50, LJ: Osvaldo Frigerio 7.54, TJ: Angel Gagliano 14.84, SP/DT: Gerardo Carucci 16.20/46.04, HT: Andrés Charadia 58.40, JT: Walter Franzantti 66.28 (old).
**WOMEN**
100m: Deborah Bell 12.2, 200m: Olga Conte 24.84, 400m/800m: Carmen Mosegui (Uru) 55.5/ 2:14.3, 1500m: Liliana Gongora 4:38.98, 3000m: Adriana Calvo 10:38.4, 10000m: Elizabeth Cobanea 38:16.3, 100mh: Graciela Pguliese 15.20, 400mh: Ana Laura Paz 63.85, HJ: Nancy Piva 1.66, LJ: Ana Vizioli 5.74, SP: Berenice da Silva (Uru) 14.43, DT: Liliana Olguin 41.60, JT: Ana Campillay 42.66.

# AUSTRALIA

**Governing body**: Amateur Athletic Union of Australia, P.O.Box 254, Moonee Ponds, Victoria 3039. Founded 1897.
**National Championships** first held in 1893 (men), 1930 (women)
**1986 Champions: MEN**
100m: Gerrard Keating 10.51, 200m: Robert Stone 20.97, 400m: Darren Clark 45.69, 800m: Alan Ozolins 1:48.45, 1500m: Mike Hillardt 3:38.50, 5000m: Malcolm Norwood 14:11.81, 10000m: Lars-Erik Nilssen (Swe) 28:37.73, Mar: Eloi Schleder (Bra) 2:12:54, 3000mSt: Gary Zeuner 8:41.53, 110mh: Don Wright 13.72, 400mh: Ken Gordon 50.74, HJ: Lee Balkin (USA) 2.25, PV: Larry Jessee (USA) 5.25, LJ: Gary Honey 8.08, TJ: Peter Beames 16.47, SP: Stuart Gyngell 18.52, DT: Paul Nandapi 61.28, HT: Joe Quigley 72.86, JT: Murray Keen 76.42, Dec: Simon Shirley 7438, 5kmW(t)/30kmW: David Smith 19:23.34/2:05:59, 50kmW: Willi Sawall 3:59:48.

**WOMEN**
100m/200m: Diane Holden 11.74/23.71, 400m/ 400mh: Debbie Flintoff 52.03/54.28 800m: Wendy Old 2:00.81, 1500m: Penny Just 4:18.02, 3000m: Jacquie Perkins 9:15.76, 10000m: Tania Turney 34:16.94, Mar: Ngaire Drake (NZ) 2:38:52, 100mh: Glynis Nunn 13.48, HJ: Christine Stanton 1.94, LJ: Robyn Lorraway 6.55, TJ: Ann Turnbull 12.25, SP/DT: Gael Martin 18.69/ 57.14, JT: Sue Howland 61.74, Hep: Jane Flemming 5882, 5kmW(t)/10kmW/20kmW: Kerry Saxby 22:29.25/44:53/1:38:27.

# Men

**Simon BAKER** b.6 Feb 1958 Oakleigh, Vic. 1.86m 70kg. Club: Oakleigh. Teacher.
At 30kmW: CG: '86- 1. At 20kmW: OG: '84- 14; WCh: '83- 29; LT: '83- 14, '85- 12.
Track pbs: 3kmW: 11:51.45 '85, 5kmW: 19:46.01 '86, 10kmW: 41:06.0 '85, 1HrW: 14609m '86. Road pbs: 20kmW: 1:23:13 '86, 30kmW: 2:07:47 '86.

**Darren CLARK** b.6 Sep 1965 Sydney 1.80m 78kg. Club: Randwick Botany (NSW).
At 400m: OG: '84- 4; WCh: '83- sf; CG: '86- 2 (2 4x400mR); WCp: '85- 4 (3 at 200m). Australian champion 1986, AAA champion 1983-6.
Three Australian 400m records 1984-6. Two Commonwealth 300m bests 1985-6.
Progression at 400m: 1982- 46.62, 1983- 45.05, 1984- 44.75, 1985- 44.80, 1986- 44.72. pbs: 100m: 10.47/10.3 '83, 200m: 20.49 '83, 300m: 31.88 '86.
Set world age-17 best to win AAA title in 1983. Ran a 43.86 relay leg in 1984 Olympics.

**Robert de CASTELLA** b.27 Feb 1957 Melbourne 1.80m 65kg. Club: Mazda. Biophysicist with the Australian Institute of Sport, Canberra. Married to Gayelene Clews, pb 10000m: 33:53.1 '85 and cross-country international.
At Mar: OG: '80- 10, '84- 5; WCh: '83- 1; CG: '82- 1, '86- 1. Australian champion 1979. World CC: 6th 1981 and 1983. Pacific Conference 10000m champion 1977.
Commonwealth records at 20km (58:37.2) and 1 hour (20516m) in 1982, and world marathon best 1981. Further Australian record 1986.
Progression at Mar: 1979- 2:13:23, 1980- 2:10:44, 1981- 2:08:18, 1982- 2:09:18, 1983- 2:08:37, 1984- 2:09:09, 1985- 2:08:48, 1986- 2:07:50. pbs: 1500m: 3:48.0 '86, 3000m: 8:03.81 '85, 5000m: 13:34.28 '81, 10000m: 28:02.73 '83. 'Deke', as 1984 Olympic favourite, was a little disappointed with his fifth place, but came back strongly in 1986 to win at Boston and take his

Darren Clark. *ASP*

second Commonwealth title, before third at New York. Has run 15 marathons, six sub 2:10 and all sub 2:15, winning eight of them. Very strong runner, who has stayed clear of injuries. His younger brother Nick ran a 2:15:04 marathon in 1983.

**Michael HILLARDT** b.22 Jan 1961 Brisbane 1.80m 68kg. Club: St.Stephens Harriers (Vic). Was at University of Queensland. Storeman.
At 1500m: OG: '84- sf; CG: '82- 5, '86- 8; WCp: '85- 5; WIG: '85- 1. At 800m: WCh: '83- sf, WCp: '81- 4. Australian champion at 800m 1981 and 1983, 1500m 1980, 1982-6. Austrian champion at 800m 1979-80, 1500m 1980.
Australian records at 1000m (3), 1500m (3), 1 mile (5) 1982-5.
Progression at 1500m/1M: 1978- 3:46.0, 1979- 4:01.6M, 1980- 3:39.67, 1981- 3:41.74/3:56.6, 1982- 3:38.04/3:53.33, 1983- 3:41.51/3:57.09, 1984- 3:34.20/3:52.34, 1985- 3:33.39/3:51.82. 1986- 3:34.51/3:56.6i. pbs: 400m: 47.8 '80, 800m: 1:45.74 '83, 1000m: 2:17.49 '84, 2000m: 5:06.0 '85, 3000m: 7:52.17 '84, 5000m: 13:38.31 '86. Has disappointed in major championships.

**Gary HONEY** b.26 Jul 1959 Thomastown, Melbourne 1.83m 70kg. Club: Ivanhoe (Vic). Physical education teacher.
At LJ: OG: '80- dnq, '84- 2; WCh: '83- 6; CG: '82- 1, '86- 1 (4 TJ); WCp: '79- 5, '81- 2, '85- 4. Australian champion 1979, 1981-6.
Five Australian long jump records 1981-4, including two Commonwealth records 1984.
Progression at LJ: 1977- 7.32, 1978- 7.64, 1979-

7.97/8.09w, 1980- 7.98/8.10w, 1981- 8.11/8.13w, 1982- 8.13, 1983- 8.12, 1984- 8.27/8.39w, 1985- 8.05/8.08w, 1986- 8.08/8.12w. pbs 100m: 10.4 '85, 400m: 46.9, TJ: 16.16 '86.

**Don WRIGHT** b.26 Apr 1959 Warwick, Queensland 1.83m 80kg. Club: Woden Valley (ACT). Sports administrator.
At 110mh: OG: '84- sf; WCh: '83- sf; CG: '78- 8, '82- 3, '86- 3; WCp: '85- 4. Australian champion 1983-6.
Progression at 110mh: 1977- 14.2/14.0, 1978- 13.76, 1979- 14.66, 1980- 14.27/14.15w/13.9, 1981- 14.04, 1982- 13.58, 1983- 13.75/13.79w/ 13.5, 1984- 13.72/13.7, 1985- 13.72/13.6, 1986- 13.65/13.64w. pb 400mh: 51.88 '82.

# Women

**Debbie FLINTOFF** b.20 Apr 1960 Melbourne 1.71m 56kg. Club: Glenhuntly. Teller.
At 400mh (R- 4x100m relay): OG: '84- 6; WCh: '83- sf; CG: '82- 1 (2R), '86- 1 (3R, 1 at 400m); WCp: '85- 3. Australian champion 400m 1985-6, 400mh 1982-6. 3rd GP 1985.
Nine Australian, including seven Commonwealth, 400mh records 1982-6; two Australian 400m records 1985-6.
Progression at 400mh: 1980- 59.34, 1981- 57.94, 1982- 55.89, 1983- 56.22, 1984- 56.02, 1985- 54.80, 1986- 53.76. pbs: 100m: 11.5 '86, 200m: 23.51 '86, 400m: 50.78 '86, 800m: 2:06.0 (mixed) '86, 100mh: 14.2w '79, HJ: 1.69 '79.
Married her coach Phil King in 1986.

Debbie Flintoff. *ASP*

**Sue HOWLAND** b.4 Sep 1960 Mackay, Queensland 1.80m 78kg. Club: Belconnen Striders West (ACT). Security guard.
At JT: CG: '82- 1, '86- 3; WCp: '85- 4. Australian champion 1986.
Australian javelin record 1986.
Progression at JT: 1978- 46.88, 1979- 50.68, 1980- 62.30, 1981- 61.42, 1982- 65.74, 1985- 63.58, 1986- 69.80. pbs: HJ: 1.68 '76, SP: 14.73 '80.

**Gael MARTIN** b.27 Aug 1956 Melbourne 1.72m 90kg. née Mulhall, married to weightlifter Nigel Martin. Club: South Canberra Tuggers (ACT). Clerk.
At SP/DT: OG: '80- 12/dnq, '84- 3/8; WCh: '83- 11/-; CG: '74- 10/9, '78- 1/2, '82- 2/2, '86- 1/1; WCp:'77- 6 DT, '79- 5 DT, '85- 4 SP. Australian champion SP: 1976-81, 1983-5; DT: 1977-81, 1983-4, 1986.
Thirteen Commonwealth shot records 1978-84, Australian records: 15 shot 1977-84, 5 discus 1977-9.
Progression at SP: 1972- 13.68, 1973- 13.93, 1974- 13.61, 1975- 12.90, 1976- 13.92, 1977- 16.48, 1978- 18.16, 1979- 18.17, 1980- 18.55, 1981- 18.37, 1982- 18.85, 1983- 18.98, 1984- 19.74, 1985- 18.96, 1986- 19.59. pb DT: 63.08 '79.
World powerlifting record holder for 90kg and 90+kg classes. Suspended for drugs abuse 1981.

**Lisa MARTIN** b.12 May 1960 Gawler, SA 1.67m 45kg. née O'Dea, married to Kenny Martin (USA, 3kmSt: AAA champion 1981, pb 8:20.97 '80; marathon: US champion 1984-5, pb 2:11:24 '84). Club: Nike TC, USA; was at University of Oregon.
At Mar: OG: '84- 7, CG: '86- 1. TAC champion 1985, 2nd New York 1985-6. At 10km: WCp: '85- dnf.
Commonwealth marathon best 1986, four Australian records at marathon and 10000m 1983-6.
Progression at Mar: 1983- 2:32:22, 1984- 2:27:40, 1985- 2:29:48, 1986- 2:26:07. pbs: 1500m: 4:21.2 '83, 3000m: 9:09.67 '85, 5000m: 15:34.7 '85, 10000m: 32:17.86 '85, 400mh: 60.5 '79.
Started as a hurdler, switching to distance running in 1981. Has won five out of ten marathons to second at Osaka 1987. Ran Commonwealth half marathon best of 1:09:45 to win Great North Run 1986.

**Glynis NUNN** b.4 Dec 1960 Toowoomba 1.68m 58kg. née Saunders, married to Christopher Nunn (7130 decathlon '82). Club: Combined

Lisa Martin. *Mark Shearman*

Teachers' College (SA). Physical education teacher.
At 100mh/Hep: OG: '84- 5/1 (7 at LJ); WCh: '83- sf/7; CG: '78- dnf Pen, '82- 6/1 (7 at LJ), '86- 3/-; WCp: '85- 5/-. Australian champion: 100mh: 1982-6, Pen/Hep: 1978, 1980-2, 1984. Won WAAA 100mh 1985.
Commonwealth heptathlon record 1984, Australian record holder since 1980.
Progression at Pen (p)/Hep: 1975- 3538p, 1976- 3897p, 1977- 4180p, 1978- 4006p, 1979- 3963p, 1980- 4251p, 1981- 5721w, 1982- 6254, 1983- 6131, 1984- 6387. pbs: 100m: 11.9 '84, 200m: 24.02 '83, 800m: 2:10.57 '84, 100mh: 13.02 '84, 400mh: 57.23 '83, HJ: 1.83 '84, LJ: 6.66 '84, TJ: 12.21 '86, SP: 13.93 '82, JT: 36.06 '84.
Uniquely a finalist at three events in both Commonwealth and Olympic Games.

**Kerry SAXBY** b.2 Jun 1961 1.63m 57kg. Student at Australian Institute of Sport, Canberra.
At 10kmW: WCp: '85- 10. Australian champion 5kmW, 10kmW and 20kmW 1986.
World road walking bests: 15km: 1:09:33 '85, 20km: 1:33:30 '85; world track best: 1500mW: 6:03.3 '85. Commonwealth bests: track: 5kmW: 21:53.36 '86, 10kmW: 45:08.13 '86. Other pbs: track: 3km: 12:49.9 '85, road: 10kmW: 44:53 '86. Won Goodwill Games 10km walk 1986.

**Christine STANTON** b.12 Dec 1959 Cottesloe, WA 1.83m 66kg. née Annison. Club: Karrinyup (WA). Media manager.
At HJ: OG: '80- 6=, '84- 11=; WCh: '83- dnq; CG: '82- 2, '86- 1; WCp: '77- 6, '81- 4, '85- 5. Australian champion HJ 1976-7, 1980-1, 1983 and 1985; LJ 1981.
Four Australian high jump records 1984-5 and Commonwealth heptathlon record 1981.
Progression at HJ: 1974- 1.69, 1975- 1.79, 1976-

1.83, 1977- 1.88, 1978- 1.88, 1980- 1.91, 1981-
1.92, 1982- 1.88, 1983- 1.92, 1984- 1.95, 1985-
1.96, 1986- 1.94. pbs: 200m: 24.6 '85, 100mh:
13.82 '85, LJ: 6.40/6.45w '81, SP: 13.25 '85,
Hep: 5938 '85.

# AUSTRIA

**Governing body**: Osterreichischer Leichtathletik
Verband, Vienna 1040, Prinz Eugenstrasse 12.
Founded 1900.
**National Championships** first held in 1911
(men), 1918 (women)
**1986 Champions: MEN**
100m/200m: Andreas Berger 10.42/21.04, 400m:
Klaus Ehrle 47.17, 800m: Peter Svaricek 1:49.49,
1500m: Karl Blaha 3:55.20, 5000m: Gerhard
Hartmann 14:13.52, 10000m: Robert Nemeth
29:40.58, Mar: Hansjörg Randl 2:22:44,
3000mSt: Wolfgang Konrad 8:50.59, 110mh:
Thomas Weimann 14.21w, 400mh: Thomas
Futterknecht 50.41, HJ: Gottfried Wittgruber 2.14,
PV: Hermann Fehringer 5.66, LJ: Teddy Stein-
mayr 7.78, TJ: Alfred Stummer 16.35, SP/DT:
Erwin Weitzl 18.78/60.66, HT: Johann Lindner
72.92, JT: Otto Petrovic 68.18, Dec: Georg
Werthner 7375, 20kmW: Martin Toporek 1:28:12,
50kmW: Wilfried Siegele 4:38:13.
**WOMEN**
100m/200m/400m/400mh: Gerda Haas 11.68/
23.62w/52.67/58.92, 800m: Karoline Käfer
2:05.82, 1500m/3000m: Anni Müller 4:29.86/
9:32.06, 10000m: Carina Weber-Leutner
35:18.20, Mar: Ida Hellwagner 2:59:37, 100mh:
Sabine Seitl 13.68, HJ/Hep: Sigrid Kirchmann
1.86/5449, LJ: Regina Helfenbein 6.27, SP:
Veronika Längle 14.52, DT: Ursula Weber 53.68,
JT: Lisbeth Kucher 53.14.

**Dietmar MILLONIG** b.1 Jun 1955 Villach 1.69m
56kg. Club: Villach. Works for Adidas.
At 5000m: OG: '80- 6; WCh: '83- 8; ECh: '78- ht (ht
1500m), '82- 5; EJ: '73- 5. At 3000m: EI: '86- 1.
Austrian champion: 1500m 1973, 1976, 1978-9;
5000m 1975-7, 1980-4; 10km 1979-82, 1984-5.
Austrian records (1976-82): 5 at 5000m, 4
3000m, 3 10000m, 2 1M, 1 each at 1500m,
2000m, 15km, 20km, 1 Hr.
Progression at 5000m: 1972- 14:45.8, 1973-
14:25.0, 1974- 14:15.0, 1975- 14:06.6, 1976-
14:34.46, 1977- 13:47.59, 1978- 13:40.4, 1979-
13:31.4, 1980- 13:23.25, 1981- 13:22.68, 1982-
13:15.31, 1983- 13:27.01, 1984- 13:27.13, 1985-
13:17.91, 1986- 13:30.86. pbs: 800m: 1:49.72
'81, 1000m: 2:21.3 '78, 1500m: 3:38.38 '82, 1M:
3:57.7 '79, 3000m: 7:43.66 '80, 10000m:
27:42.98 '82, 15000m: 44:54.0 '82, 1 hour:
19898m '82, 20km: 1:00:19.5 '82, 3kmSt: 9:05.6
'76.

# BAHAMAS

**Governing body**: Bahamas Amateur Athletic
Association, P.O.Box S.S.5517, Nassau.

**Brad COOPER** b.30 Jun 1957 1.88m 132kg. Was
at Florida State University, USA.
At DT: OG: '84- dnq; WCh: '83- 12; CG: '78- 2 (14
SP), '82- 1; PAm: '79- 2, '83- 2; CAmG: '78- 3, '82-
2, '86- 3. CAC champion 1983, won NCAA 1979,
AAA 1982.
Progression at DT: 1977- 57.48, 1978- 57.60,
1979- 64.78, 1980- 62.44, 1981- 66.14, 1982-
66.72, 1983- 63.24, 1984- 64.08, 1985- 60.10,
1986- 67.10. pb SP: 18.35 '79.

# BAHRAIN

**Governing body**: Bahrain Amateur Athletic
Association, PO Box 29269, Manama. Founded
1974.

**Ahmed HAMADA** b.18 Aug 1961 Manama
1.85m 73kg. Soldier.
At 400mh: OG: '84- h; WCh: '83- sf; WCp: '85- 6;
AsG: '82- 3, '86- 1; AsCh: '83- 1 (3 110mh), '85-1.
AAA champion 1985.
Two Asian 400mh records 1983-6.
Progression at 400mh: 1979- 54.0, 1980- 51.8,
1981- 51.83, 1982- 50.02, 1983- 49.43, 1984-
50.62, 1985- 49.82, 1986- 49.31. pbs (all Bahrain
records): 400m: 46.9 '82, 800m: 1:49.6 '84,
110mh: 14.17 '83.

# BELGIUM

**Governing bodies**: Ligue Royale Belge d'Ath-
léetisme, Rue St.Laurent 14-26 (Bte 6), 1000
Bruxelles (KBAB). Vlaamse Atletiek Liga (VAL);
Ligue Belge Francophone d'Athlétisme (LBFA).
Original governing body founded 1889.
**National Championships** first held in 1889
(men), 1921 (women)
**1986 Champions: MEN**
100m/LJ: Ronald Desruelles 10.43/7.94, 200m:
Jeroen Fischer 21.13, 400m: Peter Pieters 46.92,
800m: Marc Corstjens 1:49.63, 1500m: Vincent
Rousseau 3:53.77, 5000m: Willy Goddaert
13:55.28, 10000m: Alex Hagelsteens 29:04.00,
Mar: Dick Vanderherten 2:14:22, 3000mSt:
William van Dijck 8:28.93, 110mh: Roland Mar-
loye 14.12, 400mh: Rik Tommelein 49.55, HJ:
Patrick Steemans 2.14, PV: Kris De Ridder 5.20,
TJ: Didier Falise 16.86, SP: Noel Legros 15.83,
DT: Robert Van Schoor 48.92, HT: Marnix Ver-
hegghe 65.68, JT: Frank Stockmans 68.36.

## WOMEN

100m/200m: Tonia Oliviers 12.06/24.35, 400m: Regine Berg 52.50, 800m: Isabelle De Bruycker 2:07.53, 1500m: Corine Debaets 4:15.87, 3000m: Ria Van Landeghem 9:20.73, Mar: Agnes Pardaens 2:37:05, 100mh: Sylvia Dethier 13.71, 400mh: Nathalie Nisen 58.62, HJ: Christine Soetewey 1.81, LJ: Hilda Vervaet 6.38, SP: Marie-Paule Geldhof 14.00, DT:Ingrid Engelen 49.74, JT: Martine Florent 47.90.

**Eddy ANNYS** b.15 Dec 1958 Wilrijk 1.87m 70kg. Club: AV Toekomst.
At HJ: OG: '84- dnq; WCh: '83- 14; EI: '86- 3=; WSG: '83- 2.
Seven Belgian high jump records 1981-5. Belgian champion 1983, 1985.
Progression at HJ: 1972- 1.45, 1973- 1.70, 1976- 1.90, 1977- 2.15, 1978- 2.20, 1979- 2.21, 1980- 2.18, 1981- 2.25, 1982- 2.24i, 1983- 2.34, 1984- 2.32, 1985- 2.36, 1986- 2.31. pb LJ: 6.78 '82.

**Ronald DESRUELLES** b.14 Feb 1955 1.86m 80kg. Club: AV Toekomst.
At LJ: OG: '76- dnq; ECh: '78 & '82- dnq; EI: '78- 2. Won AAA 1979. At 100m: OG: '84- qf; ECh: '78- h, '86- sf. At 60m: EI: '84- 3, '85- 3, '86- 1. WIG: '85- 3. Belgian champion at LJ 1975-9, 1981-4, 1986; 100m 1978-9, 1982, 1984-6; 200m 1985.
Belgian records: 3 at 100m 1984-5, 1 200m 1984, 5 LJ 1976-80.
Progression at 100m: 1971- 11.4, 1972- 11.0, 1973- 10.7, 1974- 10.6, 1975- 10.5, 1976- 10.4, 1977- 10.2, 1978- 9.9/10.43, 1979- 10.2/10.42, 1980- 10.5, 1981- 10.3, 1982- 10.47, 1983- 10.2, 1984- 10.25/10.0, 1985- 10.34/10./1/10.02?w, 1986- 10.27/10.16w. pbs: 200m: 20.66 '84, 20.5w '85; 400m: 49.0 '84, HJ: 2.02 '82, PV: 4.10 '74, Dec: 7217 '84.
After winning 1980 European Indoor LJ title was disqualified on a positive drugs test. Is now concentrating on sprints rather than long jump. His brother Patrick is Belgian pole vault record holder (5.60m in 1981).

**Vincent ROUSSEAU** b.29 Jul 1962 1.76m 60kg. 'Club: Moha. Soldier.
At 5000m: ECh: '86- 13. 2nd GP 1986. At 10000m: WCp: '85- 5. Belgian champion 5000m 1984, 1500m 1985-6.
Progression at 5000m: 1980- 14:30.5, 1981- 14:08.32, 1982- 13:40.21, 1983- 13:33.2, 1984- 13:24.81, 1985- 13:18.94, 1986- 13:15.01. pbs: 1500m: 3:36.38 '85, 1M: 3:54.69 '85, 3000m: 7:42.15 '86, 10000m: 28:40.63 '85.
An inconsistent runner, who had many wins at cross-country and on the track over the past couple of years, but also bad losses in several important races.

**William VAN DIJCK** b.24 Jan 1961 1.85m 65kg. Club: Looise. Teacher.
At 3km St: OG: '84- sf; WCh: '83- sf; ECh: '86- 5. Belgian champion 1983, 1985-6. Won GP 1986. Eight Belgian 3kmSt records 1983-6.
Progression at 3kmSt: 1981- 8:44.92, 1982- 8:36.40, 1983- 8:21.73, 1984- 8:18.75, 1985- 8:13.77, 1986- 8:10.01. pbs: 800m: 1:51.8 '83, 1500m: 3:41.2 '85, 1M: 3:57.59 '85, 3000m: 7:49.7 '84, 5000m: 13:23.40 '85.
Won the 1986 Grand Prix at 3000m steeplechase, with a series of fine wins, although he disappointed with fifth place at Stuttgart.

---

# BRAZIL

---

**Governing body**: Confederacao Brasileira de Atletismo (CBAT), Avenida Graca Aranha, 81-Conj 808/811, 20030 Rio de Janeiro. Founded 1914. National Championships are held bienially (not in 1986).

**José Luis BARBOSA** b.27 May 1961 Tres Lagoas 1.84m 68kg. Student in the USA.
At 800m: OG: '84- sf; WCh: '83- sf; PAm: '83- 2 (2 4x400mR); SACh: '83- 1. AAA champion 1985.
Progression at 800m: 1979- 1:53.0, 1980- 1:50.0, 1981- 1:48.3, 1982- 1:47.4, 1983- 1:44.3, 1984- 1:44.98, 1985- 1:44.79, 1986- 1:44.10. pbs: 400m: 45.9 '83, 1000m: 2:17.36 '85.
A very consistent 800m runner, he has ten sub-1:45 times.

**Robson CAETANO da SILVA** b.4 Sep 1964 Rio de Janeiro 1.87m 74kg.
At 200m (R- 4x100m relay): OG: '84- sf; WCp: '85- 1 (2R); PAm: '83- 3R; SACh: '85- 1.
South American records: two at 100m, one 200m 1985-6.
Progression at 100m/200m: 1982- 10.34/10.2/21.46, 1983- 10.40/10.3/20.95, 1984- 10.50/10.3/20.71, 1985- 10.22/10.1/20.44, 1986- 10.02/20.28. pb 400m: 46.5 '85.

**Joaquim CRUZ** b.12 Mar 1963 Taguatinga, Brasilia 1.88m 77kg. Club: Team Nike. Student at Oregon University.
At 800m: OG: '84- 1 (sf 1500m); WCh: '83- 3; WCp: '81- 6. Won NCAA 800m 1983-4, 1500m 1984. South American record holder at 800m, 1000m, 1500m and 1 mile. World junior 800m record 1981.
Progression at 800m: 1978- 1:51.4, 1979- 1:49.8, 1980- 1:47.85, 1981- 1:44.3, 1982- 1:46.95, 1983- 1:44.04, 1984- 1:41.77, 1985- 1:42.49. pbs: 400m: 47.17 '80, 1000m: 2:14.09 '84, 1500m: 3:35.70 '85, 1M: 3:53.00 '84.

Has six of the twelve sub 1:43 800m times ever run. Missed 1986 season due to Achilles tendinitis.

**Agberto GUIMARAES** b.18 Aug 1957 Belem 1.75m 64kg. Was at Brigham Young University, USA.
At 800m: OG: '80- 4, '84- sf; WCh: '83- 6; PAm: '79- 3, '83- 1 (2 4x400mR); WCp: '79- 5, '85- 3; SACh: '75- 3, '77- 1; WSG: '77- 4. At 1500m: OG: '84- sf; PAm: '79- 3, '83- 1.
Progression at 800m: 1976- 1:49.4, 1977- 1:46.0, 1978- 1:47.7, 1979- 1:45.94, 1980- 1:46.20, 1981- 1:47.52, 1982- 1:45.13, 1983- 1:45.15, 1984- 1:43.63, 1985- 1:43.78, 1986- 1:45.11. pbs: 400m: 46.34 '80, 1000m: 2:15.81 '83, 1500m: 3:39.9 '84, 1M: 4:00.0 '84.

# BULGARIA

**Governing body**: Bulgarian Athletics Federation, 18 Tolboukhine Bd, Sofia. Founded 1924
**National Championships** first held in 1926 (men), 1938 (women)
**1986 Champions: MEN**
100m: Valentin Atanassov 10.32, 200m: Nikolai Markov 21.14, 400m: Memchil Kharizanov 45.6, 800m: Binko Kolev 1:51.40, 1500m/5000m: Evgeni Ignatov 3:42.99/13:45.52, 10000m: Emil Stoyanov 30:06.2, Mar: Stanimir Pentschev 2:17:00, 3000mSt: Anton Tomov 8:49.87, 110mh: Plamen Krastev 13.70, 400mh: Toma Tomov 50.80, HJ: Georgi Dakov 2.18, PV: Atanas Tarev 5.77, LJ: Atanas Chochev 7.94, TJ: Khristo Markov 17.62, SP: Georgi Todorov 20.48, DT: Kamen Dimitrov 64.92, HT: Emanuil Dyulgerov 77.86, JT: Emil Tzvetanov 74.98, Dec: Tzetzko Mitrakiev 7487, 50kmW: Bontscho Lapkov 4:20:38.
**WOMEN**
100m/200m: Anelia Nuneva 10.9/22.78, 400m: Pepa Pavlova 51.40, 800m/1500m/10000m: Nikolina Shtereva 2:02.64/4:16.29/33:25.7, 3000m: Katya Krasteva 9:29.18, Mar: Rosiza Zoneva 3:07:37, 100m: Yordanka Donkova 12.36, 400mh: Bonka Peneva 57.03, HJ: Stefka Kostadinova 2.01, LJ: Lyudmila Ninova 6.88, SP: Svetla Mitkova 19.04, DT: Tsvetanka Khristova 69.10, JT: Ivanka Vancheva 60.68, Hep: Tanya Tarkalanova 6001, 5kmW/10kmW: Atanaska Dtzivkova 23:18/51:38.0.

**Evgeniy IGNATOV** b.25 Jun 1959 Ruse 1.83m 66kg. Club: Lokomotif, Ruse.
At 5000m: ECh: '82- 4, '86- 4. Balkan champion 1985.
Bulgarian records 1980-6: 4 at 5000m, 3 at 2000m, 1 each at 1500m, 3000m, 10000m.

Progression at 5000m: 1978- 14:18.4, 1979- 13:58.9, 1980- 13:48.4, 1981- 13:30.82, 1982- 13:27.78, 1983- 14:03.9, 1984- 13:26.35, 1985- 13:30.09, 1986- 13:13.15. pbs: 800m: 1:51.6 '80, 1500m: 3:39.53 '82, 2000m: 4:59.02 '85, 3000m: 7:47.54 '84, 10000m: 28:24.73 '84.

**Khristo MARKOV** b.27 Jan 1965 Bozovo/Ruse 1.85m 76kg. Club: ZSKA Sofia. Sports student.
At TJ: WCh: '83- dnq; ECh: '86- 1; EJ: '83-1; EI: '85- 1; WIG: '85- 1. Balkan champion 1985, Bulgarian 1984-5. 2nd GP 1986.
World Junior record 1984 and five European Junior records in 1983-4. Six Bulgarian TJ records 1983-6, the last two also European records. Equalled European indoor LJ best 1985.
Progression at TJ: 1981- 15.72, 1983- 16.88, 1984- 17.42, 1985- 17.77, 1986- 17.80. pb LJ: 8.23i '85, 8.16w/8.04 '86.

**Georgi POMASHKI** b.10 Jan 1960 Plevin 1.90m 80kg. Club: CSKA Septemvryisko zname, Sofia.
At TJ: ECh: '86- 4.
Progression at TJ: 1979- 15.65, 1980- 15.43, 1981- 16.23, 1982- 16.02, 1983- 16.91, 1984- 16.55i/16.54, 1985- 16.94, 1986- 16.99. pb LJ: 7.76i '86.

**Atanas TAREV** b.31 Jan 1958 Bolyarzi, Plovdiv 1.80m 75kg. Club: Trakja, Plovdiv. Physical education student.
At PV: WCh: '83- 3; OG: '80- dnq; ECh: '82- 3, '86- 4; EJ: '77- 3; EI: '85- 3, '86- 1. Balkan champion 1979-80, 1985, Bulgarian 1976-85.
18 Bulgarian pole vault records from 5.07m in 1977.
Progression at PV: 1975- 4.50, 1976- 4.90, 1977- 5.15, 1978- 5.22, 1979- 5.40, 1980- 5.44, 1981- 5.51, 1982- 5.70, 1983- 5.71, 1984- 5.72, 1985- 5.75, 1986- 5.80.

**Toma TOMOV** b.6 May 1958 Jambol 1.79m 68kg. Club: Levski Spartak, Sofia. Physical education student.
At 400mh: WCh: '83- sf; ECh: '82- 8, '86- 4. Balkan and Bulgarian champion 1984-6.
Bulgarian records at 400mh (7) and 400m (1) 1982-6.
Progression at 400mh: 1981- 51.81, 1982- 49.74, 1983- 49.24, 1984- 48.99, 1985- 49.49, 1986- 48.48. pb 400m: 45.86 '84.

# Women

**Yordanka DONKOVA** b.28 Sep 1961 Dolni Bogrov, Sofia 1.75m 67kg. Club: Levski Spartak. Physical education student.
At 100mh: OG: '80- sf; ECh: '82- 2, '86- 1 (2R); EJ:

Khristo Markov. *Janko Garov*

Ataras Tarev. *Janko Garov*

Yordanka Donkova. *ASP*

'79- 8; ECp: '81- 5. At Hep: ECp: '83- 7. At 60mh: EI: '82- 3, '84- 3. Balkan champion 1980, 1984, 1986; Bulgarian 1984, 1986. Won GP 100mh and overall 1986.
Nine Bulgarian 100mh records 1982-6, including four world records 1986.
Progression at 100mh: 1977- 14.84, 1978- 13.91, 1979- 13.57, 1980- 13.24, 1981- 13.39/12.9, 1982- 12.44, 1983- 12.65, 1984- 12.50, 1985- 13.24, 1986- 12.26/12.0w, pbs: 100m: 11.27 '82, 200m: 22.95 '82, HJ: 1.78 '82, LJ: 6.39 '82, Hep: 6187 '83.
Displayed the finest ever sprint hurdling by a woman in 1986, with very sharp speed and technique, running ten sub-12.50 times. By the end of the year of the fastest times ever, she had the three best, 7/8 and 11/20. She had had a knee injury in 1985. She lost three fingers on her right hand in an accident on her fifth birthday.

**Svetlana ISSAEVA** b.18 Mar 1967 Pleven 1.76m 60kg. Club: Spartak, Pleven.
At HJ: ECh: '86- 2; EJ: '83- 4=, '85- 3.
Progression at HJ: 1981- 1.80, 1982- 1.79, 1983- 1.87, 1984- 1.84, 1985- 1.93, 1986- 1.97.

**Silvia KHRISTOVA** b.22 Aug 1965 1.65m 59kg. Now MONEVA.
At LJ: ECh: '86- 6; WSG: '85- 2.
Bulgarian long jump record 1986.
Progression at LJ: 1983- 6.29, 1984- 6.64, 1985- 6.76, 1986- 7.00. pb 100m: 11.85 '85.

**Tsvetanka KHRISTOVA** b.14 Mar 1962 Kazanlak 1.75m 80kg. Club: Rozova dolina, Kazanlak.
At DT: WCh: '83- 4; ECh: '82- 1, '86- 2; EJ: '79- 3; WSG: '85- 2; ECp: '85- 3. Balkan champion 1984, 1986. Bulgarian champion 1985-6. Won GP 1986.
Two Bulgarian discus records 1986.
Progression at DT: 1977- 46.90, 1978- 48.84, 1979- 54.76, 1980- 58.44, 1981- 64.38, 1982- 70.64, 1983- 66.88, 1984- 68.34, 1985- 68.68, 1986- 72.52.

**Stefka KOSTADINOVA** b.5 Mar 1965 Plovdiv 1.80m 58kg. Club: Tralija Plovdiv. Physical education student.
At HJ: ECh: '86- 1; EJ: '81- 10; EI: '85- 1; WCp: '85- 1; ECp: '85- 1, WIG: '85- 1. Balkan and Bulgarian champion 1985-6. Won GP 1985.
World records at 2.07 and 2.08 in 1986. World indoor best 2.04m 1987.
Progression at HJ: 1977- 1.45, 1978- 1.66, 1979- 1.75, 1980- 1.84, 1981- 1.86, 1982- 1.90, 1983- 1.83i, 1984- 2.00, 1985- 2.06, 1986- 2.08.
Won 34 successive high jump competitions 1984-6, her one loss (to Heike Redetzky) in the latter year was then followed by 10 further wins.

**Svetla MITKOVA** b.17 Jun 1964 1.78m 90kg. Club: Rozova dolina, Kazanlak.
At SP/DT: WCh: '83- 10 DT; ECh: '86- 12/5; EJ: '81: 3/2; ECp: SP '83- 5, '85- 5. Bulgarian champion shot 1984-6, discus 1983. 2nd GP DT 1986.
Progression at SP/DT: 1980- 14.10/50.70, 1981- 17.16/59.84, 1982- 18.03/60.58, 1983- 18.83/66.80, 1984- 19.11/64.84, 1985- 18.87/54.34, 1986- 20.05/68.90.

**Lyudmila NINOVA** b.25 Jun 1960 Vidin 1.71m 56kg. Club: Akademik, Sofia.
At LJ: ECh: '86- 5. Balkan champion 1986.
Three Bulgarian long jump records 1984-6.
Progression at LJ: 1983- 6.23, 1984- 6.80, 1985- 6.64, 1986- 6.88. pb Hep: 5248* '84.

**Anelia NUNEVA** b.30 Jun 1962 Bjala 1.67m 57kg. Club: Lokomotif, Ruse. Physical education student. Now VECHERNIKOVA.
At 100m (200m): WCh: '83- sf (6); ECh: '82- 4 (6), '86- 2 (2R); WCp: '85- 4; ECp: '83- 2 (4), '85- 3; WSG: '85- 2. At 60m: EI: '84- 2. Balkan champion 100m 1984-6, 200m 1986.
Three Bulgarian 100m records 1982-6.
Progression at 100m/200m: 1978- 12.23/25.60, 1979- 12.10/25.90, 1981- 11.34/11.31w/23.58, 1982- 11.14/22.93, 1983- 11.07/22.58, 1984- 11.10/22.67, 1985- 11.14/22.73, 1986- 11.04/10.9/22.58.

**Ginka ZAGORCHEVA** b.12 Apr 1958 Rakovski, Plovdiv 1.72m 53kg. Club: Levski Spartak. Physical education student. Now BOYCHEVA.
At 100mh (R- 4x100m relay): WCh: '83- 3; ECh: '82- 8, '86- 3 (2R); WSG: '85- 1; WCp: '85- 2 (3R); ECp: '83- 3, '85- 1. Balkan champion 1985, Bulgarian 1983, 1985. 3rd GP 1986. At 60mh: EI: '85- 2. Bulgarian 100mh record 1985.
Progression at 100mh: 1975- 13.9, 1977- 13.90, 1978- 13.39, 1979- 13.22, 1981- 13.74, 1982- 12.73, 1983- 12.49, 1984- 12.62, 1985- 12.42, 1986- 12.39/12.1w. pbs: 100m: 11.38 '83, 200m: 24.13 '85.

# CANADA

**Governing body**: Canadian Track and Field Association, 333 River Road, Ottawa, Ontario K1L 8H9. Formed as the Canadian AAU in 1884.
**National Championship** first held in 1884 (men), 1925 (women).
**1986 champions: MEN**
100m: Ben Johnson 10.07, 200m: Atlee Mahorn 20.40, 400m: John Graham 46.44, 800m: Simon Hoogewerf 1:48.61, 1500m: Dave Campbell 3:42.17, 5000m: Paul Williams 13:41.86, 10000m: Paul McCloy 28:29.16, Mar: Antonio

Graham Fell. *Mark Shearman*

Diaz Romero 2:20:35, 3000mSt: Graeme Fell 8:25.82, 110mh: Mark McKoy 13.68, 400mh: Pierre Leveille 50.84, HJ: Milt Ottey 2.33, PV: Robert Ferguson 5.15, LJ: Ian James 7.93, TJ: Edrick Floreal 16.37, SP:* Mike Spiritoso 19.88 (Luby Chambul 17.94), DT:* Rob Gray 59.42 (Raymond Lazdins 56.00), HT: Darren McFee 59.92, JT: Peter Massfeller 68.74, Dec: Dave Steen 8118, 20kmW: Guillaume Leblanc 1:29:52.
* Spiritoso and Gary subsequently disqualified for failing doping controls.

**WOMEN**

100m/200m: Angella Issajenko 11.08/22.88, 400m: Charmaine Crooks 51.36, 800m: Renée Belanger 2:06.34, 1500m: Brit McRoberts 4:10.85, 3000m: Lynn Williams 9:07.55, 10000m: Carole Rouillard 32:30.93, Mar: Ellen Rochefort 2:35:15, 100mh: Faye Blackwood 13.47, 400mh: Gwen Wall 57.32, HJ: Shari Orders 1.81, LJ: Sharon Clark 6.45w, SP: Melody Torcolacci 16.08, DT: Gale Zaphiropoulos 51.58, JT: Kristy Evans 55.98, Hep: Linda Spenst 5578, 5kmW: Anne Peel 22:18.5.

**Dave EDGE** b.12 Nov 1954 Blackpool, England 1.75m 61kg. Club: Etobicoke Huskies-Striders. National accounts magager for clothing company.
At marathon: OG: '84- dnf; WCh: '83- 24; CG: '86- 2. Canadian champion 1984.

Progression at Mar: 1982- 2:12:25, 1983- 2:11:04, 1984- 2:13:20, 1985- 2:12:24, 1986- 2:11:08. pb 10000m: 29:27.29 '84.

**Graeme FELL** b.19 Mar 1959 Romford, England 1.84m 73kg. Club: Valley Royals. UK international, married middle distance runner Debbie Campbell. Canadian citizenship 1986.
At 3kmSt: WCh: '83- 6; ECh: '82- 10; CG: '82- 2, '86- 1; WCp: '85- 3. Canadian champion 1985-6. 3rd GP 1986.
Records at 3kmSt: UK 1983, Canadian (twice) 1985.
Progression at 3kmSt: 1975- 9:57.2, 1976- 9:32.4, 1977- 8:56.6, 1978- 8:48.43, 1979- 8:36.94, 1980- 8:49.92, 1981- 8:31.80, 1982- 8:19.72, 1983- 8:15.16, 1984- 8:17.71, 1985- 8:12.58, 1986- 8:14.57. pbs: 1500m: 3:39.3 '85, 1M: 3:57.5 '83, 2000m: 5:07.54 '82, 3000m: 7:42.26 '83, 5000m: 13:39.0 '86.

**Ben JOHNSON** b.30 Dec 1961 Falmouth, Jamaica 1.80m 75kg. Club: York Optimists. Came to Canada in 1976.
At 100m (R- 4x100m relay): OG: '84- 3 (3R); WCh: '83- sf; CG: '82- 2 (2R), '86- 1 (1R, 3 200m); PAm: '83- 6; WSG: '83- 5 (2R); WCp: '85- 1 (2R). 2nd GP 1986. Member 1980 Olympic team. At 60m: WIG: '85- 1. Canadian champion 100m 1984-6, 200m 1985.
Two Canadian, 1984, and two Commonwealth records, 1985-6, at 100m, the last a world low altitude best. Commonwealth 60m best 6.56 '85, world indoor bests: 60m: 6.50 '86 (twice), 6.44 '87; 50m: 5.55 '87.
Progression at 100m: 1978- 10.79/10.4, 1979- 10.66, 1980- 10.62/10.38w/10.2, 1981- 10.25, 1982- 10.30/10.05w, 1983- 10.19, 1984- 10.12/ 10.01w, 1985- 10.00, 1986- 9.95. pb 200m: 20.41 '85, 20.37w '82.
The first Canadian to win an Olympic medal since 1964, he has continued to improve to claim the title of the world's fastest man. Lost just once in 1986, when he had ten sub 10.10 times, the most ever run in a season. Started 1987 by smashing world indoor sprint records.

**Guillaume LEBLANC** b.14 Apr 1982 Sept-Iles 1.84m 75kg. Club d'Athlétisme de Sept-Isles.
At 20kmW: OG: '84- 4 (dnf 50kmW); WCh: '83- 8; WSG: '83- 1, '85- 3; PAm: '86- 1; LT: '83- 11, '85- 5; CG 30kmW: '82- 3, '86- 2. Member 1980 Olympic team. Canadian champion 1985-6.
Commonwealth 20km track walk record, 1:23:17, 1986.
Progression at 20kmW: 1979- 1:33:35, 1981- 1:26:32, 1982- 1:24:28, 1983- 1:22.04, 1984- 1:24:29, 1985- 1:23:51, 1986- 1:21:13. pbs: 30kmW: 2:08:38 '86, 50kmW: 3:58:33 '83.

Ben Johnson. *ASP*

**Mark McKOY** b.10 Dec 1961 Georgetown, Guyana 1.81m 70kg. Club: York U.Optimists; Pacific Coast Club, USA.
At 110mh (R- 4x100m relay): OG: '84- 4; WCh: '83- 4; CG: '82- 1 (2R), '86- 1 (1R); WSG: '83- 3; PAm: '83- 6. Member 1980 Olympic team. Canadian champion 1981-6. Won GP 1985.
Eight Canadian, including four Commonwealth 110mh records 1982-5. World indoor records: 50mh: 6.25 '86, 60mh: 7.47 '86. Commonwealth indoor record 50yh: 5.95 '85.
Progression at 110mh: 1979- 14.19, 1980- 14.02, 1981- 13.97, 1982- 13.37, 1983- 13.53/13.51w, 1984- 13.27/13.16w, 1985- 13.27, 1986- 13.35/13.31w. pbs: 100m: 10.21 '86, 200m: 20.96 '85, 400mh: 53.75 '79.

**Atlee MAHORN** b.27 Oct 1965 Jamaica 1.87m 77kg. Club: York U.Optimists. Political science student at University of California, Berkeley, USA.
At 200m (R- 4x100m relay): OG: '84- sf; WCh: '83- qf; CG: '86- 1 (1R, 3 4x400mR); WSG: '85- 2 (2R). Canadian champion 1986.
Canadian 400m record 1986.
Progression at 200m: 1982- 21.63, 1983- 20.65, 1984- 20.69, 1985- 20.65, 1986- 20.34/20.31w. pbs: 100m: 10.26 '86, 10.19w '85; 400m: 45.62 '86.

**Milt OTTEY** b.29 Dec 1959 May Pen, Jamaica 1.78m 66kg. Club: York U.Optimists and Pacific Coast Club, USA. Moved to Canada at age of ten. Was at University of Texas at El Paso, now studying at University of Toronto.
At HJ: OG: '84- 6; WCh: '83- 9; CG: '82- 1, '86- 1; PAm: '79- 3; WCp: '79- 5, '81- 5. Won TAC and NCAA 1982. Member 1980 Olympic team. Canadian champion 1981-4, 1986.
Three Commonwealth high jump records 1982-6.
Progression at HJ: 1977- 1.95, 1978- 2.11, 1979- 2.19, 1980- 2.20i, 1981- 2.24, 1982- 2.32, 1983- 2.30, 1984- 2.29, 1985- 2.31, 1986- 2.33.

**Dave STEEN** b.14 Nov 1959 New Westminster, BC 1.85m 80kg. University of Toronto Track Club. Student at the Univerity of Toronto.
At Dec: OG: '84- 8; CG: '82- 2, '86- 2 (4 PV); WSG: '81- 5, '83- 1; PAm: '83- 1. Member 1980 Olympic team. Canadian champion Dec 1982, 1986; LJ 1977.
Six Canadian records at decathlon 1981-5.
Progression at Dec: 1977- 6917*, 1978- 6860*, 1979- 7543, 1980- 7654, 1981- 7923, 1982- 8003, 1983- 8213, 1984- 8248, 1985- 8316w, 1986- 8254w. pbs: 100m: 10.91 '86, 10.8 '85, 10.7w '84; 400m: 47.58 '85, 1500m: 4:14.10 '83, 110mh: 14.80/14.72w '86, 14.7w '84; HJ: 2.15i '83, PV: 5.30 '85, LJ: 7.72 '86, SP: 14.36 '84, DT: 51.58 '83, JT: 67.20 '82.
Uncle Dave won Commonwealth shot title in 1966 and 1970, father Don was Canadian decathlon champion in 1956.

# Women

**Angela BAILEY** b.28 Feb 1962 Coventry, UK 1.57m 52kg. Student at UCLA.
At 100m/200m (4x100m relay): OG: '84- 6/sf (2R); WCh: '83- 5/7; CG: '78- sf/h (2R), '82- 4/8 (2R), '86- 4/- (2R). Member 1980 Olympic team. Canadian 100m/200m champion 1985.
Progression at 100m, 200m: 1976- 11.8, 24.7; 1977- 11.66, 24.2; 1978- 11.52, 23.91; 1979- 11.49, 24.12; 1980- 11.44/11.27w, 23.42/23.19w; 1981- 11.21, 22.86; 1982- 11.23, 23.44/22.75w;

1983- 11.17, 22.64; 1984- 11.25, 22.75; 1985-
11.21, 23.02, 1986- 11.50/11.23w, 23.02. pb
400m: 51.96 '83.

**Debbie BOWKER** b.16 Dec 1958 Victoria, BC
1.63m 52kg. née Scott. Club: Vikes. Education
student.
At 3000m (1500m): OG: '84- (10); CG: '78- 9, '82-
12 (sf), '86- 2 (2); WCp: '77- 6; WIG: '85- 1.
Canadian champion 1500m 1982-5, 3000m
1982. Canadian records at 1M, 3000m, 5000m
1982; 2000m 1986.
Progression at 3000m: 1976- 9:41.8, 1977-
9:18.7, 1978- 9:18.3, 1979- 9:16.6, 1980- 9:03.9,
1981- 8:58.30, 1982- 8:48.85, 1984- 8:58.5,
1985- 8:49.80, 1986- 8:53.28. pbs: 800m: 2:03.1
'85, 1000m: 2:39.76 '84, 1500m: 4:06.89 '83, 1M:
4:29.67 '82, 2000m: 5:39.96 '86, 5000m:
15:48.99 '82.

**Debbie BRILL** b.10 Mar 1953 Mission, BC 1.77m
60kg. Vancouver Olympic Club.
At HJ: OG: '72- 8, '76- dnq, '84- 5; WCh: '83- 6;
CG: '70- 1, '78- 2, '82- 1, '86- 5; PAm: '71- 1, '75-
4, '79- 3; WCp: '77- 3, '79- 1; WSG: '77- 2.
Member 1980 Olympic team. Won US HJ 1979 &
1982. Canadian champion 1968-71, 1974, 1976,
1978, 1980, 1982-4.
17 Commonwealth high jump records 1970-84 as
well as eight indoor marks equalling or bettering
the record, the most for any athlete at any event.
Progression at HJ: 1966- 1.41, 1967- 1.63, 1968-
1.71, 1969- 1.76, 1970- 1.83, 1971- 1.85, 1972-
1.86, 1974- 1.87, 1975- 1.89, 1976- 1.90, 1977-
1.91, 1978- 1.92i/1.91, 1979- 1.96, 1980- 1.97,
1982- 1.99i/1.95, 1983- 1.95, 1984- 1.98, 1985-
1.96, 1986- 1.97i/1.89.
First woman to use flop style effectively as she
pioneered the 'Brill bend' in the late 1960s.
Youngest ever Commonwealth champion in 1970
at 17 years 137 days in 1970, and won again in
1982. Gave birth to son, Neil in 1981 and returned
to set world indoor best at 1.99m in 1982.

**Charmaine CROOKS** b.8 Aug 1961 Mandeville,
Jamaica 1.70m 60kg. Club: York U. Optimists.
University of Texas at El Paso.
At 400m (4x400m relay): OG: '84- 7 (2R); WCh:
'83-sf (4R); CG: '82- 7 (1R), '86- 5 (1R); PAm: '83-
1; WSG: '83- 4 (2R), '85- 6 (2R); WCp: '81- 3R;
WIG: '85- 3. Canadian champion 1980, 1986.
Progression at 400m: 1979- 53.12, 1980- 52.33,
1981- 52.32, 1982- 52.01, 1983- 51.49, 1984-
50.45, 1985- 52.70, 1986- 50.84. pb 200m: 23.30
'83.

**Angella ISSAJENKO** b.28 Sep 1958 Jamaica
1.65m 61kg. née Taylor. Club: York U. Optimists.
At 100m/200m (R- 4x100mR): OG: '84- 8 at 200m

(2R); WCh: '83- 7 at 100m; CG: '78- ht 200m, '82-
1/3 (2R, 1 4x400mR), '86- 3/1 (2R); PAm: '79- 3/2;
WCp: '79- 5/5, '81- 4/4; WSG: '83- 3/4 (2R).
Member 1980 Olympic team. Canadian champion 100m/200m 1979-84, 1986.
Commonwealth 100m record 1982; world indoor
bests: 300m: 36.91 '80, 50m: 6.06 '87. Canadian
records: four 100m and seven 200m 1979-82.
Progression at 100m, 200m: 1977- 12.4; 1978-
12.07, 23.87; 1979- 11.20, 22.80/22.74w; 1980-
11.23/11.03w, 22.61; 1981- 11.12, 22.55/22.46w;
1982- 11.00/10.92w, 22.25/22.19w; 1983- 11.22/
11.17w, 22.81; 1984- 11.16/11.09w, 22.61/
22.44w, 1986- 11.24/11.08w/11.0A, 22.80. pb
400m: 51.81 '81.
Gave birth to daughter, Sasha, September 1985.

**Marita PAYNE** b.7 Oct 1960 Barbados 1.72m
57kg. Came to Canada as 9-year-old. Club: York
U. Optimists, Canada & Bud Light Track America.
Florida State University.
At 400m: OG: '84- 4 (2 at 4x100mR, 4 x400mR);
WCh: '83- 5; CG: '82- sf (2 at 4x100mR), '86- 4
(1R); PAm: '79- 7; WCp: '79- 4, '81- 3 at
4x400mR. WSG: '83- 2 at 200m, 4x100mR and
4x400mR. Won NCAA 1984. Member 1980
Olympic team. Canadian champion 1981.
Commonwealth 400m record 1983.
Progression at 400m: 1979- 53.01, 1981- 52.01,
1982- 51.99, 1983- 50.06, 1984- 49.91, 1986-
51.77. pbs: 100m: 11.43, 11.34w '83; 200m:
22.62 '83, 300m: 37.20 '86.
Married Houston basketball player Mitchell
Wiggins 7 Sep 1985.

**Jillian RICHARDSON** b.10 Mar 1965 Trinidad
1.72m 59kg. Club: Calgary Spartans. Physical
education student.
At 400m (R- 4x400m relay): OG: '84- 2R; WCh:
'83- 4R; CG: '82- 1R, '86- 2 (1R); PAm: '83- 2R (3
4x100mR); WSG: '83- 2R.
Progression at 400m: 1980- 53.70, 1981- 52.95,
1982- 52.70, 1983- 51.91, 1984- 51.58, 1985-
53.19, 1986- 51.55. pbs: 100m: 11.90 '84, 200m:
23.53/23.25w '86.

**Lynn WILLIAMS** b.11 Jul 1960 Regina, Saska-
toon 1.55m 49kg. Club: Valley Royals. née
Kanuka, married to Paul Williams (Canadian
10km record holder). Graduate of San Diego
State University, USA.
At 3000m: OG: '84- 3; WCh: '83- 10; CG: '86- 1 (3
1500m); WSG: '83- 3. Canadian champion 1983-
4, 1986. 3rd GP 1985.
Commonwealth 5000m record 1985. Canadian
records: 3000m (3), 5000m (2), 1000m, 1500m,
1M, 2000m (1 each) 1983-5.
Progression at 3000m: 1979- 9:47.0, 1980-
9:21.1, 1981- 9:13.13, 1982- 9:13.1, 1983-

8:50.20, 1984- 8:42.14, 1985- 8:37.38, 1986-
8:52.91. pbs: 800m: 2:02.90 '85, 1000m: 2:39.23
'84, 1500m: 4:00.27 '85, 1M: 4:27.77i '86, 4:28.03
'85, 2000m: 5:43.9 '85, 5000m: 15:07.71 '85.

# CHILE

**Governing body**: Federation Atlética de Chile,
Calle Santo Toribio No 660 - Castilla 820,
Santiago de Chile. Founded 1917.

**Gert WEIL** b.3 Jan 1960 1.97m 115kg.
At SP: OG: '84- 10; PAm: '83- 2; WCp: '85- 5.
SACh 1st 1979-81-83-85.
Nine S.American shot records 1984-6.
Progression at SP: 1978- 14.88, 1979- 16.42,
1980- 16.77, 1981- 17.48, 1982- 17.54, 1983-
18.29, 1984- 19.94, 1985- 20.47, 1986- 20.90. pb
DT: 52.26 '84.

# CHINA

**Governing body**: Athletic Association of the
People's Republic of China, 9 Tiyuguan Road,
Beijing.

**ZHU JIANHUA** b.29 May 1963 Shanghai 1.96m
74kg. Physical education student
At HJ: OG: '84- 3; WCh: '83- 3; WSG: '81- 2; AsG:
'82- 1, '86- 1; AsCh: '81- 1, '83- 1; WCp: '81- 9.
Three world high jump records: 2.37m and 2.38m
in 1983, 2.39m in 1984. Seven Chinese records
1981-4.
Progression at HJ: 1975- 1.51, 1976- 1.69, 1977-
1.83, 1978- 1.95, 1979- 2.13, 1980- 2.25, 1981-
2.30, 1982- 2.33, 1983- 2.38, 1984- 2.39, 1985-
2.35, 1986- 2.31.

# Women

**GUAN PING** b.1966
At 10kmW: AsG: '86- 1; WCp: '83- 6, '85- 2.
World 5000m and 10000m walk records 1986.
World junior best for 10kmW (road): 46:38.7 '83.
Track pbs: 5kmW: 21:26.5 '86, 10kmW: 44:42.2
'86. Road 10kmW: 44:28 '85.

**WANG YAN** b.9 Apr 1971 Liaoning 1.61m 46kg.
World walk records 1986: 3km: 12:39.1, 5km:
21:33.8, the latter on 9 March was at age 14 years
334 days, as she became the youngest ever to set
a world record. World junior record at 10km walk:
44:59.3 '86.

**XU YONGJIU** b.29 Oct 1964 Liaoning 1.58m
46kg.

At 10kmW: AsG: '86- 2; WCp: '83- 1, '85- 5.
Two world records at 10km walk: 45:31.9 and
44:59.2 in 1986.
Track pbs: 3kmW: 13:05.0 '84, 5kmW: 21:41.0
'84. Road 10kmW: 44:45 '85.

**YAN HONG** b.23 Oct 1966 Liaoning 1.54m 44kg.
At 10kmW: WCp: '83- dq(1st), '85- 1. 2nd WIG
3kmW 1985.
World walk records: 5km 21:40.3 and 10km
45:39.5 in 1984. Three world junior 5km walk
records 1983-4. World road best 44:14 for 10km
walk 1985.
Track pbs: 3kmW: 13:05.56i '85, 5kmW: 21:40.3
'84, 10kmW: 45:32.4 '86.

**ZHENG DAZHEN** b.22 Sep 1959 Xiamen 1.75m
60kg. Physical education student
At HJ: OG: '84- 7; WCh: '83- 18; WCp: '79- 7;
AsG: '78- 1, '82- 1, '86- 2; AsCh: '79- 1, '81- 2, '83-
1. Three Asian high jump records 1980-2.
Progression at HJ: 1972- 1.34, 1973- 1.48, 1974-
1.52, 1975- 1.69, 1976- 1.76, 1977- 1.78, 1978-
1.88, 1979- 1.89, 1980- 1.92, 1981- 1.91, 1982-
1.93, 1983- 1.90, 1984- 1.91, 1985- 1.87i, 1986-
1.90.

# CUBA

**Governing body**: Federacion Cubana de Atletismo, Calle 13 No.601, Zona Postale 4, Vedado,
Ciudad de la Habana. Founded 1922

**National Champions 1986: MEN**
100m: Osvaldo Lara 10.53, 200m: Sergio Querol
21.25, 400m: Felix Stevens 44.77, 800m:
Roberto Ramos 1:47.76, 1500m: Felix Mesa
3:48.1, 5000m: Juan Linares 14:21.41, 10000m:
Alberto Cuba 29:52.0, Mar: Andres Chavez
2:19:02, 3kmSt: Juan Conde 8:37.6, 110mh:
Juan Saborit 14.21, 400mh: Francisco Velazco
49.64, HJ: Javier Sotomayor 2.36, PV: Ruben
Camino 5.10, LJ: Jaime Jefferson 8.47, TJ:
Lazaro Betancourt 17.45, SP: Paul Ruiz 19.14,
DT: Raul Calderon 57.36, HT: Vicente Sanchez
67.42, JT: Ramon Gonzalez 85.16, Dec: Ernseto
Betancourt 7729, 20kmW/50kmW: Edel Oliva
1:27:31/4:03:23.
**WOMEN**
100m: Idania Pino 12.29, 200m: Ester Petiton
24.03, 400m: Migdalia Pena 53.74, 800m: Idalmis
Lopez 2:07.0, 1500m: Eloina Kerr 4:23.2, 3000m:
Sergia Martinez 9:50.84, 10000m: Lucia Conde
39:53.8, 100mh: Alinska Lopez 13.92, 400mh:
Odalys Hernandez 58.1, HJ: Silvia Costa 1.85,
LJ: Adelinna Polledo 6.53, SP: Marcelina
Rodriguez 17.41, DT: Maritza Marten 60.76, JT:
Maria Caridad Colon 68.32, Hep: Caridad Bal-
sindes 5400.

# Men

**Lazaro BETANCOURT** b.18 Mar 1963 Habana 1.89m 83kg. Sports student.
At TJ: PAm: '83- 2, CAmG: '82- 2, '86- 1; WIG: '85- 2. Cuban champion 1983-4. Won AAA 1984.
Four Cuban triple jump records 1983-6. World low altitude TJ best at 17.57m 1985.
Progression at TJ: 1979- 14.96, 1980- 15.56/ 15.78w, 1981- 16.11, 1982- 16.64, 1983- 17.40/ 17.50w, 1984- 17.45, 1985- 17.57, 1986- 17.78. pb LJ: 7.48 '83.
Suspended after failing doping test at Florence 1986. His father, also Lazaro Betancourt, was Cuban record holder for 110mh at 14.0 in 1964 and CAmG champion in 1962.

**Francisco CENTELLES** b.26 Jan 1961 1.96m 81kg.
At HJ: OG: '80- dnq; WCh: '83- 15; PAm: '79-4, '83- 1; CAmG: '82- 1, '86- 1; WSG: '85- 2.
Progression at HJ: 1975- 1.90, 1976- 2.00, 1977- 2.11, 1978- 2.15, 1979- 2.18, 1980- 2.24, 1981- 2.22, 1982- 2.28, 1983- 2.32, 1984- 2.30, 1985- 2.31, 1986- 2.30.

**Luis Mariano DELIS** b.6 Dec 1957 Guantanamo 1.85m 106kg.
At DT: OG: '80- 3; WCh: '83- 2; PAm: '79- 3, '83- 1 (1 at SP); WCp: '79- 3, '81- 2, '85- 3; WSG: '83- 1, '85- 1; CAmG: '78- 1, '82- 1 (1 at SP), '86- 1. Won US title 1982. CAC champion 1985. Cuban champion 1978-83.
Progression at DT: 1973- 43.54, 1974- 49.02, 1975- 50.70, 1976- 56.82, 1977- 61.02, 1978- 62.14, 1979- 66.52, 1980- 68.04, 1981- 67.28, 1982- 70.58, 1983- 71.06, 1984- 69.74, 1985- 70.00, 1986- 68.00. pb SP: 19.89 '82.

**Roberto HERNANDEZ** b.6 Mar 1967 Matanzas 1.72m 72kg. Student.
At 400m (R- 4x400m relay): WJ: '86- 2 (1R); WSG: '85- 2 (1R). CAC champion 1985.
Progression at 400m: 1983- 48.0, 1984- 46.44, 1985- 45.14, 1986- 45.05. pbs: 200m: 20.37 '86, 20.2 '85; 300m: 32.34 '85.

**Jaime JEFFERSON** b.17 Jan 1962 Guantanamo 1.89m 78kg.
At LJ: PAm: '83- 1; CAmG: '86- 1; WSG: '85- 1. CAC champion 1985.
Four Cuban long jump records 1984-6.
Progression at LJ: 1981- 7.25, 1982- 7.50, 1983- 8.05, 1984- 8.37, 1985- 8.24/8.28w, 1986- 8.47. pbs: 100m: 10.2/10.35/10.33w '85, TJ: 16.28 '85.

**Osvaldo LARA** b.13 Jul 1955 Habana 1.71m 72kg. Sports student.
At 100m (R- 4x100m relay): OG: '80- 5 (8 at 200m); WCh: '83- sf; PAm: '79- 6 (7 at 200m, 2R), '83- 4 (2R); CAmG: '78- 2, '82- 2 (1R), '86- 1R; WSG: '77- 3.
Progression at 100m: 1976- 10.43/10.0, 1977- 10.20/10.1/10.0w , 1978- 10.11, 1979- 10.27/ 10.23w, 1980- 10.21/10.1, 1981- 10.1/10.29w, 1982- 10.26/9.7w/10.2, 1983- 10.21, 1984- 10.14/10.0, 1985- 10.13, 1986- 10.33. pb 200m: 20.1 '78, 20.76 '85.

**Juan MARTINEZ** b.17 May 1958 Habana 1.86m 122kg.
At DT: WCh: '83- 7; WSG: '85- 3; PAm: '79- 4, '83- 3; CAmG: '86- 2. Won AAA 1985.
Progression at DT: 1975- 47.90, 1976- 53.98, 1977- 57.24, 1978- 60.34, 1979- 64.88, 1980- 66.46, 1982- 63.70, 1983- 70.00, 1984- 67.32, 1985- 69.32, 1986- 68.40. pb SP: 15.98 '76.

**Leandro PENALVER** b.23 May 1961 Matanzas 1.75m 71kg.
At 100m/200m (R- 4x100m relay): WCh: '83- sf/-; PAm: '83- 1/2 (2R); WCp: '85- 2R; CAmG: '82- 1/1 (1R, 1 4x400mR), '86- -/1 (1R); WSG: '85- 1 at 200m and both relays. CAC 200m champion 1985. Cuban 400m champion 1985.
Progression at 100m, 200m: 1981- 10.61/ 10.24w/10.4, 20.92; 1982- 10.16/10.1, 20.42/ 20.3; 1983- 10.06, 20.45; 1984- 10.14, 20.65; 1985- 10.22, 20.56/20.53w; 1986- 10.23, 20.53. pb 400m: 45.35 '85.

**Andres SIMON** b.15 Sep 1961 Guantanamo 1.60m 67kg. Student.
At 100m (R- 4x100mR): CAmG: '86- 1 (1R); WSG: '85- 2 (1R). CAC champion 1985.
Progression at 100m: 1983- 10.60, 1984- 10.25, 1985- 10.10/9.97w, 1986- 10.18.

**Javier SOTOMAYOR** b.13 Oct 1967 Limonar, Matanzas 1.96m 76kg.
At HJ: WJ: '86- 1; WCp: '85- 3; WIG: '85- 2. Cuban champion 1984. CAC champion 1985.
Three Cuban records 1984-6. World junior high jump record 1986.
Progression at HJ: 1982- 2.00, 1983- 2.17, 1984- 2.33, 1985- 2.34, 1986- 2.36.

**Felix STEVENS** b.8 Mar 1964 1.90m 72kg.
At 400m (R- 4x400m relay): CAmG: '86- 1 (1R). Cuban champion 1986.
Progression at 400m: 1985- 45.51, 1986- 44.77. pbs: 100m: 10.52 '85, 10.5 '83; 200m: 20.65 '85.

# Women

**Maria Caridad COLON** b.25 Mar 1958 Baracoa 1.75m 70kg.
At JT: OG: '80- 1; WCh: '83- 8; PAm: '79- 1, '83- 1; WSG: '85- 3; CAmG: '78- 1, '82- 1, '86- 1; WCp: '79- 3, '85- 7. Six times Cuban javelin champion.
Progression at JT: 1974- 42.24, 1975- 43.62, 1976- 49.74, 1977- 54.32, 1978- 63.50, 1979- 64.38, 1980- 68.40, 1982- 62.80, 1983- 65.70, 1984- 69.96, 1985- 68.20, 1986- 70.14.
Has steadily regained the form that won her the Olympic javelin gold medal in 1980. Married to her coach Angel Salcedo. Had a baby in 1981.

**Silvia COSTA** b.4 May 1964 Pinar del Rio 1.79m 60kg.
At HJ: WCh: '83- 10=; PAm: '83- 2; WSG: '83- 2, '85- 1; WCp: '85- 4; CAmG: '82- 1, '86- 1; WIG: '85- 3=. CAC champion 1985.
Two world junior high jump records 1982. Cuban record holder since 1980.
Progression at HJ: 1977- 1.57, 1978- 1.64, 1979- 1.82, 1980- 1.90, 1981- 1.88, 1982- 1.95, 1983- 1.98, 1984- 1.99, 1985- 2.01, 1986- 1.99. pb 100mh: 14.48 '83, 14.3 '80.

**Ivonne LEAL** b.27 Feb 1966 San Nicolas, Habana 1.64m 64kg.
At JT: CAmG: '86- 2; WSG: '85- 1.
Cuban javelin record 1985.
Progression at JT: 1980- 40.20, 1981- 47.00, 1982- 55.00, 1983- 56.82, 1984- 58.54, 1985- 71.82, 1986- 69.82.

**Maritza MARTEN** b.17 Aug 1963 Habana 1.77m 83kg.
At DT: PAm: '83- 2; CAmG: '86- 2; WCp: '85- 3; WSG: '85- 1. CAC champion 1985, Cuban champion 1984-5.
Cuban discus record 1985.
Progression at DT: 1977- 41.34, 1978- 47.46, 1979- 53.30, 1980- 54.94, 1981- 53.70, 1982- 59.54, 1983- 63.94, 1984- 67.76, 1985- 70.50, 1986- 66.86. pb SP: 15.52 '85.

**Ana Fidelia QUIROT** b.23 Mar 1963 Santiago de Cuba 1.65m 59kg.
At 400m/800m (R- 4x400m relay): WCp: '85- 4/4; PAm: '79- 2R, '83- 2 (3R); WSG: '85- 2/3; CAmG: '78- 1R, '82- 4 (1R), '86- 1/1 (1R). Double CAC champion 1985.
Cuban records: three 800m 1985-6, one 400m 1986.
Progression at 400m/800m: 1980- 55.0, 1981- 54.2, 1982- 52.61, 1983- 51.83, 1984- 50.87, 1985- 50.86/1:59.45, 1986- 50.41/1:58.80. pb 200m: 23.16/22.9 '84.

**Hilda Elisa RAMOS** b.1 Sep 1964 1.76m 80kg.
At DT: CAmG: '86- 1.
Progression at DT: 1980- 45.32, 1981- 50.04, 1982- 52.62, 1983- 63.60, 1984- 67.56, 1985- 67.52, 1986- 67.92. pb SP: 16.36 '85.

# CZECHOSLOVAKIA

**Governing body**: Ceskoslovensky atléticky svaz, Na Porici 12, 115 30 Praha 1. Founded 1897 (AAU of Bohemia).
**National Championships** first held in 1907 (Bohemia), 1919 (CS)
**1986 Champions: MEN**
100m: Lubos Chochlik 10.56, 200m: Josef Lomicky 21.46, 400m: Petr Brecka 46.87, 800m: Milan Drahonovsky 1:48.01, 1500m: Jan Kraus 3:43.60, 5000m: Lubomir Tesacek 13:40.61, 10000m: Martin Vrabel 28:46.80, Mar, Miroslaw Becker 2:19:13, 3000mSt: Stanislav Stit 8:35.80, 110mh: Pavel Sada 14.13, 400mh: Josef Kucej 50.11, HJ: Jan Zvara 2.26, PV: Zdenek Lubensky 5.72, LJ: Zdenek Hanacek 7.78, TJ: Jan Cado 17.04, SP: Jozef Kubes 19.77, DT: Imrich Bugar 66.64, HT: Zdenek Bednar 70.58, JT: Jan Zelezny 79.36, Dec: Roman Hraban 7866w, 20kmW: Jozef Pribilinec 1:28:07, 50kmW: Pavel Szikora 3:49:00.
**WOMEN**
100m/LJ: Eva Murkova 11.63/6.70, 200m: Tatana Kocembova 23.63, 400m: Jana Mrovcova 53.01, 800m: Petra Pokorna 2:05.13, 1500m: Ivana Walterova 4:11.67, 3000m: Jana Kucerikova 9:15.54, 10000m: Ludmila Melicherova 33:31.03, Mar, Hana Horakova 2:40:17, 100mh: Milena Tebichova 13.74, 400mh: Blanka Hakova 59.67, HJ: Daniela Chvalkova 1.86, LJ: Eva Murkova 6.70, SP: Sona Vasickova 19.70, DT: Gabriela Hanulakova 56.94, JT: Elena Burgarova 56.44, Hep: Zuzana Lajbnerova 5916w, 10kmW: Dana Vavracova 50:07.

**Pavol BLAZEK** b.9 Jul 1958 Trnava 1.68m 57kg. Club: Dukla B.Bystrica. Soldier.
At 20kmW (50kmW): OG: '80- 14 (10); WCh: '83- 6 (17); ECh: '78- 14, '82- 3 (dnf), '86- 6; LT: '83- 9, '85- 10. CS 20kmW champion 1981.
Progression at 20kmW: 1977- 1:33:34, 1978- 1:27:50, 1979- 1:25:14, 1980- 1:25:00t, 1981- 1:24:07, 1982- 1:23:59, 1983- 1:21:37, 1984- 1:21:24t, 1985- 1:22:30, 1986- 1:21:21. Track pbs: 3kmW: 11:36.7i '85, 5kmW: 18:58.1i '86, 10kmW: 39:31.83i '86; Road pb 50kmW: 4:03:22 '83.

**Imrich BUGAR** b.14 Apr 1955 Dunajska Streda 1.95m 120kg. Club: Dukla Praha. Civil servant.
At DT: OG: '80- 2; WCh: '83- 1; ECh: '78- 3, '82- 1,

'86- 8; WCp: '81- 3, '85- 4; ECp: '85- 1. CS champion 1978-86. Won GP 1985.
Six CS discus records 1981-5.
Progression at DT: 1972- 44.42, 1973- 48.22, 1974- 51.38, 1975- 53.88, 1976- 57.52, 1977- 62.54, 1978- 65.96, 1979- 64.88, 1980- 66.38, 1981- 67.48, 1982- 68.60, 1983- 70.72, 1984- 70.26, 1985- 71.26, 1986- 67.18. pb SP: 15.19 '82.
World and European discus champion who competes often and throws consistently well. He was a handball prospect at school, but learned to throw the discus in a few weeks at the age of 17 in 1972.

**Jan CADO** b.7 May 1963 Trstena 1.82m 75kg. Club: Slavia Praha IPS. Student.
At TJ: WCh: '83- 6; ECh: '86- 14; EI: '83- 4, '84- 4, '85- 2; ECp: '85- 4. CS champion 1986.
CS triple jump record 1984.
Progression at TJ: 1979- 14.14, 1980- 14.85, 1981- 15.40, 1982- 16.31/16.66w, 1983- 17.06, 1984- 17.34, 1985- 17.23i/17.03, 1986- 17.04. pbs: 100m: 10.60 '84, LJ: 8.09 '84.

**Jan LEITNER** b.14 Sep 1953 Znojmo 1.86m 87kg. Club: Dukla Praha. Civil servant.
At LJ: OG: '80- dnq; WCh: '83- 10; ECh: '78- 11, '82- 3; EI: '84- 1, '86- 3; ECp: '85- 2; WIG: '85- 1. CS champion 1975, 1977-82, 1984-5.
Four CS long jump records 1977-82.
Progression at LJ: 1970- 6.22, 1971- 6.45, 1972- 7.13, 1973- 7.25, 1974- 7.61, 1975- 7.74/7.88w, 1976- 7.76/7.90w, 1977- 7.95/8.04w, 1978- 8.03, 1979- 7.78/7.86w, 1980- 7.95, 1981- 8.07, 1982- 8.10, 1983- 7.94/7.96w, 1984- 8.10, 1985- 8.03/8.17i, 1986- 8.04/8.15w/8.17i. pbs: 100m: 10.75 '85, TJ: 16.21 '82.

**Zdenek LUBENSKY** b.3 Dec 1962 Kutna Hora 1.85m 75kg. Club: VS Praha. Student.
At PV: ECh: '86- 6; ECp: '85- 4. CS champion 1985-6. Two CS pole vault records 1985-6.
Progression at PV: 1980- 4.30, 1981- 4.90, 1982- 5.05, 1983- 5.20, 1984- 5.30, 1985- 5.66, 1986- 5.72.

**Jozef PRIBILINEC** b.6 Jul 1960 Kremnica 1.68m 66kg. Club: Dukla B.Bystrica. Soldier.
At 20kmW: OG: '80- 20; WCh: '83- 2; ECh: '82- 2, '86- 1; LT: '83- 1, '85- dq; EJ: '79- 1 at 10kmW. CS 20kmW champion 1979, 1982-5.
World track bests: 3kmW: 11:00.2 '85, 5kmW: 18:51.2 '81, 10kmW: 38:02.60 '85, 15kmW: 58:22.4 '86, 1 hour: 15447m '86. World junior records: 3kmW: 11:13.2, 10kmW: 40:55.4 in 1979. World road best for 20kmW in 1983.
Progression at 20kmW: 1978- 1:33:07, 1979- 1:22:44, 1980- 1:21:39.2l, 1981- 1:21:56, 1982-

1:22:27, 1983- 1:19:30, 1984- 1:25:07, 1985- 1:20:40, 1986- 1:21:15. pb 50kmW: 4:16:41 '84.
Disqualified after finishing first in the 1985 Lugano Cup race.

**Pavol SZIKORA** b.26 Mar 1952 Lucenec 1.76m 65kg. Club: Dukla Banska Bystrica. Technician.
At 50kmW: WCh: '83- 11; ECh: '86- 8. CS champion 1983, 1985-6.
Progression at 50kmW: 1980- 4:01:03, 1981- 4:19:46, 1982- 4:02:42, 1983- 3:56:14, 1984- 3:45:53, 1985- 3:54:58, 1986- 3:49:00. pb 20kmW: 1:24:29 '81.

**Gejza VALENT** b.3 Oct 1953 Praha 1.96m 120kg. Club: Vitkovice. Technician.
At DT: WCh: '83- 3; ECh: '82- 6, '86- 5. 3rd GP 1985.
Progression at DT: 1970- 44.76, 1971- 46.38, 1972- 49.44, 1973- 49.94, 1974- 54.00, 1975- 54.96, 1976- 56.64, 1977- 56.10, 1978- 53.04, 1979- 55.56, 1980- 58.64, 1981- 65.42, 1982- 67.56, 1983- 67.26, 1984- 69.70, 1985- 68.40, 1986- 65.58. pb SP: 15.98 '81.
Leapt into world class in the 1980s after a decade of little progress. His father, Gejza, had a personal best discus mark of 53.84m in 1956, which ranked him 16th in the world.

**Jan ZVARA** b.12 Feb 1963 Banska Bystrica 1.90m 85kg. Club: Sparta Praha. Mechanic.
At HJ: ECh: '86- 9=; ECp: '85- 1. CS champion 1985-6. Six CS high jump records 1985.
Progression at HJ: 1979- 1.85, 1980- 1.95, 1981- 2.01, 1983- 2.12, 1984- 2.20, 1985- 2.35, 1986- 2.34. pb TJ: 14.90/15.02w '82.

# Women

**Helena FIBINGEROVA** b.13 Jul 1949 Vicemerice 1.79m 99kg. Club: Vitkovice. Married (1977) Jaroslav Smid (18.82m shot in 1970).
At SP: OG: '72- 7, '76- 3; WCh: '83- 1; ECh: '69- 10, '71- 12, '74- 3, '78- 2, '82- 2, '86- 10; EI: 1st '73-4, '77-8, '80, '83-5, 2nd '75, '81-2. WCp: '77- 2, '79- 2, '81- 2, '85- 3; ECp: '83- 1, '85- 2. CS champion 1970-9, 1981-5. Won GP 1985.
World records: 21.99m in 1976 and 22.32m in 1977, as well four world indoor bests, headed by 22.50m in 1977. 21 CS records 1970-77.
Progression at SP: 1966- 13.61, 1967- 14.60, 1968- 15.29, 1969- 16.01, 1970- 16.77, 1971- 16.57, 1972- 19.18, 1973- 20.80, 1974- 21.57, 1975- 21.43, 1976- 21.99, 1977- 22.32/22.50i, 1978- 21.87, 1979- 21.18, 1980- 21.53, 1981- 21.57, 1982- 21.55, 1983- 21.46, 1984- 21.60, 1985- 21.47i/21.03, 1986- 20.80. pb DT: 50.28 '73.

She scored an emotional triumph in Helsinki in 1983, for it was her first win outdoors in a long major championships career. In 1986 she competed in a record sixth European Championships. Indoors she holds the record for the most European titles.

**Tatana KOCEMBOVA** b.2 May 1962 Ostrava-Vitkovice 1.69m 55kg. Club: Vitkovice. Clerk.
At 400m (R- 4x400m relay): WCh: '83- 2 (2R); ECh: '82- 3 (2R), '86- 6; EI: '84- 1; EJ: '79- 8; ECp: '83- 1 (1R, 4 at 100m). CS champion at 100m 1985; 200m 1983-4, 1986; 400m 1981.
Progression at 200m/400m: 1977- 26.2/60.4, 1978- 25.64/59.0, 1979- 25.12/54.02, 1980- 55.99, 1981- 23.95/52.41, 1982- 23.10/50.41, 1983- 22.50/48.59, 1984- 22.47/48.73, 1985- 22.65/50.74, 1986- 22.92/49.83. pbs: 100m: 11.31 '83, 500m: 65.9 '84.
In 1984 ran a 47.84 relay last leg and had her first success over Kratochvilova at 400m, beating her three times.

**Eva MURKOVA** b.29 May 1962 Bojnica 1.68m 56kg. Club: Slavia PF B.Bystrica. Student.
At LJ: WCh: '83- 7; ECh: '82- dnq, '86- 14; EI: '83- 1, '84- 2, '85- 2; ECp: '83- 2, ECp: '85- 6. CS champion 100m 1983, 1986; LJ 1983 and 1985-6. Three CS long jump records 1983-4.
Progression at LJ: 1977- 5.14, 1978- 5.13, 1979- 5.76, 1980- 6.10, 1981- 6.42, 1982- 6.74, 1983- 6.92, 1984- 7.17w/7.01, 1985- 6.76/6.99i, 1986- 6.93. pbs: 100m: 11.38 '86, 200m: 24.21 '83.

**Milena STRNADOVA** b.23 May 1961 Usti n.Labem 1.61m 53kg. née Matejkovicova. Club: VS Praha. Student.
At 800m (R- 4x400m relay): WCh: '83- 7 (2R); ECh: '82- 2R, '86- 5; EI: '84- 1. 3rd GP 1985. At 1500m: ECp: '85- 5.
Progression at 800m: 1981- 2:07.17, 1982- 2:05.14, 1983- 1:57.28, 1984- 1:59.43i, 1985- 1:58.42, 1986- 1:57.90. pb 400m: 51.88 '83, 1000m: 2:39.5 '85, 1500m: 4:07.35 '85.

**Ivana WALTEROVA** b.26 May 1962 Sumperk 1.74m 61kg. née Kleinova. Club: VS Praha.
At 1500m: WCh: '83- 11; ECh: '86- 4; EI: '83- 3, '84- 3. At 3000m: WCh: '83- h; ECp: '83- 4. CS champion 1500m 1984, 1986; 3000m 1983.
CS records 1500m (2) 1984-6, 1M 1986, 3000m (2) 1983.
Progression at 1500m: 1977- 4:44.2, 1978- 4:30.03, 1979- 4:24.4, 1980- 4:26.8, 1981- 4:26.10, 1982- 4:15.13, 1983- 4:10.82, 1984- 4:05.52, 1985- 4:14.80i, 1986- 4:01.84. pbs: 800m: 2:01.12 '86, 1000m: 2:42.89i '86, 1M: 4:22.82 '86, 3000m: 8:55.54 '83.

Tatana Kocembova. *ASP*

# DENMARK

**Governing body**: Dansk Athletik Forbund, Idraettens Hus, Brondby Stadion 20, DK-2605 Brondby.
**National Championships** first held in 1894
1986 Champions: MEN
100m: Morten Kjems 10.48w, 200m: Lars Pedersen 21.57, 400m: Jesper Carlsen 47.67, 800m: Mogens Guldberg 1:49.01, 1500m: Niels Kim Hjorth 3:45.6, 5000m/3000mSt: Allan Zachariasen 13:53.10/8:49.18, 10000m: Keld Johnsen 28:59.9, Mar: Svend Erik Kristensen 2:15:04, 110mh: Erik S.Jensen 14.17w, 400mh: Martin Lauersen 53.44, HJ: Rene T.Nielsen 2.10, PV: Martin Lind 5.00, LJ/Dec: Lars Warming 7.33w/ 7734, TJ: Rene Dålfogt 14.49, SP: Michael Henningsen 16.28, DT: Kjeld Andresen 49.03, HT: Peter Christensen 59.87, JT: Kenneth Pedersen 74.26, 20kmW: Stan Barbuzynski 1:43:45, 50kmW: Mogens Christensen 4:52:26.
WOMEN
100m/LJ: Lene Demsitz 11.44w/6.42w, 200m/ 400m: Betina Wilhjelm 24.1/55.84, 800m/1500m: Tina Krebs 2:06.38/4:17.59, 3000m: Dorthe Rasmussen 9:18.23, 10000m: Kersti Jakobsen 33:50.47, Mar: Joan Carstensen 2:48:31, 100mh: Dorthe Wolfsberg 13.75w, 400mh: Helle Vinkler 60.10, HJ: Birgitte Kristensen 1.71, SP: Birthe Kofoed 12.89, DT: Liselotte Hansen 47.01, JT: Simone Frandsen 54.85, Hep: Lisbeth Larsen 4941 5kmW/10kmW: Gunhild Kristiansen 24:52/ 49:05.

# DJIBOUTI

**Governing body**: Fédération Djiboutienne d'Athlétisme, BP 16, Djibouti.

**Djama ROBLEH Djama** b.1958 Ali Sabieh 1.69m 52kg. Army sub-officer.
At Mar: OG: '84- 8; WCh: '83- 47, WCp: '85- 3; AfCh: '82- 2. Second Chicago marathon 1985 in African record.
Progression at Mar: 1982- 2:31:06, 1983- 2:16:49, 1984- 2:11:25, 1985- 2:08:08, 1986- 2:14:25. pbs: 3000m: 8:16.30 '84, 5000m: 13:53.8 '83, 10km: 29:07.73 '84.
Has won two of his eight marathons.

**Ahmed SALAH Houssain** b.1956 Ali Sabieh 1.82m 60kg. Army sub-officer.
At Mar: OG: '84- 20; WCh: '83- dnf; WCp: '85- 1; AfCh: '85- 1. At 10km: AfCh: '82- 6, '84- 2. Won Paris marathon 1984, 1986. 2nd New York 1985, Chicago 1986. African marathon record to win World Cup marathon 1985.

Progression at Mar: 1983- 2:17:29, 1984- 2:11:58, 1985- 2:08:09, 1986- 2:09:57. pbs: 3000m: 8:08.62 '84, 5000m: 13:51.5 '85, 10km: 28:17.40 '84.
Has won four of his 12 marathons.

# ETHIOPIA

**Governing body**: National Ethiopian Athletic Federation, Addis Ababa Stadium, PO Box 3241, Addis Ababa.

**Kebede BALCHA** b.7 Sep 1951 1.67m 52kg. Soldier.
At Mar: WCh: '83- 2; OG: '80- dnf; WCp: '85- 11; AfCh: '82- dnf, '85- 2.
Progression at Mar: 1977- 2:14:41, 1979- 2:11:35, 1981- 2:11:11, 1983- 2:10:04, 1984- 2:11:40, 1985- 2:11:19, 1986- 2:14:11. pb 10000m: 30:30.7 '82.
Of his 23 marathons, has won five: Athens 1977, Montreal 1979, 1981, 1983, 1985.

**Wodajo BULTI** b.11 Mar 1957 Gione 1.85m 60kg. Soldier.
At 5000m: WCh: '83- 7; WCp: '85- 3 (1 at 10000m); AfCh: '82- 1 (3 at 1500m), '85- 1 (1 at 10000m). World CC: '85- 3.
Progression at 5000m/10000m: 1981- 13:40.20, 1982- 13:07.29, 1983- 13:22.32, 1984- 13:10.08/ 27:58.24, 1985- 13:31.02/28:22.43, 1986- 28:33.90. pbs: 1500m: 3:40.08 '82, 3000m: 7:40.64 '83.

**Bekele DEBELE** b.12 Mar 1963 1.70m 55kg. Soldier.
At 10000m: WCh: '83- 10. World CC: '83-1, '84- 8, 85- 4, '86- 4. pbs: 3000m: 8:11.4 '84, 5000m: 13:33.74 '84, 10000m: 27:49.30 '83.

**Belaine DINSAMO** b.28 Jun 1957. Policeman.
Progression at Mar: 1985- 2:28:26, 1986- 2:08:29.
Second in 1986 Tokyo and Rotherham marathons, and won at the Goodwill Games.

**Abebe MEKONNEN** b.1964. Army.
At Mar: WCp: '85-5; AfCh: '85- 5. World CC: '86- 2.
Progression at Mar: 1984- 2:11:30, 1985- 2:09:05, 1986- 2:08:39.
Has won three of his 13 marathons, all in 1986: Rotterdam, Addis Abada, Montreal.

**Dereje NEDI** b.10 Oct 1955 1.75m 55kg. Soldier.
At Mar: OG: '80- 7; WCh: '83- dnf; WCp: '85- 16; AfG: '78- 2; AfCh: '79- dnf, '82- dnf, '85- 3.
Ethiopian marathon records in 1983 and 1984.

Progression at Mar: 1976- 2:17:07, 1977-
2:14:49, 1978- 2:23:08, 1979- 2:22:13, 1980-
2:12:44, 1981- 2:12:14, 1982- 2:13:25, 1983-
2:10:39, 1984- 2:10:32, 1985- 2:12:22, 1986-
2:16:20.
Won Frankfurt and Moscow marathons in 1984,
Abebe Bikila marathon 1984-5.

# FINLAND

**Governing body**: Suomen Urheiluliitto, Radio-
katu, SF-00240 Helsinki. Founded 1906.
**National Championships** first held in 1907
(men), 1913 (women)
**1986 Champions: MEN**
100m/200m: Kimmo Saaristo 10.76/21.29, 400m:
Jari Niemelä 46.98, 800m/1500m: Ari Suhonen
1:50.12/3:46.87, 5000m/3000mSt: Tommy
Ekblom 13:37.70/8:28.12, 10000m: Martti Vainio
28:25.38, Mar: Jouni Kortelainen 2:14:29,
110mh: Arto Bryggare 13.73, 400mh: Jari Rauta-
palo 51.35, HJ: Timo Ruuskanen 2.18, PV:
Kimmo Kuusela 5.35, LJ: Petri Keskitalo 7.70, TJ:
Harri Pesonen 15.97, SP: Jari Kuoppa 19.36, DT:
Raimo Vento 60.08, HT: Harri Huhtala 77.68, JT:
Seppo Räty 80.02, Dec: Henrik Broman 7491,
20kmW/50kmW: Reima Salonen 1:21:51/
3:42:36.
**WOMEN**
100m/200m: Sisko Markkanen 11.83/24.12,
400m: Sonja Finell 54.91, 800m: Kaisa Ylimäki
2:03.63, 1500m: Marjo-Riitta Lakka 4:26.94,
3000m: Päivi Tikkanen 9:10.96, 10000m: Sinikka
Keskitalo 33:51.78, Mar: Sirkku Kumpulainen
2:36:05, 100mh: Saila Purho 13.96, 400mh: Tuija
Helander 56.77, HJ: Minna Rantanen 1.81, LJ:
Ringa Ropo 6.18, SP: Asta Hovi 17.74, DT: Anne
Känsäkangas 56.38, JT: Tiina Lillak 64.42, Hep:
Ragne Backman 5686, 5kmW: Mirva Hämäläinen
22:38.79, 10kmW Rd: Sirkka Oikarinen 46:46.

**Jyrki BLOM** b.11 May 1962 Vehkalähti 1.83m
83kg. Club: Vehkalahden Veikot. Student.
At JT: ECh: '86- 4.
Progression at JT: 1979- 62.76, 1980- 70.84,
1981- 74.80, 1982- 76.86, 1983- 79.40, 1984-
83.94, 1985- 85.30, new: 1986- 80.48.

**Arto BRYGGARE** b.26 May 1958 Kouvola 1.94m
82kg. Club: Lappeenrannan Urheilu-Miehet.
Economics student.
At 110mh: OG: '80- 6, '84- 3; WCh: '83- 2; ECh:
'78- 3, '82- 3, '86- 2; EJ: '75- 7, '77- 1; ECp: '77- 4.
At 50mh/60mh: EI: '77- 3, '79- 2, '81- 1, '83- 2.
Finnish 110mh champion 1977-86.
11 Finnish 110mh records 1976-84. European
junior 110mh record in 1977 and world indoor
best of 13.58 in 1983.

Progression at 110mh: 1975- 14.46, 1976- 14.04,
1977- 13.66/13.55w, 1978- 13.56, 1979- 13.81,
1980- 13.76, 1981- 13.77, 1982- 13.57, 1983-
13.44, 1984- 13.35, 1985- 13.63/13.61w, 1986-
13.42. pbs: 100m: 10.5/10.60 '77, 200m: 21.3 '77,
200mh: 23.1 '78.
Very consistent hurdler in the major events. He
won his tenth successive Finnish 110mh title in
1986.

**Tommy EKBLOM** b.20 Sep 1959 Porvoo 1.78m
67kg. Club: Porvoon Urheilijat. Sports instructor.
At 3kmSt: OG: '80- 12, '84- 9; WCh: '83- 12; ECh:
'82- 8, '86- 10; WSG: '81- 2. Finnish champion at
3kmSt 1979, 1981-2, 1984, 1986; 5000m 1983,
1986.
Progression at 3kmSt: 1976- 9:29.4, 1977-
9:11.8, 1978- 8:39.8, 1979- 8:37.31, 1980-
8:20.20, 1981- 8:21.93, 1982- 8:21.4, 1983-
8:19.40, 1984- 8:20.54, 1985- 8:30.26, 1986-
8:24.05. pbs: 1500m: 3:44.87 '81, 3000m:
7:49.59 '83, 5000m: 13:29.23 '85, 10000m:
28:30.14 '81.

**Harri HUHTALA** b.13 Aug 1952 Paattinen 1.87m
108kg. Club: Tampereen Pyrintö. Policeman
At HT: OG: '80- 9, '84- 6; WCh: '83- 10; ECh: '78-
11, '82- 5, '86- 10; ECp: '75- 5. Finnish champion
1975-6, 1980, 1982-3, 1985-6.
Six Finnish hammer records 1978-83.
Progression at HT: 1968- 44.98, 1969- 49.22,
1970- 55.92, 1971- 59.12, 1972- 60.30, 1973-
66.04, 1974- 69.10, 1975- 71.04, 1976- 71.40,
1977- 72.68, 1978- 73.66, 1979- 74.22, 1980-
75.94, 1981- 76.76, 1982- 77.02, 1983- 78.68,
1984- 78.74, 1985- 76.74, 1986- 78.38.

**Seppo RÄTY** b.27 Apr 1962 Helsinki 1.88m
98kg. Club: Tohmajärven Urheilijat. Railwayman.
At JT: ECh: '86- 17. Finnish champion 1985-6.
Finnish best with new javelin 1986.
Progression at JT: 1979- 63.20, 1980- 71.14,
1981- 75.44, 1982- 72.74, 1983- 74.38, 1984-
82.60, 1985- 85.72, new: 1986- 81.72.

**Reima SALONEN** b.19 Nov 1955 Taivassalo
1.77m 70kg. Club: Turun Weikot. Fireman.
At 50kmW (20kmW): OG: '80- dnf (9), '84- 4;
WCh: '76- 3, '83- 4 (12); ECh: '82- 1 (8), '86- 5
(dq). EJ: '73- 13 at 10kmW. Finnish champion
20kmW: 1973-83, 1985-6; 50kmW 1974-5, 1977-
9, 1981-2, 1986-6.
World road best 20km walk 1979. World indoor
bests: 1500mW 5:28.7 '77, 3kmW: 11:05.1 '77,
5kmW: 19:44.8 and 19:35.8 '78, 10kmW: 39:58.0
'89.
Progression at 20kmW/50kmW: 1974- 1:29:34t/
4:35:48, 1975- 1:29:36/4:37:47, 1976- 1:27:32/
3:58:53, 1977- 1:27:19/4:12:28, 1978- 1:24:51/

3:51:38, 1979- 1:21:01/3:49:52, 1980- 1:19:35 short, 1981- 4:03:23, 1982- 1:25:56/3:49:47, 1983- 1:22:26/3:52:53, 1984- 1:23:04/3:48:36, 1985- 1:23:06/3:47:40, 1986- 1:19:52/3:42:36. Track pbs: 3kmW: 10:56.88i '84, 5kmW: 19:14.8 '80, 10kmW: 39:58.0i '80.
Undefeated by a Finnish walker since 1973; disqualified only twice in career.

**Juha TIAINEN** b.5 Dec 1955 Uukuniemi 1.82m 107kg. Club: Lappeenrannan Urheilu-Miehet. Policeman.
At HT: OG: '80- 10, '84- 1; WCh: '83- 9; ECh: '82-12, '86- 18; ECp: '77- 6. Finnish hammer champion 1977, 1979, 1981, 1984.
Eight Finnish records 1976-84.
Progression at HT: 1972- 40.94, 1973- 49.62, 1974- 51.64, 1975- 65.12, 1976- 71.80, 1977-72.62, 1978- 71.08, 1979- 74.42, 1980- 75.88, 1981- 76.64, 1982- 78.34, 1983- 81.02, 1984-81.52, 1985- 78.10, 1986- 79.32. pb SP: 15.14 '76.
Finland's first ever Olympic champion at the hammer.

Juha Tiainen. *ASP*

**Martti VAINIO** b.30 Dec 1950 Vehkalahti 1.90m 74kg. Club: Lapuan Virkiä. Businessman.
At 10000m (5000m): OG: '76- h, '80- 13 (11), '84-dq; WCh: '83- 4 (3); ECh: '78- 1 (6), '82- 3 (8), '86-7 (6); WCp: '81- 5; ECp: '77- 4. Finnish champion: 5000m 1978, 1980-2, 1984; 10000m 1977-8, 1980-4, 1986.
Finnish 10000m record 1978.
Progression at 5000m/10000m: 1973- 14:55.6, 1974- 13:55.6/29:09.6, 1975- 13:47.4/29:00.0, 1976- 13:35.26 / 28:07.43, 1977- 13:40.6 / 28:07.23, 1978- 13:28.03 / 27:30.99, 1979-13:21.85 / 28:04.24, 1980- 13:29.54 / 28:00.64, 1981- 13:28.79 / 27:45.50, 1982- 13:24.89 / 27:42.51, 1983- 13:20.07 / 28:01.37, 1984-13:16.02 / 27:41.75*, 1986- 13:22.67 / 27:44.57.
At Mar: 1974- 2:33:46, 1979- 2:24:51, 1984-2:13:05, 1986- 2:16:44. pbs: 1500m: 3:41.09 '83, 2000m: 5:17.5 '80, 3000m: 7:44.42 '84, 3000mSt: 8:55.0 '75
Did not start athletics until 21 years old. Failed drugs test (*) after finishing second in the 1984 Olympic 10000m; reinstated to compete in 1986. Has said that he intends to concentrate on the marathon in future.

# Women

**Tuija HELANDER** b.23 May 1961 Eura 1.72m 63kg. Club: Euran Raiku. Economics student.
At 400mh: OG: '84- 7; WCh: '83- ht; ECh: '86- sf. Finnish champion 400mh 1977, 1980, 1982-6 and 400m 1985.
Eight Finnish 400mh records 1980-5.
Progression at 400mh: 1977- 60.29, 1978- 59.78, 1979- 59.81, 1980- 57.84, 1981- 60.11, 1982-59.17, 1983- 58.81, 1984- 56.55, 1985- 55.21, 1986- 56.17. pbs: 100m: 12.10/11.96w '85, 200m: 24.57 '86, 400m: 52.32 '85, 800m: 2:11.8 '80, 100mh: 13.87 '84, HJ: 1.65 '78, LJ: 5.69 '77, Pen: 3729* '78.

**Sinikka KESKITALO** b.29 Jan 1951 Jalasjärvi 1.53m 46kg. née Leppälä. Club: Tampereen Urheilijat. Dressmaker.
At Mar: OG: '84- 15; ECh: '86- 4; ECp: '85- 5. Finnish champion Mar 1983 & 1985, 10000m 1986.
Progression at Mar: 1982- 2:42:11, 1983-2:37:07, 1984- 2:35:15, 1985- 2:33:53, 1986-2:33:18. pbs: 1500m: 4:37.4 '83, 3000m: 9:20.47 '84, 5000m: 16:12.27 '84, 10000m: 33:01.27 '84.
Did not start running until 1981 at the age of 30.

**Tuula LAAKSALO** b.21 Apr 1953 Rovaniemi 1.70m 70kg. née Hyytiäinen. Club: Virtain Urheilijat. Bank officer.
At JT: OG: '84- 4; WCh: '83- 6; ECh: '82- 12, '86- 15. Finnish champion 1982 and 1984.
Progression at JT: 1969- 43.80, 1971- 48.52, 1972- 51.84, 1978- 49.26, 1979- 54.12, 1980- 56.34, 1981- 63.82, 1982- 64.48, 1983- 67.40, 1984- 67.38, 1985- 63.36, 1986- 63.68.

**Tiina LILLAK** b.15 Apr 1961 Helsinki 1.81m 74kg. Club: Esbo IF. Student.
At JT: OG: '80- dnq, '84- 2; WCh: '83- 1; ECh: '82- 4, '86- 4; EJ: '79- 14. Finnish champion 1980-1, 1983, 1985-6.
Eleven Finnish records 1980-3, including two world records 1982-3, the first ever set by a Finnish woman thrower.
Progression at JT: 1976- 44.94, 1977- 47.92, 1978- 51.60, 1979- 56.36, 1980- 61.02 , 1981- 66.34, 1982- 72.40, 1983- 74.76, 1984- 74.24, 1985- 70.62, 1986- 72.42. pb SP: 14.31 '83.
Full name Ilse Kristiina Lillak. Her win on the final throw in Helsinki in 1983, and the attendant roar of the crowd will long be remembered as one of the great moments in athletics history. In 1984 she was held back by a broken bone in her foot, but still managed to gain the Olympic silver medal.

# FRANCE

**Governing body**: Fédération Française d'Athlétisme, 10 rue du Faubourg Poissonnière, 75480 Paris Cedex 10. Founded 1920.
**National Championships** first held in 1888 (men), 1918 (women)
**1986 Champions: MEN**
100m: Antoine Richard 10.09, 200m: Bruno Marie-Rose 20.69, 400m: Yann Quentrec 45.83, 800m: Claude Diomar 1:46.65, 1500m: Pascal Thiébaut 3:39.18, 5000m: Paul Arpin 13:51.14, 10000m: Jean-Louis Prianon 28:35.85, Mar: Alain Lazare 2:14:14, 3kmSt: Pascal Debacker 8:29.03, 110mh: Stéphane Caristan 13.46, 400mh: Philippe Gonigam 49.82, HJ: Franck Verzy 2.24, PV: Thierry Vigneron 5.70, LJ: Norbert Brige 8.08, TJ: Serge Helan 16.93, SP: Luc Viudes 18.08, DT: Frederic Selle 59.76, HT: Walter Ciofani 74.12, JT: Michel Bertimon 79.24, Dec: Alain Blondel 8118, 20kmW: Martial Fesselier 1:27:07, 50kmW: Eric Neisse 4:14:52.
**WOMEN**
100m: Laurence Bily 11.33, 200m: Marie-Christine Cazier 22.95, 400m: Nathalie Simon 52.35, 800m: Natalie Thoumas 2:03.87, 1500m: Nathalie Froget 4:10.81, 3000m: Francoise Bonnet 9:10.88, 10000m: Jocelyne Villeton

33:11.69, Mar: Françoise Bonnet 2:32:32, 100mh: Laurence Elloy 12.94, 400mh: Chantal Beaugeant 57.23, HJ: Brigitte Rougeron 1.84, LJ: Nadine Fourcade 6.73, SP: Simone Creantor 16.56, DT: Isabelle Devaluez 54.84, JT: Evelyne Giardino 54.16, Hep: Liliane Menissier 6165, 5kmW/10kmW: Suzanne Griesbach 23:31.0/ 49:13.51.

**Stéphane CARISTAN** b.31 May 1964 Créteil 1.87m 75kg. Club: AC Paris. Student.
At 110mh: OG: '84- 6; WCh: '83- h; ECh: '86- 1. French champion 1983-6. At 60mh: WIG: '85- 1.
Two European 110mh records 1986.
Progression at 110mh: 1981- 14.95, 1982- 14.35, 1983- 13.86, 1984- 13.43, 1985- 13.47/13.4, 1986- 13.20/13.0. pbs: 100m: 10.51 '84, PV: 5.00 '83, LJ: 7.79i '84, JT: 62.38 '83.

**Philippe COLLET** b.13 Dec 1963 Nancy 1.76m 70kg. Club: ASPTT Grenoble.
At PV: ECh: '86- 3; EI: '86- 3; WCp: '85- 2; EJ: '81- 11; ECp: '85- 2; WSG: '85- 2. French champion 1985.
Progression at PV: 1978- 3.30, 1980- 4.90, 1981- 5.10, 1982- 5.20, 1983- 5.60, 1984- 5.60, 1985- 5.80, 1986- 5.85. pbs: 100m: 10.81 '85, Dec: 7011 '86.

**Joseph MAHMOUD** b.13 Dec 1955 Safi, Morocco 1.74m 65kg. Club: CMS Marignane. Sports monitor.
At 3kmSt: OG: '84- 2; WCh: '83- 4; ECh: '82- h, '86- 6; WCp: '85- 6; ECp: '81- 6, '83- 3. French champion 1980-5.
Five French steeplechase records 1982-4, including European record in 1984.
Progression at 3kmSt: 1975- 9:00.0, 1976- 8:43.4, 1977- 8:43.5, 1978- 8:40.3, 1979- 8:32.88, 1980- 8:30.78, 1981- 8:24.75, 1982- 8:20.54, 1983- 8:15.59, 1984- 8:07.62, 1985- 8:11.07, 1986- 8:20.25. pbs: 1500m: 3:38.39 '84, 3000m: 7:45.26 '85, 5000m: 13:48.19 '84.

**Bruno MARIE-ROSE** b.20 May 1965 Bordeaux 1.93m 83kg. Club: CA Ouest (St Germain). Student.
At 100m (R- 4x100m relay): OG: '84- qf (6R); ECh: '86- 3 (sf 200m/4R); EJ: '83- dnf. At 60m: EI: '85- 3. French champion: 100m 1984, 200m 1986.
Progression at 100m/200m: 1981- 10.78, 1982- 10.88/22.01, 1983- 10.43/10.33w/21.65, 1984- 10.29/21.26, 1985- 10.38/20.94/20.8, 1986- 10.18/20.53.

**William MOTTI** b.25 Jul 1964 Bondy 1.99m 92kg. Club: Racing Club de France. Was at Mt. St Mary's College, USA.

Stéphane Caristan. *Mark Shearman*

At Dec: OG: '84- 5; ECH: '86- dnf; EJ: '81- 2 at HJ, '83- dnf Dec. French champion 1985.
Two French decathlon records 1984-5. US collegiate record 1984.
Progression at Dec: 1982- 7739, 1983- 7315, 1984- 8278, 1985- 8306, 1986- 8006. pbs: 100m: 11.03/10.96w '85, 400m: 48.01 '84, 1500m: 4:35.15 '84, 110mh: 14.67/14.5 '84, HJ: 2.22i/2.20 '82, PV: 4.60 '84, LJ: 7.63 '85, SP: 15.11 '85, DT: 50.92 '84, JT: 70.38 '82.

**Pierre QUINON** b.20 Feb 1962 Lyon 1.80m 74kg. Club: Racing Club de France. Business student.
At PV: OG: '84- 1; WCh: '83- nh; ECh: '82- 12=; EI: '84- 2; EJ: '81- 2. French champion 1982-4. 2nd GP 1985.
World pole vault record at 5.82m in 1983.
Progression at PV: 1976- 3.40, 1977- 3.90, 1978- 4.50, 1979- 5.00, 1980- 5.10i, 1981- 5.50, 1982- 5.70, 1983- 5.82, 1984- 5.80, 1985- 5.90, 1986- 5.72i/5.70.

**Thierry VIGNERON** b.9 Mar 1960 Gennevilliers, Paris 1.81m 73kg. Racing Club de France. Physical education student.
At PV: OG: '80- 7, '84- 3=; WCh: '83- 8=; ECh: '82- 5=, '86- nh; EI: '81- 1, '84- 1; EJ: '77- 9, '79- 3; WSG: '81- 4, '83- 2; WIG: '85- 2. French champion 1980, 1986. 3rd GP 1985.
Five world pole vault records: 5.75m twice in 1980, 5.80m (world's first 19ft vault) in 1981, 5.83m in 1983 and 5.91m in 1984. Also three world indoor bests: 5.70m twice in 1981 and 5.85m in 1984, and four world junior records from 5.45m to 5.61m in 1979.
Progression at PV: 1974- 3.70, 1975- 4.20, 1976- 4.95i, 1977- 5.10, 1978- 5.30, 1979- 5.61, 1980- 5.75, 1981- 5.80, 1982- 5.71, 1983- 5.83, 1984- 5.91, 1985- 5.80, 1986- 5.90. pbs: LJ: 6.99 '78, TJ: 15.70i '86.
A prolific vaulter, who has set many records, but until recently did not have the championship results to match. His latest world record lasted just ten minutes for it came in his epic duel with Sergey Bubka in Rome in 1984.

# Women

**Marie-Christine CAZIER** b.23 Aug 1963 Paris 1.78m 59kg. Club: Stade Messin. Student.
At 200m (R- 4x100m relay): WCh: '83- qf; ECh: '82- 8 (3R), '86- 2 (4R); EI: '84- 2; EJ: '81- 5 (2R); WIG: '85- 2. French champion 100m 1985, 200m 1985-6.
Three French 200m records 1986.
Progression at 100m, 200m: 1978- 25.57; 1979- 24.96; 1980- 12.02, 24.97; 1981- 11.92, 23.76/23.53w; 1982- 11.47, 22.94; 1983- 11.34/11.1, 23.21; 1984- 11.70, 23.48i/23.4; 1985- 11.26/11.12w, 22.75/22.7, 1986- 11.23/11.1, 22.32. pbs: 400m: 54.18i '86, 55.5 '83; 400mh: 57.2/57.71 '85.

**Laurence ELLOY** b.3 Dec 1959 Rouen 1.69m 62kg. Previous married name Machabey. Club: Stade Français. Secretary.
At 100mh: OG: '80- sf, '84- h; WCh: '83- sf; ECh: '78- h, '82- sf, '86- 6; EJ: '77- 4. French champion 1979, 1982, 1984-6. At 60mh: WIG: '85- 2.
Four French 100mh records 1982-6.
Progression at 100mh: 1976- 14.9, 1977- 13.82, 1978- 13.47, 1979- 13.33, 1980- 13.13, 1981- 13.19, 1982- 12.90/12.81w, 1983- 12.95, 1984- 12.94/12.72w, 1985- 12.79/12.72w, 1986- 12.69. pb 100m: 11.94 '82, 11.93w/11.8 '76.

**Maryse EWANJE-EPÉE** b.4 Sep 1964 Poitiers 1.76m 62kg. Club: Montpellier UC. Student of literature and drama.
At HJ: OG: '84- 4; WCh: '83- 12=; ECh: '82- 10, '86- dnq; EI: '83- 3, '84- 2; WSG: '83- 3. French champion 1982-5. At Hep: EJ: '81- 6.
Four French high jump records 1983-5.
Progression at HJ: 1977- 1.52, 1978- 1.61, 1979- 1.69, 1980- 1.76, 1981- 1.87, 1982- 1.89, 1983- 1.95, 1984- 1.95i/1.94, 1985- 1.96, 1986- 1.94i/1.92. pbs: 100m: 12.1 '84; 200m: 24.85w '85; 100mh: 13.71 '85, 13.6 '84; LJ: 6.26 '85; Hep: 5867 '85.
Her younger sister Monique (b.11 Jul 1967) won the 1985 European Junior 100mh title in a European Junior record 13.10.

**Maria LELUT** b.Ilhavo, Portugal 29 Jan 1956 1.59m 47kg. née Rebello. Club: Viry-Chatillon.
At Mar: ECh: '86- 9.
French marathon best 1986.
Progression at Mar: 1981- 2:45:59, 1982- 2:45:16, 1983- 2:42:02, 1984- 2:38:58, 1985- 2:34:02, 1986- 2:29:51. pbs: 1500m: 4:18.83 '83, 3000m: 9:13.15 '85, 5000m: 16:15.9 '85, 10000m: 34:10.78 '85.
Won Paris, second Chicago marathons 1986. Her husband, Michel, has a marathon best of 2:14:58 '81.

**Anne PIQUEREAU** b.Poitiers 15 Jun 1964 1.72m 65kg. Club: Stade Clermont-Ferrand. Student.
At 100mh: ECh: '86- sf; EJ: '81- 3; WSG: '85- 3. At 60mh: EJ: '85- 3, '86- 2; WIG: '85- 3.
Progression at 100mh: 1981- 13.76/13.67w, 1982- 13.64/13.5w, 1983- 13.22/13.0, 1984- 13.39/13.30w, 1985- 12.89, 1986- 12.95. pbs: 100m: 11.9 '83, LJ: 6.40 '85.

**Annette SERGENT** b.Chambéry 17 Nov 1962 1.57m 46kg. Club: ASU Lyon. Student.
At 3000m: OG: '84- h; ECh: '86- 8 (8 at 1500m). French champion 1500m 1984-5, 3000m 1983-5. World CC: '86- 3. French records: 3000m (3) 1985-6, 2000m & 5000m 1986.
Progression at 3000m: 1979- 11:19.7, 1980- 10:14.7, 1981- 9:48.16, 1982- 9:19.76, 1983- 9:12.74, 1984- 9:02.05, 1985- 8:50.56, 1986- 8:46.94. pbs: 800m: 2:07.96 '85, 1000m: 2:41.5 '85, 1500m: 4:10.14 '85, 2000m: 5:39.00 '86, 5000m: 15:32.92 '86.

**Jocelyne VILLETON** b.Vals-les/Bains 17 Sep 1954 1.70m 55kg. Club: Saint-Etienne. Office worker.
At Mar: ECh: '86- 5. French champion 10000m 1986. French 10000m record 1986.
Progression at Mar: 1982- 3:00:46, 1983- 2:50:09, 1984- 2:47:09, 1985- 2:35:50, 1986- 2:32:22. pbs: 1500m: 4:28.2 '85, 3000m: 9:24.65 '85, 10000m: 32:59.67 '86.
Second Paris and fourth New York marathons 1986.

# GERMAN DEMOCRATIC REPUBLIC

**Governing body**: Deutscher Verband für Leichtathletik der DDR, 1005 Berlin, Storkower Strasse 118. Founded 1950.
**National Championships** first held in 1950.
**1986 Champions: MEN**
100m/200m: Thomas Schröder 10.10/20.57, 400m: Mathias Schersing 45.19, 800m: Hans-Joachim Mogalle 1:46.56, 1500m: Andreas Busse 3:36.97, 5000m/10000m: Hansjörg Kunze 13:31.05/27:34.68, Mar: Uwe Koch 2:17:04, 3kmSt: Hagen Melzer 8:19.48, 110mh: Holger Pohland 13.56, 400mh: Ingo Krüger 50.46, HJ: Gerd Wessig 2.30, PV: Uwe Langhammer 5.50, LJ: Ron Beer 8.13w, TJ: Dirk Gamlin 17.11w, SP: Udo Beyer 22.14, DT: Jürgen Schult 64.84, HT: Gunther Rodehau 80.16, JT: Detlef Michel 82.84, 20kmW/50kmW: Hartwig Gauder 1:25:55/3:43:52, Dec: Uwe Freimuth 8248.

## WOMEN

100m: Silke Gladisch 10.96, 200m/LJ: Heike Drechsler 21.71/7.35w, 400m: Petra Müller 50.67, 800m: Sigrun Wodars 1:57.05, 1500m/3000m Ines Bibernell 4:07.64/8:49.80, 10000m: Ulrike Bruns 32:13.41, Mar: Uta Pippig 2:37:56, 100mh: Cornelia Oschkenat 12.56, 400mh: Sabine Busch 53.85, HJ: Andreas Bienias 1.97, SP: Ines Müller 20.72, DT: Martina Hellmann 71.02, JT: Petra Felke 67.76, Hep: Anke Behmer 6444, 10kmW: Ines Estedt 50:08.

**Udo BEYER** b.9 Aug 1955 Eisenhüttenstadt 1.94m 135kg. Club: ASK Vorwärts Potsdam. Sports student.
At SP: OG: '76- 1, '80- 3; WCh: '83- 6; ECh: '74- 8, '78- 1, '82- 1, '86- 3; EJ: '73- 1; WSG: '79- 1; WCp and ECp: '77- 1, '79- 1, '81- 1, ECp: '85- 3; WIG: '85- 2. GDR champion 1977-86.
Six GDR shot records, the last three also world records in 1978, 1983, and 1986; five European junior records 1973-4.
Progression at SP: 1971- 15.71, 1972- 17.08, 1973- 19.65, 1974- 20.20, 1975- 20.97, 1976- 21.12, 1977- 21.74, 1978- 22.15, 1979- 21.74, 1980- 21.98, 1981- 21.69, 1982- 21.94, 1983- 22.22, 1984- 22.04, 1985- 21.88, 1986- 22.64. pbs: DT: 56.42 '74, HT: 66.84 '73.
Ranked as the world's number one shot putter seven times 1977-82 and 1984 after winning the 1976 Olympic title at the age of 20, losing only a handful of times in the past decade. A pulled back muscle cost him the chance of winning the 1980 Olympic title.

**Steffen BRINGMANN** b.11 Mar 1964 Leipzig 1.83m 78kg. Club: SC DHfK Leipzig. Sports student.
At 100m (R- 4x100m relay): ECh: '86- 2 (2R); EJ: '81- sf (1R); WCp: '85- 4R; ECp: '85- 2R. At 60m: '86- 2.
European indoor best 6.54 for 60m and world indoor best 9.50 for 100y 1986.
Progression at 100m: 1976- 13.0, 1977- 12.5, 1978- 11.63, 1979- 11.52, 1980- 10.86/10.7, 1981- 10.60, 1982- 10.83, 1983- 10.27/10.25w, 1984- 10.43/10.30w, 1985- 10.22/10.17w, 1986- 10.13. pb 200m: 20.80 '83.

**Andreas BUSSE** b.6 May 1959 Dresden 1.85m 69kg. Club: SC Einheit Dresden. Student. Engineer.
At 1500m: OG: '80- 4; WCh: '83- 7; ECh: '82- 11, '86- h; ECp: '83- 2. At 800m: OG: '80- 5; ECh: '78- 6; EJ: '75- 4, '77- 1. GDR 1500m champion 1983-4, 1986.
World junior records at 1000m in 1977 and 800m in 1978, and GDR 1000m record 1983.
Progression at 1500m: 1974- 3:52.1, 1975-

3:51.1, 1978- 3:40.3, 1979- 3:38.6, 1980- 3:38.6, 1981- 3:42.51, 1982- 3:38.92, 1983- 3:37.19, 1984- 3:34.10, 1985- 3:37.19, 1986- 3:35.52. pbs: 400m: 47.95 '80, 800m: 1:44.72 '80, 1000m: 2:15.25 '83, 1M: 3:55.63 '86, 2000m: 5:08.71 '85, 3000m: 8:05.51 '86.

**Lutz DOMBROWSKI** b.25 Jun 1959 Karl-Marx-Stadt 1.88m 87kg. Club: SC Karl-Marx-Stadt. Machine fitter.
At LJ: OG: '80- 1; ECh: '82- 1; WCp: '79- 2; ECp: '79- 1. GDR champion 1979 and 1984. At TJ: EJ: '77- 4; WCp: '81- 7; ECp: '81- 5.
Two European long jump records 1980.
Progression at LJ: 1971- 5.25, 1972- 5.46, 1973- 6.41, 1974- 6.35, 1975- 7.13, 1976- 7.55, 1977- 7.80i, 1979- 8.31, 1980- 8.54, 1982- 8.30/8.41w, 1984- 8.50, 1985- 8.02, 1986- 8.11/8.12w. pbs: 100m: 10.4; TJ: 16.61i '77 (European junior best).
Won the 1980 Olympic title with the world's first 28ft long jump (Beamon of course had jumped over 29ft). His father Helmut was German youth 100m champion in 1939.

**Frank EMMELMANN** b.15 Sep 1961 Schneidlingen 1.85m 78kg. Club: SC Magdeburg. Fitter. Married Kirsten Siemon (qv) in 1984.
At 100m/200m (R- 4x100m relay): WCh: '83- sf/5; ECh: '82- 1/3 (2R), '86- -/8 (2R); WCp: '81- 3/3 (2R), '85- 3/2; ECp: '81- 2/1, '83- 1/-, '85- 3/1. GDR champion: 100m 1981-2, 1985; 200m 1981 and 1984-5.
Two GDR records each at 100m 1984-5, 200m 1981-5.
Progression at 100m, 200m: 1977- 10.9; 1978- 10.70, 22.00; 1979- 10.42/10.2, 20.90; 1980- 10.39; 1981- 10.19/10.15w, 20.33/20.23w; 1982- 10.20/10.11w, 20.47; 1983- 10.18, 20.55; 1984- 10.11, 20.46; 1985- 10.06, 20.23, 1986- 10.32, 20.62.
Has compiled a fine championships record in the sprints.

**Uwe FREIMUTH** b.10 Sep 1961 Rathenow 1.91m 93kg. Club: ASK Vorwärts Potsdam. Sports instructor.
At Dec: WCh: '83- 4; ECh: '86- 6; ECp: '81- 3, '83- 1, '85- 7. GDR champion 1985-6.
Four GDR decathlon records 1983-4.
Progression at Dec: 1978- 7221, 1979- 7449, 1980- 7733, 1981- 8221, 1982- 8026, 1983- 8551, 1984- 8792, 1985- 8504, 1986- 8322. pbs: 100m: 10.82 '86, 10.98w '85, 400m: 47.90 '86, 1500m: 4:23.25 '83, 110mh: 14.54 '83, HJ: 2.15 '81, PV: 5.15 '84, LJ: 7.79 '83, SP: 16.42 '84, DT: 51.54 '84, JT: 73.02 '84.

**Dirk GAMLIN** b.26 Oct 1963 Granzin 1.88m 83kg. Club: SC Traktor Schwerin. Mechanic. At TJ: ECh: '86- 5. GDR champion 1985-6.
Progression at TJ: 1979- 13.73, 1980- 14.55, 1981- 15.35, 1982- 15.40, 1983- 16.17/16.37w, 1984- 16.64i/16.42, 1985- 17.44, 1986- 17.17. pb LJ: 7.93w '85.

**Hartwig GAUDER** b.10 Nov 1954 Vaihingen, FGR 1.86m 70kg. Club: SC Turbine Erfurt. Architectural student.
At 50kmW: OG: '80- 1; ECh: '82- 4, '86- 1; LT: '81- 2, '85- 1. At 20kmW: ECh: '78- 7; LT: '79- 7. At 10kmW: EJ: '73- 1. GDR champion: 20kmW 1975-6, 1985-6; 50kmW 1979, 1982, 1986.
World indoor best 1 hour walk 14906m 1986.
Progression at 20kmW/50kmW: 1972- 1:34:19, 1973- 1:32:55, 1974- 1:28:47, 1975- 1:26:29, 1976- 1:26:25, 1977- 1:27:07, 1978- 1:24:22.7t, 1979- 1:21:39/4:01:20, 1980- 1:23:36.6i/3:48:15, 1981- 3:46:57, 1982- 1:29:29/3:49:44, 1983- 1:21:33/3:43:23, 1984- 1:22:53/3:41:24, 1985- 1:23:03/3:43:33, 1986- 1:21:15/3:40:55. Track pbs: 3kmW: 11:20.0 '84, 5kmW: 19:08.59i '81, 10kmW: 39:16.30i '86.
Family moved from West Germany when he was aged five.

**Ralf HABER** b.18 Aug 1962 Altenburg 1.89m 110kg. Club: SC Karl-Marx-Stadt. Sports student. At HT: ECh: '86- 6; EJ: '81- 4. GDR champion 1984. GDR hammer record in 1983.
Progression at HT: 1979- 52.18, 1980- 66.44, 1981- 70.88, 1982- 76.42, 1983- 79.02, 1984- 79.38, 1985- 78.68, 1986- 80.60.

**Michael HEILMANN** b.26 Oct 1961 Kleinmachnow 1.75m 53kg. Club: TSC Berlin. Economics student.
At Mar: ECh: '86- dnf; WCp: '85- 4; ECp: '83- 5, '85- 1. GDR marathon record 1985.
Progression at Mar: 1981- 2:18:19, 1982- 2:18:25, 1983- 2:11:49, 1984- 2:09:30, 1985- 2:09:03, 1986- 2:10:27. pbs: 1500m: 3:50.88 '86, 5000m: 13:43.80 '85, 10000m: 28:23.76 '85.

**Uwe HOHN** b.16 Jul 1962 Rheinsberg 1.98m 116kg. Club: ASK Potsdam. Sports student. At JT: ECh: '82- 1; EJ: '81- 1; WCp: '85- 1; ECp: '85- 1. GDR champion 1984-5.
The only man to throw the javelin over 100 metres, with 104.80m in East Berlin on 20 Jul 1984. This, at 5.08m, was the biggest ever improvement on a world javelin record. Two months earlier he set a European record 99.52m. European Junior record in 1981.
Progression at JT: 1975- 41.92, 1976- 54.38, 1977- 63.52, 1978- 72.76, 1979- 74.06, 1980- 85.52, 1981- 86.56, 1982- 91.34, 1984- 104.80,

1985- 96.96. pb DT: 59.80 '85.
Had a back operation and missed the 1986 season.

**Ralf KOWALSKY** b.22 Mar 1962 Elgersburg 1.80m 66kg. Club: TSC Berlin. Sports student. At 20kmW: WCh: '83- 14; ECh: '86- dq. GDR champion 1981 and 1983. At 10kmW: EJ: '81- 1.
Two world junior records at both 10km and 20km track walks in 1980-1, world records at 2 hours (28358m) and 30km (2:06:54) in 1982, world best 5km 1984. World indoor best 1 hour walk 14754m 1984.
Progression at 20kmW: 1978- 1:32:34, 1979- 1:29:30, 1980- 1:24:07.2i, 1981- 1:21:39.1t, 1982- 1:22:52, 1983- 1:21:52, 1984- 1:20:35, 1985- 1:23:31, 1986- 1:20:31. Track pbs: 3kmW: 11:21.0 '84, 5kmW: 18:42.66 '84, 10kmW: 38:54.75 '81.

**Hansjörg KUNZE** b.28 Dec 1959 Rostock 1.79m 63kg. Club: SC Empor Rostock. Medical student. At 10000m: WCh: '83- 3. At 5000m: OG: '80- sf; ECh: '82- 9, '86- dnf; WCp: '79- 4, '81- 2; ECp: '79- 1, '81- 3, '83- 4. At 3000m: EJ: '73- 3. World CC: '82- 4. GDR champion at 5000m 1981, 1983-4, 1986; 10000m 1984, 1986.
European 5000m record 1981, world indoor 5000m best 13:13.3 1983, world junior 3000m record 7:56.4 1976.
Progression at 5000m/10000m: 1974- 15:14.6, 1975- 14:20.4, 1978- 13:42.2/29:57.9, 1979- 13:27.7, 1980- 13:26.4/28:00.73, 1981- 13:10.40/28:12.25, 1982- 13:12.53, 1983- 13:13.3i/27:30.69, 1984- 13:33.90i/27:33.10, 1986- 13:31.05/27:34.68. pbs: 1500m: 3:40.04 '79, 3000m: 7:44.05 '83 (GDR record).

**Volker MAI** b.3 May 1966 Templin 1.94m 72kg. Club: SC Neubrandenburg. Medical student. At TJ: ECh: '86- 7, EI: '85- 3; EJ: '83- 5, '85- 1 (1 LJ); WCp: '85- 4; ECp: '85- 2.
World junior and GDR TJ record in 1985.
Progression at TJ: 1981- 14.72, 1982- 15.90, 1983- 16.20/16.22w, 1984- 17.12, 1985- 17.50, 1986- 17.02. pbs: 100m: 10.9 '86, 200m: 21.91 '85, LJ: 8.04 '85.

**Dietmar MEISCH** b.10 Feb 1959 Weida 1.78m 65kg. Club: TSC Berlin. Electronics student. At 50kmW: OG: '80- dnf; WCh: '83- dq; ECh: '82- dnf, '86- 6; LT: '79- 8, '81- 4, '85- 6.
Progression at 50kmW: 1979- 3:50:02, 1980- 3:47:38, 1981- 3:48:57, 1982- 3:48:01, 1983- 3:46:12, 1984- 3:43:33, 1985- 3:49:44, 1986- 3:48:01. pb 20kmW: 1:22:38 '83.

Hagen Melzer. *ASP*

**Hagen MELZER** b.16 Jun 1959 Bautzen 1.78m 62kg. Club: SC Einheit Dresden. Electrician.
At 3000mSt: WCh: '83- 11; ECh: '82- 4, '86- 1; WCp: '85- 5; ECp: '79- 5, '83- 4, '85- 6. GDR champion 1980, 1983, 1985-6. At 2000mSt: EJ: '77- 6.
Progression at 3000mSt: 1978- 8:38.66, 1979- 8:31.7, 1980- 8:27.7, 1981- 8:27.68, 1982- 8:21.27, 1983- 8:20.28, 1984- 8:21.32, 1985- 8:28.56, 1986- 8:16.65. pbs: 1500m: 3:40.68 '84, 3000m: 7:51.43 '82.

**Detlef MICHEL** b.13 Oct 1955 Berlin 1.84m 96kg. Club: TSC Berlin. Water and gas installer.
At JT: OG: '80- dnq; WCh: '83- 1; ECh: '78- 4, '82- 3, '86- 2; WCp: '81- 2; ECp: '75- 4, '81- 1, '83- 1. GDR champion 1975, 1979-80, 1982-3, 1986.
Five GDR javelin records 1981-3, the last equalled the European record at 96.72m.
Progression at JT: 1970- 64.08, 1971- 67.96, 1972- 75.80, 1973- 72.48, 1974- 76.70, 1975- 84.58, 1976- 84.72, 1977- 82.44, 1978- 86.12, 1979- 89.74, 1980- 90.98, 1981- 92.48, 1982- 94.52, 1983- 96.72, 1984- 93.68, 1985- 84.74, new: 1986- 83.52. pb LJ: 7.20 '77.

**Matthias MODER** b.17 Jun 1963 Torgau 1.84m 110kg. Club: SC Dynamo Berlin. Mechanic.
At HT: ECh: '86- 7; EJ: '81- 7; ECp: '85- 3. GDR champion 1985.
GDR hammer record 1985.

Progression at HT: 1980- 62.24, 1981- 69.88, 1982- 74.78, 1983- 73.94, 1984- 79.38, 1985- 80.92, 1986- 80.30. pb SP: 15.98 '80.

**Axel NOACK** b.23 Sep 1961 Gorlitz 1.82m 74kg. Club: TSC Berlin. Architectural student.
At 50kmW: LT: '85- 3. GDR champion 1984. At 20kmW: ECh: '86- dq.
Progression at 20kmW/50kmW: 1981- 1:35:23, 1982- 1:33:23, 1983- 1:24:19/4:22:41, 1984- 1:26:20/4:00.41, 1985- 1:26:54/3:56.22, 1986- 1:21:55.

**Gunther RODEHAU** b.6 Jul 1959 Meissen 1.79m 113kg. Club: SC Einheit Dresden. Vehicle mechanic.
At HT: WCh: '83- 5; ECh: '86- 4; WCp: '85- 2; ECp: '83- 3. GDR champion 1986.
Two GDR hammer records 1984-5.
Progression at HT: 1977- 49.94, 1978- 60.84, 1979- 68.90, 1980- 74.02, 1981- 74.42, 1982- 72.18, 1983- 78.14, 1984- 80.20, 1985- 82.64, 1986- 81.70.

**Mathias SCHERSING** b.7 Oct 1964 Halle 1.85m 68kg. Club: SC Chemie Halle. Student.
At 400m (R- 4x400m relay): ECh: '86- 3; EJ: '83- 1R; EI: '86- 3; WCp: '85- 2R. GDR champion 1986.
Progression at 400m: 1982- 47.91, 1983- 47.06, 1984- 44.86, 1985- 45.12, 1986- 44.85. pbs: 100m: 10.5 '82, 200m: 20.80 '86.

**Werner SCHILDHAUER** b.5 Jun 1959 Dessau 1.83m 65kg. Club: SC Chemie Halle. Electrician.
At 10000m (5000m): OG: '80- 7; WCh: '83- 2/2; ECh: '82- 2/2; WCp: '79- 6, '81- 1, '85- 3; ECp: '79- 4, '81- 1, '83- 1, '85- 2; EJ: '77- 2 at 3000m. World CC: '82- 8. GDR champion: 5000m 1982 and 1985, 10000m 1981-3 and 1985.
Three GDR 10000m records 1981-3.
Progression at 5000m/10000m: 1978- 13:54.0, 1979- 13:30.1/28:23.6, 1980- 13:30.2/27:53.51, 1981- 13:31.59/27:38.43, 1982- 13:12.54/27:33.66, 1983- 13:26.36/27:24.95, 1984- 13:26.23/28:09.05, 1985- 13:27.16/28:24.84, 1986- 13:40.24/28:32.49. pbs: 1500m: 3:38.57 '82, 2000m: 5:06.18 '81, 3000m: 7:46.5i '82, Mar: 2:17:20 '80. Also GDR records at 15km: 43:50.2, 20km: 58:30.2, 1 hour: 20536m in 1983.

**Thomas SCHÖNLEBE** b.6 Aug 1965 Frauenstein 1.85m 72kg. Club: SC Karl-Marx-Stadt. Sports student.
At 400m: WCh: '83- 6; ECh: '86- 2; EJ: '83- 1 (1R); WCp: '85- 2; ECp: '83- 2, '85- 1; EI: '86- 1; WIG: '85- 1. GDR champion 1983-5.
Three European Junior 400m records 1983-4 and world indoor bests: 45.60 '85, 45.41 '86. Two

GDR 400m records 1985.
Progression at 400m: 1981- 47.50, 1982- 46.71, 1983- 45.29, 1984- 45.01, 1985- 44.62, 1986- 44.63. pbs: 100m: 10.98 '82, 200m: 20.91 '86, 800m: 1:57.7 '81, LJ: 6.83 '81.

**Thomas SCHRÖDER** b.23 Aug 1962 Waren 1.77m 75kg. Club: SC Neubrandenburg. Law student.
At 100m (200m, R- 4x100m relay): WCh: '83- sf (4R); ECh: '82- sf, '86- 4 (4, 2R); EJ: '79- 1 (2), '81- 1 (1, 2R). GDR champion at 100m 1983-4, 1986; 200m 1986.
World indoor 100 yards best of 9.50 twice in 1984.
Progression at 100m: 1977- 11.15/10.9, 1978- 10.89, 1979- 10.41, 1980- 10.42, 1981- 10.35/10.14w, 1982- 10.39/10.38w, 1983- 10.22, 1984- 10.27, 1985- 10.27, 1986- 10.10. pb 200m: 20.54 '86.

**Jürgen SCHULT** b.11 May 1960 Neuhaus, Kr. Hagenow 1.93m 110kg. Club: SC Traktor Schwerin. Machine fitter.
At DT: WCh: '83- 5; ECh: '86- 7; EJ: '79- 1; WCp: '85- 2; ECp: '83- 1, '85- 4. GDR champion 1983-6.
World discus record 1986.
Progression at DT: 1978- 51.82, 1979- 57.22, 1980- 61.26, 1981- 61.56, 1982- 63.18, 1983- 66.78, 1984- 68.82, 1985- 69.74, 1986- 74.08. pb SP: 18.59 '84.

**Ulf TIMMERMANN** b.1 Nov 1962 Berlin 1.94m 118kg. Club: TSC Berlin. Mechanical engineering student.
At SP: WCh: '83- 2; ECh: '86- 2; EI: '85- 2; EJ: '81- 2 (9 at DT); WCp: '85- 1; ECp: '83- 2.
World record 22.62m and European indoor shot best 21.87m 1985.
Progression at SP: 1979- 16.23, 1981- 19.00, 1982- 20.22, 1983- 21.36, 1984- 21.75, 1985- 22.62, 1986- 22.60. pb DT: 52.68 '81.

**Torsten VOSS** b.24 Mar 1963 Güstrow 1.86m 86kg. Club: SC Traktor Schwerin. Mechanic.
At Dec: WCh: '83- 7; ECh: '82- dnf, '86- 4; EJ: '81- 2, ECp: '85- 1. GDR champion 1982-3.
World junior decathlon record 1982.
Progression at Dec: 1977- 5083*, 1978- 6325*, 1979- 7160, 1980- 7518, 1981- 8003, 1982- 8397, 1983- 8335, 1984- 8543, 1985- 8559, 1986- 8450. pbs: 100m: 10.54 '84, 10.53w '86; 400m: 47.50 '84, 1500m: 4:17.00 '81, 110mh: 13.94 '85, HJ: 2.11 '81, PV: 5.15i '86, LJ: 8.02 '84, SP: 15.39 '84, DT: 44.74 '84, JT: 62.90 '82.

**Ronald WEIGEL** b.8 Aug 1959 Hildburghausen 1.76m 61kg. Club: ASK Vorwärts Potsdam. Student of journalism.
At 50kmW: WCh: '83- 1; ECh: '86- dq. At 10kmW:

EJ: '77- 2. GDR champion 20kmW 1984, 50kmW 1983, 1985.
At 20km walk: European track record 1:20:54.9 1983, world indoor best 1:20:40 1980. World fastest 50km road walk 1984 and 1986; GDR road bests at 30km (2:12:41) and 35km (2:34:40) 1984.
Progression at 20kmW/50kmw: 1975- 1:40:56, 1976- 1:30:49, 1977- 1:27:51, 1978- 1:27:00, 1979- 1:25:00, 1980- 1:20:40i/1:22:50, 1981- 1:22:40/3:49:53, 1982- 1:29:36/3:44:20, 1983- 1:20:55/3:41:31, 1984- 1:19:56/3:38:31, 1985- 1:22:12/3:47.15, 1986- 1:20:39/3:38:17. Track pbs: 3kmW: 11:18.0 '84, 5kmW: 18:53.38 '84, 10kmW: 38:35.5i '80 1hrW: 14750mi '84

**Gerald WEISS** b.8 Jan 1960 Lübz 1.91m 104kg. Club: SC Traktor Schwerin. Mechanic.
At JT: ECh: '86- 11; EJ: '79- nt; WSG: '81- 2. GDR champion 1981.
Progression at JT: 1974- 49.82, 1975- 58.12, 1976- 70.80, 1977- 71.82, 1978- 73.42, 1979- 82.02, 1980- 85.92, 1981- 89.56, 1982- 83.26, 1983- 86.28, 1984- 90.06, 1985- 82.84, new: 81.40.

**Gerd WESSIG** b.16 Jul 1959 Lübz 2.01m 88kg. Club: SC Traktor Schwerin. Cook/gastronomic student.
At HJ: OG: '80- 1; ECh: '86- 7=; ECp: '85- 2. GDR champion 1980, 1984-6.
World record 2.36m to win 1980 Olympic high jump.
Progression at HJ: 1976- 2.06, 1977- 2.13, 1978- 2.19, 1979- 2.23i, 1980- 2.36, 1982- 2.26, 1983- 2.21, 1984- 2.30, 1985- 2.29, 1986- 2.30. pbs: Dec: 7974 '83, 100m: 10.77 '83, 110mh: 14.96 '83, PV: 4.60 '83, LJ: 7.24 '83, 7.31w '82, DT: 45.70 '83.

# Women

**Ingrid AUERSWALD** b.2 Sep 1957 Jena 1.68m 59kg. née Brestrich. Club: SC Motor Jena. Sports student.
At 100m (R- 4x100m relay): OG: '80- 3 (1R); WCh: '83- 1R; ECh: '86- 5 (1R); WCp: '85- 1R; ECp: '77- 1R, '79- 1R, '83- 1R, '85- 1R.
Ran on seven world record 4x100m teams 1979-85.
Progression at 100m: 1975- 11.9, 1976- 11.71, 1977- 11.29, 1978- 11.36, 1979- 11.28, 1980- 11.08/10.93w, 1981- 11.34, 1982- 11.77, 1983- 11.17, 1984- 11.04, 1985- 11.12; 1986- 11.11. pb 200m: 22.60 '80.

**Anke BEHMER** b.5 Jun 1961 Stavenhagen 1.74m 62kg. née Vater. Club: SC Neubranden-burg. Medical student.
At Hep: WCh: '83- 3; ECh: '82- 4, '86- 1; ECp: '81-5; EJ: '79- 3 (Pen). GDR champion 1983, 1986.
Progression at Pen (p)/Hep: 1977- 3648p, 1978-4114p, 1979- 4321p, 1980- 5792, 1981- 6251, 1982- 6371, 1983- 6531, 1984- 6775, 1986-6717. pbs: 200m: 23.20w/23.26 '84, 800m: 2:03.76 '84, 100mh: 13.25 '86, HJ: 1.87 '86, LJ: 6.84 '84, SP: 15.26 '82, JT: 40.24 '86.
Missed 1985 season due to pregnancy.

**Kerstin BEHRENDT** b.2 Sep 1967 Leisnig/Kreis Döbeln 1.77m 62kg. Club: SC DHfK Leipzig. Medical student.
European Junior gold medallist 1985 at 100m, 200m, 4x100mR.
Progression at 100m/200m: 1981- 12.36, 1983-12.04/24.8, 1984- 11.86/24.44, 1985- 11.21/23.21, 1986- 11.62/23.89.

**Susanne BEYER** b.24 Jun 1961 Suhl 1.78m 58kg. née Helm. Club: SC Dynamo Berlin. Physiotherapy student.
At HJ: WCh: '83- 7; ECh: '86- 4=; EI: '85- 2; WCp: '85- 3; ECp: '85- 3. GDR champion 1983 and 1985.
Progression at HJ: 1977- 1.55, 1978- 1.77, 1979-1.83, 1980- 1.88, 1981- 1.88, 1982- 1.91, 1983-1.97, 1984- 1.96, 1985- 1.97, 1986- 1.96, 1987-2.00i.

**Ines BIBERNELL** b.21 Jul 1965 Querfurt 1.68m 59kg. Club: SC Chemie Halle. Administrator.
At 3000m: EI: '86- 1. At 10000m: WCp: '85- 4; ECp: '85- 2. GDR champion 3000m 1985-6, 1500m 1986.
Progression at 3000m/10000m: 1982- 9:34.0, 1983- 9:17.29, 1984- 9:14.31i, 1985- 9:00.30/32:45.58, 1986- 8:49.80/32:32.28. pbs: 800m: 2:05.4 '83, 1500m: 4:05.64 '85, 2000m: 5:47.98 '85, 5000m: 15:27.05 '86.

**Andrea BIENIAS** b.11 Nov 1959 Leipzig 1.80m 67kg. née Reichstein. Club: SC DHfK Leipzig. Sports student.
At HJ: OG: '80- 6=; WCh: '83- 10=; ECh: '82- 6=, '86- 4=; ECp: '82- 2, '86- 1; EJ: '77- 6; ECp: '81- 5=. GDR champion 1981-2, 1984, 1986.
European indoor high jump best 1.99m in 1982.
Progression at HJ: 1972- 1.43, 1973- 1.53, 1974-1.65, 1975- 1.70i, 1976- 1.83, 1977- 1.90, 1978-1.85, 1979- 1.86, 1980- 1.94, 1981- 1.95, 1982-1.99i/1.96, 1983- 1.97, 1984- 1.96, 1985- 1.91, 1986- 1.98i/1.97.

**Ulrike BRUNS** b.17 Nov 1953 Cottbus 1.73m 56kg. née Klapezynski. Club: ASK Vorwärts Pots-dam. Medical technician.
At 10000m: ECh: '86- 3. At 1500m: OG: '76- 2, '80- 5; ECh: '74- 6, '78- 7, '82- 5; WCp: '77- 3, '81-3; ECp: '77- 2, '81- 2. At 3000m: WCp: '77- 4, '85-1; ECp: '83- 2, '85- 3. At 800m: ECh: '78- 7; ECp: '75- 2; EI: '78- 1. GDR champion: 1500m 1978, 1982, 1984-5; 3000m 1976, 1981, 1984.
GDR records (1976-86): 5 at 3000m, 2 at 10000m, 1 each at 800m, 1500m, 1M, 2000m.
Progression at 1500m/3000m: 1968- 4:59.0, 1969- 4:43.4, 1970- 4:28.0, 1971- 4:28.8, 1972-4:25.1, 1973- 4:16.3, 1974- 4:09.9, 1975- 4:08.8, 1976- 3:59.9/8:55.6, 1977- 4:04.52/8:49.2, 1978-4:01.95, 1980- 4:00.62, 1981- 4:01.44/8:49.67, 1982- 4:00.78/8:54.09, 1983- 4:04.25/8:44.88, 1984- 4:01.38/8:36.38, 1985- 4:01.95/8:36.51, 1986- 4:04.85/8:48.22. At 10000m: 1984-32:46.08, 1986- 31:19.76. pbs: 400m: 54.5 '77, 800m: 1:57.06 '76, 1000m: 2:31.95 '78, 1M: 4:21.59 '85, 2000m: 5:37.62 '85.
Long and distinguished career, has gradually moved up in distances run. Unbeaten in 1984. Gave birth to a daughter in 1979.

**Sabine BUSCH** b.21 Nov 1962 Erfurt 1.77m 66kg. Club: SC Turbine Erfurt. Sports student.
At 400mh (R- 4x400m relay): ECh: '86- 2 (1R); WCp: '85- 1 (1R); ECp: '85- 1 (2R). At 400m: WCh: '83- sf (1R); ECh: '82- 4 (1R); EI: '85- 1, '86-1; ECp: '83- 4. GDR champion 400m 1983, 400mh 1985-6.
Ran on 4x400m world record team 1984. In 1985 set world record of 53.55 for 400mh, having run GDR record of 53.83 on her debut at the event.
Progression at 400m: 1978- 62.4, 1979- 53.97, 1980- 51.41/51.0, 1981- 52.03, 1982- 50.57, 1983- 50.26, 1984- 49.24, 1985- 51.07, 1986-50.43. At 400mh: 1985- 53.55, 1986- 53.60. pbs: 100m: 11.80 '82, 200m: 22.83 '83.
In 1985-6 ran 9 sub-54.00 times.

**Katrin DÖRRE** b.6 Oct 1961 Leipzig 1.70m 57kg. Club: SC DHfK Leipzig. Medical student.
At Mar: ECh: '86- dnf; WCp: '85- 1; ECp: '85- 1. GDR champion 3000m 1980, Mar 1982.
Six GDR marathons records.
Progression at Mar: 1982- 2:43:19, 1983-2:37:41, 1984- 2:26:52, 1985- 2:30:11, 1986-2:29:33. pbs: 800m: 2:05.4 '80, 1000m: 2:44.8 '80, 1500m: 4:18.7 '79, 3000m: 9:04.01 '84, 10000m: 33:00.0 '84.
Has won 10 of her 13 marathons, including Osaka 1984, Tokyo 1984-5, Nagoya and Karl-Marx-Stadt 1986.

Sabine Busch. *ASP*

**Heike DRECHSLER** b.16 Dec 1964 Gora 1.81m 69kg. née Daute. Married Andreas Drechsler 28 July 1984. Club: SC Motor Jena. Optical instrument maker.
At LJ: WCh: '83- 1; ECh: '82- 4, '86- 1 (1 200m); EI: '83- 3, '85- 3, '86- 1; EJ: '81- 1; WCp: '85- 1; ECp: '83- 1, '85- 2. GDR champion LJ 1981, 1983-6, 200m 1986.
Seven GDR long jump records, including three world, 1983-6. Two world records at 200m 1986. Four world indoor LJ bests: 6.88 '83, 6.99 '84 and '85, 7.29 '86. World junior LJ records in 1981 and 1982 and at heptathlon in 1981.
Progression at LJ: 1977- 4.46, 1978- 5.69, 1979- 5.90, 1980- 6.64/6.70w, 1981- 6.91/7.01w, 1982- 6.98, 1983- 7.14/7.27w, 1984- 7.40, 1985- 7.44, 1986- 7.45. At 100m/200m: 1981- 11.75/24.16, 1985- /23.19, 1986- 10.91/10.80w/21.71. pbs: 800m: 2:17.07 '81, 100mh: 14.12 '80, HJ: 1.81 '80, SP: 13.31 '81, Hep: 5812 '81.
The youngest gold medallist of the 1983 world championships, she has jumped consistently over 7 metres ever since. She made a sensational breakthrough in 1986 into a great sprinter, starting with the GDR indoor 100 yards title in 10.24;

she set world records at long jump and equalled Marita Koch over 200 metres.

**Kirsten EMMELMANN** b.19 Apr 1961 Warnemünde 1.73m 63kg. née Simeon. Married to Frank Emmelmann (qv). Club: SC Magdeburg. Student.
At 400m (R = 4x400m relay): ECh: '82- 1R, '86- 4 (1R); EI: '83- 2, '85- 2; ECp: '85- 2. WCp '85- 1R, '81- 1 4x100mR. GDR champion 1985. At 200m: EI: '86- 3; EJ: '79- 5 (2 at 100m, 1 at 4x100mR).
Progression at 400m: 1981- 52.03, 1982- 51.14, 1983- 51.32, 1984- 50.62, 1985- 50.07, 1986- 50.43. pbs: 100m: 11.23 '82, 11.2 '79; 200m: 22.50 '81.

**Petra FELKE** b.30 Jul 1959 Saalfeld 1.72m 63kg. Club: SC Motor Jena.
At JT: WCh: '83- 9; ECh: '82- 7, '86- 2; EJ: '77- 2; WSG: '81- 1; WCp: '81- 2, '85- 2; ECp: '85- 1. GDR champion 1984-6. Won GP 1986.
GDR javelin record 1984, and in 1985 two world records (75.26 & 75.40) in one competition.
Progression at JT: 1973- 36.07, 1974- 42.10, 1975- 50.40, 1976- 49.32, 1977- 61.24, 1978-

61.90, 1979- 61.38, 1980- 62.10, 1981- 66.60, 1982- 65.56, 1983- 69.02, 1984- 74.72, 1985- 75.40, 1986- 75.04.
Won 26 successive competions from May 1984 to September 1985. In 1984-6 won 42 out of 47 competitions.

**Cornelia FEUERBACH** b.26 Apr 1963 Halberstadt 1.72m 59kg. Club: SC Magdeburg. Student.
At 400mh: ECh: '86- 3. At 4x400mR: EJ: '81- 1.
Progression at 400mh: 1985- 54.64, 1986- 54.13.
pbs: 100m: 11.48/11.31w '84, 200m: 23.50 '82, 400m: 53.21i '85, 100mh: 12.86 '83.
Moved up from 100mh to 400mh with great success in 1985-6.

Cornelia Feuerbach. *ASP*

**Ellen FIELDER** b.26 Nov 1958 Demmin 1.76m 66kg. née Neumann. Club: SC Dynamo Berlin. Agricultural student.
At 400mh: WCh: '80- 2, '83- 3; ECh: '86- 6; WCp: '81- 1; ECp: '81- 1, '83- 1. GDR 400mh champion 1981-3. GDR 400mh record 1983.
Progression at 400mh: 1978- 58.12, 1980- 54.56, 1981- 54.79, 1982- 54.96, 1983- 54.20, 1984- 55.40, 1985- 55.20, 1986- 54.76. pbs: 200m: 23.58/23.44w '81, 400m: 52.13 '83, 100mh: 13.4 '75.

**Diana GANSKY** b.14 Dec 1963 Bergen 1.84m 92kg. née Sachse. Club: ASK Vorwärts Potsdam. Sports student.
At DT: ECh: '86- 1; EJ: '83- 1.
Progression at DT: 1977- 36.36, 1979- 44.46,

1980- 57.36, 1981- 59.00, 1982- 60.80, 1983- 61.88, 1984- 66.36, 1985- 69.14, 1986- 73.26.
Married Frank Gansky on 5 Sep 1986, a week after winning the European discus gold medal.

**Silke GLADISCH** b.20 Jun 1964 Stralsund 1.68m 59kg. Club: SC Empor Rostock. Student.
At 100m (R- 4x100m relay): WCh: '83- sf (1R); ECh: '86- 4 (3 200m, 1R); WCp: '85- 1R; ECp: '83- 1R, '85- 1R; EJ: '81- 1R. GDR champion 1986. At 60m: EI: '83- 2, '86- 3; WIG: '85- 1.
Ran on two world record 4x100m teams 1983-5.
Progression at 100m/200m: 1978- 12.6, 1979- 12.39/25.51, 1980- 11.8/24.6, 1981- 11.63/23.69, 1982- 11.54/11.33w/23.30, 1983- 11.03/22.72, 1984- 11.10/22.70, 1985- 10.99/22.12, 1986- 10.96/22.07.

**Marlies GÖHR** b.21 Mar 1958 Gera 1.65m 55kg. née Oelsner. Club: SC Motor Jena. Psychology student.
At 100m: (R- 4x100m relay): OG: '76- 8 (1R), 80- 2 (1R); WCh: '83- 1 (1R); ECh: '78- 1 (3R, 2 at 200m), '82- 1 (1R), '86- 1 (1R); EJ: '75- 2 (1R); WSG: '79- 1; WCp: '77- 1, '79- 2 (2R), '81- 3 (1R), '85- 1 (1R); ECp: '77, '79, '81, '83, '85- all 1 (1R). EI 60m: 1st '77-9, '82-3; 2nd '85-6. GDR champion 100m 1977-85, 200m 1978, 1981, 1984.
World records: three 100m, nine 4x100m and one 4x200m, 1977-85. World indoor bests at 60m (7.12 in 1978 and 7.10 in 1980), 100y (10.41 1978, 10.35 1979, 10.29 in 1980 and 1983) and 100m (11.37 1977, 11.29 1979 and 11.16 in 1980). World junior 100m record 1976.
Progression at 100m/200m: 1971- 12.8, 1972- 12.1/24.8, 1973- 11.8/24.5, 1974- 11.6/11.81/24.3, 1975- 11.54/11.42w/23.8, 1976- 11.17/23.26, 1977- 10.88/23.23, 1978- 10.94/22.38, 1979- 10.97/22.36, 1980- 10.93/10.79w/22.45, 1981- 11.09, 1982- 10.88/22.78, 1983- 10.81, 1984- 10.84/21.74, 1985- 10.86, 1986- 10.91.
Her outstanding sprinting career includes a record number of European Cup Final victories, and five European outdoor gold medals, including a hat-trick of 100m titles. The first woman to run a sub 11-second 100 metres, to the end of 1986 she had run a record 30 such times, including two with excess wind assistance.

**Sabine GÜNTHOR** b.6 Nov 1963 Jena 1.70m 60kg. née Rieger. Club: SC Motor Jena.
At 200m (R- 4x100m relay): ECh: '82- 3 (1R), '86- 7 (1R); EJ: '81- 1 (1R); WCp: '85- 1R.
Ran on world record 4x100m team 1985.
Progression at 200m: 1978- 25.04, 1979- 24.31, 1980- 23.90, 1981- 23.10/22.91w, 1982- 22.37, 1983- 23.29, 1984- 22.65, 1985- 22.79, 1986- 22.76. pb 100m: 11.19 '85.

**Heike HARTWIG** b.30 Dec 1962 1.80m 95kg. née Dittrich. Club: SC Dynamo Berlin.
At SP: ECh: '86- 5; WCp: '85- 2.
Progression at SP: 1978- 13.38, 1979- 14.06, 1980- 15.76, 1981- 17.60, 1982- 19.48, 1983- 19.50, 1984- 20.28, 1985- 20.65, 1986- 20.72. pb DT: 63.12 '86.

**Martina HELLMANN** b.12 Dec 1960 Leipzig 1.78m 85kg. née Opitz. Club: SC DHfK Leipzig. Sociology student.
At DT: WCh: '83- 1; ECh: '86- 3; WCp: '85- 1; ECp: '83- 1, '85- 2. GDR champion 1985-6.
Held GDR discus record for a week in 1984.
Progression at DT: 1974- 34.67, 1975- 41.42, 1976- 44.92, 1977- 55.00, 1978- 57.82, 1979- 64.50, 1980- 64.32, 1981- 52.12, 1982- 64.32, 1983- 70.26, 1984- 72.32, 1985- 69.78, 1986- 72.52. pb SP: 17.10 '78.

**Kerstin KNABE** b.7 Jul 1959 Oschatz 1.80m 70kg. née Claus. Club: SC DHfK Leipzig. Administrator.
At 100mh: OG: '80-4; WCh: '83- 2; ECh: '82- 3; EJ: '77- 1 (1R); WCp: '79- 3, '81- 2; ECp: '81- 2. GDR champion 1979, 1981. At 60mh: EI: '82- 1, '83- 2, '86- 3.
Progression at 100mh: 1974- 14.0, 1975- 13.7, 1976- 14.25, 1977- 13.32, 1978- 13.28, 1979- 12.87, 1980- 12.60, 1981- 12.85, 1982- 12.54, 1983- 12.62, 1984- 12.98, 1985- 12.98, 1986- 12.64. pbs: 100m: 11.51/11.44w '82, 200m: 23.29 '85.

**Heidi KRIEGER** b.20 Jul 1965 1.87m 98kg. Club: SC Dynamo Berlin.
At SP: ECh: '86- 1; EI: '84- 3, '86- 2; EJ: '83- 1 (1 at DT).
Progression at SP: 1980- 11.93, 1981- 14.05, 1982- 16.82, 1983- 19.03i, 1984- 20.51i/20.24, 1985- 20.39i/19.82, 1986- 21.10. pb DT: 61.98 '83.

**Silvia MADETZKY** b.24 Jun 1962 Schkopau 1.85m 95kg. Club: SC Chemie Halle.
At DT: ECh: '82- 5; EJ: '79- 2.
Progression at DT: 1976- 39.04, 1977- 45.10, 1978- 51.74, 1979- 59.26, 1981- 59.04, 1982- 68.24, 1983- 62.46, 1984- 65.20, 1985- 66.52, 1986- 67.08. pb SP: 18.28 '80.

**Gabriele MARTINS** b.1 Jun 1962 Aschersieben 1.70m 53kg. née Riemann. Club: SC Dynamo Berlin.
At Mar: ECp: '85- 2.
Progression at Mar: 1985- 2:32:23, 1986- 2:32:38. pbs: 1500m: 4:04.00 '82, 3000m: 8:48.46 '84, 10000m: 33:19.91 '85.

Silvia Madetzky. *ASP*

**Irina MESZYNSKI** b.24 Mar 1962 Berlin 1.75m 97kg. Club: TSC Berlin. Law student.
At DT: ECh: '82- 8, '86- 4; EJ: '79- 1. GDR champion 1982. World discus record 1984 and two world junior records 1980.
Progression at DT: 1975- 44.12, 1976- 45.00, 1977- 48.48, 1978- 50.54, 1979- 62.42, 1980- 64.86, 1981- 67.38, 1982- 71.40, 1984- 73.36, 1985- 68.18, 1986- 68.74. pb SP: 17.33 '81.
Her world discus record at the Friendship Games in 1984 followed a year out of competition when she had a knee operation.

**Ines MÜLLER** b.2 Jan 1959 Grimmen 1.82m 90kg. née Reichenbach. Club: SC Empor Rostock. Sports student.
At SP: OG: '80- 8; ECh: '86- 2; ECp: '85- 3; WIG: '85- 2. GDR champion 1985-6. At DT: EJ: '77- 1.
Progression at SP: 1975- 13.03, 1976- 13.07, 1977- 17.30, 1978- 18.24, 1979- 20.81, 1980- 21.00, 1981- 21.14, 1982- 20.93, 1983- 20.54, 1984- 21.32, 1985- 21.26i/20.68, 1986- 21.45. pb DT: 66.40 '85.

**Petra MÜLLER** b.18 Jul 1965 Quedlingen 1.80m 64kg. Club: SC Chemie Halle. Student of botany.
At 400m (R- 4x400mR): ECh: '86- 3 (1R); EJ: '83- 1 (1R); EI: '86- 2; ECp: '85- 2R. GDR champion 1986.
Progression at 400m: 1983- 51.79, 1982- 51.38, 1985- 50.14, 1986- 49.79. pbs: 100m: 11.91 '83, 200m: 23.36 '85.

**Dagmar NEUBAUER** b.3 Jun 1962 Suhl 1.70m 58kg. née Rübsam. Club: SC Turbine Erfurt. Student.
At 400m (R- 4x400m relay): WCh: '83- 7 (1R); ECh: '82- 6 (1R); EI: '82- 2, '85- 2; EJ: '79- 1 (1R); WCp: '81- 1R, '85- 1R; ECp: '81- 1R, '85- 2R. GDR champion 1982.
Ran on two world record 4x400m teams, 1982 and 1984.
Progression at 400m: 1977- 58.6, 1979- 51.55, 1980- 51.01, 1981- 50.98, 1982- 50.52, 1983- 50.48, 1984- 49.58, 1985- 50.38, 1986- 50.92. pbs: 100m: 11.73 '80, 200m: 22.87 '84, 800m: 1:58.36 '84.

**Cornelia OSCHKENAT** b.29 Oct 1961 Neubrandenburg 1.78m 67kg. née Riefstahl. Married Andreas Oschkenat (2nd EJ 1981, 5th ECh 1986 at 110mh, pb 13.50 '83) in 1984. Club: SC Dynamo Berlin. Agricultural student.
At 100mh: WCh: '83- 7; ECh: '82- h, '86- 2; WCp: '85- 1; ECp: '85- 3. GDR champion 1984-6. 2nd GP 1986. At 60mh: EI: '85- 1, '86- 1.
World indoor best of 6.73 for 50mh 1986.
Progression at 100mh: 1978- 14.36, 1979- 14.36, 1980- 13.78/13.73w, 1981- 13.25/13.09w, 1982- 12.90, 1983- 12.72, 1984- 12.57, 1985- 12.70/ 12.56w, 1986- 12.50. pbs: 100m: 11.31 '86, 11.10w '84; 200m: 23.15 '84.

**Sabine PAETZ** b.16 Oct 1957 Döbeln 1.74m 68kg. née Möbius. Club: SC DHfK Leipzig. Sports student.
At Pen/Hep: WCh: '83- 2; ECh: '82- 2; ECp: '79- 4, '81- 4, '85- 1.
GDR pentathlon record 1979, world heptathlon record 1984. World indoor pentathlon best, 4862* points in 1984.
Progression at 100mh/Pen (p) or Hep: 1972- 14.8, 1973- 14.5, 1974- 14.1, 1975- 14.4, 1976- 13.9, 1977- 13.50, 1978- 13.40/4154p, 1979- 13.41/4619p, 1980- 13.21/4627p, 1981- 13.36/ 6200, 1982- 12.83/6629, 1983- 13.06/6713, 1984- 12.54/6946, 1985- 12.97/12.78w/6595, 1986- 12.89/6456. pbs: 100m: 11.46 '84, 200m: 23.23w/23.37 '84, 800m: 2:07.03 '84, HJ: 1.83 '82, LJ: 7.12 '84, SP: 16.16 '84, JT: 44.62 '84.

**Helga RADTKE** b.16 May 1962 Sanitz 1.71m 64kg. Club: SC Empor Rostock. Sports student.
At LJ: WCh: '83- 12; ECh: '86- 3; EI: '83- 2, '86- 2; EJ: '79- 1; WIG: '85- 1.
Progression at LJ: 1977- 5.68, 1978- 5.74, 1979- 6.63, 1980- 6.71, 1982- 6.83, 1983- 6.83, 1984- 7.21, 1985- 7.19, 1986- 7.17. pbs: 100m: 11.6 '85, 100mh: 14.67 '79, HJ: 1.75 '82.

**Heike THEELE** b.4 Oct 1964 Magdeburg 1.72m 63kg. née Terpe. Club: SC Magdeburg. Physiotherapy student.
At 100mh: ECh: '86- 4.
European junior 100mh record 1982.
Progression at 100mh: 1981- 13.69, 1982- 13.17, 1983- 13.05, 1984- 13.02/12.99w, 1985- 13.03, 1986- 12.63. pbs: 100m: 11.53 '86, 200m: 23.70 '86, 400mh: 62.42 '81.

**Sibylle THIELE** b.6 Mar 1965 Meiningen 1.77m 74kg. Club: SC Dynamo Berlin. Student.
At Hep: EJ: '83- 1; ECp: '83- 9, '85- 3.
Three world junior heptathlon records 1982-3. GDR champion 1985.
Progression at Hep: 1980- 5304, 1981- 5705, 1982- 6046, 1983- 6465, 1984- 6387, 1985- 6487, 1986- 6635. pbs: 200m: 24.07 '83, 800m: 2:14.47 '83, 100mh: 13.14 '86, HJ: 1.90 '83, LJ: 6.77 '85, SP: 16.00 '86, JT: 48.68 '86.
Missed 1986 European Championships through injury.

**Gloria UIBEL** b. 13 Jan 1964 1.72m 57 kg. née Kovarik. Club: SC Cottbus.
At 100mh: EJ: '81- 2.
Progression at 100mh: 1979- 14.29, 1981- 13.26, 1983- 13.00, 1984- 12.79, 1985- 13.12, 1986- 12.91. pbs: 100m: 11.46w/11.60 '84, 200m: 24.34 '81.

**Christine WACHTEL** b.6 Jan 1965 Altentreptow 1.66m 56kg. Club: SC Neubrandenberg. Economics student.
At 800m: ECh: '86- 8; EJ: '83- 2 (1 4x400mR); WCp: '85- 1; ECp: '85- 3. GDR champion 1983, 1985. World junior 800m record 1983.
Progression at 800m: 1976- 2:29.5, 1977- 2:19.8, 1978- 2:16.4, 1979- 2:09.1, 1980- 2:04.7, 1981- 2:03.35, 1982- 2:01.16, 1983- 1:59.40, 1984- 1:58.24, 1985- 1:56.71, 1986- 1:58:59. pbs: 400m: 52.19 '84, 1500m: 4:18.03 '82, 400mh: 58.08 '82.

**Sigrun WODARS** b.7 Nov 1965 Eldena 1.66m 54kg. née Ludwigs. Club: SC Neubrandenburg. Sports student.
At 800m: ECh: '86- 2; EI: '86- 1. EJ '81- 4 400mh, '83- 5 400, 1 4x400mR. GDR 800m champion 1986.
Progression at 800m: 1982- 2:05.09, 1983- 2:03.40, 1984- 1:59.53, 1985- 1:58.32, 1986- 1:57.05. pbs: 200m: 24.36 '83, 400m: 51.95 '86, 1000m: 2:40.42 '85, 400mh: 56.18 '85.

**Katrin WUHN** b.19 Nov 1965 Berlin 1.70m 58kg. Club: SC Chemie Halle.
At 800m: EJ: '83- 1.
Progression at 800m: 1982- 2:08.4, 1983-

Sigrun Wodars (116) with Lyubov Gurina (USSR-831). Between them is Mitica Junghiatu (Rom), and on left is Gaby Bussmann (FRG).

2:00.18, 1984- 1:57.86, 1985- 2:00.56i, 1986- 1:58.80. pbs: 400m: 54.24 '83, 1000m: 2:35.4 '84, 1500m: 4:05.96 '86.

**Ilke WYLUDDA** b.28 Mar 1969 Leipzig 1.84m 88kg. Club: SC Chemie Halle. Schoolgirl.
At DT: WJ: '86- 1; EJ: '85- 1 (2 SP).
Progression at SP/DT: 1982- 13.72/46.54, 1983- 15.18/51.12, 1984- 16.42/57.74, 1985- 18.27/62.36, 1986- 19.08/65.86.

**Antje ZÖLLKAU** b.23 Jun 1963 Saalfeld 1.72m 71kg. née Kempe. Club: SC Motor Jena. Student.
At JT: WCh: '83- 11; ECh: '82- 2; EJ: '81- 2; ECp: '83- 2.
GDR javelin champion and record 1983.
Progression at JT: 1976- 38.24, 1977- 44.58, 1978- 49.66, 1979- 55.54, 1980- 53.92, 1981- 64.62, 1982- 68.38, 1983- 71.00, 1984- 72.16, 1985 - 65.96, 1986 - 65.18.

# FEDERAL REPUBLIC OF GERMANY

**Governing body**: Deutscher Leichtathletik Verband (DLV), Julius Reiber Strasse 19, 6100 Darmstadt. Founded in 1898.
**National Championships** first held in 1891.
**1986 champions: MEN**
100m: Christian Haas 10.18w, 200m/400m: Ralf Lübke 20.50/44.98, 800m: Matthias Assmann 1:46.35, 1500m: Uwe Mönkemeyer 3:38.59, 5000m: Dieter Baumann 13:45.00, 10000m: Christoph Herle 28:34.39, Mar: Wolfgang Krüger 2:15:20, 3000mSt: Patriz Ilg 8:28.34, 110mh: Siegfried Wentz 13.76, 400mh: Harald Schmid

48.59, HJ: Carlo Thränhardt 2.25, PV: Wladyslaw Kozakiewicz 5.55, LJ: Dietmar Haaf 7.97, TJ: Peter Bouschen 16.80w, SP: Karsten Stolz 19.92, DT: Alois Hannecker 65.28, HT: Christoph Sahner 79.56, JT: Wolfram Gambke 81.30, Dec: Jens Schulze 8032, 20kmW(t): Wolfgang Wiedemann 1:26:01, 50kmW: Alfons Schwarz 4:01:28.
**WOMEN**
100m/200m: Heide-Elke Gaugel 11.56/23.20, 400m: Gisela Kinzel 51.56, 800m: Gaby Bussmann 2:02.11, 1500m/3000m: Brigitte Kraus 4:13.39/8:47.83, 10000m: Kerstin Pressler 32:47.80, Mar: Heidi Hutterer 2:36:44, 100mh: Edith Oker 13.28w, 400mh: Gudrun Abt 56.94, HJ: Heike Redetzky 1.90, LJ: Monika Hirsch 6.66, SP/DT: Claudia Losch 20.92/62.36, JT: Beate Peters 69.56, Hep: Birgit Dressel 6377, 5kmW: Renate Warz 24:10.

**Peter BRAUN** b.1 Aug 1962 Tuttlingen 1.83m 64kg. Club: LG Tuttlingen-Fridingen.
At 800m: ECh: '86- 6; EI: '86- 1; ECp: '85- 3.
Progression at 800m: 1982- 1:52.24, 1983- 1:47.10, 1984- 1:45.62, 1985- 1:44.15, 1986- 1:44.03. pb 400m: 47.19 '86.

**Rolf DANNEBERG** b.1 Mar 1953 Hamburg 1.98m 112kg. Club: LG Wedel/Pinneberg. Teacher.
At DT: OG: '84- 1; ECh: '82- dnq, '86- 11. FRG champion 1980.
Progression at DT: 1974- 50.56, 1975- 55.30, 1976- 55.96, 1977- 56.02, 1978- 61.12, 1979- 61.02, 1980- 62.86, 1981- 62.50, 1982- 63.74, 1983- 62.84, 1984- 67.40, 1985- 64.94, 1986- 66.16. pb SP: 17.80 '86.
Caused major upset to win Olympic discus title.

**Jürgen EVERS** b.29 Apr 1965 Stuttgart 1.83m 66kg. Club: Salamander Kornwestheim. Student. At 100m/200m (R- 4x100m relay): OG: '84- qf/qf (5R); WCh: '83- 5R; ECh: '86- sf/2; EJ: '83- 4/1 (1R). European junior 200m record 1983.
Progression at 200m: 1982- 21.24, 1983- 20.37, 1984- 21.02/20.95w, 1985- 21.11, 1986- 20.58. pbs: 100m: 10.31 '83, 400m: 46.5 '84.
The 1983 European Junior champion caused a surprise when he won the European silver medal in the city of his birth.

**Wolfgang GAMBKE** b.2 Nov 1959 Pinneberg 1.81m 87kg. Club: LG Wedel/Pinneberg. Biology student.
At JT: OG: '84- 4; ECh: '86- 6; WSG: '85- 2. FRG champion 1986.
Progression at JT: 1975- 63.06, 1976- 68.62, 1977- 65.60, 1978- 71.50, 1979- 76.00, 1980-81.48, 1981- 85.64, 1982- 84.02, 1983- 81.76, 1984- 85.80, 1985- 84.48, new: 1986- 81.30.

**Jürgen HINGSEN** b.25 Jan 1958 Duisburg 2.00m 102kg. Club: LAV Bayer Uerdingen/ Dormagen. Physical education student.
At Dec: OG: '84- 2; WCh: '83- 2; ECh: '78- 13, '82-2, '86- 2; WSG: '79- 2; ECp: '79- 10, '81- 2. FRG champion at decathlon 1982 and long jump 1983.
Three decathlon world records: one each year 1982-4.
Progression at Dec: 1977- 7483, 1978- 7944, 1979- 8218, 1980- 8409, 1981- 8146, 1982-8741, 1983- 8825, 1984- 8832, 1985- dnf, 1986-8730. pbs: 100m: 10.70w '84, 10.74 '82, 200m: 21.66 '82, 400m: 47.65 '82, 1500m: 4:12.3 '79, 110mh: 14.07/13.84w '84, 13.8w '83, HJ: 2.18 '78, PV: 5.10 '84, LJ: 8.04 '82, SP: 16.57 '86, DT: 50.82 '84, JT: 67.42 '83.
Great decathlete who has ranked as world number two five times 1981-6.

**Patriz ILG** b.5 Dec 1957 Aalen-Oberalfingen 1.73m 63kg. Club: LAC Quelle Fürth. Physical education and crafts teacher.
At 3kmSt: WCh: '83- 1; ECh: '78- 2, '82- 1, '86- 3; ECp: '81- 3, '85- 1. At 3000m: EI: '82- 1; EJ: '75- 2. FRG steeplechase champion 1978, 1980-2, 1985-6.
Progression at 3kmSt: 1977- 8:40.4, 1978-8:16.92, 1980- 8:25.89, 1981- 8:21.13, 1982-8:17.04, 1983- 8:15.06, 1984- 8:40.53, 1985-8:16.14, 1986- 8:16.92. pbs: 1500m: 3:40.53 '83, 3000m: 7:45.06 '78, 5000m: 13:24.4 '83, 10000m: 28:47.6 '78.
Injuries caused the World and European steeple-chase champion to miss most of the 1979 and 1984 seasons. A great finisher who has not run all out for fast times. He is the only steeplechaser to win medals at three European Championships.

**Wladyslaw KOZAKIEWICZ** b.8 Dec 1953 Solecznikach, near Vilnius, Lithuania 1.87m 86kg. Club: TK Hannover. Left Poland 1984 and granted FRG citizenship 1986.
At PV: OG: '76- 11, '80- 1; WCh: '83- 8=; ECh: '74- 2, '78- 4; EI: '75- 3, '77- 1, '79- 1, '82- 3; WSG: '77- 1, '79- 1; WCp: '77- 2; ECp: '75- 1, '77- 1, '79-3, '81- nh. Polish champion 1973, 1976-9, 1981, 1984.
Seven Polish pole vault records 1973-80, of which four were European records 1975-7 and then two world records in 1980: 5.72m and 5.78m, the latter when he won the Olympic title. Five FRG records 1986.
Progression at PV: 1968- 2.95, 1969- 3.85, 1970-4.26, 1971- 4.65, 1972- 5.02, 1973- 5.35i, 1974-5.38, 1975- 5.60, 1976- 5.62, 1977- 5.66, 1978-5.62, 1979- 5.61, 1980- 5.78, 1981- 5.62, 1982-5.60, 1983- 5.62, 1984- 5.75, 1985- 5.70, 1986-5.70. pb Dec: 7692 '77.
Brother Eduard had a decathlon pb of 7633 points in 1974.

**Guido KRATSCHMER** b.10 Jan 1953 Gross-heubach 1.86m 94kg. Club: USC Mainz. Physical education teacher.
At Dec: OG: '76- 2, '84- 4; WCh: '83- 9; ECh: '74-3, '78- dnf, '82- 9, '86- dnf; ECp: 75- 9, '77- 3, '79-2, '81- 5, '83- 11. FRG champion at decathlon 1975-80, and 110mh 1978.
World decathlon record 1980, European record 1978 and two other FRG records 1976.
Progression at Dec: 1972- 7379, 1973- 7306, 1974- 8108, 1975- 7866, 1976- 8407, 1977-8061, 1978- 8493, 1979- 8476, 1980- 8667, 1981- 8069, 1982- 8194, 1983- 8460, 1984-8429, 1985- 8223, 1986- 8519. pbs: 100m: 10.54/ 10.4w '79, 200m: 21.58 '84, 21.4 '81; 400m: 47.64 '78, 1500m: 4:21.21 '80, 110mh: 13.85/13.6 '78, HJ: 2.03 '76, PV: 4.90 '84, LJ: 7.84 '78, SP: 16.94 '85, DT: 49.74 '78, JT: 69.40 '84.
Has been fated in European Championships, having to withdraw in both 1978 and 1986 when in prime form. Won at Götzis in 1986.

**Ralf LÜBKE** b.17 Jun 1965 Mülheim/Ruhr 1.92m 80kg. Club: LG Bayer Leverkusen. Student, currently doing military service.
At 200m: OG: '84- 5; EJ: '83- 2 (1 at 4 x 100mR); ECp: '85- 3 (1 at 4x400mR). At 400m (R- 4x400m relay): ECh: '86- 5 (2R). FRG champion 100m 1984, 200m 1984-6, 400m 1986.
World indoor bests for 200m at 20.98 and 20.77 in 1983, and 20.67 and 20.57 in 1984.
Progression at 200m/400m: 1980- 22.04/50.2, 1981- 21.43, 1982- 21.04, 1983- 20.50, 1984-20.51, 1985- 20.38/45.06, 1986- 20.50/44.98. pb 100m: 10.42/10.40w '84.

**Dietmar MÖGENBURG** b.15 Aug 1961 Leverkusen 2.01m 78kg. Club: OSC Berlin. Architectural student.
At HJ: OG: '84- 1; WCh: '83- 4; ECh: '82- 1, '86- 4; EI: '80- 1, '81- 2=, '82- 1, '84- 1, '86- 1; EJ: '79- 1; ECp: '79- 1, '83- 3. FRG champion 1980-5.
Six FRG high jump records, including a world, and world junior, record 2.35m in 1980 and two European records at 2.36m in 1983.
Progression at HJ: 1972- 1.41, 1973- 1.67, 1974- 1.74, 1975- 1.90, 1976- 2.05, 1977- 2.10, 1978- 2.23, 1979- 2.32, 1980- 2.35, 1981- 2.30, 1982- 2.34i/2.30, 1983- 2.32, 1984- 2.36, 1985- 2.39i/2.31, 1986- 2.34i/2.30. pb LJ: 7.76 '80.
A supreme competitor, who has made a habit of winning the important competitions, since his first major success when he won the 1979 European Cup Final high jump at the age of 17 in 1979.

**Klaus PLOGHAUS** b.31 Jan 1956 Gelnhausen 1.86m 110kg. Club: Bayer Leverkusen. Architectural student.
At HT: OG: '84- 3; WCh: '83- 6; ECh: '78- 12, '82- 8, '86- 9; EJ: '73- 4, '75- 2; WSG: '79- 1, '81- 1. FRG champion 1982.
Progression at HT: 1973- 59.72, 1974- 65.40, 1975- 69.30, 1976- 71.62, 1977- 71.88, 1978- 73.14, 1979- 76.76, 1980- 77.60, 1981- 80.56, 1982- 77.44, 1983- 80.04, 1984- 79.36, 1985- 80.20, 1986- 81.32.

**Christoph SAHNER** b.23 Sept 1963 Illingen 1.80m 103kg. Club: TV Wattenscheid. Mining mechanic.
At HT: OG: '84- nt; WCh: '83- 11; ECh: '82- dnq, '86- 8; EJ: '81- 1; ECp: '85- 4. FRG champion 1985-6.
Progression at HT: 1980- 61.34, 1981- 72.06, 1982- 75.24, 1983- 77.88, 1984- 78.04, 1985- 81.56, 1986- 80.38.

**Jörg SCHAEFER** b.17 Jul 1959 Leckingsen 1.98m 116kg. Club: TV Wattenscheid. Student.
At HT: ECh: '82- 9, '86- 5.
Progression at HT: 1978- 50.00, 1979- 59.64, 1980- 67.68, 1981- 72.56, 1982- 76.32, 1983- 75.38, 1984- 76.58, 1985- 78.90, 1986- 79.92.

**Ralf SALZMANN** b.6 Feb 1955 Kassel 1.72m 58kg. Club: PSV Grün-Weiss Kassel. Policeman.
At Mar: OG: '84- 18; WCh: '83- dnf; ECh: '82- 22, '86- 4. FRG champion 1980-4.
Progression at Mar: 1979- 2:17:56 1980- 2:16:22, 1981- 2:15:42, 1982- 2:14:33, 1983- 2:12:57, 1984- 2:11:21, 1985- 2:10:56, 1986- 2:11:41.
pbs: 3000m: 7:58.19 '82, 5000m: 13:37.74 '84, 10000m: 28:11.49 '85.

**Harald SCHMID** b.29 Sep 1957 Hanau 1.87m 82kg. Club: TV Gelnhausen. Physical education student. Married to Elzbieta Rabsztyn (7th European 100mh 1978 for Poland).
At 400mh (R- 4 x 400m relay): OG: '76- sf (3R), '84- 3; WCh: '83- 2 (2R); ECh: '78- 1 (1R), '82- 1 (1R), '86- 1 (2R); WCp: '77- 3 (1R), '79- 2, '85- 3; ECp: '77- 2, '79- 1, '81- 2, '83- 1, '85- 1 (1R). At 400m: EJ: '75- 7 (2R); ECp: '79- 1 (1R). FRG champion at 400mh 1977-8, 1980-6 and at 400m 1979.
Four FRG 400mh records, the last two European records, 1977-82. World junior record in 1976.
Progression at 400mh: 1974- 54.9, 1975- 51.8, 1976- 49.81, 1977- 48.85, 1978- 48.43, 1979- 47.85, 1980- 48.05, 1981- 48.64, 1982- 47.48, 1983- 48.49, 1984- 47.69, 1985- 47.85, 1986- 47.89. pbs: 100m: 10.3 '78, 200m: 20.69 '80, 400m: 44.92 '79, 500m: 1:01.22 '78, 800m: 1:44.84 '79, 110mh: 14.7 '78.
He is the last man to have defeated Edwin Moses at 400mh (at the ISTAF meeting in 1977), and has been consistently in the world's top three since then. He has a men's record of five European gold medals; in 1986 he completed a hat-trick of titles at 400mh, and added a silver to his two relay golds.

**Rainer SCHWARZ** b.5 Jun 1959 München 1.81m 63kg. Club: LG Buchendorf.
At 3kmSt: WCh: '83- sf; ECh: '82- 12, '86- 7. FRG champion 1983.
FRG 3kmSt record 1985.
Progression at 3kmSt: 1978- 8:56.1, 1979- 8:48.5, 1980- 8:33.53, 1981- 8:25.64, 1982- 8:25.51, 1983- 8:19.64, 1984- 8:31.8, 1985- 8:11.93, 1986- 8:20.90. pbs: 1500m: 3:45.5 '83, 3000m: 7:54.09 '85, 5000m: 13:39.53 '83.

**Erwin SKAMRAHL** b.8 Mar 1958 Oberg 1.78m 67kg. Club: VfL Wolfsburg. Policeman.
At 400m (R- 4x400m relay): OG: '84- qf; WCh: '83- 4 (2R); ECh: '82- 1R, '86- 8; ECp: '85- 4 (1R). At 200m: ECh: '82- 4; EI: '82- 1; ECp: '81- 3, '83- 3. FRG champion at 200m 1981-3, 400m 1980, 1982, 1984-5.
European 400m record 1983. World indoor bests: 200m: 20.99 '82, 300m: 32.72 '86.
Progression at 400m: 1974- 52.3, 1975- 48.3, 1976- 47.05, 1977- 47.2, 1978- 46.75, 1979- 45.84, 1980- 45.80, 1981- 45.3, 1982- 45.09, 1983- 44.50, 1984- 45.74, 1985- 44.92, 1986- 45.46. pbs: 100m: 10.47 '83, 200m: 20.44 '83, 20.25w '81, 300m: 32.74 '80.

**Herbert STEFFNY** b.5 Sep 1953 Trier 1.79m 67kg. Club: Post Jahn Freiburg. Biologist.
At Mar: ECh: '86- 3; WCp: '85- 14. FRG champion 1985. 5th Chicago 1986.

Harald Schmid. *ASP*

Progression at Mar: 1983- 2:20:05, 1984-2:14:30, 1985- 2:11:49, 1986- 2:11:17. pbs: 3000m: 8:05.95 '86, 5000m: 13:46.74 '86, 10000m: 28:35.00 '86.

**Klaus TAFELMEIER** b.12 Apr 1958 Singen 1.90m 94kg. Club: Bayer Leverkusen. Physical education student.
At JT: OG: '84- dnq; WCh: '83- 8; ECh: '82- 13, '86- 1; EJ: '75- 6, '77- 1; ECp: '81- 4, '83- 3, '85- 7. FRG champion 1982-5.
World best, two European and four FRG records for new javelin 1986.
Progression at JT: 1974- 62.46, 1975- 77.82, 1976- 82.12, 1977- 84.14, 1978- 86.00, 1979-89.78, 1980- 88.34, 1981- 88.48, 1982- 87.30, 1983- 91.44, 1984- 90.10, 1985- 89.38, new: 1986- 85.74.
Many long throws, but he failed to place well in major events from his European Junior win in 1977 until he triumphed in Stuttgart with the gold medal and European record.

Klaus Tafelmeier. *Mark Shearman*

Carlo Thränhardt. *Mark Shearman*

**Carlo THRÄNHARDT** b.5 Jul 1957 Bad Lauch-städt 1.99m 85kg. Club: ASV Köln. Student of journalism.
At HJ: OG: '84- 10; WCh: '83- 7; ECh: '78- 5, '86-3; EI: '81- 2=, '83- 1, '84- 2=, '86- 2; WCp: '77- 4; ECp: '77- 5, '85- 4. FRG champion 1986. Won AAA title 1980.
Seven FRG high jump records 1977-84, including European records 2.36m and 2.37m in 1984. World indoor bests: 2.37m 1984, 2.40m 1987.
Progression at HJ: 1975- 2.09, 1976- 2.15, 1977-2.25, 1978- 2.26i, 1979- 2.30, 1980- 2.31, 1981-2.28i, 1982- 2.30, 1983- 2.34, 1984- 2.37, 1985-2.30, 1986- 2.36i/2.32, 1987- 2.40i.
Although less consistent at 2.30m or above than in previous years, he won his first outdoor major championships medal and first FRG title in 1986.

**Siegfried WENTZ** b.7 Mar 1960 Röthenbach 1.93m 93kg. Club: USC Mainz. Medical student.
At Dec: OG: '84- 3; WCh: '83- 3; ECh: '82- 20, '86-3; EJ: '79- 1; ECp: '81- 4, '83- 3, '85- 5. FRG champion 1985 (and 110mh 1986).
Progression at Dec: 1977- 6907, 1978- 7391, 1979- 7775, 1980- 7876, 1981- 8178, 1982-8301, 1983- 8762, 1984- 8497, 1985- 8440,

1986- 8676. pbs: 100m: 10.76 '86, 400m: 47.38 '83, 1500m: 4:19.78 '82, 110mh: 13.76 '86, HJ: 2.12 '86, PV: 4.90 '86, LJ: 7.63 '85, SP: 16.11 '85, DT: 51.28 '86, JT: 75.08 '83.

**Thomas WESSINGHAGE** b.22 Feb 1952 Hagen 1.83m 69kg. Club: ASV Köln. Doctor of medicine.
At 1500m: OG: '72-sf, '76- sf (sf at 800m); ECh: '74- 3, '78- 4; EI: 1st '75, '80, '81, 2nd '74, '76, '78, '79, 3rd '84; EJ: '70- 8; WCp: '77- 2, '79- 1; ECp: '75- 1, '77- 2, '79- 2; WSG: '75- 1. At 3000m: EI: '85- 2. At 5000m: WCh: '83- 6; ECh: '82- 1, '86- h; ECp: '81- 5, '83- 1, '85- 2. 3rd GP 1985, FRG champion at 1500m 1975, 1977-82 and 5000m 1982, 1985.
FRG records at 1500m (5), 1M, 3000m, 5000m (2). European records at 1M: 3:53.10 in 1976 and 3:52.50 in 1978, and at 2000m in 1982. Record 63 internationals for FRG 1972-86.
Progression at 1500m/5000m: 1969- 3:58.2, 1970- 3:47.6, 1971- 3:42.2, 1972- 3:40.5, 1973-3:39.47, 1974- 3:39.30, 1975- 3:36.37, 1976-3:34.78, 1977- 3:36.0, 1978- 3:37.19/13:37.30, 1979- 3:34.77/13:19.87, 1980- 3:31.58/13:19.76, 1981- 3:33.49/13:13.47, 1982- 3:32.85/13:12.78, 1983- 3:34.72/13:18.86, 1984- 3:38.61/13:53.09,

1985- 3:37.53/13:22.44, 1986- 3:39.31/13:21.98.
pbs: 800m: 1:46.56 '76, 1000m: 2:16.4 '77, 1M:
3:49.98 '83, 2000m: 4:52.20 '82, 3000m: 7:36.75
'81.

# Women

**Sabine BRAUN** b.19 Jun 1965 Essen 1.72m
60kg. Club: Bayer Leverkusen. Student of sport
and biology.
At Hep: OG: '84- 6; EJ: '83- 2; ECp: '85- 4. At LJ:
WCp: '85- 5; ECp: '85- 3. FRG LJ champion 1985.
Progression at Hep: 1982- 5477, 1983- 6254,
1984- 6436, 1985- 6323, 1986- 6418. pbs: 100m:
11.59 '85, 200m: 23.60 '85, 800m: 2:09.41 '84,
100mh: 13.34 '85, HJ: 1.81 '83, LJ: 6.73 '85, SP:
13.09 '84, JT: 54.10 '86.
Missed 1986 European Championships through
injury.

**Gabriele BUSSMANN** b.8 Oct 1959 Haltern/
Westfalia 1.70m 55kg. Club: SC Eintracht Hamm.
Student of psychology.
At 800m: ECh: '86- 4. At 400m (R- 4 x 400m
relay): OG: '84- sf (3R); WCh: '83- 4; ECh: '78- sf,
'82- 7; EI: '82- 3; EJ: '77- 1 (1R); ECp: '81- 2, '83-
3. FRG champion 400m 1978, 1980, 1982-3;
800m 1986.
Five FRG 400m records 1981-3.
Progression at 400m/800m: 1975- 55.4, 1976-
53.31, 1977- 52.33, 1978- 51.74, 1979- 51.77,
1980- 51.10, 1981- 50.83, 1982- 50.64, 1983-
49.75, 1984- 50.98, 1985- 2:03.47, 1986- 51.71/
1:58.11. pbs: 100m: 11.65 '81, 11.4 '83; 200m:
23.15 '83.

**Birgit DRESSEL** b.4 May 1960 Bremen 1.72m
65kg. Club: USC Mainz. Physical education
teacher.
At Hep: OG: '84- 9; ECh: '86- 4. FRG champion
1986.
Progression at Hep: 1980- 5248, 1981- 5547,
1982- 5845, 1983- 5969, 1984- 6144, 1985-
6056, 1986- 6487. pbs: 200m: 24.68 '86, 800m:
2:14.30 '84, 100mh: 13.52 '86, 400mh: 59.87 '86,
HJ: 1.92 '86, LJ: 6.41 '86, SP: 14.84i '87, JT:
45.70 '86.

**Sabine EVERTS** b.4 Mar 1961 Düsseldorf 1.69m
55kg. Club: Bayer Uerdingen/Dormagen. Student
of physical education and philology.
At Pen/Hep: OG: '84- 3; WCh: '83- 4; ECh: '82- 3;
EJ: '79- 1; ECp: '79- 7, '81- 3, '85- 6. At LJ: ECh:
'82- 6; EI: '82- 1; ECp: '83- 5. At 400mh: ECp: '83-
5, '85- 4. FRG titles at Pen/Hep 1980-3, 1985, LJ
1979-80, 1982, 400mh 1985.
World junior pentathlon record 1979. Five FRG

heptathlon records 1981-2.
Progression at LJ/Pen (p) or Hep: 1974- 5.26,
1975- 5.38, 1976- 6.20, 1977- 6.28/4225p, 1978-
6.21/4366p, 1979- 6.57, 6.69w/4627p, 1980-
6.64i/4657p, 1981- 6.66/6363, 1982- 6.77/6523,
1983- 6.66/6388, 1984- 6.77/6388, 1985- 6.71w/
6.70/6368, 1986- 6.32. pbs: 100m: 11.81/11.72w
'82, 11.5 '80; 200m: 23.43 '82; 400m: 52.35i '81;
800m: 2:06.17 '83; 100mh: 13.17 '82; 400mh:
55.48 '85; HJ: 1.89 '82; SP: 12.86 '81; JT: 38.70.
Injured in 1986.

**Heidi-Elke GAUGEL** b.11 Jul 1959 Schönaich
1.67m 54kg. Club: VfL Sindelfingen. Shorthand
clerk.
At 100m/200m (R- 4x400m relay): OG: '84- sf/sf
(3R); ECh: '82- h/h, '86- 8/- (2R); EI: '82- -/3; ECp:
'85- 4/4. FRG champion at 100m & 200m 1984-6.
Progression at 100m, 200m: 1973- 12.8; 1974-
12.8; 1975- 12.6; 1976- 12.17; 24.6; 1977- 11.87,
24.6; 1978- 11.75/11.7, 24.21/23.7; 1979- 11.79,
23.70/23.60w; 1980- 11.53, 23.60i/23.65; 1981-
11.54/11.35w, 23.02; 1982- 11.39, 23.03; 1983-
11.46/11.3, 23.36i/23.66; 1984- 11.24/22.72,
1985- 11.15/22.56, 1986- 11.20/22.91. pb 400m:
52.83 '85.

**Margrit KLINGER** b.22 Jun 1960 Hönebach/
Hessen 1.65m 55kg. Club: TV Obersuhl. Admin-
istrative clerk.
At 800m: OG: '84- 7; WCh: '83- 4; ECh: '82- 3;
ECp: '81- 4, '83- 3, '85- dnf. FRG champion at
800m 1980-82, 1984-5, 1500m 1984.
FRG 800m record 1982.
Progression at 800m: 1973- 2:16.9, 1974- 2:15.1,
1975- 2:13.1, 1976- 2:11.3, 1977- 2:06.7, 1978-
2:02.6, 1979- 1:59.48, 1980- 1:59.20, 1981-
1:59.54, 1982- 1:57.22, 1983- 1:58.01, 1984-
2:00.00, 1985- 1:57.58, 1986- 1:59.98. pbs:
400m: 53.4 '80, 1000m: 2:34.94 '83, 1500m:
4:02.66 '83, 5000m: 16:47.97 '85, 400mh: 61.6
'78.

**Brigitte KRAUS** b.12 Aug 1956 Bensberg 1.80m
58kg. Club: ASV Köln. Draughtswoman.
At 3000m: OG: '84- dnf; WCh: '83- 2; ECh: '82- 7,
'86- h; EI '84- 1; ECp: '77- 5. At 1500m: OG: '76-
sf; ECh: '78- sf; EI: '76- 1, '78- 3, '82- 2, '83- 1, '85-
3; ECp: '79- 6, '81- 4, '85- 6. At 800m: ECp '75- 7.
Has won a record 58 FRG junior and senior titles
indoors and out. Senior outdoor titles: 800m
1976; 1500m 1976, 1978-9, 1981, 1983, 1985-6;
3000m 1976-7, 1979, 1983-6.
FRG records at 1000m (3), 1500m (3), 1M (1) and
3000m (5) 1976-85. World indoor 1000m best of
2:34.8 in 1978. Women's record 54 internationals
for FRG 1973-86.
Progression at 1500m/3000m: 1971- 4:38.4,
1972- 4:22.97, 1973- 4:24.0, 1974- 4:17.4, 1975-

4:13.91, 1976- 4:04.21/9:05.6, 1977- 4:08.7/
9:01.29, 1978- 4:01.54/9:29.7, 1979- 4:04.8/
8:54.4, 1980- 4:06.62/9:26.2, 1981- 4:05.47/
9:16.6, 1982- 4:04.22i/8:44.43, 1983- 4:02.42/
8:35.11, 1984- 4:06.00/8:40.90, 1985- 4:03.64i/
8:58.55, 1986- 4:04.65/8:47.83. pbs: 400m: 55.6
'78, 800m: 1:59.28 '83, 1000m: 2:33.44 '79, 1M:
4:25.03 '85.

**Claudia LOSCH** b.10 Jan 1960 Wanne-Eickel
1.81m 84kg. Club: LAC Quelle Fürth. Optician.
At SP: OG: '84- 1; WCh: '83- 7; ECh: '86- 4 (9 DT);
EI: '84- 2, '85- 2, '86- 1; WSG: '83- 2. FRG
champion 1982-6 (and DT 1986).
Progression at SP: 1975- 12.58, 1976- 13.14,
1977- 13.71, 1978- 14.14, 1979- 15.00, 1980-
15.85, 1981- 15.50, 1982- 18.51, 1983- 20.08,
1984- 20.55, 1985- 20.59i/19.96, 1986- 21.46i/
20.92. pb DT: 63.12 '85.
Rapid progress to the status of top Western shot-
putter.

**Beate PETERS** b.12 Oct 1959 Marl 1.78m 80kg.
Club: TV Wattenscheid. Student of PE and biology.
At JT: OG: '84- 7; WCh: '83- 7; ECh: '86- 3; WSG:
'81- 2, '83- 1, '85- 2; ECp: '83- 4, '85- 4. FRG
champion 1985-6.
FRG javelin record 1986.
Progression at JT: 1976- 40.18, 1977- 46.84,
1978- 56.64, 1979- 57.16, 1980- 50.50, 1981-
56.98, 1982- 60.24, 1983- 66.86, 1984- 63.02,
1985- 64.40, 1986- 69.56. pb SP: 14.63 '78.

**Heike REDETZKY** b.5 May 1964 Kiel 1.81m
64kg. Club: LG Bayer Leverkusen. Student.
At HJ: OG: '84- 11=; ECh: '86- 6; EJ: '81- 5; ECp:
'85- 6. FRG champion 1984-6.
Progression at HJ: 1979- 1.69, 1980- 1.85, 1981-
1.87i, 1982- 1.89, 1983- 1.87i, 1984- 1.91, 1985-
1.92, 1986- 1.93. pbs: 100mh: 14.04/14.0 '81, LJ:
6.13 '81.

**Ute THIMM** b.10 Jul 1958 Bochum 1.67m 53kg.
Club: TV Wattenscheid. Sociology student.
At 400m (R- 4x400m relay): OG: '86- 6 (3R);
WCh: '83- 6R (qf 200m); ECh: '82- 4R, '86- 5 (2R).
FRG champion 1981, 1984.
Progression at 400m: 1977- 55.4, 1980- 54.6,
1981- 52.32, 1982- 51.47, 1983- 50.78, 1984-
50.37, 1985- 53.53, 1986- 51.15. pbs: 100m:
11.31 '85, 200m: 22.88 '86.

**Ingrid THYSSEN** b.9 Jan 1956 Aachen. 1.71m
71kg. Club: LG Bayer Leverkusen. Physical
education teacher.
At JT: OG: '84- 6; WCh: '83- 14; ECh: '78- 7, '82-
9, '86- 7; WSG: '81- 4; ECp: '81- 3. FRG champion
1978-84.

Two FRG javelin records 1982-5.
Progression at JT: 1970- 35.50, 1971- 39.66,
1972- 46.08, 1973- 49.38, 1974- 51.90, 1975-
55.72, 1976- 60.00, 1977- 57.14, 1978- 60.42,
1979- 60.40, 1980- 64.04, 1981- 65.56, 1982-
68.10, 1983- 65.80, 1984- 66.12, 1985- 68.84,
1986- 67.34. pb HJ: 1.76 '71.
German schools four-event (75m, LJ, SP, HJ)
champion 1970.

# GREECE

**Governing body**: Hellenic Amateur Athletic
Association (SEGAS), 137 Syngrou Avenue,
Athens 171 21. Founded 1896.
**National Championships** first held in 1896
(men), 1930 (women).
**1986 Champions: MEN**
100m: Kosmas Stratos 10.46, 200m: Theodoros
Gatzios 21.12, 400m: Vassilis Kalipossis 47.16,
800m: Sotirios Moutsanas 1:49.61, 1500m: Niko-
laos Tsiakoulas 3:43.33, 5000m/10000m:
Spiridon Andriopoulos 14:01.08/29:13.03, Mar:
Anastassios Psathas 2:17:12, 3000mSt: Kyria-
kos Moutessidis 8:35.83, 110mh: Grigoris
Zagoras 14.46, 400mh: Thanassis Kalogiannis
49.53, HJ: Kosmas Mihalopoulos 2.20, PV:
Andreas Tsonis 5.00, LJ: Giorgios Tsiantas 7.62,
TJ: Charalambos Giannoulis 16.47, SP: Dimitrios
Koutsoukis 19.45, DT: Konstantinos Georgako-
poulos 59.72, HT: Triantafillos Apostolidis 66.00,
JT: Antonios Papadimitriou 71.58, Dec: Than-
assis Pambaliaris 7226, 20kmW: Christos Kara-
georgos 1:28:35.8.
**WOMEN**
100m/200m: Marina Skordi 11.87/24.34, 400m:
Artemis Vassilikopoulou 55.68, 800m/1500m:
Irini Theodoridou 2:07.32/4:32.53, 5000m:
Dimitra Papaspyrou 17:08.41, Mar: Georgia
Papanastassiou 3:04:04, 100mh: Elisabeth
Pantazi 14.00, 400mh: Chionati Kapeti 59.29, HJ:
Niki Gavera 1.80, LJ: Paraskevi Patoulidou 6.01,
SP: Eleni Tsedemeidou 13.85, DT: Georgia
Giannakidou 48.96, JT: Anna Verouli 58.48,
10kmW: Konstantina Bornivelli 55:23.2.

**Thanassis KALOGIANNIS** b.10 Sep 1965 Volos
1.93m 77kg. Dental student at Athens University.
At 400mh: OG: '84- h; EC: '82- h, '86- 8.
Greek 400mh record 1986.
Progression at 400mh: 1982- 54.1, 1983- 51.67,
1984- 50.22, 1986- 48.88. pbs: 200m: 21.48 '86,
400m: 45.90 '84.

# Women

**Sofia SAKORAFA** b.29 Apr 1957 Trilaka 1.77m 73kg. Physical education teacher. Married her coach Dimitrios Kostavelis in 1983.
At JT: OG: '76- dnq, '80- dnq; ECh: '78- dnq, '82-3; EJ: '75- 5. Balkan champion 1986.
World javelin record 1982, 16 Greek records 1972-82.
Progression at JT: 1972- 41.32, 1973- 49.70, 1974- 51.94, 1975- 56.04, 1976- 57.40, 1977- 55.74, 1978- 59.76, 1979- 58.82, 1980- 59.34, 1981- 63.46, 1982- 74.20, 1983- 72.28, 1986- 62.50. pb SP: 14.60 '82.
After a shoulder operation, she did not compete in 1984-5.

**Anna VEROULI** b.13 Nov 1956 Kavala 1.66m 75kg. Physical education teacher.
At JT: OG: '84- dnq; WCh: '83- 3; ECh: '82- 1, '86- 10. Five Greek javelin records 1973-82.
Progression at JT: 1971- 34.90, 1972- 40.96, 1973- 45.50, 1974- 48.94, 1975- 50.22, 1976- 54.24, 1977- 49.94, 1978- 48.42, 1979- 53.62, 1980- 57.70, 1981- 62.28, 1982- 70.02, 1983- 70.90, 1984- 72.70, 1986- 64.30. pb SP: 15.24 '82.
There were emotional scenes in 1982 in her home-town of Athens, where she won the first European Championships gold medal by a Greek woman. She was disqualified at the 1984 Olympics for illegal drug use.

# HUNGARY

**Governing body**: Magyar Atlétikai Szövetség, 1143 Budapest, Dozsa György utca 1-3. Founded 1897.
**National Championships** first held in 1896 (men), 1932 (women)
**1986 Champions: MEN**
100m: Attila Kovacs 10.29, 200m: György Fetter 20.78, 400m: Gusztav Menczer 45.97, 800m: Andras Paroczai 1:49.20, 1500m/5000m/10000m: Gabor K.Szabo 3:40.64/14:08.18/28:55.25, Mar: Istvan Kerekjarto 2:13:35, 3000mSt: Gabor Marko 8:36.74, 110mh: György Bakos 13.74, 400mh: Istvan Simon Balla 49.62, HJ: Gyula Nemeth 2.25, PV: Gabor Molnar 5.30, LJ: Gyula Paloczi 8.02, TJ: Bela Bakosi 16.59w, SP: Laszlo Szabo 18.83, DT: Csaba Hollo 60.50, HT: Tibor Gecsek 77.24, JT: Tamas Bolgar 76.84, Dec: Bela Vago 7516, 20kmW: Sandor Urbanik 1:26:04, 50kmW: Rudolf Vereb 3:57:32.

**WOMEN**
100m: Juhasz Ecsekine 11.71, 200m/400m: Judit Forgacs 23.89/51.81, 800m: Elvira Biacsics 2:05.62, 3000m/10000m/Mar: Karolina Szabo 9:10.12/32:07.64/2:30:31, 5000m: Erika Vereb 15:38.93, 100mh: Xenia Siska 12.92, 400mh: Eva Balazs 59.88, HJ: Katalin Sterk 1.98, LJ: Ildiko Fekete 6.56, SP/DT: Marta Kripli 17.49/62.36, JT: Zsuzsa Malovecz 61.46, Hep: Margit Palombi 6001, 10kmW: Rudolfne Hudi 49:00.

**György BAKOS** b.6 Jul 1960 Zalaegerszeg 1.88m 77kg. Club: U.Dozsa. Student of economics at Budapest University.
At 110mh: WCh: '83- 6; ECh: '82- sf, '86- 8; EJ: '79- 2; WSG: '85- 2; WCp: '85- 5=. Hungarian champion 1980, 1983-4, 1986. At 60mh: EI: '84-2, '85- 1.
Eight Hungarian 110mh records 1981-5.
Progression at 110mh: 1979- 14.21, 1980- 14.12, 1981- 13.77/13.5w, 1982- 13.80, 1983- 13.49, 1984- 13.45, 1985- 13.45, 1986- 13.60. pbs: 100m: 10.69 '81, 200m: 21.21 '83, 300m: 33.03 '81, 400m: 48.11 '78, 400mh: 52.25 '79.

**Bela BAKOSI** b.18 Jun 1957 Kemecse 1.80m 67kg. Nyiregyhaza Club.
At TJ: WCh: '83- 7; OG: '80- 7; ECh: '78- 15, '82-3; EI: '80- 1, '82- 1, '83- 3, '84- 3, '86- 3; WSG: '81-2; WCp: '81- 5; ECp: '83- 3. Hungarian champion: TJ 1979-82 and 1984-6, LJ 1979.
Four Hungarian triple jump records 1979-85.
Progression at TJ: 1975- 15.25, 1976- 15.74, 1977- 16.04, 1978- 16.45, 1979- 16.90, 1980- 16.88, 1981- 17.13/17.21w, 1982- 17.20/17.29w, 1983- 17.13, 1984- 17.15i, 1985- 17.23, 1986- 16.93i. pbs: 100m: 10.7 '80, HJ: 2.08 '75, LJ: 7.88 '79.

**Laszlo SZALMA** b.21 Oct 1957 Nagymaros 1.90m 80kg. Club: Vasas.
At LJ: OG: '80- 4; WCh: '83- 4; ECh: '78- dnq, '82-11; EI: '78- 1, '83- 1, '85- 2, '86- 2; WSG: '81- 1; WCp: '81- 7, '85- 3. Hungarian champion 1978, 1980-3, 1985.
Eight Hungarian long jump records 1977-85.
Progression at LJ: 1975- 7.50, 1976- 7.81, 1977- 7.97, 1978- 8.00i, 1979- 7.82i, 1980- 8.13/8.25w, 1981- 8.12/8.23w, 1982- 8.20, 1983- 8.24, 1984- 8.27, 1985- 8.30, 1986- 8.24i/8.03/8.07w. pb 100m: 10.4 '80, 10.54 '85.

# Women

**Marta KRIPLI** b.1 Oct 1960 1.80m 108kg. Club: MTK VM.
Hungarian champion SP 1986, DT 1984-6.
Three Hungarian discus records 1985-6.

Progression at DT: 1976- 45.50, 1977- 48.70, 1978- 50.82, 1979- 52.64, 1980- 57.02, 1981- 57.74, 1982- 57.70, 1983- 60.06, 1984- 61.00, 1985- 65.34, 1986- 66.48. pb SP: 18.16 '86.
Married at end of 1986, and now BACSKAI.

**Xenia SISKA** b.3 Nov 1957 Budapest 1.75m 57kg. Club: Vasas.
At 100mh: OG: '80- sf; WCh: '83- sf; ECh: '78- sf, '86- sf; EJ: '75- 3; ECp: '81- 7, '83- 7. At 60mh: WIG: '85- 1. Hungarian champion 100m 1984, 100mh 1980-4, 1986.
Nine Hungarian 100mh records 1978-84.
Progression at 100mh: 1974- 14.3, 1975- 13.78, 1976- 13.7, 1977- 13.95, 1978- 13.36/13.2, 1979- 13.57/13.44w/13.3, 1980- 13.17, 1981- 13.50, 1982- 13.37/13.05w, 1983- 13.16, 1984- 12.76, 1985- 12.99/12.85w, 1986- 12.77. pbs: 100m: 11.60 '84, 200m: 24.2 '78, 400mh: 58.18 '84, LJ: 6.10 '75.

**Katalin STERK** b.30 Sep 1961 1.78m 64kg. Club: TBSC. Civil servant.
At HJ: WCh: '83- 12=; ECh: '82- 8, '86- dnq; EI: '82- 3. Hungarian champion 1982, 1986.
Two Hungarian high jump records 1982-6.
Progression at HJ: 1975- 1.63, 1976- 1.74, 1977- 1.75, 1978- 1.78, 1979- 1.81, 1980- 1.87, 1981- 1.93, 1982- 1.99i/1.96, 1983- 1.90, 1986- 1.98.
Missed 1984 and 1985 seasons.

# ITALY

**Governing Body**: Federazione Italiana di Atletica Leggera (FIDAL), via Tevere 1/A, Roma. Constituted 1926. First governing body formed 1896.
**National Championships** first held in 1906 (men), 1927 (women).

**1986 champions: MEN**
100m/200m: Stefano Tilli 10.48/20.72, 400m: Mauro Zuliani 46.05, 800m: Alberto Barsotti 1:47.88, 1500m/3kmSt: Alessandro Lambruschini 3:46.36/8:33.14, 5000m: Stefano Mei 13:56.61, 10000m: Francesco Panetta 28:00.20, Mar: Osvaldo Faustini 2:16:03, 110mh: Daniele Fontecchio 13.86, 400mh: Luca Cosi 50.99, HJ: Gianni Davito 2.24, PV: Gianni Stecchi 5.40, LJ: Giovanni Evangelisti 8.13, TJ: Dario Badinelli 16.25, SP: Alessandro Andrei 21.29, DT: Marco Martino 63.14, HT: Lucio Serrano 74.80, JT: Agostino Ghesini 74.92, Dec: Marco Rossi 7490, 10kmW: Carlo Mattioli 40:13.50, 20kmW/50kmW: Maurizio Damilano 1:23:55/3:51:50.

**WOMEN**
100m: Rossella Tarolo 11.69, 200m: Daniela Ferrian 23.73, 400m: Cosetta Campana 54.06, 800m: Nicoletta Tozzi 2:04.57, 1500m/3000m: Roberta Brunet 4:21.84/9:06.74, 10000m: Cristina Tomasini 33:12.01, Mar: Paolo Moro 2:38:10, 100mh: Mary Massarin 13.64, 400mh: Giuseppina Cirulli 57.80, HJ: Sandra Fossati 1.86, LJ: Antonella Capriotti 6.47, SP: M.Assunta Chiumariello 15.91, DT: Sandra Benedet 52.78, JT: Fausta Quintavalla 59.80, Hep: Claudia Del Fabbro 5441, 5kmW: M.Grazia Cogoli 23:08.68, 10kmW: Nadia Forestan 50:10.

**Alessandro ANDREI** b.3 Jan 1959 Firenze 1.91m 118kg. Club: Fiamme Oro, Padova. Policeman.
At SP: OG: '84- 1; WCh: '83- 7; ECh: '82- 10, '86- 4; EI: '84- 3; EJ: '77- 9; WSG: '85- 1; WCp: '81- 7, '85- 3; ECp: '83- 4, '85- 2. Italian champion 1983- 6. Seventeen Italian shot records 1982-6.
Progression: 1976- 15.32, 1977- 17.46, 1978- 17.38i, 1979- 18.41, 1980- 19.58, 1981- 19.92, 1982- 20.35, 1983- 20.19, 1984- 21.50, 1985- 21.95, 1986- 22.06. pb DT: 47.54 '79.

**Salvatore ANTIBO** b.7 Feb 1962 Altofonte, Palermo 1.70m 52kg. Club: Pro Sport FI. Policeman.
At 5000m/10000m: OG: '84- sf/4; ECh: '82- h/6, '86- 10/3. At 5000m: WCh: '83- 13; EJ: '81- 2.
Progression at 10000m: 1981- 30:16.4, 1982- 28:16.25, 1983- 29:32.47, 1984- 27:48.02, 1985- 28:27.49, 1986- 27:39.52. pbs: 2000m: 5:05.92 '86, 3000m: 7:49.4 '85, 5000m: 13:21.26 '85.

**Walter ARENA** b.30 May 1964 Catania 1.73m 67kg. Club: Fiamme Azzurre.
At 20kmW: ECh: '86- 5. 10kmW: EJ: '81- 5, '83-1.
Progression at 20kmW: 1984- 1:24:36, 1985- 1:25:14, 1986- 1:22:42. Track pbs: 3kmW: 11:38.2i '84, 5kmW: 18:51.04 '86, 10kmW: 39:52.99 '86.

**Alessandro BELLUCCI** b.21 Feb 1955 Lanuvio, Roma 1.70m 55kg. Club: Fiamme Gialle. Accountant.
At 50kmW: OG: '84- 3; WCh: '83- 7; ECh: '78- 7, '82- dq, '86- 11; LT: '79- 11, '81- 3, '85- 4. At 20kmW: ECh: '74- 7; LT: '77- 11.
Progression at 50kmW: 1976- 4:21:02, 1977- 4:15:53, 1978- 3:58:26, 1979- 3:51:20, 1980- 3:56:48, 1981- 3:54:57, 1982- 3:54:52, 1983- 3:55:38, 1984- 3:53:45, 1985- 3:58:22, 1986- 3:54:10. pb 20kmW: 1:23:16 '82.

**Gelindo BORDIN** b.2 Apr 1959 Longare 1.80m 68kg. Club: Eccosasa Verona.
At Mar: ECh: '86- 1; WCp: '85- 12; ECp: '85- 7.

Progression at Mar: 1984- 2:13:20, 1985-
2:11:29, 1986- 2:10:54. pbs: 5000m: 14:06.6 '79,
10000m: 29:00.65 '83, 3kmSt: 8:49.2 '83.
His European gold medal was his first win in six
marathons.

**Alberto COVA** b.1 Dec 1958 Inverigo, Como
1.76m 58kg. Club: Pro Patria Freedent.
At 10km: OG: '84- 1; WCh: '83- 1; ECh: '82- 1, '86-
2; ECp: '83- 2, '85- 1. At 5km: ECh: '82- dq, '86- 8;
ECp: '81- 6, '83- 3, '85- 1; EJ: '77- 5. At 3km: EI:
'82- 2. World CC: '82- 7, '83- 10, '84- 13, '86- 9.
Italian champion 5000m 1980, 1982-3, 1985;
10000m 1981-2, CC 1982-6.
Italian records at 5000m 1982 and 1985.
Progression at 5km/10km: 1976- 14:38.4, 1977-
14:04.0, 1978- 14:07.4, 1979- 13:58.2, 1980-
13:40.4/29:20.5, 1981- 13:27.20/28:19.12, 1982-
13:13.71/27:41.03, 1983- 13:38.13/27:37.59,
1984- 13:18.24/27:47.54, 1985- 13:10.06/
27:49.36, 1986- 13:15.86/27:57.93. pbs: 800m:
1:53.2 '78, 1500m: 3:40.6 '85, 2000m: 5:09.0 '86,
3000m: 7:46.40 '83, 3000mSt: 8:37.2 '80.
Famed for the blistering finish that has brought
him great success at 10000 metres.

**Maurizio DAMILANO** b.6 Apr 1957 Scarnafigi
1.83m 70kg. Club: Sisport Torino.
At 20kmW (50kmW): OG: '80- 1, '84- 3 (dnf);
WCh: '83- 7; ECh: '78- 6, '82- dq (dq), '86- 2 (dnf);
WSG: '81- 1, '83- 2; LT: '77- 4, '81- 6, '83- 4, '85- 2.
At 10kmW: EJ: '75- 4. At 3kmW: WIG: '85- 2. 15
Italian championships (6 at 10kmW, 7 at 20kmW,
2 at 50kmW) 1978-86.
Three Italian 20kmW records. World records at
25km, 30km and 2 hours walk 1985 world best
3kmW 1980.
Progression at 20kmW: 1976- 1:29:15, 1977-
1:25:33, 1978- 1:24:58, 1979- 1:22:59.1t, 1980-
1:21:47.8t, 1981- 1:22:26, 1982- 1:22:06, 1983-
1:20:10, 1984- 1:20:09, 1985- 1:21:43, 1986-
1:21:17. pb 50kmW: 3:51:50 '86. Track pbs:
3kmW: 11:07.75 '81, 5kmW: 19:07.96i '84,
10kmW: 39:21.92 '81, 25kmW: 1:44:54.0t '85,
30kmW: 2:06:07.3t '85, 1hr: 14932m '84, 2hr:
28565m '85.
When he won the 1980 Olympic 20km walk title,
his twin brother Giorgio was 11th.

**Giovanni EVANGELISTI** b.11 Sep 1961 Rimini
1.79m 70kg. Club: PP Freedent. Architectural
student.
At LJ: OG: '84- 3; WCh: '83- dnq; ECh: '82- 6, '86-
3; EI: '82- 3; WCp: '81- 6; ECp: '81- 8, '83- 6, '85-
8; WIG: '85- 3. Italian champion 1981-2.
Six Italian long jump records 1982-6.
Progression at LJ: 1976- 5.40, 1977- 6.10, 1978-
6.68, 1979- 7.30, 1980- 7.84, 1981- 7.94, 1982-

8.10i/8.07/8.21w, 1983- 8.09/8.11w, 1984- 8.24,
1985- 8.14i/8.01, 1986- 8.24. pbs: 100m: 10.4
'81, 10.73 '84; TJ: 16.30 '80.

**Carlo MATTIOLI** b.23 Oct 1954 Pergola 1.78m
68kg. Club: GS Caribinieri Bologna. Soldier
At 20kmW: OG: '84- 5; WCh: '83-18; ECh: '82- 6,
'86- 11; LT: '83- 7, '85- 8; WSG: '81- 2. Italian
10kmW champion 1986.
World indoor bests at 3kmW and 5kmW (19:06.8
and 18:59.2) in 1980.
Progression at 20kmW: 1978- 1:30:45, 1979-
1:24:56, 1980- 1:24:53, 1981- 1:23:54, 1982-
1:22:34, 1983- 1:21:11, 1984- 1:22:07, 1985-
1:24:14, 1986- 1:24:30. Track pbs: 3kmW:
10:54.61i '80, 5kmW: 18:48.88 '86, 10kmW:
39:52.4 '85.

**Stefano MEI** b.3 Feb 1963 La Spezia 1.82m
66kg. Club: Fiamme Oro Padova. Policeman.
At 1500m: OG: '84- sf; WCh: '83- sf; ECh: '82- h;
ECp: '85- 3. At 3000m: EI: '86- 2; EJ: '79- 8, '81- 4.
At 5000m: ECh: '86- 2; WSG: '85- 1; WCp: '85- 2.
3rd GP 1986. At 10000m: ECh: '86- 1. Italian
champion 5000m 1984, 1986; 1500m 1985.
Italian 1500m and 2 miles records 1986.
Progression at 5000m/10000m: 1979- 14:36.7,
1980- 13:55.91, 1981- 13:52.51, 1982- 13:45.48,
1983- 13:32.06, 1984- 13:29.61, 1985- 13:21.05,
1986- 13:11.57/27:43.97. pbs: 800m: 1:48.1 '85,
1500m: 3:34.57 '86, 1M: 3:58.65 '86, 3000m:
7:42.85 '86, 2M: 8:28.49 '86..
World age 16 best for 3000m (8:08.6) in 1979.

**Francesco PANETTA** b.10 Jan 1963 Siderno
1.75m 64kg. Club: PP Freedent. Student.
At 3kmSt: OG: '84- sf (h 10000m); ECh: '86- 2. At
2kmSt: EJ: '81- 7. World CC:'84- 10. Italian
champion 3kmSt 1985, 10000m 1986.
Progression at 3kmSt/10000m: 1981- 9:09.3,
1982- 8:33.24/29:31.6, 1983- 8:35.39/28:41.2,
1984- 8:26.90/28:03.99, 1985- 8:21.60/27:44.65,
1986- 8:16.85/27:51.05. pbs: 1500m: 3:45.2 '85,
2000m: 5:09.2 '86, 3000m: 7:49.90 '85, 2M:
8:30.7 '86, 5000m: 13:20.93 '85.
Made a brave attempt to run away from the field in
the European steeplechase final in 1986. Despite
being caught he rallied for the silver medal.

**Orlando PIZZOLATO** b.30 Jul 1958 Thiene
1.79m 61kg. Club: Cus Universo Ferrera. Student.
At Mar: ECh: '86- 2; WSG: '85- 1; WCp: '85- 6.
Progression at Mar: 1978- 2:22:50, 1979-
2:17:28, 1980- 2:15:07, 1982- 2:14:42, 1983-
2:15:28, 1984- 2:14:53, 1985- 2:10:23, 1986-
2:10:57. pbs: 1500m: 3:48.3 '82, 3000m: 8:05.73
'83, 5000m: 13:45.0 '83, 10000m: 28:22.9 '83.
The surprise winner of the 1984 New York mara-

thon confirmed his status in 1985, when he triumphed in hot conditions to win the World Student Games title before again winning in New York; these three are his only wins in 23 marathons. Moved up from 57th at half-way to 6th in World Cup marathon.

**Gianni POLI** b.5 Nov 1957 Lumezzane 1.80m 61kg. Club: S.Rocchino BS.
At Mar: WCh: '83- 7; ECh: '82- 13, '86- 13; ECp: '81- 9; '83- 3. Italian champion 1984.
Three Italian marathon records 1981-5.
Progression at Mar: 1979- 2:20:10, 1980- 2:14:12, 1981- 2:11:19, 1982- 2:15:38, 1983- 2:11:05, 1984- 2:11:05, 1985- 2:09:57, 1986- 2:11:06. pbs: 5000m: 14:05.1 '79, 10000m: 28:58.5 '86.
Has won two of his 17 marathons 1979-86, at Milan in 1984 and New York 1986.

# Women

**Gabriella DORIO** b.27 Jun 1957 Veggiano 1.67m 55kg. Club: Fiat Parflu Torino. Physical education instructor.
At 1500m (800m): OG: '76- 6(sf), '80- 4(8), '84- 1(4); WCh: '83- 7; ECh: '74- 9, '78- 6(sf), '82- 3; EI: '82--/1; EJ: '73- 8 at 800m, '75- 3; WSG: '79- 5(4), '81- 1(2), '83- 1; WCp: '81- 2(4); ECp: '79- 7. World CC: '75- 4, '76- 3.
19 Italian championships (7 at 800m, 10 1500m, 2 CC) 1973-84, 61 internationals. Italian records: 4 at 800m, 4 1500m, 1 each 1M, 2000m, 3000m 1976-86.
Progression at 800m/1500m/3000m: 1972- 2:10.8; 1973- 2:05.9/4:27.6, 1974- 2:07.5/4:12.1/ 9:40.0, 1975-    2:04.5/4:07.27/9:19.0,    1976- 2:01.63/4:07.27,  1977-  2:05.53/4:10.84/9:54.8, 1978-   2:00.38/4:01.25/9:13.3,   1979-   2:00.8/ 4:06.03/9:05.4,  1980-  1:57.66/3:59.82/8:49.96, 1981-  1:58.82/4:03.27/8:48.65,  1982-  1:59.13/ 3:58.65/9:30.22,  1983-  2:00.05/4:02.43/9:04.96, 1984-  1:59.05/4:01.96,  1986-  2:03.03/4:07.61. pbs: 400m: 54.9 '80, 1000m: 2:33.18 '82, 1M: 4:23.29 '80, 2000m: 5:43.30 '86.
Gave birth to a daughter, Anna Chiara, in 1985.

**Laura FOGLI** b.5 Oct 1959 Comacchio 1.68m 50kg. Club: Snia Milano. Housewife.
At Mar: OG: '84- 9; WCh: '83- 6; ECh: '82- 2, '86- 2; WCp: '85- 4; ECp: '81- 5, '85- 6. Italian champion 1980. At 10km: ECp: '85- 6.
Three Italian marathon bests 1981-4.
Progression at Mar: 1981- 2:45:41/2:34:48sh, 1982-  2:33:01/2:31:08 short,  1983-  2:31:49, 1984- 2:29:28, 1985- 2:31:36, 1986- 2:29:44. pbs: 800m: 2:11.4 '79, 1500m: 4:19.8 '80, 3000m: 9:17.3 '78, 5000m: 16:06.19 '85, 10000m:

Laura Fogli. *ASP*

33:39.04 '84.
Her New York marathon positions (4th 1981-2, 3rd 1983-6) and two European silver medals point to her consistency, but of her sixteen marathons, she has only won two, Rome 1982 and Pittsburgh 1986.

Giuliana **SALCE** b.16 Jun 1955 Roma 1.69m 52kg. Club: Team Eclas Ostia.
Won WIG 3000m 1985. Italian champion 5kmW 1982-4, 10kmW 1984.
World records at 5km walk 1983 and 3km walk 1984. European 5km walk record 1986. World indoor bests: 1MW: 6:43.59 '84, 6:28.46 '85; 3kmW: 13:08.09 and 12:56.7 '84, 12:31.57 '85; 5kmW: 21:44.52 '85.
Progression at 3kmW/5kmW: 1979- 25:55.1, 1980- 14:12.5, 1981- 14:45.0i, 1982- 13:42.6/ 23:59.1, 1983- 13:03.83/21:51.85, 1984- 12:42.33/22:28.3, 1985- 12:31.57i/21:44.52i, 1986- 12:48.96i/21:35.25. Track pbs: 1MW: 6:28.46i '84, 10kmW: 47:38.4 '86, 1hrW: 12644m '86. Road pb: 10kmW: 46:30 '86.

# IVORY COAST

**Governing body**: Fédération Ivoirienne d'Athlétisme, Boulevard Lagunaire, BP 2844, Abidjan 01. Founded 1960.

René **DJÉDJÉMEL** b.5 June 1958 1.86m 80kg. Military fireman.
At 400mh: WSG: '85- 3; AfCh: '85- 1 (1 at 110mh). Progression at 400mh: 1982- 52.3, 1983- 52.3, 1984- 50.27/50.2, 1985- 49.13, 1986- 48.94. pbs: 100m: 10.6 '84, 200m: 21.3 '84, 400m: 46.8 '86, 110mh: 14.14 '85, 14.1 '86.

Gabriel **TIACOH** b.10 Sep 1963 1.80m 75kg. Student at Washington State University, USA.
At 400m: OG: '84- 2; WCh: '83- qf; AfCh: '84- 1, '85- 2. Won French 400m 1984.
Seven Ivory Coast inc. three African 400m records 1983-6. African 300m best 1986.
Progression at 400m: 1981- 48.79, 1982- 46.94, 1983- 45.86, 1984- 44.54, 1985- 44.87, 1986- 44.30. pbs: 100m: 10.7 '82, 200m: 20.71 '84, 300m: 31.74 '86.
Won first ever Olympic medal for the Ivory Coast. Was the world's best 400m runner in 1986, when he lost just once, to Darrell Robinson in Berlin. He has a career record 13 sub-45 second times, with a season's record nine in 1986.

# JAMAICA

**Governing body**: Jamaica Amateur Athletic Association, PO Box 272, Kingston 5. Founded 1932.
**1986 Champions: MEN**
100m: Raymond Stewart 10.35, 200m: Leroy Reid 20.83, 400m: Bert Cameron 46.15, 800m: Henry Record 1:52.38, 1500m: Linton McKenzie 3:52.38, 5000m/10000m: Mike Feurtado

14:40.76/30:42.8, 110mh: Richard Bucknor 14.4, 400mh: Winthrop Graham 50.41, HJ: Errol Braham 1.98, LJ: Ronald Chambers 7.44, TJ: Devon Dixon 15.68, SP: Rohan Webb 15.07, DT: Michael Hill 43.38.
**WOMEN**
100m: Camille Coates 11.33, 200m: Grace Jackson 22.92, 400m: Ilrey Oliver 52.28, 800m: Cathy Rattray-Williams 2:05.73, 100mh: Michelle Freeman 14.85, HJ: Mable Thomas 1.80, LJ: Cynthia Henry 6.75.

Bert **CAMERON** b.16 Nov 1959 Spanish Town 1.88m 79kg. Club: Converse TC, USA. Graduate of University of Texas at El Paso.
At 400m (R- 4x400m relay): OG: '80- qf, '84- dns; WCh: '83- 1; CG: '78- qf (2R), '82- 1 (2R); PAm: '79- 4 (2R); WCp: '81- 3 (3R); CAmG: '78- 1R, '82- 1. NCAA champion 1980-1, 1983 (also indoors 1980-1).
Five Jamaican inc. one Commonwealth 400m records 1980-1.
Progression at 400m: 1978- 47.20, 1979- 45.97, 1980- 45.23, 1981- 44.58, 1982- 44.69, 1983- 44.62, 1984- 45.07, 1985- 44.94, 1986- 44.66. pbs: 200m: 20.74 '83, 800m: 1:49.57 '82.
The World and Commonwealth champion produced a devastating burst of speed to qualify for the Olympic 400m final after pulling up with a suspected injury in his semi-final. Alas the injury was sustained and he could not run the final.

# Women

Grace **JACKSON** b.14 Jun 1961 St.Ann 1.78m 59kg. Atoms Track Club, USA.
At 100m/200m (R- 4x100m relay): OG: '84- 5/5; WCh: '83:-/5; CG: '82- sf/7 (3R); WSG: '83- 6/3, '85- 3/1; WCp: '85- 2=/2. CAmG: '78- 2 at HJ.
Jamaican 400m record 1986.
Progression at 100m, 200m: 1981- 11.86/11.7/ 11.81w; 1982- 11.68/11.45w, 22.92; 1983- 11.27/ 11.22w, 22.46; 1984- 11.24, 22.20; 1985- 11.24w/11.26/11.0, 22.57/22.48w; 1986- 11.31/ 11.2, 22.39. pbs: 400m: 50.94 '86, 100mh: 14.06 '81, 400mh: 59.49 '84, HJ: 1.75 '81.

Merlene **OTTEY** b.10 May 1960 Jamaica 1.74m 57kg. Club: Mazda TC, USA. Graduate of Nebraska University. Married Nat Page (US - HJ: 2.28i '81 and 1979 NCAA champion, 400mh: 49.21 '86) on 3 Feb 1984.
At 100m/200m (R- 4x100m relay): OG: '80- -/3, '84- 3/3; WCh: '83- 4/2 (3R); CG: '82- 2/1 (3R); PAm: '79- -/3. Won NCAA 100m 1982-3, 200m 1983; TAC 100m 1984-5, 200m 1982 and 1984-5; CAC 100m & 200m 1985. 2nd GP 100m 1985.
Five Commonwealth records at 200m and three

Grace Jackson. *ASP*

at 100m, 1980-5. World indoor bests for 300y (32.63 '82) and 300m (35.83 '81).
Progression at 100m, 200m: 1975- ,25.9; 1976- 12.0, 24.7; 1977- 12.2, 25.1; 1978- 12.6, 24.5; 1979- 11.59/11.4, 23.10/22.79w, 1980- 11.36/11.0, 22.20; 1981- 11.07/10.97w, 22.35; 1982- 11.03/10.97w, 22.17; 1983- 11.07/10.98w, 22.19/22.11w, 1984- 11.01, 22.09, 1985- 10.92/21.93, 1986- 11.06/10.7w/22.43. pb 400m: 51.12 '83.
Graceful sprinter, who has been consistently in the medals in major championships.

# JAPAN

**Governing body**: Nippon Rikujo-Kyogi Renmei, 1-1-1 Jinnan, Shibuya-Ku, Tokyo 150. Founded 1911.
**National Championships** first held in 1914 (men), 1925 (women)
**1986 Champions: MEN**
100m: Hirofumi Miyazaki 10.62, 200m: Hirobumi Koike 21.15, 400m: Susumu Takano 45.90, 800m: Toru Shioda 1:52.47, 1500m: Masami Ohtsuka 3:47.37, 5000m: Yutaka Kanai 13:50.33, 10000m: Masanari Shintaku 28:22.15, Mar: Toshihiro Shibutani 2:14:55, 3kmSt: Shigeyuki

Aikyo 8:38.22, 110mh: Hiroshi Kakimoti 14.24, 400mh: Ryoichi Yoshida 49.95, HJ: Shuji Ujino 2.24, PV: Toshiyuki Hashioka 5.40, LJ: Junichi Usui 7.87, TJ: Norifumi Yamashita 17.15, SP: Yoshihisa Urita 16.97, DT: Hirotaka Maeda 55.06, HT: Shigenobu Murofushi 70.20, JT: Masanori Amano 78.54, Dec: Takeshi Kojyo 7220, 20kmW: Takehiro Sonohara 1:30:46, 50kmW: Shuichi Takashima 4:23:36.
**WOMEN**
100m: Emiko Konishi 12.24, 200m: Hiromi Isozaki 24.29, 400m: Hitomi Koshimoto 54.66, 800m: Ayako Arai 2:08.91, 1500m: Toyoko Takada 4:29.42, 3000m: Yuka Terunuma 9:32.35, 10000m: Misako Miyahara 34:53.89, 100mh: Chizuko Akimoto 13.89, 400mh: Yoko Satoh 59.65, HJ: Masami Matsui 1.84, LJ/Hep: Minako Isogai 6.20/5315, SP: Aya Suzuki 15.23, DT: Ikuko Kitamori 50.96, JT: Emi Matsui 55.54.

**Kunimitsu ITOH** b.6 Jan 1955 Nagano Pre. 1.63m 53kg. Clerk, Kanebo.
At Mar: WCp: '85- 77. At 10000m: WCh: '83- h; AsCh: '79- 2, '81- 1; WCp: '81- 7; Japanese champion 1980. At 5000m: AsCh: '75- 1.
Progresion at Mar: 1976- 2:21:25, 1977- 2:18:57, 1978- 2:13:25, 1979- 2:12:08, 1980- 2:10:05, 1981- 2:09:37, 1982- 2:11:45, 1983- 2:09:35, 1984- 2:12:04, 1985- 2:11:19, 1986- 2:07:57.
pbs: 1500m: 4:00.5 '72, 5000m: 13:39.86 '81, 10000m: 27:47.35 '80, 30km: 1:29:12 '80.

**Taisuke KODAMA** b.26 Jul 1958 Kagoshima Pre. 1.65m 49kg. Clerk, Asahi Kasei Chemical.
At Mar: WCp: '85- 52.
Asian marathon best 1986.
Progression at Mar: 1982- 2:16:20, 1983- 2:12:51, 1984- 2:10:36, 1985- 2:16:51, 1986- 2:07:35. pbs: 5000m: 13:46.36 '83, 10000m: 28:44.23 '83.
Won Beppu and Beijing Marathons in 1986.

**Takeyuki NAKAYAMA** b.20 Dec 1959 Nagano Pre. 1.80m 58kg. Clerk, Daiei Store.
At Mar: AsG: '86- 1; WCp: '85- 2.
Progression at Mar: 1983- 2:14:15, 1984- 2:10:00, 1985- 2:08:15, 1986- 2:08:21. pbs: 5000m: 13:43.80 '85, 10000m: 28:07.0 '86, 30km: 1:31:50 '83.
Big marathon wins at Fukuoka 1984 and Seoul 1985. In 1986 was fourth in Tokyo and won Asian Games.

**Toshihiko SEKO** b.15 Jul 1956 Yokkaiichi City 1.70m 59kg. Graduate of Waseda University, clerk, SB Foods.
At Mar: OG: '84- 14; Japanese champion 1979, 1983. At 10000m: AsG: '86- 3.
Four Asian marathon bests 1979-83. World

Toshihiko Seko. *ASP*

records for 25km, 1:13:55.8 and 30km, 1:29:18.8 in 1981. Asian records for 5000m 1986, 10000m 1980 and 1985.
Progression at Mar: 1977- 2:15:01, 1978- 2:10:21, 1979- 2:10:12, 1980- 2:09:45, 1981- 2:09:26, 1983- 2:08:38, 1984- 2:14:13, 1986- 2:08:27. pbs: 800m: 1:51.7 '76, 1500m: 3:50.9 '78, 5000m: 13:24.29 '86, 10000m: 27:42.17 '85, 20km: 57:48.7 '85, 30km: 1:29:18.8 '81, 1Hr: 20280m '81.
He disappointed in the 1984 Olympics after single-minded preparation and five successive marathon wins since 1979, but made a successful return to the marathon in 1986. Of his thirteen marathons he has won eight, including Fukuoka 1978-80, 1983; Boston 1981; Tokyo 1983; London and Chicago 1986.

**Masanari SHINTAKU** b.20 Dec 1957 Hiroshima Pre. 1.74m 57kg. Graduate of Hihon Taiiku University, clerk, SB Foods.
At 10000m: OG: '84- 16; AsG: '86- 1. At 3kmSt: WCp: '77- 6, '79- 5, '81- 3; AsG: '78- 1; AsCh: '79- 1, '81- 1. At 5000m: AsG: '82- 1, '86- 2. Japanese champion 10000m 1981, 1984, 1986; 3kmSt 1977-80; 5000m: 1980-3; Mar 1985.
Japanese records: 1 at 5000m, 2 15km, and 1 3000mSt 1977-82.

Marathon debut in 1985: 2:12:23 third Tokyo, then won at Fukuoka in 2:09:51.
Progression at 10000m: 1976- 30:18.0, 1977- 29:20.6, 1978- 29:33.5, 1979- 28:56.1, 1981- 28:24.77, 1983- 27:44.5, 1984- 27:59.59, 1985- 27:50.05, 1986- 28:09.47. pbs: 800m: 1:56.1 '78, 1500m: 3:43.4 '78, 5000m: 13:24.69 '82, 15km: 44:17.1 '81, 30km: 1:29:57.3 '81, 3kmSt: 8:19.52 '80.

**Susumu TAKANO** b.21 May 1961 Shizuoka Pre. 1.78m 67kg. Graduate student at Tokai University.
At 400m (R- 4x400mR): OG: '84- sf; WCh: '83- qf; AsG: '82- 1 (1R), '86- 1 (1R); WSG: '83- 5. Japanese champion 1982, 1985-6.
Four Asian 400m records 1985-6.
Progression at 400m: 1979- 48.6, 1980- 48.02, 1981- 47.01, 1982- 46.51, 1983- 45.86, 1984- 45.69, 1985- 45.30, 1986- 45.00. pbs: 100m: 10.6 '83, 200m: 20.88 '84.

**Norifumi YAMASHITA** b.10 Sep 1962 Mie Pre. 1.77m 63kg. Graduate of Tsukaba University, clerk, Nihon Electric.
At TJ: AsG: '86- 1. Japanese champion 1985-6.
Three Japanese triple jump records 1985-6.
Progression at TJ: 1978- 14.38, 1979- 14.98, 1980- 15.49, 1981- 15.49, 1982- 15.69, 1983- 15.89, 1984- 16.50, 1985- 16.92, 1986- 17.15.

## Women

**Megumi SATOH** b.13 Sep 1966 Niigata Pre. 1.75m 57kg. Student at Fukuoka University.
At HJ: OG: '84- dnq; WCh: '83- dnq; AsG: '82- 4, '86- 1; AsCh: '81- 3. Japanese champion 1981, 1983, 1985.
Progression at HJ: 1979- 1.60, 1980- 1.79, 1981- 1.87, 1982- 1.83, 1983- 1.90, 1984- 1.87, 1985- 1.92, 1986- 1.91i/1.89. pb LJ: 6.01 '86.

Pre. = Prefecture.

## KENYA

**Governing body**: Kenya Amateur Athletic Association, Nyayo National Stadium, PO Box 46722, Uhuru-High-Way, Nairobi. Founded 1951.
**National Championships**
**1986 Champions: MEN**
100m: Peter Wekesa 10.3, 200m: Alfred Nyambane 21.3, 400m: John Anzrah 45.6, 800m/1500m: Joseph Chesire 1:46.6/3:41.4, 5000m: Paul Kipkoech 13:47.0, 10000m: Jackson Ruto

29:03.1, 3000mSt: Boniface Merande 8:27.0, 110mh: Charles Kokoyo 14.5, 400mh: Joseph Maritim 50.7, HJ: Nathan Rotich 2.05, PV: S.C.Maina 3.80, LJ: John Kipngetich 7.26, TJ: Ben K.Mugun 15.87, SP: Simon Murei 15.02, DT: John Pondo 46.24, HT: Philip Maritim 46.80, JT (old): George Odera 73.10, 10kmW: Philip Kipkemboi 43:35.6.

## WOMEN

100m/200m/LJ: Joyce Odhiambo 11.7/24.2/6.13, 400m: Esther Kavaya 53.2, 800m: Mary Chemweno-Koskei 2:07.0, 1500m/5000m: Susan Sirma 4:23.7/17:05.0, 100mh: Marcella Mbunde 15.0, 400mh: Rose Tata-Muya 59.8, HJ: Rosa Chepkoskei 1.65, SP: Mary Chelagat 11.47, DT: Philis Macharia 37.16, JT: Martha Johnson 43.67, 5kmW: Agnetha Chelimo 27:00.3.

**Charles CHERUIYOT** b.2 Dec 1964 1.65m 54kg. Mount St.Mary's College, USA.
At 5000m: OG: '84- 6. Kenyan champion at 3000mSt 1981, 5000m 1983.
World junior record for 5000m and African junior record for 3000m in 1983.
Progression at 5000m: 1982- 14:01.5, 1983-13:25.33, 1984- 13:18.41, 1985- 13:34.80, 1986-13:33.55. pbs: 800m: 1:50.4 '82, 1500m: 3:41.83 '83, 1M: 3:57.76 '86, 2000m: 5:05.1 '86, 3000m: 7:44.10 '86, 10000m: 28:34.74 '84, 3000mSt: 8:51.6 '80.
Twin brother Kipkoech Cheruiyot was the 1982 African 1500m champion and set the world junior record for 1500m at 3:34.92 in 1983. He improved to a Kenyan 1500m record 3:33.07 in 1986.

**Joseph CHESIRE** b.12 Nov 1957 1.67m 57kg. Soldier.
At 1500m: OG: '84- 4; WIG: '85- 3; AfCh: '85- 3. Kenyan champion 800m 1986, 1500m 1985-6.
Progression at 1500m: 1984- 3:34.52, 1985-3:37.67, 1986- 3:34.32. pbs: 800m: 1:45.10 '86, 1M: 4:00.45 '86, 3000m: 7:49.4 '84.

**Julius KARIUKI** b.12 Apr 1961 1.81m 62kg. Civil servant.
At 3000mSt: OG: '84- 7; AfCh: '85- 1; WCp: '85- 1.
Progression at 3000mSt: 1981- 9:34.5, 1984-8:17.47, 1985- 8:20.74, 1986- 8:15.92. pbs: 1500m: 3:37.79 '86, 1M: 4:00.43 '86, 2000m: 5:04.71 '86, 3000m: 7:47.35 '86, 5000m: 13:59.02 '85.

**Paul KIPKOECH** b.6 Jan 1963 1.73m 58kg. Soldier.
At 5000m (at 10000m): OG: '84- 5; WCh: '83- 9; AfCh: '82- 4 (5), '85- 2 (3). World CC: '85- 2, '86- 5. Kenyan champion at 10000m 1983 and 1985; 5000m 1984, 1986.

Progression at 5000m: 1982- 13:51.03/29:35.56, 1983- 13:25.08/28:36.05, 1984- 13:14.40/28:05.4, 1985- 13:17.64/27:58.26, 1986-13:18.91/27:43.31. pbs: 1500m: 3:41.41 '86, 2000m: 5:05.0 '86, 3000m: 7:39.38 '86, 3000mSt: 8:56.4 '83.

**Edwin KOECH** b.23 Jul 1961 1.74m 64kg. Atlantic Coast Club, USA. Was at Richmond University.
At 800m: OG: '84- 6.
Progression at 800m: 1981- 1:54.1, 1982- 1:47.2, 1983- 1:48.59, 1984- 1:44.12, 1985- 1:45.31, 1986- 1:45.26. pbs: 100m/200m/400m: 10.9/22.0/47.7 '80, 1000m: 2:20.80 '86, 1500m: 3:49.8 '84.

**Peter KOECH** b.18 Feb 1958 Kiliburani, Nandi district 1.80m 67kg. Was at Washington State University, USA.
CG: '82- 3 at 5km, 15 10km. Won NCAA 3000mSt 1985.
Progression at 5000m/3000mSt: 1981- 13:57.23, 1982- 13:09.50, 1983- 13:44.0, 1984- 13:30.59/8:29.09, 1985- 13:24.5/8:19.84, 1986- 13:34.2/8:13.33. pbs: 1500m: 3:35.67 '86, 2000m: 5:02.79 '82, 3000m: 7:39.09 '82, 10000m: 28:07.28 '82, Mar: 2:18:56 '86.

**Billy KONCHELLAH** b.20 Oct 1961 1.88m 74kg. Club: Mazda TC, USA.
At 800m: OG: '84- 4.
African junior 800m record 1980.
Progression at 800m: 1980- 1:46.79, 1981-1:49.79, 1982- 1:51.3, 1984- 1:44.03, 1985-1:43.72. pbs: 200m: 21.2/21.20w '80, 400m: 45.38 '79, 600m: 1:17.4 '82, 1000m: 2:16.71 '85, 1500m: 3:44.5 '85.

**Julius KORIR** b.21 Apr 1960 Nandi district 1.72m 64kg. Student at Washington State University, USA.
At 3000mSt: OG: '84- 1; WCh: '83- 7; CG: '82- 1; AfCh: '82- 2. Kenyan champion 1982. Won NCAA 5000m 1984, 3kmSt 1986.
Progression at 3000mSt: 1981- 8:44.0, 1982-8:23.94, 1983- 8:20.02, 1984- 8:11.80, 1986-8:12.74. pbs: 800m: 1:48.42 '84, 1500m: 3:40.31 '83, 1M: 4:04.4i '84, 3000m: 7:48.90 '86, 5000m: 13:38.7 '82.
While his Commonwealth victory was a surprise, he confirmed his status with a clear Olympic win. Missed 1985 outdoor season through injury.

**Sammy KOSKEI** b.14 May 1961 Nandi district 1.83m 68kg. Club: Mazda TC, USA. Was at Southern Methodist University, now at North Texas State University, USA studying for a business degree.

At 800m: WCh: '83- sf; CG: '82- 9; AfCh: '84- 1, '85- 1; WCp: '85- 1. Won NCAA 1981.
African records: two at 800m 1984, one 1000m 1985.
Progression at 800m: 1980- 1:46.90, 1981- 1:45.32, 1982- 1:44.93, 1983- 1:46.40, 1984- 1:42.28, 1985- 1:43.78, 1986- 1:45.89. pbs: 1000m: 2:14.95 '85, 1500m: 3:40.14 '85, 1M: 3:56.79 '82.

**Mike MUSYOKI** b.28 May 1956 1.68m 54kg. Club: Mazda TC, USA.
At 10000m (5000m): OG: '84- 3; CG: '78- 2 (2); AfG: '78- 2 (2). Won NCAA 10000m 1978 while at the University of Texas at El Paso.
World half-marathon best of 60:43 to win Great North Run in 1986. African junior 10000m record in 1975.
Progression at 10000m/Mar: 1975- 29:05.2, 1976- 28:40.0, 1977- 27:41.92, 1978- 28:05.2, 1979- 28:03.25, 1980- 28:20.5, 1981- 28:34.43, 1982- 28:13.86, 1983- 28:06.7, 1984- 27:46.0, 1985- 27:54.8/2:17:36, 1986- 27:55.6/2:10:30. pb 5000m: 13:24.89 '78.
Has had great success in US road running for several years, including 42:27.55 world best for 15km in 1983. Fourth Chicago marathon 1986.

**John NGUGI** b.1962 1.78m 62kg. Kikuyu. Civil servant in Nairobi.
At 5000m: AfCh: '85- 3. Won East & Central African 1500m 1985, 5000m 1986. World CC: '86- 1.
Progression at 1500m/5000m: 1984- 3:51.0, 1985- 3:37.02/13:18.99, 1986- 13:29.0. pbs: 2000m: 5:06.50 '86, 3000m: 7:49.35 '86, 10000m: 28:37.38 '86.

**Samson OBWOCHA** b.1954
World 2000m steeplechase best 1986.
Progression at 3000mSt: 1985- 8:38.86, 1986- 8:14.17. pbs: 800m: 1:48.5 '78, 1500m: 3:39.55 '81, 3000m: 7:54.48 '85, 2M: 8:29.01 '86, 5000m: 13:41.01 '85, 10000m: 29:05.44 '84, 2000mSt: 5:19.68 '86.
Suddenly burst to prominence as a steeplechaser in 1986 at the age of 32.

**Wilson WAIGWA** b.15 Feb 1949 1.72m 64kg. Club: El Paso TC, USA. Graduate of University of Texas at El Paso
At 5000m: OG: '84- 10; CG: '82- 13. Won AAA 1982. At 1500m: CG: '78- 5, '82- 9; AfrG: '78- 2. Won NCAA 1977. 5th world CC 1984.
Progression at 5000m: 1976- 13:48.29, 1977- 14:02.4, 1978- 13:24.43, 1979- 13:42.1, 1980- 13:20.36, 1981- 13:57.14, 1982- 13:29.32, 1983- 13:21.98, 1984- 13:27.34, 1985- 13:30.26, 1986- 13:23.18. pbs: 800m: 1:49.1 '77, 1500m: 3:35.0 '83, 1M: 3:50.7 '83, 2000m: 5:05.41 '82, 3000m: 7:40.52 '83, 10000m: 28:44.75 '86.

# KOREA

**Governing body**: Korea Amateur Athletic Federation, PO Box 566, K.W.M. Seoul. Founded 1945.

**CHANG JAE-KEUN** b.2 Jan 1962 1.84m 64kg.
At 200m: OG: '84- qf; WCh: '83- qf; WSG: '85- 3; WCp: '85- 4; AsG: '82- 1, '86- 1; AsCh: '83- 3, '85- 1 (3 at 100m).
Two Asian 200m records 1985.
Progression at 200m: 1981- 21.09, 1982- 20.89, 1983- 20.93, 1984- ?, 1985- 20.41, 1986- 20.71. pb 100m: 10.35 '85.

# MEXICO

**Governing body**: Federacion Mexicana de Atletismo, Puerta Numero 9, Ciudad Deportiva 08010, Mexico 8 D.F. Founded 1933.

**Arturo BARRIOS** b.12 Dec 1963 Mexico City 1.74m 60kg.
Mechanical engineering graduate of Texas A&M University, USA.
Progression at 10000m: 1985- 28:42.77, 1986- 27:50.28. pbs: 3000m: 7:48.22 '86, 2M: 8:24.99 '86, 5000m: 13:25.83 '86, Mar: 2:14:09 '86, 3kmSt: 8:47.8 '84.
Had an outstanding season on the 1986 US road running circuit. He set a world 10km road best for a loop course of 27:41 at Phoenix and also had important 15km wins at Jacksonville and Portland.

**Martin BERMUDEZ** b.19 Jul 1958 1.74m 74kg.
At 50kmW: OG: '80- dnf, '84- disq; WCh: '83- disq; PAm: '79- 2, '83- 2, '86- 1; LT: '79- 1, '81- 6; CAmG: '86- 1. CAC champion 1985.
Progression at 50kmW: 1977- 4:19:07, 1978- 3:58:48, 1979- 3:43:36, 1980- 3:48:22, 1981- 3:53:10, 1982- 3:53:00, 1983- 3:50:43, 1984- 3:48:03, 1985- 4:22:33, 1986- 3:56:21. pbs: Track: 3kmW: 11:51.0 '83, 10kmW: 39:58.0 '85, 20kmW: 1:23:44 '86, 1hrW: 14742m '86. Road: 10kmW: 39:29 '86, 20kmW: 1:22:22 '80.

**Ernesto CANTO** b.18 Oct 1959 1.70m 58kg.
At 20kmW: OG: '84- 1 (10 at 50kmW); WCh: '83- 1; PAm: '83- 2; LT: '79- 6, '81- 1, '83- 2; CAmG: '82- 1, '86- 1. CAC champion 1985.
World walking records at 20km, 1:18:40.0 and 1 hour, 15253m in 1984.
Progression at 20kmW: 1979- 1:21:12, 1980- 1:19:02, 1981- 1:23:08, 1982- 1:23:13, 1983-

1:19:41, 1984- 1:18:40t, 1985- 1:28:26, 1986-
1:22:58. pbs: Track: 3kmW: 11:50.0 '83, 5kmW:
19:40.6 '81, 10kmW: 39:29.2 '84. Road 50kmW:
3:51:10 '82.

# MOROCCO

**Governing Body**: Fédération Royale Marocaine
d'Athlétisme, Centre National des Sports, Bellevue Avenue, Ibn sina Agdal, Rabat. Founded
1957.

**Saïd AOUITA** b.2 Nov 1960 Kenitra 1.75m 58kg.
At 5000m: OG: '84- 1. At 1500m: WCh: '83- 3;
WSG: '83- 1; AfCh: '79- 9, '82- 2; '84- 1. Won GP
1986. At 800m: AfCh: '82- 3. Pan-Arab 1500m
champion 1985.
African records: 1500m- 3, 1M- 1, 2000m- 3,
5000m- 3 in 1984-6, including world records at
1500m and 5000m in 1985.
Progression at 1500m/5000m: 1978- -/14:10.0,
1979- 3:42.3/13:48.5, 1980- 3:37.08, 1981-
3:37.69/13:39.0?, 1982- 3:37.37/14:05.7, 1983-
3:32.54, 1984- 3:31.54/13:04.78, 1985- 3:29.46/
13:00.40, 1986- 3:36.1/13:00.86. pbs: 800m:
1:44.38 '83, 1000m: 2:15.71 '83, 1M: 3:46.92 '85,
2000m: 4:51.98 '86, 3000m: 7:32.23 '86, 2M:
8:14.81 '86, 10000m: 27:26.11 '86, 3000mSt:
8:40.2 '79.
Was at INSEP, Paris in 1981, and moved from
Morocco to Marignane, near Marseille, France in
1982, then to Florence, Italy 1983. Unbeaten at
5000m since 1979, and at any event in 1984 and
1986, and only by Steve Cram in his world record
1500m at Nice in 1985. Had an amazing sequence of near misses at world records in 1986
when he won the overall Grand Prix. Of the fastest
ever times has 2/3 at 1500m, 4/6 at 3000m, 5/7 at
5000m. First notable performance was 37th in
world junior cross-country 1978.

# Women

**NAWAL EL MOUTAWAKIL** b.15 Apr 1962
Casablanca 1.62m 50kg. Physical education
student at Iowa State University.
At 400mh: OG: '84- 1; WCh: '83- sf; WSG: '85- 3;
AfCh: '82- 1 (1 at 100mh, 2 100m), '84- 1 (1 at
200m), '85- 1; WCp: '81- 8 at 100m, '85- 4. NCAA
champion 1984.
Four African records at 400mh 1983-4 and one at
400m 1984. African junior record for 100m, 11.89
in 1979.
Progression at 400mh: 1981- 60.1, 1982- 58.3,
1983- 56.23, 1984- 54.61, 1985- 55.11, 1986-
55.7/55.83. pbs: 100m: 11.4 '83, 11.2w '84, 11.85

'85; 200m: 23.67 '85; 400m: 51.84 '84; 100mh:
13.4 '83 (all national records).
First Moroccan and first African woman, apart
from South Africans, to win an Olympic gold
medal. Second smallest ever Olympic champion.
Underwent operation on right knee to remove
bone fragment in January 1985. Won six gold
medals at 1985 Pan Arab Games: 100m, 200m,
400m, 400mh and both relays.

# NETHERLANDS

**Governing body**: Koninklijke Nederlandse
Atletiek-Unie (KNAU), Nachtegaalstraat 67, P.O.
Box 14444, 3508 SM Utrecht. Founded 1901.
**National Championships** first held in 1910
(men), 1921 (women)
**1986 Champions: MEN**
100m/200m: Ahmed de Kom 10.49/20.88w,
400m: Arjan Visserman 46.33, 800m: Jaap van
Treyen 1:51.04, 1500m: Han Kulker 3:48.70,
5000m: Rob de Brouwer 14:07.42, 10000m:
Martin ten Kate 28:43.82, Mar: Adri Hartveld
2:15:32, 3000mSt: Hans Koeleman 8:35.83,
110mh: Robert de Wit 14.46, 400mh: Marco
Beukenkamp 51.16, HJ: Ruud Wielart 2.17, PV:
Chris Leewenburgh 5.20, LJ: Emiel Mellaard
7.98, TJ: Paul Lucassen 16.05w, SP/DT: Erik de
Bruin 18.81/65.10, HT: Peter van Noort 62.96, JT:
Marcel Bunck 71.04, Dec: Niek Mosselman 7072,
20kmW: Harold van Beek 1:36:54, 50kmW: Jan
Cortenbach 4:14:54.
**WOMEN**
100m: Nellie Fiere 11.15, 200m: Els Vader
22.55w, 400m: Marjo van Agt 53.61, 800m/
1500m/3000m: Elly van Hulst 2:07.66/4:29.73/
9:34.09, 10000m: Janine v.d.Bolt 34:48.39, Mar:
Eefje van Wissen 2:40:07, 100mh/Hep: Tineke
Hidding 13.81/5896, 400mh: Evelien van Hees
60.06, HJ: Ella Wijnants 1.75, LJ: Edine van
Heezik 6.49w, SP: Deborah Dunant 16.29, DT:
Bea Wiarda 53.96, JT: Bernadet Fransen 56.96.

**Erik DE BRUIN** b.25 May 1963 Hardinxveld
1.86m 110kg. Club: VLTC'86. Student.
AT SP/DT: OG: '84- 8/9; ECh: '86:-/6; EJ: '81- 8/3.
Dutch records: 16 shot, 6 discus 1982-6.
Progression at SP/DT: 1979- 14.71/48.04, 1980-
16.22/55.76, 1981- 17.36/55.94, 1982- 17.99/
57.88, 1983- 19.49i/18.95/56.70, 1984- 20.58i/
20.20/63.66, 1985- 20.60i/20.24/66.38, 1986-
20.95/66.78.

**Rob DRUPPERS** b.29 Apr 1962 1.86m 70kg.
Club: Hellas.
At 800m: WCh: '83- 2; ECh: '82- 5, '86- 4; EJ: '81-
h; WCp: '85- 5.
Dutch records 1982-5: 800m (4), 1000m (4),

1500m (2).
Progression at 800m: 1976- 2:10.5, 1977- 2:03.9, 1978- 1:59.1, 1979- 1:52.6, 1980- 1:48.8, 1981- 1:46.88, 1982- 1:44.54, 1983- 1:44.20, 1984- 1.44.60, 1985- 1:43.56, 1986- 1:45.29. pbs: 400m: 47.1 '83, 1000m: 2:15.23 '85, 1500m: 3:35.07 '85, 1M: 3:57.22 '85.

**HAN KULKER** b.15 Aug 1959 Den Haag 1.83m 64kg. Club: Bataven.
At 1500m: ECh: '86- 3; EI: '86- 3.
Dutch 1 mile record 1986.
Progression at 1500m: 1982- 3:52.0, 1984- 3:42.98, 1985- 3:39.3, 1986- 3:36.54. pbs: 400m: 48.8 '85, 800m: 1:46.85 '83, 1000m: 2:18.07 '86, 1M: 3:53.93 '86, 3000m: 8:10.31 '85.
A surprise European 1500m bronze medallist both indoors and out in 1986.

**Emil MELLAARD** b.21 Mar 1966 Spijkenisse 1.89m 74kg. Club: AAC. Student.
At LJ: ECh: '86- 4; EJ: '85- 3. Dutch champion 1984-6. Two Dutch long jump records 1986.
Progression at LJ: 1981- 6.55, 1982- 7.01, 1983- 7.48/7.67w, 1984- 7.84, 1985- 7.99i/7.97, 1986- 7.98. pbs: 100m: 10.87 '85, 10.82w '86, 200m: 21.8 '85, 110mh: 14.4 '84, 14:44 '86.

**Gerard NIJBOER** b.18 Aug 1955 Uffelte 1.82m 70kg. Club: Daventria. Male nurse.
At Mar: OG: '80- 2, '84- dnf; WCh: '83- 29; ECh: '82- 1, '86- 6.
Progression at Mar: 1979- 2:16:48, 1980- 2:09:01, 1982- 2:15:16, 1983- 2:16:59, 1984- 2:10:53, 1985- 2:14:27, 1986- 2:12:46. pbs: 3000m: 8:05.6 '79, 5000m: 13:56.2 '79, 10000m: 28:49.2 '80, 1hr: 19663m '80.
Ran sixteen marathons 1979-86, winning three, including a European best at Amsterdam in 1980. Has been troubled by knee injuries.

# Women

**Carla BEURSKENS** b.15 Feb 1952 Tegelen 1.65m 45kg. now Roemerman. Club: Festina.
At Mar: OG: '84- 22; WCh: '83- 17; ECh: '82- 5, '86- 7. At 3000m: ECh: '78- 21. World road 15km: '86- 3.
Dutch records 1981-5: 3 10000m and marathon, 2 5000m, 1 half-marathon (70:44 '85).
Progression at Mar: 1981- 2:42:56, 1982- 2:34:14, 1983- 2:39:25, 1984- 2:32:53, 1985- 2:27:50, 1986- 2:27:35. pbs: 800m: 2:14.5 '79, 1000m: 2:54.2 '81, 1500m: 4:23.9i '81, 4:24.1 '79; 3000m: 9:08.32 '81, 5000m: 15:46.20 '85, 10000m: 32:28.28 '85.
Major marathon wins: Frankfurt 1985, Honolulu 1986. 2nd Boston 1986.

**Nellie FIERE-COOMAN** b.6 Jun 1964 Paramaribo, Surinam 1.57m 60kg. née Cooman. Club: AV Rotterdam.
At 100m: ECh: '86- 3; EJ: '81- 7. At 60m: EI: '84- 3, '85- 1, '86- 1. Dutch champion 1985-6.
World indoor best of 7.00 for 60m 1986. Three Dutch 100m records 1986.
Progression at 100m: 1981- 11.74/11.52w, 1982- 11.54/11.48w, 1983- 11.58, 1984- 11.39/11.26w, 1985- 11.46/11.39w/11.2, 1986- 11.08. pbs: 200m: 23.79/23.03w '86, LJ: 6.12 '83.
After making her name as a 60m sprinter indoors, reached top class outdoors at 100m in 1986.

**Elly VAN HULST** b.9 Jun 1959 Culemborg 1.78m 58kg. Club: PAC.
At 1500m (800m): OG: '84- 12 (sf); ECh: '82- 8 (sf), '86- 11 (9- 3000m); EI: '84- 2; WIG: '85- 1. At 800m: EJ: '77- 4. Dutch champion at 800m 1978-9, 1981-6; 1500m 1981-6, 3000m 1982-6, 5000m 1983-4, 10000m 1984.
Dutch records 1981-6: 4 at 3000m; 2 each 800m, 1000m, 1M, 2000m; 1 each 1500m, 5000m.
Progression at 1500m: 1976- 4:45.5, 1977- 4:34.1, 1978- 4:20.8, 1979- 4:21.6, 1980- 4:21.6, 1981- 4:08.86, 1982- 4:03.78, 1983- 4:10.50, 1984- 4:05.44, 1985- 4:08.30i, 1986- 4:04.32. pbs: 400m: 54.66 '77, 800m: 1:59.62 '81, 1000m: 2:36.70 '81, 1M: 4:22.40 '86, 2000m: 5:39.52 '86, 3000m: 8:48.25 '86, 5000m: 15:42.5 '85, 10000m: 34:55.98 '84.

# NEW ZEALAND

**Governing body**: New Zealand Amateur Athletic Association, PO Box 741, Wellington.
**National Championships** first held in 1888 (men), 1926 (women)
**1986 Champions: MEN**
100m/200m: Dale McClunie 10.85/21.39, 400m: Paul Cuff 47.67, 800m: Chris Rodgers 1:49.74, 1500m: John Walker 3:42.88, 5000m: David Rush 14:01.41, 10000m: Kerry Rodger 28:55.04, Mar: John Campbell 2:15:19, 3000mSt: Gregor Cameron 8:41.47, 110mh/PV/Dec: Simon Poelman 14.42/4.82/7872, 400mh: Wayne Paul 51.54, HJ: Roger TePuni 2.14, LJ: Steven Walsh 7.56, TJ: Even Peterson 15.14, SP/DT: Henry Smith 16.94/53.02;, HT: Angus Cooper 62.84, JT: John Staplyton-Smith 73.76, 5kmW/30kmW(Rd): Murray Day 20:50.67/2:20:22.
**WOMEN**
100m/200m: Bev Peterson 11.62/23.56, 400m: Carlene Dillimore 54.40, 800m: Gail Metzger 2:05.24, 1500m: Chrissy Pfitzinger 4:11.44, 3000m: Anne Audain 9:03.32, 5000m: Debbie Elsmore 16:03.70, 10000m: Christine Morriss 35:36.43, Mar: Sharon Higgins 2:45:44, 100mh:

Lynette Stock 13.4, 400mh: Kim Peterson 60.33, HJ: Trudy Painter 1.89, LJ: Jayne Mitchell 6.24, SP: Glenda Hughes 15.70, DT: Elizabeth Ryan 46.78, JT: Kaye Nordstrom 45.26, Hep: Terry Genge 5274, 5kmW: Jane Jackson 26:46.92.

**Simon POELMAN** b.27 May 1963 1.87m 90kg.
At decathlon: CG: '86- 3. NZ champion 1984, 1986 (and 110mh and PV 1986).
Four NZ decathlon records 1985-6.
Progression at Dec: 1984- 7499*, 1985- 7854, 1986- 8158. pbs: 100m: 10.78 '86, 400m: 49.74 '86, 1500m: 4:24.35 '84, 110mh: 14.42 '86, HJ: 2.05 '86, PV: 4.80 '86, LJ: 7.36 '86, SP: 14.73 '86, DT: 44.40 '86, JT: 59.68 (old) '85.

**Peter RENNER** b.27 Oct 1959 Mosgiel, near Dunedin 1.86m 75kg. Club: New Brighton. Bushman.
At 3000mSt: OG: '84- 11; WCh: '83- sf; CG: '82- 5, '86- 4 (h 1500m); WCp: '85- 7. At 5000m: CG: '82- 8; WCp '81- 9. NZ champion at 3kmSt 1982-5, 5000m 1984.
Two NZ steeplechase records 1984.

Progression at 3kmSt: 1980- 8:36.6, 1981- 8:37.63, 1982- 8:28.4, 1983- 8:23.38, 1984- 8:14.05, 1985- 8:21.68, 1986- 8:20.16. pbs: 1500m: 3:42.8 '85, 1M: 3:59.7 '85, 5000m: 13:45.00 '82, 10000m: 28:56.69 '85.

**John WALKER** b.12 Jan 1952 Papakura 1.83m 74kg. Sports co-ordinator.
At 1500m: OG: '76- 1 (h 800m); WCh: '83- 9; CG: '74- 2 (3 at 800m), '82- 2 (4 at 800m); WCp: '77- dnf, '81- 2. At 5000m: OG: '84- 8; CG: '86- 5. World CC: '75- 4. NZ champion 800m 1972-3, 1977, 1980-2; 1500m 1974, 1979-83, 1986.
World records at 1M in 1975 and 2000m in 1976.
Progression at 1500m/1M: 1970- 3:52.4, 1972- 3:46.4, 1973- 3:38.0/3:58.8, 1974- 3:32.52/3:54.9, 1975- 3:32.4/3:49.4, 1976- 3:34.19/3:53.07, 1977- 3:32.72/3:52.0, 1978- 3:40.3/3:56.4, 1979- 3:37.0/3:52.85, 1980- 3:33.31/3:52.7, 1981- 3:34.5/3:50.12, 1982- 3:33.7/3:49.08, 1983- 3:33.84/3:49.73, 1984- 3:35.93/3:49.73, 1985- 3:34.97/3:53.20, 1986- 3:35.74/3:53.72. At 5000m: 1981- 13:20.89, 1984- 13:24.46, 1985- 13:47.87, 1986- 13:19.28. pbs:

Anne Audain leads Liz Lynch in the 1986 Commonwealth 10 000 metres. *Mark Shearman*

400m: 48.9 '73, 800m: 1:44.94 '74, 1000m: 2:16.57 '80, 2000m: 4:51.4 '76, 3000m: 7:37.49 '82, 2M: 8:20.57 '75.
The first sub 3:50 miler ran his 100th sub four-minute mile on 17 Feb 1985. Although no longer the world's number one that he was in the mid-70s, he remains a top class runner.

## Women

**Anne AUDAIN** b.1 Nov 1955 Auckland 1.68m 53kg. née Garrett. Club: Otahuhu, Team Nike, USA. Qualified as teacher.
At Mar: OG: '84- dnf. At 10000m: CG: '86- 2. At 3000m: CG: '82- 1. At 1500m: OG: '76- h (h 800m); CG: '74- 6; WCp: '77- 8. NZ champion 800m 1979; 1500m 1976, 1979-80; 3000m 1982, 1986.
Commonwealth records: 3000m 1982, 10000m 1983 and 1986, 5000m 1982, the latter also a world record. Has set NZ records from 1500m to 10000m 1976-86.
Progression at 3000m/Mar: 1975- 9:14.9, 1980- 8:59.2, 1982- 8:45.53, 1983- 2:32:14, 1984- 2:32:07, 1986- 9:03.32. At 10000m: 1983- 32:21.47, 1985- 32:57.40, 1986- 31:53.31. pbs: 800m: 2:04.1 '80, 1500m: 4:10.68 '76, 1M: 4:33.93 '83, 5000m: 15:13.22 '82.
Has had considerable success in recent years on the US road running circuit. Ran the then fastest debut marathon for fourth at Chicago in 1983.

**Lorraine MOLLER** b.1 Jun 1955 Putaruru 1.74m 58kg. Housewife, former school teacher. PE diploma from University of Otago. Married marathoner Ron Daws in 1981.
At Mar: OG: '84- 5; CG: '86- 2. At 3000m: WCh: '83- 14; CG: '82- 3 (3 at 1500m), '86- 5. At 800m: CG: '74- 5.
Two Commonwealth marathon bests 1979-80, further NZ best 1986.
Progression at Mar: 1979- 2:37:37, 1980- 2:31:42, 1981- 2:29:36, 1982- 2:36:13, 1984- 2:28:34, 1985- 2:34:55, 1986- 2:28:17. pbs: 800m: 2:03.6 '74, 1500m: 4:10.35 '85, 1M: 4:32.97 '85, 2000m: 5:47.97 '85, 3000m: 8:51.78 '83, 5000m: 15:32.90 '86, 10000m: 32:40.61 (mx) '86.
Won her first eight marathons, before second to Joyce Smith at London in 1982. Of 19 marathons she has now won 12, including Avon 1980, 1982 and 1984; Boston 1984; Osaka 1986-7.

# NIGERIA

**Governing body**: Amateur Athletic Association of Nigeria, P.O.Box 211, Lagos. Founded 1944.
**National Championships**
**1986 Champions: MEN**
100m: Chidi Imo 10.0, 200m: Gabriel Okon 20.8, 400m: Moses Ugbisien 46.1, 800m: Ado Maude 1:52.6, 1500m/3000mSt: Okandeji Kuranga 3:53.4/9:09.6, 5000m: Ibrahim Kabir 16:05.8, 10000m: Josaiah Adamu 31:26.4, 110mh: Mbanefo Akpom 14.0, 400mh: Henry Amike 50.1, LJ: Yussuf Alli 8.05, TJ: Ajayi Agbebaku 16.76, SP: Adewale Olokoju 17.27, DT: Ken Onuagu-luchi 52.92, HT: Louis Nwabude 44.20, JT (old): J.Okaegbu 60.24.
**WOMEN**
100m/200m: Mary Onyeali 11.3/23.3, 400m: Sadia Sowunmi 53.0, 800m/1500m: Ngozi Ohaechesi 2:18.9/4:53.5, 3000m: Zenaibu Mamudu 11:05.5, 100mh/400mh: Maria Usifo 13.3/61.2, LJ: Lynda Omagbemi 6.26, SP: T.Iwobi 12.60, DT: Otoyo Iguo 38.32, JT: K.Nwani 38.85.

**Ajayi AGBEBAKU** b.6 Dec 1955 1.85m 80kg. Club: El Paso TC, USA. Was at Missouri University, USA.
At TJ: OG: '84- 7; WCh: '83- 3; WSG: '83- 1; AfCh: '79- 1 (1 at LJ), '84- 2; WCp: '79- 7, '81- 8.
Five African triple jump records 1981-3.
At TJ: 1974- 14.66, 1975- 15.14, 1976- 14.98i, 1977- 16.10, 1978- 16.60i, 1979- 16.57/16.82w, 1980- 16.48i, 1981- 16.88, 1982- 17.00i, 1983- 17.26, 1984- 16.96, 1985- 16.23i, 1986- 17.12. pb LJ: 7.94 '79.

**Henry AMIKE** b.4 Oct 1961 1.85m 71kg. Club: All Star International, USA. Was at University of Missouri.
At 400mh: OG: '84- 8; WSG: '85- 2; AfCh: '84- 2, '85- 2.
Progression at 400mh: 1981- 50.9, 1982- 52.07, 1983- 51.34, 1984- 49.33, 1985- 48.88, 1986- 49.13. pbs: 200m: 21.55 '84, 21.5 '81, 400m: 46.29 '84, 800m: 1:51.89 '85.

**Innocent EGBUNIKE** b.30 Nov 1961 1.74m 68kg. Club: Puma TC, USA. Was at Azusa Pacific College.
At 400m: OG: '84- 7 (3 at 4x400mR); WCp: '85- 3. At 200m: WCh: '83- 7 (qf 100m); WSG: '83- 1, '85- 1; AfCh: '84- 1, '85- 1 (2 at 200m).
Commonwealth 400m record 1986, African records: 200m 1983 and 100m 1984. Commonwealth indoor 300m best of 33.35 in 1983, and Nigerian records at 100m, 200m and 400m in 1983-6.

Innocent Egbunike. *Mark Shearman*

Progression at 400m: 1982- 47.99, 1984- 44.81, 1985- 44.66, 1986- 44.50. pbs: 100m: 10.15/10.12w '84; 200m: 20.42/20.4 '83, 20.23w '84; 800m: 1:54.0 '85..
Most unluckily had the baton knocked out of his hand at the end of the 1985 World Cup 4x400m relay in Canberra.

**Paul EMORDI** b.25 Dec 1965 1.89m 80kg. Student at Texas Southern University, USA.
At LJ/TJ: OG: '84--/dnq; AfCh: '84- 1/-, '85- 1/1; WCp: '85- 8/5.
Progression at LJ, TJ: 1981- 7.62, 15.72; 1982- 7.78, 15.85; 1983- 15.86w; 1984- 7.90, 16.78; 1985- 8.07, 16.89/17.15w; 1986- 8.15/8.22w, 17.05/17.31w.

**Chidi IMO** b.27 Aug 1963 1.88m 77kg. University of Missouri, USA.
At 100m: OG: '84- qf; WCh: '83- qf; WSG: '83- 1, '85- 1; AfCh: '84- 1, '85- 1; WCp: '85- 2. 2nd NCAA 1986. Won GP 100m 1986.
Three African 100m records 1985-6.
Progression at 100m: 1981- 10.6, 1982- 10.2, 1983- 10.23, 1984- 10.30/10.25w, 1985- 10.11/10.04w, 1986- 10.00. pb 200m: 20.36 '86, 19.9w '85.
Had a splendidly consistent season in 1986, when he won the Grand Prix for 100m. Was runner-up to Ben Johnson in the Grand Prix Final, the Goodwill Games and at Zürich.

**Joseph TAIWO** b.24 Aug 1959 1.83m 74kg. Was at Washington State University, USA.
At TJ: OG: '84- 9; AfCh: '84- 1. AAA champion 1986. 2nd NCAA 1981 & 1984. 3rd GP 1986.
Progression at TJ: 1979- 15.77, 1980- 16.13w/15.72, 1981- 16.68, 1982- 16.91, 1983- 16.42, 1984- 17.19, 1985- 16.80, 1986- 17.18/17.26w. pb LJ: 7.50i '82.

**Sunday UTI** b.23 Oct 1962 1.75m 68kg. Was at Iowa State University, USA
At 400m (R- 4x400m relay): OG: '80- h, '84- 6 (3R); WCh: '83- dq h; WSG: '83- 1, '85- 3; AfCh: '84- 2. 2nd NCAA 1985.
Progression at 400m: 1979- 48.6, 1981- 45.9, 1982- 45.84, 1983- 44.96, 1984- 44.83, 1985- 44.91, 1986- 45.38. pbs: 100m: 10.4 '84, 200m: 20.79 '85, 20.6 '84.

# NORWAY

**Governing body**: Norges Fri-Idrettsforbund, Tollbugt.11, 0152 Oslo 1. Founded 1896.
**National Championships** first held in 1897 (men), 1947 (women).
**1986 Champions: MEN**
100m/200m Einar Sagli 10.71/21.19, 400m: Svein Erik Storlien 47.59, 800m: Espen Borge 1:48.07, 1500m: Lars Ove Strømø 3:47.65, 5000m/3000mSt: Are Nakkim 13:38.18/8:33.02, 10000m: John Halvorsen 28:27.33, Mar: Atle Joakimsen 2:21:32, 110mh: Robert Ekpete 14.30, 400mh: Geirmund Holsen 51.49, HJ: Hakon Sarnbloom 2.13, PV: Trond Skramstad 4.80, LJ/TJ: Lars Hansen 7.44/15.50, SP: Jan Sagedal 20.49, DT: Knut Hjeltnes 65.72, HT: Køre Sagedal 67.72, JT: Øystein Slettevold 76.88, Dec: Trond Skramstad 7375, 10kmW/20kmW: Erling Andersen 40:39.0/1:26:19.1.

**WOMEN**
100m/200m: Sølvi Olsen 11.83/24.10, 400m/
400mh: Anne Gundersen 53.44/58.21, 800m:
Langøigjelten Bjørn 2:03.61, 1500m: Ingrid Kristiansen 4:05.97, 3000m: Christin Sorum 9:06.49
5000m: Grete Kirkeberg 15:45.98, Mar: Oddrun
Hovsengen 2:51:07, 100mh/LJ: Hilde Fredriksen
14.14/6.18, HJ: Hanne Haugland 1.78, SP: Stine
Lerdahl 15.12, DT: Mette Bergmann 55.12, JT:
Trine Solberg 60.50, Hep: Anne Brit Skjaeveland
5133, 3kmW/5kmW: Kjersti Tysse 13:27.6/
22:26.8, 10kmW: Mona Iversen 49:18.0.

**Erling ANDERSEN** b.22 Sep 1960 Bergen
1.82m 66kg. Club: Søfteland IL.
At 20kmW: OG: '84- 8; WCh: '83- 21; ECh: '78-
23. At 50kmW: disq OG '84 and WCh '83; ECh:
'82- dnf, '86- 10. At 10kmW: EJ: '75- 10, '77- 11,
'79- 2.
European 20km walk records in 1980 and 1984.
World junior records at 5kmW, 19:56.9 and
10kmW, 40:50.0 in 1979.
Progression at 20kmW/50kmW: 1978- 1:27:47,
1979- 1:23:59, 1980- 1:20:57t, 1981- 1:23:47/
3:58:19, 1982- 1:23:54/4:03:40, 1983- 1:23:50t/
3:54:00, 1984- 1:20:36.7t/3:53:16, 1985- 1:22:26/
3:44:24, 1986- 1:21:08t/3:49:49. pbs: track:
3kmW: 11:11.2 '81, 5kmW: 19:16.5 '82, 10kmW:
39:53.4 '84, 1 hrW: 14957m '84; road: 30kmW:
2:13:36 '85.

**Knut HJELTNES** b.8 Dec 1951 Ulvik 1.92m
120kg. Club: IL Gular. Was at Western Maryland
and Penn State Universities, USA.
At DT: OG: '76- 7, '84- 4; WCh: '83- 9; ECh: '78- 5,
'82- 12, '86- 4; WCp: '79- 4. Norwegian champion
at DT: 1975-6, 1979-84, 1986; SP 1975-6, 1978-
84. 2nd GP DT 1985.
Norwegian records: 9 DT 1975-85, 4 SP 1975-80.
Progression at DT: 1968- 41.90, 1969- 49.00,
1970- 51.52, 1971- 50.68, 1972- 58.96, 1973-
58.92, 1974- 56.70, 1975- 61.52, 1976- 64.64,
1977- 65.66, 1978- 65.44, 1979- 69.50, 1980-
67.66, 1981- 67.64, 1982- 64.24, 1983- 66.74,
1984- 67.30, 1985- 69.62, 1986- 68.50. pb SP:
20.55 '80, JT: 77.86 '76.
Suspended for drugs abuse in 1977.

**Lars Arvid NILSEN** b.15 Apr 1965 Notodden
1.93m 110kg. Club: IF Uraedd Porsgrunn. Student at Southern Methodist University, USA.
At SP: ECh: '86- 5; EJ: '83- 10.
Four Norwegian shot records 1986.
Progression at SP: 1982- 15.66, 1983- 16.48,
1984- 17.87, 1985- 19.13, 1986- 21.22. pb DT:
47.76 '85.

# Women

**Ingrid KRISTIANSEN** b.21 Mar 1956 Trondheim
1.69m 50kg. née Christensen. Club: IL i Bul, Oslo.
At Mar: OG: '84- 4; ECh: '82- 3. At 10000m: ECh:
'86- 1. At 3000m: WCh: '80- 3; ECh: '78- 10, '82-
8. At 1500m: ECh: '71- ht. World CC: '82- 6, '84- 4,
'85- 3. Major marathon wins: Stockholm 1980-2,
Houston 1983-4, London 1984 (in European best
time) and 1985 (in world best time), Boston and
Chicago 1986.
World records: 5000m (3) 1981, 1984 and 1986;
10000m (2) 1985-6. World road bests in 1986 at
10km: 30:45.7 and half marathon 1:07:59.
Progression at Mar: 1977- 2:45:15, 1980-
2:34:25, 1981- 2:30:09sh/2:41:34, 1982- 2:33:36,
1983- 2:33:27, 1984- 2:24:26, 1985- 2:21:06,
1986- 2:24:55. At 5000m/10000m: 1981-
15:28.43, 1982- 15:21.81, 1984- 14:58.89, 1985-
14:57.43/30:59.42, 1986- 14:37.33/30:13.74.
pbs: 800m: 2:09.7 '81, 1500m: 4:05.97 '86,
3000m: 8:34.10 '86.
Won Houston marathon just five months after
giving birth to son, Gaute in August 1983. Has
won 10/19 marathons. At cross-country skiing
was 15th in the 1978 world championships. Ran
10km on the road in 30:39 in the 1986 Ekiden
Relay, much the fastest ever by a woman, then
took 45.68 sec off the world 10000m record on the
track. She also smashed the world record for
5000m and improved her bests at 1500m and
3000m in 1986. She is the only man or woman to
hold world records at 5000m, 10000m and marathon.

**Trine SOLBERG** b.18 Apr 1966 Lorenskog
1.72m 65kg. Club: IF Minerva. Bank clerk.
At JT: OG: '84- 5; ECh: '82- dnq, '86- 9; EJ: '81- 5,
'83- 2. Norwegian champion 1983-6. 3rd GP
1986.
Seven Norwegian javelin records 1981-5.
Progression at JT: 1978- 31.04, 1979- 44.08,
1980- 49.54, 1981- 56.06, 1982- 58.02, 1983-
61.58, 1984- 65.02, 1985- 68.94, 1986- 67.80.
Full name Else Katrine Solberg. She was the top
goalscorer in Norwegian second divsion handball
in 1984, and but for her interest in the javelin
would have been a candidate for the national
team.

**Grete WAITZ** b.1 Oct 1953 Oslo 1.72m 52kg. née
Andersen, she married Jack Nilsen, who is now
her coach, in 1975 and together they took the
name Waitz. Club: SK Vidar.
At marathon: OG: '84- 2; WCh: '83- 1. At 3000m:
ECh: '78- 3; WCp: '77- 1, '79- 2. At 1500m: OG:
'72- h, '76- sf; ECh: '71- h (h 800m), '74- 3, '78- 5.

World CC: record five wins 1978-81 and 1983, third in 1982 and 1984.
Two world records at 3000m: 8:46.6 in 1975 and 8:45.4 in 1976, European 5000m record: 15:08.80 in 1982, and European junior 1500m record: 4:17.0 in 1971. Has set four world bests for the marathon. The first three came each year from 1978 to 1980 when in her first three marathons she won in New York, and the fourth when she won the 1983 London marathon. She won the New York marathon again each year 1982-6 and the London 1986. Of her 14 marathons she has won 11, was second in Los Angeles and did not finish twice.
World road bests for 15km: 47:52 in 1984, 10 miles: 53:05 in 1979, 20 miles: 1:51:23 in 1980. 24 Norwegian records, 800m to marathon 1971-83.
Progression at marathon: 1978- 2:32:30, 1979- 2:27:33, 1980- 2:25:41, 1982- 2:27:14, 1983- 2:25:29, 1984- 2:26:18, 1985- 2:28:34, 1986- 2:24:54. pbs: 400m: 57.6 '72, 800m: 2:03.1 '75, 1500m: 4:00.55 '78, 1M: 4:26.90 '79, 3000m: 8:31.75 '79, 5000m: 15:08.80 '82, HJ: 1.61 '71.
Unbeaten for twelve years in cross-country races, and her first ever loss on the road was to Maricica Puica in 1981. A statue of her was erected outside the Bislett Stadium in Oslo in 1984.

# POLAND

**Governing body**: Polski Zwiazek Lekkiej Atletyki (PZLA), 00-372 Warszawa, ul.Foksal 19. Founded 1919.
**National Championships** first held in 1920 (men), 1922 (women)
**1986 Champions: MEN**
100m/200m: Czeslaw Pradzynski 10.32/20.72, 400m: Andrzej Stepien 46.27, 800m: Rafal Jerzy 1:49.72, 1500: Waldemar Lisicki 3:40.75, 5000m/10000m: Boguslaw Psujek 14:10.47/29:26.46, Mar: Antoni Niemczak 2:10:34, 3kmSt: Henryk Jankowski 8:43.45, 110mh: Romuald Giegiel 13.75, 400mh: Ryszard Stoch 49.93, HJ: Dariusz Zielke 2.25, PV: Mariusz Klimczyk 5.40, LJ: Stanislaw Jaskulka 8.16w, TJ: Jacek Pastusinski 16.72, SP: Helmut Krieger 21.30, DT: Dariusz Juzyszyn 63.52, HT: Waclaw Filek 73.46, JT: Stanislaw Gorak 77.78, Dec: Janusz Lesniewicz 7827, 20kmW/50kmW: Grzegorz Ledzion 1:24:50/3:52:23.
**WOMEN**
100m/200m: Ewa Kasprzyk 10.93/22.54, 400m: Marzena Wojdecka 51.44, 800m: Grazyna Kowina 2:02.52, 1500m: Barbara Klepka 4:19.31, 3000m/5000m/10000m: Renata Kokowska 9:00.24/15:56.19/33:27.95, Mar: Renata Walendziak 2:32:30, 100mh: Malgorzata Nowak 13.57, 400mh: Genowefa Blaszak 55.56, HJ:

Danuta Bulkowska 1.95, LJ: Agata Karczmarek 6.92w, SP: Malgorzata Wolska 17.46, DT: Renata Katewicz 61.16, JT: Genowefa Olejarz 61.04, Hep: Lidia Bierka 5913w, 5kmW: Zofia Wolan 24:02.68, 10kmW: Renata Rogoz 49:21.

**Zdzislaw HOFFMANN** b. 27 Aug 1959 Swiebodzin 1.91m 87kg. Club: Legia Warszawa. Mechanic.
At TJ: OG: '80- dnq; WCh: '83- 1; ECp: '81- 7, '83- 2, '85- 5. Polish champion 1981, 1983-4.
Six Polish triple jump records 1983-5.
Progression at TJ: 1974- 13.32, 1975- 13.60, 1976- 14.50, 1977- 15.80, 1978- 15.84, 1979- 16.40, 1980- 16.48, 1981- 16.58, 1982- 16.49, 1983- 17.42, 1984- 17.34/17.55w, 1985- 17.53, 1986- 16.46. pb LJ: 8.09 '83.

**Stanislaw JASKULKA** b.25 Aug 1958 Puck 1.82m 76kg. Club: AZS Warszawa. Student.
At LJ: OG: '80- 5; ECh: '78- 10, '82- dnq, '86- 5; EJ: '77- 1; WSG:'85- 3; ECp: '81- 5. Polish champion 1980-2, 1984, 1986.
Progression at LJ: 1973- 6.83, 1974- 7.57, 1975- 7.82, 1976- 7.97, 1977- 7.83, 1978- 8.02, 1979- 7.85, 1980- 8.13, 1981- 8.11, 1982- 8.10, 1983- 7.92, 1984- 8.06, 1985- 8.11, 1986- 8.00/8.16w. pb 100m: 10.62 '80.

**Marian KOLASA** b.12 Aug 1959 Gdansk 1.95m 90kg. Club: Baltyk Gdynia. Political economist.
At PV: EI: '86- 2; ECp: '85- 3. Polish champion 1985. Polish PV record 1985.
Progression at PV: 1972- 3.00, 1973- 3.50, 1974- 4.00, 1975- 4.40, 1976- 4.95, 1977- 5.13, 1978- 5.20i, 1979- 5.10, 1980- 5.40, 1981- 5.50, 1982- 5.30, 1983- 5.50, 1984- 5.60, 1985- 5.80, 1986- 5.50/5.71exh/5.81i.
His brother Ryszard has a PV best of 5.60 '85 and 5.71exh '86.

**Krzysztof KRAWCZYK** b.28 Jan 1962 Walbrzych 1.86m 74kg. Club: AZS Wroclaw. Student.
At HJ: ECh: '86- 5; EJ: '81- 1.
Progression at HJ: 1976- 1.55, 1977- 1.70, 1978- 1.90, 1979- 2.06, 1980- 2.21, 1981- 2.26, 1983- 2.20, 1984- 2.27i, 1985- 2.26, 1986- 2.31.

**Boguslaw MAMINSKI** b.18 Dec 1955 Kamien Pomorski 1.81m 68kg. Club: Atletico Bojanese, Italy. Mechanic.
At 3kmSt: OG: '80- 7; WCh: '83- 2; ECh: '82- 2, '86- dnf; WCp: '81- 1; ECp: '81- 2, '83- 1, '85- 2 ('79- 6 at 1500m). Polish champion 3kmSt 1979, 1985; 5000m 1983.
Polish 2000m record 1982.
Progression at 3kmSt: 1978- 8:34.8, 1979- 8:23.0, 1980- 8:18.78, 1981- 8:16.66, 1982- 8:17.41, 1983- 8:12.62, 1984- 8:09.18, 1985-

8:15.70, 1986- 8:20.56. pbs: 1000m: 2:20.8 '78, 1500m: 3:38.93 '80, 2000m: 5:02.12 '82, 3000m: 7:45.12 '85, 5000m: 13:26.09 '80.

**Ryszard OSTROWSKI** b.6 Feb 1961 Poznan 1.76m 62kg. Club: AZS Poznan. Student.
At 800m: ECh: '85- 5; WSG: '83- 1, '85- 1. Polish champion 1982-4. At 1500m: ECp: '85- 5.
Polish records: 800m (2) 1985, 1000m 1982..
Progression at 800m: 1979- 1:51.1, 1980- 1:48.5, 1981- 1:47.44, 1982- 1:47.06, 1983- 1:45.90, 1984- 1:45.68, 1985- 1:44.38, 1986- 1:45.14.
pbs: 400m: 46.73 '84, 1000m: 2:18.56 '82, 1500m: 3:40.69 '85.

**Edward SARUL** b.16 Nov 1958 Nowy Kosciol 1.95m 117kg. Club: Gornik Zabrze. Miner.
At SP: WCh: '83- 1; ECh: '82- 11; ECp: '83- 1. Polish champion 1979-80, 1982-3.
Two Polish shot records 1983.
Progression at SP: 1975- 13.20, 1976- 14.93, 1977- 16.74, 1978- 18.24, 1979- 19.06, 1980- 19.80, 1981- 18.44, 1982- 20.64, 1983- 21.68, 1984- 20.89, 1985- 20.02, 1986- 20.74.

**Marian WORONIN** b.13 Aug 1956 Grodzisk Mazowiecki 1.86m 90kg. Club: Legia Warszawa. Mechanic.
At 100m (200m, R- 4x100m relay): OG: '76- sf (4R), '80- 7 (7, 2R); WCh: '83- qf; ECh: '74- h (h), '78- sf (1R), '82- 3, '86- h; EJ: '75- 3; WCp: '79- 3, '81- 1R, '85- 7; ECp: '77- 8, '79- 2 (3, 1R), '81- 4 (1R), '85- 1 (4). At 50m/60m: EI: '77- 3, '79- 1, '80- 1, '81- 1, '82- 1. Polish champion 100m 1978-83, 1985; 200m 1983.
European 100m record in 1984. Polish records: 4 at 100m 1979-84, 2 at 200m 1978-79.
Progression at 100m/200m: 1972- 11.2; 1973- 10.7, 21.8; 1974- 10.47/10.3, 21.29/21.1; 1975- 10.55/10.3, 21.4/21.56; 1976- 10.38/10.2, 20.8/ 20.73w; 1977- 10.61, 21.48; 1978- 10.25, 20.77/ 20.73w; 1979- 10.16, 20.50/20.43w; 1980- 10.19/ 10.13w, 20.49; 1981- 10.28/10.15w, 20.55; 1982- 10.17, 20.83; 1983- 10.23/10.10w, 20.64; 1984- 10.00, 20.78; 1985- 10.14, 20.50 1986- 10.11, 20.88.
Was back in top form at 100m, but pulled up with a groin injury at European Championships.

**Jacek WSZOLA** b.30 Dec 1956 Warszawa 1.94m 74kg. Club: AZS Warszawa. Instructor.
At HJ: OG: '76- 1, '80- 2; WCh: '83- 13; ECh: '74- 5, '78- 6, '82- dnc; EJ: '75- 1; EI: '77- 1, '80- 2; WSG: '77- 1, '79- 4; WCp: '77- 3, '79- 2; ECp: '75- 5, '77- 2, '83- 5=, '85- 5. Polish champion 1974- 80, 1982, 1984-5 (he was the youngest ever in 1974 at the age of 17).
Ten Polish high jump records 1974-80, including a European record 2.29m in 1976 and a world

record 2.35m in 1980.
Progression at HJ: 1971- 1.60, 1972- 1.80, 1973- 2.08, 1974- 2.20, 1975- 2.23, 1976- 2.29, 1977- 2.30, 1978- 2.24, 1979- 2.29, 1980- 2.35, 1981- 2.28i, 1982- 2.28, 1983- 2.28, 1984- 2.31, 1985- 2.32, 1986- 2.25/2.33i.

# Women

**Genowefa BLASZAK** b.22 Aug 1957 Ksiaz Wielkopolski 1.68m 57kg. née Nowaczyk. Club: Chemik Kedzierzyn.
At 400mh (R- 4x400m relay): ECh: '78- 8 (3R), '82- 8, '86- 5 (3R); WCp: '81- 2, '85- 7; ECp: '81- 3, '83- 8, '85- 3. 2nd GP 1985. Polish champion 400m 1976, 1982, 1984; 400mh 1976, 1981, 1983, 1985-6.
Four Polish 400mh records 1984-5.
Progression at 400mh: 1975- 58.8, 1976- 59.59, 1978- 56.67, 1981- 55.78, 1982- 55.76, 1983- 55.97, 1984- 54.78, 1985- 54.27, 1986- 54.47.
pbs: 100m: 11.64 '84, 200m: 22.90 '85, 400m: 50.70 '86.

**Danuta BULKOWSKA** b.31 Jan 1959 Olszanka 1.78m 57kg. Club: AZS Wroclaw. Student.
At HJ: OG: '80- dnq; ECh: '86- 7; EI: '84- 3, '85- 3; EJ: '79- 3=; ECp: '85- 4; WSG: '85- 3. Polish champion 1977, 1983-6.
Polish high jump record 1984.
Progression at HJ: 1974- 1.65, 1975- 1.68, 1976- 1.73, 1977- 1.86, 1978- 1.87, 1979- 1.86i, 1980- 1.90, 1981- 1.88i, 1982- 1.85, 1983- 1.91, 1984- 1.97, 1985- 1.94, 1986- 1.96.

**Ewa KASPRZYK** b.7 Sep 1957 Poznan 1.64m 56kg. née Witkowska. Club: Olimpia Poznan. Student.
At 200m (R- 4x100m relay): WCh: '83- 8; ECh: '86- 5 (3 at 4x400mR); EI: '86- 2; EJ: '75- 2R; WCp: '85- 4 (3R); ECp: '83- 8 (6 at 100m), '85- 3. 2nd GP 1986. Polish champion 100m 1986, 200m 1983-6.
Polish records: 100m, 200m (2) 1986.
Progression at 100m, 200m: 1972- 25.5; 1973- 24.2; 1974- 23.7; 1975- 11.90/11.3, 24.05/23.5; 1976- 11.77, 23.85; 1977- 12.09, 23.79; 1979- 24.32; 1980- 11.97, 24.01; 1981- 24.85; 1982- 11.65/11.4, 23.59; 1983- 11.53, 22.79; 1984- 11.22, 22.42; 1985- 11.32, 22.61/22.60w; 1986- 10.93, 22.13. pb 400m: 51.30 '86.

**Malgorzata NOWAK** b.9 Feb 1959 Bialystok 1.80m 70kg. née Guzowska. Club: Gwardia Warszawa. Teacher.
At Hep: OG: '80- 12; ECh: '82- 13, '86- 3; EJ: '13 pen; WSG: '81- 1, '85- 1. Polish champion Hep 1980-4, 100mh 1986.

Nine Polish heptathlon records 1980-5.
Progression at Pen(p)/Hep: 1976- 4096p, 1977-
3929p, 1978- 4043p, 1979- 4430p, 1980- 5752,
1981- 6333, 1982- 6371, 1983- 5863, 1984-
6332, 1985- 6616, 1986- 6352. pbs: 100m: 11.88
'85, 200m: 24.20 '85, 800m: 2:14.87 '85, 100mh:
13.31/13.27w '85, HJ: 1.95 '85, LJ: 6.53 '81, SP:
16.59 '86, JT: 45.06 '86.

**Genowefa OLEJARZ** b.17 Oct 1962 Jezowa
1.74m 74kg. Club: AZS Warszawa. Student.
At JT: ECh: '82- dnq, '86- 5; EJ: '79- 12; ECp: '83-
3, '85- 6. Polish champion 1982-6.
Two Polish records 1983-4.
Progression at JT: 1979- 49.76, 1980- 48.84,
1981- 53.96, 1982- 60.82, 1983- 63.12, 1984-
65.52, 1985- 60.84, 1986- 64.90. pb SP: 13.10
'83.

# PORTUGAL

**Governing body**: Federacao Portuguesa de
Atletismo, Av.Infante Santo, 68-E-F, 1300
Lisboa. Founded 1921.
**National Championships** first held in 1910
(men), 1937 (women)
**1986 Champions: MEN**
100m/200m: Arnaldo Abrantes 10.52/21.44,
400m/800m: Alvaro Silva 46.81/1:47.58, 1500m:
Antonio Monteiro 3:42.58, 5000m/10000m:
Domingos Castro 13:24.89/28:25.20, Mar: Telmo
Fernandes 2:19:57, 3000mSt: José Regalo
8:24.40, 110mh: Joao Lima 14.4, 400mh:
Joaquim Carvalho 53.57, HJ: Luis Marto 2.10,
PV: Manuel Miguel 4.85, LJ: Carlos Medeiros
7.33, TJ: José Leitao 16.06, SP: Mario Pinto
15.72, DT: Paulo Santos 51.12, HT: José
Pedroso 53.38, JT: Carlos Cunha 70.32, Dec:
Paulo Barrigana 6399, 20kmW: José Urbano
1:29:19.
**WOMEN**
100m: Virginia Gomes 11.67, 200m: Graziela
Guerreiro 24.34, 400m: Maria Joao Lopes 54.81,
800m: Carla Sacramento 2:11.65, 1500m:
Fernanda Marques 4:17.08, 3000m: Albertina
Dias 9:17.96, 10000m: Maria Conceicao Ferreira
33:21.25, Mar: Ermelinda Cunha 2:59:05,
100mh: Cristina Eduardo 15.29, 400mh: Marta
Moreira 59.81, HJ/Hep: Graca Borges 1.65/4473,
LJ: Ana Oliveira 6.02w, SP: Adilia Silvério 13.84,
DT: Teresa Machado 46.30, JT: Ana Morais
44.26, 10kmW: Ana Bela Aires 53:57.

**Domingos CASTRO** b.22 Nov 1963 1.67m 55kg.
Club: Sporting Club de Portugal. Student.
At 10000m: ECh: '86- 5. Portugese 5000m and
10000m champion 1986.

Domingos Castro.

Progression at 5000m/10000m: 1983- 13:48.52/
30:29:1, 1984- 13:52.54/30:39.6, 1985- 13:38.60,
1986- 13:19.03/28:01.62. pbs: 1500m: 3:39.2 '86,
3000m: 7:59.73 '84.
Made enormous progress in 1986; as well as his
European 10km fifth place, he had important wins
at 10000m in the Goodwill Games and at 5000m
in Brussels. His twin brother Dionisio ran 13:22.94
and 28:12.04 in 1986 and was 11th in the European 10000m.

**Antonio LEITAO** b.22 Jul 1960 Espinho 1.76m
68kg. Club: S.L.Benfica. Student.
At 5000m: OG: '84- 3; WCh: '83- 10; ECh: '82- h,
'86- 5; EJ: '79- 3. Two Portugese titles: one each

Antonio Leitao (623) leads the 1986 European 5000m field. Other leaders are 341 Tim Hutchings, 323 Jack Buckner, 429 Alberto Cova.

at 5000m and 3000mSt.
Portugese records at 5000m in 1982, 3000m in 1983 and 3kmSt in 1984.
Progression at 5000m: 1977- 14:14.3, 1978- 14:12.6, 1979- 13:54.83, 1980- 13:52.1, 1981- 13:42.5, 1982- 13:07.70, 1983- 13:14.13, 1984- 13:09.20, 1985- 13:19.75, 1986- 13:15.18. pbs: 800m: 1:53.7 '81, 1500m: 3:38.2 '82, 2000m: 5:09.74 '85, 3000m: 7:39.69 '83, 2M: 8:20.86 '84, 10000m: 29:07.59 '85, 3kmSt: 8:26.19 '84.
Had posted several fast times but little major success until the Olympics, when he ensured that the pace was fast in the final, and reaped his reward with a bronze medal.

**Carlos LOPES** b.18 Feb 1947 Viseu 1.67m 56kg. Club: Albufeira. Bank employee and owner of sports store.
At Mar: OG: '84- 1. At 10000m: OG: '72- h (h 5000m), 76- 2; WCh: '83- 6; ECh: '71- 33 (h 3kmSt), '74- dnf, '82- 4. World CC: '76- 1, '77- 2, '83- 3, '84- 1, '85- 1. Portugese titles: 2 at 5000m and 10000m, 1 3kmSt, 9 CC.
World marathon best 1985. European 10000m

record 1982 and marathon best 1983. Portugese records (1971-83): 9 at 5000m, 8 10000m, 2 3000m, 1 each 2M, 15km, 20km, 1 hour, also two marathon bests.
Progression at 10000m/Mar: 1967- 30:52.0, 1968- 30:45.6, 1969- 30:40.6, 1970- 30:26.6, 1971- 29:28.0, 1972- 28:53.6, 1973- 28:37.0, 1974- 28:38.8, 1975- 28:30.6, 1976- 27:42.65, 1977- 28:44.6, 1978- 28:05.0, 1979- 28:44.3, 1981- 27:47.8, 1982- 27:24.39, 1983- 27:23.44/ 2:08:39, 1984- 27:17.48/2:09:06, 1985- 2:07:12. pbs: 1500m: 3:41.4 '82, 3000m: 7:48.8 '76, 5000m: 13:16.38 '84, 3kmSt: 8:39.6 '73
Of his seven marathons, he has won two, when he was the oldest to be Olympic champion in 1984 and when he was the oldest to set a world best at Rotterdam in 1985. His first marathon was a failure to finish at New York in 1982. He is also the oldest ever world cross-country champion. Sidelined with injuries for much of 1986.

**Fernando MAMEDE** b.1 Nov 1951 Beja 1.75m 59kg. Sporting Club of Lisbon. Bank employee.
At 10000m: OG: '84- dnf; WCh: '83- 14. At 5000m:

ECh: '78- 15. At 800m/1500m: OG: '72- h/h, '76-h/sf; ECh: '71- h/h, '74- sf/h. At 800m: EJ: '70- h. World CC: '81- 3. Portuguese titles: 1 800m, 4 1500m, 2 10000m, 5 CC.
At 10000m set world record in 1984, and European records in 1981 and 1982. Portuguese records: 7 at 1500m, 5 800m, 4 10000m, 2 each 1000m, 3000m and 5000m, 1 each 1 mile and 2000m.
Progression at 5000m/10000m: 1973- 14:24.8, 1974- 13:55.2, 1975- 14:19.8, 1976- 13:49.4, 1977- 13:38.7/29:10.6, 1978- 13:17.76/28:39.6, 1979- 13:26.0/28:16.4, 1980- 13:20.0/27:37.88, 1981- 13:19.2/27:27.7, 1982- 13:14.6/27:22.95, 1983- 13:08.54/27:25.13, 1984- 13:12.83/27:13.81, 1985- 13:23.71/27:41.09, 1986- 13:28.4/27:47.84. pbs: 400m: 48.2 '71, 800m: 1:47.47 '74, 1500m: 3:37.98 '76, 2000m: 5:00.8 '84, 3000m: 7:43.94 '83.
A great distance runner who sadly has totally failed to produce his form in major track finals. Ran off the track in the 1984 Olympic final, unable to control his nerves.

# Women

**Aurora CUNHA** b.31 May 1959 Ronfe, near Guimaraes 1.55m 48kg. Club: FC Oporto. Textiles worker.
At 10000m: ECh: '86- 4. At 3000m: OG: '84- 6; WCh: '83- 9; ECh: '82- 10 (10 at 1500m). At 10000m: WCp: '85- 1. World road: 10km '84-1, 15km '85- 1, '86- 1. Won 19 Portuguese titles: 6 each 1500m and 3000m, 5 5000m, 4 CC.
42 Portuguese records (1976-86): 15 at 3000m, 12 1500m, 6 5000m, 3 each 2000m and 10000m, 2 1000m, 1 800m.
Progression at 3000m/5000m: 1976- 9:54.0, 1977- 9:42.35, 1978- 9:28.4, 1979- 9:16.7, 1980-9:04.7/16:41.6, 1981- 9:30.2, 1982- 8:54.5/15:35.2, 1983- 8:50.20/15:31.7, 1984- 8:46.37/15:09.07, 1985- 8:48.10/15:06.96, 1986- 8:57.31/15:25.59. At 10000m: 1983- 31:52.85, 1984-32:30.91, 1985- 31:35.45, 1986- 31:29.41. pbs: 800m: 2:05.4 '82, 1000m: 2:45.8 '82, 1500m: 4:09.31 '83, 2000m: 5:54.0 '82.

**Rosa MOTA** b.29 Jun 1958 Foz do Douro 1.57m 45kg. Club: Porto.
At Mar: OG: '84- 3; WCh: '83- 4; ECh: '82- 1 (12 at 3000m), '86- 1. World road: 10km '84- 2, 15km '86- 2; World CC: '86- 5. Portuguese titles: 1 800m, 3 1500m, 2 3000m, 1 5000m, 7 CC.
Portuguese records (1974-85): 6 at 1500m, 5 3000m, 2 5000m, 1 each 1000m, 15km, 20km, 1 hour; also seven marathon bests.
Progression at Mar: 1982- 2:36:04, 1983-2:31:12, 1984- 2:26:01, 1985- 2:23:29, 1986-

2:27:15. pbs: 800m: 2:10.76 '85, 1500m: 4:19.53 '83, 3000m: 8:53.84 '84, 5000m: 15:22.97 '85, 10000m: 32:33.51 '85, 20km: 1:06:55.5 '83 (world best), 1 hour: 18027m '83.
Has won six of her nine marathons, including the European gold in her first marathon in 1982, and again in 1986. She improved her best in each of her first seven marathons and won the first ever Olympic medal by a Portugese woman. Her other marathon wins: Rotterdam 1983, Chicago 1983-4, Tokyo 1986. In 1985 she won the Great North Run half marathon in 1:09:54.

# ROMANIA

**Governing body**: Federation Romana de Atletism, Str. Vasile Conta 16, 70139 Bucaresti. Founded 1912.
**National Championships** first held in 1921 (men), 1925 (women)
**1986 Champions: MEN**
100m: Paul Stanciu 10.61, 200m: Constantin Ivan 21.28, 400m/400mh: Horia Toboc 47.60/51.81, 800m: Victor Iacoban 1:48.54, 1500m: Constantin Rosu 3:44.37, 5000m: Corneliu Scurt 14:10.81, 10000m: Gyorgy Marko 29:53.87, 3000mSt: Augustin Barbu 8:58.36, 110mh: Liviu Giurgean 13.60, HJ: Sorin Matei 2.31, PV: Ravzan Stanescu 5.00, LJ: Laurentiu Budur 7.75, TJ: Daniel Ciobanu 16.73, SP: Sorin Tirichita 19.39, DT: Marcel Tirle 62.12, HT: Nicolae Bindar 74.64, JT: Nicu Roata 79.58, Dec: Aurel Astileanu 7714.
**WOMEN**
100m: Doina Carutasu 11.64, 200m: Elena Lina 23.43, 400m: Mihaela Ene 51.67, 800m/1500m: Ilinca Mitrea 1:59.71/4:13.93, 3000m: Elena Fidatov 9:12.88, 10000m: Elena Murgoci 32:24.69, 100mh: Mihaela Pogacian 12.90, 400mh: Christieana Matei 55.05, HJ: Galina Astafei 1.93, LJ: Vali Ionescu 7.03, SP: Mihaela Loghin 20.57, DT: Daniela Costian 68.52, JT: Eva Raduly-Zorgo 57.98, Hep: Petra Vaidean 6217, 5kmW: Victoria Oprea 23:02.67.

**Sorin MATEI** b.6 Jul 1963 Bucaresti 1.84m 71kg. Student.
At HJ: WCh: '83- 17; ECh: '82- dnq, '86- 14; EJ: '81- 5.
Seven Romanian high jump records 1980-5.
Progression at HJ: 1977- 1.88, 1978- 2.03, 1979-2.12i, 1980- 2.27, 1981- 2.22, 1982- 2.28, 1983-2.30, 1984- 2.34, 1985- 2.35, 1986- 2.32.

**Eugen POPESCU** b.12 Aug 1962 Bucaresti 1.94m 78kg.
At HJ: ECh: '86- 7=. Balkan champion 1986.
Progression at HJ: 1979- 2.13, 1980- 2.18, 1981- 2.18i, 1982- 2.15, 1983- 2.23, 1984- 2.25, 1985- 2.26, 1986- 2.31.

# Women

**Daniela COSTIAN** b.30 Apr 1965 Braila 1.82m 92kg.
Club: Dinamo Bucaresti.
At DT: ECh: '86- 7; EJ: '83- 5; WSG:'85- 3.
Romanian discus record 1986.
Progression at DT: 1979- 32.30, 1980- 40.16, 1981- 40.60, 1982- 55.08, 1983- 60.50, 1984- 65.22, 1985- 67.54, 1986- 69.66.

**Florenta CRACIUNESCU** b.7 May 1955 Craiova 1.81m 95kg. née Ionescu, formerly Tacu.
At DT: OG: '80- 6, '84- 3 (8 at SP); WCh: '83- 9; ECh: '82- 7; EJ: '73- 4; WSG: '79- 3, '81- 1, '83- 1; ECp: '79- 4. Balkan champion 1979, 1982, 1985.
Two Romanian discus records 1981-5.
Progression at DT: 1971- 36.50, 1972- 47.70, 1973- 50.82, 1974- 56.70, 1975- 59.26, 1976- 60.10, 1977- 57.28, 1978- 58.34, 1979- 65.06, 1980- 67.02, 1981- 68.98, 1982- 68.24, 1983- 67.74, 1984- 66.08, 1985- 69.50, 1986- 65.50. pb SP: 17.71i '80.

**Valeria 'Vali' IONESCU** b.21 Aug 1960 Tumu Magurele 1.72m 64kg.
At LJ: OG: '84- 2; WCh: '83- 9; ECh: '82- 1, '86- 4; EI: '82- 3; WSG: '81- 3, '83- 3. Romanian champion 1980-3, 1986. Balkan champion 1984.
World record long jump 1982.
Progression at LJ: 1976- 5.52, 1977- 5.49, 1978- 5.58, 1979- 6.07, 1980- 6.54, 1981- 6.75, 1982- 7.20, 1983- 6.92, 1984- 7.11, 1985- 6.97, 1986- 7.10.

**Mitica JUNGHIATU** b.18 Aug 1962 Silistea 1.73m 55kg. Student.
At 800m: ECh: '86- 6. At 1500m: EI: '86- 3. Balkan champion 1985-6.
Progression at 800m: 1979- 2:05.9, 1982- 2:02.39, 1983- 2:01.99, 1984- 2:03.52, 1985- 1:59.20, 1986- 1:57.87. pb 1500m: 4:06.61 '86.

**Ella KOVACS** b.11 Dec 1964 1.68m 52kg.
At 800m: EI: '85- 1.
Progression at 800m: 1982- 2:04.55, 1984- 1:58.42, 1985- 1:55.68, 1986- 1:59.91. pbs: 400m: 53.44 '84, 1500m: 4:06.38 '84.

**Mihaela LOGHIN** b.1 Jun 1952 Roman 1.70m 78kg. Physical Training instructor.
At SP: OG: '84- 2; WCh: '83- 6; ECh: '78- 8, '82- 8,

'86- 8; EI: '86- 3; WSG: '75- 2, '79- 3; ECp: '79- 5.
Balkan champion 1982-6. 3rd GP 1985.
12 Romanian shot records 1975-84.
Progression at SP: 1968- 12.94, 1969- 13.70, 1970- 14.61, 1971- 16.11, 1972- 16.07, 1973- 15.94, 1974- 16.77, 1975- 19.15, 1976- 19.02, 1977- 18.63, 1978- 19.13, 1979- 19.41, 1980- 19.55, 1981- 19.92, 1982- 19.98, 1983- 20.95, 1984- 21.00, 1985- 20.97, 1986- 20.62. pb JT: 51.20 '76.

**Cristieana MATEI** b.2 Jan 1962 Cusmir 1.71m 62kg. née Cojocaru.
At 400mh: OG: '84- 3; WCh: '83- 8; ECh: '82- h, '86- 7; WSG: '85- 2. Balkan champion 1982-3, 1985. At 800m: EI: '84- 3, '85- 3, '86- 2; WSG: '85- 2; WIG: '85- 1. At 1500m: EJ: '79- 3.
Eleven Romanian 400mh records 1982-6.
Progression at 400mh: 1977- 61.59, 1978- 61.3, 1979- 62.39, 1981- 57.67, 1982- 56.50, 1983- 56.26, 1984- 55.24, 1985- 55.10, 1986- 54.55. pbs: 400m: 51.44 '86, 800m: 1:59.06 '85, 1500m: 4:12.2 '79, 3000m: 9:28.4 '79.

**Doina MELINTE** b.27 Dec 1956 Hudesti 1.73m 59kg. née Besliu.
At 800m/1500m: OG: '80- sf 800m, '84- 1/2; WCh: '83- 6/6; ECh: '82- 6/9, '86- -/3 (dnf h 3000m); WSG: '81- 1/2, '83- 3/2; EI: 800m: '82- 1, '84- 2; 1500m: '85- 1. Balkan champion 1500m 1982, 1984. 2nd GP 800m 1985, 1500m 1986.
Romanian 800m record in 1982.
Progression at 800m/1500m: 1976- 2:13.4/ 4:43.4, 1977- 2:11.8/4:38.4, 1978- 2:06.1, 1979- 2:04.4/4:18.6, 1980- 2:00.5/4:00.68, 1981- 1:57.81/4:03.70, 1982- 1:55.05/4:01.40, 1983- 1:57.06/4:01.49, 1984- 1:56.53/3:58.1, 1985- 1:56.81/3:59.88, 1986- 1:56.2/3:56.7. pbs: 400m: 52.5 '85, 600m: 1:23.5 '86 (world best), 3000m: 8:37.11 '86.

**Mihaela POGACIAN** b.27 Jan 1958 Bucharest 1.65m 60kg. née Stoica, formerly Dumitrescu.
At 100mh: WCh: '83- qf; ECh: '86- 5; EJ: '77- 5.
Two Romanian 100mh records 1985 6.
Progression at 100mh: 1973- 14.6, 1974- 13.8, 1975- 13.6, 1976- 13.6, 1977- 14.4, 1978- 13.29, 1979- 13.27, 1980- 13.21/12.9w, 1981- 13.42, 1982- 13.15, 1983- 12.92, 1985- 12.79, 1986- 12.75. pb LJ: 6.23 '83.

**Maricica PUICA** b.29 Jul 1950 Iasi 1.68m 54kg. née Luca, married to trainer Ion Puica.
At 3000m (1500m): OG: '76- (h), '80- (7), '84- 1 (3); ECh: '78- 4 (11), '82- 2 (4), '86- 2 (5); EI: '82- 2; WSG: '77- (3); WCp: '81- 2; ECp: '77- 2, '79- 2. Balkan champion 1500m 1978, 3000m 1978, 1981-2, 1984. World CC: 1st 1982, 1984; 3rd

Maricica Puica. *ASP*

1978. 2nd 3000m GP 1985, Won 1500m and 2nd overall GP 1986.
World records: 1 mile 1982, 2000m 1986; European 1M record 1981. Romanian records at 1500m 1984 and at 1M, 2000m, 3000m (2), 5000m in 1985, 1000m and 2000m 1986.
Progression at 1500m/3000m: 1969- 4:35.8, 1970- 4:34.1, 1971- 4:28.8, 1972- 4:28.7, 1973- 4:22.6/9:33.0, 1974- 4:18.2/9:19.0, 1975- 4:12.8, 1976- 4:06.1/9:18.4, 1977- 4:05.1/8:46.44, 1978- 4:05.13/8:40.94, 1979- 3:59.8/8:49.1, 1980- 3:59.3/9:00.2, 1981- 3:58.29/8:34.30, 1982- 3:57.48/8:31.67, 1983- 4:10.91/9:04.20, 1984- 3:57.22/8:33.57, 1985- 3:57.73/8:27.83, 1986- 3:59.62/8:35.92. pbs: 800m: 1:57.8 '79, 1000m: 2:31.5 '86, 1M: 4:17.33 '85, 2000m: 5:28.69 '86, 5000m: 15:06.04 '85.

**Mariana STANESCU** b.7 Sep 1964 Redea 1.68m 51kg.
Progression at 3000m: 1983- 9:23.6, 1984- 9:00.10, 1985- 8:48.52, 1986- 8:38.83. pbs:

800m: 2:00.49 '86, 1500m: 4:04.69 '86, 1M: 4:25.52 '86, 5000m: 15:41.36 '86, 10000m: 33:43.35 '86, Mar: 3:05:48 '84.
Won Goodwill Games 3000m 1986.

## SENEGAL

**Governing body**: Fédération Sénégalaise d'Athlétisme, B.P.1737, Dakar.

**Amadou Dia BÂ** b.22 Aug 1958 1.90m 82kg.
At 400mh: OG: '84- 5; WCh: '83- 7; WSG: '83- 2; AfG: '78- 3 at HJ, '82- 1 (1 at 400m); AfCh: '84- 1; WCp: '85- 4, and '81- 7 at HJ.
Progression at 400mh: 1982- 49.55, 1983- 49.03, 1984- 48.73, 1985- 48.29, 1986- 48.07. pbs: 100m: 10.7 '84, 200m: 21.51/21.3w '85, 400m: 45.78 '86, HJ: 2.18 '81.
Switched from high jump to 400m hurdles with immediate success in 1981.

**Moussa FALL** b.28 Aug 1963 1.78m 67kg.
At 800m: OG: '84- sf; AfCh: '84- 2, '85- 2. At 400m: WCh: '83- h.
Progression at 800m: 1982- 1:51.7, 1983- 1:49.0, 1984- 1:45.03, 1985- 1:44.68, 1986- 1:44.86. pbs: 400m: 47.3 '83, 1000m: 2:18.1 '85, 1500m: 3:44.86 '86, 1M: 3:59.44 '86.

## SOMALIA

**Governing body**: Somali Amateur Athletic Association, P.O.Box 523, Mogadiscio. Founded 1959.

**Abdi BILE Abdi** b.1963 1.85m 75kg. George Mason University, USA.
At 1500m: OG: '84- sf (qf 800m); AfCh: '85- 2. NCAA champion 1985.
Progression at 1500m: 1982- 3:51.6, 1984- 3:39.86/3:36.0dq, 1985- 3:34.24, 1986- 3:34.01. pbs: 800m: 1:46.1 '84, 1000m: 2:17.15 '85, 1M: 3:53.08 '85.

## SOUTH AFRICA

**Governing body**: South African Amateur Athletic Union, P.O. Box 1261, Pretoria 0001. Founded 1894. Membership of the IAAF terminated in 1976.
**National Championships** first held in 1894 (men), 1929 (women)
**1986 Champions: MEN**
100m: Peter Ngobeni 10.39, 200m: Wessel Oosthuizen 20.52, 400m: Henry Mohoanyane 45.72, 800m/1500m: Johan Fourie 1:48.18/

3:47.50, 5000m: Matthews Temane 14:04.36, 10000m: Xolile Yawa 29:10.76, Mar: Zithulele Sinqe 2:08:04*, 3000mSt: Johan Schnetler 8:48.72, 110mh: Ralf Schroeder 13.94, 400mh: Hannes Pienaar 49.75, HJ: Christo de Wet 2.15, PV: Theo Pellissier 5.00, LJ: Francois Fouché 7.88, TJ: Willie Olivier 16.70w, SP: Eugene Nysschen 18.16, DT: John van Reenen 17.51/ 55.26, HT: Charlie Koen 66.02, JT: Chris de Beer 80.56, Dec: Bertus de Klerk 7085, 20kmW: Chris Britz 1:33:13.
* marathon course dropped 150 metres.

**WOMEN**
100m/200m: Evette Armstrong 11.27/22.55, 400m/400mh: Myrtle Bothma 50.12/53.98, 800m: Zelda Botes 2:03.95, 1500m: Ermyntrude Vermeulen 4:16.33, 3000m: Nicole Landmann 9:36.58, Mar: Cassandra Mihailovic 2:45:18, 100mh: Ina van Rensburg 13.51, HJ: Desiré du Plessis 1.98, LJ: Maryna van Niekerk 6.50w, SP: Rouxnel White 15.01, DT: Nanette van der Walt 51.42, JT: Susan Lio--Cachet 57.90, Hep: Annie le Roux 5796.

**Johan FOURIE** b.2 Dec 1959 Springs 1.80m 70kg. Sergeant in South African Police, Pretoria.
SA champion at 1500m 1979-86, 800m 1984-6.
SA records at 1500m (4), 1 mile (2), 2000m (3), 3000m (2).
Progression at 1500m/1 mile: 1977- 3:49.00, 1978- 3:43.6/4:00.6, 1979- 3:40.2/3:56.3, 1980- 3:40.1/4:00.35, 1981- 3:38.3/3:54.4, 1982- 3:37.02/3:53.29, 1983- 3:35.2/3:52.31, 1984- 3:34.3/3:51.23, 1985- 3:34.59/3:56.65, 1986- 3:34.38/3:52.14. pbs: 800m: 1:46.9 '86, 1000m: 2:17.0 '85, 2000m: 4:56.41 '85, 3000m: 7:44.0 '85, 5000m: 13:51.8 '81.

# Women

**Myrtle BOTHMA** b.18 Feb 1964 East London 1.74m 57kg. née Simpson.
SA champion 400m and 400mh 1984-6.
SA records 1986: 1 at 400m, 4 at 400mh.
Progression at 400mh: 1983- 55.74, 1984- 56.25, 1985- 56.10, 1986- 53.74. pbs: 200m: 24.17 '85, 400m: 50.12 '86.

**Charmaine GALE** b.27 Feb 1964 Estcourt 1.78m 65kg. Policewoman.
SA HJ champion 1980.
Two world junior high jump bests 1981; seven SA records 1980-5.
Progression at HJ: 1977- 1.72, 1978- 1.77, 1979- 1.83, 1980- 1.92, 1981- 1.96, 1982- 1.90, 1983- 1.90, 1984- 1.88, 1985- 2.00, 1986- 1.99.

**Desiré DU PLESSIS** b.20 May 1965 Westonaria 1.84m 64kg. Student at Rand Afrikaans University, Johannesburg.
SA high jump champion 1983-6.
SA high jump record 1986.
Progression at HJ: 1980- 1.70, 1981- 1.80, 1982- 1.81, 1983- 1.90, 1984- 1.87, 1985- 1.93, 1986- 2.01.

# SPAIN

**Governing body**: Real Federacion Española de Atletismo, Calle Miguel Angel 16, Madrid 28010. Founded 1920.
**National Championships** first held in 1917 (men), 1931 (women)
**1986 Champions: MEN**
100m: José J.Arques 10.48, 200m: Antonio Sanchez 21.20, 400m: Angel Heras 46.86, 800m: Coloman Trabado 1:48.91, 1500m: José Luis Gonzalez 3:44.98, 5000m: Pedro Arco 14:21.90, 10000m: Santiago Llorente 29:58.35, Mar: Santiago de la Parte 2:16:37, 3000mSt: Francisco Sanchez 8:35.36, 110mh: Carlos Sala 13.81, 400mh: José Alonso 49.98, HJ: Gustavo A. Becker 2.19, PV: Alberto Ruiz 5.40, LJ: Antonio Corgos 7.96, TJ: Alberto Solanas 16.24, SP: Martin Vara 16.97, DT: Sinesio Garrachon 55.72, HT: Raul Jimeno 72.36, JT: Julian Sotelo 66.14, Dec: Miguel Barahona 7048, 20kmW(t): Daniel Plaza 1:26:50.5, 50kmW: Jorge Llopart 3:50:26.
**WOMEN**
100m/200m: Blanca Lacambra 11.64/23.74, 400m: Esther Lahoz 54.55, 800m: Rosa Colorado 2:06.10, 1500m: Gloria Palle 4:32.52, 3000m: Asuncion Sinovas 9:39.56, 5000m: Carmen Valero 16:48.95, 10km/Mar: Mercedes Calleja 34:23.4/2:40:24, 100mh: Ana-Isabel Guerra 14.17, 400mh: Cristina Perez 57.41, HJ: Covadonga Mateos 1.84, LJ: Maria J.Fernandez 6.20, SP: Margarita Ramos 14.82, DT: Angeles Barreiro 50.70, JT: Natividad Vizcaino 54.72, Hep: Ana Perez 5390, 5kmW/10kmW (road): Maria Cruz Diaz 22:30.90/48:12.

**José Manuel ABASCAL** b.17 Mar 1958 Alceda, Santander 1.82m 67kg. Club: Independiente. Physical education teacher.
At 1500m: OG: '80- h, '84- 3; WCh: '83- 5; ECh: '78- h, '82- 3, '86- h; WCp: '85- 4; EI: '82- 2, '83- 2; EJ: '75- 8, '77- 1 at 3000m. Spanish 1500m champion 1978, 1981-2, 1984-5. 3rd GP 1985.
Eight Spanish records 1977-86: 5 2000m, 3 1500m.
Progression at 1500m/1M: 1974- 4:02.2, 1975- 3:48.8, 1976- 3:47.7, 1977- 3:38.2, 1978- 3:40.0, 1979- 3:37.93/4:02.5, 1980- 3:37.4, 1981- 3:36.6, 1982- 3:33.12/3:53.64, 1983- 3:33.18/3:51.71,

1984- 3:33.69/3:55.69i, 1985- 3:31:69/3:58.33, 1986- 3:31.13/3:50.54. pbs: 800m: 1:49.5 '80, 1000m: 2:19.57 '81, 2000m: 4:52.40 '86, 3000m: 7:54.56 '84, 5000m: 13:17.71 '86, 3000mSt: 8:38.8 '81.

**José ALONSO** b.12 Feb 1957 Vendrell, Tarragona 1.83m 75kg. Club: FC Barcelona. Physical education teacher.
At 400mh: OG: '84- h; WCh: '83- sf; ECh: '78- 7, '82- sf, '86- 6; EJ: '75- 3. Spanish champion 1977-8, 1980, 1984-6. At 400m: EI: '85- 3, '86- 2.
Three Spanish 400mh records 1981-5.
Progression at 400mh: 1974- 57.3, 1975- 51.57, 1976- 50.6, 1977- 51.2/51.48, 1978- 50.19, 1969- 51.5, 1980- 50.1, 1981- 49.81, 1982- 50.02, 1983- 49.75/49.7, 1984- 49.94, 1985- 49.39, 1986- 49.45. pbs: 100m: 10.8 '76, 200m: 21.52 '85, 400m: 46.52i '85, 110mh: 14.6 '76.

**José Luis CARREIRA** b.30 Mar 1962 Madrid 1.70m 62kg. Club: FC Barcelona. Student.
At 1500m: ECh: '86- 9; EI: '85- 3, '86- 2; EJ: '81- sf 800m.
Progression at 1500m: 1981- 3:59.7, 1982- 3:57.3, 1983- 3:45.81, 1984- 3:38.79, 1985- 3:40.27i, 1986- 3:35.56. pbs: 800m: 1:48.2 '84, 1000m: 2:21.09 '84, 1M: 3:57.01 '86, 2000m: 4:57.53 '86, 3000m: 7:59.49i '86.

**Antonio CORGOS** b.10 Mar 1960 Barcelona 1.83m 78kg. Club: FC Barcelona. Student.
At LJ: OG: '80- 7, '84- 10; WCh: '83- 7; ECh: '82- 2, '86- dnq; EI: '81- 2. Spanish champion 1980, 1982-6. At TJ: EJ: '77- 9.
Four Spanish long jump records 1978-80 and European junior records in 1978 and 1979.
Progression at LJ: 1975- 6.03, 1976- 6.87, 1977- 7.30/7.35w, 1978- 8.05, 1979- 8.09, 1980- 8.23, 1981- 7.97i, 1982- 8.13, 1983- 8.06, 1984- 8.02, 1985- 8.20, 1986- 8.08/8.12i. pbs: 100m: 10.62/10.57w '83, 10.4/10.2w '84; HJ: 2.08 '78; TJ: 16.33i '80.

**José Luis GONZALEZ** b.8 Dec 1957 Villaluenga de la Sagra, Toledo 1.80m 63kg. Club: Real Madrid CF.
At 1500m: OG: '80- sf, '84- h; WCh: '83- sf; ECh: '86- 4; EI: '82- 1, '85- 1 '86- 1; WIG: '85- 2. At 3000m: EJ: '75- 3. Spanish champion at 1500m 1976, 1979-80, 1986 and CC 1980-1. 2nd GP 1M 1986.
12 Spanish records 1979-86: 4 1500m & 1M, 3 3000m, 1 5000m.
Progression at 1500m/1M: 1974- 3:51.3, 1975- 3:46.1, 1976- 3:45.8, 1977- 3:49.1, 1978- 3:43.4, 1979- 3:36.32/3:55.47, 1980- 3:35.1/3:57.82, 1981- 3:34.41/3:49.67, 1982- 3:38.70i/3:56.12i, 1983- 3:33.44/3:50.76, 1984- 3:34.61/3:56.41,

1985- 3:30.92/3:47.79, 1986- 3:32.90/3:50.59. pbs: 800m: 1:46.6 '83, 2000m: 5:02.25 '85, 3000m: 7:44.25 '86, 5000m: 13:15.90 '85, 10000m: 29:03.5 '80.

**Jorge LLOPART** b.5 May 1952 El Prat de Llobregat, Barcelona 1.69m 59kg. Club: CGR La Seda. Textile factory worker.
At 50kmW: OG: '80- 2, '84- 7; WCh: '83- dnf (28 at 20kmW); ECh: '78- 1, '82- 6, '86- 9; LT: '83- 4, '85-8. Spanish champion 1978-9, 1981, 1985-6.
Progression at 50kmW: 1975- 4:30:11, 1976- 4:22:43, 1978- 3:53:30, 1979- 3:44:33, 1980- 3:45:55, 1981- 3:48:17, 1982- 3:51:12, 1983- 3:47:48, 1984- 4:03:09, 1985- 3:52:28, 1986- 3:50:26. pbs: 20kmW: 1:25:20 '80, 30kmW: 2:08:39 '79, 2hrW: 27986m '79. track pbs: 5kmW: 19:51.1 '85, 10kmW: 41:17.8 '85, 1hrW: 14285m '86.

**José MARIN** b.21 Jan 1950 El Prat de Llobregat, Barcelona 1.64m 60kg. Club: CN Barcelona. Electrician.
At 20kmW/50kmW: OG: '80- 5/6, '84- 6/-; WCh: '83- 4/2; ECh: '78- 5/dnf, '82- 1/2, '86- dq/-; LT: 50kmW: '79- 7; 20kmW: '81- 5, '85- 1. Spanish champion at 20kmW: 1974-5, 1977, 1979, 1981, 1985; 50kmW: 1980, 1982-4.
World records for 2 hours (28165m) and 30km (2:07:59.8) in 1979.
Progression at 20kmW/50kmW: 1973- 1:35:12t, 1974- 1:33:27t, 1975- 1:31:17t/4:23:30, 1976- 1:29:16t/4:13:43, 1977- 1:33:24t, 1978- 1:24:39/4:10:48, 1979- 1:24:18/3:49:46, 1980- 1:23:52/3:43:35, 1981- 1:23:54/3:55:37, 1982- 1:23:43/3:49:08, 1983- 1:20:00/3:40:46, 1984- 1:25:17/3:50:12, 1985- 1:21:42, 1986- 1:29:00. Track pbs: 3kmW: 11:40.1i '79, 5kmW: 19:24.5 '80, 10kmW: 40:18.7 '81, 1hrW: 14420m '83.

**Miguel Angel PRIETO** b.20 Sep 1964 Segovia 1.87m 81kg. Club: Real Club Deportivo Coruna.
At 20kmW: ECh: '86- 3; LT: '85- 7.
Progression at 20kmW: 1982- 1:38:51, 1983- 1:27:54, 1984- 1:30:27, 1985- 1:24:04, 1986- 1:21:36. Track pbs: 5kmW: 19:41.00i '86, 10kmW: 39:51.1 '86 (Spanish record). Road pb: 50kW: 3:55:57 '85.

**Carlos SALA** b.20 Mar 1960 Barcelona 1.86m 75kg. Club: FC Barcelona. Student.
At 110mh: OG: '80- sf, '84- 7; ECh: '86- 3; EJ: '79-5. Spanish champion 1986.
Progression at 110mh: 1978- 14.7, 1979- 14.23/13.8w, 1980- 13.84, 1981- 13.90, 1982- 13.93, 1983- 13.64/13.55w, 1984- 13.56, 1985- 13.62/13.4, 1986- 13.50.

There was a Spanish 1-2 in the 1986 European Indoor 1500 metres. No. 63 José Luis Gonzales won from 59 José Luis Carreira. No. 65 Adelino Kidalgo finished sixth. *Mark Shearman*

## Women

**Maria CRUZ DIAZ** b.24 Oct 1969 Barcelona 1.60m 46kg. Club: CN Barcelona. Public relations student.
At 10kmW: ECh: '86- 1; WCp: '83- 29, '85- 22. At 5kmW: WJ: '86- 4; EJ: '85- 1=. Spanish champion 5kmW 1984-6, 10kmW 1985-6.
European junior 5km walk record 1985, and road best for 10kmW 1986.
Progression at 10kmW: 1983- 50:18.2, 1984- 48:51, 1985- 47:26, 1986- 46:09. Track pbs: 3kmW: 13:32.4 '86, 5kmW: 22:30.90 '86.
Was the youngest ever Spanish international at age 13 in the 1983 World Race Walking Cup and the youngest ever individual European champion in 1986.

## SUDAN

**Governing body**: Sudan Amateur Athletic Association, P.O.Box 1938, Khartoum. Founded 1959.

**OMER KHALIFA** b.1953? 1.77m 63kg. Formerly at Loughborough University, England.
At 800m/1500m: OG: '84- sf/8; WCh: '83- h/h; AfrG: '78- 8/6; AfrCh: '79- 2/4, '82- 5/4, '84- 3/2, '85--/1; WCp: '81- 5 at 800m, '85- 1 at 1500m. At 800m won AAA 1980, Pan-Arab 1985.
Progression at 1500m: 1975- 3:51.2, 1976- 3:39.8, 1977- 3:37.7, 1978- 3:39.96, 1979- 3:38.8, 1980- 3:34.11, 1981- 3:34.96, 1982- 3:43.4, 1983- 3:37.30, 1984- 3:34.59, 1985- 3:34.07, 1986- 3:33.28. pbs: 800m: 1:44.75 '86, 1000m: 2:18.92 '80, 1M: 3:53.74 '84, 2000m: 5:02.55 '84, 3000m: 7:50.02 '77, 5000m: 13:56.45 '86, Mar: 2:26:40 '81.
As the torch bearer in the Sport Aid run 1986, he set out from a relief camp in the Sudan to reach the United Nations via 12 European cities in eight days.

# SWEDEN

**Governing body**: Svenska Fri-Idrottsförbundet, Sofiatornet, Stadion, S-114 33 Stockholm. Founded 1895.
**National Championships** first held in 1896 (men), 1927 (women)
**1986 Champions: MEN**
100m/110mh: Peter Eriksson 10.63/14.00, 200m/400m: Tommy Björnquist 21.22/46.98, 800m: Ronny Olsson 1:47.24, 1500m: Johnny Kroon 3:45.73, 5000m: Mats Erixon 13:55.33, 10000m: Patrik Wallin 29:27.74, Mar: Kjell-Erik Ståhl 2:12:33, 3000mSt: Håkan Mattisson 8:46.61, 400mh: Ulf Sedlacek 50.71, HJ: Patrik Sjöberg 2.30, PV: Kasimir Zalar 5.51, LJ: Anders Hoffström 7.74, TJ: Claes Rahm 16.50, SP: Anders Skärvstrand 18.44, DT: Göran Bergqvist 58.28, HT: Tore Gustafsson 74.06, JT: Dag Wennlund 81.86, Dec: Mikael Olander 7669, 10kmW: Jan Staaf 41:18.4, 20kmW/50kmW: Bo Gustafsson 1:27:23/4:04:39.
**WOMEN**
100m: Lena Möller 11.69, 200m/100mh: Ann-Louise Skoglund 23.32/13.23w, 400m: Monica Strand 54.25, 800m: Jill McCabe 2:06.77, 1500m: Gunilla Andrén 4:21.19, 3000m: Eva Ernström 9:08.35, 10000m: Birgit Bringslid 33:50.02, Mar: Evy Palm 2:34:42, 400mh: Christina Wennberg 57.15, HJ: Susanne Lorentzon 1.86, LJ/Hep: Eva Karblom 6.44/5785, SP: Siv Tornegård 15.15, DT: Gunnel Hettman 47.92, JT: Elisabet Nagy 58.16, 3kmW/5kmW/10kmW: Ann Jansson 13:01.2/22:33.2/46:13.2.

**Mats ERIXON** b.19 Mar 1958 Nässjö 1.75m 61kg. Club: Mölndals AIK. Recreational officer.
At 5000m: OG: '84- 12; ECh: '82- 14. At 10000m: ECh: '82- 12, '86- 4. Swedish champion 5000m 1981-2, 1984-6; 10000m 1984-5.
Swedish 10000m record 1982.
Progression at 10000m: 1979- 29:53.64, 1980- 29:05.95, 1981- 29:21.04, 1982- 27:56.56, 1984- 28:07.49, 1985- 28:42.45, 1986- 28:01.50. pbs: 800m: 1:51.60 '84, 1500m: 3:41.49 '81, 3000m: 7:48.20 '85, 5000m: 13:26.96 '84, Mar: 2:13:29 '85, 3kmSt: 8:48.30 '82.

**Stefan FERNHOLM** b.2 Jul 1959 Norrköping 1.86m 114kg. Club: Bellevue IK. Student. Was at Brigham Young University, USA.
At DT: OG: '84- 8; ECh: '86- 10. Swedish champion 1984.
Progression at DT: 1979- 44.82, 1980- 57.08, 1981- 41.18, 1982- 50.66, 1983- 62.08, 1984- 67.00, 1985- 67.72, 1986- 65.08. pbs: SP: 19.99 '81, HT: 54.42 '84.
Switched main event from shot to discus from 1983.

**Bo GUSTAFSSON** b.29 Sep 1954 Strömstad 1.76m 64kg. Club: Enhörna IF.
At 50kmW: OG: '80- dnf (dq 20kmW), '84- 2; WCh: '83- dnf; ECh: '78- 10 at 20kmW, '82- 3 (dq 20kmW), '86- 7. Swedish champion 10kmW 1975-7, 1980-4; 20kmW 1980-5; 50kmW 1983 and 1985.
Progression at 50kmW: 1979- 4:14:57, 1981- 4:03:55, 1982- 3:53:22, 1983- 3:51:49, 1984- 3:53:19, 1985- 3:48:35, 1986- 3:50:13. pbs: 20kmW: 1:21:38 '83, Mar: 2:30:38 '83.

**Sven NYLANDER** b.1 Jan 1962 Varberg 1.93m 85kg. Club: IF Göta. Student. Was at Southern Methodist University, USA.
At 400mh: OG: '84- 4; WCh: '83- 4; ECh: '82- 7, '86- 3; Won NCAA 1983. At 110mh: EJ: 79- 6. Swedish champion at 400mh 1982, 110mh 1979 and 1983.
Three Swedish 400mh records 1982-6.
Progression at 400mh: 1978- 54.8, 1979- 52.62, 1981- 51.58, 1982- 49.64, 1983- 48.88, 1984- 48.97, 1985- 50.39, 1986- 48.83. pbs: 100m: 10.89 '83, 200m: 21.18 '86, 400m: 47.8i '81, 48.10 '82; 110mh: 13.98/13.73w '86, LJ: 6.82i '79.

**Patrik SJÖBERG** b.5 Jan 1965 Göteborg 2.00m 79kg. Club: Örgryte IS.
At HJ: OG: '84- 2; WCh: '83- 11; ECh: '82- 10=, '86- 6; EI: '85- 1; EJ: '81- 8, '83- 3; WCp: '85- 1; WIG: '85- 1. Swedish champion 1981-6.
Ten Swedish high jump records 1982-5, European record 1985. World indoor bests: 2.38 '85, 2.41 '87.
Progression at HJ: 1976- 1.40, 1977- 1.59, 1978- 1.80, 1979- 1.91, 1980- 2.07, 1981- 2.21, 1982- 2.26, 1983- 2.33, 1984- 2.33, 1985- 2.38, 1986- 2.34, 1987- 2.41i. pbs: LJ: 7.67 '86, TJ: 15.87 '83.

**Dag WENNLUND** b.9 Oct 1963 Mariestad 1.88m 97kg. Club: Mariestads AIF. Student at Texas University, USA.
At JT: ECh: '86- 15; EJ: '81- 12. Swedish champion 1985-6.
Two Swedish javelin records 1985-6.
Progression at JT: 1980- 65.06, 1981- 70.50, 1982- 78.20, 1983- 81.06, 1984- 82.34, 1985- 92.20. new 1986- 81.86. pbs: SP: 13.09 '82, DT: 40.74 '84, HT: 41.70 '84.

# Women

**Ann JANSSON** b.1 Jul 1958 Norrby 1.70m 53kg. Club: Brunflo IF. Student.
At 10kmW: ECh: '86- 2; WCp: '81- 2, '85- 11. At 10km track walk: world record 47:58.2 '81, European records 47:49.3 '82, 46:14.3 '85.

Swedish record holder at 3km, 5km, 10km and 20km walks.
Track pbs: 1MW: 6:47.0 '85 (world best), 3kmW: 13:01.2 '86, 5kmW: 22:17.1 '85, 10kmW: 46:13.2 '86. Road pbs: 20kmW: 1:36:18 '86.

**Ann-Louise SKOGLUND** b.28 Jun 1962 Karlstad 1.74m 58kg. Club: IF Göta. Clerk.
At 400mh: OG: '84- 5; WCh: '83- 6; ECh: '82- 1. At 400m: OG: '80- ht, EI: '86- 3; EJ: '79- 6. Swedish champion 100m 1980, 200m 1982-5, 400m 1980-1, 100mh 1981 and 1984-5, 400mh 1978 and 1980.
Three world junior 400mh records 1978-80. Swedish records (1978-86): 400m (5), 100mh (2), 400mh (10).
Progression at 400mh: 1977- 62.6, 1978- 57.58, 1979- 57.87, 1980- 56.68, 1981- 56.00, 1982- 54.57, 1983- 54.80, 1984- 55.17, 1985- 55.44, 1986- 54.15. pbs: 100m: 11.70/11.57w '85, 11.5w '77; 200m: 23.27 '85, 400m: 51.69 '86. 100mh: 13.25 '85, 13.23w '86; LJ: 5.59 '82.
Has met peak form at the European Championships. She won in 1982 and improved the Swedish record she set then in 1986 when she was fourth.

**Siw VERA-YBANEZ** b.9 Jul 1957 Strägnäs 1.70m 55kg. née Gustafsson. Club: Enhörna IF. Teacher. Married to Enrique Vera (Mex) (50kmW: WCh: '76- 2, LT: '79- 2; pb 3:43:59 '79).
At 10kmW: ECh: '86- 3; WCp: '83- 5.
World track walk bests: 3km: 13:39.6 '77, 5km 23:25.0 '77; 10km 49:46.8 '76 and 48:40.3 '77; world road bests: 5km: 23:30 '76, 22:57.5 '77, 22:03.2 '83.
Track pbs: 1MW: 7:09.4 '78, 3kmW: 13:23.5 '84, 5kmW: 23:18.6 '81, 10kmW: 47:35.6 '84. Road pbs: 5kmW: 22:03.2 '83, 10kmW: 46:19 '86, 20kmW: 1:44:53 '86.

# SWITZERLAND

**Governing body**: Schweizerischer Leichtathletikverband (SLV), Case Postale 2233, CH 3001, Berne. Formed in 1905 as the Athletischer Ausschuss des Schweizerischen Fussball-Verbandes.
**National Championships** first held in 1906 (men), 1934 (women).
**1986 Champions: MEN**
100m: Stefan Burkart 10.62, 200m: René Gloor 21.36, 400m: Marcel Arnold 45.69, 800m: Gert Kilbert 1:47.31, 1500m: Peter Wirz 3:46.10, 5000m: Markus Ryffel 14:06.14, 10000m: Fredi Griner 29:27.97, Mar: Michael Longthorn (UK) 2:17:57, 3kmst: Roland Hertner 8:48.47, 110mh: Fabien Niederhauser 14.08, 400mh: Thomas

Wild 51.49, HJ: Roland Dalhäuser 2.21, PV: Daniel Aebischer 4.80, LJ: Grégoire Ulrich 7.62, TJ: Peter von Stokar 15.36, SP: Werner Günthör 21.12, DT: Christian Erb 54.04, HT: Daniel Obrist 63.12, JT: Rudolf Steiner 75.52, 10kmW: Thierry Giroud 44:35.77, Dec: Beat Gähwiler 8089.
**WOMEN**
100m/200m: Vroni Werthmüller 11.39/23.59, 400m: Patricia Duboux 54.23, 800m: Sandra Gasser 2:04.93, 1500m: Cornelia Bürki 4:13.45, 3000m: Martine Oppliger 9:27.85, 10000m: Margrit Isenegger 35:22.39, Mar: Helen Comsa 2:41:09, 100mh/LJ: Rita Heggli 13.41/6.35, 400mh: Caroline Plüss 57.47, HJ: Anja Barelkowski (FRG) 1.87, SP: Ursula Stäheli 16.96, DT: Claudia Elsener 51.46, JT: Denise Thièmard 62.10, Hep: Esther Suter 5473, 5kmW: Margot Vetterli 25:56.07.

**Pierre DÉLÈZE** b.25 Sep 1958 Nendaz 1.75m 62kg. Club: LC Zürich. Arts graduate.
At 1500m: OG: '80- ht, '84- ht; WCh: '83- 6; ECh: '78- h, '82- 7; EI: '80- 3; EJ: '77- 3; WSG: '79- 2. 2nd GP 1985. At 5000m: ECh: '86- 7. Swiss champion at 1500m 1978-81, 5000m 1985.
Nine Swiss records 1979-83: 4 1500m, 3 1M, 1 1000m & 2000m.
Progression at 1500m/5000m: 1974- 4:01.82, 1975- 3:49.84, 1976- 3:49.8, 1977- 3:41.8, 1978- 3:39.82, 1979- 3:36.7, 1980- 3:33.80, 1981- 3:36.90, 1982- 3:34.40/13:28.27, 1983- 3:32.97, 1984- 3:33.64, 1985- 3:31.75/13:53.97, 1986- 3:38.38/13:15.31. pbs: 800m: 1:48.92 '82, 1000m: 2:16.87 '83, 1M: 3:50.38 '82, 2000m: 4:56.51 '83, 3000m: 7:44.08 '80.
Moved up to 5000 metres in 1986, and ran fast times in Helsinki and Zürich for first and second places respectively. Disappointed with seventh in the Europeans. Fast finisher.

**Werner GÜNTHÖR** b.1 Jun 1961 Magglingen 2.00m 125kg. Club: STV Bern.
At SP: OG: '84- 5; WCh: '83- dnq; ECh: '86- 1; EI: '84- 2, '85- 3, '86- 1. Swiss champion 1981-6. Won GP 1986.
Eight Swiss shot records 1984-6.
Progression at SP: 1977- 12.12, 1978- 13.60, 1979- 15.08, 1980- 16.42, 1981- 16.65, 1982- 17.51i, 1983- 20.01, 1984- 20.80, 1985- 21.55i/21.26, 1986- 22.22. pbs: DT: 54.48 '85, JT: 74.88 '81.
Had a brilliant season in 1986, with European titles both indoors and out. In the latter he added 56cm to his Swiss record.

**Markus RYFFEL** b.5 Feb 1955 Stafa 1.68m 56kg. Club: STV Bern. Shop-keeper, formerly a typographer.
At 5000m: OG: '76- ht, '80- 5 (dnf 10km), '84- 2;

WCh: '83- 12 (dnf 10km); ECh: '78- 2=, '82- 10, '86- dnf; EJ: '73- 7. At 3000m: EI: '77- 3, '78- 1, '79- 1, '84- 2. Swiss champion: 1500m 1974; 5000m 1976-79, 1981-83, 1986; 10000m 1976, 1985.
17 Swiss records 1976-85: 7 5000m, 4 3000m & 10000m, 2 2000m.
Progression at 5000m/10000m: 1972- 15:15.8, 1973- 14:03.1, 1974- 14:08.8/30:21.8, 1975- 13:50.8/28:54.04, 1976- 13:32.65/28:05.37, 1977- 13:23.93/28:36.0, 1978- 13:19.97/28:21.55, 1979- 13:13.32/28:41.7, 1980- 13:23.03/28:47.8, 1981- 13:19.74/27:54.99, 1982- 13:17.80/28:19.9, 1983- 13:19.38/27:54.88, 1984- 13:07.54/29:05.89, 1985- 13:17.27/27:54.29, 1986- 13:16.28. pbs: 1500m: 3:38.6 '79, 1M: 3:58.05 '84, 2000m: 4:59.54 '78, 3000m: 7:41.00 '79, Mar: 2:16:40 '83.

**Peter WIRZ** b.29 Jul 1960 Brienz 1.81m 68kg. Club: STV Bern. Operations planner.
At 1500m: OG: '84- 6; WCh: '83- h; ECh: '86- 10; EI: '84- 1; EJ: '79- 3.
Swiss 800m champion 1983-4.
Progression at 1500m: 1977- 4:01.33, 1978- 3:50.4, 1979- 3:42.7, 1980- 3:45.00, 1982- 3:40.61, 1983- 3:36.81, 1984- 3:35.83, 1985- 3:37.83, 1986- 3:37.75. pbs: 800m: 1:47.98 '84, 1000m: 2:18.37 '83, 1M: 3:55.68 '86, 2000m: 4:58.29 '84, 3000m: 7:55.68 '83.

Werner Günthör. *Mark Shearman*

# Women

**Cornelia BÜRKI** b.3 Oct 1953 Humansdorp, South Africa 1.60m 53kg. née de Vos. Swiss national by marriage. Club: LC Rapperswil-Jona.
At 1500m: OG: '80- ht; WCh: '83- 10; ECh: '78- 8, '86- 8. 3rd GP 1986. At 3000m: OG: '84- 5; WCh: '83- 11; ECh: '78- 6, '82- 11, '86- 7. World CC 5th 1978 and 1985. Swiss champion 1975-86: 12 at 1500m, 9 CC, 8 3000m, 4 800m.
25 Swiss records 1976-86: 8 3000m, 7 1500m, 6 800m, 3 1M, 1 1000m & 2000m.
Progression at 1500m/3000m: 1974: 4:32.20/-, 1975- 4:14.5/9:15.4, 1976- 4:09.9/9:33.8, 1977- 4:12.14/9:07.56, 1978- 4:04.60/8:46.13, 1979- 4:06.3/-, 1980- 4:04.39/8:53.76, 1981- 4:09.65/9:16.02, 1982- 4:07.88/8:55.67, 1983- 4:07.85/8:46.94, 1984- 4:05.67/8:45.20, 1985- 4:02.05/8:38.71, 1986- 4:03.38/8:44.44. pbs: 800m: 2:00.99 '86, 1000m: 2:39.67 '77, 1M: 4:24.85 '86, 2000m: 5:35.59 '86, Mar: 2:42:33 '84.
Her two daughters, Sorita and Esther, were born in 1972, before she began her running career.

Cornelia Bürki. *Mark Shearman*

# TANZANIA

**Governing body**: Tanzania Amateur Athletic Association, PO Box 2172, Dar es Salaam. Founded 1954.

**Juma IKANGAA** b.19 Jul 1957 Dodoma 1.63m 58kg.
At Mar: OG: '84- 6; WCh: '83- 15; CG: '82- 2; AfrCh: '82- 1; WCp: '85- 10.
Progression at Mar: 1982- 2:09:30, 1983- 2:08:55, 1984- 2:10:49, 1985- 2:11:06, 1986- 2:08:10. pbs: 5000m: 13:41.0 '86, 10000m: 28:15.13 '86.
First African to better 2hrs 10min for marathon, when second to de Castella in epic Commonwealth duel in 1982. Improved his African best when second at Fukuoka in 1983. Has won six of his 15 marathons including Melbourne 1983-4, Tokyo 1984 and 1986, Fukuoka 1986.

**Gidamis SHAHANGA** b.4 ep 1957 Katesh 1.80m 57kg. Club: Team Adidas, UA. Was at University of Texas at El Paso.
At Mar: OG: '80- 15, '84- 22 (h 10000m); CG: '78- 1, '82- 6 (1 at 10000m); AfrG: '78- 7; AfrCh: '79- 2.
At 10000m: WCh: '83- 5. Won NCAA 5000m and 10000m 1983.
Progression at 10000m/Mar: 1978- 2:15:40, 1979- 30:15.0/2:18:50, 1980- 2:16:47, 1981- 28:12.6, 1982- 27:38.1/2:14:25, 1983- 27:46.93/ 2:11:05, 1984- 28:03.24/2:10:19, 1985- 2:15:41, 1986- 2:09:39. pbs: 3000m: 7:48.26 '83, 5000m: 13:34.18 '83.
Shahanga was the first African ever to win the Commonwealth title and also the youngest ever medallist at the event when he scored a major upset in 1978. Won a second Commonwealth gold at 10000m in 1982. Won Los Angeles and Rotterdam marathons in 1984. Ran a pb for fourth at Beijing 1986 in at least his 24th marathon.

# UNITED KINGDOM

**Governing body**: British Amateur Athletic Board, Francis House, Francis Street, London SW1P 1DL. Founded 1932. The Amateur Athletic Association was founded in 1880 and the Women's Amateur Athletic Association in 1922.
National Championships (first were English Championships 1863-79):
**UK National Championships** first held in 1977.
**1986 Champions: MEN**
100m: Jamie Henderson 10.49, 200m: John Regis 21.34, 400m: Phil Brown 45.29, 800m: Peter Elliott 1:46.66, 1500m: Rob Harrison 3:35.74, 5000m: Jack Buckner 13:52.30, 10000m: Karl Harrison 28:21.93, 3000mSt: Kevin Capper 8:36.14, 110mh: Colin Jackson 13.73, 400mh: Max Robertson 49.99, HJ: Geoff Parsons 2.24, PV: Andrew Ashurst 5.30, LJ: Derrick Brown 7.69, TJ: John Herbert 16.96w, SP: Billy Cole 18.68, DT: Graham Savory 58.10, HT: Phil Head 67.48, JT: Michael Hill 73.74, 10kmW: Phil Vesty 41:54.87.
**WOMEN**
100m: Paula Dunn 11.65, 200m: Kathy Cook 23.80, 400m: Angela Piggford 53.09, 800m: Anne Purvis 2:01.63, 1500m: Christina Boxer 4:08.68, 3000m: Wendy Sly 8:52.94, 10000m: Elizabeth Lynch 32:59.59, 100mh: Sally Gunnell 13.50, 400mh: Yvette Wray 57.88, HJ: Diana Davies 1.88, LJ: Kim Hagger 6.39, SP: Judy Oakes 19.00, DT: Venissa Head 55.74, JT: Fatima Whitbread 68.98, 5kmW: Lisa Langford 24:38.99.

**National Road Walk Champions:** MEN 20kmW: Ian McCombie 1:27:14, 50kmW: Godfried De Jonckheere (Bel) 4:10:21. WOMEN 5kmW: Beverley Allen 23:29, 10kmW: Susan Ashforth 53:08.

**AAA Championships** first held in 1880.
**1986 Champions:**
100m: Linford Christie 10.22, 200m: John Regis 20.41, 400m: Darren Clark (Aus) 44.94, 800m: Steve Cram 1:46.15, 1500m: John Gladwin 3:35.93, 5000m: Tim Hutchings 13:25.03, 10000m: Jonathan Solly 27:51.76, Mar: Hugh Jones 2:11:42, 3000mSt: Edison Wedderburn 8:33.03, 110mh: Colin Jackson 13.51, 400mh: Max Robertson 49.53, HJ: Geoff'Parsons 2.23, PV: Brian Hooper 5.30, LJ: Derrick Brown 8.07w, TJ: Joseph Taiwo (Nig) 16.99w, SP: Billy Cole 19.01, DT: Richard Slaney 59.62, HT: David Smith 68.72, JT: David Ottley 80.24, Dec: Greg Richards 7336, 3kmW: Murray Day (NZ) 12:04.0, 10kmW: Ian McCombie 41:42.28.

**WAAA Championships** first held in 1922.
**1986 Champions:**
100m: Paula Dunn 11.34, 200m: Simone Jacobs 23.34, 400m: Kathy Cook 53.50, 800m: Diane Edwards 2:04.26, 1500m: Zola Budd 4:01.93 3000m: Christine Benning 9:05.13, 5000m: Marina Samy 16:22.36, 10000m: Jill Clarke 33:27.69, 100mh: Sally Gunnell 13.13w, 400mh: Yvette Wray 59.11, HJ: Diana Davies 1.80, LJ: Mary Berkeley 6.35, SP: Judy Oakes 18.70, DT: Kathryn Farr 51.20, JT: Fatima Whitbread 69.02, Hep: Terri Genge (NZ) 5547, 5kmW/10kmW: Helen Elleker 24:27.17/49:21.8.

A 44.4 leg from Todd Bennett brings England victory over the USA (Ray Armstead) at Gateshead in 1986.
*Mark Shearman*

**Todd BENNETT** b.6 Jul 1962 Southampton 1.70m 66kg. Club: Southampton & Eastleigh. Clerical officer.
At 400m (R- 4x400m relay): OG: '84- qf (2R); WCh: '83- sf (3R); ECh: '82- sf (2R), '86- dnf h 200; CG: '82- 5 (1R), '86- 1R (2 at 200m); EJ: '81- 1 (2R); ECp: '83- 1R, '85- 3R; EI: '85- 1; WIG: '85- 2. At 200m won UK and AAA titles 1984.
Commonwealth and European 300m best 1984, world indoor 400m best (45.56) 1985.
Progression at 200m, 400m: 1978- 50.9; 1979- 22.6, 48.8; 1980- 21.7, 47.54; 1981- 21.77/21.4/ 21.3w, 46.6; 1982- 21.11/21.0w, 45.89; 1983- 21.02/20.86w, 45.58; 1984- 20.36, 45.45; 1985- 20.81/20.7/20.6w, 45.35; 1986- 20.50, 45.62. pbs: 100m: 10.46 '86, 300m: 32.14 '84, 400mh: 51.5 '85, LJ: 7.01 '82.

**Steve BINNS** b.25 Aug 1960 Keighley 1.70m 57kg. Club: Bingley H.
At 10000m: WCh: '83- h; ECh: '86- 12; CG: '86- 2. UK champion 1986. At 5000m: EJ: '79- 1.
World junior 5000m record, 13:27.04 in 1979.
Progression at 10000m: 1982- 28:20.76, 1983- 27:55.66, 1984- 28:53.22, 1985- 27:59.06, 1986- 27:58.01. pbs: 1500m: 3:46.1 '86, 1M: 4:02.28 '83, 2000m: 5:09.14 '83, 3000m: 7:51.84 '79, 2M: 8:26.54 '86, 5000m: 13:26.86 '83.

**Roger BLACK** b.31 Mar 1966 Portsmouth 1.90m 83kg. Club: Southampton & Eastleigh. Has post-poned medical studies.
At 400m (R- 4x400mR): ECh: '86- 1(1R); CG: '86- 1 (1R); EJ: '85- 1 (1R).
UK 400m record and European 300m best 1986.

Progression at 400m: 1984- 47.7, 1985- 45.36, 1986- 44.59. pbs: 100m: 10.65 '86, 10.6 '84; 200m: 20.63 '86, 300m: 32.08 '86.

In two years of serious competition he has won six gold medals, both 400m and 4x400m relay in three international championships. First notable performance was third in English Schools 200m 1983.

**Roald BRADSTOCK** b.24 Jun 1962 Hertford Heath 1.80m 95kg. Club: Borough of Enfield Harriers. Southern Methodist University, USA.

At JT: OG: '84- 7; ECh: '86- 16; EJ: '81- 2.

One Commonwealth (1985) and five UK javelin records 1984-5. New javelin world best 81.74m 1986.

Progression at JT: 1977- 46.02, 1978- 53.64, 1979- 66.06, 1980- 72.72, 1981- 83.20, 1982- 78.74, 1983- 85.34, 1984- 88.26, 1985- 91.40, 1986 (new)- 81.74.

**Jack BUCKNER** b.22 Sep 1961 Wells, Somerset 1.73m 59kg. Club: Charnwood. Geography graduate of Loughborough University.

At 5000m: CG: '86- 2. UK champion 1986. Won AAA 10km road 1985.

Progression at 5000m: 1984- 13:45.57, 1985- 13:21.06, 1986- 13:10.15. pbs: 800m: 1:49.8 '81, 1000m: 2:18.88 '82, 1500m: 3:35.28 '86, 1M: 3:51.57 '84, 2000m: 5:01.90 '83, 3000m: 7:40.43 '86, 2M: 8:17.12 '86, 10km (road): 28:13 '85.

After an impressive start to the 1985 season he was sidelined by injuries, but having committed himself to moving up in distance, consolidated his 5000m experience in 1986. He learnt with every race, before triumphing at the European Championships, having earlier shown his class with a brilliant win at 3000m in the Bislett Games.

**Linford CHRISTIE** b.2 Apr 1960 St.Andrews, Jamaica 1.89m 77kg.

Club: Thames Valley Harriers. Youth worker.

At 100m (R- 4x100m relay): ECh: '86- 1 (3R); CG: '86- 2 (2R); AAA champion 1986. At 200m: EI: '86- 1. UK 100m & 200m champion 1985.

UK 100m record 1986.

Progression at 100m: 1977- 10.9, 1979- 10.7/10.6w, 1980- 10.73/10.6/10.5w, 1981- 10.85/10.7, 1982- 10.50, 1983- 10.46/10.4, 1984- 10.44/10.31w, 1985- 10.42/10.20w, 1986- 10.04. pb 200m: 20.51 '86.

**Sebastian COE** b.29 Sep 1956 Chiswick, London 1.77m 54kg. Club: Haringey. Graduate of Loughborough University.

At 800m: OG: '80- 2, '84- 2; ECh: '78- 3, '82- 2, '86- 1; EI: '77- 1; WCp: '81- 1; ECp: '77- 4, '79- 1, '81- 1. At 1500m: OG: '80- 1, '84- 1; ECh: '86- 2; EJ: '75- 3. UK 800m champion 1978. Won AAA 800m 1981.

Britain's most prolific world record setter: 800m (2), 1000m (2), 1500m (1), 1M (3), 4x800mR (1) 1979-82. World indoor records: 800m: 1:46.0 '81, 1:44.91 '83; 1000m: 2:18.58 '83. UK records: 800m (5), 1000m (2), 1500m (2), 1M (3) 1977-81.

Progression at 800m, 1500m/1M: 1970- 4:31.8; 1971- 2:08.4, 4:18.0; 1972- 1:59.9, 4:05.9; 1973- 1:56.0, 3:55.0; 1975- 1:53.8, 3:45.2; 1976- 1:47.7, 3:42.67/3:58.35; 1977- 1:44.95, 3:57.67M; 1978- 1:43.97, 4:02.17M; 1979- 1:42.33, 3:32.03/3:48.95; 1980- 1:44.7, 3:32.19; 1981- 1:41.73, 3:31.95/3:47.33; 1982- 1:44.48, 3:39.1/3:59.5; 1983- 1:43.80, 3:35.17/3:52.93; 1984- 1:43.64, 3:32.39/3:54.6, 1985- 1:43.07, 3:32.13/3:49.22; 1986- 1:44.10, 3:29.77. pbs: 400m: 46.87 '79, 600m: 1:16.2 '78, 1000m: 2:12.18 '81, 2000m: 4:58.84 '82, 3000m: 7:54.32i

Closely matched Loughborough graduates Jack Buckner (l) and Tim Hutchings (r). *Mark Shearman*

'86, 5000m: 14:06.2 '80.

Made wonderful recovery from serious illness in 1983 to retain Olympic 1500m title. Was undefeated in a 1500m or 1 mile final from 14 Sep 1976 to 24 Jun 1983. Missed 1986 Commonwealth 800m final and 1500m through virus illness, but came back to share titles with Steve Cram at the Europeans and then narrowly missed the 1500m world record at Rieti. Appointed vicechairman of the Sports Council 1986.

**Steve CRAM** b.14 Oct 1960 Gateshead 1.86m 69kg. Club: Jarrow & Hebburn.
At 1500m: OG: '80- 8, '84- 2; WCh: '83- 1; CG: '78- h, '82- 1, '86- 1 (1 at 800m); ECh: '82- 1, '86- 1 (3 at 800m); ECp: '81- 3, '83- 1, '85- 1. At 3000m: EJ: '79- 1. AAA champion at 1500m 1981-3, 800m 1984, 1986.
World records at 1500m, 1M and 2000m 1985, and on 4 x 800m relay team 1982.
Progression at 800m, 1500m/1M: 1973- 4:31.5; 1974- 2:11.0, 4:22.3; 1975- 2:07.1, 4:13.9; 1976- 1:59.7, 4:07.1; 1977- 1:56.3, 3:47.7; 1978- 1:53.5, 3:40.09/3:57.43; 1979- 1:48.5, 3:42.5/ 3:57.03; 1980- 1:48.41, 3:34.74/3:53.8; 1981- 1:46.29, 3:34.81/3:49.95; 1982- 1:44.45, 3:33.66/ 3:49.90; 1983- 1:43.61, 3:31.66/3:52.56; 1984- 1:46.0, 3:33.13/3:49.65; 1985- 1:42.88, 3:29.67/ 3:46.32; 1986- 1:43.22, 3:30.15/3:48.31. pbs: 400m: 49.1 '82, 600m: 1:16.79 '83, 1000m: 2:12.88 '85, 2000m: 4:51.39 '85, 3000m: 7:43.1 '83, 2M: 8:14.9 '83, 5000m: 13:48.0 '84.
Set world age 17 mile best in 1978. Despite severe injury problems completed a major championship treble in 1983 and went on to gain Olympic silver before his wonderful 1985 season. In 1986 became third man to win Commonwealth 800m/1500m double and then won gold and bronze at the Europeans.

**Peter ELLIOTT** b.Rawmarsh, Rotherham 1.81m 67kg. Club: Rotherham. Joiner with British Steel.
At 800m: OG: '84- sf; WCh: '83- 4; CG: '86- 3; EI: '83- 2; EJ: '81- 4; ECp: '83- 3. UK 800m champion 1983-4, 1986. Won AAA 800m 1982, 1500m 1984. Ran on world record 4 x 800m team 1982.
Progression at 800m: 1975- 2:20.8, 1976- 2:05.9, 1977- 2:01.9, 1978- 1:52.05, 1979- 1:50.7, 1980- 1:51.3, 1981- 1:47.35, 1982- 1:45.61, 1983- 1:43.98, 1984- 1:45.49, 1985- 1:49.4, 1986- 1:44.06. pbs: 400m: 48.2 '84, 600m: 1:16.6 '83, 1000m: 2:17.65 '83, 1500m: 3:35.62 '86, 1M: 3:54.22 '86.
In 1984 became the first British runner to beat Seb Coe at 1500m since 1976. Missed most of 1985 season through injury.

Linford Christie. *ASP*

**John GLADWIN** b.7 May 1963 Wimbledon, London 1.88m 70kg.
Club: Belgrave Harriers. Shop assistant.
At 1500m: CG: '86- 2; ECh: '86- 5. UK champion 1983, AAA champion 1986.
Progression at 1500m: 1979 - 4:09.0, 1981- 4:02.0, 1983- 3:45.09, 1984- 3:39.47, 1986- 3:35.26. pbs: 400m: 48.9 '82, 800m: 1:45.14 '86, 1000m: 2:19.14 '84, 1M: 3:54.52 '86, 3000m: 8:03.3 '86.

**Roger HACKNEY** b.2 Sep 1957 Swansea 1.83m 74kg. Club: Aldershot, Farnham & District. Doctor in the Royal Air Force. Graduate of Birmingham University.
At 3kmSt: OG: '80- sf, '84- 10; WCh: '83- 5; ECh: '82- h, '86- 8; CG: '82- 4 (11 at 5000m), '86- 2;

John Gladwin. *ASP*

LJ); ECp: '85- 1; WSG: '83- 3, '85- 3. UK champion LJ 1982, TJ 1986.
Progression at TJ: 1978- 14.27, 1979- 15.28/15.30w, 1980- 15.30/15.45w, 1981- 16.03, 1982-16.91, 1983- 17.05, 1984- 16.77, 1985- 17.41, 1986- 16.85/17.27w. pbs: 400m: 48.13 '86, LJ: 7.74 '85, 7.94w '83.

**Tim HUTCHINGS** b.4 Dec 1958 London 1.83m 71kg. Club: Crawley. Graduate of Loughborough University.
At 5000m: OG: '84- 4; ECh: '82- 7, '86- 3; CG: '82-14, '86- 3. At 1500m: CG: '78- 10. UK champion 1982, AAA 1986.
World CC: '84- 2. English National CC champion 1983, 1986.
Progression at 5000m: 1979- 14:06.76, 1981-14:18.4, 1982- 13:25.08, 1983- 13:24.10, 1984-13:11.50, 1985- 13:33.24, 1986- 13:12.88. pbs: 800m: 1:51.8 '77, 1000m: 2:22.6 '82, 1500m: 3:38.06 '84, 1M: 3:54.53 '82, 2000m: 5:00.37 '83, 3000m: 7:44.55 '84, 2M: 8:15.53 '86.

**Colin JACKSON** b.18 Feb 1967 Cardiff 1.82m 73kg. Club: Cardiff AAC. Student.
At 110mh: WJ: '86- 1; CG: '86- 2; EJ: '85- 2. UK and AAA champion 1986.
European junior 110mh record 1986.
Progression at 110mh: 1984- 13.92, 1985- 13.69, 1986- 13.44/13.42w. pbs: 100m: 10.49 '86, HJ: 1.81 '82, LJ: 7.96w '86, 7.56 '85; JT: 52.86 '84.
Injury cost him the chance of medal at the 1986 European Championships.

**Hugh JONES** b.1 Nov 1955 North London 1.79m 60kg. Club: Ranelagh H. Graduate of Liverpool University.
At Mar: OG: '84- 12; WCh: '83- 8; ECh: '86- 5; ECp: '81- 5.
Progression at Mar: 1978- 2:25:13, 1979-2:20:28, 1980- 2:18:56, 1981- 2:11:00, 1982-2:09:24, 1983- 2:09:45, 1984- 2:11:54, 1985-2:10:36, 1986- 2:11:42. pbs: 5000m: 14:04.2 '78, 10000m: 28:49.51 '78.
Has run 18 marathons, winning six including AAA 1981 and London 1982. 2nd London 1986. Much troubled by Achilles tendon injuries, but a consistently top-class runner.

**Steve JONES** b.4 Aug 1955 Tredegar, Gwent 1.78m 62kg. Club: Newport H. Corporal in the Royal Air Force (air frame technician).
At marathon: ECh: '86- 20. At 10000m: OG: '84-8; WCh: '83- 12; ECh: '82- 7; CG: '82- 11, '86- 3; ECp: '83- 5. At 5000m: CG: '78- 11. World CC: '79- 7, '80- 9, '84- 3. AAA champion at 10000m on track and road 1984, half marathon 1985.
World marathon best in 1984 and a further Commonwealth record in 1985. UK half marathon

ECp: '81- 7. UK champion 1982, AAA champion 1980 and 1982.
Progression at 3kmSt: 1977- 9:10.0, 1978-8:47.60, 1979- 8:32.97, 1980- 8:27.12, 1981-8:29.71, 1982- 8:21.41, 1983- 8:19.38, 1984-8:20.16, 1985- 8:30.37, 1986- 8:20.97. pbs: 1500m: 3:43.65 '82, 1M: 3:58.77 '86, 2000m: 5:07.99 '83, 3000m: 7:49.47 '84, 5000m: 13:44.04 '86, 2000mSt: 5:23.6 '82 (UK best), 400mh: 56.8 '81
Wife Gillian has 400m pb of 54.9 '84.

**John HERBERT** b. 20 Apr 1962 Nottingham 1.88m 76kg. Club: Haringey. Graphic design student.
At TJ: OG: '84- 10; WCh: '83- 18; ECh: '82- 12, '86- 17; CG: '82- 5 (4 at LJ), '86- 1; EJ: '81- 9 (4 at

best (1:00:59) 1986.
Progression at 10000m: 1980- 28:13.25, 1981-
28:00.58, 1982- 28:05.74, 1983- 27:39.14, 1984-
27:58.64, 1985- 27:53.91, 1986- 28:02.48; at
Mar: 1984- 2:08:05, 1985- 2:07:13, 1986-
2:22:12. pbs: 1500m: 3:42.3 '82, 1M: 4:00.6* '80,
3000m: 7:49.80 '84, 2M: 8:26.71 '80, 5000m:
13:18.6 '82, 3000mSt: 8:32.00 '80.
He moved sensationally into the limelight by winning the 1984 Chicago marathon in the world's
best time. His only previous attempt at the event
had resulted in him dropping out at Chicago in
1983. In 1985 he won at London (2:08:16) and at
Chicago, when just a second outside Lopes's
world best. In 1986 won his first major championships medal at 10000m at the Commonwealth
Games, but after leading by two minutes before
halfway fell back sharply in the European marathon.

**Tom McKEAN** b.27 Oct 1963 1.83m 71kg. Club:
Bellshill YMCA. Labourer.
At 800m: CG: '86- 2; ECh: '86- 3; ECp: '85- 1; UK
champion 1985.
Progression at 800m: 1977- 2:05.0, 1978- 1:58.6,
1979- 1:55.3, 1980- 1:56.15, 1981- 1:53.2?,
1982- 1:49.01, 1983- 1:49.48, 1984- 1:48.40,
1985- 1:46.05, 1986- 1:44.80. pbs: 200m: 22.3
'82, 400m: 47.60 '86, 1000m: 2:18.91 '85.
Made a great debut in international athletics in
1985, when, in the absence of other top UK 800m
runners, he had a string of successes, culminat-
ing in his win in the European Cup Final. He
earlier completed a remarkable 34 successive
wins at 800m. Won medals in both his major races
in 1986.

**David OTTLEY** b.5 Aug 1955 Thurrock 1.88m
95kg. Club: Telford. Youth Training Scheme
supervisor, former school teacher. Was at
Borough Road College.
At JT: OG: '80- dnq, '84- 2; ECh: '82- 12, '86- 10;
CG: '78- 5, '82- 7, '86- 1; WSG: '77- 2; WCp: '85-
4; ECp: '79- 4, '81- 5, '83- 4, '85- 4. UK champion
1978-82 and won AAA 1977, 1982, 1984-6. 2nd
GP 1986.
UK javelin record in 1980.
Progression at JT: 1970- 54.94, 1971- 62.20,
1972- 66.34, 1973- 66.52, 1974- 72.10, 1975-
74.74, 1976- 80.08, 1977- 81.50, 1978- 79.20,
1979- 80.82, 1980- 85.52, 1981- 84.40, 1982-
85.36, 1983- 84.76, 1984- 85.86, 1985- 90.70,
(new) 1986- 80.62. pb SP: 14.49 '81.
Won Olympic silver medal on his 29th birthday
and has progressed further to top world class.

**Steve OVETT** b.9 Oct 1955 Brighton 1.83m 70kg.
Club: Phoenix, Brighton.
At 800m: OG: '76- 5, '80- 1, '84- 8; ECh: '74- 2,

Tom McKean. *ASP*

'78- 2; EJ: '73- 1; ECp: '75- 1. At 1500m: OG: '76-
sf, '80- 3, '84- dnf; WCh: '83- 4; ECh: '78- 1; WCp:
'77- 1, '81- 1; ECp: '77- 1. At 5000m: CG: '86- 1;
ECh: '86- dnf. UK 1500m champion 1977 and
1981. Won AAA 800m 1974-6, 1500m 1979-80.
World records: 3 at 1500m 1980-3, 2 at 1 mile
1980-1. World 2 miles best 1978. UK records:
800m (1), 1000m (1), 1500m (4), 1M (4), 2000m
(2) 1977-83. European junior 800m record 1974.
Progression at 1500m/1M, 5000m: 1970- 4:10.7;
1972- 4:01.5; 1973- 3:44.8/4:00.0; 1974- 3:46.2/
3:59.4; 1975- 3:39.5/3:57.00; 1976- 3:37.89;
1977- 3:34.45/3:54.69, 13:25.0; 1978- 3:35.59/
3:52.8; 1979- 3:32.11/3:49.57; 1980- 3:31.36/
3:48.8, 13:27.87; 1981- 3:31.57/3:48.40; 1982-
3:38.48; 1983- 3:30.77/3:50.49; 1984- 3:34.50,
1985- 3:37.74/3:55.01; 1986- 3:33.78/3:52.99,
13:20.06. pbs: 400m: 47.5 '74, 600m: 1:16.0 '79,

800m: 1:44.09 '78, 1000m: 2:15.91 '79, 2000m: 4:57.71 '82, 3000m: 7:41.3 '77, 2M: 8:13.51 '78.
Started his championship success at 400m with the English Schools Junior title in 1970 and AAA Youth titles in 1971 and 1972. Bravely failed to overcome bronchial problems at the 1984 Olympics. Won 45 successive races at 1500m or 1 mile 1977-80. With the 1986 Commonwealth title, achieved major championship wins from 800m to 5000m.

**Geoff PARSONS** b.14 Aug 1964 Margate 2.03m 78kg.
Club: London AC. Student of mineral process engineering at the Royal School of Mines.
At HJ: OG: '84- dnq; ECh: '82- dnq, '86- 9=; CG: '82- 7, '86- 2; EI: '86- 3=; EJ: '83- 7; ECp: '83- 7=.
UK champion 1985-6, AAA champion 1986.
Seven UK high jump records (and four indoor bests) 1983-6.
Progression at high jump: 1979- 1.86, 1980- 2.06, 1981- 2.05, 1982- 2.21, 1983- 2.25, 1984- 2.26, 1985- 2.25, 1986- 2.28/2.30i
The tallest ever UK international, he achieved the unique feat, in 1983, of setting a UK senior record when winning an English Schools title.

**Derek REDMOND** b. 3 Sep 1965 Bletchley 1.83m 67kg. Club: Birchfield H.
At 400m (R- 4x400m relay); ECh: '86- 4 (1R); EJ: '83- sf (4R); ECp: '85- 3 (3R).
UK 400m record 1985.
Progression at 400m: 1980- 53.6, 1981- 52.8, 1982- 49.5, 1983- 47.55, 1984- 46.32, 1985- 44.82, 1986- 45.25. pbs: 100m: 10.8 '85, 200m: 21.4/21.0w '85, 300m: 32.50 '85, 800m: 1:55.3 '84.
At the age of 19 in 1985 broke David Jenkins' ten-year-old British record. Missed 1986 Commonwealth Games due to a serious hamstring injury, but returned in fine style for the Europeans.

**Colin REITZ** b.6 Apr 1960 Clapton, London 1.86m 73kg. Club: Newham & Essex Beagles.
At 3kmSt: OG: '80- sf, '84- 5; WCh: '83- 3; ECh: '82- 9, '86- 4; CG: '82- 8 (6 at 1500m), '86- 3. At 2000mSt: EJ: '79- 2. AAA 3kmSt champion 1983.
Five UK steeplechase records 1982-6.
Progression at 3kmSt: 1975- 9:43.8, 1976- 9:16.6, 1977- 9:03.27, 1978- 9:01.54, 1979- 8:42.75, 1980- 8:29.75, 1981- 8:29.31, 1982- 8:18.80, 1983- 8:17.75, 1984- 8:13.78, 1985- 8:13.50, 1986- 8:12.11. pbs: 800m: 1:50.0 '80, 1500m: 3:37.55 '85, 1M: 3:55.41 '82, 2000m: 5:04.86 '82, 3000m: 7:44.40 '83, 2M: 8:25.52 '86, 2000mSt: 5:23.87 '84.

**Jonathan SOLLY** b.28 Jun 1963 Wimbledon 1.83m 66kg.
Club: Bingley Harriers. Economics graduate of Durham University.
At 10000m: CG: '86- 1. AAA champion 1986.
Progression at 5000m, 10000m: 1983- 14:15.7; 1984- 13:30.91; 1986- 13:22.39, 27:51.76. pbs: 800m: 1:56.5 '84, 1500m: 3:45.00 '86, 3000m: 7:50.20 '86.
Displayed great promise in 1984, when he took 40 seconds off his 5000m pb in May, and improved a further six seconds to place ninth in the Olympic Trials. After missing the 1985 season through injury, he emerged in 1986 with second at the AAA 10km road race (28:03) and a brilliant win at the AAAs in his first ever track 10km, when he ran away from the field with six laps to go. His Commonwealth gold medal made it two out of two at his new event

**Charlie SPEDDING** b.19 May 1952 Bishop Auckland, Co.Durham 1.74m 63kg. Club: Gateshead H. Product services manager for Nike. Qualified as pharmacist.
At Mar: OG: '84- 3, CG: '86- dnf. At 10000m: ECh: '82- 8; CG: '82- 4. AAA champion at 10000m 1983, marathon 1984.
Progression at Mar: 1984- 2:09:57, 1985- 2:08:33, 1986- 2:10:13. pbs: 1500m: 3:45.36 '73, 1M: 4:03.5 '76, 2000m: 5:12.02 '82, 3000m: 7:54.0 '75, 2M: 8:26.87 '76, 5000m: 13:28.7 '78, 10000m: 28:08.12 '83.
Major success since the age of 30, but he has had a long career, placing second in the 1971 English Schools 1500m, but had many injuries in the 1970s. Won his first two marathons, Houston and London, in 1984. Second at London 1985, third Chicago 1986.

**Daley THOMPSON** b.30 Jul 1958 Notting Hill, London 1.84m 88kg. Club: Newham & Essex Beagles.
At Dec: OG: '76- 18, '80- 1, '84- 1; WCh: '83- 1; ECh: '78- 2, '82- 1, '86- 1; CG: '78- 1, '82- 1, '86- 1; EJ: '77-1 (5 at LJ). UK long jump champion 1979.
Won AAA decathlon 1976 and LJ 1977.
Four world decathlon records (8648 in 1980, 8730 and 8774 in 1982, 8847 in 1984), three world junior records 1976-7, ten UK and Commonwealth records 1976-84.
Progression at Dec: 1975- 6941, 1976- 7748, 1977- 8082, 1978- 8470w, 1979- 6949dnf, 1980- 8648, 1981- 7797, 1982- 8774, 1983- 8714, 1984- 8847, 1986- 8811. pbs: 100m: 10.26 '86, 200m: 20.88 '79, 300m: 33.94 '81, 400m: 46.86 '82, 1500m: 4:20.3 '76, 110mh: 14.04 '86, 400mh: 52.14 '86, HJ: 2.14i '82, PV: 5.20 '81, LJ: 8.01 '84, 8.11w '78, SP: 16.10 '84, DT: 49.10 '86, JT: 65.38 '80.

His supreme competitive ability has brought him unparalleled decathlon success. In his career, from 1975 to 1986, he has won 19 of the 28 decathlons that he has contested. He did not finish two decathlons, one in 1979 and one in 1984, but has otherwise won ten in succession from his European second place in 1978. Has never contested a decathlon in England!

**Nigel WALKER** b.15 Jun 1963 Cardiff 1.80m 75kg. Club: Cardiff AAC. Civil servant.
At 110mh: OG: '84- sf; ECh: '86- 4; CG: '86- 4; EJ: '81- ht. Won UK 1983, AAA 1984.
Progression at 110mh: 1980- 15.07, 1981- 14.47, 1982- 14.24, 1983- 14.19, 1984- 13.78, 1985- 13.88/13.70w, 1986- 13.52. pbs: 100m: 10.55/10.38w/10.5 '86, 200m: 21.35 '83, 400mh: 57.1 '82.

**Allan WELLS** b.3 May 1952 Edinburgh 1.83m 83kg. Club: Edinburgh Southern H. Laboratory assistant, qualified as a marine engineer.
At 100m/200m (R- 4x400m relay): OG: '80- 1/2 (4R), '84- sf 100m; WCh: '83- 4/4; ECh: '78- 6/-, '86- 5/5; CG: '78- 2/1 (1R), '82- 1/1= (3R); WCp:

Allan Wells. *Mark Shearman*

'81- 1/2; ECp: '79- 3/1, '81- 1/2, '83- 2/1. Won IAAF Golden Sprints 1981.
UK records at 100m (3) and 200m (5) 1978-80.
Progression at 100m, 200m: 1971- 11.1; 1972- 10.9w, 22.1w; 1973- 11.1, 22.4; 1975- 11.0, 22.2w; 1976- 10.55/10.4w, 21.42/21.2w; 1977- 10.62/10.52w, 21.10/20.9/20.7w; 1978- 10.15/10.07w, 20.61/20.12w; 1979- 10.19/10.0w, 20.42/20.19w; 1980- 10.11/10.05w, 20.21/20.11w; 1981- 10.17/10.15w, 20.26/20.15w; 1982- 10.20/10.02w, 20.43; 1983- 10.15, 20.52; 1984- 10.18, 20.62/20.55w; 1986- 10.22/20.53. pbs: 400m: 49.1 '75, LJ: 7.32 '72.
Only took up sprinting seriously at the age of 24. After missing the 1986 Commonwealth Games in his hometown, returned in sensational style.

# Women

**Zola BUDD** b.Bloemfontein, South Africa 26 May 1966 1.61m 43kg. British citizenship by parentage obtained 6 April 1984. Club: Aldershot, Farnham & District.
At 3000m: OG: '84- 7; ECh: '86- 4 (9 at 1500m); ECp: '85- 1. World CC: '85- 1, '86- 1. South African champion at 1500m and 3000m 1982 and 1983. Won UK 1500m 1984, WAAA 3000m 1985, 1500m 1986.
While in South Africa set world 5000m best of 15:01.83 in 1984 and world junior bests at 1500m (2), 1M (1), 2000m (2), 3000m (3) and 5000m (4). Since taking up British citizenship: world record at 5000m 1985, and in 1984: world best at 2000m, world junior best at 1M, European junior records at 1500m (4:04.39) and 3000m (8:40.22). Commonwealth indoor records: 3000m 1985-6; 1500m 1986. UK & Commonwealth records at 1500m, 1M, 3000m (2) and 5000m 1985.
Progression at 1500m/3000m/5000m: 1980- 4:24.3/10:06.5, 1981- 4:19.0, 1982- 4:09.1/8:59.2, 1983- 4:06.87/8:39.00/15:10.65, 1984- 4:01.81/8:37.5/15:01.83, 1985- 3:59.96/8:28.83/14:48.07, 1986- 4:01.93/8:34.43. pbs: 800m: 2:00.9 '84, 1000m: 2:45.16 '86, 1M: 4:17.57 '85, 2000m: 5:30.19 '86.
Not permitted to run in the 1986 Commonwealth Games.

**Christina CAHILL** b.25 Mar 1957 Northolt, Middlesex 1.63m 51kg. née Boxer, married Sean Cahill (3:56.95 1M 1979) in 1986. Club: Aldershot, Farnham & District. Promotions manageress, sports goods.
At 1500m: OG: '84- 6; WCh: '83- 9; ECh: '86- h; CG: '78- 11, '82- 1, '86- 4; ECp: '85- 2. At 800m: OG: '80- sf; ECp: '79- 6, '81- 5. Won UK 800m 1979-80, 1984, 1500m 1986; WAAA 800m 1977-8 and 1985, 1500m 1982.

Commonwealth records at 1500m and 1 mile 1984; UK records at 800m and 1 mile 1979.
Progression at 1500m: 1970- 4:44.1, 1971- 4:39.1, 1972- 4:29.0, 1977- 4:20.7, 1978- 4:10.0, 1979- 4:07.06, 1980- 4:09.15, 1981- 4:10.22, 1982- 4:04.48, 1983- 4:06.74, 1984- 4:00.57, 1985- 4:02.58, 1986- 4:08.68. pbs: 400m: 55.14 '79, 800m: 1:59.05 '79, 1000m: 2:34.92 '85, 1M: 4:22.64 '84, 2000m: 5:33.85 '84, 3000m: 8:49.89 '85.
Won National junior cross-country title in 1971.

**Kathy COOK** b.3 May 1960 Winchester 1.80m 67kg. Club: Wolverhampton & Bilston. née Smallwood. Married to Garry Cook (1:44.55 '84 for 800m). Bank liason officer. Graduate of Borough Road College.
At 400m: OG: '84- 3; CG: '86- 3 (2 4x400mR). At 200m (100m, R- 4x100m relay): OG: '80- 5 (6, 2R), 84- 4 (3R); WCh: '83- 3 (2R); ECh: '78- sf (2R), '82- 2 (2R), '86- sf (5R); CG: '78- 5 (1R), '82- 2 (1R), '86- 2 (1R); EJ: '77- 3 (3, 3R); WSG: '79- 2 (2, 2R), '81- 1 (2R); WCp: '81- 2 at 100m; ECp: '79- 4 (3R), '81- 2 (2, 2R), '83- 3 (3, 3R), '85- 5. UK champion 100m 1983; 200m 1980, 1983, 1985-6. WAAA champion 100m 1978, 1980, 1983-4; 200m 1978-80, 1982, 1984-5; 400m 1986.
UK & Commonwealth 400m records in 1982 and 1984, UK 100m record 1981, and four UK 200m records 1979-84, including a Commonwealth record in 1982. World 300m best 1984.
Progression at 200m, 400m: 1974- 25.1; 1975- 24.46; 1976- 24.57/24.3; 1977- 23.22/23.1w, 56.0; 1978- 22.99/22.73w; 1979- 22.70, 54.5; 1980- 22.31, 54.3; 1981- 22.58/22.57w, 51.08; 1982- 22.13, 50.46; 1983- 22.26, 50.95; 1984- 22.10, 49.43; 1985- 22.87, 51.36; 1986- 23.12, 51.88. pbs: 100m: 11.10 '81, 11.08w '83; 300m: 35.46 '84, HJ: 1.63 '75.
By far Britain's biggest medal winner ever at major Games (23), she struggled to recapture her form in 1986, and the Europeans was the first championships at which she failed to win a sprint relay medal.

**Elizabeth LYNCH** b.24 May 1964 Dundee 1.68m 45kg. Club: Dundee Hawkhill H. Engaged to steeplechaser Peter McColgan.
At 10000m: CG: '86- 1; ECh: '86- 7 (12 at 3000m); WSG: '86- 3; UK champion 1986. NCAA indoor mile champion 1986, while at University of Alabama.
Commonwealth 10000m record 1986.
Progression at 3000m/10000m: 1979- 11:15.1, 1980- 10:41.8, 1982- 9:42.3, 1983- 9:34.5, 1984- 9:49.2, 1985- 9:03.80/33:19.14, 1986- 8:46.53/ 31:41.42. pbs: 800m: 2:07.6 '82, 1000m: 2:45.95i '86, 1500m: 4:13.13 '86, 1M: 4:33.91 '86, 2000m: 5:43.40 '86, 5000m: 15:41.58 '86.

Liz Lynch started 1987 in magnificent style. Her wins included a UK 10km road record of 31:07. *ASP*

**Yvonne MURRAY** b.4 Oct 1964 Musselburgh. 1.73m 50kg. Club: Edinburgh AC. Clerk.
At 3000m: ECh: '86- 3; CG: '82- 10 (10 at 1500m), '86- 3 (5 1500m); EJ: '81- 6; EI: '84- 3, '85- 2. UK champion 3000m 1985, 5000m 1983.
Commonwealth 2000m record 1986. UK junior 3000m record 1982.
Progression at 3000m: 1980- 10:11.8, 1981- 9:30.0, 1982- 9:07.77, 1983- 9:04.14, 1984- 8:58.54, 1985- 9:00.97, 1986- 8:37.15. pbs: 800m: 2:03.60 '86, 1000m: 2:37.75 '86, 1500m: 4:05.76 '86, 1M: 4:23.08 '86, 2000m: 5:29.58 '86, 5000m: 15:50.54 '84, 10000m: 33:43.80 '85.
Surged into the lead with two and a half laps to go in the Commonwealth 3000m, and had enormous home crowd support but had to settle for the bronze medal. In the European Championships she improved her 3000m pb by 5.76 sec. in the heat and a further 12.41 sec. in the final.

**Heather OAKES** b.14 Aug 1959 London 1.66m 63kg. née Hunte, married to Gary Oakes (3rd Olympic 400mh 1980 in 49.11). Club: Haringey. Clerical officer.

At 100m (R- 4x100m relay): OG: '80- 8 (3R), '84- 7 (3R); WCh: '83- sf; ECh: '86- sf (sf 200m); CG: '82- 7, '86- 1 (1R); EJ: '77- 4 (3R); WCp: '79- 1R; ECp: '79- 4 (3R), '85- 6. At 60m: EI: '85- 3; WIG: '85- 2. UK champion 100m 1979-80, 1982, 1984 and 200m 1979, 1984. Won WAAA 100m 1979.
Progression at 100m: 1972- 12.5, 1973- 12.5/ 12.3w, 1974- 12.0w, 1975- 12.02/11.8/11.7w, 1976- 11.79/11.6, 1977- 11.58, 1978- 11.60/11.3, 1979- 11.30/11.26w, 1980- 11.20/11.01w/11.1, 1981- 12.2, 1982- 11.36/11.32w, 1983- 11.37/ 11.35w, 1984- 11.27/11.08w, 1985- 11.33, 1986- 11.22/11.20w. pb 200m: 22.92 '86, 22.9 '80.

**Judy OAKES** b.14 Feb 1958 Lewisham, London 1.63m 81kg. Club: Croydon H. Gymnasium assistant.

At SP: OG: 84- 4; WCh: '83- 12; ECh: '86- 14; CG: '78- 3, '82- 1, '86- 2; EI: '79- 3; ECp: '77- 7, '85- 4. UK champion 1978, 1982, 1984-5. Won WAAA 1979-80, 1982-6 and record nine indoor titles.
Four UK shot records 1979-86.
Progression at SP: 1973- 11.73, 1974- 12.50, 1975- 14.22, 1976- 15.94, 1977- 16.24i, 1978- 16.74i, 1979- 16.72, 1980- 17.20, 1981- 16.88, 1982- 17.92, 1983- 18.28, 1984- 18.35i/18.28, 1985- 18.10i/18.02, 1986- 19.00. pbs: DT: 52.96 '85, JT: 46.66 '86.
Won world powerlifting titles at 75kg in 1981 and 82kg in 1982 and set world records at these weights.

**Tessa SANDERSON** b.St.Elizabeth, Jamaica 14 Mar 1956 1.68m 72kg. Club: Wolverhampton & Bilston. Sports promotion assistant in Leeds.

At JT: OG: '76- 9, '80- dnq, '84- 1; WCh: '83- 4; ECh: '74- 13, '78- 2; CG: '74- 5, '78- 1, '86- 1; EJ: '73- 12; WCp: '77- 2; ECp: '75- 7, '77- 2, '79- 3, '81- 2. UK champion 1977-78 and won WAAA 1975-7, 1979-80, 1985.
Ten UK, including five Commonwealth javelin records 1976-83; also two UK & Commonwealth heptathlon records 1981.
Progression at JT: 1970- 31.86, 1971- 42.02, 1972- 43.06, 1973- 51.34, 1974- 55.04, 1975- 54.40, 1976- 57.20, 1977- 67.20, 1978- 64.00, 1979- 65.34, 1980- 69.70, 1981- 68.86, 1982- 66.00, 1983- 73.58, 1984- 69.56, 1985- 71.18, 1986- 69.80. pbs: 200m: 24.89 '81, 400m: 57.3 '72, 800m: 2:26.20 '81, 100mh: 13.46 '81, 400mh: 60.46 '77, HJ: 1.69 '73, LJ: 5.97 '81, SP: 13.27 '81, Hep: 6140 '81.

Judy Simpson. *ASP*

**Judy SIMPSON** b.Kingston, Jamaica 14 Nov 1960 1.82m 72kg. née Livermore, married to Robin Simpson (4.60m PV). Club: Birchfield H.

At Pen/Hep: OG: '80- 13, '84- 5 (dnq HJ); WCh: '83- dnf (sf 100mh); ECh: '82- 7, '86- 3; CG: '82- 2 (5 at 100mh), '86- 1; WSG: '81- 4, '83- 3, '85- 3; ECp: '83- 5, '85- 9. WAAA champion 1982-3.
Four Commonwealth heptathlon records 1981-6.
Progression at Hep (p Pen): 1977- 3870p, 1978- 4028wp, 1979- 4908/4090p, 1980- 4357p, 1981- 5844, 1982- 6259, 1983- 6347, 1984- 6264, 1985- 6082, 1986- 6623. pbs: 200m: 24.75 '83, 400m: 53.76 '81, 800m: 2:11.49 '82, 100mh: 13.05 '86, HJ: 1.92 '83, LJ: 6.40 '84, 6.56w '86; SP: 14.73 '86, JT: 40.92 '86.
Had a marvellous European Championships in 1986 with five pbs in seven events. Former UK champion at Tae Kwan Do.

**Wendy SLY** b.5 Nov 1959 Hampton, Middlesex 1.66m 51kg. née Smith, married to Chris Sly (2nd European Junior 1500m 1977). Club: Hounslow and Brooks Racing Team, USA.
At 3000m: OG: '84- 2; WCh: '80- dnf, '83- 5; CG: '82- 2, '86- 8. At 1500m: WCh: '83- 5; ECp: '83- 4; EJ: '77- 11; WSG: '81- 6. Won IAAF world road 10km 1983, UK 3000m 1983, English national CC 1981.
UK & Commonwealth records at 3000m 1982 and 1983, 1M 1984.
Progression at 3000m: 1977- 9:32.0, 1978- 9:21.8, 1980- 8:53.78, 1981- 8:56.7i, 1982- 8:46.01, 1983- 8:37.06, 1984- 8:39.47, 1986- 8:47.00. pbs: 400m: 57.9 '78, 800m: 2:02.89 '83, 1000m: 2:39.94 '80, 1500m: 4:04.14 '83, 1M: 4:28.07 '84, 2000m: 5:42.15 '82. UK road bests: 10km: 31:29 '83, 15km: 48:17 '85.
Has fared most successfully at road running in the USA. Troubled by injuries and had a knée operation in 1985.

**Angela TOOBY** b.24 Oct 1960 Woolhope, Hereford 1.66m 51kg. Club: Cardiff. Teacher.
At 10000m: CG: '86- 3; ECh: '86- 9; ECp: '85- 3. UK champion at 5000m 1984. World CC: '84- 8, '85- 6.
Progression at 10000m: 1984- 32:58.07, 1985- 33:04.66, 1986- 31:56.59. pbs: 1500m: 4:14.3 '85, 3000m: 8:52.59 '84, 5000m: 15:22.50 '84, Mar: 3:29 '81.
Twin sister Susan has pbs of 3000m: 8:57.17 '84 and 5000m: 15:32.19 '85.

**Kirsty WADE** b. 6 Aug 1962 Girvan, Scotland 1.69m 56kg. née McDermott. Club: Blaydon H. Was at Loughborough University. Runs a fitness centre at Rowlands Gill, Tyne & Wear.
At 800m: CG: '82- 1, '86- 1; EJ: '79- 6; ECp: '85- 4; WSG: '83- 8. At 1500m: CG: '86- 1; ECh: '86- 7. UK & Commonwealth records at 800m, 1000m and 1M 1985.
Progression at 800m/1500m: 1975- 2:16.2, 1976- 2:11.1, 1977- 2:11.20, 1978- 2:07.74, 1979- 2:04.8/4:34.9, 1980- 2:05.42/4:58.49M, 1981- 2:02.88i/2:04.01/4:21.3, 1982- 2:00.56/4:22.9, 1983- 2:01.88, 1984- 2:02.34/4:14.81, 1985- 1:57.42/4:02.83, 1986- 2:00.01/4:03.74. pbs: 100m: 12.2 '78, 200m: 25.1 '78, 400m: 54.50 '81, 600m: 1:26.5 '85, 1000m: 2:33.70 '85, 1M: 4:19.41 '85, 3000m: 10:01.8 '82.
In 1986 became the first woman ever to win the Commonwealth 800m/1500m double.

**Fatima WHITBREAD** b.Hackney, London 3 Mar 1961 1.67m 77kg. Club: Thurrock H. Born of Cypriot parents and adopted by Margaret Whitbread, UK javelin coach and ex-international (45.18m in 1959).

At JT: OG: '80- dnq, '84- 3; WCh: '83- 2; ECh: '82- 8, '86- 1; CG: '78- 6, '82- 3; EJ: '79- 1; WCp: '85- 3; ECp: '83- 1, '85- 2. WAAA champion 1981-4, 1986; UK champion 1981-5. 2nd GP 1986.
World javelin record 1986.
Progression at JT: 1975- 34.94, 1976- 41.20, 1977- 48.34, 1978- 53.88, 1979- 58.20, 1980- 60.14, 1981- 65.82, 1982- 66.98, 1983- 69.54, 1984- 71.86, 1985- 72.98, 1986- 77.44. pbs: 200m: 24.38 '84, SP: 15.41 '84.
Threw the javelin over 70 metres 22 times in 12 competitions in 1986 and produced a staggering world record at 9.18am at the 1986 European Championships. Having defeated Petra Felke in the final she then threw the world's second best ever to seal that victory. Has made continuous improvement for twelve successive seasons.

# USA

**Governing body**: TAC- The Athletics Congress of the USA, P.O.Box 120, Indianapolis, Indiana 46206. Founded 1979, when it replaced the AAU (founded 1888) as the governing body.
**National Championships** first held in 1876 (men), 1923 (women)
**1986 Champions: MEN**
100m/LJ: Carl Lewis 9.91w/8.67w, 200m: Floyd Heard 20.03w, 400m: Darrell Robinson 44.47, 800m: Johnny Gray 1:44.73, 1500m: Steve Scott 3:42.41, 5000m: Doug Padilla 13:46.69, 10000m: Gerard Donakowski 28:21.11, Mar: Bill Donakowski 2:10:40, 3000mSt: Henry Marsh 8:19.16, 110mh: Greg Foster 13.26, 400mh: Danny Harris 48.90, HJ: Doug Nordquist 2.33, PV: Mike Tully 5.80, TJ: Charlie Simpkins 17.91w, SP: John Brenner 21.09, DT: John Powell 65.94, HT: Bill Green 76.20, JT: Tom Petranoff 76.32, Dec: Dave Johnson 8203w, 20kmW: Tim Lewis 1:25:22, 50kmW: Marco Evoniuk 4:13:32.
**WOMEN**
100m/200m: Pam Marshall 10.80w/22.24w, 400m: Diane Dixon 50.41, 800m: Claudette Groenendaal 1:59.79, 1500m: Linda Detlefsen 4:08.00, 3000m: Mary Knisely 8:46.18, 5000m: Betty Springs 15:30.99, 10000m: Nanette Doak 32:29.86, Mar: Kim Rosenquist 2:32:30, 100mh: Benita Fitzgerald-Brown 12.83w, 400mh: Judi Brown-King 55.46, HJ: Louise Ritter 1.93, LJ: Carol Lewis 6.93w, TJ: Wendy Brown 13.78w, SP: Ramona Pagel 18.63, DT: Carol Cady 62.72, JT: Helena Uusitalo (Fin) 58.44, Hep: Jane Frederick 6230, 10kmW: Debbie Lawrence 50:28.86.

# Men

**Kevin AKINS** b.27 Jan 1960 Rochester, NY 1.96m 136kg. New York AC. Was at Ohio State University.
At SP: WCh: '83- 13. Won TAC 1982.
Progression at SP: 1979- 17.96, 1980- 18.67, 1981- 20.08i, 1982- 21.38i, 1983- 21.61, 1984- 20.70i, 1985- 21.49, 1986- 21.06.

**Ray ARMSTEAD** b.27 May 1960 St Louis, Missouri 1.87m 76kg. Club: Accusplit. Was at Northeast Missouri University.
At 400m (R- 4x400m relay): OG: '84- 1R; WCp: '85- 1R. 2nd GP 1986.
Progression at 400m: 1982- 46.13, 1984- 44.83, 1985- 44.91, 1986- 44.98. pb 300m: 32.60 '86.
Ran 43.97 second leg on US 4x400m Olympic team 1984.

Ray Armstead. *ASP*

**Ron BACKES** b.19 Feb 1963 1.90m 116kg. Club: New York AC. University of Minnesota.
NCAA indoor shot champion 1986.
Progression at SP: 1984- 19.58, 1985- 20.25, 1986- 21.01i/20.92. pb DT: 59.90 '86.

**Willie BANKS** b.11 Mar 1956 Travis Air Force Base, California 1.90m 77kg. Club: Mazda TC. Graduate of UCLA. Sports consultant.
At TJ: OG: '84- 6; WCh: '83- 2; PAm: '79- 2; WCp: '79- 5, '81- 3, '85- 1; WSG: '77- 3, '79- 1. Won US Olympic Trials 1980, TAC 1983, 1985.
Five US records 1981-5, including world low-altitude bests of 17.56m 1981, 17.67m 1985, and world record 17.97m 1985. World indoor best 17.41m 1982.
Progression at TJ: 1973- 15.02, 1974- 15.62, 1975- 16.79, 1976- 16.66/16.88w, 1977- 16.88, 1978- 17.05, 1979- 17.23/17.43w, 1980- 17.13/ 17.36w, 1981- 17.56, 1982- 17.41i, 1983- 17.26/ 17.32w, 1984- 17.39, 1985- 17.97, 1986- 17.58/ 17.82w. pb LJ: 8.11 '81.
The ebullient Banks has made the triple jump into a star event by the force of his own personality, encouraging crowds to clap him down the runway to an accelerating tempo. Married Louise Romo (pbs 800m 1:59.63 '85, 1500m 4:09.29 '84) on 15 Nov 1986.

**Kirk BAPTISTE** b.20 Jun 1963 Beaumont, Texas 1.84m 79kg. Club: Athletics West. Student at Houston University.
At 200m: OG: '84- 2; WCp: dq (4 at 100m, 1 4x100mR). Won NCAA 200m 1984 & 1985, TAC 100m and 200m 1985. 2nd GP 200m 1985.
World 300m best: 31.70 in 1984.
Progression at 100m, 200m: 1982- 21.29; 1983- 10.34, 20.38; 1984- 10.16/10.13w, 19.96; 1985- 10.11/10.09w, 20.11/20.03w; 1986- 10.17, 20.25/ 20.14w/20.2. pb 400m: 45.93 '86.

**Randy BARNES** b.16 Jun 1966 Charleston, W.Virginia 1.95m 121kg. Student at Texas A&M University.
Pogression at SP: 1986- 21.88. pb DT: 61.18 '86.
From a 1985 best of 20.36m with the 12lb shot, he made a sensational start to his senior career, moving from 19.83 indoors to 21.08 and 21.88 in April 1986, the latter improving Randy Matson's university record (the world record 21.78 '67). Then a finger injury cut short his season.

**Earl BELL** b.25 Aug 1955 Ancon, Panama Canal Zone 1.91m 75kg. Pacific Coast Club. Graduate of Arkansas State University.
At PV: OG: '76- 6, '84-3=; PAm: '75- 1. US champion 1976 and 1984. Won NCAA 1975-7, AAA 1981. World record 5.67m 1976 and US record 5.80m 1984.

Progression at PV: 1968- 3.22, 1969- 3.50, 1970-
3.85, 1971- 4.11, 1972- 4.40, 1973- 4.72, 1974-
5.09, 1975- 5.51, 1976- 5.67, 1977- 5.60, 1978-
5.50, 1979- 5.48i, 1980- 5.60, 1981- 5.65, 1982-
5.65i, 1983- 5.65, 1984- 5.80, 1985- 5.60/5.61i,
1986- 5.81.

**Bruce BICKFORD** b.12 Mar 1957 Benton, Maine
1.80m 60kg. Club: New Balance TC. Graduate of
Northeastern University.
TAC 10000m champion 1985.
Progression at 5km/10km: 1980- 13:06.7i(3M),
1981- 13:35.2i/13:38.08, 1982- 13:45.67i, 1983-
13:30.5i / 28:48.2, 1984- 13:33.78 / 27:47.91,
1985- 13:13.49 / 27:37.17, 1986- 13:45.29i /
28:42.54. pbs: 1M: 4:00.6i '84, 3000m: 7:51.34
'84, 2M: 8:29.8i '85, 3kmSt: 8:25.36 '82.
Ran US junior record (8:38.67) for 3km steeplechase in 1976, his main event until 1984.

**John BRENNER** b.4 Jan 1961 Long Beach
1.92m 130kg. Club: Mazda TC. Was at UCLA.
Won NCAA shot and discus 1984, TAC shot
1986. 3rd GP 1986.
Progression at SP: 1979- 16.75, 1980- 17.10,
1981- 18.08, 1982- 19.71, 1983- 20.80, 1984-
21.92, 1985- 21.05, 1986- 21.78. pbs: DT: 66.62
'86, HT: 66.62 '86, JT: 69.86 '84.

**Art BURNS** b.19 Jul 1954 Washington, DC
1.86m 118kg. Club: Athletics West. Graduate of
University of Colorado. Systems analyst.
At DT: OG: '84- 5; WCh: '83- 8. 2nd TAC 1985.
Progression at DT: 1975- 55.06, 1976- 59.28,
1977- 63.88, 1979- 64.44, 1980- 66.90, 1981-
67.86, 1982- 68.20, 1983- 70.36, 1984- 70.98,
1985- 69.10, 1986- 68.72.

**Tonie CAMPBELL** b.14 Jun 1960 Los Angeles
1.90m 75kg. Club: Stars & Stripes TC. Graduate
of University of Southern California.
At 110mh: OG: '84- 5; PAm: '83- 2; WSG: '81- 4;
WCp: '85- 1. Won TAC 1984. US Olympic Trials:
3rd 1980, 2nd 1984. 3rd GP 1986.
US indoor 60mh record: 7.58 '84.
Progression at 110mh: 1979- 14.31, 1980- 13.44,
1981- 13.44, 1982- 13.48/13.46w, 1983- 13.32/
13.1, 1984- 13.23/13.1, 1985- 13.27, 1986-
13.39/13.0/13.29w. pb 400mh: 50.28 '81.
Made great recovery after surgery to repair
snapped ligaments and torn cartilege in right knee
in April 1985.

**Cletus CLARK** b.20 Jan 1962 Austin, Texas
1.93m 86kg. Club: Houston TC. Graduated from
University of Houston.
At 110mh: WSG: '85- 1. 2nd TAC 1985.
Progression at 110mh: 1980- 14.13, 1981- 13.81/
13.79w, 1982- 13.68, 1983- 13.56, 1984- 13.41/
13.39w, 1985- 13.38, 1986- 13.57.

**Mike CONLEY** b.5 Oct 1962 Chicago 1.85m
78kg. Club: Tyson International. University of
Arkansas.
At TJ: OG: '84- 2; WCh: '83- 4; WSG: '83- 2. At LJ:
WCh: '83- 3; WCp: '85- 1. Won US Trials TJ 1984,
NCAA LJ/TJ double in 1984 and 1985 (also 2nd
200m). 1st LJ, 2nd TJ TAC 1985. Won AAA TJ
1983. Won GP LJ 1985, TJ 1986.
Progression at LJ, TJ: 1979- 7.14, 13.99; 1980-
6.84, 15.13; 1981- 7.46/7.56w, 15.80/15.83w;
1982- 8.19, 17.01; 1983- 8.38w/8.28, 17.23i/
17.37w; 1984- 8.21/8.23w, 17.50; 1985- 8.43/
8.53w, 17.71/17.72w; 1986- 8.33/8.63w, 17.69/
17.84w. pbs: 100m: 10.36 '86, 200m: 20.21/
20.12w '85, 20.0 '84.
At the NCAAs won the LJ/TJ double indoors and
out 1984-5. Exceeded 17m in all triple jump
competitions 1985-6, winning 9/14 in 1985, 10/15
in 1986.

**Brian CROUSER** b.9 Jul 1962 1.88m 102kg.
Club: New York AC. University of Oregon.
NCAA javelin champion 1982 and 1985.
Inaugural world best 79.86m with new javelin
1986.
Progression at JT: 1979- 66.20, 1980- 72.50,
1982- 86.24, 1983- 85.50, 1984- 89.20, 1985-
95.10, new: 1986- 79.86.
Brother Dean's pbs: SP: 21.07 '82, DT: 65.88 '83.

**Lorenzo DANIEL** b.23 Mar 1966 Wrens, Georgia
1.88m 77kg. Club: Nike TC. Mississippi State
University.
World junior 200m record 1985.
Progression at 200m: 1984- 21.3, 1985- 20.07,
1986- 20.17/20.11w. pbs: 100m: 10.08/10.00w
'86, LJ: 7.25 '84.

**Joe DIAL** b.26 Oct 1962 Marlow, Oklahoma
1.75m 68kg. Club: Athletics West. Graduate of
Oklahoma State University.
NCAA pole vault champion 1984 and 1985. TAC
champion 1985.
Five US pole vault records 1985-6. World indoor
best 5.91m 1986.
Progression at PV: 1976- 2.77, 1977- 3.83, 1978-
4.47, 1979- 4.94, 1980- 5.31, 1981- 5.52, 1982-
5.60, 1983- 5.62i/5.60, 1984- 5.66, 1985- 5.85,
1986- 5.90/5.91i.
Set US high school record in 1981. One of the
smallest ever top-class vaulters.

**Bill DONAKOWSKI** b.21 Jun 1956 1.68m 59kg.
Club: Brooks TC. Was at University of Michigan.
TAC marathon champion 1986.
Progression at Mar: 1985- 2:14:07, 1986-
2:10:41. pbs: 5000m: 13:32.15 '78, 10000m:
28:13.9 '79.
Won New Jersey and Twin Cities marathons in

1986. His brother Gerard (b.20 Feb 1960) was TAC champion and ran a pb 27:58.41 at 10000m, and 13:25.75 at 5000m in 1986; their sister Donna ran 10:01.96i for 3000m in 1986.

**Dwayne EVANS** b.13 Oct 1958 Phoenix, Arizona 1.86m 75kg. Club: Stars & Stripes. Was at Arizona State University. Teacher.
At 200m: OG: '76- 3. US champion 1979, won NCAA 1981. WCp '85- 1 4x100mR.
World junior 200m record 1976.
Progression at 200m: 1973- 22.5 (220y), 1974- 21.3, 1975- 20.9, 1976- 20.22, 1977- 21.04, 1979- 20.28, 1980- 20.68/20.62w, 1981- 20.34/20.20w, 1982- 20.84, 1983- 20.76/20.74w, 1984- 20.38/20.21w, 1985- 20.44/20.36w, 1986- 20.36/20.09w. pbs: 100y: 9.44 '76, 100m: 10.20/10.07w '81, 10.1 '78, 300m: 32.75 '84.
With the bronze at the age of 17 in 1976, he is the youngest ever Olympic 200m medallist. More than ten years on he remains a world-class sprinter.

**Derrick FLORENCE** b.15 Jun 1968 1.78m 70kg. Student at Texas A&M University.
At 100m/200m: WJ: '86- 1/2.
Progression at 100m: 1985- 10.4, 1986- 10.13/10.1. pb 200m: 20.63 '86.
US high school 100m record in 1986 while at Ball High, Galveston.

**Greg FOSTER** b.4 Aug 1958 Maywood, Illinois 1.90m 85kg. Club: World Class AC. Graduate of UCLA.
At 110mh: OG: '84- 2; WCh: '83- 1; WCp: '81- 1. Won TAC 110mh 1981, 1983, 1986; NCAA 110mh 1978, 1981 and 200m 1979; US Olympic Trials 1984.
US 110mh record 13.22 in 1978, and world indoor bests: 50yh: 5.88 '86, 50mh: 6.35 '85.
Progression at 110mh: 1977- 13.54 (120yh), 1978- 13.22, 1979- 13.28/13.0, 1980- 13.27, 1981- 13.03, 1982- 13.22, 1983- 13.11, 1984- 13.15, 1985- 13.24, 1986- 13.25. pbs: 100m: 10.28 '79, 200m: 20.20 '79.
Ten successive years in the world top ten 1977- 86, eight of them in the top two. Has run a record 32 (and 2 wa) sub 13.30 times, including 8 sub 13.20. His 7.36 for 60mh indoors in January 1987 was ruled to have been with a flying start.

**Michael FRANKS** b.23 Sep 1963 St Louis, Missouri 1.80m 68kg. Club: Athletics West. Southern Illinois University.
At 400m (R- 4x400m relay): WCh: '83- 2; WCp: '85- 1 (1R). Won GP 400m and second overall 1985.
Progression at 400m: 1981- 48.74, 1983- 44.96, 1984- 45.20, 1985- 44.47, 1986- 45.33. pbs:

100m: 10.25 '84, 200m: 20.62/20.58w '83, 300m: 32.26 '85, 800m: 1:52.25 '85.

**Harvey GLANCE** b.28 Mar 1957 Phenix City, Alabama 1.71m 67kg. Club: Pollitabs SC. Graduate of Auburn University.
At 100m (R- 4x100m relay): OG: '76- 4 (1R); PAm: '79- 2 (1R); WCp: '79- 2R, '85- 1R. NCAA champion 100m 1976-7, 200m 1977. US Olympic Trials 100m: 1st 1976, 2nd 1980, 7th 1984. 3rd GP 1986.
In 1976: at 100m two world records at 9.9, and world junior records: hand-timed 10.0 and 9.9 twice, auto-timed 10.12 and 10.11, and 20.1 for 200m.
Progression at 100m (y 100 yards): 1972- 9.9y, 1973- 9.7y, 1974- 9.5y, 1975- 10.3/9.4y, 1976- 10.11/9.9, 1977- 10.16/9.8, 1978- 10.15/10.07w/9.9, 1979- 10.13, 1980- 10.14/10.07w, 1981- 10.20w/10.38/9.8, 1982- 10.31, 1983- 10.42, 1984- 10.09/10.07w, 1985- 10.05, 1986- 10.09/10.04w. pbs: 200m: 20.39 '79, 20.1 '76; LJ: 7.87 '77.

**Sam GRADDY** b.10 Feb 1964 Gaffney, S.Carolina 1.78m 68kg. Tennessee University.
At 100m (R- 4x100m relay): OG: '84- 2 (1R); PAm: '83- 3 (1R); WSG: '83- 3. Won NCAA and TAC, 2nd US Trials 1984. At 60m: WIG: '85- 2.
Progression at 100m (y 100 yards): 1981- 10.23y, 1982- 9.61y/10.4, 1983- 10.18/10.16w, 1984- 10.09/10.08w, 1985- 10.19, 1986- 10.12/10.08w. pb 200m: 20.57 '86.

**Johnny GRAY** b.19 Jun 1960 Los Angeles 1.92m 76kg. Club: Santa Monica TC. Was at Arizona State University. Married Judy Terrel on 4 Sep 1984.
At 800m: OG: '84- 7. Won TAC 1985.
Five US 800m records 1984-5. Two 600m world bests 1984-6. World indoor 1000y best 2:04.39 in 1986.
Progression at 800m: 1977- 2:06.0y, 1978- 1:51.8, 1979- 1:49.39, 1980- 1:47.06, 1982- 1:45.41, 1983- 1:45.50, 1984- 1:42.96, 1985- 1:42.60, 1986- 1:43.46. pbs: 400m: 46.3 '83, 600m: 1:12.81 '86, 1000m: 2:17.27 '84, 1500m: 3:43.98 '84.
Ran fastest ever 800m relay leg, 1:43.3, on 6 Apr 1985 at Tempe. has 11 sub 1:44 times for 800m.

**Roddie HALEY** b.6 Dec 1964 Texarkana, Texas 1.78m 64kg. Club: World Class AC. University of Arkansas.
At 400m: Won NCAA 1985, 2nd NCAA and TAC 1986.
World indoor 500m best 61.18 (and short course 1:00.69 and 59.82) 1986.
Progression at 400m: 1983- 48.3, 1984- 45.66, 1985- 44.67, 1986- 44.48. pb 200m: 20.99 '86.

Johnny Gray (3) leads José Luis Barbosa (8) and William Wuyka (4). *Mark Shearman*

**Danny HARRIS** b.7 Sep 1965 1.83m 77kg. Club: Athletics West. Was at Iowa State University.
At 400mh: OG: '84- 2. Won NCAA 1984-6, TAC 1986. 2nd GP 1986.
Progression at 400mh: 1984- 48.02, 1985- 47.63, 1986- 47.82. pbs: 100m: 10.5 '84, 9.9w '85; 200m: 20.91 '84; 400m: 45.3 '84, 45.46 '85.
US high school record at 35.52 for 300mh in 1983. Made his debut at 400mh on 24 Mar 1984, set world junior records in his 3rd, 4th, 6th, 9th and 11th races at the event, taking the record from 49.55 to 48.02! Also good footballer, but now concentrating on track.

**Tranel HAWKINS** b.17 Sep 1962 Dayton, Ohio 1.95m 81kg. Club: Accusplit SC. Angelo State University, Texas.
At 400mh: OG: '84- 6. 2nd NCAA and 3rd US Olympic Trials 1984.
Progression at 400mh: 1983- 50.35, 1984- 48.28, 1985- 49.03, 1986- 49.56.
Recruited to Angelo State as basketball player, made remarkable progress at 400mh in 1984.

**Floyd HEARD** b.24 Mar 1966 West Point, Miss. 1.78m 74kg. Student at Texas A&M University.
At 200m: TAC and NCAA champion 1986.
Progression at 200m: 1983- 21.43, 1984- 21.00/20.7w, 1985- 20.61, 1986- 20.12/20.03w. pb 100m: 10.20/10.09w '86.
Shot to the fore in 1986 with a championship double and victory at the Goodwill Games over 200m.

Danny Harris. *ASP*

**Jim HOWARD** b.11 Sep 1959 Texas City 1.96m 80kg. Club: Mazda TC. Graduate of Texas A&M University. Chemical engineer.
At HJ: WCp: '85- 2. Won TAC 1984. 3rd US Olympic Trials 1980. Won GP 1986.
Three US indoor high jump records: 2.34 '85 to 2.36 '86. US outdoor record 1985.
Progression at HJ: 1978- 2.11, 1979- 2.21i, 1980- 2.23, 1981- 2.26, 1982- 2.19i, 1983- 2.30, 1984- 2.33, 1985- 2.35, 1986- 2.36i/2.34.
Won USA/Mobil Indoor Grand Prix overall title 1985 and 1986.

**Thomas JEFFERSON** b.6 Aug 1962 1.83m 75kg. Club: Mazda TC. Kent State University.
At 200m: OG: '84- 3. WSG: '85- 2 4x100mR.
Progression at 200m: 1980- 21.4, 1981- 21.2, 1982- 21.11, 1983- 20.90, 1984- 20.26/20.21w, 1985- 20.45, 1986- 20.36. pb 100m: 10.17 '86, 10.08w '85, 9.9w '84.

**Earl JONES** b.17 Jul 1964 Chicago 1.81m 73kg. Club: Santa Monica TC. Was at Eastern Michigan University.
At 800m: OG: '84- 3. Won US Olympic Trials 800m in US record of 1:43.74 in 1984. In 1985 won NCAA and third TAC. 2nd NCAA 1500m in 1983. 2nd GP 1986.
Progression at 800m: 1982- 1:52.3, 1983- 1:48.6, 1984- 1:43.74, 1985- 1:44.58, 1986- 1:43.62. pbs: 400m: 46.33 '84, 600m: 1:13.80 '86, 1000m: 2:20.1i '85, 1500m: 3:36.19 '86; 1M: 3:58.76 '86.
Exciting front runner who made tremendous breakthrough to the top in 1984.

**Al JOYNER** b.19 Jan 1960 East St.Louis, Illinois 1.86m 77kg. Club: Athletics West. Graduate of Arkansas State University.
At TJ: OG: '84- 1; WCh: '83- 8. Won TAC and 2nd US Trials 1984.
Progression at TJ: 1978- 15.30, 1979- 15.76, 1980- 15.80, 1981- 16.27, 1982- 16.78i, 1983- 17.12/17.14w, 1984- 17.19/17.26w, 1985- 17.46, 1986- 16.97/17/11w. pbs: 110mh: 13.51 '85, 400mh: 52.43 '83, LJ: 7.59 '83.
Won Olympic gold while sister Jackie (qv) won silver.

**Emmit KING** b.24 Mar 1959 Alabama 1.76m 78kg. Club: New Balance TC. Was at University of Alabama.
At 100m (R- 4x100m relay): WCh: '83- 3 (1R); PAm: '79- 3. Won NCAA 1983.
Progression at 100m (y 100 yards): 1977- 9.5y, 1978- 9.5y, 1979- 10.16/10.0, 1980- 10.30, 1981- 10.18/10.14w, 1982- 10.13, 1983- 10.06/10.05w, 1984- 10.18/10.17w, 1985- 10.32, 1986- 10.07/10.0. pb 200m: 20.86 '82.
Overall winner of USA/Mobil Indoor Grand Prix 1984 (won TAC 60y).

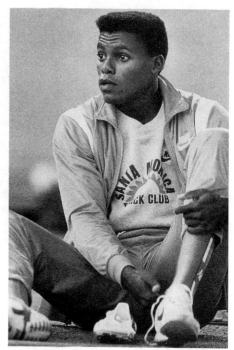

Carl Lewis. *ASP*

**Roger KINGDOM** b.26 Aug 1962 Vienna, Georgia 1.83m 86kg. Club: New Image TC. University of Pittsburgh.
At 110mh: OG: '84- 1; PAm: '83- 1. Won NCAA 1983, 2nd TAC and 3rd US Trials 1984. Won TAC 1985.
Progression at 110mh: 1982- 14.07, 1983- 13.44, 1984- 13.16/13.1/13.00w, 1985- 13.14, 1986- 13.40/13.39w. pbs: 200m: 21.08w '84, HJ: 2.14i '84.
The Olympic champion has been hampered a a left hamstring injury in 1985 and 1986.

**Carl LEWIS** b.1 Jul 1961 Birmingham, Alabama 1.88m 77kg. Club: Santa Monica TC. Was at Houston University.
At 100m/LJ (R- 4 x100m relay): OG: '84- 1/1 (1R, 1 at 200m); WCh: '83- 1/1 (1R); PAm: '79- -/3; WCp: '81- 9/1. Won TAC 100m 1981-3, 1986; 200m 1983; LJ 1981-3, 1986. Won NCAA 100m 1980-1, LJ 1981. Won 100m/200m/LJ treble at US Olympic Trials 1984.
Two world records at 4x100mR 1983-4. Low altitude world bests at 100m (3), 200m, LJ (4). World indoor bests: 60y: 6.02 '83, long jump: 8.49m '81, 8.56m '81, 8.79m '84. US 200m record 1983.

Progression at 100m, 200m, LJ: 1974- 5.77 LJ; 1975- 6.01 LJ; 1976- 11.1y, -, 6.93; 1977- 10.6y, -, 7.26; 1978- 10.5/9.3yw, -, 7.57/7.85w; 1979- 10.3, 20.9, 8.13; 1980- 10.21/10.16w, 20.66, 8.11/8.35w; 1981- 10.00/9.99w, 20.73, 8.62/8.73w; 1982- 10.00, 20.27, 8.76; 1983- 9.97/9.93w, 19.75, 8.79; 1984- 9.99, 19.80, 8.79i/8.71; 1985- 9.98/9.90w, 20.69/20.3w, 8.62/8.77w; 1986- 10.06/9.91w, 20.41/20.23w/20.1, 8.67w/8.37i/8.35. pb 300m: 32.18 '84.

Has won 48 successive long jump competitions 1981-6, and has 29 of the 39 long jumps in history over 28ft (8.53m). Emulated Jesse Owens in winning four Olympic gold medals. Sullivan Award winner 1981. Numerous awards as best athlete of the year 1982-3-4.

**Jud LOGAN** b.19 Jul 1959 North Canton, Ohio 1.93m 125kg. Club: New York AC. Was at Kent State University. Nautilus instructor.
At HT: OG: '84-dnq; WCp: '85-3. TAC champion 1984-5.
Nine US hammer records 1984-6. Six US indoor 35lb weight records.
Progression at HT: 1979- c48.50, 1980- c56.10, 1981- 59.64, 1982- 64.06, 1983- 67.66, 1984- 74.56, 1985- 77.24, 1986- 80.88. pb 35lb Wt: 23.71 '86.

**David MACK** b.25 May 1961 Lynwood, Cal. 1.80m 68kg. Club: Santa Monica TC. Was at University of Oregon.
At 800m: WCh: '83- sf. Won NCAA 1985.
Progression at 800m: 1977- 1:56.7y, 1978- 1:51.8y, 1979- 1:50.2y, 1980- 1:46.67, 1981- 1:46.03, 1982- 1:45.55, 1983- 1:44.39, 1984- 1:49.21, 1985- 1:43.35, 1986- 1:44.17. pbs: 400m: 47.11 '83, 600m: 1:14.15 '86, 1000m: 2:16.90 '85, 1500m: 3:43.8 '82, 1M: 4:01.20 '82.
Had operation for compartment syndrome 1984.

**Walter McCOY** b.15 Nov 1958 Daytona Beach, Florida 1.78m 75kg. Club: Mazda TC. Graduate of Florida State University.
At 400m (R- 4x400m relay): WSG: '79- 3 (1R), '81- 2 (2R); WCp: '81- 1R, '85- 1R. 3rd US Olympic Trials 1980, 2nd TAC 1984.
Progression at 400m: 1976- 47.8y, 1977- 46.52, 1978- 45.56, 1979- 45.16, 1980- 45.49, 1981- 44.99, 1982- 44.97, 1983- 44.97, 1984- 44.76, 1985- 45.12, 1986- 45.07. pbs: 200m: 20.86 '84, 20.7w '83; 300m: 32.16 '84.
Prodigiously consistent 400m runner, who has run 104 sub-46 sec. races 1978-85.

**Antonio McKAY** b.9 Feb 1964 1.83m 80kg. Club: Mazda TC. Georgia Tech University.
At 400m (R-4x400m relay): OG: '84- 3 (1R).

Won NCAA (indoors and out) and US Trials in 1984.
World indoor bests: 300m: 32.52 '87, 400m: 45.79 '84, 440y, 45.45 '86.
Progression at 400m: 1981- 47.84y, 1982- 45.9, 1984- 44.71, 1985- 46.47i, 1986- 44.69.
Underwent surgery on a torn cartilage in his right knee in 1982, and missed the 1983 season, but stormed through first indoors and then out in 1984. Passed 1985 outdoor season.

**Lee McRAE** b.23 Jan 1966 Pembroke, NC 1.76m 60kg. Club: Karamu Flyers. Student at Pitt University.
At 100m: Won NCAA, 2nd TAC 1986.
World indoor 55m best: 6.00 '86.
Progression at 100m: 1982- 10.63, 1983- 10.53, 1984- 10.45, 1985- 10.27/10.07w, 1986- 10.11/10.02w. pb 200m: 21.17 '83.
Came to the fore in the 1986 indoor season, when he won the TAC 60y in 6.06.

**Sydney MAREE** b.9 Sep 1956 Atteridgeville, Pretoria, S.Africa 1.80m 66kg. Club: Puma TC. Graduate of Villanova University. Left South Africa for the USA in 1978, permanent resident from 1981 and granted full US citizenship on 1 May 1984.
At 1500m: WCh:'83- sf; WCp: '81- 5. US champion at 1500m 1981, 5000m 1984. Won NCAA 1500m 1980-1, 5000m 1979. 2nd TAC 5000m 1985. 2nd GP 5000m 1985.
World 1500m record in 1983. US records at 1500m, 2000m and 5000m in 1985.
Progression at 1500m/1 mile, 5000m: 1976- 3:42.0/3:57.9; 1977- 3:41.2/3:57.2; 1978- 3:38.87/3:56.0, 13:50.2; 1979- 3:38.2i/3:53.7, 13:20.63; 1980- 3:38.64/3:55.9; 1981- 3:32.30/3:48.83, 13:38.3i; 1982- 3:32.12/3:48.85, 13:32.40; 1983- 3:31.24/3:50.30; 1984- 3:37.02, 13:51.31; 1985- 3:29.77/3:50.34, 13:01.15; 1986- 3:32.56/3:53.29, 13:14.62. pbs: 800m: 1:48.11 '82, 1000m: 2:19.2 '85, 2000m: 4:54.20 '85, 3000m: 7:33.37 '82, 10000m: 28:21.46 '80.
Third in US Olympic 1500m Trials 1984 but had to withdraw from the Olympics due to injury.

**Henry MARSH** b.15 Mar 1954 Boston 1.78m 72kg. Club: Athletics West. Graduate of Brigham Young University.
At 3kmSt: OG: '76- 10, '84- 4; WCh: '83- 8; PAm: '79- 1; WCp: '79- 4, '81- dq, '85- 2. Won eight US titles 1978-79, 1981-6; and US Olympic Trials 1980 and 1984. 2nd GP 1986.
Four US steeplechase records 1977-85.
Progression at 3kmSt: 1973- 9:25.0, 1975- 9:35.0, 1976- 8:23.99, 1977- 8:21.55, 1978- 8:22.5, 1979- 8:23.51, 1980- 8:15.68, 1981- 8:18.58, 1982- 8:16.17, 1983- 8:12.37, 1984-

Sidney Maree. *ASP*

8:14.25, 1985- 8:09.17, 1986- 8:13.15. pbs: 1500m: 3:43.52 '85, 1M: 3:59.31 '85, 3000m: 7:56.2 '85, 2M: 8:33.90i '84, 5000m: 13:45.2 '84. Has met with ill fortune in major events: in the 1981 World Cup he ran inside a barrier and was disqualified, and in the 1983 World Championships tripped over the final barrier.

**Roy MARTIN** b.25 Dec 1966 Dallas 1.85m 79kg. Student at Southern Methodist University.
4th US Olympic Trials 200m 1984. 2nd TAC 200m 1985. World junior 200m record 1985.
Progression at 200m: 1981- 21.9, 1982- 21.69/21.33w, 1983- 21.00/20.28w, 1984- 20.28, 1985- 20.13, 1986- 20.16/19.86w. pbs: 100m: 10.12/9.97w '86, 10.0 '85; 400m: 48.3 '82.

**Eric METCALF** b.23 Jan 1968 Virginia 1.75m 76kg. Texas University.
Won NCAA long jump 1986 in a world age 18 best. Progression at LJ: 1984- 7.50, 1985- 7.75i, 1986- 8.24.

**Edwin MOSES** b.31 Aug 1955 Dayton, Ohio 1.87m 77kg. Club: Team Adidas. Graduate of Morehouse College, Atlanta, Georgia; now lives at Laguna Hills, California.
At 400mh: OG: '76- 1, '84- 1; WCh: '83- 1; WCp: '77- 1, '79- 1, '81- 1. US champion 1977, 1979, 1981, 1983; AAA champion 1979. Won US Trials 1976, 1980 and 1984.
Four world 400mh records 1976-83.
Progression at 400mh: 1975- 52.0 (440y), 1976- 47.63, 1977- 47.45, 1978- 47.94, 1979- 47.53, 1980- 47.13, 1981- 47.14, 1983- 47.02, 1984- 47.32, 1986- 47.38. pbs: 400m: 45.60 '77, 800m: 1:48.98 '83, 110mh: 13.64/13.5 '78.
Has dominated his event for nearly a decade, and has set up the greatest ever winning streak by a track athlete, 119 successive 400mh races (104

finals) since beaten by Harald Schmid in Berlin on 26 Aug 1977. His total career record at 400mh, 1975-84, is 149 wins in 155 races. Has run the 11 fastest times to the end of 1986. Sullivan Award winner 1983. Missed 1982 and 1985 seasons through injury.

**Larry MYRICKS** b.10 Mar 1956 Clinton, Mississippi 1.86m 77kg. Club: Southern California Cheetahs. Was at Mississippi College.
At LJ: OG: '76- nj, '84- 4; WCp: '79- 1. US champion 1979-80, won NCAA 1976 and 1979, AAA 1981. Won US Olympic Trials 1980, 2nd 1976 and 1984. 2nd GP 1985. At 200m: WCh: '83- h.
Progression at LJ: 1974- 7.17i, 1975- 7.83, 1976- 8.09i/8.26w, 1978- 8.05, 1979- 8.52, 1980- 8.38i, 1981- 8.45, 1982- 8.56, 1983- 8.23/8.64w, 1984- 8.59, 1985- 8.44, 1986- 8.50/8.55w. pbs: 100m: 10.31 '83, 200m: 20.03 '83, 400m: 46.74 '84.
Broke his leg warming up for the 1976 Olympic long jump final, but returned to Montreal to win at the 1979 World Cup with world low altitude best.

**Renaldo NEHEMIAH** b.24 Mar 1959 Newark, NJ 1.85m 77kg.
At 110mh: WCp: '79- 1; PAm: '79- 1. Won AAU 1978-80, NCAA 1979, AAA 1981, Olympic Trials 1980.
Three world 110m hurdles records 1979-81 and the fastest ever hand timed 110mh 1979. Five world junior 110mh records 1978. World indoor bests 1979-82 with best times: 50yh (4) 5.92 '82, 50mh (1) 6.36 '79, 60yh (5) 6.82 '82, 60mh (1) 7.62 '79.
Progression at 110mh: 1976- 14.2, 1977- 13.89/13.5, 1978- 13.23, 1979- 13.00/12.91w/12.8, 1981- 12.93, 1986- 13.48. pbs: 100m: 10.24/10.18w '79, 200m: 20.37 '79, LJ: 7.61 '77.
'Skeets' Nehemiah, arguably the finest high hurdler ever, achieved his long-sought wish in 1986, when he was readmitted to international competition by the IAAF. He had turned professional footballer with the San Francisco 49ers in 1982. He won his only race in 1986 on his return at Viareggio on 6 August. He had world ranked four times, number one each year 1978-81.

**Mark NENOW** b.16 Nov 1957 Fargo, N.Dakota 1.74m 59kg. Club: Puma TC. Accountancy degree from University of Kentucky.
At 10000m: WCh: '83- 12; PAm: '83- 3. 2nd TAC 1985-6.
US 10000m record 1986. World road 10km best (point-to-point) of 27:22 in 1984.
Progression at 10000m: 1978- 28:46.5, 1979- 30:55.9, 1980- 28:32.7, 1981- 28:45.86, 1982- 27:36.7, 1983- 27:52.41, 1984- 27:40.56, 1985- 27:40.85, 1986- 27:20.56. pbs: 3000m: 7:52.94 '85, 5000m: 13:18.54 '84.

**Sunder NIX** b.2 Dec 1961 Birmingham, Alabama 1.75m 65kg. Club: Athletics West. Was at Indiana University.
At 400m (R- 4x400m relay): OG: '84- 5 (1R); WCh: '83- 3; WSG: '83- 3 (1R). Won TAC 1983.
Progression at 400m: 1979- 48.8, 1980- 46.6, 1981- 45.66, 1982- 44.68, 1983- 44.87, 1984- 44.75, 1985- 46.22, 1986- 44.84.

**Doug NORDQUIST** b.20 Dec 1958 1.93m 84kg. Club: Tiger International. Graduate of Washington State University. Bandmaster.
At HJ: OG: '84- 5. 2nd US Olympic Trials. 2nd GP 1986.
Progression at HJ: 1979- 2.19, 1980- 2.13, 1981- 2.24, 1982- 2.19i, 1983- 2.22, 1984- 2.31, 1985- 2.27i/2.25, 1986- 2.34.

**Brian OLDFIELD** b.1 Jun 1945 Elgin, Illinois 1.95m 125kg. Club: University of Chicago TC. Graduate of Middle Tennessee State.
At SP: OG: '72- 6. US champion 1980. Won AAA shot and discus 1980.
World bests as an ITA pro in 1975 with 22.11i, 22.25 and 22.86. As a reinstated amateur set two US records, 1982 and 1984.
Progression at SP: (p- professional marks): 1964- 16.38, 1965- 17.28, 1966- 18.03, 1968- 18.65, 1969- 19.68, 1970- 19.47i, 1971- 18.59i, 1972- 20.97, 1973- 21.60ip, 1974- 21.12p, 1975- 22.86p, 1976- 22.45p, 1977- 19.95, 1979- 21.02, 1980- 21.82, 1981- 22.02, 1982- 20.71, 1983- 21.22, 1984- 22.19, 1985- 21.41, 1986- 20.63. pb DT: 62.26 '75.
His astonishing performances as a professional in 1975-6 remain unapproached but, although as a reinstated amateur he was ineligible for the Olympics, Oldfield topped the world list in 1984 at the age of 39.

**Billy OLSON** b.19 Jul 1958 Abilene, Texas 1.88m 73kg. Pacific Coast Club. Graduate of Abilene Christian University.
At PV: WCh: '83- nh; WCp: '81- 3. US champion 1981 and 1982 (tie).
One US pole vault record outdoors (5.72m in 1982) and eleven world indoor bests from 5.71m in 1982 to 5.93m 1986.
Progression at PV: 1975- 4.49, 1976- 4.82, 1977- 5.18, 1978- 5.45, 1979- 5.50, 1980- 5.67, 1981- 5.60, 1982- 5.74i/5.72, 1983- 5.80i/5.70, 1984- 5.80i/5.54, 1985- 5.86i/5.70, 1986- 5.93i/5.50.
USA/Mobil Indoor Grand Prix overall winner 1982 and 1983.

**Doug PADILLA** b.4 Oct 1956 Oakland, California 1.76m 60kg. Club: Athletics West. Graduate of Brigham Young University, studying for Masters degree in electrical engineering.

At 5000m: OG: '84- 7; WCh: '83- 5; WSG: '81- 1; WCp: '85- 1. US champion 1983 and 1985, and won US Olympic Trials 1984. Won 5000m and overall Grand Prix 1985.
US 3000m record 1983.
Progression at 5000m: 1975- 15:14.0, 1979- 13:43.0, 1980- 13:36.50, 1981- 13:33.'5, 1982- 13:20.55i, 1983- 13:17.69, 1984- 13:23.56, 1985- 13:15.44, 1986- 13:42.45/13:32.64i. pbs: 800m: 1:48.30 '85, 1500m: 3:37.95 '83, 1M: 3:56.3i '82, 3:56.66 '83; 2000m: 5:03.84 '83, 3000m: 7:35.84 '83, 2M: 8:15.3i '85.
Went on Mormon mission to El Salvador 1976-8.

**David PATRICK** b.12 Jun 1960 Centralia, Illinois 1.83m 74kg. Club: Team Adidas. Graduate of University of Tennessee.
At 800m: WCh: '83- 8. At 400mh: WSG: '81- 5. Won TAC 400mh 1982 and 1984, 800m 1983; NCAA 400mh 1982.
Progression at 400mh: 1979- 54.26, 1980- 50.90, 1981- 49.25, 1982- 48.44, 1983- 48.05, 1984- 48.80, 1985- 49.01, 1986- 48.59. pb: 800m: 1:44.70 '83.

David Patrick. *ASP*

**Tom PETRANOFF** b.8 Apr 1958 Aurora, Illinois 1.86m 98kg. Club: Athletics West. Shoe consultant.
At JT: OG: '84- 10; WCh: '83- 2, '85- 3. Won TAC 1985-6. Won GP 1985.
World javelin record 1983. Three US bests, the last also a world best with new javelin 1986.
Progression at JT: 1977- 77.48, 1978- 79.74, 1979- 78.18, 1980- 85.44, 1981- 76.04, 1982- 88.40, 1983- 99.72, 1984- 89.50, 1985- 91.56, new: 1986- 85.38.
Imparts strong negative rotation to the javelin, a legacy of pitching skills. Attended Palomar College, California, where he went to play baseball.

**Andre PHILLIPS** b.5 Sep 1959 Milwaukee 1.88m 79kg. Club: World Class AC. Graduate of UCLA. At 400mh: WCh: '83- 5; WCp: '85- 1 (1 at 4x400mR). Won NCAA 1981, TAC 1985. 2nd GP 1985.
Progression at 110mh/400mh: 1977- 53.41 (440yh), 1978- 50.67, 1979- 14.32/49.47, 1980- 14.01/49.30, 1981- 13.95/48.10, 1982- 48.45, 1983- 47.78, 1984- 48.42, 1985- 13.25/47.67, 1986- 47.51. pbs: 100m: 10.4 '86, 200m: 20.55 '86, 400m: 44.71 '86.
Has been the closest American challenger to Ed Moses, and is the only other US athlete to break 48 sec. for 400mh. Also developed into a world class high hurdler in 1985. Had a great season in 1986, losing just one of his seven 400mh races, to Danny Harris in Oslo in his slowest time of the year, 48.15!

**Pat PORTER** b.31 May 1959 Wadena, Minn. 1.83m 61kg. Club: Athletics West. Graduate of Adams State College. Lives in Alamosa, Colorado.
At 10000m: OG: '84- 15; WCp: '85- 2. 3rd US Trials '84. World CC: '83- 9, '84- 4, '86- 6. US CC champion 1982-6.
Progression at 10000m: 1982- 28:26.27, 1983- 28:04.31, 1984- 27:49.5, 1985- 28:12.46, 1986- 27:57.3. pb 5000m: 13:34.98 '85.

**John POWELL** b.25 Jun 1947 San Francisco 1.88m 110kg. Club: Mazda TC. Graduate of San Jose State University. Real Estate Broker, former San Jose policeman.
At DT: OG: '72- 4, '76- 3, '84- 3; WCh: '83- dnq; PAm: '75- 1; WCp: '85- 5. US champion 1974-5, 1983-6, AAA champion 1974, 1976, 1979, 1981. Won US Olympic Trials 1984, 2nd 1972, 1976, 1980.
World discus record 69.08m in 1975.
Progression at DT: 1966- 42.98, 1967- 50.01, 1968- 57.12, 1969- 59.44, 1970- 61.42, 1971- 63.12, 1972- 64.22, 1973- 66.66, 1974- 68.08, 1975- 69.08, 1976- 67.54, 1977- 67.98, 1978- 58.16, 1979- 67.34, 1980- 68.20, 1981- 69.98, 1982- 68.32, 1983- 68.30, 1984- 71.26, 1985- 65.50, 1986- 65.94. pbs: SP: 17.09 '76, HT: 58.50 '84.

**Brad PURSLEY** b.24 May 1960 1.85m 77kg. Pacific Coast Club. Graduate of Abilene Christian University.
Progression at PV: 1977- 4.26, 1978- 4.26, 1979- 5.18, 1980- 5.50, 1981- 5.50, 1982- 5.62, 1983- 5.75, 1984- 5.65, 1985- 5.70, 1986- 5.65/5.70i.

**Mike RAMOS** b.1 Nov 1962 1.83m 86kg. Club: Puma TC. University of Washington.
At Dec: WSG: '85- 1. Won NCAA 1986.

Progression at Dec: 1981- 6955*, 1982- 7579, 1983- 7789w, 1984- 7987, 1985- 8294, 1986- 8322. pbs: 100m: 10.77/10.69w '85, 400m: 49.25 '86, 1500m: 4:43.29 '85, 110mh: 14.98 '86, 14.90w '85, HJ: 2.16 '86, PV: 5.00 '85, LJ: 7.47 '86, SP: 15.33 '85, DT: 50.98 '86, JT: 66.52 '84.

**Darrell ROBINSON** b.23 Dec 1963 Chinon, France 1.86m 62kg. Club: Mazda TC. Dancer. 2nd TAC 400m 1982 and 1985.
World junior 400m record 1982.
Progression at 400m: 1980- 47.26, 1981- 46.8, 1982- 44.69, 1983- 45.29, 1984- 45.40, 1985- 44.71, 1986- 44.45. pbs: 200m: 20.48/20.41w '86, 300m: 32.17 '86.
Ran six sub-45 sec 400m races 1986.

**Steve SCOTT** b.5 May 1956 Upland, California 1.86m 73kg. Club: Tiger TC. Graduate of University of California at Irvine.
At 1500m: OG: '84- 10; WCh: '83- 2; WCp: '77- 2, '79- 4. US champion 1977-9, 1982-3, 1986. Won US Trials 1980, NCAA 1978 at 1500m and AAA 1979 at 800m.
US records at 1500m (2), 1 mile (4), 2000m (2), 3000m (1). World indoor best for 2000m: 4:58.6 in 1981. Won GP 1500m 1985, 1 mile 1986.
Progression at 1500m/1 mile: 1973- 4:25.0M, 1974- 3:56.8/4:15.0, 1975- 3:47.5/4:08.0, 1976- 3:40.43/4:05.5, 1977- 3:36.13/3:55.21, 1978- 3:36.0/3:52.93, 1979- 3:34.6/3:51.11, 1980- 3:33.33/3:52.7, 1981- 3:31.96/3:49.68, 1982- 3:32.33/3:47.69, 1983- 3:32.71/3:49.21, 1984- 3:33.46/3:52.99, 1985- 3:31.76/3:49.93, 1986- 3:33.71/3:48.73. pbs: 800m: 1:45.05 '82, 1000m: 2:16.40 '81, 2000m: 4:54.71 '82, 3000m: 7:36.69 '81, 5000m: 13:38.4 '79, Mar: 2:32:32 '77.
America's top miler of recent years, with prolific fast times, ran his 100th sub-four-minute mile in May 1985 and has a record eight sub 3:50 miles. He has a fine competitive record, but he faded disappointingly in the Olympic final.

**Charlie SIMPKINS** b.19 Oct 1963 Aiken, S. Carolina 1.85m 70kg. Club: Team Nike. Student at Baptist College.
At TJ: WSG: '85- 1. Won TAC 1986.
World indoor triple jump best: 17.50i '86.
Progression at TJ: 1982- 15.23, 1983- 16.64, 1984- 16.76/17.18w, 1985- 17.86, 1986- 17.50i/ 17.42/17.91w. pb HJ: 2.18 '85.
Produced third best ever TJ to win World Student Games title, after dramatic improvement in 1985, when he was TAC third and beat Willie Banks at the National Sports Festival. Won a great TAC competition in 1986 but lost form thereafter through injury.

**Calvin SMITH** b.8 Jan 1961 Bolton, Mississippi 1.78m 64kg. Club: Team Adidas. Was at University of Alabama.
At 100m/200m (R- 4x100m relay): OG: '84- 1R; WCh: '83- 2/1 (1R); WSG: '81: 2/- (1R); WCp: '85- 1R. Won TAC 200m 1982. 3rd TAC 100m & 200m 1985. Won GP 200m 1985.
World records: 100m 1983 and twice at 4x100m relay 1983-4.
Progression at 100m, 200m: (y 100y/220y): 1978- 9.6y, 21.5y; 1979- 10.36/10.30w, 20.7; 1980- 10.17/10.12w, 20.64; 1981- 10.21, 21.00; 1982- 10.05/9.91w, 20.31/20.20w; 1983- 9.93, 19.99; 1984- 10.11/9.94w, 20.33; 1985- 10.10, 20.14; 1986- 10.14, 20.29. pb 400m: 46.43 '82.

**Jim SPIVEY** b.7 Mar 1960 Schiller Park, Illinois 1.78m 61kg. Club: Athletics West. Graduate of Indiana University. School teacher in Indiana.
At 1500m: OG: '84- 5; WSG: '81- 4. Won NCAA 1982, TAC 1984-5. 3rd GP 1M 1986. At 5000m: WCh: '83- sf.
Progression at 1500m/1M: 1976- 4:35.5M, 1977- 4:18.3M, 1978- 4:08.0*M, 1979- 3:44.66, 1980- 3:38.56/3:58.9i, 1981- 3:37.24/3:57.0, 1982- 3:37.34/3:55.56, 1983- 3:36.4/3:50.59, 1984- 3:34.19/3:53.88, 1985- 3:35.15/3:52.95, 1986- 3:34.4/3:49.80. pbs: 800m: 1:46.5 '82, 1000m: 2:16.54 '84, 2000m: 5:05.79i '86, 3000m: 7:51.47 '86, 2M: 8:24.14 '86, 5000m: 13:19.24 '83.
Has a renowned finishing kick, as he showed when he outsprinted Steve Scott to win the 1984 US Olympic Trials 1500m.

**Milan STEWART** b.31 Oct 1960 Los Angeles 1.81m 79kg. Club: Southern California Cheetahs. Was at USC (won NCAA 110mh 1982).
Progression at 110mh: 1977- 14.4, 1978- 14.42, 1979- 13.85/13.70w, 1980- 13.72, 1981- 13.65, 1982- 13.46/13.44w, 1983- 13.58, 1984- 13.48/13.4, 1985- 13.68, 1986- 13.37. pb: 400mh: 51.01 '82.

**Gregg TAFRALIS** b.9 Apr 1958 1.83m 120kg. Club: NYAC.
At SP: 2nd TAC 1986.
Progression at SP: 1981- 18.24, 1982- 20.12, 1983- 20.20, 1984- 21.25, 1985- 21.32, 1986- 21.45. pb DT: 62.38 '86.

**Keith TALLEY** b.28 Jan 1964 Indianapolis 1.93m 88kg. Club: Team Nike. University of Alabama. NCAA 110mh champion 1986.
Progression at 110mh: 1983- 14.1, 1984- 13.69/13.50w, 1985- 13.59/13.33w, 1986- 13.31. pbs: 100m: 10.28/10.24w '86, LJ: 8.05 '86, 8.44w '85.

**Henry THOMAS** b.10 Jul 1967 1.88m 77kg. Student at UCLA.
Progression at 200m, 400m: 1982- 48.57; 1983- 21.02, 48.5; 1984- 20.73, 45.82; 1985- 20.69/20.4, 45.09; 1986- 20.49, 45.42. pbs: 100m: 10.25/10.0w '85, 300m: 32.49 '85.
Brilliant high school career at Hawthorne, California.

**Mike TULLY** b.21 Oct 1956 Long Beach, Cal. 1.90m 86 kg. Club: Mazda TC. Graduate of UCLA.
At PV: OG: '84- 2; PAm: '83- 1; WCp: '77-1, '79- 1. US champion 1977, 1979, 1986; won NCAA 1978, AAA 1976 and 1979. Won US Olympic Trials 1984 (2nd= 1980).
Two world junior records 1975, unratified world pole vault best of 5.71m and indoor world bests 5.59m and 5.62m in 1978. Three US records 1984.
Progression at PV: 1972- 3.50, 1973- 4.31, 1974- 5.10, 1975- 5.43, 1976- 5.44, 1977- 5.60, 1978- 5.71, 1979- 5.56, 1980- 5.65, 1982- 5.60, 1983- 5.49, 1984- 5.82, 1985- 5.80, 1986- 5.80.

**Sam TURNER** b.17 Jun 1957 1.91m 80kg. Club: Mazda TC. Was at Cal State Los Angeles.
At 110mh: WCh: '83- 8.
Progression at 110mh: 1978- 13.89, 1979- 13.90w/13.8, 1980- 13.82/13.6w, 1981- 13.38, 1982- 13.31, 1983- 13.17, 1984- 13.49/13.38w, 1985- 13.34, 1986- 13.54/13.53w. pbs 100m: 10.41w '83, 200m: 20.52 '84, 400m: 46.73 '78, 400mh: 49.04 '78.

**Kevin YOUNG** b.16 Sep 1966 1.90m 75kg. Student at UCLA.
Second NCAA 400mh 1986.
Progression at 400mh: 1985- 51.09, 1986- 48.77. pbs: 110mh: 13.84 '86, LJ: 7.73 '86.
Great improvement in 1986; regularly uses 12 strides for first six hurdles and has even used only eleven at some stages.

# Women

**Evelyn ASHFORD** b.15 Apr 1957 Shreveport, Louisiana 1.65m 52kg. Club: Mazda TC. Was at UCLA. Married to basketball player Ray Washington.
At 100m (200m, R- 4x100m relay): OG: '76- 5, '84- 1 (1R); WCh: '83- dnf; PAm: '79- 1 (1); WCp: '77- 5 (4), '79- 1 (1), '81- 1 (1). US champion at 100m 1977, 1979, 1981-3; 200m 1977-9, 1981, 1983. Won GP 100m 1986.
World records for 100m in 1983 and 1984. US records at 100m (5) and 200m (4) 1977-84. World indoor bests: 50y: 5.77 & 5.74 '83; 60y: 6.54 '82.

Jeanette Bolden. *ASP*

**Jeanette BOLDEN** b.26 Jan 1960 Los Angeles 1.74m 62kg. Club: World Class AC. Graduate of UCLA.
At 100m (R- 4x100m relay): OG: '84- 4 (1R); WCp: '81- 1R. TAC indoor 60y champion 1986.
World indoor bests: 50y: 5.80 '82; 60y: 6.60 '82, 6.54 '86.
Progression at 100m: 1976- 12.24w, 1977- 11.68, 1978- 12.12, 1980- 11.41, 1981- 11.18, 1982- 11.16/11.12w, 1983- 11.48, 1984- 11.15, 1985- 11.09, 1986- 11.08. pbs: 200m: 23.49 '82, 23.02w '84; 400m: 54.64 '84; 100mh: 13.31 '85.

**Cindy BREMSER** b.5 May 1953 Milwaukee 1.62m 51kg. Club: Wisconsin United. Graduate of the University of Wisconsin. Has taken Masters degree in pediatric nursing and is employed by a health insurance company.
At 3000m: OG: '84- 4; WCh: '83- h; WCp: '85- 3.
At 1500m: PAm: '75- 4, '83- 2.
Has 15 2nd or 3rd placings in US championships at 1500m and 3000m but no wins.
Progression at 3000m: 1975- 9:13.4, 1976- 9:27.6, 1977- 9:03.97, 1978- 9:04.78, 1979- 8:59.93, 1980- 9:16.21, 1981- 8:55.39, 1982- 8:51.11, 1983- 8:55.48, 1984- 8:38.60, 1985- 8:49.66, 1986- 8:46.56. pbs: 800m: 2:04.20 '83, 1500m: 4:04.09 '85, 1M: 4:29.21 '82, 2000m: 5:47.89 '84, 2M: 9:28.29i '86, 5000m: 15:11.78 '86.

**Valerie BRISCO-HOOKS** b.6 Jul 1960 Greenwood, Miss. 1.70m 61kg. Club: World Class AC. Married to Alvin Hooks (10.36 for 100m in 1980), with one child (Alvin Jr.).
At 200m: OG: '84- 1 (1 at 400m, 4x400mR); PAm: '79- 4 (1 at 4x100mR). US 400m champion 1984. 2nd GP 400m, 3rd 200m 1986.
US 200m and 400m (2) records in 1984. World indoor bests at 220y, 440y, 500y 1985.
Progression at 100m, 200m/400m: 1977- 11.00y, 24.4/54.19; 1978- 11.57, 23.77/53.70; 1979- 11.69, 23.16/22.53w/52.08; 1980- 56.56i; 1981- 11.56, 23.49/52.62; 1983- 11.39, 23.10/53.61; 1984- 11.08/11.02w, 21.81/48.83; 1985- 11.01, 21.98/49.56; 1986- 10.99, 22.24/50.21.
Won three Olympic gold medals in 1984, a feat previously achieved by only three other women. Her victory celebration with coach Bob Kersee will long be remembered! USA/Mobil Indoor Grand Prix overall winner 1985.

**Alice BROWN** b.20 Sep 1960 Jackson, Mississippi 1.57m 56kg. Club: World Class AC. Attends Cal State Northridge.
At 100m (R- 4x100m relay): OG: '84- 2 (1R); WCh: '83- sf; WCp: '81- 2R. Won TAC and US Trials in 1980 and 2nd at both in 1984. Won GP 100m 1985. World indoor 60y best: 6.62 '81.

Progression at 100m, 200m: 1975- 11.5/24.2, 1976- 11.21/23.9w, 1977- 11.25/22.62, 1978- 11.16/22.66, 1979- 10.97/21.83, 1980- 11.33, 1981- 10.90/21.84, 1982- 10.93/22.10, 1983- 10.79/21.88, 1984- 10.76/22.75, 1986- 10.88/10.85w/21.97. pbs: 400m: 51.08 '84, 800m: 2:13.07 '84.
After giving birth to daughter, Raina Ashley Washington on 30 May 1985, she had a brilliant season in 1986, losing once each at 100m and at 200m, the latter, to Brisco-Hooks at the Grand Prix final was her first loss at that event for eight years after 27 finals wins. With automatic timing has run 25 sub-11 second times (including 7 wa).

Progression at 100m: 1976- 12.20, 1977- 11.86, 1978- 11.64, 1979- 11.73/11.65w, 1980- 11.21/11.17w, 1981- 11.28/11.13w, 1982- 11.37, 1983- 11.08, 1984- 11.13/11.07w, 1985- 11.02, 1986- 11.06/10.84w. pbs: 200m: 22.41 '83, 400m: 53.90 '85.

**Judi BROWN-KING** b.14 Jul 1961 Milwaukee 1.80m 67kg. Club: Athletics West. Michigan State University.
At 400mh: OG: '84- 2; WCh: '83- sf; PAm: '83- 1 (1 at 4x400m relay); WCp: '85- 2. Won NCAA 1983, TAC 1984-6 and US Trials 1984. Won GP 1985. Four US 400mh records 1984-5.
Progression at 400mh: 1980- 59.95, 1981- 59.49, 1982- 57.80, 1983- 56.03, 1984- 54.93, 1985- 54.38, 1986- 55.20. pbs: 100m: 11.3 '86; 200m: 23.53 '84, 23.2 '86; 400m: 52.33 '85, 800m: 2:06.6 '85, 100mh: 13.60/13.5w '85.
Her uncle, Bill Brown won a silver medal at 800m and gold at 4x400m relay in the 1951 Pan-American Games. Married Garland King August 1984.

**Chandra CHEESEBOROUGH** b.10 Jan 1959 Jacksonville, Florida 1.65m 59kg. Club: Athletics West. Graduate of Tennessee State University. Married Leon Shellman on 7 Jan 1985.
At 400m: OG: '84- 2 (1 at 4x100mR & 4x400mR). At 200m (R- 4x100m relay): OG: '76- sf (6 at 100m); PAm: '75- 1 (1R), '79- 1R. US champion at 100m 1976. Won US Olympic Trials at 200m 1980, 400m 1984.
World junior record for 100m in 1976. World 60y indoor best: 6.68 '79. US 200m record 1975 and two US 400m records 1984.
Progression at 200m/400m: 1975- 22.77, 1976- 23.18/22.64w, 1977- 22.89, 1978- 23.40, 1979- 23.34/22.84w, 1980- 22.84/22.70w, 1981- 22.65, 1982- 23.05, 1983- 51.00, 1984- 22.47/49.05, 1985- 23.13/22.92w, 1986- 23.14/51.57. pbs: 100m: 11.13 '76 & '84, 10.99w '83, 300m: 35.46 '84 (US best).
US international since she won the 1975 Pan-American 200m gold medal aged 16 in 1975. Moved up most successfully to 400m in 1984.

**Diane DIXON** b.23 Sep 1964 New York 1.65m 54kg. Club: Atoms TC. Was at Ohio State University.
At 400m: WIG: '85- 1. 3rd TAC 1985. Won GP 1986.
Progression at 400m: 1979- 56.1, 1980- 55.34, 1981- 53.91, 1982- 51.75, 1983- 51.60, 1984- 51.19, 1985- 50.29, 1986- 50.24. pbs: 100m: 11.27 '86, 200m: 22.53 '86.
USA/Mobil Indoor Grand Prix overall winner 1986.

**Benita FITZGERALD-BROWN** b.6 Jul 1961 Warrenton, Va. 1.79m 64kg. Club: Mazda TC. Degree in industrial engineering from University of Tennessee. Married Laron Brown (45.45 for 400m 1983) in 1984.
At 100mh: OG: '84- 1; WCh: '83- 8; PAm: '83- 1; WSG: '83- 3. Won TAC 1983, 1986; NCAA 1982- 3. 2nd US Trials 1980 and 1984.
Progression at 100mh: 1978- 14.00, 1979- 13.33, 1980- 13.11, 1981- 13.10, 1982- 12.92, 1983- 12.84, 1984- 12.84, 1985- 12.97, 1986- 12.84/12.83w. pbs: 100m: 11.36/11.2/11.13w '82, 200m: 23.22 '81, 23.0 '83.

**Jane FREDERICK** b.7 Apr 1952 Oakland, Cal. 1.82m 72kg. Club: Athletics West. Graduate of the University of Colorado.
At Pen/Hep: OG: '72- 21, '76- 7; WCh: '83- dnf, PAm: '79- dnf; WSG: '75- 1, '77- 2. US champion at Pen/Hep: 1972-3, 1975-6, 1979, 1981, 1983, 1986; 100mh: 1975-6. At LJ: WCp: '77- 7; PAm: '79- 5.
Six US heptathlon records, from a world best of 6104 in 1981 to 1984. Also eight US pentathlon records 1972-9. World indoor best (hand-timed) of 7.3 for 60y hurdles 1977.
Progression at Pen (p)/Hep: 1972- 4284p, 1973- 4281p, 1974- 4391p, 1975- 4676p, 1976- 4732p, 1977- 4625p, 1978- 4704p, 1979- 4708p, 1981- 6291, 1982- 6491, 1983- 6471, 1984- 6803, 1985- 6666, 1986- 6230. pbs: 200m: 23.9/24.13 '76, 800m: 2:10.25 '84, 100mh: 13.25 '78, HJ: 1.89 '83, LJ: 6.56/6.58w '78, SP: 16.18 '78, JT: 52.74 '84.
Missed 1984 Olympics due to injury at US Trials.

**Florence GRIFFITH** b.21 Dec 1959 Los Angeles 1.69m 59kg. Club: World Class AC. Graduate of UCLA.
At 200m: OG: '84- 2; WCh: '83- 4. At 4x100mR:

Florence Griffith. *ASP*

WCp: '81- 2. 3rd GP 1985. Won NCAA 200m 1982, 400m 1983.
Progression at 100m, 200m: 1978- 10.85yw, 24.4y; 1980- 11.51, 23.55/23.02w; 1981- 11.23, 22.81/22.61w; 1982- 11.12, 22.39/22.23w; 1983- 11.06/10.96w, 22.23; 1984- 10.99, 22.04; 1985- 11.00, 22.46; 1986- 11.42, 23.51/23.57yi. pb 400m: 50.94 '83.
Has four-inch fingernails on her left hand! Engaged to Greg Foster (qv).

**Stephanie HIGHTOWER** b.19 Jul 1958 Fort Knox, Kentucky 1.64m 54kg. Married J.Douglas Leftwich 26 Jul 1986. Graduate of Ohio State University.
At 100mh: WSG: '81- 1; WCp: '81- 4. US champion 1980-2, 1984. Won US Olympic Trials 1980. Two US 100mh records 1982. Three world indoor bests for 60y hurdles 1980-3, best of 7.36.
Progression at 100mh: 1975- 15.0, 1976- 14.60, 1977- 14.27w, 1978- 13.50, 1979- 13.09, 1980- 12.90, 1981- 13.03, 1982- 12.79, 1983- 13.00, 1984- 12.90/12.78w, 1985- 12.92, 1986- 12.96/12.90w. pb 100m: 11.56 '78.
Missed US Olympic selection in 1984 by the narrowest of margins. USA/Mobil Indoor Grand Prix overall winner 1983 and 1984.

**Lynn JENNINGS** b.1 Jul 1960 1.65m 50kg. Club: Athletics West. Graduate of Princeton University. World CC: '86- 2. TAC CC champion 1985.
World indoor 2 miles best 9:28.15 to win 1986 TAC title.
Progression at 3000m: 1979- 9:51.2, 1982- 9:35.6, 1983- 9:01.44, 1984- 9:45.4, 1985- 8:49.86, 1986- 8:53.19i. pbs: 800m: 2:06.54 '86, 1500m: 4:10.87 '86, 1M: 4:31.86 '85, 2000m: 5:52.62 '86, 2M: 9:28.15i '86, 5000m: 15:08.36 '86, 10000m: 32:03.37 '85.
TAC junior 1500m champion 1977.

**Jackie JOYNER** b.3 Mar 1962 East St.Louis, Illinois 1.78m 70kg. Club: World Class AC. UCLA. Sister of triple jumper Al Joyner. Married coach Bobby KERSEE on 11 Jan 1986.
At Hep: OG: '84- 2 (5 LJ); WCh: '83- dnf. Won TAC 1982, NCAA 1982-3. At NCAA 1985: 2nd 400mh & TJ, 3rd 100mh. 3rd GP LJ 1985.
Two world heptathlon records 1986. US records: LJ 1985, heptathlon (3) 1986.
Progression at LJ, Hep: 1974- 5.10, 1975- 5.22, 1976- 5.31, 1977- 5.69, 1978- 6.06; 1979- 6.28/6.30w; 1980- 6.34/6.42w; 1981- 6.39/6.47w, 5754w; 1982- 6.44/6.61w, 6066; 1983- 6.74/6.77w, 6390; 1984- 6.81, 6579; 1985- 7.24, 6718; 1986- 7.12/7.15w, 7158. pbs: 100m: 11.71 '86, 200m: 22.85 '86, 400m: 54.0 '83, 800m: 2:09.32 '82, 100mh: 12.84 '86; 400mh: 55.05 '85, HJ: 1.88 '86, TJ: 13.20 '85, SP: 15.20 '86, JT: 50.12 '86.

**Mary KNISELY** b.29 May 1959 Wilmington, Delaware 1.62m 48kg. née Schilly. Club: New Balance TC. Physical therapy graduate of University of Delaware.
At 10000m: WCp: '85- 2. TAC 3000m champion 1986. 3rd GP 5000m 1986.
Progression at 3000m/10000m: 1982- 9:11.99, 1983- 9:07.65, 1984- 8:51.9, 1985- 8:43.82/32:19.93, 1986- 8:46.18. pbs: 800m: 2:05.45 '85, 1500m: 4:05.70 '85, 1M: 4:31.71 '86, 2000m: 5:40.50 '86, 5000m: 15:22.33 '86.

**Lillie LEATHERWOOD** b.6 Jul 1964 Ralph, Alabama 1.67m 56kg. Club: New Balance TC. University of Alabama.
At 400m (R- 4x400m relay): OG: '84- 5 (1R); WCp: '85- 3. Won TAC 1985, NCAA 1986. 3rd GP 1986.
Progression at 400m: 1983- 53.2, 1984- 50.19, 1985- 50.43, 1986- 50.18. pbs: 100m: 11.74/11.42w '84, 200m: 23.16 '86, 22.84w '85, 300m: 36.15 '85.

**Carol LEWIS** b.8 Aug 1963 Birmingham, Alabama 1.78m 68kg. Santa Monica Track Club. University of Houston. Sister of Carl Lewis.
At LJ: OG: '84- 9; WCh: '83- 3; WCp: '85- 3. Won TAC 1982-3, 1985-6, NCAA 1983, US Trials 1984 (3rd 1980).
Two US long jump records 1985.
Progression at LJ: 1975- 4.65, 1976- 5.29, 1977- 5.71, 1978- 6.22/6.23w, 1979- 6.37, 1980- 6.60, 1981- 6.59i, 1982- 6.81, 1983- 6.97/7.04w, 1984- 6.97/7.03w, 1985- 7.04, 1986- 6.90/6.93w. pbs: 200m: 24.51w '85, 100mh: 13.46/13.45w '83, 13.2w '85; HJ: 1.83 '85, SP: 12.61 '85, JT: 42.40 '85, Hep: 5716w '85.
Won record five Junior TAC titles.

**Pam MARSHALL** b.16 Aug 1960 Hazelhurst, Michigan 1.78m 63kg. Club: Mazda TC.
At 200m: WCp: '85- 5. TAC champion 100m and 200m 1986.
Progression at 100m/200m: 1978- 11.78, 23.82; 1980- 11.86, 23.56/23.31w; 1981- 11.69, 23.66; 1982- 11.44, 23.34; 1984- 11.43, 22.67/22.59w; 1985- 11.15, 22.39; 1986- 11.21/10.80w/10.9, 22.12. pb 400m: 49.99 '86.

**Patti Sue PLUMER** b.27 Apr 1962 1.62m 49kg. Club: Puma TC. Graduate of Stanford University.
At 5000m: NCAA champion 1984. 2nd GP 1986. 2nd NCAA 3000m 1982-4.
Progression at 3000m/5000m: 1981- 9:42.02, 1982- 8:55.98, 1983- 8:53.54i/8:53.81/15:49.7, 1984- 8:54.91/15:29.0, 1985- 9:01.85i, 1986- 8:46.24/15:20.88. pbs: 1500m: 4:11.36 '84, 1M: 4:33.36i '86, 2000m: 5:44.48 '84.

**Louise RITTER** b.18 Feb 1958 Dallas, Texas 1.78m 60kg. Pacific Coast Club. Graduate of Texas Woman's University.
At HJ: OG: '84- 8; WCh: '83- 3; PAm: '79- 1; WCp: '77- 4, '79- 5. US champion 1978, 1985-6, won US Olympic Trials 1980 and 1984. Won AIAW 1977- 9. 2nd GP 1985.
Seven US high jump records 1978-83.
Progression at HJ: 1973- 1.74, 1974- 1.78, 1975- 1.80, 1976- 1.82, 1977- 1.86, 1978- 1.90, 1979- 1.93, 1980- 1.95, 1981- 1.94, 1982- 1.93i, 1983- 2.01, 1984- 1.96i, 1985- 2.00, 1986- 1.93.
Switched to 'flop' in 1977, straddle best 1.82m.

**Joan SAMUELSON** b.16 May 1957 Cape Elizabeth, Maine 1.60m 47kg. née Benoit. Club: Athletics West. Graduate of Bowdoin College.
At Mar: OG: '84- 1. At 3000m: PAm: '83- 1. World CC: '83- 4.
Five US marathon records 1979-85, including world best in 1983. US road bests: 10M: 53:18 '86, half marathon: 1:08:34 '84.
Progression at Mar: 1979- 2:35:15, 1980- 2:31:23, 1981- 2:30:16, 1982- 2:26:11, 1983- 2:22:43, 1984- 2:24:52, 1985- 2:21:21. pbs: 1500m: 4:24.0i '83, 1M: 4:36.48i '83, 3000m: 8:53.49 '83, 5000m: 15:40.42 '82, 10000m: 32:07.41 '84.
Has won eight of her thirteen marathons, climaxed by her sensational Olympic victory, made possible by winning the US Trials race just 17 days after undergoing arthroscopic surgery on her right knee. She won the 1985 Chicago marathon in a time just 14 seconds outside the world best. Sullivan Award winner 1985.

**Mary SLANEY** b.4 Aug 1958 Flemington, New Jersey 1.68m 49kg. née Decker. Club: Athletics West. Was at University of Colorado. Married British discus thrower Richard Slaney (pb 64.66m in 1984, CG: 4th at SP and DT 1982, 6th DT 1986) on 1 Jan 1985. Formerly married to 2:09:32 marathon runner Ron Tabb.
At 3000m: OG: '84- dnf; WCh: '83- 1. At 1500m: WCh: '83- 1; PAm: '79- 1. US champion at 800m 1974, 1500m 1982-3, 3000m 1983. Won US Olympic Trials at 1500m 1980, 3000m 1984. Won GP 3000m 1986.
World records: 3 at 1M 1980-5, 1 each at 5000m and 10000m 1982. 21 US records at eight distances from 800m to 10000m. World junior records at 800m: 2:02.43 '74 and 2:02.29 '74, 1 mile: 4:37.4 '73. 13 world indoor bests 1974-85, no. with best times: 880y (1) 1:59.7 '80, 1000y (2) 2:23.8 '78, 1500m (2) 4:00.2 '80 (oversized track), 1M (4) 4:17.55 '80 (oversized track), 2000m (2) 5:34.52 '85, 3000m (1) 8:47.3 '82, 2M (1) 9:31.7 '83.

Progression at 1500m (M 1 mile)/3000m: 1971- 5:04.8M, 1972- 4:35.9, 1973- 4:37.4M, 1974- 5:00.8M, 1978- 4:08.9, 1979- 4:05.0, 1980- 3:59.43/8:38.73, 1982- 4:01.7/8:29.71, 1983- 3:57.12/8:34.62, 1984- 3:59.19/8:34.91, 1985- 3:57.24/8:25.83, 1986- 4:42.64M. pbs: 400m: 53.84 '73, 800m: 1:56.90 '85, 1M: 4:16.71 '85, 2000m: 5:32.7 '84, 5000m: 15:06.53 '85, 10000m: 31:35.3 '82.
USA/Mobil Indoor Grand Prix overall winner 1982. Decker became the youngest ever US international at 14 years 224 days when she ran 1M indoors against the USSR in 1973. Later that year she won at 800m v USSR, and she set a world indoor best for 880y at 2:02.3 in 1974. However for the next four years she competed rarely due to a series of injuries. She overcame these to dominate US distance running, and score double success at the 1983 world championships. Seeking to add Olympic success, she fell in the 3000m final in Los Angeles. Came back in invincible form in 1985 and won the women's overall Grand Prix title. Gave birth to a daughter, Ashley Lynn, on 30 May 1986 and returned to racing with sixth place in the 5th Avenue Mile on 13 Sep 1986.

**Gwen TORRENCE** b.12 Jun 1965 Atlanta 1.68m 52kg. Club: Georgia TC. University of Georgia.
NCAA indoor 55m champion 1986. 2nd NCAA 100m 1985-6, 200m 1986.
Progression at 100m, 200m: 1982- 24.2; 1983- 11.92, 24.34/23.9y; 1984- 11.41/11.37w, 23.54; 1985- 11.40/11.11w, 22.96; 1986- 11.30/11.01w, 22.53.
Shot to prominince indoors in 1986, winning the Millrose 60y in 6.57.

**Diane WILLIAMS** b.14 Dec 1961 Chicago 1.62m 56kg. Club: Puma TC. Was at Cal State University, Los Angeles.
At 100m: WCh: '83- 3.
Progression at 100m: 1980- 11.37/11.32w, 1982- 11.14/11.13w, 1983- 10.94, 1984- 11.04, 1985- 11.23, 1986- 11.18/10.92w. pb 200m: 22.60 '86.

# USSR

**Governing body**: Light Athletic Federation of the USSR, Luzhnetskaya Naberezhnaya 8, 119270 Moscow.
**National Championships** first held in 1920 (men), 1922 (women)
**1986 Champions: MEN**
100m: Viktor Bryzgin 10.28, 200m: Aleksandr Yevgenyev 20.50, 400m: Aleksandr Kurochkin 45.89, 800m: Viktor Zemlyanskiy 1:45.05, 1500m: Nikolay Afanasyev 3:39.52, 5000m:

Mikhail Dasko 13:32.19, 10000m: Oleg Strizhakov 28:38.85, 3000mSt: Ivan Konovalov 8:27.77, 110mh: Andrey Prokofyev 13.46, 400mh: Aleksandr Vasilyev 48.55, HJ: Valeriy Sereda 2.34, PV: Rodion Gataullin 5.85, LJ: Sergey Layevskiy 8.14, TJ: Oleg Protsenko 17.59, SP: Sergey Smirnov 22.16, DT: Romas Ubartas 67.28, HT: Benjaminas Viluckis 79.28, JT: Marek Kaleta 82.00, Dec: Grigoriy Degtyarov 8322.

## WOMEN

100m: Irina Slyussar 11.22, 200m: Marina Molokova 22.46, 400m: Maria Pinigina 50.50, 800m: Lyubov Kiryukhina 1:57.18, 1500m: Tatyana Samolenko 3:59.45, 3000: Regina Chistyakova 8:40.74, 5000m: Svetlana Ulmasova 15:26.56, 100mh: Vera Akimova 12.68, 400mh: Marina Stepanova 53.84, HJ: Olga Turchak 1.97, LJ: Yelena Byelevskaya 7.31, SP: Natalya Lisovskaya 21.38, DT: Ellina Zvereva 66.06, JT: Natalya Kolenchukova 65.56, Hep: Natalya Shubenkova 6631.

**Aleksandr APAYCHEV** b.6 May 1961 Kirov 1.87m 90kg. Club: Trudovye Rezervy, Brovary. Sports student.
At Dec: ECh: '86- 5; ECp: '85- 6.
Two USSR decathlon records 1984.
Progression at Dec: 1978- 7028*, 1979- 7387, 1980- 7576, 1981- 7962, 1982- 8104, 1983- 8270, 1984- 8709, 1985- 8112, 1986- 8244. pbs: 100m: 10.87 '84, 400m: 48.40 '84, 1500m: 4:18.78 '84, 110mh: 13.93 '84, HJ: 2.00 '84, PV: 5.00i '84, LJ: 7.61 '83, SP: 16.30i '86, 16.20 '84, DT: 48.72 '84, JT: 76.52 '81.

**Gennadiy AVDEYENKO** b.4 Nov 1963 Odessa 2.02m 82kg. Refrigeration mechanic.
At HJ: WCh: '83- 1.
Progression at HJ: 1980- 2.06, 1981- 2.21, 1982- 2.22, 1983- 2.32, 1984- 2.31, 1985- 2.35, 1986- 2.35. pb TJ: 15.57 '80.
Perhaps the most surprising world champion of 1983.

**Janis BOJARS** b.12 May 1956 Ilukste, Latvia 1.85m 127kg. Sports instructor.
At SP: WCh: '83- 5; ECh: '82- 2; EI: '83- 1, '84- 1; ECp: '83- 3; WIG: '85- 3. USSR champion 1983.
Progression at SP: 1973- 14.83, 1974- 16.64, 1975- 16.63, 1976- 16.97, 1977- 17.75, 1978- 18.88, 1979- 19.42, 1980- 20.02, 1981- 20.36, 1982- 21.31, 1983- 21.40, 1984- 21.74, 1985- 21.31, 1986- 20.98.

**Maris BRUZHIKS** b.25 Aug 1962 Stuchka, Latvia 1.86m 70kg. Club: SKA Riga. Sports student.
At TJ: ECh: '86- 2; EI: '86- 1.
World indoor TJ best 17.54m 1986.

Progression at TJ: 1977- 11.60, 1978- 13.57, 1979- 14.60, 1980- 15.43, 1981- 15.48i, 1982- 15.55, 1983- 16.47, 1984- 17.15, 1985- 17.38, 1986- 17.54i/17.33. pbs: HJ: 2.15, LJ: 7.91 '84.

**Viktor BRYZGIN** b.22 Aug 1962 Voroshilovgrad 1.80m 72kg. Teacher.
At 100m (R- 4x100m relay): WCh: '83- qf (3R); ECh: '86- 9 (1R); ECp: '83- 4. USSR champion 1986.
Progression at 100m: 1982- 10.54/10.2, 1983- 10.20, 1984- 10.18/10.0, 1985- 10.24/10.0, 1986- 10.03?w/10.11.
Has looked very good at times, less so at others, as in the contrast between heats and final of the 1986 European 100m.

**Sergey BUBKA** b.4 Dec 1963 Voroshilovgrad, Ukraine 1.83m 80kg. Club: Donyetsk. Student.
At PV: WCh: '83- 1; ECh: '86- 1; EJ: '81- 7=; EI: '85- 1; WCp: '85- 1; ECp: '85- 1; WIG: '85- 1. USSR champion 1984. Won GP 1986.
Six world pole vault records 1984-6, including the world's first six-metre jump. Eight world indoor pole vault bests from 1984 to 5.96m in January 1987.
Progression at PV: 1975- 2.70, 1976- 3.50, 1977- 3.60, 1978- 4.40, 1979- 4.80, 1980- 5.10, 1981- 5.40, 1982- 5.55, 1983- 5.72, 1984- 5.94, 1985- 6.00, 1986- 6.01.
The surprise world champion in 1983 has gone on to dominate the world of pole vaulting. Has the speed and strength to manage a very high hold on the pole.

**Vasiliy BUBKA** b.26 Nov 1960 Voroshilovgrad, Ukraine 1.84m 76kg. Club: Donyetsk. Teacher. Elder brother of Sergey.
At PV: WIG: '85- 3. USSR champion 1985.
Progression at PV: 1975- 3.25, 1976- 4.20, 1977- 4.90, 1978- 5.09, 1979- 5.20i, 1980- 5.20, 1981- 5.30, 1982- 5.50, 1983- 5.60i, 1984- 5.70i, 1985- 5.85, 1986- 5.80.

**Grigoriy DEGTYAROV** b.16 Aug 1958 Vorkuta 1.90m 90kg. Club: Trud, Kirov. Teacher.
At Dec: WCh: '83- dnf; ECh: '82- 6, '86- dnf; ECp: '85-3. USSR champion 1983-4, 1986.
USSR decathlon records: 8538 in 1983, 8579 and 8652 in 1984.
Progression at Dec: 1974- 4780*, 1975- 5000*, 1976- 6340*, 1977- 7228*, 1978- 7419*, 1979- 7360*, 1980- 7646, 1981- 8095, 1982- 8233, 1983- 8580, 1984- 8698, 1985- 8206, 1986- 8322. pbs: 100m: 10.87 '84, 400m: 49.40 '83, 1500m: 4:14.25 '81, 110mh: 14.45 '84, HJ: 2.10 '84, PV: 5.10 '84, LJ: 7.75 '83, SP: 16.14 '86, DT: 51.56 '85, JT: 67.08 '84.
Won Goodwill Games decathlon 1986.

The brothers Bubka – Sergey (left), Vasily (right). *ASP*

**Robert EMMIYAN** b.16 Feb 1965 Leninaken 1.78m 69kg. Soviet army, Leninaken - Instructor.
At LJ: ECh: '86- 1; EJ: '83- 3; EI: '84- 3, '86- 1; WSG: '85- 2; WCp: '85- 2.
At long jump: European record 1986, European junior record 1984, European indoor record 8.34m 1986.
Progression at LJ: 1980- 7.70, 1981- 7.77, 1982- 7.91, 1983- 8.01, 1984- 8.13, 1985- 8.30/8.38w, 1986- 8.61. pb TJ: 14.47 '80.
Has come through over the last couple of years as a major talent. Only Bob Beamon and Carl Lewis have legal jumps better than his 1986 European record of 8.61m. Lost only once in 1986.

**Andrey FEDORIV** b.10 Aug 1963 Lvov 1.79m 71kg. Soldier.
At 200m: ECh: '86- 3.
Progression at 200m: 1983- 20.70/20.4, 1984- 20.84, 1985- 20.90, 1986- 20.53. pb 100m: 10.36 '86, 10.0 '86.
Perhaps the most surprising European medallist of 1986.

**Rodion GATAULLIN** b.23 Nov 1965 Tashkent 1.91m 78kg. Club: Burevestnik, Tashkent. Medical student.
At PV: ECh: '86- nh; EJ: '83- 1; WSG: '85- 1. USSR champion 1985.
World junior pole vault record when second in USSR championships 1984.
Progression at PV: 1978 - 3.10, 1979- 3.80, 1980- 4.20, 1981- 4.80, 1982- 5.20, 1983- 5.55, 1984- 5.65, 1985- 5.75, 1986- 5.85. pb 110mh: 14.4.

**Sergey GAVRYUSHIN** b.27 Jun 1959 Karaganda 1.92m 125kg. Club: Trud, Moskva. Teacher.
At SP: WSG: '85- 3.
Progression at SP: 1975- 15.20, 1976- 16.97, 1977- 17.52, 1978- 17.97, 1980- 18.89, 1981- 19.99, 1982- 21.03, 1983- 20.97, 1984- 21.60, 1985- 20.96, 1986- 22.10.

**Vyacheslav IVANENKO** b.3 Mar 1961 Kemerova 1.64m 58kg. Teacher.
At 50kmW: ECh: '86- 2.
Progression at 20kmW/50kmW: 1985- 1:22:36, 1986- 1:22:18/3:41:54.

**Marek KALETA** b.17 Dec 1961 Estonia 1.80m 82kg. Teacher.
At JT: ECh: '86- 9. USSR champion 1986.
Progression at JT: 1983- 75.50, 1984- 83.30, 1985- 86.24, new: 1986- 82.00.

**Viktor KALINKIN** b.23 Feb 1960 Kirilovo 1.80m 70kg. Club: Penza Burevestnik. Engineer.
At 800m: WCh: '83- sf; ECh: '86- 8; WCp: '85- 2; WSG: '85- 2. USSR champion 1983-4.

Progression at 800m: 1979- 1:52.2, 1980-1:50.20, 1981- 1:48.82, 1980- 1:46.74, 1983-1:45.6, 1984- 1:44.73, 1985- 1:45.21, 1986-1:45.08. pbs: 400m: 46.9 '84, 1000m: 2:19.21 '85, 1500m: 3:37.1 '84.

**Sergey KASNAUSKAS** b.20 Apr 1961 Minsk 1.92m 126kg. Sports instructor.
At SP: EJ: '79- 3.
Two European indoor bests (21.43m and 21.46m) in 1984.
Progression at SP: 1977- 14.35, 1978- 17.25, 1979- 18.03, 1980- 18.50i, 1981- 18.67?, 1982-18.52, 1983- 21.17, 1984- 22.09, 1986- 21.23.

**Vaclavas KIDIKAS** b.17 Oct 1961 Klaipeda, Lithuania 1.97m 103kg. Teacher.
At DT: ECh: '86- 3.
Progression at DT: 1982- 55.48, 1983- 61.42, 1984- 62.60, 1985- 67.34, 1986- 67.00.

**Georgiy KOLNOOTCHENKO** b.7 May 1959 Manychkoye, Stavropol 1.97m 115kg. Club: Dynamo, Minsk. Serviceman.
At DT: WCh: '83- 6; ECh: '82- 5, '86- 2; WCp: '85-1; ECp: '83- 3, '85- 2. USSR champion 1983 and 1985.
Two USSR discus records 1980 and 1982.
Progression at DT: 1975- 44.24, 1976- 51.36, 1977- 55.10, 1978- 55.88, 1979- 60.72, 1980-67.36, 1981- 64.08, 1982- 69.44, 1983- 65.42, 1984- 66.52, 1985- 69.08, 1986- 67.02.

**Mikhail KOSTIN** b.10 May 1959 1.94m 120kg.
Progression at SP: 1982- 18.40, 1983- 19.74, 1984- 20.96, 1985- 21.24, 1986- 21.96.

**Aleksandr KOTOVICH** b.6 Jan 1961 1.83m 76kg.
At HJ: EI: '85- 2.
Progression at HJ: 1980- 2.15, 1981- 2.18, 1982-2.24, 1983- 2.26, 1984- 2.33, 1985- 2.35i/2.29, 1986- 2.34i/2.32.

**Aleksandr KRUPSKIY** b.4 Jan 1960 Irkutsk 1.85m 77kg. Club: Lokomotiv, Irkutsk. Railway engineer.
At PV: ECh: '82- 1; EI: '81- 2, '84- 3, '85- 2; EJ: '79-2; ECp: '83- 2.
Progression at PV: 1974- 3.00, 1975- 4.10, 1976-4.80, 1977- 5.00, 1978- 5.20, 1979- 5.50, 1980-5.50, 1981- 5.70, 1982- 5.70, 1983- 5.74, 1984-5.82, 1985- 5.75, 1986- 5.75.

**Vladimir KRYLOV** b.26 Feb 1964 Sengiley 1.84m 75kg. Student.
At 200m (R- 4x400m relay): ECh: '86- 2 (2R). At 400m: WCp: '85- 5; ECp: '85- 2. USSR champion 1984-5.

Progression at 200m/400m: 1982- 20.9, 1983-21.76/48.52, 1984- 46.05, 1985- 20.61/45.22, 1986- 20.50/45.20. pb 100m: 10.25 '86, 9.9 '85.

**Sergey LAYEVSKIY** b.3 Mar 1959 Dnepropetrovsk 1.84m 72kg. Club: Burevestnik, Dnepropetrovsk. Metallurgy engineer.
At LJ: ECh: '86- 2; EI: '85- 3; ECp: '85- 1. USSR champion 1984-6. 3rd GP 1985.
Progression at LJ: 1977- 7.18, 1978- 7.22, 1979-7.55, 1980- 7.59, 1981- 7.91, 1982- 8.13, 1983-7.87, 1984- 8.32, 1985- 8.20, 1986- 8.20. pbs: 100m: 10.65, 400m: 47.8.

**Sergey LITVINOV** b.23 Jan 1958 Tsukarov, Krasnodar 1.80m 110kg. Teacher.
At HT: OG: '80- 2; WCh: '83- 1; ECh: '82- 3, '86- 2; EJ: '75- 3, '77- 2; WCp: '79- 1; ECp: '79- 2, '83- 1.
USSR champion 1979 and 1983. 2nd GP 1986.
Three world hammer records, in 1980, 1982 and 1983; two world junior records 1976-7.
Progression at HT: 1974- 60.68, 1975- 65.32, 1976- 72.38, 1977- 74.32, 1978- 76.22, 1979-79.82, 1980- 81.66, 1981- 79.60, 1982- 83.98, 1983- 84.14, 1984- 85.20, 1985- 76.94, 1986-86.04.
Only two men have thrown the hammer more than 85m, yet Litvinov has twice thrown over this distance and yet lost to Yuriy Sedykh: at Cork in 1984 and at the 1986 European Championships, when he opened with 85.74.

**Igor LOTAREV** b.30 Aug 1964 Kursk 1.81m 66kg. Serviceman in Kursk.
At 1500m: ECh: '86- 11, EJ: '83- 2; WCp: '85- 3 ECp: '85- 4. USSR champion 1985.
USSR records 1500m (2) 1984-5, 2000m 1986.
Progression at 1500m: 1979- 4:17.7, 1980-4:00.7, 1981- 3:53.0, 1982- 3:43.2, 1983- 3:38.3, 1984- 3:34.88, 1985- 3:34.49, 1986- 3:37.53. pbs: 800m: 1:46.18 '85, 1000m: 2:21.14 '84, 2000m: 5:01.35 '86, 3000m: 7:52.15 '84, 5000m: 13:55.84 '86.

**Sergey MALCHENKO** b.2 Nov 1963 Tula 1.90m 74kg. Soldier.
At HJ: ECh: '86- 2.
Progression at HJ: 1982- 2.11, 1983- 2.29, 1984-2.25, 1985- 2.31, 1986- 2.33.

**Nikolay MATYUSHENKO** b.4 Jan 1966 Kharkov 1.75m 62kg. Soldier.
At 3kmSt: ECh: '86- dnf. At 2kmSt: EJ: '83- 1, '85-1.
Progression at 3kmSt: 1984- 8:52.1, 1985-8:41.06, 1986- 8:25.73. pbs: 3000m: 7:54.74 '86, 2kmSt: 5:28.31 '85.
Only the fourth athlete ever to retain a European junior title.

Sergey Malchenko in the 1986 European high jump. *Mark Shearman*

**Viktor MOSTOVIK** b.7 Jan 1963 Moldavia 1.79m 58kg. Student.
At 20kmW: ECh: '86- 4; LT: '85- 3; WSG: '85- 1. EJ: '81- 3 at 10kmW. USSR champion 1985.
Progression at 20kmW: 1982- 1:26:04, 1983- 1:23:57, 1984- 1:22:57, 1985- 1:21:33, 1986- 1:21:52.

**Vladimir MURAVYEV** b.30 Sep 1959 Karaganda 1.78m 75kg. Serviceman.
At 200m (R- 4x100mR): WCh: '83- sf (2R); ECh: '82- 7; WSG: '81- 5 (2R), '83- 4; WCp: '81- 4R, '85- 6 (3R); ECp: '83- 6. At 100m: OG: 6 (1R); ECh: '82- sf, '86- sf (1R); ECp: '81- 5 (2R), '85- 2; EJ: '77- 4R. EI: '81- 2 at 50m. USSR champion at 100m 1985, 200m 1983.
Progression at 200m: 1984- 12.3, 1975- 11.1, 1976- 10.6, 1977- 10.64/10.4, 1978- 10.4, 1979- 10.44/10.3, 1980- 10.34, 1981- 10.36, 1982- 10.48, 1983- 10.36, 1984- 10.23, 1985- 10.22, 1986- 10.19?w/10.20. pb 200m: 20.34 '84.

**Nikolay MUSIYENKO** b.16 Dec 1959 1.83m 79kg.
At TJ: ECh: '86- 6; EI: '82- 3, '83- 1. European triple jump record 1986.
Progression at TJ: 1977- 15.64, 1978- 16.07,

1979- 16.03, 1980- 16.26i, 1981- 16.91, 1982- 17.16i, 1983- 17.12i/17.00, 1984- 17.24, 1985- 17.26, 1986- 17.78. pb LJ: 7.58.

**Aleksandr NEVSKIY** b.21 Feb 1958 Severny, Tomsk 1.90m 88kg. Club: Dynamo, Kiev. Student.
At Dec: WCh: '83- 6; ECp: '79- 3, '85- 2. USSR champion 1981.
Progression at Dec: 1978- 7615, 1979- 8014, 1980- 8007, 1981- 8133, 1982- 8114, 1983- 8420, 1984- 8491, 1985- 8409, 1986- 8143. pbs: 100m: 10.7 '78, 10.92 '85, 400m: 48.44 '84, 1500m: 4:17.03 '83, 110mh: 14.67 '84, 14.63w '83, HJ: 2.14i '80, PV: 4.70 '84, LJ: 7.58 '83, SP: 16.11i '86, DT: 49.08 '83, JT: 69.56 '84.

**Igor NIKULIN** b.14 Aug 1960 Moscow 1.92m 118kg. Teacher.
At HT: WCh: '83- 4; ECh: '82- 2, '86- 3; EJ: '79- 1; WSG: '81- 3, '85- 3. USSR champion 1981 and 1984.
Progression at HT: 1975- 48.50, 1976- 58.14, 1977- 63.40, 1978- 71.60, 1979- 75.20, 1980- 80.34, 1981- 77.50, 1982- 83.54, 1983- 82.92, 1984- 82.56, 1985 78.88, 1986- 82.34.

He became the youngest ever 80m hammer thrower in 1980. His father Yuriy was fourth in the 1964 Olympic hammer.

**Igor PAKLIN** b.15 Jun 1963 Frunze, Kirghizia 1.93m 71kg. Club: Burevestnik Frunze. Student at Polytechnic Institute, Frunze.
At HJ: WCh: '83- 4=; ECh: '86- 1; EJ: '81- 4; WCp: '85- 4; ECp: '85- 3; WSG: '83- 1, '85- 1. USSR champion 1985. 3rd GP 1986.
World high jump record at 2.41m 1985, and world indoor best of 2.36 in 1984.
Progression at HJ: 1978- 1.85, 1979- 2.06, 1980- 2.18, 1981- 2.21, 1982- 2.24, 1983- 2.33, 1984- 2.36i/2.30, 1985- 2.41, 1986- 2.38.
Following his world record at the end of the 1985 season, he became the world's most consistent jumper in the major events of 1986.

**Andrey PERLOV** b.12 Dec 1961.
At 50kmW: LT: '85- 2. USSR champion 1984-5. At 20 kmW: WSG: '85- 2.
World junior record at 20km track walk with 1:22:42.8 in 1980.

Progression at 50kmW: 1981- 4:05:29, 1983- 3:45:49, 1984- 3:43:06, 1985- 3:39:47. Track pbs: 10kmW: 39:40.8 '83, 20kmW: 1:21:16 '80.

**Aleksey PERSHIN** b.8 Mar 1962 Kzyl-Orda 1.75m 65kg. Teacher.
At 20kmW: ECh: '86- 7.
Progression at 20kmW: 1982- 1:27:12, 1984- 1:24:04, 1985- 1:22:54, 1986- 1:23:29.

**Vladimir PLEKHANOV** b.11 Apr 1958 1.85m 80kg. At TJ: EI: '86- 2.
Progression at TJ: 1981- 16.24, 1982- 16.79, 1983- 16.79, 1984- 17.09i, 1985- 17.60, 1986- 17.21i/17.07.

**Vladimir POLYAKOV** b.17 Apr 1960 Aleksin, Tula region 1.90m 75kg. Club: Spartak, Moscow.
At PV: WCh: '83- 10=, ECh: '82- 2; EI: '80- 2, '83- 1; EJ: '79- 1; WSG: '81- 2. USSR champion 1983. Soviet pole vault records at 5.72m and 5.81m in 1981, the latter was a world record.
Progression at PV: 1973- 3.00, 1974- 3.80, 1975-

Igor Paklin. *Mark Shearman*

4.50, 1976- 4.90, 1977- 5.00, 1978- 5.20, 1979-
5.40, 1980- 5.60, 1981- 5.81, 1982- 5.60, 1983-
5.73i, 1984- 5.80, 1985- 5.50, 1986- 5.65.

**Rudolf POVARNITSIN** b.12 Jul 1962 Votkinsk,
Udmurt ASR 2.01m 75kg. Club: Trud Kiev.
World record high jump 1985 with 14cm improvement in personal best.
Progression at HJ: 1980- 2.02, 1981- 2.15, 1982-
2.18, 1983- 2.22, 1984- 2.21, 1985- 2.40, 1986-
2.30.

**Andrey PROKOFYEV** b.6 Jun 1959 Sverdlovsk
1.87m 83kg. At 110mh (R- 4x100m relay): OG:
'80- 4 (1R); WCh: '83- sf (3R); ECh: '82- 2 (1R),
'86- h; WSG: '79- 1, '83- 1; ECp: '83- 5. USSR
champion 1978-9, 1982-3, 1986.
European 110mh record 1986.
Progression at 110mh: 1974- 16.3, 1975- 15.8,
1976- 14.4, 1977- 14.1, 1978- 13.77, 1979-
13.50/13.3, 1980- 13.49, 1981- 13.79/13.6, 1982-
13.46, 1983- 13.46, 1984- 13.57, 1986- 13.28.
pbs: 100m: 10.33/10.1 '82, 10.13dt '80; 200m:
20.9 '77.

**Oleg PROTSENKO** b.11 Aug 1963 Soltsy,
Novgorod 1.91m 82kg. Club: Dynamo Zhukovski.
Sports student.
At TJ: ECh: '86- 3; WCp: '85- 2; ECp: '85- 3.
USSR champion 1985-6.
European TJ record 1985, world indoor best
17.67m 1987.
Progression at TJ: 1979- 15.05i, 1980- 15.94,
1981- 16.68, 1982- 16.59, 1983- 17.27, 1984-
17.52, 1985- 17.67, 1986- 17.59. pb LJ: 8.00i '86.

**Sergey PROTSISHIN** b.17 Apr 1959 Kherson
1.77m 70kg. Club: Avangaard, Lvov. Mechanic.
At 20kmW: LT: '83- 10, '85- 6. At 50kmW: ECh:
'86- 4.
Progression at 20kmW: 1977- 1:34:26, 1978-
1:28:51, 1979- 1:28:50, 1980- 1:29:50, 1981-
1:27:20, 1982- 1:25:09/1:23:04Sh, 1983-
1:22:03, 1984- 1:21:57, 1985- 1:22:33, 1986-
1:23:54. At 50kmW: 1982- 4:04:58, 1986-
3:45.51. pbs: track: 5kmW: 19:34.29i '84,
10kmW: 39:42.7 '83.

**Heino PUUSTE** b.7 Sep 1955 Lagedi, Estonia
1.88m 90kg. Club: Trud, Talinn. Teacher.
At JT: OG: '80- 4; WCh: '83- 4; ECh: '82- 2, '86- 5;
WSG: '79- 3, '81- 3; WCp: '85- 2; ECp: '83- 2.
USSR champion 1979.
Progression at JT: 1973- 64.70, 1974- 72.86,
1975- 76.62, 1976- 80.54, 1977- 82.56, 1978-
84.06, 1979- 84.42, 1980- 89.32, 1981- 87.22,
1982- 90.72, 1983- 94.20, 1984- 91.86, 1985-
88.58, new: 1986- 83.20.

**Yuriy SEDYKH** b.11 Jun 1955 Novocherkassk
1.85m 110kg. Graduate of the Kiev Institute of
Physical Culture.
At HT: OG: '76- 1, '80- 1; WCh: '83- 2; ECh: '78- 1,
'82- 1, '86- 1; EJ: '73-1; WSG: '75- 3, '77- 2, '79- 3;
WCp: '77- 4, '81- 1; ECp: '77- 3, '81- 1. USSR
hammer champion 1976, 1978, 1980.
World junior records in 1973 and 1974, and eight
Soviet records, including six world records: 80.38,
80.64 and 81.80 in 1980, 86.34 in 1984, 86.66
and 86.74 in 1986.
Progression at HT: 1971- 57.02, 1972- 62.96,
1973- 69.04, 1974- 70.86, 1975- 75.00, 1976-
78.86, 1977- 76.60, 1978- 79.76, 1979- 77.58,
1980- 81.80, 1981- 80.18, 1982- 81.66, 1983-
80.94, 1984- 86.34, 1985- 82.70, 1986- 86.74. pb
35lb Wt: 23.46 '79 (former world indoor best).
The greatest hammer thrower of all-time, who
reached new peaks in 1984, throwing consistently over 85 metres, and even better in 1986. At
the European Championships he responded to
Litvinov's opening 85.74 with five throws averaging 86.16 following the world record of 86.74 with
86.68 and 86.62! Coached by his predecessor as
Olympic champion, Anatoliy Bondarchuk. Won
the 1980 Olympic title by setting a new world
record with the first throw of the competition.

**Valeriy SEREDA** b.30 Jun 1959 Pyatigorsk
1.86m 76kg.
Serviceman based in Leningrad.
At HJ: WCh: '83- 8; ECh: '82- 5, '86- 11=; WCp:
'81- 4; ECp: '81- 1, '83- 2. USSR champion 1983,
1986. European high jump record 1984.
Progression at HJ: 1972- 1.60, 1973- 1.80, 1974-
1.85, 1975- 2.00, 1976- 2.09, 1977- 2.15, 1978-
2.16, 1979- 2.20i, 1980- 2.18, 1981- 2.30, 1982-
2.28i, 1983- 2.35, 1984- 2.37, 1985- 2.31i, 1986-
2.34.

**Sergey SMIRNOV** b.17 Sep 1960 Leningrad
1.92m 126kg. Engineer.
At SP: WCh: '83- dnq; ECh: '86- dnc; WSG: '83- 3;
EI: '86- 2; WCp: '85- 2; ECp: '85- 1. USSR cham-
pion 1985-6.
Two USSR shot records 1985-6.
Progression at SP: 1980- 16.31, 1981- 18.86,
1982- 20.42, 1983- 21.00, 1984- 21.63, 1985-
22.05, 1986- 22.24.
Although he qualified, did not take part in the
European shot final in 1986.

**Valeriy SUNTSOV** b.10 Jul 1955 Debessy,
Udmurt ASSR 1.76m 65kg. Club: Burevestnik,
Izhevsk. Engineer.
At 50kmW: ECh: '82- 7, '86- 3; LT: '81- 7, '85- 7. At
20kmW: WSG: '81- 5.
Progression at 50kmW: 1979- 3:56:31, 1980-
3:37:59 (short), 1981- 3:54:14, 1982- 3:46:58,

1983- 3:46:34, 1984- 3:47:44, 1985- 3:42:37, 1986- 3:42:38. pb 20kmW: 1:22:34 '80.

**Juri TAMM** b.5 Feb 1957 Parnu, Estonia 1.93m 120kg. Club: Burevestnik Kiev. Teacher.
At HT: OG: '80- 3; WCp: '85- 1; ECp: '85- 1; WSG: '81- 2, '83- 1.
World hammer record in 1980, only to be overtaken by Yuriy Sedykh in same competition.
Progression at HT: 1974- 49.16, 1975- 54.76, 1976- 66.86, 1977- 72.44, 1978- 74.58, 1979- 75.18, 1980- 80.46, 1981- 77.26, 1982- 74.82, 1983- 79.18, 1984- 84.40, 1985- 84.08, 1986- 80.88.

**Yuriy TARASYUK** b.11 Apr 1957 Minsk 1.88m 101kg. Club: Minsk Burevestnik.
Progression at HT: 1975- 64.50, 1976- 68.52, 1977- 71.20, 1978- 72.70, 1979- 75.46, 1980- 74.78, 1981- 74.86, 1982- 80.72, 1983- 81.18, 1984- 81.44, 1985- 80.22, 1986- 79.34.

**Romas UBARTAS** b.26 May 1960 Lithuania 2.02m 120kg. Teacher.
At DT: ECh: '86- 1. USSR champion 1986.
Progression at DT: 1980- 57.52, 1981- 65.62,

1982- 59.80, 1983- 66.64, 1984- 66.92, 1985- 63.86, 1986- 67.88.

**Sergey USOV** b.14 Jan 1964 Tashkent 1.88m 87kg. Club: Dynamo, Tashkent.
At 110mh: EJ: '83- 2; WCp: '85- 2; ECp: '85- 1. USSR champion 1985.
Progression at 110mh: 1982- 14.29/13.8i, 1983- 13.96/13.8, 1984- 13.74, 1985- 13.56.

**Gennadiy VALYUKEVICH** b.1 Jun 1958 Brest Litovsk 1.82m 74kg. At TJ: WCh: '83- 10; ECh: '78- 5, '82- 4; EI: '79- 1, '82- 2, '83- 2; EJ: '77- 1; WCp: '79- 2. USSR champion 1979 and 1984.
World indoor triple jump bests: 17.18m and 17.29m 1979.
Progression at TJ: 1974- 13.65, 1975- 14.71, 1976- 15.68, 1977- 16.60, 1978- 17.02, 1979- 17.29i, 1980- 16.61, 1981- 17.18, 1982- 17.42, 1983- 17.23, 1984- 17.47, 1985- 17.48, 1986- 17.53/17.75w. pb 100m: 10.4, LJ: 7.41.
Married to Irina Valyukevich (qv). His 17.75m in 1986 exceeded the then European record, but there was no wind gauge.

Aleksandr Vasilyev. *Mark Shearman*

**Aleksandr VASILYEV** b.26 Jul 1961 Shostka, Ukraine 1.91m 83kg.
Club: Soviet Army, Minsk. Soldier.
At 400mh: ECh: '86- 2; WCp: '85- 2; ECp: '85- 2. USSR champion 1985-6.
Three USSR 400mh records 1985.
Progression at 400mh: 1977- 55.6, 1978- 53.69, 1979- 52.06, 1980- 51.51, 1981- 49.84, 1982- 49.64/49.4, 1983- 49.07, 1984- 48.45, 1985- 47.92, 1986- 48.24. pbs: 400m: 46.76 '85, 110mh: 14.31.

**Benjaminas VILUCKIS** b.20 Mar 1961 1.87m 118kg.
USSR hammer champion 1986.
Progression at HT: 1980- 67.80, 1981- 69.82, 1982- 74.12, 1983- 77.50, 1984- 78.20, 1984- 78.20, 1985- 80.42, 1986- 82.24.

**Konstantin VOLKOV** b.28 Feb 1960 Irkutsk 1.85m 79kg. Serviceman based in Irkutsk
At PV: OG: '80- 2=; WCh: '83- 2; EI: '79- 2, '80- 1, '82- 2; WSG: '81- 1, '83- 1; WCp: '79- 3, '81- 1; ECp: '79- 1, '81- 1=. USSR champion 1979.
World junior pole vault records at 5.55m and 5.60m in 1979 and four USSR records 1980-4.
Progression at PV: 1971- 2.80, 1972- 3.10, 1973- 3.20, 1974- 3.70, 1975- 4.40, 1976- 4.60, 1977- 4.90, 1978- 5.35, 1979- 5.60, 1980- 5.70i, 1981- 5.75, 1982- 5.65i, 1983- 5.70, 1984- 5.85, 1985- 5.50, 1986- 5.65i.
Excellent competitor. A mark of 5.84m in 1981, in excess of the then world record, was described as an exhibition mark. His father Yuriy vaulted 5.16i in 1970.

**Aleksandr YAKOVLEV** b.8 Sep 1957 Irpen, Kiev 1.82m 74kg.
At TJ: EI: '78- 3; WSG: '85- 2.
Progression at TJ: 1972- 13.76, 1973- 14.41, 1974- 15.56, 1975- 15.80, 1976- 16.60, 1977- 16.83, 1978- 16.89, 1979- 16.95, 1980- 16.73, 1981- 16.63, 1982- 16.93, 1983- 17.05i, 1984- 17.50, 1985- 17.43, 1986- 17.26. pb LJ: 8.10i '84.

**Aleksandr YEVGENYEV** b.20 Jul 1961 Leningrad 1.74m 70kg. Club: Dynamo, Leningrad. Teacher.
At 200m (R- 4x100m relay): ECh: '86- 6 (1R); EI: '83- 1, '84- 1, '85- 3, '86- 2; WIG: '85- 1; WCp: '85- 3R. USSR champion 1986. At 100m: ECh: '82- sf.
Progression at 200m: 1976- 23.7, 1977- 22.5, 1978- 21.84, 1980- 21.4, 1981- 21.19, 1982- 21.06, 1983- 20.72, 1984- 20.41, 1985- 20.42, 1986- 20.50. pb 100m: 10.22 '84.

**Viktor YEVSYUKOV** b.6 Oct 1956 Donetsk 1.90m 100kg. Teacher.
At JT: ECh: '86- 3; ECp: '85-2. USSR champion

1984. World new javelin best 1986.
Progression at JT: 1977- 79.32, 1978- 76.76, 1979- 84.48, 1980- 85.20, 1981- 84.42, 1982- 87.50, 1983- 88.10, 1984- 90.94, 1985- 93.70, new: '86- 83.68.

**Tagir ZEMSKOV** b.6 Aug 1962 Leningrad 1.82m 67kg. Student.
At 400mh: ECh: '86- 5; EJ: '81- 4; WSG: '85- 1 (2 4x400mR); ECp: '85- 5. USSR champion 1985.
Progression at 400mh: 1980- 52.8, 1981- 50.79, 1982- 50.13, 1983- 49.53, 1984- 49.7/50.05, 1985- 49.33/49.2, 1986- 49.07.

# Women

**Nunu ABASHIDZE** b.27 Mar 1955 Novo-Volyansk 1.68m 105kg. Club: Dynamo, Odessa. Sports instructor.
At SP: OG: '80- 4; WCh: '83- 4; ECh: '82- 3, '86- 6; EJ: '73- 4; ECp: '79- 2, '83- 3; WIG: '85- 3. USSR champion 1979, 1982 and 1984.
Progression at SP: 1970- 12.04, 1971- 13.15, 1972- 14.71, 1973- 16.64, 1974- 17.72, 1975- 17.59, 1976- 19.08, 1978- 18.62, 1979- 20.25, 1980- 21.37, 1981- 18.57i, 1982- 21.23, 1983- 20.94, 1984- 21.53, 1985- 20.45, 1986- 20.90.
Suspended for drugs use at the 1981 European Indoors.

**Ravilya AGLETDINOVA** b.10 Feb 1960 Kurgan-Tyube, Tadzhikstan 1.69m 57kg. Club: Urozhai, Minsk. Teacher.
At 1500m: WCh: '83- 4; ECh: '86- 1; EJ: '77- 10; WCp: '85- 2, ECp: '85- 1. At 800m: ECh: '82- 4. USSR champion 800m & 1500m 1985.
Progression at 800m/1500m: 1974- 2:24.8, 1975- 2:10.8/4:39.6, 1976- 2:06.01/4:21.5, 1977- 2:04.0/4:14.42, 1978- 2:03.6/4:16.1, 1979- 2:04.2/4:11.5, 1980- 2:02.0/4:06.6, 1981- 1:58.65/4:04.40, 1982- 1:56.1/4:07.41, 1983- 1:57.0/3:59.31, 1984- 1:58.08/3:58.70, 1985- 1:56.24/3:58.40, 1986- 1:59.37/3:59.84. pb 1000m: 2:37.18i '84.

**Natalya AKHRIMENKO** b.12 May 1955 Novo-kuybyshevsk 1.84m 90kg. née Petrova. Teacher.
At SP: OG: '80- 7; ECh: '86- 3; WSG: '83- 3 (2 DT).
Progression at SP: 1973- 14.34, 1974- 16.13, 1977- 18.18, 1978- 19.09, 1979- 18.24, 1980- 20.44, 1981- 17.44, 1982- 20.34, 1983- 20.25, 1984- 20.10, 1985- 21.08, 1986- 21.39. pb DT: 64.60 '80.

**Vera AKIMOVA** b.5 Jun 1959 Tashkent 1.68m 58kg. née Yeremeryeva, then Tinkova. Teacher.
At 100mh: ECh: '86- sf; ECp: '85- 2. USSR champion 1985-6. EI 60mh: '84- 2.

Ravilya Ageltdinova. *Mark Shearman*

Progression at 100mh: 1975- 14.5, 1976- 13.8, 1977- 13.6, 1978- 13.4, 1979- 13.28/12.9, 1980- 13.4, 1981- 13.2, 1982- 13.2/13.63, 1983- 13.03/ 12.7/12.88w, 1984- 12.50, 1985- 12.59, 1986- 12.68. pb 100m: 11.7.

**Natalya ARTYEMOVA** b.5 Jan 1963 Rostov-on-Don 1.66m 49kg. Club: Dynamo, Leningrad. Student.
At 3000m: WCh: '83- 8. USSR champion 1983.
Set unratified world 1 mile record at 4:15.8 in 1984, USSR record at 5000m 1985.
Progression at 1500m/3000m: 1979- 5:00.6, 1980- 4:36.0, 1981- 4:32.2, 1982- 4:10.6/9:15.0, 1983- 4:02.63/8:47.98, 1984- 4:00.68/8:38.84, 1985- 3:59.28/8:46.1. pbs: 400m: 53.5 '84, 800m: 1:58.05 '85, 1000m: 2:37.45i '84, 1M: 4:15.8 '84, 5000m: 14:54.80 '85.

**Elvira BARBASHINA** b.25 Feb 1963 1.66m 57kg.
At 200m (R- 4x100m relay): WCp: '85- 2R; ECp: '85- 2 (2R). USSR champion 1985.
Progression at 100m/200m: 1983- 11.61/11.37w/ 11.3/23.66, 1984- 11.39/23.23, 1985- 11.21/ 22.50, 1986- 11.12/22.27.

**Natalya BOCHINA** b.4 Jan 1962 Leningrad 1.74m 59kg. Club: Dynamo, Leningrad. Student.
At 100m/200m (R- 4x100m relay): OG: '80- sf/2 (2R); ECh: '86- -/6 (3R); EJ: '79- -/3= (2R); WCp: '81- 5/5 (3R), '85- 2R; ECp: '81- -/3 (3R). At 400m: EI: '81- 2. USSR 100m & 200m champion 1981.
Four world junior 200m records 1980.
Progression at 200m: 1978- 23.72, 1979- 23.22, 1980- 22.19, 1981- 22.90/22.5, 1984- 22.45/22.1, 1985- 22.73, 1986- 22.60. pbs: 100m: 11.22/11.0 '80, 400m: 51.47 '81.

**Olga BONDARENKO** b.2 Jun 1960 Altay 1.53m 41kg. née Krentser. Teacher.
At 3000m: ECh: '86- 1; EI: '85- 2. At 10000m: ECh: '86- 2; WCp: '85- 3; ECp: '85- 1. USSR champion 3000m and 5000m 1985. 7th world CC 1985.
World records at 10000m in 1981 and 1984, USSR records: 5000m 1985, 10000m (3) 1981-6.
Progression at 3000m/10000m: 1978- 9:24.8, 1979- 9:08.2, 1980- 8:52.5, 1981- 8:51.5/ 32:30.80, 1982- 8:57.73i/35:08.0, 1983- 8:47.02/ 31:35.61, 1984- 8:36.20/31:13.78, 1985- 8:42.19/ 31:25.18, 1986- 8:33.99/30:57.21. pbs: 1500m: 4:05.99 '86, 2000m: 5:40.15 '86, 5000m: 14:55.76 '85, Mar: 2:43:24 '84.
Misjudged the finish of the 1985 World Cup 10000m to mar a great season, but returned to another fine year in 1986 with gold and silver at the Europeans.

**Yelena BYELEVSKAYA** b.11 Oct 1963 Evpatoria 1.77m 57kg. née Mityayeva. Student.
At LJ: ECh: '86- 7. USSR champion 1986.
Progression at LJ: 1980- 6.23, 1981- 6.41, 1982- 6.61, 1983- 6.76, 1984- 6.88, 1985- 7.00, 1986- 7.31.

**Tamara BYKOVA** b.21 Dec 1958 Azov, near Rostov-on-Don 1.80m 58kg. Club: Burevestnik, Rostov-on-Don. Student of education.
At HJ: OG: '80- 9; WCh: '83- 1; ECh: '82- 2, '86- dnq; EI: '83- 1; WSG: '81- 3, '83- 1; WCp: '81- 2, '85- 2; ECp: '83- 2, '85- 2. USSR champion 1980, 1982-3, 1985. 3rd GP 1985.
World indoor high jump bests: 2.02m and 2.03m 1983. World records: 2.03m and 2.04m 1983, 2.05m 1984. Eight USSR records.
Progression at HJ: 1974- 1.50, 1975- 1.72, 1976- 1.70, 1977- 1.70, 1978- 1.85, 1979- 1.88, 1980-

1.97, 1981- 1.96, 1982- 1.98, 1983- 2.04, 1984- 2.05, 1985- 2.02, 1986- 1.96.

**Galina CHISTYAKOVA** b.26 Jul 1962 Izmail, Ukraine 1.69m 55kg. Club: Moskva Burevestnik. Sports student. Married to Aleksandr Beskrovniy (TJ: 17.53m '84, 1 EJ '79, 5 ECh '82).
At LJ: ECh: '86- 2; EI: '85- 1; WCp: '85- 2, ECp: '85- 1. Won GP 1985.
Three USSR long jump records 1984-6.
Progression at LJ: 1973- 3.75, 1974- 4.20, 1975- 4.96, 1976- 5.25, 1977- 5.80, 1978- 6.04, 1979- 6.43, 1980- 6.43, 1981- 6.36/6.54w, 1982- 6.43, 1984- 7.29, 1985- 7.28, 1986- 7.34. pb 100m: 11.6 '84.
Gave birth to a daughter in 1983.

**Olga GAVRILOVA** b. 8 Feb 1957 Svobodny 1.76m 75kg. Club: Spartak, Leningrad. Sports instructor.
At JT: WCp: '85- 1.
Progression at JT: 1981- 53.90, 1982- 58.20, 1983- 63.10, 1984- 63.52, 1985- 66.80, 1986- 59.82.

**Aleksandra GRIGORYEVA** b.1 Jan 1960 Chuvashia 1.68m 56kg. Teacher.
At 5kmW: WSG: '85- 1. At 10kmW: ECh: ECh: '86- 7; WCp: '85- 3=.
Track pbs: 3kmW: 12:31 '86, 5kmW: 21:55.99 '85, 10kmW: 46:00.27 '86. Road pbs: 5kmW: 21:42 '86, 10kmW: 45:33 '86.

**Natalya GRIGORYEVA** b.3 Dec 1962 Ishimbay 1.73m 60kg. née Dorofeyeva. Student.
At 100mh: ECh: '86- 7.
Progression at 100mh: 1982- 13.77/13.4, 1983- 13.26, 1984- 13.20/12.7, 1985- 12.89/12.8, 1986- 12.61. pb 400mh: 57.9 '83.

**Lyubov GURINA** b.6 Aug 1957 Matushkino, Kirov region 1.67m 55kg. Club: Trud, Kirov. Sports instructor.
At 800m: WCh: '83- 2; ECh: '86- 3.
World record at 4x800m relay 1984.
Progression at 800m: 1976- 2:15.7, 1977- 2:08.0, 1978- 2:04.6, 1979- 2:00.2, 1980- 1:59.9, 1981- 1:58.72, 1982- 1:57.3, 1983- 1:56.11, 1984- 1:56.26, 1986- 1:57.52. pbs: 400m: 51.38 '83, 1000m: 2:37.60i '83, 1500m: 4:06.34 '86.
Goodwill Games winner 1986.

**Svetlana GUSAROVA** b.29 May 1959 Murmansk 1.64m 56kg. Servicewoman in Alma Ata.
At 100mh: WCp: '85- 3.
Progression at 100mh: 1977- 13.97, 1978- 13.6, 1979- 13.90, 1980- 13.21, 1981- 13.50, 1982- 13.16/12.8, 1983- 12.86, 1984- 12.74, 1985- 12.61. pbs: 100m: 11.52 '85, 200m: 23.3 '82.

**Svetlana GUSKOVA** b.19 Aug 1959 Tiraspol, Moldavia 1.63m 49kg. Club: Trudovye Rezervy, Tiraspol. Sports instructor.
At 10000m: ECh: '86- 5; WSG: '85- 2. At 3000m: ECp: '79- 1. At 1500m: EI: '79- 3. Won GP 5000m 1986.
Progression at 3000m/10000m: 1976- 9:14.8, 1977- 9:12.54, 1978- 8:47.6, 1979- 8:46.8, 1982- 8:29.36, 1983- 8:35.06, 1984- 8:29.59/35:05.6, 1985- 8:51.14/31:57.80, 1986- 8:42.04/31:42.43.
pbs: 800m: 1:59.5 '78, 1000m: 2:38.69i '84, 1500m: 3:57.05 '82, 2000m: 5:44.64 '84, 5000m: 15:02.12 '86.

**Yekaterina KHRAMENKOVA** b.6 Oct 1956 Minsk 1.70m 49kg. University lecturer.
At Mar: ECh: '86- 3; ECp: '85- 8.
Progression at Mar: 1984- 2:36:39, 1985- 2:32:24, 1986- 2:34:18.

**Margarita KHROMOVA** b.19 Jun 1963 Balkhash, Kazakhstan 1.78m 58kg. née Ponomaryeva. Club: Trudovye Reservy, Leningrad. Student of economics.
At 400mh: ECh: '86- 8; EJ: '81- 3 (2 at 4x400mR); WCp: '85- 6.
World record for 400mh in 1984.
Progression at 400mh: 1981- 57.45, 1983- 56.9, 1984- 53.58, 1985- 55.48, 1986- 54.57. pb 400m: 52.05 '84, 52.0 '86.

**Lyubov KIRYUKHINA** b.10 May 1963 Fergana 1,65m 65kg. Student.
At 800m: ECh: '86- 7; EJ: '81- 3 (2 4x400mR).
USSR champion 1986.
Progression at 800m: 1980- 2:04.76, 1981- 2:01.36, 1982- 2:00.65, 1983- 1:59.46, 1984- 1:58.87, 1986- 1:57.18. pbs: 400m: 52.9 '83, 1000m: 2:39.73i '85, 1500m: 4:07.18 '82.

**Svetlana KITOVA** b.25 Jun 1960 Dushanbe 1.68m 60kg. Club: Trudovye Reservye, Moskva.
At 1500m: ECh: '86- 6; EI: '86- 1; WSG: '85- 1. At 800m: EI: '83- 1; WSG: '85- 4.
Progression at 800m/1500m: 1978- 2:07.1, 1979- 2:06.5, 1980- 2:01.3, 1981- 2:02.1, 1982- 1:59.51, 1983- 1:58.82, 1984- 1:58.08, 1985- 1:59.6/4:05.77, 1986- 2:01.43i/4:01.83. pb 1000m: 2:37.93i '85.

**Yelena KOKONOVA** b.4 Aug 1963 1.71m 64kg. née Stetsura.
At LJ: EI: '86- 3. USSR champion 1984-5.
USSR LJ record 1985.
Progression at LJ: 1981- 6.20, 1982- 6.50, 1983- 6.83, 1984- 7.09, 1985- 7.31, 1986- 7.00i.

**Nadezhda KORSHUNOVA** b.13 Jul 1961
Gissar, Tadzikistan SSR 1.69m 56kg. Club:
Spartak Kharkov. Student.
At 100mh: WSG: '85- 2 (2 4x100mR).
Progression at 100mh: 1978 - 14.1, 1979- 13.92,
1980- 13.4, 1981- 13.60/13.2, 1982- 13.48/12.9,
1983- 12.99/12.97w, 1984- 12.65, 1985- 12.71.


**Larisa KOSITSYNA** b.14 Dec 1963 Ashkhabad
1.82m 67kg. Student.
At HJ: WCh: '83- 17; ECh: '86- 9=; EJ: '81- 3; EI:
'83- 2, '86- 3.
Progression at HJ: 1980- 1.83i, 1981-1.86, 1982-
1.95, 1983- 1.98, 1984- 1.90i, 1985- 1.97, 1986-
1.98i/1.94.


**Olga KRISHTOP** b.23 Jun 1957.
At 10kmW: WCp: '85- 3=.
World record for 5kmW in 1985.
Track pbs: 5kmW: 21:36.2 '84, 10kmW: 47:21.47
'86. Road: 10kmW: 44:43 '86.


**Lidia LEVANDOVSKAYA** b.5 Oct 1962 Ivano-
Frankovsk 1.70m 56kg. Student.
At 10kmW: ECh: '86- 6.
Track pbs: 3kmW: 12:46 '86, 5kmW: 22:20.8 '85,
10kmW: 45:20.8 '86. Road pbs: 5kmW: 22:12 '85,
20kmW: 1:41:19 '86.


**Natalya LISOVSKAYA** b.16 Jul 1962 Alegazy,
Bashkir ASSR 1.88m 94kg. Club: Spartak, Moscow. Student.
At SP: WCh: '83- 5; ECh: '86- 9; EI: '82- 3; WCp:
'85- 1; ECp: '85- 1; WSG: '83- 1; WIG: '85- 1.
USSR champion 1981, 1983, 1985-6. 2nd GP
1986. World shot record in 1984.
Progression at SP: 1978- 13.22, 1979- 14.50,
1980- 14.91, 1981- 18.66, 1982- 19.84, 1983-
20.85, 1984- 22.53, 1985- 21.73, 1986- 21.70. pb
DT: 63.44 '82.


**Marianna MASLENNIKOVA** b.17 May 1961
Leningrad 1.73m 66kg. Student.
At Hep: ECh: '86- 5; ECp: '85- 5.
Progression at Hep: 1981- 5333, 1982- 6079,
1983- 5863, 1984- 6374, 1985- 6264, 1986-
6416. pbs: 200m: 24.09 '85, 800m: 2:04.44 '85,
100mh: 13.37 '85, HJ: 1.88 '86, LJ: 6.44 '84, SP:
13.35 '86, JT: 38.96 '85.


**Marina MOLOKOVA** b.24 Aug 1962 Irkutsk
1.73m 61kg. Student.
At 200m: ECh: '86- 4. USSR champion 1986.

Progression at 200m: 1982- 24.02/23.7, 1983-
23.33, 1984- 22.97, 1985- 22.76, 1986- 22.46. pb
100m: 11.22 '86.

Nadezhda OLIZARENKO. *ASP*


**Nadezhda OLIZARENKO** b.28 Nov 1953
Bryansk 1.65m 54kg. née Mushta. Married to
Sergey Olizarenko (3kmSt 8:24.0 '78). Sports
instructor in Odessa.
At 800m: OG: '80- 1 (3 at 1500m); ECh: '78- 2 (2 at
4x400mR), '86- 1; EI: '85- 2; WSG: '79- 1; WCp:
'79- 2, '85- 3; ECp: '85- 2 (2R). USSR champion
1980.
Two world records for 800m in 1980, 1:54.85 and
1:53.43, the latter in winning the Olympic title, and
also ran on the world record 4x800m team 1984.
Progression at 800m: 1970- 2:11.4, 1972- 2:08.6,
1974- 2:05.0, 1975- 2:03.3, 1976- 2:05.8, 1977-
1:59.76, 1978- 1:55.82, 1979- 1:57.5, 1980-
1:53.43, 1983- 1:58.16, 1984- 1:56.09, 1985-
1:56.25, 1986- 1:57.15. pbs: 400m: 50.96 '80,
1500m: 3:56.8 '80.

**Maria PINIGINA** b.9 Feb 1958 Ivanovo, Frunze, Kirghizia 1.71m 57kg. née Kulchunova. Club: Spartak, Kiev. Sports instructor.
At 400m (R- 4x400m relay): WCh: '83- 3 (3R); ECh: '78- 4 (2R), '86- dnc sf; EJ: '75- 4; WSG: '79- 1, '83- 1(1R); WCp: '79- 2, '85- 2R; ECp: '79- 2 (2R), '83- 2 (2R), '85- 1R. USSR champion 1978- 9, 1983, 1986.
Four USSR 400m records 1979-84.
Progression at 400m: 1971- 64.4, 1972- 64.3, 1973- 57.4, 1974- 54.47, 1975- 52.62, 1976- 51.80, 1977- 52.92, 1978- 50.83, 1979- 49.63, 1980- 51.2/51.45, 1983- 49.19, 1984- 49.74, 1985- 49.61, 1986- 50.29. pbs: 100m: 11.4 '76, 200m: 22.80 '83, 800m: 2:08.4.

**Irina PODYALOVSKAYA** b.19 Oct 1959 Vishenka, Mogilev region 1.65m 53kg. Club: Trudovye Reservy, Moscow. Student.
At 800m: WSG: '83- 1. USSR champion 1983.
World record at 4x800m relay 1984.
Progression at 800m: 1975- 2:08.2, 1976- 2:06.03, 1977- 2:03.65, 1979- 2:01.6, 1981- 2:00.2, 1982- 1:59.64, 1983- 1:57.99, 1984- 1:55.69, 1985- 1:57.6, 1986- 1:57.86. pb 400m: 51.67 '84.

**Yelena POLITIKA** b.24 Aug 1964 Akhtyrka 1.72m 64kg. née Kudinova. Student.
At 100mh: ECh: '86- sf.
Progression at 100mh: 1982- 13.5, 1983- 13.47, 1984- 13.21/12.8, 1985- 13.10/13.0, 1986- 12.71.

**Marina RODCHENKOVA** b.30 Jul 1961 Moskva.
At 10000m: WSG: '85- 1. At 1500m: EJ: '79- 5.
World road 15km: '86- 9. pbs: 1500m: 4:07.27 '84, 3000m: 8:48.54 '84, 5000m: 15:19.26 '85, 10000m: 32:32.55 '85.

**Yelena RODIONOVA** b.7 May 1965 Chelyabinsk 1.72m 60kg.
At 10kmW: ECh: '86- 4.
Track pbs: 10kmW: 46:21.13 '86. Road pbs: 5kmW: 22:13 '85, 10kmW: 46:02 '86.

**Tatyana SAMOLENKO** b.12 Aug 1961 Orenburg 1.66m 57kg. née Khamitova. Teacher.
At 1500m/3000m: ECh: '86- 2/5. USSR 1500m champion 1986.
Progression at 1500m/3000m: 1980- 4:25.2, 1983- 4:10.85, 1984- 4:02.41, 1985- 4:02.41, 1986- 3:59.45/8:36.00. pbs: 400m: 53.5 '86, 800m: 1:58.56 '85, 1000m: 2:39.4i '84..
The European silver medal was her only loss at 1500m in 1986.

**Natalya SHUBENKOVA** b.25 Sep 1957 Srosty, Altay province. 1.72m 64kg. Club: Dynamo, Barnaul. Teacher.

At Hep: WCh: '83- dnf; ECh: '82- 5, '86- 2; ECp: '81- 7, '85- 2. USSR champion 1983-6.
USSR heptathlon record 1984.
Progression at Hep: 1980- 5332, 1981- 5993, 1982- 6524, 1983- 6517, 1984- 6859, 1985- 6510, 1986- 6645. pbs: 200m: 23.57 '84, 800m: 2:03.61 '86, 100mh: 12.93 '84, HJ: 1.83 '84, LJ: 6.73 '84, SP: 13.94 '86, JT: 51.42 '85.

**Irina SLYUSSAR** b.19 Mar 1963 Dneprodzerzhinsk 1.66m 56kg. Student.
At 100m/200m: ECh: '86- sf/-; WSG: '85- 1/3 (2R).
USSR 100m champion 1986.
Progression at 100m, 200m: 1982- 11.5, 25.34; 1983- 11.2/11.52w, 23.1; 1984- 11.27, 22.76; 1985- 11.11/10.8, 22.59; 1986- 11.09, 22.98.

Marina Stepanova. *ASP*

**Marina STEPANOVA** b.1 May 1950 Meglevo 1.70m 60kg. née Makeyeva. Club: Leningrad. Sports instructress.
At 400mh: ECh: '78- 6, '86- 1; WCp: '79- 2; ECp: '79- 1, '85- 2. USSR champion 1979 and 1985.
Three world 400mh records 1979-86.
Progression at 400mh: 1976- 60.80, 1977- 58.75, 1978- 56.16, 1979- 54.78, 1980- 55.21, 1983- 56.03, 1984- 53.67, 1985- 54.37, 1986- 52.94. pbs: 300m: 37.68i '86, 400m: 51.25 '80, 800m: 1:59.8 '80.
Gave birth to daughter Marina in December 1981.
Won the 1986 European 400mh title in a world record 53.32, the oldest woman ever to set a world record. She improved further to 52.94 at Tashkent on 17 September at the age of 36 years 139 days.

**Olga TURCHAK** b.5 Mar 1967 Alma-Ata 1.90m 60kg. Student.
At HJ: ECh: '86- 3; EJ: '85- 2. USSR champion

1986. World junior high jump record 1984.
Progression at HJ: 1983- 1.84, 1984- 1.96, 1985-
1.95, 1986- 2.01.

**Svetlana ULMASSOVA** b.4 Feb 1953 Novo
Balakhly, Uzbek SSR 1.61m 53kg. née Glukhar-
yeva.
At 3000m: WCh: '83- 4; ECh: '78- 1, '82- 1; WSG:
'75- 3; WCp: '79- 1. USSR champion 3000m
1978-9, 1982; 5000m 1986. World 3000m record
1982, also USSR record 1976.
Progression at 3000m/5000m: 1973- 10:23.5,
1974- 9:18.6, 1975- 8:55.88, 1976- 8:48.4, 1977-
8:58.6, 1978- 8:33.16, 1979- 8:36.32, 1981-
8:33.16, 1982- 8:26.78, 1983- 8:35.55, 1986-
8:39.19/15:05.50. pbs: 800m: 2:00.8 '79, 1000m:
2:33.6 '79, 1500m: 3:58.76 '82, 1M: 4:23.8 '81,
10000m: 32:14.83 '86.
Returned to top-class competition in 1986 after
two years out.

**Irina VALYUKEVICH** b.19 Nov 1959 Kaliningrad
1.70m 60kg. Shopkeeper. née Apollonova, married to Gennadiy Valyukevich (qv).
At LJ: ECh: '86- 15, WSG: '85- 1.
Progression at LJ: 1983- 6.46, 1984- 6.95, 1985-
7.07, 1986- 7.07/7.10w.

**Olga VLADYKINA** b.30 Jun 1963 Krasnokamsk,
Perm 1.70m 62kg. Club: Dynamo, Voroshilovgrad. Economics student.
At 400m: ECh: '86- 2; WCp: '85- 2 (2R); ECp: '85-
1 (1R). USSR champion 1984-5.
Four USSR 400m records 1984-5.
Progression at 400m: 1977- 63.0, 1978- 59.8,
1979- 57.8, 1980- 55.49, 1981- 54.23, 1982-
51.89, 1983- 50.48, 1984- 48.98, 1985- 48.27,
1986- 49.67. pbs: 100m: 11.3 '85, 200m: 22.44
'85.

**Galina YERMAKOVA** b.15 Jul 1953 Kemerovo
1.82m 98kg. née Savinkova. Club: Dynamo,
Moscow. Sports instructor.
At DT: WCh: '83- 11; ECh: '82- 3, '86- 6; WCp: '81-
3, '85- 2; ECp: '81- 2, '85- 1. USSR champion
1984.
Three USSR discus records 1983-4, including a
world record in 1983.
Progression at DT: 1971- 33.00, 1972- 41.10,
1973- 55.72, 1974- 59.78, 1976- 76.60, 1977-
61.48, 1978- 62.18, 1979- 65.78, 1980- 67.22,
1981- 69.70, 1982- 69.90, 1983- 73.26, 1984-
73.28, 1985- 72.96, 1986- 68.32. pb SP: 16.50
'80.

**Natalya YERMOLOVICH** b.29 Apr 1964 Gomel
1.75m 80kg. Student née Kolenchukovo.
At JT: ECh: '86- 6; ECp: '85- 3. USSR champion
1985.

Olga Vladykina. *ASP*

Progression at JT: 1981- 49.86, 1982- 56.96,
1983- 61.62, 1984- 64.26, 1985- 69.86, 1986-
65.68, 1986- 66.64.

**Marina ZHIROVA** b.6 Jun 1963 Yegoryevsk,
Moskva 1.72m 62kg. née Titova. Club: Trud.
Moscow. Student.
At 100m (R- 4x100m relay): WCp: '85- 2= (2R, 3
200m); ECp: '85- 2 (2R). At 200m: ECh: '86- 8
(3R). USSR champion 1985.
USSR 100m record 1985.
Progression at 100m, 200m: 1977- 12.4, 25.4;
1978- 11.9/11.4w, 24.9; 1979- 11.97/11.6/
11.72w, 24.31; 1980- 11.8, 24.6; 1981- 11.5,
24.3; 1982- 11.4, 23.4; 1983- 11.80, 23.4/23.71;
1984- 11.24, 23.20; 1985- 10.98, 22.46; 1986-
11.44, 22.93.

**Yelena ZHUPIYEVA** b.18 Apr 1960 Arkhangelsk
1.58m 46kg. née Durshan. Engineer.
At 3000m/10000m: ECh: '86- 6/6.
Progression at 3000m/10000m: 1979- 9:31.1,
1981- 8:55.8/33:18.12, 1984- 8:39.52, 1985-
8:38.1/32:25.37, 1986- 8:40.74/31:42.99. pbs:
1500m: 4:04.44 '84, 5000m: 15:23.25 '86.

**Lyubov ZVERKOVA** b.14 Jun 1955 1.80m
101kg. née Krakova. Then Urakova.
USSR discus champion 1985.

Progression at DT: 1973- 52.74, 1974- 50.86, 1975- 53.18, 1979- 59.34, 1980- 57.12, 1981- 59.64, 1982- 64.00, 1983- 64.68, 1984- 68.58, 1985- 66.64, 1986- 66.84.

**Ellina ZVERYEVA** b.16 Nov 1960 Dolgoprudny 1.82m 90kg. formerly Kisheyeva. Student.
At DT: USSR champion 1986.
Progression at DT: 1981- 59.88, 1982- 62.52, 1983- 65.18, 1984- 68.56, 1985- 66.64, 1986- 68.96.

---

# VENEZUELA

**Governing body**: Federacion Venezolana de Atletismo, Instituto Nacional de Deportes la Vega, Caracas.

**William WUYKE** b.21 May 1958 1.73m 63kg. Was at University of Alabama, USA.
At 800m: OG: '80- qf, '84- sf; WCh: '83- h; SACh: '77- 2, '79- 2; CAmG: '82- 2. Won AAA 1983.
Progression at 800m: 1976- 1:52.3, 1977- 1:47.1, 1978- 1:48.9, 1979- 1:47.9, 1980- 1:47.0, 1981- 1:48.9, 1982- 1:45.75, 1983- 1:45.07, 1984- 1:43.93, 1986- 1:43.54. pbs: 400m: 46.69 '84, 600m: 1:17.5 '86, 1000m: 2:16.56 '83, 1500m: 3:44.53 '84.

---

# YUGOSLAVIA

**Governing body**: Atletski Savez Jugoslavije, Stahinica Bana 73a, 11000 Beograd. Founded in 1921.
**National Championships** first held in 1920 (men) and 1923 (women)
**1986 champions: MEN**
100m/200m: Mladen Nikolic 10.62/21.29, 400m: Ismail Macev 46.60, 800m: Slobodan Popovic 1:48.23, 1500m/5000m: Romeo Zivko 3:45.59/ 14:18.20, 10000m: Milorad Paunovic 30:23.45, Mar: Tomislav Askovic 2:18:56, 3kmSt: Slobodan Crnokrak 8:48.22, 110mh: Ales Kolar 14.42, 400mh: Rok Kopitar 51.51, HJ: Novica Canovic 2.22, PV: Zelimir Sarcevic 5.00, LJ: Lahor Marinovic 7.60, TJ: Djordje Kozul 16.18, SP: Vladimir Milic 19.54, DT: Zeljko Tarabaric 55.26, HT: Srecko Stiglic 64.36 (his 21st successive title), JT: Darko Cujnik 74.08, Dec: Sasa Karan 7337, 20kmW: Edvard Kolar 1:38:19.

**WOMEN**
100m: Marina Flajsman 11.78, 200m: Dijana Istvanovic 24.03, 400m/800m: Slobodanka Colovic 53.41/1:59.63, 1500m/3000m: Snezana Pajkic 4:15.75/9:23.33, Mar: Marija Kusnjacic 3:32:59, 100mh: Gordana Cotric 14.45, 400mh: Irena Dominc 59.95, HJ: Biljana Petrovic 1.87, LJ: Snezana Dancetovic 6.22, SP/JT: Danica Zivanov 16.67/55.86, DT: Snezana Golubic 54.02, Hep: Marina Mihajlova 5207.

**Sejad KRDZALIC** b.5 Jan 1960 Zenica 1.86m 93kg. Club: Partizan, Beograd. Electrician and student of physical education.
At JT: OG: '84- dnq; ECh: '86- 7. Balkan champion 1986.
Four Yugoslav javelin records 1984-5, six with new javelin 1986.
Progression at JT: 1977- 51.06, 1978- 63.86, 1979- 61.26, 1980- 66.24, 1981- 69.16, 1982- 71.90, 1983- 80.86, 1984- 83.70, 1985- 85.10, new: 1986- 82.34.

**Nenad STEKIC** b.7 Mar 1951 Beograd 1.81m 73kg. Club: Crvena zvezda, Beograd. Commercial agent. Economics graduate of University of Beograd.
At LJ: OG: '76- 6, '80- dnq, '84- dnq; WCh: '83- 5; ECh: '69- 10, '71- dnq, '74- 2, '78- 2, '82- 5; EI: '80- 2; EJ: '70- 3; WSG: '75- 2, '77- 1; WCp: '77- 4; ECp: '79- 4, '81- 7. Balkan champion 1973-4, 1976, 1978-80; Yugoslav champion 1972-7, 1983, 1985.
Five Yugoslav long jump records 1969-75, including European record 8.45m 1975.
Progression at LJ: 1965- 6.27, 1966- 6.49, 1968- 7.34, 1969- 7.73/7.78w, 1970- 7.71/7.75w, 1971- 7.85, 1972- 7.60, 1973- 7.96/8.12w, 1974- 8.24, 1975- 8.45, 1976- 8.12/8.39w, 1977- 8.27/8.32w, 1978- 8.32, 1979- 8.27, 1980- 8.11/8.19w, 1981- 8.01, 1982- 8.12, 1983- 8.11, 1984- 8.10, 1985- 8.07, 1986- 8.19. pbs: 100m: 10.4 '74, HJ: 1.95 '68, TJ: 14.93 '77.
47 Internationals 1969-86, and 116 8-metre plus jumps in 52 competitions. At 35 in 1986 he is the oldest 8m long jumper ever.

---

# Women

**Slobodanka COLOVIC** b.10 Jan 1965 Osijek 1.73m 56kg. Club: Slavonija, Osijek. Student.
At 800m: ECh: '86- sf; EJ: '83- 4. EI: '86- 3. Balkan champion 1986.
Progression at 800m: 1978- 2:15.8, 1979- 2:13.9, 1980- 2:10.1, 1981- 2:08.21, 1982- 2:04.65, 1983- 2:02.47, 1984- 2:03.04, 1985- 2:01.37, 1986- 1:59.63. pbs: 100m: 12.3 '83, 200m: 25.29 '83, 400m: 53.41 '86.

# WORLD AND CONTINENTAL RECORDS
# WORLD LISTS AND INDEX
## Introduction

## RECORDS

World, World Junior, Olympic, Continental and Area records are listed. In running events up to and including 400 metres, only fully automatic times are shown. Marks listed are those which are considered statistically acceptable by the ATFS, and thus may differ from official records where, for instance the performance was set indoors or while the athlete was a professional.

## WORLD ALL-TIME and WORLD YEAR LISTS

These lists are presented in the following format: Mark, Wind reading (where appropriate), Name, Nationality (abbreviated), Year of birth (last two digits), Position in competition, Meeting name (if significant), Venue, Date of performance.

Position, meet and venue details have been omitted for reasons of space beyond 50th place in all-time lists and 100th in year lists.

## INDEX

These lists contain the names of all athletes ranked with full details in the World year lists. The format of the index is as follows:

Family name, First Name, Nationality, Birthdate, Height (cm) and Weight (kg), 1986 best mark, Lifetime best as at the end of 1985 and the relevant year.

## Meeting abbreviations

The following abbreviations have been used for meetings with, in parentheses, the first year that they were held.

| | |
|---|---|
| AAA | (UK) Amateur Athletic Association Championships (1880) |
| AAU | (USA) Amateur Athletic Union Championships (1888) (now TAC) |
| AfrC | African Championships (1979) |
| AfrG | African Games (1965) |
| AsiC | Asian Championships (1973) |
| AsiG | Asian Games (1951) |
| ASV | Weltklasse in Köln, ASV Club meeting (1934) |
| Balk | Balkan Games (1929) |
| Barr | (Cuba) Barrientos Memorial |
| BGP | Budapest Grand Prix (1978) |
| Bisl | Bislett Games, Oslo |
| CAC | Central American and Caribbean Championships (1967) |
| CAG | Central American and Caribbean Games (1926) |
| CalR | California Relays (1942) |
| CISM | International Military Championships (1946) |

| | |
|---|---|
| Coke | Coca Cola Invitational (IAC meeting), London (1968) |
| CommG | Commonwealth Games (1930) |
| DNG | DN Galan, Stockholm (1966) |
| DrakeR | Drake Relays (1910) |
| Druz | Druzhba, Youth Meet of Socialist Countries |
| Drz | Druzhba/Friendship Games, Moskva (men), Praha (women) (1984) |
| EC | European Championships (1934) |
| EJ | European Junior Championships (1970) |
| EP | European Cup – track & field (1965), multi-events (1973) |
| EP/sf | European Cup semi-final |
| FBK | Fanny Blankers-Koen Memorial, Hengelo |
| FlaR | Florida Relays (1939) |
| FOT | (USA) Final Olympic Trials (1920) |
| GGala | Golden Gala, Roma (1980) |
| GO | Golden Oval, GDR |
| GP | IAAF Grand Prix final (1985) |

| | |
|---|---|
| GS | Golden Spikes, Ostrava (1969) |
| GWG | Goodwill Games, Moskva (1986) |
| HB | Hanns Braun Memorial, München (1930) |
| IAAF-g | IAAF Golden events (1978) |
| IbAm | Ibero-American Championships |
| ISTAF | Internationales Stadionfest, Berlin (1921) |
| IWG | Indoor World Games (1985) |
| Izv | (SU) Izvestia Cup |
| Jenner | Bruce Jenner Classic, San Jose (1979) |
| Jerome | Harry Jerome Memorial (1984) |
| JO | Jesse Owens Memorial (1981) |
| KansR | Kansas Relays, Lawrence (1923) |
| King | Martin Luther King Games (1969) |
| Kuso | Janusz Kusocinski Memorial (1954) |
| Kuts | Vladimir Kuts Memorial |
| LB | Liberty Bell, Philadelphia |
| MedG | Mediterranean Games (1951) |
| MSR | Mt.San Antonio College Relays (1959) |
| Nar | Narodna Mladesh, Sofia (1955) |
| NC | National Championships |
| NC-j | National Junior Championships |
| NC-y | National Youth Championships |
| NCAA | National Collegiate Athletic Association Championships (1921) |
| Nik | Nikaia, Nice (1976) |
| OD | (GDR) Olympischer Tag (Olympic Day) |
| OG | Olympic Games (1896) |
| OT | Olympic Trials |
| PAG | Pan American Games (1951) |
| PennR | Pennsylvania Relays (1895) |
| Pepsi | Pepsi Cola Invitational |
| PNG | Paavo Nurmi Games (1957) |
| PO | Pre Olympic Meet |
| Prav | (SU) Pravda Cup |
| PTG | Peugeot Talbot Games (1980) |
| PTS | Pravda Televizia Slovnaft, Bratislava (1960) |
| Pre | Steve Prefontaine Memorial (1976) |
| Ros | Evzen Rosicky Memorial (1947) |
| RumIC | Rumanian International Championships (1948) |
| SGP | Softeland Grand Prix (walking) |
| SoAmC | South American Championships (1919) |
| Spart | (SU) Spartakiad (1956) |
| SW | S & W Invitational, Modesto |
| TAC | (USA) The Athletics Congress Championships (1980) |

| | |
|---|---|
| TexR | Texas Relays (1925) |
| USOF | US Olympic Festival |
| VD | Ivo Van Damme Memorial, Brussels (1977) |
| WA | West Athletic Meet (AUT/BEL/DEN/HOL/IRL/POR/SPA/SWZ) |
| WAAA | (UK) Women's Amateur Athletic Association Champs. (1922) |
| WC | World Championships (1983) |
| WG | World Games, Helsinki (1961) |
| WJ | World Junior Championships (1986) |
| WK | Weltklasse, Zürich (1962) |
| WP | World Cup – track & field (1977), marathon (1985) |
| WPT | World Cup Trials (1977) |
| WUG | World University Games (1923) |
| Znam | Znamenskiy Brothers Memorial (1958) |

Dual and triangular matches are indicated by 'v' (versus) followed by the name(s) of the opposition. Quadrangular and larger inter-nation matches are denoted by the number of nations and -N; viz 8-N designates an 8-nation meeting.

## Miscellaneous abbreviations

| | |
|---|---|
| A | Made at an altitude of 1000m or higher |
| D | Made in decathlon competition |
| H | Made in heptathlon competition |
| h | Made in heat |
| i | Indoor mark |
| m | Manual timing in events beyond 400 metres |
| Q | Mark made in qualifying round |
| q | Mark made in quarter-final |
| r | Race number in a series of races |
| s | Semi-final |
| w | Wind-assisted |
| = | Tie (ex-aequo) |
| * | Converted time from yards to metres: |

For 200m: 220 yards less 0.11 second
For 400m: 440 yards less 0.26 second
For 110mh: 120yh plus 0.03 second

# GENERAL NOTES

## Altitude Aid

Marks set at an altitude of 1000m or higher have been prefixed by the letter 'A'.

Although there are not separate world records for altitude assisted events, it is understood by experts that in all events up to 400m in length (with the possible exclusion of the 110m hurdles), and in the horizontal jumps, altitude gives a material benefit to performances. As yet there is no scientific formula for quantifying such aid. For events beyond 400m, however, the thinner air of high altitude has a detrimental effect.

Supplementary lists are included in relevant events for athletes with seasonal bests at altitude who have low altitude marks qualifying for the main list.

## Automatic Timing

In the main lists for sprints and hurdles, only times recorded by fully automatic timing devices are included. Such a timing device is one which is started automatically by the firing of the starter's gun, with the finish recorded photographically with a strip camera or a movie camera and linked back electronically to the start.

## Hand Timing

In the sprints and hurdles supplementary lists are included for races which are hand timed. Any athlete with a hand timed best 0.01 seconds or more better than his or her automatically timed best has been included. Hand timed lists have been terminated close to the differential levels considered by the IAAF to be equivalent to automatic times, i.e. 0.24 sec. for 100m, 200m, 100mh, 110mh, and 0.14 sec. for 400m and 400mh.

In events beyond 400m, automatically timed marks are integrated with hand timed marks, with the latter designated with the symbol 'm'. All-time lists also include some auto times in tenths of a second, where the 1/100th time is not known, but the reader can differentiate these from hand timed marks as they do not have the suffix 'm'.

## Indoor Marks

Indoor marks are included in the main lists for field events and straightway track events, but not for other track events. This is because there is no curb for indoor races and theoretically this can enable athletes to run less than full distance, and, more importantly, because track sizes vary greatly in circumference and banking, while outdoor tracks are far more standardized. Athletes whose seasonal bests were set indoors are shown in a supplemental list if they also have outdoor marks qualifying for the world list.

## Supplementary Marks

Non-winning marks in a field event series which, had they been winning marks, would have qualified for the top 30 performances list are included in a supplement at the end of the relevant events.

## Wind Assistance

In the lists for 100m, 200m, 100mh, 110mh, long jump and triple jump, anemometer readings have been shown where available. The readings are given in metres per second to one decimal place. Where the figure was given originally to two decimal places, it has been rounded to the next tenth upwards, e.g. a wind reading of +2.01 m/s, beyond the IAAF legal limit of 2.0, is rounded to +2.1; or –1.22 m/s is rounded up to –1.2.

## Amendments

Keen observers may spot errors in the lists. They are invited to send corrections to the editor, who will pass them on to the relevant compilers.

**Peter Matthews, 10 Madgeways Close, Great Amwell, Ware, Herts SG12 9RU, England**

# WORLD & CONTINENTAL RECORDS: MEN

(as at 31 Dec 1986)

Key:    W = World;    I = I.A.A.F. (if different);    C = Commonwealth
        Afr = Africa;  Asi = Asia;    CAC = Central America & Caribbean
        E = Europe;  NAm = N.America;  Oce = Oceania;  SAm = S.America
                OG = Olympic Games;    WJ = World Junior

        A = altitude over 1000m;    + = timing by photo-electric-cell
        * = awaiting ratification;    £ = not officially ratified

| Record | Mark | Name | Nat | Venue | Date |
|--------|------|------|-----|-------|------|

## 100 METRES

| Record | Mark | Name | Nat | Venue | Date |
|--------|------|------|-----|-------|------|
| W,NAm | 9.93A | Calvin SMITH | USA | Colorado Springs | 3 Jul 83 |
| C | 9.95 | Ben JOHNSON | Can | Moskva | 9 Jul 86 |
| CAC | 9.98A | Silvio LEONARD | Cub | Guadalajara | 11 Aug 77 |
| E | 10.00 | Marian WORONIN | Pol | Warszawa | 9 Jun 84 |
| Afr | 10.00 | Chidi IMO | Nig | Moskva | 9 Jul 86 |
| SAm | 10.02 | Robson DA SILVA | Bra | Habana | 27 Sep 86 |
| Oce | 10.22 | Gerard KEATING | Aus | Canberra | 4 Oct 85 |
| Asi | 10.26 | LI Tao | Chn | Jakarta | 5 Dec 86 |
| OG | 9.95A | Jim HINES | USA | Ciudad de México | 14 Oct 68 |
| WJ | 10.07 | Stanley FLOYD | USA | Austin | 24 May 80 |

## 200 METRES

| Record | Mark | Name | Nat | Venue | Date |
|--------|------|------|-----|-------|------|
| W,E | 19.72A | Pietro MENNEA | Ita | Ciudad de México | 12 Sep 79 |
| NAm | 19.75 | Carl LEWIS | USA | Indianapolis | 19 Jun 83 |
| C,CAC | 19.86A | Donald QUARRIE | Jam | Cali | 3 Aug 71 |
| Oce | 20.06A | Peter NORMAN | Aus | Ciudad de México | 16 Oct 68 |
| SAm | 20.28 | Robson DA SILVA | Bra | Madrid | 4 Jun 86 |
| Afr | 20.41A | Wessel OOSTHUIZEN | RSA | Pretoria | 16 Mar 85 |
| Asi | 20.41 | CHANG Jae Keun | SKo | Jakarta | 27 Sep 85 |
| OG | 19.80 | Carl LEWIS | USA | Los Angeles | 8 Aug 84 |
| WJ | 20.07 | Lorenzo DANIEL | USA | Starkville | 18 May 85 |

## 400 METRES

| Record | Mark | Name | Nat | Venue | Date |
|--------|------|------|-----|-------|------|
| W,NAm | 43.86A | Lee EVANS | USA | Ciudad de México | 18 Oct 68 |
| CAC | 44.26 | Alberto JUANTORENA | Cub | Montréal | 29 Jul 76 |
| Afr | 44.30 | Gabriel TIACOH | IvC | Indianapolis | 7 Jun 86 |
| E | 44.50 | Erwin SKAMRAHL | FRG | München | 26 Jul 83 |
| C | 44.50 | Innocent EGBUNIKE | Nig | Zürich | 13 Aug 86 |
| Oce | 44.72 | Darren CLARK | Aus | Zürich | 13 Aug 86 |
| Asi | 45.00 | Susumu TAKANO | Jap | Seoul | 1 Oct 86 |
| SAm | 45.21 | Gerson SOUZA | Bra | Rieti | 16 Sep 82 |
| OG | 43.86A | Lee EVANS | USA | Ciudad de México | 18 Oct 68 |
| WJ | 44.69 | Darrell ROBINSON | USA | Indianapolis | 24 Jul 82 |

## 800 METRES

| Record | Mark | Name | Nat | Venue | Date |
|--------|------|------|-----|-------|------|
| W,C,E | 1:41.73+ | Sebastian COE | UK | Firenze | 10 Jun 81 |
| SAm | 1:41.77 | Joaquim CRUZ | Bra | Köln | 26 Aug 84 |
| Afr | 1:42.28 | Sammy KOSKEI | Ken | Köln | 26 Aug 84 |
| NAm | 1:42.60 | Johnny GRAY | USA | Koblenz | 28 Aug 85 |
| CAC | 1:43.44 | Alberto JUANTORENA | Cub | Sofiya | 21 Aug 77 |
| Oce | 1:44.3 m | Peter SNELL | NZ | Christchurch | 3 Feb 62 |
| Asi | 1:45.77 | Sri Ram SINGH | Ind | Montréal | 25 Jul 76 |
| OG | 1:43.00 | Joaquim CRUZ | Bra | Los Angeles | 6 Aug 84 |
| WJ | 1:44.9 ym | Jim RYUN | USA | Terre Haute | 10 Jun 66 |
|  | 1:44.3 m | Joaquim CRUZ | Bra | Rio de Janeiro | 27 Jun 81 |

| Record | Mark | Name | Nat | Venue | Date |
|---|---|---|---|---|---|

## 1500 METRES

| | | | | | |
|---|---|---|---|---|---|
| W | 3:29.46 | Saïd AOUITA | Mar | W.Berlin | 23 Aug 85 |
| E,C | 3:29.67 | Steve CRAM | UK | Nice | 16 Jul 85 |
| NAm | 3:29.77 | Sydney MAREE | USA | Köln | 25 Aug 85 |
| Oce | 3:32.4 m | John WALKER | NZ | Oslo | 30 Jul 75 |
| SAm | 3:35.70 | Joaquim CRUZ | Bra | Eugene | 1 Jun 85 |
| Asi | 3:38.24 | Takashi ISHII | Jap | Düsseldorf | 3 Sep 77 |
| CAC | 3:38.85 | Eduardo CASTRO | Mex | Ciudad Bolívar | 14 Aug 81 |
| OG | 3:32.53 | Sebastian COE | UK | Los Angeles | 11 Aug 84 |
| WJ | 3:34.92 | Kipkoech CHERUIYOT | Ken | München | 26 Jul 83 |

## 1 MILE

| | | | | | |
|---|---|---|---|---|---|
| W,C,E | 3:46.32 | Steve CRAM | UK | Oslo | 27 Jul 85 |
| Afr | 3:46.92 | Saïd AOUITA | Mar | Zürich | 21 Aug 85 |
| NAm | 3:47.69 | Steve SCOTT | USA | Oslo | 7 Jul 82 |
| Oce | 3:49.08 | John WALKER | NZ | Oslo | 7 Jul 82 |
| SAm | 3:53.00 | Joaquim CRUZ | Bra | Los Angeles | 13 May 84 |
| CAC | 3:57.34 | Byron DYCE | Jam | Stockholm | 1 Jul 74 |
| Asi | 3:59.7 m | Takashi ISHII | Jap | Melbourne | 10 Dec 77 |
| WJ | 3:51.3 m | Jim RYUN | USA | Berkeley | 17 Jul 66 |

## 3000 METRES

| | | | | | |
|---|---|---|---|---|---|
| W,C,Afr | 7:32.1 m | Henry RONO | Ken | Oslo | 27 Jun 78 |
| (W,Afr) | 7:32.23 | Saïd AOUITA | Mar | Köln | 17 Aug 86 |
| E | 7:32.79 | Dave MOORCROFT | UK | London | 17 Jul 82 |
| NAm | 7:33.37 | Sydney MAREE | USA | London | 17 Jul 82 |
| Oce | 7:37.49 | John WALKER | NZ | London | 17 Jul 82 |
| CAC | 7:47.44 | Rodolfo GÓMEZ | Mex | Köln | 22 Jun 77 |
| SAm | 7:53.0 m | José DA SILVA | Bra | Gateshead | 26 Jul 75 |
| Asi | 7:54.0 m | Takao NAKAMURA | Jap | Troisdorf | 11 Jul 79 |
| WJ | 7:43.20 | Ari PAUNONEN | Fin | Köln | 22 Jun 77 |

## 5000 METRES

| | | | | | |
|---|---|---|---|---|---|
| W,Afr | 13:00.40 | Saïd AOUITA | Mar | Oslo | 27 Jul 85 |
| C,E | 13:00.41 | Dave MOORCROFT | UK | Oslo | 7 Jul 82 |
| NAm | 13:01.15 | Sydney MAREE | USA | Oslo | 27 Jul 85 |
| Oce | 13:12.87 | Dick QUAX | NZ | Stockholm | 5 Jul 77 |
| CAC | 13:22.4 m | Maurizio GONZÁLEZ | Mex | Walnut | 27 Apr 85 |
| Asi | 13:24.29 | Toshihiko SEKO | Jap | London | 11 Sep 86 |
| SAm | 13:29.67 | Domingo TIBADUIZA | Col | Zürich | 16 Aug 78 |
| OG | 13:05.59 | Saïd AOUITA | Mar | Los Angeles | 11 Aug 84 |
| WJ | 13:25.33 | Charles CHERUIYOT | Ken | München | 26 Jul 83 |

## 10 000 METRES

| | | | | | |
|---|---|---|---|---|---|
| W,E | 27:13.81 | Fernando MAMEDE | Por | Stockholm | 2 Jul 84 |
| NAm | 27:20.56 | Mark NENOW | USA | Bruxelles | 5 Sep 86 |
| C,Afr | 27:22.47+ | Henry RONO | Ken | Wien | 11 Jun 78 |
| Oce | 27:39.89 | Ron CLARKE | Aus | Oslo | 14 Jul 65 |
| Asi | 27:42.17 | Toshihiko SEKO | Jap | Stockholm | 2 Jul 85 |
| CAC | 27:45.0 m | Jesus HERRERA | Mex | Walnut | 27 Apr 85 |
| SAm | 27:53.02+ | Domingo TIBADUIZA | Col | Wien | 11 Jun 78 |
| OG | 27:38.35 | Lasse VIREN | Fin | München | 3 Sep 72 |
| WJ | 28:29.32 | Habte NEGASH | Eth | Moskva | 9 Jun 85 |

| Record | Mark | Name | Nat | Venue | Date |
|--------|------|------|-----|-------|------|

## 3000 METRES STEEPLECHASE

| Record | Mark | Name | Nat | Venue | Date |
|--------|------|------|-----|-------|------|
| W,C,Afr | 8:05.4 m | Henry RONO | Ken | Seattle | 13 May 78 |
| E | 8:07.62 | Joseph MAHMOUD | Fra | Bruxelles | 24 Aug 84 |
| NAm | 8:09.17 | Henry MARSH | USA | Koblenz | 28 Aug 85 |
| Oce | 8:14.05 | Peter RENNER | NZ | Koblenz | 29 Aug 84 |
| Asi | 8:19.52 | Masanari SHINTAKU | Jap | Stockholm | 8 Jul 80 |
| SAm | 8:26.01 | Adauto DOMINGUES | Bra | La Coruna | 6 Aug 86 |
| CAC | 8:30.23 | Carmelo RIOS | PRc | Eugene | 1 Jun 85 |
| OG | 8:08.02 | Anders GÄRDERUD | Swe | Montréal | 28 Jul 76 |
| WJ | 8:29.50 | Ralf PÖNITZSCH | GDR | Warszawa | 19 Aug 76 |

## 110 METRES HURDLES

| Record | Mark | Name | Nat | Venue | Date |
|--------|------|------|-----|-------|------|
| W,NAm | 12.93 | Renaldo NEHEMIAH | USA | Zürich | 19 Aug 81 |
| E | 13.20 | Stéphane CARISTAN | Fra | Stuttgart | 30 Aug 86 |
| CAC | 13.21 | Alejandro CASAÑAS | Cub | Sofiya | 21 Aug 77 |
| C | 13.27 | Mark McKOY | Can | Walnut | 25 Jul 84 |
|  | 13.27 | Mark McKOY | Can | Ottawa | 3 Aug 85 |
| Oce | 13.58 | Don WRIGHT | Aus | Brisbane | 4 Oct 82 |
| Afr | 13.69 | Fatwel KIMAIYO | Ken | Christchurch | 26 Jan 74 |
|  | 13.69 | Godwin OBASOGIE | Nig | Austin | 3 Apr 76 |
| Asi | 13.82 | YU Chicheng | Chn | Barcelona | 8 Jul 85 |
| SAm | 13.87 | Pedro CHIAMULERA | Bra | Santiago | 13 Sep 85 |
| OG | 13.20 | Roger KINGDOM | USA | Los Angeles | 6 Aug 84 |
| WJ | 13.23 | Renaldo NEHEMIAH | USA | Zürich | 16 Aug 78 |

## 400 METRES HURDLES

| Record | Mark | Name | Nat | Venue | Date |
|--------|------|------|-----|-------|------|
| W,NAm | 47.02 | Edwin MOSES | USA | Koblenz | 31 Aug 83 |
| E | 47.48 | Harald SCHMID | FRG | Athínai | 8 Sep 82 |
| C,Afr | 47.82 | John AKII-BUA | Uga | München | 2 Sep 72 |
| CAC | 49.17 | Karl SMITH | Jam | Houston | 15 May 82 |
| SAm | 49.24 | Antonio FERREIRA | Bra | Kobe | 30 Aug 85 |
| Asi | 49.31 | Ahmad HAMADA | Bhn | Seoul | 30 Sep 86 |
| Oce | 49.32 | Bruce FIELD | Aus | Christchurch | 29 Jan 74 |
| OG | 47.63 | Edwin MOSES | USA | Montréal | 25 Jul 76 |
| WJ | 48.02 | Danny HARRIS | USA | Los Angeles | 17 Jun 84 |

## HIGH JUMP

| Record | Mark | Name | Nat | Venue | Date |
|--------|------|------|-----|-------|------|
| W,E | 2.41 | Igor PAKLIN | SU | Kobe | 4 Sep 85 |
| Asi | 2.39 | ZHU Jianhua | Chn | Eberstadt | 10 Jun 84 |
| NAm | 2.36iA | Jimmy HOWARD | USA | Albuquerque | 25 Jan 86 |
|  | 2.35 | Jimmy HOWARD | USA | Houston | 25 May 85 |
| CAC | 2.36 | Javier SOTOMAYOR | Cub | Habana | 22 Feb 86 |
| C | 2.33 | Milt OTTEY | Can | Ottawa | 21 Jun 86 |
| Afr | 2.28 | Othmane BELFAA | Alg | Amman | 20 Aug 83 |
| Oce | 2.28- | John ATKINSON | Aus | Melbourne | 31 Mar 84 |
| SAm | 2.25 | Claudio FREIRE | Bra | Rio de Janeiro | 10 Oct 82 |
| OG | 2.36 | Gerd WESSIG | GDR | Moskva | 1 Aug 80 |
| WJ | 2.36 | Javier SOTOMAYOR | Cub | Habana | 22 Mar 86 |

## POLE VAULT

| Record | Mark | Name | Nat | Venue | Date |
|--------|------|------|-----|-------|------|
| W,E | 6.01 | Sergey BUBKA | SU | Moskva | 8 Jul 86 |
| NAm | 5.93i | Billy OLSON | USA | East Rutherford | 8 Feb 86 |
|  | 5.90* | Joe DIAL | USA | Norman | 25 Apr 86 |
| SAm | 5.76 | Tom HINTNAUS | Bra | Zürich | 21 Aug 85 |
| C | 5.65 | Keith STOCK | Eng | Stockholm | 7 Jul 81 |
| Asi | 5.55 | LIANG Xueren | Chn | Beijing | 16 Aug 86 |
|  | 5.55* | Toshiyuki HASHIOKA | Jap | Kofu | 14 Oct 86 |
| Oce | 5.53 | Don BAIRD | Aus | Long Beach | 16 Apr 77 |
| CAC | 5.45 | Ruben CAMINO | Cub | San Juan | 21 Sep 85 |
| Afr | 5.34 | Lakhdar RAHAL | Alg | Paris | 4 Jun 79 |
| OG | 5.78 | Władysław KOZAKIEWICZ | Pol | Moskva | 30 Jul 80 |
| WJ | 5.65 | Rodion GATAULLIN | SU | Donetsk | 8 Sep 84 |

| Record | Mark | Name | Nat | Venue | Date |
|--------|------|------|-----|-------|------|

# LONG JUMP

| | | | | | |
|--------|--------|------------------------|-----|----------------------|-----------|
| W,NAm | 8.90A | Bob BEAMON | USA | Ciudad de México | 18 Oct 68 |
| E | 8.61* | Robert EMMIYAN | SU | Moskva | 6 Jul 86 |
| CAC | 8.37 | Jaime JEFFERSON | Cub | Moskva | 17 Aug 84 |
| SAm | 8.36 | Joao Carlos DE OLIVEIRA | Bra | Rieti | 21 Jul 79 |
| C,Oce | 8.27 | Gary HONEY | Aus | Budapest | 20 Aug 84 |
| Afr | 8.26i | Charlton EHIZEULEN | Nig | Bloomington | 7 Mar 75 |
| | 8.21 | Yussuf ALLI | Nig | Edmonton | 7 Jul 83 |
| Asi | 8.23 | CHEN Zunrong | Chn | Beijing | 12 Apr 86 |
| OG | 8.90A | Bob BEAMON | USA | Ciudad de México | 18 Oct 68 |
| WJ | 8.34 | Randy WILLIAMS | USA | München | 8 Sep 72 |

# TRIPLE JUMP

| | | | | | |
|--------|--------|------------------------|-----|----------------------|-----------|
| W,NAm | 17.97 | Willie BANKS | USA | Indianapolis | 16 Jun 85 |
| SAm | 17.89A | Joao Carlos DE OLIVEIRA | Bra | Ciudad de México | 15 Oct 75 |
| E | 17.80 | Khristo MARKOV | Bul | Budapest | 11 Aug 86 |
| CAC | 17.78 | Lazaro BETANCOURT | Cub | Habana | 15 Jun 86 |
| C | 17.57A | Keith CONNOR | UK | Provo | 5 Jun 82 |
| Oce | 17.46 | Ken LORRAWAY | Aus | London | 7 Aug 82 |
| Asi | 17.34 | ZOU Zhenxian | Chn | Roma | 5 Sep 81 |
| Afr | 17.26 | Ajayi AGBEBAKU | Nig | Edmonton | 8 Jul 83 |
| OG | 17.39A | Viktor SANYEYEV | SU | Ciudad de México | 17 Oct 68 |
| WJ | 17.50 | Volker MAI | GDR | Erfurt | 23 Jun 85 |

# SHOT PUT

| | | | | | |
|--------|--------|------------------------|-----|----------------------|-----------|
| W | 22.86p | Brian OLDFIELD | USA | El Paso | 10 May 75 |
| I,E | 22.64 | Udo BEYER | GDR | E.Berlin | 20 Aug 86 |
| NAm | 22.86p | Brian OLDFIELD | USA | El Paso | 10 May 75 |
| | 22.19 | Brian OLDFIELD | USA | San Jose | 27 May 84 |
| C | 21.68 | Geoff CAPES | Eng | Cwmbrân | 18 May 80 |
| SAm | 20.90 | Gert WEIL | Chl | Wirges | 17 Aug 86 |
| Afr | 20.71 | Nagui ASAAD | Egy | Praha | 21 Jun 72 |
| CAC | 19.89 | Luis DELIS | Cub | Santaigo de Cuba | 7 Mar 82 |
| Oce | 19.80 | Les MILLS | NZ | Honolulu | 3 Jul 67 |
| Asi | 18.87 | GONG Yitian | Chn | Beijing | 7 Sep 86 |
| OG | 21.35 | Volodymyr KISELYOV | SU | Moskva | 30 Jul 80 |
| WJ | 21.05i | Terry ALBRITTON | USA | New York | 22 Feb 74 |
| | 20.65 | Mike CARTER | USA | Boston | 4 Jul 79 |

# DISCUS

| | | | | | |
|--------|---------|------------------------|-----|----------------------|-----------|
| W,E | 74.08 | Jurgen SCHULT | GDR | Neubrandenburg | 6 Jun 86 |
| NAm | 72.34dq | Ben PLUCKNETT | USA | Stockholm | 7 Jul 81 |
| | 71.32 | Ben PLUCKNETT | USA | Eugene | 4 Jun 83 |
| CAC | 71.06 | Luis DELIS | Cub | Habana | 21 May 83 |
| Afr | 68.48 | John VAN REENEN | RSA | Stellenbosch | 14 Mar 75 |
| C | 67.32 | Rob GRAY | Can | Etobicoke | 30 Apr 84 |
| Oce | 65.08 | Wayne MARTIN | Aus | Newcastle | 3 Jan 79 |
| Asi | 61.06 | Djalal-Ali KESHMIRI | Irn | Lancaster | 19 May 74 |
| SAm | 57.10 | José SOUZA | Bra | Eugene | 3 May 86 |
| OG | 68.28 | Mac WILKINS | USA | Montréal | 24 Jul 76 |
| WJ | 63.64 | Werner HARTMANN | FRG | Strasbourg | 25 Jun 78 |

| Record | Mark | Name | Nat | Venue | Date |
|--------|------|------|-----|-------|------|

## HAMMER

| Record | Mark | Name | Nat | Venue | Date |
|--------|------|------|-----|-------|------|
| W,E | 86.74 | Yuriy SEDYKH | SU | Stuttgart | 30 Aug 86 |
| NAm | 80.88 | Jud LOGAN | USA | Walnut | 27 Apr 86 |
| C | 77.54 | Martin GIRVAN | NI | Wolverhampton | 12 May 84 |
| Asi | 75.94 | Shigenobu MUROFUSHI | Jap | Walnut | 15 Jul 84 |
| Oce | 75.90 | Peter FARMER | Aus | Vanves | 14 Aug 79 |
| CAC | 74.74 | Armando OROZCO | Cub | Habana | 25 May 80 |
| Afr | 73.86 | Adam BARNARD | RSA | Johannesburg | 26 Mar 76 |
| SAm | 66.04 | José VALLEJO | Arg | Bahía Blanca | 8 Dec 74 |
| OG | 81.80 | Yuriy SEDYKH | SU | Moskva | 31 Jul 80 |
| WJ | 78.14 | Roland STEUK | GDR | Leipzig | 30 Jun 78 |

## JAVELIN (1986 model)

| Record | Mark | Name | Nat | Venue | Date |
|--------|------|------|-----|-------|------|
| W,E | 85.74 | Klaus TAFELMEIER | FRG | Como | 21 Sep 86 |
| NAm | 85.38* | Tom PETRANOFF | USA | Helsinki | 7 Jul 86 |
| Asi | 81.90 | Kazuhiro MIZOGUCHI | Jap | Tokyo | 15 Sep 86 |
| C | 81.74 | Roald BRADSTOCK | Eng | Tucson | 3 May 86 |
| Oce | 79.58 | Gavin LOVEGROVE | NZ | Nouméa | 25 Nov 86 |
| CAC | 77.32 | Raúl GONZÁLEZ | Cub | Santiago de Cuba | 4 Jul 86 |
| Afr | 76.48 | Zakayo MALEKWA | Tan | Arlington | 10 May 86 |
| SAm |  |  |  |  |  |
| OG | – |  |  |  |  |
| WJ | 79.58 | Gavin LOVEGROVE | NZ | Nouméa | 25 Nov 86 |

## DECATHLON (1962/1984 Tables)

| Record | Mark | Name | Nat | Venue | Date |
|--------|------|------|-----|-------|------|
| C | 8798 /8847 | Daley THOMPSON | Eng | Los Angeles | 9 Aug 84 |
| NAm | 8617 /8634 | Bruce JENNER | USA | Montréal | 30 Jul 76 |
| SAm | 8377m/8291 | Tito STEINER | Arg | Provo | 23 Jun 83 |
|  | 8124 /8105 | Tito STEINER | Arg | Austin | 5 Apr 79 |
| Oce | 8158 | Simon POELMAN | NZ | Christchurch | 29 Mar 86 |
| Asi | 8089m/8009 | YANG Chuan-Kuang | Tai | Walnut | 28 Apr 63 |
| Afr | 8006m/7922 | Ahmed MANSOUR BALCHA | Alg | Alger | 3 Jun 82 |
| CAC | 7881m/7749 | Rigoberto SALAZAR | Cub | Habana | 25 May 79 |
|  | 7726 /7734 | Douglas FERNÁNDEZ | Ven | Caracas | 27 Aug 83 |
| OG | 8798 /8847 | Daley THOMPSON | UK | Los Angeles | 9 Aug 84 |
| WJ | 8387 /8397 | Torsten VOSS | GDR | Erfurt | 7 Jul 82 |

## MARATHON

| Record | Mark | Name | Nat | Venue | Date |
|--------|------|------|-----|-------|------|
| W,E | 2:07:12 | Carlos LOPES | Por | Rotterdam | 20 Apr 85 |
| C | 2:07:13 | Steve JONES | Wal | Chicago | 20 Oct 85 |
| Asi | 2:07:35 | Taisuke KODAME | Jap | Beijing | 19 Oct 86 |
| Oce | 2:07:51 | Rob DE CASTELLA | Aus | Boston | 21 Apr 86 |
| Afr | 2:08:08 | Djama ROBLEH | Dji | Chicago | 20 Oct 85 |
| NAm | 2:08:52 | Alberto SALAZAR | USA | Boston | 19 Apr 82 |
| CAC | 2:09:12 | Rodolfo GÓMEZ | Mex | Tokyo | 13 Feb 83 |
| SAm | 2:11:21 | Domingo TIBADUIZA | Col | New York | 23 Oct 83 |
| OG | 2:09:21 | Carlos LOPES | Por | Los Angeles | 12 Aug 84 |
| WJ | 2:15:28 | Paul GOMPERS | USA | Huntsville | 10 Dec 83 |

## 20 KM WALK (ROAD)

| Record | Mark | Name | Nat | Venue | Date |
|--------|------|------|-----|-------|------|
| W,E | 1:19:30 | Jozef PRIBILINEC | CS | Bergen | 24 Sep 83 |
| CAC | 1:19:35 | Domingo COLIN | Mex | Cherkassy | 27 Apr 80 |
| C,Oce | 1:19:52 | Dave SMITH | Aus | Jiading | 16 Mar 85 |
| NAm | 1:21:13 | Guillaume LEBLANC | Can | St.Leonard | 5 Oct 86 |
| Asi | 1:21:29 | LIU Jianli | Chn | Jiading | 16 Mar 85 |
| SAm | 1:22:11 | Querubim MORENO | Col | Barcelona | 28 Apr 85 |
| Afr | 1:27:08 | Hassen SHEMZU | Eth | Moskva | 17 Aug 84 |
| OG | 1:23:13 | Ernesto CANTO | Mex | Los Angeles | 3 Aug 84 |
| WJ | 1:21:33 | Carlos MERCENARIO | Mex | St.Leonard | 5 Oct 86 |

RECORDS

| Record | Mark | Name | Nat | Venue | Date |
|---|---|---|---|---|---|

## 20 000M WALK (TRACK)

| | | | | | |
|---|---|---|---|---|---|
| W,CAC | 1:18:40.0 | Ernesto CANTO | Mex | Fana | 5 May 84 |
| E | 1:20:36.7 | Erling ANDERSEN | Nor | Fana | 5 May 84 |
| C,NAm | 1:23:17 £ | Guillaume LEBLANC | Can | Québec | 22 May 86 |
| | 1:24:58.8 | Marcel JOBIN | Can | Québec | 12 May 84 |
| Asi | 1:24:02.6 | JIANG Shaohong | Chn | Jiangsi | 8 Mar 86 |
| Oce | 1:26:07.8 | Dave SMITH | Aus | Melbourne | 27 Jun 81 |
| Afr | 1:26:39.93 | Benamar KACHKOUCHE | Alg | Thonon-les-Bains | 20 Jun 84 |
| SAm | 1:32:27.0 | Clodimiro MORENO | Col | Tunja | 19 May 85 |
| WJ | 1:22:42 | Andrey PERLOV | SU | Donetsk | 6 Sep 80 |

## 50KM WALK (ROAD)

| | | | | | |
|---|---|---|---|---|---|
| W,E | 3:38:17 | Ronald WEIGEL | GDR | Potsdam | 25 May 86 |
| CAC | 3:41:20 | Raúl GONZÁLEZ | Mex | Praha-Podebrady | 11 Jun 78 |
| C,Oce | 3:46:34 | Willi SAWALL | Aus | Adelaide | 6 Apr 80 |
| NAm | 3:47:48 | Marcel JOBIN | Can | Québec | 20 Jun 81 |
| Asi | 3:53:51 | SUN Xiaoguang | Chn | Jiangsi | 10 Mar 86 |
| Afr | 4:14:30 | Eddie MICHAELS | RSA | Cape Town | 11 Mar 67 |
| SAm | 4:18:08 | Ernesto ALFARO | Col | Mixhuca | 23 Apr 78 |
| OG | 3:47:26 | Raúl GONZÁLEZ | Mex | Los Angeles | 11 Aug 84 |

## 50 000M WALK (TRACK)

| | | | | | |
|---|---|---|---|---|---|
| W,CAC | 3:41:38.4 | Raúl GONZÁLEZ | Mex | Fana | 25 May 79 |
| E | 3:46:11 * | Mykola UDOVENKO | SU | Uzhgorod | 3 Oct 80 |
| | 3:48:59 | Vladimir REZAYEV | SU | Fana | 2 May 80 |
| C | 4:05:47.3 | Chris MADDOCKS | Eng | Birmingham | 22 Sep 84 |
| Oce | 4:06:39 | Willi SAWALL | Aus | Melbourne | 14 Aug 76 |
| NAm | 4:12:44.5 | Dan O'CONNOR | USA | Irvine | 19 Nov 83 |
| SAm | 4:17:11.0 | Mauricio CORTEZ | Col | Caracas | 16 Nov 86 |
| Asi | 4:20:45 | Kazuo SHIRAI | Jap | Tokyo | 9 Mar 80 |
| Afr | 4:21:44.5 | Abdelwahab FERGUENE | Alg | Toulouse | 25 Mar 84 |

## 4x100 METRES RELAY

| | | | | | |
|---|---|---|---|---|---|
| W,NAm | 37.83 | USA (Graddy, Brown, C.Smith, Lewis) | | Los Angeles | 11 Aug 84 |
| E | 38.19* | SU (Yevgenyev,Yushmanov,Muravyov,Bryzgin) | Moskva | 9 Jul 86 |
| CAC | 38.39A | Jam (Stewart, Fray, Forbes, Miller) | | C.de México | 19 Oct 68 |
| | 38.39A | Cub (Ramírez, Morales, Montes, Figuerola) | C.de México | 20 Oct 68 |
| C | 38.39A | Jam (Stewart, Fray, Forbes, Miller) | | C.de México | 19 Oct 68 |
| Afr | 38.73A | IvC (Ouré, Meité, Nogboum, Kablan) | | C.de México | 13 Sep 79 |
| SAm | 38.8 | Bra (Oliveira, da Silva, Nakaya, Correia) | São Paulo | 1 May 84 |
| | 39.02A | Bra (de Castro, dos Santos, Pegado,Filho) | C.de México | 4 Sep 79 |
| Asi | 39.17 | Chn (Cai, Li, Yu, Zheng) | | Seoul | 5 Oct 86 |
| Oce | 39.31 | Aus (Lewis, D'Arcy, Ratcliffe, Haskell) | | Christchurch | 2 Feb 74 |
| OG | 37.83 | USA (Graddy, Brown, C.Smith, Lewis) | | Los Angeles | 11 Aug 84 |
| WJ | 39.00A | USA (Jessie, Franklin, Blalock, Mitchell) | Col.Springs | 18 Jul 83 |

## 4x400 METRES RELAY

| | | | | | |
|---|---|---|---|---|---|
| W,NAm | 2:56.16A | USA (Matthews, Freeman, James, Evans) | | C.de México | 20 Oct 68 |
| E,C | 2:59.13 | UK (Akabusi, Cook, Bennett, Brown) | | Los Angeles | 11 Aug 84 |
| Afr | 2:59.32 | Nig (Uti, Ugbusie, Peters, Egbunike) | | Los Angeles | 11 Aug 84 |
| Oce | 2:59.70 | Aus (Frayne, Clark, Minihan, Mitchell) | | Los Angeles | 11 Aug 84 |
| CAC | 3:01.60 | Bar (Louis, Peltier, Edwards, Forde) | | Los Angeles | 11 Aug 84 |
| Asi | 3:02.33 | Jap (Konakatomi,Yamauchi,Kawasumi,Takano) | Seoul | 5 Oct 86 |
| SAm | 3:02.79 | Bra (da Silva, Barbosa, Guimarães, Souza) | Caracas | 28 Aug 83 |
| OG | 2:56.16A | USA (Matthews, Freeman, James, Evans) | | C.de México | 20 Oct 68 |
| WJ | 3:01.90 | USA (Campbell, Rish, Waddle, Reed) | | Athínai | 20 Jul 86 |

# WORLD & CONTINENTAL RECORDS: WOMEN

(as at 31 Dec 1986)

Key:  W = World;   I = I.A.A.F. (if different);   C = Commonwealth
      Afr = Africa;  Asi = Asia;   CAC = Central America & Caribbean
      E = Europe;  NAm = N.America;  Oce = Oceania;  SAm = S.America
            OG = Olympic Games;   WJ = World Junior

      A = altitude over 1000m;   + = timing by photo—electric—cell
      * = awaiting ratification;   £ = not officially ratified

| Record | Mark | Name | Nat | Venue | Date |
|--------|------|------|-----|-------|------|

## 100 METRES

| Record | Mark | Name | Nat | Venue | Date |
|--------|------|------|-----|-------|------|
| W,NAm | 10.76 | Evelyn ASHFORD | USA | Zürich | 22 Aug 84 |
| E | 10.81 | Marlies GÖHR | GDR | E.Berlin | 8 Jun 83 |
| C,CAC | 10.92 | Merlene OTTEY-PAGE | Jam | Walnut | 28 Apr 85 |
| Oce | 11.20A | Raelene BOYLE | Aus | Ciudad de México | 15 Oct 68 |
| Asi | 11.22 | CHI Cheng | Tai | Wien | 18 Jul 70 |
| Afr | 11.22A | Evette ARMSTRONG | RSA | Johannesburg | 18 Apr 86 |
| SAm | 11.31 | Esmeralda GARCÍA | Bra | Caracas | 24 Aug 83 |
| OG | 10.97 | Evelyn ASHFORD | USA | Los Angeles | 5 Aug 84 |
| WJ | 11.13 | Chandra CHEESEBOROUGH | USA | Eugene | 21 Jun 76 |

## 200 METRES

| Record | Mark | Name | Nat | Venue | Date |
|--------|------|------|-----|-------|------|
| W,E | 21.71 | Marita KOCH | GDR | Karl-Marx-Stadt | 10 Jun 79 |
|  |  | Marita KOCH | GDR | Potsdam | 21 Jul 84 |
|  |  | Heike DRECHSLER | GDR | Jena | 29 Jun 86 |
|  |  | Heike DRECHSLER | GDR | Stuttgart | 29 Aug 86 |
| NAm | 21.81 | Valerie BRISCO-HOOKS | USA | Los Angeles | 9 Aug 84 |
| C,CAC | 21.93 | Merlene OTTEY-PAGE | Jam | Indianapolis | 16 Jun 85 |
| Oce | 22.35 | Denise BOYD | Aus | Sydney | 23 Mar 80 |
| Afr | 22.42A | Evette ARMSTRONG | RSA | Johannesburg | 18 Apr 86 |
| Asi | 22.62 | CHI Cheng | Tai | München | 12 Jul 70 |
| SAm | 22.94A | Beatriz ALLOCCO | Arg | La Paz | 11 Nov 78 |
| OG | 21.81 | Valerie BRISCO-HOOKS | USA | Los Angeles | 9 Aug 84 |
| WJ | 22.19 | Natalya BOCHINA | SU | Moskva | 30 Jul 80 |

## 400 METRES

| Record | Mark | Name | Nat | Venue | Date |
|--------|------|------|-----|-------|------|
| W,E | 47.60 | Marita KOCH | GDR | Canberra | 6 Oct 85 |
| NAm | 48.83 | Valerie BRISCO-HOOKS | USA | Los Angeles | 6 Aug 84 |
| C | 49.43 | Kathy COOK | UK | Los Angeles | 6 Aug 84 |
| Afr | 50.12A | Myrtle BOTHMA | RSA | Germiston | 11 Apr 86 |
| CAC | 50.41 | Ana QUIROT | Cub | Habana | 14 Jun 86 |
| Oce | 50.78 | Debbie FLINTOFF | Aus | London | 11 Jul 86 |
| Asi | 51.2 m | SHIN Keum Dan | NKo | Pyongyang | 31 Oct 64 |
|  | 51.61 | P.T.Usha | Ind | Canberra | 6 Oct 85 |
| SAm | 52.40 | Norfalia CARABALI | Col | Stockholm | 12 Aug 86 |
| OG | 48.83 | Valerie BRISCO-HOOKS | USA | Los Angeles | 6 Aug 84 |
| WJ | 49.77 | Christina BREHMER/LATHAN | GDR | Dresden | 9 May 76 |

## 800 METRES

| Record | Mark | Name | Nat | Venue | Date |
|--------|------|------|-----|-------|------|
| W,E | 1:53.28 | Jarmila KRATOCHVÍLOVÁ | CS | München | 26 Jul 83 |
| NAm | 1:56.90 | Mary SLANEY | USA | Bern | 16 Aug 85 |
| C | 1:57.42* | Kirsty McDERMOTT/WADE | Wal | Belfast | 24 Jun 85 |
| Asi | 1:58.0 m | SHIN Keum Dan | NKo | Pyongyang | 5 Sep 64 |
| CAC | 1:58.80 | Ana QUIROT | Cub | Habana | 15 Jun 86 |
| Oce | 1:59.0 m | Charlene RENDINA | Aus | Melbourne | 28 Feb 76 |
| Afr | 1:59.39 | Ilze VENTER | RSA | Stellenbosch | 25 Mar 83 |
| SAm | 2:01.55 | Soraya TELLES | Bra | Habana | 28 Sep 86 |
| OG | 1:53.43 | Nadyezhda OLIZARENKO | SU | Moskva | 27 Jul 80 |
| WJ | 1:59.40 | Christine WACHTEL | GDR | Los Angeles | 26 Jun 83 |

| Record | Mark | Name | Nat | Venue | Date |
|--------|------|------|-----|-------|------|

## 1500 METRES

| Record | Mark | Name | Nat | Venue | Date |
|--------|------|------|-----|-------|------|
| W,E | 3:52.47 | Tatyana KAZANKINA | SU | Zürich | 13 Aug 80 |
| NAm | 3:57.12 | Mary DECKER/SLANEY | USA | Stockholm | 26 Jul 83 |
| C | 3:59.96 | Zola BUDD | Eng | Bruxelles | 30 Aug 85 |
| Afr | 4:01.81 | Zola BUDD | RSA | Port Elizabeth | 21 Mar 84 |
| Oce | 4:08.06 | Jenny ORR | Aus | München | 4 Sep 72 |
| SAm | 4:13.09 | Alejandra RAMOS | Chl | Kobe | 30 Aug 85 |
| Asi | 4:13.1 m | YANG Liuxia | Chn | Guangzhou | 22 Mar 86 |
| CAC | 4:14.7 | Charlotte BRADLEY | Mex | Sofiya | 23 Aug 77 |
| OG | 3:56.56 | Tatyana KAZANKINA | SU | Moskva | 1 Aug 80 |
| WJ | 4:01.81 | Zola BUDD | RSA | Port Elizabeth | 21 Mar 84 |

## 1 MILE

| Record | Mark | Name | Nat | Venue | Date |
|--------|------|------|-----|-------|------|
| W,E | 4:15.8 # | Natalya ARTYOMOVA | SU | Leningrad | 6 Aug 84 |
| I,NAm | 4:16.71 | Mary SLANEY | USA | Zürich | 21 Aug 85 |
| (E) | 4:17.44 | Maricica PUICA | Rom | Rieti | 16 Sep 82 |
| C | 4:17.57 | Zola BUDD | Eng | Zürich | 21 Aug 85 |
| Afr | 4:28.4 m | Sarina CRONJE | RSA | Stellenbosch | 15 Nov 80 |
| Oce | 4:29.28 | Penny JUST | Aus | Oslo | 27 Jul 85 |
| WJ | 4:30.7 | Zola BUDD | UK | London | 13 Jul 84 |

## 3000 METRES

| Record | Mark | Name | Nat | Venue | Date |
|--------|------|------|-----|-------|------|
| W,E | 8:22.62 | Tatyana KAZANKINA | SU | Leningrad | 26 Aug 84 |
| NAm | 8:25.83 | Mary SLANEY | USA | Roma | 7 Sep 85 |
| C | 8:28.83 | Zola BUDD | Eng | Roma | 7 Sep 85 |
| Afr | 8:37.5 | Zola BUDD | RSA | Stellenbosch | 29 Feb 84 |
| Oce | 8:44.1 # | Donna GOULD | Aus | Eugene | 13 Jul 84 |
|  | 8:45.43 | Anne AUDAIN | NZ | Brisbane | 4 Oct 82 |
| Asi | 9:02.70 | WANG Huabi | Chn | Zhengzhou | 22 Oct 86 |
| SAm | 9:22.08 | Monica REGONESI | Chl | Los Angeles | 26 Jun 83 |
| CAC | 9:30.0 | Genoveva DOMINGUEZ | Mex | Nassau | 24 Aug 84 |
| OG | 8:35.96 | Maricica PUICA | Rom | Los Angeles | 10 Aug 84 |
| WJ | 8:37.5 | Zola BUDD | RSA | Stellenbosch | 29 Feb 84 |

## 5000 METRES

| Record | Mark | Name | Nat | Venue | Date |
|--------|------|------|-----|-------|------|
| W,E | 14:37.33 | Ingrid KRISTIANSEN | Nor | Stockholm | 5 Aug 86 |
| C | 14:48.07 | Zola BUDD | UK | London | 26 Aug 85 |
| Afr | 15:01.83 | Zola BUDD | RSA | Stellenbosch | 5 Jan 84 |
| NAm | 15:06.53* | Mary SLANEY | USA | Eugene | 1 Jun 85 |
| Oce | 15:13.23 | Anne AUDAIN | NZ | Auckland | 17 Mar 82 |
| Asi | 15:37.17 | HOU Juhua | Chn | Zhengzhou | 24 Oct 86 |
| SAm | 16:31.2 | Ena GUEVARAMORA | Per | Tallahassee | 21 Apr 85 |
| CAC | 16:53.97 | Sergía MARTÍNEZ | Cub | Bratislava | 14 Jun 85 |
| WJ | 15:01.83 | Zola BUDD | RSA | Stellenbosch | 5 Jan 84 |

## 10 000 METRES

| Record | Mark | Name | Nat | Venue | Date |
|--------|------|------|-----|-------|------|
| W,E | 30:13.74 | Ingrid KRISTIANSEN | Nor | Oslo | 5 Jul 86 |
| NAm | 31:35.3 m | Mary DECKER/SLANEY | USA | Eugene | 16 Jul 82 |
| C | 31:41.42 | Liz LYNCH | Sco | Edinburgh | 28 Jul 86 |
| Oce | 31:53.31 | Anne AUDAIN | NZ | Edinburgh | 28 Jul 86 |
| Asi | 32:47.77 | WANG Xiuting | Chn | Seoul | 1 Oct 86 |
| Afr | 32:50.25 | Esther KIPLAGAT | Ken | Kobe | 30 Apr 84 |
| SAm | 34:04.42 | Monica REGONESI | Chl | Canberra | 5 Oct 85 |
| CAC | 36:06.8 | Maricela HURTADO | Mex | Ciudad de México | 24 Jun 84 |
| WJ | 32:48.1 | Akemi MASUDA | Jap | Kobe | 2 May 82 |

| Record | Mark | Name | Nat | Venue | Date |
|--------|------|------|-----|-------|------|

## 100 METRES HURDLES

| Record | Mark | Name | Nat | Venue | Date |
|--------|------|------|-----|-------|------|
| W,E | 12.26 | Yordanka DONKOVA | Bul | Ljubljana | 7 Sep 86 |
| NAm | 12.79 | Stephanie HIGHTOWER | USA | Karl-Marx-Stadt | 10 Jul 82 |
| C | 12.87 | Shirley STRONG | Eng | Zürich | 24 Aug 83 |
| Asi | 12.93 | CHI Cheng | Tai | München | 12 Jul 70 |
| | 12.93 | Esther ROT | Isr | W.Berlin | 20 Aug 76 |
| Oce | 12.93 | Pam RYAN | Aus | München | 4 Sep 72 |
| Afr | 13.14A | Ina VAN RENSBURG | RSA | Germiston | 23 Apr 82 |
| CAC | 13.18 | Grisel MACHADO | Cub | Habana | 8 Aug 82 |
| SAm | 13.25 | Nancy VALLECILLA | Ecu | Schweinfurt | 9 Aug 86 |
| OG | 12.56 | Vera KOMISOVA | SU | Moskva | 28 Jul 80 |
| WJ | 12.95 | Candy YOUNG | USA | Walnut | 16 Jun 79 |

## 400 METRES HURDLES

| Record | Mark | Name | Nat | Venue | Date |
|--------|------|------|-----|-------|------|
| W,E | 52.94* | Marina STEPANOVA | SU | Tashkent | 17 Sep 86 |
| Afr | 53.74A | Myrtle BOTHMA | RSA | Johannesburg | 18 Apr 86 |
| C,Oce | 53.76 | Debbie FLINTOFF | Aus | Oslo | 5 Jul 86 |
| NAm | 54.38 | Judy BROWN-KING | USA | Roma | 7 Sep 85 |
| Asi | 55.42 | P.T.Usha | Ind | Los Angeles | 8 Aug 84 |
| CAC | 55.75 | Sandra FARMER | Jam | Los Angeles | 18 May 85 |
| SAm | 57.4 m | Conceição GEREMIAS | Bra | Rio de Janeiro | 27 Jun 81 |
| | 57.61 | Conceição GEREMIAS | Bra | Ciudad Bolívar | 15 Aug 81 |
| OG | 54.61 | Nawal EL MOUTAWAKIL | Mar | Los Angeles | 8 Aug 84 |
| WJ | 55.20 | Leslie MAXIE | USA | San Jose | 9 Jun 84 |

## HIGH JUMP

| Record | Mark | Name | Nat | Venue | Date |
|--------|------|------|-----|-------|------|
| W,E | 2.08 | Stefka KOSTADINOVA | Bul | Sofiya | 31 May 86 |
| NAm | 2.01* | Louise RITTER | USA | Roma | 1 Sep 83 |
| CAC | 2.01 | Silvia COSTA | Cub | Kobe | 3 Sep 85 |
| Afr | 2.01 | Desirée DU PLESSIS | RSA | Johannesburg | 15 Sep 86 |
| C | 1.99i | Debbie BRILL | Can | Edmonton | 23 Jan 82 |
| | 1.98 | Debbie BRILL | Can | Rieti | 2 Sep 84 |
| Oce | 1.96 | Chris STANTON | Aus | Adelaide | 26 Jan 85 |
| Asi | 1.96 | YANG Wenqin | Chn | Beijing | 26 May 85 |
| SAm | 1.90 | Liliana ARIGONI | Arg | Santa Fe | 5 May 84 |
| OG | 2.02 | Ulrike MEYFARTH | FRG | Los Angeles | 10 Aug 84 |
| WJ | 1.96 | Charmaine GALE | RSA | Bloemfontein | 4 Apr 81 |
| | | Olga TURCHAK | SU | Donetsk | 7 Sep 84 |

## LONG JUMP

| Record | Mark | Name | Nat | Venue | Date |
|--------|------|------|-----|-------|------|
| W,E | 7.45 | Heike DRECHSLER | GDR | Tallinn | 21 Jun 86 |
| | | Heike DRECHSLER | GDR | Dresden | 3 Jul 86 |
| NAm | 7.24 | Jackie JOYNER/KERSEE | USA | Zürich | 21 Aug 85 |
| C | 6.90 | Beverley KINCH | Eng | Helsinki | 14 Aug 83 |
| Oce | 6.86 | Robyn LORRAWAY | Aus | Canberra | 23 Feb 86 |
| CAC | 6.82 | Jennifer INNIS | Guy | Nice | 14 Aug 82 |
| Afr | 6.80 | Maryna VAN NIEKERK | RSA | Johannesburg | 25 Oct 86 |
| Asi | 6.65 | HUANG Donghuo | Chn | Hiroshima | 4 May 85 |
| SAm | 6.58 | Esmeralda GARCÍA | Bra | Austin | 31 May 85 |
| OG | 7.06 | Tatyana KALPAKOVA | SU | Moskva | 31 Jul 80 |
| WJ | 6.98 | Heike DAUTE/DRESCHLER | GDR | Potsdam | 18 Aug 82 |

| Record | Mark | Name | Nat | Venue | Date |
|--------|------|------|-----|-------|------|

## SHOT PUT

| | | | | | |
|--------|------|------|-----|-------|------|
| W,E | 22.53 | Natalya LISOVSKAYA | SU | Sochi | 27 May 84 |
| CAC | 20.61 | María SARRÍA | Cub | Habana | 22 Jul 82 |
| C,Oce | 19.74 | Gael MARTIN | Aus | Berkeley | 14 Jul 84 |
| NAm | 19.13 | Ramona PAGEL | USA | Westwood | 26 May 85 |
| Asi | 18.93 | CONG Yuzhen | Chn | Beijing | 8 Sep 85 |
| Afr | 17.32 | Mariette VAN HEERDEN | RSA | Germiston | 29 Nov 80 |
| SAm | 16.32 | Maria-Nilba FERNANDES | Bra | Manaus | 2 Jul 83 |
| OG | 22.41 | Ilona BRIESENICK | GDR | Moskva | 24 Jul 80 |
| WJ | 19.57 | Grit HAUPT | GDR | Gera | 7 Jul 84 |

## DISCUS

| | | | | | |
|--------|------|------|-----|-------|------|
| W,E | 74.56 | Zděnka ŠILHAVÁ | CS | Nitra | 26 Aug 84 |
| CAC | 70.50 | Maritza MARTEN | Cub | Habana | 21 Mar 85 |
| C | 67.48 | Meg RITCHIE | Sco | Walnut | 26 Apr 81 |
| NAm | 66.10 | Carol CADY | USA | San Jose | 31 May 86 |
| Asi | 63.48 | HOU Xuemei | Chn | Beijing | 12 Apr 86 |
| Oce | 63.08 | Gael MULHALL/MARTIN | Aus | Melbourne | 11 Jan 79 |
| Afr | 58.80 | Nanette VAN DER WALT | RSA | Port Elizabeth | 15 Feb 86 |
| SAm | 56.84 | María URRUTIA | Col | Habana | 28 Sep 86 |
| OG | 69.96 | Evelin JAHL | GDR | Moskva | 1 Aug 80 |
| WJ | 65.96 | Grit HAUPT | GDR | Leipzig | 13 Jul 84 |

## JAVELIN

| | | | | | |
|--------|------|------|-----|-------|------|
| W,E,C | 77.44 | Fatima WHITBREAD | Eng | Stuttgart | 28 Aug 86 |
| CAC | 71.82 | Ivonne LÉAL | Cub | Kobe | 30 Aug 85 |
| Oce | 69.80 | Sue HOWLAND | Aus | Belfast | 30 Jun 86 |
| NAm | 69.32 | Kate SCHMIDT | USA | Fürth | 11 Sep 77 |
| Asi | 64.92 | LI Baolian | Chn | Beijing | 10 May 86 |
| Afr | 61.28 | Nellie BASSON | RSA | Stellenbosch | 31 Oct 83 |
| SAm | 56.90 | Marli DOS SANTOS | Bra | Nice | 21 Aug 77 |
| OG | 69.56 | Tessa SANDERSON | UK | Los Angeles | 6 Aug 84 |
| WJ | 71.88 | Antoaneta TODOROVA | Bul | Zagreb | 15 Aug 81 |

## HEPTATHLON (1971/1984 Tables)

| | | | | | |
|--------|------|------|-----|-------|------|
| W,NAm | 7158* | Jackie JOYNER/KERSEE | USA | Houston | 2 Aug 86 |
| E | 6867/6946 | Sabine MÖBIUS | GDR | Potsdam | 6 May 84 |
| C | 6623 | Judy SIMPSON | Eng | Stuttgart | 30 Aug 86 |
| Oce | 6390/6387 | Glynis NUNN | Aus | Los Angeles | 4 Aug 84 |
| SAm | 6084/6017 | Conceição GEREMIAS | Bra | Caracas | 25 Aug 83 |
| CAC | 5973/5930 | Hildelise DESPAIGNE | Cub | Praha | 17 Aug 84 |
| Afr | 5796 | Annie LEROUX | RSA | Germiston | 12 Apr 86 |
| Asi | 5611 | ZHU Yuqing | Chn | Nanjing | 3 Jun 86 |
| OG | 6390(6387) | Glynis NUNN | Aus | Los Angeles | 4 Aug 84 |
| | (6363)6388 | Sabine EVERTS | FRG | Los Angeles | 4 Aug 84 |
| WJ | 6421/6465 | Sybille THIELE | GDR | Schwechat | 28 Aug 83 |

## MARATHON

| | | | | | |
|--------|------|------|-----|-------|------|
| W,E | 2:21:06 | Ingrid KRISTIANSEN | Nor | London | 21 Apr 85 |
| NAm | 2:21:21 | Joan BENOIT/SAMUELSON | USA | Chicago | 20 Oct 85 |
| C,Oce | 2:26:06 | Lisa MARTIN | NZ | Edinburgh | 1 Aug 86 |
| Asi | 2:30:30 | Akemi MASUDA | Jap | Eugene | 11 Sep 83 |
| Afr | 2:35:43 | Sonja LAXTON | RSA | Stellenbosch | 13 Sep 86 |
| SAm | 2:36:17 | Elisabeth OBERLI-SCHUH | Ven | Frankfurt/Main | 13 May 84 |
| CAC | 2:37:10 | María TRUJILLO | Mex | Chicago | 20 Oct 85 |
| OG | 2:24:52 | Joan BENOIT/SAMUELSON | USA | Los Angeles | 5 Aug 84 |
| WJ | 2:34:24 | Cathy SCHIRO | USA | Washington | 12 May 84 |

| Record | Mark | Name | Nat | Venue | Date |
|--------|------|------|-----|-------|------|

## 5000 METRES WALK (TRACK)

| | | | | | |
|--------|------|------|-----|-------|------|
| W,Asi | 21:26.5 * | GUAN Ping | Chn | Qingdao | 17 Oct 86 |
| E | 21:35.25 | Giuliana SALCE | Ita | Verona | 19 Jun 86 |
| C,Oce | 21:53.36 | Kerry SAXBY | Aus | Melbourne | 16 Feb 86 |
| NAm | 22:17.5 | Ann PEEL | Can | Fana | 5 May 84 |
| CAC | 23:38.25 | María DE LA CRUZ/COLIN | Mex | Monterrey | 9 Apr 86 |
| Afr | 26:29.5 | Cheruiyot DARMAO | Ken | Nairobi | 15 Jun 84 |
| SAm | | | | | |
| WJ | 21:33.8 | WANG Yan | Chn | Jian | 8 Mar 86 |

## 10 000 METRES WALK (TRACK)

| | | | | | |
|--------|------|------|-----|-------|------|
| W,E | 44:32.50* | Yelena KUZNETSOVA | SU | Bryansk | 16 Aug 86 |
| Asi | 44:42.2 | GUAN Ping | Chn | Qingdao | 18 Oct 86 |
| C,Oce | 45:08.13 | Kerry SAXBY | Aus | Moskva | 7 Jul 86 |
| NAm | 46:12.79 | Ann PEEL | Can | Karl-Marx-Stadt | 13 Jul 86 |
| CAC | 51:08.0 | María DE LA CRUZ/COLIN | Mex | Ciudad de México | 13 Apr 85 |
| SAm | 53:26.33 | Elsa ABRIL | Col | Medellín | 29 Jun 85 |
| Afr | 56:54.9 | Sahiba MANSOURI | Alg | Alger | 11 Apr 85 |
| WJ | 44:59.3 | WANG Yan | Chn | Fuxin | 30 Mar 86 |

## 10KM WALK (ROAD)

| | | | | | |
|--------|------|------|-----|-------|------|
| W,Asi | 44:14 | YAN Hong | Chn | Jiading | 16 Mar 85 |
| E | 44:38 | Irina STRAKHOVA | SU | Zhytomyr | 26 Sep 86 |
| C,Oce | 44:53 | Kerry SAXBY | Aus | Canberra | 10 May 86 |
| CAC | 45:23 | Graciella MENDOZA | Mex | St.Leonard | 4 Oct 86 |
| NAm | 45:26 | Ann PEEL | Can | St.Leonard | 4 Oct 86 |
| SAm | 53:22 | Elsa ABRIL | Col | Chiquinquira | 6 Sep 86 |
| Afr | 70:18 | Mercy NYAMBURA | Ken | Nakuru | 1 Oct 83 |
| WJ | 45:59 | JIN Bingjie | Chn | Jiading | 16 Mar 85 |

## 4x100 METRES RELAY

| | | | | | |
|--------|------|------|-------|------|------|
| W, E | 41.37 | GDR (Gladisch, Rieger, Auerswald, Göhr) | Canberra | 6 Oct 85 |
| NAm | 41.61A | USA (Brown,Williams,Cheeseborough,Ashford) | Col.Springs | 3 Jul 83 |
| C | 42.43 | Eng (Oakes, Cook, Callender, Lannaman) | Moskva | 1 Aug 80 |
| CAC | 42.73 | Jam (Hodges, Pusey, Cuthbert, Ottey-Page) | Helsinki | 10 Aug 83 |
| Oce | 43.18 | Aus (Wilson, Wells, Boyd, Boyle) | Montreal | 31 Jul 76 |
| Afr | 43.71 | Nig (Soneye, Eseimokumoh, Onyali, Usifo) | Indianapolis | 6 Jun 86 |
| Asi | 44.77 | Chn (Pan, Shao, Luo, Tian) | Beijing | 7 Sep 86 |
| SAm | 44.90A | Arg (Fava, Godoy, Cragno, Allocco) | C.de México | 20 Oct 75 |
| OG | 41.60 | GDR (Müller, Wöckel, Auerswald, Göhr) | Moskva | 1 Aug 80 |
| WJ | 43.73A | USA (Gilmore, Finn, Simmons, Vereen) | Col.Springs | 19 Jul 83 |

## 4x400 METRES RELAY

| | | | | | |
|--------|------|------|-------|------|------|
| W,E | 3:15.92 | GDR (Walther, Busch, Rübsam, Koch) | Erfurt | 3 Jun 84 |
| NAm | 3:18.29 | USA (Leatherwood,Howard,Brisco,Cheeseb') | Los Angeles | 11 Aug 84 |
| C | 3:21.21 | Can (Crooks,Richardson,Killingbeck,Payne) | Los Angeles | 11 Aug 84 |
| Oce | 3:25.56 | Aus (Canty, Burnard, Rendina, Nail) | Montréal | 31 Jul 76 |
| CAC | 3:26.56 | Jam (Oliver, Green, Rattray, Jackson) | Los Angeles | 10 Aug 84 |
| Asi | 3:32.49 | Ind (Valsamma, Rao, Abraham, Usha) | Los Angeles | 11 Aug 84 |
| Afr | 3:34.41 | Nig (Sowunmi, Bakare, Ubah, Vaughan) | Kobe | 4 Sep 85 |
| SAm | 3:38.38 | Bra (Miranda, da Costa, Fialho, Ribeira) | São Paulo | 13 Jul 86 |
| OG | 3:18.29 | USA (Leatherwood,Howard,Brisco,Cheeseb') | Los Angeles | 11 Aug 84 |
| WJ | 3:30.39 | GDR (Feuerbach,Witzel,Vogelgesang,Bohne) | Utrecht | 23 Aug 81 |

RECORDS

# ALL-TIME WORLD LISTS

| Mark | Wind | Name | | Nat | Yr | Pos | Meet | Venue | Date |
|------|------|------|---|-----|-----|-----|------|-------|------|

## 100 METRES

| Mark | Wind | Name | | Nat | Yr | Pos | Meet | Venue | Date |
|------|------|------|---|-----|-----|-----|------|-------|------|
| A9.93 | 1.4 | Calvin | Smith | USA | 61 | 1 | USOF | Air Force Acad. | 3 Jul 83 |
| A9.95 | 0.3 | Jim | Hines | USA | 46 | 1 | OG | Ciudad México | 14 Oct 68 |
| 9.95 | 0.8 | Ben | Johnson | CAN | 61 | 1r1 | GWG | Moskva | 9 Jul 86 |
| 9.96 | 0.1 | Mel | Lattany | USA | 59 | 1r1 | | Athens, Ga. | 5 May 84 |
| 9.97 | 1.5 | Carl | Lewis | USA | 61 | 1 | SW | Modesto | 14 May 83 |
| 9.97 | 1.6 | | Smith | | | 1 | WK | Zürich | 24 Aug 83 |
| A9.98 | 0.6 | Silvio | Leonard | CUB | 55 | 1 | WPT | Guadalajara | 11 Aug 77 |
| 9.98 | 1.6 | | Lewis | | | 1r1 | SW | Modesto | 11 May 85 |
| 9.99 | 1.3 | | Lewis | | | 1r1 | | Houston | 6 May 84 |
| 9.99 | 0.2 | | Lewis | | | 1 | OG | Los Angeles | 4 Aug 84 |
| | | | | | | | | | |
| 9.99 | 0.9 | | Lewis | | | 1 | WK | Zürich | 22 Aug 84 |
| 10.00 | 0.0 | | Lewis | | | 1 | | Dallas | 16 May 81 |
| 10.00 | 1.9 | | Lewis | | | 1 | CalR | Modesto | 15 May 82 |
| 10.00 | 2.0 | Marian | Woronin | POL | 56 | 1 | Kuso | Warszawa | 9 Jun 84 |
| 10.00 | -0.4 | | Johnson | | | 1 | WP | Canberra | 4 Oct 85 |
| 10.00 | 1.0 | Chidi | Imoh | NIG | 63 | 1 | ISTAF | Berlin | 15 Aug 86 |
| A10.01 | 0.9 | Pietro | Mennea | ITA | 52 | 1 | | Ciudad México | 4 Sep 79 |
| 10.01 | 1.1 | | Johnson | | | 1 | Jenner | San José | 31 May 86 |
| A10.02 | 2.0 | Charlie | Greene (10) | USA | 44 | 1q4 | OG | Ciudad México | 13 Oct 68 |
| 10.02 | 1.0 | James | Sanford | USA | 57 | 1 | Pepsi | Westwood | 11 May 80 |
| | | | | | | | | | |
| 10.02 | 1.1 | | Johnson | | | 1 | GP | Roma | 10 Sep 86 |
| 10.02 | 1.8 | Robson | da Silva | BRA | 64 | 1 | IbAm | Habana | 27 Sep 86 |
| 10.03 | 0.8 | | Hines | | | 1s1 | AAU | Sacramento | 20 Jun 68 |
| 10.03 | | | Leonard | | | 1 | | Habana | 13 Sep 77 |
| A10.03 | 1.6 | | Sanford | | | 1 | | El Paso | 19 Apr 80 |
| A10.03 | 1.9 | Stanley | Floyd | USA | 61 | 1r1 | NCAA | Provo | 5 Jun 82 |
| 10.03 | 1.6 | | Lattany | | | 2 | WK | Zürich | 24 Aug 83 |
| 10.03 | -0.7 | | Johnson | | | 1 | WK | Zürich | 13 Aug 86 |
| A10.04 | 0.3 | Lennox | Miller | JAM | 46 | 2 | OG | Ciudad México | 14 Oct 68 |
| 10.04 | 1.0 | | Lattany | | | 1 | | Athens, Ga. | 11 Apr 81 |
| | | | | | | | | | |
| 10.04 | 0.8 | | Lewis | | | 1q5 | OG | Los Angeles | 3 Aug 84 |
| 10.04 | 1.4 | | Johnson | | | 1 | WPT | San Juan | 20 Sep 85 |
| 10.04 | 1.8 | Linford | Christie | UK | 60 | 1 | | Madrid | 4 Jun 86 |
| 10.04 | 0.8 | | Imoh | | | 2r1 | GWG | Moskva | 9 Jul 86 |
| (34 performances by 15 athletes) | | | | | | | | | |
| | | | | | | | | | |
| 10.05 | -1.1 | Steve | Riddick | USA | 51 | 1 | WK | Zürich | 20 Aug 75 |
| 10.05 | 1.8 | Harvey | Glance | USA | 57 | 1r1 | FlaR | Tampa | 30 Mar 85 |
| 10.06 | 1.1 | Bob | Hayes | USA | 42 | 1 | OG | Tokyo | 15 Oct 64 |
| 10.06 | 0.0 | Hasely | Crawford | TRI | 50 | 1 | OG | Montréal | 24 Jul 76 |
| 10.06 | 1.6 | Ron | Brown | USA | 61 | 3 | WK | Zürich | 24 Aug 83 |
| | | (20) | | | | | | | |
| 10.06 | 1.6 | Emmit | King | USA | 59 | 4 | WK | Zürich | 24 Aug 83 |
| 10.06 | 2.0 | Leandro | Peñalver | CUB | 61 | 1 | PAG | Caracas | 24 Aug 83 |
| 10.06 | 1.9 | Frank | Emmelmann | GDR | 61 | 1 | | Berlin | 22 Sep 85 |
| 10.07 | 0.0 | Valeriy | Borzov | SU | 49 | 1q3 | OG | München | 31 Aug 72 |
| 10.07 | 0.0 | Don | Quarrie | JAM | 51 | 2 | OG | Montreal | 24 Jul 76 |
| 10.07 | 1.7 | Clancy | Edwards | USA | 55 | 1 | NCAA | Eugene | 2 Jun 78 |
| A10.07 | 1.8 | Eddie | Hart | USA | 49 | 1 | USOF | Air Force Acad. | 30 Jul 78 |
| 10.07 | -0.1 | Steve | Williams | USA | 53 | 1 | WK | Zürich | 16 Aug 78 |
| A10.07 | 0.6 | Mike | Roberson | USA | 56 | 1s1 | WUG | Ciudad México | 8 Sep 79 |
| 10.08 | 0.1 | Darrell | Green | USA | 60 | 1 | | San Angelo | 13 Apr 83 |
| | | (30) | | | | | | | |

| Mark | Wind | Name | | Nat | Yr | Pos | Meet | Venue | Date |
|---|---|---|---|---|---|---|---|---|---|
| 10.08 | 1.6 | Terry | Scott | USA | 64 | 1h3 | NCAA | Austin | 30 May 85 |
| 10.08 | 0.1 | Lorenzo | Daniel | USA | 66 | 1h2 | | Knoxville | 17 May 86 |
| 10.09 | 1.4 | Sam | Graddy | USA | 64 | 1h2 | | Baton Rouge | 12 May 84 |
| 10.09 | 1.3 | Antoine | Richard | FRA | 60 | 1 | NC | Aix-les-Bains | 10 Aug 86 |
| A10.10 | 0.5 | Hermes | Ramirez | CUB | 48 | 1q2 | OG | Ciudad México | 13 Oct 68 |
| A10.10 | 1.9 | Willie | Gault | USA | 60 | 2rl | NCAA | Provo | 5 Jun 82 |
| 10.10 | | Andrés | Simón | CUB | 61 | 1 | Barr | Habana | 30 Mar 85 |
| 10.10 | 1.6 | Darwin | Cook | USA | 62 | 2rl | SW | Modesto | 11 May 85 |
| 10.10 | 1.8 | Thomas | Schröder | GDR | 62 | 1 | NC | Jena | 27 Jun 86 |
| 10.10 | 1.9 | Stanley | Kerr | USA | 67 | 1 | TAC-j | Towson | 28 Jun 86 |
| | | (40) | | | | | | | |
| A10.11 | 1.6 | Roger | Bambuck | FRA | 45 | 2sl | OG | Ciudad México | 14 Oct 68 |
| 10.11 | 1.7 | Curtis | Dickey | USA | 56 | 2 | NCAA | Eugene | 2 Jun 78 |
| A10.11 | | Osvaldo | Lara | CUB | 55 | 2 | CAG | Medellin | 16 Jul 78 |
| A10.11 | 1.8 | Don | Coleman | USA | 51 | 3 | USOF | Air Force Acad. | 30 Jul 78 |
| 10.11 | 1.4 | Allan | Wells | UK | 52 | 1ql | OG | Moskva | 24 Jul 80 |
| 10.11 | 1.8 | Jeff | Phillips | USA | 57 | 1s3 | NCAA | Baton Rouge | 5 Jun 81 |
| A10.11 | 1.9 | Mike | Miller | USA | 59 | 3rl | NCAA | Provo | 5 Jun 82 |
| 10.11 | 0.0 | Kirk | Baptiste | USA | 63 | 1 | TAC | Indianapolis | 15 Jun 85 |
| 10.11 | 1.4 | Lee | McRae | USA | 66 | 1 | NCAA | Indianapolis | 7 Jun 86 |
| 10.11 | 1.9 | Viktor | Bryzgin | SU | 62 | 1 | vGDR | Tallinn | 21 Jun 86 |
| | | (50) | | | | | | | |

| Mark | Wind | Name | | Nat | Yr |
|---|---|---|---|---|---|
| 10.12 | 0.0 | Eugen | Ray | GDR | 1977 |
| 10.12 | 1.4 | Mike | Morris | USA | 1985 |
| 10.12 | | Roy | Martin | USA | 1986 |
| 10.13 | 0.5 | Houston | McTear | USA | 1977 |
| 10.13 | 1.4 | Petar | Petrov | BUL | 1980 |
| 10.13 | 1.8 | Steffen | Bringmann | GDR | 1986 |
| 10.13 | 1.9 | Derrick | Florence | USA | 1986 |
| 10.14 | 0.8 | Ronnie R. | Smith | USA | 1968 |
| A10.14 | 0.6 | Pablo | Montes | CUB | 1968 |
| A10.14 | 1.6 | James | Butler | USA | 1982 |
| 10.14* | 2.0 | Juan | Nuñez | DOM | 1983 |
| 10.14 | 1.4 | Lee | McNeill | USA | 1986 |
| 10.15 | 0.8 | Mel | Pender | USA | 1968 |
| 10.15 | 0.0 | Colin | Bradford | JAM | 1981 |
| 10.15 | 1.9 | Valentin | Atanasov | BUL | 1982 |
| 10.15 | | Innocent | Egbunike | NIG | 1984 |
| A10.15 | 1.6 | Wessel | Oosthuizen | RSA | 1986 |
| 10.16 | 0.0 | Robert | Taylor | USA | 1972 |
| 10.16 | 1.3 | Guy | Abrahams | PAN | 1978 |
| 10.16 | | Peter | Okodogbe | NIG | 1978 |
| 10.16 | 2.0 | Christian | Haas | FRG | 1983 |
| 10.16 | 1.7 | Stefano | Tilli | ITA | 1984 |
| 10.16 | | Nikolay | Yushmanov | SU | 1985 |
| A10.17 | 1.6 | Harry | Jerome | CAN | 1968 |
| A10.17 | 0.9 | Desai | Williams | CAN | 1983 |
| 10.17 | 1.4 | Rod | Richardson | USA | 1983 |
| 10.17 | 1.8 | Thomas | Jefferson | USA | 1986 |
| 10.18 | 0.8 | Larry | Questad | USA | 1968 |
| A10.18 | 2.0 | Jean-Louis Ravelomanantsoa | | MAD | 1968 |
| 10.18 | 2.0 | Jerome | Deal | USA | 1980 |
| 10.18 | 0.6 | Rudy | Levarity | BAH | 1981 |
| 10.18 | 1.7 | Harvey | McSwain | USA | 1983 |
| 10.18 | -0.4 | Attila | Kovács | HUN | 1984 |
| 10.18 | 0.8 | Roscoe | Tatum | USA | 1985 |

| Mark | Wind | Name | | Nat | Yr |
|---|---|---|---|---|---|
| 10.18 | 1.5 | Bruno | Marie-Rose | FRA | 1986 |
| 10.19 | 0.8 | James | Gilkes | GUY | 1978 |
| A10.19 | 1.9 | Mark | McNeil | USA | 1982 |
| A10.19 | 1.9 | Tony | Sharpe | CAN | 1982 |
| A10.19 | 1.4 | Bernie | Jackson | USA | 1983 |
| 10.19 | 1.6 | Marty | Krulee | USA | 1983 |
| 10.19 | | Ray | Stewart | JAM | 1984 |
| A10.19 | 1.0 | Ken | Henderson | USA | 1986 |
| 10.19 | 1.3 | Charles-Louis Seck | | SEN | 1986 |
| 10.20 | 0.2 | Eric | Brown | USA | 1979 |
| 10.20 | 1.8 | Soren | Schlegel | GDR | 1980 |
| 10.20 | 0.0 | Dwayne | Evans | USA | 1981 |
| 10.20 | | Elliston | Stinson | USA | 1983 |
| 10.20 | 1.6 | Cameron | Sharp | UK | 1983 |
| 10.20 | 1.4 | Andrew | Smith | JAM | 1985 |
| 10.20 | 1.5 | Elliot | Bunney | UK | 1986 |
| 10.20 | 0.4 | Floyd | Heard | USA | 1986 |
| 10.20 | 0.4 | Vladimir | Muravyev | SU | 1986 |
| A10.21 | | Gaoussou | Kone | IVC | 1967 |
| 10.21 | 0.8 | Kirk | Clayton | USA | 1968 |
| 10.21 | 0.9 | Cliff | Wiley | USA | 1977 |
| 10.21 | | James | Mallard | USA | 1979 |
| A10.21 | 0.6 | Ainsley | Bennett | UK | 1979 |
| 10.21 | 0.6 | Ernest | Obeng | GHA | 1980 |
| 10.21 | | Mark | Duper | USA | 1983 |
| 10.21 | 1.6 | Luis | Morales | USA | 1983 |
| 10.21 | 0.0 | Norman | Edwards | JAM | 1984 |
| 10.21 | 2.0 | Dennis | Mitchell | USA | 1985 |
| 10.21 | 0.0 | Joe | DeLoach | USA | 1985 |
| 10.21 | 1.5 | Mark | McKoy | CAN | 1986 |
| 10.21 | 1.8 | José | Arques | SPA | 1986 |
| 10.21 | 1.0 | Wallace | Spearmon | USA | 1986 |
| 10.21 | 0.4 | Andrey | Shlyapnikov | SU | 1986 |

* Subsequently disqualified for drug abuse.

| Mark | Wind | Name | | Nat | Yr | Pos | Meet | Venue | | Date |
|------|------|------|------|-----|----|----|------|-------|---|------|

**Doubtful wind reading**

| Mark | Wind | Name | | Nat | Yr | Pos | Meet | Venue | Date |
|------|------|------|------|-----|----|-----|------|-------|------|
| 10.02 | 1.2 | Ronald | Desruelles | BEL | 55 | 1 | | Naimette -X. | 11 May 85 |
| 10.03 | -2.5 | Viktor | Bryzgin | SU | 62 | 1r1 | Znam | Leningrad | 7 Jun 86 |
| 10.04 | -2.2 | | C.Smith | | | 1 | VD | Bruxelles | 26 Aug 83 |
| 10.10 | -0.4 | Nikolay | Yushmanov | SU | 61 | 1r2 | Znam | Leningrad | 7 Jun 86 |

**Low altitude marks for athletes with best marks at altitude**

| | Name | Mark | Wind | Pos | Meet | Venue | Date | |
|---|------|------|------|-----|------|-------|------|---|
| | Floyd | 10.07 | 2.0 | 1 | | Austin | 24 May 80 | 10.03A |
| | Greene | 10.10 | 0.9 | 1s2 | AAU | Sacramento | 20 Jun 68 | 10.02A |

| | Mark | Wind | Yr | Alt | Name | Mark | Wind | Yr | Alt |
|---|------|------|----|-----|------|------|------|----|-----|
| Roberson | 10.12 | 1.1 | 80 | 10.07A | Gault | 10.17 | -0.7 | 83 | 10.10A |
| Lara | 10.13 | 0.9 | 85 | 10.11A | L.Miller | 10.18 | 0.9 | 68 | 10.04A |
| M.Miller | 10.14 | 1.5 | 82 | 10.11A | Hart | 10.20 | 1.8 | 79 | 10.07A |
| Coleman | 10.15 | 1.6 | 79 | 10.11A | Bambuck | 10.21 | 0.9 | 68 | 10.11A |
| Mennea | 10.15 | 1.3 | 79 | 10.01A | D.Williams | 10.21 | 1.4 | 85 | 10.17A |

**Wind-assisted marks**

| Mark | Wind | Name | | Nat | Yr | Pos | Meet | Venue | Date |
|------|------|------|------|-----|----|-----|------|-------|------|
| 9.87 | 11.2 | William | Snoddy | USA | 57 | 1 | | Dallas | 1 Apr 78 |
| 9.88 | 2.3 | James | Sanford | USA | 57 | 1 | | Westwood | 3 May 80 |
| 9.90 | 2.5 | Carl | Lewis | USA | 61 | 1 | MSR | Walnut | 28 Apr 85 |
| 9.91 | 5.3 | Bob | Hayes | USA | 42 | 1s1 | OG | Tokyo | 15 Oct 64 |
| 9.91 | 4.5 | | Lewis | | | 1 | TAC | Eugene | 20 Jun 86 |
| 9.91 | 2.1 | Calvin | Smith | USA | 61 | 1 | vGDR | Karl Marx St | 9 Jul 82 |
| 9.93 | 2.3 | | Lewis | | | 1 | MSR | Walnut | 24 Apr 83 |
| 9.94 | 4.6 | | C.Smith | | | 1 | | Sacramento | 21 Jul 84 |
| 9.95 | 8.9 | Willie | Gault | USA | 60 | 1 | | Knoxville | 2 Apr 83 |
| 9.95 | 2.4 | Mel | Lattany | USA | 59 | 1 | | Athens | 7 May 83 |
| 9.97 | 8.9 | | C.Smith | | | 2 | | Knoxville | 2 Apr 83 |
| 9.97 | 7.7 | Andrés | Simón | CUB | 61 | 1s1 | WUG | Kobe | 30 Aug 85 |
| 9.97 | 3.4 | Roy | Martin | USA | 66 | 1 | | Houston | 18 May 86 |
| 9.98 | 11.2 | Cole | Doty (10) | CAN | 55 | 2 | | Dallas | 1 Apr 78 |
| 9.99 | 7.2 | Pietro | Mennea | ITA | 52 | 1 | vGRE | Bari | 13 Sep 78 |
| 9.99 | 2.6 | | Lewis | | | 1 | NCAA | Baton Rouge | 5 Jun 81 |
| 9.99 | 8.5 | | Lattany | | | 1 | | Edinburgh | 26 Jun 83 |
| 9.99 | 4.1 | | C.Smith | | | 1 | | Knoxville | 14 Apr 84 |
| 10.00 | 3.4 | | Sanford | | | 1h3 | NCAA | Austin | 5 Jun 80 |
| 10.00 | 2.6 | Jeff | Phillips | USA | 57 | 2 | NCAA | Baton Rouge | 5 Jun 81 |
| 10.00 | 2.1 | | Lewis | | | 1 | Jenner | San José | 26 May 84 |
| 10.01 | 2.3 | Ron | Brown | USA | 61 | 2 | MSR | Walnut | 24 Apr 83 |
| 10.00 | 2.6 | Lorenzo | Daniel | USA | 66 | 1 | | Knoxville | 18 May 86 |
| 10.01 | 4.0 | | Lattany | | | 1r1 | SW | Modesto | 12 May 84 |
| 10.01 | 5.5 | | B.Johnson | | | 1 | NC | Winnipeg | 30 Jun 84 |
| 10.01 | 2.4 | | Lewis | | | 1s1 | TAC | Eugene | 20 Jun 86 |
| 10.02 | 5.9 | Allan | Wells | UK | 52 | 1 | CommG | Brisbane | 4 Oct 82 |
| 10.02 | 3.4 | | Brown | | | 1 | Jenner | San José | 28 May 83 |
| 10.02 | 2.9 | Terry | Scott | USA | 64 | 1 | NCAA | Austin | 1 Jun 85 |
| 10.02 | 2.3 | | B.Johnson | | | 1 | NC | Ottawa | 3 Aug 85 |
| 10.02 | 4.5 | Lee | McRae | USA | 66 | 2 | TAC | Eugene | 20 Jun 86 |
| A10.02 | 6.2 | Aaron | Thigpen | USA | 64 | 1 | | Provo | 10 May 86 |
| 10.03 | 7.6 | Don | Quarrie | JAM | 51 | 1 | CommG | Edmonton | 7 Aug 78 |
| 10.03 | 4.2 | | Sanford | | | 1 | USOC | Syracuse | 25 Jul 81 |
| 10.03 | 2.6 | | C.Smith | | | 1 | vFRG, AFR | Durham | 26 Jun 82 |
| 10.03 | 3.4 | | Lewis | | | 2 | Jenner | San José | 28 May 83 |
| (36/19) | | | | | | | | | |
| 10.04 | 11.2 | Ray | Brooks | USA | 56 | 3 | | Dallas | 1 Apr 78 |
| 10.04 | 4.5 | Harvey | Glance | USA | 57 | 3 | TAC | Eugene | 20 Jun 86 |

MEN All-time

| Mark | Wind | Name | | Nat | Yr | Pos | Meet | Venue | Date | | |
|---|---|---|---|---|---|---|---|---|---|---|---|
| 10.05 | 2.3 | Emmit | King | USA | 59 | 1h1 | NCAA | Houston | 2 | Jun | 83 |
| A10.06 | 8.8 | Jerome | Deal | USA | 58 | 1 | | El Paso | 6 | May | 78 |
| 10.06 | 4.3 | Stefano | Tilli | ITA | 62 | 1 | | Cagliari | 9 | Oct | 83 |
| 10.06 | 7.7 | Arnaldo S. | de Oliveira | BRA | 64 | 2s1 | WUG | Kobe | 30 | Aug | 85 |
| 10.07 | 3.8 | Dwayne | Evans | USA | 58 | 1 | CalR | Modesto | 16 | May | 81 |
| 10.07 | 5.9 | Cameron | Sharp | UK | 58 | 3 | CommG | Brisbane | 4 | Oct | 82 |
| 10.08 | 4.0 | Johnny | Jones | USA | 58 | 1 | | Austin | 20 | May | 77 |
| 10.08 | 8.3 | Mike | Miller | USA | 59 | 1 | | Lexington | 17 | Apr | 82 |
| 10.08 | 2.4 | Sam | Graddy | USA | 64 | 1 | | Knoxville | 19 | May | 84 |
| 10.08 | >4.5 | Mike | McFarlane | UK | 60 | 1 | NC | Cwmbran | 27 | May | 84 |
| 10.08 | 2.3 | Peter | Ngobeni | RSA | 62 | 1 | | Durban | 23 | Feb | 85 |
| 10.08 | 2.9 | Thomas | Jefferson | USA | 62 | 3 | NCAA | Austin | 1 | Jun | 85 |
| 10.08 | 4.0 | Roscoe | Tatum | USA | 66 | 1r2 | | Houston | 18 | May | 86 |
| 10.09 | 2.4 | Eugen | Ray | GDR | 57 | 1s1 | NC | Dresden | 1 | Jul | 77 |
| 10.09 | | Ellison | Portis | USA | | 1s1 | | Abilene | 23 | May | 80 |
| 10.09 | 2.1 | Rod | Richardson | USA | 62 | 1 | | College St. | 20 | Mar | 82 |
| 10.09 | 5.9 | Paul | Narracott | AUS | 59 | 4 | CommG | Brisbane | 4 | Oct | 82 |
| 10.09 | 4.1 | Stanley | Blalock | USA | 64 | 1 | | Athens | 19 | Mar | 83 |
| 10.09 | 5.5 | Tony | Sharpe | CAN | 61 | 2 | NC | Winnipeg | 30 | Jun | 84 |
| 10.09 | 6.0 | Kirk | Baptiste | USA | 63 | 2 | TexR | Austin | 6 | Apr | 85 |
| 10.09 | 3.1 | Mike | Morris | USA | 63 | 1 | | University P. | 19 | May | 85 |
| 10.09 | 4.5 | Floyd | Heard | USA | 66 | 4 | TAC | Eugene | 20 | Jun | 86 |
| 10.10 | 4.8 | Herschel | Walker | USA | 62 | 1 | | Athens | 20 | Mar | 82 |
| 10.10 | 8.5 | Donovan | Reid | UK | 63 | 2 | | Edinburgh | 26 | Jun | 83 |
| 10.11 | 4.0 | Bill | Collins | USA | 50 | 2 | | Austin | 20 | May | 77 |
| 10.11 | 11.2 | Mike | Kelley | USA | 57 | 4 | | Dallas | 1 | Apr | 78 |
| 10.11 | 2.3 | Billy | Mullins | USA | 58 | 2 | | Westwood | 3 | May | 80 |
| 10.11 | 8.5 | Drew | McMaster | UK | 57 | 3 | | Edinburgh | 26 | Jun | 83 |
| 10.11 | 2.9 | Lee | McNeill | USA | 64 | 4 | NCAA | Austin | 1 | Jun | 85 |

| Mark | Wind | Name | | Nat | Yr |
|---|---|---|---|---|---|
| 10.12 | 2.8 | Christian | Haas | FRG | 1980 |
| 10.12 | 3.2 | Desai | Williams | CAN | 1980 |
| A10.12 | | Jerome | Harrison | USA | 1981 |
| 10.12 | | William | Davis | USA | 1983 |
| 10.12 | 3.4 | Innocent | Egbunike | NIG | 1984 |
| 10.12 | 6.5 | Carl | Carter | USA | 1984 |
| 10.12 | >4.5 | Luke | Watson | UK | 1984 |
| 10.12 | | Desmond | Ross | USA | 1985 |
| A10.12 | 6.2 | Ken | Henderson | USA | 1986 |
| 10.13 | | Alvin | Matthias | USA | 1980 |
| 10.13 | 4.7 | James | Butler | USA | 1982 |
| 10.14 | 3.7 | Eric | Brown | USA | 1980 |
| 10.14 | 2.3 | Hermann | Panzo | FRA | 1981 |
| 10.14 | 2.7 | Verril | Young | USA | 1983 |
| A10.14 | 6.2 | Gabriel | Okon | NIG | 1986 |
| 10.14 | 4.5 | Wallace | Spearmon | USA | 1986 |
| 10.15 | 5.3 | Wieslaw | Maniak | POL | 1964 |
| 10.15 | | Felix | Mata | VEN | 1973 |
| 10.15 | 7.6 | James | Gilkes | GUY | 1978 |
| 10.15 | 2.8 | Gerrard | Keating | AUS | 1985 |
| 10.15 | 3.0 | Mark | Witherspoon | USA | 1986 |
| 10.16 | 2.5 | Vassilios | Papageorgopoulos | GRE | 1972 |
| 10.16 | 4.0 | Dwayne | Strozier | USA | 1978 |
| 10.16 | 4.0 | Ron | Ingram | USA | 1981 |
| 10.16 | 4.0 | Herkie | Walls | USA | 1981 |
| 10.16 | 2.3 | Phil | Epps | USA | 1982 |
| 10.16 | | Al | Miller | USA | 1983 |
| 10.16 | >4.0 | Greg | Sholars | USA | 1984 |
| 10.16 | 3.5 | Bruce | Davis | USA | 1984 |
| 10.16 | 2.4 | Claude | Magee | USA | 1984 |
| 10.16 | 3.2 | Elliston | Stinson | USA | 1984 |
| 10.16 | 4.0 | Norman | Edwards | JAM | 1984 |
| 10.16 | 2.3 | Greg | Meghoo | JAM | 1986 |
| 10.16 | 4.0 | Jason | Leach | USA | 1986 |
| 10.16 | 2.2 | John | Mair | JAM | 1986 |
| 10.16 | 2.8 | Ronald | Desruelles | BEL | 1986 |
| 10.17 | 2.4 | Cliff | Wiley | USA | 1977 |
| 10.17 | | Wylie | Turner | USA | 1978 |
| 10.17 | 2.9 | Efrem | Coley | USA | 1979 |
| 10.17 | 3.1 | Vincent | Courville | USA | 1982 |
| 10.17 | | Paul | Warren | USA | 1983 |
| 10.17 | 4.0 | Jere | Wheeler | USA | 1984 |
| 10.17 | | Edgar | Washington | USA | 1985 |
| A10.18 | 8.8 | Doug | Parrell | USA | 1978 |
| 10.18 | 4.2 | Renaldo | Nehemiah | USA | 1978 |
| 10.18 | 2.7 | Rich | Edwards | USA | 1979 |
| 10.18 | | Charles | Pickens | USA | 1980 |
| 10.18 | 4.2 | Luis | Morales | USA | 1983 |
| 10.18 | 2.3 | Bobby | Bankston | USA | 1986 |
| 10.18 | 3.4 | Andrew | Smith | JAM | 1986 |

| Mark | Wind | Name | | Nat | Yr | Pos | Meet | Venue | | Date |
|------|------|------|---|-----|----|----|------|-------|---|------|

**Short course (98.5m)**

| 9.84 | 2.2 | Verril | Young | USA | 60 | 1r2 | | Baton Rouge | 21 Apr 84 |

**Doubtful timing**

| 10.07 | 1.8 | Ed | Preston | USA | 55 | 1 | TexR | Austin | 3 Apr 76 |

| 10.13 | 1.5 | Andrey | Prokofyev | SU | 1980 | 10.19 | 1.5 | Aleksandr | Aksinin | SU | 1980 |
| 10.14 | 1.8 | Robert | Woods | USA | 1976 | 10.20 | 1.8 | Albert | Lomotey | GHA | 1976 |

**Rolling start**

| 10.16 | 0.9 | Armin | Hary | FRG | 1960 |

**Hand timing**

| 9.8 | | Harvey | Glance | USA | 57 | 1 | | Auburn | 9 Apr 77 |
| 9.8 | -0.8 | | Glance | | | 1 | FlaR | Gainesville | 28 Mar 81 |
| 9.8 | 0.4 | Jeff | Phillips | USA | 57 | 1 | | Knoxville | 22 May 82 |

| 9.9 | 0.9 | Eddie | Hart | USA | 1972 | 9.9 | 1.5 | Ronald | Desruelles | BEL | 1978 |
| 9.9 | 0.9 | Rey | Robinson | USA | 1972 | 9.9 | 1.5 | Aleksandr | Aksinin | SU | 1980 |
| 9.9 | 1.3 | Steve | Williams | USA | 1974 | 9.9 | | Carl | Lewis | USA | 1982 |
| 9.9 | 1.7 | Silvio | Leonard | CUB | 1975 | 9.9 | 1.6 | Mel | Lattany | USA | 1982 |
| 9.9 | 1.7 | Don | Quarrie | JAM | 1976 | 9.9 | 1.2 | Paul | Narracott | AUS | 1984 |
| 9.9 | 1.8 | Johnny | Jones | USA | 1977 | 9.9 | -0.4 | Darwin | Cook | USA | 1985 |
| 9.9 | | Mike | Roberson | USA | 1978 | 9.9 | 1.2 | Vladimir | Krylov | SU | 1985 |

**Wind-assisted marks**

| 9.7 | 3.8 | Osvaldo | Lara | CUB | 55 | 1 | | Santiago de Cuba | 24 Feb 82 |
| 9.8 | 2.8 | Jim | Hines | USA | 46 | 1h1 | AAU | Sacramento | 20 Jun 68 |
| 9.8 | 4.1 | Steve | Williams | USA | 53 | 1 | | Arima | 29 May 75 |
| 9.8 | 4.1 | Hasely | Crawford | TRI | 50 | 2 | | Arima | 29 May 75 |
| 9.8 | 3.8 | Silvio | Leonard | CUB | 55 | 2 | | Santiago de Cuba | 24 Feb 82 |
| A9.8 | | Willie | Gault | USA | 60 | 1 | | El Paso | 26 Mar 83 |
| 9.8 | | Mike | Taylor | USA | 65 | 1 | | Shreveport | 11 Apr 83 |
| 9.8 | 3.3 | Mel | Lattany | USA | 59 | 1r1 | | Paris | 24 Jun 83 |
| 9.8 | | Elliot | Hanna | USA | 63 | 1 | | Ames | 4 May 85 |

## 200 METRES

| A19.72 | 1.8 | Pietro | Mennea | ITA | 52 | 1 | WUG | Ciudad México | 12 Sep 79 |
| 19.75 | 1.5 | Carl | Lewis | USA | 61 | 1 | TAC | Indianapolis | 19 Jun 83 |
| 19.80 | -0.9 | | Lewis | | | 1 | OG | Los Angeles | 8 Aug 84 |
| A19.83 | 0.9 | Tommie | Smith | USA | 44 | 1 | OG | Ciudad México | 16 Oct 68 |
| 19.84 | 0.2 | | Lewis | | | 1q3 | FOT | Los Angeles | 19 Jun 84 |
| A19.86 | 1.0 | Don | Quarrie | JAM | 51 | 1 | PAG | Cali | 3 Aug 71 |
| 19.86 | -0.2 | | Lewis | | | 1 | FOT | Los Angeles | 21 Jun 84 |
| A19.92 | 1.9 | John | Carlos | USA | 45 | 1 | FOT | Echo Summit | 12 Sep 68 |
| A19.96 | 0.2 | | Mennea | | | 1h9 | WUG | Ciudad México | 10 Sep 79 |
| 19.96 | 0.0 | | Mennea | | | 1 | | Barletta | 17 Aug 80 |

| 19.96 | -0.9 | Kirk | Baptiste | USA | 63 | 2 | OG | Los Angeles | 8 Aug 84 |
| 19.99 | 0.6 | Calvin | Smith | USA | 61 | 1 | WK | Zürich | 24 Aug 83 |
| 20.00 | 0.0 | Valeriy | Borzov | SU | 49 | 1 | OG | München | 4 Sep 72 |
| 20.01 | 0.0 | | Mennea | | | 1 | GGala | Roma | 5 Aug 80 |
| 20.03 | 1.6 | Clancy | Edwards | USA | 55 | 1 | | Westwood | 29 Apr 78 |
| 20.03 | 0.4 | | Mennea | | | 1 | 8-N | Tokyo | 20 Sep 80 |
| 20.03 | -0.1 | | Mennea | | | 1 | | Beijing | 27 Sep 80 |
| 20.03 | 1.5 | Larry | Myricks(10) | USA | 56 | 2 | TAC | Indianapolis | 19 Jun 83 |
| A20.04 | 0.0 | | Mennea | | | 1s1 | WUG | Ciudad México | 11 Sep 79 |
| 20.05 | 0.4 | | Mennea | | | 1 | VD | Bruxelles | 22 Aug 80 |

MEN All-time

| Mark | Wind | Name | | Nat | Yr | Pos | Meet | Venue | Date |
|------|------|------|------|-----|----|----|------|-------|------|
| 20.05 | -0.2 | | Baptiste | | | 2 | FOT | Los Angeles | 21 Jun 84 |
| A20.06 | 0.9 | Peter | Norman | AUS | 42 | 2 | OG | Ciudad México | 16 Oct 68 |
| 20.06 | 0.4 | | Quarrie | | | 1 | WK | Zürich | 16 Aug 74 |
| 20.06 | 0.9 | | Edwards | | | 1 | | Corvallis | 20 May 78 |
| 20.06 | 1.7 | Silvio | Leonard | CUB | 55 | 1 | Kuso | Warszawa | 19 Jun 78 |
| 20.07 | | James | Mallard | USA | 57 | 1 | | Tuscaloosa | 20 Apr 79 |
| 20.07 | | | Mennea | | | 1 | | Rovereto | 13 Sep 80 |
| 20.07 | 0.3 | Albert | Robinson | USA | 64 | 1 | | Indianapolis | 5 May 84 |
| 20.07 | 1.2 | | Mennea | | | 1 | | Brindisi | 3 Oct 84 |
| 20.07 | 1.5 | Lorenzo | Daniel | USA | 66 | 1 | | Starkville | 18 May 85 |
| (30/15) | | | | | | | | | |
| 20.08 | 0.9 | LaMonte | King | USA | 59 | 1 | TAC | Walnut | 15 Jun 80 |
| 20.10 | 1.7 | Millard | Hampton | USA | 56 | 1 | FOT | Eugene | 22 Jun 76 |
| 20.12 | 0.7 | Floyd | Heard | USA | 66 | 1 | GWG | Moskva | 7 Jul 86 |
| 20.13 | 1.7 | Roy | Martin | USA | 66 | 1r1 | | Austin | 11 May 85 |
| 20.14 | 1.8 | James | Gilkes | USA | 52 | 1 | | Ingelheim | 12 Sep 78 |
| (20) | | | | | | | | | |
| A20.15 | 0.3 | Mike | Miller | USA | 59 | 1h2 | NCAA | Provo | 2 Jun 82 |
| 20.16 | -0.1 | Steve | Williams | USA | 53 | 1 | | Stuttgart | 26 Aug 75 |
| 20.16 | 1.5 | Elliott | Quow | USA | 62 | 3 | TAC | Indianapolis | 19 Jun 83 |
| 20.19 | 0.0 | Larry | Black | USA | 51 | 2 | OG | München | 4 Sep 72 |
| 20.19 | 0.7 | James | Sanford | USA | 57 | 1 | | Westwood | 28 Apr 79 |
| 20.19 | 1.9 | Phil | Epps | USA | 59 | 1 | | College St. | 20 Mar 82 |
| 20.19 | 0.6 | John | Dinan | AUS | 59 | 1 | | Canberra | 6 Mar 86 |
| 20.20 | 0.7 | Greg | Foster | USA | 58 | 2 | | Westwood | 28 Apr 79 |
| 20.21 | 0.9 | Allan | Wells | UK | 52 | 2 | OG | Moskva | 28 Jul 80 |
| 20.21 | 0.1 | Mel | Lattany | USA | 59 | 1 | WP | Roma | 6 Sep 81 |
| (30) | | | | | | | | | |
| 20.21 | 1.3 | Mike | Conley | USA | 62 | 2 | | Fayetteville | 18 May 85 |
| 20.22 | 1.7 | Dwayne | Evans | USA | 58 | 2 | FOT | Eugene | 22 Jun 76 |
| A20.22 | 0.4 | Tony | Sharpe | CAN | 61 | 1 | | Colorado Spr. | 20 Jul 82 |
| A20.23 | 0.3 | James | Butler | USA | 60 | 2h2 | NCAA | Provo | 2 Jun 82 |
| 20.23 | 0.2 | Frank | Emmelmann | GDR | 61 | 1 | EP | Moskva | 18 Aug 85 |
| 20.23 | 0.5 | Mike | Timpson | USA | 67 | 1 | | University Pk | 16 May 86 |
| A20.24 | 1.8 | Leszek | Dunecki | POL | 56 | 2 | WUG | Ciudad México | 12 Sep 79 |
| 20.24 | 0.2 | Joe | DeLoach | USA | 67 | 3 | Arco | Los Angeles | 8 Jun 85 |
| 20.26 | 1.5 | Bernie | Jackson | USA | 61 | 5 | TAC | Indianapolis | 19 Jun 83 |
| 20.26 | -0.9 | Thomas | Jefferson | USA | 62 | 3 | OG | Los Angeles | 8 Aug 84 |
| (40) | | | | | | | | | |
| 20.27 | 0.9 | Wardell | Gilbreath | USA | 54 | 1 | | Tucson | 1 May 76 |
| A20.27 | 1.6 | William | Snoddy | USA | 57 | 1 | USOF | Colorado Spr. | 30 Jul 78 |
| 20.27 | 0.2 | Jeff | Phillips | USA | 57 | =1 | Jenner | San José | 17 Apr 82 |
| A20.28 | 1.9 | Larry | Questad | USA | 43 | 3 | FOT | Echo Summit | 12 Sep 68 |
| 20.28 | 1.2 | Robson C. | da Silva | BRA | 64 | 1 | | Madrid | 4 Jun 86 |
| A20.29 | 1.9 | Jerry | Bright | USA | 47 | 4 | FOT | Echo Summit | 12 Sep 68 |
| A20.29 | 1.9 | Tom | Randolph | USA | 42 | 5 | FOT | Echo Summit | 12 Sep 68 |
| A20.29 | -0.1 | Desai | Williams | CAN | 59 | 1 | | Provo | 21 May 83 |
| 20.29 | 1.5 | Clinton | Davis | USA | 65 | 1 | TAC-j | University Pk | 26 Jun 83 |
| 20.29 | 1.5 | Daron | Council | USA | 64 | 2 | | Starkville | 18 May 85 |
| (50) | | | | | | | | | |

| Mark | Wind | Name | | Nat | Yr | | Mark | Wind | Name | | Nat | Yr |
|------|------|------|------|-----|----|---|------|------|------|------|-----|----|
| 20.30 | -0.9 | João B. | da Silva | BRA | 1984 | | A20.34* | 0.9 | Lennox | Miller | JAM | 1967 |
| 20.30 | -1.3 | Sam | Graddy | USA | 1985 | | A20.34 | 1.8 | Wessel | Oosthuizen | RSA | 1986 |
| 20.30 | 0.0 | Harvey | McSwain | USA | 1986 | | 20.34 | 0.7 | Atlee | Mahorn | CAN | 1986 |
| 20.31# | 0.5 | Steve | Riddick | USA | 1975 | | 20.35 | | Efrem | Coley | USA | 1980 |
| 20.32 | 0.4 | Brady | Crain | USA | 1985 | | 20.35 | | Rod | Barksdale | USA | 1984 |
| 20.33 | -1.4 | Darwin | Cook | USA | 1985 | | 20.36 | -0.8 | Henry | Carr | USA | 1964 |
| 20.33 | | Larry | Jackson | USA | 1976 | | 20.36 | 0.3 | Dwight | Williams | USA | 1984 |
| 20.33 | 0.0 | Wallace | Spearmon | USA | 1986 | | 20.36 | 1.8 | Todd | Bennett | UK | 1984 |
| A20.34 | 0.9 | Edwin | Roberts | TRI | 1968 | | A20.36 | 0.1 | Chidi | Imoh | NIG | 1986 |
| 20.34 | -1.2 | Vladimir | Muravyev | SU | 1984 | | 20.37 | 0.0 | Larry | Burton | USA | 1972 |
| (60) | | | | | | | (70) | | | | | |

| Mark | Wind | Name | | Nat | Yr | Pos | Meet | Venue | | Date |
|---|---|---|---|---|---|---|---|---|---|---|
| 20.37 | -1.2 | Eugen | Ray | GDR | 1977 | | | | | |
| 20.37 | | Renaldo | Nehemiah | USA | 1979 | | | | | |
| 20.37 | 1.0 | Jurgen | Evers | FRG | 1983 | | | | | |
| 20.37 | 1.6 | Donald | Bly | USA | 1984 | | | | | |
| 20.37 | 0.2 | Roberto | Hernández | CUB | 1986 | | | | | |
| 20.38* | 0.0 | Mark | Lutz | USA | 1973 | | | | | |
| 20.38 | 0.8 | Pascal | Barre | FRA | 1979 | | | | | |
| 20.38 | -1.4 | Eric | Brown | USA | 1981 | | | | | |
| 20.38 | 0.5 | Ralf | Lübke | FRG | 1985 | | | | | |
| A20.39 | 0.0 | Mike | Fray | JAM | 1968 | | | | | |
| | | (80) | | | | | | | | |
| A20.39 | 1.0 | Marshall | Dill | USA | 1971 | | | | | |
| 20.39 | | Harvey | Glance | USA | 1979 | | | | | |
| 20.39 | 1.8 | Don | Coleman | USA | 1979 | | | | | |
| 20.39 | 0.2 | Cliff | Wiley | USA | 1979 | | | | | |
| 20.39 | 0.9 | Bernhard | Hoff | GDR | 1980 | | | | | |
| A20.39 | 1.6 | Ronnie | Taylor | USA | 1982 | | | | | |
| 20.39 | 1.7 | Terron | Wright | USA | 1982 | | | | | |

| Mark | Wind | | | | | | Name | | Nat | Yr |
|---|---|---|---|---|---|---|---|---|---|---|
| A20.39 | | Peter | Ngobeni | RSA | 1985 |
| 20.39 | 0.9 | Stanley | Kerr | USA | 1986 |
| 20.40 | 0.5 | Stefano | Tilli | ITA | 1984 |
| | | (90) | | | |
| 20.41 | 0.0 | Stanley | Floyd | USA | 1981 |
| 20.41 | 1.6 | J.-Jacques | Boussemart | FRA | 1984 |
| 20.41 | -1.2 | Aleksandr | Yevgenyev | SU | 1984 |
| 20.41 | 0.1 | Greg | Moses | USA | 1985 |
| 20.41 | -1.1 | Antonio | Manning | USA | 1985 |
| 20.41 | 1.3 | Elliston | Stinson | USA | 1985 |
| 20.41 | 1.5 | Ben | Johnson | CAN | 1985 |
| 20.41 | 1.0 | Chang | Jae-Keun | SKO | 1985 |
| 20.41 | 1.4 | John | Regis | UK | 1986 |
| 20.42 | 1.8 | Hans-Joachim Zenk | | GDR | 1974 |
| | | (100) | | | |
| A20.42 | 1.8 | Ainsley | Bennett | UK | 1979 |
| 20.42 | 0.6 | Leandro | Peñalver | CUB | 1982 |
| 20.42 | 0.6 | Innocent | Egbunike | NIG | 1983 |

Low altitude marks for athletes with lifetime bests at high altitude

| | | | | | | | | | |
|---|---|---|---|---|---|---|---|---|---|
| Quarrie | 20.06 | 0.4 | 1 | WK | Zurich | 16 Aug 74 | 19.86A |
| Snoddy | 20.28 | 1.4 | 2 | NCAA | Eugene | 3 Jun 78 | 20.27A |
| | | | | | | | |
| Butler | 20.31 | 0.9 | 1984 | 20.23A | D.Williams | 20.39 | 1983 | 20.29A |
| Carlos | 20.34 | 1.5 | 1968 | 19.92A | Dill | 20.44* | 0.0 | 1973 | 20.39A |

Wind-assisted marks

| Mark | Wind | Name | | Nat | Yr | Pos | Meet | Venue | Date |
|---|---|---|---|---|---|---|---|---|---|
| 19.86 | 4.6 | Roy | Martin | USA | 66 | 1 | | Houston | 18 May 86 |
| 19.94 | 4.0 | James | Sanford | USA | 57 | 1s1 | NCAA | Austin | 7 Jun 80 |
| 19.95 | 3.4 | Mike | Roberson | USA | 56 | 1h3 | NCAA | Austin | 5 Jun 80 |
| 19.96 | 2.8 | | Roberson | | | 1 | NCAA | Austin | 7 Jun 80 |
| 20.01 | 2.5 | Derald | Harris | USA | 58 | 1 | | San José | 9 Apr 77 |
| 20.01 | 2.1 | C. | Lewis | | | 1 | Jenner | San José | 26 May 84 |
| 20.03 | 2.7 | K. | Baptiste | | | 1 | NCAA | Austin | 31 May 85 |
| 20.03 | 3.2 | Floyd | Heard | USA | 66 | 1 | TAC | Eugene | 21 Jun 86 |
| 20.04 | 2.5 | | Baptiste | | | 1 | MSR | Walnut | 28 Apr 85 |
| | | (9/7-5) | | | | | | | |
| A20.07 | 2.1 | James | Butler | USA | 60 | 1r1 | NCAA | Provo | 4 Jun 82 |
| 20.09 | 3.7 | Brady | Crain | USA | 56 | 1 | TAC | San José | 9 Jun 80 |
| 20.10 | 4.6 | Stanley | Kerr | USA | 67 | 2 | | Houston | 18 May 86 |
| 20.11 | 3.7 | Allan | Wells | UK | 52 | 1 | | Edinburgh | 20 Jun 80 |
| 20.12 | 3.6 | Mike | Conley | USA | 62 | 1h3 | NCAA | Austin | 30 May 85 |
| 20.20 | 2.5 | Dwayne | Evans | USA | 58 | 1 | NCAA | Baton Rouge | 6 Jun 81 |
| 20.21 | 3.8 | Thomas | Jefferson | USA | 62 | 1s2 | TAC | San José | 9 Jun 84 |
| A20.22 | 2.1 | Eric | Brown | USA | 60 | 4r1 | NCAA | Provo | 4 Jun 82 |
| 20.22 | 5.9 | Dave | Smith | JAM | 60 | 1 | | Bozeman | 19 May 84 |
| 20.22 | | Vincent | Coleman | USA | 65 | 1 | | Arlington | 26 Apr 86 |
| | | | | | | | | | |
| 20.23* | 4.1 | Reggie | Jones | USA | 53 | 1s2 | NCAA | Austin | 8 Jun 74 |
| 20.23 | 4.5 | Innocent | Egbunike | NIG | 61 | 1 | | Pomona | 31 Mar 84 |
| 20.25 | 3.2 | Erwin | Skamrahl | FRG | 58 | 1 | NC | Gelsenkirchen | 19 Jul 81 |
| 20.27 | 4.3 | Steve | Morgan | JAM | 65 | 1 | | University Pk | 19 May 85 |
| A20.27 | | Ken | Henderson | USA | 66 | 1 | | Provo | 10 May 86 |
| 20.27 | 4.9 | Wallace | Spearmon | USA | 62 | 2s1 | TAC | Eugene | 21 Jun 86 |

| | | | | | | | | | | | |
|---|---|---|---|---|---|---|---|---|---|---|---|
| A20.34 | 2.2 | Marshall | Dill | USA | 1971 | 20.39 | 4.5 | Olaf | Prenzler | GDR | 1979 |
| 20.37 | | Tony | Dees | USA | 1983 | 20.39 | 3.3 | Stanley | Floyd | USA | 1980 |
| 20.38 | 3.4 | Byron | Howell | USA | 1985 | 20.39 | 3.0 | David | Walker | USA | 1981 |
| 20.38 | 4.6 | Leroy | Reid | JAM | 1986 | | | | | | |

* 220 yards less 0.12 seconds

| Mark | Wind | Name | | Nat | Yr | Pos | Meet | Venue | Date |
|------|------|------|---|-----|----|----|------|-------|------|

**Hand timing**

| Mark | Wind | Name | | Nat | Yr | Pos | Meet | Venue | Date |
|------|------|------|---|-----|----|----|------|-------|------|
| A19.7 | | James | Sanford | USA | 57 | 1 | | El Paso | 19 Apr 80 |
| 19.8" | 1.3 | Don | Quarrie | JAM | 51 | 1 | Pre | Eugene | 7 Jun 75 |
| 19.8* | 1.3 | Steve | Williams | USA | 53 | 2 | Pre | Eugene | 7 Jun 75 |
| 19.8 | | James | Mallard | USA | 57 | 1 | | Tuscaloosa | 13 May 79 |
| A19.8 | 0.8 | P. | Mennea | | | 1r1 | | Ciudad México | 3 Sep 79 |
| 19.9* | 0.1 | T. | Smith | | | 1 | | Sacramento | 11 Jun 66 |
| 19.9 | 0.0 | | Williams | | | 1 | King | Kingston | 17 May 75 |
| 19.9 | 1.4 | | Williams | | | 1 | | Gainesville | 17 Apr 76 |
| 19.9 | -0.9 | | Williams | | | 1 | King | Atlanta | 22 May 76 |
| 19.9 | | Mel | Lattany | USA | 59 | 2 | | Tuscaloosa | 13 May 79 |
| 20.0 | 1.9 | Larry | Black | USA | 51 | 1s1 | | Billings | 2 Jun 72 |
| 20.0 | -0.2 | Clancy | Edwards | USA | 55 | 1 | | Tucson | 4 Mar 78 |
| 20.0 | 1.9 | LaMonte | King | USA | 59 | 1 | | San José | 12 May 79 |
| 20.0 | -0.8 | Mike | Conley | USA | 62 | 1h3 | | Austin | 11 May 84 |
| 20.1* | 0.5 | Henry | Carr | USA | 42 | 1 | | Tempe | 4 Apr 64 |
| 20.1* | 1.8 | Willie | Turner -1 | USA | 48 | 2 | | Sacramento | 10 Jun 67 |
| 20.1* | 0.0 | Mike | Fray | JAM | 47 | 1 | | Mesa | 23 Mar 68 |
| 20.1 | -1.6 | Paul | Nash | RSA | 47 | 1 | | Zurich | 2 Jul 68 |
| A20.1 | | Clyde | Glosson | USA | 47 | 1r1 | | Echo Summit | 31 Aug 68 |
| 20.1* | 0.9 | Willie | Deckard | USA | 51 | 1 | | Westwood | 8 May 71 |
| 20.1 | | Marshall | Dill | USA | 52 | 1 | | Windsor | 1 Jul 71 |
| 20.1* | | Carl | Lawson | JAM | 47 | 1h1 | | Moscow | 18 May 73 |
| 20.1 | 1.4 | Harvey | Glance | USA | 57 | 1 | | Auburn | 17 Apr 76 |
| A20.1 | | Mike | Roberson | USA | 56 | 1r9 | | Ciudad México | 3 Sep 79 |
| A20.1 | | Wessel | Oosthuizen | RSA | 61 | 1 | | Germiston | 29 Mar 83 |

| Mark | | Name | | Nat | Yr | | Mark | Wind | Name | | Nat | Yr |
|------|---|------|---|-----|----|---|------|------|------|---|-----|----|
| 20.2* | | Jim | Hines | USA | 1967 | | 20.2 | 1.4 | Stanley | Harris | USA | 1976 |
| A20.2 | | Wayne | Collett | USA | 1968 | | 20.2* | 1.5 | Bill | Collins | USA | 1976 |
| 20.2* | | Lennox | Miller | JAM | 1969 | | 20.2 | 1.5 | Hasely | Crawford | TRI | 1976 |
| 20.2* | | Larry | Burton | USA | 1972 | | 20.2* | 1.3 | Johnny | Jones | USA | 1977 |
| 20.2* | | Ivory | Crockett | USA | 1972 | | A20.2 | | Willie | Smit | RSA | 1980 |
| 20.2 | 1.2 | H.-Jürgen | Bombach | GDR | 1973 | | A20.2 | | Paulo | Correia | BRA | 1981 |
| 20.2 | 1.2 | Siegfried | Schenke | GDR | 1973 | | 20.2 | 1.8 | Brad | MacDonald | USA | 1984 |

**Wind-assisted marks**

| Mark | Wind | Name | | Nat | Yr | Pos | Meet | Venue | Date |
|------|------|------|---|-----|----|----|------|-------|------|
| 19.8* | | Carl | Lawson | JAM | 47 | 1 | | Moscow | 19 May 73 |
| 19.8* | 3.4 | James | Gilkes | GUY | 52 | 1 | NCAA | Austin | 8 Jun 74 |
| 19.8 | 4.4 | Desmond | Ross | USA | 61 | 1 | | Manhattan | 11 May 85 |
| 19.9* | | Gerald | Tinker | USA | 51 | 1 | | Kent | 5 May 73 |
| 19.9* | 3.4 | Reggie | Jones | USA | 53 | 2 | NCAA | Austin | 8 Jun 74 |
| 19.9 | | Silvio | Leonard | CUB | 55 | 1 | | Habana | 22 May 77 |
| 19.9 | 4.4 | Chidi | Imoh | NIG | 63 | 2 | | Manhattan | 11 May 85 |
| A20.0* | 3.4 | Seraphino | Antao | KEN | 37 | 1 | | Nairobi | 22 Sep 62 |
| 20.0* | 3.4 | Wardell | Gilbreath | USA | 54 | 3 | NCAA | Austin | 8 Jun 74 |
| 20.0 | 6.6 | Perry | Williams | USA | 61 | 1 | | Raleigh | 9 Apr 82 |
| 20.0 | 4.4 | Leroy | Dixson | USA | 63 | 3 | | Manhattan | 11 May 85 |
| 20.0 | 4.4 | Anthony | Small | CAN | 64 | 4 | | Manhattan | 11 May 85 |
| 20.1 | | Charles | Joseph | TRI | 52 | 1 | | Arima | 15 Jun 74 |
| A20.1* | 2.1 | Larry | Brown | USA | 51 | 1 | | Salt Lake C. | 10 May 75 |
| 20.1 | 2.1 | Steve | Riddick | USA | 51 | 1 | | Fort de France | 2 May 76 |
| 20.1 | 4.4 | Aubrey | Jones | USA | 63 | 5 | | Manhattan | 11 May 85 |
| 20.1 | 4.4 | Dennis | Wallace | JAM | 62 | 6 | | Manhattan | 11 May 85 |
| A20.1 | | Gabriel | Okon | NIG | 66 | 1 | | Flagstaff | 3 May 86 |

" during 220 yards race; * 220 yards less 0.1 seconds

| Mark | Name | | Nat | Yr | Pos | Meet | Venue | Date | |
|------|------|--|-----|----|----|------|-------|------|--|

## 400 METRES

| Mark | Name | | Nat | Yr | Pos | Meet | Venue | Date | |
|------|------|--|-----|----|-----|------|-------|------|--|
| A43.86 | Lee | Evans | USA | 47 | 1 | OG | Ciudad México | 18 Oct | 68 |
| A43.97 | Larry | James | USA | 47 | 2 | OG | Ciudad México | 18 Oct | 68 |
| A44.06 | | Evans | | | 1 | FOT | Echo Summit | 14 Sep | 68 |
| A44.19 | | James | | | 2 | FOT | Echo Summit | 14 Sep | 68 |
| 44.26 | Alberto | Juantorena | CUB | 50 | 1 | OG | Montreal | 29 Jul | 76 |
| A44.27 | | Juantorena | | | 1 | CAG | Medellin | 16 Jul | 78 |
| 44.27 | Alonzo | Babers | USA | 61 | 1 | OG | Los Angeles | 8 Aug | 84 |
| 44.30 | Gabriel | Tiacoh | IVC | 63 | 1 | NCAA | Indianapolis | 7 Jun | 86 |
| 44.32 | | Tiacoh | | | 1 | Pepsi | Westwood | 17 May | 86 |
| 44.40 | Fred | Newhouse | USA | 48 | 2 | OG | Montreal | 29 Jul | 76 |
| | | | | | | | | | |
| A44.41 | Ron | Freeman | USA | 47 | 3 | OG | Ciudad México | 18 Oct | 68 |
| A44.45 | Ronnie | Ray | USA | 54 | 1 | PAG | Ciudad México | 18 Oct | 75 |
| 44.45 | Darrell | Robinson | USA | 63 | 2 | Pepsi | Westwood | 17 May | 86 |
| 44.46 | | Tiacoh | | | 1 | WK | Zürich | 13 Aug | 86 |
| 44.47 | Michael | Franks (10) | USA | 63 | 1 | WP | Canberra | 5 Oct | 85 |
| 44.47 | | Robinson | | | 1 | TAC | Eugene | 21 Jun | 86 |
| 44.48 | Roddie | Haley | USA | 65 | 1 | | Houston | 18 May | 86 |
| 44.50 | Erwin | Skamrahl | FRG | 58 | 1 | | München | 26 Jul | 83 |
| 44.50 | | Haley | | | 2 | TAC | Eugene | 21 Jun | 86 |
| 44.50 | Innocent | Egbunike | NIG | 61 | 2 | WK | Zürich | 13 Aug | 86 |
| | | | | | | | | | |
| 44.54 | | Tiacoh | | | 2 | OG | Los Angeles | 8 Aug | 84 |
| 44.58 | Bert | Cameron | JAM | 59 | 1 | NCAA | Baton Rouge | 6 Jun | 81 |
| 44.58 | | Tiacoh | | | 1 | | Los Angeles | 24 May | 86 |
| 44.59 | Roger | Black | UK | 66 | 1 | EC | Stuttgart | 29 Aug | 86 |
| A44.60 | John | Smith | USA | 50 | 1 | PAG | Cali | 1 Aug | 71 |
| 44.60 | Viktor | Markin | SU | 57 | 1 | OG | Moskva | 30 Jul | 80 |
| A44.62 | | Freeman | | | 3 | FOT | Echo Summit | 14 Sep | 68 |
| 44.62 | | Cameron | | | 1 | NCAA | Houston | 4 Jun | 83 |
| 44.62 | Thomas | Schönlebe | GDR | 65 | 1 | vSU | Erfurt | 22 Jun | 85 |
| 44.63 | | Schönlebe | | | 2 | EC | Stuttgart | 29 Aug | 86 |
| 44.64 | | Tiacoh | | | 1s2 | OG | Los Angeles | 6 Aug | 84 |
| (31/18) | | | | | | | | | |
| | | | | | | | | | |
| 44.66 | Vince | Matthews | USA | 47 | 1 | OG | München | 7 Sep | 72 |
| 44.68 | Sunder | Nix | USA | 61 | 1 | USOF | Indianapolis | 24 Jul | 82 |
| (20) | | | | | | | | | |
| 44.69 | Antonio | McKay | USA | 64 | 4= | WK | Zürich | 13 Aug | 86 |
| 44.70 | Karl | Honz | FRG | 51 | 1 | NC | München | 20 Jul | 72 |
| 44.70 | Cliff | Wiley | USA | 55 | 1 | TAC | Sacramento | 21 Jun | 81 |
| 44.71 | Andre | Phillips | USA | 59 | 3 | Pepsi | Westwood | 17 May | 86 |
| 44.72 | Hartmut | Weber | FRG | 60 | 1 | EC | Athinai | 9 Sep | 82 |
| 44.72 | Darren | Clark | AUS | 65 | 5 | WK | Zürich | 13 Aug | 86 |
| 44.73 | Willie | Smith | USA | 56 | 1 | | Tuscaloosa | 15 Apr | 78 |
| A44.73 | James | Rolle | USA | 64 | 1 | USOF | Air Force Acad. | 2 Jul | 83 |
| A44.76 | El Kashief | Hassan | SUD | 56 | 1h4 | NCAA | Provo | 3 Jun | 82 |
| 44.76 | Walter | McCoy | USA | 58 | 2 | WK | Zürich | 22 Aug | 84 |
| (30) | | | | | | | | | |
| 44.77 | Felix | Stevens | CUB | 64 | 1 | NC | Santiago de Cu. | 23 Feb | 86 |
| 44.80 | Wayne | Collett | USA | 49 | 2 | OG | München | 7 Sep | 72 |
| A44.80 | Chris | Whitlock | USA | 59 | 2 | USOF | Air Force Acad. | 2 Jul | 83 |
| 44.82* | Wendell | Mottley | TRI | 41 | 1 | CommG | Kingston | 11 Aug | 66 |
| 44.82 | Maxie | Parks | USA | 51 | 1 | AAU | Westwood | 12 Jun | 76 |
| 44.82 | Derek | Redmond | UK | 65 | 1 | Bisl | Oslo | 27 Jul | 85 |
| 44.83 | Sunday | Uti | NIG | 62 | 2s2 | OG | Los Angeles | 6 Aug | 84 |
| 44.83 | Ray | Armstead | USA | 60 | 3 | WK | Zürich | 22 Aug | 84 |
| 44.84 | Billy | Mullins | USA | 58 | 1 | Pepsi | Westwood | 11 May | 80 |
| 44.84 | Rick | Mitchell | AUS | 55 | 2 | OG | Moskva | 30 Jul | 80 |
| (40) | | | | | | | | | |

MEN All-time

| Mark | Name | | Nat | Yr | Pos | Meet | Venue | Date | |
|------|------|--|-----|----|-----|------|-------|------|--|
| 44.85* | Maurice | Peoples | USA | 50 | 1 | NCAA | Baton Rouge | 9 Jun 73 |
| 44.85 | Mathias | Schersing | GDR | 64 | 3 | EC | Stuttgart | 29 Aug 86 |
| 44.86 | Zeke | Jefferson | USA | 61 | 1 | | Dallas | 16 May 81 |
| 44.87 | Frank | Schaffer | GDR | 58 | 3 | OG | Moskva | 30 Jul 80 |
| 44.87 | Mark | Rowe | USA | 60 | 1 | TAC | Indianapolis | 16 Jun 85 |
| 44.88 | Mike | Paul | TRI | 57 | 2 | ASV | Köln | 22 Aug 82 |
| 44.89 | Harold | Madox | USA | 65 | 1s2 | | Odessa, Tex. | 16 May 86 |
| 44.89 | Clarence | Daniel | USA | 61 | 1s1 | TAC | Eugene | 20 Jun 86 |
| 44.90 | Leslie | Kerr | USA | 58 | 2 | | Dallas | 16 May 81 |
| 44.92 | Julius | Sang | KEN | 46 | 3 | OG | München | 7 Sep 72 |
| | (50) | | | | | | | |
| 44.92 | Harald | Schmid | FRG | 57 | 1 | NC | Stuttgart | 11 Aug 79 |
| 44.92 | Howard | Henley | USA | 61 | 1 | Pepsi | Westwood | 10 May 81 |
| 44.92 | Laron | Brown | USA | 62 | 1 | | Knoxville | 24 May 86 |

| Mark | Name | | Nat | Yr | | Mark | Name | | Nat | Yr |
|------|------|--|-----|----|--|------|------|--|-----|----|
| 44.93 | David | Jenkins | UK | 1975 | | 45.09 | Aldo | Canti | FRA | 1984 |
| A44.94 | Eddie | Carey | USA | 1983 | | 45.09 | Kevin | Robinzine | USA | 1985 |
| 44.94 | Rod | Jones | USA | 1984 | | | (80) | | | |
| 44.95 | Herman | Frazier | USA | 1976 | | 45.09 | Henry | Thomas | USA | 1985 |
| 44.95 | Jens | Carlowitz | GDR | 1984 | | 45.10 | Bernd | Herrmann | FRG | 1974 |
| 44.98* | Larance | Jones | USA | 1974 | | 45.10 | Willie | Caldwell | USA | 1985 |
| 44.98 | Charlie | Phillips | USA | 1983 | | 45.10 | Danny | Everett | USA | 1986 |
| | (60) | | | | | 45.11 | Robert | Taylor | USA | 1976 |
| 44.98 | Ralf | Lubke | FRG | 1986 | | A45.11 | Ludwig | Myburgh | RSA | 1985 |
| 44.99 | Ken | Randle | USA | 1976 | | 45.12 | Darrol | Gatson | USA | 1979 |
| A45.00 | Eliot | Tabron | USA | 1982 | | A45.12 | Nikolay | Chernyetskiy | SU | 1979 |
| 45.00 | Susumu | Takano | JAP | 1986 | | A45.12 | Franz-Peter Hofmeister | | FRG | 1979 |
| A45.01 | Amadou | Gakou | SEN | 1968 | | 45.12 | Mathias | Schersing | GDR | 1985 |
| 45.01 | Charles | Asati | KEN | 1970 | | | (90) | | | |
| 45.01 | Tony | Darden | USA | 1981 | | 45.13 | Andrew | Valmon | USA | 1985 |
| A45.01 | Jaco | Reinach | RSA | 1983 | | 45.14 | Mike | Cannon | USA | 1985 |
| 45.02 | Ian | Morris | TRI | 1986 | | 45.15 | Mike | Larrabee | USA | 1964 |
| 45.04 | Fons | Brijdenbach | BEL | 1976 | | 45.19 | Darnell | Chase | USA | 1986 |
| | (70) | | | | | 45.19 | Danny | Harris | USA | 1986 |
| 45.05 | Yevgeniy | Lomtyev | SU | 1984 | | A45.20* | Mike | Sands | BAH | 1975 |
| 45.05 | Roberto | Hernández | CUB | 1986 | | 45.20 | Vladimir | Krylov | SU | 1986 |
| A45.06 | Martin | Jellinghaus | FRG | 1968 | | 45.21 | Emmett | Taylor | USA | 1968 |
| 45.07 | Otis | Davis | USA | 1960 | | 45.21 | Adrian | Rodgers | USA | 1978 |
| 45.07 | Bill | Green | USA | 1981 | | A45.21 | James | Atuti | KEN | 1979 |
| 45.07 | Devon | Morris | JAM | 1986 | | | (100) | | | |
| 45.08 | Carl | Kaufmann | FRG | 1960 | | 45.21 | Gerson A. | Souza | BRA | 1982 |
| A45.08* | Benny | Brown | USA | 1975 | | 45.21 | Bruce | Frayne | AUS | 1984 |

Low altitude marks for athletes with altitude bests

| | | | | | | | |
|--|--|--|--|--|--|--|--|
| Evans | | 44.95 | 1967 | 43.86A | Tabron | 45.17 | 1983 | 45.00A |
| Whitlock | | 45.04 | 1983 | 44.80A | Hassan | 45.18 | 1979 | 44.76A |
| J.Smith | | 45.15* | 1975 | 44.60A | Carey | 45.20 | 1983 | 44.94A |

* 440 yards less 0.26 seconds

Hand timing

| Mark | Name | | Nat | Yr | Pos | Meet | Venue | Date | Auto best |
|------|------|--|-----|----|-----|------|-------|------|-----------|
| 44.1 | Wayne | Collett | USA | 49 | 1 | FOT | Eugene | 9 Jul 72 | 44.80 |
| 44.2 | John | Smith | USA | 50 | 1 | AAU | Eugene | 26 Jun 71 | 44.60 |
| 44.2 | Fred | Newhouse | USA | 48 | 1s1 | FOT | Eugene | 7 Jul 72 | 44.40 |
| 44.3 | | J.Smith | | | 2 | FOT | Eugene | 9 Jul 72 | |
| A44.4 | Vince | Matthews | USA | 47 | 1 | | Echo Summit | 31 Aug 68 | 44.66 |
| 44.4* | Curtis | Mills | USA | 48 | 1 | NCAA | Knoxville | 21 Jun 69 | - |
| 44.4* | | Collett | | | 2 | AAU | Eugene | 26 Jun 71 | |
| A44.4* | | J.Smith | | | 1 | ITA | El Paso | 22 May 76 | |
| A44.4 | A. | Juantorena | | | 1 | | Ciudad México | 3 Jul 76 | 44.26 |
| 44.5" | Tommie | Smith | USA | 44 | 1 | | San José | 20 May 67 | 45.25 |

| Mark | Name | | Nat | Yr | Pos | Meet | Venue | | Date | |
|------|------|--|-----|----|-----|------|-------|--|------|--|
| A44.5" | L. | Evans | | | 1 | | Echo Summit | 12 Sep 69 | | 43.86 |
| 44.5 | | J.Smith | | | 1 | NCAA | Eugene | 3 Jun 72 | | |
| (12/8-6) | | | | | | | | | | |
| 44.6 | Adolph | Plummer | USA | 38 | 1 | | Tempe | 25 May 63 | | - |
| 44.7* | Benny | Brown | USA | 53 | 1 | | Westwood | 5 May 73 | | 45.08 |
| 44.8* | Ken | Randle | USA | 54 | 1 | | Westwood | 3 May 75 | | 44.99 |
| 44.8* | Warren | Edmondson | USA | 50 | 2 | ITA | Atlanta | 25 Apr 76 | | 45.51 |

| Mark | Name | | Nat | Yr | Date | | Mark | Name | | Nat | Yr | Date |
|------|------|--|-----|----|------|--|------|------|--|-----|----|------|
| 44.9 | Mike | Larrabee | USA | 1964 | 45.15 | | 45.0 | Ulis | Williams | USA | 1964 | - |
| 44.9* | Theron | Lewis | USA | 1966 | - | | 45.0 | Fons | Brijdenbach | BEL | 1974 | 45.04 |
| A44.9* | Steve | Williams | USA | 1972 | - | | 45.0* | Evis | Jennings | USA | 1976 | 45.54 |
| 44.9* | Darwin | Bond | USA | 1974 | 45.37 | | A45.0 | Bill | Green | USA | 1981 | 45.07 |
| A44.9 | David | Kitur | KEN | 1986 | 45.62 | | | | | | | |

* 440 yards less 0.3 seconds, " during 440 yards race

MEN All-time

# 800 METRES

| Mark | Name | | Nat | Yr | Pos | Meet | Venue | | Date |
|------|------|--|-----|----|-----|------|-------|--|------|
| 1:41.73" | Sebastian | Coe | UK | 56 | 1 | | Firenze | 10 Jun 81 | |
| 1:41.77 | Joaquim C. | Cruz | BRA | 63 | 1 | ASV | Köln | 26 Aug 84 | |
| 1:42.28 | Sam | Koskei | KEN | 61 | 2 | ASV | Köln | 26 Aug 84 | |
| 1:42.33 | | Coe | | | 1 | Bisl | Oslo | 5 Jul 79 | |
| 1:42.34 | | Cruz | | | 1rl | WK | Zürich | 22 Aug 84 | |
| 1:42.41 | | Cruz | | | 1 | VD | Bruxelles | 24 Aug 84 | |
| 1:42.49 | | Cruz | | | 1 | | Koblenz | 28 Aug 85 | |
| 1:42.54 | | Cruz | | | 1 | ASV | Köln | 25 Aug 85 | |
| 1:42.60 | Johnny | Gray | USA | 60 | 2 | | Koblenz | 28 Aug 85 | |
| 1:42.88 | Steve | Cram | UK | 60 | 1rl | WK | Zürich | 21 Aug 85 | |
| 1:42.96 | | Gray | | | 1 | | Koblenz | 29 Aug 84 | |
| 1:42.98 | | Cruz | | | 1rl | ISTAF | Berlin | 23 Aug 85 | |
| 1:43.00 | | Cruz | | | 1 | OG | Los Angeles | 6 Aug 84 | |
| 1:43.07 | | Coe | | | 2 | ASV | Köln | 25 Aug 85 | |
| 1:43.19 | | Cram | | | 1 | | Rieti | 7 Sep 86 | |
| 1:43.22 | | Cram | | | 1 | CommG | Edinburgh | 31 Jul 86 | |
| 1:43.23 | | Cruz | | | 2rl | WK | Zürich | 21 Aug 85 | |
| 1:43.28 | | Gray | | | 2 | VD | Bruxelles | 24 Aug 84 | |
| 1:43.28 | | Gray | | | 3 | ASV | Köln | 26 Aug 84 | |
| 1:43.28 | | Koskei | | | 2 | | Koblenz | 29 Aug 84 | |
| 1:43.33 | | Gray | | | 3 | ASV | Köln | 25 Aug 85 | |
| 1:43.35 | David | Mack | USA | 61 | 3rl | | Koblenz | 28 Aug 85 | |
| 1:43.43 | | Gray | | | 3rl | WK | Zürich | 21 Aug 85 | |
| 1:43.44 | Alberto | Juantorena | CUB | 50 | 1 | WUG | Sofia | 21 Aug 77 | |
| 1:43.46 | | Cram | | | 1rl | WK | Zürich | 13 Aug 86 | |
| 1:43.50 | | Juantorena | | | 1 | OG | Montréal | 25 Jul 76 | |
| 1:43.5 m* | Rick | Wohlhuter | USA | 48 | 1 | | Eugene | 8 Jun 74 | |
| 1:43.51 | | Koskei | | | 2rl | WK | Zürich | 22 Aug 84 | |
| 1:43.54 | William | Wuyke | VEN | 58 | 2 | | Rieti | 7 Sep 86 | |
| 1:43.56 | Rob | Druppers (10) | HOL | 62 | 4 | ASV | Köln | 25 Aug 85 | |
| 1:43.57 | Mike | Boit | KEN | 49 | 1 | ISTAF | Berlin | 20 Aug 76 | |
| 1:43.59 | | Gray | | | 1 | | Rieti | 2 Sep 84 | |
| (32/11) | | | | | | | | | |
| 1:43.62 | Earl | Jones | USA | 64 | 2rl | WK | Zürich | 13 Aug 86 | |
| 1:43.63 | Agberto | Guimarães | BRA | 57 | 3 | | Koblenz | 29 Aug 84 | |
| 1:43.65 | Willi | Wülbeck | FRG | 54 | 1 | WC | Helsinki | 9 Aug 83 | |
| 1:43.7 m | Marcello | Fiascanaro | ITA | 49 | 1 | vCS | Milano | 27 Jun 73 | |
| 1:43.72 | Billy | Konchellah | KEN | 61 | 4rl | | Koblenz | 28 Aug 85 | |
| 1:43.84 | Olaf | Beyer | GDR | 57 | 1 | EC | Praha | 31 Aug 78 | |
| 1:43.85 | John | Kipkurgat | KEN | 44 | 1 | CommG | Christchurch | 29 Jan 74 | |

| Mark | Name | | Nat | Yr | Pos | Meet | Venue | Date | |
|---|---|---|---|---|---|---|---|---|---|
| 1:43.86 | Ivo | Van Damme | BEL | 54 | 2 | OG | Montreal | 25 Jul | 76 |
| 1:43.88 | Donato | Sabia | ITA | 63 | 1 | | Firenze | 13 Jun | 84 |
| | (20) | | | | | | | | |
| 1:43.9 m | José | Marajo | FRA | 54 | 1 | | Saint Maur | 12 Sep | 79 |
| 1:43.92 | John | Marshall | USA | 63 | 3 | FOT | Los Angeles | 19 Jun | 84 |
| 1:43.92 | James | Robinson | USA | 54 | 4 | FOT | Los Angeles | 19 Jun | 84 |
| 1:43.98 | Peter | Elliott | UK | 62 | 2 | | Oslo | 23 Aug | 83 |
| 1:44.03 | Peter | Braun | FRG | 62 | 1rl | | Koblenz | 6 Aug | 86 |
| 1:44.07 | Luciano | Sušanj | YUG | 48 | 1 | EC | Roma | 4 Sep | 74 |
| 1:44.09 | Steve | Ovett | UK | 55 | 2 | EC | Praha | 31 Aug | 78 |
| 1:44.10 | José Luis | Barbosa | BRA | 61 | 4 | | Rieti | 7 Sep | 86 |
| 1:44.12 | Edwin | Koech | KEN | 61 | 2sl | OG | Los Angeles | 5 Aug | 84 |
| 1:44.20 | Juma | N'diwa | KEN | 60 | 1 | | München | 26 Jul | 83 |
| | (30) | | | | | | | | |
| 1:44.24 | James | Maina Boi | KEN | 54 | 1 | WK | Zürich | 15 Aug | 79 |
| 1:44.25 | Vasiliy | Matveyev | SU | 62 | 1 | Izv | Kiev | 22 Jun | 84 |
| 1:44.29 | Don | Paige | USA | 56 | 1 | | Rieti | 4 Sep | 83 |
| 1:44.3 m" | Peter | Snell | NZ | 38 | 1 | | Christchurch | 3 Feb | 62 |
| 1:44.3 m* | Jim | Ryun | USA | 47 | 1 | USTFF | Terre Haute | 10 Jun | 66 |
| 1:44.3 m | Dave | Wottle | USA | 50 | 1 | FOT | Eugene | 1 Jul | 72 |
| 1:44.38 | Said | Aouita | MOR | 60 | 1 | | Lausanne | 30 Jun | 83 |
| 1:44.38 | Ryszard | Ostrowski | POL | 61 | 1 | WUG | Kobe | 4 Sep | 85 |
| A1:44.40 | Ralph | Doubell | AUS | 45 | 1 | OG | Ciudad México | 15 Oct | 68 |
| 1:44.5 m | Pekka | Vasala | FIN | 48 | 1 | vSWE | Helsinki | 20 Aug | 72 |
| | (40) | | | | | | | | |
| 1:44.5 m* | Danie | Malan | RSA | 50 | 2 | | Los Angeles | 27 May | 73 |
| 1:44.55 | Garry | Cook | UK | 58 | 4 | | Koblenz | 29 Aug | 84 |
| A1:44.57 | Wilson | Kiprugut | KEN | 38 | 2 | OG | Ciudad México | 15 Oct | 68 |
| 1:44.59 | Matthias | Assmann | FRG | 57 | 4rl | | Koblenz | 6 Aug | 86 |
| 1:44.61 | Tom | McKean | UK | 63 | 2 | EC | Stuttgart | 28 Aug | 86 |
| 1:44.62 | James | Mays | USA | 59 | 1 | DNG | Stockholm | 2 Jul | 84 |
| 1:44.65 | Ikem | Billy | UK | 64 | 1 | OsloG | Oslo | 21 Jul | 84 |
| 1:44.66 | Faouzi | Lahbi | ALG | 58 | 5rl | | Koblenz | 6 Aug | 86 |
| 1:44.68 | Moussa | Fall | SEN | 63 | 1 | | Rovereto | 1 Sep | 85 |
| 1:44.70 | David | Patrick | USA | 60 | 1 | TAC | Indianapolis | 19 Jun | 83 |
| 1:44.70 | Babacar | Niang | SEN | 58 | 1 | | Paris | 22 Jul | 86 |
| | (51) | | | | | | | | |

| Mark | Name | | Nat | Yr | | Mark | Name | | Nat | Yr |
|---|---|---|---|---|---|---|---|---|---|---|
| 1:44.7 m | Dicky | Broberg | RSA | 1971 | | 1:45.14 | John | Gladwin | UK | 1986 |
| 1:44.72 | Andreas | Busse | GDR | 1980 | | 1:45.15 | Coloman | Trabado | SPA | 1984 |
| 1:44.73 | Viktor | Kalinkin | SU | 1984 | | 1:45.17 | Aleksandr | Kostetskiy | SU | 1984 |
| 1:44.75 | Omer | Khalifa | SUD | 1986 | | 1:45.20 | Dragan | Zivotić | YUG | 1979 |
| 1:44.78 | Peter | Bourke | AUS | 1982 | | 1:45.2 m | Juris | Luzins | USA | 1971 |
| 1:44.80 | Ken | Swenson | USA | 1970 | | | (80) | | | |
| 1:44.81 | Detlef | Wagenknecht | GDR | 1981 | | 1:45.2 m | Seymour | Newman | JAM | 1977 |
| 1:44.84 | Mark | Enyeart | USA | 1977 | | 1:45.2 m | Tom | McLean | USA | 1977 |
| 1:44.84 | Harald | Schmid | FRG | 1979 | | 1:45.21 | Randy | Wilson | USA | 1985 |
| | (60) | | | | | 1:45.25 | Eugene | Sanders | USA | 1985 |
| 1:44.87 | Stanley | Redwine | USA | 1984 | | 1:45.29 | Ocky | Clark | USA | 1985 |
| 1:44.90 | Walter | Adams | FRG | 1970 | | 1:45.3 m* | Byron | Dyce | JAM | 1969 |
| 1:44.9 m | Franz-Josef | Kemper | FRG | 1966 | | 1:45.3 m | Ron | Phillips | USA | 1972 |
| 1:44.93 | Hans-Joachim | Mogalle | GDR | 1982 | | 1:45.3 m | Yevgeniy | Arzhanov | SU | 1972 |
| 1:44.93 | Hans-Peter | Ferner | FRG | 1983 | | 1:45.3 | Filbert | Bayi | TAN | 1974 |
| 1:44.93 | Viktor | Zemlyanskiy | SU | 1985 | | 1:45.3 m | Carlo | Grippo | ITA | 1976 |
| 1:44.94 | John | Walker | NZ | 1974 | | | (90) | | | |
| 1:45.0 m | Wade | Bell | USA | 1967 | | 1:45.3 m | Mark | Handelsman | RSA | 1981 |
| 1:45.05 | Steve | Scott | USA | 1982 | | 1:45.3 m | Konstantin | Russkikh | SU | 1985 |
| 1:45.08 | Leonid | Masunov | SU | 1984 | | 1:45.3 m | Alberto | Barsotti | ITA | 1986 |
| | (70) | | | | | 1:45.31 | Rob | Harrison | UK | 1984 |
| 1:45.10 | Philippe | Collard | FRA | 1986 | | 1:45.32 | Valeriy | Starodubtsev | SU | 1986 |
| 1:45.10 | Joseph | Chesire | KEN | 1986 | | 1:45.34 | Joel | N'getich | KEN | 1981 |
| 1:45.11 | Nikolay | Kirov | SU | 1981 | | 1:45.36 | Bill | Hooker | AUS | 1973 |
| 1:45.12 | Andy | Carter | UK | 1973 | | 1:45.38 | Cosmas | Silei | KEN | 1973 |
| 1:45.14 | Chris | McGeorge | UK | 1983 | | 1:45.4 | four men | | | |

| Mark | Name | | Nat | Yr | Pos | Meet | Venue | Date | |
|------|------|--|-----|-----|-----|------|-------|------|---|

| Mark | Name | | Nat | Yr | Pos | Meet | Venue | Date | |
|------|------|--|-----|-----|-----|------|-------|------|---|
| 2:12.18 | Sebastian | Coe | UK | 56 | 1 | OsloG | Oslo | 11 Jul | 81 |
| 2:12.88 | Steve | Cram | UK | 60 | 1 | | Gateshead | 9 Aug | 85 |
| 2:13.40 | | Coe | | | 1 | Bisl | Oslo | 1 Jul | 80 |
| 2:13.9 m | Rick | Wohlhuter | USA | 48 | 1 | King | Oslo | 30 Jul | 74 |
| 2:14.09 | Joaquim C. | Cruz | BRA | 63 | 1 | Nik | Nice | 20 Aug | 84 |
| 2:14.53 | Willi | Wülbeck | FRG | 54 | 2 | Bisl | Oslo | 1 Jul | 80 |
| 2:14.54 | | Cruz | | | 1 | Pre | Eugene | 21 Jul | 84 |
| 2:14.95 | Sam | Koskei | KEN | 61 | 1 | VD | Bruxelles | 30 Aug | 85 |
| 2:14.90 | | Coe | | | 1 | | London (Har.) | 16 Jul | 86 |
| 2:15.09 | | Cram | | | 1 | | Edinburgh | 23 Jul | 85 |
| 2:15.11 | | Cruz | | | 1 | | Bern | 16 Aug | 85 |
| 2:15.12 | | Cram | | | 1 | Coke | London | 17 Sep | 82 |
| 2:15.23 | Rob | Druppers | HOL | 62 | 1 | | Utrecht | 17 Aug | 85 |
| 2:15.25 | Andreas | Busse | GDR | 59 | 1 | | Berlin | 31 Jul | 83 |
| 2:15.28 | | Cruz | | | 1 | | Bern | 29 Jul | 83 |
| 2:15.3 | Mike | Boit | KEN | 49 | 1 | | Wattenscheid | 23 Sep | 77 |
| 2:15.33 | | Druppers | | | 2 | VD | Bruxelles | 30 Aug | 85 |
| 2:15.5 m | Ivo | Van Damme (10) | BEL | 54 | 1 | | Namur | 14 Jul | 76 |
| 2:15.75 | Said | Aouita | MOR | 60 | 1 | | Grosseto | 18 Aug | 83 |
| 2:15.77 | | Cram | | | 1 | PTG | London | 11 Jul | 86 |
| 2:15.81 | Agberto | Guimarães | BRA | 57 | 2 | | Bern | 29 Jul | 83 |
| 2:15.84 | | Cram | | | 1 | | London | 7 Aug | 82 |
| 2:15.86 | | Cram | | | 1 | | Birmingham | 19 Jul | 86 |
| 2:15.89 | Juma | N'diwa | KEN | 60 | 3 | VD | Bruxelles | 30 Aug | 85 |
| 2:15.91 | Steve | Ovett | UK | 55 | 1 | | Koblenz | 6 Sep | 79 |
| 2:15.98 | | Boit | | | 1 | Nik | Nice | 20 Aug | 78 |
| 2:15.98 | | Cram | | | 1 | | Loughborough | 17 Jun | 84 |
| 2:16.0 | Danie | Malan | RSA | 49 | 1 | HB | München | 24 Jun | 73 |
| 2:16.0 m | Vladimir | Malozemlin | SU | 56 | 1 | | Kiev | 11 Jun | 81 |
| 2:16.0 m | | Cruz | | | 1 | | Paris | 13 Jul | 85 |
| 2:16.03 | | Boit | | | 1 | Nik | Nice | 23 Aug | 81 |
| (31/16) | | | | | | | | | |
| 2:16.1 m | Tom | Byers | USA | 55 | 1 | | København | 6 Aug | 81 |
| 2:16.2 m | Jürgen | May | GDR | 42 | 1 | | Erfurt | 20 Jul | 65 |
| 2:16.2 m | Franz-Josef | Kemper | FRG | 45 | 1 | | Hannover | 21 Sep | 66 |
| 2:16.25 | James | Maina Boi | KEN | 54 | 3 | | Koblenz | 6 Sep | 79 |
| (20) | | | | | | | | | |
| 2:16.3 m | James | Robinson | USA | 54 | 2 | | København | 6 Aug | 81 |
| 2:16.3 m | Andreas | Hauck | GDR | 60 | 1 | | Potsdam | 12 Jul | 84 |
| 2:16.40 | Steve | Scott | USA | 56 | 2 | Nik | Nice | 23 Aug | 81 |
| 2:16.4 | Thomas | Wessinghage | FRG | 52 | 3 | | Wattenscheid | 23 Sep | 77 |
| 2:16.4 m | Nikolay | Shirokov | SU | 55 | 2 | | Kiev | 11 Jun | 81 |
| 2:16.5 m | Bodo | Tummler | FRG | 43 | 2 | | Hannover | 21 Sep | 66 |
| 2:16.54 | Jim | Spivey | USA | 60 | 2 | Pre | Eugene | 21 Jul | 84 |
| 2:16.56 | William | Wuyke | VEN | 58 | 3 | | Bern | 29 Jul | 83 |
| 2:16.57 | John | Walker | NZ | 52 | 3 | Bisl | Oslo | 1 Jul | 80 |
| 2:16.6 m | Peter | Snell | NZ | 38 | 1 | | Auckland | 12 Nov | 64 |
| (30) | | | | | | | | | |
| 2:16.6 m | Philippe | Collard | FRA | 60 | 1 | | Parilly | 18 Jul | 86 |
| 2:16.64 | Antonio | Paez | SPA | 56 | 4 | Bisl | Oslo | 1 Jul | 80 |
| 2:16.7 m | Siegfried | Valentin | GDR | 36 | 1 | | Potsdam | 19 Jul | 60 |
| 2:16.7 m | Detlef | Wagenknecht | GDR | 59 | 1 | | Berlin | 26 May | 82 |
| 2:16.7 m | John | Marshall | USA | 63 | 2 | | Paris | 13 Jul | 85 |
| 2:16.71 | Billy | Konchellah | KEN | 61 | 4 | VD | Bruxelles | 30 Aug | 85 |
| 2:16.8 m | José | Marajo | FRA | 54 | 1 | | Paris | 17 Jun | 80 |
| 2:16.8 m | Vitaliy | Tishchenko | SU | 57 | 3 | | Kiev | 11 Jun | 81 |

MEN All-time

| Mark | Name | | Nat | Yr | Pos | Meet | Venue | Date | |
|------|------|--|-----|----|-----|------|-------|------|--|
| 2:16.82 | Graham | Williamson | UK | 60 | 1 | | Edinburgh | 17 Jul | 84 |
| 2:16.87 | Pierre | Délèze | SWZ | 58 | 4 | | Bern | 29 Jul | 83 |
| | (40) | | | | | | | | |
| 2:16.90 | David | Mack | USA | 61 | 2 | | Edinburgh | 23 Jul | 85 |
| 2:16.9 m | Francesco | Arese | ITA | 44 | 1 | | Torino | 11 Oct | 70 |
| 2:16.92 | Jurgen | Straub | GDR | 53 | 1 | | Potsdam | 13 Jul | 80 |
| 2:17.0 m | Marcel | Philippe | FRA | 51 | 1 | | Paris | 28 Jun | 73 |
| 2:17.0 m | Byron | Dyce | JAM | 48 | 2 | | København | 15 Aug | 73 |
| 2:17.0 m | Lutz | Zauber | GDR | 58 | 2 | | Berlin | 26 May | 82 |
| 2:17.0 mA | Johan | Fourie | RSA | 59 | 1 | | Bloemfontein | 28 Jan | 85 |
| 2:17.01 | Edwin | Koech | KEN | 61 | 1 | Nik | Nice | 15 Jul | 86 |
| 2:17.14 | Riccardo | Materazzi | ITA | 63 | 1 | | Pisa | 20 Jun | 84 |
| 2:17.15 | Abdi | Bile | SOM | 63 | 3 | | Edinburgh | 23 Jul | 85 |
| | (50) | | | | | | | | |

# 1500 METRES

| Mark | Name | | Nat | Yr | Pos | Meet | Venue | Date | |
|------|------|--|-----|----|-----|------|-------|------|--|
| 3:29.46 | Saïd | Aouita | MOR | 60 | 1 | ISTAF | Berlin | 23 Aug | 85 |
| 3:29.67 | Steve | Cram | UK | 60 | 1 | Nik | Nice | 16 Jul | 85 |
| 3:29.71 | | Aouita | | | 2 | Nik | Nice | 16 Jul | 85 |
| 3:29.77 | Sydney | Maree | USA | 56 | 1 | ASV | Köln | 25 Aug | 85 |
| 3:29.77 | Sebastian | Coe | UK | 56 | 1 | | Rieti | 7 Sep | 86 |
| 3:30.15 | | Cram | | | 1 | VD | Bruxelles | 5 Sep | 86 |
| 3:30.77 | Steve | Ovett | UK | 55 | 1 | | Rieti | 4 Sep | 83 |
| 3:30.92 | José Luis | Gonzalez | SPA | 57 | 3 | Nik | Nice | 16 Jul | 85 |
| 3:31.13 | José Manuel | Abascal | SPA | 58 | 1 | | Barcelona | 16 Aug | 86 |
| 3:31.24 | | Maree | | | 1 | ASV | Köln | 28 Aug | 83 |
| 3:31.34 | | Cram | | | 1 | OsloG | Oslo | 27 Jun | 85 |
| 3:31.36 | | Ovett | | | 1 | | Koblenz | 27 Aug | 80 |
| 3:31.54 | | Aouita | | | 1 | FBK | Hengelo | 6 Jul | 84 |
| 3:31.57 | | Ovett | | | 1 | BGP | Budapest | 29 Jul | 81 |
| 3:31.58 | Thomas | Wessinghage | FRG | 52 | 2 | | Koblenz | 27 Aug | 80 |
| 3:31.66 | | Cram | | | 1 | VD | Bruxelles | 26 Aug | 83 |
| 3:31.69 | | Abascal | | | 1 | | Barcelona | 13 Aug | 85 |
| 3:31.7+ | | Aouita | | | 1 | WK | Zürich | 21 Aug | 85 |
| 3:31.75 | Pierre | Délèze | SWZ | 58 | 1 | WK | Zürich | 21 Aug | 85 |
| 3:31.76 | Steve | Scott (10) | USA | 56 | 4 | Nik | Nice | 16 Jul | 85 |
| 3:31.95 | | Coe | | | 1 | DNG | Stockholm | 7 Jul | 81 |
| 3:31.95 | | Ovett | | | 1 | | Milano | 8 Jul | 81 |
| 3:31.96 | Harald | Hudak | FRG | 57 | 3 | | Koblenz | 27 Aug | 80 |
| 3:31.96 | | Scott | | | 1 | | Koblenz | 26 Aug | 81 |
| 3:32.03 | | Coe | | | 1 | WK | Zürich | 15 Aug | 79 |
| 3:32.09 | | Ovett | | | 1 | OsloG | Oslo | 15 Jul | 80 |
| 3:32.11 | | Ovett | | | 1 | VD | Bruxelles | 4 Sep | 79 |
| 3:32.12 | | Maree | | | 1 | VD | Bruxelles | 27 Aug | 82 |
| 3:32.13 | | Coe | | | 2 | WK | Zürich | 21 Aug | 85 |
| 3:32.16 | Filbert | Bayi | TAN | 53 | 1 | CommG | Christchurch | 2 Feb | 74 |
| 3:32.19 | | Coe | | | 1 | WK | Zürich | 13 Aug | 80 |
| (31/12) | | | | | | | | | |
| 3:32.4 m | John | Walker | NZ | 52 | 1 | OsloG | Oslo | 30 Jul | 75 |
| 3:33.07 | Kipkoech | Cheruiyot | KEN | 64 | 1 | | Grosseto | 10 Aug | 86 |
| 3:33.1 m | Jim | Ryun | USA | 47 | 1 | vComm | Los Angeles | 8 Jul | 67 |
| 3:33.16 | Ben | Jipcho | KEN | 43 | 3 | CommG | Christchurch | 2 Feb | 74 |
| 3:33.28 | Omer | Khalifa | SUD | 56 | 2 | | Grosseto | 10 Aug | 86 |
| 3:33.39 | Mike | Hillardt | AUS | 61 | 4 | ISTAF | Berlin | 23 Aug | 85 |
| 3:33.5 m+ | Ray | Flynn | IRL | 57 | 2 | OsloG | Oslo | 7 Jul | 82 |
| 3:33.67+ | Mike | Boit | KEN | 49 | 2 | VD | Bruxelles | 28 Aug | 81 |
| | (20) | | | | | | | | |

| Mark | Name | | Nat | Yr | Pos | Meet | Venue | Date |
|------|------|--|-----|----|----|------|-------|------|
| 3:33.68 | Jürgen | Straub | GDR | 53 | 1 | | Potsdam | 31 Aug 79 |
| 3:33.74 | Willi | Wülbeck | FRG | 54 | 4 | | Koblenz | 27 Aug 80 |
| 3:33.79 | David | Moorcroft | UK | 53 | 1 | FBK | Hengelo | 27 Jul 82 |
| 3:33.83 | John | Robson | UK | 57 | 2 | VD | Bruxelles | 4 Sep 79 |
| 3:33.89 | Rod | Dixon | NZ | 50 | 4 | CommG | Christchurch | 2 Feb 74 , |
| 3:33.99 | Steve | Lacy | USA | 56 | 4 | OsloG | Oslo | 15 Jul 80 |
| 3:33.99 | Todd | Harbour | USA | 59 | 2 | WK | Zürich | 18 Aug 82 |
| 3:34.0 m | Jean | Wadoux | FRA | 52 | 1 | | Colombes | 23 Jul 70 |
| 3:34.01 | Graham | Williamson | UK | 60 | 3 | Bisl | Oslo | 28 Jun 83 |
| 3:34.01 | Abdi | Bile | SOM | 63 | 4 | ASV | Köln | 17 Aug 86 |
| | (30) | | | | | | | |
| 3:34.02 | Frank | O'Mara | IRL | 61 | 2 | VD | Bruxelles | 30 Aug 85 |
| 3:34.10 | Andreas | Busse | GDR | 59 | 1 | OD | Potsdam | 21 Jul 84 |
| 3:34.19 | Jim | Spivey | USA | 60 | 5 | WK | Zürich | 22 Aug 84 |
| 3:34.22 | Graham | Crouch | AUS | 48 | 5 | CommG | Christchurch | 2 Feb 74 |
| 3:34.3 m | Johan | Fourie | RSA | 59 | 1 | | P.Elizabeth | 21 Mar 84 |
| 3:34.32 | Joseph | Chesire | KEN | 57 | 4 | | Grosseto | 10 Aug 86 |
| 3:34.49 | Igor | Lotarev | SU | 64 | 4 | VD | Bruxelles | 30 Aug 85 |
| 3:34.52 | Philippe | Dien | FRA | 57 | 2 | | Viareggio | 27 Jul 83 |
| 3:34.57 | Stefano | Mei | ITA | 63 | 3 | | Rieti | 7 Sep 86 |
| 3:34.7+ | Chuck | Aragon | USA | 59 | 3 | OsloG | Oslo | 21 Jul 84 |
| | (40) | | | | | | | |
| 3:34.84 | Uwe | Becker | FRG | 55 | 3 | | Koblenz | 31 Aug 83 |
| 3:34.85 | Dragan | Zdravković | YUG | 59 | 2 | EP/B | Praha | 20 Aug 83 |
| 3:34.87 | Jan | Kubista | CS | 60 | 3 | EP/B | Praha | 20 Aug 83 |
| 3:34.91 | Kipchoge | Keino | KEN | 40 | 1 | OG | Ciu.México | 20 Oct 68 |
| 3:34.93 | José | Marajo | FRA | 54 | 3 | | Rieti | 4 Sep 83 |
| 3:35.0+ | Wilson | Waigwa | KEN | 49 | 2 | | Koblenz | 31 Aug 83 |
| 3:35.07 | Alex | Gonzalez | FRA | 51 | 3 | VD | Bruxelles | 4 Sep 79 |
| 3:35.07 | Rob | Druppers | HOL | 62 | 7 | ISTAF | Berlin | 23 Aug 85 |
| 3:35.16 | Steve | Crabb | UK | 63 | 4 | Bisl | Oslo | 28 Jun 84 |
| 3:35.26 | Uwe | Mönkemeyer | FRG | 59 | 5 | ASV | Köln | 17 Aug 86 |
| 3:35.26 | John | Gladwin | UK | 63 | 4 | VD | Bruxelles | 5 Sep 86 |
| | (51) | | | | | | | |

MEN All-time

| | | | | | |
|--|--|--|--|--|--|
| :35.28 | Craig | Masback | USA | 1982 | |
| :35.28 | Jack | Buckner | UK | 1986 | |
| :35.29 | Tim | Hacker | USA | 1985 | |
| :35.3m+ | John | Gregorek | USA | 1982 | |
| :35.4m+ | Vladimir | Malozemlin | SU | 1980 | |
| :35.50 | Pascal | Thiébaut | FRA | 1985 | |
| :35.56 | José Luis | Carreira | SPA | 1986 | |
| :35.58 | Olaf | Beyer | GDR | 1981 | |
| :35.6 m | Herb | Elliott | AUS | 1960 | |
| | (60) | | | | |
| :35.62 | Peter | Elliott | UK | 1986 | |
| :35.66 | Frank | Clement | UK | 1978 | |
| :35.67 | Peter | Koech | KEN | 1986 | |
| :35.70 | Joaquim C. | Cruz | BRA | 1985 | |
| :35.74 | Rob | Harrison | UK | 1986 | |
| :35.75 | Tom | Byers | USA | 1982 | |
| :35.76 | Marcus | O'Sullivan | IRL | 1986 | |
| :35.79 | Riccardo | Materazzi | ITA | 1984 | |
| :35.8 | Suleiman | Nyambui | TAN | 1979 | |
| :35.8 m | Vitaliy | Tishchenko | SU | 1980 | |
| | (70) | | | | |
| :35.8 m+ | Robert | Nemeth | AUT | 1981 | |
| :35.83 | Peter | Wirz | SWZ | 1984 | |
| :35.86 | Andrés | Vera | SPA | 1986 | |
| :35.93+ | Vittorio | Fontanella | ITA | 1981 | |
| :35.98 | Danie | Malan | RSA | 1976 | |
| :35.98 | Klaus-Peter | Nabein | FRG | 1986 | |

| | | | | |
|--|--|--|--|--|
| 3:36.0 m | Marty | Liquori | USA | 1971 |
| 3:36.01 | Niels Kim | Hjorth | DEN | 1986 |
| 3:36.04 | Kevin | Johnson | USA | 1984 |
| 3:36.05 | Rich | Harris | USA | 1984 |
| | (80) | | | |
| 3:36.08 | Claudio | Patrignani | ITA | 1983 |
| 3:36.19 | Mirosław | Zerkowski | POL | 1980 |
| 3:36.19 | Earl | Jones | USA | 1986 |
| 3:36.2 m | Dave | Wottle | USA | 1973 |
| 3:36.2 | Karl | Fleschen | FRG | 1977 |
| 3:36.2 | Francis | Gonzalez | FRA | 1979 |
| 3:36.2m+ | Eamonn | Coghlan | IRL | 1983 |
| 3:36.23 | Paul-Heinz | Wellmann | FRG | 1976 |
| 3:36.26 | Ivo | Van Damme | BEL | 1976 |
| 3:36.26 | Abderrahmane | Morceli | ALG | 1977 |
| | (90) | | | |
| 3:36.3 m | Michel | Jazy | FRA | 1966 |
| 3:36.3 m | Francesco | Arese | ITA | 1971 |
| 3:36.3 m | Nikolay | Kirov | SU | 1980 |
| 3:36.3 m | Antti | Loikkanen | FIN | 1980 |
| 3:36.31 | Eddy | Stevens | BEL | 1986 |
| 3:36.33 | Pekka | Vasala | FIN | 1972 |
| 3:36.34 | Paul | Rugut | KEN | !1983 |
| 3:36.35 | Uerry | Brahl | USA | 1986 |
| 3:36.36 | Anatnliy | Kalutskiy | SU | 1984 |
| 3:36.37 | Cyrille | Laventure | FRA | 1986 |
| | (100) | | | |
| 3;36.38 | Vincent | Rousseau | BEL | 1985 |

Indoors : 3:25.6 m+ Eamonn Coghlan I RL 1980

| Mark | Name | | Nat | Yr | Pos | Meet | Venue | Date | |
|------|------|---|-----|-----|-----|------|-------|------|---|

# 1 MILE

| 3:46.32 | Steve | Cram | UK | 60 | 1 | Bisl | Oslo | 27 Jul 8! |
| 3:46.92 | Saïd | Aouita | MOR | 60 | 1 | WK | Zürich | 21 Aug 8! |
| 3:47.33 | Sebastian | Coe | UK | 56 | 1 | VD | Bruxelles | 28 Aug 8! |
| 3:47.69 | Steve | Scott | USA | 56 | 1 | OsloG | Oslo | 7 Jul 8! |
| 3:47.79 | José Luis | Gonzalez | SPA | 57 | 2 | Bisl | Oslo | 27 Jul 8 |
| 3:48.31 | | Cram | | | 1 | Bisl | Oslo | 5 Jul 8● |
| 3:48.40 | Steve | Ovett | UK | 55 | 1 | | Koblenz | 26 Aug 8 |
| 3:48.53 | | Coe | | | 1 | WK | Zürich | 19 Aug 8 |
| 3:48.53 | | Scott | | | 1 | Bisl | Oslo | 26 Jun 8! |
| 3:48.73 | | Scott | | | 2 | Bisl | Oslo | 5 Jul 8● |
| | | | | | | | | |
| 3:48.8 m | | Ovett | | | 1 | Bisl | Oslo | 1 Jul 8● |
| 3:48.83 | Sydney | Maree | USA | 56 | 1 | | Rieti | 9 Sep 8 |
| 3:48.85 | | Maree | | | 2 | Bisl | Oslo | 26 Jun 8 |
| 3:48.95 | | Coe | | | 1 | OsloG | Oslo | 17 Jul 7 |
| 3:49.08 | John | Walker | NZ | 52 | 2 | OsloG | Oslo | 7 Jul 8 |
| 3:49.21 | | Scott | | | 1 | ISTAF | Berlin | 17 Aug 8 |
| 3:49.22 | | Coe | | | 3 | Bisl | Oslo | 27 Jul 8 |
| 3:49.25 | | Ovett | | | 1 | OsloG | Oslo | 11 Jul 8 |
| 3:49.31 | | Cram | | | 1 | | London | 12 Sep 8 |
| 3:49.34 | David | Moorcroft | UK | 53 | 3 | Bisl | Oslo | 26 Jun 8 |
| | | | | | | | | |
| 3:49.4m | | Walker | | | 1 | | Göteborg | 12 Aug 7 |
| 3:49.42 | | Maree | | | 1 | | Cork | 13 Jul 8 |
| 3:49.45 | Mike | Boit (10) | KEN | 49 | 2 | VD | Bruxelles | 28 Aug 8 |
| 3:49.49 | | Scott | | | 1 | OsloG | Oslo | 9 Jul 8 |
| 3:49.49 | | Cram | | | 1 | | London | 12 Sep 8 |
| 3:49.50 | | Walker | | | 4 | Bisl | Oslo | 26 Jun 8 |
| 3:49.54 | | Aouita | | | 1 | WK | Zürich | 22 Aug 8● |
| 3:49.57 | | Ovett | | | 1 | | London | 31 Aug 7 |
| 3:49.65 | | Cram | | | 1 | | Koblenz | 29 Aug 8● |
| 3:49.66 | | Ovett | | | 1 | | Lausanne | 14 Jul 8● |
| 3:49.67 | | Gonzalez | | | 2 | OsloG | Oslo | 11 Jul 8● |
| 3:49.68 | | Scott | | | 3 | OsloG | Oslo | 11 Jul 8● |
| (32/10) | | | | | | | | |
| | | | | | | | | |
| 3:49.77 | Ray | Flynn | IRL | 57 | 3 | OsloG | Oslo | 7 Jul 8 |
| 3:49.80 | Jim | Spivey | USA | 60 | 3 | Bisl | Oslo | 5 Jul 8● |
| 3:49.98 | Thomas | Wessinghage | FRG | 52 | 3 | ISTAF | Berlin | 17 Aug 8 |
| 3:50.34 | Todd | Harbour | USA | 59 | 5 | OsloG | Oslo | 11 Jul 8● |
| 3:50.38 | Pierre | Délèze | SWZ | 58 | 4 | | Koblenz | 25 Aug 8 |
| 3:50.59 | José Manuel | Abascal | SPA | 58 | 2 | GP-GG | Roma | 10 Sep 8 |
| 3:50.64 | Graham | Williamson | UK | 60 | 4 | | Cork | 13 Jul 8 |
| 3:50.73 | Wilson | Waigwa | KEN | 49 | 2 | | Koblenz | 31 Aug 8 |
| 3:50.84 | Tom | Byers | USA | 55 | 6 | | Koblenz | 25 Aug 8 |
| 3:50.98 | José | Marajo | FRA | 54 | 4 | OsloG | Oslo | 9 Jul 8 |
| (20) | | | | | | | | |
| 3:51.0 m | Filbert | Bayi | TAN | 53 | 1 | King | Kingston | 17 May 7 |
| 3:51.06 | Frank | O'Mara | IRL | 60 | 4 | GP-GG | Roma | 10 Sep 8 |
| 3:51.1 m | Jim | Ryun | USA | 47 | 1 | AAU | Bakersfield | 23 Jun ● |
| 3:51.23 | Johan | Fourie | RSA | 59 | 1 | | Pt.Elizabeth | 7 Mar ! |
| 3:51.34 | John | Gregorek | USA | 60 | 6 | Bisl | Oslo | 26 Jun ! |
| 3:51.39 | Rich | Harris | USA | 59 | 3 | | Koblenz | 29 Aug ● |
| 3:51.57 | Jack | Buckner | UK | 61 | 4 | | Koblenz | 29 Aug 8 |
| 3:51.59 | Eamonn | Coghlan | IRL | 52 | 5 | OsloG | Oslo | 9 Jul ! |
| 3:51.62 | Chuck | Aragon | USA | 59 | 3 | OsloG | Oslo | 21 Jul ! |
| 3:51.82 | Mike | Hillardt | AUS | 61 | 1 | | Koblenz | 28 Aug ! |
| (30) | | | | | | | | |

| Mark | Name | | Nat | Yr | Pos | Meet | Venue | Date |
|------|------|---|-----|----|----|------|-------|------|
| 3:51.94 | Suleiman | Nyambui | TAN | 53 | 4 | | Lausanne | 14 Jul 81 |
| 3:52.02 | Craig | Masback | USA | 55 | 3 | OsloG | Oslo | 17 Jul 79 |
| 3:52.02 | Pascal | Thiebaut | FRA | 59 | 4 | OsloG | Oslo | 21 Jul 84 |
| 3:52.17 | Ben | Jipcho | KEN | 43 | 1 | DNG | Stockholm | 2 Jul 73 |
| 3:52.2 m | Marty | Liquori | USA | 49 | 2 | King | Kingston | 17 May 75 |
| 3:52.24 | Dragan | Zdravković | YUG | 59 | 5 | ISTAF | Berlin | 17 Aug 83 |
| 3:52.31 | Vittorio | Fontanella | ITA | 53 | 6 | WK | Zürich | 19 Aug 81 |
| 3:52.36 | Uwe | Becker | FRG | 55 | 7 | | Koblenz | 25 Aug 82 |
| 3:52.42 | Robert | Nemeth | AUT | 58 | 3 | | Rieti | 9 Sep 81 |
| 3:52.44 | John | Robson | UK | 57 | 8 | OsloG | Oslo | 11 Jul 81 |
| | (40) | | | | | | | |
| 3:52.59 | Jozef | Plachý | CS | 49 | 2 | DNG | Stockholm | 3 Jul 78 |
| 3:52.64 | Marcus | O'Sullivan | IRL | 61 | 2 | | Cork | 9 Jul 85 |
| 3:52.78 | Alex | Gonzalez | FRA | 51 | 6 | | Lausanne | 14 Jul 81 |
| 3:52.99 | Mark | Rowland | UK | 63 | 7 | GP-GG | Roma | 10 Sep 86 |
| 3:53.00 | Joaquim C. | Cruz | BRA | 63 | 2 | Pepsi | Westwood | 13 May 84 |
| 3:53.02 | Francis | Gonzalez | FRA | 52 | 8 | | Lausanne | 14 Jul 81 |
| 3:53.08 | Abdi | Bile | SOM | 63 | 5 | WK | Zürich | 21 Aug 85 |
| 3:53.1 m | Kipchoge | Keino | KEN | 40 | 1 | NC | Kisumu | 10 Sep 67 |
| 3:53.20 | Ian | Stewart -2 | UK | 60 | 8 | | Koblenz | 25 Aug 82 |
| 3:53.2 m | Tony | Waldrop | USA | 51 | 1 | PennR | Philadelphia | 27 Apr 74 |
| | (50) | | | | | | | |

| Mark | Name | | Nat | Yr |
|------|------|---|-----|----|
| 3:53.3 m | Dave | Wottle | USA | 1973 |
| 3:53.3 m | Rick | Wohlhuter | USA | 1975 |
| 3:53.55 | Andreas | Busse | GDR | 1982 |
| 3:53.6 m | Michel | Jazy | FRA | 1965 |
| 3:53.62 | Rod | Dixon | NZ | 1975 |
| 3:53.74 | Omer | Khalifa | SUD | 1984 |
| 3:53.8 m | Jürgen | May | GDR | 1965 |
| 3:53.8 m | Bodo | Tummler | FRG | 1968 |
| 3:53.85 | Rob | Harrison | UK | 1986 |
| 3:53.92 | Kipkoech | Cheruiyot | KEN | 1983 |
| | (60) | | | |
| 3:53.93 | Han | Kulker | HOL | 1985 |
| 3:54.03 | Peter | Snell | NZ | 1964 |
| 3:54.06 | Kevin | Johnson | USA | 1984 |
| 3:54.11 | Klaus-Peter | Nabein | FRG | 1986 |
| 3:54.19 | Don | Paige | USA | 1982 |
| 3:54.2 m | Frank | Clement | UK | 1978 |
| 3:54.22 | Peter | Elliott | UK | 1986 |
| 3:54.36 | Steve | Crabb | UK | 1984 |
| 3:54.39 | Neil | Horsfield | UK | 1986 |
| 3:54.45 | Anders | Gärderud | SWE | 1975 |
| | (70) | | | |
| 3:54.48 | David | Taylor | IRL | 1983 |
| 3:54.5 m | Herb | Elliott | AUS | 1958 |
| 3:54.52 | Ulf | Högberg | SWE | 1974 |
| 3:54.52 | John | Gladwin | UK | 1986 |
| 3:54.53 | Tim | Hutchings | UK | 1982 |
| 3:54.56 | Terry | Brahm | USA | 1984 |
| 3:54.6 m | Steve | Prefontaine | USA | 1973 |
| 3:54.6 m | Danie | Malan | RSA | 1975 |
| 3:54.63 | Abderrahmane | Morceli | ALG | 1983 |
| 3:54.63 | Gerry | O'Reilly | IRL | 1986 |
| | (80) | | | |
| 3:54.65 | Tom | Smith | USA | 1984 |
| 3:54.68 | Tom | Moloney | IRL | 1986 |
| 3:54.69 | Vincent | Rousseau | BEL | 1985 |
| 3:54.7 m | John | Hartnett | IRL | 1973 |
| 3:54.7 m | Karl | Fleschen | FRG | 1977 |
| 3:54.78 | Tom B. | Hansen | DEN | 1975 |
| 3:54.84 | Steve | Lacy | USA | 1980 |
| 3:54.94 | Matt | Centrowitz | USA | 1982 |
| 3:55.0 m | Dennis | Fikes | USA | 1974 |
| 3:55.0 m | Jim | McGuinness | UK | 1977 |
| | (90) | | | |
| 3:55.1 m | Steve | Foster | USA | 1977 |
| 3:55.13 | Istvan | Knipl | HUN | 1984 |
| 3:55.16 | Jeff | Atkinson | USA | 1986 |
| 3:55.17 | Johnny | Kroon | SWE | 1986 |
| 3:55.18 | Tony | Rogers | NZ | 1984 |
| 3:55.2 m | Ken | Hall | AUS | 1975 |
| 3:55.2 m | Pat | Scammell | AUS | 1985 |
| 3:55.26 | Ross | Donoghue | USA | 1984 |
| 3:55.3 m | Peter | Stewart | UK | 1972 |
| 3:55.3 m | Jürgen | Straub | GDR | 1977 |
| | (100) | | | |
| 3:55.31 | Dub | Myers | USA | 1986 |
| 3:55.33 | Andrés | Vera | SPA | 1984 |

indoor marks

| Mark | Name | | Nat | Yr | Pos | Venue | Date |
|------|------|---|-----|----|----|-------|------|
| 3:49.78 | Eamonn | Coghlan | IRL | 52 | 1 | E.Rutherford | 27 Feb 83 |
| 3:54.40 | Jay | Woods | USA | 1983 | | | |
| 3:54.93 | Dick | Buerkle | USA | 1978 | | | |

MEN All-time

| Mark | Name | | Nat | Yr | Pos | Meet | Venue | Date |
|---|---|---|---|---|---|---|---|---|

## 2000 METRES

| Mark | Name | | Nat | Yr | Pos | Meet | Venue | Date |
|---|---|---|---|---|---|---|---|---|
| 4:51.39 | Steve | Cram | UK | 60 | 1 | BGP | Budapest | 4 Aug 8 |
| 4:51.52 | John | Walker | NZ | 52 | 1 | Bisl | Oslo | 30 Jun 7 |
| 4:51.98 | Saïd | Aouita | MOR | 60 | 1 | VD | Bruxelles | 5 Sep 8 |
| 4:52.20 | Thomas | Wessinghage | FRG | 52 | 1 | | Ingelheim | 31 Aug 8 |
| 4:52.40 | José Manuel | Abascal | SPA | 58 | 1 | | Santander | 7 Sep 8 |
| 4:54.02 | | Aouita | | | 1 | | Rieti | 4 Sep 8 |
| 4:54.20 | Sydney | Maree | USA | 56 | 2 | | Rieti | 4 Sep 8 |
| 4:54.71 | Steve | Scott | USA | 56 | 2 | | Ingelheim | 31 Aug 8 |
| 4:54.88 | | Abascal | | | 1 | | Santander | 3 Sep 8 |
| 4:54.98 | | Aouita | | | 1 | | Madrid | 4 Jun 8 |
| | | | | | | | | |
| 4:55.82 | | Scott | | | 3 | | Rieti | 4 Sep 8 |
| 4:56.1 m | Michel | Jazy | FRA | 36 | 1 | | Saint Maur | 12 Oct 6 |
| 4:56.41 | Johan | Fourie | RSA | 59 | 1 | | Stellenbosch | 22 Apr 8 |
| 4:56.5 m | | Fourie | | | 1 | | Stellenbosch | 23 Apr 8 |
| 4:56.51 | Pierre | Délèze (10) | SWZ | 58 | 1 | | Bern | 3 Aug 8 |
| 4:56.8 m | | Walker | | | 1 | | Göteborg | 30 Aug 7 |
| 4:57.1 m | Willy | Polleunis | BEL | 47 | 1 | | Louvain | 21 Sep 7 |
| 4:57.2 m | | Fourie | | | 1 | | Stellenbosch | 22 Feb 8 |
| 4:57.27 | | Délèze | | | 1 | | Langenthal | 27 Jul 8 |
| 4:57.53 | José Luis | Carreira | SPA | 62 | 2 | | Santander | 7 Sep 8 |
| | | | | | | | | |
| 4:57.66 | Eamonn | Coghlan | IRL | 52 | 1 | | London | 29 Aug 8 |
| 4:57.71 | Steve | Ovett | UK | 55 | 1 | OsloG | Oslo | 7 Jul 8 |
| 4:57.8 m | Harald | Norpoth | FRG | 42 | 1 | | Hagen | 10 Sep 6 |
| 4:57.82 | | Ovett | | | 1 | | London | 3 Jun 7 |
| 4:58.1 m | | Polleunis | | | 1 | | Saint Maur | 27 Sep 7 |
| 4:58.1 m | Francis | Gonzalez | FRA | 52 | 1 | | Rennes | 22 Jun 7 |
| 4:58.29 | Peter | Wirz | SWZ | 60 | 2 | | Langenthal | 27 Jul 8 |
| 4:58.38 | Graham | Williamson | UK | 60 | 2 | | London | 29 Aug 8 |
| 4:58.4 m | | Jazy | | | 1 | | Chambery | 24 Sep 6 |
| 4:58.42 | | Wessinghage | | | 2 | OsloG | Oslo | 7 Jul 8 |
| (30/18) | | | | | | | | |
| | | | | | | | | |
| 4:58.65 | Stefano | Mei | ITA | 63 | 1 | | Viareggio | 15 Aug 8 |
| 4:58.84 | Sebastian | Coe | UK | 56 | 1 | | Bordeaux | 5 Jun 8 |
| (20) | | | | | | | | |
| 4:59.02 | Evgeni | Ignatov | BUL | 59 | 4 | | Rieti | 4 Sep 8 |
| 4:59.04 | Rich | Harris | USA | 59 | 2 | | Viareggio | 15 Aug 8 |
| 4:59.21 | Filbert | Bayi | TAN | 53 | 1 | | Schaan | 17 Sep 7 |
| 4:59.28 | Todd | Harbour | USA | 59 | 3 | Nik | Nice | 14 Aug 8 |
| 4:59.40 | Ray | Flynn | IRL | 57 | 1 | | Stuttgart | 29 Aug 8 |
| 4:59.43 | Mike | Boit | KEN | 49 | 5 | | Rieti | 4 Sep 8 |
| 4:59.54 | Markus | Ryffel | SWZ | 55 | 2 | | Schaan | 17 Sep 7 |
| 4:59.56 | Robert | Nemeth | AUT | 58 | 1 | | Klagenfurt | 8 Aug 8 |
| 4:59.57 | Nick | Rose | UK | 51 | 2 | | London | 3 Jun 7 |
| 4:59.59 | Alex | Gonzalez | FRA | 51 | 2 | | Bordeaux | 5 Jun 8 |
| (30) | | | | | | | | |
| 4:59.6 m | Jürgen | Straub | GDR | 53 | 1 | | Potsdam | 5 Jul 8 |
| 4:59.71 | Suleiman | Nyambui | TAN | 53 | 3 | | Schaan | 17 Sep 7 |
| 4:59.8 m | Emiel | Puttemans | BEL | 47 | 1 | | Landen | 12 Aug 7 |
| 4:59.1 m | Peter | Daenens | BEL | 60 | 1 | | Neerpelt | 19 Aug 8 |
| 5:00.0 m | Gianni | Del Buono | ITA | 43 | 1 | | Reggio Emil. | 24 Sep 7 |
| 5:00.11 | Craig | Masback | USA | 55 | 5 | | Bordeaux | 5 Jun 8 |
| 5:00.19 | John | Gregorek | USA | 60 | 3 | OsloG | Oslo | 7 Jul 8 |
| 5:00.37 | Tim | Hutchings | UK | 58 | 3 | | London | 29 Aug 8 |
| 5:00.4 m | Karl | Fleschen | FRG | 55 | 2 | Bisl | Oslo | 30 Jun 7 |
| 5:00.6 m | Klaus-Peter | Hildenbrand | FRG | 52 | 3 | Bisl | Oslo | 30 Jun 7 |
| (40) | | | | | | | | |

| Mark | Name | | Nat | Yr | Pos | Meet | Venue | Date | |
|------|------|--|-----|-----|-----|------|-------|------|--|
| 5:00.8 m | Fernando | Mamede | POR | 51 | 1 | | Lisboa | 10 | Jun 84 |
| 5:00.8 m | João | Campos | POR | 58 | 2 | | Lisboa | 10 | Jun 84 |
| 5:00.9 m | Bob | Verbeeck | BEL | 60 | 2 | | Neerpelt | 19 | Aug 83 |
| 5:01.0 m | Dragan | Zdravković | YUG | 59 | 1 | | Titovo Uziče | 24 | Sep 82 |
| 5:01.09 | Eamonn | Martin | UK | 58 | 1 | | Belfast | 19 | Jun 84 |
| 5:01.2 m | Josef | Odlozil | CS | 38 | 1 | | Stara Boles. | 8 | Sep 65 |
| 5:01.27 | Joost | Borm | HOL | 56 | 7 | | Bordeaux | 5 | Jun 82 |
| 5:01.3 m | Steve | Foley | AUS | 57 | 1 | | Adelaide | 22 | Dec 79 |
| 5:01.4 m | Steve | Prefontaine | USA | 51 | 1 | | Coos Bay | 9 | May 75 |
| 5:01.67 | Rod | Dixon | NZ | 50 | 2 | | London | 4 | Jul 75 |
| | (50) | | | | | | | | |

# 3000 METRES

**MEN All-time**

| Mark | Name | | Nat | Yr | Pos | Meet | Venue | Date | |
|------|------|--|-----|-----|-----|------|-------|------|--|
| 7:32.1 m | Henry | Rono | KEN | 52 | 1 | Bisl | Oslo | 27 | Jun 78 |
| 7:32.23 | Saïd | Aouita | MOR | 60 | 1 | ASV | Köln | 17 | Aug 86 |
| 7:32.54 | | Aouita | | | 1 | WK | Zürich | 13 | Aug 86 |
| 7:32.79 | David | Moorcroft | UK | 53 | 1 | | London | 17 | Jul 82 |
| 7:32.94 | | Aouita | | | 1 | VD | Bruxelles | 30 | Aug 85 |
| 7:33.3 m | | Aouita | | | 1 | VD | Bruxelles | 24 | Aug 84 |
| 7:33.37 | Sydney | Maree | USA | 56 | 2 | | London | 17 | Jul 82 |
| 7:35.2 m | Brendan | Foster | UK | 48 | 1 | | Gateshead | 3 | Aug 74 |
| 7:35.84 | Doug | Padilla | USA | 56 | 1 | OsloG | Oslo | 9 | Jul 83 |
| 7:36.69 | Steve | Scott | USA | 56 | 1 | | Ingelheim | 1 | Sep 81 |
| 7:36.75 | Thomas | Wessinghage | FRG | 52 | 2 | | Ingelheim | 1 | Sep 81 |
| 7:37.49 | John | Walker | NZ | 52 | 3 | | London | 17 | Jul 82 |
| 7:37.6 m | Emiel | Puttemans (10) | BEL | 47 | 1 | | Aarhus | 14 | Sep 72 |
| 7:37.60 | Eamonn | Coghlan | IRL | 52 | 1 | Bisl | Oslo | 1 | Jul 80 |
| 7:37.70 | Rudy | Chapa | USA | 57 | 1 | | Eugene | 10 | May 79 |
| 7:38.25 | | Padilla | | | 1 | | Lausanne | 10 | Jul 85 |
| 7:38.26 | | Maree | | | 2 | WK | Zürich | 13 | Aug 86 |
| 7:38.39 | | Coghlan | | | 1 | VD | Bruxelles | 26 | Aug 83 |
| 7:38.53 | | Scott | | | 2 | | Lausanne | 10 | Jul 85 |
| 7:38.89 | | Wessinghage | | | 2 | Bisl | Oslo | 1 | Jul 80 |
| 7:39.08 | | Coghlan | | | 1 | Bisl | Oslo | 5 | Jul 79 |
| 7:39.09 | Peter | Koech | KEN | 58 | 4 | | London | 17 | Jul 82 |
| 7:39.27 | Filbert | Bayi | TAN | 53 | 3 | Bisl | Oslo | 1 | Jul 80 |
| 7:39.34 | | Wessinghage | | | 1 | ASV | Köln | 22 | Aug 82 |
| 7:39.38 | Paul | Kipkoech | KEN | 63 | 2 | ASV | Köln | 17 | Aug 86 |
| 7:39.5 m | Kipchoge | Keino | KEN | 40 | 1 | | Hälsingborg | 27 | Aug 65 |
| 7:39.69 | António | Leitão | POR | 58 | 2 | VD | Bruxelles | 26 | Aug 83 |
| 7:39.71 | | Wessinghage | | | 3 | VD | Bruxelles | 26 | Aug 83 |
| | (28/17) | | | | | | | | |
| 7:40.19 | Bill | McChesney | USA | 59 | 2 | ASV | Köln | 22 | Aug 82 |
| 7:40.3 m | Suleiman | Nyambui | TAN | 53 | 2 | Bisl | Oslo | 27 | Jun 78 |
| 7:40.4 m | Nick | Rose | UK | 51 | 3 | Bisl | Oslo | 27 | Jun 78 |
| | (20) | | | | | | | | |
| 7:40.43 | Jack | Buckner | UK | 61 | 1 | Bisl | Oslo | 5 | Jul 86 |
| 7:40.49 | Dragan | Zdravković | YUG | 59 | 2 | OsloG | Oslo | 9 | Jul 83 |
| 7:40.52 | Wilson | Waigwa | KEN | 49 | 4 | VD | Bruxelles | 26 | Aug 83 |
| 7:40.64 | Wodajo | Bulti | ETH | 57 | 5 | VD | Bruxelles | 26 | Aug 83 |
| 7:40.94 | Eamonn | Martin | UK | 58 | 3 | OsloG | Oslo | 9 | Jul 83 |
| 7:41.00 | Francis | Gonzalez | FRA | 52 | 2 | | Lausanne | 18 | Jul 79 |
| 7:41.00 | Markus | Ryffel | SWZ | 55 | 3 | | Lausanne | 18 | Jul 79 |

| Mark | Name | | Nat | Yr | Pos | Meet | Venue | Date |
|---|---|---|---|---|---|---|---|---|
| 7:41.0 m | Rod | Dixon | NZ | 50 | 1 | | Milano | 2 Jul 74 |
| 7:41.22 | Karl | Fleschen | FRG | 55 | 1 | ASV | Köln | 22 Jun 77 |
| 7:41.3 m | Steve | Ovett | UK | 55 | 1 | | Wattenscheid | 23 Sep 77 |
| (30) | | | | | | | | |
| 7:41.60 | Ray | Flynn | IRL | 57 | 1 | PTG | London | 13 Jul 84 |
| 7:42.05 | Dmitriy | Dmitriyev | SU | 56 | 2 | PTG | London | 13 Jul 84 |
| 7:42.1 m | Boris | Kuznetsov | SU | 48 | 1 | | Podolsk | 20 Aug 78 |
| 7:42.11 | Ralph | King | USA | 56 | 4 | | Lausanne | 18 Jul 79 |
| 7:42.15 | Vincent | Rousseau | BEL | 62 | 1 | Nik | Nice | 15 Jul 86 |
| 7:42.24 | Dan | Glans | SWE | 47 | 4 | Bisl | Oslo | 5 Jul 79 |
| 7:42.26 | Graeme | Fell | UK | 59 | 4 | OsloG | Oslo | 9 Jul 83 |
| 7:42.38 | Peter | Weigt | FRG | 48 | 2 | ASV | Köln | 22 Jun 77 |
| 7:42.4 m | Bronisław | Malinowski | POL | 51 | 3 | Bisl | Oslo | 4 Jul 74 |
| 7:42.4 m | Knut | Kvalheim | NOR | 50 | 4 | Bisl | Oslo | 4 Jul 74 |
| (40) | | | | | | | | |
| 7:42.47 | Dave | Lewis | UK | 61 | 5 | OsloG | Oslo | 9 Jul 83 |
| 7:42.6 m | Steve | Prefontaine | USA | 51 | 2 | | Milano | 2 Jul 74 |
| 7:42.85 | Stefano | Mei | ITA | 63 | 2 | Nik | Nice | 15 Jul 86 |
| 7:43.1 m+ | Steve | Cram | UK | 60 | 1 | | London | 29 Aug 83 |
| 7:43.15 | Terry | Brahm | USA | 62 | 2 | | Paris | 22 Jul 86 |
| 7:43.18 | Eshetu | Tura | ETH | 50 | 1 | | Viareggio | 3 Aug 72 |
| 7:43.20 | Ari | Paunonen | FIN | 58 | 3 | ASV | Köln | 22 Jun 77 |
| 7:43.2 m | Lasse | Viren | FIN | 49 | 1 | | Oulu | 27 Jul 72 |
| 7:43.23 | Marty | Liquori | USA | 49 | 2 | Coke | London | 9 Sep 77 |
| 7:43.66 | Dietmar | Millonig | AUT | 55 | 2 | | Lausanne | 15 Aug 81 |
| (50) | | | | | | | | |

| Mark | Name | | Nat | Yr |
|---|---|---|---|---|
| 7:43.76 | Jacques | Boxberger | FRA | 1976 |
| 7:43.79 | Alberto | Salazar | USA | 1979 |
| 7:43.90 | Ian | Stewart -2 | UK | 1982 |
| 7:43.94 | Fernando | Mamede | POR | 1983 |
| 7:44.0 m | Johan | Fourie | RSA | 1985 |
| 7:44.05 | Hansjörg | Kunze | GDR | 1983 |
| 7:44.08 | Pierre | Délèze | SWZ | 1980 |
| 7:44.08 | Robert | Nemeth | AUT | 1984 |
| 7:44.10 | Charles | Cheruiyot | KEN | 1986 |
| 7:44.25 | Jose Luis | Gonzalez | SPA | 1986 |
| (60) | | | | |
| 7:44.35 | Willi | Polleunis | BEL | 1976 |
| 7:44.39 | Dominique | Bouchard | FRA | 1985 |
| 7:44.40 | Colin | Reitz | UK | 1983 |
| 7:44.4 m | Ben | Jipcho | KEN | 1973 |
| 7:44.4 m | Jos | Hermens | HOL | 1974 |
| 7:44.42 | Martti | Vainio | FIN | 1984 |
| 7:44.55 | Tim | Hutchings | UK | 1984 |
| 7:44.76 | Paul | Davies-Hale | UK | 1985 |
| 7:44.8 m | Arne | Kvalheim | NOR | 1974 |
| 7:45.06 | Patriz | Ilg | FRG | 1978 |
| (70) | | | | |
| 7:45.11 | Dick | Quax | NZ | 1977 |
| 7:45.17 | Frank | Zimmermann | FRG | 1978 |
| 7:45.2 m | Harald | Norpoth | FRG | 1967 |
| 7:45.2 m | Yohannes | Mohamed | ETH | 1973 |
| 7:45.2 m | Vittorio | Fontanella | ITA | 1981 |
| 7:45.2+ | Geoff | Turnbull | UK | 1986 |

| Mark | Name | | Nat | Yr |
|---|---|---|---|---|
| 7:45.22 | John | Treacy | IRL | 1980 |
| 7:45.26 | Joseph | Mahmoud | FRA | 1985 |
| 7:45.28 | Richard | Tuwei | KEN | 1983 |
| 7:45.29 | Dennis | Coates | UK | 1977 |
| (80) | | | | |
| 7:45.59 | Detlef | Uhlemann | FRG | 1977 |
| 7:45.61 | Mike | Boit | KEN | 1982 |
| 7:45.81 | John | Robson | UK | 1984 |
| 7:46.0 m | Siegfried | Herrmann | GDR | 1965 |
| 7:46.17 | Féthi | Baccouche | TUN | 1986 |
| 7:46.2 m | Dave | Bedford | UK | 1972 |
| 7:46.2 m | Franco | Fava | ITA | 1977 |
| 7:46.3 | Aleksandr | Fedotkin | SU | 1978 |
| 7:46.30 | Niels Kim | Hjort | DEN | 1983 |
| 7:46.33 | Bill | McCullough | USA | 1979 |
| (90) | | | | |
| 7:46.39 | Adrian | Royle | UK | 1983 |
| 7:46.40 | Alberto | Cova | ITA | 1983 |
| 7:46.42 | Mike | Musyoki | KEN | 1977 |
| 7:46.42 | Don | Clary | USA | 1982 |
| 7:46.48 | Alberto | Cova | ITA | 1985 |
| 7:46.54 | Frank | O'Mara | IRL | 1984 |
| 7:46.6 m+ | Dave | Black | UK | 1973 |
| 7:46.67 | Josh | Kimeto | KEN | 1977 |
| 7:46.76 | Kipsubai | Koskei | KEN | 1981 |
| 7:46.79 | Garry | Bjorklund | USA | 1976 |
| (100) | | | | |

Indoor marks

| Mark | Name | | Nat | Yr | Pos | Meet | Venue | Date |
|---|---|---|---|---|---|---|---|---|
| 7:39.2 m+ | | Puttemans | | | 1 | | Berlin | 18 Feb 73 |
| 7:42.97 | Christoph | Herle | FRG | 55 | 1 | NC | Dortmund | 16 Feb 85 |
| 7:45.50 | Aleksandr | Fedotkin | SU | 55 | 3 | EC | Wien | 25 Feb 79 |
| 7:45.51 | Andreas | Bäsig | GDR | 55 | 4 | EC | Wien | 25 Feb 79 |
| 7:46.5 m | Werner | Schildhauer | GDR | 59 | 1 | | Senftenberg | 6 Feb 82 |

+ time during 2 miles race

| ark | Name | | Nat | Yr | Pos | Meet | Venue | Date | |
|---|---|---|---|---|---|---|---|---|---|
| 8:13.51 | Steve | Ovett | UK | 55 | 1 | Coke | London | 15 Sep 78 |
| 8:13.68 | Brendan | Foster | UK | 48 | 1 | | London | 27 Jul 73 |
| 8:14.0 m | Lasse | Viren | FIN | 49 | 1 | | Stockholm | 14 Aug 72 |
| 8:14.32 | Rod | Dixon | NZ | 50 | 1 | | Stockholm | 18 Jul 74 |
| 8:14.66 | Henry | Rono | KEN | 52 | 2 | Coke | London | 15 Sep 78 |
| 8:14.81 | Saïd | Aouita | MOR | 60 | 1 | | London | 12 Sep 86 |
| 8:14.93 | Steve | Cram | UK | 60 | 1 | | London | 29 Aug 83 |
| 8:15.18 | | Dixon | | | 1 | OsloG | Oslo | 17 Jul 79 |
| 8:15.53 | Tim | Hutchings | UK | 58 | 2 | | London | 12 Sep 86 |
| 8:15.98 | Geoff | Turnbull | UK | 61 | 3 | | London | 12 Sep 86 |
| | | | | | | | | | |
| 8:16.31 | Emiel (10) | Puttemans | BEL | 47 | 1 | | Stockholm | 25 Jul 73 |
| 8:16.55 | | Puttemans | | | 2 | | Stockholm | 18 Jul 74 |
| 8:16.38 | Ben | Jipcho | KEN | 43 | 2 | | Stockholm | 25 Jul 73 |
| 8:16.75 | David | Moorcroft | UK | 53 | 1 | | London | 20 Aug 82 |
| 8:16.78 | | Dixon | | | 1 | | Stockholm | 19 Aug 75 |
| 8:16.94 | | Foster | | | 2 | OsloG | Oslo | 17 Jul 79 |
| (16/12) | | | | | | | | | |
| 8:17.05 | Peter | Koech | KEN | 58 | 2 | | London | 20 Aug 82 |
| 8:17.1 m | Dick | Quax | NZ | 48 | 1 | LB | Philadelphia | 4 Aug 76 |
| 8:17.12 | Marty | Liquori | USA | 49 | 1 | | Stockholm | 17 Jul 75 |
| 8:17.12 | Jack | Buckner | UK | 61 | 4 | | London | 12 Sep 86 |
| 8:18.29 | Steve | Prefontaine | USA | 51 | 3 | | Stockholm | 18 Jul 74 |
| 8:18.43 | Bronislaw | Malinowski | POL | 51 | 3 | Coke | London | 15 Sep 78 |
| 8:19.37 | Nat | Muir | UK | 58 | 2 | | London | 27 Jun 80 |
| 8:19.45 | Filbert | Bayi | TAN | 53 | 3 | | London | 27 Jun 80 |
| | (20) | | | | | | | | |
| 8:19.6 m | Ron | Clarke | AUS | 37 | 1 | | London | 24 Aug 68 |
| 8:19.9 m | Duncan | MacDonald | USA | 49 | 2 | LB | Philadelphia | 4 Aug 76 |

| | | | | | | | | | |
|---|---|---|---|---|---|---|---|---|---|
| 8:20.28 | David | James | UK | 1980 | 8:21.86 | Dave | Black | UK | 1973 |
| 8:20.57 | John | Walker | NZ | 1975 | 8:22.00 | Craig | Virgin | USA | 1979 |
| 8:20.6 m | Anders | Gärderud | SWE | 1972 | 8:22.0 m | George | Young | USA | 1968 |
| 8:20.66 | Dave | Lewis | UK | 1984 | 8:22.0 m | Ian | Stewart -1 | UK | 1972 |
| 8:20.8 m | Jos | Hermens | HOL | 1975 | 8:22.15 | Willy | Polleunis | BEL | 1978 |
| 8:20.86 | António | Leitão | POR | 1984 | 8:22.41 | Nick | Rose | UK | 1978 |
| 8:21.09 | Barry | Smith | UK | 1980 | 8:22.6 m | Michel | Jazy | FRA | 1965 |
| 8:21.8 m | Dick | Buerkle | USA | 1976 | 8:22.98 | Geoff | Smith | UK | 1980 |
| 8:21.8 m | Paul | Geis | USA | 1976 | 8:23.16 | Bill | McChesney | USA | 1981 |

ndoor marks

| | | | | | | | | | |
|---|---|---|---|---|---|---|---|---|---|
| 8:13.2 m | Emiel | Puttemans | BEL | 47 | 1 | | Berlin | 18 Feb 73 |
| 8:15.3 m | Doug | Padilla | USA | 56 | 1 | | San Diego | 15 Feb 85 |
| 8:15.9 m | H. | Rono | | | 1 | | San Diego | 22 Feb 80 |
| 8:16.5 m | | Padilla | | | 1 | | San Diego | 18 Feb 83 |
| 8:16.8 m | | Padilla | | | 1 | | San Diego | 19 Feb 82 |
| (3/3-2) | | | | | | | | | |
| 8:17.9 m | Suleiman | Nyambui | TAN | 53 | 1 | | San Diego | 17 Feb 78 |
| 8:18.4 m | Nick | Rose | UK | 51 | 2 | | San Diego | 17 Feb 78 |
| 8:19.2 m | Kerry | O'Brien | AUS | 46 | 1 | | San Diego | 19 Feb 71 |
| 8:20.6 m | Kerry | Pearce | AUS | 46 | 2 | | San Diego | 19 Feb 71 |
| 8:20.84 | Eamonn | Coghlan | IRL | 52 | 1 | | Dallas | 2 Feb 85 |

| | | | | | | | | | |
|---|---|---|---|---|---|---|---|---|---|
| 8:22.2 m | Steve | Lacy | USA | 1980 | 8:22.7 m | Graeme | Fell | UK | 1982 |
| 8:22.4 m | Dick | Tayler | NZ | 1974 | 8:23.16 | Ed | Eyestone | USA | 1985 |

**2 MILES**

MEN All-time

| Mark | Name | | Nat | Yr | Pos | Meet | Venue | Date |
|------|------|--|-----|----|----|------|-------|------|

## 5000 METRES

| Mark | Name | | Nat | Yr | Pos | Meet | Venue | Date | |
|------|------|--|-----|----|----|------|-------|------|--|
| 13:00.40 | Saïd | Aouita | MOR | 60 | 1 | Bisl | Oslo | 27 Jul | 8 |
| 13:00.41 | David | Moorcroft | UK | 53 | 1 | OsloG | Oslo | 7 Jul | 8 |
| 13:00.86 | | Aouita | | | 1 | | La Coruna | 6 Aug | 8 |
| 13:01.15 | Sydney | Maree | USA | 56 | 2 | Bisl | Oslo | 27 Jul | 8 |
| 13:04.52 | | Aouita | | | 1 | OsloG | Oslo | 27 Jun | 8 |
| 13:04.78 | | Aouita | | | 1 | | Firenze | 13 Jun | 8 |
| 13:05.59 | | Aouita | | | 1 | OG | Los Angeles | 11 Aug | 8 |
| 13:06.20 | Henry | Rono | KEN | 52 | 1 | | Knarvik | 13 Sep | 8 |
| 13:07.29 | Wodajo | Bulti | ETH | 57 | 1 | | Rieti | 16 Sep | 8 |
| 13:07.54 | Markus | Ryffel | SWZ | 55 | 2 | OG | Los Angeles | 11 Aug | 8 |
| 13:07.70 | António | Leitão | POR | 60 | 2 | | Rieti | 16 Sep | 8 |
| 13:08.4 m | | Rono | | | 1 | | Berkeley | 8 Apr | 7 |
| 13:08.54 | Fernando | Mamede | POR | 51 | 1 | | Tokyo | 17 Sep | 8 |
| 13:08.97 | | Rono | | | 1 | DNG | Stockholm | 6 Jul | 8 |
| 13:09.20 | | Leitao | | | 3 | OG | Los Angeles | 11 Aug | 8 |
| 13:09.50 | Peter | Koech | KEN | 58 | 2 | DNG | Stockholm | 6 Jul | 8 |
| 13:09.92 | | Mamede | | | 1 | | Rieti | 4 Sep | 8 |
| 13:10.06 | Alberto | Cova (10) | ITA | 58 | 3 | Bisl | Oslo | 27 Jul | 8 |
| 13:10.08 | | Bulti | | | 2 | | Firenze | 13 Jun | 8 |
| 13:10.15 | Jack | Buckner | UK | 61 | 1 | EC | Stuttgart | 31 Aug | 8 |
| 13:10.40 | Hansjörg | Kunze | GDR | 59 | 1 | | Rieti | 9 Sep | 8 |
| 13:11.50 | Tim | Hutchings | UK | 58 | 4 | OG | Los Angeles | 11 Aug | 8 |
| 13:11.57 | Stefano | Mei | ITA | 63 | 2 | EC | Stuttgart | 31 Aug | 8 |
| 13:11.93 | Alberto | Salazar | USA | 58 | 3 | DNG | Stockholm | 6 Jul | 8 |
| 13:11.99 | Valeriy | Abramov | SU | 56 | 2 | | Rieti | 9 Sep | 8 |
| 13:12.15 | | Rono | | | 1 | | Koblenz | 26 Aug | 8 |
| 13:12.29 | Suleiman | Nyambui | TAN | 53 | 1 | | Stockholm | 18 Jun | 7 |
| 13:12.34 | | Rono | | | 1 | Coke | London | 11 Sep | 8 |
| 13:12.47 | | Rono | | | 3 | | Rieti | 9 Sep | 8 |
| 13:12.51 | | Aouita | | | 1 | | Lausanne | 10 Jul | 8 |
| 13:12.53 | | Kunze | | | 1 | WK | Zürich | 18 Aug | 8 |
| 13:12.54 | Werner | Schildhauer | GDR | 59 | 2 | WK | Zürich | 18 Aug | 8 |
| (32/18) | | | | | | | | | |
| 13:12.78 | Thomas | Wessinghage | FRG | 52 | 3 | WK | Zürich | 18 Aug | 8 |
| 13:12.86 | Dick | Quax | NZ | 48 | 1 | DNG | Stockholm | 5 Jul | 7 |
| | (20) | | | | | | | | |
| 13:12.91 | Matt | Centrowitz | USA | 55 | 1 | Pre | Eugene | 5 Jun | 8 |
| 13:13.0 m | Emiel | Puttemans | BEL | 47 | 1 | | Bruxelles | 20 Sep | 7 |
| 13:13.15 | Evgeni | Ignatov | BUL | 59 | 4 | EC | Stuttgart | 31 Aug | 8 |
| 13:13.49 | Bruce | Bickford | USA | 57 | 2 | OsloG | Oslo | 27 Jun | 8 |
| 13:13.69 | Klaus-Peter | Hildenbrand | FRG | 52 | 2 | | Stockholm | 5 Jul | 7 |
| 13:13.82 | Miruts | Yifter | ETH | 44 | 1 | WP | Düsseldorf | 4 Sep | 7 |
| 13:13.88 | Karl | Fleschen | FRG | 55 | 2 | DNG | Stockholm | 5 Jul | 7 |
| 13:14.40 | Paul | Kipkoech | KEN | 63 | 5 | OG | Los Angeles | 11 Aug | 8 |
| 13:14.4 | Ben | Jipcho | KEN | 43 | 1 | CommG | Christchurch | 29 Jan | 7 |
| 13:14.54 | Peter | Weigt | FRG | 48 | 3 | DNG | Stockholm | 5 Jul | 7 |
| | (30) | | | | | | | | |
| 13:14.6 | Brendan | Foster | UK | 48 | 2 | CommG | Christchurch | 29 Jan | |
| 13:14.80 | Bill | McChesney | USA | 59 | 5 | WK | Zürich | 18 Aug | 8 |
| 13:15.0 | Ilie | Floroiu | RUM | 52 | 1 | NC | Bucuresti | 23 Jul | |
| 13:15.01 | Vincent | Rousseau | BEL | 62 | 4 | GP-GG | Roma | 10 Sep | |
| 13:15.06 | Marty | Liquori | USA | 49 | 2 | WP | Düsseldorf | 4 Sep | |
| 13:15.31 | Dietmar | Millonig | AUT | 55 | 6 | WK | Zürich | 18 Aug | 8 |
| 13:15.31 | Pierre | Délèze | SWZ | 58 | 1 | WG | Helsinki | 7 Jul | |
| 13:15.44 | Doug | Padilla | USA | 56 | 1 | WG | Helsinki | 4 Jul | |

| Mark | Name | | Nat | Yr | Pos | Meet | Venue | Date |
|------|------|---|-----|----|----|------|-------|------|
| 13:15.59 | Julian | Goater | UK | 53 | 2 | Coke | London | 11 Sep 81 |
| 13:15.90 | José Luis | Gonzalez | SPA | 57 | 3 | OsloG | Oslo | 27 Jun 85 |
| | (40) | | | | | | | |
| 13:16.02 | Martti | Vainio | FIN | 50 | 2 | Bisl | Oslo | 28 Jun 84 |
| 13:16.38 | Carlos | Lopes | POR | 47 | 3 | Bisl | Oslo | 28 Jun 84 |
| 13:16.4 m | Lasse | Viren | FIN | 49 | 1 | | Helsinki | 14 Sep 72 |
| 13:16.6 m | Ron | Clarke | AUS | 37 | 1 | | Stockholm | 5 Jul 66 |
| 13:16.81 | John | Treacy | IRL | 57 | 4 | Bisl | Oslo | 28 Jun 84 |
| 13:17.2 m | Enn | Sellik | SU | 54 | 1 | | Podolsk | 28 Jun 76 |
| 13:17.21 | Dave | Bedford | UK | 49 | 1 | AAA | London | 14 Jul 72 |
| 13:17.27 | Rod | Dixon | NZ | 50 | 3 | | Stockholm | 5 Jul 76 |
| 13:17.37 | Dmitriy | Dmitriyev | SU | 56 | 1 | Izv | Kiev | 23 Jun 84 |
| 13:17.42 | David | Fitzsimons | AUS | 50 | 3 | WP | Düsseldorf | 4 Sep 77 |
| | (50) | | | | | | | |

| Mark | Name | | Nat | Yr |
|------|------|---|-----|----|
| 13:17.5 | Mohamed | Kedir | ETH | 1980 |
| 13:17.59 | Anders | Gärderud | SWE | 1976 |
| 13:17.66 | Aleksandr | Fedotkin | SU | 1979 |
| 13:17.69 | Bronislaw | Malinowski | POL | 1976 |
| 13:17.71 | José Manuel | Abascal | SPA | 1986 |
| 13:17.9 | Aleksandr | Antipov | SU | 1979 |
| 13:17.9 m | Nat | Muir | UK | 1980 |
| 13:18.0 m | Boris | Kuznetsov | SU | 1976 |
| 13:18.19 | Lasse | Orimus | FIN | 1976 |
| 13:18.19 | Ralph | King | USA | 1982 |
| | (60) | | | |
| 13:18.20 | Frank | Zimmermann | FRG | 1978 |
| 13:18.2 m | Filbert | Bayi | TAN | 1980 |
| 13:18.41 | Charles | Cheruiyot | KEN | 1980 |
| 13:18.46 | Gennadiy | Fishman | SU | 1984 |
| 13:18.53 | Antonio | Prieto | SPA | 1983 |
| 13:18.54 | Mark | Nenow | USA | 1984 |
| 13:18.6 m | Steve | Jones | UK | 1982 |
| 13:18.91 | Nick | Rose | UK | 1984 |
| 13:18.99 | John | Ngugi | KEN | 1985 |
| 13:19.03 | Domingos | Castro | POR | 1986 |
| | (70) | | | |
| 13:19.10 | João | Campos | POR | 1984 |
| 13:19.1 m | Craig | Virgin | USA | 1980 |
| 13:19.13 | Eamonn | Coghlan | IRL | 1981 |
| 13:19.19 | Venanzio | Ortis | ITA | 1981 |
| 13:19.22 | Rudy | Chapa | USA | 1979 |
| 13:19.24 | George Kip | Rono | KEN | 1980 |
| 13:19.24 | Jim | Spivey | USA | 1983 |
| 13:19.25 | Christoph | Herle | FRG | 1985 |
| 13:19.28 | John | Walker | NZ | 1986 |
| 13:19.37 | Steve | Plasencia | USA | 1985 |
| | (80) | | | |
| 13:19.40 | Duncan | MacDonald | USA | 1976 |
| 13:19.51 | Manfred | Kuschmann | GDR | 1977 |
| 13:19.52 | Ray | Flynn | IRL | 1984 |
| 13:19.62 | Paul | Cummings | USA | 1982 |
| 13:19.66 | Ian | McCafferty | UK | 1972 |
| 13:19.73 | Jim | Hill | USA | 1983 |
| 13:20.06 | Steve | Ovett | UK | 1986 |
| 13:20.24 | Francis | Gonzalez | FRA | 1979 |
| 13:20.36 | Wilson | Waigwa | KEN | 1980 |
| 13:20.49 | Harald | Norpoth | FRG | 1973 |
| | (90) | | | |
| 13:20.54 | Knut | Kvalheim | NOR | 1974 |
| 13:20.6 m | John | N'geno | KEN | 1976 |
| 13:20.93 | Francesco | Panetta | ITA | 1985 |
| 13:20.94 | Eamonn | Martin | UK | 1983 |
| 13:21.07 | Detlef | Uhlemann | FRG | 1976 |
| 13:21.1 | Yohannes | Mohamed | ETH | 1979 |
| 13:21.14 | Barry | Smith | UK | 1981 |
| 13:21.14 | Uwe | Mönkemeyer | FRG | 1986 |
| 13:21.2 m | Tony | Simmons | UK | 1976 |
| 13:21.2 m | Anatoliy | Krakhmalyuk | SU | 1983 |
| | (100) | | | |

# 10 000 METRES

| Mark | Name | | Nat | Yr | Pos | Meet | Venue | Date |
|------|------|---|-----|----|----|------|-------|------|
| 7:13.81 | Fernando | Mamede | POR | 51 | 1 | DNG | Stockholm | 2 Jul 84 |
| 7:17.48 | Carlos | Lopes | POR | 47 | 2 | DNG | Stockholm | 2 Jul 84 |
| 7:20.56 | Mark | Nenow | USA | 57 | 2 | VD | Bruxelles | 5 Sep 86 |
| 7:22.47+ | Henry | Rono | KEN | 52 | 1 | | Wien | 11 Jun 78 |
| 7:22.95 | | Mamede | | | 1 | | Paris | 9 Jul 82 |
| 7:23.44 | | Lopes | | | 1 | OsloG | Oslo | 9 Jul 83 |
| 7:24.39 | | Lopes | | | 1 | Bisl | Oslo | 26 Jun 82 |
| 7:24.95 | Werner | Schildhauer | GDR | 59 | 1 | NC | Jena | 28 May 83 |
| 7:25.13 | | Mamede | | | 2 | OsloG | Oslo | 9 Jul 83 |
| 7:25.61 | Alberto | Salazar | USA | 58 | 2 | Bisl | Oslo | 26 Jun 82 |
| 7:26.11 | Saîd | Aouita | MOR | 60 | 1 | Bisl | Oslo | 5 Jul 86 |
| 7:26.95 | Alex | Hagelsteens | BEL | 56 | 3 | Bisl | Oslo | 26 Jun 82 |
| 7:27.7 m | | Mamede | | | 1 | | Lisboa | 30 May 81 |
| 7:28.67 | | Rono | | | 4* | Bisl | Oslo | 26 Jun 82 |
| 7:28.80 | | Nenow | | | 2 | Bisl | Oslo | 5 Jul 86 |

| Mark | Name | | Nat | Yr | Pos | Meet | Venue | Date | |
|---|---|---|---|---|---|---|---|---|---|
| 27:29.06 | | Salazar | | | 2 | | Paris | 9 Jul | 82 |
| 27:29.16 | Craig | Virgin | USA | 55 | 1 | | Paris | 17 Jul | 80 |
| 27:29.90 | | Rono | | | 1 | | Eugene | 10 Apr | 82 |
| 27:30.00 | | Salazar | | | 2 | | Eugene | 10 Apr | 82 |
| 27:30.3 | Brendan | Foster (10) | UK | 48 | 1 | AAA | London | 23 Jun | 78 |
| | | | | | | | | | |
| 27:30.47 | Samson | Kimobwa | KEN | 55 | 1 | WG | Helsinki | 30 Jun | 77 |
| 27:30.69 | Hansjörg | Kunze | GDR | 59 | 2 | NC | Jena | 28 May | 83 |
| 27:30.80 | Dave | Bedford | UK | 49 | 1 | AAA | London | 13 Jul | 73 |
| 27:30.99 | Martti | Vainio | FIN | 50 | 1 | EC | Praha | 29 Aug | 78 |
| 27:31.19 | Nick | Rose | UK | 51 | 3 | OsloG | Oslo | 9 Jul | 83 |
| 27:31.48 | Venanzio | Ortis | ITA | 55 | 2 | EC | Praha | 29 Aug | 78 |
| 27:31.50 | Aleksandr | Antipov | SU | 55 | 3 | EC | Praha | 29 Aug | 78 |
| 27:31.68 | | Rono | | | 1 | | Melbourne | 6 Feb | 80 |
| 27:32.65 | | Foster | | | 4 | EC | Praha | 29 Aug | 78 |
| 27:32.85 | | Mamede | | | 1 | EP/C | Lisboa | 20 Aug | 83 |
| (30/17) | | | | | | | | | |
| | | | | | | | | | |
| 27:34.58 | Julian | Goater | UK | 53 | 5 | Bisl | Oslo | 26 Jun | 81 |
| 27:36.2 m | Gabriel | Kamau | KEN | 57 | 1 | MSR | Walnut | 24 Apr | 82 |
| 27:36.27 | David | Black | UK | 52 | 5 | EC | Praha | 29 Aug | 78 |
| | | (20) | | | | | | | |
| 27:36.64 | Gerard | Tebroke | HOL | 49 | 6 | EC | Praha | 29 Aug | 78 |
| 27:36.8 m | Karl | Fleschen | FRG | 55 | 1 | | Troisdorf | 28 Apr | 78 |
| 27:37.17 | Bruce | Bickford | USA | 57 | 1 | DNG | Stockholm | 2 Jul | 85 |
| 27:37.59 | Alberto | Cova | ITA | 58 | 2 | | Lausanne | 30 Jun | 83 |
| 27:38.1 m | Gidamas | Shahanga | TAN | 57 | 3 | MSR | Walnut | 24 Apr | 82 |
| 27:38.35 | Lasse | Viren | FIN | 49 | 1 | OG | München | 3 Sep | 72 |
| 27:38.6 m | Zakariah | Barie | TAN | 53 | 4 | MSR | Walnut | 24 Apr | 82 |
| 27:39.14 | Steve | Jones | UK | 55 | 4 | OsloG | Oslo | 9 Jul | 83 |
| 27:39.44 | Mohamed | Kedir | ETH | 53 | 2 | WP | Roma | 4 Sep | 81 |
| 27:39.52 | Salvatore | Antibo | ITA | 62 | 3 | Bisl | Oslo | 5 Jul | 84 |
| | | (30) | | | | | | | |
| 27:39.58 | Emiel | Puttemans | BEL | 47 | 2 | OG | München | 3 Sep | 72 |
| 27:39.76 | Mike | McLeod | UK | 51 | 1 | VD/IAAF | Bruxelles | 4 Sep | 79 |
| 27:39.89 | Ron | Clarke | AUS | 37 | 1 | | Oslo | 14 Jul | 65 |
| 27:40.06 | Ilie | Floroiu | RUM | 52 | 7 | EC | Praha | 29 Aug | 78 |
| 27:40.61 | Enn | Sellik | SU | 54 | 8 | EC | Praha | 29 Aug | 78 |
| 27:40.96 | Miruts | Yifter | ETH | 44 | 3 | OG | München | 3 Sep | 72 |
| 27:41.05 | Ed | Eyestone | USA | 61 | 1 | MSR | Walnut | 27 Apr | 85 |
| 27:41.25 | Jos | Hermens | HOL | 50 | 2 | DNG | Stockholm | 4 Jul | 77 |
| 27:41.26 | Knut | Kvalheim | NOR | 50 | 9 | EC | Praha | 29 Aug | 78 |
| 27:41.34 | Leon | Schots | BEL | 47 | 3 | VD/IAAF | Bruxelles | 4 Sep | 79 |
| | | (40) | | | | | | | |
| 27:41.89 | Aleksandr | Fedotkin | SU | 55 | 4 | VD/IAAF | Bruxelles | 4 Sep | 79 |
| 27:41.92 | Mike | Musyoki | KEN | 56 | 2 | WG | Helsinki | 30 Jun | 77 |
| 27:41.95 | Dick | Quax | NZ | 48 | 4 | Coke | London | 9 Sep | 77 |
| 27:42.09 | Detlef | Uhlemann | FRG | 49 | 3 | DNG | Stockholm | 4 Jul | 77 |
| 27:42.17 | Toshihiko | Seko | JAP | 56 | 4 | DNG | Stockholm | 2 Jul | 85 |
| 27:42.65 | Franco | Fava | ITA | 52 | 3 | WG | Helsinki | 30 Jun | 77 |
| 27:42.8 m | Frank | Zimmermann | FRG | 55 | 2 | | Troisdorf | 28 Apr | 78 |
| 27:42.98 | Dietmar | Millonig | AUT | 55 | 6 | Bisl | Oslo | 26 Jun | 81 |
| 27:43.03 | Ian | Stewart -1 | UK | 49 | 6 | Coke | London | 9 Sep | 77 |
| 27:43.31 | Paul | Kipkoech | KEN | 62 | 1 | | Aachen | 30 May | 84 |
| | | (50) | | | | | | | |

| Mark | Name | | Nat | Yr | | Mark | Name | | Nat | Yr |
|---|---|---|---|---|---|---|---|---|---|---|
| 27:43.59 | Tony | Simmons | UK | 1977 | | 27:43.76 | Geoff | Smith | UK | 1981 |
| 27:43.6 m | Steve | Prefontaine | USA | 1974 | | 27:43.89 | Frank | Heine | GDR | 1986 |
| 27:43.66 | Antonio | Prieto | SPA | 1983 | | 27:43.9 m | Simeon | Kigen | KEN | 1985 |
| 27:43.7 m | Paul | Cummings | USA | 1984 | | 27:43.97 | Stefano | Mei | ITA | 1986 |
| 27:43.74 | Bernie | Ford | UK | 1977 | | 27:44.28 | Kaarlo | Maaninka | FIN | 1980 |
| | | | | | | | | (60) | | |

| Mark | Name | | Nat | Yr | Pos | Meet | Venue | Date |
|------|------|--|-----|-----|-----|------|-------|------|
| 27:44.5 m | Masanari | Shintaku | JAP | 1983 | 27:49.30 | Bekele | Debele | ETH | 1983 |
| 27:44.53 | Some | Muge | KEN | 1986 | 27:49.35 | Gerhard | Hartmann | AUT | 1986 |
| 27:44.65 | Francesco | Panetta | ITA | 1985 | 27:49.5 m | Pat | Porter | USA | 1984 |
| 27:45.0 m | Jesus | Herrera | MEX | 1985 | 27:50.0 m | Sosthenes | Bitok | KEN | 1984 |
| 27:45.8 m | Martin | Pitayo | MEX | 1985 | 27:50.19 | Paul | Williams | CAN | 1986 |
| 27:45.91 | Frank | Shorter | USA | 1975 | 27:50.25 | Joel | Cheruiyot | KEN | 1979 |
| 27:46.4 | Richard | Tayler | NZ | 1974 | 27:50.27 | Christoph | Herle | FRG | 1985 |
| 27:46.47 | Tolossa | Kotu | ETH | 1980 | 27:50.28 | Arturo | Barrios | MEX | 1986 |
| 27:46.71 | Bill | Scott | AUS | 1980 | 27:50.30 | Pierre | Levisse | FRA | 1985 |
| 27:46.9 m | Garry | Bjorklund | USA | 1984 | 27:50.7 | Gerard | Barrett | AUS | 1979 |
| | (70) | | | | | (90) | | | |
| 27:47.0 m | Tony | Sandoval | USA | 1984 | 27:51.70 | Steve | Plasencia | USA | 1986 |
| 27:47.16 | Adrian | Royle | UK | 1982 | 27:51.73 | Suleiman | Nyambui | TAN | 1981 |
| 27:47.25 | Bill | McChesney | USA | 1981 | 27:51.76 | Jon | Solly | UK | 1986 |
| 27:47.35 | Kunimitsu | Itoh | JAP | 1980 | 27:52.48 | Jean-Louis | Prianon | FRA | 1986 |
| 27:48.14 | Mariano | Haro | SPA | 1972 | 27:52.78 | Juha | Vaatainen | FIN | 1971 |
| 27:48.2 m | Matthews | Motshwarateu | BOT | 1979 | 27:53.02+ | Domingo | Tibaduiza | COL | 1978 |
| 27:48.50 | Marc | Smet | BEL | 1976 | 27:53.1 m | Greg | Meyer | USA | 1983 |
| 27:48.59 | Hideki | Kita | JAP | 1980 | 27:53.30 | Steve | Austin | AUS | 1981 |
| 27:48.63 | Toshiaki | Kamata | JAP | 1977 | 27:53.36 | Jurgen | Haase | GDR | 1971 |
| 27:48.7 | John | Treacy | IRL | 1980 | 27:53.61 | Jerzy | Kowol | POL | 1978 |
| | (80) | | | | | (100) | | | |

\* disqualified as an unsanctioned competitor, + photoelectric cell time

**MEN All-time** (side tab)

# MARATHON

| | | | | Nat | Yr | Pos | | Meet/Venue | Date |
|--|--|--|--|-----|-----|-----|--|------------|------|
| 2:07:12 | Carlos | Lopes | | POR | 47 | 1 | | Rotterdam | 20 Apr 85 |
| 2:07:13 | Steve | Jones | | UK | 55 | 1 | | Chicago | 20 Oct 85 |
| 2:07:35 | Taisuke | Kodama | | JAP | 58 | 1 | | Beijing | 19 Oct 86 |
| 2:07:51 | Robert | de Castella | | AUS | 57 | 1 | | Boston | 21 Apr 86 |
| 2:07:57 | Kunimitsu | Itoh | | JAP | 55 | 2 | | Beijing | 19 Oct 86 |
| 2:08:05 | | Jones | | | | 1 | | Chicago | 21 Oct 84 |
| 2:08:08 | Djama | Robleh | | DJI | 58 | 2 | | Chicago | 20 Oct 85 |
| 2:08:09 | Ahmed | Salah | | DJI | 56 | 1 | WP | Hiroshima | 14 Apr 85 |
| 2:08:10 | Juma | Ikangaa | | TAN | 57 | 1 | | Tokyō | 9 Feb 86 |
| 2:08:15 | Takeyuki | Nakayama | | JAP | 59 | 2 | WP | Hiroshima | 14 Apr 85 |
| 2:08:16 | | Jones | | | | 1 | | London | 21 Apr 85 |
| 2:08:18 | | de Castella | | | | 1 | | Fukuoka | 6 Dec 81 |
| 2:08:21 | | Nakayama | | | | 1 | AsG | Seoul | 5 Oct 86 |
| 2:08:26 | | Robleh | | | | 3 | WP | Hiroshima | 14 Apr 85 |
| 2:08:27 | Toshihiko | Seko | (10) | JAP | 56 | 1 | | Chicago | 26 Oct 86 |
| 2:08:29 | Belaine | Dinsamo | | ETH | 57 | 2 | | Tokyō | 9 Feb 86 |
| 2:08:33 | Charles | Spedding | | UK | 52 | 2 | | London | 21 Apr 85 |
| 2:08:34 | Derek | Clayton | | AUS | 42 | 1 | | Antwerpen | 30 May 69 |
| 2:08:37 | | de Castella | | | | 1 | | Rotterdam | 9 Apr 83 |
| 2:08:38 | | Seko | | | | 1 | | Tokyō | 13 Feb 83 |
| 2:08:39 | | Lopes | | | | 2 | | Rotterdam | 9 Apr 83 |
| 2:08:39 | Abebe | Mekonnen | | ETH | 64 | 3 | | Tokyō | 9 Feb 86 |
| 2:08:39 | | Ikangaa | | | | 3 | | Beijing | 19 Oct 86 |
| 2:08:43 | | Nakayama | | | | 4 | | Tokyō | 9 Feb 86 |
| 2:08:48 | | de Castella | | | | 3 | | Chicago | 20 Oct 85 |
| 2:08:51 | Alberto | Salazar | | USA | 58 | 1 | | Boston | 19 Apr 82 |
| 2:08:52 | | Seko | | | | 1 | | Fukuoka | 4 Dec 83 |
| 2:08:53 | Dick | Beardsley | | USA | 56 | 2 | | Boston | 19 Apr 82 |
| 2:08:55 | Takeshi | Soh | | JAP | 53 | 2 | | Tokyō | 13 Feb 83 |
| 2:08:55 | | Ikangaa | | | | 2 | | Fukuoka | 4 Dec 83 |
| 2:08:59p | Rod | Dixon | | NZ | 50 | 1 | | New York | 23 Oct 83 |
| (31/18) | | | | | | | | | |

| Mark | Name | | Nat | Yr | Pos | Meet | Venue | Date |
|---|---|---|---|---|---|---|---|---|
| 2:09:00 | Greg | Meyer | USA | 55 | 1 | | Boston | 18 Apr 83 |
| 2:09:01 | Gerard | Nijboer | HOL | 55 | 1 | | Amsterdam | 26 Apr 80 |
| | (20) | | | | | | | |
| 2:09:03 | Michael | Heilmann | GDR | 61 | 4 | WP | Hiroshima | 14 Apr 85 |
| 2:09:06 | Shigeru | Soh | JAP | 53 | 1 | | Beppu | 5 Feb 78 |
| 2:09:08p | Geoff | Smith | UK | 53 | 2 | | New York | 23 Oct 83 |
| 2:09:12 | Ian | Thompson | UK | 49 | 1 | CommG | Christchurch | 31 Jan 74 |
| 2:09:12 | Rodolfo | Gomez | MEX | 50 | 3 | | Tokyo | 13 Feb 83 |
| 2:09:14 | Jörg | Peter | GDR | 55 | 1 | | Grünau | 21 Jul 84 |
| 2:09:16 | Allister | Hutton | UK | 54 | 3 | | London | 21 Apr 85 |
| 2:09:23 | Christoph | Herle | FRG | 55 | 4 | | London | 21 Apr 85 |
| 2:09:24 | Hugh | Jones | UK | 55 | 1 | | London | 9 May 82 |
| 2:09:27 | Bill | Rodgers | USA | 47 | 1 | | Boston | 16 Apr 79 |
| | (30) | | | | | | | |
| 2:09:28 | Ron | Hill | UK | 38 | 1 | CommG | Edinburgh | 23 Jul 70 |
| 2:09:28 | John | Graham | UK | 56 | 1 | | Rotterdam | 23 May 81 |
| 2:09:32 | Ron | Tabb | USA | 54 | 2 | | Boston | 18 Apr 83 |
| 2:09:39 | Gidamis | Shahanga | TAN | 57 | 4 | | Beijing | 19 Oct 86 |
| 2:09:43 | Mike | Gratton | UK | 54 | 1 | | London | 17 Apr 83 |
| 2:09:43 | Henrik | Jørgensen | DEN | 61 | 5 | | London | 21 Apr 85 |
| 2:09:44 | Joseph | Nzau | KEN | 50 | 1 | | Chicago | 16 Oct 83 |
| 2:09:51 | Masanari | Shintaku | JAP | 57 | 1 | | Fukuoka | 1 Dec 85 |
| 2:09:55 | Waldemar | Cierpinski | GDR | 50 | 1 | OG | Montreal | 31 Jul 76 |
| 2:09:56 | John | Treacy | IRL | 57 | 2 | OG | Los Angeles | 12 Aug 84 |
| | (40) | | | | | | | |
| 2:09:57 | Armand | Parmentier | BEL | 54 | 4 | | Rotterdam | 9 Apr 83 |
| 2:09:57 | Gianni | Poli | ITA | 57 | 4 | | Chicago | 20 Oct 85 |
| 2:09:58 | Benji | Durden | USA | 51 | 3 | | Boston | 18 Apr 83 |
| 2:10:00 | Marc | Smet | BEL | 51 | 1 | | Berchem | 10 Sep 79 |
| 2:10:01 | Hiromi | Taniguchi | JAP | 60 | 2 | | Fukuoka | 1 Dec 85 |
| 2:10:03 | Kebede | Balcha | ETH | 51 | 1 | | Montréal | 25 Sep 83 |
| 2:10:05 | Gabriel | Kamau | KEN | 57 | 4 | | Chicago | 21 Oct 84 |
| 2:10:06 | Phil | Coppess | USA | 54 | 1 | | Minneapolis | 6 Oct 85 |
| 2:10:07 | Ed | Mendoza | USA | 52 | 4 | | Boston | 18 Apr 83 |
| 2:10:09 | Jerome | Drayton | CAN | 45 | 1 | | Fukuoka | 7 Dec 75 |
| | (50) | | | | | | | |

| Mark | Name | | Nat | Yr | Mark | Name | | Nat | Yr |
|---|---|---|---|---|---|---|---|---|---|
| 2:10:09 | Garry | Henry | AUS | 1980 | 2:10:47 | Dick | Quax | NZ | 1980 |
| 2:10:12 | Gerry | Helme | UK | 1983 | 2:10:48 | Bill | Adcocks | UK | 1968 |
| 2:10:15 | Jeff | Wells | USA | 1978 | 2:10:48 | Yakov | Tolstikov | SU | 1984 |
| 2:10:15 | Paul | Ballinger | NZ | 1982 | 2:10:49 | Jacques | Boxberger | FRA | 1985 |
| 2:10:18 | Simeon | Kigen | KEN | 1984 | 2:10:51 | Bernie | Ford | UK | 1979 |
| 2:10:19 | Tony | Sandoval | USA | 1980 | 2:10:51p | John | Tuttle | USA | 1983 |
| 2:10:20 | Garry | Bjorklund | USA | 1980 | 2:10:52 | Goe Chun Son | | PRK | 1980 |
| 2:10:21 | Dave | Chettle | AUS | 1975 | | (80) | | | |
| 2:10:23 | Orlando | Pizzolato | ITA | 1985 | 2:10:54 | John | Lodwick | USA | 1979 |
| 2:10:26 | Craig | Virgin | USA | 1981 | 2:10:54 | Gelindo | Bordin | ITA | 1986 |
| | (60) | | | | 2:10:55 | Kyle | Heffner | USA | 1980 |
| 2:10:29 | Kirk | Pfeffer | USA | 1980 | 2:10:55 | Chris | Bunyan | UK | 1983 |
| 2:10:29 | Martin | Pitayo | MEX | 1984 | 2:10:56 | Ralf | Salzmann | FRG | 1985 |
| 2:10:30 | Frank | Shorter | USA | 1972 | 2:10:56 | Peter | Butler | CAN | 1985 |
| 2:10:30 | Hideki | Kita | JAP | 1983 | 2:10:58 | Vladimir | Kotov | SU | 1980 |
| 2:10:30 | Mike | Musyoki | KEN | 1986 | 2:10:59 | Robert | Hodge | USA | 1980 |
| 2:10:32 | Dereje | Nedi | ETH | 1984 | 2:11:00 | Jesus | Herrera | MEX | 1984 |
| 2:10:33 | Vadim | Sidorov | SU | 1982 | 2:11:02 | Tommy | Persson | SWE | 1980 |
| 2:10:33 | Charmake | Abdillahi | DJI | 1985 | | (90) | | | |
| 2:10:34 | Antoni | Niemczak | POL | 1986 | 2:11:02 | Massimo | Magnani | ITA | 1985 |
| 2:10:38 | Akio | Usami | JAP | 1970 | 2:11:02 | Cor | Lambregts | HOL | 1985 |
| | (70) | | | | 2:11:03 | Bogusław | Psujek | POL | 1986 |
| 2:10:38 | Kjell-Erik | Ståhl | SWE | 1983 | 2:11:04 | Dave | Edge | CAN | 1983 |
| 2:10:41 | Bill | Donakowski | USA | 1986 | 2:11:04 | Fumiaki | Abe | JAP | 1985 |
| 2:10:42 | Agapius | Masong | TAN | 1983 | 2:11:05 | Allan | Zachariasen | DEN | 1983 |

| Mark | Name | | Nat | Yr | Pos | Meet | Venue | Date | |
|---|---|---|---|---|---|---|---|---|---|
| *:11:08 | Don | Norman | USA | 1985 | | 2:11:09 Dave | Smith | USA | 1980 |
| *:11:08 | Jose | Gomez | MEX | 1985 | | 2:11:09 Hiroshi | Sunaga | JAP | 1985 |
| | (100) | | | | | | | | |

Short course
| 2:08:13 | Alberto | Salazar | USA | 58 | 1 | | New York | 25 Oct 81 |
|---|---|---|---|---|---|---|---|---|
| 2:10:53 | Jukka | Toivola | FIN | 1981 | | | | |

Downhill course
| 2:08:04 | Zithulele | Singe | RSA | 63 | 1 | NC | Port Elizabeth | 3 May 86 |
|---|---|---|---|---|---|---|---|---|
| 2:08:15 | Willie | Mtolo | RSA | 65 | 2 | NC | Port Elizabeth | 3 May 86 |
| 2:08:58 | Mark | Plaatjes | RSA | 62 | 1 | NC | Port Elizabeth | 4 May 85 |
| 2:09:41 | Ernest | Seleke | RSA | 59 | 1 | | Port Elizabeth | 31 May 84 |
| 2:10:39 | Thompson Magawana | | RSA | 1985 | | 2:11:00 Ernest Tjela | | RSA | 1986 |

p pending remeasurement

# 3000 METRES STEEPLECHASE

| Mark | Name | | Nat | Yr | Pos | Meet | Venue | Date |
|---|---|---|---|---|---|---|---|---|
| 8:05.4 m | Henry | Rono | KEN | 52 | 1 | | Seattle | 13 May 78 |
| 8:07.62 | Joseph | Mahmoud | FRA | 55 | 1 | VD | Bruxelles | 24 Aug 84 |
| 8:08.02 | Anders | Gärderud | SWE | 46 | 1 | OG | Montreal | 28 Jul 76 |
| 8:09.11 | Bronislaw | Malinowski | POL | 51 | 2 | OG | Montreal | 28 Jul 76 |
| 8:09.17 | Henry | Marsh | USA | 54 | 1 | | Koblenz | 28 Aug 85 |
| 8:08.18 | Boguslaw | Mamiński | POL | 55 | 2 | VD | Bruxelles | 24 Aug 84 |
| 8:09.70 | | Gärderud | | | 1 | DNG | Stockholm | 1 Jul 75 |
| 8:09.70 | | Malinowski | | | 1 | OG | Moskva | 31 Jul 80 |
| 8:10.01 | William | van Dijck | BEL | 61 | 1 | VD | Bruxelles | 5 Sep 86 |
| 8:10.36 | Frank | Baumgartl | GDR | 55 | 3 | OG | Montreal | 28 Jul 76 |
| 8:10.4 m | | Gärderud | | | 1 | vGDR, NOR | Oslo | 25 Jun 75 |
| 8:11.04 | Krzysztof | Wesolowski | POL | 56 | 1 | VD | Bruxelles | 30 Aug 85 |
| 8:11.07 | | Mahmoud | | | 2 | VD | Bruxelles | 30 Aug 85 |
| 8:11.52 | | van Dijck | | | 1 | Nik | Nice | 15 Jul 86 |
| 8:11.63 | | Malinowski | | | 1 | ISTAF | Berlin | 18 Aug 78 |
| 8:11.64 | | Mahmoud | | | 1 | | Koblenz | 29 Aug 84 |
| 8:11.80 | Julius | Korir    (10) | KEN | 60 | 1 | OG | Los Angeles | 10 Aug 84 |
| 8:11.93 | Rainer | Schwarz | FRG | 59 | 2 | | Koblenz | 28 Aug 85 |
| 8:12.0 | George Kip | Rono | KEN | 58 | 1 | GGala | Roma | 5 Aug 80 |
| 8:12.11 | Colin | Reitz | UK | 60 | 2 | VD | Bruxelles | 5 Sep 86 |
| 8:12.23 | | Malinowski | | | 1 | DNG | Stockholm | 10 Aug 76 |
| 8:12.37 | | Marsh | | | 1 | ISTAF | Berlin | 17 Aug 83 |
| 8:12.39 | | H.Rono | | | 1 | NCAA | Eugene | 3 Jun 78 |
| 8:12.48 | Filbert | Bayi | TAN | 53 | 2 | OG | Moskva | 31 Jul 80 |
| 8:12.5 | Mariano | Scartezzini | ITA | 54 | 2 | GGala | Roma | 5 Aug 80 |
| 8:12.58 | Graeme | Fell | CAN | 59 | 3 | | Koblenz | 28 Aug 85 |
| 8:12.60 | Tapio | Kantanen | FIN | 49 | 4 | OG | Montreal | 28 Jul 76 |
| 8:12.62 | | Malinowski | | | 2 | DNG | Stockholm | 1 Jul 75 |
| 8:12.62 | | Mamiński | | | 2 | ISTAF | Berlin | 17 Aug 83 |
| 8:12.74 | | Korir | | | 2 | Nik | Nice | 15 Jul 86 |
| (30/17) | | | | | | | | |
| 8:13.16 | Brian | Diemer | USA | 61 | 2 | | Koblenz | 29 Aug 84 |
| 8:13.33 | Peter | Koech | KEN | 58 | 3 | Nik | Nice | 15 Jul 86 |
| 8:13.57 | Eshetu | Tura | ETH | 50 | 3 | OG | Moskva | 31 Jul 80 |
| | (20) | | | | | | | |
| 8:13.91 | Ben | Jipcho | KEN | 43 | 1 | WG | Helsinki | 27 Jun 73 |
| 8:14.05 | Michael | Karst | FRG | 52 | 1 | DNG | Stockholm | 5 Jul 77 |
| 8:14.05 | Peter | Renner | NZ | 59 | 3 | | Koblenz | 29 Aug 84 |
| 8:14.13 | Joshua | Kipkemboi | KEN | 60 | 1 | | Koblenz | 6 Aug 86 |
| 8:14.17 | Samson | Obwocha | KEN | 54 | 2 | | Koblenz | 6 Aug 86 |
| 8:15.06 | Patriz | Ilg | FRG | 57 | 1 | WC | Helsinki | 12 Aug 83 |
| 8:15.32 | Dan | Glans | SWE | 47 | 3 | DNG | Stockholm | 10 Aug 76 |

MEN All-time

| Mark | Name | | Nat | Yr | Pos | Meet | Venue | Date | |
|------|------|--|-----|----|----|------|-------|------|--|
| 8:15.74 | Domingo | Ramón | SPA | 58 | 4 | OG | Moskva | 31 Jul | 80 |
| 8:15.92 | Julius | Kariuki | KEN | 61 | 4 | VD | Bruxelles | 5 Sep | 86 |
| 8:16.10 | Gheorge | Cefan | RUM | 47 | 2 | | Stockholm | 8 Jun | 76 |
| | (30) | | | | | | | | |
| 8:16.25 | Juan | Torres | SPA | 57 | 4 | | Koblenz | 29 Aug | 84 |
| 8:16.59 | Francisco | Sanchez | SPA | 58 | 4 | ISTAF | Berlin | 17 Aug | 83 |
| 8:16.59 | Ivan | Huff | USA | 59 | 5 | VD | Bruxelles | 5 Sep | 86 |
| 8:16.65 | Hagen | Melzer | GDR | 59 | 1 | EC | Stuttgart | 29 Aug | 86 |
| 8:16.85 | Francesco | Panetta | ITA | 63 | 2 | EC | Stuttgart | 29 Aug | 86 |
| 8:17.22 | Wolfgang | Konrad | AUT | 58 | 2 | ISTAF | Berlin | 20 Aug | 82 |
| 8:17.97 | Gabor | Markó | HUN | 60 | 1 | OD | Potsdam | 21 Jul | 84 |
| 8:18.02 | Hans | Koeleman | HOL | 57 | 2 | BGP | Budapest | 4 Aug | 85 |
| 8:18.22 | Richard | Tuwei | KEN | 54 | 1 | FBK | Hengelo | 12 Jul | 83 |
| 8:18.29 | Ismo | Toukonen | FIN | 54 | 3 | EC | Praha | 3 Sep | 78 |
| | (40) | | | | | | | | |
| 8:18.39 | Alessandro | Lambruschini | ITA | 65 | 1 | | Cesenatico | 27 Jun | 86 |
| 8:18.45 | John | Gregorek | USA | 60 | 3 | FOT | Los Angeles | 23 Jun | 84 |
| 8:18.47 | Giuseppe | Gerbi | ITA | 55 | 6 | OG | Moskva | 31 Jul | 80 |
| 8:18.54 | Pascal | Debacker | FRA | 60 | 5 | Nik | Nice | 15 Jul | 86 |
| 8:18.57 | Amos | Korir | KEN | 56 | 1 | Pre | Eugene | 6 Jun | 81 |
| 8:18.70 | Féthi | Baccouche | TUN | 60 | 6s2 | OG | Los Angeles | 8 Aug | 84 |
| 8:18.82 | Raymond | Pannier | FRA | 61 | 6 | Nik | Nice | 15 Jul | 86 |
| 8:18.85 | Franco | Fava | ITA | 52 | 4 | EC | Roma | 7 Sep | 74 |
| 8:18.95 | Dennis | Coates | UK | 53 | 1h2 | OG | Montreal | 25 Jul | 76 |
| 8:19.02 | Mirosław | Zerkowski | POL | 56 | 1 | PTS | Bratislava | 14 Jun | 86 |
| | (50) | | | | | | | | |

| Mark | Name | | Nat | Yr |
|------|------|--|-----|-----|
| 8:19.05 | Greg | Duhaime | CAN | 1982 |
| 8:19.27 | Farley | Gerber | USA | 1984 |
| 8:19.29 | Doug | Brown | USA | 1978 |
| 8:19.38 | Roger | Hackney | UK | 1983 |
| 8:19.38 | Ivan | Konovalov | SU | 1985 |
| 8:19.40 | Tommy | Ekblom | FIN | 1983 |
| 8:19.44 | Gerd | Frähmcke | FRG | 1976 |
| 8:19.52 | Masanari | Shintaku | JAP | 1980 |
| 8:19.57 | Yohannes | Mohamed | ETH | 1975 |
| 8:19.75 | Anatoliy | Dimov | SU | 1980 |
| | (60) | | | |
| 8:19.8 m | Jurgen | Straub | GDR | 1975 |
| 8:19.88 | Jim | Cooper | USA | 1986 |
| 8:20.2 | Boualem | Rahoui | ALG | 1975 |
| 8:20.40 | Ken | Martin | USA | 1984 |
| 8:20.41 | Paul | Copu | RUM | 1978 |
| 8:20.7 m | Peter | Daenens | BEL | 1984 |
| 8:20.83 | Paul | Davies-Hale | UK | 1984 |
| 8:21.00 | António | Campos | SPA | 1976 |
| 8:21.08 | Evan | Robertson | NZ | 1976 |
| 8:21.08 | Norbert | Brötzmann | GDR | 1983 |
| | (70) | | | |
| 8:21.20 | Eddie | Wedderburn | UK | 1985 |
| 8:21.41 | José | Regalo | POR | 1986 |
| 8:21.59 | James | Munyala | KEN | 1977 |
| 8:21.6 m | Takashi | Koyama | JAP | 1974 |
| 8:21.72 | George | Malley | USA | 1978 |
| 8:21.72 | Nollie | Meintjies | RSA | 1983 |
| 8:21.75 | Andrey | Popelyayev | SU | 1984 |

| Mark | Name | | Nat | Yr |
|------|------|--|-----|-----|
| 8:21.98 | Kerry | O'Brien | AUS | 1970 |
| 8:22.18 | Czesław | Mojzysz | POL | 1985 |
| 8:22.2 m | Vladimir | Dudin | SU | 1969 |
| | (80) | | | |
| 8:22.33 | Henryk | Jankowski | POL | 1986 |
| 8:22.4 | Hillary | Tuwei | KEN | 1980 |
| 8:22.45 | Patrick | Sang | KEN | 1984 |
| 8:22.47 | Willi | Maier | FRG | 1976 |
| 8:22.48 | John | Davies | UK | 1974 |
| 8:22.49 | Sergey | Yepishin | SU | 1981 |
| 8:22.49 | Roland | Hertner | SWZ | 1986 |
| 8:22.51 | Vasile | Bichea | RUM | 1980 |
| 8:22.54 | Kelly | Jensen | USA | 1983 |
| 8:22.6 m | Ilkka | Äyräväinen | FIN | 1982 |
| | (90) | | | |
| 8:22.63 | Julian | Marsay | UK | 1978 |
| 8:22.8 | Vladimir | Lissovskiy | SU | 1976 |
| 8:22.8 | Paul | Thijs | BEL | 1978 |
| 8:22.81 | Randy | Jackson | USA | 1980 |
| 8:22.82 | John | Bicourt | UK | 1976 |
| 8:22.83 | Ron | Addison | USA | 1977 |
| 8:22.9 m | Vesa | Laukkanen | FIN | 1982 |
| 8:23.14 | Ralf | Pönitzsch | GDR | 1981 |
| 8:23.34 | Solomon | Chebor | KEN | 1981 |
| 8:23.4 m | Aleksandr | Morozov | SU | 1969 |
| 8:23.4 m | Kazimierz | Maranda | POL | 1975 |
| 8:23.4 m | Vladimir | Filonov | SU | 1976 |
| | (102) | | | |

| Mark | Wind | Name | | Nat | Yr | Pos | Meet | Venue | Date |
|------|------|------|---|-----|----|----|------|-------|------|

## 110 METRES HURDLES

| Mark | Wind | Name | | Nat | Yr | Pos | Meet | Venue | Date |
|------|------|------|---|-----|----|----|------|-------|------|
| 12.93 | -0.2 | Renaldo | Nehemiah | USA | 59 | 1 | WK | Zürich | 19 Aug 81 |
| 13.00 | 0.9 | | Nehemiah | | | 1 | Pepsi | Westwood | 6 May 79 |
| 13.03 | -0.2 | Greg | Foster | USA | 58 | 2 | WK | Zürich | 19 Aug 81 |
| 13.04 | 0.0 | | Nehemiah | | | 1 | | Koblenz | 26 Aug 81 |
| 13.07 | -0.1 | | Nehemiah | | | 1 | ASV | Koln | 23 Aug 81 |
| 13.07 | 0.3 | | Nehemiah | | | 1 | VD | Bruxelles | 28 Aug 81 |
| 13.10 | 0.8 | | Foster | | | 1 | Pepsi | Westwood | 10 May 81 |
| 13.11 | -0.4 | | Foster | | | 1 | Pepsi | Westwood | 15 May 83 |
| 13.14 | 0.6 | Roger | Kingdom | USA | 62 | 1 | SW | Modesto | 11 May 85 |
| 13.15 | -0.7 | | Foster | | | 1 | TAC | Indianapolis | 18 Jun 83 |
| 13.15 | -1.1 | | Foster | | | 1 | WK | Zürich | 22 Aug 84 |
| 13.16 | 1.7 | | Nehemiah | | | 1 | Jenner | San Jose | 14 Apr 79 |
| 13.16 | -0.1 | | Foster | | | 1 | ISTAF | Berlin | 17 Aug 84 |
| 13.16 | -1.1 | | Kingdom | | | 2 | WK | Zürich | 22 Aug 84 |
| 13.17 | 0.8 | | Nehemiah | | | 1 | AAA | London | 8 Aug 81 |
| 13.17 | -0.4 | Sam | Turner | USA | 57 | 2 | Pepsi | Westwood | 15 May 83 |
| 13.17 | -0.1 | | Kingdom | | | 2 | ISTAF | Berlin | 17 Aug 84 |
| 13.18 | 2.0 | | Foster | | | 1 | CalR | Modesto | 16 May 81 |
| 13.19 | 1.5 | | Nehemiah | | | 1 | AAU | Walnut | 16 Jun 79 |
| 13.19 | 0.5 | | Foster | | | 1h1 | FOT | Los Angeles | 18 Jun 84 |
| 13.19 | 0.6 | | Kingdom | | | 1 | Nik | Nice | 20 Aug 84 |
| 13.20 | 2.0 | | Nehemiah | | | 1 | PAG | San Juan | 11 Jul 79 |
| 13.20 | -1.3 | | Foster | | | 1 | vGDR | Los Angeles | 26 Jun 83 |
| 13.20 | -0.2 | | Foster | | | 1 | | Koblenz | 31 Aug 83 |
| 13.20 | -0.4 | | Kingdom | | | 1 | OG | Los Angeles | 6 Aug 84 |
| 13.20 | 2.0 | Stéphane | Caristan | FRA | 64 | 1 | EC | Stuttgart | 30 Aug 86 |
| 13.21 | 0.6 | Alejandro | Casañas | CUB | 52 | 1 | WUG | Sofia | 21 Aug 77 |
| 13.21 | -0.6 | | Nehemiah | | | 1 | WK | Zürich | 13 Aug 80 |
| 13.21 | 1.1 | | Foster | | | 1 | Pepsi | Westwood | 13 May 84 |
| 13.21 | -1.1 | | Foster | | | 1 | FOT | Los Angeles | 19 Jun 84 |
| | | (30/6) | | | | | | | |
| 13.23 | 1.1 | Tonie | Campbell | USA | 60 | 2 | Pepsi | Westwood | 13 May 84 |
| 13.24 | 0.3 | Rod | Milburn | USA | 50 | 1 | OG | München | 7 Sep 72 |
| 13.25 | 0.1 | Andre | Phillips | USA | 59 | 1 | USOCF | Baton Rouge | 28 Jul 85 |
| 13.26 | 1.6 | Willie | Gault | USA | 60 | 1 | USOCF | Indianapolis | 25 Jul 82 |
| | | (10) | | | | | | | |
| 13.27 | 1.5 | Mark | McKoy | CAN | 61 | 1 | | Walnut | 25 Jul 84 |
| 13.28 | 1.1 | Guy | Drut | FRA | 50 | 1 | NC | St. Etienne | 29 Jun 75 |
| 13.28 | 1.0 | Andrey | Prokofyev | SU | 59 | 1r2 | GWG | Moskva | 6 Jul 86 |
| 13.31 | | Keith | Talley | USA | 64 | 2r1 | GWG | Moskva | 6 Jul 86 |
| 13.33 | 0.0 | Willie | Davenport | USA | 43 | 1 | OG | Ciudad México | 17 Oct 68 |
| 13.34 | 1.8 | Dedy | Cooper | USA | 56 | 2 | | Houston | 3 May 80 |
| 13.35 | 2.0 | Arto | Bryggare | FIN | 58 | 1h1 | OG | Los Angeles | 5 Aug 84 |
| 13.36 | 0.1 | Jack | Pierce | USA | 62 | 2 | USOCF | Baton Rouge | 28 Jul 85 |
| 13.37 | 2.0 | Thomas | Munkelt | GDR | 52 | 1 | EP | Helsinki | 14 Aug 77 |
| 13.37 | 0.2 | Milan | Stewart | USA | 60 | 2 | | Paris | 22 Jul 86 |
| | | (20) | | | | | | | |
| 13.38 | 1.8 | Ervin | Hall | USA | 47 | 1s1 | OG | Ciudad México | 17 Oct 68 |
| 13.38 | 1.6 | Jerry | Wilson | USA | 50 | 1 | AAU | Eugene | 20 Jun 75 |
| 13.38 | 0.6 | Cletus | Clark | USA | 62 | 2 | SW | Modesto | 11 May 85 |
| 13.39 | 1.9 | Larry | Cowling | USA | 60 | 1 | vGDR | Karl Marx St. | 10 Jul 82 |
| 13.39 | 1.1 | Aleksandr | Markin | SU | 62 | 1 | | Sochi | 24 May 86 |
| 13.40 | 2.0 | Holger | Pohland | GDR | 63 | 1 | vSU | Tallinn | 21 Jun 86 |
| 13.41 | 0.0 | Charles | Foster | USA | 53 | 4 | OG | Montreal | 28 Jul 76 |
| 13.42* | 0.0 | Tom | Hill | USA | 49 | 1 | AAU | Bakersfield | 26 Jun 70 |
| 13.42 | -0.9 | Igor | Kazanov | SU | 63 | 1 | Spart | Tashkent | 20 Sep 86 |

| Mark | Wind | Name | | Nat | Yr | Pos | Meet | Venue | Date |
|---|---|---|---|---|---|---|---|---|---|
| 13.43 | 1.8 | Earl | McCullough | USA | 46 | 1 | | Minneapolis | 16 Jul 67 |
| | | (30) | | | | | | | |
| 13.43* | 0.0 | Marcus | Walker | USA | 49 | 2 | AAU | Bakersfield | 26 Jun 70 |
| 13.43 | 1.9 | Mark | Holtom | UK | 58 | 2 | CommG | Brisbane | 4 Oct 82 |
| 13.44 | 0.9 | Aleksandr | Puchkov | SU | 57 | 3 | OG | Moskva | 27 Jul 80 |
| 13.44 | -0.8 | Colin | Jackson | UK | 67 | 1 | WJ | Athinai | 19 Jul 86 |
| 13.45* | 0.7 | Leon | Coleman | USA | 44 | 1= | AAU | Miami | 28 Jun 69 |
| A13.45 | 1.6 | Kerry | Bethel | USA | 57 | 1 | USOCF | Air Force Ac. | 30 Jul 78 |
| 13.45 | 1.8 | Henry | Andrade | USA | 62 | 3s2 | FOT | Los Angeles | 19 Jun 84 |
| 13.45 | 1.4 | György | Bakos | HUN | 60 | 2 | 8-N | Tokyō | 14 Sep 84 |
| A13.46 | 0.0 | Eddy | Ottoz | ITA | 44 | 3 | OG | Ciudad México | 17 Oct 68 |
| 13.46 | 1.8 | James | Owens | USA | 55 | 3 | NCAA | Eugene | 2 Jun 78 |
| | | (40) | | | | | | | |
| 13.46 | -0.3 | Plamen | Krastev | BUL | 58 | 1 | 4-N | Athinai | 10 Jul 84 |
| 13.46 | 1.4 | Al | Lane | USA | 62 | 4 | | Villanova | 9 Jun 85 |
| 13.46 | 1.8 | Jonathan | Ridgeon | UK | 67 | 1 | EJ | Cottbus | 23 Aug 85 |
| 13.47 | 1.8 | Frank | Siebeck | GDR | 49 | 1 | DNG | Stockholm | 1 Jul 75 |
| 13.47 | 1.8 | Viktor | Myasnikov | SU | 48 | 2 | vUSA | Berkeley | 7 Jul 78 |
| 13.47 | 1.6 | John | Johnson | USA | 60 | 1h4 | NCAA | Eugene | 31 May 84 |
| 13.47 | 0.0 | Sansiski | Daniels | USA | 63 | 2 | NCAA | Indianapolis | 7 Jun 86 |
| 13.47 | 0.5 | Liviu | Giurgian | RUM | 62 | 1 | | Bucuresti | 15 Jun 86 |
| 13.47 | 1.0 | Igor | Perevedentsev | SU | 64 | 2r2 | GWG | Moskva | 6 Jul 86 |
| 13.48 | 1.7 | Garnett | Edwards | USA | 56 | 2s1 | NCAA | Champaign | 1 Jun 79 |
| 13.48 | 1.8 | John | Timpson | USA | 62 | 1r1 | | Baton Rouge | 21 Apr 84 |
| | | (51) | | | | | | | |

| | | | | | | | | | | | |
|---|---|---|---|---|---|---|---|---|---|---|---|
| 13.49 | 2.0 | Javier | Moracho | SPA | 1985 | | 13.57 | 1.8 | Gary | Burl | USA 1976 |
| 13.50 | 0.9 | Andreas | Oschkenat | GDR | 1983 | | 13.57 | 1.4 | Robert | Gaines | USA 1976 |
| 13.50 | 2.0 | Wayne | Roby | USA | 1985 | | 13.57 | 1.0 | Romuald | Giegiel | POL 1982 |
| 13.50 | 1.0 | Vladimir | Shishkin | SU | 1986 | | | | (80) | | |
| 13.50 | 2.0 | Carlos | Sala | SPA | 1986 | | 13.57 | 0.3 | Vyacheslav | Ustinov | SU 1984 |
| 13.51 | 0.8 | Al | Joyner | USA | 1985 | | 13.57 | | Arthur | Blake | USA 1986 |
| 13.51 | 0.0 | Martin | Booker | USA | 1986 | | 13.57 | 0.0 | Thomas | Wilcher | USA 1986 |
| 13.52 | 0.0 | Eric | Reid | USA | 1986 | | 13.58 | 1.9 | Don | Wright | AUS 1982 |
| 13.52 | 0.0 | Nigel | Walker | UK | 1986 | | 13.59 | | Tommy Lee | White | USA 1968 |
| | | (60) | | | | | 13.59 | 0.8 | Lance | Babb | USA 1980 |
| A13.53* | -0.2 | Richmond | Flowers | USA | 1967 | | 13.59 | 1.3 | John | Lenstrohm | USA 1982 |
| 13.53 | 0.6 | Jan | Pusty | POL | 1977 | | 13.59 | 1.5 | Venzislav | Radev | BUL 1983 |
| 13.53 | 0.9 | Dan | Lavitt | USA | 1980 | | A13.60 | 0.0 | Werner | Trzmiel | FRG 1968 |
| 13.53 | 0.4 | James | Quinn | USA | 1984 | | 13.60 | 0.6 | Wayne | Mason | USA 1980 |
| 13.53 | 1.6 | William | Skinner | USA | 1986 | | | | (90) | | |
| 13.54 | -0.3 | Yuriy | Chervanev | SU | 1980 | | 13.60 | 0.9 | Andreas | Schlisske | GDR 1983 |
| 13.54 | 0.8 | Karl Werner | Dönges | FRG | 1982 | | 13.60 | 1.8 | Jacek | Rutkowski | POL 1983 |
| 13.54 | 1.2 | Nikolay | Shilev | BUL | 1984 | | 13.60 | 0.8 | Wilbert | Greaves | UK 1985 |
| 13.55* | 0.0 | Ricky | Stubbs | USA | 1973 | | A13.61 | 1.8 | Pat | Pomphrey | USA 1968 |
| 13.55* | 0.9 | Larry | Shipp | USA | 1975 | | 13.61 | | Eduard | Pereverzev | SU 1977 |
| | | (70) | | | | | 13.61 | 0.9 | Greg | Robertson | USA 1978 |
| 13.55 | | Mirosław | Wodzynski | POL | 1975 | | 13.62 | 1.7 | Dan | Oliver | USA 1979 |
| 13.55 | 0.6 | Vyacheslav | Kulebyakin | SU | 1977 | | 13.62 | | Reggie | Davis | USA 1986 |
| 13.55 | 0.0 | Julius | Ivan | CS | 1981 | | 13.63* | | Hayes | Jones | USA 1963 |
| 13.55 | 1.3 | James | McCraney | USA | 1984 | | 13.63 | -0.3 | Reggie | Towns | USA 1983 |
| 13.56 | 1.9 | Martin | Lauer | FRG | 1959 | | 13.63 | 0.1 | Stefan | Baker | USA 1984 |
| 13.56 | 0.6 | Sergey | Usov | SU | 1985 | | | | (101) | | |
| 13.56 | | Reyna | Thompson | USA | 1986 | | | | | | |

Doubtful wind reading

| | | | | | | | | | | |
|---|---|---|---|---|---|---|---|---|---|---|
| 13.48 | -0.9 | Igor | Podmaryov | SU | 1986 | | 13.63 | -0.6 | Gennadiy | Chugunov | SU 1986 |
| 13.55 | -0.9 | Jonas | Jakstis | SU | 1986 | | 13.63 | -0.9 | Sergey | Novikov | SU 1986 |

Low altitude bests

| | | | | | | | | | | |
|---|---|---|---|---|---|---|---|---|---|---|
| Davenport | | 13.38 | 0.0 | 3 | OG | Montréal | 28 Jul 76 | 13.33A |
| Hall | | 13.46* | 0.7 | 3 | AAU | Miami | 28 Jun 69 | 13.38A |
| Bethel | 13.52 | 0.4 | 1978 | 13.45A | Ottoz | 13.59 | 0.0 | 1969 | 13.46A |

| Mark | Wind | Name | | Nat | Yr | Pos | Meet | Venue | Date |
|------|------|------|------|-----|-----|-----|------|-------|------|

**Wind-assisted marks**

| Mark | Wind | Name | | Nat | Yr | Pos | Meet | Venue | Date |
|------|------|------|------|-----|-----|-----|------|-------|------|
| 12.91 | 3.5 | Renaldo | Nehemiah | USA | 59 | 1 | NCAA | Champaign | 1 Jun 79 |
| 13.00 | 3.5 | | Nehemiah | | | 1 | USOCF | Syracuse | 26 Jul 81 |
| 13.00 | 2.7 | Roger | Kingdom | USA | 62 | 1 | | Sacramento | 21 Jul 84 |
| 13.14 | 2.9 | Igor | Kazanov | SU | 63 | 1rl | Znam | Leningrad | 8 Jun 86 |
| 13.16 | 2.7 | Mark | McKoy | CAN | 61 | 2 | | Sacramento | 21 Jul 84 |
| 13.18 | 2.1 | | Nehemiah | | | 1 | ISTAF | Berlin | 21 Aug 81 |
| (6/4) | | | | | | | | | |
| 13.25 | 2.9 | Aleksandr | Markin | SU | 62 | 2rl | Znam | Leningrad | 8 Jun 86 |
| 13.28 | 2.7 | Henry | Andrade | USA | 62 | 3 | | Sacramento | 21 Jul 84 |
| 13.33 | 2.9 | Gennadiy | Chugunov | SU | 63 | 3rl | Znam | Leningrad | 8 Jun 86 |
| 13.36* | 3.5 | Ricky | Stubbs | USA | 51 | 1 | TexR | Austin | 13 Apr 74 |
| 13.36 | 2.9 | Vladimir | Shishkin | SU | 64 | 4rl | Znam | Leningrad | 8 Jun 86 |
| 13.38* | 2.3 | Charles | Foster | USA | 53 | 1 | NCAA | Austin | 7 Jun 74 |
| 13.38 | 3.4 | Al | Lane | USA | 62 | 1h3 | NCAA | Eugene | 31 May 84 |
| 13.39 | | Colin | Williams | USA | | 1 | | Dallas | 1 Apr 78 |
| 13.39 | 3.1 | Arthur | Blake | USA | 66 | 3sl | TAC | Eugene | 19 Jun 86 |
| 13.40 | 3.4 | Liviu | Giurgian | RUM | 62 | 1 | | Beograd | 27 Jun 86 |
| | | | | | | | | | |
| 13.41* | 3.5 | Efrem | Gipson | USA | 49 | 2 | TexR | Austin | 13 Apr 74 |
| 13.42 | 4.5 | Colin | Jackson | UK | 67 | 2 | CommG | Edinburgh | 27 Jul 86 |
| 13.43 | 3.2 | James | McCraney | USA | 55 | 4rl | SW | Modesto | 12 May 84 |
| 13.44 | 4.5 | Milan | Stewart | USA | 60 | 1 | CalR | Modesto | 15 May 82 |
| 13.46 | 2.3 | Rod | Wilson | USA | 61 | 1 | | Houston | 28 May 83 |
| 13.46 | 4.0 | Wayne | Roby | USA | 62 | 2 | NCAA | Austin | 1 Jun 85 |
| 13.46 | 2.9 | Anatoliy | Titov | SU | 56 | 5rl | Znam | Leningrad | 8 Jun 86 |

| Mark | | Name | | Nat | Yr | | Mark | | Name | | Nat | Yr |
|------|---|------|---|-----|-----|---|------|---|------|---|-----|-----|
| 13.48* | 2.3 | Larry | Shipp | USA | 1974 | | 13.59 | | Anthony | Coleman | USA | 1977 |
| 13.52 | 4.2 | Thomas | Wilcher | USA | 1985 | | 13.59 | 4.1 | Eugene | Miller | USA | 1980 |
| 13.52 | 2.9 | Aleš | Höffer | CS | 1986 | | 13.59 | 4.0 | Jacek | Rutkowski | POL | 1983 |
| 13.53 | 3.0 | Orlando | McDaniel | USA | 1980 | | 13.59 | 3.4 | Axel | Schaumann | FRG | 1983 |
| 13.53 | 2.3 | Reyna | Thompson | USA | 1986 | | | | | | | |
| 13.53 | 2.6 | James | Purvis | USA | 1986 | | 13.59 | 5.7 | Charles | James | USA | 1985 |
| 13.53 | 2.9 | Igor | Khitrakov | SU | 1986 | | 13.59 | | Harold | Morton | USA | 1986 |
| 13.54 | 4.3 | Julius | Ivan | CS | 1981 | | 13.60 | 3.5 | James | Walker | USA | 1979 |
| 13.54 | 2.3 | Malcolm | Dixon | USA | 1983 | | 13.60 | | Dennis | Brantley | USA | 1981 |
| | | | | | | | 13.60 | 3.4 | Albert | Jones | USA | 1984 |
| 13.54 | 4.0 | Romuald | Giegiel | POL | 1983 | | 13.60 | | Kevin | McKinley | USA | 1986 |
| 13.55 | 3.5 | Dan | Oliver | USA | 1979 | | A13.60 | 2.2 | Ralf | Schroeder | RSA | 1986 |
| 13.55 | 5.2 | Carlos | Sala | SPA | 1983 | | 13.61* | 3.5 | Vance | Roland | USA | 1974 |
| 13.56 | 3.0 | Reggie | Towns | USA | 1983 | | 13.61 | 2.4 | Leszek | Wodzynski | POL | 1974 |
| 13.57 | 2.6 | Stefan | Baker | USA | 1984 | | 13.61 | | Jim | Kelley | USA | 1978 |
| 13.58 | 2.9 | Anton | Isayev | SU | 1986 | | 13.61 | 3.5 | Doc | King | USA | 1979 |

120 yards time plus 0.03 seconds

**and timing**

| Mark | Wind | Name | | Nat | Yr | Pos | Meet | Venue | Date |
|------|------|------|------|-----|-----|-----|------|-------|------|
| 12.8 | | Renaldo | Nehemiah | USA | 59 | 1 | | Kingston | 11 May 79 |
| 13.0 | 1.8 | Guy | Drut | FRA | 50 | 1 | ISTAF | Berlin | 22 Aug 75 |
| 13.0 | | Greg | Foster | USA | 58 | 2 | | Kingston | 11 May 79 |
| 13.0* | 2.0 | Rod | Milburn | USA | 50 | 1sl | AAU | Eugene | 25 Jun 71 |
| 13.0* | 1.0 | | Milburn | | | 1 | | Eugene | 20 Jun 73 |
| 13.0* | 0.9 | | Milburn | | | 1 | ITA | El Paso | 10 May 75 |
| 13.0 | 0.8 | Mark | McKoy | CAN | 61 | 1 | Nik | Nice | 16 Jul 85 |
| 13.0 | | Stéphane | Caristan | FRA | 64 | 1 | | Creteil | 3 May 86 |
| (9/6) | | | | | | | | | |
| 13.1 | | Tonie | Campbell | USA | 60 | 1 | | Nassau | 7 May 83 |
| 13.1 | -0.9 | Roger | Kingdom | USA | 62 | 1rl | | Tillsonburg | 7 Jul 84 |
| 13.1* | 0.9 | Lance | Babb | USA | 50 | 2 | ITA | El Paso | 10 May 75 |
| 13.2 | 0.0 | Lee | Calhoun | USA | 33 | 1 | | Bern | 21 Aug 60 |
| 13.2 | -0.9 | Willie | Davenport | USA | 43 | 1 | | Zürich | 4 Jul 69 |
| 13.2 | 1.2 | Alejandro | Casañas | CUB | 54 | 1 | Kuso | Warszawa | 20 Jun 75 |

MEN All-time

| Mark | Wind | Name | | Nat | Yr | Pos | Meet | Venue | | Date |
|---|---|---|---|---|---|---|---|---|---|---|
| 13.2 | 1.8 | Charles | Foster | USA | 53 | 2 | ISTAF | Berlin | | 22 Aug 75 |
| 13.2 | 1.7 | Karl Werner | Dönges | FRG | 58 | 1 | | Albstadt | | 14 Jun 81 |
| 13.2* | 1.7 | Tom | Hill | USA | 49 | 1 | USTFF | Wichita | | 13 Jun 70 |
| 13.2 | | Modesto | Castillo | DOM | 59 | 1 | | S.Domingo | | 26 May 84 |
| 13.2 | 0.8 | Henry | Andrade | USA | 62 | 2 | Nik | Nice | | 16 Jul 85 |
| 13.2 | 0.8 | Gyorgy | Bakos | HUN | 60 | 3 | Nik | Nice | | 16 Jul 85 |
| 13.3 | 1.2 | Frank | Siebeck | GDR | 1972 | 13.3* | | Jack | Davis | USA | 1956 |
| 13.3 | 1.7 | Leszek | Wodzynski | POL | 1974 | 13.3* | | Jerry | Tarr | USA | 1962 |
| 13.3 | | Stepan | Kuziv | SU | 1980 | 13.3* 0.9 | Earl | McCullough | USA | 1968 |
| 13.3 | | Aleksandr | Puchkov | SU | 1982 | 13.3* 1.6 | Richmond | Flowers | USA | 1968 |
| 13.3 | 0.8 | Carlos | Sala | SPA | 1985 | 13.3*-1.3 | Ervin | Hall | USA | 1969 |
| 13.3 | 0.8 | Igor | Kazanov | SU | 1985 | 13.3* 1.9 | Charles | Rich | USA | 1974 |
| 13.3 | 0.2 | Anatoliy | Titov | SU | 1985 | A13.3* 0.9 | Paul | Gibson | USA | 1975 |

Wind-assisted marks

| Mark | Wind | Name | | Nat | Yr | Pos | Meet | Venue | | Date |
|---|---|---|---|---|---|---|---|---|---|---|
| 13.0 | | Alejandro | Casañas | CUB | 54 | 1 | Barr | Habana | | 22 May 77 |
| 13.0* | 2.2 | | R.Milburn | | | 1 | | Billings | | 4 Jun 7 |
| 13.0* | 3.2 | | Milburn | | | 1 | | Lafayette | | 15 Apr 72 |
| 13.0* | 2.5 | | Milburn | | | 1 | CalR | Modesto | | 27 May 72 |
| 13.0 | | Tonie | Campbell | USA | 60 | 1 | | Los Angeles | | 16 Jul 8 |
| (5/3-1) | | | | | | | | | | |
| 13.1* | 3.2 | Tom | Hill | USA | 49 | 1sl | USTFF | Wichita | | 13 Jun 70 |
| 13.1* | 4.5 | Larry | Shipp | USA | 54 | 1 | KansR | Lawrence | | 20 Apr 7 |
| 13.1 | | Ronnie | McCoy | USA | 63 | 1 | | Naperville | | 10 May 8 |
| 13.2 | 2.6 | Dedy | Cooper | USA | 56 | 1 | | San Jose | | 2 May 8 |
| 13.2 | | Gene | Norman | USA | 61 | 1 | | New York | | 29 May 8 |
| 13.2* | | Danny | Smith | BAH | 52 | 1 | | Baton Rouge | | 19 Apr 7 |
| 13.3 | 3.2 | Marcus | Walker | USA | 1970 | 13.3 | | Reyna | Thompson | USA | 1986 |
| 13.3 | 2.4 | Juan | Morales | CUB | 1971 | 13.3* 2.5 | Ron | Draper | USA | 1971 |
| 13.3 | | Kerry | Bethel | USA | 1978 | 13.3* | | Ricky | Stubbs | USA | 1974 |
| 13.3 | 4.3 | Vitaliy | Sklyarov | SU | 1983 | 13.3* | | Clim | Jackson | USA | 1975 |
| 13.3 | | Keith | Talley | USA | 1985 | 13.3* | | Donnie | Taylor | USA | 1976 |

* 120 yards time

# 400 METRES HURDLES

| Mark | | Name | | Nat | Yr | Pos | Meet | Venue | | Date |
|---|---|---|---|---|---|---|---|---|---|---|
| 47.02 | Edwin | | Moses | USA | 55 | 1 | | Koblenz | | 31 Aug 8 |
| 47.13 | | | Moses | | | 1 | | Milano | | 3 Jul 8 |
| 47.14 | | | Moses | | | 1 | | Lausanne | | 14 Jul 8 |
| 47.17 | | | Moses | | | 1 | ISTAF | Berlin | | 8 Aug 8 |
| 47.27 | | | Moses | | | 1 | ISTAF | Berlin | | 21 Aug 8 |
| 47.32 | | | Moses | | | 1 | | Koblenz | | 29 Aug 8 |
| 47.37 | | | Moses | | | 1 | WP | Roma | | 4 Sep 8 |
| 47.37 | | | Moses | | | 1 | WK | Zürich | | 24 Aug 8 |
| 47.38 | | | Moses | | | 1 | | Lausanne | | 2 Sep 8 |
| 47.43 | | | Moses | | | 1 | ASV | Koln | | 28 Aug 8 |
| 47.45 | | | Moses | | | 1 | AAU | Westwood | | 11 Jun 7 |
| 47.48 | Harald | | Schmid | FRG | 57 | 1 | EC | Athinai | | 8 Sep 8 |
| 47.50 | | | Moses | | | 1 | WC | Helsinki | | 9 Aug 8 |
| 47.51 | Andre | | Phillips | USA | 59 | 1 | VD | Bruxelles | | 5 Sep 8 |
| 47.53 | | | Moses | | | 1 | WP | Montréal | | 24 Aug 7 |
| 47.53 | | | Moses | | | 1 | ISTAF | Berlin | | 15 Aug 8 |
| 47.58 | | | Moses | | | 1 | WP | Düsseldorf | | 2 Sep 7 |
| 47.58 | | | Moses | | | 1sl | FOT | Los Angeles | | 17 Jun 8 |
| 47.59 | | | Moses | | | 1 | TAC | Sacramento | | 21 Jun 8 |
| 47.63 | | | Moses | | | 1 | OG | Montréal | | 25 Jul 7 |

| Mark | Name | | Nat | Yr | Pos | Meet | Venue | Date |
|------|------|---|-----|----|----|------|-------|------|
| 47.63 | Danny | Harris | USA | 65 | 1 | WK | Zürich | 21 Aug 85 |
| 47.64 | | Moses | | | 1 | WK | Zürich | 19 Aug 81 |
| 47.66 | | Moses | | | 1 | | Paris | 22 Jul 86 |
| 47.67 | | Moses | | | 1 | OsloG | Oslo | 17 Jul 79 |
| 47.67 | | Phillips | | | 1 | TAC | Indianapolis | 16 Jun 85 |
| 47.69 | | Moses | | | 1 | | Durham | 19 May 79 |
| 47.69 | | Schmid | | | 1 | | Lausanne | 10 Jul 84 |
| 47.69 | | Phillips | | | 1 | WK | Zürich | 13 Aug 86 |
| 47.75 | | Moses | | | 1 | OG | Los Angeles | 5 Aug 84 |
| 47.76 | | Moses | | | 1 | FOT | Los Angeles | 18 Aug 84 |
| 47.76 | | Moses | | | 1 | BGP | Budapest | 11 Aug 86 |
| (31/4) | | | | | | | | |
| 47.82 | John | Akii-Bua | UGA | 49 | 1 | OG | München | 2 Sep 72 |
| 47.92 | Aleksandr | Vasilyev | SU | 61 | 2 | EP | Moskva | 17 Aug 85 |
| 48.05 | David | Patrick | USA | 60 | 2 | WK | Zürich | 24 Aug 83 |
| 48.07 | Amadou | Dia Bâ | SEN | 58 | 2 | ISTAF | Berlin | 15 Aug 86 |
| 48.12 | David | Hemery | UK | 44 | 1 | OG | Ciudad México | 15 Oct 68 |
| 48.16 | Tony | Rambo | USA | 60 | 3sl | FOT | Los Angeles | 17 Jun 84 |
| (10) | | | | | | | | |
| 48.28 | Tranel | Hawkins | USA | 62 | 3 | FOT | Los Angeles | 18 Jun 84 |
| 48.34 | Vasiliy | Arkhipenko | SU | 57 | 2 | EP | Torino | 4 Aug 79 |
| 48.39 | Quentin | Wheeler | USA | 55 | 2 | AAU | Walnut | 17 Jun 79 |
| 48.42 | David | Lee | USA | 59 | 4 | WK | Zürich | 24 Aug 83 |
| 48.44 | Harry | Schulting | HOL | 56 | 1 | WUG | Ciudad México | 12 Sep 79 |
| 48.46 | Larry | Cowling | USA | 60 | 2 | NCAA | Provo | 4 Jun 82 |
| 48.48 | James | Walker | USA | 57 | 1 | | Tuscaloosa | 13 May 79 |
| 48.48 | Toma | Tomov | BUL | 58 | 2 | BGP | Budapest | 11 Aug 86 |
| 48.50 | Uwe | Ackermann | GDR | 60 | 1 | vUSA | Karl-Marx-Stadt | 9 Jul 82 |
| 48.51 | Ralph | Mann | USA | 49 | 2 | OG | München | 2 Sep 72 |
| (20) | | | | | | | | |
| 48.55 | Jim | Bolding | USA | 49 | 1 | | Paris | 8 Jul 75 |
| 48.55 | Tom | Andrews | USA | 54 | 1 | AAU | Westwood | 12 Jun 76 |
| 48.58 | Volker | Beck | GDR | 56 | 3 | EP | Torino | 4 Aug 79 |
| 48.59 | Alan | Pascoe | UK | 47 | 1 | DNG | Stockholm | 30 Jun 75 |
| 48.60 | Aleksandr | Yatsevich | SU | 56 | 2 | EC | Athinai | 8 Sep 82 |
| 48.63 | Bart | Williams | USA | 56 | 2 | | Lausanne | 10 Jul 84 |
| 48.64 | Jim | Seymour | USA | 49 | 4 | OG | München | 2 Sep 72 |
| 48.69 | Mike | Shine | USA | 53 | 2 | OG | Montreal | 25 Jul 76 |
| 48.71 | Vladimir | Budko | SU | 65 | 1 | Spart | Tashkent | 18 Sep 86 |
| 48.72 | Dale | Laverty | USA | 65 | 2 | | El Paso | 20 Apr 86 |
| (30) | | | | | | | | |
| 48.73 | Paul | Montgomery | USA | 61 | 3 | NCAA | Provo | 4 Jun 82 |
| 48.77 | Kevin | Young | USA | 66 | 2 | NCAA | Indianapolis | 6 Jun 86 |
| 48.78 | Aleksandr | Kharlov | SU | 58 | 1 | Spart | Moskva | 20 Jun 83 |
| 48.81 | Hannes | Pienaar | RSA | 60 | 1 | | Pretoria | 15 Feb 86 |
| 48.83 | Sven | Nylander | SWE | 62 | 2s2 | EC | Stuttgart | 27 Aug 86 |
| 48.88 | Henry | Amike | NIG | 61 | 2 | NCAA | Austin | 31 May 85 |
| 48.88 | Athanassios | Kalogiannis | GRE | 65 | 1r2 | GWG | Moskva | 9 Jul 86 |
| 48.90 | Reggie | Davis | USA | 64 | 2 | DrakeR | Des Moines | 26 Apr 85 |
| 48.94 | Geoff | Vanderstock | USA | 46 | 1 | FOT | Echo Summit | 11 Sep 68 |
| 48.94 | Jean-Claude | Nallet | FRA | 47 | 2 | EC | Roma | 4 Sep 74 |
| (40) | | | | | | | | |
| 48.94 | R.Meledje | Djédjémel | IVC | 58 | 4 | WK | Zürich | 13 Aug 86 |
| 48.95 | Jon | Thomas | USA | 63 | 1 | | Evanston | 19 May 85 |
| 48.98 | Nikolay | Vasilyev | SU | 56 | 1s2 | WUG | Ciudad México | 11 Sep 79 |
| 48.98 | Nikolay | Ilchenko | SU | 63 | 2 | Spart | Tashkent | 18 Sep 86 |
| 49.00 | Wes | Williams | USA | 48 | 5 | AAU | Westwood | 12 Jun 76 |
| 49.00 | James | King | USA | 49 | 2 | | Bratislava | 7 Sep 79 |
| 49.02 | Gerhard | Hennige | FRG | 40 | 2 | OG | Ciudad México | 15 Oct 68 |
| 49.02 | Yevgeniy | Gavrilenko | SU | 51 | 1 | vFRG | München | 30 May 76 |
| 49.03 | John | Sherwood | UK | 45 | 3 | OG | Ciudad México | 15 Oct 68 |
| 49.04 | Sam | Turner | USA | 57 | 3 | | Lausanne | 13 Jul 78 |
| (50) | | | | | | | | |

| Mark | Name | | Nat | Yr | | Pos | Meet | Venue | | Date |
|------|------|--|-----|----|-|-----|------|-------|--|------|
| A49.06 | Ron | Whitney | USA | 1968 | | 49.34 | Christian | Rudolph | GDR | 1971 |
| 49.07 | Tagir | Zemskov | SU | 1986 | | 49.34 | William | Koskei | KEN | 1974 |
| 49.10 | Hartmut | Weber | FRG | 1982 | | 49.34 | Mirosław | Kodejs | CS | 1974 |
| A49.10 | Bernie | Holloway | USA | 1982 | | 49.34 | Olivier | Gui | FRA | 1985 |
| 49.11 | Rok | Kopitar | YUG | 1980 | | | (80) | | | |
| 49.11 | Gary | Oakes | UK | 1980 | | 49.34 | Paulo | Chiamulera | BRA | 1985 |
| A49.12 | Vyacheslav | Skomorokhov | SU | 1968 | | 49.35 | Sergey | Melnikov | SU | 1983 |
| A49.14 | Roberto | Frinolli | ITA | 1968 | | 49.36 | Rick | Walker | USA | 1977 |
| A49.15 | Rainer | Schubert | FRG | 1968 | | 49.37* | Robert | Primeaux | USA | 1973 |
| 49.16 | Kevin | Henderson | USA | 1985 | | 49.37 | Garry | Brown | AUS | 1982 |
| | (60) | | | | | 49.39 | Dennis | Otono | NIG | 1979 |
| 49.17 | Karl | Smith | JAM | 1982 | | 49.39 | José | Alonso | SPA | 1985 |
| 49.17 | Ryszard | Szparak | POL | 1983 | | 49.39 | Uwe | Schmitt | FRG | 1985 |
| 49.18 | Ray | Smith | USA | 1984 | | A49.40 | Hugo | Pont | HOL | 1979 |
| 49.20 | Daniel | Kimaiyo | KEN | 1978 | | 49.40 | Valeriy | Vikhrov | SU | 1984 |
| 49.21 | Dieter | Buttner | FRG | 1972 | | | (90) | | | |
| 49.21 | Nat | Page | USA | 1986 | | 49.40 | Ryōichi | Yoshida | JAP | 1986 |
| 49.24 | António | Diaz Ferreira | BRA | 1985 | | 49.41 | Jesus | Aguilasocho | MEX | 1985 |
| A49.26 | Hennie | Kotze | RSA | 1983 | | 49.42 | Franz | Meier | SWZ | 1984 |
| A49.27 | Boyd | Gittins | USA | 1968 | | 49.45 | Peter | Scholz | FRG | 1984 |
| 49.29 | Belfred | Clark | USA | 1986 | | 49.46* | Gerhardus | Potgieter | RSA | 1958 |
| | (70) | | | | | 49.46 | Chris | Person | USA | 1980 |
| 49.31 | Rich | Graybehl | USA | 1978 | | 49.46 | Greg | Rolle | BAH | 1983 |
| 49.31 | Ahmed | Hamada | BHN | 1986 | | A49.47 | Tom | Wyatt | USA | 1968 |
| 49.32 | Bruce | Field | AUS | 1974 | | 49.47 | Georgios | Vamvakas | GRE | 1985 |
| 49.33 | Dmitriy | Shkarupin | SU | 1983 | | 49.48 | Frank | Nusse | HOL | 1975 |
| 49.33 | Leander | McKenzie | USA | 1985 | | | (100) | | | |
| 49.33 | Thomas | Futterknecht | AUT | 1985 | | | | | | |

* 440 yards time less 0.26 seconds

Low altitude bests for athletes with high altitude marks

|  |  |  |  |  |  |  |  |  |
|--|--|--|--|--|--|--|--|--|
| | Hemery | 48.52 | 3 | OG | München | 2 Sep 82 | A48.12 |
| | Schulting | 48.71 | 2 | WK | Zürich | 15 Aug 79 | A48.44 |
| | Cowling | 48.87 | 1 | | Berkeley | 12 Jun 83 | A48.46 |
| Montgomery | 49.14 | 1983 | A48.73 | | N.Vasilyev | 49.34 | 1980 | A48.98 |
| Laverty | 49.27 | 1985 | A48.72 | | Holloway | 49.35 | 1983 | A49.10 |
| Pienaar | 49.27 | 1986 | A48.81 | | Schubert | 49.39 | 1972 | A49.15 |

Hand timing

| | | | | | | | | | |
|--|--|--|--|--|--|--|--|--|--|
| 48.1 | Jim | Bolding | USA | 49 | 1 | | Milano | | 2 Jul 7 |
| 48.4 | Ralph | Mann | USA | 49 | 1 | FOT | Eugene | | 2 Jul 7 |
| 48.5 | Aleksandr | Yatsevich | SU | 56 | 1 | | Kiev | | 9 Aug 8 |
| 48.6 | Jean-Claude | Nallet | FRA | 47 | 1 | vUSA | Colombes | | 8 Jul 7 |
| 48.6 | Dick | Bruggeman | USA | 47 | 2 | FOT | Eugene | | 2 Jul 7 |
| 48.7 | Aleksandr | Cheshko | SU | 58 | 1 | | Cherkassy | | 3 Sep 8 |
| 48.9* | Wayne | Collet | USA | 49 | 2 | NCAA | Des Moines | | 20 Jun 7 |

| | | | | | | | | | |
|--|--|--|--|--|--|--|--|--|--|
| A49.0* | Gerhardus | Potgieter | RSA | 1960 | | 49.2 | Glenn | Davis | USA | 1958 |
| A49.0 | William | Koskei | KEN | 1972 | | 49.2 | Salvatore | Morale | ITA | 1962 |
| 49.1 | Rex | Cawley | USA | 1964 | | 49.2 | Nick | Lee | USA | 1969 |
| 49.1 | Vyacheslav | Skomorokhov | SU | 1969 | | 49.3 | Christian | Rudolph | GDR | 1971 |
| 49.1 | Bruce | Collins | USA | 1972 | | 49.3 | Gary | Knoke | AUS | 1972 |
| 49.1 | Miroslav | Kodejs | CS | 1974 | | 49.3 | Viktor | Savchenko | SU | 1972 |

* 440 yards less 0.3 seconds, + during 440 yards race

| Mark | Name | | Nat | Yr | Pos | Meet | Venue | Date |
|---|---|---|---|---|---|---|---|---|

# HIGH JUMP

| Mark | Name | | Nat | Yr | Pos | Meet | Venue | Date |
|---|---|---|---|---|---|---|---|---|
| 2.41 | Igor | Paklin | SU | 63 | 1 | WUG | Kobe | 4 Sep 85 |
| 2.40 | Rudolf | Povarnitsin | SU | 62 | 1 | | Donyetsk | 11 Aug 85 |
| 2.39 | Zhu Jianhua | | CHN | 63 | 1 | | Eberstadt | 10 Jun 84 |
| 2.39i | Dietmar | Mögenburg | FRG | 61 | 1 | | Köln | 24 Feb 85 |
| 2.38 | | Zhu | | | 1 | NC | Shanghai | 22 Sep 83 |
| 2.38i | Patrik | Sjöberg | SWE | 65 | 1 | | Berlin | 22 Feb 85 |
| 2.38 | | Sjöberg | | | 1 | | Eberstadt | 16 Jun 85 |
| 2.38 | | Paklin | | | 1 | | Rieti | 7 Sep 86 |
| 2.37 | | Zhu | | | 1 | | Beijing | 11 Jun 83 |
| 2.37i | Carlo | Thränhardt | FRG | 57 | 1 | | Berlin | 24 Feb 84 |
| 2.37 | Valeriy | Sereda | SU | 59 | 1 | | Rieti | 2 Sep 84 |
| 2.37 | | Thränhardt | | | 2 | | Rieti | 2 Sep 84 |
| 2.37 | | Paklin | | | 1 | ASV | Köln | 17 Aug 86 |
| 2.36 | Gerd | Wessig | GDR | 59 | 1 | OG | Moskva | 1 Aug 80 |
| 2.36i | | Paklin | | | 1 | vITA, SPA | Milano | 1 Feb 84 |
| 2.36 | Sergey | Zasimovich | SU | 62 | 1 | | Tashkent | 5 May 84 |
| 2.36 | | Thränhardt | | | 2 | | Eberstadt | 10 Jun 84 |
| 2.36 | | Mögenburg | | | 3 | | Eberstadt | 10 Jun 84 |
| 2.36 | Eddy | Annys (10) | BEL | 58 | 1 | | Ghent | 26 May 85 |
| 2.36i | Jim | Howard | USA | 59 | 1 | | Albuquerque | 26 Jan 86 |
| 2.36i | | Thränhardt | | | 1 | | Berlin | 14 Feb 86 |
| 2.36 | Javier | Sotomayor | CUB | 67 | 1 | NC | Santiago de Cu. | 23 Feb 86 |
| 2.35i | Vladimir | Yashchenko | SU | 59 | 1 | EC | Milano | 12 Mar 78 |
| 2.35 | Jacek | Wszola | POL | 56 | 1 | | Eberstadt | 25 May 80 |
| 2.35 | | Mögenburg | | | 1 | | Rehlingen | 26 May 80 |
| 2.35 | | Sereda | | | 1 | Spart | Moskva | 19 Jun 83 |
| 2.35 | | Zhu | | | 1 | | Guangzhou | 5 Mar 84 |
| 2.35 | | Mögenburg | | | 1 | OG | Los Angeles | 11 Aug 84 |
| 2.35 | | Zhu | | | 1 | | Shanghai | 22 Sep 84 |
| 2.35i | Aleksandr | Kotovich | SU | 61 | 1 | | Vilnius | 13 Jan 85 |
| 2.35i | | Howard | | | 1 | | Richfield | 17 Feb 85 |
| 2.35i | | Sjöberg | | | 1 | EC | Athinai | 2 Mar 85 |
| 2.35 | | Zhu | | | 1 | | Guangzhou | 23 Mar 85 |
| 2.35 | | Howard | | | 1 | | Houston | 25 May 85 |
| 2.35 | Sorin | Matei | RUM | 63 | 1 | Rum IC | Bucuresti | 1 Jun 85 |
| 2.35 | Gennadiy | Avdeyenko | SU | 63 | 1 | | Leningrad | 26 Jul 85 |
| 2.35 | | Sjöberg | | | 1 | | Rieti | 4 Sep 85 |
| 2.35 | Jan | Zvara | CS | 63 | 1 | | Praha | 14 Sep 85 |
| 2.35i | | Howard | | | 1 | | Toronto | 31 Jan 86 |
| 2.35 | | Avdeyenko | | | 1 | Nar | Sofia | 1 Jun 86 |
| (40/18) | | | | | | | | |
| 2.34 | Paul | Frommeyer | FRG | 57 | 1 | | Recke | 17 Jun 83 |
| 2.34 | Dwight | Stones | USA | 53 | 1 | FOT | Los Angeles | 24 Jun 84 |
| (20) | | | | | | | | |
| 2.34i | Yuriy | Sergiyenko | SU | 65 | 1 | | Kiev | 2 Feb 85 |
| 2.34 | Dennis | Lewis | USA | 59 | 1 | | Los Angeles | 30 Mar 85 |
| 2.34 | Jerome | Carter | USA | 63 | 1 | | Villanova | 14 Jun 86 |
| 2.34 | Doug | Nordquist | USA | 58 | 1 | GWG | Moskva | 9 Jul 86 |
| 2.33i | Jeff | Woodard | USA | 58 | 1 | TAC | New York | 27 Feb 81 |
| 2.33 | Aleksey | Demyanyuk | SU | 58 | 1 | | Leningrad | 11 Jul 81 |
| 2.33 | Tyke | Peacock | USA | 61 | 1 | ISTAF | Berlin | 17 Aug 83 |
| 2.33 | Vladimir | Granyenkov | SU | 59 | 1 | | Moskva | 5 Aug 84 |
| 2.33 | Brian | Whitehead | USA | 62 | 1 | JO | Columbus | 5 May 85 |
| 2.33 | Milton | Ottey | CAN | 59 | 1 | NC | Ottawa | 21 Jun 86 |
| (30) | | | | | | | | |

| Mark | Name | | Nat | Yr | Pos | Meet | Venue | Date |
|------|------|------|-----|----|-----|------|-------|------|
| 2.33 | Andrey | Morozov | SU | 60 | 1 | | Lipetsk | 19 Jul 86 |
| 2.33 | Sergey | Malchenko | SU | 63 | 3 | Spart | Tashkent | 20 Sep 86 |
| 2.32i | Franklin | Jacobs | USA | 57 | 1 | | New York | 27 Jan 78 |
| 2.32i | Janusz | Trzepizur | POL | 59 | 2 | EC | Milano | 6 Mar 82 |
| 2.32i | Roland | Dalhäuser | SWZ | 58 | 3 | EC | Milano | 6 Mar 82 |
| 2.32 | Gennadiy | Belkov | SU | 56 | 1 | | Tashkent | 29 May 82 |
| 2.32 | Del | Davis | USA | 60 | 2 | NCAA | Provo | 4 Jun 82 |
| 2.32 | J.Francisco | Centelles | CUB | 61 | 1 | PTS | Bratislava | 4 Jun 83 |
| 2.32 | Franck | Verzy | FRA | 61 | 1 | EP | London | 20 Aug 83 |
| 2.32 | Thomas | Eriksson | SWE | 63 | 1 | NCAA | Austin | 1 Jun 85 |
| | (40) | | | | | | | |
| 2.32 | Tom | McCants | USA | 62 | 2 | NCAA | Austin | 1 Jun 85 |
| 2.31 | Rolf | Beilschmidt | GDR | 53 | 1 | EP | Helsinki | 13 Aug 77 |
| 2.31i | Greg | Joy | CAN | 56 | 1 | | College Park | 13 Jan 78 |
| 2.31 | Jorg | Freimuth | GDR | 61 | 3 | OG | Moskva | 1 Aug 80 |
| 2.31 | Gerd | Nagel | FRG | 57 | 2 | | Eberstadt | 7 Jun 81 |
| 2.31i | Milton | Goode | USA | 60 | 1 | | New York | 12 Feb 82 |
| 2.31 | Steve | Wray | BAH | 62 | 2 | CommG | Brisbane | 7 Oct 82 |
| 2.31i | Constantin | Militaru | RUM | 63 | 1 | | Sofia | 11 Feb 84 |
| 2.31 | Dariusz | Zielke | POL | 60 | 1 | | Warszawa | 12 Aug 84 |
| 2.31 | Andreas | Sam | GDR | 60 | 1 | | Praha | 28 Aug 8 |
| | (50) | | | | | | | |
| 2.31 | Brent | Harken | USA | 61 | 2 | GGala | Roma | 31 Aug 8 |
| 2.31 | Brian | Stanton | USA | 61 | 2 | Arco | Los Angeles | 8 Jun 8 |
| 2.31 | Anatoliy | Korobenko | SU | 57 | 1 | | Odessa | 26 Jul 8 |
| 2.31i | Vadim | Oganyan | SU | 63 | 2 | | Moskva | 6 Feb 8 |
| 2.31 | Eugen | Popescu | RUM | 62 | 2 | NC | Pitesti | 8 Aug 8 |
| 2.31 | Krzysztof | Krawczyk | POL | 62 | 3 | BGP | Budapest | 11 Aug 8 |

| Mark | Name | | Nat | Yr | | Mark | Name | | Nat | Yr |
|------|------|------|-----|----|---|------|------|------|-----|----|
| 2.30 | Aleksandr | Grigoryev | SU | 1977 | | 2.29i | Adrian | Proteasa | RUM | 1980 |
| 2.30 | Henry | Lauterbach | GDR | 1978 | | 2.29 | James | Frazier | USA | 1980 |
| 2.30 | Benn | Fields | USA | 1978 | | 2.29 | Leo | Williams | USA | 1982 |
| 2.30 | Andre | Schneider | FRG | 1979 | | | (80) | | | |
| | (60) | | | | | 2.29 | Cai Shu | | CHN | 1982 |
| 2.30 | Massimo | Di Giorgio | ITA | 1981 | | 2.29 | Liu Yunpeng | | CHN | 1984 |
| 2.30i | Nick | Saunders | BER | 1983 | | 2.29i | Yuriy | Shevchenko | SU | 1985 |
| 2.30 | Ricky | Thompson | USA | 1983 | | 2.29i | Yuriy | Gotovskiy | SU | 1985 |
| 2.30 | James | Barrineau | USA | 1983 | | 2.29 | Jindrich | Vondra | CS | 1985 |
| 2.30 | Takao | Sakamoto | JAP | 1984 | | 2.29 | Igor | Ivliyev | SU | 1985 |
| 2.30i | Brian | Tietjens | USA | 1985 | | 2.29i | Gennadiy | Martsinovich | SU | 1986 |
| 2.30i | Dariusz | Biczysko | POL | 1985 | | 2.29 | Vic | Smalls | USA | 1986 |
| 2.30 | Lee | Balkin | USA | 1985 | | 2.29 | Ron | Lee | USA | 1986 |
| 2.30 | Joe | Patrone | USA | 1985 | | 2.29 | Georgi | Dakov | BUL | 1986 |
| 2.30 | Dothel | Edwards | USA | 1985 | | | (90) | | | |
| | (70) | | | | | 2.29 | Gennadiy | Vaskevich | SU | 1986 |
| 2.30i | Geoff | Parsons | UK | 1986 | | 2.285i | John | Radetich | USA | 1976 |
| 2.30 | Jake | Jacoby | USA | 1986 | | 2.285i | Kyle | Arney | USA | 1977 |
| 2.30 | Greg | Jones | USA | 1986 | | 2.285i | Nat | Page | USA | 1981 |
| 2.30 | Kenny | Banks | USA | 1986 | | 2.285i | Jeff | Loescher | USA | 1985 |
| 2.29 | Ni Chihchin | | CHN | 1970 | | 2.285 | Bill | Jasinski | USA | 1985 |
| 2.29 | Pat | Matzdorf | USA | 1971 | | 2.285 | Hollis | Conway | USA | 1986 |
| 2.29 | Rory | Kotinek | USA | 1977 | | 2.28 | 22 athletes from Valeriy Brumel | | | 1963 |

Best outdoor marks for athletes with indoor best
| | | | | | | | | | |
|---|---|---|---|---|---|---|---|---|---|
| Yashchenko | 2.34 | 1 | Prav Tbilisi | 16 Jun 78 | Dalhauser | 2.31 | 1 | Eberstadt | 7 Jun 8 |
| Kotovich | 2.33 | 1 | Nar Sofia | 20 May 84 | Militaru | 2.31 | 1 | Bucuresti | 25 May 8 |
| Woodard | 2.32 | 1 | NCAA Austin | 7 Jun 80 | | | | | |

Ancillary jumps
| | | | | | | | |
|---|---|---|---|---|---|---|---|
| Zhu | 2.36 | 10 Jun 84 | | Mögenburg | 2.35 | 24 Feb 85 | |
| Povarnitsin | 2.35 | 11 Aug 85 | | Paklin | 2.35 | 4 Sep 85 | |

| Mark | Name | | Nat | Yr | Pos | Meet | Venue | Date |
|------|------|------|-----|-----|-----|------|-------|------|

## POLE VAULT

| Mark | Name | | Nat | Yr | Pos | Meet | Venue | Date |
|------|------|------|-----|-----|-----|------|-------|------|
| 6.01 | Sergey | Bubka | SU | 63 | 1 | GWG | Moskva | 8 Jul 86 |
| 6.00 | | S.Bubka | | | 1 | | Paris | 13 Jul 85 |
| 5.95 | | S.Bubka | | | 1 | Nik | Nice | 16 Jul 85 |
| 5.95i | | S.Bubka | | | 1 | TAC | New York | 28 Feb 86 |
| 5.94 | | S.Bubka | | | 1 | GGala | Roma | 31 Aug 84 |
| 5.94i | | S.Bubka | | | 1 | | Inglewood | 21 Feb 86 |
| 5.93i | Billy | Olson | USA | 58 | 1 | | East Rutherford | 8 Feb 86 |
| 5.92i | | S.Bubka | | | 1 | NC | Moskva | 8 Feb 86 |
| 5.91 | Thierry | Vigneron | FRA | 60 | 2 | GGala | Roma | 31 Aug 84 |
| 5.91i | Joe | Dial | USA | 62 | 1 | | Columbia | 1 Feb 86 |
| 5.90 | | Bubka | | | 1 | PTG | London | 13 Jul 84 |
| 5.90 | Pierre | Quinon | FRA | 62 | 2 | Nik | Nice | 16 Jul 85 |
| 5.90 | | Dial | | | 1 | | Norman | 25 Apr 86 |
| 5.90 | | Vigneron | | | 1 | | Paris | 22 Jul 86 |
| 5.89i | | Olson | | | 1 | | Albuquerque | 25 Jan 86 |
| 5.88 | | Bubka | | | 1 | | Saint Denis | 2 Jun 84 |
| 5.88i | | Olson | | | 1 | | Los Angeles | 17 Jan 86 |
| 5.88 | | Dial | | | 1 | | El Paso | 20 Apr 86 |
| 5.87i | | S.Bubka | | | 1 | | Osaka | 15 Jan 86 |
| 5.86i | | Olson | | | 1 | | Saskatoon | 28 Dec 85 |
| 5.86 | | Dial | | | 1 | | Norman | 12 Apr 86 |
| 5.85i | | Vigneron | | | 1 | EC | Göteborg | 4 Mar 84 |
| 5.85 | | Bubka | | | 1 | PTS | Bratislava | 26 May 84 |
| 5.85 | Konstantin | Volkov | SU | 60 | 1 | Izv | Kiev | 22 Jun 84 |
| 5.85 | | Dial | | | 1 | | Norman | 19 May 85 |
| 5.85 | | S.Bubka | | | 1 | | Donyetsk | 11 Aug 85 |
| 5.85 | Vasiliy | Bubka | SU | 60 | 1 | | Donyetsk | 29 Aug 85 |
| 5.85 | | S.Bubka | | | 1 | GP | Roma | 7 Sep 85 |
| 5.85 | | S.Bubka | | | 1 | WP | Canberra | 5 Oct 85 |
| 5.85 | Rodion | Gataullin | SU | 65 | 1 | NC | Kiev | 16 Jul 86 |
| 5.85 | Philippe | Collet | FRA | 63 | 2 | | Paris | 22 Jul 86 |
| 5.85 | | Gataullin | | | 1 | WK | Zürich | 13 Aug 86 |
| 5.85 | | S.Bubka | | | 1 | EC | Stuttgart | 29 Aug 86 |
| | (33/9) | | | | | | | |
| 5.82 | Mike | Tully | USA | 56 | 1 | Pre | Eugene | 21 Jul 84 |
| | | (10) | | | | | | |
| 5.82 | Aleksandr | Krupskiy | SU | 60 | 1 | BGP | Budapest | 20 Aug 84 |
| 5.82 | Aleksandr | Parnov | SU | 59 | 1 | | Sumgait | 21 Aug 85 |
| 5.81 | Vladimir | Polyakov | SU | 60 | 1 | vGDR | Tbilisi | 26 Jun 81 |
| 5.81i | Marian | Kolasa | POL | 59 | 1 | | Praha | 13 Feb 86 |
| 5.81 | Earl | Bell | USA | 55 | 1 | USOF | Houston | 2 Aug 86 |
| 5.80 | Pavel | Bogatyryov | SU | 61 | 1 | | Schwechat | 19 Jun 85 |
| 5.80i | Dave | Volz | USA | 62 | 2 | | New York | 14 Feb 86 |
| 5.80 | Atanas | Tarev | BUL | 58 | 2 | | Lausanne | 2 Sep 86 |
| 5.78 | Władysław | Kozakiewicz | POL | 53 | 1 | OG | Moskva | 30 Jul 80 |
| 5.77 | Philippe | Houvion | FRA | 57 | 1 | | Paris | 17 Jul 80 |
| | | (20) | | | | | | |
| 5.77 | Doug | Fraley | USA | 65 | 1 | MSR | Walnut | 27 Apr 86 |
| 5.76 | Jeff | Buckingham | USA | 60 | 1 | | Lawrence | 16 Jul 83 |
| 5.76 | Tom | Hintnaus | BRA | 58 | 1 | WK | Zürich | 21 Aug 85 |
| 5.75 | Jean-Michel | Bellot | FRA | 53 | 1 | | Colombes | 25 Sep 82 |
| 5.75 | Brad | Pursley | USA | 60 | 1 | | Abilene | 29 Mar 83 |
| 5.74i | Aleksandr | Obizhayev | SU | 59 | 1 | | Moskva | 12 Feb 83 |
| 5.73 | Larry | Jessee | USA | 52 | 1 | | Vanves | 27 Apr 84 |
| 5.72 | Dan | Ripley | USA | 53 | 1= | TAC | Knoxville | 20 Jun 82 |

MEN All-time

| Mark | Name | | Nat | Yr | Pos | Meet | Venue | Date | |
|------|------|---|-----|----|----|------|-------|------|---|
| 5.72i | Serge | Ferreira | FRA | 59 | 1 | | Paris | 3 Feb 85 | |
| 5.72 | Doug | Lytle (30) | USA | 62 | 1 | KansR | Lawrence | 19 Apr | 8 |
| 5.72 | Zdeněk | Lubenský | CS | 62 | 1 | NC | Bratislava | 12 Jul | 8 |
| 5.71 | Felix | Bohni | SWZ | 58 | 1 | | Bern | 11 Jun | 8 |
| 5.71 | Aleksandr | Chernyayev | SU | 60 | 1 | | Chernigov | 2 Jul | 8 |
| 5.71 | Vladimir | Shulgin | SU | 61 | 3 | | Riga | 2 Jun | 8 |
| 5.70 | Dave | Roberts | USA | 51 | 1 | FOT | Eugene | 22 Jun | 7 |
| 5.70 | Sergey | Kulibaba | SU | 59 | 1 | vUSA | Leningrad | 10 Jul | 8 |
| 5.70i | Viktor | Spasov | SU | 59 | 1 | EC | Milano | 7 Mar | 8 |
| 5.70 | Nikolay | Selivanov | SU | 58 | 1 | | Moskva | 16 Jun | 8 |
| 5.70 | Patrick | Abada | FRA | 54 | 1 | VD | Bruxelles | 26 Aug | 8 |
| 5.70 | Tadeusz | Ślusarski (40) | POL | 50 | 2 | VD | Bruxelles | 26 Aug | 8 |
| 5.70 | Sergey | Smolyakov | SU | 62 | 3 | | Moskva | 19 Jul | 8 |
| 5.70 | Hermann | Fehringer | AUT | 62 | 1 | | Amstetten | 6 Jun | 8 |
| 5.70 | Tim | Bright | USA | 60 | 1 | SW | Modesto | 10 May | 8 |
| 5.70 | Dale | Jenkins | USA | 63 | 2 | SW | Modesto | 10 May | 8 |
| 5.70 | Scott | Davis | USA | 61 | 1 | | Eugene | 17 May | 8 |
| 5.70 | Kasimir | Zalar | SWE | 57 | 1 | | Nyköpping | 2 Jul | 8 |
| 5.70 | Vadim | Kodentsev | SU | 64 | 1 | | Omsk | 14 Jul | 8 |
| 5.70 | Stanimir | Penchev | BUL | 59 | 1 | | Sofia | 3 Aug | 8 |
| 5.70 | Kory | Tarpenning | USA | 62 | 3 | WK | Zürich | 13 Aug | 8 |
| 5.69 | Steve | Stubblefield (50) | USA | 61 | 2 | KansR | Lawrence | 20 Apr | 8 |

| Mark | Name | | Nat | Yr | | Mark | Name | | Nat | Yr |
|------|------|---|-----|----|---|------|------|---|-----|----|
| 5.67i | Miroslaw | Chmara | POL | 1986 | | 5.61 | Todd | Cooper | USA | 1985 |
| 5.66 | Antti | Kalliomaki | FIN | 1980 | | 5.61i | Grigoriy | Yegorov | SU | 1986 |
| 5.66 | Jurgen | Winkler | FRG | 1983 | | 5.61 | Alberto | Ruiz | SPA | 1986 |
| 5.65 | Keith | Stock | UK | 1981 | | 5.61 | Ferenc | Salbert | HUN/FRA | 1986 |
| 5.65 | Gunther | Lohre | FRG | 1982 | | 5.60 | Yuriy | Prokhorenko | SU | 1980 |
| 5.65 | Ivo | Yanchev | BUL | 1982 | | 5.60 | Rauli | Pudas | FIN | 1980 |
| 5.65i | Peter | Volmer | FRG | 1984 | | 5.60 | Mariusz | Klimczyk | POL | 1980 |
| 5.65i | Andrey | Pogoreliy | SU | 1985 | | 5.60i | Patrick | Desruelles (80) | BEL | 1981 |
| 5.65 | Arkadiy | Shkvira | SU | 1985 | | 5.60 | Viktor | Sobolev | SU | 1981 |
| 5.65 | Valentin | Videv (60) | BUL | 1985 | | 5.60 | Greg | Woepse | USA | 1984 |
| 5.65i | Valeriy | Ishutin | SU | 1986 | | 5.60 | Anton | Paskalev | BUL | 1984 |
| 5.65 | Gennadiy | Sukharev | SU | 1986 | | 5.60i | Nat | Durham | USA | 1984 |
| 5.65 | Aleksey | Nikitin | SU | 1986 | | 5.60 | Serge | Leveur | FRA | 1985 |
| 5.65 | Nikolay | Nikolov | BUL | 1986 | | 5.60 | Asko | Peltoniemi | FIN | 1985 |
| 5.63 | Bob | Seagren | USA | 1972 | | 5.60 | David | Hodge | USA | 1985 |
| 5.62 | František | Jansa | CS | 1983 | | 5.60 | Mikhail | Voronin | SU | 1985 |
| 5.62 | Scott | Huffman | USA | 1985 | | 5.60 | Gerald | Kager | AUT | 1986 |
| 5.62 | Greg | Duplantis | USA | 1986 | | 5.60 | Timo | Kuusisto (90) | FIN | 1986 |
| 5.62 | Sergey | Gavrikov | SU | 1986 | | | | | | |
| 5.62 | Dave | Kenworthy (70) | USA | 1986 | | 5.60 | Paul | Benavides | USA | 1986 |
| | | | | | | 5.60 | Yevgeniy | Bondarenko | SU | 1986 |
| 5.61i | Steve | Smith | USA | 1975 | | 5.59 | Kjell | Isaksson | SWE | 1980 |
| 5.61 | Vladimir | Trofimenko | SU | 1978 | | 5.59 | Brian | Hooper | UK | 1980 |

Best outdoor marks for athletes with lifetime bests indoors    5.55 by 20 men

| | | | | | | | |
|---|---|---|---|---|---|---|---|
| Kolasa | 5.80 | 1 | | Kamp-Lintfort | 1 Sep 86 | 5.81 |
| Volz | 5.75 | 1 | Nik | Nice | 14 Aug 82 | 5.80 |
| Olson | 5.72 | 1= | TAC | Knoxville | 20 Jun 82 | 5.93 |
| Obizhayev | 5.72 | 2 | | Tallinn | 28 Jun 86 | 5.74 |
| Ferreira | 5.71 | 1 | | Creteil | 23 Jun 84 | 5.72 |

Spasov    5.65   1983 (5.70i)    Ishutin    5.65   1986 (5.65i)    Smith   5.59   1983 (5.61i)
Pogoreliy  5.65   1985 (5.65i)    Desruelles 5.60   1981 (5.60i)

| Exhibition | | | | | | Ancillary jumps | | | |
|-----------|---|---|---|---|---|----------------|---|---|---|
| Jessee | 5.86i | 1 | Newcastle | 16 Oct 85 | | S.Bubka | 5.85 | 16 Jul | 8 |
| S.Bubka | 5.85 | 1 | St.Ghislain | 7 Jul 85 | | S.Bubka | 5.85i | 28 Feb | 8 |
| R.Kolasa | 5.71 | 2 | Sopot | 2 Aug 86 | | S.Bubka | 5.85 | 8 Jul | 8 |
| Leveur | 5.66i | | 1985 | | | | | | |

| Mark | Wind | Name | | Nat | Yr | Pos | Meet | Venue | Date |
|---|---|---|---|---|---|---|---|---|---|
| A8.90 | 2.0 | Bob | Beamon | USA | 45 | 1 | OG | Ciudad México | 18 Oct 68 |
| 8.79 | 1.9 | Carl | Lewis | USA | 61 | 1 | TAC | Indianapolis | 19 Jun 83 |
| 8.79i | - | | Lewis | | | 1 | | New York | 27 Jan 84 |
| 8.76 | 1.0 | | Lewis | | | 1 | USOF | Indianapolis | 24 Jul 82 |
| 8.71 | -0.4 | | Lewis | | | 1 | Pepsi | Westwood | 13 May 84 |
| 8.71 | 0.1 | | Lewis | | | 1 | FOT | Los Angeles | 19 Jun 84 |
| 8.65 | 0.2 | | Lewis | | | 1 | VD | Bruxelles | 24 Aug 84 |
| 8.62 | 0.8 | | Lewis | | | 1 | TAC | Sacramento | 20 Jun 81 |
| 8.62 | -0.1 | | Lewis | | | 1 | VD | Bruxelles | 30 Aug 85 |
| 8.61 | 0.5 | | Lewis | | | 1 | Pepsi | Westwood | 16 May 82 |
| 8.61 | -0.3 | Robert | Emmiyan | SU | 65 | 1 | GWG | Moskva | 6 Jul 86 |
| 8.59 | 1.3 | Larry | Myricks | USA | 56 | 1 | | Rhede | 5 Sep 84 |
| 8.58 | 0.0 | | Lewis | | | 1 | WK | Zürich | 18 Aug 82 |
| 8.56i | - | | Lewis | | | 1 | | E.Rutherford | 16 Jan 82 |
| 8.56 | 0.5 | | Myricks | | | 1 | | Rhede | 1 Sep 82 |
| 8.56 | 1.0 | | Lewis | | | 1 | Pepsi | Westwood | 15 May 83 |
| 8.55i | - | | Lewis | | | 1 | TAC | New York | 26 Feb 82 |
| 8.55 | 1.2 | | Lewis | | | 1 | WC | Helsinki | 10 Aug 83 |
| 8.55i | - | | Lewis | | | 1 | | E.Rutherford | 11 Feb 84 |
| 8.54 | 0.9 | Lutz | Dombrowski | GDR | 59 | 1 | OG | Moskva | 28 Jul 80 |
| 8.54i | - | | Lewis | | | 1 | | New York | 28 Jan 83 |
| 8.54 | -1.6 | | Lewis | | | 1 | OG | Los Angeles | 6 Aug 84 |
| 8.53 | 1.2 | | Lewis | | | 1 | | Houston | 5 May 85 |
| 8.52 | 0.0 | | Myricks | | | 1 | WP | Montréal | 26 Aug 79 |
| 8.52 | -2.0 | | Lewis | | | 1 | WK | Zürich | 19 Aug 81 |
| 8.50i | - | | Lewis | | | 1 | TAC | New York | 24 Feb 84 |
| 8.50 | 2.0 | | Dombrowski | | | 1 | | Dresden | 27 Jul 84 |
| 8.50i | - | | Lewis | | | 1 | | New York | 25 Jan 85 |
| 8.50 | | | Myricks | | | 1 | | Rhede | 2 Jul 86 |
| 8.49i | - | | Lewis | | | 1 | | Fort Worth | 20 Feb 81 |
| 8.49 | 1.4 | | Lewis | | | - | JO | Westwood | 7 Aug 82 |
| 8.49 | 0.9 | | Myricks | | | 1 | USOF | Houston | 3 Aug 86 |
| | | (32/5) | | | | | | | |
| 8.47 | | Jaime | Jefferson | CUB | 62 | 1 | NC | Santiago de C. | 22 Feb 86 |
| 8.45 | 2.0 | Nenad | Stekić | YUG | 51 | 1 | PO | Montreal | 25 Jul 75 |
| 8.43 | 0.8 | Jason | Grimes | USA | 59 | - | TAC | Indianapolis | 16 Jun 85 |
| 8.43 | 1.6 | Mike | Conley | USA | 62 | 1 | | Lausanne | 10 Jul 85 |
| 8.38 | 0.4 | Konstantin | Semykin | SU | 60 | 1 | Drz | Moskva | 17 Aug 84 |
| | | (10) | | | | | | | |
| 8.37 | | Sergey | Rodin | SU | 63 | 1 | | Moskva | 6 Jul 84 |
| 8.36 | 1.0 | João C. | de Oliveira | BRA | 54 | 1 | | Rieti | 21 Jul 79 |
| 8.36 | 1.6 | Frank | Pashchek | GDR | 56 | 1 | OD | Berlin | 28 May 80 |
| 8.35 | 0.0 | Ralph | Boston | USA | 39 | 1 | CalR | Modesto | 29 May 65 |
| 8.35 | 0.0 | Igor | Ter-Ovanesyan | SU | 38 | 1 | PO | Ciudad México | 19 Oct 67 |
| 8.35 | 0.8 | Josef | Schwarz | FRG | 35 | 1 | vUSA | Stuttgart | 15 Jul 70 |
| 8.35 | -0.6 | Arnie | Robinson | USA | 48 | 1 | OG | Montreal | 29 Jul 76 |
| 8.35 | 2.0 | Henry | Lauterbach | GDR | 57 | 1 | | Erfurt | 2 Aug 81 |
| 8.34 | 0.0 | Randy | Williams | USA | 53 | Q | OG | München | 8 Sep 72 |
| 8.33i | - | Reggie | Kelly | USA | 62 | 1 | | Jackson | 3 Dec 83 |
| | | (20) | | | | | | | |
| 8.32 | 0.1 | Sergey | Layevskiy | SU | 59 | 1 | NC | Donyetsk | 8 Sep 84 |
| 8.32 | | Ubaldo | Duany | CUB | 60 | 2 | NC | Santiago de C. | 22 Feb 86 |
| 8.31 | 0.7 | Atanas | Atanasov | BUL | 56 | 1 | | Sofia | 4 Jul 84 |
| 8.30 | 1.8 | László | Szalma | HUN | 57 | 1 | | Budapest | 7 Jul 85 |
| 8.29 | | Grigoriy | Petrosyan | SU | 58 | 1 | | Yerevan | 20 Oct 86 |

| Mark | Wind | Name | | Nat | Yr | Pos | Meet | Venue | Date |
|---|---|---|---|---|---|---|---|---|---|
| 8.28 | | Aleksandr | Beskrovniy | SU | 60 | 1 | | Moskva | 29 May 83 |
| 8.28 | 0.1 | Vadim | Kobylyanskiy | SU | 61 | 2 | NC | Donyetsk | 8 Sep 84 |
| 8.27 | 0.5 | Grzegorz | Cybulski | POL | 51 | 1 | Kuso | Warszawa | 20 Jun 75 |
| 8.27 | 2.0 | Mike | McRae | USA | 55 | 1 | TAC | San Jose | 9 Jun 84 |
| 8.27 | 1.2 | Gary | Honey | AUS | 59 | 1 | BGP | Budapest | 20 Aug 84 |
| | | (30) | | | | | | | |
| 8.26i | - | Charlton | Ehizuelen | NIG | 53 | 1 | | Bloomington | 7 Mar 75 |
| 8.26 | 1.4 | Jacques | Rousseau | FRA | 51 | - | NC | Lille | 26 Jun 76 |
| 8.25i | - | Henry | Hines | USA | 49 | 1 | ITA | New York | 6 Jun 73 |
| 8.25 | 1.7 | Gyula | Pálóczi | HUN | 62 | 1 | BGP | Budapest | 4 Aug 85 |
| 8.25 | 1.9 | Luis | Bueno | CUB | 69 | 1 | IbAm | Habana | 28 Sep 86 |
| 8.24 | 1.7 | James | McAlister | USA | 51 | 1 | | Westwood | 5 May 73 |
| 8.24 | -0.7 | Giovanni | Evangelisti | ITA | 61 | 3 | OG | Los Angeles | 6 Aug 84 |
| 8.24 | 0.2 | Eric | Metcalfe | USA | 68 | 1 | NCAA | Indianapolis | 6 Jun 86 |
| 8.23 | 2.0 | Lynn | Davies | UK | 42 | 1 | vSWZ | Bern | 30 Jun 68 |
| 8.23 | 2.0 | James | Lofton | USA | 56 | 2 | AAU | Westwood | 9 Jun 78 |
| | | (40) | | | | | | | |
| 8.23 | 0.2 | Antonio | Corgos | SPA | 60 | 1 | NC | Madrid | 24 Aug 80 |
| 8.23 | 0.0 | Yuriy | Samarin | SU | 60 | 3 | NC | Donyetsk | 8 Sep 84 |
| 8.23i | - | Khristo | Markov | BUL | 65 | 1 | | Sofia | 10 Feb 85 |
| 8.23 | | Chen Zunrong | | CHN | 62 | 1 | | Beijing | 12 Apr 84 |
| 8.22 | 0.1 | Preston | Carrington | USA | 49 | Q | OG | München | 8 Sep 72 |
| 8.22 | | Larry | Doubley | USA | 58 | 1 | NCAA | Champaign | 3 Jun 77 |
| 8.22 | | LaMonte | King | USA | 59 | 1 | | San Jose | 12 May 79 |
| 8.22 | 0.6 | David | Giralt | CUB | 59 | 3 | WP | Montréal | 26 Aug 79 |
| 8.22 - | 1.6 | Uwe | Lange | GDR | 54 | 1 | | Dresden | 19 May 84 |
| 8.22 | | Yuriy | Kharitonov | SU | 59 | 1 | | Gorkiy | 11 Aug 84 |
| | | (50) | | | | | | | |

| Mark | Wind | Name | | Nat | Yr |
|---|---|---|---|---|---|
| 8.21 | 1.9 | Waldemar | Stepień | POL | 1969 |
| 8.21 | | Aleksey | Pereverzev | SU | 1976 |
| 8.21i | - | Winfried | Klepsch | FRG | 1981 |
| A8.21 | 2.0 | Vance | Johnson | USA | 1982 |
| 8.21 | 1.5 | Yussuf | Alli | NIG | 1983 |
| 8.21 | 0.6 | Ron | Beer | GDR | 1985 |
| 8.20 | 1.5 | James | Moore | USA | 1974 |
| 8.20 | 1.9 | Andrzej | Klimaszewski | POL | 1980 |
| 8.20 | 1.3 | Viktor | Belskiy | SU | 1982 |
| 8.20 | -0.8 | Vernon | George | USA | 1985 |
| | | (60) | | | |
| 8.20 | | Valeriy | Bakunin | SU | 1986 |
| A8.19 | 0.0 | Klaus | Beer | GDR | 1968 |
| 8.19 | 1.4 | Atanas | Chochev | BUL | 1981 |
| 8.19i | - | Greg | Artis | USA | 1982 |
| 8.18 | 0.5 | Hans | Baumgartner | FRG | 1972 |
| 8.18 | 1.9 | Max | Klauss | GDR | 1974 |
| 8.18 | 2.0 | Frank | Wartenberg | GDR | 1976 |
| 8.18 | 1.2 | Valeriy | Podluzhniy | SU | 1980 |
| A8.18i | - | George | Gaffney | USA | 1983 |
| 8.18 | | Ralph | Spry | USA | 1983 |
| | | (70) | | | |
| 8.17i | - | J.François | Bonheme | FRA | 1974 |
| 8.17i | - | Jan | Leitner | CS | 1985 |
| 8.17 | | Mike | Powell | USA | 1985 |
| 8.17i | - | Kenny | Harrison | USA | 1986 |
| 8.17 | | Martin | Digno | CUB | 1986 |
| 8.16 | 1.3 | Gayle | Hopkins | USA | 1964 |
| 8.16 | | Clarence | Robinson | USA | 1965 |
| 8.16 | | Rainer | Stenius | FIN | 1966 |
| A8.16 | | Phil | Shinnick | USA | 1968 |
| 8.16 | 0.8 | Jacques | Pani | FRA | 1969 |
| | | (80) | | | |
| 8.16 | | Shamil | Abbyasov | SU | 1981 |
| 8.16 | 0.5 | Marco | Delonge | GDR | 1986 |
| 8.15 | 0.1 | Paul | Emordi | NIG | 1986 |
| 8.15 | 1.2 | Leroy | Burrell | USA | 1986 |
| 8.15 | 1.8 | Oleg | Semiraz | SU | 1986 |
| 8.14 | | Stan | Whitley | USA | 1969 |
| 8.14 | 1.0 | Tommy | Haynes | USA | 1974 |
| 8.14 | 1.4 | Jens | Knipphals | FRG | 1980 |
| 8.14 | 1.6 | Rolf | Bernhard | SWZ | 1981 |
| A8.14 | | Cilliers | Botha | RSA | 1982 |
| | | (90) | | | |
| 8.14 | | Liu Yuhuang | | CHN | 1982 |
| 8.14 | | Ken | Frazier | USA | 1984 |
| 8.14 | | Mike | Davis | USA | 1985 |
| 8.14 | | Vladimir | Potapenko | SU | 1985 |
| 8.14 | | Juan | Ortiz | CUB | 1986 |
| 8.13 | 1.5 | Jesse | Owens | USA | 1935 |
| 8.13 | | Danny | Seay | USA | 1975 |
| 8.13 | | Lutz | Franke | GDR | 1979 |
| 8.13 | 0.5 | Stanislaw | Jaskulka | POL | 1980 |
| A8.13 | | Steve | Bridges | USA | 1982 |
| | | (100) | | | |
| 8.13 | | Vladimir | Tsepelyov | SU | 1982 |
| 8.13 | 0.9 | Vesco | Bradley | USA | 1983 |
| 8.13 | | Viktor | Savinykh | SU | 1983 |
| 8.13 | 2.0 | Andre | Reichelt | GDR | 1984 |
| 8.13 | 0.3 | Gennadiy | Danilov | SU | 1985 |

Low altitude marks for athletes with high altitude bests

| | Mark | Wind | Pos | Meet | Venue | Date | |
|---|---|---|---|---|---|---|---|
| Beamon | 8.33 | 1.3 | 1 | AAU | Sacramento | 20 Jun 68 | 8.90 |
| Ter-Ovanesyan | 8.23 | | 1 | | Leselidze | 23 Apr 66 | 8.35 |

| Mark | Wind | Name | | Nat | Yr | Pos | Meet | Venue | Date |
|------|------|------|------|-----|----|-----|------|-------|------|

Best outdoor marks for athletes with indoor bests
Chizuelen   A8.20   1975   (8.26i)          Hines      8.19   1972   (8.25i)

Note: Sergey  Rodin 8.37 not ratified as USSR record (no wind gauge), but
      considered wind legal. Next best: 8.33  1.0  1  Leningrad  27 Jul 83
Not confirmed:    8.15  Steve Hanna  BAH 581983

Supplementary (non-winning) marks
Lewis  8.71  0.6   19 Jun 83   Lewis  8.52i  -    28 Jan 83   Wind-assisted
Lewis  8.61  0.6   16 May 82   Lewis  8.51  0.3   15 May 83   Lewis  8.73  2.4  18 May 85
Lewis  8.59  0.3   24 Aug 84   Lewis  8.50i  -    11 Feb 84   Lewis  8.51  2.7   5 May 85
Lewis  8.55        24 Jul 82

Wind-assisted marks

| Mark | Wind | Name | | Nat | Yr | Pos | Meet | Venue | Date |
|------|------|------|------|-----|----|-----|------|-------|------|
| 8.77 | 3.9 | | C.Lewis | | | 1 | Pepsi | Westwood | 18 May 85 |
| 8.73 | 4.6 | | Lewis | | | Q | TAC | Sacramento | 19 Jun 81 |
| 8.73 | 3.2 | | Lewis | | | Q | TAC | Indianapolis | 17 Jun 83 |
| 8.67 | 3.3 | | Lewis | | | 1 | TAC | Eugene | 20 Jun 86 |
| 8.64 | 3.1 | Larry | Myricks | USA | 56 | 1 | USOF | Air Force Ac. | 2 Jul 83 |
| 8.63 | 2.1 | | Lewis | | | 1 | Pepsi | Westwood | 10 May 81 |
| 8.63 | 3.9 | Mike | Conley | USA | 62 | 2 | TAC | Eugene | 20 Jun 86 |
| 8.57 | 5.2 | Jason | Grimes | USA | 59 | 1 | vFRG, AFR | Durham | 27 Jun 82 |
| 8.56 | 8.9 | | Lewis | | | 1 | | Sacramento | 21 Jul 84 |
| 8.55 | 2.5 | | Myricks | | | 1 | SW | Modesto | 10 May 86 |
| 8.53 | 2.7 | | Conley | | | 1 | TAC | Indianapolis | 16 Jun 85 |
| 8.51 | 5.3 | | Grimes | | | 1 | vSU | Indianapolis | 3 Jul 82 |
| 8.50 | 2.4 | | Lewis | | | 1 | JO | Westwood | 7 Aug 82 |
| 8.50 | 4.4 | | Grimes | | | 2 | TAC | Indianapolis | 16 Jun 85 |
| 8.49 | 2.6 | Ralph | Boston | USA | 39 | 1 | FOT | Los Angeles | 12 Sep 64 |
| 8.46 | 3.4 | Randy | Williams | USA | 53 | 1 | | Eugene | 18 May 73 |
| 8.44 | | Keith | Talley | USA | 64 | Q | | Odessa | 16 May 85 |
| 8.42 | | Anthony | Bailous | USA | 65 | Q | | Odessa | 16 May 85 |
| 8.41 | 4.3 | Shamil | Abbyasov | SU | 57 | 2 | vUSA | Indianapolis | 3 Jul 82 |
| 8.40 | 4.3 | Henry | Hines | USA | 49 | 1 | CalR | Modesto | 27 May 72 |
| 8.39 | 6.2 | Gary | Honey | AUS | 59 | 2 | | Sacramento | 21 Jul 84 |
| 8.37 | 3.5 | Arnie | Robinson | USA | 48 | 1 | FOT | Eugene | 25 Jun 76 |
| 8.37 | 2.8 | Jacques | Rousseau | FRA | 51 | 1 | NC | Lille | 25 Jun 76 |
| 8.36 | 5.2 | Ralph | Spry | USA | 60 | 1 | NCAA | Houston | 3 Jun 83 |
| 8.34 | | Mike | McRae | USA | 55 | 1 | SW | Modesto | 12 May 84 |
| 8.33 | | Phil | Shinnick | USA | 43 | 1 | CalR | Modesto | 25 May 63 |
| 8.33 | 2.1 | Charlton | Ehizuelen | NIG | 53 | 1 | KansR | Lawrence | 19 Apr 75 |
| 8.33 | 3.7 | Andrzej | Klimaszewski | POL | 60 | 1 | Kuso | Warszawa | 13 Jun 80 |
| 8.32 | 3.8 | David | Giralt | CUB | 59 | 1 | WPT | Quebec City | 11 Aug 79 |
| 8.31 | | Mike | Davis | USA | 64 | 1 | | Houston | 18 May 86 |
| 8.28 | | Yuriy | Samarin | SU | 60 | 1 | | Kharkov | 8 Jul 84 |
| 8.28 | 4.0 | Mike | Powell | USA | 63 | 3 | TAC | Indianapolis | 16 Jun 85 |
| 8.26 | 4.0 | Carl | Williams | USA | 57 | 1 | | Abilene | 19 May 78 |
| 8.26 | 3.4 | Larry | Doubley | USA | 58 | 1 | | Los Angeles | 15 Mar 80 |
| 8.25 | | LaMonte | King | USA | 59 | 1 | | Tempe | 26 May 79 |
| 8.24 | | Gordon | Laine | USA | 58 | 2 | | Knoxville | 19 May 84 |
| 8.23 | | Norm | Tate | USA | 42 | 1 | | El Paso | 22 May 71 |
| 8.22 | 5.9 | Darrell | Horn | USA | 1964 | | | | |
| 8.22 | 3.0 | Jerry | Proctor | USA | 1969 | | | | |
| 8.22 | 3.0 | Jacques | Pani | FRA | 1969 | | | | |
| 8.22 | | Liu Yuhaung | | CHN | 1981 | | | | |
| 8.22 | | Paul | Emordi | NIG | 1986 | | | | |
| 8.21 | | Danny | Seay | USA | 1975 | | | | |
| 8.21 | 2.1 | Atanas | Chochev | BUL | 1986 | | | | |
| 8.21 | 2.3 | Tyrus | Jefferson | USA | 1986 | | | | |
| 8.20 | | Josh | Owusu | GHA | 1971 | | | | |
| 8.20 | 3.6 | Valeriy | Podluzhniy | SU | 1973 | | | | |
| 8.20 | 2.2 | Rolf | Bernhard | SWZ | 1977 | | | | |
| 8.20 | | Moses | Kiyai | KEN | 1985 | | | | |
| 8.19 | 2.8 | J.François | Bonheme | FRA | 1973 | | | | |
| 8.19 | | Ron | Waynes | USA | 1985 | | | | |
| 8.18 | | Theo | Hamilton | USA | 1975 | | | | |
| 8.18 | 2.2 | Philippe | Deroche | FRA | 1976 | | | | |
| 8.18 | 3.7 | Włodzimierz | Włodarczyk | POL | 1984 | | | | |
| 8.17 | | Thomas | Selmon | USA | 1984 | | | | |

| Mark | | Name | | Nat | Yr | Pos | Meet | Venue | | Date |
|---|---|---|---|---|---|---|---|---|---|---|
| A8.16 | 4.0 | Charles | Mays | USA | 1968 | 8.15 | | Phil | May | AUS 1970 |
| 8.16 | 3.0 | Murray | Tolbert | AUS | 1972 | 8.15 | 6.4 | Alan | Lerwill | UK 1972 |
| 8.16 | | Danny | Brabham | USA | 1973 | A8.15 | 2.4 | Skeeter | Jackson | USA 1983 |
| 8.16 | 2.8 | Roy | Mitchell | UK | 1976 | 8.14 | 3.2 | Manfred | Steinbach | FRG 1960 |
| 8.16 | 2.5 | Ed | Tave | USA | 1983 | 8.14 | 2.7 | Anthony | Carter | USA 1977 |
| 8.16 | 6.4 | Stanisław | Jaskulka | POL | 1986 | A8.14 | 8.9 | Dannie | Jackson | USA 1978 |
| 8.15 | 3.9 | Pentti | Eskola | FIN | 1963 | A8.14 | 2.3 | Gilbert | Smith | USA 1982 |

# TRIPLE JUMP

| Mark | | Name | | Nat | Yr | Pos | Meet | Venue | | Date |
|---|---|---|---|---|---|---|---|---|---|---|
| 17.97 | 1.5 | Willie | Banks | USA | 56 | 1 | TAC | Indianapolis | 16 | Jun 8 |
| A17.89 | 0.0 | Joao C. | de Oliveira | BRA | 54 | 1 | PAG | Ciudad México | 15 | Oct 7 |
| 17.86 | 1.3 | Charles | Simpkins | USA | 63 | 1 | WUG | Kobe | 2 | Sep 8 |
| 17.80 | 0.6 | Khristo | Markov | BUL | 65 | 1 | BGP | Budapest | 11 | Aug 8 |
| 17.78 | 1.0 | Nikolay | Musiyenko | SU | 59 | 1 | Znam | Leningrad | 7 | Jun 8 |
| 17.78 | 0.6 | Lázaro | Betancourt | CUB | 63 | 1 | Barr | Habana | 15 | Jun 8 |
| 17.77 | 1.9 | | Markov | | | 1 | EP-B | Budapest | 11 | Aug 8 |
| 17.71 | 1.9 | Mike | Conley | USA | 62 | 2 | TAC | Indianapolis | 16 | Jun 8 |
| 17.71 | 2.0 | | Banks | | | 1 | | Barcelona | 8 | Jul 8 |
| 17.69 | 1.0 | Oleg | Protsenko | SU | 63 | 1 | NC | Leningrad | 4 | Aug 8 |
| 17.69 | 0.2 | | Conley | | | 1 | GWG | Moskva | 9 | Jul 8 |
| 17.67 | 0.0 | | Banks | | | 1 | Arco | Los Angeles | 8 | Jun 8 |
| 17.66 | 1.9 | | Markov | | | 1 | EC | Stuttgart | 30 | Aug 8 |
| 17.62 | | | Markov | | | 1 | NC | Sofia | 14 | Aug 8 |
| 17.60 | 0.6 | Vladimir | Plekhanov | SU | 58 | 2 | NC | Leningrad | 4 | Aug 8 |
| 17.59 | -2.1 | | Protsenko | | | 1 | NC | Kiev | 17 | Jul 8 |
| 17.58 | -0.3 | | Banks | | | 1 | VD | Bruxelles | 30 | Aug 8 |
| 17.58 | 1.5 | | Banks | | | 1 | WP | Canberra | 4 | Oct 8 |
| A17.58 | 0.0 | | Banks | | | 1 | | El Paso | 20 | Apr 8 |
| A17.57 | 0.0 | Keith | Connor (10) | UK | 57 | 1 | NCAA | Provo | 5 | Jun 8 |
| 17.57 | 0.5 | | Betancourt | | | 1 | | Habana | 23 | Mar 8 |
| 17.56 | 0.8 | | Banks | | | 1 | TAC | Sacramento | 21 | Jun 8 |
| 17.55 | -0.5 | | Banks | | | 1 | DNG | Stockholm | 8 | Jul 8 |
| 17.55 | 0.3 | Vasiliy | Grischenkov | SU | 58 | 1 | SPA | Moskva | 19 | Jun 8 |
| 17.55 | -0.6 | | Conley | | | 1 | WK | Zürich | 13 | Aug 8 |
| 17.54 | -1.5 | | Conley | | | - | NCAA | Austin | 1 | Jun 8 |
| 17.54i | - | Maris | Bružiks | SU | 62 | 1 | EC | Madrid | 23 | Feb 8 |
| 17.53 | 1.0 | Aleksandr | Beskrovniy | SU | 60 | 2 | SPA | Moskva | 19 | Jun 8 |
| 17.53 | 1.6 | Zdzislaw | Hoffmann | POL | 59 | 1 | | Madrid | 4 | Jun 8 |
| 17.53 | 1.0 | Gennadiy | Valyukevich | SU | 58 | 1 | | Erfurt | 1 | Jun 8 |
| (30/15) | | | | | | | | | | |
| 17.50 | 2.0 | Aleksandr | Yakovlev | SU | 57 | 1 | Znam | Sochi | 10 | Jun 8 |
| 17.50 | 0.4 | Volker | Mai | GDR | 66 | 1 | vSU | Erfurt | 23 | Jun 8 |
| 17.46 | 1.7 | Ken | Lorraway | AUS | 56 | 1 | | London | 7 | Aug 8 |
| 17.46 | 0.9 | Al | Joyner | USA | 60 | 4 | TAC | Indianapolis | 16 | Jun 8 |
| 17.44 | | Viktor | Saneyev | SU | 45 | 1 | | Sukhumi | 17 | Oct 7 |
| | | (20) | | | | | | | | |
| 17.44 | 2.0 | Dirk | Gamlin | GDR | 63 | 1 | | Dresden | 7 | Jul 8 |
| 17.43i | - | Vladimir | Inozemtsev | SU | 64 | 1 | | Kiev | 26 | Jan 8 |
| 17.41 | 0.0 | John | Herbert | UK | 62 | 3 | WUG | Kobe | 2 | Sep 8 |
| A17.40 | 0.4 | Pedro | Perez Duenas | CUB | 52 | 1 | PAG | Cali | 5 | Aug 7 |
| 17.37 | 0.7 | Vyacheslav | Bordukov | SU | 59 | 2 | Nar | Sofia | 19 | May 8 |
| 17.35 | -0.3 | Jaak | Uudmae | SU | 54 | 1 | OG | Moskva | 25 | Jul 8 |
| 17.35 | 0.7 | Vladimir | Chernikov | SU | 59 | 4 | NC | Leningrad | 4 | Aug 8 |
| 17.34 | 0.3 | Zou Zhenxian | | CHN | 55 | 2 | WP | Roma | 5 | Sep 8 |
| 17.34 | 0.1 | Ján | Čado | CS | 63 | 1 | PTS | Bratislava | 26 | May 8 |
| 17.33 | 0.8 | Peter | Bouschen | FRG | 60 | 1 | NC | Bremen | 25 | Jun 8 |
| | | (30) | | | | | | | | |

| ark | Wind | Name | | Nat | Yr | Pos | Meet | Venue | Date |
|---|---|---|---|---|---|---|---|---|---|
| 17.33i | – | Grigoriy | Yemets | SU | 57 | 1 | EC | Göteborg | 3 Mar 84 |
| 17.31 | 1.5 | Jörg | Drehmel | GDR | 45 | 2 | OG | München | 4 Sep 72 |
| 17.30i | – | Shamil | Abbyasov | SU | 57 | 1 | EC | Grenoble | 21 Feb 81 |
| 17.30 | 1.9 | Jörg | Elbe | GDR | 64 | 1 | | Dresden | 2 Aug 85 |
| 17.29 | -0.6 | Ralf | Jaros | FRG | 65 | 1 | | Rhede | 5 Jul 85 |
| 17.27 | 2.0 | Nelson | Prudencio | BRA | 44 | 2 | OG | Ciudad México | 17 Oct 68 |
| 17.27 | 1.2 | Bedros | Bedrosian | RUM | 58 | 1 | | Bucuresti | 9 Jun 84 |
| 17.26 | 1.5 | Ajayi | Agbebaku | NIG | 56 | 1 | WUG | Edmonton | 8 Jul 83 |
| 17.25 | | Aleksandr | Kovalenko | SU | 63 | 1 | | Moskva | 11 May 86 |
| 17.24 | 0.8 | James | Butts | USA | 50 | 1 | WG | Helsinki | 29 Jun 78 |
| | | (40) | | | | | | | |
| 17.23 | | Jaroslav | Priščák | CS | 56 | 1 | | Praha | 13 May 84 |
| 17.23 | 1.8 | Bela | Bakosi | HUN | 57 | 1 | NC | Budapest | 29 Jul 85 |
| 17.22 | 0.0 | Giuseppe | Gentile | ITA | 43 | 3 | OG | Ciudad México | 17 Oct 68 |
| 17.22 | 1.9 | Vasiliy | Isayev | SU | 59 | 4 | Znam | Sochi | 10 Jun 84 |
| 17.22 | | Yevgeniy | Anikin | SU | 58 | 1 | | Sochi | 26 Apr 86 |
| 17.22 | 2.0 | Aleksandr | Leonov | SU | 62 | 3 | Znam | Leningrad | 7 Jun 86 |
| 17.21 | 1.6 | Aleksandr | Pokusayev | SU | 60 | 1 | | Krasnodar | 26 May 83 |
| 17.21 | 0.9 | Vlastimil | Mařinec | CS | 57 | 1 | PTS | Bratislava | 4 Jun 83 |
| 17.20 | 0.1 | Mikhail | Bariban | SU | 49 | 1 | WUG | Moskva | 19 Aug 73 |
| 17.20 | 0.0 | Tommy | Haynes | USA | 52 | 2 | PAG | Ciudad México | 15 Oct 75 |
| | | (50) | | | | | | | |
| 17.20 | | Vladimir | Brigadniy | SU | 55 | 1 | | Ashkabad | 2 May 83 |
| 17.20 | 0.7 | Igor | Lapshin | SU | 63 | 4 | Znam | Leningrad | 7 Jun 86 |

| | | | | | | | | | | | | |
|---|---|---|---|---|---|---|---|---|---|---|---|---|
| 17.19 | 1.0 | Ron | Livers | USA | 1977 | | 17.05 | | Paul | Emordi | NIG | 1986 |
| 17.19 | -0.3 | Paul | Jordan | USA | 1984 | | 17.05 | | Frank | Rutherford | BAH | 1986 |
| 17.19 | | Joseph | Taiwo | NIG | 1984 | | 17.05 | 1.2 | Sergey | Tkachev | SU | 1986 |
| 17.18 | 0.7 | Robert | Cannon | USA | 1982 | | 17.04 | | Steve | Hanna | BAH | 1981 |
| 17.18 | 1.3 | Mamed | Akhundov | SU | 1985 | | | | (80) | | | |
| 17.18 | | Jorge | Reyna | CUB | 1986 | | 17.04 | 0.0 | Dimitrios | Mihas | GRE | 1981 |
| 17.17 | 0.8 | Mike | Marlow | USA | 1981 | | 17.04 | 0.3 | Vasif | Asadov | SU | 1986 |
| 17.15 | 0.9 | Norifumi | Yamashita | JAP | 1986 | | 17.03 | 1.0 | Jozef | Szmidt | POL | 1960 |
| | | (60) | | | | | 17.03i | – | Vince | Parrette | USA | 1980 |
| 17.13 | 0.0 | Serge | Helan | FRA | 1986 | | 17.03 | | Aleksandr | Lisichonok | SU | 1981 |
| 17.12 | | Carol | Corbu | RUM | 1981 | | 17.03 | | Vadim | Kobylyanskiy | SU | 1982 |
| 17.12 | 0.0 | Oleg | Sokirkin | SU | 1986 | | 17.03 | | Vladimir | Bereglazov | SU | 1983 |
| 17.12 | 2.0 | Dario | Badinelli | ITA | 1986 | | 17.03 | | Sergey | Belevskiy | SU | 1984 |
| 17.11 | 1.1 | Jacek | Pastusinski | POL | 1986 | | A17.02 | 2.0 | Phil | May | AUS | 1968 |
| 17.10 | | Nate | Cooper | USA | 1979 | | 17.02 | | Igor | Usov | SU | 1982 |
| 17.10 | | Aleksey | Roganin | SU | 1982 | | | | (90) | | | |
| 17.10 | | Viktor | Gerasimenya | SU | 1984 | | 17.02 | | Boris | Khoklov | SU | 1982 |
| 17.09 | 0.5 | Ian | Campbell | AUS | 1980 | | 17.02 | 0.6 | Andrey | Kayukov | SU | 1986 |
| 17.09 | 1.1 | Dan | Simion | RUM | 1983 | | 17.01 | | Nikolay | Dudkin | SU | 1970 |
| | | (70) | | | | | 17.01 | 0.0 | Miloš | Srejović | YUG | 1981 |
| 17.09 | -0.3 | Stoitsa | Iliev | BUL | 1984 | | 17.01 | 2.0 | Eric | McCalla | UK | 1984 |
| 17.07 | 0.3 | Dave | Smith | USA | 1972 | | 17.01 | | Norbert | Elliott | BAH | 1986 |
| 17.07 | | Anatoliy | Piskulin | SU | 1978 | | 17.00 | 1.6 | Pertti | Pousi | FIN | 1968 |
| 17.07 | | Viktor | Panych | SU | 1983 | | 17.00 | | Gustavo | Platt | CUB | 1973 |
| 17.07 | | Kenny | Harrison | USA | 1986 | | 17.00 | | Sergey | Klimin | SU | 1983 |
| 17.06 | 1.6 | Michal | Joachimowski | POL | 1973 | | 17.00 | 1.3 | Mihai | Ene | RUM | 1985 |
| | | | | | | | | | (100) | | | |

ow altitude marks for athletes with high-altitude bests

| Connor | 17.30 | 1.2 | 1 | | London | 9 Jun 82 | 17.57A |
|---|---|---|---|---|---|---|---|
| Haynes | 17.12 | | 1 | CISM | Al Jazair | 6 Jul 79 | 17.20A |
| Prudencio | 17.05 | 1.4 | | 1972 | (17.27A) | | |

est outdoor marks for athletes with lifetime bests set indoors

| Bružiks | 17.38 | 0.5 | 1 | | Alma-Ata | 14 Sep 85 | 17.54i |
|---|---|---|---|---|---|---|---|
| Yemets | 17.30 | 0.2 | 2 | NC | Donyetsk | 9 Sep 84 | 17.33i |
| Abbyasov | 17.27 | | 1 | | Tashkent | 15 May 83 | 17.30i |
| Inozemtsev | 17.16 | 0.2 | | 1986 | (17.43i) | | |

MEN All-time

| Mark | Wind | Name | | Nat | Yr | Pos | Meet | Venue | Date |
|---|---|---|---|---|---|---|---|---|---|

**Wind-assisted marks**

| Mark | Wind | Name | | Nat | Yr | Pos | Meet | Venue | Date |
|---|---|---|---|---|---|---|---|---|---|
| 17.91 | 3.2 | Charles | Simpkins | USA | 63 | 1 | TAC | Eugene | 21 Jun 8 |
| 17.84 | 2.3 | Mike | Conley | USA | 62 | 2 | TAC | Eugene | 21 Jun 8 |
| 17.82 | 3.6 | | W.Banks | | | 1 | Jenner | San Jose | 31 May 8 |
| 17.81 | 4.6 | Keith | Connor | UK | 57 | 1 | CommG | Brisbane | 9 Oct 8 |
| 17.75 | | Gennadiy | Valyukevich | SU | 58 | 1 | | Uzhgorod | 27 Apr 8 |
| 17.72 | 3.2 | | Conley | | | 1 | NCAA | Austin | 1 Jun 8 |
| 17.64 | 3.2 | | O.Protsenko | SU | 63 | 1 | | Sao Paulo | 11 May 8 |
| 17.56 | 3.7 | Ron | Livers | USA | 55 | 1 | AAU | Walnut | 17 Jun 7 |
| 17.55 | 3.6 | Zdzislaw | Hoffmann | POL | 59 | 1 | Kuso | Warszawa | 9 Jun 8 |
| 17.55 | 2.6 | | Banks | | | 2 | | Sao Paulo | 11 May 8 |
| 17.54 | 3.2 | Ken | Lorraway | AUS | 56 | 2 | CommG | Brisbane | 9 Oct 8 |
| | | | | | | | | | |
| 17.41 | 3.2 | Kenny | Harrison | USA | 65 | 4 | TAC | Eugene | 21 Jun 8 |
| 17.38 | 4.2 | Milan | Tiff | USA | 49 | 1 | AAU | Westwood | 11 Jun 7 |
| 17.31 | | Paul | Emordi | NIG | 65 | 1 | DrakeR | Des Moines | 26 Apr 8 |
| 17.30 | 3.2 | Anatoliy | Piskulin | SU | 52 | 1 | WUG | Sofia | 22 Aug 7 |
| 17.30 | 3.7 | David | McFadgen | USA | 60 | 2 | USOF | Houston | 2 Aug 8 |
| 17.29 | 2.9 | James | Butts | USA | 50 | 1 | FOT | Eugene | 26 Jun 7 |
| 17.29 | 3.4 | Bela | Bakosi | HUN | 57 | 1 | | Hiroshima | 6 May 8 |
| 17.23 | 2.5 | Henry | Ellard | USA | 61 | 1 | | Fresno | 1 May 8 |
| 17.21 | 2.2 | Ray | Kimble | USA | 53 | 1 | | Berkeley | 12 Jun 8 |

| Mark | Wind | Name | | Nat | Yr | | Mark | Wind | Name | | Nat | Yr |
|---|---|---|---|---|---|---|---|---|---|---|---|---|
| 17.20 | 2.2 | Mike | Marlow | USA | 1981 | | A17.09 | 3.0 | Nikolay | Dudkin | SU | 196 |
| 17.19 | 4.7 | Ian | Campbell | AUS | 1980 | | 17.08 | | Byron | Criddle | USA | 198 |
| 17.16 | 3.3 | Arne | Holm | SWE | 1986 | | 17.03 | 2.4 | Greg | Caldwell | USA | 198 |
| A17.12 | 2.5 | Art | Walker | USA | 1968 | | 17.02 | 4.9 | Aston | Moore | UK | 198 |
| 17.12 | 2.4 | John | Craft | USA | 1972 | | 17.01 | 2.8 | Rayfield | Dupree | USA | 197 |
| 17.10 | 3.0 | Phil | May | AUS | 1971 | | | | | | | |

**Ancillary marks**

| | | | | | | | | | | |
|---|---|---|---|---|---|---|---|---|---|---|
| Markov | 17.74 | 1.2 | 11 Aug 86 | | **Wind-assisted** | | | | | |
| Simpkins | 17.68 | 1.0 | 2 Sep 85 | | Connor | 17.72 | 3.8 | 9 Oct 82 | | |
| Banks | 17.64 | 1.1 | 16 Jun 85 | | Simpkins | 17.70 | 3.9 | 21 Jun 86 | | |
| Markov | 17.64 | 1.4 | 11 Aug 86 | | Simpkins | 17.62 | 3.4 | 21 Jun 86 | | |
| Betancourt | 17.54 | | 15 Jun 86 | | Conley | 17.54 | 2.8 | 21 Jun 86 | | |

# SHOT PUT

| Mark | Name | | Nat | Yr | Pos | Meet | Venue | Date |
|---|---|---|---|---|---|---|---|---|
| 22.86 | Brian | Oldfield | USA | 45 | 1 | ITA | El Paso | 10 May |
| 22.64 | Udo | Beyer | GDR | 55 | 1 | | Berlin | 20 Aug |
| 22.62 | Ulf | Timmermann | GDR | 62 | 1 | | Berlin | 22 Sep |
| 22.60 | | Timmermann | | | 1 | vSU | Tallinn | 21 Jun |
| 22.51 | | Timmermann | | | 1 | | Erfurt | 1 Jun |
| 22.47 | | Timmermann | | | 1 | | Dresden | 17 Aug |
| 22.45 | | Oldfield | | | 1 | ITA | El Paso | 22 May |
| 22.28 | | Oldfield | | | 1 | ITA | Edinburgh | 18 Jun |
| 22.24 | Sergey | Smirnov | SU | 60 | 2 | vGDR | Tallinn | 21 Jun |
| 22.22 | | Beyer | | | 1 | vUSA | Los Angeles | 25 Jun |
| | | | | | | | | |
| 22.22 | Werner | Günthör | SWZ | 61 | 1 | EC | Stuttgart | 28 Aug |
| 22.19 | | Oldfield | | | 1 | Jenner | San José | 26 May |
| 22.16 | | Smirnov | | | 1 | NC | Kiev | 16 Jul |
| 22.16 | | Günthör | | | 1 | | St. Gallen | 20 Sep |
| 22.15 | | Beyer | | | 1 | | Göteborg | 6 Jul |
| 22.15i | | Timmermann | | | 1 | NC | Senftenberg | 16 Feb |
| 22.14 | | Beyer | | | 1 | NC | Jena | 27 Jun |
| 22.11i | | Oldfield | | | 1 | ITA | Daly City | 4 Apr |
| 22.10 | Sergey | Gavryushin | SU | 59 | 1 | | Tbilisi | 31 Aug |
| 22.09 | Sergey | Kasnauskas | SU | 61 | 1 | | Staiki | 23 Aug |

| ark | Name | | Nat | Yr | Pos | Meet | Venue | Date |
|---|---|---|---|---|---|---|---|---|
| 2.08 | | Timmermann | | | 1 | vSU | Erfurt | 22 Jun 85 |
| 2.06 | Alessandro | Andrei | ITA | 59 | 1 | | Viareggio | 6 Aug 86 |
| 2.05 | | Smirnov | | | 1 | EP | Moskva | 17 Aug 85 |
| 2.05 | | Beyer | | | 3 | vSU | Tallinn | 21 Jun 86 |
| 2.04 | | Beyer | | | 1 | | Rehlingen | 11 Jun 84 |
| 2.02i | George | Woods | USA | 43 | 1 | | Inglewood | 8 Feb 74 |
| 2.02 | | Oldfield | | | 1 | CalR | Modesto | 16 May 81 |
| 2.02 | Dave | Laut | USA | 56 | 1 | | Koblenz | 25 Aug 82 |
| 2.01 | | Smirnov | | | 1 | vUSA, JAP | Tokyō | 21 Sep 85 |
| 2.00 | Aleksandr | Baryshnikov | SU | 48 | 1 | vFRA | Colombes | 10 Jul 76 |
| 2.00 | | Beyer | | | 1 | | Dresden | 26 Jul 84 |
| 2.00 | | Timmermann | | | 1 | WP | Canberra | 5 Oct 86 |
| 2.00 | | Timmermann | | | 2 | NC | Jena | 27 Jun 86 |
| (33/10) | | | | | | | | |
| 1.96 | Mikhail | Kostin | SU | 59 | 1 | | Vitebsk | 20 Jul 86 |
| 1.92 | John | Brenner | USA | 61 | 1 | NCAA | Eugene | 2 Jun 84 |
| 1.88* | Remigius | Machura | CS | 60 | 1 | WK | Zürich | 21 Aug 85 |
| 1.88 | Randy | Barnes | USA | 66 | 1 | | Waco | 18 Apr 86 |
| 1.85 | Terry | Albritton | USA | 55 | 1 | | Honolulu | 21 Feb 76 |
| 1.82 | Al | Feuerbach | USA | 48 | 1 | | San José | 5 May 73 |
| 1.78 | Randy | Matson | USA | 45 | 1 | | College Station | 22 Apr 67 |
| 1.76 | Mike | Carter | USA | 60 | 2 | NCAA | Eugene | 2 Jun 84 |
| 1.74 | Janis | Bojars | SU | 56 | 1 | | Riga | 14 Jul 84 |
| (20) | | | | | | | | |
| 1.73 | Augie | Wolf | USA | 61 | 1 | | Leverkusen | 12 Apr 84 |
| 1.69 | Reijo | Stahlberg | FIN | 52 | 1 | WCR | Fresno | 5 May 79 |
| 1.68 | Geoff | Capes | UK | 49 | 1 | 4-N | Cwmbran | 18 May 80 |
| 1.68 | Edward | Sarul | POL | 58 | 1 | | Sopot | 31 Jul 83 |
| 1.67 | Hartmut | Briesenick | GDR | 49 | 1 | | Potsdam | 1 Sep 73 |
| 1.61 | Kevin | Akins | USA | 60 | 1 | CalR | Modesto | 14 May 83 |
| 1.58 | Vladimir | Kiselyov | SU | 57 | 3 | Drz | Moskva | 17 Aug 84 |
| 1.53 | Yevgeniy | Mironov | SU | 49 | 1 | NC | Kiev | 24 Jun 76 |
| 1.51 | Ralf | Reichenbach | FRG | 50 | 1 | ISTAF | Berlin | 8 Aug 80 |
| 1.45 | Gregg | Tafralis | USA | 58 | 3 | MSR | Walnut | 27 Apr 86 |
| (30) | | | | | | | | |
| 1.44 | Mikhail | Domorosov | SU | 55 | 2 | | Staiki | 23 Aug 84 |
| 1.43 | Mike | Lehmann | USA | 60 | 2 | Jenner | San Jose | 28 May 83 |
| 1.42i | Fred | DeBernardi | USA | 49 | 1 | ITA | Portland | 20 Apr 74 |
| 1.35 | Ron | Semkiw | USA | 54 | 1 | | Mesa | 5 Mar 74 |
| 1.33 | Hans | Hoglund | SWE | 52 | 1 | NCAA | Provo | 6 Jun 75 |
| 1.32 | Heinz-Joachim | Rothenburg | GDR | 44 | 1 | | Potsdam | 3 Jun 72 |
| 1.31 | Hans-Peter | Gies | GDR | 47 | 2 | | Potsdam | 25 Aug 72 |
| 1.30 | Helmut | Krieger | POL | 58 | 1 | NC | Grudziądz | 27 Jun 86 |
| 1.29 | Jim | Doehring | USA | 62 | 1 | | Walnut | 1 Jun 86 |
| 1.25 | Hans-Jürg. | Jacobi | GDR | 50 | 2 | NC | Cottbus | 16 Jul 80 |
| (40) | | | | | | | | |
| 1.24i | Soren | Tallhem | SWE | 64 | 1 | NCAA | Syracuse | 9 Mar 85 |
| 1.22 | Lars | Nilsen | NOR | 65 | 1 | NCAA | Indianapolis | 6 Jun 86 |
| 1.20 | Josef | Kubes | CS | 57 | 2 | NC | Praha | 24 Jul 83 |
| 1.19 | Wladysław | Komar | POL | 40 | 1 | | Warszawa | 17 Aug 74 |
| 1.19 | Vladimir | Milić | YUG | 55 | 1 | | Beograd | 18 Aug 82 |
| 1.12 | John | Campbell | USA | 62 | 1 | NCAA | Austin | 1 Jun 85 |
| 1.11* | Zlatan | Saračević | YUG | 56 | 1 | | Zagreb | 16 Jun 84 |
| 1.10 | Pete | Shmock | USA | 50 | 1 | Pre | Eugene | 5 Jun 76 |
| 1.10 | Donatas | Stukonis | SU | 57 | 1 | | Kaunas | 20 Jul 85 |
| 1.09 | Hreinn | Halldorsson | ICE | 49 | 1 | DNG | Stockholm | 4 Jul 77 |
| (50) | | | | | | | | |
| 1.09 | Sergey | Donskikh | SU | 56 | 1 | | Leningrad | 13 Aug 84 |

| Mark | Name | | Nat | Yr | Pos | Meet | Venue | Date |
|------|------|------|-----|----|-----|------|-------|------|
| 21.08 | Colin | Anderson | USA | 1980 | | | | |
| 21.07 | Dean | Crouser | USA | 1982 | | | | |
| 21.06i | Mac | Wilkins | USA | 1977 | | | | |
| 21.04 | Jaroslav | Brabeć | CS | 1973 | | | | |
| 21.04 | Peter | Block | GDR | 1982 | | | | |
| 21.04 | Nikolay | Borodkin | SU | 1985 | | | | |
| 21.02 | Sergey | Solomko | SU | 1984 | | | | |
| 21.02i | Jesse | Stuart | USA | 1985 | | | | |
| 21.01 | Neal | Steinhauer | USA | 1967 | | | | |
| | (60) | | | | | | | |
| 21.01i | Ron | Backes | USA | 1986 | | | | |
| 20.98 | Janusz | Gassowski | POL | 1985 | | | | |
| 20.97i | Karl | Salb | USA | 1973 | | | | |
| 20.95 | Anatoliy | Yarosh | SU | 1980 | | | | |
| 20.95 | Erik | de Bruin | HOL | 1986 | | | | |
| 20.92 | Mathias | Schmidt | GDR | 1981 | | | | |
| 20.90· | Mike | Smith | USA | 1984 | | | | |
| 20.90 | Marco | Montelatici | ITA | 1985 | | | | |
| 20.90 | Gert | Weil | CHL | 1986 | | | | |
| 20.85 | Bishop | Dolegiewicz | CAN | 1978 | | | | |
| | (70) | | | | | | | |
| 20.84 | Matti | Yrjölä | FIN | 1976 | | | | |
| 20.84 | Jeff | Stover | USA | 1980 | | | | |
| 20.83 | Ventislav | Khristov | BUL | 1985 | | | | |
| 20.83 | Mike | Spiritoso | CAN | 1986 | | | | |
| 20.81 | Grigoriy | Skorikov | SU | 1983 | | | | |
| 20.80 | Vladimir | Yaryshkin | SU | 1986 | | | | |
| 20.78 | Valeriy | Voykin | SU | 1979 | | | | |
| 20.78 | Gary | Williky | USA | 1982 | | | | |
| 20.77 | Steve | Summers | USA | 1980 | | | | |
| 20.77 | Ivan | Ivančić | YUG | 1983 | | | | |
| | (80) | | | | | | | |
| 20.76 | Wolfgang | Schmidt | GDR | 1978 | | | | |
| 20.76 | Jan | Sagedal | NOR | 1986 | | | | |
| 20.76 | Viktor | Stepanskiy | SU | 1986 | | | | |
| 20.73 | Rob | Suelflohn | USA | 1985 | | | | |
| 20.72 | Valcho | Stoev | BUL | 1980 | | | | |
| 20.71 | Nagui | Assaad | EGY | 1972 | | | | |
| 20.71 | Algis | Pusinaitis | SU | 1984 | | | | |
| 20.70i | Scott | Lofquist | USA | 1985 | | | | |
| 20.68 | Dallas | Long | USA | 1964 | | | | |
| 20.68 | Igor | Avrunin | SU | 1983 | | | | |
| | (90) | | | | | | | |
| 20.67 | Vyacheslav | Yemelyanov | SU | 1985 | | | | |
| 20.65 | Nikolay | Valakhanovich | SU | 1983 | | | | |
| 20.62 | Aleksandr | Nosenko | SU | 1976 | | | | |
| 20.61 | Mikhail | Gusyev | SU | 1981 | | | | |
| 20.61 | Oskar | Jakobsson | ICE | 1982 | | | | |
| 20.61 | Bruno | Pauletto | CAN | 1983 | | | | |
| 20.60 | Dieter | Hoffmann | GDR | 1969 | | | | |
| 20.59 | Dimitrios | Koutsoukis | GRE | 1986 | | | | |
| 20.58 | Brian | Muir | USA | 1984 | | | | |
| 20.58 | Torsten | Pelzer | GDR | 1986 | | | | |
| | (100) | | | | | | | |

* Disqualified for failing dope test.   4-N Capes 21.68  Eng v Wal v HUN v HOL

Best outdoor marks for athletes with lifetime bests indoors

| Machura | | 21.74 | 1 | Ros | Praha | | 16 Aug 82 | 21.79 |
|---------|--|-------|---|-----|-------|--|-----------|-------|
| Woods | | 21.63 | 2 | CalR | Modesto | | 22 May 76 | 22.02 |
| DeBernardi | | 21.41 | 1 | ITA | El Paso | | 27 Apr 74 | 21.42 |
| Backes | 20.92 | 1986 | | (21.01i) | Salb | 20.73 | 1974 | (20.97i |
| Stuart | 20.84 | 1973 | | (21.02i) | Wilkins | 20.64 | 1976 | (21.06i |

Ancillary marks at 22.01 or better

| Beyer | 22.58 | 20 Aug 86 | Timmermann 22.12 | 21 Jun 86 | Timmermann 22.05 | 21 Jun 86 |
|-------|-------|-----------|------------------|-----------|------------------|-----------|
| Oldfield | 22.24 | 10 May 75 | Smirnov 22.10 | 21 Jun 86 | Kasnauskas 22.02 | 23 Aug 84 |
| Beyer | 22.24 | 20 Aug 86 | Smirnov 22.09 | 21 Jun 86 | Timmermann 22.01 | 21 Jun 86 |
| Beyer | 22.15 | 20 Aug 86 | Timmermann 22.08 | 17 Aug 86 | Timmermann 22.01 | 17 Aug 86 |

# DISCUS

| 74.08 | Jürgen | Schult | GDR | 60 | 1 | | Neubrandenburg | 6 Jun |
|-------|--------|--------|-----|----|---|---|----------------|-------|
| 72.34* | Ben | Plucknett | USA | 54 | 1 | DNG | Stockholm | 7 Jul |
| 71.86 | Yuriy | Dumchev | SU | 58 | 1 | | Moskva | 29 May |
| 71.32 | | Plucknett | | | 1 | Pre | Eugene | 4 Jun |
| 71.26 | John | Powell | USA | 47 | 1 | TAC | San José | 9 Jun |
| 71.26 | Rickard | Bruch | SWE | 46 | 1 | | Malmö | 15 Nov |
| 71.26 | Imrich | Bugár | CS | 55 | 1 | Jenner | San José | 25 May |
| 71.20* | | Plucknett | | | 1 | CalR | Modesto | 16 May |
| 71.18 | Art | Burns | USA | 54 | 1 | | San José | 19 Jul |
| 71.16 | Wolfgang | Schmidt | GDR | 54 | 1 | | Berlin | 9 Aug |
| | | | | | | | | |
| 71.14 | | Plucknett | | | 1 | | Berkeley | 12 Jun |
| 71.06 | Luis M. | Delis | CUB | 57 | 1 | Barr | Habana | 21 May |
| 71.00 | | Bruch | | | 1 | | Malmö | 14 Oct |
| 70.98 | Mac | Wilkins (10) | USA | 50 | 1 | WG | Helsinki | 9 Jul |
| 70.98 | | Burns | | | 1 | Pre | Eugene | 21 Jul |

| ark | Name | | Nat | Yr | Pos | Meet | Venue | Date |
|---|---|---|---|---|---|---|---|---|
| 0.86 | | Wilkins | | | 1 | | San José | 1 May 76 |
| 0.82 | | Plucknett | | | 1 | | Salinas | 1 Jun 83 |
| 0.72 | | Bugár | | | 1 | vHUN, AUT | Schwechat | 18 Jun 83 |
| 0.66 | | Wilkins | | | 1 | AAU | Walnut | 16 Jun 79 |
| 0.58 | | Delis | | | 1 | | Salinas | 19 May 82 |
| 0.48 | | Wilkins | | | 1 | | San José | 29 Apr 78 |
| 0.48 | | Wilkins | | | 1 | Pre | Eugene | 31 May 78 |
| 0.48 | | Bruch | | | 1 | | Malmo | 12 Sep 84 |
| 0.44 | | Wilkins | | | 2 | TAC | San José | 9 Jun 84 |
| 0.38 | Jay | Silvester | USA | 37 | 1 | | Lancaster | 16 May 71 |
| 0.36 | | Wilkins | | | 1 | SW | Modesto | 14 May 83 |
| 0.26 | | Bugár | | | 1 | vITA | Cagliari | 8 Sep 84 |
| 0.24 | | Schmidt | | | 1 | | Potsdam | 18 Aug 78 |
| 0.24 | | Bugár | | | 1 | | Nitra | 26 Aug 84 |
| 0.20 | | Delis | | | 1 | CAC | Habana | 8 Aug 82 |
| (30/11) | | | | | | | | |
| 0.00 | Juan | Martínez | CUB | 58 | 2 | Barr | Habana | 21 May 83 |
| 9.70 | Gejza | Valent | CS | 53 | 2 | | Nitra | 26 Aug 84 |
| 9.62 | Knut | Hjeltnes | NOR | 51 | 2 | Jenner | San José | 25 May 85 |
| 9.46 | Al | Oerter | USA | 36 | 1 | TFA | Wichita | 31 May 80 |
| 9.44 | Georgiy | Kolnootchenko | SU | 59 | 1 | vUSA | Indianapolis | 3 Jul 82 |
| 9.40 | Art | Swarts | USA | 45 | 1 | | Scotch Plains | 8 Dec 79 |
| 9.26 | Ken | Stadel | USA | 52 | 2 | AAU | Walnut | 16 Jun 79 |
| 8.64 | Dmitriy | Kovtsun | SU | 55 | 1 | | Riga | 6 Jul 84 |
| 8.52 | Igor | Duginyets | SU | 56 | 1 | NC | Kiev | 21 Aug 82 |
| (20) | | | | | | | | |
| 8.50 | Armin | Lemme | GDR | 55 | 1 | vUSA | Karl Marx St. | 10 Jul 82 |
| 8.48 | John | van Reenen | RSA | 47 | 1 | | Stellenbosch | 14 Mar 75 |
| 8.12 | Markku | Tuokko | FIN | 51 | 1 | WCR | Fresno | 5 May 79 |
| 8.12 | Iosif | Nagy | RUM | 46 | 2 | | Zaragoza | 22 May 83 |
| 8.08 | Hein-Direck | Neu | FRG | 44 | 1 | | Bremerhaven | 27 May 77 |
| 8.00 | Svein Inge | Valvik | NOR | 56 | 1 | | Juarez | 31 May 82 |
| 7.88 | Romas | Ubartas | SU | 60 | 1 | vGDR | Tallinn | 21 Jun 86 |
| 7.82 | Velko | Velev | BUL | 48 | 1 | | Riga | 13 Aug 78 |
| 7.76 | Vitaliy | Pishchalnikov | SU | 58 | 1 | | Stavropol | 9 May 84 |
| 7.72 | Stefan | Fernholm | SWE | 59 | 1 | | Provo | 22 May 85 |
| (30) | | | | | | | | |
| 7.56 | Wolfgang | Warnemünde | GDR | 53 | 1 | | Rostock | 2 Jun 80 |
| .54 | Siegfried | Pachale | GDR | 49 | 1 | | Karl Marx St. | 29 May 76 |
| .54 | Hilmar | Hossfeld | GDR | 54 | 2 | OT | Jena | 17 May 80 |
| .54 | Werner | Hartmann | FRG | 59 | 1 | | Georgsheil | 29 Apr 82 |
| .40 | Rolf | Danneberg | FRG | 53 | 1 | | Stade | 5 May 84 |
| 7.38 | Tim | Vollmer | USA | 46 | 2 | | Lancaster | 16 May 71 |
| .38 | Ferenc | Tégla | HUN | 47 | 1 | | Szentes | 12 Oct 77 |
| .34 | Vaclavas | Kidikas | SU | 61 | 1 | | Leningrad | 26 Jul 85 |
| .32 | Rob | Gray | CAN | 56 | 1 | | Etobicoke | 30 Apr 84 |
| .30 | Ion | Zamfirache | RUM | 53 | 1 | | Bucuresti | 19 May 85 |
| (40) | | | | | | | | |
| .22 | Mitch | Crouser | USA | 57 | 1 | | Eugene | 5 Aug 85 |
| .18 | Ludvík | Danek | CS | 37 | 1 | | Praha | 10 Jul 74 |
| .14 | Borislav | Tashev | BUL | 56 | 1 | | Pleven | 31 Jul 82 |
| .14 | Igor | Avrunin | SU | 57 | 1 | | Smolininkay | 9 May 84 |
| .10 | Alwin | Wagner | FRG | 50 | 1 | | Felsberg | 7 Sep 82 |
| .10 | Brad | Cooper | BAH | 57 | 1 | NC | Nassau | 14 Jun 86 |
| .98 | Greg | McSeveney | USA | 59 | 1 | | Walnut | 2 Jun 85 |
| .96 | Marco | Bucci | ITA | 60 | 2 | | Formia | 30 Jun 84 |
| .92 | Géza | Fejér | HUN | 45 | 1 | vRUM | Budapest | 3 Jul 71 |
| .90 | Norbert | Thiede | GDR | 49 | 1 | | Rostock | 25 Apr 76 |
| .90 | Marco | Martino | ITA | 60 | 3 | | Formia | 30 Jun 84 |
| (51) | | | | | | | | |

MEN All-time

| Mark | Name | | Nat | Yr | Pos | Meet | Venue | Date | |
|------|------|--|-----|----|-----|------|-------|------|--|
| 66.82 | Pentti | Kahma | FIN | 1975 | | | | | |
| 66.78 | Erik | de Bruin | HOL | 1986 | | | | | |
| 66.70 | Vladimir | Zinchenko | SU | 1983 | | | | | |
| 66.64 | Viktor | Rashchupkin | SU | 1980 | | | | | |
| 66.64 | Sergey | Lukashok | SU | 1983 | | | | | |
| 66.62 | John | Brenner | USA | 1986 | | | | | |
| 66.60 | Vitaliy | Sokolov | SU | 1986 | | | | | |
| 66.42 | Mike | Buncic | USA | 1985 | | | | | |
| 66.38 | János | Murányi | HUN | 1971 | | | | | |
| | (60) | | | | | | | | |
| 66.36 | Anatoliy | Lang | SU | 1982 | | | | | |
| 66.32 | Öystein | Bjørbaek | NOR | 1983 | | | | | |
| 66.22 | Göran | Svensson | SWE | 1981 | | | | | |
| 66.16 | Stan | Cain | USA | 1981 | | | | | |
| 66.16 | Dave | Voorhees | USA | 1982 | | | | | |
| 66.16 | Gennadiy | Samarin | SU | 1984 | | | | | |
| 66.04 | Vladimir | Lyakhov | SU | 1976 | | | | | |
| 66.04 | Velislav | Prokhaska | BUL | 1981 | | | | | |
| 65.92 | Jon | Cole | USA | 1972 | | | | | |
| 65.92 | Pyotr | Mikhailov | SU | 1979 | | | | | |
| | (70) | | | | | | | | |
| 65.92 | Aleksandr | Klimenko | SU | 1979 | | | | | |
| 65.88 | Dirk | Wippermann | FRG | 1971 | | | | | |
| 65.88 | Dean | Crouser | USA | 1983 | | | | | |
| 65.86 | Rick | Meyer | USA | 1986 | | | | | |
| 65.84 | Mike | Hoffman | USA | 1971 | | | | | |
| 65.84 | Janos | Farago | HUN | 1976 | | | | | |

| Mark | Name | | Nat | Yr |
|------|------|--|-----|----|
| 65.78 | Georgi | Taushanski | BUL | 1984 |
| 65.60 | Threinn | Hafsteinsson | ICE | 1983 |
| 65.58 | Jim | McGoldrick | USA | 1977 |
| 65.54 | Hans-Jürgen | Jacobi | GDR | 1976 |
| | (80) | | | |
| 65.44 | Ari | Huumonen | FIN | 1983 |
| 65.40 | Borys | Chambul | CAN | 1976 |
| 65.40 | Kenth | Gardenkrans | SWE | 1980 |
| 65.40 | Kamen | Dimitrov | BUL | 1986 |
| 65.36 | Mike | Buncic | USA | 1985 |
| 65.34 | Kalev | Külv | SU | 1981 |
| 65.32 | Bishop | Dolegiewicz | CAN | 1975 |
| 65.32 | Randy | Heisler | USA | 1986 |
| 65.28 | Emil | Vladimirov | BUL | 1980 |
| 65.28 | Marcus | Gordien | USA | 1984 |
| | (90) | | | |
| 65.28 | Alois | Hannecker | FRG | 1986 |
| 65.24 | Aleksandr | Nazhimov | SU | 1980 |
| 65.22 | Viktor | Penzikov | SU | 1974 |
| 65.16 | Randy | Matson | USA | 1967 |
| 65.16 | Richard | Slaney | UK | 1985 |
| 65.14 | Kenneth | Akesson | SWE | 1975 |
| 65.14 | Vitaliy | Gaslenko | SU | 1986 |
| 65.12 | Vladimir | Rayev | SU | 1976 |
| 65.12 | Dan | Gardner | ISR | 1980 |
| 65.12 | Dariusz | Juzyszyn | POL | 1985 |
| | (100) | | | |

Technical irregularity

| 67.02 | Lothar | Milde | GDR | 34 | 1 | | Halle | 27 May |
|-------|--------|-------|-----|----|---|--|-------|--------|

\* Disqualified for drug abuse.

Ancillary marks

| Plucknett | 71.10 | 4 Jun 83 | Wilkins | 70.24 | 1 May 76 | Bruch | 70.18 | 14 Oct 8√ |
|-----------|-------|----------|---------|-------|----------|-------|-------|-----------|
| Wilkins | 70.40 | 31 May 78 | Wilkins | 70.20 | 9 Jul 80 | Wilkins | 70.10 | 29 Apr 7√ |

# HAMMER

| Mark | Name | | Nat | Yr | Pos | Meet | Venue | Date | |
|------|------|--|-----|----|-----|------|-------|------|--|
| 86.74 | Yuriy | Sedykh | SU | 55 | 1 | EC | Stuttgart | 30 Aug | |
| 86.66 | | Sedykh | | | 1 | vGDR | Tallinn | 22 Jun | |
| 86.34 | | Sedykh | | | 1 | | Cork | 3 Jul | |
| 86.04 | Sergey | Litvinov | SU | 58 | 1 | OD | Dresden | 3 Jul | |
| 85.74 | | Litvinov | | | 2 | EC | Stuttgart | 30 Aug | |
| 85.68 | | Sedykh | | | 1 | BGP | Budapest | 11 Aug | |
| 85.60 | | Sedykh | | | 1 | PTG | London | 13 Jul | |
| 85.60 | | Sedykh | | | 1 | Drz | Moskva | 17 Aug | |
| 85.20 | | Litvinov | | | 2 | | Cork | 3 Jul | |
| 85.14 | | Litvinov | | | 1 | PTG | London | 11 Jul | |
| 85.02 | | Sedykh | | | 1 | BGP | Budapest | 20 Aug | |
| 84.92 | | Sedykh | | | 2 | OD | Dresden | 3 Jul | |
| 84.88 | | Litvinov | | | 1 | GP-GG | Roma | 10 Sep | |
| 84.72 | | Sedykh | | | 1 | GWG | Moskva | 9 Jul | |
| 84.64 | | Litvinov | | | 2 | GWG | Moskva | 9 Jul | |
| 84.60 | | Sedykh | | | 1 | | Tokyo | 14 Sep | |
| 84.58 | | Sedykh | | | 1 | Znam | Leningrad | 8 Jun | |
| 84.40 | Juri | Tamm | SU | 57 | 1 | | Banska Bystrica | 9 Sep | |
| 84.36 | | Litvinov | | | 2 | vGDR | Tallinn | 22 Jun | |
| 84.26 | | Sedykh | | | 1 | Nik | Nice | 15 Jul | |

| Mark | Name | | Nat | Yr | Pos | Meet | Venue | Date |
|---|---|---|---|---|---|---|---|---|
| 84.14 | | Litvinov | | | 1 | Spart | Moskva | 21 Jun 83 |
| 84.14 | | Sedykh | | | 1 | WG | Helsinki | 7 Jul 86 |
| 84.08 | | Tamm | | | 1 | BGP | Budapest | 4 Aug 85 |
| 84.02 | | Litvinov | | | 2 | WG | Helsinki | 7 Jul 86 |
| 83.98 | | Litvinov | | | 1 | | Moskva | 4 Jun 82 |
| 83.90 | | Sedykh | | | 1 | GGala | Roma | 31 Aug 84 |
| 83.66 | | Tamm | | | 1 | vUSA, JAP | Tokyo | 22 Sep 85 |
| 83.58 | | Litvinov | | | 1 | | Moskva | 8 Jul 84 |
| 83.54 | Igor | Nikulin | SU | 60 | 1 | | Athinai | 2 Sep 82 |
| 83.40 | | Tamm | | | 1 | | Adler | 25 May 85 |
| (30/4) | | | | | | | | |
| | | | | | | | | |
| 82.64 | Günther | Rodehau | GDR | 59 | 1 | | Dresden | 3 Aug 85 |
| 82.24 | Benjaminas | Vilučkis | SU | 61 | 1 | | Klaipeda | 24 Aug 86 |
| 81.56 | Christoph | Sahner | FRG | 63 | 1 | | Rehlingen | 27 May 85 |
| 81.52 | Juha | Tiainen | FIN | 55 | 1 | | Tampere | 11 Jun 84 |
| 81.44 | Yuriy | Tarasyuk | SU | 57 | 1 | | Minsk | 10 Aug 84 |
| 81.32 | Klaus | Ploghaus | FRG | 56 | 1 | | Paderborn | 25 May 86 |
| (10) | | | | | | | | |
| 81.20 | Igor | Grigorash | SU | 59 | 1 | | Kiev | 23 Aug 84 |
| 80.92 | Matthias | Moder | GDR | 63 | 1 | | Halle | 11 Jun 85 |
| 80.88 | Jud | Logan | USA | 59 | 1 | MSR | Walnut | 27 Apr 86 |
| 80.80 | Karl-Hans | Riehm | FRG | 51 | 1 | | Rhede | 30 Jul 80 |
| 80.70 | Vasiliy | Sidorenko | SU | 61 | 1 | | Tiraspol | 9 Aug 86 |
| 80.68 | Viktor | Litvinenko | SU | 57 | 2 | | Kiev | 23 Aug 84 |
| 80.68 | Igor | Astapkovich | SU | 63 | 1 | | Minsk | 1 Jun 86 |
| 80.60 | Ralf | Haber | GDR | 62 | 2 | | Dresden | 16 Aug 86 |
| 80.64 | Emanuil | Dyulgherov | BUL | 55 | 1 | | Sofia | 25 Aug 84 |
| 80.50 | Detlef | Gerstenberg | GDR | 57 | 1 | | Berlin | 15 Jul 84 |
| (20) | | | | | | | | |
| 80.48 | Boris | Zaychuk | SU | 47 | 2 | | Sochi | 24 May 80 |
| 80.38 | František | Vrbka | CS | 58 | 2 | EP | Moskva | 18 Aug 85 |
| 80.24 | Grigoriy | Shevtsov | SU | 58 | 1 | | Volgograd | 9 May 83 |
| 80.20 | Igor | Shchegolev | SU | 60 | 1 | | Volgograd | 6 Sep 86 |
| 80.18 | Zdzisław | Kwasny | POL | 60 | 2 | EP | London | 21 Aug 83 |
| 80.16 | Anatoliy | Chyuzhas | SU | 56 | 2 | | Klaipeda | 27 May 84 |
| 79.92 | Jörg | Schaefer | FRG | 59 | 1 | ISTAF | Berlin | 15 Aug 86 |
| 79.90 | Roland | Steuk | GDR | 59 | 1 | | Sofia | 16 Jun 84 |
| 79.84 | Sergey | Alay | SU | 65 | 2 | | Minsk | 4 Sep 86 |
| 79.70 | Ivan | Tanev | BUL | 57 | 1 | | Sofia | 24 May 86 |
| (30) | | | | | | | | |
| 79.66 | Donatas | Plunge | SU | 60 | 2 | | Klaipeda | 24 Aug 86 |
| 79.56 | Anatoliy | Yefimov | SU | 56 | 1 | | Adler | 24 Apr 83 |
| 79.46 | Mariusz | Tomaszewski | POL | 56 | 1 | | Zabrze | 1 Jul 84 |
| 79.30 | Walter | Schmidt | FRG | 48 | 1 | | Frankfurt/Main | 14 Aug 75 |
| 79.28 | Johann | Lindner | AUT | 56 | 1 | | Hainfeld | 27 May 85 |
| 79.22 | Igor | Kuprishchenkov | SU | 59 | 1 | | Smolensk | 20 Jul 85 |
| 79.16 | Manfred | Hüning | FRG | 53 | 1 | | Dortmund | 22 Aug 79 |
| 79.12 | Albert | Sinka | HUN | 62 | 2 | BGP | Budapest | 11 Aug 86 |
| 79.06 | József | Vida | HUN | 63 | 1 | | Szombathely | 28 Aug 84 |
| 79.00 | Sergey | Ivanov | SU | 62 | 1 | | Lipetsk | 19 Jul 86 |
| (40) | | | | | | | | |
| 78.92 | Valeriy | Kocherga | SU | 63 | 1 | | Yalta | 12 Oct 86 |
| 78.84 | Imre | Szitás | HUN | 61 | 1 | | Miskolc-Diosgyor | 26 Aug 84 |
| 78.74 | Harri | Huhtala | FIN | 52 | 2 | PNG | Turku | 26 Jun 84 |
| 78.64 | Yuriy | Esayan | SU | 62 | 2 | | Yalta | 12 Oct 86 |
| 78.62 | Aleksey | Spiridonov | SU | 51 | 1 | vUK | Kiev | 22 May 76 |
| 78.62 | Sergey | Dvoretskiy | SU | 57 | 1 | | Gorkiy | 12 Aug 84 |
| 78.60 | Henryk | Krolak | POL | 60 | 1 | Kuso | Warszawa | 9 Jun 84 |
| 78.58 | Aleksandr | Kozlov | SU | 52 | 5 | | Sochi | 24 May 80 |
| 78.56 | Aleksandr | Buneyev | SU | 50 | 1 | | Togliatti | 28 Aug 82 |
| 78.54 | Vladimir | Gudilin | SU | 52 | 1 | | Rovno | 7 Sep 85 |
| (50) | | | | | | | | |

| Mark | Name | | Nat | Yr | Pos | Meet | Venue | | Date |
|------|------|--|-----|----|----|------|-------|--|------|
| 78.52 | Aleksey | Malyukov | SU | 1980 | | | | | |
| 78.50 | Walter | Ciofani | FRA | 1985 | | | | | |
| 78.46 | Plamen | Minev | BUL | 1985 | | | | | |
| 78.46 | Sergey | Dorozhon | SU | 1986 | | | | | |
| 78.34 | Ken | Flax | USA | 1986 | | | | | |
| 78.32 | Igor | Kucherenko | SU | 1986 | | | | | |
| 78.28 | Viktor | Bobryshev | SU | 1983 | | | | | |
| 78.18 | Heinz | Weis | FRG | 1985 | | | | | |
| 78.16 | Giampaolo | Urlando | ITA | 1984 | | | | | |
| 78.12 | Grigoriy | Vovk | SU | 1985 | | | | | |
| (60) | | | | | | | | | |
| 78.12 | Yevgeniy | Gribov | SU | 1985 | | | | | |
| 78.08 | Aleksandr | Puchkov | SU | 1986 | | | | | |
| 78.04 | Valeriy | Reshetnikov | SU | 1986 | | | | | |
| 78.02 | Vladimir | Kuprovskiy | SU | 1985 | | | | | |
| 77.94 | Orlando | Bianchini | ITA | 1984 | | | | | |
| 77.84 | Pavel | Repin | SU | 1981 | | | | | |
| 77.80 | Yuriy | Kashchenko | SU | 1983 | | | | | |
| 77.80 | Declan | Hegarty | IRL | 1985 | | | | | |
| 77.80 | Michael | Beierl | AUT | 1986 | | | | | |
| 77.76 | Tore | Gustafsson | SWE | 1986 | | | | | |
| (70) | | | | | | | | | |
| 77.70 | Oleg | Dyatlov | SU | 1985 | | | | | |
| 77.66 | Tibor | Gecsek | HUN | 1986 | | | | | |
| 77.64 | Dzhumber | Pkhakadze | SU | 1975 | | | | | |
| 77.60 | Vladimir | Lesovoy | SU | 1977 | | | | | |
| 77.58 | Valentin | Dmitrenko | SU | 1975 | | | | | |
| 77.56 | Yuriy | Pastukhov | SU | 1983 | | | | | |

| Mark | Name | | Nat | Yr |
|------|------|--|-----|----|
| 77.54 | Martin | Girvan | UK | 1984 |
| 77.50 | Nicolae | Bindar | RUM | 1985 |
| 77.48 | Giuliano | Zanello | ITA | 1986 |
| 77.48 | Norbert | Radefeld | FRG | 1986 |
| (80) | | | | |
| 77.42 | Anatoliy | Bondarchuk | SU | 1976 |
| 77.40 | Sergey | Abramov | SU | 1982 |
| 77.38 | Anatoliy | Prokopenko | SU | 1983 |
| 77.32 | Vyacheslav | Korovin | SU | 1984 |
| 77.30 | Dave | Smith | UK | 1985 |
| 77.20 | Bill | Green | USA | 1986 |
| 77.16 | Gennadiy | Volik | SU | 1983 |
| 77.12 | Vladimir | Dubinin | SU | 1983 |
| 77.12 | Maco | Gerloff | GDR | 1986 |
| 77.08 | Ireneusz | Golda | POL | 1983 |
| (90) | | | | |
| 77.02 | Matt | Mileham | UK | 1984 |
| 77.00 | Aleksandr | Gurmazhenko | SU | 1982 |
| 77.00 | Nikolay | Pichugin | SU | 1984 |
| 76.96 | Sergey | Vashchenko | SU | 1984 |
| 76.96 | Aleksandr | Seleznyev | SU | 1985 |
| 76.94 | Sergey | Ishchenko | SU | 1983 |
| 76.94 | Vladimir | Nagurniy | SU | 1984 |
| 76.88 | Leszek | Woderski | POL | 1984 |
| 76.80 | Tibor | Tanczi | HUN | 1984 |
| 76.70 | Marc | Odenthal | FRG | 1985 |
| (100) | | | | |

Extra trial

| 81.04 | Mariusz | Tomaszewski | POL | 56 | - | | Zabrze | 1 Jul 8 |
|-------|---------|-------------|-----|----|----|--|--------|---------|

Chain exceeding maximum legal length

| 81.12 | Grigoriy | Shevtsov | SU | 58 | 1 | | Sochi | 12 May 8 |
|-------|----------|----------|----|----|----|--|-------|----------|

Ancillary marks

| | | | | | | | | |
|--|--|--|--|--|--|--|--|--|
| Sedykh | 86.68 | 30 Aug 86 | Sedykh | 84.58 | 14 Sep 84 | Sedykh | 83.82 | 7 Jul 86 |
| Sedykh | 86.62 | 30 Aug 86 | Litvinov | 84.58 | 11 Jul 86 | Sedykh | 83.80 | 7 Jul 86 |
| Sedykh | 86.00 | 3 Jul 84 | Sedykh | 84.48 | 14 Sep 84 | Litvinov | 83.74 | 3 Jul 84 |
| Sedykh | 86.00 | 22 Jun 86 | Sedykh | 84.44 | 17 Aug 84 | Litvinov | 83.72 | 9 Jul 86 |
| Sedykh | 85.82 | 22 Jun 86 | Sedykh | 84.34 | 9 Jul 86 | Tamm | 83.68 | 9 Sep 84 |
| Sedykh | 85.52 | 13 Jul 84 | Sedykh | 84.18 | 3 Jul 84 | Litvinov | 83.66 | 11 Jul 86 |
| Sedykh | 85.46 | 30 Aug 86 | Sedykh | 84.18 | 3 Jul 86 | Litvinov | 83.66 | 10 Sep 86 |
| Sedykh | 85.42 | 11 Aug 86 | Sedykh | 84.12 | 22 Jun 86 | Litvinov | 83.64 | 10 Sep 86 |
| Litvinov | 85.42 | 3 Jul 86 | Sedykh | 84.02 | 7 Jul 86 | Litvinov | 83.58 | 22 Jun 86 |
| Sedykh | 85.28 | 30 Aug 86 | Sedykh | 84.02 | 9 Jul 86 | Litvinov | 83.58 | 3 Jul 86 |
| Sedykh | 85.26 | 11 Aug 86 | Sedykh | 83.98 | 15 Jul 86 | Sedykh | 83.52 | 20 Aug 84 |
| Sedykh | 85.24 | 11 Aug 86 | Sedykh | 83.94 | 30 Aug 86 | Litvinov | 83.52 | 22 Jun 86 |
| Sedykh | 85.20 | 3 Jul 84 | Sedykh | 83.90 | 31 Aug 84 | Sedykh | 83.50 | 31 Aug 84 |
| Sedykh | 85.04 | 13 Jul 84 | Sedykh | 83.90 | 11 Aug 86 | Litvinov | 83.50 | 11 Jul 84 |
| Litvinov | 84.92 | 3 Jul 86 | Sedykh | 83.88 | 17 Aug 84 | Sedykh | 83.44 | 31 Aug 84 |
| Litvinov | 84.84 | 3 Jul 84 | Sedykh | 83.86 | 20 Aug 84 | Tamm | 83.42 | 4 Aug 8? |
| Sedykh | 84.84 | 17 Aug 84 | Sedykh | 83.86 | 15 Jul 86 | Tamm | 83.40 | 4 Aug 8? |
| Sedykh | 84.64 | 11 Aug 86 | Sedykh | 83.84 | 31 Aug 84 | | | |

# JAVELIN

No all-time list is published as 1986 was the first year of the new
specification javelin. Thus the 1986 yearlist can be used as the all-time
list. A 100-deep all-time list was published in last year's annual.

## DECATHLON

The list that follows is 50 deep. A 100-deep list was published last year.

| oints | Pos | Meet | Name | | Nat | Yr | Venue | | | Date |
|---|---|---|---|---|---|---|---|---|---|---|

**DECATHLON**

| 847 | 1 | OG | Daley | Thompson | UK | 58 | Los Angeles | | | 9 Aug 84 |
| | | | 10.44 | 8.01 | 15.72 | 2.03 | 46.97 | 14.33 | 46.56 | 5.00 | 65.24 | 4:35.00 |
| 832 | 1 | | Jürgen | Hingsen | FRG | 58 | Mannheim | | | 9 Jun 84 |
| | | | 10.70w | 7.76 | 16.42 | 2.07 | 48.05 | 14.07 | 49.36 | 4.90 | 59.86 | 4:19.75 |
| 825 | 1 | | | Hingsen | | | Bernhausen | | | 5 Jun 83 |
| | | | 10.92 | 7.74 | 15.94 | 2.15 | 47.89 | 14.10 | 46.80 | 4.70 | 67.26 | 4:19.74 |
| 811 | 1 | EC | | Thompson | | | Stuttgart | | | 28 Aug 86 |
| | | | 10.26 | 7.72 | 15.73 | 2.00 | 47.02 | 14.04 | 43.38 | 5.10 | 62.78 | 4:26.16 |
| 792 | 1 | OD | Uwe | Freimuth | GDR | 61 | Potsdam | | | 21 Jul 84 |
| | | | 11.06 | 7.79 | 16.30 | 2.03 | 48.43 | 14.66 | 46.58 | 5.15 | 72.42 | 4:25.19 |
| 774 | 1 | EC | | Thompson | | | Athinai | | | 8 Sep 82 |
| | | | 10.51 | 7.80 | 15.44 | 2.03 | 47.11 | 14.39 | 45.48 | 5.00 | 63.56 | 4:23.71 |
| 762 | 2 | | Siegfried | Wentz | FRG | 60 | Bernhausen | | | 5 Jun 83 |
| | | | 10.89 | 7.49 | 15.35 | 2.09 | 47.38 | 14.00 | 46.90 | 4.80 | 70.68 | 4:24.90 |
| 741 | 1 | | | Hingsen | | | Ulm | | | 15 Aug 82 |
| | | | 10.74w | 7.85 | 16.00 | 2.15 | 47.65 | 14.64 | 44.92 | 4.60 | 63.10 | 4:15.13 |
| 730 | 1 | | | Thompson | | | Götzis | | | 23 May 82 |
| | | | 10.50w | 7.95 | 15.31 | 2.08 | 46.86 | 14.31 | 44.34 | 4.90 | 60.52 | 4:30.55 |
| 730 | 2 | EC | | Hingsen | | | Stuttgart | | | 28 Aug 86 |
| | | | 10.87w | 7.89w | 16.46 | 2.12 | 48.79 | 14.52 | 48.42 | 4.60 | 64.38 | 4:21.61 |
| 714 | 1 | WC | | Thompson | | | Helsinki | | | 13 Aug 83 |
| | | | 10.60 | 7.88 | 15.35 | 2.03 | 48.12 | 14.37w | 44.46 | 5.10 | 65.24 | 4:29.72 |
| 709 | 1 | vGDR | Aleksandr | Apaychev | SU | 61 | Neubrandenburg | | | 3 Jun 84 |
| | | | 10.96 | 7.57 | 16.00 | 1.97 | 48.72 | 13.93 | 48.00 | 4.90 | 72.24 | 4:26.51 |
| 698 | 1 | NC | Grigoriy | Degtyaryev | SU | 58 | Kiev | | | 22 Jun 84 |
| | | | 10.87 | 7.42 | 16.03 | 2.10 | 49.75 | 14.53 | 51.20 | 4.90 | 67.08 | 4:23.09 |
| 695 | 2 | OG | | Hingsen | | | Los Angeles | | | 9 Aug 84 |
| | | | 10.91 | 7.80 | 15.87 | 2.12 | 47.69 | 14.29 | 50.82 | 4.50 | 60.44 | 4:22.60 |
| 676 | 3 | EC | | Wentz | | | Stuttgart | | | 28 Aug 86 |
| | | | 10.83 | 7.60 | 15.45 | 2.12 | 47.57 | 14.07 | 45.66 | 4.90 | 65.34 | 4:35.00 |
| 667 | 1 | | Guido | Kratschmer | FRG | 53 | Bernhausen | | | 14 Jun 80 |
| | | | 10.58w | 7.80 | 15.47 | 2.00 | 48.04 | 13.92 | 45.52 | 4.60 | 66.50 | 4:24.15 |
| 667 | 1 | vFRA | | Thompson | | | Arles | | | 18 May 86 |
| | | | 10.56 | 7.81 | 15.39 | 1.98 | 47.52 | 14.35 | 47.62 | 4.90 | 63.68 | 4:30.04 |
| 663 | 1 | CommG | | Thompson | | | Edinburgh | | | 28 Jul 86 |
| | | | 10.37 | 7.70w | 15.01 | 2.08 | 47.30 | 14.22 | 43.72 | 5.10 | 60.82 | 4:39.63 |
| 648 | 1 | | | Thompson | | | Götzis | | | 18 May 80 |
| | | | 10.55 | 7.72 | 14.46 | 2.11 | 48.04 | 14.37 | 42.98 | 4.90 | 65.38 | 4:25.49 |
| 634 | 1 | OG | Bruce | Jenner | USA | 49 | Montreal | | | 30 Jul 76 |
| | | | 10.94 | 7.22 | 15.35 | 2.03 | 47.51 | 14.84 | 50.04 | 4.80 | 68.52 | 4:12.61 |
| 617 | 1 | | | Degtyaryev | | | Götzis | | | 20 May 84 |
| | | | 11.05 | 7.73 | 16.14 | 2.08 | 49.76 | 14.45 | 49.40 | 4.90 | 60.70 | 4:20.49 |
| 616 | 2 | vSU | | Freimuth | | | Neubrandenburg | | | 3 Jun 84 |
| | | | 11.10 | 7.79 | 16.42 | 1.94 | 48.93 | 14.54 | 51.54 | 4.90 | 66.32 | 4:27.95 |
| 599 | 2 | WC | | Hingsen | | | Helsinki | | | 13 Aug 83 |
| | | | 10.95 | 7.75 | 15.66 | 2.00 | 48.08 | 14.36w | 43.30 | 4.90 | 67.42 | 4:21.59 |
| 597 | 1 | NC | | Freimuth | | | Potsdam | | | 6 May 84 |
| | | | 11.06 | 7.69 | 16.06 | 1.97 | 48.78 | 14.75 | 47.54 | 4.80 | 73.02 | 4:24.46 |
| 592 | 1 | | | Apaychev | | | Kiev | | | 6 May 84 |
| | | | 10.97 | 7.61 | 15.91 | 1.95 | 48.40 | 14.11 | 45.08 | 4.80 | 68.88 | 4:18.78 |
| 590 | 1 | | | Wentz | | | Bernhausen | | | 15 Jun 86 |
| | | | 10.97 | 7.17 | 16.03 | 2.06 | 48.09 | 14.11 | 48.16 | 4.90 | 67.42 | 4:32.25 |
| 580 | 1 | Spart | | Degtyaryev | | | Moskva | | | 19 Jun 83 |
| | | | 11.13 | 7.75 | 15.97 | 2.09 | 49.40 | 14.51 | 49.66 | 5.00 | 58.56 | 4:25.53 |
| 572 | 1 | Drz | | Degtyaryev | | | Moskva | | | 18 Aug 84 |
| | | | 10.99 | 7.58 | 15.54 | 2.09 | 50.29 | 14.60 | 49.20 | 5.10 | 63.20 | 4:27.14 |
| 559 | 1 | vSU | Torsten | Voss | GDR | 63 | Dresden | | | 7 Jul 85 |
| | | | 10.66 | 8.00 | 14.73 | 2.06 | 48.28 | 14.50w | 43.28 | 4.90 | 61.28 | 4:28.80 |

| Points | Pos | Meet | Name | | Nat | Yr | Venue | | | Date |
|---|---|---|---|---|---|---|---|---|---|---|

8551 1 EP     Freimuth     Sofia     11 Sep 8
  11.24   7.37   16.00   2.01   48.17   14.54   48.16   4.90   70.26   4:27.04
  (30/9)

8547 2 NC   Igor     Sobolevskiy   SU 62   Kiev     22 Jun 8
  10.64   7.71   15.93   2.01   48.24   14.82   50.54   4.40   67.40   4:32.84
  (10)

8534 1   Siegfried   Stark    GDR 55   Halle     4 May 8
  11.10w 7.64   15.81   2.03   49.53   14.86w   47.20   5.00   68.70   4:27.70

8519 3 NC   Yuriy     Kutsenko    SU 52   Kiev     22 Jun 8
  11.07   7.54   15.11   2.13   49.07   14.94   50.38   4.60   61.70   4:12.68

8491 2   Aleksandr   Nevskiy    SU 58   Götzis     20 May 8
  10.97   7.24   15.04   2.08   48.44   14.67   46.06   4.70   69.56   4:19.62

8485 1 NC   Konstantin   Akhapkin   SU 56   Moskva     2 Aug 8
  11.10   7.72   15.25   2.02   49.14   14.38   45.68   4.90   62.42   4:19.60

8466 1 OG   Nikolay    Avilov     SU 48   München     8 Sep 7
  11.00   7.68   14.36   2.12   48.45   14.31   46.98   4.55   61.66   4:22.82

8417 4 NC   Sergey    Zhelanov    SU 57   Kiev     22 Jun 8
  11.04   7.50   14.31   2.13   48.94   14.40   43.44   5.00   65.90   4:37.24

8400 1 NC   Aleksandr   Grebenyuk   SU 51   Riga     3 Jul 7
  10.7   7.12   15.50   2.02   48.8   14.3   45.52   4.70   71.52   4:27.3

8397 1 vSU   Fred     Dixon     USA 49   Bloomington   14 Aug 7
  10.85   7.44   15.20   2.04   48.54   14.94   47.14   4.60   67.88   4:30.21

8381w 1 TAC   John     Sayre     USA 61   Indianapolis   18 Jun 8
  10.86W 7.41w   14.22   2.00   49.98   14.84W   46.08   5.30   67.68   4:37.07

8366 1   Vadim     Podmaryov    SU 58   Tashkent     26 May 8
  11.09   7.56   15.28   2.08   50.00   14.89   48.58   4.60   67.46   4:32.31
  (20)

8356 5 NC   Viktor    Gruzenkin    SU 51   Kiev     22 Jun 8
  10.92   7.67   15.98   2.07   50.06   14.65   46.70   4.60   65.74   4:43.00

8334 1 EP   Rainer    Pottel     GDR 53   Birmingham   30 Aug 8
  11.06   7.68   14.38   2.01   48.35   14.57   39.52   4.80   67.46   4:22.67

8334 1 NC   Stefan    Niklaus    SWZ 58   Lausanne     3 Jul 8
  10.82   7.32   15.44   2.01   47.47   14.79   48.68   4.40   67.84   4:41.29

8326 4   Andreas    Rizzi     FRG 59   Bernhausen   5 Jun 8
  10.52   7.71   14.78   2.00   46.82   14.91   43.62   4.70   50.92   4:21.04

8322 1   Mike     Ramos     USA 62   Los Angeles   21 May 8
  10.77   7.39   14.67   2.16   50.16   14.98   49.04   4.80   63.52   4:48.06

8316w 1   Dave     Steen     CAN 59   University Park   20 Apr 8
  10.8W   7.59W   13.01   2.01   48.7   15.0   43.68   5.30   64.98   4:24.6

8315 1 Spart Mikhail   Medved     SU 64   Alma-Ata     19 Sep 8
  11.13   7.50   16.06   2.11   49.98   14.47   43.78   4.90   64.46   4:48.18

8309 1   Bill     Toomey     USA 39   Los Angeles   11 Dec 8
  10.3   7.76   14.38   1.93   47.1   14.3   46.49   4.27   65.74   4:39.4

8306 1 NC   William    Motti     FRA 64   Athis-Mons   7 Jul 8
  11.03   7.63   15.11   2.16   48.43   14.75   45.98   4.40   63.38   4:43.06

8304w 1 NCAA Tito   Steiner    ARG 52   Baton Rouge   3 Jun 8
  11.19W 7.37   15.20   2.09   49.85   14.97   45.28   4.70   70.28   4:31.98
  (30)

8302 1   Tim     Bright     USA 60   Fresno     26 Mar 8
  10.94   7.15   14.38   2.04   48.72   14.0   43.02   5.51   57.86   4:42.28

8288 2 NC   Valeriy    Kachanov    SU 54   Moskva     21 Jun 8
  11.08   7.54   14.53   2.08   48.70   14.61   46.10   4.50   58.10   4:17.4

8282 1 vGDR Aleksandr   Shablenko   SU 57   Potsdam     1 Jun 8
  10.95   7.25   15.23   2.03   48.85   14.25   47.14   5.00   50.64   4:25.9

8267 1 MSR   Mark     Anderson    USA 58   Walnut     22 Apr 8
  11.11   7.03   14.86   2.10   49.21   15.77   42.50   4.70   76.42   4:21.7

8261 1   Steffen    Grummt    GDR 59   Halle     20 Jun 8
  10.99w 7.62   16.32   1.91   49.16   14.38w   48.76   4.40   63.56   4:24.6

8255 4   Jens     Schulze    FRG 56   Mannheim     9 Jun 8
  10.56w 7.33   15.00   2.01   48.58   14.44w   45.32   4.60   53.70   4:22.95

| ints | Pos | Meet | Name | | Nat | Yr | Venue | | | Date |
|------|-----|------|------|---|-----|-----|-------|---|---|------|
| 248 | 1 | | Bob | Coffman | USA | 51 | Quebec City | | | 12 Aug 79 |
| | | | 10.71 | 7.37 | 15.92 | 1.90 | 48.85 | 13.91 | 49.52 | 4.50 | 56.36 | 4:36.5 |
| 235 | 2 | NC | Jörg-Peter | Schäperkötter | GDR | 58 | Neubrandenburg | | | 22 May 83 |
| | | | 10.93 | 7.62 | 15.46 | 2.03 | 47.74 | 14.58 | 49.72 | 4.40 | 47.62 | 4:25.73 |
| 234 | 1 | | Kurt | Bendlin | FRG | 43 | Heidelberg | | | 14 May 67 |
| | | | 10.6 | 7.55 | 14.50 | 1.84 | 47.9 | 14.8 | 46.31 | 4.10 | 74.85 | 4:19.4 |
| 232 | 1 | | Sven | Reintak | SU | 63 | Tartu | | | 18 May 86 |
| | | | 10.9 | 7.20 | 14.82 | 2.04 | 50.2 | 14.4 | 44.64 | 5.10 | 61.36* | 4:26.2 |
| | | | (40) | | | | | | | | |
| 230 | 1 | EC | Ryszard | Skowronek | POL | 49 | Roma | | | 7 Sep 74 |
| | | | 10.97 | 7.49 | 13.10 | 1.95 | 47.90 | 14.79 | 43.26 | 5.10 | 64.14 | 4:30.9 |
| 227 | 2 | Spart | Andrey | Fomochkin | SU | 63 | Tashkent | | | 19 Sep 86 |
| | | | 10.71 | 7.48 | 14.27 | 1.99 | 46.74 | 14.43 | 43.46 | 4.60 | 51.52 | 4:20.97 |
| 224 | 1 | | Georg | Werthner | AUT | 56 | Schielleiten | | | 8 Aug 82 |
| | | | 11.12 | 7.13 | 14.84 | 2.07 | 49.68 | 14.89 | 40.46 | 4.70 | 68.86 | 4:15.89 |
| 224 | 1 | | Igor | Kolovanov | SU | 58 | Kiev | | | 12 May 83 |
| | | | 10.9 | 7.53 | 14.48 | 2.07 | 49.9 | 14.4 | 44.24 | 4.80 | 61.70 | 4:28.3 |
| 19 | 2 | | Josef | Zeilbauer | AUT | 52 | Götzis | | | 16 May 76 |
| | | | 10.9 | 7.21 | 14.68 | 2.10 | 49.4 | 14.2 | 44.62 | 4.70 | 64.04 | 4:32.6 |
| 17 | 4 | OG | Raimo | Pihl | SWE | 49 | Montréal | | | 30 Jul 76 |
| | | | 10.93 | 6.99 | 15.55 | 2.00 | 47.97 | 15.81 | 44.30 | 4.40 | 77.34 | 4:28.76 |
| 17 | 2 | | Sergey | Popov | SU | 57 | Kiev | | | 6 May 84 |
| | | | 11.50 | 7.27 | 14.64 | 2.01 | 50.30 | 15.12 | 49.60 | 4.80 | 66.78 | 4:19.00 |
| 14 | 1 | | Pavel | Tarnovetskiy | SU | 61 | Sochi | | | 25 May 86 |
| | | | 11.14 | 7.35 | 14.72 | 2.08 | 49.61 | 14.82 | 46.62 | 5.00 | 53.10 | 4:23.57 |
| 12 | 1 | | Mikhail | Romanyuk | SU | 62 | Kiev | | | 11 Aug 84 |
| | | | 10.8 | 7.29 | 14.24 | 1.80 | 48.0 | 14.3 | 46.52 | 4.80 | 63.50 | 4:12.8 |
| 11w | 1 | EP-B | Christian | Plaziat | FRA | 63 | Arles | | | 8 Sep 85 |
| | | | 10.78W | 7.17w | 15.02 | 2.16 | 50.95 | 15.03w | 46.88 | 4.80 | 59.90 | 4:37.71 |
| | | | (50) | | | | | | | | | |

cathlon marks are not allowed as records if the wind-assistance for 100m,
Omh or LJ is above 4.0 metres per second. Such marks are indicated with w. For
dividual events: w wind 2.1 to 4.0 m/s, W wind in excess of 4 m/s.
tes: Dates given are those of second day of competition. All pre-1986 marks
nieved with old javelin.

## 400 METRES RELAY

| 37.83 | USA | | 1 | OG | Los Angeles | 11 Aug 84 |
|-------|-----|---|---|-----|-------------|-----------|
| (Graddy, | R.Brown, | C.Smith, | Lewis) | | | |
| 37.86 | USA | | 1 | WC | Helsinki | 10 Aug 83 |
| (E.King, | Gault, | C.Smith, | Lewis) | | | |
| 37.98 | USA | | 1 | GWG | Moskva | 9 Jul 86 |
| (McRae, | Heard, | Glance, | Lewis) | | | |
| 38.03 | USA | | 1 | WP | Düsseldorf | 3 Sep 77 |
| (Collins, | Riddick, | Wiley, | S.Williams) | | | |
| 38.10 | USA | | 1 | WP | Canberra | 5 Oct 85 |
| (Glance, | Baptiste, | C.Smith, | Evans) | | | |
| 38.13 | USA | | 1 | WK | Zürich | 18 Aug 82 |
| (Lattany, | Floyd, | C.Smith, | Lewis) | | | |
| 38.19 | USA | | 1 | OG | München | 10 Sep 72 |
| (Black, | R.Taylor, | Tinker, | Hart) | | | |
| 38.19 | SU | | 2 | GWG | Moskva | 9 Jul 86 |
| (Yevgenyev, | Yushmanov, | Muravyev, | Bryzgin) | | | |
| 38.22 | USA | | 1 | vGDR | Karl-Marx-Stadt | 9 Jul 82 |
| (T.Wright, | M.Miller, | Cook, | C.Smith) | | | |
| 38.24 | USA | | 1 | OG | Ciudad México | 20 Oct 68 |
| (Greene, | Pender, | R.R.Smith, | Hines) | | | |

| Mark | Nat | Pos | Meet | Venue | Date |
|---|---|---|---|---|---|
| 38.24 | USA | 1 | ISTAF | Berlin | 20 Aug 82 |
| (Lattany, Floyd, C.Smith, Lewis) | | | | | |
| 38.26 | SU | 1 | OG | Moskva | 1 Aug 80 |
| (Muravyev, Sidorov, Aksinin, Prokofyev) | | | | | |
| 38.27 | USA - USOC South | 1 | USOF | Indianapolis | 24 Jul 82 |
| (M.Miller, Lewis, C.Smith, Floyd) | | | | | |
| 38.28 | SU | 1 | EP | Moskva | 17 Aug 85 |
| (Shlyapnikov, Semenov, Yevgenyev, Muravyev) | | | | | |
| 38.28 | USA | 1 | vSU, JAP | Tokyo | 21 Sep 85 |
| (Glance, Baptiste, C.Smith, Lewis) | | | | | |
| 38.29 | GDR | 2 | vUSA | Karl-Marx-Stadt | 9 Jul 82 |
| (Schröder, Kübeck, Prenzler, Emmelmann) | | | | | |
| 38.29 | SU | 1 | EC | Stuttgart | 31 Aug 86 |
| (Yevgenyev, Yushmanov, Muravyev, Bryzgin) | | | | | |
| A38.30 | USA - USOC South | 1 | USOF | Air Force Acad. | 30 Jul 79 |
| (Roberson, Glance, Collins, Lattany) | | | | | |
| 38.30 | GDR | 1 | OD | Berlin | 8 Jun 83 |
| (Schröder, Bringmann, Prenzler, Emmelmann) | | | | | |
| A38.31 | USA | 1 | PAG | Ciudad México | 20 Oct 75 |
| (C.Edwards, L.Brown, Merrick, Collins) | | | | | |
| 38.31 | AMERICAS | 2 | WP | Canberra | 5 Oct 85 |
| (D.Williams/CAN, Simon/CUB, Ro.da Silva/BRA, Johnson/CAN) | | | | | |
| 38.32 | SU | 1 | Drz | Moskva | 17 Aug 84 |
| (Yevgenyev, A.Fedoriv, Muravyev, Sokolov) | | | | | |
| 38.33 | USA | 1 | OG | Montreal | 31 Jul 76 |
| (Glance, J.Jones, Hampton, Riddick) | | | | | |
| 38.33 | POL | 2 | OG | Moskva | 1 Aug 80 |
| (Zwolinski, Licznerski, Dunecki, Woronin) | | | | | |
| 38.35 | SU | 3 | WP | Canberra | 5 Oct 85 |
| (Yushmanov, Semenov, Yevgenyev, Muravyev) | | | | | |
| 38.36 | SU | 1 | vGDR | Tallinn | 21 Jun 86 |
| (Yevgenyev, Yushmanov, Muravyev, Bryzgin) | | | | | |
| 38.37 | ITA | 2 | WC | Helsinki | 10 Aug 83 |
| (Tilli, Simionato, Pavoni, Mennea) | | | | | |
| A38.39 | JAM | 1s1 | OG | Ciudad México | 19 Oct 68 |
| (Stewart, Fray, Forbes, L.Miller) | | | | | |
| 38.39 | GDR | 4 | WP | Canberra | 5 Oct 85 |
| (Trüppel, Bringmann, Heimrath, Emmelmann) | | | | | |
| A38.40 | CUB | 2 | OG | Ciudad México | 20 Oct 68 |
| (Ramirez, Morales, Montes, Figuerola) | | | | | |
| (30/7) | | | | | |
| A38.43 | FRA | 3 | OG | Ciudad México | 20 Oct 68 |
| (Fenouil, Delecour, Piquemal, Bambuck) | | | | | |
| A38.43 | CAN | 1 | | Colorado Spr. | 19 Jul 8. |
| (Johnson, Sharpe, D.Williams, S.Hinds) | | | | | |
| 38.56 | FRG | 5 | WC | Helsinki | 10 Aug 8. |
| (Bastians, Haas, Evers, A.Rizzi) | | | | | |
| 38.62 | UK | 4 | OG | Moskva | 1 Aug 8. |
| (McFarlane, Wells, Sharp, McMaster) | | | | | |
| A38.73 | IvC | 2 | WUG | Ciudad México | 13 Sep 7. |
| (Ouré, Meité, Nogboum, Kablan) | | | | | |
| 38.82 | CS | 4 | OG | München | 10 Sep 7. |
| (Matousek, Demeć, Kynos, Bohman) | | | | | |
| 38.87 | HUN | 1 | | Budapest | 23 Jul 8. |
| (Kiss, Nagy, Babály, Tatár) | | | | | |
| A38.97 | TRI | 3h1 | OG | Ciudad México | 19 Oct 6. |
| (Fabien, Short, Archer, Roberts) | | | | | |
| 38.98 | NIG | 5s2 | OG | Los Angeles | 11 Aug 8. |
| (Adeyanju, Ikpoto, Oyeledun, Imoh) | | | | | |
| 38.99 | BUL | 5 | OG | Moskva | 1 Aug 8. |
| (Pavlov, Ivanov, Karaniotov, Petrov) | | | | | |

| Mark | Nat | Pos | Meet | Venue | Date |
|------|-----|-----|------|-------|------|
| A39.02 | BRA | 1 | | Ciudad México | 4 Sep 79 |
| | (de Castro, Rocha dos Santos, Pegado, de Araujo) | | | | |
| 39.17 | CHN | 1 | AsG | Seoul | 5 Oct 86 |
| | (Cai Jian Ming, Li Feng, Yu Zhuang Hui, Zheng Chen) | | | | |
| 39.19 | SWZ | 1 | | Bern (Wa.) | 5 Aug 78 |
| | (Fähndrich, U.Gisler, Muster, Ziegler) | | | | |
| 39.24 | GHA | 1 | AfrG | Algiers | 27 Jul 78 |
| | (Enchill, Karikari, Lomotey, Obeng) | | | | |
| 39.30 | FIN | 5s2 | OG | München | 9 Sep 72 |
| | (Rajamaki, Vilen, Gustafsson, Juhola) | | | | |
| 39.31 | AUS | 1 | CommG | Christchurch | 2 Feb 74 |
| | (G.Lewis, D'Arcy, Ratcliffe, Haskell) | | | | |
| 39.31 | JAP | 2 | AsG | Seoul | 5 Oct 86 |
| | (Arikawa, Miyazaki, Koike, Fuwa) | | | | |
| A39.45 | BAH | 4h1 | OG | Ciudad México | 19 Oct 68 |
| | (Wisdom, Robinson, Nottage, Johnson) | | | | |
| 39.53 | VEN | 6 | OG | Tokyo | 21 Oct 64 |
| | (Herrera, Murad, Romero, Fusil) | | | | |
| A39.54 | CON | 1s1 | WUG | Ciudad México | 12 Sep 79 |
| | (Ntsana, Kanza, Nkounkou, Pauletto) | | | | |
| 39.55 | SPA | 1 | | Zürich | 10 Jul 76 |
| | (Paraiso, Martinez, Garcia Lopez, Sarria) | | | | |
| 39.56 | DOM | 3 | CAG | Santiago (Dom) | 3 Jul 86 |
| | (Mendez, Suero, Reynoso, Nunez) | | | | |
| 39.59 | SWE | 1 | vFIN | Helsinki | 17 Aug 74 |
| | (Trulsson, Sjöberg, Grama, Garpenborg) | | | | |
| A39.59 | GUY | 6 | PAG | Ciudad México | 20 Oct 75 |
| | (Schultz, Wilson, Callison, Gilkes) | | | | |

MEN All-time

# 1600 METRES RELAY

| Mark | Nat | Pos | Meet | Venue | Date |
|------|-----|-----|------|-------|------|
| A2:56.16 | USA | 1 | OG | Ciudad México | 20 Oct 68 |
| | (Matthews 45.0, Freeman 43.2, James 43.9, Evans 44.1) | | | | |
| 2:57.91 | USA | 1 | OG | Los Angeles | 11 Aug 84 |
| | (Nix 45.59, Armstead 43.97, Babers 43.75, McKay 44.60) | | | | |
| 2:58.65 | USA | 1 | OG | Montréal | 31 Jul 76 |
| | (Frazier 45.3, B.Brown 44.62, Newhouse 43.8, Parks 45.00) | | | | |
| 2:59.12 | USA | 1 | WP | Roma | 6 Sep 81 |
| | (McCoy 45.20, Wiley 44.41, W.Smith 44.58, Darden 44.93) | | | | |
| 2:59.13 | UK | 2 | OG | Los Angeles | 11 Aug 84 |
| | (Akabusi 45.87, Cook 44.74, T.Bennett 44.17, P.Brown 44.35) | | | | |
| 2:59.32 | NIG | 3 | OG | Los Angeles | 11 Aug 84 |
| | (Uti 45.34, Ugbisie 44.48, Peters 44.94, Egbunike 44.56) | | | | |
| 2:59.52 | USA | 1h1 | OG | Montréal | 30 Jul 76 |
| | (Frazier 45.5, B.Brown 45.3, Newhouse 43.63, Parks 45.1) | | | | |
| 2:59.6m | USA | 1 | | Los Angeles | 24 Jul 66 |
| | (Frey 46.3, Evans 44.5, T.Smith 43.8, T.Lewis 45.0) | | | | |
| A2:59.64 | KEN | 2 | OG | Ciudad México | 20 Oct 68 |
| | (Asati 44.6, Nyamau 45.5, Bon 45.1, Rudisha 44.4) | | | | |
| 2:59.70 | AUS | 4 | OG | Los Angeles | 11 Aug 84 |
| | (Frayne 45.38, Clark 43.86, Minihan 45.07, Mitchell 45.39) | | | | |
| | (10) | | | | |
| 2:59.83 | KEN | 1 | OG | München | 10 Sep 72 |
| | (Asati 45.3, Nyamau 45.8, Ouko 45.2, Sang 43.5) | | | | |
| 2:59.85 | UK | 1 | EC | Stuttgart | 31 Aug 86 |
| | (Redmond 45.4, Akabusi 45.4, Whittle 45.2, Black 43.9) | | | | |
| 2:59.86 | GDR | 1 | vSU | Erfurt | 23 Jun 85 |
| | (Möller 45.8, Schersing 44.8, Carlowitz 45.3, Schönlebe 44.1) | | | | |
| A2:59.91 | USA - USOC South | 1 | USOF | Air Force Academy | 3 Jul 83 |
| | (L.Brown, Brooks, Rolle, McCoy) | | | | |

| Mark | Nat | Pos | Meet | Venue | Date |
|------|-----|-----|------|-------|------|
| 3:00.04 | USA - USOC North | 1 | USOF | Baton Rouge | 28 Jul 85 |
| | (Franks 45.0, Armstead 45.2, Dixson 44.8, Harris 45.1) | | | | |
| 3:00.07 | GDR | 1 | | Erfurt | 3 Jun 84 |
| | (Lieske, Schersing, Carlowitz, Schönlebe) | | | | |
| 3:00.11 | USA | 1 | | Berkeley | 14 Jul 84 |
| | (W.Smith, Armstead, Babers, McCoy) | | | | |
| 3:00.16 | SU | 1 | Drz | Moskva | 18 Aug 84 |
| | (Lovachov, Lomtyev, Kurochkin, Markin 43.9) | | | | |
| 3:00.17 | FRG | 2 | EC | Stuttgart | 31 Aug 86 |
| | (Just 46.1, Itt 45.0, Schmid 44.5, Lübke 44.6) | | | | |
| A3:00.18 | USA - USOF North | 2 | USOF | Air Force Academy | 3 Jul 83 |
| | (Wiley, S.Davis, Bradley, Babers) | | | | |
| | (20) | | | | |
| 3:00.19 | USA | 1sl | OG | Los Angeles | 10 Aug 84 |
| | (Nix 45.93, McCoy 44.65, W.Smith 44.81, McKay 44.80) | | | | |
| 3:00.27 | GDR | 1 | | Dresden | 27 Jul 84 |
| | (Niestadt, Schersing, Schönlebe, Carlowitz) | | | | |
| 3:00.33 | FRG | 1 | EP | Moskva | 18 Aug 85 |
| | (Skamrahl 45.7, Just 45.0, Schmid 45.1, Lübke 44.6) | | | | |
| 3:00.42 | USA - USOF South | 2 | USOF | Baton Rouge | 28 Jul 85 |
| | (Rowe 45.7, Caldwell 45.0, Robinzine 44.7, Haley 45.1) | | | | |
| 3:00.46 | UK | 2 | OG | München | 10 Sep 72 |
| | (Reynolds 46.3, Pascoe 45.1, Hemery 45.0, Jenkins 44.1) | | | | |
| 3:00.47 | USA | 1 | PAG | Caracas | 28 Aug 83 |
| | (Babers 45.2, Bradley 45.7, Rolle 44.6, Carey 45.0) | | | | |
| 3:00.47 | GDR | 2 | Drz | Moskva | 18 Aug 84 |
| | (Niestadt, Schersing, Schönlebe, Carlowitz) | | | | |
| 3:00.47 | SU | 3 | EC | Stuttgart | 31 Aug 86 |
| | (Prosin 45.8, Krylov 44.6, Kornilov 45.5, Kurochkin 44.6) | | | | |
| 3:00.48 | GDR | 2 | EP | Moskva | 18 Aug 85 |
| | (Lieske, Carlowitz, Schersing, Schönlebe 44.7) | | | | |
| 3:00.50 | FRG | 1 | EC | Athinai | 11 Sep 82 |
| | (Skamrahl 45.9, Schmid 44.9, Giessing 45.6, Weber 44.2) | | | | |
| | (30/8) | | | | |
| A3:00.58 | POL | 4 | OG | Ciudad México | 20 Oct 68 |
| | (Gredziński 46.8, Balachowski 44.7, Werner 44.5, Badeński 44.5) | | | | |
| 3:00.65 | FRA | 3 | OG | München | 10 Sep 72 |
| | (Bertould 46.2, Velasquez 45.0, Kerbiriou 45.2, Carette 44.3) | | | | |
| 3:01.12 | FIN | 6 | OG | München | 10 Sep 72 |
| | (Lonnqvist 46.7, Salin 45.1, Karttunen 44.8, Kukkoaho 44.5) | | | | |
| 3:01.37 | ITA | 4 | EC | Stuttgart | 31 Aug 86 |
| | (Bongiorni 46.2, Zuliani 45.0, Petrella 45.3, Ribaud 44.9) | | | | |
| 3:01.60 | BAR | 6 | OG | Los Angeles | 11 Aug 84 |
| | (Louis 46.67, Peltier 44.97, Edwards 45.04, Forde 44.92) | | | | |
| 3:01.7 | TRI | 3 | OG | Tokyo | 21 Oct 64 |
| | (Skinner 46.0, Bernard 45.3, Roberts 45.4, Mottley 45.0) | | | | |
| 3:02.09 | UGA | 7 | OG | Los Angeles | 11 Aug 84 |
| | (Govile 46.72, Kyeswa 44.60, Rwamu 46.40, Okot 44.37) | | | | |
| 3:02.20 | CUB | 1 | WUG | Kobe | 4 Sep 85 |
| | (Martinez, Peñalver, Ramos, Hernández) | | | | |
| 3:02.3 | JAM | 4 | OG | Tokyo | 21 Oct 64 |
| | (Kahn 46.1, Mal Spence 45.4, Mel Spence 45.2, Kerr 45.6) | | | | |
| 3:02.33 | JAP | 1 | AsG | Seoul | 5 Oct 86 |
| | (Konakatoni, Yamauchi, Kawasumi, Takano) | | | | |
| 3:02.57 | SWE | 7 | OG | München | 10 Sep 72 |
| | (Carlgren 46.0, Faager 45.5, Öhlman 45.3, Rönner 45.8) | | | | |
| 3:02.64 | CAN | 4 | OG | Montréal | 31 Jul 76 |
| | (Seale 47.0, Domansky 45.3, Hope 45.5, Saunders 44.8) | | | | |
| 3:02.79 | BRA | | PAG | Caracas | 28 Aug 83 |
| | (E.da Silva, Barbosa, Guimaraes, Gerson Souza) | | | | |

| Mark | Nat | Pos | Meet | Venue | Date |
|------|-----|-----|------|-------|------|
| 3:02.82 | CS | 5 | EC | Athinai | 11 Sep 82 |
| (Brecka 46.9, Malovec 44.9, Zahorak 45.4, Sajdok 45.6) | | | | | |
| A3:03.18 | HOL | 2 | WUG | Ciudad Mexico | 13 Sep 79 |
| (Pont, Gijsbers, Klarenbeek, Schulting) | | | | | |
| 3:03.36 | RSA | 1 | | Stellenbosch | 25 Apr 83 |
| (Reinach, Myburgh, Kotze, J.Oosthuizen) | | | | | |
| 3:03.50 | IVC | 3h3 | OG | Los Angeles | 10 Aug 84 |
| (Kablam 46.5, Nogboum 46.3, Melejde 46.3, Tiacoh 44.4) | | | | | |
| 3:03.68 | BEL | 2 | EP/s | Lille | 5 Jul 81 |
| (DeLeeuw, Roelandt, Van den Berghe, Brijdenbach) | | | | | |
| 3:04.04 | SPA | 1 | EP-B | Budapest | 11 Aug 85 |
| (Prado, Sanchez, Heras, Alonso) | | | | | |
| 3:04.29 | SWZ | 4 | EC | Praha | 3 Sep 78 |
| (Strittmatter, Haas, Vost, R.Gisler 45.56) | | | | | |
| 3:04.70 | HUN | 1 | vAUT, GRE | Linz | 29 Jun 86 |
| (Menczer, Szabo, I.Takács, Martina) | | | | | |
| 3:04.76 | SEN | 1 | AfrC | Rabat | 15 Jul 84 |
| (Diallo, Niang, Fall, Dia Ba 44.8) | | | | | |
| 3:04.77 | YUG | 2 | EP-B | Budapest | 11 Aug 85 |
| (Branković, Popović, Magov, Knapić) | | | | | |

# 20 000 METRES WALK (Track)

| Mark | Name | Nat | Pos | Meet | Venue | Date |
|------|------|-----|-----|------|-------|------|
| 1:18:40.0 | Ernesto Canto | MEX 59 | 1 | SGP | Fana | 5 May 84 |
| 1:20:06.8 | Daniel Bautista | MEX 52 | 1 | | Montreal | 17 Oct 79 |
| 1:20:36.7 | Erling Andersen | NOR 60 | 2 | SGP | Fana | 5 May 84 |
| 1:20:37.8 | Valdas Kazlauskas | SU 58 | 1 | | Moskva | 16 Sep 83 |
| 1:20:41.6 | Yevgeniy Misyulya | SU 64 | 1 | SGP | Fana | 26 Apr 86 |
| 1:20:47.0 | Bautista | | 1 | | Formia | 13 Apr 80 |
| 1:20:54.9 | Ronald Weigel | GDR 59 | 1 | | East Berlin | 27 Mar 83 |
| 1:20:57.0 | Andersen | | 1 | | Trois-Rivières | 24 Sep 80 |
| 1:20:58.6 | Domingo Colin | MEX 52 | 1 | SGP | Fana | 26 May 79 |
| 1:21:05.8 | Bautista | | 1 | SGP | Fana | 3 May 80 |
| 1:21:08.0 | Andersen | | 2 | SGP | Fana | 26 Apr 86 |
| 1:21:13.2 | Weigel | | 1 | | Potsdam | 24 Mar 84 |
| 1:21:21.3 | Roland Wieser | GDR 56 | 1 | | Leipzig | 23 Jun 79 |
| 1:21:23.5 | Pavol Blažek | CS 58 | 3 | SGP | Fana | 5 May 84 |
| 1:21:24.5 | Feliz Gómez | MEX 55 | 2 | | Montréal | 17 Oct 79 |
| 1:21:25.0 | Blažek | | 3 | SGP | Fana | 26 Apr 86 |
| 1:21:30 | Pyotr Pochenchuk | SU 54 | 1 | | Leningrad | 16 Aug 80 |
| 1:21:39.2 | Jozef Pribilinec | CS 60 | 2 | SGP | Fana | 3 May 80 |
| 1:21:47 | Mykola Vynnychenko | SU 58 | 1 | | Donetsk | 6 Sep 80 |
| 1:21:47.8 | Maurizio Damilano | ITA 57 | 2 | | Formia | 13 Apr 80 |
| (20/14) | | | | | | |
| 1:21:48.8 | Raúl González | MEX 52 | 4 | SGP | Fana | 5 May 84 |
| 1:21:56.0 | Yevgeniy Yevsyukov | SU 50 | 2 | | Donetsk | 6 Sep 80 |
| 1:22:13.1 | Werner Heyer | GDR 56 | 1 | | East Berlin | 29 Mar 80 |
| 1:22:14.0 | Gérard Lelièvre | FRA 49 | 1 | | Epinay/Seine | 15 Apr 84 |
| 1:22:23 | Anatoliy Solomin | SU 52 | 3 | | Donetsk | 6 Sep 80 |
| 1:22:37.1 | Valeriy Suntsov | SU 55 | 4 | SGP | Fana | 26 Apr 86 |
| (20) | | | | | | |
| 1:22:40.8 | Boris Yakovlev | SU 45 | 4 | SGP | Fana | 26 May 79 |
| 1:22:42.8 | Andrey Perlov | SU 61 | 1 | | Novosibirsk | 28 Aug 82 |
| 1:22:49.4 | Bo Gustafsson | SWE 54 | 2 | SGP | Fana | 15 May 82 |
| 1:22:50.0 | Viktor Mostovik | SU 63 | 2 | | Moskva | 16 Sep 83 |
| 1:22:53 | Nikolay Matveyev | SU 55 | 2 | | Leningrad | 16 Aug 80 |
| 1:23:00 | Ivan Sankovskiy | SU 58 | 5 | | Donetsk | 6 Sep 80 |

| Mark | Name | Nat | Yr | Pos | Meet | Venue | Date |
|------|------|-----|----|----|------|-------|------|

## 20 000 METRES WALK (Road)

| Mark | Name | Nat | Yr | Pos | Meet | Venue | Date |
|------|------|-----|----|----|------|-------|------|
| 1:19:30 | Jozef Pribilinec | CS | 60 | 1 | LT | Bergen | 24 Sep 83 |
| 1:19:35 | Domingo Colin | MEX | 52 | 1 | | Cherkassy | 27 Apr 80 |
| 1:19:41 | Ernesto Canto | MEX | 59 | 2 | LT | Bergen | 24 Sep 83 |
| 1:19:43 | Anatoliy Solomin | SU | 52 | 3 | LT | Bergen | 24 Sep 83 |
| 1:19:49 | Pribilinec | | | 1 | | Barcelona | 17 Apr 83 |
| 1:19:52 | David Smith | AUS | 55 | 1 | | Jiading | 16 Mar 85 |
| 1:19:52 | Reima Salonen | FIN | 55 | 1 | IM | Pihtipudas | 21 Jun 86 |
| 1:19:53 | Yevgeniy Yevsyukov | SU | 50 | 2 | | Cherkassy | 27 Apr 80 |
| 1:19:56 | Ronald Weigel | GDR | 59 | 1 | | East Berlin | 27 Jul 84 |
| 1:20:00 | José Marin | SPA | 50 | 2 | | Barcelona | 17 Apr 83 |
| 1:20:02 | Salonen | | | 1 | GP | Russe | 20 Apr 86 |
| 1:20:09 | Maurizio Damilano | ITA | 57 | 1 | | Piacenza | 13 May 84 |
| 1:20:10 | Damilano | | | 4 | LT | Bergen | 24 Sep 83 |
| 1:20:18 | Alessandro Pezzatini | ITA | 57 | 2 | | Piacenza | 13 May 84 |
| 1:20:23 | Smith | | | 1 | | Melbourne | 18 Dec 83 |
| 1:20:30 | Yevsyukov | | | 5 | LT | Bergen | 24 Sep 83 |
| 1:20:31 | Ralf Kowalsky | GDR | 62 | 1 | IM | Potsdam | 24 May 86 |
| 1:20:35 | Solomin | | | 4 | | Cherkassy | 27 Apr 80 |
| 1:20:35 | Kowalsky | | | 1 | | East Berlin | 20 Jul 84 |
| 1:20:39 | Weigel | | | 1 | | East Berlin | 11 Jun 86 |
| (20/12) | | | | | | | |
| 1:20:40 | Marcelino Colin | MEX | 61 | 6 | LT | Bergen | 24 Sep 83 |
| 1:20:50 | Nikolay Polozov | SU | 51 | 5 | | Cherkassy | 27 Apr 80 |
| 1:20:53 | Aivars Rumbenieks | SU | 51 | 6 | | Cherkassy | 27 Apr 80 |
| 1:21:00 | Daniel Bautista | MEX | 52 | 1 | | Xalapa | 30 Mar 80 |
| 1:21:00 | Aleksandr Boyarshinov | SU | 63 | 1 | | Bryansk | 14 Aug 86 |
| 1:21:11 | Carlo Mattioli | ITA | 54 | 7 | LT | Bergen | 24 Sep 83 |
| 1:21:13 | Guillaume Leblanc | CAN | 62 | 1 | PAC | St.Leonard | 5 Oct 86 |
| 1:21:15 | Hartwig Gauder | GDR | 54 | 1 | | Varnamo | 9 May 86 |
| (20) | | | | | | | |
| 1:21:16 | Andrey Perlov | SU | 61 | 7 | | Cherkassy | 27 Apr 80 |
| 1:21:18 | Nikolay Matveyev | SU | 55 | 1 | | Ruse | 17 Apr 83 |
| 1:21:19 | Feliz Gómez | MEX | 55 | 2 | | Vretstorp | 9 Jun 79 |
| 1:21:21 | Aleksandr Potashov | SU | 62 | 8 | | Cherkassy | 27 Apr 80 |
| 1:21:21 | Pavol Blažek | CS | 58 | 1 | | Trnava | 25 May 86 |
| 1:21:26 | Anatoliy Gorshkov | SU | 52 | 8 | LT | Bergen | 24 Sep 83 |
| 1:21:33 | Viktor Mostovik | SU | 63 | 1 | | Leningrad | 1 Aug 85 |
| 1:21:33 | Carlos Mercenario | MEX | 67 | 2 | PAC | St.Leonard | 5 Oct 86 |
| 1:21:36 | Willi Sawall | AUS | 41 | 1 | | Melbourne | 4 Jul 82 |
| 1:21:36 | Miguel A.Prieto | SPA | 63 | 3 | EC | Stuttgart | 27 Aug 86 |
| (30) | | | | | | | |
| 1:21:37 | Gérard Lelièvre | FRA | 49 | 5 | WCh | Helsinki | 7 Aug 83 |
| 1:21:38 | Bo Gustafsson | SWE | 54 | 1 | | København | 16 Jul 83 |
| 1:21:39 | Liu Jianli | CHN | | 2 | | Jiading | 16 Mar 85 |
| 1:21:40 | Maris Petersons | SU | 48 | 9 | | Cherkassy | 27 Apr 80 |
| 1:21:41 | Mykola Vynnychenko | SU | 58 | 2 | | Xalapa | 30 Mar 80 |
| 1:21:41 | Roman Mrazek | CS | 62 | 2 | | Trnava | 25 May 86 |
| 1:21:43 | Ivan Sankovskiy | SU | 58 | 1 | | Moskva | 13 May 84 |
| 1:21:44 | Aleksandr Pankov | SU | 52 | 10 | | Cherkassy | 27 Apr 80 |
| 1:21:45 | Michael Bönke | GDR | 57 | 2 | | East Berlin | 29 May 83 |
| 1:21:48 | Uwe Dünkel | GDR | 60 | 3 | | East Berlin | 29 May 83 |
| (40) | | | | | | | |
| 1:21:48 | Tim Lewis | USA | 62 | 3 | PAC | St.Leonard | 5 Oct 86 |
| 1:21:55 | Axel Noack | GDR | 61 | 2 | IM | Potsdam | 24 May 86 |
| 1:21:57 | Sergey Protsyshin | SU | 59 | 1 | | Moskva | 17 Aug 84 |
| 1:22:03 | Lyubomir Ivanov | BUL | 60 | 2 | | East Berlin | 20 Jul 84 |
| 1:22:05 | Yevgeniy Zaikin | SU | 57 | 11 | | Cherkassy | 27 Apr 80 |
| 1:22:08 | Aleksandr Starchenko | SU | 50 | 1 | | Chelyabinsk | 7 Oct 79 |

| Mark | Name | Nat | Yr | Pos | Meet | Venue | Date |
|------|------|-----|----|----|------|-------|------|
| 1:22:09 | Frants Kostyukovich | SU | 63 | 1 | | Novopolotsk | 22 Apr 85 |
| 1:22:11 | Querubin Moreno | COL | 59 | 1 | | Barcelona | 28 Apr 85 |
| 1:22:11 | Sandor Urbanik | HUN | 64 | 1 | | Tatabanya | 7 Sep 86 |
| 1:22:12 | Roland Wieser | GDR | 56 | 2 | | Naumberg | 1 May 81 |
| | (50) | | | | | | |

## 50 000 METRES WALK (Track)

| Mark | Name | Nat | Yr | Pos | Meet | Venue | Date |
|------|------|-----|----|----|------|-------|------|
| 3:41:38.4 | Raúl González | MEX | 52 | 1 | SGP | Fana | 25 May 79 |
| 3:43:42.4 | González | | | 1 | SGP | Fana | 2 May 80 |
| 3:45:38.0 | González | | | 1 | SGP | Fana | 14 May 82 |
| 3:46:11 | Mykola Udovenko | SU | 56 | 1 | | Uzhgorod | 3 Oct 80 |
| 3:48:59 | Vadim Rezayev | SU | 50 | 2 | SGP | Fana | 2 May 80 |
| 3:52:15.0 | Jorge Llopart | SPA | 52 | 1 | SGP | Fana | 28 May 81 |
| 3:52:23.5 | Gonzalez | | | 1 | | Førde | 19 May 78 |
| 3:52:40 | Vyacheslav Fursov | SU | 54 | 3 | SGP | Fana | 2 May 80 |
| 3:53:56.9 | Gérard Lelièvre | FRA | 49 | 1 | | St.Quentin | 27 Mar 83 |
| 3:56:35.4 | Bo Gustafsson | SWE | 54 | 1 | | Borås | 12 Oct 85 |
| | (10/7) | | | | | | |

## 50 000 METRES WALK (Road)

| Mark | Name | Nat | Yr | Pos | Meet | Venue | Date |
|------|------|-----|----|----|------|-------|------|
| 3:38:17 | Ronald Weigel | GDR | 59 | 1 | IM | Potsdam | 25 May 86 |
| 3:38:31 | Weigel | | | 1 | | East Berlin | 20 Jul 84 |
| 3:39:47 | Andrey Perlov | SU | 61 | 1 | | Leningrad | 3 Aug 85 |
| 3:40:46 | Jose Marin | SPA | 50 | 1 | | Valencia | 13 Mar 83 |
| 3:40:55 | Hartwig Gauder | GDR | 54 | 1 | EC | Stuttgart | 31 Aug 86 |
| 3:41:20 | Raúl González | MEX | 52 | 1 | | Poděbrady | 11 Jun 78 |
| 3:41:24 | Gauder | | | 2 | | East Berlin | 20 Jul 84 |
| 3:41:31 | Weigel | | | 1 | | Naumberg | 1 May 83 |
| 3:41:51 | Venyamin Nikolayev | SU | 58 | 2 | | Leningrad | 3 Aug 85 |
| 3:41:54 | Vyacheslav Ivanenko | SU | 61 | 2 | EC | Stuttgart | 31 Aug 86 |
| 3:42:04 | Yevgeniy Yevsyukov | SU | 50 | 3 | | Leningrad | 3 Aug 85 |
| 3:42:36 | Reima Salonen | FIN | 55 | 1 | NC | Vantaa | 24 May 86 |
| 3:42:37 | Valeriy Suntsov | SU | 55 | 4 | | Leningrad | 3 Aug 85 |
| 3:42:38 | Suntsov | | | 3 | EC | Stuttgart | 31 Aug 86 |
| 3:43:06 | Perlov | | | 1 | | Moskva | 17 Aug 84 |
| 3:43:08 | Weigel | | | 1 | WCh | Helsinki | 12 Aug 83 |
| 3:43:23 | Gauder | | | 2 | | Naumberg | 1 May 83 |
| 3:43:25 | Weigel | | | 1 | | Naumberg | 1 May 84 |
| 3:43:33 | Dietmar Meisch | GDR | 59 | 3 | | East Berlin | 20 Jul 84 |
| 3:43:33 | Gauder | | | 1 | WCp-s | Borås | 15 Jun 85 |
| | (20/11) | | | | | | |
| 3:43:36 | Martin Bermúdez | MEX | 58 | 1 | LT | Eschborn | 30 Sep 79 |
| 3:43:59 | Enrique Vera-Ybáñez | MEX | 54 | 2 | LT | Eschborn | 30 Sep 79 |
| 3:44:08 | Viktor Dorovskikh | SU | 50 | 5 | | Leningrad | 3 Aug 85 |
| 3:44:24 | Erling Andersen | NOR | 60 | 2 | WCp-s | Borås | 15 Jun 85 |
| 3:44:33 | Jorge Llopart | SPA | 52 | 1 | | Reus | 26 Aug 79 |
| 3:45:51 | Uwe Dunkel | GDR | 60 | 1 | | East Berlin | 18 Jul 81 |
| 3:45:51 | Sergey Protsyshin | SU | 59 | 4 | EC | Stuttgart | 31 Aug 86 |
| 3:45:53 | Pavol Szikora | CS | 52 | 2 | | Moskva | 17 Aug 84 |
| 3:46:28 | Valeriy Yarets | SU | 56 | 6 | | Leningrad | 3 Aug 85 |
| | (20) | | | | | | |
| 3:46:34 | Willi Sawall | AUS | 41 | 1 | | Adelaide | 6 Apr 80 |
| 3:46:55 | Vyacheslav Fursov | SU | 54 | 5 | LT | Eschborn | 30 Sep 79 |
| 3:46:57 | Vladimir Rezayev | SU | 50 | 2 | | Moskva | 27 Jul 79 |
| 3:47:13 | Pyotr Gaus | SU | 52 | 3 | | Moskva | 3 Jul 82 |
| 3:47:16 | Sergey Yung | SU | 55 | 4 | | Moskva | 3Jul 82 |
| 3:47:18 | Domingo Colin | MEX | 52 | 1 | | Valencia | 20 May 79 |

MEN All-time

| Mark | Name | Nat | Yr | Pos | Meet | Venue | Date |
|------|------|-----|----|----|------|-------|------|
| 3:47:20 | Nikolay Frolov | SU | 56 | 7 | | Leningrad | 3 Aug 85 |
| 3:47:25 | Aleksandr Starchenko | SU | 51 | 2 | | Sochi | 17 Apr 83 |
| 3:47:48 | Marcel Jobin | CAN | 42 | 2 | | Quebec | 20 Jun 81 |
| 3:47:54 | Vitaliy Popovich (30) | SU | 57 | 8 | | Leningrad | 3 Aug 85 |
| 3:47:59 | Viktor Shchernov | SU | 52 | 1 | | Cherkassy | 8 Oct 82 |
| 3:48:19 | Pyotr Melnyk | SU | 51 | 4 | | Moskva | 27 Jul 79 |
| 3:48:35 | Bo Gustafsson | SWE | 54 | 4 | WCp-s | Borås | 15 Jun 85 |
| 3:49:06 | Felix Gómez | MEX | 55 | 2 | | Mixhuca | 18 Apr 82 |
| 3:49:08 | Vladimir Nefyodov | SU | 55 | 1 | | Kiev | 29 Aug 83 |
| 3:49:25 | Mykola Udovenko | SU | 56 | 3 | | Mixhuca | 18 Apr 82 |
| 3:49:52 | Ivan Tikhonov | SU | 50 | 3 | | Sochi | 17 Apr 83 |
| 3:49:58 | Viktor Grodovchuk | SU | 52 | 5 | | Moskva | 3 Jul 82 |
| 3:49:58 | Artur Sumak | SU | 63 | 4 | | Zhitomir | 30 Sep 84 |
| 3:50:24 | Yevgeniy Ivchenko (40) | SU | 38 | 5 | | Moskva | 27 Jul 79 |
| 3:50:24 | Leonid Sivakov | SU | 56 | 9 | | Leningrad | 3 Aug 85 |
| 3:50:51 | Paolo Gregucci | Ita | 51 | 9 | LT | Eschborn | 30 Sep 79 |
| 3:50:51 | Vladimir Dusko | SU | 56 | 5 | | Sochi | 10 Jun 84 |
| 3:50:53 | Sergey Tsimbalyuk | SU | 58 | 2 | | Smolensk | 28 Sep 85 |
| 3:50:59 | Vadim Tsevetkov | SU | 46 | 7 | | Moskva | 3 Jul 82 |
| 3:51:10 | Ernesto Canto | MEX | 59 | 1 | | Poděbrady | 12 Jun 82 |
| 3:51:17 | Aleksandr Potashev | SU | 62 | 4 | NC | Alitus | 31 May 86 |
| 3:51:20 | Sandro Bellucci | ITA | 55 | 11 | LT | Eschborn | 30 Sep 79 |
| 3:51:27 | Horst-Joachim Matern | GDR | 54 | 2 | | Naumberg | 1 May 81 |
| 3:51:28 | Anatoliy Ovchinnikov | SU | 57 | 8 | | Moskva | 3 Jul 82 |

| Mark | Wind | Name | | Nat | Yr | Pos | Meet | Venue | Date |
|------|------|------|------|-----|----|----|------|-------|------|

## 100 METRES

| Mark | Wind | Name | | Nat | Yr | Pos | Meet | Venue | Date |
|------|------|------|------|-----|----|----|------|-------|------|
| 9.95 | 0.8 | Ben | Johnson | CAN | 61 | 1r1 | GWG | Moskva | 9 Jul |
| 10.00 | 1.0 | Chidi | Imoh | NIG | 63 | 1r1 | ISTAF | W Berlin | 15 Aug |
| 10.01 | 0.9 | | Johnson | | | 1 | Jenner | San Jose | 31 May |
| 10.02 | 1.1 | | Johnson | | | 1 | GP | Roma | 10 Sep |
| 10.02 | 1.8 | Robson C | da Silva | BRA | 64 | 1 | IbAm | Habana | 27 Sep |
| 10.03 | -0.7 | | Johnson | | | 1 | WK | Zürich | 13 Aug |
| 10.04 | 1.8 | Linford | Christie | UK | 60 | 1 | | Madrid | 4 Jun |
| 10.04 | 0.8 | | Imoh | | | 2r1 | GWG | Moskva | 9 Jul |
| A10.06 | 0.1 | | Johnson | | | 1r1 | | Provo | 24 May |
| 10.06 | 0.8 | Carl | Lewis | USA | 61 | 3r1 | GWG | Moskva | 9 Jul |
| | | | | | | | | | |
| 10.06 | 1.8 | | Johnson | | | 1 | | Birmingham | 18 Jul |
| 10.06 | 0.3 | | Johnson | | | 1 | VD | Bruxelles | 5 Sep |
| 10.07 | -0.1 | Emmit | King | USA | 59 | 1 | | Sevilla | 24 May |
| 10.07 | 1.6 | | Johnson | | | 1 | NC | Ottawa | 21 Jun |
| 10.07 | 1.6 | | Johnson | | | 1 | CG | Edinburgh | 27 Jul |
| 10.08 | 0.1 | Lorenzo | Daniel | USA | 66 | 1h2 | | Knoxville | 17 May |
| 10.08 | 1.3 | | Lewis | | | 1 | Pre | Eugene | 7 Jun |
| 10.08 | 1.1 | | Imoh | | | 2 | GP | Roma | 10 Sep |
| A10.09 | 0.2 | | Johnson | | | 1r2 | | Provo | 24 May |
| 10.09 | -0.5 | Harvey | Glance | USA | 57 | 1 | OD | Dresden | 3 Jul |
| | | | | | | | | | |
| 10.09 | 1.3 | Antoine | Richard | FRA | 60 | 1 | NC | Aix-les-Bains | 9 Aug |
| 10.10 | 1.5 | | King | | | 1 | | Tuscaloosa | 29 Mar |
| 10.10 | 1.8 | Thomas | Schröder (10) | GDR | 62 | 1 | NC | Jena | 27 Jun |
| 10.10 | 1.9 | Stanley | Kerr | USA | 67 | 1 | TAC-j | Towson, MD | 28 Jun |
| 10.11 | 1.4 | Lee | McRae | USA | 66 | 1 | NCAA | Indianapolis | 7 Jun |
| 10.11 | 1.9 | Viktor | Bryzgin | SU | 62 | 1 | v GDR | Tallinn | 21 Jun |
| 10.11 | 1.0 | Marian | Woronin | POL | 56 | 2r1 | ISTAF | W Berlin | 15 Aug |
| 10.12 | 1.5 | | Daniel | | | 2 | | Tuscaloosa | 29 Mar |
| 10.12 | | Roy | Martin | USA | 66 | 2 | | Dallas | 12 Apr |
| 10.12 | 0.0 | Sam | Graddy | USA | 64 | 1 | | Knoxville | 24 May |
| | | | | | | | | | |
| 10.12 | -1.8 | | Johnson | | | 1 | | Burnaby | 10 Jun |
| 10.12 | 0.8 | | McRae | | | 4r1 | GWG | Moskva | 9 Jul |
| 10.12 | 1.8 | | Imoh | | | 2 | | Birmingham | 18 Jul |
| 10.12 | 0.0 | | Imoh (34/16) | | | 1 | ASV | Köln | 17 Aug |
| | | | | | | | | | |
| 10.13 | 1.8 | Steffen | Bringmann | GDR | 64 | 2 | NC | Jena | 27 Jun |
| 10.13 | 1.9 | Derrick | Florence | USA | 68 | 2 | TAC-j | Towson, MD | 28 Jun |
| 10.14 | 1.4 | Lee | McNeill | USA | 64 | 3 | NCAA | Indianapolis | 7 Jun |
| 10.14 | 1.0 | Calvin | Smith (20) | USA | 61 | 3r1 | ISTAF | W Berlin | 15 Aug |
| | | | | | | | | | |
| A10.15 | 1.6 | Wessel | Oosthuizen | RSA | 61 | 1 | | Secunda | 15 Nov |
| 10.17 | 1.8 | Thomas | Jefferson | USA | 62 | 2 | | Madrid | 4 Jun |
| 10.17 | 0.3 | Kirk | Baptiste | USA | 63 | 2h3 | TAC | Eugene | 19 Jun |
| 10.18 | 1.8 | Andrés | Simón | CUB | 61 | 3 | | Madrid | 4 Jun |
| 10.18 | 1.9 | Nikolay | Yushmanov | SU | 61 | 3 | v GDR | Tallinn | 21 Jun |
| 10.18 | 1.5 | Bruno | Marie-Rose | FRA | 65 | 2s1 | EC | Stuttgart | 27 Aug |
| A10.19 | 1.0 | Ken | Henderson | USA | 66 | 1 | | Provo | 12 Apr |
| 10.19 | 1.3 | Charles-L | Seck | SEN | 65 | 2 | FraC | Aix-les-Bains | 9 Aug |
| 10.20 | 1.5 | Elliot | Bunney | UK | 66 | 1 | | Edinburgh | 14 Jun |
| 10.20 | 0.4 | Floyd | Heard (30) | USA | 66 | 1h1 | TAC | Eugene | 19 Jun |
| | | | | | | | | | |
| 10.20 | 0.4 | Vladimir | Muravyov | SU | 59 | 1r2 | GWG | Moskva | 9 Jul |
| 10.21 | 1.5 | Mark | McKoy | CAN | 61 | 1 | | Baton Rouge | 13 Apr |
| 10.21 | 0.0 | Harvey | McSwain | USA | 63 | 2 | | Knoxville | 24 May |

| Mark | Wind | Name | | Nat | Yr | Pos | Meet | Venue | Date |
|------|------|------|---|-----|-----|-----|------|-------|------|
| 10.21 | 1.8 | José Javier | Arques | SPA | 60 | 4 | | Madrid | 4 Jun |
| 10.21 | 0.2 | Mike | Morris | USA | 63 | 1h2 | TAC | Eugene | 19 Jun |
| 10.21 | 1.0 | Wallace | Spearmon | USA | 62 | 2h4 | TAC | Eugene | 19 Jun |
| 10.21 | 0.4 | Andrey | Shlyapnikov | SU | 59 | 2r2 | GWG | Moskva | 9 Jul |
| 10.21 | 1.2 | Desai | Williams | CAN | 59 | 1 | BGP | Budapest | 11 Aug |
| 10.22 | 0.1 | Albert | Robinson | USA | 64 | 2 | | Knoxville | 12 Apr |
| 10.22 | 1.8 | Mike | McFarlane(40) | UK | 60 | 1s1 | AAA | London | 20 Jun |
| 10.22 | 1.9 | Mike | Marsh | USA | 67 | 3 | TAC-j | Towson, MD | 28 Jun |
| 10.22 | 1.5 | Allan | Wells | UK | 52 | 3s1 | EC | Stuttgart | 27 Aug |
| 10.22 | 1.8 | P Francesco | Pavoni | ITA | 63 | 1 | CISM | Ostia | 11 Sep |
| 10.23 | 1.2 | Leandro | Peñalver | CUB | 61 | 2 | BGP | Budapest | 11 Aug |
| 10.24 | 1.8 | Ricardo | Chacón | CUB | 63 | 5 | | Madrid | 4 Jun |
| 10.25 | 1.5 | Darwin | Cook | USA | 62 | 1 | | Eugene | 24 May |
| 10.25 | 1.9 | Vladimir | Krylov | SU | 64 | 4 | v GDR | Tallinn | 21 Jun |
| A10.25 | | Joel | Isasi | CUB | 67 | 1h | CAC-j | México, D.F. | 26 Jun |
| 10.25 | | Dirk | Schweisfurth | FRG | 65 | 1 | | Gelnhausen | 12 Sep |
| 10.26 | 0.2 | Manley | Waller    (50) | USA | 64 | 2h2 | TAC | Eugene | 19 Jun |
| 10.26 | 1.2 | Atlee | Mahorn | CAN | 65 | 2 | v GDR | Karl-Marx-Stadt | 12 Jul |
| 10.26 | 2.0 | Daley | Thompson | UK | 58 | 2 | EC | Stuttgart | 27 Aug |
| 10.26 | 0.9 | Tao | Li | CHN | 68 | 1 | AsiC-j | Djakarta | 5 Dec |
| 10.27 | -1.6 | Daron | Council | USA | 64 | 1 | | Auburn | 19 Apr |
| 10.27 | 0.4 | Marty | Krulee | USA | 56 | 3h1 | TAC | Eugene | 19 Jun |
| 10.27 | 1.8 | Sören | Schlegel | GDR | 60 | 3s1 | NC | Jena | 27 Jun |
| 10.27 | 1.3 | Ronald | Desruelles | BEL | 55 | 1 | | Hechtel | 5 Jul |
| 10.27 | -1.1 | Mark | Mitchell | USA | 67 | 1 | | Budapest | 12 Jul |
| 10.27 | 1.5 | Christian | Haas | FRG | 58 | 5s1 | EC | Stuttgart | 27 Aug |
| 10.28 | 1.5 | Keith | Talley    (60) | USA | 64 | 3 | | Tuscaloosa | 29 Mar |
| 10.29 | -0.5 | Luis | Morales | PR | 64 | 1 | | San Diego | 1 Mar |
| 10.29 | 1.9 | Ray | Stewart | JAM | 65 | 1h2 | | Baton Rouge | 21 Mar |
| 10.29 | 0.0 | Greg | Moses | USA | 65 | 3 | | Knoxville | 24 May |
| 10.29 | 1.9 | Brady | Crain | USA | 56 | 2 | | Villanova | 8 Jun |
| 10.29 | -0.3 | Attila | Kovács | HUN | 60 | 1 | NC | Budapest | 15 Aug |
| 10.30 | | Jorge | Aguilera | CUB | 66 | 1h | | Santiago/Cuba | 21 Feb |
| 10.30 | | Greg | Sholars | USA | 66 | 2 | | Dallas | 12 Apr |
| 10.30 | 0.3 | Tallal | Mansour | QAT | 64 | 1 | AsiG | Seoul | 30 Sep |
| 10.31 | | Aatron | Kenney | USA | 63 | 1ro | TexR | Austin | 4 Apr |
| 10.31 | 0.8 | Andreas | Berger    (70) | AUT | 61 | 1 | v Bul, | Gre,Hun Linz | 28 Jun |
| 10.31 | 0.2 | Juan | Nunez | DOM | 59 | 1s1 | CAC | Santiago/Dom | 29 Jun |
| 10.31 | 2.0 | Larry | Myricks | USA | 56 | 2r3 | ISTAF | W Berlin | 15 Aug |
| 10.32 | 1.4 | Robert | Hackett | USA | 64 | 1 | | Madison | 24 May |
| 10.32 | 0.3 | Volker | Schulz | GDR | 64 | 2 | | Neubrandenburg | 6 Jun |
| 10.32 | 0.5 | Frank | Emmelmann | GDR | 61 | 2h1 | PTS | Bratislava | 14 Jun |
| 10.32 | 1.9 | Czesław | Pradzyński | POL | 60 | 1 | NC | Grudziadz | 27 Jun |
| 10.32 | 0.0 | Max | Morinière | FRA | 64 | 1 | | Cannes | 13 Jul |
| 10.32 | 1.2 | Lincoln | Asquith | UK | 64 | 3 | BGP | Budapest | 11 Aug |
| 10.32 | 0.3 | Valentin | Atanasov | BUL | 61 | 1 | NC | Sofia | 13 Aug |
| 10.32 | 0.4 | Jürgen | Evers    (80) | FRG | 65 | 1r2 | ISTAF | W Berlin | 15 Aug |
| 10.33 | | Osvaldo | Lara | CUB | 55 | 1h | | Santiago/Cuba | 21 Feb |
| 10.33 | | Dennis | Mitchell | USA | 66 | 1 | | Gainesville | 19 Apr |
| 10.33 | 1.7 | Dwayne | Evans | USA | 58 | 1 | | Walnut, CA | 1 Jun |
| 10.33 | 1.5 | Jamie | Henderson | UK | 69 | 2 | | Edinburgh | 14 Jun |
| 10.33 | 1.9 | Nikolay | Markov | BUL | 60 | 1 | | Sofia | 3 Aug |

| Mark | Wind | Name | | Nat | Yr | Pos | Meet | Venue | Date |
|------|------|------|------|-----|----|----|------|-------|------|
| 10.33 | -0.9 | František | Ptáčník | CS | 62 | 1 | | Praha | 17 Aug |
| 10.34 | -1.6 | Stanley | Blalock | USA | 64 | 2 | | Auburn | 19 Apr |
| 10.34 | | Dave | Smith | JAM | 60 | 3 | | Kingston | 3 May |
| 10.34 | 0.1 | Ray | Hill | USA | 67 | 1 | | Odessa, TX | 16 May |
| 10.34 | 2.0 | Torsten | Heimrath (90) | GDR | 63 | 1r2 | | Jena | 31 May |
| 10.34 | 0.8 | Piotr | Waszek | POL | 60 | 1 | | Słupsk | 7 Jun |
| 10.34 | 1.7 | Chris | Perry | AUS | 59 | 4 | AAA | London | 20 Jun |
| 10.35 | 0.6 | Viktor | Panov | SU | 60 | 1 | | Sochi | 17 May |
| 10.35 | 0.0 | Hiroki | Fuwa | JAP | 66 | 1 | | Tokyo | 7 Jun |
| 10.35 | | Greg | Meghoo | JAM | 65 | 2 | NC | Kingston | 20 Jun |
| 10.35 | 1.8 | Heiko | Truppel | GDR | 64 | 5 | NC | Jena | 27 Jun |
| 10.35 | 1.9 | Anri | Grigorov | BUL | 64 | 3 | | Sofia | 3 Aug |
| 10.35 | 1.2 | István | Tatár | HUN | 58 | 5 | BGP | Budapest | 11 Aug |
| 10.36 | | Sergio | Querol | CUB | 65 | h | | Santiago/Cuba | 21 Feb |
| 10.36 | | Earle | Laing (100) | JAM | 64 | 3 | | Dallas | 12 Apr |
| 10.36 | 0.6 | Aleksandr | Shishov | SU | 59 | 2 | | Sochi | 17 May |
| 10.36 | 0.1 | Mike | Dexter | USA | 64 | 1h2 | | Los Angeles | 23 May |
| 10.36 | 1.0 | Hurvie | Milner | USA | 61 | 4h4 | TAC | Eugene | 19 Jun |
| 10.36 | 1.3 | Andrey | Fyodorov | SU | 63 | 1 | | Moskva | 27 Jun |
| 10.36 | 0.3 | Krasimir | Bozhinovski | BUL | 67 | 1 | NC-j | Sofia | 5 Jul |
| 10.36 | -0.5 | Aleksandr | Semyonov | SU | 62 | 1s2 | NC | Kiev | 14 Jul |
| 10.36 | 2.0 | Mike | Conley | USA | 62 | 4r3 | ISTAF | W Berlin | 15 Aug |
| A10.36 | 1.6 | Tsahakile | Nzimande | RSA | 61 | 2 | | Secunda | 15 Nov |
| A10.36 | 1.6 | Raoul | Karp (109) | RSA | 67 | 3 | | Secunda | 15 Nov |

| 10.37 | | Jason | Leach (110) | USA | 66 | 22 Mar |
|-------|---|-------|-------------|-----|----|--------|
| A10.37 | 1.7 | Johan | Rossouw | RSA | 65 | 11 Apr |
| 10.37 | | Ken | Robinson | USA | 63 | 19 Apr |
| 10.37 | | Pierre | Goode | USA | 67 | 2 May |
| 10.37 | | Keith | Thomas | USA | 68 | 24 May |
| 10.37 | | Andrew | Smith | JAM | 64 | 20 Jun |
| 10.37 | 1.2 | Endre | Havas | HUN | 66 | 25 Jun |
| 10.37 | -0.5 | Pyotr | Vorobyov | SU | 58 | 14 Jul |
| A10.38 | | Peter | Ngobeni | RSA | 62 | 7 Feb |
| 10.38 | | Andre | Cason | USA | 69 | 12 Apr |
| 10.38 | | Greg | Walker (120) | USA | 63 | 26 Apr |
| 10.38 | 0.8 | Anthony | Miller | USA | | 17 May |
| 10.38 | 0.7 | Bobby | Bankston | USA | 63 | 22 May |
| 10.38 | 0.0 | Roscoe | Tatum | USA | 66 | 5 Jun |
| 10.38 | | John | Mair | JAM | | 20 Jun |
| 10.38 | 1.9 | Leszek | Dunecki | POL | 56 | 27 Jun |
| 10.38 | -0.3 | Fabian | Whymns | BAH | 61 | 29 Jun |
| 10.38 | -0.3 | Gerardo | Suero | DOM | 57 | 29 Jun |
| 10.39 | | Henry | Thomas | USA | 67 | 22 Mar |
| 10.39 | | Vincent | Coleman | USA | 65 | 4 Apr |
| 10.39 | | Walker | Watkins (130) | USA | 67 | 9 May |
| A10.39 | | Gabriel | Okon | NIG | 66 | 9 May |
| 10.39 | | José | Campanioni | CUB | 64 | 30 May |
| 10.39 | 0.4 | Joe | DeLoach | USA | 67 | 19 Jun |
| 10.39 | 2.0 | Clarence | Callender | UK | 61 | 20 Jun |
| 10.39 | 1.6 | Mike | Dwyer | CAN | 62 | 21 Jun |

| 10.39 | 1.8 | Steffen | Schwabe | GDR | 64 | 27 Jun |
|-------|-----|---------|---------|-----|----|--------|
| 10.39 | 1.8 | Jörg | Treffer | GDR | 65 | 27 Jun |
| 10.39 | 1.4 | Ernest | Obeng | UK | 56 | 5 Jul |
| 10.39 | 1.9 | István | Nagy | HUN | 59 | 11 Aug |
| 10.40 | 0.6 | Gerrard | Keating (140) | AUS | 62 | 6 Mar |
| 10.40 | 1.9 | Brian | Cooper | USA | 65 | 21 Mar |
| 10.40 | | Desmond | Ross | USA | 61 | 12 Apr |
| 10.40 | | Chris | Stokes | JAM | | 19 Apr |
| 10.40 | 1.4 | Greg | Richardson | USA | 64 | 4 May |
| 10.40 | | Everton | Wanliss | JAM | | 10 May |
| 10.40 | 0.6 | Konstantin | Osadchenko | SU | 62 | 17 May |
| 10.40 | 0.8 | William | Trott | BER | 65 | 17 May |
| 10.40 | 0.8 | Krzysztof | Zwóliński | POL | 59 | 7 Jun |
| 10.40 | 0.0 | Stefano | Tilli | ITA | 62 | 26 Jun |
| 10.40 | | Kosmas | Stratos (150) | GRE | 59 | 7 Aug |
| 10.40 | -0.9 | Luboš | Chochlík | CS | 59 | 17 Aug |
| 10.41 | | Carl | Carter | USA | 64 | 22 Mar |
| 10.41 | | William | Snoddy | USA | 57 | 12 Apr |
| 10.41 | -0.2 | Danny | Peebles | USA | 66 | 19 Apr |
| 10.41 | -1.6 | Norman | Edwards | JAM | 62 | 19 Apr |
| 10.41 | 0.9 | Antonio | Manning | USA | 65 | 3 May |
| 10.41 | 0.1 | Harold | Madox | USA | 65 | 16 May |
| 10.41 | | Jarrett | Cooper | USA | 67 | 24 May |
| 10.41 | | Terry | Scott | USA | 64 | 30 May |
| 10.41 | 0.2 | Olaf | Prenzler (160) | GDR | 58 | 14 Jun |

| Mark | Wind | Name | | Nat | Yr | Pos | Meet | Venue | Date |
|------|------|------|------|-----|----|-----|------|-------|------|
| 10.41 | 1.1 | Nikolay | Antonov | BUL | 68 | | | | 21 Jun |
| 10.41 | 2.0 | Thierry | Lauret | FRA | 65 | | | | 22 Jun |
| 10.41 | | Amadou | Mbaye | SEN | 64 | | | | 9 Jul |
| 10.42 | | Keith | Stanford | USA | 64 | | | | 21 Mar |
| A10.42 | 1.0 | Gerald | Johnson | USA | | | | | 12 Apr |
| A10.42 | | Victor | Edet | NIG | 65 | | | | 17 May |
| 10.42 | 0.8 | Christian | Mark | AUT | 62 | | | | 18 Jun |
| 10.42 | 1.5 | Dirk | Assenheimer | GDR | 66 | | | | 27 Jun |
| 10.42 | 1.9 | Matthias | Schlicht | FRG | 67 | | | | 17 Jul |
| 10.43 | | Ricky | Turner (170) | USA | 68 | | | | 3 May |
| 10.43 | | Wenzhen | Wang | CHN | 67 | | | | 7 May |
| 10.43 | | Jeff | Williams | USA | 64 | | | | 9 May |
| 10.43 | | Clive | Wright | JAM | | | | | 17 May |
| A10.43 | 0.1 | Rick | Jones | CAN | 63 | | | | 24 May |
| 10.43 | 2.0 | Clayton | Kearney | AUS | 64 | | | | 20 Jun |

| Mark | Wind | Name | | | Nat | Yr | Pos | Meet | Venue | | Date |
|------|------|------|------|------|-----|----|-----|------|-------|------|------|
| 10.43 | 1.9 | Marek | | Hulbój | POL | 63 | | | | | 27 Jun |
| 10.43 | 1.4 | Peter | | Klein | FRG | 59 | | | | | 29 Jun |
| 10.43 | 1.0 | Gerd | | Umlauft | GDR | 67 | | | | | 26 Jul |
| 10.43 | 1.0 | Vadim | | Davydov | SU | 60 | | | | | 1 Aug |
| 10.43 | 1.3 | Gilles | | Quenehervé | FRA | 66 | | | | | 8 Aug |
| | | | | | | | | (180) | | | |
| 10.43 | 0.2 | John | | Regis | (181) UK | 66 | | | | | 12 Sep |

Best low altitude mark:

| 10.39 | 1.8 | K | | Henderson | | | | | | | 22 Mar |
|------|------|------|------|------|------|------|------|------|------|------|------|
| 10.39 | -0.3 | K | | Henderson | | | | | | | 19 Apr |

---

| | 1 | 10 | 20 | 30 | 50 | 100 | Under 10.30 | Under 10.40 |
|------|-------|-------|-------|-------|-------|-------|-------------|-------------|
| 1982 | 10.00 | 10.15 | 10.20 | 10.26 | 10.32 | 10.40 | 41 | 91 |
| 1983 | 9.93 | 10.15 | 10.19 | 10.22 | 10.30 | 10.37 | 48 | 111 |
| 1984 | 9.96 | 10.14 | 10.20 | 10.25 | 10.29 | 10.36 | 53 | 129 |
| 1985 | 9.98 | 10.11 | 10.20 | 10.23 | 10.27 | 10.35 | 62 | 132 |
| 1986 | 9.95 | 10.10 | 10.14 | 10.20 | 10.26 | 10.36 | 65 | 139 |

---

Marks made with assisting wind > 2 m/s :

| Mark | Wind | Name | | Nat | Yr | Pos | Meet | Venue | Date |
|------|------|------|------|-----|----|-----|------|-------|------|
| 9.91 | 4.5 | Carl | Lewis | USA | 61 | 1 | TAC | Eugene | 20 Jun |
| 9.97 | 3.4 | Roy | Martin | USA | 66 | 1r1 | | Houston | 18 May |
| 10.00 | 2.6 | Lorenzo | Daniel | USA | 66 | 1 | | Knoxville | 18 May |
| 10.01 | 2.4 | | Lewis | | | 1s1 | TAC | Eugene | 20 Jun |
| A10.02 | 6.4 | Aaron | Thigpen | USA | 64 | 1 | | Provo | 10 May |
| 10.02 | 4.5 | Lee | McRae | USA | 66 | 2 | TAC | Eugene | 20 Jun |
| 10.04 | 4.5 | Harvey | Glance | USA | 57 | 3 | TAC | Eugene | 20 Jun |
| 10.07 | 2.4 | | Glance | | | 1 | | Modesto, CA | 10 May |
| 10.08 | 2.6 | Sam | Graddy | USA | 64 | 2 | | Knoxville | 18 May |
| 10.08 | 4.0 | Roscoe | Tatum | USA | 66 | 1r2 | | Houston | 18 May |
| 10.09 | 2.4 | | Glance | | | 2s1 | TAC | Eugene | 20 Jun |
| 10.09 | 4.5 | Floyd | Heard | USA | 66 | 4 | TAC | Eugene | 20 Jun |
| 10.10 | 2.2 | Mike | Morris (10) | USA | 63 | 1 | | Univ Park, PA | 16 May |
| 10.10 | 4.5 | | Morris | | | 5 | TAC | Eugene | 20 Jun |
| 10.10 | 2.8 | | Glance | | | 1 | | Catania | 13 Sep |
| 10.11 | 2.9 | | Graddy | | | 1 | King | Atlanta | 20 Apr |
| 10.11 | 2.8 | | Imoh | | | 2 | | Catania | 13 Sep |
| A10.12 | 6.4 | Ken | Henderson | USA | 66 | 2 | | Provo | 10 May |
| 10.12 | 3.4 | | Heard | | | 2r1 | | Houston | 18 May |
| 10.12 | 2.5 | | McRae (20/12) | | | 1s2 | TAC | Eugene | 20 Jun |
| A10.14 | 6.4 | Gabriel | Okon | NIG | 66 | 3 | | Provo | 10 May |
| 10.14 | 4.5 | Wallace | Spearmon | USA | 62 | 6 | TAC | Eugene | 20 Jun |
| 10.15 | 3.0 | Mark | Witherspoon | USA | 63 | 1r2 | MSR | Walnut, CA | 27 Apr |

| Mark | Wind | Name | | Nat | Yr | Pos | Meet | Venue | Date |
|------|------|------|--|-----|----|----|------|-------|------|
| 10.16 | 2.3 | Greg | Meghoo | JAM | 65 | 1 | | San Angelo | 26 Apr |
| 10.16 | 2.2 | John | Mair | JAM | | 2 | | Univ Park, PA | 16 May |
| 10.16 | 4.0 | Jason | Leach | USA | 66 | 2r2 | | Houston | 18 May |
| 10.16 | 2.8 | Ronald | Desruelles | BEL | 55 | 3 | | Catania | 13 Sep |
| 10.18 | 2.3 | Bobby | Bankston (20) | USA | 63 | 2 | | San Angelo | 26 Apr |
| 10.18 | 3.4 | Andrew | Smith | JAM | 64 | 4r1 | | Houston | 18 May |
| 10.18 | 2.9 | Christian | Haas | FRG | 58 | 1 | NC | W Berlin | 11 Jul |
| 10.19 | 5.1 | Ray | Hill | USA | 67 | 1h4 | | Odessa, TX | 15 May |
| 10.21 | 5.4 | Stanley | Blalock | USA | 64 | 1 | FlaR | Gainesville | 29 Mar |
| 10.21 | | Kevin | Loyd | USA | 66 | 1h2 | | Arlington | 25 Apr |
| 10.21 | | Robert | Hackett | USA | 64 | 1 | | Madison | 9 May |
| 10.21 | | Benny | Mitchell | USA | 65 | 1 | | Arlington | 10 May |
| 10.21 | 3.4 | Ray | Stewart | JAM | 65 | 5r1 | | Houston | 18 May |
| 10.22 | | Brian | Cooper | USA | 65 | 1 | | Arlington | 26 Apr |
| 10.22 | 3.0 | Ernest | Obeng (30) | UK | 56 | 2r2 | MSR | Walnut, CA | 27 Apr |
| 10.22 | 3.4 | Greg | Sholars | USA | 66 | 6r1 | | Houston | 18 May |
| 10.23 | 5.4 | Dennis | Mitchell | USA | 66 | 2 | FlaR | Gainesville | 29 Mar |
| 10.23 | | Vincent | Coleman | USA | 65 | 2 | | Arlington | 26 Apr |
| 10.23 | 2.6 | Daron | Council | USA | 64 | 3 | | Knoxville | 18 May |
| 10.24 | 2.4 | Marty | Krulee | USA | 56 | 4 | | Modesto, CA | 10 May |
| 10.24 | 2.6 | Keith | Talley | USA | 64 | 4 | | Knoxville | 18 May |
| 10.25 | 2.3 | Max | Morinière | FRA | 64 | 1 | | Fort-de-France | 15 Mar |
| 10.26 | | Alrick | Munroe | JAM | 60 | 2 | | Arlington | 10 May |
| 10.26 | 4.0 | Earle | Laing | JAM | 64 | 3r2 | | Houston | 18 May |
| 10.26 | 2.1 | Attila | Kovács (40) | HUN | 60 | 2s2 | EC | Stuttgart | 27 Aug |
| 10.27 | 4.5 | Everton | Wanliss | JAM | | 1r2 | | Modesto, CA | 10 May |
| 10.27 | 2.4 | Frank | Emmelmann | GDR | 61 | 1r1 | | Jena | 31 May |
| 10.29 | 4.1 | Calvin | Long | USA | 66 | 1h2 | | Odessa, TX | 15 May |
| 10.29 | 2.9 | Chris | Perry | AUS | 59 | 2s3 | AAA | London | 20 Jun |
| 10.29 | 3.0 | Jamie | Henderson | UK | 69 | 2h2 | CG | Edinburgh | 26 Jul |
| 10.30 | | Merrick | Robinson | USA | 63 | 1 | | San Marcos | 26 Apr |
| 10.30 | 4.5 | Hurvie | Milner | USA | 61 | 2r2 | | Modesto, CA | 10 May |
| 10.30 | 2.4 | István | Tatár | HUN | 58 | 1 | | Budapest | 6 Jul |
| 10.31 | 4.1 | Byron | Morrow | USA | 65 | 1r3 | | Houston | 18 May |
| 10.31 | 2.4 | Volker | Schulz (50) | GDR | 64 | 2r1 | | Jena | 31 May |
| 10.32 | | Carl | Carter | USA | 64 | 1 | | Abilene | 8 Mar |
| 10.32 | 3.0 | Leroy | Burrell | USA | 67 | 3r2 | MSR | Walnut, CA | 27 Apr |
| 10.32 | 3.1 | William | Trott | BER | 65 | 1h3 | | Walnut, CA | 5 May |
| A10.32 | 6.4 | Rex | Brown | USA | 64 | 4 | | Provo | 10 May |
| 10.32 | 3.2 | Clarence | Callender | UK | 61 | 4s2 | CG | Edinburgh | 27 Jul |
| 10.32 | 2.4 | Fabian | Whymns | BAH | 61 | 1 | | Gävle | 28 Jul |
| 10.33 | 2.5 | Gerrard | Keating | AUS | 62 | 1 | | Canberra | 23 Feb |
| 10.33 | | Floyd | Dixon | USA | 64 | 2 | | San Marcos | 26 Apr |
| 10.33 | 3.1 | Don | Young | USA | 64 | 2h3 | | Walnut, CA | 5 May |
| 10.33 | 3.3 | Harold | Madox (60) | USA | 65 | 1s2 | | Odessa, TX | 16 May |
| 10.33 | 2.9 | Werner | Zaske | FRG | 61 | 3 | NC | W Berlin | 11 Jul |
| 10.34 | 4.2 | Phil | Davies | UK | 60 | 1 | | Swansea | 13 Jul |
| 10.35 | | Bobby | Johnson | USA | 67 | 1 | | Dallas | 22 Apr |
| 10.35 | 2.3 | Granvel | Holmes | USA | 66 | 3 | | San Angelo | 26 Apr |
| 10.35 | | Elliott | Hanna | USA | 63 | 1 | | Ames | 3 May |
| 10.35 | 4.5 | Chris | Stokes (66) | JAM | | 3r2 | | Modesto, CA | 10 May |

| Mark | Wind | Name | | Nat | Yr | Date |
|---|---|---|---|---|---|---|
| 10.36 | 2.9 | Terry | McDaniel | USA | 65 | 20 Apr |
| 10.36 | | Derwin | Hall | USA | | 22 Apr |
| 10.36 | | Sansiski | Daniels | USA | 64 | 26 Apr |
| 10.36 | | Burns | Andama (70) | UGA | 62 | 10 May |
| | | | | | | |
| 10.36 | 2.8 | Anthony | Barnes | USA | | 10 May |
| 10.36 | 2.6 | Greg | Richardson | USA | 64 | 18 May |
| 10.36 | 4.0 | Ned | Pucek | USA | 67 | 18 May |
| A10.36 | 3.2 | Luis | Smith | PAN | 68 | 13 Sep |
| 10.37 | | Antonio | Manning | USA | 65 | 12 Apr |
| 10.37 | | Al | Edwards | USA | 67 | 26 Apr |
| A10.37 | 6.4 | Chris | Leeuwenburgh | HOL | 62 | 10 May |
| 10.37 | 2.7 | Rick | Jones | CAN | 63 | 10 May |
| 10.37 | 2.4 | Dirk | Assenheimer | GDR | 66 | 31 May |
| 10.37 | 2.9 | Peter | Klein (80) | FRG | 59 | 11 Jul |
| | | | | | | |
| 10.37 | 2.9 | Matthias | Schlicht | FRG | 67 | 11 Jul |
| 10.37 | 4.4 | Alain | Mazella | FRA | 66 | 19 Jul |
| 10.38 | | Tim | Martin | USA | 65 | 26 Apr |
| 10.38 | 2.3 | Darren | Williams | USA | 64 | 26 Apr |
| 10.38 | 4.5 | Greg | Holmes | USA | 55 | 10 May |
| 10.38 | 4.0 | John | Simpson | USA | 66 | 18 May |
| | | | | | | |
| 10.38 | 4.2 | Nigel | Walker | UK | 63 | 13 Jul |
| 10.38 | 3.8 | Jae-Keun | Chang | SKO | 62 | 30 Sep |
| 10.39 | 3.4 | Keith | Stanford | USA | 64 | 5 Apr |
| 10.39 | | Marshall | Malone (90) | USA | 67 | 25 Apr |
| | | | | | | |
| 10.39 | 2.3 | Tarrell | Carpenter | USA | 67 | 28 Jun |
| 10.40 | | David | Rhodes | USA | 64 | 10 May |
| 10.40 | 2.5 | Marek | Hulbój | POL | 63 | 27 Jun |
| 10.40 | 3.0 | Simon | Baird | UK | 63 | 26 Jul |
| 10.41 | 2.8 | Haywood | Taylor | USA | | 25 Apr |
| 10.41 | | Steve | Lofton | USA | | 3 May |
| A10.41 | 6.4 | Darryl | Hudson | USA | 64 | 10 May |
| 10.41 | 4.5 | Tim | Williams | USA | | 10 May |
| 10.41 | 2.7 | Shinji | Aoto | JAP | 67 | 13 Jul |
| 10.41 | 3.8 | Kamel | Selmi (100) | ALG | 65 | 7 Aug |
| | | | | | | |
| 10.42 | 5.4 | Everard | Samuels | JAM | 58 | 29 Mar |
| 10.42 | | Mike | Taylor | USA | 65 | 25 Apr |
| 10.42 | 5.0 | Aleksandr | Kutepov | SU | 68 | 23 May |
| 10.42 | 3.5 | Roman | Osipenko | SU | 67 | 23 May |
| 10.42 | 2.5 | David | Kirton | UK | 67 | 16 Jul |
| 10.42 | 4.4 | Daniel | Sangouma (106) | FRA | 65 | 19 Jul |

Doubtful wind readings:

| Mark | Wind | Name | | Nat | Yr | Pos | Meet | Venue | Date |
|---|---|---|---|---|---|---|---|---|---|
| 10.03 | -2.5 | Viktor | Bryzgin | SU | 62 | 1h1 | Znam | Leningrad | 7 Jun |
| 10.07 | -1.2 | | Bryzgin | | | 1r1 | Znam | Leningrad | 7 Jun |
| 10.10 | -0.4 | Nikolay | Yushmanov | SU | 61 | 1r2 | Znam | Leningrad | 7 Jun |
| | | | | | | | | | |
| 10.19 | -1.2 | Vladimir | Muravyov | SU | 59 | 2r1 | Znam | Leningrad | 7 Jun |
| 10.29 | -2.5 | Gennadiy | Mirzoyan | SU | 64 | 2h1 | Znam | Leningrad | 7 Jun |
| 10.32 | 0.2 | Aleksandr | Semyonov | SU | 62 | 1h | Znam | Leningrad | 7 Jun |
| 10.32 | -2.5 | Nikolay | Razgonov | SU | 64 | 3h1 | Znam | Leningrad | 7 Jun |
| 10.33 | -1.2 | Boris | Nikulin | SU | 60 | 6r1 | Znam | Leningrad | 7 Jun |
| 10.35 | -0.4 | Igor | Groshev | SU | 64 | 2r2 | Znam | Leningrad | 7 Jun |
| 10.35 | -0.4 | Aleksandr | Pugovkin | SU | 64 | 2r2 | Znam | Leningrad | 7 Jun |
| 10.35 | -0.4 | Vladimir | Shershen | SU | 61 | 4r2 | Znam | Leningrad | 7 Jun |
| 10.36 | -1.2 | Yuriy | Petrov | SU | 63 | 7r1 | Znam | Leningrad | 7 Jun |
| | | | | | | | | | |
| 10.41 | -2.5 | Vadim | Samoilenko | SU | 63 | | 7 | Jun | |
| 10.41 | -0.4 | | Samoilenko | | | | 7 | Jun | |
| 10.41 | -1.7 | Anatoliy | Kalinichev | SU | 61 | | 7 | Jun | |

Hand timing:

| Mark | Wind | Name | | Nat | Yr | Pos | Venue | Date |
|---|---|---|---|---|---|---|---|---|
| 10.0 | | Emmit | King | USA | 59 | 1 | Tempe | 5 Apr |
| 10.0 | | Luis | Morales | PR | 64 | 2 | Tempe | 5 Apr |
| 10.0 | | Dana | Gardner | USA | | 1 | Cape Girardeau | 19 Apr |
| 10.0 | | Viktor | Bryzgin | SU | 62 | 1 | Stakhanov | 26 Apr |
| 10.0 | | Andrey | Fyodorov | SU | 63 | 1 | Moskva | 9 May |
| 10.0 | | William | Reed | USA | 70 | 1 | Philadelphia | 30 May |
| 10.1 | 1.0 | Marty | Krulee | USA | 56 | 1 | Pomona, CA | 22 Mar |
| 10.1 | | Anthony | Monroe | TRI | 64 | 1 | Irvine, CA | 22 Mar |
| 10.1 | 1.8 | Aatron | Kenney | USA | 63 | 1 | San Angelo | 10 Apr |
| 10.1 | | Ken | Robinson (10) | USA | 63 | 1 | Lincoln | 3 May |

| Mark | Wind | Name | | Nat | Yr | Pos | Meet | Venue | Date |
|------|------|------|------|-----|----|----|------|-------|------|
| 10.1 | 1.9 | Clyde | Bishop | USA | 62 | 1h1 | | Houston | 9 May |
| 10.1 | | Max | Morinière | FRA | 64 | 1 | | St John's | 31 May |
| 10.1 | | Igor | Zhaivoronok | SU | 62 | | | Omsk | 13 Jun |
| 10.1 | | Viktor | Khrishchuk | SU | 58 | | | Omsk | 13 Jun |
| 10.1 | | Aleksandr | Pugovkin | SU | 64 | 1 | | Stakhanov | 13 Jun |
| 10.1 | | Stanley | Floyd | USA | 61 | 1 | | Houston | 13 Jun |
| 10.1 | | Boris | Nikulin | SU | 60 | 1 | | Ryazan | 28 Jun |
| 10.1 | | Albert | Salimov | SU | 62 | 1 | | Novotroitsk | 28 Jun |
| 10.1 | | Andrey | Razin | SU | 62 | 2 | | Novotroitsk | 28 Jun |
| 10.1 | 1.8 | Aleksandr | Shishov (20) | SU | 59 | 1 | | Novosibirsk | 28 Jun |
| 10.1 | | Vladimir | Kravtsov | SU | 56 | h | | Lipetsk | 18 Jul |
| 10.1 | | Geldy | Redzhepov | SU | 62 | 1 | | Lipetsk | 18 Jul |
| A10.1 | | Katsuiko | Nakaya | BRA | 57 | 1 | | México, D.F. | 8 Aug |
| A10.1 | | Frankie | Fredericks | RSA | 67 | 1 | | Windhoek | 18 Oct |

(24)

Marks made with assisting wind > 2 m/s :

| Mark | Wind | Name | | Nat | Yr | Pos | Meet | Venue | Date |
|------|------|------|------|-----|----|----|------|-------|------|
| 9.9 | | Alrick | Munroe | JAM | 60 | 1 | | Plainview, TX | 22 Mar |
| 10.0 | | Richard | Ross | USA | | 1 | | Lubbock | 8 Mar |
| 10.0 | | Ed | Moxey | BAH | 66 | 1 | | Mobile | 29 Mar |
| 10.0 | | Carl | Carter | USA | 64 | 1 | | Lubbock | 29 Mar |
| 10.0 | 3.6 | Hiroki | Fuwa | JAP | 66 | 1 | | Shizuoka | 27 Apr |
| A10.0 | | Anthony | Monroe | TRI | 64 | 1 | | Flagstaff | 3 May |
| 10.0 | | Aatron | Kenney | USA | 63 | | | | |
| 10.1 | | Derwin | Hall | USA | | 1h | | Dallas | 8 Mar |
| 10.1 | | James | Glenn | USA | 69 | 1 | | Dallas | 8 Mar |
| 10.1 | | Bobby | Johnson (10) | USA | 67 | 2 | | Dallas | 8 Mar |
| 10.1 | | Perry | Cartlidge | USA | 63 | 1 | | Jonesboro | 29 Mar |
| 10.1 | | Greg | Meghoo | JAM | 65 | 3 | | Lubbock | 29 Mar |
| 10.1 | 3.6 | Leroy | Burrell | USA | 67 | 1h3 | TexR | Austin | 4 Apr |
| 10.1 | 3.6 | Andrew | Smith | JAM | 64 | 1h4 | TexR | Austin | 4 Apr |
| A10.1 | | Gabriel | Okon | NIG | 66 | 1 | | Albuquerque | 12 Apr |
| A10.1 | | Chris | Leeuwenburgh | HOL | 62 | 2 | | Albuquerque | 12 Apr |
| A10.1 | | Andrew | Brass | USA | | 3 | | Albuquerque | 12 Apr |
| 10.1 | 3.6 | Hirofumi | Miyazaki | JAP | 59 | 2 | | Shizuoka | 27 Apr |
| 10.1 | 6.5 | Harold | Madox | USA | 65 | 1h1 | | Odessa, TX | 15 May |
| 10.1 | 3.5 | Oleg | Kucherov (20) | SU | 66 | 1 | | Leningrad | 25 Jun |
| A10.1 | | Luis | Smith | PAN | 68 | 1h | | Quito | 13 Sep |
| 10.1 | | Dmitriy | Vanyaykin(22) | SU | 66 | 1 | v Rum-j | Rovno | 4 Oct |

| Mark | Wind | Name | | Nat | Yr | Pos | Meet | Venue | Date |
|------|------|------|---|-----|-----|-----|------|-------|------|

## 200 METRES

| Mark | Wind | Name | | Nat | Yr | Pos | Meet | Venue | Date |
|------|------|------|---|-----|-----|-----|------|-------|------|
| 20.12 | 0.6 | Floyd | Heard | USA | 66 | 1r1 | GWG | Moskva | 7 Jul |
| 20.16 | | Roy | Martin | USA | 66 | 1 | | Dallas | 12 Apr |
| 20.17 | 0.3 | Lorenzo | Daniel | USA | 66 | 1 | King | Atlanta | 20 Apr |
| 20.19 | 1.6 | John | Dinan | AUS | 59 | 1 | | Canberra | 6 Mar |
| 20.23 | 0.5 | Mike | Timpson | USA | 67 | 1 | | Univ Park, PA | 16 May |
| 20.25 | 1.2 | Kirk | Baptiste | USA | 63 | 1 | BGP | Budapest | 11 Aug |
| 20.28 | 1.2 | Robson C | da Silva | BRA | 64 | 1 | | Madrid | 4 Jun |
| 20.29 | 0.3 | Calvin | Smith | USA | 61 | 1 | | Paris | 22 Jul |
| 20.30 | 0.0 | Harvey | McSwain | USA | 63 | 1 | | Knoxville | 24 May |
| 20.30 | -1.2 | | Smith | | | 1r1 | WK | Zürich | 13 Aug |
| 20.33 | 0.0 | Wallace | Spearmon (10) | USA | 62 | 2 | | Knoxville | 24 May |
| 20.33 | -1.2 | | Baptiste | | | 2r1 | WK | Zürich | 13 Aug |
| A20.34 | 1.8 | Wessel | Oosthuizen | RSA | 61 | 1 | | Secunda | 1 Feb |
| 20.34 | 0.2 | | Heard | | | 1 | NCAA | Indianapolis | 6 Jun |
| 20.34 | 0.7 | Atlee | Mahorn | CAN | 65 | 1 | Nik | Nice | 15 Jul |
| 20.35 | 1.2 | | Baptiste | | | 1h3 | TAC | Eugene | 19 Jun |
| 20.35 | -1.2 | | Heard | | | 3r1 | WK | Zürich | 13 Aug |
| A20.36 | 0.1 | Chidi | Imoh | NIG | 63 | 1 | | Boulder | 18 May |
| 20.36 | 1.2 | Thomas | Jefferson | USA | 62 | 2 | | Madrid | 4 Jun |
| 20.36 | 0.1 | Dwayne | Evans | USA | 58 | 1h2 | TAC | Eugene | 19 Jun |
| 20.37 | 0.2 | Roberto | Hernandez | CUB | 67 | 1 | | Sevilla | 24 May |
| 20.37 | 1.8 | | Heard | | | 1h4 | TAC | Eugene | 19 Jun |
| 20.38 | 0.0 | | Heard | | | 1 | | Austin | 3 May |
| 20.39 | 1.2 | | Daniel | | | 2h3 | TAC | Eugene | 19 Jun |
| 20.39 | 0.9 | Stanley | Kerr | USA | 67 | 1 | TAC-j | Towson, MD | 29 Jun |
| 20.40 | 1.4 | | Spearmon | | | 1h1 | TAC | Eugene | 19 Jun |
| 20.40 | 1.0 | | Mahorn | | | 1 | NC | Ottawa | 22 Jun |
| 20.41 | 1.8 | Carl | Lewis | USA | 61 | 2h4 | TAC | Eugene | 19 Jun |
| 20.41 | 1.4 | John | Regis | UK | 66 | 1 | AAA | London | 21 Jun |
| 20.41 | 0.7 | | Smith | | | 2 | Nik | Nice | 15 Jul |
| 20.41 | -1.6 | | Baptiste | | | 1 | USOCF | Houston | 1 Aug |
| 20.41 | -0.3 | | Baptiste | | | 1 | | Koblenz | 6 Aug |
| | | | (32/19) | | | | | | |
| 20.48 | 1.8 | Darrell | Robinson (20) | USA | 63 | 1r2 | | Modesto, CA | 10 May |
| 20.49 | | Henry | Thomas | USA | 67 | 1 | | Westwood | 22 Mar |
| 20.49 | -0.9 | Mike | Dexter | USA | 64 | 1 | | Los Angeles | 24 May |
| 20.50 | 1.2 | Brady | Crain | USA | 56 | 3h3 | TAC | Eugene | 19 Jun |
| 20.50 | 1.4 | Todd | Bennett | UK | 62 | 2 | AAA | London | 21 Jun |
| 20.50 | 1.7 | Ralf | Lübke | FRG | 65 | 1 | NC | W Berlin | 13 Jul |
| 20.50 | 0.0 | Aleksandr | Yevgenyev | SU | 61 | 1 | NC | Kiev | 16 Jul |
| 20.50 | 0.9 | Attila | Kovács | HUN | 60 | 1 | | Budapest | 13 Sep |
| 20.50 | -0.5 | Vladimir | Krylov | SU | 64 | 1 | Spart | Tashkent | 20 Sep |
| 20.51 | 1.4 | Linford | Christie | UK | 60 | 3 | AAA | London | 21 Jun |
| 20.52 | | Dennis | Mitchell (30) | USA | 66 | 1 | FlaR | Gainesville | 29 Mar |
| 20.52 | 1.9 | Daron | Council | USA | 64 | 2 | | Tampa | 12 Apr |
| 20.53 | | Albert | Robinson | USA | 64 | 1 | | Austin | 22 Mar |
| 20.53 | 0.0 | Leandro | Peñalver | CUB | 61 | 1s1 | CAC | Santiago/Dom | 2 Jul |
| 20.53 | 0.6 | Andrey | Fyodorov | SU | 63 | 4r1 | GWG | Moskva | 7 Jul |
| 20.53 | 1.2 | Allan | Wells | UK | 52 | 3 | BGP | Budapest | 11 Aug |
| 20.53 | 0.7 | Bruno | Marie-Rose | FRA | 65 | 1 | | Rieti | 7 Sep |
| 20.54 | 0.0 | Thomas | Schröder | GDR | 62 | 1s2 | EC | Stuttgart | 28 Aug |
| 20.55 | | Andre | Phillips | USA | 59 | 1 | | Los Angeles | 1 Aug |

| Mark | Wind | Name | | Nat | Yr | Pos | Meet | Venue | Date |
|------|------|------|------|-----|----|----|------|-------|------|
| 20.56 | | Earle | Laing | JAM | 64 | 2 | | Austin | 22 Mar |
| 20.56 | | Leroy | Reid (40) | JAM | 63 | 2 | | Dallas | 12 Apr |
| | | | | | | | | | |
| 20.56 | 0.2 | Danny | Peebles | USA | 66 | 4 | NCAA | Indianapolis | 6 Jun |
| 20.57 | | Luís | Morales | PR | 64 | 1 | | Los Angeles | 22 Mar |
| 20.57 | 0.3 | Sam | Graddy | USA | 64 | 3 | King | Atlanta | 20 Apr |
| 20.57 | 0.7 | Stefano | Tilli | ITA | 62 | 2 | | Rieti | 7 Sep |
| 20.58 | 0.4 | James | Butler | USA | 60 | 2 | | Fort-de-France | 4 May |
| 20.58 | 1.1 | Olaf | Prenzler | GDR | 58 | 2 | NC | Jena | 29 Jun |
| 20.58 | 2.0 | Christian | Haas | FRG | 58 | 1 | | Regensburg | 29 Jun |
| 20.58 | 0.0 | Jürgen | Evers | FRG | 65 | 2s2 | EC | Stuttgart | 28 Aug |
| 20.60 | -0.8 | Lee | McNeill | USA | 64 | 1 | | Charlottesville | 10 May |
| 20.60 | 0.2 | Roscoe | Tatum (50) | USA | 66 | 1r1 | | Houston | 18 May |
| | | | | | | | | | |
| 20.61 | 1.8 | István | Nagy | HUN | 59 | 1 | | Budapest | 25 May |
| 20.61 | -0.7 | Roland | Jokl | AUT | 62 | 1 | | Südstadt/Wien | 5 Jul |
| 20.62 | 0.9 | Nikolay | Razgonov | SU | 64 | 1s2 | NC | Kiev | 16 Jul |
| 20.62 | 1.1 | Frank | Emmelmann | GDR | 61 | 1 | GO | Dresden | 17 Aug |
| 20.63 | | Derrick | Florence | USA | 68 | 1 | | Pasadena, TX | 3 May |
| 20.63 | 1.8 | Roger | Black | UK | 66 | 1 | | London | 12 Sep |
| A20.65 | 0.6 | Ken | Henderson | USA | 66 | 1 | | Provo | 12 Apr |
| 20.65 | 2.0 | Danny | Everett | USA | 66 | 1 | | Westwood | 19 Apr |
| 20.67 | 0.3 | Terry | McDaniel | USA | 65 | 4 | King | Atlanta | 20 Apr |
| 20.67 | 0.2 | Patrick | Gordon (60) | USA | 65 | 2r1 | | Houston | 18 May |
| | | | | | | | | | |
| 20.67 | 0.0 | Robert | Hackett | USA | 64 | 1 | | Madison | 24 May |
| 20.67 | 1.4 | Felix | Stevens | CUB | 64 | 1 | Barr | Habana | 15 Jun |
| 20.67 | 1.4 | Clayton | Kearney | AUS | 64 | 4 | AAA | London | 21 Jun |
| 20.68 | 0.5 | Mike | Morris | USA | 63 | 2 | | Univ Park, PA | 16 May |
| A20.69 | | Peter | Ngobeni | RSA | 62 | 1 | | Potchefstroom | 7 Feb |
| 20.69 | 2.0 | Mike | Marsh | USA | 67 | 2 | | Westwood | 19 Apr |
| 20.69 | 0.2 | Steve | Morgan | JAM | 65 | 2 | IC4A | Villanova | 25 May |
| 20.69 | 1.1 | Torsten | Heimrath | GDR | 63 | 3 | NC | Jena | 29 Jun |
| 20.70 | -0.2 | Stanley | Blalock | USA | 64 | 1 | | Knoxville | 12 Apr |
| A20.70 | 0.1 | Devlon | Dunn (70) | USA | | 2 | | Boulder | 18 May |
| | | | | | | | | | |
| 20.70 | 0.0 | Laron | Brown | USA | 62 | 5 | | Knoxville | 24 May |
| 20.70 | 0.3 | Desai | Williams | CAN | 59 | 2 | | Paris | 22 Jul |
| 20.71 | 1.8 | Marty | Krulee | USA | 56 | 5r2 | | Modesto, CA | 10 May |
| 20.71 | -0.1 | P Francesco | Pavoni | ITA | 63 | 1 | CISM | Ostia | 13 Sep |
| 20.71 | 1.9 | Jae-Keun | Chang | SKO | 62 | 1s1 | AsiG | Seoul | 1 Oct |
| 20.72 | -0.3 | Czesław | Pradzyński | POL | 60 | 1 | NC | Grudziadz | 28 Jun |
| 20.74 | | William | Snoddy | USA | 57 | 1 | | Norman | 12 Apr |
| 20.74 | -0.4 | Susumu | Takano | JAP | 61 | 1s2 | | Kofu | 15 Oct |
| A20.74 | 1.5 | Tsahakile | Nzimande | RSA | 61 | 2 | | Bloemfontein | 5 Nov |
| 20.75 | 1.6 | Robert | Stone (80) | AUS | 65 | 2 | | Canberra | 6 Mar |
| | | | | | | | | | |
| 20.75 | | Carl | Carter | USA | 64 | 3 | | Austin | 22 Mar |
| 20.75 | 1.0 | Greg | Moses | USA | 65 | 1 | | Atlanta | 10 May |
| 20.75 | 1.8 | Gusztáv | Menczer | HUN | 59 | 2 | | Budapest | 25 May |
| 20.76 | 0.3 | Miles | Murphy | AUS | 67 | 1h2 | | Canberra | 21 Feb |
| 20.76 | | Sergio | Querol | CUB | 65 | 1h | | Santiago/Cuba | 22 Feb |
| 20.76 | 0.1 | Ian | Morris | TRI | 61 | 1 | | Los Angeles | 23 May |
| 20.76 | 0.2 | John | Mair | JAM | | 3 | IC4A | Villanova | 25 May |
| 20.77 | 1.4 | Tony | Dees | USA | 63 | 2r2 | | Columbus | 4 May |
| 20.77 | 0.0 | Nikolay | Yushmanov | SU | 61 | 1r2 | GWG | Moskva | 7 Jul |
| 20.78 | 1.6 | Michael | Newbold (90) | BAH | 67 | 1 | | Abymes | 31 Mar |

| Mark | Wind | Name | | Nat | Yr | Pos | Meet | Venue | Date |
|---|---|---|---|---|---|---|---|---|---|
| A20.78 | | Robin | McLean | RSA | 59 | 2 | | Johannesburg | 18 Apr |
| 20.78˙ | 0.4 | Aldo | Canti | FRA | 61 | 3 | | Fort-de-France | 4 May |
| 20.78 | 0.4 | Donny | Young | USA | 62 | 1 | | Tallahassee | 31 May |
| 20.78 | 1.0 | Ben | Johnson | CAN | 61 | 2 | NC | Ottawa | 22 Jun |
| 20.78 | 1.9 | Erwin | Skamrahl | FRG | 58 | 3s2 | NC | W Berlin | 13 Jul |
| 20.78 | -2.5 | György | Fetter | HUN | 63 | 1 | NC | Budapest | 16 Aug |
| 20.79 | -0.6 | Juan | Nunez | DOM | 59 | 2 | CAC | Santiago/Dom | 3 Jul |
| 20.79 | 0.1 | Ronald | Desruelles | BEL | 55 | 1 | | Hechtel | 5 Jul |
| 20.79 | 1.9 | Rolf | Kistner | FRG | 62 | 4s2 | NC | W Berlin | 13 Jul |
| 20.79 | 0.0 | Pascal | Barré (100) | FRA | 59 | 1 | | Bern | 20 Aug |
| 20.80 | 1.5 | Vincent | Coleman | USA | 65 | 1h1 | | Arlington | 25 Apr |
| 20.80 | 1.1 | Mathias | Schersing | GDR | 64 | 4 | NC | Jena | 29 Jun |
| 20.81 | 1.4 | Mike | St Louis(103) | UK | 64 | 5 | AAA | London | 21 Jun |

| Mark | Wind | Name | | Nat | Yr | Date |
|---|---|---|---|---|---|---|
| 20.82 | -1.6 | Neal | Jessie | USA | 64 | 5 Apr |
| 20.82 | | João B | da Silva | BRA | 63 | 13 Jul |
| 20.82 | 0.3 | Antoine | Richard | FRA | 60 | 22 Jul |
| 20.83 | 1.1 | Dwight | Johnson | USA | 64 | 22 Mar |
| A20.83 | 2.0 | Raoul | Karp | RSA | 67 | 12 Apr |
| 20.83 | 0.0 | Anthony | Miller | USA | 65 | 17 May |
| A20.83 | 1.5 | Eugene | van Niekerk | RSA | 65 | 5 Nov |
| | | | (110) | | | |
| 20.84 | 1.8 | Bernard | Whyte | CAN | 65 | 13 Apr |
| 20.85 | 1.5 | Brian | Cooper | USA | 65 | 24 May |
| 20.85 | -1.4 | Volker | Westhagemann | FRG | 64 | 17 Jun |
| 20.85 | 1.8 | J-Jacques | Boussemart | FRA | 63 | 10 Aug |
| A20.86 | 0.1 | Kevin | Young | USA | 65 | 18 May |
| 20.86 | | Dave | Smith | JAM | 60 | 24 May |
| 20.86 | 1.1 | Heiko | Truppel | GDR | 64 | 29 Jun |
| 20.86 | -0.8 | Larry | Myricks | USA | 56 | 13 Aug |
| 20.87 | 1.6 | Dazel | Jules | TRI | 67 | 31 Mar |
| 20.87 | 1.0 | Gilles | Quenehervé | FRA | 66 | 21 Jun |
| | | | (120) | | | |
| 20.88 | -2.5 | Willie | Smith | USA | 56 | 19 Apr |
| 20.88 | -0.9 | Gabriel | Tiacoh | IVC | 63 | 3 May |
| 20.88 | 0.2 | Nikolay | Antonov | BUL | 68 | 29 Jun |
| 20.88 | 1.8 | Peter | Klein | FRG | 59 | 13 Jul |
| 20.88 | | Marian | Woronin | POL | 56 | 12 Sep |
| 20.88 | -0.1 | Andrijus | Komikas | SU | 64 | 19 Sep |
| 20.89 | | Greg | Walker | USA | 63 | 26 Apr |
| 20.89 | -1.4 | Norbert | Dobeleit | FRG | 64 | 17 Jun |
| 20.89 | 0.2 | Tallal | Mansour | QAT | 64 | 9 Aug |
| 20.90 | -0.8 | Willie | Parker (130) | USA | 65 | 10 May |
| 20.90 | 0.0 | Norman | Edwards | JAM | 62 | 24 May |
| 20.90 | 0.0 | Aleksandr | Knysh | SU | 64 | 16 Jul |
| 20.91 | | Ricardo | Chacón | CUB | 63 | 22 Feb |
| A20.91 | 2.0 | Ludwig | Myburgh | RSA | 62 | 12 Apr |
| 20.91 | 1.3 | Oleg | Fatun | SU | 59 | 8 Jun |
| 20.91 | 0.4 | Giovanni | Bongiorni | ITA | 56 | 24 Jul |
| 20.91 | 1.9 | Thomas | Schönlebe | GDR | 65 | 20 Aug |
| 20.92 | | Michael | Franks | USA | 63 | 12 Apr |
| 20.92 | 0.1 | Dana | Gardner | USA | | 23 May |
| 20.92 | -1.6 | Darren | Clark (140) | AUS | 65 | 5 Aug |

| Mark | Wind | Name | | Nat | Yr | Date |
|---|---|---|---|---|---|---|
| 20.93 | | Jason | Leach | USA | 66 | 22 Mar |
| 20.93* | | Walker | Watkins | USA | 67 | 9 May |
| 20.93 | 1.3 | Gennadiy | Gureyev | SU | 66 | 8 Jun |
| 20.93 | -2.8 | Harlan | Davis | USA | | 14 Jun |
| 20.93 | 0.8 | Harouna | Pale | BFA | 55 | 9 Aug |
| 20.94 | 2.0 | Leroy | Burrell | USA | 67 | 19 Apr |
| 20.94 | 1.8 | Brad | McDonald | USA | 58 | 10 May |
| 20.94 | -0.2 | Mark | Mitchell | USA | 67 | 24 Jun |
| 20.95 | | C | Walker | USA | | 30 May |
| 20.95 | 1.7 | Einar | Sagli (150) | NOR | 58 | 21 Jun |
| A20.96 | 1.8 | Andre | Muller | RSA | 66 | 1 Feb |
| 20.96 | | Joel | Isasi | CUB | 67 | 22 Feb |
| 20.96 | | Andre | Freeman | USA | 64 | 22 Mar |
| 20.96 | | Anatoliy | Litvinov | SU | 59 | 18 May |
| 20.96 | 0.6 | Yann | Quentrec | FRA | 62 | 14 Jun |
| 20.96 | | Clive | Wright | JAM | | 21 Jun |
| 20.97 | 0.3 | Everard | Samuels | JAM | 58 | 20 Apr |
| 20.97 | 0.0 | Quincy | Watts | USA | 70 | 23 May |
| 20.97 | 0.7 | Cyprean | Enweani | CAN | 64 | 30 May |
| 20.97 | 0.4 | Arthur | Blake (160) | USA | 66 | 31 May |
| 20.97 | 0.6 | Peter | Howard | USA | 63 | 21 Jun |
| 20.97 | 1.3 | Steffen | Bringmann | GDR | 64 | 22 Jun |
| 20.97 | 1.0 | Harald | Schmid | FRG | 57 | 28 Jun |
| 20.97 | -1.5 | Leszek | Dunecki | POL | 56 | 3 Aug |
| 20.97 | 1.8 | Feng | Li | CHN | 65 | 3 Oct |
| A20.97 | | Gerhard | Barnard | RSA | 67 | 6 Dec |
| 20.98 | | Rod | Richardson | USA | 68 | 3 May |
| 20.99 | | Roddie | Haley | USA | 65 | 12 Apr |
| 20.99 | 1.0 | Mike | Dwyer | CAN | 62 | 22 Jun |
| 20.99 | 1.0 | Edgar | Itt (170) | FRG | 67 | 28 Jun |
| 20.99 | 1.3 | Dirk | Schweisfurth | FRG | 65 | 7 Sep |
| 20.99 | -0.6 | Sergey | Zhukov (172) | SU | 65 | 19 Sep |

Best low altitude marks:

| Mark | Wind | Name | | | | Date |
|---|---|---|---|---|---|---|
| 20.47 | -0.3 | | Imoh | 2 | Koblenz | 6 Aug |
| 20.87 | 1.8 | K | Henderson | | | 22 Mar |
| 20.91 | | | Oosthuizen | | | 21 Apr |

| Mark | Wind | Name | | Nat | Yr | Pos | Meet | Venue | Date |
|------|------|------|--|-----|----|-----|------|-------|------|

| | 1 | 10 | 20 | 30 | 50 | 100 | Under 20.70 | Under 20.90 |
|---|---|----|----|----|----|-----|-------------|-------------|
| 1982 | 20.15 | 20.39 | 20.47 | 20.58 | 20.74 | 20.88 | 43 | 108 |
| 1983 | 19.75 | 20.32 | 20.46 | 20.52 | 20.65 | 20.85 | 53 | 117 |
| 1984 | 19.80 | 20.34 | 20.41 | 20.52 | 20.62 | 20.78 | 79 | 144 |
| 1985 | 20.07 | 20.32 | 20.41 | 20.49 | 20.59 | 20.80 | 72 | 140 |
| 1986 | 20.12 | 20.33 | 20.48 | 20.52 | 20.60 | 20.79 | 68 | 129 |

Marks made with assisting wind > 2  m/s :

| Mark | Wind | Name | | Nat | Yr | Pos | Meet | Venue | Date |
|------|------|------|--|-----|----|-----|------|-------|------|
| 19.86 | 4.6 | Roy | Martin | USA | 66 | 1r2 | | Houston | 18 May |
| 20.03 | 3.2 | Floyd | Heard | USA | 66 | 1 | TAC | Eugene | 21 Jun |
| 20.09 | 2.2 | Dwayne | Evans | USA | 58 | 1 | | Walnut, CA | 1 Jun |
| 20.10 | 4.6 | Stanley | Kerr | USA | 67 | 2r2 | | Houston | 18 May |
| 20.11 | 2.8 | Lorenzo | Daniel | USA | 66 | 1 | | Knoxville | 18 May |
| 20.12 | 3.2 | | Evans | | | 2 | TAC | Eugene | 21 Jun |
| 20.14 | 3.2 | Kirk | Baptiste | USA | 63 | 3 | TAC | Eugene | 21 Jun |
| 20.19 | 2.6 | | Evans | | | 1s2 | TAC | Eugene | 21 Jun |
| 20.22 | | Vincent | Coleman | USA | 65 | 1 | | Arlington | 26 Apr |
| 20.23 | 2.1 | Carl | Lewis | USA | 61 | 1 | | Houston | 4 May |
| 20.23 | 4.9 | | Baptiste | | | 1s1 | TAC | Eugene | 21 Jun |
| 20.24 | 2.6 | | Heard | | | 2s2 | TAC | Eugene | 21 Jun |
| 20.25 | 4.6 | | Heard | | | 3r2 | | Houston | 18 May |
| A20.27 | 2.8 | Ken | Henderson | USA | 66 | 1 | | Provo | 10 May |
| 20.27 | 4.9 | Wallace | Spearmon (10) | USA | 62 | 2s1 | TAC | Eugene | 21 Jun |
| 20.28 | 2.1 | | Baptiste | | | 2 | | Houston | 4 May |
| 20.30 | 2.2 | | Dinan | | | 1 | | Canberra | 22 Feb |
| 20.30 | 3.2 | | Lewis | | | 4 | TAC | Eugene | 21 Jun |
| 20.31 | 2.2 | Atlee | Mahorn | CAN | 65 | 1 | CG | Edinburgh | 31 Jul |
| 20.32 | 2.6 | | Lewis | | | 3s2 | TAC | Eugene | 21 Jun |
| 20.34 | 2.6 | | McSwain | | | 4s2 | TAC | Eugene | 21 Jun |
| 20.36 | 3.2 | | McSwain | | | 5 | TAC | Eugene | 21 Jun |
| 20.38 | | | Heard | | | 1 | | College Sta, TX | 29 Mar |
| 20.38 | 4.6 | Leroy | Reid | JAM | 63 | 4r2 | | Houston | 18 May |
| 20.38 | 4.9 | | Daniel | | | 3s1 | TAC | Eugene | 21 Jun |
| 20.40 | | | Heard | | | 1h1 | | College Sta, TX | 29 Mar |
| 20.41 | 2.1 | Darrell | Robinson | USA | 63 | 1r2 | MSR | Walnut, CA | 27 Apr |
| | | | (27/15) | | | | | | |
| A20.45 | 2.8 | Aaron | Thigpen | USA | 64 | 2 | | Provo | 10 May |
| 20.46 | 2.4 | Ian | Morris | TRI | 61 | 1 | | San Angelo | 26 Apr |
| A20.46 | 2.8 | Andre | Freeman | USA | 64 | 3 | | Provo | 10 May |
| 20.50 | 2.1 | Mark | Witherspoon | USA | 63 | 2r2 | MSR | Walnut, CA | 27 Apr |
| 20.55 | 3.5 | Marty | Krulee (20) | USA | 56 | 1 | | San Jose | 19 Apr |
| 20.60 | 4.6 | Jason | Leach | USA | 66 | 5r2 | | Houston | 18 May |
| 20.63 | | Brian | Cooper | USA | 65 | 2 | | Arlington | 26 Apr |
| 20.64 | 2.2 | Ben | Johnson | CAN | 61 | 3 | CG | Edinburgh | 31 Jul |
| 20.65 | | Carl | Carter | USA | 64 | 1 | | Lubbock | 29 Mar |
| 20.65 | | Harold | Madox | USA | 65 | 1s1 | | Odessa, TX | 16 May |

MEN 1986

| Mark | Wind | Name | | Nat | Yr | Pos | Meet | Venue | Date |
|------|------|------|------|-----|----|-----|------|-------|------|
| 20.66 | 2.3 | Erwin | Skamrahl | FRG | 58 | 1 | | Lage | 13 Jun |
| A20.67 | 2.8 | Gabriel | Okon | NIG | 66 | 4 | | Provo | 10 May |
| A20.67 | 2.8 | Rex | Brown | USA | 64 | 5 | | Provo | 10 May |
| 20.69 | 2.6 | Cameron | Sharp | UK | 58 | 2r1 | MSR | Walnut, CA | 27 Apr |
| 20.71 | 2.4 | Greg | Meghoo (30) | JAM | 65 | 2 | | San Angelo | 26 Apr |
| 20.71 | 2.1 | Leroy | Burrell | USA | 67 | 3 | | Houston | 4 May |
| 20.71 | 5.1 | Anthony | Miller | USA | 65 | 1h1 | | Walnut, CA | 5 May |
| 20.72 | | Kevin | Young | USA | 65 | 1h2 | | College Sta, TX | 29 Mar |
| 20.73 | 3.1 | Fred | Simmons | USA | | 1h4 | | Walnut, CA | 5 May |
| 20.76 | 2.6 | John | Johnson | USA | 60 | 3r1 | MSR | Walnut, CA | 27 Apr |
| 20.76 | 2.8 | Norman | Edwards | JAM | 62 | 5 | | Knoxville | 18 May |
| 20.77 | | Andrew | Smith | JAM | 64 | 2h1 | | College Sta, TX | 29 Mar |
| 20.78 | 2.1 | Willie | Smith | USA | 56 | 6r2 | MSR | Walnut, CA | 27 Apr |
| 20.80 | 4.9 | Dana | Gardner | USA | | 1h3 | | Los Angeles | 21 May |
| 20.80 | 2.7 | Innocent | Egbunike (40) | NIG | 61 | 1 | | Santa Monica | 7 Jun |

| Mark | Wind | Name | | Nat | Yr | Date | Mark | Wind | Name | | Nat | Yr | Date |
|------|------|------|------|-----|----|------|------|------|------|------|-----|----|------|
| 20.81 | 4.2 | Calvin | Long | USA | 66 | 10 May | 20.91 | | Steve | Lofton | USA | | 3 May |
| 20.82 | 9.0 | Don | Young | USA | 64 | 5 May | 20.91 | 2.3 | Andreas | Knötgen | FRG | 64 | 13 Jun |
| 20.82 | | Volker | Westhagemann | FRG | 64 | 28 Jun | 20.92 | | Ray | Hill | USA | 67 | 17 May |
| 20.82 | 3.4 | Arnaldo | Abrantes | POR | 61 | 25 Jul | 20.93 | 2.7 | | Hedgepath(60) | USA | | 19 Apr |
| 20.83 | 2.4 | Aatron | Kenney | USA | 63 | 26 Apr | | | | | | | |
| 20.83 | 2.7 | Greg | Moore | USA | 59 | 7 Jun | 20.95 | | Archie | Roberts | USA | | 29 Mar |
| 20.84 | 2.7 | Brad | McDonald | USA | 58 | 19 Apr | 20.95 | 2.5 | Stewart | Weathers | UK | 65 | 4 Jun |
| 20.84 | | Lonnie | Hooker | USA | 64 | 17 May | 20.95 | 3.4 | Luis | Cunha | POR | 64 | 25 Jul |
| 20.85 | | Mark | Senior | JAM | 63 | 29 Mar | 20.96 | | Greg | Sholars | USA | 66 | 29 Mar |
| 20.85 | 3.1 | Jeff | Williams (50) | USA | 64 | 9 May | 20.96 | 2.8 | Greg | Richardson | USA | 64 | 18 May |
| | | | | | | | 20.96 | 3.9 | Mike | McFarlane | UK | 60 | 21 Jun |
| 20.87 | | Devon | Morris | JAM | 61 | 29 Mar | 20.96 | 2.2 | Simon | Baird | UK | 63 | 31 Jul |
| 20.87 | | Tim | Martin | USA | 65 | 26 Apr | 20.97 | 2.6 | Courtney | Brown | CAN | 65 | 27 Apr |
| 20.88 | 2.1 | Ahmed | de Kom | HOL | 59 | 12 Jul | 20.97 | | David | Rhodes | USA | 64 | 10 May |
| 20.90 | | Antonio | Manning | USA | 65 | 12 Apr | 20.97 | 2.6 | Mike | Dwyer (70) | CAN | 62 | 31 Jul |
| 20.90 | | | DeWitt | USA | 66 | 27 Apr | | | | | | | |
| 20.90 | | Clyde | Bishop | USA | 62 | 9 May | 20.98 | 3.9 | Bruce | Frayne | AUS | 58 | 23 Jan |
| | | | | | | | 20.98 | | Chip | Rish (72) | USA | 67 | 29 Mar |

Hand timing:

| Mark | Wind | Name | | Nat | Yr | Pos | Meet | Venue | Date |
|------|------|------|------|-----|----|-----|------|-------|------|
| 20.1 | 0.5 | Carl | Lewis | USA | 61 | 1 | Jenner | San Jose | 31 May |
| 20.2 | 0.5 | Kirk | Baptiste | USA | 63 | 2 | Jenner | San Jose | 31 May |
| 20.3 | 0.9 | Marty | Krulee | USA | 56 | 1 | | Pomona, CA | 22 Mar |
| 20.3 | 0.8 | Daron | Council | USA | 64 | 1 | | Starkville | 3 May |
| 20.4 | 0.8 | Ronnie | Dennis | USA | 64 | 2 | | Starkville | 3 May |
| 20.5 | 0.9 | Mark | Witherspoon | USA | 63 | 2 | | Pomona, CA | 22 Mar |
| 20.5 | | Marcus | Black | USA | | 1 | | Columbia, SC | 5 Apr |
| A20.5 | | George | Crunkleton | USA | 56 | 1 | | Albuquerque | 5 Apr |
| A20.5 | | Gabriel | Okon | NIG | 66 | 1 | | Albuquerque | 19 Apr |
| 20.5 | | William | Reed (10) | USA | 70 | 1 | | Philadelphia | 30 May |
| 20.5 | | Nikolay | Antonov | BUL | 68 | 1 | NC-j | Sofia | 6 Jul |
| 20.5 | | Krasimir | Bozhinovski | BUL | 67 | 2 | NC-j | Sofia | 6 Jul |
| 20.5 | 0.2 | Nikolay | Razgonov (13) | SU | 64 | 1 | | Kiev | 30 Aug |

| Mark | | Name | | Nat | Yr | Pos | Meet | Venue | | Date |
|------|---|------|---|-----|----|----|------|-------|---|------|
| 20.6 | 0.9 | Innocent | Egbunike | NIG 61 | 22 Mar | 20.7 | | Dana | Gardner | USA | 19 Apr |
| 20.6 | | Fedya | Yakubov | BUL 60 | 18 May | 20.7 | 0.8 | Wayne | Banks | USA 65 | 3 May |
| 20.6 | | Mike | Dwyer | CAN 62 | 1 Jun | 20.7 | 0.1 | John | Mair | JAM | 10 May |
| 20.6 | | Ian | Morris | TRI 61 | 8 Jun | 20.7 | 1.4 | Gilles | Quenehervé | FRA 66 | 22 May |
| 20.6 | 1.2 | Sergey | Klenov | SU 67 | 26 Jun | 20.7 | | Tony | Sharpe | CAN 61 | 1 Jun |
| 20.6 | | Aleksey | Golovin | SU 62 | 19 Jul | 20.7 | | Vadim | Samoilenko | SU 63 | 19 Jul |
| 20.6 | -0.3 | Ali | Bakhta (20) | ALG 61 | 25 Jul | 20.7 | | Ronald | Desruelles | BEL 55 | 27 Sep |
| 20.6 | 0.2 | Dmitriy | Vanyaykin | SU 66 | 30 Aug | | | | (29) | | |
| A20.6 | | Frankie | Fredericks | RSA 67 | 18 Oct | | | | | | |

Marks made with assisting wind > 2 m/s :

| | | | | | | | | | | |
|---|---|---|---|---|---|---|---|---|---|---|
| A20.1 | | Gabriel | Okon | NIG 66 | 1 | | | Flagstaff | | 3 May |
| 20.2 | | Alrick | Munroe | JAM 60 | 1 | | | Plainview, TX | | 22 Mar |
| A20.2 | | Anthony | Monroe | TRI 64 | 2 | | | Flagstaff | | 3 May |
| A20.3 | | Jason | Leach | USA 66 | 2 | | | Albuquerque | | 29 Mar |
| 20.6 | 3.2 | Everard | Samuels | JAM 58 | 12 Apr | 20.7 | 5.5 | Robert | Stone | AUS 65 | 1 Feb |
| 20.6 | | Earl | Walker | USA | 3 May | 20.7 | | John | Story (9) | USA 66 | 19 Apr |
| 20.6 | | Desmond | Ross | USA 61 | 3 May | | | | | | |

**MEN 1986**

# 400 METRES

| | | | | | | | | | |
|------|---------|-----------|------|----|-----|-----|-------------|----|-----|
| 44.30 | Gabriel | Tiacoh | IVC 63 | 1 | NCAA | Indianapolis | 7 Jun |
| 44.32 | | Tiacoh | | 1 | Pepsi | Westwood | 17 May |
| 44.45 | Darrell | Robinson | USA 63 | 2 | Pepsi | Westwood | 17 May |
| 44.46 | | Tiacoh | | 1r1 | WK | Zürich | 13 Aug |
| 44.47 | | Robinson | | 1 | TAC | Eugene | 21 Jun |
| 44.48 | Roddie | Haley | USA 65 | 1 | | Houston | 18 May |
| 44.50 | | Haley | | 2 | TAC | Eugene | 21 Jun |
| 44.50 | Innocent | Egbunike | NIG 61 | 2r1 | WK | Zürich | 13 Aug |
| 44.58 | | Tiacoh | | 1 | | Los Angeles | 24 May |
| 44.59 | Roger | Black | UK 66 | 1 | EC | Stuttgart | 29 Aug |
| 44.63 | Thomas | Schönlebe | GDR 65 | 2 | EC | Stuttgart | 29 Aug |
| 44.66 | Bert | Cameron | JAM 59 | 3r1 | WK | Zürich | 13 Aug |
| 44.69 | Antonio | McKay | USA 64 | =4r1 | WK | Zürich | 13 Aug |
| 44.69 | | Robinson | | =4r1 | WK | Zürich | 13 Aug |
| 44.71 | Andre | Phillips | USA 59 | 3 | Pepsi | Westwood | 17 May |
| 44.72 | Darren | Clark (10) | AUS 65 | 6r1 | WK | Zürich | 13 Aug |
| 44.74 | | Tiacoh | | 1h1 | NCAA | Indianapolis | 5 Jun |
| 44.75 | | Tiacoh | | 1 | Nik | Nice | 15 Jul |
| 44.77 | Felix | Stevens | CUB 64 | 1 | | Santiago/Cuba | 21 Feb |
| 44.79 | | McKay | | 1 | BGP | Budapest | 11 Aug |
| 44.80 | | Stevens | | 1 | | Habana | 5 Feb |
| 44.82 | | Egbunike | | 4 | Pepsi | Westwood | 17 May |
| 44.82 | | Robinson | | 1 | VD | Bruxelles | 5 Sep |
| 44.84 | Sunder | Nix | USA 61 | 1 | DNG | Stockholm | 1 Jul |
| 44.85 | Mathias | Schersing | GDR 64 | 3 | EC | Stuttgart | 29 Aug |

| Mark | Name | | Nat | Yr | Pos | Meet | Venue | Date |
|---|---|---|---|---|---|---|---|---|
| 44.86 | | Robinson | | | 1r1 | ISTAF | W Berlin | 1b Aug |
| 44.87 | | Tiacoh | | | 2r1 | ISTAF | W Berlin | 15 Aug |
| 44.89 | Harold | Madox | USA | 65 | 1s2 | | Odessa, TX | 16 May |
| 44.89 | Clarence | Daniel | USA | 61 | 1s1 | TAC | Eugene | 20 Jun |
| 44.89 | | McKay (30/15) | | | 1 | IAC | London | 8 Aug |
| 44.92 | Laron | Brown | USA | 62 | 1 | | Knoxville | 24 May |
| 44.98 | Ralf | Lübke | FRG | 65 | 1 | NC | W Berlin | 12 Jul |
| 44.98 | Ray | Armstead | USA | 60 | 1r2 | WK | Zürich | 13 Aug |
| 45.00 | Susumu | Takano | JAP | 61 | 1 | AsiG | Seoul | 1 Oct |
| 45.02 | Ian | Morris (20) | TRI | 61 | 2 | CAC | Santiago/Dom | 2 Jul |
| 45.05 | Roberto | Hernández | CUB | 67 | 2 | | Santiago/Cuba | 21 Feb |
| 45.07 | Devon | Morris | JAM | 61 | 1 | | Russellville | 24 May |
| 45.07 | Walter | McCoy | USA | 58 | 3 | TAC | Eugene | 21 Jun |
| 45.10 | Danny | Everett | USA | 66 | 1s2 | TAC | Eugene | 20 Jun |
| 45.19 | Darnell | Chase | USA | 65 | 2 | | Houston | 18 May |
| 45.19 | Danny | Harris | USA | 65 | 1 | | Catania | 13 Sep |
| 45.20 | Vladimir | Krylov | SU | 64 | 1 | Spart | Tashkent | 18 Sep |
| 45.25 | Kevin | Robinzine | USA | 66 | 3 | NCAA | Indianapolis | 7 Jun |
| 45.25 | Derek | Redmond | UK | 65 | 4 | EC | Stuttgart | 29 Aug |
| 45.26 | Dennis | Mitchell (30) | USA | 66 | 1 | | Tampa | 12 Apr |
| 45.29 | Phil | Brown | UK | 62 | 1 | NC | Cwmbran | 26 May |
| 45.33 | Michael | Franks | USA | 63 | 1 | FBK | Hengelo | 27 Jun |
| 45.36 | Butch | Reynolds | USA | 64 | 1 | | Columbus | 4 May |
| 45.38 | Brian | Whittle | UK | 64 | 2 | NC | Cwmbran | 26 May |
| 45.38 | Michael | Cannon | USA | 64 | 4 | NCAA | Indianapolis | 7 Jun |
| 45.38 | Súnday | Uti | NIG | 62 | 2 | | München | 17 Jun |
| 45.41 | Antonio | Sanchez | SPA | 63 | 6 | EC | Stuttgart | 29 Aug |
| 45.42 | Henry | Thomas | USA | 67 | 6 | Pepsi | Westwood | 17 May |
| 45.43 | Clifton | Campbell | USA | 67 | 1 | | Knoxville | 18 May |
| 45.46 | Erwin | Skamrahl (40) | FRG | 58 | 3 | | München | 17 Jun |
| 45.47 | Yann | Quentrec | FRA | 62 | 1r3 | ASV | Köln | 17 Aug |
| 45.49 | Perry | Cartlidge | USA | 63 | 1h1 | | Knoxville | 17 May |
| 45.49 | Mark | Witherspoon | USA | 63 | 7 | Pepsi | Westwood | 17 May |
| 45.50 | Peter | Howard | USA | 63 | 3 | | Los Angeles | 24 May |
| A45.53 | Ludwig | Myburgh | RSA | 62 | 1 | | Germiston | 2 Apr |
| 45.53 | Gerson A | Souza | BRA | 59 | 1 | | Sao Paulo | 13 Jul |
| A45.57 | Pierre | le Roux | RSA | 65 | 2 | | Germiston | 2 Apr |
| 45.58 | Aleksandr | Kurochkin | SU | 61 | 2 | v GDR | Tallinn | 21 Jun |
| 45.59 | Mark | Senior | JAM | 63 | 1 | | Tempe | 19 Apr |
| 45.61 | Andrew | Valmon (50) | USA | 65 | 1 | King | Atlanta | 20 Apr |
| 45.62 | Atlee | Mahorn | CAN | 65 | 1 | | Tempe | 12 Apr |
| 45.62 | Todd | Bennett | UK | 62 | 2 | | Fürth | 15 Jun |
| 45.62 | Aldo | Canti | FRA | 61 | 3s1 | EC | Stuttgart | 28 Aug |
| 45.64 | Davison | Lishebo | ZAM | 55 | 2 | King | Atlanta | 20 Apr |
| 45.64 | Miles | Murphy | AUS | 67 | 1 | WC-j | Athínai | 18 Jul |
| 45.65 | Kriss | Akabusi | UK | 58 | 4 | NC | Cwmbran | 26 May |
| 45.65 | Elvis | Forde | BAR | 59 | 3 | CAC | Santiago/Dom | 2 Jul |
| 45.67 | Rod | Jones | USA | 64 | 4 | | Houston | 18 May |
| 45.68 | Jorge | Valentin | CUB | 64 | 3 | | Santiago/Cuba | 21 Feb |
| 45.68 | Arjen | Visserman(60) | HOL | 65 | 3 | FBK | Hengelo | 27 Jun |

| Mark | Name | | Nat | Yr | Pos | Meet | Venue | Date |
|------|------|---|-----|----|----|------|-------|------|
| 45.69 | Thomas | Johnson | USA | 65 | 5 | | Tampa | 12 Apr |
| 45.69 | Tyrone | Harrell | USA | 63 | 1 | | Raleigh | 17 May |
| 45.69 | Charlie | Jenkins | USA | 64 | 4 | USOCF | Houston | 2 Aug |
| 45.69 | Marcel | Arnold | SWZ | 62 | 1 | NC | Winterthur | 10 Aug |
| 45.69 | Roberto | Ribaud | ITA | 61 | 2h4 | EC | Stuttgart | 27 Aug |
| 45.71 | Jesus | Malave | VEN | 65 | 2 | Barr | Habana | 14 Jun |
| A45.72 | Henry | Mohoanyane | RSA | 63 | 1 | NC | Germiston | 11 Apr |
| 45.72 | Edgar | Itt | FRG | 67 | 3 | WC-j | Athinai | 18 Jul |
| 45.73 | Derek | O'Connor | IRL | 65 | 3h2 | NCAA | Indianapolis | 5 Jun |
| 45.75 | Robert | Stone (70) | AUS | 65 | 1 | | Melbourne | 23 Feb |
| 45.78 | Harald | Schmid | FRG | 57 | 4r1 | | Koblenz | 6 Aug |
| 45.78 | Amadou | Dia Ba | SEN | 58 | 3 | | Catania | 13 Sep |
| A45.78 | Japie | de Jongh | RSA | 64 | 1 | | Bloemfontein | 5 Dec |
| 45.80 | Ken | Lowery | USA | 61 | 1 | | Evanston | 11 Apr |
| 45.80 | Arkadiy | Kornilov | SU | 63 | 1h | NC | Kiev | 14 Jul |
| 45.82 | Gary | Duncan | USA | 64 | 2 | | Knoxville | 18 May |
| 45.83 | Chip | Rish | USA | 67 | 4 | | Los Angeles | 24 May |
| 45.83 | Yuriy | Dudkin | SU | 64 | 2 | Spart | Tashkent | 18 Sep |
| 45.87 | Mark | Rowe | USA | 60 | 1 | | Houston | 24 May |
| A45.88 | Ian | Small-Smith (80) | RSA | 67 | 1 | | Bloemfontein | 24 Feb |
| 45.88 | Tim | Simon | USA | 66 | 1 | | W Lafayette | 11 May |
| 45.91 | Roberto | Ramos | CUB | 59 | 4 | | Santiago/Cuba | 21 Feb |
| 45.91 | Oliver | Bridges | USA | 62 | 5 | | Knoxville | 24 May |
| 45.91 | Johnny | Thomas | USA | 63 | 2h4 | NCAA | Indianapolis | 5 Jun |
| 45.91 | Mike | Paul | TRI | 57 | 3 | | Birmingham | 19 Jul |
| 45.91 | Dimitar | Rangelov | BUL | 63 | 1 | | Sofia | 3 Aug |
| 45.92 | Jörg | Vaihinger | FRG | 62 | 3 | NC | W Berlin | 12 Jul |
| 45.92 | Momchil | Kharizanov | BUL | 61 | 2 | | Sofia | 3 Aug |
| 45.93 | Bruce | Frayne | AUS | 58 | 2 | | Canberra | 6 Mar |
| 45.93 | Kirk | Baptiste (90) | USA | 63 | 2 | | Houston | 21 Mar |
| 45.94 | Carter | Williams | USA | 65 | 6 | | Tampa | 12 Apr |
| 45.94 | Edwin | Modibedi | RSA | 61 | 1 | IC4A | Villanova | 25 May |
| 45.94 | Vladimir | Prosin | SU | 59 | 5r1 | GWG | Moskva | 7 Jul |
| 45.95 | João B | da Silva | BRA | 63 | 2 | | Saõ Paulo | 13 Jul |
| 45.96 | Isidro | del Prado | PHI | 59 | 2 | AsiG | Seoul | 1 Oct |
| 45.97 | Alfonzo | Henson | USA | 65 | 2 | | Baton Rouge | 4 May |
| 45.97 | Gusztáv | Menczer | HUN | 59 | 1 | NC | Budapest | 15 Aug |
| 45.98 | David | Johnston | AUS | 61 | 3 | | Canberra | 6 Mar |
| 45.98 | Agustin | Pavó | CUB | 62 | 3 | Barr | Habana | 14 Jun |
| 46.01 | Sean | Banks (100) | USA | | 1s1 | | Odessa, TX | 16 May |
| 46.01 | Vyacheslav | Kocheryagin | SU | 62 | 1h | Znam | Leningrad | 7 Jun |
| 46.01 | Moses | Kyeswa | UGA | 58 | 1 | | Växjö | 21 Aug |
| A46.02 | Jimmy | Jones | USA | 66 | 1r2 | | El Paso | 20 Apr |
| 46.02 | Hartmut | Weber (104) | FRG | 60 | 4 | | München | 17 Jun |

| Mark | Name | | | | | Mark | Name | | | |
|------|------|---|---|---|---|------|------|---|---|---|
| 46.03 | Dwyan | Biggers | USA 63 27 Apr | | | 46.06 | Angel | Heras | SPA 58 24 May | |
| 46.03 | Hector | Daley | PAN 61 4 May | | | 46.07 | Aaron | Baynes | USA 67 16 May | |
| 46.04 | Moses | Ugbisie | NIG 64 24 May | | | 46.08 | Eulogio | Mordoche | CUB 67 14 Jun | |
| 46.04 | John | Patterson | USA 65 5 Jun | | | 46.09 | Jeff | Reynolds | USA 16 May | |
| A46.05 | Mark | Thomas | UK 65 18 May | | | 46.09 | Willie | Caldwell | USA 63 24 May | |
| 46.05 | Klaus | Just | (110) FRG 64 12 Jul | | | 46.11 | Todd | Steverson | USA 64 30 May | |
| | | | | | | 46.12 | Raymond | Pierre | USA 67 3 May | |
| 46.05 | Mauro | Zuliani | ITA 59 23 Jul | | | 46.12 | Allen | Ingraham(120) | BAH 62 21 Aug | |
| 46.05 | Vladimir | Volodko | SU 63 18 Sep | | | | | | | |

| Mark | Name | | Nat | Yr | Pos | Meet | Venue | | | Date |
|------|------|------|-----|----|-----|------|-------|---|---|------|
| 46.13 | Omar | Davidson | USA | 66 | 23 | May | | | | |
| 46.15 | Malcolm | Walters | USA | | 29 | Mar | | | | |
| 46.16 | Michael | Greene | USA | 66 | 10 | May | | | | |
| 46.18 | Patrick | Gordon | USA | 65 | 12 | Apr | | | | |
| 46.19 | Mon | White | USA | | 12 | Apr | | | | |
| 46.19 | Tony | Allen | USA | 67 | 10 | May | | | | |
| 46.19 | Ramiro | Gonzalez | CUB | 68 | 3 | Aug | | | | |
| A46.19 | Samuel | van Aswegen | RSA | 65 | 1 | Nov | | | | |
| 46.20 | David | Peltier | BAR | 63 | 26 | Apr | | | | |
| 46.20 | Steve | Heard (130) | UK | 62 | 21 | Jun | | | | |
| 46.23 | Mike | Armour | USA | 62 | 31 | May | | | | |
| 46.23 | Ismail | Mačev | YUG | 60 | 11 | Aug | | | | |
| 46.25 | István | Takács | HUN | 59 | 15 | Aug | | | | |
| 46.25 | Mike | Okot | UGA | 58 | 21 | Aug | | | | |
| 46.27 | Andrzej | Stepień | POL | 53 | 28 | Jun | | | | |
| 46.27 | Frank | Möller | GDR | 60 | 4 | Jul | | | | |
| 46.29 | Paul | Harmsworth | UK | 63 | 26 | May | | | | |
| 46.29 | Norbert | Dobeleit | FRG | 64 | 4 | Jul | | | | |
| 46.29 | Nikolay | Chernetskiy | SU | 59 | 7 | Jul | | | | |
| 46.30 | Greg | Henderson (140) | USA | 63 | 17 | May | | | | |
| 46.30 | Ryszard | Wichrowski | POL | 59 | 28 | Jun | | | | |
| 46.33 | Carsten | Petters | GDR | 59 | 11 | Jun | | | | |
| 46.34 | Steve | Griffiths | JAM | 64 | 12 | Apr | | | | |
| 46.35 | Kris | Durr | USA | 64 | 5 | Apr | | | | |
| 46.36 | Vyacheslav | Stukalov | SU | 62 | 23 | May | | | | |
| 46.37 | Darrell | Hadden | USA | 64 | 3 | May | | | | |
| 46.37 | László | Kiss | HUN | 64 | 15 | Aug | | | | |
| 46.38 | Carlos | Reyté | CUB | 56 | 5 | Feb | | | | |
| 46.39 | Gary | Pervis | USA | | 15 | Mar | | | | |
| 46.39 | Alan | Slack (150) | UK | 60 | 26 | May | | | | |
| A46.39 | Andre | Smith | CAN | 62 | 26 | May | | | | |
| 46.39 | Frank | Seybold | FRG | 64 | 12 | Jul | | | | |
| 46.39 | Vladimír | Petrov | SU | 64 | 17 | Sep | | | | |
| 46.41 | Willie | Smith | USA | 56 | 23 | May | | | | |
| 46.41 | Željko | Knapić | YUG | 57 | 30 | Jul | | | | |

| Mark | Name | | Nat | Yr | Pos | Meet | Venue | |
|------|------|------|-----|----|-----|------|-------|---|
| 46.41 | Athanassios | Kalogiannis | GRE | 65 | 6 | Sep | | |
| 46.42 | Héctor | Herrera | CUB | 59 | 5 | Feb | | |
| 46.42 | Koichi | Konakatomi | JAP | 65 | 11 | May | | |
| A46.42 | John | Graham | CAN | 65 | 24 | May | | |
| 46.42 | Lázaro | Martínez(160) | CUB | 62 | 8 | Jun | | |
| 46.42 | J-Jacques | Boussemart | FRA | 63 | 27 | Jul | | |
| 46.42 | Vladimir | Zavgorodny | SU | 65 | 17 | Sep | | |
| 46.42 | Mohamed | al Malky | OMA | 59 | 1 | Oct | | |
| 46.43 | Curtis | Chappell | USA | | 10 | May | | |
| 46.43 | Yuriy | Kozlov | SU | 58 | 14 | Jul | | |
| 46.43 | Olurotimi | Peters | NIG | 54 | 19 | Aug | | |
| A46.45 | Gerhard | Barnard | RSA | 67 | 11 | Apr | | |
| 46.45 | Walt | Jones | USA | 64 | 24 | May | | |
| 46.45 | Harold | Leonard | USA | 67 | 31 | May | | |
| 46.45 | Devon | Whaley (170) | BER | | 5 | Aug | | |
| 46.47 | | McKinley | USA | | 24 | May | | |
| 46.48 | Vladimir | Popov | SU | 66 | 17 | Sep | | |
| A46.49 | Nicholas | Mabu | RSA | 65 | 18 | Apr | | |
| 46.49 | Maksim | Marchenko | SU | 62 | 7 | Jun | | |
| 46.49 | Wolfgang | Schierer(175) | FRG | 63 | 12 | Jul | | |

Indoor mark:

| 46.49 i | Sam | Koduah | GHA | | | 15 | Feb |
|---------|-----|--------|-----|---|---|----|-----|

Best low altitude marks:

| 46.32 | M | Thomas | | | 31 | May |
|-------|---|--------|---|---|----|-----|
| 46.35 | | le Roux | | | 19 | Mar |
| 46.41 | | Myburgh | | | 19 | Mar |
| 46.48 | A | Smith | | | 22 | Jun |

---

| | 1 | 10 | 20 | 30 | 50 | 100 | Under 46.00 | Under 46.30 |
|------|------|------|------|------|------|------|------|------|
| 1982 | 44.68 | 45.09 | 45.46 | 45.65 | 45.89 | 46.23 | 65 | 106 |
| 1983 | 44.50 | 44.98 | 45.29 | 45.48 | 45.74 | 46.16 | 80 | 117 |
| 1984 | 44.27 | 44.83 | 45.19 | 45.37 | 45.62 | 46.03 | 98 | 157 |
| 1985 | 44.47 | 44.91 | 45.11 | 45.30 | 45.52 | 45.99 | 102 | 139 |
| 1986 | 44.30 | 44.72 | 45.02 | 45.26 | 45.61 | 46.01 | 99 | 139 |

---

| Mark | Name | | Nat | Yr | Pos | Meet | Venue | | Date |
|------|------|--|-----|----|----|------|-------|--|------|

Hand timing:

| A44.9 | David | Kitur | KEN 62 | 1 | | Kisumu | 3 May |
| 45.4 | William | Reed | USA 70 | 1 | | Philadelphia | 27 May |
| A45.6 | John | Anzrah | KEN 54 | 1 | NC | Nairobi | 14 Jun |
| A45.6 | Tito | Sawe | KEN 62 | 1 | | Nairobi | 28 Jun |
| 45.6 | Momchil | Kharizanov | BUL 61 | 1 | NC | Sofia | 13 Aug |
| A45.7 | David | Kiprotich | KEN 60 | 2 | | Nairobi | 28 Jun |
| 45.8 | Johnny | Thomas | USA 63 | 1 | | Arlington | 10 May |
| 45.9 | Earle | Laing | JAM 64 | 1 | | Austin | 30 May |
| A45.9 | Samuel | van Aswegen | RSA 65 | 1 | | Johannesburg | 18 Oct |
| | | (9) | | | | | |

| 46.0 | John | Patterson | USA 65 | 22 Mar | 46.2 | Mike | Okot | UGA 58 | 12 Apr |
| | | (10) | | | 46.2 | Elijah | Sogomo | KEN 54 | 3 May |
| 46.0 | Darrell | Hadden | USA 64 | 10 Apr | 46.2 | Derwin | Graham | USA 64 | 30 May |
| 46.0 | Hartmut | Weber | FRG 60 | 26 Jul | A46.2 | Alfred | Nyambane | KEN 56 | 5 Jul |
| 46.1 | Predrag | Melnjak | YUG 69 | 17 May | 46.2 | Mikhail | Ivanov | (19) SU 62 | 18 Jul |
| 46.1 | Lucas | Sang | KEN 61 | | | | | | |

## 800 METRES

MEN 1986

| 1:43.19 | Steve | Cram | UK | 60 | 1 | | Rieti | 7 Sep |
| 1:43.22 | | Cram | | | 1 | CG | Edinburgh | 31 Jul |
| 1:43.46 | Johnny | Gray | USA | 60 | 1r1 | WK | Zürich | 13 Aug |
| 1:43.54 | William | Wuyke | VEN | 58 | 2 | | Rieti | 7 Sep |
| 1:43.62 | | Cram | | | 1 | Nik | Nice | 15 Jul |
| 1:43.62 | Earl | Jones | USA | 64 | 2r1 | WK | Zürich | 13 Aug |
| 1:43.84 | | Gray | | | 1r1 | DNG | Stockholm | 1 Jul |
| 1:43.97 | | Wuyke | | | 3r1 | WK | Zürich | 13 Aug |
| 1:44.03 | Peter | Braun | FRG | 62 | 1r1 | | Koblenz | 6 Aug |
| 1:44.06 | Peter | Elliott | UK | 62 | 3 | | Rieti | 7 Sep |
| | | | | | | | | |
| 1:44.10 | Sebastian | Coe | UK | 56 | 1 | PTG | London | 11 Jul |
| 1:44.10 | José Luis | Barbosa | BRA | 61 | 4 | | Rieti | 7 Sep |
| 1:44.12 | | Barbosa | | | 4r1 | WK | Zürich | 13 Aug |
| 1:44.17 | | Coe | | | 2r1 | DNG | Stockholm | 1 Jul |
| 1:44.17 | David | Mack | USA | 61 | 2r1 | | Koblenz | 6 Aug |
| 1:44.19 | | Barbosa | | | 3r1 | | Koblenz | 6 Aug |
| 1:44.28 | | Coe | | | 1 | | London | 12 Sep |
| 1:44.50 | | Coe | | | 1 | EC | Stuttgart | 28 Aug |
| 1:44.59 | Matthias | Assmann (10) | FRG | 57 | 4r1 | | Koblenz | 6 Aug |
| 1:44.61 | Tom | McKean | UK | 63 | 2 | EC | Stuttgart | 28 Aug |
| | | | | | | | | |
| 1:44.62 | | Barbosa | | | 3r1 | DNG | Stockholm | 1 Jul |
| 1:44.66 | Faouzi | Lahbi | MOR | 58 | 5r1 | | Koblenz | 6 Aug |
| 1:44.66 | | Barbosa | | | 1 | VD | Bruxelles | 5 Sep |
| 1:44.68 | | Barbosa | | | 1 | | Catania | 13 Sep |
| 1:44.70 | | Jones | | | 1 | Bisl | Oslo | 5 Jul |
| 1:44.70 | Babacar | Niang | SEN | 58 | 1 | | Paris | 22 Jul |
| 1:44.70 | | Wuyke | | | 1r1 | ASV | Köln | 17 Aug |
| 1:44.71 | | Jones | | | 2 | Nik | Nice | 15 Jul |
| 1:44.72 | | Gray | | | 2 | PTG | London | 11 Jul |
| 1:44.73 | | Gray (30/13) | | | 1 | TAC | Eugene | 21 Jun |

| Mark | Name | | Nat | Yr | Pos | Meet | Venue | Date |
|------|------|--|-----|----|-----|------|-------|------|
| 1:44.75 | Omer | Khalifa | SUD | 56 | 2 | | Catania | 13 Sep |
| 1:44.86 | Moussa | Fall | SEN | 63 | 2 | VD | Bruxelles | 5 Sep |
| 1:45.05 | Viktor | Zemlyanskiy | SU | 63 | 1 | NC | Kiev | 16 Jul |
| 1:45.10 | Philippe | Collard | FRA | 60 | 2 | | Lausanne | 2 Sep |
| 1:45.10 | Joseph | Chesire | KEN | 57 | 3 | | Catania | 13 Sep |
| 1:45.11 | Agberto | Guimarães | BRA | 57 | 6r1 | | Koblenz | 6 Aug |
| 1:45.14 | Ryszard | Ostrowski(20) | POL | 61 | 5 | Nik | Nice | 15 Jul |
| | | | | | | | | |
| 1:45.14 | John | Gladwin | UK | 63 | 3 | | Paris | 22 Jul |
| 1:45.18 | Viktor | Kalinkin | SU | 60 | 2 | OD | Dresden | 3 Jul |
| 1:45.23 | Andreas | Busse | GDR | 59 | 3 | OD | Dresden | 3 Jul |
| 1:45.24 | H-Joachim | Mogalle | GDR | 59 | 1r2 | WK | Zürich | 13 Aug |
| 1:45.26 | Edwin | Koech | KEN | 61 | 2r2 | WK | Zürich | 13 Aug |
| 1:45.29 | Rob | Druppers | HOL | 62 | 1 | | Vught | 3 Aug |
| 1:45.3 m | Alberto | Barsotti | ITA | 64 | 1 | | Pisa | 9 Jul |
| 1:45.32 | Valeriy | Starodubtsev | SU | 62 | 2 | NC | Kiev | 16 Jul |
| 1:45.64 | David | Sharpe | UK | 67 | 5 | VD | Bruxelles | 5 Sep |
| 1:45.73 | Thomas | Giessing (30) | FRG | 61 | 1r2 | | Koblenz | 6 Aug |
| | | | | | | | | |
| 1:45.74 | Hans-Peter | Ferner | FRG | 56 | 4 | BGP | Budapest | 11 Aug |
| 1:45.80 | Vladimir | Graudyn | SU | 63 | 3 | NC | Kiev | 16 Jul |
| 1:45.86 | Stanley | Redwine | USA | 61 | 2 | TAC | Eugene | 21 Jun |
| 1:45.86 | Pat | Scammell | AUS | 61 | 4 | CG | Edinburgh | 31 Jul |
| 1:45.89 | Sammy | Koskei | KEN | 61 | 5 | | Paris | 22 Jul |
| 1:45.90 | Marc | Corstjens | BEL | 65 | 7 | VD | Bruxelles | 5 Sep |
| 1:45.93 | Tony | Morrell | UK | 62 | 6 | PTG | London | 11 Jul |
| 1:45.96 | Willi | Wülbeck | FRG | 54 | 1 | | Aachen | 30 May |
| 1:45.96 | Anatoliy | Millin | SU | 59 | 1 | Znam | Leningrad | 8 Jun |
| 1:45.97 | Petru | Drăgoescu(40) | RUM | 62 | 5r2 | WK | Zürich | 13 Aug |
| | | | | | | | | |
| 1:46.01 | Luis | Migueles | ARG | 65 | 4 | PTS | Bratislava | 14 Jun |
| 1:46.01 | Rob | Harrison | UK | 59 | 5 | PTS | Bratislava | 14 Jun |
| 1:46.07 | Robin | van Helden | HOL | 65 | 3r2 | | Koblenz | 6 Aug |
| 1:46.09 | Coloman | Trabado | SPA | 58 | 1r3 | WK | Zürich | 13 Aug |
| 1:46.10 | Mike | Hillardt | AUS | 61 | 1 | | Canberra | 6 Mar |
| 1:46.10 | Ralph | Schumann | GDR | 66 | 5 | Bisl | Oslo | 5 Jul |
| 1:46.1 m | Jeff | Roberson | USA | 64 | 1 | | San Jose | 19 Apr |
| 1:46.12 | James | Robinson | USA | 54 | 3 | TAC | Eugene | 21 Jun |
| 1:46.18 | Leonid | Masunov | SU | 62 | 2= | Znam | Leningrad | 8 Jun |
| 1:46.18 | Bo | Breigan (50) | NOR | 58 | 6 | Bisl | Oslo | 5 Jul |
| | | | | | | | | |
| 1:46.19 | Ocky | Clark | USA | 60 | 1h3 | NCAA | Indianapolis | 4 Jun |
| 1:46.21 | Pablo | Squella | CHL | 63 | 2h3 | NCAA | Indianapolis | 4 Jun |
| 1:46.39 | Anatoliy | Ivanov | SU | 62 | 4 | NC | Kiev | 16 Jul |
| 1:46.48 | Kipkoech | Cheruiyot | KEN | 64 | 4 | | Caorle | 27 Jul |
| 1:46.49 | Oslen | Barr | GUY | 61 | 1 | | Houston | 10 May |
| 1:46.50 | Butch | Brown | USA | 61 | 1r2 | | Washington,D.C. | 31 May |
| 1:46.52 | Martin | Enholm | SWE | 65 | 6r1 | DNG | Stockholm | 1 Jul |
| 1:46.53 | Axel | Harries | FRG | 64 | 8 | FBK | Hengelo | 27 Jun |
| 1:46.57 | Jack | Armour | USA | 61 | 6 | TAC | Eugene | 21 Jun |
| 1:46.59 | Rainer | Thau (60) | FRG | 62 | 1 | | Menden | 11 Jun |
| | | | | | | | | |
| 1:46.59 | Chris | McGeorge | UK | 62 | 7r1 | DNG | Stockholm | 1 Jul |
| 1:46.60 | Gert | Kilbert | SWZ | 65 | 1r2 | DNG | Stockholm | 1 Jul |
| 1:46.60 | Marco | Mayr | SWZ | 60 | 4r2 | | Koblenz | 6 Aug |
| 1:46.6 m | Ahmed | Belkessam | ALG | 62 | 1 | | Alger | 26 May |
| 1:46.61 | Fred | Williams | RSA | 62 | 1 | NCAA | Indianapolis | 6 Jun |

| Mark | Name | | Nat | Yr | Pos | Meet | Venue | Date |
|------|------|--|-----|----|----|------|-------|------|
| 1:46.63 | Igor | Lotarev | SU | 64 | 7 | PTS | Bratislava | 14 Jun |
| 1:46.63 | Jürgen | Herms | GDR | 63 | 2h2 | NC | Jena | 27 Jun |
| 1:46.65 | Claude | Diomar | FRA | 61 | 1 | NC | Aix-les-Bains | 10 Aug |
| 1:46.66 | Milan | Drahoňovský | CS | 66 | 8 | PTS | Bratislava | 14 Jun |
| 1:46.68 | Viktor | Sapetchenkov | SU | 65 | 3 | Spart | Tashkent | 18 Sep |
| | | (70) | | | | | | |
| 1:46.70 | Ibrahim | Okash | SOM | 64 | 2r2 | DNG | Stockholm | 1 Jul |
| 1:46.7 m | Stefano | Cecchini | ITA | 61 | 1 | | Viterbo | 22 Jun |
| 1:46.73 | Hauke | Fuhlbrügge | GDR | 66 | 2 | GO | Dresden | 16 Aug |
| 1:46.74 | Alvaro | Silva | POR | 65 | 3h3 | EC | Stuttgart | 26 Aug |
| 1:46.80 | Randy | Moore | USA | 64 | =1s1 | TAC | Eugene | 20 Jun |
| 1:46.8 m | Joey | Bunch | USA | 65 | 2 | | San Jose | 19 Apr |
| 1:46.82 | Andrey | Ponomaryov | SU | 64 | 4 | Spart | Tashkent | 18 Sep |
| 1:46.88 | Ronny | Olsson | SWE | 61 | 9 | PTS | Bratislava | 14 Jun |
| 1:46.90 | Alan | Ozolins | AUS | 64 | 2 | | Melbourne | 20 Mar |
| 1:46.9 m | André | Lavie    (80) | FRA | 59 | 1 | | Saint-Maur | 9 Jul |
| 1:46.91 | Markus | Trinkler | SWZ | 62 | 4 | | Bern | 20 Aug |
| 1:46.92 | Simon | Hoogewerf | CAN | 63 | 5 | Pre | Eugene | 7 Jun |
| 1:46.94 | Sergey | Kutsebo | SU | 61 | 1h3 | Znam | Leningrad | 7 Jun |
| 1:46.96 | István | Szalai | HUN | 62 | 1 | | Budapest | 10 May |
| 1:46.96 | Herbert | Wursthorn | FRG | 57 | 4 | | Fürth | 15 Jun |
| 1:46.96 | Philippe | Fargère | FRA | 64 | 3 | | Saint-Denis | 21 Jun |
| 1:46.96 | Jens | Behmer | GDR | 65 | 3h2 | NC | Jena | 27 Jun |
| 1:46.97 | Lorenzo | Brown | USA | 61 | 1 | | Walnut, CA | 17 May |
| 1:46.99 | Tracy | Baskin | USA | 65 | 1r1 | | Washington,D.C. | 31 May |
| 1:46.99 | Klaus-Peter | Nabein    (90) | FRG | 60 | 7r2 | | Koblenz | 6 Aug |
| 1:47.00 | Doug | Herron | USA | 66 | 4 | Pepsi | Westwood | 17 May |
| 1:47.0 m | Sisa | Kirati | KEN | 57 | 2 | | Nairobi | 17 May |
| 1:47.0 m | Gert | de Bruyn | RSA | 65 | 1 | | Welkom | 22 Nov |
| 1:47.02 | Andreas | Kaliebe | GDR | 62 | 3 | GO | Dresden | 16 Aug |
| 1:47.04 | Ari | Suhonen | FIN | 65 | 1r2 | ISTAF | W Berlin | 15 Aug |
| 1:47.05 | Paul | Schnyder | AUS | 62 | 3 | | Melbourne | 20 Mar |
| 1:47.05 | Samuel | Tirop | KEN | | 1r2 | GWG | Moskva | 8 Jul |
| 1:47.08 | Ken | Washington | USA | 61 | 8r2 | | Koblenz | 6 Aug |
| 1:47.11 | Ray | Brown | USA | 61 | 2h3 | TAC | Eugene | 19 Jun |
| 1:47.12 | Slobodan | Popović (100) | YUG | 62 | 5 | Znam | Leningrad | 8 Jun |
| 1:47.14 | Steve | Crabb | UK | 63 | 3 | NC | Cwmbran | 26 May |
| 1:47.15 | Holger | Böttcher | FRG | 63 | 5 | | Fürth | 15 Jun |
| 1:47.17 | John | Marshall | USA | 63 | 5s1 | TAC | Eugene | 20 Jun |
| 1:47.17 | Thomas | Lauterbach | GDR | 66 | 4 | GO | Dresden | 16 Aug |
| | | (104) | | | | | | |

| 1:47.20 | Detlef | Wagenknecht | GDR 59 27 Jun | | 1:47.4 m | Charles | Onsare | KEN 62 May |
|---------|--------|-------------|----------------|--|----------|---------|--------|------------|
| 1:47.2 m | Predrag | Melnjak | YUG 69 8 Jun | | 1:47.41 | Scott | Davis | USA 61 24 May |
| 1:47.2 m | Thierry | Tonnellier | FRA 59 30 Jul | | 1:47.42 | Han | Kulker | HOL 59 3 Aug |
| 1:47.23 | Derwin | Graham | USA 64 18 May | | 1:47.46 | Andrey | Sudnik | SU 67 15 Jun |
| 1:47.27 | Brian | Thompson | CAN 63 10 Jun | | 1:47.46 | Mike | Armour (120) | USA 62 19 Jun |
| 1:47.27 | Malcolm | Edwards (110) | UK 58 31 Jul | | | | | |
| 1:47.28 | Dave | Campbell | USA 66 17 May | | 1:47.46 | Vadim | Laushkin | SU 65 16 Jul |
| 1:47.30 | Henning | Gericke | RSA 60 10 Mar | | 1:47.48 | Mike | Elliott | USA 64 20 Jun |
| 1:47.3 m | Hervé | Phélippeau | FRA 62 30 Jul | | 1:47.49 | James | Mays | USA 59 17 Aug |
| 1:47.33 | Peter | Bourke | AUS 58 6 Mar | | 1:47.50 | Aleksandr | Karchevskiy | SU 64 25 May |
| 1:47.40 | Krzysztof | Pradzyński | POL 58 19 Jun | | 1:47.50 | Eckhardt | Rüter | FRG 63 6 Aug |

MEN 1986

| Mark | Name | | | Nat | Yr | Pos | Meet | Venue | | Date | |
|------|------|---|---|-----|----|-----|------|-------|---|------|---|
| 1:47.5 m | Vladimir | Samoilenko | | SU | 61 | 20 Jul | | | | | |
| 1:47.51 | Aleksandr | Shevchenko | | SU | 64 | 25 May | | | | | |
| 1:47.51 | Said | Mhand | | MOR | 58 | 30 Jul | | | | | |
| 1:47.52 | Calvin | Harris | | USA | 62 | 4 Jun | | | | | |
| 1:47.53 | Darryl | Taylor | (130) | UK | 65 | 26 May | | | | | |
| 1:47.54 | Carlos | Ward | | USA | 63 | 4 Jun | | | | | |
| 1:47.58 | Nixon | Kiprotich | | KEN | | 8 Jul | | | | | |
| 1:47.58 | Dan | Futrell | | USA | 56 | 2 Aug | | | | | |
| 1:47.60 | Andreas | Hauck | | GDR | 60 | 6 Jun | | | | | |
| 1:47.6 m | Jean | Malan | | RSA | 64 | 12 Mar | | | | | |
| 1:47.6 m | David | Kiplimo | | KEN | 59 | 17 May | | | | | |
| 1:47.61 | Steffen | Oehme | | GDR | 63 | 16 Aug | | | | | |
| 1:47.62 | András | Paróczai | | HUN | 56 | 11 Aug | | | | | |
| 1:47.63 | Nikolay | Dobrovolskiy | | SU | 66 | 25 May | | | | | |
| 1:47.63 | Jaap | van Treyen | | HOL | 64 | 30 May | | | | | |
| 1:47.64 | Alex | Geissbühler | (140) | SWZ | 64 | 13 Aug | | | | | |
| 1:47.65 | Francisco | Martin | | SPA | 61 | 12 Jul | | | | | |
| 1:47.66 | Piotr | Piekarski | | POL | 64 | 17 Aug | | | | | |
| 1:47.66 | Sergey | Kamayev | | SU | 63 | 17 Sep | | | | | |
| 1:47.69 | Michael | Damberg | | FRG | 58 | 21 May | | | | | |
| 1:47.70 | Johnny | Walker | | USA | 63 | 4 Jun | | | | | |
| 1:47.7 m | David | Moore | | USA | 67 | 10 May | | | | | |
| 1:47.7 m | Bruno | Migliorini | | ITA | 64 | 22 Jun | | | | | |
| 1:47.7 m | Petrus | Tunisi | | RSA | | 22 Nov | | | | | |
| 1:47.73 | Marcus | Sanders | (150) | USA | 63 | 4 May | | | | | |
| 1:47.74 | Mike | Okot | | UGA | 58 | 2 Jul | | | | | |
| 1:47.74 | Ferenc | Reichnach | | HUN | 64 | 10 Sep | | | | | |
| 1:47.76 | Roberto | Ramos | | CUB | 59 | 23 Feb | | | | | |
| 1:47.76 | Angel | Osoria | | CUB | 65 | 9 Jun | | | | | |
| 1:47.77 | Ulrich | Kniehase | | FRG | 64 | 23 Aug | | | | | |
| 1:47.78 | Vladimir | Skutov | | SU | 59 | 26 Jul | | | | | |
| 1:47.79 | Eero | Kytölä | | FIN | 62 | 3 Aug | | | | | |
| 1:47.80 | Mario | Silva | | POR | 61 | 10 Aug | | | | | |
| 1:47.8 m | Andrey | Vansovskiy | | SU | 62 | 8 May | | | | | |
| 1:47.8 m | Alex | Vétillard | (160) | FRA | 62 | 18 Jun | | | | | |
| 1:47.8 m | Renzo | Piccin | | ITA | 59 | 9 Jul | | | | | |
| 1:47.8 m | Joël | Hégésippe | | FRA | 63 | 9 Jul | | | | | |
| 1:47.8 m | Didier | Le Guillou | | FRA | 60 | 30 Jul | | | | | |
| 1:47.81 | José | Isaac | | CUB | 66 | 9 Jun | | | | | |
| 1:47.81 | Alessandro | Lambruschini | | ITA | 65 | 11 Jun | | | | | |
| 1:47.81 | Markus | Trines | | FRG | 63 | 17 Aug | | | | | |
| 1:47.83 | Barbaro | Serrano | | CUB | 58 | 15 Jun | | | | | |
| 1:47.84 | Andrew | Alphonse | | TRI | | 28 Jul | | | | | |
| 1:47.85 | Cedric | Matterson | | USA | 65 | 30 May | | | | | |
| 1:47.85 | Heiko | Mätzig | (170) | FRG | 66 | 2 Jul | | | | | |
| 1:47.86 | Philippe | Detaellenaere | | BEL | 62 | 3 Aug | | | | | |
| 1:47.87 | Mark | Rodholm | | USA | 66 | 3 May | | | | | |
| 1:47.89 | Tamás | Pócsái | | HUN | 62 | 10 Sep | | | | | |
| 1:47.90 | Raul | Mesa | | CUB | 65 | 20 Jun | | | | | |
| 1:47.90 | Vladimir | Zdobnov | | SU | 65 | 18 Sep | | | | | |
| 1:47.90 | Victor | Radebe | | RSA | | 6 Dec | | | | | |
| 1:47.92 | Christian | Skoog | | SWE | 65 | 29 May | | | | | |
| 1:47.92 | Zsolt | Szabó | | HUN | 61 | 10 Sep | | | | | |
| 1:47.95 | Vasiliy | Matveyev | | SU | 62 | 13 Sep | | | | | |
| 1:47.96 | Marcel | Theer | (180) | CS | 65 | 11 Aug | | | | | |
| 1:47.97 | Gary | Marlow | | UK | 63 | 25 May | | | | | |
| 1:47.98 | Chris | Mills | | USA | 66 | 31 May | | | | | |
| 1:47.99 | Dave | Anderton | | USA | 64 | 3 May | | | | | |
| 1:47.99 | Mark | Kirk | | UK | 63 | 30 Jun | | | | | |
| 1:47.99 | Joachim | Heydgen | (185) | FRG | 63 | 30 Jul | | | | | |

Indoor mark:

| 1:47.94i | Jussi | Udelhoven | | | | FRG | 66 | 8 Feb |
|----------|-------|-----------|---|---|---|-----|----|-------|

---

| | 1 | 10 | 20 | 30 | 50 | 100 | Under 1:46.0 | Under 1:47.0 |
|------|---|----|----|----|----|-----|--------------|--------------|
| 1982 | 1:44.45 | 1:45.05 | 1:45.44 | 1:45.90 | 1:46.5 | 1:47.33 | 31 | 76 |
| 1983 | 1:43.61 | 1:44.32 | 1:45.13 | 1:45.58 | 1:46.29 | 1:47.14 | 42 | 89 |
| 1984 | 1:41.77 | 1:43.93 | 1:44.87 | 1:45.17 | 1:46.04 | 1:46.97 | 46 | 101 |
| 1985 | 1:42.49 | 1:44.15 | 1:45.21 | 1:45.6 | 1:46.08 | 1:47.17 | 46 | 91 |
| 1986 | 1:43.19 | 1:44.59 | 1:45.14 | 1:45.73 | 1:46.18 | 1:47.12 | 40 | 90 |

---

| Mark | Name | | Nat | Yr | Pos | Meet | Venue | Date |
|------|------|--|-----|----|-----|------|-------|------|

## 1000 METRES

| 2:14.90 | Sebastian | Coe | UK | 56 | 1 | | Haringey | 16 Jul |
| 2:15.77 | Steve | Cram | UK | 60 | 1 | PTG | London | 11 Jul |
| 2:15.86 | | Cram | | | 1 | | Birmingham | 19 Aug |
| 2:16.6 m | Philippe | Collard | FRA | 60 | 1 | | Parilly | 18 Jul |
| 2:17.01 | Sammy | Koskei | KEN | 61 | 1 | Nik | Nice | 15 Jul |
| 2:17.25 | Earl | Jones | USA | 64 | 2 | PTG | London | 11 Jul |
| 2:17.47 | Tony | Morrell | UK | 62 | 2 | | Birmingham | 19 Aug |
| 2:17.49 | Hauke | Fuhlbrügge | GDR | 66 | 1 | BGP | Budapest | 11 Aug |
| 2:17.66 | Vladimir | Graudyn | SU | 63 | 2 | BGP | Budapest | 11 Aug |
| 2:17.7 m | Ari | Suhonen | FIN | 65 | 1 | | Porvoo | 7 Sep |
| | | (10/9) | | | | | | |
| 2:17.81 | James | Robinson (10) | USA | 54 | 3 | PTG | London | 11 Jul |
| | | | | | | | | |
| 2:17.87 | Enda | Fitzpatrick | IRL | 65 | 3 | BGP | Budapest | 11 Aug |
| 2:17.99 | Rob | Harrison | UK | 59 | 1 | v USA | Gateshead | 27 Jun |
| 2:18.07 | Han | Kulker | HOL | 59 | 4 | BGP | Budapest | 11 Aug |
| 2:18.14 | Babacar | Niang | SEN | 58 | 2 | Nik | Nice | 15 Jul |
| 2:18.18 | Malcolm | Edwards | UK | 58 | 4 | PTG | London | 11 Jul |
| 2:18.3 m | Marc | Corstjens | BEL | 65 | 1 | | Neerpelt | 19 Sep |
| 2:18.35 | Paul | Larkins | UK | 63 | 2 | v USA | Gateshead | 27 Jun |
| 2:18.54 | Johan | Fourie | RSA | 59 | 1 | | Potchefstroom | 7 Mar |
| 2:18.72 | Vladimír | Slouka | CS | 62 | 5 | BGP | Budapest | 11 Aug |
| 2:18.73 | Chris | McGeorge (20) | UK | 62 | 5 | | Birmingham | 19 Aug |
| | | | | | | | | |
| 2:18.76 | Uwe | Mönkemeyer | FRG | 59 | 1 | | Lage | 13 Jun |
| 2:18.78 | Ahmed | Belkessam | ALG | 62 | 3 | Nik | Nice | 15 Jul |
| 2:18.86 | Uwe | Becker | FRG | 55 | 2 | | Lage | 13 Jun |
| 2:18.96 | Ray | Brown | USA | 61 | 4 | v Eng | Gateshead | 27 Jun |
| 2:18.97 | László | Tóth | HUN | 55 | 6 | BGP | Budapest | 11 Aug |
| 2:18.98 | David | Sharpe (26) | UK | 67 | 6 | | Birmingham | 19 Aug |

| 2:19.04 | Eckhardt | Rüter | FRG 63 | 23 Aug | 2:19.8 m | Rob | Druppers | HOL 62 | 1 Aug |
| 2:19.11 | Andrés | Vera | SPA 60 | 26 Jun | 2:19.82 | Moussa | Fall (40) | SEN 63 | 19 Aug |
| 2:19.12 | Markus | Trines | FRG 63 | 23 Aug | | | | | |
| 2:19.4 m | Jens-Peter | Herold (30) | GDR 65 | 22 May | 2:19.84 | Bo | Breigan | NOR 58 | 11 Jul |
| | | | | | 2:19.87 | Ralf | Stewing | FRG 62 | 13 Jun |
| 2:19.51 | José | Moya | SPA 62 | 26 Jun | 2:19.89 | Steve | Crabb | UK 63 | 5 Jul |
| 2:19.54 | Sotirios | Moutsanas | GRE 58 | 26 Jun | 2:19.95 | Hans | Allmandinger | FRG 58 | 4 Jul |
| 2:19.54 | Marco | Mayr | SWZ 60 | 20 Aug | 2:19.96 | Rainer | Thau | FRG 62 | 27 Apr |
| 2:19.70 | Markus | Hacksteiner | SWZ 64 | 20 Aug | 2:19.97 | Klaus | Klein (46) | FRG 65 | 4 Jul |
| 2:19.74 | István | Knipl | HUN 61 | 11 Aug | | | | | |
| 2:19.76 | Randy | Moore | USA 62 | 11 Jul | Indoor marks : | | | | |
| 2:19.79 | Simon | Hoogewerf | CAN 63 | 11 Aug | | | | | |
| 2:19.8 m | Andreas | Hauck | GDR 60 | 22 May | 2:19.64i | Doug | Consiglio | CAN 64 | 17 Jan |
| | | | | | 2:19.73i | Gawain | Guy | USA 62 | 1 Mar |

## 1500 METRES

| 3:29.77 | Sebastian | Coe | UK | 56 | 1 | | Rieti | 7 Sep |
| 3:30.15 | Steve | Cram | UK | 60 | 1 | VD | Bruxelles | 5 Sep |
| 3:31.13 | José Manuel | Abascal | SPA | 58 | 1 | | Barcelona | 16 Aug |
| 3:32.56 | Sydney | Maree | USA | 56 | 1 | ASV | Köln | 17 Aug |
| 3:32.90 | José Luis | González | SPA | 57 | 2 | ASV | Köln | 17 Aug |
| 3:33.06+ | | Cram | | | 1 | Bisl | Oslo | 5 Jul |
| 3:33.07 | Kipkoech | Cheruiyot | KEN | 64 | 1 | | Grosseto | 10 Aug |
| 3:33.28 | Omer | Khalifa | SUD | 56 | 2 | | Grosseto | 10 Aug |
| 3:33.34 | | Maree | | | 2 | | Rieti | 7 Sep |
| 3:33.38 | | Maree | | | 3 | | Grosseto | 10 Aug |

| Mark | Name | | Nat | Yr | Pos | Meet | Venue | Date |
|---|---|---|---|---|---|---|---|---|
| 3:33.61+ | | Cram | | | 1 | | London | 12 Sep |
| 3:33.71 | Steve | Scott | USA | 56 | 3 | ASV | Köln | 17 Aug |
| 3:33.78 | Steve | Ovett | UK | 55 | 1r1 | | Koblenz | 6 Aug |
| 3:33.9 m+ | | Scott | | | 2 | Bisl | Oslo | 5 Jul |
| 3:33.98 | | Abascal | | | 2 | VD | Bruxelles | 5 Sep |
| 3:34.01 | Abdi | Bile | (10) SOM | 63 | 4 | ASV | Köln | 17 Aug |
| 3:34.03 | | González | | | 1 | | La Coruña | 6 Aug |
| 3:34.32 | | Coe | | | 1 | FBK | Hengelo | 27 Jun |
| 3:34.32 | Joseph | Chesire | KEN | 57 | 4 | | Grosseto | 10 Aug |
| 3:34.32 | | González | | | 3 | VD | Bruxelles | 5 Sep |
| 3:34.33 | | Bile | | | 2r1 | | Koblenz | 6 Aug |
| 3:34.38 | Johan | Fourie | RSA | 59 | 1 | | Stellenbosch | 17 Feb |
| 3:34.4 m+ | Jim | Spivey | USA | 60 | 3 | Bisl | Oslo | 5 Jul |
| 3:34.50 | | Ovett | | | 1 | | Paris | 22 Jul |
| 3:34.51 | Mike | Hillardt | AUS | 61 | 1 | DNG | Stockholm | 1 Jul |
| 3:34.57 | Stefano | Mei | ITA | 63 | 3 | | Rieti | 7 Sep |
| 3:34.68 | | Hillardt | | | 2 | | Paris | 22 Jul |
| 3:34.70 | | Maree | | | 1 | | Malmö | 19 Aug |
| 3:34.70+ | | Abascal | | | 1 | GP | Roma | 10 Sep |
| 3:35.0 m+ | | González | | | 4 | Bisl | Oslo | 5 Jul |
| 3:35.0 m+ | | Scott | | | 2 | GP | Roma | 10 Sep |
| 3:35.04 | Frank | O'Mara | IRL | 61 | 2 | DNG | Stockholm | 1 Jul |
| 3:35.09 | | Coe (33/16) | | | 1 | | Bern | 20 Aug |
| 3:35.26 | Uwe | Mönkemeyer | FRG | 59 | 5 | ASV | Köln | 17 Aug |
| 3:35.26 | John | Gladwin | UK | 63 | 4 | VD | Bruxelles | 5 Sep |
| 3:35.28 | Jack | Buckner | UK | 61 | 3 | DNG | Stockholm | 1 Jul |
| 3:35.50 | Steve | Crabb (20) | UK | 63 | 3 | | Paris | 22 Jul |
| 3:35.52 | Andreas | Busse | GDR | 59 | 4 | DNG | Stockholm | 1 Jul |
| 3:35.54 | Pascal | Thiébaut | FRA | 59 | 1 | | Nancy | 26 Jun |
| 3:35.56 | José Luis | Carreira | SPA | 62 | 2 | | La Coruña | 6 Aug |
| 3:35.62 | Peter | Elliott | UK | 62 | 2 | WG | Helsinki | 7 Jul |
| 3:35.67 | Peter | Koech | KEN | 58 | 4 | FBK | Hengelo | 27 Jun |
| 3:35.74 | Rob | Harrison | UK | 59 | 1 | NC | Cwmbran | 26 May |
| 3:35.74 | John | Walker | NZ | 52 | 3 | | La Coruña | 6 Aug |
| 3:35.76 | Marcus | O'Sullivan | IRL | 61 | 6 | ASV | Köln | 17 Aug |
| 3:35.86 | Andrés | Vera | SPA | 60 | 4 | | La Coruña | 6 Aug |
| 3:35.98 | Klaus-Peter | Nabein (30) | FRG | 60 | 5 | FBK | Hengelo | 27 Jun |
| 3:36.01 | Niels Kim | Hjort | DEN | 59 | 4r1 | | Koblenz | 6 Aug |
| 3:36.1 m+ | Said | Aouita | MOR | 60 | 1 | ISTAF | W Berlin | 15 Aug |
| 3:36.19 | Earl | Jones | USA | 64 | 6 | FBK | Hengelo | 27 Jun |
| 3:36.31 | Eddy | Stevens | BEL | 61 | 5r1 | | Koblenz | 6 Aug |
| 3:36.35 | Terry | Brahm | USA | 62 | 5 | DNG | Stockholm | 1 Jul |
| 3:36.37 | Cyrille | Laventure | FRA | 64 | 5 | | Paris | 22 Jul |
| 3:36.40 | Dieter | Baumann | FRG | 60 | 6r1 | | Koblenz | 6 Aug |
| 3:36.52 | Richie | Harris | USA | 59 | 7 | FBK | Hengelo | 27 Jun |
| 3:36.54 | Han | Kulker | HOL | 59 | 8 | FBK | Hengelo | 27 Jun |
| 3:36.60 | Bruno | Levant (40) | FRA | 60 | 6 | | Paris | 22 Jul |
| 3:36.62 | Chuck | Aragon | USA | 59 | 7r1 | | Koblenz | 6 Aug |
| 3:36.74 | Rainer | Thau | FRG | 62 | 8r1 | | Koblenz | 6 Aug |
| 3:36.89 | Peter | Bourke | AUS | 58 | 1 | v Bel, | Eng Woluwe | 13 Jul |
| 3:36.96 | Teòfilo | Benito | SPA | 66 | 5 | | La Coruña | 6 Aug |

| Mark | Name | | Nat | Yr | Pos | Meet | Venue | Date |
|------|------|--|-----|-----|-----|------|-------|------|
| 3:37.2 m+ | Mark | Rowland | UK | 63 | | GP | Roma | 10 Sep |
| 3:37.35 | Alessandro | Lambruschini | ITA | 65 | 1 | | Grosseto | 12 Jun |
| 3:37.40 | Jürgen | Grothe | FRG | 60 | 10r1 | | Koblenz | 6 Aug |
| 3:37.53 | Igor | Lotarev | SU | 64 | 4h3 | EC | Stuttgart | 29 Aug |
| 3:37.58 | Dave | Taylor | IRL | 59 | 2 | | Dublin | 4 Aug |
| 3:37.75 | Peter | Wirz  (50) | SWZ | 60 | 6h3 | EC | Stuttgart | 29 Aug |
| 3:37.79 | Julius | Kariuki | KEN | 61 | 2 | | Rovereto | 30 Jul |
| 3:37.92 | Jens-Peter | Herold | GDR | 65 | 2 | NC | Jena | 29 Jun |
| 3:37.95 | Mogens | Guldberg | DEN | 63 | 12 | FBK | Hengelo | 27 Jun |
| 3:37.95 | Ray | Flynn | IRL | 57 | 6 | | La Coruña | 6 Aug |
| 3:38.00 | Mario | Silva | POR | 61 | 7 | | La Coruña | 6 Aug |
| 3:38.02 | Paul | Larkins | UK | 63 | 2 | v Bel, | Aus Woluwe | 13 Jul |
| 3:38.21 | Neil | Horsfield | UK | 66 | 4 | AAA | London | 21 Jun |
| 3:38.38 | Pierre | Délèze | SWZ | 58 | 2 | | Madrid | 20 Jun |
| 3:38.4 m | Pat | Scammell | AUS | 61 | 1 | | Canberra | 4 Feb |
| 3:38.44 | Markus | Hacksteiner  (60) | SWZ | 64 | 3 | WG | Helsinki | 7 Jul |
| 3:38.45+ | Gerry | O'Reilly | IRL | 64 | | | Cork | 8 Jul |
| 3:38.5 m+ | Tom | Moloney | IRL | 60 | | | Cork | 8 Jul |
| 3:38.56 | Joseph | LeBon | FRA | 64 | 8 | | Paris | 22 Jul |
| 3:38.68 | Willi | Wülbeck | FRG | 54 | 1 | | Essen | 3 Jun |
| 3:38.70 | Vincent | Rousseau | BEL | 62 | 4 | | Madrid | 20 Jun |
| 3:38.7 m | Emmanuel | Goulin | FRA | 62 | 1 | | Saint-Maur | 30 Jul |
| 3:38.79 | Krzysztof | Pradzyński | POL | 58 | 1 | | Zabrze | 9 Aug |
| 3:38.80 | Uwe | Becker | FRG | 55 | 2 | NC | W Berlin | 12 Jul |
| 3:38.81 | Doug | Padilla | USA | 56 | 1 | Nurmi | Turku | 3 Jul |
| 3:38.87 | Hauke | Fuhlbrügge  (70) | GDR | 66 | 1 | GO | Dresden | 17 Aug |
| 3:38.91 | Torsten | Lenhardt | GDR | 63 | 2 | GO | Dresden | 17 Aug |
| 3:39.01 | Adrian | Passey | UK. | 64 | 4 | v Bel, | Aus Woluwe | 13 Jul |
| 3:39.02 | Sisa | Kirati | KEN | 57 | 3 | | Essen | 3 Jun |
| 3:39.06 | Robert | Nemeth | AUT | 58 | 9 | | Paris | 22 Jul |
| 3:39.07 | Wolfgang | Konrad | AUT | 58 | 6 | | Bern | 20 Aug |
| 3:39.15 | Östen | Buskas | SWE | 62 | 2 | Bisl | Oslo | 5 Jul |
| 3:39.18 | Enda | Fitzpatrick | IRL | 65 | 1 | ISTAF | W Berlin | 15 Aug |
| 3:39.2 m | Domingos | Castro | POR | 63 | 1 | | Lisboa | 30 Jul |
| 3:39.28 | Luca | Vandi | ITA | 62 | 6 | | Rieti | 7 Sep |
| 3:39.30 | Alberto | Corvo  (80) | ITA | 63 | 5 | | Grosseto | 10 Aug |
| 3:39.31 | Thomas | Wessinghage | FRG | 52 | 7 | | Bern | 20 Aug |
| 3:39.36 | Marco | Mayr | SWZ | 60 | 5 | | Essen | 3 Jun |
| 3:39.38 | Marek | Adamski | POL | 61 | 1 | | Łódź | 21 Jun |
| 3:39.39 | Josphat | Muraya | KEN | 57 | 6 | | Essen | 3 Jun |
| 3:39.39 | Johnny | Kroon | SWE | 60 | 1 | | Gävle | 28 Jul |
| 3:39.4 m | Renat | Altynguzhin | SU | 56 | 1 | | Novotroitsk | 28 Jun |
| 3:39.41 | Chris | McGeorge | UK | 62 | 4r2 | WK | Zürich | 13 Aug |
| 3:39.52 | Sergey | Afanasyev | SU | 64 | 1 | NC | Kiev | 17 Jul |
| 3:39.56 | Volker | Welzel | FRG | 61 | 8 | | Bern | 20 Aug |
| 3:39.57 | Walter | Merlo  (90) | ITA | 65 | 7 | | Rieti | 7 Sep |
| 3:39.58 | Luciano | Carchesio | ITA | 61 | 2 | | Grosseto | 12 Jun |
| 3:39.61 | Mike | Stahr | USA | 64 | 2 | USOCF | Houston | 3 Aug |
| 3:39.66 | Ronny | Olsson | SWE | 61 | 4 | | Malmö | 19 Aug |
| 3:39.69 | Pascal | Clouvel | FRA | 60 | 2 | | Dijon | 14 Jun |
| 3:39.80 | Harald | Olbrich | FRG | 59 | 9 | | Bern | 20 Aug |
| 3:39.8 m | Grzegorz | Basiak | POL | 62 | 1 | | Stargard | 14 Jun |

MEN 1986

| Mark | Name | | Nat | Yr | Pos | Meet | Venue | | Date |
|------|------|--|-----|----|----|------|-------|--|------|
| 3:39.82 | Ari | Suhonen | FIN | 65 | 1 | | Varkaus | | 22 Jul |
| 3:39.86 | Vasiliy | Matveyev | SU | 62 | 3 | NC | Kiev | | 17 Jul |
| 3:39.88 | Marc | Borghans | HOL | 60 | 2r2 | | Koblenz | | 6 Aug |
| 3:39.9 m | Vladimir | Vorontsov | SU | 58 | 2 | | Novotroitsk | | 28 Jun |
| | | (100) | | | | | | | |
| 3:39.9 m | Vladimír | Slouka | CS | 62 | 1 | | Praha | | 2 Aug |
| 3:39.91 | Vince | Draddy | USA | 61 | 1 | | Eugene | | 24 May |
| 3:39.96 | Pavel | Yakovlev | SU | 58 | 1r2 | GWG | Moskva | | 8 Jul |
| 3:39.98 | Raffaele | Alliegro | ITA | 64 | 3 | | Grosseto | | 12 Jun |
| 3:39.99 | Abel | Anton (105) | SPA | 62 | 3 | | Barcelona | | 16 Aug |

| Mark | Name | | Nat | Yr | Pos |
|------|------|--|-----|----|-----|
| 3:40.02 | Anatoliy | Kalutskiy | SU | 60 | 8 Jun |
| 3:40.02 | Yuriy | Kiselyov | SU | 64 | 8 Jun |
| 3:40.03 | László | Tóth | HUN | 55 | 6 Aug |
| 3:40.03 | Dave | Campbell | CAN | 60 | 13 Aug |
| 3:40.04 | Eckhardt | Rüter (110) | FRG | 63 | 12 Jul |
| 3:40.05 | Adelino | Hidalgo | SPA | 63 | 6 Aug |
| 3:40.22 | Hans | van der Veen | RSA | 66 | 19 Mar |
| 3:40.25 | Gary | Staines | UK | 63 | 14 Jun |
| 3:40.26 | Claudio | Patrignani | ITA | 59 | 20 Jun |
| 3:40.26 | Jim | McKeon | USA | 62 | 3 Jul |
| 3:40.28 | Lars | Stene | NOR | 61 | 28 Jun |
| 3:40.29 | Antonio | Fernández | SPA | 61 | 16 Aug |
| 3:40.3 m+ | Tim | Hutchings | UK | 58 | 5 Aug |
| 3:40.43 | István | Knipl | HUN | 61 | 20 Jun |
| 3:40.46 | Wałdemar | Lisicki (120) | POL | 62 | 2 Aug |
| 3:40.48 | Kevin | Curtin | USA | 62 | 24 May |
| 3:40.48 | Anatoliy | Legeda | SU | 62 | 17 Jul |
| 3:40.50 | Carey | Nelson | CAN | 63 | 6 Aug |
| 3:40.5 m | João | Campos | POR | 58 | 16 Aug |
| 3:40.5 m+ | Monde | Tutani | RSA | 62 | 13 Dec |
| 3:40.52 | Sergey | Lapetin | SU | 60 | 31 May |
| 3:40.54 | Gábor K | Szabó | HUN | 62 | 18 Jul |
| 3:40.54 | Harri | Hänninen | FIN | 63 | 22 Jul |
| 3:40.56 | Ralf | Stewing | FRG | 62 | 12 Jul |
| 3:40.60 | Alistair | Currie (130) | UK | 65 | 14 Jun |
| 3:40.6 m | Getahun | Ayana | ETH | 65 | 5 Jul |
| 3:40.62 | Willy | Goddaert | BEL | 59 | 13 Jul |
| 3:40.64 | Steffen | Oehme | GDR | 63 | 17 Aug |
| 3:40.64 | Olaf | Beyer | GDR | 57 | 20 Aug |
| 3:40.65 | Dub | Myers | USA | 64 | 3 Aug |
| 3:40.69 | Gareth | Brown | UK | 61 | 21 Jun |
| 3:40.7 m | Rachid | Kram | ALG | 63 | 10 Apr |
| 3:40.7 m | Lorenzo | Hidalgo | SPA | 65 | 22 Aug |
| 3:40.71 | Vladimir | Samoilenko | SU | 61 | 17 Jul |
| 3:40.74 | Petru | Drăgoescu | RUM | 62 | 6 Sep |
| | | (140) | | | |

| Mark | Name | | Nat | Yr | Pos |
|------|------|--|-----|----|-----|
| 3:40.76 | Lars Ove | Strømø | NOR | 63 | 28 Jul |
| 3:40.79 | Nikolaos | Tsiakoulas | GRE | 59 | 6 Sep |
| 3:40.8 m | Borislav | Dević | YUG | 63 | 7 Jun |
| 3:40.8 m | Oanda | Kirochi | KEN | 69 | 5 Jul |
| 3:40.81 | Malcolm | Edwards | UK | 58 | 14 Jun |
| 3:40.85 | Bruno | Lafranchi | SWZ | 55 | 20 Aug |
| 3:40.86 | Steve | Plasencia | USA | 56 | 24 May |
| 3:40.86 | Karl | Blaha | AUT | 65 | 10 Aug |
| 3:40.88 | Eamonn | Coghlan | IRL | 52 | 4 Aug |
| 3:40.89 | Dominique | Bouchard(150) | FRA | 63 | 14 Aug |
| 3:40.90 | Stefano | Cecchini | ITA | 61 | 28 May |
| 3:40.9 m | Evgeni | Ignatov | BUL | 59 | 20 Aug |
| 3:40.94 | Ari | Paunonen | FIN | 58 | 26 Jun |
| 3:40.98 | Alan | Mottershead | UK | 55 | 14 Jun |
| 3:40.98 | Suleiman | Nyambui | TAN | 53 | 5 Aug |
| 3:40.98 | Romeo | Živko | YUG | 62 | 6 Sep |
| 3:41.00 | Tamás | Szabó | HUN | 61 | 18 Jul |
| 3:41.0 m | Ildar | Romanov | SU | 61 | 28 Jun |
| 3:41.0 m | Rob | Druppers | HOL | 62 | 25 Jul |
| 3:41.03 | Mark | Scruton (160) | UK | 58 | 14 Jun |
| 3:41.04 | Maurice | Smith | USA | 62 | 3 Aug |
| 3:41.08 | Dick | Oldfield | USA | 60 | 24 May |
| 3:41.1 m | Gerard | Ryan | AUS | 60 | 4 Feb |
| 3:41.11 | Yvan | Perré | FRA | 61 | 22 Jul |
| 3:41.11 | Klaus | Klein | FRG | 65 | 6 Aug |
| 3:41.12 | Deon | Brummer | RSA | 59 | 17 Feb |
| 3:41.17 | Lars | Brechtel | FRG | 61 | 12 Jul |
| 3:41.20 | Aleksandr | Mukhlynin | SU | 65 | 8 Jun |
| 3:41.20 | Johan | Engholm (169) | SWE | 62 | 5 Jul |

Indoor marks :

| Mark | Name | | Nat | Yr | Pos |
|------|------|--|-----|----|-----|
| 3:38.73i | Doug | Consiglio | CAN | 64 | 1 Mar |
| 3:39.68i | Abel | Anton | SPA | 62 | 1 Mar |
| 3:40.2 mi | Jim | McKeon | USA | 62 | 16 Feb |

| | 1 | 10 | 20 | 30 | 50 | 100 | Under 3:38.0 | Under 3:40.0 |
|------|---|----|----|----|----|-----|--------------|--------------|
| 1982 | 3:32.12 | 3:34.40 | 3:37.02 | 3:37.96 | 3:38.88 | 3:40.32 | 30 | 85 |
| 1983 | 3:30.77 | 3:34.01 | 3:35.2 | 3:36.77 | 3:38.18 | 3:39.86 | 49 | 100 |
| 1984 | 3:31.54 | 3:34.20 | 3:35.16 | 3:36.36 | 3:37.1 | 3:38.89 | 65 | 136 |
| 1985 | 3:29.46 | 3:33.91 | 3:35.29 | 3:36.88 | 3:38.38 | 3:40.32 | 47 | 84 |
| 1986 | 3:29.77 | 3:34.01 | 3:35.50 | 3:35.98 | 3:37.75 | 3:39.9 | 54 | 105 |

| Mark | Name | | Nat | Yr | Pos | Meet | Venue | Date |
|---|---|---|---|---|---|---|---|---|

## 1 MILE

| Mark | Name | | Nat | Yr | Pos | Meet | Venue | Date |
|---|---|---|---|---|---|---|---|---|
| 3:48.31 | Steve | Cram | UK | 60 | 1 | Bisl | Oslo | 5 Jul |
| 3:48.73 | Steve | Scott | USA | 56 | 2 | Bisl | Oslo | 5 Jul |
| 3:49.49 | | Cram | | | 1 | | London | 12 Sep |
| 3:49.80 | Jim | Spivey | USA | 60 | 3 | Bisl | Oslo | 5 Jul |
| 3:50.28 | | Scott | | | 1 | GP | Roma | 10 Sep |
| 3:50.33 | Said | Aouita | MOR | 60 | 1 | ISTAF | W Berlin | 15 Aug |
| 3:50.54 | José Manuel | Abascal | SPA | 58 | 2 | GP | Roma | 10 Sep |
| 3:50.59 | José Luis | González | SPA | 57 | 2 | ISTAF | W Berlin | 15 Aug |
| 3:50.82 | | González | | | 4 | Bisl | Oslo | 5 Jul |
| 3:50.93 | John | Walker | NZ | 52 | 3 | GP | Roma | 10 Sep |
| 3:51.06 | Frank | O'Mara | IRL | 61 | 4 | GP | Roma | 10 Sep |
| 3:51.20 | | González | | | 5 | GP | Roma | 10 Sep |
| 3:51.32 | | O'Mara | | | 3 | ISTAF | W Berlin | 15 Aug |
| 3:51.43 | | Cram | | | 1 | v USA | Gateshead | 27 Jun |
| 3:51.56 | | Walker | | | 4 | ISTAF | W Berlin | 15 Aug |
| 3:51.86 | | Aouita | | | 1 | | Lausanne | 2 Sep |
| 3:52.03 | | González | | | 2 | | Lausanne | 2 Sep |
| 3:52.13 | | Scott | | | 1 | Nik | Nice | 15 Jul |
| 3:52.14 | Johan | Fourie | RSA | 59 | 1 | | Port Elizabeth | 21 Apr |
| 3:52.72 | | Spivey | | | 6 | GP | Roma | 10 Sep |
| 3:52.92 | | Abascal | | | 3 | | Lausanne | 2 Sep |
| 3:52.99 | Steve | Ovett (10) | UK | 55 | 1 | | Cork | 8 Jul |
| 3:52.99 | Mark | Rowland | UK | 63 | 7 | GP | Roma | 10 Sep |
| | | (23/11) | | | | | | |
| 3:53.29 | Sydney | Maree | USA | 56 | 1 | | Villanova | 8 Jun |
| 3:53.55 | Marcus | O'Sullivan | IRL | 61 | 2 | | Cork | 8 Jul |
| 3:53.85 | Rob | Harrison | UK | 59 | 4 | Nik | Nice | 15 Jul |
| 3:54.06 | Pascal | Thiébaut | FRA | 59 | 5 | Nik | Nice | 15 Jul |
| 3:54.11 | Klaus-Peter | Nabein | FRG | 60 | 5 | | Lausanne | 2 Sep |
| 3:54.22 | Peter | Elliott | UK | 62 | 2 | v USA | Gateshead | 27 Jun |
| 3:54.39 | Neil | Horsfield | UK | 66 | 4 | | Cork | 8 Jul |
| 3:54.52 | John | Gladwin | UK | 63 | 3 | | London | 12 Sep |
| 3:54.63 | Gerry | O'Reilly (20) | IRL | 64 | 2 | | Villanova | 8 Jun |
| 3:54.68 | Tom | Moloney | IRL | 60 | 5 | | Cork | 8 Jul |
| 3:55.16 | Jeff | Atkinson | USA | 63 | 4 | PTG | London | 11 Jul |
| 3:55.17 | Johnny | Kroon | SWE | 60 | 5 | ISTAF | W Berlin | 15 Aug |
| 3:55.31 | Dub | Myers | USA | 64 | 1 | | Eugene | 17 May |
| 3:55.63 | Andreas | Busse | GDR | 59 | 6 | ISTAF | W Berlin | 15 Aug |
| 3:55.68 | Peter | Wirz | SWZ | 60 | 5 | PTG | London | 11 Jul |
| 3:55.77 | Tim | Hutchings | UK | 58 | 3 | | Gateshead | 5 Aug |
| 3:56.12 | Monde | Tutani | RSA | 62 | 2 | | Port Elizabeth | 13 Dec |
| 3:56.36 | Steve | Martin | UK | 59 | 4 | | Gateshead | 5 Aug |
| 3:56.48 | Jim | McKeon (30) | USA | 62 | 7 | PTG | London | 11 Jul |
| 3:56.66 | Han | Kulker | HOL | 59 | 1 | | Barcelona | 16 Jul |
| 3:56.68 | David | Moorcroft | UK | 53 | 3 | IAC | London | 8 Aug |
| 3:56.84 | Uwe | Mönkemeyer | FRG | 59 | 7 | ISTAF | W Berlin | 15 Aug |
| 3:56.88 | Eamonn | Coghlan | IRL | 52 | 4 | | Villanova | 8 Jun |
| 3:56.97 | Dave | Taylor | IRL | 59 | 7 | | Cork | 8 Jul |
| 3:57.01 | José Luis | Carreira | SPA | 62 | 2 | | Barcelona | 16 Jul |
| 3:57.07 | Neil | Ovington | UK | 63 | 9 | PTG | London | 11 Jul |
| 3:57.09 | Andrés | Vera | SPA | 60 | 3 | | Barcelona | 16 Jul |
| 3:57.11 | Steve | Crabb | UK | 63 | 5 | IAC | London | 8 Aug |
| 3:57.24 | Richie | Harris (40) | USA | 59 | 6 | Nik | Nice | 15 Jul |

MEN 1986

| Mark | Name | | Nat | Yr | Pos | Meet | Venue | Date |
|------|------|---|-----|----|----|------|-------|------|
| 3:57.25 | Mike | Stahr | USA | 64 | 10 | PTG | London | 11 Jul |
| 3:57.29 | Jack | Buckner | UK | 61 | 6 | IAC | London | 8 Aug |
| 3:57.46 | Pat | Scammell | AUS | 61 | 4 | | Barcelona | 16 Jul |
| 3:57.53 | Peter | Bourke | AUS | 58 | 11 | PTG | London | 11 Jul |
| 3:57.60 | Tom | Byers | USA | 55 | 3 | Pepsi | Westwood | 17 May |
| 3:57.66 | Geoff | Turnbull | UK | 61 | 2 | | Birmingham | 18 Jul |
| 3:57.76 | Charles | Cheruiyot | KEN | 64 | 1 | PennR | Philadelphia | 26 Apr |
| 3:57.76 | Ray | Wicksell | USA | 56 | 8 | | Cork | 8 Jul |
| 3:58.00 | Paul | Donovan | IRL | 63 | 1 | | Tillsonburg | 28 Jun |
| 3:58.01 | Dave | Campbell (50) | CAN | 60 | 3 | | Birmingham | 18 Jul |

| | | | | | | | | | | | | | | |
|--|--|--|--|--|--|--|--|--|--|--|--|--|--|--|
| 3:58.10 | Rob | Lonergan | CAN | 59 | 5 Aug | | 3:58.65 | Stefano | Mei | | ITA | 63 | 6 Aug |
| 3:58.28 | Adrian | Callan | UK | 62 | 13 Jul | | 3:58.76 | Earl | Jones | (60) | USA | 64 | 17 May |
| 3:58.31 | Kevin | King | USA | 63 | 8 Jun | | | | | | | | |
| 3:58.35 | Mike | Blackmore | USA | 61 | 17 May | | 3:58.77 | Roger | Hackney | | UK | 57 | 13 Jul |
| 3:58.38 | Adrian | Passey | UK | 64 | 18 Jul | | 3:58.77 | Alan | Mottershead | | UK | 55 | 13 Jul |
| 3:58.42 | Ralf | Eckert | FRG | 59 | 8 Jul | | 3:58.82 | Enda | Fitzpatrick | | IRL | 65 | 12 Sep |
| 3:58.54 | Eugene | Curran | IRL | 64 | 8 Jul | | 3:58.84 | Rachid | Kram | | ALG | 63 | 18 Jul |
| 3:58.6 m | Colin | Reitz | UK | 60 | 20 Sep | | 3:58.88 | Kelly | Britz | | CAN | 58 | 17 May |
| | | | | | | | 3:58.97 | Chris | McGeorge | | UK | 62 | 27 Jun |
| | | | | | | | 3:58.97 | Kipkoech | Cheruiyot(67) | | KEN | 64 | 6 Aug |

Indoor marks :

| 3:52.30i | | O'Mara | | | 1 | | Fayetteville | 25 Jan |
|----------|--|--------|--|--|---|--|--------------|--------|

| 3:55.771 | Abdi | Bile | SOM | 63 | 2 | | Johnson City | 18 Jan |
|----------|------|------|-----|----|----|--|--------------|--------|
| 3:55.91i | Doug | Consiglio | CAN | 64 | 2 | | Fayetteville | 25 Jan |
| 3:56.34i | Eamonn | Coghlan | IRL | 52 | 2 | | New York | 14 Feb |
| 3:56.39i | Paul | Donovan | IRL | 63 | 3 | | Fayetteville | 25 Jan |
| 3:56.6 m1 | Mike | Hillardt | AUS | 61 | 1 | | San Diego | 23 Feb |
| 3:56.74i | Kipkoech | Cheruiyot | KEN | 64 | 3 | | Johnson City | 18 Jan |
| 3:57.8 m1 | Tom | Smith | USA | 57 | 1 | | Rosemont, IL | 16 Feb |
| 3:57.91i | Ray | Flynn | IRL | 57 | 2 | | Inglewood, CA | 21 Feb |

Indoor marks :

| 3:58.26i | Gary | Taylor | UK | 63 | 17 Jan | | 3:58.98i | Kevin | Johnson | (12) | USA | 60 | 28 Feb |
|----------|------|--------|----|----|--------|--|----------|-------|---------|------|-----|----|--------|
| 3:58.98i | Mark | Fricker | USA | 59 | 28 Feb | | | | | | | | |

# 2000 METRES

| 4:51.98 | Said | Aouita | MOR | 60 | 1 | VD | Bruxelles | 5 Sep |
|---------|------|--------|-----|----|----|----|-----------|-------|
| 4:52.40 | José Manuel | Abascal | SPA | 58 | 1 | | Santander | 7 Sep |
| 4:57.43 | José Luis | Carreira | SPA | 62 | 2 | | Santander | 7 Sep |
| 4:58.88 | John | Walker | NZ | 52 | 2 | VD | Bruxelles | 5 Sep |
| 5:01.27 | Johan | Fourie | RSA | 59 | 1 | | Port Elizabeth | 13 Oct |
| 5:01.33 | | Walker | | | 1 | | Birmingham | 19 Jul |
| 5:01.35 | Igor | Lotarev | SU | 64 | 1 | | Tallinn | 28 Jun |
| 5:01.47 | Steve | Ovett | UK | 55 | 1 | | Sevilla | 24 May |
| 5:01.52 | Pierre | Délèze | SWZ | 58 | 2 | | Sevilla | 24 May |
| 5:02.20 | | Abascal | | | 3 | | Sevilla | 24 May |
| 5:02.41+ | | Aouita | | | 1 | WK | Zürich | 13 Aug |
| 5:02.43+ | Sydney | Maree | (12/9) | USA | 56 | 2 | WK | Zürich | 13 Aug |
| 5:02.60 | Teófilo | Benito | (10) | SPA | 66 | 4 | | Sevilla | 24 May |

| Mark | Name | | Nat | Yr | Pos | Meet | Venue | Date |
|---|---|---|---|---|---|---|---|---|
| 5:02.78 | Andrés | Vera | SPA | 60 | 5 | | Sevilla | 24 May |
| 5:02.86 | David | Moorcroft | UK | 53 | 2 | | Birmingham | 19 Jul |
| 5:02.95 | Tim | Hutchings | UK | 58 | 3 | | Birmingham | 19 Jul |
| 5:03.16 | Joseph | LeBon | FRA | 64 | 3 | VD | Bruxelles | 5 Sep |
| 5:03.94 | Uwe | Becker | FRG | 55 | 4 | VD | Bruxelles | 5 Sep |
| 5:04.05 | Peter | Koech | KEN | 58 | 4 | | Birmingham | 19 Jul |
| 5:04.21 | Mike | Gilchrist | NZ | 60 | 5 | | Birmingham | 19 Jul |
| 5:04.71 | Julius | Kariuki | KEN | 61 | 1 | | Catania | 13 Sep |
| 5:04.75+ | Volker | Welzel | FRG | 61 | 1 | ASV | Köln | 17 Aug |
| 5:05.0 m+ | Paul | Kipkoech (20) | KEN | 63 | | ASV | Köln | 17 Aug |
| 5:05.1 m+ | Charles | Cheruiyot | KEN | 64 | | ASV | Köln | 17 Aug |
| 5:05.16 | Adelino | Hidalgo | SPA | 63 | 6 | | Sevilla | 24 May |
| 5:05.35 | Johnny | Kroon | SWE | 60 | 5 | VD | Bruxelles | 5 Sep |
| 5:05.78 | Suleiman | Nyambui | TAN | 53 | 1 | | Stockholm | 23 Jul |
| 5:05.85 | Alessandro | Lambruschini | ITA | 65 | 2 | | Milano | 17 May |
| 5:05.92 | Salvatore | Antibo | ITA | 62 | 2 | | Catania | 13 Sep |
| 5:06.04 | Mauricio | González | MEX | 60 | 3 | | Catania | 13 Sep |
| 5:06.43 | John | Gregorek | USA | 60 | 6 | | Birmingham | 19 Jul |
| 5:06.50 | John | Ngugi | KEN | 62 | 4 | | Catania | 13 Sep |
| 5:06.95 | Franco | Boffi (30) | ITA | 58 | 5 | | Catania | 13 Sep |
| 5:06.96 | Carey | Nelson | CAN | 63 | 7 | | Birmingham | 19 Jul |
| 5:06.98 | Jama | Aden (32) | SOM | 62 | 2 | | Stockholm | 23 Jul |

| Mark | Name | | Nat | Yr | Date | Mark | Name | | | Nat | Date |
|---|---|---|---|---|---|---|---|---|---|---|---|
| 5:07.08 | Vince | Draddy | USA 61 | 13 Sep | 5:09.2 m | Klaus-Peter | Nabein | | FRG 60 | 14 May |
| 5:07.33 | Stefano | Cecchini | ITA 61 | 17 May | 5:09.2 m | Francesco | Panetta | | ITA 63 | 24 May |
| 5:07.66 | Alberto | Corvo | ITA 63 | 17 May | 5:09.3 m | Eddy | De Pauw | | BEL 60 | 1 Aug |
| 5:07.72 | Walter | Merlo | ITA 65 | 13 Sep | 5:09.36 | Jonny | Danielson | | SWE 64 | 23 Jul |
| 5:08.45 | Deon | Brummer | RSA 59 | 13 Oct | 5:09.4 m | Willy | Goddaert | | BEL 59 | 1 Aug |
| 5:08.48+ | Jack | Buckner | UK 61 | 5 Jul | 5:09.5 m | Alejandro | Gomez | | SPA 67 | 3 Sep |
| 5:08.92 | Mauro | Pregnolato | ITA 64 | 17 May | 5:09.77 | Monde | Tutani (47) | | RSA 62 | 13 Oct |
| 5:09.0 m | Alberto | Cova (40) | ITA 58 | 24 May | | | | | | |

Indoor marks :

| Mark | Name | | Nat | Yr | Pos | Venue | Date |
|---|---|---|---|---|---|---|---|
| 5:03.3 mi | Walter | Merlo | ITA | 65 | 1 | Torino | 16 Feb |
| 5:05.771 | Terry | Brahm | USA | 62 | 1 | Bloomington | 31 Jan |
| 5:05.791 | Jim | Spivey | USA | 60 | 2 | Bloomington | 31 Jan |
| 5:06.101 | Marcus | Pingpank | RSA | 64 | 2 | Dortmund | 15 Feb |

# 3000 METRES

| Mark | Name | | Nat | Yr | Pos | Meet | Venue | Date |
|---|---|---|---|---|---|---|---|---|
| 7:32.23 | Said | Aouita | MOR | 60 | 1 | ASV | Köln | 17 Aug |
| 7:32.54 | | Aouita | | | 1 | WK | Zürich | 13 Aug |
| 7:38.26 | Sydney | Maree | USA | 56 | 2 | WK | Zürich | 13 Aug |
| 7:39.38 | Paul | Kipkoech | KEN | 63 | 2 | ASV | Köln | 17 Aug |
| 7:40.43 | Jack | Buckner | UK | 61 | 1 | Bisl | Oslo | 5 Jul |
| 7:42.15 | Vincent | Rousseau | BEL | 62 | 1 | Nik | Nice | 15 Jul |
| 7:42.32 | | Aouita | | | 1 | | Paris | 22 Jul |
| 7:42.85 | Stefano | Mei | ITA | 63 | 2 | Nik | Nice | 15 Jul |
| 7:43.15 | Terry | Brahm | USA | 62 | 2 | | Paris | 22 Jul |
| 7:44.10 | Charles | Cheruiyot | KEN | 64 | 3 | WK | Zürich | 13 Aug |
| 7:44.25 | José Luis | González | SPA | 57 | 3 | Nik | Nice | 15 Jul |
| 7:44.53 | António | Leitão (10) | POR | 60 | 4 | Nik | Nice | 15 Jul |

MEN 1986

| Mark | Name | | Nat | Yr | Pos | Meet | Venue | Date |
|------|------|------|-----|----|-----|------|-------|------|
| 7:44.78 | | Maree | | | 1 | IAC | London | 8 Aug |
| 7:44.88 | Tim | Hutchings | UK | 58 | 1 | | Loughborough | 14 Jun |
| 7:45.2 m+ | Geoff | Turnbull | UK | 61 | 1 | | London | 12 Sep |
| 7:45.33 | Johan | Fourie | RSA | 59 | 1 | | Stellenbosch | 6 Jan |
| 7:45.4 m+ | | Aouita | | | 2= | | London | 12 Sep |
| 7:45.4 m+ | | Hutchings | | | 2= | | London | 12 Sep |
| 7:45.6 m+ | | Buckner | | | 4 | | London | 12 Sep |
| 7:46.15 | Colin | Reitz (20/14) | UK | 60 | 4 | WK | Zürich | 13 Aug |
| 7:46.17 | Féthi | Baccouche | TUN | 60 | 3 | | Paris | 22 Jul |
| 7:46.82 | Pierre | Délèze | SWZ | 58 | 2 | IAC | London | 8 Aug |
| 7:46.87 | Doug | Padilla | USA | 56 | 1 | FBK | Hengelo | 27 Jun |
| 7:46.87 | Richie | Harris | USA | 59 | 4 | | Paris | 22 Jul |
| 7:47.35 | Julius | Kariuki | KEN | 61 | 1 | | Caorle | 27 Jul |
| 7:47.39 | Suleiman | Nyambui (20) | TAN | 53 | 2 | FBK | Hengelo | 27 Jun |
| 7:47.83 | Bogusław | Maminski | POL | 55 | 3 | FBK | Hengelo | 27 Jun |
| 7:47.90 | Ezequiel | Canário | POR | 60 | 1 | | Västerås | 26 Jun |
| 7:48.04 | Carey | Nelson | CAN | 63 | 5 | | Paris | 22 Jul |
| 7:48.18 | Eamonn | Coghlan | IRL | 52 | 1 | Jenner | San Jose | 31 May |
| 7:48.20 | Raymond | Pannier | FRA | 61 | 1 | | Marseille | 1 Jul |
| 7:48.22 | Arturo | Barrios | MEX | 63 | 4 | IAC | London | 8 Aug |
| 7:48.90 | Julius | Korir | KEN | 60 | 6 | | Paris | 22 Jul |
| 7:49.17 | Rob | Lonergan | CAN | 59 | 4 | FBK | Hengelo | 27 Jun |
| 7:49.35 | John | Ngugi | KEN | 62 | 4 | | Caorle | 27 Jul |
| 7:49.41 | Vince | Draddy (30) | USA | 61 | 5 | Nik | Nice | 15 Jul |
| 7:49.48 | Franco | Boffi | ITA | 58 | 2 | | Marseille | 1 Jul |
| 7:49.50 | Gennadiy | Temnikov | SU | 61 | 1 | | Sochi | 24 May |
| 7:49.61 | Frank | O'Mara | IRL | 61 | 5 | WK | Zürich | 13 Aug |
| 7:49.70 | Paul | Arpin | FRA | 60 | 3 | | Marseille | 1 Jul |
| 7:49.93 | John | Gregorek | USA | 60 | 7 | | Paris | 22 Jul |
| 7:50.01 | Steve | Ovett | UK | 55 | 5 | IAC | London | 8 Aug |
| 7:50.09 | Marcus | O'Sullivan | IRL | 61 | 6 | WK | Zürich | 13 Aug |
| 7:50.19 | Francesco | Panetta | ITA | 63 | 4 | | Marseille | 1 Jul |
| 7:50.20 | Jon | Solly | UK | 63 | 6 | IAC | London | 8 Aug |
| 7:50.28 | Pascal | Clouvel (40) | FRA | 60 | 5 | | Marseille | 1 Jul |
| 7:50.29 | Ray | Wicksell | USA | 56 | 3 | Bisl | Oslo | 5 Jul |
| 7:50.31 | Gerhard | Hartmann | AUT | 55 | 7 | WK | Zürich | 13 Aug |
| 7:50.33 | John | Walker | NZ | 52 | 1 | PTG | London | 11 Jul |
| 7:50.37 | Paul | Davies-Hale | UK | 62 | 6 | Nik | Nice | 15 Jul |
| 7:50.44 | Alberto | Cova | ITA | 58 | 6 | | Marseille | 1 Jul |
| 7:50.5 m | Jos | Maes | BEL | 61 | 2 | | Kortessem | 6 Aug |
| 7:50.54 | Gennadiy | Fishman | SU | 59 | 2 | | Sochi | 24 May |
| 7:50.58 | Mauricio | González | MEX | 60 | 4 | ASV | Köln | 17 Aug |
| 7:50.71 | Ray | Flynn | IRL | 57 | 7 | IAC | London | 8 Aug |
| 7:50.89 | William | Van Dijck(50) | BEL | 61 | 7 | ASV | Köln | 17 Aug |

| 7:51.0 m | José | Albentosa | SPA 64 | 16 Aug | | 7:51.59 | João | Campos | | POR 58 | 24 Jun |
| 7:51.19 | Markus | Ryffel | SWZ 55 | 15 Aug | | 7:51.70 | Dionísio | Castro | (60) | POR 63 | 1 Jun |
| 7:51.45 | Wilson | Waigwa | KEN 49 | 17 Aug | | | | | | | |
| 7:51.47 | Jim | Spivey | USA 60 | 19 Aug | | 7:51.79 | Jonny | Danielson | | SWE 64 | 24 Jun |
| 7:51.47 | Evgeni | Ignatov | BUL 59 | 2 Sep | | 7:51.99 | Cyrille | Laventure | | FRA 64 | 15 Jul |
| 7:51.49 | Markus | Hacksteiner | SWZ 64 | 2 Sep | | 7:52.04 | Patriz | Ilg | | FRG 57 | 15 Aug |
| 7:51.50 | Igor | Lotarev | SU 64 | 24 May | | 7:52.21 | Joseph | Mahmoud | | FRA 55 | 22 Jul |
| 7:51.50 | Robert | Nemeth | AUT 58 | 5 Jul | | 7:52.24 | Dieter | Baumann | | FRG 65 | 15 Aug |

| Mark | Name | | Nat | Yr | Pos | Meet | Venue | | Date |
|------|------|--|-----|----|----|------|-------|--|------|
| 7:52.27 | Steve | Plasencia | USA 56 | | 31 May | | Volker | Welzel | FRG 61 | 15 Aug |
| 7:52.39 | John | Easker | USA 63 | | 27 Jun | | Herbert | Stephan | FRG 59 | 15 Aug |
| 7:52.42 | Steve | Scott | USA 56 | | 26 Jun | | Mats | Erixon | SWE 58 | 24 Jun |
| 7:52.60 | Pavel | Yakovlev | SU 58 | | 24 May | | Jama | Aden | SOM 62 | 19 Aug |
| 7:52.75 | Jim | Hill (70) | USA 61 | | 17 May | | Mark | Rowland | UK 63 | 27 Jun |
| | | | | | | | Dan | Henderson(90) | USA 58 | 31 May |
| 7:52.91 | Matthews | Temane | RSA 60 | | 6 Jan | | | | | |
| 7:52.92 | Don | Clary | USA 57 | | 17 May | | Gerard | Donakowski | USA 60 | 15 Aug |
| 7:52.98 | Nat | Muir | UK 58 | | 3 Jul | | Francisco | Pacheco | MEX 61 | 31 May |
| 7:53.0 m | Jean-Pierre | Paumen | BEL 56 | | 9 Jul | | Lars-Erik | Nilsson | SWE 61 | 24 Jun |
| 7:53.1 m | Erwin | Naessens | BEL 61 | | 9 Jul | | Nick | Peach | UK 59 | 11 Jul |
| 7:53.18 | Matti | Valkonen | FIN 60 | | 3 Jul | | Greg | Lautenslager | USA 57 | 17 May |
| 7:53.20 | Bill | Krohn | USA 58 | | 3 Jul | | Billy | Dee | UK 61 | 5 Sep |
| 7:53.21 | Jim | Cooper | USA 59 | | 3 Jul | | Marco | Gozzano | ITA 63 | 1 Jul |
| 7:53.23 | Claudio | Patrignani | ITA 59 | | 1 Jul | | Craig | Mochrie | UK 62 | 5 Sep |
| 7:53.29 | Deon | Brummer (80) | RSA 59 | | 6 Jan | | Mogens | Guldberg | DEN 63 | 2 Sep |
| | | | | | | | Nikolay | Matyushenko | SU 66 | 24 May |
| 7:53.30 | Kipsubai | Koskei | KEN 51 | | 17 Aug | | | (100) | | |
| 7:53.38 | Roger | Hackney | UK 57 | | 11 Jul | | Keith | Brantly (101) | USA 62 | 17 May |
| 7:53.50 | Tommy | Ekblom | FIN 59 | | 26 Jun | | | | | |
| 7:53.5 m | Eddy | De Pauw | BEL 60 | | 6 Aug | | | | | |

Indoor marks :

| 7:47.61i | Walter | Merlo | ITA 65 | 2 | v Hun | Budapest | 1 Feb |
|----------|--------|-------|---------|---|-------|----------|-------|
| 7:48.81i | Gábor K | Szabó | HUN 62 | 3 | v Ita | Budapest | 1 Feb |
| 7:49.61i | Dave | Lewis | UK 61 | 1 | NC | Cosford | 25 Jan |
| 7:49.83i | Raf | Wijns | BEL 64 | 1 | | Gainesville | 9 Mar |
| 7:49.97i | Billy | Dee | UK 61 | 2 | NC | Cosford | 25 Jan |

| 7:51.59i | Lubomír | Tesáček | CS 57 | | 26 Jan | | 7:54.32i | Sebastian | Coe | UK 56 | 8 Mar |
|----------|---------|---------|--------|--|--------|--|----------|-----------|--------|--------|-------|
| 7:52.50i | David | Reid | CAN 63 | | 9 Mar | | 7:54.48i | Peter | McColgan | UK 63 | 9 Mar |
| 7:53.03i | Steve | Binns | UK 60 | | 8 Feb | | 7:54.66i | Brian | Abshire (13) | USA 63 | 2 Feb |
| 7:53.42i | Mark | Roberts | UK 59 | | 8 Feb | | | | | | |
| 7:54.09i | Mikhail | Dasko (10) | SU 61 | | 8 Feb | | | | | | |

## 2 MILES

| 8:14.81 | Said | Aouita | MOR 60 | 1 | | London | | 12 Sep |
|---------|------|--------|--------|---|--|--------|--|--------|
| 8:15.53 | Tim | Hutchings | UK 58 | 2 | | London | | 12 Sep |
| 8:15.98 | Geoff | Turnbull | UK 61 | 3 | | London | | 12 Sep |
| 8:17.12 | Jack | Buckner | UK 61 | 4 | | London | | 12 Sep |

| 8:24.14 | Jim | Spivey | USA 60 | 19 Jul | | 8:26.30 | Paul | Kipkoech | KEN 63 | 19 Aug |
|---------|-----|--------|--------|--------|--|---------|------|----------|--------|--------|
| 8:24.99 | Arturo | Barrios | MEX 63 | 19 Jul | | 8:26.54 | Steve | Binns | UK 60 | 19 Jul |
| 8:25.15 | Steve | Plasencia | USA 56 | 19 Jul | | 8:26.58 | Dave | Lewis (11) | UK 61 | 19 Aug |
| 8:25.52 | Colin | Reitz | UK 60 | 19 Aug | | | | | | |

## 5000 METRES

| 13:00.86 | Said | Aouita | MOR 60 | 1 | | La Coruña | 6 Aug |
|----------|------|--------|--------|---|----|-----------|-------|
| 13:10.15 | Jack | Buckner | UK 61 | 1 | EC | Stuttgart | 31 Aug |
| 13:11.57 | Stefano | Mei | ITA 63 | 2 | EC | Stuttgart | 31 Aug |
| 13:12.88 | Tim | Hutchings | UK 58 | 3 | EC | Stuttgart | 31 Aug |
| 13:13.13 | | Aouita | | 1 | GP | Roma | 10 Sep |
| 13:13.15 | Evgeni | Ignatov | BUL 59 | 4 | EC | Stuttgart | 31 Aug |
| 13:14.29 | | Mei | | 2 | GP | Roma | 10 Sep |
| 13:14.62 | Sydney | Maree | USA 56 | 3 | GP | Roma | 10 Sep |
| 13:15.01 | Vincent | Rousseau | BEL 62 | 4 | GP | Roma | 10 Sep |
| 13:15.18 | António | Leitão | POR 60 | 5 | GP | Roma | 10 Sep |

| Mark | Name | | Nat | Yr | Pos | Meet | Venue | Date | |
|------|------|--|-----|----|----|------|-------|------|--|
| 13:15.31 | Pierre | Délèze | SWZ | 58 | 1 | WG | Helsinki | 7 | Jul |
| 13:15.86 | Alberto | Cova     (10) | ITA | 58 | 1 | WK | Zürich | 13 | Aug |
| 13:16.00 |  | Délèze |  |  | 2 | WK | Zürich | 13 | Aug |
| 13:16.02 |  | Leitão |  |  | 2 |  | La Coruña | 6 | Aug |
| 13:16.28 |  | Mei |  |  | 3 | WK | Zürich | 13 | Aug |
| 13:16.28 | Markus | Ryffel | SWZ | 55 | 4 | WK | Zürich | 13 | Aug |
| 13:16.49 |  | Buckner |  |  | 5 | WK | Zürich | 13 | Aug |
| 13:16.66 |  | Rousseau |  |  | 2 | WG | Helsinki | 7 | Jul |
| 13:17.67 |  | Leitão |  |  | 5 | EC | Stuttgart | 31 | Aug |
| 13:17.71 | José Manuel | Abascal | SPA | 58 | 1 |  | Cork | 8 | Jul |
| 13:18.33 |  | Leitão |  |  | 1 |  | Rieti | 7 | Sep |
| 13:18.91 | Paul | Kipkoech | KEN | 63 | 6 | GP | Roma | 10 | Sep |
| 13:19.03 | Domingos | Castro | POR | 63 | 1 | VD | Bruxelles | 5 | Sep |
| 13:19.26 |  | Rousseau |  |  | 2 | VD | Bruxelles | 5 | Sep |
| 13:19.28 | John | Walker | NZ | 52 | 2 |  | Cork | 8 | Jul |
| 13:19.31 |  | Kipkoech |  |  | 6 | WK | Zürich | 13 | Aug |
| 13:19.43 |  | Aouita |  |  | 1 | DNG | Stockholm | 1 | Jul |
| 13:19.45 |  | Hutchings |  |  | 3 | VD | Bruxelles | 5 | Sep |
| 13:19.63 |  | Aouita |  |  | 1 |  | Rovereto | 30 | Jul |
| 13:20.04 |  | Leitão |  |  | 3 | WG | Helsinki | 7 | Jul |
| 13:20.06 | Steve | Ovett | UK | 55 | 1 |  | Belfast | 30 | Jun |
| 13:20.06 |  | Kipkoech |  |  | 2 |  | Rovereto | 30 | Jul |
|  |  | (32/16) |  |  |  |  |  |  |  |
| 13:21.14 | Uwe | Mönkemeyer | FRG | 59 | 1 |  | Koblenz | 6 | Aug |
| 13:21.33 | Mark | Nenow | USA | 57 | 2 |  | Belfast | 30 | Jun |
| 13:21.41 | Salvatore | Antibo | ITA | 62 | 7 | GP | Roma | 10 | Sep |
| 13:21.73 | Geoff | Turnbull (20) | UK | 61 | 5 | VD | Bruxelles | 5 | Sep |
| 13:21.98 | Thomas | Wessinghage | FRG | 52 | 8 | WK | Zürich | 13 | Aug |
| 13:22.11 | John | Treacy | IRL | 57 | 9 | WK | Zürich | 13 | Aug |
| 13:22.30 | Gerhard | Hartmann | AUT | 55 | 2 |  | Koblenz | 6 | Aug |
| 13:22.35 | Eamonn | Coghlan | IRL | 52 | 3 |  | Cork | 8 | Jul |
| 13:22.39 | Jon | Solly | UK | 63 | 4 | WG | Helsinki | 7 | Jul |
| 13:22.67 | Martti | Vainio | FIN | 50 | 6 | EC | Stuttgart | 31 | Aug |
| 13:22.90 | Steve | Plasencia | USA | 56 | 3 |  | Koblenz | 6 | Aug |
| 13:22.94 | Dionísio | Castro | POR | 63 | 6 | VD | Bruxelles | 5 | Sep |
| 13:23.18 | Wilson | Waigwa | KEN | 49 | 4 |  | Cork | 8 | Jul |
| 13:24.29 | Toshihiko | Seko     (30) | JAP | 56 | 1 | PTG | London | 11 | Jul |
| 13:24.35 | Paul | Donovan | IRL | 63 | 5 |  | Cork | 8 | Jul |
| 13:24.70 | Frank | O'Mara | IRL | 61 | 1 | Pre | Eugene | 7 | Jun |
| 13:25.13 | Petr | Klimeš | UK | 58 | 6 |  | Cork | 8 | Jul |
| 13:25.15 | Matthews | Temane | RSA | 60 | 1 |  | Stellenbosch | 8 | Nov |
| 13:25.62 | Lubomír | Tesáček | CS | 57 | 7 |  | Cork | 8 | Jul |
| 13:25.75 | Gerard | Donakowski | USA | 60 | 2 |  | Dedham | 7 | Jun |
| 13:25.83 | Arturo | Barrios | MEX | 63 | 3 |  | La Coruña | 6 | Aug |
| 13:25.90 | José Luis | González | SPA | 57 | 6 | DNG | Stockholm | 1 | Jul |
| 13:25.90 | Pavel | Klimeš | UK | 58 | 8 |  | Cork | 8 | Jul |
| 13:25.97 | Bruno | Lafranchi(40) | SWZ | 55 | 12 | WK | Zürich | 13 | Aug |
| 13:26.43 | Jim | Hill | USA | 61 | 2 | Pre | Eugene | 7 | Jun |
| 13:26.88 | Terry | Thornton | RSA | 67 | 2 |  | Stellenbosch | 8 | Nov |
| 13:27.40 | Vince | Draddy | USA | 61 | 4 | Pre | Eugene | 7 | Jun |
| 13:27.41 | Don | Clary | USA | 57 | 5 | Pre | Eugene | 7 | Jun |
| 13:27.55 | Paul | Williams | CAN | 56 | 6 | Pre | Eugene | 7 | Jun |

| Mark | Name | | Nat | Yr | Pos | Meet | Venue | Date |
|------|------|---|-----|----|----|------|-------|------|
| 13:27.65 | Paul | McCloy | CAN | 63 | 7 | Pre | Eugene | 7 Jun |
| 13:28.23 | Dan | Henderson | USA | 58 | 8 | Pre | Eugene | 7 Jun |
| 13:28.36 | Ezequiel | Canário | POR | 60 | 7 | DNG | Stockholm | 1 Jul |
| 13:28.4 m | Fernando | Mamede | POR | 51 | 1 | | Lisboa | 17 May |
| 13:28.7 m | Jean-Louis | Prianon (50) | FRA | 60 | 1 | | Saint-Maur | 16 Jul |
| 13:28.81 | João | Campos | POR | 58 | 8 | DNG | Stockholm | 1 Jul |
| 13:28.88 | Masanari | Shintaku | JAP | 57 | 3 | PTG | London | 11 Jul |
| 13:28.91 | José | Regalo | POR | 63 | 3 | NC | Lisboa | 10 Aug |
| 13:29.0 m | John | Ngugi | KEN | 62 | 1 | | Hiroshima | 3 May |
| 13:29.12 | Nick | Rose | UK | 51 | 9 | | Cork | 8 Jul |
| 13:29.21 | Marcus | O'Sullivan | IRL | 61 | 4 | | Dedham | 7 Jun |
| 13:29.27 | Mikhail | Dasko | ·SU | 61 | 1 | | Banská Bystrica | 5 Sep |
| 13:29.53 | Mauricio | González | MEX | 60 | 3 | | Rieti | 7 Sep |
| 13:29.60 | Kipsubai | Koskei | KEN | 51 | 4 | | Koblenz | 6 Aug |
| 13:29.63 | Fernando | Couto (60) | POR | 59 | 7h2 | EC | Stuttgart | 28 Aug |
| 13:29.78 | Steve | Binns | UK | 60 | 4 | PTG | London | 11 Jul |
| 13:29.87 | Shuichi | Yoneshige | JAP | 61 | 1 | FBK | Hengelo | 27 Jun |
| 13:30.0 m | Kerry | Rodger | NZ | 62 | 1 | | Auckland | 18 Feb |
| 13:30.51 | John | Easker | USA | 63 | 3 | | Belfast | 30 Jun |
| 13:30.60 | Steve | Jones | UK | 55 | 5 | PTG | London | 11 Jul |
| 13:30.69 | Cyrille | Laventure | FRA | 64 | 6 | PTG | London | 11 Jul |
| 13:30.83 | Dave | Clarke | UK | 58 | 7 | PTG | London | 11 Jul |
| 13:30.86 | Dietmar | Millonig | AUT | 55 | 9 | DNG | Stockholm | 1 Jul |
| 13:31.01 | Guowei | Zhang | CHN | 59 | 8 | PTG | London | 11 Jul |
| 13:31.05 | Hansjörg | Kunze (70) | GDR | 59 | 1 | NC | Jena | 28 Jun |
| 13:31.2 m | Paul | Arpin | FRA | 60 | 2 | | Saint-Maur | 16 Jul |
| 13:31.52 | Ray | Flynn | IRL | 57 | 13 | WK | Zürich | 13 Aug |
| 13:31.62 | Steve | Harris | UK | 61 | 11 | DNG | Stockholm | 1 Jul |
| 13:31.77 | Bruno | Levant | FRA | 60 | 9 | VD | Bruxelles | 5 Sep |
| 13:31.92 | Ivan | Uvízl | CS | 58 | 8h2 | EC | Stuttgart | 28 Aug |
| 13:32.24 | José | Albentosa | SPA | 64 | 4 | | Sevilla | 24 May |
| 13:32.31 | Frank | Heine | GDR | 63 | 2 | NC | Jena | 28 Jun |
| 13:32.34 | Ray | Wicksell | USA | 56 | 10 | Pre | Eugene | 7 Jun |
| 13:32.61 | Abel | Anton | SPA | 62 | 9h2 | EC | Stuttgart | 28 Aug |
| 13:32.65 | Francisco | Pacheco (80) | MEX | 61 | 3 | 1AC | London | 8 Aug |
| 13:32.7 m | Dave | Burridge | NZ | 62 | 2 | | Auckland | 18 Feb |
| 13:32.92 | Jim | Cooper | USA | 59 | 5 | | Dedham | 7 Jun |
| 13:33.09 | Dave | Lewis | UK | 61 | 4 | AAA | London | 21 Jun |
| 13:33.32 | Christoph | Herle | FRG | 55 | 13 | DNG | Stockholm | 1 Jul |
| 13:33.46 | Kozo | Akutsu | JAP | 60 | 2 | FBK | Hengelo | 27 Jun |
| 13:33.55 | Charles | Cheruiyot | KEN | 64 | 1 | | Viareggio | 6 Aug |
| 13:33.58 | Carey | Nelson | CAN | 63 | 10 | | Cork | 8 Jul |
| 13:33.89 | Kurt | Hürst | SWZ | 51 | 15 | WK | Zürich | 13 Aug |
| 13:33.90 | Greg | Lautenslager | USA | 57 | 11 | Pre | Eugene | 7 Jun |
| 13:33.98 | Lars-Erik | Nilsson (90) | SWE | 61 | 1 | | Göteborg | 12 Jun |
| 13:34.00 | Billy | Dee | UK | 61 | 2 | | Göteborg | 12 Jun |
| 13:34.10 | Gennadiy | Temnikov | SU | 61 | 2 | NC | Kiev | 14 Jul |
| 13:34.2 m | Peter | Koech | KEN | 58 | 1 | MSR | Walnut, CA | 26 Apr |
| 13:34.34 | Barry | Smith | UK | 53 | 10 | PTG | London | 11 Jul |
| 13:34.45 | Rob | Lonergan | CAN | 59 | 12 | Pre | Eugene | 7 Jun |
| 13:34.66 | Gábor K | Szabó | HUN | 62 | 6 | | Koblenz | 6 Aug |
| 13:34.7 m | Suleiman | Nyambui | TAN | 53 | 2 | MSR | Walnut, CA | 26 Apr |

| Mark | Name | | Nat | Yr | Pos | Meet | Venue | Date |
|------|------|--|-----|----|-----|------|-------|------|
| 13:35.04 | Dieter | Baumann | FRG | 65 | 2 | | Koblenz | 21 May |
| 13:35.19 | Eirik | Hansen | NOR | 63 | 7 | | Koblenz | 6 Aug |
| 13:35.34 | Matti | Valkonen(100) | FiN | 60 | 7 | WG | Helsinki | 7 Jul |
| | | | | | | | | |
| 13:35.49 | Bogusław | Psujek | POL | 56 | 1 | | Sopot | 2 Aug |
| 13:35.50 | Rob | de Castella | AUS | 57 | 1 | | Canberra | 1 Mar |
| 13:35.6 m | Luis M | Barreto | MEX | 60 | 3 | MSR | Walnut, CA | 26 Apr |
| 13:35.73 | Mats | Erixon | SWE | 58 | 3 | | Göteborg | 12 Jun |
| 13:35.75 | John | Gregorek(105) | USA | 60 | 6 | | Dedham | 7 Jun |

| Mark | Name | | Nat | Yr | Date | Mark | Name | | Nat | Yr | Date |
|------|------|--|-----|----|------|------|------|--|-----|----|------|
| 13:36.02 | Malcolm | Norwood | AUS | 64 | 20 Mar | 13:40.42 | Niels Kim | Hjort | DEN | 59 | 3 Jun |
| 13:36.51 | John | Woods | IRL | 55 | 8 Jul | 13:40.50 | Volker | Welzel | FRG | 61 | 6 Aug |
| 13:36.78 | Gennadiy | Fishman | SU | 59 | 25 Jul | 13:40.58 | David | Moorcroft | UK | 53 | 22 Jun |
| 13:36.8 m | Kevin | King | USA | 63 | 24 Apr | 13:40.7 m | Jim | Norris | USA | 63 | 24 Apr |
| 13:36.9 m | Grant | Whitney (110) | USA | 64 | 24 Apr | 13:40.86 | Xolile | Yawa | RSA | 62 | 13 Dec |
| | | | | | | 13:40.92 | Nat | Muir | UK | 58 | 31 Jul |
| 13:36.92 | Henrik | Jørgensen | DEN | 61 | 12 Jun | 13:41.0 m | Juma | Ikangaa | TAN | 57 | 3 May |
| 13:36.94 | Nasser | Ben Larbi | FRA | 62 | 22 Jul | 13:41.01 | Sławomir | Kondraszewski | POL | 62 | 2 Aug |
| 13:37.01 | Dmitriy | Dmitriyev | SU | 56 | 5 Sep | 13:41.08 | Axel | Krippschock | GDR | 62 | 11 Jun |
| 13:37.04 | Troy | Billings | USA | 60 | 7 Jun | 13:41.20 | Kari | Kananen (160) | FIN | 63 | 7 Jul |
| 13:37.05 | Pascal | Thiébaut | FRA | 59 | 3 Jun | | | | | | |
| 13:37.2 m | Are | Nakkim | NOR | 64 | 24 Apr | 13:41.32 | Bogusław | Maminski | POL | 55 | 6 Aug |
| 13:37.3 m | José Luis | Serrano | SPA | 60 | 17 May | 13:41.37 | Sergey | Kiselyov | SU | 60 | 30 May |
| 13:37.4 m | Martin | Redmond | IRL | | 24 Apr | 13:41.42 | Francesco | Panetta | ITA | 63 | 20 Jun |
| 13:37.49 | Herbert | Stephan | FRG | 59 | 6 Aug | 13:41.63 | Dave | Taylor | IRL | 59 | 30 Jun |
| 13:37.70 | Tommy | Ekblom (120) | FIN | 59 | 27 Jul | 13:41.65 | Rob | de Brouwer | HOL | 62 | 22 Jul |
| | | | | | | 13:41.7 m | Eddy | De Pauw | BEL | 60 | 15 Aug |
| 13:37.81 | Geoff | Shaw | NZ | 57 | 11 Jan | 13:41.93 | Vladimir | Solovyov | SU | 59 | 25 Jul |
| 13:38.00 | Jonny | Danielson | SWE | 64 | 28 Aug | 13:42.0 m | Umbe | Slaa | TAN | 51 | 3 May |
| 13:38.0 m | Greg | Beardsley | USA | 61 | 24 Apr | 13:42.15 | Allan | Zachariassen | DEN | 55 | 31 May |
| 13:38.04 | Terry | Brahm | USA | 62 | 11 Apr | 13:42.16 | Alejandro | Gomez (170) | SPA | 67 | 6 Aug |
| 13:38.04 | Cor | Lambregts | HOL | 58 | 21 May | | | | | | |
| 13:38.05 | Art | Boileau | CAN | 57 | 24 May | 13:42.4 m | Steve | Pinard | USA | | 24 Apr |
| 13:38.17 | Andrey | Kuznetsov | SU | 62 | 25 Jul | 13:42.43 | Brendan | Quinn | IRL | 60 | 30 Jun |
| 13:38.29 | Vitaliy | Tishchenko | SU | 57 | 7 Jun | 13:42.45 | Romas | Sausaitis | SU | 55 | 30 May |
| 13:38.3 m | Roberto | Lopez | MEX | 65 | 26 Apr | 13:42.45 | Doug | Padilla | USA | 56 | 7 Jun |
| 13:38.31 | Mike | Hillardt(130) | AUS | 61 | 2 Dec | 13:42.6 m | Andrew | Lloyd | AUS | 59 | 9 Dec |
| | | | | | | 13:42.63 | Adauto | Domingues | BRA | 61 | 14 Aug |
| 13:38.66 | Richard | O'Flynn | IRL | 62 | 30 Jun | 13:42.68 | John | Robson | UK | 57 | 27 Jun |
| 13:38.78 | Gerard | Ryan | AUS | 60 | 2 Dec | 13:42.73 | Jon | Richards | UK | 64 | 28 Jul |
| 13:38.8 m | Brian | Abshire | USA | 63 | 24 Apr | 13:42.94 | Jon | Sinclair | USA | 57 | 11 Jan |
| 13:38.88 | Noel | Harvey | IRL | 60 | 8 Jul | 13:43.18 | Joseph | Chelelgo(180) | KEN | 63 | 22 Jul |
| 13:38.93 | Dave | Murphy | UK | 57 | 11 Jul | | | | | | |
| 13:39.0 m | Graeme | Fell | CAN | 59 | 17 May | 13:43.2 m | Chris | Fox | USA | 58 | 26 Apr |
| 13:39.02 | Stanisław | Zdunek | POL | 56 | 2 Aug | 13:43.26 | Robert | Schneider | FRG | 60 | 20 Jun |
| 13:39.09 | Randy | Reina | USA | 59 | 10 May | 13:43.43 | Valeriy | Mishechkin | SU | 62 | 25 Jul |
| 13:39.1 m | Joaquim | Pinheiro | POR | 60 | 17 May | 13:43.50 | Nikolay | Chameyev | SU | 62 | 30 May |
| 13:39.11 | Terry | Greene (140) | UK | 60 | 31 Jul | 13:43.5 m | Martin | Flynn | IRL | | 3 Jun |
| | | | | | | 13:43.6 m | Carlos | Capítulo | POR | 57 | 17 May |
| 13:39.24 | Some | Muge | KEN | 59 | 3 Jun | 13:43.6 m | Jos | Maes | BEL | 61 | 15 Aug |
| 13:39.33 | Tsukasa | Endoh | JAP | 61 | 8 Jul | 13:43.67 | Engelbert | Franz | FRG | 63 | 6 Aug |
| 13:39.48 | Gianni | Truschi | ITA | 56 | 20 Jun | 13:43.69 | Patriz | Ilg | FRG | 57 | 21 May |
| 13:39.51 | Elisio | Rios | POR | 61 | 10 Aug | 13:43.8 m | Tony | Dirks (190) | HOL | 61 | 15 Aug |
| 13:39.57 | Martin | Vrábel | CS | 55 | 27 Jun | | | | | | |
| 13:39.71 | Franco | Boffi | ITA | 58 | 20 Jun | 13:43.88 | Dominique | Delattre | FRA | 58 | 5 Sep |
| 13:40.24 | Werner | Schildhauer | GDR | 59 | 28 Jun | 13:43.93 | Robert | Nemeth | AUT | 58 | 7 Jul |
| 13:40.34 | Stanislav | Rozman | YUG | 60 | 27 Jun | 13:43.95 | Mark | Boucher | AUS | 62 | 2 Dec |
| 13:40.35 | Algis | Dabulskis | SU | 61 | 7 Jun | 13:44.0 m | Ivan | Huff | USA | 59 | 26 Apr |
| 13:40.42 | Jim | Spivey (150) | USA | 60 | 23 May | 13:44.04 | Roger | Hackney | UK | 57 | 14 Jun |

| Mark | Name | | Nat | Yr | Pos | Meet | Venue | Date |
|------|------|---|-----|----|----|------|-------|------|
| 13:44.1 m | Thierry | Pantel | FRA 64 | 16 Jul | | 13:44.59 | Fyodor Gogolyuk | SU 62 14 Jul |
| 13:44.22 | Ranieri | Carenza | ITA 63 | 12 Sep | | 13:44.7 m | Michael Scheytt | FRG 59 15 Aug |
| 13:44.27 | Thomas | Sørensen | DEN 63 | 31 May | | 13:44.76 | Candido Alario | SPA 57 14 Aug |
| 13:44.43 | Kurt | Stenzel | FRG 62 | 21 May | | 13:44.84 | Mike McLeod | UK 52 8 Jul |
| 13:44.56 | Raymond | Pannier (200) | FRA 61 | 21 Jun | | 13:44.9 m | Dirk Lakeman | USA 58 7 Jun |
| | | | | | | 13:44.95 | Martyn Brewer | UK 56 11 Apr |
| | | | | | | 13:44.97 | Bob Verbeeck(207) | BEL 60 3 Jun |

-------------------------------------------------------------------------

| | 1 | 10 | 20 | 30 | 50 | 100 | Under 13:30.0 | Under 13:40.0 |
|------|---|----|----|----|----|-----|------|------|
| 1982 | 13:00.41 | 13:12.91 | 13:19.62 | 13:26.8 | 13:30.88 | 13:39.74 | 41 | 103 |
| 1983 | 13:08.54 | 13:20.94 | 13:22.67 | 13:26.61 | 13:31.43 | 13:38.8 | 39 | 109 |
| 1984 | 13:04.78 | 13:16.81 | 13:23.56 | 13:25.78 | 13:27.95 | 13:35.1 | 57 | 144 |
| 1985 | 13:00.40 | 13:18.47 | 13:21.13 | 13:24.5 | 13:32.7 | 13:38.5 | 40 | 117 |
| 1986 | 13:00.86 | 13:15.86 | 13:21.73 | 13:24.29 | 13:28.7 | 13:35.34 | 62 | 146 |

-------------------------------------------------------------------------

Indoor marks :

| 13:32.64i | Doug | Padilla | USA 56 | 1 | | E Rutherford | 8 Feb |
|-----------|------|---------|--------|---|---|-------------|-------|
| 13:33.58i | John | Gregorek | USA 60 | 2 | | E Rutherford | 8 Feb |
| 13:34.23i | Sosthenes | Bitok | KEN 57 | 4 | | E Rutherford | 8 Feb |
| 13:40.49i | Axel | Krippschock | GDR 62 | | 1 Feb | | |
| 13:42.49i | Pat | Petersen | USA 59 | | 8 Feb | | |

MEN 1986

# 10 000 METRES

| 27:20.56 | Mark | Nenow | | USA 57 | 1 | VD | Bruxelles | 5 Sep |
|----------|------|-------|---|--------|---|----|-----------|-------|
| 27:26.11 | Said | Aouita | | MOR 60 | 1 | Bisl | Oslo | 5 Jul |
| 27:28.80 | | Nenow | | | 2 | Bisl | Oslo | 5 Jul |
| 27:34.68 | Hansjörg | Kunze | | GDR 59 | 1 | NC | Jena | 31 May |
| 27:39.52 | Salvatore | Antibo | | ITA 62 | 3 | Bisl | Oslo | 5 Jul |
| 27:43.31 | Paul | Kipkoech | | KEN 63 | 1 | | Aachen | 30 May |
| 27:43.89 | Frank | Heine | | GDR 63 | 2 | NC | Jena | 31 May |
| 27:43.97 | Stefano | Mei | | ITA 63 | 4 | Bisl | Oslo | 5 Jul |
| 27:44.53 | Some | Muge | | KEN 59 | 2 | | Aachen | 30 May |
| 27:44.57 | Martti | Vainio | | FIN 50 | 5 | Bisl | Oslo | 5 Jul |
| 27:45.45 | Toshihiko | Seko | (10) | JAP 56 | 6 | Bisl | Oslo | 5 Jul |
| 27:47.84 | Fernando | Mamede | | POR 51 | 1 | WA | Barcelona | 15 Jun |
| 27:49.35 | Gerhard | Hartmann | | AUT 55 | 7 | Bisl | Oslo | 5 Jul |
| 27:50.19 | Paul | Williams | | CAN 56 | 8 | Bisl | Oslo | 5 Jul |
| 27:50.28 | Arturo | Barrios | | MEX 63 | 1 | | Paris | 22 Jul |
| 27:51.05 | Francesco | Panetta | | ITA 63 | 9 | Bisl | Oslo | 5 Jul |
| 27:51.70 | Steve | Plasencia | | USA 56 | 10 | Bisl | Oslo | 5 Jul |
| 27:51.76 | Jon | Solly | | UK 63 | 1 | AAA | London | 20 Jun |
| 27:52.48 | Jean-Louis | Prianon | | FRA 60 | 2 | | Paris | 22 Jul |
| 27:53.72 | Ezequiel | Canário | | POR 60 | 11 | Bisl | Oslo | 5 Jul |
| 27:54.8 m | Gerardo | Alcala | (20) | MEX 61 | 1 | MSR | Walnut, CA | 26 Apr |
| 27:55.6 m | Mike | Musyoki | | KEN 56 | 2 | MSR | Walnut, CA | 26 Apr |

| Mark | Name | | Nat | Yr | Pos | Meet | Venue | Date |
|------|------|---|-----|----|----|------|-------|------|
| 27:56.0 m | Francisco | Pacheco | MEX | 61 | 3 | MSR | Walnut, CA | 26 Apr |
| 27:56.4 m | Ed | Eyestone | USA | 61 | 4 | MSR | Walnut, CA | 26 Apr |
| 27:56.79 | | Mei | | | 1 | EC | Stuttgart | 26 Aug |
| 27:56.8 m | Paul | McCloy | CAN | 63 | 5 | MSR | Walnut, CA | 26 Apr |
| 27:57.3 m | Pat | Porter | USA | 59 | 6 | MSR | Walnut, CA | 26 Apr |
| 27:57.42 | | Solly | | | 1 | CG | Edinburgh | 26 Jul |
| 27:57.53 | Cor | Lambregts | HOL | 58 | 3 | | Aachen | 30 May |
| 27:57.93 | Alberto | Cova | ITA | 58 | 2 | EC | Stuttgart | 26 Aug |
| 27:58.01 | Steve | Binns | UK | 60 | 2 | CG | Edinburgh | 26 Jul |
| 27:58.41 | Gerard | Donakowski | USA | 60 | 12 | Bisl | Oslo | 5 Jul |
| 27:58.69 | | Binns | | | 2 | AAA | London | 20 Jun |
| 27:58.70 | Lars-Erik | Nilsson (30) | SWE | 61 | 4 | | Aachen | 30 May |
| 27:59.12 | Allister | Hutton | UK | 54 | 5 | | Aachen | 30 May |
| 27:59.33 | Steve | Harris | UK | 61 | 3 | | Paris | 22 Jul |
| | | (36/32) | | | | | | |
| 28:01.50 | Mats | Erixon | SWE | 58 | 4 | EC | Stuttgart | 26 Aug |
| 28:01.62 | Domingos | Castro | POR | 63 | 5 | EC | Stuttgart | 26 Aug |
| 28:02.13 | Xolile | Yawa | RSA | 62 | 1 | | Port Elizabeth | 13 Oct |
| 28:02.48 | Steve | Jones | UK | 55 | 3 | CG | Edinburgh | 26 Jul |
| 28:02.5 m | Shuichi | Yoneshige | JAP | 61 | 1 | | Isezaki | 20 Apr |
| 28:02.83 | Mike | McLeod | UK | 52 | 3 | AAA | London | 20 Jun |
| 28:03.68 | Carl | Thackery | UK | 62 | 4 | AAA | London | 20 Jun |
| 28:04.10 | John | Treacy (40) | IRL | 57 | 6 | EC | Stuttgart | 26 Aug |
| 28:04.4 m | Ivan | Uvízl | CS | 58 | 1 | | Praha | 6 Aug |
| 28:05.5 m | Kozo | Akutsu | JAP | 60 | 1 | | Kyoto | 26 Oct |
| 28:06.37 | Nick | Rose | UK | 51 | 5 | AAA | London | 20 Jun |
| 28:07.0 m | Takeyuki | Nakayama | JAP | 59 | 2 | | Kyoto | 26 Oct |
| 28:07.29 | Paul | Arpin | FRA | 60 | 4 | | Paris | 22 Jul |
| 28:07.51 | Andrew | Lloyd | AUS | 59 | 1 | | Melbourne | 18 Dec |
| 28:08.19 | Henrik | Jørgensen | DEN | 61 | 13 | Bisl | Oslo | 5 Jul |
| 28:08.78 | Dave | Clarke | UK | 58 | 6 | AAA | London | 20 Jun |
| 28:09.4 m | Lubomír | Tesáček | CS | 57 | 2 | | Praha | 6 Aug |
| 28:09.4 m | Kazuya | Nishimoto(50) | JAP | 62 | 3 | | Kyoto | 26 Oct |
| 28:09.47 | Masanari | Shintaku | JAP | 57 | 15 | Bisl | Oslo | 5 Jul |
| 28:10.3 m | Keith | Brantly | USA | 62 | 7 | MSR | Walnut, CA | 26 Apr |
| 28:11.07 | Karl | Harrison | UK | 56 | 7 | AAA | London | 20 Jun |
| 28:11.25 | Peter | Brett | AUS | 62 | 2 | | Melbourne | 18 Dec |
| 28:11.89 | Julian | Goater | UK | 53 | 8 | AAA | London | 20 Jun |
| 28:12.04 | Dionísio | Castro | POR | 63 | 3 | GWG | Moskva | 9 Jul |
| 28:13.3 m | David | Barney | USA | 60 | 8 | MSR | Walnut, CA | 26 Apr |
| 28:13.61 | Kurt | Stenzel | FRG | 62 | 6 | | Aachen | 30 May |
| 28:14.08 | Jon | Richards | UK | 64 | 9 | AAA | London | 20 Jun |
| 28:14.21 | Ralf | Salzmann (60) | FRG | 55 | 7 | | Aachen | 30 May |
| 28:15.00 | Danny | Boltz | AUS | 62 | 3 | | Melbourne | 18 Dec |
| 28:15.1 m | José | Gomez | MEX | 56 | 9 | MSR | Walnut, CA | 26 Apr |
| 28:15.13 | Juma | Ikangaa | TAN | 57 | 1 | | Kobe | 29 Apr |
| 28:15.13 | Geir | Kvernmo | NOR | 55 | 8 | | Aachen | 30 May |
| 28:15.58 | Martin | McLoughlin | UK | 58 | 10 | AAA | London | 20 Jun |
| 28:15.68 | Michael | Scheytt | FRG | 59 | 9 | | Aachen | 30 May |
| 28:15.90 | Kurt | Hürst | SWZ | 51 | 10 | | Aachen | 30 May |
| 28:16.19 | Jamie | Harrison | AUS | 63 | 4 | | Melbourne | 18 Dec |
| 28:17.12 | Douglas | Wakhihuru | KEN | 63 | 16 | Bisl | Oslo | 5 Jul |
| 28:18.6 m | Dan | Henderson(70) | USA | 58 | 10 | MSR | Walnut, CA | 26 Apr |

| Mark | Name | | Nat | Yr | Pos | Meet | Venue | Date |
|------|------|------|-----|----|----|------|-------|------|
| 28:19.15 | Gerard | Barrett | AUS | 56 | 5 | | Melbourne | 18 Dec |
| 28:19.3 m | Eamonn | Coghlan | IRL | 52 | 1 | PennR | Philadelphia | 24 Apr |
| 28:20.11 | Kipsubai | Koskei | KEN | 51 | 11 | | Aachen | 30 May |
| 28:20.78 | John | Woods | IRL | 55 | 11 | AAA | London | 20 Jun |
| 28:20.95 | Steve | Moneghetti | AUS | 62 | 18 | Bisl | Oslo | 5 Jul |
| 28:21.26 | Adam | Hoyle | AUS | 63 | 6 | | Melbourne | 18 Dec |
| 28:21.9 m | Randy | Reina | USA | 59 | 2 | PennR | Philadelphia | 24 Apr |
| 28:21.92 | Are | Nakkim | NOR | 64 | 19 | Bisl | Oslo | 5 Jul |
| 28:22.56 | Mark | Dalloway | UK | 63 | 2 | NC | Cwmbran | 25 May |
| 28:22.74 | Jim | Hill (80) | USA | 61 | 1 | | Eugene | 3 May |
| 28:22.94 | Christoph | Herle | FRG | 55 | 20 | Bisl | Oslo | 5 Jul |
| 28:23.04 | Mark | Scrutton | UK | 60 | 12 | AAA | London | 20 Jun |
| 28:23.45 | Matthews | Temane | RSA | 60 | 2 | | Port Elizabeth | 13 Oct |
| 28:23.50 | Lawrie | Whitty | AUS | 60 | 7 | | Melbourne | 18 Dec |
| 28:24.32 | Umbe | Slaa | TAN | 51 | 4 | | Tokyo | 11 May |
| 28:24.52 | Roy | Andersen | NOR | 55 | 13 | | Aachen | 30 May |
| 28:24.78 | Algis | Dabulskis | SU | 61 | 1 | | Kiev | 26 Jul |
| 28:24.85 | Guowei | Zhang | CHN | 59 | 3 | | Kobe | 29 Apr |
| 28:26.29 | Peter | Tootell | UK | 63 | 3 | NC | Cwmbran | 25 May |
| 28:27.01 | Graham | Payne (90) | UK | 57 | 4 | NC | Cwmbran | 25 May |
| 28:27.14 | Habib | Romdhani | TUN | 60 | 6 | | Paris | 22 Jul |
| 28:27.23 | Spiridon | Andriopoulos | GRE | 62 | 6 | GWG | Moskva | 9 Jul |
| 28:27.33 | John | Halvorsen | NOR | 66 | 1 | NC | Sandnes | 10 Aug |
| 28:27.71 | Fumiaki | Abe | JAP | 58 | 6 | | Tokyo | 11 May |
| 28:28.44 | Martín | Vrábel | CS | 55 | 1 | PTS | Bratislava | 14 Jun |
| 28:28.53 | Bogusław | Psujek | POL | 56 | 1 | | Sopot | 24 Aug |
| 28:28.55 | Dmitriy | Dmitriyev | SU | 56 | 2 | | Kiev | 26 Jul |
| 28:28.74 | Alan | Guilder | UK | 61 | 6 | NC | Cwmbran | 25 May |
| 28:28.93 | Tetsuo | Urakawa | JAP | 61 | 7 | | Tokyo | 11 May |
| 28:29.41 | John | Bowden (100) | NZ | 56 | 1 | | Auckland | 11 Jan |
| 28:29.93 | Richard | Mulligan | IRL | 61 | 13 | AAA | London | 20 Jun |
| 28:29.97 | Andrew | Garnham (102) | AUS | 60 | 9 | | Melbourne | 18 Dec |

| Mark | | | Nat | Yr | Date | | Mark | | | Nat | Yr | Date |
|------|---|---|-----|----|------|---|------|---|---|-----|----|------|
| 28:30.3 m | Mark | Conover | USA | 60 | 26 Apr | | 28:35.20 | Konrad | Dobler | FRG | 57 | 30 May |
| 28:30.54 | Jong-Yoon | Kim | SKO | 60 | 29 Sep | | 28:35.2 m | Ken | Halla | USA | 63 | 24 Apr |
| 28:30.9 m | Tsukasa | Endoh | JAP | 61 | 26 Oct | | 28:35.72 | Theo | Vanden Abeele | BEL | 60 | 30 May |
| 28:31.0 m | Joaquim | Pinheiro | POR | 60 | 20 Jul | | 28:35.8 m | Charlie | Bevier | USA | 59 | 26 Apr |
| 28:31.29 | Ivan | Parlui | SU | 51 | 26 Jul | | 28:35.91 | Bekele | Debele | ETH | 63 | 12 Sep |
| 28:31.41 | Greg | Meyer | USA | 55 | 7 Jun | | 28:36.00 | Salvatore | Nicosia | ITA | 63 | 28 May |
| 28:31.6 m | Rob | de Brouwer | HOL | 62 | 18 Jun | | 28:36.53 | Herbert | Stephan | FRG | 59 | 30 May |
| 28:31.85 | Barry | Smith (110) | UK | 53 | 20 Jun | | 28:36.75 | Giovanni | D'Aleo (130) | ITA | 59 | 28 May |
| 28:32.22 | Mick | Fromant | UK | 52 | 25 May | | 28:36.79 | Shozo | Shimoju | JAP | 57 | 11 May |
| 28:32.49 | Werner | Schildhauer | GDR | 59 | 9 Jul | | 28:37.0 m | Takao | Nakamura | JAP | 58 | 26 Oct |
| 28:33.03 | Peter | Butler | CAN | 58 | 22 Jun | | 28:37.30 | Anatoliy | Krakhmalyuk | SU | 60 | 26 Jul |
| 28:33.27 | Alex | Hagelsteens | BEL | 56 | 5 Sep | | 28:37.38 | John | Ngugi | KEN | 62 | 11 May |
| 28:33.28 | Mark | Boucher | AUS | 62 | 18 Dec | | 28:37.98 | Rob | de Castella | AUS | 57 | 6 Mar |
| 28:33.38 | Malcolm | Norwood | AUS | 64 | 18 Dec | | 28:38.85 | Oleg | Strizhakov | SU | 63 | 17 Jul |
| 28:33.88 | Alain | Capovani | ITA | 63 | 28 May | | 28:39.34 | Gennadiy | Fishman | SU | 59 | 17 Jul |
| 28:33.90 | Wodajo | Bulti | ETH | 57 | 12 Sep | | 28:39.35 | Chris | Robison | UK | 61 | 20 Jun |
| 28:34.30 | Simon | Malibeng | RSA | 62 | 13 Oct | | 28:39.4 m | Jean-Pierre | N'Dayisenga | BEL | 62 | 28 Mar |
| 28:34.62 | Gianni | Truschi (120) | ITA | 56 | 28 May | | 28:39.41 | Viktor | Chumakov (140) | SU | 57 | 17 Jul |
| 28:34.75 | Steve | Emson | UK | 56 | 25 May | | 28:39.50 | Ravil | Kashchapov | SU | 56 | 17 Jul |
| 28:35.00 | Herbert | Steffny | FRG | 53 | 30 May | | 28:39.69 | Nat | Muir | UK | 58 | 25 May |

MEN 1986

| Mark | Name | | Nat | Yr | Pos | Meet | Venue | | Date |
|------|------|--|-----|----|-----|------|-------|--|------|
| 28:40.20 | Giuseppe | Denti | ITA | 60 | 28 May | | | | |
| 28:40.9 m | Thierry | Watrice | FRA | 57 | 6 Aug | | | | |
| 28:41.37 | Hans-Jürgen | Orthmann | FRG | 54 | 11 Jul | | | | |
| 28:41.50 | Pete | Pfitzinger | USA | 57 | 10 May | | | | |
| 28:41.51 | Greg | Oman | USA | 60 | 11 Apr | | | | |
| 28:42.02 | Renat | Altynguzhin | SU | 56 | 26 Jul | | | | |
| 28:42.15 | Dave | Murphy | UK | 57 | 20 Jun | | | | |
| 28:42.38 | Satoshi | Katoh (150) | JAP | 61 | 11 May | | | | |
| 28:42.43 | Leonid | Tikhonov | SU | 56 | 26 Jul | | | | |
| 28:42.54 | Bruce | Bickford | USA | 57 | 10 May | | | | |
| 28:42.58 | Yutaka | Kanai | JAP | 59 | 5 Jul | | | | |
| 28:42.80 | Eric | Carter | USA | 66 | 11 Apr | | | | |
| 28:43.01 | Rolando | Vera | ECU | 65 | 9 Jul | | | | |
| 28:43.39 | Greg | Beardsley | USA | 61 | 11 Apr | | | | |
| 28:43.40 | Larry | Greene | USA | 60 | 11 Apr | | | | |
| 28:43.6 m | Raf | Wijns | BEL | 64 | 18 Jun | | | | |
| 28:43.69 | Oddmund | Roalkvam | NOR | 58 | 5 Jul | | | | |
| 28:43.8 m | Carlos | Retiz (160) | MEX | 61 | 26 Apr | | | | |
| 28:43.82 | Martin | ten Kate | HOL | 58 | 14 May | | | | |
| 28:43.9 m | Ian | Cherry | USA | 64 | 24 Apr | | | | |
| 28:43.98 | Peter | Chumba | KEN | 68 | 16 Jul | | | | |
| 28:44.0 m | Shangyan | Cai | CHN | 62 | 5 Oct | | | | |
| 28:44.23 | Ildar | Denikeyev | SU | 61 | 8 Jun | | | | |
| 28:44.29 | Richard | O'Flynn | IRL | 62 | 6 Aug | | | | |
| 28:44.75 | Wilson | Waigwa | KEN | 49 | 5 Sep | | | | |
| 28:44.78 | Tom | Ratcliffe | USA | 59 | 10 May | | | | |
| 28:44.8 m | Gidabit | Shahanga | TAN | 65 | 26 Apr | | | | |
| 28:44.90 | Stephens | Morake (170) | RSA | 54 | 13 Oct | | | | |
| 28:45.14 | Juma | Mnyampanda | TAN | 67 | 16 Jul | | | | |
| 28:45.41 | Sergey | Skorinov | SU | 58 | 26 Apr | | | | |
| 28:45.50 | Sergey | Kharkin | SU | 63 | 26 Apr | | | | |
| 28:45.80 | Sergey | Makarov | SU | 59 | 8 Jun | | | | |
| 28:45.97 | Tony | Dirks | HOL | 61 | 14 May | | | | |
| 28:46.43 | Klaas | Lok | HOL | 55 | 14 May | | | | |
| 28:46.44 | Pär | Wallin | SWE | 55 | 9 Aug | | | | |
| 28:46.83 | Jan | Marchewka | POL | 62 | 3 Jun | | | | |
| 28:47.08 | Vladimir | Solovyov | SU | 59 | 8 Jun | | | | |
| 28:47.18 | Terry | Greene (180) | UK | 60 | 26 Jul | | | | |
| 28:47.45 | David | Krafsur | USA | 65 | 11 Apr | | | | |
| 28:47.6 m | Mikhail | Dasko | SU | 61 | 18 Aug | | | | |
| 28:48.02 | Ryszard | Kopijasz | POL | 52 | 3 Jun | | | | |
| 28:49.09 | Debebe | Demisse | ETH | 68 | 16 Jul | | | | |
| 28:49.15 | Abderrazak | Gtari | TUN | 60 | 22 Jul | | | | |
| 28:49.91 | Nikolay | Levdanskiy | SU | 61 | 26 Jul | | | | |
| | | (186) | | | | | | | |

|      | 1 | 10 | 20 | 30 | 50 | 100 | Under 28:00.0 | Under 28:30.0 |
|------|---|----|----|----|----|-----|---------------|---------------|
| 1982 | 27:22.95 | 27:38.1 | 28:01.00 | 28:09.7 | 28:17.71 | 28:35.01 | 19 | 87 |
| 1983 | 27:23.44 | 27:46.93 | 27:59.15 | 28:06.7 | 28:19.97 | 28:38.40 | 22 | 68 |
| 1984 | 27:13.81 | 27:47.0 | 27:57.68 | 28:02.41 | 28:07.49 | 28:26.1 | 25 | 115 |
| 1985 | 27:37.17 | 27:49.36 | 27:58.56 | 28:06.5 | 28:23.40 | 28:39.2 | 21 | 66 |
| 1986 | 27:20.56 | 27:45.45 | 27:54.8 | 27:58.70 | 28:09.4 | 28:29.41 | 32 | 102 |

# 3000 METRES STEEPLECHASE

| Mark | Name | | Nat | Yr | Pos | Meet | Venue | Date |
|------|------|--|-----|----|-----|------|-------|------|
| 8:10.01 | William | Van Dijck | BEL | 61 | 1 | VD | Bruxelles | 5 Sep |
| 8:11.52 | | Van Dijck | | | 1 | Nik | Nice | 15 Jul |
| 8:12.11 | Colin | Reitz | UK | 60 | 2 | VD | Bruxelles | 5 Sep |
| 8:12.74 | Julius | Korir | KEN | 60 | 2 | Nik | Nice | 15 Jul |
| 8:13.15 | Henry | Marsh | USA | 54 | 3 | VD | Bruxelles | 5 Sep |
| 8:13.33 | Peter | Koech | KEN | 58 | 3 | Nik | Nice | 15 Jul |
| 8:14.13 | Joshua | Kipkemboi | KEN | 60 | 1 | | Koblenz | 6 Aug |
| 8:14.17 | Samson | Obwocha | KEN | 54 | 2 | | Koblenz | 6 Aug |
| 8:14.57 | Graeme | Fell | CAN | 59 | 4 | Nik | Nice | 15 Jul |
| 8:14.61 | | Marsh | | | 3 | | Koblenz | 6 Aug |
| 8:15.41 | | Korir | | | 1 | FBK | Hengelo | 27 Jun |
| 8:15.92 | Julius | Kariuki | KEN | 61 | 4 | VD | Bruxelles | 5 Sep |
| 8:16.59 | Ivan | Huff (10) | USA | 59 | 5 | VD | Bruxelles | 5 Sep |
| 8:16.65 | Hagen | Melzer | GDR | 59 | 1 | EC | Stuttgart | 29 Aug |
| 8:16.85 | Francesco | Panetta | ITA | 63 | 2 | EC | Stuttgart | 29 Aug |

| Mark | Name | | Nat | Yr | Pos | Meet | Venue | Date | |
|---|---|---|---|---|---|---|---|---|---|
| 8:16.92 | Patriz | Ilg | FRG | 57 | 3 | EC | Stuttgart | 29 | Aug |
| 8:17.24 | | Van Dijck | | | 1 | WK | Zürich | 13 | Aug |
| 8:17.64 | | Kariuki | | | 2 | WK | Zürich | 13 | Aug |
| 8:18.12 | | Reitz | | | 4 | EC | Stuttgart | 29 | Aug |
| 8:18.39 | Alessandro | Lambruschini | ITA | 65 | 1 | | Cesenatico | 27 | Jun |
| 8:18.54 | Pascal | Debacker | FRA | 60 | 5 | Nik | Nice | 15 | Jul |
| 8:18.82 | Raymond | Pannier | FRA | 61 | 6 | Nik | Nice | 15 | Jul |
| 8:18.86 | | Panetta | | | 2 | | Cesenatico | 27 | Jun |
| 8:18.90 | | Korir | | | 1 | DNG | Stockholm | 1 | Jul |
| 8:18.90 | | Reitz | | | 7 | Nik | Nice | 15 | Jul |
| 8:18.99 | | Debacker | | | 3 | WK | Zürich | 13 | Aug |
| 8:19.02 | Mirosław | Żerkowski | POL | 56 | 1 | PTS | Bratislava | 14 | Jun |
| 8:19.16 | | Marsh | | | 1 | TAC | Eugene | 21 | Jun |
| 8:19.29 | | Obwocha | | | 4 | WK | Zürich | 13 | Aug |
| 8:19.33 | | Kariuki | | | 1 | | Lausanne | 2 | Sep |
| | | (30/17) | | | | | | | |
| 8:19.44 | Francisco | Sánchez | SPA | 58 | 5 | WK | Zürich | 13 | Aug |
| 8:19.52 | Gábor | Markó | HUN | 60 | 4 | | Koblenz | 6 | Aug |
| 8:19.88 | Jim | Cooper (20) | USA | 59 | 2 | TAC | Eugene | 21 | Jun |
| 8:20.07 | Farley | Gerber | USA | 60 | 3 | TAC | Eugene | 21 | Jun |
| 8:20.16 | Peter | Renner | NZ | 59 | 8 | Nik | Nice | 15 | Jul |
| 8:20.25 | Joseph | Mahmoud | FRA | 55 | 6 | EC | Stuttgart | 29 | Aug |
| 8:20.56 | Bogusław | Maminski | POL | 55 | 9 | Nik | Nice | 15 | Jul |
| 8:20.90 | Rainer | Schwarz | FRG | 59 | 7 | EC | Stuttgart | 29 | Aug |
| 8:20.97 | Roger | Hackney | UK | 57 | 8 | EC | Stuttgart | 29 | Aug |
| 8:21.41 | José | Regalo | POR | 63 | 9 | EC | Stuttgart | 29 | Aug |
| 8:22.33 | Henryk | Jankowski | POL | 61 | 1 | | Sopot | 2 | Aug |
| 8:22.34 | Hans | Koeleman | HOL | 57 | 7 | VD | Bruxelles | 5 | Sep |
| 8:22.49 | Roland | Hertner (30) | SWZ | 57 | 6 | | Koblenz | 6 | Aug |
| 8:22.85 | Czesław | Mojżysz | POL | 58 | 3 | PTS | Bratislava | 14 | Jun |
| 8:23.69 | Féthi | Baccouche | TUN | 60 | 3 | WG | Helsinki | 7 | Jul |
| 8:24.05 | Tommy | Ekblom | FIN | 59 | 1h1 | EC | Stuttgart | 27 | Aug |
| 8:25.04 | Wiesław | Ziembicki | POL | 60 | 2 | | Sopot | 2 | Aug |
| 8:25.73 | Nikolay | Matyushenko | SU | 66 | 3r1 | GWG | Moskva | 8 | Jul |
| 8:25.89 | Ivan | Konovalov | SU | 59 | 1 | Znam | Leningrad | 7 | Jun |
| 8:25.90 | Bret | Hyde | USA | 59 | 5 | TAC | Eugene | 21 | Jun |
| 8:25.92 | Bruno | Le Stum | FRA | 59 | 6 | | Lausanne | 2 | Sep |
| 8:26.01 | Adauto | Domingues | BRA | 61 | 1 | | La Coruña | 6 | Aug |
| 8:26.46 | Brian | Abshire (40) | USA | 63 | 1 | | Tallahassee | 5 | Apr |
| 8:27.0 m | Boniface | Merande | KEN | 62 | 1 | NC | Nairobi | 14 | Jun |
| 8:27.07 | Eddie | Wedderburn | UK | 60 | 5 | BGP | Budapest | 11 | Aug |
| 8:27.24 | Jorge | Bello | SPA | 63 | 7 | | Lausanne | 2 | Sep |
| 8:28.20 | Are | Nakkim | NOR | 64 | 3 | FBK | Hengelo | 27 | Jun |
| 8:28.20 | Micah | Boinet | KEN | 65 | 4r1 | GWG | Moskva | 8 | Jul |
| 8:28.36 | Wolfgang | Konrad | AUT | 58 | 3 | WA | Barcelona | 15 | Jun |
| 8:28.64 | Ivan | Danu | SU | 59 | 3 | Znam | Leningrad | 7 | Jun |
| 8:28.85 | Frank | Ruhkieck | GDR | 61 | 2 | NC | Jena | 27 | Jun |
| 8:28.89 | Ricardo | Vera | URU | 62 | 4 | | La Coruña | 6 | Aug |
| 8:29.00 | Roger | Gjøvåg (50) | NOR | 56 | 4 | FBK | Hengelo | 27 | Jun |
| 8:29.00 | Lars | Sörensen | FIN | 59 | 5 | WG | Helsinki | 7 | Jul |
| 8:29.14 | Luciano | Carchesio | ITA | 61 | 2 | v FRG, | Hun Milano | 19 | Jun |
| 8:29.25 | Brendan | Quinn | IRL | 60 | 9 | | Koblenz | 6 | Aug |

| Mark | Name | | Nat | Yr | Pos | Meet | Venue | Date |
|------|------|------|-----|----|-----|------|-------|------|
| 8:29.27 | Tomasz | Zimny | POL | 63 | 3 | | Sopot | 2 Aug |
| 8:29.35 | Peter | McColgan | UK | 63 | 3 | NCAA | Indianapolis | 6 Jun |
| 8:29.51 | Lev | Glinskikh | SU | 62 | 1r2 | GWG | Moskva | 8 Jul |
| 8:29.52 | Valeriy | Vandyak | SU | 61 | 2 | NC | Kiev | 17 Jul |
| 8:29.66 | Kurt | Russell | USA | 63 | 1 | | Baton Rouge | 22 Mar |
| 8:29.75 | Mike | Fadil | USA | 63 | 7 | WG | Helsinki | 7 Jul |
| 8:29.8 m | Kieran | Stack    (60) | IRL | 63 | 1 | IC4A | Villanova | 25 May |
| | | | | | | | | |
| 8:29.84 | Mark | Smith | USA | 63 | 4 | USOCF | Houston | 2 Aug |
| 8:29.98 | Joseph | Chelelgo | KEN | 63 | 8 | WG | Helsinki | 7 Jul |
| 8:30.45 | Krzysztof | Wesołowski | POL | 56 | 1 | | Wrocław | 7 Sep |
| 8:30.46 | Michael | Heist | FRG | 65 | 10 | | Koblenz | 6 Aug |
| 8:30.77 | Domingo | Ramón | SPA | 58 | 5 | | La Coruña | 6 Aug |
| 8:30.87 | Igor | Pavlov | SU | 60 | 4 | NC | Kiev | 17 Jul |
| 8:31.10 | Vesa | Siivonen | FIN | 63 | 10 | WG | Helsinki | 7 Jul |
| 8:31.1 m | Patrick | Sang | KEN | 64 | 1 | PennR | Philadelphia | 26 Apr |
| 8:31.49 | Shigeyuki | Aikyo | JAP | 64 | 5 | FBK | Hengelo | 27 Jun |
| 8:31.6 m | Mike | Gilchrist(70) | NZ | 60 | 1 | | Christchurch | 6 Apr |
| | | | | | | | | |
| 8:31.75 | Jiří | Švec | CS | 63 | 4 | Kuso | Warszawa | 17 Jun |
| 8:31.96 | Luboš | Gaisl | CS | 63 | 4 | PTS | Bratislava | 14 Jun |
| 8:32.35 | Rickey | Pittman | USA | 61 | 5 | Pre | Eugene | 7 Jun |
| 8:32.46 | Sławomir | Gurny | POL | 64 | 1 | | Grudziadz | 15 Aug |
| 8:32.49 | Juan | Conde | CUB | 65 | 1 | | Habana | 8 Jun |
| 8:32.51 | Piotr | Zgarda | POL | 56 | 5 | Kuso | Warszawa | 17 Jun |
| 8:32.82 | Franco | Boffi | ITA | 58 | 1 | | Udine | 8 Jun |
| 8:32.87 | Christian | Schieber | FRG | 59 | 11 | | Koblenz | 6 Aug |
| 8:33.0 m | Mike | Vanatta | USA | 61 | 1 | MSR | Walnut, CA | 26 Apr |
| 8:33.06 | Boris | Pruss    (80) | SU | 58 | 6 | NC | Kiev | 17 Jul |
| | | | | | | | | |
| 8:33.2 m | Nathan | Morris | USA | 64 | 2 | | Los Angeles | 29 Mar |
| 8:33.26 | Liam | O'Brien | IRL | 54 | 5 | WA | Barcelona | 15 Jun |
| 8:33.42 | Karol | Dołega | POL | 63 | 4 | | Sopot | 2 Aug |
| 8:33.55 | Herman | Hofstee | HOL | 63 | 12 | | Koblenz | 6 Aug |
| 8:33.89 | Nick | Peach | UK | 59 | 2 | AAA | London | 21 Jun |
| 8:34.03 | Juan | Linares | CUB | 62 | 2 | | Habana | 8 Jun |
| 8:34.04 | Vitaliy | Surin | SU | 63 | 7 | NC | Kiev | 17 Jul |
| 8:34.19 | Engelbert | Franz | FRG | 63 | 3 | NC | W Berlin | 12 Jul |
| 8:34.2 m | Aleksandr | Zagoruiko | SU | 55 | 2 | | Dnepropetrovsk | 29 Jun |
| 8:34.60 | Augustin | Barbu    (90) | RUM | 63 | 1 | | București | 25 May |
| | | | | | | | | |
| 8:34.72 | Aivar | Tsarskiy | SU | 62 | 8 | NC | Kiev | 17 Jul |
| 8:34.74 | Martin | ten Kate | HOL | 58 | 6 | FBK | Hengelo | 27 Jun |
| 8:34.8 m | Gyula | Balogh | HUN | 61 | 1 | | Miskolc | 18 May |
| 8:34.87 | Yevgeniy | Volgin | SU | 62 | 9 | NC | Kiev | 17 Jul |
| 8:34.99 | Dave | Daniels | USA | 58 | 4h1 | TAC | Eugene | 19 Jun |
| 8:35.03 | Phil | Laheurte | CAN | 57 | 14 | | Koblenz | 6 Aug |
| 8:35.05 | Elisio | Rios | POR | 61 | 2 | NC | Lisboa | 9 Aug |
| 8:35.51 | Vyacheslav | Groshev | SU | 58 | 1 | | Sochi | 27 Apr |
| 8:35.62 | Juan | Espino | SPA | 59 | 4 | | Sevilla | 24 May |
| 8:35.65 | Greg | Beardsley (100) | USA | 61 | 10 | TAC | Eugene | 21 Jun |
| 8:35.80 | Stanislav | Štít | CS | 58 | 1 | NC | Bratislava | 12 Jul |
| 8:35.83 | Kyriakos | Moutesidis | GRE | 63 | | | | |
| 8:35.92 | Mohamed | Mestour (103) | MOR | 61 | 6 | | La Coruña | 6 Aug |

| Mark | Name | | Nat | Yr | Pos | Meet | Venue | Date |
|------|------|--|-----|----|----|------|-------|------|
| 8:36.11 | David | Barney | USA 60 | | 7 Jun | | | |
| 8:36.14 | Kevin | Capper | UK 59 | | 26 May | | | |
| 8:36.17 | Carmelo | Rios | PR 59 | | 19 Jun | | | |
| 8:36.4 m | Alejandro | Gomez | SPA 67 | | 5 Sep | | | |
| 8:36.43 | Dariusz | Kaczmarski | POL 62 | | 2 Aug | | | |
| 8:36.44 | Bruno | Coutant | FRA 63 | | 16 Jul | | | |
| 8:36.57 | João Lopes | da Silva(110) | POR 61 | | 19 Mar | | | |
| 8:36.63 | Kari | Hänninen | FIN 62 | | 26 Jul | | | |
| 8:36.84 | Béla | Vágó | HUN 63 | | 14 Jun | | | |
| 8:37.00 | Jos | Maes | BEL 61 | | 9 Aug | | | |
| 8:37.10 | César | Sánchez | SPA 63 | | 6 Aug | | | |
| 8:37.23 | Angelo | Carosi | ITA 64 | | 23 Jul | | | |
| 8:37.33 | Shouguo | Cheng | CHN 60 | | 30 Sep | | | |
| 8:37.5 m | Manuel | Matias | POR 62 | | 30 Jul | | | |
| 8:37.67 | Thomas | Spiegelberger | FRG 63 | | 6 Aug | | | |
| 8:37.70 | Matthias | Kohls | FRG 61 | | 12 Jul | | | |
| 8:37.80 | Karl | Van Calcar (120) | USA 65 | | 7 Jun | | | |
| 8:37.87 | Colin | Walker | UK 62 | | 26 May | | | |
| 8:37.89 | Andrew | Taylor | UK 60 | | 26 May | | | |
| 8:37.99 | Jakab | Lamuth | HUN 64 | | 17 Sep | | | |
| 8:38.0 m | Zablon | Mose | KEN 60 | | 16 May | | | |
| 8:38.01 | Mati | Uusmaa | SU 59 | | 14 Jun | | | |
| 8:38.11 | Antanas | Stancius | SU 58 | | 25 May | | | |
| 8:38.28 | Filippos | Filippou | CYP 56 | | 18 May | | | |
| 8:38.37 | Rafael | Colmenares | VEN 61 | | 14 Mar | | | |
| 8:38.4 m | Alain | Boucher | CAN 63 | | 10 Aug | | | |
| 8:38.45 | Bob | Rice (130) | CAN 65 | | 22 Jun | | | |
| 8:38.67 | John | Hartigan | UK 65 | | 21 Jun | | | |
| 8:38.97 | David | Baptiste | UK 65 | | 21 Jun | | | |
| 8:39.01 | Mark | Junkermann | USA 65 | | 23 May | | | |
| 8:39.38 | Dan | Nelson | USA 64 | | 12 Apr | | | |
| 8:39.4 m | Greg | Cameron | NZ 64 | | 19 Mar | | | |
| 8:39.4 m | Gary | Zeuner | AUS 53 | | 20 Mar | | | |
| 8:39.51 | Hajime | Nagasato | JAP 60 | | 1 Jun | | | |
| 8:39.58 | Karl-Heinz | Seck | FRG 54 | | 3 Jun | | | |
| 8:39.63 | Johan | Schnetler | RSA 66 | | 19 Mar | | | |
| 8:39.66 | Martin | Fiz (140) | SPA 63 | | 6 Aug | | | |
| 8:39.69 | Vasiliy | Koromyslov | SU 57 | | 27 Apr | | | |
| 8:39.8 m | Aleksandr | Khudyakov | SU 60 | | 23 Aug | | | |
| 8:39.93 | Daniel | Prinsloo | RSA 61 | | 19 Mar | | | |
| 8:39.99 | Mark | Wayment | USA 61 | | 4 Jun | | | |
| 8:40.0 m | Valeriy | Kachan | SU 60 | | 29 Jun | | | |
| 8:40.12 | Sergio | Magonara | ITA 65 | | 23 Jul | | | |
| 8:40.20 | Valeriy | Gryaznov | SU 61 | | 15 Jul | | | |
| 8:40.27 | Thomas | Peucker | GDR 66 | | 27 Jun | | | |
| 8:40.28 | Tadeusz | Markowski | POL 60 | | 27 Jun | | | |
| 8:40.3 m | Wilson | Musonik (150) | KEN 56 | | 15 May | | | |
| 8:40.32 | Dariusz | Rudzik | POL 63 | | 27 Jun | | | |
| 8:40.45 | Aleksandr | Chepasov | SU 63 | | 7 Jun | | | |
| 8:40.53 | Brent | Barnhill | USA 61 | | 24 May | | | |
| 8:40.80 | Azzeddine | Brahmi | ALG 66 | | 13 Sep | | | |
| 8:40.81 | Fernando | Couto | POR 59 | | 20 Jul | | | |
| 8:40.9 m | Arlindo | Macedo (156) | POR 61 | | 30 Jul | | | |

Zagoruiko (8:34.2 m) also did 8:34.27 4 Znam Leningrad 7 Jun.

| | 1 | 10 | 20 | 30 | 50 | 100 | Under 8:30.0 | Under 8:35.0 |
|---|---|-----|-----|-----|-----|------|------|------|
| 1982 | 8:16.17 | 8:21.15 | 8:23.94 | 8:27.36 | 8:31.0 | 8:35.7 | 42 | 94 |
| 1983 | 8:12.37 | 8:19.38 | 8:21.72 | 8:25.05 | 8:28.77 | 8:36.09 | 60 | 94 |
| 1984 | 8:07.62 | 8:17.27 | 8:20.40 | 8:25.13 | 8:28.95 | 8:35.35 | 55 | 97 |
| 1985 | 8:09.17 | 8:18.02 | 8:21.99 | 8:24.90 | 8:30.23 | 8:35.95 | 49 | 87 |
| 1986 | 8:10.01 | 8:16.59 | 8:19.88 | 8:22.49 | 8:29.00 | 8:35.65 | 62 | 95 |

MEN 1986

| Mark | Name | | Nat | Yr | Pos | Meet | Venue | Date |
|------|------|--|-----|----|----|------|-------|------|

# MARATHON

| Mark | Name | | Nat | Yr | Pos | Meet | Venue | Date |
|------|------|--|-----|----|----|------|-------|------|
| 2:07:35 | Taisuke | Kodama | JAP | 58 | 1 | | Beijing | 19 Oct |
| 2:07:51 | Rob | de Castella | AUS | 57 | 1 | | Boston | 21 Apr |
| 2:07:57 | Kunimitsu | Itoh | JAP | 55 | 2 | | Beijing | 19 Oct |
| 2:08:10 | Juma | Ikangaa | TAN | 57 | 1 | | Tokyo | 9 Feb |
| 2:08:21 | Takeyuki | Nakayama | JAP | 59 | 1 | AG | Seoul | 5 Oct |
| 2:08:27 | Toshihiko | Seko | JAP | 56 | 1 | | Chicago | 26 Oct |
| 2:08:29 | Belaine | Dinsamo | ETH | 57 | 2 | | Tokyo | 9 Feb |
| 2:08:39 | Abebe | Mekonnen | ETH | 64 | 3 | | Tokyo | 9 Feb |
| 2:08:39 | | Ikangaa | | | 3 | | Beijing | 19 Oct |
| 2:08:43 | | Nakayama | | | 4 | | Tokyo | 9 Feb |
| 2:09:08 | | Mekonnen | | | 1 | | Rotterdam | 19 Apr |
| 2:09:09 | | Dinsamo | | | 2 | | Rotterdam | 19 Apr |
| 2:09:39 | Gidamis | Shahanga | TAN | 57 | 4 | | Beijing | 19 Oct |
| 2:09:57 | Ahmed | Salah | DJI | 56 | 2 | | Chicago | 26 Oct |
| | (10) | | | | | | | |
| 2:10:02 | | Seko | | | 1 | | London | 20 Apr |
| 2:10:06 | | Ikangaa | | | 1 | | Fukuoka | 7 Dec |
| 2:10:08 | Hirmoi | Taniguchi | JAP | 60 | 2 | AG | Seoul | 5 Oct |
| 2:10:13 | Charlie | Spedding | GBR | 52 | 3 | | Chicago | 26 Oct |
| 2:10:15 | | de Castella | | | 1 | CG | Edinburgh | 1 Aug |
| 2:10:27 | Michael | Heilmann | GDR | 61 | 5 | | Tokyo | 9 Feb |
| 2:10:30 | Mike | Musyoki | KEN | 56 | 4 | | Chicago | 26 Oct |
| 2:10:31 | | Mekonnen | | | 1 | | Montreal | 28 Sep |
| 2:10:34 | | Kodama | | | 1 | | Beppu | 2 Feb |
| 2:10:34 | Antoni | Niemczak | POL | 55 | 1 | NC | Debno | 6 Apr |
| 2:10:39 | Geoff | Smith | GBR | 53 | 5 | | Beijing | 19 Oct |
| 2:10:41 | Bill | Donakowski | USA | 56 | 1 | TAC | St Paul | 12 Oct |
| 2:10:54 | Gelindo | Bordin | ITA | 59 | 1 | EC | Stuttgart | 30 Aug |
| 2:10:57 | Orlando | Pizzolato | ITA | 58 | 2 | EC | Stuttgart | 30 Aug |
| 2:11:03 | Bogulaw | Psujek | POL | 56 | 1 | | W Berlin | 28 Sep |
| | (20) | | | | | | | |
| 2:11:06 | Gianni | Poli | ITA | 57 | 1 | | New York | 2 Nov |

30 performances/ 21 performers

| Mark | Name | | Nat | Yr | Pos | Meet | Venue | Date |
|------|------|--|-----|----|----|------|-------|------|
| 2:11:08 | Dave | Edge | CAN | 54 | 2 | CG | Edinburgh | 1 Aug |
| 2:11:10 | Masayuki | Nishi | JAP | 64 | 6 | | Beijing | 19 Oct |
| 2:11:15 | Art | Boileau | CAB | 57 | 2 | | Boston | 21 Apr |
| 2:11:17 | Herbert | Steffny | FRG | 53 | 5 | | Chicago | 26 Oct |
| 2:11:18 | Wiktor | Sawicki | POL | 55 | 2 | NC | Debno | 6 Apr |
| 2:11:18 | Steve | Moneghetti | AUS | 62 | 3 | CG | Edinburgh | 1 Aug |
| 2:11:19 | Yuichiro | Osuda | JAP | 61 | 2 | | Fukuoka | 7 Dec |
| 2:11:25 | Bruno | Lafranchi | SUi | 55 | 3 | | Fukuoka | 7 Dec |
| 2:11:27 | John | Burra | TAN | 62 | 6 | | Tokyo | 9 Feb |
| | (30) | | | | | | | |
| 2:11:31 | Paul | Cummings | USA | 53 | 1 | | Houston | 19 Jan |
| 2:11:34 | Czeslaw | Wilczewski | POL | 58 | 2 | | Beppu | 2 Feb |
| 2:11:41 | Ralf | Salzmann | FRG | 55 | 4 | EC | Stuttgart | 30 Aug |
| 2:11:42 | Jerzy | Skarzynski | POL | 56 | 3 | NC | Debno | 6 Apr |
| 2:11:42 | Hugh | Jones | GBR | 55 | 2 | | London | 20 Apr |
| 2:11:43 | Yakov | Tolstikov | SOV | 59 | 1 | | Uzhgorod | 7 Oct |
| 2:11:44 | Ibrahim | Hussein | KEN | 58 | 1 | | Honolulu | 7 Dec |
| 2:11:49 | Henrik | Jorgensen | DEN | 61 | 2 | | W Berlin | 28 Sep |
| 2:11:56 | Allan | Zachariassen | DEN | 55 | 3 | | Rotterdam | 19 Apr |
| 2:11:58 | Don | Janicki | USA | 60 | 2 | TAC | St Paul | 12 Oct |
| | (40) | | | | | | | |

| Mark | Name | | Nat | Yr | Pos | Meet | Venue | Date |
|------|------|------|-----|-----|-----|------|-------|------|
| 2:11:58 | Kazuyoshi | Kudo | Jap | 61 | 4 | | Fukuoka | 7 Dec |
| 2:11:59 | Isamu | Sennai | JAP | 60 | 5 | | Fukuoka | 7 Dec |
| 2:12:02 | Chiaki | Harumatsu | JAP | 58 | 6 | | Fukuoka | 7 Dec |
| 2:12:07 | Ryszard | Misiewicz | POL | 57 | 4 | NC | Debno | 6 Apr |
| 2:12:08 | David | Gordon | USA | 59 | 3 | TAC | St Paul | 12 Oct |
| 2:12:10 | John | Graham | GBR | 56 | 4 | CG | Edinburgh | 1 Aug |
| 2:12:12 | Karel | Lismont | BEL | 49 | 1 | | Hamburg | 25 May |
| 2:12:14 | Thom | Hunt | USA | 58 | 2 | | Jersey C | 4 May |
| 2:12:14 | Tetsuo | Urukawa | JAP | 61 | 7 | | Fukuoka | 7 Dec |
| 2:12:21 | Zbigniew | Pierzynka | POL | 51 | 5 | NC | Debno | 6 Apr |
| 2:12:22 | Gerhard | Hartmann | AUT | 55 | 1 | | Wien | 13 Apr |
| | (50) | | | | | | | |
| 2:12:27 | Cor | Lambregts | HOL | 58 | 4 | | Rotterdam | 19 Apr |
| 2:12:33 | Kjell-Erik | Stahl | SWE | 56 | 1 | NC | Stockholm | 7 Jun |
| 2:12:35 | Gabriel | Kamau | KEN | 57 | 3 | | W Berlin | 28 Sep |
| 2:12:36 | Allister | Hutton | GBR | 54 | 3 | | London | 20 Apr |
| 2:12:37 | Frank | Plasso | USA | 60 | 1 | | Las Vegas | 1 Feb |
| 2:12:39 | Delfim | Moreira | POR | 55 | 4 | | W Berlin | 28 Sep |
| 2:12:44 | Gerry | Kiernan | IRE | 53 | 3 | | Houston | 19 Jan |
| 2:12:46 | Gerhard | Nijboer | HOL | 55 | 6 | EC | Stuttgart | 30 Aug |
| 2:12:48 | Kiyoji | Hayashi | JAP | 61 | 8 | | Tokyo | 9 Feb |
| 2:12:53 | Joseph | Kipsang | KEN | 62 | 1 | | Duluth | 21 Jun |
| | (60) | | | | | | | |
| 2:12:53 | Jacques | Lefrand | FRA | 52 | 7 | EC | Stuttgart | 30 Aug |
| 2:12:54 | Eloi | Schleder | BRZ | 51 | 1 | | Sydney | 8 Jun |
| 2:12:56 | Pat | Petersen | USA | 59 | 4 | | London | 20 Apr |
| 2:12:57 | Roy | Andersen | NOR | 55 | 4 | | Houston | 19 Jan |
| 2:12:59 | Ric | Sayre | USA | 53 | 1 | | Los Angeles | 9 Mar |
| 2:13:00 | Akiro | Ono | JAP | 60 | 3 | | Beppu | 2 Feb |
| 2:13:00 | Takeshi | Kondo | JAP | 59 | 9 | | Fukuoka | 7 Dec |
| 2:13:01 | Henryk | Lupa | POL | 56 | 6 | NC | Debno | 6 Apr |
| 2:13:02 | Mehmet | Terzi | TUR | 55 | 5 | | London | 20 Apr |
| 2:13:05 | Sergey | Rudenko | SOV | 58 | 1 | | Vilnius | 26 Apr |
| | (70) | | | | | | | |
| 2:13:05 | Pawel | Lorens | POL | 58 | 6 | | W Berlin | 28 Sep |
| 2:13:09 | Igor | Braslavskiy | SOV | 59 | 2 | | Vilnius | 26 Apr |
| 2:13:10 | Loris | Pimazzoni | ITA | 56 | 10 | | Fukuoka | 7 Dec |
| 2:13:11 | Danny | Grimes | USA | 59 | 4 | TAC | St Paul | 12 Oct |
| 2:13:12 | Jean-Pierre | Paumen | BEL | 56 | 5 | | Rotterdam | 19 Apr |
| 2:13:14 | Bill | Reifsnyder | USA | 62 | 4 | | Jersey C | 4 May |
| 2:13:15 | Pär | Wallin | SWE | 55 | 2 | NC | Stockholm | 7 Jun |
| 2:13:15 | Fekere Mariam | Wolde | ETH | | 7 | | Beijing | 19 Oct |
| 2:13:15 | Zhu | Shuchun | PRC | 60 | 8 | | Beijing | 19 Oct |
| 2:13:17 | Shozo | Nakajima | JAP | | 1 | | Chichibu | 7 Dec |
| | (80) | | | | | | | |
| 2:13:18 | Tomio | Sueyoshi | JAP | 59 | 5 | | Beppu | 2 Feb |
| 2:13:19 | Michael | O'Reilly | GBR | 58 | 1 | | Columbus | 16 Nov |
| 2:13:20 | Danny | Gonzalez | USA | 62 | 1 | | Sacramento | 7 Dec |
| 2:13:21 | Ieuan | Ellis | GBR | 60 | 9 | | Beijing | 19 Oct |
| 2:13:24 | Thomas | Eickmann | FRG | 62 | 7 | | W Berlin | 28 Sep |
| 2:13:26 | Marty | Froelick | USA | 58 | 6 | | Houston | 19 Jan |
| 2:13:26 | Agapius | Masong | TAN | 60 | 2 | | San Diego | 13 Dec |
| 2:13:27 | Phil | Coppess | USA | 54 | 5 | | Jersey C | 4 May |
| 2:13:27 | Yuriy | Porotov | SOV | 50 | 2 | | Uzhgorod | 7 Oct |
| 2:13:27 | Masayuki | Tsubo | JAP | | 10 | | Beijing | 19 Oct |
| | (90) | | | | | | | |
| 2:13:27 | Salvatore | Bettiol | ITA | 61 | 6 | | New York | 2 Nov |
| 2:13:27 | Alessio | Faustini | ITA | 60 | 11 | | Fukuoka | 7 Dec |
| 2:13:29 | Pete | Pfitzinger | USA | 57 | 1 | | San Fransisco | 20 Jul |
| 2:13:29 | Dirk | van der Herten | BEL | 57 | 10 | EC | Stuttgart | 30 Aug |

| Mark | Name | | Nat | Yr | Pos | Meet | Venue | Date |
|------|------|--|-----|----|----|------|-------|------|
| 2:13:32 | Hiroshi | Munakata | JAP | 59 | 9 | | Tokyo | 9 Feb |
| 2:13:35 | Istvan | Kerekjarto | HUN | 53 | 1 | NC | Szeged | 16 Mar |
| 2:13:36 | Bill | Rodgers | USA | 47 | 4 | | Boston | 21 Apr |
| 2:13:36 | Alex | Gonzales | FRA | 51 | 11 | EC | Stuttgart | 30 Aug |
| 2:13:37 | Kazimierz | Lasecki | POL | 58 | 7 | NC | Debno | 6 Apr |
| 2:13:38 | Santiago | de la Parte | SPA | 48 | 10 | | Tokyo | 9 Feb |
| | (100) | | | | | | | |
| 2:13:38 | Zeng | Zhaoxue | PRC | 59 | 11 | | Beijing | 19 Oct |
| | (101) | | | | | | | |

| | | | | | | | | | | |
|--|--|--|--|--|--|--|--|--|--|--|
| 2:13:39 | Jacek | Konieczny | POL | 59 | | 2:14:03 | Osvaldo | Faustini | ITA | 57 |
| 2:13:40 | Jarl Gaute | Aase | NOR | 59 | | 2:14:04 | Svend Erik | Kristensen | DEN | 56 |
| 2:13:41 | Viktor | Nedybalyuk | SOV | 56 | | 2:14:04 | Kenny | Stuart | GBR | 57 |
| 2:13:42 | Yutaka | Kanai | JAP | 59 | | 2:14:06 | Yoo | Jae-Sung | SKO | 60 |
| 2:13:44 | George | Malley | USA | 55 | | | (130) | | | |
| 2:13:44 | Li | Jong-Gil | NKO | 57 | | 2:14:06 | Yu | Sun-Ho | NKO | 65 |
| 2:13:45 | Gyula | Borka | HUN | 59 | | 2:14:09 | Linn | Whatcott | USA | 61 |
| 2:13:45 | Eddy | Hellebuyk | BEL | 62 | | 2:14:09 | Zoltan | Kiss | HUN | 56 |
| 2:13:47 | David | Olds | USA | 61 | | 2:14:09 | Arturo | Barrios | MEX | 63 |
| | (110) | | | | | 2:14:10 | Jung | Man-Hwa | SKO | 60 |
| 2:13:48 | Tadeusz | Lawicki | POL | 56 | | 2:14:11 | Kebede | Balcha | ETH | 51 |
| 2:13:49 | Wu | Zhihan | PRC | 58 | | 2:14:12 | Johan | Geinaert | BEL | 51 |
| 2:13:51 | Vladimir | Kotov | SOV | 58 | | 2:14:13 | Luc | Waegeman | BEL | 58 |
| 2:13:51 | Alexsandr | Baza | SOV | 53 | | 2:14:14 | Alain | Lazare | FRA | 52 |
| 2:13:52 | Yoshihiro | Nishimura | JAP | 57 | | 2:14:14 | Hiroshi | Nagashina | JAP | 59 |
| 2:13:53 | Oddmund | Roaldkvam | NOR | 58 | | | (140) | | | |
| 2:13:54 | Wojciech | Ratkowski | POL | 54 | | 2:14:15 | Zoltan | Lantos | HUN | 63 |
| 2:13:55 | Henrik | Albahn | DEN | 60 | | 2:14:15 | Vladimir | Nikityuk | SOV | 56 |
| 2:13:55 | Kingston | Mills | IRE | 55 | | 2:14:15 | Cai | Shangyan | PRC | |
| 2:13:56 | Andrzej | Sajkowski | POL | 52 | | 2:14:16 | Thompson | Magawana | RSA | 59 |
| | (120) | | | | | 2:14:17 | Fumiaki | Abe | JAP | 58 |
| 2:13:56 | Zenon | Poniatowski | POL | 54 | | 2:14:18 | Jacky | Boxberger | FRA | 49 |
| 2:13:57 | Jozef | Machalek | SWE | 48 | | 2:14:19 | Sergey | Krestyaninov | SOV | 62 |
| 2:13:58 | Frederik | Van der Vennet | BEL | 52 | | 2:14:19 | Toru | Mimura | JAP | 62 |
| 2:13:59 | Paul | Williams | CAN | 56 | | 2:14:20 | Zoltan | Nalasnyik | HUN | 57 |
| 2:14:00 | Janos | Papp | HUN | 59 | | 2:14:22 | Katsushi | Matsuda | JAP | 59 |
| 2:14:02 | Rich | Brownsberger | USA | 63 | | | (150) | | | |

Downhill

| 2:08:04 | Zithuele | Sinque | RSA | 63 | 1 | | Port Elizabeth | 3 May |
|---------|----------|--------|-----|----|----|--|----------------|-------|
| 2:08:15 | Willie | Mtolo | RSA | 64 | 2 | | Port Elizabeth | 3 May |
| 2:11:00 | Ernest | Tjela | RSA | 54 | 3 | | Port Elizabeth | 3 May |

The course at Port Elizabeth is point to point and drops 149' between start and finish.

| Mark | Wind | Name | | Nat | Yr | Pos | Meet | Venue | Date |
|------|------|------|------|-----|----|----|------|-------|------|

## 110 METRES HURDLES

| 13.20 | 2.0 | Stéphane | Caristan | FRA | 64 | 1 | EC | Stuttgart | 30 Aug |
|-------|-----|----------|----------|-----|----|----|------|-----------|--------|
| 13.25 |     | Greg     | Foster   | USA | 58 | 1r1 | GWG | Moskva | 6 Jul |
| 13.25 | 0.8 |          | Foster   |     |    | 1 |      | Birmingham | 19 Aug |
| 13.26 | 1.6 |          | Foster   |     |    | 1 | TAC | Eugene | 20 Jun |
| 13.27 | 2.0 |          | Foster   |     |    | 1 | Pepsi | Westwood | 17 May |
| 13.28 | 1.0 | Andrey   | Prokofyev | SU | 59 | 1r2 | GWG | Moskva | 6 Jul |
| 13.28 | 0.9 |          | Caristan |     |    | 1s1 | EC | Stuttgart | 29 Aug |
| 13.31 |     | Keith    | Talley   | USA | 64 | 2r1 | GWG | Moskva | 6 Jul |
| 13.32 | 1.7 |          | Foster   |     |    | 1 | Pre | Eugene | 7 Jun |
| 13.33 | 0.2 |          | Caristan |     |    | 1 |      | Paris | 22 Jul |
| | | | | | | | | | |
| 13.35 | -1.1 | Mark    | McKoy    | CAN | 61 | 1 |      | Papeete | 27 Mar |
| 13.36 | 0.0 |          | Talley   |     |    | 1 | NCAA | Indianapolis | 7 Jun |
| 13.37 | 0.5 |          | McKoy    |     |    | 1 |      | Barcelona | 16 Jul |
| 13.37 | 0.2 | Milan    | Stewart  | USA | 60 | 2 |      | Paris | 22 Jul |
| 13.38 | -0.5 |         | Foster   |     |    | 1 | WK | Zürich | 13 Aug |
| 13.39 | 1.1 | Aleksandr | Markin | SU | 62 | 1 |      | Sochi | 24 May |
| 13.39 | 1.7 | Tonie    | Campbell | USA | 60 | 2 | Pre | Eugene | 7 Jun |
| 13.39 | 1.0 |          | McKoy    |     |    | 1 |      | Lappeenranta | 26 Jun |
| 13.39 | -0.1 |         | Foster   |     |    | 1 | PTG | London | 11 Jul |
| 13.39 | 0.6 |          | Caristan |     |    | 1 |      | Lausanne | 2 Sep |
| | | | | | | | | | |
| 13.40 | 2.0 | Roger    | Kingdom  | USA | 62 | 2 | Pepsi | Westwood | 17 May |
| 13.40 | 2.0 | Holger   | Pohland (10) | GDR | 63 | 1 | v SU | Tallinn | 21 Jun |
| 13.40 | 0.0 |          | Stewart  |     |    | 1r1 | BGP | Budapest | 11 Aug |
| 13.41 | 0.1 |          | McKoy    |     |    | 1 |      | Baton Rouge | 13 Apr |
| 13.41 | 1.4 |          | McKoy    |     |    | 1 |      | Baton Rouge | 4 May |
| 13.41 | 0.7 |          | Talley   |     |    | 1h2 | TAC | Eugene | 19 Jun |
| 13.42 | 1.2 |          | Caristan |     |    | 1 |      | Creteil | 14 Jun |
| 13.42 | -0.5 |         | Caristan |     |    | 1 |      | Saint-Denis | 21 Jun |
| 13.42 | 2.0 | Arto     | Bryggare | FIN | 58 | 2 | EC | Stuttgart | 30 Aug |
| 13.42 | -0.9 | Igor    | Kazanov  | SU | 63 | 1 | Spart | Tashkent | 20 Sep |
| | | (30/12) | | | | | | | |
| 13.44 | -0.8 | Colin   | Jackson  | UK | 67 | 1 | WC-j | Athinai | 19 Jul |
| 13.47 | 0.0 | Sansiski | Daniels | USA | 64 | 2 | NCAA | Indianapolis | 7 Jun |
| 13.47 | 0.9 | Liviu    | Giurgian | RUM | 62 | 1 | RumIC | Bucureşti | 14 Jun |
| 13.47 | 1.0 | Igor     | Perevedentsev | SU | 64 | 2r2 | GWG | Moskva | 6 Jul |
| 13.48 | 0.0 | Renaldo  | Nehemiah | USA | 59 | 1 |      | Viareggio | 6 Aug |
| 13.50 | 1.0 | Vladimir | Shishkin | SU | 64 | 3r2 | GWG | Moskva | 6 Jul |
| 13.50 | 2.0 | Carlos   | Sala     | SPA | 60 | 3 | EC | Stuttgart | 30 Aug |
| 13.51 | 0.0 | Martin   | Booker (20) | USA | 63 | 3 | NCAA | Indianapolis | 7 Jun |
| | | | | | | | | | |
| 13.52 | 0.0 | Eric     | Reid     | USA | 65 | 4 | NCAA | Indianapolis | 7 Jun |
| 13.52 | 0.7 | Andreas  | Oschkenat | GDR | 62 | 1s2 | EC | Stuttgart | 29 Aug |
| 13.52 | 2.0 | Nigel    | Walker   | UK | 63 | 4 | EC | Stuttgart | 30 Aug |
| 13.53 | 1.6 | William  | Skinner  | USA | 64 | 1 | IC4A | Villanova | 25 May |
| 13.54 | 2.0 | Sam      | Turner   | USA | 57 | 4 | Pepsi | Westwood | 17 May |
| 13.55 | 1.0 | Jack     | Pierce   | USA | 62 | 1 |      | Belfast | 30 Jun |
| 13.56 |     | Reyna    | Thompson | USA | 63 | 1 |      | Waco | 18 Apr |
| 13.57 |     | Arthur   | Blake    | USA | 66 | 1 |      | Tampa | 12 Apr |
| 13.57 | 0.0 | Thomas   | Wilcher  | USA | 64 | 5 | NCAA | Indianapolis | 7 Jun |
| 13.57 | 1.0 | Cletus   | Clark (30) | USA | 62 | 2 |      | Belfast | 30 Jun |
| | | | | | | | | | |
| 13.59 | 1.9 | Plamen   | Krastev  | BUL | 58 | 1 |      | Sofia | 3 Aug |
| 13.60 | 0.7 | György   | Bakos    | HUN | 60 | 4s2 | EC | Stuttgart | 29 Aug |
| 13.62 |     | Reggie   | Davis    | USA | 64 | 2 |      | Tampa | 12 Apr |
| 13.63 | -0.6 | Gennadiy | Chugunov | SU | 63 | 1h | Znam | Leningrad | 8 Jun |

MEN 1986

| Mark | Wind | Name | | Nat | Yr | Pos | Meet | Venue | Date |
|------|------|------|--|-----|-----|-----|------|-------|------|
| 13.64 | 1.1 | Don | Wright | AUS | 59 | 1r2 | BGP | Budapest | 11 Aug |
| 13.64 | -0.9 | Viktor | Batrachenko | SU | 63 | 2 | Spart | Tashkent | 20 Sep |
| 13.65 | 0.7 | Tony | Dees | USA | 63 | 1 | PennR | Philadelphia | 26 Apr |
| 13.66 | 0.0 | Jonathan | Ridgeon | UK | 67 | 6 | NCAA | Indianapolis | 7 Jun |
| 13.66 | 0.8 | Malcolm | Dixon | USA | 59 | 1h4 | TAC | Eugene | 19 Jun |
| 13.67 | | Andrew | Parker (40) | JAM | 65 | 1 | | Tempe | 22 Mar |
| | | | | | | | | | |
| 13.67 | 1.1 | Anatoliy | Titov | SU | 56 | 4 | | Sochi | 24 May |
| 13.68 | -0.1 | Ron | Stewart | USA | 63 | 1 | | Raleigh | 29 Mar |
| 13.68 | 1.3 | Al | Joyner | USA | 60 | 1 | | Fresno | 5 Apr |
| 13.68 | 2.0 | Anton | Isayev | SU | 62 | 1h | | Riga | 30 May |
| 13.69 | 0.9 | Mikael | Ylöstalo | FIN | 63 | 5s1 | EC | Stuttgart | 29 Aug |
| 13.70 | 0.1 | Sergey | Strelchenko | SU | 61 | 5 | NC | Kiev | 16 Jul |
| 13.70 | 1.0 | Piotr | Wójcik | POL | 65 | 1 | | Poznan | 7 Sep |
| 13.71 | 0.0 | James | Purvis | USA | 66 | 7 | NCAA | Indianapolis | 7 Jun |
| 13.72 | -1.2 | Romuald | Giegiel | POL | 57 | 1 | Kuso | Warszawa | 17 Jun |
| 13.72 | 0.0 | Al | Lane (50) | USA | 62 | 3 | USOCF | Houston | 3 Aug |
| | | | | | | | | | |
| 13.73 | 2.0 | Frank | Barnett | USA | 66 | 6 | Pepsi | Westwood | 17 May |
| A13.74 | | Ralf | Schroeder | RSA | 62 | 1 | | Germiston | 22 Mar |
| 13.74 | 1.3 | Krzysztof | Płatek | POL | 62 | 1 | | Słupsk | 8 Jun |
| 13.74 | 2.0 | Vyacheslav | Ustinov | SU | 57 | 1 | | Moskva | 3 Aug |
| 13.75 | 1.8 | Chris | Branham | USA | 62 | 1 | | Modesto, CA | 10 May |
| 13.75 | 1.5 | Vitaliy | Sklyarov | SU | 60 | 1h | | Riga | 30 May |
| 13.75 | -0.9 | Igor | Khitryakov | SU | 65 | 2s | Spart | Tashkent | 20 Sep |
| 13.76 | 1.4 | Siegfried | Wentz | FRG | 60 | 1 | NC | W Berlin | 12 Jul |
| 13.78 | 0.8 | Charles | James | USA | 64 | 3h4 | NCAA | Indianapolis | 5 Jun |
| 13.79 | 1.9 | Rodney | Cooper (60) | USA | 65 | 1 | | Odessa, TX | 16 May |
| | | | | | | | | | |
| 13.79 | 0.9 | Robert, | Thomas | USA | 60 | 2 | | Houston | 24 May |
| 13.79 | 1.2 | Aleš | Höffer | CS | 62 | 3h2 | Znam | Leningrad | 8 Jun |
| 13.79 | -0.4 | Ventsislav | Radev | BUL | 61 | 2 | NC | Sofia | 13 Aug |
| 13.79 | 1.8 | Gianni | Tozzi | ITA | 62 | 1 | | Chieti | 5 Sep |
| 13.79 | 0.0 | Luigi | Bertocchi | ITA | 65 | 1 | CISM | Ostia | 13 Sep |
| 13.80 | | Mark | Boyd | USA | 65 | 2 | | Tempe | 22 Mar |
| 13.80 | 1.8 | Daniele | Fontecchio | ITA | 60 | 2 | | Chieti | 5 Sep |
| 13.81 | 1.8 | John | Lenstrohm | USA | 61 | 2 | | Modesto, CA | 10 May |
| 13.81 | 2.0 | Bernard | Williams | USA | 65 | 1h1 | | Knoxville | 17 May |
| A13.82 | 1.1 | Kobus | Schoeman (70) | RSA | 65 | 1h | NC | Germiston | 11 Apr |
| | | | | | | | | | |
| 13.82 | | Rod | Jett | USA | 66 | 1 | | Berkeley | 3 May |
| 13.82 | 1.1 | Vladimir | Zaika | SU | 57 | 6 | | Sochi | 24 May |
| 13.82 | -1.2 | Robert | Kurnicki | POL | 65 | 1 | | Poznan | 26 Aug |
| 13.83 | 0.0 | Robert | Reading | USA | 67 | 1h1 | | Los Angeles | 23 May |
| 13.83 | 0.0 | Javier | Moracho | SPA | 57 | 1 | | Sevilla | 24 May |
| 13.84 | 2.0 | Kevin | Young | USA | 66 | 7 | Pepsi | Westwood | 17 May |
| 13.84 | | Walt | Foster | USA | 64 | 1 | | Knoxville | 30 May |
| 13.84 | 1.6 | Michael | Radzey | FRG | 60 | 1 | | Stuttgart | 28 Jun |
| 13.84 | 1.2 | Béla | Bodó | HUN | 59 | 1 | | Budapest | 6 Jul |
| 13.84 | -0.9 | Sergey | Krasovskiy (80) | SU | 63 | 7 | Spart | Tashkent | 20 Sep |
| | | | | | | | | | |
| 13.85 | 1.5 | Mike | Timpson | USA | 67 | 2 | | Univ Park, PA | 16 May |
| 13.85 | -0.5 | Franck | Chevallier | FRA | 64 | 2 | | Saint-Denis | 21 Jun |
| 13.85 | 1.5 | Jean-Marc | Muster | SWZ | 61 | 1 | | Chaux-de-Fonds | 25 Jun |
| 13.86 | 0.6 | Jeff | Powell | USA | 63 | 1 | | Knoxville | 12 Apr |
| 13.86 | 1.8 | John | Johnson | USA | 60 | 2r1 | MSR | Walnut, CA | 27 Apr |
| 13.86 | 1.5 | Carl | Campbell | USA | 63 | 2h1 | NCAA | Indianapolis | 5 Jun |

| Mark | Wind | Name | | Nat | Yr | Pos | Meet | Venue | Date |
|---|---|---|---|---|---|---|---|---|---|
| 13.86 | -0.1 | Angel | Bueno | CUB | 63 | 1 | CAC | Santiago/Dom | 2 Jul |
| 13.87 | | James | Quinn | USA | 63 | 1 | | Charleston, SC | 18 Mar |
| 13.87 | 1.5 | Calvin | Holmes | USA | 65 | 3 | | Univ Park, PA | 16 May |
| 13.87 | 1.9 | Earl | Diamond (90) | USA | 66 | 2 | | Odessa, TX | 16 May |
| 13.87 | 0.0 | Kevin | McKinley | USA | 64 | 1 | | Russellville | 23 May |
| 13.87 | | Damon | Polk | USA | 65 | 1 | | Norman | 22 May |
| 13.87 | 0.5 | Daniel | Darien | FRA | 61 | 1 | | Nantes | 7 Jun |
| 13.87 | 1.8 | Jeff | Glass | CAN | 62 | 3h2 | CG | Edinburgh | 26 Jul |
| 13.87 | 1.5 | Zhicheng | Yu | CHN | 63 | 1 | | Beijing | 7 Sep |
| 13.88 | 0.6 | Chris | Lancaster | USA | 65 | 2 | | Knoxville | 12 Apr |
| A13.88 | 0.8 | Mike | Cole | USA | 61 | 2 | | El Paso | 20 Apr |
| 13.88 | 0.6 | Dirk | Morris | USA | 65 | 5h2 | NCAA | Indianapolis | 5 Jun |
| 13.89 | 0.8 | Alex | Washington | USA | 62 | 4h4 | TAC | Eugene | 19 Jun |
| 13.90 | | Leander | McKenzie(100) | USA | 63 | 1 | | Indianapolis | 3 May |
| 13.90 | | Ion | Oltean | RUM | 58 | 1 | | Piteşti | 28 Jun |
| 13.90 | 1.4 | Guido | Kratschmer | FRG | 53 | 2 | NC | W Berlin | 12 Jul |
| 13.90 | 0.2 | Philippe | Aubert (103) | FRA | 57 | 4 | | Paris | 22 Jul |

| Mark | Wind | Name | | Nat | Yr | Date |
|---|---|---|---|---|---|---|
| 13.91 | | Reggie | Jones | USA | 65 | 12 Apr |
| 13.91 | 1.4 | David | Nelson | UK | 67 | 21 Jun |
| 13.91 | -0.1 | Juan | Saborit | CUB | 56 | 2 Jul |
| 13.92 | 1.1 | Sergey | Novikov | SU | 63 | 30 May |
| 13.92 | 1.5 | Pat | Duffy | USA | 65 | 5 Jun |
| 13.92 | 1.2 | Pavel | Šáda | CS | 64 | 6 Jul |
| 13.92 | 0.9 | Wilbert | Greaves (110) | UK | 56 | 12 Sep |
| 13.93 | 2.0 | Steve | Kerho | USA | 64 | 17 May |
| 13.93 | 0.0 | Paweł | Grzegorzewski | POL | 66 | 17 Aug |
| 13.93 | -0.9 | Gennadiy | Dashkevich | SU | 66 | 20 Sep |
| 13.93 | -0.7 | Gela | Veshapidze | SU | 66 | 20 Sep |
| 13.94 | 0.1 | James | Collins | USA | 65 | 5 Jun |
| 13.94 | 0.7 | Ulf | Söderman | SWE | 63 | 29 Aug |
| 13.95 | -0.1 | Courtney | Hawkins | USA | 67 | 29 Mar |
| 13.95 | | John | Register | USA | 65 | 3 May |
| 13.95 | 1.9 | Lamont | Frazier | USA | 66 | 24 May |
| 13.96 | | Elliott | White (120) | USA | 63 | 12 Apr |
| 13.96 | 0.7 | Ronnie | McCoy | USA | 63 | 26 Apr |
| 13.96 | -1.5 | Steve | Buckeridge | UK | 65 | 31 May |
| 13.97 | | Andre | Phillips | USA | 59 | 23 Mar |
| 13.97 | 1.8 | Willie | Goldsmith | USA | | 27 Apr |
| 13.97 | | Ed | Cooper | USA | 63 | 23 May |
| 13.97 | | Emilio | Valle | CUB | 67 | 14 Jun |
| 13.97 | 2.0 | Wayne | Roby | USA | 62 | 19 Jun |
| 13.98 | | Geoff | Calderone | USA | 64 | 17 May |
| 13.98 | 1.9 | Tomasz | Nagórka | POL | 67 | 25 May |
| 13.98 | 1.2 | Igor | Podmaryov | SU | 61 | 8 Jun |
| | | | (130) | | | |
| 13.98 | 1.8 | Jonas | Jakstis | SU | 59 | 8 Jun |
| 13.98 | -0.2 | Sven | Nylander | SWE | 62 | 9 Aug |
| 13.98 | 1.8 | Wojciech | Zawiła | POL | 61 | 30 Aug |
| 13.98 | -0.7 | Vladimir | Mozharovskiy | SU | 64 | 20 Sep |
| A13.98 | | Wessel | Bosman | RSA | 58 | 29 Nov |
| 13.99 | | David | Parker | USA | 65 | 19 Apr |
| 13.99 | | Chris | Havner | USA | | 19 Apr |
| 13.99 | 1.9 | Lyndon | Pereira Campos | BRA | 66 | 27 Sep |
| 14.00 | 0.4 | Angel | Martin | SPA | 64 | 18 May |
| 14.00 | 0.6 | Danny | Harris (140) | USA | 65 | 18 May |

| Mark | Wind | Name | | Nat | Yr | Date |
|---|---|---|---|---|---|---|
| 14.00 | -0.3 | Hugh | Teape | UK | 63 | 13 Jul |
| 14.00 | -0.7 | Peter | Eriksson | SWE | 64 | 1 Aug |
| A14.01 | | Jurie | van der Walt | RSA | 60 | 22 Mar |
| 14.01 | | Albert | Jones | USA | 62 | 12 Apr |
| 14.01 | 0.0 | Everett | White | USA | 63 | 17 May |
| 14.01 | | Maynard | Hurd | USA | | 24 May |
| 14.01 | 1.6 | Harold | Morton | USA | 64 | 25 May |
| 14.01 | -0.1 | Olivier | Saint-Gilles | FRA | 63 | 12 Jul |
| 14.01 | 0.4 | Jürgen | Betz | FRG | 65 | 23 Aug |
| 14.02 | | Mike | Lee (150) | USA | 65 | 29 Mar |
| 14.02 | 0.4 | Sergey | Polishchuk | SU | 62 | 17 May |
| 14.02 | 0.0 | Kenny | Hall | USA | | 17 May |
| 14.02 | -0.3 | Jörg | Naumann | GDR | 63 | 6 Jun |
| 14.02 | 1.9 | Andrzej | Siwek | POL | 58 | 21 Jun |
| 14.02 | 1.4 | Jürgen | Schoch | FRG | 62 | 12 Jul |
| 14.02 | 0.9 | Roland | Marloye | BEL | 62 | 29 Aug |
| 14.02 | -0.9 | Oleg | Degtyar | SU | 64 | 20 Sep |
| 14.03 | | Quanbin | Lu | CHN | 60 | 4 Jun |
| 14.03 | 1.0 | Harri | Ylinen | FIN | 64 | 5 Jun |
| 14.03 | -0.3 | Yuriy | Myshkin (160) | SU | 63 | 8 Jun |
| 14.03 | 0.0 | Gheorghe | Boroi | RUM | 64 | 6 Sep |
| 14.04 | 1.8 | Ricky | Alexander | USA | 60 | 27 Apr |
| 14.04 | 1.5 | George | Ifill | USA | | 16 May |
| 14.04 | -0.3 | Daley | Thompson | UK | 58 | 28 Aug |
| 14.04 | 0.0 | Mike | Benjamin | USA | 61 | 13 Sep |
| 14.05 | 1.8 | Lawrence | Felton | USA | 67 | 27 Apr |
| 14.05 | 0.4 | Antonio | Lanau | SPA | 66 | 18 May |
| 14.05 | 0.9 | Vernon | George | USA | 64 | 24 May |
| 14.05 | -0.7 | Vyacheslav | Vasilyev | SU | 64 | 20 Sep |
| 14.06 | | Jacinto | Alvarez (170) | CUB | 66 | 21 Feb |
| 14.06 | 0.0 | Mbanefo | Akpom | NIG | 66 | 23 May |
| 14.06 | 0.6 | Heiko | Buss | FRG | 63 | 19 Jun |
| 14.06 | -1.1 | Nikolay | Shilev | BUL | 63 | 21 Jun |
| 14.06 | 2.0 | Martin | Wiechert | FRG | 65 | 28 Jun |
| 14.06 | 1.1 | Balázs | Villányi | HUN | 61 | 11 Aug |
| 14.07 | 1.8 | James | McCraney | USA | 55 | 10 May |
| 14.07 | 1.8 | Dmitriy | Kaladze | SU | 61 | 8 Jun |

| Mark | Wind | Name | | Nat | Yr | Pos | Meet | Venue | | Date |
|------|------|------|------|-----|-----|-----|------|-------|------|------|
| 14.07 | 0.5 | Alain | Blondel | FRA | 62 | | | | | 8 Aug |
| 14.07 | 0.1 | Eric | Spence | CAN | 61 | | | | | 9 Aug |
| 14.07 | | Carlos Amorim dos Santos | | BRA | 61 | | | | | 11 Oct |
| | | | (180) | | | | | | | |
| 14.08 | | Raymond | Young | USA | 66 | | | | | 12 Apr |
| 14.08 | 0.0 | Dannie | Jackson | USA | 58 | | | | | 4 May |
| 14.08 | | Randy | Cox | USA | 64 | | | | | 11 May |
| 14.08 | | Ike | Mbadugha | NIG | 68 | | | | | 16 May |
| 14.08 | 0.8 | Thomas | Weimann | AUT | 67 | | | | | 15 Jun |
| 14.08 | 1.7 | Michael | Neugebauer | FRG | 62 | | | | | 12 Jul |
| 14.08 | 1.1 | Arturas | Malionis | SU | 63 | | | | | 16 Jul |
| 14.08 | 0.9 | Thierry | Richard | FRA | 61 | | | | | 9 Aug |
| 14.08 | 0.1 | Michel | Brodeur | CAN | 61 | | | | | 9 Aug |
| 14.08 | -0.1 | Fabien | Niederhäuser | SWZ | 61 | | | | | 10 Aug |
| | | | (190) | | | | | | | |
| 14.08 | 1.7 | Serge | Liegeois | BEL | 64 | | | | | 15 Aug |
| 14.09 | | Manuel | Mayor | CUB | 67 | | | | | 21 Feb |
| 14.09 | | Pat | McGhee | USA | 66 | | | | | 22 Mar |
| 14.09 | 0.8 | Ron | Lee | USA | 62 | | | | | 22 May |
| 14.09 | 0.8 | Jörg | Reichel | FRG | 66 | | | | | 20 Jun |
| 14.09 | 0.2 | Sergey | Tsyvashov | SU | 62 | | | | | 6 Sep |
| 14.09 | | Jailton | Bonfim | (197) | BRA | 65 | | | | | 11 Oct |

Blake (13.57) also did 13.57 0.0 1 Tallahassee
26 Apr; Bodó (13.84 1.2) also did 13.84 0.4 2 NC
Budapest 15 Aug; Neugebauer (14.08 1.7) also did
14.08 1.4 12 Jul.

Best low altitude marks:

| 13.76 | | Schroeder | 1 Port Elizabeth | 21 Apr |
|-------|--|-----------|------------------|--------|
| 14.08 | | Schoeman | | 21 Apr |

----------------------------------------------------------------------------

| | 1 | 10 | 20 | 30 | 50 | 100 | Under 13.80 | Under 14.00 |
|------|------|------|------|------|------|------|------|------|
| 1982 | 13.22 | 13.46 | 13.65 | 13.72 | 13.82 | 14.01 | 45 | 94 |
| 1983 | 13.11 | 13.50 | 13.60 | 13.68 | 13.79 | 13.96 | 50 | 106 |
| 1984 | 13.15 | 13.45 | 13.55 | 13.64 | 13.74 | 13.91 | 59 | 138 |
| 1985 | 13.14 | 13.46 | 13.59 | 13.65 | 13.75 | 13.94 | 57 | 115 |
| 1986 | 13.20 | 13.40 | 13.51 | 13.57 | 13.72 | 13.90 | 65 | 138 |

----------------------------------------------------------------------------

Marks made with assisting wind > 2 m/s:

| Mark | Wind | Name | | | Nat | Yr | Pos | Meet | Venue | Date |
|------|------|------|------|------|-----|-----|-----|------|-------|------|
| 13.14 | | Igor | Kazanov | | SU | 63 | 1r1 | Znam | Leningrad | 8 Jun |
| 13.25 | | Aleksandr | Markin | | SU | 62 | 2r1 | Znam | Leningrad | 8 Jun |
| 13.29 | 3.1 | Tonie | Campbell | | USA | 60 | 1s2 | TAC | Eugene | 19 Jun |
| 13.30 | 3.1 | | Foster | | | | 2s2 | TAC | Eugene | 19 Jun |
| 13.31 | 4.5 | Mark | McKoy | | CAN | 61 | 1 | CG | Edinburgh | 27 Jul |
| 13.33 | 2.7 | | Talley | | | | 1 | | Knoxville | 18 May |
| 13.33 | | Gennadiy | Chugunov | | SU | 63 | 3r1 | Znam | Leningrad | 8 Jun |
| 13.36 | | Vladimir | Shishkin | | SU | 64 | 4r1 | Znam | Leningrad | 8 Jun |
| 13.39 | 4.4 | Roger | Kingdom | | USA | 62 | 1 | Jenner | San Jose | 31 May |
| 13.39 | 3.1 | Arthur | Blake | (10) | USA | 66 | 3s2 | TAC | Eugene | 19 Jun |
| 13.40 | 3.4 | Liviu | Giurgian | | RUM | 62 | 1 | | Beograd | 27 Jun |
| 13.42 | 4.5 | Colin | Jackson | | UK | 67 | 2 | CG | Edinburgh | 27 Jul |
| 13.42 | 2.3 | | Stewart | (13) | | | 1 | | La Coruña | 6 Aug |
| 13.46 | | Anatoliy | Titov | | SU | 56 | 5r1 | Znam | Leningrad | 8 Jun |
| 13.52 | | Aleš | Höffer | | CS | 62 | 6r1 | Znam | Leningrad | 8 Jun |
| 13.53 | 3.0 | Sam | Turner | | USA | 57 | 1r2 | MSR | Walnut, CA | 27 Apr |
| 13.53 | 2.4 | Jack | Pierce | | USA | 62 | 1 | | Columbus | 4 May |
| 13.53 | 2.6 | James | Purvis | | USA | 66 | 1 | | Atlanta | 10 May |
| 13.53 | 2.3 | Reyna | Thompson | | USA | 63 | 1 | | Houston | 18 May |
| 13.53 | | Igor | Khitryakov | | SU | 65 | 7r1 | Znam | Leningrad | 8 Jun |
| | | | (20) | | | | | | | |

| Mark | Wind | Name | | Nat | Yr | Pos | Meet | Venue | Date |
|------|------|------|---|-----|----|----|------|-------|------|
| 13.57 | 4.4 | Malcolm | Dixon | USA | 59 | 3 | Jenner | San Jose | 31 May |
| 13.58 | | Anton | Isayev | SU | 62 | 8r1 | Znam | Leningrad | 8 Jun |
| 13.59 | | Harold | Morton | USA | 64 | 1 | | N Little Rock | 12 Apr |
| 13.60 | | Kevin | McKinley | USA | 64 | 1 | | Prairie View,TX | 29 Mar |
| A13.60 | 2.2 | Ralf | Schroeder | RSA | 62 | 1 | | Johannesburg | 18 Apr |
| 13.64 | 3.1 | Alex | Washington | USA | 62 | 6s2 | TAC | Eugene | 19 Jun |
| A13.66 | 2.2 | Kobus | Schoeman | RSA | 65 | 2 | | Johannesburg | 18 Apr |
| 13.67 | 2.5 | Romuald | Giegiel | POL | 57 | 3 | v Fra, | Ita,Spa Monaco | 6 Jul |
| 13.68 | | John | Register | USA | 65 | 2 | | N Little Rock | 12 Apr |
| 13.69 | 7.9 | Jörg | Naumann (30) | GDR | 63 | 4 | PTS | Bratislava | 13 Jun |
| 13.70 | 2.7 | Wilbert | Greaves | UK | 56 | 1h3 | AAA | London | 20 Jun |
| 13.73 | 2.3 | Sven | Nylander | SWE | 62 | 2 | | Houston | 18 May |
| 13.73 | 3.1 | Krzysztof | Płatek | POL | 62 | 1 | | Heidelberg | 24 May |
| 13.76 | 2.2 | Earl | Diamond | USA | 66 | 1s1 | | Odessa, TX | 16 May |
| A13.77 | 2.8 | Wessel | Bosman | RSA | 58 | 2 | | Secunda | 15 Nov |
| 13.79 | | Craig | Bradford | USA | 64 | 2 | | Arlington | 26 Apr |
| 13.79 | 4.4 | John | Johnson | USA | 60 | 4 | Jenner | San Jose | 31 May |
| 13.81 | 7.9 | Juan | Saborit | CUB | 56 | 6 | PTS | Bratislava | 13 Jun |
| 13.82 | 3.0 | Bill | Brown | USA | 65 | 1 | | Boise | 19 Apr |
| 13.82 | 3.0 | Carl | Campbell (40) | USA | 63 | 5r2 | MSR | Walnut, CA | 27 Apr |
| 13.82 | | David | Nelson | UK | 67 | 2 | | Wigan | 5 Jul |
| 13.83 | 5.2 | James | Quinn | USA | 63 | 4 | FlaR | Gainesville | 29 Mar |
| 13.83 | 3.8 | James | Collins | USA | 65 | 1 | | San Angelo | 26 Apr |
| 13.85 | 3.5 | Pat | Duffy | USA | 65 | 2 | | Walnut, CA | 1 Jun |
| 13.86 | 2.6 | Dirk | Morris | USA | 65 | 2 | | Atlanta | 10 May |
| 13.87 | 2.3 | Leander | McKenzie | USA | 63 | 2 | | Tallahassee | 22 Mar |
| 13.87 | 2.7 | Vernon | George | USA | 64 | 2 | | Houston | 4 May |
| 13.88 | 3.2 | Ron | Lee (48) | USA | 62 | 1 | | Los Angeles | 24 May |

| Mark | Wind | Name | | | Nat | Yr | Date | | Mark | Wind | Name | | | Nat | Yr | Date |
|------|------|------|---|---|-----|----|------|---|------|------|------|---|---|-----|----|------|
| 13.91 | 3.0 | Everett | White | | USA | 63 | 10 May | | 13.95 | 2.3 | Charles | Powell | | USA | 64 | 18 May |
| 13.91 | 2.3 | Lawrence | Felton | (50) | USA | 67 | 18 May | | 13.97 | 3.0 | Angel | Martin | (60) | SPA | 64 | 12 Jul |
| 13.91 | | Henry | Andrade | | USA | 62 | 30 May | | 13.98 | 5.2 | Mike | Lee | | USA | 65 | 29 Mar |
| 13.91 | 7.9 | Pavel | Šáda | | CS | 64 | 13 Jun | | 13.98 | 3.8 | Bobby | Bankston | | USA | 63 | 26 Apr |
| 13.92 | 3.0 | Albert | Jones | | USA | 62 | 26 Apr | | 13.98 | 3.9 | Heiko | Buss | | FRG | 63 | 29 Jun |
| 13.92 | 2.2 | Elliott | White | | USA | 63 | 18 May | | 14.00 | | Don | Allen | | USA | | 29 Mar |
| 13.93 | 3.0 | James | McCraney | | USA | 55 | 26 Apr | | 14.01 | 2.3 | Hiroshi | Kakimori | | JAP | 68 | 12 Jul |
| 13.94 | 2.5 | Gheorghe | Boroi | | RUM | 64 | 9 Aug | | 14.02 | 3.5 | Raymond | Young | | USA | 66 | 1 Jun |
| 13.95 | 2.9 | Olivier | Vallaeys | | FRA | 66 | 15 May | | 14.02 | 3.0 | Antonio | Lanau | | SPA | 66 | 12 Jul |
| 13.95 | 2.7 | Belfred | Clark | | USA | 65 | 18 May | | 14.06 | | Anthony | Jarrett | (68) | UK | 68 | 5 Jul |

Doubtful wind readings:

| Mark | Wind | Name | | Nat | Yr | Pos | Meet | Venue | Date |
|------|------|------|---|-----|----|----|------|-------|------|
| 13.48 | -0.9 | Igor | Podmaryov | SU | 61 | 1r2 | Znam | Leningrad | 8 Jun |
| 13.55 | -0.9 | Jonas | Jakstis | SU | 59 | 2r2 | Znam | Leningrad | 8 Jun |
| 13.63 | -0.9 | Sergey | Novikov | SU | 63 | 3r2 | Znam | Leningrad | 8 Jun |
| 13.67 | -0.9 | Yuriy | Myshkin | SU | 63 | 5r2 | Znam | Leningrad | 8 Jun |
| 13.77 | -0.9 | Dmitriy | Kaladze | SU | 61 | 6r2 | Znam | Leningrad | 8 Jun |

Hand timing:

| Mark | Name | | Nat | Yr | Pos | Venue | Date |
|------|------|---|-----|----|----|-------|------|
| 13.0 | Stéphane | Caristan | FRA | 64 | 1 | Creteil | 3 May |
| 13.0 | Tonie | Campbell | USA | 60 | 1 | Los Angeles | 16 Jul |

MEN 1986

| Mark | Wind | Name | | Nat | Yr | Pos | Meet | Venue | Date |
|------|------|------|---|-----|----|----|------|-------|------|
| 13.4 | -0.2 | Jack | Pierce | USA | 62 | 2 | | Tempe | 5 Apr |
| 13.4 | 0.2 | Igor | Kazanov | SU | 63 | 1h | | Minsk | 30 May |
| 13.4 | 1.5 | Igor | Perevedentsev | SU | 64 | 1 | | Kazan | 29 Jun |
| 13.4 | | Gennadiy | Chugunov | SU | 63 | 1 | | Lvov | 9 Aug |
| 13.5 | -0.2 | Andrew | Parker | JAM | 65 | 3 | | Tempe | 5 Apr |
| 13.5 | -0.2 | Al | Lane | USA | 62 | 4 | | Tempe | 5 Apr |
| 13.5 | | Alex | Washington | USA | 62 | 1 | | Toledo, OH | 24 May |
| 13.5 | | Anton | Isayev | SU | 62 | 1 | | Leningrad | 15 Jun |
| 13.5 | | Jonas | Jakstis | SU | 59 | 2 | | Lvov | 9 Aug |
| 13.5 | 1.1 | Igor | Khitryakov | SU | 65 | 1 | | Alma-Ata | 29 Aug |
| 13.5 | 0.2 | Viktor | Batrachenko | SU | 63 | 1 | | Kiev | 31 Aug |
| 13.6 | 0.0 | Frank | Barnett | USA | 66 | 1 | | Tucson | 15 Feb |
| A13.6 | | Kobus | Schoeman | RSA | 65 | 1 | | Pretoria | 14 Mar |
| 13.6 | | John | Lenstrohm | USA | 61 | 1 | | Long Beach | 16 May |
| 13.6 | | Aleksey | Matveyev | SU | 63 | 1 | | Novotroitsk | 28 Jun |
| 13.6 | | Oleg | Zhdanov | SU | 62 | 2 | | Novotroitsk | 28 Jun |
| 13.6 | | Vyacheslav | Ustinov | SU | 57 | 1 | | Lipetsk | 18 Jul |
| 13.6 | | Sergey | Strelchenko | SU | 61 | 3 | | Lvov | 9 Aug |
| | | | (20) | | | | | | |
| 13.6 | 0.2 | Oleg | Degtyar (21) | SU | 64 | 2 | | Kiev | 31 Aug |

| Mark | Wind | Name | | Nat | Yr | Date | Mark | Wind | Name | | Nat | Yr | Date |
|------|------|------|---|-----|----|------|------|------|------|---|-----|----|------|
| 13.7 | 0.0 | John | Johnson | USA | 60 | 3 May | 13.8 | -0.2 | Ronnie | McCoy | USA | 63 | 5 Apr |
| 13.7 | 1.1 | Dmitriy | Kaladze | SU | 61 | 30 May | 13.8 | 1.8 | Daniel | Darien | FRA | 61 | 27 Apr |
| 13.7 | 0.2 | Vladimir | Mozharovskiy | SU | 64 | 15 Jun | 13.8 | 0.2 | Aleksey | Korolyov | SU | 66 | 25 Jun |
| 13.7 | | German | Ivanov | SU | 62 | 28 Jun | 13.8 | | Vladimir | Zaika | SU | 57 | |
| 13.7 | | Philippe | Aubert | FRA | 57 | 28 Jun | 13.8 | 0.2 | Andrey | Koroteyev | SU | 66 | 31 Aug |
| 13.7 | 0.2 | Sergey | Krasovskiy | SU | 63 | 31 Aug | 13.8 | 0.2 | Mikhail | Ryabukhin | SU | 67 | 31 Aug |
| 13.8 | | Frank | Mene | NIG | 68 | 22 Feb | 13.8 | | Arturas | Malionis (39) | SU | 63 | 7 Sep |
| A13.8 | | Wessel | Bosman | RSA | 58 | 14 Mar | | | | | | | |
| 13.8 | -0.7 | Kevin | McKinley (30) | USA | 64 | 22 Mar | | Indoor mark: | | | | | |
| 13.8 | -0.7 | Vernon | George | USA | 64 | 22 Mar | 13.7 i | | Zhicheng | Yu | CHN | 63 | 15 Mar |
| 13.8 | -0.7 | Albert | Jones | USA | 62 | 22 Mar | | | | | | | |

Marks made with assisting wind > 2 m/s:

| Mark | Wind | Name | | Nat | Yr | Pos | Meet | Venue | Date |
|------|------|------|---|-----|----|----|------|-------|------|
| 13.3 | | Reyna | Thompson | USA | 63 | 1 | | Arlington | 10 May |
| 13.4 | | Sansiski | Daniels | USA | 64 | 2 | | Arlington | 10 May |
| 13.4 | | Carl | Campbell | USA | 63 | 3 | | Arlington | 10 May |
| 13.4 | 4.3 | Aleksey | Korolyov | SU | 66 | 1h | | Leningrad | 25 Jun |
| 13.5 | | Al | Joyner | USA | 60 | 1h4 | KansR | Lawrence | 18 Apr |
| 13.5 | | Henry | Andrade | USA | 62 | 4 | | Arlington | 10 May |
| 13.5 | | Mike | Cole | USA | 61 | 5 | | Arlington | 10 May |
| 13.5 | 11.2 | Earl | Diamond | USA | 66 | 1h3 | | Odessa, TX | 15 May |
| 13.6 | | Albert | Jones (9) | USA | 62 | 1 | | Wichita | 3 May |

| Mark | | Name | | Nat | Yr | Date | Mark | Wind | Name | | Nat | Yr | Date |
|------|---|------|---|-----|----|------|------|------|------|---|-----|----|------|
| 13.7 | | Damon | Polk | USA | 65 | 18 Apr | 13.8 | 2.9 | John | Caliguri | AUS | 62 | 7 Jan |
| 13.7 | | Solomon | Branch | USA | 66 | 9 May | 13.8 | | Mauro | Re (14) | ITA | 67 | 27 Apr |
| 13.7 | | Mikhail | Ryabukhin | SU | 67 | 4 Oct | | | | | | | |

| Mark | Name | | Nat | Yr | Pos | Meet | Venue | Date |
|------|------|--|-----|-----|-----|------|-------|------|

# 400 METRES HURDLES

| Mark | Name | | Nat | Yr | Pos | Meet | Venue | Date |
|------|------|--|-----|-----|-----|------|-------|------|
| 47.38 | Edwin | Moses | USA | 55 | 1 | | Lausanne | 2 Sep |
| 47.51 | Andre | Phillips | USA | 59 | 1 | VD | Bruxelles | 5 Sep |
| 47.53 | | Moses | | | 1r1 | ISTAF | W Berlin | 15 Aug |
| 47.66 | | Moses | | | 1 | | Paris | 22 Jul |
| 47.69 | | Phillips | | | 1r1 | WK | Zürich | 13 Aug |
| 47.76 | | Moses | | | 1r1 | BGP | Budapest | 11 Aug |
| 47.82 | Danny | Harris | USA | 65 | 1 | Bisl | Oslo | 5 Jul |
| 47.84 | | Phillips | | | 1r1 | ASV | Köln | 17 Aug |
| 47.89 | Harald | Schmid | FRG | 57 | 2r1 | WK | Zürich | 13 Aug |
| 47.94 | | Moses | | | 1r1 | GWG | Moskva | 9 Jul |
| 47.95 | | Phillips | | | 1 | Jenner | San Jose | 31 May |
| 48.04 | | Harris | | | 1 | PTG | London | 11 Jul |
| 48.07 | Amadou | Dia Ba | SEN | 58 | 2r1 | ISTAF | W Berlin | 15 Aug |
| 48.08 | | Phillips | | | 1 | | Bern | 20 Aug |
| 48.11 | | Dia Ba | | | 2 | | Paris | 22 Jul |
| 48.14 | | Phillips | | | 1 | GP | Roma | 10 Sep |
| 48.15 | | Phillips | | | 2 | Bisl | Oslo | 5 Jul |
| 48.21 | | Moses | | | 1 | | Birmingham | 19 Jul |
| 48.21 | | Moses | | | 1 | IAC | London | 8 Aug |
| 48.23 | | Harris | | | 1 | Nik | Nice | 15 Jul |
| 48.24 | Aleksandr | Vasilyev | SU | 61 | 2r1 | GWG | Moskva | 9 Jul |
| 48.28 | | Harris | | | 1 | DrakeR | Des Moines | 25 Apr |
| 48.28 | | Moses | | | 1 | | Malmö | 19 Aug |
| 48.33 | | Harris | | | 1 | NCAA | Indianapolis | 6 Jun |
| 48.40 | | Schmid | | | 2 | Nik | Nice | 15 Jul |
| 48.42 | | Harris | | | 2 | VD | Bruxelles | 5 Sep |
| 48.47 | | Dia Ba | | | 2 | GP | Roma | 10 Sep |
| 48.48 | Toma | Tomov | BUL | 58 | 2r1 | BGP | Budapest | 11 Aug |
| 48.55 | | Vasilyev | | | 1 | NC | Kiev | 16 Jul |
| 48.57 | | Harris | | | 1 | | Tempe | 5 Apr |
| 48.57 | | Dia Ba | | | 3 | VD | Bruxelles | 5 Sep |
| 48.59 | David | Patrick | USA | 60 | 3r1 | GWG | Moskva | 9 Jul |
| 48.59 | | Schmid (33/8) | | | 1 | NC | W Berlin | 13 Jul |
| A48.64 | Tranel | Hawkins | USA | 62 | 1 | | El Paso | 20 Apr |
| 48.71 | Vladimir | Budko (10) | SU | 65 | 1 | Spart | Tashkent | 18 Sep |
| A48.72 | Dale | Laverty | USA | 65 | 2 | | El Paso | 20 Apr |
| 48.77 | Kevin | Young | USA | 66 | 2 | NCAA | Indianapolis | 6 Jun |
| A48.81 | Hannes | Pienaar | RSA | 60 | 1 | | Pretoria | 15 Feb |
| 48.83 | Sven | Nylander | SWE | 62 | 2s2 | EC | Stuttgart | 27 Aug |
| 48.88 | Athanassios | Kalogiannis | GRE | 65 | 1r2 | GWG | Moskva | 9 Jul |
| 48.94 | René | Djedjemel | IVC | 58 | 4r1 | WK | Zürich | 13 Aug |
| 48.97 | Reggie | Davis | USA | 64 | 2 | | Columbus | 4 May |
| 48.98 | Nikolay | Ilchenko | SU | 63 | 2 | Spart | Tashkent | 18 Sep |
| 49.07 | Tagir | Zemskov | SU | 62 | 2r1 | Znam | Leningrad | 8 Jun |
| 49.13 | Henry | Amike (20) | NIG | 61 | 3 | | Lausanne | 2 Sep |
| 49.21 | Nat | Page | USA | 57 | 4r1 | BGP | Budapest | 11 Aug |
| 49.29 | Belfred | Clark | USA | 65 | 1 | | Knoxville | 18 May |
| 49.31 | Ahmed | Hamada | BHN | 61 | 1 | AsiG | Seoul | 30 Sep |
| 49.38 | Oleg | Azarov | SU | 62 | 2r2 | GWG | Moskva | 9 Jul |
| 49.40 | Ryoichi | Yoshida | JAP | 65 | 2 | AsiG | Seoul | 30 Sep |
| 49.41 | Kevin | Henderson | USA | 65 | 2r1 | PennR | Philadelphia | 25 Apr |

| Mark | Name | | Nat | Yr | Pos | Meet | Venue | Date | |
|------|------|--|-----|-----|-----|------|-------|------|--|
| 49.45 | José | Alonso | SPA | 57 | 2s1 | EC | Stuttgart | 27 | Aug |
| 49.46 | Bernie | Holloway | USA | 61 | 1 | | Burnaby | 10 | Jun |
| 49.50 | Charles | Powell | USA | 64 | 1r2 | DrakeR | Des Moines | 25 | Apr |
| 49.52 | Valeriy | Vikhrov (30) | SU | 61 | 3r1 | Znam | Leningrad | 8 | Jun |
| 49.52 | Peter | Scholz | FRG | 59 | 2r2 | ISTAF | W Berlin | 15 | Aug |
| 49.53 | Max | Robertson | UK | 63 | 1 | AAA | London | 21 | Jun |
| 49.55 | Rik | Tommelein | BEL | 62 | 1 | NC | Bruxelles | 10 | Aug |
| 49.60 | Phil | Beattie | UK | 63 | 1 | CG | Edinburgh | 28 | Jul |
| 49.61 | Charles | Moss | USA | 63 | 2 | | Knoxville | 24 | May |
| 49.62 | István | Simon-Balla | HUN | 58 | 1 | NC | Budapest | 16 | Aug |
| 49.64 | Francisco | Velazco | CUB | 61 | 1 | | Santiago/Cuba | 22 | Feb |
| 49.65 | Bernard | Williams | USA | 65 | 3r1 | PennR | Philadelphia | 25 | Apr |
| 49.65 | Pat | McGhee | USA | 66 | 2h2 | TAC | Eugene | 19 | Jun |
| 49.66 | Leander | McKenzie (40) | USA | 63 | 1 | | Tallahassee | 17 | May |
| 49.68 | Ed | Cooper | USA | 63 | 2 | MSR | Walnut, CA | 27 | Apr |
| 49.68 | Aleksandr | Kharlov | SU | 58 | 1 | | Kiev | 27 | Jul |
| 49.68 | Edgar | Itt | FRG | 67 | 1 | NC-j | Wetzlar | 7 | Sep |
| 49.69 | Michel | Zimmerman | BEL | 60 | 2 | NC | Bruxelles | 10 | Aug |
| 49.71 | Thomas | Futterknecht | AUT | 62 | 1 | | Dingolfing | 26 | Jul |
| 49.72 | Tony | Rambo | USA | 60 | 1 | FlaR | Gainesville | 29 | Mar |
| 49.78 | Nikolay | Taletskiy | SU | 62 | 1r2 | Znam | Leningrad | 8 | Jun |
| 49.79 | Uwe | Schmitt | FRG | 61 | 2 | | Koblenz | 6 | Aug |
| 49.80 | Matthias | Kaulin | FRG | 63 | 3r2 | ISTAF | W Berlin | 15 | Aug |
| 49.81 | John | Graham (50) | CAN | 65 | 4 | | Birmingham | 19 | Aug |
| 49.82 | Philippe | Gonigam | FRA | 63 | 1 | NC | Aix-les-Bains | 10 | Aug |
| 49.85 | Bozhidar | Konstantinov | BUL | 63 | 2 | Nar | Sofia | 31 | May |
| 49.86 | Jon | Thomas | USA | 63 | 1h1 | | Knoxville | 23 | May |
| 49.90 | Craig | Calk | USA | 65 | 6 | NCAA | Indianapolis | 6 | Jun |
| 49.90 | Jozef | Kucej | CS | 65 | 1 | | Nicosia | 13 | Sep |
| 49.90 | Sergey | Dobrovolskiy | SU | 66 | 3 | Spart | Tashkent | 18 | Sep |
| 49.92 | Georgios | Vamvakas | GRE | 60 | 2 | NC | Athinai | 8 | Aug |
| 49.93 | Tony | Valentine | USA | 64 | 1 | IC4A | Villanova | 25 | May |
| 49.93 | Ryszard | Stoch | POL | 62 | 1 | NC | Grudziadz | 28 | Jun |
| 49.95 | Ryszard | Szparak (60) | POL | 51 | 2 | | La Coruña | 6 | Aug |
| 49.98 | Jörg | Reichel | FRG | 66 | 1r2 | | München | 17 | Jun |
| 49.98 | Attila | Spiriev | HUN | 64 | 2 | NC | Budapest | 16 | Aug |
| 49.99 | Gordon | Bugg | USA | 66 | 5 | MSR | Walnut, CA | 27 | Apr |
| 50.02 | Emilio | Valle | CUB | 67 | 1 | WC-j | Athinai | 18 | Jul |
| 50.03 | Winthrop | Graham | JAM | | 1 | CAC | Santiago/Dom | 30 | Jun |
| 50.05 | Hiroshi | Kakimori | JAP | 68 | 1s1 | WC-j | Athinai | 17 | Jul |
| 50.09 | Kevin | McKinley | USA | 64 | 2 | DrakeR | Des Moines | 25 | Apr |
| 50.10 | Igor | Yatsyk | SU | 62 | s | Spart | Tashkent | 17 | Sep |
| 50.11 | Julio | Prado | CUB | 60 | 2 | | Santiago/Cuba | 22 | Feb |
| 50.14 | Vladimir | Titov (70) | SU | 59 | 1 | | Krasnodar | 22 | Jun |
| 50.14 | David | Charlton | BAH | 62 | 2 | CAC | Santiago/Dom | 30 | Jun |
| 50.15 | Alain | Cuypers | BEL | 67 | 3 | NC | Bruxelles | 10 | Aug |
| 50.16 | Leszek | Rzepakowski | POL | 57 | 2 | NC | Grudziadz | 28 | Jun |
| 50.16 | Lloyd | Guss | CAN | 59 | 6r2 | WK | Zürich | 13 | Aug |
| 50.17 | Pablo | Squella | CHL | 63 | 2 | IbAm | Habana | 28 | Sep |
| 50.19 | Shigenori | Ohmori | JAP | 60 | 2 | | Tokyo | 11 | May |
| 50.20 | Gary | Oakes | UK | 58 | 2 | | London | 7 | Jun |
| 50.21 | Franck | Jonot | FRA | 61 | 2 | NC | Aix-les-Bains | 10 | Aug |

| Mark | Name | | | Nat | Yr | Pos | Meet | Venue | Date |
|------|------|--|--|-----|----|-----|------|-------|------|
| 50.21 | Yassem | Al Douwaila | | KUW | 63 | 4 | CISM | Ostia | 11 Sep |
| 50.25 | Sansiski | Daniels | (80) | USA | 64 | 4h1 | NCAA | Indianapolis | 4 Jun |
| A50.26 | Kobus | Burger | | RSA | 62 | 2 | NC | Germiston | 12 Apr |
| 50.27 | Sergey | Kutsebo | | SU | 61 | h | NC | Kiev | 15 Jul |
| 50.27 | Joseph | Maritim | | KEN | 68 | 1s2 | WC-j | Athinai | 17 Jul |
| A50.28 | Dries | Vorster | | RSA | 62 | 3 | NC | Germiston | 12 Apr |
| 50.28 | Luca | Cosi | | ITA | 63 | 5s1 | EC | Stuttgart | 27 Aug |
| 50.29 | Valeriy | Dauksha | | SU | 66 | s | Spart | Tashkent | 17 Sep |
| 50.30 | Daniel | Ogidi | | NIG | 63 | 5h3 | NCAA | Indianapolis | 4 Jun |
| A50.31 | Hawie | Engels | | RSA | 62 | 2 | | Johannesburg | 18 Apr |
| A50.33 | Pierre | Leveille | | CAN | 62 | 2 | | Provo | 26 May |
| 50.33 | Patrick | Mann | (90) | USA | 66 | 4h4 | TAC | Eugene | 19 Jun |
| 50.33 | Mark | Holtom | | UK | 58 | 3 | AAA | London | 21 Jun |
| 50.34 | Emmanuel | Gonigam | | FRA | 63 | 5 | v Ita, | Pol,Spa Monaco | 5 Jul |
| 50.35 | Dave | Chesarek | | USA | 64 | 2 | | Los Angeles | 24 May |
| 50.36 | Thomas | Nyberg | | SWE | 62 | 3 | DNG | Stockholm | 1 Jul |
| A50.37 | Steve | Patterson | | USA | 63 | 2 | | Boulder | 18 May |
| 50.39 | Pascal | Maran | | FRA | 67 | 3 | WC-j | Athinai | 18 Jul |
| 50.39 | István | Takács | | HUN | 59 | 3 | NC | Budapest | 16 Aug |
| 50.40 | Ron | Stewart | | USA | 63 | 2r2 | PennR | Philadelphia | 25 Apr |
| 50.40 | Michael | Graham | | USA | 67 | 1 | TAC-j | Towson, MD | 29 Jun |
| 50.41 | Kevin | Mason | (100) | USA | 67 | 2 | TAC-j | Towson, MD | 29 Jun |
| 50.45 | Gilles | Vimbert | | FRA | 66 | 3 | NC | Aix-les-Bains | 10 Aug |
| 50.46 | Tommy | Robbins | | USA | | 1 | | Raleigh | 17 May |
| 50.46 | Rod | Guillory | | USA | 64 | 1 | | Houston | 24 May |
| 50.46 | Ingo | Krüger | | GDR | 66 | 1 | NC | Jena | 28 Jun |
| 50.47 | Ken | Gordon | | AUS | 62 | 1 | v Bel, | Eng Woluwe | 13 Jul |
| 50.47 | Ahmed | Abdel Halim | | EGY | 59 | 2 | | Nicosia | 13 Sep |
| 50.48 | Jesus | Aguilasocho | | MEX | 60 | 3 | CAC | Santiago/Dom | 30 Jun |
| 50.49 | Richard | Curtis | (108) | USA | 65 | 3 | | Los Angeles | 24 May |

| Mark | Name | | | Nat | Yr | Date |
|------|------|--|--|-----|----|------|
| 50.50 | Vladimir | Smerichinskiy | | SU | 62 | 15 Jul |
| A50.51 | Steve | Jackson | (110) | USA | 65 | 24 May |
| 50.51 | Bart | Williams | | USA | 56 | 14 Jun |
| 50.51 | Carlos | Amorim dos Santos | | BRA | 61 | 13 Jul |
| 50.51 | Giorgio | Rucli | | ITA | 63 | 10 Aug |
| 50.52 | Bruce | Tiller | | USA | | 25 Apr |
| 50.52 | Marek | Helinurm | | SU | 63 | 24 May |
| 50.52 | James | Ferreira | | USA | 65 | 4 Jun |
| 50.52 | Stanislav | Náveshák | | CS | 65 | 14 Jun |
| 50.52 | Uwe | Ackermann | | GDR | 60 | 28 Jun |
| 50.53 | Richard | Bucknor | | JAM | | 21 Mar |
| 50.53 | Sergey | Mironov | (120) | SU | 63 | 24 May |
| 50.53 | Hans-Jürgen | Ende | | GDR | 62 | 28 Jun |
| 50.55 | Markus | König | | FRG | 62 | 29 Jun |
| 50.57 | Nikolay | Boiko | | SU | 68 | 17 Jul |
| 50.58 | Izel | Jenkins | | USA | 64 | 17 May |
| 50.58 | Carsten | Köhrbrück | | FRG | 67 | 18 Jul |
| 50.59 | Dirk | Morris | | USA | 65 | 10 May |
| 50.60 | Daniel | Hejret | | CS | 62 | 13 Jul |
| 50.63 | Klaus | Ehrle | | AUT | 66 | 4 Jun |
| 50.63 | Martin | Booker | | USA | 63 | 4 Jun |
| 50.65 | Francisco | Moret | (130) | CUB | 64 | 22 Feb |
| 50.69 | Ulf | Sedlacek | | SWE | 65 | 18 Aug |
| 50.69 | Krasimir | Demirev | | BUL | 62 | 7 Sep |
| 50.70 | Wayne | Paul | | NZ | 57 | 26 Mar |
| 50.70 | Andri | Hargrove | | USA | 58 | 18 May |
| 50.72 | Dolph | Francis | | AUS | 67 | 17 Jul |
| 50.73 | Lájos | Csapó | | HUN | 62 | 29 Jun |
| 50.73 | Christian | Walter | | FRG | 64 | 3 Aug |
| 50.74 | Artur | Pisarev | | SU | 64 | 18 Sep |
| 50.74 | German | Petrov | | SU | 67 | 18 Sep |
| 50.76 | Sylvester | Davis | (140) | USA | 62 | 17 May |
| 50.76 | Charles | DeRousselle | | USA | | 24 May |
| 50.77 | Philippe | Garnier | | FRA | 63 | 14 Jun |
| 50.77 | Vyacheslav | Myts | | SU | 61 | 15 Jul |
| 50.78 | René | Barrientos | | CUB | 66 | 22 Feb |
| 50.80 | Hideo | Numazawa | | JAP | 63 | 30 May |
| 50.80 | Oleg | Zhdanov | | SU | 62 | 7 Sep |
| 50.81 | Yongzhi | Yao | | CHN | 62 | 3 Jun |
| 50.81 | Aleksey | Bazarov | | SU | 63 | 18 Sep |
| 50.83 | Jan | Majewicz | | POL | 64 | 28 Jun |
| 50.84 | Yuriy | Matyushev | (150) | SU | 65 | 24 May |
| 50.84 | Aleš | Maňásek | | CS | 65 | 28 Jun |
| 50.85 | Garry | Brown | | AUS | 54 | 20 Mar |

MEN 1986

| Mark | Name | | Nat | Yr | Pos | Meet | Venue | | Date |
|------|------|--|-----|----|----|------|-------|--|------|
| A50.85 | Antonio | Smith | VEN | 67 | 27 Jun | | | | |
| 50.85 | Angelo | Locci | ITA | 62 | 30 Jul | | | | |
| 50.86 | Bryan | Leturgez | USA | 62 | 25 Apr | | | | |
| 50.86 | Payton | Hines | USA | 59 | 4 May | | | | |
| 50.87 | Marvin | Parnell | USA | | 4 May | | | | |
| 50.87 | Jesus | Ariño | SPA | 63 | 3 Aug | | | | |
| A50.88 | Hennie | Kotze | RSA | 60 | 18 Jan | | | | |
| 50.89 | Patrick | Cheruiyot | KEN | 65 | 12 Apr | | | | |
| | | (160) | | | | | | | |
| 50.90 | Sergey | Sedov | SU | 60 | 22 Jun | | | | |
| 50.91 | Harold | Morton | USA | 64 | 12 Apr | | | | |
| 50.91 | Mark | Boyd | USA | 65 | 19 Apr | | | | |
| 50.91 | Aleksandr | Cheshko | SU | 58 | 15 Jul | | | | |
| 50.92 | Hamish | Halley | AUS | 66 | 6 Mar | | | | |
| 50.92 | Peter | Eriksson | SWE | 64 | 28 Jul | | | | |
| 50.93 | Shunqi | Guo | CHN | 63 | 24 Oct | | | | |
| 50.94 | Sergey | Dedukhov | SU | 63 | 18 Sep | | | | |
| 50.95 | Greg | Rolle | BAH | 59 | | | | | |
| 50.96 | Dominique | Duvigneau | FRA | 60 | 10 Aug | | | | |
| | | (170) | | | | | | | |
| 50.97 | Barry | Johnson | USA | 65 | 10 May | | | | |
| 50.97 | Zhenbin | Huang | CHN | 64 | 4 Jun | | | | |
| 50.97 | Neville | Douglas | CAN | 65 | 22 Jun | | | | |
| 50.99 | Dave | Johnson | USA | | 10 May | | | | |
| 51.00 | Dale | Horrobin | AUS | 60 | 16 Mar | | | | |
| 51.01 | Carsten | Fischer | FRG | 62 | 12 Jul | | | | |
| 51.01 | Stefan | Schnabel | FRG | 63 | 13 Jul | | | | |
| 51.01 | Jörg | Steinbrecher | GDR | 63 | 16 Aug | | | | |
| A51.03 | Poena | Prinsloo | RSA | 67 | 7 Mar | | | | |
| A51.03 | Chris | McGowan (180) | USA | 66 | 17 May | | | | |
| 51.03 | | | | | | Martin | Gillingham | UK 63 | 14 Jun |
| 51.03 | | | | | | Jean-Michel | Serres | FRA 61 | 10 Aug |
| 51.04 | | | | | | James | Purvis | USA 66 | 19 Apr |
| 51.04 | | | | | | Willie | Parker | USA 65 | 17 May |
| 51.05 | | | | | | Rok | Kopitar | YUG 59 | 7 Sep |
| 51.06 | | | | | | Ladrick | Trusty | JAM 62 | 10 May |
| 51.06 | | | | | | Sam | Spiller | USA | 24 May |
| 51.06 | | | | | | József | Szalai | HUN 61 | 16 Aug |
| 51.06 | | | | | | Hamidou | Mbaye | SEN 60 | 30 Aug |
| 51.07 | | | | | | Raymond | Young (190) | USA 66 | 24 May |
| 51.07 | | | | | | Carlos | Azulay | SPA 58 | 3 Aug |
| 51.08 | | | | | | Vladislav | Pecen | CS 60 | 24 Jun |
| 51.09 | | | | | | Brent | Walker | USA | 17 May |
| 51.09 | | | | | | Xinliang | Song | CHN 64 | 24 Oct |
| 51.10 | | | | | | Tony | McKinney | USA 67 | 26 Apr |
| 51.10 | | | | | | Marc | Blin | FRA 62 | 14 Jun |
| 51.10 | | | | | | Aleksandr | Gutnik | SU 62 | 7 Sep |
| 51.11 | | | | | | Rudik | Matevosyan | SU 62 | 24 May |
| 51.11 | | | | | | Dennis | Moore | USA 65 | 24 May |
| 51.12 | | | | | | Han-Ju | Chung (200) | SKO 65 | 25 May |
| 51.12 | | | | | | Derrick | Peynado | JAM 60 | 21 Jun |
| 51.13 | | | | | | Sergey | Politiko | SU 64 | 18 Sep |
| 51.14 | | | | | | José | Duany | CUB 65 | 22 Feb |
| 51.14 | | | | | | Jean-Pascal | Valentian | FRA 60 | 10 Jul |
| 51.14 | | | | | | Hartmut | Weber (205) | FRG 60 | 12 Sep |

---

| | 1 | 10 | 20 | 30 | 50 | 100 | Under 50.00 | Under 51.00 |
|------|-------|-------|-------|-------|-------|-------|-------|-------|
| 1982 | 47.48 | 48.90 | 49.64 | 49.88 | 50.19 | 50.89 | 34 | 111 |
| 1983 | 47.02 | 49.03 | 49.35 | 49.59 | 50.02 | 50.72 | 48 | 137 |
| 1984 | 47.32 | 48.74 | 49.40 | 49.63 | 49.92 | 50.53 | 52 | 162 |
| 1985 | 47.63 | 49.03 | 49.34 | 49.49 | 49.91 | 50.65 | 56 | 144 |
| 1986 | 47.38 | 48.71 | 49.13 | 49.52 | 49.81 | 50.41 | 63 | 174 |

---

Best low altitude marks:

| 49.27 | | Pienaar | | 1 | | Stellenbosch | 17 Feb |
|-------|--|---------|--|---|--|--------------|--------|
| 49.56 | | Laverty | | 4 | | Tempe | 5 Apr |
| 49.56 | | Hawkins | | 1 | | Modesto, CA | 10 May |
| 50.62 | | Vorster | 19 Mar | 50.85 | | Engels | 19 Mar |
| 50.70 | | Patterson | 4 Jun | 51.00 | | Burger | 22 Mar |
| 50.84 | | Leveille | 22 Jun | 51.02 | | Jackson | 3 May |

Hand timing:

| 50.1 | Sansiski | Daniels | USA | 64 | 2 | TexR | Austin | 4 Apr |
|------|----------|---------|-----|----|----|------|--------|-------|
| 50.1 | Oleg | Zhdanov | SU | 62 | 1 | | Lipetsk | 19 Jul |
| 50.2 | Anthony | Bennon | USA | 66 | 1 | | Columbia, SC | 5 Apr |
| 50.2 | Daniel | Ogidi | NIG | 63 | 2 | NC | Lagos | 22 Jun |

| Mark | Name | | Nat | Yr | Pos | Meet | Venue | | Date |
|------|------|---|-----|----|----|------|-------|---|------|
| A50.2 | Simon | Kitur | KEN | 59 | 1 | | Nairobi | | 5 Jul |
| 50.3 | German | Petrov | (6) SU | 67 | 1 | | Leningrad | | 26 Jun |
| | | | | | | | | | |
| 50.4 | Sergey | Dedukhov | SU 63 29 Aug | | | A50.6 | Paul | Rop | KEN 60 5 Jul |
| 50.5 | Elvis | Cedeno | VEN 64 19 Apr | | | 50.6 | Sergey | Sedov | SU 60 19 Jul |
| 50.5 | Andri | Hargrove | USA 58 19 Apr | | | 50.7 | Rhan | Sheffield | USA 55 19 Apr |
| 50.5 | Aleksandr | Cheshko | (10) SU 58 26 Jun | | | 50.8 | Aleksey | Bazarov | SU 63 10 Aug |
| | | | | | | 50.8 | Sergey | Politiko | SU 64 29 Aug |
| 50.5 | Yuriy | Matyushev | SU 65 29 Aug | | | 50.9 | Valeriy | Solovushkov | SU 62 15 Jun |
| 50.6 | Efrain | Williams | PR 19 Apr | | | 50.9 | Yuriy | Poteyev (20) | SU 66 29 Aug |
| 50.6 | Domingo | Cordero | PR 19 Apr | | | | | | |

# HIGH JUMP

| Mark | Name | | Nat | Yr | Pos | Meet | Venue | Date |
|------|------|---|-----|----|----|------|-------|------|
| 2.38 | Igor | Paklin | SU | 63 | 1 | | Rieti | 7 Sep |
| 2.37 | | Paklin | | | 1 | ASV | Köln | 17 Aug |
| 2.36 i | Jim | Howard | USA | 59 | 1 | | Albuquerque | 25 Jan |
| 2.36 i | Carlo | Thränhardt | FRG | 57 | 1 | | W Berlin | 14 Feb |
| 2.36 | Javier | Sotomayor | CUB | 67 | 1 | | Santiago/Cuba | 23 Feb |
| 2.35 i | | Howard | | | 1 | | Toronto | 31 Jan |
| 2.35 | Gennadiy | Avdeyenko | SU | 63 | 1 | Nar | Sofia | 1 Jun |
| 2.35 | | Paklin | | | 1 | Spart | Tashkent | 20 Sep |
| 2.34 i | | Thränhardt | | | 1 | | Simmerath | 17 Jan |
| 2.34 i | Aleksandr | Kotovich | SU | 61 | 1 | | Minsk | 18 Jan |
| | | | | | | | | |
| 2.34 i | | Howard | | | 1 | | New York | 14 Feb |
| 2.34 i | Dietmar | Mögenburg | FRG | 61 | 1 | EC | Madrid | 22 Feb |
| 2.34 i | | Howard | | | 1 | TAC | New York | 28 Feb |
| 2.34 | Jerome | Carter | USA | 63 | 1 | | Villanova | 8 Jun |
| 2.34 | Ján | Zvara | CS | 63 | 1 | PTS | Bratislava | 14 Jun |
| 2.34 | | Paklin | | | 1 | DNG | Stockholm | 1 Jul |
| 2.34 | Doug | Nordquist(10) | USA | 58 | 1 | GWG | Moskva | 9 Jul |
| 2.34 | Valeriy | Sereda | SU | 59 | 1 | NC | Kiev | 15 Jul |
| 2.34 | | Howard | | | 1 | WK | Zürich | 13 Aug |
| 2.34 | | Avdeyenko | | | 1 | | Kiev | 31 Aug |
| | | | | | | | | |
| 2.34 | | Paklin | | | 1 | EC | Stuttgart | 31 Aug |
| 2.34 | | Paklin | | | 1 | GP | Roma | 10 Sep |
| 2.34 | Patrik | Sjöberg | SWE | 65 | 1 | | Catania | 13 Sep |
| 2.33 i | | Howard | | | 1 | | Portland | 24 Jan |
| 2.33 i | Jacek | Wszoła | POL | 56 | 1 | NC | Zabrze | 9 Feb |
| 2.33 | Milton | Ottey | CAN | 59 | 1 | NC | Ottawa | 21 Jun |
| 2.33 | | Nordquist | | | 1 | TAC | Eugene | 21 Jun |
| 2.33 | | Howard | | | 2 | TAC | Eugene | 21 Jun |
| 2.33 | Andrey | Morozov | SU | 60 | 1 | | Lipetsk | 19 Jul |
| 2.33 | | Sjöberg | | | 1 | v Fin | Helsinki | 9 Aug |
| | | | | | | | | |
| 2.33 | | Howard | | | 1 | BGP | Budapest | 11 Aug |
| 2.33 | | Avdeyenko | | | 2 | Spart | Tashkent | 20 Sep |
| 2.33 | Sergey | Malchenko | SU | 63 | 3 | Spart | Tashkent | 20 Sep |
| | | (33/16) | | | | | | |
| 2.32 i | Dennis | Lewis | USA | 59 | 2 | | Toronto | 31 Jan |
| 2.32 | Sorin | Matei | RUM | 63 | 3 | GWG | Moskva | 9 Jul |
| 2.31 i | Eddy | Annijs | BEL | 58 | 3 | | Simmerath | 17 Jan |
| 2.31 i | Vadim | Oganyan (20) | SU | 63 | 2 | NC | Moskva | 6 Feb |

| Mark | Name | | Nat | Yr | Pos | Meet | Venue | Date |
|------|------|------|-----|----|----|------|-------|------|
| 2.31 i | Jianhua | Zhu | CHN | 63 | 1 | | Kobe | 5 Mar |
| 2.31 | Aleksey | Demyanyuk | SU | 58 | 1 | | Uzhgorod | 8 May |
| 2.31 | Constantin | Militaru | RUM | 63 | 1 | | București | 24 May |
| 2.31 | Eugen | Popescu | RUM | 62 | 2 | NC | Pitești | 8 Aug |
| 2.31 | Krzysztof | Krawczyk | POL | 62 | 3 | BGP | Budapest | 11 Aug |
| 2.30 i | Geoff | Parsons | UK | 64 | 1 | NC | Cosford | 25 Jan |
| 2.30 i | Brian | Stanton | USA | 61 | 2 | | Albuquerque | 25 Jan |
| 2.30 i | Gerd | Nagel | FRG | 57 | 4 | | W Berlin | 14 Feb |
| 2.30 i | Andreas | Sam | GDR | 60 | 1 | NC | Senftenberg | 15 Feb |
| 2.30 | Jake | Jacoby    (30) | USA | 61 | 1 | | Houston | 4 May |
| | | | | | | | | |
| 2.30 | Juan | Centelles | CUB | 61 | 2 | | Habana | 9 Jun |
| 2.30 | Greg | Jones | USA | 65 | 3 | TAC | Eugene | 21 Jun |
| 2.30 | Kenny | Banks | USA | 66 | 4 | TAC | Eugene | 21 Jun |
| 2.30 | Rudolf | Povarnitsyn | SU | 62 | 1 | v GDR | Tallinn | 22 Jun |
| 2.30 | Gerd | Wessig | GDR | 59 | 1 | NC | Jena | 28 Jun |
| 2.29 i | Gennadiy | Martsinovich | SU | 61 | 2 | | Vilnius | 11 Jan |
| 2.29 | Victor | Smalls | USA | 64 | 1 | | Atlanta | 10 May |
| 2.29 | Georgi | Dakov | BUL | 67 | 2 | Nar | Sofia | 1 Jun |
| 2.29 | Gennadiy | Vaskevich | SU | 66 | 2 | | Kiev | 31 Aug |
| 2.29 | Yuriy | Sergiyenko | SU | 65 | 4 | Spart | Tashkent | 20 Sep |
| | | (40) | | | | | | |
| 2.285 | Hollis | Conway | USA | 67 | 1 | | Lafayette, LA | 12 Apr |
| 2.285 | Ron | Lee | USA | 62 | 1 | | Pomona, CA | 10 May |
| 2.28 i | Dariusz | Zielke | POL | 60 | 1 | | Handen | 26 Jan |
| 2.28 i | Novica | Čanović | YUG | 61 | 4= | | Solna | 25 Feb |
| 2.28 | Sergey | Zasimovich | SU | 62 | 1 | | Alma-Ata | 11 May |
| 2.28 | Markus | Einberger | AUT | 64 | 1 | | Schwechat | 18 May |
| 2.28 | Joey | Johnson | USA | 67 | 1 | v Rum-j | Pitești | 12 Jul |
| 2.28 | Jindřich | Vondra | CS | 57 | 1 | | Praha | 21 Aug |
| 2.27 i | Lee | Balkin | USA | 61 | 5 | | W Berlin | 14 Feb |
| 2.27 | James | Lott    (50) | USA | 65 | 1 | | Austin | 3 May |
| | | | | | | | | |
| 2.27 | Bernhard | Bensch | FRG | 64 | 4 | | Eberstadt | 15 Jun |
| 2.27 | Yunpeng | Liu | CHN | 62 | 2 | AsiG | Seoul | 4 Oct |
| 2.265i | Tom | McCants | USA | 62 | 1 | | Bloomington | 1 Feb |
| 2.265i | Dothel | Edwards | USA | 66 | 1 | | Gainesville | 16 Feb |
| 2.26 i | Brian | Whitehead | USA | 62 | 3= | | New York | 14 Feb |
| 2.26 | Mark | Reed | USA | 65 | 1 | TexR | Austin | 5 Apr |
| 2.26 | Maurice | Crumby | USA | 65 | 2 | TexR | Austin | 5 Apr |
| 2.26 | Bill | Jasinski | USA | 64 | 3 | TexR | Austin | 5 Apr |
| 2.26 | Normunds | Sietins | SU | 67 | 1 | | Murjani | 11 May |
| 2.26 | Nick | Saunders (60) | BER | 63 | 1 | | Paris | 22 Jul |
| | | | | | | | | |
| 2.26 | Rick | Noji | USA | 67 | 1 | | México, D.F. | 9 Aug |
| 2.25 i | Greg | Gonsalves | USA | 63 | 1 | | Allston | 1 Feb |
| 2.25 i | Peter | Blank | FRG | 62 | 1 | | Zweibrücken | 4 Feb |
| 2.25 i | Yuriy | Gotovskiy | SU | 61 | 1 | | Leningrad | 23 Feb |
| 2.25 | Brian | Tietjens | USA | 62 | 1 | | Ames | 3 May |
| 2.25 | Grigoriy | Chorny | SU | 62 | 2 | | Uzhgorod | 8 May |
| 2.25 | Vladimir | Korniyenko | SU | 66 | 1 | | Alma-Ata | 30 May |
| 2.25 | Kenny | Smith | USA | 62 | 1 | | Tallahassee | 31 May |
| 2.25 | Yuriy | Shevchenko | SU | 60 | 3 | Znam | Leningrad | 8 Jun |
| 2.25 | Sergey | Serebryanskiy | SU | 62 | 3 | | Dnepropetrovsk | 28 Jun |
| | | (70) | | | | | | |
| 2.25 | Roland | Dalhäuser | SWZ | 58 | 2 | | Boswil | 5 Jul |
| 2.25 | Sergey | Maly | SU | 65 | 1 | | Poltava | 20 Jul |

| Mark | Name | | Nat | Yr | Pos | Meet | Venue | Date |
|------|------|------|-----|-----|-----|------|-------|------|
| 2.25 | Gyula | Németh | HUN | 59 | 1 | NC | Budapest | 16 Aug |
| 2.25 | Gustavo | Becquer | SPA | 66 | 1 | | Ordizia | 20 Sep |
| 2.25 | Yang | Cao | CHN | 68 | | | Qingdao | 3 Oct |
| 2.24 i | Gianni | Davito | ITA | 57 | 1 | | Torino | 15 Jan |
| 2.24 i | Gian Piero | Palomba | ITA | 63 | 2 | | Torino | 15 Jan |
| 2.24 i | Hans | Burchard | FRG | 59 | 5 | | Simmerath | 17 Jan |
| 2.24 i | Matthias | Grebenstein | GDR | 64 | 3 | | Arnstadt | 22 Jan |
| 2.24 i | Maris | Reinsons (80) | SU | 64 | 1 | | Riga | 24 Jan |
| 2.24 i | Wolfgang | Neuhoff | FRG | 58 | 1 | | Düsseldorf | 25 Jan |
| 2.24 i | Andre | Schneider | FRG | 58 | 3 | | Stuttgart | 2 Feb |
| 2.24 | Tyke | Peacock | USA | 61 | 1 | MSR | Walnut, CA | 27 Apr |
| 2.24 | Milton | Goode | USA | 60 | 2 | MSR | Walnut, CA | 27 Apr |
| 2.24 | Igor | Ivliyev | SU | 63 | 2 | | Sochi | 18 May |
| 2.24 | Oleg | Azizmuradov | SU | 62 | 3 | | Sochi | 18 May |
| 2.24 | Vyacheslav | Galushko | SU | 67 | 1 | | Simferopol | 23 May |
| 2.24 | Eric | Monnerais | FRA | 65 | 1 | | Laval | 25 May |
| 2.24 | Brian | Marshall | CAN | 65 | 1 | | Los Angeles | 24 May |
| 2.24 | Shuji | Ujino (90) | JAP | 60 | 1 | NC | Tokyo | 1 Jun |
| 2.24 | Leo | Williams | USA | 60 | 1 | | Santa Monica | 7 Jun |
| 2.24 | Ben | Lucero | USA | 62 | 2 | | Santa Monica | 7 Jun |
| 2.24 | Dominique | Hernandez | FRA | 60 | 2 | | Saint-Denis | 21 Jun |
| 2.24 | Marcello | Benvenuti | ITA | 64 | 3 | | Caorle | 27 Jul |
| 2.24 | Franck | Verzy | FRA | 61 | 1 | | Mâcon | 1 Aug |
| 2.24 | Dany | Dhaneus | FRA | 65 | 1 | | Recklinghausen | 3 Aug |
| 2.235 | Natty | Crooks | CAN | 63 | 3 | | El Paso | 20 Apr |
| 2.23 i | Larry | Helwig | CAN | 63 | 1 | NC | Edmonton | 23 Feb |
| 2.23 | Sašo | Apostolovski | YUG | 63 | 1 | | Nova Gorica | 10 May |
| 2.23 | Hrvoje | Fižuleto(100) | YUG | 63 | 1 | | Dijon | 14 Jun |
| 2.23 | Evgeni | Peev | BUL | 65 | 1 | | Sofia | 21 Jun |
| 2.23 | Uwe | Martin | FRG | 62 | 1 | | Aschaffenburg | 21 Jun |
| 2.23 | Ilya | Chernov | SU | 67 | 1 | NC-j | Kaunas | 21 Jul |
| 2.23 | Sergey | Ilnitskiy | SU | 62 | 1 | | Chelyabinsk | 9 Aug |
| 2.23 | Oleg | Urmakayev | SU | 65 | D | Spart | Tashkent | 18 Sep |
| 2.23 | Vladimir | Sokolov (106) | SU | 63 | 6 | Spart | Tashkent | 20 Sep |

| Mark | Name | | Nat | Yr | Date |
|------|------|------|-----|-----|------|
| 2.22 i | Vladimir | Zybalov | SU | 64 | 4 Jan |
| 2.22 i | Neal | Guidry | USA | 67 | 11 Jan |
| 2.22 i | Dave | Glassburn | USA | | 18 Jan |
| 2.22 i | Gennadiy | Belkov (110) | SU | 56 | 25 Jan |
| 2.22 i | Mark | Gooden | USA | | 26 Jan |
| 2.22 i | Miguel | Moral | SPA | 61 | 8 Feb |
| 2.22 i | Dave | Sampson | USA | 63 | 22 Feb |
| 2.22 | Christo | de Wet | RSA | 61 | 24 Feb |
| 2.22 i | Darrell | Wills | USA | | 1 Mar |
| 2.22 i | Alain | Metellus | CAN | 65 | 8 Mar |
| 2.22 | Brad | Speer | USA | 65 | 5 Apr |
| 2.22 | Marshall | Broadway | USA | 62 | 5 Apr |
| 2.22 | Troy | Kemp | BAH | 66 | 5 Apr |
| 2.22 | Mark | Trujillo(120) | USA | 66 | 12 Apr |
| 2.22 | Troy | Haines | USA | 64 | 19 Apr |
| 2.22 | James | Barrineau | USA | 55 | 3 May |
| 2.22 | Jon | Shelton | USA | 67 | 3 May |
| 2.22 | Ernie | Patterson | USA | 61 | 10 May |
| 2.22 | Bogusław | Glinkowski | POL | 63 | 3 Jun |
| 2.22 | Marcin | Chudak | POL | 66 | 3 Jun |
| 2.22 | Phil | Henderson | AUS | 67 | 28 Jun |
| 2.22 | Sergey | Zaitsev | SU | 65 | 14 Jul |
| 2.22 | Ivars | Zankovskis | SU | 65 | 14 Jul |
| 2.22 | Gennadiy | Balandinskiy (130) | SU | 65 | 19 Jul |
| 2.22 | Almas | Tleuliyev | SU | 64 | 19 Jul |
| 2.22 | Thomas | Müller | GDR | 67 | 20 Jul |
| 2.22 | Christian | Klemenczak | FRA | 57 | 30 Jul |
| 2.22 | Sergey | Churikov | SU | 66 | 7 Sep |
| 2.22 | Bennie | Joubert | RSA | 65 | 9 Sep |
| 2.22 | Oleg | Kulikovskiy | SU | 63 | 19 Sep |
| 2.22 i | Andrey | Mukhin | SU | 65 | 28 Dec |
| 2.215 | Joe | Patrone | USA | 62 | 17 May |
| 2.21 | Frank | Eatmon | USA | 64 | 11 Jan |
| 2.21 | Maury | Burnett (140) | USA | 64 | 11 Jan |
| 2.21 i | Carsten | Siebert | GDR | 62 | 18 Jan |
| 2.21 i | Pier Paolo | Montalto | ITA | 63 | 22 Jan |
| 2.21 i | Vasiliy | Makhonin | SU | 60 | 25 Jan |
| 2.21 i | J-Charles | Gicquel | FRA | 67 | 1 Feb |

MEN 1986

| Mark | Name | | Nat | Yr | Pos | Meet | Venue | | Date |
|------|------|--|-----|----|-----|------|-------|--|------|
| 2.21 1 | Vincent | Gouzalch | FRA | 63 | 1 Feb | 2.21 | Vladimír | Štalmach | CS 65 28 Jun |
| 2.21 1 | Mirosław | Włodarczyk | POL | 59 | 9 Feb | 2.21 | Andrea | Liverani | ITA 64 1 Jul |
| 2.21 1 | Jorge | Alfaro | CUB | 62 | 12 Feb | 2.21 | Torsten | Marschner | GDR 68 2 Jul |
| 2.21 | Ron | Kamaka | USA | 63 | 26 Mar | 2.21 | Matti | Luostarinen | FIN 61 13 Jul |
| 2.21 | Mike | Burns | USA | 64 | 4 May | 2.21 | Josef | Hrabal | CS 58 13 Jul |
| 2.21 | Thomas | Eriksson(150) | SWE | 63 | 24 May | 2.21 | Andreas | Surbeck | FRG 59 20 Jul |
| | | | | | | 2.21 | Daniele | Pagani (160) | ITA 66 23 Jul |
| 2.21 | Takao | Sakamoto | JAP | 58 | 1 Jun | | | | |
| 2.21 | Zhongwei | Hao | CHN | 64 | 7 Jun | 2.21 | Luca | Toso | ITA 64 23 Jul |
| 2.21 | Fayyaz | Ahmed | UK | 66 | 21 Jun | 2.21 | Jeff | Martinez | USA 68 27 Jul |
| | | | | | | 2.21 | Tao | Ni (163) | CHN 69 23 Aug |

| | 1 | 10 | 20 | 30 | 50 | 100 | Over 2.25 | Over 2.21 |
|------|------|------|------|-------|------|------|------|------|
| 1982 | 2.34 | 2.31 | 2.28 | 2.27 | 2.25 | 2.22 | 57 | 146 |
| 1983 | 2.38 | 2.32 | 2.30 | 2.285 | 2.27 | 2.24 | 83 | 187 |
| 1984 | 2.39 | 2.33 | 2.31 | 2.30 | 2.28 | 2.24 | 98 | 184 |
| 1985 | 2.41 | 2.35 | 2.32 | 2.30 | 2.27 | 2.24 | 85 | 171 |
| 1986 | 2.38 | 2.34 | 2.31 | 2.30 | 2.27 | 2.23 | 75 | 163 |

Best outdoor marks:

| 2.32 | Kotovich | | 1 | Znam | Leningrad | 8 Jun |
|------|----------|--|---|------|-----------|-------|
| 2.32 | Thränhardt | | 1 | | Eberstadt | 24 Sep |
| 2.31 | Annijs | | 1 | | Louvain | 25 May |
| 2.31 | Zhu | | 1 | AsiG | Seoul | 4 Oct |
| 2.30 | Mögenburg | | 2= | WK | Zürich | 13 Aug |
| 2.30 | Nagel | | 1 | | Forbach | 21 Sep |
| 2.29 | Oganyan | | 5 | Spart | Tashkent | 20 Sep |
| 2.28 | Parsons | | 1 | | London | 17 May |
| 2.28 | Čanović | | 3 | PTS | Bratislava | 14 Jun |
| 2.27 | Sam | (10) | 2 | NC | Jena | 28 Jun |
| | | | | | | |
| 2.265 | McCants | | 4 | | Knoxville | 24 May |
| 2.26 | Edwards | | 1 | | Knoxville | 12 Apr |
| 2.26 | Zielke | | 1 | | Łódź | 6 Sep |
| 2.25 | Balkin | | 1 | AusC | Adelaide | 15 Mar |
| 2.25 | Martsinovich | | 1 | | Vitebsk | 6 Jul |
| 2.25 | Whitehead | | 3 | USOCF | Houston | 3 Aug |
| 2.25 | Wszoła | | 5= | IAC | London | 8 Aug |
| 2.24 | Schneider | | 8 | | Eberstadt | 15 Jun |
| 2.24 | Neuhoff | | 1 | | Mönchengladbach | 17 Jun |
| 2.24 | Davito | (20) | 1 | v FRG, | Hun Milano | 20 Jun |
| | | | | | | |
| 2.24 | Stanton | | Q | TAC | Eugene | 20 Jun |
| 2.24 | Grebenstein | | 3 | NC | Jena | 28 Jun |
| | | (22) | | | | |

| 2.22 | Gonsalves | 10 May | 2.22 | | Gotovskiy(28) | 14 Jul' |
|------|-----------|--------|------|--|---------------|--------|
| 2.22 | Moral | 18 May | | | | |
| 2.22 | Belkov | 31 May | Ancillary jump /over 2.33/: | | | |
| 2.22 | Metellus | 21 Jun | | | | |
| 2.22 | Blank | 12 Jul | 2.33 | | Paklin | 7 Sep |

| Mark | Name | | Nat | Yr | Pos | Meet | Venue | Date |
|------|------|---|-----|----|----|------|-------|------|

## POLE VAULT

| Mark | Name | | Nat | Yr | Pos | Meet | Venue | Date |
|------|------|---|-----|----|----|------|-------|------|
| 6.01 | Sergey | Bubka | SU | 63 | 1 | GWG | Moskva | 8 Jul |
| 5.95 i | | Bubka | | | 1 | TAC | New York | 28 Feb |
| 5.94 i | | Bubka | | | 1 | | Inglewood, CA | 21 Feb |
| 5.93 i | Billy | Olson | USA | 58 | 1 | | E Rutherford | 8 Feb |
| 5.92 i | | Bubka | | | 1 | NC | Moskva | 8 Feb |
| 5.91 i | Joe | Dial | USA | 62 | 1 | | Columbia, MO | 1 Feb |
| 5.90 | | Dial | | | 1 | | Norman | 25 Apr |
| 5.90 | Thierry | Vigneron | FRA | 60 | 1 | | Paris | 22 Jul |
| 5.89 i | | Olson | | | 1 | | Albuquerque | 25 Jan |
| 5.88 i | | Olson | | | 1 | | Los Angeles | 17 Jan |
| 5.88 | | Dial | | | 1 | | El Paso | 20 Apr |
| 5.87 i | | Bubka | | | 1 | | Osaka | 15 Jan |
| 5.86 | | Dial | | | 1 | | Norman | 12 Apr |
| 5.85 | Rodion | Gataullin | SU | 65 | 1 | NC | Kiev | 16 Jul |
| 5.85 | Philippe | Collet | FRA | 63 | 2 | | Paris | 22 Jul |
| 5.85 | | Gataullin | | | 1 | WK | Zürich | 13 Aug |
| 5.85 | | Bubka | | | 1 | EC | Stuttgart | 29 Aug |
| 5.84 | | Gataullin | | | 1 | | Tashkent | 13 Jun |
| 5.81 i | Marian | Kolasa | POL | 59 | 1 | | Praha | 13 Feb |
| 5.81 i | | Bubka | | | 1 | | Rosemont, IL | 16 Feb |
| 5.81 | Earl | Bell | USA | 55 | 1 | USOCF | Houston | 2 Aug |
| 5.81 i | | Gataullin | | | 1 | | Tashkent | Dec |
| 5.80 i | Dave | Volz | USA | 62 | 2* | | New York | 14 Feb |
| 5.80 i | | Dial | | | 1 | | San Diego | 23 Feb |
| 5.80 i | | Dial | | | 1 | | Boulder | 8 Mar |
| 5.80 | | Gataullin | | | 1 | | Sochi | 23 May |
| 5.80 | | Gataullin | | | 1 | Znam | Leningrad | 7 Jun |
| 5.80 | Mike | Tully (10) | USA | 56 | 1 | TAC | Eugene | 21 Jun |
| 5.80 | | Gataullin | | | 2 | GWG | Moskva | 8 Jul |
| 5.80 | Vasiliy | Bubka | SU | 60 | 2 | NC | Kiev | 16 Jul |
| 5.80 | | Bell | | | 2 | WK | Zürich | 13 Aug |
| 5.80 | | Collet | | | 1 | | Lausanne | 2 Sep |
| 5.80 | Atanas | Tarev | BUL | 58 | 2 | | Lausanne | 2 Sep |
| 5.80 i | | Vigneron | | | 1 | | Colombes | 20 Dec |
| | | (34/12) | | | | | | |
| 5.77 | Doug | Fraley | USA | 65 | 1 | MSR | Walnut, CA | 27 Apr |
| 5.75 | Aleksandr | Krupskiy | SU | 60 | 1 | | Sochi | 17 May |
| 5.72 i | Pierre | Quinon | FRA | 62 | 3 | | New York | 14 Feb |
| 5.72 | Doug | Lytle | USA | 62 | 1 | KansR | Lawrence | 19 Apr |
| 5.72 | Aleksandr | Obizhayev | SU | 59 | 2 | | Tallinn | 28 Jun |
| 5.72 | Zdeněk | Lubenský | CS | 62 | 1 | NC | Bratislava | 12 Jul |
| 5.70 i | Brad | Pursley | USA | 60 | 2 | | Albuquerque | 25 Jan |
| 5.70 i | Władysław | Kozakiewicz | FRG | 53 | 1 | | Toronto | 31 Jan |
| | | (20) | | | | | | |
| 5.70 | Felix | Böhni | SWZ | 58 | 3 | MSR | Walnut, CA | 27 Apr |
| 5.70 | Tim | Bright | USA | 60 | 1 | | Modesto, CA | 10 May |
| 5.70 | Dale | Jenkins | USA | 63 | 2 | | Modesto, CA | 10 May |
| 5.70 | Sergey | Kulibaba | SU | 59 | 2 | | Sochi | 17 May |
| 5.70 | Scott | Davis | USA | 61 | 1 | | Eugene | 17 May |
| 5.70 | Kasimir | Zalar | SWE | 57 | 1 | | Nyköping | 2 Jul |
| 5.70 | Vadim | Kodentsov | SU | 64 | 1 | | Omsk | 14 Jul |
| 5.70 | Larry | Jessee | USA | 52 | 1 | | El Paso | 30 Jul |
| 5.70 | Stanimir | Penchev | BUL | 59 | 1 | | Sofia | 3 Aug |
| 5.70 | Kory | Tarpenning (30) | USA | 62 | 3 | WK | Zürich | 13 Aug |

| Mark | Name | | Nat | Yr | Pos | Meet | Venue | Date |
|---|---|---|---|---|---|---|---|---|
| 5.67 i | Mirosław | Chmara | POL | 64 | 1 | | Madrid | 12 Feb |
| 5.67 | Dave | Kenworthy | USA | 60 | 1 | | Foggia | 18 Sep |
| 5.66 | Hermann | Fehringer | AUT | 62 | 1 | NC | Linz | 13 Jul |
| 5.65 i | Valeriy | Ishutin | SU | 65 | 2 | | Minsk | 19 Jan |
| 5.65 i | Konstantin | Volkov | SU | 60 | 4 | NC | Moskva | 8 Feb |
| 5.65 | Vladimir | Polyakov | SU | 60 | 2 | | Sochi | 23 May |
| 5.65 | Aleksey | Nikitin | SU | 58 | 1 | | Moskva | 27 Jun |
| 5.65 | Gennadiy | Sukharev | SU | 65 | 3 | | Tallinn | 28 Jun |
| 5.65 | Viktor | Spasov | SU | 59 | 4 | | Tallinn | 28 Jun |
| 5.65 | Andrey | Pogorely (40) | SU | 59 | 2 | | Omsk | 14 Jul |
| 5.65 | Nikolay | Nikolov | BUL | 64 | 1 | | Stara Zagora | 19 Jul |
| 5.65 | Sergey | Smolyakov | SU | 62 | 1 | | Moskva | 9 Aug |
| 5.62 i | Pavel | Bogatyryov | SU | 61 | 1 | | Vilnius | 12 Jan |
| 5.62 | Greg | Duplantis | USA | 62 | 2 | | El Paso | 20 Apr |
| 5.62 | Sergey | Gavrikov | SU | 64 | 1 | | Leningrad | 15 Jun |
| 5.61 i | Grigoriy | Yegorov | SU | 67 | 1 | v GDR-j | Moskva | 16 Feb |
| 5.61 | Alberto | Ruiz | SPA | 61 | 1 | | Manresa | 26 Jun |
| 5.61 | Ferenc | Salbert | FRA | 60 | 1 | | Suresnes | 17 Jul |
| 5.60 | Gerald | Kager | AUT | 63 | 1 | | Lisboa | 1 Jun |
| 5.60 | Jürgen | Winkler  (50) | FRG | 59 | 3 | | München | 17 Jun |
| 5.60 | Scott | Huffman | USA | 64 | 4 | TAC | Eugene | 21 Jun |
| 5.60 | František | Jansa | CS | 62 | 1 | RoŠ | Praha | 24 Jun |
| 5.60 | Asko | Peltoniemi | FIN | 63 | 3 | | Somero | 13 Jul |
| 5.60 | Timo | Kuusisto | FIN | 59 | 4 | | Somero | 13 Jul |
| 5.60 | Serge | Leveur | FRA | 57 | 5 | | Paris | 22 Jul |
| 5.60 | Ivo | Yanchev | BUL | 60 | 2 | | Sofia | 26 Jul |
| 5.60 | Paul | Benavides | USA | 64 | 2 | | El Paso | 30 Jul |
| 5.60 | Serge | Ferreira | FRA | 59 | 3 | NC | Aix-les-Bains | 10 Aug |
| 5.60 | Yevgeniy | Bondarenko | SU | 66 | 2 | Spart | Tashkent | 18 Sep |
| 5.56 i | Jeff | Buckingham | USA | 60 | 1 | | Johnson City | 18 Jan |
| | | (60) | | | | | | |
| 5.55 i | Tadeusz | Slusarski | POL | 50 | 3 | NC | Zabrze | 9 Feb |
| 5.55 i | Vasiliy | Trofimenko | SU | 62 | 1 | | Leningrad | 23 Feb |
| 5.55 | Mark | Heppner | USA | 64 | 3 | | San Jose | 1 Mar |
| 5.55 | Delko | Lesov | BUL | 67 | 2 | Nar | Sofia | 31 May |
| 5.55 | Xueren | Liang | CHN | 65 | 1 | | Beijing | 16 Aug |
| 5.55 | Kimmo | Kuusela | FIN | 62 | 5 | EC | Stuttgart | 29 Aug |
| 5.55 | Toshiyuki | Hashioka | JAP | 64 | 1 | | Kofu | 14 Oct |
| 5.54 i | Steve | Stubblefield | USA | 61 | 1 | | Richfield | 23 Feb |
| 5.52 i | Lane | Lohr | USA | 64 | 1 | | W Lafayette | 1 Mar |
| 5.51 | Philippe | Sivillon (70) | FRA | 58 | | | Walnut, CA | 26 Jan |
| 5.51 | Terry | Womack | USA | 65 | 2 | | Norman | 25 Apr |
| 5.51 | Cam | Miller | USA | 66 | 1 | | San Angelo | 26 Apr |
| 5.50 i | Aleksandr | Parnov | SU | 59 | 3 | | Vilnius | 12 Jan |
| 5.50 i | Igor | Trandenkov | SU | 66 | 1 | | Klaipeda | 18 Jan |
| 5.50 i | Oleg | Isakin | SU | 60 | 1 | | Volgograd | 25 Jan |
| 5.50 i | Helmar | Schmidt | FRG | 63 | 3 | | Sindelfingen | 29 Jan |
| 5.50 i | Philippe | Houvion | FRA | 57 | 2 | v GDR | Lievin | 1 Feb |
| 5.50 i | Aleksandr | Morozov | SU | 63 | 2 | | Moskva | 2 Feb |
| 5.50 i | Ryszard | Kolasa | POL | 64 | 1 | | Piraeus | 2 Feb |
| 5.50 i | Gerhard | Schmidt  (80) | FRG | 61 | 2 | | Zweibrücken | 4 Feb |
| 5.50 i | Peter | Volmer | FRG | 58 | 2 | | Nördlingen | 16 Feb |
| 5.50 | Steve | Thaxton | USA | 64 | 1 | | Abilene | 8 Mar |

| Mark | Name | | Nat | Yr | Pos | Meet | Venue | Date |
|---|---|---|---|---|---|---|---|---|
| 5.50 | David | Hodge | USA | 62 | 1 | | Baton Rouge | 22 Mar |
| 5.50 | Steve | Klassen | USA | 65 | 1 | | San Jose | 19 Apr |
| 5.50 | Sergey | Fomenko | SU | 67 | 1 | | Sochi | 26 Apr |
| 5.50 | Rumen | Stoyanov | BUL | 59 | 1 | | Varna | 17 May |
| 5.50 | Jay | Davis | USA | 67 | 2 | | Eugene | 17 May |
| 5.50 | Baker | Vinci | USA | 62 | 2 | | Eugene | 24 May |
| 5.50 | Jeff | Pascoe | USA | 64 | 1 | NCAA | Indianapolis | 6 Jun |
| 5.50 | Anton | Paskalev (90) | BUL | 58 | 1 | | Sofia | 7 Jun |
| 5.50 | Alain | Donias | FRA | 60 | 1 | | Nantes | 7 Jun |
| 5.50 | Patrick | Abada | FRA | 54 | 3 | | Dijon | 14 Jun |
| 5.50 | István | Bagyula | HUN | 69 | 1 | v Ita, | FRG Milano | 19 Jun |
| 5.50 | Uwe | Langhammer | GDR | 65 | 1 | NC | Jena | 27 Jun |
| 5.50 | Christoph | Pietz | GDR | 64 | 2 | NC | Jena | 27 Jun |
| 5.50 | Bernhard | Zintl | FRG | 65 | 2 | NC | W Berlin | 12 Jul |
| 5.50 | Igor | Potapovich | SU | 67 | 1 | WC-j | Athinai | 17 Jul |
| 5.50 | Stoyan | Peev | BUL | 65 | 3 | | Stara Zagora | 19 Jul |
| 5.50 | Vladimir | Legchenko | SU | 65 | 1 | | Donetsk | 29 Jul |
| 5.50 | Kimmo | Pallonen(100) | FIN | 59 | 2 | | Lohja | 3 Aug |
| 5.50 | Chris | Leeuwenburgh | HOL | 62 | | | Hechtel | 15 Aug |
| 5.50 | Sergey | Dzhemiyev | SU | 64 | | | | |
| 5.50 | Aleksandr | Zhukov (103) | SU | 65 | 3 | Spart | Tashkent | 18 Sep |

| Mark | Name | | Nat | Yr | Date |
|---|---|---|---|---|---|
| 5.49 i | Todd | Cooper | USA | 63 | 8 Feb |
| 5.49 | Pat | Manson | USA | 67 | 24 Jun |
| 5.48 i | Chris | Bohannon | USA | 65 | 14 Mar |
| 5.45 1 | Mauro | Barella | ITA | 56 | 22 Jan |
| 5.45 | Jerry | Mulligan | USA | 58 | 2 Mar |
| 5.45 | Tim | Canfield | USA | 63 | 26 Apr |
| 5.45 | Kelly | Rodrigues (110) | USA | 63 | 9 May |
| 5.45 | Steve | Glander | USA | 64 | 15 May |
| 5.45 | Bob | Dandino | USA | 61 | 16 May |
| 5.45 | Tim | McMichael | USA | 67 | 22 May |
| 5.45 | Valeriy | Bukreyev | SU | 64 | 28 May |
| 5.45 | Mike | Shafe | USA | 63 | 30 May |
| 5.45 | Dave | Watson | USA | 64 | 31 May |
| 5.45 | Tapani | Haapakoski | FIN | 53 | 3 Jun |
| 5.45 | Mike | Thiede | GDR | 67 | 26 Jul |
| 5.43 | Javier | Garcia | SPA | 66 | 16 Jul |
| 5.41 | Charles | Suey (120) | USA | 60 | 20 Jun |
| 5.40 i | Roman | Troshin | SU | 65 | 11 Jan |
| 5.40 i | Leonid | Ivanushkin | SU | 61 | 19 Jan |
| 5.40 i | Mariusz | Klimczyk | POL | 56 | 19 Jan |
| 5.40 1 | Sergey | Ponomarenko | SU | 63 | 26 Jan |
| 5.40 1 | Gerald | Heinrich | FRG | 56 | 29 Jan |
| 5.40 1 | Manfred | Reichert | FRG | 58 | 4 Feb |
| 5.40 1 | Marco | Andreini | ITA | 61 | 5 Feb |
| 5.40 1 | Vladimir | Naimushin | SU | 67 | 7 Feb |
| 5.40 1 | Enrico | Mann | GDR | 65 | 8 Feb |
| 5.40 | Greg | West (130) | USA | 67 | 12 Apr |
| 5.40 | Ricky | Wright | USA | 64 | 13 Apr |
| 5.40 | Brandon | Richards | USA | 67 | 19 Apr |
| 5.40 | Tom | Hintnaus | BRA | 58 | 27 Apr |
| 5.40 | Viktor | Komarov | SU | 66 | 15 May |
| 5.40 | Gerard | Pineau | FRA | 62 | 7 Jun |
| 5.40 | Karsten | Wichert | GDR | 68 | 27 Jun |
| 5.40 | Aleksandr | Chernyayev | SU | 60 | 16 Jul |
| 5.40 | Gianni | Stecchi | ITA | 58 | 22 Jul |
| 5.40 | Mikhail | Voronin | SU | 60 | 26 Jul |
| 5.40 | Zhivko | Zhechev (140) | BUL | 66 | 26 Jul |
| 5.40 | Alain | Auclair | FRA | 62 | 27 Jul |
| 5.40 | Yevgeniy | Ryutin | SU | 65 | 29 Jul |
| 5.40 | Daniil | Ivanov | BUL | 65 | 3 Aug |
| 5.40 | Viktor | Ryzhenkov | SU | 66 | 10 Aug |
| 5.40 | Zbigniew | Radzikowski | FRG | 60 | 10 Aug |
| 5.40 | Vadim | Tsepilov | SU | 64 | 15 Aug |
| 5.40 | Andrey | Gurov | SU | 66 | 16 Aug |
| 5.40 | Mikhail | Kashnov | SU | 66 | 20 Aug |
| 5.40 | Gábor | Molnár | HUN | 64 | 6 Sep |
| 5.40 | Igor | Yanchevskiy (150) | SU | 68 | 7 Sep |
| 5.40 | Zebiao | Ji | CHN | 64 | 30 Sep |
| 5.40 | Gennadiy | Kachkovskiy | SU | 64 | 5 Oct |
| 5.38 i | Matt | Kolb | USA | | 14 Mar |
| 5.38 | Dean | Starkey | USA | 67 | 11 May |
| 5.37 i | Roy | Hix | USA | 64 | 15 Feb |
| 5.35 | Randy | Hall | USA | 59 | 30 May |
| 5.35 | Keith | Stock | UK | 57 | 15 Jun |
| 5.35 | Pavel | Sluka | CS | 64 | 28 Jun |
| 5.35 | Jari | Holttinen | FIN | 65 | 13 Jul |
| 5.35 | Alain | Morineau(160) | FRA | 60 | 27 Jul |
| 5.35 | Leszek | Holownia | FRG | 57 | 12 Aug |
| 5.35 | Mark | Strawderman | USA | 60 | 12 Jan |
| 5.33 i | Bob | Phillips | USA | 59 | 22 Feb |
| 5.33 i | Tom | Riether | CHL | 64 | 26 Apr |
| 5.33 | Mike | Ledsome | USA | 62 | 26 Apr |
| 5.33 | Brent | Burns | USA | 69 | 31 Jul |
| 5.31 | Jeff | Gutteridge | UK | 56 | 7 Sep |

MEN 1986

| Mark | Name | | Nat | Yr | Pos | Meet | Venue | | Date |
|---|---|---|---|---|---|---|---|---|---|
| 5.30 i | Andrew | Ashurst | UK | 65 | 11 Jan | | | | |
| 5.30 i | Chisato | Itakura | JAP | 61 | 15 Jan | | | | |
| 5.30 i | Marc | Maes (170) | BEL | 59 | 22 Jan | | | | |
| 5.30 i | Yevgeniy | Laptev | SU | 62 | 25 Jan | | | | |
| 5.30 i | Aleksandr | Isachenko | SU | 65 | 25 Jan | | | | |
| 5.30 i | Andreas | Kramss | GDR | 62 | 25 Jan | | | | |
| 5.30 i | Oleg | Kritarov | SU | 64 | 26 Jan | | | | |
| 5.30 i | Dietmar | Wesp | FRG | 59 | 29 Jan | | | | |
| 5.30 i | Chet | Clodfelter | USA | 63 | 1 Mar | | | | |
| 5.30 | Doug | Jones | USA | 65 | 22 Mar | | | | |
| 5.30 | Doug | Wicks | USA | 63 | 12 Apr | | | | |
| 5.30 | David | Gatch | USA | 64 | 19 Apr | | | | |
| 5.30 | Bo | Verbick (180) | USA | 63 | 26 Apr | | | | |
| 5.30 | Eric | White | USA | | 26 Apr | | | | |
| 5.30 | Rainer | Lewin | GDR | 67 | 11 May | | | | |
| 5.30 | Jean-Marc | Tailhardat | FRA | 66 | 17 May | | | | |
| 5.30 | Craig | Hagan | USA | 64 | 17 May | | | | |
| 5.30 | Perry | Hottel | USA | 65 | 22 May | | | | |
| 5.30 | Valentin | Videv | BUL | 63 | 24 May | | | | |
| 5.30 | Todd | Verbick | USA | 65 | 24 May | | | | |
| 5.30 | Anthony | Curran | USA | 59 | 1 Jun | | | | |
| 5.30 | Enfa | Huang | CHN | 63 | 3 Jun | | | | |
| 5.30 | Harri | Palola (190) | FIN | 66 | 5 Jun | | | | |
| 5.30 | Sigurdur | | | | | | Sigurdsson | ICE 57 | 8 Jun |
| 5.30 | Ruben | | | | | | Camino | CUB 59 | 8 Jun |
| 5.30 | Aarne | | | | | | Rämö | FIN 58 | 10 Jun |
| 5.30 | Roman | | | | | | Rumyantsev | SU 66 | 15 Jun |
| 5.30 | Igor | | | | | | Burltikov | SU 62 | 20 Jun |
| 5.30 | Galin | | | | | | Nikolov | BUL 68 | 21 Jun |
| 5.30 | Brian | | | | | | Hooper | UK 53 | 21 Jun |
| 5.30 | Corrado | | | | | | Alagona | ITA 60 | 22 Jun |
| 5.30 | Vlastimil | | | | | | Jukl | CS 65 | 28 Jun |
| 5.30 | Oleg | | | | | | Shkerdin(200) | SU 68 | 1 Jul |
| 5.30 | Detlef | | | | | | de Raad | FRG 60 | 2 Jul |
| 5.30 | Antonio | | | | | | Colella | ITA 64 | 2 Jul |
| 5.30 | Aleksandr | | | | | | Gorbatenko | SU 66 | 26 Jul |
| 5.30 | Aleksey | | | | | | Starushchenko | SU 66 | 26 Jul |
| 5.30 | Bobby | | | | | | Williams | USA 61 | 28 Jul |
| 5.30 | Arkadiy | | | | | | Shkvira | SU 60 | 29 Jul |
| 5.30 | Giorgio | | | | | | Grassi | ITA 63 | 30 Jul |
| 5.30 | Vyacheslav | | | | | | Aristov | SU 66 | 10 Aug |
| 5.30 | Konstantin | | | | | | Adnachov | SU 66 | 6 Sep |
| 5.30 | Andrey | | | | | | Burov (210) | SU 64 | 7 Sep |

* Olson 5.80i 1 14 Feb; height remeasured as 5.79.

--------------------------------------------------------------------------------

| | 1 | 10 | 20 | 30 | 50 | 100 | Over 5.50 | Over 5.40 |
|---|---|---|---|---|---|---|---|---|
| 1982 | 5.75 | 5.70 | 5.60 | 5.55 | 5.51 | 5.33 | 64 | 85 |
| 1983 | 5.83 | 5.71 | 5.65 | 5.60 | 5.50 | 5.36 | 65 | 97 |
| 1984 | 5.94 | 5.75 | 5.66 | 5.60 | 5.55 | 5.41 | 84 | 129 |
| 1985 | 6.00 | 5.80 | 5.71 | 5.65 | 5.60 | 5.40 | 84 | 124 |
| 1986 | 6.01 | 5.80 | 5.70 | 5.70 | 5.60 | 5.50 | 103 | 152 |

--------------------------------------------------------------------------------

Best outdoor marks:

| Mark | | Name | | Pos | Meet | Venue | Date |
|---|---|---|---|---|---|---|---|
| 5.70 | | Quinon | | 1 | | Dôle | 26 Jun |
| 5.70 | | Kozakiewicz | | 4 | | Paris | 22 Jul |
| 5.65 | | Ishutin | | 2 | | Tashkent | 13 Jun |
| 5.65 | | Pursley | | 4 | WK | Zürich | 13 Aug |
| 5.59 | | Volz | | 2 | KansR | Lawrence | 19 Apr |
| 5.50 | | Parnov | | 1 | | Moskva | 9 May |
| 5.50 | | Yegorov | | 1 | | Alma-Ata | 31 May |
| 5.50 | | Stubblefield | | 2 | Jenner | San Jose | 31 May |
| 5.50 | | Houvion | | 4 | | Dijon | 14 Jun |
| 5.50 | G | Schmidt (10) | | 1 | | Salzburg | 20 Jun |
| 5.50 | M | Kolasa | | 5 | ISTAF | W Berlin | 15 Aug |
| 5.50 | | Olson (12) | | 3 | VD | Bruxelles | 5 Sep |
| 5.49 | | Lohr | 19 Apr | 5.40 | | Mann | 11 Jun |
| 5.40 | | Isakin | 17 May | 5.40 | R | Kolasa | 17 Jun |
| 5.40 | | Volmer | 29 May | 5.40 | | Troshin | 26 Jun |
| 5.40 | | Andreini | 4 Jun | 5.40 | | Klimczyk (20) | 27 Jun |

| Mark | Wind | Name | | Nat | Yr | Pos | Meet | Venue | Date |
|------|------|------|---|-----|-----|-----|------|-------|------|
| 5.40 | | | Ivanushkin | 28 Jun | | Ancillary jumps /over 5.80/: | | | |
| 5.40 | | | Bogatyryov | 16 Jul | | | | | |
| 5.40 | | | Trofimenko | 9 Aug | | 5.85 i | S | Bubka | 21 Feb |
| 5.40 | | | Heinrich | 20 Aug | | 5.85 i | S | Bubka | 28 Feb |
| 5.40 | | | Trandenkov | 18 Sep | | 5.85 | S | Bubka | 8 Jul |
| 5.30 | | | Clodfelter | 29 Mar | | 5.80 i | S | Bubka | 15 Jan |
| 5.30 | | | Strawderman | 26 Apr | | 5.80 i | S | Bubka | 8 Feb |
| 5.30 | | | Hix | 4 May | | 5.80 | | Dial | 20 Apr |
| 5.30 | | | Ashurst | 25 May | | 5.80 | | Dial | 25 Apr |
| 5.30 | | | Barella (30) | 19 Jul | | 5.80 | | Vigneron | 22 Jul |
| 5.30 | | | Itakura (31) | 14 Oct | | | | | |

Extra trial:

| | | | | | | | | | |
|------|------|------|---|-----|-----|-----|------|-------|------|
| 5.71 | | Hermann | Fehringer | AUT | 62 | - | | Vöcklabruck | 16 Aug |

Exhibition:

| | | | | | | | | | |
|------|------|------|---|-----|-----|-----|------|-------|------|
| 5.80 i | | Marian | Kolasa | POL | 59 | - | | Zweibrücken | 4 Feb |
| 5.71 ^ | | M | Kolasa | | | 1 | | Sopot | 2 Aug |
| 5.71 ^ | | Ryszard | Kolasa | POL | 64 | 2 | | Sopot | 2 Aug |
| 5.70 ^ | | Dave | Kenworthy | USA | 60 | 1 | | Mirano | 14 Sep |

| | | | | | | | |
|--------|---------|---------|------------|---------|----|----|----|
| 5.43^ | Günther | Lohre | FRG 53 24 May | ^made in irregular conditions | | | |
| 5.40^ | Andrea | Pegoraro | ITA 66 14 Sep | (Market squares /out of stadium) | | | |
| 5.35^ | Antonio | Colella | ITA 64 3 Sep | | | | |

**MEN 1986**

## LONG JUMP

| | | | | | | | | | |
|------|------|------|---|-----|-----|-----|------|-------|------|
| 8.61 | -0.3 | Robert | Emmiyan | SU | 65 | 1 | GWG | Moskva | 6 Jul |
| 8.50 | | Larry | Myricks | USA | 56 | 1 | | Rhede | 2 Jul |
| 8.49 | 0.9 | | Myricks | | | 1 | USOCF | Houston | 3 Aug |
| 8.47 | | Jaime | Jefferson | CUB | 62 | 1 | | Santiago/Cuba | 22 Feb |
| 8.41 | -0.2 | | Myricks | | | 2 | GWG | Moskva | 6 Jul |
| 8.41 | 0.0 | | Emmiyan | | | 1 | EC | Stuttgart | 29 Aug |
| 8.38 | 1.9 | | Emmiyan | | | 1 | v GDR | Tallinn | 21 Jun |
| 8.37 i | - | Carl | Lewis | USA | 61 | 1 | | E Rutherford | 8 Feb |
| 8.37 i | - | | Myricks | | | 1 | | New York | 14 Feb |
| 8.37 | -0.3 | | Emmiyan | | | 1 | Spart | Tashkent | 19 Sep |
| 8.35 | 1.5 | | Lewis | | | - | TAC | Eugene | 20 Jun |
| 8.34 i | - | | Emmiyan | | | 1 | NC | Moskva | 8 Feb |
| 8.34 | 0.1 | | Jefferson | | | 1 | CAC | Santiago/Dom | 30 Jun |
| 8.33 | 1.9 | Mike | Conley | USA | 62 | - | TAC | Eugene | 20 Jun |
| 8.32 i | - | | Emmiyan | | | 1 | EC | Madrid | 22 Feb |
| 8.32 | | Ubaldo | Duany | CUB | 60 | 2 | | Santiago/Cuba | 22 Feb |
| 8.31 i | - | | Conley | | | 1 | | Rosemont, IL | 16 Feb |
| 8.30 i | - | | Myricks | | | 2 | | E Rutherford | 8 Feb |
| 8.30 | 1.4 | | Myricks | | | 1 | ISTAF | W Berlin | 15 Aug |
| 8.29 i | - | | Conley | | | 2 | | New York | 14 Feb |
| 8.29 | | Grigoriy | Petrosyan | SU | 58 | 1 | | Yerevan | 20 Oct |
| 8.27 i | - | | Conley | | | 1 | TAC | New York | 28 Feb |
| 8.27 | 1.0 | | Myricks | | | 1 | BGP | Budapest | 11 Aug |
| 8.25 | 1.9 | Luis | Bueno | CUB | 69 | 1 | IbAm | Habana | 28 Sep |
| 8.24 i | - | László | Szalma | HUN | 57 | 2 | EC | Madrid | 22 Feb |

| Mark | Wind | Name | | Nat | Yr | Pos | Meet | Venue | Date |
|------|------|------|--|-----|----|-----|------|-------|------|
| 8.24 | 0.2 | Eric | Metcalf (10) | USA | 68 | 1 | NCAA | Indianapolis | 6 Jun |
| 8.24 | 1.0 | Giovanni | Evangelisti | ITA | 61 | 1 | | Caorle | 27 Jul |
| 8.24 | 1.9 | | Emmiyan | | | Q | EC | Stuttgart | 28 Aug |
| 8.23 | | | Lewis | | | - | | Houston | 4 May |
| 8.23 | | Zunrong | Chen (30/12) | CHN | 62 | 1 | | Beijing | 12 Apr |
| | | | | | | | | | |
| 8.20 | 0.7 | Sergey | Layevskiy | SU | 59 | 1 | Znam | Leningrad | 8 Jun |
| 8.20 | 0.2 | Yuriy | Samarin | SU | 60 | 1 | | Krasnodar | 22 Jun |
| 8.20 | | Valeriy | Bakunin | SU | 62 | 1 | | Volgograd | 6 Sep |
| 8.19 | | Nenad | Stekić | YUG | 51 | 1 | | Formia | 13 Jul |
| 8.17 i | - | Jan | Leitner | CS | 53 | 3 | EC | Madrid | 22 Feb |
| 8.17 i | - | Kenny | Harrison | USA | 65 | 1 | NCAA | Oklahoma City | 14 Mar |
| 8.17 | | Martin | Digno | CUB | 65 | 2 | | Habana | 8 Jun |
| 8.16 | 0.1 | Paul | Emordi (20) | NIG | 65 | 1 | | Houston | 21 Mar |
| | | | | | | | | | |
| 8.16 | 0.5 | Marco | Delonge | GDR | 66 | 1 | OD | Dresden | 3 Jul |
| 8.15 | 1.2 | Leroy | Burrell | USA | 67 | 1 | | Westwood | 19 Apr |
| 8.15 | 1.8 | Oleg | Semiraz | SU | 61 | 1· | | Kharkov | 14 May |
| 8.15 | 1.5 | Ron | Beer | GDR | 65 | 2 | OD | Dresden | 3 Jul |
| 8.14 | | Juan | Ortiz | CUB | 64 | 3 | | Santiago/Cuba | 22 Feb |
| 8.13 | 1.9 | Vadim | Kobylyanskiy | SU | 61 | 1 | | Poltava | 20 Jul |
| 8.12 i | - | Antonio | Corgos | SPA | 60 | 4 | EC | Madrid | 22 Feb |
| 8.12 | 0.5 | Mathias | Koch | GDR | 62 | 3 | OD | Dresden | 3 Jul |
| 8.12 | 1.8 | Gordon | Laine | USA | 58 | 1 | | Budapest | 6 Jul |
| 8.12 | 0.1 | Ralph | Spry (30) | USA | 60 | 1 | CISM | Ostia | 13 Sep |
| | | | | | | | | | |
| 8.11 | 0.7 | Lutz | Dombrowski | GDR | 59 | 4 | OD | Dresden | 3 Jul |
| 8.11 | 1.9 | Yuriy | Sharapanyuk | SU | 62 | 2 | | Poltava | 20 Jul |
| 8.11 | | Aleksandr | Aushev | SU | 60 | 1 | | Chelyabinsk | 9 Aug |
| 8.10 i | - | Ray | Humphrey | USA | 65 | 2 | NCAA | Oklahoma City | 14 Mar |
| 8.09 | 1.6 | Norbert | Brige | FRA | 64 | 1 | RoŠ | Praha | 24 Jun |
| 8.09 | 1.1 | Ian | James | CAN | 63 | 1 | v GDR | Karl-Marx-Stadt | 13 Jul |
| 8.09 | 0.5 | Gary | Honey | AUS | 59 | 1 | | Melbourne | 6 Dec |
| 8.08 | 1.0 | Mirosław | Hydel | POL | 63 | 2 | | Granada | 17 May |
| 8.08 | 1.0 | Igor | Kharitonov | SU | 62 | 2 | | Volgograd | 6 Sep |
| 8.07 | 0.2 | Andrzej | Klimaszewski (40) | POL | 60 | 3 | | Granada | 17 May |
| | | | | | | | | | |
| 8.07 | 1.9 | Tyrus | Jefferson | USA | 65 | - | TAC | Eugene | 20 Jun |
| 8.07 | 0.3 | Vladimir | Potapenko | SU | 61 | 2 | | Krasnodar | 22 Jun |
| 8.07 | 1.7 | Vladimir | Bobylev | SU | 66 | 3 | | Volgograd | 6 Sep |
| 8.06 | 0.2 | Sergey | Sorokin | SU | 63 | 4 | | Krasnodar | 22 Jun |
| 8.06 | -0.3 | Leonid | Voloshin | SU | 66 | 2 | Spart | Tashkent | 19 Sep |
| 8.05 | | Keith | Talley | USA | 64 | 1 | | Tuscaloosa | 29 Mar |
| 8.05 | 0.9 | Mike | Powell | USA | 63 | 1 | | Los Angeles | 23 May |
| 8.05 | | Yusuf | Alli | NIG | 50 | 1 | NC | Lagos | 22 Jun |
| 8.04 | 1.5 | Mike | McRae | USA | 55 | 1 | | San Jose | 19 Apr |
| 8.04 | 0.8 | Khristo | Markov (50) | BUL | 65 | - | Nar | Sofia | 31 May |
| | | | | | | | | | |
| 8.04 | 1.2 | Zdeněk | Hanáček | CS | 62 | 1 | GS | Ostrava | 11 Jun |
| 8.04 | | Fabrizio | Secchi | ITA | 58 | 1 | | Ravenna | 22 Jun |
| 8.03 | | Sergey | Podgainy | SU | 63 | 3 | | Lipetsk | 19 Jul |
| 8.03 | 0.4 | Jens | Hirschberg | GDR | 64 | 2 | GO | Dresden | 16 Aug |
| 8.02 | 1.6 | Gyula | Pálóczi | HUN | 62 | 1 | NC | Budapest | 16 Aug |
| 8.02 | -0.3 | Vakhtang | Minashvili | SU | 65 | 3 | Spart | Tashkent | 19 Sep |
| 8.00 i | - | Jesus | Olivan | SPA | 68 | 2 | v UK | Madrid | 1 Feb |
| 8.00 | 0.2 | Claude | Morinière | FRA | 60 | 1 | | Lisboa | 31 May |
| 8.00 | 1.0 | Stanisław | Jaskułka | POL | 58 | 2 | Kuso | Warszawa | 17 Jun |

| Mark | Wind | Name | | Nat | Yr | Pos | Meet | Venue | Date |
|------|------|------|------|-----|-----|-----|------|-------|------|
| 8.00 | 0.1 | Konstantin | Semykin (60) | SU | 60 | 5 | | Krasnodar | 22 Jun |
| 8.00 i | - | Oleg | Protsenko | SU | 63 | 1 | | Moskva | Dec |
| 7.99 | 1.8 | Uwe | Vogel | GDR | 58 | 5 | OD | Dresden | 3 Jul |
| 7.98 | | Ron | Waynes | USA | 60 | 1 | | Tempe | 5 Apr |
| 7.98 | 0.8 | Aleksandr | Yakovlev | SU | 57 | 2 | GS | Ostrava | 11 Jun |
| 7.98 | | Aleksey | Starkov | SU | 64 | 1 | | Leningrad | 14 Jun |
| 7.98 | 1.4 | Emil | Mellaard | HOL | 66 | 1 | NC | Amsterdam | 13 Jul |
| 7.98 | 2.0 | Atanas | Atanasov | BUL | 56 | 2 | | Sofia | 3 Aug |
| 7.98 | 2.0 | Vladimir | Ratushkov | SU | 65 | 2 | | Baku | 5 Oct |
| A7.97 | | Francois | Fouche | RSA | 63 | 1 | | Germiston | 22 Mar |
| 7.97 | 0.1 | Dietmar | Haaf (70) | FRG | 67 | 1 | NC | W Berlin | 13 Jul |
| 7.97 | 1.0 | Fred | Salle | UK | 64 | 1 | v Bel, | Aus Woluwe | 13 Jul |
| 7.96 | 0.4 | Jerzy | Żeligowski | POL | 58 | 4 | | Granada | 17 May |
| 7.95 | 0.3 | Atanas | Chochev | BUL | 57 | - | Nar | Sofia | 31 May |
| 7.95 | 0.5 | Igor | Dovoino | SU | 64 | 1 | | Kiev | 31 Aug |
| 7.94 i | - | Claudio | Cherubini | ITA | 60 | 2 | | Firenze | 22 Jan |
| 7.94 | | Uchenna | Agu | USA | 64 | 3 | TexR | Austin | 4 Apr |
| 7.94 | | Olivier | Cadier | BRA | 60 | 1 | | Sao Paulo | 13 Jul |
| 7.94 | 1.8 | Ronald | Desruelles | BEL | 55 | 1 | NC | Bruxelles | 10 Aug |
| 7.94 | -0.8 | Jong-Il | Kim | SKO | 62 | 1 | AsiG | Seoul | 4 Oct |
| 7.93 i | - | Dannie | Jackson (80) | USA | 58 | 4 | TAC | New York | 28 Feb |
| 7.93 | · | Malcolmb | Branham | USA | 66 | 1 | | Clarksville | 2 May |
| 7.93 | 1.8 | Dragan | Despotović | YUG | 62 | 1 | | Maribor | 24 May |
| 7.93 | | Lahor | Marinović | YUG | 67 | 1 | | Split | 7 Jun |
| 7.93 | 0.8 | Krzysztof | Kaniecki | POL | 65 | 1 | | Poznan | 25 Aug |
| 7.92 | | Mike | Davis | USA | 64 | 1 | | N Little Rock | 12 Apr |
| 7.92 | 1.7 | Yuhuang | Liu | CHN | 59 | 3 | | Kohriyama | 4 May |
| 7.92 | 0.8 | Yan | Pang | CHN | 63 | 5 | RoŠ | Praha | 24 Jun |
| 7.92 | 1.1 | Eduard | Belozerskikh | SU | 65 | 1 | | Alma-Ata | 30 Aug |
| 7.92 | 0.6 | Vladimir | Cherkasov | SU | 63 | 5 | | Volgograd | 6 Sep |
| 7.92 | 0.3 | Junichi | Usui (90) | JAP | 57 | 2 | AsiG | Seoul | 4 Oct |
| 7.92 | | Michael | Morgan | AUS | 66 | 1 | | Brisbane | 8 Nov |
| 7.91 | | Frans | Maas | HOL | 64 | 2 | | Tempe | 5 Apr |
| 7.91 | | Shijie | Wang | CHN | 63 | | | Beijing | 12 Apr |
| 7.91 | 1.1 | Vladimir | Zubrilin | SU | 63 | 2 | | Moskva | 9 Aug |
| 7.91 | 1.1 | Ivo | Krsek | CS | 67 | 1 | | Praha | 19 Aug |
| 7.90 i | - | Greg | Neal | USA | 63 | 1 | | Fairfax, VA | 1 Feb |
| 7.90 i | - | Brian | Cooper | USA | 65 | 1 | | Monroe, LA | 14 Feb |
| 7.90 i | - | David | Coney | USA | 63 | 1 | | Univ Park, PA | 1 Mar |
| 7.90 | | Eric | Barber | USA | 63 | 1 | | Natchitoches | 8 Mar |
| 7.90 | | Lyndon | Sands (100) | BAH | 64 | 5 | NCAA | Indianapolis | 6 Jun |
| 7.90 | 0.7 | Gian Carlo | Biscarini | ITA | 62 | 1 | | Perugia | 11 Jun |
| 7.90 | 0.9 | Derrick | Brown (102) | UK | 63 | 2 | WG | Helsinki | 7 Jul |

| Mark | Wind | Name | | | | | Mark | | Name | | |
|------|------|------|------|-----|-----|-----|------|------|------|-----|-----|
| 7.89 | 1.2 | Markus | Kessler | FRG 62 | 13 Jun | | 7.86 | | Mihail | Rodosthenous | CYP 59 | 25 May |
| A7.88 i | - | Greg | Foster II | USA 64 | 1 Feb | | 7.86 | | Rob | Boulware | USA 64 | 31 May |
| 7.88 | | Lisandro | Milhet | CUB 67 | 22 Feb | | 7.86 | | Joakim | Assenmacher | FRG 63 | 28 Jun |
| 7.88 | | Andre | Ester | USA 65 | 25 Apr | | 7.86 | | Teddy | Steirmayr | AUT 64 | 15 Aug |
| 7.87 | | Moses | Kiyai | KEN 60 | 6 Jun | | 7.86 | | Badara | Mbengue | SEN 66 | 31 Aug |
| 7.86 i | - | Sergey | Zaozerskiy | SU 64 | 12 Jan | | 7.85 i | - | Scott | Sanders | USA 67 | 31 Jan |
| 7.86 i | - | Eugene | Profit | USA 64 | 8 Mar | | 7.85 i | - | Maris | Bruziks | SU 62 | 12 Feb |
| 7.86 | 0.0 | Sharrieff | Hazim (110) | USA 64 | 23 May | | 7.85 i | - | Noboru | Sasano | JAP 59 | 5 Mar |
| | | | | | | | 7.85 | | J R | Alexander | USA 63 | 12 Apr |
| | | | | | | | 7.85 | | Won-Jin | Kim (120) | SKO 68 | 24 May |

MEN 1986

| Mark | Wind | Name | | Nat | Yr | Pos | Meet | Venue | | Date |
|------|------|------|---|-----|----|----|------|-------|---|------|
| 7.85 | 2.0 | Włodzimierz | Włodarczyk | POL | 57 | | | 3 | | Jun |
| 7.85 | 0.0 | Sergey | Vasilenko | SU | 65 | | | 28 | | Jun |
| 7.85 | | Christian | Thomas | FRG | 65 | | | 3 | | Aug |
| 7.85 | 1.9 | Nobuo | Toyota | JAP | 67 | | | 5 | | Dec |
| 7.84 i | - | Leotha | Stanley | USA | 56 | | | 16 | | Feb |
| 7.84 | | Shamil | Abbyasov | SU | 57 | | | 19 | | Jul |
| 7.84 | 1.5 | Thomas | Wolf | GDR | 67 | | | 9 | | Aug |
| 7.84 | 1.4 | Ján | Čado | CS | 63 | | | 6 | | Sep |
| 7.83 | | Joey | Wells | BAH | 65 | | | 19 | | Apr |
| 7.83 | | Krzysztof | Zuch    (130) | POL | 62 | | | 17 | | May |
| 7.83 | 0.0 | René | Gloor | SWZ | 56 | | | 20 | | Aug |
| 7.83 | | Torsten | Murr | FRG | 63 | | | 20 | | Sep |
| 7.83 | 2.0 | Christian | Plaziat | FRA | 63 | | | 24 | | Oct |
| 7.82 i | - | Artem | Tsygankov | SU | 64 | | | 8 | | Feb |
| 7.82 | | Kevin | Adkins | USA | 68 | | | 14 | | Jun |
| 7.82 | | Albert | Sagdeyev | SU | 63 | | | 30 | | Jun |
| 7.82 | | Oleg | Mamayev | SU | 58 | | | 19 | | Jul |
| 7.82 | 0.0 | Winfried | Klepsch | FRG | 56 | | | 26 | | Jul |
| 7.82 | | Sergey | Borisevich | SU | 63 | | | 31 | | Aug |
| 7.81 i | - | Ivan | Mafienya(140) | SU | 57 | | | 11 | | Jan |
| 7.81 i | - | Vadim | Pugachov | SU | 63 | | | 1 | | Feb |
| 7.81 | 1.4 | David | Culbert | AUS | 67 | | | 16 | | Mar |
| 7.81 | | Daley | Thompson | UK | 58 | | | 17 | | May |
| 7.81 | -0.3 | Edrick | Floreal | CAN | 66 | | | 21 | | Jun |
| 7.81 | -1.1 | Elmer | Williams | PR | 64 | | | 30 | | Jun |
| 7.81 | 1.2 | Arunas | Voitovich | SU | 65 | | | 15 | | Jul |
| 7.81 | 1.3 | Béla | Vágó | HUN | 62 | | | 16 | | Aug |
| A7.81 | | Nico | Schutte | RSA | 64 | | | 1 | | Nov |
| 7.80 | | Kayode | Elegbede | NIG | 55 | | | 7 | | Apr |
| 7.80 | | Haralambos | Giannoulis | GRE | 63 | | | | | |
| | | | (150) | | | | | | | |
| 7.80 | | Aivo | Möttus | SU | 61 | | | 18 | | Jun |
| 7.80 | | Jens | Petersson | GDR | 64 | | | 6 | | Jul |
| 7.80 | -0.6 | Viktor | Rudenik | SU | 64 | | | 16 | | Jul |
| 7.80 | 0.0 | Robert | Cannon | USA | 58 | | | 22 | | Jul |
| 7.79 i | - | Chris | Bean | USA | 62 | | | 17 | | Jan |
| 7.79 | | Dimitrios | Araouzos | CYP | 61 | | | 16 | | May |
| 7.79 | | Thomas | Weatherspoon | USA | 62 | | | 29 | | May |
| 7.79 | | Andreas | Schlindwein | FRG | 65 | | | 16 | | Aug |
| 7.79 | | Sergey | Kargin | SU | 62 | | | 6 | | Sep |
| 7.79 | | Aleksandr | Shevchuk | SU | 65 | | | 11 | | Oct |
| | | | (160) | | | | | | | |
| 7.78 i | - | John | Register | USA | 65 | | | 25 | | Jan |
| 7.78 | | Julius | Meekins | USA | | | | | 19 | | Apr |
| 7.78 | 1.1 | Frank-Peter | Külske | GDR | 60 | | | 1 | | Jun |
| 7.78 | | Antonio | Zuncheddu | ITA | 65 | | | 28 | | Jun |
| 7.78 | 1.2 | Rod | Tolbert | USA | 67 | | | 28 | | Jun |
| 7.78 | | Valeriy | Sukhanov | SU | 60 | | | 30 | | Jun |
| 7.78 | 0.2 | Jeroen | Fischer | BEL | 66 | | | 10 | | Aug |
| 7.78 | | Osvaldo | Larrondo | CUB | 64 | | | 28 | | Sep |
| 7.77 i | - | Rainer | Sonnenburg | FRG | 60 | | | 8 | | Feb |
| 7.77 | | Verdell | Oliver (170) | USA | 66 | | | 5 | | Apr |
| 7.77 | 0.5 | Sergey | Rodin | SU | 63 | | | 9 | | May |
| 7.77 | | Dezalya | Manns | USA | 64 | | | 17 | | May |
| 7.77 | | John | Alexander | USA | | | | | 17 | | May |
| 7.77 | | Aleksey | Khomich | SU | 63 | | | 26 | | May |
| 7.77 | | Aleksandr | Nesterenko | SU | 63 | | | 14 | | Jun |
| 7.77 | 0.6 | Javier | San Adrian | SPA | 67 | | | 15 | | Jun |
| 7.77 | 1.2 | Alfonz | Hertelendi | HUN | 62 | | | 16 | | Aug |
| 7.77 | | Lianghua | Li | CHN | 63 | | | 23 | | Oct |
| 7.76 i | - | Georgi | Pomashki | BUL | 60 | | | 12 | | Jan |
| 7.76 i | - | Gennadiy | Danilov (180) | SU | 61 | | | 19 | | Jan |
| 7.76 i | - | Danny | Holland | USA | 66 | | | 21 | | Feb |
| 7.76 | | Juris | Tone | SU | 61 | | | 13 | | May |
| 7.76 | | Igor | Aleksandrov | SU | 57 | | | 14 | | Jun |
| 7.76 | | Babou | Saine | GAM | 67 | | | 28 | | Jun |
| 7.76 | | Michael | Becker | FRG | 65 | | | 28 | | Jun |
| 7.75 i | - | Oleg | Kurbatov | SU | 67 | | | 25 | | Jan |
| 7.75 i | - | Ray | Hawkins | USA | | | | | 28 | | Feb |
| 7.75 | 1.9 | Grigoriy | Degtyarov | SU | 58 | | | 24 | | May |
| 7.75 | | Edward | Manderson | CAY | 68 | | | 21 | | Jun |
| 7.75 | 1.2 | Kyle | McDuffie(190) | CAN | 60 | | | 21 | | Jun |
| 7.75 | | Jörg | Klocke | FRG | 60 | | | 28 | | Jun |
| 7.75 | | Igor | Streltsov | SU | 65 | | | | | |
| 7.75 | | Nikolay | Mamchur | SU | 63 | | | | | |
| 7.75 | 0.0 | Jürgen | Hingsen | FRG | 58 | | | 13 | | Jul |
| 7.75 | | Peter | Rouhi | FRG | 66 | | | 3 | | Aug |
| 7.75 | | Laurentiu | Budur | RUM | 63 | | | 8 | | Aug |
| 7.75 | 0.7 | Ivan | Tuparov | BUL | 59 | | | 14 | | Aug |
| 7.75 | 0.0 | Aleksandr | Savenok (198) | SU | 67 | | | 6 | | Sep |

T Jefferson (8.07 1.9) also did 8.07 1.1 2 USOCF Houston 3 Aug; Mellaard (7.98 1.4) also did 7.98 -0.9 1 Koblenz 6 Aug; Wang (7.91) also did 7.91 1.8 6 Roš Praha 24 Jun; Kim (7.85) also did 7.85 5 Dec.

---

| | 1 | 10 | 20 | 30 | 50 | 100 | Over 8.00 | Over 7.80 |
|------|------|------|------|------|------|------|------|------|
| 1982 | 8.76 | 8.19 | 8.12 | 8.07 | 7.95 | 7.85 | 42 | 125 |
| 1983 | 8.79 | 8.19 | 8.10 | 8.06 | 7.99 | 7.86 | 47 | 135 |
| 1984 | 8.79 | 8.27 | 8.14 | 8.10 | 8.02 | 7.90 | 58 | 157 |
| 1985 | 8.62 | 8.23 | 8.14 | 8.11 | 8.03 | 7.89 | 60 | 149 |
| 1986 | 8.61 | 8.24 | 8.16 | 8.12 | 8.04 | 7.90 | 61 | 154 |

---

| Mark | Wind | Name | | Nat | Yr | Pos | Meet | Venue | | Date |
|------|------|------|------|-----|----|-----|------|-------|------|------|

Best outdoor marks:

| | | | | | | | | | |
|---|---|---|---|---|---|---|---|---|---|
| 8.11 | | | Harrison | | | 1 | KansR | Lawrence | 18 Apr |
| 8.08 | -0.4 | | Corgos | | | 1 | | Granada | 17 May |
| 8.04 | 0.0 | | Leitner | | | 3 | Roš | Praha | 24 Jun |
| 8.03 | 2.0 | | Szalma | | | – | | Budapest | 12 Jul |
| 7.92 | 2.0 | | Jackson | | | 5 | TAC | Eugene | 20 Jun |
| 7.84 | 0.6 | Neal | 17 May | 7.77 | 0.8 | | | Tsygankov | 18 Sep |
| 7.81 | 2.0 | Zaozerskiy | 6 Sep | 7.76 | -0.8 | | | Profit | 25 Apr |
| 7.78 | 0.8 | Sasano | 31 May | 7.76 | | | | Bean (11) | 16 May |

Ancillary jumps /over 8.23/:

| | | | | | | | | | |
|---|---|---|---|---|---|---|---|---|---|
| 8.39 | | Myricks | 2 Jul | 8.27 | i – | | | Myricks | 14 Feb |
| 8.37 | | Myricks | 2 Jul | | | | | | |
| 8.37 | -0.1 | Myricks | 6 Jul | 8.25 | 0.2 | | | Emmiyan | 6 Jul |
| 8.35 | 1.8 | Lewis | 20 Jun | 8.25 | 0.1 | | | Myricks | 3 Aug |
| 8.34 | 0.1 | Myricks | 3 Aug | 8.24 | 2.0 | | | Emmiyan | 21 Jun |
| 8.31 | | Myricks | 2 Jul | 8.24 | 0.0 | | | Myricks | 11 Aug |
| 8.29 | i – | Emmiyan | 8 Feb | 8.24 | 0.6 | | | Myricks | 11 Aug |
| 8.29 | i – | Emmiyan | 22 Feb | 8.23 | 0.7 | | | Myricks | 15 Aug |
| 8.29 | 0.0 | Emmiyan | 29 Aug | | | | | | |

Marks made with assisting wind > 2 m/s :

| | | | | | | | | | |
|---|---|---|---|---|---|---|---|---|---|
| 8.67 | 3.3 | Carl | Lewis | USA | 61 | 1 | TAC | Eugene | 20 Jun |
| 8.63 | 3.9 | Mike | Conley | USA | 62 | 2 | TAC | Eugene | 20 Jun |
| 8.55 | 2.3 | Larry | Myricks | USA | 56 | 1 | | Modesto, CA | 10 May |
| 8.47 | 3.4 | | Myricks | | | 3 | TAC | Eugene | 20 Jun |
| 8.34 | 3.6 | | Lewis | | | Q | TAC | Eugene | 19 Jun |
| 8.33 | 3.0 | | Lewis | | | 1 | MSR | Walnut, CA | 27 Apr |
| 8.31 | | Mike | Davis | USA | 64 | 1 | | Houston | 18 May |
| 8.26 | | | Lewis (8/4) | | | 1 | | Houston | 4 May |
| 8.22 | 3.0 | Mike | Powell | USA | 63 | 2 | MSR | Walnut, CA | 27 Apr |
| 8.22 | | Paul | Emordi | NIG | 65 | 1 | | Houston | 9 May |
| 8.21 | 2.1 | Atanas | Chochev | BUL | 57 | 1 | Nar | Sofia | 31 May |
| 8.21 | 2.3 | Tyrus | Jefferson | USA | 65 | 4 | TAC | Eugene | 20 Jun |
| 8.20 | | Moses | Kiyai | KEN | 60 | 1 | DrakeR | Des Moines | 25 Apr |
| 8.16 | 2.9 | Khristo | Markov (10) | BUL | 65 | 2 | Nar | Sofia | 31 May |
| 8.16 | 6.4 | Stanisław | Jaskułka | POL | 58 | 1 | NC | Grudziadz | 29 Jun |
| 8.12 | 2.3 | Gary | Honey | AUS | 59 | 1 | | Melbourne | 23 Feb |
| 8.12 | | Derrick | Brown | UK | 63 | 1 | | Loughborough | 14 Jun |
| 8.12 | 5.8 | Jerzy | Żeligowski | POL | 58 | 2 | NC | Grudziadz | 29 Jun |
| 8.12 | 4.7 | Lutz | Dombrowski | GDR | 59 | 3 | NC | Jena | 29 Jun |
| 8.11 | 3.4 | Andrzej | Klimaszewski | POL | 60 | 1 | Kuso | Warszawa | 17 Jun |
| 8.08 | 2.4 | Dannie | Jackson | USA | 58 | 1 | | Kohriyama | 4 May |
| 8.07 | 2.3 | Aivo | Mõttus | SU | 61 | 1 | | Riga | 14 Jun |
| 8.06 | 2.8 | Jong-Il | Kim | SKO | 62 | 4 | MSR | Walnut, CA | 27 Apr |
| 8.06 | 6.3 | Scott | Sanders (20) | USA | 67 | 2 | TAC-j | Towson, MD | 28 Jun |
| 8.06 | 5.4 | Włodzimierz | Włodarczyk | POL | 57 | 5 | NC | Grudziadz | 29 Jun |
| 8.04 | 3.6 | Yuhuang | Liu | CHN | 59 | 1 | | Shizuoka | 27 Apr |
| 8.04 | | Kerry | Therwhanger | USA | 63 | 1 | | Abilene | 15 May |
| 8.04 | 4.0 | Ivo | Krsek | CS | 67 | 1 | | Recklinghausen | 3 Aug |
| 8.02 | | Ray | Mitchell | USA | 63 | 1 | | Wichita | 3 May |

| Mark | Wind | Name | | Nat | Yr | Pos | Meet | Venue | Date |
|------|------|------|--|-----|----|-----|------|-------|------|
| A8.02 | 5.0 | Francois | Fouche | RSA | 63 | 1 | | Welkom | 22 Nov |
| 8.01 | 2.7 | Michael | Morgan | AUS | 66 | 2 | | Melbourne | 6 Dec |
| 8.00 | 3.0 | Sergey | Zaozerskiy | SU | 64 | 4 | | Volgograd | 6 Sep |
| 7.98 | | Lyndon | Sands | BAH | 64 | 3 | | Houston | 18 May |
| 7.97 | | Chris | Walker (30) | USA | 65 | 1 | | College Sta, TX | 29 Mar |
| | | | | | | | | | |
| 7.97 | 2.6 | Vernon | George | USA | 64 | Q | TAC | Eugene | 19 Jun |
| 7.96 | | Joey | Wells | BAH | 65 | 2 | | Arlington | 10 May |
| 7.96 | 4.4 | Colin | Jackson | UK | 67 | 1 | | Vic/Barcelona | 17 May |
| 7.94 | 3.9 | John | King | UK | 63 | 2 | AAA | London | 20 Jun |
| 7.93 | 2.8 | Arunas | Voitovich | SU | 65 | 2 | | Riga | 14 Jun |
| 7.93 | 2.2 | David | Burgess | UK | 62 | 1 | | Hendon | 15 Jun |
| 7.93 | 3.4 | Nobuo | Toyota | JAP | 67 | 1 | AsiC-j | Djakarta | 5 Dec |
| 7.92 | | Sharrieff | Hazim | USA | 64 | 2 | | Wichita | 3 May |
| 7.91 | 3.0 | Lisandro | Milhet | CUB | 67 | 1 | | Salamanca | 12 Jul |
| 7.91 | | Albert | Sagdeyev (40) | SU | 63 | 6 | | Volgograd | 6 Sep |

| Mark | Wind | Name | | Nat | Yr | Date | Mark | Wind | Name | | Nat | Yr | Date |
|------|------|------|--|-----|----|------|------|------|------|--|-----|----|------|
| 7.90 | | John | Bodine | USA | 63 | 3 May | 7.79 | 2.5 | John | Tillman | USA | 65 | 17 May |
| 7.90 | 2.5 | Viktor | Rudenik | SU | 64 | 14 Jun | 7.79 | 2.5 | Kyle | McDuffie | CAN | 60 | 31 Jul |
| 7.90 | 4.8 | Zbigniew | Maksymiuk | POL | 61 | 29 Jun | 7.78 | | Phil | Morris | JAM | 63 | 29 Mar |
| 7.89 | | Edrick | Floreal | CAN | 66 | 25 Apr | 7.78 | | Greg | Henderson | USA | | 11 Apr |
| 7.89 | 4.0 | John | Shepherd | UK | 61 | 20 Jun | 7.78 | 5.6 | Konstantin | Krause | GDR | 67 | 4 May |
| 7.89 | 2.8 | Jürgen | Hingsen | FRG | 58 | 27 Aug | 7.78 | 2.8 | Stoyan | Stanchev | BUL | 67 | 31 May |
| 7.87 | | Craig | Stewart | USA | 62 | 10 May | 7.78 | 2.3 | Tomm | Wislǿff | NOR | 62 | 21 Jun |
| 7.86 | 2.4 | Sergey | Vasilenko | SU | 65 | 23 May | 7.78 | | Róbert | Széli | CS | 65 | 3 Aug |
| 7.85 | 2.2 | Koji | Umemoto | JAP | 61 | 31 May | 7.77 | | Dennis | McWhinney | JAM | | 9 May |
| 7.85 | 2.3 | Kevin | Adkins (50) | USA | 68 | 14 Jun | 7.77 | | Steve | Pope (70) | USA | | 15 May |
| | | | | | | | | | | | | | |
| 7.85 | 2.7 | Torsten | Voss | GDR | 63 | 27 Aug | 7.76 | 2.7 | Guido | Kratschmer | FRG | 53 | 24 May |
| 7.84 | | Rickey | Dobbins | USA | | 1 Mar | | | | (71) | | | |
| 7.84 | 2.8 | Ivan | Tuparov | BUL | 59 | 31 May | | | | | | | |
| 7.83 | | Bernd | Rebischke | FRG | 55 | 13 Jun | Ancillary jumps /over 8.23/: | | | | | | |
| 7.83 | 2.5 | Vasile | Dima | RUM | 58 | 6 Jul | | | | | | | |
| 7.83 | | Osvaldo | Larrondo | CUB | 64 | 28 Sep | 8.44 | | | Myricks | | | 10 May |
| 7.82 | 4.0 | Femi | Abejide | UK | 65 | 20 Jun | 8.29 | | | Myricks | | | 10 May |
| 7.82 | 3.3 | Einar | Sagli | NOR | 58 | 12 Sep | 8.29 | 3.3 | | Emmiyan | | | 21 Jun |
| 7.80 | 3.0 | Krzysztof | Chlond | POL | 65 | 7 Sep | 8.28 | 2.5 | | Lewis | | | 27 Apr |
| 7.79 | | Don | Carter (60) | USA | | 18 Apr | | | | | | | |

# TRIPLE JUMP

| Mark | Wind | Name | | Nat | Yr | Pos | Meet | Venue | Date |
|------|------|------|--|-----|----|-----|------|-------|------|
| 17.80 | 0.6 | Khristo | Markov | BUL | 65 | 1 | BGP | Budapest | 11 Aug |
| 17.78 | 1.0 | Nikolay | Musiyenko | SU | 59 | 1 | Znam | Leningrad | 7 Jun |
| 17.78 | 0.6 | Lazaro | Betancourt | CUB | 63 | 1 | Barr | Habana | 15 Jun |
| 17.69 | 0.2 | Mike | Conley | USA | 62 | 1 | GWG | Moskva | 9 Jul |
| 17.66 | 1.9 | | Markov | | | 1 | EC | Stuttgart | 30 Aug |
| 17.62 | 1.1 | | Markov | | | 1 | NC | Sofia | 14 Aug |
| 17.59 | -2.1 | Oleg | Protsenko | SU | 63 | 1 | NC | Kiev | 17 Jul |
| A17.58 | 0.0 | Willie | Banks | USA | 56 | 1 | | El Paso | 20 Apr |
| 17.55 | -0.6 | | Conley | | | 1 | WK | Zürich | 13 Aug |
| 17.54 | i - | Maris | Bruziks | SU | 62 | 1 | EC | Madrid | 23 Feb |
| | | | | | | | | | |
| 17.53 | 1.0 | Gennadiy | Valyukevich | SU | 58 | 1 | | Erfurt | 1 Jun |
| 17.50 | i - | Charles | Simpkins | USA | 63 | 1 | | Los Angeles | 17 Jan |
| 17.50 | 0.1 | | Conley | | | 1 | USOCF | Houston | 2 Aug |
| 17.45 | | | Betancourt | | | 1 | | Santiago/Cuba | 23 Feb |
| 17.43 | i - | Vladimir | Inozemtsev (10) | SU | 64 | 1 | | Kiev | 26 Jan |

| Mark | Wind | Name | | Nat | Yr | Pos | Meet | Venue | Date |
|------|------|------|------|-----|----|----|------|-------|------|
| 17.43 | 0.4 | | Valyukevich | | | 2 | NC | Kiev | 17 Jul |
| 17.42 | i - | | Simpkins | | | 1 | | San Diego | 23 Feb |
| 17.42 | 1.7 | | Simpkins | | | - | TAC | Eugene | 21 Jun |
| 17.42 | 0.9 | | Simpkins | | | 1 | Bisl | Oslo | 5 Jul |
| 17.41 | 1.4 | | Conley | | | 1 | | Cagliari | 14 Sep |
| 17.35 | i - | | Musiyenko | | | 1 | NC | Moskva | 7 Feb |
| 17.35 | 1.2 | | Valyukevich | | | - | Znam | Leningrad | 7 Jun |
| 17.35 | -0.1 | | Markov | | | 2 | GWG | Moskva | 9 Jul |
| 17.34 | i - | | Conley | | | 1 | TAC | New York | 28 Feb |
| 17.34 | 0.5 | | Musiyenko | | | 1 | v GDR | Tallinn | 22 Jun |
| 17.33 | -0.1 | | Musiyenko | | | 3 | GWG | Moskva | 9 Jul |
| 17.33 | 1.1 | | Bruziks | | | 2 | EC | Stuttgart | 30 Aug |
| 17.32 | i - | | Bruziks | | | 1 | | Vilnius | 11 Jan |
| 17.32 | -1.6 | | Protsenko | | | 2 | WK | Zürich | 13 Aug |
| 17.31 | | | Banks (30/10) | | | - | Jenner | San Jose | 31 May |
| 17.26 | 0.2 | Aleksandr | Yakovlev | SU | 57 | 1 | PTS | Bratislava | 14 Jun |
| 17.25 | | Aleksandr | Kovalenko | SU | 63 | 1 | | Moskva | 11 May |
| 17.22 | | Yevgeniy | Anikin | SU | 58 | 1 | | Sochi | 26 Apr |
| 17.22 | 2.0 | Aleksandr | Leonov | SU | 62 | 3 | Znam | Leningrad | 7 Jun |
| 17.22 | 0.0 | Vyacheslav | Bordukov | SU | 59 | 1 | | Donetsk | 7 Sep |
| 17.21 | i - | Vladimir | Plekhanov | SU | 58 | 2 | EC | Madrid | 23 Feb |
| 17.20 | 0.7 | Igor | Lapshin | SU | 63 | 4 | Znam | Leningrad | 7 Jun |
| 17.18 | | Jorge | Reyna | CUB | 63 | 2 | | Santiago/Cuba | 23 Feb |
| 17.18 | -0.7 | Joseph | Taiwo | NIG | 59 | 2 | ASV | Köln | 17 Aug |
| 17.17 | 1.0 | Dirk | Gamlin (20) | GDR | 63 | 1 | GO | Dresden | 16 Aug |
| 17.15 | 0.9 | Norifumi | Yamashita | JAP | 62 | 1 | NC | Tokyo | 1 Jun |
| 17.13 | 1.9 | Aleksandr | Pokusayev | SU | 60 | 1 | | Taganrog | 6 Jul |
| 17.13 | 0.0 | Serge | Hélan | FRA | 64 | 3 | ASV | Köln | 17 Aug |
| 17.12 | 0.0 | Oleg | Sokirkin | SU | 66 | 1 | | Alma-Ata | 11 May |
| 17.12 | | Nikolay | Mamchur | SU | 63 | | | | |
| 17.12 | -0.3 | Ajayi | Agbebaku | NIG | 55 | 4 | WK | Zürich | 13 Aug |
| 17.12 | 2.0 | Dario | Badinelli | ITA | 60 | 2 | | Cagliari | 14 Sep |
| 17.11 | 1.1 | Jacek | Pastusinski | POL | 64 | 1 | Kuso | Warszawa | 17 Jun |
| 17.07 | | Kenny | Harrison | USA | 65 | 1 | NCAA | Indianapolis | 7 Jun |
| 17.05 | | Paul | Emordi (30) | NIG | 65 | Q | NCAA | Indianapolis | 5 Jun |
| 17.05 | | Frank | Rutherford | BAH | 64 | 2 | NCAA | Indianapolis | 7 Jun |
| 17.05 | 1.2 | Sergey | Tkachov | SU | 58 | 2 | | Taganrog | 6 Jul |
| 17.04 | 0.3 | Vasif | Asadov | SU | 65 | 5 | Znam | Leningrad | 7 Jun |
| 17.04 | 1.6 | Ján | Čado | CS | 63 | 1 | NC | Bratislava | 12 Jul |
| 17.02 | | Norbert | Elliott | BAH | 62 | 1 | NC | Nassau | 14 Jun |
| 17.02 | 1.6 | Robert | Cannon | USA | 58 | 2 | | Gavle | 28 Jul |
| 17.02 | 0.9 | Volker | Mai | GDR | 66 | 2 | GO | Dresden | 16 Aug |
| 17.02 | 0.6 | Andrey | Kayukov | SU | 64 | 1 | | Volgograd | 7 Sep |
| 17.00 | | Igor | Usov | SU | 61 | 2 | | Alma-Ata | 11 May |
| 16.99 | | Al | Joyner (40) | USA | 60 | 4 | Pre | Eugene | 7 Jun |
| 16.99 | 0.3 | Georgi | Pomashki | BUL | 60 | 4 | EC | Stuttgart | 30 Aug |
| 16.98 | -0.2 | Parkev | Grigoryan | SU | 65 | 4 | Spart | Tashkent | 17 Sep |
| 16.97 | 0.2 | Igor | Parygin | SU | 67 | 1 | WC-j | Athinai | 20 Jul |
| 16.97 | 0.5 | Jörg | Elbe | GDR | 64 | 3 | GO | Dresden | 16 Aug |
| 16.97 | 0.3 | Ravil | Aminov | SU | 63 | 2 | | Volgograd | 7 Sep |
| 16.96 | -1.5 | Vasiliy | Grishchenkov | SU | 58 | 5 | NC | Kiev | 17 Jul |
| 16.96 | 0.9 | Arne | Holm | SWE | 61 | - | v Fin | Helsinki | 10 Aug |

MEN 1986

| Mark | Wind | Name | | Nat | Yr | Pos | Meet | Venue | Date |
|------|------|------|--|-----|----|----|------|-------|------|
| 16.94 | -0.9 | Ralf | Jaros | FRG | 65 | 1 | | Fürth | 15 Jun |
| 16.94 | 0.8 | Ivan | Slanař | CS | 61 | 1 | | Praha | 17 Aug |
| 16.93 | i - | Béla | Bakosi (50) | HUN | 57 | 3 | EC | Madrid | 23 Feb |
| | | | | | | | | | |
| 16.93 | 1.1 | Wolfgang | Zinser | FRG | 64 | 1 | | Düsseldorf | 18 May |
| 16.92 | -0.1 | Mihai | Ene | RUM | 60 | 1 | RumIC | Bucureşti | 15 Jun |
| 16.92 | 2.0 | Milan | Mikuláš | CS | 63 | 2 | NC | Bratislava | 12 Jul |
| 16.91 | | Ray | Kimble | USA | 53 | - | | Modesto, CA | 10 May |
| 16.88 | | Barbaro | Torres | CUB | 63 | 3 | | Santiago/Cuba | 23 Feb |
| 16.88 | 1.3 | Vladimir | Chernikov | SU | 59 | 3 | WG | Helsinki | 7 Jul |
| 16.87 | 1.7 | Michael | Makin | UK | 62 | 2 | CG | Edinburgh | 2 Aug |
| 16.86 | 1.5 | Dmitriy | Litvinenko | SU | 63 | 2 | | Sochi | 24 May |
| 16.86 | 1.2 | Didier | Falise | BEL | 61 | 1 | NC | Bruxelles | 9 Aug |
| 16.85 | i - | Grigoriy | Yemets (60) | SU | 57 | 3 | | Kiev | 26 Jan |
| | | | | | | | | | |
| 16.85 | -0.3 | John | Herbert | UK | 62 | 2 | PTG | London | 11 Jul |
| 16.84 | | John | Tillman | USA | 65 | 4 | NCAA | Indianapolis | 7 Jun |
| 16.83 | -0.1 | Boris | Khokhlov | SU | 58 | 4 | | Kiev | 27 Jul |
| 16.82 | | Byron | Criddle | USA | 62 | 1 | | Houston | 4 May |
| 16.82 | | Lazaro | Balcindes | CUB | 63 | 2 | Barr | Habana | 15 Jun |
| 16.81 | i - | Yuriy | Gorbachenko | SU | 66 | 4 | | Kiev | 26 Jan |
| 16.81 | -2.0 | Juan | Lopez | CUB | 67 | - | WC-j | Athinai | 20 Jul |
| 16.80 | 0.0 | Mamed | Akhundov | SU | 64 | 2 | | Donetsk | 7 Sep |
| 16.79 | -0.4 | Aleksandr | Vinokurov | SU | 63 | 6 | Spart | Tashkent | 17 Sep |
| 16.78 | | Héctor | Marquetti(70) | CUB | 68 | 5 | | Santiago/Cuba | 23 Feb |
| | | | | | | | | | |
| 16.78 | | Mihai | Bran | RUM | 62 | 1 | | Bucureşti | 25 May |
| 16.78 | 0.7 | Peter | Bouschen | FRG | 60 | - | NC | W Berlin | 12 Jul |
| 16.78 | 0.1 | Vyacheslav | Shkarpov | SU | 66 | 3 | | Kiev | 29 Aug |
| 16.73 | i - | Marios | Hatziandreou | CYP | 62 | | | | |
| 16.73 | | Henry | Ellard | USA | 61 | 1 | | Fresno | 29 May |
| 16.73 | 0.2 | Haralambos | Giannoulis | GRE | 63 | 1 | | Lisboa | 1 Jun |
| 16.73 | | Steve | Hanna | BAH | 58 | 3 | NC | Nassau | 14 Jun |
| 16.73 | | Daniel | Ciobanu | RUM | 65 | 1 | NC | Piteşti | 9 Aug |
| 16.72 | 1.2 | Djordje | Kožul | YUG | 63 | 5 | BGP | Budapest | 11 Aug |
| 16.71 | | Vernon | Samuels (80) | UK | 64 | 1 | | Houston | 18 May |
| | | | | | | | | | |
| 16.70 | | Damir | Tashpulatov | SU | 64 | 2 | | Alma-Ata | 30 May |
| 16.69 | | David | McFadgen | USA | 60 | 1 | | Charlottesville | 10 May |
| 16.69 | 0.5 | Vladimir | Bereglazov | SU | 59 | 3 | | Riga | 30 May |
| 16.68 | | Francisco | Santos | BRA | 60 | 1 | | Sao Paulo | 13 Jul |
| 16.62 | | Ivo | Bilík | CS | 62 | 1 | | Poznan | 19 Jun |
| 16.62 | 1.0 | Andrey | Kruzhakov | SU | 61 | 3 | | Volgograd | 7 Sep |
| 16.60 | 1.1 | Nikolay | Avramov | BUL | 67 | 1 | | Pleven | 28 Jun |
| 16.59 | i - | Ray | Humphrey | USA | 65 | 1 | IC4A | Princeton | 9 Mar |
| 16.59 | 1.8 | Alain | René-Corail | FRA | 62 | 2 | | Fort-de-France | 3 May |
| 16.59 | | Joshua | Kio (90) | NIG | 57 | 3 | NC | Lagos | 22 Jun |
| | | | | | | | | | |
| 16.58 | | Andrzej | Grabarczyk | POL | 64 | 2 | | Poznan | 19 Jun |
| 16.57 | | Vitaliy | Yakuba | SU | 65 | 2 | | Ryazan | 28 Jun |
| 16.56 | 1.7 | Claes | Rahm | SWE | 64 | 3 | v Fin | Helsinki | 10 Aug |
| 16.55 | 1.5 | Andrey | Kurdinovskiy | SU | 65 | 1 | | Baku | 31 May |
| 16.55 | | Peter | Beames | AUS | 63 | - | AAA | London | 21 Jun |
| 16.55 | 0.3 | Klaus | Kübler | FRG | 59 | 4 | | Stuttgart | 6 Jul |
| 16.54 | i - | Edrick | Floreal | CAN | 66 | 1 | | Lincoln | 7 Feb |
| 16.54 | 0.0 | Vasiliy | Isayev | SU | 59 | 2 | | Leningrad | 20 Aug |
| 16.53 | 0.6 | Erich | Gotman | SU | 63 | 2 | | Alma-Ata | 31 Aug |

| Mark | Wind | Name | | Nat | Yr | Pos | Meet | Venue | Date |
|---|---|---|---|---|---|---|---|---|---|
| 16.52 | 1.3 | Heiko | Reski (100) | FRG | 63 | 3 | | Düsseldorf | 18 May |
| 16.50 | i - | Vladimir | Popov | SU | 65 | 9 | NC | Moskva | 7 Feb |
| 16.50 | i - | Dan | Simion (102) | RUM | 58 | 2 | NC | Bacău | 9 Feb |
| 16.49 | 1.0 | Krzysztof | Zuch | POL | 62 | 28 Jun | | | |
| 16.48 | i - | Vladimir | Zubrilin | SU | 63 | 2 Feb | | | |
| 16.48 | 2.0 | Zhenxian | Zou | CHN | 55 | 27 Apr | | | |
| 16.47 | | José | Salazar | VEN | 57 | 20 Apr | | | |
| A16.47 | | Willie | Olivier | RSA | 58 | 5 Nov | | | |
| 16.46 | | Francisco | Olivares | MEX | 62 | 12 Apr | | | |
| 16.46 | | Jaak | Uudmäe | SU | 54 | 15 Jun | | | |
| 16.46 | 1.7 | Zdzisław | Hoffmann(110) | POL | 59 | 17 Jun | | | |
| 16.46 | 0.5 | Aleksandr | Maletskiy | SU | 66 | 27 Jun | | | |
| 16.44 | 0.8 | Nikolay | Ivanov | BUL | 63 | 31 May | | | |
| 16.44 | 1.4 | Aston | Moore | UK | 56 | 21 Jun | | | |
| 16.43 | 2.0 | Thomas | Eriksson | SWE | 63 | 4 May | | | |
| 16.43 | -0.2 | Garfield | Anselm | FRA | 66 | 9 Aug | | | |
| 16.42 | 0.6 | Sergey | Frolenkov | SU | 62 | 7 Sep | | | |
| 16.41 | | Stanislav | Bobkov | SU | 68 | 25 May | | | |
| 16.41 | 0.3 | Thomas | Rex | GDR | 65 | 12 Jun | | | |
| 16.40 | | Danyel | Kelly | USA | 61 | 8 Feb | | | |
| 16.40 | | Lahor | Marinović | YUG | 67 | 8 Jun | | | |
| | | | (120) | | | | | | |
| 16.39 | | Stanisław | Oporski | POL | 59 | 27 Apr | | | |
| 16.39 | | Ioannis | Kiriazis | GRE | 62 | 29 Jun | | | |
| 16.39 | 1.7 | Paolo | Challancin | ITA | 63 | 14 Sep | | | |
| A16.38 | | Dudson | Higgins | BAH | 67 | 29 Jun | | | |
| 16.38 | -0.4 | Ernesto | Torres | PR | 59 | 4 Jul | | | |
| 16.38 | 1.1 | Francis | Dodoo | GHA | 60 | 28 Jul | | | |
| 16.38 | | Yanping | Chen | CHN | 66 | 24 Oct | | | |
| 16.37 | 0.4 | Mikhail | Kusturov | SU | 62 | 7 Sep | | | |
| 16.37 | | Dainis | Berzins | SU | 66 | 5 Oct | | | |
| 16.37 | | Benzhong | Du (130) | CHN | 67 | 11 Oct | | | |
| 16.36 | i - | Yasushi | Ueta | JAP | 55 | 8 Mar | | | |
| 16.36 | i - | Arthur | Ogedegbe | NIG | | 9 Mar | | | |
| 16.36 | 0.9 | Zdravko | Dimitrov | BUL | 67 | 28 Jun | | | |
| 16.35 | 1.2 | Igor | Kolomagin | SU | 62 | 24 May | | | |
| 16.35 | 1.2 | Alfred | Sturmer | AUT | 62 | 13 Jul | | | |
| 16.35 | | Vasiliy | Sokov | SU | 68 | 21 Jul | | | |
| 16.34 | i - | Jorge | Vila | SPA | 55 | 23 Feb | | | |
| 16.33 | i - | Roberto | Mazzucato | ITA | 54 | 22 Jan | | | |
| 16.33 | | Changjiang | Sun | CHN | 64 | 2 May | | | |
| 16.33 | | Dimitrios | Mihas (140) | GRE | 58 | | | | |
| 16.32 | i - | Nikolay | Prokhorov | SU | 64 | 12 Jan | | | |
| 16.32 | | Andrey | Shaykovskiy | SU | 63 | 11 May | | | |
| 16.32 | -0.1 | Waldemar | Golanko | POL | 61 | 24 May | | | |
| 16.32 | | Andrey | Stepin | SU | 67 | 25 May | | | |
| 16.32 | 1.3 | Dancho | Boshnakov | BUL | 68 | 1 Aug | | | |
| 16.31 | i - | Jaroslav | Priščák | CS | 56 | 9 Feb | | | |
| 16.31 | | Gianni | Cecconi | ITA | 64 | 14 Jun | | | |
| 16.30 | | Bedros | Bedrosian | RUM | 55 | 9 Aug | | | |
| 16.30 | 1.1 | Stanislav | Zubar | SU | 64 | 29 Aug | | | |
| 16.29 | i - | Yuriy | Svistunov | SU | 61 | 12 Jan | | | |
| | | | (150) | | | | | | |
| 16.29 | | Nenad | Velimirović | YUG | 60 | 17 May | | | |
| 16.29 | 1.1 | Gian Carlo | Biscarini | ITA | 62 | 27 Jun | | | |
| 16.29 | 1.8 | Markku | Rokala | FIN | 60 | 10 Aug | | | |
| 16.28 | i - | Keith | Presberry | USA | 63 | 21 Feb | | | |
| 16.28 | i - | Pierre | Camara | FRA | 65 | 23 Feb | | | |
| 16.28 | 1.0 | Wolfgang | Knabe | FRG | 59 | 7 Jun | | | |
| 16.28 | 2.0 | Andrey | Kamozharskiy | SU | 60 | 27 Jun | | | |
| A16.27 | | Moses | Kiyai | KEN | 60 | 18 May | | | |
| 16.27 | 1.4 | Valeriy | Klimenko | SU | 66 | 6 Jul | | | |
| 16.26 | | Sergey | Naryzhny(160) | SU | 65 | 25 May | | | |
| 16.25 | i - | Sergey | Tarasov | SU | 62 | 24 Jan | | | |
| 16.25 | 0.4 | Esa | Viitasalo | FIN | 60 | 10 Jun | | | |
| 16.25 | 2.0 | Ryszard | Juszczak | POL | 58 | 3 Aug | | | |
| 16.24 | i - | Sergo | Akhvlediani | SU | 62 | 7 Feb | | | |
| 16.24 | 1.7 | Ed | Roskiewicz | USA | 60 | 23 May | | | |
| 16.24 | 2.0 | Alberto | Solanas | SPA | 55 | 1 Aug | | | |
| 16.23 | i - | Sergey | Belevskiy | SU | 59 | 19 Jan | | | |
| 16.23 | i - | Aleksey | Roganin | SU | 59 | 25 Jan | | | |
| 16.23 | | Ken | Frazier | USA | 63 | 7 Jun | | | |
| 16.23 | | Viktor | Mikhailov | SU | 64 | | | | |
| | | | (170) | | | | | | |
| 16.23 | 1.6 | Milan | Šimunič | YUG | 52 | 27 Sep | | | |
| 16.22 | i - | Mike | Hanks | USA | 64 | 25 Jan | | | |
| 16.21 | i - | Mikhail | Ageyev | SU | 60 | 18 Jan | | | |
| 16.21 | 1.7 | Abcelvio | Rodrigues | BRA | 57 | 21 Sep | | | |
| | | | (174) | | | | | | |

Kayukov (17.02 0.6) also did 17.02 - 0.1 2 Spart Tashkent 17 Sep.

MEN 1986

| | 1 | 10 | 20 | 30 | 50 | 100 | Over 17.00 | Over 16.50 |
|---|---|---|---|---|---|---|---|---|
| 1982 | 17.57 | 17.16 | 17.02 | 16.91 | 16.69 | 16.38 | 24 | 74 |
| 1983 | 17.55 | 17.27 | 17.12 | 17.05 | 16.74 | 16.43 | 33 | 87 |
| 1984 | 17.52 | 17.34 | 17.19 | 17.02 | 16.78 | 16.42 | 32 | 91 |
| 1985 | 17.97 | 17.48 | 17.29 | 17.04 | 16.88 | 16.51 | 31 | 103 |
| 1986 | 17.80 | 17.43 | 17.17 | 17.05 | 16.93 | 16.52 | 39 | 102 |

| Mark | Wind | Name | | Nat | Yr | Pos | Meet | Venue | Date |
|------|------|------|---|-----|----|----|------|-------|------|

**Best outdoor marks:**

| | | | | | | | |
|--|--|--|--|--|--|--|--|
| 17.16 | 0.2 | | Inozemtsev | 4 | PTS | Bratislava | 14 Jun |
| 17.07 | 1.3 | | Plekhanov | 3 | NC | Kiev | 17 Jul |
| 16.75 | | | Yemets | 1 | | Kharkov | 15 May |
| 16.61 | | | Hatziandreou | 1 | | Limassol | 2 Jul |
| A16.51 | 0.2 | | Floreal | 2 | | Boulder | 18 May |

| | | | | | | |
|--|--|--|--|--|--|--|
| 16.45 | 1.6 | Bakosi | 17 Aug | | | |
| 16.32 | 1.8 | Ueta | 1 Jun | **Best low altitude mark:** | | |
| 16.30 | 0.6 | Zubrilin | 29 Jun | | | |
| 16.21 | | Simion (9) | 9 Aug | 16.37 0.2 | Floreal | 22 Jun |

**Ancillary jumps /over 17.31/:**

| | | | | | | | |
|--|--|--|--|--|--|--|--|
| 17.74 | 1.2 | Markov | 11 Aug | 17.40 | 1.4 | Musiyenko | 7 Jun |
| 17.64 | 1.4 | Markov | 11 Aug | 17.38 | | Betancourt | 23 Feb |
| 17.54 | | Betancourt | 15 Jun | | | | |
| 17.53 | | Valyukevich | 1 Jun | 17.36 | 1.2 | Simpkins | 5 Jul |
| 17.52 | 1.2 | Musiyenko | 7 Jun | 17.35 | 0.9 | Markov | 30 Aug |
| 17.51 | -0.1 | Conley | 13 Aug | 17.34 | 1.1 | Markov | 30 Aug |
| 17.47 | -0.5 | Protsenko | 17 Jul | 17.32 | | Simpkins | 5 Jul |
| 17.47 | 0.1 | Markov | 30 Aug | 17.31 | 0.9 | Valyukevich | 17 Jul |

**Marks made with assisting wind > 2 m/s:**

| Mark | Wind | | Name | Nat | Yr | Pos | Meet | Venue | Date |
|------|------|--|------|-----|----|----|------|-------|------|
| 17.91 | 3.2 | Charles | Simpkins | USA | 63 | 1 | TAC | Eugene | 21 Jun |
| 17.84 | 2.3 | Mike | Conley | USA | 62 | 2 | TAC | Eugene | 21 Jun |
| 17.82 | 3.6 | Willie | Banks | USA | 56 | 1 | Jenner | San Jose | 31 May |
| 17.75 | | Gennadiy | Valyukevich | SU | | 1 | | Uzhgorod | 27 Apr |
| 17.59 | | | Conley | | | 2 | Jenner | San Jose | 31 May |
| 17.52 | 4.5 | | Banks | | | 3 | TAC | Eugene | 21 Jun |
| 17.51 | | | Banks | | | 1 | Pre | Eugene | 7 Jun |
| 17.41 | 3.2 | Kenny | Harrison | USA | 65 | 4 | TAC | Eugene | 21 Jun |
| 17.40 | 2.1 | | Valyukevich | | | 2 | Znam | Leningrad | 7 Jun |
| 17.31 | | Paul | Emordi (10/6) | NIG | 65 | 1 | DrakeR | Des Moines | 26 Apr |
| | | | | | | | | | |
| 17.30 | 3.7 | David | McFadgen | USA | 60 | 2 | USOCF | Houston | 2 Aug |
| 17.27 | 2.8 | John | Herbert | UK | 62 | 1 | CG | Edinburgh | 2 Aug |
| 17.26 | 3.7 | Joseph | Taiwo | NIG | 59 | 1 | | Koblenz | 6 Aug |
| 17.16 | 3.3 | Arne | Holm (10) | SWE | 61 | 1 | v Fin | Helsinki | 10 Aug |
| | | | | | | | | | |
| 17.11 | 2.6 | Al | Joyner | USA | 60 | 1 | | Knoxville | 23 May |
| 17.08 | 2.5 | Robert | Cannon | USA | 58 | 5 | TAC | Eugene | 21 Jun |
| 17.02 | | Ray | Kimble | USA | 53 | 3 | | Modesto, CA | 10 May |
| 16.94 | 2.2 | Juan | Lopez | CUB | 67 | 2 | WC-j | Athinai | 20 Jul |
| 16.90 | 2.8 | Peter | Beames | AUS | 63 | 2 | AAA | London | 21 Jun |
| 16.83 | 3.0 | Béla | Bakosi | HUN | 57 | Q | EC | Stuttgart | 29 Aug |
| 16.82 | 2.5 | Jorge Jose | dos Santos | BRA | 62 | 1 | | Sao Paulo | 21 Sep |
| 16.80 | 3.4 | Peter | Bouschen | FRG | 60 | 1 | NC | W Berlin | 12 Jul |
| 16.79 | 2.3 | Francisco | Santos | BRA | 60 | 2 | | Shizuoka | 27 Apr |
| 16.78 | 2.7 | Edrick | Floreal (20) | CAN | 66 | 3 | DrakeR | Des Moines | 26 Apr |
| | | | | | | | | | |
| A16.70 | 4.0 | Willie | Olivier | RSA | 58 | 1 | NC | Germiston | 12 Apr |
| 16.66 | 2.1 | Gennadiy | Kakhno | SU | 64 | Q | | Sochi | 23 May |
| 16.64 | 2.1 | Yasushi | Ueta | JAP | 55 | 2 | NC | Tokyo | 1 Jun |
| 16.64 | 2.9 | Claes | Rahm | SWE | 64 | 3 | | Gävle | 28 Jul |
| 16.64 | 3.2 | Thomas | Eriksson | SWE | 63 | 2 | v Fin | Helsinki | 10 Aug |

| Mark | Wind | Name | | Nat | Yr | Pos | Meet | Venue | Date |
|------|------|------|------|-----|----|-----|------|-------|------|
| 16.61 | 2.3 | Nikolay | Ivanov | BUL | 63 | 1 | | Sofia | 10 May |
| 16.56 | | José | Salazar | VEN | 57 | 3 | | Houston | 4 May |
| 16.51 | 2.2 | Francis | Dodoo (28) | GHA | 60 | 5 | | Gävle | 28 Jul |

| Mark | Wind | Name | | Nat | Yr | Pos | Meet | Venue | Date |
|------|------|------|------|-----|----|-----|------|-------|------|
| 16.47 | 2.1 | Guido | Schumann | GDR | 68 | 1 Aug | | | |
| 16.44 | | Derek | McKinley (30) | USA | | 4 May | | | |
| 16.37 | | Sergey | Borisevich | SU | 63 | 15 Jun | | | |
| 16.37 | 3.4 | Tomohiro | Kafuku | JAP | 62 | 13 Jul | | | |
| 16.35 | | Ed | Roskiewicz | USA | 60 | 11 Apr | | | |
| 16.35 | | Darryl | Taylor | USA | | 7 Jun | | | |
| 16.27 | 3.9 | Gyula | Novák | HUN | 60 | 8 Jun | | | |

| Mark | Wind | Name | | Nat | Yr | Date |
|------|------|------|------|-----|----|------|
| 16.26 | | Nikolay | Tuparov | BUL | 64 | 10 May |
| 16.25 | | Francis | Agyepong | UK | 65 | 10 Aug |
| 16.24 | 2.5 | Enrico | Chierici | ITA | 61 | 1 Jun |
| 16.24 | 2.1 | Craig | Duncan | UK | 65 | 21 Jun |
| 16.24 | 3.9 | Ulrich | Wrede (40) | FRG | 63 | 12 Jul |
| 16.21 | 4.2 | Gábor | Simon | HUN | 60 | 8 Jun |
| 16.21 | 3.0 | Kálmán | Sári | HUN | 60 | 17 Aug |

Ancillary jumps /over 17.31/:

| Mark | Wind | Name | Date |
|------|------|------|------|
| 17.70 | 3.9 | Simpkins | 21 Jun |
| 17.62 | 3.4 | Simpkins | 21 Jun |
| 17.54 | 2.8 | Conley | 21 Jun |
| 17.46 | | Valyukevich | 27 Apr |
| 17.43 | | Banks | 31 May |
| 17.42 | | Valyukevich | 27 Apr |

| Mark | Wind | Name | Date |
|------|------|------|------|
| 17.41 | | Valyukevich | 27 Apr |
| 17.41 | 3.1 | Simpkins | 21 Jun |
| 17.41 | 5.8 | Conley | 21 Jun |
| 17.40 | | Conley | 31 May |
| 17.37 | | Conley | 31 May |
| 17.33 | | Conley | 31 May |

## SHOT PUT

MEN 1986

| Mark | Name | | Nat | Yr | Pos | Meet | Venue | Date |
|------|------|------|-----|----|-----|------|-------|------|
| 22.64 | Udo | Beyer | GDR | 55 | 1 | | Berlin | 20 Aug |
| 22.60 | Ulf | Timmermann | GDR | 62 | 1 | v SU | Tallinn | 21 Jun |
| 22.51 | | Timmermann | | | 1 | | Erfurt | 1 Jun |
| 22.47 | | Timmermann | | | 1 | GO | Dresden | 17 Aug |
| 22.24 | Sergey | Smirnov | SU | 60 | 2 | v GDR | Tallinn | 21 Jun |
| 22.22 | Werner | Günthör | SWZ | 61 | 1 | EC | Stuttgart | 28 Aug |
| 22.16 | | Smirnov | | | 1 | NC | Kiev | 16 Jul |
| 22.16 | | Günthör | | | 1 | | St Gallen | 20 Sep |
| 22.14 | | Beyer | | | 1 | NC | Jena | 27 Jun |
| 22.10 | Sergey | Gavryushin | SU | 59 | 1 | | Moskva | 31 Aug |
| 22.06 | Alessandro | Andrei | ITA | 59 | 1 | | Viareggio | 6 Aug |
| 22.05 | | Beyer | | | 3 | v SU | Tallinn | 21 Jun |
| 22.00 | | Timmermann | | | 2 | NC | Jena | 27 Jun |
| 21.96 | Mikhail | Kostin | SU | 59 | 1 | | Vitebsk | 2 Jul |
| 21.88 | Randy | Barnes | USA | 66 | 1 | | Waco | 18 Apr |
| 21.86 | | Beyer | | | 1 | | Neubrandenburg | 7 Jun |
| 21.84 | | Timmermann | | | 2 | EC | Stuttgart | 28 Aug |
| 21.83 | | Timmermann | | | 1 | | Plovdiv | 17 May |
| 21.80 i | | Günthör | | | 1 | | Magglingen | 26 Jan |
| 21.79 | | Smirnov | | | 1 | Znam | Leningrad | 7 Jun |
| 21.79 | | Smirnov | | | 1 | GWG | Moskva | 8 Jul |
| 21.78 | John | Brenner | USA | 61 | 1 | MSR | Walnut, CA | 27 Apr |
| 21.77 | | Andrei | | | 1 | | Formia | 13 Jul |
| 21.72 | | Gavryushin | | | 1 | | Krasnodar | 22 Jun |
| 21.70 | | Timmermann | | | 1 | | Sofia | 11 May |
| 21.69 | | Beyer | | | 1 | | Umeå | 2 Sep |
| 21.68 | | Beyer | | | 1 | DNG | Stockholm | 1 Jul |
| 21.67 | | Timmermann | | | 1 | GP | Roma | 10 Sep |

| Mark | Name | | Nat | Yr | Pos | Meet | Venue | Date |
|------|------|------|-----|----|----|------|-------|------|
| 21.66 | | Günthör | | | 1 | | Langenthal | 4 Jun |
| 21.65 | | Beyer (30/9) | | | 2 | | Erfurt | 1 Jun |
| 21.49 | Sergey | Kasnauskas | SU | 62 | 1 | | Minsk | 31 Aug |
| | | (10) | | | | | | |
| 21.45 | Gregg | Tafralis | USA | 58 | 3 | MSR | Walnut, CA | 27 Apr |
| 21.30 | Helmut | Krieger | POL | 58 | 1 | NC | Grudziadz | 27 Jun |
| 21.29 | Jim | Doehring | USA | 62 | 1 | | Walnut, CA | 1 Jun |
| 21.22 | Lars Arvid | Nilsen | NOR | 65 | 1 | NCAA | Indianapolis | 6 Jun |
| 21.06 | Kevin | Akins | USA | 60 | 1 | | Columbus | 4 May |
| 21.01 i | Ron | Backes | USA | 63 | 1 | NCAA | Oklahoma City | 15 Mar |
| 20.98 | Dave | Laut | USA | 56 | 1 | | Goleta, CA | 3 May |
| 20.98 | Janis | Bojars | SU | 56 | 4 | v GDR | Tallinn | 21 Jun |
| 20.95 | Erik | de Bruin | HOL | 63 | 1 | | Leiden | 14 May |
| 20.90 | Gert | Weil (20) | CHL | 60 | 1 | | Wirges | 17 Aug |
| 20.83 | Mike | Spiritoso | CAN | 63 | 2 | NCAA | Indianapolis | 6 Jun |
| 20.80 | Vladimir | Yaryshkin | SU | 63 | 1 | | Baku | 5 Oct |
| 20.76 | Jan | Sagedal | NOR | 60 | 1 | | Bodø | 4 Jun |
| 20.76 | Viktor | Stepanskiy | SU | 59 | 1 | | Ternopol | 19 Jul |
| 20.74 | Edward | Sarul | POL | 58 | 1 | | Zabrze | 14 Jun |
| 20.66 | Janusz | Gassowski | POL | 58 | 1 | | Białystok | 14 Sep |
| 20.65 i | Marco | Montelatici | ITA | 53 | 1 | NC | Genova | 6 Feb |
| 20.65 | Jesse | Stuart | USA | 51 | 1 | | Caorle | 27 Jul |
| 20.63 | Brian | Oldfield | USA | 45 | 4 | Pepsi | Westwood | 17 May |
| 20.59 | Dimitrios | Koutsoukis | GRE | 62 | 4 | NCAA | Indianapolis | 6 Jun |
| | | (30) | | | | | | |
| 20.58 | Torsten | Pelzer | GDR | 63 | 1 | | Potsdam | 11 Jun |
| 20.57 | Karsten | Stolz | FRG | 64 | 1 | | Mönchengladbach | 24 May |
| 20.57 | Nikolay | Borodkin | SU | 55 | 4 | NC | Kiev | 16 Jul |
| 20.55 | Sergey | Kot | SU | 60 | 1 | | Kiev | 27 Jul |
| 20.48 | Georgi | Todorov | BUL | 60 | 1 | NC | Sofia | 13 Aug |
| 20.46 | Jari | Kuoppa | FIN | 60 | 1 | | Teuva | 29 Jun |
| 20.46 | Maris | Petrashko | SU | 61 | 1 | | Riga | 20 Sep |
| 20.44 | Klaus | Görmer | GDR | 63 | 1 | | Regis-Breitingen | 25 May |
| 20.40 | Art | McDermott | USA | 61 | 5 | | Modesto, CA | 10 May |
| 20.39 | Josef | Kubeš (40) | CS | 57 | 1 | | Praha | 28 Apr |
| 20.38 | Vitalius | Mitkus | SU | 65 | 1 | | Donetsk | 4 Oct |
| 20.37 | Ventsislav | Khristov | BUL | 62 | 1 | v Aut, | Gre,Hun Linz | 28 Jun |
| 20.36 | Jozef | Lacika | CS | 61 | 1 | | Praha | 24 May |
| 20.33 i | Sergey | Donskikh | SU | 56 | 3 | NC | Moskva | 7 Feb |
| 20.33 i | Mike | Smith | USA | 58 | 4 | TAC | Princeton | 28 Feb |
| 20.33 | Udo | Gelhausen | FRG | 56 | 1 | | Mönchengladbach | 9 Aug |
| 20.28 | Vladimir | Milić | YUG | 55 | 2 | | Fürth | 15 Jun |
| 20.25 | Saulius | Kleisa | SU | 64 | 3 | | Donetsk | 6 Sep |
| 20.24 | Rob | Suelflohn | USA | 59 | 2 | | San Jose | 19 Apr |
| 20.24 | Arne | Pedersen (50) | NOR | 61 | 2 | | Long Beach | 3 May |
| 20.23 | Piotr | Perżyło | POL | 61 | 1 | | Rzeszów | 7 Jun |
| 20.21 | Janne | Ronkainen | FIN | 63 | 1 | | Kuusankoski | 10 Jun |
| 20.15 | Steve | Cate | USA | 63 | Q | NCAA | Indianapolis | 4 Jun |
| 20.15 | Garry | Frank | USA | 64 | 5 | NCAA | Indianapolis | 6 Jun |
| 20.13 | Yuriy | Kuyumdzhan | SU | 61 | 2 | | Moskva | 11 May |
| 20.13 | Karel | Šula | CS | 59 | 1 | | Bratislava | 2 Jun |
| 20.05 | Kari | Töyrylä | FIN | 56 | 2 | | Kauhajoki | 2 Jul |
| 20.05 | Sergey | Sinitsa | SU | 66 | 2 | | Minsk | 31 Aug |

| Mark | Name | | Nat | Yr | Pos | Meet | Venue | Date |
|------|------|------|-----|----|----|------|-------|------|
| 20.02 i | Richard | Navara | CS | 64 | 1 | | Praha | 25 Jan |
| 20.01 | Algis | Pusinaitis | SU | 57 | 1 | | Lvov | 9 Aug |
| | | (60) | | | | | | |
| 20.00 | Jovan | Lazarević | YUG | 52 | 1 | | Subotica | 24 Aug |
| 19.98 i | Vyacheslav | Yemelyanov | SU | 57 | 1 | | Volgograd | 24 Jan |
| 19.97 | Klaus | Bodenmüller | AUT | 62 | 2 | WA | Barcelona | 14 Jun |
| 19.95 | Jim | Camp | USA | 63 | 2 | DrakeR | Des Moines | 26 Apr |
| 19.94 | Anatoliy | Samolyuk | SU | 58 | 2 | | Donetsk | 4 Oct |
| 19.91 i | Marty | Kobza | USA | 62 | 1 | | Fayetteville | 25 Jan |
| 19.90 | Jim | Banich | USA | 63 | Q | NCAA | Indianapolis | 4 Jun |
| 19.90 | Tariel | Bitsadze | SU | 66 | 3 | | Baku | 5 Oct |
| 19.89 | Mikhail | Kulish | SU | 64 | 2 | | Krasnodar | 22 Jun |
| 19.88 | Brian | Faul (70) | USA | 60 | 1 | | Long Beach | 16 May |
| | | | | | | | | |
| 19.84 | Luc | Viudes | FRA | 56 | 1 | | Joinville | 12 Jul |
| 19.79 | Eugeniusz | Bałło | POL | 60 | 2 | | Sevilla | 24 May |
| 19.79 | Zlatan | Saračević | YUG | 56 | 2 | | Beograd | 27 Jun |
| 19.75 | Sergey | Solomko | SU | 58 | 1 | | Tiraspol | 10 Aug |
| 19.72 i | Donatas | Stukonis | SU | 57 | 1 | | Vilnius | 12 Jan |
| 19.70 | Sören | Tallhem | SWE | 64 | 1 | | Tucson | 22 Mar |
| 19.66 | Stefan | Schröfel | FRG | 61 | 3 | | Kamp-Lintfort | 14 Sep |
| 19.64 | Lars | Sundin | SWE | 61 | 1 | | Provo | 24 May |
| 19.64 | Georg | Andersen | NOR | 63 | Q | EC | Stuttgart | 27 Aug |
| 19.59 i | John | Smith (80) | USA | 61 | 2 | | Champaign | 8 Feb |
| | | | | | | | | |
| 19.58 | Arnold | Campbell | USA | 66 | 4 | | Stanford | 29 Mar |
| 19.57 | Vladimir | Kisheyev | SU | 62 | 4 | | Moskva | 28 Jun |
| 19.54 | Viktor | Bely | SU | 64 | 5 | Spart | Tashkent | 18 Sep |
| 19.53 i | Vyacheslav | Lykho | SU | 67 | 1 | | Moskva | Dec |
| 19.51 | Rolf | Saalfrank | FRG | 62 | 1 | | Schwabmünchen | 3 Aug |
| 19.50 | John | Frazier | USA | 63 | 9 | | Modesto, CA | 10 May |
| 19.48 i | Anders | Skärvstrand | SWE | 60 | 1 | | Lidingö | 16 Feb |
| 19.46 | Ahmed Kamel | Shatta | EGY | 61 | 1 | | Los Angeles | 24 May |
| 19.46 | Erwin | Weitzl | AUT | 60 | 2 | | Bludenz | 7 Jun |
| 19.46 | Mikhail | Ivanov (90) | SU | 62 | 3 | | Donetsk | 4 Oct |
| | | | | | | | | |
| 19.45 i | Ed | Wade | USA | 64 | 1 | | Lincoln | 1 Mar |
| 19.43 i | Igor | Palchikov | SU | 60 | | | Barnaul | 11 Jan |
| 19.41 i | Fernando | Baroni | ITA | 57 | 2 | v Hun | Budapest | 1 Feb |
| 19.41 | Pat | Reid | USA | 65 | Q | NCAA | Indianapolis | 4 Jun |
| 19.41 | Sorin | Tirichiţă | RUM | 60 | 1 | | Poiana Brașov | 26 Jul |
| 19.40 | Greg | Aitkenhead | USA | 66 | 2 | | Los Angeles | 23 May |
| 19.36 i | Mikhail | Domorosov | SU | 55 | 2 | | Minsk | 26 Jan |
| 19.36 | Aleksandr | Bagach | SU | 66 | 2 | | Kiev | 28 Aug |
| 19.34 i | Peter | Kassubek | FRG | 59 | 3 | NC | Sindelfingen | 7 Feb |
| 19.33 | Gennadiy | Vlasyuk (100) | SU | 61 | 1 | | Vinnitsa | 11 May |
| | | | | | | | | |
| 19.32 i | Aleksey | Terenko | SU | 61 | 7 | NC | Moskva | 7 Feb |
| 19.32 | Brian | Blutreich | USA | 67 | 4 | | Tempe | 5 Apr |
| 19.30 | Paul | Ruiz (103) | CUB | 62 | 1 | | Habana | 31 May |

| | | | | | | | | | |
|------|------|------|-----|----|----|------|------|------|----|
| 19.29 | Sven | Buder | GDR 66 27 Jun | | 19.22 | Aleksandr | Baryshnikov | SU | 48 13 May |
| 19.27 | Mark | Colligan | USA 63 18 May | | | | (110) | | |
| 19.27 | Claus-Dieter | Föhrenbach | FRG 55 4 Jul | | 19.22 | Viktor | Sosnin | SU | 54 28 Jun |
| 19.27 | Knut | Hjeltnes | NOR 51 9 Aug | | 19.22 | Yngve | Wahlander | SWE | 58 22 Jul |
| 19.25 | Gennadiy | Mikhailov | SU 56 13 May | | 19.21 i | Bruce | Anderson | USA | 62 25 Jan |
| 19.23 | Joe | Zelezniak | USA 51 3 Aug | | 19.20 | Valeriy | Sotin | SU | 60 26 Apr |

| Mark | Name | | | Nat | Yr | Pos | Meet | Venue | | Date |
|------|------|--|--|-----|----|-----|------|-------|--|------|
| 19.20 | Frank | Schneider | | GDR | 60 | 27 Jun | 18.88 | Mieczysław | Kropelnicki | POL 51 17 Sep |
| 19.18 | Trond | Ulleberg | | NOR | 62 | 9 Jul | 18.87 | Yitian | Gong | CHN 63 7 Sep |
| 19.10 | Ron | McKee | | USA | 59 | 22 Apr | 18.86 | Narciso | Boue | CUB 62 18 May |
| 19.10 | Maik | Prollius | | GDR | 66 | 27 Jun | 18.84 | German | Geyger | SU 62 6 Sep |
| 19.10 | Nikolay | Gemizhev | | BUL | 56 | 29 Jun | 18.82 i | Scott | Karr | USA 8 Feb |
| 19.06 | Aleksey | Lukashenko | | SU | 67 | 9 Aug | 18.82 | Zsigmond | Ladányi | HUN 61 14 Sep |
| | | | (120) | | | | 18.80 | Edward | Ellis | USA 64 29 Mar |
| 19.04 | Mike | Schnebel | | USA | 64 | 18 May | 18.78 i | John | Turco (140) | USA 16 Feb |
| 19.02 1 | Gerry | Donini | | USA | | 23 Feb | | | | |
| 19.02 | Dennis | DeSoto | | USA | 62 | 8 Mar | 18.78 i | Scott | Eriksson | USA 61 22 Feb |
| 19.02 | László | Szabó | | HUN | 55 | 7 Jun | 18.77 i | Mike | Judge | USA 64 1 Mar |
| 19.01 | Billy | Cole | | UK | 65 | 21 Jun | 18.77 | Terry | Thomas | USA 64 14 May |
| 19.01 | Marius | Andruşcă | | RUM | 61 | 7 Aug | 18.75 | Ivan | Ivančič | YUG 37 7 Sep |
| 19.00 | Kalman | Konya | | FRG | 61 | 20 Jul | 18.74 i | Sean | Purcell | USA 64 15 Mar |
| 18.98 | Randy | Heisler | | USA | 61 | 17 May | 18.72 | Jeff | Braun | USA 57 9 Aug |
| 18.95 | Marvin | Lewis | | USA | 63 | 26 Apr | 18.71 | Balwinder | Singh | IND 59 5 Aug |
| 18.92 | Aigars | Dronka (130) | | SU | 61 | 16 May | 18.70 i | Brian | Donahue | USA 62 12 Jan |
| | | | | | | | 18.70 | John | van Reenen | RSA 47 7 Mar |
| 18.91 | Aleksey | Malakhov | | SU | 61 | 1 Jun | 18.70 | Eugene | Nysschen(150) | RSA 64 19 Mar |
| 18.91 | Yaroslav | Malinin | | SU | 61 | 17 Aug | | | | |

---

| | 1 | 10 | 20 | 30 | 50 | 100 | Over 20.00 | Over 19.00 |
|------|-------|-------|-------|-------|-------|-------|------------|------------|
| 1982 | 22.02 | 21.04 | 20.62 | 20.32 | 19.99 | 19.22 | 48 | 113 |
| 1983 | 22.22 | 21.20 | 20.81 | 20.64 | 20.13 | 19.37 | 64 | 149 |
| 1984 | 22.19 | 21.63 | 21.09 | 20.70 | 20.23 | 19.48 | 66 | 145 |
| 1985 | 22.62 | 21.32 | 20.98 | 20.64 | 20.07 | 19.34 | 54 | 119 |
| 1986 | 22.64 | 21.49 | 20.90 | 20.59 | 20.24 | 19.33 | 61 | 127 |

---

Best outdoor marks:

| | | | | | | | |
|-------|---|------------|--------|---|-----|-----------------|--------|
| 20.92 | | Backes | | 1 | | Knoxville | 12 Apr |
| 20.27 | M | Smith | | 1 | | Long Beach | 3 May |
| 19.89 | | Navara | | 1 | | Beograd | 27 Jun |
| 19.83 | | Kobza | | Q | NCAA | Indianapolis | 4 Jun |
| 19.68 | | Yemelyanov | | 1 | | Sochi | 26 Apr |
| 19.61 | | Stukonis | | 2 | | Tallinn | 28 Jun |
| 19.44 | | Montelatici | | 2 | | Lisboa | 31 May |
| 19.34 | | Lykho | | 1 | | Dnepropetrovsk | 27 Sep |
| 19.31 | | Kassubek | | 1 | | Norden | 21 Sep |
| | | | | | | | |
| 19.27 | | Wade | 18 Apr | 18.84 | | Palchikov | 26 Apr |
| 19.24 | | Baroni | 6 Sep | 18.82 | | Donini | 17 May |
| 18.97 | J | Smith | 11 May | 18.81 | | Terenko (16) | 28 Jun |
| 18.87 | | Skärvstrand | 21 Jun | | | | |

Ancillary marks /over 21.85/:

| | | | | | | |
|-------|------------|--------|-------|------------|--------|
| | | | 22.01 | Timmermann | 17 Aug |
| 22.58 | Beyer | 20 Aug | 21.98 | Beyer | 21 Jun |
| 22.24 | Beyer | 20 Aug | 21.96 | Andrei | 6 Aug |
| 22.15 | Beyer | 20 Aug | 21.95 | Andrei | 6 Aug |
| 22.12 | Timmermann | 21 Jun | 21.92 | Beyer | 27 Jun |
| 22.10 | Smirnov | 21 Jun | 21.90 | Timmermann | 21 Jun |
| 22.09 | Smirnov | 21 Jun | 21.89 | Timmermann | 27 Jun |
| 22.08 | Timmermann | 17 Aug | 21.89 | Günthör | 20 Sep |
| 22.05 | Timmermann | 21 Jun | 21.88 | Andrei | 6 Aug |
| 22.01 | Timmermann | 21 Jun | 21.85 | Timmermann | 17 Aug |

| Mark | Name | | Nat | Yr | Pos | Meet | Venue | Date |
|---|---|---|---|---|---|---|---|---|

## DISCUS THROW

| Mark | Name | | Nat | Yr | Pos | Meet | Venue | Date |
|---|---|---|---|---|---|---|---|---|
| 74.08 | Jürgen | Schult | GDR | 60 | 1 | | Neubrandenburg | 6 Jun |
| 68.72 | Art | Burns | USA | 54 | 1 | | Salinas, CA | 12 Apr |
| 68.50 | Knut | Hjeltnes | NOR | 51 | 2 | | Salinas, CA | 12 Apr |
| 68.40 | Juan | Martinez | CUB | 58 | 1 | | Habana | 19 Jun |
| 68.32 | | Burns | | | 1 | Jenner | San Jose | 19 Apr |
| 68.00 | Luis | Delis | CUB | 57 | 1 | | Zaragoza | 29 May |
| 67.88 | Romas | Ubartas | SU | 60 | 1 | v GDR | Tallinn | 21 Jun |
| 67.76 | Armin | Lemme | GDR | 55 | 2 | | Neubrandenburg | 6 Jun |
| 67.58 | | Hjeltnes | | | 1e1 | | Modesto, CA | 10 May |
| 67.44 | | Burns | | | 1 | | San Jose | 22 Apr |
| 67.38 | Imrich | Bugár | CS | 55 | 1 | | Praha | 17 Aug |
| 67.28 | | Ubartas | | | 1 | NC | Kiev | 15 Jul |
| 67.22 | | Hjeltnes | | | 1 | Bisl | Oslo | 5 Jul |
| 67.18 | | Bugár | | | 1 | Pepsi | Westwood | 17 May |
| 67.18 | | Schult | | | 1 | | Schwerin | 4 Jun |
| 67.16 | | Hjeltnes | | | 1 | v Swz, | Swe Luzern | 21 Jun |
| 67.12 | | Ubartas | | | 1 | GWG | Moskva | 6 Jul |
| 67.10 | Brad | Cooper | BAH | 57 | 1 | NC | Nassau | 14 Jun |
| 67.08 | | Ubartas | | | 1 | EC | Stuttgart | 31 Aug |
| 67.02 | | Burns | | | 2 | Pepsi | Westwood | 17 May |
| 67.02 | Georgiy | Kolnootchenko | SU | 59 | 2 | EC | Stuttgart | 31 Aug |
| 67.00 | | Martinez | | | 1 | Barr | Habana | 14 Jun |
| 67.00 | Vaclovas | Kidikas | SU | 61 | 2 | v GDR | Tallinn | 21 Jun |
| 66.94 | Dmitriy | Kovtsun | SU | 55 | 1 | | Tallinn | 18 Jun |
| 66.90 | | Burns | | | 1 | | Long Beach | 3 May |
| 66.82 | | Kidikas | | | 1 | | Moskva | 9 Aug |
| 66.82 | | Ubartas | | | 2 | | Moskva | 9 Aug |
| 66.80 | | Burns | | | 2e1 | | Modesto, CA | 10 May |
| 66.78 | Erik | de Bruin | HOL | 63 | 1 | | Vught | 3 Aug |
| 66.74 | | Bugár | | | 1 | | Praha | 9 Aug |
| 66.72 | | Hjeltnes | | | 1 | MSR | Walnut, CA | 27 Apr |
| | | (31/13) | | | | | | |
| 66.62 | John | Brenner | USA | 61 | 3 | | Salinas, CA | 12 Apr |
| 66.60 | Vitaliy | Sokolov | SU | 55 | 1 | | Vitebsk | 6 Jul |
| 66.48 | Svein Inge | Valvik | NOR | 56 | 1 | | Klagshamn | 8 Oct |
| 66.16 | Rolf | Danneberg | FRG | 53 | 1 | | Dingolfing | 26 Jul |
| 65.94 | John | Powell | USA | 47 | 1 | TAC | Eugene | 21 Jun |
| 65.86 | Marco | Martino | ITA | 60 | 1 | | Caravaggio | 4 Jun |
| 65.86 | Rick | Meyer (20) | USA | 61 | 2 | TAC | Eugene | 21 Jun |
| 65.58 | Gejza | Valent | CS | 53 | 1 | | Opava | 5 Aug |
| 65.40 | Kamen | Dimitrov | BUL | 62 | 1 | | Plovdiv | 17 May |
| 65.34 | Randy | Heisler | USA | 61 | 1 | | Bloomington | 17 May |
| 65.28 | Sergey | Lukashok | SU | 58 | 1 | | Tallinn | 28 Jun |
| 65.28 | Alois | Hannecker | FRG | 61 | 1 | NC | W Berlin | 12 Jul |
| 65.28 | Georgi | Taushanski | BUL | 57 | 2 | | Sofia | 20 Aug |
| 65.16 | Igor | Duginets | SU | 56 | 2 | | Leselidze | 18 May |
| 65.14 | Vitaliy | Gaslenko | SU | 62 | 1 | | Chelyabinsk | 9 Aug |
| 65.10 | Mike | Buncic | USA | 62 | 1 | | Columbus | 4 May |
| 65.10 | Raul | Calderon (30) | CUB | 62 | 2 | | Habana | 8 Jun |
| 65.08 | Stefan | Fernholm | SWE | 59 | 1 | | Norrköping | 19 Aug |
| 65.08 | Jonas | Siaudinis | SU | 58 | 1 | | Baku | 5 Oct |
| 65.00 | Vitaliy | Pishchalnikov | SU | 58 | 3 | | Leselidze | 18 May |

| Mark | Name | | Nat | Yr | Pos | Meet | Venue | Date |
|---|---|---|---|---|---|---|---|---|
| 64.94 | Art | Swarts | USA | 45 | 1 | | Scotch Plains | 8 Mar |
| 64.58 | Georgi | Georgiev | BUL | 61 | 2 | | Sofia | 3 Aug |
| 64.52 | Greg | McSeveney | USA | 59 | 1 | | Long Beach | 16 May |
| 64.34 | Dariusz | Juzyszyn | POL | 57 | 1 | | Białystok | 27 Jul |
| 64.32 | Alwin | Wagner | FRG | 50 | 1 | ISTAF | W Berlin | 15 Aug |
| 64.24 | Vladislav | Popov | SU | 62 | 2 | | Chelyabinsk | 9 Aug |
| 64.16 | Andreas | Becker (40) | GDR | 62 | 3 | | Neubrandenburg | 6 Jun |
| 64.12 | John | van Reenen | RSA | 47 | 1 | | Stellenbosch | 10 Feb |
| 63.98 | Vesteinn | Hafsteinsson | ICE | 60 | 1 | | Tuscaloosa | 29 Mar |
| 63.98 | Lutz | Friedrich | GDR | 61 | 1 | | Cottbus | 22 Jun |
| 63.72 | Marcus | Gordien | USA | 55 | 4 | | Salinas, CA | 12 Apr |
| 63.68 | Art | McDermott | USA | 61 | 2 | | Columbus | 4 May |
| 63.42 | Manfred | Schmitz | FRG | 60 | 1e2 | | Norden | 20 Sep |
| 63.30 | Vladimir | Turanok | SU | 57 | 1 | | Riga | 14 Jun |
| 63.28 | Mieczysław | Szpak | POL | 61 | 2 | | Słupsk | 18 Sep |
| 63.26 | Vladimir | Zinchenko | SU | 59 | 1 | | Adler | 24 Feb |
| 63.24 | Judd | Binley (50) | USA | 55 | 1 | | Eugene | 24 May |
| 63.22 | József | Ficsor | HUN | 65 | 3 | v CS | Praha | 18 Sep |
| 63.18 | Wulf | Brunner | FRG | 62 | 1 | | Bürstadt | 29 Jun |
| 63.16 | Mirosław | Jasinski | FRG | 59 | 3 | | Rhede | 2 Jul |
| 63.14 | Yuriy | Dumchev | SU | 58 | 1 | | Riga | 31 May |
| 63.08 | Christian | Okoye | NIG | 61 | 3 | | Walnut, CA | 1 Jun |
| 63.02 | Jay | Kovar | USA | 60 | 1e2 | | Modesto, CA | 10 May |
| 62.96 | Andrey | Kuzyanin | SU | 60 | 2 | | Riga | 31 May |
| 62.94 | Yevgeniy | Burin | SU | 64 | 1 | | Leningrad | 5 Jul |
| 62.74 | Richard | Slaney | UK | 56 | 5 | MSR | Walnut, CA | 27 Apr |
| 62.66 | Ed | Wade (60) | USA | 64 | 1 | | Wichita | 3 May |
| 62.58 | Csaba | Holló | HUN | 58 | 2 | v Aut, | Bul,Gre Linz | 28 Jun |
| 62.54 | Jacek | Strychalski | POL | 62 | 1 | | Warszawa | 8 Jun |
| 62.48 | Olaf | Többen | FRG | 62 | 1e1 | | Norden | 20 Sep |
| 62.46 | Mike | Gravelle | USA | 65 | 1 | | San Bruno, CA | 26 Apr |
| 62.42 | Rüdiger | Pudenz | GDR | 66 | 1 | v Can | Karl-Marx-Stadt | 13 Jul |
| 62.42 | Eggert | Bogason | ICE | 60 | 1 | | Hafnarfjordur | 22 Jul |
| 62.40 | Al | Oerter | USA | 36 | 2 | | Ewing, NJ | 14 Jun |
| 62.38 | Gregg | Tafralis | USA | 58 | 1 | | San Bruno, CA | 2 Apr |
| 62.18 | Werner | Hartmann | FRG | 59 | 5 | NC | W Berlin | 12 Jul |
| 62.14 | Velko | Velev (70) | BUL | 48 | 3 | | Sofia | 3 Aug |
| 62.12 | Wolfgang | Warnemünde | GDR | 53 | 2 | | Berlin | 4 Jul |
| 62.12 | Ion | Zamfirache | RUM | 53 | 1 | | Pitești | 20 Jul |
| 62.12 | Marcel | Târle | RUM | 66 | 1 | NC | Pitești | 9 Aug |
| 62.10 | Georg | Andersen | NOR | 63 | 1 | | Bodø | 4 Jun |
| 62.02 | Rickard | Bruch | SWE | 46 | 1 | | Lund | 5 Jun |
| 62.02 | Eligiusz | Pukownik | POL | 62 | 1 | | Słupsk | 7 Jun |
| 62.02 | Olav | Jenssen | NOR | 62 | 1 | | Malmö | 19 Aug |
| 61.88 | Ferenc | Tégla | HUN | 47 | 1 | | Budapest | 8 Jun |
| 61.86 | Bernd | Kneissler | FRG | 62 | 1 | | Los Angeles | 24 May |
| 61.82 | Uldis | Meijers (80) | SU | 63 | 1 | | Riga | 2 May |
| 61.80 | Saveliy | Khaustov | SU | 61 | 1 | | Nalchik | 24 Aug |
| 61.66 | Gary | Kostrubala | USA | 64 | 1 | TexR | Austin | 4 Apr |
| 61.62 | Kari | Nisula | FIN | 63 | 2e2 | | Modesto, CA | 10 May |
| 61.52 | Tadeusz | Majewski | POL | 54 | 1 | | Warszawa | 16 Jun |
| 61.40 | Paul | Mardle | UK | 62 | 1 | | Birmingham | 15 Jun |

| Mark | Name | | Nat | Yr | Pos | Meet | Venue | Date |
|------|------|--|-----|----|----|------|-------|------|
| 61.36 | Rob | Gray | CAN | 56 | 1 | | Univ Park, PA | 3 May |
| 61.34 | Paul | Nandapi | AUS | 61 | 1 | | Sydney | 9 Mar |
| 61.34 | Valeriy | Murashov | SU | 64 | 2 | | Budapest | 27 Jul |
| 61.34 | Sergey | Pachin | SU | 68 | 2 | v GDR-j | Karl-Marx-Stadt | 10 Aug |
| 61.18 | Randy | Barnes (90) | USA | 66 | 1 | | Houston | 17 May |
| 61.18 | Raimo | Vento | FIN | 54 | 1 | | Lappeenranta | 9 Jun |
| 61.16 | Lars | Sundin | SWE | 61 | 1e2 | | Provo | 24 May |
| 61.16 | Stanisław | Grabowski | POL | 55 | 2 | NC | Grudziadz | 29 Jun |
| 61.08 | Alfonz | Saskói | HUN | 58 | 1 | | Szeged | 19 Aug |
| 61.08 | Aleksandr | Grechko | SU | 62 | 1 | | Donetsk | 4 Oct |
| 61.02 | Ray | Lazdins | CAN | 64 | 1 | | Etobicoke | 29 Apr |
| 61.02 | Marek | Polewany | POL | 61 | 2 | | Białystok | 14 Sep |
| 61.02 | Andrzej | Maliszewski | POL | 57 | 1 | | Tarnów | 20 Sep |
| 61.02 | László | Németh | HUN | 60 | 1 | | Székesfehérvár | 30 Sep |
| 60.96 | Scott | Eriksson(100) | USA | 61 | 1 | | Ann Arbor | 17 May |

| Mark | Name | | Nat | Yr | Date | | Mark | Name | | Nat | Yr | Date |
|------|------|--|-----|----|------|--|------|------|--|-----|----|------|
| 60.92 | Jim | Banich | USA | 63 | 8 Mar | | 59.90 | Ron | Backes | USA | 63 | 11 Apr |
| 60.92 | Graham | Savory | UK | 60 | 10 May | | 59.84 | Øystein | Bjørbaek | NOR | 53 | 9 Jul |
| 60.88 | Scott | Lofquist | USA | 60 | 17 May | | 59.70 | Josef | Kubeš | CS | 57 | 20 May |
| 60.84 | Rob | James | USA | 61 | 5 Apr | | 59.70 | Vasiliy | Petrov | SU | 66 | 26 Jul |
| 60.76 | Attila | Horváth | HUN | 67 | 27 Jul | | 59.70 | Dietmar | Krause | GDR | 63 | 20 Aug |
| 60.70 | Sándor | Katona | FRA | 53 | 30 Aug | | 59.68 | Pavel | Popov | SU | 65 | 5 Jul |
| 60.66 | Todd | Kaufman | USA | 61 | 5 Apr | | 59.68 | Angelos | Nikolaidis | GRE | 56 | |
| 60.66 | Erwin | Weitzl | AUT | 60 | 13 Jul | | 59.66 | Sergey | Seregin | SU | 59 | 6 Sep |
| 60.66 | Ferenc | Szegletes | HUN | 48 | 13 Sep | | 59.54 | Mitch | Crouser | USA | 57 | 26 Jul |
| 60.62 | Kevin | Carr (110) | USA | 64 | 26 Apr | | 59.52 | Patrick | Journoud(140) | FRA | 64 | 8 May |
| 60.60 | Vasil | Baklarov | BUL | 67 | 17 Jul | | 59.52 | Marty | Kobza | USA | 62 | 17 May |
| 60.56 | Frédéric | Selle | FRA | 57 | 14 Jun | | 59.50 | J R | Quinn | USA | 65 | 30 May |
| 60.54 | Paul | Bender | USA | 61 | 28 May | | 59.46 | Vlad | Slavnic | AUS | 58 | 27 Nov |
| 60.50 | Edward | Rikert | POL | 61 | 1 Jun | | 59.34 | Albert | Reinaste | SU | 59 | 28 Jun |
| 60.48 | Yuriy | Seskin | SU | 66 | 25 Jun | | 59.30 | Robert | Sippio | USA | 62 | 26 Apr |
| 60.48 | Konstantinos | Georgakopoulos | GRE | 63 | 31 Jul | | 59.22 | Rosen | Velinov | BUL | 67 | 1 Jun |
| 60.48 | Iosif | Nagy | RUM | 46 | 9 Aug | | 59.20 | Sergey | Gorislavtsev | SU | 62 | 14 May |
| 60.36 | Jim | Seifert | USA | 62 | 13 May | | 59.14 | Peter | Kassubek | FRG | 59 | 20 Sep |
| 60.36 | Mac | Wilkins | USA | 50 | 28 May | | 59.08 | Gabriel | Pedroso | CUB | 68 | 9 May |
| 60.34 | Bo | Henriksson (120) | SWE | 63 | 10 Jun | | 59.04 | Marty | Davenport (150) | USA | 63 | 4 Apr |
| 60.24 | Vasiliy | Kaptyukh | SU | 67 | 28 Sep | | 59.04 | Roberto | Moya | CUB | 65 | 28 Sep |
| 60.10 | Sergey | Kot | SU | 60 | 26 Jul | | 59.02 | Igor | Novitskiy | SU | 62 | 19 Jul |
| 60.08 | Wim | de Wolff | HOL | 58 | 9 Jul | | 59.00 | Andrey | Kokhanovskiy | SU | 68 | 16 Jul |
| 60.04 | Roger | Bakowski | FRG | 64 | 20 Sep | | 59.00 | Ari | Huumonen(154) | FIN | 56 | 14 Aug |
| 60.02 | Ferenc | Csiszár | HUN | 55 | 24 Aug | | | | | | | |
| 60.00 | Rolando | Ribalta | CUB | 68 | 14 Jun | | | | | | | |
| 60.00 | Domenico | Polato | ITA | 60 | 15 Jun | | Exhibition: | | | | | |
| 60.00 | Jürgen | Riese | FRG | 62 | 2 Aug | | | | | | | |
| 59.92 | Antonio | Roccabella | ITA | 59 | 27 Jun | | 61.84 | Sándor | Katona | FRA | 53 | |
| 59.92 | Stefan | Schröfel(130) | FRG | 61 | 2 Aug | | | | | | | Szentes 20 Sep |

Ancillary marks /over 67.00/:

| | | | | | |
|------|------|------|------|------|------|
| 67.74 | | Delis | 29 May | 67.26 | Ubartas | 21 Jun |
| 67.68 | | Ubartas | 21 Jun | 67.20 | Schult | 6 Jun |

MEN 1986

| Mark | Name | | Nat | Yr | Pos | Meet | Venue | | Date |
|------|------|--|-----|----|-----|------|-------|--|------|

| | 1 | 10 | 20 | 30 | 50 | 100 | Over 62.00 | Over 60.00 |
|------|------|------|------|------|------|------|------|------|
| 1982 | 70.58 | 68.20 | 66.36 | 64.62 | 62.92 | 60.26 | 62 | 104 |
| 1983 | 71.86 | 68.12 | 66.24 | 64.56 | 62.98 | 60.48 | 73 | 119 |
| 1984 | 71.26 | 67.76 | 66.90 | 65.70 | 63.66 | 60.96 | 80 | 129 |
| 1985 | 71.26 | 67.36 | 66.38 | 65.06 | 63.02 | 60.54 | 70 | 121 |
| 1986 | 74.08 | 67.02 | 65.86 | 65.10 | 63.24 | 60.96 | 77 | 128 |

# HAMMER THROW

| Mark | Name | | Nat | Yr | Pos | Meet | Venue | Date |
|------|------|------|-----|----|-----|------|-------|------|
| 86.74 | Yuriy | Sedykh | SU | 55 | 1 | EC | Stuttgart | 30 Aug |
| 86.66 | | Sedykh | | | 1 | v GDR | Tallinn | 22 Jun |
| 86.04 | Sergey | Litvinov | SU | 58 | 1 | OD | Dresden | 3 Jul |
| 85.74 | | Litvinov | | | 2 | EC | Stuttgart | 30 Aug |
| 85.68 | | Sedykh | | | 1 | BGP | Budapest | 11 Aug |
| 85.14 | | Litvinov | | | 1 | PTG | London | 11 Jul |
| 84.92 | | Sedykh | | | 2 | OD | Dresden | 3 Jul |
| 84.88 | | Litvinov | | | 1 | GP | Roma | 10 Sep |
| 84.72 | | Sedykh | | | 1 | GWG | Moskva | 9 Jul |
| 84.64 | | Litvinov | | | 2 | GWG | Moskva | 9 Jul |
| 84.58 | | Sedykh | | | 1 | Znam | Leningrad | 8 Jun |
| 84.36 | | Litvinov | | | 2 | v GDR | Tallinn | 22 Jun |
| 84.26 | | Sedykh | | | 1 | Nik | Nice | 15 Jul |
| 84.14 | | Sedykh | | | 1 | WG | Helsinki | 7 Jul |
| 84.02 | | Litvinov | | | 2 | WG | Helsinki | 7 Jul |
| 83.02 | | Sedykh | | | 1 | | Adler | 24 May |
| 82.90 | | Sedykh | | | Q | EC | Stuttgart | 29 Aug |
| 82.34 | Igor | Nikulin | SU | 60 | 3 | OD | Dresden | 3 Jul |
| 82.24 | Benjaminas | Viluckis | SU | 61 | 1 | | Klaipeda | 24 Aug |
| 82.10 | | Litvinov | | | 2 | Znam | Leningrad | 8 Jun |
| 82.00 | | Nikulin | | | 3 | EC | Stuttgart | 30 Aug |
| 81.98 | | Sedykh | | | 2 | GP | Roma | 10 Sep |
| 81.70 | Günther | Rodehau | GDR | 59 | 1 | GO | Dresden | 16 Aug |
| 81.58 | | Viluckis | | | 1 | | Krasnodar | 21 Jun |
| 81.32 | Klaus | Ploghaus | FRG | 56 | 1 | | Paderborn | 24 May |
| 81.30 | | Nikulin | | | 2 | | Adler | 24 May |
| 81.26 | | Nikulin | | | 1 | | Kiev | 27 Jul |
| 81.02 | | Nikulin | | | 1 | | Adler | 24 Feb |
| 80.88 | Jud | Logan | USA | 59 | 1 | MSR | Walnut, CA | 27 Apr |
| 80.88 | Jüri | Tamm | SU | 57 | 1 | | Leselidze | 18 May |
| | | (30/8) | | | | | | |
| 80.70 | Vasiliy | Sidorenko | SU | 61 | 1 | | Tiraspol | 10 Aug |
| 80.68 | Igor | Astapkovich | SU | 63 | 1 | | Minsk | 1 Jun |
| | | (10) | | | | | | |
| 80.60 | Ralf | Haber | GDR | 62 | 2 | GO | Dresden | 16 Aug |
| 80.38 | Christoph | Sahner | FRG | 63 | 1 | | Rhede | 2 Jul |
| 80.30 | Matthias | Moder | GDR | 63 | 1 | | Berlin | 20 Aug |

| Mark | Name | | Nat | Yr | Pos | Meet | Venue | Date |
|------|------|---|-----|-----|-----|------|-------|------|
| 80.20 | Igor | Shchegolev | SU | 60 | 1 | | Volgograd | 6 Sep |
| 79.92 | Jörg | Schaefer | FRG | 59 | 1 | ISTAF | W Berlin | 15 Aug |
| 79.84 | Sergey | Alai | SU | 65 | 2 | | Minsk | 31 Aug |
| 79.70 | Ivan | Tanev | BUL | 57 | 1 | | Sofia | 24 May |
| 79.66 | Donatas | Plunge | SU | 60 | 2 | | Klaipeda | 24 Aug |
| 79.32 | Juha | Tiainen | FIN | 55 | 2 | v FRG, | Can Rehlingen | 19 May |
| 79.30 | Yuriy | Tarasyuk (20) | SU | 57 | 2 | | Minsk | 1 Jun |
| | | | | | | | | |
| 79.12 | Albert | Sinka | HUN | 62 | 2 | BGP | Budapest | 11 Aug |
| 79.00 | Sergey | Ivanov | SU | 63 | 1 | | Lipetsk | 19 Jul |
| 78.92 | Valeriy | Kocherga | SU | 63 | 1 | | Yalta | 12 Oct |
| 78.64 | Yuriy | Esayan | SU | 62 | 2 | | Yalta | 12 Oct |
| 78.46 | Johann | Lindner | AUT | 59 | 1 | | Hainfeld | 19 May |
| 78.46 | Sergey | Dorozhon | SU | 64 | 2 | | Tiraspol | 10 Aug |
| 78.38 | Harri | Huhtala | FIN | 52 | 2 | | Lappeenranta | 26 Jun |
| 78.34 | Ken | Flax | USA | 63 | 1 | NCAA | Indianapolis | 7 Jun |
| 78.34 | Anatoliy | Chyuzhas | SU | 56 | 3 | | Kiev | 27 Jul |
| 78.32 | Igor | Kucherenko (30) | SU | 60 | 1 | | Taganrog | 5 Jul |
| 78.30 | Emanuil | Dyulgerov | BUL | 55 | 1 | | Sofia | 3 Aug |
| 78.08 | Aleksandr | Puchkov | SU | 60 | 1 | | Minsk | 20 Jul |
| 78.04 | Valeriy | Reshetnikov | SU | 59 | 3 | | Tiraspol | 10 Aug |
| 78.00 | Igor | Grigorash | SU | 58 | 3 | | Krasnodar | 21 Jun |
| 77.80 | Michael | Beierl | AUT | 63 | 1 | CISM | Ostia | 12 Sep |
| 77.76 | Tore | Gustafsson | SWE | 62 | 1 | | Pullman | 10 May |
| 77.66 | Tibor | Gécsek | HUN | 64 | 1 | | Szombathely | 11 Oct |
| 77.60 | Nicolae | Bindar | RUM | 56 | 1 | | București | 1 Jun |
| 77.48 | Giuliano | Zanello | ITA | 63 | 1 | | Meretto | 25 May |
| 77.48 | Norbert | Radefeld (40) | FRG | 62 | 3 | NC | W Berlin | 13 Jul |
| | | | | | | | | |
| 77.28 | Imre | Szitás | HUN | 61 | 1 | | Maribor | 24 May |
| 77.20 | Bill | Green | USA | 60 | 2 | | Los Angeles | 18 May |
| 77.12 | Maco | Gerloff | GDR | 64 | 2 | | Potsdam | 12 Jun |
| 76.86 | Walter | Ciofani | FRA | 62 | 1 | | Saint-Denis | 21 Jun |
| 76.60 | David | Smith | UK | 62 | 1 | | Hull | 6 Sep |
| 76.54 | Valeriy | Gubkin | SU | 67 | 2 | | Minsk | 27 Jun |
| 76.42 | Henryk | Królak | POL | 60 | 1 | | Poznan | 19 Jun |
| 76.34 | Anatoliy | Yefimov | SU | 56 | 1 | | Leningrad | 18 Aug |
| 76.22 | Viktor | Apostolov | BUL | 62 | 2 | | Sofia | 26 Jul |
| 76.14 | Marc | Odenthal (50) | FRG | 63 | 1 | | Rovereto | 30 Jul |
| | | | | | | | | |
| 76.08 | Heinz | Weis | FRG | 63 | 1e2 | | Rehlingen | 19 May |
| 75.96 | Albert | Meheş | RUM | 60 | 1 | | Pitești | 20 Jul |
| 75.92 | Ajet | Toska | ALB | 61 | 1 | | Tirane | 22 Aug |
| 75.90 | Aleksandr | Seleznev | SU | 64 | 3 | Spart | Tashkent | 17 Sep |
| 75.86 | Viktor | Bobryshev | SU | 57 | 3 | | Leningrad | 18 Aug |
| 75.54 | Sergey | Dvoretskiy | SU | 57 | 2 | | Lipetsk | 19 Jul |
| 75.42 | Yevgeniy | Gribov | SU | 62 | 1 | | Sochi | 26 Apr |
| 75.16 | Nikolay | Lysenko | SU | 66 | 5 | | Kiev | 27 Jul |
| 75.10 | Eduard | Piskunov | SU | 67 | 1 | | Grodno | 5 Jul |
| 75.04 | Kjell | Bystedt (60) | SWE | 60 | 1 | | Västerås | 23 Jul |
| | | | | | | | | |
| 75.02 | Jens | Geisensetter | GDR | 64 | 1 | | Potsdam | 15 May |
| 74.98 | Vyacheslav | Korovin | SU | 62 | 3 | | Lvov | 9 Aug |
| 74.86 | Vladimir | Stepochkin | SU | 64 | 3 | | Kiev | 29 Aug |
| 74.84 | Thomas | Grogorick | GDR | 62 | 1 | | Eisenhüttenstadt | 27 Apr |
| 74.80 | Lucio | Serrani | ITA | 61 | 1 | NC | Torino | 22 Jul |

MEN 1986

| Mark | Name | | Nat | Yr | Pos | Meet | Venue | Date |
|---|---|---|---|---|---|---|---|---|
| 74.76 | Andrey | Abduvaliyev | SU | 66 | 5 | Spart | Tashkent | 17 Sep |
| 74.70 | Sándor | Vörös | HUN | 56 | 1 | | Budapest | 18 May |
| 74.68 | Orlando | Bianchini | ITA | 55 | 1 | | Roma | 25 May |
| 74.66 | Lance | Deal | USA | 61 | 2 | | Corvallis | 29 May |
| 74.60 | Zdeněk | Bednář (70) | CS | 57 | 1 | | Banská Bystrica | 31 May |
| 74.42 | Boris | Kotelnikov | SU | 65 | 3 | | Volgograd | 6 Sep |
| 74.30 | Mariusz | Tomaszewski | POL | 56 | 2 | | Warszawa | 17 Aug |
| 73.92 | Martin | Girvan | UK | 60 | 1 | | Haringey | 16 Jul |
| 73.90 | Ivan | Petkov | BUL | 60 | 1 | | Kazanlık | 8 Mar |
| 73.90 | Pavel | Repnikov | SU | 64 | 3 | | Leningrad | 18 Aug |
| 73.80 | Sergey | Gula | SU | 63 | 2 | | Poltava | 19 Jul |
| 73.68 | József | Vida | HUN | 63 | 3 | | Szombathely | 14 May |
| 73.68 | Dave | McKenzie | USA | 49 | 1 | | Stanford | 14 Jun |
| 73.54 | Aivar | Räni | SU | 63 | 1 | | Tallinn | 7 Jun |
| 73.52 | Vladimir | Zotov (80) | SU | 63 | 6 | | Volgograd | 6 Sep |
| 73.48 | Panagiotis | Kremastiotis | GRE | 60 | 1 | | Athinai | 27 Apr |
| 73.46 | Aleksandr | Gurmazhenko | SU | 57 | 5 | | Dnepropetrovsk | 29 Jun |
| 73.46 | Wacław | Filek | POL | 59 | 1 | NC | Grudziadz | 29 Jun |
| 73.22 | Vitaliy | Alisevich | SU | 67 | 2 | | Simferopol | 23 May |
| 73.14 | Mikhail | Pyryalov | SU | 63 | | | Moskva | 14 Jun |
| 73.12 | Sándor | Füzesi | HUN | 59 | 3 | | Budapest | 3 Aug |
| 73.10 | Valentin | Doshev | BUL | 63 | 3 | | Sofia | 24 May |
| 73.10 | Mikhail | Lavrenyev | SU | 62 | 1 | | Leningrad | 13 Jul |
| 72.92 | Leszek | Woderski | POL | 58 | 2 | NC | Grudziadz | 29 Jun |
| 72.86 | Joe | Quigley (90) | AUS | 61 | 1 | NC | Adelaide | 16 Mar |
| 72.82 | Matt | Mileham | UK | 56 | 1 | | Fresno | 5 Apr |
| 72.80 | Rumen | Koprivchin | BUL | 62 | 5 | NC | Sofia | 14 Aug |
| 72.70 | Vasiliy | Rymaryuk | SU | 61 | 6 | | Dnepropetrovsk | 29 Jun |
| 72.66 | Georgi | Minchev | BUL | 62 | 6 | NC | Sofia | 14 Aug |
| 72.60 | Yaroslav | Chmyr | SU | 66 | 8 | | Kiev | 27 Jul |
| 72.54 | Andrey | Skvaruk | SU | 67 | 2 | v Rum-j | Rovno | 5 Oct |
| 72.46 | Pavel | Dashkin | SU | 64 | | | Moskva | 27 Jun |
| 72.46 | Mikhail | Popel | SU | 66 | 4 | | Minsk | 31 Aug |
| 72.40 | Aleksey | Afanasyev | SU | 65 | 1 | | Moskva | 15 Jun |
| 72.36 | Raul | Jimeno (100) | SPA | 59 | 1 | NC | Madrid | 1 Aug |
| 72.36 | Romeo | Budai | ITA | 58 | 2 | | Gorizia | 21 Sep |
| 72.28 | Pat | Egan | USA | 62 | 2 | | Dedham | 7 Jun |
| 72.26 | Viktor | Baigush | SU | 63 | 3 | | Yalta | 12 Oct |
| 72.22 | Grigoriy | Vovk | SU | 62 | | | Donetsk | 10 May |
| 72.10 | Francisco | Fuentes | SPA | 63 | 1 | | Madrid | 23 Mar |
| 72.02 | Vasiliy | Populyak(106) | SU | 64 | | | Kiev | 13 Aug |

| Mark | | | | | | Mark | | | | |
|---|---|---|---|---|---|---|---|---|---|---|
| 71.98 | Sergey | Vorobyov | SU | 64 | 18 Aug | 71.34 | Greg | Gassner | USA 60 | 29 May |
| 71.80 | Sergey | Koptilov | SU | 60 | 12 May | 71.34 | Christoph | Koch | FRG 65 | 31 May |
| 71.72 | Klaus-Bernd | Leitges | FRG | 66 | 13 Jul | 71.34 | Dave | Huxley (120) | AUS 58 | 13 Dec |
| 71.70 | Steffen | Raschick(110) | GDR | 66 | 30 Jul | | | | | |
| | | | | | | 71.32 | Enrico | Sgrulletti | ITA 65 | 13 Jul |
| 71.54 | Yuriy | Pastukhov | SU | 61 | 10 Aug | 71.32 | Károly | Povázson | HUN 60 | 17 Aug |
| 71.52 | Hakim | Toumi | ALG | 61 | 6 Jun | 71.30 | Jan | DeSoto | USA 54 | 14 Jun |
| 71.48 | John | McArdle | USA | 57 | 17 May | 71.28 | Björn-Peter | Fuhrmann | GDR 67 | 11 May |
| 71.44 | Jukka | Olkkonen | FIN | 58 | 15 Jun | 71.22 | Zdzisław | Kwasny | POL 60 | 17 Jun |
| 71.44 | Ari | Taavitsainen | FIN | 58 | 8 Jul | 71.10 | Rainer | Schons | FRG 62 | 11 May |
| 71.38 | Vladimir | Kuprovskiy | SU | 57 | 12 Jun | 71.10 | Marnix | Verhegghe | BEL 61 | 21 Sep |
| 71.38 | Yuriy | Melnik | SU | 62 | 20 Jun | 71.02 | Vilnis | Sudars | SU 63 | 2 May |

| Mark | Name | | | Nat | Yr | Pos | Meet | Venue | | Date | |
|---|---|---|---|---|---|---|---|---|---|---|---|
| 70.94 | Phil | Spivey | | AUS | 61 | 5 Jul | 70.42 | Marcel | Mangra | RUM 63 | 1 Jun |
| 70.82 | Lutz | Anne | (130) | GDR | 66 | 12 Jun | 70.32 | Declan | Hegarty | IRL 60 | 5 Apr |
| | | | | | | | 70.24 | Aleksandr | Shorokhov | SU 62 | 1 Jun |
| 70.82 | Tsvetan | Stoyanov | | BUL | 62 | 28 Jun | 70.20 | Conor | McCullough | IRL 61 | 27 Apr |
| 70.82 | Ryszard | Jakubowski | | POL | 59 | 27 Jul | 70.20 | Gary | Halpin | IRL 66 | 24 May |
| 70.78 | Vladimir | Knigin | | SU | 64 | 29 Jun | 70.20 | Shigenobu | Murofushi | JAP 45 | 30 May |
| 70.76 | Aleksandr | Drigol | | SU | 66 | 29 Aug | 70.14 | Pasi | Heikkilä | FIN 65 | 21 Jun |
| 70.68 | Vladimir | Mishin | | SU | 62 | 27 Jun | 70.10 | Michael | Jones | UK 63 | 26 Jul |
| 70.66 | Aleksandr | Tsvetikov | | SU | 62 | 29 Jun | 70.10 | Lech | Kowalski | POL 61 | 6 Sep |
| 70.66 | Kare | Sagedal | | NOR | 60 | 4 Aug | 70.08 | Jun | Luo | (150) CHN 64 | 28 Jul |
| 70.60 | Giovanni | Zichichi | | ITA | 64 | 25 Apr | | | | | |
| 70.52 | Mike | Maynard | | USA | 59 | 22 Mar | 70.06 | Plamen | Minev | (151) BUL 65 | 24 May |
| 70.52 | Fred | Schumacher | | SWE | 61 | 7 Jun | | | | | |
| | | | (140) | | | | | | | | |

Ancillary marks /over 84.00/:

| | | | | | | | | |
|---|---|---|---|---|---|---|---|---|
| 86.68 | Sedykh | 30 Aug | 84.92 | | Litvinov | | 3 Jul |
| 86.62 | Sedykh | 30 Aug | 84.64 | | Sedykh | | 11 Aug |
| 86.00 | Sedykh | 22 Jun | 84.58 | | Litvinov | | 11 Jul |
| 85.82 | Sedykh | 22 Jun | 84.34 | | Sedykh | | 9 Jul |
| 85.46 | Sedykh | 30 Aug | 84.18 | | Sedykh | | 3 Jul |
| 85.42 | Litvinov | 3 Jul | 84.12 | | Sedykh | | 22 Jun |
| 85.42 | Sedykh | 11 Aug | 84.02 | | Sedykh | | 7 Jul |
| 85.28 | Sedykh | 30 Aug | 84.02 | | Sedykh | | 9 Jul |
| 85.26 | Sedykh | 11 Aug | | | | | |
| 85.24 | Sedykh | 11 Aug | | | | | |

MEN 1986

| | 1 | 10 | 20 | 30 | 50 | 100 | Over 75.00 | Over 72.00 |
|---|---|---|---|---|---|---|---|---|
| 1982 | 83.98 | 77.92 | 76.60 | 75.90 | 74.56 | 71.62 | 43 | 94 |
| 1983 | 84.14 | 80.00 | 77.98 | 77.30 | 75.30 | 72.40 | 55 | 109 |
| 1984 | 86.34 | 80.50 | 79.06 | 77.94 | 76.34 | 73.08 | 64 | 122 |
| 1985 | 84.08 | 80.20 | 78.50 | 78.10 | 76.48 | 72.96 | 69 | 116 |
| 1986 | 86.74 | 80.68 | 79.30 | 78.32 | 76.14 | 72.36 | 61 | 106 |

## JAVELIN THROW

| | | | | | | | |
|---|---|---|---|---|---|---|---|
| 85.74 | Klaus | Tafelmeier | FRG | 58 | 1 | | Como | 21 Sep |
| 85.38 | Tom | Petranoff | USA | 58 | 1 | WG | Helsinki | 7 Jul |
| 84.76 | | Tafelmeier | | | 1 | EC | Stuttgart | 27 Aug |
| 83.68 | Viktor | Yevsyukov | SU | 56 | 1 | Znam | Leningrad | 8 Jun |
| 83.52 | Detlef | Michel | GDR | 55 | 1 | | Berlin | 18 Jun |
| 83.48 | | Tafelmeier | | | 1 | | Lausanne | 2 Sep |
| 83.46 | | Petranoff | | | 1 | GWG | Moskva | 6 Jul |
| 83.44 | | Petranoff | | | 1 | | Pihtipudas | 13 Jul |
| 83.40 | | Yevsyukov | | | 1 | v GDR | Tallinn | 22 Jun |
| 83.20 | Heino | Puuste | SU | 55 | 2 | v GDR | Tallinn | 22 Jun |

| Mark | Name | | Nat | Yr | Pos | Meet | Venue | Date | |
|------|------|--|-----|----|-----|------|-------|------|--|
| 83.12 | | Puuste | | | 2 | GWG | Moskva | 6 | Jul |
| 82.90 | | Tafelmeier | | | 1 | | Ingelheim | 5 | Aug |
| 82.84 | | Michel | | | 1 | NC | Jena | 29 | Jun |
| 82.70 | | Petranoff | | | 1 | | Gävle | 28 | Jul |
| 82.68 | | Tafelmeier | | | Q | EC | Stuttgart | 26 | Aug |
| 82.54 | | Puuste | | | Q | EC | Stuttgart | 26 | Aug |
| 82.48 | Jan | Železný | CS | 66 | 1 | | Praha | 17 | Aug |
| 82.40 | | Petranoff | | | 1 | DNG | Stockholm | 1 | Jul |
| 82.34 | Sejad | Krdžalić | YUG | 60 | 1 | | Beograd | 27 | Jun |
| 82.24 | | Tafelmeier | | | 1 | | Hannover | 7 | Jun |
| 82.00 | Marek | Kaleta | SU | 61 | 1 | NC | Kiev | 15 | Jul |
| 81.92 | | Puuste | | | 2 | NC | Kiev | 15 | Jul |
| 81.90 | | Michel | | | 2 | EC | Stuttgart | 27 | Aug |
| 81.90 | Kazuhiro | Mizoguchi | JAP | 62 | 1 | | Tokyo | 15 | Sep |
| 81.86 | Dag | Wennlund (10) | SWE | 63 | 1 | NC | Karlskrona | 2 | Aug |
| 81.80 | | Yevsyukov | | | 3 | EC | Stuttgart | 27 | Aug |
| 81.74 | Roald | Bradstock | UK | 62 | 1 | | Tucson | 3 | May |
| 81.72 | Seppo | Räty | FIN | 62 | 1 | | Parkano | 11 | May |
| 81.50 | | Räty | | | 2 | WG | Helsinki | 7 | Jul |
| 81.44 | Sergey | Gavras(30/13) | SU | 57 | 3 | GWG | Moskva | 6 | Jul |
| 81.40 | Gerald | Weiss | GDR | 60 | Q | NC | Stuttgart | 26 | Aug |
| 81.30 | Wolfram | Gambke | FRG | 59 | 1 | NC | W Berlin | 13 | Jul |
| 81.02 | Volker | Hadwich | GDR | 64 | 1 | | Erfurt | 1 | Jun |
| 80.94 | Sergey | Glebov | SU | 64 | 1 | Spart | Tashkent | 17 | Sep |
| 80.76 | Charlus | Bertimon | FRA | 57 | 1 | | Sarrebourg | 7 | Sep |
| 80.74 | Peter | Borglund | SWE | 64 | 1 | | Södertälje | 4 | Jun |
| 80.66 | Masami | Yoshida (20) | JAP | 58 | 1 | | Kawasaki | 23 | Sep |
| 80.62 | David | Ottley | UK | 55 | 1 | CG | Edinburgh | 2 | Aug |
| 80.56 | László | Stefán | HUN | 63 | 1 | v Aut, | Bul,Gre Linz | 29 | Jun |
| 80.56 | Jorma | Markus | FIN | 52 | 3 | | Pihtipudas | 13 | Jul |
| 80.48 | Jyrki | Blom | FIN | 62 | 4 | EC | Stuttgart | 27 | Aug |
| 80.28 | Einar | Vilhjalmsson | ICE | 60 | 2 | | Växjö | 21 | Aug |
| 79.86 | Brian | Crouser | USA | 62 | 1 | | Papeete | 27 | Mar |
| 79.86 | Thomas | Schäffner | GDR | 63 | 3 | NC | Jena | 29 | Jun |
| 79.74 | Normunds | Pildavs | SU | 64 | 1 | | Riga | 15 | Jun |
| 79.74 | Sigurdur | Einarsson | ICE | 62 | 1 | | Kvarnsveden | 24 | Jun |
| 79.58 | Nicu | Roata (30) | RUM | 61 | 1 | NC | Pitești | 8 | Aug |
| 79.58 | Gavin | Lovegrove | NZ | 67 | 2 | | Noumea | 25 | Oct |
| 79.54 | Yuriy | Smirnov | SU | 61 | 1 | | Ventspils | 28 | Sep |
| 79.52 | Štefan | Lengyel | CS | 61 | 1 | v Hun | Praha | 17 | Sep |
| 79.14 | Bob | Roggy | USA | 56 | 1 | Pre | Eugene | 7 | Jun |
| 79.04 | Mike | Mahovlich | CAN | 60 | 1 | | Seattle | 26 | Apr |
| 78.96 | Klaus-Jörg | Murawa | GDR | 64 | 4 | NC | Jena | 29 | Jun |
| 78.96 | Eero | Heikkinen | FIN | 55 | Q | NC | Vaasa | 26 | Jul |
| 78.84 | Vladimir | Sasimovich | SU | 68 | 1 | WC-j | Athinai | 18 | Jul |
| 78.64 | Yuriy | Zhirov | SU | 60 | 1 | | Bratislava | 4 | Sep |
| 78.56 | Mike | Hill (40) | UK | 64 | 2 | CG | Edinburgh | 2 | Aug |
| 78.54 | Masanori | Amano | JAP | 65 | 1 | NC | Tokyo | 1 | Jun |
| 78.50 | Vladimir | Furdylo | SU | 58 | 2 | | Riga | 15 | Jun |
| 78.36 | Jan-Olov | Johansson | SWE | 62 | 1 | | Pullman | 19 | Apr |
| 78.32 | Stanisław | Górak | POL | 59 | Q | EC | Stuttgart | 26 | Aug |
| 78.18 | Matti | Korte | FIN | 56 | 1 | | Koski | 1 | Jun |

| Mark | Name | | Nat | Yr | Pos | Meet | Venue | Date |
|------|------|--|-----|----|-----|------|-------|------|
| 77.96 | Andrey | Maznichenko | SU | 66 | 1 | | Dnepropetrovsk | 27 Jun |
| 77.96 | Zdeněk | Adamec | CS | 56 | 2 | NC | Bratislava | 13 Jul |
| 77.64 | Aimo | Aho | FIN | 51 | 5 | | Pihtipudas | 13 Jul |
| 77.62 | Reidar | Lorentzen | NOR | 56 | 1 | | Lisboa | 31 May |
| 77.38 | Arto | Manninen (50) | FIN | 62 | 3 | Nurmi | Turku | 3 Jul |
| 77.32 | Ferenc | Paragi | HUN | 53 | 2 | v Aut, | Bul,Gre Linz | 29 Jun |
| 77.32 | Ramon | González | CUB | 65 | 1 | CAC | Santiago/Dom | 4 Jul |
| 77.30 | Viktor | Bochin | SU | 60 | 1 | | Budapest | 11 Sep |
| 77.28 | Vladimir | Gavrilyuk | SU | 61 | 2 | | Sochi | 24 May |
| 77.14 | Jean-Paul | Lakafia | FRA | 61 | 2 | NC | Aix-les-Bains | 10 Aug |
| 76.94 | Vladimir | Polishko | SU | 59 | 4 | | Dnepropetrovsk | 27 Jun |
| 76.90 | Marcis | Strobinders | SU | 66 | 2 | Spart | Tashkent | 17 Sep |
| 76.88 | Peter | Schreiber | FRG | 64 | 3 | NC | W Berlin | 13 Jul |
| 76.88 | Øystein | Slettevold | NOR | 62 | 1 | NC | Sandnes | 8 Aug |
| 76.84 | Tamás | Bolgár (60) | HUN | 55 | 1 | NC | Budapest | 17 Aug |
| 76.70 | Constantin | Chiriac | RUM | 60 | 2 | NC | Pitești | 8 Aug |
| 76.70 | Virginius | Kuzminskas | SU | 61 | 1 | | Kaunas | 12 Sep |
| 76.64 | Pascal | Lefevre | FRA | 65 | 3 | NC | Aix-les-Bains | 10 Aug |
| 76.54 | Andreas | Linden | FRG | 65 | 4 | NC | W Berlin | 13 Jul |
| 76.48 | Peter | Yates | UK | 57 | 1 | | Walnut, CA | 1 Feb |
| 76.48 | Zakayo | Malekwa | TAN | 51 | 1 | | Arlington | 10 May |
| 76.34 | Hans-Joachim | Lange | GDR | 60 | 4 | | Potsdam | 12 Jun |
| 76.26 | Maximo | Driggs | CUB | 62 | 4 | PTS | Bratislava | 13 Jun |
| 76.22 | Dionisio | Quintana | CUB | 57 | 1 | | Habana | 20 Jun |
| 76.16 | Janis | Zirnis (70) | SU | 47 | 2 | | Riga | 30 May |
| 76.12 | Yki | Laine | FIN | 65 | 3 | NC | Vaasa | 27 Jul |
| 76.12 | Dainis | Kula | SU | 59 | Q | | Ventspils | 27 Sep |
| 76.06 | Fabio | De Gaspari | ITA | 66 | 2 | v Fra, | Pol,Spa Monaco | 6 Jul |
| 76.04 | Kari | Ihalainen | FIN | 54 | 2 | | Keuruu | 20 Jun |
| 76.02 | Mike | Barnett | USA | 61 | 1 | | Walnut, CA | 1 Jun |
| 75.96 | Rudolf | Steiner | SWZ | 51 | 1 | | Bern | 5 Sep |
| 75.92 | Yuriy | Novikov | SU | 58 | 5 | NC | Kiev | 15 Jul |
| 75.90 | John | Amabile | USA | 62 | 1 | | Ewing, NJ | 14 Jun |
| 75.88 | Kenneth | Pedersen | DEN | 65 | 5 | | Gävle | 28 Jul |
| 75.86 | Bogdan | Patelka (80) | POL | 66 | 1 | | Grudziadz | 3 Jun |
| 75.84 | Ming | Zhao | CHN | 63 | 1 | | Beijing | 17 May |
| 75.80 | Craig | Christianson | USA | 61 | 1 | | Eugene | 1 Aug |
| 75.76 | Mirosław | Szybowski | POL | 60 | 2 | | Grudziadz | 3 Jun |
| 75.76 | Emil | Tsvetanov | BUL | 63 | 2 | Balk | Ljubljana | 7 Sep |
| 75.74 | Ken | Asakura | JAP | 61 | 3 | | Tokyo | 11 May |
| 75.72 | Bob | Erskine | USA | 64 | 2 | | Houston | 17 May |
| 75.70 | Hannu | Holopainen | FIN | 58 | 1 | | Hämeenlinna | 29 Jun |
| 75.58 | Narve | Hoff | NOR | 57 | 3 | | Byrkjelo | 28 Jun |
| 75.52 | Knut | Hempel | FRG | 65 | 1 | | Hamburg | 11 Oct |
| 75.48 | Francois | Demontigny | FRA | 65 | 4 | NC | Aix-les-Bains | 10 Aug |
| | | (90) | | | | | | |
| 75.46 | Rick | Simoncic | USA | 63 | 1 | | Russellville | 22 May |
| 75.46 | Nikolay | Kosyanok | SU | 58 | 1 | | Minsk | 30 May |
| 75.42 | Sören | Tallhem | SWE | 64 | 2 | TexR | Austin | 4 Apr |
| 75.40 | Stefan | Stoikov | BUL | 51 | 1 | | Sofia | 11 May |
| 75.40 | Juha | Hentunen | FIN | 60 | 3 | | Keuruu | 20 Jun |
| 75.38 | Uwe | Tefs | GDR | 68 | 1 | v CS, | Hun-j Praha | 1 Jul |

| Mark | Name | | Nat | Yr | Pos | Meet | Venue | Date | |
|------|------|--|-----|----|-----|------|-------|------|--|
| 75.38 | Ivan | Mustapić | YUG | 66 | 3 | Balk | Ljubljana | 7 | Sep |
| 75.36 | Dave | Stephens | USA | 62 | 1 | | Long Beach | 16 | May |
| 75.30 | Mikhail | Shishkov | SU | 60 | 5 | | Adler | 24 | Feb |
| 75.30 | Mark | Babich (100) | USA | 63 | 2 | | Pullman | 19 | Apr |
| | | | | | | | | | |
| 75.28 | Karl-Friedrich Michel | | FRG | 65 | 1 | | Stuttgart | 5 | Oct |
| 75.26 | Philippe | Lecurieux | FRA | 58 | 2 | | Sarrebourg | 7 | Sep |
| 75.24 | Ron | Bahm | USA | 65 | 1 | | Wichita | 12 | Apr |
| 75.06 | Steve | Feraday | CAN | 59 | 5 | v FRG, | Fin Rehlingen | 19 | May |
| 75.06 | Leif | Lundmark | SWE | 53 | 2 | | Boden | 20 | Jul |
| 75.00 | Fabiano | Fakataulavelua | FRA | 62 | 2 | | Saint-Denis | 21 | Jun |
| | | (106) | | | | | | | |

Ancillary marks /over 82.00/:

| | | | | |
|------|------------|--|----|-----|
| 83.34 | Tafelmeier | | 2 | Sep |
| 82.46 | Tafelmeier | | 21 | Sep |
| 82.42 | Tafelmeier | | 5 | Aug |
| 82.26 | Petranoff | | 6 | Jul |
| 82.22 | Tafelmeier | | 21 | Sep |
| 82.00 | Tafelmeier | | 2 | Sep |

Marks made with old implement:

| Mark | Name | | Nat | Yr | Pos | Venue | Date | |
|------|------|--|-----|----|-----|-------|------|--|
| 92.38 | Tom | Petranoff | USA | 58 | 1 | San Diego | 1 | Mar |
| 87.94 | Chris | de Beer | RSA | 61 | 1 | Bloemfontein | 12 | Feb |
| 87.14 | Ramon | González | CUB | 65 | 1 | Habana | 14 | Feb |
| 86.28 | Darryl | Brand | UK | 63 | 1 | Hendon | 15 | Jun |
| 84.74 | Martin | Alvarez | CUB | 60 | 2 | Santiago/Cuba | 23 | Feb |
| 84.40 | Stanisław | Górak | POL | 59 | 1 | Słupsk | 8 | Jun |
| 83.70 | Mike | O'Rourke | NZ | 55 | 1 | Auckland | 11 | Jan |
| 82.66 | Orlando | Hernandez | CUB | 62 | 3 | Santiago/Cuba | 23 | Feb |
| 82.28 | Zbigniew | Bednarski | POL | 60 | 1 | Rzeszów | 25 | May |
| 82.18 | Andrey | Maznichenko | SU | 66 | 1 | Moskva | 10 | Aug |
| | | | | | | | | |
| 82.08 | John | Amabile | USA | 62 | 1 | San Juan | 19 | Apr |
| 82.04 | Mike | Hill | UK | 64 | 1 | Cleckheaton | 20 | Apr |
| 81.94 | Stanisław | Witek | POL | 60 | 1 | Bialogard | 27 | Sep |
| 81.00 | Reinaldo | Patterson | CUB | 56 | 2 | Habana | 6 | Feb |
| 80.98 | Murray | Keen | AUS | 65 | 1 | Perth | 12 | Feb |
| 80.60 | Lev | Shatilo | SU | 63 | 1 | Leselidze | 11 | May |
| 80.44 | Maximo | Driggs | CUB | 62 | 4 | Habana | 6 | Feb |
| 80.00 | Gavin | Lovegrove | NZ | 67 | 1 | Auckland | 18 | Jan |

| Points | Name | | Nat | Yr | Pos | Meet | Venue | Date |
|---|---|---|---|---|---|---|---|---|

## DECATHLON

**MEN 1986**

| 8811 | Daley | Thompson | UK | 58 | 1 | EC | Stuttgart | 27/28 Aug |
|---|---|---|---|---|---|---|---|---|
| | 10.26 7.72 15.73 2.00 47.02 / 14.04 43.38 5.10 62.78 4:26.16 | | | | | | | | |
| 8730 | Jürgen | Hingsen | FRG | 58 | 2 | EC | Stuttgart | 27/28 Aug |
| | 10.87w 7.89w 16.46 2.12 48.79 / 14.52 48.42 4.60 64.38 4:21.61 | | | | | | | | |
| 8676 | Siegfried | Wentz | FRG | 60 | 3 | EC | Stuttgart | 27/28 Aug |
| | 10.83 7.60 15.45 2.12 47.57 / 14.07 45.66 4.90 65.34 4:35.00 | | | | | | | | |
| 8667 | | Thompson | | | 1 | v Fra,Can | Arles | 17/18 May |
| | 10.56 7.81 15.39 1.98 47.52 / 14.35 47.62 4.90 63.28 4:30.04 | | | | | | | | |
| 8663 | | Thompson | | | 1 | CG | Edinburgh | 27/28 Jul |
| | 10.37 7.70w 15.01 2.08 47.30 / 14.22 43.72 5.10 60.82 4:39.63 | | | | | | | | |
| 8590 | | Wentz | | | 1 | | Bernhausen | 14/15 Jun |
| | 10.97 7.17 16.03 2.06 48.09 / 14.11 48.16 4.90 67.42 4:32.25 | | | | | | | | |
| 8519 | Guido | Kratschmer | FRG | 53 | 1 | | Götzis | 24/25 May |
| | 10.82 7.76w 16.62 1.93 48.75 / 14.09 48.42 4.60 63.82 4:32.36 | | | | | | | | |
| 8485 | | Hingsen | | | 2 | | Bernhausen | 14/15 Jun |
| | 10.98 7.62 16.57 2.00 50.05 / 14.42 47.50 4.80 63.78 4:25.94 | | | | | | | | |
| 8450 | Torsten | Voss | GDR | 63 | 4 | EC | Stuttgart | 27/28 Aug |
| | 10.53w 7.85w 14.93 2.09 48.03 / 14.91 43.64 5.10 57.76 4:47.15 | | | | | | | | |
| 8322 | Mike | Ramos | USA | 62 | 1 | | Los Angeles | 19/20 May |
| | 10.77 7.39 14.67 2.16 50.16 / 14.98 49.06 4.80 63.52 4:48.06 | | | | | | | | |
| 8322 | Uwe | Freimuth | GDR | 61 | 2 | | Götzis | 24/25 May |
| | 11.23 7.57w 15.80 1.93 49.50 / 14.79 47.98 4.90 64.78 4:29.22 | | | | | | | | |
| 8322 | Grigoriy | Degtyarov | SU | 58 | 1 | GWG | Moskva | 6/ 7 Jul |
| | 10.90 7.52 15.33 2.02 50.10 / 14.65 48.56 4.80 59.28 4:29.34 | | | | | | | | |
| 8315 | Mikhail | Medved | SU | 64 | 1 | Spart | Tashkent | 18/19 Sep |
| | 11.13 7.50 16.06 2.11 49.99 / 14.47 43.78 4.90 64.46 4:48.18 | | | | | | | | |
| 8302 m | Tim | Bright (10) | USA | 60 | 1 | | Fresno | 25/26 Mar |
| | 10.94 7.15 14.38 2.04 48.72 / 14.0 m 43.02 5.51 57.76 4:42.28 | | | | | | | | |
| 8261 | | Ramos | | | 1 | NCAA | Indianapolis | 6/ 7 Jun |
| | 10.89 7.08 14.07 2.07 49.25 / 14.74w 50.98 5.00 62.42 4:47.00 | | | | | | | | |
| 8254 W | Dave | Steen | CAN | 59 | 1 | v USA | Saskatoon | 16/17 Aug |
| | 10.91w 7.72w 13.50 1.93 48.91 / 14.82W 43.32 5.15 59.98 4:24.53 | | | | | | | | |
| 8248 | | Freimuth | | | 1 | NC | Potsdam | 11/12 Jun |
| | 11.23 7.35 16.01 1.97 50.00 / 14.68 45.96 5.00 63.58 4:33.90 | | | | | | | | |
| 8243 | | Steen | | | 1 | | Eagle Rock, CA | 22/23 Mar |
| | 11.14 7.64 13.24 2.03 48.15 / 14.84 42.52 4.90 62.66 4:23.86 | | | | | | | | |
| 8244 | Aleksandr | Apaichev | SU | 58 | 2 | GWG | Moskva | 6/ 7 Jul |
| | 11.09 7.35 15.66 1.96 50.23 / 14.19 44.80 4.60 67.12 4:28.46 | | | | | | | | |
| 8232 M | Sven | Reintak | SU | 63 | 1 | | Tartu | 17/18 May |
| | 10.9 m 7.20 14.82 2.04 50.2 m/ 14.4 m 44.64 5.10 61.36¯4:26.2 m | | | | | | | | |
| 8227 | Andrey | Fomochkin | SU | 63 | 2 | Spart | Tashkent | 18/19 Sep |
| | 10.71 7.48 14.27 1.99 46.74 / 14.43 43.46 4.60 51.52 4:20.97 | | | | | | | | |
| 8214 | Pavel | Tarnovetskiy | SU | 61 | 1 | | Sochi | 23/24 May |
| | 11.14 7.35 14.72 2.08 49.61 / 14.82 46.62 5.00 53.10 4:23.57 | | | | | | | | |
| 8205 | | Reintak | | | 1 | v Swe,Fin,Swz | Uppsala | 14/15 Jun |
| | 11.19 7.17 14.32 2.03 49.99 / 14.93 44.86 5.10 62.08 4:20.85 | | | | | | | | |
| 8203 | Gary | Armstrong | USA | 60 | 1 | | Tallahassee | 26/27 Apr |
| | 10.85 7.40 13.96 2.00 47.68 / 14.61 44.70 4.80 54.46 4:24.16 | | | | | | | | |
| 8203 W | Dave | Johnson | USA | 63 | 1 | TAC | Eugene | 18/19 Jun |
| | 11.23 7.30W 14.08 2.07 49.53 / 14.79 46.16 4.90 62.78 4:30.06 | | | | | | | | |
| 8199 | | Apaichev | | | 5 | EC | Stuttgart | 27/28 Aug |
| | 11.14 7.25 15.57 1.88 49.45 / 14.29 45.82 4.80 64.84 4:28.66 | | | | | | | | |
| 8197 | | Freimuth | | | 6 | EC | Stuttgart | 27/28 Aug |
| | 11.02 7.25 15.28 1.97 48.35 / 14.85 45.94 4.90 60.36 4:34.54 | | | | | | | | |

| Points | Name | | Nat | Yr | Pos | Meet | Venue | Date |
|--------|------|---|-----|----|----|------|-------|------|
| 8196 | Christian | Plaziat | FRA | 63 | 7 | EC | Stuttgart | 27/28 Aug |
| | 10.84w 7.36w 14.73  2.15 | | 50.03 / | 14.83 | 45.40 | 4.70 | 57.10 | 4:35.20 |
| 8185 | Alain | Blondel | FRA | 62 | 8 | EC | Stuttgart | 27/28 Aug |
| | 10.74w 7.42  13.27  2.00 | | 47.79 / | 14.34 | 39.22 | 4.90 | 55.18 | 4:18.97 |
| 8173 | | Steen (30/19) | | | 2 | CG | Edinburgh | 27/28 Jul |
| | 11.14  7.40  13.22  2.02 | | 48.45 / | 14.91 | 43.62 | 5.00 | 60.18 | 4:22.65 |
| 8170 | Thomas | Fahner  (20) | GDR | 66 | 3 | | Götzis | 24/25 May |
| | 10.82  7.29  13.96  1.90 | | 47.90 / | 14.96 | 43.52 | 5.10 | 61.88 | 4:31.47 |
| 8168 | Valter | Külvet | SU | 64 | 1e2 | NC | Moskva | 6/ 7 Jul |
| | 11.30  7.04  15.50  1.99 | | 49.45 / | 15.03 | 49.94 | 4.90 | 61.32 | 4:30.29 |
| 8159 | Chris | Branham | USA | 62 | 1 | MSR | Walnut, CA | 24/25 Apr |
| | 11.02  7.42w 14.69  2.11 | | 50.66 / | 14.14 | 42.32 | 4.80 | 62.82 | 4:48.33 |
| 8158 | Simon | Poelman | NZ | 63 | 1 | | Christchurch | 29/30 Mar |
| | 10.84  7.36w 14.23  2.05 | | 49.74 / | 14.59 | 43.56 | 4.80 | 57.22 | 4:27.66 |
| 8143 | Aleksandr | Nevskiy | SU | 58 | 2e2 | NC | Moskva | 6/ 7 Jul |
| | 11.04  7.24  15.57  1.99 | | 49.48 / | 14.70 | 46.40 | 4.70 | 54.40 | 4:20.67 |
| 8114 | Yevgeniy | Ovsyannikov | SU | 63 | 3 | Spart | Tashkent | 18/19 Sep |
| | 11.11  7.54  14.13  2.11 | | 49.68 / | 14.82 | 47.12 | 4.80 | 48.10 | 4:26.17 |
| 8112 | Michael | Neugebauer | FRG | 62 | 1 | | Ingolstadt | 21/22 Jun |
| | 10.82  7.30  14.13  2.02 | | 48.37 / | 14.11 | 43.14 | 4.50 | 57.04 | 4:31.60 |
| 8108 | Richardas | Malahovskis | SU | 65 | 1 | v FRG | Bernhausen | 14/15 Jun |
| | 11.16  6.92  13.68  2.09 | | 47.97 / | 14.93 | 42.10 | 4.70 | 63.40 | 4:20.56 |
| 8089 | Beat | Gähwiler | SWZ | 65 | 1 | NC | Wil | 5/ 6 Jul |
| | 11.00  7.48w 14.35  1.95 | | 48.43 / | 14.71 | 39.42 | 4.70 | 60.64 | 4:21.95 |
| 8082 | Aleksey | Lyakh | SU | 62 | 3 | GWG | Moskva | 6/ 7 Jul |
| | 11.18  7.71  14.97  2.05 | | 50.60 / | 14.85 | 44.40 | 4.60 | 61.28 | 4:40.10 |
| 8079 | Sergey | Popov  (30) | SU | 57 | 3e2 | NC | Moskva | 6/ 7 Jul |
| | 11.18  7.45  14.49  1.96 | | 49.76 / | 15.18 | 48.60 | 4.90 | 58.78 | 4:34.34 |
| 8076 | John | Sayre | USA | 61 | 2 | MSR | Walnut, CA | 24/25 Apr |
| | 11.23w 6.93w 14.53  1.99 | | 49.32 / | 14.82 | 48.52 | 5.00 | 64.90 | 4:47.29 |
| 8060 | Jens | Petersson | GDR | 64 | 4 | GWG | Moskva | 6/ 7 Jul |
| | 10.72  7.80  14.59  1.99 | | 48.56 / | 14.71 | 42.82 | 4.50 | 50.66 | 4:33.84 |
| 8045 | Sergey | Zhelanov | SU | 57 | 1 | SU P | Dnepropetrovsk | 6/ 7 Sep |
| | 11.35  7.27  14.17  2.11 | | 50.03 / | 15.28 | 44.84 | 4.90 | 58.72 | 4:29.84 |
| 8041 | Bart | Goodell | USA | 61 | 1 | | Los Gatos, CA | 25/26 Aug |
| | 10.73  7.05  15.88  1.97 | | 49.50 / | 15.62 | 52.90 | 4.60 | 61.30 | 4:56.41 |
| 8032 | Jens | Schulze | FRG | 56 | 1 | NC | Hannover | 19/20 Jul |
| | 11.10  7.05  15.23  2.00 | | 48.64 / | 14.33 | 46.28 | 4.60 | 51.28 | 4:27.73 |
| 8030 | Steve | Erickson | USA | 61 | 2 | TAC | Eugene | 18/19 Jun |
| | 11.23  7.06w 14.50  1.92 | | 48.83 / | 14.82 | 44.32 | 5.00 | 61.08 | 4:29.89 |
| 8021 M | Igor | Pupchonok | SU | 63 | 1 | | Alma-Ata | 28/29 Aug |
| | 11.1 m 7.04  15.83  2.15 | | 49.5 m/ | 14.8 m | 41.58 | 4.20 | 66.10⁻ | 4:29.0 m |
| 8006 | William | Motti | FRA | 62 | 2 | v Can,UK | Arles | 17/18 May |
| | 11.25  7.24w 14.77  2.16 | | 48.98 / | 14.73 | 42.32 | 4.50 | 62.54 | 4:51.71 |
| 8001 M | Andrey | Nazarov | SU | 65 | 2 | | Tartu | 17/18 May |
| | 10.7 m 7.39  12.83  2.13 | | 50.1 m/ | 14.3 m | 39.24 | 4.20 | 67.80⁻ | 4:29.4 m |
| 8000 | Hans-Ulrich | Riecke  (40) | GDR | 63 | 5 | GWG | Moskva | 6/ 7 Jul |
| | 10.60  7.74  14.58  1.90 | | 49.31 / | 14.81 | 42.96 | 4.40 | 57.90 | 4:37.94 |
| 7998 W | Gary | Kinder | USA | 62 | 2 | USOCF | Houston | 2/ 3 Aug |
| | 11.02  6.91W 15.45  1.99 | | 51.35 / | 14.92W | 46.86 | 5.00 | 66.74 | 4:57.90 |
| 7991 | Steve | Odgers | USA | 61 | 3 | MSR | Walnut, CA | 24/25 Apr |
| | 11.14  7.22w 15.00  1.93 | | 48.68 / | 15.01 | 46.80 | 4.40 | 61.30 | 4:29.33 |

| Points | Name | | Nat | Yr | Pos | Meet | Venue | Date |
|--------|------|--|-----|----|-----|------|-------|------|
| 7990 | Sten | Ekberg | SWE | 64 | 2 | NCAA | Indianapolis | 6/ 7 Jun |
| | 11.08  7.26   14.04    2.07 | | 48.86 / 15.36w 45.00   4.50  58.66  4:28.86 | | | | | |
| 7966 M | Vladimir | Obukhov | SU | 59 | 1 | | Lipetsk | 20/21 Jul |
| | 10.9 m 7.24   15.81    1.97 | | 50.2 m/ 14.9 m 43.50   4.70  57.56  4:27.5 m | | | | | |
| 7962 | Robert | de Wit | HOL | 62 | 9 | EC | Stuttgart | 27/28 Aug |
| | 11.07w 7.05   14.04    2.00 | | 49.35 / 14.58  43.34   4.80  54.74  4:26.09 | | | | | |
| 7950 | Wojciech | Podsiadlo | POL | 58 | 1 | | Poznan | 5/ 6 Sep |
| | 11.01  7.10   14.21    1.98 | | 50.26 / 14.72  42.06   4.80  60.98  4:31.93 | | | | | |
| 7949 | Sergey | Gazyura | SU | 64 | 5 | Spart | Tashkent | 18/19 Sep |
| | 11.11  6.67   14.90    1.99 | | 48.96 / 14.81  45.48   4.80  54.70  4:24.85 | | | | | |
| 7945 M | Tiit | Pahker | SU | 58 | 3 | | Tartu | 17/18 May |
| | 10.9 m 7.14   14.10    2.04 | | 49.7 m/ 15.6 m 43.34   5.00  60.46⁻4:31.8 m | | | | | |
| 7930 W | Tony | Allen-Cooksey | USA | 56 | 2 | v Can | Saskatoon | 16/17 Aug |
| | 11.12w 7.64w 14.42    1.93 | | 49.92 / 14.71W 42.96   4.75  56.38  4:39.13 | | | | | |
| 7920 | Nikolay | Reka (50) | SU | 63 | 6 | Spart | Tashkent | 18/19 Sep |
| | 11.30  6.94   13.48    1.93 | | 48.66 / 14.63  45.28   4.90  54.22  4:19.72 | | | | | |
| 7918 M | Vladimir | Romanov | SU | 61 | 2 | | Lipetsk | 20/21 Jul |
| | 10.6 m 7.32   14.56    2.00 | | 49.6 m/ 15.7 m 48.52   4.40  58.50  4:35.2 m | | | | | |
| 7905 | Věroslav | Valenta | CS | 65 | 1 | | | 7/ 8 Jun |
| | 11.32  7.21w 15.13    1.98 | | 49.90 / 14.41  48.78   4.40  52.42  4:32.89 | | | | | |
| 7904 | Aleksandr | Tsyoma | SU | 61 | 6 | | Sochi | 23/24 May |
| | 11.03  7.21   14.53    1.99 | | 51.19 / 14.49  43.94   4.70  54.14  4:30.02 | | | | | |
| 7896 | Patrick | Vetterli | SWZ | 61 | 1 | | Balgach | 2/ 3 Aug |
| | 11.25w 7.25w 14.80    2.07 | | 49.35 / 14.77  46.06   4.30  60.44  4:50.93 | | | | | |
| 7895 | Patrick | Gellens | FRA | 59 | 3 | v Can,UK | Arles | 17/18 May |
| | 11.21w 7.28   13.61    2.04 | | 49.43 / 15.66  46.08   4.90  51.66  4:27.46 | | | | | |
| 7891 | Thomas | Halamoda | GDR | 66 | 9 | GWG | Moskva | 6/ 7 Jul |
| | 10.98  7.58   14.84    1.87 | | 49.46 / 15.16  41.22   4.40  64.28  4:35.08 | | | | | |
| 7889 | Eugene | Gilkes | UK | 62 | 4 | v Fra,Can | Arles | 17/18 May |
| | 10.82  7.20   14.88    1.95 | | 47.12 / 15.26  44.76   4.20  47.00  4:16.36 | | | | | |
| 7888 | Mikael | Olander | SWE | 63 | 11= | EC | Stuttgart | 27/28 Aug |
| | 11.29w 6.78w 15.62    1.97 | | 50.85 / 16.16  46.30   4.60  72.50  4:33.46 | | | | | |
| 7874 | Vladimir | Kryuchkov | SU | 62 | 7 | | Sochi | 23/24 May |
| | 11.41  7.00   14.71    2.08 | | 49.37 / 15.33  42.24   4.60  56.14  4:21.00 | | | | | |
| 7868 | Ivan | Bably (60) | SU | 63 | 8 | | Sochi | 23/24 May |
| | 11.18  6.95   14.42    2.05 | | 49.87 / 14.20  42.26   4.60  51.70  4:28.20 | | | | | |
| 7866 W | Roman | Hrabaň | CS | 62 | 1 | NC | Bratislava | 12/13 Jul |
| | 10.87W 7.16   15.32    1.90 | | 50.12 / 14.99  45.08   4.80  60.82  4:57.55 | | | | | |
| 7866 | Igor | Marin | SU | 65 | 8 | Spart | Tashkent | 18/19 Sep |
| | 11.13  7.21   14.05    2.05 | | 49.91 / 15.14  44.08   4.70  52.22  4:29.45 | | | | | |
| 7864 | Frédéric | Sacco | FRA | 61 | 5 | v Can,UK | Arles | 17/18 May |
| | 11.36  7.14   16.20    1.98 | | 51.40 / 15.21  45.38   4.70  58.06  4:35.62 | | | | | |
| 7855 | Wolfgang | Muders | FRG | 57 | 1 | | Wuppertal | 21/22 Jun |
| | 11.28  6.82   15.09    2.02 | | 50.47 / 14.44  42.42   4.70  52.74  4:22.43 | | | | | |
| 7845 | Nikolay | Afanasyev | SU | 65 | 4 | v FRG | Bernhausen | 14/15 Jun |
| | 11.16  6.87   13.27    1.91 | | 49.62 / 14.69  41.86   4.90  63.46  4:30.79 | | | | | |
| 7844 | Christian | Deick | FRG | 65 | 5 | v SU | Bernhausen | 14/15 Jun |
| | 10.93  7.23   14.82    1.91 | | 49.61 / 15.15  44.72   4.10  60.94  4:25.38 | | | | | |
| 7842 | Krzysztof | Krakowiak | POL | 61 | 2 | | Poznan | 5/ 6 Sep |
| | 11.16  7.37   14.83    1.92 | | 50.11 / 14.77  49.86   4.20  61.78  4:51.28 | | | | | |
| 7838 | Aleksandr | Areshin | SU | 61 | 10 | | Sochi | 23/24 May |
| | 11.32  7.34w 15.09    1.96 | | 49.10 / 14.78  42.52   4.40  53.12  4:25.60 | | | | | |
| 7833 | Aleksandr | Stavro | SU | 63 | 10 | Spart | Tashkent | 18/19 Sep |
| | 11.16  6.97   13.70    1.99 | | 48.78 / 15.29  41.42   4.50  59.22  4:17.19 | | | | | |

MEN 1986

| Points | Name | Nat | Yr | Pos | Meet | Venue | Date |
|---|---|---|---|---|---|---|---|
| 7827 | Janusz  Lesniewicz (70) | POL | 55 | 1 | NC | Grudziadz | 27/28 Jun |
| | 11.12  7.13w 13.61  2.04  49.23 / 15.21  44.08  4.50  55.14  4:28.09 | | | | | | |
| 7814 M | Andrey     Krovotyntsev | SU | 65 | 1 | | Moskva | 23/24 May |
| 7813 = | 11.3 m 6.97  15.08  1.96  51.0 m/ 15.0 m 46.70  4.80  58.90  4:30.1 m | | | | | | |
| 7802 | Andre     Preysing | GDR | 66 | 2 | | Berlin | 19/20 Aug |
| | 11.07  7.26w 13.19  2.13  48.47 / 15.04  40.96  4.60  48.02  4:34.94 | | | | | | |
| 7776 | Lars     Warming | DEN | 63 | 14 | EC | Stuttgart | 27/28 Aug |
| | 10.82w 7.03  13.52  1.94  47.76 / 14.54  40.48  4.60  44.00  4:19.49 | | | | | | |
| 7776 | Roman     Terekhov | SU | 63 | 11 | Spart | Tashkent | 18/19 Sep |
| | 11.28  7.08  12.05  1.96  48.15 / 14.57  40.38  4.40  59.28  4:16.79 | | | | | | |
| 7769 | Vadim     Podmaryov | SU | 58 | 5e2 | NC | Moskva | 6/ 7 Jul |
| | 11.18  7.26  14.31  2.05  50.88 / 15.15  46.42  4.60  54.44  4:48.34 | | | | | | |
| 7768 | Jim     Connolly | USA | 63 | 4 | NCAA | Indianapolis | 6/ 7 Jun |
| | 11.06  6.87  14.56  2.01  49.82 / 15.71  40.54  4.40  69.46  4:39.21 | | | | | | |
| 7763 | Shannon     Sullivan | USA | 59 | 2 | | San Diego | 16/17 May |
| | 11.26  6.84  13.57  1.94  49.89 / 15.42  41.64  5.20  56.52  4:28.10 | | | | | | |
| 7755 | Felix     Haas | SWZ | 59 | 2 | | Balgach | 2/ 3 Aug |
| | 11.01w 6.80w 14.25  1.89  48.65 / 14.70  41.90  4.30  60.56  4:26.72 | | | | | | |
| 7749 | Sergey     Pogrebnyuk | SU | 61 | 2 | | Kiev | 25/26 Jul |
| 7748 = | 11.29  7.28  13.84  1.92  50.91 / 15.20  41.72  4.70  60.88  4:28.86 | | | | | | |
| 7746 W | Rob     Muzzio (80) | USA | 64 | 3 | USOCF | Houston | 2/ 3 Aug |
| | 11.21  7.17w 16.61  1.96  50.87 / 15.22W 45.64  4.00  60.28  4:39.28 | | | | | | |
| 7743 | Andrzej     Wyzykowski | POL | 60 | 3 | | Poznan | 5/ 6 Sep |
| | 11.15  7.05  14.93  1.95  50.35 / 15.19  47.26  4.40  61.90  4:51.24 | | | | | | |
| 7742 | Hans-Joachim Häberle | FRG | 59 | 9 | | Götzis | 24/25 May |
| | 11.23  7.29  14.28  1.81  48.96 / 15.57  44.36  4.40  61.46  4:25.03 | | | | | | |
| 7737 | Sheldon     Blockberger | USA | 64 | 1 | | Knoxville | 15/16 May |
| | 10.89  7.69  13.03  2.01  49.53 / 14.83  39.54  4.20  54.94  4:38.22 | | | | | | |
| 7737 | Staffan     Blomstrand | SWE | 60 | 5 | NCAA | Indianapolis | 6/ 7 Jun |
| | 11.25  6.96  14.15  1.98  48.22 / 16.53w 43.46  4.60  61.02  4:28.66 | | | | | | |
| 7736 M | Viktor     Gartung | SU | 60 | 1 | | Minsk | 26/27 Jun |
| | 10.8 m 6.81  13.91  1.93  49.3 m/ 15.7 m 45.04  4.70  60.92  4:31.9 m | | | | | | |
| 7729 | Ed     Brown | USA | 58 | 1 | | Goleta, CA | 17/18 May |
| | 11.14  6.83  12.43  2.10  50.25 / 14.47  40.20  4.30  59.82  4:25.82 | | | | | | |
| 7727 M | Nikolay     Petrashkevich | SU | 62 | 1 | | Leningrad | 25/26 Jun |
| | 10.8 m 6.92  15.27  1.95  50.3 m/ 14.4 m 46.86  4.70  51.64⁻54.6 m | | | | | | |
| 7727 | Christian     Gugler | SWZ | 60 | 2 | NC | Wil | 5/ 6 Jul |
| | 11.60  7.05  14.08  1.98  51.81 / 14.92  46.26  4.60  63.42  4:38.99 | | | | | | |
| 7726 | Marek     Kubiszewski | POL | 55 | 3 | NC | Grudziadz | 27/28 Jun |
| | 11.26  6.91  15.05  1.98  50.01 / 14.80  44.48  4.10  63.80  4:41.98 | | | | | | |
| 7725 | Jon  Hallingstad (90) | USA | 58 | 2 | | Tallahassee | 26/27 Apr |
| | 11.59  6.78  14.23  1.91  50.03 / 16.13  43.62  4.70  65.28  4:13.32 | | | | | | |
| 7721 m | Ernesto     Betancourt | CUB | 62 | 1 | | Santiago/Cuba | 21/22 Feb |
| | 10.70  6.81  14.61  1.93  48.5 m/ 15.34  46.36  3.70  65.56⁻4:40.4 m | | | | | | |
| 7720 M | Heinz     Heinrichs | USA | 61 | 1 | | Northridge | 31 May/ 1 Jun |
| 7715 | Martin     Grundmann | FRG | 65 | 6 | v SU | Bernhausen | 14/15 Jun |
| | 11.53  7.42  13.51  2.03  50.94 / 14.73  39.72  4.40  57.12  4:23.75 | | | | | | |
| 7714 | Aurel     Astilean | RUM | 62 | 1 | NC | Pitesti | 8/ 9 Aug |
| 7712 = | 10.94  7.19  12.85  2.00  49.65 / 15.23  39.30  4.60  54.98  4:27.29 | | | | | | |
| 7703 M | Sergey     Potapov | SU | 62 | 2 | | Leningrad | 25/26 Jun |
| | 10.9 m 7.42  15.25  1.95  52.0 m/ 15.3 m 47.16  4.80  60.50⁻5:13.2 m | | | | | | |
| 7698 | Andreas     Rizzi | FRG | 59 | 10 | | Götzis | 24/25 May |
| | 10.83  7.29  15.35  1.90  49.32 / 15.37  46.00  4.30  48.60  4:39.50 | | | | | | |

| Points | Name | | Nat | Yr | Pos | Meet | Venue | Date |
|---|---|---|---|---|---|---|---|---|
| 7696 | Marco | Rossi | ITA | 63 | 1 | | Bolzano | 27/28 Sep |
| | 10.89 | 6.91   13.21   1.95   50.02 / 14.88  41.60  4.60  52.74  4:23.60 | | | | | | |
| 7691 | Keith | Robinson | USA | 64 | 6 | NCAA | Indianapolis | 6/ 7 Jun |
| | 11.09 | 6.68w  13.66   1.92   48.98 / 14.88  43.94  4.30  59.74  4:26.98 | | | | | | |
| 7686 | Stephan | Niklaus | SWZ | 58 | 1 | | Olten | 13/14 Sep |
| | 10.90 | 6.72   14.68   1.95   49.18 / 14.99  45.68  4.30  67.02  5:11.35 | | | | | | |
| 7672 | Xiashun | Xi   (100) | CHN | 62 | 1 | | Nanjing | 6/ 7 Jun |
| | 11.18 | 7.25   12.93   2.08   49.60 / 15.03  36.02  4.80  55.62  4:44.53 | | | | | | |

| Points | | Name | Nat | Yr | Date | Points | | Name | Nat | Yr | Date |
|---|---|---|---|---|---|---|---|---|---|---|---|
| 7664 mW | Harry | Clark | USA | 65 | 2/ 3 Apr | 7523 | Mike | Smith | CAN | 67 | 16/17 Jul |
| 7660 M | Andrey | Atsuta | SU | 62 | 5/ 6 Aug | 7517 | Jürgen | Hoppe   (130) | FRG | 65 | 19/20 Jul |
| 7646 | Jürgen | Mandl | AUT | 65 | 24/25 May | 7517 | Georg | Manke-Reimers | FRG | 64 | 19/20 Jul |
| 7641 m | Stefan | Haigis | FRG | 67 | 14/15 Jun | 7517 M | Rudolf | Pastukhov | SU | 62 | 5/ 6 Aug |
| 7637 | Igor | Drobyshevskiy | SU | 66 | 18/19 Sep | 7517 | Vadim | Drapeza | SU | 65 | 18/19 Sep |
| 7631 | Béla | Vágó | HUN | 62 | 24/25 May | 7516 M | Aleksandr | Adamov | SU | 63 | 30/31 May |
| 7623 | Petri | Keskitalo | FIN | 67 | 16/17 Jul | 7512 | Stuart | Andrews | AUS | 62 | 27/28 Jul |
| 7619 | Trond | Skramstad | NOR | 60 | 14/15 Jun | 7509 | Nikolay | Zayats | SU | 67 | 16/17 Jul |
| 7615 | Jann | Trefny | SWZ | 66 | 5/ 6 Jul | 7507 | Greg | Richards | UK | 56 | 23/24 Aug |
| 7609 M | Carlos | O'Connell(110) | IRL | 63 | 2/ 3 Aug | 7505 | Nikolay | Savko | SU | 64 | / 1 Jun |
| 7601 | Dariusz | Grad | POL | 63 | 27/28 Jun | 7500 M | Aleksandr | Tarasov | SU | 62 | 13/14 Jun |
| 7599 | Jay | Thorson | USA | 63 | 6/ 7 Jun | 7499 M | Andrey | Zhurikov (140) | SU | 64 | 20/21 Jun |
| 7597 | Rolf | Müller | FRG | 61 | 19/20 Jul | | | | | | |
| 7584 | Simon | Shirley | AUS | 66 | 19/20 May | 7494 | Joe | Farinella | USA | | 18/19 Jun |
| 7584 M | Igor | Kolovanov | SU | 58 | | 7491 | Henrik | Broman | FIN | 61 | 19/20 Jul |
| 7581 | Norbert | Demmel | FRG | 63 | 19/20 Jul | 7489 M | Sergey | Mikish | SU | 66 | 27/28 Aug |
| 7580 | Martin | Szafranski | FRG | 58 | 14/15 Jun | 7488 M | Aleksandr | Kolyadov | SU | 62 | 14/15 Jun |
| 7564 | Andreas | Poser | GDR | 64 | 6/ 7 Jul | 7487 M | Zebin | Chen | CHN | 63 | 25/26 Apr |
| 7563 | Brad | McStravick | UK | 56 | 27/28 Jul | 7487 | Tsetsko | Mitrakiev | BUL | 56 | 2/ 3 Aug |
| 7560 | Kevin | McGorty (120) | USA | 65 | 6/ 7 Jun | 7476 | Nikolay | Botev | BUL | 63 | 2/ 3 Aug |
| | | | | | | 7476 M | Sergey | Sinegubov | SU | 66 | 5/ 6 Aug |
| 7554 M | Andrey | Nevadovskiy | SU | 61 | 2/ 3 Aug | 7475 | René | Günther | GDR | 65 | 19/20 Aug |
| 7552 | Ralf | Oberhofer | FRG | 66 | 19/20 Jul | 7473 M | Mark | Sanders (150) | USA | 63 | 21/22 Mar |
| 7547 M(=7550) | Viktor | Bondarenko | SU | 63 | 27/28 Aug | | | | | | |
| 7538 M | Mikhail | Aliyevskiy | SU | 65 | 23/24 May | 7473 M | Derek | Huff | USA | 66 | 22/23 Apr |
| 7536 | Vasiliy | Potapenko | SU | 64 | 14/15 Jun | 7472 | Kris | Szabadhegy | USA | 64 | 19/20 Mar |
| 7531 M | Michael | Rückel | FRG | 63 | 14/15 Jun | 7468 | Sergey | Belyayev | SU | 63 | 18/19 Sep |
| 7527 | Mikhail | Ivanov | SU | 64 | 2/ 3 Aug | 7467 | Doug | Hedrick | USA | 65 | 15/16 May |
| 7524 M | Martin | Otte | FRG | 67 | 27/28 Sep | 7466 | Gerald | Borchert(155) | FRG | 66 | 14/15 Jun |

MEN 1986

Best non-windy performances:

| 8171 | | Johnson | - | TAC | Eugene | 18/19 Jun |
|---|---|---|---|---|---|---|
| | 11.23 | 7.17w 14.08  2.07  49.53 / 14.79  46.16  4.90  62.78  4:30.06 | | | | |
| 7857 | | Kinder | 3 | TAC | Eugene | 18/19 Jun |
| | 11.34 | 7.08w 16.04  1.98  51.45 / 15.57  47.24  4.70  68.16  4:57.35 | | | | |
| 7839 | | Allen-Cooksey | 4 | TAC | Eugene | 18/19 Jun |
| | 11.54 | 7.60  14.49  2.01  49.80 / 15.00  42.24  4.80  56.14  4:44.73 | | | | |
| 7614 | | Hraban | | | | 19/20 Aug |

Auto-timed marks for athletes with hand-timed bests:

| 7972 | | Bright | 6 | GWG | Moskva | 6/ 7 Jul |
|---|---|---|---|---|---|---|
| | 11.05 | 6.79  12.96  2.11  49.02 / 14.40  39.22  5.40  53.16  4:39.35 | | | | |

| Points | Name | Nat | Yr | Pos | Meet | Venue | Date |
|--------|------|-----|----|----|------|-------|------|
| 7628 | Romanov | | | 6/ 7 Jul | | W = assisting wind > 4.00 m/s | |
| 7625 | Potapov | | | 17/18 Aug | | w = assisting wind between 2.00 and 4.00 m/s | |
| 7621 | Obukhov | | | 31 May/ 1 Jun | | M = hand-timed 100m, 400m, 110mH and 1500m | |
| 7611 | Krovotyntsev | | | 2/ 3 Aug | | m = hand-timed 100m or 400m or 110mH | |
| 7580 | Gartung | | | 6/ 7 Sep | | ¬ = old javelin | |
| 7575 | Atsuta | | | 6/ 7 Sep | | | |
| 7477 | Heinrichs | | | 18/19 Jun | | | |
| 7470 | Sinegubov | | | 15/16 Aug | | | |

# 4 x 100 METRES RELAY

| | | | | | | |
|---|---|---|---|---|---|---|
| 37.98 | USA | | 1 | GWG | Moskva | 9 Jul |
| | (McRae, Heard, Glance, Lewis) | | | | | |
| 38.19 | SU | | 2 | GWG | Moskva | 9 Jul |
| | (Yevgenyev, Yushmanov, Muravyov, Bryzgin) | | | | | |
| 38.29 | SU | | 1 | EC | Stuttgart | 31 Aug |
| | (Yevgenyev, Yushmanov, Muravyov, Bryzgin) | | | | | |
| 38.36 | SU | | 1 | v GDR | Tallinn | 21 Jun |
| | (Yevgenyev, Yushmanov, Muravyov, Bryzgin) | | | | | |
| 38.46 | TCU | USA | 1 | NCAA | Indianapolis | 6 Jun |
| | (Tatum, A.Smith/JAM, Reid/JAM, Sholars) | | | | | |
| 38.56 | TCU | USA | 1h1 | NCAA | Indianapolis | 4 Jun |
| | (Tatum, A.Smith/JAM, Morrow, Sholars) | | | | | |
| 38.59 | SU | | 1 | Znam | Leningrad | 7 Jun |
| | (Yevgenyev, Yushmanov, Muravyov, Bryzgin) | | | | | |
| 38.60 | GDR | | 1 | OD | Dresden | 3 Jul |
| | (Schlegel, Bringmann, Prenzler, Schröder) | | | | | |
| 38.63 | Texas A&M | USA | 2 | NCAA | Indianapolis | 6 Jun |
| | (Felton, Heard, Roberts, Kerr) | | | | | |
| 38.64 | USOC East | USA | 1 | USOCF | Houston | 2 Aug |
| | (McRae, Pierce, Dees, Morris) | | | | | |
| 38.64 | GDR | | 2 | EC | Stuttgart | 31 Aug |
| | (Schröder, Bringmann, Prenzler, Emmelmann) | | | | | |
| 38.67 | USA | | 2 | OD | Dresden | 3 Jul |
| | (McRae, Heard, Glance, Morris) | | | | | |
| 38.67 | Hungary | | 1 | BGP | Budapest | 11 Aug |
| | (Karaffa, Nagy, Tatár, Kovács) | | | | | |
| 38.71 | UK | | 3 | EC | Stuttgart | 31 Aug |
| | (Bunney, Thompson, McFarlane, Christie) | | | | | |
| 38.74 | Cuba | | 1 | CAC | Santiago/Dom | 3 Jul |
| | (Lara, Peñalver, Querol, Simón) | | | | | |
| 38.76 | FRG | | 1 | | Recklinghausen | 3 Aug |
| | (Haas, Zaske, Klein, Dobeleit) | | | | | |
| 38.81 | GDR | | 1h2 | EC | Stuttgart | 30 Aug |
| | (Schröder, Bringmann, Prenzler, Emmelmann) | | | | | |
| 38.81 | France | | 4 | EC | Stuttgart | 31 Aug |
| | (Francois, Quenehervé, Richard, Marie-Rose) | | | | | |
| 38.86 | Italy | | 5 | EC | Stuttgart | 31 Aug |
| | (Ullo, Simionato, Pavoni, Tilli) | | | | | |
| 38.90 | USC | USA | 3 | NCAA | Indianapolis | 6 Jun |
| | (Reading, Manning, Dexter, Morales/PR) | | | | | |

| Mark | Name | Nat | Yr | Pos | Meet | Venue | Date |
|------|------|-----|----|----|------|-------|------|
| 38.92 | France | | | 1 | | Bern | 20 Aug |
| | (Pas.Barré, Quenehervé, Richard, Marie-Rose) | | | | | | |
| 38.95 | Hungary | | | 1 | PTS | Bratislava | 14 Jun |
| | (Karaffa, Nagy, Tatár, Kovács) | | | | | | |
| 38.96 | Cuba | | | 1 | Nar | Sofia | 31 May |
| | (Lara, Chacón, Querol, Simón) | | | | | | |
| 38.96 | Jamaica | | | 2 | CAC | Santiago/Dom | 3 Jul |
| | (Meghoo, A.Smith, Stewart, Reid) | | | | | | |
| 38.97 | TCU | USA | | 1 | TexR | Austin | 5 Apr |
| | (Tatum, A.Smith/JAM, Reid/JAM, Sholars) | | | | | | |
| 38.97 | France | | | 1h1 | EC | Stuttgart | 30 Aug |
| | (Francois, Quenehervé, Richard, Marie-Rose) | | | | | | |
| 38.98 | SU | | | 2 | Nar | Sofia | 31 May |
| | (Yevgenyev, Yushmanov, Muravyov, Razgonov) | | | | | | |
| 39.00 | FRG | | | 1 | | Koblenz | 6 Aug |
| | (Haas, Zaske, Klein, Dobeleit) | | | | | | |
| 39.01 | Honved | HUN | | 1 | NC | Budapest | 17 Aug |
| | (Hobinka, Karaffa, Karlik, Tatár) | | | | | | |
| 39.02 | TCU | USA | | 1 | | Houston | 18 May |
| | (Tatum, A.Smith/JAM, Reid/JAM, Sholars) | | | | | | |
| 39.02 | GDR | (31/10) | | 1 | | Neubrandenburg | 7 Jun |
| | (Schulz, Bringmann, Schröder, Prenzler) | | | | | | |
| 39.07 | Bulgaria | | | 1 | NC | Sofia | 13 Aug |
| | (Markov, Grigorov, Bozhinovski, Atanasov) | | | | | | |
| 39.15 | Canada | | | 1 | CG | Edinburgh | 2 Aug |
| | (McKoy, Mahorn, D.Williams, Johnson) | | | | | | |
| 39.17 | China | | | 1 | AsiG | Seoul | 5 Oct |
| | (Jianming Cai, Feng Li, Zhuanghui Yu, Chen Zheng) | | | | | | |
| 39.27 | Poland | | | 1 | Kuso | Warszawa | 17 Jun |
| | (Zwólinski, J.Licznerski, Dunecki, Waszek) | | | | | | |
| 39.30 | Brazil | | | 1 | IbAm | Habana | 28 Sep |
| | (Santos, Nakaya, de Oliveira, R. da Silva) | | | | | | |
| 39.31 | Japan | | | 2 | AsiG | Seoul | 5 Oct |
| | (Arikawa, Miyazaki, Koike, Fuwa) | | | | | | |
| 39.48 | Czechoslovakia | | | 1 | Roš | Praha | 24 Jun |
| | (Lomický, Ptáčník, Mezihorák, Chochlík) | | | | | | |
| 39.56 | DOM | | | 3 | CAC | Santiago/Dom | 3 Jul |
| | (Mendez, Suero, Reynoso, Nunez) | | | | | | |
| 39.61 | Puerto Rico | | | 4 | CAC | Santiago/Dom | 3 Jul |
| | (Andino, E.Williams, Guilbe, Morales) | | | | | | |
| 39.63 | Austria | (20) | | 2 | v Bul,Gre,Hun | Linz | 28 Jun |
| | (Gründl, Mark, Berger, Jokl) | | | | | | |
| 39.66 | South Korea | | | 3 | AsiG | Seoul | 5 Oct |
| | (Nak-Kun Sung, Jae-Keun Chang, Jong-Il Kim, Duk-Sup Shim) | | | | | | |
| 39.74 | Portugal | | | 8 | EC | Stuttgart | 31 Aug |
| | (Abrantes, Curvelo, Cunha, Agostinho) | | | | | | |
| 40.00 | Holland | | | 1 | | Vught | 3 Aug |
| | (Mellaard, Jorissen, Leeuwenburgh, de Kom) | | | | | | |
| 40.01 | Greece | | | | | | |
| | (Tefas, Gatzios, Vagenas, Stratos) | | | | | | |
| 40.05 | Spain | | | 1 | | Madrid | 4 Jun |
| | (Gascon, Prado, Heras, Arques) | | | | | | |
| 40.07 | Taiwan | | | 1 | | Taipeh | 8 Oct |
| | (Cheng-Chuen Lai, Shun-Long Li, Yi-Cheng Tsai, Hsin-Fu Chen) | | | | | | |

MEN 1986

| Mark | Name | Nat | Yr | Pos | Meet | Venue | Date |
|------|------|-----|----|----|------|-------|------|
| 40.20 | Switzerland | | | 1 | v Nor,Swe | Luzern | 21 Jun |
| | (Kiser, Gloor, Mangold, Breitenmoser) | | | | | | |
| 40.24 | Thailand | | | 2 | CISM | Ostia | 12 Sep |
| | (Bookerd, Promna, Sermsiri, Watcharakupt) | | | | | | |
| 40.25 | Yugoslavia | | | 2 | Balk | Ljubljana | 6 Sep |
| | (Bogdanović, Nikolić, A.Popović, Petaković) | | | | | | |
| 40.27 | Victoria | (30) AUS | | 1 | NC | Adelaide | 15 Mar |
| | (Stone, Climpson, Douglas, Perry) | | | | | | |
| 40.27 | Indonesia | (31) | | 2 | | Taipeh | 8 Oct |
| | (Affar, Purnomo, Nenepath, Indra) | | | | | | |

Hand timing:

| Mark | Name | Nat | Yr | Pos | Meet | Venue | Date |
|------|------|-----|----|----|------|-------|------|
| A39.9 | Kenya | | | 1 | | Nairobi | 5 Jul |
| | (Nyambane, Nyangau, S.Kıpkemboi, Wekesa) | | | | | | |

# 4 x 400 METRES RELAY

| Mark | Name | Nat | Yr | Pos | Meet | Venue | Date |
|------|------|-----|----|----|------|-------|------|
| 2:59.84 | UK | | | 1 | EC | Stuttgart | 31 Aug |
| | (Redmond, Akabusi, Whittle, Black) | | | | | | |
| 3:00.17 | FRG | | | 2 | EC | Stuttgart | 31 Aug |
| | (Just, Itt, Schmid, Lübke) | | | | | | |
| 3:00.47 | SU | | | 3 | EC | Stuttgart | 31 Aug |
| | (Prosin, Krylov, Kornilov, Kurochkin) | | | | | | |
| 3:01.25 | SU | | | 1 | GWG | Moskva | 8 Jul |
| | (Krylov, Prosin, Volodko, Kurochkin) | | | | | | |
| 3:01.26 | UK | | | 1 | v Comm | Gateshead | 5 Aug |
| | (Akabusi, Black, T.Bennett, Brown) | | | | | | |
| 3:01.37 | Italy | | | 4 | EC | Stuttgart | 31 Aug |
| | (Bongiorni, Zuliani, Petrella, Ribaud) | | | | | | |
| 3:01.45 | Baylor | USA | | 1 | TexR | Austin | 5 Apr |
| | (Chase, Pierre, D.Graham, J.Thomas) | | | | | | |
| 3:01.47 | USA | | | 2 | GWG | Moskva | 8 Jul |
| | (McCoy, Daniel, Everett, Robinson) | | | | | | |
| 3:01.62 | SMU | USA | | 1 | NCAA | Indianapolis | 7 Jun |
| | (Spells, R.Jones, Martin, Robinzine) | | | | | | |
| 3:01.67 | USOC East | USA | | 1 | USOCF | Houston | 3 Aug |
| | (Valmon, Bridges, Jenkins, Reed) | | | | | | |
| 3:01.90 | USA - j | | | 1 | WC-j | Athinai | 20 Jul |
| | (Campbell, Rish, Waddle, Reed) | | | | | | |
| 3:01.95 | UCLA | USA | | 2 | NCAA | Indianapolis | 7 Jun |
| | (A.Washington, K.Young, Stanich, Everett) | | | | | | |
| 3:02.33 | Japan | | | 1 | AsiG | Seoul | 5 Oct |
| | (Konakatomi, Yamauchi, Kawasumi, Takano) | | | | | | |
| 3:02.4 m | Odessa CC | USA | | 1jc | TexR | Austin | 5 Apr |
| | (Carter, Johnson, Long, Madox) | | | | | | |
| 3:02.41 | Cuba | | | 1 | CAC | Santiago/Dom | 4 Jul |
| | (Peñalver, Pavó, Valentín, Stevens) | | | | | | |
| 3:02.44 | Commonwealth | | | 2 | v UK | Gateshead | 5 Aug |
| | (Clark/AUS, Cameron/JAM, Murphy/AUS, Paul/TRI) | | | | | | |

| Mark | Name | Nat | Yr | Pos | Meet | Venue | Date |
|------|------|-----|----|----|------|-------|------|
| 3:02.50 | SMU                  USA | | 1 | | Modesto, CA | 10 May |
| | (Spells, R.Jones, Martin, Robinzine) | | | | | | |
| 3:02.54 | England              UK | | 1 | v USA | Gateshead | 27 Jun |
| | (M.Thomas, Heard, Akabusi, T.Bennett) | | | | | | |
| 3:02.56 | Baylor               USA | | 3 | NCAA | Indianapolis | 7 Jun |
| | (Chase, Pierre, D.Graham, J.Thomas) | | | | | | |
| 3:02.59 | USA                  | | 2 | v Eng | Gateshead | 27 Jun |
| | (Daniel, Page, Nix, Armstead) | | | | | | |
| 3:02.70 | SMU                  USA | | 1h2 | NCAA | Indianapolis | 5 Jun |
| | (Spells, Martin, R.Jones, Robinzine) | | | | | | |
| 3:02.72 | Baylor               USA | | 1 | | Houston | 18 May |
| | (Chase, Pierre, D.Graham, J.Thomas) | | | | | | |
| 3:02.74 | TCU                  USA | | 1 | | Westwood | 19 Apr |
| | (Alexander, Burnett, Cannon, Allen) | | | | | | |
| 3:02.82 | Commonwealth         | | 3 | v Eng,USA | Gateshead | 27 Jun |
| | (D.Morris/JAM, Johnston/AUS, Clark/AUS, Cameron/JAM) | | | | | | |
| 3:02.95 | Villanova            USA | | 4 | NCAA | Indianapolis | 7 Jun |
| | (G.Davis, Valentine, Modibedi/RSA, Jenkins) | | | | | | |
| 3:02.96 | Iowa State           USA | | 1 | | Knoxville | 24 May |
| | (P.Cheruiyot/KEN, M.Thomas/UK, Dixson, D.Harris) | | | | | | |
| 3:03.04 | UCLA                 USA | | 2 | | Westwood | 19 Apr |
| | (A.Washington, Stanich, K.Young, Everett) | | | | | | |
| 3:03.23 | Baylor               USA | | 1h1 | NCAA | Indianapolis | 5 Jun |
| | (Chase, Pierre, D.Graham, J.Thomas) | | | | | | |
| 3:03.24 | USA                  | | 1 | | Fort-de-France | 4 May |
| | (Daniel, M.Armour, Mitchell, McCoy) | | | | | | |
| 3:03.24 | Villanova            USA | | 2h1 | NCAA | Indianapolis | 5 Jun |
| | (G.Davis, Valentine, Modibedi/RSA, Jenkins) | | | | | | |
| 3:03.27 | TCU              (31/7) USA | | 2 | TexR | Austin | 5 Apr |
| | (Cannon, Burnett, Alexander, Allen) | | | | | | |
| A3:03.90 | RSA                  | | 1 | | Johannesburg | 18 Apr |
| 3:04.12 | Spain                | | 5 | EC | Stuttgart | 31 Aug |
| | (Prado, Sanchez, Alonso, Heras) | | | | | | |
| A3:04.4 m | Kenya             (10) | | 1 | | Nairobi | 5 Jul |
| | (Nyambane, D.Kiprotich, Sogomo, Anzrah) | | | | | | |
| 3:04.53 | Yugoslavia           | | 1 | Balk | Ljubljana | 7 Sep |
| | (Branković, S.Popović, Melnjak, Knapić) | | | | | | |
| 3:04.57 | Trinidad             | | 2 | CAC | Santiago/Dom | 4 Jul |
| | (St Louis, I.Morris, Paul, Bernard) | | | | | | |
| 3:04.70 | Hungary              | | 1 | v Aut,Bul,Gre | Linz | 29 Jun |
| | (Menczer, I.Szabó, I.Takács, Martina) | | | | | | |
| 3:04.87 | GDR                  | | 6 | EC | Stuttgart | 31 Aug |
| | (Möller, Niestädt, Schönlebe, Schersing) | | | | | | |
| 3:05.10 | BRA                  | | 1 | | Sao Paulo | 13 Jul |
| 3:05.16 | Jamaica - j          | | 3 | WC-j | Athinai | 20 Jul |
| | (Christie, Mason, Davis, Patterson) | | | | | | |
| 3:05.45 | Bulgaria             | | 1 | | Sofia | 3 Aug |
| | (Konstantinov, Rangelov, Kharizanov, Tomov) | | | | | | |
| 3:06.00 | Australia            | | 1 | v Bel,Eng | Woluwe | 13 Jul |
| | (Frayne, Gordon, Clark, Johnston) | | | | | | |

MEN 1986

| Mark | Name | Nat | Yr | Pos | Meet | Venue | Date |
|------|------|-----|----|----|------|-------|------|
| 3:06.23 | Greece | | | 2 | Balk | Ljubljana | 7 Sep |
| | (Vamvakas, V.Kalliposis, S.Kalliposis, Kalogiannis) | | | | | | |
| 3:06.40 | France | (20) | | 4h2 | EC | Stuttgart | 30 Aug |
| | (Quentrec, Pas.Barré, Boussemart, Canti) | | | | | | |
| 3:06.88 | Barbados | | | 3 | CAC | Santiago/Dom | 4 Jul |
| | (Atkins, Carter, Catwell, Forde) | | | | | | |
| 3:07.10 | Nigeria - j | | | 2h3 | WC-j | Athinai | 19 Jul |
| | (Falaye, Vincent, Bosso, Bakare) | | | | | | |
| 3:07.15 | Poland | | | 2 | v Fra,Ita,Spa | Monaco | 6 Jul |
| | (Szparak, Stoch, Wichrowski, Stepień) | | | | | | |
| 3:07.26 | Holland | | | 2 | WA | Barcelona | 15 Jun |
| | (Donners, Druppers, Ellsworth, Visserman) | | | | | | |
| 3:07.28 | Iraq | | | 2 | AsiG | Seoul | 5 Oct |
| | (Youseif, Saihan, Lafta, Mahdi) | | | | | | |
| 3:07.65 | Switzerland | | | 1 | v Nor,Swe | Luzern | 21 Jun |
| | (Kaufmann, Notz, Kehl, Gloor) | | | | | | |
| 3:08.28 | Canada | | | 1 | v GDR | Karl-Marx-Stadt | 13 Jul |
| | (Skerritt, A.Smith, Guss, Graham) | | | | | | |
| 3:08.33 | Belgium | | | 3 | v Aus,Eng | Woluwe | 13 Jul |
| 3:08.60 | Ivory Coast | | | 1 | CISM | Ostia | 13 Sep |
| | (Djetenan, Kpidi, Kuya, Djedjemel) | | | | | | |
| 3:08.90 | Sweden | (30) | | 2 | v Swz,Nor | Luzern | 21 Jun |
| | (T.Johansson, Granat, P.Johansson, Sedlacek) | | | | | | |

Disqualified:

| Mark | Name | Nat | Yr | Pos | Meet | Venue | Date |
|------|------|-----|----|----|------|-------|------|
| 3:01.07 | SMU | USA | | - | TexR | Austin | 5 Apr |
| | (Robinzine, Satterwhite, R.Jones, Martin) | | | | | | |
| 3:01.93 | SMU | USA | | - | PennR | Philadelphia | 26 Apr |
| | (R.Jones, Martin, Spells, Robinzine) | | | | | | |

# 3000 METRES WALK (Track)

| | | | | | | | |
|------|------|-----|----|----|----|------|------|
| 11:26.9' | Carlo Mattioli | ITA | 54 | 1 | | Udine | 3 Sep |
| 11:34.9 | Andrew Jachno | AUS | 62 | 1 | | Melbourne | 1 Mar |
| 11:35.0' | Jozef Pribilinec | CS | 60 | 1 | | Hildesheim | 6 Sep |
| 11:35.2 | Phil Vesty | UK | 63 | 1 | | Melbourne | 13 Feb |
| 11:36.2' | David Smith | AUS | 55 | 2 | | Hildesheim | 6 Sep |
| 11:37.0' | Martin Bermudez | MEX | 58 | 3 | | Hildesheim | 6 Sep |
| 11:38.0 | Ronald Weigel | GDR | 59 | 1 | | Potsdam | 11 May |
| 11:41.02 | Ian McCombie | UK | 61 | 2 | IM | Swansea | 13 Jul |
| 11:46.0' | Roman Mrazek | CS | 62 | 4 | | Hildesheim | 6 Sep |
| 11:47.5' | Mikhail Shchennikov | SU | 67 | 1 | | Karl-Marx-Stadt | 9 Aug |
| Indoor marks | | | | | | | |
| 11:30.5' | Jozef Pribilinec | CS | 60 | 1 | | Jablonec | 1 Feb |
| 11:31.6 | Pauli Pirjeta | FIN | 57 | 1 | | Laukaa | 15 Mar |
| 11:40.5' | Pavol Blazek | CS | 58 | 2 | | Jablonec | 1 Feb |
| 11:45.0 | Alessandro Pezzatini | ITA | 57 | 2 | | Torino | 15 Jan |

# 5000 METRES WALK (Track)

| | | | | | | |
|------|------|-----|----|----|------|------|
| 18:48.88 | Carlo Mattioli | ITA | 54 | 1 | Udine | 3 Sep |
| 18:51.04 | Walter Arena | ITA | 64 | 2 | Udine | 3 Sep |
| 18:52.87 | David Smith | AUS | 55 | 1 | Canberra | 21 Feb |
| 19:15.0 | Ronald Weigel | GDR | 59 | 1 | Potsdam | 11 May |

| Mark | Name | Nat | Yr | Pos | Meet | Venue | Date |
|---|---|---|---|---|---|---|---|
| 19:19.3 | Mikhail Shchennikov | SU | 67 | 1 | | Karl-Marx-Stadt | 9 Aug |
| 19:23.0 | Jozef Pribilinec | CS | 60 | 1 | | Hildesheim | 6 Sep |
| 19:34.0 | Martin Bermudez | MEX | 58 | 3 | | Hildesheim | 6 Sep |
| 19:38.95 | Salvatore Cacia | ITA | 67 | 3 | | Udine | 3 Sep |
| 19:42.0 | Miguel Angel Prieto | SPA | 64 | 1 | | Pontevedra | 13 Jul |
| 19:43.00 | Sandro Bellucci | ITA | 55 | 4 | | Udine | 3 Sep |
| 19:46.01 | Simon Baker | AUS | 58 | 2 | | Adelaide | 15 Mar |
| Indoor marks | | | | | | | |
| 18:58.1 | Pavol Blazek | CS | 58 | 1 | | Banska Bystrica | 28 Feb |
| 19:41.40 | Miguel Angel Prieto | SPA | 64 | 1 | | Madrid | 25 Jan |
| 19:42.0' | Hartwig Gauder | GDR | 54 | 1 | | Senftenberg | 15 Feb |
| 19:42.3 | Ivo Pitak | CS | 58 | 2 | | Jablonec | 1 Feb |
| 19:42.4 | Roman Mrazek | CS | 62 | 3 | | Jablonec | 1 Feb |

# 20 000 METRES WALK (Track)

| Mark | Name | Nat | Yr | Pos | Meet | Venue | Date |
|---|---|---|---|---|---|---|---|
| 1:20:41.6 | Yevgeniy Misyulya | SU | 64 | 1 | SGP | Fana | 26 Apr |
| 1:21:08.0 | Erling Andersen | NOR | 60 | 2 | SGP | Fana | 26 Apr |
| 1:21:25.0 | Pavol Blazek | CS | 58 | 3 | SGP | Fana | 26 Apr |
| 1:22:37.1 | Valeriy Suntsov | SU | 55 | 4 | SGP | Fana | 26 Apr |
| 1:23:17.0 | Guillaume Leblanc | CAN | 62 | 1 | IM | Montreal | 22 May |
| 1:23:18.4 | Axel Noack | GDR | 61 | 1 | | Potsdam | 22 Mar |
| 1:23:32.0 | Ernesto Canto | MEX | 59 | 2 | IM | Montreal | 22 May |
| 1:23:32.3 | Bo Gustafsson | SWE | 54 | 5 | SGP | Fana | 26 Apr |
| 1:23:33.7 | Dietmar Meisch | GDR | 59 | 2 | | Potsdam | 22 Mar |
| 1:23:44.0 | Martin Bermudez | MEX | 58 | 3 | IM | Montreal | 22 May |
| | (10) | | | | | | |
| 1:23:45.0 | Andrei Rubarth | GDR | 62 | 3 | | Potsdam | 22 Mar |
| 1:23:57.0 | Venyamin Nikolayev | SU | 58 | 6 | SGP | Fana | 26 Apr |
| 1:23:57.2 | Timothy Lewis | USA | 62 | 4 | IM | Montreal | 22 May |
| 1:24:02.6 | Jian Shaohong | CHN | 60 | 1 | NC | Jian | 8 Mar |
| 1:24:10.0 | Francois Lapointe | CAN | 61 | 5 | IM | Montreal | 22 May |
| 1:24:14.6 | Sergey Pasko | SU | 61 | 1 | | Zhytomyr | 6 Sep |
| 1:24:15.5 | Martin Fesselier | FRA | 61 | 7 | SGP | Fana | 26 Apr |
| 1:24:55.0 | Volodymyr Pishko | SU | 62 | 2 | | Zhytomyr | 6 Sep |
| 1:25:03.0 | Sergey Svets | SU | 60 | 3 | | Zhytomyr | 6 Sep |
| 1:25:15.0 | Frants Kostyukevich | SU | 63 | 1 | | Kiyev | 25 Jul |
| | (20) | | | | | | |
| 1:25:21.0 | Mikhail Narizniy | SU | 64 | 4 | | Zhytomyr | 6 Sep |
| 1:25:21.5 | Sergey Kozika | SU | 65 | 5 | | Zhytomyr | 6 Sep |
| 1:25:23.6 | Zhou Zhaowen | CHN | 68 | 1 | NC | Qingdao | 17 Oct |
| 1:25:31.0 | Antanas Grigulianas | SU | 61 | 1 | RC | Birshton | 27 Sep |
| 1:25:31.5 | Martin Toporek | AUT | 61 | 8 | SGP | Fana | 26 Apr |
| 1:25:36.5 | Lars Ove Moen | NOR | 59 | 9 | SGP | Fana | 26 Apr |
| 1:25:40.6 | Marcello Villa | ITA | 61 | 1 | | Colleferro | 12 Oct |
| 1:25:42.0 | Nikolay Kalinka | SU | 62 | 6 | | Zhytomyr | 6 Sep |
| 1:25:42.7 | Sandor Urbanik | HUN | 64 | 1 | | Tatabanya | 4 Oct |
| 1:25:43.0 | Sergio Spagnulo | ITA | 62 | 1 | | Boviso M | 11 Oct |
| | (30) | | | | | | |
| 1:25:57.0 | Jozef Pribilinec | CS | 60 | 1 | | Banska Bystrica | 29 Jun |
| 1:26:01.0 | Roman Mrazek | CS | 62 | 2 | | Banska Bystrica | 29 Jun |
| 1:26:04.2 | Ivo Pitak | CS | 58 | 1 | | Praha | 14 Jun |
| 1:26:06.0 | Lio Baojin | CHN | 59 | 2 | NC | Qingdao | 17 Oct |
| 1:26:15.0 | Volodymyr Tokarev | SU | 60 | 7 | | Zhytomyr | 6 Sep |
| 1:26:16.4 | Carlo Mattioli | ITA | 54 | 1 | | Bologna | 12 Oct |
| 1:26:24.7 | Torsten Hafemeister | GDR | 65 | 4 | | Potsdam | 22 Mar |
| 1:26:26.4 | Nikolay Polosov | SU | 51 | 1 | | Chebokosary | 27 Apr |

MEN 1986

| Mark | Name | Nat | Yr | Pos | Meet | Venue | Date |
|------|------|-----|-----|-----|------|-------|------|

## 20 000 METRES WALK (ROAD)

| Mark | Name | Nat | Yr | Pos | Meet | Venue | Date |
|------|------|-----|-----|-----|------|-------|------|
| 1:19:52 | Reima Salonen | FIN | 55 | 1 | IM | Pihtipudas | 21 Jun |
| 1:20:02 | Salonen | | | 1 | GP | Ruse | 20 Apr |
| 1:20:31 | Ralf Kowalsky | GDR | 62 | 1 | IM | Potsdam | 24 May |
| 1:20:39 | Weigel | | | 1 | | Berlin | 11 Jun |
| 1:21:00 | Aleksandr Boyarshinov | SU | 63 | 1 | | Bryansk | 14 Aug |
| 1:21:13 | Guillaume Leblanc | CAN | 62 | 1 | PAC | St.Leonard | 5 Oct |
| 1:21:15 | Hartwig Gauder | GDR | 54 | 1 | | Varnamo | 9 May |
| 1:21:15 | Jozef Pribilinec | CS | 60 | 1 | EC | Stuttgart | 27 Aug |
| 1:21:17 | Maurizio Damilano | ITA | 57 | 2 | EC | Stuttgart | 27 Aug |
| 1:21:21 | Pavol Blazek | CS | 58 | 1 | | Trnava | 25 May |
| 1:21:27 | David Smith | AUS | 55 | 1 | NC | Canberra | 10 May |
| 1:21:33 | Carlos Mercenario | MEX | 67 | 2 | PAC | St.Leonard | 5 Oct |
| 1:21:36 | Miguel A.Prieto | SPA | 63 | 3 | EC | Stuttgart | 27 Aug |
| 1:21:41 | Roman Mrazek | CS | 62 | 2 | | Trnava | 25 May |
| 1:21:48 | Timothy Lewis | USA | 62 | 3 | PAC | St.Leonard | 5 Oct |
| 1:21:51 | Salonen | | | 1 | NC | Vaasa | 25 Jul |
| 1:21:52 | Viktor Mostovik | SU | 63 | 4 | EC | Stuttgart | 27 Aug |
| 1:21:55 | Axel Noack | GDR | 61 | 2 | IM | Potsdam | 24 May |
| 1:22:08 | Kowalsky | | | 1 | GP | Naumberg | 1 May |
| 1:22:08 | Pribilinec | | | 1 | GPH | Hospitalet | 11 May |
| 1:22:10 | Mostovik | | | 2 | GPH | Hospitalet | 11 May |
| 1:22:11 | Sandor Urbanik | HUN | 64 | 1 | | Tatabanya | 7 Sep |
| 1:22:14 | Smith | | | 1 | | Melbourne | 16 Feb |
| 1:22:17 | Salonen | | | 3 | GPH | Hospitalet | 11 May |
| 1:22:18 | Vyacheslav Ivanenko | SU | 61 | 2 | | Varnamo | 9 May |
| 1:22:22 | Noack | | | 2 | | Berlin | 11 Jun |
| 1:22:36 | Sergey Tsymbalyuk | SU | 58 | 1 | | Moskva | 2 May |
| 1:22:39 | Jan Klos | POL | 60 | 1 | IM | Warszawa | 13 Sep |
| 1:22:39 | Vikulfo Andablo | MEX | 65 | 4 | PAC | St.Leonard | 5 Oct |
| 1:22:42 | Walter Arena | ITA | 64 | 5 | EC | Stuttgart | 27 Aug |
| (30/22) | | | | | | | |
| 1:22:45 | Alessandro Pezzatini | ITA | 57 | 3 | IM | Potsdam | 24 May |
| 1:22:49 | Yevgeniy Zaykin | SU | 57 | 2 | | Moskva | 2 May |
| 1:22:58 | Ernesto Canto | MEX | 59 | 5 | GPH | Hospitalet | 11 May |
| 1:23:09 | Andrei Rubarth | GDR | 62 | 4 | IM | Potsdam | 24 May |
| 1:23:13 | Simon Baker | AUS | 58 | 2 | IM | Eschborn | 14 Sep |
| 1:23:17 | Martin Bermudez | MEX | 58 | 6 | GPH | Hospitalet | 11 May |
| 1:23:24 | Bo Gustafsson | SWE | 54 | 3 | | Varnamo | 9 May |
| 1:23:24 | Ian McCombie | UK | 61 | 5 | IM | Potsdam | 24 May |
| (30) | | | | | | | |
| 1:23:29 | Aleksey Pershin | SU | 62 | 1 | GWG | Moskva | 7 Jul |
| 1:23:40 | Valdas Kazlauskas | SU | 58 | 1 | NC | Alitus | 21 May |
| 1:23:41 | Alfons Schwarz | FRG | 54 | 1 | | Rheinsabern | 5 Apr |
| 1:23:42 | Ivo Pitak | CS | 58 | 3 | | Praha | 10 Aug |
| 1:23:46 | Aleksandr Starchenko | SU | 51 | 3 | | Moskva | 2 May |
| 1:23:46 | Anatoliy Gorshkov | SU | 52 | 2 | NC | Alitus | 21 May |
| 1:23:53 | Yevgeniy Misyulya | SU | 64 | 3 | GWG | Moskva | 7 Jul |
| 1:23:54 | Sergey Protsishin | SU | 59 | 4 | | Varnamo | 9 May |
| 1:23:58 | Sergio Spagnulo | ITA | 62 | 1 | | Romont | 24 Aug |
| 1:23:59 | Zbigniew Wisniowski | POL | 60 | 1 | | Gdansk | 31 Aug |
| (40) | | | | | | | |
| 1:24:02 | Hector Moreno | COL | 65 | 5 | PAC | St.Leonard | 5 Oct |

| Mark | Name | Nat | Yr | Pos | Meet | Venue | Date |
|------|------|-----|----|----|------|-------|------|
| 1:24:03 | Yevgeniy Yevsyukov | SU | 50 | 4 | | Moskva | 2 May |
| 1:24:10 | Dietmar Meisch | GDR | 59 | 3 | | Berlin | 11 Jun |
| 1:24:13 | Frants Kostyukevich | SU | 63 | 4 | NC | Alitus | 31 May |
| 1:24:16 | Vasiliy Matveyev | SU | 57 | 5 | NC | Alitus | 31 May |
| 1:24:16 | Alik Basriev | BUL | 59 | 1 | | Tolbuchin | 8 Jun |
| 1:24:16 | Querubin Moreno | COL | 59 | 6 | PAC | St.Leonard | 5 Oct |
| 1:24:17 | Grzegorz Ledzion | POL | 57 | 8 | GPH | Hospitalet | 11 May |
| 1:24:19 | Jacek Bednarek | POL | 64 | 2 | IM | Warszawa | 13 Sep |
| 1:24:20 | Jerzy Wroblewicz (50) | POL | 61 | 3 | IM | Warszawa | 13 Sep |
| 1:24:24 | Francisco Vargas | COL | 61 | 7 | PAC | St.Leonard | 5 Oct |
| 1:24:25 | Torsten Hafemeister | GDR | 65 | 5 | | Berlin | 11 Jun |
| 1:24:25 | Jan Staaf | SWE | 62 | 9 | EC | Stuttgart | 27 Aug |
| 1:24:30 | Carlo Mattioli | ITA | 54 | 1 | | Scauri | 20 Apr |
| 1:24:37 | Zoltan Farkas | HUN | 60 | 1 | | Budapest | 8 Jun |
| 1:24:41 | Pauli Pirjeta | FIN | 58 | 1 | | Lapinlahti | 13 Sep |
| 1:24:42 | Jonas Szalas | HUN | 56 | 2 | | Budapest | 8 Jun |
| 1:24:49 | Zdzislaw Szlapkin | POL | 61 | 2 | GP | Ruse | 20 Apr |
| 1:24:49 | Vitaliy Matsko | SU | | 1 | | Leningrad | 17 Aug |
| 1:24:50 | Ptotr Pochenchuk (60) | SU | 54 | 6 | NC | Alitus | 31 May |
| 1:24:55 | Boguslaw Duda | POL | 53 | 2 | | Mielec | 17 May |
| 1:24:57 | Ivan Sankovskiy | SU | 58 | 6 | | Moskva | 2 May |
| 1:24:58 | Ray Sharp | USA | 59 | 8 | PAC | St.Leonard | 5 Oct |
| 1:25:01 | Erling Andersen | NOR | 60 | 5 | IM | Warszawa | 13 Sep |
| 1:25:04 | Giorgio Damilano | ITA | 57 | 7 | IM | Potsdam | 24 May |
| 1:25:04 | Carl Schueler | USA | 56 | 9 | PAC | St.Leonard | 5 Oct |
| 1:25:06 | Pyotr Kakhnovits | SU | 61 | 7 | NC | Alitus | 31 May |
| 1:25:06 | Wolfgang Wiedemann | FRG | 57 | 4 | IM | Eschborn | 14 Sep |
| 1:25:09 | Willie Sawall | AUS | 41 | 1 | | Melbourne | 19 Apr |
| 1:25:13 | Costel Sofran (70) | ROM | 61 | 3 | GP | Ruse | 20 Apr |
| 1:25:20 | Sergey Shildkret | SU | 62 | 7 | | Moskva | 2 May |
| 1:25:21 | Jaroslav Makovec | CS | 60 | 4 | | Praha | 10 Aug |
| 1:25:21 | Anatoliy Solomin | SU | 52 | 1 | | Zhytomyr | 26 Sep |
| 1:25:23 | Zbigniew Sadlej | POL | 61 | 4 | GP | Ruse | 20 Apr |
| 1:25:38 | Yuriy Bogoyavlenskiy | SU | 59 | 8 | | Moskva | 2 May |
| 1:25:46 | Andrew Jachno | AUS | 62 | 2 | | Melbourne | 19 Apr |
| 1:25:46 | Sun Xiaoguang | CHN | 65 | 1 | AsiG | Seoul | 29 Sep |
| 1:25:49 | Andrey Popov | SU | 64 | 2 | | Leningrad | 17 Aug |
| 1:25:49 | Thorsten Zervas | FRG | 61 | 1 | | Hahnstattern | 21 Sep |
| 1:25:50 | Dorel Firica (80) | ROM | | 1 | | Mamaia | 29 Mar |
| 1:25:50 | Franz-Josef Weber | FRG | 62 | 2 | | Rheinzabern | 5 Apr |
| 1:25:50 | Alessandro Bellucci | ITA | 55 | 3 | NC | Piacenza | 14 Sep |
| 1:25:50 | Joel Sanchez | MEX | | 10 | PAC | St.Leonard | 5 Oct |
| 1:25:51 | Stefan Johansson | SWE | 67 | 1 | NC-J | Varnamo | 9 May |
| 1:25:51 | Felix Gomez | MEX | 55 | 12 | GPH | Hospitalet | 11 May |
| 1:25:52 | Pavel Szikora | CS | 52 | 5 | | Praha | 10 Aug |
| 1:26:12 | Endre Andrasfay | HUN | 44 | 3 | | Budapest | 8 Jun |
| 1:26:13 | Marcello Villa | ITA | 61 | 4 | NC | Piacenza | 14 Sep |
| 1:26:19 | Rajmund Wollherr | POL | 62 | 1 | | Norderstedt | 12 Oct |
| 1:26:20 | Martial Fesselier (90) | FRA | 61 | 10 | EC | Stuttgart | 27 Aug |
| 1:26:22 | Oleg Plastun | SU | 63 | 3 | | Leningrad | 17 Aug |
| 1:26:28 | Dimitri Orfanopoulos | GRE | 64 | 2 | Balk | Ljubljana | 6 Sep |

MEN 1986

| Mark | Name | Nat | Yr | Pos | Meet | Venue | Date |
|------|------|-----|----|----|------|-------|------|

# 50 000 METRES WALK (ROAD)

| Mark | Name | Nat | Yr | Pos | Meet | Venue | Date |
|------|------|-----|----|----|------|-------|------|
| 3:38:17 | Ronald Weigel | GDR | 59 | 1 | IM | Potsdam | 25 May |
| 3:40:55 | Hartwig Gauder | GDR | 54 | 1 | EC | Stuttgart | 31 Aug |
| 3:41:54 | Vyacheslav Ivanenko | SU | 61 | 2 | EC | Stuttgart | 31 Aug |
| 3:42:36 | Reima Salonen | FIN | 55 | 1 | NC | Vantaa | 24 May |
| 3:42:38 | Valeriy Suntsov | SU | 55 | 3 | EC | Stuttgart | 31 Aug |
| 3:43:42 | Gauder | | | 1 | IM | Naumberg | 1 May |
| 3:45:51 | Sergey Protsyshin | SU | 59 | 4 | EC | Stuttgart | 31 Aug |
| 3:45:55 | Suntsov | | | 1 | NC | Alitus | 31 May |
| 3:46:01 | Ivanenko | | | 2 | NC | Alitus | 31 May |
| 3:46:14 | Salonen | | | 5 | EC | Stuttgart | 31 Aug |
| 3:47:05 | Gauder | | | 2 | IM | Potsdam | 25 May |
| 3:47:38 | Protsyshin | | | 3 | NC | Alitus | 21 May |
| 3:48:00 | Nikolay Frolov | SU | 56 | 1 | PP | Podebrady | 1 Jun |
| 3:48:01 | Dietmar Meisch | GDR | 59 | 6 | EC | Stuttgart | 31 Aug |
| 3:48:37 | Meisch | | | 3 | IM | Potsdam | 25 May |
| 3:49:00 | Pavol Szikora | CS | 52 | 2 | PP | Podebrady | 1 Jun |
| 3:49:49 | Erling Andersen | NOR | 60 | 1 | INC | Madrid | 16 Mar |
| 3:50:13 | Bo Gustafsson | SWE | 54 | 7 | EC | Stuttgart | 31 Aug |
| 3:50:26 | Jorge Llopart | SPA | 52 | 2 | INC | Madrid | 16 Mar |
| 3:51:15 | Salonen | | | 2 | IM | Naumberg | 1 May |
| 3:51:17 | Aleksandr Potashev | SU | 62 | 4 | NC | Alitus | 31 May |
| 3:51:33 | Szikora | | | 3 | IM | Naumberg | 1 May |
| 3:51:35 | Szikora | | | 8 | EC | Stuttgart | 31 Aug |
| 3:51:43 | Ivo Pitak | CS | 58 | 1 | | Dudince | 6 Apr |
| 3:51:50 | Maurizio Damilano | ITA | 57 | 1 | NC | Canicatti | 6 Apr |
| 3:52:12 | Llopart | | | 9 | EC | Stuttgart | 31 Aug |
| 3:52:23 | Grzegorz Ledzion | POL | 57 | 1 | NC | Rzeszow | 20 Apr |
| 3:52:54 | Gustaffsson | | | 4 | IM | Potsdam | 25 May |
| 3:53:42 | Andersen | | | 10 | EC | Stuttgart | 31 Aug |
| 3:53:51 | Sun Xiaoguang | CHN | 65 | 1 | | Jian | 10 Mar |
| (30/17) | | | | | | | |
| 3:54:08 | Qian Ku | CHN | 62 | 2 | | Jian | 10 Mar |
| 3:54:10 | Alessandro Bellucci | ITA | 55 | 11 | EC | Stuttgart | 31 Aug |
| 3:54:44 | Pavol Jati | CS | 59 | 3 | PP | Podebrady | 1 Jun |
| (20) | | | | | | | |
| 3:55:12 | Sergey Shildkret | SU | 62 | 5 | NC | Alitus | 21 May |
| 3:55:27 | Miguel A.Prieto | SPA | 63 | 3 | INC | Madrid | 16 Mar |
| 3:55:30 | Bernd Gummelt | GDR | 63 | 4 | IM | Naumberg | 1 May |
| 3:55:50.8t | Vitaliy Popovich | SU | 62 | 1 | SGP | Fana | 26 Apr |
| 3:56:08 | Stanislav Vezel | SU | 62 | 6 | NC | Alitus | 21 May |
| 3:56:21 | Martin Bermudez | MEX | 58 | 1 | PAC | St.Leonard | 5 Oct |
| 3:56:23 | Giacomo Poggi | ITA | 60 | 6 | IM | Potsdam | 25 May |
| 3:56:25 | Felix Gomez | MEX | 55 | 1 | | Chapultepec | 13 Apr |
| 3:56:42 | Raffaello Ducceschi | ITA | 62 | 13 | EC | Stuttgart | 31 Aug |
| 3:57:04 | Yonat Olikh | SU | 58 | 2 | NC | Zhytomyr | 27 Sep |
| (30) | | | | | | | |
| 3:57:08 | Bohdan Bulakowski | POL | 50 | 4 | PP | Podebrady | 1 Jun |
| 3:57:22 | Rudolf Vereb | HUN | 61 | 1 | NC | Bekescsaba | 20 Apr |
| 3:57:31 | Vladimir Vasilenko | SU | 61 | 3 | NC | Zhytomyr | 27 Sep |
| 3:58:28 | Mykola Udovenko | SU | 56 | 1 | | Kiyev | 27 Jul |
| 3:58:45 | Francois Lapointe | CAN | 61 | 1 | | Columbus | 2 Nov |
| 3:58:46 | Leonid Sivakov | SU | 56 | 7 | NC | Alitus | 21 May |
| 3:59:07 | Laszlo Sator | HUN | 53 | 1 | | Budapest | 12 Jul |
| 3:59:11 | Alain Lemercier | FRA | 57 | 14 | EC | Stuttgart | 31 Aug |

| Mark | Name | Nat | Yr | Pos | Meet | Venue | Date |
|------|------|-----|----|----|------|-------|------|
| 3:59:29 | Andrey Popov | SU | 64 | 4 | NC | Zhytomyr | 27 Sep |
| 3:59:34 | Antonio Gonzalez | SPA | 62 | 4 | NC | Madrid | 16 Mar |
| | (40) | | | | | | |
| 3:59:44 | Vitaliy Matsko | SU | 60 | 8 | NC | Alitus | 21 May |
| 3:59:44 | Zoltan Czukor | HUN | 62 | 2 | | Budapest | 12 Jul |
| 3:59:44 | Martial Fesselier | FRA | 61 | 15 | EC | Stuttgart | 31 Aug |
| 3:59:45 | Jose Pinto | POR | 56 | 1 | | Woluwe | 22 Jun |
| 3:59:48 | Willie Sawall | AUS | 41 | 1 | | Adelaide | 17 Aug |
| 4:00:14 | Jozef Hudak | CS | 62 | 5 | PP | Podebrady | 1 Jun |
| 4:00:47 | Les Morton | UK | 58 | 5 | INC | Madrid | 16 Mar |
| 4:01:01 | Giorgio Damilano | ITA | 57 | 4 | NC | Canicatti | 6 Apr |
| 4:01:07 | Santiago Fonseca | HON | | 1 | | Guatemala | 12 Jan |
| 4:01:28 | Alfons Schwarz | FRG | 54 | 1 | NC | Ichenhausen | 20 Apr |
| | (50) | | | | | | |
| 4:01:30 | Roland Nilsson | SWE | 48 | 6 | INC | Madrid | 16 Mar |
| 4:01:31 | Vitaliy Nefyodov | SU | 55 | 9 | NC | Alitus | 21 May |
| 4:01:45 | Manuel Alcalde | SPA | 56 | 8 | IM | Potsdam | 25 May |
| 4:02:03 | Zhang Fuxin | CHN | 61 | 3 | | Jian | 10 Mar |
| 4:02:42 | Robert Mildenberger | FRG | 50 | 2 | NC | Ichenhausen | 20 Apr |
| 4:02:50 | Miklos Domjan | HUN | 54 | 3 | NC | Bekescsaba | 20 Apr |
| 4:02:56 | Kastutis Staciunas | SU | 62 | 11 | NC | Alitus | 31 May |
| 4:03:01 | Zhao Jianping | CHN | 65 | 4 | | Jian | 10 Mar |
| 4:03:08 | Dennis Jackson | UK | 45 | 8 | INC | Madrid | 16 Mar |
| 4:03:11 | Jaroslav Makovec | CS | 60 | 6 | PP | Podebrady | 1 Jun |
| | (60) | | | | | | |
| 4:03:23 | Edel Oliva | CUB | 65 | 1 | NC | Habana | 2 Feb |
| 4:03:32 | Sergey Tsymbalyuk | SU | 58 | 12 | NC | Alitus | 21 May |
| 4:03:42.2t | Jerzy Wroblewicz | POL | 61 | 1 | | Warszawa | 11 Oct |
| 4:03:53 | Antanas Grigaliunas | SU | 61 | 6 | NC | Zhytomyr | 27 Sep |
| 4:03:59 | Detlef Heitmann | FRG | 52 | 3 | NC | Ichenhausen | 20 Apr |
| 4:04:06 | Venyamin Nikolayev | SU | 58 | 1 | | Penza | 23 Aug |
| 4:04:15 | Aleksandr Turov | SU | 62 | 7 | NC | Zhytomyr | 27 Sep |
| 4:04:22 | Andres Marin | SPA | 61 | 10 | IM | Potsdam | 25 May |
| 4:04:27 | Michael Harvey | AUS | 62 | 2 | | Adelaide | 17 Aug |
| 4:04:41 | Thierry Toutain | FRA | 62 | 11 | IM | Potsdam | 25 May |
| | (70) | | | | | | |
| 4:04:59 | Guillaume Leblanc | CAN | 62 | 4 | | Chapultepec | 13 Apr |
| 4:04:59 | Thomas Pomozi | SWE | 63 | 2 | NC | Brunflo | 2 Aug |
| 4:05:00 | Fritz Helms | FRG | 60 | 4 | NC | Ichenhausen | 20 Apr |
| 4:05:01 | Lars Ove Moen | NOR | 59 | 16 | EC | Stuttgart | 31 Aug |
| 4:05:03 | Pauli Pirjeta | FIN | 58 | 2 | NC | Vantaa | 24 May |
| 4:05:30.2t | Jean-Claude Corre | FRA | 61 | 4 | SGP | Fana | 26 Apr |
| 4:05:56 | Marco Evoniuk | USA | 57 | 2 | PAC | St.Leonard | 5 Oct |
| 4:06:06 | Aleksandr Korotkov | SU | 59 | 2 | | Penza | 23 Aug |
| 4:06:23 | Aleksandr Khmelnitskiy | SU | 64 | 13 | NC | Alitus | 21 May |
| 4:06:36 | Paul Blagg | UK | 60 | 14 | IM | Potsdam | 25 May |
| | (80) | | | | | | |
| 4:06:38 | Pyotr Palagitskiy | SU | 62 | 9 | NC | Zhytomyr | 27 Sep |
| 4:07:23 | Aleksandr Volgin | SU | 68 | 10 | NC | Zhytomyr | 27 Sep |
| 4:07:30.0t | Maurice Dumont | FRA | 55 | 2 | | Marseille | 23 Mar |
| 4:07:36 | Virginius Pilauskas | SU | 62 | 11 | NC | Zhytomyr | 27 Sep |
| 4:07:51 | Samuel Gines | SPA | 58 | 10 | INC | Madrid | 16 Mar |
| 4:07:53 | Jaime Lopez | MEX | 62 | 3 | PAC | St.Leonard | 5 Oct |
| 4:08:10 | Matti Heikkila | FIN | 64 | 3 | NC | Vantaa | 24 May |
| 4:08:19 | Constantin Ispas | ROM | 54 | 1 | | Mamaia | 30 Mar |
| 4:08:19 | Karoly Farago | HUN | 61 | 4 | NC | Bekescsaba | 20 Apr |
| 4:08:34 | Peter Scholle | GDR | 66 | 15 | IM | Potsdam | 25 May |
| | (90) | | | | | | |
| 4:08:35 | Li Baojin | CHN | 60 | 5 | | Jian | 10 Mar |

MEN 1986

| Mark | Name | Nat | Yr | Pos | Meet | Venue | Date |
|------|------|-----|-----|-----|------|-------|------|
| 4:08:39 | Sergey Nazarenko | SU | 63 | 12 | NC | Zhytomyr | 27 Sep |
| 4:08:40 | Andrey Plotnikov | SU | 67 | 1 | Spa | Tashkent | 18 Sep |
| 4:09:02 | Endre Andrasfay | HUN | 44 | 2 | | Bekescsaba | 20 Apr |
| 4:09:08 | Yan Wenping | CHN | 63 | 6 | | Jian | 10 Mar |
| 4:09:21 | Deng Dongmin | CHN | 66 | 7 | | Jian | 10 Mar |
| 4:09:28 | Aleksandr Aleksandrov | SU | 63 | 2 | Spa | Tashkent | 18 Sep |
| 4:09:31 | Martin Arcambould | CAN | 61 | 2 | | Columbus | 2 Nov |
| 4:09:34 | Pedro Aroche | MEX | 46 | 5 | | Chapultepec | 13 Apr |
| 4:09:39.5t | Michel Viardot | FRA | 52 | 3 | | Marseille | 22 Mar |
| | (100) | | | | | | |

# 1986 WORLD JUNIOR LISTS

| Mark | Wind | Name | Nat | Yr | Pos | Meet | Venue | Date |
|------|------|------|-----|-----|-----|------|-------|------|

## 100 METRES

| Mark | Wind | Name | Nat | Yr | Pos | Meet | Venue | Date |
|------|------|------|-----|-----|-----|------|-------|------|
| 10.10 | 1.9 | Stanley Kerr | USA | 19.6.67 | 1 | TAC-j | Towson | 28 Jun |
| 10.13 | 1.9 | Derrick Florence | USA | 19.6.68 | 2 | TAC-j | Towson | 28 Jun |
| 10.22 | 1.9 | Michael Marsh | USA | 4.8.67 | 3 | TAC-j | Towson | 28 Jun |
| A10.25 | | Joel Isasi | CUB | 31.7.67 | 1s | | Ciudad México | 26 Jun |
| 10.26 | 0.9 | Li Tao | CHN | 15.1.68 | 1 | Asi-j | Djakarta | 5 Dec |
| 10.27 | -1.1 | Mark Mitchell | USA | 22.4.67 | 1 | | Budapest | 12 Jul |
| 10.33 | 1.5 | Jamie Henderson | UK | 29.3.67 | 2 | RC | Edinburgh | 14 Jun |
| 10.34 | 0.1 | Ray Hill | USA | 24.6.67 | 1 | | Odessa | 16 May |
| 10.36 | 0.3 | Krasimir Bozhinovski | BUL | 1.7.67 | 1 | NC-J | Sofia | 5 Jul |
| A10.36 | 2.0 | Raoul Karp | RSA | 30.9.67 | 3 | | Secunda | 15 Nov |
| 10.37 | | Pierre Goode | USA | 28.1.67 | 1h2 | | Troy | 2 May |
| 10.37 | | Keith Thomas | USA | 12.9.68 | 1 | | Charleston | 24 May |
| 10.38 | | Andre Cason | USA | 20.1.69 | 1 | | Charlottesville | 12 Apr |
| 10.39 | | Henry Thomas | USA | 7.7.67 | 1 | | Westwood | 22 Mar |
| 10.39 | | Walker Watkins | USA | 29.9.67 | 1 | | Winter Park | 9 May |
| 10.39 | 0.3 | Joe De Loach | USA | 5.6.67 | 5h1 | TAC | Eugene | 19 Jun |
| 10.41 | | Jarrett Cooper | USA | 10.11.67 | 2 | | Charleston | 24 May |
| 10.41 | 0.3 | Nikolay Andonov | BUL | 17.8.68 | 2 | NC-J | Sofia | 5 Jul |
| 10.42 | 1.9 | Matthias Schlicht | FRG | 3.5.67 | 3s1 | WJ | Athinai | 17 Jul |
| 10.43 | | Ricky Turner | USA | 31.7.68 | 1 | | Brenham | 3May |
| 10.43 | 1.0 | Gerd Umlauft | GDR | 13.6.67 | 1 | NC-J | Cottbus | 26 Jul |
| 10.43 | | Wang Wenzhen | PRC | -.-.67 | | | Beijing | 7 Sep |

### Wind-assisted
| Mark | Wind | Name | Nat | Yr | Pos | Meet | Venue | Date |
|------|------|------|-----|-----|-----|------|-------|------|
| 10.19 | 5.1 | Ray Hill | USA | 24.6.67 | 1h4 | | Odessa | 15 May |
| 10.29 | 3.0 | Jamie Henderson | UK | 29.3.69 | 2h2 | CG | Edinburgh | 26 Jul |
| A10.31 | 3.2 | Luis Smith | PAN | 3.1.68 | 1 | | Quito | 28 Sep |
| 10.32 | 3.0 | Leroy Burrell | USA | 21.2.67 | 3r2 | | Walnut | 27 Apr |
| 10.35 | | Bobby Johnson | USA | 15.7.67 | 1 | | Dallas | 22 Apr |
| 10.36 | | Derwin Hall | USA | -.-.69 | 1 | | Dallas | 22 Apr |
| 10.37 | | Al Edwards | USA | 18.5.67 | | | San Marcos | 26 Apr |
| 10.37 | 2.9 | Matthias Schlicht | FRG | 3.5.67 | 5 | | Berlin | 11 Jul |
| 10.39 | 2.3 | Tarrell Carpenter | USA | 10.7.67 | 3h2 | TAC-j | Towson | 28 Jun |
| 10.41 | | Steve Lofton | USA | -.-.68 | 1 | | Palestine | 3 May |
| 10.41 | 2.7 | Shinji Aoto | JAP | 7.3.67 | 1h | | Helsingborg | 13 Jul |
| 10.42 | 5.0 | Aleksandr Kutepov | SU | 10.1.68 | 1 | | Simferopol | 23 May |
| 10.42 | 3.5 | Roman Osipenko | SU | 12.11.67 | 1s | | Simferopol | 24 May |
| 10.42 | 2.5 | David Kirton | UK | 7.12.67 | 1h7 | WJ | Athinai | 16 Jul |

### Hand-timed
| Mark | Wind | Name | Nat | Yr | Pos | Meet | Venue | Date |
|------|------|------|-----|-----|-----|------|-------|------|
| 10.0 | | William Reed | UK | 1.4.70 | 1 | | Philadelphia | 30 May |
| A10.1 | | Frank Fredericks | RSA | 2.10.67 | 1 | | Windhoek | 18 Oct |
| 10.0w | | Richard Ross | USA | | 1 | | Lubbock | 8 Mar |
| 10.1w | | Derwin Hall | USA | -.-.69 | 1h | | Dallas | 8 Mar |
| 10.1w | | James Glenn | USA | 1.1.69 | 1 | | Dallas | 8 Mar |
| 10.1w | | Bobby Johnson | USA | 15.7.67 | 2 | | Dallas | 8 Mar |
| 10.1w | 3.6 | Leroy Burrell | USA | 21.2.67 | 1h3 | | Austin | 4Apr |
| A10.1w | | Luis Smith | PAN | 3.1.68 | 1h2 | | Quito | 13 Sep |

| Mark | Wind | Name | Nat | Yr | Pos | Meet | Venue | Date |
|------|------|------|-----|-----|-----|------|-------|------|

# 200 METRES

| Mark | Wind | Name | Nat | Yr | Pos | Meet | Venue | Date |
|------|------|------|-----|-----|-----|------|-------|------|
| 20.23 | 0.5 | Michael Timpson | USA | 6.6.67 | 1 | | University Park | 16 May |
| 20.37 | 0.2 | Roberto Hernández | CUB | 6.3.67 | 1 | | Sevilla | 24 May |
| 20.39 | 0.9 | Stanley Kerr | USA | 19.6.67 | 1 | TAC-j | Towson | 29 Jun |
| 20.49 | 0.9 | Henry Thomas | USA | 7.7.67 | 1 | | Westwood | 22 Mar |
| 20.63 | | Derrick Florence | USA | 19.6.68 | 1 | | Pasadena | 3 May |
| 20.69 | 2.0 | Michael Marsh | USA | 4.8.67 | 2 | | Los Angeles | 19 Apr |
| 20.76 | 0.3 | Miles Murphy | AUS | 19.5.67 | 1h2 | | Canberra | 21 Feb |
| 20.78 | 1.6 | Mike Newbold | BAH | 4.1.67 | 1 | | Les Abymes | 31 Mar |
| 20.80 | | Raoul Karp | RSA | 30.9.67 | 1 | | Durban | 20 Dec |
| 20.88 | 0.2 | Nikolay Andonov | BUL | 17.8.68 | 1 | | Linz | 29 Jun |
| 20.92 | | Ray Hill | USA | 24.6.67 | | | Odessa | |
| 20.93* | | Walker Watkins | USA | 29.9.67 | 1h | | Winter Park | 9 May |
| 20.93 | −2.8 | Harlan Davis | USA | −.−.67 | 1 | | Sacramento | 14 Jun |
| 20.94 | −0.3 | Mark Mitchell | USA | 22.4.67 | 1 | | Praha | 24 Jun |
| 20.94 | | Leroy Burrell | USA | 21.2.67 | 3 | | Los Angeles | 19 Apr |
| 20.96 | | Joel Isasi | CUB | 31.7.67 | 1s | | Santiago de Cuba | 22 Feb |
| 20.97 | 0.0 | Quincy Watts | USA | 19.6.70 | 1h1 | | Van Nuys | 23 May |
| A20.97 | | Gerhard Barnard | RSA | 8.5.67 | 2 | | Bloemfontein | 6 Dec |
| 20.98 | | Roderick Richardson | USA | 22.11.68 | 1 | | Selma | 3 May |
| 20.99 | 1.0 | Edgar Itt | FRG | 8.6.67 | 2 | | Bürstadt | 28 Jun |
| 21.01 | | Andre Cason | USA | 20.1.69 | 1h | | Charlotteville | 23 May |
| A21.02 | | Frank Fredericks | USA | 2.10.67 | 1 | | Germiston | 11 Oct |

Wind-assisted
| Mark | Wind | Name | Nat | Yr | Pos | Meet | Venue | Date |
|------|------|------|-----|-----|-----|------|-------|------|
| 20.10 | 4.6 | Stanley Kerr | USA | 19.6.67 | 2r3 | | Houston | 18 May |
| 20.71 | 2.1 | Leroy Burrell | USA | 21.3.67 | 3 | | Houston | 4 May |
| 20.91 | | Steve Lofton | USA | −.−.68 | 1 | | Palestine | 3 May |
| 20.98 | | Chip Rush | USA | 28.4.67 | 3h2 | | College Station | 29 Mar |

Hand-timed
| Mark | Wind | Name | Nat | Yr | Pos | Meet | Venue | Date |
|------|------|------|-----|-----|-----|------|-------|------|
| 20.5 | | William Reed | USA | 1.4.70 | 1 | | Philadelphia | 30 May |
| 20.5 | | Nikolay Andonov | BUL | 17.8.68 | 1 | NC-j | Sofia | 6 Jul |
| 20.5 | | Krasimir Bozhinovski | BUL | 1.7.67 | 2 | NC-j | Sofia | 6 Jul |
| 20.6 | 1.2 | Sergey Klyonov | SU | 11.7.67 | h | | Leningrad | 26 Jun |
| A20.6 | | Frank Fredericks | RSA | 2.10.67 | 2 | | Windhoek | 18 Oct |
| 20.8 | | Columbus Wise | USA | 6.5.68 | 1 | | Orange | 19 Apr |
| 20.8 | 1.6 | Oleg Kutscherov | SU | 22.1.68 | 2 | | Leningrad | 22 Jul |

# 400 METRES

| Mark | Wind | Name | Nat | Yr | Pos | Meet | Venue | Date |
|------|------|------|-----|-----|-----|------|-------|------|
| 45.05 | | Roberto Hernández | CUB | 6.3.67 | 2 | | Santiago de Cuba | 21 Feb |
| 45.42 | | Henry Thomas | USA | 7.7.67 | 6 | Pepsi | Los Angeles | 17 May |
| 45.43 | | Clifton Campbell | USA | 18.6.67 | 1 | | Knoxville | 18 May |
| 45.64 | | Miles Murphy | AUS | 19.5.67 | 1 | WJ | Athinai | 18 Jul |
| 45.72 | | Edgar Itt | FRG | 8.6.67 | 3 | WJ | Athinai | 18 Jul |
| 45.83 | | Chip Rish | USA | 28.4.67 | 4 | | Los Angeles | 24 May |
| A45.88 | | Ian Small-Smith | RSA | 3.2.67 | 1 | | Bloemfontein | 24 Feb |
| 46.07 | | Aaron Baynes | USA | 10.2.67 | 2s2 | | Odessa | 16 May |
| 46.08 | | Eulogio Mordoche | CUB | 13.9.67 | 4 | | Habana | 14 Jun |
| 46.12 | | Raymond Pierre | USA | 18.9.67 | 2 | | Austin | 3 May |
| 46.19 | | Tony Allen | USA | 21.6.67 | 1h2 | | Arlington | 10 May |
| 46.19 | | Mon White | USA | −.−.67 | | | | |
| 46.19 | | Ramiro González | CUB | 3.8.68 | 1 | Drz | Neubrandenburg | 3 Aug |
| 46.39 | | Gary Purvis | USA | | 1 | | Houston | 15 Mar |
| A46.45 | | Gerhard Barnard | RSA | 8.5.67 | 5 | | Germiston | 11 Apr |
| 46.45 | | Harold Leonard | USA | 1.8.67 | 1 | | Evanston | 31 May |
| 46.50 | | Steve Lewis | USA | 16.5.67 | 1h3 | | Norwalk | 6 Jun |
| 46.50 | | William Reed | USA | 1.4.67 | 1v | Rum-j | Pitesti | 11 Jul |
| 46.51 | | Guy Scott | USA | 29.5.67 | 3 | | Knoxville | 12 Apr |
| 46.51 | | Joseph Falaye | NIG | 24.4.68 | 2s2 | WJ | Athinai | 17 Jul |

| Mark | Wind | Name | Nat | Yr | Pos | Meet | Venue | Date |
|---|---|---|---|---|---|---|---|---|

Hand-timed

| 45.4 | | William Reed | USA | 1.4.70 | 1 | | Philadelphia | 27 May |
| 46.1 | | Predrag Melnjak | YUG | 17.3.69 | 1 | | Rijeka | 17 May |
| 46.4 | | Joseph Falaye | NIG | 24.4.68 | 1 | | Lagos | 17 May |

## 800 METRES

| 1:45.64 | | David Sharpe | UK | 8.7.67 | 5 | VD | Bruxelles | 5 Sep |
| 1:47.2 | | Predrag Melnjak | YUG | 17.3.69 | 1 | | Split | 8 Jun |
| 1:47.46 | | Andrey Sudnik | SU | 20.8.67 | 2 | | Bucuresti | 15 Jun |
| 1:47.7 | | David Moore | USA | 12.9.67 | 2 | | Pittsburgh | 10 May |
| 1:48.20 | | Paul Williams | UK | 3.5.67 | 3h1 | NC | Cwmbran | 25 May |
| 1:48.31 | | Alexander Adam | FRG | 10.5.68 | 6r1 | | Rhede | 2 Jul |
| 1:48.58 | | Tibor Martina | HUN | 23.7.68 | 1v | YugJ | Miskolc | 8 Jun |
| 1:48.60 | | Aaron Baynes | USA | 10.2.67 | 1 | | Lawrence | 19 Apr |
| 1:48.67 | | Ionel Tomescu | ROM | 13.6.67 | 4 | | Bucureşti | 15 Jun |
| 1:48.69 | | John-Henry May | GDR | 8.12.67 | 1 | | Cottbus | 17 May |
| 1:48.70 | | Samir Benfares | FRA | 6.6.68 | | | St Maur | 9 Jul |
| 1:48.71 | | Geoffrey Seurei | KEN | 5.5.67 | 2s2 | WJ | Athinai | 17 Jul |
| 1:48.75 | | Bruce Harris | USA | 13.1.67 | 1 | | Washington | 31 May |
| 1:48.71 | | Guy Scott | USA | 29.5.67 | 1 | | Madison | 24 May |
| 1:48.85 | | Bernd Müller | FRG | 6.6.67 | 3 | NC-j | Wetzlar | 7 Sep |
| 1:48.86 | | George Kersh | USA | 3.7.68 | 1 | TAC-j | Towson | 29 Jun |
| 1:48.90 | | Sean Kelly | USA | 6.7.67 | 4 | | Austin | 30 May |
| 1:48.91 | | Manuel Balmaceda | CHL | 5.5.67 | 2 | WJ | Athinai | 18 Jul |
| 1:48.95 | | Kevin McKay | UK | 9.2.69 | 3h3 | NC | Cwmbran | 25 May |
| 1:48.95 | | Sergey Timofeyev | SU | 4.1.68 | 3s2 | WJ | Athinai | 17 Jul |
| 1:49.00 | | Pavol Stenko | CS | 22.1.67 | 1r3 | PTS | Bratislava | 14 jun |

## 1500 METRES

| 3:40.8 | | William Oanda Kirochi | KEN | 12.12.69 | 1 | NC-j | Nairobi | 5 Jul |
| 3:41.35 | | Angel Fariñas | SPA | 21.5.67 | 1 | | Barcelona | 16 Aug |
| 3:42.14 | | Rüdiger Horn | GDR | 28.7.67 | 1 | | Potsdam | 11 May |
| 3:42.2 | | Peter Rono | KEN | 31.7.67 | 2 | NC-j | Nairobi | 5 Jul |
| 3:42.77 | | David Sharpe | UK | 8.7.67 | 11 | Bisl | Oslo | 5 Jul |
| 3:43.21 | | Zoltán Sári | HUN | 21.4.67 | 6 | | Budapest | 18 Jul |
| 3:43.53 | | Alexandros Gotzis | GRE | | | | | |
| 3:43.8 | | John Nuttall | UK | 11.1.67 | 5 | | Stretford | 24 Jun |
| 3:43.92 | | Johan Boakes | UK | 12.4.68 | 3h1 | NC | Cwmbran | 25 May |
| 3:44.29 | | Calvin Gaziano | USA | 6.1.67 | | | Austin | 3 May |
| 3:44.37 | | Naude Jordaan | RSA | 7.7.67 | 5 | | Stellenbosch | 17 Feb |
| 3:44.43 | | John Quade | USA | 1.3.67 | | | | |
| 3:44.58 | | Mark Deady | USA | 2.10.67 | 6 | | Indianapolis | 3 May |
| 3:44.67 | | Raimundo Santos | POR | 24.8.67 | 5 | NC | Lisboa | 9 Aug |
| 3:44.91 | | Jacques Van Rennsburg | RSA | 24.1.68 | 4 | | Stellenbosch | 19 Mar |
| 3:45.00 | | Branko Zorko | YUG | -.-.67 | 3 | | Nova Gorica | 10 May |
| 3:45.00 | | Karol Miżkowski | POL | 3.2.67 | 4r1 | | Warszawa | 16 Jun |
| 3:45.15 | | Radim Kunčický | CS | 18.5.67 | 2r2 | GS | Ostrava | 11 Jun |
| 3:45.37 | | Sergey Melnikov | SU | -.-.68 | | | Tallinn | 28 Jun |
| 3:45.55 | | Eyob Muller | HOL | 8.9.67 | 2 | | Papendal | 19 May |

| Mark | Wind | Name | Nat | Yr | Pos | Meet | Venue | Date |
|------|------|------|-----|-----|-----|------|-------|------|

# 3000 METRES

| Mark | Name | Nat | Yr | Pos | Meet | Venue | Date |
|------|------|-----|-----|-----|------|-------|------|
| 7:57.84 | Alejandro Gómez | SPA | 11.4.67 | 5 | | Bern | 20 Aug |
| 8:03.13 | Terry Thonrton | RSA | 23.9.67 | 1 | | Durban | 4 Oct |
| 8:04.94 | Jacques Van Rensburg | RSA | 24.1.68 | 1 | | Stellenbosch | 29 Oct |
| 8:05.03 | Manuel Carrera | SPA | 3.2.67 | 11 | | Manresa | 26 Jun |
| 8:05.8 | John Trautmann | USA | 29.6.68 | 1 | | Philadelphia | 25 Apr |
| 8:06.32 | Moulay Brahim Boutayeb | MOR | -.-.67 | 7 | | Grosseto | 10 Aug |
| 8:07.60 | Eric Mastalir | USA | 11.1.68 | 1 | | Sacramento | 14 Jun |
| 8:07.7 | Simon Mugglestone | UK | 24.7.68 | 3 | | Derby | 16 Jul |
| 8:07.8 | Gino Van Geyte | BEL | 12.3.67 | | | | |
| 8:09.02i | Scott Fry | USA | 30.6.67 | 2 | | West Lafayette | 28 Feb |
| 8:09.65 | John Nuttall | UK | 11.1.67 | 1v | Aus-j | Swansea | 28 Jun |
| 8:09.93 | Darren Mead | UK | 4.10.68 | 1 | AAA-j | London | 21 Jun |
| 8:09.98 | Anacleto Jiménez | SPA | 24.2.67 | 7 | | Zaragoza | 29 May |
| 8:10.53 | James Starling | UK | 17.8.67 | 2 | AAA-j | London | 21 Jun |
| 8:10.54 | Mark Mastalir | USA | 11.1.68 | 2 | | Sacramento | 14 Jun |
| 8:10.55 | Greg Andersen | CAN | 1.3.68 | 1 | | Ottawa | 7 Jun |
| 8:10.6 | Darrell Smith | UK | 10.4.67 | 3 | | Tonbridge | 20 Aug |
| 8:11.25 | Naude Jordaan | RSA | 7.7.67 | 1 | | Stellenbosch | 19 Mar |
| 8:11.36 | Tony Ford | AUS | 13.8.67 | 1 | | Melbourne | 18 Dec |
| 8:11.58 | Olaf Kattluhn | GDR | 1.3.67 | 1 | | Berlin | 10 Jul |

# 5000 METRES

| Mark | Name | Nat | Yr | Pos | Meet | Venue | Date |
|------|------|-----|-----|-----|------|-------|------|
| 13:26.88 | Terry Thornton | RSA | 23.9.67 | 2 | | Stellenbosch | 8 Nov |
| 13:42.16 | Alejandro Gómez | SPA | 11.4.67 | 7 | | La Coruna | 6 Aug |
| 13:45.15 | Habte Negash | ETH | -.-.67 | | | | |
| 13:50.1 | Scott Fry | USA | 30.6.67 | 6 | Penn R | Philadelphia | 24 Apr |
| 13:52.15 | Debebe Demisse | ETH | -.-.68 | | | | |
| 13:52.49 | Moulay Brahim Boutayeb | MOR | -.-.67 | 4 | | Rovereto | 30 Jul |
| 13:53.0 | Juma Mnyampanda | TAN | -.-.67 | 1 | | Dar es Salaam | 30 Apr |
| 13:55.12 | Araresso Fufa | ETH | -.-.68 | | | | |
| 13:55.25 | Peter Chumba | KEN | -.-.68 | 1 | WJ | Athinai | 19 Jul |
| 13:56.45 | Melese Feyisa | ETH | -.9.67 | 3 | WJ | Athinai | 19 Jul |
| 13:58.0 | Kamel Bouhaloufa | FRA | 2.10.67 | | | St Maur | 15 Oct |
| 13:58.6 | Kenji Ayabe | JAP | 25.3.68 | 1 | | Kyoto | 26 Oct |
| 14:00.36 | Anacleto Jimenez | SPA | 24.2.67 | 7 | WJ | Athinai | 19 Jul |
| 14:00;46 | Aboukar Hassan-Adani | SOM | -.-.68 | 8 | WJ | Athinai | 19 Jul |
| 14:01;40 | Eric Mastalir | USA | 1.1.68 | 9 | WJ | Athinai | 19 Jul |
| 14:02.14 | Guo Yijiang | CHN | -.-.68 | | | Beijing | 7 Sep |
| 14:01.4 | Peter Rono | KEN | 31.7.67 | 1 | NC-j | Nairobi | 4 Jul |
| 14:03.4 | Juan Viudes | SPA | 19.1.67 | 5v | Sco | Lloret de Mar | 8 Jun |
| 14:04.02 | Niklas Johnsson | SWE | 7.3.68 | 4 | | Södertälje | 4 Jun |
| 14:05.0 | Martin Rono | KEN | -.-.68 | 3 | NC-j | Nairobi | 4 Jul |

# 10 000 METRES

| Mark | Name | Nat | Yr | Pos | Meet | Venue | Date |
|------|------|-----|-----|-----|------|-------|------|
| 28:32.32 | Debebe Demisse | ETH | -.-.68 | 3 | | Budapest | 12 Sep |
| 28:44.00 | Peter Chumba | KEN | -.-.68 | 1 | WJ | Athinai | 16 Jul |
| 28:45.14 | Juma Mnyampanda | TAN | -.-.67 | 2 | WJ | Athinai | 16 Jul |
| 28:57.1 | Harry Green | USA | 18.7.67 | 4 | Penn R | Philadelphia | 24 Apr |
| 29:02;43 | Stephan Freigang | GDR | 27.9.67 | 6 | NC | Jena | 31 May |
| 29:02.86 | Lemma Bekele | ETH | 29.10.67 | 6 | | Budapest | 12 Sep |
| 29:14.4 | Sammy Kibiwot | KEN | -.-.67 | 2 | NC-j | Nairobi | 4 Jul |
| 29:20.26 | Terry Thornton | RSA | 23.9.67 | 5 | | Port Elizabeth | 13 Oct |
| 29:23.10 | Sandor Barcza | HUN | 15.1.67 | 14 | NC | Budapest | 1 Jun |
| 29:29.43 | Moulay Brahim Boutayeb | MOR | -.-.67 | 6 | PTS | Bratislava | 14 Jun |
| 29:35.65 | József Kovács | HUN | 6.6.67 | 17 | NC | Budapest | 1 Jun |
| 29:36.70 | Akira Nakamura | JAP | 26.6.67 | | | Chiba | |
| 29:41.9 | Gino Van Geyten | BEL | 16.3.67 | | | Leuven | 18 Jun |
| 29:42.08 | Olaf Kattluhn | GDR | 1.3.67 | 11 | NC | Jena | 31 May |
| 29:47.69 | Chris Borsa | USA | 12.3.67 | | | Madison | 23 May |

| Mark | Wind | Name | Nat | Yr | Pos | Meet | Venue | Date |
|------|------|------|-----|-----|-----|------|-------|------|

## 2000 METRES STEEPLECHASE

| Mark | Wind | Name | Nat | Yr | Pos | Meet | Venue | Date |
|------|------|------|-----|-----|-----|------|-------|------|
| 5:28.56 | | Juan Azkueta | SPA | 2.7.67 | 1 | WJ | Athinai | 20 Jul |
| 5:29.56 | | Johnstone Kipkoech | KEN | 20.12.68 | 2 | WJ | Athinai | 20 Jul |
| 5:29.60 | | Jens Volkmann | FRG | 31.5.67 | 3 | WJ | Athinai | 20 Jul |
| 5:32.84 | | Tom Hanlon | UK | 2.5.67 | 4 | WJ | Athinai | 20 Jul |
| 5:33.83 | | José-Luis Civera | SPA | 10.2.67 | 5 | WJ | Athinai | 20 Jul |
| 5:34.86 | | Vyascheslav Koshelev | SU | 20.1.68 | 6 | WJ | Athinai | 20 Jul |
| 5:35.99 | | Angel Rodriguez | CUB | 14.10.67 | 7 | WJ | Athinai | 20 Jul |
| 5:36.80 | | Steve Conwell | CAN | 10.6.67 | 8 | WJ | Athinai | 20 Jul |
| 5:37.7 | | Vittorio Di Saverio | ITA | 17.1.67 | | | | |
| 5:38.79 | | Jaroslav Folta | POL | 1.4.67 | 5h1 | WJ | Athinai | 18 Jul |
| 5:38.91 | | Viktor Shevlyakov | SU | 9.11.67 | 6h1 | WJ | Athinai | 18 Jul |
| 5:39.05 | | Dmitriy Rizhukhin | SU | -.-.67 | 1 | | Kaunas | 19 Jul |
| 5:39.13 | | Oliver Hamsch | GDR | 6.4.67 | 1 | | Jena | 31 May |
| 5:39.76 | | John Gill | CAN | 10.6.67 | 2 | NC-j | St Johns | 28 Jun |
| 5:40.12 | | Róbert Banai | HUN | 28.2.67 | | | | |
| 5:40.68 | | Andreas Fischer | FRG | 11.4.68 | 8 | | Lübeck | 3 May |
| 5:40.88 | | Reinhold Rogen | ITA | 1.3.67 | 1 | | Grosseto | 12 Jun |
| 5:40.95 | | Taoufik Boukrouma | TAN | -.-.67 | 9 | WJ | Athinai | 20 Jul |
| 5:40.96 | | Abdelmalek Amanallah | MOR | 68 | 10 | WJ | Athinai | 20 jul |
| 5:41.04 | | Anatoliy Reznik | SU | 3.3.68 | 2 | NC-j | Kaunas | 19 Jul |

## 3000 METRES STEEPLECHASE

| Mark | Wind | Name | Nat | Yr | Pos | Meet | Venue | Date |
|------|------|------|-----|-----|-----|------|-------|------|
| 8:36.4 | | Alejandro Gómez | SPA | 11.4.67 | 1 | | Pontevedra | 5 Sep |
| 8:42.85 | | Jens Volkmann | FRG | 31.5.67 | 2 | NC-j | Wetzlar | 7 Sep |
| 8:44.77 | | Angel Rodríguez | CUB | 14.10.67 | 3 | | Habana | 8 Jun |
| 8:47.49 | | Tom Hanlon | UK | 2.5.67 | 4 | VSPA | Lloret de Mar | 8 Jun |
| 8:47.74 | | Vyascheslav Koshelev | SU | 20.1.68 | | Znam | Leningrad | 7 Jun |
| 8:48.8 | | Johnstone Kipkoech | KEN | 20.12.68 | 3 | NC-j | Nairobi | 4 Jul |
| 8:48.80 | | Anton Nicolaisen | RSA | 25.1.68 | 3 | | Port Elizabeth | 13 Feb |
| 8:49.4 | | William Mutwol | KEN | -.-.67 | 4 | NC-j | Nairobi | 4 Jul |
| 8:52.93 | | Vittorio Di Saverio | ITA | 17.1.67 | 3 | | Roma | 8 Sep |
| 8:57.43 | | Koichi Morishita | JAP | | 10h2 | | Kofu | 14 Oct |
| 8:58.18 | | Atsuyuki Okada | JAP | 25.8.67 | 3 | | Tokyo | 17 May |
| 8:58.48 | | Yoshinori Kosugi | JAP | | 4 | | Tokyo | 17 May |
| 8:58.87 | | Juan Azkueta | SPA | 2.7.67 | 3s3 | NC | Madrid | 1 Aug |
| 8:59.10 | | Róbert Banai | HUN | 28.2.67 | 2 | | Miskolc | 26 Jul |
| 8:59.65 | | Matthias Hoher | FRG | -.-.67 | 5 | NC-j | Wetzlar | 7 Sep |
| 9:01.83 | | José Ramon Pestana | CUB | 27.3.68 | 4 | | Habana | 15 Jun |
| 9:01.94 | | Yasunori Kiuchi | JAP | | 1 | | Niigata | 21 Jun |
| 9:02.40 | | Masao Ueno | JAP | 4.10.68 | 2 | | Nagoya | 29 Jun |
| 9:02.57 | | Takahiro Kiyota | JAP | | 3 | | Nagoya | 29 Jun |
| 9:02.92 | | Hiroshi Tako | JAP | | 2 | | Niigata | 21 Jun |

## 110 METRES HURDLES

| Mark | Wind | Name | Nat | Yr | Pos | Meet | Venue | Date |
|------|------|------|-----|-----|-----|------|-------|------|
| 13.44 | -0.8 | Colin Jackson | UK | 18.2.67 | 1 | WJ | Athinai | 19 Jul |
| 13.66 | 0.0 | Jon Ridgeon | UK | 14.2.67 | 6 | NCAA | Indianapolis | 7 Jun |
| 13.83 | 0.0 | Robert Reading | USA | 9.6.67 | 1h1 | | Los Angeles | 23 May |
| 13.85 | 1.5 | Mike Timpson | USA | 6.6.67 | 2 | | University Park | 16 May |
| 13.91 | 1.4 | David Nelson | UK | 11.3.67 | 3 | AAA | London | 21 jun |
| 13.95 | -0.1 | Courtney Hawkins | USA | 11.7.67 | 2 | | Tuscaloosa | 29 Mar |
| 13.97 | | Emilio Valle | CUB | 21.4.67 | 1 | | Habana | 14 Jun |
| 13.98 | 1.9 | Tomasz Nagórka | POL | 3.10.67 | 1h1 | | Lodz | 25 May |
| 14.05 | 1.8 | Lawrence Felton | USA | 21.2.67 | 6 | MSR | Walnut | 27 Apr |
| 14.08 | 1.9 | Ike Mbadugha | NIG | -.-.68 | 3 | | Odessa, USA | 16 May |

Jnr MEN 1986

| Mark | Wind | Name | Nat | Yr | Pos | Meet | Venue | Date |
|------|------|------|-----|-----|-----|------|-------|------|
| 14.08 | 0.8 | Thomas Weimann | AUT | 12.10.67 | 2 | WA | Barcelona | 15 Jun |
| 14.09 | | Manuel Mayor | CUB | 9.2.67 | 3s | | Santiago de Cuba | 21 Feb |
| 14.11 | -0.8 | Philippe Tourret | FRA | 8.7.67 | 4 | WJ | Athinai | 19 Jul |
| 14.11 | 1.7 | Dimitriy Buldov | SU | 12.3.68 | 1 | NC-j | Kaunas | 20 Jul |
| 14.13 | 1.2 | Florian Schwarthoff | FRG | 7.5.68 | 1v | UK-j | Göttingen | 16 Aug |
| 14.14 | 1.2 | Anthony Jarrett | UK | 13.8.68 | 2v | UK-j | Göttingen | 16 Aug |
| 14.14 | -1.9 | Hiroshi Kakimori | JAP | 31.3.68 | 1s2 | | Kofu | 15 Oct |
| 14.16 | 1.7 | Brett St Louis | UK | 16.9.68 | 1 | | London | 14 Sep |
| 14.18 | 0.7 | Vladimir Belokon | SU | 13.2.69 | 1 | | Dnepropetrovsk | 28 Sep |
| 14.20 | -0.4 | Vyacheslaw Ivashchenko | SU | 19.3.67 | 5h1 | Znam | Leningrad | 8 Jun |

Wind-assisted marks

| Mark | Wind | Name | Nat | Yr | Pos | Meet | Venue | Date |
|------|------|------|-----|-----|-----|------|-------|------|
| 13.42 | 4.5 | Colin Jackson | UK | 18.2.67 | 2 | CG | Edinburgh | 27 Jul |
| 13.82 | | David Nelson | UK | 11.3.67 | 2 | | Wigan | 5 Jul |
| 13.91 | 2.3 | Lawrence Felton | USA | 21.2.67 | 5 | | Houston | 18 May |
| 13.95 | 2.3 | Gerry Guster | USA | 15.3.67 | 6 | | Houston | 18 May |
| 14.01 | 2.3 | Hiroshi Kakimori | JAP | 31.3.68 | 1 | | Helsingborg | 12 Jul |
| 14.06 | | Anthony Jarrett | UK | 13.8.68 | 1r2 | | Wigan | 5 Jul |
| 14.10 | 3.1 | Jamie Hence | USA | 7.6.67 | 1 | TAC-j | Towson | 29 Jun |
| 14.10 | 2.4 | Vyacheslav Ivashchenko | SU | 19.3.67 | 1 | GDR-j | Karl-Marx-Stadt | 10 Aug |
| 14.12 | 3.2 | Brett St. Louis | UK | 16.9.68 | 1 | | Edinburgh | 16 Aug |
| 14.13 | 3.1 | Herman Clark | USA | 8.5.67 | 2 | TAC-J | Towson | 29 Jun |

Hand-timed

| Mark | Wind | Name | Nat | Yr | Pos | Meet | Venue | Date |
|------|------|------|-----|-----|-----|------|-------|------|
| 13.8 | | Mikhail Ryabukhin | SU | 25.3.67 | 5 | | Kiev | 31 Aug |
| 13.8 | | Frank Mene | NIG | 13.5.68 | 1 | | Ilorin | 22 Feb |
| 13.8 | | Thomas Weimann | AUT | 12.10.67 | | | | |
| 13.9i | | Vyacheslav Ivashchenko | SU | 19.3.67 | 1 | | Lipetsk | 8 Feb |
| A13.9 | | Emilio Valle | CUB | 21.4.67 | 1s | | Ciudad México | 20 Jun |
| 13.7w | | Mikhail Ryabukhin | SU | 25.3.67 | 1 | | Kiev | 5 Oct |
| 13.8w | | Mario Re | ITA | 28.3.67 | 1 | | Castelfranco | 27 Apr |

# 400 METRES HURDLES

| Mark | Wind | Name | Nat | Yr | Pos | Meet | Venue | Date |
|------|------|------|-----|-----|-----|------|-------|------|
| 49.68 | | Edgar Itt | FRG | 8.6.67 | 1 | NC-J | Wetzlar | 7 Sep |
| 50.02 | | Emilio Valle | CUB | 21.4.67 | 1 | WJ | Athinai | 18 Jul |
| 50.05 | | Hiroshi Kakimori | JAP | 31.3.68 | 1s1 | WJ | Athinai | 17 Jul |
| 50.15 | | Alain Cuypers | BEL | 29.11.67 | 3 | NC | Bruxelles | 10 Aug |
| 50.27 | | Joseph Maritim | KEN | 22.10.68 | 1s2 | WJ | Athinai | 17 Jul |
| 50.39 | | Pascal Maran | FRA | 21.3.67 | 3 | WJ | Athinai | 18 Jul |
| 50.40 | | Michael Graham | USA | 13.2.67 | 1 | TAC-J | Towson | 29 Jun |
| 50.41 | | Kevin Mason | USA | 17.6.67 | 2 | TAC-J | Towson | 29 Jun |
| 50.57 | | Nikolay Boiko | SU | 16.2.68 | 3s1 | WJ | Athinai | 17 Jul |
| 50.58 | | Carsten Köhrbrück | FRG | 26.6.67 | 4 | WJ | Athinai | 18 Jul |
| 50.72 | | Dolph Francis | AUS | 6.5.67 | 2s2 | WJ | Athinai | 17 Jul |
| 50.74 | | German Petrov | SU | 26.3.67 | 2r2 | | Tashkent | 18 Sep |
| 50.76 | | Milton Davis | USA | -.-.67 | 1h1 | | Knoxville | 17 May |
| A51.03 | | Poena Prinsloo | RSA | 7.1.67 | 3 | | Potchefstroom | 7 Mar |
| 51.10 | | Tony McKennie | USA | 26.10.67 | 1 | | Huntingdon | 26 Apr |
| A51.18 | | Ferrins Pieterse | RSA | 22.3.67 | 1 | | Bloemfontein | 4 Apr |
| 51.23 | | Róbert Bágyi | HUN | 15.1.67 | 5s2 | WJ | Athinai | 17 Jul |
| 51.36 | | Dmitriy Bagryanou | SU | -.-.67 | 1 | NC-J | Kaunas | 21 Jul |
| A51.37 | | Paul Weyer | RSA | 15.3.68 | 2 | | Bloemfontein | 4 Apr |

Hand-timed

| Mark | Wind | Name | Nat | Yr | Pos | Meet | Venue | Date |
|------|------|------|-----|-----|-----|------|-------|------|
| 50.3 | | German Petrov | SU | 26.3.67 | 1 | | Leningrad | 28 Jun |
| 51.0 | | Paul Tanui | KEN | | 2 | NC-J | Nairobi | 5 Jul |
| 51.1 | | Emil Peshev | BUL | 4.1.68 | 1 | NC-j | Sofi | 6 Jun |
| 51.2 | | Peter Cherimoi | KEN | -.-.67 | 2 | | Meru | 3 Aug |

| Mark | Wind | Name | Nat | Yr | Pos | Meet | Venue | Date |
|------|------|------|-----|----|----|------|-------|------|

## HIGH JUMP

| Mark | Wind | Name | Nat | Yr | Pos | Meet | Venue | Date |
|------|------|------|-----|----|-----|------|-------|------|
| 2.36 | | Javier Sotomayor | CUB | 13.10.67 | 1 | | Santiago de Cuba | 23 Feb |
| 2.29 | | Hollis Conway | USA | 8.1.67 | 1 | | Lafayette | 12 Apr |
| 2.29 | | Georgi Dakov | BUL | 27.10.67 | 2 | Nar | Sofia | 1 Jun |
| 2.28 | | Joey Johnson | USA | 12.5.67 | 1 | v Rum–j | Pitesti | 11 Jul |
| 2.26 | | Normunds Sietins | SU | 17.7.67 | 1 | | Murjani | 11 May |
| 2.26 | | Rick Noji | USA | 22.10.67 | 1 | | Ciudad México | 9 Aug |
| 2.28 | | Cao Yang | CHN | –.–.68 | 1 | | Qingdao | 3 Oct |
| 2.24 | | Vyacheslav Galushko | SU | 3.9.67 | 1 | GDR–j | Karl–Marx–Stadt | 9 Aug |
| 2.23 | | Ilya Chernov | SU | 12.6.67 | 1 | NC–j | Kaunas | 21 Jul |
| 2.22i | | Neal Guidry | USA | 3.4.67 | 1 | | Gainesville | 11 Jan |
| 2.22 | | Jon Shelton | USA | 5.2.67 | 2 | | Austin | 3 May |
| 2.22 | | Phillip Henderson | AUS | 15.1.67 | 1 | v UK–j | Swansea | 28 Jun |
| 2.22 | | Thomas Müller | GDR | 5.11.67 | 3 | WJ | Athinai | 20 Jul |
| 2.21i | | Jean–Charles Gicquel | FRA | 24.2.67 | 3 | v GDR | Lievin | 1 Feb |
| 2.21 | | Torsten Marschner | GDR | 17.11.68 | 1 | v CS–j | Praha | 2 Jul |
| 2.21 | | Jeff Martinez | USA | 12.4.68 | 1 | | Lincoln | 25 Jul |
| 2.21 | | Ni Tao | CHN | –.–.69 | 1 | v JAP | Beijing | 23 Aug |
| 2.20i | | Dimitry Vasilchenko | SU | 6.8.67 | 1 | | Lipetsk | 4 Jan |
| 2.20i | | Petr Kratochvíl | CS | 20.2.68 | 1 | | Praha | 2 Feb |
| 2.20 | | Marino Drake | CUB | 16.2.67 | 3 | | Habana | 23 Feb |
| 2.20 | | Tom Smith | USA | 10.7.67 | 4 | | Knoxville | 12 Apr |
| 2.20 | | Uwe Bellmann | GDR | 8.6.68 | 1 | | Cottbus | 17 May |
| 2.20 | | José Mendez | BRA | | 1 | | Quito | 15 Sep |

## POLE VAULT

| Mark | Wind | Name | Nat | Yr | Pos | Meet | Venue | Date |
|------|------|------|-----|----|-----|------|-------|------|
| 5.61i | | Grigoriy Yegorov | SU | 12.1.67 | 1v | GDR–j | Moskva | 16 Feb |
| 5.50 | | | | | 1 | | Alma Ata | 31 May |
| 5.55 | | Delko Lesov | BUL | 6.1.67 | 2 | Nar | Sofia | 31 May |
| 5.50 | | Sergey Fomenko | SU | 7.6.67 | 1 | | Sochi | 26 Apr |
| 5.50 | | Jay Davis | SU | 29.7.67 | 2 | | Eugene | 17 May |
| 5.50 | | István Bagyula | HUN | 2.1.69 | 1 | | Milano | 19 Jun |
| 5.50 | | Igor Potapovich | SU | 6.9.67 | 1 | WJ | Athinai | 17 Jul |
| 5.49 | | Pat Manson | USA | 29.11.67 | 1 | | Lakewood | 24 Jun |
| 5.45 | | Tim McMichael | USA | 22.2.67 | i | | Norman | 25 May |
| 5.45 | | Mike Thiede | GDR | 20.5.67 | 1 | NC–j | Cottbus | 26 Jul |
| 5.40i | | Vladimir Naymushin | SU | 4.2.67 | 3 | NC–j | Lipetsk | 7 Feb |
| 5.40 | | Greg West | USA | 19.5.67 | 2 | | Dallas | 12 Apr |
| 5.40 | | Brandon Richards | USA | 6.2.67 | 1 | | Westwood | 19 Apr |
| 5.40 | | Karsten Wichert | GDR | 1.4.68 | 3 | NC | Jena | 27 Jun |
| 5.40 | | Igor Yanchevskiy | SU | –.–.68 | | | Volgograd | 7 Sep |
| 5.38 | | Dean Starkey | USA | 27.3.67 | 1 | | W. Lafayette | 11 May |
| 5.33 | | Brent Burns | USA | 2.5.69 | 1 | | Los Gatos | 31 Jul |
| 5.30 | | Rainer Lewin | GDR | 5.3.67 | 1 | | Potsdam | 11 May |
| 5.30 | | Galin Nikolov | BUL | 25.1.68 | 6 | | Sofia | 21 Jun |
| 5.30 | | Oleg Shkerdin | SU | –.–.68 | 1 | | Vitebsk | 1 Jul |
| 5.28i | | Simeon Anastassiadis | GRE | 6.8.68 | 1 | VFra–j | Vittel | 22 Feb |
| 5.28 | | Tim Bihm | USA | 4.1.68 | 1 | | Markoville | 2 May |

## LONG JUMP

| Mark | Wind | Name | Nat | Yr | Pos | Meet | Venue | Date |
|------|------|------|-----|----|-----|------|-------|------|
| 8.25 | | Luis A. Bueno | CUB | 22.5.69 | 1 | | Habana | 28 Sep |
| 8.24 | 0.2 | Eric Metcalf | USA | 23.1.68 | 1 | NCAA | Indianapolis | 6 Jun |
| 8.15 | 1.2 | Leroy Burrell | USA | 21.2.67 | 1 | | Los Angeles | 19 Apr |
| 8.00i | | Jesús Olivan | SPA | 5.7.68 | 2v | UK | Madrid | 1 Feb |
| 7.97 | 0.1 | Dietmar Haaf | FRG | 6.3.67 | 1 | NC | W Berlin | 13 Jul |

| Mark | Wind | Name | Nat | Yr | Pos | Meet | Venue | Date |
|------|------|------|-----|----|----|------|-------|------|
| 7.93 | | Lahor Marinović | YUG | 29.6.67 | 1 | | Split | 7 Jun |
| 7.91 | 1.1 | Ivo Krsek | CS | 21.3.67 | 1 | | Praha | 19 Aug |
| 7.88 | | Lisandro Milhet | CUB | 20.1.67 | 4 | | Santiago de Cuba | 22 Feb |
| 7.85i | | Scott Sanders | USA | 2.9.67 | 1 | | Bloomington | 31 Jan |
| 7.85 | | Kim Weu-Jin | SKO | 1.12.68 | 2 | Asi-j | Djakarta | 5 Dec |
| 7.85 | 1.9 | Nobuo Toyota | JAP | -.-.67 | - | Asi-j | Djakarta | 5 Dec |
| 7.84 | 1.5 | Thomas Wolf | GDR | 18.8.67 | 1 | v SU-j | Karl-Marx-Stadt | 9 Aug |
| 7.82 | | Kevin Adkins | USA | 22.2.68 | | | Sacramento | 14 Jun |
| 7.81 | 1.4 | David Culbert | AUS | 17.3.67 | 2 | NC | Adelaide | 16 Mar |
| 7.78 | | Roderick Tolbert | USA | 11.6.67 | 3 | TAC-j | Towson | 28 Jun |
| 7.77 | 0.6 | Javier San Adrián | SPA | 17.11.67 | 1 | | San Sebastián | 15 Jun |
| 7.76 | | Babou Saine | GAM | 12.9.69 | 1 | | Banjul | 28 Jun |
| 7.75i | | Oleg Kurbatov | SU | 3.3.67 | 1 | | Moskva | 25 Jan |
| 7.75 | | Edward Manderson | CAY | 18.6.68 | 1 | | Elmhurst | 21 Jun |
| 7.75 | | Aleksandr Savenok | SU | 14.2.67 | 6 | | Donetsk | 6 Sep |

Wind-assisted
| 8.06w | | Scott Sanders | USA | 2.9.67 | 2 | TAC-j | Towson | 28 Jun |
| 8.04 | 4.0 | Ivo Krsek | CS | 21.3.67 | 1v | FRG-j | Recklinghausen | 3 Aug |
| 7.96 | 4.4 | Colin Jackson | UK | 18.2.67 | 1v | Cat | Barcelona | 17 May |
| 7.93 | 3.4 | Nobuo Toyota | JAP | -.-.67 | 1 | Asi-j | Djakarta | 5 Dec |
| 7.91 | 3.0 | Lisandro Milhet | CUB | 20.1.67 | 1 | | Salamanca | 12 Jul |
| 7.85 | 2.3 | Kevin Adkins | USA | 22.2.68 | 1 | | Sacramento | 14 Jun |
| 7.78 | 5.3 | Konstantin Krause | GDR | 8.10.67 | 1 | | Neubrandenburg | 3 May |

# TRIPLE JUMP

| Mark | Wind | Name | Nat | Yr | Pos | Meet | Venue | Date |
|------|------|------|-----|----|----|------|-------|------|
| 16.97 | 0.2 | Igor Parigin | SU | 3.2.67 | 1 | WJ | Athinai | 20 Jul |
| A16.80 | | Juan M.Lopez | CUB | 7.4.67 | 1 | PAG-j | Ciudad México | 29 Jun |
| 16.78 | | Hector Marquetti | CUB | 7.4.68 | 5 | | Santiago de Cuba | 23 Feb |
| 16.60 | 1.1 | Nikolay Avramov | BUL | 25.2.67 | 1 | | Pleven | 28 Jun |
| 16.41 | | Stanislav Bobkov | SU | 28.7.68 | 1 | | Simferopol | 25 May |
| 16.40 | | Lahor Marinović | YUG | 29.6.67 | 1 | | Split | 8 Jun |
| A16.38 | | Dudson Higgins | BAH | | 2 | CAC-j | Ciudad México | 29 Jun |
| 16.37 | | Du Benzhong | CHN | 15.5.67 | 1 | | Nanjing | 11 Oct |
| 16.36 | 0.9 | Zdravko Dimitrov | BUL | 21.1.67 | 2 | | Pleven | 28 Jun |
| 16.35 | | Vasiliy Sokov | SU | -.-.67 | 1 | | Kaunas | 21 Jun |
| 16.32 | | Andrey Stepin | SU | -.-.67 | 2 | | Simferopol | 25 May |
| 16.32 | 1.3 | Dantcho Boschnakov | BUL | 14.2.68 | 2 | DRz | Neubrandenburg | 1 Aug |
| 16.18 | | Brian Wellman | BER | 8.9.67 | 2 | PAG-j | Winter Park | 6 Jul |
| 16.13 | | James Williams | USA | 30.3.67 | 1 | | Fresno | 9 May |
| 16.13 | | Oleg Kilochko | SU | -.-.69 | 1 | | Dnepropetrovsk | 28 Sep |
| 16.11 | 1.5 | Guido Schumann | GDR | 20.3.68 | 3 | v SU-j | Karl-Marx-Stadt | 9 Aug |
| 16.09 | | Roman Sintelev | SU | 12.10.68 | 4 | v GDR-j | Karl-Marx-Stadt | 9 Aug |
| 16.09 | 1.1 | Zhou Qi | CHN | -.-.67 | 2 | v JAP | Beijing | 23 Aug |
| 16.08 | | Zheng SiXin | CHN | -.-.67 | 2 | | Nanjing | 11 Oct |
| 16.03 | | Luo JiCheng | CHN | -.-.67 | 1 | | Qingdao | 5 Oct |

Wind-assisted
| 16.41 | 2.1 | Guido Schumann | GDR | 20.3.68 | 1 | Drz | Neubrandenburg | 1 Aug |
| 16.09 | 2.8 | Goran Trifunović | YUG | -.-.68 | 1 | v Fra-j | Thonon Les Bains | 12 Jul |
| 16.07 | | Hollis Conway | USA | 8.1.67 | 1 | | Houston | 24 May |

Disqualified for drug usage
| 16.94 | 2.2 | Juan M.Lopez | CUB | 7.4.67 | (2) | WJ | Athinai | 20 Jul |
| 16.81 | -2.1 | | | | - | WJ | Athinai | 20 Jul |

| Mark | Wind | Name | Nat | Yr | Pos | Meet | Venue | Date |
|------|------|------|-----|-----|-----|------|-------|------|

## SHOT

| Mark | Wind | Name | Nat | Yr | Pos | Meet | Venue | Date |
|------|------|------|-----|-----|-----|------|-------|------|
| 19.53i | | Vyacheslav Lykho | SU | 16.1.67 | | | Moskva | Dec |
| 19.34 | | | | | 1 | | Dnepropetrovsk | 27 Sep |
| 19.32 | | Brian Blutreich | USA | 5.1.67 | 4 | | Tempe | 5 Apr |
| 19.06 | | Aleksey Lukashenko | SU | 29.3.67 | 1 | GDR-j | Karl-Marx-Stadt | 9 Aug |
| 18.62 | | Radoslav Despotov | BUL | 8.8.68 | 3 | | Sofia | 22 Jun |
| 18.46i | | Tino Bonk | GDR | 1.3.67 | 1 | | Potsdam | 11 Jan |
| 17.92 | | | | | 5 | | Erfurt | 1 Jun |
| 18.45 | | Jenó Kóczián | HUN | 5.4.67 | 2 | | Budapest | 15 Aug |
| 18.44 | | John Minns | AUS | 31.5.67 | 1 | | Melbourne | 18 Dec |
| 18.03 | | Darren Crawford | USA | 8.11.67 | | | Albuquerque | 5 Apr |
| 17.95 | | Andrew Papathanassiou | USA | 14.7.67 | | | | |
| 17.71 | | Steffen Benzin | GDR | 3.8.67 | 6 | | Erfurt | 1 Jun |
| 17.61 | | Oliver Dück | FRG | 7.2.67 | 1 | | Vaterstetten | 26 Sep |
| 17.56 | | Pavel Zhelezko | SU | 4.6.67 | 3 | | Simferopol | 25 May |
| 17.35 | | Danis Davydov | SU | 8.7.67 | | | | |
| 17.33 | | Adewale Olukoju | NIG | 27.7.68 | 1 | | Ibadan | 8 Apr |
| 17.26 | | Costel Grasu | ROM | 5.7.67 | 1 | | Pitesti | 6 Jul |
| 17.23 | | Bentley Laidler | AUS | 15.6.68 | 1 | v UK-j | Swansea | 28 Jun |
| 17.17 | | Pyotr Pogoreliy | SU | 28.4.68 | 2 | | Grodno | 5 Jul |
| 17.12 | | Svetozar Donev | BUL | -.-.68 | 2 | Drz | Neubrandenburg | 2 Aug |
| 17.08 | | Tony Sylvester | USA | 17.12.67 | 2 | v Rom-j | Pitesti | 11 Jul |
| 17.04 | | Karsten Nuelken | GDR | 12.4.68 | 3 | Drz | Neubrandenburg | 2 Aug |

## DISCUS

| Mark | Wind | Name | Nat | Yr | Pos | Meet | Venue | Date |
|------|------|------|-----|-----|-----|------|-------|------|
| 61.34 | | Sergey Pachin | SU | 24.5.68 | 2 | GDR-j | Karl-Marx-Stadt | 10 Aug |
| 60.78 | | Attila Horváth | HUN | 28.7.67 | 1 | | Miskolc | 27 Jul |
| 60.60 | | Vasil Baklarov | BUL | 1.1.67 | 1 | WJ | Athinai | 17 Jul |
| 60.24 | | Vasiliy Kaptyukh | SU | 276.67 | 1 | | Dnepropetrovsk | 28 Sep |
| 60.00 | | Rolando Ribalta | CUB | 30.4.68 | 4 | | Habana | 14 Jun |
| 59.22 | | Rosen Velinov | BUL | 7.8.67 | 6 | Nar | Sofia | 1 Jun |
| 59.08 | | Gabriel Pedroso | CUB | 12.1.68 | 1 | | Habana | 9 May |
| 59.00 | | Andrey Kokhanovsky | SU | 11.1.68 | Q | WJ | Athinai | 16 Jul |
| 58.66 | | Lars Riedel | GDR | 28.6.67 | 1 | | Neubrandenburg | 3 May |
| 58.64 | | Werner Reiterer | AUS | 27.1.68 | 2 | WJ | Athinai | 17 Jul |
| 58.26 | | Igor Yanushko | SU | -.-.68 | | | | 24 Aug |
| 58.04 | | Vyascheslav Demakov | SU | -.-.68 | 3 | | Chelyabinsk | 9 Aug |
| 57.80 | | Karsten Nuelken | GDR | 12.4.68 | 2 | | Neubrandenburg | 3 May |
| 57.74 | | Peter Thompson | USA | 21.10.67 | 2 | | Tucson | 8 Mar |
| 57.30 | | Veselin Efrimov | BUL | 22.7.67 | 3 | | Warszawa | 16 Jun |
| 57.30 | | Dmitriy Zinchenko | SU | -.-.68 | | | | 2 Jul |
| 56.96 | | Brian Blutreich | USA | 5.1.67 | 1 | | Walnut | 26 Apr |
| 56.70 | | Yuriy Nesteres | SU | -.-.69 | | | | 29 Jun |
| 56.38 | | Glenn Schneider | USA | 24.1.67 | 2 | | Berkley | 3 May |
| 56.34 | | Zdeněk Kohout | CS | 14.5.67 | 5 | PTS | Bratislava | 13 Jun |
| 56.24 | | Bentley Laidler | AUS | 15.6.68 | 2v | UK-j | Swansea | 28 Jun |

## HAMMER

| Mark | Wind | Name | Nat | Yr | Pos | Meet | Venue | Date |
|------|------|------|-----|-----|-----|------|-------|------|
| 76.54 | | Valeriy Gubkin | SU | 3.9.67 | 2 | | Minsk | 27 Jun |
| 75.10 | | Eduard Piskunov | SU | -.-.67 | 1 | | Grodno | 10 Jul |
| 73.22 | | Vitaliy Alisyevich | SU | 20.11.67 | 1 | | Simferopol | 23 May |
| 72.54 | | Andrey Skvaruk | SU | 9.3.67 | 2 | | Rovno | 5 Oct |
| 71.28 | | Björn-Peter Fuhrmann | GDR | 4.9.67 | 1 | | Potsdam | 11 May |
| 70.42 | | Aleksander Grininchenko | SU | 23.1.67 | | | Grodno | 5 Jul |
| 70.24 | | Aleksander Shorokhov | SU | -.-.- | | | Minsk | 1 Jun |

| Mark | Wind | Name | Nat | Yr | Pos | Meet | Venue | Date |
|------|------|------|-----|-----|-----|------|-------|------|
| 69.80 | | Valeriy Khoyatelov | SU | -.-.67 | | | | |
| 69.58 | | Viktor Melnik | SU | 22.4.67 | | | | |
| 69.40 | | René Fox | FRG | 9.11.67 | 1 | | Rehlingen | 19 May |
| 69.24 | | Sabin Khristov | BUL | 21.2.67 | 1 | | Ruse | 7 Jun |
| 68.98 | | Sean Carlin | AUS | 29.11.67 | 1 | | Athinai | 12 Jul |
| 68.66 | | Raphael Piolanti | FRA | 14.11.67 | 1 | v Yug-j | Athinai | 18 Aug |
| 68.62 | | Jörn Hubner | GDR | 22.1.68 | 3 | v SU-j | Karl-Marx-Stadt | 10 Aug |
| 68.34 | | Aleksandr Krikun | SU | 1.3.68 | 6 | | Kiyev | 29 Aug |
| 67.92 | | Fréderic Kuhn | FRA | 10.7.68 | 1 | | Courbevoie | 21 Oct |
| 67.74 | | Valentin Grokholskiy | SU | -.-.68 | | | Kiyev | 28 Nov |
| 67.50 | | Sergey Garkusha | SU | 24.1.67 | | | Yalta | 12 May |
| 67.30 | | Vadim Kolesnik | SU | -.-.69 | | | Tarnopol | |
| 67.00 | | Vadim Kalugin | SU | -.-.68 | 3 | | Adler | 24 Feb |

# JAVELIN

| Mark | Wind | Name | Nat | Yr | Pos | Meet | Venue | Date |
|------|------|------|-----|-----|-----|------|-------|------|
| 79.58 | | Gavin Lovegrove | NZ | 21.10.67 | 2 | | Nouméa | 26 Oct |
| 78.84 | | Vladimir Zasimovich | SU | 14.9.68 | 1 | WJ | Athinai | 18 Jul |
| 75.40 | | Kim Jae Sang | SKO | 23.9.68 | 1 | Asi-j | Djakarta | 4 Dec |
| 75.38 | | Uwe Tefs | GDR | 2.1.68 | 1 | CS-j | Praha | 1 Jul |
| 74.64 | | Steffen Thrän | GDR | 8.6.67 | 1 | | Karl-Marx-Stadt | 24 May |
| 74.54 | | Gary Jenson | UK | 14.2.67 | 1 | | Thurrock | 19 Sep |
| 74.40 | | Juha Laukkanen | FIN | 6.1.69 | 1 | | Pielavesi | 30 Jul |
| 74.24 | | Mark Roberson | UK | 13.3.67 | 2 | WJ | Athinai | 18 Jul |
| 73.94 | | Miroslaw Witek | POL | 24.4.67 | 1 | v 3-j | Bad Reichenhall | 21 Jun |
| 73.92 | | Uwe Ludwig | GDR | 22.7.67 | 1 | | Neubrandenburg | 4 May |
| 73.70 | | Anatoliy Yukhimenko | SU | 15.8.67 | 2 | | Kiev | 28 Aug |
| 73.48 | | Patrik Boden | SWE | 30.6.67 | 1 | | Karlstad | 13 May |
| 73.00 | | Arnis Shimkuss | SU | 31.5.67 | 4 | | Riga | 30 May |
| 72.78 | | Silvio Warsönke | GDR | 2.8.67 | 3 | | Neubrandenburg | 4 May |
| 72.20 | | Juan Oxamendi | CUB | 16.8.68 | 2 | Drz | Neubrandenburg | 3 Aug |
| 72.04 | | Takahiro Yamada | JAP | 20.4.68 | 1 | | Kofu | 14 Oct |
| 71.92 | | Markus Galanski | FRG | 22.1.67 | 1 | | Haguneau | 27 Sep |
| 71.71 | | Kimmo Kinnunen | FIN | 31.3.68 | 1 | | Ylivieska | 2 Aug |
| 71.10 | | Jan Ungureanu | RUM | 9.2.68 | 3 | Drz | Neubrandenburg | 3 Aug |
| 71.08 | | Raymond Hecht | GDR | 11.11.68 | 5 | | Karl-Marx-Stadt | 24 May |

# DECATHLON

| | | | | | | | | |
|------|------|------|-----|-----|-----|------|-------|------|
| 7641 | | Stefan Haigis | FRG | 12.3.67 | 1 | v FRA-j | Antony | 15 Jun |
| (11.38w, | 7.35, | 14.15, | 2.04, | 50.6 / | 15.44w, | 41.50, | 4.10, 65.36, | 4:44.79) |
| 7623 | | Petri Keskitalo | FIN | 10.3.67 | 1 | WJ | Athinai | 17 Jul |
| (10.93, | 7.40, | 13.98, | 1.97, | 50.00 / | 15.02, | 35.52, | 4.70, 56.52, | 4:54.34) |
| 7524 | | Martin Otte | FRG | 3.5.67 | 1 | | Gelsenkirchen | 28 Sep |
| (10.6, | 6.94, | 13.76, | 2.02, | 49.8 / | 15.1 | 43.48 | 4.00, 54.90, | 4:44.5) |
| 7523 | | Mike Smith | CAN | 16.9.67 | 2 | WJ | Athinai | 17 Jul |
| (11.11, | 7.20, | 13.62, | 1.97, | 48.58 / | 15.45, | 38.20 | 3.70, 60.94, | 4:28.95) |
| 7509 | | Nikolay Zajats | SU | 3.2.67 | 3 | WJ | Athinai | 17 Jul |
| (11.12w, | 7.05, | 12.49, | 1.97, | 49.27 / | 15.33, | 39.82, | 4.80, 50.46, | 4:41.10) |
| 7362 | | René Schmidheiny | SWI | 4.1.67 | 3 | | Landquart | 25 May |
| (11.26, | 6.93, | 14.17, | 1.87, | 51.38 / | 14.79, | 44.92, | 4.00, 58.78, | 4:52.11) |
| 7358 | | Michael Kühne | GDR | 14.12.68 | 5 | WJ | Athinai | 17 Jul |
| (11.41w, | 6.90, | 12.08, | 1.91, | 49.63 / | 15.64, | 38.02, | 4.40, 56.52, | 4:19.31) |
| 7349 | | Andres Aavik | SU | 3.7.67 | 1 | | Kaunas | 20 Jul |
| (11.52, | 6.78, | 13.05, | 1.87, | 50.93 / | 15.14, | 39.58, | 4.80, 50.46, | 4:25.18) |
| 7330 | | Deszö Szabó | HUN | 4.9.67 | 1 | | Miskolc | 25 May |
| (11.41, | 7.19, | 12.02, | 1.91, | 49.30 / | 15.63, | 39.84, | 4.60, 46.72, | 4:27.37) |
| 7316 | | Oleg Semyonov | SU | 24.3.67 | 6 | WJ | Athinai | 17 Jul |

| Mark | Wind | Name | Nat | Yr | Pos | Meet | Venue | Date |
|---|---|---|---|---|---|---|---|---|

| | (10.99w, | 6.79, | 13.47, | 1.91, | 50.39 / | 15.58, | 44.88, | 4.00, | 59.26, | 4:55.85) |
|---|---|---|---|---|---|---|---|---|---|---|
| 7311 | | Miguel Valle | | CUB | 29.9.68 | 1 | | Habana | 9 Jun |
| | (11.01, | 7.11, | 12.63, | 1.83, | 49.77 / | 14.92, | 39.20, | 4.00, | 57.12, | 4:41.55) |
| 7278 | | Dietmar Koszewski | | FRG | 26.7.67 | 2 | v Fra j | Antony | 15 Jun |
| | (11.25, | 7.42w, | 11.70, | 1.86, | 49.4 / | 14.47, | 32.30, | 4.30, | 52.42, | 4:36.43) |
| 7272 | | Jari Näki | | FIN | 23.1.67 | 6 | | Uppsala | 15 jun |
| | (11.26, | 6.75, | 13.08, | 2.00, | 51.13 / | 15.69, | 41.00, | 4.20, | 62.18, | 4:56.89) |
| 7233 | | Andrey Chernyavskiy | | SU | -.-.68 | 2 | | Kaunas | 20 Jul |
| | (11.48, | 7.17, | 12.01, | 1.96, | 49.95 / | 15.52, | 34.74, | 4.20, | 48.72, | 4:15.55) |
| 7229 | | Antonio Peñalver | | SPA | 1.12.68 | 7 | WJ | Athinai | 17 Jul |
| | (11.38w, | 6.93, | 12.56, | 2.03, | 51.41 / | 15.85, | 40.30, | 48.74, | 4:30.84) |
| 7228 | | Andrey Obyedkin | | SU | -.-.67 | 3 | | Kaunas | 20 Jul |
| | (11.62, | 6.85, | 13.06, | 1.96, | 50.66 / | 16.16, | 37.88, | 4.30, | 51.94, | 4:15.25) |
| 7225 | | Mike Beyer | | GDR | 25.7.68 | 1 | | Neubrandenburg | 1 Jun |
| | (11.49, | 7.12, | 11.42, | 2.04, | 51.43 / | 15.12, | 38.90, | 4.30, | 48.22, | 4:32.84) |
| 7210 | | Aleksandr Kovalenko | | SU | 1.5.68 | 1 | | Neubrandenburg | 2 Aug |
| | (11.12, | 7.32w, | 11.71, | 1.95, | 50.46 / | 15.59, | 36.58, | 4.10, | 47.58, | 4:26.00) |

## 10 000 METRES WALK

| Mark | Name | Nat | Yr | Pos | Meet | Venue | Date |
|---|---|---|---|---|---|---|---|
| 40:31.1 | Giovanni De Benedictis | ITA | 8.12.68 | 1 | | Pescara | 19 Apr |
| 40:38.01 | Mikhail Shchennikov | SU | 24.12.67 | 1 | WJ | Athinai | 18 Apr |
| 40:40.73 | Salvatore Cacia | ITA | 22.7.67 | 2 | WJ | Athinia | 18 Jul |
| 40:41.05 | Ricardo Pueyo | SPA | 1.3.67 | 3 | WJ | Athinai | 18 Jul |
| 41:12.6 | Stefan Johansson | SWE | 11.4.67 | 1 | | Brunflo | 31 Jul |
| 41:15.96 | Wolfram Kienast | GDR | 2.10.67 | 5 | WJ | Athinai | 18 Jul |
| 41:50.20 | Carlos Mercenario | MEX | 3.5.67 | 7 | WJ | Athinai | 18 Jul |
| 42:03.17 | Wu Chaocai | CHN | 25.10.68 | 8 | WJ | Athinai | 18 Jul |
| 42:06.77 | Mikhail Orlov | SU | 25.6.67 | 2 | | Simferopol | 23 May |
| 42:12.78 | Andrey Plotnikov | SU | -.-.67 | 3 | | Simferopol | 23 May |
| 42:18.54 | André Kowalsky | GDR | 15.6.67 | 1 | | Potsdam | 11 May |
| 42:29.78 | Giovanni Perricelli | ITA | 25.8.67 | 6 | | Torino | 23 Jul |
| 42:31.57 | Edoardo Redolfi | ITA | -.-.67 | 1 | | Lugo de Ravenna | 24 Jun |
| 42:40.89 | Sergey Katurayev | SU | -.-.67 | 4 | | Simferopol | 23 May |
| 42:44.7 | Walter Bottarelli | ITA | -.-.67 | 3 | | Bovisio Masciago | 2 Jul |

_ndoors_
| 40:24.4 | Mikhail Shchennikov | SU | 24.12.67 | 1 | NC-J | Lipetsk | 7 Feb |
| 42:06.7 | Mikhail Orlov | SU | 25.6.67 | 2 | NC-J | Lipetsk | 7 Feb |
| 42:45.3 | Mikhail Golubnichiy | SU | -.-.68 | 3 | NC-J | Lipetsk | 7 Feb |

## 4 X 100 METRES RELAY

| Mark | Nat | Name | Pos | Meet | Venue | Date |
|---|---|---|---|---|---|---|
| 39.53 | USA | Marsh, Florence, Reed, Kerr | 1h2 | WJ | Athinai | 19 Jul |
| 39.80 | UK | Henderson, Goedluck, Kirton, Ridgeon | 1 | WJ | Athinai | 20 Jul |
| 39.81 | FRG | Schlicht, Kobor, Schmidt, Todt | 2 | WJ | Athinai | 20 Jul |
| 39.93 | POL | Kaniecki, Jedrusik, Konoka, Parjaszewski | 1H3 | WJ | Athinai | 19 Jul |
| 40.19 | FRA | Laude, Theophile, Theophile, Chatam | 2h2 | WJ | Athinai | 19 Jul |
| 40.21 | CUB | Isasi, Valle, Gonzalez, Martinez | 3h2 | WJ | Athinai | 19 Jul |
| 40.34 | BAH | Johnson, Newbold, Miller, Miller | 4h2 | WJ | Athinai | 19 Jul |

## 4 X 400 METRES RELAY

| Mark | Nat | Name | Pos | Meet | Venue | Date |
|---|---|---|---|---|---|---|
| 01.90 | USA | Campbell, Rish, Waddle, Reed | 1 | WJ | Athinai | 20 Jul |
| 04.22 | CUB | Cadogan, Mordoche, Gonzalez, Hernández | 2 | WJ | Athinai | 20 Jul |
| 05.16 | JAM | Christie, Mason, Davis, Patterson | 3 | WJ | Athinai | 20 Jul |
| 05.89 | UK | Patterson, Bakewell, Crampton, Tyler | 4 | WJ | Athinai | 20 Jul |
| 06.97 | USSR | Ovchinnikov, Lytkin, Koltovich, Krasnikov | 5 | WJ | Athinai | 19 Jul |
| 07.10 | NIG | Falaye, Vincent, Bosso, Bakare | 2h3 | WJ | Athinai | 19 Jul |
| 07.94 | FRG | Groen, Möschele, Maier, Itt | 1 | | Bad Reichenhall | 21 Jun |

LATE AMENDMENTS TO 1986 MEN'S LISTS

MEN'S ALL-TIME LISTS
400m    amend   44.67*  Curtis Mills USA 48   1 NCAA Knoxville 21 Jun 69 (44.4*)

MEN'S LISTS
100m    add     10.1  1.8  Labay            USA        1    San Antonio   29 Mar
                10.1       Gerardo Suero    DOM        1    Santo Domingo 26 Apr
                10.1       Zheng Chen       CHN 65     1    Beijing       12 Apr
200m    add     A20.6      John Anzrah      KEN 54     1    Nairobi        2 Aug
        delete  20.90w     DeWitt (was 20.9)
100m/200m  10.38/20.87     Tim Martin on 26 Apr both OK, not wind assisted
800m    amend   A1:47.0m   Charles Onsare   KEN 58          Nairobi        2 Aug
                A1:47.1m   Geoffrey Seurey  KEN 67          Nairobi        2 Aug
3000m St add    8:38.49    Emilio Ulloa     CHL 54   6 Dec
110m hurdles  13.64 1.2    Malcolm Dixon 1= Jenner 19 Apr San Jose (from 13.66)
        amend 13.59w  Harold Morton to 13.6 legal wind
              13.68w  John Register to 13.7 legal wind
        add   13.84w  Mike Cole        USA 61     1    Lubbock       29 Mar
              13.90w  Geoff Caldarone  USA 64     1    Allston        5 Apr
        add   13.5    Yu Zhicheng      CHN 63     1    Beijing       12 Apr
              13.6    Lu Quanbin       CHN 60     1    Beijing        2 May
              13.7    Wu Jiang         CHN 64    12 Apr
400m hurdles  add  50.99 Sidney dos Santos BRA 62 13 Jul,
              51.17 P.L.Lopez BRA 66 13 Jul, A50.6 John S.Ruto KEN 62 2 Aug
High jump   add  2.21     Georges Archanjo BRA 61   13 Jul

JUNIOR MEN'S LISTS
100m    add     10.36w  4.0  Ned Pucek       USA       .67   4    Houston    18 May
                10.39w       Marshall Malone USA  30.6.67   4h2  Arlington  25 Apr
200m    add     20.87   1.6  Dazel Jules     TRI  10.8.67    2   Les Abymes 31 Mar
                20.92w       Ray Hill        USA  24.6.67    1   Odessa     16 May
800m    add     A1:47.1      Geoffrey Suerey KEN       .67        Nairobi     2 Aug
2000m St   5:37.7           Vitterio Di Saverio            1   Rieti      25 Jun
110mh   amend  13.97  0.1   Emilio Valle (also to senior list)
        add    13.9          Herwig Röttl    AUT  30.1.68    1   Kranj       9 Sep
400mh   add    50.53         Richard Bucknor JAM            1   Kingston   21 Mar
               A50.85        Antonio Smith   VEN   3.1.67        Ciu.México 29 Jun
               51.06         Sam Spiler      USA            3   Houston    24 May
               51.2          Dmitriy Bagryanov BUL      .67        Grodno      6 Jul
High jump   amend  2.20     José Luis Mendez BRA      .67
Pole vault  amend  5.50     Sergey Fomenko             1   Sochi      26 Apr
Long jump   amend  8.25  1.9  Luis Bueno
            add  7.78  2.8  Stoyan Stanchev BUL   7.7.67    5   Sofia      31 May
Shot    delete  17.71  by Benzin (6.25kg shot)
Hammer  amend   75.10  by Piskunov on 5 Jul
Javelin amend  74.66  Patrik Boden     SWE  30.6.67    1   Uddevalla  25 Sep
               73.22  Juan Oxamendi    CUB  16.8.68    2   Ciu.México 21 Jun
10 km walk   40:30.1 Giovanni De Benedictis  at Pescara 21 Apr
             42:31.57 Redolfi was 2nd, and 42:44.7 Bottarelli 4th

AMENDMENTS TO RECORDS SECTION
Revise African records as follows:
MEN
200m           20.36A  Chidi IMO          NIG    Boulder          18 May 86
WOMEN
100m hurdles   13.09A  Ina VAN RENSBURG   RSA    Johannesburg     18 Apr 86

| ame | | Nat | Yr | Ht/Wt | Event | 1986 Mark | Pre-1986 best | |
|---|---|---|---|---|---|---|---|---|
| Athletes suspended for drug abuse are denoted by -# after their name) | | | | | | | | |
| bada | Patrick | FRA | 20Mar54 | 189/80 | PV | 5.50 | 5.70 | -83 |
| bascal | José Man. | SPA | 17Mar58 | 182/67 | 1500 | 3:31.13 | 3:31.69 | -85 |
| | | | | | Mile | 3:50.54 | 3:51.71 | -83 |
| | | | | | 2k | 4:52.40 | 4:54.88 | -85 |
| | | | | | 5k | 13:17.71 | 13:39.27 | -84 |
| oduvaliyev | Andrey | SU | 30Jun66 | | HT | 74.76 | 73.20 | -85 |
| be | Fumiaki | JAP | 31Jul58 | 167/49 | 10k | 28:27.71 | 28:45.4 | -82 |
| bshire | Brian | USA | 14Nov63 | 180/57 | 3kSt | 8:26.46 | 8:34.0 | -85 |
| damec | Zdeněk | CS | 9Jan56 | 181/93 | JT | 77.96 | 92.94* | -85 |
| damski | Marek | POL | 30Jan61 | 176/64 | 1500 | 3:39.38 | 3:38.28 | -84 |
| den | Jama | SOM | 62 | 180/68 | 2k | 5:06.98 | -0- | |
| anasyev | Aleksey | SU | 65 | | HT | 72.40 | 71.50 | -84 |
| anasyev | Nikolay | SU | 11Aug65 | 187/80 | Dec | 7845 | 8090 | -85 |
| anasyev | Sergey | SU | 28Aug64 | 178/71 | 1500 | 3:39.52 | 3:39.49 | -85 |
| bebaku | Ajayi | NIG | 6Dec56 | 185/80 | TJ | 17.12 | 17.26 | -83 |
| du | Uchenna | USA | 12May64 | 188/79 | LJ | 7.94 | 7.59w | -85 |
| uilasocho | Jesus | MEX | 2Mar60 | 173/65 | 400h | 50.48 | 49.41 | -85 |
| uilera | Jorge | CUB | 16Jan66 | 172/64 | 100 | 10.30 | 10.59,10.5 | -85 |
| o | Aimo | FIN | 31May51 | 185/89 | JT | 77.64 | 89.42* | -77 |
| kyō | Shigeyuki | JAP | 29Jan64 | 168/57 | 3kSt | 8:31.49 | 8:31.27 | -83 |
| tkenhead | Greg | USA | 25May66 | 190/110 | SP | 19.40 | 18.61 | -85 |
| abusi | Kriss | UK | 28Nov58 | 185/79 | 400 | 45.65 | 45.43 | -84 |
| hundov | Mamed | SU | 9Oct64 | 180/68 | TJ | 16.80 | 17.18 | -85 |
| ins | Kevin | USA | 27Jan60 | 196/136 | SP | 21.06 | 21.61 | -83 |
| utsu | Kōzō | JAP | 11Nov60 | 162/50 | 5k | 13:33.46 | 13:48.67 | -85 |
| | | | | | 10k | 28:05.5 | | |
| ay | Sergey | SU | 65 | | HT | 79.84 | 75.02 | -85 |
| bentosa | José M. | SPA | 21Jan64 | 172/56 | 5k | 13:32.24 | 13:38.30 | -85 |
| cala | Gerardo | MEX | 28Jun61 | 170/57 | 10k | 27:54.8 | 28:25.3 | -85 |
| Duaill | Yassem | KUW | 9Mar63 | | 400h | 50.21 | 50.74 | -85 |
| isyevich | Vitaliy | SU | 20Nov67 | 186/116 | HT | 73.22 | 70.20 | -85 |
| li | Yussuf | NIG | 28Jul60 | 185/80 | LJ | 8.05 | 8.21-83,8.25w | -82 |
| liegro | Raffaele | ITA | 30May64 | | 1500 | 3:39.98 | 3:44.9 | -85 |
| onso | José | SPA | 12Feb57 | 183/75 | 400h | 49.45 | 49.39 | -85 |
| tynguzhin | Renat | SU | 19Sep56 | 170/66 | 1500 | 3:39.4 | 3:43.7 | -81 |
| varez | Martin | CUB | 29Sep60 | | JT | 84.74* | 83.80* | -84 |
| abile | John | USA | 23Apr62 | 185/93 | JT | 75.90,82.08* | 74.72* | -84 |
| ano | Masanori | JAP | 26Feb65 | 178/78 | JT | 78.54 | 77.38* | -85 |
| ike | Henry | NIG | 40ct61 | 185/71 | 400h | 49.13 | 48.88 | -85 |
| inov | Ravil | SU | 20Feb63 | | TJ | 16.97 | | |
| dersen | Georg | NOR | 7Jan63 | 190/110 | SP | 19.64 | 18.60 | -85 |
| | | | | | DT | 62.10 | 56.68 | -85 |
| dersen | Roy | NOR | 2Apr55 | 172/55 | 10k | 28:24.52 | 28:15.1 | -83 |
| | | | | | Mar | 2:12:57 | -0- | |
| donov | Nikolay | BUL | 17Aug68 | 193/80 | 200 | 20.5 | 21.43 | -85 |
| drade | Henry | USA | 17Apr62 | 180/73 | 110h | 13.5w | 13.45,13.28w | -84 |
| | | | | | | | 13.2 | -85 |
| drei | Alessandro | ITA | 3Jan59 | 191/118 | SP | 22.06 | 21.95 | -85 |
| driopoulos | Spiridon | GRE | 1Aug62 | 180/70 | 10k | 28:27.23 | 28:30.1 | -83 |
| ikin | Yevgeniy | SU | 13Mar58 | 188/73 | TJ | 17.22 | 17.07 | -80 |
| ays | Eddy | BEL | 15Dec58 | 187/73 | HJ | 2.31i,2.31 | 2.36 | -85 |
| tibo | Salvatore | ITA | 7Feb62 | 170/52 | 2k | 5:05.92 | | |
| | | | | | 5k | 13:21.41 | 13:21.26 | -85 |
| | | | | | 10k | 27:39.52 | 27:48.02 | -84 |
| on | Abel | SPA | 24Oct62 | 179/63 | 1500 | 3:39.93, 3:39.68i | 3:37.5 | -85 |
| | | | | | 5k | 13:32.61 | 13:25.81 | -85 |
| zrah | John | KEN | 27Oct54 | 176/70 | 400 | 45.6A | 45.67,45.3A | -84 |

| Name | | Nat | Yr | Ht/Wt | Event | 1986 Mark | Pre-1986 best | |
|---|---|---|---|---|---|---|---|---|
| Aouita | Saïd | MOR | 2Nov60 | 175/58 | 1500 | 3:36.1 | 3:29.46 | -8 |
| | | | | | Mile | 3:50.33 | 3:46.92 | -8 |
| | | | | | 2k | 4:51.98 | 4:54.02 | -8 |
| | | | | | 3k | 7:32.23 | 7:32.94 | -8 |
| | | | | | 2M | 8:14.81 | -0- | |
| | | | | | 5k | 13:00.86 | 13:00.40 | -8 |
| | | | | | 10k | 27:26.11 | -0- | |
| Apaychev | Aleksandr | SU | 6May61 | 187/90 | Dec | 8244 | 8709 | -8 |
| Apostolov | Viktor | BUL | 1Oct62 | 181/110 | HT | 76.22 | 69.80 | -8 |
| Apostolovski | Sašo | YUG | 20Jan63 | 193/70 | HJ | 2.23 | 2.28i,2.24 | -8 |
| Aragon | Chuck | USA | 29Mar59 | 183/67 | 1500 | 3:36.62 | 3:34.7 | -8 |
| Areshin | Aleksandr | SU | 9Mar61 | 188/83 | Dec | 7838 | 8071 | -8 |
| Armour | Jack | USA | 10Feb61 | 178/73 | 800 | 1:46.57 | 1:47.77 | -8 |
| Arnold | Marcel | SWZ | 17Jan62 | 183/78 | 400 | 45.69 | 45.37 | -8 |
| Armstead | Ray | USA | 27May60 | 187/76 | 400 | 44.98 | 44.83 | -8 |
| Armstrong -# | Gary | USA | 31Dec60 | 185/79 | Dec | 8203 | 7609 | -8 |
| Arpin | Paul | FRA | 20Feb60 | 170/56 | 3k | 7:49.70 | 7:49.2 | -8 |
| | | | | | 5k | 13:31.2 | 13:52.36 | -8 |
| | | | | | 10k | 28:07.29 | -0- | |
| Arques | José | SPA | 16May60 | 182/74 | 100 | 10.21 | 10.34 | -8 |
| Asadov | Vasif | SU | 27Aug65 | 180/69 | TJ | 17.04 | 16.62 | -8 |
| Asakura | Ken | JAP | 11May61 | 186/80 | JT | 75.74 | 79.10* | -8 |
| Asquith | Lincoln | UK | 3Apr64 | 175/75 | 100 | 10.32 | 10.33,10.20w | -8 |
| Assmann | Matthias | FRG | 2Feb57 | 191/84 | 800 | 1:44.59 | 1:44.93 | -8 |
| Astapkovich | Igor | SU | 63 | | HT | 80.68 | 80.16 | -8 |
| Astilean | Aurel | ROM | 1Apr62 | 187/79 | Dec | 7714 | 7467 | -8 |
| Atanasov | Atanas | BUL | 7Oct56 | 185/76 | LJ | 7.98 | 8.31 | -8 |
| Atanasov | Valentin | BUL | 7May61 | 188/84 | 100 | 10.32 | 10.15,10.1 | -8 |
| Atkinson | Jeff | USA | 24Feb63 | 185/68 | Mile | 3:55.16 | | |
| Atsutsa | Andrey | SU | 20Jan62 | 189/91 | Dec | 7660 | 7756 | -8 |
| Aushev | Aleksandr | SU | 14May60 | 181/71 | LJ | 8.11 | 8.12 | -8 |
| Avdeyenko | Gennadiy | SU | 4Nov63 | 202/82 | HJ | 2.35 | 2.35 | -8 |
| Avramov | Nikolay | BUL | 25Feb67 | 188/76 | TJ | 16.60 | 15.84 | -8 |
| Azarov | Oleg | SU | 16Feb62 | 185/76 | 400h | 49.38 | 51.07,51.0 | -8 |
| Azizmuradov | Oleg | SU | 26Jan62 | 193/74 | HJ | 2.24 | 2.26 | -8 |
| Babich | Mark | USA | 7Aug63 | 190/86 | JT | 75.30 | 80.88* | -8 |
| Babiy | Ivan | SU | 22Jul63 | 183/82 | Dec | 7868 | 7944 | -8 |
| Baccouche | Féthi | TUN | 16Nov60 | 171/59 | 3k | 7:46.17 | 7:50.02 | -8 |
| | | | | | 3kSt | 8:23.69 | 8:18.70 | -8 |
| Backes | Ron | USA | 2Jan63 | 190/116 | SP | 21.01i,20.92 | 20.25 | -8 |
| Badinelli | Dario | ITA | 10Aug60 | 185/68 | TJ | 17.12 | 17.04 | -8 |
| Bagach | Aleksandr | SU | 21Nov66 | 194/120 | SP | 19.36 | 18.79 | -8 |
| Bagyula | István | HUN | 2Jan69 | 183/75 | PV | 5.50 | 5.10 | -8 |
| Bahm | Ron | USA | 9Feb65 | 183/86 | JT | 75.24 | 73.14* | -8 |
| Bakos | György | HUN | 6Jul60 | 188/77 | 110h | 13.60 | 13.2-85,13.45 | -8 |
| Bakosi | Béla | HUN | 18Jun57 | 180/67 | TJ | 16.93i | 17.23 | -8 |
| | | | | | | 16.83w | 17.29w | -8 |
| Bakunin | Valeriy | SU | 13Feb62 | | LJ | 8.20 | 8.00i-85,7.91 | -8 |
| Balcindes | Lázaro | CUB | 8Feb63 | 177/73 | TJ | 16.82 | 16.96 | -8 |
| Balkin | Lee | USA | 7Jun61 | 192/75 | HJ | 2.27i,2.25 | 2.30 | -8 |
| Bałło | Eugeniusz | POL | 1Jul60 | 191/126 | SP | 19.79 | 19.92i | -8 |
| | | | | | | | 19.54 | -8 |
| Balogh | Gyula | HUN | 15Feb61 | 186/68 | 3kSt | 8:34.8 | 8:30.57 | -8 |
| Banich | Jim | USA | 12Sep63 | 191/110 | SP | 19.90 | 19.45 | -8 |
| | | | | | DT | 60.92 | 58.52 | -8 |
| Banks | Kenny | USA | 12Nov66 | | HJ | 2.30 | 2.185 | -8 |
| Banks | Sean | USA | | | 400 | 46.01 | 47.21 | -8 |
| Banks | Willie | USA | 11Mar56 | 190/77 | TJ | 17.58A,17.82w | 17.97 | -8 |
| Bankston | Bobby | USA | 20Jan63 | 173/75 | 100 | 10.18w | 10.31,10.24w | -8 |
| | | | | | | | 10.0w | -8 |

| me | | Nat | Yr | Ht/Wt | Event | 1986 Mark | Pre-1986 best |
|---|---|---|---|---|---|---|---|
| aptiste | Kirk | USA | 20Jun63 | 184/79 | 100 | 10.17    10.11,10.09w | -85 |
| | | | | | 200 | 20.25,20.14w 19.96 | -84 |
| | | | | | 400 | 45.93    46.0A-85,46.38 | -84 |
| arber | Eric | USA | 24Jun63 | 188/86 | LJ | 7.90    8.00 | -85 |
| arbosa | José Luis | BRA | 27May61 | 184/68 | 800 | 1:44.10    1:44.3 | -83 |
| arbu | Agustin | RUM | 21Apr63 | 168/54 | 3kSt | 8:34.60    8:32.83 | -84 |
| arella | Mauro | ITA | 12Dec56 | 178/70 | PV | 5.45i    5.50 | -84 |
| arnes | Randy | USA | 16Jun66 | 196/121 | SP | 21.88    18.56 | -85 |
| | | | | | DT | 61.18 | |
| arnett | Mike | USA | 21May61 | 185/102 | JT | 76.02    90.34* | -83 |
| arnett | Frank | USA | 17Jan66 | 180/82 | 110h | 13.73,13.6   14.15 | -85 |
| arney | David | USA | 18Jan60 | 175/58 | 10k | 28:13.3 | |
| aroni | Fernando | ITA | 3Sep57 | | SP | 19.41i    19.67 | -84 |
| arr | Oslen | GUY | 3Apr61 | 165/67 | 800 | 1:46.49    1:46.42 | -84 |
| arré | Pascal | FRA | 12Apr59 | 174/66 | 200 | 20.79    20.38 | -79 |
| arreto | Luis M. | MEX | 25Apr60 | 177/63 | 5k | 13:35.6    13:42.98 | -85 |
| arrett | Gerard | AUS | 31Dec56 | 176/62 | 10k | 28:19.15   27:50.7 | -79 |
| arrios | Arturo | MEX | 12Dec63 | 174/60 | 3k | 7:48.22 | |
| | | | | | 5k | 13:25.83    13:46.37 | -85 |
| | | | | | 10k | 27:50.28    28:42.77 | -85 |
| arsotti | Alberto | ITA | 29Feb64 | 186/70 | 800 | 1:45.3    1:46.86 | -85 |
| asiak | Grzegorz | POL | 22Jun62 | 180/68 | 1500 | 3:39.8    3:39.59 | -84 |
| askin | Tracy | USA | 3Nov65 | 190/77 | 800 | 1:46.99    1:49.54 | -85 |
| atrachenko | Viktor | SU | 6Jan63 | 186/78 | 110h | 13.64,13.5  13.92,13.6 | -82 |
| aumann | Dieter | FRG | 15Feb65 | 176/63 | 1500 | 3:36.40    3:40.48 | -85 |
| | | | | | 5k | 13:35.04    13:48.0 | -85 |
| ames | Peter | AUS | 13Sep63 | 180/70 | TJ | 16.55,16.90w 16.22 | -84 |
| ardsley | Greg | USA | 14Dec61 | 179/64 | 3kSt | 8:35.65    8:29.65 | -85 |
| attie | Phil | UK | 8Sep63 | 178/74 | 400h | 49.60    50.43 | -84 |
| cker | Andreas | GDR | 15Aug62 | 195/107 | DT | 64.16    60.96 | -85 |
| cker | Uwe | FRG | 10Dec55 | 188/70 | 1k | 2:18.86    2:18.80 | -83 |
| | | | | | 1500 | 3:38.80    3:34.84 | -83 |
| | | | | | 2k | 5:03.94    5:02.00 | -84 |
| cker | Gustavo | SPA | 17Jun66 | 184/70 | HJ | 2.25    2.23 | -85 |
| dnář | Zdeněk | CS | 1Mar57 | 195/110 | HT | 74.60    74.12 | -83 |
| dnarski | Zbigniew | POL | 4Jun60 | 173/81 | JT | 82.26*    86.70* | -85 |
| er | Ron | GDR | 29Aug65 | 183/78 | LJ | 8.15    8.21 | -85 |
| hmer | Jens | GDR | 11Sep65 | 182/66 | 800 | 1:46.96    1:48.00 | -85 |
| ierl | Michael | AUT | 27Dec63 | 186/110 | HT | 77.80    73.36 | -85 |
| lkessam | Ahmed | ALG | 27Mar62 | | 800 | 1:46.6    1:45.6 | -85 |
| | | | | | 1k | 2:18.78    2:20.8 | -82 |
| ll | Earl | USA | 25Aug55 | 191/75 | PV | 5.81    5.80 | -84 |
| llo | Jorge | SPA | 28Mar63 | 187/70 | 3kSt | 8:27.24    8:28.36 | -85 |
| lozerskikh | Eduard | SU | 65 | | LJ | 7.92    7.59 | -83 |
| lyi | Viktor | SU | 64 | | SP | 19.54    20.07 | -85 |
| navides | Paul | USA | 5Nov64 | | PV | 5.60    5.45 | -85 |
| nito | Teófilo | SPA | 22Jul66 | 175/64 | 1500 | 3:36.96    3:38.92 | -85 |
| | | | | | 2k | 5:02.60    5:15.78 | -85 |
| nnett | Todd | UK | 6Jul62 | 171/66 | 200 | 20.50    20.36 | -84 |
| | | | | | 400 | 45.62    45.35 | -85 |
| nnon | Anthony | USA | 15Mar66 | 180/75 | 400h | 50.2 | |
| nsch | Bernhard | FRG | 22Sep64 | 197/83 | HJ | 2.27i,2.27  2.22 | -82 |
| nvenuti | Marcello | ITA | 26Apr64 | | HJ | 2.24    2.26 | -85 |
| reglazov | Vladimir | SU | 59 | | TJ | 16.69    17.03 | -83 |
| rger | Andreas | AUT | 9Jun61 | 173/74 | 100 | 10.31    10.41 | -85 |
| rtimon | Charlus-Mi | FRA | 1Jan57 | 187/87 | JT | 80.76    88.52* | -85 |
| rtocchi | Luigi | ITA | 10Jun65 | | 110h | 13.79    14.02-85,13.6 | -84 |
| tancourt | Ernesto | CUB | 5Nov63 | 186/83 | Dec | 7721    6446 | -85 |
| tancourt -# | Lázaro | CUB | 18Mar63 | 189/81 | TJ | 17.78    17.57 | -85 |
| ttiol | Salvatore | ITA | 28Nov61 | 178/57 | Mar | 2:13:27    2:14:17 | -85 |
| yer | Udo | GDR | 9Aug55 | 194/140 | SP | 22.64    22.22 | -83 |
| anchini | Orlando | ITA | 4Jun55 | 193/130 | HT | 74.68    77.94 | -84 |

| Name | | Nat | Yr | Ht/Wt | Event | 1986 Mark | Pre-1986 best |
|---|---|---|---|---|---|---|---|
| Bile | Abdi | SOM | 63 | 185/75 | 1500 | 3:34.01 | 3:34.24 | -8 |
| | | | | | Mile | 3:55.77i | 3:53.08 | -8 |
| Bilík | Ivo | CS | 2Aug62 | 185/76 | TJ | 16.62 | 16.38i,16.27 | -8 |
| Bindar | Nicolae | RUM | 14Mar56 | 177/113 | HT | 77.60 | 77.50 | -8 |
| Binley | Judd | USA | 4Jan55 | 186/102 | DT | 63.24 | 64.64 | -8 |
| Binns | Steve | UK | 25Aug60 | 170/57 | 5k | 13:29.78 | 13:26.86 | -8 |
| | | | | | 10k | 27:58.01 | 27:55.66 | -8 |
| Biscarini | G.Carlo | ITA | 19Oct62 | 176/64 | LJ | 7.90i | 7.87 | -8 |
| Bishop | Clyde | USA | 29May62 | 183/82 | 100 | 10.34w | 10.34w-82,10.1 | -8 |
| Bitok | Sosthenes | KEN | 23Mar57 | 188/68 | 5k | 13:34.23i | 13:29.02i, | |
| | | | | | | | 13:43.47 | -8 |
| Bitsadze | Tariel | SU | 12Jan66 | 194/110 | SP | 19.90 | 18.44 | -8 |
| Black | Marcus | USA | | 180/73 | 200 | 20.5 | | |
| Black | Roger | UK | 31Mar66 | 190/83 | 200 | 20.63 | 21.6,21.89 | -8 |
| | | | | | 400 | 44.59 | 45.36 | -8 |
| Blake | Arthur | USA | 19Aug66 | 183/66 | 110h | 13.57,13.39w | 13.84 | -8 |
| Blalock | Stanley | USA | 18Mar64 | 175/71 | 100 | 10.34, | 10.30 | -8 |
| | | | | | | 10.21w | 10.09w | -8 |
| | | | | | 200 | 20.70 | 20.50 | -8 |
| | | | | | | | 20.4,20.3w | -8 |
| Blank | Peter | FRG | 10Apr62 | 194/81 | HJ | 2.25 | 2.24i-85,2.23 | -8 |
| Blockberger | Sheldon | USA | 19Sep64 | 188/82 | Dec | 7737 | 7361 | -8 |
| Blom | Jyrki | FIN | 11May62 | 183/83 | JT | 80.48 | 85.30* | -8 |
| Blomstrand | Staffan | SWE | 3Aug60 | 187/82 | Dec | 7737 | 7630 | -8 |
| Blondel | Alain | FRA | 7Dec62 | 185/76 | Dec | 8185 | 7763 | -8 |
| Blutreich | Brian | USA | 5Jan67 | | SP | 19.32 | -0- | |
| Bobryshev | Viktor | SU | 28May57 | 187/120 | HT | 75.86 | 78.28 | -8 |
| Bobylev | Vladimir | SU | 12Jun66 | | LJ | 8.07 | 8.06 | -8 |
| Bochin | Viktor | SU | 60 | | JT | 77.30 | 90.04* | -8 |
| Bodine | John | USA | 20Sep63 | | LJ | 7.90w | 7.62 | -8 |
| Bodenmüller | Klaus | AUT | 6Sep62 | 194/100 | SP | 19.97 | 18.24 | -8 |
| Bodó | Bela | HUN | 19Jan59 | 185/80 | 110h | 13.84 | 13.68-83,13.6 | -8 |
| Böhni | Felix | SWZ | 14Feb58 | 189/82 | PV | 5.70 | 5.71 | -8 |
| Böttcher | Holger | FRG | 27Jul63 | 183/73 | 800 | 1:47.15 | 1:46.20 | -8 |
| Boffi | Franco | ITA | 2Nov58 | 186/70 | 2k | 5:06.95 | 5:06.65 | -8 |
| | | | | | 3k | 7:49.48 | 7:52.78 | -8 |
| | | | | | 3kSt | 8:32.82 | 8:27.66 | -8 |
| Bogasson | Egert | ICE | 19Jul60 | 191/115 | DT | 62.42 | 58.84 | -8 |
| Bogatyryov | Pavel | SU | 19Mar61 | 194/84 | PV | 5.62i | 5.80 | -8 |
| Bohannon | Chris | USA | 23Sep65 | 180/73 | PV | 5.48i | 5.18 | -8 |
| Boileau | Art | CAN | 9Oct57 | 176/67 | Mar | 2:11:15 | 2:11:30 | -8 |
| Boinet | Micah | KEN | 65 | | 3kSt | 8:28.20 | 8:37.6A | -8 |
| Bojars | Janis | SU | 12May56 | 185/127 | SP | 20.98 | 21.74 | -8 |
| Bolgár | Tamás | HUN | 24Aug55 | 185/102 | JT | 76.84 | 84.86* | -8 |
| Boltz | Danny | AUS | 17Jul62 | | 10k | 28:15.00 | 29:18.5 | -8 |
| Bondarenko | Yevgeniy | SU | 80ct66 | | PV | 5.60 | 5.30 | -8 |
| Booker | Martin | USA | 8Mar63 | 185/82 | 110h | 13.51 | 13.76,13.68w | -8 |
| Bordin | Gelindo | ITA | 2Apr59 | 180/68 | Mar | 2:10:54 | 2:11:29 | -8 |
| Bordukov | Vyacheslav | SU | 1Jan59 | 184/69 | TJ | 17.22 | 17.37 | -8 |
| Borghans | Marc | HOL | 1Apr60 | | 1500 | 3:39.88 | 3:47.2 | -7 |
| Borglund | Peter | SWE | 29Jan64 | 183/84 | JT | 80.74 | 82.26* | -8 |
| Borodkin | Nikolay | SU | 20Jan55 | 190/127 | SP | 20.57 | 21.04 | -8 |
| Bosman | Wessel | RSA | 24Jun58 | 181/75 | 110h | 13.77Aw | 13.71A-81,13.5A | -8 |
| Bourke | Peter | AUS | 23Apr58 | 182/73 | 1500 | 3:36.89 | 3:42.81 | -8 |
| | | | | | Mile | 3:57.53 | 3:58.0 | -8 |
| Bouschen | Peter | FRG | 16May60 | 181/78 | TJ | 16.78,16.80w | 17.33 | -8 |
| Bowden | John | NZ | 19Jun56 | 180/64 | 10k | 28:29.41 | | |
| Boyd | Mark | USA | 19May65 | 187/89 | 110h | 13.80 | 13.98 | -8 |
| Bozhinovski | Krasimir | BUL | 1Jul67 | 178/70 | 100 | 10.36 | 10.68 | -8 |
| | | | | | 200 | 20.5 | | |
| Bradford | Craig | USA | 4Jun64 | 185/77 | 110h | 13.79w | 14.11 | -8 |
| Bradstock | Roald | UK | 24Apr62 | 180/95 | JT | 81.74 | 91.40* | -8 |

| ␀e | | Nat | Yr | Ht/Wt | Event | 1986 Mark | Pre-1986 best | |
|---|---|---|---|---|---|---|---|---|
| ahm | Terry | USA | 21Nov62 | 180/68 | 1500 | 3:36.35 | 3:38.0 | -84 |
| | | | | | 2k | 5:05.71i | | |
| | | | | | 3k | 7:43.15 | 7:59.28 | -84 |
| an | Mihai | RUM | 12Jan62 | 189/82 | TJ | 16.78 | 16.97 | -85 |
| and | Darryl | UK | 6Aug63 | | JT | 86.28* | 80.22* | -85 |
| anham | Chris | USA | 24Jan62 | 193/86 | 110h | 13.75 | 13.9 | -85 |
| | | | | | Dec | 8159w | 7708 | -85 |
| anham | Malcolmb | USA | 3May66 | 183/75 | LJ | 7.93 | 7.84 | -85 |
| antly | Keith | USA | 23May62 | 179/63 | 10k | 28:10.3 | 28:14.0 | -85 |
| aslavskiy | Igor | SU | 19Aug59 | | Mar | 2:13:09 | 2:14:55 | -85 |
| ass | Andrew | USA | | | 100 | 10.1Aw | | |
| aun | Peter | FRG | 1Aug62 | 183/64 | 800 | 1:44.03 | 1:44.15 | -85 |
| eigan | Bo | NOR | 17Dec58 | 190/85 | 800 | 1:46.18 | 1:46.08 | -85 |
| enner | John | USA | 4Jan61 | 192/130 | SP | 21.78 | 21.92 | -84 |
| | | | | | DT | 66.62 | 63.44 | -84 |
| ett | Peter | AUS | 14Nov62 | 178/70 | 10k | 28:11.25 | 28:44.5 | -85 |
| idges | Oliver | USA | 30Jun62 | 192/86 | 400 | 45.91 | 45.35A-82,45.45 | -84 |
| ige | Norbert | FRA | 9Jan64 | 183/78 | LJ | 8.09 | 8.08 | -85 |
| ight | Tim | USA | 28Jul60 | 188/79 | PV | 5.70 | 5.52 | -85 |
| | | | | | Dec | 8302 | 8221 | -85 |
| ingmann | Steffen | GDR | 11Mar64 | 184/78 | 100 | 10.13 | 10.22,10.17w | -85 |
| own | Bill | USA | 24May65 | 188/79 | 110h | 13.82w | 13.94w | -85 |
| own | Butch | USA | 27Apr61 | 188/75 | 800 | 1:46.50 | 1:47.39 | -83 |
| own | Derrick | UK | 21Nov63 | 180/77 | LJ | 7.90,8.12w | 8.00 | -85 |
| own | Ed | USA | 20Jul58 | 188/81 | Dec | 7729 | 7676 | -85 |
| own | Laron | USA | 3Jun62 | 185/76 | 200 | 20.70 | 21.0-82,20.5Aw | -83 |
| | | | | | 400 | 44.92 | 45.45 | -83 |
| own | Lorenzo | USA | 16Mar61 | | 800 | 1:46.97 | | |
| own | Phil | UK | 6Jan62 | 180/73 | 400 | 45.29 | 45.26 | -85 |
| own | Ray | USA | 11Aug61 | 185/73 | 800 | 1:47.11 | 1:46.74 | -83 |
| | | | | | 1k | 2:18.96 | | |
| own | Rex | USA | 12Feb64 | 178/77 | 100 | 10.32Aw | 10.4w | -85 |
| | | | | | 200 | 20.67Aw | | |
| uch | Ricky | SWE | 2Jul46 | 199/130 | DT | 62.02 | 71.26 | -84 |
| uin | Erik de | HOL | 25May63 | 186/110 | SP | 20.95 | 20.60i,20.24 | -85 |
| | | | | | DT | 66.78 | 66.38 | -85 |
| nner | Wulf | FRG | 20Mar62 | 187/110 | DT | 63.18 | 60.72 | -84 |
| uziks | Maris | SU | 25Aug62 | 186/70 | TJ | 17.54i,17.33 | 17.38 | -85 |
| ggare | Arto | FIN | 26May58 | 194/82 | 110h | 13.42 | 13.35 | -84 |
| zgin | Viktor | SU | 22Aug62 | 180/72 | 100 | 10.11, | 10.18, | |
| | | | | | | 10.03dwr,10.0 | 10.0 | -84 |
| ka | Sergey | SU | 4Dec63 | 183/80 | PV | 6.01 | 6.00 | -85 |
| ka | Vasiliy | SU | 26Nov60 | 184/76 | PV | 5.80 | 5.85 | -85 |
| kingham | Jeff | USA | 14Jun60 | 172/68 | PV | 5.56i | 5.76 | -83 |
| kner | Jack | UK | 22Sep61 | 173/59 | 1500 | 3:35.28 | 3:36.73 | -85 |
| | | | | | Mile | 3:57.29 | 3:51.57 | -84 |
| | | | | | 3k | 7:40.43 | 7:45.19 | -84 |
| | | | | | 2M | 8:17.12 | 8:21.4i | -85 |
| | | | | | 5k | 13:10.15 | 13:21.06 | -85 |
| ai | Romeo | ITA | 7Jun58 | | HT | 72.36 | 72.68 | -84 |
| ko | Vladimir | SU | 4Feb65 | 186/79 | 400h | 48.71 | 48.74 | -84 |
| no | Angel | CUB | 2Mar63 | 176/70 | 110h | 13.86 | 13.81-83,13.7w | -82 |
| no | Luis A. | CUB | 22May69 | 174/67 | LJ | 8.25 | 7.62 | -85 |
| ár | Imrich | CS | 14Apr55 | 196/120 | DT | 67.38 | 71.26 | -85 |
| g | Gordon | USA | 24Jun66 | 168/61 | 400h | 49.99 | 50.27 | -85 |
| reyev | Valeriy | SU | 15Jun64 | 181/67 | PV | 5.45 | 5.39 | -84 |
| ch | Joey | USA | 29Mar65 | 175/62 | 800 | 1:46.8 | 1:47.47 | -85 |
| cic | Mike | USA | 25Jul62 | 193/111 | DT | 65.10 | 66.42 | -85 |
| ney | Elliott | UK | 11Dec66 | 182/80 | 100 | 10.20 | 10.38-85,10.29w | -84 |
| chard | Hans | FRG | 17Aug59 | 198/87 | HJ | 2.24i | 2.27i-83,2.21 | -81 |
| ger | Kobus | RSA | 7Nov62 | 187/85 | 400h | 50.26A | 49.95 | -85 |
| gess | David | UK | 19Dec62 | 186/69 | LJ | 7.93w | 7.66,7.74w | -83 |

| Name | | Nat | Yr | Ht/Wt | Event | 1986 Mark | Pre-1986 best | |
|---|---|---|---|---|---|---|---|---|
| Burin | Yevgeniy | SU | 4Mar64 | 190/110 | DT | 62.94 | 62.18 | — |
| Burns | Art | USA | 19Jul54 | 185/118 | DT | 68.72 | 71.18 | — |
| Burra | John | TAN | 60 | | Mar | 2:11:27 | 2:15:59 | — |
| Burrell | Leroy | USA | 21Feb67 | 180/79 | 100 | 10.32w,10.1w | 10.43 | — |
| | | | | | 200 | 20.71w | 21.51 | — |
| | | | | | LJ | 8.15 | 7.18 | — |
| Burridge | David | NZ | 20Jan62 | 187/68 | 5k | 13:32.7 | | |
| Busse | Andreas | GDR | 6May59 | 185/68 | 800 | 1:45.23 | 1:44.72 | — |
| | | | | | 1500 | 3:35.52 | 3:34.10 | — |
| | | | | | Mile | 3:55.63 | 3:53.55 | — |
| Buskas | Östen | SWE | 3Dec62 | 175/62 | 1500 | 3:39.15 | 3:46.52 | — |
| Butler | James | USA | 21Jun60 | 175/66 | 200 | 20.58 | 20.31 | — |
| | | | | | | | 20.23A,20.07Aw | |
| Byers | Tom | USA | 12May55 | 185/71 | Mile | 3:57.60 | 3:50.84 | — |
| Bystedt | Kjell | SWE | 24May60 | 189/112 | HT | 75.04 | 75.84 | — |
| Cadier | Olivier | BRA | 5Aug60 | | LJ | 7.94 | 7.81 | |
| Čado | Ján | CS | 7May63 | 182/75 | TJ | 17.04 | 17.34 | — |
| Calk | Craig | USA | 31Jan65 | 188/78 | 400h | 49.90 | | |
| Calderon | Raul | CUB | 27Nov62 | 183/105 | DT | 65.10 | 63.18 | — |
| Callender | Clarence | UK | 16Nov61 | 181/73 | 100 | 10.32w | 10.60,10.48w | — |
| Cameron | Bert | JAM | 16Nov59 | 188/79 | 400 | 44.66 | 44.58 | — |
| Camp | Jim | USA | 16Dec63 | 189/105 | SP | 19.95 | 18.78,18.81i | — |
| Campbell | Arnold | USA | 15Nov66 | 180/115 | SP | 19.58 | 19.40 | — |
| Campbell | Carl | USA | 11Mar63 | 188/79 | 110h | 13.86, | 13.94, | — |
| | | | | | | 13.82w,13.4w | 13.91w | |
| Campbell | Clifton | USA | 18Jun67 | 185/66 | 400 | 45.43 | 47.4* | — |
| Campbell | Dave | CAN | 31Aug60 | 177/65 | Mile | 3:58.01 | 3:59.61 | — |
| Campbell | Tonie | USA | 14Jun60 | 188/77 | 110h | 13.39,13.29w | 13.23 | — |
| | | | | | | 13.0 | 13.1 | — |
| Campos | João | POR | 22Sep58 | 173/55 | 5k | 13:28.81 | 13:19.10 | — |
| Canário | Ezequiel | POR | 10Apr60 | 181/60 | 3k | 7:47.90 | 7:49.8 | — |
| | | | | | 5k | 13:28.36 | 13:26.50 | — |
| | | | | | 10k | 27:53.72 | | |
| Canfield | Tim | USA | 16Nov63 | 188/79 | PV | 5.45 | 5.28 | |
| Cannon | Mike | USA | 26Oct64 | 175/64 | 400 | 45.38 | 45.14 | — |
| Cannon | Robert | USA | 9Jul58 | 186/74 | TJ | 17.02,17.08w | 17.18 | — |
| Canović | Novica | YUG | 29Nov61 | 193/75 | HJ | 2.28i,2.28 | 2.28 | — |
| Canti | Aldo | FRA | 9Mar61 | 185/80 | 200 | 20.78 | 20.69 | — |
| | | | | | 400 | 45.62 | 45.09 | — |
| Cao Yang | | CHN | 68 | | HJ | 2.25 | | |
| Carchesio | Luciano | ITA | 7Jan61 | 178/65 | 1500 | 3:39.58 | 3:42.52 | — |
| | | | | | 3kSt | 8:29.14 | 8:27.94 | — |
| Caristan | Stèphane | FRA | 31Mar64 | 187/75 | 110h | 13.20, | 13.43 | — |
| | | | | | | 13.0 | 13.4 | — |
| Carreira | José Luis | SPA | 30Mar62 | 170/62 | 1500 | 3:35.56 | 3:38.79 | — |
| | | | | | Mile | 3:57.01 | 3:59.32 | — |
| | | | | | 2k | 4:57.53 | 5:14.29 | — |
| Carter | Carl | USA | 7Mar64 | 180/82 | 100 | 10.32w,10.0w | 10.12w | — |
| | | | | | 200 | 20.75,20.65w | 20.69w | — |
| Carter | Jerome | USA | 25Mar63 | 185/66 | HJ | 2.34 | 2.31i-83,2.30 | — |
| Cartlidge | Perry | USA | 29Mar63 | 175/75 | 100 | 10.1w | | |
| | | | | | 400 | 45.49 | 45.75 | — |
| Castro | Dionisio | POR | 22Nov63 | 167/56 | 5k | 13:22.94 | 13:38.85 | — |
| | | | | | 10k | 28:12.04 | 28:54.0 | — |
| Castro | Domingos | POR | 22Nov63 | 167/56 | 1500 | 3:39.2 | 3:44.8 | — |
| | | | | | 5k | 13:19.03 | 13:38.60 | — |
| | | | | | 10k | 28:01.62 | 30:39.6 | — |
| Cate | Steve | USA | 23Nov63 | 190/107 | SP | 20.15 | 18.79,18.83i | — |
| Cecchini | Stefano | ITA | 20Oct61 | 172/52 | 800 | 1:46.7 | 1:46.60 | — |
| Centelles | J.Francisco | CUB | 26Jan61 | 196/81 | HJ | 2.30 | 2.32 | — |
| Chacón | Ricardo | CUB | 8Jan63 | 175/73 | 100 | 10.24 | 10.31 | — |

| me | | Nat | Yr | Ht/Wt | Event | 1986 Mark | Pre-1986 best | |
|---|---|---|---|---|---|---|---|---|
| ang | Jae-Keun | SKO | 2Jan62 | 184/64 | 200 | 20.71 | 20.41 | -85 |
| arlton | David | BAH | 6Jan62 | 183/70 | 400h | 50.14 | 50.07 | -83 |
| ase | Darnell | USA | 13Dec65 | 175/71 | 400 | 45.19 | 46.11 | -85 |
| atta | Ahmed Kamel | EGY | 23Jan61 | 190/115 | SP | 19.46dq | 19.62 | -85 |
| elelgo | Joseph | KEN | 24Apr63 | 170/61 | 3kSt | 8:29.98 | 8:32.35 | -85 |
| en Zunrong | | CHN | 25Aug62 | 178/68 | LJ | 8.23 | 7.89 | -85 |
| erkasov | Vladimir | SU | 63 | | LJ | 7.92 | | |
| ernikov | Vladimir | SU | 3Aug59 | 188/74 | TJ | 16.88 | 17.35 | -85 |
| ernov | Ilya | SU | 12Jun67 | | HJ | 2.23 | 2.19 | -85 |
| eruiyot | Charles | KEN | 2Dec64 | 165/54 | Mile | 3:57.76 | -0- | |
| | | | | | 2k | 5:05.1 | 5:06.37 | -85 |
| | | | | | 3k | 7:44.10 | 7:47.47 | -83 |
| | | | | | 5k | 13:33.55 | 13:18.41 | -84 |
| eruiyot | Kipkoech | KEN | 2Dec64 | 164/55 | 800 | 1:46.48 | 1:47.8 | -84 |
| | | | | | 1500 | 3:33.07 | 3:34.92 | -83 |
| | | | | | Mile | 3:56.74i | 3:53.92 | -83 |
| erubini | Claudio | ITA | 29Apr60 | 183/74 | LJ | 7.94i | 7.69,7.77w | -85 |
| esarek | Dave | KEN | 3Jul64 | 185/75 | 400h | 50.35 | 51.05 | -85 |
| esire | Joseph | KEN | 12Nov57 | 167/57 | 800 | 1:45.10 | 1:45.36 | -85 |
| | | | | | 1500 | 3:34.32 | 3:34.52 | -84 |
| evallier | Franck | FRA | 3Jan64 | 185/71 | 110h | 13.85 | 13.85,13.84w | -84 |
| iriac | Constantin | RUM | 70ct60 | 186/85 | JT | 76.70 | 79.00* | -83 |
| mara | Mirosław | POL | 9May64 | 201/86 | PV | 5.67i | 5.40 | -85 |
| myr | Jaroslav | SU | 29Nov66 | 188/110 | HT | 72.60 | 75.22 | -85 |
| ochev | Atanas | BUL | 17Jan57 | 180/74 | LJ | 7.95,8.21w | 8.19 | -81 |
| ornyi | Grigoriy | SU | 27Mar62 | 188/82 | HJ | 2.25 | 2.25 | -85 |
| ristianson | Craig | USA | 1Apr61 | | JT | 77.44 | 83.46* | -85 |
| ristie | Linford | UK | 2Apr60 | 189/77 | 100 | 10.04 | 10.42,10.20w | -85 |
| | | | | | 200 | 20.51 | 21.0-84,21.37 | -85 |
| ugunov | Gennadiy | SU | 26Nov63 | 188/80 | 110h | 13.67,13.33w | 14.01 | -84 |
| | | | | | | 13.63dwr,13.4 13.8 | | -85 |
| yuzhas | Anatoliy | SU | 18Apr56 | 180/103 | HT | 78.34 | 80.16 | -84 |
| d | Ramon | SPA | 15Aug54 | 181/72 | TJ | 16.66i | 16.69 | -80 |
| | | | | | | | 16.71Aw | -79 |
| obanu | Daniel | RUM | 30Jan65 | 190/65 | TJ | 16.73 | 16.70i,16.70 | -85 |
| ofani | Walter | FRA | 17Feb62 | 185/105 | HT | 76.86 | 78.50 | -85 |
| ark | Belfred | USA | 19Aug65 | 183/79 | 400h | 49.29 | 49.45 | -84 |
| ark | Cletus | USA | 20Jan62 | 193/86 | 110h | 13.57 | 13.38 | -85 |
| ark | Darren | AUS | 6Sep65 | 179/76 | 400 | 44.72 | 44.75 | -84 |
| ark | Harry | USA | 3Feb65 | 185/77 | Dec | 7664w | 7022h* | -84 |
| ark | Ocky | USA | 14Nov60 | 180/69 | 800 | 1:46.19 | 1:45.29 | -85 |
| arke | Dave | UK | 1Jan58 | 183/68 | 5k | 13:30.83 | 13:22.54 | -83 |
| | | | | | 10k | 28:08.78 | 27:55.77 | -82 |
| ary | Don | USA | 29Jul57 | 175/74 | 5k | 13:27.41 | 13:28.62 | -84 |
| ouvel | Pascal | FRA | 12Nov60 | 187/75 | 1500 | 3:39.69 | 3:45.32 | -85 |
| | | | | | 3k | 7:50.28 | | |
| e | Sebastian | UK | 29Sep56 | 175/54 | 800 | 1:44.10 | 1:41.73 | -81 |
| | | | | | 1k | 2:14.90 | 2:12.18 | -81 |
| | | | | | 1500 | 3:29.77 | 3:31.95 | -81 |
| ghlan | Eamonn | IRL | 24Nov52 | 177/63 | Mile | 3:56.88, | 3:51.59, | |
| | | | | | | 3:56.34i | 3:49.78i | -83 |
| | | | | | 3k | 7:48.18 | 7:37.60 | -80 |
| | | | | | 5k | 13:22.85 | 13:19.13 | -81 |
| | | | | | 10k | 28:19.3 | -0- | |
| le | Mike | USA | 30Jan61 | | 110h | 13.88,13.5w | 13.5dt | -85 |
| eman | Vincent | USA | 28Jun65 | 185/75 | 100 | 10.23w | 10.43,10.25w | -85 |
| | | | | | 200 | 20.81, | 20.89, | |
| | | | | | | 20.22w | 20.84w | -85 |
| lard | Philippe | FRA | 26Feb60 | 176/65 | 800 | 1:45.10 | 1:47.12 | -85 |
| | | | | | 1k | 2:16.6 | 2:19.5 | -85 |
| llet | Philippe | FRA | 13Dec63 | 176/70 | PV | 5.85 | 5.80 | -85 |
| lins | James | USA | 19Feb65 | 190/102 | 110h | 13.83w | 14.20,14.09w | -85 |

| Name | | Nat | Yr | Ht/Wt | Event | 1986 Mark | Pre-1986 best |
|------|--|-----|----|----|-------|-----------|---------------|
| Conde | Juan | CUB | 30Apr65 | 175/65 | 3kSt | 8:32.49 | 8:36.8 – |
| Coney | Dave | USA | 4May63 | 188/88 | LJ | 7.90i | 7.85,7.90w – |
| Conley | Mike | USA | 5Oct62 | 185/78 | 100 | 10.36 | 10.39w – |
| | | | | | LJ | 8.33,8.63w | 8.43,8.53w – |
| | | | | | TJ | 17.69, | 17.71, |
| | | | | | | 17.84w | 17.72w – |
| Connolly | Jim | USA | 24Mar63 | 185/88 | Dec | 7768 | 7771 – |
| Conover | Mark | USA | 28May60 | 178/60 | 10k | 28:30.3 | 28:43.45 – |
| Consiglio | Doug | CAN | 10Jan64 | 193/68 | 1500 | 3:38.73i | 3:43.6 – |
| | | | | | Mile | 3:55.91i | 4:10.95 – |
| Conway | Hollis | USA | 8Jan67 | 183/66 | HJ | 2.29 | 2.185 – |
| Cook | Darwin | USA | 16Jul62 | 178/75 | 100 | 10.25 | 10.10,9.9 – |
| Cooksey | Tony | USA | 7Jul56 | 183/79 | Dec | 7930W | 7972 – |
| Cooper | Brad | BAH | 30Jun57 | 188/132 | DT | 67.10 | 66.72 – |
| Cooper | Brian | USA | 21Aug65 | 183/79 | 100 | 10.22w | 10.45 – |
| | | | | | 200 | 20.63w | |
| | | | | | LJ | 7.90i | 7.97 – |
| Cooper | Ed | USA | 4Sep63 | 185/68 | 400h | 49.68 | 49.69 – |
| Cooper | Jim | USA | 6Oct59 | 180/65 | 5k | 13:32.92 | |
| | | | | | 3kSt | 8:19.88 | 8:23.82 – |
| Cooper | Rodney | USA | 15Oct65 | | 110h | 13.79 | |
| Cooper | Todd | USA | 4Mar63 | 178/64 | PV | 5.49i | 5.61 – |
| Coppess | Phil | USA | 2Sep54 | 180/65 | Mar | 2:13:27 | 2:10:05 – |
| Corgos | Antonio | SPA | 10Mar60 | 183/76 | LJ | 8.12i,8.08 | 8.23 – |
| Corstjens | Marc | BEL | 31Aug65 | 175/65 | 800 | 1:45.90 | 1:47.89 – |
| | | | | | 1k | 2:18.3 | 2:19.7 – |
| Corvo | Alberto | ITA | 14Apr63 | 174/66 | 1500 | 3:39.30 | 3:40.02 – |
| Cosi | Luca | ITA | 16Apr63 | 174/66 | 400h | 50.28 | 50.70 – |
| Council | Daron | USA | 26Dec64 | 188/73 | 100 | 10.27, | 10.23, |
| | | | | | | 10.23w | 10.22w – |
| | | | | | 200 | 20.52,20.3 | 20.29 – |
| Couto | Fernando | POR | 4Dec59 | 165/59 | 5k | 13:29.63 | 13:38.3 – |
| Cova | Alberto | ITA | 1Dec58 | 176/58 | 3k | 7:50.44 | 7:46.40 – |
| | | | | | 5k | 13:15.86 | 13:10.06 – |
| | | | | | 10k | 27:57.93 | 27:37.59 – |
| Crabb | Steve | UK | 30Nov63 | 179/64 | 800 | 1:47.14 | 1:45.80 – |
| | | | | | 1500 | 3:35.50 | 3:35.16 – |
| | | | | | Mile | 3:57.11 | 3:54.36 – |
| Crain | Brady | USA | 8Aug56 | 168/62 | 100 | 10.29 | 10.43-84,10.0w – |
| | | | | | 200 | 20.50 | 20.32-85,20.09w– |
| Cram | Steve | UK | 14Oct60 | 186/69 | 800 | 1:43.19 | 1:42.88 – |
| | | | | | 1000 | 2:15.77 | 2:12.88 – |
| | | | | | 1500 | 3:30.15 | 3:29.67 – |
| | | | | | Mile | 3:48.31 | 3:46.32 – |
| Criddle | Byron | USA | 21Feb62 | 179/74 | TJ | 16.82 | 16.86-83,17.08w– |
| Crooks | Natty | CAN | 24Aug63 | 185/75 | HJ | 2.235 | 2.20 – |
| Crouser | Brian | USA | 9Jul62 | 188/102 | JT | 79.86 | 95.10* – |
| Crumby | Maurice | USA | 31May63 | 196/75 | HJ | 2.26 | 2.26 – |
| Crunkleton | George | USA | 5Feb56 | 192/84 | 200 | 20.5A | 20.74A-84,20.82– |
| Cummings | Paul | USA | 5Sep53 | 177/63 | Mar | 2:11:31 | 2:12:39 – |
| Curtis | Richard | USA | 31Mar65 | 178/73 | 400h | 50.49 | 51.10 – |
| Cuypers | Alain | BEL | 29Nov67 | 180/68 | 400h | 50.15 | 51.94 – |
| Dabulskis | Algis | SU | 15Dec61 | | 10k | 28:24.78 | 28:24.13 – |
| Dakov | Georgi | BUL | 27Oct67 | 195/78 | HJ | 2.29 | 2.24 – |
| Dalhäuser | Roland | SWZ | 12Apr58 | 191/86 | HJ | 2.25 | 2.32i-82,2.31 – |
| Dalloway | Mark | UK | 28Oct63 | | 10k | 28:22.56 | -0- – |
| Dandino | Bob | USA | 14Dec61 | 178/73 | PV | 5.45 | 5.50 – |
| Daniel | Clarence | USA | 11Jun61 | 183/79 | 400 | 44.89 | 45.39 – |
| Daniel | Lorenzo | USA | 23Mar66 | 188/77 | 100 | 10.08, | 10.29, |
| | | | | | | 10.00w | 10.14w – |
| | | | | | 200 | 20.17,20.11w | 20.07 – |

| me | | Nat | Yr | Ht/Wt | Event | 1986 Mark | Pre-1986 best |
|---|---|---|---|---|---|---|---|
| aniels | Dave | USA | 28Oct58 | 188/73 | 3kSt | 8:34.99 | 8:23.56 -85 |
| aniels | Sansiski | USA | 31May64 | 183/73 | 110h | 13.47,13.4w | 13.58,13.5-85 |
| | | | | | 400h | 50.25,50.1 | 51.12 -84 |
| anneberg | Rolf | FRG | 1Mar53 | 198/112 | DT | 66.16 | 67.40 -84 |
| anu | Ivan | SU | 17Oct59 | | 3kSt | 8:28.64 | 8:29.6 -81 |
| arien | Daniel | FRA | 18Oct61 | 180/77 | 110h | 13.87 | 14.14-85,14.0 -82 |
| ashkin | Pavel | SU | 64 | | HT | 72.46 | 70.48 -84 |
| a Silva | João Batista | BRA | 22Aug63 | 178/74 | 400 | 45.95 | 46.7-84,46.99 -85 |
| a Silva | Robson Caetano | BRA | 4Sep64 | 187/74 | 100 | 10.02 | 10.22-85,10.2 -82 |
| | | | | | 200 | 20.28 | 20.44 -85 |
| asko | Mikhail | SU | 26Jan61 | 174/61 | 5k | 13:29.27 | 13:40.60 -85 |
| auksha | Valeriy | SU | 14Feb66 | 183/72 | 400h | 50.29 | 51.67 -84 |
| avies | Phil | UK | 18Nov60 | | 100 | 10.34w | 10.71,10.59w -85 |
| avies-Hale | Paul | UK | 21Jun62 | 176/60 | 3k | 7:50.37 | 7:44.76 -85 |
| avis | Jay | USA | 29Jul67 | 178/71 | PV | 5.50 | 5.28 -85 |
| avis | Mike | USA | 5Jan64 | 187/72 | LJ | 7.92,8.31w | 8.14 -85 |
| avis | Reggie | USA | 17Jan64 | 189/80 | 110h | 13.62 | 13.69,13.67w -85 |
| | | | | | 400h | 48.97 | 48.90 -85 |
| avis | Scott | USA | 12Dec61 | 188/77 | PV | 5.70 | 5.52 -85 |
| avito | Gianni | ITA | 19Aug57 | 193/78 | HJ | 2.24i, | 2.27i -82 |
| | | | | | | 2.24 | 2.27 -83 |
| al | Lance | USA | 21Aug61 | 188/108 | HT | 74.66 | 68.48 -85 |
| backer | Pascal | FRA | 8Apr60 | 170/58 | 3kSt | 8:18.54 | 8:20.34 -84 |
| e Beer | Chris | RSA | 18Aug61 | | JT | 87.94* | 85.18* -85 |
| e Bruyn | Gert | RSA | 26Aug65 | | 800 | 1:47.0A | 1:49.28 -85 |
| e Castella | Robert | AUS | 27Feb57 | 180/65 | 5k | 13:35.50 | 13:34.2 -81 |
| | | | | | Mar | 2:07:51 | 2:08:18 -81 |
| e | Billy | UK | 18Dec61 | 171/55 | 3k | 7:49.97i | 7:47.61 -85 |
| | | | | | 5k | 13:34.00 | 13:39.88 -85 |
| es | Tony | USA | 6Aug63 | 193/91 | 200 | 20.77 | 20.54 -84 |
| | | | | | | | 20.37w,20.2w -83 |
| | | | | | 110h | 13.65 | 13.65-84,13.6 -83 |
| Gaspari | Fabio | ITA | 4Dec66 | | JT | 76.06 | 74.90* -85 |
| gtyar | Oleg | SU | 7Aug64 | 191/82 | 110h | 13.6 | 13.5 -85 |
| gtyaryev | Grigoriy | SU | 10Aug58 | 190/90 | Dec | 8322 | 8698 -84 |
| ick | Christian | FRG | 8Jun65 | | Dec | 7844 | 7367 -85 |
| e Jongh | Japie | RSA | 6Dec64 | 192/87 | 400 | 45.78A | 45.87A -85 |
| lèze | Pierre | SWZ | 25Sep58 | 175/62 | 1500 | 3:38.38 | 3:31.75 -85 |
| | | | | | 2k | 5:01.52 | 4:56.51 -83 |
| | | | | | 3k | 7:46.82 | 7:44.08 -80 |
| | | | | | 5k | 13:15.31 | 13:28.77 -82 |
| lis | Luis M. | CUB | 6Dec57 | 185/106 | DT | 68.00 | 71.06 -83 |
| longe | Marco | GDR | 16Jun66 | 194/82 | LJ | 8.16 | 7.92-85,7.96w -84 |
| l Prado | Isidro | PHI | 15May59 | 176/73 | 400 | 45.96 | 45.57 -84 |
| montigny | Francois | FRA | 30Jul65 | 188/78 | JT | 75.48 | 78.74* -85 |
| myanyuk | Aleksey | SU | 30Jul58 | 188/80 | HJ | 2.31 | 2.33 -81 |
| nnis | Ronnie | USA | 24Oct64 | 175/64 | 200 | 20.4 | 20.47,20.44w -85 |
| spotović | Dragan | YUG | 18Nov62 | 190/79 | LJ | 7.93 | 7.71w -85 |
| sruelles | Ronald | BEL | 14Feb55 | 186/80 | 100 | 10.27, | 10.25 -84 |
| | | | | | | 10.16w | 10.02dwr-85,9.9-78 |
| | | | | | 200 | 20.79 | 20.66 -84 |
| | | | | | LJ | 7.94 | 8.08 -79 |
| xter | Mike | USA | 31Dec64 | 185/77 | 100 | 10.36 | 10.42,10.35w -85 |
| | | | | | 200 | 20.49 | 20.57 -85 |
| | | | | | | | 20.56w-83,20.5 -84 |
| aneus | Dany | FRA | 26Mar65 | 185/69 | HJ | 2.24 | 2.20 -85 |
| a Bâ | Amadou | SEN | 22Sep58 | 188/72 | 400 | 45.78 | 45.8-82,46.04 -84 |
| | | | | | 400h | 48.07 | 48.29 -85 |
| al | Joe | USA | 26Oct62 | 174/59 | PV | 5.91i,5.90 | 5.85 -85 |
| amond | Earl | USA | 21Jul66 | | 110h | 13.87,13.83dt, | |
| | | | | | | 13.76w,13.5w | |
| gno | Martin | CUB | 21Dec65 | | LJ | 8.17 | 7.79 -85 |

| Name | | Nat | Yr | Ht/Wt | Event | 1986 Mark | Pre-1986 best | |
|---|---|---|---|---|---|---|---|---|
| Dimitrov | Kamen | BUL | 18Jan62 | 194/90 | DT | 65.40 | 64.56 | -8 |
| Dinan | John | AUS | 18Nov59 | 183/85 | 200 | 20.19 | 21.09 | -8 |
| Dinsamo | Belaine | ETH | 28Jun57 | | Mar | 2:08:29 | 2:28:26A | -8 |
| Diomar | Claude | FRA | 4Dec61 | 175/62 | 800 | 1:46.65 | 1:49.29 | -£ |
| Dixon | Floyd | USA | 9Apr64 | 175/73 | 100 | 10.33w | 10.52 | -£ |
| Dixon | Malcolm | USA | 11Oct59 | 188/84 | 110h | 13.66, | 13.75, | |
| | | | | | | 13.57w | 13.54w | -£ |
| Djédjémel | René M. | IVC | 5Jun58 | 186/80 | 400h | 48.94 | 49.13 | -£ |
| Dmitriyev | Dmitriy | SU | 3Mar56 | 175/65 | 10k | 28:28.55 | 29:01.5 | -£ |
| Dobrovolskiy | Sergey | SU | 7Mar66 | 184/76 | 400h | 49.90 | 50.77 | -£ |
| Doehring | Jim | USA | 27Jan62 | 183/114 | SP | 21.29 | 20.62 | -£ |
| Dołega | Karol | POL | 19Jul63 | 184/70 | 3kSt | 8:33.42 | 8:35.37 | -£ |
| Dombrowski | Lutz | GDR | 25Jun59 | 187/87 | LJ | 8.11,8.12w | 8.54 | -£ |
| Domingues | Adauto | BRA | 20May61 | 173/62 | 3kSt | 8:26.01 | 8:32.97 | -£ |
| Donakowski | Bill | USA | 21Jun56 | 168/59 | Mar | 2:10:41 | 2:14:07 | -£ |
| Donakowski | Gerard | USA | 20Feb60 | 172/58 | 5k | 13:25.75 | 13:36.0 | -£ |
| | | | | | 10k | 27:58.41 | 28:03.92 | -£ |
| Donias | Alain | FRA | 15Jan60 | 184/75 | PV | 5.50 | 5.50 | -£ |
| Donovan | Paul | IRL | 11Jul63 | 179/63 | Mile | 3:56.39i, | 3:55.82 | -£ |
| | | | | | | 3:58.00 | | |
| | | | | | 5k | 13:24.35 | 14:00.0 | -£ |
| Donskikh | Sergey | SU | 25Jan56 | 196/128 | SP | 20.33i | 21.09 | -£ |
| Dorozhon | Sergey | SU | 17Feb64 | 184/110 | HT | 78.46 | 78.00 | -£ |
| Doshev | Valentin | BUL | 12Apr63 | 180/110 | HT | 73.10 | 73.16 | -£ |
| dos Santos | Jorge José | BRA | 14Dec62 | | TJ | 16.82w | | |
| Dovoyno | Igor | SU | 27Aug64 | 178/64 | LJ | 7.95 | | |
| Draddy | Vince | USA | 19Apr61 | 184/66 | 1500 | 3:39.91 | 3:40.33 | -£ |
| | | | | | 3k | 7:49.41 | 7:49.55 | -£ |
| | | | | | 5k | 13:27.40 | 13:26.79 | -£ |
| Drăgoescu | Petru | RUM | 22Jul62 | 183/69 | 800 | 1:45.97 | 1:45.41 | -£ |
| Drahoňovský | Milan | CS | 18Jun66 | 180/65 | 800 | 1:46.66 | 1:48.20 | -£ |
| Driggs | Maximo | CUB | 9Jun62 | | JT | 76.26 | 79.18* | -£ |
| Druppers | Rob | HOL | 29Apr62 | 186/70 | 800 | 1:45.29 | 1:43.56 | -£ |
| Duany | Ubaldo | CUB | 16May60 | 183/73 | LJ | 8.32 | 8.14-84,8.18w | -£ |
| Dudkin | Yuriy | SU | 64 | | 400 | 45.83 | 47.05 | -£ |
| Duffy | Pat | USA | 4May65 | 188/79 | 110h | 13.85w | 13.86 | -£ |
| Duginyets | Igor | SU | 20May56 | 196/100 | DT | 65.16 | 68.52 | -£ |
| Dumchev | Yuriy | SU | 5Aug58 | 200/128 | DT | 63.14 | 71.86 | -£ |
| Duncan | Gary | USA | 25May64 | 196/79 | 400 | 45.82 | 46.62 | -£ |
| Dunn | Devlon | USA | | | 200 | 20.70A | 20.9w | -£ |
| Duplantis | Greg | USA | 22Jan62 | 173/61 | PV | 5.62 | 5.48 | -£ |
| Dvoretskiy | Sergey | SU | 30Apr57 | 191/108 | HT | 75.54 | 78.62 | -£ |
| Dwyer | Mike | CAN | 10Oct62 | 183/75 | 200 | 20.6 | 20.83 | -£ |
| Dyulgherov | Emanuil | BUL | 7Feb55 | 178/95 | HT | 78.30 | 80.64 | -£ |
| Dzhemiyev | Sergey | SU | 3Apr64 | 181/62 | PV | 5.50 | 5.40i-83,5.30 | -£ |
| Easker | John | USA | 30May63 | 178/67 | 5k | 13:30.51 | 13:37.2 | -£ |
| Edge | Dave | CAN | 11Nov54 | 170/55 | Mar | 2:11:08 | 2:11:04 | -£ |
| Edwards | Dothel | USA | 9Sep66 | 193/72 | HJ | 2.27i,2.26 | 2.30 | -£ |
| Edwards | Mal | UK | 7Jan58 | 185/70 | 1k | 2:18.18 | 2:23.8 | -£ |
| Edwards | Norman | JAM | 24Sep62 | 185/82 | 200 | 20.76w | 20.91w | -£ |
| Egan | Pat | USA | 21Jan62 | 185/107 | HT | 72.28 | 68.58 | -£ |
| Egbunike | Innocent | NIG | 30Nov61 | 174/68 | 200 | 20.80w | 20.42,20.4 | -£ |
| | | | | | | 20.6 | 20.23w | -£ |
| | | | | | 400 | 44.50 | 44.66 | -£ |
| Eickmann | Thomas | FRG | 16Mar62 | | Mar | 2:13:24 | 2:17:47 | -£ |
| Einarsson | Sigurdur | ICE | 28Sep62 | 190/102 | JT | 79.74 | 87.80* | -£ |
| Einberger | Markus | AUT | 5Feb64 | 198/82 | HJ | 2.28 | 2.20,2.24i | -£ |
| Ekberg | Sten | SWE | 25Dec64 | 190/86 | Dec | 7990 | 7886 | -£ |
| Ekblom | Tommy | FIN | 20Sep59 | 176/62 | 3kSt | 8:24.05 | 8:19.40 | -£ |
| Elbe | Jörg | GDR | 11Apr64 | 187/77 | TJ | 16.97 | 17.30 | -£ |
| Ellard | Henry | USA | 21Jul61 | 180/77 | TJ | 16.73 | 16.71,17.23w | -£ |

| ne | | Nat | Yr | Ht/Wt | Event | 1986 Mark | Pre-1986 best | |
|---|---|---|---|---|---|---|---|---|
| lliott | Norbert | BAH | 6Nov62 | 183/78 | TJ | 17.01 | 16.79i,16.55 | -85 |
| lliott | Peter | UK | 9Oct62 | 181/67 | 800 | 1:44.06 | 1:43.98 | -83 |
| | | | | | 1500 | 3:35.62 | 3:36.97 | -84 |
| | | | | | Mile | 3:54.22 | 3:55.71 | -84 |
| llis | Ieuan | UK | 11May60 | | Mar | 2:13:21 | 2:15:02 | -85 |
| nmelmann | Frank | GDR | 15Sep61 | 185/78 | 100 | 10.32,10.27w | 10.06 | -85 |
| | | | | | 200 | 20.62 | 20.23 | -85 |
| miyan | Robert | SU | 16Feb65 | 178/69 | LJ | 8.61 | 8.30,8.38w | -85 |
| nordi | Paul | NIG | 25Dec65 | 189/80 | LJ | 8.15,8.22w | 8.07 | -85 |
| | | | | | TJ | 17.05, | 16.89, | |
| | | | | | | 17.31w | 17.15Aw | -85 |
| ado | Tsukasa | JAP | 9Nov61 | 164/50 | 10k | 28:30.9 | | |
| e | Mihai | RUM | 24Jul60 | 183/69 | TJ | 16.92 | 17.00 | -85 |
| gels | Hawie | RSA | 27Dec62 | 178/74 | 400h | 50.31 | 50.10A,50.45 | -85 |
| holm | Martin | SWE | 7Feb65 | 176/74 | 800 | 1:46.52 | 1:47.76 | -85 |
| ickson | Steve | USA | 13Jan61 | 190/86 | Dec | 8030w | 8063w | -85 |
| iksson | Thomas | SWE | 1May63 | 183/77 | TJ | 16.64w | 16.43,16.51w | -84 |
| ixon | Mats | SWE | 19Mar58 | 175/61 | 5k | 13:35.73 | 13:26.96 | -84 |
| | | | | | 10k | 28:01.50 | 27:56.56 | -82 |
| skine | Bob | USA | 29Feb64 | 190/102 | JT | 75.72 | 75.20 | -85 |
| ayan | Yuriy | SU | 3Apr62 | 180/100 | HT | 78.64 | 76.36 | -85 |
| pino | Juan | SPA | 24Jun59 | 168/50 | 3kSt | 8:35.62 | 8:36.2 | -83 |
| angelisti | Giovanni | ITA | 11Sep61 | 179/70 | LJ | 8.24 | 8.24 | -84 |
| ans | Dwayne | USA | 13Oct58 | 187/75 | 100 | 10.33 | 10.20,10.07w | -81 |
| | | | | | 200 | 20.36, | 20.22 | -76 |
| | | | | | | 20.09w | 20.20w | -81 |
| erett | Danny | USA | 1Nov66 | 187/61 | 200 | 20.65 | 20.97 | -85 |
| | | | | | 400 | 45.10 | 45.76 | -85 |
| ers | Jürgen | FRG | 29Apr65 | 183/65 | 100 | 10.32 | 10.31 | -83 |
| | | | | | 200 | 20.58 | 20.37 | -83 |
| estone | Ed | USA | 15Jun61 | 185/66 | 10k | 27:56.4 | 27:41.05 | -85 |
| dil | Mike | USA | 22Jun63 | 172/63 | 3kSt | 8:29.75 | 8:29.01 | -85 |
| hner | Thomas | GDR | 18Jul66 | 187/82 | Dec | 8170 | 7815 | -85 |
| kataulavelua | Fabiano | FRA | 15Jan62 | 182/97 | JT | 75.00 | 79.04* | -85 |
| lise | Didier | BEL | 3Mar61 | 185/75 | TJ | 16.86 | 16.51 | -85 |
| ll | Moussa | SEN | 28Aug63 | 178/67 | 800 | 1:44.86 | 1:44.68 | -85 |
| rgere | Philippe | FRA | 20Mar64 | 183/70 | 800 | 1:46.96 | 1:46.4 | -85 |
| ul | Brian | USA | 5Mar60 | 190/115 | SP | 19.88 | 19.52 | -85 |
| ustini | Alessio | ITA | 10Jun60 | 165/48 | Mar | 2:13:27 | 2:13:55 | -85 |
| doriv | Andrey | SU | 10Aug63 | 179/71 | 100 | 10.36,10.0 | 10.42 | -85 |
| | | | | | 200 | 20.53 | 20.70,20.4 | -83 |
| nringer | Hermann | AUT | 8Dec62 | 181/81 | PV | 5.66,5.71xt | 5.70 | -85 |
| l | Graeme | CAN | 19Mar59 | 184/73 | 3kSt | 8:14.57 | 8:12.58 | -85 |
| raday | Steve | CAN | 5Apr59 | | JT | 75.06 | 81.34* | -85 |
| rner | Hans-Peter | FRG | 6Jun56 | 176/72 | 800 | 1:45.74 | 1:44.93 | -83 |
| nholm | Stefan | SWE | 2Jul59 | 186/118 | DT | 65.08 | 67.72 | -85 |
| reira | Serge | FRA | 11Aug59 | 183/72 | PV | 5.60 | 5.72i-85,5.71 | -84 |
| ter | György | HUN | 2Oct63 | 179/72 | 200 | 20.78 | 21.23-85,21.13w | -82 |
| sor | József | HUN | 29Jul65 | 196/110 | DT | 63.22 | 60.30 | -85 |
| ek | Wacław | POL | 2Apr59 | 188/115 | HT | 73.46 | 74.64 | -85 |
| shman | Gennadiy | SU | 7Sep59 | 182/68 | 3k | 7:50.54 | 7:52.39 | -84 |
| zpatrick | Enda | IRL | 28Apr65 | 183/66 | 1k | 2:17.87 | | |
| | | | | | 1500 | 3:39.18 | 3:42.05 | -85 |
| zuleto | Hrvoje | YUG | 15Jan63 | 191/69 | HJ | 2.23 | 2.26 | -84 |
| ax | Ken | USA | 20Apr63 | 178/100 | HT | 78.34 | 74.50 | -85 |
| real | Edrick | CAN | 5Oct66 | | TJ | 16.54i, | 16.44 | -85 |
| | | | | | | 16.51A,16.78w | | |
| rence | Derrick | USA | 19Jun68 | 178/70 | 100 | 10.13,10.1 | 10.4 | -85 |
| | | | | | 200 | 20.63,20.5 | 21.19 | -85 |
| yd | Stanley | USA | 23Jun61 | 178/74 | 100 | 10.1 | 10.07,10.0 | -80 |
| | | | | | | | 10.03A | -82 |

| Name | | Nat | Yr | Ht/Wt | Event | 1986 Mark | Pre-1986 best | |
|---|---|---|---|---|---|---|---|---|
| Flynn | Ray | IRL | 22Jan57 | 182/65 | 1500 | 3:37.95 | 3:33.5 | -8 |
| | | | | | Mile | 3:57.91i | 3:49.77 | -8 |
| | | | | | 3k | 7:50.71 | 7:41.60 | -8 |
| | | | | | 5k | 13:31.52 | 13:19.52 | -8 |
| Fomenko | Sergey | SU | 7Jun67 | | PV | 5.50 | 5.10i,5.10 | -8 |
| Fomochkin | Andrey | SU | 24May63 | 182/83 | Dec | 8227 | 8109 | -8 |
| Fontecchio | Daniele | ITA | 29Dec60 | 188/80 | 110h | 13.80 | 13.66,13.4 | -8 |
| Forde | Elvis | BAR | 18Nov59 | 180/74 | 400 | 45.65 | 45.32 | -8 |
| Foster | Greg | USA | 4Aug58 | 190/84 | 110h | 13.25 | 13.03-81,13.0 | -8 |
| Foster | Walt | USA | 16Apr64 | | 110h | 13.84 | 14.19 | -8 |
| Fouche | François | RSA | 5Jun63 | 194/73 | LJ | 7.97A,8.02Aw | 8.04A | -8 |
| Fourie | Johan | RSA | 2Dec59 | 180/70 | 1k | 2:18.54 | 2:17.0A | -8 |
| | | | | | 1500 | 3:34.38 | 3:34.3 | -8 |
| | | | | | Mile | 3:52.14 | 3:51.23 | -8 |
| | | | | | 2k | 5:01.27 | 4:56.41 | -8 |
| | | | | | 3k | 7:45.33 | 7:44.0 | - |
| Fraley | Doug | USA | 7Mar65 | 188/81 | PV | 5.77 | 5.56 | - |
| Frank | Garry | USA | 20Dec64 | 193/126 | SP | 20.15 | 19.08 | - |
| Franks | Michael | USA | 23Sep63 | 180/70 | 400 | 45.33 | 44.47 | - |
| Franz | Engelbert | FRG | 24Nov63 | | 3kSt | 8:34.19 | 8:44.61 | - |
| Frayne | Bruce | AUS | 24Jan58 | 179/66 | 400 | 45.97 | 45.21 | - |
| Frazier | John | USA | 27Apr63 | 187/109 | SP | 19.50 | 19.88 | - |
| Fredericks | Frankie | RSA | 2Oct67 | | 100 | 10.1A | 10.73 | - |
| Freeman | Andre | USA | 21May64 | 170/70 | 200 | 20.46Aw | 21.14-85,20.9 | - |
| Freimuth | Uwe | GDR | 10Sep61 | 191/93 | Dec | 8322 | 8792 | - |
| Friedrich | Lutz | GDR | 8Aug61 | 196/115 | DT | 63.98 | 62.40 | - |
| Froelick | Marty | USA | 12Mar58 | 178/62 | Mar | 2:13:26 | 2:11:13 | - |
| Fuhlbrügge | Hauke | GDR | 21Mar66 | 181/67 | 800 | 1:46.73 | 1:46.91 | - |
| | | | | | 1k | 2:17.49 | -0 - | - |
| | | | | | 1500 | 3:38.87 | 3:43.68 | - |
| Furdylo | Vladimir | SU | 6Apr58 | | JT | 78.50 | 85.42* | - |
| Füzesi | Sándor | HUN | 15Dec59 | 186/120 | HT | 73.12 | 74.62 | - |
| Futterknecht | Thomas | AUT | 24Dec62 | 177/68 | 400h | 49.71 | 49.33 | - |
| Fuwa | Hiroki | JAP | 9Jul66 | 171/60 | 100 | 10.35,10.0w | 10.34 | - |
| Gahwiler | Beat | SWZ | 26Jan65 | 185/89 | Dec | 8089m | 7570 | - |
| Gaisl | Luboš | CS | 11Mar63 | 180/65 | 3kSt | 8:31.96 | 8:34.04 | - |
| Galushko | Vyacheslav | SU | 23May67 | 194/75 | HJ | 2.24 | 2.22 | - |
| Gambke | Wolfram | FRG | 2Nov59 | 180/80 | JT | 81.30 | 85.80* | - |
| Gamlin | Dirk | GDR | 26Oct63 | 188/83 | TJ | 17.17 | 17.44 | - |
| Gardner | Dana | USA | 3Jun63 | 188/79 | 100 | 10.0 | | - |
| | | | | | 200 | 20.80w | | - |
| Garnham | Andrew | AUS | 6Feb60 | | 10k | 28:29.97 | 29:45.21 | - |
| Gartung | Viktor | SU | 18May60 | 189/88 | Dec | 7736m | 7993 | - |
| Gaslenko | Vitaliy | SU | 15Mar62 | | DT | 65.14 | 63.28 | - |
| Gassowski | Janusz | POL | 1Mar58 | 191/125 | SP | 20.66 | 20.98 | - |
| Gataullin | Rodion | SU | 23Nov65 | 191/78 | PV | 5.85 | 5.75 | - |
| Gavras | Sergey | SU | 16Apr57 | 185/95 | JT | 81.44,81.76* | 86.24 | - |
| Gavrikov | Sergey | SU | 19Apr64 | 189/78 | PV | 5.62 | 5.30 | - |
| Gavrilyuk | Vladimir | SU | 17Jun61 | 182/78 | JT | 77.28 | 83.40* | - |
| Gavryushin | Sergey | SU | 27Jun59 | 192/125 | SP | 22.10 | 21.60 | - |
| Gazyura | Anatoliy | SU | 17Mar64 | 188/84 | Dec | 7949 | 7112m# | - |
| Gécsek | Tibor | HUN | 22Sep64 | 182/94 | HT | 77.66 | 77.62 | - |
| Geisensetter | Jens | GDR | 30Jul64 | 189/112 | HT | 75.02 | 73.72 | - |
| Gelhausen | Udo | FRG | 5Jul56 | 188/127 | SP | 20.33 | 20.00 | - |
| Gellens | Patrick | FRA | 8Feb59 | 184/74 | Dec | 7895 | 7942 | - |
| George | Vernon | USA | 6Oct64 | 190/75 | 110h | 13.87w,13.78dt | 13.95 | - |
| | | | | | LJ | 7.97w | 8.20 | - |
| Georgiev | Kiril | BUL | 22May57 | 189/110 | DT | 64.58 | 63.54 | - |
| Gerber | Farley | USA | 25Apr60 | 178/68 | 3kSt | 8:20.07 | 8:19.27 | - |
| Gerloff | Maco | GDR | 19Jul64 | 189/110 | HT | 77.12 | 76.92 | - |
| Giannoulis | Haralambis | GRE | 63 | 190/79 | TJ | 16.73 | 16.68 | - |

| ame | | Nat | Yr | Ht/Wt | Event | 1986 Mark | Pre-1986 best |
|---|---|---|---|---|---|---|---|
| iegiel | Romuald | POL | 8May57 | 186/78 | 110h | 13.72, | 13.57 | -82 |
| | | | | | | 13.67w | 13.54w | -83 |
| iessing | Thomas | FRG | 19Mar61 | 197/85 | 800 | 1:45.73 | 1:47.54 | -85 |
| ilchrist | Mike | NZ | 9Aug60 | 178/69 | 2k | 5:04.21 | | |
| | | | | | 3kSt | 8:34.62 | | |
| ilkes | Eugene | UK | 5Mar62 | 193/90 | Dec | 7889 | 7752 | -85 |
| irvan | Martin | UK | 17Apr60 | 194/118 | HT | 73.92 | 77.54 | -84 |
| iurgian | Liviu | RUM | 26Jul62 | 192/79 | 110h | 13.47,13.40w | 13.54 | -85 |
| jøvaag | Roger | NOR | 7Sep56 | 192/83 | 3kSt | 8:29.00 | 8:34.70 | -84 |
| ladwin | John | UK | 7May63 | 190/70 | 800 | 1:45.14 | 1:46.11 | -85 |
| | | | | | 1500 | 3:35.26 | 3:39.47 | -84 |
| | | | | | Mile | 3:54.52 | 4:02.20 | -83 |
| lance | Harvey | USA | 28Mar57 | 171/67 | 100 | 10.09, | 10.05 | -85 |
| | | | | | | 10.04w | 9.8 | -77 |
| lander | Steve | USA | | | PV | 5.45 | | |
| lass | Jeff | CAN | 21Apr62 | 185/82 | 110h | 13.87 | 13.73A,13.79 | -84 |
| lebov | Sergey | SU | 26Jan64 | 184/88 | JT | 80.94 | 80.52* | -85 |
| lenn | James | USA | | | 100 | 10.1 | | |
| linskikh | Lev | SU | 25Jul62 | | 3kSt | 8:29.51 | 8:33.8 | -83 |
| oater | Julian | UK | 12Jan53 | 183/66 | 10k | 28:11.89 | 27:34.58 | -82 |
| örmer | Klaus | GDR | 5Jul63 | 194/115 | SP | 20.44 | 20.06 | -83 |
| omez | José | MEX | 19Mar56 | 165/55 | 10k | 28:15.1 | 27:56.74 | -83 |
| onigam | Emmanuel | FRA | 21Feb63 | 177/70 | 400h | 50.34 | 51.25 | -85 |
| onigam | Philippe | FRA | 21Feb63 | 178/71 | 400h | 49.82 | 50.36 | -85 |
| onsalves | Greg | USA | 3Aug63 | 188/70 | HJ | 2.25i | 2.27 | -85 |
| onzález | Alex | FRA | 16Mar51 | 183/71 | Mar | 2:13:36 | 2:15:09 | -85 |
| onzalez | Danny | USA | 29Apr64 | 175/59 | Mar | 2:13:23 | -0- | |
| onzález | Jose Luis | SPA | 8Dec57 | 180/61 | 1500 | 3:32.90 | 3:30.92 | -85 |
| | | | | | Mile | 3:50.59 | 3:47.79 | -85 |
| | | | | | 3k | 7:44.25 | 7:45.44 | -84 |
| | | | | | 5k | 13:25.90 | 13:15.90 | -85 |
| onzález | Mauricio | MEX | 16Oct60 | 180/67 | 2k | 5:06.04 | | |
| | | | | | 3k | 7:50.58 | 7:47.78 | -85 |
| | | | | | 5k | 13:29.53 | 13:22.4 | -85 |
| onzález | Ramon | CUB | 24Aug65 | 182/83 | JT | 77.32,87.14* | 87.90* | -83 |
| ode | Milton | USA | 16Feb60 | 183/73 | HJ | 2.24 | 2.28-84,2.31i | -82 |
| odell | Bart | USA | 4Oct61 | 193/95 | Dec | 8041 | 7720 | -85 |
| rak | Stanisław | POL | 24Feb59 | 182/92 | JT | 78.32,84.40 | 88.10* | -84 |
| rbachenko | Yuriy | SU | 19Jul66 | 188/75 | TJ | 16.81i | 16.86 | -85 |
| rdien | Marcus | USA | 20Apr55 | 194/116 | DT | 63.74 | 65.28 | -84 |
| rdon | Dave | USA | 30Aug59 | 175/58 | Mar | 2:12:08 | 2:11:41 | -83 |
| rdon | Ken | AUS | 19May62 | 183/72 | 400h | 50.47 | 50.23 | -85 |
| rdon | Pat | USA | 20Aug65 | | 200 | 20.67 | 21.22 | -85 |
| tman | Erich | SU | 16Oct63 | | TJ | 16.53 | | |
| tovskiy | Yuriy | SU | 31May61 | 191/80 | HJ | 2.25 | 2.25,2.29i | -85 |
| ulin | Emmanuel | FRA | 5Mar62 | 178/62 | 1500 | 3:38.7 | 3:40.27 | -84 |
| abarczyk | Andrzej | POL | 12Jan64 | 186/71 | TJ | 16.58 | 16.43 | -85 |
| abowski | Stanisław | POL | 26Apr55 | 190/109 | DT | 61.16 | 64.38 | -83 |
| addy | Sam | USA | 10Feb64 | 178/70 | 100 | 10.12, | 10.09, | |
| | | | | | | 10.08w | 10.08w | -84 |
| | | | | | 200 | 20.57 | 20.30 | -85 |
| aham | John | CAN | 20Nov65 | 186/81 | 400h | 49.81 | 49.86 | -85 |
| aham | John | UK | 18Jun56 | 180/66 | Mar | 2:12:10 | 2:09:28 | -81 |
| aham | Mike | USA | 13Feb67 | 178/70 | 400h | 50.40 | 53.76 | -84 |
| aham | Winthrop | JAM | 67 | 180/64 | 400h | 50.03 | | |
| avelle | Mike | USA | 13Apr65 | | DT | 62.46 | 52.18 | -85 |
| audyn | Vladimir | SU | 26Aug63 | 182/70 | 800 | 1:45.80 | 1:48.26 | -84 |
| | | | | | 1k | 2:17.66 | -0- | |
| ay | Johnny | USA | 19Jun60 | 190/76 | 800 | 1:43.46 | 1:42.60 | -85 |
| ay   -# | Rob | CAN | 5Oct56 | 188/120 | DT | 61.36 | 67.32 | -84 |
| eaves | Wilbert | UK | 23Dec56 | 187/77 | 110h | 13.70w | 13.60 | -85 |
| ebenstein | Matthias | GDR | 12Jan64 | 186/72 | HJ | 2.24i,2.24 | 2.27 | -84 |

| Name | | Nat | Yr | Ht/Wt | Event | 1986 Mark | Pre-1986 best | |
|------|---|-----|----|-------|-------|-----------|---------------|---|
| Grechko | Aleksandr | SU | 17Mar62 | 184/100 | DT | 61.08 | 59.60 | -8 |
| Green | Bill | USA | 28Apr60 | 186/109 | HT | 77.20 | 76.52 | -8 |
| Gregorek | John | USA | 15Apr60 | 185/75 | 2k | 5:06.43 | | |
| | | | | | 3k | 7:49.93 | 7:47.85 | -8 |
| | | | | | 5k | 13:35.75, | 13:29.3i | -8 |
| | | | | | | 13:33.58i | | |
| Gribov | Yevgeniy | SU | 18Apr62 | | HT | 75.42 | 78.12 | -8 |
| Grigorash | Igor | SU | 18Aug59 | 184/104 | HT | 78.00 | 81.20 | -8 |
| Grigorov | Anri | BUL | 18Oct64 | 177/63 | 100 | 10.35 | 10.41 | -8 |
| Grigoryan | Parkev | SU | 65 | | TJ | 16.97 | 15.78 | -8 |
| Grimes | Dan | USA | 30Jan59 | 170/57 | Mar | 2:13:11 | 2:14:10 | -8 |
| Grishchenkov | Vasiliy | SU | 23Jan58 | 181/78 | TJ | 16.96 | 17.55 | -8 |
| Grogorick | Thomas | GDR | 10May62 | 188/108 | HT | 74.84 | 74.12 | -8 |
| Groshev | Igor | SU | 15Mar64 | 176/74 | 100 | 10.35dwr | 10.37 | -8 |
| Groshev | Vyacheslav | SU | 17Aug58 | | 3kSt | 8:35.51 | 8:32.0 | -8 |
| Grothe | Jürgen | FRG | 14Apr60 | 182/69 | 1500 | 3:37.40 | 3:39.37 | -8 |
| Grundmann | Martin | FRG | 6Jan65 | 189/82 | Dec | 7715 | 7623 | -8 |
| Grzegorzewski | Pawel | POL | 2Jul66 | 185/70 | 110h | 13.87 | 14.34 | -8 |
| Gubkin | Valeriy | SU | 11Jan67 | 194/100 | HT | 76.54 | 69.66 | -8 |
| Günthör | Werner | SWZ | 1Jun61 | 200/124 | SP | 22.22 | 21.55i,21.25, | |
| | | | | | | | 21.26uns | -8 |
| Gugler | Christian | SWZ | 1Aug60 | 186/83 | Dec | 7727 | 8046 | -8 |
| Guilder | Alan | UK | 10Dec61 | | 10k | 28:28.74 | 30:25.2 | -8 |
| Guillory | Rod | USA | 8Aug64 | | 400h | 50.46 | 50.84 | -8 |
| Guimarães | Agberto | BRA | 18Aug57 | 175/57 | 800 | 1:45.11 | 1:43.63 | -8 |
| Gula | Sergey | SU | 2Jun63 | 180/96 | HT | 73.80 | 72.50 | -8 |
| Guldberg | Mogens | DEN | 2Aug63 | 184/65 | 1500 | 3:37.95 | 3:42.15 | -8 |
| Gurmazhenko | Aleksandr | SU | 23May57 | 191/115 | HT | 73.46 | 76.60 | -8 |
| Gurny | Slawomir | POL | 2Sep64 | 181/72 | 3kSt | 8:32.46 | 8:31.97 | -8 |
| Guss | Lloyd | CAN | 22Jan59 | 188/81 | 400h | 50.16 | 49.83A,50.24 | -8 |
| Gustafsson | Tore | SWE | 11Feb62 | 181/111 | HT | 77.76 | 76.46 | -8 |
| Haaf | Dietmar | FRG | 6Mar67 | 173/64 | LJ | 7.97 | 7.78 | -8 |
| Haapakoski | Tapani | FIN | 14Jun53 | 178/72 | PV | 5.45 | 5.55 | -8 |
| Haas | Christian | FRG | 22Aug58 | 181/76 | 100 | 10.27, | 10.16 | -8 |
| | | | | | | 10.18w | 10.1-85,10.12w- | 8 |
| | | | | | 200 | 20.58 | 20.46 | -8 |
| Haas | Felix | SWZ | 24Apr59 | 182/85 | Dec | 7755 | 7654 | -8 |
| Haber | Ralf | GDR | 18Aug62 | 189/110 | HT | 80.60 | 79.38 | -8 |
| Hackett | Robert | USA | 3Aug64 | 172/68 | 100 | 10.32, | 10.34, | |
| | | | | | | 10.21w | 10.25w | -8 |
| | | | | | 200 | 20.67 | 20.59 | -8 |
| Hackney | Roger | UK | 2Sep57 | 183/74 | 3kSt | 8:20.97 | 8:19.38 | -8 |
| Hacksteiner | Markus | SWZ | 18Nov64 | 185/72 | 1500 | 3:38.44 | 3:42.52 | -8 |
| Häberle | Hans-Joach. | FRG | 7Apr59 | 185/80 | Dec | 7742 | 8020 | -8 |
| Hadwich | Volker | GDR | 23Sep64 | 196/98 | JT | 81.02 | 84.70* | - |
| Hafsteinsson | Vestein | ICE | 12Dec60 | 190/113 | DT | 63.98 | 65.60 | - |
| Halamoda | Thomas | GDR | 15Jul66 | 187/85 | Dec | 7891 | 6312m | - |
| Haley | Roddie | USA | 6Dec65 | 178/64 | 400 | 44.48 | 44.67 | - |
| Halim | Ahmed | EGY | 2Jan59 | 175/77 | 400h | 50.47 | 49.74 | - |
| Hall | Derwin | USA | 69 | | 100 | 10.1 | | |
| Hallingstad | Jon | USA | 30Oct58 | 184/83 | Dec | 7725 | 7609 | - |
| Halvorsen | John | NOR | 17Aug66 | | 10k | 28:27.33 | -0- | - |
| Hamada | Ahmed | BHN | 18Sep61 | 183/70 | 400h | 49.31 | 49.43 | - |
| Hanáček | Zdeněk | CS | 11Jan62 | 183/72 | LJ | 8.04 | 8.02 | - |
| Hanna | Elliott | USA | 10May63 | 170/68 | 100 | 10.35w | 10.3-84,9.8w | - |
| Hanna | Steve | BAH | 30Oct58 | 180/68 | TJ | 16.73 | 17.04-81,17.07w- | - |
| Hannecker | Alois | FRG | 10Jul61 | 190/110 | DT | 65.28 | 64.82 | - |
| Hansen | Eirik | NOR | 18May63 | 180/65 | 5k | 13:35.19 | 13:51.5 | - |
| Harrell | Tyrone | USA | 26Nov63 | | 400 | 45.69 | 46.37 | - |
| Harries | Axel | FRG | 19Sep64 | 186/76 | 800 | 1:46.53 | 1:45.80 | - |

| ame | | Nat | Yr | Ht/Wt | Event | 1986 Mark | Pre-1986 best |
|---|---|---|---|---|---|---|---|
| arris | Danny | USA | 7Sep65 | 183/77 | 400 | 45.19 | 45.46-85,45.3 -84 |
| | | | | | 400h | 47.82 | 47.63 -85 |
| arris | Rich | USA | 4Mar59 | 175/61 | 1500 | 3:36.52 | 3:36.05 -84 |
| | | | | | Mile | 3:57.24 | 3:51.39 -84 |
| | | | | | 3k | 7:46.87 | 7:47.87 -84 |
| arris | Steve | UK | 17Nov61 | 175/60 | 5k | 13:31.62 | 13:30.79 -83 |
| | | | | | 10k | 27:59.33 | -0- |
| arrison | Jamie | AUS | 63 | | 10k | 28:16.19 | 29:28.6 -85 |
| arrison | Karl | UK | 16Oct56 | 175/57 | 10k | 28:11.07 | 28:21.92 -83 |
| arrison | Kenny | USA | 13Feb65 | 175/68 | LJ | 8.17i, | 7.84i -85 |
| | | | | | | 8.11 | 7.83 -84 |
| | | | | | TJ | 17.07,17.41w | 16.50 -84 |
| arrison | Rob | UK | 5Jun59 | 180/70 | 800 | 1:46.01 | 1:45.31 -84 |
| | | | | | 1k | 2:17.99 | 2:17.20 -84 |
| | | | | | 1500 | 3:35.74 | 3:43.2 -84 |
| | | | | | | | 3:42.95i -85 |
| | | | | | Mile | 3:53.85 | 3:56.76 -84 |
| artmann | Gerhard | AUT | 12Jan55 | 180/64 | 3k | 7:50.31 | 7:59.02 -85 |
| | | | | | 5k | 13:22.30 | 13:34.20 -85 |
| | | | | | 10k | 27:49.35 | 28:30.21 -85 |
| | | | | | Mar | 2:12:22 | 2:14:59 -85 |
| artmann | Werner | FRG | 20Apr59 | 189/115 | DT | 62.18 | 67.54 -82 |
| arumatsu | Chiaki | JAP | 5Mar58 | 167/54 | Mar | 2:12:02 | |
| ashioka | Toshiyuki | JAP | 18Jan64 | 182/72 | PV | 5.55 | 5.30 -85 |
| atziandreou | Marios | CYP | 19Sep62 | 183/76 | TJ | 16.61 | 16.69 -85 |
| awkins | Tranel | USA | 17Sep62 | 196/80 | 400h | 48.64A,49.56 | 48.28 -84 |
| ayashi | Kijoyi | JAP | 5Jun61 | 166/54 | Mar | 2:12:48 | 2:12:47 -84 |
| azim | Sharrieff | USA | 1Nov64 | 185/73 | LJ | 7.92w | 7.32i -84 |
| eard | Floyd | USA | 24Mar66 | 178/71 | 100 | 10.20, | 10.27 -85 |
| | | | | | | 10.09w | 10.1w -84 |
| | | | | | 200 | 20.12,20.03w | 20.61 -85 |
| eikkinen | Eero | FIN | 22Jul55 | 178/82 | JT | 78.96 | 82.12* -85 |
| eilmann | Michael | GDR | 26Oct61 | 174/54 | Mar | 2:10:27 | 2:09:03 -85 |
| eimrath | Torsten | GDR | 14May63 | 180/78 | 100 | 10.34 | 10.39 -85 |
| | | | | | 200 | 20.69 | 20.87 -85 |
| ine | Frank | GDR | 21Aug63 | 182/68 | 5k | 13:32.31 | 13:34.32 -85 |
| | | | | | 10k | 27:43.89 | 28:35.71 -85 |
| einrichs | Heinz | USA | 22Mar61 | 190/91 | Dec | 7720m | 7535 -84 |
| isler | Randy | USA | 7Aug61 | 192/111 | DT | 65.34 | 62.22 -84 |
| eist | Michael | FRG | 2May65 | | 3kSt | 8:30.46 | 8:40.56 -85 |
| elan | Serge | FRA | 24Feb64 | 176/70 | TJ | 17.13 | 16.69 -85 |
| elwig | Larry | CAN | 26Sep63 | | HJ | 2.23i | 2.18 -85 |
| empel | Knut | FRG | 26May65 | | JT | 75.52 | 70.70* -85 |
| enderson | Dan | USA | 26Jun58 | 183/66 | 5k | 13:28.23 | 13:23.57 -85 |
| | | | | | 10k | 28:18.6 | 28:02.41 -84 |
| enderson | Jamie | UK | 29Mar69 | 178/64 | 100 | 10.33,10.29 | 10.6w -85 |
| enderson | Ken | USA | 5Dec66 | 173/66 | 100 | 10.19A, | 10.49, |
| | | | | | | 10.12Aw | 10.27Aw -85 |
| | | | | | 200 | 20.65A,20.27Aw | 20.85A -85 |
| enderson | Kevin | USA | 4Feb65 | 183/73 | 400h | 49.41 | 49.16 -85 |
| nson | Alfonzo | USA | 65 | | 400 | 45.97 | 46.26 -84 |
| ntunen | Juha | FIN | 29Nov60 | 181/84 | JT | 75.40 | 81.56* -81 |
| ppner | Mark | USA | 24Apr64 | 180/74 | PV | 5.55 | 5.33 -85 |
| rbert | John | UK | 20Apr62 | 188/76 | TJ | 16.85,17.27w | 17.41 -85 |
| rle | Christoph | FRG | 19Nov55 | 183/68 | 5k | 13:33.32 | 13:19.25 -85 |
| | | | | | 10k | 28:22.94 | 27:50.27 -85 |
| rms | Jürgen | FRG | 17Oct63 | 177/69 | 800 | 1:46.63 | 1:47.22 -85 |
| rnandez | Dominique | FRA | 1Aug60 | 178/66 | HJ | 2.24 | 2.23 -85 |
| rnández | Orlando | CUB | 21May62 | | JT | 82.66* | 80.20* -85 |
| rnández | Roberto | CUB | 6Mar67 | 172/62 | 200 | 20.37 | 20.59,20.2 -85 |
| | | | | | 400 | 45.05 | 45.14 -85 |
| rold | Jens-Peter | GDR | 25Oct65 | 180/64 | 1500 | 3:37.92 | 3:43.9 -85 |

MEN: INDEX

| Name | | Nat | Yr | Ht/Wt | Event | 1986 Mark | Pre-1986 best | |
|---|---|---|---|---|---|---|---|---|
| Herron | Doug | USA | 15Dec66 | 180/66 | 800 | 1:47.00 | 1:48.09 | -8! |
| Hertner | Roland | SWZ | 21Mar57 | 169/62 | 3kSt | 8:22.49 | 8:25.26 | -8! |
| Hidalgo | Adelino | SPA | 8Mar63 | 181/70 | 2k | 5:05.16 | 5:12.9 | -8. |
| Hill | Jim | USA | 1Jul61 | 180/63 | 5k | 13:26.43 | 13:19.73 | -8: |
| | | | | | 10k | 28:22.74 | 27:55.23 | -8: |
| Hill | Mike | UK | 22Oct64 | 190/100 | JT | 78.56,82.04* | 82.30* | -8! |
| Hill | Ray | USA | 24Jun67 | | 100 | 10.34,10.19w | 10.53 | -8: |
| Hillardt | Mike | AUS | 22Jan61 | 180/70 | 800 | 1:46.10 | 1:45.74 | -8 |
| | | | | | 1500 | 3:34.51 | 3:33.39 | -8! |
| | | | | | Mile | 3:56.90, | 3:51.82 | -8! |
| | | | | | | 3:56.6i | | |
| Hingsen | Jürgen | FRG | 25Jan58 | 200/102 | Dec | 8730 | 8832 | -8. |
| Hirschberg | Jens | GDR | 6May64 | 191/78 | LJ | 8.03 | 7.42 | -8 |
| Hjeltnes | Knut | NOR | 8Dec51 | 190/116 | DT | 68.50 | 69.62 | -8 |
| Hjort | Niels Kim | DEN | 29Jun59 | 182/62 | 1500 | 3:36.01 | 3:37.71 | -8 |
| Hodge | David | USA | 1Oct62 | 183/73 | PV | 5.50 | 5.60 | -8 |
| Höffer | Aleš | CS | 9Dec62 | 182/75 | 110h | 13.79, | 13.87,13.86w | -8 |
| | | | | | | 13.52w | 13.6 | -8. |
| Hoff | Narve | NOR | 10Jul57 | 194/99 | JT | 75.58 | 83.64* | -8. |
| Hoffmann | Zdzisław | POL | 27Aug59 | 190/85 | TJ | 16.56 | 17.55w-84,17.53 | -8 |
| Hofstee | Herman | HOL | 17Jul63 | | 3kSt | 8:33.55 | 8:48.4 | -8 |
| Holló | Csaba | HUN | 6Jul58 | 190/112 | DT | 62.58 | 63.02 | -8 |
| Holloway | Bernie | USA | 20Nov61 | 180/73 | 400h | 49.46 | 49.35-83,49.10A | -8 |
| Holm | Arne | SWE | 22Dec61 | 186/80 | TJ | 16.96,17.16w | 16.62i | -8 |
| Holmes | Calvin | USA | 13Sep65 | 180/70 | 110h | 13.87 | 13.94w | -8 |
| Holmes | Granvel | USA | 22May66 | 188/79 | 100 | 10.35w | | |
| Holopainen | Hannu | FIN | 25Jun58 | 184/88 | JT | 75.70 | 84.02* | -8 |
| Holtom | Mark | UK | 6Feb58 | 188/84 | 400h | 50.33 | 49.49 | -8 |
| Honey | Gary | AUS | 26Jul59 | 183/70 | LJ | 8.09,8.12w | 8.27,8.39w | -8 |
| Hoogewerf | Simon | CAN | 11May63 | 175/66 | 800 | 1:46.92 | 1:45.95 | -8 |
| Horsfield | Neil | UK | 7Dec66 | 190/73 | 1500 | 3:38.21 | 3:44.49 | -8 |
| | | | | | Mile | 3:54.39 | 4:01.7 | -8 |
| Houvion | Philippe | FRA | 5Oct57 | 180/80 | PV | 5.50i,5.50 | 5.77 | -8 |
| Howard | Jim | USA | 11Sep59 | 196/80 | HJ | 2.36i,2.34 | 2.35i,2.35 | -8 |
| Howard | Peter | USA | 17Oct63 | 180/68 | 400 | 45.50 | 45.46 | -8 |
| Hoyle | Adam | AUS | 20Aug63 | | 10k | 28:21.26 | 29:13.7 | -8 |
| Hrabaň | Roman | CS | 28Jun62 | 186/81 | Dec | 7866W | 7629 | -8 |
| Hürst | Kurt | SWZ | 12Nov51 | 184/66 | 5k | 13:33.89 | 13:39.69 | -8 |
| | | | | | 10k | 28:15.90 | 28:26.19 | -8 |
| Huff | Ivan | USA | 31Jul59 | 178/70 | 3kSt | 8:16.59 | 8:22.80 | -8 |
| Huffman | Scott | USA | 30Nov64 | 175/73 | PV | 5.60 | 5.62 | -8 |
| Huhtala | Harri | FIN | 13Aug52 | 187/110 | HT | 78.38 | 78.74 | -8 |
| Humphrey | Ray | USA | 31Aug65 | 180/72 | LJ | 8.10i | 8.04 | -8 |
| | | | | | TJ | 16.59i | 15.82, | |
| | | | | | | | 16.03i,16.31w | -8 |
| Hunt | Thom | USA | 17Mar58 | 173/55 | Mar | 2:12:14 | 2:13:39 | -8 |
| Hussein | Ibrahim | KEN | 3Jun58 | 170/57 | Mar | 2:11:44 | 2:12:08 | -8 |
| Hutchings | Tim | UK | 4Dec58 | 183/72 | Mile | 3:55.77 | 3:54.53 | -8 |
| | | | | | 2k | 5:02.95 | 5:00.37 | -8 |
| | | | | | 3k | 7:44.88 | 7:44.55 | -8 |
| | | | | | 2M | 8:15.53 | 8:19.46 | -8 |
| | | | | | 5k | 13:12.88 | 13:11.50 | -8 |
| Hutton | Allister | UK | 18Jul54 | 167/54 | 10k | 27:59.12 | 28:13.09 | -7 |
| | | | | | Mar | 2:12:36 | 2:09:16 | -8 |
| Hyde | Bret | USA | 3Jul59 | 193/81 | 3kSt | 8:25.90 | 8:25.39 | -8 |
| Hydel | Mirosław | POL | 24Jul63 | 187/74 | LJ | 8.08 | 7.97 | -8 |
| Ignatov | Evgeni | BUL | 25Jun59 | 183/66 | 5k | 13:13.15 | 13:26.35 | -8 |
| Ihalainen | Kari | FIN | 24Jul54 | 181/95 | JT | 76.04 | 87.04* | -8 |
| Ikangaa | Juma | TAN | 19Jul57 | 163/58 | 10k | 28:15.13 | 28:23.29 | -8 |
| | | | | | Mar | 2:08:10 | 2:08:55 | -8 |
| Ilg | Patriz | FRG | 5Dec57 | 173/63 | 3kSt | 8:16.92 | 8:15.06 | -8 |

| me | | Nat | Yr | Ht/Wt | Event | 1986 Mark | Pre-1986 best | |
|---|---|---|---|---|---|---|---|---|
| lchenko | Nikolay | SU | 12Aug63 | | 400h | 48.98 | 49.43 | -85 |
| lnitskiy | Sergey | SU | 22Sep62 | 189/80 | HJ | 2.23 | 2.26i,2.25 | -84 |
| noh | Chidi | NIG | 27Aug63 | 188/77 | 100 | 10.00 | 10.11,10.04w,10.1 | -85 |
| | | | | | 200 | 20.36A,20.47 | 20.59,19.9w | -85 |
| nozemtsev | Vladimir | SU | 25May64 | 184/75 | TJ | 17.43i, | 16.86, | |
| | | | | | | 17.16 | 16.93i | -85 |
| sakin | Oleg | SU | 10Aug60 | 174/70 | PV | 5.50 | 5.40 | -84 |
| sasi | Joel | CUB | 31Jul67 | 167/69 | 100 | 10.25A | 10.60 | -85 |
| sayev | Anton | SU | 25Jun62 | 178/70 | 110h | 13.68 | 13.74 | -85 |
| | | | | | | 13.58w,13.5 | 13.4 | -84 |
| sayev | Vasiliy | SU | 1Feb59 | 188/78 | TJ | 16.54 | 17.22 | -84 |
| shutin | Valeriy | SU | 5Dec65 | | PV | 5.65i,5.65 | 5.60 | -85 |
| toh | Kunimitsu | JAP | 6Jan55 | 163/53 | Mar | 2:07:57 | 2:09:35 | -83 |
| t | Edgar | FRG | 8Jun67 | 186/73 | 400 | 45.72 | 47.20 | -85 |
| | | | | | 400h | 49.68 | 54.3 | -84 |
| vanov | Anatoliy | SU | 28Feb62 | | 800 | 1:46.39 | 1:45.9 | -85 |
| vanov | Mikhail | SU | 26Dec62 | | SP | 19.46 | | |
| vanov | Nikolay | BUL | 6Aug63 | 183/74 | TJ | 16.52,16.61w | | |
| vanov | Sergey | SU | 3Jan62 | 182/120 | HT | 79.00 | 76.48 | -85 |
| vliyev | Igor | SU | 63 | | HJ | 2.24 | 2.29 | -85 |
| ckson | Colin | UK | 18Feb67 | 182/74 | 110h | 13.44,13.42w | 13.69 | -85 |
| | | | | | LJ | 7.96w | 7.56,7.58w | -85 |
| ckson | Dannie | USA | 11May58 | 187/83 | LJ | 7.93i,7.92 | 8.09 | -85 |
| | | | | | | | 8.14w | -78 |
| coby | Jake | USA | 24Sep61 | 198/82 | HJ | 2.30 | 2.285 | -84 |
| kstis | Jonas | SU | 2Oct59 | 182/74 | 110h | 13.55dwr, | 13.85 | -84 |
| | | | | | | 13.5 | 13.6 | -85 |
| mes | Charles | USA | 19Jul64 | 180/77 | 110h | 13.78 | 13.66,13.59w | -85 |
| mes | Ian | CAN | 17Jul63 | 178/73 | LJ | 8.09 | 7.80,7.83w | -83 |
| nicki | Don | USA | 23Apr60 | 178/72 | Mar | 2:11:58 | 2:11:16 | -85 |
| nkowski | Henryk | POL | 15Oct61 | 180/67 | 3kSt | 8:22.33 | 8:26.90 | -85 |
| nsa | František | CS | 12Sep62 | 180/76 | PV | 5.60 | 5.62 | -83 |
| ros | Ralf | FRG | 13Dec65 | 193/83 | TJ | 16.94 | 17.29 | -85 |
| sinski | Bill | USA | 13Feb64 | 190/77 | HJ | 2.26 | 2.285 | -85 |
| sinski | Mirosław | FRG | 5May59 | 189/105 | DT | 63.16 | 60.08 | -82 |
| skulka | Stanisław | POL | 25Aug58 | 182/76 | LJ | 8.00,8.16w | 8.13 | -80 |
| fferson | Jaime | CUB | 17Jan62 | 189/78 | LJ | 8.47 | 8.37 | -84 |
| fferson | Thomas | USA | 8Jun62 | 183/75 | 100 | 10.17 | 10.25,9.9w | -84 |
| | | | | | | | 10.1,10.08w | -85 |
| | | | | | 200 | 20.36 | 20.26,20.21w | -84 |
| fferson | Tyrus | USA | 2Feb65 | | LJ | 8.07,8.21w | 7.78 | -85 |
| nkins | Charley | USA | 9Apr64 | 185/75 | 400 | 45.69 | 46.47 | -85 |
| nkins | Dale | USA | 27Feb63 | 178/66 | PV | 5.70 | 5.69 | -85 |
| nssen | Olav | NOR | 11May62 | 193/112 | DT | 62.02 | 60.60 | -85 |
| ssee | Larry | USA | 31Mar52 | 178/79 | PV | 5.70 | 5.73-84,5.86iex | -85 |
| tt | Rod | USA | 28Oct66 | 183/75 | 110h | 13.82 | 14.04 | -85 |
| meno | Raul | SPA | 18May59 | 186/100 | HT | 72.56 | 71.48 | -85 |
| hansson | Jan-Olov | SWE | 9Sep62 | 184/90 | JT | 78.36 | 83.42* | -85 |
| hnson | Ben | CAN | 30Dec61 | 180/75 | 100 | 9.95 | 10.00 | -85 |
| | | | | | 200 | 20.78, | 20.41 | -85 |
| | | | | | | 20.64w | 20.37Aw | -82 |
| hnson | Bobby | USA | 15Jul67 | | 100 | 10.35w | 10.47w | -85 |
| hnson | Dave | USA | 7Apr63 | 189/86 | Dec | 8203 | 7948 | -85 |
| hnson | Joey | USA | 12May67 | 193/84 | HJ | 2.28 | -0- | |
| hnson | John | USA | 20Jan60 | 188/82 | 200 | 20.76w | | |
| | | | | | 110h | 13.86,13.79w | 13.47 | -84 |
| hnson | Thomas | USA | 7Jun65 | 170/68 | 400 | 45.69 | 46.39 | -85 |
| hnston | David | AUS | 8Nov61 | 187/75 | 400 | 45.98 | 46.17 | -84 |
| kl | Roland | AUT | 26Jul62 | 177/77 | 200 | 20.61 | 20.78 | -85 |
| nes | Albert | USA | 8Oct62 | 183/81 | 110h | 13.80dt, | 13.78 | -83 |
| | | | | | | 13.6w | 13.60w | -84 |

| Name | | Nat | Yr | Ht/Wt | Event | 1986 Mark | Pre-1986 best | |
|---|---|---|---|---|---|---|---|---|
| Jones | Earl | USA | 17Jul64 | 180/73 | 800 | 1:43.62 | 1:43.74 | -8 |
| | | | | | 1k | 2:17.25 | 2:20.1i | -8 |
| | | | | | 1500 | 3:36.19 | 3:40.64 | -8 |
| Jones | Greg | USA | 21Aug65 | | HJ | 2.30 | 2.21,2.235i | -8 |
| Jones | Hugh | UK | 1Nov55 | 180/64 | Mar | 2:11:42 | 2:09:24 | -8 |
| Jones | Jim | USA | 25Mar66 | 185/73 | 400 | 46.02A | | |
| Jones | Rod | USA | 31Mar64 | 178/73 | 400 | 45.67 | 44.94 | -8 |
| Jones | Steve | UK | 4Aug55 | 178/62 | 5k | 13:30.60 | 13:18.6 | -8 |
| | | | | | 10k | 28:02.48 | 27:39.14 | -8 |
| Jonot | Franck | FRA | 1Apr61 | 187/75 | 400h | 50.21 | 50.07 | -8 |
| Jørgensen | Henrik | DEN | 10Oct61 | 178/59 | 10k | 28:08.19 | 27:57.98 | -8 |
| | | | | | Mar | 2:11:49 | 2:09:43 | -8 |
| Joyner | Al | USA | 19Jan60 | 186/77 | 110h | 13.68,13.5w | 13.51 | -8 |
| | | | | | TJ | 16.99,17.11w | 17.46 | -8 |
| Juzyszyn | Dariusz | POL | 20Mar57 | 200/123 | DT | 64.34 | 65.98 | -8 |
| Kager | Gerald | AUT | 13May63 | 181/77 | PV | 5.60 | 5.55i,5.50 | -8 |
| Kakhno | Gennadiy | SU | 30Apr64 | 180/69 | TJ | 16.66w | 16.49 | -8 |
| Kakimori | Hiroshi | JAP | 31Mar68 | 181/75 | 400h | 50.05 | 50.03 | -8 |
| Kaladze | Dmitriy | SU | 21Feb61 | 188/85 | 110h | 13.77dwr | 14.13,13.8 | -8 |
| Kaleta | Marek | SU | 17Dec61 | 182/80 | JT | 82.00 | 86.24* | -8 |
| Kaliebe | Andreas | GDR | 17Sep62 | 183/69 | 800 | 1:47.02 | 1:47.09 | -8 |
| Kalinkin | Viktor | SU | 23Feb60 | 180/70 | 800 | 1:45.08 | 1:44.73 | -8 |
| Kalogiannis | Athanassios | GRE | 10Sep65 | 193/77 | 400h | 48.88 | 50.22 | -8 |
| Kamau | Gabriel | KEN | 20Mar57 | 172/64 | Mar | 2:11:49 | 2:10:05 | -8 |
| Kaniecki | Krzysztof | POL | 23Jun65 | 183/73 | LJ | 7.93 | 7.78 | -8 |
| Kariuki | Julius | KEN | 12Apr61 | 181/62 | 1500 | 3:37.79 | 3:42.58 | -8 |
| | | | | | 2k | 5:04.71 | | |
| | | | | | 3k | 7:47.35 | 7:52.87 | -8 |
| | | | | | 3kSt | 8:15.92 | 8:17.47 | -8 |
| Karp | Raoul | RSA | 30Sep67 | | 100 | 10.36A | 10.61A | -8 |
| Kasnauskas | Sergey | SU | 20Apr61 | 192/126 | SP | 21.23 | 22.09 | -8 |
| Kassubek | Peter | FRG | 10Jun59 | 195/122 | SP | 19.34i,19.31 | 18.96 | -8 |
| Katona | Sándor | FRA | 24Sep63 | 178/100 | DT | 61.84ex | 60.30 | -8 |
| Kaulin | Matthias | FRG | 3Feb63 | 187/76 | 400h | 49.80 | 49.87 | -8 |
| Kayukov | Andrey | SU | 12Apr64 | 187/75 | TJ | 17.02 | 16.95 | -8 |
| Kazanov | Igor | SU | 24Sep63 | 186/81 | 110h | 13.42,13.14w | 13.59 | -8 |
| | | | | | | 13.4 | 13.3 | -8 |
| Kearney | Clayton | AUS | 11Apr64 | 184/83 | 200 | 20.67 | 20.64 | -8 |
| Keating | Gerrard | AUS | 3Dec62 | 185/82 | 100 | 10.33w | 10.22-85,10.18w | -8 |
| Kenney | Aatron | USA | 6Sep63 | 178/79 | 100 | 10.31,10.1 | | |
| Kenworthy | Dave | USA | 27Jun60 | 183/75 | PV | 5.62 | 5.61 | -8 |
| Kerékjártó | István | HUN | 13Jun53 | 172/61 | Mar | 2:13:35 | 2:14:33 | -8 |
| Kerr | Stanley | USA | 19Jun67 | 173/70 | 100 | 10.10 | 10.41,10.1w | -8 |
| | | | | | 200 | 20.39,20.10w | 20.66,20.4 | -8 |
| Khalifa | Omer | SUD | 1Jan56 | 174/64 | 800 | 1:44.75 | 1:44.87 | -8 |
| | | | | | 1500 | 3:33.28 | 3:34.07 | -8 |
| Kharitonov | Igor | SU | 7Dec62 | | LJ | 8.08 | 7.83 | -8 |
| Kharizanov | Momchil | BUL | 29May61 | 177/65 | 400 | 45.92,45.6 | 46.45 | -8 |
| Kharlov | Aleksandr | SU | 18Mar58 | 194/80 | 400h | 49.68 | 48.78 | - |
| Khaustov | Saveli | SU | 17Feb61 | 196/102 | DT | 61.80 | 60.40 | - |
| Khrishchuk | Viktor | SU | 58 | | 100 | 10.1 | 10.2-82,10.46 | - |
| Khitryakov | Igor | SU | 15Jul65 | | 110h | 13.75, | 14.25 | - |
| | | | | | | 13.53w,13.5 | | |
| Khoklov | Boris | SU | 20Dec58 | 186/69 | TJ | 16.83 | 17.02 | - |
| Khristov | Ventsislav | BUL | 18May62 | 188/110 | SP | 20.37 | 20.83 | - |
| Kidikas | Vaclavas | SU | 17Oct61 | 197/103 | DT | 67.00 | 67.34 | - |
| Kiernan | Gerry | IRL | 31May53 | 183/66 | Mar | 2:12:44 | 2:12:20 | - |
| Kilbert | Gert | SWZ | 21Sep65 | 164/54 | 800 | 1:46.60 | 1:46.33 | - |
| Kim | Jae Sang | KOR | 23Sep68 | 174/75 | JT | 75.40 | | |
| Kim | Yong Il | KOR | 11Sep62 | 178/68 | LJ | 7.94, | 7.94-82,7.98A | - |
| | | | | | | 8.06w | 8.09w | - |

| Name | | Nat | Yr | Ht/Wt | Event | 1986 Mark | Pre-1986 best | |
|------|------|-----|-----|-------|-------|-----------|---------------|---|
| Kim | Yong Yun | KOR | 21Jan60 | | 10k | 28:30.54 | 29:51.60 | -85 |
| Kimble | Ray | USA | 19Apr53 | 183/84 | TJ | 16.91, | 16.99 | -84 |
| | | | | | | 17.02w | 17.21w | -83 |
| Kinder | Gary | USA | 25Oct62 | 183/85 | Dec | 7998W | 7965w | -85 |
| King | Emmit | USA | 24Mar59 | 175/78 | 100 | 10.07, | 10.06,10.05w | -83 |
| | | | | | | 10.0 | 10.0 | -79 |
| King | John | UK | 13Feb63 | 183/78 | LJ | 7.94w | 7.89 | -85 |
| Kingdom | Roger | USA | 26Aug62 | 185/84 | 110h | 13.40, | 13.14 | -85 |
| | | | | | | 13.39w | 13.1,13.00w | -84 |
| Kio | Joshua | NIG | 7Sep57 | 176/72 | TJ | 16.59 | 16.69 | -82 |
| Kipkemboi | Joshua | KEN | 22Feb60 | 165/60 | 3kSt | 8:14.13 | 8:21.70 | -85 |
| Kipkoech | Paul | KEN | 6Jan63 | 173/58 | 2k | 5:05.0 | 5:18.32 | -84 |
| | | | | | 3k | 7:39.38 | 7:46.18 | -83 |
| | | | | | 5k | 13:18.91 | 13:14.40 | -84 |
| | | | | | 10k | 27:43.31 | 27:58.26 | -85 |
| Kiprotich | James | KEN | 60 | | 400 | 45.7A | 46.9A | -85 |
| Kipsang | Joseph | KEN | 25Sep62 | 162/57 | Mar | 2:12:52 | -0- | |
| Kirati | Sisa | KEN | 57 | | 1500 | 3:39.02 | 3:40.0A | -85 |
| Kisheyev | Vladimir | SU | 4Dec62 | 193/108 | SP | 19.57 | 20.07 | -84 |
| Kistner | Rolf | FRG | 4Oct62 | 179/75 | 200 | 20.79 | 20.87 | -83 |
| Kitur | David | KEN | 12Oct62 | 183/72 | 400 | 44.9 | 45.62,45.1A | -84 |
| Kitur | Simon | KEN | 12Jun59 | 182/74 | 400h | 50.2A | 49.70 | -84 |
| Kiyai | Moses | KEN | 60 | 185/75 | LJ | 8.20w | 8.20w-85,8.08 | -84 |
| Klassen | Steve | USA | 15Feb65 | 180/77 | PV | 5.50 | 5.30 | -85 |
| Kleisa | Saulius | SU | 64 | | SP | 20.25 | 18.88 | -85 |
| Klimaszewski | Andrzej | POL | 14May60 | 185/78 | LJ | 8.07,8.11w | 8.20,8.33w | -80 |
| Klimeš | Pavel | UK | 27Oct58 | 177/60 | 5k | 13:25.90 | 13:33.30 | -85 |
| Klimeš | Petr | UK | 27Oct58 | 178/61 | 5k | 13:25.13 | 13:34.36 | -85 |
| Kneissler | Bernd | FRG | 13Sep62 | 198/130 | DT | 61.86 | 61.62 | -84 |
| Kobylyanskiy | Vadim | SU | 8Aug61 | 180/73 | LJ | 8.13 | 8.28 | -84 |
| Kobza | Marty | USA | 6Mar62 | 194/118 | SP | 19.91i,19.83 | 20.36 | -85 |
| Koch | Mathias | GDR | 3Sep62 | 188/75 | LJ | 8.12 | 8.09i,8.08 | -84 |
| Kocherga | Valeriy | SU | 9Dec63 | 191/118 | HT | 78.92 | 74.58 | -85 |
| Kocheryagin | Vyacheslav | SU | 23Apr62 | 188/74 | 400 | 46.01 | 46.51-83,46.3-85 | |
| Kodama | Taisuke | JAP | 26Jul58 | 165/49 | Mar | 2:07:35 | 2:10:36 | -84 |
| Kodentsev | Vadim | SU | 2Feb64 | | PV | 5.70 | 5.20i | -83 |
| Koech | Edwin | KEN | 23Jul61 | 174/64 | 800 | 1:45.26 | 1:44.12 | -84 |
| Koech | Peter | KEN | 18Feb58 | 180/67 | 1500 | 3:35.67 | 3:38.46 | -85 |
| | | | | | 2k | 5:04.05 | 5:02.79 | -82 |
| | | | | | 5k | 13:34.2 | 13:09.50 | -82 |
| | | | | | 3kSt | 8:13.33 | 8:19.84 | -85 |
| Koeleman | Hans | HOL | 5Oct57 | 181/67 | 3kSt | 8:22.34 | 8:18.02 | -85 |
| Kolasa | Marian | POL | 12Aug59 | 195/90 | PV | 5.81i,5.50,5.71ex | 5.80 | -85 |
| Kolasa | Ryszard | POL | 17Apr64 | 185/84 | PV | 5.71ex,5.50i | 5.60 | -85 |
| Kolnootchenko | Georgiy | SU | 7May59 | 197/115 | DT | 67.02 | 69.44 | -82 |
| Kondo | Takashi | JAP | 13Nov59 | 175/56 | Mar | 2:13:00 | | |
| Konovalov | Ivan | SU | 6Jul59 | 175/64 | 3kSt | 8:25.89 | 8:19.38 | -85 |
| Konrad | Wolfgang | AUT | 22Dec58 | 184/65 | 1500 | 3:39.07 | 3:40.86 | -79 |
| | | | | | | | 3:39.56i | -80 |
| | | | | | 3kSt | 8:28.36 | 8:17.22 | -82 |
| Konstantinov | Bozhidar | BUL | 1Sep63 | 188/70 | 400h | 49.85 | 50.03 | -84 |
| Koprivichin | Rumen | BUL | 20Oct62 | 188/90 | HT | 72.80 | 72.20 | -85 |
| Korir | Julius | KEN | 21Apr60 | 172/64 | 3k | 7:48.90 | 7:54.77 | -83 |
| | | | | | 3kSt | 8:12.74 | 8:11.80 | -84 |
| Kornilov | Arkadiy | SU | 20Dec63 | 185/74 | 400 | 45.80 | 46.12 | -84 |
| Korniyenko | Vladimir | SU | 28Jan66 | 178/70 | HJ | 2.25 | 2.19i | -85 |
| Korobenko | Anatoliy | SU | 12Aug57 | 183/71 | HJ | 2.25 | 2.31 | -85 |
| Korolyov | Aleksey | SU | 66 | | 110h | 13.4w | 14.92,14.6 | -85 |
| Korovin | Vyacheslav | SU | 8Sep62 | | HT | 74.98 | 77.32 | -84 |
| Korte | Matti | FIN | 20Aug56 | 188/82 | JT | 78.18 | 84.80* | -84 |
| Koskei | Kipsubai | KEN | 51 | 172/57 | 5k | 13:29.60 | 13:26.86 | -81 |
| | | | | | 10k | 28:20.11 | 28:07.40 | -80 |

| Name | | Nat | Yr | Ht/Wt | Event | 1986 Mark | Pre-1986 best | |
|------|--|-----|-----|-------|-------|-----------|----------------|--|
| Koskei | Sam | KEN | 14May61 | 183/68 | 800 | 1:45.89 | 1:42.28 | -84 |
| | | | | | 1000 | 2:17.01 | 2:14.95 | -85 |
| Kostin | Mikhail | SU | 10May59 | 194/120 | SP | 21.96 | 21.24 | -85 |
| Kostrubala | Gary | USA | 30Jun64 | 188/105 | DT | 61.66 | 58.22 | -85 |
| Kot | Sergey | SU | 7Jan60 | | SP | 20.55 | 20.12 | -85 |
| Kotelnikov | Boris | SU | 65 | | HT | 74.42 | 71.58 | -85 |
| Kotovich | Aleksandr | SU | 6Jan61 | 183/76 | HJ | 2.34i, | 2.35i | -85 |
| | | | | | | 2.32 | 2.33 | -84 |
| Koutsoukis | Dimitrios | GRE | 8Dec62 | 193/120 | SP | 20.59 | 20.51 | -84 |
| Kovács | Attila | HUN | 2Sep60 | 182/72 | 100 | 10.29,10.26 | 10.18 | -84 |
| | | | | | 200 | 20.50 | 20.60,20.51w | -84 |
| Kovalenko | Aleksandr | SU | 8May63 | 179/70 | TJ | 17.25 | 16.58 | -85 |
| Kovar | Jay | USA | 15May60 | 193/114 | DT | 63.02 | 61.26 | -84 |
| Kovtsun | Dmitriy | SU | 29Sep55 | 191/116 | DT | 66.94 | 68.64 | -84 |
| Kozakiewicz | Władysław | FRG | 8Dec53 | 187/86 | PV | 5.70i,5.70 | 5.78 | -80 |
| Kožul | Djordje | YUG | 31Dec63 | 186/72 | TJ | 16.72 | 16.33 | -85 |
| Krakowiak | Krzysztof | POL | 5Feb61 | 182/80 | Dec | 7842 | 7908 | -85 |
| Krasovskiy | Sergey | SU | 18May63 | 192/85 | 110h | 13.84 | 13.84-85,13.6 | -84 |
| Krastev | Plamen | BUL | 18Nov58 | 187/76 | 110h | 13.59 | 13.46,13.4 | -84 |
| Kratschmer | Guido | FRG | 10Jan53 | 186/94 | Dec | 8519 | 8667 | -80 |
| Kravtsov | Vladimir | SU | 10Mar56 | 184/78 | 100 | 10.1 | 10.23-85,10.1 | -79 |
| Krawczyk | Krzysztof | POL | 28Jan62 | 186/74 | HJ | 2.31 | 2.27i-84,2.26 | -81 |
| Krdžalić | Sejad | YUG | 5Jan60 | 186/93 | JT | 82.34 | 85.10* | -85 |
| Kremastiotis | Panagiotis | GRE | 60 | | HT | 73.48 | 70.12 | -81 |
| Krieger | Helmut | POL | 17Jul58 | 196/137 | SP | 21.30 | 21.07 | -85 |
| Królak | Henryk | POL | 15Jan60 | 186/104 | HT | 76.42 | 78.60 | -84 |
| Kroon | Johnny | SWE | 6Jan60 | 185/67 | 1500 | 3:39.39 | 3:36.49 | -85 |
| | | | | | Mile | 3:55.17 | 4:00.98 | -82 |
| | | | | | 2k | 5:05.35 | -0- | |
| Krovotintsev | Andrey | SU | 18Jun65 | | Dec | 7814m | 7454 | -85 |
| Krsek | Ivo | CS | 21Mar67 | 184/76 | LJ | 7.91,8.04w | 7.83 | -85 |
| Krüger | Ingo | GDR | 6Jul66 | 179/78 | 400h | 50.46 | 51.99 | -8. |
| Krulee | Marty | USA | 4Nov56 | 170/68 | 100 | 10.27, | 10.19,10.0, | |
| | | | | | | 10.24w,10.1 | 10.16w | -8. |
| | | | | | 200 | 20.71, | 20.51 | -8. |
| | | | | | | 20.55w,20.3 | 20.4 | -8 |
| Krupskiy | Aleksandr | SU | 4Jan60 | 185/77 | PV | 5.75 | 5.82 | -84 |
| Kruzhakov | Andrey | SU | 19Oct61 | | TJ | 16.62 | | |
| Krylov | Vladimir | SU | 26Feb64 | 184/73 | 100 | 10.25 | 9.9 | -8 |
| | | | | | 200 | 20.50 | 20.61 | -8 |
| | | | | | 400 | 45.20 | 45.22 | -8 |
| Kryuchkov | Vladimir | SU | 27Jul62 | 189/80 | Dec | 7874 | 7816 | -8 |
| Kubeš | Josef | CS | 2Sep57 | 190/110 | SP | 20.39 | 21.20 | -8 |
| Kubiszewski | Marek | POL | 7Oct55 | 181/87 | Dec | 7726 | 8105 | -8 |
| Kucej | Jozef | CS | 23Mar65 | 181/68 | 400h | 49.90 | 51.82 | -8 |
| Kucherenko | Igor | SU | 12May60 | | HT | 78.32 | 77.36 | -8 |
| Kucherov | Oleg | SU | 22Jan66 | 172/68 | 100 | 10.1w | 10.3 | -8 |
| Kudō | Kazuyoshi | JAP | 27Feb61 | 169/54 | Mar | 2:11:58 | | |
| Kübler | Klaus | FRG | 17Apr59 | 185/76 | TJ | 16.55 | 16.91 | -8 |
| Külvet | Valter | SU | 19Feb64 | 191/85 | Dec | 8168 | 8132 | -8 |
| Kula | Dainis | SU | 28Apr59 | 190/98 | JT | 76.12 | 92.06* | -8 |
| Kulibaba | Sergey | SU | 24Jul59 | 178/70 | PV | 5.70 | 5.70 | -8 |
| Kulish | Mikhail | SU | 20Mar64 | 191/103 | SP | 19.89 | 19.62 | -8 |
| Kulker | Han | HOL | 15Aug59 | 183/64 | 1k | 2:18.07 | | |
| | | | | | 1500 | 3:36.54 | 3:39.3,3:39.39 | -8 |
| | | | | | Mile | 3:56.66 | 3:53.93 | -8 |
| Kunze | Hansjörg | GDR | 28Dec59 | 179/63 | 5k | 13:31.05 | 13:10.40 | -8 |
| | | | | | 10k | 27:34.68 | 27:30.69 | -8 |
| Kuoppa | Jari | FIN | 25Jun60 | 190/105 | SP | 20.46 | 19.57 | -8 |
| Kurdinovskiy | Aleksandr | SU | 20Mar65 | | TJ | 16.55 | 16.63 | -8 |
| Kurnicki | Robert | POL | 27Mar65 | 189/78 | 110h | 13.82 | 14.15 | -8 |
| Kurochkin | Aleksandr | SU | 23Jul61 | 192/89 | 400 | 45.58 | 45.52,45.3 | -8 |

| ame | | Nat | Yr | Ht/Wt | Event | 1986 Mark | Pre-1986 best | |
|---|---|---|---|---|---|---|---|---|
| :utsebo | Sergey | SU | 7Feb61 | 181/74 | 800 | 1:46.94 | 1:45.81 | -85 |
| | | | | | 400h | 50.27 | 49.92 | -82 |
| :uusela | Kimmo | FIN | 7Oct62 | 181/74 | PV | 5.55 | 5.51 | -84 |
| :uusisto | Timo | FIN | 28Jun59 | 181/68 | PV | 5.60 | 5.55 | -82 |
| :uyumdzhyan | Yuriy | SU | 29May61 | | SP | 20.13 | 19.90i,19.83 | -83 |
| uzyanin | Andrey | SU | 60 | | DT | 62.96 | 59.48 | -84 |
| vernmo | Geir | NOR | 29Oct55 | 184/66 | 10k | 28:15.13 | 28:53.5 | -83 |
| yeswa | Moses | UGA | 12Apr58 | 178/68 | 400 | 46.01 | 45.85 | -85 |
| acika | Jozef | CS | 8Jun61 | 193/125 | SP | 20.36 | 20.02 | -84 |
| afranchi | Bruno | SWZ | 19Jul55 | 178/60 | 5k | 13:25.97 | 13:34.93 | -85 |
| | | | | | Mar | 2:11:25 | 2:11:12 | -82 |
| ahbi | Faouzi | MOR | 2Mar58 | 176/60 | Mar | 1:44.66 | 1:45.67 | -84 |
| aheurte | Phil | CAN | 4Jun57 | 180/64 | 3kSt | 8:35.03 | 8:29.3 | -85 |
| aine | Gordon | USA | 24Feb58 | 183/69 | LJ | 8.12 | 7.98-85,8.24w | -84 |
| aine | Yki | FIN | 16May65 | 185/85 | JT | 76.12 | 76.42* | -85 |
| aing | Earle | JAM | 24Sep64 | 186/81 | 100 | 10.36,10.26 | 10.33,10.25w | -83 |
| | | | | | 200 | 20.56 | 20.58,20.51w | -85 |
| | | | | | 400 | 45.9 | 46.74 | -85 |
| akafia | Jean-Paul | FRA | 29Jun61 | 192/103 | JT | 77.14 | 86.60* | -85 |
| ambregts | Cor | HOL | 4Aug58 | 178/66 | 10k | 27:57.53 | 28:03.19 | -85 |
| | | | | | Mar | 2:12:27 | 2:11:02 | -85 |
| ambruschini | Alessandro | ITA | 7Jan65 | 178/63 | 1500 | 3:37.35 | 3:40.61 | -85 |
| | | | | | 2k | 5:05.85 | | |
| | | | | | 3kSt | 8:18.39 | 8:36.09 | -85 |
| ancaster | Chris | USA | 23Dec65 | 183/75 | 110h | 13.88 | | |
| ane | Al | USA | 27Apr62 | 184/88 | 110h | 13.72 | 13.46 | -85 |
| | | | | | | 13.5 | 13.38w | -84 |
| ange | Joachim | GDR | 25Jan60 | 189/95 | JT | 76.34 | 87.42* | -84 |
| anghammer | Uwe | GDR | 12Jun65 | 191/81 | PV | 5.50 | 5.40 | -85 |
| apshin | Igor | SU | 8Aug63 | 186/74 | TJ | 17.20 | 17.17 | -85 |
| ara | Osvaldo | CUB | 13Jul55 | 171/72 | 100 | 10.3 | 10.11A-78,10.0 | -76 |
| | | | | | | | 10.13-85,9.7w | -82 |
| arkins | Paul | UK | 19May63 | 183/67 | 1k | 2:18.35 | 2:23.04 | -85 |
| | | | | | 1500 | 3:38.02 | 3:38.44 | -84 |
| asecki | Kazimierz | POL | 3Feb58 | 178/66 | Mar | 2:13:37 | 2:16:06 | -84 |
| aut | Dave | USA | 21Dec56 | 193/114 | SP | 20.98 | 22.02 | -82 |
| autenslager | Greg | USA | 15Oct57 | 180/64 | 5k | 13:33.90 | 13:44.1 | -80 |
| auterbach | Thomas | GDR | 24Nov66 | 181/74 | 800 | 1:47.17 | 1:48.40 | -84 |
| venture | Cyrille | FRA | 29Mar64 | 187/62 | 1500 | 3:36.37 | 3:37.04 | -85 |
| | | | | | 5k | 13:30.69 | -0- | |
| verty | Dale | USA | 30Apr65 | 183/81 | 400h | 48.72A,49.56 | 49.27 | -85 |
| vie | Andrie | FRA | 28Jun59 | 180/68 | 800 | 1:46.9 | 1:46.90 | -83 |
| yevskiy | Sergey | SU | 3Mar59 | 184/72 | LJ | 8.20 | 8.32 | -84 |
| zarević | Jovan | YUG | 3May52 | 194/114 | SP | 20.00 | 20.49 | -81 |
| zdins | Ray | CAN | 29Sep64 | 196/102 | DT | 61.02 | 58.36-85,61.02dh | -84 |
| ach | Jason | USA | 11Mar66 | 175/64 | 100 | 10.16w | 10.26,10.22w | -85 |
| | | | | | | | 10.1w | -84 |
| | | | | | 200 | 20.60w,20.3Aw | 20.79w | -85 |
| Bon | Joseph | FRA | 30May64 | 184/69 | 1500 | 3:38.56 | 3:44.14 | -85 |
| | | | | | 2k | 5:03.16 | | |
| curieux | Philippe | FRA | 22May58 | 187/90 | JT | 75.26 | 82.54* | -85 |
| e | Ron | USA | 4Jan62 | 193/73 | 110h | 13.88w | | |
| | | | | | HJ | 2.285 | 2.235 | -83 |
| euwenburgh | Chris | HOL | 4Oct62 | 183/78 | 100 | 10.1Aw | 10.5A,10.3w | -85 |
| | | | | | PV | 5.50 | 5.38 | -85 |
| fèvre | Pascal | FRA | 25Jan65 | | JT | 76.64 | 79.02* | -85 |
| frand | Jacques | FRA | 16May52 | 174/56 | Mar | 2:12:53 | 2:13:50 | -85 |
| gchenko | Vladimir | SU | 65 | | PV | 5.50 | 5.20 | -85 |
| itão | António | POR | 22Jul60 | 176/68 | 3k | 7:44.53 | 7:39.69 | -83 |
| | | | | | 5k | 13:15.18 | 13:07.70 | -82 |

| Name | | Nat | Yr | Ht/Wt | Event | 1986 Mark | Pre-1986 best | |
|---|---|---|---|---|---|---|---|---|
| Leitner | Ján | CS | 14Sep53 | 186/87 | LJ | 8.17i, | 8.17i | -8⁵ |
| | | | | | | 8.04,8.15w | 8.10 | -8² |
| Lemme | Armin | GDR | 28Oct55 | 199/120 | DT | 67.76 | 68.50 | -8² |
| Lengyel | Stefan | CS | 8Jun61 | 184/88 | JT | 79.52 | 82.20* | -8⁵ |
| Lenhardt | Thorsten | GDR | 17Aug63 | 176/63 | 1500 | 3:38.91 | 3:42.08 | -8 |
| Lenstrohm | John | USA | 27Feb61 | 185/77 | 110h | 13.81,13.6 | 13.59 | -8² |
| Leonov | Aleksandr | SU | 7Feb62 | | TJ | 17.22 | 16.76 | -8 |
| le Roux | Pierre | RSA | 16Dec65 | 190/78 | 400 | 45.57A | 45.83A | -8 |
| Lesniewicz | Janusz | POL | 14Apr55 | 185/81 | Dec | 7827 | 8019 | -8 |
| Lesov | Delko | BUL | 6Jan67 | 182/69 | PV | 5.55 | 5.30 | -8 |
| Le Stum | Bruno | FRA | 25Dec59 | 179/57 | 3kSt | 8:25.92 | 8:32.67 | -8 |
| Levant | Bruno | FRA | 24Jan60 | 180/69 | 1500 | 3:36.60 | 3:38.38 | -8 |
| | | | | | 5k | 13:31.77 | | |
| Leveur | Serge | FRA | 17Jun57 | 182/76 | PV | 5.60 | 5.60,5.66iex | -8 |
| Leveille | Pierre | CAN | 19Feb62 | 183/73 | 400h | 50.33A | 50.32A,51.22 | -8 |
| Lewis | Carl | USA | 1Jul61 | 188/80 | 100 | 10.06, | 9.97 | -8 |
| | | | | | | 9.91w | 9.90w-85,9.9 | -8 |
| | | | | | 200 | 20.41,20.23w,20.1 | 19.75 | -8 |
| | | | | | LJ | 8.37i,8.35,8.67w | 8.79 | -8 |
| Lewis | Dave | UK | 15Oct61 | 180/68 | 3k | 7:49.61i | 7:42.47 | -8 |
| | | | | | 5k | 13:33.09 | 13:21.13 | -8 |
| Lewis | Dennis | USA | 20Mar59 | 193/81 | HJ | 2.32i | 2.34 | -8 |
| Li Tao | | CHN | 15Jan68 | | 100 | 10.26 | | |
| Liang Xuereng | | CHN | 7Mar65 | 186/60 | PV | 5.55 | 5.48 | -8 |
| Linares | Juan | CUB | 8Mar62 | | 3kSt | 8:34.03 | 8:39.2 | -8 |
| Linden | Andreas | FRG | 20Feb65 | | JT | 76.54 | 76.28* | -8 |
| Lindner | Johann | AUT | 3May59 | 188/110 | HT | 78.46 | 79.28 | -8 |
| Lishebo | Davison | ZAM | 1Oct55 | 184/73 | 400 | 45.64 | 45.57 | -8 |
| Lismont | Karel | BEL | 8Mar49 | 168/62 | Mar | 2:12:12 | 2:11:13 | -7 |
| Litvinenko | Dmitriy | SU | 12Aug63 | 184/72 | TJ | 16.86 | 16.78i-83,16.74 | -8 |
| Litvinov | Sergey | SU | 23Jan58 | 180/110 | HT | 86.04 | 85.20 | -8 |
| Liu Yuhuang | | CHN | 25Jul59 | 176/67 | LJ | 7.92, | 8.14 | -8 |
| | | | | | | 8.04w | 8.22w | -8 |
| Liu Yunpeng | | CHN | 24Oct62 | 192/85 | HJ | 2.27 | 2.29 | -8 |
| Lloyd | Andrew | AUS | 14Feb59 | 172/53 | 10k | 28:07.51 | 28:16.7 | -8 |
| Lofquist | Scott | USA | 20Mar60 | 201/133 | DT | 60.88 | 62.58 | -8 |
| Logan | Jud | USA | 19Jul59 | 193/122 | HT | 80.88 | 77.24,77.72ic | -8 |
| Lohr | Lane | USA | 10Sep64 | 188/75 | PV | 5.52,5.49i | 5.50 | -8 |
| Lonergan | Rob | CAN | 8Oct59 | 175/61 | 3k | 7:49.17 | 7:50.44 | -8 |
| | | | | | 5k | 13:34.45 | 13:35.76 | -8 |
| Long | Calvin | USA | 2Jul66 | 193/86 | 100 | 10.29w | 10.28 | -8 |
| Lopez -# | Juan M. | CUB | 7Apr67 | 189/81 | TJ | 16.81,16.94w | 16.25 | -8 |
| Lorens | Pawel | POL | 19Mar58 | 174/61 | Mar | 2:13:05 | 2:14:25 | -8 |
| Lorentzen | Reidar | NOR | 22Sep56 | 180/85 | JT | 77.62 | 88.54* | -8 |
| Lotarev | Igor | SU | 30Aug64 | 181/66 | 800 | 1:46.63 | 1:46.18 | -8 |
| | | | | | 1500 | 3:37.53 | 3:34.49 | -8 |
| Lott | James | USA | 13Oct65 | 186/83 | HJ | 2.27 | 2.27 | -8 |
| Lovegrove | Gavin | NZ | 21Oct67 | 187/90 | JT | 79.58 | 79.12* | -8 |
| Lowery | Ken | USA | 13Aug61 | 192/80 | 400 | 45.80 | 45.69 | -8 |
| Loyd | Kevin | USA | 20Jun66 | 175/68 | 100 | 10.21w | 10.44w | -8 |
| Lubenský | Zdeněk | CS | 3Dec62 | 185/73 | PV | 5.72 | 5.66 | -8 |
| Lübke | Ralf | FRG | 17Jun65 | 192/80 | 200 | 20.50 | 20.38 | -8 |
| | | | | | 400 | 44.98 | 45.06 | -8 |
| Lucero | Ben | USA | 22Jun62 | 186/70 | HJ | 2.24 | 2.25 | -8 |
| Lukashok | Sergey | SU | 20Jun58 | 202/120 | DT | 65.28 | 66.64 | -8 |
| Lundmark | Leif | SWE | 7Sep53 | 178/90 | JT | 75.06 | 89.92* | - |
| Lupa | Henryk | POL | 17Jul56 | 178/69 | Mar | 2:13:01 | 2:12:49 | - |
| Lyach | Aleksey | SU | 4May62 | 187/83 | Dec | 8082 | 8108 | - |
| Lykho | Vyacheslav | SU | 16Jan67 | 194/110 | SP | 19.53i | 16.40i,15.83- | - |
| Lysenko | Nikolay | SU | 14Jul66 | 185/100 | HT | 75.16 | 69.72 | -8 |
| Lytle | Doug | USA | 7Aug62 | 185/80 | PV | 5.72 | 5.71 | - |

| ame | | Nat | Yr | Ht/Wt | Event | 1986 Mark | Pre-1986 best | |
|---|---|---|---|---|---|---|---|---|
| aas | Frans | HOL | 13Jul64 | 196/89 | LJ | 7.91 | 7.70 | -84 |
| cCants | Tom | USA | 27Nov62 | 185/79 | HJ | 2.27i,2.27 | 2.32 | -85 |
| cCloy | Paul | CAN | 6Nov63 | 187/70 | 5k | 13:27.65 | 13:37.27 | -84 |
| | | | | | 10k | 27:56.8 | 28:11.72 | -84 |
| cColgan | Peter | UK | 20Feb63 | | 3kSt | 8:29.35 | 8:42.54 | -85 |
| cCoy | Walter | USA | 15Nov58 | 178/75 | 400 | 45.07 | 44.76 | -84 |
| cDaniel | Terry | USA | 8Feb65 | 183/79 | 200 | 20.67 20.62w | -85,21.05 | -84 |
| cDermott | Art | USA | 7Nov61 | 183/111 | SP | 20.40 | 19.76i,19.68 | -84 |
| | | | | | DT | 63.68 | 64.04 | -84 |
| cFadgen | David | USA | 22Sep60 | 187/78 | TJ | 16.69, | 16.64 | -82 |
| | | | | | | 17.30w | 17.21w | -83 |
| cFarlane | Mike | UK | 2May60 | 178/75 | 100 | 10.22 | 10.27,10.08w | -84 |
| cGeorge | Chris | UK | 13Jan62 | 176/65 | 800 | 1:46.59 | 1:45.14 | -83 |
| | | | | | 1000 | 2:18.73 | 2:17.45 | -84 |
| | | | | | 1500 | 3:39.41 | 3:41.46 | -85 |
| cGhee | Pat | USA | 24Jun66 | 190/76 | 400h | 49.65 | 50.22 | -85 |
| ack | David | USA | 30May61 | 178/67 | 800 | 1:44.17 | 1:43.35 | -85 |
| cKay | Antonio | USA | 9Feb64 | 183/77 | 400 | 44.69 | 44.71 | -84 |
| cKean | Tom | UK | 27Oct63 | 183/71 | 800 | 1:44.61 | 1:46.05 | -85 |
| cKenzie | Dave | USA | 10May49 | 188/111 | HT | 73.68 | 74.98 | -84 |
| cKenzie | Leander | USA | 27Jan63 | 180/73 | 110h | 13.87w | 13.81,13.7w | -84 |
| | | | | | 400h | 49.66 | 49.33 | -85 |
| cKeon | Jim | USA | 8Sep62 | 185/66 | Mile | 3:56.48 | 3:58.4,3:58.36i | -85 |
| cKinley | Kevin | USA | 17Dec64 | | 110h | 13.87,13.75dt | 13.72dt | -85 |
| | | | | | | 13.60w | 13.7-83,14.10 | -84 |
| | | | | | 400h | 50.09 | | |
| cKoy | Mark | CAN | 10Dec61 | 181/70 | 100 | 10.21 | 10.44 | -81 |
| | | | | | 110h | 13.35, | 13.0 | -85 |
| | | | | | | 13.31w | 13.27,13.16w | -84 |
| cLean | Robin | RSA | 5Jul59 | 180/64 | 200 | 20.78A | 20.86A | -85 |
| cLeod | Mike | UK | 25Jan52 | 180/63 | 10k | 28:02.83 | 27:39.76 | -79 |
| cLoughlin | Martin | UK | 23Dec58 | | 10k | 28:15.58 | 29:05.9 | -85 |
| cMichael | Tim | USA | 22Dec67 | 172/64 | PV | 5.45 | 4.87 | -85 |
| cNeill | Lee | USA | 2Dec64 | 168/64 | 100 | 10.14 | 10.17,10.11w | -85 |
| | | | | | 200 | 20.60 | | |
| cRae | Lee | USA | 23Jan66 | 176/71 | 100 | 10.11, | 10.27, | |
| | | | | | | 10.02w | 10.07w | -85 |
| cRae | Mike | USA | 9Jul55 | 185/82 | LJ | 8.04 | 8.27,8.34w | -84 |
| cSeveney -# | Greg | USA | 29May59 | 190/118 | DT | 64.52 | 66.98 | -85 |
| cSwain | Harvey | USA | 10Mar63 | 172/71 | 100 | 10.21 | 10.18,10.1 | -83 |
| | | | | | 200 | 20.30 | 20.36 | -85 |
| adox | Harold | USA | 26Dec65 | 188/73 | 100 | 10.33w,10.1w | | |
| | | | | | 200 | 20.65w | | |
| | | | | | 400 | 44.89 | 45.43,45.3A | -85 |
| es | Jos | BEL | 11Apr61 | | 3k | 7:50.5 | 7:56.7 | -85 |
| hmoud | Joseph | FRA | 13Dec55 | 174/65 | St | 8:20.25 | 8:07.62 | -84 |
| horn | Atlee | CAN | 27Oct65 | 187/77 | 100 | 10.26 | 10.19w,10.39 | -85 |
| | | | | | 200 | 20.34,20.31w | 20.65 | -85 |
| | | | | | 400 | 45.62 | | |
| hovlich -# | Mike | CAN | 27Aug60 | 188/110 | JT | 79.04 | 83.46* | -85 |
| i | Volker | GDR | 3May66 | 194/72 | TJ | 17.02 | 17.50 | -85 |
| ir | John | JAM | | | 100 | 10.31, | 10.41 | -84 |
| | | | | | | 10.16w | 10.1 | -85 |
| | | | | | 200 | 20.76 20.73,20.66w,20.6 | | -85 |
| kin | Michael | UK | 1Mar62 | 183/76 | TJ | 16.87 | 16.47 | -84 |
| jewski | Tadeusz | POL | 14Jul54 | 195/118 | DT | 61.52 | 61.58 | -83 |
| ksymiuk | Zbigniew | POL | 25Feb61 | 176/70 | LJ | 7.90w | 7.65 | -85 |
| lakhovskis | Richardas | SU | 28Apr65 | 193/83 | Dec | 8108 | 7690 | -85 |
| lave | Jesus | VEN | 24Oct65 | 170/64 | 400 | 45.71 | 46.8 | -83 |

| Name | | Nat | Yr | Ht/Wt | Event | 1986 Mark | Pre-1986 best | |
|---|---|---|---|---|---|---|---|---|
| Malchenko | Sergey | SU | 2Nov63 | 190/74 | HJ | 2.33 | 2.31 | -8 |
| Malekwa | Zakayo | TAN | 2Feb51 | 183/84 | JT | 76.48 | 87.68* | -8 |
| Maliszewski | Andrzej | POL | 22May57 | 187/105 | DT | 61.02 | 58.62 | -8 |
| Malyi | Sergey | SU | 5Aug65 | | HJ | 2.25 | 2.25 | -8 |
| Mamchur | Nikolay | SU | 9Oct63 | 189/74 | TJ | 16.96 | 16.61 | -8 |
| Mamede | Fernando | POR | 1Nov51 | 175/59 | 5k | 13:28.4 | 13:08.54 | -8 |
| | | | | | 10k | 27:47.84 | 27:13.81 | -8 |
| Mamiński | Bogusław | POL | 18Dec55 | 181/68 | 3k | 7:47.83 | 7:47.12 | -8 |
| | | | | | St | 8:20.56 | 8:09.18 | -8 |
| Mandl | Jurgen | AUT | 19Aug65 | 182/80 | Dec | 7646 | 7500 | -8 |
| Mann | Patrick | USA | 24Apr66 | 180/77 | 400h | 50.33 | 50.06 | -8 |
| Manninen | Arto | FIN | 2Jan62 | 198/97 | JT | 77.38 | 85.62* | -8 |
| Manson | Pat | USA | 29Nov67 | 178/70 | PV | 5.49 | 5.10 | -8 |
| Mansour | Tallal | QAT | 64 | | 100 | 10.30 | 10.36 | -8 |
| Maran | Pascal | FRA | 21Mar67 | 182/73 | 400h | 50.39 | 51.53 | -8 |
| Mardle | Paul | UK | 10Nov62 | 192/108 | DT | 61.40 | 61.86 | -8 |
| Maree | Sydney | USA | 9Sep56 | 180/66 | 1500 | 3:32.56 | 3:29.77 | -8 |
| | | | | | Mile | 3:53.29 | 3:48.83 | -8 |
| | | | | | 2k | 5:02.6 | 4:54.20 | -8 |
| | | | | | 3k | 7:38.26 | 7:33.37 | -8 |
| | | | | | 5k | 13:14.62 | 13:01.15 | -8 |
| Marie-Rose | Bruno | FRA | 20May65 | 193/83 | 100 | 10.18 | 10.29 | -8 |
| | | | | | 200 | 20.53 | 20.94,20.8 | -8 |
| Marinović | Lahor | YUG | 29Jun67 | 186/75 | LJ | 7.93 | 7.48 | -8 |
| Maritim | Joseph | KEN | 22Oct68 | 180/70 | 400h | 50.27 | 50.6A | -8 |
| Markin | Aleksandr | SU | 8Sep62 | 185/78 | 110h | 13.39, | 13.84 | -8 |
| | | | | | | 13.25w | 13.7i | -8 |
| Markó | Gábor | HUN | 7Feb60 | 184/63 | St | 8:19.52 | 8:17.97 | -8 |
| Markov | Khristo | BUL | 27Jan65 | 185/76 | LJ | 8.04, | 7.95 | -8 |
| | | | | | | 8.16w | 8.23i | -8 |
| | | | | | TJ | 17.80 | 17.77 | -8 |
| Markov | Nikolay | BUL | 9Jun60 | 180/74 | 100 | 10.33 | 10.40 | -8 |
| Markus | Jorma | FIN | 28Nov52 | 178/78 | JT | 80.56 | 90.18* | -8 |
| Marquetti | Hector | CUB | 7Apr68 | 175/70 | TJ | 16.78 | 16.25 | -8 |
| Marsh | Henry | USA | 15Mar54 | 178/72 | St | 8:13.15 | 8:09.17 | -8 |
| Marsh | Michael | USA | 4Aug67 | 178/68 | 100 | 10.22 | 10.6 | -8 |
| | | | | | 200 | 20.69 | 20.82 | -8 |
| Marshall | Brian | CAN | 1Apr65 | 194/80 | HJ | 2.24 | 2.22 | -8 |
| Marshall | John | USA | 5Nov63 | 190/74 | 800 | 1:47.17 | 1:43.92 | -8 |
| Martin | Roy | USA | 25Dec66 | 185/79 | 100 | 10.12, | 10.18 | -8 |
| | | | | | | 9.97w | 10.14w,10.1w | -8 |
| | | | | | 200 | 20.16 | 20.13 | - |
| Martin | Steve | UK | 16Jul59 | 192/75 | Mile | 3:56.36 | 3:56.71 | -8 |
| Martin | Uwe | FRG | 14Aug62 | 191/76 | HJ | 2.23 | 2.20 | -8 |
| Martínez | Juan | CUB | 17May58 | 186/122 | DT | 68.40 | 70.00 | -8 |
| Martino | Marco | ITA | 21Feb60 | 190/108 | DT | 65.86 | 66.90 | -8 |
| Martsinovich | Gennadiy | SU | 4May61 | 195/80 | HJ | 2.29i | 2.25 | -8 |
| Maryin | Igor | SU | 28Apr65 | | Dec | 7866 | 8147 | -8 |
| Mason | Kevin | USA | 17Jun67 | 188/70 | 400h | 50.41 | 50.82 | -8 |
| Masong | Agapius | TAN | 12Apr60 | 179/67 | Mar | 2:13:26 | 2:10:42 | -8 |
| Masunov | Leonid | SU | 62 | 177/61 | 800 | 1:46.18 | 1:45.08 | -8 |
| Matei | Sorin | RUM | 6Jul63 | 184/71 | HJ | 2.32 | 2.35 | -8 |
| Matveyev | Aleksey | SU | 62 | | 110h | 13.6 | | |
| Matveyev | Vasiliy | SU | 4Feb62 | 174/60 | 1500 | 3:39.86 | 3:38.1 | -8 |
| Matyushenko | Nikolay | SU | 4Jan66 | 175/62 | St | 8:25.73 | 8:41.06 | -8 |
| Mayr | Marco | SWZ | 19Jul60 | 178/59 | 800 | 1:46.60 | 1:45.75 | -8 |
| | | | | | 1500 | 3:39.36 | 3:42.28 | -8 |
| Maznichenko | Andrey | SU | 29Sep66 | | JT | 82.18*,77.96 | 82.32* | -8 |
| Medved | Mikhail | SU | 30Jan64 | 199/89 | Dec | 8315 | 8105 | -8 |
| Meghoo | Greg | JAM | 11Aug65 | 180/74 | 100 | 10.35, | 10.36 | -8 |
| | | | | | | 10.16w,10.1 | 10.24w | -8 |
| | | | | | 200 | 20.71w | 20.6w | -8 |

| Name | | Nat | Yr | Ht/Wt | Event | 1986 Mark | Pre-1986 best | |
|------|---|-----|-----|-------|-------|-----------|---------------|---|
| Meheş | Albert | RUM | 10Apr60 | 186/120 | HT | 75.96 | 76.14 | -85 |
| Mei | Stefano | ITA | 3Feb63 | 181/62 | 1500 | 3:34.57 | 3:36.30 | -85 |
|  |  |  |  |  | 3k | 7:42.85 | 7:47.32 | -85 |
|  |  |  |  |  | 5k | 13:11.57 | 13:21.05 | -85 |
|  |  |  |  |  | 10k | 27:43.97 | -0- |  |
| Meijers | Uldis | SU | 11Jun63 | 197/100 | DT | 61.82 | 58.50 | -84 |
| Mekonnen | Abebe | ETH | 64 | 158/59 | Mar | 2:08:39 | 2:09:05 | -85 |
| Mellaard | Emiel | HOL | 21Mar66 | 189/74 | LJ | 7.98 | 7.99i,7.97 | -85 |
| Melzer | Hagen | GDR | 16Jun59 | 178/63 | St | 8:16.65 | 8:20.28 | -83 |
| Menczer | Gusztáv | HUN | 15Oct59 | 185/72 | 200 | 20.75 | 20.79 | -85 |
|  |  |  |  |  |  |  | 20.65w | -84 |
|  |  |  |  |  | 400 | 45.97 | 45.81 | -85 |
| Merande | Boniface | KEN | 62 |  | St | 8:27.0A | 8:33.0 | -85 |
| Merlo | Walter | ITA | 18Jul65 | 178/58 | 1500 | 3:39.57 | 3:40.29 | -85 |
|  |  |  |  |  | 2k | 5:03.3i |  |  |
|  |  |  |  |  | 3k | 7:47.61i | 7:50.16 | -85 |
| Mestour | Mohamed | MOR | 61 |  | St | 8:35.92 | 8:39.55 | -85 |
| Metcalf | Eric | USA | 23Jan68 | 175/76 | LJ | 8.24 | 7.65,7.75i | -85 |
| Meyer -# | Rick | USA | 21Oct61 | 196/114 | DT | 65.86 | 63.96 | -83 |
| Michel | Detlef | GDR | 13Oct55 | 188/97 | JT | 83.52 | 96.72* | -83 |
| Michel | Karl-Friedrich | FRG | 9May65 |  | JT | 75.28 | 75.42* | -85 |
| Migueles | Luis | ARG | 1Apr65 | 180/71 | 800 | 1:46.01 | 1:46.90 | -85 |
| Mikuláš | Milan | CS | 1Apr63 | 190/70 | TJ | 16.92 | 16.03 | -85 |
| Mileham | Matt | UK | 27Dec56 | 188/109 | HT | 72.82 | 77.02 | -84 |
| Milhet | Lisandro | CUB | 20Jan67 | 170/ | LJ | 7.98 | 7.34 | -84 |
| Milić | Vladimir | YUG | 23Oct55 | 190/115 | SP | 20.28 | 21.19 | -82 |
| Militaru | Constantin | RUM | 17Feb63 | 188/69 | HJ | 2.31 | 2.30-85,2.31i | -84 |
| Miller | Anthony | USA | 15Apr65 | 183/82 | 200 | 20.71w |  |  |
| Miller | Cam | USA | 13Nov66 | 183/77 | PV | 5.51 | 5.18 | -85 |
| Millin | Anatoliy | SU | 11Oct59 | 176/65 | 800 | 1:45.96 | 1:45.50 | -85 |
| Millonig | Dietmar | AUT | 1Jun55 | 169/57 | 5k | 13:30.86 | 13:15.31 | -82 |
| Milner | Hurvie | AUS | 26Sep61 | 172/68 | 100 | 10.36,10.30w | 10.22w | -85 |
| Minashvili | Vakhtang | SU | 9Jun65 |  | LJ | 8.02 | 7.91 | -85 |
| Minchev | Georgi | BUL | 8Sep62 | 187/100 | HT | 72.66 | 71.46 | -85 |
| Mirzoyan | Gennadiy | SU | 64 |  | 100 | 10.29dwr | 10.26 | -85 |
| Misiewicz | Ryszard | POL | 10Mar57 | 170/61 | Mar | 2:12:07 | 2:13:15 | -84 |
| Mitchell | Benny | USA | 2May65 | 178/73 | 100 | 10.21w | 10.5 | -85 |
| Mitchell | Dennis | USA | 20Feb66 | 175/67 | 100 | 10.33, | 10.21 | -85 |
|  |  |  |  |  |  | 10.23w | 10.2 | -83 |
|  |  |  |  |  | 200 | 20.52 | 20.49,20.47w | -85 |
|  |  |  |  |  | 400 | 45.26 | 45.99 | -85 |
| Mitchell | Mark | USA | 22Apr67 | 182/75 | 100 | 10.27 | 10.4 | -85 |
| Mitchell | Ray | USA | 14Dec63 | 185/77 | LJ | 8.02w | 8.02w | -85 |
| Mitkus | Vitalius | SU | 65 |  | SP | 20.38 | 19.12 | -85 |
| Miyazaki | Hirofumi | JAP | 14Jul59 | 167/60 | 100 | 10.1w | 10.54 | -85 |
| Mizoguchi | Kazuhiro | JAP | 18Mar62 | 182/83 | JT | 81.90 | 85.56* | -85 |
| Moder | Matthias | GDR | 17Jun63 | 184/110 | HT | 80.30 | 80.92 | -85 |
| Modibedi | Edwin | RSA | 14Jun64 | 188/77 | 400 | 45.94 | 45.45 | -85 |
| Mogalle | Hans-Joachim | GDR | 28Aug59 | 185/65 | 800 | 1:45.24 | 1:44.93 | -82 |
| Mögenburg | Dietmar | FRG | 15Aug61 | 201/78 | HJ | 2.34i,2.30 | 2.39i-85,2.36 | -84 |
| Mohoanyane | Henry | LES | 11Aug63 |  | 400 | 45.72A | 46.4 | -85 |
| Mojzysz | Czeslaw | POL | 3Aug58 | 180/65 | St | 8:22.85 | 8:22.18 | -85 |
| Moloney | Tom | IRL | 11Mar60 | 183/70 | 1500 | 3:38.5 | 3:40.77 | -84 |
|  |  |  |  |  | Mile | 3:54.68 | 3:57.70 | -83 |
| Moneghetti | Steve | AUS | 26Sep62 | 176/60 | 10k | 28:20.95 | 28:56.0 | -84 |
|  |  |  |  |  | Mar | 2:11:18 | -0- |  |
| Mönkemeyer | Uwe | FRG | 22Sep59 | 183/70 | 1k | 2:18.76 | 2:19.80 | -82 |
|  |  |  |  |  | 1500 | 3:35.26 | 3:36.95 | -84 |
|  |  |  |  |  | Mile | 3:56.84 | 3:56.84 | -84 |
|  |  |  |  |  | 5k | 13:21.14 | 13:27.05 | -84 |
| Monnerais | Eric | FRA | 4Apr65 | 190/84 | HJ | 2.24 | 2.22 | -85 |

| Name | | Nat | Yr | Ht/Wt | Event | 1986 Mark | Pre-1986 best |
|------|--|-----|-----|-------|-------|-----------|---------------|
| Monroe | Anthony | TRI | 18Oct64 | | 100 | 10.1, | 10.42, |
| | | | | | | 10.0Aw | 10.1,10.39w -85 |
| | | | | | 200 | 20.2Aw | |
| Montelatici | Marco | ITA | 25Aug53 | 188/126 | SP | 20.65i,19.44 | 20.90 -85 |
| Moorcroft | David | UK | 10Apr53 | 180/68 | Mile | 3:56.68 | 3:49.34 -82 |
| | | | | | 2k | 5:02.86 | 5:02.89 -82 |
| Moore | Randy | USA | 18Nov62 | 180/73 | 800 | 1:46.80 | 1:45.96 -85 |
| Moracho | Javier | SPA | 18Aug57 | 180/74 | 110h | 13.83 | 13.49,13.4 -85 |
| Morales | Luis | PR | 4Mar64 | 168/64 | 100 | 10.29,10.0 | 10.21,10.18w-83 |
| | | | | | 200 | 20.57 | 20.67,20.42w -84 |
| Moreira | Delfim | POR | 11Dec55 | 174/67 | Mar | 2:12:35 | 2:12:54 -82 |
| Morgan | Michael | AUS | 30Jul66 | 181/83 | LJ | 7.92,8.01w | 7.68 -85 |
| Morgan | Steve | JAM | 65 | 188/64 | 200 | 20.69 | 20.27w-85,20.93-84 |
| Moriniére | Claude | FRA | 10Jan60 | 177/74 | LJ | 8.00 | 7.89 -80 |
| Moriniére | Max | FRA | 16Feb64 | 183/78 | 100 | 10.32,10.25w, | 10.33 -85 |
| | | | | | | 10.1 | 10.32w -84 |
| Morozov | Aleksandr | SU | 63 | | PV | 5.50i | 5.30 -85 |
| Morozov | Andrey | SU | 14Jun60 | 185/78 | HJ | 2.33 | 2.28 -8 |
| Morrell | Tony | UK | 30May62 | 193/74 | 800 | 1:45.93 | 1:48.10 -85 |
| | | | | | 1k | 2:17.47 | 2:20.08 -82 |
| Morris | Devon | JAM | 22Jan61 | 180/75 | 400 | 45.07 | 45.25 -8 |
| Morris | Dirk | USA | 9Jan65 | 188/82 | 110h | 13.88, | 13.83, |
| | | | | | | 13.86w | 13.68w -85 |
| Morris | Ian | TRI | 30Nov61 | 173/64 | 200 | 20.76,20.46w | 20.6 -8 |
| | | | | | 400 | 45.02 | 45.38,45.1-8 |
| Morris | Mike | USA | 7May63 | 173/74 | 100 | 10.21, | 10.12, |
| | | | | | | 10.10w | 10.09w,9.9w-8 |
| | | | | | 200 | 20.68 | 20.52 -8 |
| Morris | Nathan | USA | 6Jun64 | 175/68 | St | 8:33.2 | 8:36.79 -8 |
| Morrow | Byron | USA | 13Nov65 | 175/73 | 100 | 10.31w | 10.40 -8 |
| Morton | Harold | USA | 16Jan64 | 188/81 | 110h | 13.59w | 14.41w -8 |
| Moses | Edwin | USA | 31Aug55 | 188/77 | 400h | 47.38 | 47.02 -8 |
| Moses | Greg | USA | 29Dec65 | 178/75 | 100 | 10.29 | 10.23 -8 |
| | | | | | 200 | 20.75 | 20.41 -8 |
| Moss | Charles | USA | 24Apr63 | 175/72 | 400h | 49.61 | 50.35 -8 |
| Motti | William | FRA | 25Jul64 | 199/92 | Dec | 8006 | 8306 -8 |
| Möttus | Aivo | SU | 21Oct61 | | LJ | 8.07w | 7.84 -8 |
| Moxey | Edmondo | USA | 14Oct66 | 178/70 | 100 | 10.0w | 10.4 -8 |
| Mozharovskiy | Vladimir | SU | 64 | | 110h | 13.6 | 14.0 -8 |
| Mtolo | Willie | RSA | 24Apr64 | | Mar | 2:08:15dh | 2:10:32dh-8 |
| Muders | Wolfgang | FRG | 5Nov57 | 194/91 | Dec | 7855 | 8065 -8 |
| Muge | Some | KEN | 59 | 174/60 | 10k | 27:44.53 | 28:30.07 -8 |
| Mulligan | Jerry | USA | 9Apr58 | 183/77 | PV | 5.45 | 5.50 -8 |
| Mulligan | Richard | IRL | 19Apr61 | | 10k | 28:29.93 | 29:08.9 -8 |
| Munakata | Hiroshi | JAP | 5Apr59 | 166/54 | Mar | 2:13:32 | |
| Munroe | Alrick | JAM | 13Nov60 | 178/74 | 100 | 10.26w,9.9w | 10.46 -8 |
| | | | | | 200 | 20.2w | 20.9 -8 |
| Murashov | Valeriy | SU | 64 | | DT | 61.34 | 58.30 -8 |
| Muravyev | Vladimir | SU | 30Sep59 | 178/75 | 100 | 10.20,10.19dwr | 10.22 -8 |
| Murawa | Klaus-Jörg | GDR | 5Jun64 | 190/90 | JT | 78.96 | 89.86* -8 |
| Muraya | Josphat | KEN | 25Dec57 | 168/57 | 1500 | 3:39.39 | 3:37.49 -8 |
| Murphy | Miles | AUS | 19May67 | 185/75 | 200 | 20.76 | 20.93 -8 |
| | | | | | 400 | 45.64 | 46.20 -8 |
| Musiyenko | Nikolay | SU | 16Dec59 | 183/79 | TJ | 17.78 | 17.26 -8 |
| Mustapic | Ivan | YUG | 9Jul66 | 195/105 | JT | 75.38 | 77.96* -8 |
| Muster | Jean-Marc | SWZ | 1Nov61 | 188/75 | 110h | 13.85 | 13.74 -8 |
| Musyoki | Mike | KEN | 28May56 | 168/54 | 10k | 27:55.6 | 27:41.92 -7 |
| | | | | | Mar | 2:10:30 | 2:17:36 -8 |
| Muzzio | Rob | USA | 25Jun64 | 188/86 | Dec | 7747w | 8205 -8 |
| Myburgh | Ludwig | RSA | 26Apr62 | 182/74 | 400 | 45.53A | 45.11A -8 |
| | | | | | | | 45.62 -8 |
| Myers | Dub | USA | 4Apr64 | 183/70 | Mile | 3:55.31 | 3:57.06 -8 |

| ame | | Nat | Yr | Ht/Wt | Event | 1986 Mark | Pre-1986 best | |
|---|---|---|---|---|---|---|---|---|
| Myricks | Larry | USA | 10Mar56 | 186/82 | 100 | 10.31 | 10.31 | -83 |
| | | | | | LJ | 8.50 | 8.64Aw-83,8.59 | -84 |
| Myshkin | Yuriy | SU | 21Apr63 | 182/75 | 110h | 13.67dw | 13.89,13.4 | -85 |
| Nabein | Klaus-Peter | FRG | 10May60 | 186/75 | 800 | 1:46.99 | 1:46.03 | -82 |
| | | | | | 1500 | 3:35.98 | 3:36.24 | -83 |
| | | | | | Mile | 3:54.11 | | |
| Nagel | Gerd | FRG | 22Oct57 | 188/74 | HJ | 2.30i,2.30 | 2.31 | -81 |
| Nagy | István | HUN | 28Apr59 | 176/70 | 200 | 20.61 | 20.43w-85,20.62 | -82 |
| Nakaya | Katshuiko | BRA | 22Apr57 | 178/70 | 100 | 10.1A | 10.25,10.1 | -83 |
| | | | | | | | 10.1A | -79 |
| Nakajima | Shūzō | JAP | 11Jan61 | 171/54 | Mar | 2:13:17 | | |
| Nakayama | Takeyuki | JAP | 20Dec59 | 179/56 | 10k | 28:07.0 | 28:26.9 | -85 |
| | | | | | Mar | 2:08:21 | 2:08:15 | -85 |
| Nakkim | Are | NOR | 13Feb64 | 181/66 | 10k | 28:21.92 | 29:44.18 | -84 |
| | | | | | St | 8:28.20 | 8:38.70 | -85 |
| Nandapi | Paul | AUS | 21Dec61 | 185/109 | DT | 61.34 | 61.86 | -85 |
| Naumann | Jörg | GDR | 2Jan63 | 182/75 | 110h | 13.69w | 13.65-85,13.6 | -82 |
| Navara | Richard | CS | 13Jan64 | 194/120 | SP | 20.02i,19.89 | 19.80 | -85 |
| Nazarov | Andrey | SU | 9Jan65 | 190/80 | Dec | 8001 | 7269 | -85 |
| Neal | Greg | USA | 22Jan63 | 188/75 | LJ | 7.90i | 7.89 | -82 |
| Nehemiah | Renaldo | USA | 24Mar59 | 185/78 | 110h | 13.48 | 12.93 | -81 |
| | | | | | | | 12.8,12.91w | -79 |
| Nelson | Carey | CAN | 4Jun63 | 179/64 | 2k | 5:06.96 | | |
| | | | | | 3k | 7:48.04 | 8:06.2 | -84 |
| | | | | | 5k | 13:33.58 | 13:40.4 | -85 |
| Nelson | David | UK | 11Mar67 | 188/76 | 110h | 13.82 | 14.42,14.19w | -85 |
| Nemeth | Gyula | HUN | 26Sep59 | 184/71 | HJ | 2.25 | 2.24 | -80 |
| Nemeth | László | HUN | 14Apr60 | 190/100 | DT | 61.02 | 61.66 | -85 |
| Nemeth | Robert | AUT | 5Jun58 | 189/70 | 1500 | 3:39.06 | 3:35.80 | -84 |
| Nenow | Mark | USA | 16Nov57 | 172/57 | 5k | 13:21.33 | 13:18.54 | -84 |
| | | | | | 10k | 27:20.56 | 27:36.7 | -82 |
| Neugebauer | Michael | FRG | 7Apr62 | 188/77 | Dec | 8112 | 8062 | -85 |
| Neuhoff | Wolfgang | FRG | 8Jul58 | 189/74 | HJ | 2.24i,2.24 | 2.23 | -82 |
| Nevskiy | Aleksandr | SU | 21Feb58 | 190/88 | Dec | 8143 | 8491 | -84 |
| Newbold | Mike | BAH | 4Jan67 | 178/70 | 200 | 20.78 | | |
| Nobeni | Peter | RSA | 23May62 | 176/72 | 200 | 20.69A | 20.39A,20.3A | -85 |
| Nugi | John | KEN | 62 | 178/62 | 2k | 5:06.50 | | |
| | | | | | 3k | 7:49.35 | 8:08.2 | -85 |
| | | | | | 5k | 13:29.0 | 13:18.99 | -85 |
| Nang | Babacar | SEN | 9Sep58 | 178/63 | 800 | 1:44.70 | 1:45.30 | -83 |
| | | | | | 1k | 2:18.14 | 2:18.06 | -83 |
| Nemczak -# | Antoni | POL | 17Nov55 | 176/68 | Mar | 2:10:34 | 2:12:17 | -84 |
| Njboer | Gerard | HOL | 18Aug55 | 182/70 | Mar | 2:12:46 | 2:09:01 | -80 |
| Nikitin | Aleksey | SU | 58 | | PV | 5.65 | 5.50 | -85 |
| Niklaus | Stephan | SWZ | 17Apr58 | 189/90 | Dec | 7686 | 8334 | -83 |
| Nikolov | Nikolay | BUL | 15Oct64 | 182/78 | PV | 5.65 | 5.50 | -85 |
| Nikulin | Boris | SU | 7Apr60 | | 100 | 10.36,10.1, | 10.32, | |
| | | | | | | 10.33dwr | 10.0 | -84 |
| Nikulin | Igor | SU | 14Aug60 | 192/118 | HT | 82.34 | 83.54 | -82 |
| Nilsen | Lars Arvid | NOR | 15Apr65 | 190/105 | SP | 21.22 | 19.13 | -85 |
| Nilsson | Lars-Erik | SWE | 1Feb61 | 175/60 | 5k | 13:33.98 | 13:44.43 | -84 |
| | | | | | 10k | 27:58.70 | 28:09.22 | -84 |
| Nishi | Masayuki | JAP | 25Jan64 | 166/54 | Mar | 2:11:10 | | |
| Nishimoto | Kazuya | JAP | 2Jun62 | 170/53 | 10k | 28:09.4 | | |
| Nisula | Kari | FIN | 9Sep63 | 195/100 | DT | 61.62 | 59.92 | -85 |
| Nix | Sunder | USA | 2Dec61 | 175/65 | 400 | 44.84 | 44.68 | -82 |
| Noji | Rick | USA | 22Oct67 | 173/54 | HJ | 2.26 | 2.25 | -84 |
| Nordquist | Doug | USA | 20Dec58 | 193/79 | HJ | 2.34 | 2.31 | -84 |
| Novikov | Sergey | SU | 22Jun63 | 184/75 | 110h | 13.63dwr | 14.17,13.8 | -85 |
| Novikov | Yuriy | SU | 23Apr58 | | JT | 75.92 | 86.06* | -85 |

| Name | | Nat | Yr | Ht/Wt | Event | 1986 Mark | Pre-1986 best | |
|------|------|-----|-----|-------|-------|-----------|---------------|---|
| Nunez | Juan | DOM | 19Nov59 | 178/73 | 100 | 10.31 | 10.16,10.14dq | -8 |
| | | | | | 200 | 20.79 | 20.75-81,20.5 | -8 |
| Nyambui | Suleiman | TAN | 13Feb53 | 182/68 | 2k | 5:05.78 | 4:59.71 | -7 |
| | | | | | 3k | 7:47.39 | 7:40.3 | -7 |
| | | | | | 5k | 13:34.7 | 13:12.29 | -7 |
| Nyberg | Thomas | SWE | 17Apr62 | 195/84 | 400h | 50.36 | 50.34 | -8 |
| Nylander | Sven | SWE | 1Jan62 | 193/85 | 110h | 13.73w | 14.07,13.99w | -8 |
| | | | | | 400h | 48.83 | 48.88 | -8 |
| Nzimande | Tsanakile | RSA | 19Nov61 | | 100 | 10.36A | 10.61A | -8 |
| | | | | | 200 | 20.74A | 21.32A | -8 |
| Oakes | Gary | UK | 21Sep58 | 178/69 | 400h | 50.20 | 49.11 | -8 |
| Obeng | Ernest | UK | 8Apr56 | 167/60 | 100 | 10.22w | 10.21 | -8 |
| | | | | | | | 10.1,10.20w | -7 |
| Obizhayev | Aleksandr | SU | 16Sep59 | 185/85 | PV | 5.72 | 5.74i-83,5.71 | -8 |
| O'Brien | Liam | IRL | 11Oct54 | 179/66 | St | 8:33.26 | 8:27.24 | -8 |
| Obukhov | Vladimir | SU | 59 | | Dec | 7966 | 7435 | -8 |
| Obwocha | Samson | KEN | 54 | | St | 8:14.17 | 8:38.86 | -8 |
| O'Connor | Derek | IRL | 14Jun65 | 192/80 | 400 | 45.73 | -0- | |
| Odenthal | Marc | FRG | 19Feb63 | 194/110 | HT | 76.14 | 76.70 | -8 |
| Odgers | Steve | USA | 9Nov61 | 183/79 | Dec | 7991w | 7575w | -8 |
| Oerter | Al | USA | 19Sep36 | 193/125 | DT | 62.40 | 69.46 | -8 |
| Oganyan | Vadim | SU | 9Apr63 | 185/74 | HJ | 2.31i,2.29 | 2.30 | -8 |
| Ogidi | Daniel | NIG | 9Aug63 | 175/72 | 400h | 50.30,50.2 | 49.51 | -8 |
| Ohmori | Shigenobu | JAP | 9Jul60 | 184/72 | 400h | 50.19 | 49.74 | -8 |
| Ohsuda | Yichiro | JAP | 26Oct61 | 168/51 | Mar | 2:11:19 | | |
| Okash | Ibrahim | SOM | 18Sep64 | 180/65 | 800 | 1:46.70 | 1:46.54 | -8 |
| Okon | Gabriel | NIG | 66 | | 100 | 10.14Aw, | 10.68 | -8 |
| | | | | | | 10.1Aw | 10.2 | -8 |
| | | | | | 200 | 20.67Aw, | 20.9 | -8 |
| | | | | | | 20.5A,20.1Aw | | |
| Okoye | Christian | NIG | 61 | | DT | 63.06 | 64.72 | -8 |
| Olander | Mikael | SWE | 11Jun63 | 188/89 | Dec | 7888 | 7570W | -5 |
| Olbrich | Harald | FRG | 3Feb59 | | 1500 | 3:39.80 | 3:38.71 | -8 |
| Oldfield | Brian | USA | 1Jun45 | 196/125 | SP | 20.63 | 22.86 | - |
| Olivan | Jesus | SPA | 9Jul68 | 188/77 | LJ | 8.00i | 7.71 | - |
| Olivier | Willie | RSA | 27Sep58 | 192/88 | TJ | 16.70Aw | 16.77w,16.49A | - |
| Olson | Billy | USA | 19Jul58 | 188/73 | PV | 5.93i, | 5.86i | - |
| | | | | | | 5.50 | 5.72 | - |
| Olsson | Ronny | SWE | 10ct61 | 185/68 | 800 | 1:46.88 | 1:46.28 | - |
| | | | | | 1500 | 3:39.66 | 3:44.76 | - |
| O'Mara | Frank | IRL | 17Jul61 | 176/61 | 1500 | 3:35.04 | 3:34.02 | - |
| | | | | | Mile | 3:51.06 | 3:52.50 | - |
| | | | | | 3k | 7:49.61 | 7:46.54 | - |
| | | | | | 5k | 13:24.70 | 14:04.02 | - |
| Ono | Akira | JAP | 2Jan60 | 170/54 | Mar | 2:13:00 | | |
| Oosthuizen | Wessel | RSA | 23Feb61 | 184/75 | 100 | 10.15A | 10.29A,10.35- | |
| | | | | | | | 10.1A,10.16Aw- | |
| | | | | | 200 | 20.34A | 20.41A,20.68, | |
| | | | | | | | 20.1A | - |
| O'Reilly | Gerry | IRL | 1Jul64 | 188/70 | 1500 | 3:38.45 | 3:44.65 | - |
| | | | | | Mile | 3:54.63 | 4:02.66 | - |
| O'Reilly | Mike | IRL | 23Apr58 | | Mar | 2:13:19 | 2:15:54 | - |
| Ortiz | Juan | CUB | 23Aug64 | 175/68 | LJ | 8.14 | 8.04 | - |
| O'Rourke | Mike | NZ | 21Aug55 | 190/100 | JT | 83.70* | 90.58* | - |
| Oschkenat | Andreas | GDR | 9Jun62 | 191/82 | 110h | 13.52 | 13.50 | - |
| Ostrowski | Ryszard | POL | 6Feb61 | 176/62 | 800 | 1:45.14 | 1:44.38 | - |
| O'Sullivan | Marcus | IRL | 22Dec61 | 175/60 | 1500 | 3:35.76 | 3:37.20 | - |
| | | | | | Mile | 3:53.55 | 3:52.64 | - |
| | | | | | 3k | 7:50.09 | 8:02.6 | - |
| | | | | | 5k | 13:29.21 | 13:33.0 | - |
| Ottey | Milton | CAN | 29Dec59 | 178/66 | HJ | 2.33 | 2.32 | - |

| Name | | Nat | Yr | Ht/Wt | Event | 1986 Mark | Pre-1986 best | |
|------|--|-----|-----|-------|-------|-----------|---------------|--|
| Ottley | David | UK | 5Aug55 | 188/95 | JT | 80.62 | 90.70* | -85 |
| Ovett | Steve | UK | 9Oct55 | 183/70 | 1500 | 3:33.78 | 3:30.77 | -83 |
| | | | | | Mile | 3:52.99 | 3:48.40 | -81 |
| | | | | | 2k | 5:01.47 | 4:57.71 | -82 |
| | | | | | 3k | 7:50.01 | 7:41.3 | -77 |
| | | | | | 5k | 13:20.06 | 13:25.0 | -77 |
| Ovington | Neil | UK | 26Jan63 | | Mile | 3:57.07 | 4:04.6 | -85 |
| Ovsyannikov | Yevgeniy | SU | 10Jul63 | 183/85 | Dec | 8114 | 8069 | -84 |
| Ozolins | Alan | AUS | 1Feb64 | 182/74 | 800 | 1:46.90 | 1:47.30 | -85 |
| Pacheco | Francisco | MEX | 10Oct61 | 168/51 | 5k | 13:32.65 | 13:46.9 | -85 |
| | | | | | 10k | 27:56.0 | 28:21.8 | -84 |
| Pachin | Sergey | SU | 24May68 | 190/90 | DT | 61.34 | 54.06 | -85 |
| Padilla | Doug | USA | 4Oct56 | 176/60 | 1500 | 3:38.81 | 3:37.95 | -83 |
| | | | | | 3kSt | 7:46.87 | 7:35.84 | -83 |
| | | | | | 5k | 13:32.64i | 13:15.44 | -85 |
| Page | Nat | USA | 26Jan57 | 193/81 | 400h | 49.21 | 49.47 | -85 |
| Pahker | Tiit | SU | 22Dec58 | 190/85 | Dec | 7945 | 7976 | -82 |
| Paklin | Igor | SU | 15Jun63 | 193/71 | HJ | 2.38 | 2.41 | -85 |
| Palchikov | Igor | SU | 61 | | SP | 19.43i | 20.25 | -84 |
| Pallonen | Kimmo | FIN | 17Jan59 | 190/81 | PV | 5.50 | 5.56 | -82 |
| Pálóczi | Gyula | HUN | 13Sep62 | 185/67 | LJ | 8.02 | 8.25 | -85 |
| Palomba | Gian Piero | ITA | 13Aug63 | 191/64 | HJ | 2.24i | 2.23i | -85 |
| Panetta | Francesco | ITA | 10Jan63 | 175/64 | 3kSt | 7:50.19 | 7:49.90 | -85 |
| | | | | | 10k | 27:51.05 | 27:44.65 | -85 |
| | | | | | St | 8:16.85 | 8:21.60 | -85 |
| Pang | Yan | CHN | 15Jan63 | 185/70 | LJ | 7.92 | 7.99 | -84 |
| Pannier | Raymond | FRA | 12Feb61 | 174/63 | 3kSt | 7:48.20 | 7:54.15 | -85 |
| | | | | | St | 8:18.82 | 8:22.36 | -85 |
| Panov | Viktor | SU | 16Feb60 | | 100 | 10.35 | 10.1-85,10.51 | -84 |
| Paragi | Ferenc | HUN | 21Aug53 | 179/104 | JT | 77.32 | 96.72* | -80 |
| Parker | Andrew | JAM | 11Jan65 | 190/77 | 110h | 13.67,13.5 | 13.93w | -84 |
| Parlui | Ivan | SU | 19Apr51 | 182/63 | 10k | 28:31.29 | 28:00.47 | -76 |
| Parnov | Aleksandr | SU | 10May59 | 187/69 | PV | 5.50i,5.50 | 5.82 | -85 |
| Parsons | Geoff | UK | 14Aug64 | 203/75 | HJ | 2.30i,2.28 | 2.26 | -84 |
| Parygin | Igor | SU | 3Feb67 | 187/73 | TJ | 16.97 | 14.29 | -84 |
| Pascoe | Jeff | USA | 24May64 | 188/77 | PV | 5.50 | 5.18 | -85 |
| Paskalev | Anton | BUL | 6Nov58 | 185/74 | PV | 5.50 | 5.60 | -84 |
| Passey | Adrian | UK | 2Sep64 | 178/64 | 1500 | 3:39.01 | 3:45.4 | -85 |
| Pastusinski | Jacek | POL | 8Sep64 | 200/90 | TJ | 17.11 | 17.09 | -85 |
| Patelka | Bogdan | POL | 12Jun66 | 182/74 | JT | 75.86 | 79.10* | -85 |
| Patrick | David | USA | 12Jun60 | 183/72 | 400h | 48.59 | 48.05 | -83 |
| Patterson | Reinaldo | CUB | 7Feb56 | 178/84 | JT | 81.00* | 84.64* | -84 |
| Patterson | Steve | USA | 26Feb63 | 180/76 | 400h | 50.37A | 51.05 | -84 |
| Paul | Mike | TRI | 28Mar57 | 185/77 | 400 | 45.91 | 44.88 | -82 |
| Paumen | Jean-Pierre | BEL | 16Dec56 | | Mar | 2:13:12 | -0- | |
| Pavlov | Igor | SU | 4Sep60 | | St | 8:30.87 | 8:34.25 | -84 |
| Pavó | Agustín | CUB | 28May62 | 178/67 | 400 | 45.98 | 45.71 | -82 |
| Pavoni | Pier-Francesco | ITA | 21Feb63 | 182/70 | 100 | 10.22 | 10.25 | -82 |
| | | | | | 200 | 20.71 | 20.49 | -83 |
| Payne | Graham | UK | 10Sep57 | | 10k | 28:27.01 | 28:44.4 | -84 |
| Peach | Nick | UK | 18Oct59 | 178/64 | St | 8:33.89 | 8:46.97 | -85 |
| Peacock | Tyke | USA | 24Feb61 | 188/78 | HJ | 2.24 | 2.33 | -83 |
| Pedersen | Arne | NOR | 19Apr61 | 191/115 | SP | 20.24 | 19.28 | -85 |
| Pedersen | Kenneth | DEN | 18Dec65 | 188/98 | JT | 75.88 | 81.28* | -85 |
| Peebles | Danny | USA | 30May66 | 180/76 | 200 | 20.56 | 20.55 | -85 |
| Peev | Evgeni | BUL | 25Feb65 | 197/79 | HJ | 2.23 | 2.25 | -83 |
| Peev | Stoyan | BUL | 12May65 | 190/78 | PV | 5.50 | | |
| Peltoniemi | Asko | FIN | 7Feb63 | 182/70 | PV | 5.60 | 5.60 | -85 |
| Pelzer | Torsten | GDR | 26Jun63 | 198/120 | SP | 20.58 | 20.39 | -84 |
| Peñalver | Leandro | CUB | 23May61 | 175/71 | 100 | 10.23 | 10.06 | -83 |
| | | | | | 200 | 20.53 | 20.42,20.3 | -82 |

| Name | | Nat | Yr | Ht/Wt | Event | 1986 Mark | Pre-1986 best | |
|---|---|---|---|---|---|---|---|---|
| Penchev | Stanimir | BUL | 19Feb59 | 181/72 | PV | 5.70 | 5.61 | -8' |
| Perevdentsev | Igor | SU | 4Jan64 | 187/77 | 110h | 13.47,13.4 | 13.87,13.6 | -84 |
| Perry | Chris | AUS | 21Feb59 | 180/79 | 100 | 10.34,10.29 | 10.3 | -8! |
| Perzyło | Piotr | POL | 15Nov61 | | SP | 20.23 | 18.51 | -8! |
| Petersen | Pat | USA | 3Dec59 | 183/67 | Mar | 2:12:56 | 2:11:23 | -8! |
| Petersson | Jens | GDR | 8Sep64 | 196/92 | Dec | 8060 | 7710 | -8! |
| Petkov | Ivan | BUL | 15Feb60 | 182/95 | HT | 73.90 | 75.38 | -84 |
| Petranoff | Tom | USA | 8Apr58 | 186/98 | JT | 85.38,92.38* | 99.72* | -8. |
| Petrashkevich | Nikolay | SU | 3Aug62 | 187/88 | Dec | 7727 | 7661 | -8! |
| Petrashko | Maris | SU | 6Mar61 | 186/100 | SP | 20.46 | 19.37 | -8 |
| Petrosyan | Grigoriy | SU | 21Feb58 | 168/66 | LJ | 8.29 | 7.99 | -84 |
| Petrov | German | SU | 26Mar67 | 184/70 | 400h | 50.3 | 52.35 | -8 |
| Petrov | Yuriy | SU | 10Aug63 | | 100 | 10.36dwr | 10.48,10.2 | -8 |
| Pfitzinger | Pete | USA | 29Aug57 | 174/60 | Mar | 2:13:29 | 2:11:43 | -8 |
| Phillips | Andre | USA | 5Sep59 | 188/81 | 200 | 20.55 | 21.2* | -8 |
| | | | | | 400 | 44.71 | 45.17 | -8 |
| | | | | | 400h | 47.51 | 47.67 | -8 |
| Pienaar | Hannes | RSA | 23Aug60 | 183/78 | 400h | 48.81A, | 49.32A | -8 |
| | | | | | | 49.27 | 49.62 | -8 |
| Pierce | Jack | USA | 23Sep62 | 185/75 | 110h | 13.55, | 13.36 | -8 |
| | | | | | | 13.53w,13.4 | | |
| Pierzynska | Zbigniew | POL | 21Oct51 | 171/61 | Mar | 2:12:21 | 2:12:53 | -8 |
| Pietz | Christoph | GDR | 15Jul64 | 185/80 | PV | 5.50 | 5.42i,5.40 | -8 |
| Pildavs | Normunds | SU | 12Apr64 | 178/79 | JT | 79.74 | 79.02* | -8 |
| Pimazzoni | Loris | ITA | 6Jul56 | | Mar | 2:13:10 | 2:16:56 | -8 |
| Pingpank | Marcus | RSA | 5Feb64 | | 2k | 5:06.10i | 5:07.80 | -8 |
| Pishchalnikov | Vitaliy | SU | 1Apr58 | 198/110 | DT | 65.00 | 67.76 | -8 |
| Piskunov | Eduard | SU | 67 | | HT | 75.10 | 69.56 | -8 |
| Pittman | Rickey | USA | 4Oct61 | 175/61 | St | 8:32.35 | 8:23.66 | -8 |
| Pizzolato | Orlando | ITA | 30Jul58 | 179/61 | Mar | 2:10:57 | 2:10:23 | -8 |
| Plasencia | Steve | USA | 28Oct56 | 178/64 | 5k | 13:22.90 | 13:19.37 | -8 |
| | | | | | 10k | 27:51.70 | 27:58.56 | -8 |
| Plasso | Frank | USA | 15Jun60 | 175/61 | Mar | 2:12:37 | 2:13:38 | -8 |
| Płatek | Krzysztof | POL | 13Jan62 | 187/75 | 110h | 13.74, | 13.91,13.83w | -8 |
| | | | | | | 13.73w | 13.7w | -8 |
| Plaziat | Christian | FRA | 28Oct63 | 190/83 | Dec | 8196 | 8211w | -8 |
| Plekhanov | Vladimir | SU | 11Apr58 | 185/80 | TJ | 17.21i,17.0 | 17.60 | -8 |
| Ploghaus | Klaus | FRG | 31Jan56 | 186/110 | HT | 81.32 | 80.56 | -8 |
| Plunge | Donatas | SU | 11Nov60 | 195/118 | HT | 79.66 | 79.08 | -8 |
| Podchainyiy | Sergey | SU | 4Jan63 | | LJ | 8.03 | 7.81 | -8 |
| Podmaryov | Igor | SU | 8Dec61 | 182/74 | 110h | 13.48dwr | 13.95 | -8 |
| | | | | | | | 13.7 | -8 |
| Podmaryov | Vadim | SU | 4Sep58 | 180/80 | Dec | 7769 | 8366 | -8 |
| Podsiadło | Wojciech | POL | 22Apr58 | 188/84 | Dec | 7950 | 7987 | -8 |
| Poelman | Simon | NZ | 27May63 | 187/91 | Dec | 8158 | 7854 | -8 |
| Pogoreliy | Andrey | SU | 59 | | PV | 5.65 | 5.65i,5.65 | -8 |
| Pogrebnyuk | Sergey | SU | 29Mar61 | 185/85 | Dec | 7749 | 7599 | -8 |
| Pohland | Holger | GDR | 5Apr63 | 182/78 | 110h | 13.40 | 13.47 | -8 |
| Pokusayev | Aleksandr | SU | 30Apr60 | 181/77 | TJ | 17.13 | 17.21 | -8 |
| Polewany | Marek | POL | 1Jan61 | 193/115 | DT | 61.02 | 60.92 | -8 |
| Poli | Giovanni | ITA | 5Nov57 | 180/68 | Mar | 2:11:06 | 2:09:57 | -8 |
| Polishko | Vladimir | SU | 12Jun59 | 180/80 | JT | 76.94 | 81.92* | -8 |
| Polk | Damon | USA | 17Jun65 | 183/75 | 110h | 13.87 | 13.94-85,13.72w | -8 |
| Polyakov | Vladimir | SU | 17Apr60 | 190/75 | PV | 5.65 | 5.81 | -8 |
| Pomashki | Georgi | BUL | 10Jan60 | 190/80 | TJ | 16.99 | 16.94 | -8 |
| Ponomaryev | Andrey | SU | 28Jan64 | | 800 | 1:46.82 | | |
| Popescu | Eugen | RUM | 12Aug62 | 194/78 | HJ | 2.31 | 2.26 | -8 |
| Popov | Sergey | SU | 2Dec57 | 191/85 | Dec | 8079 | 8217 | -8 |
| Popov | Vladimir | SU | 65 | | TJ | 16.50i | | |
| Popov | Vladislav | SU | 12Jun62 | | DT | 64.24 | 61.32 | -8 |
| Popović | Slobodan | YUG | 28Sep62 | 178/66 | 800 | 1:47.12 | 1:46.09 | -8 |
| Populyakh | Vasiliy | SU | 64 | | HT | 72.02 | | |

| ame | | Nat | Yr | | Ht/Wt | Event | 1986 Mark | Pre-1986 best | |
|---|---|---|---|---|---|---|---|---|---|
| ²orotov | Yuriy | SU | 9Nov50 | | | Mar | 2:13:27 | 2:14:11 | -80 |
| ²orter | Pat | USA | 31May59 | | 183/60 | 10k | 27:57.3 | 27:49.5 | -84 |
| ²otapenko | Vladimir | SU | 7Mar61 | | 190/78 | LJ | 8.07 | 8.14 | -85 |
| ²otapov | Sergey | SU | 15Jul62 | | 193/90 | Dec | 7703 | 7701 | -84 |
| ²otapovich | Igor | SU | 6Sep67 | | 185/79 | PV | 5.50 | 5.20 | -85 |
| ²ovarnitsin | Rudolf | SU | 12Jul62 | | 201/75 | HJ | 2.30 | 2.40 | -85 |
| ²owell | Charles | USA | 18Nov64 | | 185/79 | 400h | 49.50 | 51.38 | -84 |
| ²owell | Jeff | USA | 27May63 | | 178/79 | 110h | 13.86 | 13.88w-85,13.90 | -84 |
| ²owell | John | USA | 25Jun47 | | 188/110 | DT | 65.94 | 71.26 | -84 |
| ²owell | Mike | USA | 10Nov63 | | 190/75 | LJ | 8.04,8.22w | 8.17,8.28w | -85 |
| ²rado | Julio | CUB | 27Jul60 | | 191/71 | 400h | 50.11 | 49.61 | -84 |
| ²radzyński | Czeslaw | POL | 24Aug60 | | 177/75 | 100 | 10.32 | 10.50,10.32w | -84 |
| | | | | | | 200 | 20.72 | 20.70-84,20.5 | -83 |
| radzyński | Krzysztof | POL | 6Apr58 | | 181/66 | 1500 | 3:38.79 | 3:38.85 | -84 |
| renzler | Olaf | GDR | 24Aug58 | | 182/77 | 200 | 20.58 | 20.46-82,20.39w | -79 |
| reysing | Andre | GDR | 6Oct66 | | 189/80 | Dec | 7802 | 7538 | -85 |
| riáñon | Jean-Louis | FRA | 22Feb60 | | 176/58 | 5k | 13:28.7 | 13:33.77 | -85 |
| | | | | | | 10k | 27:52.48 | 28:06.02 | -85 |
| rokofyev | Andrey | SU | 6Jun59 | | 187/83 | 110h | 13.28 | 13.3-79,13.46 | -82 |
| rosin | Vladimir | SU | 15Aug59 | | 186/75 | 400 | 45.94 | 45.47 | -84 |
| rotsenko | Oleg | SU | 11Aug63 | | 191/82 | LJ | 8.00i | 7.35,7.74w | -82 |
| | | | | | | TJ | 17.59 | 17.69 | -85 |
| russ | Boris | SU | 9Feb58 | | 182/72 | St | 8:33.06 | 8:24.8 | -82 |
| ryalov | Mikhail | SU | 63 | | | HT | 73.14 | | |
| sujek | Bogusław | POL | 22Nov56 | | 182/69 | 5k | 13:35.49 | 13:38.65 | -85 |
| | | | | | | 10k | 28:28.53 | 28:42.63 | -85 |
| | | | | | | Mar | 2:11:03 | -0- | |
| táčník | František | CS | 27Feb62 | | 183/80 | 100 | 10.33 | 10.25 | -85 |
| ɹchkov | Aleksandr | SU | 30Apr60 | | 177/100 | HT | 78.08 | 77.28 | -84 |
| ɹdenz | Rüdiger | GDR | 22Dec66 | | 198/110 | DT | 62.42 | 58.74 | -85 |
| ɹgovkin | Aleksandr | SU | 28Sep64 | | 180/80 | 100 | 10.1,10.35dwr | 10.0 | -85 |
| ɹkownik | Eligiusz | POL | 30Jun62 | | 195/112 | DT | 62.02 | 64.34 | -85 |
| ɹrsley | Brad | USA | 24May60 | | 185/77 | PV | 5.70i,5.65 | 5.75 | -83 |
| ɹpchonok | Igor | SU | 61 | | | Dec | 8021m | 7501 | -84 |
| ɹrvis | James | USA | 4Sep66 | | 190/88 | 110h | 13.71,13.53 | 13.74 | -85 |
| ɹśinaitis | Algis | SU | 15Feb57 | | 195/110 | SP | 20.01 | 20.71 | -84 |
| ɹuste | Heino | SU | 7Sep55 | | 188/90 | JT | 83.20 | 94.20* | -83 |
| ɹentrec | Yann | FRA | 17Feb62 | | 190/75 | 400 | 45.47 | 46.24 | -85 |
| ɹerol | Sergio | CUB | 12Apr65 | | 177/72 | 100 | 10.36 | 10.1,10.28 | -85 |
| | | | | | | 200 | 20.76 | 21.16,20.8 | -85 |
| ɹigley | Joe | AUS | 5Dec61 | | 187/110 | HT | 72.86 | 72.00 | -85 |
| ɹinn | Brendan | IRL | 26Jul60 | | 188/73 | St | 8:29.25 | 8:24.09 | -85 |
| ɹinn | James | USA | 30Sep63 | | 187/86 | 110h | 13.87, | 13.53 | -84 |
| | | | | | | | 13.83w | 13.5 | -85 |
| ɹinon | Pierre | FRA | 20Feb62 | | 180/74 | PV | 5.72i,5.70 | 5.90 | -85 |
| ɹintana | Dionisio | CUB | 9Oct57 | | 180/78 | JT | 76.22 | 83.32* | -81 |
| defeld | Norbert | FRG | 3Mar62 | | 192/96 | HT | 77.48 | 73.36 | -85 |
| dev | Venzislav | BUL | 9Jan61 | | 187/70 | 110h | 13.79 | 13.59,13.5 | -83 |
| dzey | Michael | FRG | 31Aug60 | | 194/77 | 110h | 13.84 | 13.77-85,13.7 | -83 |
| ni | Aivar | SU | 4Mar63 | | 177/102 | HT | 73.54 | 72.24 | -85 |
| hm | Claes | SWE | 18Feb64 | | 182/73 | TJ | 16.56, | 16.30 | -84 |
| | | | | | | | 16.64w | 16.59w | -83 |
| mbo | Tony | USA | 30May60 | | 175/78 | 400h | 49.72 | 48.16 | -84 |
| món | Domingo | SPA | 10Mar58 | | 162/57 | St | 8:30.77 | 8:15.74 | -80 |
| mos | Mike | USA | 1Nov62 | | 183/86 | Dec | 8322 | 8294 | -85 |
| mos | Roberto | CUB | 6Aug59 | | 198/75 | 400 | 45.91 | 45.84 | -83 |
| ngelov | Dimitar | BUL | 14Nov63 | | 181/68 | 400 | 45.91 | 46.08 | -84 |
| tushkov | Vladimir | SU | 1Jan65 | | 187/75 | LJ | 7.98 | 8.10 | -85 |
| ty | Seppo | FIN | 27Apr62 | | 186/81 | JT | 81.72 | 85.72* | -85 |

| Name | | Nat | Yr | Ht/Wt | Event | 1986 Mark | Pre-1986 best | |
|---|---|---|---|---|---|---|---|---|
| Razgonov | Nikolay | SU | 16Jan64 | 187/77 | 100 | 10.32dwr | 10.42 | -85 |
| | | | | | 200 | 20.62,20.5 | 21.10 | -85 |
| Razin | Andrey | SU | 10May62 | | 100 | 10.1 | 10.2-82,10.44 | -85 |
| Reading | Robert | USA | 9Jun67 | 193/88 | 110h | 13.83 | | |
| Redmond | Derek | UK | 3Sep65 | 183/67 | 400 | 45.25 | 44.82 | -85 |
| Redwine | Stanley | USA | 10Apr61 | 186/73 | 800 | 1:45.86 | 1:44.87 | -84 |
| Redzhepov | Geldy | SU | 62 | | 100 | 10.1 | 10.2,10.50 | -83 |
| Reed | Mark | USA | 22May65 | 190/76 | HJ | 2.26 | 2.24 | -85 |
| Reed | Sidney | USA | 28Mar65 | 193/83 | 110h | 13.87 | 14.55 | -85 |
| Reed | William | USA | 1Apr70 | 181/77 | 100 | 10.0 | | |
| | | | | | 200 | 20.5 | 21.38,21.33w | -85 |
| | | | | | 400 | 45.4 | 46.55 | -85 |
| Regalo | José | POR | 22Nov63 | 180/60 | 5k | 13:28.91 | 13:37.53 | -8* |
| | | | | | St | 8:21.41 | 8:32.10 | -8 |
| Regis | John | UK | 13Oct66 | 181/86 | 200 | 20.41 | 20.78 | -8* |
| Register | John | USA | 9Mar65 | 183/81 | 110h | 13.68w | 14.09 | -8 |
| Reichel | Jörg | FRG | 14Aug66 | | 400h | 49.98 | 51.39 | -84 |
| Reid | Eric | USA | 17Feb65 | 188/85 | 110h | 13.52 | 13.80w-85,14.01-8 | |
| Reid | Leroy | JAM | 3Aug63 | 187/77 | 200 | 20.56, | 20.62, | |
| | | | | | | 20.38w | 20.53w,20.4-8 | |
| Reid | Pat | USA | 65 | 190/136 | SP | 19.41i | 19.21 | -8 |
| Reifsnyder | Bill | USA | 30Apr62 | 173/59 | Mar | 2:13:14 | 2:14:39 | -8 |
| Reina | Randy | USA | 31Dec59 | 168/54 | 10k | 28:21.9 | 28:51.5 | -8 |
| Reinsons | Maris | SU | 27Jul64 | 188/78 | HJ | 2.24i | 2.22 | -8 |
| Reintak | Sven | SU | 17Jun63 | 195/87 | Dec | 8232m | 8176 | -8 |
| Reitz | Colin | UK | 6Apr60 | 186/73 | 3kSt | 7:46.15 | 7:44.40 | -8 |
| | | | | | St | 8:12.11 | 8:13.50 | -8 |
| Reka | Nikolay | SU | 12May63 | 183/81 | Dec | 7920 | 7707 | -8 |
| René-Corail | Alain | FRA | 21Apr62 | 186/70 | TJ | 16.59 | 16.73 | -8 |
| Renner | Peter | NZ | 27Oct59 | 186/75 | St | 8:20.16 | 8:14.05 | -8 |
| Repnikov | Pavel | SU | 26Jan64 | 184/86 | HT | 73.90 | 71.24 | -8 |
| Reshetnikov | Valeriy | SU | 25Mar59 | 180/100 | HT | 78.04 | 76.72 | -8 |
| Reski | Heiko | GDR | 22Aug63 | 191/77 | TJ | 16.52 | 16.08 | -8 |
| Reyna | Jorge | CUB | 10Jan63 | 179/68 | TJ | 17.18 | 17.05 | -8 |
| Reynolds | Butch | USA | 8Aug64 | 193/84 | 400 | 45.36 | 45.47 | -8 |
| Ribaud | Roberto | ITA | 30Jun61 | 175/65 | 400 | 45.69 | 45.96 | -8 |
| Richard | Antoine | FRA | 8Sep60 | 174/63 | 100 | 10.09 | 10.20 | -8 |
| Richards | Jon | UK | 19May64 | 173/57 | 10k | 28:14.08 | -0- | |
| Ridgeon | Jonathan | UK | 14Feb67 | 186/77 | 110h | 13.66 | 13.46 | -8 |
| Riecke | Hans-Ulrich | GDR | 3Oct63 | 192/90 | Dec | 8000 | 8181 | -8 |
| Rios | Elísio | POR | 3Apr61 | 167/58 | St | 8:35.05 | 8:34.75 | -8 |
| Rish | Chip | USA | 28Apr67 | 175/68 | 400 | 45.83 | 46.04,45.7 | -8 |
| Rizzi | Andreas | FRG | 6May59 | 183/86 | Dec | 7698 | 8326 | -8 |
| Roată | Nicu | RUM | 6Jul61 | 188/83 | JT | 79.58 | 85.86* | -8 |
| Robbins | Tommy | USA | | | 400h | 50.46 | 52.97 | -8 |
| Roberson | Jeff | USA | 12Aug64 | 190/74 | 800 | 1:46.1 | 1:50.02 | -8 |
| Robertson | Max | UK | 27Dec63 | 185/77 | 400h | 49.53 | 49.75 | -8 |
| Robinson | Albert | USA | 28Nov64 | 187/84 | 100 | 10.22 | 10.24,10.23w | -8 |
| | | | | | 200 | 20.53 | 20.07 | -8 |
| Robinson | Darrell | USA | 23Dec63 | 186/66 | 200 | 20.48 | 20.80, | |
| | | | | | | 20.41w | 20.74w | -8 |
| | | | | | 400 | 44.45 | 44.69 | -8 |
| Robinson | James | USA | 27Aug54 | 178/65 | 800 | 1:46.12 | 1:43.92 | -8 |
| | | | | | 1k | 2:17.81 | 2:16.3 | -8 |
| Robinson | Keith | USA | 29Apr64 | 188/84 | Dec | 7691 | 7638 | -8 |
| Robinson | Ken | USA | 15Jul63 | 176/70 | 100 | 10.1 | 10.27-82,10.24w | -8 |
| Robinson | Merrick | USA | 2Mar63 | 180/75 | 100 | 10.30w | 10.4 | -8 |
| Robinzine | Kevin | USA | 12Apr66 | 178/64 | 400 | 45.25 | 45.09 | -8 |
| Rodehau | Gunther | GDR | 6Jul59 | 179/113 | HT | 81.70 | 82.64 | -8 |
| Rodger | Kerry | NZ | 13Mar62 | 184/67 | 5k | 13:30.0 | | |
| Rodgers | Bill | USA | 23Dec47 | 175/60 | Mar | 2:13:36 | 2:09:27 | - |
| Rodriques | Kelly | USA | 13Sep63 | 180/77 | PV | 5.45 | 5.20 | - |

| me | | Nat | Yr | Ht/Wt | Event | 1986 Mark | Pre-1986 best | |
|---|---|---|---|---|---|---|---|---|
| oggy | Bob | USA | 6Aug56 | 194/109 | JT | 79.14 | 95.80* | -82 |
| omanov | Vladimir | SU | 25Sep61 | 183/88 | Dec | 7918m | 7784 | -85 |
| omdhani | Habib | TUN | 4Mar60 | | 10k | 28:27.14 | 28:38.71 | -85 |
| onkainen | Janne | FIN | 5Feb63 | 180/98 | SP | 20.21 | 19.50 | -85 |
| ose | Nick | UK | 30Dec51 | 174/60 | 5k | 13:29.12 | 13:18.91 | -84 |
| | | | | | 10k | 28:06.37 | 27:31.19 | -83 |
| oss | Richard | USA | | | 100 | 10.0w | | |
| ossi | Marco | ITA | 7Jul63 | 188/86 | Dec | 7696 | 7729 | -85 |
| ousseau | Vincent | BEL | 29Jul62 | 176/60 | 1500 | 3:38.70 | 3:36.38 | -85 |
| | | | | | 3kSt | 7:42.15 | 7:50.3 | -84 |
| | | | | | 5k | 13:15.01 | 13:18.94 | -85 |
| owe | Mark | USA | 28Jul60 | 192/79 | 400 | 45.87 | 44.87 | -85 |
| owland | Mark | UK | 7Mar63 | 183/72 | 1500 | 3:37.2 | 3:42.6 | -84 |
| | | | | | Mile | 3:52.99 | 4:00.16 | -85 |
| denik | Viktor | SU | 64 | | LJ | 7.90 | | |
| denko | Sergey | SU | 14Oct58 | | Mar | 2:13:05 | 2:14:36 | -84 |
| hkieck | Frank | GDR | 23Nov61 | 176/60 | St | 8:28.85 | 8:29.93 | -84 |
| iz | Alberto | SPA | 22Dec61 | 178/76 | PV | 5.61 | 5.60 | -85 |
| ssell | Kurt | USA | 28Jul63 | 188/69 | St | 8:29.66 | 8:43.62 | -85 |
| therford | Frank | BAH | 23Nov64 | 185/79 | TJ | 17.05 | 16.49 | -85 |
| ffel | Markus | SWZ | 5Feb55 | 167/55 | 5k | 13:16.28 | 13:07.54 | -84 |
| maryuk | Vasiliy | SU | 9Mar61 | 184/86 | HT | 72.70 | 73.04 | -85 |
| epakowski | Leszek | POL | 25Apr57 | 181/74 | 400h | 50.16 | 50.40 | -85 |
| alfrank | Rolf | FRG | 9Mar62 | | SP | 19.51 | 18.69 | -85 |
| borit | Juan | CUB | 6May56 | 185/74 | 110h | 13.81w | 13.78w, | |
| | | | | | | | 13.7,13.6w | -82 |
| cco | Fréderic | FRA | 22Aug61 | 185/88 | Dec | 7864 | 7857w-85,7704 | -84 |
| gdeyev | Albert | SU | 63 | | LJ | 7.91w | | |
| gedål | Jan | NOR | 19Jun60 | 189/107 | SP | 20.76 | 19.66 | -85 |
| hner | Christoph | FRG | 23Sep63 | 180/103 | HT | 80.38 | 81.56 | -85 |
| la | Carlos | SPA | 20Mar60 | 186/76 | 110h | 13.50 | 13.56 | -84 |
| | | | | | | | 13.4-85,13.55w | -83 |
| lazar | Jose | VEN | 12Sep57 | 182/67 | TJ | 16.56w | 16.54,16.85w | -85 |
| lbert | Ferenc | FRA | 5Aug60 | 190/80 | PV | 5.61 | 5.55 | -82 |
| lah | Ahmed | DJI | 56 | 180/54 | Mar | 2:09:57 | 2:08:09 | -85 |
| limov | Albert | SU | 62 | | 100 | 10.1 | | |
| lle | Fred | UK | 10Sep64 | 188/84 | LJ | 7.97 | 7.92w-85,7.73 | -84 |
| lzmann | Ralf | FRG | 6Feb55 | 172/58 | 10k | 28:14.21 | 28:11.49 | -85 |
| | | | | | Mar | 2:11:41 | 2:10:56 | -85 |
| n | Andreas | GDR | 5Feb60 | 186/81 | HJ | 2.30i,2.27 | 2.31 | -84 |
| marin | Yuriy | SU | 27Dec60 | 179/74 | LJ | 8.20 | 8.23,8.28w | -84 |
| nolyuk | Anatoliy | SU | 2Jul58 | 186/115 | SP | 19.94 | 19.60i,19.47 | -85 |
| nuels | Vernon | UK | 5Oct64 | 188/80 | TJ | 16.71 | 16.26 | -84 |
| chez | António | SPA | 22Sep63 | 181/72 | 400 | 45.41 | 45.54 | -85 |
| chez | Francisco | SPA | 18May58 | 175/64 | 3kSt | 8:19.44 | 8:16.59 | -83 |
| nders | Scott | USA | 2Sep67 | 183/77 | LJ | 8.00,8.06w | 7.55 | -85 |
| ds | Lyndon | BAH | 6Feb64 | 178/62 | LJ | 7.90,7.98w | 7.93 | -84 |
| g | Patrick | KEN | 11Apr64 | 175/64 | 3kSt | 8:31.1 | 8:22.45 | -84 |
| etchenkov | Viktor | SU | 18Apr65 | 182/70 | 800 | 1:46.68 | 1:49.9 | -84 |
| ačević | Zlatan | YUG | 27Jul56 | 196/145 | SP | 19.79 | 21.11 | -84 |
| ul | Edward | POL | 16Nov58 | 195/117 | SP | 20.74 | 21.68 | -83 |
| köi | Alfonz | HUN | 12Jun58 | 186/96 | DT | 61.08 | 63.24 | -84 |
| nders | Nick | BER | 14Sep63 | 188/75 | HJ | 2.26 | 2.30i,2.27 | -83 |
| ory | Graham | UK | 11Oct60 | 190/120 | DT | 60.92 | 56.90 | -84 |
| e | Tito | KEN | 61 | | 400 | 45.6A | 45.7A | -85 |
| icki | Wiktor | POL | 20May55 | 171/66 | Mar | 2:11:18 | 2:13:35 | -84 |
| re | John | USA | 25Mar61 | 190/88 | Dec | 8076 | 8381w | -85 |
| re | Ric | USA | 9Aug53 | 180/66 | Mar | 2:12:59 | 2:13:50 | -83 |
| mmell | Pat | AUS | 15Apr61 | 189/67 | 800 | 1:45.86 | 1:45.74 | -84 |
| | | | | | 1500 | 3:38.4 | 3:37.86 | -84 |
| | | | | | Mile | 3:57.46 | 3:55.2 | -85 |

| Name | | Nat | Yr | Ht/Wt | Event | 1986 Mark | Pre-1986 best | |
|---|---|---|---|---|---|---|---|---|
| Schaefer | Jörg | FRG | 17Jul59 | 198/116 | HT | 79.92 | 78.90 | -8 |
| Schäffner | Thomas | GDR | 3Aug63 | 191/88 | JT | 79.86 | 83.50* | -8 |
| Schersing | Mathias | GDR | 7Oct64 | 182/68 | 200 | 20.80 | 20.91 | -8 |
| | | | | | 400 | 44.85 | 44.86 | -8 |
| Scheytt | Michael | FRG | 16Jun59 | 181/59 | 10k | 28:15.68 | 28:18.55 | -8 |
| Schieber | Christian | FRG | 18Sep59 | | 3kSt | 8:32.87 | 8:33.82 | -8 |
| Schleder | Eloi | BRA | 26Jul51 | 176/64 | Mar | 2:12:54 | 2:13:08 | -8 |
| Schlegel | Sören | GDR | 28Dec60 | 180/76 | 100 | 10.27 | 10.20 | -8 |
| Schmid | Harald | FRG | 29Sep57 | 187/82 | 400 | 45.78 | 44.92 | -7 |
| | | | | | 400h | 47.89 | 47.48 | -8 |
| Schmidt | Gerhard | FRG | 12Jan61 | 183/70 | PV | 5.50i | 5.55i-83,5.52 | -8 |
| Schmidt | Helmar | FRG | 11Sep63 | 184/67 | PV | 5.50i | 5.35 | -8 |
| Schmitt | Uwe | FRG | 17Aug61 | 184/74 | 400h | 49.79 | 49.39 | -8 |
| Schmitz | Manfred | FRG | 13Mar60 | 197/110 | DT | 63.42 | 62.54 | -8 |
| Schneider-Laub | André | FRG | 12Aug58 | 194/76 | HJ | 2.24i,2.24 | 2.30 | -7 |
| Schnyder | Paul | AUS | 8Apr62 | | 800 | 1:47.05 | 1:46.86 | -8 |
| Schoeman | Kobus | RSA | 16Nov65 | | 110h | 13.82A, | 14.00, | |
| | | | | | | 13.66Aw,13.6A | 13.8 | -8 |
| Schönlebe | Thomas | GDR | 6Aug65 | 185/76 | 400 | 44.63 | 44.62 | -8 |
| Scholz | Peter | FRG | 31Oct59 | 184/75 | 400h | 49.52 | 49.45 | -8 |
| Schreiber | Peter | FRG | 9Aug64 | 195/90 | JT | 76.88 | 79.28* | -8 |
| Schröder | Thomas | GDR | 23Aug62 | 177/75 | 100 | 10.10 | 10.22-83,10.14w | -8 |
| | | | | | 200 | 20.54 | 20.56 | -8 |
| Schroeder | Ralf | RSA | 6Nov62 | | 110h | 13.74A | 13.78A, | |
| | | | | | | 13.76,13.60Aw | 13.5A | -8 |
| Schröfel | Stefan | FRG | 4Feb61 | 190/99 | SP | 19.66 | 19.33 | -8 |
| Schult | Jurgen | GDR | 11May60 | 193/110 | DT | 74.08 | 69.74 | -8 |
| Schulz | Volker | GDR | 8Jul64 | 178/82 | 100 | 10.32, | 10.50 | -8 |
| | | | | | | 10.31w | 10.47w | -8 |
| Schulze | Jens | FRG | 6Apr56 | 183/84 | Dec | 8032 | 8255 | -8 |
| Schumann | Ralph | GDR | 26May66 | 186/73 | 800 | 1:46.10 | 1:46.69 | -8 |
| Schwarz | Rainer | FRG | 5Jun59 | 181/63 | 3kSt | 8:20.90 | 8:11.93 | -8 |
| Schweisfurth | Dirk | FRG | 24Oct65 | 183/78 | 100 | 10.25 | 10.47,10.3- | 8 |
| Scott | Steve | USA | 5May56 | 186/73 | 1500 | 3:33.71 | 3:31.76 | -8 |
| | | | | | Mile | 3:48.73 | 3:47.69 | -8 |
| Scrutton | Mark | UK | 14Apr60 | 185/69 | 10k | 28:23.04 | 28:25.6 | -8 |
| Secchi | Fabrizio | ITA | 9Aug58 | 174/64 | LJ | 8.04 | 7.89 | - |
| Seck | Charles-L. | SEN | 11May65 | 167/70 | 100 | 10.19 | 10.1-85,10.36 | -8 |
| Sedykh | Yuriy | SU | 11Jun55 | 185/110 | HT | 86.74 | 86.34 | - |
| Seko | Toshihiko | JAP | 15Jul56 | 170/59 | 5k | 13:24.29 | 13:30.94 | - |
| | | | | | 10k | 27:45.45 | 27:42.17 | - |
| | | | | | Mar | 2:08:27 | 2:08:38 | - |
| Seleznyev | Aleksandr | SU | 64 | 180/100 | HT | 75.90 | 76.96 | - |
| Semiraz | Oleg | SU | 15Oct61 | 171/64 | LJ | 8.15 | 8.12 | - |
| Semykin | Konstantin | SU | 26May60 | 180/76 | LJ | 8.00 | 8.38 | - |
| Semyonov | Aleksandr | SU | 25Mar62 | | 100 | 10.32 | 10.34-84,10.3- | |
| Senior | Mark | JAM | 13Dec63 | 170/67 | 400 | 45.59 | 45.75 | - |
| Sennai | Isamu | JAP | 11Aug60 | 172/57 | Mar | 2:11:59 | 2:12:20 | - |
| Serebryanskiy | Sergey | SU | 14Dec62 | 184/76 | HJ | 2.25 | 2.23i,2.23 | - |
| Sereda | Valeriy | SU | 30Jun59 | 186/76 | HJ | 2.34 | 2.37 | - |
| Sergiyenko | Yuriy | SU | 19Mar65 | 190/73 | HJ | 2.29 | 2.34i,2.31 | - |
| Serrani | Lucio | ITA | 11Mar61 | 190/120 | HT | 74.80 | 75.84 | - |
| Shafe | Mike | USA | 7Dec63 | 175/70 | PV | 5.45,5.52ex | 5.50 | - |
| Shahanga | Gidamis | TAN | 4Sep57 | 180/57 | Mar | 2:09:39 | 2:10:19 | - |
| Sharapanyuk | Yuriy | SU | 62 | | LJ | 8.11 | | |
| Sharp | Cameron | UK | 3Jun58 | 182/77 | 200 | 20.69w | 20.47 | - |
| Sharpe | David | UK | 8Jul67 | 180/66 | 800 | 1:45.64 | 1:48.47 | - |
| | | | | | 1k | 2:18.98 | 2:23.43i | - |
| Shchegolev | Igor | SU | 26Oct60 | 186/95 | HT | 80.20 | 78.46 | - |
| Shershen | Vladimir | SU | 8Nov61 | 182/67 | 100 | 10.35dwr | 10.35-85,10.2- | |
| Shevchenko | Yuriy | SU | 18Apr60 | 190/78 | HJ | 2.25 | 2.29i-85,2.26- | |

| me | | Nat | Yr | Ht/Wt | Event | 1986 Mark | Pre-1986 best |
|---|---|---|---|---|---|---|---|
| ⴑintaku | Masanari | JAP | 21Dec57 | 175/60 | 5k | 13:28.88 | 13:24.69 -82 |
| | | | | | 10k | 28:09.47 | 27:44.5 -83 |
| ⴑishkin | Vladimir | SU | 16Jun64 | | 110h | 13.50, | 13.6 -85 |
| | | | | | | 13.36w | 13.94 -84 |
| ⴑishkov | Mikhail | SU | 27Aug60 | 183/82 | JT | 75.30 | 79.82* -85 |
| ⴑishov | Aleksandr | SU | 4Apr59 | | 100 | 10.36, | 10.45 -84 |
| | | | | | | 10.1 | 10.2 -83 |
| ⴑkarpov | Vyacheslav | SU | 6Sep66 | 187/87 | TJ | 16.78 | 15.48 -84 |
| ⴑlyapnikov | Andrey | SU | 13Jan59 | 178/74 | 100 | 10.21  10.26 | -83,10.1 -85 |
| ⴑolars | Greg | USA | 8Feb66 | 172/66 | 100 | 10.30, | 10.35 -85 |
| | | | | | | 10.22w | 10.16w -84 |
| ⴑtrobinders | Marcis | SU | 12Jun66 | 185/85 | JT | 76.90 | 79.82* -85 |
| ⴑaudinis | Jonas | SU | 24Feb58 | 188/110 | DT | 65.08 | 63.34 -83 |
| ⴑdorenko | Vasiliy | SU | 1May61 | 186/100 | HT | 80.70 | 80.40 -85 |
| ⴑetins | Normunds | SU | 17Jul67 | 191/76 | HJ | 2.26 | 2.25 -85 |
| ⴑivonen | Vesa | FIN | 21Dec63 | | 3kSt | 8:31.10 | 8:33.77 -85 |
| ⴑlva | Alvaro | POR | 21Apr65 | | 800 | 1:46.74 | 1:48.6 -85 |
| ⴑlva | Mário | POR | 23Jul61 | 174/56 | 1500 | 3:38.00 | 3:43.4 -84 |
| ⴑmion | Dan | RUM | 28Jan58 | 188/78 | TJ | 16.50i | 17.09 -83 |
| ⴑmmons | Fred | USA | | | 200 | 20.73w | |
| ⴑmón | Andrés | CUB | 15Sep61 | 160/67 | 100 | 10.18 | 10.10,9.97w-85 |
| ⴑmon | Tim | USA | 11Sep66 | 188/73 | 400 | 45.88 | 45.75 -85 |
| ⴑmon-Balla | István | HUN | 9Feb58 | 186/69 | 400h | 49.62 | 49.75 -85 |
| ⴑmoncic | Rick | USA | 25Oct63 | | JT | 75.46 | 75.66* -85 |
| ⴑmpkins | Charles | USA | 19Oct63 | 185/70 | TJ | 17.50i, | 17.86 -85 |
| | | | | | | 17.42,17.91w | |
| ⴑnka | Albert | HUN | 22Nov62 | 187/95 | HT | 79.12 | 75.26 -85 |
| ⴑnnitsa | Sergey | SU | 66 | | SP | 20.05 | 18.64 -85 |
| ⴑnqe | Zithulele | RSA | 9Jun63 | | Mar | 2:08:14dh | 2:15:08 -85 |
| ⴑvillon | Philippe | FRA | 25May58 | 182/76 | PV | 5.45 | 5.52 -82 |
| ⴑöberg | Patrik | SWE | 5Jan65 | 200/79 | HJ | 2.34 | 2.38i,2.38 -85 |
| ⴑamrahl | Erwin | FRG | 8Mar58 | 178/67 | 200 | 20.78 | 20.44 -83 |
| | | | | | | 20.66w | 20.25w -81 |
| | | | | | 400 | 45.46 | 44.50 -83 |
| ⴑarzynski | Jerzy | POL | 13Jan56 | 176/61 | Mar | 2:11:42 | 2:12:37 -84 |
| ⴑinner | William | USA | 30Sep64 | | 110h | 13.53 | 13.9w -85 |
| ⴑlyarov | Vitaliy | SU | 31Jan60 | 187/75 | 110h | 13.75 | 13.66-85,13.5-84 |
| | | | | | | | 13.3w -83 |
| ⴑvarstrand | Anders | SWE | 24Jul60 | 189/120 | SP | 19.48i | 19.74 -85 |
| ⴑvaryuk | Andrey | SU | 9Mar67 | 187/90 | HT | 72.54 | 65.42 -85 |
| ⴑaa | Umbe | TAN | 51 | | 10k | 28:24.32 | 29:27.98 -83 |
| ⴑanař | Ivan | CS | 11Jan61 | 191/84 | TJ | 16.94 | 16.98 -85 |
| ⴑaney | Richard | UK | 16May56 | 201/130 | DT | 62.74 | 65.16 -85 |
| ⴑettevold | Øystein | NOR | 26Nov62 | 192/94 | JT | 76.88 | 78.76* -84 |
| ⴑouka | Vladimír | CS | 7May62 | 176/66 | 1k | 2:18.72 | 2:23.6 -85 |
| | | | | | 1500 | 3:39.9 | 3:51.17 -84 |
| ⴑusarski | Tadeusz | POL | 19May50 | 178/79 | PV | 5.55i | 5.70,5.71ex -85 |
| ⴑalls | Vic | USA | 20Sep64 | 186/75 | HJ | 2.29 | 2.26 -85 |
| ⴑall-Smith | Ian | RSA | 3Feb67 | | 400 | 45.88A | 45.97A -85 |
| ⴑirnov | Sergey | SU | 17Sep60 | 192/126 | SP | 22.24 | 22.05 -85 |
| ⴑirnov | Yuriy | SU | 6Apr61 | 191/90 | JT | 79.54 | 87.10* -84 |
| ⴑith | Andrew | JAM | 29Jan64 | 178/79 | 100 | 10.18w,10.1 | 10.20 -85 |
| | | | | | 200 | 20.77w | 20.83 -85 |
| ⴑith | Barry | UK | 16Apr53 | 168/60 | 5k | 13:34.34 | 13:21.14 -81 |
| ⴑith | Calvin | USA | 8Jan61 | 178/64 | 100 | 10.14 | 9.93A,9.97 -83 |
| | | | | | 200 | 20.29 | 19.99 -83 |
| ⴑith | Dave | JAM | 15Oct60 | 174/71 | 100 | 10.34 | 10.35,10.23w -85 |
| ⴑith | Dave | UK | 21Jun62 | 190/118 | HT | 76.60 | 77.30 -85 |
| ⴑith | Geoff | UK | 24Oct53 | 173/61 | Mar | 2:10:39 | 2:09:08 -83 |
| ⴑith | John | USA | 16Apr61 | 185/109 | SP | 19.59i | 19.58 -85 |
| ⴑith | Kenny | USA | 22Nov62 | 186/70 | HJ | 2.25 | 2.24 -84 |
| ⴑith | Luis | PAN | 3Jan68 | 170/67 | 100 | 10.1Aw | |

| Name | | Nat | Yr | Ht/Wt | Event | 1986 Mark | Pre-1986 best | |
|------|---|-----|-----|-------|-------|-----------|---------------|---|
| Smith | Mark | USA | 22Feb63 | 180/62 | 3kSt | 8:29.84 | 8:37.44 | -8 |
| Smith | Mike | USA | 4Jun58 | 183/118 | SP | 20.33i,20.27 | 20.90 | -8 |
| Smith | Tom | USA | 9Oct57 | 180/60 | Mile | 3:57.8i | 3:54.65 | -8 |
| Smith | Willie | USA | 28Feb56 | 173/73 | 200 | 20.78w | 20.5-74,20.78-7 | |
| Smolyakov | Sergey | SU | 12Oct62 | | PV | 5.65 | 5.70 | -8 |
| Snoddy | William | USA | 6Dec57 | 180/76 | 200 | 20.74 | 20.27A,20.28-7 | |
| Sörensen | Lars | FIN | 13Feb59 | 181/65 | 3kSt | 8:29.00 | 8:27.27 | -8 |
| Sokirkin | Oleg | SU | 2 Jan66 | 182/72 | TJ | 17.12 | 16.39 | -8 |
| Sokolov | Vitaliy | SU | 23Aug55 | 183/115 | DT | 66.60 | 65.06 | -8 |
| Sokolov | Vladimir | SU | 5Oct63 | 196/75 | HJ | 2.23 | 2.23 | -8 |
| Solly | Jon | UK | 28Jun63 | 183/66 | 3k | 7:50.20 | 7:54.97 | -8 |
| | | | | | 5k | 13:22.39 | 13:30.91 | -8 |
| | | | | | 10k | 27:51.76 | -0- | |
| Solomko | Sergey | SU | 28May58 | 192/110 | SP | 19.75 | 21.02 | -8 |
| Sorokin | Sergey | SU | 29Jul63 | | LJ | 8.06 | 7.79 | -8 |
| Sotomayor | Javier | CUB | 13Oct67 | 195/82 | HJ | 2.36 | 2.34 | -8 |
| Souza | Gerson A. | BRA | 2Jan59 | 176/74 | 400 | 45.53 | 45.21-82,45.2-8 | |
| Spasov | Viktor | SU | 19Jul59 | 185/75 | PV | 5.65 | 5.65,5.70i | -8 |
| Spearmon | Wallace | USA | 3Sep62 | 188/76 | 100 | 10.21, | 10.23 | -8 |
| | | | | | | 10.14w | 10.0w | -8 |
| | | | | | 200 | 20.33,20.27w | 20.36 | -8 |
| Spedding | Charles | UK | 19May52 | 173/63 | Mar | 2:10:13 | 2:08:33 | -8 |
| Spiriev | Attila | HUN | 8Feb64 | 181/63 | 400h | 49.98 | 50.7-85,51.15-8 | |
| Spiritoso -# | Mike | CAN | 3Jul63 | 181/114 | SP | 20.83 | 20.02 | -8 |
| Spivey | Jim | USA | 7Mar60 | 178/61 | 1500 | 3:34.4 | 3:34.19 | -8 |
| | | | | | Mile | 3:49.80 | 3:50.59 | -8 |
| | | | | | 2k | 5:05.79i | | |
| Spry | Ralph | USA | 16Jun60 | 173/70 | LJ | 8.12 | 8.18,8.36w | -8 |
| Squella | Pablo | CHL | 14Aug63 | 178/64 | 800 | 1:46.21 | 1:49.30 | -8 |
| | | | | | 400h | 50.16 | 50.31 | -8 |
| St Louis | Mike | UK | 26Mar64 | 178/73 | 200 | 20.81 | 21.03,20.9 | -8 |
| Stack | Kieran | IRL | 11May63 | | 3kSt | 8:29.8 | 8:29.60 | -8 |
| Ståhl | Kjell-Erik | SWE | 17Feb46 | 188/71 | Mar | 2:12:33 | 2:10:38 | -8 |
| Stahr | Mike | USA | 9Dec64 | 180/63 | 1500 | 3:39.61 | 3:43.06 | -8 |
| | | | | | Mile | 3:57.25 | | |
| Stanton | Brian | USA | 19Feb61 | 196/82 | HJ | 2.30i,2.24 | 2.31 | -8 |
| Starkov | Aleksey | SU | 2Apr64 | 177/78 | LJ | 7.98 | | |
| Starodubtsev | Valeriy | SU | 14Feb62 | 187/75 | 800 | 1:45.32 | 1:46.24 | -8 |
| Stavro | Aleksandr | SU | 5Jan63 | 186/82 | Dec | 7833 | 7717 | -8 |
| Stecchi | Gianni | ITA | 3Mar58 | 178/80 | PV | 5.55ex | 5.40 | -8 |
| Steen | Dave | CAN | 14Nov59 | 185/80 | Dec | 8254W | 8317 | -8 |
| Stefán | László | HUN | 4Nov63 | 190/87 | JT | 80.56 | 81.08* | -8 |
| Steffny | Herbert | FRG | 5Sep53 | 179/67 | Mar | 2:11:17 | 2:11:49 | -8 |
| Steiner | Rudolf | SWZ | 16Jan51 | 177/87 | JT | 75.96 | 77.86* | -8 |
| Stekić | Nenad | YUG | 7Mar51 | 181/73 | LJ | 8.19 | 8.45 | -8 |
| Stenzel | Helmut | FRG | 27Jun56 | | 10k | 28:13.61 | 29:45.7 | -8 |
| Stepanskiy | Viktor | SU | 25Apr59 | 184/118 | SP | 20.76 | 20.61i,20.55- | |
| Stephens | Dave | USA | 8Feb62 | 193/89 | JT | 75.36 | 79.70* | -8 |
| Stevens | Eddy | BEL | 26Apr61 | 185/65 | 1500 | 3:36.31 | 3:36.9 | -8 |
| Stevens | Felix | CUB | 8Mar64 | 190/72 | 200 | 20.67 | 20.65 | -8 |
| | | | | | 400 | 44.77 | 45.51 | -8 |
| Stewart | Milan | USA | 31Oct60 | 183/79 | 110h | 13.37 | 13.46,13.44w | -8 |
| | | | | | | | 13.4 | -8 |
| Stewart | Ray | JAM | 18Mar65 | 178/73 | 100 | 10.29,10.21w | 10.19 | -8 |
| Stewart | Ron | USA | 13Jan63 | 190/78 | 110h | 13.68 | 14.26,14.09w- | |
| Stít | Stanislav | CS | 16Jul58 | 181/68 | 3kSt | 8:35.80 | 8:36.77 | -8 |
| | | | | | 400h | 50.40 | 50.04 | -8 |
| Stoch | Ryszard | POL | 24Mar62 | 180/78 | 400h | 49.93 | 50.17 | -8 |
| Stoikov | Stefan | BUL | 18Mar51 | 184/85 | JT | 75.40 | 86.24* | -8 |
| Stokes | Chris | JAM | | | 100 | 10.35w | 10.45,10.39w- | |
| Stolz | Karsten | FRG | 23Jul64 | 208/142 | SP | 20.57 | 19.73 | -8 |

| me | | Nat | Yr | Ht/Wt | Event | 1986 Mark | Pre-1986 best | |
|---|---|---|---|---|---|---|---|---|
| tone | Robert | AUS | 5Jan65 | 176/71 | 200 | 20.76 | 20.95 | -85 |
| | | | | | 400 | 45.75 | 47.21 | -84 |
| toyanov | Rumen | BUL | 21Apr59 | 181/74 | PV | 5.50 | 5.55i-85,5.50 | -83 |
| trelchenko | Sergey | SU | 21Dec61 | 188/75 | 110h | 13.70,13.6 | 13.81,13.5 | -85 |
| trychalski | Jacek | POL | 6Mar62 | 198/100 | DT | 62.54 | 61.50 | -85 |
| tuart | Jesse | USA | 18Mar51 | 190/120 | SP | 20.65 | 21.02i-85,20.84 | -83 |
| tubblefield | Steve | USA | 30Dec61 | 183/77 | PV | 5.54i,5.45 | 5.69 | -85 |
| tukonis | Donatas | SU | 19Nov57 | 192/108 | SP | 19.72i,19.6 | 21.10 | -85 |
| tyopochkin | Vladimir | SU | 3Jul64 | 188/100 | HT | 74.86 | 75.76 | -85 |
| uelflohn | Rob | USA | 15Feb59 | 190/118 | SP | 20.24 | 20.73 | -85 |
| ueyoshi | Tomio | JAP | 5Feb59 | 160/52 | Mar | 2:13:18 | | |
| uhonen | Ari | FIN | 19Dec65 | 183/70 | 800 | 1:47.04 | 1:48.37 | -85 |
| | | | | | 1k | 2:17.7 | 2:18.72 | -85 |
| | | | | | 1500 | 3:39.82 | 3:49.83 | -85 |
| ukharev | Gennadiy | SU | 5Jun65 | | PV | 5.65 | 5.53i,5.30 | -84 |
| ula | Karel | CS | 30Jun59 | 189/104 | SP | 20.13 | 20.30 | -85 |
| ullivan | Shannon | USA | 15Oct59 | 183/86 | Dec | 7763 | 7717 | -84 |
| undin -# | Lars | SWE | 21Jul61 | 193/120 | SP | 19.60 | 19.54 | -85 |
| | | | | | DT | 61.16 | 60.86 | -85 |
| urin | Vitaliy | SU | 5Jan63 | | 3kSt | 8:34.04 | 8:38.23 | -85 |
| uec | Jiří | CS | 14Aug64 | 182/69 | 3kSt | 8:31.75 | 8:37.29 | -85 |
| uarts -# | Art | USA | 14Feb45 | 193/116 | DT | 64.94 | 69.40 | -79 |
| abó | Gábor K. | HUN | 19Jun62 | 182/66 | 3k | 7:48.81i | 7:47.4 | -83 |
| | | | | | 5k | 13:34.66 | 13:33.07 | -85 |
| alai | István | HUN | 25May62 | 181/65 | 800 | 1:46.96 | 1:46.54 | -84 |
| alma | Laszlo | HUN | 21Oct57 | 190/80 | LJ | 8.24i, | 8.30 | -85 |
| | | | | | | 8.03,8.07w | | |
| itás | Imre | HUN | 4Sep61 | 185/110 | HT | 77.28 | 78.84 | -84 |
| pak | Mieczysław | POL | 10Jul61 | 191/106 | DT | 63.28 | 62.46 | -85 |
| parak | Ryszard | POL | 2Jul51 | 178/70 | 400h | 49.95 | 49.17 | -83 |
| ybowski | Mirosław | POL | 15Sep60 | 178/90 | JT | 75.76 | 87.56* | -85 |
| felmeier | Klaus | FRG | 12Apr58 | 190/94 | JT | 85.74 | 91.44* | -83 |
| fralis | Gregg | USA | 9Apr58 | 183/120 | SP | 21.45 | 21.32 | -85 |
| | | | | | DT | 62.38 | 58.28 | -85 |
| iwo | Joseph | NIG | 24Aug59 | 183/74 | TJ | 17.18,17.26w | 17.19 | -84 |
| kács | István | HUN | 20Jan59 | 183/69 | 400h | 50.39 | 50.23 | -84 |
| kano | Susumu | JAP | 21May61 | 178/65 | 200 | 20.74 | 20.88 | -84 |
| | | | | | 400 | 45.00 | 45.30 | -85 |
| letskiy | Nikolay | SU | 61 | | 400h | 49.78 | 50.51 | -83 |
| lley | Keith | USA | 28Jan64 | 193/88 | 100 | 10.28, | 10.34, | |
| | | | | | | 10.24w | 10.25w | -85 |
| | | | | | 110h | 13.31 | 13.59, | |
| | | | | | | | 13.3w-85,13.50w | -84 |
| | | | | | LJ | 8.05 | 7.98,8.44w | -85 |
| llhem | Sören | SWE | 16Feb64 | 192/110 | SP | 19.70 | 21.24i,20.91 | -85 |
| | | | | | JT | 75.42 | 78.86* | -84 |
| mm | Juri | SU | 5Feb57 | 193/120 | HT | 80.88 | 84.40 | -84 |
| nev | Ivan | BUL | 1May57 | 187/105 | HT | 79.70 | 77.40 | -85 |
| niguchi | Hiromi | JAP | 5Apr60 | 171/56 | Mar | 2:10:08 | 2:10:01 | -85 |
| rasyuk | Yuriy | SU | 11Apr57 | 188/101 | HT | 79.34 | 81.44 | -84 |
| rev | Atanas | BUL | 31Jan58 | 180/75 | PV | 5.80 | 5.75 | -85 |
| rnavetskiy | Pavel | SU | 22Feb61 | 188/85 | Dec | 8214 | 8207 | -84 |
| rpenning | Kory | USA | 27Feb62 | 180/75 | PV | 5.70 | 5.65 | -85 |
| shpulatov | Damir | SU | 29Jan64 | 189/75 | TJ | 16.70 | 16.32 | -84 |
| tár | István | HUN | 24Mar58 | 174/68 | 100 | 10.35,10.30w | 10.25 | -85 |
| tum | Roscoe | USA | 13Feb66 | 183/91 | 100 | 10.08w | 10.18,10.0w | -85 |
| | | | | | 200 | 20.60 | 20.73 | -85 |
| ushanski | Georgi | BUL | 26Dec57 | 192/108 | DT | 65.28 | 65.78 | -84 |
| ylor | Dave | IRL | 7Mar59 | 183/64 | 1500 | 3:37.58 | 3:38.41 | -83 |
| | | | | | Mile | 3:56.97 | 3:54.48 | -83 |
| fs | Uwe | GDR | 2Jan68 | 190/86 | JT | 75.38 | 70.06* | -85 |
| gla | Ferenc | HUN | 15Jul47 | 185/98 | DT | 61.88 | 67.38 | -77 |

| Name | | Nat | Yr | Ht/Wt | Event | 1986 Mark | Pre-1986 best | |
|------|--|-----|-----|-------|-------|-----------|---------------|--|
| Temane | Matthews | RSA | 14Dec60 | 171/55 | 5k | 13:25.15 | 13:36.92 | -8 |
| | | | | | 10k | 28:23.45 | 28:34.92 | -8 |
| Temnikov | Gennadiy | SU | 13Sep61 | | 3k | 7:49.50 | 7:54.06 | -8 |
| | | | | | 5k | 13:34.10 | 13:35.63 | -8 |
| ten Kate | Martin | HOL | 16Dec58 | 164/62 | 3kSt | 8:34.74 | 8:38.80 | -8 |
| Terekhov | Roman | SU | 30Apr63 | | Dec | 7776 | 7719 | -8 |
| Terenko | Aleksey | SU | 11Aug61 | | SP | 19.32 | | |
| Terzi | Mehmat | TUR | 5May55 | 176/59 | Mar | 2:13:02 | 2:12:54 | -8 |
| Tesáček | Lubomír | CS | 9Feb57 | 171/54 | 5k | 13:25.62 | 13:30.42 | -8 |
| | | | | | 10k | 28:09.4 | 30:44.63 | -8 |
| Thackery | Carl | UK | 14Oct62 | 176/63 | 10k | 28:03.68 | 28:54.90 | -8 |
| Thau | Rainer | FRG | 2Dec62 | 186/73 | 800 | 1:46.59 | 1:45.8 | -8 |
| | | | | | 1500 | 3:36.74 | 3:37.83 | -8 |
| Thaxton | Steve | USA | 29Jul64 | 187/82 | PV | 5.50 | 5.41 | -8 |
| Therwanger | Kerry | USA | 27May63 | 180/66 | LJ | 8.04w | 7.66-83,7.95w | -8 |
| Thiebaut | Pascal | FRA | 6Jun59 | 175/61 | 1500 | 3:35.54 | 3:35.50 | -8 |
| | | | | | Mile | 3:54.06 | 3:52.02 | -8 |
| Thiede | Mike | GDR | 20May67 | 191/77 | PV | 5.45 | 5.35 | -8 |
| Thigpen | Aaron | USA | 18Sep64 | 170/65 | 100 | 10.02Aw | 10.30Aw | -8 |
| | | | | | 200 | 20.45Aw | 21.41 | -8 |
| Thomas | Henry | USA | 10Jul67 | 188/77 | 200 | 20.49 | 20.69,20.4 | -8 |
| | | | | | 400 | 45.42 | 45.09 | -8 |
| Thomas | Johnny | USA | 3Aug63 | 175/80 | 400 | 45.91,45.8 | 46.97 | -8 |
| Thomas | Jon | USA | 1Feb63 | 190/81 | 400h | 49.86 | 48.95 | -8 |
| Thomas | Robert | USA | 25Jul60 | 178/70 | 110h | 13.79 | 13.84,13.76dt | -8 |
| | | | | | | | 13.8-81,13.7 | -8 |
| Thompson | Daley | UK | 31Jul58 | 184/88 | 100 | 10.26 | 10.36,10.28w | -8 |
| | | | | | Dec | 8811 | 8847 | -8 |
| Thompson | Reyna | USA | 28Aug63 | 185/82 | 110h | 13.56, | 13.75,13.5 | -8 |
| | | | | | | 13.53w,13.3w | 13.64w | -8 |
| Thornton | Terry | RSA | 23Sep67 | | 5k | 13:26.78 | 14:06.3 | -8 |
| Thränhardt | Carlo | FRG | 5Jul57 | 199/85 | HJ | 2.36i,2.32 | 2.37 | -8 |
| Tiacoh | Gabriel | IVC | 10Sep63 | 180/75 | 400 | 44.30 | 44.54 | -8 |
| Tiainen | Juha | FIN | 5Dec55 | 182/107 | HT | 79.32 | 81.52 | -8 |
| Tietjens | Brian | USA | 21Sep62 | 196/77 | HJ | 2.25 | 2.285-84,2.30i | -8 |
| Tilli | Stefano | ITA | 22Aug62 | 175/65 | 200 | 20.57 | 20.40 | -8 |
| Tillman | John | USA | 11Feb65 | 183/75 | TJ | 16.84 | 16.94 | -8 |
| Timmermann | Ulf | GDR | 1Nov62 | 194/118 | SP | 22.60 | 22.62 | -8 |
| Timpson | Michael | USA | 6Jun67 | 179/75 | 200 | 20.23 | 20.76 | -8 |
| | | | | | 110h | 13.85 | -0- | |
| Tiritichă | Sorin | RUM | 10Feb60 | 192/125 | SP | 19.41 | 19.16 | -8 |
| Tîrle | Marcel | RUM | 19Oct66 | 194/105 | DT | 62.12 | 57.52 | -8 |
| Tirop | Samuel | KEN | | | 800 | 1:47.05 | | |
| Titov | Anatoliy | SU | 3Mar56 | 183/73 | 110h | 13.67, | 13.70 | -8 |
| | | | | | | 13.46w | 13.3 | -8 |
| Titov | Vladimir | SU | 24Apr59 | 186/76 | 400h | 50.14 | 49.90 | -8 |
| Tjela | Ernest | RSA | 16Oct54 | | Mar | 2:11:00 | 2:15:11 | -8 |
| Tkachev | Sergey | SU | 7Oct58 | | TJ | 17.05 | 17.02 | -8 |
| Todorov | Georgi | BUL | 7Mar60 | 193/112 | SP | 20.48 | 20.30 | -8 |
| Többen | Olaf | FRG | 19Dec62 | | DT | 62.48 | 60.44 | -8 |
| Töyrylä | Kari | FIN | 17Aug56 | 195/120 | SP | 20.05 | 19.79 | -8 |
| Tolstikov | Yakov | SU | 20May59 | | Mar | 2:11:43 | 2:10:58 | -8 |
| Tomaszewski | Mariusz | POL | 23Apr56 | 190/122 | HT | 74.30 | 79.46,81.46ex | -8 |
| Tommelein | Rik | BEL | 1Nov62 | 178/66 | 400h | 49.55 | 49.64 | -8 |
| Tomov | Toma | BUL | 6May58 | 179/68 | 400h | 48.48 | 48.99 | -8 |
| Tonnelier | Thierry | FRA | 28Dec59 | 176/67 | 800 | 1:47.0 | 1:47.1 | -8 |
| Tootell | Peter | UK | 12Mar63 | | 10k | 28:26.29 | -0- | |
| Torres | Barbaro | CUB | 21Apr63 | | TJ | 16.88 | 16.30 | -8 |
| Toska | Ajet | ALB | 61 | | HT | 75.92 | 73.72 | -8 |
| Tóth | László | HUN | 31Aug55 | 177/61 | 1k | 2:18.97 | 2:22.4 | -8 |
| Toyota | Noburo | JAP | 67 | 172/58 | LJ | 7.93w | | |
| Tozzi | Gianni | ITA | 6May62 | 182/65 | 110h | 13.79 | 13.84 | - |

| me | | Nat | Yr | Ht/Wt | Event | 1986 Mark | Pre-1986 best | |
|---|---|---|---|---|---|---|---|---|
| rabado | Coloman | SPA | 2Jan58 | 182/71 | 800 | 1:46.09 | 1:45.15 | -84 |
| randenkov | Igor | SU | 17Aug66 | 191/72 | PV | 5.50i | 5.45 | -85 |
| reacy | John | IRL | 4Jun57 | 175/59 | 5k | 13:22.11 | 13:16.81 | -84 |
| | | | | | 10k | 28:04.10 | 27:48.7 | -80 |
| rinkler | Markus | SWZ | 11Dec62 | 181/70 | 800 | 1:46.91 | 1:48.34 | -85 |
| rofimenko | Vasiliy | SU | 28Jan62 | 195/80 | PV | 5.55i | 5.40 | -81 |
| rott | William | BER | 20Mar65 | | 100 | 10.32w | 10.38,10.27w | -85 |
| ruppel | Heiko | GDR | 3Jul64 | 182/70 | 100 | 10.35 | 10.35,10.25w | -85 |
| sarskiy | Aivar | SU | 15Jun62 | 177/61 | 3kSt | 8:34.72 | 8:36.77 | -85 |
| subo | Masayuki | JAP | | 168/53 | Mar | 2:13:27 | | |
| svetanov | Emil | BUL | 14Mar63 | 175/82 | JT | 75.76 | 82.12* | -83 |
| syoma | Aleksandr | SU | 31Mar61 | | Dec | 7904 | 7798 | -85 |
| ully | Mike | USA | 21Oct56 | 190/86 | PV | 5.80 | 5.82 | -84 |
| uranok | Vladimir | SU | 5Jun57 | 185/100 | DT | 63.30 | 64.56 | -85 |
| urnbull | Geoff | UK | 15Apr61 | 173/60 | Mile | 3:57.66 | 3:58.44 | -83 |
| | | | | | 3k | 7:45.2 | 7:47.88 | -84 |
| | | | | | 2M | 8:15.98 | | |
| | | | | | 5k | 13:21.73 | 13:33.86 | -84 |
| urner | Sam | USA | 17Jun57 | 191/80 | 110h | 13.54,13.53w | 13.17 | -83 |
| utani | Monde | RSA | 22Feb62 | | Mile | 3:56.12 | | |
| artas | Romas | SU | 26May60 | 202/120 | DT | 67.88 | 66.92 | -84 |
| eta | Yasushi | JAP | 13Nov55 | 180/69 | TJ | 16.64w | 16.71 | -84 |
| jino | Shuji | JAP | 15Jan60 | 181/75 | HJ | 2.24 | 2.28 | -84 |
| akawa | Tetsuo | JAP | 10Dec61 | 160/48 | 10k | 28:28.93 | 28:34.49 | -84 |
| rmakayev | Oleg | SU | 65 | | HJ | 2.23 | 2.20 | -84 |
| sov | Igor | SU | 28Mar61 | 181/75 | TJ | 17.00 | 17.02 | -82 |
| stinov | Vyacheslav | SU | 10May57 | 190/86 | 110h | 13.74, | 13.57 | -84 |
| | | | | | | 13.6 | 13.5 | -83 |
| sui | Junichi | JAP | 5Oct57 | 178/70 | LJ | 7.92 | 8.10 | -79 |
| i | Sunday | NIG | 23Oct62 | 175/68 | 400 | 45.38 | 44.83 | -84 |
| ízl | Ivan | CS | 16Aug58 | 171/57 | 5k | 13:31.92 | 13:33.1 | -80 |
| | | | | | 10k | 28:04.4 | 29:15.21 | -84 |
| ihinger | Jörg | FRG | 8Oct62 | 191/84 | 400 | 45.92 | 45.52 | -85 |
| inio | Martti | FIN | 30Dec50 | 190/74 | 5k | 13:22.67 | 13:16.02 | -84 |
| | | | | | 10k | 27:44.57 | 27:30.99 | -78 |
| lent | Gejza | CS | 3Oct53 | 196/120 | DT | 65.58 | 69.70 | -84 |
| lenta | Véroslav | CS | 25Mar65 | 197/88 | Dec | 7905 | 7398 | -85 |
| lentín | Jorge | CUB | 16Aug64 | 184/76 | 400 | 45.68 | 47.34 | -85 |
| lentine | Tony | USA | 6Sep64 | 190/77 | 400h | 49.93 | 49.66 | -84 |
| lle | Emilio | CUB | 21Apr67 | 182/70 | 400h | 50.02 | 52.44 | -85 |
| lmon | Andrew | USA | 1Jan65 | 185/75 | 400 | 45.61 | 45.13 | -85 |
| lvik | Svein-Inge | NOR | 20Sep56 | 190/112 | DT | 66.48 | 68.00 | -82 |
| lkonen | Matti | FIN | 17Sep60 | 179/63 | 5k | 13:35.34 | 14:06.42 | -84 |
| lyukevich | Gennadiy | SU | 1Jun58 | 182/74 | TJ | 17.53,17.75w | 17.48 | -85 |
| mvakas | Georgios | GRE | 1Jan60 | 185/76 | 400h | 49.92 | 49.47 | -85 |
| n Aswegen | Samuel | RSA | 5Nov65 | | 400 | 45.9A | 46.55 | -85 |
| natta | Mike | USA | 18Oct61 | 175/63 | 3kSt | 8:33.0 | 8:31.14 | -84 |
| n d. Herten | Dirk | BEL | 9Mar57 | 170/60 | Mar | 2:13:29 | 2:12:21 | -84 |
| ndi | Luca | ITA | 21Jun62 | | 1500 | 3:39.28 | 3:40.00 | -85 |
| n Dijck | William | BEL | 24Jan61 | 180/59 | 3k | 7:50.89 | 7:49.7 | -84 |
| | | | | | 3kSt | 8:10.01 | 8:13.77 | -85 |
| ndyak | Valeriy | SU | 9Jan61 | 182/71 | 3kSt | 8:29.52 | 8:34.44 | -83 |
| n Helden | Rob | HOL | 6Feb65 | 180/73 | 800 | 1:46.07 | 1:49.09 | -85 |
| n Reenen | John | RSA | 26Mar47 | 202/125 | DT | 64.12 | 68.48 | -75 |
| nyaykin | Dmitriy | SU | 66 | | 100 | 10.1 | 10.6 | -85 |
| skevich | Gennadiy | SU | 20Aug66 | 184/78 | HJ | 2.29 | 2.16 | -85 |
| silyev | Aleksandr | SU | 26Jul61 | 191/83 | 400h | 48.24 | 47.92 | -85 |
| lazco | Francisco | CUB | 4Oct61 | 183/74 | 400h | 49.64 | 52.03 | -85 |
| lev | Velko | BUL | 4Jan48 | 189/118 | DT | 62.14 | 67.82 | -78 |
| nto | Raimo | FIN | 15Sep54 | 187/108 | DT | 61.18 | 59.50 | -80 |

| Name | | Nat | Yr | Ht/Wt | Event | 1986 Mark | Pre-1986 best | |
|---|---|---|---|---|---|---|---|---|
| Vera | Andrés | SPA | 31Dec60 | 186/72 | 1500 | 3:35.86 | 3:36.55 | -8 |
| | | | | | Mile | 3:57.09 | 3:55.33 | -8 |
| | | | | | 2k | 5:02.78 | | |
| Vera | Ricardo | URU | 16Sep62 | 186/71 | 3kSt | 8:28.89 | 8:43.31 | -8 |
| Verzy | Franck | FRA | 13May61 | 181/66 | HJ | 2.24 | 2.32 | -8 |
| Vetterli | Patrick | SWZ | 6Oct61 | 200/100 | Dec | 7896 | 7827 | -8 |
| Vida | József | HUN | 9Jan63 | 192/108 | HT | 73.68 | 79.06 | -8 |
| Vigneron | Thierry | FRA | 9Mar60 | 181/73 | PV | 5.90 | 5.91 | -8 |
| Vikhrov | Valeriy | SU | 61 | | 400h | 49.52 | 49.40 | -8 |
| Vilhjalmsson | Einar | ICE | 1Jun60 | 188/97 | JT | 80.28 | 92.42* | -8 |
| Vilučkis | Benjaminas | SU | 20Mar61 | 187/118 | HT | 82.24 | 80.42 | -8 |
| Vimbert | Gilles | FRA | 27Jul66 | 179/70 | 400h | 50.45 | 51.73 | -8 |
| Vinci | Baker | USA | 19Oct62 | 183/73 | PV | 5.50 | 5.43 | -8 |
| Vinokurov | Aleksandr | SU | 1Jul63 | 186/72 | TJ | 16.79 | | |
| Visserman | Arjen | HOL | 20Aug65 | 187/74 | 400 | 45.68 | 46.40 | -8 |
| Viudes | Luc | FRA | 31Jan56 | 192/132 | SP | 19.84 | 19.67 | -7 |
| Vlasyuk | Gennadiy | SU | 22Apr61 | 180/105 | SP | 19.33 | 19.49 | -8 |
| Vogel | Uwe | GDR | 6Jul58 | 187/78 | LJ | 7.99 | 8.05 | -8 |
| Voitovich | Arunas | SU | 65 | | LJ | 7.93w | 8.00 | -8 |
| Volgin | Yevgeniy | SU | 62 | | 3kSt | 8:34.87 | 8:39.4 | -8 |
| Volkov | Konstantin | SU | 28Feb60 | 185/79 | PV | 5.65i | 5.85 | -8 |
| Volmer | Peter | FRG | 14Jan58 | 180/69 | PV | 5.50i | 5.65i-84,5.55-8 |
| Voloshin | Leonid | SU | 14May66 | 180/74 | LJ | 8.06 | 7.79 | -8 |
| Volz | Dave | USA | 2May62 | 180/82 | PV | 5.80i,5.59 | 5.75 | -8 |
| Vondra | Jindrich | CS | 15Apr57 | 198/82 | HJ | 2.28 | 2.29 | -8 |
| Vorontsov | Vladimir | SU | 1Jan58 | 178/67 | 1500 | 3:39.9 | 3:42.2 | -8 |
| Vörös | Sándor | HUN | 19Jan58 | 196/115 | HT | 74.96 | 74.62 | -8 |
| Vorster | Dries | RSA | 25Oct62 | | 400h | 50.28A | 50.77 | -8 |
| Voss | Torsten | GDR | 24Mar63 | 186/88 | Dec | 8450 | 8559 | -8 |
| Vovk | Grigoriy | SU | 16Jun62 | 182/94 | HT | 72.22 | 78.12 | -8 |
| Vrábel | Martin | CS | 21Sep55 | 165/55 | 10k | 28:28.44 | 28:19.66 | -8 |
| Wade | Ed | USA | 10Dec64 | 193/105 | SP | 19.45i | 18.06 | -8 |
| | | | | | DT | 62.66 | 60.36 | -8 |
| Wagner | Alwin | FRG | 11Aug50 | 196/122 | DT | 64.32 | 67.10 | -8 |
| Waigwa | Wilson | KEN | 15Feb49 | 172/64 | 5k | 13:23.18 | 13:20.36 | -8 |
| Wakiihuru | Douglas | KEN | 62 | | 10k | 28:17.12 | 28:24.45 | -8 |
| Walker | Chris | USA | 1Aug65 | 193/81 | LJ | 7.97w | 7.87 | - |
| Walker | John | NZ | 12Jan52 | 183/74 | 1500 | 3:35.74 | 3:32.4 | - |
| | | | | | Mile | 3:50.93 | 3:49.08 | - |
| | | | | | 2k | 4:58.88 | 4:51.52 | - |
| | | | | | 3k | 7:50.33 | 7:37.49 | - |
| | | | | | 5k | 13:19.28 | 13:20.89 | - |
| Walker | Nigel | UK | 15Jun63 | 180/72 | 110h | 13.52 | 13.70w-85,13.78- |
| Waller | Manley | USA | 21Jul64 | 178/77 | 100 | 10.26 | 10.29w-85,10.47- |
| Wallin | Par | SWE | 6Mar55 | 189/66 | Mar | 2:13:15 | | |
| Wang Shijie | | CHN | 24Dec63 | 181/73 | LJ | 7.91 | 8.01 | - |
| Wanliss | Everton | JAM | | | 100 | 10.27w | 10.38w | - |
| Warnemünde | Wolfgang | GDR | 8May53 | 202/117 | DT | 62.12 | 67.56 | - |
| Warming | Lars | DEN | 21Jun63 | 192/84 | Dec | 7776 | 7422w | - |
| Washington | Alex | USA | 28Dec62 | 187/77 | 110h | 13.89 | 13.75,13.6, | |
| | | | | | | | 13.64w 13.5w-85,13.64w- | |
| Washington | Ken | USA | 16Jan61 | 190/84 | 800 | 1:47.08 | 1:46.75 | - |
| Waszek | Piotr | POL | 26Jun60 | 185/81 | 100 | 10.34 | 10.44 | - |
| Waynes | Ron | USA | 2Sep60 | 183/73 | LJ | 7.98 | 8.19w-85,8.03 | - |
| Wedderburn | Eddie | UK | 6Dec60 | 183/66 | 3kSt | 8:27.07 | 8:21.20 | - |
| Weil | Gert | CHL | 3Jan60 | 197/115 | SP | 20.90 | 20.47 | - |
| Weis | Heinz | FRG | 14Jul63 | 193/105 | HT | 76.08 | 78.18 | - |
| Weiss | Gerald | GDR | 8Jan60 | 191/104 | JT | 81.40 | 90.06* | - |
| Weitzl | Erwin | AUT | 17Jul60 | 194/125 | SP | 19.46 | 20.04 | - |

| ame | | Nat | Yr | Ht/Wt | Event | 1986 Mark | Pre-1986 best | |
|---|---|---|---|---|---|---|---|---|
| ells | Allan | UK | 3May52 | 183/86 | 100 | 10.22 | 10.11 | −80 |
| | | | | | | | 1Q.02w-82,10.0w-79 | |
| | | | | | 200 | 20.53 | 20.21,20.11w | −80 |
| ells | Joey | BAH | 22Dec65 | 170/64 | LJ | 7.96w | 8.04 | −83 |
| elzel | Volker | FRG | 23Sep61 | | 1500 | 3:39.56 | 3:41.20 | −85 |
| | | | | | 2k | 5:04.75 | | |
| ennlund | Dag | SWE | 9Oct63 | 188/96 | JT | 81.86 | 92.20* | −85 |
| entz | Siegfried | FRG | 7Mar60 | 193/93 | 110h | 13.76 | 13.90 | −85 |
| | | | | | Dec | 8676 | 8762 | −83 |
| esołowski | Krzysztof | POL | 9Dec56 | 179/64 | 3kSt | 8:30.45 | 8:11.04 | −85 |
| essig | Gerd | GDR | 16Jul59 | 201/88 | HJ | 2.30 | 2.36 | −80 |
| essinghage | Thomas | FRG | 22Feb52 | 183/69 | 1500 | 3:39.31 | 3:31.58 | −80 |
| | | | | | 5k | 13:21.98 | 13:12.78 | −82 |
| hitehead | Brian | USA | 24Feb62 | 180/70 | HJ | 2.26i,2.25 | 2.33 | −85 |
| hittle | Brian | UK | 24Apr64 | 188/76 | 400 | 45.38 | 46.60 | −85 |
| hitty | Laurie | AUS | 5Feb60 | 178/69 | 10k | 28:23.50 | 28:26.34 | −83 |
| hymns | Fabian | BAH | 11Jun61 | 173/68 | 100 | 10.32w | 10.28,10.21Aw | −82 |
| icksell | Ray | USA | 24Apr56 | 183/70 | Mile | 3:57.76 | 3:56.23 | −81 |
| | | | | | 3k | 7:50.29 | 7:50.9 | −85 |
| | | | | | 5k | 13:32.34 | 13:35.8 | −85 |
| ijns | Raf | BEL | 7Jan64 | 180/67 | 3k | 7:49.83i | 7:52.40 | −85 |
| ilcher | Thomas | USA | 11Apr64 | 180/84 | 110h | 13.57 | 13.75,13.52w | −85 |
| ilczewski | Tadeusz | POL | 26Dec58 | 179/68 | Mar | 2:11:34 | 2:15:12 | −84 |
| illiams | Bernard | USA | 23May65 | 185/77 | 110h | 13.81 | 13.73 | −85 |
| | | | | | 400h | 49.65 | 49.88 | −85 |
| illiams | Carter | USA | 29Aug65 | 178/68 | 400 | 45.94 | 45.84 | −85 |
| illiams | Desai | CAN | 12Jun59 | 175/72 | 100 | 10.21 | 10.21,10.0 | −85 |
| | | | | | | | 10.17A-83,10.12w | −80 |
| | | | | | 200 | 20.70 | 20.29A,20.39 | −83 |
| | | | | | | | 20.35w | −80 |
| illiams | Fred | RSA | 24Feb62 | 170/62 | 800 | 1:46.61 | 1:46.08 | −85 |
| | | | | | 1k | 2:18.74i | | |
| illiams | Leo | USA | 28Apr60 | 193/83 | HJ | 2.24 | 2.29 | −82 |
| illiams | Paul | CAN | 7Aug56 | 178/63 | 5k | 13:27.55 | 13:29.18 | −84 |
| | | | | | 10k | 27:50.19 | 27:55.92 | −84 |
| inkler | Jürgen | FRG | 1Mar59 | 188/78 | PV | 5.60 | 5.66 | −83 |
| irz | Peter | SWZ | 29Jul60 | 181/68 | 1500 | 3:37.75 | 3:35.83 | −84 |
| | | | | | Mile | 3:55.68 | 3:57.74 | −83 |
| it | Robert de | HOL | 7Aug62 | 186/88 | Dec | 7962 | 7875 | −83 |
| itek | Stanislaw | POL | 24Apr60 | 180/93 | JT | 81.94* | 85.10* | −84 |
| therspoon | Mark | USA | 3Sep63 | 190/85 | 100 | 10.15w | 10.36-85,10.27w-84 | |
| | | | | | 200 | 20.50w,20.5 | 20.63,20.5w-84 | |
| | | | | | 400 | 45.49 | 45.37 | −84 |
| odarczyk | Włodzimierz | POL | 23Aug57 | 187/74 | LJ | 8.06w | 8.09,8.17u | −85 |
| | | | | | | | 8.18w | −84 |
| oderski | Leszek | POL | 4Apr58 | 188/110 | HT | 72.92 | 76.88 | −84 |
| jcik | Piotr | POL | 7Feb65 | 190/74 | 110h | 13.70 | 13.93 | −85 |
| lde | Fekere | ETH | | | Mar | 2:13:13 | | |
| mack | Terry | USA | 29Oct65 | 193/84 | PV | 5.51 | 5.45 | −85 |
| ods | John | IRL | 8Dec55 | 170/60 | 10k | 28:20.78 | 28:27.28 | −82 |
| ronin | Marian | POL | 13Aug56 | 186/90 | 100 | 10.11 | 10.00 | −84 |
| ight | Don | AUS | 26Apr59 | 183/76 | 110h | 13.46 | 13.58-82,13.5 | −83 |
| zoła | Jacek | POL | 30Dec56 | 194/79 | HJ | 2.33i,2.25 | 2.35 | −80 |
| ilbeck | Willi | FRG | 18Dec54 | 186/69 | 800 | 1:45.96 | 1:43.65 | −83 |
| | | | | | 1500 | 3:38.68 | 3:33.74 | −80 |
| rsthorn | Herbert | FRG | 22Jun57 | 179/69 | 800 | 1:46.96 | 1:46.5 | −85 |
| yke | William | VEN | 21May58 | 173/63 | 800 | 1:43.54 | 1:43.93 | −84 |
| zykowski | Andrzej | POL | 7Nov60 | 190/85 | Dec | 7742 | 7852 | −84 |
| | Xiashun | CHN | 5Oct62 | | Dec | 7672 | 7331 | −85 |

| Name | | Nat | Yr | Ht/Wt | Event | 1986 Mark | Pre-1986 best | |
|------|---|-----|-----|-------|-------|-----------|---------------|---|
| Yakovlev | Aleksandr | SU | 8Sep57 | 182/74 | LJ | 7.98 | 8.10i-83,7.85 | -8 |
| | | | | | TJ | 17.26 | 17.50 | -8 |
| Yakovlev | Pavel | SU | 16Jan58 | 183/70 | 1500 | 3:39.96 | 3:36.4 | -8 |
| Yakuba | Vitaliy | SU | 22May65 | | TJ | 16.57 | | |
| Yamashita | Norifumi | JAP | 10Sep62 | 177/63 | TJ | 17.15 | 16.92 | -8 |
| Yanchev | Ivo | BUL | 5Sep60 | 186/78 | PV | 5.60 | 5.65-83,5.70ex | -8 |
| Yaryshkin | Vladimir | SU | 28Feb63 | | SP | 20.80 | 19.67 | -8 |
| Yates | Peter | UK | 15Jun57 | 181/84 | JT | 76.48 | 85.92* | -8 |
| Yatsyk | Igor | SU | 63 | | 400h | 50.10 | 50.6 | -8 |
| Yawa | Xolile | RSA | 29Sep62 | 169/50 | 10k | 28:02.13 | 28:13.64 | -8 |
| Yefimov | Anatoliy | SU | 18Jun56 | 185/108 | HT | 76.34 | 79.56 | -8 |
| Yegorov | Grigoriy | SU | 12Jan67 | 185/75 | PV | 5.61i,5.50 | 5.55 | -8 |
| Yemelyanov | Vyacheslav | SU | 6Jan57 | | SP | 19.98i,19.68 | 20.64 | -8 |
| Yemets | Grigoriy | SU | 8Oct57 | 192/80 | TJ | 16.85i, | 17.33i, | |
| | | | | | | 16.75 | 17.30 | -8 |
| Yevgenyev | Aleksandr | SU | 20Jul61 | 174/70 | 200 | 20.50 | 20.41 | -8 |
| Yevsyukov | Viktor | SU | 6Oct56 | 190/100 | JT | 83.68 | 93.70* | -8 |
| Ylöstalo | Mikael | FIN | 2May63 | 187/75 | 110h | 13.69 | 14.02-84,13.96w | -8 |
| Yoneshige | Shuichi | JAP | 24Jun61 | 172/57 | 5k | 13:29.87 | 13:40.22 | -8 |
| | | | | | 10k | 28:02.5 | 28:17.0 | -8 |
| Yoshida | Masami | JAP | 14Jun58 | 179/85 | JT | 80.66 | 87.18* | -8 |
| Yoshida | Ryoichi | JAP | 2Mar65 | 175/63 | 400h | 49.40 | 49.75 | -8 |
| Young | Don | USA | 31Mar64 | | 100 | 10.33w | 10.34 | -8 |
| | | | | | | | 10.29w,10.1w | -8 |
| Young | Donnie | USA | 62 | 185/75 | 200 | 20.78 | 20.64 | -8 |
| Young | Kevin | USA | 9Jun65 | 188/77 | 200 | 20.72w | 21.00 | -8 |
| Young | Kevin | USA | 16Sep66 | 190/75 | 110h | 13.84 | 14.12 | -8 |
| | | | | | 400h | 48.77 | 51.09 | -8 |
| Yu Zhicheng | | CHN | 23Jul63 | 187/75 | 110h | 13.87 | 13.82 | -8 |
| Yushmanov | Nikolay | SU | 18Dec61 | 184/80 | 100 | 10.18, | 10.16 | -8 |
| | | | | | | 10.10dwr | 10.1 | |
| | | | | | 200 | 20.77 | 20.99-82,20.9 | -8 |
| | | | | | | | | |
| Zachariassen | Alan | DEN | 4Nov55 | 170/58 | Mar | 2:11:56 | 2:11:05 | -8 |
| Zagoruyko | Aleksandr | SU | 4Nov55 | 175/64 | 3kSt | 8:34.27, | 8:26.73 | -8 |
| | | | | | | 8:34.2 | | |
| Zaika | Vladimir | SU | 3Aug57 | 190/82 | 110h | 13.82 | 13.71,13.5 | -8 |
| Zalar | Kasimir | SWE | 24Mar57 | 180/76 | PV | 5.70 | 5.61 | -8 |
| Zamfirache | Ion | RUM | 23Aug53 | 190/120 | DT | 62.12 | 67.30 | -8 |
| Zanello | Giuliano | ITA | 22May63 | 184/110 | HT | 77.48 | 75.00 | -8 |
| Zaozerskiy | Sergey | SU | 28Jan64 | | LJ | 8.00w | 7.96 | -8 |
| Zasimovich | Sergey | SU | 6Sep62 | 188/73 | HJ | 2.28 | 2.36 | -8 |
| Zasimovich | Vladimir | SU | 14Sep68 | 178/81 | JT | 78.84 | 77.60* | -8 |
| Zaske | Werner | FRG | 28Feb61 | 189/75 | 100 | 10.33w | 10.35 | -8 |
| Železný | Ján | CS | 16Jun66 | 186/77 | JT | 82.48 | 84.68* | -8 |
| Zeligowski | Jerzy | POL | 29Apr58 | 180/72 | LJ | 7.96,8.12w | 7.98 | -8 |
| Zemlyanskiy | Viktor | SU | 10Feb63 | 183/68 | 800 | 1:45.05 | 1:44.93 | -8 |
| Zemskov | Tagir | SU | 6Aug62 | 182/67 | 400h | 49.07 | 49.33,49.2 | -8 |
| Zerkowski | Mirosław | POL | 20Aug56 | 171/59 | 3kSt | 8:19.02 | 8:27.61 | -8 |
| Zgarda | Piotr | POL | 18Jun56 | 174/62 | 3kSt | 8:32.51 | 8:27.2 | - |
| Zhang Guowei | | CHN | 27Apr59 | | 5k | 13:31.01 | 13:50.77 | -8 |
| | | | | | 10k | 28:24.85 | 28:52.73 | -8 |
| Zhayvoronok | Igor | SU | 62 | | 100 | 10.1 | 10.64 | -8 |
| Zhdanov | Oleg | SU | 19Oct62 | | 110h | 13.6 | 14.35 | -8 |
| | | | | | 400h | 50.1 | 51.2 | -8 |
| Zhelanov | Sergey | SU | 14Jun57 | 190/82 | Dec | 8045 | 8417 | -8 |
| Zhirov | Yuriy | SU | 1Jan60 | 177/80 | JT | 78.64 | 83.98* | -8 |
| Zhu Jianhua | | CHN | 29May63 | 193/70 | HJ | 2.31i,2.31 | 2.39 | -8 |
| Zhu Shuchun | | CHN | 5Apr60 | | Mar | 2:13:15 | 2:17:12 | -8 |
| Zhukov | Aleksandr | SU | 18Mar65 | 185/67 | PV | 5.50 | 5.30 | -8 |
| Zielke | Dariusz | POL | 21Oct60 | 192/77 | HJ | 2.28i,2.26 | 2.31 | -8 |

| ne | | Nat | Yr | Ht/Wt | Event | 1986 Mark | Pre-1986 best | |
|---|---|---|---|---|---|---|---|---|
| iembicki | Wiesław | POL | 17Jan60 | 175/64 | 3kSt | 8:25.04 | 8:29.91 | -83 |
| immerman | Michel | BEL | 1Jan60 | 186/70 | 400h | 49.69 | 49.64 | -84 |
| imny | Tomasz | POL | 24Dec63 | 180/67 | 3kSt | 8:29.27 | 8:35.27 | -85 |
| inchenko | Vladimir | SU | 25Jul59 | 192/115 | DT | 63.26 | 66.70 | -83 |
| inser | Wolfgang | FRG | 26Mar64 | 185/69 | TJ | 16.93 | 16.93 | -85 |
| intl | Bernhard | FRG | 16Jun65 | 185/76 | PV | 5.50 | 5.35 | -85 |
| irnis | Janis | SU | 28Nov47 | 190/94 | JT | 76.16 | 89.48* | -81 |
| otov | Vladimir | SU | 7Mar63 | | HT | 73.52 | 74.80 | -85 |
| ubrilin | Vladimir | SU | 15Jun63 | 191/80 | LJ | 7.91 | 7.93 | -85 |
| vara | Jan | CS | 12Feb63 | 190/85 | HJ | 2.34 | 2.35 | -85 |

MEN: INDEX

# ALL-TIME WORLD LISTS

| Mark | Wind | Name | Nat | Yr | Pos | Meet | Venue | Date |
|------|------|------|-----|----|----|------|-------|------|

## 100 METRES

| Mark | Wind | Name | Nat | Yr | Pos | Meet | Venue | Date |
|------|------|------|-----|----|----|------|-------|------|
| 10.76 | 1.7 | Evelyn Ashford | USA | 57 | 1 | WK | Zürich | 22 Aug 84 |
| A10.79 | 0.6 | Ashford | | | 1 | USOF | A.F.Academy | 3 Jul 83 |
| 10.81 | 1.7 | Marlies Göhr' | GDR | 58 | 1 | OD | Berlin | 8 Jun 83 |
| 10.83 | 1.7 | Marita Koch | GDR | 57 | 2 | OD | Berlin | 8 Jun 83 |
| 10.84 | 1.7 | Göhr | | | 2 | WK | Zürich | 22 Aug 84 |
| 10.86 | 0.4 | Göhr | | | 1 | | Potsdam | 5 May 84 |
| 10.86 | 2.0 | Göhr | | | 1 | | Berlin | 22 Sep 85 |
| 10.87 | 1.9 | Göhr | | | 1 | | Dresden | 26 Jul 84 |
| 10.88 | 2.0 | Oelsner' | | | 1 | NC | Dresden | 1 Jul 77 |
| 10.88 | 1.9 | Göhr | | | 1 | v USA | Karl-Marx-St. | 9 Jul 82 |
| 10.88 | 1.9 | Ashford | | | 1 | | Rieti | 7 Sep 86 |
| 10.89 | 0.7 | Göhr | | | 1 | NC | Erfurt | 1 Jun 84 |
| A10.90 | 0.6 | Ashford | | | 1r1 | USOF | Colorado Spr. | 22 Jul 81 |
| 10.90 | 1.1 | Göhr | | | 1 | NC | Karl-Marx-St. | 16 Jun 83 |
| 10.91 | 1.0 | Göhr | | | 1 | NC | Dresden | 1 Jul 82 |
| 10.91 | 0.6 | Göhr | | | 1 | | Berlin | 31 Jul 83 |
| 10.91 | -0.5 | Göhr | | | 1 | OD | Berlin | 20 Jul 84 |
| 10.91 | 0.2 | Ashford | | | 1 | GWG | Moskva | 6 Jul 86 |
| 10.91 | 0.2 | Heike Drechsler' | GDR | 64 | 2 | GWG | Moskva | 6 Jul 86 |
| 10.91 | 0.8 | Göhr | | | 1 | EC | Stuttgart | 27 Aug 86 |
| 10.92 | 1.3 | Ashford | | | 1h2 | ISTAF | Berlin | 17 Aug 84 |
| 10.92 | 1.0 | Merlene Ottey-Page | JAM | 60 | 1 | MSR | Walnut | 28 Apr 85 |
| 10.92 | 1.2 | Göhr | | | 1 | | Halle | 11 Jun 85 |
| 10.93 | 2.0 | Göhr | | | 1 | OT | Dresden | 24 May 80 |
| 10.93 | 0.1 | Ashford | | | 1 | | Westwood | 7 Aug 82 |
| 10.93 | 1.6 | Ashford | | | 1 | GG | Roma | 31 Aug 84 |
| 10.93 | 1.1 | Ottey-Page | | | 1 | | Los Angeles | 8 Jun 85 |
| 10.93 | 1.8 | Ewa Kasprzyk | POL | 57 | 1 | NC | Grudziądz | 27 Jun 86 |
| 10.93 | 1.6 | Ashford | | | 1 | ISTAF | Berlin | 15 Aug 86 |

( 29 Performances by 6 Athletes)

| Mark | Wind | Name | Nat | Yr | Pos | Meet | Venue | Date |
|------|------|------|-----|----|----|------|-------|------|
| A10.94 | 0.6 | Diane Williams | USA | 60 | 2 | USOF | A.F.Academy | 3 Jul 83 |
| 10.95 | 1.0 | Bärbel Wöckel' | GDR | 55 | 2 | NC | Dresden | 1 Jul 82 |
| 10.96 | 0.8 | Silke Gladisch | GDR | 64 | 1 | NC | Jena | 27 Jun 86 |
| 10.98 | 0.1 | Marina Zhirova (10) | SU | 63 | 2 | EP | Moskva | 17 Aug 85 |
| 10.99 | 0.0 | Florence Griffith | USA | 59 | 2 | ISTAF | Berlin | 17 Aug 84 |
| 10.99 | 1.3 | Valerie Brisco-Hooks | USA | 69 | 1 | | Westwood | 17 May 86 |
| 11.00 | 1.4 | Angella Taylor' | CAN | 58 | 1 | CommG | Brisbane | 4 Oct 82 |
| 11.01 | 0.6 | Annegret Richter | FRG | 50 | 1s1 | OG | Montréal | 25 Jul 76 |
| 11.02 | 2.0 | Romy Müller' | GDR | 58 | 3 | OT | Dresden | 24 May 80 |
| 11.02 | -0.1 | Lyudmila Kondratyeva | SU | 58 | 2 | Drz | Praha | 16 Aug 84 |
| 11.02 | 0.0 | Alice Brown | USA | 60 | 1 | | Koblenz | 28 Aug 85 |
| 11.03 | 2.0 | Monika Hamann' | GDR | 54 | 2 | NC | Dresden | 1 Jul 77 |
| 11.04 | 0.6 | Inge Helten | FRG | 50 | 1h1 | | Fürth | 13 Jun 76 |
| 11.04 | 1.7 | Ingrid Auerswald (20) | GDR | 57 | 4 | WK | Zürich | 22 Aug 84 |
| 11.04 | 0.8 | Anelia Nuneva' | BUL | 62 | 2 | EC | Stuttgart | 27 Aug 86 |
| 11.07 | -0.2 | Renate Stecher' | GDR | 50 | 1 | OG | München | 2 Sep 72 |

| Mark | Wind | Name | Nat | Yr | Pos | Meet | Venue | Date |
|------|------|------|-----|----|----|------|-------|------|
| A11.08 | 1.2 | Wyomia Tyus | USA | 45 | 1 | OG | México | 15 Oct 68 |
| 11.08 | 2.0 | Brenda Morehead | USA | 57 | 1 | FOT | Eugene | 21 Jun 76 |
| 11.08 | -0.1 | Jeanette Bolden | USA | 60 | 2 | WK | Zürich | 13 Aug 86 |
| 11.08 | 0.8 | Nelli Cooman-Fiere | HOL | 64 | 3 | EC | Stuttgart | 27 Aug 86 |
| 11.09 | 1.7 | Jarmila Kratochvílová | CS | 51 | 1 | PTS | Bratislava | 6 Jun 81 |
| 11.09 | 1.7 | Nadezhda Georgieva | BUL | 61 | 1 | NC | Sofia | 4 Jun 83 |
| 11.09 | -1.4 | Irina Slyusar | SU | 63 | 1 | Znam | Leningrad | 7 Jun 86 |
| 11.10 | 0.1 | Kathy Smallwood' | UK | 60 | 2 | WP | Roma | 5 Sep 81 |
|       |      | (30) |     |    |    |      |       |      |
| 11.11 | 1.7 | Bärbel Schölzel | GDR | 59 | 5 | OD | Berlin | 8 Jun 83 |
| A11.11 | 0.6 | Jackie Washington | USA | 62 | 3 | USOF | A.F.Academy | 3 Jul 83 |
| A11.12 | 0.6 | Barbara Ferrell | USA | 47 | 1q1 | OG | México | 14 Oct 68 |
| 11.12 | 0.1 | Gail Devers | USA | 66 | 1h2 | NCAA | Indianapolis | 5 Jun 86 |
| 11.12 | 0.2 | Elvira Barbashina | SU | 63 | 3 | GWG | Moskva | 6 Jul 86 |
| 11.13 | -1.2 | Irena Szewińska' | POL | 46 | 1 | EC | Roma | 3 Sep 74 |
| 11.13 | 2.0 | Chandra Cheeseborough | USA | 59 | 2 | FOT | Eugene | 21 Jun 76 |
| 11.13 | 1.8 | Gesine Walther | GDR | 62 | 1h2 |  | Cottbus | 21 Aug 82 |
| 11.13 | 0.9 | Helinä Marjamaa' | FIN | 56 | 1 |  | Lahti | 19 Jul 83 |
| 11.14 | 1.7 | Lilieth Hodges | JAM | 53 | =1h1 | AAU | Westwood | 8 Jun 78 |
|       |      | (40) |     |    |    |      |       |      |
| 11.15 | 2.0 | Chantal Rega | FRA | 55 | 1 | NC | Lille | 26 Jun 76 |
| 11.15 | 1.4 | Sofka Popova | BUL | 53 | 1 | Balk | Sofia | 13 Jun 80 |
| 11.15 | 0.6 | Pam Marshall | USA | 60 | 3 |  | Modesto | 11 May 85 |
| 11.15 | 0.7 | Heidi-Elke Gaugel | FRG | 59 | 1 | NC | Stuttgart | 2 Aug 85 |
| 11.15 | 0.0 | Sheila Echols | USA | 64 | 1 |  | Knoxville | 24 May 86 |
| 11.16 | 0.4 | Andrea Lynch | UK | 52 | 1 |  | London | 11 Jun 75 |
| 11.16 | 1.2 | Silvia Chivas | CUB | 54 | 1s1 | WUG | Sofia | 20 Aug 77 |
| 11.16 | 1.0 | Linda Haglund | SWE | 56 | 4 | OG | Moskva | 26 Jul 80 |
| 11.16 | 1.8 | Rose-Aimée Bacoul | FRA | 52 | 1s1 | NC | Bordeaux | 23 Jul 83 |
| 11.16 | 0.0 | Tatyana Alexeyeva | SU | 63 | 1 |  | Sochi | 19 May 84 |
|       |      | (50) |     |    |    |      |       |      |

Marks made with assisting wind > 2m/s

| Mark | Wind | Name | Nat | Yr | Pos | Meet | Venue | Date |
|------|------|------|-----|----|----|------|-------|------|
| 10.78 | 3.1 | Ashford |  |  | 1 |  | Modesto | 12 May 84 |
| 10.79 | 3.3 | Marlies Göhr' | GDR | 58 | 1 | NC | Cottbus | 16 Jul 80 |
| 10.80 | 2.9 | Pam Marshall | USA | 60 | 1 | TAC | Eugene | 20 Jun 86 |
| 10.80 | 2.8 | Heike Drechsler' | GDR | 64 | 1 | Bisl | Oslo | 5 Jul 86 |
| 10.84 | 2.9 | Alice Brown | USA | 60 | 2 | TAC | Eugene | 20 Jun 86 |
| 10.85 | 5.2 | Ashford |  |  | 1 |  | Norwalk | 14 Jun 81 |
| 10.85 | 2.4 | Ashford |  |  | 1 |  | Modesto | 14 May 83 |
| 10.85 | 2.9 | Ashford |  |  | 3 | TAC | Eugene | 20 Jun 86 |
| 10.88 | 3.0 | Ashford |  |  | 1 | MSR | Walnut | 29 Apr 84 |
| 10.92 | 3.3 | Bärbel Wöckel' | GDR | 55 | 2 | NC | Cottbus | 16 Jul 80 |
| 10.92 | 4.3 | Wöckel |  |  | 1 |  | Cottbus | 21 Aug 82 |
| 10.92 | 3.4 | Angella Taylor' | CAN | 58 | 1s2 | CG | Brisbane | 4 Oct 82 |
| 10.92 | 4.1 | Göhr |  |  | 1 | v UK | Birmingham | 6 Jul 85 |
| 10.92 | 2.9 | Diane Williams | USA | 60 | 4 | TAC | Eugene | 20 Jun 86 |
| 10.93 | 3.8 | Sonia Lannaman | UK | 56 | 1 | EP/sf | Dublin | 17 Jul 77 |
| 10.93 | 3.3 | Ingrid Auerswald | GDR | 57 | 3 | NC | Cottbus | 16 Jul 80 |

( 19 Performances by 9 Athletes )

| Mark | Wind | Name | Nat | Yr | Pos | Meet | Venue | Date |
|------|------|------|-----|----|----|------|-------|------|
| 10.94 | 3.9 | Jackie Washington | USA | 62 | 1 |  | Houston | 18 May 86 |
|       |      | (10) |     |    |    |      |       |      |
| 10.96 | 2.9 | Brenda Morehead | USA | 57 | 1s2 | AAU | Walnut | 16 Jun 79 |
| 10.96 | 2.9 | Florence Griffith | USA | 59 | 1 | WK | Zürich | 24 Aug 83 |
| 10.96 | 2.8 | Gail Devers | USA | 66 | 2s1 | TAC | Eugene | 20 Jun 86 |

| Mark | Wind | Name | Nat | Yr | Pos | Meet | Venue | Date |
|------|------|------|-----|----|-----|------|-------|------|
| 10.97 | 3.3 | Gesine Walther | GDR | 62 | 4 | NC | Cottbus | 16 Jul 80 |
| 10.97 | 3.9 | Juliet Cuthbert | JAM | 64 | 2 | | Houston | 18 May 86 |
| 10.99 | 2.4 | Chandra Cheeseborough | USA | 59 | 2 | | Modesto | 14 May 83 |
| 11.01 | 4.0 | Heather Hunte' | UK | 59 | 1 | | London | 21 May 80 |
| 11.01 | 5.8 | Gwen Torrence | USA | 65 | 1 | FlaR | Gainesville | 29 Mar 86 |
| 11.04 | 3.0 | Michelle Finn | USA | 65 | 1 | NCAA | Austin | 1 Jun 85 |
| A11.05 | 2.2 | Silvia Chivas | CUB | 54 | 1 | WPT | Guadalajara | 12 Aug 77 |
| | | (20) | | | | | | |
| 11.06 | 2.8 | Linda Haglund | SWE | 56 | 1 | ISTAF | Berlin | 21 Aug 81 |
| 11.06 | 3.7 | Randy Givens | USA | 62 | 1 | NCAA | Eugene | 1 Jun 84 |
| 11.08 | 2.9 | Kathy Cook' | UK | 60 | 4 | WK | Zürich | 24 Aug 83 |
| 11.09 | 2.7 | Olga Antonova' | SU | 60 | 1 | | Leningrad | 26 Jul 83 |
| 11.09 | | Angela Williams | TRI | 65 | 1 | | Nashville | 14 Apr 84 |
| 11.09 | | Wanda Fort | USA | 63 | 2 | | Nashville | 14 Apr 84 |
| 11.11 | 2.4 | Pauline Davis | BAH | 66 | 1 | | Knoxville | 18 May 86 |
| 11.12 | 2.9 | Marie-Chr. Cazier | FRA | 63 | 1 | | Joinville | 12 Jun 85 |
| A11.13 | 3.1 | Benita Fitzgerald' | USA | 61 | 3 | NCAA | Provo | 4 Jun 82 |
| 11.13 | 2.2 | Beverley Kinch | UK | 64 | 1 | WUG | Edmonton | 6 Jul 83 |
| | | (30) | | | | | | |
| 11.13 | 3.3 | Shirley Thomas | UK | 63 | 2 | NC | Cwmbran | 27 May 84 |
| 11.14 | | Esther Hope | TRI | 60 | 1 | | Houston | 2 May 81 |
| 11.14 | 3.7 | Brenda Cliette | USA | 63 | 2 | NCAA | Eugene | 1 Jun 84 |
| 11.14 | 2.5 | Paula Dunn | UK | 64 | 1s1 | CommG | Edinburgh | 27 Jul 86 |
| 11.15 | | Sheila LaBome | USA | 60 | 2 | | Houston | 2 May 81 |
| | | (35) | | | | | | |

Doubtful automatic timing

| Mark | Wind | Name | Nat | Yr | Pos | Meet | Venue | Date |
|------|------|------|-----|----|-----|------|-------|------|
| 10.87 | 1.9 | Lyudmila Kondratyeva | SU | 58 | 1 | | Leningrad | 3 Jun 80 |
| 10.99 | 1.9 | Natalya Bochina | SU | 62 | 2 | | Leningrad | 3 Jun 80 |

## 200 METRES

| Mark | Wind | Name | Nat | Yr | Pos | Meet | Venue | Date |
|------|------|------|-----|----|-----|------|-------|------|
| 21.71 | 0.7 | Marita Koch | GDR | 57 | 1 | v Can | Karl-Marx-St. | 10 Jun 79 |
| 21.71 | 0.3 | Koch | | | 1 | OD | Potsdam | 21 Jul 84 |
| 21.71 | 1.2 | Heike Drechsler' | GDR | 64 | 1 | NC | Jena | 29 Jun 86 |
| 21.71 | -0.8 | Drechsler | | | 1 | EC | Stuttgart | 29 Aug 86 |
| 21.74 | 0.4 | Marlies Göhr' | GDR | 58 | 1 | NC | Erfurt | 3 Jun 84 |
| 21.76 | 0.3 | Koch | | | 1 | NC | Dresden | 3 Jul 82 |
| 21.78 | -1.3 | Koch | | | 1 | NC | Leipzig | 11 Aug 85 |
| 21.81 | -0.1 | Valerie Brisco-Hooks | USA | 60 | 1 | OG | Los Angeles | 9 Aug 84 |
| 21.82 | 1.3 | Koch | | | 1 | NC | Karl-Marx-St. | 18 Jun 83 |
| 21.83 | -0.2 | Evelyn Ashford | USA | 57 | 1 | WP | Montréal | 24 Aug 79 |
| 21.84 | -1.1 | Ashford | | | 1 | VD | Bruxelles | 28 Aug 81 |
| 21.85 | 0.3 | Bärbel Wöckel' | GDR | 55 | 2 | OD | Potsdam | 21 Jul 84 |
| 21.87 | 0.0 | Koch | | | 1 | WK | Zürich | 22 Aug 84 |
| 21.88 | 0.9 | Ashford | | | 1 | TAC | Indianapolis | 19 Jun 83 |
| 21.90 | 1.9 | Koch | | | 1 | | Dresden | 3 Aug 85 |
| 21.90 | -0.7 | Koch | | | 1 | WP | Canberra | 4 Oct 85 |
| A21.91 | 1.9 | Koch | | | 1 | WUG | México | 12 Sep 79 |
| 21.93 | 0.4 | Merlene Ottey-Page | JAM | 60 | 1 | TAC | Indianapolis | 16 Jun 85 |
| 21.97 | 1.9 | Jarmila Kratochvílová | CS | 51 | 1 | PTS | Bratislava | 6 Jun 81 |
| 21.97 | -1.4 | Ashford | | | 1 | WK | Zürich | 13 Aug 86 |
| 21.98 | -1.1 | Brisco-Hooks | | | 1r2 | WK | Zürich | 21 Aug 85 |

WOMEN All-time

| Mark | Wind | Name | Nat | Yr | Pos | Meet | Venue | Date |
|------|------|------|-----|-----|-----|------|-------|------|
| 21.99 | 0.9 | Chandra Cheeseborough | USA | 59 | 2 | TAC | Indianapolis | 19 Jun 83 |
| 22.01 | 0.6 | Wöckel | | | 1 | NC | Cottbus | 18 Jul 80 |

( 23 Performances by 9 Athletes )

| Mark | Wind | Name | Nat | Yr | Pos | Meet | Venue | Date |
|------|------|------|-----|-----|-----|------|-------|------|
| 22.04 | -0.1 | Florence Griffith | USA | 59 | 2 | OG | Los Angeles | 9 Aug 84 |
| | | (10) | | | | | | |
| 22.07 | 1.2 | Silke Gladisch | GDR | 64 | 2 | NC | Jena | 29 Jun 86 |
| 22.10 | -0.1 | Kathy Cook' | UK | 60 | 4 | OG | Los Angeles | 9 Aug 84 |
| 22.12 | 1.2 | Pam Marshall | USA | 60 | 1 | GWG | Moskva | 8 Jul 86 |
| 22.13 | 1.2 | Ewa Kasprzyk | POL | 57 | 2 | GWG | Moskva | 8 Jul 86 |
| 22.19 | 1.5 | Natalya Bochina | SU | 62 | 2 | OG | Moskva | 30 Jul 80 |
| 22.20 | -0.1 | Grace Jackson | JAM | 61 | 5 | OG | Los Angeles | 9 Aug 84 |
| 22.21 | 1.9 | Irena Szewińska' | POL | 46 | 1 | | Potsdam | 13 Jun 74 |
| 22.24 | 0.3 | Gesine Walther | GDR | 62 | 2 | NC | Dresden | 3 Jul 82 |
| A22.25 | 0.8 | Angella Taylor' | CAN | 58 | 1 | | Colorado Spr. | 20 Jul 82 |
| 22.27 | 1.2 | Elvira Barbashina | SU | 63 | 3 | GWG | Moskva | 8 Jul 86 |
| | | (20) | | | | | | |
| 22.31 | 0.1 | Lyudmila Kondratyeva | SU | 58 | 1 | | Moskva | 12 Jun 80 |
| 22.31 | 0.9 | Randy Givens | USA | 62 | 4 | TAC | Indianapolis | 19 Jun 83 |
| 22.32 | -0.8 | Marie-Chr. Cazier | FRA | 63 | 2 | EC | Stuttgart | 29 Aug 86 |
| 22.35 | 1.8 | Denise Boyd' | AUS | 52 | 1 | NC | Sydney | 23 Mar 80 |
| 22.37 | 1.3 | Sabine Rieger' | GDR | 63 | 2 | v SU | Cottbus | 26 Jun 82 |
| 22.38 | 1.6 | Renate Stecher' | GDR | 50 | 1 | NC | Dresden | 21 Jul 73 |
| 22.38 | 1.7 | Brenda Morehead | USA | 57 | 1 | | Nashville | 12 Apr 80 |
| 22.39 | 0.6 | Mona-Lisa Pursiainen' | FIN | 51 | 1 | WUG | Moskva | 20 Aug 73 |
| 22.39 | 0.0 | Annegret Richter | FRG | 50 | 2 | OG | Montréal | 28 Jul 76 |
| 22.41 | 0.9 | Alice Brown | USA | 60 | 5 | TAC | Indianapolis | 19 Jun 83 |
| | | (30) | | | | | | |
| 22.42 | 1.2 | Nadezhda Georgieva | BUL | 61 | 1 | Nar | Sofia | 22 May 83 |
| A22.42 | | Evette Armstrong' | RSA | 65 | 1 | | Johannesburg | 18 Apr 86 |
| 22.44 | 1.3 | Olga Vladykina | SU | 63 | 1 | | Donyetsk | 29 Aug 85 |
| 22.45 | 1.1 | Raelene Boyle | AUS | 51 | 2 | OG | München | 7 Sep 72 |
| 22.46 | 0.2 | Marina Zhirova | SU | 63 | 1 | v Jap,USA | Tokyo | 22 Sep 85 |
| 22.46 | 0.1 | Marina Molokova | SU | 62 | 1 | NC | Kiev | 16 Jul 86 |
| 22.47 | 1.5 | Romy Müller' | GDR | 58 | 4 | OG | Moskva | 30 Jul 80 |
| 22.47 | 0.2 | Taťána Kocembová | CS | 62 | 1 | | Barcelona | 8 Jul 84 |
| 22.50 | 0.0 | Kirsten Siemon' | GDR | 61 | 2 | NC | Jena | 9 Aug 81 |
| 22.51 | -0.1 | Maya Azarashivili | SU | 64 | 1 | Spart | Tashkent | 20 Sep 86 |
| | | (40) | | | | | | |
| 22.53 | 1.4 | Rose-Aimée Bacoul | FRA | 52 | 4s2 | OG | Los Angeles | 9 Aug 84 |
| 22.53 | 0.3 | Diane Dixon | USA | 64 | 3 | Jenn | San Jose | 31 May 86 |
| 22.53 | 1.2 | Gwen Torrence | USA | 65 | 4 | GWG | Moskva | 8 Jul 86 |
| 22.56 | -0.4 | Heidi-Elke Gaugel | FRG | 59 | 1 | NC | Stuttgart | 4 Aug 85 |
| 22.58 | 1.5 | Sonia Lannaman | UK | 56 | 1 | | Cwmbran | 18 May 80 |
| 22.58 | 1.2 | Anelia Nuneva' | BUL | 62 | 1 | v Hun,Pol | Sofia | 24 Jul 83 |
| 22.59 | 1.4 | Irina Slyusar | SU | 63 | 1s2 | WUG | Kobe | 31 Aug 85 |
| 22.60 | 1.1 | Ingrid Auerswald | GDR | 57 | 2 | OT | Erfurt | 18 May 80 |
| 22.60 | 2.0 | Diane Williams | USA | 60 | 2r2 | MSR | Walnut | 27 Apr 86 |
| 22.61 | 1.9 | Christina Brehmer' | GDR | 58 | 2 | | Halle | 14 Jun 79 |
| | | (50) | | | | | | |

Marks made with assisting wind > 2 m/s

| Mark | Wind | Name | Nat | Yr | Pos | Meet | Venue | Date |
|------|------|------|-----|-----|-----|------|-------|------|
| 21.85 | 2.6 | Koch | | | 1 | | Karl-Marx-St. | 27 May 79 |
| 21.85 | 2.6 | Bärbel Wöckel' | GDR | 55 | 1 | v USA | Karl-Marx-St. | 10 Jul 82 |
| A22.19 | 3.1 | Angella Taylor' | CAN | 58 | 1 | | Colorado Spr. | 21 Jul 82 |
| 22.35 | 2.1 | Juliet Cuthbert | JAM | 64 | 1r3 | | Houston | 18 May 86 |
| A22.39 | 2.9 | Evette Armstrong' | RSA | 65 | 1h | NC | Germiston | 12 Apr 86 |

| Mark | Wind | Name | Nat | Yr | Pos | Meet | Venue | Date |
|------|------|------|-----|----|----|------|-------|------|
| 22.48 | 4.0 | Michelle Scutt' | UK | 60 | 1 | WA | Dublin | 4 Jul 82 |
| 22.55 | 3.3 | Els Vader | HOL | 59 | 1 | NC | Amsterdam | 12 Jul 86 |
|  |  | (6) |  |  |  |  |  |  |

## 400 METRES

| Mark | Name | Nat | Yr | Pos | Meet | Venue | Date |
|------|------|-----|----|----|------|-------|------|
| 47.60 | Marita Koch | GDR | 57 | 1 | WP | Canberra | 6 Oct 85 |
| 47.99 | Jarmila Kratochvílová | CS | 51 | 1 | WC | Helsinki | 10 Aug 83 |
| 48.16 | Koch |  |  | 1 | EC | Athínai | 8 Sep 82 |
| 48.16 | Koch |  |  | 1 | Drz | Praha | 16 Aug 84 |
| 48.22 | Koch |  |  | 1 | EC | Stuttgart | 28 Aug 86 |
| 48.26 | Koch |  |  | 1 |  | Dresden | 27 Jul 84 |
| 48.27 | Olga Vladykina | SU | 63 | 2 | WP | Canberra | 6 Oct 85 |
| 48.45 | Kratochvílová |  |  | 1 | NC | Praha | 23 Jul 83 |
| 48.59 | Taťána Kocembová | CS | 62 | 2 | WC | Helsinki | 10 Aug 83 |
| 48.60 | Koch |  |  | 1 | EP | Torino | 4 Aug 79 |
| 48.60 | Vladykina |  |  | 1 | EP | Moskva | 17 Aug 85 |
| 48.61 | Kratochvílová |  |  | 1 | WP | Roma | 6 Sep 81 |
| 48.73 | Kocembová |  |  | 2 | Drz | Praha | 16 Aug 84 |
| 48.77 | Koch |  |  | 1 | v USA | Karl-Marx-St. | 9 Jul 82 |
| 48.82 | Kratochvílová |  |  | 1 | Roš | Praha | 23 Jun 83 |
| 48.83 | Valerie Brisco-Hooks | USA | 60 | 1 | OG | Los Angeles | 6 Aug 84 |
| 48.85 | Kratochvílová |  |  | 2 | EC | Athínai | 8 Sep 82 |
| 48.86 | Kratochvílová |  |  | 1 | WK | Zürich | 18 Aug 82 |
| 48.86 | Koch |  |  | 1 | NC | Erfurt | 2 Jun 84 |
| 48.87 | Koch |  |  | 1 | VD | Bruxelles | 27 Aug 82 |
| 48.88 | Koch |  |  | 1 | OG | Moskva | 28 Jul 80 |

( 21 Performances by 5 Athletes )

| Mark | Name | Nat | Yr | Pos | Meet | Venue | Date |
|------|------|-----|----|----|------|-------|------|
| 49.05 | Chandra Cheeseborough | USA | 59 | 2 | OG | Los Angeles | 6 Aug 84 |
| 49.19 | Maria Pinigina' | SU | 58 | 3 | WC | Helsinki | 10 Aug 83 |
| 49.24 | Sabine Busch | GDR | 62 | 2 | NC | Erfurt | 2 Jun 84 |
| 49.28 | Irena Szewińska' | POL | 46 | 1 | OG | Montréal | 29 Jul 76 |
| 49.43 | Kathy Cook' | UK | 60 | 3 | OG | Los Angeles | 6 Aug 84 |
|  | (10) |  |  |  |  |  |  |
| 49.56 | Bärbel Wöckel' | GDR | 55 | 1 |  | Erfurt | 30 May 82 |
| 49.58 | Dagmar Rübsam' | GDR | 62 | 3 | NC | Erfurt | 2 Jun 84 |
| 49.66 | Christina Lathan' | GDR | 58 | 3 | OG | Moskva | 28 Jul 80 |
| 49.75 | Gaby Bussmann | FRG | 59 | 4 | WC | Helsinki | 10 Aug 83 |
| 49.79 | Petra Müller | GDR | 65 | 2 | GO | Dresden | 16 Aug 86 |
| 49.91 | Marita Payne | CAN | 60 | 4 | OG | Los Angeles | 6 Aug 84 |
| 49.99 | Pam Marshall | USA | 60 | 1 | Pepsi | Westwood | 17 May 86 |
| 50.03 | Gesine Walther | GDR | 62 | 2 |  | Jena | 13 May 84 |
| 50.07 | Irina Nazarova' | SU | 57 | 4 | OG | Moskva | 28 Jul 80 |
| 50.07 | Kirsten Emmelmann' | GDR | 61 | 2 | ISTAF | Berlin | 23 Aug 85 |
|  | (20) |  |  |  |  |  |  |
| A50.12 | Myrtle Bothma' | RSA | 64 | 1 | NC | Germiston | 11 Apr 86 |
| 50.14 | Riita Salin | FIN | 50 | 1 | EC | Roma | 4 Sep 74 |
| 50.15 | Ellen Streidt' | GDR | 52 | 2 |  | Berlin | 10 Jul 76 |
| 50.17 | Nina Zyuskova | SU | 52 | 5 | OG | Moskva | 28 Jul 80 |
| 50.18 | Lillie Leatherwood | USA | 64 | 1 | GP | Roma | 11 Jul 86 |
| 50.19 | Irina Baskakova | SU | 56 | 2 | Spart | Moskva | 21 Jun 83 |
| 50.24 | Diane Dixon | USA | 64 | 1 | Bisl | Oslo | 5 Jul 86 |

| Mark | Name | Nat | Yr | Pos | Meet | Venue | Date |
|------|------|-----|----|----|------|-------|------|
| 50.26 | Brigitte Rohde' | GDR | 54 | 1r2 | v UK, | Yug Split | 1 May 76 |
| 50.28 | Lilia Novoseltseva' | SU | 62 | 2 | | Moskva | 20 Jul 84 |
| 50.34 | Doris Maletzki | GDR | 52 | 4 | OT | Berlin | 10 Jul 76 |
| | (30) | | | | | | |
| 50.37 | Ute Thimm' | FRG | 58 | 6 | OG | Los Angeles | 6 Aug 84 |
| 50.40 | Sherri Howard | USA | 62 | 4 | FOT | Los Angeles | 19 Jun 84 |
| 50.41 | Ana Fidelia Quirot | CUB | 63 | 1 | Barr | Habana | 14 Jun 86 |
| 50.45 | Charmaine Crooks | CAN | 61 | 7 | OG | Los Angeles | 6 Aug 84 |
| 50.49 | Tatyana Goyshchik' | SU | 52 | 3 | Spart | Moskva | 24 Jul 79 |
| 50.56 | Pirjo Häggman | FIN | 51 | 4 | OG | Montréal | 29 Jul 76 |
| A50.56 | Aurelia Penton | CUB | 43 | 1 | CAG | Medellin | 16 Jul 78 |
| A50.57 | Evette Armstrong' | RSA | 65 | 1 | | Germiston | 2 Apr 86 |
| 50.60 | Larisa Krylova | SU | 55 | 1 | | Kiev | 14 Aug 82 |
| 50.62 | Rosalyn Bryant | USA | 56 | 1s2 | OG | Montréal | 28 Jul 76 |
| | (40) | | | | | | |
| 50.62 | Karoline Käfer | AUT | 54 | 1 | | Klagenfurt | 18 Jun 77 |
| 50.63 | Michelle Scutt' | UK | 60 | 1 | NC | Cwmbran | 31 May 82 |
| 50.63 | Marina Ivanova' | SU | 62 | 4 | Spart | Moskva | 21 Jun 83 |
| 50.63 | Lyudmila Byelova | SU | 58 | 3 | | Moskva | 4 Aug 84 |
| 50.70 | Gabriele Kotte' | GDR | 58 | 2 | NC | Karl-Marx-St. | 12 Aug 79 |
| 50.70 | Genowefa Błaszak | POL | 57 | 3 | ISTAF | Berlin | 15 Aug 86 |
| 50.75 | Joslyn Hoyte-Smith | UK | 54 | 1 | v GDR, | Bel London | 18 Jun 82 |
| 50.77 | Yelena Korban' | SU | 61 | 1 | | Leningrad | 27 Jul 83 |
| 50.78 | Gisela Anton | GDR | 54 | 1 | | Halle | 27 Jul 76 |
| 50.78 | Olga Mineyeva | SU | 52 | 2 | | Moskva | 12 Jun 80 |
| | (50) | | | | | | |
| 50.78 | Debbie Flintoff | AUS | 60 | 3 | GP | Roma | 11 Jul 86 |

Hand timing

| | | | | | | | |
|------|------|-----|----|----|------|-------|------|
| 50.3 | Olga Mineyeva | SU | 52 | 1 | | Kharkov | 9 Aug 80 |
| 50.6 | Tatyana Prorochenko | SU | 52 | 1 | | Alushta | 8 Sep 77 |
| 50.6 | Inna Yevseyeva | SU | 64 | 1 | | Kiev | 29 Aug 86 |

# 800 METRES

| | | | | | | | |
|------|------|-----|----|----|------|-------|------|
| 1:53.28 | Jarmila Kratochvílová | CS | 51 | 1 | | München | 26 Jul 83 |
| 1:53.43 | Nadezhda Olizarenko' | SU | 53 | 1 | OG | Moskva | 27 Jul 80 |
| 1:54.68 | Kratochvílová | | | 1 | WC | Helsinki | 9 Aug 83 |
| 1:54.81 | Olga Mineyeva | SU | 52 | 2 | OG | Moskva | 27 Jul 80 |
| 1:54.85 | Olizarenko | | | 1 | | Moskva | 12 Jun 80 |
| 1:54.94 | Tatyana Kazankina | SU | 51 | 1 | OG | Montréal | 26 Jul 76 |
| 1:55.04 | Kratochvílová | | | 1 | | Oslo | 23 Aug 83 |
| 1:55.05 | Doina Melinte | RUM | 56 | 1 | NC | Bucureşti | 1 Aug 82 |
| 1:55.1 | Mineyeva | | | 1 | Znam | Moskva | 6 Jul 80 |
| 1:55.41 | Mineyeva | | | 1 | EC | Athínai | 8 Sep 82 |
| 1:55.42 | Nikolina Shtereva | BUL | 55 | 2 | OG | Montréal | 26 Jul 76 |
| 1:55.46 | Tatyana Providokhina | SU | 53 | 3 | OG | Moskva | 27 Jul 80 |
| 1:55.5 m | Mineyeva | | | 1 | Kuts | Podolsk | 21 Aug 82 |
| 1:55.60 | Elfi Zinn | GDR | 53 | 3 | OG | Montréal | 26 Jul 76 |
| 1:55.68 | Ella Kovacs | RUM | 64 | 1 | RumIC | Bucureşti | 2 Jun 85 |
| 1:55.69 | Irina Podyalovskaya | SU | 59 | 1 | | Kiev | 22 Jun 84 |
| 1:55.74 | Anita Weiss' | GDR | 55 | 4 | OG | Montréal | 26 Jul 76 |
| 1:55.80 | Providokhina | | | 1 | EC | Praha | 31 Aug 78 |
| 1:55.82 | Mushta' | | | 2 | EC | Praha | 31 Aug 78 |
| 1:55.9 | Providokhina | | | 2 | Znam | Moskva | 6 Jul 80 |

| Mark | Name | Nat | Yr | Pos | Meet | Venue | Date |
|------|------|-----|----|----|------|-------|------|
| 1:55.91 | Kratochvílová | | | 1 | EP | Moskva | 17 Aug 85 |
| 1:55.96 | Lyudmila Veselkova | SU | 50 | 2 | EC | Athínai | 8 Sep 82 |
| 1:55.95 | Yekaterina Podkopayeva' | SU | 52 | 1 | | Leningrad | 27 Jul 83 |

( 23 Performances by 13 Athletes )

| | | | | | | | |
|------|------|-----|----|----|------|-------|------|
| 1:56.0 m | Valentina Gerasimova | SU | 48 | 1 | NC | Kiev | 12 Jun 76 |
| 1:56.1 m | Ravilya Agletdinova | SU | 60 | 2 | Kuts | Podolsk | 21 Aug 82 |
| 1:56.11 | Lyubov Gurina | SU | 57 | 2 | WC | Helsinki | 9 Aug 83 |
| 1:56.2 | Totka Petrova | BUL | 56 | 1 | | Paris | 6 Jul 79 |
| 1:56.2 m | Tatyana Mishkel | SU | 52 | 3 | Kuts | Podolsk | 21 Aug 82 |
| 1:56.21 | Martina Kämpfert' | GDR | 59 | 4 | OG | Moskva | 27 Jul 80 |
| 1:56.21 | Zamira Zaytseva | SU | 53 | 2 | | Leningrad | 27 Jul 83 |
| | (20) | | | | | | |
| 1:56.44 | Svetlana Styrkina | SU | 49 | 5 | OG | Montréal | 26 Jul 76 |
| 1:56.57 | Zoya Rigel | SU | 52 | 3 | EC | Praha | 31 Aug 78 |
| 1:56.6 m | Tamara Sorokina' | SU | 50 | 5 | Kuts | Podolsk | 21 Aug 82 |
| 1:56.67 | Fita Lovin' | RUM | 51 | 2 | | Moskva | 12 Jun 80 |
| 1:56.71 | Christine Wachtel | GDR | 65 | 3 | EP | Moskva | 17 Aug 85 |
| 1:56.78 | Lyudmila Borisova | SU | 59 | 3 | | Kiev | 19 Jul 84 |
| 1:56.84 | Nina Ruchayeva | SU | 56 | 2 | | Moskva | 19 Jul 84 |
| 1:56.90 | Mary Decker-Slaney | USA | 58 | 1 | | Bern | 16 Aug 85 |
| 1:56.9 m | Olga Dvirna | SU | 53 | 6 | Kuts | Podolsk | 21 Aug 82 |
| 1:56.95 | Jolanta Januchta | POL | 55 | 1 | BGP | Budapest | 11 Aug 80 |
| | (30) | | | | | | |
| 1:56.96 | Zuzana Moravčíková | CS | 56 | 1 | | Leipzig | 27 Jul 83 |
| 1:56.97 | Valentina Zhukova' | SU | 59 | 5 | | Kiev | 22 Jun 84 |
| 1:57.0 | Olga Vakhrusheva | SU | 47 | 3 | | Moskva | 12 Jun 80 |
| 1:57.05 | Sigrun Wodars' | GDR | 65 | 1 | NC | Jena | 28 Jun 86 |
| 1:57.06 | Ulrike Klapezynski' | GDR | 53 | 1 | OT | Berlin | 10 Jul 76 |
| 1:57.08 | Galina Zakharova | SU | 56 | 1 | NP | Baku | 16 Sep 84 |
| 1:57.18 | Lyubov Kiryukhina | SU | 63 | 1 | NC | Kiev | 16 Jul 86 |
| 1:57.20 | Hildegard Ullrich' | GDR | 59 | 5 | OG | Moskva | 27 Jul 80 |
| 1:57.21 | Svetla Zlateva-Koleva | BUL | 52 | 6 | OG | Montréal | 26 Jul 76 |
| 1:57.22 | Margrit Klinger | FRG | 60 | 3 | EC | Athínai | 8 Sep 82 |
| | (40) | | | | | | |
| 1:57.26 | Elżbieta Katolik | POL | 49 | 2 | BGP | Budapest | 11 Aug 80 |
| 1:57.28 | Milena Matějkovičová' | CS | 61 | 2 | | Leipzig | 27 Jul 83 |
| 1:57.39 | Ileana Silai | RUM | 41 | 1 | NC | Bucureşti | 28 Aug 77 |
| 1:57.42 | Kirsty McDermott' | UK | 62 | 2 | | Belfast | 24 Jun 85 |
| 1:57.47 | Nadezhda Zvyagintseva | SU | 61 | 6 | | Kiev | 22 Jun 84 |
| 1:57.5 m | Tatyana Pozdnyakova | SU | 56 | 9 | Kuts | Podolsk | 21 Aug 82 |
| 1:57.54 | Nadezhda Zabolotnyeva | SU | 61 | 2 | GWG | Moskva | 6 Jul 86 |
| 1:57.57 | Antje Schröder | GDR | 63 | 3 | | Leipzig | 27 Jul 83 |
| 1:57.6 | Christiane Wartenberg' | GDR | 56 | 1 | | Potsdam | 29 Jul 79 |
| 1:57.66 | Gabriella Dorio | ITA | 57 | 1 | | Pisa | 5 Jul 80 |
| | (50) | | | | | | |

## 1000 METRES

| | | | | | | | |
|------|------|-----|----|----|-------|------|
| 2:30.6 | Tatyana Providokhina | SU | 53 | 1 | Podolsk | 20 Aug 78 |
| 2:30.85 | Martina Kämpfert' | GDR | 59 | 1 | Berlin | 9 Jul 80 |
| 2:31.5 m | Maricica Puica | RUM | 50 | 1 | Poiana Brasov | 1 Jun 86 |
| 2:31.6 | Beate Liebich | GDR | 58 | 2 | Berlin | 9 Jul 80 |
| 2:31.65 | Olga Dvirna | SU | 53 | 1 | Athínai | 1 Sep 82 |

| Mark | Name | Nat | Yr | Pos | Meet | Venue | Date |
|------|------|-----|----|----|------|-------|------|
| 2:31.74 | Anita Weiss' | GDR | 55 | 1 | | Potsdam | 13 Jul 80 |
| 2:31.8 | Dvirna | | | 1 | Kuts | Podolsk | 5 Aug 79 |
| 2:31.95 | Ulrike Bruns' | GDR | 53 | 1 | ISTAF | Berlin | 18 Aug 78 |
| 2:32.29 | Christiane Wartenberg' | GDR | 56 | 2 | | Potsdam | 13 Jul 80 |
| 2:32.6 | Raisa Byelousova | SU | 52 | 2 | Kuts | Podolsk | 5 Aug 79 |

( 10 Performers by 9 Athletes )

| Mark | Name | Nat | Yr | Pos | Meet | Venue | Date |
|------|------|-----|----|----|------|-------|------|
| 2:32.70 | Jolanta Januchta | POL | 55 | 1 | WK | Zürich | 19 Aug 81 |
| | (10) | | | | | | |
| 2:32.8 m | Tamara Sorokina' | SU | 50 | 1 | | Podolsk | 24 Jul 76 |
| 2:32.9 | Lyudmila Kalnitskaya | SU | 53 | 2 | | Podolsk | 20 Aug 78 |
| 2:33.0 m | Totka Petrova | BUL | 56 | 1 | | Sofia | 13 Aug 78 |
| 2:33.2 m | Gabriella Dorio | ITA | 57 | 1 | | Formia | 28 Aug 82 |
| 2:33.44 | Brigitte Kraus | FRG | 56 | 1 | ISTAF | Berlin | 17 Aug 79 |
| 2:33.6 | Svetlana Ulmasova | SU | 53 | 3 | Kuts | Podolsk | 5 Aug 79 |
| 2:33.70 | Kirsty McDermott' | UK | 62 | 1 | | Gateshead | 9 Aug 85 |
| 2:33.8 m | Nikolina Shtereva | BUL | 55 | 1 | | Sofia | 4 Jul 76 |
| 2:34.1 | Valentina Ilyinykh | SU | 56 | 4 | Kuts | Podolsk | 5 Aug 79 |
| 2:34.13 | Tatyana Pozdnyakova | SU | 56 | 2 | | Athínai | 1 Sep 82 |
| | (20) | | | | | | |
| 2:34.6 m | Heike Oehme | GDR | 63 | 1 | | Cottbus | 14 May 86 |
| 2:34.8 m | Christina Liebetrau' | GDR | 53 | 1 | | Dresden | 7 Aug 77 |
| 2:34.8 m | Hildegard Ullrich' | GDR | 59 | 2 | | Potsdam | 12 Jul 84 |
| 2:34.8 m | Mary Decker-Slaney | USA | 58 | 1 | | Eugene | 4 Jul 85 |
| 2:34.92 | Christina Boxer | UK | 57 | 2 | | Gateshead | 9 Aug 85 |
| 2:34.94 | Margrit Klinger | FRG | 60 | 1 | | Letter | 8 Sep 83 |
| 2:35.0 m | Karin Krebs' | GDR | 43 | 1 | | Potsdam | 28 Aug 74 |
| 2:35.2 m | Rositsa Pekhlivanova | BUL | 55 | 2 | | Sofia | 4 Jul 76 |
| 2:35.32 | Shireen Bailey | UK | 59 | 1 | | Birmingham | 19 Jul 86 |
| 2:35.4 | Irina Nikitina' | SU | 61 | 5 | Kuts | Podolsk | 5 Aug 79 |
| | (30) | | | | | | |
| 2:35.4 m | Katrin Wühn | GDR | 65 | 3 | | Potsdam | 12 Jul 84 |
| | (31) | | | | | | |

# 1500 METRES

| Mark | Name | Nat | Yr | Pos | Meet | Venue | Date |
|------|------|-----|----|----|------|-------|------|
| 3:52.47 | Tatyana Kazankina | SU | 51 | 1 | WK | Zürich | 13 Aug 80 |
| 3:54.23 | Olga Dvirna | SU | 53 | 1 | NC | Kiev | 27 Jul 82 |
| 3:55.0 | Kazankina | | | 1 | Znam | Moskva | 6 Jul 80 |
| 3:56.0 | Kazankina | | | 1 | | Podolsk | 28 Jun 76 |
| 3:56.14 | Zamira Zaytseva | SU | 53 | 2 | NC | Kiev | 27 Jul 82 |
| 3:56.50 | Tatyana Pozdnyakova | SU | 56 | 3 | NC | Kiev | 27 Jul 82 |
| 3:56.56 | Kazankina | | | 1 | OG | Moskva | 1 Aug 80 |
| 3:56.63 | Nadezhda Ralldugina | SU | 57 | 1 | Drz | Praha | 18 Aug 84 |
| 3:56.65 | Yekaterina Podkopayeva' | SU | 52 | 1 | | Rieti | 2 Sep 84 |
| 3:56.7 | Lyubov Smolka | SU | 52 | 2 | Znam | Moskva | 6 Jul 80 |
| 3:56.7 m | Doina Melinte | RUM | 56 | 1 | | Bucureşti | 12 Jul 86 |
| 3:56.8 | Nadezhda Olizarenko' | SU | 53 | 3 | Znam | Moskva | 6 Jul 80 |
| 3:56.9 | Zaytseva | | | 4 | Znam | Moskva | 6 Jul 80 |
| 3:57.05 | Svetlana Guskova | SU | 59 | 4 | NC | Kiev | 27 Jul 82 |
| 3:57.12 | Mary Decker-Slaney | USA | 58 | 1 | vScan | Stockholm | 26 Jul 83 |
| 3:57.22 | Maricica Puica | RUM | 50 | 1 | | Bucureşti | 1 Jul 84 |
| 3:57.24 | Decker | | | 1 | VD | Bruxelles | 30 Aug 85 |
| 3:57.4 | Totka Petrova | BUL | 56 | 1 | Balk | Athínai | 11 Aug 79 |

| Mark | Name | Nat | Yr | Pos | Meet | Venue | Date |
|------|------|-----|-----|-----|------|-------|------|
| 3:57.4 | Podkopayeva | | | 5 | Znam | Moskva | 6 Jul 80 |
| 3:57.48 | Puica | | | 1 | NC | București | 31 Jul 82 |
| 3:57.70 | Pozdnyakova | | | 2 | | Rieti | 2 Sep 84 |
| 3:57.71 | Christiane Wartenberg' | GDR | 56 | 2 | OG | Moskva | 1 Aug 80 |
| 3:57.72 | Galina Zakharova | SU | 56 | 1 | NP | Baku | 14 Sep 84 |
| 3:57.73 | Puica | | | 2 | VD | Bruxelles | 30 Aug 85 |
| 3:57.78 | Dvirna | | | 1 | BGP | Budapest | 29 Jul 81 |
| 3:57.80 | Dvirna | | | 1 | EC | Athínai | 11 Sep 82 |
| 3:57.82 | Puica | | | 1 | | Tirrenia | 25 Aug 82 |

( 27 Performances by 15 Athletes )

| Mark | Name | Nat | Yr | Pos | Meet | Venue | Date |
|------|------|-----|-----|-----|------|-------|------|
| 3:58.2 | Natalia Maraşescu' | RUM | 52 | 1 | NC | București | 13 Jul 79 |
| 3:58.37 | Tatyana Providokhina | SU | 53 | 1 | Kuts | Podolsk | 22 Aug 82 |
| 3:58.40 | Ravilya Agletdinova | SU | 60 | 1 | EP | Moskva | 18 Aug 85 |
| 3:58.5 | Ileana Silai | RUM | 41 | 2 | NC | București | 13 Jul 79 |
| 3:58.65 | Gabriella Dorio | ITA | 57 | 2 | | Tirrenia | 25 Aug 82 |
| | (20) | | | | | | |
| 3:58.76 | Svetlana Ulmasova | SU | 53 | 2 | Kuts | Podolsk | 22 Aug 82 |
| 3:58.89 | Tamara Sorokina' | SU | 50 | 1 | Znam | Leningrad | 26 Jul 81 |
| 3:59.01 | Giana Romanova | SU | 55 | 1 | EC | Praha | 3 Sep 78 |
| 3:59.28 | Natalya Artyemova | SU | 63 | 2 | NC | Leningrad | 2 Aug 85 |
| 3:59.45 | Tatyana Samolyenko' | SU | 61 | 1 | NC | Kiev | 17 Jul 86 |
| 3:59.48 | Yelena Sipatova | SU | 55 | 4 | Kuts | Podolsk | 22 Aug 82 |
| 3:59.67 | Anna Bukis | POL | 53 | 3 | BGP | Budapest | 29 Jul 81 |
| 3:59.8 m | Raisa Katyukova' | SU | 50 | 2 | | Podolsk | 28 Jun 76 |
| 3:59.90 | Angelika Zauber | GDR | 58 | 1 | NC | Jena | 9 Aug 81 |
| 3:59.9 m | Ulrike Klapezynski' | GDR | 53 | 1 | | Potsdam | 14 Jul 76 |
| | (30) | | | | | | |
| 3:59.9 m | Beate Liebich | GDR | 58 | 1 | OT | Potsdam | 5 Jul 80 |
| 3:59.96 | Zola Budd | UK | 66 | 3 | VD | Bruxelles | 30 Aug 85 |
| 4:00.12 | Fita Lovin' | RUM | 51 | 1 | RumIC | București | 4 Jun 83 |
| 4:00.18 | Valentina Ilyinykh | SU | 56 | 4 | EC | Praha | 3 Sep 78 |
| 4:00.18 | Irina Nikitina' | SU | 61 | 5 | Kuts | Podolsk | 22 Aug 82 |
| 4:00.18 | Ruth Wysocki | USA | 57 | 1 | FOT | Los Angeles | 24 Jun 84 |
| 4:00.26 | Alla Yushina | SU | 58 | 3 | Znam | Leningrad | 26 Jul 81 |
| 4:00.27 | Lynn Williams | CAN | 60 | 4 | VD | Bruxelles | 30 Aug 85 |
| 4:00.3 | Lyudmila Shesterova | SU | 56 | 7 | Znam | Moskva | 6 Jul 80 |
| 4:00.42 | Lyudmila Medvedyeva | SU | 57 | 3 | NP | Baku | 14 Sep 84 |
| | (40) | | | | | | |
| 4:00.53 | Svetlana Popova | SU | 59 | 6 | NC | Kiev | 27 Jul 82 |
| 4:00.55 | Grete Waitz' | NOR | 53 | 5 | EC | Praha | 3 Sep 78 |
| 4:00.57 | Christina Boxer | UK | 57 | 1 | | Gateshead | 6 Jul 84 |
| 4:00.62 | Maria Radu | RUM | 59 | 2 | RumIC | București | 4 Jun 83 |
| 4:00.62 | Natalya Boborova' | SU | 59 | 2 | | Moskva | 20 Jul 84 |
| 4:01.22 | Galina Kireyeva | SU | 56 | 8 | NC | Kiev | 27 Jul 82 |
| 4:01.38 | Lyudmila Bragina | SU | 43 | 1 | OG | München | 9 Sep 72 |
| 4:01.4 m | Gunhild Hoffmeister | GDR | 44 | 2 | | Potsdam | 14 Jul 76 |
| 4:01.53 | Christine Benning | UK | 55 | 3 | WK | Zürich | 15 Aug 79 |
| 4:01.54 | Brigitte Kraus | FRG | 56 | 1 | v SU | Dortmund | 1 Jul 78 |
| | (50) | | | | | | |

WOMEN All-time

| Mark | Name | Nat | Yr | Pos | Meet | Venue | Date |
|------|------|-----|-----|-----|------|-------|------|

# 1 MILE

| Mark | Name | Nat | Yr | Pos | Meet | Venue | Date |
|------|------|-----|-----|-----|------|-------|------|
| 4:15.8 m | Natalya Artyemova | SU | 63 | 1 | | Leningrad | 5 Aug 84 |
| 4:16.71 | Mary Decker-Slaney | USA | 58 | 1 | WK | Zürich | 21 Aug 85 |
| 4:17.33 | Maricica Puica | RUM | 50 | 2 | WK | Zürich | 21 Aug 85 |
| 4:17.44 | Puica | | | 1 | | Rieti | 16 Sep 82 |
| 4:17.57 | Zola Budd | UK | 66 | 3 | WK | Zürich | 21 Aug 85 |
| 4:18.08 | Decker | | | 1 | | Paris | 9 Jul 82 |
| 4:18.25 | Puica | | | 1 | Nik | Nice | 15 Jul 86 |
| 4:19.18 | Decker | | | 1 | Bisl | Oslo | 27 Jul 85 |
| 4:19.41 | Kirsty McDermott' | UK | 62 | 2 | Bisl | Oslo | 27 Jul 85 |
| 4:19.59 | Decker | | | 1 | IAC | London | 2 Aug 85 |
| 4:20.89 | Lyudmila Veselkova | SU | 50 | 1 | | Bologna | 12 Sep 81 |
| 4:20.89 | Puica | | | 1 | | Paris | 22 Jul 86 |
| 4:21.40 | Fita Lovin' | RUM | 51 | 2 | | Bologna | 12 Sep 81 |
| 4:21.46 | Decker | | | 1 | Bisl | Oslo | 26 Jun 82 |
| 4:21.52 | Vesela Yatzinska | BUL | 51 | 1 | BGP | Budapest | 30 Jun 82 |
| 4:21.59 | Ulrike Bruns' | GDR | 53 | 4 | WK | Zürich | 21 Aug 85 |
| 4:21.61 | Wade' | | | 1 | VD | Bruxelles | 5 Sep 86 |
| 4:21.65 | Decker | | | 1 | | Westwood | 15 may 83 |
| 4:21.68 | Decker | | | 1 | | Auckland | 26 Jan 80 |
| 4:21.78 | Vanya Stoyanova | BUL | 58 | 2 | BGP | Budapest | 30 Jun 82 |
| 4.21.78 | Ruth Wysocki | USA | 57 | 1 | Coke | London | 7 Sep 84 |

( 21 Performances by 11 Athletes )

| Mark | Name | Nat | Yr | Pos | Meet | Venue | Date |
|------|------|-----|-----|-----|------|-------|------|
| 4:21.88 | Doina Melinte | RUM | 56 | 2 | VD | Bruxelles | 5 Sep 86 |
| 4:21.89 | Tamara Sorokina' | SU | 50 | 3 | BGP | Budapest | 30 Jun 82 |
| 4:22.09 | Natalia Maraşescu' | RUM | 52 | 1 | | Auckland | 27 Jan 79 |
| 4:22.40 | Elly van Hulst | HOL | 59 | 4 | VD | Bruxelles | 5 Sep 86 |
| 4:22.5 m | Zamira Zaytseva | SU | 53 | 1 | | Kiev | 15 Jun 81 |
| 4:22.64 | Christina Boxer | UK | 57 | 2 | Coke | London | 7 Sep 84 |
| 4:22.82 | Ivana Walterová' | CS | 62 | 5 | VD | Bruxelles | 5 Sep 84 |
| 4:23.08 | Yvonne Murray | UK | 64 | 6 | VD | Bruxelles | 5 Sep 84 |
| 4:23.29 | Gabriella Dorio | ITA | 57 | 1 | | Viareggio | 14 Aug 80 |
| | (20) | | | | | | |
| 4:23.8 m | Svetlana Ulmasova | SU | 53 | 2 | | Kiev | 15 Jun 81 |
| 4:23.93 | Sue Addison | USA | 56 | 2 | Nik | Nice | 15 Jul 86 |
| 4:24.57 | Christine Benning | UK | 55 | 3 | Coke | London | 7 Sep 84 |
| 4:24.6 m | Silvana Cruciata | ITA | 53 | 1 | DNG | Stockholm | 8 Jul 81 |
| 4:24.69 | Brit McRoberts | CAN | 57 | 3 | Nik | Nice | 15 Jul 86 |
| 4:24.85 | Cornelia Bürki | SWZ | 53 | 7 | VD | Bruxelles | 5 Sep 86 |
| 4:25.03 | Brigitte Kraus | FRG | 56 | 5 | WK | Zürich | 21 Aug 85 |
| 4:25.29 | Claudette Groenendaal | USA | 63 | 8 | VD | Bruxelles | 5 Sep 86 |
| 4:25.52 | Mariana Stanescu | RUM | 64 | 4 | Nik | Nice | 15 Jul 86 |
| 4:25.57 | Lynn Williams | CAN | 60 | 5 | Nik | Nice | 15 Jul 86 |
| | (30) | | | | | | |
| 4:26.90 | Grete Waitz' | NOR | 53 | 1 | | Gateshead | 9 Jul 78 |
| 4:27.52 | Francie Larrieu-Smith | USA | 52 | 2 | | Philadelphia | 30 Jun 79 |
| 4:27.52 | Margherita Gargano | ITA | 52 | 3 | | Rieti | 16 Sep 82 |
| 4:27.97 | Irina Lebedinskaya' | SU | 61 | 2 | | Edinburgh | 23 Jul 85 |
| 4:28.07 | Wendy Sly' | UK | 59 | 1 | | London | 18 Aug 84 |
| | (35) | | | | | | |

| Mark | Name | Nat | Yr | Pos | Meet | Venue | Date |
|------|------|-----|-----|-----|------|-------|------|

## 3000 METRES

| Mark | Name | Nat | Yr | Pos | Meet | Venue | Date |
|------|------|-----|-----|-----|------|-------|------|
| 8:22.62 | Tatyana Kazankina | SU | 51 | 1 | | Leningrad | 26 Aug 84 |
| 8:25.83 | Mary Decker-Slaney | USA | 58 | 1 | GP | Roma | 7 Sep 85 |
| 8:26.78 | Svetlana Ulmasova | SU | 53 | 1 | NC | Kiev | 25 Jul 82 |
| 8:27.12 | Lyudmila Bragina | SU | 43 | 1 | v USA | College Park | 7 Aug 76 |
| 8:27.83 | Maricica Puica | RUM | 50 | 2 | GP | Roma | 7 Sep 85 |
| 8:28.83 | Zola Budd | UK | 59 66 | 3 | GP | Roma | 7 Sep 85 |
| 8:29.36 | Svetlana Guskova | SU | 59 | 2 | NC | Kiev | 5 Jul 82 |
| 8:29.59 | Guskova | | | 1 | | Moskva | 6 Aug 84 |
| 8:29.69 | Decker | | | 1 | | Köln | 25 Aug 85 |
| 8:29.71 | Decker | | | 1 | | Oslo | 7 Jul 82 |
| 8:30.28 | Ulmasova | | | 1 | EC | Athínai | 9 Sep 82 |
| 8:30.32 | Puica | | | 2 | | Köln | 25 Aug 85 |
| 8:31.67 | Puica | | | 1 | Balk | Bucureşti | 14 Aug 82 |
| 8:31.75 | Grete Waitz' | NOR | 53 | 1 | | Oslo | 17 Jul 79 |
| 8:32.0 m | Tatyana Pozdnyakova | SU | 56 | 1 | | Ryazan | 11 Aug 84 |
| 8:32.08 | Kazankina | | | 1 | | Leningrad | 27 Jul 83 |
| 8:32.1 m | Waitz | | | 1 | | Oslo | 27 Jun 78 |
| 8:32.91 | Decker | | | 1 | PTG | London | 20 Jul 85 |
| 8:33.01 | Kazankina | | | 1 | Drz | Praha | 16 Aug 84 |
| 8:33.16 | Ulmasova | | | 1 | EC | Praha | 29 Aug 78 |

( 20 Performances by 9 Athletes )

| Mark | Name | Nat | Yr | Pos | Meet | Venue | Date |
|------|------|-----|-----|-----|------|-------|------|
| 8:33.40 | Galina Zakharova | SU | 56 | 3 | NC | Kiev | 25 Jul 82 |
| | (10) | | | | | | |
| 8:33.53 | Natalia Maraşescu' | RUM | 52 | 2 | EC | Praha | 29 Aug 78 |
| 8:33.53 | Yelena Sipatova | SU | 55 | 1 | | Moskva | 12 Jul 80 |
| 8:33.9 | Tatyana Sycheva | SU | 57 | 2 | | Moskva | 12 Jul 80 |
| 8:33.99 | Olga Bondarenko' | SU | 60 | 1 | EC | Stuttgart | 28 Aug 86 |
| 8:34.0 | Faina Krasnova' | SU | 57 | 3 | | Moskva | 12 Jul 80 |
| 8:34.02 | Alla Yushina | SU | 58 | 2 | | Leningrad | 27 Jul 83 |
| 8:34.10 | Ingrid Kristiansen' | NOR | 58 | 1 | WK | Zürich | 13 Aug 86 |
| 8:35.11 | Brigitte Kraus | FRG | 56 | 2 | WC | Helsinki | 10 Aug 83 |
| 8:35.74 | Alla Libutina | SU | 53 | 6 | NC | Kiev | 25 Jul 82 |
| 8:35.74 | Zamira Zaytseva | SU | 53 | 2 | EP | Moskva | 17 Aug 85 |
| | (20) | | | | | | |
| 8:36.0 | Lyubov Smolka | SU | 52 | 4 | | Moskva | 12 Jul 80 |
| 8:36.00 | Tatyana Samolyenko' | SU | 61 | 1 | v GDR | Tallinn | 22 Jun 86 |
| 8:36.38 | Ulrike Bruns' | GDR | 53 | 1 | OD | Berlin | 20 Jul 84 |
| 8:36.40 | Olga Dvirna | SU | 53 | 1 | | Sochi | 30 May 82 |
| 8:37.06 | Wendy Sly' | UK | 59 | 5 | WC | Helsinki | 10 Aug 83 |
| 8:37.11 | Doina Melinte | RUM | 56 | 1 | v Eng, Rus | Bucureşti | 15 Jun 86 |
| 8:37.15 | Yvonne Murray | UK | 64 | 3 | EC | Stuttgart | 28 Aug 86 |
| 8:37.38 | Lynn Williams | CAN | 60 | 3 | ASV | Köln | 25 Aug 85 |
| 8:37.96 | Agnese Possamai | ITA | 53 | 6 | WC | Helsinki | 10 Aug 83 |
| 8:38.1 m | Yelena Zhupiyeva | SU | 60 | 1 | | Kharkov | 11 Aug 85 |
| | (30) | | | | | | |
| 8:38.22 | Olga Kuzyukova | SU | 53 | 8 | | Leningrad | 27 Jul 83 |
| 8:38.60 | Cindy Bremser | USA | 53 | 2 | WK | Zürich | 22 Aug 84 |
| 8:38.71 | Cornelia Bürki | SWZ | 53 | 2 | PTG | London | 20 Jul 85 |
| 8:38.83 | Mariana Stanescu | RUM | 64 | 1 | GWG | Moskva | 6 Jul 86 |
| 8:38.84 | Natalya Artyemova | SU | 63 | 1 | | Kiev | 20 Jun 84 |
| 8:39.25 | Regina Chistyakova | SU | 61 | 3 | GWG | Moskva | 6 Jul 86 |

| Mark | Name | Nat | Yr | Pos | Meet | Venue | Date |
|------|------|-----|----|-----|------|-------|------|
| 8:40.4 | Nina Yapeyeva | SU | 56 | 5 | | Moskva | 12 Jul 80 |
| 8:41.05 | Raisa Sadreydinova | SU | 52 | 9 | | Leningrad | 27 Jul 83 |
| 8:41.07 | Zhanna Tursunova | SU | 57 | 6 | | Kiev | 20 Jun 84 |
| 8:41.43 | Joan Hansen | USA | 58 | 3 | FOT | Los Angeles | 23 Jun 84 |
| | (40) | | | | | | |
| 8:41.77 | Raisa Katyukova' | SU | 50 | 2 | v USA | College Park | 7 Aug 76 |
| 8:41.8 | Giana Romanova | SU | 55 | 6 | | Moskva | 12 Jul 80 |
| 8:42.3 m | Loa Olafsson | DEN | 58 | 2 | | Oslo | 17 Jun 78 |
| 8:42.6 m | Jan Merrill | USA | 56 | 3 | | Oslo | 17 Jun 78 |
| 8:42.84 | Irina Bondarchuk | SU | 52 | 3 | | Sochi | 30 May 82 |
| 8: 3.65 | Birgit Friedmann | FRG | 60 | 5 | EC | Athínai | 9 Sep 82 |
| 8:43.82 | Mary Knisely' | USA | 59 | 3 | Nik | Nice | 16 Jul 85 |
| 8:44.46 | Christine Benning | UK | 55 | 3 | WK | Zürich | 22 Aug 84 |
| 8:44.7 | Raisa Byelousova | SU | 52 | 4 | Znam | Kaunas | 11 Aug 79 |
| 8:44.86 | Lesley Welch | USA | 63 | 4 | Nik | Nice | 15 Jul 86 |
| | (50) | | | | | | |

# 5000 METRES

| Mark | Name | Nat | Yr | Pos | Meet | Venue | Date |
|------|------|-----|----|-----|------|-------|------|
| 14:37.33 | Ingrid Kristiansen' | NOR | 56 | 1 | | Stockholm | 5 Aug 86 |
| 14:48.07 | Zola Budd | UK | 66 | 1 | | London | 26 Aug 85 |
| 14:54.08 | Natalya Artyemova | SU | 63 | 1 | | Podolsk | 9 Sep 85 |
| 14:55.76 | Olga Bondarenko' | SU | 60 | 2 | | Podolsk | 9 Sep 85 |
| 14:57.43 | Kristiansen | | | 2 | | London | 26 Aug 85 |
| 14:58.70 | Kristiansen | | | 1 | FBK | Hengelo | 27 Jul 86 |
| 14:58.89 | Kristiansen | | | 1 | Bisl | Oslo | 28 Jun 84 |
| 15:01.83 | Budd | | | 1 | | Stellenbosch | 5 Jan 84 |
| 15:02.12 | Svetlana Guskova | SU | 59 | 1 | v GDR | Tallinn | 21 Jun 86 |
| 15:03.51 | Bondarenko | | | 1 | GWG | Moskva | 8 Jul 86 |
| 15:05.31 | Bondarenko | | | 1 | NC | Leningrad | 1 Aug 85 |
| 15:05.50 | Svetlana Ulmasova | SU | 53 | 2 | GWG | Moskva | 8 Jul 86 |
| 15:06.04 | Maricica Puica | RUM | 50 | 1 | WG | Helsinki | 4 Jul 85 |
| 15:06.18 | Bondarenko | | | 2 | v GDR | Tallinn | 21 Jun 86 |
| 15:06.53 | Mary Decker-Slaney | USA | 58 | 1 | Pre | Eugene | 1 Jun 85 |
| 15:06.96 | Aurora Cunha | POR | 59 | 2 | WG | Helsinki | 4 Jul 85 |
| 15:07.56 | Cathy Branta-Easker | USA | 63 | 3 | WG | Helsinki | 4 Jul 85 |
| 15:07.71 | Lynn Williams | CAN | 60 | 4 | WG | Helsinki | 4 Jul 85 |
| 15:07.76# | Kristiansen | | | 1 | EC | Stuttgart | 30 Aug 86 |
| 15:08.26 | Decker | | | 1 | Pre | Eugene | 5 Jun 82 |
| 15:08.36 | Lynn Jennings | USA | 60 | 2 | FBK | Hengelo | 27 Jun 86 |
| 15:08.80 | Grete Waitz' | NOR | 53 | 1 | Bisl | Oslo | 26 Jun 82 |
| 15:09.07 | Cunha | | | 2 | Bisl | Oslo | 28 Jun 84 |
| 15:09.86 | Budd | | | 1 | | Pt. Elizabeth | 7 Mar 84 |

( 24 Performances by 13 Athletes )

| Mark | Name | Nat | Yr | Pos | Meet | Venue | Date |
|------|------|-----|----|-----|------|-------|------|
| 15:11.78 | Cindy Bremser | USA | 53 | 3 | GWG | Moskva | 8 Jul 86 |
| 15:12.62 | Irina Bondarchuk | SU | 52 | 1 | Znam | Moskva | 11 Jun 82 |
| 15:13.22 | Anne Audain' | NZ | 55 | 1 | | Auckland | 17 Mar 82 |
| 15:14.51 | Paula Fudge | UK | 52 | 1 | | Knarvik | 13 Sep 81 |
| 15:16.27 | Lyudmila Matveyeva | SU | 57 | 2 | NC | Leningrad | 1 Aug 85 |
| 15:19.0 m | Anna Domoratskaya | SU | 53 | 1 | | Kiev | 30 Sep 83 |
| 15:19.26 | Marina Rodchenkova | SU | 61 | 3 | NC | Leningrad | 1 Aug 85 |
| | (20) | | | | | | |

| Mark | Name | Nat | Yr | Pos | Meet | Venue | Date |
|------|------|-----|-----|-----|------|-------|------|
| 15:19.54 | Charlotte Teske | FRG | 49 | 2 | Bisl | Oslo | 26 Jun 82 |
| 15:20.88 | PattiSue Plumer | USA | 62 | 5 | GWG | Moskva | 8 Jul 86 |
| 15:21.0 | Margherita Gargano | ITA | 52 | 1 | | Partinico | 22 Sep 82 |
| 15:21.90 | Gabriele Veith' | GDR | 56 | 6 | GWG | Moskva | 8 Jul 86 |
| 15:21.92 | Anna Pedan | SU | 61 | 5 | NC | Leningrad | 1 Aug 85 |
| 15:22.33 | Mary Knisely' | USA | 59 | 3 | GP | Roma | 10 Sep 86 |
| 15:22.37 | Cathy Twomey | USA | 56 | 4 | Pre | Eugene | 1 Jun 85 |
| 15:22.50 | Angela Tooby | UK | 60 | 3 | Bisl | Oslo | 28 Jun 84 |
| 15:22.96 | Sue French-Lee | CAN | 60 | 1 | | Knoxville | 13 Apr 84 |
| 15:22.97 | Rosa Mota | POR | 58 | 3 | | Oslo | 27 Jun 85 |
| | (30) | | | | | | |
| 15:23.03 | Kathy Hayes | USA | 62 | 1 | | Eugene | 4 May 85 |
| 15:23.12 | Tatyana Kazankina | SU | 51 | 1 | | Paris | 4 Sep 84 |
| 15:23.25 | Yelena Zhupiyeva | SU | 60 | 7 | GWG | Moskva | 8 Jul 86 |
| 15:23.54 | Erika Veréb | HUN | 63 | 4 | GP | Moskva | 10 Sep 86 |
| 15:24.6 m | Yelena Sipatova | SU | 55 | 1 | Kuts | Podolsk | 6 Sep 81 |
| 15:25.13 | Yelena Tsukhlo | SU | 54 | 2 | Znam | Moskva | 11 Jun 82 |
| 15:25.24 | Betty Springs | USA | 61 | 7 | Pre | Eugene | 1 Jun 85 |
| 15:27.05 | Ines Bibernell | GDR | 65 | 1 | OD | Dresden | 3 Jul 86 |
| 15:27.5 m | Monica Joyce | IRL | 58 | 1 | | San Diego | 20 May 83 |
| 15:27.96 | Marie-Louise Hamrin | SWE | 57 | 4 | Bisl | Oslo | 28 Jun 84 |
| | (40) | | | | | | |
| 15:28.33 | Lesley Welch | USA | 63 | 8 | Pre | Eugene | 1 Jun 85 |
| 15:28.44 | Krishna Wood | AUS | 66 | 1 | | Melbourne | 2 Dec 86 |
| 15:28.55 | Natalya Sorokivskaya | SU | 62 | 3 | NC | Kiev | 14 Jul 86 |
| 15:29.65 | Barbara Moore | NZ | 57 | 2 | | Auckland | 17 Mar 82 |
| 15:29.7 m | Dorthe Rasmussen | DEN | 60 | 1 | | Vallensbaek | 31 May 83 |
| 15:30.6 | Jan Merrill | USA | 56 | 1 | | Palo Alto | 22 Mar 80 |
| 15:30.84 | Ille Kukk | SU | 57 | 7 | NC | Leningrad | 1 Aug 85 |
| 15:31.09 | Stephanie Herbst | USA | 65 | 1 | | San Diego | 29 Mar 86 |
| 15:31.45 | Nina Yapeyeva | SU | 56 | 8 | NC | Leningrad | 1 Aug 85 |
| 15:32.19 | Susan Tooby | UK | 60 | 2 | NC | Antrim | 26 May 85 |
| | (50) | | | | | | |

## 10 000 METRES

| | | | | | | | |
|------|------|-----|-----|-----|------|-------|------|
| 30:13.74 | Ingrid Kristiansen' | NOR | 56 | 1 | Bisl | Oslo | 5 Jul 86 |
| 30:23.25 | Kristiansen | | | 1 | EC | Stuttgart | 30 Aug 86 |
| 30:57.21 | Olga Bondarenko' | SU | 60 | 2 | EC | Stuttgart | 30 Aug 86 |
| 30:59.42 | Kristiansen | NOR | 56 | 1 | Bisl | Oslo | 27 Jul 85 |
| 31:13.78 | Bondarenko | | | 1 | | Kiev | 24 Jun 84 |
| 31:15.00 | Galina Zakharova | SU | 56 | 2 | | Kiev | 24 Jun 84 |
| 31:19.76 | Ulrike Bruns' | GDR | 53 | 3 | EC | Stuttgart | 30 Aug 86 |
| 31:25.18 | Bondarenko | | | 1 | Znam | Moskva | 9 Jun 85 |
| 31:27.58 | Raisa Sadreydinova | SU | 52 | 1 | NC | Odessa | 7 Sep 83 |
| 31:29.41 | Aurora Cunha | POR | 59 | 2 | Bisl | Oslo | 5 Jul 86 |
| 31:35.01 | Lyudmila Baranova | SU | 50 | 1 | | Krasnodar | 29 May 83 |
| 31:35.3 m | Mary Decker-Slaney | USA | 58 | 1 | | Eugene | 16 Jul 82 |
| 31:35.45 | Cunha | | | 2 | Bisl | Oslo | 27 Jul 85 |
| 31:35.61 | Bondarenko | | | 2 | | Krasnodar | 29 May 83 |
| 31:38.64 | Bondarenko | | | 2 | NC | Odessa | 7 Sep 83 |
| 31:39.35 | Cunha | | | 4 | EC | Stuttgart | 30 Aug 86 |
| 31:41.42 | Liz Lynch | UK | 64 | 1 | CommG | Edinburgh | 28 Jul 86 |
| 31:42.43 | Svetlana Guskova | SU | 59 | 5 | EC | Stuttgart | 30 Aug 86 |
| 31:42.99 | Yelena Zhupiyeva | SU | 60 | 6 | EC | Stuttgart | 30 Aug 86 |

| Mark | Name | Nat | Yr | Pos | Meet | Venue | Date |
|------|------|-----|-----|-----|------|-------|------|
| 31:47.38 | Bondarenko | | | 1 | EP | Moskva | 18 Aug 85 |
| 31:48.23 | Anna Domoratskaya | SU | 53 | 1 | NC | Kiev | 27 Jul 82 |
| 31:48.94 | Tatyana Pozdnyakova | SU | 56 | 3 | NC | Odessa | 7 Sep 83 |
| 31:49.44 | Bondarenko | | | 1 | | Kiev | 28 Aug 83 |

( 23 Performances by 13 Athletes)

| Mark | Name | Nat | Yr | Pos | Meet | Venue | Date |
|------|------|-----|-----|-----|------|-------|------|
| 31:53.31 | Anne Audain' | NZ | 55 | 2 | CommG | Edinburgh | 28 Jul 86 |
| 31:53.53 | Zhanna Tursunova | SU | 57 | 3 | | Kiev | 24 Jun 84 |
| 31:55.93 | Karolina Szabó | HUN | 61 | 8 | EC | Stuttgart | 30 Aug 86 |
| 31:56.59 | Angela Tooby | UK | 60 | 9 | EC | Stuttgart | 30 Aug 86 |
| 31:56.01 | Lyubov Konyukhova | SU | 56 | 4 | | Kiev | 24 Jun 84 |
| 31:59.70 | Raisa Smekhnova' | SU | 50 | 6 | | Kiev | 24 Jun 84 |
| 32:00.26 | Charlotte Teske | FRG | 49 | 2 | IAAFg | Knarvik | 4 Sep 83 |
| | (20) | | | | | | |
| 32:02.89 | Dorthe Rasmussen | DEN | 60 | 3 | IAAFg | Knarvik | 4 Sep 83 |
| 32:03.37 | Lynn Jennings | USA | 60 | 3 | Bisl | Oslo | 27 Jul 85 |
| 32:04.34 | Maria Curatolo | ITA | 63 | 10 | EC | Stuttgart | 30 Aug 86 |
| 32:06.38 | Natalya Sorokivskaya | SU | 62 | 3 | Znam | Leningrad | 8 Jun 86 |
| 32:07.41 | Joan Benoit' | USA | 57 | 1 | FOT | Los Angeles | 17 Jun 84 |
| 32:14.83 | Svetlana Ulmasova | SU | 53 | 5 | Znam | Leningrad | 8 Jun 86 |
| 32:15.56 | Erika Veréb | HUN | 63 | 11 | EC | Stuttgart | 30 Aug 86 |
| 32:16.97 | Danièle Kaber | LUX | 60 | 12 | EC | Stuttgart | 30 Aug 86 |
| 32:17.19 | Yelena Sipatova | SU | 55 | 1 | NC | Moskva | 19 Sep 81 |
| 32:17.22 | Gabriele Veith' | GDR | 56 | 13 | EC | Stuttgart | 30 Aug 86 |
| | (30) | | | | | | |
| 32:17.86 | Lisa Martin' | AUS | 60 | 4 | Bisl | Oslo | 27 Jul 85 |
| 32:18.29 | Francie Larrieu-Smith | USA | 52 | 1 | TAC | Indianapolis | 14 Jun 85 |
| 32:18.40 | Marie-Louise Hamrin | SWE | 57 | 14 | EC | Stuttgart | 30 Aug 86 |
| 32:19.93 | Mary Knisely' | USA | 59 | 2 | WP | Canberra | 5 Oct 85 |
| 32:20.40 | Yelena Tsukhlo | SU | 54 | 2 | NC | Moskva | 19 Sep 83 |
| 32:22.63 | Marina Byelyayeva | SU | 58 | 7 | Znam | Leningrad | 8 Jun 86 |
| 32:25.99 | Lyudmila Matveyeva | SU | 57 | 7 | | Kiev | 24 Jun 84 |
| 32:23.04 | Nancy Rooks | CAN | 59 | 4 | IAAFg | Knarvik | 4 Sep 83 |
| 32:23.1 m | Tuija Toivonen' | FIN | 58 | 1 | | Vantaa | 7 Sep 83 |
| 32:24.09 | Elena Murgoci | RUM | 60 | 1 | NC | Pitești | 9 Aug 86 |
| | (40) | | | | | | |
| 32:25.19 | Nadezhda Styepanova | SU | 59 | 8 | Znam | Leningrad | 8 Jun 86 |
| 32:25.62 | Elisabet Bradu | SU | 52 | 3 | Znam | Moskva | 9 Jun 85 |
| 32:25.99 | Christine Loiseau | FRA | 60 | 15 | EC | Stuttgart | 30 Aug 86 |
| 32:26.58 | Viorica Ghican | RUM | 65 | 2 | NC | Pitești | 9 Aug 86 |
| 32:26.90 | Lieve Slegers | BEL | 65 | 16 | EC | Stuttgart | 30 Aug 86 |
| 32:28.28 | Carla Beurskens | HOL | 52 | 5 | Bisl | Oslo | 27 Jul 85 |
| 32:29.39 | Tatyana Gridnyeva | SU | 58 | 2 | | Kiev | 25 Jul 86 |
| 32:29.73 | Rita Van Landeghem | BEL | 57 | 4 | Bisl | Oslo | 5 Jul 86 |
| 32:29.84 | Nan Doak | USA | 62 | 1 | TAC | Eugene | 19 Jun 86 |
| 32:30.24 | Lynn Nelson | USA | 62 | 2 | TAC | Eugene | 19 Jun 86 |
| | (50) | | | | | | |

## MARATHON

| | | | | | | | |
|------|------|-----|-----|-----|------|-------|------|
| 2:21:06 | Ingrid Kristiansen' | NOR | 56 | 1 | | London | 21 Apr 85 |
| 2:21:21 | Joan Benoit' | USA | 57 | 1 | | Chicago | 20 Oct 85 |
| 2:22:43 | Benoit | | | 1 | | Boston | 18 Apr 83 |
| 2:23:05 | Kristiansen | | | 2 | | Chicago | 20 Oct 85 |

| Mark | Name | Nat | Yr | Pos | Meet | Venue | Date |
|------|------|-----|----|----|------|-------|------|
| 2:23:29 | Rosa Mota | POR | 58 | 3 | | Chicago | 20 Oct 85 |
| 2:24:26 | Kristiansen | | | 1 | | London | 13 May 84 |
| 2:24:52 | Benoit | | | 1 | OG | Los Angeles | 5 Aug 84 |
| 2:24:54 | Grete Waitz' | NOR | 53 | 1 | | London | 20 Apr 86 |
| 2:24:55 | Kristiansen | | | 1 | | Boston | 21 Apr 86 |
| 2:25:29 | Waitz | | | 1 | | London | 17 Apr 83 |
| 2:25:42 | Waitz | | | 1 | | New York | 26 Oct 80 |
| 2:26:01 | Mota | | | 1 | | Chicago | 21 Oct 84 |
| 2:26:07 | Lisa Martin' | AUS | 60 | 1 | CommG | Edinburgh | 1 Aug 86 |
| 2:26:11 | Benoit | | | 1 | Nike | Eugene | 12 Sep 82 |
| 2:26:18 | Waitz | | | 2 | OG | Los Angeles | 5 Aug 84 |
| 2:26:26 | Julie Brown | USA | 55 | 1 | Avon | Los Angeles | 5 Jun 83 |
| 2:26:46 | Alison Roe | NZ | 56 | 1 | | Boston | 20 Apr 81 |
| 2:26:52 | Katrin Dörre | GDR | 61 | 1 | OT | Berlin | 21 Jul 84 |
| 2:26:57 | Mota | | | 3 | OG | Los Angeles | 5 Aug 84 |
| 2:27:00 | Waitz | | | 1 | | New York | 23 Oct 83 |
| 2:27:08 | Kristiansen | | | 1 | | Chicago | 26 Oct 86 |
| 2:27:14 | Waitz | | | 1 | | New York | 24 Oct 82 |
| 2:27:33 | Waitz | | | 1 | | New York | 21 Oct 79 |
| 2:27:34 | Kristiansen | | | 4 | OG | Los Angeles | 5 Aug 84 |
| 2:27:15 | Mota | | | 1 | | Tokyo | 16 Nov 86 |

( 25 Performances by 8 Athletes )

| Mark | Name | Nat | Yr | Pos | Meet | Venue | Date |
|------|------|-----|----|----|------|-------|------|
| 2:27:35 | Carla Beurskens | HOL | 52 | 2 | | Boston | 21 Apr 86 |
| 2:27:51 | Patricia Catalano' | USA | 53 | 2 | | Boston | 20 Apr 81 |
| | (10) | | | | | | |
| 2:28:04 | Veronique Marot | UK | 55 | 4 | | Chicago | 20 Oct 85 |
| 2:28:06 | Sarah Rowell | UK | 62 | 2 | | London | 21 Apr 85 |
| 2:28:07 | Carey May' | IRL | 59 | 1 | | Osaka | 27 Jan 85 |
| 2:28:17 | Lorraine Moller | NZ | 55 | 2 | CommG | Edinburgh | 1 Aug 86 |
| 2:28:20 | Mary O'Connor / | NZ | 55 | 2 | | London | 17 Apr 83 |
| 2:28:32 | Charlotte Teske | FRG | 49 | 1 | | Frankfurt | 15 May 83 |
| 2:28:36 | Sylvia Ruegger | CAN | 61 | 1 | Tenn | Houston | 6 Jan 85 |
| 2:28:38 | Sally-Ann Hales | UK | 61 | 3 | | London | 21 Apr 85 |
| 2:28:51 | Ágnes Öze-Sipka | HUN | 54 | 1 | | Budapest | 26 Oct 86 |
| 2:28:54 | Priscilla Welch | UK | 44 | 6 | OG | Los Angeles | 5 Aug 84 |
| | (20) | | | | | | |
| 2:29:10 | Raisa Smekhnova' | SU | 50 | 1 | NP | Vilnius | 7 Oct 84 |
| 2:29:28 | Jacqueline Gareau | CAN | 53 | 2 | | Boston | 18 Apr 83 |
| 2:29:28 | Laura Fogli | ITA | 59 | 9 | OG | Los Angeles | 5 Aug 84 |
| 2:29:43 | Joyce Smith | UK | 37 | 1 | | London | 9 May 82 |
| 2:29:51 | Maria Lelut | FRA | 56 | 2 | | Chicago | 26 Oct 86 |
| 2:30:30 | Akemi Masuda | JAP | 64 | 1 | Nike | Eugene | 11 Sep 83 |
| 2:30:31 | Karolina Szabó | HUN | 61 | 1 | | Szeged | 22 Mar 86 |
| 2:30:36 | Nadezhda Usmanova | SU | 56 | 2 | NP | Vilnius | 7 Oct 84 |
| 2:30:42 | Dorthe Rasmussen | DEN | 60 | 4 | | Chicago | 21 Oct 84 |
| 2:30:50 | Natalya Bardina | SU | 61 | 1 | | Krasnodar | 28 Oct 84 |
| | (30) | | | | | | |
| 2:30:54 | Julie Shea | USA | 59 | 4 | | Boston | 20 Apr 81 |
| 2:31:09 | Marianne Dickerson | USA | 60 | 2 | WC | Helsinki | 7 Aug 83 |
| 2:31:11 | Zoya Ivanova | SU | 51 | 1 | NC | Baku | 13 May 84 |
| 2:31:19 | Ann Ford | UK | 52 | 4 | | London | 21 Apr 85 |
| 2:31:28 | Deborah Raunig | USA | 55 | 4 | | Chicago | 26 Oct 86 |
| 2:31:31 | Lisa Larsen' | USA | 61 | 5 | | Chicago | 21 Oct 84 |
| 2:31:36 | Nancy Ditz | USA | 54 | 1 | TAC | Sacramento | 8 Dec 85 |
| 2:31:37 | Monika Lövenich | FRG | 55 | 2 | | Frankfurt | 15 May 83 |
| 2:31:43 | Sylvie Bornet | FRA | 60 | 4 | | London | 20 Apr 86 |
| 2:31:44 | Glenys Quick | NZ | 57 | 6 | | Chicago | 20 Oct 85 |
| | (40) | | | | | | |

WOMEN All-time

| Mark | Name | Nat | Yr | Pos | Meet | Venue | Date |
|---|---|---|---|---|---|---|---|
| 2:31:48 | Odette Lapierre | CAN | 55 | 3 | CommG | Edinburgh | 1 Aug 86 |
| 2:31:53 | Janis Klecker | USA | 60 | 2 | TAC | Sacramento | 8 Dec 85 |
| 2:32:06 | Tatyana Gridnyeva | SU | 58 | 1 | | Uzhorod | 7 Oct 86 |
| 2:32:07 | Anne Audain' | NZ | 55 | 2 | | Los Angeles | 19 Feb 84 |
| 2:32:07 | Tuija Toivonen' | FIN | 58 | 10 | OG | Los Angeles | 5 Aug 84 |
| 2:32:08 | Kristina Garlipp | GDR | 61 | 2 | | Budapest | 26 Oct 86 |
| 2:32:16 | Lizanne Bussières | CAN | 63 | 3 | | Boston | 21 Apr 86 |
| 2:32:21 | Lyubov Svirskaya | SU | 60 | 2 | | Uzhorod | 7 Oct 86 |
| 2:32:22 | Jocelyne Villeton | FRA | 54 | 2 | | Paris | 4 May 86 |
| 2:32:23 | Gabriele Martins' | GDR | 62 | 2 | EP | Roma | 15 Sep 85 |
| | (50) | | | | | | |

# 100 METRES HURDLES

| Mark | | Name | Nat | Yr | Pos | Meet | Venue | Date |
|---|---|---|---|---|---|---|---|---|
| 12.26 | 1.5 | Yordanka Donkova | BUL | 61 | 1 | Balk | Ljubljana | 7 Sep 86 |
| 12.29 | -0.4 | Donkova | | | 1 | ASV | Köln | 17 Aug 86 |
| 12.34 | 0.1 | Donkova | | | 1h2 | ASV | Köln | 17 Aug 86 |
| 12.36 | 1.9 | Grażyna Rabsztyn | POL | 52 | 1 | Kuso | Warszawa | 13 Jun 80 |
| 12.36 | -0.6 | Donkova | | | 1 | NC | Sofia | 13 Aug 86 |
| 12.37 | 1.4 | Donkova | | | 1r1 | ISTAF | Berlin | 15 Aug 86 |
| 12.38 | 0.0 | Donkova | | | 1 | BGP | Budapest | 11 Aug 86 |
| 12.38 | -0.7 | Donkova | | | 1 | EC | Stuttgart | 29 Aug 86 |
| 12.39 | 1.5 | Vera Komisova' | SU | 53 | 1 | GGala | Roma | 5 Aug 80 |
| 12.39 | 1.5 | Ginka Zagorcheva | BUL | 58 | 2 | Balk | Ljubljana | 7 Sep 86 |
| 12.40 | 0.4 | Donkova | | | 1 | GWG | Moskva | 8 Jul 86 |
| 12.42 | 1.8 | Bettine Jahn | GDR | 58 | 1 | OD | Berlin | 8 Jun 83 |
| 12.42 | 1.0 | Zagorcheva | | | 1 | | Sofia | 14 Aug 85 |
| 12.42 | -0.2 | Donkova | | | 1 | VD | Bruxelles | 5 Sep 86 |
| 12.43 | -0.9 | Lucyna Kalek' | POL | 56 | 1 | | Hannover | 19 Aug 84 |
| 12.44 | 1.9 | Langer' | | | 2 | Kuso | Warszawa | 13 Jun 80 |
| 12.44 | 1.0 | Donkova | | | 1 | | Sofia | 7 Aug 82 |
| 12.45 | 1.5 | Kalek | | | 1h1 | EC | Athínai | 8 Sep 82 |
| 12.45 | 0.4 | Kalek | | | 1 | EC | Athínai | 9 Sep 82 |
| 12.47 | 0.6 | Donkova | | | 1 | GP | Roma | 10 Sep 86 |
| 12.48 | 1.9 | Rabsztyn | | | 1 | | Fürth | 10 Jun 78 |
| 12.48 | 1.2 | Rabsztyn | | | 1 | Kuso | Warszawa | 18 Jun 79 |
| 12.48 | 0.5 | Jahn | | | 1 | | Berlin | 31 Jul 83 |
| 12.48 | -0.2 | Zagorcheva | | | 2 | VD | Bruxelles | 5 Sep 86 |

( 24 Performances by 6 Athletes )

| 12.50 | 0.0 | Vera Akimova' | SU | 59 | 1 | | Sochi | 19 May 84 |
|---|---|---|---|---|---|---|---|---|
| 12.50 | 0.3 | Cornelia Oschkenat' | GDR | 61 | 1 | PTS | Bratislava | 14 Jun 86 |
| 12.54 | 0.4 | Kerstin Knabe | GDR | 59 | 3 | EC | Athínai | 9 Sep 82 |
| 12.54 | 0.9 | Sabine Paetz | GDR | 57 | 1 | | Berlin | 15 Jul 84 |
| | | (10) | | | | | | |
| 12.56 | 1.2 | Johanna Klier' | GDR | 52 | 1r1 | NC | Cottbus | 17 Jul 80 |
| 12.59 | -0.6 | Anneliese Ehrhardt | GDR | 50 | 1 | OG | München | 8 Sep 72 |
| 12.61 | 0.3 | Svetlana Gusarova | SU | 59 | 2 | NC | Leningrad | 3 Aug 85 |
| 12.61 | 1.9 | Natalya Grigoryeva | SU | 62 | 1s1 | NC | Kiev | 15 Jul 86 |
| 12.63 | 1.8 | Zofia Bielczyk | POL | 58 | 1h1 | Kuso | Warszawa | 18 Jun 79 |
| 12.63 | 1.4 | Heike Theele' | GDR | 64 | 2 | NC | Jena | 27 Jun 86 |
| A12.65 | 0.0 | Danuta Perka | POL | 56 | 1h3 | WUG | México | 9 Sep 79 |
| 12.65 | 0.0 | Nadezhda Korshunova | SU | 61 | 2 | | Sochi | 19 May 84 |

| Mark | Wind | Name | Nat | Yr | Pos | Meet | Venue | Date |
|------|------|------|-----|----|----|------|-------|------|
| 12.66 | 0.0 | Yelena Biserova | SU | 62 | 3 | | Sochi | 19 May 84 |
| 12.67 | 0.6 | Tatyana Anisimova | SU | 49 | 2 | EC | Praha | 2 Sep 78 |
| | | (20) | | | | | | |
| 12.69 | 0.2 | Laurence Elloy | FRA | 59 | 2h1 | GWG | Moskva | 8 Jul 86 |
| 12.71 | -0.7 | Yelena Politika | SU | 64 | 2 | NC | Kiev | 15 Jul 86 |
| 12.73 | 0.6 | Gudrun Berend' | GDR | 55 | 3 | EC | Praha | 2 Sep 78 |
| 12.75 | 0.8 | Mihaela Pogacian' | RUM | 58 | 1 | | Bucureşti | 25 May 86 |
| 12.76 | | Nina Derbina' | SU | 56 | 1 | | Leningrad | 22 Jun 80 |
| 12.76 | 1.7 | Xénia Siska | HUN | 57 | 3 | BGP | Budapest | 20 Aug 84 |
| 12.78 | -0.7 | Yelizav. Chernysheva | SU | 58 | 4 | NC | Kiev | 15 Jul 86 |
| 12.79 | 1.9 | Stephanie Hightower | USA | 58 | 3 | v GDR | Karl-Marx-St. | 10 Jul 82 |
| 12.79 | 0.9 | Gloria Kovarik' | GDR | 64 | 4 | | Berlin | 15 Jul 84 |
| 12.80 | 0.0 | Natalya Lebedyeva | SU | 49 | 3 | OG | Montréal | 29 Jul 76 |
| | | (30) | | | | | | |
| 12.80 | 1.9 | Elżbieta Rabsztyn | POL | 56 | 5 | Kuso | Warszawa | 13 Jun 80 |
| 12.81 | 1.0 | Maria Merchuk' | SU | 59 | 3 | v GDR | Cottbus | 26 Jun 82 |
| 12.83 | 1.5 | Natalya Petrova | SU | 57 | 2s2 | WC | Helsinki | 13 Aug 83 |
| 12.84 | 0.0 | Valeria Bufanu | RUM | 46 | 1s1 | OG | München | 7 Sep 72 |
| 12.84 | 1.2 | Irina Litovchenko' | SU | 50 | 3s2 | OG | Moskva | 28 Jul 80 |
| 12.84 | 1.1 | Benita Fitzgerald' | USA | 61 | 1 | NCAA | Houston | 4 Jun 83 |
| 12.84 | 1.1 | Ulrike Denk | FRG | 64 | 1 | NC | Stuttgart | 3 Aug 85 |
| 12.84 | 0.6 | Jackie Joyner | USA | 62 | 5 | GP | Roma | 10 Sep 86 |
| 12.85 | 0.1 | Rhonda Blanford | USA | 63 | 1 | TAC | Indianapolis | 15 Jun 85 |
| 12.85 | -2.0 | Liliana Nastase | RUM | 62 | 1h2 | Znam | Leningrad | 7 Jun 86 |
| | | (40) | | | | | | |
| 12.86 | 1.5 | Deby LaPlante | USA | 53 | 1 | AAU | Walnut | 16 Jun 79 |
| 12.86 | 0.4 | Cornelia Feuerbach | GDR | 63 | 3r1 | | Leipzig | 27 Jul 83 |
| 12.87 | 0.3 | Lyubov Kononova | SU | 48 | 3 | WP | Düsseldorf | 3 Sep 77 |
| 12.87 | 1.1 | Shirley Strong | UK | 58 | 1 | WK | Zürich | 24 Aug 83 |
| 12.89 | 0.2 | Annerose Fiedler' | GDR | 51 | 2 | EC | Roma | 7 Sep 74 |
| 12.89 | 0.4 | Candy Young | USA | 62 | 2 | VD | Bruxelles | 27 Aug 82 |
| 12.89 | 1.7 | Anne Piquereau | FRA | 64 | 2 | | Joinville | 12 Jun 85 |
| 12.90 | -0.6 | Karin Balzer | GDR | 38 | 3 | OG | München | 8 Sep 72 |
| 12.91 | 0.5 | Danuta Straszyńska | POL | 42 | 2s2 | OG | München | 7 Sep 72 |
| 12.91 | 0.2 | Teresa Nowak | POL | 42 | 3 | EC | Roma | 7 Sep 74 |
| | | (50) | | | | | | |
| 12.91 | 0.2 | Bożena Nowakowska' | POL | 55 | 1 | | v GDR,CS-j,Ziel.Góra | 9 Aug 75 |
| | | (51) | | | | | | |

Low altitude mark                                                        A-best

| 12.69 | 1.9 | | Perka | | 4 | Kuso | Warszawa | 13 Jun 80 | A12.65 |
|-------|-----|--|-------|--|---|------|----------|-----------|--------|

Marks made with assisting wind > 2 m/s

| 12.35 | 2.4 | Bettine Jahn | GDR | 58 | 1 | WC | Helsinki | 13 Aug 83 |
|-------|-----|--------------|-----|----|---|----|----------|-----------|
| 12.39 | 2.8 | Rabsztyn | | | 1 | 4-N | Bremen | 24 Jun 79 |
| 12.42 | 2.4 | Kerstin Knabe | GDR | 59 | 2 | WC | Helsinki | 13 Aug 83 |
| 12.45 | 2.8 | Rabsztyn | | | 1h2 | Kuso | Warszawa | 13 Jun 80 |

( 4 Performances by 2 Athletes )

| 12.51 | 3.2 | Johanna Klier' | GDR | 52 | 1 | NC | Cottbus | 17 Jul 80 |
|-------|-----|----------------|-----|----|---|------|----------|-----------|
| 12.51 | 3.6 | Sabine Paetz | GDR | 57 | 1 | | Dresden | 27 Jul 84 |
| 12.67 | 2.4 | Natalya Petrova | SU | 57 | 4 | WC | Helsinki | 13 Aug 83 |
| 12.70 | 4.1 | Rhonda Blanford | USA | 63 | 1 | NCAA | Austin | 1 Jun 85 |
| 12.78 | 4.5 | Shirley Strong | UK | 58 | 1 | CommG | Brisbane | 8 Oct 82 |
| 12.78 | 4.6 | Stephanie Hightower | USA | 58 | 1 | | Modesto | 12 May 84 |
| 12.83 | 2.5 | Benita Fitzgerald' | USA | 61 | 1 | TAC | Eugene | 20 Jun 86 |

| Mark | Wind | Name | Nat | Yr | Pos | Meet | Venue | Date |
|------|------|------|-----|-----|-----|------|-------|------|
| 12.89 | 2.5 | Lyudmila Oliyar | SU | 58 | 1h | | Leningrad | 26 Jul 83 |
| | | (10) | | | | | | |
| 12.90 | 4.5 | Lorna Boothe | UK | 54 | 2 | CommG | Brisbane | 8 Oct 82 |
| 12.91 | 2.9 | Michele Chardonnet | FRA | 56 | 2 | NC | Lille | 1 Jul 84 |
| 12.91 | 2.5 | Rosalind Council' | USA | 65 | 3 | TAC | Eugene | 20 Jun 86 |
| 12.91 | 2.5 | Pam Page | USA | 56 | 4 | TAC | Eugene | 20 Jun 86 |
| | | (14) | | | | | | |

# 400 METRES HURDLES

| | | | | | | | | |
|------|------|------|-----|-----|-----|------|-------|------|
| 52.94 | | Marina Styepanova' | SU | 50 | 1s | Spart | Tashkent | 17 Sep 86 |
| 53.32 | | Styepanova | | | 1 | EC | Stuttgart | 30 Aug 86 |
| 53.55 | | Sabine Busch | GDR | 62 | 1 | | Berlin | 22 Sep 85 |
| 53.58 | | Margarita Ponomaryova' | SU | 63 | 1 | | Kiev | 22 Jun 84 |
| 53.60 | | Busch | | | 2 | EC | Stuttgart | 30 Aug 86 |
| 53.62 | | Busch | | | 1h2 | NC | Jena | 27 Jun 86 |
| 53.64 | | Busch | | | 1 | VD | Bruxelles | 5 Sep 86 |
| 53.67 | | Styepanova | | | 1 | Drz | Praha | 17 Aug 84 |
| 53.72 | | Styepanova | | | 1h | Spart | Tashkent | 16 Sep 86 |
| A53.74 | | Myrtle Bothma' | RSA | 64 | 1 | | Johannesburg | 18 Apr 86 |
| 53.75 | | Busch | | | 1 | | Jena | 31 May 86 |
| 53.76 | | Debbie Flintoff | AUS | 60 | 1 | Bisl | Oslo | 5 Jul 86 |
| 53.81 | | Styepanova | | | 1rl | GWG | Moskva | 7 Jul 86 |
| 53.83 | | Busch | | | 1 | | Jena | 12 Jun 85 |
| 53.83 | | Styepanova | | | 1s2 | EC | Stuttgart | 29 Aug 86 |
| 53.84 | | Styepanova | | | 1 | NC | Kiev | 16 Jul 86 |
| 53.85 | | Busch | | | 1 | NC | Jena | 28 Jun 86 |
| 53.92 | | Styepanova | | | 1h | Znam | Leningrad | 7 Jun 86 |
| 53.93 | | Busch | | | 1 | v SU | Erfurt | 23 Jun 85 |
| A53.95 | | Bothma | | | 1 | NC | Germiston | 12 Apr 86 |
| 53.97 | | Busch | | | 2s2 | EC | Stuttgart | 29 Aug 86 |

( 21 Performances by 5 Athletes )

| | | | | | | | | |
|------|------|------|-----|-----|-----|------|-------|------|
| 54.02 | | Anna Ambraziene' | SU | 55 | 1 | Znam | Moskva | 11 Jun 83 |
| 54.13 | | Cornelia Feuerbach | GDR | 63 | 3 | EC | Stuttgart | 30 Aug 86 |
| 54.14 | | Yekaterina Fesenko-Grun | SU | 58 | 1 | WC | Helsinki | 10 Aug 83 |
| 54.15 | | Ann-Louise Skoglund | SWE | 62 | 4 | EC | Stuttgart | 30 Aug 86 |
| 54.20 | | Ellen Fiedler' | GDR | 58 | 1 | EP | London | 20 Aug 83 |
| | | (10) | | | | | | |
| 54.27 | | Genowefa Błaszak' | POL | 57 | 1 | DNG | Stockholm | 2 Jul 85 |
| 54.28 | | Karin Rossley | GDR | 57 | 1 | OT | Jena | 17 May 80 |
| 54.34 | | Tatyana Pavlova' | SU | 58 | 1h1 | NC | Leningrad | 2 Aug 85 |
| 54.38 | | Judi Brown-King | USA | 61 | 1 | GP | Roma | 7 Sep 85 |
| 54.55 | | Bärbel Broschat | GDR | 57 | 1 | WC | Sittard | 16 Aug 80 |
| 54.55 | | Cristeana Matei' | RUM | 62 | 2rl | GWG | Moskva | 7 Jul 86 |
| 54.56 | | Yelena Filipishina | SU | 62 | 2 | | Moskva | 20 Jul 84 |
| 54.61 | | Nawal el Moutawakil | MOR | 62 | 1 | OG | Los Angeles | 8 Aug 84 |
| 54.64 | | Petra Pfaff | GDR | 60 | 4 | WC | Helsinki | 10 Aug 83 |
| 54.66 | | Latanya Sheffield | USA | 63 | 1 | NCAA | Austin | 31 May 85 |
| | | (20) | | | | | | |
| 54.68 | | Birgit Uibel | GDR | 61 | 1 | | Dresden | 19 May 84 |
| 54.76 | | Petra Krug | GDR | 63 | 5 | WC | Helsinki | 10 Aug 83 |
| 54.78 | | Marina Sereda' | SU | 64 | 2 | Spart | Tashkent | 18 Sep 86 |

| Mark | Name | Nat | Yr | Pos | Meet | Venue | Date |
|------|------|-----|----|----|------|-------|------|
| 54.80 | Tatyana Storozheva | SU | 54 | 1 | | Moskva | 12 Jun 80 |
| 54.86 | Tonja Brown | USA | 60 | 3 | GP | Roma | 7 Sep 85 |
| 54.89 | Tatyana Zelentsova' | SU | 48 | 1 | EC | Praha | 2 Sep 78 |
| 54.90 | Sharrieffa Barksdale | USA | 61 | 1 | | Knoxville | 24 May 86 |
| 54.93 | Chantal Rega | FRA | 55 | 3 | EC | Athínai | 10 Sep 82 |
| 54.93 | Yelena Goncharova | SU | 63 | 1 | | Sochi | 18 May 86 |
| 55.02 | Margarita Navickaite | SU | 61 | 6 | | Kiev | 22 Jun 84 |
| | (30) | | | | | | |
| 55.05 | Jackie Joyner | USA | 62 | 4 | VD | Bruxelles | 30 Aug 85 |
| 55.14 | Silvia Hollmann | FRG | 55 | 2 | EC | Praha | 2 Sep 78 |
| 55.16 | Nicoleta Carutasu' | RUM | 64 | 2 | | Bucureşti | 24 May 86 |
| 55.16 | Maria Usifo | NIG | 64 | 1 | NCAA | Indianapolis | 6 Jun 86 |
| 55.19 | Mary Wagner | FRG | 61 | 1 | | Fürth | 21 May 83 |
| 55.20 | Leslie Maxie | USA | 67 | 2 | TAC | San Jose | 9 Jun 84 |
| 55.21 | Tuija Helander | FIN | 61 | 2 | EP-B | Budapest | 10 Aug 85 |
| 55.33 | Angela Wright-Scott | USA | 64 | 2 | FOT | Los Angeles | 21 Jun 84 |
| 55.38 | Schowonda Williams | USA | 66 | 2 | | Knoxville | 24 May 86 |
| 55.42 | P.T. Usha | IND | 64 | 4 | OG | Los Angeles | 8 Aug 84 |
| | (40) | | | | | | |
| 55.44 | Krystyna Kacperczyk | POL | 48 | 1 | ISTAF | Berlin | 18 Aug 78 |
| 55.46 | Brigitte Köhn' | GDR | 54 | 4 | EC | Praha | 2 Sep 78 |
| 55.48 | Sabine Everts | FRG | 61 | 1 | NC | Stuttgart | 4 Aug 85 |
| 55.49 | Natalya Tsiruk | SU | 55 | 1 | NC | Moskva | 18 Sep 81 |
| A55.49 | Charmaine Fick | RSA | 59 | 1 | NC | Bloemfontein | 16 Apr 83 |
| 55.53 | Radostina Dimitrova | BUL | 66 | 3 | OD | Potsdam | 21 Jul 84 |
| 55.57 | Marina Balabanova | SU | 64 | 4 | Spart | Tashkent | 18 Sep 86 |
| 55.60 | Lori McCauley | USA | 61 | 4 | FOT | Los Angeles | 21 Jun 84 |
| 55.62 | Olga Nazarova' | SU | 62 | .h | NC | Kiev | 15 Jul 86 |
| 55.63 | Anita Weiss' | GDR | 55 | 6 | EC | Praha | 2 Sep 78 |
| | (50) | | | | | | |

Low altitude mark                                    A-best

| 54.86 | | Bothma | | 1 | | Pt. Elizabeth | 21 Apr 86 | A53.74 |

# HIGH JUMP

| | | | | | | | |
|------|------|-----|----|----|------|-------|------|
| 2.08 | Stefka Kostadinova | BUL | 65 | 1 | Nar | Sofia | 31 May 86 |
| 2.07 | Lyudmila Andonova | BUL | 60 | 1 | OD | Berlin | 20 Jul 84 |
| 2.07 | Kostadinova | | | 1 | | Sofia | 25 May 86 |
| 2.06 | Kostadinova | | | 1 | EP | Moskva | 18 Aug 85 |
| 2.06 | Kostadinova | | | 1 | | Fürth | 15 Jun 86 |
| 2.06 | Kostadinova | | | 1 | | Cagliari | 14 Sep 86 |
| 2.05 | Tamara Bykova | SU | 58 | 1 | | Kiev | 22 Jun 84 |
| 2.05 | Kostadinova | | | 1 | | Wörrstadt | 14 Jun 86 |
| 2.05 | Kostadinova | | | 1 | | Rieti | 7 Sep 86 |
| 2.04 | Bykova | | | 1 | | Pisa | 25 Aug 83 |
| 2.04 | Kostadinova | | | 1 | VD | Bruxelles | 30 Aug 85 |
| 2.04 | Kostadinova | | | 1 | | Rieti | 4 Sep 85 |
| 2.04 | Kostadinova | | | 1 | | Bern | 20 Aug 86 |
| 2.03i | Bykova | | | 1 | EC | Budapest | 6 Mar 83 |
| 2.03 | Ulrike Meyfarth | FRG | 56 | 1 | EP | London | 21 Aug 83 |
| 2.03 | Bykova | | | 2 | EP | London | 21 Aug 83 |
| 2.03 | Bykova | | | 1 | | Moskva | 6 Aug 84 |
| 2.03 | Andonova | | | 1 | | Rieti | 2 Sep 84 |
| 2.03 | Kostadinova | | | 1 | GWG | Moskva | 7 Jul 86 |

| Mark | Name | Nat | Yr | Pos | Meet | Venue | Date |
|------|------|-----|----|-----|------|-------|------|
| 2.02 | Meyfarth | | | 1 | EC | Athínai | 8 Sep 82 |
| 2.02 | Meyfarth | | | 1 | OG | Los Angeles | 10 Aug 84 |
| 2.02 | Andonova | | | 1 | GGala | Roma | 31 Aug 84 |
| 2.02 | Bykova | | | 2 | EP | Moskva | 18 Aug 85 |

( 23 Performances by 4 Athletes )

| Mark | Name | Nat | Yr | Pos | Meet | Venue | Date |
|------|------|-----|----|-----|------|-------|------|
| 2.01 | Sara Simeoni | ITA | 53 | 1 | v Pol | Brescia | 4 Aug 78 |
| 2.01 | Louise Ritter | USA | 58 | 1 | GGala | Roma | 1 Sep 83 |
| 2.01 | Silvia Costa | CUB | 64 | 1 | WUG | Kobe | 3 Sep 85 |
| 2.01 | Olga Turchak | SU | 67 | 2 | GWG | Moskva | 7 Jul 86 |
| 2.01 | Desireé du Plessis | RSA | 65 | 1 | | Johannesburg | 16 Sep 86 |
| 2.00 | Rosemarie Ackermann' | GDR | 52 | 1 | ISTAF | Berlin | 26 Aug 77 |
| | (10) | | | | | | |
| 2.00i | Coleen Sommer' | USA | 60 | 1 | | Ottawa | 14 Feb 82 |
| 2.00 | Charmaine Gale | RSA | 64 | 1 | | Pretoria | 25 Mar 85 |
| 1.99i | Debbie Brill | CAN | 53 | 1 | | Edmonton | 23 Jan 82 |
| 1.99i | Andrea Bienias' | GDR | 59 | 2 | EC | Milano | 7 Mar 82 |
| 1.99i | Katalin Sterk | HUN | 61 | 3 | EC | Milano | 7 Mar 82 |
| 1.99 | Kerstin Brandt' | GDR | 61 | 3 | EP | London | 21 Aug 83 |
| 1.98i | Andrea Mátay | HUN | 55 | 1 | NC | Budapest | 17 Feb 79 |
| 1.98 | Larisa Kositsyna | SU | 63 | 2 | Nar | Sofia | 21 May 83 |
| 1.98 | Valentina Poluyko | SU | 55 | 1 | | Leningrad | 26 Jul 83 |
| 1.98 | Lyudmila Butuzova | SU | 57 | 2 | Znam | Sochi | 10 Jun 84 |
| | (20) | | | | | | |
| 1.98 | Niculina Vasile | RUM | 58 | 1 | RumIC | București | 2 Jun 85 |
| 1.98i | Gabriele Günz | GDR | 61 | 1 | | Berlin | 25 Jan 86 |
| 1.97 | Pam Spencer | USA | 57 | 1 | VD | Bruxelles | 28 Aug 81 |
| 1.97i | Zhanna Nyekrasova | SU | 57 | 1 | NP | Moskva | 13 Feb 82 |
| 1.97 | Jutta Kirst | GDR | 54 | 1 | v USA | Karl-Marx-St. | 10 Jul 82 |
| 1.97 | Yelena Popkova | SU | 55 | 2 | NC | Kiev | 21 Aug 82 |
| 1.97 | Susanne Helm | GDR | 61 | 1 | OD | Berlin | 8 Jun 83 |
| 1.97 | Olga Juha | HUN | 62 | 4 | EP | London | 21 Aug 83 |
| 1.97i | Marina Doronina | SU | 61 | 1 | | Vilnius | 14 Jan 84 |
| 1.97 | Danuta Bułkowska | POL | 59 | 2 | | Wörrstadt | 9 Jun 84 |
| | (30) | | | | | | |
| 1.97 | Olga Byelkova | SU | 55 | 2 | | Kiev | 22 Jun 84 |
| 1.97 | Joni Huntley | USA | 56 | 3 | OG | Los Angeles | 10 Aug 84 |
| 1.97 | Svetlana Isaeva | BUL | 67 | 2 | | Sofia | 25 May 86 |
| 1.96 | Nina Serbina | SU | 52 | 1 | | Chernigov | 3 Jun 80 |
| 1.96 | Chris Stanton' | AUS | 59 | H | | Adelaide | 26 Jan 85 |
| 1.96 | Yang Wenqin | CHN | 60 | 1 | | Beijing | 26 May 85 |
| 1.96 | Maryse Ewanje-Epée | FRA | 64 | 1 | NC | Colombes | 21 Jul 85 |
| 1.96 | Galina Brigadnaya | SU | 58 | 1 | | Alma-Ata | 13 Sep 85 |
| 1.95 | Brigitte Holzapfel | FRG | 58 | 1 | NC | Köln | 12 Aug 78 |
| 1.95 | Kristine Nitzsche | GDR | 59 | P | EP/sf | Schielleiten | 14 Jul 79 |
| | (40) | | | | | | |
| 1.95 | Urszula Kielan | POL | 60 | 1 | | Grudziądz | 28 May 80 |
| 1.95 | Diana Elliott' | UK | 61 | 1 | Bisl | Olso | 26 Jun 82 |
| 1.95 | Lyudmila Petrus' | SU | 63 | 3 | | Kiev | 22 Jun 84 |
| 1.95 | Jolanta Komsa | POL | 58 | 1 | | Zabrze | 14 Sep 84 |
| 1.95 | Marina Degtyar | SU | 62 | 1 | | Krivoy Rog | 15 Jun 85 |
| 1.95 | Małgorzata Nowak' | POL | 59 | H | WUG | Kobe | 30 Aug 85 |

Best outdoor marks                                                    Indoo

| | | | Pos | Meet | Venue | Date | |
|------|------|--|-----|------|-------|------|------|
| 1.98 | Sommer | | 1 | v FRG,Afr | Durham | 26 Jun 82 | 2.00i |
| 1.98 | Brill | | 1 | | Rieti | 2 Sep 84 | 1.99i |
| 1.97 | Bienias | | 1 | | Leipzig | 27 Jul 83 | 1.99i |
| 1.98 | Sterk | | 1 | NC | Budapest | 17 Aug 86 | 1.99i |

| Mark | Wind | Name | Nat | Yr | Pos | Meet | Venue | Date | |
|------|------|------|-----|----|-----|------|-------|------|---|

## LONG JUMP

| Mark | Wind | Name | Nat | Yr | Pos | Meet | Venue | Date |
|------|------|------|-----|----|-----|------|-------|------|
| 7.45 | 0.9 | Heike Drechsler' | GDR | 64 | 1 | v SU | Tallinn | 21 Jun 86 |
| 7.45 | 1.1 | Drechsler | | | 1 | OD | Dresden | 3 Jul 86 |
| 7.44 | 2.0 | Drechsler | | | 1 | | Berlin | 22 Sep 85 |
| 7.43 | 1.4 | Anişoara Cuşmir' | RUM | 62 | 1 | RumIC | Bucuresti | 4 Jun 83 |
| 7.40 | 1.8 | Daute' | | | 1 | | Dresden | 26 Jul 84 |
| 7.39 | 0.3 | Drechsler | | | 1 | WK | Zürich | 21 Aug 85 |
| 7.34 | 1.6 | Daute' | | | 1 | | Dresden | 19 May 84 |
| 7.34 | 1.4 | Galina Chistyakova | SU | 62 | 2 | v GDR | Tallinn | 21 Jun 86 |
| 7.33 | 0.4 | Drechsler | | | 1 | v SU | Erfurt | 22 Jun 85 |
| 7.33 | 2.0 | Drechsler | | | 1 | | Dresden | 2 Aug 85 |
| 7.32 | -0.2 | Daute' | | | 1 | OD | Berlin | 20 Jul 84 |
| 7.31 | 1.5 | Yelena Kokonova | SU | 63 | 1 | | Alma-Ata | 12 Sep 85 |
| 7.31 | 1.3 | Drechsler | | | 1 | | Jena | 31 May 86 |
| 7.31 | -0.2 | Yelena Byelevskaya' | SU | 63 | 1 | NC | Kiev | 15 Jul 86 |
| 7.29 | 0.0 | Daute' | | | 1 | | Jena | 13 May 84 |
| 7.29 | -0.5 | Chistyakova | | | 1 | | Moskva | 6 Aug 84 |
| 7.29 | 1.8 | Drechsler | | | 1 | | Neubrandenburg | 7 Jun 85 |
| 7.29i | - | Drechsler | | | 1 | | Berlin | 25 Jan 86 |
| 7.29 | 1.5 | Drechsler | | | - | NC | Jena | 28 Jun 86 |
| 7.28 | 0.9 | Chistyakova | | | 1 | EP | Moskva | 18 Aug 85 |
| 7.27 | 1.0 | Stanciu' | | | 1 | v Bul,GDR | Sofia | 17 Jun 84 |
| 7.27 | 1.3 | Chistyakova | | | 2 | v GDR | Erfurt | 22 Jun 85 |
| 7.27 | 0.7 | Drechsler | | | 1 | WP | Canberra | 6 Oct 85 |
| 7.27 | 0.8 | Chistyakova | | | 1 | GWG | Moskva | 7 Jul 86 |
| 7.27 | 0.3 | Drechsler | | | 1 | EC | Stuttgart | 27 Aug 86 |

( 25 Performances by 5 Athletes )

| Mark | Wind | Name | Nat | Yr | Pos | Meet | Venue | Date |
|------|------|------|-----|----|-----|------|-------|------|
| 7.24 | -0.1 | Jackie Joyner | USA | 62 | 2 | WK | Zürich | 21 Aug 85 |
| 7.21 | 1.6 | Helga Radtke | GDR | 62 | 2 | | Dresden | 26 Jul 84 |
| 7.20 | -0.5 | Vali Ionescu | RUM | 60 | 1 | NC | Bucureşti | 1 Aug 82 |
| 7.20 | 2.0 | Irena Ozhenko' | SU | 62 | 1 | | Budapest | 12 Sep 86 |
| 7.19 | 1.3 | Larisa Berezhnaya | SU | 61 | 1 | | Krasnodar | 22 Jun 86 |
| | | (10) | | | | | | |
| 7.12 | 1.6 | Sabine Paetz | GDR | 57 | 2 | | Dresden | 19 May 84 |
| 7.09 | 0.0 | Vilma Bardauskiene | SU | 53 | Q | EC | Praha | 29 Aug 78 |
| 7.07 | 0.4 | Irina Valyukevich | SU | 59 | 2 | NC | Leningrad | 1 Aug 85 |
| 7.06 | 0.4 | Tatyana Kalpakova | SU | 59 | 1 | OG | Moskva | 31 Jul 80 |
| 7.04 | 0.5 | Brigitte Wujak' | GDR | 55 | 2 | OG | Moskva | 31 Jul 80 |
| 7.04 | 2.0 | Svetlana Zorina | SU | 60 | 1 | Spart | Moskva | 20 Jun 83 |
| 7.04 | 0.9 | Tatyana Proskuryakova' | SU | 56 | 1 | | Kiev | 25 Aug 83 |
| 7.04 | 2.0 | Yelena Yatsuk | SU | 61 | 1 | Znam | Moskva | 8 Jun 85 |
| 7.04 | 0.3 | Carol Lewis | USA | 63 | 5 | WK | Zürich | 21 Aug 85 |
| 7.02 | 0.5 | Niole Medvedyeva | SU | 60 | 4 | Drz | Praha | 17 Aug 84 |
| | | (20) | | | | | | |
| 7.01 | -0.4 | Tatyana Skachko | SU | 54 | 3 | OG | Moskva | 31 Jul 80 |
| 7.01 | -0.3 | Eva Murková | CS | 62 | 1 | PTS | Bratislava | 26 May 84 |
| 7.01 | | Yelena Ivanova | SU | 61 | 2 | | Moskva | 9 Jul 84 |
| 7.01 | -1.0 | Marina Kibakina' | SU | 60 | 1 | | Krasnoyarsk | 10 Aug 85 |
| 7.00 | 2.0 | Jodi Anderson | USA | 57 | 1 | FOT | Eugene | 28 Jun 80 |
| 7.00 | | Margarita Butkiene | SU | 49 | 1 | | Vilnius | 25 May 83 |
| 7.00 | -0.2 | Birgit Grosshennig | GDR | 65 | 2 | | Berlin | 9 Jun 84 |

| Mark | Wind | Name | Nat | Yr | Pos | Meet | Venue | Date |
|------|------|------|-----|----|----|------|-------|------|
| 7.00 | 0.6 | Silvia Khristova' | BUL | 65 | 1 | | Sofia | 3 Aug 86 |
| 6.99 | 2.0 | Siegrun Siegl' | GDR | 54 | 1 | OD | Dresden | 19 May 76 |
| 6.96 | 2.0 | Anna Włodarczyk | POL | 51 | 1 | NC | Lublin | 22 Jun 84 |
| | | (30) | | | | | | |
| 6.96 | 1.8 | Christine Schima | GDR | 62 | 3 | | Dresden | 26 Jul 84 |
| 6.94 | 1.3 | Yelena Chicherova | SU | 58 | 2 | | Kiev | 21 Jun 84 |
| 6.92 | 1.6 | Angela Voigt' | GDR | 51 | 1 | | Dresden | 9 May 76 |
| 6.92 | | Vera Olenchenko | SU | 59 | 1 | | Baku | 22 Sep 85 |
| 6.91 | 1.8 | Heike Duwe | GDR | 60 | 3 | | Berlin | 9 Jun 84 |
| 6.90 | 1.8 | Ramona Neubert | GDR | 58 | - | v UK | Dresden | 14 Jun 81 |
| 6.90 | | Tatyana Turulina | SU | 58 | 1 | | Krasnodar | 26 May 83 |
| 6.90 | 1.4 | Beverley Kinch | UK | 64 | - | WC | Helsinki | 14 Aug 83 |
| 6.89 | -0.3 | Sigrid Ulbricht | GDR | 58 | 2 | NC | Jena | 9 Aug 81 |
| 6.89 | 1.8 | Jarmila Strejčková' | CS | 53 | 1 | | Praha | 18 Sep 82 |
| | | (40) | | | | | | |
| 6.88 | 0.6 | Natalya Shevchenko | SU | 66 | 2 | | Sochi | 26 May 84 |
| 6.88 | -0.8 | Lyudmila Ninova | BUL | 60 | 1 | NC | Sofia | 14 Aug 86 |
| 6.88 | 1.6 | Galina Salo | SU | 59 | 2 | | Volgograd | 6 Sep 86 |
| 6.87 | | Marieta Ilcu | RUM | 62 | 1 | | Poiana Brasov | 10 Aug 85 |
| 6.86 | 1.5 | Robyn Lorraway' | AUS | 61 | 1 | | Canberra | 23 Feb 86 |
| 6.85 | | Valentina Kovalyeva | SU | 60 | 1 | | Gorkiy | 24 Aug 85 |
| 6.85 | | Valentina Kurochkina | SU | 59 | H | | Alma-Ata | 14 Sep 85 |
| 6.84 | 0.0 | Heidemarie Rosendahl | FRG | 47 | 1 | WUG | Torino | 3 Sep 70 |
| 6.84 | 0.0 | Lidiya Alfeyeva | SU | 46 | 2 | OT | Moskva | 12 Jun 80 |
| 6.84 | -0.6 | Natalya Alyoshina | SU | 56 | 2 | Spart | Moskva | 20 Jun 83 |
| | | (50) | | | | | | |
| 6.84 | | Larisa Baluta | SU | 65 | 2 | | Krasnodar | 6 Aug 83 |
| 6.84 | | Natalya Chemidronova | SU | 59 | 1 | | Kazan | 14 Jul 84 |
| 6.84 | 0.5 | Anke Vater' | GDR | 61 | H | OD | Potsdam | 21 Jul 84 |
| | | (53) | | | | | | |

Marks made with assisiting wind > 2 m/s

| | | | | | | | | |
|------|------|------|-----|----|----|------|-------|------|
| 7.35 | 3.4 | Drechsler | | | 1 | NC | Jena | 29 Jun 86 |
| 7.33 | 3.5 | Drechsler | | | 1 | | Jena | 12 Jun 85 |
| 7.27 | 2.2 | Daute' | | | 1 | WC | Helsinki | 14 Aug 83 |
| 7.17 | 3.6 | Eva Murková | CS | 62 | 1 | | Nitra | 26 Aug 84 |
| 7.10 | 3.7 | Irina Valyukevich | SU | 59 | 4 | v GDR | Tallinn | 21 Jun 86 |
| 7.00 | 3.8 | Ramona Neubert | GDR | 58 | 1 | v UK | Dresden | 14 Jun 81 |
| 7.00 | 4.2 | Sue Hearnshaw' | UK | 58 | 1 | NC | Cwmbran | 27 May 84 |
| 6.99 | 4.6 | Beverley Kinch | UK | 64 | 5 | WC | Helsinki | 14 Aug 83 |
| 6.98 | 3.4 | Ines Schmidt | GDR | 60 | 2 | | Nitra | 26 Aug 84 |
| 6.97 | 2.7 | Anna Włodarczyk | POL | 51 | 1 | 4-N | Warszawa | 15 Jul 84 |
| 6.96 | | Tatyana Shchelkanova | SU | 37 | P | NC | Dnepropetrovsk | 14 Aug 66 |
| 6.92 | 4.0 | Agata Karczmarek | POL | 63 | 1 | NC | Grudziądz | 29 Jun 86 |
| 6.91 | | Kathy McMillan | USA | 57 | 1 | | Houston | 3 May 80 |
| | | (10) | | | | | | |
| 6.91 | 2.7 | Shonel Ferguson | BAH | 57 | 1 | CommG | Brisbane | 8 Oct 82 |
| 6.90 | 2.6 | Robyn Lorraway' | AUS | 61 | 1 | | Adelaide | 4 Feb 84 |
| 6.89 | 3.7 | Sheila Echols | USA | 64 | 2 | TAC | Eugene | 21 Jun 86 |
| 6.86 | 5.6 | Heidemarie Wycisk | GDR | 49 | 2 | | Dresden | 9 May 76 |
| 6.85 | 2.4 | Jennifer Inniss | USA/GUY | 59 | 2 | TAC | Indianapolis | 18 Jun 83 |
| 6.85 | | Gwen Loud | USA | 61 | 1 | NCAA | Eugene | 2 Jun 84 |
| 6.84 | 3.2 | Susan Reeve | UK | 51 | 1 | | Edinburgh | 25 Jun 77 |
| | | (18) | | | | | | |

| Mark | Name | Nat | Yr | Pos | Meet | Venue | Date |
|------|------|-----|-----|-----|------|-------|------|

**SHOT PUT**

WOMEN All-time

| | | | | | | | |
|------|------|-----|-----|-----|------|-------|------|
| 22.53 | Natalya Lisovskaya | SU | 62 | 1 | | Sochi | 27 May 84 |
| 22.50i | Helena Fibingerová | CS | 49 | 1 | | Jablonec | 19 Feb 77 |
| 22.45 | Ilona Slupianek' | GDR | 56 | 1 | OT | Potsdam | 11 May 80 |
| 22.41 | Slupianek | | | 1 | OG | Moskva | 24 Jul 80 |
| 22.40 | Slupianek | | | 1 | | Berlin | 3 Jun 83 |
| 22.38 | Slupianek | | | 1 | OT | Karl-Marx-St. | 25 May 80 |
| 22.36 | Slupianek | | | 1 | | Celje | 2 May 80 |
| 22.34 | Slupianek | | | 1 | | Berlin | 7 May 80 |
| 22.34 | Slupianek | | | 1 | NC | Cottbus | 18 Jul 80 |
| 22.32 | Fibingerová | | | 1 | | Nitra | 20 Aug 77 |
| | | | | | | | |
| 22.22 | Slupianek | | | 1 | | Potsdam | 13 Jul 80 |
| 22.13 | Slupianek | | | 1 | | Split | 29 Apr 80 |
| 22.06 | Slupianek | | | 1 | | Berlin | 15 Aug 78 |
| 22.05 | Slupianek | | | 1 | OD | Berlin | 28 May 80 |
| 22.05 | Slupianek | | | 1 | OT | Potsdam | 31 May 80 |
| 22.04 | Slupianek | | | 1 | | Potsdam | 4 Jul 79 |
| 22.04 | Slupianek | | | 1 | | Potsdam | 29 Jul 79 |
| 21.99 | Fibingerová | | | 1 | | Opava | 26 Sep 76 |
| 21.98 | Slupianek | | | 1 | | Berlin | 17 Jul 79 |
| 21.96 | Fibingerová | | | 1 | GS | Ostrava | 8 Jun 77 |
| | | | | | | | |
| 21.96 | Lisovskaya | | | 1 | Drz | Praha | 16 Aug 84 |

( 21 Performances by 3 Athletes )

| | | | | | | | |
|------|------|-----|-----|-----|------|-------|------|
| 21.89 | Ivanka Khristova-Todorova | BUL | 41 | 1 | | Belmeken | 4 Jul 76 |
| 21.86 | Marianne Adam | GDR | 51 | 1 | v SU | Leipzig | 23 Jun 79 |
| 21.61 | Verzhinia Veselinova | BUL | 57 | 1 | | Sofia | 21 Aug 82 |
| 21.58 | Margitta Droese' | GDR | 52 | 1 | | Erfurt | 28 May 78 |
| 21.53 | Nunu Abashidze | SU | 55 | 2 | | Kiev | 20 Jun 84 |
| 21.46i | Claudia Losch | FRG | 60 | 1 | | Zweibrücken | 4 Feb 86 |
| 21.45 | Nadezhda Chizhova | SU | 45 | 1 | | Varna | 29 Sep 73 |
| | (10) | | | | | | |
| 21.45 | Ines Müller' | GDR | 59 | 1 | | Schwerin | 4 Jun 86 |
| 21.43 | Eva Wilms | FRG | 52 | 2 | HB | München | 17 Jun 77 |
| 21.42 | Svetlana Krachevskaya' | SU | 44 | 2 | OG | Moskva | 24 Jul 80 |
| 21.39 | Natalya Akhrimenko | SU | 55 | 2 | v GDR | Tallinn | 21 Jun 86 |
| 21.27 | Liane Schmuhl | GDR | 61 | 1 | | Cottbus | 26 Jun 82 |
| 21.19 | Helma Knorscheidt | GDR | 56 | 1 | | Berlin | 24 May 84 |
| 21.10 | Heidi Krieger | GDR | 65 | 1 | EC | Stuttgart | 26 Aug 86 |
| 21.05 | Zdeňka Šilhavá' | CS | 54 | 2 | NC | Praha | 23 Jul 83 |
| 21.01 | Ivanka Petrova-Stoycheva | BUL | 51 | 1 | NC | Sofia | 28 Jul 79 |
| 21.00 | Mihaela Loghin | RUM | 52 | 1 | | Formia | 30 Jun 84 |
| | (20) | | | | | | |
| 21.00 | Cordula Schulze | GDR | 59 | 4 | OD | Potsdam | 21 Jul 84 |
| 20.95 | Elena Stoyanova-Simeonova | BUL | 52 | 2 | Balk | Sofia | 14 Jun 80 |
| 20.72 | Heike Hartwig' | GDR | 62 | 1 | GO | Dresden | 16 Aug 86 |
| 20.61 | María Elena Sarría | CUB | 54 | 1 | | Habana | 22 Jul 82 |
| 20.60 | Marina Antonyuk | SU | 62 | 1 | | Chelyabinsk | 10 Aug 86 |
| 20.47 | Nina Isayeva | SU | 50 | 1 | | Bryansk | 28 Aug 82 |
| 20.44 | Tatyana Orlova | SU | 55 | 1 | | Staiki | 28 May 83 |
| 20.24 | Lyudmila Voyevudskaya | SU | 58 | 1 | | Dnepropetrovsk | 5 Aug 84 |
| 20.22 | Margitta Gummel' | GDR | 41 | 2 | OG | München | 7 Sep 72 |
| 20.21 | Svetlana Melnikova | SU | 51 | 1 | | Riga | 5 Jun 82 |
| | (30) | | | | | | |

| Mark | Name | Nat | Yr | Pos | Meet | Venue | Date |
|------|------|-----|----|----|------|-------|------|
| 20.21 | Lyudmila Savina | SU | 55 | 2 | Znam | Sochi | 9 Jun 84 |
| 20.20 | Danguole Bimbaite | SU | 62 | 1 | | Leselidze | 18 May 86 |
| 20.12 | Vera Tsapkalenko | SU | 54 | 2 | Prav | Sochi | 29 May 77 |
| 20.12 | Rimma Muzikevičiene | SU | 52 | 1 | | Vilnius | 16 Aug 80 |
| 20.07 | Tatyana Shcherbanos | SU | 60 | 4 | NC | Donyetsk | 7 Sep 84 |
| 20.06 | Raisa Taranda | SU | 47 | 2 | NC | Kiev | 23 Jun 76 |
| 20.05 | Svetla Mitkova | BUL | 64 | 2 | | Plovdiv | 17 May 86 |
| 20.04 | Gabriele Retzlaff | GDR | 54 | 5 | NC | Cottbus | 18 Jul 80 |
| 20.03 | Faina Melnik | SU | 45 | 2 | PTS | Bratislava | 2 Jun 76 |
| 19.96i | Simone Rüdrich | GDR | 61 | 2 | NC | Senftenberg | 20 Feb 83 |
| | (40) | | | | | | |
| 19.94 | Natalya Zubekhina | SU | 51 | 1 | | Tula | 14 Jul 84 |
| 19.94 | Yelena Kozlova | SU | 62 | 2 | | Kiev | 14 Aug 84 |
| 19.92 | Tamara Bufetova | SU | 51 | 1 | Prav | Tbilisi | 17 Jun 78 |
| 19.91 | Nina Samsonova | SU | 51 | 2 | NC | Kiev | 20 Aug 82 |
| 19.90 | Natalya Nosenko | SU | 51 | 2 | v UK | Kiev | 23 May 76 |
| 19.85 | Alexandra Mititelu | SU | 59 | 2 | | Tallinn | 28 Jun 84 |
| 19.81 | Alexandra Abashidze | SU | 58 | 3 | NC | Kiev | 20 Aug 82 |
| 19.80 | Lyubov Koftunova | SU | 59 | 1 | | Alma-Ata | 12 Sep 85 |
| 19.78 | Konstanze Simm' | GDR | 64 | 1 | | Karl-Marx-St. | 11 Jul 84 |
| 19.78 | Lyubov Vasilyeva | SU | 57 | . | | Moskva | 31 Aug 86 |
| | (50) | | | | | | |

Best outdoor marks                                                        Indoor

| 20.96 | | Losch | 1 | NC | Berlin | 13 Jul 86 | 21.46i |
|-------|--|-------|---|----|--------|-----------|--------|
| 19.83 | | Rüdrich | 1 | | Cottbus | 13 Aug 83 | 19.96i |

# DISCUS THROW

| 74.56 | Zdeňka Šilhavá' | CS | 54 | 1 | | Nitra | 26 Aug 84 |
|-------|------|-----|----|----|------|-------|------|
| 73.36 | Irina Meszynski | GDR | 62 | 1 | Drz | Praha | 17 Aug 84 |
| 73.28 | Galina Savinkova' | SU | 53 | 1 | NC | Donyetsk | 8 Sep 84 |
| 73.26 | Savinkova | | | 1 | | Leselidze | 21 May 83 |
| 73.26 | Diana Sachse | GDR | 63 | 1 | | Neubrandenburg | 6 Jun 86 |
| 73.10 | Gisela Beyer | GDR | 60 | 1 | OD | Berlin | 20 Jul 84 |
| 72.96 | Savinkova | | | 1 | v GDR | Erfurt | 23 Jun 85 |
| 72.52 | Martina Hellmann' | GDR | 60 | 1 | | Frohburg | 15 Jun 86 |
| 72.52 | Tsvetanka Khristova | BUL | 62 | 1 | BGP | Budapest | 11 Aug 86 |
| 72.32 | Opitz' | GDR | 60 | 1 | | Leipzig | 13 Jul 84 |
| 72.30 | Sachse | | | 1 | | Potsdam | 22 May 86 |
| 72.30 | Sachse | | | 1 | | Erfurt | 1 Jun 86 |
| 72.28 | Beyer | | | 1 | | Berlin | 15 Jul 84 |
| 72.14 | Galina Murashova | SU | 55 | 2 | Drz | Praha | 17 Aug 84 |
| 72.12 | Sachse | | | 1 | v SU | Tallinn | 21 Jun 86 |
| 72.02 | Meszynski | | | 2 | OD | Berlin | 20 Jul 84 |
| 72.00 | Šilhavá | | | 1 | | Litomyšl | 28 Jul 84 |
| 71.90 | Khristova | | | 1 | | Stara Zagora | 19 Jul 86 |
| 71.80 | Maria Vergova-Petkova | BUL | 50 | 1 | NC | Sofia | 13 Jul 80 |
| 71.80 | Khristova | | | 1 | PTS | Bratislava | 14 Jun 86 |
| 71.60 | Opitz' | | | 3 | OD | Berlin | 20 Jul 84 |
| 71.50 | Evelin Jahl' | GDR | 56 | 1 | OT | Potsdam | 10 May 80 |
| 71.46 | Jahl | | | 1 | OD | Berlin | 10 Jun 81 |
| 71.40 | Meszynski | | | 1 | v USA | Karl-Marx-St. | 10 Jul 82 |

| Mark | Name | Nat | Yr | Pos | Meet | Venue | Date |
|---|---|---|---|---|---|---|---|
| 71.36 | Sachse | | | 1 | EC | Stuttgart | 28 Aug 86 |
| 71.30 | Petkova | | | 1 | | Sofia | 1 Aug 81 |

( 26 Performances by 10 Athletes )

| Mark | Name | Nat | Yr | Pos | Meet | Venue | Date |
|---|---|---|---|---|---|---|---|
| 71.22 | Ria Stalman | HOL | 52 | 1 | | Walnut | 15 Jul 84 |
| 70.50 | Faina Melnik | SU | 45 | 1 | Znam | Sochi | 24 Apr 76 |
| 70.50 | Maritza Marten | CUB | 63 | 1 | | Habana | 21 Mar 85 |
| 69.86 | Valentina Kharchenko | SU | 49 | 1 | | Feodosia | 16 May 81 |
| 69.66 | Daniela Costian | RUM | 65 | 1 | | Piteşti | 19 Jul 86 |
| 69.50 | Florenta Craciunescu' | RUM | 55 | 1 | Balk | Stara Zagora | 2 Aug 85 |
| 69.08 | Carmen Romero | CUB | 50 | 1 | NC | Habana | 17 Apr 76 |
| 69.08 | Mariana Lengyel' | RUM | 53 | 1 | | Constanta | 19 Apr 86 |
| 68.96 | Ellina Zvereva' | SU | 60 | 1 | | Minsk | 2 Sep 86 |
| 68.92 | Sabine Engel | GDR | 54 | 1 v | SU,Pol | Karl-Marx-St. | 25 Jun 77 |
| | (20) | | | | | | |
| 68.90 | Svetla Mitkova | BUL | 64 | 2 | BGP | Budapest | 11 Aug 86 |
| 68.64 | Margitta Pufe' | GDR | 52 | 1 | ISTAF | Berlin | 17 Aug 79 |
| 68.60 | Nadezhda Kugayevskikh | SU | 60 | 1 | | Oryol | 30 Aug 83 |
| 68.58 | Lyubov Zverkova | SU | 55 | 1 | | Kiev | 22 Jun 84 |
| 68.24 | Silvia Madetzky | GDR | 62 | 1 | | Potsdam | 27 Aug 82 |
| 68.18 | Tatyana Lesovaya | SU | 56 | 1 | | Alma-Ata | 23 Sep 82 |
| 67.96 | Argentina Menis | RUM | 48 | 1 | RumIC | Bucureşti | 15 May 76 |
| 67.92 | Hilda Elisa Ramos | CUB | 64 | 2 | Nar | Sofia | 31 May 86 |
| 67.90 | Petra Sziegaud | GDR | 58 | 1 | | Berlin | 19 May 82 |
| 67.54 | Svetlana Petrova | SU | 51 | 1 | | Brest | 20 Sep 78 |
| | (30) | | | | | | |
| 67.48 | Meg Ritchie | UK | 52 | 1 | MSR | Walnut | 26 Apr 81 |
| 67.40 | Brigitte Michel | GDR | 56 | 2 | | Halle | 14 Jun 79 |
| 67.32 | Natalya Gorbacheva | SU | 47 | 1 | | Leningrad | 4 Jun 83 |
| 67.26 | Svetla Bozhkova | BUL | 51 | 2 | | Sofia | 5 Jul 80 |
| 67.16 | Simona Andrusca | RUM | 62 | 2 | RumIC | Bucureşti | 1 Jun 85 |
| 67.06 | Ingra-Anne Manecke | FRG | 56 | 1 | | Fürth | 29 May 82 |
| 67.02 | Gabriele Hinzmann | GDR | 47 | 1 | | Potsdam | 1 Sep 73 |
| 67.02 | Ulla Lundholm | FIN | 57 | 1 | | Helsinki | 23 Aug 83 |
| 66.94 | Nadezhda Yerokha | SU | 52 | 1 | | Leselidze | 23 Mar 80 |
| 66.54 | María Cristina Betancourt | CUB | 47 | 1 | | Habana | 13 Feb 81 |
| | (40) | | | | | | |
| 66.48 | Márta Kripli | HUN | 60 | 3 | BGP | Budapest | 11 Aug 86 |
| 66.42 | Anna Khorina-Salak | SU | 59 | 1 | | Tallinn | 18 Jun 86 |
| 66.40 | Ines Müller' | GDR | 59 | 3 | | Berlin | 22 Sep 85 |
| 66.30 | Lyudmila Isayeva | SU | 49 | 1 | Znam | Kaunas | 11 Aug 79 |
| 66.10 | Carol Cady | USA | 62 | 1 | Jenn | San Jose | 31 May 86 |
| 66.06 | Svetlana Melnikova | SU | 51 | 2 | EP | Torino | 4 Aug 79 |
| 65.96 | Grit Haupt | GDR | 66 | 3 | | Leipzig | 13 Jul 84 |
| 65.94 | Tatyana Berezhnaya | SU | 56 | 3 | NC | Donyetsk | 9 Sep 80 |
| 65.86 | Ilke Wyludda | GDR | 69 | 1 | Druz | Neubrandenburg | 1 Aug 86 |
| 65.78 | Gabriele Reinsch | GDR | 63 | 1 | | Dresden | 7 Jul 85 |
| | (50) | | | | | | |

## JAVELIN THROW

| Mark | Name | Nat | Yr | Pos | Meet | Venue | Date |
|---|---|---|---|---|---|---|---|
| 77.44 | Fatima Whitbread | UK | 61 | Q | EC | Stuttgart | 28 Aug 86 |
| 76.32 | Whitbread | | | 1 | EC | Stuttgart | 29 Aug 86 |
| 75.40 | Petra Felke | GDR | 59 | 1 | | Schwerin | 4 Jun 85 |
| 75.04 | Felke | | | 1 | GO | Dresden | 17 Aug 86 |

| Mark | Name | Nat | Yr | Pos | Meet | Venue | Date |
|------|------|-----|-----|-----|------|-------|------|
| 74.94 | Felke | | | 1 | v SU | Erfurt | 22 Jun 85 |
| 74.90 | Felke | | | 1 | OD | Berlin | 27 Jun 85 |
| 74.76 | Tiina Lillak | FIN | 61 | 1 | | Tampere | 13 Jun 83 |
| 74.72 | Felke | | | 1 | | Celje | 5 May 84 |
| 74.70 | Felke | | | 1 | | Berlin | 22 Sep 85 |
| 74.56 | Felke | | | 1 | ISTAF | Berlin | 23 Aug 85 |
| 74.24 | Lillak | | | 1 | | Fresno | 7 Apr 84 |
| 74.24 | Felke | | | 1 | OD | Potsdam | 21 Jul 84 |
| 74.20 | Sofia Sakorafa | GRE | 57 | 1 | NC | Chania | 26 Sep 82 |
| 74.14 | Lillak | | | 1 | NC | Pori | 3 Jul 83 |
| 74.10 | Felke | | | 1 | | Berlin | 20 Aug 86 |
| 73.92 | Lillak | | | 1 | v UK,Swz | Lappeenranta | 18 Jun 83 |
| 73.80 | Lillak | | | 1 | | Thessaloniki | 23 Sep 83 |
| 73.74 | Felke | | | 1 | | Praha | 28 Aug 84 |
| 73.58 | Tessa Sanderson | UK | 56 | 1 | | Edinburgh | 26 Jun 83 |
| 73.54 | Felke | | | 1 | | Umeå | 2 Sep 86 |
| 73.30 | Felke | | | 1 | Drz | Praha | 16 Aug 84 |
| 73.20 | Felke | | | 1 | EP | Moskva | 17 Aug 85 |
| 73.08 | Felke | | | 1 | | Berlin | 2 Apr 86 |

( 23 Performances by 5 Athletes )

| Mark | Name | Nat | Yr | Pos | Meet | Venue | Date |
|------|------|-----|-----|-----|------|-------|------|
| 72.70 | Anna Verouli | GRE | 56 | 1 | | Chania | 20 May 84 |
| 72.16 | Antje Kempe-Zöllkau | GDR | 63 | 2 | | Celje | 5 May 84 |
| 71.88 | Antoaneta Todorova | BUL | 63 | 1 | EP | Zagreb | 15 Aug 81 |
| 71.82 | Ivonne Leal | CUB | 66 | 1 | WUG | Kobe | 30 Aug 85 |
| 70.14 | Mayra Vila | CUB | 60 | 2 | | Madrid | 14 Jun 85 |
| | (10) | | | | | | |
| 70.14 | María Caridad Colón | CUB | 58 | 1 | Barr | Habana | 15 Jun 86 |
| 70.08 | Tatyana Biryulina | SU | 55 | 1 | | Podolsk | 12 Jul 80 |
| 69.96 | Ruth Fuchs | GDR | 46 | 1 | | Split | 29 Apr 80 |
| 69.86 | Natalya Kolenchukova' | SU | 64 | 1 | NC | Leningrad | 3 Aug 85 |
| 69.80 | Sue Howland | AUS | 60 | 2 | | Belfast | 30 Jun 86 |
| 69.56 | Beate Peters | FRG | 59 | 1 | NC | Berlin | 12 Jul 86 |
| 69.32 | Kate Schmidt | USA | 53 | 1 | | Fürth | 11 Sep 77 |
| 69.28 | Petra Rivers | AUS | 52 | 1 | NC | Brisbane | 20 Mar 82 |
| 68.94 | Trine Solberg | NOR | 66 | 1 | v SU | Oslo | 16 Jul 85 |
| 68.84 | Ingrid Thyssen | FRG | 56 | 1 | | Lüdenscheid | 5 Oct 85 |
| | (20) | | | | | | |
| 68.80 | Eva Raduly-Zörgö | RUM | 54 | 1 | Znam | Moskva | 5 Jul 80 |
| 68.28 | Saida Gunba | SU | 59 | 2 | Znam | Moskva | 5 Jul 80 |
| 67.90 | Dulce Maria García | CUB | 65 | 3 | Barr | Habana | 15 Jun 86 |
| 67.84 | Jadviga Putiniene | SU | 45 | 3 | Znam | Moskva | 5 Jul 80 |
| 67.40 | Tuula Laaksalo | FIN | 53 | 2 | | Pihtipudas | 24 Jul 83 |
| 67.32 | Regine Kemptner | GDR | 67 | 2 | NC | Jena | 27 Jun 86 |
| 67.24 | Ute Hommola | GDR | 52 | 1 | v UK | Dresden | 13 Jun 81 |
| 67.20 | Fausta Quintavalla | ITA | 59 | 1 | | Milano | 22 Jun 83 |
| 67.00 | Corina Girbea' | RUM | 59 | 1 | v Hun | Debrecen | 13 Jun 82 |
| 67.00 | Zinaida Gavrilina | SU | 61 | 1 | NC | Donyetsk | 9 Sep 84 |
| | (30) | | | | | | |
| 66.96 | Ute Richter | GDR | 58 | 1 | | Neubrandenburg | 21 May 83 |
| 66.80 | Olga Gavrilova | SU | 57 | 1 | WP | Canberra | 4 Oct 85 |
| 66.80 | Jana Köpping | GDR | 66 | 3 | NC | Jena | 27 Jun 86 |
| 66.64 | Zsuzsa Malovecz | HUN | 63 | 1 | | Rehlingen | 19 May 86 |
| 66.56 | Elena Burgárová | CS | 52 | 2 | | Nitra | 26 Aug 84 |
| 66.52 | Alexandra Beck | GDR | 68 | 1 | | Chania | 24 May 86 |
| 66.48 | Eva Helmschmidt | FRG | 57 | 1 | v Hol,Bel | Bielefeld | 4 Jun 83 |
| 66.08 | Rositha Potreck | GDR | 59 | 1 | NC | Jena | 9 Aug 81 |

| Mark | Name | Nat | Yr | Pos | Meet | Venue | Date |
|------|------|-----|-----|-----|------|-------|------|
| 66.08 | Susanne Jung | GDR | 63 | 2 | | Neubrandenburg | 7 Jun 85 |
| 65.74 | Pam Matthews | AUS | 58 | 1 | | Brisbane | 16 Dec 79 |
| | (40) | | | | | | |
| 65.68 | Yelena Medvedyeva | SU | 65 | 2 | NC | Leningrad | 3 Aug 85 |
| 65.56 | Irina Kostyuchenkova | SU | 61 | 1 | NC | Kiev | 17 Jul 86 |
| 65.52 | Genowefa Olejarz | POL | 62 | 1 | | Zabrze | 20 May 84 |
| 65.46 | Sabine Sebrowski | GDR | 51 | 1 | OT | Karl-Marx-St. | 30 May 76 |
| 65.38 | Ivanka Vancheva | BUL | 53 | 5 | OG | Moskva | 25 Jul 80 |
| 65.26 | Olga Chistyakova | SU | 50 | 2 | Znam | Sochi | 10 Jun 84 |
| 65.14 | Marion Becker' | FRG | 50 | Q | OG | Montréal | 23 Jul 76 |
| 65.02 | Nina Nikanorova | SU | 47 | 1 | | Sochi | 23 May 80 |
| 65.00 | Zoya Karepina | SU | 61 | 2 | NP | Alma-Ata | 14 Sep 85 |
| 64.92 | Li Baolian | CHN | 63 | 1 | | Beijing | 10 May 86 |
| | (50) | | | | | | |

# HEPTATHLON

| | | | | | | | |
|---|---|---|---|---|---|---|---|
| 7158 | Jackie Joyner | USA 62 | 1 | USOF | Houston | | 2 Aug 86 |
| | 13.18/-0.5 1.88 15.20 22.85/+1.2 7.03/+2.9 50.12 2:09.69 | | | | | | |
| 7148 | Joyner | | 1 | GWG | Moskva | | 7 Jul 86 |
| | 12.85/+0.2 1.88 14.76 23.00/ 7.01/-0.5 49.86 2:10.02 | | | | | | |
| 6946 | Sabine Paetz | GDR 57 | 1 | NC | Potsdam | | 6 May 84 |
| | 12.64/+0.3 1.80 15.37 23.37/+0.7 6.86/-0.2 44.62 2:08.93 | | | | | | |
| 6935 | Ramona Neubert | GDR 58 | 1 | v SU | Moskva | | 19 Jun 83 |
| | 12.42/ 1.82 15.25 23.49/ 6.79/+0.7 49.94 2:07.51 | | | | | | |
| 6910 | Joyner | | 1 | MSR | Walnut | | 25 Apr 86 |
| | 12.9 / 1.86 14.75 23.24/+2.8 6.85/+2.1 48.28 2:14.11 | | | | | | |
| 6859 | Natalya Shubenkova | SU 57 | 1 | NC | Kiev | | 21 Jun 84 |
| | 12.93/+1.0 1.83 13.66 23.57/-0.3 6.73/+0.4 46.26 2:04.60 | | | | | | |
| 6845 | Neubert | | 1 | v SU | Halle | | 20 Jun 82 |
| | 13.58/ 1.83 15.10 23.14/ 6.84w 42.54 2:06.16 | | | | | | |
| 6841 | Joyner | | 1 | | Götzis | | 25 May 86 |
| | 13.09/-1.3 1.87 14.34 23.63/-0.8 6.76/-0.3 48.88 2:14.58 | | | | | | |
| 6813 | Paetz | | 1 | OD | Potsdam | | 21 Jul 84 |
| | 12.71/+0.4 1.74 16.16 23.23w 6.58/ 41.94 2:07.03 | | | | | | |
| 6803 | Jane Frederick | USA 52 | 1 | | Talence | | 16 Sep 84 |
| | 13.27/+1.2 1.87 15.49 24.15/+1.6 6.43/+0.2 51.74 2:13.55 | | | | | | |
| 6789 | Neubert | | 2 | OD | Potsdam | | 21 Jul 84 |
| | 13.48/+0.4 1.74 15.03 23.47w 6.71/ 47.88 2:04.73 | | | | | | |
| 6788 | Neubert | | 1 | v SU | Kiev | | 28 Jun 81 |
| | 13.70/ 1.86 15.41 23.58/ 6.82/+0.2 40.62 2:06.72 | | | | | | |
| 6775 | Anke Vater' | GDR 61 | 3 | OD | Potsdam | | 21 Jul 84 |
| | 13.30/+0.4 1.86 14.86 23.20w 6.84/+0.5 34.04 2:03.76 | | | | | | |
| 6772 | Neubert | | 1 | EP-A | Sofia | | 11 Sep 83 |
| | 13.39/ 1.78 15.21 23.52/ 6.69/ 45.30 2:06.70 | | | | | | |
| 6770 | Neubert | | 1 | WC | Helsinki | | 9 Aug 83 |
| | 13.29/+0.3 1.80 15.38 23.27/-0.1 6.67/-0.4 45.12 2:11.34 | | | | | | |
| 6718 | Joyner | | 1 | USOF | Baton Rouge | | 28 Jul 85 |
| | 13.32/-2.2 1.82 14.72 23.59/-1.3 6.69/ 45.04 2:11.46 | | | | | | |
| 6717 | Behmer' | | 1 | EC | Stuttgart | | 30 Aug 86 |
| | 13.25/+0.8 1.77 14.50 23.46/-0.1 6.79/+1.4 40.24 2:03.96 | | | | | | |
| 6713 | Paetz | | 2 | WC | Helsinki | | 9 Aug 83 |
| | 13.11/+0.3 1.83 14.23 23.60/-0.1 6.68/-0.9 44.52 2:11.59 | | | | | | |
| 6678 | Frederick | | 4 | OD | Potsdam | | 21 Jul 84 |
| | 13.76/ 1.86 15.91 24.86/ 6.21/ 52.74 2:10.25 | | | | | | |

| Points | Name | Nat | Yr | Pos | Meet | Venue | Date |
|--------|------|-----|----|----|------|-------|------|
| 6670 | Neubert | | | 1 | NC | Halle | 24 May 81 |
| | 13.58/    1.80 14.75 23.70/    6.82/+2.0 40.98 2:07.55 | | | | | | |
| 6666 | Frederick | | | 1 | | Götzis | 26 May 85 |
| | 13.54/+1.3 1.84 15.22 24.19/+3.2 6.39/+1.9 50.98 2:12.25 | | | | | | |
| 6664 | Neubert | | | 1 | EC | Athínai | 10 Sep 82 |
| | 13.61/-1.0 1.83 15.02 23.40/-0.3 6.63/-0.2 42.48 2:11.06 | | | | | | |
| 6646 | Natalya Grachova | SU | 52 | 1 | NC | Moskva | 2 Aug 82 |
| | 13.80/    1.80 16.18 23.86/    6.65/+3.5 39.42 2:06.59 | | | | | | |
| 6645 | Shubenkova | | | 2 | EC | Stuttgart | 30 Aug 86 |
| | 13.33/-1.6 1.80 13.68 23.92/-0.1 6.54/+2.2 44.98 2:04.40 | | | | | | |
| 6635 | Sibylle Thiele | GDR | 65 | 2 | GWG | Moskva | 7 Jul 86 |
| | 13.14/+0.6 1.76 16.00 24.18/    6.62/    45.74 2:15.30 | | | | | | |

( 25 Performances by 8 Athletes )

| Points | Name | Nat | Yr | Pos | Meet | Venue | Date |
|--------|------|-----|----|----|------|-------|------|
| 6623 | Judy Simpson' | UK | 60 | 3 | EC | Stuttgart | 30 Aug 86 |
| | 13.05/+0.8 1.92 14.73 25.09/+0.0 6.56/+2.5 40.92 2:11.70 | | | | | | |
| 6616 | Małgorzata Nowak' | POL | 59 | 1 | WUG | Kobe | 31 Aug 85 |
| | 13.27/+4.0 1.95 15.35 24.20/+0.0 6.37/+3.9 43.36 2:20.39 | | | | | | |
| | (10) | | | | | | |
| 6552 | Nadezhda Vinogradova | SU | 59 | 2 | NC | Kiev | 21 Jun 84 |
| | 13.92/+1.0 1.80 15.19 23.94/+0.2 6.67/+0.1 38.60 2:06.80 | | | | | | |
| 6541 | Mila Kolyadina | SU | 60 | 4 | v GDR | Moskva | 19 Jun 83 |
| | 14.05/    1.82 16.28 24.81/    6.48/+0.8 48.26 2:15.26 | | | | | | |
| 6536 | Yekaterina Smirnova | SU | 56 | 3 | v GDR | Moskva | 19 Jun 83 |
| | 13.41/    1.82 14.82 24.84/    6.56/+1.1 45.66 2:13.38 | | | | | | |
| 6523 | Sabine Everts | FRG | 61 | 1 | v SU | Mannheim | 10 Jun 82 |
| | 13.45/    1.89 12.39 23.73/    6.75/    36.02 2:07.73 | | | | | | |
| 6487 | Birgit Dressel | FRG | 60 | 4 | EC | Stuttgart | 30 Aug 86 |
| | 13.56/-1.6 1.92 14.12 24.68/+0.0 6.28/+1.1 45.70 2:15.78 | | | | | | |
| 6461 | Valentina Kurochkina | SU | 59 | 1 | | Tallinn | 11 Aug 83 |
| | 13.89/    1.85 14.40 24.51/    6.63/+1.2 43.98 2:15.94 | | | | | | |
| 6453 | Valentina Dimitrova | BUL | 56 | 2 | | Götzis | 29 May 83 |
| | 14.31/+0.8 1.86 16.07 24.78/+1.0 6.26/+1.4 42.26 2:08.74 | | | | | | |
| 6436 | Sabine Braun | FRG | 65 | 1 | v Bul | Mannheim | 9 Jun 84 |
| | 13.68/    1.78 13.09 23.88/    6.03/    52.14 2:09.41 | | | | | | |
| 6427M | Antonina Sukhova | SU | 59 | 1 | | Tula | 26 Aug 84 |
| | 13.0 /    1.82 13.79 24.8 /    6.41/    45.88 2:13.5 | | | | | | |
| 6424 | Jodi Anderson | USA | 57 | 2 | FOT | Los Angeles | 17 Jun 84 |
| | 13.52/    1.80 13.40 24.49/    6.36/    48.52 2:13.20 | | | | | | |
| | (20) | | | | | | |
| 6423M | Lyubov Racu | SU | 61 | 1 | | Kishinyev | 28 Aug 83 |
| | 13.6 /    1.80 14.75 24.2 /    6.53/    41.86 2:11.6 | | | | | | |
| 6416 | Marianna Maslennikova | SU | 61 | 5 | GWG | Moskva | 7 Jul 86 |
| | 13.41/    1.88 13.30 24.40/    6.38/    36.04 2:06.09 | | | | | | |
| 6408 | Tatyana Shpak | SU | 60 | 1 | | Donyetsk | 28 Aug 85 |
| | 13.92/+0.4 1.77 14.93 23.80/+1.3 6.65/+0.0 26.50 2:09.98 | | | | | | |
| 6403 | Emilia Dimitrova | BUL | 67 | 6 | GWG | Moskva | 7 Jul 86 |
| | 13.73/    1.76 13.46 23.17/    6.29/    43.30 2:09.85 | | | | | | |
| 6399 | Olga Yakovleva | SU | 57 | 1 | NP | Tashkent | 27 Sep 82 |
| | 13.53/    1.79 15.14 24.26/    6.13/    41.42 2:09.20 | | | | | | |
| 6387 | Glynis Nunn' | AUS | 60 | 1 | OG | Los Angeles | 4 Aug 84 |
| | 13.02/-1.5 1.80 12.82 24.06/-1.3 6.66/-0.8 35.58 2:10.57 | | | | | | |
| 6377 | Kristine Nitzsche | GDR | 59 | 4 | EP-A | Sofia | 11 Sep 83 |
| | 13.96/    1.90 16.10 24.28/    6.10/    41.54 2:20.16 | | | | | | |
| 6366 | Heike Tischler | GDR | 64 | 5 | OD | Potsdam | 21 Jul 84 |
| | 14.41/    1.77 14.18 24.23w    6.12/    50.18 2:07.67 | | | | | | |
| 6349 | Valda Ruškite | SU | 62 | 7 | GWG | Moskva | 7 Jul 86 |
| | 13.34/    1.70 14.63 24.74/    6.45/    43.48 2:11.16 | | | | | | |

| Points | Name | Nat | Yr | Pos | Meet | Venue | Date |
|--------|------|-----|-----|-----|------|-------|------|
| 6333 | Nadine Debois | FRA | 61 | 1 | | Clamart | 27 Apr 86 |
| | 13.62/ | 1.81 | 13.74 | 24.37/ | 6.59/ | 32.48 | 2:05.77 |
| | (30) | | | | | | |
| 6327 | Svetlana Filatyeva | SU | 64 | 1 | v FRG | Bernhausen | 15 Jun 86 |
| | 13.63/ | 1.82 | 13.51 | 24.62/ | 6.38/ | 45.30 | 2:16.47 |
| 6319M | Tamara Moshicheva | SU | 62 | 1 | | Kharkov | 7 Jul 85 |
| | 13.7 / | 1.78 | 12.78 | 24.2 / | 6.35/ | 44.96 | 2:07.3 |
| 6316 | Larisa Nikitina | SU | 65 | 1 | | Sochi | 25 May 86 |
| | 14.25/ | 1.86 | 15.00 | 25.38/ | 6.37/ | 47.70 | 2:19.91 |
| 6307 | Vera Yurchenko | SU | 59 | 1 | NP | Dnepropetrovsk | 7 Sep 86 |
| | 13.68/+1.5 | 1.66 | 15.45 | 24.47/+0.5 | 6.48/+0.6 | 42.42 | 2:12.02 |
| 6305 | Chantal Beaugeant | FRA | 61 | 1 | EP-B | Arlès | 8 Sep 85 |
| | 13.42/+3.5 | 1.75 | 12.12 | 24.53/+4.0 | 6.27/+3.8 | 48.24 | 2:09.76 |
| 6295 | Yekaterina Gordiyenko | SU | 51 | 1 | v USA | Leningrad | 2 Aug 81 |
| | 13.58/ | 1.74 | 15.37 | 24.44/ | 6.45/ | 34.80 | 2:09.67 |
| 6269 | Olga Nemogayeva' | SU | 59 | 7 | v GDR | Moskva | 19 Jun 83 |
| | 13.53/ | 1.82 | 13.15 | 24.56/ | 6.34/ | 37.40 | 2:08.79 |
| 6265 | Corinne Schneider | SWZ | 62 | 1 | v Est | Zug | 16 Jun 85 |
| | 14.03/-0.2 | 1.87 | 12.68 | 25.23/-0.2 | 6.09/+1.3 | 52.54 | 2:16.94 |
| 6259 | Kim Hagger | UK | 61 | 1 | v Fra,Can | Arlès | 18 May 86 |
| | 13.46/-1.0 | 1.90 | 12.63 | 24.67/+2.0 | 6.57/+2.5 | 36.06 | 2:17.72 |
| 6256 | Helga Nusko | FRG | 65 | 1 | NC-j | Ulm | 14 Jul 85 |
| | 14.00/ | 1.78 | 15.09 | 25.11/ | 6.23/ | 49.92 | 2:21.63 |
| | (40) | | | | | | |
| 6251 | Svetlana Ovchinnikova | SU | 56 | 5 | NC | Leningrad | 3 Aug 85 |
| | 13.55/ | 1.74 | 16.80 | 24.75/ | 5.91/ | 40.20 | 2:13.11 |
| 6250M | Marina Spirina | SU | 55 | 1 | | Kharkov | 16 Jul 85 |
| | 13.5 / | 1.76 | 12.30 | 24.1 / | 6.42/ | 41.76 | 2:07.9 |
| 6250 | Ines Schulz | GDR | 59 | 1 | | Berlin | 20 Aug 86 |
| | 13.84/+2.0 | 1.81 | 13.51 | 25.02/+1.4 | 6.36/+1.5 | 42.66 | 2:12.22 |
| 6249 | Cindy Greiner | USA | 57 | 4 | OG | Los Angeles | 4 Aug 84 |
| | 13.71/-1.5 | 1.83 | 13.36 | 24.40/-1.3 | 6.15/+0.2 | 40.86 | 2:11.75 |
| 6248 | Natalya Alyoshina | SU | 56 | 3 | NP | Tashkent | 27 Sep 82 |
| | 13.65/ | 1.79 | 12.91 | 23.80/ | 6.69/ | 36.20 | 2:16.68 |
| 6247 | Nina Vashchenko | SU | 60 | 2 | NP | Tashkent | 27 Sep 82 |
| | 13.74/ | 1.82 | 13.02 | 24.68/ | 6.50/ | 40.02 | 2:13.88 |
| 6234 | Heidrun Geissler | GDR | 61 | 2 | EP-A | Birmingham | 30 Aug 81 |
| | 14.42/ | 1.87 | 13.12 | 24.67/ | 6.69/+1.9 | 36.18 | 2:12.22 |
| 6223 | Olga Permyakova | SU | 64 | 2 | NP | Alma-Ata | 14 Sep 85 |
| | 14.35/ | 1.81 | 14.02 | 24.55/ | 6.40/ | 42.32 | 2:15.05 |
| 6218 | Lyudmila Serbul | SU | 60 | 7 | NC | Kiev | 21 Jun 84 |
| | 14.02/+1.0 | 1.74 | 14.37 | 24.77/+0.2 | 6.00/+0.1 | 43.38 | 2:05.60 |
| 6218 | Jana Sobotka | GDR | 65 | 6 | OD | Potsdam | 21 Jul 84 |
| | 14.40/ | 1.74 | 13.28 | 24.19/ | 6.27/ | 43.64 | 2:06.83 |
| | (50) | | | | | | |

Marks made with assisting wind > 4 m/s

| | | | | | | | |
|--------|------|-----|-----|-----|------|-------|------|
| 6313 | Liliana Nastase | RUM | 62 | 2 | WUG | Kobe | 31 Aug 85 |
| | 13.06/+4.6 | 1.71 | 12.35 | 23.68/+0.0 | 6.78/+7.9 | 41.26 | 2:18.41 |
| 6278 | Jane Flemming | AUS | 65 | 2 | CommG | Edinburgh | 28 Jul 86 |
| | 13.32/+4.7 | 1.79 | 12.70 | 24.17/ | 6.33/ | 43.12 | 2:15.63 |

# 4x100 METRES RELAYS

| | | | | | |
|-------|------|---|-----|----------|-----------|
| 41.37 | GDR | | 1 | WP | Canberra | 6 Oct 85 |

(Gladisch, Rieger, Auerswald, Göhr)

WOMEN All-time

| Mark | Name | Pos | Meet | Venue | Date |
|------|------|-----|------|-------|------|
| 41.53 | GDR | 1 | | Berlin | 31 Jul 83 |
| | (Gladisch, Koch, Auerswald, Göhr) | | | | |
| 41.60 | GDR | 1 | OG | Moskva | 1 Aug 80 |
| | (Müller, Wöckel, Auerswald, Göhr) | | | | |
| A41.61 | USA | 1 | USOF | A.F. Academy | 3 Jul 83 |
| | (Brown, Williams, Cheeseborough, Ashford) | | | | |
| 41.63 | USA | 1 | v GDR | Los Angeles | 25 Jun 83 |
| | (Brown, Williams, Cheeseborough, Ashford) | | | | |
| 41.65 | USA | 1 | OG | Los Angeles | 11 Aug 84 |
| | (Brown, Bolden, Cheeseborough, Ashford) | | | | |
| 41.65 | GDR | 1 | EP | Moskva | 17 Aug 85 |
| | (Gladisch, Koch, Auerswald, Göhr) | | | | |
| 41.69 | GDR | 1 | OD | Potsdam | 21 JUl 84 |
| | (Gladisch, Koch, Auerswald, Göhr) | | | | |
| 41.76 | GDR | 1 | WC | Helsinki | 10 Aug 83 |
| | (Gladisch, Koch, Auerswald, Göhr) | | | | |
| 41.84 | GDR | 1 | EC | Stuttgart | 31 Aug 86 |
| | (Gladisch, Günther, Auerswald, Göhr) | | | | |
| | (10) | | | | |
| 41.85 | GDR | 1 | OT | Potsdam | 13 Jul 80 |
| | (Müller, Wöckel, Auerswald, Göhr) | | | | |
| 41.85 | GDR | 1 | WK | Zürich | 22 Aug 84 |
| | (Gladisch, Koch, Auerswald, Göhr) | | | | |
| 41.94 | GDR | 1 | NC | Cottbus | 17 Jul 80 |
| | (Müller, Wöckel, Auerswald, Göhr) | | | | |
| 41.97 | GDR | 1 | | Potsdam | 28 Aug 82 |
| | (G.Walther, Wöckel, Schölzel, Göhr) | | | | |
| 41.97 | GDR | 1 | | Leipzig | 27 Jul 83 |
| | (Gladisch, Koch, Auerswald, Göhr) | | | | |
| 41.98 | GDR | 1 | GO | Dresden | 17 Aug 86 |
| | (Gladisch, Günther, Auerswald, Göhr) | | | | |
| 41.99 | GDR | 1 | v USA | Karl-Marx-St. | 9 Jul 82 |
| | (G.Walther, Wöckel, Schölzel, Göhr) | | | | |
| 42.00 | SU | 2 | EP | Moskva | 17 Aug 85 |
| | (Nastoburko, Pomoshchnikova, Zhirova, Barbashina) | | | | |
| 42.07 | GDR | 1 | v SU | Erfurt | 22 Jun 85 |
| | (Gladisch, Koch, Auerswald, Göhr) | | | | |
| 42.09 | GDR | 1 | EP | Torino | 4 Aug 79 |
| | (Brehmer, Schneider, Auerswald, Göhr) | | | | |
| | (20) | | | | |
| 42.09 | GDR | 1 | OT | Berlin | 9 Jul 80 |
| | (Müller, Wöckel, Auerswald, Göhr) | | | | |
| 42.09 | GDR | 2 | v USA | Los Angeles | 25 Jun 83 |
| | (Koch, Wöckel, Gladisch, Göhr) | | | | |
| 42.09 | GDR | 1 | GO | Dresden | 3 Aug 85 |
| | (Gladisch, Koch, Auerswald, Göhr) | | | | |
| 42.10 | GDR | 1 | v Can | Karl-Marx-St. | 10 Jun 79 |
| | (Koch, Schneider, Auerswald, Göhr) | | | | |
| 42.10 | SU | 2 | OG | Moskva | 1 Aug 80 |
| | (Komisova, Maslakova, V.Anisimova, Bochina) | | | | |
| 42.12 | USA | 1 | GWG | Moskva | 9 Jul 86 |
| | (Finn, Williams, Givens, Ashford) | | | | |
| 42.13 | GDR | 1h1 | EC | Stuttgart | 30 Aug 86 |
| | (Gladisch, Günther, Auerswald, Göhr) | | | | |
| 42.15 | USA | 1 | | Walnut | 25 Jul 84 |
| | (Brown, Griffith, Cheeseborough, Ashford) | | | | |
| 42.15 | GDR | 1 | | Dresden | 27 Jul 84 |
| | (G.Walther, Wöckel, Auerswald, Göhr) | | | | |
| 42.16 | GDR | 1 | | Karl-Marx-St. | 17 Jun 83 |
| | (Koch, Wöckel, Gladisch, Göhr) | | | | |
| | (30) | | | | |

| Mark | Name | Pos | Meet | Venue | Date |
|------|------|-----|------|-------|------|
| 42.17 | GDR | 1 | | Berlin | 26 Jul 79 |
| | (Brehmer, Schneider, Auerswald, Göhr) | | | | |
| 42.19 | Europe | 1 | WP | Montréal | 26 Aug 79 |
| | (Haglund/Swe, Rega/Fra, Richter/FRG, Hunte/UK) | | | | |
| 42.19 | GDR | 1 | EC | Athínai | 11 Sep 82 |
| | (G.Walther, Wöckel, Rieger, Göhr) | | | | |
| 42.20 | SC Motor Jena | 1 | NC | Erfurt | 2 Jun 84 |
| | (Schmidt, Wöckel, Auerswald, Göhr) | | | | |
| | (34) | | | | |

# 4x400 METRES RELAYS

| Mark | Name | Pos | Meet | Venue | Date |
|------|------|-----|------|-------|------|
| 3:15.92 | GDR | 1 | NC | Erfurt | 3 Jun 84 |
| | (G.Walther, Busch, Rübsam, Koch) | | | | |
| 3:16.87 | GDR | 1 | EC | Stuttgart | 31 Aug 86 |
| | (Emmelmann, Busch, Müller, Koch) | | | | |
| 3:18.29 | USA | 1 | OG | Los Angeles | 11 Aug 84 |
| | (Leatherwood, S.Howard, Brisco-Hooks, Cheeseborough) | | | | |
| 3:18.58 | SU | 1 | EP | Moskva | 18 Aug 85 |
| | (I.Nazarova, Olizarenko, Pinigina, Vladykina) | | | | |
| 3:19.04 | GDR | 1 | EC | Athínai | 11 Sep 82 |
| | (Siemon, Busch, Rübsam, Koch) | | | | |
| 3:19.12 | SU | 1 | Drz | Praha | 18 Aug 84 |
| | (Baskakova, I.Nazarova, Pinigina, Vladykina) | | | | |
| 3:19.23 | GDR | 1 | OG | Montréal | 31 Jul 76 |
| | (Maletzki, Rohde, Streidt, Brehmer) | | | | |
| 3:19.49 | GDR | 1 | WP | Canberra | 4 Oct 85 |
| | (Emmelmann, Busch, Neubauer, Koch) | | | | |
| 3:19.60 | USA | 1 | | Walnut | 25 Jul 84 |
| | (Leatherwood, S.Howard, Brisco-Hooks, Cheeseborough) | | | | |
| 3:19.62 | GDR | 1 | EP | Torino | 5 Aug 79 |
| | (Kötte, Brehmer, Köhn, Koch) | | | | |
| | (10) | | | | |
| 3:19.73 | GDR | 1 | WC | Helsinki | 14 Aug 83 |
| | (K.Walther, Busch, Koch, Rübsam) | | | | |
| 3:19.83 | GDR | 1 | EP | Zagreb | 16 Aug 81 |
| | (Rübsam, Steuk, Wöckel, Koch) | | | | |
| 3:20.10 | GDR | 2 | EP | Moskva | 18 Aug 85 |
| | (Emmelmann, Busch, Neubauer, Müller) | | | | |
| 3:20.12 | SU | 1 | OG | Moskva | 1 Aug 80 |
| | (Prorochenko, Goyshchik, Zyuskova, I.Nazarova) | | | | |
| 3:20.21 | GDR | 1 | v SU | Erfurt | 23 Jun 85 |
| | (Emmelmann, Busch, Müller, Neubauer) | | | | |
| 3:20.23 | GDR | 1 | v USA | Karl-Marx-St. | 10 Jul 82 |
| | (Siemon, Busch, Rübsam, Koch) | | | | |
| 3:20.32 | CS | 2 | WC | Helsinki | 14 Aug 83 |
| | (Kocembová, Moravčíková, Matějkovičová, Kratochvílová) | | | | |
| 3:20.35 | GDR | 2 | OG | Moskva | 1 Aug 80 |
| | (Löwe, Krug, Lathan, Koch) | | | | |
| 3:20.37 | GDR | 1 | WP | Montréal | 24 Aug 79 |
| | (Kotte, Brehmer, Köhn, Koch) | | | | |
| 3:20.39 | SU | 2 | EP | Torino | 5 Aug 79 |
| | (Bagryantseva, Zyuskova, Prorochenko, Kulchunova) | | | | |
| | (20) | | | | |
| 3:20.60 | SU | 2 | WP | Canberra | 4 Oct 85 |
| | (Alexeyeva, I.Nazarova, Pinigina, Vladykina) | | | | |

WOMEN All-time

| Mark | Name | Pos | Meet | Venue | Date |
|------|------|-----|------|-------|------|
| 3:20.62 | GDR<br>(Rübsam, Steuk, Wöckel, Koch) | 1 | WP | Roma | 4 Sep 81 |
| 3:20.79 | CS<br>(Moravčíková, Kocembová, Matějkovičová, Kratochvílová) | 1 | EP | London | 21 Aug 83 |
| 3:21.16 | SU<br>(Korban, Ivanova, Baskakova, Pinigina) | 3 | WC | Helsinki | 14 Aug 83 |
| 3:21.20 | GDR<br>(Marquardt, Krug, Brehmer, Koch) | 1 | EC | Praha | 3 Sep 78 |
| 3:21.21 | CAN<br>(Crooks, Richardson, Killingbeck, Payne) | 2 | OG | Los Angeles | 11 Aug 84 |
| 3:21.22 | USA<br>(Cheeseborough, Cliette, Leatherwood, Dixon) | 1 | GWG | Moskva | 8 Jul 86 |
| 3:21.71 | SU<br>(Korban, Ivanova, Baskakova, Pinigina) | 2 | EP | London | 21 Aug 83 |
| 3:21.89 | CS<br>(Bulířova, Moravčíková, Kratochvílová, Kocembová) | 2 | Drz | Praha | 18 Aug 84 |
| 3:21.94 | Ukraine<br>(Dzhigalova, Olizarenko, Pinigina, Vladykina)<br>(30) | 1 | NC | Kiev | 17 Jul 86 |
| 3:21.99 | SU<br>(Styepanova, Pinigina, Dzhigalova, Vladykina) | 2 | GWG | Moskva | 8 Jul 86 |
| 3:22.17 | CS<br>(Tylová, Matějkovičová, Kocembová, Kratochvílová) | 2 | EC | Athínai | 11 Sep 82 |
| 3:22.53 | SU<br>(Prorochenko, Mushta, Providokhina, Kulchunova) | 2 | EC | Praha | 3 Sep 78 |
| 3:22.70 | GDR<br>(K.Walther, Busch, Bremer, Rübsam)<br>(34) | 3 | EP | London | 21 Aug 83 |

# WOMEN – NAME CHANGES

Indicated by ' in the all-time lists are women who have competed with distinction under two or more names. The following list shows the names for these competitors.

| ORIGINAL | MARRIED NAME | ORIGINAL | MARRIED NAME | ORIGINAL | MARRIED NAME |
|---|---|---|---|---|---|
| Andrei | Maraşescu | Kleinová | Walterová | Reichenbach | I.Müller |
| Andersen | Waitz | Klimchuk | Zelentsova | Reichstein | Bienias |
| Annison | Stanton | Kolenchukova | Yermolovich | Riefstahl | Oschkenat |
| Bagryantseva | Nazarova | Kotenyeva | Sereda | Rieger | Gunther |
| Barkusky | Weiss | Kotte | Löwe | Riemann | Martins |
| Bartoňová | Šilhavá | Kovarik | Uibel | Rienstra | Sommer |
| Benoit | Samuelson | Krentser | Bondarenko | Robertson | Boyd |
| Berend | Wakan | Krumpholtz | Fiedler | Rodina | Boborova |
| Bondareva | Litovchenko | Kulchunova | Pinigina | Rohde | Köhn |
| Brehmer | Lathan | Künzel | Wujak | Rübsam | Neubauer |
| Burneleit | Krebs | Kuragina | Nemogayeva | Saunders | Nunn |
| Christensen | Kristiansen | Laihorinne | Marjamaa | Savinkova | Yermakova |
| Cojocaru | Matei | Langer | Kalek | Schaller | Klier |
| Cuşmir | Stanciu | Larsen | Weidenbach | Schilly | Knisely |
| Daute | Drechsler | Livermore | Simpson | Schlaak | Jahl |
| Decker | Slaney | Ludwigs | Wodars | Schmalfeld | Voigt |
| de Klerk | Armstrong | Lyons | Catalano | Schmidt | R.Kirst |
| Didilenko | Korban | McDermott | Wade | Schneider | R.Müller |
| Dittrich | Hartwig | Makeyeva | Styepanova | Schoknecht | Slupianek |
| Dolzhenko | Krachevskaya | Matějkovičová | Strnadová |  | – Briesenick |
| Droese | Pufe | May | Edge | Siemon | Emmelmann |
| Duzhnovich | Ozhenko | Meinel | Lehmann | Simm | Kleeberg |
| Eckert | Wöckel |  | – Veith | Simpson | M.Bothma |
| Elliott | Davies | Meissner | Stecher | Smallwood | Cook |
| Finger | Thimm | Meyer | Hamann | Smith | Sly |
| Fitzgerald | Brown | Mityayeva | Byelevskaya | Steiner | M.Becker |
| Garrett | Audain | Mobius | Paetz | Stoica | Pogacian |
| Girbea | C.Ivan | Morgulina | Derbina | Stoll | Wartenberg |
| Grigoryeva | O.Nazarova | Mushta | Olizarenko | Strandvall | Pursiainen |
| Guzowska | M.Nowak | Nasonova | O.Antonova | Strong | R.Lorraway |
| Hearnshaw | Telfer | Nasonova | Goyshchik | Strophal | Streidt |
| Helm | S.Beyer | Neumann | E.Fiedler | Tacu | Craciunescu |
| Helmboldt | Gummel | Neumann | C.Liebetrau | Taylor | Issajenko |
| Hunte | H.Oakes | Nikitina | V.Komissova | Terpe | Theele |
| Ionescu | M.Lengyel | Nowaczyk | Blaszak | Thon | Siegl |
| Ivanova | M.Kharlamova | Nowakowska | Swierczyńska | Toivonen | Jousimaa |
| Jahn | Wilden | Nuneva | Vechernikova | Ullrich | H.Körner |
| Kämpfert | Steuk | Nygrýnová | Strejčková | Vater | Behmer |
| Kastetskaya | Ambraziene | O'Dea | L.Martin | Vornicu | Carutasu |
| Katyukova | Smekhnova | Oelsner | Göhr | Witschas | Ackermann |
| Kazachkova | Sorokina | Opitz | Hellmann | Yeremeyeva | Tinkova |
| Kemenchedzi | Merchuk | Pendergraft | Council |  | – Akimova |
| Khamitova | Samolyenko | Petrus | Avdeyenko | Zubova | T.Pavlova |
| Khristova | I.Moneva | Ponomaryova | Khromova | Zuyeva | Chervyakova |
| Kibakina | Sluzhkina | Poryvkina | Podkopayeva | Zverkova | Kisheyeva |
| Kirszenstein | Szewińska | Probert | Scutt |  |  |
| Kisheyeva | Zvereva | Proskuryakova | Rodionova |  |  |
| Klapezynski | Bruns | Rafira | Lovin |  |  |

| Mark | Wind | Name | | Nat | Yr | Pos | Meet | Venue | Date |
|------|------|------|---|-----|----|----|------|-------|------|

## 100 METRES

| Mark | Wind | Name | | Nat | Yr | Pos | Meet | Venue | Date |
|------|------|------|---|-----|----|-----|------|-------|------|
| 10.88 | 1.9 | Evelyn | Ashford | USA | 57 | 1 | | Rieti | 7 Sep |
| 10.91 | 0.2 | | Ashford | | | 1 | GWG | Moskva | 6 Jul |
| 10.91 | 0.2 | Heike | Drechsler | GDR | 64 | 2 | GWG | Moskva | 6 Jul |
| 10.91 | 0.8 | Marlies | Göhr | GDR | 58 | 1 | EC | Stuttgart | 27 Aug |
| 10.93 | 1.8 | Ewa | Kasprzyk | POL | 57 | 1 | NC | Grudziadz | 27 Jun |
| 10.93 | 1.6 | | Ashford | | | 1r1 | ISTAF | W Berlin | 15 Aug |
| 10.94 | 1.0 | | Drechsler | | | 1 | GO | Dresden | 16 Aug |
| 10.95 | -0.1 | | Ashford | | | 1 | WK | Zürich | 13 Aug |
| 10.96 | 0.8 | Silke | Gladisch | GDR | 64 | 1 | NC | Jena | 27 Jun |
| 10.96 | 0.9 | | Drechsler | | | 1h1 | GO | Dresden | 16 Aug |
| | | | | | | | | | |
| 10.97 | 1.9 | | Drechsler | | | 1 | | Potsdam | 11 Jun |
| 10.98 | 1.2 | | Göhr | | | 1s2 | EC | Stuttgart | 27 Aug |
| 10.99 | 1.3 | Valerie | Brisco-Hooks | USA | 60 | 1 | Pepsi | Westwood | 17 May |
| 11.01 | 0.7 | | Göhr | | | 1 | | Berlin | 20 Aug |
| 11.01 | 1.9 | | Göhr | | | 2 | | Rieti | 7 Sep |
| 11.02 | 0.3 | | Drechsler | | | 1 | | Neubrandenburg | 6 Jun |
| 11.02 | 1.1 | | Gladisch | | | 1s1 | NC | Jena | 27 Jun |
| 11.02 | 1.0 | | Göhr | | | 2 | GO | Dresden | 16 Aug |
| 11.04 | 0.8 | Anelia | Nuneva | BUL | 62 | 2 | EC | Stuttgart | 27 Aug |
| 11.05 | 0.0 | | Ashford | | | 1 | | Grosseto | 10 Aug |
| | | | | | | | | | |
| 11.05 | 1.2 | | Gladisch | | | 2s2 | EC | Stuttgart | 27 Aug |
| 11.06 | 1.3 | Alice | Brown | USA | 60 | 2 | Pepsi | Westwood | 17 May |
| 11.06 | 0.4 | Merlene | Ottey-Page | JAM | 60 | 1 | | Sevilla | 24 May |
| 11.06 | 0.3 | | Drechsler | | | 1h | | Potsdam | 11 Jun |
| 11.06 | -0.1 | | Göhr | | | 1h2 | EC | Stuttgart | 26 Aug |
| 11.07 | 1.6 | | Ottey-Page | | | 2r1 | ISTAF | W Berlin | 15 Aug |
| 11.08 | 0.8 | | Gladisch | | | 1 | v SU | Tallinn | 21 Jun |
| 11.08 | -0.1 | Jeanette | Bolden (10) | USA | 60 | 2 | WK | Zürich | 13 Aug |
| 11.08 | 1.2 | | Nuneva | | | 3s2 | EC | Stuttgart | 27 Aug |
| 11.08 | 0.8 | Nelli | Cooman | HOL | 64 | 3 | EC | Stuttgart | 27 Aug |
| | | | | | | | | | |
| 11.08 | 0.0 | | Ashford | | | 1 | | Catania | 13 Sep |
| | | | (31/11) | | | | | | |
| 11.09 | -1.4 | Irina | Slyusar | SU | 63 | 1 | Znam | Leningrad | 7 Jun |
| 11.11 | 0.8 | Ingrid | Auerswald | GDR | 57 | 5 | EC | Stuttgart | 27 Aug |
| 11.12 | 0.1 | Gail | Devers | USA | 66 | 1h2 | NCAA | Indianapolis | 5 Jun |
| 11.12 | 0.2 | Elvira | Barbashina | SU | 63 | 3 | GWG | Moskva | 6 Jul |
| 11.15 | 0.0 | Sheila | Echols | USA | 64 | 1 | | Knoxville | 24 May |
| 11.17 | 1.2 | Els | Vader | HOL | 59 | 1 | WA | Barcelona | 14 Jun |
| 11.18 | 1.6 | Diane | Williams | USA | 60 | 5r1 | ISTAF | W Berlin | 15 Aug |
| 11.19 | 1.8 | Jolanta | Janota | POL | 64 | 2 | NC | Grudziadz | 27 Jun |
| 11.20 | | Michelle | Finn (20) | USA | 65 | 1 | | Indianapolis | 3 May |
| | | | | | | | | | |
| 11.20 | 1.8 | Urszula | Jaros | POL | 56 | 3 | NC | Grudziadz | 27 Jun |
| 11.20 | 1.6 | Heidi-Elke | Gaugel | FRG | 59 | 6r1 | ISTAF | W Berlin | 15 Aug |
| 11.20 | 1.9 | Natalya | Pomoshchnikova | SU | 65 | 1s2 | Spart | Tashkent | 17 Sep |
| 11.20 | -0.1 | Maya | Azarashvili | SU | 64 | 1 | Spart | Tashkent | 17 Sep |
| 11.21 | -2.1 | Olga | Zolotaryova | SU | 61 | 1h | Znam | Leningrad | 7 Jun |
| 11.21 | 0.6 | Pam | Marshall | USA | 60 | 1h1 | TAC | Eugene | 19 Jun |
| A11.22 | | Evette | Armstrong | RSA | 65 | 1 | | Johannesburg | 18 Apr |
| 11.22 | 1.4 | Marina | Molokova | SU | 62 | 1h1 | NC | Kiev | 14 Jul |
| 11.22 | 2.0 | Heather | Oakes | UK | 59 | 1h2 | CG | Edinburgh | 27 Jul |
| 11.23 | 0.3 | M-Christine | Cazier (30) | FRA | 63 | 3 | | Paris | 22 Jul |
| | | | | | | | | | |
| 11.24 | 0.0 | Juliet | Cuthbert | JAM | 64 | 1h1 | | Houston | 17 May |
| 11.24 | -0.1 | Angella | Issajenko | CAN | 58 | 4 | WK | Zürich | 13 Aug |

| Mark | Wind | Name | | Nat | Yr | Pos | Meet | Venue | Date |
|------|------|------|------|-----|----|-----|------|-------|------|
| 11.25 | 0.6 | Jackie | Washington | USA | 62 | 1 | | Houston | 12 Apr |
| 11.25 | 0.8 | Paula | Dunn | UK | 64 | 7 | EC | Stuttgart | 27 Aug |
| 11.27 | 1.1 | Pauline | Davis | BAH | 66 | 1h2 | | Knoxville | 17 May |
| 11.27 | 0.0 | Diane | Dixon | USA | 64 | 3 | | Knoxville | 24 May |
| 11.27 | -0.2 | Antonina | Nastoburko | SU | 59 | 2 | NC | Kiev | 14 Jul |
| 11.27 | 1.1 | Nadezhda | Georgieva | BUL | 61 | 2 | | Sofia | 3 Aug |
| 11.28 | -0.6 | Mary | Onyali | NIG | 68 | 1h2 | | Houston | 9 May |
| 11.28 | 1.0 | Tatyana | Papilina (40) | SU | 67 | 1 | NC-j | Kaunas | 19 Jul |
| 11.29 | 1.3 | Sabine | Günther | GDR | 63 | 1 | | Jena | 31 May |
| 11.30 | 0.8 | Gwen | Torrence | USA | 65 | 2 | NCAA | Indianapolis | 7 Jun |
| 11.30 | 0.5 | Pepa | Pavlova | BUL | 61 | 1 | | Sofia | 21 Jun |
| 11.30 | 0.7 | Heike | Morgenstern | GDR | 62 | 3 | | Berlin | 20 Aug |
| 11.31 | 1.1 | Dannette | Young | USA | 64 | 1 | | Los Angeles | 24 May |
| 11.31 | 1.6 | Cornelia | Oschkenat | GDR | 61 | 3h2 | GO | Dresden | 16 Aug |
| 11.31 | 1.9 | Grace | Jackson | JAM | 61 | 4 | | Rieti | 7 Sep |
| 11.33 | 1.3 | Jeanette | Düring | GDR | 65 | 2 | | Jena | 31 May |
| 11.33 | | Camille | Coates | JAM | 66 | 1 | NC | Kingston | 20 Jun |
| 11.33 | 1.5 | Laurence | Bily (50) | FRA | 63 | 1 | NC | Aix-les-Bains | 9 Aug |
| 11.34 | -0.8 | Lyubov | Aleksandrova | SU | 65 | 1r2 | Znam | Leningrad | 7 Jun |
| 11.34 | 0.9 | Tina | Iheagwan | NIG | 68 | 1 | WC-j | Athinai | 17 Jul |
| 11.34 | 1.9 | Lidia | Yelagina | SU | 64 | 1 | | Bryansk | 14 Aug |
| 11.34 | 1.5 | Ute | Thimm | FRG | 58 | 2r3 | ISTAF | W Berlin | 15 Aug |
| 11.36 | 0.0 | Mary | Bolden | USA | 64 | 2h1 | | Houston | 17 May |
| 11.36 | -0.8 | Svetlana | Chervyakova | SU | 63 | 2r2 | Znam | Leningrad | 7 Jun |
| 11.36 | 1.9 | Natalya | German | SU | 63 | 2s2 | Spart | Tashkent | 17 Sep |
| 11.38 | 1.3 | Jennifer | Inniss | USA | 59 | 4 | Pepsi | Westwood | 17 May |
| 11.38 | 1.6 | Eva | Murkova | CS | 62 | 1 | | Banska Bystrica | 31 May |
| 11.38 | 1.0 | Valya | Valova (60) | BUL | 61 | 2 | | Sofia | 9 Aug |
| 11.39 | 1.0 | Angela | Phipps | CAN | 64 | 2 | | Baton Rouge | 13 Apr |
| 11.39 | 0.3 | Gillian | Forde | TRI | 67 | 3 | King | Atlanta | 20 Apr |
| 11.39 | 1.6 | Ewa | Pisiewicz | POL | 62 | 2 | | Hania | 24 May |
| 11.39 | 1.3 | Stefanie | Jacob | GDR | 65 | 4 | | Jena | 31 May |
| 11.39 | 0.8 | Vroni | Werthmüller | SWZ | 59 | 1 | NC | Winterthur | 9 Aug |
| 11.40 | 1.1 | Wendy | Vereen | USA | 66 | 2 | PennR | Philadelphia | 26 Apr |
| 11.40 | 1.6 | Taťána | Kocembová | CS | 62 | 2 | | Banská Bystrica | 31 May |
| 11.40 | -0.4 | Angela | Bailey | CAN | 62 | 1s | NC | Ottawa | 21 Jun |
| 11.41 | 0.0 | Brenda | Cliette | USA | 63 | 2 | | Tallahassee | 22 Mar |
| 11.41 | -1.5 | Olga | Frolova (70) | SU | 64 | 1s1 | Spart | Tashkent | 17 Sep |
| 11.42 | | Angela | Thacker | USA | 64 | 1 | KansR | Lawrence | 19 Apr |
| 11.42 | 1.5 | Florence | Griffith | USA | 59 | 3r3 | ISTAF | W Berlin | 15 Aug |
| A11.43 | 1.5 | Maryke | Smith | RSA | 66 | 2 | NC | Germiston | 11 Apr |
| 11.43 | 0.8 | Odessa | Smalls | USA | 64 | 1 | | Columbus | 4 May |
| 11.43 | 1.5 | Francoise | Leroux | FRA | 61 | 2 | NC | Aix-les-Bains | 9 Aug |
| 11.44 | | Klavdia | Salyga | SU | 64 | 1h | | Sochi | 17 May |
| 11.44 | -1.2 | Yordanka | Donkova | BUL | 61 | 2 | Nar | Sofia | 31 May |
| 11.44 | -1.3 | Marita | Koch | GDR | 57 | 1h | | Neubrandenburg | 6 Jun |
| 11.44 | 0.0 | Marina | Zhirova | SU | 63 | 1 | | Tallinn | 18 Jun |
| 11.45 | 0.7 | Rossella | Tarolo (80) | ITA | 64 | 1 | | Bolzano | 25 May |
| 11.45 | 0.0 | Randy | Givens | USA | 62 | 3 | | Grosseto | 10 Aug |
| 11.46 | 1.1 | LaVonna | Martin | USA | 66 | 2h2 | | Knoxville | 17 May |
| 11.46 | 0.9 | Caryl | Smith | USA | 69 | 2 | WC-j | Athinai | 17 Jul |
| A11.46 | | Elinda | Rademeyer | RSA | 65 | 1 | | Bloemfontein | 6 Dec |

| Mark | Wind | Name | | Nat | Yr | Pos | Meet | Venue | Date |
|---|---|---|---|---|---|---|---|---|---|
| 11.47 | | Debbie | Greene | BAH | 64 | 1 | | Tempe | 22 Mar |
| 11.47 | -1.8 | Monika | Hirsch | FRG | 59 | 1 | | Fürth | 15 Jun |
| 11.48 | | Rufina | Ubah | NIG | 59 | 2 | KansR | Lawrence | 19 Apr |
| 11.48 | 0.3 | Olga | Antonova | SU | 60 | 4s2 | NC | Kiev | 14 Jul |
| 11.49 | -1.4 | Elvira | Kotoviene | SU | 58 | 6 | Znam | Leningrad | 7 Jun |
| 11.49 | 1.2 | Blanca | Lacambra (90) | SPA | 65 | 2 | WA | Barcelona | 14 Jun |
| | | | | | | | | | |
| 11.49 | 0.9 | Maicel | Malone | USA | 69 | 3 | WC-j | Athinai | 17 Jul |
| 11.49 | 0.9 | Katrin | Krabbe | GDR | 69 | 4 | WC-j | Athinai | 17 Jul |
| 11.49 | -1.5 | Olga | Naumkina | SU | 64 | 2s1 | Spart | Tashkent | 17 Sep |
| 11.50 | 0.7 | Vineta | Ikauniece | SU | 62 | 1h | | Riga | 30 May |
| 11.50 | 1.0 | Sandra | Whittaker | UK | 63 | 1 | | Edinburgh | 14 Jun |
| 11.50 | 0.0 | Olga | Kvast | SU | 63 | 1h3 | | Tallinn | 28 Jun |
| 11.50 | 1.2 | Resi | März | FRG | 60 | 1 | | Regensburg | 28 Jun |
| 11.50 | 0.3 | Svetlana | Zhizdrikova | SU | 60 | 5s2 | NC | Kiev | 14 Jul |
| 11.51 | | Muriel | Leroy | FRA | 68 | 2s3 | WC-j | Athinai | 17 Jul |
| 11.51 | 2.0 | Natalya | Kovtun (100) | SU | 64 | h | | Bryansk | 14 Aug |
| | | | | | | | | | |
| 11.51 | 1.4 | Carla | Mercurio | ITA | 60 | 1 | | Chieti | 5 Sep |
| 11.51 | | Ratjai | Sripet | THA | 66 | 1 | | Taipeh | 8 Oct |
| 11.52 | 1.1 | Sandra | Dennis | JAM | | 3 | PennR | Philadelphia | 26 Apr |
| 11.52 | 1.8 | Pippa | Windle | UK | 61 | 3 | WAAA | Birmingham | 6 Jun |
| 11.52 | -0.4 | Anke | Köninger | FRG | 61 | 2h2 | | Fürth | 15 Jun |
| 11.52 | 0.9 | Lena | Möller | SWE | 57 | 1 | | Västerås | 26 Jun |
| 11.52 | 1.8 | Bianca | Betz | FRG | 60 | 1s | | Essen | 28 Jun |
| 11.52 | 0.0 | Kirsten | Emmelmann | GDR | 61 | 1 | | Linz | 10 Sep |
| A11.52 | | Ansie | Basson (109) | RSA | 66 | 1 | | Bloemfontein | 5 Nov |

11.53 1.3 Tsvetanka Ilieva (110) BUL 63 24 May
11.53 1.4 Yelena Vinogradova SU 64 14 Jul
11.53 1.5 Magali Seguin FRA 64 9 Aug
11.53 1.6 Heike Theele GDR 64 16 Aug
11.53 0.7 Ulrike Sarvari FRG 64 27 Aug
11.53 0.5 Lydia de Vega PHI 64 4 Oct
11.54 0.6 Inger Peterson USA 64 12 Apr
11.54 0.3 Michelle King USA 64 20 Apr
11.54 0.9 Eldece Clarke BAH 65 22 May
11.55 Kim Dunlap USA 64 24 May
11.55 Manuela Braun (120) GDR 66 6 Jun
11.55 -2.1 Lyudmila Khristosenko SU 66 7 Jun
11.55 0.5 Amparo Caicedo COL 65 29 Jun
11.55 1.4 Christelle Bulteau FRA 63 8 Aug
11.55 0.9 Marina Vladimirova SU 67 14 Aug
11.55 -0.2 Irina Kot SU 67 17 Sep
11.56 1.1 Diane Holden AUS 63 22 Feb
11.56 0.9 Vivianne Spence JAM 22 May
11.56 Vivien McKenzie USA 64 23 May
11.56 1.8 Wendy Hoyte UK 57 6 Jun
11.56 1.2 Virginia Gomes (130) POR 64 14 Jun
11.56 0.9 Claudia Lepping FRG 68 17 Jul
11.56 1.2 Violetta Kaminska POL 63 8 Aug
11.57 Marie-France Loval FRA 64 22 Mar
11.57 Lisa Ford USA 66 12 Apr
11.57 0.0 Angela Curry USA 62 26 Apr
11.57 Davera Taylor USA 65 23 May
11.57 -0.4 Vera Sevalnikova SU 63 17 Sep

11.58 0.6 Pam Qualls USA 66 19 Jun
11.58 1.4 Rimma Nurmukhomyatova SU 59 27 Jun (140)
11.58 0.7 Marina Kleyankina SU 62 1 Aug
11.58 -0.2 Marina Krivosheina SU 67 17 Sep
A11.59 Mari Lise Furstenberg RSA 66 22 Mar
11.59 1.8 Linda Eseimokumoh NIG 66 4 Apr
11.59 Carlette Guidry USA 68 3 May
11.59 1.0 Janis Neilson UK 63 14 Jun
11.59 Celena Mondie USA 68 28 Jun
A11.59 Madele Naude RSA 66 5 Nov
11.60 -2.0 Nellina Lofton USA 67 19 Apr
11.60 Anita Howard USA 69 8 May
11.60 Angela McClatchey USA 67 23 May (150)
11.60 0.7 Daniela Ferrian ITA 61 25 May
11.60 1.4 Nadezhda Rashchupkina SU 63 14 Jul
11.60 1.2 Radislava Nagy CS 59 2 Aug
11.60 1.2 Mihaela Chindea RUM 67 2 Aug
11.61 Janice Marshall USA 12 Apr
11.61 Lorinda Richardson USA 65 3 May
11.61 0.8 Ethlyn Tate JAM 66 4 May
11.61 1.1 Patricia Davis USA 65 24 May
11.61 1.8 Joanna Smolarek POL 65 27 Jun
11.61 0.8 Joan Baptiste (160) UK 59 12 Sep
11.62 -0.7 Beverley Peterson NZ 56 8 Mar
11.62 1.0 Alicia Bass USA 65 13 Apr
11.62 1.0 Dorothea Brown USA 64 13 Apr
A11.62 Cynthia Henry JAM 62 20 Apr
11.62 Nedrea Williams USA 65 17 May

WOMEN 1986

| Mark | Wind | Name | | Nat | Yr | Pos | Meet | Venue | Date |
|------|------|------|------|-----|----|-----|------|-------|------|
| 11.62 | | Kerstin | Behrendt | GDR 67 | 6 Jun | 11.64 1.2 | Erzsébet | Ecseki | HUN 58 2 Aug |
| 11.62 | 1.6 | Krasimira | Ilieva | BUL 58 | 21 Jun | 11.64 1.8 | Nicoleta | Carutasu | RUM 64 7 Aug |
| 11.62 | 1.8 | Ewa | Kiedrowska | POL 65 | 27 Jun | 11.65 -0.5 | Wanda | Eades | USA 29 Mar |
| 11.62 | 1.1 | Corinne | Blanchard | FRA 65 | 5 Jul | 11.65 0.0 | Janet | Levy | USA 64 26 Apr |
| 11.62 | 0.3 | Odiah | Sidibe (170) | FRA 70 | 16 Jul | A11.65 | Leisa | Davis-Knowles | USA 63 18 May (190) |
| 11.63 | | Frenchie | Holmes | USA 69 | 3 May | 11.65 | Sybil | Perry | USA 63 23 May |
| 11.63 | | Patricia | Bille | GDR 68 | 10 Jul | A11.65 -0.1 | Esmie | Lawrence | CAN 61 26 May |
| 11.63 | 1.0 | Lidia | Okolo-Kulak | SU 67 | 19 Jul | 11.65 | Peifeng | Weng | CHN 61 6 Jun |
| 11.63 | -0.4 | Yelena | Kelchevskaya | SU 55 | 9 Aug | 11.65 1.8 | Ramona | Steici | RUM 67 7 Aug |
| 11.63 | 1.0 | Natalya | Potapova | SU 65 | 14 Aug | 11.65 1.5 | Marie-France | Johanssen | FRA 60 9 Aug |
| 11.64 | 1.9 | Nicole | Williams | USA 67 | 12 Apr | 11.65 | Gloria | Uibel | GDR 64 16 Aug |
| 11.64 | 0.6 | Paula | Ready | USA 66 | 12 Apr | 11.66 1.1 | Terri | Dendy | USA 65 26 Apr |
| 11.64 | 0.6 | Bertha | Dooley | USA 67 | 12 Apr | 11.66 | Ellen | Schlieben | GDR 66 6 Jun |
| 11.64 | 0.3 | Carla | McLaughlin | USA 67 | 20 Apr | 11.66 -0.8 | Olga | Kosyakova | SU 68 7 Jun |
| 11.64 | | Francine | Landre (180) | FRA 70 | 9 May | 11.66 1.1 | Gabi | Lippe (200) | FRG 67 29 Jun |
| 11.64 | 1.8 | Helen | Barnett | UK 58 | 6 Jun | 11.66 | Christiane | Prajet | FRA 57 29 Jun |
| 11.64 | | Corina | Rosioru | RUM 68 | 7 Jun | 11.66 1.9 | Jane | Flemming | AUS 65 5 Jul |
| 11.64 | 0.9 | Maria | Fernström | SWE 67 | 26 Jun | 11.66 1.4 | Irina | Skibinskikh | SU 61 14 Jul |
| 11.64 | 0.0 | Marina | Shmonina | SU 65 | 14 Jul | 11.66 0.0 | Marisa | Masullo (204) | ITA 59 13 Sep |
| 11.64 | -0.3 | Martha | Grossenbacher | HOL 59 | 26 Jul | | | | |

Intermediate time during 200 m race :
11.00          Drechsler-EC Stuttgart, 29 Aug

--------------------------------------------------------------------------------

| | 1 | 10 | 20 | 30 | 50 | 100 | Under 11.50 | Under 11.60 |
|------|------|------|------|------|------|------|------|------|
| 1982 | 10.88 | 11.14 | 11.28 | 11.33 | 11.43 | 11.58 | 67 | 106 |
| 1983 | 10.79 | 11.09 | 11.22 | 11.30 | 11.41 | 11.54 | 79 | 122 |
| 1984 | 10.76 | 11.10 | 11.21 | 11.26 | 11.36 | 11.51 | 86 | 140 |
| 1985 | 10.86 | 11.11 | 11.21 | 11.27 | 11.38 | 11.54 | 85 | 121 |
| 1986 | 10.88 | 11.08 | 11.20 | 11.23 | 11.33 | 11.51 | 93 | 147 |

--------------------------------------------------------------------------------

Marks made with assisting wind > 2 m/s:

| | | | | | | | | | |
|------|------|------|------|------|----|-----|------|------|------|
| 10.80 | 2.9 | Pam | Marshall | USA 60 | 1 | TAC | | Eugene | 20 Jun |
| 10.80 | 2.8 | Heike | Drechsler | GDR 64 | 1 | Bisl | | Oslo | 5 Jul |
| 10.84 | 2.9 | Alice | Brown | USA 60 | 2 | TAC | | Eugene | 20 Jun |
| 10.85 | 2.9 | Evelyn | Ashford | USA 57 | 3 | TAC | | Eugene | 20 Jun |
| 10.92 | 2.9 | Diane | Williams | USA 60 | 4 | TAC | | Eugene | 20 Jun |
| 10.94 | 3.9 | Jackie | Washington | USA 62 | 1 | | | Houston | 18 May |
| 10.95 | 2.8 | | Ashford | | 1s1 | TAC | | Eugene | 20 Jun |
| 10.96 | 2.8 | Gail | Devers | USA 66 | 2s1 | TAC | | Eugene | 20 Jun |
| 10.97 | 3.9 | Juliet | Cuthbert | JAM 64 | 2 | | | Houston | 18 May |
| 10.97 | 2.6 | | Brown | | 1s2 | TAC | | Eugene | 20 Jun |
| 10.98 | 3.0 | | Marshall | | 1 | | | Modesto, CA | 10 May |
| 11.00 | 2.9 | | Devers | | 5 | TAC | | Eugene | 20 Jun |
| 11.01 | 5.8 | Gwen | Torrence | USA 65 | 1 | FlaR | | Gainesville | 29 Mar |
| 11.02 | | | Brown | | 1 | | | Irvine, CA | 3 May |
| 11.02 | 2.6 | | Marshall | | 2s2 | TAC | | Eugene | 20 Jun |
| 11.04 | 5.8 | Michelle | Finn (10) | USA 65 | 2 | FlaR | | Gainesville | 29 Mar |
| 11.06 | 2.1 | | Ashford | | 1h2 | TAC | | Eugene | 19 Jun |
| 11.08 | 2.5 | | Ashford | | 1 | | | Pomona, CA | 19 Apr |

| Mark | Wind | Name | | Nat | Yr | Pos | Meet | Venue | Date |
|------|------|------|------|-----|-----|-----|------|-------|------|
| 11.08 | 2.6 | | Williams | | | 3s2 | TAC | Eugene | 20 Jun |
| 11.08 | 3.3 | Angella | Issajenko | CAN | 58 | 1 | NC | Ottawa | 21 Jun |
| | | (20/11) | | | | | | | |
| 11.11 | 2.4 | Pauline | Davis | BAH | 66 | 1 | | Knoxville | 18 May |
| 11.14 | 2.5 | Paula | Dunn | UK | 64 | 1h1 | CG | Edinburgh | 27 Jul |
| 11.17 | 3.9 | Mary | Bolden | USA | 64 | 3 | | Houston | 18 May |
| 11.18 | 3.2 | Maicel | Malone | USA | 69 | 1 | TAC-j | Towson, MD | 28 Jun |
| 11.20 | 2.3 | Heather | Oakes | UK | 59 | 1 | CG | Edinburgh | 27 Jul |
| 11.23 | 3.3 | Angela | Bailey | CAN | 62 | 2 | NC | Ottawa | 21 Jun |
| 11.27 | 2.6 | Jennifer | Inniss | USA | 59 | 5s2 | TAC | Eugene | 20 Jun |
| A11.28 | 4.4 | Debbie | Greene | BAH | 64 | 1 | | Provo | 10 May |
| 11.28 | 3.2 | Caryl | Smith (20) | USA | 69 | 2 | TAC-j | Towson, MD | 28 Jun |
| | | | | | | | | | |
| 11.37 | 5.0 | Irina | Privalova | SU | 68 | 1 | | Simferopol | 23 May |
| 11.37 | 2.6 | Odessa | Smalls | USA | 64 | 6s2 | TAC | Eugene | 20 Jun |
| 11.38 | 2.9 | Michelle | King | USA | 64 | 2r1 | MSR | Walnut, CA | 27 Apr |
| A11.39 | 3.2 | Maryke | Smith | RSA | 66 | 1 | | Secunda | 15 Nov |
| 11.41 | | Marie-France | Johanssen | FRA | 60 | 1h1 | | Chambery | 26 Apr |
| 11.42 | 2.6 | Rossella | Tarolo | ITA | 64 | 1h3 | | Bolzano | 25 May |
| 11.42 | 2.8 | Randy | Givens | USA | 62 | 6s1 | TAC | Eugene | 20 Jun |
| 11.45 | 3.3 | Esmie | Lawrence | CAN | 61 | 3 | NC | Ottawa | 21 Jun |
| 11.46 | | Maria | Usifo | NIG | 64 | 1 | | College Sta, TX | 29 Mar |
| 11.46 | | Zelda | Johnson (30) | USA | 64 | 2 | | Irvine, CA | 3 May |
| | | | | | | | | | |
| 11.47 | 2.9 | Inger | Peterson | USA | 64 | 3r1 | MSR | Walnut, CA | 27 Apr |
| 11.47 | 3.9 | Ursula | Younger | USA | | 4 | | Houston | 18 May |
| 11.47 | 2.4 | Daniela | Ferrian | ITA | 61 | 1 | | Donnas | 9 Jul |
| 11.48 | | Lisa | Ford | USA | 66 | 2 | | College Sta, TX | 29 Mar |
| 11.48 | 3.2 | Carlette | Guidry | USA | 68 | 3 | TAC-j | Towson, MD | 28 Jun |
| A11.49 | 4.4 | Lola | Ogunde | NIG | 64 | 2 | | Provo | 10 May |
| 11.51 | | Janice | Marshall (37) | USA | | 1 | | Arlington | 10 May |

| | | | | | | | | | |
|--|--|--|--|--|--|--|--|--|--|
| 11.53 3.2 Denise | Liles | USA 68 28 Jun | 11.60 2.4 Carla | McLaughlin | USA 67 18 May |
| 11.53 2.6 Sharon | Dolby | UK 68 16 Aug | 11.60 | Sabine | Richter | FRG 66 13 Jun |
| 11.54 2.3 Simone | Jacobs (40) UK 66 18 Jul | 11.60 2.1 Kornelija Šinković | YUG 64 27 Jun |
| | | | 11.60 3.9 Corina | Roșioru | RUM 68 11 Jul |
| A11.54 3.2 Michelle | du Toit | RSA 64 15 Nov | 11.60 2.5 Sallyanne Short | UK 68 27 Jul |
| 11.55 2.5 Kaye | Jeffrey | UK 63 27 Jul | 11.61 2.3 Kathy | Cook | UK 60 18 Jul |
| 11.56 5.0 Olga | Kosyakova | SU 68 23 May | 11.62 3.9 Katrice | Harris | USA 64 18 May |
| A11.57 4.4 Cynthia | Henry | JAM 62 10 May | 11.63 4.8 Patrice | Carpenter | USA 65 10 May |
| 11.58 2.1 Dijana | Ištvanović | YUG 57 27 Jun | 11.63 3.2 Tami | Stiles (60) USA 68 28 Jun |
| 11.58 3.2 Ulrike | Sommer | FRG 59 28 Jun | | |
| 11.58 2.4 Christiane Prajet | FRA 57 9 Jul | 11.63 2.5 Helen | Miles | UK 67 27 Jul |
| 11.59 | Alma | Dickerson | USA 26 Apr | 11.63 4.5 Monique | Dunstan | AUS 70 13 Dec |
| 11.59 2.8 Corinne | Blanchard | FRA 65 19 Jul | 11.65 2.6 Kerry | Johnson | AUS 63 1 Feb |
| 11.59 2.9 Gina | Tovo (50) AUS 70 13 Dec | 11.65 | Alesia | Turner | USA 67 8 Mar |
| | | | 11.65 4.6 Vickie | Williams | USA 18 May |
| 11.60 | Comfort | Igeh | NIG 63 7 Mar | 11.65 5.0 Lyudmila | Lapshina (66) SU 69 23 May |

Hand timing:

| | | | | | | | | | |
|------|------|------|------|------|------|------|------|------|------|
| 10.9 | | Pam | Marshall | USA | 60 | 1 | | Tempe | 5 Apr |
| 10.9 | | Anelia | Nuneva | BUL | 62 | 1 | NC | Sofia | 13 Aug |
| 11.0 | | Natalya | PomoshchnikovaSU | | 65 | 1 | | Moskva | 9 May |
| A11.0 | 0.1 | Angella | Issajenko | CAN | 58 | 1r1 | | Provo | 24 May |
| A11.0 | 0.1 | Diane | Williams | USA | 60 | 2r2 | | Provo | 24 May |
| 11.0 | | Lidia | Yelagina | SU | 64 | 1 | | Lipetsk | 18 Jul |
| 11.1 | | Gillian | Forde | TRI | 67 | 1 | | Pt-a-Pierre | 18 Apr |

| Mark | Wind | Name | | Nat | Yr | Pos | Meet | Venue | Date |
|------|------|------|--|-----|----|----|------|-------|------|
| 11.1 | 1.7 | M-Christine | Cazier | FRA | 63 | 1 | | Nantes | 7 Jun |
| 11.1 | | Almira | Nizamova | SU | 62 | 2 | | Lipetsk | 18 Jul |
| 11.1 | | Yelena | Kelchevskaya | SU | 55 | 3 | | Lipetsk | 18 Jul |
| | | | (10) | | | | | | |
| 11.1 | 0.9 | Lyubov | Aleksandrova | SU | 65 | 1 | | Alma-Ata | 28 Aug |
| 11.1 | 2.0 | Natalya | German | SU | 63 | 1 | | Kiev | 29 Aug |
| 11.2 | | Dannette | Young | USA | 64 | 1h | | Tallahassee | 15 Mar |
| 11.2 | | Wendy | Vereen | USA | 66 | 2 | | Tempe | 5 Apr |
| 11.2 | | Olga | Vladykina | SU | 63 | | | Stakhanov | 26 Apr |
| 11.2 | | Irina | Skibinskikh | SU | 61 | 1 | | Odessa | 3 May |
| 11.2 | | Larisa | Shlykova | SU | 60 | 2 | | Moskva | 9 May |
| 11.2 | | Elvira | Kotoviene | SU | 58 | 1 | | Vilnius | 24 May |
| 11.2 | 1.7 | Laurence | Bily | FRA | 63 | 2 | | Nantes | 7 Jun |
| 11.2 | | Pauline | Davis   (20) | BAH | 66 | 1 | NC | Nassau | 14 Jun |
| 11.2 | | Lyudmila | Khristosenko | SU | 66 | | | | |
| 11.2 | 2.0 | Marina | Shmonina | SU | 65 | 1 | | Tiraspol | 9 Aug |
| 11.2 | | Valya | Valova | BUL | 61 | 2 | NC | Sofia | 13 Aug |
| 11.2 | 0.9 | Olga | Kvast | SU | 63 | 2 | | Alma-Ata | 28 Aug |
| 11.2 | 2.0 | Irina | Kot    (25) | SU | 67 | 2 | | Kiev | 29 Aug |

| 11.3i | | Irina | Privalova | SU | 68 | 1Mar | | 11.3 | 1.7 Magali | | Seguin | FRA 64 | 7 Jun |
|-------|--|-------|-----------|----|----|------|--|------|------------|--|--------|--------|-------|

11.3i   Irina   Privalova   SU 68  1 Mar    11.3  1.7 Magali      Seguin       FRA 64  7 Jun
11.3    Marie-France Loval  FRA 64 22 Mar   11.3      Marina     Vladimirova  SU 67 15 Jun
11.3  2.0 Mary    Bolden    USA 64  4 Apr   11.3      Natalya    Kovtun       SU 64 28 Jun
11.3  2.0 Camille Coates    JAM 66  4 Apr   A11.3     Joyce      Odhiambo     KEN 62 28 Jun
11.3  2.0 Lisa    Ford  (30) USA 66 4 Apr   11.3  1.0 Tatyana    Sergiyenko   SU 64  5 Jul
                                                                    (40)
11.3    Judi    Brown-King  USA 61  5 Apr   11.3      Yelena     Ruzina       SU 64 18 Jul
11.3    Yelena  Petrova     SU 62  3 May    11.3      Natalya    Potapova     SU 65 18 Jul
11.3    Tsvetanka Ilieva    BUL 63  3 May   11.3      Nadezhda   Rashchupkina SU 63  9 Aug
A11.3 0.1 Randy  Givens     USA 62 24 May   11.3      Tatyana    Oksimets     SU 64 14 Aug
11.3 1.7 Christelle Bulteau FRA 63  7 Jun   11.3  0.9 Vera       Sevalnikova  SU 63 28 Aug
                                                                    (45)

Marks made with assisting wind > 2 m/s:

| Mark | Wind | Name | | Nat | Yr | Pos | | Venue | Date |
|------|------|------|--|-----|----|-----|--|-------|------|
| 10.7 | 3.4 | Merlene | Ottey-Page | JAM | 60 | 1h2 | | Shizuoka | 27 Apr |
| 10.9 | | Sheila | Echols | USA | 64 | 1 | | New Orleans | 5 Apr |
| 11.2 | | Camille | Coates | JAM | 66 | 1 | | Lubbock | 29 Mar |
| A11.2 | 4.3 | Debbie | Greene | BAH | 64 | 1 | | Albuquerque | 12 Apr |
| A11.2 | 4.3 | Cynthia | Henry | JAM | 62 | 2 | | Albuquerque | 12 Apr |
| 11.2 | | Davera | Taylor | USA | 65 | 1 | | Ames | 3 May |
| 11.2 | | Silke | Knoll | FRG | 67 | 1 | | Celle | 4 May |

11.3    Tracy   Mayfield   USA 68 26 Apr
11.3    Vivien  McKenzie   USA 64  3 May
11.3    Marina  Flajšman (10) YUG 63 19 May

Mark made in mixed race with men:

| 11.0 | 4.0 | Diane | Holden | AUS | 63 | - | | Sydney | 5 Apr |
|------|-----|-------|--------|-----|----|----|--|--------|-------|

| Mark | Wind | Name | | Nat | Yr | Pos | Meet | Venue | Date |
|------|------|------|--|-----|----|----|----|-------|------|

| Mark | Wind | Name | | Nat | Yr | Pos | Meet | Venue | Date |
|------|------|------|--|-----|----|----|----|-------|------|
| 21.71 | 1.2 | Heike | Drechsler | GDR | 64 | 1 | NC | Jena | 29 Jun |
| 21.71 | -0.8 | | Drechsler | | | 1 | EC | Stuttgart | 29 Aug |
| 21.97 | -1.4 | Evelyn | Ashford | USA | 57 | 1 | WK | Zürich | 13 Aug |
| 22.06 | 0.3 | | Ashford | | | 1 | VD | Bruxelles | 5 Sep |
| 22.07 | 1.2 | Silke | Gladisch | GDR | 64 | 2 | NC | Jena | 29 Jun |
| 22.10 | 0.3 | | Drechsler | | | 2 | VD | Bruxelles | 5 Sep |
| 22.12 | 1.2 | Pam | Marshall | USA | 60 | 1 | GWG | Moskva | 8 Jul |
| 22.13 | 1.3 | | Drechsler | | | 1 | v SU | Tallinn | 22 Jun |
| 22.13 | 1.2 | Ewa | Kasprzyk | POL | 57 | 2 | GWG | Moskva | 8 Jul |
| 22.17 | 0.0 | | Ashford | | | 1 | | Viareggio | 6 Aug |
| 22.19 | 0.8 | | Kasprzyk | | | 1 | | Słupsk | 8 Jun |
| 22.20 | 1.7 | Marita | Koch | GDR | 57 | 1r1 | | Berlin | 20 Aug |
| 22.24 | -0.3 | Valerie | Brisco-Hooks | USA | 60 | 1 | DNG | Stockholm | 1 Jul |
| 22.26 | 0.0 | | Ashford | | | 1 | PTG | London | 11 Jul |
| 22.26 | -1.4 | | Brisco-Hooks | | | 2 | WK | Zürich | 13 Aug |
| 22.27 | 1.2 | Elvira | Barbashina | SU | 63 | 3 | GWG | Moskva | 8 Jul |
| 22.28 | 2.0 | | Marshall | | | 1r2 | MSR | Walnut, CA | 27 Apr |
| 22.29 | 0.5 | | Gladisch | | | 1s1 | EC | Stuttgart | 28 Aug |
| 22.30 | 0.3 | | Ashford | | | 1 | Jenner | San Jose | 31 May |
| 22.30 | 0.8 | | Brisco-Hooks | | | 1 | GP | Roma | 10 Sep |
| 22.31 | 0.0 | | Gladisch | | | 1 | | Erfurt | 1 Jun |
| 22.31 | -0.3 | | Ashford | | | 1r1 | ASV | Köln | 17 Aug |
| 22.31 | 0.8 | | Ashford | | | 2 | GP | Roma | 10 Sep |
| 22.32 | -0.8 | M-Christine | Cazier | FRA | 63 | 2 | EC | Stuttgart | 29 Aug |
| 22.33 | 0.3 | | Drechsler | | | 1s2 | EC | Stuttgart | 28 Aug |
| 22.34 | 0.9 | | Kasprzyk | | | 1 | BGP | Budapest | 11 Aug |
| 22.37 | -0.7 | | Gladisch | | | 1 | PTS | Bratislava | 14 Jun |
| 22.38 | -0.7 | | Ashford | | | 1 | Nik | Nice | 15 Jul |
| 22.38 | -1.7 | | Ashford | | | 1 | IAC | London | 8 Aug |
| 22.38 | 1.7 | | Gladisch | | | 2r1 | | Berlin | 20 Aug |
| 22.39 | 0.3 | Grace | Jackson | JAM | 61 | 2 | Jenner | San Jose | 31 May |
| | | | (31/10) | | | | | | |
| A22.42 | | Evette | Armstrong | RSA | 65 | 1 | | Johannesburg | 18 Apr |
| 22.43 | 0.9 | Merlene | Ottey-Page | JAM | 60 | 2 | BGP | Budapest | 11 Aug |
| 22.46 | 0.1 | Marina | Molokova | SU | 62 | 1 | NC | Kiev | 16 Jul |
| 22.51 | -0.1 | Maya | Azarashvili | SU | 64 | 1 | Spart | Tashkent | 20 Sep |
| 22.53 | 0.3 | Diane | Dixon | USA | 64 | 3 | Jenner | San Jose | 31 May |
| 22.53 | 1.2 | Gwen | Torrence | USA | 65 | 4 | GWG | Moskva | 8 Jul |
| 22.58 | -0.1 | Olga | Vladykina | SU | 63 | 1h3 | Znam | Leningrad | 8 Jun |
| 22.58 | -0.4 | Anelia | Nuneva | BUL | 62 | 1 | Balk | Ljubljana | 7 Sep |
| 22.59 | 0.3 | Randy | Givens | USA | 62 | 4 | Jenner | San Jose | 31 May |
| 22.60 | 2.0 | Diane | Williams (20) | USA | 60 | 2r2 | MSR | Walnut, CA | 27 Apr |
| 22.60 | 0.1 | Natalya | Bochina | SU | 62 | 2 | NC | Kiev | 16 Jul |
| 22.68 | 2.0 | Jackie | Washington | USA | 62 | 1 | | Houston | 4 May |
| 22.68 | -0.4 | Pepa | Pavlova | BUL | 61 | 2 | Balk | Ljubljana | 7 Sep |
| 22.71 | 1.1 | Juliet | Cuthbert | JAM | 64 | 1 | NCAA | Indianapolis | 6 Jun |
| 22.76 | 1.2 | Sabine | Günther | GDR | 63 | 3 | NC | Jena | 29 Jun |
| 22.80 | 0.3 | Angella | Issajenko | CAN | 58 | 6 | VD | Bruxelles | 5 Sep |
| 22.81 | -0.1 | Yelena | Vinogradova | SU | 64 | 2h3 | Znam | Leningrad | 8 Jun |
| 22.83 | 1.3 | Pauline | Davis | BAH | 66 | 1h3 | NCAA | Indianapolis | 4 Jun |
| 22.85 | 1.2 | Jackie | Joyner | USA | 62 | H | USOCF | Houston | 1 Aug |
| 22.86 | 0.3 | Els | Vader (30) | HOL | 59 | 1 | | Saint-Denis | 21 Jun |
| 22.88 | 2.0 | Alice | Brown | USA | 60 | 4r2 | MSR | Walnut, CA | 27 Apr |

| Mark | Wind | Name | | Nat | Yr | Pos | Meet | Venue | Date | |
|------|------|------|--|-----|----|----|----|------|------|--|
| 22.88 | -0.3 | Ute | Thimm | FRG | 58 | 6r1 | ASV | Köln | 17 | Aug |
| 22.90 | 1.9 | Sheila | Echols | USA | 64 | 1 | | Baton Rouge | 30 | May |
| 22.90 | 1.3 | Mary | Onyali | NIG | 68 | 2h3 | NCAA | Indianapolis | 4 | Jun |
| 22.90 | 1.2 | Jolanta | Janota | POL | 64 | 2 | v Fra, | Spa Epinal | 5 | Jul |
| 22.91 | 0.5 | Heidi-Elke | Gaugel | FRG | 59 | 1 | | Schweinfurt | 9 | Aug |
| 22.92 | -0.8 | Taťána | Kocembová | CS | 62 | 1 | GS | Ostrava | 11 | Jun |
| 22.92 | 0.3 | Heather | Oakes | UK | 59 | 5s2 | EC | Stuttgart | 28 | Aug |
| 22.93 | 0.9 | Tsvetanka | Ilieva | BUL | 63 | 2 | | Sofia | 25 | May |
| 22.93 | 0.5 | Marina | Zhirova (40) | SU | 63 | 3s1 | EC | Stuttgart | 28 | Aug |
| | | | | | | | | | | |
| 22.95 | -0.1 | Svetlana | Chervyakova | SU | 63 | 2 | Spart | Tashkent | 20 | Sep |
| A22.95 | | Elinda | Rademeyer | RSA | 65 | 1 | | Bloemfontein | 5 | Dec |
| 22.96 | | Wendy | Vereen | USA | 66 | 2 | | Columbus | 4 | May |
| 22.97 | | Michelle | Finn | USA | 65 | 1 | | Tampa | 12 | Apr |
| 22.97 | -0.3 | Heike | Morgenstern | GDR | 62 | 2 | GO | Dresden | 17 | Aug |
| 22.98 | -0.1 | Irina | Slyusar | SU | 63 | 3 | Spart | Tashkent | 20 | Sep |
| 22.99 | -1.0 | Yordanka | Donkova | BUL | 61 | 1 | | Schwechat | 18 | May |
| 23.00 | 0.8 | Urszula | Jaros | POL | 56 | 2 | | Słupsk | 8 | Jun |
| A23.02 | 1.2 | Angela | Bailey | CAN | 62 | 3r2 | | Provo | 24 | May |
| 23.02 | 1.7 | Annett | Hesselbarth | GDR | 66 | 4r1 | | Berlin | 20 | Aug |
| | | | (50) | | | | | | | |
| 23.02 | -0.1 | Natalya | Pomoshchnikova | SU | 65 | 4 | Spart | Tashkent | 20 | Sep |
| 23.04 | 0.3 | Svetlana | Zhizdrikova | SU | 60 | 4s2 | NC | Kiev | 16 | Jul |
| A23.06 | 1.1 | Debbie | Greene | BAH | 64 | 1 | | Provo | 10 | May |
| 23.06 | -0.3 | Olga | Frolova | SU | 64 | 1s | Spart | Tashkent | 19 | Sep |
| 23.07 | | Brenda | Cliette | USA | 63 | 3 | | Columbus | 4 | May |
| 23.09 | 2.0 | Rossella | Tarolo | ITA | 64 | 1 | v FRG, | Hun Verona | 19 | Jun |
| A23.10 | 1.6 | Madele | Naude | RSA | 63 | 2 | NC | Germiston | 12 | Apr |
| 23.11 | 1.4 | Vineta | Ikauniece | SU | 62 | 1h5 | Znam | Leningrad | 8 | Jun |
| 23.11 | 0.6 | Falilat | Ogunkoya | NIG | 68 | 1 | WC-j | Athinai | 19 | Jul |
| 23.11 | -1.1 | Kathy | Cook (60) | UK | 60 | 4h3 | EC | Stuttgart | 28 | Aug |
| | | | | | | | | | | |
| A23.12 | | Mari Lise | Furstenberg | RSA | 66 | 2 | | Germiston | 22 | Mar |
| 23.12 | -2.9 | Marita | Payne | CAN | 62 | 2 | | Houston | 29 | Mar |
| 23.12 | 1.9 | Dannette | Young | USA | 64 | 1 | | Nashville | 12 | Apr |
| 23.12 | | Maicel | Malone | USA | 69 | 1h3 | | Indianapolis | 30 | May |
| 23.13 | 0.1 | Mary | Bolden | USA | 64 | 1h1 | | Knoxville | 23 | May |
| A23.13 | 0.1 | Esmie | Lawrence | CAN | 61 | 1r1 | | Provo | 26 | May |
| 23.14 | 1.3 | Gillian | Forde | TRI | 67 | 1 | | Abymes | 31 | Mar |
| 23.14 | 0.4 | Chandra | Cheeseborough | USA | 59 | 2 | Bisl | Oslo | 5 | Jul |
| 23.16 | 0.0 | Lillie | Leatherwood | USA | 64 | 4 | | Knoxville | 24 | May |
| 23.17 | 0.4 | Emilia | Dimitrova(70) | BUL | 67 | H | GWG | Moskva | 6 | Jul |
| | | | | | | | | | | |
| 23.18 | 1.8 | Nedrea | Williams | USA | 65 | 1 | | Tucson | 31 | May |
| 23.18 | 1.0 | Claudia | Lepping | FRG | 68 | 1 | | Trier | 2 | Aug |
| 23.19 | 0.3 | Sherri | Howard | USA | 62 | 7 | Jenner | San Jose | 31 | May |
| 23.21 | 1.2 | Olga | Zolotaryova | SU | 61 | 1 | | Kiev | 26 | Jul |
| 23.21 | 0.0 | Nadezhda | Georgieva | BUL | 61 | 2r3 | ASV | Köln | 17 | Aug |
| 23.23 | 1.7 | Kerry | Johnson | AUS | 63 | 1 | | Canberra | 6 | Mar |
| 23.23 | -0.1 | Lyubov | Aleksandrova | SU | 65 | 5 | Spart | Tashkent | 20 | Sep |
| A23.25 | 0.1 | Jillian | Richardson | CAN | 65 | 2r1 | | Provo | 26 | May |
| A23.25 | | Ansie | Basson | RSA | 66 | 2 | | Bloemfontein | 5 | Dec |
| 23.26 | 1.3 | Angela | Phipps (80) | CAN | 64 | 1 | | Baton Rouge | 13 | Apr |
| | | | | | | | | | | |
| 23.27 | -1.2 | Gervaise | McCraw | USA | 64 | 1 | | Los Angeles | 22 | Mar |
| 23.27 | | Odessa | Smalls | USA | 64 | 3h1 | NCAA | Indianapolis | 4 | Jun |
| 23.27 | | Maryke | Smith | RSA | 66 | 1 | | Durban | 20 | Dec |
| 23.29 | 1.8 | Dagmar | Neubauer | GDR | 62 | 1r2 | | Berlin | 20 | Aug |

| Mark | Wind | Name | | Nat | Yr | Pos | Meet | Venue | Date |
|------|------|------|------|-----|----|-----|------|-------|------|
| 23.30 | 0.1 | LaVonna | Martin | USA | 66 | 2h1 | | Knoxville | 17 May |
| 23.30 | | Ana | Quirot | CUB | 63 | 1 | | Habana | 9 Jun |
| 23.31 | 0.3 | Laurence | Bily | FRA | 63 | 3 | | Saint-Denis | 21 Jun |
| 23.31 | 0.6 | Katrin | Krabbe | GDR | 69 | 3 | WC-j | Athinai | 19 Jul |
| 23.32 | 0.8 | Ann-Louise | Skoglund | SWE | 62 | 1 | NC | Karlskrona | 3 Aug |
| 23.33 | -0.1 | Natalya | German (90) | SU | 63 | 1h | NC | Kiev | 15 Jul |
| 23.34 | 0.6 | Kim | Dunlap | USA | 64 | 2 | | Madison | 24 May |
| 23.34 | 0.9 | Katya | Ilieva | BUL | 63 | 3 | | Sofia | 25 May |
| 23.35 | -2.8 | Lydia | de Vega | PHI | 64 | 1 | | Walnut, CA | 10 May |
| 23.35 | 1.4 | Maria | Pinigina | SU | 58 | 1 | | Riga | 31 May |
| 23.35 | -0.9 | Joan | Baptiste | UK | 59 | 5 | | Gateshead | 5 Aug |
| 23.35 | -0.3 | Irina | Kot | SU | 67 | 3s | Spart | Tashkent | 19 Sep |
| 23.36 | 1.7 | Sharon | Stewart | AUS | 65 | 2 | | Canberra | 6 Mar |
| A23.36 | 0.1 | Charmaine | Crooks | CAN | 61 | 3r1 | | Provo | 26 May |
| 23.36 | 0.0 | Cornelia | Oschkenat | GDR | 61 | 4 | | Erfurt | 1 Jun |
| 23.36 | 1.2 | Christelle | Bulteau (100) | FRA | 63 | 3 | v Pol, | Spa Epinal | 5 Jul |
| 23.36 | 1.2 | Oksana | Kovalyova (101) | SU | 69 | 1 | v GDR-j | Karl-Marx-Stadt | 10 Aug |

23.37 -0.3 Ilrey Oliver JAM 62 17 May
23.37 0.3 Marina Kleyankina SU 62 16 Jul
A23.38 Angela Thacker USA 64 1 May
23.38 -0.5 Gail Devers USA 66 3 May
23.38 Pam Qualls USA 66 4 Jun
A23.39 Fransie Pieterse RSA 61 19 Feb
23.39 Terri Dendy USA 65 17 May
23.39 0.3 Yelena Nasonkina SU 62 16 Jul
23.39 1.1 Jennifer Stoute (110) UK 65 28 Jul

23.39 -1.7 Sandra Whittaker UK 63 28 Aug
23.40 0.5 Tracey Cofield USA 67 31 May
23.40 0.3 Olga Kvast SU 63 16 Jul
23.41 0.3 Anke Behmer GDR 61 6 Jul
23.41 1.1 Fabienne Ficher FRA 66 7 Sep
23.42 1.7 Sue Alton AUS 66 6 Mar
23.42 2.0 Carla Mercurio ITA 60 19 Jun
23.42 0.7 Vroni Werthmüller SWZ 59 21 Jun
23.42 Tatyana Papilina SU 67 20 Jul
23.43 Denise Blackman (120) BAR 65 19 Apr

23.43 Iolanda Oanţă RUM 65 25 May
23.43 1.2 Undine Bremer GDR 61 29 Jun
23.43 0.5 Marina Shmonina SU 65 16 Jul
23.43 1.1 Maree Chapman AUS 63 28 Jul
23.43 1.8 Ronny Uebel GDR 63 20 Aug
23.44 -0.4 Nelli Cooman HOL 64 4 Jun
23.44 1.2 Kornelija Šinković YUG 64 27 Jun
23.44 0.4 Camille Coates JAM 66 3 Jul
23.44 0.3 Vera Zaitseva SU 63 10 Aug
23.44 0.2 P.T. Usha (130) IND 64 1 Oct

23.45 Janet Davis USA 65 12 Apr
23.45 2.0 Janice Marshall USA 4 May
A23.45 1.3 Cathie Chrusch CAN 60 26 May
23.46 Kerstin Walther GDR 61 1 Jun
23.46 0.5 Yelena Petrova SU 62 16 Jul
23.46 0.6 Carlette Guidry USA 68 19 Jul
A23.47 1.1 Angela Bridgeman UK 63 10 May

23.48 0.2 Muriel Leroy FRA 68 18 Jul
23.48 -0.1 Marina Krivosheina SU 67 20 Sep
23.49 -0.1 Antonina Nastoburko SU 59 15 Jul
(140)
23.50 1.7 Martha Grossenbacher HOL 59 12 Jul
23.51 -1.4 Florence Griffith USA 59 13 Aug
23.52 0.0 Michelle King USA 64 27 Apr
23.52 Tamaris Fiebig GDR 70 18 May
23.52 0.4 Amparo Caicedo COL 65 3 Jul
23.52 -1.7 Genowefa Błaszak POL 57 8 Aug
A23.53 Natasha Kaiser USA 67 17 May
23.54 0.0 Simone Jacobs UK 66 11 Jul
23.54 -0.4 Mihaela Ene RUM 62 7 Sep
23.55 1.2 Marina Stepanova SU 50 18 May
(150)
23.55 0.5 Anke Köninger FRG 61 13 Jul
23.55 0.5 Resi März FRG 60 13 Jul
23.55 1.6 Natalya Potapova SU 65 16 Aug
23.55 -0.8 Tatyana Ledovskaya SU 66 19 Sep
23.56 0.0 Beverley Peterson NZ 56 9 Mar
A23.56 1.1 Cynthia Henry JAM 62 10 May
23.56 Bridgette Tate USA 66 23 May
23.56 0.3 Galina Rakhmetova SU 61 16 Jul
23.56 1.7 Cornelia Feuerbach GDR 63 20 Aug
23.57 2.0 Irma Kőnye (160) HUN 54 9 Aug
23.57 2.0 Joanna Smolarek POL 65 17 Aug
A23.58 1.1 Lola Ogunde NIG 64 10 May
23.58 0.6 Blanca Lacambra SPA 65 16 Jul
23.59 0.9 Linetta Wilson USA 67 24 May
23.59 -1.2 Ewa Pisiewicz POL 62 25 May
23.59 -1.0 Ina Cordes FRG 68 18 Jul
23.59 -0.3 Magali Seguin FRA 64 10 Aug
23.60 -0.3 Jeanette Düring GDR 65 17 Aug
23.61 Angela McClatchey USA 67 23 May
23.61 0.9 Valya Valova (170) BUL 61 25 May
23.61 0.0 Tami Stiles USA 68 30 May
A23.61 Michelle du Toit RSA 64 5 Dec

WOMEN 1986

| Mark | Wind | Name | | Nat | Yr | Pos | Meet | Venue | Date |
|------|------|------|------|-----|----|----|------|-------|------|
| 23.63 | | Carla | McLaughlin | USA | 67 | 3 May | | | |
| 23.63 | | Robin | Benjamin | USA | 66 | 4 May | | | |
| 23.64 | 0.0 | Rufina | Ubah | NIG | 59 | 27 Apr | | | |
| 23.65 | -1.2 | Iwona | Pakula | POL | 62 | 25 May | | | |
| 23.65 | -0.1 | Elvira | Kotoviene | SU | 58 | 8 Jun | | | |
| 23.65 | 1.2 | Dijana | Ištvanović | YUG | 57 | 27 Jun | | | |
| 23.66 | 1.3 | Sandie | Richards | JAM | 68 | 31 Mar | | | |
| 23.66 | 1.4 | Natalya | Grigoryeva | SU | 62 | 8 Jun | | | |
| | | | (180) | | | | | | |
| 23.66 | 1.3 | Gisela | Kinzel | FRG | 61 | 28 Jun | | | |
| A23.66 | | Elise | van Vuuren | RSA | 64 | 5 Dec | | | |
| 23.67 | 0.3 | Natalya | Shubenkova | SU | 57 | 6 Jul | | | |
| 23.67 | 1.2 | Anett | Walter | GDR | 68 | 10 Aug | | | |
| 23.67 | 0.9 | Silke | Knoll | FRG | 67 | 7 Sep | | | |
| 23.68 | | Anita | Howard | USA | 69 | 9 May | | | |
| A23.68 | 0.1 | Molly | Killingbeck | CAN | 59 | 26 May | | | |
| 23.69 | -2.9 | Robin | Stephens | USA | 63 | 29 Mar | | | |
| 23.69 | -3.3 | Alice | Jackson | USA | 58 | 20 Apr | | | |
| 23.69 | | Comfort | | Igeh | (190) | | | NIG | 63 24 May |
| 23.69 | | Corina | | Rosioru | | | | RUM | 68 25 May |
| 23.69 | 1.3 | Helga | | Arendt | | | | FRG | 64 28 Jun |
| 23.70 | | Leisa | | Davis-Knowles | | | | USA | 63 12 Apr |
| 23.70 | 0.0 | Zelda | | Johnson | | | | USA | 64 27 Apr |
| 23.70 | 2.0 | Linda | | Coleman | | | | USA | 66 4 May |
| 23.70 | | Heike | | Theele | | | | GDR | 64 1 Jun |
| 23.71 | -1.0 | Debbie | | Flintoff | | | | AUS | 60 21 Jan |
| 23.71 | -1.1 | Diane | | Holden | | | | AUS | 63 16 Mar |
| 23.71 | -2.3 | Rositsa | | Stamenova | | | | BUL | 55 22 Jun |
| 23.72 | 0.6 | Sonja | | Fridy | (200) | | | USA | 65 19 Apr |
| 23.72 | -2.8 | Andrea | | Rolfe | | | | USA | 66 10 May |
| 23.72 | 0.9 | Alice | | Bell | | | | USA | 24 May |
| 23.72 | | Marie-Jose | | Hontas | | | | FRA | 65 29 Jun |
| 23.72 | 2.0 | Kaye | | Jeffrey | (204) | | | UK | 63 17 Aug |

Indoor marks :

| | | | | | | | | | |
|--|--|--|--|--|--|--|--|--|--|
| 22.33 | i - | | Koch | | | 1 | NC | Senftenberg | 16 Feb |
| 22.77 | i - | Kirsten | Emmelmann | GDR | 61 | 2 | NC | Senftenberg | 16 Feb |
| 22.81 | i - | Ewa | Pisiewicz | POL | 62 | 1 | | Stuttgart | 2 Feb |
| 23.44 | i*- | Florence | Griffith | USA | 59 | 28 Feb | | | |
| 23.51 | i - | Jeanette | Düring | GDR | 65 | 16 Feb | | | |

Best low altitude marks :

| | | | | | | | | |
|--|--|--|--|--|--|--|--|--|
| 23.17 | | Armstrong | | 1 | | | Port Elizabeth | 21 Apr |
| 23.32 | | Naude | | 2 | | | Port Elizabeth | 21 Apr |
| 23.34 | 0.7 | Bailey | | 2 | NC | | Ottawa | 22 Jun |
| 23.36 | | Greene | | 1 | | | Houston | 24 May |
| 23.40 | 0.7 | Lawrence | 22 Jun | 23.53 0.7 | | | Richardson | 22 Jun |
| 23.47 | | Thacker | 18 Apr | 23.71 | | | Kaiser | 3 May |

---

| | 1 | 10 | 20 | 30 | 50 | 100 | Under 23.00 | Under 23.50 |
|------|------|------|------|------|------|------|------|------|
| 1982 | 21.76 | 22.39 | 22.91 | 22.96 | 23.23 | 23.56 | 31 | 95 |
| 1983 | 21.82 | 22.42 | 22.79 | 22.97 | 23.15 | 23.54 | 32 | 94 |
| 1984 | 21.71 | 22.36 | 22.65 | 22.75 | 22.98 | 23.39 | 51 | 116 |
| 1985 | 21.78 | 22.55 | 22.75 | 22.92 | 23.19 | 23.58 | 35 | 89 |
| 1986 | 21.71 | 22.39 | 22.60 | 22.86 | 23.02 | 23.36 | 47 | 140 |

---

Marks made with assisting wind > 2 m/s:

| | | | | | | | | |
|--|--|--|--|--|--|--|--|--|
| 22.24 | 2.2 | | Marshall | | | 1 | TAC | Eugene | 21 Jun |
| 22.35 | 2.1 | Juliet | Cuthbert | JAM | 64 | 1 | | Houston | 18 May |
| A22.39 | 2.9 | Evette | Armstrong | RSA | 65 | 1h | NC | Germiston | 12 Apr |

| Mark | Wind | Name | | Nat | Yr | Pos | Meet | Venue | Date |
|------|------|------|------|-----|----|-----|------|-------|------|
| 22.55 | 3.3 | Els | Vader | HOL | 59 | 1 | NC | Amsterdam | 12 Jul |
| 22.77 | 2.7 | Mary | Onyali | NIG | 68 | 1 | | Houston | 9 May |
| 22.84 | 2.1 | Dannette | Young | USA | 64 | 1 | | Los Angeles | 23 May |
| 23.03 | 3.3 | Nelli | Cooman | HOL | 64 | 2 | NC | Amsterdam | 12 Jul |
| 23.04 | 2.1 | Blanca | Lacambra | SPA | 65 | 1 | | Salamanca | 12 Jul |
| A23.05 | 3.3 | Angela | Thacker | USA | 64 | 1h1 | | Boulder | 17 May |
| 23.15 | 2.3 | Odessa | Smalls (10) | USA | 64 | 3h1 | TAC | Eugene | 21 Jun |
| | | | | | | | | | |
| 23.18 | 2.1 | Joan | Baptiste | UK | 59 | 1 | | Cwmbran | 13 Sep |
| 23.21 | 4.9 | Pam | Qualls | USA | 66 | 1 | | Pullman | 10 May |
| 23.22 | | Maria | Usifo | NIG | 64 | 1 | | College Sta, TX | 29 Mar |
| 23.23 | | Lisa | Ford | USA | 66 | 2 | | College Sta, TX | 29 Mar |
| 23.23 | 2.1 | Vivianne | Spence | JAM | | 2 | | Los Angeles | 23 May |
| 23.23 | 2.1 | Paula | Dunn | UK | 64 | 2 | | Cwmbran | 13 Sep |
| 23.25 | 2.1 | Katrin | Krabbe | GDR | 69 | 1 | | Berlin | 10 Jul |
| 23.29 | | Camille | Coates | JAM | 66 | 1 | | Arlington | 10 May |
| 23.30 | 2.1 | Patrice | Carpenter | USA | 65 | 3 | | Los Angeles | 23 May |
| 23.34 | 2.1 | Simone | Jacobs (20) | UK | 66 | 1 | WAAA | Birmingham | 7 Jun |

| 23.37 | 3.9 | Muriel | Leroy | FRA 68 | 6 Jul | | 23.61 | 2.1 | Helen | Barnett | UK 58 | 7 Jun |
|-------|-----|--------|-------|--------|-------|---|-------|-----|-------|---------|-------|-------|
| 23.38 | | Sally | Gunnell | UK 66 | 11 Jul | | 23.62 | 2.4 | Davera | Taylor | USA 65 | 29 Mar |
| A23.39 | | Angela | Bridgeman | UK 63 | 12 Apr | | 23.62 | | Gerda | Haas | AUT 65 | 12 Jul |
| 23.43 | | Elena | Lina | RUM 54 | 9 Aug | | 23.63 | | Ramona | Steici | RUM 67 | 9 Aug |
| 23.44 | 4.9 | Donna | Dennis | USA 64 | 10 May | | 23.63 | 2.6 | Wendy | Jeal | UK 60 | 14 Sep |
| 23.46* | | Kim | Walker | USA 68 | 3 May | | 23.66 | 2.1 | Eldece | Clarke | BAH 65 | 23 May |
| 23.54 | 2.2 | Diane | Holden | AUS 63 | 2 Feb | | 23.67 | 4.1 | Rita | Angotzi | ITA 67 | 25 May |
| 23.54 | 2.7 | Mosunmola | Soneye | NIG 64 | 9 May | | 23.69 | 2.1 | Katrice | Harris | USA 64 | 18 May |
| 23.55* | | Chryste | Gaines | USA 68 | 3 May | | 23.70 | | Marie-France | Johanssen | FRA 60 | 26 Apr |
| 23.58 | 2.7 | Evan | Williams (30) | USA 65 | 9 May | | | | | (40) | | |
| | | | | | | | 23.70 | | Tatyana | Sergiyenko | SU 64 | 16 Aug |
| 23.60 | 2.1 | Cristina | Perez | SPA 65 | 12 Jul | | 23.71 | 2.7 | Gwen | Williams (42) | USA | 9 May |

**Hand timing:**

| 22.5 | 1.5 | Marina | Stepanova | SU | 50 | 1 | Leningrad | 27 Jun |
|------|-----|--------|-----------|----|----|---|-----------|--------|
| 22.5 | 0.7 | Natalya | German | SU | 63 | 1 | Kiev | 30 Aug |
| 22.8 | | Tsvetanka | Ilieva | BUL | 63 | 1 | Sofia | 4 May |
| 22.9 | | Carlette | Guidry | USA | 68 | 1 | Houston | 20 Jun |
| 22.9 | 1.7 | Olga | Frolova | SU | 64 | h | Leningrad | 26 Jun |
| 22.9 | 0.0 | Lyubov | Aleksandrova | SU | 65 | 1 | Alma-Ata | 30 Aug |
| 23.0 | | Katya | Ilieva | BUL | 63 | 2 | Sofia | 4 May |
| 23.0 | 0.0 | Natalya | Pomoshchnikova | SU | 65 | 1 | Moskva | 10 May |

| 23.2 | | Judi | Brown-King | USA 61 | 5 Apr | 23.3 | 0.3 | Antonina | Nastoburko | SU 59 | 28 Jun |
|------|---|------|------------|--------|-------|------|-----|----------|------------|-------|--------|
| 23.2 | | Linetta | Wilson (10) | USA 67 | 3 May | 23.3 | | Vera | Zaitseva | SU 63 | 29 Jun |
| | | | | | | 23.3 | | Yelena | Kelchevskaya | SU 55 | 19 Jul |
| 23.2 | | Yelena | Petrova | SU 62 | 16 May | 23.3 | | Gisela | Kinzel | FRG 61 | 9 Aug |
| 23.2 | | Cynthia | Titus | USA 69 | 17 May | 23.3 | 0.0 | Vera | Sevalnikova | SU 63 | 30 Aug |
| 23.2 | 1.4 | Kornelija | Šinković | YUG 64 | 8 Jun | 23.3 | 0.0 | Natalya | Miljauskiene | SU 63 | 30 Aug |
| 23.2 | 0.0 | Marina | Shmonina | SU 65 | 14 Jun | 23.4 | | Lisa | Ford | USA 66 | 12 Apr |
| 23.2 | | Daniela | Ferrian | ITA 61 | 14 Jun | A23.4 | 1.9 | Cynthia | Henry (30) | JAM 62 | 12 Apr |
| 23.2 | 0.3 | Tatyana | Kruglova | SU 63 | 27 Jun | | | | | | |
| 23.2 | 1.5 | Larisa | Lesnykh | SU 64 | 27 Jun | 23.4 | | Kim | Walker | USA 68 | 17 May |
| 23.2 | | P.T. | Usha | IND 64 | 14 Aug | 23.4 | | Pauline | Darkenteil | USA 68 | 17 May |
| 23.2 | 1.1 | Olga | Kvast | SU 63 | 29 Aug | 23.4 | 0.0 | Galina | Rakhmetova | SU 61 | 14 Jun |
| 23.2 | 0.7 | Tatyana | Oksimets (20) | SU 64 | 30 Aug | 23.4 | | Yelena | Kuzina | SU 66 | 29 Jun |
| | | | | | | 23.4 | | Lidia | Yelagina | SU 64 | 19 Jul |
| 23.3 | 2.0 | Maria | Pinigina | SU 58 | 15 May | 23.4 | -0.8 | Blanca | Lacambra | SPA 65 | 3 Aug |
| 23.3 | | Marina | Sereda | SU 64 | 13 Jun | 23.4 | | Irina | Skibinskikh | SU 61 | |
| | | | | | | | | | (37) | | |

WOMEN 1986

| Mark | Wind | Name | | Nat | Yr | Pos | Meet | Venue | Date |
|------|------|------|--|-----|-----|-----|------|-------|------|

Marks made with assisting wind > 2 m/s:

| Mark | Wind | Name | | Nat | Yr | Pos | | | Meet | Venue | Date |
|------|------|------|--|-----|-----|-----|--|--|------|-------|------|
| 22.9 | 3.3 | Marina | Shmonina | SU | 65 | 1 | | | | Tiraspol | 10 Aug |
| 23.2 | 4.0 | Sandra | Whittaker | UK | 63 | 1 Jun | 23.3 | 4.0 Janis | | Neilson | UK 63 1 Jun |
| A23.3 | | Angela | Bridgeman | UK | 63 | 29 Mar | | | | | |

# 400 METRES

| Mark | | Name | | Nat | Yr | Pos | Meet | Venue | Date |
|------|--|------|--|-----|-----|-----|------|-------|------|
| 48.22 | Marita | Koch | | GDR | 57 | 1 | EC | Stuttgart | 28 Aug |
| 49.17 | | Koch | | | | 1 | GP | Roma | 10 Sep |
| 49.24 | | Koch | | | | 1 | GO | Dresden | 16 Aug |
| 49.28 | | Koch | | | | 1 | VD | Bruxelles | 5 Sep |
| 49.67 | Olga | Vladykina | | SU | 63 | 2 | EC | Stuttgart | 28 Aug |
| 49.76 | | Vladykina | | | | 1 | v GDR | Tallinn | 21 Jun |
| 49.79 | Petra | Müller | | GDR | 65 | 2 | GO | Dresden | 16 Aug |
| 49.83 | Tatána | Kocembová | | CS | 62 | 1 | PTS | Bratislava | 14 Jun |
| 49.84 | | Müller | | | | 1 | OD | Dresden | 3 Jul |
| 49.84 | | Müller | | | | 1s1 | EC | Stuttgart | 27 Aug |
| 49.85 | | Müller | | | | 2 | v SU | Tallinn | 21 Jun |
| 49.88 | | Müller | | | | 3 | EC | Stuttgart | 28 Aug |
| 49.96 | | Vladykina | | | | 1 | GWG | Moskva | 9 Jul |
| 49.99 | Pam | Marshall | | USA | 60 | 1 | Pepsi | Westwood | 17 May |
| A50.12 | Myrtle | Bothma | | RSA | 64 | 1 | NC | Germiston | 11 Apr |
| 50.18 | Lillie | Leatherwood | | USA | 64 | 1 | PTG | London | 11 Jul |
| 50.18 | | Vladykina | | | | 1 | Spart | Tashkent | 18 Sep |
| 50.21 | Valerie | Brisco-Hooks | | USA | 60 | 2 | GP | Roma | 10 Sep |
| 50.23 | | Vladykina | | | | 2s1 | EC | Stuttgart | 27 Aug |
| 50.24 | Diane | Dixon | | USA | 64 | 1 | Bis1 | Oslo | 5 Jul |
| 50.29 | Maria | Pinigina (10) | | SU | 58 | 2 | GWG | Moskva | 9 Jul |
| 50.29 | | Leatherwood | | | | 1 | WK | Zürich | 13 Aug |
| 50.29 | | Brisco-Hooks | | | | 2 | VD | Bruxelles | 5 Sep |
| 50.31 | | Müller | | | | 1 | | Neubrandenburg | 7 Jun |
| 50.31 | | Brisco-Hooks | | | | 1 | ISTAF | W Berlin | 15 Aug |
| 50.41 | Ana | Quirot | | CUB | 63 | 1 | Barr | Habana | 14 Jun |
| 50.41 | | Dixon | | | | 1 | TAC | Eugene | 21 Jun |
| 50.43 | Sabine | Busch | | GDR | 62 | 2 | PTS | Bratislava | 14 Jun |
| 50.43 | Kirsten | Emmelmann | | GDR | 61 | 4 | EC | Stuttgart | 28 Aug |
| 50.47 | | Leatherwood | | | | 3 | GWG | Moskva | 9 Jul |
| | | (30/13) | | | | | | | |
| A50.57 | Evette | Armstrong | | RSA | 65 | 1 | | Germiston | 2 Apr |
| 50.70 | Genowefa | Błaszak | | POL | 57 | 3 | ISTAF | W Berlin | 15 Aug |
| 50.78 | Debbie | Flintoff | | AUS | 60 | 3 | PTG | London | 11 Jul |
| 50.80 | Inna | Yevseyeva | | SU | 64 | 2 | Spart | Tashkent | 18 Sep |
| 50.83 | Gisela | Kinzel | | FRG | 61 | 4 | ISTAF | W Berlin | 15 Aug |
| 50.84 | Charmaine | Crooks | | CAN | 61 | 2 | Pepsi | Westwood | 17 May |
| 50.92 | Dagmar | Neubauer (20) | | GDR | 62 | 4 | GO | Dresden | 16 Aug |
| 50.94 | Grace | Jackson | | JAM | 61 | 1 | | Knoxville | 24 May |
| 51.01 | Aelita | Yurchenko | | SU | 65 | 3 | Spart | Tashkent | 18 Sep |
| 51.15 | Ute | Thimm | | FRG | 58 | 5 | EC | Stuttgart | 28 Aug |
| A51.16 | Madele | Naude | | RSA | 63 | 2 | NC | Germiston | 11 Apr |
| 51.19 | Annett | Hesselbarth | | GDR | 66 | 5 | GO | Dresden | 16 Aug |
| 51.20 | Irina | Chapala | | SU | 64 | 4 | Spart | Tashkent | 18 Sep |
| 51.30 | Ewa | Kasprzyk | | POL | 57 | 1 | | Hania | 25 May |

| Mark | Name | | Nat | Yr | Pos | Meet | Venue | Date |
|---|---|---|---|---|---|---|---|---|
| 51.40 | Pepa | Pavlova | BUL | 61 | 1 | NC | Sofia | 13 Aug |
| 51.44 | Delisa | Walton-Floyd | USA | 61 | 1r2 | MSR | Walnut, CA | 27 Apr |
| 51.44 | Marzena | Wojdecka (30) | POL | 63 | 1 | NC | Grudziadz | 28 Jun |
| 51.44 | Olga | Nazarova | SU | 65 | 2h1 | NC | Kiev | 14 Jul |
| 51.44 | Cristieana | Matei | RUM | 62 | 5 | WK | Zürich | 13 Aug |
| 51.45 | Rositsa | Stamenova | BUL | 55 | 1 | Balk | Ljubljana | 6 Sep |
| A51.48 | Natasha | Kaiser | USA | 67 | 1 | | Boulder | 18 May |
| 51.48 | Olga | Pesnopevtseva | SU | 68 | s | Spart | Tashkent | 17 Sep |
| 51.53 | Blanca | Lacambra | SPA | 65 | 1 | | Madrid | 20 Jun |
| 51.55 | Denean | Howard | USA | 64 | 2h2 | TAC | Eugene | 19 Jun |
| 51.55 | Jillian | Richardson | CAN | 65 | 2 | NC | Ottawa | 21 Jun |
| 51.55 | Vineta | Ikauniece | SU | 62 | 2 | NC | Kiev | 15 Jul |
| 51.56 | Lyudmila | Belova (40) | SU | 58 | 3h1 | NC | Kiev | 14 Jul |
| 51.57 | Chandra | Cheeseborough | USA | 59 | 5 | PTG | London | 11 Jul |
| 51.60 | Larisa | Dzhigalova | SU | 62 | 1 | | Sochi | 24 May |
| 51.60 | Nadezhda | Olizarenko | SU | 53 | 6 | GWG | Moskva | 9 Jul |
| 51.66 | Maree | Chapman | AUS | 63 | 6 | PTG | London | 11 Jul |
| 51.66 | Mihaela | Ene | RUM | 62 | 2 | Balk | Ljubljana | 6 Sep |
| 51.69 | Marina | Stepanova | SU | 50 | 1 | | Sochi | 18 May |
| 51.69 | Ann-Louise | Skoglund | SWE | 62 | 4 | DNG | Stockholm | 1 Jul |
| 51.70 | Molly | Killingbeck | CAN | 59 | 4 | Nik | Nice | 15 Jul |
| 51.71 | Gaby | Bussmann | FRG | 59 | 2 | NC | W Berlin | 12 Jul |
| 51.74 | Larisa | Lesnykh (50) | SU | 64 | 6 | Spart | Tashkent | 18 Sep |
| 51.75 | Brenda | Cliette | USA | 63 | 3 | Jenner | San Jose | 31 May |
| 51.76 | Ilrey | Oliver | JAM | 62 | 2 | | Knoxville | 18 May |
| 51.77 | Marita | Payne | CAN | 60 | 2 | | Paris | 22 Jul |
| 51.81 | Judit | Forgács | HUN | 59 | 1 | NC | Budapest | 15 Aug |
| 51.83 | Airat | Bakare | NIG | 66 | 1 | | Russellville | 24 May |
| 51.85 | Fabienne | Ficher | FRA | 66 | 4 | | Paris | 22 Jul |
| 51.85 | Karin | Lix | FRG | 65 | 1 | NC-j | Wetzlar | 6 Sep |
| 51.87 | Tatyana | Ledovskaya | SU | 66 | 7 | Spart | Tashkent | 18 Sep |
| 51.88 | Kathy | Cook | UK | 60 | 3 | CG | Edinburgh | 27 Jul |
| 51.90 | Rochelle | Stevens (60) | USA | 66 | 1r1 | King | Atlanta | 20 Apr |
| 51.92 | Els | Vader | HOL | 59 | 1 | FBK | Hengelo | 27 Jun |
| 51.94 | Marina | Kharlamova | SU | 62 | 5h1 | NC | Kiev | 14 Jul |
| 51.95 | Natalya | Bochina | SU | 62 | h | NC | Kiev | 14 Jul |
| 51.95 | Sigrun | Wodars | GDR | 65 | 1 | | Berlin | 20 Aug |
| 52.00 | Malena | Andonova | BUL | 57 | 1 | NC | Sofia | 13 Aug |
| 52.02 | Susann | Sieger | GDR | 68 | 1 | WC-j | Athinai | 18 Jul |
| 52.03 | Nadezhda | Zabolotneva | SU | 61 | 2 | | Moskva | 9 Aug |
| 52.05 | Ronny | Uebel | GDR | 63 | 8 | OD | Dresden | 3 Jul |
| 52.05 | Juliana | Marinova | BUL | 67 | 2 | | Sofia | 3 Aug |
| 52.10 | Alice | Jackson (70) | USA | 58 | 2s2 | TAC | Eugene | 20 Jun |
| 52.12 | Terri | Dendy | USA | 65 | 3 | NCAA | Indianapolis | 7 Jun |
| 52.13 | Katya | Ilieva | BUL | 63 | 1 | | Sofia | 24 May |
| 52.16 | P.T. | Usha | IND | 64 | 1 | AsiG | Seoul | 4 Oct |
| 52.18 | Sandie | Richards | JAM | 68 | 1 | | Abymes | 30 Mar |
| 52.18 | Nathalie | Simon | FRA | 62 | 1 | v Gre, | Yug Athinai | 16 Aug |
| 52.22 | Helga | Arendt | FRG | 64 | 1r2 | ASV | Köln | 17 Aug |
| 52.23 | Yordanka | Stoyanova | BUL | 59 | 3 | NC | Sofia | 13 Aug |
| 52.24 | Gervaise | McCraw | USA | 64 | 4 | NCAA | Indianapolis | 7 Jun |
| 52.25 | Tsvetanka | Ilieva | BUL | 63 | 3 | Nar | Sofia | 31 May |
| 52.25 | Janeene | Vickers (80) | USA | 68 | 4 | WC-j | Athinai | 18 Jul |

| Mark | Name | | Nat | Yr | Pos | Meet | Venue | Date |
|---|---|---|---|---|---|---|---|---|
| 52.26 | Leisa | Davis-Knowles | USA | 63 | 1 | KansR | Lawrence | 19 Apr |
| 52.26 | Chewuakii | Knighten | USA | 67 | 1 | | Los Angeles | 3 May |
| 52.26 | Iolanda | Oanţă | RUM | 65 | 1h | NC | Piteşti | 7 Aug |
| 52.27 | Sharon | Stewart | AUS | 65 | 1 | | Melbourne | 6 Feb |
| A52.28 | Ansie | Basson | RSA | 66 | 2 | | Bloemfontein | 5 Nov |
| 52.29 | Elena | Lina | RUM | 54 | 2 | NC | Piteşti | 7 Aug |
| 52.30 | Ute | Lix | FRG | 65 | 2 | NC-j | Wetzlar | 6 Sep |
| 52.32 | Irina | Zaitseva | SU | 63 | 2 | | Kiev | 25 Jul |
| 52.37 | Cathy | Rattray | JAM | 63 | 2 | | Villanova | 8 Jun |
| A52.38 | Linetta | Wilson        (90) | USA | 67 | 2 | | Boulder | 18 May |
| 52.40 | Margarita | Khromova | SU | 63 | 3 | | Moskva | 9 Aug |
| 52.40 | Norfalia | Carabali | COL | 67 | 1 | | Stockholm | 12 Aug |
| 52.41 | Jearl | Miles | USA | 66 | 1 | | Tallahassee | 31 May |
| 52.42 | Maicel | Malone | USA | 69 | 1 | | Indianapolis | 31 May |
| 52.43 | Sadia | Sowunmi | NIG | 64 | 2 | | Houston | 24 May |
| 52.46 | Helen | Barnett | UK | 58 | 5h3 | EC | Stuttgart | 26 Aug |
| 52.47 | Lilia | Nurutdinova | SU | 63 | 1 | | Volgograd | 7 Sep |
| 52.48 | Larisa | Glavenko | SU | 63 | 1 | | Tallinn | 28 Jun |
| 52.50 | Tracey | Cofield | USA | 67 | 2 | | Tallahassee | 31 May |
| 52.50 | Regine | Berg        (100) | BEL | 58 | 1 | NC | Bruxelles | 10 Aug |

| Mark | Name | | Nat | Yr | Date |
|---|---|---|---|---|---|
| 52.51 | Ilona | Pál | HUN | 54 | 15 Aug |
| 52.52 | Judi | Brown-King | USA | 61 | 31 May |
| 52.53 | Małgorzata | Dunecka | POL | 56 | 28 Jun |
| A52.54 | Michelle | Maxey | USA | 64 | 18 May |
| 52.55 | Sherri | Howard | USA | 62 | 5 Jun |
| 52.58 | Elżbieta | Kapusta | POL | 60 | 28 Jun |
| 52.60 | Barbara | Flowers | USA | 66 | 18 May |
| 52.60 | Christine | Näthler | GDR | 66 | 3 Jul |
| 52.61 | Yelena | Didilenko | SU | 61 | 14 Jun |
| 52.61 | Yelena | Golesheva | SU | 66 | 17 Sep |
| | | (110) | | | |
| 52.63 | Yelena | Goncharova | SU | 63 | 26 Apr |
| 52.63 | Vera | Zaitseva | SU | 63 | 14 Aug |
| 52.65 | Adina | Valdez | TRI | | 10 May |
| 52.66 | Svobodka | Damyanova | BUL | 55 | 13 Aug |
| 52.67 | Gerda | Haas | AUT | 65 | 13 Jul |
| 52.68 | Evelyne | Elien | FRA | 64 | 16 Aug |
| 52.68 | Ellen | Fiedler | GDR | 58 | 12 Sep |
| A52.69 | Esmie | Lawrence | CAN | 61 | 24 May |
| 52.71 | Schowonda | Williams | USA | 66 | 30 May |
| 52.75 | Janice | Kelly (120) | STK | | 17 May |
| 52.76 | Adriane | Diamond | USA | 65 | 24 May |
| 52.78 | Milena | Strnadová | CS | 61 | 31 May |
| 52.79 | Andrea | Thomas | JAM | 68 | 20 Apr |
| 52.80 | Althea | Thomas | JAM | 67 | 24 May |
| 52.82 | Marina | Kleyankina | SU | 62 | 9 Aug |
| 52.86 | Sharieffa | Barksdale | USA | 61 | 17 Aug |
| 52.87 | Nawal | El Moutawakil | MOR | 62 | 19 Apr |
| 52.88 | Undine | Bremer | GDR | 61 | 27 Jun |
| A52.91 | Angela | Bailey | CAN | 62 | 26 May |
| A52.93 | Fransie | Pieterse (130) | RSA | 61 | 19 Feb |
| 52.93 | Cosetta | Campana | ITA | 61 | 19 Jun |
| 52.93 | Marjo | van Agt | HOL | 58 | 27 Jun |
| 52.96 | Patrice | Carpenter | USA | 65 | 24 May |
| 52.96 | Lyubov | Kiryukhina | SU | 63 | 25 Jul |
| 52.98 | Cheryl | Thibedeau | CAN | 66 | 21 Jun |

| Mark | Name | | Nat | Yr | Date |
|---|---|---|---|---|---|
| 53.00 | Robin | Stephens | USA | 63 | 12 Apr |
| 53.00 | Cristina | Perez | SPA | 65 | 20 Jun |
| 53.01 | Jana | Mrovcová | CS | 67 | 12 Jul |
| 53.01 | Erica | Rossi | ITA | 55 | 7 Sep |
| 53.03 | Joetta | Clark    (140) | USA | 62 | 8 Jun |
| 53.05 | Maria | Figueredo | BRA | 63 | 13 Jul |
| 53.06 | Renee | Ross | USA | 63 | 27 Apr |
| 53.06 | Denise | Mitchell | USA | 66 | 18 May |
| 53.07 | Sonja | Fridy | USA | 65 | 10 May |
| 53.08 | Lăcrămioara | Andrei | RUM | 68 | 14 Jun |
| 53.08 | Iulia | State | RUM | 59 | 7 Aug |
| 53.09 | Angela | Piggford | UK | 63 | 26 May |
| 53.10 | Sandra | Farmer | JAM | 62 | 24 May |
| 53.10 | Easter | Gabriel | USA | 60 | 24 May |
| 53.11 | Leaha | Walker (150) | USA | 70 | 24 May |
| 53.12 | Jolanta | Stalmach | POL | 60 | 17 Jun |
| 53.12 | Gudrun | Abt | FRG | 62 | 17 Jun |
| 53.14 | Tatyana | Smeyan | SU | 59 | 14 Jun |
| 53.15 | Zelda | Botes | RSA | 68 | 19 Feb |
| 53.15 | Lawanda | Cabell | USA | 64 | 3 May |
| 53.15 | Galina | Rakhmetova | SU | 61 | 14 Jul |
| 53.16 | Maria | Costencu | RUM | 64 | 24 May |
| 53.20 | Merlene | Ottey-Page | JAM | 60 | 4 Jun |
| 53.21 | Tasha | Downing | USA | 70 | 18 Jul |
| 53.22 | Gwen | Williams (160) | USA | | 10 May |
| 53.23 | Wendy | Old | AUS | 60 | 18 Jan |
| 53.26 | Linda | Keough | UK | 63 | 14 Jun |
| 53.27 | Tatyana | Kruglova | SU | 63 | 7 Jun |
| 53.30 | Kim | Dunlap | USA | 64 | 30 May |
| 53.31 | Yelena | Kuzina | SU | 66 | 30 May |
| 53.32 | Ann | Middle | UK | 62 | 6 Aug |
| 53.32 | Yelena | Potapenko | SU | 65 | 6 Sep |
| 53.32 | Shiny | Abraham | IND | 65 | 4 Oct |
| 53.33 | Věra | Tylová | CS | 60 | 11 Jun |
| 53.34 | Fiona | Hargreaves | UK | 62 | 25 May |
| | | (170) | | | |

| Mark | Name | Nat | Yr | Pos | Meet | Venue | Date |
|---|---|---|---|---|---|---|---|

```
53.34   Ewa         Marcinkowska POL 66 28 Jun   53.51   Stela     Popa         RUM 62 24 May
53.34   Heike       Böckmann     GDR 69  3 Aug    53.52   Valentina Grishkina    SU  56 25 Jul
53.39   Janet       Davis        USA 65 12 Apr    53.52   Phyllis   Watt         UK  65 13 Sep
53.40   Suzanne     Guise        UK  62 26 May    53.53   Vivianne  Spence       JAM    22 May
53.41   Heike       Schulte-Mattler FRG 58 11 Jul 53.54   Galina    Prokofyeva   SU  58  7 Sep
53.41   Slobodanka  Čolović      YUG 65  2 Aug    53.56   Jenny     Laurendet    AUS 62  8 Feb
53.41   Cornelia    Feuerbach    GDR 63 10 Sep    53.56   Toni      Midderhoff   USA    24 May
53.42   Sylvia      Deniau       FRA 64 10 Aug    53.58   Christine Wachtel      GDR 65  7 Jun
53.43   Sally       Fleming      AUS 61  9 Mar    53.59   Sabine    Alber        FRG 65  6 Sep
53.43   Astrid      Brun   (180) NOR 57  1 Jul    53.60   Tudoriţa  Chidu  (200) RUM 67  7 Jun

53.44   Tatyana     Grebenchuk   SU  60 25 Jul    53.60   Gabriela  Sedláková    CS  68 19 Aug
53.44   Anne        Gundersen    NOR 66 10 Aug                              (201)
53.45   Sabine      Zwiener      FRG 67 17 Jun   Indoor marks :
53.45   Ulrike      Sommer       FRG 59 29 Jun
53.47   Patricia    Walsh        IRL 66  8 Jul   52.87 i  Petra     Pfaff        GDR 60 26 Jan
53.48   Yelena      Poida        SU  64  6 Sep   52.89 i  Astrid    Ortel        FRG 65  7 Feb
53.49   Trina       Creekmore    USA 66 24 May   53.02 i  Cornelia  Feuerbach    GDR 63 26 Jan
53.49   Princess    Bennett      USA 68 24 May   53.27 i  Lilia     Novoseltsova SU  62  7 Feb
53.49   Daniela     Gămălie      RUM 67 28 Jun   53.42 i  Nadine    Debois       FRA 61 26 Jan
53.50   Denise      Blackman(190) BAR 65  3 May
```

Best low altitude marks:

```
51.74              Bothma              1              Stellenbosch    19 Mar
51.98              Naude               2              Stellenbosch    19 Mar
52.29              Kaiser              5    NCAA      Indianapolis     7 Jun

52.78              Wilson         5 Jun 53.12          Maxey          19 Jun
```

Disqualified:

```
51.75    Alice      Jackson       USA 58   -    USOCF   Houston        2 Aug
```

----------------------------------------------------------------------------

| | 1 | 10 | 20 | 30 | 50 | 100 | Under 52.00 | Under 53.00 |
|---|---|---|---|---|---|---|---|---|
| 1982 | 48.16 | 50.63 | 51.18 | 51.79 | 52.08 | 52.95 | 42 | 108 |
| 1983 | 47.99 | 50.63 | 50.99 | 51.37 | 51.89 | 52.77 | 56 | 116 |
| 1984 | 48.16 | 49.74 | 50.56 | 51.19 | 51.89 | 52.63 | 56 | 130 |
| 1985 | 47.60 | 50.38 | 51.12 | 51.61 | 52.21 | 52.89 | 40 | 109 |
| 1986 | 48.22 | 50.29 | 50.92 | 51.44 | 51.74 | 52.50 | 64 | 135 |

----------------------------------------------------------------------------

Hand timing:

```
50.6     Inna        Yevseyeva    SU  64  1        Kiev             29 Aug
51.6     Marina      Stepanova    SU  50  1h       Sochi            17 May
51.7     Marina      Kharlamova   SU  62  1        Kazan            29 Jun
52.0     Tsvetanka   Ilieva       BUL 63  1        Sofia             3 May
52.0     Terri       Dendy        USA 65  1        Charlottesville  10 May
52.0     Margarita   Khromova     SU  64  h        Sochi            17 May
52.4     Maicel      Malone       USA 69  1        Indianapolis     26 Apr
52.5     Althea   Thomas   JAM 67 19 Apr  52.5   Margarita Navickaite  SU  61 30 Aug
52.5     Yelena   Gorbenko  SU  66 24 May                        (10)
```

| Mark | Name | | Nat | Yr | Pos | Meet | Venue | | Date |
|------|------|---|-----|----|-----|------|-------|---|------|
| 52.6 | Galina | Rodina | SU | 61 | | | | | 31 Jul |
| 52.6 | Tatyana | Smeyan | SU | 59 | | | | | 1 Aug |
| 52.6 | Yelena | Potapenko | SU | 65 | | | | | 29 Aug |
| 52.7 | Fransie | Pieterse | RSA | 61 | | | | | 12 Mar |
| 52.7 | Tatyana | Balukhina | SU | 65 | | | | | 9 Aug |
| 52.8 | Galina | Prokofyeva | SU | 58 | | | | | 21 Jun |
| 52.8 | Anfisa | Bikbulatova | SU | 65 | | | | | 28 Jun |
| 52.9 | Easter | Gabriel | USA | 60 | | | | | 30 May |
| 52.9 | Věra | Tylová | CS | 60 | | | | | 24 Jun |

| Mark | Name | | Venue | | Nat | Yr | Date |
|------|------|---|-------|---|-----|----|------|
| 52.9 | Yelena | Kuzina | (20) | SU | 66 | | 28 Jun |
| 53.0 | Irina | Skibinskikh | | SU | 61 | | 6 Jun |
| 53.0 | Gladys | Taylor | | UK | 53 | | 29 Jun |
| 53.1 | Yelena | Poida | | SU | 64 | | 9 Aug |
| 53.1 | Juliet | Cuthbert | | JAM | 64 | | 22 Mar |
| 53.2 | Tatyana | Sacheva | | SU | 64 | | 24 Jun |
| 53.2 | Mirian | Knijn | | HOL | 66 | | 12 Apr |
| 53.2 | Lyudmila | Gaman | | SU | 60 | | 6 Jun |
| A53.2 | Esther | Kavaya | (28) | KEN | 58 | | 14 Jun |

# 800 METRES

| Mark | Name | | Nat | Yr | Pos | Meet | Venue | Date |
|------|------|---|-----|----|-----|------|-------|------|
| 1:56.2 m | Doina | Melinte | RUM | 56 | 1 | | București | 13 Jul |
| 1:57.05 | Sigrun | Wodars | GDR | 65 | 1 | NC | Jena | 28 Jun |
| 1:57.15 | Nadezhda | Olizarenko | SU | 53 | 1 | EC | Stuttgart | 28 Aug |
| 1:57.18 | Lyubov | Kiryukhina | SU | 63 | 1 | NC | Kiev | 16 Jul |
| 1:57.42 | | Olizarenko | | | 1 | | Moskva | 9 Aug |
| 1:57.42 | | Wodars | | | 2 | EC | Stuttgart | 28 Aug |
| 1:57.52 | Lyubov | Gurina | SU | 57 | 1 | GWG | Moskva | 6 Jul |
| 1:57.54 | Nadezhda | Zabolotneva | SU | 61 | 2 | GWG | Moskva | 6 Jul |
| 1:57.73 | | Gurina | | | 3 | EC | Stuttgart | 28 Aug |
| 1:57.86 | Irina | Podyalovskaya | SU | 59 | 2 | NC | Kiev | 16 Jul |
| 1:57.87 | Mitica | Junghiatu | RUM | 62 | 3 | GWG | Moskva | 6 Jul |
| 1:57.90 | Milena | Strnadová | CS | 61 | 4 | GWG | Moskva | 6 Jul |
| 1:57.92 | | Strnadová | | | 1 | GS | Ostrava | 11 Jun |
| 1:57.98 | | Wodars | | | 1 | v SU | Tallinn | 22 Jun |
| 1:58.11 | Gaby | Bussmann (10) | FRG | 59 | 1 | ISTAF | W Berlin | 15 Aug |
| 1:58.16 | Heike | Oehme | GDR | 63 | 2 | ISTAF | W Berlin | 15 Aug |
| 1:58.17 | | Kiryukhina | | | 1 | Znam | Leningrad | 8 Jun |
| 1:58.18 | | Olizarenko | | | 3 | NC | Kiev | 16 Jul |
| 1:58.26 | | Wodars | | | 1s2 | EC | Stuttgart | 27 Aug |
| 1:58.36 | Vera | Chuvashova | SU | 59 | 4 | NC | Kiev | 16 Jul |
| 1:58.42 | | Bussmann | | | 1 | BGP | Budapest | 11 Aug |
| 1:58.43 | Vera | Dodika | SU | 59 | 1h1 | | Krasnodar | 21 Jun |
| 1:58.47 | | Gurina | | | 2 | Znam | Leningrad | 8 Jun |
| 1:58.52 | Laima | Baikauskaite | SU | 56 | 1 | | Kiev | 26 Jul |
| 1:58.55 | Claudette | Groenendaal | USA | 63 | 3 | ISTAF | W Berlin | 15 Aug |
| 1:58.57 | | Bussmann | | | 4 | EC | Stuttgart | 28 Aug |
| 1:58.59 | Christine | Wachtel | GDR | 65 | 1 | GO | Dresden | 16 Aug |
| 1:58.60 | | Wodars | | | 1 | VD | Bruxelles | 5 Sep |
| 1:58.63 | | Wodars | | | 1 | | Potsdam | 11 Jun |
| 1:58.66 | | Strnadová | | | 1 | Ros | Praha | 24 Jun |
| 1:58.67 | | Gurina(31/16) | | | 2 | v GDR | Tallinn | 22 Jun |
| 1:58.7 m | Violeta | Beclea | RUM | 65 | 2 | | București | 13 Jul |
| 1:58.78 | Irina | Zaitseva | SU | 63 | 2 | | Kiev | 26 Jul |
| 1:58.80 | Ana | Quirot | CUB | 63 | 1 | Barr | Habana | 15 Jun |
| 1:58.80 | Katrin | Wühn (20) | GDR | 65 | 3 | v SU | Tallinn | 22 Jun |
| 1:59.1 m | Lyubov | Kremleva | SU | 62 | 1 | | Ryazan | 29 Jun |
| 1:59.13 | Maria | Pintea | RUM | 67 | 1 | RumIC | București | 15 Jun |
| 1:59.21 | Tatyana | Samolenko | SU | 61 | 1 | | Rieti | 7 Sep |

| Mark | Name | | Nat | Yr | Pos | Meet | Venue | Date |
|------|------|------|-----|-----|-----|------|-------|------|
| 1:59.32 | Florence | Giolitti | FRA | 66 | 1 | Nik | Nice | 15 Jul |
| 1:59.37 | Ravilya | Agletdinova | SU | 60 | 2 | | Rieti | 7 Sep |
| 1:59.41 | Svetlana | Prodan | SU | 62 | 7 | NC | Kiev | 16 Jul |
| 1:59.43 | Yvette | Bletsch | GDR | 65 | 3 | | Berlin | 20 Aug |
| 1:59.45 | Cristieana | Matei | RUM | 62 | 2 | BGP | Budapest | 11 Aug |
| 1:59.50 | Svetlana | Meleshkova | SU | 62 | 3 | | Kiev | 26 Jul |
| 1:59.63 | Slobodanka | Čolović (30) | YUG | 65 | 1 | NC | Beograd | 3 Aug |
| 1:59.67 | Diana | Richburg | USA | 63 | 1 | IAC | London | 8 Aug |
| 1:59.67 | Lorraine | Baker | UK | 64 | 5 | ISTAF | W Berlin | 15 Aug |
| 1:59.71 | Ilinca | Mitrea | RUM | 64 | 1 | NC | Pitești | 8 Aug |
| 1:59.74 | Yelena | Zavadskaya | SU | 64 | 1s1 | Spart | Tashkent | 17 Sep |
| 1:59.79 | Aurora | Miu | RUM | 62 | 3 | RumIC | București | 15 Jun |
| 1:59.80 | Nikolina | Shtereva | BUL | 55 | 3 | | Lausanne | 2 Sep |
| 1:59.85 | Shireen | Bailey | UK | 59 | 2 | VD | Bruxelles | 5 Sep |
| 1:59.90 | Ellen | Schulz | GDR | 62 | 3h1 | NC | Jena | 27 Jun |
| 1:59.91 | Ella | Kovacs | RUM | 64 | 4 | RumIC | București | 15 Jun |
| 1:59.98 | Margrit | Klinger (40) | FRG | 60 | 1 | | Paris | 22 Jul |
| 2:00.00 | Delisa | Walton-Floyd | USA | 61 | 2 | TAC | Eugene | 21 Jun |
| 2:00.01 | Kirsty | Wade | UK | 62 | 2 | WG | Helsinki | 7 Jul |
| 2:00.1 m | Nadezhda | Vazhenina | SU | 63 | 1 | | Chelyabinsk | 23 Aug |
| 2:00.17 | Fatima | Aouam | MOR | 59 | 6 | ISTAF | W Berlin | 15 Aug |
| 2:00.2 m | Joetta | Clark | USA | 62 | 3 | Pepsi | Westwood | 17 May |
| 2:00.28 | Aurica | Mitrea | RUM | 59 | 6 | RumIC | București | 15 Jun |
| 2:00.31 | Sue | Addison | USA | 56 | 7 | ISTAF | W Berlin | 15 Aug |
| 2:00.49 | Mariana | Stănescu | RUM | 64 | 1 | Kuso | Warszawa | 17 Jun |
| 2:00.56 | Andrea | Lange | GDR | 66 | 4 | | Potsdam | 11 Jun |
| 2:00.60 | Diane | Edwards (50) | UK | 66 | 5 | IAC | London | 8 Aug |
| 2:00.6 m | Inna | Yevseyeva | SU | 64 | 1h | | Kiev | 28 Aug |
| 2:00.61 | Gabriela | Sedláková | CS | 68 | 5s2 | EC | Stuttgart | 27 Aug |
| 2:00.66 | Tudorița | Chidu | RUM | 67 | 7 | RumIC | București | 15 Jun |
| 2:00.68 | Nathalie | Thoumas | FRA | 62 | 2 | | Saint-Denis | 21 Jun |
| 2:00.68 | Svetlana | Kharkova | SU | 65 | 6 | | Kiev | 26 Jul |
| 2:00.7 m | Nadezhda | Gizatullina | SU | 59 | 3 | | Chelyabinsk | 23 Aug |
| 2:00.72 | Galina | Rakova | SU | 59 | 7 | | Kiev | 26 Jul |
| 2:00.8 m | Irina | Kolmakova | SU | 64 | 4 | | Chelyabinsk | 23 Aug |
| 2:00.8 m | Svetlana | Yurlina | SU | 64 | 1 | | Tashkent | 29 Aug |
| 2:00.81 | Wendy | Old (60) | AUS | 60 | 1 | NC | Adelaide | 16 Mar |
| 2:00.83 | Valentina | Parkhuta | SU | 59 | h | Znam | Leningrad | 7 Jun |
| 2:00.85 | Karen | Bakewell | USA | 65 | 1 | NCAA | Indianapolis | 6 Jun |
| 2:00.90 | Yelena | Vlasova | SU | 66 | 8 | | Kiev | 26 Jul |
| 2:00.94 | Brit | McRoberts | CAN | 57 | 8 | ISTAF | W Berlin | 15 Aug |
| 2:00.99 | Cornelia | Bürki | SWZ | 53 | 6 | IAC | London | 8 Aug |
| 2:01.00 | Mihaela | Ene | RUM | 62 | 1 | | Pitești | 29 Jun |
| 2:01.0 m | Nadezhda | Stepanova | SU | 59 | 1 | | Novotroitsk | 29 Jun |
| 2:01.0 m | Tatyana | Sachova | SU | 64 | 6 | | Chelyabinsk | 23 Aug |
| 2:01.02 | Tina | Parrott | USA | 64 | 2 | NCAA | Indianapolis | 6 Jun |
| 2:01.1 m | Natalya | Betekhtina | SU | 61 | 2 | | Novotroitsk | 29 Jun |
| | | (70) | | | | | | |
| 2:01.12 | Ivana | Walterova | CS | 62 | 3 | GS | Ostrava | 11 Jun |
| 2:01.19 | Elena | Lina | RUM | 54 | 2 | | Pitești | 19 Jul |
| 2:01.23 | Svetlana | Andreyeva | SU | 65 | 3 | Spart | Tashkent | 18 Sep |
| 2:01.34 | Kim | Gallagher | USA | 64 | 9 | ISTAF | W Berlin | 15 Aug |
| 2:01.36 | Grażyna | Kowina | POL | 62 | 3 | Kuso | Warszawa | 17 Jun |
| 2:01.40 | Selina | Chirchir | KEN | 68 | 1 | WC-j | Athinai | 18 Jul |

| Mark | Name | | Nat | Yr | Pos | Meet | Venue | Date |
|------|------|------|-----|----|-----|------|-------|------|
| 2:01.40 | Christina | Boxer | UK | 57 | 4 | | Paris | 22 Jul |
| 2:01.4 m | Zelda | Botes | RSA | 68 | 1 | | Port Elizabeth | 12 Mar |
| 2:01.4 m | Olga | Dogadina | SU | 59 | | | Chelyabinsk | 23 Aug |
| 2:01.48 | Debbie | Bowker (80) | CAN | 58 | 10 | ISTAF | W Berlin | 15 Aug |
| 2:01.5 m | Regine | Berg | BEL | 58 | 1 | | Hechtel | 15 Aug |
| 2:01.54 | Svetlana | Guskova | SU | 59 | 11 | ISTAF | W Berlin | 15 Aug |
| 2:01.55 | Julie | Jenkins | USA | 64 | 4 | TAC | Eugene | 21 Jun |
| 2:01.55 | Soraya | Vieira | BRA | 58 | 2 | IbAm | Habana | 28 Sep |
| 2:01.6 m | Nonna | Kharinskaya | SU | 64 | | | Chelyabinsk | 23 Aug |
| 2:01.63 | Anne | Purvis | UK | 59 | 1 | NC | Cwmbran | 26 May |
| 2:01.63 | Birgit | Schmidt | FRG | 63 | 1 | | Rhede | 2 Jul |
| 2:01.66 | Tamara | Koba | SU | 57 | 9 | | Kiev | 26 Jul |
| 2:01.83 | Ronelle | Roodt | RSA | 64 | 1 | | Stellenbosch | 19 Mar |
| 2:01.93 | Renee | Belanger (90) | CAN | 62 | 2 | v GDR | Karl-Marx-Stadt | 12 Jul |
| 2:01.93 | Adriana | Dumitru | RUM | 68 | 3 | WC-j | Athinai | 18 Jul |
| 2:01.96 | Yelena | Didilenko | SU | 61 | | | Sochi | 25 May |
| 2:01.98 | Evelyn | Adiru | UGA | 64 | 3 | NCAA | Indianapolis | 6 Jun |
| 2:01.98 | Tatyana | Mamayeva | SU | 62 | h | NC | Kiev | 14 Jul |
| 2:01.99 | Anushka | Dimitrova | BUL | 62 | 2 | | Praha | 24 Aug |
| 2:02.0 m | Zukhra | Mukhamatova | SU | 61 | 3 | | Novotroitsk | 29 Jun |
| 2:02.02 | Helen | Thorpe | UK | 63 | 2 | NC | Cwmbran | 26 May |
| 2:02.03 | Brigitte | Brückner | FRG | 56 | 3 | | Fürth | 15 Jun |
| 2:02.04 | Karol | Davidson | USA | 65 | 1h1 | NCAA | Indianapolis | 4 Jun |
| 2:02.04 | Martina | Steuk (100) | GDR | 59 | 5 | GO | Dresden | 16 Aug |
| 2:02.05 | Regina | Jacobs | USA | 63 | 1 | | Los Angeles | 1 Aug |
| 2:02.07 | Julie | Schwass | AUS | 57 | 2 | NC | Adelaide | 16 Mar |
| 2:02.10 | Galina | Afonina | SU | 59 | h | | Krasnodar | 21 Jun |
| 2:02.12 | Angelita | Lind | PR | 59 | 2 | CAC | Santiago/Dom | 3 Jul |
| 2:02.12 | Kaisa | Ylimäki | FIN | 60 | 1 | | Jyväskylä | 5 Aug |
| 2:02.18 | Lynne | Robinson | UK | 69 | 4 | WC-j | Athinai | 18 Jul |
| 2:02.19 | Sandra | Gasser (107) | SWZ | 62 | 3 | | Bern | 20 Aug |

| Mark | Name | | Nat Yr Date | Mark | Name | | Nat Yr Date |
|------|------|------|------|------|------|------|------|
| 2:02.2 m | Lenuţa | Raţă | RUM 66 13 Jul | 2:02.75 | Alisa | Harvey (130) | USA 65 18 May |
| 2:02.25 | Christine | Whittingham | UK 56 19 Jun | | | | |
| 2:02.26 | Imekda | Gonzalez (110) | MEX 67 3 Jul | 2:02.78 | Galina | Bochkaryova | SU 63 26 Jul |
| | | | | 2:02.79 | Louise | Romo | USA 63 4 Jun |
| 2:02.31 | Chris | Gregorek | USA 59 28 Jul | 2:02.8 m | Natalya | Strelnikova | SU 59 19 Jul |
| 2:02.33 | Aldona | Sutiene | SU 61 14 Jul | 2:02.81 | Birute | Skurdelite | SU 63 15 Jul |
| 2:02.39 | Brygida | Bak | POL 61 17 Jun | 2:02.81 | Irina | Nikitina | SU 61 26 Jul |
| 2:02.47 | Essie | Washington | USA 57 21 Jun | 2:02.85 | Natalya | Knyazkova | SU 63 7 Jun |
| 2:02.50 | Rosa | Colorado | SPA 54 20 Jun | 2:02.89 | Yelena | Cherepanova | SU 64 24 May |
| 2:02.55 | Tatyana | Grebenchuk | SU 60 26 Jul | 2:02.90 | Elize | Fouche | RSA 60 19 Mar |
| 2:02.56 | Olga | Nelyubova | SU 64 18 Sep | 2:02.9 m | Galina | Rodina | SU 61 29 Jul |
| 2:02.60 | Margareta | Ghile | RUM 61 8 Aug | 2:02.94 | Renee | Ross (140) | USA 63 4 Jun |
| 2:02.6 m | Irina | Lebedinskaya | SU 61 6 Jul | | | | |
| 2:02.6 m | Tatyana | Gudz (120) | SU 66 20 Jul | 2:02.95 | Katja | Prochnow | GDR 68 31 May |
| | | | | 2:02.95 | Ute | Schmidt | GDR 65 27 Jun |
| 2:02.6 m | Galina | Skvortsova | SU 61 1 Aug | 2:02.99 | Camille | Cato | CAN 63 24 May |
| 2:02.62 | Margit | Schultheiss | FRG 56 2 Jul | 2:02.99 | Vesna | Bajer | YUG 63 3 Aug |
| 2:02.64 | Nery | McKeen | CUB 57 15 Jun | 2:02.99 | Elvira | Biacsics | HUN 64 10 Sep |
| 2:02.66 | Magda | Maiocchi | ITA 62 13 Jul | 2:03.0 m | Alla | Moskotina | SU 60 29 Jun |
| 2:02.68 | Elly | van Hulst | HOL 59 15 Aug | 2:03.0 m | Marina | Galavatskikh | SU 64 29 Jun |
| 2:02.7 m | Birgit | Barth | GDR 62 22 Jun | 2:03.0 m | Catherine | Guerrero | FRA 60 13 Jul |
| 2:02.7 m | Olga | Parlyuk | SU 63 5 Jul | 2:03.03 | Linda | Detlefsen | USA 62 8 Jun |
| 2:02.72 | Bronwyn | Fleming | AUS 62 16 Mar | 2:03.03 | Gabriella | Dorio (150) | ITA 57 10 Aug |
| 2:02.72 | Anna | Rybicka | POL 63 28 Jun | | | | |

| Mark | Name | | Nat | Yr | Pos | Meet | Venue | | Date |
|------|------|--|-----|----|-----|------|-------|--|------|
| 2:03.06 | Wendy | Sly | UK | 59 | 2 Sep | 2:03.59 | Denisa | Zavelca | RUM 70 3 Aug |
| 2:03.07 | Claire S | Nichols | AUS 64 16 Mar | | | 2:03.60 | Yvonne | Murray | UK 64 14 Jun |
| 2:03.09 | Wanda | Wojtowiec | POL 60 24 Jun | | | 2:03.6 m | Nathalie | Froget | FRA 64 13 Jul |
| 2:03.10 | Yelena | Medvedyeva | SU 59 31 May | | | 2:03.61 | Teena | Colebrook | UK 56 27 Apr |
| 2:03.10 | Celestine | N'Drin | IVC 63 4 Jun | | | 2:03.61 | Natalya | Shubenkova | SU 57 7 Jul |
| 2:03.11 | Gabriele | Lesch | FRG 64 6 Aug | | | | | (180) | |
| 2:03.13 | Maria | Ribeaux | CUB 58 15 Jun | | | 2:03.61 | Randi | Bjørn | NOR 57 9 Aug |
| 2:03.2 m | Sarah | Collins | AUS 65 13 Dec | | | 2:03.62 | Tatyana | Tokina | SU 66 15 Aug |
| 2:03.21 | Galina | Reznikova | SU 61 26 Jul | | | 2:03.64 | Ellen | Kiessling | GDR 68 10 Jul |
| 2:03.24 | Katrin | Stuhlmacher | GDR 67 27 Jun | | | 2:03.65 | Larisa | Yakubovich | SU 28 Jun |
| | | (160) | | | | 2:03.69 | Rose | Monday (185) | USA 59 1 Aug |
| 2:03.29 | Livia | Pocornicu | RUM 63 15 Jun | | | | | | |
| 2:03.30 | Lyudmila | Borisova | SU 59 25 May | | | Botes (2:01.4 m) also did 2:01.46 1 Stellenbosch | | | |
| 2:03.30 | Rositsa | Stamenova | BUL 55 25 May | | | 10 Feb; Lebedinskaya (2:02.6 m) also did 2:02.66 | | | |
| 2:03.34 | Svetlana | Masterkova | SU 68 27 Jun | | | 15 Jun; Hanon (2:03.4 m) also did 2:03.50 21 Jun. | | | |
| 2:03.37 | Debbie | Grant | USA 65 4 Jun | | | | | | |
| 2:03.4 m | Christine | Hanon | FRA 60 13 Jul | | | Marks made in mixed race with men: | | | |
| 2:03.4 m | Vera | Vinogradova | SU 64 23 Aug | | | | | | |
| 2:03.45 | Tina | Krebs | DEN 63 24 May | | | 2:00.55 | Zola Budd | | UK 66 Meilen 21 Jun |
| 2:03.46 | Antonina | Babushkina | SU 64 17 Sep | | | 2:00.8 m | Essie Washington USA 57 Houston 13 Jun | | |
| 2:03.48 | Flavia | Gaviglio (170) | ITA 63 13 Jul | | | | | | |
| | | | | | | Indoor marks: | | | |
| 2:03.50 | Ermyntrude | Vermeulen | RSA 68 19 Mar | | | | | | |
| 2:03.50 | Nicoletta | Tozzi | ITA 66 13 Jul | | | 2:01.431 | Svetlana Kitova SU 60 1 Moskva 2 Feb | | |
| 2:03.52 | Jill | McCabe | SWE 62 28 Jul | | | | | | |
| 2:03.56 | Zhanna | Safonova | SU 63 28 Jun | | | 2:02.3 mi | Katrin | Stuhlmacher | GDR 67 8 Feb |
| 2:03.59 | Sandra | Speers | AUS 64 16 Mar | | | | | | |

WOMEN 1986

| | 1 | 10 | 20 | 30 | 50 | 100 | Under 2:00.0 | Under 2:02.0 |
|------|------|------|------|------|------|------|------|------|
| 1982 | 1:55.05 | 1:57.3 | 1:59.0 | 1:59.93 | 2:00.9 | 2:02.8 | 30 | 83 |
| 1983 | 1:53.28 | 1:57.4 | 1:58.5 | 1:59.28 | 2:00.1 | 2:01.91 | 45 | 101 |
| 1984 | 1:55.69 | 1:57.20 | 1:58.08 | 1:58.65 | 1:59.6 | 2:01.50 | 54 | 113 |
| 1985 | 1:55.68 | 1:57.42 | 1:58.42 | 1:59.61 | 2:00.73 | 2:02.43 | 34 | 84 |
| 1986 | 1:56.2 | 1:58.11 | 1:58.80 | 1:59.63 | 2:00.60 | 2:02.04 | 40 | 95 |

# 1000 METRES

| Mark | Name | | Nat | Yr | Pos | Venue | Date |
|------|------|--|-----|----|-----|-------|------|
| 2:31.5 m | Maricica | Puică | RUM | 50 | 1 | Poiana Braşov | 1 Jun |
| 2:34.6 m | Heike | Oehme | GDR | 63 | 1 | Cottbus | 14 May |
| 2:35.32 | Shireen | Bailey | UK | 59 | 1 | Birmingham | 19 Jul |
| 2:35.48 | Kirsty | Wade | UK | 62 | 2 | Birmingham | 19 Jul |
| 2:35.51 | Lorraine | Baker | UK | 64 | 3 | Birmingham | 19 Jul |
| 2:35.84 | Christina | Boxer | UK | 57 | 4 | Birmingham | 19 Jul |
| 2:36.66 | Florence | Giolitti | FRA | 66 | 1 | Marseille | 1 Jul |
| 2:37.05 | Christine | Whittingham | UK | 56 | 2 | Gateshead | 27 Jun |
| 2:37.75 | Yvonne | Murray | UK | 64 | 4 | Gateshead | 27 Jun |
| 2:38.10 | Gillian | Dainty (10) | UK | 58 | 5 | Gateshead | 27 Jun |
| 2:38.16 | Diana | Richburg | USA | 63 | 6 | Gateshead | 27 Jun |
| 2:38.30 | Debbie | Bowker | CAN | 58 | 5 | Birmingham | 19 Jul |
| 2:38.56 | Brit | McRoberts | CAN | 57 | 3 | Gateshead | 5 Aug |

| Mark | Name | | Nat | Yr | Pos | Meet | Venue | Date |
|------|------|------|-----|----|-----|------|-------|------|
| 2:38.6 m | Andrea | Lange | GDR | 66 | 1 | | Potsdam | 22 May |
| 2:38.67 | Lynne | McDougall | UK | 65 | 6 | | Birmingham | 19 Jul |
| 2:38.8 m | Nikolina | Shtereva | BUL | 55 | 1 | | Sofia | 3 Aug |
| 2:38.81 | Lynn | Williams | CAN | 60 | 7 | | Birmingham | 19 Jul |
| 2:38.88 | Margrit | Klinger (18) | FRG | 60 | 1 | | Koblenz | 21 May |

Indoor marks:

| | | | | | | | | |
|------|------|------|-----|----|-----|------|-------|------|
| 2:37.741 | Tatyana | Petrova | SU | 64 | 1 | | Moskva | 1 Feb |
| 2:37.9 mi | Joetta | Clark | USA | 62 | 1 | | Gainesville | 9 Mar |
| 2:38.121 | Svetlana | Kitova | SU | 60 | 2 | | Moskva | 1 Feb |
| 2:38.581 | Yekaterina | Podkopayeva | SU | 52 | 3 | | Moskva | 1 Feb |
| 2:38.631 | Regina | Chistyakova | SU | 61 | 4 | | Moskva | 1 Feb |

## 1500 METRES

| | | | | | | | | |
|------|------|------|-----|----|-----|------|-------|------|
| 3:56.7 m | Doina | Melinte | RUM | 56 | 1 | | Bucureşti | 12 Jul |
| 3:59.25 | | Melinte | | | 1 | | Piteşti | 28 Jun |
| 3:59.45 | Tatyana | Samolenko | SU | 61 | 1 | NC | Kiev | 17 Jul |
| 3:59.62 | Maricica | Puică | RUM | 50 | 1 | RumIC | Bucureşti | 14 Jun |
| 3:59.84 | Ravilya | Agletdinova | SU | 60 | 2 | NC | Kiev | 17 Jul |
| 4:00.38 | | Puică | | | 1 | DNG | Stockholm | 1 Jul |
| 4:01.10 | | Melinte | | | 1 | ASV | Köln | 17 Aug |
| 4:01.15+ | | Puică | | | 1 | Nik | Nice | 15 Jul |
| 4:01.19 | | Agletdinova | | | 1 | EC | Stuttgart | 31 Aug |
| 4:01.20 | | Puică | | | 1 | Bisl | Oslo | 5 Jul |
| 4:01.57 | Lyubov | Kremleva | SU | 62 | 3 | NC | Kiev | 17 Jul |
| 4:01.83 | Svetlana | Kitova | SU | 60 | 4 | NC | Kiev | 17 Jul |
| 4:01.84 | Ivana | Walterová | CS | 62 | 1 | BGP | Budapest | 11 Aug |
| 4:01.93 | Zola | Budd | UK | 66 | 1 | WAAA | Birmingham | 7 Jun |
| 4:01.95 | | Melinte | | | 2 | BGP | Budapest | 11 Aug |
| 4:02.36 | | Samolenko | | | 2 | EC | Stuttgart | 31 Aug |
| 4:02.44 | | Melinte | | | 3 | EC | Stuttgart | 31 Aug |
| 4:02.48 | | Samolenko | | | 1 | Znam | Leningrad | 8 Jun |
| 4:02.71 | | Samolenko | | | 1 | GP | Roma | 10 Sep |
| 4:02.90 | Heike | Oehme | GDR | 63 | 1 | v SU | Tallinn | 21 Jun |
| 4:02.92 | Laima | Baikauskaite | SU | 56 | 5 | NC | Kiev | 17 Jul |
| 4:03.09 | Natalya | Boborova | SU | 59 | 6 | NC | Kiev | 17 Jul |
| 4:03.09 | | Walterová | | | 4 | EC | Stuttgart | 31 Aug |
| 4:03.3 m+ | | Puică | | | 1 | | Paris | 22 Jul |
| 4:03.38 | Cornelia | Bürki | SWZ | 53 | 2 | ASV | Köln | 17 Aug |
| 4:03.46 | Olga | Parlyuk | SU | 63 | 7 | NC | Kiev | 17 Jul |
| 4:03.55 | | Puică | | | 2 | GP | Roma | 10 Sep |
| 4:03.74 | Kirsty | Wade | UK | 62 | 3 | GP | Roma | 10 Sep |
| 4:03.77 | | Kitova | | | 2 | v GDR | Tallinn | 21 Jun |
| 4:03.90 | | Puică | | | 5 | EC | Stuttgart | 31 Aug |
| 4:03.92 | Elena | Fidatov | RUM | 60 | 2 | | Piteşti | 28 Jun |
| 4:03.98 | Nikolina | Shtereva | BUL | 55 | 3 | BGP | Budapest | 11 Aug |
| | | (32/16) | | | | | | |
| 4:04.29 | Vera | Michallek | FRG | 58 | 3 | ASV | Köln | 17 Aug |
| 4:04.32 | Elly | van Hulst | HOL | 59 | 2 | DNG | Stockholm | 1 Jul |
| 4:04.49 | Margareta | Keszeg | RUM | 65 | 3 | | Piteşti | 28 Jun |
| 4:04.56 | Violeta | Beclea (20) | RUM | 65 | 4 | | Piteşti | 28 Jun |

| Mark | Name | | Nat | Yr | Pos | Meet | Venue | Date |
|------|------|------|-----|----|----|------|-------|------|
| 4:04.60 | Yelena | Romanova | SU | 63 | 2 | RumIC | București | 14 Jun |
| 4:04.65 | Brigitte | Kraus | FRG | 56 | 1 | FBK | Hengelo | 27 Jun |
| 4:04.69 | Mariana | Stǎnescu | RUM | 64 | 5 | | Pitești | 28 Jun |
| 4:04.85 | Ulrike | Bruns | GDR | 53 | 1 | GO | Dresden | 17 Aug |
| 4:04.86 | Claudette | Groenendaal | USA | 63 | 4 | ASV | Köln | 17 Aug |
| 4:05.07 | Ilinca | Mitrea | RUM | 64 | 1 | | Pitești | 19 Jul |
| 4:05.12 | Yvette | Bletsch | GDR | 65 | 4 | BGP | Budapest | 11 Aug |
| 4:05.13 | Sue | Addison | USA | 56 | 2 | FBK | Hengelo | 27 Jun |
| 4:05.19 | Irina | Lebedinskaya | SU | 61 | 3 | RumIC | București | 14 Jun |
| 4:05.19 | Paula | Ivan        (30) | RUM | 63 | 6 | | Pitești | 28 Jun |
| 4:05.28 | Debbie | Bowker | CAN | 58 | 6 | ASV | Köln | 17 Aug |
| 4:05.36 | Brit | McRoberts | CAN | 57 | 2 | Bisl | Oslo | 5 Jul |
| 4:05.46 | Tamara | Koba | SU | 57 | 8 | NC | Kiev | 17 Jul |
| 4:05.49 | Fatima | Aouam | MOR | 59 | 7 | ASV | Köln | 17 Aug |
| 4:05.76 | Yvonne | Murray | UK | 64 | 3 | Bisl | Oslo | 5 Jul |
| 4:05.81 | Yelena | Zhupiyeva | SU | 60 | h | | Moskva | 28 Jun |
| 4:05.86 | Wendy | Sly | UK | 59 | 9 | ASV | Köln | 17 Aug |
| 4:05.96 | Katrin | Wühn | GDR | 65 | 3 | GO | Dresden | 17 Aug |
| 4:05.97 | Ingrid | Kristiansen | NOR | 56 | 1 | NC | Sandnes | 10 Aug |
| 4:05.99 | Olga | Bondarenko | SU | 60 | h | | Moskva | 28 Jun |
| | | (40) | | | | | | |
| 4:06.02 | Ana | Pǎdurean | RUM | 69 | 7 | | Pitești | 28 Jun |
| 4:06.19 | Maria | Pîntea | RUM | 67 | 8 | | Pitești | 28 Jun |
| 4:06.24 | Christine | Whittingham | UK | 56 | 4 | Bisl | Oslo | 5 Jul |
| 4:06.33 | Valentina | Parkhuta | SU | 59 | 9 | NC | Kiev | 17 Jul |
| 4:06.34 | Lyubov | Gurina | SU | 57 | 10 | NC | Kiev | 17 Jul |
| 4:06.45 | Viorica | Ghican | RUM | 65 | 5 | | Pitești | 19 Jul |
| 4:06.47 | Diana | Richburg | USA | 63 | 4 | WK | Zürich | 13 Aug |
| 4:06.72 | Anne Jorun | Flaten | NOR | 61 | 6 | Bisl | Oslo | 5 Jul |
| 4:06.81 | Mitica | Junghiatu | RUM | 62 | 5 | RumIC | București | 14 Jun |
| 4:06.81 | Galina | Rakova     (50) | SU | 59 | 1 | | Moskva | 2 Aug |
| 4:07.26 | Ana | Barbu | RUM | 63 | 6 | | Pitești | 19 Jul |
| 4:07.35 | Lynn | Williams | CAN | 60 | 8 | Bisl | Oslo | 5 Jul |
| 4:07.61 | Gabriella | Dorio | ITA | 57 | 9 | GP | Roma | 10 Sep |
| 4:07.64 | Ines | Bibernell | GDR | 65 | 1 | NC | Jena | 29 Jun |
| 4:07.74 | Christina | Boxer | UK | 57 | 6h1 | EC | Stuttgart | 29 Aug |
| 4:08.00 | Linda | Detlefsen | USA | 62 | 1 | TAC | Eugene | 21 Jun |
| 4:08.02 | Chris | Gregorek | USA | 59 | 2 | TAC | Eugene | 21 Jun |
| 4:08.17 | Svetlana | Ulmasova | SU | 53 | h | | Moskva | 28 Jun |
| 4:08.18 | Regina | Jacobs | USA | 63 | 7 | WK | Zürich | 13 Aug |
| 4:08.19 | Birgit | Schmidt     (60) | FRG | 63 | 12 | ASV | Köln | 17 Aug |
| 4:08.34 | Alla | Yushina | SU | 58 | 1 | | Moskva | 29 Jun |
| 4:08.50 | Andrea | Lange | GDR | 66 | 3 | | Potsdam | 12 Jun |
| 4:08.54 | Lesley | Welch | USA | 63 | 1 | | Dedham | 10 May |
| 4:08.54 | Lenuța | Rațǎ | RUM | 66 | 11 | RumIC | București | 14 Jun |
| 4:08.7 m | Florence | Giolitti | FRA | 66 | 1 | | Parilly | 18 Jul |
| 4:08.76 | Regina | Chistyakova | SU | 61 | 2 | | Krasnodar | 22 Jun |
| 4:08.85 | Simona | Staicu | RUM | 71 | | | Pitești | 28 Jun |
| 4:08.94 | Margareta | Ghile | RUM | 61 | 12 | RumIC | București | 14 Jun |
| 4:08.95 | Alisa | Harvey | USA | 65 | 4 | TAC | Eugene | 21 Jun |
| 4:09.20 | Suzanne | Girard     (70) | USA | 62 | 1 | | Barcelona | 16 Jul |
| 4:09.3 m | Nadezhda | Stepanova | SU | 59 | 1 | | Chelyabinsk | 24 Aug |
| 4:09.35 | Mary | Knisely | USA | 59 | 8 | DNG | Stockholm | 1 Jul |
| 4:09.61 | Evelyn | Adiru | UGA | 64 | 5 | TAC | Eugene | 21 Jun |

WOMEN 1986

| Mark | Name | | Nat | Yr | Pos | Meet | Venue | Date |
|------|------|--|-----|----|----|------|-------|------|
| 4:09.62 | Iulia | Beşliu | RUM | 65 | | RumIC | Bucureşti | 14 Jun |
| 4:09.64 | Cristina | Misaroş | RUM | 69 | 2 | NC-j | Bucureşti | 7 Jun |
| 4:10.08 | Ruth | Wysocki | USA | 57 | 6 | FBK | Hengelo | 27 Jun |
| 4:10.23 | Lynne | MacDougall | UK | 65 | 1 | | Edinburgh | 14 Jun |
| 4:10.39 | Sabine | Leist | GDR | 66 | 6 | Znam | Leningrad | 8 Jun |
| 4:10.4 m | Annette | Sergent | FRA | 62 | 2 | | Parilly | 18 Jul |
| 4:10.63 | Luminiţa | Zăiţuc (80) | RUM | 68 | 3 | NC-j | Bucureşti | 7 Jun |
| 4:10.78 | Shireen | Bailey | UK | 59 | 3 | v Pol, | Sco/Wal Hendon | 17 Aug |
| 4:10.81 | Svetlana | Guskova | SU | 59 | 10 | Bisl | Oslo | 5 Jul |
| 4:10.81 | Nathalie | Froget | FRA | 64 | 1 | NC | Aix-les-Bains | 10 Aug |
| 4:10.84 | Adriana | Dumitru | RUM | 68 | | | Bucureşti | 24 May |
| 4:10.87 | Lynn | Jennings | USA | 60 | 6 | TAC | Eugene | 21 Jun |
| 4:11.08 | Yelena | Tyurina | SU | 64 | 11 | NC | Kiev | 17 Jul |
| 4:11.09 | Gillian | Dainty | UK | 58 | | RumIC | Bucureşti | 14 Jun |
| 4:11.29 | Gabriele | Veith | GDR | 56 | 4 | NC | Jena | 29 Jun |
| 4:11.3 m | Anne | Hare | NZ | 64 | 1 | | Hamilton | 1 Feb |
| 4:11.3 m | Marina | Pluzhnikova | SU | 63 | 1 | | Kazan | 29 Jun |
| | | (90) | | | | | | |
| 4:11.32 | Ellen | Schulz | GDR | 62 | 6 | OD | Dresden | 3 Jul |
| 4:11.37 | Cindy | Bremser | USA | 53 | 3 | USOCF | Houston | 3 Aug |
| 4:11.44 | Christine | Pfitzinger | NZ | 59 | 1 | NC | Christchurch | 9 Mar |
| 4:11.48 | Suzanne | Morley | UK | 57 | 3 | NC | Cwmbran | 26 May |
| 4:11.52 | Svetlana | Meleshkova | SU | 62 | 3 | | Kiev | 25 Jul |
| 4:11.64 | Marie-Pierre | Duros | FRA | 67 | 1 | v Gre, | Yug Athinai | 16 Aug |
| 4:11.64 | Nadezhda | Vazhenina | SU | 63 | 1 | | Bryansk | 17 Aug |
| 4:11.77 | Missy | Kane | USA | 55 | 8 | TAC | Eugene | 21 Jun |
| 4:11.88 | Doina | Homneac | RUM | 69 | | RumIC | Bucureşti | 14 Jun |
| 4:12.00 | Yelena | Medvedyeva | SU | 59 | 2 | | Sochi | 25 May |
| | | (100) | | | | | | |

| 4:12.07 | Sandra | Gasser | SWZ 62 30 May | 4:13.74 | Irina | Kolmakova | SU 64 28 Jun |
|---------|--------|--------|----------------|---------|--------|-----------|--------------|
| 4:12.07 | Iris | Biba | FRG 64 17 Aug | 4:13.76 | Snežana | Pajkić | YUG 70 29 Aug |
| 4:12.13 | Ines | Deselaers | FRG 63 17 Aug | 4:13.8 m | Tatyana | Sokolova (130) | SU 58 28 Jun |
| 4:12.19 | Renee | Odom | USA 56 21 Jun | | | | |
| 4:12.2 m | Larisa | Yemelyanenko | SU 64 10 Aug | 4:13.8 m | Irina | Shestunkina | SU 64 29 Jun |
| 4:12.27 | Agnese | Possamai | ITA 53 9 Jul | 4:13.85 | Cathie | Twomey | USA 56 7 Jun |
| 4:12.4 m | Natalya | Betekhtina | SU 61 28 Jun | 4:13.90 | Zita | Agoston | HUN 65 28 Jun |
| 4:12.44 | Nathalie | Thoumas | FRA 62 14 Jun | 4:13.9 m | Natalya | Linkova | SU 59 18 Jul |
| 4:12.5 m | Natalya | Lagunkova | SU 59 27 Jun | 4:13.9 m | Olga | Dogadina | SU 59 24 Aug |
| 4:12.67 | Ermyntrude | Vermeulen | RSA 68 19 Mar | 4:13.94 | Corinne | Debaets | BEL 63 30 May |
| | | (110) | | 4:14.00 | Claudia | Borgschulze | FRG 64 30 May |
| 4:12.69 | Susanne | Fischer | GDR 68 26 Jul | 4:14.02 | Gunilla | Andrén | SWE 61 1 Jul |
| 4:12.72 | Jacqueline | Lefeuvre | FRA 58 10 Aug | 4:14.06 | Camelia | Ionescu | RUM 62 14 Jun |
| 4:12.84 | Penny | Just | AUS 57 9 Mar | 4:14.17 | Veronique | Collard (140) | BEL 63 30 May |
| 4:13.03 | Mirela | Šket | YUG 65 16 Aug | | | | |
| 4:13.07 | Roberta | Brunet | ITA 65 9 Jul | 4:14.2 m | Yekaterina Skvortsova | | SU 61 |
| 4:13.10 | Sabrina | Dornhoefer | USA 63 7 Jun | 4:14.24 | Irina | Podyalovskaya | SU 59 25 May |
| 4:13.1 m | Liuxia | Yang | CHN 62 22 Mar | 4:14.26 | Svetlana | Prodan | SU 62 7 Sep |
| 4:13.12 | Natalya | Sorokivskaya | SU 62 7 Sep | 4:14.27 | Lidia | Camberg | POL 62 30 Aug |
| 4:13.13 | Elizabeth | Lynch | UK 64 14 Jun | 4:14.28 | Martine | Fays | FRA 59 10 Aug |
| 4:13.19 | Marina | Loseva (120) | SU 61 7 Jun | 4:14.4 m | Irina | Karbolina | SU 60 28 Jun |
| | | | | 4:14.43 | Erika | Veréb | HUN 63 3 Jul |
| 4:13.32 | Beatrix | Neuhaus | FRG 63 17 Aug | 4:14.45 | Andri | Avraam | CYP 63 16 Aug |
| 4:13.38 | Darlene | Beckford | USA 61 3 Aug | 4:14.47 | Marjorie | van der Merwe | RSA 68 19 Mar |
| 4:13.5 m | Xiujuan | Geng | CHN 64 22 Mar | 4:14.5 m | Maria | Vasilyuk (150) | SU 62 19 Jul |
| 4:13.58 | Věra | Vinogradova | SU 64 17 Aug | | | | |
| 4:13.59 | Birgit | Barth | GDR 62 29 Jun | 4:14.51 | Tanya | Peckham | RSA 66 23 Feb |
| 4:13.66 | Věra | Nožičková | CS 66 13 Jul | 4:14.52 | Christin | Sørum | NOR 68 20 May |
| 4:13.70 | Jill | Jones | USA 61 7 Jun | 4:14.6 m | Irina | Matrosova | SU 62 14 Jun |

| Mark | Name | | Nat | Yr | Pos | Meet | Venue | Date |
|------|------|---|-----|----|-----|------|-------|------|
| 4:14.61 | Jane | Shields | UK | 60 | 27 Jun | 4:14.95 | Galina Bochkaryova | SU 63 25 Jul |
| 4:14.63 | Patricia | Demilly | FRA | 59 | 14 Jun | | | (164) |
| 4:14.70 | Irina | Nikitina | SU | 61 | 25 Jul | | | |
| 4:14.86 | Heidrun | Vetter | FRG | 61 | 10 Aug | Yemelyanenko (4:12.2 m) also did 4:12.22 17 Aug | | |
| 4:14.88 | Lyudmila | Borisova | SU | 66 | 20 Sep | Shestunkina (4:13.8 m) also did 4:13.86 25 May | | |
| 4:14.9 m | Ronelle | Roodt | RSA | 64 | 12 Mar | | | |
| 4:14.9 m | Tatyana | Kazankina | SU | 51 | 24 May | Marks made in mixed race with men: | | |
| | | (160) | | | | | | |
| 4:14.9 m | Irina | Mozharova | SU | 58 | 29 Jun | 4:02.6 m | Regina Jacobs USA 63 Los Angeles 30 Jul | |
| 4:14.91 | Asuncion | Sinovas | SPA | 61 | 6 Aug | 4:14.0 m | Jackie Perkins AUS 65 28 Jan | |
| 4:14.95 | Jill | McCabe | SWE | 62 | 1 Jul | | | |

Indoor marks:

| | | | | | | | | |
|------|------|---|---|----|----|----|-----------|--------|
| 4:07.621 | Ines | Bibernell | GDR | 65 | 1 | NC | Senftenberg | 16 Feb |
| 4:07.641 | Tatyana | Petrova | SU | 64 | 2 | NC | Moskva | 6 Feb |
| 4:08.191 | Regina | Chistyakova | SU | 61 | 5 | NC | Moskva | 6 Feb |
| 4:10.871 | Gabriele | Veith | GDR | 56 | 2 | NC | Senftenberg | 16 Feb |

4:13.591   Yekaterina Podkopayeva SU 52 6 Feb   4:13.831   Iva Jurková   CS 66 26 Jan

-------------------------------------------------------------------------------

| | 1 | 10 | 20 | 30 | 50 | 100 | Under 4:05.0 | Under 4:10.0 |
|------|------|------|------|------|------|------|------|------|
| 1982 | 3:54.23 | 3:59.24 | 4:03.05 | 4:05.33 | 4:07.72 | 4:13.25 | 28 | 65 |
| 1983 | 3:57.12 | 4:01.4 | 4:03.36 | 4:04.77 | 4:08.32 | 4:12.2 | 32 | 63 |
| 1984 | 3:56.63 | 4:00.18 | 4:01.83 | 4:03.2 | 4:06.09 | 4:10.38 | 38 | 95 |
| 1985 | 3:57.24 | 4:02.05 | 4:04.73 | 4:06.65 | 4:09.54 | 4:12.3 | 21 | 53 |
| 1986 | 3:56.7 | 4:02.92 | 4:04.56 | 4:05.19 | 4:06.81 | 4:12.00 | 25 | 75 |

-------------------------------------------------------------------------------

## ONE MILE

| | | | | | | | | |
|------|------|---------|-----|----|---|-----|-----------|--------|
| 4:18.25 | Maricica | Puică | RUM | 50 | 1 | Nik | Nice | 15 Jul |
| 4:20.89 | | Puică | | | 1 | | Paris | 22 Jul |
| 4:21.61 | Kirsty | Wade | UK | 62 | 1 | VD | Bruxelles | 5 Sep |
| 4:21.88 | Doina | Melinte | RUM | 56 | 2 | VD | Bruxelles | 5 Sep |
| 4:22.11 | | Puică | | | 3 | VD | Bruxelles | 5 Sep |
| 4:22.40 | Elly | van Hulst | HOL | 59 | 4 | VD | Bruxelles | 5 Sep |
| 4:22.82 | Ivana | Walterova | CS | 62 | 5 | VD | Bruxelles | 5 Sep |
| 4:23.08 | Yvonne | Murray | UK | 64 | 6 | VD | Bruxelles | 5 Sep |
| 4:23.93 | Sue | Addison | USA | 56 | 2 | Nik | Nice | 15 Jul |
| 4:24.69 | Brit | McRoberts | CAN | 57 | 3 | Nik | Nice | 15 Jul |
| 4:24.85 | | Melinte | | | 1 | IAC | London | 8 Aug |
| 4:24.85 | Cornelia | Bürki (12/9) | SWZ | 53 | 7 | VD | Bruxelles | 5 Sep |
| 4:25.29 | Claudette | Groenendaal | USA | 63 | 8 | VD | Bruxelles | 5 Sep |
| | | (10) | | | | | | |
| 4:25.52 | Mariana | Stănescu | RUM | 64 | 4 | Nik | Nice | 15 Jul |
| 4:25.57 | Lynn | Williams | CAN | 60 | 5 | Nik | Nice | 15 Jul |
| 4:27.5 m+ | Zola | Budd | UK | 66 | 1 | PTG | London | 11 Jul |
| 4:28.1 m | Diana | Richburg | USA | 63 | 1 | | Amherst | 10 Jul |

| Mark | Name | | Nat | Yr | Pos | Meet | Venue | Date |
|------|------|------|-----|----|----|------|-------|------|
| 4:28.18 | Wendy | Sly | UK | 59 | 9 | VD | Bruxelles | 5 Sep |
| 4:28.72 | Florence | Giolitti | FRA | 66 | 2 | | Paris | 22 Jul |
| 4:29.40 | Regina | Jacobs | USA | 63 | 5 | IAC | London | 8 Aug |
| 4:29.49 | Linda | Detlefsen | USA | 62 | 6 | Nik | Nice | 15 Jul |
| 4:30.69 | Fatima | Aouam | MOR | 59 | 10 | VD | Bruxelles | 5 Sep |
| 4:31.71 | Mary | Knisely (20) | USA | 59 | 6 | IAC | London | 8 Aug |
| | | | | | | | | |
| 4:33.06 | Alisa | Harvey | USA | 65 | 1 | PennR | Philadelphia | 26 Apr |
| 4:33.27 | Lesley | Welch | USA | 63 | 2 | PennR | Philadelphia | 26 Apr |
| 4:33.85 | Tanya | Peckham | RSA | 66 | 1 | | Stellenbosch | 6 Jan |
| 4:34.10 | Lynne | MacDougall | UK | 65 | 7 | IAC | London | 8 Aug |
| 4:34.21 | Suzanne | Girard | USA | 62 | 3 | PennR | Philadelphia | 26 Apr |
| 4:34.46 | Christine | Benning | UK | 55 | 8 | IAC | London | 8 Aug |
| 4:34.55 | Mary Ellen | McGowan (27) | USA | 63 | 4 | PennR | Philadelphia | 26 Apr |

Mark made in mixed race with men:

| | | | | | | | | |
|------|------|------|-----|----|----|------|-------|------|
| 4:31.2 m | Krishna | Wood | AUS | 66 | - | | Canberra | 15 Nov |

Indoor marks:

| | | | | | | | | |
|------|------|------|-----|----|----|------|-------|------|
| 4:33.351 | Cindy | Bremser | USA | 53 | 6 | | New York | 14 Feb |
| 4:33.361 | PattiSue | Plumer | USA | 62 | 7 | | New York | 14 Feb |
| 4:33.741 | Lynn | Jennings | USA | 60 | 1 | | Allston | 26 Jan |
| 4:34.8 mi | Renee | Odom | USA | 56 | 2 | | San Diego | 23 Feb |

## 2000 METRES

| | | | | | | | | |
|------|------|------|-----|----|----|------|-------|------|
| 5:28.69 | Maricica | Puică | RUM | 50 | 1 | PTG | London | 11 Jul |
| 5:29.58 | Yvonne | Murray | UK | 64 | 2 | PTG | London | 11 Jul |
| 5:30.19 | Zola | Budd | UK | 66 | 3 | PTG | London | 11 Jul |
| 5:35.59 | Cornelia | Bürki | SWZ | 53 | 4 | PTG | London | 11 Jul |
| 5:37.86 | Lesley | Welch | USA | 63 | 5 | PTG | London | 11 Jul |
| 5:39.00 | Annette | Sergent | FRA | 62 | 6 | PTG | London | 11 Jul |
| 5:39.52 | Elly | van Hulst | HOL | 59 | 7 | PTG | London | 11 Jul |
| 5:39.96 | Debbie | Bowker | CAN | 58 | 1 | | Gateshead | 5 Aug |
| 5:40.15 | Olga | Bondarenko | SU | 60 | 1 | | Rieti | 7 Sep |
| 5:40.50 | Mary | Knisely (10) | USA | 59 | 8 | PTG | London | 11 Jul |

Disqualified:

| | | | | | | | | |
|------|------|------|-----|----|----|------|-------|------|
| 5:39.19 | Sue | Addison | USA | 56 | - | PTG | London | 11 Jul |

## 3000 METRES

| | | | | | | | | |
|------|------|------|-----|----|----|------|-------|------|
| 8:33.99 | Olga | Bondarenko | SU | 60 | 1 | EC | Stuttgart | 28 Aug |
| 8:34.10 | Ingrid | Kristiansen | NOR | 56 | 1 | WK | Zürich | 13 Aug |
| 8:34.43 | Zola | Budd | UK | 66 | 1 | | Belfast | 30 Jun |
| 8:34.9 m | | Bondarenko | | | 1 | | Podolsk | 12 Aug |
| 8:35.88 | | Kristiansen | | | 1 | Nik | Nice | 15 Jul |
| 8:35.92 | Maricica | Puică | RUM | 50 | 2 | EC | Stuttgart | 28 Aug |
| 8:36.00 | Tatyana | Samolenko | SU | 61 | 1 | v GDR | Tallinn | 22 Jun |
| 8:37.11 | Doina | Melinte | RUM | 56 | 1 | RumIC | Bucureşti | 15 Jun |
| 8:37.15 | Yvonne | Murray | UK | 64 | 3 | EC | Stuttgart | 28 Aug |
| 8:37.84 | | Puică | | | 1 | ASV | Köln | 17 Aug |

| Mark | Name | | Nat | Yr | Pos | Meet | Venue | Date | |
|------|------|------|-----|-----|-----|------|-------|------|---|
| 8:38.20 | | Budd | | | 4 | EC | Stuttgart | 28 | Aug |
| 8:38.83 | Mariana | Stănescu | RUM | 64 | 1 | GWG | Moskva | 6 | Jul |
| 8:38.91 | | Puică | | | 2 | RumIC | Bucureşti | 15 | Jun |
| 8:39.06 | | Puică | | | 2 | WK | Zürich | 13 | Aug |
| 8:39.19 | Svetlana | Ulmasova | SU | 53 | 2 | GWG | Moskva | 6 | Jul |
| 8:39.25 | Regina | Chistyakova | SU | 61 | 3 | GWG | Moskva | 6 | Jul |
| 8:40.34 | | Bondarenko | | | 2 | Nik | Nice | 15 | Jul |
| 8:40.35 | | Samolenko | | | 5 | EC | Stuttgart | 28 | Aug |
| 8:40.72 | | Puică | | | 1 | WG | Helsinki | 7 | Jul |
| 8:40.74 | | Chistyakova | | | 1 | NC | Kiev | 16 | Jul |
| 8:40.74 | Yelena | Zhupiyeva | SU | 60 | 6 | EC | Stuttgart | 28 | Aug |
| 8:41.68 | | Ulmasova | | | 2 | v GDR | Tallinn | 22 | Jun |
| 8:42.04 | Svetlana | Guskova | SU | 59 | 3 | Nik | Nice | 15 | Jul |
| 8:42.09 | | Zhupiyeva | | | 2 | NC | Kiev | 16 | Jul |
| 8:43.46 | | Zhupiyeva | | | 4 | GWG | Moskva | 6 | Jul |
| 8:44.44 | Cornelia | Bŭrki | SWZ | 53 | 7 | EC | Stuttgart | 28 | Aug |
| 8:44.86 | Lesley | Welch | USA | 63 | 4 | Nik | Nice | 15 | Jul |
| 8:45.00 | | Bŭrki | | | 5 | Nik | Nice | 15 | Jul |
| 8:45.76 | | Budd | | | 3 | WK | Zürich | 13 | Aug |
| 8:45.93 | Alla | Yushina | SU | 58 | 1 | | Krasnodar | 21 | Jun |
| | | (30/15) | | | | | | | |
| 8:46.18 | Mary | Knisely | USA | 59 | 1 | TAC | Eugene | 21 | Jun |
| 8:46.24 | PattiSue | Plumer | USA | 62 | 5 | GWG | Moskva | 6 | Jul |
| 8:46.53 | Elizabeth | Lynch | UK | 64 | 1 | | Birmingham | 18 | Jul |
| 8:46.56 | Cindy | Bremser | USA | 53 | 2 | TAC | Eugene | 21 | Jun |
| 8:46.94 | Annette | Sergent (20) | FRA | 62 | 6 | Nik | Nice | 15 | Jul |
| 8:47.00 | Wendy | Sly | UK | 59 | 3 | RumIC | Bucureşti | 15 | Jun |
| 8:47.83 | Brigitte | Kraus | FRG | 56 | 1 | NC | W Berlin | 13 | Jul |
| 8:48.15 | Natalya | Lagunkova | SU | 59 | 3 | NC | Kiev | 16 | Jul |
| 8:48.22 | Ulrike | Bruns | GDR | 53 | 1 | | Potsdam | 11 | Jun |
| 8:48.25 | Elly | van Hulst | HOL | 59 | 3 | WG | Helsinki | 7 | Jul |
| 8:49.12 | Marina | Rodchenkova | SU | 61 | 4 | NC | Kiev | 16 | Jul |
| 8:49.15 | Natalya | Sorokivskaya | SU | 62 | 5 | NC | Kiev | 16 | Jul |
| 8:49.71 | Nadezhda | Stepanova | SU | 59 | 6 | NC | Kiev | 16 | Jul |
| 8:49.80 | Ines | Bibernell | GDR | 65 | 1 | NC | Jena | 27 | Jun |
| 8:49.91 | Marina | Pluzhnikova | SU | 63 | 7 | NC | Kiev | 16 | Jul |
| | | (30) | | | | | | | |
| 8:50.26 | Elena | Fidatov | RUM | 60 | 4 | RumIC | Bucuresti | 15 | Jun |
| 8:50.68 | Gabriele | Veith | GDR | 56 | 2 | NC | Jena | 27 | Jun |
| 8:50.82 | Yelena | Sipatova | SU | 55 | 8 | NC | Kiev | 16 | Jul |
| 8:50.99 | Vera | Michallek | FRG | 58 | 2 | | Belfast | 30 | Jun |
| 8:51.54 | Margareta | Keszeg | RUM | 65 | 7 | GWG | Moskva | 6 | Jul |
| 8:52.45 | Martine | Fays | FRA | 59 | 9 | Nik | Nice | 15 | Jul |
| 8:52.47 | Jackie | Perkins | AUS | 65 | 1 | | Melbourne | 18 | Dec |
| 8:52.91 | Lynn | Williams | CAN | 60 | 4 | WG | Helsinki | 7 | Jul |
| 8:53.03 | Krishna | Wood | AUS | 66 | 2 | | Melbourne | 18 | Dec |
| 8:53.10 | Leslie | Seymour (40) | USA | 60 | 5 | TAC | Eugene | 21 | Jun |
| 8:53.23 | Ruth | Wysocki | USA | 57 | 3 . | | Belfast | 30 | Jun |
| 8:53.28 | Debbie | Bowker | CAN | 58 | 10 | Nik | Nice | 15 | Jul |
| 8:54.0 m | Ana | Barbu | RUM | 63 | 1 | | Bucureşti | 13 | Jul |
| 8:54.53 | Viorica | Ghican | RUM | 65 | 6 | RumIC | Bucureşti | 15 | Jun |
| 8:54.99 | Iris | Biba | FRG | 64 | 2 | NC | W Berlin | 13 | Jul |
| 8:55.50 | Paula | Ivan | RUM | 63 | 3 | | Bucureşti | 25 | May |
| 8:55.97 | Corinne | Debaets | BEL | 63 | 5 | | Belfast | 30 | Jun |

| Mark | Name | | Nat | Yr | Pos | Meet | Venue | Date | |
|---|---|---|---|---|---|---|---|---|---|
| 8:56.08 | Brenda | Webb | USA | 54 | 6 | TAC | Eugene | 21 | Jun |
| 8:56.30 | Christine | Benning | UK | 55 | 3 | NC | Cwmbran | 25 | May |
| 8:56.34 | Yelena | Romanova (50) | SU | 63 | 3 | Znam | Leningrad | 7 | Jun |
| 8:56.49 | Jana | Kučeríková | CS | 64 | 2 | | Cork | 8 | Jul |
| 8:56.61 | Jane | Shields | UK | 60 | 4 | NC | Cwmbran | 25 | May |
| 8:56.72 | Adriana | Dumitru | RUM | 68 | 8 | RumIC | Bucureşti | 15 | Jun |
| 8:56.83 | Christine | Pfitzinger | NZ | 59 | | | Auckland | 12 | Mar |
| 8:57.22 | Larisa | Yemelyanenko | SU | 64 | 3 | | Kiev | 26 | Jul |
| 8:57.27 | Maria | Vasilyuk | SU | 62 | 9 | NC | Kiev | 16 | Jul |
| 8:57.31 | Aurora | Cunha | POR | 59 | 1 | WA | Barcelona | 15 | Jun |
| 8:57.71 | Sabrina | Dornhoefer | USA | 63 | 6 | WG | Helsinki | 7 | Jul |
| 8:59.0 m | Susan | Bruce | NZ | 64 | 2 | | Auckland | 25 | Feb |
| 8:59.15 | Carole | Rouillard(60) | CAN | 60 | 5 | | Birmingham | 18 | Jul |
| 8:59.24 | Ingrid | Delagrange | BEL | 58 | 4 | | Koblenz | 6 | Aug |
| 8:59.70 | Eva | Kadas | RUM | 59 | 5 | | Bucureşti | 25 | May |
| 8:59.72 | Iulia | Beşliu | RUM | 65 | 9 | RumIC | Bucureşti | 15 | Jun |
| 9:00.03 | Antje | Winkelmann | FRG | 65 | 2 | | Lage | 13 | Jun |
| 9:00.12 | Ille | Kukk | SU | 57 | 11 | NC | Kiev | 16 | Jul |
| 9:00.13 | Christin | Sørum | NOR | 68 | 8h1 | EC | Stuttgart | 26 | Aug |
| 9:00.16 | Sandra | Gasser | SWZ | 62 | 5 | WK | Zürich | 13 | Aug |
| 9:00.24 | Renata | Kokowska | POL | 58 | 1 | NC | Grudziadz | 27 | Jun |
| 9:00.32 | Anne Jorun | Flaten | NOR | 61 | 6 | | Birmingham | 18 | Jul |
| 9:00.43 | Martine | Oppliger (70) | SWZ | 57 | 6 | WK | Zürich | 13 | Aug |
| 9:00.45 | Suzanne | Girard | USA | 62 | 3 | USOCF | Houston | 1 | Aug |
| 9:00.64 | Lyudmila | Matveyeva | SU | 57 | 10 | RumIC | Bucureşti | 15 | Jun |
| 9:01.06 | Betty | Springs | USA | 61 | 3 | | Knoxville | 23 | May |
| 9:01.14 | Yekaterina | Skvortsova | SU | 61 | 4 | | Donetsk | 6 | Sep |
| 9:01.2 m | Alison | Wiley | CAN | 63 | 1 | | Watford | 13 | Aug |
| 9:01.29 | Ria | Van Landeghem | BEL | 57 | 7 | | Belfast | 30 | Jun |
| 9:01.34 | Liz | Natale | USA | 64 | 2 | | Tallahassee | 19 | Apr |
| 9:01.55 | Roberta | Brunet | ITA | 65 | 7 | WK | Zürich | 13 | Aug |
| 9:01.71 | Wanda | Panfil | POL | 59 | 2 | NC | Grudziadz | 27 | Jun |
| 9:01.75 | Tuija | Jousimaa (80) | FIN | 58 | 10 | WG | Helsinki | 7 | Jul |
| 9:01.75 | Rasa | Verbickiene | SU | 62 | 12 | NC | Kiev | 16 | Jul |
| 9:01.76 | Cleopatra | Pălăcian | RUM | 68 | 6 | | Bucureşti | 25 | May |
| 9:02.08 | Nancy | Rooks | CAN | 59 | 7 | | Birmingham | 18 | Jul |
| 9:02.11 | Christina | Mai | FRG | 61 | 6 | | Koblenz | 6 | Aug |
| 9:02.32 | Marie-Louise | Hamrin | SWE | 57 | 7h2 | EC | Stuttgart | 26 | Aug |
| 9:02.36 | Nadezhda | Vazhenina | SU | 63 | 2 | | Bryansk | 14 | Aug |
| 9:02.38 | Cathie | Twomey | USA | 56 | 7 | TAC | Eugene | 21 | Jun |
| 9:02.50 | Albina | Tarasova | SU | 58 | 5 | | Donetsk | 6 | Sep |
| 9:02.70 | Huabi | Wang | CHN | 66 | 1 | | Zhengzhou | 22 | Oct |
| 9:02.78 | Ruth | Partridge(90) | UK | 60 | 12 | RumIC | Bucureşti | 15 | Jun |
| 9:03.00 | Anna | Pedan | SU | 61 | 13 | NC | Kiev | 16 | Jul |
| 9:03.32 | Anne | Audain | NZ | 55 | 1 | NC | Christchurch | 7 | Mar |
| 9:03.32 | Christine | McMiken | NZ | 63 | 1 | | Eugene | 3 | May |
| 9:03.35 | Philippa | Mason | UK | 69 | 2 | WC-j | Athinai | 19 | Jul |
| 9:03.49 | Tatyana | Pentukova | SU | 65 | 3 | | Bryansk | 14 | Aug |
| 9:03.77 | Sabine | Kunkel | FRG | 64 | 3 | NC | W Berlin | 13 | Jul |
| 9:03.89 | Lorraine | Moller | NZ | 55 | 5 | CG | Edinburgh | 27 | Jul |
| 9:03.95 | Shelly | Steely | USA | 62 | 8 | TAC | Eugene | 21 | Jun |
| 9:03.96 | Maria | Lantsova | SU | 62 | 1 | | Moskva | 1 | Aug |
| 9:04.04 | Ludmila | Melicherová | CS | 64 | 1 | | Praha | 9 | Aug |

(100)

| Mark | Name | | Nat | Yr | Pos | Meet | Venue | Date |
|---|---|---|---|---|---|---|---|---|
| 9:04.20 | Juhua | Hou | CHN | 67 | 2 | | Zhengzhou | 22 Oct |
| 9:04.21 | Nina | Yapeyeva | SU | 56 | 4 | | Kiev | 26 Jul |
| 9:04.33 | Joan | Nesbit | USA | 62 | 10 | | Birmingham | 18 Jul |
| 9:04.45 | Annette | Hand | USA | 65 | 9 | TAC | Eugene | 21 Jun |
| 9:04.58 | Claudia | Borgschulze | FRG | 64 | 4 | NC | W Berlin | 13 Jul |
| 9:04.85 | Dorina | Calenic (106) | RUM | 69 | | | Piteşti | 29 Jun |

| Mark | Name | | Nat | Yr | Date |
|---|---|---|---|---|---|
| 9:05.11 | Marina | Belyayeva | SU | 58 | 26 Jul |
| 9:05.30 | Roisin | Smyth | IRL | 63 | 8 Jul |
| 9:05.35 | Irina | Mozharova | SU | 58 | 23 May |
| 9:05.94 | Jingmin | Li (110) | CHN | 64 | 7 Jun |
| 9:06.14 | Ulrike | Beck | FRG | 61 | 6 Aug |
| 9:06.19 | Lisa | Breiding | USA | 66 | 23 May |
| 9:06.27 | Monika | Kukel | GDR | 66 | 20 Aug |
| 9:06.40 | Sue | French-Lee | CAN | 60 | 24 May |
| 9:06.43 | Jeanette | Hain | GDR | 66 | 27 Jun |
| 9:06.52 | Svetlana | Kuznetsova | SU | 61 | 27 Jun |
| 9:06.56 | Irina | Karbolina | SU | 60 | 26 Jul |
| 9:06.88 | Christine | Loiseau | FRA | 60 | 17 Aug |
| 9:06.90 | Simona | Staicu | RUM | 71 | 8 Jun |
| 9:06.93 | Irina | Matrosova | SU | 62 | 16 Jul |
| | | (120) | | | |
| 9:07.0 m | Dorthe | Rasmussen | DEN | 60 | 26 Jul |
| 9:07.18 | Inna | Pushkareva | SU | 65 | 23 May |
| 9:07.44 | Snežana | Pajkić | YUG | 70 | 26 Aug |
| 9:07.49 | Marion | Josefsen | NOR | 67 | 8 Aug |
| 9:07.60 | Eva | Ernström | SWE | 61 | 9 Aug |
| 9:07.63 | Zita | Agoston | HUN | 65 | 11 Jun |
| 9:07.67 | Sue | Schroeder | USA | 63 | 21 Jun |
| 9:07.74 | Jurate | Urbanaviciute | SU | 61 | 26 Jul |
| 9:07.78 | Päivi | Tikkanen | FIN | 60 | 7 Jul |
| 9:08.28 | Xiuting | Wang (130) | CHN | 65 | 7 Sep |
| 9:08.34 | Sissel | Grottenberg | NOR | 56 | 8 Aug |
| 9:08.4 m | Lyudmila | Nikolayeva | SU | 64 | 28 Aug |

| Mark | Name | | Nat | Yr | Date |
|---|---|---|---|---|---|
| 9:08.59 | Lynn | Jennings | USA | 60 | 7 Jun |
| 9:08.64 | Stephanie | Herbst | USA | 65 | 24 May |
| 9:08.74 | Marzanna | Ulidowska | POL | 61 | 27 Jun |
| 9:08.82 | Mary | Donoghue | IRL | 62 | 8 Jul |
| 9:08.85 | Erika | Vereb | HUN | 63 | 18 Sep |
| 9:08.93 | Olga | Matselyukh | SU | 65 | 26 Jul |
| 9:09.00 | Maria | Curatolo | ITA | 63 | 27 Jun |
| 9:09.3 m | Monica | Joyce (140) | IRL | 58 | 26 Apr |
| 9:09.39 | Fernanda | Ribeiro | POR | 69 | 19 Jul |
| 9:09.4 m | Yelena | Plastinina | SU | 63 | 28 Aug |
| 9:09.59 | Julie-Ann | Laughton | UK | 59 | 28 May |
| 9:09.66 | Yanling | Wang | CHN | 64 | 7 Jun |
| 9:09.78 | Karolina | Szabó | HUN | 61 | 18 Sep |
| 9:09.81 | Ragnheidur | Olafsdottir | ICE | 63 | 23 May |
| 9:09.92 | Kathrin | Ullrich | GDR | 67 | 13 Jul |
| 9:10.09 | Mioara | Bicu | RUM | 59 | 15 Jun |
| 9:10.3 m | Olga | Parlyuk | SU | 63 | 28 Jun |
| 9:10.34 | Grete | Kirkeberg | NOR | 64 | 8 Aug |
| | | (150) | | | |
| 9:10.36 | Gitte | Karlshøj | DEN | 59 | 14 Aug |
| 9:10.50 | Angela | Tooby | UK | 60 | 17 Aug |
| 9:10.57 | Kathrin | Kley | GDR | 68 | 24 May |
| 9:10.72 | Rosanna | Munerotto | ITA | 62 | 27 Jun |
| 9:10.80 | Elisabeth | Franzis | FRG | 62 | 21 May |
| 9:10.88 | Francoise | Bonnet | FRA | 57 | 8 Aug |
| 9:10.92 | Cristina | Tomasini | ITA | 58 | 25 May |
| 9:10.96 | Tatyana | Polovinskaya | SU | 65 | 26 Jul |
| | | (158) | | | |

WOMEN 1986

Indoor marks:

| Mark | Name | | Nat | Yr | Pos | Meet | Venue | Date |
|---|---|---|---|---|---|---|---|---|
| 8:39.79i | | Budd | | | 1 | v Hun | Cosford | 8 Feb |
| 8:42.3 mi | | Bondarenko | | | 1 | | Volgograd | 26 Jan |
| 8:44.86i | | Samolenko | | | 1 | NC | Moskva | 8 Feb |
| 8:47.00i | Gabriele | Veith | GDR | 56 | 1 | | Tokyo | 8 Mar |
| 8:47.79i | Yelena | Romanova | SU | 63 | 3 | NC | Moskva | 8 Feb |
| 8:53.19i | Lynn | Jennings | USA | 60 | 2 | | E Rutherford | 8 Feb |
| 8:55.61i | Cathy | Easker | USA | 63 | 4 | | E Rutherford | 8 Feb |
| 8:57.05i | Iulia | Beşliu | RUM | 65 | 1 | NC | Bacău | 8 Feb |
| 9:02.64i | Zita | Ágoston | HUN | 65 | 2 | v UK | Cosford | 8 Feb |

| Mark | Name | | Nat | Yr | Date |
|---|---|---|---|---|---|
| 9:06.29i | Christina | Boxer | UK | 57 | 25 Feb |
| 9:06.61i | Nikolina | Shtereva | BUL | 55 | 16 Feb |
| 9:06.89i | Iva | Jurková | CS | 66 | 2 Feb |
| 9:07.06i | Nan | Doak | USA | 62 | 19 Jan |

| Mark | Name | | Nat | Yr | Date |
|---|---|---|---|---|---|
| 9:07.91i | Kathryn | Carter | UK | 59 | 8 Feb |
| 9:08.42i | Stephanie | Herbst | USA | 65 | 28 Feb |
| 9:08.51i | Karolina | Szabó | HUN | 61 | 6 Feb |
| 9:09.6 mi | Lyubov | Smolka | SU | 62 | 26 Jan |
| 9:10.77i | Michele | Bush (18) | USA | 61 | 8 Feb |

| Mark | Name | | | Nat | Yr | Pos | Meet | Venue | Date |
|------|------|--|--|-----|----|-----|------|-------|------|

| | 1 | 10 | 20 | 30 | 50 | 100 | Under 8:55.0 | Under 9:05.0 |
|--|---|----|----|----|----|-----|--------------|--------------|
| 1982 | 8:26.78 | 8:36.54 | 8:46.01 | 8:51.79 | 8:55.98 | 9:08.02 | 42 | 88 |
| 1983 | 8:32.08 | 8:37.40 | 8:47.36 | 8:50.36 | 8:55.09 | 9:05.7 | 49 | 97 |
| 1984 | 8:22.62 | 8:37.76 | 8:42.14 | 8:47.94 | 8:52.49 | 9:01.5 | 61 | 115 |
| 1985 | 8:25.83 | 8:42.19 | 8:48.52 | 8:51.10 | 8:58.55 | 9:05.94 | 36 | 89 |
| 1986 | 8:33.99 | 8:39.25 | 8:46.94 | 8:49.91 | 8:56.34 | 9:04.04 | 45 | 106 |

# 5000 METRES

| Mark | Name | | Nat | Yr | Pos | Meet | Venue | Date |
|------|------|--|-----|----|-----|------|-------|------|
| 14:37.33 | Ingrid | Kristiansen | NOR | 56 | 1 | | Stockholm | 5 Aug |
| 14:58.70 | | Kristiansen | | | 1 | FBK | Hengelo | 27 Jun |
| 15:02.12 | Svetlana | Guskova | SU | 59 | 1 | v GDR | Tallinn | 21 Jun |
| 15:03.51 | Olga | Bondarenko | SU | 60 | 1 | GWG | Moskva | 8 Jul |
| 15:05.50 | Svetlana | Ulmasova | SU | 53 | 2 | GWG | Moskva | 8 Jul |
| 15:06.18 | | Bondarenko | | | 2 | v GDR | Tallinn | 21 Jun |
| 15:07.89+ | | Kristiansen | | | 1 | EC | Stuttgart | 30 Aug |
| 15:08.36 | Lynn | Jennings | USA | 60 | 2 | FBK | Hengelo | 27 Jun |
| 15:11.27 | | Guskova | | | 1 | | Sochi | 25 May |
| 15:11.33+ | | Kristiansen | | | 1 | Bisl | Oslo | 5 Jul |
| 15:11.78 | Cindy | Bremser | USA | 53 | 3 | GWG | Moskva | 8 Jul |
| 15:16.84 | | Bondarenko | | | 1 | GP | Roma | 10 Sep |
| 15:17.90 | | Guskova | | | 4 | GWG | Moskva | 8 Jul |
| 15:17.95 | | Guskova | | | 2 | GP | Roma | 10 Sep |
| 15:18.68 | | Guskova | | | 1 | PTS | Bratislava | 14 Jun |
| 15:20.88 | PattiSue | Plumer | USA | 62 | 5 | GWG | Moskva | 8 Jul |
| 15:21.90 | Gabriele | Veith | GDR | 56 | 6 | GWG | Moskva | 8 Jul |
| 15:22.33 | Mary | Knisely | USA | 59 | 3 | GP | Roma | 10 Sep |
| 15:23.25 | Yelena | Zhupiyeva(10) | SU | 60 | 7 | GWG | Moskva | 8 Jul |
| 15:23.54 | Erika | Veréb | HUN | 63 | 4 | GP | Roma | 10 Sep |
| 15:25.10 | | Veith | | | 3 | v SU | Tallinn | 21 Jun |
| 15:25.59 | Aurora | Cunha | POR | 59 | 3 | FBK | Hengelo | 27 Jun |
| 15:26.56 | | Ulmasova | | | 1 | NC | Kiev | 14 Jul |
| 15:27.05 | Ines | Bibernell | GDR | 65 | 1 | OD | Dresden | 3 Jul |
| 15:27.70 | | Plumer | | | 5 | GP | Roma | 10 Sep |
| 15:28.16 | Angela | Tooby | UK | 60 | 6 | GP | Roma | 10 Sep |
| 15:28.40 | Marina | Rodchenkova | SU | 61 | 2 | NC | Kiev | 14 Jul |
| 15:28.55 | Natalya | Sorokivskaya | SU | 62 | 3 | NC | Kiev | 14 Jul |
| 15:28.61 | | Knisely | | | 1 | VD | Bruxelles | 5 Sep |
| 15:28.64 | Krishna | Wood | AUS | 66 | 1 | | Melbourne | 2 Dec |
| 15:28.74 | | Plumer | | | 2 | OD | Dresden | 3 Jul |
| 15:29.36 | Lyudmila | Matveyeva | SU | 57 | 4 | NC | Kiev | 14 Jul |
| | | (32/18) | | | | | | |
| 15:30.60 | Yelena | Sipatova | SU | 55 | 5 | NC | Kiev | 14 Jul |
| 15.30.99 | Betty | Springs (20) | USA | 61 | 1 | TAC | Eugene | 20 Jun |
| 15:31.09 | Stephanie | Herbst | USA | 65 | 1 | | San Diego | 29 Mar |
| 15:32.11 | Anna | Domoradskaya | SU | 53 | 6 | NC | Kiev | 14 Jul |

| Mark | Name | | Nat | Yr | Pos | Meet | Venue | Date |
|---|---|---|---|---|---|---|---|---|
| 15:32.76 | Maricica | Puică | RUM | 50 | 1 | | Paris | 22 Jul |
| 15:32.90 | Lorraine | Moller | NZ | 55 | 2 | TAC | Eugene | 20 Jun |
| 15:32.92 | Annette | Sergent | FRA | 62 | 2 | | Paris | 22 Jul |
| 15:33.57 | Maria | Vasilyuk | SU | 62 | 7 | NC | Kiev | 14 Jul |
| 15:34.69 | Karolina | Szabó | HUN | 61 | 1 | v Aut, | Bul Linz | 29 Jun |
| 15:36.68 | Iris | Biba | FRG | 64 | 1 | | Gelnhausen | 12 Sep |
| 15:37.17 | Juhua | Hou | CHN | 67 | 1 | | Zhengzhou | 24 Oct |
| 15:38.09 | Christine | Loiseau (30) | FRA | 60 | 3 | | Paris | 22 Jul |
| 15:38.34 | Jackie | Perkins | AUS | 65 | 2 | | Melbourne | 2 Dec |
| 15:39.44 | Brenda | Webb | USA | 54 | 1 | King | Atlanta | 20 Apr |
| 15:40.49 | Valentina | Vasilyeva | SU | 64 | 3 | | Sochi | 25 May |
| 15:41.36 | Mariana | Stănescu | RUM | 64 | 1 | Roš | Praha | 24 Jun |
| 15:41.36 | Susan | Tooby | UK | 60 | 5 | VD | Bruxelles | 5 Sep |
| 15:41.46+ | Ulrike | Bruns | GDR | 53 | 6 | EC | Stuttgart | 30 Aug |
| 15:41.58+ | Elizabeth | Lynch | UK | 64 | 7 | EC | Stuttgart | 30 Aug |
| 15:41.68 | Vera | Michallek | FRG | 58 | 3 | | Gelnhausen | 12 Sep |
| 15:41.77 | Suzanne | Girard | USA | 62 | 4 | TAC | Eugene | 20 Jun |
| 15:41.83 | Elena | Fidatov (40) | RUM | 60 | 2 | Roš | Praha | 24 Jun |
| 15:42.38 | Daniele | Kaber | LUX | 60 | 6 | VD | Bruxelles | 5 Sep |
| 15:42.45 | Ille | Kukk | SU | 57 | 8 | NC | Kiev | 14 Jul |
| 15:42.69 | Wanda | Panfil | POL | 59 | 3 | PTS | Bratislava | 14 Jun |
| 15:44.27 | Sue | Schroeder | USA | 63 | 2 | NCAA | Indianapolis | 7 Jun |
| 15:44.30 | Sabrina | Dornhoefer | USA | 63 | 4 | FBK | Hengelo | 27 Jun |
| 15:45.4 m | Galina | Ikonnikova | SU | 62 | 1 | | Moskva | 11 May |
| 15:45.89 | Lieve | Slegers | BEL | 65 | 7 | VD | Bruxelles | 5 Sep |
| 15:45.98 | Grete | Kirkeberg | NOR | 64 | 1 | NC | Sandnes | 10 Aug |
| 15:46.99 | Alla | Yushina | SU | 58 | 1 | | Moskva | 3 Aug |
| 15:48.10 | Tatyana | Sokolova (50) | SU | 58 | 4 | | Sochi | 25 May |
| 15:48.21 | Patty | Murray | USA | | 3 | NCAA | Indianapolis | 7 Jun |
| 15:48.25 | Kerstin | Pressler | FRG | 62 | 3 | Roš | Praha | 24 Jun |
| 15:49.43 | Eva | Ernström | SWE | 61 | 4 | PTS | Bratislava | 14 Jun |
| 15:49.56 | Marleen | Renders | BEL | 68 | 8 | VD | Bruxelles | 5 Sep |
| 15:50.64 | Ute | Jamrozy | FRG | 64 | 5 | FBK | Hengelo | 27 Jun |
| 15:50.91 | Sun-Me | Kim | NKO | 68 | 4 | Roš | Praha | 24 Jun |
| 15:51.0 m | Christin | Sørum | NOR | 68 | 1 | | Sola | 8 Oct |
| 15:51.13 | Suzie | Tuffey | USA | 67 | 1 | | Raleigh | 17 May |
| 15:52.11 | Antje | Winkelmann | FRG | 65 | 4 | | Gelnhausen | 12 Sep |
| 15:52.19 | Huabi | Wang (60) | CHN | 66 | 2 | | Zhengzhou | 24 Oct |
| 15:52.36 | Joan | Nesbit | USA | 62 | 1 | | Dedham | 7 Jun |
| 15:52.5 m | Sylvia | Mosqueda | USA | 66 | 1 | | Walnut, CA | 16 May |
| 15:52.71+ | Anne | Audain | NZ | 55 | 1 | CG | Edinburgh | 28 Jul |
| 15:53.38 | Ria | Van Landeghem | BEL | 57 | 12 | GWG | Moskva | 8 Jul |
| 15:53.83 | Carla | Beurskens | HOL | 52 | 7 | FBK | Hengelo | 27 Jun |
| 15:54.01 | M Conceicao | Ferreira | POR | 62 | 13 | GWG | Moskva | 8 Jul |
| 15:54.12 | Jacque | Struckhoff | USA | 65 | 3 | DrakeR | Des Moines | 26 Apr |
| 15:54.94 | Lion-Sun | Kim | NKO | 69 | 5 | Roš | Praha | 24 Jun |
| 15:55.3 m | Chris | Vanatta | USA | 64 | 1 | | Baton Rouge | 21 Mar |
| 15:55.55 | Jana | Kučeríková | CS | 64 | 6 | PTS | Bratislava | 14 Jun |
| | | (70) | | | | | | |
| 15:55.82 | Sabine | Knetsch | FRG | 66 | 5 | | Gelnhausen | 12 Sep |
| 15:56.19 | Renata | Kokowska | POL | 58 | 1 | | Grudziadz | 3 Jun |
| 15:56.41 | Patty | Matava | USA | 65 | 2 | | Charlottesville | 10 May |
| 15:57.08 | Anna | Pedan | SU | 61 | 6 | | Sochi | 25 May |
| 15:57.44 | Lyudmila | Nikolayeva | SU | 64 | 9 | NC | Kiev | 14 Jul |

WOMEN 1986

| Mark | Name | | Nat | Yr | Pos | Meet | Venue | Date |
|---|---|---|---|---|---|---|---|---|
| 15:57.52 | Ulrike | Beck | FRG | 61 | 6 | | Gelnhausen | 12 Sep |
| 15:58.05 | Christine | McMiken | NZ | 63 | 1 | TexR | Austin | 4 Apr |
| 15:58.53 | Yelizaveta | Bradu | SU | 54 | 7 | | Sochi | 25 May |
| 15:58.77 | Margaret | Thomas | USA | 59 | 3 | King | Atlanta | 20 Apr |
| 15:58.90 | Anne | Schweitzer | USA | 65 | 1 | | Houston | 18 May |
| | | (80) | | | | | | |
| 15:58.94 | Lidia | Alekseyeva | SU | 61 | 8 | | Sochi | 25 May |
| 15:59.77 | Inna | Pushkareva | SU | 65 | 1 | | Leningrad | 19 Aug |
| | | (82) | | | | | | |
| 16:00.12+ | Maria | Curatolo | ITA | 63 | 30 Aug | | Natale | USA 64 29 Mar |
| 16:00.49 | Cristina | Tomasini | ITA | 58 | 3 Jun | | Fukao | JAP 61 11 May |
| 16:01.1m | Hisano | Yokosuka | JAP | 65 | 25 Oct | | Palm | SWE 42 5 Aug |
| 16:01.3m | Francie | Larrieu-Smith | USA | 52 | 10 May | | Yamauchi | JAP 66 25 Oct |
| 16:01.57 | Lisa | Breiding | USA | 66 | 4 Apr | | Ormsby | USA 64 18 Apr |
| 16:02.19 | Yekaterina | Skvortsova | SU | 61 | 7 Sep | | Terakoshi | JAP 69 11 May |
| 16:02.20 | Dorthe | Rasmussen | DEN | 60 | 5 Aug | | O'Connor | NZ 55 22 Jul |
| 16:02.35 | Albina | Tarasova (90) | SU | 58 | 7 Sep | | Ágoston | HUN 65 11 Aug |
| 16:02.61 | Hongyan | Xiao | CHN | 65 | 4 Jun | | Bonnet (120) | FRA 57 22 Jul |
| 16:03.68 | Yelena | Provorova | SU | 64 | 19 Aug | | Reynolds | USA 64 18 Apr |
| 16:03.70 | Debbie | Elsmore | NZ | 58 | 1 Feb | | Kunkel | FRG 64 23 Apr |
| 16:04.02 | Kumi | Araki | JAP | 65 | 15 Sep | | Oppliger | SWZ 57 6 Jun |
| 16:04.32 | Wendy | Renner | NZ | 60 | 1 Feb | | Conz | USA 57 7 Jun |
| 16:04.33 | Marie-Louise | Hamrin | SWE | 57 | 4 Apr | | Asai | JAP 59 11 May |
| 16:04.43 | Alison | Wiley | CAN | 63 | 3 May | | Wolter | USA 67 24 May |
| 16:04.46 | Maria | Lantsova | SU | 62 | 29 Jun | | Keogh | USA 69 10 May |
| 16:04.68 | Sue | King | USA | 58 | 8 Jul | | Forsythe | USA 63 21 Mar |
| 16:04.7m | Leslie | Seymour (100) | USA | 60 | 31 May | | Lelut | FRA 56 4 Jun |
| 16:05.56 | Jingmin | Li | CHN | 64 | 4 Jun | | Sirma (130) | KEN 66 5 Jul |
| 16:05.60 | Claudia | Borgschulze | FRG | 64 | 23 Aug | | Camberg | POL 62 3 Jun |
| 16:07.48 | Yuki | Tamura | JAP | 67 | 15 Sep | | Wood | USA 67 12 Apr |
| 16:08.08 | Márta | Visnyei | HUN | 62 | 10 May | | Mozharova | SU 58 25 May |
| 16:08.41 | Sissel | Grottenberg | NOR | 56 | 5 Aug | | Ulidowska | POL 61 3 Jun |
| 16:08.6m | Xiuxia | Li | CHN | 67 | 2 May | | Belyayeva | SU 57 25 May |
| 16:09.2m | Stacy | Prey | USA | 67 | 24 Apr | | McGrann | USA 65 12 Apr |
| 16:09.26 | Jenny | Spangler | USA | 63 | 21 Mar | | Polo | USA 64 24 Apr |
| 16:09.53 | Huandi | Zhong | CHN | 66 | 24 Oct | | Sipka-Óze | HUN 54 10 May |
| 16:09.61 | Janet | Smith (110) | USA | 65 | 18 Apr | | Clarke | UK 58 26 May |
| 16:09.66 | Miyuki | Yamashita | JAP | 64 | 15 Sep | | Villeton(140) | FRA 54 4 Jun |

Second column marks:

| Mark | | Name | |
|---|---|---|---|
| 16:10.13 | Liz | Natale | USA 64 29 Mar |
| 16:10.61 | Mami | Fukao | JAP 61 11 May |
| 16:10.97 | Evy | Palm | SWE 42 5 Aug |
| 16:11.0m | Tomoko | Yamauchi | JAP 66 25 Oct |
| 16:11.06 | Kathy | Ormsby | USA 64 18 Apr |
| 16:11.25 | Saori | Terakoshi | JAP 69 11 May |
| 16:11.56 | Mary | O'Connor | NZ 55 22 Jul |
| 16:11.59 | Zita | Ágoston | HUN 65 11 Aug |
| 16:12.04 | Francoise | Bonnet (120) | FRA 57 22 Jul |
| 16:12.42 | Ellen | Reynolds | USA 64 18 Apr |
| 16:12.7m | Sabine | Kunkel | FRG 64 23 Apr |
| 16:13.48 | Martine | Oppliger | SWZ 57 6 Jun |
| 16:13.99 | Nancy | Conz | USA 57 7 Jun |
| 16:14.23 | Eriko | Asai | JAP 59 11 May |
| 16:14.29 | Lori | Wolter | USA 67 24 May |
| 16:14.69 | Erin | Keogh | USA 69 10 May |
| 16:15.5m | Sandy | Forsythe | USA 63 21 Mar |
| 16:15.63 | Maria | Lelut | FRA 56 4 Jun |
| 16:16.4m | Susan | Sirma (130) | KEN 66 5 Jul |
| 16:16.71 | Lidia | Camberg | POL 62 3 Jun |
| 16:16.89 | Sally | Wood | USA 67 12 Apr |
| 16:17.35 | Irina | Mozharova | SU 58 25 May |
| 16:17.52 | Marzanna | Ulidowska | POL 61 3 Jun |
| 16:17.66 | Lucia | Belyayeva | SU 57 25 May |
| 16:18.46 | Beth | McGrann | USA 65 12 Apr |
| 16:19.2m | Roxann | Polo | USA 64 24 Apr |
| 16:19.30 | Ágnes | Sipka-Óze | HUN 54 10 May |
| 16:19.4m+ | Jill | Clarke | UK 58 26 May |
| 16:19.83 | Jocelyne | Villeton(140) | FRA 54 4 Jun |

Indoor marks:

| 15:37.5 mi | Brenda | Webb | USA 54 | 1 | | Gainesville | 2 Feb |
|---|---|---|---|---|---|---|---|
| 16:17.1mi | Andrea | Everett | UK 64 25 Jan | | | | |
| 16:18.291 | Sheri | Reid | USA 63 15 Feb | | | | |

16:19.5mi Carole Rouillard CAN 60 11 Jan

Mark made in mixed race with men:

| 15:19.841 | Lesley | Welch | USA 63 | - | | Boston | 25 Jan |
|---|---|---|---|---|---|---|---|

# 10 000 METRES

| Mark | Name | | Nat | Yr | Pos | Meet | Venue | Date |
|---|---|---|---|---|---|---|---|---|
| 30:13.74 | Ingrid | Kristiansen | NOR | 56 | 1 | Bisl | Oslo | 5 Jul |
| 30:23.25 | | Kristiansen | | | 1 | EC | Stuttgart | 30 Aug |
| 30:57.21 | Olga | Bondarenko | SU | 60 | 2 | EC | Stuttgart | 30 Aug |
| 31:19.76 | Ulrike | Bruns | GDR | 53 | 3 | EC | Stuttgart | 30 Aug |
| 31:29.41 | Aurora | Cunha | POR | 59 | 2 | Bisl | Oslo | 5 Jul |

| Mark | Name | | Nat | Yr | Pos | Meet | Venue | Date | |
|------|------|--|-----|----|----|------|-------|------|--|
| 31:39.35 | | Cunha | | | 4 | EC | Stuttgart | 30 | Aug |
| 31:41.42 | Elizabeth | Lynch | UK | 64 | 1 | CG | Edinburgh | 28 | Jul |
| 31:42.43 | Svetlana | Guskova | SU | 59 | 5 | EC | Stuttgart | 30 | Aug |
| 31:42.99 | Yelena | Zhupiyeva | SU | 60 | 6 | EC | Stuttgart | 30 | Aug |
| 31:49.46 | | Lynch | | | 7 | EC | Stuttgart | 30 | Aug |
| 31:53.31 | Anne | Audain | NZ | 55 | 2 | CG | Edinburgh | 28 | Jul |
| 31:55.93 | Karolina | Szabó | HUN | 61 | 8 | EC | Stuttgart | 30 | Aug |
| 31:56.59 | Angela | Tooby (10) | UK | 60 | 9 | EC | Stuttgart | 30 | Aug |
| 31:56.66 | | Guskova | | | 1 | Znam | Leningrad | 8 | Jun |
| 31:57.00 | | Zhupiyeva | | | 2 | Znam | Leningrad | 8 | Jun |
| 32:04.34 | Maria | Curatolo | ITA | 63 | 10 | EC | Stuttgart | 30 | Aug |
| 32:06.38 | Natalya | Sorokivskaya | SU | 62 | 3 | Znam | Leningrad | 8 | Jun |
| 32:07.64 | | Szabó | | | 1 | NC | Budapest | 1 | Jun |
| 32:11.89 | Anna | Domoradskaya | SU | 53 | 4 | Znam | Leningrad | 8 | Jun |
| 32:13.41 | | Bruns | | | 1 | NC | Erfurt | 1 | Jun |
| 32:14.83 | Svetlana | Ulmasova | SU | 53 | 5 | Znam | Leningrad | 8 | Jun |
| 32:15.00 | Galina | Zakharova | SU | 56 | 6 | Znam | Leningrad | 8 | Jun |
| 32:15.56 | Erika | Veréb | HUN | 63 | 11 | EC | Stuttgart | 30 | Aug |
| 32:16.97 | Daniele | Kaber | LUX | 60 | 12 | EC | Stuttgart | 30 | Aug |
| 32:17.1 m | | Audain | | | 1 | | Auckland | 20 | Feb |
| 32:17.22 | Gabriele | Veith | GDR | 56 | 13 | EC | Stuttgart | 30 | Aug |
| 32:18.40 | Marie-Louise | Hamrin | SWE | 57 | 14 | EC | Stuttgart | 30 | Aug |
| 32:18.95 | | Veith | | | 2 | NC | Erfurt | 1 | Jun |
| 32:19.86 | | Veréb | | | 3 | Bisl | Oslo | 5 | Jul |
| 32:21.68 | | Sorokivskaya | | | 1 | | Kiev | 25 | Jul |
| | | (30/19) | | | | | | | |
| 32:22.63 | Marina | Belyayeva(20) | SU | 58 | 7 | Znam | Leningrad | 8 | Jun |
| 32:24.69 | Elena | Murgoci | RUM | 60 | 1 | NC | Piteşti | 9 | Aug |
| 32:25.19 | Nadezhda | Stepanova | SU | 59 | 8 | Znam | Leningrad | 8 | Jun |
| 32:25.99 | Christine | Loiseau | FRA | 60 | 15 | EC | Stuttgart | 30 | Aug |
| 32:26.58 | Viorica | Ghican | RUM | 65 | 2 | NC | Piteşti | 9 | Aug |
| 32:26.90 | Lieve | Slegers | BEL | 65 | 16 | EC | Stuttgart | 30 | Aug |
| 32:29.39 | Tatyana | Gridneva | SU | 58 | 2 | | Kiev | 25 | Jul |
| 32:29.73 | Ria | Van Landeghem | BEL | 57 | 4 | Bisl | Oslo | 5 | Jul |
| 32:29.86 | Nan | Doak | USA | 62 | 1 | TAC | Eugene | 19 | Jun |
| 32:30.24 | Lynn | Nelson | USA | 62 | 2 | TAC | Eugene | 19 | Jun |
| 32:30.71 | Nancy | Rooks (30) | CAN | 59 | 4 | CG | Edinburgh | 28 | Jul |
| 32:30.75 | Sue | French-Lee | CAN | 60 | 5 | CG | Edinburgh | 28 | Jul |
| 32:30.93 | Carole | Rouillard | CAN | 60 | 1 | NC | Ottawa | 20 | Jun |
| 32:31.00 | Marina | Pluzhnikova | SU | 63 | 9 | Znam | Leningrad | 8 | Jun |
| 32:32.28 | Ines | Bibernell | GDR | 65 | 3 | NC | Erfurt | 1 | Jun |
| 32:32.75 | Stephanie | Herbst | USA | 65 | 1 | NCAA | Indianapolis | 4 | Jun |
| 32:33.19 | Yelizaveta | Bradu | SU | 54 | 11 | Znam | Leningrad | 8 | Jun |
| 32:33.73 | Nina | Yapeyeva | SU | 56 | 3 | | Kiev | 25 | Jul |
| 32:34.73 | Marty | Cooksey | USA | 54 | 3 | TAC | Eugene | 19 | Jun |
| 32:36.2 m | Kathy | Ormsby | USA | 64 | 1 | PennR | Philadelphia | 24 | Apr |
| 32:37.99 | Grete | Kirkeberg(40) | NOR | 64 | 5 | Bisl | Oslo | 5 | Jul |
| 32:38.96 | Marina | Rodchenkova | SU | 61 | 12 | Znam | Leningrad | 8 | Jun |
| 32:40.22 | Cristina | Tomasini | ITA | 58 | 6 | Bisl | Oslo | 5 | Jul |
| 32:40.6 m | Ellen | Reynolds | USA | 64 | 2 | PennR | Philadelphia | 24 | Apr |
| 32:40.69 | Carla | Beurskens | HOL | 52 | 7 | Bisl | Oslo | 5 | Jul |
| 32:41.9 m | Lisa | Welch | USA | 63 | 3 | PennR | Philadelphia | 24 | Apr |
| 32:43.49 | Sue | Berenda | CAN | 61 | 4 | NC | Ottawa | 20 | Jun |

WOMEN 1986

| Mark | Name | | Nat | Yr | Pos | Meet | Venue | Date | |
|------|------|--|-----|----|-----|------|-------|------|--|
| 32:45.4 m | Joan | Samuelson | USA | 57 | 1 | | Chestnut Hill | 17 | Apr |
| 32:46.24 | Kerstin | Pressler | FRG | 62 | 2 | | Essen | 3 | Jun |
| 32:47.24 | Ludmila | Melicherová | CS | 64 | 17 | EC | Stuttgart | 30 | Aug |
| 32:47.25 | Evy | Palm (50) | SWE | 42 | 9 | Bisl | Oslo | 5 | Jul |
| | | | | | | | | | |
| 32:47.77 | Xiuting | Wang | CHN | 65 | 1 | AsiG | Seoul | 1 | Oct |
| 32:48.71 | Martine | Oppliger | SWZ | 57 | 10 | Bisl | Oslo | 5 | Jul |
| 32:48.80 | Anna | Pedan | SU | 61 | 13 | Znam | Leningrad | 8 | Jun |
| 32:50.29 | Lizanne | Bussieres | CAN | 61 | 5 | NC | Ottawa | 20 | Jun |
| 32:51.59 | Eva | Ernström | SWE | 61 | 11 | Bisl | Oslo | 5 | Jul |
| 32:51.71 | Christine | McMiken | NZ | 63 | 2 | NCAA | Indianapolis | 4 | Jun |
| 32:52.93 | Ellen | Wessinghage | FRG | 48 | 12 | Bisl | Oslo | 5 | Jul |
| 32:53.04 | Dorthe | Rasmussen | DEN | 60 | 18 | EC | Stuttgart | 30 | Aug |
| 32:56.78 | Susan | Tooby | UK | 60 | 6 | CG | Edinburgh | 28 | Jul |
| 32:59.67 | Jocelyne | Villeton (60) | FRA | 54 | 15 | Bisl | Oslo | 5 | Jul |
| | | | | | | | | | |
| 33:02.21 | Katrin | Dörre | GDR | 61 | 4 | NC | Erfurt | 1 | Jun |
| 33:05.41 | Yelena | Tolstoguzova | SU | 62 | | | Kiev | 25 | Jul |
| 33:06.0 m | Lyudmila | Matveyeva | SU | 57 | | | Ufa | 4 | Jul |
| 33:08.10 | Natalya | Boborova | SU | 59 | 14 | Znam | Leningrad | 8 | Jun |
| 33:10.25 | Shireen | Samy | UK | 60 | 16 | Bisl | Oslo | 5 | Jul |
| 33:10.62 | Magda | Ilands | BEL | 50 | 22 | EC | Stuttgart | 30 | Aug |
| 33:10.8 m | Janet | Smith | USA | 65 | 4 | PennR | Philadelphia | 24 | Apr |
| 33:10.94 | Marina | Samy | UK | 60 | 7 | CG | Edinburgh | 28 | Jul |
| 33:11.12 | Hongyan | Xiao | CHN | 65 | 1 | | Nanjing | 6 | Jun |
| 33:11.77 | Xiuxia | Li (70) | CHN | 67 | | | Nanjing | 6 | Jun |
| | | | | | | | | | |
| 33:12.1 m | Elena | Evanoff | CAN | 64 | 5 | MSR | Walnut, CA | 26 | Apr |
| 33:13.23 | Monika | Schäfer | FRG | 59 | 3 | NC | W Berlin | 11 | Jul |
| 33:13.30 | Gulnara | Faizulina | SU | 65 | 16 | Znam | Leningrad | 8 | Jun |
| 33:14.07 | Marit | Uglem | NOR | 61 | 17 | Bisl | Oslo | 5 | Jul |
| 33:14.10 | Yelena | Sipatova | SU | 55 | 17 | Znam | Leningrad | 8 | Jun |
| 33:14.83 | Ute | Jamrozy | FRG | 64 | 4 | NCAA | Indianapolis | 4 | Jun |
| 33:15.00 | Marina | Malukhina | SU | 62 | 18 | Znam | Leningrad | 8 | Jun |
| 33:15.0 m | Debbie | Elsmore | NZ | 58 | 2 | | Auckland | 20 | Feb |
| 33:18.0 m | Natalya | Lagunkova | SU | 59 | 1 | | Yalta | 11 | Oct |
| 33:19.5 m | Albina | Tarasova (80) | SU | 58 | 2 | | Chelyabinsk | 24 | Aug |
| | | | | | | | | | |
| 33:19.67 | Kathrin | Kley | GDR | 68 | 1 | WC-j | Athinai | 18 | Jul |
| 33:20.30 | Kathy | Pfiefer | USA | 59 | 6 | TAC | Eugene | 19 | Jun |
| 33:20.58 | Zita | Ágoston | HUN | 65 | 3 | NC | Budapest | 1 | Jun |
| 33:20.66 | Yelena | Gorbulya | SU | 65 | 19 | Znam | Leningrad | 8 | Jun |
| 33:20.66 | Nadezhda | Gumerova | SU | 49 | 20 | Znam | Leningrad | 8 | Jun |
| 33:20.68 | Mercedes | Calleja | SPA | 58 | 24 | EC | Stuttgart | 30 | Aug |
| 33:20.75 | Kumi | Araki | JAP | 65 | 2 | AsiG | Seoul | 1 | Oct |
| 33:21.25 | M Conceicao | Ferreira | POR | 62 | 1 | NC | Lisboa | 26 | Apr |
| 33:22.30 | Astrid | Schmidt | FRG | 63 | 3 | | Essen | 3 | Jun |
| 33:22.5 m | Jacque | Struckhoff | USA | 65 | 2 | FlaR | Gainesville | 29 | Mar |
| | | (90) | | | | | | | |
| 33:22.71 | Odette | Lapierre | CAN | 55 | 6 | NC | Ottawa | 20 | Jun |
| 33:22.92 | Maria | Lantsova | SU | 62 | 1 | | Moskva | 22 | Aug |
| 33:23.02 | Carol | McLatchie | USA | 51 | 7 | TAC | Eugene | 19 | Jun |
| 33:23.6 m | Genoveva | Dominguez | MEX | 63 | 6 | MSR | Walnut, CA | 26 | Apr |
| 33:25.7 m | Nikolina | Shtereva | BUL | 55 | 1 | NC | Sofia | 27 | Apr |
| 33:27.45 | Mami | Fukao | JAP | 61 | 1 | | Kobe | 29 | Apr |
| 33:27.50 | Lyudmila | Medvedeva | SU | 57 | 2 | | Moskva | 22 | Aug |
| 33:27.69 | Jill | Clarke | UK | 58 | 1 | WAAA | Hull | 22 | Jun |

| Mark | Name | | Nat | Yr | Pos | Meet | Venue | Date |
|------|------|---|-----|----|----|------|-------|------|
| 33:27.95 | Renata | Kokowska | POL | 58 | 1 | | Sopot | 2 Aug |
| 33:29.46 | Tatyana | Pentukova | SU | 65 | 1 | | Bryansk | 16 Aug |
| | (100) | | | | | | | |
| 33:31.40 | Connie Jo | Robinson | USA | 64 | 4 Jun | | | |
| 33:31.58 | Huandi | Zhong | CHN | 66 | 6 Jun | | | |
| 33:31.9 m | Lori | Wolter | USA | 67 | 26 Apr | | | |
| 33:32.2 m | Patty | Matava | USA | 65 | 24 Apr | | | |
| 33:32.33 | Galina | Ikonnikova | SU | 62 | 22 Aug | | | |
| 33:34.03 | Lynn | Everington | UK | 62 | 26 May | | | |
| 33:34.20 | Ille | Kukk | SU | 57 | 8 Jun | | | |
| 33:34.77 | Debbie | Peel | UK | 58 | 22 Jun | | | |
| 33:34.81 | Qinghuan | Wang | CHN | 65 | 6 Jun | | | |
| 33:35.24 | Tatyana | Polovinskaya | SU | 65 | 25 Jul | | | |
| | (110) | | | | | | | |
| 33:35.43 | Gina | McMenamin | USA | 64 | 4 Jun | | | |
| 33:36.26 | Ágnes | Sipka-Őze | HUN | 54 | 1 Jun | | | |
| 33:36.7 m | Brenda | Webb | USA | 54 | 2 Apr | | | |
| 33:37.20 | Tatyana | Sokolova | SU | 58 | 8 Jun | | | |
| 33:38.07 | Huabi | Wang | CHN | 66 | 6 Jun | | | |
| 33:39.20 | Nadezhda | Ilyina | SU | 64 | 16 Aug | | | |
| 33:39.48 | Maria | Lelut | FRA | 56 | 14 Jun | | | |
| 33:39.9 m | Veronique | Marot | UK | 55 | 5 Apr | | | |
| 33:40.6 m | Andrea | Everett | UK | 64 | 5 Apr | | | |
| 33:41.05 | Kate | Wiley (120) | CAN | 62 | 20 Jun | | | |
| 33:41.13 | Marleen | Renders | BEL | 68 | 26 Apr | | | |
| 33:41.5 m | Katie | Ishmael | USA | 64 | 26 Apr | | | |
| 33:42.24 | Monika | Kukel | GDR | 66 | 1 Jun | | | |
| 33:42.55 | Nina | Yedovina | SU | 60 | 25 Jul | | | |
| 33:42.56 | Juhua | Hou | CHN | 67 | 6 Jun | | | |
| 33:43.01 | Jana | Kučeríková | CS | 64 | 31 May | | | |
| 33:43.35 | Sue | King | USA | 58 | 19 Jun | | | |
| 33:43.35 | Mariana | Stănescu | RUM | 64 | 9 Aug | | | |
| 33:44.01 | Tammy | Donnelly | USA | 66 | 21 May | | | |
| 33:44.1 m | Sandy | Blakeslee | USA | 65 | 24 Apr | | | |
| | (130) | | | | | | | |
| 33:45.0 m | Agnes | Pardaens | BEL | 56 | | | | |
| 33:49.00 | Sinikka | Keskitalo | FIN | 51 | 10 Aug | | | |
| 33:50.02 | Birgit | Bringslid | SWE | 45 | 3 Aug | | | |
| 33:50.19 | Elisabeth | Franzis | FRG | 62 | 3 Jun | | | |
| 33:50.47 | Kersti | Jacobsen | DEN | 56 | 3 Jul | | | |
| 33:51.83 | Yelena | Uskova | SU | 67 | 20 Jul | | | |
| 33:54.0 m | Chris | Vanatta | USA | 64 | 29 Mar | | | |
| 33:54.78 | Rita | Marchisio | ITA | 50 | 22 Jul | | | |
| 33:55.5 m | Saori | Terakoshi | JAP | 69 | 21 Sep | | | |
| 33:55.98 | Irina | Bondarchuk | SU | 52 | 17 Aug | | | |
| | (140) | | | | | | | |
| 33:56.20 | Bente | Moe | NOR | 60 | 15 Mar | | | |
| 33:56.97 | Olga | Durynina | SU | 64 | 16 Aug | | | |
| 33:57.64 | Alevtina | Chasova | SU | 61 | 8 Jun | | | |
| 33:57.99 | Norah | Maraga | KEN | 71 | 18 Jul | | | |
| 33:58.47 | Emma | Scaunich | ITA | 54 | 22 Jul | | | |
| 33:58.84 | Catherine | Spradley | USA | 66 | 4 Jun | | | |
| 33:59.27 | Irina | Kazakova | SU | 67 | 17 Aug | | | |
| 33:59.4 m | Jody | Pease | USA | 63 | 26 Apr | | | |
| 33:59.90 | Christine | Price | UK | 52 | 28 Jul | | | |
| 34:00.12 | Jeanette | Nordgren-Ling | SWE | 61 | 3 Aug | | | |
| | (150) | | | | | | | |
| 34:00.37 | Jutta | Helmich | FRG | 61 | 6 Sep | | | |
| 34:00.4 m | Sherrie | Roach | USA | | 26 Apr | | | |
| 34:01.60 | Sue | Schroeder | USA | 63 | 9 May | | | |
| 34:01.8 m | Holly | Hering | USA | | 26 Apr | | | |
| 34:01.93 | Zhourong | Jiang | CHN | 62 | 6 Jun | | | |
| 34:02.22 | Jenny | Spangler | USA | 63 | 23 May | | | |
| 34:03.37 | Sissel | Grottenberg | NOR | 56 | 5 Jul | | | |
| 34:04.63 | Uta | Pippig | GDR | 65 | 1 Jun | | | |
| 34:04.74 | Susan | Crehan | UK | 56 | 22 Jun | | | |
| 34:04.93 | Albina | Galyamova | SU | 64 | 17 Aug | | | |
| | (160) | | | | | | | |
| 34:05.05 | Alena | Palmquist | USA | | 23 May | | | |
| 34:06.6 m | Eriko | Asai | JAP | 59 | 4 May | | | |
| 34:06.63 | Lyubov | Fyodorova | SU | 65 | 16 Aug | | | |
| 34:07.13 | Anuța | Cătuna | RUM | 68 | 9 Aug | | | |
| 34:07.5 m | Hisano | Yokosuka | JAP | 65 | 10 Oct | | | |
| 34:07.66 | Sirkku | Kumpulainen | FIN | 56 | 27 Jul | | | |
| 34:08.0 m | Vera | Michallek | FRG | 58 | 5 Apr | | | |
| 34:08.0 m | Michele | Hallett | USA | 64 | 24 Apr | | | |
| 34:08.64 | Marion | Götte | FRG | 60 | 3 Jun | | | |
| 34:08.9 m | Erin | Gillespie | USA | 67 | 9 May | | | |
| | (170) | | | | | | | |
| 34:09.24 | Tuija | Jousimaa | FIN | 58 | 10 Aug | | | |
| 34:09.46 | Kristina | Garlipp (172) | GDR | 61 | 2 Aug | | | |

Marks made in mixed race with men:

| Mark | Name | | Nat | Yr | Pos | Meet | Venue | Date |
|------|------|---|-----|----|----|------|-------|------|
| 32:17.1 m | Christine | McMiken | NZ | 63 | - | | Warrensburg | 19 Apr |
| 32:40.61 | Lorraine | Moller | NZ | 55 | - | | Auckland | 11 Jan |
| 33:20.78 | Mary | O'Connor | NZ | 55 | - | | Christchurch | 18 Jan |
| 33:45.2 m | Donna | Gould | AUS | 66 | 3 Jan | | | |
| 33:58.6 m | Tania | Turney | AUS | 65 | | | | 22 Feb |
| 33:47.4 m | Gayelene | Clews | AUS | 60 | 22 Feb | | | |

| | 1 | 10 | 20 | 30 | 50 | 100 | Under 33:00.0 | Under 34:00.0 |
|------|---|----|----|----|----|-----|---------------|---------------|
| 1982 | 31:35.3 | 32:36.96 | 33:14.6 | 33:48.1 | 34:15.5 | | 16 | 38 |
| 1983 | 31:27.58 | 32:23.04 | 33:02.37 | 33:14.45 | 33:40.5 | | 18 | |
| 1984 | 31:13.78 | 32:30.91 | 32:50.6 | 33:02.61 | 33:34.7 | 34:26.36 | 27 | 70 |
| 1985 | 30:59.42 | 32:25.62 | 32:45.58 | 33:07.66 | 33:28.36 | 33:59.39 | 25 | 100 |
| 1986 | 30:13.74 | 31:56.59 | 32:22.63 | 32:30.71 | 32:47.25 | 33:29.46 | 60 | 149 |

WOMEN 1986

| Mark | Name | | Nat | Yr | Pos | Meet | Venue | Date |
|------|------|------|-----|----|-----|------|-------|------|

# MARATHON

| Mark | Name | | Nat | Yr | Pos | Meet | Venue | Date |
|------|------|------|-----|----|-----|------|-------|------|
| 2:24:54 | Grete | Waitz | NOR | 53 | 1 | | London | 20 Apr |
| 2:24:55 | Ingrid | Kristiansen | NOR | 56 | 1 | | Boston | 21 Apr |
| 2:26:07 | Lisa | Martin | AUS | 60 | 1 | CG | Edinburgh | 1 Aug |
| 2:27:08 | | Kristiansen | | | | | Chicago | 26 Oct |
| 2:27:15 | Rosa | Mota | POR | 58 | 1 | | Tokyo | 16 Nov |
| 2:27:35 | Carla | Beurskens | HOL | 52 | 2 | | Boston | 21 Apr |
| 2:28:06 | | Waitz | | | | | New York | 2 Nov |
| 2:28:17 | Lorraine | Moller | NZL | 55 | 2 | CG | Edinburgh | 1 Aug |
| 2:28:38 | | Mota | | | | EC | Stuttgart | 26 Aug |
| 2:28:51 | Agnes | Sipka | HUN | 54 | 1 | | Budapest | 26 Oct |
| 2:29:12 | | Martin | | | 2 | | New York | 2 Nov |
| 2:29:33 | Katrin | Dörre | GDR | 61 | 1 | | Nagoya | 2 Mar |
| 2:29:44 | Laura | Fogli | ITA | 59 | 3 | | New York | 2 Nov |
| 2:29:51 | Maria | Lelut | FRA | 56 | 2 | | Chicago | 26 Oct |
| | (10) | | | | | | | |
| 2:30:24 | | Moller | | | 1 | | Osaka | 26 Jan |
| 2:30:31 | Karolina | Szabo | HUN | 61 | 1 | NC | Szeged | 22 Mar |
| 2:30:52 | Mary | O'Connor | NZL | 55 | 2 | | London | 20 Apr |
| 2:31:02 | | Beurskens | | | 1 | | Honolulu | 7 Dec |
| 2:31:14 | Priscilla | Welch | GBR | 44 | 3 | | Chicago | 26 Oct |
| 2:31:28 | Debbie | Raunig | USA | 55 | 4 | | Chicago | 26 Oct |
| 2:31:31 | | Sipka | | | 2 | NC | Szeged | 22 Mar |
| 2:31:33 | Veronique | Marot | GBR | 55 | 1 | | Houston | 19 Jan |
| 2:31:40 | Ann | Ford | GBR | 52 | 3 | | London | 20 Apr |
| 2:31:43 | Sylvie | Bornet | FRA | 60 | 4 | | London | 20 Apr |
| 2:31:48 | Odette | Lapierre | CAN | 55 | 3 | CG | Edinburgh | 1 Aug |
| 2:31:54 | | Dörre | | | 2 | | Tokyo | 16 Nov |
| 2:32:06 | Tatyana | Gridneva | SOV | 58 | 1 | | Uzhgorod | 7 Oct |
| 2:32:08 | Kristina | Garlipp | GDR | 61 | 2 | | Budapest | 26 Oct |
| | (20) | | | | | | | |
| 2:32:10 | Charlotte | Teske | FRG | 49 | 1 | | W Berlin | 28 Sep |
| 2:32:16 | Lizanne | Bussieres | CAN | 61 | 3 | | Boston | 21 Apr |
| 2:32:16 | | Lelut | | | 1 | | Paris | 4 May |

31 Performances/22 performers

| Mark | Name | | Nat | Yr | Pos | Meet | Venue | Date |
|------|------|------|-----|----|-----|------|-------|------|
| 2:32:23 | Jocelyne | Villeton | FRA | 54 | 2 | | Paris | 4 May |
| 2:32:25 | Paula | Fudge | GBR | 52 | 5 | | London | 20 Apr |
| 2:32:30 | Renata | Walendziak | POL | 50 | 1 | NC | Debno | 6 Apr |
| 2:32:31 | Lyubov | Svirskaya | SOV | 60 | 2 | | Uzhgorod | 7 Oct |
| 2:32:31 | Kim | Rosenquist | USA | 58 | 1 | TAC | St Paul | 12 Oct |
| 2:32:32 | Francoise | Bonnet | FRA | 57 | 1 | NC | Lyon | 25 Oct |
| 2:32:38 | Gabriele | Martins | GDR | 62 | 2 | | Nagoya | 2 Mar |
| 2:32:46 | Raisa | Smekhnova | SOV | 50 | 1 | | Vilnius | 26 Apr |
| | (30) | | | | | | | |
| 2:32:47 | Evy | Palm | SWE | 42 | 4 | | Boston | 21 Apr |
| 2:32:53 | Kersti | Jakobsen | DEN | 56 | 6 | | London | 20 Apr |
| 2:32:54 | Irinia | Ruban | SOV | 62 | 3 | | Uzhgorod | 7 Oct |
| 2:33:02 | Valentina | Ustinova | SOV | 57 | 4 | | Uzhgorod | 7 Oct |
| 2:33:18 | Sinikka | Keskitalo | FIN | 51 | 5 | | Boston | 21 Apr |
| 2:33:24 | Gabriela | Gorzynska | POL | 56 | 2 | NC | Debno | 6 Apr |
| 2:33:35 | Nadezhda | Gumerova | SOV | 49 | 1 | NC/GWG | Moscow | 5 Jul |
| 2:33:36 | Francie | Larrieu-Smith | USA | 52 | 2 | | Houston | 19 Jan |
| 2:33:39 | Bente | Moe | NOR | 60 | 3 | | Houston | 19 Jan |
| 2:33:40 | Julie | Isphording | USA | 61 | 6 | | Boston | 21 Apr |
| | (40) | | | | | | | |
| 2:33:44 | Grazyna | Mierzejewska | POL | 57 | 3 | NC | Debno | 6 Apr |
| 2:33:49 | Midde | Hamrin | SWE | 57 | 1 | | Columbus | 16 Nov |
| 2:33:53 | Magda | Ilands | BEL | 50 | 2 | | W Berlin | 28 Sep |
| 2:33:58 | Chantal | Langlace | FRA | 55 | 1 | | Lille | 7 Sep |
| 2:34:05 | Monika | Schäfer | FRG | 59 | 3 | | W Berlin | 28 Sep |

| Mark | Name | | Nat | Yr | Pos | Meet | Venue | Date |
|------|------|------|-----|-----|-----|------|-------|------|
| 2:34:09 | Irina | Bogacheva | SOV | 62 | 2 | NC/GWG | Moscow | 5 Jul |
| 2:34:18 | Yekaterina | Khramenkova | SOV | 56 | 3 | EC | Stuttgart | 26 Aug |
| 2:34:34 | Janine | Aiello | USA | 59 | 1 | | San Diego | 13 Dec |
| 2:34:40 | Sylviane | Geffray | FRA | 53 | 3 | | Paris | 4 May |
| 2:34:41 | Maureen | Custy | USA | 55 | 5 | | Chicago | 26 Oct |
| | (50) | | | | | | | |
| 2:34:47 | Eriko | Asai | JAP | 59 | 2 | | Osaka | 26 Jan |
| 2:34:50 | Christa | Vahlensieck | FRG | 49 | 7 | | Boston | 21 Apr |
| 2:34:50 | Nancy | Ditz | USA | 54 | 2 | TAC | St Paul | 12 Oct |
| 2:35:07 | Irina | Petrova | SOV | 62 | 4 | NC/GWG | Moscow | 5 Jul |
| 2:35:20 | Tatyana | Zuyeva | SOV | 58 | 3 | | Vilnius | 26 Apr |
| 2:35:26 | Connie | Prince | USA | 57 | 3 | TAC | St Paul | 12 Oct |
| 2:35:37 | Rita | Borralho | POR | 54 | 1 | | Jersey C | 4 May |
| 2:35:41 | Rita | Marchisio | ITA | 50 | 3 | | Osaka | 26 Jan |
| 2:35:42 | Cathie | Twomey | USA | 56 | 4 | TAC | St Paul | 12 Oct |
| 2:35:42 | Lisa | Weidenbach | USA | 61 | 2 | | Honolulu | 7 Dec |
| | (60) | | | | | | | |
| 2:35:43 | Sonja | Laxton | RSA | 48 | 1 | | Stellenbosch | 13 Sep |
| 2:35:43 | Gail | Kingma | USA | 60 | 6 | | Chicago | 26 Oct |
| 2:35:51 | Ellen | Rochefort | CAN | 54 | 1 | NC | Montreal | 28 Sep |
| 2:35:55 | Heidi | Hutterer | FRG | 59 | 5 | | Houston | 19 Jan |
| 2:36:05 | Sirkku | Kumpulainen | FIN | 56 | 1 | NC | Jyväskylä | 25 May |
| 2:36:06 | Tani | Ruckle | AUS/CAN | 62 | 1 | | Melbourne | 12 Oct |
| 2:36:11 | Renata | Kokowska | POL | 58 | 4 | | W Berlin | 28 Sep |
| 2:36:13 | Luzia | Sahli | SUI | 56 | 1 | NC | Zurich | 13 Apr |
| 2:36:18 | Lyubov | Klocko | SOV | 62 | 5 | | Uzhgorod | 7 Oct |
| 2:36:19 | Patti | Gray | USA | 62 | 3 | | Honolulu | 7 Dec |
| | (70) | | | | | | | |
| 2:36:22 | Katy | Schilly-Laetsch | USA | 56 | 6 | GWG | Moscow | 5 Jul |
| 2:36:23 | Lyutsia | Belyayeva | SOV | 57 | 4 | | Vilnius | 26 Apr |
| 2:36:24 | Laurie | Crisp | USA | 61 | 4 | | Osaka | 26 Jan |
| 2:36:26 | Sue | Schneider | USA | 56 | 5 | | Houston | 19 Jan |
| 2:36:31 | Julia | Gates | GBR | 59 | 7 | | London | 20 Apr |
| 2:36:33 | Kerstin | Pressler | FRG | 62 | 1 | | Tiberias | 17 Dec |
| 2:36:34 | Gaby | Wolf | FRG | 60 | 6 | | Houston | 19 Jan |
| 2:36:34 | Lorna | Irving | GBR | 47 | 5 | CG | Edinburgh | 1·Aug |
| 2:36:41 | Genoveva | Eichmann | SWI | 57 | 2 | NC | Zurich | 13 Apr |
| 2:36:43 | Angelika | Dunke | FRG | 55 | 2 | | Hamburg | 25 May |
| | (80) | | | | | | | |
| 2:36:44 | Helen | Comsa | SWI | 52 | 3 | NC | Zurich | 13 Apr |
| 2:36:48 | Tuija | Jousimaa | FIN | 58 | 7 | | Chicago | 26 Oct |
| 2:36:52 | Tatyana | Polovinskaya | SOV | 65 | 5 | | Vilnius | 26 Apr |
| 2:36:55 | Wen | Yanmin | PRC | 66 | 1 | | Hong Kong | 26 Jan |
| 2:37:05 | Agnes | Pardaens | BEL | 56 | 1 | NC | Lommel | 19 May |
| 2:37:06 | Irina | Sklyarenko | SOV | 64 | 6 | | Uzhgorod | 7 Oct |
| 2:37:08 | Doris | Schlosser | FRG | 44 | 4 | | Hamburg | 25 May |
| 2:37:09 | Karina | Weber | AUT | 60 | 8 | | Chicago | 26 Oct |
| 2:37:11 | Elena | Murgoci | ROM | 60 | 1 | | Pyongyang | 17 Apr |
| 2:37:23 | Birgit | Schuckmann | GDR | 60 | 3 | | Budapest | 26 Oct |
| | (90) | | | | | | | |
| 2:37:23 | Janice | Ettle | USA | 58 | 5 | TAC | St Paul | 12 Oct |
| 2:37:27 | Ria | van Landeghem | BEL | 57 | 5 | | Osaka | 26 Jan |
| 2:37:29 | Sandra | Branney | GBR | 54 | 1 | | Glasgow | 21 Sep |
| 2:37:30 | Nadyezhda | Yerokhina | SOV | 57 | 6 | | Vilnius | 26 Apr |
| 2:37:43 | Nadia | Usmanova | SOV | 56 | 8 | NC/GWG | Moscow | 5 Jul |
| 2:37:43 | Melinda | Ireland | USA | 51 | 4 | | San Diego | 13 Dec |
| 2:37:50 | Emma | Scaunich | ITA | 54 | 7 | | New York | 2 Nov |
| 2:37:56 | Uta | Pippig | GDR | 65 | 1 | NC | Leipzig | 22 Jun |
| 2:37:57 | Angela | Pain | GBR | 62 | 6 | CG | Edinburgh | 1 Aug |
| 2:37:58 | Maria | Trujillo | MEX | 59 | 1 | | San Fransisco | 20 Jul |
| 2:38:00 | Irina | Hulanicka | POL | 56 | 4 | NC | Debno | 6 Apr |
| | (101) | | | | | | | |

| Mark | Wind | Name | | Nat | Yr | Pos | Meet | Venue | Date |
|------|------|------|--|-----|----|-----|------|-------|------|

# 100 METRES HURDLES

| Mark | Wind | Name | | Nat | Yr | Pos | Meet | Venue | Date |
|------|------|------|--|-----|----|-----|------|-------|------|
| 12.26 | 1.5 | Yordanka | Donkova | BUL | 61 | 1 | Balk | Ljubljana | 7 Sep |
| 12.29 | -0.4 | | Donkova | | | 1 | ASV | Köln | 17 Aug |
| 12.34 | 0.1 | | Donkova | | | 1h2 | ASV | Köln | 17 Aug |
| 12.36 | -0.6 | | Donkova | | | 1 | NC | Sofia | 13 Aug |
| 12.37 | 1.4 | | Donkova | | | 1r1 | ISTAF | W Berlin | 15 Aug |
| 12.38 | 0.0 | | Donkova | | | 1 | BGP | Budapest | 11 Aug |
| 12.38 | -0.7 | | Donkova | | | 1 | EC | Stuttgart | 29 Aug |
| 12.39 | 1.5 | Ginka | Zagorcheva | BUL | 58 | 2 | Balk | Ljubljana | 7 Sep |
| 12.40 | 0.4 | | Donkova | | | 1 | GWG | Moskva | 8 Jul |
| 12.42 | -0.2 | | Donkova | | | 1 | VD | Bruxelles | 5 Sep |
| | | | | | | | | | |
| 12.47 | 0.6 | | Donkova | | | 1 | GP | Roma | 10 Sep |
| 12.48 | -0.2 | | Zagorcheva | | | 2 | VD | Bruxelles | 5 Sep |
| 12.49 | 0.1 | | Donkova | | | 1s2 | EC | Stuttgart | 28 Aug |
| 12.49 | 0.6 | | Zagorcheva | | | 2 | GP | Roma | 10 Sep |
| 12.50 | 0.3 | Cornelia | Oschkenat | GDR | 61 | 1 | PTS | Bratislava | 14 Jun |
| 12.51 | 0.3 | | Donkova | | | 2 | PTS | Bratislava | 14 Jun |
| 12.51 | 0.4 | | Donkova | | | 1h2 | GWG | Moskva | 8 Jul |
| 12.51 | 1.0 | | Oschkenat | | | 1h2 | GO | Dresden | 17 Aug |
| 12.51 | 0.5 | | Zagorcheva | | | 1h2 | VD | Bruxelles | 5 Sep |
| 12.51 | 1.1 | | Zagorcheva | | | 1 | | London | 12 Sep |
| | | | | | | | | | |
| 12.52 | 1.0 | | Oschkenat | | | 1 | GO | Dresden | 17 Aug |
| 12.52 | 0.1 | | Oschkenat | | | 2s2 | EC | Stuttgart | 28 Aug |
| 12.55 | -1.9 | | Oschkenat | | | 1 | | Potsdam | 11 Jun |
| 12.55 | -0.4 | | Zagorcheva | | | 2 | ASV | Köln | 17 Aug |
| 12.55 | -0.7 | | Oschkenat | | | 2 | EC | Stuttgart | 29 Aug |
| 12.55 | 1.1 | | Donkova | | | 2 | | London | 12 Sep |
| 12.56 | 1.4 | | Oschkenat | | | 1 | NC | Jena | 27 Jun |
| 12.56 | 2.0 | | Oschkenat | | | 1h2 | EC | Stuttgart | 27 Aug |
| 12.57 | 1.4 | | Zagorcheva | | | 2r1 | ISTAF | W Berlin | 15 Aug |
| 12.58 | 2.0 | | Zagorcheva | | | 2h2 | EC | Stuttgart | 27 Aug |
| | | | | | | | | | |
| 12.58 | -0.2 | | Donkova | | | 1h1 | VD | Bruxelles | 5 Sep |
| | | | (31/3) | | | | | | |
| 12.61 | 1.9 | Natalya | Grigoryeva | SU | 62 | 1s1 | NC | Kiev | 15 Jul |
| 12.63 | 1.4 | Heike | Theele | GDR | 64 | 2 | NC | Jena | 27 Jun |
| 12.64 | 1.4 | Kerstin | Knabe | GDR | 59 | 3 | NC | Jena | 27 Jun |
| 12.68 | -0.7 | Vera | Akimova | SU | 59 | 1 | NC | Kiev | 15 Jul |
| 12.69 | 0.2 | Laurence | Elloy | FRA | 59 | 2h1 | GWG | Moskva | 8 Jul |
| 12.71 | -0.7 | Yelena | Politika | SU | 64 | 2 | NC | Kiev | 15 Jul |
| 12.75 | 0.8 | Mihaela | Pogăcian (10) | RUM | 58 | 1 | | Bucureşti | 25 May |
| | | | | | | | | | |
| 12.77 | 1.3 | Xénia | Siska | HUN | 57 | 1 | | Budapest | 2 Aug |
| 12.78 | -0.7 | Yelizaveta | Chernyshova | SU | 58 | 4 | NC | Kiev | 15 Jul |
| 12.84 | 0.6 | Benita | Fitzgerald-Brown | USA | 61 | 4 | GP | Roma | 10 Sep |
| 12.84 | 0.6 | Jackie | Joyner | USA | 62 | 5 | GP | Roma | 10 Sep |
| 12.85 | -1.9 | Liliana | Năstase | RUM | 62 | 1h2 | Znam | Leningrad | 7 Jun |
| 12.89 | 1.4 | Sabine | Paetz | GDR | 57 | 4 | NC | Jena | 27 Jun |
| 12.91 | 1.3 | Gloria | Uibel | GDR | 64 | 4h | | Potsdam | 11 Jun |
| 12.94 | 0.5 | Lyudmila | Khristosenko | SU | 66 | 1s | Spart | Tashkent | 17 Sep |
| 12.95 | -0.1 | LaVonna | Martin | USA | 66 | 1 | | Tempe | 5 Apr |
| 12.95 | 0.6 | Anne | Piquereau(20) | FRA | 64 | 2 | NC | Aix-les-Bains | 10 Aug |
| | | | | | | | | | |
| 12.96 | 1.4 | Stephanie | Hightower | USA | 58 | 3r1 | ISTAF | W Berlin | 15 Aug |
| 13.01 | 1.3 | Pam | Page | USA | 58 | 1h2 | TAC | Eugene | 19 Jun |
| 13.03 | 1.1 | Rosalind | Council | USA | 65 | 1 | NCAA | Indianapolis | 7 Jun |
| 13.03 | -0.7 | Lyudmila | Oliyar | SU | 58 | 5 | NC | Kiev | 15 Jul |

| Mark | Wind | Name | | Nat | Yr | Pos | Meet | Venue | Date |
|------|------|------|---|-----|----|----|------|-------|------|
| 13.05 | 0.8 | Judy | Simpson | UK | 60 | H | EC | Stuttgart | 29 Aug |
| 13.07 | -0.8 | Marjan | Olijslager | HOL | 62 | 4 | OD | Dresden | 3 Jul |
| 13.07 | 0.2 | Monique | Ewanje-Epée | FRA | 67 | 2 | | Paris | 22 Jul |
| 13.08 | 0.1 | Gail | Devers | USA | 66 | 1h3 | NCAA | Indianapolis | 5 Jun |
| 13.08 | 0.2 | Irina | Mylnikova | SU | 65 | 3 | Spart | Tashkent | 17 Sep |
| A13.09 | | Ina | van Rensburg | RSA | 56 | 1 | | Johannesburg | 18 Apr |
| | | | (30) | | | | | | |
| 13.10 | -0.8 | Eva | Sokolova | SU | 61 | 2h4 | Znam | Leningrad | 7 Jun |
| 13.10 | -0.7 | Heike | Tillack | GDR | 68 | 1 | WC-j | Athinai | 18 Jul |
| 13.11 | -0.8 | Oksana | Sukhareva | SU | 63 | 3h4 | Znam | Leningrad | 7 Jun |
| 13.11 | 0.2 | Florence | Colle | FRA | 65 | 3 | | Paris | 22 Jul |
| 13.11 | 0.4 | Sally | Gunnell | UK | 66 | 1 | v Pol, | Sco/Wal Hendon | 17 Aug |
| 13.11 | 1.5 | Rita | Heggli | SWZ | 62 | 1 | | Dübendorf | 20 Sep |
| 13.13 | 1.1 | Maria | Usifo | NIG | 64 | 3 | NCAA | Indianapolis | 7 Jun |
| 13.14 | 0.6 | Sibylle | Thiele | GDR | 65 | H | GWG | Moskva | 6 Jul |
| 13.14 | 1.9 | Galina | Kazakova | SU | 61 | 3s1 | NC | Kiev | 15 Jul |
| 13.14 | -0.7 | Aliuska | Lopez    (40) | CUB | 69 | 2 | WC-j | Athinai | 18 Jul |
| | | | | | | | | | |
| 13.16 | 1.2 | Wendy | Jeal | UK | 60 | 5h1 | EC | Stuttgart | 27 Aug |
| 13.17 | -0.6 | Galina | Makarova | SU | 60 | 2h3 | Znam | Leningrad | 7 Jun |
| 13.17 | 0.7 | Lidia | Okolo-Kulak | SU | 67 | 1 | NC-j | Kaunas | 20 Jul |
| 13.19 | 1.8 | Margit | Palombi | HUN | 61 | H | | Miskolc | 24 May |
| 13.19 | 1.0 | Natalya | Gorbunova | SU | 64 | 1r2 | Znam | Leningrad | 7 Jun |
| 13.19 | 0.4 | Patrizia | Lombardo | ITA | 58 | 5h2 | GWG | Moskva | 8 Jul |
| 13.19 | 1.9 | Galina | Khaustova | SU | 65 | 4s1 | NC | Kiev | 15 Jul |
| 13.20 | 0.8 | Patricia | Davis | USA | 64 | 1 | | Los Angeles | 24 May |
| 13.21 | 0.7 | Irina | Svetonosova | SU | 58 | 1 | | Donetsk | 6 Sep |
| 13.23 | 1.0 | Natalya | Kolovanova | SU | 64 | 2r2 | Znam | Leningrad | 7 Jun |
| | | | (50) | | | | | | |
| 13.23 | 0.2 | Natalya | Shubenkova | SU | 57 | H | GWG | Moskva | 6 Jul |
| 13.23 | 1.3 | Kristin | Patzwahl | GDR | 65 | 3 | | Budapest | 2 Aug |
| 13.24 | -0.2 | Claudia | Reidick | FRG | 62 | 1 | | Schweinfurt | 9 Aug |
| 13.25 | 1.3 | Yolanda | Johnson | USA | 68 | 4h2 | TAC | Eugene | 19 Jun |
| 13.25 | -0.2 | Nancy | Vallecilla | EQU | 57 | 2 | | Schweinfurt | 9 Aug |
| 13.25 | 2.0 | Anke | Behmer | GDR | 61 | H | | Berlin | 19 Aug |
| 13.26 | 1.6 | Alicia | Bass | USA | 65 | 1 | TexR | Austin | 5 Apr |
| 13.26 | 1.1 | Marina | Sluzhkina | SU | 60 | 1 | | Baku | 4 Oct |
| 13.27 | 1.9 | Natalya | Bordyugova | SU | 61 | 6s1 | NC | Kiev | 15 Jul |
| 13.27 | 1.1 | Kim | Hagger    (60) | UK | 61 | 4 | | London | 12 Sep |
| | | | | | | | | | |
| 13.28 | 1.9 | Natalya | Tochilova | SU | 64 | 1 | | Bryansk | 14 Aug |
| 13.28 | -0.3 | Yelena | Ziatdinova | SU | 64 | 2s | Spart | Tashkent | 17 Sep |
| 13.29 | 1.4 | Edith | Oker | FRG | 61 | 8r1 | ISTAF | W Berlin | 15 Aug |
| 13.30 | 0.6 | Shirley | Strong | UK | 58 | 3 | | Dijon | 14 Jun |
| 13.30 | 1.0 | Lyubov | Stolyar | SU | 61 | 1 | | Moskva | 22 Aug |
| 13.31 | | Mary | Massarin | ITA | 63 | 1 | | Trento | 22 Jun |
| 13.31 | 0.2 | Tatyana | Filatova | SU | 59 | 2h2 | | Tallinn | 28 Jun |
| 13.32 | 1.1 | Jackie | Humphrey | USA | 65 | 5 | NCAA | Indianapolis | 7 Jun |
| 13.32 | -1.5 | Ulrike | Denk | FRG | 64 | 1 | | Hannover | 7 Jun |
| 13.32 | 1.0 | Daniela | Bizbac    (70) | RUM | 67 | 1 | v USA-j | Pitești | 12 Jul |
| | | | | | | | | | |
| 13.33 | 0.9 | Sophia | Hunter | JAM | 65 | 3h1 | NCAA | Indianapolis | 5 Jun |
| 13.33 | -0.4 | Tanya | Tarkalanova | BUL | 65 | H | NC | Sofia | 2 Aug |
| 13.34 | 0.2 | Valda | Ruskite | SU | 62 | H | GWG | Moskva | 6 Jul |
| 13.35 | 1.0 | Svetlana | Yermilova | SU | 59 | 5r2 | Znam | Leningrad | 7 Jun |
| 13.38 | 2.0 | Candy | Young | USA | 62 | 1r2 | ISTAF | W Berlin | 15 Aug |
| 13.38 | -0.2 | Tatyana | Reshetnikova | SU | 66 | s | Spart | Tashkent | 17 Sep |
| 13.39 | 0.4 | Jitka | Tesárková | CS | 65 | 1 | GS | Ostrava | 11 Jun |

WOMEN 1986

| Mark | Wind | Name | | Nat | Yr | Pos | Meet | Venue | Date |
|------|------|------|------|-----|----|-----|------|-------|------|
| 13.39 | 1.5 | Marina | Sukhareva | SU | 62 | 2 | | Moskva | 3 Aug |
| 13.39 | -0.3 | Ann-Louise | Skoglund | SWE | 62 | 1 | v Fin | Helsinki | 9 Aug |
| 13.39 | 0.8 | Małgorzata | Nowak (80) | POL | 59 | H | EC | Stuttgart | 29 Aug |
| A13.40 | 1.9 | Karen | Cannon | USA | 58 | 2 | | El Paso | 20 Apr |
| 13.40 | 1.4 | Glynis | Nunn | AUS | 60 | 1 | | Hechtel | 5 Jul |
| 13.40 | 1.0 | Tanya | Davis | USA | 68 | 2 | v Rum-j | Pitești | 12 Jul |
| 13.40 | 0.1 | Svetlana | Besprozvannaya | SU | 65 | H | Spart | Tashkent | 16 Sep |
| 13.41 | 1.0 | Marina | Smirnova | SU | 60 | 6r2 | Znam | Leningrad | 7 Jun |
| 13.41 | 0.5 | Brigitte | Gerstenmaier | FRG | 60 | 2h1 | | Fürth | 15 Jun |
| 13.41 | 0.6 | Marianna | Maslennikova | SU | 61 | H | GWG | Moskva | 6 Jul |
| 13.41 | 1.5 | Heike | Filsinger | FRG | 61 | 2s1 | NC | W Berlin | 12 Jul |
| 13.41 | 1.9 | Lyudmila | Narozhilenko | SU | 63 | 3 | | Bryansk | 14 Aug |
| 13.42 | 1.0 | Bettine | Jahn (90) | GDR | 58 | 5 | GO | Dresden | 17 Aug |
| 13.42 | 0.2 | Natalya | Belenkova | SU | 65 | 6 | Spart | Tashkent | 17 Sep |
| 13.43 | 1.9 | Irina | Tyukhai | SU | 67 | 4 | | Bryansk | 14 Aug |
| 13.44 | | Irina | Dudkova | SU | 61 | H | | Minsk | 30 May |
| 13.44 | | Yinghua | Feng | CHN | 66 | 1 | | Nanjing | 6 Jun |
| 13.45 | 1.2 | Jane | Flemming | AUS | 65 | 2h1 | CG | Edinburgh | 31 Jul |
| 13.46 | 0.8 | Latanya | Sheffield | USA | 63 | 1 | | Fresno | 10 May |
| 13.46 | -0.4 | Julie | Rocheleau | CAN | 64 | 2 | | Tillsonburg | 28 Jun |
| 13.47 | | Faye | Barrett | USA | | 1 | KansR | Lawrence | 19 Apr |
| 13.47 | 0.0 | Gayle | Watkins | USA | 58 | 3 | MSR | Walnut, CA | 27 Apr |
| 13.47 | 0.8 | Ilona | Dumitrașcu (100) | RUM | 62 | 3 | | București | 25 May |
| 13.47 | 0.5 | Michèle | Chardonnet | FRA | 56 | 1 | | Créteil | 14 Jun |
| 13.47 | 1.8 | Faye | Blackwood (102) | CAN | 57 | 1 | NC | Ottawa | 21 Jun |

| Mark | Wind | Name | | Nat | Yr | Date |
|------|------|------|------|-----|----|------|
| 13.48 | -1.8 | Schowonda | Williams | USA | 66 | 26 Apr |
| 13.48 | | Leticia | Beverly | USA | 67 | 24 May |
| 13.48 | 1.2 | Angelika | Kuhmann | FRG | 57 | 19 Jul |
| 13.48 | 1.2 | Judith | Rodgers | UK | 64 | 31 Jul |
| 13.49 | 0.4 | Alina | Grecu | RUM | 65 | 15 Jun |
| 13.49 | -0.1 | Natalya | Dudina | SU | 66 | 17 Sep |
| 13.49 | 1.9 | Odalys | Adams | CUB | 67 | 27 Sep |
| 13.50 | 1.4 | Lesley-Ann | Skeete (110) | UK | 67 | 6 Jun |
| 13.50 | 2.0 | Barbara | Latos | POL | 65 | 5 Jul |
| 13.50 | | Antonina | Sukhova | SU | 59 | 6 Jul |
| A13.51 | | Annemarie | le Roux | RSA | 63 | 22 Mar |
| 13.51 | 0.6 | Isabelle | Kaftandjian | FRA | 64 | 14 Jun |
| 13.51 | 1.6 | Svetlana | Chistyakova | SU | 61 | 2 Aug |
| A13.51 | 1.3 | Sanet | Grobler | RSA | 64 | 15 Nov |
| 13.52 | 0.7 | Cheryl | Wilson | USA | 66 | 4 May |
| 13.52 | 1.1 | Arnita | Epps | USA | 64 | 7 Jun |
| 13.52 | | Zdravka | Georgieva | BUL | 69 | 5 Jul |
| 13.52 | 1.3 | Birgit | Dressel (120) | FRG | 60 | 12 Jul |
| 13.52 | -0.7 | Birgit | Wolf | FRG | 69 | 18 Jul |
| 13.53 | 0.7 | Jenny | Laurendet | AUS | 62 | 15 Mar |
| A13.53 | | Annie | le Roux | RSA | 65 | 2 Apr |
| 13.53 | -0.2 | Svetlana | Filatyeva | SU | 64 | 24 May |
| 13.53 | 1.4 | Christine | Sallaz | FRA | 61 | 25 May |
| 13.53 | 0.9 | Nicolle | Thompson | USA | 67 | 31 May |
| 13.53 | 1.0 | Irina | Gritsenko | SU | 65 | 7 Jun |
| 13.53 | -0.6 | Diana | Ruskova | BUL | 67 | 13 Aug |
| A13.54 | 1.4 | Sylvia | Forgrave | CAN | 57 | 26 May |
| 13.54 | | Wen-Ying | Chen (130) | TAI | | 28 Jun |
| 13.54 | 0.2 | Veronique | Truwant | FRA | 65 | 29 Jun |
| 13.54 | 0.6 | Cindy | Greiner | USA | 57 | 6 Jul |
| A13.54 | 1.3 | Ilse | Luneburg | RSA | 65 | 15 Nov |
| 13.55 | -0.2 | Sabine | Braun | FRG | 65 | 24 May |
| 13.55 | 1.8 | Yolanda | Jones | CAN | 67 | 21 Jun |
| 13.55 | -0.4 | Ivanka | Valkova | BUL | 65 | 2 Aug |
| 13.55 | 1.6 | Cornelia | Feuerbach | GDR | 63 | 7 Sep |
| 13.56 | 0.0 | Grisel | Machado | CUB | 59 | 1 Jul |
| 13.56 | 0.7 | Svetlana | Gerevich | SU | 66 | 6 Sep |
| 13.57 | | Vanda | Nováková (140) | CS | 58 | 30 Aug |
| 13.57 | | Emilia | Dimitrova | BUL | 67 | 20 Sep |
| 13.58 | | Bridgette | Tate | USA | 66 | 24 May |
| 13.58 | 1.0 | Lenuța | Bîrzu | RUM | 69 | 12 Jul |
| 13.59 | 1.6 | Karen | Nelson | CAN | 63 | 5 Apr |
| 13.59 | 0.0 | Antonella | Bellutti | ITA | 68 | 12 Jun |
| 13.59 | -0.2 | Gudrun | Lattner | FRG | 59 | 9 Aug |
| 13.60 | | Sybil | Perry | USA | 63 | 24 May |
| 13.60 | -0.1 | Eva | Riekstina | SU | 64 | 17 Sep |
| 13.61 | 0.0 | Lynda | Tolbert | USA | 67 | 17 May |
| 13.61 | | Olga | Kutsakova (150) | SU | 68 | 23 May |
| 13.61 | 0.2 | Nadezhda | Korshunova | SU | 61 | 22 Jun |
| 13.62 | 0.0 | Nadine | Debois | FRA | 61 | 26 Apr |
| 13.62 | 1.0 | Iwona | Parucka | POL | 63 | 25 May |
| 13.62 | 2.0 | Laura | Rosati | ITA | 60 | 8 Jul |
| 13.62 | 0.5 | Gabi | Lippe | FRG | 67 | 7 Sep |
| 13.62 | 1.8 | Chantal | Beaugeant | FRA | 61 | 20 Sep |
| 13.63 | 1.9 | Cecelia | Branch | CAN | 57 | 17 May |
| 13.63 | | Svetla | Trichkova | BUL | 68 | 5 Jul |

| Mark | Wind | Name | | Nat | Yr | Pos | Meet | Venue | Date |
|------|------|------|---|-----|-----|-----|------|-------|------|
| 13.63 | 0.2 | Jane | Frederick | USA | 52 | 6 Jul | 13.69 -1.2 Rimma | Nurmukhomyatova SU 59 | 26 Jul |
| A13.64 | | Isabel | Campher (160) | RSA | 58 | 2 Apr | 13.70 -0.4 Jill | Kirk UK 59 | 14 Jun |
| | | | | | | | 13.70 Heather | Platt UK 59 | 18 Jul |
| 13.64 | | Cheryl | Henry | USA | 64 | 12 Apr | 13.71 Burgel | Assmann GDR 68 | 25 May |
| 13.64 | | Hilsa | van Heerden | RSA | 61 | 21 Apr | A13.71 1.4 Sue | Kameli CAN 56 | 26 May |
| 13.64 | 0.7 | Sabine | Seitl | AUT | 65 | 19 May | 13.71 1.8 Sylvia | Dethier BEL 65 | 9 Aug |
| 13.64 | 1.9 | Zsuzsa | Gazdag | HUN | 64 | 12 Jul | 13.71 2.0 Rhonda | Blanford(190) USA 63 | 15 Aug |
| 13.64 | 0.0 | Corinne | Grimont | FRA | 63 | 13 Jul | | | |
| 13.65 | 0.8 | Felicia | Zǎrescu | RUM | 60 | 25 May | 13.72 Alina | Barthelemy CUB 65 | 13 Feb |
| 13.65 | 1.9 | Ildikó | Baranyai | HUN | 58 | 27 Jun | 13.72 0.1 Debbie | DaCosta USA 64 | 4 May |
| 13.65 | -0.4 | Kathy | Freeman | USA | 62 | 28 Jun | 13.72 -0.8 Tatyana | Kirichenko SU 65 | 7 Jun |
| 13.65 | 1.0 | Florina | Neder | RUM | 70 | 12 Jul | 13.72 Svetlana | Ovchinnikova SU 56 | 26 Jul |
| 13.65 | 1.0 | Jutta | Fundel (170) | FRG | 68 | 26 Jul | 13.73 2.0 Susan | DeVries USA 66 | 4 Apr |
| | | | | | | | 13.73 0.2 Marion | Weser GDR 62 | 6 Jul |
| 13.65 | | Claudia | Bartl | GDR | 68 | 27 Jul | 13.73 1.1 Lidia | Bierka POL 60 | 2 Aug |
| 13.65 | -0.3 | Annika | Lorentzon | SWE | 64 | 9 Aug | 13.74 1.4 Kerry | Robin-Millerchip UK 61 | 6 Jun |
| 13.66 | 0.9 | Donna | Waller | USA | 64 | 5 Jun | 13.74 1.5 Jocelyne | Junod SWZ 65 | 25 Jun |
| 13.66 | 1.5 | Kay | Morley | UK | 63 | 14 Jun | 13.74 Remigia | Zablovskaite SU 67 | 6 Jul |
| 13.66 | 1.6 | Tatyana | Dolgaya | SU | 64 | 2 Aug | | (200) | |
| 13.66 | -0.1 | Valentina | Bushuyeva | SU | 63 | 9 Aug | 13.74 0.8 Milena | Tebichová CS 62 | 12 Jul |
| 13.66 | 1.9 | Julieta | Rousseaux | CUB | 66 | 27 Sep | 13.74 0.5 Angela | Weiss SWZ 53 | 10 Aug |
| 13.67 | 0.8 | Natalie | Day | USA | 63 | 24 May | 13.74 1.3 Stefanie | Hühn FRG 66 | 16 Aug |
| 13.67 | 1.2 | Lynette | Stock | NZ | 62 | 31 Jul | 13.74 1.1 Heather | Ross (204) UK 62 | 12 Sep |
| 13.68 | | Jackie | Browne (180) | USA | 65 | 24 May | | | |

Behmer (13.25 2.0) also did 13.25 0.8 H EC

| 13.68 | 1.5 | Vera | Yurchenko | SU | 59 | 6 Sep | Stuttgart 29 Aug; Rocheleau(13.46 -0.4) also did |
|------|------|------|---|-----|-----|-----|------|
| A13.69 | | Karen | Wilkenson | RSA | 66 | 28 Feb | 13.46 -1.1 4 CG Edinburgh 1 Aug. |
| 13.69 | | Zifang | Xiao | CHN | 64 | 7 Jun | |

Best low altitude marks:

| 13.23 | | | van Rensburg | 1 | | Port Elizabeth | 21 Apr |
|-------|---|---|--------------|---|---|----------------|--------|
| 13.48 | 1.3 | | Cannon | 19 Jun | 13.72 1.8 | Forgrave | 21 Jun |
| 13.62 | | Annie | le Roux | 21 Apr | | | |

---

| | 1 | 10 | 20 | 30 | 50 | 100 | Under 13.30 | Under 13.70 |
|------|-------|-------|-------|-------|-------|-------|------|------|
| 1982 | 12.44 | 12.88 | 13.09 | 13.17 | 13.42 | 13.68 | 37 | 102 |
| 1983 | 12.42 | 12.86 | 13.00 | 13.13 | 13.25 | 13.55 | 55 | 145 |
| 1984 | 12.43 | 12.74 | 13.01 | 13.13 | 13.33 | 13.48 | 42 | 163 |
| 1985 | 12.42 | 12.85 | 12.99 | 13.10 | 13.24 | 13.48 | 56 | 161 |
| 1986 | 12.26 | 12.75 | 12.95 | 13.09 | 13.23 | 13.47 | 63 | 184 |

---

Marks made with assisting wind > 2 m/s:

| 12.57 | 2.4 | | Oschkenat | | | 1 | v SU | Tallinn | 21 Jun |
|-------|-----|------|-----------|-----|-----|-----|------|---------|--------|
| 12.83 | 2.5 | Benita | Fitzgerald-Brown | USA | 61 | 1 | TAC | Eugene | 20 Jun |
| 12.90 | 2.5 | Stephanie | Hightower | USA | 58 | 2 | TAC | Eugene | 20 Jun |
| 12.91 | 2.5 | Rosalind | Council | USA | 65 | 3= | TAC | Eugene | 20 Jun |
| 12.91 | 2.5 | Pam | Page | USA | 58 | 3= | TAC | Eugene | 20 Jun |
| 13.06 | 2.5 | Sophia | Hunter | JAM | 65 | 6 | TAC | Eugene | 20 Jun |
| 13.08 | 2.5 | Patricia | Davis | USA | 65 | 7 | TAC | Eugene | 20 Jun |
| 13.18 | 3.0 | Gayle | Watkins | USA | 58 | 3h1 | TAC | Eugene | 19 Jun |
| 13.22 | 3.1 | Edith | Oker | FRG | 61 | 2h2 | | Fürth | 15 Jun |

WOMEN 1986

| Mark | Wind | Name | | Nat | Yr | Pos | Meet | Venue | Date |
|------|------|------|------|-----|-----|-----|------|-------|------|
| 13.23 | 2.1 | Ann-Louise | Skoglund (10) | SWE | 62 | 1 | NC | Karlskrona | 2 Aug |
| 13.24 | 2.7 | Lesley-Ann | Skeete | UK | 67 | 2 | WAAA | Birmingham | 7 Jun |
| 13.25 | 2.5 | Mary | Massarin | ITA | 63 | 2 | | Bolzano | 25 May |
| 13.31 | 2.3 | Glynis | Nunn | AUS | 60 | 2h2 | CG | Edinburgh | 31 Jul |
| A13.32 | | Annie | le Roux | RSA | 65 | H | NC | Germiston | 11 Apr |
| 13.32 | 2.7 | Schowonda | Williams | USA | 66 | 2 | | Knoxville | 18 May |
| 13.32 | 4.7 | Jane | Flemming | AUS | 65 | H | CG | Edinburgh | 26 Jul |
| 13.32 | 2.3 | Julie | Rocheleau | CAN | 64 | 3h2 | CG | Edinburgh | 31 Jul |
| 13.36 | 3.0 | Natalie | Day | USA | 63 | 6h1 | TAC | Eugene | 19 Jun |
| 13.37 | 2.2 | Birgit | Dressel | FRG | 60 | 3 | NC | W Berlin | 12 Jul |
| 13.39 | | Karen | Cannon (20) | USA | 58 | 4 | | Modesto | 10 May |
| 13.43 | 2.5 | Karin | Malmbratt | SWE | 66 | 2 | | Falkenberg | 11 Jul |
| 13.43 | 2.2 | Angelika | Kuhmann | FRG | 57 | 4 | NC | W Berlin | 12 Jul |
| 13.44 | 2.7 | Flora | Hyacinth (23) | UVI | 66 | 4 | | Knoxville | 18 May |

| Mark | | Name | | Nat | Yr | Date | | Mark | | Name | | Nat | Yr | Date |
|------|------|------|------|-----|-----|------|------|------|------|------|------|-----|-----|------|
| 13.50 | | Lynda | Tolbert | USA | 67 | 10 May | | 13.60 | 2.4 | Olga | Kutsakova | SU | 68 | 10 Aug |
| 13.50 | 2.6 | Veronique | Truwant | FRA | 65 | 20 Jul | | 13.62 | 2.8 | Susan | DeVries | USA | 66 | 22 Mar |
| 13.51 | 3.1 | Gudrun | Lattner | FRG | 59 | 15 Jun | | 13.62 | 2.2 | Heike | Ulbrich | FRG | 63 | 10 Aug |
| 13.52 | | Jenny | Laurendet | AUS | 62 | 23 Feb | | 13.63 | 2.3 | Liliane | Ménissier | FRA | 60 | 12 Jul |
| 13.52 | 2.3 | Kay | Morley | UK | 63 | 31 Jul | | 13.67 | | Heidi | van Staden | RSA | 59 | 11 Apr |
| 13.54 | 2.7 | Jill | Kirk | UK | 59 | 7 Jun | | 13.68 | 4.6 | Zuzana | Lajbnerová | CS | 63 | 12 Jul |
| 13.55 | 2.1 | Annika | Lorentzon (30) | SWE | 64 | 2 Aug | | 13.72 | 3.2 | Anne | Dalmoro (40) | FRA | 63 | 15 Jun |
| 13.58 | 3.6 | Karen | Nelson | CAN | 63 | 18 May | | 13.73 | 2.2 | Helen | Pirovano | NZ | 67 | 1 Feb |
| 13.60 | 3.6 | Debbie | DaCosta | USA | 64 | 18 May | | 13.73 | 4.9 | Chewuakii | Knighten | USA | 67 | 29 Mar |
| 13.60 | 2.3 | Ann | Girvan | UK | 65 | 31 Jul | | 13.73 | 2.8 | Maria | Asenova (43) | BUL | 67 | 21 Jun |

Hand timing:

| Mark | Wind | Name | | Nat | Yr | Pos | Meet | Venue | Date |
|------|------|------|------|-----|-----|-----|------|-------|------|
| 12.9 | | Lidia | Okolo-Kulak | SU | 67 | 1h | | Minsk | 1 Aug |
| 12.9 | 0.3 | Lyudmila | Khristosenko | SU | 66 | 1h | | Kiev | 28 Aug |
| 13.0 | | Galina | Khaustova | SU | 65 | 1 | | Leningrad | 12 May |
| 13.0 | 0.2 | Natalya | Gorbunova | SU | 64 | 1 | | Leningrad | 27 Jun |
| 13.0 | 0.2 | Yelena | Ziatdinova | SU | 64 | | | Leningrad | 27 Jun |
| 13.0 | -1.0 | Eva | Sokolova | SU | 61 | 1 | | Leningrad | 6 Jul |
| 13.0 | | Irina | Svetonosova | SU | 58 | 1 | | Lipetsk | 18 Jul |
| 13.0 | 1.4 | Natalya | Kolovanova | SU | 64 | 1 | | Poltava | 19 Jul |
| 13.0 | | Irina | Mylnikova | SU | 65 | 2 | | Minsk | 2 Aug |
| 13.1 | 1.8 | Alicia | Bass (10) | USA | 65 | 2 | | Baton Rouge | 13 Apr |
| 13.1 | 1.8 | Schowonda | Williams | USA | 66 | 3 | | Baton Rouge | 13 Apr |
| 13.1 | | Marina | Sukhareva | SU | 62 | h | | Moskva | 10 May |
| 13.1 | -0.4 | Florence | Colle | FRA | 65 | 2 | | Montgeron | 17 May |
| 13.1 | 0.2 | Irina | Gritsenko | SU | 65 | 1h | | Kiev | 28 Aug |
| 13.1 | | Svetlana | Gerevich | SU | 66 | 2 | v Rum-j | Rovno | 4 Oct |
| 13.2 | 0.8 | Sophia | Hunter | JAM | 65 | 3 | | Columbus | 4 May |
| 13.2 | | Lyubov | Stolyar | SU | 61 | 1 | | Moskva | 10 May |
| 13.2 | 2.0 | Isabelle | Kaftandjian | FRA | 64 | | | Villeneuve d'Ascq | 10 May |
| 13.2 | | Natalya | Bordyugova | SU | 61 | H | | Kharkov | 15 May |
| 13.2 | | Tamara | Moshicheva (20) | SU | 62 | H | | Leningrad | 27 Jun |
| 13.2 | | Lyudmila | Narozhilenko | SU | 63 | 1h | | Ryazan | 28 Jun |
| 13.2 | -1.0 | Svetlana | Yermilova (22) | SU | 59 | 2 | | Leningrad | 6 Jul |

| Mark | | Name | | Nat | Yr | Date | | Mark | | Name | | Nat | Yr | Date |
|------|------|------|------|-----|-----|------|------|------|------|------|------|-----|-----|------|
| 13.3 | | Jackie | Humphrey | USA | 65 | 3 May | | 13.3 | | Antonina | Sukhova | SU | 59 | 14 Jun |
| 13.3 | | Rimma | Nurmukhomyatova | SU | 59 | 10 May | | 13.3 | | Svetlana | Ovchinnikova | SU | 56 | 27 Jun |
| 13.3 | | Olga | Kutsakova | SU | 68 | 11 May | | 13.3 | | Cindy | Greiner | USA | 57 | 25 Jul |

| Mark | | Name | | Nat | Yr | Pos | Meet | Venue | | Date |
|------|--|------|--|-----|----|----|------|-------|--|------|
| 13.3 | | Claudia | Felser | FRG | 68 | 3 Aug | 13.4 -0.5 Alla | Sorokina | SU | 66 27 Jun |
| 13.3 | | Natalya | Dudina (30) | SU | 66 | 9 Aug | 13.4  Valentina | Bushuyeva | SU | 63 28 Jun |
| | | | | | | | 13.4  Remigia | Zablovskaite | SU | 67 28 Jun |
| 13.4 | 0.9 | Lynette | Stock | NZ | 62 | 8 Mar | 13.4  Olga | Litvinova(39) | SU | 64 18 Jul |
| 13.4 | | Michèle | Chardonnet | FRA | 56 | 31 Mar | | | | |
| 13.4 | -2.2 | Birgit | Dressel | FRG | 60 | 8 May | Indoor mark: | | | |
| 13.4 | 1.6 | Birgit | Wolf | FRG | 69 | 29 May | | | | |
| 13.4 | 1.2 | Natalja | Schwandt | FRG | 68 | 29 May | 13.4 i  - Yinghua | Feng | CHN | 66 15 Mar |

Marks made with assisting wind > 2 m/s:

| 12.0 | 2.1 | Yordanka | Donkova | BUL | 61 | 1 | | Sofia | | 3 Aug |
|------|-----|----------|---------|-----|----|----|--|-------|--|-------|
| 12.1 | 2.1 | Ginka | Zagorcheva | BUL | 58 | 2 | | Sofia | | 3 Aug |
| | | | | | | | | | | |
| 13.2 | | Natasha | Thomas | USA | 67 | 1 | | Ames | | 3 May |
| 13.2 | 2.3 | Natalya | Dudina | SU | 66 | 1 | | Baku | | 30 May |
| | | | | | | | | | | |
| 13.3 | 3.3 | Birgit | Wolf | FRG | 69 | 29 May | 13.4 2.3 Zinaida | Bakulya | SU | 66 30 May |
| A13.4 | | Donna | Waller | USA | 64 | 12 Apr | 13.4 2.5 Angelika | Kuhmann | FRG | 57 1 Jun |
| 13.4 | | Faye | Barrett | USA | | 18 Apr | 13.4 2.1 Diana | Ruskova | BUL | 67 3 Aug |
| 13.4 | 4.6 | Lesley-Ann Skeete | | UK | 67 | 14 May | | | | |

# 400 METRES HURDLES

| Mark | Name | | Nat | Yr | Pos | Meet | Venue | Date |
|------|------|--|-----|----|----|------|-------|------|
| 52.94 | Marina | Stepanova | SU | 50 | 1s | Spart | Tashkent | 17 Sep |
| 53.32 | | Stepanova | | | 1 | EC | Stuttgart | 30 Aug |
| 53.60 | Sabine | Busch | GDR | 62 | 2 | EC | Stuttgart | 30 Aug |
| 53.62 | | Busch | | | 1h2 | NC | Jena | 27 Jun |
| 53.64 | | Busch | | | 1 | VD | Bruxelles | 5 Sep |
| 53.72 | | Stepanova | | | 1h | Spart | Tashkent | 16 Sep |
| A53.74 | Myrtle | Bothma | RSA | 64 | 1 | | Johannesburg | 18 Apr |
| 53.75 | | Busch | | | 1 | | Jena | 31 May |
| 53.76 | Debbie | Flintoff | AUS | 60 | 1 | Bisl | Oslo | 5 Jul |
| 53.81 | | Stepanova | | | 1 | GWG | Moskva | 7 Jul |
| | | | | | | | | |
| 53.83 | | Stepanova | | | 1s2 | EC | Stuttgart | 29 Aug |
| 53.84 | | Stepanova | | | 1 | NC | Kiev | 16 Jul |
| 53.85 | | Busch | | | 1 | NC | Jena | 28 Jun |
| 53.92 | | Stepanova | | | 1h | Znam | Leningrad | 7 Jun |
| A53.95 | | Bothma | | | 1 | NC | Germiston | 12 Apr |
| 53.97 | | Busch | | | 2s2 | EC | Stuttgart | 29 Aug |
| 54.00 | | Flintoff | | | 1 | Nik | Nice | 15 Jul |
| 54.03 | | Busch | | | 1 | OD | Dresden | 3 Jul |
| 54.04 | | Stepanova | | | 1 | Znam | Leningrad | 8 Jun |
| 54.04 | | Busch | | | 1 | GO | Dresden | 16 Aug |
| | | | | | | | | |
| 54.05 | | Busch | | | 2 | Bisl | Oslo | 5 Jul |
| 54.13 | Cornelia | Feuerbach | GDR | 63 | 3 | EC | Stuttgart | 30 Aug |
| 54.15 | Ann-Louise | Skoglund | SWE | 62 | 4 | EC | Stuttgart | 30 Aug |
| 54.21 | | Busch | | | 1 | | Berlin | 20 Aug |
| 54.27 | | Feuerbach | | | 2 | GO | Dresden | 16 Aug |
| 54.28 | | Flintoff | | | 1 | NC | Adelaide | 16 Mar |
| A54.36 | | Bothma | | | 1 | | Germiston | 2 Apr |
| 54.36 | | Busch | | | 1 | v SU | Tallinn | 22 Jun |
| 54.38 | | Feuerbach | | | 3 | Bisl | Oslo | 5 Jul |
| 54.43 | | Flintoff | | | 1 | | Melbourne | 23 Feb |

(30/6)

WOMEN 1986

| Mark | Name | | Nat | Yr | Pos | Meet | Venue | Date | |
|------|------|---|-----|----|-----|------|-------|------|---|
| 54.47 | Genowefa | Błaszak | POL | 57 | 2 | VD | Bruxelles | 5 | Sep |
| 54.55 | Cristieana | Matei | RUM | 62 | 2 | GWG | Moskva | 7 | Jul |
| 54.57 | Margarita | Khromova | SU | 63 | 1r1 | Spart | Tashkent | 18 | Sep |
| 54.76 | Ellen | Fiedler (10) | GDR | 58 | 2s1 | EC | Stuttgart | 29 | Aug |
| | | | | | | | | | |
| 54.78 | Marina | Sereda | SU | 64 | 2r1 | Spart | Tashkent | 18 | Sep |
| 54.90 | Sharieffa | Barksdale | USA | 61 | 1 | | Knoxville | 24 | May |
| 54.93 | Yelena | Goncharova | SU | 63 | 1 | | Sochi | 18 | May |
| 55.16 | Nicoleta | Căruţaşu | RUM | 64 | 2 | | Bucureşti | 24 | May |
| 55.16 | Maria | Usifo | NIG | 64 | 1 | NCAA | Indianapolis | 6 | Jun |
| 55.20 | Judi | Brown-King | USA | 61 | 1 | Pre | Eugene | 7 | Jun |
| 55.27 | Margarita | Navickaite | SU | 61 | 2 | | Sochi | 24 | May |
| 55.38 | Schowonda | Williams | USA | 66 | 2 | | Knoxville | 24 | May |
| 55.57 | Marina | Balabanova | SU | 64 | 4r1 | Spart | Tashkent | 18 | Sep |
| 55.62 | Olga | Nazarova (20) | SU | 62 | h | NC | Kiev | 15 | Jul |
| | | | | | | | | | |
| 55.74 | Latanya | Sheffield | USA | 63 | 2 | Pepsi | Westwood | 17 | May |
| 55.83 | Nawal | El Moutawakil | MOR | 62 | 1 | DrakeR | Des Moines | 25 | Apr |
| 55.84 | Valentina | Grishkina | SU | 56 | h | NC | Kiev | 15 | Jul |
| 55.85 | Inna | Yevseyeva | SU | 64 | 4 | | Sochi | 24 | May |
| 55.89 | Sandra | Farmer | JAM | 62 | 3 | Nik | Nice | 15 | Jul |
| 55.90 | Leisa | Davis-Knowles | USA | 63 | 2 | NCAA | Indianapolis | 6 | Jun |
| 55.98 | Sylvia | Kirchner | GDR | 63 | 3 | | Neubrandenburg | 6 | Jun |
| 56.08 | P.T. | Usha | IND | 64 | 1 | AsiG | Seoul | 30 | Sep |
| 56.17 | Tuija | Helander | FIN | 61 | 2 | v Swe | Helsinki | 10 | Aug |
| 56.17 | Yelena | Filipishina | SU | 62 | 1 | | Volgograd | 7 | Sep |
| | | (30) | | | | | | | |
| 56.27 | Jackie | Joyner | USA | 62 | 1 | | Long Beach | 2 | Mar |
| 56.36 | Gudrun | Abt | FRG | 62 | 1 | v Ita, | Hun Verona | 19 | Jun |
| 56.39 | Tatyana | Pavlova | SU | 58 | 1 | | Sochi | 27 | Apr |
| 56.45 | Natalya | Kalinnikova | SU | 63 | 6 | Znam | Leningrad | 8 | Jun |
| 56.48 | Jenny | Laurendet | AUS | 62 | 2 | NC | Adelaide | 16 | Mar |
| 56.48 | Lyudmila | Yushchenko | SU | 64 | 5r1 | Spart | Tashkent | 18 | Sep |
| 56.51 | Irina | Svetonosova | SU | 58 | h | Znam | Leningrad | 7 | Jun |
| 56.53 | Claudia | Bartl | GDR | 68 | 4 | | Neubrandenburg | 6 | Jun |
| 56.53 | Judita | Gendvilaite | SU | 63 | 6r1 | Spart | Tashkent | 18 | Sep |
| 56.55 | Gayle | Kellon (40) | USA | 65 | 4 | Pepsi | Westwood | 17 | May |
| | | | | | | | | | |
| 56.55 | Donalda | Duprey | CAN | 67 | 2 | CG | Edinburgh | 28 | Jul |
| 56.55 | Yelena | Stas | SU | 65 | 7r1 | Spart | Tashkent | 18 | Sep |
| 56.57 | Rosalyn | Bryant | USA | 56 | 5 | Pepsi | Westwood | 17 | May |
| 56.57 | Ana Maria | Drăghia | RUM | 68 | 1 | NC-j | Bucureşti | 7 | Jun |
| 56.61 | Arnita | Epps | USA | 64 | 1 | | Houston | 24 | May |
| 56.69 | Christina | Wennberg | SWE | 63 | 6s1 | EC | Stuttgart | 29 | Aug |
| 56.72 | Leslie | Maxie | USA | 67 | 1 | | Los Angeles | 3 | May |
| 56.74 | Sally | Fleming | AUS | 61 | 2 | | Canberra | 6 | Mar |
| A56.77 | Karen | Wilkenson | RSA | 66 | 2 | NC | Germiston | 12 | Apr |
| 56.79 | Jolanta | Stalmach (50) | POL | 60 | 2 | | Bolzano | 25 | May |
| | | | | | | | | | |
| 56.80 | Kellie | Roberts | USA | 69 | 2 | WC-j | Athinai | 18 | Jul |
| 56.88 | Anna | Ambraziene | SU | 55 | 1 | | Donetsk | 7 | Sep |
| 56.89 | Susanne | Losch | GDR | 66 | 5 | OD | Dresden | 3 | Jul |
| 56.89 | Gwen | Wall | CAN | 63 | 2 | | Gateshead | 5 | Aug |
| 56.95 | Beate | Holzapfel | FRG | 66 | 2 | NC | W Berlin | 13 | Jul |
| 56.95 | Gerda | Haas | AUT | 65 | 4h2 | EC | Stuttgart | 28 | Aug |
| 56.96 | Elina | Babich | SU | 64 | 1 | | Moskva | 24 | Aug |
| 56.98 | Bonka | Dimova | BUL | 56 | 1 | | Stara Zagora | 20 | Jul |
| 57.01 | Iolanta | Karopcikaite | SU | 64 | h | NC | Kiev | 15 | Jul |

| Mark | Name | | Nat | Yr | Pos | Meet | Venue | Date |
|------|------|------|-----|-----|-----|------|-------|------|
| 57.05 | Zhivka | Petkova (60) | BUL | 67 | 2 | Nar | Sofia | 1 Jun |
| 57.07 | Yvette | Wray | UK | 58 | 4 | | Gateshead | 5 Aug |
| 57.10 | Giuseppina | Cirulli | ITA | 59 | 1 | | Formia | 13 Jul |
| 57.11 | Yekaterina | Gaponova | SU | 64 | h | NC | Kiev | 15 Jul |
| 57.15 | Cristina | Perez | SPA | 65 | 1 | | La Coruña | 6 Aug |
| 57.15 | Caroline | Plüss | SWZ | 59 | 7s2 | EC | Stuttgart | 29 Aug |
| 57.18 | Chantal | Beaugeant | FRA | 61 | 2 | v Pol, | Spa Epinal | 5 Jul |
| 57.18 | Małgorzata | Dunecka | POL | 56 | 3 | v Fra, | Spa Epinal | 5 Jul |
| 57.18 | Monika | Klebe | SWE | 64 | 8s2 | EC | Stuttgart | 29 Aug |
| 57.21 | Natalya | Ovsyannikova | SU | 64 | 1r2 | Spart | Tashkent | 18 Sep |
| A57.24 | Elmarie | Vogel (70) | RSA | 60 | 3 | | Johannesburg | 18 Apr |
| 57.27 | Olga | Petrova | SU | 63 | 2 | | Moskva | 24 Aug |
| 57.28 | Audrone | Anjuliene | SU | 64 | h | NC | Kiev | 15 Jul |
| 57.30 | Camelia | Jianu | RUM | 67 | 3 | NC | Pitești | 9 Aug |
| 57.35 | Odalys | Hernandez | CUB | 66 | 1 | Barr | Habana | 15 Jun |
| 57.36 | Galina | Govdun | SU | 63 | 2r2 | Spart | Tashkent | 18 Sep |
| 57.39 | Sametra | King | USA | 66 | 2 | PennR | Philadelphia | 24 Apr |
| 57.39 | Hélène | Huart | FRA | 65 | 3 | | Paris | 22 Jul |
| 57.41 | Montserrat | Pujol | SPA | 61 | 5 | | Barcelona | 16 Jul |
| 57.47 | Lavonda | Luckett | USA | 65 | 4h2 | NCAA | Indianapolis | 4 Jun |
| 57.50 | Iolanda | Oanţă (80) | RUM | 65 | 1 | | București | 17 May |
| 57.51 | Kathy | Freeman | USA | 62 | 2 | | Houston | 24 May |
| 57.55 | Flora | Hyacinth | UVI | 66 | 1 | CAC | Santiago/Dom | 30 Jun |
| 57.56 | Simone | Gandy | UK | 65 | 5 | RumIC | București | 14 Jun |
| 57.57 | Erika | Szopori | HUN | 63 | 1 | v Aut, | Bul Linz | 29 Jun |
| 57.57 | Yelena | Klimova | SU | 66 | s | Spart | Tashkent | 17 Sep |
| 57.58 | Zinaida | Bakulya | SU | 66 | h | NC | Kiev | 15 Jul |
| 57.60 | Semra | Aksu | TUR | 62 | 1 | | Amsterdam | 1 Jun |
| 57.60 | Tania | Fernandez | CUB | 67 | 2 | CAC | Santiago/Dom | 30 Jun |
| 57.61 | Helga | Halldorsdottir | ICE | 63 | 1 | | Corvallis | 17 May |
| 57.70 | Carmen | Stolzenburg (90) | GDR | 66 | 3 | | Budapest | 13 Sep |
| 57.72 | Petra | Krug | GDR | 63 | 3h2 | NC | Jena | 27 Jun |
| 57.76 | Sybil | Perry | USA | 63 | 6 | NCAA | Indianapolis | 6 Jun |
| 57.76 | Aileen | Mills | UK | 62 | 5 | | Gateshead | 5 Aug |
| 57.77 | April | Cook | USA | 65 | 3 | . | Houston | 24 May |
| 57.77 | Irmgard | Trojer | ITA | 64 | 1 | | Caorle | 27 Jul |
| 57.84 | Irina | Dorofeyeva | SU | 62 | h | | Sochi | 23 May |
| 57.85 | Sabine | Zwiener | FRG | 67 | 1h4 | NC | W Berlin | 12 Jul |
| 57.87 | Zuzana | Machotková | CS | 65 | 7 | OD | Dresden | 3 Jul |
| 57.88 | Blanka | Háková | CS | 64 | 3h | Znam | Leningrad | 7 Jun |
| 57.89 | Anfisa | Bikbulatova | SU | 65 | 3 | | Kiev | 27 Jul |
| | | (100) | | | | | | |
| 57.92 | Svetlana | Lukashevich | SU | 68 | 3 | WC-j | Athinai | 18 Jul |
| 57.95 | Nadine | Debois (102) | FRA | 61 | 1 | | Montgeron | 29 Jun |

| Mark | Name | | | Mark | Name | | |
|------|------|------|------|------|------|------|------|
| 58.00 | Andrea | Page | CAN 56 22 Jun | 58.10 | Larisa | Azeyeva | SU 66 7 Sep |
| 58.00 | Jill | McDermid | CAN 68 18 Jul | 58.11 | Monika | Schediwy | SWZ 64 9 Aug |
| 58.01 | Anne | Gundersen | NOR 66 28 Aug | 58.12 | Galina | Bakhchevanova | BUL 62 1 Jun |
| 58.02 | Natalya | Baranova | SU 60 10 Aug | 58.12 | Olga | Yashnikova | SU 64 24 Aug |
| 58.03 | Lilyana | Ivanova | BUL 56 14 Aug | 58.19 | Qianqian | Zhao | CHN 61 3 Jun |
| 58.06 | Justine | Craig | NZ 64 4 Apr | 58.24 | Anzhela | Bologan | SU 66 17 Sep |
| 58.07 | Chris | Crowther | USA 63 12 Apr | 58.28 | Elaine | McLaughlin | UK 63 28 Jul |
| 58.10 | Simone | Büngener (110) | FRG 62 13 Jul | 58.28 | Svetlana | Sevryukova | SU 66 16 Sep |

| Mark | Name | | Nat | Yr | Pos | Meet | Venue | | Date |
|------|------|--|-----|-----|-----|------|-------|--|------|
| A58.29 | Leonie | Louwrens | RSA 59 | 12 Apr | 58.85 | Ina | van Rensburg | RSA 56 | 3 Mar |
| 58.31 | Alyson | Evans | (120) UK 66 | 28 Jul | 58.85 | Birgit | Wolf | (150) FRG 60 | 29 Jun |
| 58.35 | Monica | Westen | SWE 66 | 18 May | 58.85 | Sofia | Sabeva | BUL 69 | 20 Jul |
| 58.41 | Juying | Chen | CHN 63 | 7 Sep | 58.87 | Maria João | Lopes | POR 62 | 14 Jun |
| 58.46 | Margit | Grotzinger | FRG 67 | 29 Jun | 58.89 | Tatyana | Ivanova | SU 64 | 15 Jul |
| 58.50 | Debbie | DaCosta | USA 64 | 19 Apr | 58.89 | Brunella | Cherici | ITA 60 | 22 Jul |
| 58.50 | Martine | Mathiot | FRA 57 | 14 Jun | 58.90 | Marina | Kogut | SU 66 | 18 Aug |
| 58.51 | Janice | Farwell | USA 66 | 24 May | 58.91 | Barbara | Johnson | IRL 62 | 19 Jul |
| 58.52 | Christa | Vandercruyssen | BEL 61 | 15 Aug | 58.91 | Alina | Buhuşi | RUM 67 | 9 Aug |
| 58.55 | Debbie | Tomsett | AUS 60 | 16 Mar | 58.92 | Natalya | Farafonova | SU 70 | 11 Jul |
| 58.55 | Zdravka | Georgieva | BUL 69 | 22 Jun | 58.93 | Yelena | Gutnik | SU 65 | 18 Sep |
| 58.57 | Galina | Selivanova | SU 60 | 23 May | 58.94 | Svetlana | Tsybulskaya | SU 60 | 28 Jun |
| | | (130) | | | | | | (160) | |
| 58.59 | Beata | Adamczyk | POL 62 | 7 Jun | 58.96 | Mary | Parr | IRL 61 | |
| 58.60 | Tatyana | Matsuta | SU 67 | 15 Jul | 58.99 | Jennifer | Harlan | USA 66 | 24 May |
| 58.61 | Angela | Wilhelm | FRG 59 | 10 Aug | 58.99 | Catherine | Lebreton | FRA 60 | 10 Aug |
| 58.62 | Nathalie | Nisen | BEL 64 | 10 Aug | 59.00 | Deborah | Church | UK 62 | 12 Jun |
| 58.62 | Jennifer | Pearson | UK 62 | 19 Aug | 59.01 | Hitomi | Koshimoto | JAP 64 | 14 Oct |
| 58.67 | Janet | Williams | USA 63 | 21 May | 59.02 | Rodica | Dudău | RUM 58 | 14 Jun |
| 58.68 | Victoria | Lee | UK 64 | 5 Aug | 59.02 | Hionati | Kapeti | GRE 67 | 7 Sep |
| 58.71 | Carmel | Major | BAH | 24 May | 59.04 | Noris | Mozo | CUB 67 | 31 May |
| 58.72 | Viktoria | Polnyuk | SU 69 | 11 Jul | 59.04 | Carol | Dawkins | UK 60 | 10 Aug |
| 58.76 | Natasha | Thomas | (140) USA 67 | 24 May | 59.05 | Alma Delia | Vazquez | (170) MEX 63 | 30 Jun |
| 58.76 | Irena | Dominc | YUG 70 | 22 Jun | 59.06 | Birgit | Engel | FRG 62 | 12 Jul |
| 58.76 | Cristina | Moretti | SWZ 63 | 9 Aug | 59.10 | Jayne | O'Brien | USA | 24 Apr |
| 58.77 | Wendy | Truvillion | USA 64 | 24 May | 59.13 | Mirosława | Koy | POL 65 | 28 Jun |
| 58.78 | Yolanda | Henry | USA 64 | 23 May | 59.14 | Linetta | Wilson | USA 67 | 12 Apr |
| 58.79 | Yvette | Cash | USA 65 | 4 May | 59.14 | Natalie | Day | USA 63 | 23 May |
| 58.80 | Shawn | Moore | USA 68 | 18 Jul | 59.16 | Claudia | Schittenhelm | FRG 65 | 29 Jun |
| 58.81 | Lyudmila | Myachikova | SU 64 | 15 Aug | 59.16 | Anita | Lauvensteine | SU 63 | 17 Sep |
| 58.83 | Pam | Board | USA 64 | 29 May | A59.16 | Katrien | van Rooyen | RSA 65 | 5 Dec |
| | | | | | | | | (178) | |

Best low altitude marks:

| | | | | | |
|------|--|----------|---|----------------|--------|
| 54.86 | | Bothma | 1 | Port Elizabeth | 21 Apr |
| 57.63 | | Wilkenson | 2 | Port Elizabeth | 21 Apr |
| 57.90 | | Vogel | 3 | Port Elizabeth | 21 Apr |

---

| | 1 | 10 | 20 | 30 | 50 | 100 | Under 57.00 | Under 59.00 |
|------|-------|-------|-------|-------|-------|-------|-------|-------|
| 1982 | 54.57 | 55.76 | 56.48 | 57.00 | 57.86 | 58.79 | 29 | 109 |
| 1983 | 54.02 | 55.49 | 56.03 | 56.26 | 57.00 | 58.20 | 49 | 147 |
| 1984 | 53.58 | 54.93 | 55.60 | 56.08 | 56.86 | 58.07 | 52 | 160 |
| 1985 | 53.55 | 54.95 | 55.48 | 55.86 | 56.86 | 58.00 | 56 | 173 |
| 1986 | 52.94 | 54.76 | 55.62 | 56.17 | 56.79 | 57.89 | 58 | 163 |

---

Hand timing:

| | | | | | | | |
|------|------|-----------------|--------|---|-----------|---|-------|
| 55.7 | Nawal | El Moutawakil | MOR 62 | 1 | Tempe | | 5 Apr |
| 56.0 | P.T. | Usha | IND 64 | 1 | New Delhi | | 6 Aug |

| Mark | Name | | Nat | Yr | Pos | Meet | Venue | Date |
|------|------|--|-----|-----|-----|------|-------|------|
| 56.1 | Anna | Ambraziene | SU | 55 | 2 | | Kaunas | 30 Aug |
| 56.3 | Irina | Svetonosova | SU | 58 | 1 | | Lipetsk | 19 Jul |
| 56.4 | Natalya | Ovsyannikova | SU | 64 | 1 | | Alma-Ata | 28 Aug |
| 57.0 | Yekaterina | Gaponova | SU | 64 | 1 | | Novotroitsk | 29 Jun |
| A57.1 | Madele | Naude | RSA | 63 | 1 | | Bloemfontein | 24 Oct |
| 57.2 | Anfisa | Bikbulatova | SU | 65 | | | Novosibirsk | 29 Jun |
| 57.2 | Svetlana | Lukashevich | SU | 68 | 1 | | Minsk | 3 Aug |
| 57.2 | Galina | Govdun (10) | SU | 63 | 2 | | Kiev | 29 Aug |
| 57.4 | Natalya | Tsiruk | SU | 55 | 1 | | Kharkov | 4 May |
| 57.5 | Victoria | Lee | UK | 64 | 1 | | Hendon | 28 Jun |
| 57.5 | Simone | Gandy | UK | 65 | 2 | | Hendon | 28 Jun |
| 57.5 | Yelena | Gutnik | SU | 65 | 3 | | Kiev | 29 Aug |
| 57.5 | Inna | Tsud | SU | 67 | 4 | | Kiev | 29 Aug |
| 57.8 | Teresa | Hoyle | UK | 63 | 1 | | Enfield | 26 Jul |
| 57.9 | Susan | Chick (17) | UK | 60 | 1 | | Enfield | 9 Aug |

| Mark | Name | | Nat | Yr | Pos | Date | | Name | | Nat | Yr | Date |
|------|------|--|-----|-----|-----|------|--|------|--|-----|-----|------|
| 58.0 | Irina | Petrova | SU | 61 | 6 Jul | 58.5 | | Nadezhda | Solovyova(30) | SU | 63 | 19 Jul |
| 58.0 | Sabine | Alber | FRG | 65 | 14 Sep | | | | | | | |
| 58.1 | Svetlana | Sevryukova | SU | 66 | 28 Aug | 58.6 | | Yelena | Mitrukova | SU | 64 | 22 Jun |
| | | (20) | | | | 58.6 | | Marina | Gazalova | SU | 65 | 20 Jul |
| 58.2 | Jennifer | Pearson | UK | 62 | 17 May | 58.7 | | Svetlana | Azhel | SU | 63 | 30 Jun |
| 58.2 | Natalya | Ryabukhova | SU | 62 | 29 Jun | 58.7 | | Natalya | Korniyenko | SU | 63 | 20 Jul |
| 58.3 | Nadezhda | Konovalova | SU | 64 | 29 Aug | 58.7 | | Laila | Grinberga | SU | 64 | 30 Aug |
| 58.4 | Marina | Kogut | SU | 66 | 25 May | 58.8 | | Yelena | Tokar | SU | 67 | 14 Jun |
| 58.4 | Anita | Lauvensteine | SU | 63 | 23 Aug | 58.9 | | Yelena | Akisheva | SU | 67 | 29 Jun |
| 58.4 | Marina | Nikulina | SU | 63 | 29 Aug | 58.9 | | Alla | Shilkina | SU | 68 | |
| 58.5 | Belkis | Chavez | CUB | 66 | 22 Feb | 58.9 | | Inna | Gridasova | SU | 63 | 20 Jul |
| 58.5 | Noris | Mozo | CUB | 67 | 22 Feb | 58.9 | | Irina | Romanenkova | SU | 66 | 5 Oct |
| 58.5 | Viktoria | Polnyuk | SU | 69 | 1 Jul | | | | (40) | | | |

## HIGH JUMP

| Mark | Name | | Nat | Yr | Pos | Meet | Venue | Date |
|------|------|--|-----|-----|-----|------|-------|------|
| 2.08 | Stefka | Kostadinova | BUL | 65 | 1 | Nar | Sofia | 31 May |
| 2.07 | | Kostadinova | | | 1 | | Sofia | 25 May |
| 2.06 | | Kostadinova | | | 1 | | Furth | 15 Jun |
| 2.06 | | Kostadinova | | | 1 | | Cagliari | 14 Sep |
| 2.05 | | Kostadinova | | | 1 | | Wörrstadt | 14 Jun |
| 2.05 | | Kostadinova | | | 1 | | Rieti | 7 Sep |
| 2.04 | | Kostadinova | | | 1 | | Bern | 20 Aug |
| 2.03 | | Kostadinova | | | 1 | GWG | Moskva | 7 Jul |
| 2.01 | Olga | Turchak | SU | 67 | 2 | GWG | Moskva | 7 Jul |
| 2.01 | | Kostadinova | | | 1 | NC | Sofia | 13 Aug |
| 2.01 | | Kostadinova | | | 1 | Balk | Ljubljana | 6 Sep |
| 2.01 | Desiree | du Plessis | RSA | 65 | 1 | | Johannesburg | 16 Sep |
| 2.00 | | Kostadinova | | | 1 | | Saint-Denis | 21 Jun |
| 2.00 | | Kostadinova | | | 1 | EC | Stuttgart | 28 Aug |
| 2.00 | | Turchak | | | 1 | Spart | Tashkent | 19 Sep |
| 2.00 | | Kostadinova | | | 1 | | Sao Paulo | 21 Sep |
| 2.00 | | du Plessis | | | 1 | | Johannesburg | 18 Oct |
| 2.00 | | du Plessis | | | 1 | | Johannesburg | 1 Nov |
| 1.99 | Charmaine | Gale | RSA | 64 | 1 | | Johannesburg | 18 Apr |
| 1.99 | Silvia | Costa | CUB | 64 | 1 | | Tokyo | 11 May |

WOMEN 1986

| Mark | Name | | Nat | Yr | Pos | Meet | Venue | Date |
|------|------|--|-----|----|-----|------|-------|------|
| 1.98 i | Gabriele | Günz | GDR | 61 | 1 | | Berlin | 26 Jan |
| 1.98 i | Andrea | Bienias | GDR | 59 | 2 | | Berlin | 26 Jan |
| 1.98 i | Larisa | Kositsyna | SU | 63 | 1 | NC | Moskva | 7 Feb |
| 1.98 | | du Plessis | | | 1 | NC | Germiston | 12 Apr |
| 1.98 | | Gale | | | 2 | NC | Germiston | 12 Apr |
| 1.98 | | Costa | | | 1 | | Firenze | 28 May |
| 1.98 | Katalin | Sterk | HUN | 61 | 1 | NC | Budapest | 17 Aug |
| 1.98 | | du Plessis | | | 1 | | Johannesburg | 9 Sep |
| 1.98 | | du Plessis | | | 1 | | Potchefstroom | 24 Oct |
| 1.97 i | | Bienias | | | 1 | | Schwedt | 18 Jan |
| 1.97 i | | Bienias | | | 1 | | Arnstadt | 22 Jan |
| 1.97 i | | Günz | | | 1 | v Fra | Lievin | 1 Feb |
| 1.97 | | Gale | | | 1 | | Pretoria | 3 Feb |
| 1.97 i | | Bienias | | | 1 | EC | Madrid | 23 Feb |
| 1.97 i | Debbie | Brill (10) | CAN | 53 | 1 | TAC | New York | 28 Feb |
| 1.97 | Svetlana | Isaeva | BUL | 67 | 2 | | Sofia | 25 May |
| 1.97 | | Costa | | | 1 | | Bolzano | 25 May |
| 1.97 | | Turchak | | | 1 | Znam | Leningrad | 8 Jun |
| 1.97 | | Turchak | | | 1 | v GDR | Tallinn | 22 Jun |
| 1.97 | | Bienias | | | 1 | NC | Jena | 29 Jun |
| 1.97 | | Turchak | | | 1 | NC | Kiev | 17 Jul |
| 1.97 | | du Plessis | | | 1 | | Johannesburg | 21 Oct |
| 1.97 | | du Plessis | | | 1 | | Secunda | 15 Nov |
| 1.97 | | du Plessis | | | 1 | | Bloemfontein | 5 Dec |
| | | (44/11) | | | | | | |
| 1.96 i | Galina | Brigadnaya | SU | 58 | 2 | NC | Moskva | 7 Feb |
| 1.96 | Tamara | Bykova | SU | 58 | 3= | GWG | Moskva | 7 Jul |
| 1.96 | Susanne | Helm | GDR | 61 | 5 | GWG | Moskva | 7 Jul |
| 1.96 | Danuta | Bułkowska | POL | 59 | 1 | | Caorle | 27 Jul |
| 1.94 i | Marina | Doronina | SU | 61 | 1 | | Moskva | 2 Feb |
| 1.94 i | Maryse | Ewanje-Epée | FRA | 64 | 2 | | Madrid | 12 Feb |
| 1.94 | Chris | Stanton | AUS | 59 | 1 | NC | Adelaide | 16 Mar |
| 1.94 | Elvira | Yakimova | SU | 63 | 1 | | Tashkent | 27 Apr |
| 1.94 | Galina | Balgurina(20) | SU | 65 | 1 | | Sochi | 24 May |
| 1.94 | Marina | Yevstigneyeva | SU | 62 | 4 | Znam | Leningrad | 8 Jun |
| 1.94 | Elżbieta | Trylinska | POL | 60 | 1 | | Warszawa | 8 Jun |
| 1.94 | Sara | Simeoni | ITA | 53 | 1 | | Formia | 13 Jul |
| 1.94 | Svetlana | Gorbunova | SU | 62 | 1 | | Lvov | 9 Aug |
| 1.94 | Olga | Juha | HUN | 62 | 3 | BGP | Budapest | 11 Aug |
| 1.94 | Natalya | Golodnova | SU | 67 | 1 | | Alma-Ata | 31 Aug |
| 1.94 | Marina | Degtyar | SU | 62 | 1 | | Kiev | 31 Aug |
| 1.94 | Albina | Kazakova | SU | 62 | 2 | | Donetsk | 6 Sep |
| 1.93 | Louise | Ritter | USA | 58 | 1 | TexR | Austin | 4 Apr |
| 1.93 | Jan | Chesbro (30) | USA | 58 | 2 | TAC | Eugene | 20 Jun |
| 1.93 | Emilia | Petkanova | BUL | 65 | 1 | | Stara Zagora | 19 Jul |
| 1.93 | Galina | Astafei | RUM | 69 | 1 | NC | Pitești | 9 Aug |
| 1.93 | Diana | Davies | UK | 61 | 1 | | London | 12 Sep |
| 1.93 | Heike | Redetzky | FRG | 64 | 1 | | Forbach | 21 Sep |
| 1.92 i | Yelena | Duginets | SU | 59 | 1 | | Leningrad | 5 Jan |
| 1.92 i | Lyudmila | Butuzova | SU | 57 | 2 | | Minsk | 19 Jan |
| 1.92 i | Irina | Barinova | SU | 61 | 3 | | Klaipeda | 19 Jan |
| 1.92 i | Urszula | Kielan | POL | 60 | 1 | | Praha | 13 Feb |
| 1.92 | Madely | Beaugendre | FRA | 65 | 4 | Nik | Nice | 15 Jul |
| 1.92 | Karen | Scholz (40) | GDR | 69 | 1 | WC-j | Athinai | 18 Jul |

| Mark | Name | | Nat | Yr | Pos | Meet | Venue | Date |
|------|------|--|-----|----|-----|------|-------|------|
| 1.92 | Brigitte | Rougeron | FRA | 61 | 1 | | Rheinau-Freistett | 20 Jul |
| 1.92 | Nadezhda | Sharpilova | SU | 59 | 1 | | Leningrad | 29 Jul |
| 1.92 | Birgit | Dressel | FRG | 60 | H | EC | Stuttgart | 29 Aug |
| 1.92 | Judy | Simpson | UK | 60 | H | EC | Stuttgart | 29 Aug |
| 1.92 | Yelena | Chaikovskaya | SU | 63 | 2 | Spart | Tashkent | 19 Sep |
| 1.92 | Yelena | Topchina | SU | 66 | 3 | Spart | Tashkent | 19 Sep |
| 1.91 i | Vanessa | Browne | AUS | 63 | 1 | | Osaka | 15 Jan |
| 1.91 i | Megumi | Satoh | JAP | 66 | 2 | | Osaka | 15 Jan |
| 1.91 i | Ute | Kühn | GDR | 65 | 2 | | Schwedt | 18 Jan |
| 1.91 i | Tamara | Malešev (50) | YUG | 67 | 1 | v Aut, Hun | Wien | 30 Jan |
| | | | | | | | | |
| 1.91 i | Latrese | Johnson | USA | 66 | 2 | | Kobe | 5 Mar |
| 1.91 | Elena | Schromm | RUM | 60 | 1 | | Bucureşti | 25 May |
| 1.91 | Xiuling | Ni | CHN | 62 | 2 | | Formia | 13 Jul |
| 1.91 | Janet | Boyle | UK | 63 | 2 | | London | 12 Sep |
| 1.90 i | Mila | Skibicki | FRG | 64 | 1 | | Simmerath | 17 Jan |
| 1.90 i | Brigitte | Holzapfel | FRG | 58 | 2 | | Simmerath | 17 Jan |
| 1.90 i | Lyudmila | Avdeyenko | SU | 63 | 1 | | Gomel | 19 Jan |
| 1.90 i | Irina | Litvinenko | SU | 60 | 1 | | Volgograd | 24 Jan |
| 1.90 i | Susanne | Lorentzon | SWE | 61 | 1 | NC | Solna | 2 Feb |
| 1.90 i | Alessandra | Fossati (60) | ITA | 63 | 2 | NC | Genova | 5 Feb |
| | | | | | | | | |
| 1.90 i | Sigrid | Kirchmann | AUT | 66 | 1 | NC | Wien | 9 Feb |
| 1.90 i | Rosanel | Gogi | BUL | 69 | 1 | NC-j | Sofia | 2 Mar |
| 1.90 | Kim | Hagger | UK | 61 | H | v Fra, Can | Arles | 17 May |
| 1.90 | Natalya | Sergiyevich | SU | 63 | 1 | | Sochi | 18 May |
| 1.90 | Lilia | Zablotskaya | SU | 65 | 5 | Znam | Leningrad | 8 Jun |
| 1.90 | Camille | Harding | USA | 65 | 3 | TAC | Eugene | 20 Jun |
| 1.90 | Valentina | Poluiko | SU | 55 | 2 | | Minsk | 26 Jun |
| 1.90 | Sharon | McPeake | UK | 62 | 2 | CG | Edinburgh | 1 Aug |
| 1.90 | Christina | Nordström | SWE | 61 | 2 | v Fin | Helsinki | 9 Aug |
| 1.90 | Dazhen | Zheng (70) | CHN | 59 | 1 | | Beijing | 7 Sep |
| | | | | | | | | |
| 1.90 | Małgorzata | Nowak | POL | 59 | H | | Talence | 20 Sep |
| 1.90 i | Rita | Graves | USA | 64 | 1 | | Manhattan, KS | 13 Dec |
| 1.89 i | Sabine | Bramhoff | FRG | 64 | 1 | | Dortmund | 11 Jan |
| 1.89 i | Lyubov | Pakhomchik | SU | 63 | 3 | | Vilnius | 12 Jan |
| 1.89 i | Svetlana | Odintsova | SU | 62 | 4 | | Kiev | 25 Jan |
| 1.89 i | Angela | Palinske | GDR | 65 | 3 | | Berlin | 8 Feb |
| 1.89 | Deann | Bopf | AUS | 62 | 1 | | Sydney | 9 Feb |
| 1.89 i | Joni | Huntley | USA | 56 | 3 | TAC | New York | 28 Feb |
| 1.89 | Trudy | Painter | NZ | 65 | 1 | NC | Christchurch | 9 Mar |
| 1.89 | Yolanda | Henry (80) | USA | 64 | 1 | | Los Angeles | 23 May |
| | | | | | | | | |
| 1.89 | Ping | Ge | CHN | 61 | 3 | | Saint-Denis | 21 Jun |
| 1.89 | Samra | Tanović | YUG | 66 | 1 | | Sarajevo | 5 Jul |
| 1.89 | Judit | Kovács | HUN | 69 | 2 | Druzhba | Neubrandenburg | 1 Aug |
| 1.89 | Hanne | Haugland | NOR | 67 | 2 | | Birmingham | 19 Aug |
| 1.89 | Hee-Sun | Kim | SKO | 63 | 3 | AsiG | Seoul | 1 Oct |
| 1.89 | Ling | Jin | CHN | 67 | | | Zhengzhou | 23 Oct |
| 1.88 i | Tatyana | Rotar | SU | 63 | 12= | NC | Moskva | 7 Feb |
| 1.88 i | Susanne | Rössler | FRG | 63 | 4 | NC | Sindelfingen | 7 Feb |
| 1.88 i | Kym | Carter | USA | 64 | 1 | | Fort Worth | 15 Feb |
| 1.88 | Jenny | Talbot (90) | AUS | 64 | 3 | NC | Adelaide | 16 Mar |
| | | | | | | | | |
| 1.88 | Hanlie | Kotze | RSA | 60 | 3 | | Port Elizabeth | 21 Apr |
| 1.88 | Phyllis | Bluntson | USA | 59 | 1 | MSR | Walnut, CA | 27 Apr |
| 1.88 | Katrena | Johnson | USA | 64 | 2= | MSR | Walnut, CA | 27 Apr |

| Mark | Name | | Nat | Yr | Pos | Meet | Venue | Date |
|---|---|---|---|---|---|---|---|---|
| 1.88 | Mary | Moore | USA | 65 | 4= | MSR | Walnut, CA | 27 Apr |
| 1.88 | Carina | Schmidt | USA | 61 | 4= | MSR | Walnut, CA | 27 Apr |
| 1.88 | Lyudmila | Tkachenko | SU | 63 | 2 | | Kharkov | 14 May |
| 1.88 | Jolanda | Jones | USA | 65 | 1 | | Houston | 18 May |
| 1.88 | Peggy | Beer | GDR | 69 | 1 | | Karl-Marx-Stadt | 25 May |
| 1.88 | Daniela | Chválková | CS | 61 | 1 | | Banská Bystrica | 31 May |
| 1.88 | Iwona | Jakobczak | POL | 66 | 3 | | Grudziadz | 3 Jun |
| | | (100) | | | | | | |
| 1.88 | Jolanta | Komsa | POL | 58 | 3= | Kuso | Warszawa | 17 Jun |
| 1.88 | Silvia | Oswald | FRG | 68 | 1 | | Bad Reichenhall | 21 Jun |
| 1.88 | Lidija | Lapajne | YUG | 59 | 1 | | Beograd | 27 Jun |
| 1.88 | Jayne | Barnetson | UK | 68 | 1 | | Swansea | 28 Jun |
| 1.88 | Monica | Matei | RUM | 63 | 2 | | Pitești | 29 Jun |
| 1.88 | Michaela | Hübel | FRG | 69 | H | | Düsseldorf | 5 Jul |
| 1.88 | Larisa | Andreyeva | SU | 64 | 1 | | Taganrog | 6 Jul |
| 1.88 | Marianna | Maslennikova | SU | 61 | H | GWG | Moskva | 6 Jul |
| 1.88 | Jackie | Joyner | USA | 62 | H | GWG | Moskva | 6 Jul |
| 1.88 | Svetla | Dimitrova | BUL | 70 | H | WC-j | Athinai | 18 Jul |
| | | (110) | | | | | | |
| 1.88 | Yelena | Obukhova | SU | 69 | 3 | WC-j | Athinai | 18 Jul |
| 1.88 | Yelena | Davydova | SU | 67 | H | Spart | Tashkent | 16 Sep |
| 1.88 | Svetlana | Filatyeva | SU | 64 | H | Spart | Tashkent | 16 Sep |
| 1.88 | Biljana | Petrović(114) | YUG | 61 | 1 | | Split | 27 Sep |

| Mark | Name | | Nat | Yr | Date | Mark | | Mark | Name | | Nat | Yr | Date |
|---|---|---|---|---|---|---|---|---|---|---|---|---|---|
| 1.87i | Sari | Karjalainen | FIN | 68 | 26 Jan | 1.86 | | Liesel | Beytell | | RSA | 66 | 14 Mar |
| 1.87i | Tami | Lutz | CAN | 64 | 15 Mar | 1.86 | | Joanne | Lamont | | AUS | 67 | 14 Mar |
| 1.87 | Liliane | Ménissier | FRA | 60 | 17 May | 1.86 i | | Dagmar | Finke | | FRG | 66 | 20 Mar |
| 1.87 | Lisa | Bernhagen | USA | 66 | 17 May | 1.86 | | Linda | Cameron | | CAN | 63 | 20 Apr |
| 1.87 | Anke | Behmer | GDR | 61 | 24 May | 1.86 | | Boriana | Borisova | | BUL | 67 | 11 May |
| 1.87 | Larisa | Suprunova | SU | 64 | 5 Jun | 1.86 | | Jennifer | Little | | UK | 65 | 11 May |
| | | (120) | | | | 1.86 | | Larisa | Nikitina | | SU | 65 | 24 May |
| 1.87 | Andrea | Breder | FRG | 64 | 19 Jul | 1.86 | | Vesna | Luković | | YUG | 59 | 24 May |
| 1.87 | Nathalie | Said | FRA | 66 | 27 Jul | 1.86 | | Svetlana | Mokryak | | SU | 67 | 30 May |
| 1.87 | Christine | Soetewey | BEL | 57 | 3 Aug | 1.86 | | Yongjun | Liu | (150) | CHN | 65 | 2 Jun |
| 1.87 | Anja | Barelkowski | FRG | 65 | 10 Aug | | | | | | | | |
| 1.87 | Corinne | Schneider | SWZ | 62 | 10 Aug | 1.86 | | Zhongping | Cao | | CHN | 66 | 4 Jun |
| 1.87 | Marion | Weser | GDR | 62 | 19 Aug | 1.86 | | Marina | Kozminykh | | SU | 68 | 9 Jul |
| 1.87 | Ortensia | Iancu | RUM | 67 | 4 Oct | 1.86 | | Yelena | Poddubskaya | | SU | 59 | 12 Jul |
| 1.86 i | Marina | Dyuzhova | SU | 65 | 4 Jan | 1.86 | | Asuncion | Morte | | SPA | 59 | 19 Jul |
| 1.86 i | Lyudmila | Sukhoroslova | SU | 62 | 11 Jan | 1.86 | | Svetlana | Borodai | | SU | 59 | 20 Jul |
| 1.86 i | Olga | Belkova | SU | 55 | 25 Jan | 1.86 | | Alla | Fedorchuk | | SU | 57 | 26 Jul |
| | | (130) | | | | 1.86 | | Minna | Vehmasto | | FIN | 62 | 31 Jul |
| 1.86 i | Natalya | Kravchinskaya | SU | 57 | 25 Jan | 1.86 | | Tamara | Moshicheva | | SU | 62 | 5 Aug |
| 1.86 i | Priska | Tanner | SWZ | 67 | 29 Jan | 1.86 | | Camelia | Cornăteanu | | RUM | 67 | 7 Aug |
| 1.86 i | Olga | Bolshova | SU | 68 | 8 Feb | 1.86 | | Tatyana | Arychenkova | | SU | 66 | 9 Aug |
| 1.86 i | Zdeňka | Svatošová | CS | 61 | 8 Feb | | | | | (160) | | | |
| 1.86 i | Heike | Grabe | GDR | 62 | 8 Feb | 1.86 | | Ivana | Vondruskova | | CS | 64 | 9 Aug |
| 1.86 i | Covadonga | Mateos | SPA | 63 | 12 Feb | 1.86 | | Lola | Butakhanova | | SU | 64 | 15 Aug |
| 1.86 i | Candy | Cashell | USA | 63 | 16 Feb | 1.86 | | Irina | Kushenko | | SU | 65 | 28 Aug |
| 1.86 | Gai | Kapernick | AUS | 70 | 16 Feb | 1.86 | | Olga | Panchuk | | SU | 63 | 18 Sep |
| 1.86 | Leah | Cranston | AUS | 70 | 16 Feb | 1.86 | | Yelena | Latsuk | | SU | 68 | 18 Sep |
| 1.86 i | Coleen | Sommer | (140) | USA | 60 | 28 Feb | | Małgorzata | Orlowska | | POL | 63 | 21 Sep |
| | | | | | | 1.86 | | Heike | Siemers | | FRG | 70 | 4 Oct |
| | | | | | | 1.86 | | Peisu | Ye | | CHN | 58 | 24 Oct |
| | | | | | | 1.86 | | Sharon | Barber | (169) | AUS | 65 | 20 Dec |

| Mark | Name | Nat | Yr | Pos | Meet | Venue | Date |
|------|------|-----|----|----|------|-------|------|

|      | 1    | 10   | 20   | 30   | 50   | 100  | Over 1.90 | Over 1.86 |
|------|------|------|------|------|------|------|-----------|-----------|
| 1982 | 2.02 | 1.97 | 1.93 | 1.91 | 1.89 | 1.86 | 48 | 106 |
| 1983 | 2.04 | 1.97 | 1.93 | 1.91 | 1.90 | 1.87 | 56 | 124 |
| 1984 | 2.07 | 1.97 | 1.95 | 1.92 | 1.90 | 1.87 | 56 | 140 |
| 1985 | 2.06 | 1.96 | 1.94 | 1.94 | 1.91 | 1.87 | 74 | 146 |
| 1986 | 2.08 | 1.97 | 1.94 | 1.93 | 1.91 | 1.88 | 72 | 169 |

Best outdoor marks:

| 1.96 |   | Brigadnaya |   | 6 | GWG | Moskva | 7 Jul |
|------|---|------------|---|---|-----|--------|-------|
| 1.94 |   | Kositsyna | | 4 | Nar | Sofia | 31 May |
| 1.92 |   | Ewanje-Epée | | 1 | | Créteil | 14 Jun |
| 1.92 |   | Doronina | | 1 | RumIC | Bucureşti | 15 Jun |
| 1.90 |   | Browne | | 1 | | Melbourne | 20 Mar |
| 1.90 |   | Kirchmann | | H | | Götzis | 24 May |
| 1.90 |   | Günz | | 1 | | Leipzig | 22 Jun |
| 1.90 |   | Kielan | | 1 | v Fra, | Spa Epinal | 5 Jul |
| 1.90 |   | Lorentzon | | 1 | v Fin | Helsinki | 9 Aug |
| 1.89 |   | Satoh | (10) | 2 | | Tokyo | 11 May |
| 1.89 |   | Brill | | 1 | | Sevilla | 24 May |
| 1.89 |   | Duginets | | 1 | | Moskva | 9 Aug |
| 1.89 |   | Odintsova | | 2 | | Lvov | 9 Aug |
| 1.88 | L | Johnson | | 1 | | Bakersfield | 8 Feb |
| 1.88 |   | Huntley | | 2= | MSR | Walnut, CA | 27 Apr |
| 1.88 |   | Graves | | 1 | | Ames | 3 May |
| 1.88 |   | Kühn | | 3 | | Jena | 31 May |
| 1.88 |   | Bramhoff | | 4 | | Wörrstadt | 14 Jun |
| 1.88 |   | Fossati | (19) | 1 | | Cesenatico | 27 Jun |

Ancillary jumps /over 2.00/:

|      |             |        | 2.03 | Kostadinova | 25 May |
|------|-------------|--------|------|-------------|--------|
| 1.87 | Palinske (20) | 22 Jun | 2.03 | Kostadinova | 14 Jun |
|      |             |        | 2.03 | Kostadinova | 14 Sep |
| 1.86 | Malešev | 16 May | 2.01 | Kostadinova | 31 May |
| 1.86 | Sukhoroslova | 28 Jun | 2.01 | Kostadinova | 7 Jul |
| 1.86 | Belkova | 9 Aug | 2.00 | Kostadinova | 25 May |
| 1.86 | Svatošová | 9 Aug | 2.00 | Kostadinova | 14 Jun |
| 1.86 | Rotar (25) | 18 Sep | 2.00 | Kostadinova | 15 Jun |
|      |         |        | 2.00 | Kostadinova | 7 Sep |
|      |         |        | 2.00 | Kostadinova | 14 Sep |

# LONG JUMP

| 7.45 | 0.9 | Heike | Drechsler | GDR | 64 | 1 | v SU | Tallinn | 21 Jun |
|------|-----|-------|-----------|-----|----|----|------|---------|--------|
| 7.45 | 1.1 | | Drechsler | | | 1 | OD | Dresden | 3 Jul |
| 7.34 | 1.4 | Galina | Chistyakova | SU | 62 | 2 | v GDR | Tallinn | 21 Jun |
| 7.31 | 1.3 | | Drechsler | | | 1 | | Jena | 31 May |
| 7.31 | -0.2 | Yelena | Belevskaya | SU | 63 | 1 | NC | Kiev | 15 Jul |

| Mark | Wind | Name | | Nat | Yr | Pos | Meet | Venue | Date | |
|------|------|------|---|-----|----|-----|------|-------|------|---|
| 7.29 i | - | | Drechsler | | | 1 | | Berlin | 25 | Jan |
| 7.29 | 1.5 | | Drechsler | | | - | NC | Jena | 28 | Jun |
| 7.27 | 0.8 | | Chistyakova | | | 1 | GWG | Moskva | 7 | Jul |
| 7.27 | 0.3 | | Drechsler | | | 1 | EC | Stuttgart | 27 | Aug |
| 7.23 | 0.2 | | Drechsler | | | 1 | | Berlin | 20 | Aug |
| 7.23 | -0.3 | | Drechsler | | | 1 | VD | Bruxelles | 5 | Sep |
| 7.20 | 2.0 | Irena | Ozhenko | SU | 62 | 1 | | Budapest | 12 | Sep |
| 7.19 | 1.3 | Larisa | Berezhnaya | SU | 61 | 1 | | Krasnodar | 22 | Jun |
| 7.18 i | - | | Drechsler | | | 1 | EC | Madrid | 22 | Feb |
| 7.17 i | - | | Drechsler | | | 1 | NC | Senftenberg | 15 | Feb |
| 7.17 | 1.3 | | Belevskaya | | | 2 | GWG | Moskva | 7 | Jul |
| 7.17 | 1.6 | Helga | Radtke | GDR | 62 | 1 | | Rieti | 7 | Sep |
| 7.16 | 2.0 | | Belevskaya | | | 3 | v GDR | Tallinn | 21 | Jun |
| 7.16 | 1.8 | | Radtke | | | 2 | OD | Dresden | 3 | Jul |
| 7.12 | -0.1 | Jackie | Joyner | USA | 62 | 2 | VD | Bruxelles | 5 | Sep |
| 7.10 | 0.4 | | Drechsler | | | 1 | | Neubrandenburg | 7 | Jun |
| 7.10 | 1.3 | | Chistyakova | | | 2 | Znam | Leningrad | 8 | Jun |
| 7.10 | 0.5 | Vali | Ionescu | RUM | 60 | 1 | | Piteşti | 28 | Jun |
| 7.09 | 0.0 | | Chistyakova | | | 2 | EC | Stuttgart | 27 | Aug |
| 7.08 i | - | | Drechsler | | | 1 | v Fra | Lievin | 1 | Feb |
| 7.07 | 0.3 | Irina | Valyukevich | SU | 59 | 3 | GWG | Moskva | 7 | Jul |
| 7.07 | 0.8 | | Ionescu | | | 1 | | Poiana Braşov | 27 | Jul |
| 7.05 | 1.1 | | Radtke | | | 2 | NC | Jena | 28 | Jun |
| 7.04 | | | Ionescu | | | 1 | | Bucureşti | 25 | May |
| 7.03 i | - | | Drechsler | | | 1 | TAC | New York | 28 | Feb |
| 7.03 | 0.6 | | Ionescu | | | 1 | NC | Piteşti | 9 | Aug |
| 7.03 | 1.7 | | Joyner | | | - | | Rieti | 7 | Sep |
| 7.03 | | | Chistyakova | | | 1 | | Nicosia | 13 | Sep |
| | | | (33/9) | | | | | | | |
| 7.01 | 1.6 | Svetlana | Zorina (10) | SU | 60 | 1 | | Volgograd | 6 | Sep |
| 7.00 i | - | Yelena | Kokonova | SU | 63 | 1 | NC | Moskva | 6 | Feb |
| 7.00 | 0.6 | Silvia | Khristova | BUL | 65 | 1 | | Sofia | 3 | Aug |
| 6.99 | | Niole | Medvedyeva | SU | 60 | 1 | | Riga | 14 | Jun |
| 6.93 | 1.3 | Eva | Murková | CS | 62 | 1 | | Bratislava | 4 | Sep |
| 6.90 | 1.0 | Carol | Lewis | USA | 63 | 5 | GWG | Moskva | 7 | Jul |
| 6.88 | 0.5 | Yelena | Ivanova | SU | 61 | 2 | | Krasnodar | 22 | Jun |
| 6.88 | -0.8 | Lyudmila | Ninova | BUL | 60 | 1 | NC | Sofia | 14 | Aug |
| 6.88 | 1.6 | Galina | Salo | SU | 59 | 2 | | Volgograd | 6 | Sep |
| 6.86 | 1.5 | Robyn | Lorraway | AUS | 61 | 1 | | Canberra | 23 | Feb |
| 6.85 | 1.8 | Tatyana | Rodionova(20) | SU | 56 | 1 | | Riga | 30 | May |
| 6.84 | 0.2 | Vera | Olenchenko | SU | 59 | 1 | | Taganrog | 6 | Jul |
| 6.82 i | - | Heidrun | Geissler | GDR | 61 | 3 | | Berlin | 25 | Jan |
| 6.82 | 1.9 | Valentina | Kravchenko | SU | 63 | 1 | | Poltava | 20 | Jul |
| 6.81 i | - | Nadine | Debois | FRA | 61 | P | NC | Paris | 9 | Mar |
| 6.81 | -0.2 | Agata | Karczmarek | POL | 63 | 1 | | Granada | 17 | May |
| 6.80 | | Marieta | Ilcu | RUM | 62 | 2 | | Piteşti | 28 | Jun |
| 6.80 | 0.7 | Iolanda | Chen | SU | 61 | 5 | NC | Kiev | 15 | Jul |
| 6.80 | | Yelena | Chicherova | SU | 58 | 1 | | Lipetsk | 18 | Jul |
| A6.80 | 0.5 | Maryna | van Niekerk | RSA | 54 | 1 | | Johannesburg | 25 | Oct |
| 6.79 | 1.4 | Anke | Behmer (30) | GDR | 61 | H | EC | Stuttgart | 30 | Aug |
| 6.78 i | - | Nadine | Fourcade | FRA | 63 | 1 | | Paris | 12 | Jan |
| 6.75 | 1.4 | Irina | Konyukhova | SU | 59 | 1 | | Sochi | 17 | May |

| Mark | Wind | Name | | Nat | Yr | Pos | Meet | Venue | Date |
|---|---|---|---|---|---|---|---|---|---|
| 6.75 | | Cynthia | Henry | JAM | 62 | 1 | NC | Kingston | 21 Jun |
| 6.74 | 0.7 | Gaby | Ehlert | GDR | 65 | 2 | | Potsdam | 12 Jun |
| 6.73 | 0.6 | Nevena | Ignatova | BUL | 62 | 1 | | Pleven | 29 Jun |
| 6.72 | 1.9 | Zsuzsa | Vanyek | HUN | 60 | 1 | | Budapest | 8 Jun |
| 6.71 | 0.0 | Sofia | Bozhanova | BUL | 67 | 2 | BGP | Budapest | 11 Aug |
| 6.70 | 1.0 | Jennifer | Inniss | USA | 59 | 1 | Pepsi | Westwood | 17 May |
| 6.70 | -1.0 | Patricia | Bille | GDR | 68 | 1 | WC-j | Athinai | 19 Jul |
| 6.70 | 2.0 | Kim | Hagger (40) | UK | 61 | H | EC | Stuttgart | 30 Aug |
| | | | | | | | | | |
| 6.69 | | Sheila | Echols | USA | 64 | 1 | | Baton Rouge | 30 May |
| 6.68 i | - | Monika | Hirsch | FRG | 59 | 4 | EC | Madrid | 22 Feb |
| 6.68 | 0.2 | Christine | Schima | GDR | 62 | 3 | | Neubrandenburg | 7 Jun |
| 6.67 i | - | Sibylle | Thiele | GDR | 65 | 4 | | Berlin | 25 Jan |
| 6.67 | 1.3 | Lene | Demsitz | DEN | 59 | 1 | WA | Barcelona | 15 Jun |
| 6.66 | | Tatyana | Kirichenko | SU | 65 | 1 | | Alma-Ata | 11 May |
| 6.66 | -0.3 | Irina | Osipova | SU | 63 | 1 | | Bryansk | 17 Aug |
| 6.66 | -1.8 | Lidia | Bierka | POL | 60 | 1 | | Poznan | 7 Sep |
| 6.65 | | Tatyana | Pavlova | SU | 60 | 1 | | Adler | 19 Apr |
| A6.65 | | Angela | Thacker (50) | USA | 64 | 1 | | Boulder | 17 May |
| | | | | | | | | | |
| 6.65 | 1.8 | Petra | Ernst | GDR | 63 | 3 | OD | Dresden | 3 Jul |
| 6.64 | 1.3 | Anu | Kaljurand | SU | 69 | 2 | | Riga | 30 May |
| 6.63 i | - | Sabine | Braun | FRG | 65 | 1 | | Karlsruhe | 31 Jan |
| 6.63 | 2.0 | Sabrina | Williams | USA | 63 | - | TAC | Eugene | 21 Jun |
| 6.62 i | - | Jasmin | Feige | FRG | 59 | 6 | EC | Madrid | 22 Feb |
| 6.62 | | Donghuo | Huang | CHN | 61 | 1 | | Nanjing | 3 Jun |
| 6.62 | | Yelena | Obizhayeva | SU | 60 | 4 | | Lipetsk | 18 Jul |
| 6.62 | 0.2 | Yelena | Davydova | SU | 67 | 2 | Spart | Tashkent | 20 Sep |
| 6.62 | 1.6 | Alla | Nechiporets | SU | 64 | 1 | | Donetsk | 5 Oct |
| 6.61 | | Wenfen | Liao (60) | CHN | 63 | 2 | | Nanjing | 3 Jun |
| | | | | | | | | | |
| 6.61 | 0.3 | Eloina | Echevarría | CUB | 61 | 1 | CAC | Santiago/Dom | 29 Jun |
| 6.61 | 0.6 | Natalya | Shubenkova | SU | 57 | H | GWG | Moskva | 7 Jul |
| 6.61 | -0.5 | Inessa | Shulyak | SU | 66 | 3 | Spart | Tashkent | 20 Sep |
| 6.60 i | - | Anişoara | Stanciu | RUM | 62 | 3 | NC | Bacău | 9 Feb |
| 6.60 i | - | Jodi | Anderson | USA | 57 | 4 | TAC | New York | 28 Feb |
| 6.60 | | Mirela | Dulgheru | RUM | 66 | 3 | | Bucureşti | 25 May |
| 6.60 | 2.0 | Tatyana | Ter-Mesrobyan | SU | 68 | 1 | | Leningrad | 26 Jun |
| 6.59 | 0.9 | Liliana | Năstase | RUM | 62 | 3 | RumIC | Bucureşti | 14 Jun |
| 6.58 | -1.0 | Florence | Colle | FRA | 65 | 2 | | Dijon | 14 Jun |
| 6.57 i | - | Sabine | Paetz (70) | GDR | 57 | P | v SU | Senftenberg | 16 Feb |
| | | | | | | | | | |
| 6.57 | | Gail | Devers | USA | | 1 | | Los Angeles | 3 May |
| 6.57 | | Esmeralda | Garcia | BRA | 59 | 1 | | Tallahassee | 31 May |
| 6.56 | | Valentina | Kovalyova | SU | 60 | 1 | | Hania | 24 May |
| 6.56 | 1.8 | Klára | Novobáczky | HUN | 58 | 1 | | Budapest | 25 Jun |
| 6.56 | 1.2 | Ildikó | Fekete | HUN | 66 | 1 | NC | Budapest | 16 Aug |
| 6.55 i | - | Marina | Sluzhkina | SU | 60 | 7 | NC | Moskva | 6 Feb |
| 6.55 | 1.5 | Nicole | Boegman | AUS | 67 | 6 | OD | Dresden | 3 Jul |
| 6.54 i | - | Anna | Buballa | FRG | 54 | 1 | | W Berlin | 18 Jan |
| 6.54 | | Comfort | Igeh | NIG | 63 | 1 | | Cape Girardeau | 5 Apr |
| 6.54 | 1.0 | Tsetska | Kancheva (80) | BUL | 63 | 4 | | Sofia | 21 Jun |
| | | | | | | | | | |
| 6.54 | | Mirela | Belu | RUM | 70 | 3 | | Piteşti | 28 Jun |
| 6.54 | 1.9 | Viktoria | Kirpa | SU | 61 | 2 | | Tiraspol | 10 Aug |
| 6.54 | 1.8 | Margit | Palombi | HUN | 61 | 2 | NC | Budapest | 16 Aug |
| 6.53 | | Adelina | Polledo | CUB | 66 | 1 | | Santiago/Cuba | 21 Feb |

| Mark | Wind | Name | | Nat | Yr | Pos | Meet | Venue | Date |
|------|------|------|------|-----|----|----|------|-------|------|
| 6.53 | | Ludmila | Jimramovská | CS | 58 | 1 | | Brno | 17 May |
| 6.53 | 0.3 | Svetlana | Besprozvannaya | SU | 65 | 2 | | Minsk | 30 May |
| 6.53 | | Euphemia | Huggins | TRI | 66 | 1 | NC | Port-of-Spain | 7 Jun |
| 6.53 | 0.6 | Ivanka | Valkova | BUL | 65 | H | NC | Sofia | 3 Aug |
| 6.51 | | Lorinda | Richardson | USA | 66 | 1 | | Indianapolis | 3 May |
| 6.51 | 0.6 | Natalya | Shimanovich | SU | 67 | Q | Spart | Tashkent | 19 Sep |
| | | | (90) | | | | | | |
| 6.50 i | - | Mary | Berkeley | UK | 65 | 1 | v Spa | Madrid | 1 Feb |
| 6.50 i | - | Gina | Ghioroaie | RUM | 58 | 4 | NC | Bacău | 9 Feb |
| 6.50 | | Zhihui | Wang | CHN | 65 | 3 | | Nanjing | 3 Jun |
| 6.50 | | Olga | Maltseva | SU | 63 | 2 | | Kazan | 29 Jun |
| 6.50 | 0.0 | Yelena | Semiraz | SU | 65 | 3 | | Donetsk | 7 Sep |
| 6.49 | 0.1 | Jarmila | Strejčková | CS | 53 | 2 | | Schwechat | 4 Jun |
| 6.49 | 0.9 | Arja | Jussila | FIN | 53 | 1 | | Tyrnävä | 15 Jun |
| 6.49 | 0.3 | Natalya | Grishenina | SU | 66 | 1 | | Moskva | 1 Aug |
| 6.49 | 1.0 | Tatyana | Shpak | SU | 60 | H | | Dnepropetrovsk | 7 Sep |
| 6.48 | | Flora | Hyacinth(100) | UVI | 66 | 1 | | Tuscaloosa | 29 Mar |
| 6.48 | 1.7 | Anke | Schmidt | GDR | 68 | 1 | | Berlin | 10 Jul |
| 6.48 | 0.6 | Vera | Yurchenko | SU | 59 | H | | Dnepropetrovsk | 7 Sep |
| | | | (102) | | | | | | |

| 6.47 i | - | Edine | van Heezik | HOL | 61 | 22 Feb |
| 6.47 | 0.2 | Tatyana | Ilyina | SU | 68 | 22 Jun |
| 6.47 | 1.5 | Antonella | Capriotti | ITA | 62 | 23 Jul |
| 6.47 | 1.5 | Vasilya | Nurutdinova | SU | 63 | 10 Aug |
| 6.46 | 0.8 | Alessandra | Becatti | ITA | 65 | 8 Jun |
| 6.46 | | Sigal | Gonen | ISR | 63 | 12 Jul |
| 6.46 | 1.5 | Marianna | Maslennikova | SU | 61 | 30 Aug |
| Λ6.46 | | Sanet | Grobler (110) | RSA | 64 | 21 Oct |
| 6.45 | | Carla | Seldon | USA | 63 | 22 Mar |
| 6.45 | | Dorothea | Brown | USA | 64 | 3 May |
| 6.45 | | Jearl | Miles | USA | 66 | 31 May |
| 6.45 | 0.4 | Silke | Harms | FRG | 67 | 2 Jul |
| 6.45 | 0.5 | Marion | Weser | GDR | 62 | 7 Jul |
| 6.45 | 0.8 | Irina | Babakova | SU | 65 | 20 Jul |
| 6.44 | | Meledy | Smith | USA | 64 | 22 Mar |
| 6.44 | 1.3 | Eva | Karblom | SWE | 63 | 3 Aug |
| 6.44 | | Elżbieta | Klimaszewska | POL | 59 | 7 Sep |
| Λ6.44 | | Almarie | Brand (120) | RSA | 66 | 14 Oct |
| 6.43 i | - | Irina | Oreshkina | SU | 64 | 4 Jan |
| 6.43 i | - | Jacinta | Bartholomew | GRN | 65 | 25 Jan |
| 6.43 | | Jayne | Mitchell | NZ | 64 | 12 Mar |
| 6.43 | 1.7 | Rita | Heggli | SWZ | 62 | 21 Jun |
| 6.43 | -0.4 | Shonel | Ferguson | BAH | 57 | 29 Jun |
| 6.43 | 2.0 | Jolanta | Bartczak | POL | 64 | 18 Jul |
| 6.43 | 1.1 | Joyce | Oladapo | UK | 64 | 1 Aug |
| 6.43 | | Mieke | van der Kolk | HOL | 68 | 3 Aug |
| 6.43 | 0.3 | Irina | Kompaniyets | SU | 64 | 17 Aug |
| 6.42 | | Sonja | Fridy (130) | USA | 65 | 28 May |
| 6.42 | 1.2 | Carlette | Guidry | USA | 68 | 5 Jul |
| 6.42 | 0.9 | Lyudmila | Fedchenko | SU | 67 | 20 Jul |
| 6.42 | | Qiying | Xiong | CHN | 67 | 22 Oct |
| 6.41 | -1.4 | Corinne | Grimont | FRA | 63 | 21 Jun |
| 6.41 | | Tatyana | Dolgaya | SU | 64 | 27 Jun |
| 6.41 | 1.1 | Olga | Maltseva II | SU | 66 | 25 Jul |
| 6.41 | 1.9 | Birgit | Dressel | FRG | 60 | 6 Aug |

| 6.41 | 1.2 | Stefanie | Hühn | FRG | 66 | 6 Aug |
| 6.41 | 0.3 | Anette | Hellig | FRG | 64 | 9 Aug |
| 6.41 | -0.3 | Emilia | Dimitrova | BUL | 67 | 7 Sep |
| | | | | (140) | | |
| 6.41 | | Petra | Văidean | RUM | 65 | 7 Sep |
| 6.41 | 1.2 | Yelena | Selina | SU | 64 | 19 Sep |
| 6.40 | 1.6 | Tatyana | Lepota | SU | 60 | 14 May |
| 6.40 | 1.1 | Hilde | Fredriksen | NOR | 60 | 21 Jun |
| 6.40 | 0.9 | Tracey | Smith | CAN | 64 | 21 Jun |
| 6.40 | | Valentina | Uccheddu | ITA | 66 | 24 Jun |
| 6.40 | | Sharon | Bowie | UK | 66 | 28 Jun |
| 6.40 | | Zuzana | Lajbnerová | CS | 63 | 9 Aug |
| 6.40 | 0.1 | Irina | Tyukhai | SU | 67 | 17 Aug |
| 6.40 | -0.4 | Svetla | Dimitrova | BUL | 70 | 7 Sep |
| | | | | (150) | | |
| 6.40 | | Annie | le Roux | RSA | 65 | 15 Nov |
| 6.39 i | - | Regina | Ziliute | SU | 62 | 26 Jan |
| 6.39 | | Madeline | De Jesus | PR | 57 | 29 Mar |
| 6.39 | | Yvette | Bates | USA | 65 | 24 May |
| 6.39 | 1.3 | Katalina | Csapó | HUN | 69 | 15 Jun |
| 6.39 | -0.5 | Liliane | Ménissier | FRA | 60 | 21 Jun |
| 6.39 | 0.3 | Anke | Weigt | FRG | 57 | 4 Jul |
| 6.39 | -0.4 | Tanya | Tarkalanova | BUL | 65 | 3 Aug |
| 6.38 i | - | Irina | Privalova | SU | 68 | 16 Feb |
| 6.38 | 0.6 | Anna | Derevyankina | SU | 67 | 10 May |
| | | | | (160) | | |
| 6.38 | 0.1 | Wendy | Brown | USA | 66 | 6 Jun |
| 6.38 | | Svetlana | Filatyeva | SU | 64 | 15 Jun |
| 6.38 | 1.6 | Maddette | Smith | USA | 69 | 28 Jun |
| 6.38 | 1.5 | Larisa | Nikitina | SU | 65 | 7 Jul |
| 6.38 | 1.6 | Hilde | Vervaet | BEL | 64 | 9 Aug |
| 6.37 | 0.9 | Mariana | Khristova | BUL | 68 | 7 Jun |
| 6.37 | | Lyubov | Ratsu | SU | 61 | 21 Jul |
| 6.37 | -0.5 | Svetlana | Chistyakova | SU | 61 | 10 Aug |
| 6.37 | | Katrin | Sasse | GDR | 68 | 10 Aug |
| 6.37 | 0.9 | Almagul | Adilova (170) | SU | 66 | 28 Aug |
| 6.37 | | Birgit | Schertel | FRG | 68 | 5 Oct |

| Mark | Wind | Name | | Nat | Yr | Pos | Meet | Venue | Date |
|------|------|------|---|-----|-----|-----|------|-------|------|
| 6.36 | 1.7 | Megan | McLean | AUS 64 | 23 Feb | 6.35 | -0.2 Sandra | Priestley | AUS 65 15 Feb |
| 6.36 | 1.6 | Géraldine | Bonnin | FRA 64 | 27 Apr | 6.35 | Christine | Douziech(180) | FRA 61 17 May |
| 6.36 | | Dorothy | Scott | JAM 57 | 27 Apr | | | | |
| 6.36 | | Veronica | Bell | USA 61 | 17 May | 6.35 | Gillian | Regan | UK 56 18 Jul |
| 6.36 | | Olimpia | Constantea | RUM 68 | 7 Jun | 6.35 | 0.8 Yelena | Muravskaya | SU 67 20 Jul |
| 6.36 | 1.5 | Ines | Schulz | GDR 65 | 20 Aug | 6.35 | 1.8 Olga | Godunova(183) | SU 62 10 Aug |
| 6.35 | 1 - | Teresa | Allen | USA 65 | 1 Feb | | | | |

---

| | 1 | 10 | 20 | 30 | 50 | 100 | Over 6.60 | Over 6.40 |
|------|------|------|------|------|------|------|------|------|
| 1982 | 7.20 | 6.86 | 6.79 | 6.72 | 6.57 | 6.44 | 45 | 121 |
| 1983 | 7.43 | 6.90 | 6.79 | 6.73 | 6.59 | 6.47 | 48 | 126 |
| 1984 | 7.40 | 7.01 | 6.88 | 6.81 | 6.69 | 6.48 | 66 | 147 |
| 1985 | 7.44 | 7.00 | 6.81 | 6.75 | 6.64 | 6.48 | 60 | 147 |
| 1986 | 7.45 | 7.01 | 6.85 | 6.79 | 6.65 | 6.48 | 67 | 151 |

---

**Best outdoor marks:**

| 6.77 | | Fourcade | | H | | Antony | 9 Jul |
|------|------|----------|---|---|---|--------|-------|
| 6.71 | | Debois | | 1 | | Montgeron | 29 Jun |
| 6.66 | 1.0 | Hirsch | | 1 | NC | W Berlin | 12 Jul |
| 6.62 | -1.0 | Thiele | | H | GWG | Moskva | 7 Jul |
| 6.60 | | Feige | | - | | Leverkusen | 4 Jul |
| 6.58 | | Stanciu | | 4 | | Bucureşti | 25 May |
| 6.49 | 1.0 | Buballa | | 2 | | Hannover | 7 Jun |
| 6.46 | 1.6 | Geissler | 24 Jun | 6.37 | | Bartholomew | 29 Mar |
| 6.40 | -0.1 | Paetz | 7 Jul | 6.36 | | Oreshkina | 17 Aug |
| 6.40 | 0.4 | Berkeley(10) | 1 Aug | 6.35 | 0.5 | Allen | 6 Jun |
| | | | | 6.35 | | van Heezik | 6 Aug |
| 6.40 | | Anderson | 3 Aug | | | (15) | |

**Ancillary jumps / over 7.15 /:**

| 7.30 | 0.3 | Drechsler | 3 Jul | 7.20 | | Drechsler | 20 Aug |
|------|------|-----------|-------|------|------|-----------|--------|
| 7.29 | 1.6 | Drechsler | 3 Jul | 7.18 | 1 - | Drechsler | 22 Feb |
| 7.28 | 1.5 | Drechsler | 3 Jul | 7.17 | 0.0 | Drechsler | 27 Aug |
| 7.27 | 1.3 | Drechsler | 21 Jun | 7.17 | 0.2 | Drechsler | 5 Sep |
| 7.25 | 1 - | Drechsler | 25 Jan | 7.16 | | Drechsler | 31 May |
| 7.25 | -0.4 | Drechsler | 27 Aug | 7.16 | 1 - | Drechsler | 15 Feb |
| 7.24 | 0.5 | Drechsler | 3 Jul | 7.16 | 1 - | Drechsler | 22 Feb |
| 7.23 | | Drechsler | 20 Aug | 7.15 | 1 - | Drechsler | 15 Feb |
| 7.20 | 0.1 | Drechsler | 3 Jul | 7.15 | 0.2 | Drechsler | 5 Sep |

**Marks made with assisting wind > 2 m/s:**

| 7.35 | 3.4 | | Drechsler | | | 1 | NC | Jena | 28 Jun |
|------|------|--------|-----------|-----|-----|-----|-------|-----------|--------|
| 7.15 | 2.6 | Jackie | Joyner | USA | 62 | 2 | | Rieti | 7 Sep |
| 7.14 | 2.5 | | Belevskaya | | | 1 | Znam | Leningrad | 8 Jun |
| 7.10 | 3.7 | Irina | Valyukevich | SU | 59 | 4 | v GDR | Tallinn | 21 Jun |
| 7.07 | 3.8 | | Radtke | | | 5 | v SU | Tallinn | 21 Jun |
| 7.03 | 2.9 | | Joyner (6/5) | | | H | USOCF | Houston | 2 Aug |

| Mark | Wind | Name | | Nat | Yr | Pos | Meet | Venue | Date |
|------|------|------|------|-----|-----|-----|------|-------|------|
| 6.93 | 3.8 | Carol | Lewis | USA | 63 | 1 | TAC | Eugene | 21 Jun |
| 6.92 | 4.0 | Agata | Karczmarek | POL | 63 | 1 | NC | Grudziadz | 29 Jun |
| 6.89 | 3.7 | Sheila | Echols | USA | 64 | 2 | TAC | Eugene | 21 Jun |
| 6.81 | 2.3 | Anke | Behmer | GDR | 61 | 3 | NC | Jena | 28 Jun |
| 6.76 | 4.3 | Gaby | Ehlert (10) | GDR | 65 | 4 | NC | Jena | 28 Jun |
| | | | | | | | | | |
| 6.74 | 4.6 | Jolanta | Bartczak | POL | 64 | 2 | NC | Grudziadz | 29 Jun |
| 6.68 | 6.4 | Elżbieta | Klimaszewska | POL | 59 | 3 | NC | Grudziadz | 29 Jun |
| 6.68 | | Jasmin | Feige | FRG | 59 | 1 | | Leverkusen | 4 Jul |
| 6.67 | 4.7 | Jodi | Anderson | USA | 57 | 3 | TAC | Eugene | 21 Jun |
| 6.67 | 2.6 | Viktoria | Kirpa | SU | 61 | 6 | NC | Kiev | 15 Jul |
| 6.64 | 2.8 | Sabrina | Williams | USA | 63 | 5 | TAC | Eugene | 21 Jun |
| 6.63 | 5.0 | Nicole | Boegman | AUS | 67 | 1 | | Brisbane | 15 Feb |
| 6.63 | | Mary | Quisenberry | USA | 65 | 1 | | Houston | 18 May |
| 6.62 | 3.5 | Dorothea | Brown | USA | 64 | 6 | TAC | Eugene | 21 Jun |
| 6.59 | 3.7 | Lynda | Omagbemi (20) | NIG | | 1 | | Houston | 9 May |
| | | | | | | | | | |
| 6.58 | 2.4 | Megan | McLean | AUS | 64 | 1 | | Canberra | 16 Feb |
| 6.58 | | Mary | Berkeley | UK | 65 | 1 | | Haringey | 10 Aug |
| 6.56 | 3.3 | Alessandra | Becatti | ITA | 65 | 2 | | Bolzano | 25 May |
| 6.56 | 2.5 | Judy | Simpson | UK | 60 | H | EC | Stuttgart | 30 Aug |
| 6.55 | 3.3 | Jane | Mitchell | NZ | 64 | 1 | | Auckland | 8 Feb |
| 6.55 | 2.1 | Edine | van Heezik | HOL | 61 | 2 | WA | Barcelona | 15 Jun |
| 6.55 | 5.0 | Irina | Kompaniyets | SU | 64 | 4 | | Volgograd | 6 Sep |
| 6.51 | 4.8 | Anke | Schmidt | GDR | 68 | H | | Neubrandenburg | 4 May |
| 6.51 | 2.8 | Gillian | Regan | UK | 56 | 1 | | Vic/Barcelona | 17 May |
| 6.50 | 4.1 | Irina | Oreshkina(30) | SU | 64 | 6 | | Volgograd | 6 Sep |
| | | | | | | | | | |
| 6.49 | | Sharon | Clarke | CAN | 63 | 3 | NCAA | Indianapolis | 6 Jun |
| 6.49 | 2.8 | Monika | Beyer | GDR | 65 | 6 | NC | Jena | 28 Jun |
| 6.48 | 2.7 | Svetla | Dimitrova(33) | BUL | 70 | H | Druzhba | Neubrandenburg | 3 Aug |

| | | | | | | | | | | |
|------|------|------|------|------|------|------|------|------|------|------|
| 6.47 | | Maddette | Smith | USA | 69 | 17 Apr | 6.39 | | Andrea | Breder | FRG 64 15 Jun |
| 6.47 | 2.9 | Fiona | May | UK | 69 | 28 Jun | 6.39 | 4.2 | Caroline | Missoudan | FRA 68 5 Jul |
| 6.47 | 3.7 | Carlette | Guidry | USA | 68 | 28 Jun | 6.38 | 3.2 | Tonya | Sedwick | USA 69 28 Jun |
| 6.45 | 6.5 | Tammy | Stevenson | USA | 64 | 9 May | 6.37 | | Andrea | Hannemann | FRG 64 12 Jul |
| 6.45 | 2.5 | Valda | Ruskite | SU | 62 | 7 Jul | 6.36 | 6.2 | Ewa | Sliwa | POL 61 29 Jun |
| 6.45 | 2.2 | Anke | Weigt | FRG | 57 | 3 Aug | 6.35 | | Christina | Sussiek (50) | FRG 60 29 Jun |
| 6.44 | 2.2 | Lena | Wallin (40) | SWE | 58 | 10 Aug | | | | | |

Ancillary jumps/over 7.15/:

| | | | | | | | | | | |
|------|------|------|------|------|------|------|------|------|------|------|
| A6.42 | | Heidi | van Staden | RSA | 59 | 12 Apr | | | | | |
| 6.40 | 2.2 | Estrella | Roldan | SPA | 62 | 12 Jul | 7.35 | 3.1 | | Drechsler | 21 Jun |
| 6.39 | | Veronica | Bell | USA | 61 | 10 May | 7.25 | 2.1 | | Drechsler | 28 Jun |
| 6.39 | | Pam | Harper | USA | 64 | 17 May | 7.23 | 3.2 | | Chistyakova | 21 Jun |

## SHOT PUT

| | | | | | | | | | |
|------|------|------|------|------|------|------|------|------|------|
| 21.70 | | Natalya | Lisovskaya | SU | 62 | 1 | v GDR | Tallinn | 21 Jun |
| 21.48 | | | Lisovskaya | | | 1 | | Moskva | 10 Aug |
| 21.46 1 | | Claudia | Losch | FRG | 60 | 1 | | Zweibrücken | 4 Feb |
| 21.45 | | Ines | Müller | GDR | 59 | 1 | | Schwerin | 4 Jun |
| 21.39 | | Natalya | Akhrimenko | SU | 55 | 2 | v GDR | Tallinn | 21 Jun |
| 21.38 | | | Lisovskaya | | | 1 | NC | Kiev | 14 Jul |
| 21.37 | | | Lisovskaya | | | 1 | GWG | Moskva | 7 Jul |
| 21.35 | | | Lisovskaya | | | 1 | | Sochi | 24 May |
| 21.34 | | | Müller | | | 3 | v SU | Tallinn | 21 Jun |
| 21.25 | | | Akhrimenko | | | 2 | | Moskva | 10 Aug |

| Mark | Name | | Nat | Yr | Pos | Meet | Venue | Date |
|---|---|---|---|---|---|---|---|---|
| 21.10 | Heidi | Krieger | GDR | 65 | 1 | EC | Stuttgart | 26 Aug |
| 21.05 | | Müller | | | 1 | OD | Dresden | 3 Jul |
| 21.03 | Nunu | Abashidze | SU | 55 | 1 | | | |
| 20.98 | | Lisovskaya | | | 1 | Znam | Leningrad | 7 Jun |
| 20.97 | | Müller | | | 1 | | Sofia | 25 May |
| 20.92 | | Losch | | | 1 | NC | W Berlin | 13 Jul |
| 20.90 | | Müller | | | 1 | | Potsdam | 12 Jun |
| 20.90 | | Abashidze | | | 3 | | Moskva | 10 Aug |
| 20.90 | | Losch | | | 1 | | Thannhausen | 6 Sep |
| 20.88 | | Losch | | | 1 | | Ingelheim | 5 Aug |
| 20.84 | | Müller | | | 1 | | Neubrandenburg | 6 Jun |
| 20.83 | | Müller | | | 1 | | Berlin | 20 Aug |
| 20.81 | | Müller | | | 2 | EC | Stuttgart | 26 Aug |
| 20.80 | Helena | Fibingerová | CS | 49 | 1 | GS | Ostrava | 11 Jun |
| 20.78 | | Losch | | | 1 | | Kamp-Lintfort | 14 Sep |
| 20.72 | | Müller | | | 1 | NC | Jena | 29 Jun |
| 20.72 | Heike | Hartwig | GDR | 62 | 1 | GO | Dresden | 16 Aug |
| 20.71 | | Krieger | | | 2 | | Potsdam | 12 Jun |
| 20.69 | | Losch | | | 1 | | Schwabmünchen | 3 Aug |
| 20.68 | | Akhrimenko | | | 3 | EC | Stuttgart | 26 Aug |
| | | (30/8) | | | | | | |
| 20.62 | Mihaela | Loghin | RUM | 52 | 1 | | Piteşti | 29 Jun |
| 20.60 | Marina | Antonyuk (10) | SU | 62 | 1 | | Chelyabinsk | 10 Aug |
| 20.22 | Lyudmila | Voyevudskaya | SU | 59 | 2 | NC | Kiev | 14 Jul |
| 20.20 | Danguole | Bimbaite | SU | 62 | 1 | | Leselidze | 18 May |
| 20.05 | Svetla | Mitkova | BUL | 64 | 2 | | Plovdiv | 17 May |
| 19.78 | Lyubov | Vasilyeva | SU | 57 | 1 | | Moskva | 31 Aug |
| 19.76 | Iris | Plotzitzka | FRG | 66 | 2 | | Ingelheim | 5 Aug |
| 19.70 | Soňa | Vašíčková | CS | 62 | 1 | NC | Bratislava | 13 Jul |
| 19.68 | Kathrin | Neimke | GDR | 66 | 4 | GO | Dresden | 16 Aug |
| 19.67 | Simona | Andruşcǎ | RUM | 62 | 1 | | Piteşti | 20 Jul |
| 19.61 | Livia | Simon | RUM | 65 | 1 | | Constanţa | 20 Apr |
| 19.59 | Gael | Martin (20) | AUS | 56 | 1 | | Vught | 6 Jul |
| 19.58 | Cordula | Schulze | GDR | 59 | 5 | GO | Dresden | 16 Aug |
| 19.48 | Ilona | Briesenick | GDR | 56 | 6 | GO | Dresden | 16 Aug |
| 19.29 | Grit | Haupt | GDR | 66 | 4 | | Potsdam | 12 Jun |
| 19.26 | Yelena | Ortina | SU | 62 | 2 | | Chelyabinsk | 10 Aug |
| 19.26 | Larisa | Agapova | SU | 64 | 1 | Spart | Tashkent | 20 Sep |
| 19.19 1 | Valentina | Fedyushina | SU | 65 | 3 | NC | Moskva | 6 Feb |
| 19.11 | Stephanie | Storp | FRG | 68 | 3 | | Fürth | 15 Jun |
| 19.08 | Ilke | Wyludda | GDR | 69 | 1 | v SU-j | Karl-Marx-Stadt | 9 Aug |
| 19.03 | Ramona | Pagel (30) | USA | 61 | 1 | | Houston | 4 May |
| 19.03 | Marina | Burina | SU | 62 | 4 | | Sochi | 24 May |
| 19.00 | Judith | Oakes | UK | 58 | 1 | NC | Cwmbran | 25 May |
| 18.99 | Natalya | Shlyakhtich | SU | 62 | 5 | | Sochi | 24 May |
| 18.95 | Astrid | Wagner | GDR | 65 | 6 | NC | Jena | 29 Jun |
| 18.92 | Liane | Schmuhl | GDR | 61 | 7 | GO | Dresden | 16 Aug |
| 18.89 | Zhihong | Huang | CHN | 65 | 1 | | Nanjing | 7 Jun |
| 18.88 | Irina | Fedchenko | SU | 66 | 1 | | Kiev | 30 Aug |
| 18.87 1 | Petra | Leidinger | FRG | 66 | 1 | NC | Sindelfingen | 8 Feb |
| 18.87 | Xinmei | Sui | CHN | 65 | | | Zhengzhou | 24 Oct |
| 18.84 | Bonnie | Dasse (40) | USA | 59 | 2 | | Walnut, CA | 1 Jun |

| Mark | Name | | Nat | Yr | Pos | Meet | Venue | Date | |
|------|------|------|-----|----|-----|------|-------|------|---|
| 18.80 | Galina | Kalinina | SU | 62 | 3 | | Chelyabinsk | 10 | Aug |
| 18.79 | Yanqin | Yang | CHN | 66 | | | Shijiazhuang | 4 | Apr |
| 18.78 | Alena | Vitoulová | CS | 60 | 1 | | Kraków | 24 | May |
| 18.75 | Aleksandra | Abashidze | SU | 58 | 1 | | Leselidze | 11 | May |
| 18.69 | Yuzhen | Cong | CHN | 63 | | | Nanjing | 7 | Jun |
| 18.62 i | Vera | Yevko | SU | 59 | 1 | | Volgograd | 24 | Jan |
| 18.61 | Meisu | Li | CHN | 59 | 1 | | Beijing | 7 | Sep |
| 18.58 | Vera | Schmidt | FRG | 61 | 4 | | Fürth | 15 | Jun |
| 18.58 | Heike | Rohrmann | GDR | 69 | 1 | | Berlin | 10 | Jul |
| 18.54 | Lyubov | Kovtunova(50) | SU | 59 | 1 | | Sochi | 26 | Apr |
| | | | | | | | | | |
| 18.50 i | Lyudmila | Savina | SU | 55 | 1 | | Moskva | 24 | Jan |
| 18.50 | Verzhinia | Veselinova | BUL | 57 | 2 | NC | Sofia | 13 | Aug |
| 18.40 | Galina | Kurochkina | SU | 65 | 2 | | Volgograd | 6 | Sep |
| 18.37 | Ines | Wittich | GDR | 69 | 4 | | Berlin | 4 | Jul |
| 18.34 | Galina | Kuzhel | SU | 59 | 2 | | Baku | 4 | Oct |
| 18.33 i | Irina | Vidosova | SU | 61 | 2 | | Volgograd | 24 | Jan |
| 18.29 | Svetlana | Tatichek | SU | 63 | Q | Spart | Tashkent | 19 | Sep |
| 18.26 | Skaidrite | Baikova | SU | 50 | 1 | | Stuchka | 23 | Aug |
| 18.16 | Márta | Kripli | HUN | 60 | 1 | | Miskolc | 24 | May |
| 18.07 | Tatyana | Orlova    (60) | SU | 55 | 1 | | Minsk | 1 | Jun |
| | | | | | | | | | |
| 18.05 | Marcelina | Rodriguez | CUB | 60 | 1 | | Hainfeld | 19 | May |
| 18.05 | Tatyana | Khorkhuleva | SU | 64 | 2 | Spart | Tashkent | 20 | Sep |
| 18.02 | Christa | Wiese | GDR | 67 | | | Neubrandenburg | 11 | Jul |
| 18.00 | Yelena | Belovolova | SU | 65 | Q | Spart | Tashkent | 19 | Sep |
| 17.87 | Rosa | Fernandez | CUB | 57 | 1 | | Budapest | 25 | May |
| 17.85 | Belsis | Laza | CUB | 67 | 2 | | Budapest | 25 | May |
| 17.84 i | Asta | Hovi | FIN | 63 | 6 | EC | Madrid | 23 | Feb |
| 17.83 | Silvia | Madetzky | GDR | 62 | 1 | | Regis-Breitingen | 25 | May |
| 17.78 | Ursula | Stäheli | SWZ | 57 | 1 | | Dübendorf | 1 | Jun |
| 17.78 | Małgorzata | Wolska    (70) | POL | 66 | 1 | | Grudziadz | 14 | Jun |
| | | | | | | | | | |
| 17.78 | Mariana | Lengyel | RUM | 53 | 3 | | Piteşti | 29 | Jun |
| 17.75 | Myrtle | Augee | UK | 65 | 2 | | Gateshead | 5 | Aug |
| 17.74 | Assunta | Chiumariello | ITA | 58 | 1 | | Imola | 12 | Oct |
| 17.70 | Carol | Cady | USA | 62 | 2 | MSR | Walnut, CA | 27 | Apr |
| 17.70 | Regina | Cavanaugh | USA | 64 | 1 | | Houston | 18 | May |
| 17.66 | Lyudmila | Kopyatkevich | SU | 65 | | | Moskva | 31 | Aug |
| 17.64 | Olga | Uhliuc | RUM | 67 | 4 | NC | Piteşti | 9 | Aug |
| 17.58 | Peggy | Pollock | USA | 60 | 2 | | Modesto, CA | 10 | May |
| 17.58 | Miglena | Meleshkova | BUL | 67 | 1 | | Pleven | 29 | Jun |
| 17.50 i | Anna | Romanova (80) | SU | 68 | 1 | v GDR-j | Moskva | 16 | Feb |
| | | | | | | | | | |
| 17.50 | Qinyun | Peng | CHN | 63 | | | Beijing | 25 | Apr |
| 17.50 | Hajnal | Voros | HUN | 59 | 1 | | Senta | 10 | May |
| 17.48 | Nadezhda | Frantseva | SU | 61 | 3 | | Kiev | 26 | Jul |
| 17.45 | Gabriele | Reinsch | GDR | 63 | 4 | | Beijing | 7 | Sep |
| 17.41 | Snezhana | Pishmanova | BUL | 68 | 2 | | Pleven | 29 | Jun |
| 17.36 | Larisa | Yurchenko | SU | 63 | 2 | | Kiev | 30 | Aug |
| 17.36 | Inessa | Sedacheva | SU | 64 | 1 | | Donetsk | 4 | Oct |
| 17.34 | Sabine | Kruse | FRG | 66 | 5 | | Fürth | 15 | Jun |
| 17.33 i | Birgit | Petsch | FRG | 63 | 4 | NC | Sindelfingen | 8 | Feb |
| 17.32 | Viktória | Szélinger(90) | HUN | 56 | 1 | | Altötting | 23 | Aug |
| | | | | | | | | | |
| 17.32 | Natalya | Didenko | SU | 62 | 5 | | Volgograd | 6 | Sep |
| 17.31 | Yelena | Kakushkina | SU | 63 | 5 | | Kiev | 26 | Jul |

| Mark | Name | | Nat | Yr | Pos | Meet | Venue | Date |
|---|---|---|---|---|---|---|---|---|
| 17.28 | Pam | Dukes | USA | 64 | 4 | MSR | Walnut, CA | 27 Apr |
| 17.28 | Connie | Price | USA | 62 | 1 | | Cape Girardeau | 11 May |
| 17.24 | Astra | Etienne | AUS | 60 | 2 | | Sydney | 8 Feb |
| 17.24 | Mechthild | Schönleber | FRG | 63 | 3 | | Hannover | 7 Jun |
| 17.17 | Iveta | Garancha | SU | 64 | 2 | | Stuchka | 23 Aug |
| 17.15 | Nadezhda | Lukiniv | SU | 68 | 1 | | Rovno | 12 Jul |
| 17.13 | Yelena | Stupakova | SU | 67 | 5 | | Tiraspol | 10 Aug |
| 17.12 | Nadezhda | Glazova (100) | SU | 66 | 6 | | Tiraspol | 10 Aug |

| Mark | Name | | | | | Mark | Name | | | |
|---|---|---|---|---|---|---|---|---|---|---|
| 17.08 i | Carla | Garrett | USA 67 | 14 Mar | 16.97 i | Diana | Clements | USA 63 | 21 Feb |
| 17.08 | Natalya | Kozlova | SU 67 | 13 Jul | 16.97 | Simone | Créantor | FRA 48 | 12 Jul |
| 17.07 | Tatyana | Vinogradova | SU 66 | 6 Sep | 16.90 | Cuiyun | Kuang | CHN 63 | 12 Apr |
| 17.06 | Melody | Torcolacci | CAN 60 | 5 Aug | 16.87 | Monika | Andris | SU 65 | 30 Jul |
| 17.06 | Lilia | Shultz | SU 64 | 31 Aug | 16.84 i | Larisa | Baranova | SU 61 | 11 Jan |
| 17.06 | Jana | Căpățînă | RUM 68 | 31 Aug | 16.76 | Svetlana | Vernaya | SU 64 | 27 Jun |
| 17.04 | Lyudmila | Novikova | SU 64 | 16 Jul | 16.76 | Svetlana | Kriveleva | SU 69 | 9 Aug |
| 17.03 | Rose | Hauch | CAN 57 | 1 Jun | 16.75 | Anastasia | Pavlova (120) | SU 68 | 18 May |
| 17.03 | Lyubov | Khvostikova | SU 64 | 16 Jul | | | | | |
| 17.01 | Eha | Rünne (110) | SU 63 | 23 May | 16.75 | Ilona | Zakharchenko | SU 67 | 21 Jun |
| | | | | | 16.74 | Olga | Izyumskaya | SU 65 | 31 Aug |
| 17.00 i | Teresa | Williford | USA 63 | 14 Mar | 16.70 | Olga | Vdovichenko | SU 68 | 3 Jul |
| 16.99 | Veronika | Kautzsch | FRG 54 | 28 Jun | | (123) | | | |

WOMEN 1986

-------------------------------------------------------------------------------

| | 1 | 10 | 20 | 30 | 50 | 100 | Over 18.00 | Over 17.00 |
|---|---|---|---|---|---|---|---|---|
| 1982 | 21.80 | 20.55 | 19.62 | 18.85 | 17.96 | 16.82 | 49 | 96 |
| 1983 | 22.40 | 20.54 | 19.61 | 19.01 | 18.19 | 17.00 | 52 | 100 |
| 1984 | 22.53 | 20.55 | 19.94 | 19.42 | 18.42 | 17.18 | 59 | 112 |
| 1985 | 21.73 | 20.39 | 19.47 | 18.94 | 18.13 | 16.92 | 56 | 92 |
| 1986 | 21.70 | 20.60 | 19.59 | 19.03 | 18.54 | 17.12 | 64 | 111 |

-------------------------------------------------------------------------------

Best outdoor marks:

| 18.52 | Yevko | 2 | | Sochi | 26 Apr |
|---|---|---|---|---|---|
| 18.50 | Fedyushina | | | Moskva | 31 Aug |
| 17.82 | Hovi | 15 | EC | Stuttgart | 26 Aug |
| 17.43 | Romanova | 1 | | Simferopol | 23 May |
| 17.15 | Petsch | 6 | | Fürth | 15 Jun |

| 17.04 | Vidosova | 26 Apr | 16.81 | | Clements (7) | 12 Apr |
|---|---|---|---|---|---|---|

Ancillary marks /over 21.00/:

| 21.64 | Lisovskaya | 21 Jun | 21.15 | Lisovskaya | 21 Jun |
|---|---|---|---|---|---|
| 21.41 | Lisovskaya | 21 Jun | 21.15 | Akhrimenko | 10 Aug |
| 21.29 | Lisovskaya | 21 Jun | 21.14 | Lisovskaya | 10 Aug |
| 21.25 | Lisovskaya | 7 Jul | | | |
| 21.25 | Akhrimenko | 10 Aug | 21.10 | Lisovskaya | 24 May |
| 21.23 | Lisovskaya | 10 Aug | 21.08 | Müller | 21 Jun |
| 21.18 | Lisovskaya | 14 Jul | 21.03 | Krieger | 26 Aug |

| Mark | Name | | Nat | Yr | Pos | Meet | Venue | Date | |
|------|------|--|-----|----|-----|------|-------|------|--|

## DISCUS THROW

| Mark | Name | | Nat | Yr | Pos | Meet | Venue | Date | |
|------|------|--|-----|----|-----|------|-------|------|--|
| 73.26 | Diana | Sachse | GDR | 63 | 1 | | Neubrandenburg | 6 | Jun |
| 72.52 | Martina | Hellmann | GDR | 60 | 1 | | Frohburg | 15 | Jun |
| 72.52 | Tsvetanka | Khristova | BUL | 62 | 1 | BGP | Budapest | 11 | Aug |
| 72.30 | | Sachse | | | 1 | | Potsdam | 22 | May |
| 72.30 | | Sachse | | | 1 | | Erfurt | 1 | Jun |
| 72.12 | | Sachse | | | 1 | v SU | Tallinn | 21 | Jun |
| 71.90 | | Khristova | | | 1 | | Stara Zagora | 19 | Jul |
| 71.80 | | Khristova | | | 1 | PTS | Bratislava | 14 | Jun |
| 71.36 | | Sachse | | | 1 | EC | Stuttgart | 28 | Aug |
| 71.02 | | Hellmann | | | 1 | NC | Jena | 28 | Jun |
| | | | | | | | | | |
| 70.88 | | Sachse | | | 1 | | Potsdam | 11 | Jun |
| 70.82 | | Khristova | | | 1 | | Sofia | 3 | Aug |
| 70.52 | | Khristova | | | 1 | OD | Dresden | 3 | Jul |
| 70.00 | | Sachse | | | 2 | NC | Jena | 28 | Jun |
| 69.84 | | Khristova | | | 1 | VD | Bruxelles | 5 | Sep |
| 69.78 | | Khristova | | | 1 | Bisl | Oslo | 5 | Jul |
| 69.66 | Daniela | Costian | RUM | 65 | 1 | | Piteşti | 19 | Jul |
| 69.58 | | Khristova | | | 1 | Balk | Ljubljana | 7 | Sep |
| 69.54 | | Khristova | | | 1 | GWG | Moskva | 9 | Jul |
| 69.52 | | Khristova | | | 2 | EC | Stuttgart | 28 | Aug |
| | | | | | | | | | |
| 69.40 | | Hellmann | | | 1 | GO | Dresden | 16 | Aug |
| 69.10 | | Khristova | | | 1 | NC | Sofia | 13 | Aug |
| 69.08 | Mariana | Lengyel | RUM | 53 | 1 | | Constanţa | 19 | Apr |
| 69.04 | | Sachse | | | 2 | OD | Dresden | 3 | Jul |
| 69.04 | | Hellmann | | | 2 | GWG | Moskva | 9 | Jul |
| 69.02 | | Sachse | | | 2 | Bisl | Oslo | 5 | Jul |
| 68.96 | Ellina | Zvereva | SU | 60 | 1 | | Minsk | 2 | Sep |
| 68.92 | | Zvereva | | | 1 | | Sochi | 24 | May |
| 68.90 | Svetla | Mitkova | BUL | 64 | 2 | BGP | Budapest | 11 | Aug |
| 68.90 | | Khristova | | | 1 | GP | Roma | 10 | Sep |
| | | (30/7) | | | | | | | |
| 68.74 | Irina | Meszynski | GDR | 62 | 2 | GO | Dresden | 16 | Aug |
| 68.32 | Galina | Yermakova | SU | 53 | 3 | v GDR | Tallinn | 21 | Jun |
| 67.92 | Hilda | Ramos (10) | CUB | 64 | 2 | Nar | Sofia | 31 | May |
| | | | | | | | | | |
| 67.08 | Silvia | Madetzky | GDR | 62 | 3 | Bisl | Oslo | 5 | Jul |
| 66.86 | Maritza | Marten | CUB | 63 | 1 | | Hainfeld | 19 | May |
| 66.84 | Lyubov | Zverkova | SU | 55 | 1 | RumIC | Bucureşti | 14 | Jun |
| 66.48 | Márta | Kripli | HUN | 60 | 3 | BGP | Budapest | 11 | Aug |
| 66.42 | Anne | Khorina | SU | 59 | 1 | | Tallinn | 18 | Jun |
| 66.10 | Carol | Cady | USA | 62 | 1 | Jenner | San Jose | 31 | May |
| 66.04 | Simona | Andruşcă | RUM | 62 | 2 | RumIC | Bucureşti | 14 | Jun |
| 65.86 | Ilke | Wyludda | GDR | 69 | 1 | Druzhba | Neubrandenburg | 1 | Aug |
| 65.50 | Florenţa | Crăciunescu | RUM | 55 | 5 | OD | Dresden | 3 | Jul |
| 65.44 | Gabriele | Reinsch (20) | GDR | 63 | 4 | GO | Dresden | 16 | Aug |
| | | | | | | | | | |
| 65.20 | Andrea | Thieme | GDR | 64 | 1 | | Potsdam | 7 | Aug |
| 64.48 | Larisa | Mikhalchenko | SU | 63 | 1 | | Kharkov | 28 | Apr |
| 64.46 | Irina | Dmitriyeva | SU | 59 | 1 | | Donetsk | 30 | Jul |
| 64.44 | Ines | Müller | GDR | 59 | 1 | | Schwerin | 4 | Jun |
| 64.42 | Larisa | Korotkevich | SU | 67 | 1 | | Minsk | 28 | Apr |
| 64.34 | Franka | Dietzsch | GDR | 68 | 1 | | Neubrandenburg | 3 | May |
| 64.34 | Renata | Katewicz | POL | 65 | 1 | | Słupsk | 7 | Jun |
| 64.08 | Elisabeta | Neamţu | RUM | 60 | 3 | NC | Piteşti | 8 | Aug |
| 63.98 | Irina | Khval | SU | 62 | 1 | | Moskva | 3 | Aug |
| 63.48 | Xuemei | Hou (30) | CHN | 62 | 1 | | Beijing | 12 | Apr |

| Mark | Name | | Nat | Yr | Pos | Meet | Venue | Date |
|------|------|------|-----|-----|-----|------|-------|------|
| 63.42 | Jana | Günther | GDR | 68 | 1 | | Budapest | 19 Jul |
| 63.38 | Elju | Kubi | SU | 51 | 1 | | Tallinn | 14 May |
| 63.12 | Heike | Hartwig | GDR | 62 | 3 | | Budapest | 13 Sep |
| 63.02 | Larisa | Mednikova | SU | 63 | 1 | | Alma-Ata | 26 Jun |
| 62.82 | Claudia | Losch | FRG | 60 | 1 | | Schwabmünchen | 3 Aug |
| 62.50 | Gabriela | Hanuláková | CS | 57 | 3 | | Hainfeld | 19 May |
| 62.44 | Gael | Martin | AUS | 56 | 1 | | Canberra | 23 Feb |
| 62.24 | Olga | Nikishina | SU | 66 | 1 | | Kiev | 29 Aug |
| 62.08 | Houruen | Yu | CHN | 63 | | | Beijing | 14 Mar |
| 61.82 | Snežana | Golubić (40) | YUG | 62 | 1 | | Beograd | 16 May |
| | | | | | | | | |
| 61.70 | Ilga | Smeikste | SU | 66 | 1 | | Riga | 14 Jun |
| 61.58 | Ágnes | Herczeg | HUN | 50 | 1 | | Budapest | 9 Aug |
| 61.58 | Antonina | Patoka | SU | 64 | 1 | | Leningrad | 18 Aug |
| 61.22 | Iveta | Garancha | SU | 64 | 1 | | Riga | 2 May |
| 61.12 | Lorna | Griffin | USA | 56 | 2 | | Salinas, CA | 12 Apr |
| 61.06 | Ewa | Siepsiak | POL | 57 | 3 | Kuso | Warszawa | 17 Jun |
| 61.04 | Kadi | Bebber | GDR | 65 | 5 | | Neubrandenburg | 6 Jun |
| 60.82 | Olga | Cinibulková | CS | 60 | 1 | | Praha | 9 Aug |
| 60.78 | Svetlana | Savchenko | SU | 65 | 1 | | Minsk | 2 Aug |
| 60.66 | Stefenia | Simova (50) | BUL | 63 | 3 | NC | Sofia | 13 Aug |
| | | | | | | | | |
| 60.60 | Tatyana | Lesovaya | SU | 56 | 1 | | Frunze | 26 Apr |
| 60.56 | Lyudmila | Platonova | SU | 64 | 2 | | Kiev | 26 Jul |
| 60.46 | Livia | Simon | RUM | 65 | 2 | | Constanţa | 19 Apr |
| 60.42 | Penny | Neer | USA | 60 | 2 | Jenner | San Jose | 31 May |
| 60.42 | Skaidrite | Baikova | SU | 50 | 1 | | Jekabpils | 8 Jun |
| 60.26 | Larisa | Baranova | SU | 61 | | | Sochi | 9 Feb |
| 60.20 | Barbara | Beuge | FRG | 60 | 1 | | Kottern | 7 Sep |
| 60.10 | Irina | Shabanova | SU | 64 | 3 | | Kiev | 26 Jul |
| 60.08 | Svetlana | Motuzenko | SU | 54 | 1 | | Kharkov | 14 May |
| 60.04 | Ramona | Pagel (60) | USA | 61 | 1 | | Houston | 4 May |
| | | | | | | | | |
| 60.00 | Dagmar | Galler | FRG | 61 | 1 | | Ingolstadt | 11 May |
| 59.90 | Zsuzsa | Pallay | HUN | 48 | 1 | | Miskolc | 24 Sep |
| 59.80 | Galina | Dorguzheva | SU | 61 | 1 | | Taganrog | 6 Jul |
| 59.78 | Anne | Känsäkangas | FIN | 60 | 1 | | Kokkola | 10 Jun |
| 59.76 | Sonja | Rust | GDR | 66 | 2 | | Schwerin | 4 Jun |
| 59.58 | Ilona | Molnár | HUN | 65 | 1 | | Szombathely | 16 Jul |
| 59.40 | Galina | Kudryavtseva | SU | 61 | 6 | | Leselidze | 18 May |
| 59.38 | Galina | Vasilyeva | SU | 60 | 1 | | Lipetsk | 18 Jul |
| 59.28 | Doris | Gutewort | FRG | 54 | 1 | | Regensburg | 29 Jun |
| 59.06 | Larisa | Platonova(70) | SU | 66 | 2 | | Tiraspol | 9 Aug |
| | | | | | | | | |
| 59.04 | Ursula | Weber | AUT | 60 | 1 | | Linz | 27 Apr |
| 59.00 | Rita | Alvarez | CUB | 66 | 3 | Barr | Habana | 14 Jun |
| 58.96 | Zilia | Akhmetova | SU | 61 | 4 | | Kiev | 26 Jul |
| 58.94 | Lacy | Barnes | USA | 64 | 3 | | Modesto, CA | 10 May |
| 58.94 | Xiaohui | Li | CHN | 56 | 2 | AsiG | Seoul | 3 Oct |
| 58.92 | Nadezhda | Zhitkova | SU | 52 | 2 | | Dnepropetrovsk | 29 Jun |
| 58.82 | Kathrin | Neimke | GDR | 66 | 7 | NC | Jena | 28 Jun |
| 58.80 | Nanette | van der Walt | RSA | 59 | 1 | | Port Elizabeth | 15 Feb |
| 58.54 | Tatyana | Belova | SU | 61 | 2 | | Sochi | 27 Apr |
| 58.34 | Galina | Murashova(80) | SU | 55 | 1 | | Vilnius | 11 May |
| | | | | | | | | |
| 58.28 | Stephanie | Storp | FRG | 68 | 1 | | Rhede | 2 Jul |
| 58.28 | Olga | Davydova | SU | 63 | Q | Spart | Tashkent | 17 Sep |

WOMEN 1986

| Mark | Name | | Nat | Yr | Pos | Meet | Venue | Date |
|------|------|------|-----|----|----|------|-------|------|
| 58.28 | Katalin | Csoke | HUN | 57 | 2 | v CS | Praha | 18 Sep |
| 58.24 | Soňa | Vašíčková | CS | 62 | 1 | | Praha | 20 May |
| 58.24 | Malda | Lange | SU | 61 | 1 | | Riga | 29 Aug |
| 58.20 | Mette | Bergmann | NOR | 62 | 7 | Bisl | Oslo | 5 Jul |
| 58.14 | Pia | Iacovo | USA | 61 | 3 | Jenner | San Jose | 31 May |
| 58.08 | | Mikheyeva | SU | | 1 | | Kaunas | 31 Aug |
| 57.98 | Ailan | Xin | CHN | 65 | | | Nanjing | 7 Jun |
| 57.84 | Eha | Rünne (90) | SU | 63 | 2 | | Tallinn | 18 May |
| | | | | | | | | |
| 57.84 | Bonnie | Dasse | USA | 59 | Q | TAC | Eugene | 19 Jun |
| 57.84 | Yelena | Rogachevskaya | SU | 63 | 1 | | Rovno | 12 Jul |
| 57.80 | Irina | Vasyutina | SU | 59 | 1 | | Leningrad | 15 Jun |
| 57.68 | Kelly | Landry | USA | 63 | 1 | | Tallahassee | 31 May |
| 57.62 | Vilia | Zubaityte | SU | 63 | 1 | | Baku | 5 Oct |
| 57.60 | Marja-Leena | Larpi | FIN | 59 | 2 | | Oulu | 31 Jul |
| 57.58 | Irina | Yatchenko | SU | 65 | 3 | | Lvov | 9 Aug |
| 57.56 | Viktoria | Kochetova | SU | 67 | 3 | | Tashkent | 26 Jan |
| 57.54 | Maria | Marello | ITA | 61 | 2 | v FRG, | Hun Verona | 19 Jun |
| 57.48 | Becky | Levi (100) | USA | 62 | 1 | | Santa Monica | 7 Jun |

| Mark | Name | | Nat | Yr | Pos/Date | Mark | Name | | Nat | Yr | Date |
|------|------|------|-----|----|----------|------|------|------|-----|----|------|
| 57.30 | Dan | Wang | CHN | 55 | 2 May | 56.06 | Iris | Plotzitzka | FRG | 66 | 7 Sep |
| 57.20 | Bea | Wiarda | HOL | 59 | 8 Jun | 56.02 | Galina | Kvacheva | SU | 65 | 9 Feb |
| 57.20 | Ilona | Zakharchenko | SU | 67 | 21 Jun | 56.00 | Xiaoyan | Xu | CHN | 63 | 29 Mar |
| 57.16 | Lyudmila | Novikova | SU | 64 | 11 Aug | 55.90 | Satu | Sulkio (120) | FIN | 61 | 11 Jun |
| 57.14 | Yelena | Drigota | SU | 62 | 29 Jun | | | | | | |
| 56.84 | Isabel | Urrutia | COL | 64 | 28 Sep | 55.82 | Kathy | Picknell | USA | 58 | 4 May |
| 56.80 | Svetlana | Melnikova | SU | 51 | 26 Jan | 55.60 | Yan | Li | CHN | 64 | 19 Sep |
| 56.74 | Cristina | Boiţ | RUM | 68 | 24 May | 55.36 | Mária | Börzsönyi | HUN | 66 | 16 Jul |
| 56.54 | Ursula | Kreutel | FRG | 65 | 19 May | 55.26 | Guofang | Chen | CHN | 63 | 7 Jun |
| 56.44 | Floarea | Vieru (110) | RUM | 67 | 12 Jul | 55.20 | Karen | Nickerson | USA | 64 | 1 Mar |
| | | | | | | 55.16 | Vera | Schmidt | FRG | 61 | 3 Aug |
| 56.36 | Yelena | Sazanova | SU | 63 | 9 Aug | 55.10 | Chunfeng | Min | CHN | 69 | 29 Mar |
| 56.30 | Laura | DeSnoo | USA | 62 | 12 Apr | 55.10 | Irina | Grachova | SU | 63 | 26 Jul |
| 56.24 | Rouxnel | White | RSA | 63 | 21 Apr | 55.08 | Pam | Dukes | USA | 64 | 3 May |
| 56.20 | Venissa | Head | UK | 56 | 27 Jul | 55.08 | Yanling | Xiao (130) | CHN | 68 | 11 Oct |
| 56.18 | Toni | Lutjens | USA | 65 | 22 Mar | | | | | | |
| 56.18 | Deborah | Dunant | HOL | 66 | 3 Aug | 55.02 | Ines | Wittich | GDR | 69 | 26 Jul |
| | | | | | | 55.00 | Rezeda | Yarmukhina | SU | 63 | 31 May |

Ancillary marks /over 70.00/:

(132)

| 72.14 | Sachse | 22 May | 70.68 | Hellmann | 28 Jun |
|-------|--------|--------|-------|----------|--------|
| 72.00 | Sachse | 22 May | 70.54 | Sachse | 28 Aug |
| 71.74 | Khristova | 11 Aug | 70.38 | Khristova | 11 Aug |
| 71.24 | Khristova | 11 Aug | | | |
| 70.94 | Hellmann | 28 Jun | 70.28 | Sachse | 11 Jun |
| 70.84 | Sachse | 11 Jun | 70.06 | Sachse | 21 Jun |
| 70.76 | Khristova | 11 Aug | | | |

| | 1 | 10 | 20 | 30 | 50 | 100 | Over 60.00 | Over 57.00 |
|------|-------|-------|-------|-------|-------|-------|------------|------------|
| 1982 | 71.40 | 68.18 | 65.04 | 63.44 | 60.90 | 57.04 | 63 | 103 |
| 1983 | 73.26 | 67.32 | 65.10 | 64.16 | 61.98 | 58.52 | 75 | 130 |
| 1984 | 74.56 | 68.56 | 66.02 | 64.36 | 62.10 | 58.50 | 76 | 119 |
| 1985 | 72.96 | 67.52 | 65.20 | 63.12 | 60.92 | 57.14 | 59 | 102 |
| 1986 | 73.26 | 67.92 | 65.44 | 63.48 | 60.66 | 57.48 | 61 | 105 |

| Mark | Name | | Nat | Yr | Pos | Meet | Venue | Date | |
|------|------|--|-----|----|----|------|-------|------|--|

## JAVELIN THROW

| Mark | | Name | Nat | Yr | Pos | Meet | Venue | Date |
|------|--|------|-----|----|----|------|-------|------|
| 77.44 | Fatima | Whitbread | UK | 61 | Q | EC | Stuttgart | 28 Aug |
| 76.32 | | Whitbread | | | 1 | EC | Stuttgart | 29 Aug |
| 75.04 | Petra | Felke | GDR | 59 | 1 | GO | Dresden | 17 Aug |
| 74.10 | | Felke | | | 1 | | Berlin | 20 Aug |
| 73.54 | | Felke | | | 1 | | Umeå | 2 Sep |
| 73.08 | | Felke | | | 1 | | Berlin | 2 Apr |
| 72.74 | | Felke | | | 1 | DNG | Stockholm | 1 Jul |
| 72.62 | | Felke | | | Q | EC | Stuttgart | 28 Aug |
| 72.52 | | Felke | | | 2 | EC | Stuttgart | 29 Aug |
| 72.42 | Tiina | Lillak | FIN | 61 | 1 | | Iisalmi | 17 Aug |
| 72.26 | | Whitbread | | | 1 | | Gateshead | 5 Aug |
| 72.18 | | Whitbread | | | 1 | IAC | London | 8 Aug |
| 72.18 | | Whitbread | | | 1 | VD | Bruxelles | 5 Sep |
| 71.96 | | Whitbread | | | 1 | | Birmingham | 19 Aug |
| 71.78 | | Whitbread | | | 1 | | Gateshead | 27 Jun |
| 71.58 | | Whitbread | | | 1 | BGP | Budapest | 11 Aug |
| 71.40 | | Felke | | | 1 | WK | Zürich | 13 Aug |
| 71.38 | | Whitbread | | | 1 | | Belfast | 30 Jun |
| 71.28 | | Lillak | | | 1 | | Kokkola | 10 Jun |
| 71.18 | | Felke | | | 1 | OD | Dresden | 3 Jul |
| 70.84 | | Whitbread | | | 1 | | Crawley | 24 Aug |
| 70.78 | | Felke | | | 1 | GWG | Moskva | 8 Jul |
| 70.74 | | Whitbread | | | 1 | Nik | Nice | 15 Jul |
| 70.64 | | Felke | | | 1 | GP | Roma | 10 Sep |
| 70.36 | | Lillak | | | 1 | | Pihtipudas | 13 Jul |
| 70.16 | | Whitbread | | | 1 | PTG | London | 11 Jul |
| 70.14 | Maria | Colon | CUB | 58 | 1 | Barr | Habana | 15 Jun |
| 70.06 | | Felke | | | 1 | WG | Helsinki | 7 Jul |
| 69.82 | Ivonne | Leal | CUB | 66 | 1 | | Habana | 6 Feb |
| 69.80 | Sue | Howland | AUS | 60 | 2 | | Belfast | 30 Jun |
| 69.80 | Tessa | Sanderson | UK | 56 | 1 | CG | Edinburgh | 31 Jul |
| | | (31/7) | | | | | | |
| 69.56 | Beate | Peters | FRG | 59 | 1 | NC | W Berlin | 12 Jul |
| 67.90 | Dulce Maria | García | CUB | 65 | 3 | Barr | Habana | 15 Jun |
| 67.80 | Trine | Solberg (10) | NOR | 66 | 2 | Bisl | Oslo | 5 Jul |
| 67.34 | Ingrid | Thyssen | FRG | 56 | 1 | ASV | Köln | 17 Aug |
| 67.32 | Regine | Kempter | GDR | 67 | 2 | NC | Jena | 27 Jun |
| 66.80 | Jana | Köpping | GDR | 66 | 3 | NC | Jena | 27 Jun |
| 66.64 | Zsuzsa | Malovecz | HUN | 63 | 1 | | Rehlingen | 19 May |
| 66.64 | Natalya | Yermolovich | SU | 64 | 1 | | Rieti | 7 Sep |
| 66.52 | Alexandra | Beck | GDR | 68 | 1 | | Hania | 25 May |
| 65.56 | Irina | Kostyuchenkova | SU | 61 | 1 | NC | Kiev | 17 Jul |
| 65.18 | Antje | Zöllkau | GDR | 63 | 2 | GO | Dresden | 17 Aug |
| 64.98 | Zinaida | Gavrilina | SU | 61 | 1 | | Riga | 31 May |
| 64.92 | Baolian | Li (20) | CHN | 63 | 1 | | Beijing | 10 May |
| 64.90 | Genowefa | Olejarz | POL | 62 | 2 | PTS | Bratislava | 14 Jun |
| 64.56 | Xiomara | Rivera | CUB | 68 | 1 | CAC-j | México, D.F. | 26 Jun |
| 64.40 | Heike | Galle | GDR | 67 | 1 | Znam | Leningrad | 8 Jun |
| 64.30 | Anna | Verouli | GRE | 56 | 2 | | Hania | 25 May |
| 63.68 | Tuula | Laaksalo | FIN | 53 | 2 | | Saarijärvi | 21 Jun |
| 63.60 | Guohua | Liu | CHN | 61 | 1 | | Kobe | 29 Apr |
| 63.56 | Natalya | Shikolenko | SU | 64 | 3 | NC | Kiev | 17 Jul |
| 63.54 | Natalya | Cherniyenko | SU | 65 | 1 | | Baku | 4 Oct |

| Mark | Name | | Nat | Yr | Pos | Meet | Venue | Date | |
|------|------|------|-----|----|-----|------|-------|------|---|
| 63.52 | Iris | de Grasse | CUB | 64 | 4 | | Habana | 6 | Feb |
| 62.96 | Larisa | Avdeyeva (30) | SU | 61 | 1 | | Volgograd | 6 | Sep |
| 62.78 | Svetlana | Pestretsova | SU | 61 | 1 | | Moskva | 27 | Jun |
| 62.56 | Yuanxiang | Zhou | CHN | 64 | | | Zhengzhou | 23 | Oct |
| 62.50 | Sofia | Sakorafa | GRE | 57 | 3 | | Hania | 25 | May |
| 62.50 | Manuela | Alizadeh | FRG | 63 | Q | EC | Stuttgart | 28 | Aug |
| 62.48 | Zoya | Karepina | SU | 61 | 1 | | Leningrad | 13 | May |
| 62.30 | Denise | Thiemard | SWZ | 60 | 2 | v Nor, | Swe Luzern | 21 | Jun |
| 62.06 | Silke | Renk | GDR | 67 | 5 | NC | Jena | 27 | Jun |
| 61.82 | Nóra | Rockenbauer | HUN | 66 | 1 | | Budapest | 21 | Aug |
| 61.78 | Susanne | Jung | GDR | 63 | 6 | NC | Jena | 27 | Jun |
| 61.70 | Anja | Reiter (40) | GDR | 69 | 1 | | Neubrandenburg | 4 | May |
| 61.64 | Éva | Budavári | HUN | 53 | 1 | | Budapest | 6 | Jul |
| 61.48 | Saida | Gunba | SU | 59 | 2 | | Moskva | 10 | Aug |
| 61.40 | Ivanka | Vancheva | BUL | 53 | 1 | | Sofia | 20 | Aug |
| 61.40 | Terese | Nekrosaite | SU | 61 | 1 | | Kaunas | 30 | Aug |
| 61.40 | Ibolya | Torma | HUN | 55 | 1 | | Budapest | 10 | Sep |
| 61.30 | Karin | Bergdahl | SWE | 64 | 1 | | Albuquerque | 29 | Mar |
| 61.10 | Helena | Laine | FIN | 55 | 4 | | Kokkola | 10 | Jun |
| 60.94 | Xiaoyan | Xin | CHN | 66 | | | Luoyang | 19 | Sep |
| 60.86 | Sølvi | Nybu | NOR | 66 | 1 | FlaR | Gainesville | 29 | Mar |
| 60.74 | Xiurong | Sun (50) | CHN | 69 | 1 | AsiC-j | Djakarta | 6 | Dec |
| 60.66 | Elisabet | Nagy | SWE | 60 | 6 | Bisl | Oslo | 5 | Jul |
| 60.64 | Natividad | Vizcaino | SPA | 54 | 1 | v Fra, | Pol Epinal | 5 | Jul |
| 60.60 | Fenghua | Ding | CHN | 64 | | | Beijing | 26 | Apr |
| 60.58 | Danica | Živanov | YUG | 67 | 2 | Balk | Ljubljana | 6 | Sep |
| 60.58 | Jinling | Wang | CHN | 65 | | | Zhengzhou | 23 | Oct |
| 60.46 | Brigitte | Graune | FRG | 61 | 1 | | Berg. Gladbach | 9 | Sep |
| 60.36 | Katalin | Hartai | HUN | 63 | 2 | | Budapest | 7 | Jun |
| 60.36 | Eva | Raduly | RUM | 54 | 3 | Balk | Ljubljana | 6 | Sep |
| 60.20 | Cathy | Sulinski | USA | 58 | 1 | MSR | Walnut, CA | 27 | Apr |
| 60.14 | Helena | Uusitalo (60) | FIN | 62 | 1 | | Corvallis | 17 | May |
| 60.10 | Demei | Xu | CHN | 67 | | | Beijing | 10 | May |
| 60.02 | Elena | Burgárová | CS | 52 | 2 | | Bratislava | 4 | Sep |
| 59.90 | Jing | Wang | CHN | 62 | | | Beijing | 10 | May |
| 59.82 | Olga | Gavrilova | SU | 57 | 1 | | Leningrad | 15 | Jun |
| 59.80 | Fausta | Quintavalla | ITA | 59 | 1 | NC | Torino | 24 | Jul |
| 59.70 | Mária | Janák | HUN | 58 | 1 | | Miskolc | 18 | May |
| 59.60 | Yingyi | Xia | CHN | 63 | | | Guangzhou | 22 | Mar |
| 59.58 | Marina | Terenchenko | SU | 61 | 1 | | Lvov | 10 | Aug |
| 59.40 | Karen | Hough | UK | 68 | Q | EC | Stuttgart | 28 | Aug |
| 59.18 | Natalya | Nasedkina(70) | SU | 63 | 7 | NC | Kiev | 17 | Jul |
| 59.12 | Iris | Grönfeldt | ICE | 63 | 1 | | Tallahassee | 19 | Apr |
| 59.12 | Wilma | Vidotto | ITA | 65 | 1 | | Amsterdam | 1 | Jun |
| 59.06 | Celine | Chartrand | CAN | 62 | 1 | | Antony | 10 | May |
| 59.04 | Yelena | Zhilichkina | SU | 63 | 1 | | Alma-Ata | 4 | May |
| 58.88 | Beate | Koch | GDR | 67 | 5 | | Berlin | 20 | Aug |
| 58.86 | Ingrid | Lammertsma | HOL | 67 | 1 | | Krommenie | 31 | Aug |
| 58.84 | Tatyana | Korablina | SU | 64 | 1 | | Bryansk | 16 | Aug |
| 58.82 | Marina | Kochneva | SU | 63 | 1 | | Riga | 19 | Jul |
| 58.72 | Diane | Royle | UK | 59 | 1 | | Kirkby | 23 | Aug |
| 58.54 | Susanne | Hoffmann (80) | GDR | 65 | 5 | | Neubrandenburg | 7 | Jun |

| Mark | Name | | Nat | Yr | Pos | Meet | Venue | Date |
|---|---|---|---|---|---|---|---|---|
| 58.52 | Naomi | Tokuyama | JAP | 68 | 1 | | Kofu | 16 Oct |
| 58.48 | Marina | Kozoderova | SU | 64 | 2 | | Volgograd | 6 Sep |
| 58.38 | Kumi | Yamamoto | JAP | 65 | 1 | | Kunitachi | 12 Apr |
| 58.26 | Ansie | Rogers | RSA | 64 | 1 | | Pretoria | 19 Feb |
| 58.22 | Sharon | Gibson | UK | 61 | 3 | v Pol, | Sco/Wal Hendon | 17 Aug |
| 58.22 | Gerda | Blokziel | HOL | 61 | 2 | | Krommenie | 31 Aug |
| 58.12 | Herminia | Bouza | CUB | 65 | 1 | | Habana | 12 Aug |
| 58.06 | Yulia | Lichagina | SU | 65 | 1 | | Adler | 19 Apr |
| 58.06 | Zhanna | Penkova | SU | 65 | 2 | | Moskva | 27 Jun |
| 57.96 | Maria | Dzhaleva (90) | BUL | 64 | 5 | Balk | Ljubljana | 6 Sep |
| | | | | | | | | |
| 57.92 | Yekaterina | Sledneva | SU | 64 | 1 | | Leningrad | 3 Jun |
| 57.90 | Susan | Lion-Cachet | RSA | 62 | 1 | NC | Germiston | 11 Apr |
| 57.88 | Maria | Jablonska | POL | 55 | 4 | v Eng, | Sco/Wal Hendon | 17 Aug |
| 57.84 | Cristina | Dobrinoiu | RUM | 62 | 2 | NC | Pitești | 9 Aug |
| 57.76 | Karin | Smith | USA | 55 | 1 | | Corvallis | 29 May |
| 57.64 | Faye | Roblin | CAN | 64 | 1 | | North York | 1 Jun |
| 57.50 | Larisa | Vovchenko | SU | 65 | 1 | | Donetsk | 5 Oct |
| 57.44 | Lyudmila | Chaynikova | SU | 60 | | | Kashira | 24 May |
| 57.44 | Isel | Lopez | CUB | 70 | | CAC-j | México, D.F. | 26 Jun |
| 57.20 | Julie | Abel (100) | UK | 66 | 1 | | Hendon | 29 Jun |

| Mark | Name | | Nat | Yr | Date | | Mark | Name | | Nat | Yr | Date |
|---|---|---|---|---|---|---|---|---|---|---|---|---|
| 57.12 | Galina | Medvedyeva | SU | 61 | 26 Apr | | 56.02 | Kristina | Jazbinšek | YUG | 65 | 27 Sep |
| 57.12 | Bernadet | Fransen | HOL | 65 | 8 May | | 55.94 | Nadine | Schoellkopf | FRA | 64 | 8 May |
| 57.04 | Päivi | Alafrantti | FIN | 64 | 5 Aug | | 55.90 | Kristy | Evans | CAN | 59 | 21 Jun |
| 56.96 | Rita | Knoll | FRG | 64 | 11 May | | 55.82 | Tatyana | Seregina | SU | 63 | 8 Feb |
| 56.82 | Valentina | Ivanova | SU | 52 | 18 Aug | | 55.82 | Mayumi | Kagaya (130) | JAP | 65 | 13 Apr |
| 56.70 | Jeanette | Kieboom | AUS | 59 | 6 Mar | | | | | | | |
| 56.64 | Elena | Revayová | CS | 58 | 31 May | | 55.80 | Evelyne | Giardino | FRA | 61 | 18 May |
| 56.62 | Mihaela | Nicoară | RUM | 59 | 15 Jun | | 55.74 | Judit | Gal | HUN | 60 | 7 Sep |
| 56.60 | Karyn | Szarkowski | USA | 65 | 6 Jun | | 55.72 | Dace | Lace | SU | 66 | 14 Aug |
| 56.56 | Galina | Vasilyeva | SU | 64 | 28 Jun | | 55.70 | Tatyana | Shikolenko | SU | 68 | 19 Jul |
| | | (110) | | | | | 55.66 | Åsa | Westman | SWE | 53 | 15 Jun |
| 56.56 | Jinli | Han | CHN | 66 | 5 Jul | | 55.64 | Petra | Rivers | AUS | 52 | 16 Mar |
| 56.56 | Christine | Riewe | GDR | 70 | 2 Aug | | 55.60 | Todorka | Todorova | BUL | 66 | 20 Jul |
| 56.54 | Marie | Fukalova | CS | 52 | 17 Aug | | 55.56 | Carla | Dumitru | RUM | 67 | 29 Jun |
| 56.46 | Jeanne | Villegas | USA | 67 | 25 Apr | | 55.54 | Emi | Matsui | JAP | 63 | 30 May |
| 56.46 | Susanne | Riewe | GDR | 70 | 2 Aug | | 55.46 | Hongyang | Zhu (140) | CHN | 64 | 5 Jul |
| 56.38 | Lori | Mercer | USA | 63 | 4 Apr | | | | | | | |
| 56.38 | Beate | Andres | GDR | 67 | 27 Jun | | 55.38 | Christine | Gravier | FRA | 63 | 24 Jul |
| 56.32 | Simone | Frandsen | DEN | 61 | 20 Jul | | 55.36 | Natalya | Balabayeva | SU | 66 | 16 Aug |
| 56.26 | Eva | Helmschmidt | FRG | 57 | 14 Jun | | 55.26 | Chizuru | Mizuno | JAP | 67 | 6 Jul |
| 56.26 | Galya | Nikolova(120) | BUL | 65 | 14 Aug | | 55.24 | Jeanette | Rose | UK | 59 | 29 Jun |
| | | | | | | | 55.22 | Yelena | Medvedyeva | SU | 65 | 1 Jun |
| 56.24 | Nina | Mulyarevich | SU | 63 | 23 Feb | | 55.12 | Yelena | Turkhunova | SU | 68 | 5 Oct |
| 56.24 | Éva | Placsintár | HUN | 65 | 29 Apr | | 55.00 | Anna | Lockton (147) | UK | 64 | 7 Jun |
| 56.18 | Donna | Mayhew | USA | 60 | 8 Jul | | | | | | | |
| 56.14 | Meg | Warren | USA | 65 | 3 Aug | | Mark made in mixed competition with men: | | | | | |
| 56.10 | Cathie | Wilson | USA | 62 | 26 Apr | | 57.04 | Petra | Rivers | AUS | 52 | 9 Mar |

Ancillary marks / over 70.00/:

| | | | | | | |
|---|---|---|---|---|---|---|
| 74.82 | Felke | 17 Aug | 71.44 | | Felke | 17 Aug |
| 73.06 | Felke | 2 Apr | 71.0 | | Whitbread | 30 Jun |
| 72.68 | Whitbread | 29 Aug | 71.00 | | Whitbread | 11 Aug |
| 72.62 | Felke | 2 Sep | | | | |
| 72.40 | Felke | 2 Sep | 70.98 | | Whitbread | 19 Aug |
| 72.00 | Felke | 29 Aug | 70.92 | | Whitbread | 11 Aug |
| 71.94 | Whitbread | 29 Aug | 70.80 | | Felke | 17 Aug |

WOMEN 1986

| Points | Name | Nat | Yr | Pos | Meet | Venue | Date |
|---|---|---|---|---|---|---|---|
| 70.72 | Felke | 13 Aug 70.02 | | | | Whitbread | 15 Jul |
| 70.60 | Whitbread | 15 Jul | | | | | |
| 70.48 | Felke | 10 Sep 70.02 | | | | Whitbread | 5 Aug |
| 70.34 | Felke | 29 Aug 70.02 | | | | Whitbread | 5 Aug |
| 70.32 | Felke | 17 Aug 70.02 | | | | Felke | 10 Sep |
| 70.18 | Whitbread | 11 Aug | | | | | |

| | 1 | 10 | 20 | 30 | 50 | 100 | Over 60.00 | Over 56.00 |
|---|---|---|---|---|---|---|---|---|
| 1982 | 74.20 | 66.64 | 64.00 | 61.88 | 59.70 | 56.20 | 48 | 108 |
| 1983 | 74.76 | 67.20 | 64.60 | 63.12 | 60.70 | 56.82 | 57 | 122 |
| 1984 | 74.72 | 66.56 | 64.26 | 62.28 | 60.68 | 57.74 | 56 | 130 |
| 1985 | 75.40 | 68.20 | 64.18 | 62.96 | 60.66 | 57.44 | 60 | 125 |
| 1986 | 77.44 | 67.80 | 64.92 | 62.96 | 60.74 | 57.20 | 62 | 126 |

# HEPTATHLON

| Points | | Name | Nat | Yr | Pos | Meet | Venue | Date |
|---|---|---|---|---|---|---|---|---|
| 7158 | Jackie | Joyner | USA 62 | 1 | | USOCF | Houston | 1/ 2 Aug |
| | | 13.18 | 1.88 | 15.20 | 22.85 / 7.03w | 50.12 | 2:09.69 | |
| 7148 | | Joyner | | 1 | | GWG | Moskva | 6/ 7 Jul |
| | | 12.85 | 1.88 | 14.76 | 23.00 / 7.01 | 49.86 | 2:10.02 | |
| 6910 m | | Joyner | | 1 | | MSR | Walnut | 24/25 Apr |
| | | 12.9 m | 1.86 | 14.75 | 23.24w/ 6.85w | 48.30 | 2:14.11 | |
| 6841 | | Joyner | | 1 | | | Götzis | 24/25 May |
| | | 13.09 | 1.87 | 14.34 | 23.63 / 6.76 | 48.88 | 2:14.58 | |
| 6717 | Anke | Behmer | GDR 61 | 1 | | EC | Stuttgart | 29/30 Aug |
| | | 13.25 | 1.77 | 14.50 | 23.46 / 6.79 | 40.24 | 2:03.96 | |
| 6645 | Natalya | Shubenkova | SU 57 | 2 | | EC | Stuttgart | 29/30 Aug |
| | | 13.33 | 1.80 | 13.68 | 23.92 / 6.54w | 44.98 | 2:04.40 | |
| 6635 | Sibylle | Thiele | GDR 65 | 2 | | GWG | Moskva | 6/ 7 Jul |
| | | 13.14 | 1.76 | 16.00 | 24.18 / 6.62 | 45.74 | 2:15.30 | |
| 6631 | | Shubenkova | | 3 | | GWG | Moskva | 6/ 7 Jul |
| | | 13.23 | 1.70 | 13.94 | 23.67 / 6.61 | 45.88 | 2:03.61 | |
| 6623 | Judy | Simpson | UK 60 | 3 | | EC | Stuttgart | 29/30 Aug |
| | | 13.05 | 1.92 | 14.73 | 25.09 / 6.56w | 40.92 | 2:11.70 | |
| 6530 | | Behmer | | 2 | | | Götzis | 24/25 May |
| | | 13.73 | 1.87 | 14.56 | 23.73 / 6.62 | 34.20 | 2:07.22 | |
| 6487 | Birgit | Dressel | FRG 60 | 4 | | EC | Stuttgart | 29/30 Aug |
| | | 13.56 | 1.92 | 14.12 | 24.68 / 6.28 | 45.70 | 2:15.78 | |
| 6456 | Sabine | Paetz | GDR 57 | 4 | | GWG | Moskva | 6/ 7 Jul |
| | | 13.11 | 1.73 | 15.68 | 24.13 / 6.40 | 42.52 | 2:15.15 | |
| 6444 | | Behmer | | 1 | | NC | Potsdam | 11/12 Jun |
| | | 13.61 | 1.83 | 14.11 | 23.73 / 6.24 | 39.08 | 2:06.77 | |
| 6418 | Sabine | Braun | FRG 65 | 3 | | | Götzis | 24/25 May |
| | | 13.55 | 1.81 | 12.50 | 24.48 / 6.29w | 54.10 | 2:16.26 | |
| 6416 | Marianna | Maslennikova | SU 61 | 5 | | GWG | Moskva | 6/ 7 Jul |
| | | 13.41 | 1.88 | 13.30 | 24.40 / 6.38 | 36.04 | 2:06.09 | |
| 6403 | Emilia | Dimitrova(10) | BUL 67 | 6 | | GWG | Moskva | 6/ 7 Jul |
| | | 13.73 | 1.76 | 13.46 | 23.17 / 6.29 | 43.30 | 2:09.85 | |

| Points | Name | | Nat | Yr | Pos | Meet | Venue | Date |
|---|---|---|---|---|---|---|---|---|
| 6396 | | Shubenkova | | | 4 | | Götzis | 24/25 May |
| | | 13.48 | 1.78 | 13.71 | 24.34 | / 6.24 | 43.34 | 2:06.80 |
| 6396 | | Maslennikova | | | 5 | EC | Stuttgart | 29/30 Aug |
| | | 13.43 | 1.86 | 13.35 | 24.50 | / 6.46 | 38.22 | 2:09.58 |
| 6387 | | Thiele | | | 2 | NC | Potsdam | 11/12 Jun |
| | | 13.50 | 1.74 | 15.40 | 24.48 | / 6.15 | 48.68 | 2:15.90 |
| 6383 M | Lyubov | Ratsu | SU | 61 | 1 | | Lipetsk | 20/21 Jul |
| | | 13.6 m | 1.79 | 14.85 | 24.6 m/ | 6.37 | 44.04 | 2:10.8 m |
| 6377 | | Dressel | | | 1 | NC | Hannover | 19/20 Jul |
| | | 13.66 | 1.90 | 13.84 | 24.85 | / 6.24 | 43.82 | 2:14.85 |
| 6352 | Małgorzata | Nowak | POL | 59 | 6 | EC | Stuttgart | 29/30 Aug |
| | | 13.39 | 1.80 | 16.39 | 24.52 | / 6.12 | 41.90 | 2:19.36 |
| 6349 | Valda | Ruskite | SU | 62 | 7 | GWG | Moskva | 6/ 7 Jul |
| | | 13.34 | 1.70 | 14.63 | 24.74 | / 6.45w | 43.48 | 2:11.16 |
| 6333 | Nadine | Debois | FRA | 61 | 1 | | Clamart | 26/27 Apr |
| | | 13.62 | 1.81 | 13.74 | 24.37 | / 6.59 | 32.48 | 2:05.77 |
| 6331 | | Ruskite | | | 7 | EC | Stuttgart | 29/30 Aug |
| | | 13.51 | 1.77 | 14.58 | 25.64 | / 6.36w | 46.46 | 2:12.76 |
| 6327 | Svetlana | Filatyeva | SU | 64 | 1 | v FRG | Bernhausen | 14/15 Jun |
| | | 13.63 | 1.82 | 13.51 | 24.62 | / 6.38 | 45.30 | 2:16.47 |
| 6316 | Larisa | Nikitina | SU | 65 | 1 | | Sochi | 24/25 May |
| | | 14.25 | 1.86 | 15.00 | 25.38 | / 6.37 | 47.70 | 2:19.91 |
| 6307 | Vera | Yurchenko | SU | 59 | 1 | SU P | Dnepropetrovsk | 6/ 7 Sep |
| | | 13.68 | 1.66 | 15.45 | 24.47 | / 6.48 | 42.42 | 2:12.02 |
| 6307 | | Filatyeva | | | 1 | Spart | Tashkent | 16/17 Sep |
| | | 13.84 | 1.88 | 13.17 | 24.68 | / 6.19 | 44.04 | 2:13.24 |
| 6304 | | Dimitrova (30/17) | | | 1 | Balk | Ljubljana | 6/ 7 Sep |
| | | 13.75 | 1.77 | 13.58 | 23.97 | / 6.41 | 40.30 | 2:11.17 |
| 6278 W | Jane | Flemming | AUS | 65 | 2 | CG | Edinburgh | 26/27 Jul |
| | | 13.32W | 1.79 | 12.70 | 24.17 | / 6.33 | 43.12 | 2:15.63 |
| 6259 | Kim | Hagger | UK | 61 | 1 | v Fra,Can | Arles | 17/18 May |
| | | 13.46 | 1.90 | 12.63 | 24.67 | / 6.57w | 36.06 | 2:17.72 |
| 6250 | Ines | Schulz | (20) GDR | 65 | 1 | | Berlin | 19/20 Aug |
| | | 13.84 | 1.81 | 13.51 | 25.02 | / 6.36 | 42.66 | 2:12.22 |
| 6242 | Chantal | Beaugeant | FRA | 61 | 2 | v Can,UK | Arles | 17/18 May |
| | | 13.74 | 1.78 | 12.96 | 24.56 | / 6.08 | 47.26 | 2:11.67 |
| 6230 | Jane | Frederick | USA | 52 | 1 | TAC | Eugene | 18/19 Jun |
| | | 14.73 | 1.82 | 14.65 | 24.94w/ | 6.09w | 49.22 | 2:14.61 |
| 6217 | Petra | Văidean | RUM | 65 | 1 | NC | Pitești | 7/ 8 Aug |
| | | 13.98 | 1.68 | 14.68 | 24.77 | / 6.37 | 45.62 | 2:13.18 |
| 6216 M | Tamara | Moshicheva | SU | 62 | 1 | | Chelyabinsk | 5/ 6 Aug |
| | | 13.5 m | 1.86 | 12.55 | 24.2 m/ | 6.15 | 42.06 | 2:14.0 m |
| 6208 | Cindy | Greiner | USA | 57 | 2 | TAC | Eugene | 18/19 Jun |
| | | 13.71 | 1.79 | 13.67 | 24.15 | / 6.20 | 39.06 | 2:12.89 |
| 6202 | Irina | Kushenko | SU | 65 | 3 | Spart | Tashkent | 16/17 Sep |
| | | 13.88 | 1.82 | 13.71 | 24.81 | / 6.03 | 40.12 | 2:07.87 |
| 6196 | Marion | Weser | GDR | 62 | 2 | | Talence | 20/21 Sep |
| | | 13.75 | 1.84 | 12.55 | 24.36 | / 6.45 | 36.84 | 2:13.72 |
| 6194 | Svetlana | Chistyakova | SU | 61 | 1e2 | NC | Moskva | 6/ 7 Jul |
| | | 13.64 | 1.82 | 12.82 | 25.40 | / 6.31 | 45.30 | 2:15.84 |
| 6194 | Camelia | Cornățeanu | RUM | 67 | 2 | NC | Pitești | 7/ 8 Aug |
| | | 14.35 | 1.86 | 14.70 | 24.97 | / 6.15 | 38.94 | 2:11.93 |
| 6179 | Birgit | Clarius | (30) FRG | 65 | 7 | | Götzis | 24/25 May |
| | | 14.30 | 1.78 | 14.00 | 24.97 | / 5.84 | 48.80 | 2:09.79 |

WOMEN 1986

| Points | Name | | Nat | Yr | Pos | Meet | Venue | Date |
|--------|------|---|-----|-----|-----|------|-------|------|
| 6172 | Liliana | Năstase | RUM | 62 | 3 | NC | Pitești | 7/ 8 Aug |
| | | 13.31 | 1.74 | 12.65 | 23.80 | / 6.33 | 38.08 | 2:14.23 |
| 6165 | Liliane | Ménissier | FRA | 60 | 1 | NC | Athis-Mons | 12/13 Jul |
| | | 13.63w | 1.87 | 12.50 | 25.02 | / 6.26 | 40.60 | 2:15.96 |
| 6125 | Lidia | Bierka | POL | 60 | 1 | | Słupsk | 2/ 3 Aug |
| | | 13.73 | 1.75 | 12.86 | 24.95 | / 6.46 | 43.40 | 2:17.65 |
| 6118 | Yelena | Martsenyuk | SU | 61 | 1 | | Kiev | 26/27 Jul |
| | | 14.38 | 1.77 | 14.65 | 24.86 | / 6.04 | 46.12 | 2:16.76 |
| 6103 | Tatyana | Shpak | SU | 60 | 2e2 | NC | Moskva | 6/ 7 Jul |
| | | 14.21 | 1.79 | 14.21 | 24.60 | / 6.35 | 35.64 | 2:13.55 |
| 6093 | Yelena | Davydova | SU | 67 | 3 | v FRG | Bernhausen | 14/15 Jun |
| | | 14.38 | 1.85 | 12.09 | 24.49 | / 6.41 | 42.58 | 2:19.43 |
| 6077 M | Antonina | Sukhova | SU | 59 | 1 | | Rostov/Don | 14/15 Jun |
| | | 6067 = 13.3 m | 1.73 | 14.80 | 24.6 m/ | 6.24 | 38.42 | 2:20.2 m |
| 6073 | Svetlana | Besprozvannaya | SU | 65 | 4 | Spart | Tashkent | 16/17 Sep |
| | | 13.40 | 1.73 | 13.06 | 24.09 | / 6.44 | 35.58 | 2:18.58 |
| 6053 | Olga | Permyakova | SU | 64 | 1 | | Bryansk | 14/15 Aug |
| | | 14.28 | 1.74 | 14.72 | 24.54 | / 6.06 | 38.38 | 2:11.97 |
| 6048 W | Anke | Schmidt (40) | GDR | 68 | 1 | | Neubrandenburg | 3/ 4 May |
| | | 13.93 | 1.72 | 12.65 | 24.11 | / 6.51W | 35.92 | 2:13.91 |
| | | | | | | | | |
| 6041 | Svetla | Dimitrova | BUL | 70 | 1 | WC-j | Athinai | 18/19 Jul |
| | | 13.85 | 1.88 | 10.12 | 24.32 | / 6.26 | 37.16 | 2:12.29 |
| 6032 | Corinne | Schneider | SWZ | 62 | 8 | | Götzis | 24/25 May |
| | | 14.16 | 1.81 | 12.99 | 25.05 | / 6.16 | 47.26 | 2:23.99 |
| 6023 | Vera | Maloletneva | SU | 66 | 5 | Spart | Tashkent | 16/17 Sep |
| | | 14.38 | 1.79 | 14.06 | 24.29 | / 5.96 | 35.60 | 2:10.22 |
| 6004 M | Irina | Dudkova | SU | 61 | 1 | | Minsk | 26/27 Jun |
| | | 6007 = 13.5 m | 1.63 | 14.20 | 24.4 m/ | 6.15 | 40.02 | 2:12.4 m |
| 6003 | Katrin | Hochrein | GDR | 66 | 14 | GWG | Moskva | 6/ 7 Jul |
| | | 13.97 | 1.85 | 13.48 | 24.23 | / 5.91 | 31.62 | 2:12.25 |
| 6001 | Margit | Palombi | HUN | 61 | 1 | NC | Budapest | 12/13 Jul |
| | | 13.23w | 1.68 | 12.15 | 24.83 | / 6.21 | 38.84 | 2:11.17 |
| 6001 | Tanya | Tarkalanova | BUL | 65 | 1 | NC | Sofia | 2/ 3 Aug |
| | | 13.33 | 1.77 | 11.92 | 24.96 | / 6.39 | 39.52 | 2:21.05 |
| 5982 M | Marina | Pronina | SU | 63 | 2 | | Lipetsk | 20/21 Jul |
| | | 14.0 m | 1.73 | 12.96 | 24.8 m/ | 6.09 | 43.96 | 2:13.3 m |
| 5969 M | Irina | Oleinik | SU | 63 | 2 | | Kiev | 12/13 Jun |
| | | 13.8 m | 1.82 | 13.03 | 25.2 m/ | 6.21 | 39.14 | 2:18.0 m |
| 5966 | Tineke | Hidding (50) | HOL | 59 | 11 | EC | Stuttgart | 29/30 Aug |
| | | 13.78 | 1.68 | 13.62 | 24.25 | / 6.23 | 35.54 | 2:14.73 |
| | | | | | | | | |
| 5959 | Grit | Colditz | GDR | 66 | 3 | | Berlin | 19/20 Aug |
| | | 14.08 | 1.78 | 12.77 | 26.10 | / 6.09 | 47.62 | 2:18.23 |
| 5953 | Marina | Shcherbina | SU | 68 | 2 | WC-j | Athinai | 18/19 Jul |
| | | 14.46 | 1.79 | 13.01 | 25.70 | / 5.97 | 47.32 | 2:16.40 |
| 5948 | Svetlana | Ovchinnikova | SU | 56 | 2 | | Kiev | 26/27 Jul |
| | | 13.72 | 1.68 | 16.12 | 24.70 | / 5.83 | 35.96 | 2:17.30 |
| 5922 | Irina | Tyukhai | SU | 67 | 8 | Spart | Tashkent | 16/17 Sep |
| | | 13.63 | 1.76 | 12.61 | 25.30 | / 6.21 | 41.00 | 2:21.68 |
| 5916 W | Zuzana | Lajbnerová | CS | 63 | 1 | NC | Bratislava | 12/13 Jul |
| | | 13.68W | 1.73 | 14.10 | 24.86 | / 6.13 | 36.62 | 2:21.20 |
| 5914 | Renate | Pfeil | FRG | 63 | 2 | NC | Hannover | 19/20 Jul |
| | | 14.15 | 1.78 | 13.90 | 25.26 | / 6.03 | 38.76 | 2:17.99 |
| 5900 | Peggy | Beer | GDR | 69 | 2 | | Neubrandenburg | 3/ 4 May |
| | | 13.93 | 1.78 | 11.64 | 24.37 | / 5.97 | 36.88 | 2:12.44 |
| 5899 | Ivanka | Valkova | BUL | 65 | 1 | | Sofia | 5/ 6 Jul |
| | | 13.66 | 1.77 | 10.56 | 24.40 | / 6.49 | 36.62 | 2:20.60 |

| Points | Name | | Nat | Yr | Pos | Meet | Venue | Date |
|---|---|---|---|---|---|---|---|---|
| 5885 | Joanne | Mulliner | UK 66 | | 6 | | v Fra,Can Arles | 17/18 May |
| | | 14.08 | 1.78 | 11.89 | 24.64 / 6.24 | | 37.92 | 2:18.77 |
| 5880 | Rita | Heggli | (60) SWZ 62 | | 2 | v Swe,Est,Fra,Fin | Uppsala14/15 Jun | |
| | | 13.38 | 1.74 | 11.16 | 25.15 / 6.19w | | 36.72 | 2:13.21 |
| 5879 M | Nadezhda | Miromanova | SU 58 | | 2 | | Chelyabinsk | 5/ 6 Aug |
| | | 14.0 m | 1.68 | 13.17 | 24.0 m/ 6.20 | | 37.80 | 2:16.6 m |
| 5875 | Remigia | Zablovskaite | SU 67 | | 5e2 | NC | Moskva | 6/ 7 Jul |
| | | 13.74 | 1.73 | 13.07 | 24.79 / 6.03 | | 38.70 | 2:19.53 |
| 5873 | Irina | Petrashkevich | SU 63 | | 1 | | Leningrad | 17/18 Aug |
| | | 14.15 | 1.73 | 12.55 | 24.54 / 5.99 | | 37.50 | 2:12.18 |
| 5860 | Olga | Konovalenko | SU 62 | | 4 | SU P | Dnepropetrovsk | 6/ 7 Sep |
| | | 14.20 | 1.72 | 12.80 | 25.08 / 6.16 | | 39.96 | 2:16.50 |
| 5849 | Sylvie | Levecq | FRA 62 | | 7 | | v Can,UK Arles | 17/18 May |
| | | 14.36 | 1.78 | 12.20 | 24.57w/ 6.20 | | 35.00 | 2:15.69 |
| 5844 | Valya | Vasileva | BUL 61 | | 2 | NC | Sofia | 2/ 3 Aug |
| | | 13.80 | 1.74 | 13.74 | 25.37 / 6.08 | | 34.24 | 2:16.42 |
| 5830 | Coculeana | Oltean | RUM 56 | | 3 | | Pitești | 28/29 Jun |
| | | 13.94 | 1.76 | 12.91 | 25.66 / 6.17 | | 39.86 | 2:21.73 |
| 5828 mW | Eva | Karblom | SWE 63 | | 1 | TexR | Austin | 2/ 3 Apr |
| | | 14.00W | 1.75 | 12.56 | 24.20w/ 6.14 | | 36.80 | 2:23.6 m |
| 5827 | Debra | Larsen | USA 64 | | 1 | | Los Angeles | 21/22 May |
| | | 15.02 | 1.80 | 13.68 | 25.70 / 6.15 | | 41.74 | 2:20.56 |
| 5826 | Jolanda | Jones | (70) USA 65 | | 1 | NCAA | Indianapolis | 4/ 5 Jun |
| | | 14.66 | 1.83 | 11.22 | 24.62 / 5.98w | | 38.10 | 2:13.31 |
| 5819 | Alla | Yeremina | SU 56 | | 1 | | Moskva | 1/ 2 Aug |
| | | 13.98 | 1.70 | 13.32 | 24.93 / 6.03 | | 36.22 | 2:15.41 |
| 5814 | Esther | Suter | SWZ 62 | | 1 | | Zug | 30/31 Aug |
| | | 14.16 | 1.75 | 12.40 | 25.08 / 5.74 | | 41.48 | 2:13.92 |
| 5804 M | Lilia | Fastivets | SU 64 | | 3 | | Krivoy Rog | 1/ 2 Aug |
| | | 13.7 m | 1.70 | 14.80 | 24.9 m/ 5.88 | | 33.70 | 2:15.9 m |
| 5796 | Annie | le Roux | RSA 65 | | 1 | NC | Germiston | 11/12 Apr |
| | | 13.32w | 1.75 | 11.56 | 24.36 / 6.08w | | 36.60 | 2:25.60 |
| 5793 M | Olga | Lvova | SU 67 | | | | Armavir | 27/28 Sep |
| | | 14.3 m | 1.73 | 13.57 | 25.2 m/ 6.03 | | 39.20 | 2:16.2 m |
| 5784 | Taisia | Prokhorenko | SU 67 | | 2 | NC-j | Kaunas | 20/21 Jul |
| | | 13.84 | 1.73 | 12.36 | 24.51 / 5.68 | | 37.68 | 2:14.58 |
| 5784 M | Svetlana | Korolkova | SU 60 | | 3 | | Lipetsk | 20/21 Jul |
| | | 14.4 m | 1.76 | 13.60 | 24.1 m/ 6.09 | | 36.70 | 2:24.0 m |
| 5779 | Andrea | Breder | FRG 64 | | 3 | NC | Hannover | 19/20 Jul |
| | | 13.96 | 1.87 | 10.47 | 24.95 / 6.33 | | 38.54 | 2:30.59 |
| 5773 | Svetlana | Ivshina | SU 62 | | 3 | | Tallinn | 2/ 3 Aug |
| | | 15.12 | 1.83 | 12.50 | 26.36 / 5.96 | | 43.68 | 2:14.78 |
| 5773 | Iustina | Nicolescu(80) | RUM 69 | | 1 | | București | 15/16 Sep |
| | | 14.56 | 1.73 | 14.68 | 26.03 / 6.19 | | 43.72 | 2:29.47 |
| 5769 | Yelena | Babikova | SU 67 | | 3 | NC-j | Kaunas | 20/21 Jul |
| | | 14.33 | 1.82 | 12.73 | 25.90 / 5.84 | | 37.00 | 2:13.95 |
| 5766 | Janet | Nicolls | USA 63 | | 1 | | Pomona, CA | 18/19 Apr |
| | | 15.35 | 1.83 | 13.39 | 26.18 / 5.66 | | 46.86 | 2:16.32 |
| 5736 | Mila | Kolyadina | SU 60 | | 9e2 | NC | Moskva | 6/ 7 Jul |
| | | 14.01 | 1.64 | 15.71 | 25.89 / 5.88 | | 46.12 | 2:32.46 |
| 5727 M | Lyudmila | Narozhilenko | SU 64 | | | | Adler | 19/20 Apr |
| | | 13.9 m | 1.71 | 12.18 | 24.6 m/ 6.21 | | 33.64 | 2:17.0 m |
| 5726 | Daniela | Kluss | FRG 67 | | 6 | v SU | Bernhausen | 14/15 Jun |
| | | 14.45 | 173 | 13.02 | 26.08 / 5.91w | | 43.86 | 2:19.07 |

| Points | Name | | Nat | Yr | Pos | Meet | Venue | Date |
|---|---|---|---|---|---|---|---|---|
| 5721 | Urszula | Włodarczyk | POL | 65 | 1 | | Poznan | 5/ 6 Sep |
| | | 14.60 | 1.66 | 13.83 | 25.50 | / 5.84 | 45.36 | 2:19.91 |
| 5718 | Cornelia | Eckl | FRG | 63 | 2 | NCAA | Indianapolis | 4/ 5 Jun |
| | | 14.06 | 1.65 | 13.44 | 25.37 | / 5.72 | 44.48 | 2:19.88 |
| 5705 M | Tatyana | Dolgaya | SU | 64 | 2 | | Minsk | 26/27 Jun |
| | | 13.6 m | 1.72 | 11.55 | 24.8 m/ | 6.41 | 32.50 | 2:21.1 m |
| 5695 | Anke | Straschewski | FRG | 63 | 3e2 | | Bernhausen | 14/15 Jun |
| | | 14.57 | 1.73 | 13.63 | 26.22 | / 5.86w | 42.50 | 2:19.09 |
| 5694 | Małgorzata | Lisowska (90) | POL | 62 | 2 | NC | Grudziadz | 28/29 Jun |
| | | 15.12 | 1.75 | 12.63 | 26.16 | / 6.06w | 49.20 | 2:25.29 |
| 5691 M | Vera | Melnik | SU | 63 | 1 | | Kiev | 27/28 Aug |
| | | 14.0 m | 1.74 | 13.41 | 25.2 m/ | 5.68 | 38.56 | 2:18.2 m |
| 5689 | Vanda | Nováková | CS | 58 | 2 v H,A,Sc | Szekesfehérvár | 21/22 Jun |
| | | 14.18 | 1.73 | 13.17 | 25.59 | / 6.26 | 36.72 | 2:26.39 |
| 5686 | Ragne | Backman | FIN | 65 | 1 | NC | Oulu | 19/20 Jul |
| | | 14.46 | 1.74 | 12.00 | 25.29 | / 5.85 | 40.58 | 2:16.90 |
| 5680 | Corina | Tifrea | RUM | 58 | 5 | NC | Pitești | 7/ 8 Aug |
| 5678 | Hilsa | van Heerden | RSA | 61 | 2 | NC | Germiston | 11/12 Apr |
| 5670 | Sigrid | Kirchmann | AUT | 66 | 10 | | Götzis | 24/25 May |
| | | 14.17 | 1.90 | 11.93 | 26.44 | / 5.67 | 48.02 | 2:35.70 |
| 5670 | Sabine | Schwarz | FRG | 67 | 1ej | | Ingolstadt | 21/22 Jun |
| | | 14.51 | 1.73 | 13.00 | 25.75 | / 5.98 | 43.20 | 2:25.20 |
| 5660 | Monika | Krolkiewicz | FRG | 57 | 1 | | Ingolstadt | 21/22 Jun |
| | | 14.14 | 1.67 | 14.45 | 25.94 | / 5.95 | 36.94 | 2:20.67 |
| 5658 | Jocelyn | Millar-Cubit | AUS | 62 | 2 | NC | Hobart | 8/ 9 Mar |
| | | 14.13 | 1.79 | 10.72 | 25.00 | / 5.89 | 34.98 | 2:15.86 |
| 5654 | Christine | Höss (100) | FRG | 62 | 2 | | Ingolstadt | 21/22 Jun |
| | | 14.80 | 1.73 | 12.17 | 25.56 | / 5.61 | 47.64 | 2:18.74 |

| | | | | |
|---|---|---|---|---|
| 5647 | Margarita | Dunayeva | SU 68 | 24/25 May |
| 5646 MW | Sharon | Jaklofsky-Smith | AUS 68 | 8/ 9 Feb |
| 5641 M | Chris | Stanton | AUS 59 | 8/ 9 Feb |
| 5638 | Cornelia | Heinrich | FRG 60 | 19/20 Jul |
| 5636 | Ionica | Domnițeanu | RUM 69 | 7/ 8 Aug |
| 5634 M | Natalya | Potasheva | SU 62 | 26/27 Jun |
| 5634 | Linda | Spenst | CAN 62 | 26/27 Jul |
| 5633 | Marcia | Marriott | UK 56 | 17/18 May |
| 5632 | Natalya | Bagreyeva | SU 62 | 28/29 Jun |
| 5632 | Terry | Genge (110) | NZ 57 | 26/27 Jul |
| 5629 | Yelena | Petushkova | SU 69 | 24/25 May |
| 5627 mW | Cheryl | Wilson | USA 66 | 15/16 May |
| 5622 M | Regina | Ziliute | SU 62 | 27/28 Aug |
| 5619 | Kerstin | Reinhardt | FRG 69 | 14/15 Jun |
| 5618 W | Debbie | DaCosta | USA 64 | 2/ 3 Apr |
| 5615 (=5619) | Yelena | Oskirko | SU 65 | 2/ 3 Aug |
| 5613 | Lana | Zimmerman | USA 62 | 18/19 Jun |
| 5613 (=5617) | Anikó | Domonkos | HUN 65 | 12/13 Jul |
| 5611 (=5605) | Yuqing | Zhu | CHN 63 | 2/ 3 Jun |
| 5611 | Heike | Filsinger (120) | FRG 61 | 13/14 Sep |
| 5610 | Petra | Kluge | GDR 64 | 19/20 Aug |
| 5609 | Gabriele | Scholz | FRG 66 | 19/20 Jul |
| 5592 | Irina | Ilyicheva | SU 68 | 20/21 Jul |
| 5590 | Valérie | Tasiemski | FRA 66 | 12/13 Jul |
| 5584 | Lyubov | Litinskaya | SU 64 | 6/ 7 Sep |
| 5583 | Heidi | Schmidt | FRG 66 | 14/15 Jun |

| | | | | |
|---|---|---|---|---|
| 5579 | Heidi | Mann | USA 64 | 4/ 5 Jun |
| 5577 | Cathey | Tyree | USA 64 | 4/ 5 Jun |
| 5573 | Marion | Zillwich | FRG 65 | 14/15 Jun |
| 5572 | Birgit | Michl (130) | FRG 67 | 14/15 Jun |
| 5571 | Stefanie | Hühn | FRG 66 | 19/20 Jul |
| 5570 | Natalya | Tochilova | SU 64 | 24/25 May |
| 5562 M | Larisa | Zakharova | SU 64 | 20/21 Jul |
| 5562 | Cecilia | Danielsson | SWE 66 | 26/27 Jul |
| 5548 | Valerie | Walsh | UK 64 | 17/18 May |
| 5548 W | Jana | Vyštejnová | CS 65 | 12/13 Jul |
| 5547 | Eleonóra | Téglási | HUN 64 | 12/13 Jul |
| 5544 | Annette | Tännander-Bank | SWE 58 | 26/27 Jul |
| 5543 | Claudia | Dickow | FRG 63 | 14/15 Jun |
| 5541 M | Diana | Kiselovaite (140) | SU 65 | 27/28 Jun |
| 5539 | Yelena | Chicherova | SU 58 | 6/ 7 Sep |
| 5536 | Virge | Viss | SU 68 | 24/25 May |
| 5535 | Hildelisa | Despaigne | CUB 57 | 8/ 9 Jun |
| 5534 | Galina | Sadkovkina | SU 65 | 14/15 Aug |
| 5531 | Alison | Armstrong | CAN 61 | 20/21 Jun |
| 5530 | Taimi | Könn | SU 61 | 14/15 Jun |
| 5526 | Sylvia | Tornow | FRG 69 | 14/15 Jun |
| 5523 | Heidrun | Wellhöfer | FRG 64 | 19/20 Jul |
| 5523 | Irina | Stasenko | SU 66 | 17/18 Aug |
| 5521 W | Connie | Polman-Tuin | CAN 63 | 16/17 Aug |
| | | (150) | | |
| 5520 M | Yelena | Zaitseva | SU 67 | |

| Points | Name | Nat | Yr | Pos | Meet | Venue | Date |
|--------|------|-----|-----|-----|------|-------|------|
| 5519 | Marjan Goedhart | HOL 62 | 14/15 Jun 5511 | Linda | | Osmers | NZ 60 26/27 Jul |
| 5518 | Frédérique Tevelle | FRA 66 | 17/18 May 5508 | Tina | | Råttyå | FIN 68 18/19 Jul |
| 5514 M | Natalya Mostibrodskaya | SU 69 | 2/ 3 Jul 5507 | Katia | | Pasquinelli | ITA 66 2/ 3 Aug |
| 5512 | Malgorzata Lesniewicz | POL 63 | 27/28 Sep 5504 | Helena | | Otáhalová (159) | CS 59 24/25 May |

Best non-windy performances:

| 5900 | | Schmidt | | | 3 | WC-j | Athinai | 18/19 Jul |
|------|--|---------|--|--|---|------|---------|-----------|
| | | 13.81 | 1.73 | 11.86 | 23.93 / 6.30 | 30.70 | 2:12.23 | |
| 5891 | | Lajbnerová | | | - | v H,A,Sc | Szekesfehérvár | 21/22 Jun |
| | | 13.98 | 1.76 | 14.39 | 25.38 / 6.09w | 37.32 | 2:20.49 | |
| 5882 | | Flemming | | | 1 | NC | Hobart | 8/ 9 Mar |
| | | 13.73 | 1.85 | 12.68 | 24.66 / 6.00 | 36.88 | 2:26.16 | |
| 5785 | | Karblom | | | 1 | NC | Huddinge | 26/27 Jul |
| | | 13.87 | 1.75 | 13.07 | 24.74 / 6.04 | 37.08 | 2:25.09 | |
| 5578 | Wilson | | 4/ 5 Jun | | | | | |

Auto-timed marks for athletes with hand-timed bests:

| 6076 | | Ratsu | | | 3 | | Sochi | 24/25 May |
|------|--|-------|--|--|---|--|-------|-----------|
| | | 13.82 | 1.77 | 13.98 | 25.53 / 6.23 | 41.54 | 2:15.85 | |
| 6017 | | Moshicheva | | | 2 | SU P | Dnepropetrovsk | 6/ 7 Sep |
| | | 14.36 | 1.72 | 13.84 | 24.39 / 6.03 | 41.90 | 2:13.05 | |
| 5978 | | Dudkova | | | 1 | | Minsk | 30/31 May |
| | | 13.44 | 1.68 | 13.15 | 25.35 / 6.32 | 35.64 | 2:10.06 | |
| 5899 | | Oleinik | | | 3 | SU P | Dnepropetrovsk | 6/ 7 Sep |
| | | 14.37 | 1.72 | 13.65 | 25.32 / 6.28 | 38.38 | 2:15.15 | |
| 5795 | | Sukhova | | | 7e2 | NC | Moskva | 6/ 7 Jul |
| | | 13.50 | 1.73 | 14.38 | 24.92 / 6.06 | 33.16 | 2:26.58 | |
| 5721 | | Pronina | | | 3 | | Bryansk | 14/15 Aug |
| | | 14.48 | 1.62 | 13.17 | 25.88 / 6.01 | 44.86 | 2:15.26 | |
| 5705 | | Dolgaya | | | 4 | | Tallinn | 2/ 3 Aug |
| | | 13.66 | 1.74 | 11.83 | 25.20 / 6.08 | 30.36 | 2:14.58 | |
| 5649 | | Korolkova | 1/ 2 Aug | | | | | |
| 5645 | | Melnik | 16/17 Sep | | | | | |

W = assisting wind > 4.00 m/s
w = assisting wind between 2.00 and 4.00 m/s
M = hand-timed 100mH, 200m and 800m
m = hand-timed 100mH or 200m or 800m

WOMEN 1986

# 4x100 METRES RELAYS

| 41.84 | GDR | | 1 | EC | Stuttgart | 31 Aug |
|-------|-----|--|---|-----|-----------|--------|
| | (Gladisch, Günther, Auerswald, Göhr) | | | | | |
| 41.98 | GDR | | 1 | GO | Dresden | 17 Aug |
| | (Gladisch, Günther, Auerswald, Göhr) | | | | | |
| 42.12 | USA | | 1 | GWG | Moskva | 9 Jul |
| | (Finn, Williams, Givens, Ashford) | | | | | |
| 42.13 | GDR | | 1h1 | EC | Stuttgart | 30 Aug |
| | (Gladisch, Günther, Auerswald, Göhr) | | | | | |
| 42.27 | SU | | 2 | GWG | Moskva | 9 Jul |
| | (Zolotaryova, Azarashvili, Slyusar, Barbashina) | | | | | |
| 42.49 | USOC West | USA | 1 | USOCF | Houston | 2 Aug |
| | (A.Brown, Williams, Marshall, Ashford) | | | | | |

| Mark | Nat | Pos | Meet | Venue | Date |
|------|-----|-----|------|-------|------|
| 42.59 | USA | 1 | ISTAF | W Berlin | 15 Aug |
| | (A.Brown, Williams, Marshall, J.Bolden) | | | | |
| 42.68 | Bulgaria | 2 | EC | Stuttgart | 31 Aug |
| | (Zagorcheva, Nuneva, Georgieva, Donkova) | | | | |
| 42.70 | GDR | 1 | | Neubrandenburg | 7 Jun |
| | (Gladisch, Günther, Düring, Auerswald) | | | | |
| 42.70 | SU | 1 | v GDR | Tallinn | 21 Jun |
| | (Barbashina, Azarashvili, Slyusar, Zolotaryova) | | | | |
| 42.74 | SU | 3 | EC | Stuttgart | 31 Aug |
| | (Nastoburko, Bochina, Zhirova, Zolotaryova) | | | | |
| 42.75 | Bulgaria | 1 | | Sofia | 3 Aug |
| | (Zagorcheva, Nuneva, Georgieva, Valova) | | | | |
| 42.83 | USOC South | USA 2 | USOCF | Houston | 2 Aug |
| | (Finn, Washington, Cheeseborough, Torrence) | | | | |
| 42.84 | FRG | 2 | ISTAF | W Berlin | 15 Aug |
| | (März, Köninger, Gaugel, Thimm) | | | | |
| 42.97 | Ukraina | SU 1 | Spart | Tashkent | 16 Sep |
| | (Khristosenko, Kot, Slyusar, German) | | | | |
| 43.02 | Bulgaria | 1h2 | EC | Stuttgart | 30 Aug |
| | (Zagorcheva, Nuneva, Georgieva, Donkova) | | | | |
| 43.11 | France | 4 | EC | Stuttgart | 31 Aug |
| | (Leroux, Cazier, Bily, Leroy) | | | | |
| 43.15 | FRG | 1r2 | | Schweinfurt | 10 Aug |
| | (März, Köninger, Gaugel, Thimm) | | | | |
| 43.18 | SU | 1 | Znam | Leningrad | 7 Jun |
| | (Nastoburko, Barbashina, Slyusar, Zhirova) | | | | |
| 43.20 | France | 2h2 | EC | Stuttgart | 30 Aug |
| | (Leroux, Cazier, Bily, Leroy) | | | | |
| 43.27 | GDR | 1 | PTS | Bratislava | 13 Jun |
| | (Knabe, Günther, Düring, Oschkenat) | | | | |
| 43.28 | Ukraina | SU 1 | NC | Kiev | 17 Jul |
| | (Grigoryeva, Skibinskikh, Slyusar, Nastoburko) | | | | |
| 43.30 | UK | 3h2 | EC | Stuttgart | 30 Aug |
| | (Dunn, Cook, Baptiste, Hoyte) | | | | |
| 43.33 | FRG | 1r1 | | Schweinfurt | 10 Aug |
| | (März, Köninger, Gaugel, Thimm) | | | | |
| 43.35 | Kazakhstan | SU 2 | Spart | Tashkent | 16 Sep |
| | (Aleksandrova, Kvast, Miljauskiene, Sevalnikova) | | | | |
| 43.38 | UK | 1 | IAC | London | 8 Aug |
| | (Dunn, Cook, Baptiste, Oakes) | | | | |
| 43.39 | Moskva | SU 2 | NC | Kiev | 17 Jul |
| | (Kleyankina, Pomoshchnikova, Zhizdrikova, Zolotaryova) | | | | |
| 43.39 | England | UK 1 | CG | Edinburgh | 2 Aug |
| | (Dunn, Cook, Baptiste, Oakes) | | | | |
| 43.43 | RSFSR | SU 3 | Spart | Tashkent | 16 Sep |
| | (Yelagina, Papilina, Vinogradova, Chervyakova) | | | | |
| 43.44 | UK | (30/7) 5 | EC | Stuttgart | 31 Aug |
| | (Dunn, Cook, Baptiste, Hoyte) | | | | |
| 43.54 | Poland | 6 | EC | Stuttgart | 31 Aug |
| | (Smolarek, Jaros, Janota, Kasprzyk) | | | | |
| 43.71 | Nigeria/Texas Southern | USA 1 | NCAA | Indianapolis | 6 Jun |
| | (Soneye, Eseimokumoh, Onyali, Usifo) | | | | |
| 43.72 | Holland | (10) 1 | WA | Barcelona | 14 Jun |
| | (Cooman, Grossenbacher, Olijslager, Vader) | | | | |

| Mark | Nat | | Pos | Meet | Venue | Date |
|------|-----|---|-----|------|-------|------|
| 43.83 | Canada | | 2 | CG | Edinburgh | 2 Aug |
| | (Bailey, Lawrence, Phipps, Issajenko) | | | | | |
| 44.00 | Italy | | 1 | v FRG,Hun | Verona | 19 Jun |
| | (Angotzi, Mercurio, Ferrian, Tarolo) | | | | | |
| A44.40 | Oranje FS | RSA | 1 | | Bloemfontein | 5 Dec |
| | (du Toit, Rademeyer, Basson, Naude) | | | | | |
| 44.55 | Cuba | | 1 | CAC | Santiago/Dom | 3 Jul |
| | (Pino, Ferrer, Armenteros, Zamora) | | | | | |
| 44.65 | Rumania - j | | 2 | v USA-j | Piteşti | 11 Jul |
| | (Roşioru, Chindea, Steici, Constantinescu) | | | | | |
| 44.77 | China | | 1 | | Beijing | 7 Sep |
| 44.81 | Sweden | | 1 | v Fin | Helsinki | 9 Aug |
| | (Wallin, Engström, Skoglund, Fernström) | | | | | |
| 44.88 | Finland | | 2 | v Swe | Helsinki | 9 Aug |
| | (Haikkonen, Markkanen, Honkaharju, Niemi) | | | | | |
| 45.04 | Yugoslavia | | 2 | v Gre,Fra | Athinai | 16 Aug |
| | (Flajšman, Čotrić, Šinković, Ištvanović) | | | | | |
| 45.14 | Thailand | (20) | 2 | AsiG | Seoul | 5 Oct |
| | (Patarach, Srithoa, Sripet, Tangjitnusorn) | | | | | |
| 45.18 | Vítkovice | CS | 1 | | Kraków | 24 May |
| | (Mrovcová, Kocembová, Černochová, Niková) | | | | | |
| 45.25 | Ultracredi Clube | BRA | 1 | | Sao Paulo | 13 Jul |
| | (Leal, Ferreira, Lopes, Garcia) | | | | | |
| 45.49 | Bahamas | | 2 | CAC | Santiago/Dom | 3 Jul |
| | (Major, P.Davis, Greene, Ferguson) | | | | | |
| 45.54 | New South Wales | AUS | 1 | NC | Adelaide | 15 Mar |
| | (Laurendet, Sullivan, Chapman, Holden) | | | | | |
| 45.58 | México | | 3 | CAC | Santiago/Dom | 3 Jul |
| | (Garcia, Vazquez, Flores, Tavares) | | | | | |
| 45.59 | South Korea | | 3 | AsiG | Seoul | 5 Oct |
| | (Mi-Kyung Yun, Sin Young An, Mi Sun Park, Young Sook Lee) | | | | | |
| 45.61 | Hungary - y | | h | Druzhba | Neubrandenburg | 2 Aug |
| | (Hettinger, Kovács, Petrucz, Gáspár) | | | | | |
| 45.64 | India | | 4 | AsiG | Seoul | 5 Oct |
| | (Valsamma, Abraham, Joseph, Usha) | | | | | |
| 45.66 | Canterbury | NZ | 1 | NC | Christchurch | 8 Mar |
| | (Lewis, Doyle, Stock, Peterson) | | | | | |
| 45.74 | Japan | (30) | 1 | | Tokyo | 15 Sep |
| | (Konishi, Kitada, Hara, Isozaki) | | | | | |

Mark made in mixed race with men:

| 43.22 | USA | | - | Nurmi | Turku | 3 Jul |
|-------|-----|---|---|-------|-------|-------|
| | (Torrence, Williams, Givens, Ashford) | | | | | |

Hand timing:

| 44.9 | Ghana | | 1 | | Kumasi | 19 Apr |
|------|-------|---|---|---|--------|--------|

WOMEN 1986

| Mark | Nat | Pos | Meet | Venue | Date |
|------|-----|-----|------|-------|------|

# 4X400 METRES RELAY

| | | | | | | |
|------|-----|-----|------|-------|------|---|
| 3:16.87 | GDR | 1 | EC | Stuttgart | 31 Aug | |
| | (Emmelmann, Busch, Müller, Koch) | | | | | |
| 3:21.22 | USA | 1 | GWG | Moskva | 8 Jul | |
| | (Cheeseborough, Cliette, Leatherwood, Dixon) | | | | | |
| 3:21.94 | Ukraina | SU | 1 | NC | Kiev | 17 Jul |
| | (Dzhigalova, Olizarenko, Pinigina, Vladykina) | | | | | |
| 3:21.99 | SU | 2 | GWG | Moskva | 8 Jul | |
| | (Stepanova, Pinigina, Dzhigalova, Vladykina) | | | | | |
| 3:22.80 | FRG | 2 | EC | Stuttgart | 31 Aug | |
| | (Kinzel, Thimm, Gaugel, Bussmann) | | | | | |
| 3:23.25 | GDR | 1 | v SU | Tallinn | 22 Jun | |
| | (Uebel, Busch, Hesselbarth, Müller) | | | | | |
| 3:24.65 | Poland | 3 | EC | Stuttgart | 31 Aug | |
| | (Kasprzyk, Wojdecka, Kapusta, Błaszak) | | | | | |
| 3:24.70 | Leningrad | SU | 2 | NC | Kiev | 17 Jul |
| | (O.Nazarova-62, Stepanova, Khromova, Lesnykh) | | | | | |
| 3:24.73 | Moskva | SU | 3 | NC | Kiev | 17 Jul |
| | (Golesheva, Kiryukhina, O.Nazarova-65, Belova) | | | | | |
| 3:24.74 | RSFSR | SU | 4 | NC | Kiev | 17 Jul |
| | (Goncharova, Kharlamova, Chuvashova, Zabolotneva) | | | | | |
| | | | | | | |
| 3:25.25 | USOC South | USA | 1 | USOCF | Houston | 3 Aug |
| | (Cheeseborough, Cliette, A.Jackson, Leatherwood) | | | | | |
| 3:25.56 | Ukraina | SU | 1 | Spart | Tashkent | 20 Sep |
| | (Sereda, Yurchenko, Yevseyeva, Vladykina) | | | | | |
| 3:26.26 | Bulgaria | 4 | EC | Stuttgart | 31 Aug | |
| | (Marinova, Pavlova, Stoyanova, Stamenova) | | | | | |
| 3:26.48 | Moskva | SU | 2 | Spart | Tashkent | 20 Sep |
| | (Golesheva, Kiryukhina, O.Nazarova-65, Pesnopevtseva) | | | | | |
| 3:26.54 | RSFSR | SU | 3 | Spart | Tashkent | 20 Sep |
| | (V.Zaitseva, Goncharova, Nurutdinova, Chapala) | | | | | |
| 3:27.72 | Bulgaria | 1 | | Sofia | 9 Aug | |
| | (Andonova, Pavlova, Marinova, Stamenova) | | | | | |
| 3:27.97 | Rumania | 1 | v Eng,RSFSR | Bucureşti | 15 Jun | |
| | (Oanţă, Lina, Ene, Andrei) | | | | | |
| 3:28.54 | England | UK | 2 | v Rum,RSFSR | Bucureşti | 15 Jun |
| | (Cook, Keough, Piggford, Parry) | | | | | |
| 3:28.92 | Canada | 1 | CG | Edinburgh | 2 Aug | |
| | (Crooks, Payne, Killingbeck, Richardson) | | | | | |
| 3:29.35 | Tennessee | USA | 1 | NCAA | Indianapolis | 7 Jun |
| | (McLaughlin, Benjamin, Martin, Oliver/JAM) | | | | | |
| | | | | | | |
| 3:29.37 | Spain | (10) | 1 | v Fra,Pol | Epinal | 5 Jul |
| | (Lacambra, Perez, Pujol, Lahoz) | | | | | |
| 3:29.37 | SC Magdeburg | GDR | 1 | NC | Dresden | 17 Aug |
| | (Feuerbach, Bremer, Kirchner, Emmelmann) | | | | | |
| 3:29.58 | Bulgaria | 1 | v Aut,Hun | Linz | 29 Jun | |
| | (Andonova, K.Ilieva, Stamenova, Pavlova) | | | | | |
| 3:29.68 | Texas Southern | USA | 1h1 | NCAA | Indianapolis | 5 Jun |
| | (Sowunmi/NIG, Epps, Bell, Usifo/NIG) | | | | | |
| 3:29.85 | GDR | 1 | v Can | Karl-Marx-Stadt | 13 Jul | |
| | (Bremer, Neubauer, Kirchner, Uebel) | | | | | |
| 3:29.90 | Alabama | USA | 2 | NCAA | Indianapolis | 7 Jun |
| | (Hyacinth/UVI, Adiru/UGA, P.Davis/BAH, Leatherwood) | | | | | |
| 3:29.98 | Poland | 2 | v Fra,Spa | Epinal | 5 Jul | |
| | (Marcinkowska, Dunecka, Kapusta, Wojdecka) | | | | | |

| Mark | Nat | Pos | Meet | Venue | Date |
|------|-----|-----|------|-------|------|
| A3:30.22 | RSA | 1 | | Johannesburg | 18 Apr |
| | (Botes, Naude, Bothma, Armstrong) | | | | |
| 3:30.37 | Texas Southern           USA | 3 | NCAA | Indianapolis | 7 Jun |
| | (Sowunmi/NIG, Epps, Bell, Usifo/NIG) | | | | |
| 3:30.40 | USOC East          (30/11) USA | 2 | USOCF | Houston | 3 Aug |
| | (R.Stevens, Clark, Roberts, Dendy) | | | | |
| 3:30.64 | Australia | 1 | | Canberra | 21 Jan |
| | (Stewart, Flintoff, S.Fleming, Chapman) | | | | |
| 3:31.63 | France | 3 | v Pol,Spa | Epinal | 5 Jul |
| | (Jaunin, Simon, Deniau, Ficher) | | | | |
| 3:32.30 | Italy | 5 | EC | Stuttgart | 31 Aug |
| | (Masullo, Campana, Cirulli, Rossi) | | | | |
| 3:33.53 | Hungary | 2 | v Aut,Bul | Linz | 29 Jun |
| | (Könye, Forgács, Pál, Erdélyi) | | | | |
| 3:33.54 | Trinidad/Jackson State   USA | 1 | King | Atlanta | 20 Apr |
| | (Forde, Salazar, Jack, Valdez) | | | | |
| 3:33.60 | Cuba | 1 | CAC | Santiago/Dom | 4 Jul |
| | (Petiton, Hernandez, Mc Keen, Quirot) | | | | |
| 3:34.58 | India | 1 | AsiG | Seoul | 5 Oct |
| | (Valsamma, Rao, Abraham, Usha) | | | | |
| 3:34.70 | Holland | 2 | WA | Barcelona | 15 Jun |
| | (Vader, van Dorp, van der Wal, van Agt) | | | | |
| 3:34.73 | Sweden            (20) | 1 | v Swz,Nor | Luzern | 21 Jun |
| | (Bergman, Strand, Fernström, Skoglund) | | | | |
| 3:35.29 | Norway | 2 | v Swz,Swe | Luzern | 21 Jun |
| | (Lauritsen, Gundersen, Andersen, Brun) | | | | |
| 3:35.38 | Czechoslovakia - j | 1 | v FRG,Fra,Pol-j | Reck'hausen | 3 Aug |
| | (Háková, Pokorná, Raabová, Sedláková) | | | | |
| 3:35.93 | Switzerland | 3 | v Nor,Swe | Luzern | 21 Jun |
| | (Délèze, Aebi, Plüss, Duboux) | | | | |
| 3:38.38 | Pao de Acucar         BRA | 1 | | Sao Paulo | 13 Jul |
| | (Barbosa, Fialho, Costa, Miranda) | | | | |
| 3:39.20 | Yugoslavia | 3 | Balk | Ljubljana | 7 Sep |
| | (Dominc, Čolović, Bečkei, Paškulin) | | | | |
| 3:39.77 | Japan             (26) | 2 | AsiG | Seoul | 5 Oct |
| | (Honda, Koshimoto, Arai, Isozaki) | | | | |

| Mark | Name | Nat | Yr | Pos | Meet | Venue | Date |
|------|------|-----|-----|-----|------|-------|------|

# 3000 METRES WALK (TRACK)

| Mark | Name | Nat | Yr | Pos | Meet | Venue | Date |
|------|------|-----|-----|-----|------|-------|------|
| 12:31.0 | Aleksandra Grigoryeva | SU | 51 | 1 | IM | Lapinlahti | 22 Jun |
| 12:39.1 | Wang Yan | CHN | 71 | 1 | | Beijing | 29 Mar |
| 12:39.8 | Guan Ping | CHN | 66 | 1 | NC | Qingdao | 17 Oct |
| 12:42.8 | Li Sujie | CHN | 66 | 2 | NC | Qingdao | 17 Oct |
| 12:46.8 | Lidiya Levandovskaya | SU | 62 | 2 | IM | Lapinlahti | 22 Jun |
| 12:56.96 | Kerry Saxby | AUS | 61 | 1 | | Canberra | 6 Mar |
| 12:58.21 | Saxby | | | 1 | | Sydney | 9 Feb |
| 13:01.2 | Ann Jansson | SWE | 58 | 1 | NC | Brunflo | 1 Aug |
| 13:03.5 | Beverley Hayman | AUS | 61 | 1 | | Sydney | 8 Mar |
| 13:10.0 | Hayman | | | 1 | | Sydney | 1 Mar |
| (10/8) | | | | | | | |
| 13:10.8 | Zhang Min | CHN | 67 | 3 | NC | Qingdao | 17 Oct |
| 13:10.8 | Qin Huanfeng | CHN | 66 | 4 | NC | Qingdao | 17 Oct |
| (10) | | | | | | | |
| 13:11.3 | An Limei | CHN | 68 | 1 | NC | Qingdao | 17 Oct |
| 13:12.3 | Shi Xiao Ling | CHN | 60 | 5 | NC | Qingdao | 17 Oct |
| 13:12.3 | Wu Lingzhem | CHN | 67 | 6 | NC | Qingdao | 17 Oct |
| 13:12.4 | Jin Gingjie | CHN | 71 | 3 | WJ | Athinai | 20 Jul |
| 13:12.60 | Gabrielle Blythe | AUS | 69 | 1 | | Melbourne | 6 Feb |
| 13:12.6 | Mirva Hamalainen | FIN | 62 | 1 | | Lahti | 2 Jul |
| 13:13.0 | Chen Zhimin | CHN | 67 | 7 | NC | Qingdao | 17 Oct |
| 13:15.47 | Sue Cook | AUS | 58 | 2 | | Canberra | 6 Mar |
| 13:18.88 | Oksana Shchastnaya | SU | 71 | 2 | IM | Neubrandenburg | 1 Aug |
| 13:19.4 | Monica Gunnarsson | SWE | 65 | 2 | NC | Brunflo | 1 Aug |
| (20) | | | | | | | |
| 13:20.0 | Li Chuniu | CHN | 69 | 2 | NC | Qingdao | 17 Oct |
| 13:21.14 | Sirkka Oikarinen | FIN | 59 | 1 | | Vantaa | 8 Jun |
| 13:21.8 | Yan Ming Zhu | CHN | 71 | 3 | NC | Qingdao | 17 Oct |
| 13:22.6 | Kersti Tysse | NOR | 72 | 1 | IM | Pihtipudas | 30 Aug |
| 13:24.4 | Fu Liqin | CHN | 70 | 4 | NC | Qingdao | 17 Oct |
| 13:26.54 | Alison Baker | CAN | 64 | 1 | | Toronto | 15 Jun |
| 13:27.1 | Wang Li Rong | CHN | 70 | 5 | NC | Qingdao | 17 Oct |
| 13:30.95 | Katrin Born | GDR | 70 | 1 | | Berlin | 10 Jul |
| 13:31.0 | Wong Na | CHN | 60 | 6 | NC | Qingdao | 17 Oct |
| (30) | | | | | | | |

# 5000 METRES WALK (TRACK)

| Mark | Name | Nat | Yr | Pos | Meet | Venue | Date |
|------|------|-----|-----|-----|------|-------|------|
| 21:26.5 | Guan Ping | CHN | 66 | 1 | NC | Qingdao | 17 Oct |
| 21:33.8 | Wang Yan | CHN | 71 | 1 | | Jian | 9 Mar |
| 21:34.37 | Li Sujie | CHN | 66 | 1 | | Beijing | 9 Sep |
| 21:35.25 | Giuliana Salce | ITA | 55 | 1 | IM | Verona | 19 Jun |
| 21:53.36 | Kerry Saxby | AUS | 61 | 1 | | Melbourne | 16 Feb |
| 21:54.3 | Li Sujie | | | 2 | NC | Qingdao | 17 Oct |
| 21:59.1 | Chen Zhimin | CHN | 67 | 3 | NC | Qingdao | 17 Oct |
| 22:02.0 | Saxby | | | 1 | | Sydney | 14 Sep |
| 22:02.75 | Jin Bingjie | CHN | 71 | 2 | | Beijing | 9 Sep |
| 22:03.5 | Shi Xiaoling | CHN | 60 | 4 | NC | Qingdao | 17 Oct |
| 22:03.65 | Wang Yan | | | 1 | WJ | Athinai | 20 Jul |
| 22:05.72 | An Limei | CHN | 68 | 3 | | Beijing | 9 Sep |
| 22:07.6 | Zhang Min | CHN | 67 | 5 | NC | Qingdao | 17 Oct |
| 22:11.56 | Yelena Kuznetsova | SU | 66 | 1 | | Bryansk | 16 Aug |
| 22:12.0 | Lidiya Levandovskaya | SU | 62 | 1 | | Alushta | 9 Feb |
| 22:14.4 | Saxby | | | 1 | | Canberra | 21 Jan |
| 22:15.2 | Qiu Huanfen | CHN | 66 | 6 | NC | Qingdao | 17 Oct |
| 22:15.76 | Wang Yan | | | 4 | | Beijing | 9 Sep |
| 22:16.5 | Jin Bingjie | | | 1 | IM | Canberra | 21 Jan |
| 22:17.76 | Natalya Zykova | SU | 69 | 2 | WJ | Athinai | 20 Jul |
| (20/14) | | | | | | | |

| Mark | Name | Nat | Yr | Pos | Meet | Venue | Date |
|------|------|-----|-----|-----|------|-------|------|
| 22:18.5 | Ann Peel | CAN | 61 | 1 | NC | Ottawa | 20 Jun |
| 22:19.29 | Sada Eidikite | SU | 67 | 1 | | Kaunas | 27 Jul |
| 22:21.4 | Li Chunxiu | CHN | 69 | 1 | | Qingdao | 17 Oct |
| 22:23.0 | Yelena Veremeychuk | SU | 59 | 3 | | Alushta | 9 Feb |
| 22:25.95 | Galina Yezhova | SU | 62 | 1 | | Kiyev | 26 Jul |
| 22:27.87 | Mirva Hamalainen | FIN | 62 | 1 | | Esbo | 14 Aug |
| | (20) | | | | | | |
| 22:28.6 | Raisa Sinyavina | SU | 54 | 2 | | Kherson | 11 May |
| 22:29.8 | Olympiada Ivanova | SU | 70 | 1 | | Dnepropetrovsk | 27 Sep |
| 22:29.9 | Wu Lingzhen | CHN | 67 | 7 | NC | Qingdao | 17 Oct |
| 22:30.90 | Maria Cruz Diaz | SPA | 69 | 1 | | Madrid | 2 Aug |
| 22:32.0 | Fu Liqin | CHN | 70 | 2 | | Qingdao | 17 Oct |
| 22:33.2 | Ann Jansson | SWE | 58 | 1 | NC | Brunflo | 30 Jul |
| 22:34.25 | Aleksandra Grigoryeva | SU | 60 | 3 | GWG | Moskva | 7 Jul |
| 22:37.11 | Yelena Sergeyeva | SU | 68 | 2 | | Kaunas | 20 Jul |
| 22:37.39 | Marina Shupilo | SU | 60 | 2 | | Kiyev | 26 Jul |
| 22:37.46 | Gabrielle Blythe | AUS | 69 | 2 | | Melbourne | 16 Feb |
| | (30) | | | | | | |
| 22:38.50' | Vera Prudnikova | SU | 54 | 5 | GWG | Moskva | 7 Jul |
| 22:38.5 | Li Shuai | CHN | 64 | 8 | NC | Qingdao | 17 Oct |
| 22:38.81 | Yuliya Lisnik | SU | 66 | 3 | | Kiyev | 26 Jul |
| 22:40.0 | Olga Kardopoltseva | SU | 66 | 1 | | Donetsk | 5 Oct |
| 22:42.8 | Miao Shuyan | CHN | 67 | 9 | NC | Qingdao | 17 Oct |
| 22:42.81 | Beverley Hayman | AUS | 61 | 2 | NC | Adelaide | 15 Mar |
| 22:43.23 | Oksana Shchastnaya | SU | 71 | 2 | Drz | Neubrandenburg | 1 Aug |
| 22:43.48' | Olga Krishtop/Yarets | SU | 57 | 6 | GWG | Moskva | 7 Jul |
| 22:45.1 | Monica Gunnarsson | SWE | 65 | 2 | NC | Brunflo | 30 Jul |
| 22:46.8 | Kersti Tysse | NOR | 72 | 1 | NC | Fana | 30 Jul |
| | (40) | | | | | | |
| 22:47.8' | Natalya Dmitroshenko | SU | 66 | 7 | GWG | Moskva | 7 Jul |
| 22:48.3 | Liu Jinglan | CHN | 66 | 10 | NC | Qingdao | 17 Oct |
| 22:51.4 | Suzanne Griesbach | FRA | 45 | 1 | | Paris | 26 Apr |
| 22:53.66' | Vera Osipova | SU | 57 | 8 | GWG | Moskva | 7 Jul |
| 22:54.63 | Valentina Tsybulskaya | SU | 68 | 3 | | Simferopol | 24 May |
| 22:54.68 | Emilia Cano | SPA | 68 | 1 | | San Sebastian | 25 Jul |
| 22:54.9 | Yelena Rodionova | SU | 65 | 3 | | Tashkent | 16 Sep |
| 22:55.47 | Mariya Vasilko | SU | 62 | 4 | | Kiyev | 26 Jul |
| 22:56.30 | Maria Reyes Sobrino | SPA | 67 | 2 | | Madrid | 2 Aug |
| 22:56.7 | Li Shufen | CHN | 68 | 3 | | Jian | 9 Mar |
| | (50) | | | | | | |
| 22:57.3 | Yin Minfen | CHN | 66 | 11 | NC | Qingdao | 17 Oct |
| 22:57.4 | Zoya Baurdinova | SU | 54 | 3 | | Kherson | 11 May |
| 22:58.5 | Liao Liying | CHN | 65 | 1 | | Guangzhou | 22 Mar |
| 23:00.23 | Tamara Torschina | CHN | 67 | 4 | | Kaunas | 20 Jul |
| 23:00.6 | Wang Zuoling | CHN | 67 | 12 | NC | Qingdao | 17 Oct |
| 23:01.0 | Natalya Yarosenko | SU | 63 | 4 | | Alushta | 9 Feb |
| 23:02.1 | Yang Suyun | CHN | 69 | 4 | NC-J | Qingdao | 17 Oct |
| 23:02.62 | Irina Shubina | CHN | 61 | 5 | | Kiyev | 26 Jul |
| 23:02.67 | Victoria Oprea | ROM | 65 | 1 | | Pitesti | 8 Aug |
| 23:06.06 | Mihaela Daugariou | ROM | 69 | 1 | | Bucaresti | 15 Jun |
| | (60) | | | | | | |
| 23:07.2 | He Paogin | CHN | 69 | 5 | NC-J | Qingdao | 17 Oct |
| 23:08.68 | Maria Grazia Cogoli | ITA | 62 | 1 | NC | Torino | 24 Jul |
| 23:13.8 | Natalya Spiridonova | SU | 63 | 4 | | Tashkent | 16 Sep |
| 23:14.98 | Teresa Palacios | SPA | 58 | 1 | IM | Epinal | 5 Jul |
| 23:15.4 | Suzanne Narbey | AUS | 64 | 1 | | Perth | 8 Mar |
| 23:16.33' | Sue Cook | AUS | 58 | 11 | GWG | Moskva | 7 Jul |
| 23:16.34 | Irina Tolstykh | SU | 65 | 6 | | Kiyev | 26 Jul |
| 23:16.99 | Katrin Born | GDR | 70 | 1 | | Potsdam | 11 May |
| 23:18.8 | Quo Junxia | CHN | 69 | 8 | NC-J | Qingdao | 17 Oct |
| 23:19.92 | Nina Strakhova | SU | 68 | 5 | | Kaunas | 19 Jul |
| | (70) | | | | | | |

| Mark | Name | Nat | Yr | Pos | Meet | Venue | Date |
|------|------|-----|----|----|------|-------|------|
| 23:20.0 | Qiao Xiaorong | CHN | 69 | 9 | NC | Qingdao | 17 Oct |
| 23:22.0 | Svetlana Yakovleva | SU | 67 | 6 | | Kaunas | 27 Jul |
| 23:22.0 | Natalya Storozhenko | SU | 63 | 2 | | Bryansk | 16 Aug |
| 23:22.3 | Alison Baker | CAN | 64 | 2 | NC | Ottawa | 21 Jun |
| 23:24.44 | Lorraine Jachno | AUS | 59 | 4 | NC | Adelaide | 15 Mar |
| 23:25.0 | Scute Lapinskaite | SU | 65 | 2 | | Birchton | 27 Sep |
| 23:26.8 | Agneta Memes | ROM | 57 | 2 | | Pitesti | 19 Jun |
| 23:26.84' | Marina Andreyeva | SU | 60 | 14 | GWG | Moskva | 7 Jul |
| 23:27.9 | Lynn Weik | USA | 68 | 1 | | Philadelphia | 24 Apr |
| 23:28.36' | Tamara Kovalenko | SU | 64 | 15 | GWG | Moskva | 7 Jul |
| | (80) | | | | | | |

' during 10,000 metres walk

Indoor mark

| Mark | Name | Nat | Yr | Pos | Meet | Venue | Date |
|------|------|-----|----|----|------|-------|------|
| 22:44.24 | Dana Vavracova | CS | 54 | 1 | | Jablonec | 1 Feb |

# 5000 METRES WALK (ROAD)

| Mark | Name | Nat | Yr | Pos | Meet | Venue | Date |
|------|------|-----|----|----|------|-------|------|
| 21:40 | Olga Krishtop/Yarets | SU | 57 | 1 | IM | Hospitalet | 11 May |
| 21:42 | Aleksandra Grigoryeva | SU | 60 | 2 | IM | Hospitalet | 11 May |
| 21:57 | Kerry Saxby | AUS | 61 | 1 | | Canberra | 3 May |
| 21:58 | Sada Eidikite | SU | 67 | 1 | | Sochi | 20 Feb |
| 22:07 | Siw Vera-Ybanez | SWE | 57 | 1 | IM | Boras | 4 Oct |
| 22:12 | Lidiya Levandovskaya | SU | 62 | 1 | | Alitus | 9 Feb |
| 22:18 | Natalya Zykova | SU | 69 | 2 | | Sochi | 20 Feb |
| 22:18 | Saxby | | | 1 | NC | Canberra | 10 May |
| 22:18 | Monica Gunnarsson | SWE | 65 | 1 | IM | Saluzzo | 15 Jun |
| 22:21 | Vera Osipova | SU | 57 | 1 | | Volgograd | 25 Jan |
| | (10/9) | | | | | | |

Further walkers who had road times superior to their track bests:

| Mark | Name | Nat | Yr | Pos | Meet | Venue | Date |
|------|------|-----|----|----|------|-------|------|
| 22:23 | Victoria Oprea | ROM | 65 | 1 | IM | Ruse | 20 Apr |
| 22:33 | Susan Cook | AUS | 58 | 1 | | Canberra | 19 Jul |
| 22:34 | Sirkka Oikarinen | FIN | 59 | 2 | IM | Ruse | 20 Apr |
| 22:36 | Katrin Born | GDR | 70 | 1 | IM | Ruse | 20 Apr |
| 22:40 | Renata Rogoz | POL | 66 | 3 | IM | Ruse | 20 Apr |
| 22:40 | Dana Vavracova | CS | 54 | 1 | | Slivice | 10 May |
| 22:43 | Maria Lewandowska | POL | 66 | 4 | IM | Ruse | 20 Apr |
| 22:45 | Olympiada Ivanova | SU | 70 | 2 | IM | Ruse | 20 Apr |
| 22:45 | Maria Grazia Cogoli | ITA | 62 | 3 | IM | Hospitalet | 11 May |
| 22:52 | Giulliana Salce | ITA | 55 | 1 | IM | Potsdam | 24 May |
| 22:56 | Maria Reyes Sobrino | SPA | 67 | 4 | IM | Hospitalet | 11 May |
| 23:02 | Graziela Mendoza | MEX | | 1 | PAC | St.Leonard | 5 Sep |
| 23:03 | Marcelia Chanez | MEX | | 3 | PAC | St.Leonard | 5 Sep |
| 23:03 | Maria de la Cruz-Colin | MEX | | 4 | PAC | St.Leonard | 5 Sep |
| 23:04 | Grazyna Madura | POL | 60 | 5 | IM | Ruse | 20 Apr |
| 23:04 | Teresa Vaill | USA | 62 | 5 | PAC | St.Leonard | 5 Sep |
| 23:05 | Mihaela Daugariou | ROM | 69 | 3 | IM | Ruse | 20 Apr |
| 23:05 | Zofia Wolan | POL | 66 | 1 | | Mielec | 9 Aug |
| 23:11 | Tamara Kovalenko | SU | 64 | 2 | | Volgograd | 25 Jan |
| 23:11 | Yevgeniya Michayeva | SU | 69 | 4 | | Sochi | 20 Feb |
| 23:11 | Doris Kampa | GDR | 64 | 1 | | Berlin | 11 Jun |
| 23:11 | Svetlana Yakovelva | SU | 67 | 1 | | Kherson | 10 Jul |
| 23:15 | Valentina Ksenofontova | SU | 60 | 3 | | Volgograd | 25 Jan |
| 23:15 | Marina Lapeyeva | SU | 71 | 7 | | Sochi | 20 Feb |
| 23:18 | Atanaska Dszivkova | BUL | | 1 | | Sofia | 27 Jul |
| 23:19 | Galina Verzun | SU | 67 | 8 | | Sochi | 20 Feb |
| 23:22 | Irina Pratova | SU | 68 | 9 | | Sochi | 20 Feb |
| 23:23 | Irina Shubina | SU | 61 | 1 | | Leningrad | 13 May |
| 23:23 | Dagmar Grimmenstein | GDR | 67 | 6 | IM | Potsdam | 24 May |
| 23:24 | Anna Bak | POL | 61 | 3 | | Mielec | 9 Aug |

| Mark | Name | Nat | Yr | Pos | Meet | Venue | Date |
|------|------|-----|-----|-----|------|-------|------|

# 10 000 METRES WALK (TRACK)

| Mark | Name | Nat | Yr | Pos | Meet | Venue | Date |
|------|------|-----|-----|-----|------|-------|------|
| 44:32.50 | Yelena Kuznetsova | SU | 66 | 1 | | Bryansk | 16 Aug |
| 44:42.2 | Guan Ping | CHN | 66 | 1 | NC | Qingdao | 18 Oct |
| 44:42.3 | Li Sujie | CHN | 66 | 2 | NC | Qingdao | 18 Oct |
| 44:59.2 | Xu Jongjiu | CHN | 64 | 1 | | Fuxin | 30 Mar |
| 44:59.3 | Wang Yang | CHN | 72 | 2 | | Fuxin | 30 Mar |
| 45:08.13 | Kerry Saxby | AUS | 61 | 1 | GWG | Moskva | 7 Jul |
| 45:20.8 | Lidiya Levandovskaya | SU | 62 | 1 | | Zhytomyr | 6 Sep |
| 45:23.7 | Gui Jiangzi | CHN | 64 | 3 | | Fuxin | 30 Mar |
| 45:29.0 | Raisa Sinyavina | SU | 54 | 2 | | Zhytomyr | 6 Sep |
| 45:31.9 | Xu Yongjiu | | | 1 | | Jian | 10 Mar |
| 45:32.1 | Guan Ping | | | 2 | | Jian | 10 Mar |
| 45:32.4 | Yan Hong | CHN | 66 | 3 | | Jian | 10 Mar |
| 45:32.5 | Olga Veremeychuk | SU | 59 | 3 | | Zhytomyr | 6 Sep |
| 45:32.7 | Li Sujie | | | 4 | | Jian | 10 Mar |
| 45:56.50 | Guan Ping | | | 2 | GWG | Moskva | 7 Jul |
| 45:59.8 | Svetlana Kasina | SU | 62 | 1 | | Kiyev | 5 Oct |
| 46:00.27 | Aleksandra Grigoryeva | SU | 60 | 3 | GWG | Moskva | 7 Jul |
| 46:11.21 | Levandovskaya | | | 4 | GWG | Moskva | 7 Jul |
| 46:12.79 | Ann Peel | CAN | 61 | 1 | | Karl-Marx-Stadt | 13 Jul |
| 46:13.2 | Ann Jansson | SWE | 58 | 1 | NC | Brunflo | 3 Aug |
| (20/15) | | | | | | | |
| 46:14.4 | Natalya Ksenofontova | SU | 60 | 5 | | Ceboksary | 26 Apr |
| 46:19.6 | Galina Shvydkaya | SU | 60 | 4 | | Zhytomyr | 6 Sep |
| 46:20.18 | Vera Prudnikova | SU | 54 | 5 | GWG | Moskva | 7 Jul |
| 46:21.13 | Yelena Rodionova | SU | 65 | 1 | Spa | Tashkent | 16 Sep |
| 46:21.8 | Natalya Dmitroshenko | SU | 66 | 1 | | Minsk | 1 Aug |
| (20) | | | | | | | |
| 46:22.0 | Chen Xiaoling | CHN | 67 | 3 | | Qingdao | 18 Oct |
| 46:27.1 | Chen Zhimin | CHN | 67 | 4 | | Qingdao | 18 Oct |
| 46:32.2 | Shi Xiaoling | CHN | 60 | 5 | | Qingdao | 18 Oct |
| 46:34.3 | Zhang Hin | CHN | 63 | 6 | | Qingdao | 18 Oct |
| 46:35.5 | Yin Mingfen | CHN | 66 | 7 | | Qingdao | 18 Oct |
| 46:37.1 | Qiu Huanfen | CHN | 66 | 5 | | Jian | 10 Mar |
| 46:41.1 | Wu Lingchen | CHN | 67 | 8 | | Qingdao | 18 Oct |
| 46:42.0 | Tatyana Krivokhizha | SU | 56 | 5 | | Zhytomyr | 6 Sep |
| 46:42.2 | Liao Liying | CHN | 65 | 6 | | Jian | 18 Mar |
| 46:43.8 | Marina Andreyeva | SU | 59 | 2 | | Ceboksary | 26 Apr |
| (30) | | | | | | | |
| 46:45.0 | Li Chunxiu | CHN | 69 | 9 | | Qingdao | 18 Oct |
| 46:47.1 | Wu Guizhen | CHN | 67 | 7 | | Jian | 18 Mar |
| 46:49.0 | Liu Jinglan | CHN | 66 | 10 | | Qingdao | 18 Oct |
| 47:01.2 | Yuliya Lisnik | SU | 66 | 1 | | Yalta | 11 Oct |
| 47:02.65 | Monica Gunnarsson | SWE | 65 | 7 | GWG | Moskva | 7 Jul |
| 47:17.76 | Natalya Spiridonova | SU | 63 | 4 | Spa | Tashkent | 16 Sep |
| 47:21.47 | Olga Krishtop/Yarets | SU | 57 | 8 | GWG | Moskva | 7 Jul |
| 47:27.5 | Suzanne Griesbach | FRA | 45 | 1 | | Paris | 26 Apr |
| 47:28.48 | Marina Shupilo | SU | 58 | 1 | | Kiyev | 28 Jul |
| 47:29.30 | Sue Cook | AUS | 58 | 9 | GWG | Moskva | 7 Jul |
| (40) | | | | | | | |
| 47:35.45 | Vera Osipova | SU | 57 | 10 | GWG | Moskva | 7 Jul |
| 47:38.4 | Giuliana Salce | ITA | 55 | 1 | | Ostia | 25 Apr |
| 47:38.9 | Maio Shuyan | CHN | 67 | 11 | NC | Qingdao | 17 Oct |
| 47:39.5 | Svetlana Kasina | SU | 62 | 6 | | Zhytomyr | 6 Sep |
| 47:40.3 | Yang Suyun | CHN | 69 | 12 | NC | Qingdao | 17 Oct |
| 47:40.56 | Olga Kardopoltseva | SU | 66 | 6 | Spa | Tashkent | 16 Sep |
| 47:41.5 | He Ligin | CHN | 69 | 13 | NC | Qingdao | 17 Oct |
| 47:41.81 | Alison Baker | CAN | 64 | 2 | IM | Karl-Marx-Stadt | 13 Jul |

| Mark | Name | Nat | Yr | Pos | Meet | Venue | Date | |
|------|------|-----|-----|-----|------|-------|------|---|
| 47:44.5 | Yan Yulian | CHN | 66 | 14 | NC | Qingdao | 17 | Oct |
| 47:45.36 | Galina Yezhova | SU | 62 | 2 | | Kiyev | 28 | Jul |
| | (50) | | | | | | | |
| 47:46.20 | Mariya Vasilko | SU | 62 | 3 | | Kiyev | 28 | Jul |
| 47:47.88 | Doris Kampa | GDR | 64 | 3 | IM | Karl-Marx-Stadt | 13 | Jul |
| 47:51.4 | Zinaida Baurdinova | SU | 54 | 3 | | Yalta | 11 | Oct |
| 47:53.5 | Natalya Tsybulskaya | SU | 66 | 1 | | Zhytomyr | 6 | Sep |
| 47:54.26 | Tamara Kovalenko | SU | 64 | 2 | | Bryansk | 16 | Aug |
| 47:58.3 | Beverley Allen | UK | 59 | 3 | IM | Plymouth | 21 | Jun |
| 47:58.67 | Sure Mustafayeva | SU | 64 | 7 | Spa | Tashkent | 16 | Sep |

# 10 000 METRES WALK (ROAD)

| Mark | Name | Nat | Yr | Pos | Meet | Venue | Date | |
|------|------|-----|-----|-----|------|-------|------|---|
| 44:38 | Irina Strakhova | SU | 59 | 1 | | Zhytomyr | 26 | Sep |
| 44:43 | Olga Krishtop | SU | 57 | 1 | | Penza | 23 | Aug |
| 44:53 | Kerry Saxby | AUS | 61 | 1 | NC | Canberra | 19 | Jul |
| 44:56 | Krishtop | | | 2 | | Zhytomyr | 26 | Sep |
| 45:08 | Strakhova | | | 2 | | Penza | 23 | Aug |
| 45:18 | Dana Vavracova | CS | 54 | 1 | | Slivice | 10 | May |
| 45:19 | Sue Cook | AUS | 58 | 1 | | Canberra | 19 | Jul |
| 45:23 | Graciella Mendoza | MEX | 67 | 1 | PAC | St.Leonard | 4 | Oct |
| 45:26 | Ann Peel | CAN | 61 | 2 | PAC | St.Leonard | 4 | Oct |
| 45:27 | Vera Osipova | SU | 57 | 3 | | Penza | 23 | Aug |
| 45:33 | Aleksandra Grigoryeva | SU | 60 | 1 | | Sochi | 21 | Feb |
| 45:33 | Maria de la Cruz/Colin | MEX | 66 | 3 | PAC | St.Leonard | 4 | Oct |
| 45:34 | Krishtop | | | 1 | NC | Alitus | 31 | May |
| 45:41 | Osipova | | | 2 | | Sochi | 21 | Feb |
| 45:44 | Natalya Spiridonova | SU | 63 | 1 | | Moskva | 27 | Jul |
| 45:49 | Nadezhda Prudnikova | SU | 54 | 2 | | Moskva | 27 | Jul |
| 45:51 | Yelena Kuznetsova | SU | 66 | 3 | | Sochi | 21 | Feb |
| 46:00 | Saxby | | | 1 | IM | Lomello | 14 | Jun |
| 46:00 | Olga Kadapoltseva | SU | 66 | 3 | | Zhytomyr | 26 | Sep |
| 46:02 | Yelena Rodionova | SU | 65 | 1 | IM | Podebrady | 1 | Jun |
| 46:03 | Krishtop | | | 4 | | Sochi | 21 | Feb |
| 46:05 | Monica Gunnarsson | SWE | 65 | 1 | IM | Potsdam | 24 | May |
| 46:05 | Olga Veremeychuk | SU | 59 | 4 | | Zhytomyr | 26 | Sep |
| 46:07 | Grigoryeva | | | 2 | NC | Alitus | 31 | May |
| 46:09 | Gunnarsson | | | 2 | IM | Lomello | 14 | Jun |
| 46:09 | Maria Cruz Diaz | SPA | 69 | 1 | EC | Stuttgart | 26 | Aug |
| 46:14 | Peel | | | 3 | IM | Lomello | 14 | Jun |
| 46:14 | Ann Jansson | SWE | 58 | 2 | EC | Stuttgart | 26 | Aug |
| 46:16 | Grigoryeva | | | 1 | IM | Pihtipudas | 21 | Jun |
| 46:17 | Rodionova | | | 5 | | Sochi | 21 | Feb |
| | (30/19) | | | | | | | |

Further walkers who had road times superior to their track bests:

| Mark | Name | Nat | Yr | Pos | Meet | Venue | Date | |
|------|------|-----|-----|-----|------|-------|------|---|
| 46:19 | Siw Vera-Ybanez | SWE | 57 | 3 | EC | Stuttgart | 26 | Aug |
| 46:23 | Tamara Kovalenko | SU | 64 | 7 | | Sochi | 21 | Feb |
| 46:25 | Tatyana Petrova | SU | 65 | 9 | | Sochi | 21 | Feb |
| 46:30 | Giuliana Salce | ITA | 55 | 2 | IM | Potsdam | 24 | May |
| 46:30 | Natalya Gavarsina | SU | 61 | 5 | | Zhytomyr | 26 | Sep |
| 46:30 | Natalya Ksenofontova | SU | 60 | 6 | | Zhytomyr | 26 | Sep |
| 46:33 | Galina Versun | SU | 67 | 1 | | Cherboksary | 11 | May |
| 46:34 | Tatyana Krivokhizha | SU | 56 | 10 | | Sochi | 21 | Feb |
| 46:35 | Marina Andreyeva | SU | 60 | 4 | | Alitus | 31 | May |
| 46:35 | Maria Reyes Sobrino | SPA | 67 | 5 | EC | Stuttgart | 26 | Aug |
| 46:40 | Mariya Vasilko | SU | 62 | 5 | | Alitus | 31 | May |
| 46:46 | Sirkka Oikarinen | FIN | 60 | 1 | | Vantaa | 24 | May |
| 46:47 | Teresa Vaill | USA | 62 | 4 | PAC | St.Leonard | 4 | Oct |

| Mark | Name | Nat | Yr | Pos | Meet | Venue | Date |
|------|------|-----|-----|-----|------|-------|------|
| 46:50 | Beverley Hayman | AUS | 61 | 1 | | Richmond | 3 May |
| 47:00 | Yuliya Lisnik | SU | 66 | 7 | | Zhytomyr | 26 Sep |
| 47:02 | Galina Yezhova | SU | 62 | 3 | | Moskva | 3 May |
| 47:05 | Irina Shubina | SU | 61 | 8 | NC | Alitus | 31 May |
| 47:06 | Sure Mustafayeva | SU | 64 | 8 | | Zhytomyr | 26 Sep |
| 47:06 | Svetlana Kasina | SU | 62 | 9 | | Zhytomyr | 26 Sep |
| 47:07 | Suzanne Griesbach | FRA | 45 | 4 | IM | Potsdam | 24 May |
| 47:14 | Dagmar Grimmenstein | GDR | 67 | 3 | | Varnamo | 9 May |
| 47:14 | Katrin Born | GDR | 70 | 5 | IM | Potsdam | 24 May |
| 47:15 | Nina Spiridonova | SU | 63 | 14 | | Sochi | 21 Feb |
| 47:15 | Marina Shupilo | SU | 60 | 9 | NC | Alitus | 31 May |
| 47:16 | Mirva Hamalainen | FIN | 62 | 1 | | Naantalia | 4 Oct |
| 47:17 | Raisa Sinyavina | SU | 54 | 10 | NC | Alitus | 31 May |
| 47:17 | Nina Fesenko | SU | 61 | 11 | NC | Alitus | 31 May |
| 47:20 | Zinaida Baurdinova | SU | 54 | 16 | | Sochi | 21 Feb |
| 47:21 | Natalya Yarosenko | SU | 63 | 12 | NC | Alitus | 31 May |
| 47:28 | Anastasiya Prokopyeva | SU | 66 | 5 | | Penza | 23 Aug |
| 47:28 | Svetlana Vasilyeva | SU | 65 | 17 | | Sochi | 21 Feb |
| 47:30 | Yelena Kovner | SU | 59 | 6 | | Penza | 23 Aug |
| 47:31 | Alla Ahmetzanova | SU | 57 | 18 | | Sochi | 21 Feb |
| 47:34 | Rimma Makarova | SU | 63 | 1 | | Leningrad | 20 Aug |
| 47:36 | Suzanne Narbey | AUS | 64 | 1 | | Perth | 26 Apr |
| 47:37 | Irina Tolstykh | SU | 65 | 19 | | Sochi | 21 Feb |
| 47:41 | Tatyina Markina | SU | 66 | 6 | | Moskva | 2 May |
| 47:48 | Yuliya Troskina | SU | 58 | 7 | | Penza | 23 Aug |
| 47:49 | Svetlana Polovinko | SU | 56 | 13 | | Sochi | 21 Feb |
| 47:52 | Lorraine Jachno | AUS | 54 | 7 | IM | Lomello | 14 Jun |
| 47:52 | Tatyana Yumaseva | SU | 64 | 11 | | Zhytomyr | 26 Sep |
| 47:53 | Nina Musnikova | SU | 59 | 22 | | Sochi | 21 Feb |
| 47:56 | Lyudmila Kiselyova | SU | 62 | 12 | | Zhytomyr | 26 Sep |
| 47:57 | Emilia Cano | SPA | 68 | 9 | IM | Potsdam | 24 May |
| 47:59 | Tatyana Ledyayeva | SU | 60 | 14 | | Zhytomyr | 26 Sep |
| 47:59 | Larissa Voronkova | SU | 67 | 15 | | Zhytomyr | 26 Sep |
| 48:01 | Kersti Tysse | NOR | 72 | 2 | | Madrid | 16 Mar |
| 48:18 | Ildiko Illyes | HUN | 66 | 1 | | Szeged | 13 Jul |

# 1986 WORLD JUNIOR LISTS

| Mark | Wind | Name | Nat | Yr | Pos | Meet | Venue | Date |
|------|------|------|-----|-----|-----|------|-------|------|

## 100 METRES

| Mark | Wind | Name | Nat | Yr | Pos | Meet | Venue | Date |
|------|------|------|-----|-----|-----|------|-------|------|
| A11.28 | −0.6 | Mary Onyali | NIG | 3.2.68 | 1h2 | | Houston | 9 May |
| A11.30 | | Yolande Straughn | BAR | 18.3.68 | 1 | | Ciudad México | 20 Jun |
| 11.34 | 0.9 | Tina Iheagwam | NIG | 3.5.68 | 1 | WJ | Athinai | 17 Jul |
| 11.46 | 0.9 | Caryl Smith | USA | 9.4.69 | 2 | WJ | Athinai | 17 Jul |
| 11.49 | 0.9 | Maicel Malone | USA | 12.6.69 | 3 | WJ | Athinai | 17 Jul |
| 11.49 | 0.9 | Kathrin Krabbe | GDR | −.−.69 | 4 | WJ | Athinai | 17 Jul |
| 11.51 | | Muriel LeRoy | FRA | 7.7.68 | 2s3 | WJ | Athinai | 17 Jul |
| 11.56 | 0.9 | Claudia Lepping | FRG | 2.7.68 | 5 | WJ | Athinai | 17 Jul |
| 11.59 | | Carlette Guidry | USA | 4.9.68 | 1 | | Pasadena | 3 May |
| 11.59 | | Celena Mondie | USA | 6.8.68 | 1 | | Atlanta | 28 Jun |
| 11.60 | | Anita Howard | USA | 22.3.69 | 1h | | Albany | 8 May |
| 11.62 | 0.3 | Odile Sidibe | FRA | 13.1.70 | 1h5 | WJ | Athinai | 16 Jul |
| 11.63 | | Frenchie Holmes | USA | 12.4.69 | 1 | | Selma | 3 May |
| 11.63 | 0.3 | Patricia Bille | GDR | 20.12.68 | 1r2 | | Berlin | 10 Jul |
| 11.64 | | Corina Rosioru | RUM | 1.1.68 | 1 | NC−J | Bucuresti | 7 Jun |
| 11.64 | | Francine Landre | FRA | 26.7.70 | | | Los Abymes | 9 May |
| 11.66 | −0.9 | Olga Kosyakova | SU | 23.2.68 | 5r2 | Znam | Leningrad | 7 Jun |
| 11.69 | | Ina Morgenstern | GDR | 6.11.68 | 2r2 | | Berlin | 10 Jul |
| 11.70 | 0.7 | Heike Tillack | GDR | 6.1.68 | 2 | | Berlin | 10 Jul |
| 11.70 | | Esther Jones | USA | 7.4.69 | 2 | | Lincoln | 27 Jul |

### ind-assisted

| Mark | Wind | Name | Nat | Yr | Pos | Meet | Venue | Date |
|------|------|------|-----|-----|-----|------|-------|------|
| 11.18 | 3.2 | Maicel Malone | USA | 12.6.69 | 1 | TAC−j | Towson | 28 Jun |
| 11.28 | 3.2 | Caryl Smith | USA | 9.4.69 | 2 | TAC−j | Towson | 28 Jun |
| 11.37 | 5.0 | Irina Privalova | SU | 22.11.68 | 1 | | Simferopol | 23 May |
| 11.48 | 3.2 | Carlette Guidry | USA | 4.9.68 | 3 | TAC−j | Towson | 28 Jun |
| 11.53 | 3.2 | Denise Liles | USA | 26.2.68 | 4 | TAC−j | Towson | 28 Jun |
| 11.53 | 2.6 | Sharon Dolby | UK | 2.9.68 | 1 | | Edinburgh | 16 Aug |
| 11.56 | 5.0 | Olga Kosyakova | SU | 23.2.68 | 2 | | Simferopol | 23 May |
| 11.59 | 2.9 | Gina Tovo | AUS | 12.3.70 | 1 | | Sydney | 12 Dec |
| 11.60 | 3.9 | Corina Rosioru | RUM | 1.1.68 | 2 | VUS−J | Pitesti | 11 Jul |
| 11.60 | 2.5 | Sally−Anne Short | UK | 6.3.68 | 5h1 | CG | Edinburgh | 27 Jul |
| 11.63 | 3.2 | Tami Stiles | USA | 7.9.68 | 5 | TAC−j | Towson | 28 Jun |
| 11.63 | 4.5 | Monique Dunstan | AUS | −.−.70 | 1h1 | | Sydney | 12 Dec |
| 11.65 | 3.0 | Lyudmila Lapshina | SU | −.−.69 | 5 | | Simferopol | 23 May |
| 11.69 | 3,3 | Keturah Anderson | CAN | 9.1.68 | 3 | PAG−j | Winter Park | 5 Jul |
| 11.69 | 3.3 | Elena Constantinescu | ROM | −.−.68 | 1r2 | | Pitesti | 11 Jul |
| 11.70 | 4.4 | Doreen Fahrendorff | GDR | 24.7.68 | 2 | | Neubrandenburg | 4 May |

### and-timed

| Mark | Wind | Name | Nat | Yr | Pos | Meet | Venue | Date |
|------|------|------|-----|-----|-----|------|-------|------|
| 11.3i | | Irina Privalova | AU | 22.11.68 | 1 | | Moskva | 1 Mar |
| 11.4 | | Ina Cordes | FRG | 25.10.68 | 1 | | Dormagen | 7 May |
| 11.4 | | Inna Semenyuk | SU | 12.6.69 | 1 | | Oryd | 30 Jun |
| 11.4 | | Claudia Elissen | HOL | 5.7.68 | 1 | | Mijmegen | 14 Sep |
| 11.4 | | Slavica Zhivkovich | YUG | 11.7.71 | 1 | | San Giovanni | 27 Sep |
| 11.4 | | Olga Kosyakova | SU | 23.2.68 | | | | |
| 11.3w | | Tracy Mayfield | USA | 3.12.68 | 1 | | Burleson | 26 Apr |

| Mark | Wind | Name | Nat | Yr | Pos | Meet | Venue | Date |
|------|------|------|-----|----|----|------|-------|------|

## 200 METRES

| Mark | Wind | Name | Nat | Yr | Pos | Meet | Venue | Date |
|------|------|------|-----|----|----|------|-------|------|
| 22.90 | 1.3 | Mary Onyali | NIG | 3.2.68 | 2h3 | NCAA | Indianapolis | 4 Jur |
| 23.11 | 0.6 | Falilat Ogunkoya | NIG | 5.12.68 | 1 | WJ | Athinai | 19 Jul |
| 23.12 | | Maicel Malone | USA | 12.6.69 | 1h3 | | Indianapolis | 31 May |
| 23.18 | 1.0 | Claudia Lepping | FRG | 2.7.68 | 1 | | Trier | 2 Aug |
| 23.31 | 0.6 | Kathrin Krabbe | GDR | 22.11.69 | 3 | WJ | Athinai | 19 Jul |
| 23.36 | 1.2 | Oksana Kovaleva | SU | 3.9.69 | 1 | VGDR-j | Karl-Marx-Stadt | 10 Au |
| 23.46 | 0.6 | Carlette Guidry | USA | 4.9.68 | 4 | WJ | Athinai | 19 Jul |
| 23.48 | 0.2 | Muriel LeRoy | FRA | 7.7.68 | 1h5 | WJ | Athinai | 18 Jul |
| 23.52 | | Tamaris Fiebig | GDR | 7.7.70 | 1 | | Cottbus | 18 May |
| 23.59 | -1.0 | Ina Cordes | FRG | 25.10.68 | 2s3 | WJ | Athinai | 19 Jul |
| 23.61 | 0.0 | Tami Stiles | USA | 7.9.68 | 1 | | Norwalk | 30 May |
| 23.66 | 1.3 | Sandie Richards | JAM | 6.1.68 | 2 | | Les Abymes | 31 Ma |
| 23.67 | 1.2 | Anett Walter | GDR | 6.1.68 | 2 | v-SU-j | Karl-Marx-Stadt | 10 Au |
| 23.68 | | Anita Howard | USA | 22.3.69 | 1h1 | | Albany | 9 Ma |
| 23.69 | | Corina Rosioru | ROM | 1.1.68 | 2 | | Bucuresti | 25 Ma |
| 23.74 | -0.2 | Tatyana Chebykina | SU | 22.11.68 | h | Znam | Leningrad | 8 Ju |
| A23.79 | 1.9 | Yolanda Johnson | USA | 12.2.68 | 1 | | Denver | 10 Ma |
| 23.80 | | Tracy Mayfield | USA | 3.12.68 | 1h | | Lubbock | 2 Ma |
| 23.81 | | Esther Jones | USA | 7.4.69 | 1 | | Lincoln | 27 Ju |
| A23.86 | 1.9 | Caryl Smith | USA | 19.4.69 | 2 | | Denver | 10 Ma |

Wind-assisted
| Mark | Wind | Name | Nat | Yr | Pos | Meet | Venue | Date |
|------|------|------|-----|----|----|------|-------|------|
| 22.77 | 2.7 | Mary Onyali | NIG | 3.2.68 | 1 | | Houston | 10 Ma |
| 23.25 | 2.1 | Kathrin Krabbe | GDR | 22.11.69 | 1 | | Berlin | 10 Ju |
| 23.37 | 3.9 | Muriel LeRoy | FRA | 7.7.68 | 1 | NC-j | Montgeron | 6 Ju |
| 23.46† | | Kimberley Walker | USA | 23.12.68 | 1 | | Mesquite | 3 Ma |
| 23.55† | | Chryste Gaines | USA | 14.9.70 | 2 | | Mesquite | 3 Ma |
| 23.76 | 2.1 | Ximena Restrepo | COL | 10.3.69 | 1 | | Habana | 28 Se |
| 23.83 | 3.1 | Sally-Anne Short | UK | 6.3.68 | 1 | RC | Cwmbran | 15 Ju |
| 23.84 | 3.8 | Cynthia Britt | USA | 19.5.68 | 2s1 | TAC-j | Towson | 29 Ju |

Hand-timed
| Mark | Wind | Name | Nat | Yr | Pos | Meet | Venue | Date |
|------|------|------|-----|----|----|------|-------|------|
| 22.9 | | Carlette Guidry | USA | 4.9.68 | 1 | | Houston | 20 Ju |
| 23.2 | | Cynthia Titus | USA | 10.8.69 | 1r2 | | Austin | 17 Ma |
| 23.4 | | Kimberley Walker | USA | 23.12.68 | 2 | | Austin | 17 Ma |
| 23.4 | | Pauline Darkenteil | USA | 28.1.68 | 2r2 | | Austin | 17 Ma |
| 23.5 | | Cynthia Britt | USA | 19.5.68 | 1 | | Tallahassee | 12 Ap |
| 23.5 | | Donatella Dal Bianco | ITA | 7.11.68 | 1 | | S. Martino BA | 21 Ju |

## 400 METRES

| Mark | Wind | Name | Nat | Yr | Pos | Meet | Venue | Date |
|------|------|------|-----|----|----|------|-------|------|
| 51.48 | | Olga Pesnopevtseva | SU | 17.1.68 | S | | Tashkent | 17 Se |
| 52.02 | | Susanne Sieger | GDR | 25.6.68 | 1 | WJ | Athinai | 18 J |
| 52.18 | | Sandie Richards | JAM | 6.1.68 | 1 | | Les Abymes | 30 Ma |
| 52.25 | | Janeene Vickers | USA | 3.12.68 | 4 | WJ | Athinai | 18 Ju |
| 52.42 | | Maicel Malone | USA | 12.6.69 | 1 | | Indianapolis | 1 Ju |
| 52.79 | | Andrea Thomas | JAM | 18.3.68 | 4r2 | | Atlanta | 20 Ap |
| 53.08 | | Lacramioara Andrei | ROM | 13.10.68 | 5 | | Bucuresti | 14 Ju |
| 53.11 | | Leaha Walker | USA | 15.8.70 | 1 | | Shippenburg | 24 Ma |
| A53.15 | | Zelda Botes | RSA | 18.7.68 | 3 | | Pretoria | 19 Fe |
| 53.21 | | Tasha Downing | USA | 5.7.70 | 5 | WJ | Athinai | 18 Ju |
| 53.34 | | Heike Böckmann | GDR | 4.5.69 | 1 | Drz | Neubrandenburg | 3 Au |
| 53.42 | | Carmen Marin | ROM | -.-.70 | | | | |
| 53.49 | | Princess Bennett | USA | 21.9.68 | 1 | | Norwalk | 24 Ma |

| Mark | Name | Nat | Yr | Pos | Meet | Venue | Date |
|------|------|-----|-----|-----|------|-------|------|
| 53.60 | Gabriela Sedláková | CS | 2.3.68 | 1 | | Praha | 19 Aug |
| 53.66 | Gisele Harris | USA | 21.2.68 | 3 | TAC-j | Towson | 29 Jun |
| 53.72 | Tatyana Chebykina | SU | 22.11.68 | h | | Simferopol | 23 May |
| 53.82 | Marina Khripankova | SU | 28.10.69 | - | | Leningrad | 7 Jun |
| 53.87 | Malgorzata Kurach | POL | 9.1.68 | 4s1 | WJ | Athinai | 18 Jul |
| 54.02 | Trevaia Williams | USA | 7.9.68 | 1 | | Pasadena | 3 May |
| 54.06 | Kandice Pritchett | USA | 5.11.70 | 2 | v Rum j | Pitesti | 11 Jul |
| 54.06 | Sonja Finell | FIN | 17.8.68 | 2 | | Kristiansand | 23 Aug |
| 54.08 | Ann Maenhout | BEL | 8.2.69 | 1 | | Dilbeek | |
| | | | | | | | |
| 52.5 | Andrea Thomas | JAM | 18.3.68 | 2 | | Lawrence | 19 Apr |

## 800 METRES

| Mark | Name | Nat | Yr | Pos | Meet | Venue | Date |
|------|------|-----|-----|-----|------|-------|------|
| 2:00.61 | Gabriela Sedláková | CS | 2.3.68 | 5s2 | EC | Stuttgart | 27 Aug |
| 2:01.40 | Selina Chirchir | KEN | 28.8.68 | 1 | WJ | Athinai | 18 Jul |
| 2:01.4 | Zelda Botes | RSA | 18.7.68 | 1 | | Port Elizabeth | 12 Mar |
| 2:01.46 | | | | 1 | | Stellenbosch | 10 Feb |
| 2:01.93 | Adriana Dumitru | ROM | 3.5.68 | 3 | WJ | Athinai | 18 Jul |
| 2:02.18 | Lynne Robinson | UK | 21.6.69 | 4 | WJ | Athinai | 18 Jul |
| 2:02.95 | Katja Prochnow | GDR | 27.4.68 | 3r2 | | Jena | 31 May |
| 2:03.34 | Svetlana Masterkova | SU | 12.1.68 | h | | Moskva | 27 Jun |
| 2:03.50 | Ermyntrude Vermeulen | RSA | 22.11.68 | 3 | | Stellenbosch | 19 Mar |
| 2:03.59 | Denisa Závelcă | ROM | 2.10.70 | 1 | Drz | Neubrandenburg | 2 Aug |
| 2:03.64 | Ellen Kiessling | GDR | 17.2.68 | 2 | | Berlin | 10 Jul |
| 2:04.25 | Simone Weidner | GDR | 30.9.69 | 2 | | Karl-Marx-Stadt | 24 May |
| 2:04.40 | Doina Homneac | ROM | -.-.69 | 1h2 | Drz | Neubrandenburg | 2 Aug |
| 2:04.47 | Karen Hartmann | GDR | 29.4.70 | 1 | VCS-j | Praha | 2 Jul |
| 2:04.49 | Monica Magnusson | SWE | 18.3.68 | 2r1 | | Stockholm | 5 Aug |
| 2:04.7 | Marjorie van der Merwe | RSA | 9.1.68 | 1 | | Stellenbosch | 25 Mar |
| 2:04.74 | Ana Padurean | ROM | 5.5.69 | | | Bucuresti | 14 Jun |
| 2:04.80 | Eva Coqui | FRG | 30.1.68 | 5 | | Rhede | 2 Jul |
| 2:04.81 | Sasithorne Chantanuhong | THA | 9.1.68 | | | | |
| 2:04.81 | Luminita Zaituc | ROM | 9.10.68 | | | Pitesti | 29 Jun |
| 2:04.99 | Snezhana Pajkić | YUG | 23.9.70 | 4s2 | WJ | Athinai | 17 Jul |

## 1500 METRES

| Mark | Name | Nat | Yr | Pos | Meet | Venue | Date |
|------|------|-----|-----|-----|------|-------|------|
| 4:06.02 | Ana Padurean | ROM | 5.5.69 | 7 | | Pitesti | 28 Jun |
| 4:08.85 | Simona Staicu | ROM | 5.5.71 | 6 | | Pitesti | 28 Jun |
| 4:09.64 | Cristina Misaros | ROM | 1.1.69 | 2 | NC-j | Bucuresti | 7 Jun |
| 4:10.63 | Luminita Zaituc | ROM | 9.10.68 | 3 | NC-j | Bucuresti | 7 Jun |
| 4:10.84 | Adriana Dumitru | ROM | 3.5.68 | | | Bucuresti | 24 May |
| 4:11.88 | Doina Homneac | ROM | -.-.69 | 12 | | Bucuresti | 14 Jun |
| 4:12.67 | Ermyntrude Vermeulen | RSA | 22.11.68 | 1 | | Stellenbosch | 19 Mar |
| 4:12.69 | Susanne Fischer | GDR | 18.8.68 | 1 | NC-j | Cottbus | 27 Jul |
| 4:13.76 | Snezhana Pajkić | YUG | 23.9.70 | 9h1 | EC | Stuttgart | 29 Aug |
| 4:14.47 | Marjorie van der Merwe | RSA | 9.1.68 | 2 | | Stellenbosch | 19 Mar |
| 4:14.52 | Christin Sørum | NOR | 12.1.68 | 2 | | Oslo | 20 May |
| 4:15.07 | Mioara Bîcu | ROM | -.-.69 | | | Bucuresti | 14 Jun |
| 4:15.59 | Selina Chirchir | KEN | 28.8.68 | 2 | WJ | Athinai | 20 Jul |
| 4:15.6 | Larisa Tretyukhina | SU | -.-.68 | | | | |
| 4:16.20 | Zelda Kuhn | RSA | 3.8.69 | 3 | | Stellenbosch | 19 Mar |
| 4:17.67 | Simone Weidner | GDR | 30.9.69 | 2 | | Cottbus | 18 May |
| 4:17.83 | Karen Hartmann | GDR | 29.4.70 | 2 | | Berlin | 10 Jul |
| 4:18.21 | Kuthrin Nerke | GDR | 9.7.68 | 3 | | Cottbus | 18 May |

| Mark | Name | Nat | Yr | Pos | Meet | Venue | Date |
|------|------|-----|-----|-----|------|-------|------|
| 4:18.53 | Desirée Futter | RSA | 20.6.69 | 1 | | Potchefstroom | 28 Feb |
| 4:18.60 | Oksana Yakovleva | SU | 21.1.69 | | | Leningrad | 8 Jun |

# 3000 METRES

| Mark | Name | Nat | Yr | Pos | Meet | Venue | Date |
|------|------|-----|-----|-----|------|-------|------|
| 8:56.72 | Adriana Dumitru | ROM | 3.5.68 | 8 | | Bucuresti | 15 Jun |
| 9:00.13 | Christin Sørum | NOR | 12.1.68 | 8h1 | EC | Stuttgart | 26 Aug |
| 9:01.76 | Cleopatra Palacian | ROM | 3.1.68 | 6 | | Bucuresti | 25 May |
| 9:03.35 | Philippa Mason | UK | 21.3.69 | 2 | WJ | Athinai | 19 Jul |
| 9:04.5 | Dorina Calenic | ROM | 4.4.69 | | | Pitesti | 29 Jun |
| 9:06:90 | Simona Staicu | ROM | 5.5.71 | 2 | NC-j | Bucuresti | 8 Jun |
| 9:07:44 | Snežana Pajkić | YUG | 23.9.70 | 9h2 | EC | Stuttgart | 26 Aug |
| 9:09.39 | Fernanda Ribeiro | POR | 23.6.69 | 4 | WJ | Athinai | 19 Jul |
| 9:10.57 | Kathrin Kley | GDR | 19.7.68 | 1 | | Karl-Marx-Stadt | 24 May |
| 9:12.80 | Anita Hakenstad | NOR | 21.7.68 | 6 | WJ | Athinai | 19 Jul |
| 9:16.33 | Marleen Renders | BEL | 24.12.68 | 1 | | Tessenderlo | 20 Sep |
| 9:17.04 | Susanne Fischer | GDR | 18.8.68 | 1 | v SU-j | Karl-Marx-Stadt | 10 Aug |
| 9:17.10 | Satu Raimiala | FIN | 21.10.69 | 4 | NC | Vaasa | 25 Jul |
| 9:17.62 | Chun Me Kim | NKO | -.-.69 | 3 | | Ostrava | 11 Jun |
| 9:17.77 | Brigitta Lorch | FRG | 23.3.68 | 7 | WJ | Athinai | 19 Jul |
| 9:19.07 | Anke Breitenbach | FRG | 23.7.69 | 4h2 | WJ | Athinai | 17 Jul |
| 9:19.26 | Norah Maraga | KEN | 26.1.71 | 5h2 | WJ | Athinai | 17 Jul |
| 9:19.27 | Anzhela Shumeyko | SU | 16.1.69 | 6h2 | WJ | Athinai | 17 Jul |
| 9:19.61 | Sonia Barry | NZ | 13.11.69 | 8 | WJ | Athinai | 19 Jul |
| 9:19.71 | Doina Homneac | ROM | -.-.69 | 19 | | Bucuresti | 15 Jun |

In handicap race:
| | | | | | | | |
|------|------|-----|-----|-----|------|-------|------|
| 9:17.7 | Sonia Barry | | | | | | |

# 10 000 METRES

| Mark | Name | Nat | Yr | Pos | Meet | Venue | Date |
|------|------|-----|-----|-----|------|-------|------|
| 33:19.5 | Kathrin Kley | GDR | 19.7.68 | 1 | WJ | Athinai | 18 Jul |
| 33:41.13 | Marleen Renders | BEL | 24.12.68 | 2 | | Bonn | 26 Apr |
| 33:55.5 | Saori Terakoshi | JAP | 23.2.69 | 1 | | Hachioji | 21 Sep |
| 33:57.99 | Norah Maraga | KEN | 26.1.71 | 2 | WJ | Athinai | 18 Jul |
| 33:59.27 | Irina Kazakova | SU | -.-.68 | 2 | | Leningrad | 17 Aug |
| 34:07.13 | Anuta Cătuna | ROM | -.-.68 | 4 | NC | Pitesti | 9 Aug |
| 34:27.32 | Olivia Gruner | FRG | 4.3.69 | 2 | | Wetzlar | 6 Sep |
| 34:28.35 | Nadezhda Tatarenko | SU | 11.8.68 | 4 | WJ | Athinai | 18 Jul |
| 34:40.74 | Tanja Kalinowski | FRG | 18.9.68 | 10 | | Essen | 3 Jul |
| 34:41.06 | Antje Pohlmann | FRG | -.-.68 | 11 | | Essen | 3 Jul |

# 100 METRES HURDLES

| Mark | | Name | Nat | Yr | Pos | Meet | Venue | Date |
|------|-----|------|-----|-----|-----|------|-------|------|
| 13.10 | -0.8 | Heike Tillack | GDR | 6.1.68 | 1 | WJ | Athinai | 118 J |
| 13.14 | -0.8 | Aliuska Lopez | CUB | 28.8.69 | 2 | WJ | Athinai | 18 Ju |
| 13.25 | 1.3 | Yolanda Johnson | USA | 12.2.68 | 4h2 | TAC | Eugene | 19 Jun |
| 13.40 | 1.0 | Tanya Davis | USA | 29.7.68 | 2 | v RUM-j | Pitesti | 12 Ju |
| 13.52 | -2.7 | Zdravka Georgieva | BUL | 20.9.69 | 1 | NC-j | Sofia | 5 Ju |
| 13.52 | -0.8 | Birgit Wolf | FRG | 11.9.69 | 4 | WJ | Athinai | 18 Ju |
| 13.58 | 1.0 | Lenuta Birzu | ROM | 20.2.69 | 3 | v USA-j | Pitesti | 12 Ju |
| 13.59 | 0.0 | Antonella Bellutti | ITA | 7.11.68 | 1 | NC-j | Grosseto | 12 Ju |
| 13.61 | | Olga Kutsakova | SU | 23.12.68 | h | | Simferopol | 23 Ma |
| 13.63 | -2.7 | Svetlana Trichkova | BUL | 8.10.68 | 2 | NC-j | Sofia | 5 Ju |
| 13.65 | 1.0 | Florina Neder | ROM | 16.1.70 | 4 | v USA-j | Pitesti | 12 Ju |
| 13.65 | 1.0 | Jutta Fundel | FRG | -.-.68 | 2 | | Krefeld | 26 Ju |
| 13.65 | -0.7 | Claudia Bartl | GDR | 2.3.68 | 2 | NC-j | Cottbus | 27 Ju |
| 13.71 | | Burgel Assmann | GDR | 14.8.68 | 1 | | Karl-Marx-Stadt | 25 Ma |
| 13.75 | | Du Juan | CHN | -.-.68 | | | Nanjing | 11 Oc |

| Mark | Wind | Name | Nat | Yr | Pos | Meet | Venue | Date |
|---|---|---|---|---|---|---|---|---|
| 13.80 | −1.9 | Anna Barinova | SU | 25.7.68 | | | Leningrad | 7 Jun |
| 13.81 | −0.2 | Anke Schmidt | GDR | 5.2.68 | H | WJ | Athinai | 18 Jul |
| 13.81 | 1.1 | Naomi Jojima | JAP | 20.10.68 | 1 | Asi-j | Djakarta | 7 Dec |
| 13.83 | 1.0 | Daniela Neaga | ROM | 14.2.70 | 5 | v USA-j | Pitesti | 12 Jul |
| 13.84 | 0.0 | Laura Biagi | ITA | −.−.68 | 2 | NJ | Grossetto | 12 Jun |
| 13.84 | 0.1 | Pamela Doggett | USA | 8.6.68 | 1 | | Lincoln | 27 Jul |

wind-assisted
| 13.60 | 2.4 | Olga Kutsakova | SU | 23.12.68 | 2 | v GDR-j | Karl−Marx−Stadt | 10 Aug |
| 13.74 | | Amona Schneeweis | FRG | −.−.70 | 1 | | Saarbruken | 17 Aug |
| 13.77 | 2.3 | Pamela Doggett | USA | 8.6.68 | 1s3 | TAC-j | Towson | 29 Jun |

hand-timed
| A13.3 | | Olga Kutsakova | SU | 23.12.68 | | | Alma Ata | 11 May |
| 13.3 | | Claudia Felser | FRG | 5.9.68 | 1r1 | | Trier | 3 Aug |
| 13.4 | 1.2 | Natalya Schwandt | FRG | 5.9.68 | 2r1 | | Ludwigsburg | 29 May |
| A13.5 | | Aida Makrevrishvili | SU | −.−.68 | | | Alma Ata | 11 May |

# 400 METRES HURDLES

| | | | | | | | | |
|---|---|---|---|---|---|---|---|---|
| 56.53 | | Claudia Bartl | GDR | 2.5.68 | 4 | | Neubrandenburg | 6 Jun |
| 56.57 | | Ana−Maria Draghia | ROM | 14.11.68 | 1 | NC-j | Bucuresti | 7 Jun |
| 56.80 | | Kellie Roberts | USA | 16.6.69 | 2 | WJ | Athinai | 18 Jul |
| 57.92 | | Svetlana Lukashevich | SU | 1.8.68 | 3 | WJ | Athinai | 18 Jul |
| 58.00 | | Jill McDermid | CAN | 17.10.68 | 4 | WJ | Athinai | 18 Jul |
| 58.55 | | Zdravica Georgieva | BUL | 20.4.69 | 2 | | Sofia | 22 Jun |
| 58.72 | | Viktoriya Polnyun | SU | 12.2.69 | 1 | | Leningrad | 11 Jul |
| 58.76 | | Irena Dominic | YUG | 19.5.70 | 1 | | Maribor | 22 Jun |
| 58.80 | | Shawn Moore | USA | 21.4.68 | 6 | WJ | Athinai | 18 Jul |
| 58.85 | | Sofia Sabeva | BUL | 11.1.69 | 2 | | Stara Zagora | 20 Jul |
| 58.92 | | Tatyana Farafanova | SU | −.−.70 | 2 | | Leningrad | 11 Jul |
| 59.25 | | Marina Matyakina | SU | 11.12.69 | 3s1 | WJ | Athinai | 17 Jul |
| 59.30 | | Vera Ordina | SU | −.−.68 | | | Leningrad | 18 Aug |
| 59.38 | | Oksana Sorokaletova | SU | −.−.68 | h | | Simeferopol | 24 May |
| 59.45 | | Viktoriya Vlaskine | SU | −.−.68 | h | | Simeferopol | 24 May |
| 59.51 | | Heike Meissner | GDR | 29:1.70 | 3 | Drz | Neubrandenburg | 2 Aug |
| 59.54 | | Chen Bairu | CHN | −.−.68 | 1 | Asi-J | Djakarta | 6 Dec |
| 59.61 | | Gabriela Stanculescu | ROM | 21.4.70 | 1 | | Pitesti | 19 Jul |

# HIGH JUMP

| | | | | | | | | |
|---|---|---|---|---|---|---|---|---|
| 1.93 | | Galina Astafei | ROM | 7.6.69 | 1 | NC | Pitesti | 9 Aug |
| 1.92 | | Karen Scholz | GDR | 16.9.69 | 1 | WJ | Athinai | 18 Jul |
| 1.90 | | Rosanel Gogi | BUL | 12.7.69 | 1 | NC-j | Sofia | 2 Mar |
| 1.89 | | Judit Kovács | HUN | 7.6.69 | 2 | Drz | Neubrandenburg | 3 Aug |
| 1.88 | | Peggy Beer | GDR | 15.9.69 | 1 | | Karl−Marx−Stadt | 24 May |
| 1.88 | | Sylvia Oswald | FRG | 14.6.68 | 1 | v 3j | Bad Reichenall | 21 Jun |
| 1.88 | | Jayne Barnetson | UK | 21.1.68 | 1 | v Oce−j | Swansea | 28 Jun |
| 1.88 | | Michael Hübel | FRG | 6.4.69 | 1 | | Düsseldorf | 6 Jul |
| 1.88 | | Svetla Dimitrova | BUL | 27.1.70 | H | WJ | Athinai | 18 Jul |
| 1.88 | | Yelena Obukhova | SU | 9.1.69 | 3 | WJ | Athinai | 18 Jul |
| 1.87i | | Sari Karjalainen | FIN | 17.2.68 | 1 | | Turku | 26 Jan |
| 1.86 | | Yelena Latsuk | SU | −.−.68 | q | | Tashkent | 18 Sep |
| 1.86i | | Olga Bolshova | SU | 10.6.68 | 1 | NC-j | Lipetsk | 8 Feb |
| 1.86 | | Gail Kapernick | AUS | 20.9.70 | 1t | | Brisbane | 16 Feb |
| 1.86 | | Leah Cranston | AUS | 25.2.70 | 1t | | Brisbane | 16 Feb |
| 1.86 | | Marina Kuzminykh | SU | 21.5.68 | 1 | NC-j | Kaunas | 24 Jul |

Jnr WOMEN 1986

| Mark | Wind | Name | Nat | Yr | Pos | Meet | Venue | Date |
|------|------|------|-----|-----|-----|------|-------|------|
| 1.86 | | Heike Siemers | FRG | 5.1.70 | 1 | | Köln | 4 Oct |
| 1.85 | | Li Jun | CHN | -.-.69 | 1 | | Beijing | 12 Apr |
| 1.85 | | Liu Qian | CHN | -.-.68 | 1 | | Tianjing | 8 May |
| 1.85 | | Britta Vörös | GDR | 4.12.68 | 1 | | Neubrandenburg | 4 May |
| 1.85 | | Peggy Odita | USA | 2.1.68 | 1 | | Fort Wayne | 14 Jun |
| 1.85 | | Debora Marti | UK | 14.4.68 | 2 | v Oce-j | Swansea | 28 Jun |
| 1.85 | | Heike Balck | GDR | 19.8.70 | 1 | | Karl-Marx-Stadt | 25 Jul |

# LONG JUMP

| Mark | Wind | Name | Nat | Yr | Pos | Meet | Venue | Date |
|------|------|------|-----|-----|-----|------|-------|------|
| 6.70 | -1.1 | Patricia Bille | GDR | 20.12.68 | 1 | WJ | Athinai | 19 Jul |
| 6.64 | 1.3 | Anu Kalyurand | SU | 16.4.69 | 2 | | Riga | 30 May |
| 6.60 | 2.0 | Tatyana Ter-Mesrobyan | SU | 12.5.68 | | | Leningrad | 26 Jun |
| 6.54 | | Mirela Belu | ROM | 16.12.70 | 3 | | Pitesti | 28 Jun |
| 6.48 | 1.7 | Anke Schmidt | GDR | 5.2.68 | 1 | | Berlin | 10 Jul |
| 6.47 | 0.2 | Tatyana Ilyina | SU | 8.8.68 | 4 | | Krasnodar | 21 Jun |
| 6.43 | | Mieke v.d. Kolk | HOL | 15.4.68 | 2 | | Vught | 3 Aug |
| 6.42 | 1.2 | Carlette Guidry | USA | 4.9.68 | 1 | PAG-j | Winter Park | 5 Jul |
| 6.40 | -0.4 | Svetla Dimitrova | BUL | 27.1.70 | M | Balk G | Ljubljana | 7 Sep |
| 6.39 | | Katalin Csapó | HUN | 19.11.69 | 1 | v FRG-j | Miskolc | 15 Jun |
| 6.38i | | Irina Privalova | SU | 22.11.68 | 2 | v GDR-j | Moskva | 16 Feb |
| 6.38 | 1.6 | Maddette Smith | USA | 15.1.68 | 3 | TAC-j | Towson | 28 Jun |
| 6.37 | 0.9 | Mariana Khristova | BUL | 8.7.68 | 1 | | Ruse | 7 Jun |
| 6.37 | | Katrin Sasse | GDR | 3.07.68 | 2 | v SU-j | Karl-Marx-Stadt | 10 Aug |
| 6.37 | | Birgit Schertel | FRG | 28.5.68 | | | Voherstruuss | 5 Oct |
| 6.36 | | Olimpia Costantea | ROM | 15.12.68 | 1 | NC-j | Bucuresti | 7 Jun |
| 6.34 | | Gabriela Sanchea | ROM | 10.12.68 | 1 | | Bucuresti | 13 Sep |
| 6.33 | 0.8 | Caroline Missoudan | FRA | 22.4.68 | 4 | WJ | Athinai | 19 Jul |
| 6.30 | | Ulrike Kubla | FRG | 18.9.68 | 2 | vHUN-j | Mislolc | 15 Jun |
| 6.29 | | Hanna Horyd | POL | 25.1.68 | 1 | Poznan | 10 May | |
| 6.29 | | Henriette Nedelcu | ROM | 13.3.68 | | | Bucuresti | 17 May |
| A6.29 | | Niurka Montalvo | CUB | 4.6.68 | 1 | | Ciudad México | 29 Jun |

Wind-assisted

| Mark | Wind | Name | Nat | Yr | Pos | Meet | Venue | Date |
|------|------|------|-----|-----|-----|------|-------|------|
| 6.51 | 4.8 | Anke Schmidt | GDR | 5.2.68 | H | | Neubrandenburg | 4 May |
| 6.48 | | Maddete Smith | USA | 15.1.68 | 1 | | Quartz Hill | 17 Apr |
| 6.48 | 2.7 | Svetla Dimitrova | BUL | 27.1.70 | H | Drz | Neubrandenburg | 3 Aug |
| 6.47 | 2.9 | Fiona May | UK | 12.12.69 | 1 | vOce-j | Swansea | 28 Jun |
| 6.47 | 3.7 | Carlette Giudry | USA | 4.9.68 | 1 | TAC-j | Towson | 28 Jun |
| 6.39 | 4.2 | Caroline Missoudan | FRA | 22.4.68 | 1 | NC-j | Montgeron | 5 Jun |
| 6.38 | 3.2 | Tonya Sedwick | USA | 24.7.69 | 2 | TAC-j | Towson | 28 Jun |

# SHOT

| Mark | Name | Nat | Yr | Pos | Meet | Venue | Date |
|------|------|-----|-----|-----|------|-------|------|
| 19.11 | Stephanie Storp | FRG | 28.11.68 | 3 | | Fürth | 15 Jun |
| 19.08 | Ilke Wyludda | GDR | 28.3.69 | 1 | v SU-j | Karl-Marx-Stadt | 9 Aug |
| 18.58 | Heike Rohrmann | GDR | 22.2.69 | 1 | | Berlin | 10 Jul |
| 18.37 | Ines Wittich | GDR | 14.12.69 | 4 | | Berlin | 4 Jul |
| 17.50i | Anna Romanova | SU | 9.3.68 | 1 | v GDR-j | Moskva | 16 Feb |
| 17.43 | | | | 1 | | Simferopol | 23 May |
| 17.41 | Snezhana Pishmanova | BUL | 4.3.68 | 2 | | Pleven | 29 Jun |
| 17.15 | Nadezhda Lukiniv | SU | 14.5.68 | 1 | | Rovno | 12 Jun |
| 17.06 | Jana Capatina | ROM | 12.1.68 | 1 | | Bucuresti | 31 Aug |
| 16.76 | Svetlana Kriveleva | SU | 16.5.69 | 4 | v GDR-j | Karl-Marx-Stadt | 9 Aug |
| 16.75 | Anastasia Pavlova | SU | 16.6.68 | 6 | | Leselidze | 18 May |
| 16.70 | Olga Vdovichenko | SU | -.-.68 | 2 | | Kaunas | 3 Jun |
| 16.62 | Natalya Lisetskaya | SU | 9.1.68 | 2 | NC-j | Kaunas | 19 Jun |

| Mark | Name | Nat | Yr | Pos | Meet | Venue | Date |
|---|---|---|---|---|---|---|---|
| 16.12 | Natalya Scheshkina | SU | −.−.68 | 4 | | Simferopol | 24 May |
| 15.86 | Min Chunfeng | CHN | 18.3.69 | 1 | v Jap | Tianjing | 28 Aug |
| 15.73 | Viktoriya Pavlish | SU | −.−.69 | 7 | | Simferopol | 23 May |
| 15.65 | Mihaela Oana | ROM | 14.1.68 | 5 | | Pitesti | 20 Jul |
| 15.63 | Elena Ghilencea | ROM | 17.5.69 | 2 | v US−j | Pitesti | 11 Jul |
| 15.47 | Jana Günther | GDR | 7.1.68 | 3 | NC−j | Cottbus | 27 Jul |
| 15.39 | Astrid Kumbernuss | GDR | 5.2.70 | 1 | NC−y | Halle | 20 Jul |
| 15.35 | Diana Stoyanova | BUL | 5.1.69 | 3 | | Varna | 18 May |

## DISCUS

| Mark | Name | Nat | Yr | Pos | Meet | Venue | Date |
|---|---|---|---|---|---|---|---|
| 65.86 | Ilke Wyludda | GDR | 28.3.69 | 1 | Drz | Neubrandenburg | 1 Aug |
| 64.34 | Franka Dietzsch | GDR | 2.4.68 | 1 | | Neubrandenburg | 3 May |
| 63.42 | Jana Günther | GDR | 7.1.68 | 1 | | Budapest | 19 Jul |
| 58.28 | Stephanie Storp | FRG | 28.11.68 | 1B | | Rhede | 2 Jul |
| 56.74 | Cristina Boit | ROM | 14.5.68 | 5 | | Bucuresti | 24 May |
| 55.10 | Min Chunfeng | CHN | 18.3.69 | | | Beijing | 29 Mar |
| 55.08 | Xiao Yanling | CHN | −.−.68 | | | Nanjing | 11 Oct |
| 55.02 | Ines Wittich | GDR | 14.11.69 | 3 | NC−j | Cottbus | 27 Jul |
| 54.32 | Irina Yurchenko | SU | −.−.68 | | | | |
| 53.92 | Astrid Kumbernuss | GDR | 5.2.70 | 2 | Drz | Neubrandenburg | 1 Aug |
| 53.38 | Idalmis Leyva | CUB | 25.7.68 | 2 | | Habana | 30 May |
| 52.88 | Natalya Yevstifeyeva | SU | −.−.68 | | | Montelimar | 21 Sep |
| 52.76 | Agnes Teppe | FRA | 4.7.68 | 1 | | Montelimar | 21 Sep |
| 52.72 | Marion Kunze | GDR | 28.10.69 | 1 | NC−j | Halle | 12 Jul |
| 52.52 | Michelle Brotherton | CAN | 5.6.68 | 1 | | Scarborough | 20 May |
| 52.48 | Yelena Nikitenko | SU | −.−.68 | | | | |
| 52.44 | Daniela Gheorghe | ROM | 17.5.68 | 7 | | Bucuresti | 24 May |
| 51.80 | Alice Matějková | CS | 11.5.69 | 1 | v GDR−j | Praha | 2 Jul |
| 51.80 | Alla Kokhan | SU | −.−.70 | | | Vasilkiv | 6 Oct |
| 51.40 | Jana Lauren | GDR | 28.6.70 | 1 | | Berlin | 22 May |

## JAVELIN

| Mark | Name | Nat | Yr | Pos | Meet | Venue | Date |
|---|---|---|---|---|---|---|---|
| 66.52 | Alexandra Beck | GDR | 13.6.68 | 1 | | Chania | 24 May |
| 64.56 | Xiomara Rivera | CUB | 24.12.68 | 1 | | Ciudad México | 26 Jun |
| 61.70 | Anja Reiter | GDR | 15.7.69 | 1 | | Neubrandenburg | 4 May |
| 60.74 | Sun Xiurong | CHN | 27.3.69 | 1 | Asi−j | Djakarta | 5 Dec |
| 59.40 | Karen Hough | UK | 2.5.68 | Q | EC | Stuttgart | 28 Aug |
| 58.52 | Naomi Tokuyama | Jap | 22.10.68 | 1 | | Kofu | 16 Oct |
| 56.56 | Christine Riewe | GDR | 26.5.70 | 2 | Drz | Neubrandenburg | 2 Aug |
| 56.46 | Susanne Riewe | GDR | 26.5.70 | 3 | Drz | Neubrandenburg | 2 Aug |
| 55.70 | Tatyana Shikolenko | SU | 10.5.68 | 4 | WJ | Athinai | 19 Jul |
| 55.12 | Natalya Turkhunova | SU | 4.12.68 | 2 | | Donyetsk | 5 Oct |
| 54.90 | Erika Hirit | ROM | 19.1.69 | 4 | NC | Pitesti | 9 Aug |
| 54.80 | Isel López | CUB | 11.7.70 | 3 | | Habana | 31 May |
| 54.68 | Lidia Pezeva | BUL | 2.3.68 | 1 | NC−j | Sofia | 6 Jul |
| 54.56 | Irina Maslova | SU | −.−.69 | 1 | | Sochi | 23 Feb |
| 54.48 | Stefania Galbiati | ITA | 8.1.69 | 1 | | Caravaggio | 18 May |
| 54.24 | Aurica Bujnita | ROM | 13.12.68 | 5 | NC | Pitesti | 9 Aug |
| 53.88 | Valentina Sirbov | ROM | 30.6.68 | 1 | | Constanta | 30 Jun |
| 53.86 | Keiko Takeda | JAP | −.−.− | 2 | Asi−j | Djakarta | 5 Dec |
| 53.70 | Ieva Skrastina | SU | −.−.69 | 1 | | Ventspils | 28 Sep |
| 53.66 | Judit Horváth | HUN | 13.2.68 | 1 | | Budapest | 1 Jun |

| Points | Name | Nat | Yr | Pos | Meet | Venue | Date |
|--------|------|-----|-----|-----|------|-------|------|

# HEPTATHLON

| 6048w | Anke Schmidt | GDR | 5.2.68 | 1 | | Neubrandenburg | 4 May |
|-------|--------------|-----|--------|---|---|----------------|-------|
| | (13.93, 1.72, 12.65, 24.11, 6.51w, 35.92, 2:13.91) | | | | | | |
| 5900 | | | | 3 | WJ | Athinai | 19 Jul |
| | (13.81, 1.73, 11.86, 23.93, 6.30, 30.70, 2:12.23) | | | | | | |
| 6041 | Svetla Dimitrova | BUL | 27.1.70 | 1 | WJ | Athinai | 19 Jul |
| | (13.85, 1.88, 10.12, 24.32, 6.26, 37.16, 2:12.29) | | | | | | |
| 5953 | Marina Shcherbina | SU | 5.1.68 | 2 | WJ | Athinai | 19 Jul |
| | (14.46, 1.79, 13.01, 25.70, 5.97, 47.32, 2:16.40) | | | | | | |
| 5900 | Peggy Beer | GDR | 15.9.69 | 2 | | Neubrandenburg | 4 May |
| | (13.93, 1.78, 11.64, 24.37, 5.97, 36.88, 2:12.44) | | | | | | |
| 5773 | Iustina Nicolescu | ROM | 26.1.69 | 1 | | Bucuresti | 16 Sep |
| | (14.56, 1.73, 14.68, 26.03, 6.19, 43.72, 2:29.47) | | | | | | |
| 5647 | Margarita Dunayeva | SU | 14.5.68 | 2 | | Simferopol | 25 May |
| | (15.15, 1.70, 12.34, 26.40, 6.04, 49.66, 2:21.24) | | | | | | |
| 5646w | Sharon Jaklofsky-Smith | AUS | 30.9.68 | 1 | | Melbourne | 9 Feb |
| | (13.9w, 1.79, 12.59, 25.2, 6.08, 34.12, 2:25.9) | | | | | | |
| 5629 | Yelena Petushkova | SU | 19.8.69 | 3 | | Simferopol | 25 May |
| | (14.15, 1.70, 12.27, 25.78, 5.81, 37.04, 2:13.21) | | | | | | |
| 5626 | Ionica Domniteanu | ROM | 8.1.69 | 6 | NC | Pitesti | 8 Aug |
| | (14.20, 1.68, 13.82, 25.09, 5.82, 37.66, 2:24.16) | | | | | | |
| 5619 | Kerstin Reinhardt | FRG | 24.6.69 | 1 | v 3N-j | Antony | 15 Jun |
| | (14.40, 1.72, 10.05, 25.21, 5.93, 38.34, 2:25.11) | | | | | | |
| 5592 | Irina Ilyicheva | SU | 27.3.68 | 4 | NC-j | Kaunas | 21 Jul |
| | (14.23, 1.73, 11.10, 24.99, 5.97, 31.94, 2:13.64) | | | | | | |
| 5536 | Virge Viss | SU | 31.3.68 | 4 | | Simferopol | 25 May |
| | (14.55, 1.70, 10.75, 25.63, 5.81, 43.36, 2:18.38) | | | | | | |
| 5526 | Sylvia Tornow | FRG | 6.2.69 | 2 | v3N-j | Antony | 15 Jun |
| | (14.31, 1.69, 13.08, 25.03, 5.48, 38.20, 2:24.98) | | | | | | |
| 5514 | Natalya Mostibrodskaya | SU | -.-.69 | 1 | | Kiyev | 3 Jul |
| | (14.8, 1.60, 13.97, 26.0, 5.88, 42.65, 2:18.6) | | | | | | |
| 5508 | Tina Tättyä | FIN | 12.11.68 | 5 | WJ | Athinai | 19 Jul |
| | (14.39, 1.79, 12.46, 25.62, 5.72, 34.14, 2:23.59) | | | | | | |
| 5498 | Zhanna Lukyanova | SU | -.-.68 | 5 | | Kaunas | 21 Jul |
| | ( | | | | | ) | |
| 5496 | Yelena Volf | SU | 2.3.69 | 1 | | Leningrad | 11 Ju |
| | (14.36, 1.67, 11.88, 25.49, 6.11, 38.90, 2:28.19) | | | | | | |
| 5481 | Heide Zuber | FRG | 7.5.68 | 8 | | Hannover | 20 Ju |
| | (14.22, 1.75, 11.77, 25.92, 5.69, 36.26, 2:20.58) | | | | | | |

# 5000 METRES WALK

| 21:33.8 | Wang Yan | CHN | 9.4.71 | 1 | | Jian | 9 Ma |
|---------|----------|-----|--------|---|---|------|------|
| 22:02.75 | Jin Bingjie | CHN | 1.4.71 | 2 | | Beijing | 9 Se |
| 22:05.72 | An Limei | CHN | -.-.68 | 3 | | Beijing | 9 Se |
| 22:17.76 | Natalya Zykova | SU | 31.10.69 | 2 | WJ | Athinai | 20 Ju |
| 22:21.4 | Li Chunxiu | CHN | -.-.69 | 1 | NC-j | Qingdao | 17 Oc |
| 22:29.8 | Olympiada Ivanova | SU | 26.8.70 | 1 | | Dnepropetrovsk | 27 Se |
| 22:30.90 | Maria Cruz Diaz | SPA | 24.10.69 | 1 | | Madrid | 2 Au |
| 22:32.0 | Fu Liqin | CHN | -.-.70 | 2 | NC-j | Qingdao | 17 Oc |
| 22:37.11 | Yelena Sergeyeva | SU | -.-.68 | 2 | | Kaunas | 20 Ju |
| 22:37.46 | Gabrielle Blythe | AUS | 9.3.69 | 2 | | Melbourne | 16 Fe |
| 22:43.23 | Oksana Shchastnaya | SU | -.-.71 | 2 | Drz | Neubrandenburg | 1 Au |
| 22:46.8 | Kersti Tysse | NOR | 18.1.72 | 1 | NC | Fana | 30 Ju |
| 22:54.63 | Valentina Tsybulskaya | SU | -.-.68 | 3 | | Simferopol | 24 Ma |

| Mark | Name | Nat | Yr | Pos | Meet | Venue | Date |
|------|------|-----|-----|-----|------|-------|------|
| 22:54.68 | Emilia Cano | SPA | 4.3.68 | 1 | | San Sebastian | 25 Jul |
| 22.56.7 | Li Shufen | CHN | -.-.68 | 3 | | Jian | 9 Mar |
| 23:02.1 | Yang Suyun | CHN | -.-.69 | 4 | NC-j | Qingdao | 17 Oct |
| 23:06.06 | Mihaela Daugariou | ROM | 5.8.69 | 1 | | Bucuresti | 15 Jun |
| 23:07.2 | He Paogin | CHN | -.-.69 | 5 | NC-j | Qingdao | 17 Oct |
| 23:16.99 | Katrin Born | GDR | 4.12.70 | 1 | | Potsdam | 11 May |
| 23:18.8 | Quo Junxia | CHN | -.-.69 | 8 | NC-j | Qingdao | 17 Oct |

# 4x100 METRES RELAY

| | | | | | | |
|------|------|------|-----|-----|-------|------|
| 43.78 | USA | Guidry, Smith, Liles, Malone | 1 | WJ | Athinai | 20 Jul |
| 43.97 | GDR | Morgenstern, Krabbe, Beisbier, Tillack | 2 | WJ | Athinai | 20 Jul |
| 44.13 | NIG | Iheagwan, Nwajei, Ogunkoya, Onyali | 3 | WJ | Athinai | 20 Jul |
| 44.29 | FRA | Rome, Sidibe, Clachet, Leroy | 4 | WJ | Athinai | 20 Jul |
| 44.58 | USSR | Kosyakova, Kovalyeva, Chebykina, Privalova | 5 | WJ | Athinai | 20 Jul |
| 45.18 | UK | Dolby, Hogg, Clements, Short | 6 | WJ | Athinai | 20 Jul |
| 45.79 | CAN | Scringer, Anderson, Taylor, Penny | 7 | WJ | Athinai | 20 Jul |

# 4x400 METRES RELAY

| | | | | | | |
|------|------|------|-----|-----|-------|------|
| 30.45 | USA | Harris, Prichett, Downing, Vickers | 1 | WJ | Athinai | 20 Jul |
| 30.90 | GDR | Böckmann, Bartl, Prochnow, Sieger | 2 | WJ | Athinai | 20 Jul |
| 32.35 | USSR | Lukashevich, Khripankova, Chebykina, Pesnopevtseva | 4 | WJ | Athinai | 20 Jul |
| 36.61 | CAN | Allen, McDermid, Taylor, Scringer | 4 | WJ | Athinai | 20 Jul |
| 38.63 | ROM | Draghia, Zaituc, Zavelca, Andrei | 5 | WJ | Athinai | 20 Jul |
| 40.62 | AUS | Walker, Allen, O'Rourke, Scamps | 6 | WJ | Athinai | 20 Jul |
| 40.99 | HUN | Koczian, Kovács, Madai, Batori | 3h1 | WJ | Athinai | 19 Jul |

Junior relay lists compiled by Lionel Peters

Jnr WOMEN 1986

## LATE AMENDMENTS TO 1986 WOMEN'S LISTS

WOMEN'S LISTS
```
100m        add  11.2      Zhang Caihua        CHN 65   1      Beijing       16 Aug
                 11.3      Tian Yumei          CHN 65  30 Aug
10000m      add  32:51.0   Pavlino Evro        ALB 65   1      Tirana        29 Nov
400m hurdles add 58.20     M.do Carmo Fialho   BRA 60  13 Jul
                 58.64     Liliana Chala       ECU 65   5 Dec
Javelin     add  59.26     Zhu Hongyang        CHN 64   3      Zengzhou      23 Oct
                 59.12     Song Ruiling        CHN 66   q      Beijing       13 Sep
                 58.24     Deng Guo            CHN 65   4      Zengzhou      23 Oct
                 58.06     Gao Zhiying         CHN 60   7      Beijing       10 May
          56.34 Ma Lu CHN 66 18 Jun,  55.90  Yu Caiyun CHN 67 23 Oct,
          55.40 Sueli Perera BRA 65 13 Jul, 55.28 Zhang Yan CHN 61 12 Ap
```

JUNIOR WOMEN'S LISTS
```
100m    amend 11.3   not   11.30  Yolanda Straugan
1500m   amend 4:11.88 Homneac 19th (also on senior list), 4:15.07 Bicu 21st
3000m   amend  9:04.85    Dorina Calenic
10000m  add   34:10.0    Natalya Vorobyeva SU       .69   2      Alushta        1 Oc
Discus  amend  54.32    Irina Yurchenko   SU             1      Moskva         3 Au
Javelin amend  57.44    Isel Lopez        CUB            2      Ciu.Mexico 26 Ju
```

# INDEX OF 1986 WORLD LISTS

| Name | | Nat | Yr | Ht/Wt | Event | 1986 Mark | | Pre-1986 best | |
|------|------|-----|-----|-------|-------|-----------|------|---------------|------|
| Abashidze | Alexandra | SU | 14Dec58 | 176/105 | SP | 18.75 | | 19.81-82 | |
| Abashidze | Nunu | SU | 27Mar55 | 168/95 | SP | 20.90 | | 21.53-84 | |
| Abt | Gudrun | FRG | 3Aug62 | 180/59 | 400h | 56.36 | | 57.48-85 | |
| Addison | Sue | USA | 28Jul56 | 163/52 | 800 | 2:00.31 | | 2:00.98-84 | |
| | | | | | 1500 | 4:05.13 | | 4:06.91-84 | |
| | | | | | Mile | 4:23.93 | | 4:34.11-82 | |
| Adiru | Evelyn | UGA | 25Feb64 | 164/ | 800 | 2:01.98 | | 2:02.27-85 | |
| | | | | | 1500 | 4:09.61 | | 4:24.46-85 | |
| Afonina | Galina | SU | 63 | | 800 | 2:02.10 | | 1:59.59-85 | |
| Agapova | Larisa | SU | 29Feb64 | 184/80 | SP | 19.26 | | 19.30-84 | |
| - Beleshina | | | | | | | | | |
| Agletdinova | Ravilya | SU | 10Feb60 | 168/58 | 800 | 1:59.37 | | 1:56.1 -82 | |
| | | | | | 1500 | 3:59.84 | | 3:58.40-85 | |
| Ágoston | Zita | HUN | 18Mar65 | 166/52 | 3000 | 9:02.64i | | 9:09.74-84 | |
| | | | | | 10k | 33:20.58 | | 34:14.5-84 | |
| Aiello | Janine | USA | 28Jan59 | | Mar | 2:34:34 | | | |
| Akhrimenko | Natalya | SU | 12May55 | 184/90 | SP | 21.39 | | 21.08-85 | |
| Akimova | Vera | SU | 5Jun59 | 167/62 | 100h | 12.68 | | 12.50-84 | |
| Akhmetova | Zilya | SU | 2Apr61 | | DT | 58.96 | | | |
| Aksu | Semra | TUR | 31May62 | 184/75 | 400h | 57.60 | | 59.5-85 | |
| Alexandrova | Lyubov | SU | 65 | | 100 | 11.34 | | 11.80-83 | |
| | | | | | | 11.1 | | 11.4-84 | |
| | | | | | 200 | 23.23 | | 24.48-83 | |
| | | | | | | 22.9 | | 24.0-83 | |
| Alexeyeva | Lidia | SU | 61 | | 5k | 15:58.94 | | | |
| Alizadeh | Manuela | FRG | 29Jan63 | 172/77 | JT | 62.50 | | 61.20-85 | |
| Alvarez | Rita | CUB | 7Jul66 | 170/71 | DT | 59.00 | | 60.78-85 | |
| Ambraziene | Anna | SU | 14Apr55 | 173/61 | 400h | 56.88 | 56.1 | 54.02-83 | |
| Anderson | Jodi | USA | 10Nov57 | 168/57 | LJ | 6.60i | 6.67w | 7.00-80 | |
| Andonova | Malena | BUL | 6May57 | 168/58 | 400 | 52.00 | | 51.87-80 | |
| Andreyeva | Larisa | SU | 13Jan64 | | HJ | 1.88 | | 1.78-81 | |
| Andreyeva | Svetlana | SU | 24Feb65 | | 800 | 2:01.23 | | 2:02.6-85 | |
| Andruşca | Simona | RUM | 24Mar62 | 178/90 | SP | 19.67 | | 19.41-85 | |
| | | | | | DT | 66.04 | | 67.16-85 | |
| Aniuliene | Audrone | SU | 64 | | 400h | 57.28 | | 58.54-85 | |
| (Račaite) | | | | | | 57.0 | | 56.3-85 | |
| Antonova | Olga | SU | 16Feb60 | 164/54 | 100 | 11.48 | 11.24-82 | 11.09w-83 | |
| Antonyuk | Marina | SU | 12May62 | 182/91 | SP | 20.60 | | 20.19-84 | |
| Aouam | Fatima | MOR | 59 | | 800 | 2:00.17 | | 2:02.0-85 | |
| | | | | | 1500 | 4:05.49 | | 4:17.43-85 | |
| | | | | | Mile | 4:30.69 | | | |
| Araki | Kumi | JAP | 11Oct65 | 153/40 | 5k | 16:04.02 | | 16:18.8-85 | |
| | | | | | 10k | 33:20.75 | | 33:58.2-85 | |
| Arendt | Helga | FRG | 24Apr64 | 178/64 | 400 | 52.22 | | 53.57-83 | |
| Armstrong | Evette | RSA | 21Aug65 | 170/51 | 100 | A11.22 | A11.28 | A11.22w-85 | |
| (de Klerk) | | | | | 200 | A22.42 | A22.76 | 23.0-84 | |
| | | | | | | A22.39w | | A22.66w-85 | |
| | | | | | | 23.17 | | 23.34-83 | |
| | | | | | 400 | A50.57 | | A55.55-85 | |
| Asai | Eriko | JAP | 20Oct59 | 150/42 | Mar | 2:34:47 | | 2:33:43-84 | |
| Ashford | Evelyn | USA | 15Apr57 | 165/54 | 100 | 10.88 | 10.85w | 10.76-84 | |
| | | | | | 200 | 21.97 | | 21.83-79 | |
| Astafei | Galina | RUM | 7Jun69 | 181/62 | HJ | 1.93 | | 1.89-85 | |
| Audain | Anne | NZ | 1Nov55 | 168/53 | 3000 | 9:03.32 | | 8:45.53-82 | |
| | | | | | 10k | 31:53.31 | | 32:21.47-83 | |
| Auerswald | Ingrid | GDR | 2Sep57 | 168/59 | 100 | 11.11 | 11.04-84 | 10.93w-80 | |
| Augee | Myrtle | UK | 4Feb65 | 173/85 | SP | 17.75 | | 17.16-85 | |
| Avdeyenko | Lyudmila | SU | 14Nov63 | | HJ | 1.90i | | 1.95-84 | |
| (Petrus) | | | | | | | | | |

| Name | | Nat | Yr | Ht/Wt | Event | 1986 Mark | | Pre-1986 best |
|---|---|---|---|---|---|---|---|---|
| Avdeyeva | Larisa | SU | 24Oct61 | | JT | 62.96 | | 60.64-85 |
| Azarashvili | Maya | SU | 6Apr64 | 170/60 | 100 | 11.20 | | 11.67-83 |
| | | | | | 200 | 22.51 | | 22.63-84 |
| Babich | Elina | SU | 64 | | 400h | 56.96 | | 57.60-84 |
| Babikova | Yelena | SU | 11Mar67 | | Hept | 5769 | | 5680-85 |
| Backman | Ragne | FIN | 15Mar65 | 177/64 | Hept | 5686 | 5589 | 5635W-85 |
| Baikauskaite | Laima | SU | 10Jun56 | 162/58 | 800 | 1:58.52 | | 1:58.3-85 |
| | | | | | 1500 | 4:02.92 | | 4:03.5-85 |
| Baikova | Skaidrite | SU | 26Apr50 | 174/80 | SP | 18.26 | | 18.75-84 |
| | | | | | DT | 60.42 | | 64.92-81 |
| Bailey | Angela | CAN | 28Feb62 | 157/52 | 100 | 11.40 11.23w | | 11.17-83 |
| | | | | | 200 | A23.02 | | A22.64-83 |
| | | | | | | 23.34 | | 22.75-84 |
| Bailey | Shireen | UK | 27Sep59 | 173/56 | 800 | 1:59.85 | | 1:59.36-85 |
| | | | | | 1k | 2:35.32 | | 2:36.80-85 |
| | | | | | 1500 | 4:10.78 | | 4:16.6-84 |
| Bakare | Airat | NIG | 66 | | 400 | 51.83 | | 53.03-85 |
| Baker | Lorraine | UK | 9Apr64 | 160/47 | 800 | 1:59.67 | | 2:00:03-84 |
| | | | | | 1k | 2:35.51 | | 2:42.11-85 |
| Bakewell | Karen | USA | 12Apr65 | | 800 | 2:00.85 | | 0 |
| Bakulya | Zinaida | SU | 66 | | 400h | 57.58 | 59.73-85 | 59.5-84 |
| Balabanova | Marina | SU | 25Sep64 | | 400h | 55.57 | 56.74 | 56.0-85 |
| Balgurina | Galina | SU | 65 | | HJ | 1.94 | | 1.86i-85 |
| Baptiste | Joan | UK | 12Oct59 | 170/61 | 200 | 23.35 23.18w | | 22.86-84 |
| Baranova | Larisa | SU | 8Oct61 | | DT | 60.26 | | 63.46-84 |
| Barbashina | Elvira | SU | 25Feb63 | 167/58 | 100 | 11.12 | | 11.21-85 |
| | | | | | 200 | 22.27 | | 22.50-84 |
| Barbu | Ana | RUM | 17Dec65 | 164/49 | 1500 | 4:07.26 | | 4:14.45-85 |
| | | | | | 3000 | 8:54.0 | | 9:10.53-85 |
| Barinova | Irina | SU | 61 | | HJ | 1.92i | | 1.90-85 |
| Barksdale | Sharrieffa | USA | 16Feb61 | 162/54 | 400h | 54.90 | | 55.58-84 |
| Barnes | Lacy | USA | 23Dec64 | 165/70 | DT | 58.94 | | 55.70-85 |
| Barnetson | Jayne | UK | 21Jan68 | 177/58 | HJ | 1.88 | | 1.88-85 |
| Barnett – Burkart | Helen | UK | 13May58 | 170/65 | 400 | 52.46 | | 52.13-84 |
| Bartl | Claudia | GDR | 2May68 | 172/56 | 400h | 56.53 | | 56.22-85 |
| Bartzak | Jolanta | POL | 20Mar64 | 165/54 | LJ | 6.74w | | 6.12-82 |
| Bass | Alicia | USA | 4Jan65 | 159/48 | 100h | 13.26 | | 13.56-85 |
| | | | | | | 13.1 | | 13.54w-85 |
| Basson | Ansie | RSA | 31Jul66 | | 200 | A23.25 | | A24.23-84 |
| | | | | | 400 | A52.28 | 55.14 | 54.8-84 |
| Beaugeant | Chantal | FRA | 16Feb61 | 170/61 | 400h | 57.18 | 56.91 | 56.7-85 |
| | | | | | Hept | 6242 | | 6305-85 |
| Beaugendre | Madely | FRA | 22Sep65 | 172/55 | HJ | 1.92 | | 1.88-85 |
| Bebber | Kadi | GDR | 27Sep65 | 176/68 | DT | 61.04 | | 61.72-85 |
| Becatti | Alessandra | ITA | 30Apr65 | 172/56 | LJ | 6.56w | | 6.32-85 |
| Beck | Alexandra | GDR | 13Jun68 | 178/68 | JT | 66.52 | | 61.92-85 |
| Beck | Ulrike | FRG | 31Oct61 | | 5k | 15:57.52 | | |
| Beclea | Violeta | RUM | 26Mar65 | 166/50 | 800 | 1:58.7 | | 2:00.75-85 |
| | | | | | 1500 | 4:04.56 | | 4:11.01-85 |
| Beer | Peggy | GDR | 15Sep69 | 173/55 | HJ | 1.88 | | 1.86i-84 |
| | | | | | Hept | 5900 | | 5479-84 |
| Behmer (Vater) | Anke | GDR | 5Jun61 | 174/62 | 100h | 13.25 | | 13.30-84 |
| | | | | | LJ | 6.79 6.81w | | 6.84-84 |
| | | | | | Hept | 6717 | | 6775-84 |
| Belanger | Renée | CAN | 12Sep62 | | 800 | 2:01.93 | | 2:01.56-85 |
| Belu | Mirela | RUM | 26Dec70 | 172/59 | LJ | 6.54 | | |

| Name | | Nat | Yr | Ht/Wt | Event | 1986 Mark | Pre-1986 best |
|------|------|-----|-----|-------|-------|-----------|---------------|
| Benning | Christine | UK | 30Mar55 | 160/49 | 3000 | 8:56.30 | 8:44.46-84 |
| Benoit | Joan | USA | 16May57 | 160/47 | 10k | 32:35.4 | 32:07.41-84 |
| -Samuelson | | | | | | | |
| Berenda | Sue | CAN | 4Mar61 | 161/46 | 10k | 32:43.49 | 34:14.7-84 |
| Berezhnaya | Larisa | SU | 61 | | LJ | 7.19 | 6.68-83 |
| Berg | Regine | BEL | 5Oct58 | 172/58 | 400 | 52.50 | 52.29-85 |
| | | | | | 800 | 2:01.5 | 2:00.74-85 |
| Bergdahl | Karin | SWE | 6Jan64 | 177/68 | JT | 61.30 | 63.64-85 |
| Bergmann | Mette | NOR | 9Nov62 | 174/80 | DT | 58.20 | 59.40-85 |
| Berkeley | Mary | UK | 3Oct65 | 176/65 | LJ | 6.50i 6.58w | 6.58-85 |
| Besliu | Iulia | RUM | 3Jul65 | 169/51 | 1500 | 4:09.62 | 4:07.07-85 |
| | | | | | 3000 | 8:59.72 | 8:45.36-85 |
| | | | | | | 8:57.05i | |
| Besprozvannaya | Svetlana | SU | 4Sep65 | | 100h | 13.40 | 13.3-85 |
| | | | | | LJ | 6.53 | 6.29-85 |
| | | | | | Hept | 6073 | 5743M-85 |
| Betekhitina | Natalya | SU | 8Sep61 | | 800 | 2:01.1 | 2:02.7-84 |
| Beuge | Barbara | FRG | 11Aug60 | 187/81 | DT | 60.20 | 61.46-82 |
| Beurskens | Carla | HOL | 10Feb52 | 165/45 | 5k | 15:53.83 | 15:46.20-85 |
| | | | | | 10k | 32:40.69 | 32:28.28-85 |
| | | | | | Mar | 2:27:35 | 2:27:50-85 |
| Beyer | Monika | GDR | 27Jan65 | 173/54 | LJ | 6.49w | 6.53-83 |
| Biba | Iris | FRG | 27May64 | 168/44 | 3000 | 8:54.99 | 9:16.71-85 |
| | | | | | 5k | 15:36.68 | |
| Bibernell | Ines | GDR | 21Jul65 | 168/58 | 1500 | 4:07.64 | 4:05.64-85 |
| - Obst | | | | | 3000 | 8:49.80 | 9:00.30-85 |
| | | | | | 5k | 15:27.05 | 0 |
| | | | | | 10k | 32:32.28 | 32:45.58-85 |
| Bienias | Andrea | GDR | 11Nov59 | 180/68 | HJ | 1.98i | 1.99i-82 |
| | | | | | | 1.97 | 1.97-83 |
| Bierka | Lidia | POL | 13Aug60 | 178/69 | LJ | 6.66 | 6.38-84 6.57w-85 |
| | | | | | Hept | 6125 | 5785-84 |
| Bikbulatova | Anfisa | SU | 1Mar65 | | 400h | 57.89 57.2 | |
| Bille | Patricia | GDR | 20Dec68 | 174/52 | LJ | 6.70 | 6.48-85 |
| Bily | Laurence | FRA | 5May63 | 168/58 | 100 | 11.33 | 11.35-82 11.2-83 |
| | | | | | 200 | 23.31 | 23.33-82 |
| Bimbaite | Danguole | SU | 10Dec62 | 184/82 | SP | 20.20 | 19.77-84 |
| Bizbac | Daniela | RUM | 21Aug67 | 172/60 | 100h | 13.32 | 13.65-84 |
| Błaszak | Genowefa | POL | 22Aug57 | 168/56 | 400 | 50.70 | 50.89 50.7-85 |
| | | | | | 400h | 54.47 | 54.27-85 |
| Bletzsch | Yvette | GDR | 22Aug65 | 168/55 | 800 | 1:59.43 | 2:00.45-85 |
| | | | | | 1500 | 4:05.12 | 4:12.97-85 |
| Blokziel | Gerda | HOL | 11Feb61 | | JT | 58.22 | 55.32-85 |
| Bluntson | Phyllis | USA | 24Apr59 | 188/65 | HJ | 1.88 | 1.92-82 |
| Boborova | Natalya | SU | 12Feb59 | 168/53 | 1500 | 4:03.09 | 4:00.62-84 |
| | | | | | 10k | 33:08.10 | 32:38.43-82 |
| Bochina | Natalya | SU | 4Jan62 | 173/62 | 200 | 22.60 | 22.19-80 |
| | | | | | 400 | 51.95 | 51.47-81 |
| Boegman | Nicole | AUS | 5Mar67 | 174/65 | LJ | 6.55 6.63w | 6.55 6.71w-83 |
| Bogacheva | Irina | SU | 30Apr62 | 164/54 | Mar | 2:34:09 | 2:35:27-85 |
| Bolden | Jeanette | USA | 26Jan60 | 174/62 | 100 | 11.08 | 11.09-85 |
| Bolden | Mary | USA | 11Nov64 | 165/51 | 100 | 11.36 | 11.34-84 |
| | | | | | | 11.17w | 11.23w-84 |
| | | | | | 200 | 23.12 | 23.00-84 |
| Bondarenko | Olga | SU | 2Jun60 | 154/40 | 1500 | 4:05.99 | 4:06.2 -84 |
| | | | | | 2k | 5:40.15 | 5:48.0-85 |
| | | | | | 3000 | 8:33.99 | 8:36.20-85 |
| | | | | | 5k | 15:03.51 | 14:55.76-85 |
| | | | | | 10k | 30:57.21 | 31:13.78-84 |

| Name | | Nat | Yr | Ht/Wt | Event | 1986 Mark | Pre-1986 best |
|---|---|---|---|---|---|---|---|
| Bonnet | Françoise | FRA | 8Apr57 | 163/48 | Mar | 2:32:32 | 2:33:44-85 |
| Bopf | Deann | AUS | 13Feb62 | 167/47 | HJ | 1.89 | 1.90-85 |
| Bordyugova | Natalya | SU | 15Apr61 | 174/61 | 100h | 13.27 | 13.38-85 12.8-84 |
| Borgschulze | Claudia | FRG | 9Feb64 | 160/47 | 5k | 16:05.60 | |
| Bornet | Sylvie | FRA | 21Jan60 | 154/37 | Mar | 2:31:43 | 2:34:05-85 |
| Borralho | Rita | POR | 21Mar54 | 165/55 | Mar | 2:35:37 | 2:35:43-84 |
| Botes | Zelda | RSA | 18Jul68 | | 800 | 2:01.4 | 2:05.43-85 |
| Bothma | Myrtle | RSA | 18Feb64 | 174/57 | 400 | A50.12 | A51.40-85 |
| (Simpson) | | | | | | 51.74 | 52.00-85 |
| | | | | | 400h | A53.74 | A55.74-83 |
| | | | | | | 54.86 | 56.25-84 |
| Bouza | Herminia | CUB | 25Sep65 | 170/74 | JT | 58.12 | 60.10-85 |
| Boxer | Christina | UK | 25Mar57 | 164/51 | 800 | 2:01.40 | 1:59.05-79 |
| - Cahill | | | | | 1k | 2:35.84 | 2:34.92-85 |
| | | | | | 1500 | 4:07.74 | 4:00.57-84 |
| Boyle | Janet | UK | 25Jul63 | 178/58 | HJ | 1.91 | 1.86-85 |
| Bozhanova | Sofia | BUL | 4Oct67 | 172/52 | LJ | 6.71 | 6.68-85 |
| Bradu | Elisabet | SU | 27Oct54 | 157/44 | 5k | 15:58.53 | 16:08.76-85 |
| | | | | | 10k | 32:33.19 | 32:25.62-85 |
| Bramhoff | Sabine | FRG | 1Nov64 | 180/67 | HJ | 1.89i 1.88 | 1.86-84 |
| Branney | Sandra | UK | 30Apr54 | | Mar | 2:37:29 | 2:45:06-85 |
| Branta-Easker | Cathy | USA | 6Jan63 | 165/50 | 3000 | 8:55.61i | 8:49.64-85 |
| Braun | Sabine | FRG | 19Jun65 | 172/60 | LJ | 6.63i | 6.73-85 |
| | | | | | Hept | 6418 | 6436-84 |
| Breder | Andrea | FRG | 7Dec64 | 167/49 | Hept | 5779 | 5641-85 |
| Breiding | Lisa | USA | 26Nov66 | | 5k | 16:01.57 | |
| Bremser | Cindy | USA | 5May53 | 162/51 | 1500 | 4:11.37 | 4:04.09-85 |
| | | | | | 3000 | 8:46.56 | 8:38.60-84 |
| | | | | | 5k | 15:11.78 | 15:19.50-85 |
| Briesenick | Ilona | GDR | 24Sep56 | 180/94 | SP | 19.48 | 22.45-80 |
| Brigadnaya | Galina | SU | 30Oct58 | 175/57 | HJ | 1.96i 1.96 | 1.96-85 |
| Brill | Debbie | CAN | 10Mar53 | 177/60 | HJ | 1.97i | 1.99i-82 |
| | | | | | | 1.89 | 1.98-84 |
| Brisco-Hooks | Valerie | USA | 6Jul60 | 170/61 | 100 | 10.99 | 11.01-85 |
| | | | | | 200 | 22.24 | 21.81-84 |
| | | | | | 400 | 50.21 | 48.83-84 |
| Brown | Alice | USA | 20Sep60 | 157/58 | 100 | 11.06 10.84w | 11.02-85 |
| | | | | | 200 | 22.88 | 22.41-83 |
| Brown | Dorothea | USA | 15Mar64 | 160/52 | LJ | 6.62w | 6.26-83 6.59w-82 |
| Brown-King | Judi | USA | 14Jul61 | 180/67 | 400h | 55.20 | 54.38-85 |
| Browne | Vanessa | AUS | 5Jan63 | 170/53 | HJ | 1.91i 1.90 | 1.94-83 |
| Bruce | Sue | NZ | 25Jul64 | | 3000 | 8:59.0 | 8:56.2-85 |
| Brunet | Roberta | ITA | 20May65 | 168/50 | 3000 | 9:01.55 | 9:08.24-85 |
| Bruns | Ulrike | GDR | 17Nov53 | 173/56 | 1500 | 4:04.85 | 3:59.9 -76 |
| | | | | | 3000 | 8:48.22 | 8:36.38-84 |
| | | | | | 5k | 15:41.46# | 0 |
| | | | | | 10k | 31:19.76 | 32:46.08-84 |
| Bryant | Rosalyn | USA | 7Jan56 | 168/58 | 400h | 56.57 | |
| Buballa | Anna | FRG | 25Jul54 | 169/57 | LJ | 6.54i 6.49 | 6.64 6.70w-85 |
| Budavári | Éva | HUN | 30Jul53 | 166/65 | JT | 61.64 | 60.86-84 |
| Budd | Zola | UK | 26May66 | 161/43 | 800 | 2:02.55$ | 2:00.9 -84 |
| | | | | | 1500 | 4:01.93 | 3:59.96-85 |
| | | | | | Mile | 4:27.5# | 4:17.57-85 |
| | | | | | 2k | 5:30.19 | 5:33.15-84 |
| | | | | | 3000 | 8:34.43 | 8:28.83-85 |
| Bułkowska | Danuta | POL | 31Jan59 | 177/59 | HJ | 1.96 | 1.97-84 |
| Bulteau | Christelle | FRA | 23Jul63 | 159/52 | 200 | 23.36 | 23.53-85 23.39w-84 |
| Burgárová | Elena | CS | 13Nov52 | 168/65 | JT | 60.02 | 66.56-84 |
| Burina | Marina | SU | 26Feb62 | 180/90 | SP | 19.03 | 18.85-83 |
| (Chuguyevskaya) | | | | | | | |

| Name | | Nat | Yr | Ht/Wt | Event | 1986 Mark | Pre-1986 best |
|------|---|-----|-----|-------|-------|-----------|---------------|
| Bürki | Cornelia | SWZ | 3Oct53 | 160/53 | 800 | 2:00.99 | 2:01.14-79 |
| | | | | | 1500 | 4:03.38 | 4:02.05-85 |
| | | | | | Mile | 4:24.85 | 4:26.48-85 |
| | | | | | 2k | 5:35.59 | 0 |
| | | | | | 3000 | 8:44.44 | 8:38.71-85 |
| Busch | Sabine | GDR | 21Nov62 | 177/65 | 400 | 50.43 | 49.24-84 |
| | | | | | 400h | 53.60 | 53.55-85 |
| Bussières | Lizanne | CAN | 20Aug61 | 159/51 | 10k | 32:50.29 | 34:40.3-83 |
| | | | | | Mar | 2:32:16 | 2:35:53-84 |
| Bussmann | Gaby | FRG | 8Oct59 | 170/57 | 400 | 51.71 | 49.75-83 |
| | | | | | 800 | 1:58.11 | 1:59.39-83 |
| Butuzova | Lyudmila | SU | 28Feb57 | 184/71 | HJ | 1.92i | 1.98-84 |
| Byelenkova | Natalya | SU | 65 | | 100h | 13.42 | 13.48-84 |
| Byelevskaya | Yelena | SU | 11Oct63 | 174/55 | LJ | 7.31 | 7.00-85 |
| Byelova | Lyudmila | SU | 23Nov58 | 168/59 | 400 | 51.56 | 50.63-84 |
| Byelova | Tatyana | SU | 12May61 | 182/88 | DT | 58.54 | 63.26-83 |
| Byelovolova | Yelena | SU | 6Feb65 | | SP | 18.00 | 17.32-84 |
| Byelyayeva | Lutsia | SU | 22Jun57 | 160/47 | Mar | 2:36:23 | 2:33:54-84 |
| Byelyayeva | Marina | SU | 26Oct58 | | 10k | 32:22.63 | 32:59.08-85 |
| Bykova | Tamara | SU | 21Dec58 | 180/58 | HJ | 1.96 | 2.05-84 |
| | | | | | | | |
| Cady | Carol | USA | 6Jun62 | 170/80 | SP | 17.70 | 17.40-84 |
| | | | | | DT | 66.10 | 63.30-83 |
| Calleja | Mercedes | SPA | 9Jul58 | 161/45 | 10k | 33:20.68 | 33:30.71-85 |
| Cannon | Karen | USA | 19Sep58 | 170/59 | 100h | A13.40 | 13.43 13.33w-83 |
| | | | | | | 13.39w | 13.1-85 |
| Carabali | Norfalia | COL | 21Jan67 | 160/45 | 400 | 52.40 | 52.92-85 |
| Carpenter | Patrice | USA | 25Sep65 | 166/55 | 200 | 23.30w | 23.55-85 |
| Carter | Kym | USA | 12Mar63 | 187/77 | HJ | 1.88i | 1.89-82 |
| Caruţaşu | Nicoleta | RUM | 14Feb64 | 172/64 | 400h | 55.16 | 55.67-84 |
| (Vornicu) | | | | | | | |
| Cavanaugh | Regina | USA | 6Dec64 | 180/84 | SP | 17.70 | 17.26-85 |
| Cazier | Marie-Christine | FRA | 28Aug63 | 178/61 | 100 | 11.23 | 11.26 11.12w-85 |
| | | | | | | 11.1 | 10.9-85 |
| | | | | | 200 | 22.32 | 22.75-85 |
| Chapala | Irina | SU | 14Apr64 | | 400 | 51.20 | 53.82-82 |
| Chapman | Maree | AUS | 25Jul63 | 172/55 | 400 | 51.66 | 51.51-85 |
| Chartrand | Celine | CAN | 26May62 | 173/63 | JT | 59.06 | 59.46-85 |
| Chaykovskaya | Yelena | SU | 2Feb63 | 176/58 | HJ | 1.92 | 1.94-85 |
| Cheeseborough | Chandra | USA | 10Jan59 | 165/61 | 200 | 23.14 | 21.99-83 |
| | | | | | 400 | 51.57 | 49.05-84 |
| Chen | Yolanda | SU | 26Jul61 | 169/52 | LJ | 6.80 | 6.83-84 |
| Cherniyenko | Natalya | SU | 1Oct65 | 179/75 | JT | 63.54 | 62.90-84 |
| Chernysheva | Yelizaveta | SU | 26Jan58 | 169/56 | 100h | 12.78 | 12.85 12.6-85 |
| Chervyakova | Svetlana | SU | 16Mar63 | | 100 | 11.36 | 11.30-84 |
| | | | | | 200 | 22.95 | 22.91 22.63w-85 |
| Chesbro | Jan | USA | 14Jul58 | 186/67 | HJ | 1.93 | 1.91-85 |
| Chicherova | Yelena | SU | 9Aug58 | 172/58 | LJ | 6.80 | 6.94-84 |
| Chidu | Tudoriţa | RUM | 17Oct67 | 169/53 | 800 | 2:00.62 | 2:07.8-84 |
| Chirchir | Selina | KEN | 28Aug68 | 168/ | 800 | 2:01.40 | 2:03.70-85 |
| Chistyakova | Galina | SU | 26Jul62 | 169/54 | LJ | 7.34 | 7.29-84 |
| Chistyakova | Regina | SU | 8Jan61 | 166/49 | 1500 | 4:08.76 | 4:07.70-85 |
| | | | | | 3000 | 8:39.25 | 8:53.50-85 |
| Chistyakova | Svetlana | SU | 9Aug61 | 175/68 | Hept | 6194 | 5865-84 |
| Chiumariello | Assunta | ITA | 1Jan58 | 170/77 | SP | 17.74 | 16.48-84 |
| Chuvasheva | Vera | SU | 59 | | 800 | 1:58.36 | 1:58.8 -84 |
| Chválková | Daniela | CS | 14May61 | 166/50 | HJ | 1.88 | 1.87-84 |
| (Reiská) | | | | | | | |

| Name | | Nat | Yr | Ht/Wt | Event | 1986 Mark | Pre-1986 best |
|------|--|-----|----|----|----|----|----|
| Cinibulková | Olga | CS | 4Apr60 | 168/71 | DT | 60.82 | 60.00-85 |
| Cirulli | Giuseppina | ITA | 19Mar59 | 168/52 | 400h | 57.10 | 56.44-84 |
| Clarius | Birgit | FRG | 18Mar65 | 175/65 | Hept | 6179 | 5961-84 |
| Clark | Joetta | USA | 1Aug62 | 172/52 | 800 | 2:00.2 | 1:58.98-85 |
| Clarke | Jill | UK | 20Jun58 | 163/48 | 10k | 33:27.68 | 0 |
| Clarke | Sharon | CAN | 7Oct63 | 169/45 | LJ | 6.49w | 6.29 6.52w-85 |
| Cliette | Brenda | USA | 5Sep63 | 174/61 | 100 | 11.41 | 11.30-83 11.14w-84 |
|  |  |  |  |  | 200 | 23.07 | 22.81-84 |
|  |  |  |  |  | 400 | 51.75 | 51.92-84 |
| Coates | Camille | JAM | 9Mar66 | 163/52 | 100 | 11.33 | 11.44 11.43w-85 |
|  |  |  |  |  | 200 | 23.29w | 23.61-85 |
| Cofield | Tracey | USA | 28Jul67 |  | 400 | 52.50 |  |
| Colditz | Grit | GDR | 20Apr66 | 175/66 | Hept | 5959 | 5946-85 |
| Colle | Florence | FRA | 4Dec65 | 169/55 | 100h | 13.11 | 13.52-84 |
|  |  |  |  |  |  | 13.1 | 13.2w-84 |
|  |  |  |  |  | LJ | 6.58 | 6.32-84 |
| Colón | María Caridad | CUB | 25Mar58 | 175/70 | JT | 70.14 | 69.96-84 |
| Colović | Slobodanka | YUG | 19Jan65 | 174/59 | 800 | 1:59.63 | 2:01.37-85 |
| Comsa | Helen | SWZ | 1Nov52 | 167/54 | Mar | 2:36:44 | 2:43:29-84 |
| Cong | Yuzhen | CHN | 22Jan63 | 175/85 | SP | 18.69 | 18.93-85 |
| Cook | April | USA | 23Jun65 | 178/57 | 400h | 57.77 | 59.24-84 |
| Cook | Kathy | UK | 3May60 | 180/67 | 200 | 23.11 | 22.10-84 |
|  |  |  |  |  | 400 | 51.88 | 49.43-84 |
| Cooksey | Marty | USA | 18Jul54 | 165/48 | 10k | 32:34.73 | 32:52.91-84 |
| Cooman-Fiere | Nelli | HOL | 6Jun64 | 157/60 | 100 | 11.08 | 11.39-84 11.2-85 |
|  |  |  |  |  |  |  | 11.26w-84 |
|  |  |  |  |  | 200 | 23.03w | 23.95-83 |
|  |  |  |  |  |  |  | 23.54w-85 |
| Cornaţeanu | Camelia | RUM | 23Jan67 | 174/64 | Hept | 6194 | 5473-85 |
| Costa | Silvia | CUB | 4May64 | 179/60 | HJ | 1.99 | 2.01-85 |
| Costian | Daniela | RUM | 30Apr65 | 182/92 | DT | 69.66 | 67.54-85 |
| Council | Rosalind | USA | 6Mar65 | 165/55 | 100h | 13.03 | 13.24-85 |
| (Pendergraft) |  |  |  |  |  | 12.91w | 13.00w-85 |
| Craciunescu | Florenţa | RUM | 7May55 | 184/95 | DT | 65.50 | 69.50-85 |
| Crisp | Laurie | USA | 28Mar61 | 157/49 | Mar | 2:36:24 | 2:37:01-84 |
| Crooks | Charmaine | CAN | 8Aug61 | 175/64 | 200 | A23.36 | A23.30-83 |
|  |  |  |  |  | 400 | 50.84 | 50.45-84 |
| Csöke | Katalin | HUN | 26Jan57 | 173/79 | DT | 58.28 | 63.20-80 |
| Cunha | Aurora | POR | 31May59 | 155/48 | 3000 | 8:57.31 | 8:46.37-84 |
|  |  |  |  |  | 5k | 15:25.59 | 15:06.96-85 |
|  |  |  |  |  | 10k | 31:29.41 | 31:35.45-85 |
| Curatolo | Maria | ITA | 12Oct63 | 147/40 | 5k | 16:06.5 |  |
|  |  |  |  |  | 10k | 32:06.38 | 32:22.93-85 |
| Custy | Maureen | USA | 31Aug55 |  | Mar | 2:34:41 | 2:34:17-85 |
| Cuthbert | Juliet | JAM | 9Apr64 | 160/54 | 100 | 11.24 10.97w | 11.18-85 |
|  |  |  |  |  | 200 | 22.71 | 22.78-85 |
|  |  |  |  |  |  | 22.35w | 22.39w-85 |
| Dainty | Gillian | UK | 24Nov58 | 160/48 | 1k | 2:38.10 | 2:37.82-81 |
|  |  |  |  |  | 1500 | 4:11.09 | 4:07.90-84 |
| Dasse | Bonnie | USA | 22Jul59 | 178/84 | SP | 18.84 | 19.07-85 |
|  |  |  |  |  | DT | 57.84 | 51.76-85 |
| Davidson | Karol | USA | 12Aug65 | 178/53 | 800 | 2:02.04 | 2:03.95-85 |
| Davies | Diana | UK | 7May61 | 175/65 | HJ | 1.93 | 1.95-82 |
| Davis-Knowles | Leisa | USA | 17Mar63 | 168/60 | 400 | 52.26 | 53.16-85 |
|  |  |  |  |  | 400h | 55.90 | 55.70-85 |

| Name | | Nat | Yr | Ht/Wt | Event | 1986 Mark | | Pre-1986 best |
|---|---|---|---|---|---|---|---|---|
| Davis | Patricia | USA | 24Feb65 | 163/56 | 100h | 13.20 | 13.08w | 13.16-85 |
| Davis | Pauline | BAH | 9Jul66 | 168/57 | 100 | 11.27 | | 11.47-85 |
| | | | | | | 11.11w | | 11.1-84 |
| | | | | | 200 | 22.83 | | 22.97-84 |
| Davis | Tanya | USA | 27Jul68 | 155/53 | 100h | 13.40 | | 14.14-85 |
| Davydova | Olga | SU | 17Sep63 | | DT | 58.28 | | 59.20-85 |
| Davydova | Yelena | SU | 16Nov67 | 180/67 | HJ | 1.88 | | 1.86-85 |
| | | | | | LJ | 6.62 | | 6.81-85 |
| | | | | | Hept | 6093 | | 6051-85 |
| Day | Natalie | USA | 11Mar63 | 163/54 | 100h | 13.36w | | 13.72-85 |
| de Grasse | Iris | CUB | 18Aug64 | 172/72 | JT | 63.52 | | 64.90-84 |
| de Vega | Lydia | PHI | 26Dec64 | 170/52 | 200 | 23.35 | | 23.54-81 |
| Debaets | Corinne | BEL | 2Dec63 | 165/55 | 3000 | 8:55.97 | | 8:57.76-84 |
| Debois | Nadine | FRA | 25Sep61 | 173/66 | LJ | 6.81i | | 6.46-85 |
| | | | | | | 6.71 | | 6.70w-85 |
| | | | | | Hept | 6333 | | 6242-85 |
| Degtyar | Marina | SU | 17Jun62 | 183/62 | HJ | 1.94 | | 1.95-85 |
| Delagrange | Ingrid | BEL | 28Jun58 | 165/50 | 3000 | 8:59.24 | | 9:11.2-85 |
| Demsitz | Lene | DEN | 8Mar59 | 164/53 | LJ | 6.67 | | 6.72-85 |
| Dendy | Terri | USA | 8May65 | 168/53 | 400 | 52.12 52.0 | 54.30 | 52.9-85 |
| Denk | Ulrike | FRG | 10May64 | 169/61 | 100h | 13.32 | | 12.84-85 |
| Detlefsen | Linda | USA | 18Oct62 | 165/46 | 1500 | 4:08.00 | | 4:11.16-85 |
| - Sheskey | | | | | Mile | 4:29.49 | | 4:40.80i-84 |
| Devers | Gail | USA | 19Nov66 | 163/50 | 100 | 11.12 10.96w | | 11.19-85 |
| | | | | | 100h | 13.08 | 13.16 | 13.15w-85 |
| | | | | | LJ | 6.57 | | 6.31-85 |
| Didenko | Natalya | SU | 62 | | SP | 17.32 | | 17.29-85 |
| Dietzsch | Franka | GDR | 22Jan68 | 184/90 | DT | 64.34 | | 56.94-85 |
| Didilenko | Yelena | SU | 20Apr61 | 172/55 | 800 | 2:01.96 | | |
| Dimitrova | Anushka | BUL | 6Jul62 | 169/57 | 800 | 2:01.99 | | 2:06.30-85 |
| Dimitrova | Emilia | BUL | 13Nov67 | 170/60 | 200 | 23.17 | | 24.09-85 |
| | | | | | Hept | 6403 | | 6079-85 |
| Dimitrova | Svetla | BUL | 27Jan70 | 172/59 | HJ | 1.88 | | 1.62-85 |
| | | | | | LJ | 6.48w | | 5.57-85 |
| | | | | | Hept | 6041 | | 0 |
| Ding | Fenghua | CHN | 64 | | JT | 60.60 | | 59.60-84 |
| Ditz | Nancy | USA | 25Jun54 | 165/51 | Mar | 2:34:50 | | 2:31:36-85 |
| Dixon | Diane | USA | 23Sep64 | 165/54 | 100 | 11.27 | | 11.50-84 |
| | | | | | 200 | 22.53 | | 22.93-85 |
| | | | | | | | | 22.92w-85 |
| | | | | | 400 | 50.24 | | 50.29-85 |
| Dmitriyeva | Irina | SU | 59 | | DT | 64.46 | | 65.30-84 |
| Doak | Nan | USA | 3Jul62 | 150/41 | 10k | 32:29.86 | | 33:33.03-85 |
| Dogadina | Olga | SU | 28Mar59 | | 800 | 2:01.4 | | 1:59.2 -84 |
| Dodika | Vera | SU | 21Feb59 | | 800 | 1:58.43 | | 1:59.33-84 |
| Dolgaya | Tatyana | SU | 24Nov64 | 174/62 | Hept | 5705 | | 5797M-85 |
| Dominguez | Genoveva | MEX | 3Jan65 | 160/48 | 10k | 33:23.6 | | |
| Domoratskaya | Anna | SU | 17Nov53 | 164/55 | 5k | 15:32.11 | | 15:19.0-83 |
| | | | | | 10k | 32:11.89 | | 31:48.23-82 |
| Donkova | Yordanka | BUL | 28Sep61 | 175/67 | 100 | 11.44 | | 11.27-82 |
| | | | | | 200 | 22.99 | | 22.95-82 |
| | | | | | 100h | 12.26 12.0w | | 12.44-82 |
| Dorguzheva | Galina | SU | 11Feb61 | | DT | 59.80 | | 58.66-83 |
| Dorio | Gabriella | ITA | 27Jun57 | 167/55 | 1500 | 4:07.61 | | 3:58.65-82 |
| Dornhoefer | Sabrina | USA | 2Dec63 | 165/52 | 3000 | 8:57.71 | | 8:59.25-84 |
| | | | | | 5k | 15:44.30 | | 15:42.22-85 |
| Dorofeyeva | Irina | SU | 63 | | 400h | 57.84 | 56.82-84 | 56.8-85 |
| Doronina | Marina | SU | 29Jan61 | 181/60 | HJ | 1.94i 1.92 | 1.97i | 1.96-84 |
| Dörre | Katrin | GDR | 6Oct61 | 170/57 | 10k | 32:02.21 | | 33:00.0-84 |
| | | | | | Mar | 2:29:33 | | 2:26:52-84 |

| Name | | Nat | Yr | Ht/Wt | Event | 1986 Mark | Pre-1986 best |
|------|------|-----|-----|-------|-------|-----------|---------------|
| Draghia | Ana Maria | RUM | 14Nov68 | 172/54 | 400h | 56.57 | 58.16-85 |
| Drechsler | Heike | GDR | 16Dec64 | 181/69 | 100 | 10.91 10.80w | 0 |
| | | | | | 200 | 21.71 | 23.19-85 |
| | | | | | LJ | 7.45 | 7.44-85 |
| Dressel | Birgit | FRG | 4May60 | 172/65 | 100h | 13.37w | 13.84-84 |
| | | | | | HJ | 1.92 | 1.90-82 |
| | | | | | Hept | 6487 | 6144-84 |
| du Plessis | Desirée | RSA | 20May65 | 184/64 | HJ | 2.01 | 1.93-85 |
| Dudkova | Irina | SU | 7Sep59 | 172/66 | Hept | 6007M 5978 | 5968-85 |
| Duginyets | Yelena | SU | 4Dec59 | 176/66 | HJ | 1.92i 1.89 | 1.94-85 |
| Dukes | Pam | USA | 15May64 | 180/85 | SP | 17.28 | 15.72-84 |
| Dulgheru | Mirela | RUM | 5Oct66 | 172/62 | LJ | 6.60 | 6.34-84 |
| Dumitru | Adriana | RUM | 3May68 | 167/54 | 800 | 2:01.83 | 2:03.79-85 |
| | | | | | 1500 | 4:10.84 | 4:14.48-85 |
| | | | | | 3000 | 8:56.72 | 9:13.89-85 |
| Dunayeva | Margarita | SU | 6Apr68 | | Hept | 5647 | |
| Dunecka | Małgorzata | POL | 21Dec56 | 176/64 | 400h | 57.18 | 56.94 55.6-85 |
| Dunke | Angelika | FRG | 28Jun55 | | Mar | 2:36:43 | 2:39:35-85 |
| Dunlap | Kim | USA | 26Jun64 | | 200 | 23.34 | |
| Dunn | Paula | UK | 3Dec64 | 159/43 | 100 | 11.25 | 11.67-85 |
| | | | | | | 11.14w | 11.65w-85 |
| | | | | | 200 | 23.23w | 24.62-84 24.4-85 |
| Duprey | Donalda | CAN | 1Mar67 | 172/56 | 400h | 56.55 | 58.02-85 |
| Düring | Jeanette | GDR | 1Feb65 | 165/51 | 100 | 11.33 | 11.36-85 |
| Duros | Marie-Pierre | FRA | 7Jun67 | 160/45 | 1500 | 4:11.64 | 4:18.34-85 |
| Dzhaleva | Maria | BUL | 6Feb64 | 170/70 | JT | 57.96 | 60.70-83 |
| Dzhigalova | Larisa | SU | 22Oct62 | 176/61 | 400 | 51.60 | 51.60-83 |
| Echevarría | Eloína | CUB | 25Aug61 | 168/63 | LJ | 6.61 | 6.67-83 6.71w-82 |
| Echols | Sheila | USA | 2Oct64 | 165/52 | 100 | 11.15 | 11.43-85 |
| | | | | | | 10.9w | 11.41w-85 |
| | | | | | 200 | 22.90 | |
| | | | | | LJ | 6.69 6.89w | 6.57-85 |
| Eckl | Cornelia | FRG | 2Sep63 | 177/66 | Hept | 5718 | 5647-83 |
| Edwards | Diane | UK | 17Jun66 | 172/55 | 800 | 2:00.60 | 2:02.00-85 |
| Ehlert | Gaby | GDR | 30Jun65 | 179/67 | LJ | 6.74 6.76w | 6.54 6.68w-85 |
| Eichenmann | Genoveva | SWZ | 12Sep57 | 162/52 | Mar | 2:36:41 | 2:38:50-85 |
| el Moutawakil | Nawal | MOR | 15Apr62 | 162/50 | 400h | 55.83 55.7 | 54.61-84 |
| Elloy | Laurence | FRA | 3Dec59 | 169/62 | 100h | 12.69 | 12.79-85 |
| | | | | | | | 12.72w-84 |
| Elsmore | Debbie | NZ | 28Mar58 | | 5k | 16:03.70 | |
| | | | | | 10k | 33:15.0 | |
| Emmelmann | Kirsten | GDR | 19Apr61 | 173/63 | 200 | 22.77i | 22.50-81 |
| | | | | | 400 | 50.43 | 50.07-85 |
| Ene | Mihaela | RUM | 31Oct62 | 166/53 | 400 | 51.66 | 52.21-85 |
| (Rachieru) | | | | | 800 | 2:01.00 | 2:02.65-85 |
| Epps | Arnita | USA | 6Jun64 | 170/58 | 400h | 56.61 | 55.83-85 |
| Ernst | Petra | GDR | 2Aug63 | 182/69 | LJ | 6.65 | 6.51i-83 6.34-84 |
| Ernström | Eva | SWE | 2Sep61 | 170/52 | 5k | 15:49.53 | 15:34.7 -83 |
| | | | | | 10k | 32:51.59 | 0 |
| Etienne | Astra | AUS | 19Jul60 | 171/79 | SP | 17.24 | 17.39 17.75*-85 |
| Ettle | Janice | USA | 3Dec58 | 170/59 | Mar | 2:37:23 | 2:33:41-84 |
| Evanoff | Elena | CAN | 29Feb64 | | 10k | 33:12.1 | 33:59.39-85 |
| Ewanje-Epée | Maryse | FRA | 4Sep64 | 176/63 | HJ | 1.94i 1.92 | 1.96-85 |
| Ewanje-Epée | Monique | FRA | 11Jul67 | 173/62 | 100h | 13.07 | 13.10-85 |

| Name | | Nat | Yr | Ht/Wt | Event | 1986 Mark | Pre-1986 best |
|---|---|---|---|---|---|---|---|
| Faizulina | Gulnara | SU | 65 | | 10k | 33:13.30 | |
| Farmer | Sandra | JAM | 18Aug62 | 173/63 | 400h | 55.89 | 55.75-85 |
| Fastivets | Lilia | SU | 25Apr64 | 174/67 | Hept | 5804 | 5475-85 |
| Fays | Martine | FRA | 3Aug59 | 173/55 | 3000 | 8:52.45 | 9:12.93-85 |
| Fedchenko | Irina | SU | 15Jan66 | 184/95 | SP | 18.88 | 18.10-85 |
| Fedyushina | Valentina | SU | 65 | | SP | 19.19i 18.50 | 19.01-85 |
| Feige | Jasmin | FRG | 20Jun59 | 173/60 | LJ | 6.62i | 6.71i-85 |
| | | | | | | 6.60 6.68w | 6.65-81 |
| Fekete | Ildikó | HUN | 12Nov66 | 166/53 | LJ | 6.56 | 6.56-81 |
| Felke | Petra | GDR | 30Jul59 | 172/63 | JT | 75.04 | 75.40-85 |
| Fernández | Rosa | CUB | 7Oct57 | 162/84 | SP | 17.87 | 18.51-83 |
| Fernández | Tania | CUB | 26Aug67 | 181/59 | 400h | 57.60 | 0 |
| Ferreira Maria | Conceicao | POR | 13Mar62 | 148/40 | 5k | 15:54.01 | 17:11.2-83 |
| | | | | | 10k | 33:21.25 | 33:17.41-85 |
| Ferrian | Daniela | ITA | 12Sep61 | 170/52 | 100 | 11.47w 11.65-83 | 11.3-85 |
| Feuerbach | Cornelia | GDR | 26Apr63 | 172/59 | 400h | 54.13 | 54.64-85 |
| Fibingerová | Helena | CS | 13Jul49 | 179/99 | SP | 20.80 22.50i | 22.32-77 |
| Ficher | Fabienne | FRA | 25Apr66 | 175/59 | 400 | 51.85 | 52.52-85 |
| Fidatof | Elena | RUM | 24Jul60 | 169/52 | 1500 | 4:03.92 | 4:10.05-85 |
| | | | | | 3000 | 8:50.26 | 8:47.60-85 |
| | | | | | 5k | 15:41.83 | |
| Fiedler | Ellen | GDR | 26Nov58 | 176/66 | 400h | 54.76 | 54.20-83 |
| Filatova | Tatyana | SU | 59 | 174/66 | 100h | 13.31 13.43-85 | 13.3 -81 |
| Filatyeva | Svetlana | SU | 3Apr64 | 167/58 | HJ | 1.88 | 1.85-84 |
| | | | | | Hept | 6327 | 6319-84 |
| Filsinger | Heike | FRG | 19Jan61 | 170/59 | 100h | 13.41 | 13.04-83 |
| Finn | Michelle | USA | 8May65 | 165/52 | 100 | 11.20 | 11.26-85 |
| | | | | | | 11.04w | 11.04w 11.2-85 |
| | | | | | 200 | 22.97 23.32 | 22.77w-85 |
| | | | | | | | 22.9 22.6w-85 |
| Fitzgerald-Brown | Benita | USA | 6Jul61 | 179/63 | 100h | 12.84 12.83w | 12.84-83 |
| Flaten | Anne Jorum | NOR | 7May61 | 169/54 | 1500 | 4:06.72 | 4:10.80-85 |
| | | | | | 3000 | 9:00.32 | 9:10.36-85 |
| Fleming (Hamilton) | Sally | AUS | 14May61 | 180/56 | 400h | 56.74 | 57.86-79 |
| Flemming | Jane | AUS | 14Apr65 | 168/56 | 100h | 13.32w | 13.62-85 |
| | | | | | Hept | 5882 6278W | 5901-85 |
| Flintoff | Debbie | AUS | 20Apr60 | 171/56 | 400 | 50.78 | 50.93-85 |
| | | | | | 400h | 53.76 | 54.80-85 |
| Fogli | Laura | ITA | 5Oct59 | 168/50 | Mar | 2:29:44 | 2:29:28-84 |
| Ford | Ann | UK | 30Mar52 | 166/45 | Mar | 2:31:40 | 2:31:19-85 |
| Ford | Lisa | USA | 24Oct66 | 165/56 | 100 | 11.48w | 11.58w-84 |
| | | | | | 200 | 23.23w | 23.5w-84 |
| Forde | Gillian | TRI | 5Nov67 | | 100 | 11.39 11.1 | 11.55-84 |
| | | | | | 200 | 23.14 23.80 | 23.73w-84 |
| Forgács | Judit | HUN | 25May59 | 168/58 | 400 | 51.81 | 51.55-83 |
| Fossatti | Alessandra | ITA | 30Sep63 | 170/55 | HJ | 1.90i 1.88 | 1.89-81 |
| Fourcade | Nadine | FRA | 25Feb63 | 174/65 | LJ | 6.78i 6.77 | 6.79-85 |
| Frantseva | Nadyezhda | SU | 2Oct61 | | SP | 17.48 | 17.71-84 |
| Frederick | Jane | USA | 7Apr52 | 180/73 | Hept | 6230 | 6803-84 |
| Freeman | Kathy | USA | 13Jan62 | 172/54 | 400h | 57.51 | 57.57-84 |
| French-Lee | Sue | CAN | 7May60 | 157/48 | 10k | 32:30.75 | |
| Froget | Nathalie | FRA | 9Jul64 | 170/52 | 1500 | 4:10.81 | 4:18.21-85 |
| Frolova (Stroganova) | Olga | SU | 2Oct64 | 162/54 | 100 | 11.41 | 11.62-85 |
| | | | | | 200 | 23.06 | 23.67-85 |
| | | | | | | 22.9 | 23.3-85 |
| Fudge | Paula | UK | 30Mar52 | 168/54 | Mar | 2:32:25 | 2:35:10-85 |
| Fukao | Mami | JAP | 18Apr61 | 153/43 | 10k | 33:27.45 | 33:54.9-82 |
| Furstenberg | Mari-Lise | RSA | 17Jun66 | 170/58 | 200 | A23.12 | A23.06-85 |
| | | | | | | | 23.60-84 |

| Name | | Nat | Yr | Ht/Wt | Event | 1986 Mark | | Pre-1986 best |
|------|------|-----|-----|-------|-------|-----------|------|---------------|
| Gale | Charmaine | RSA | 27Feb64 | 178/65 | HJ | 1.99 | | 2.00-85 |
| Gallagher | Kim | USA | 11Jun64 | 165/47 | 800 | 2:01.34 | | 1:58.50-84 |
| Galle | Heike | GDR | 20Mar67 | 176/71 | JT | 64.40 | | 59.06-85 |
| Galler | Dagmar | FRG | 20Dec61 | 178/76 | DT | 60.00 | | 61.24-85 |
| Gandy | Simone | UK | 28Jul65 | 172/52 | 400h | 57.56 | | 58.68-85 |
| | | | | | | 57.5 | | 58.3-84 |
| Gaponova | Yekaterina | SU | 30Aug64 | | 400h | 57.11 | 57.0 | 58.95 58.6-85 |
| Garancha | Iveta | SU | 17Sep64 | 183/95 | SP | 17.17 | | 16.47-85 |
| | | | | | DT | 61.22 | | 56.20-84 |
| García | Dulce Maria | CUB | 2Jul65 | | JT | 67.90 | | 67.20-85 |
| Garcia | Esmeralda | BRA | 16Feb59 | 162/52 | LJ | 6.57 | | 6.57-85 |
| Garlipp | Kristina | GDR | 29Sep61 | 167/52 | Mar | 2:32:08 | | 2:42:16-85 |
| Gasser | Sandra | SWZ | 27Jul62 | 169/52 | 3000 | 9:00.16 | | 8:58.31-84 |
| Gates | Julie | UK | 12May59 | | Mar | 2:36:31 | | 2:41:26-85 |
| Gavrilina | Zinaida | SU | 22Sep61 | 178/79 | JT | 64.98 | | 67.00-84 |
| Gavrilova | Olga | SU | 8Feb57 | 176/75 | JT | 59.82 | | 66.80-85 |
| Gaugel | Heidi-Elke | FRG | 11Jul59 | 167/54 | 100 | 11.20 | | 11.15-85 |
| | | | | | 200 | 22.91 | | 22.56-85 |
| Ge | Ping | CHN | 11Jan61 | 169/56 | HJ | 1.89 | | 1.92-83 |
| Geffray (Levesque) | Sylviane | FRA | 6Apr53 | 159/46 | Mar | 2:34:03 | | 2:37:41-84 |
| Geissler | Heidrun | GDR | 16Nov61 | 179/70 | LJ | 6.82i | | 6.73-82 |
| Gendvilaite | Judita | SU | 63 | | 400h | 56.53 | | 61.01 60.1-82 |
| Georgieva (Ivanova) | Nadezhda | BUL | 2Sep61 | 158/48 | 100 | 11.27 | | 11.09-83 |
| | | | | | 200 | 23.21 | | 22.42-83 |
| Gerevich | Svetlana | SU | 20Aug66 | 161/58 | 100h | 13.1 | | 13.72 13.2-84 |
| German | Natalya | SU | 10Nov63 | 171/62 | 100 | 11.36 | 11.1 | 11.42 11.2-85 |
| | | | | | 200 | 23.33 | 22.5 | 23.11 22.7-85 |
| Gerstenmaier - Grönich | Brigitte | FRG | 9Jun60 | 172/58 | 100h | 13.41 | | 13.40 13.36w-83 |
| | | | | | | | | 13.1-84 |
| Ghican | Viorica | RUM | 9Jun65 | 161/47 | 1500 | 4:06.45 | | 4:11.95-85 |
| | | | | | 3000 | 8:54.53 | | 8:55.36-85 |
| | | | | | 10k | 32:26.58 | | 34:00.83-85 |
| Ghile | Margareta | RUM | 13Jul61 | 164/51 | 1500 | 4:08.94 | | 4:07.05-85 |
| Ghioroaie | Gina | RUM | 18Nov58 | 164/57 | LJ | 6.50i | | 6.76-82 |
| Gibson | Sharon | UK | 31Dec61 | 168/77 | JT | 58.22 | | 61.44-85 |
| Giolitti | Florence | FRA | 31Aug66 | 171/53 | 800 | 1:59.32 | | 2:01.77-85 |
| | | | | | 1k | 2:36.67 | | 2:40.1 -85 |
| | | | | | 1500 | 4:08.8 | | 4:10.38-85 |
| | | | | | Mile | 4:28.72 | | 0 |
| Girard | Suzanne | USA | 30Nov62 | 160/47 | 1500 | 4:09.20 | | 4:10.6#-85 |
| | | | | | 3000 | 9:00.45 | | 9:03.7-85 |
| | | | | | 5k | 15:41.77 | | 15:45.86-84 |
| Givens | Randy | USA | 27Mar62 | 165/54 | 100 | 11.45 | | 11.27-84 |
| | | | | | | 11.42w | | 11.06w-84 |
| | | | | | 200 | 22.59 | | 22.31-83 |
| Gizatullina | Nadezhda | SU | 13Mar59 | | 800 | 2:00.7 | | 2:01.5 -84 |
| Gladisch | Silke | GDR | 20Jun64 | 168/56 | 100 | 10.96 | | 10.99-85 |
| | | | | | 200 | 22.07 | | 22.12-85 |
| Glavenko | Larisa | SU | 29Nov63 | | 400 | 52.48 | | 53.86 53.0-85 |
| Gogi | Rosanel | BUL | 12Jul69 | 178/53 | HJ | 1.90i | | 1.85-85 |
| Göhr | Marlies | GDR | 21Mar58 | 165/55 | 100 | 10.91 | | 10.81-83 10.79w-80 |
| Golodnova | Natalya | SU | 14Apr67 | 179/58 | HJ | 1.94 | | 1.94-85 |
| Golubić | Snežana | YUG | 19Aug62 | 180/71 | DT | 61.82 | | 57.24-85 |
| Goncharova | Yelena | SU | 27Mar63 | 179/66 | 400h | 54.93 | | 55.20-85 |
| Gorbulya | Yelena | SU | 65 | | 10k | 33:20.66 | | |

| Name | | Nat | Yr | Ht/Wt | Event | 1986 Mark | Pre-1986 best |
|------|--|-----|----|----|-------|-----------|---------------|
| Graune | Brigitte | FRG | 14Mar61 | 180/70 | JT | 59.24 | 61.90-85 |
| Graves | Rita | USA | 15Jun64 | 176/59 | HJ | 1.90i | 1.85i-85 |
| | | | | | | 1.88 | 1.84-84 |
| Gray | Patti | USA | 27Dec62 | 155/42 | Mar | 2:36:19 | 2:38:19-83 |
| Greene | Debbie | BAH | 24Feb64 | 165/46 | 100 | 11.47 A11.28w | |
| | | | | | 200 | A23.06 23.36 | 23.77-84 |
| | | | | | | | 23.3-85 |
| Gregorek | Chris | USA | 9Jul59 | 170/57 | 1500 | 4:08.02 | 4:09.42-84 |
| Greiner | Cindy | USA | 15Feb57 | 175/62 | Hept | 6208 | 6249-84 |
| Gridnyeva | Tatyana | SU | 8Oct58 | | 10k | 32:29.39 | 32:54.2-85 |
| | | | | | Mar | 2:32:06 | 2:38:47-85 |
| Griffin | Lorna | USA | 9Jun56 | 181/82 | DT | 61.12 | 63.22-80 |
| Griffith | Florence | USA | 21Dec59 | 169/59 | 100 | 11.42  10.99-84 | 10.96w-83 |
| Grigoryeva | Natalya | SU | 3Dec62 | 171/58 | 100h | 12.61  12.89-85 | 12.7-84 |
| Grishenina | Natalya | SU | 66 | | LJ | 6.49 | 6.29-84 |
| Grishkina | Valentina | SU | 13Jul56 | | 400h | 55.84 | 55.79-84 |
| Groenendaal | Claudette | USA | 1Nov63 | 175/67 | 800 | 1:58.55 | 1:58.33-85 |
| | | | | | 1500 | 4:04.86 | 4:08.13-84 |
| | | | | | Mile | 4:25.29 | 4:33.62-85 |
| Grönfeldt | Iris | ICE | 8Feb63 | 172/64 | JT | 59.12 | 58.24-85 |
| Guidry | Carlette | USA | 4Sep68 | 173/61 | 100 | 11.48w | 11.61-85 |
| | | | | | 200 | 22.9 | 23.84-85 |
| Gumerova | Nadezhda | SU | 1Jan49 | 160/47 | 10k | 33:20.66 | 32:50.04-84 |
| | | | | | Mar | 2:33:35 | 2:34:58-85 |
| Gunba | Saida | SU | 30Aug59 | 168/85 | JT | 61.48 | 68.28-80 |
| Gunnell | Sally | UK | 29Jul66 | 167/58 | 100h | 13.11 | 13.24-84 |
| Günther | Sabine | GDR | 6Nov63 | 170/60 | 100 | 11.29 | 11.19-85 |
| (Rieger) | | | | | 200 | 22.76 | 22.37-82 |
| Günther | Jana | GDR | 7Jan68 | 184/81 | DT | 63.42 | 59.76-85 |
| Günz | Gabriele | GDR | 8Sep61 | 182/65 | HJ | 1.98i 1.90  1.96i | 1.95-85 |
| Gurina | Lyubov | SU | 6Aug57 | 166/57 | 800 | 1:57.52 | 1:56.11-83 |
| | | | | | 1500 | 4:06.34 | 4:09.40-81 |
| Guskova | Svetlana | SU | 19Aug59 | 161/50 | 800 | 2:01.54 | 1:59.5 -78 |
| | | | | | 1500 | 4:10.81 | 3:57.05-82 |
| | | | | | 3000 | 8:42.04 | 8:29.36-82 |
| | | | | | 5k | 15:02.12 | 15:19.99-85 |
| | | | | | 10k | 31:42.43 | 31:57.80-85 |
| Gutewort | Doris | FRG | 3Dec54 | 178/75 | DT | 59.28 | 63.60-82 |
| Gutnik | Yelena | SU | 26May65 | 166/52 | 400h | 57.5  60.24-84 | 59.0-85 |
| Gorbunova | Natalya | SU | 30Jan64 | 174/62 | 100h | 13.19  13.41-84 | 13.2-85 |
| Gorbunova | Svetlana | SU | 28Nov62 | 179/64 | HJ | 1.94 | 1.94-85 |
| Górzyńska | Gabriela | POL | 27Feb56 | 166/52 | Mar | 2:33:24 | 2:38:14-85 |
| Govdun | Galina | SU | 23Mar63 | | 400h | 57.36 57.2  57.24 | 56.9-83 |
| Haas | Gerda | AUT | 19Jun65 | 180/60 | 400h | 56.95 | 57.48-85 |
| Hagger | Kim | UK | 2Dec61 | 171/58 | 100h | 13.27 | 13.32-85 |
| | | | | | HJ | 1.90 | 1.88-84 |
| | | | | | LJ | 6.70  6.48-84 | 6.58w-85 |
| | | | | | Hept | 6259 | 6103-84 |

| Name | | Nat | Yr | Ht/Wt | Event | 1986 Mark | | Pre-1986 best |
|---|---|---|---|---|---|---|---|---|
| Háková | Blanka | CS | 6Apr64 | 170/58 | 400h | 57.88 | | 58.95-85 |
| Halldórsdóttir | Helga | ICE | 22Apr63 | 174/60 | 400h | 57.61 | | 58.44-85 |
| Hamrin | Marie-Louise | SWE | 19Apr57 | 167/53 | 3000 | 9:02.32 | | 8:59.11-83 |
| | | | | | 5k | 16:04.33 | | 15:27.96-84 |
| | | | | | 10k | 32:18.40 | | 33:10.11-80 |
| | | | | | Mar | 2:33:49 | | 2:33:53-84 |
| Hanuláková | Gabriela | CS | 6Mar57 | 180/98 | DT | 62.50 | | 64.00-84 |
| Harding | Camille | USA | 19Nov65 | 174/59 | HJ | 1.90 | | 1.90-85 |
| Hare | Anne | NZ | 7Jun64 | 167/56 | 1500 | 4:11.2 | | 4:10.59-85 |
| (McKenzie) | | | | | | | | |
| Hartai | Katalin | HUN | 24Mar63 | 178/67 | JT | 60.36 | | 61.88-84 |
| Hartwig | Heike | GDR | 30Dec62 | 180/95 | SP | 20.72 | | 20.65-85 |
| | | | | | DT | 63.12 | | 61.72-84 |
| Harvey | Alisa | USA | 16Sep65 | 160/48 | 1500 | 4:08.95 | | 4:11.02-85 |
| Haugland | Hanne | NOR | 14Dec67 | | HJ | 1.89 | | 1.87-85 |
| Haupt | Grit | GDR | 4Jun66 | 180/90 | SP | 19.29 | | 19.57-84 |
| Heggli | Rita | SWZ | 3Dec62 | 165/54 | 100h | 13.11 | | 13.16-85 |
| | | | | | Hept | 5880 | | 5983-85 |
| Helander | Tuija | FIN | 23May61 | 172/63 | 400h | 56.17 | | 55.21-85 |
| Hellmann | Martina | GDR | 12Dec60 | 178/85 | DT | 72.52 | | 72.32-84 |
| Helm-Beyer | Susanne | GDR | 24Jun61 | 178/58 | HJ | 1.96 | | 1.97-83 |
| Henry | Cynthia | JAM | 8Jun62 | 168/60 | LJ | 6.75 | | 6.49-85 |
| Henry | Yolanda | USA | 2Dec64 | 168/52 | HJ | 1.89 | | 1.83-85 |
| Herbst | Stephanie | USA | 27Dec65 | 170/50 | 5k | 15:31.09 | | 16:03.48-85 |
| | | | | | 10k | 32:32.75 | | 33:49.77-85 |
| Herczeg | Ágnes | HUN | 28Aug50 | 180/82 | DT | 61.58 | | 65.22-82 |
| Hernández | Odalys | CUB | 4Sep66 | 180/58 | 400h | 57.35 | | 58.43-85 |
| Hesselbarth | Annett | GDR | 4Jun66 | 176/63 | 200 | 23.02 | 23.60-84 | 23.41i-85 |
| | | | | | 400 | 51.19 | | 51.91-85 |
| Hidding | Tineke | HOL | 28Jul59 | 174/62 | Hept | 5966 | | 6104-83 |
| Hightower | Stephanie | USA | 19Jul58 | 164/54 | 100h | 12.96 | | 12.79-82 |
| | | | | | | 12.90w | | 12.78w-84 |
| Hirsch | Monika | FRG | 28Feb59 | 173/62 | 100 | 11.47 | 11.41 | 11.28w-81 |
| | | | | | LJ | 6.68i 6.66 | | 6.65-85 |
| Hochrein | Katrin | GDR | 3Oct66 | 181/70 | Hept | 6003 | | 5554-84 |
| Hoffmann | Susanne | GDR | 23Apr65 | 170/70 | JT | 58.54 | | 59.88-85 |
| Holden | Diane | AUS | 28Oct63 | 161/53 | 100 | 11.0$ | 11.39-80 | 11.22w-83 |
| Holzapfel | Beate | FRG | 9Apr66 | 177/65 | 400h | 56.95 | | 57.62-85 |
| Holzapfel | Brigitte | FRG | 10Apr58 | 183/64 | HJ | 1.90i | | 1.95-78 |
| Homneac | Doina | RUM | 69 | | 1500 | 4:11.88 | | 4:20.29-85 |
| Höss | Christine | FRG | 24Sep62 | | Hept | 5654 | | 5425-85 |
| Hou | Juhua | CHN | 67 | | 5k | 15:37.17 | | |
| Hou | Xuemei | CHN | 17Feb62 | | DT | 63.48 | | 56.70-85 |
| Hough | Karen | UK | 2May68 | 170/65 | JT | 59.40 | | 56.06-85 |
| Hovi | Asta | FIN | 29Jul63 | 181/100 | SP | 17.84i 17.82 | | 17.18-85 |
| Howard | Denean | USA | 5Oct64 | 168/52 | 400 | 51.55 | | 50.87-82 |
| Howard | Sherri | USA | 1Jun62 | 170/53 | 200 | 23.19 | 22.97 | 22.78w-84 |
| Howland | Sue | AUS | 4Sep60 | 180/78 | JT | 69.80 | | 65.74-82 |
| Huang | Donghuo | CHN | 28Aug61 | 169/55 | LJ | 6.62 | | 6.65-85 |
| Huang | Zhihong | CHN | 7May65 | | SP | 18.89 | | 17.51-85 |
| Huart | Helene | FRA | 19Jun65 | 173/60 | 400h | 57.39 | | 56.98-85 |
| Hübel | Michaela | FRG | 6Apr69 | | HJ | 1.88 | | 1.79-85 |
| Huggins | Euphemia | TRI | 24Feb66 | 175/70 | LJ | 6.53 | | 6.15-84 |
| Humphrey | Jackie | USA | 30Sep65 | 163/60 | 100h | 13.32 | | 13.48-85 |
| Hunter | Sophia | JAM | 12Sep65 | 162/50 | 100h | 13.33 | | 13.41-85 |
| | | | | | | 13.06w | | 13.01w-85 |
| Huntley | Joni | USA | 4Aug56 | 173/61 | HJ | 1.89i 1.88 | | 1.97-84 |
| Hutterer | Heidi | FRG | 5Dec59 | 157/46 | Mar | 2:35:55 | | 2:36:38-82 |
| Hyacinth | Flora | VI | 30Mar66 | 172/62 | 400h | 57.55 | | |
| | | | | | LJ | 6.48 | | |

| Name | | Nat | Yr | Ht/Wt | Event | 1986 Mark | | Pre-1986 best |
|------|---|-----|-----|-------|-------|-----------|---|---------------|
| Iacovo | Pia | USA | 24Oct61 | 170/73 | DT | 58.14 | | 58.54-83 |
| Igeh | Comfort | NIG | 63 | | LJ | 6.54 | | 5.99i-85 |
| Ignatova-Kirilova | Nevena | BUL | 1Jan62 | 172/59 | LJ | 6.73 | | 6.59-84 |
| Iheagwam | Tina | NIG | 3May68 | 153/ | 100 | 11.34 | | 11.6-85 |
| Ikauniece | Vineta | SU | 4Dec62 | 169/61 | 100 | 11.50 | | 11.0-85 |
| | | | | | 200 | 23.11 | | 23.00-85 |
| | | | | | 400 | 51.55 | | 52.84-85 |
| Ikonnikova | Galina | SU | 22Oct62 | | 5k | 15:45.4 | | 15:59.30-85 |
| Ilands | Magda | BEL | 16Jan50 | 159/53 | 10k | 33:10.62 | | 33:12.17-83 |
| | | | | | Mar | 2:33:53 | | 2:34:10-85 |
| Ilcu | Marieta | RUM | 16Oct62 | 173/62 | LJ | 6.80 | | 6.87-85 |
| Ilieva | Katya | BUL | 3Jan63 | 165/58 | 200 | 23.34 23.0 | | 23.59-83 |
| | | | | | 400 | 52.13 | | 51.27-83 |
| Ilieva | Tsvetanka | BUL | 1Mar63 | 165/52 | 200 | 22.93 22.8 | | 23.47-82 |
| | | | | | 400 | 52.25 51.8 | | 53.00-82 |
| Inniss | Jennifer | USA | 21Nov59 | 175/61 | 100 | 11.38 | 11.26-84 | 11.1-83 |
| | | | | | | 11.27w | | 11.17w-83 |
| | | | | | LJ | 6.70 | 6.82-82 | 6.85w-83 |
| Ionescu | Valy | RUM | 31Aug60 | 172/64 | LJ | 7.10 | | 7.20-83 |
| Ireland | Mindy | USA | 14Oct51 | 166/52 | Mar | 2:37:43 | | 2:39:08-83 |
| Irving | Lorna | UK | 23Mar47 | 167/54 | Mar | 2:36:34 | | 2:37:19-84 |
| Isaeva | Svetlana | BUL | 18Mar67 | 176/60 | HJ | 1.97 | | 1.93-85 |
| Isphording | Julie | USA | 5Dec61 | 165/48 | Mar | 2:33:40 | | 2:32:26-84 |
| Issajenko | Angella | CAN | 28Sep58 | 167/61 | 100 | 11.24 All.0 | | 11.00-82 |
| (Taylor) | | | | | | 11.08w | | 10.92w-82 |
| | | | | | 200 | 22.80 | A22.25 | 22.37-82 |
| | | | | | | | | A22.19w-82 |
| Ivan (Ilie) | Paula | RUM | 20Jul63 | 170/59 | 1500 | 4:05.19 | | 4:10.84-85 |
| | | | | | 3000 | 8:55.50 | | 8:47.02-85 |
| Ivanova | Yelena | SU | 23Jan61 | 173/67 | LJ | 6.88 | | 7.01-84 |
| Ivshina | Svetlana | SU | 8Jun62 | 171/62 | Hept | 5773 | | 6091M-83 |
| | | | | | | | | |
| Jackson | Alice | USA | 28Dec58 | 159/55 | 400 | 52.10 51.75dq | | 51.90-84 |
| Jackson | Grace | JAM | 14Jun61 | 183/62 | 100 | 11.31 | | 11.24-84 |
| | | | | | | | 11.0-85 | 11.22w-83 |
| | | | | | 200 | 22.39 | | 22.20-84 |
| | | | | | 400 | 50.94 | | 51.69-83 |
| Jacob | Stefanie | GDR | 27Oct65 | 172/60 | 100 | 11.39 | | 11.51-85 |
| Jacobs | Regina | USA | 26Aug63 | 169/48 | 800 | 2:02.05 | | 2:04.38-82 |
| | | | | | 1500 | 4:08.18 | | 4:11.33-84 |
| | | | | | Mile | 4:02.6$ | | |
| | | | | | | 4:29.40 | | |
| Jacobs | Simone | UK | 5Sep66 | 157/50 | 200 | 23.34w | 23.28-83 | 23.01w-84 |
| Jacobsen | Kersti | DEN | 15Feb56 | 171/56 | Mar | 2:32:53 | | 2:34:53-84 |
| Jahn | Bettine | GDR | 3Aug58 | 170/60 | 100h | 13.42 | 12.42 | 12.35w-83 |
| Jakóbczak | Iwona | POL | 5Jul66 | 184/58 | HJ | 1.88 | | 1.83-85 |
| Jakofsky-Smith | Sharon | AUS | 30Sep68 | 170/51 | Hept | 5646MW | | 5445M-84 |
| Jamrozy | Ute | FRG | 19May64 | 172/52 | 5k | 15:50.64 | | |
| | | | | | 10k | 33:14.83 | | 33:35.39-85 |
| Janák | Mária | HUN | 9Feb58 | 180/70 | JT | 59.70 | | 62.10-82 |
| Janota | Jolanta | POL | 6Jul64 | 170/58 | 100 | 11.19 | 11.88 | 11.87w-85 |
| | | | | | | | | 11.6-85 |
| | | | | | 200 | 22.90 | | 24.47-81 |

| Name | | Nat | Yr | Ht/Wt | Event | 1986 Mark | | Pre-1986 best |
|------|---|-----|-----|--------|--------|-----------|---|---------------|
| Jaros | Urszula | POL | 20Feb56 | 163/53 | 100 | 11.20 | | 11.63-85 |
| | | | | | 200 | 23.00 | | 23.08-85 |
| Jeal | Wendy | UK | 21Nov60 | 165/60 | 100h | 13.16 | 13.36 | 13.18w-84 |
| Jenkins | Julie | USA | 12Aug64 | 168/57 | 800 | 2:01.55 | | 2:03.14-85 |
| Jennings | Lynn | USA | 1Jul60 | 165/50 | 1500 | 4:10.87 | | 4:16.81-85 |
| | | | | | 3000 | 8:53.19i | | 8:49.86-85 |
| | | | | | 5k | 15:08.36 | | 15:12.96-85 |
| Jianu | Camelia | RUM | 17Nov67 | 164/50 | 400h | 57.30 | | 58.69-85 |
| Jimramovská | Ludmila | CS | 5Jun58 | 168/54 | LJ | 6.53 | | 6.62-82 |
| Jin | Ling | CHN | 67 | | HJ | 1.89 | | 1.82-85 |
| Johnson | Katrena | USA | 17Feb64 | 179/62 | HJ | 1.88 | | 1.94-85 |
| Johnson | Kerry | AUS | 23Oct63 | 163/50 | 200 | 23.23 | | 23.63-85 |
| Johnson | Latrese | USA | 24Dec66 | 178/54 | HJ | 1.91i 1.88 | | 1.90-85 |
| Johnson | Yolanda | USA | 12Feb68 | 160/56 | 100h | 13.25 | 13.60 | 13.54w-85 |
| Johnson | Zelda | USA | 5Jul64 | 157/50 | 100 | 11.46w | | 11.23-84 |
| Jones | Jolanda | USA | 6Nov65 | 178/63 | HJ | 1.88 | | 1.87-84 |
| | | | | | Hept | 5826 | 5463 | 5765W-85 |
| Jousimaa | Tuija | FIN | 22Sep58 | 171/55 | 3000 | 9:01.75 | | 8:57.00-83 |
| (Toivonen) | | | | | Mar | 2:36:48 | | 2:32:07-83 |
| Joyner-Kersee | Jackie | USA | 3Mar62 | 178/75 | 200 | 22.85 | | 23.59-85 |
| | | | | | 100h | 12.84 | 13.07 | 13.00w-85 |
| | | | | | 400h | 56.27 | | 55.05-85 |
| | | | | | HJ | 1.88 | | 1.87-85 |
| | | | | | LJ | 7.12 7.15w | | 7.24-85 |
| | | | | | Hept | 7158 | | 6718-85 |
| Juha | Olga | HUN | 22Feb62 | 174/56 | HJ | 1.94 | | 1.97-83 |
| Jung | Susanne | GDR | 17May63 | 178/72 | JT | 61.78 | | 66.08-85 |
| Junghiatu | Mitica | RUM | 18Aug62 | 173/55 | 800 | 1:57.87 | | 1:59.20-85 |
| | | | | | 1500 | 4:06.81 | | 4:14.32-83 |
| Jussila | Arja | FIN | 29Apr53 | 171/57 | LJ | 6.49 | | 6.42-83 |
| | | | | | | | | |
| Kaber | Danièle | LUX | 20Apr60 | 160/45 | 5k | 15:42.38 | | 16:12.1-85 |
| | | | | | 10k | 32:16.97 | | 34:36.54-85 |
| Kadas | Eva | RUM | 8Nov59 | 163/54 | 3000 | 8:59.70 | | 9:01.80-85 |
| Kaiser | Natasha | USA | 14May67 | 173/57 | 400 | A51.48 52.29 | | 54.09-84 |
| Kakushkina | Yelena | SU | 63 | | SP | 17.31 | | 16.95-84 |
| Kalinina | Galina | SU | 9Mar62 | | SP | 18.80 | | 17.76-84 |
| Kalinnikova | Natalya | SU | 63 | | 400h | 56.45 | | 56.79-85 |
| Kaljurand | Anu | SU | 16Apr69 | 170/56 | LJ | 6.64 | | 6.47-85 |
| Kancheva | Tsetska | BUL | 7Aug63 | 176/66 | LJ | 6.54 | | 6.71-84 |
| Kane | Missy | USA | 21Jun55 | 164/51 | 1500 | 4:11.77 | | 4:06.47-84 |
| Känsäkangas | Anne | FIN | 21Jun60 | 173/76 | DT | 59.78 | | 64.24-83 |
| (Paavolainen) | | | | | | | | |
| Karczmarek | Agata | POL | 29Nov63 | 177/59 | LJ | 6.81 6.92w | | 6.62-85 |
| Karepina | Zoya | SU | 3Jan61 | 177/77 | JT | 62.48 | | 65.00-85 |
| Karblom | Eva | SWE | 15Jan63 | 177/66 | Hept | 5785 | | 5538-82 |
| | | | | | | 5828W | | 5601W-85 |
| Karopčikaite | Iolanta | SU | 9Sep64 | 167/60 | 400h | 57.01 | | 59.4-85 |
| Kasprzyk | Ewa | POL | 7Sep57 | 164/53 | 100 | 10.93 | | 11.22-84 |
| | | | | | 200 | 22.13 | | 22.42-84 |
| | | | | | 400 | 51.30 | | 53.51-80 |
| Katewicz | Renata | POL | 2May65 | 179/85 | DT | 64.34 | | 63.26-85 |
| Katona | Patricia | FRA | 7Aug60 | 177/77 | DT | 61.86 | | 59.04-84 |
| Kazakova | Albina | SU | 5Jul62 | | HJ | 1.94 | | 1.94-84 |
| Kazakova | Galina | SU | 61 | | 100h | 13.14 | 13.40-85 | 13.1-84 |
| Kelchevskaya | Yelena | SU | 7May55 | 168/53 | 100 | 11.1 | 11.48 | 11.40w-82 |
| | | | | | | | | 11.2 -81 |

| Name | | Nat | Yr | Ht/Wt | Event | 1986 Mark | Pre-1986 best |
|------|---|-----|-----|-------|-------|-----------|---------------|
| Kellon | Gayle | USA | 29Mar65 | 176/58 | 400h | 56.55 | 57.60-83 |
| Kempter | Regine | GDR | 4Apr67 | 180/64 | JT | 67.32 | 63.06-85 |
| Keskitalo | Sinikka | FIN | 29Jan51 | 153/46 | Mar | 2:33:18 | 2:33:53-85 |
| Keszeg | Margareta | RUM | 31Aug65 | 165/51 | 1500 | 4:04.49 | 4:06.65-85 |
| | | | | | 3000 | 8:51.54 | 8:46.44-85 |
| Kharinskaya | Nona | SU | 64 | | 800 | 2:01.6 | 2:00.1-85 |
| Kharkova | Svetlana | SU | 3Jul65 | | 800 | 2:00.68 | |
| Kharlamova (Ivanova) | Marina | SU | 24May62 | 177/62 | 400 | 51.94 51.7 | 50.63-83 |
| Khaustova (Selyutskaya) | Galina | SU | 4Jul65 | | 100h | 13.19 13.0 | 13.43 13.2-85 |
| Khorina-Salak | Anne | SU | 2Aug59 | | DT | 66.42 | 62.40-85 |
| Khorkhuleva | Irina | SU | 15Jul64 | | SP | 18.05 | |
| Khramenkova | Yekaterina | SU | 6Oct56 | 170/54 | Mar | 2:34:18 | 2:32:24-85 |
| Khristosenko | Lyudmila | SU | 14Oct66 | 170/57 | 100h | 12.94 12.9 | 13.00 12.8-85 |
| Khristova-Moneva | Silvia | BUL | 22Aug65 | 168/58 | LJ | 7.00 | 6.76-85 |
| Khristova | Tsvetanka | BUL | 14Mar62 | 175/80 | DT | 72.52 | 70.64-82 |
| Khromova | Margarita | SU | 19Jun63 | 176/57 | 400 | 52.40 52.0 | 52.05-84 |
| | | | | | 400h | 54.57 | 53.58-84 |
| Khval | Irina | SU | 17May62 | | DT | 63.98 | 63.96-83 |
| Kielan | Urszula | POL | 10Oct60 | 177/58 | HJ | 1.92i 1.90 | 1.95-80 |
| Killingbeck | Molly | CAN | 3Feb59 | 170/56 | 400 | 51.70 A51.08-83 | 52.09-82 |
| Kim | Hee-Sun | SKO | 20Apr63 | | HJ | 1.89 | 1.81-82 |
| Kim | Lyon-Sun | PRK | 15Dec69 | | 5k | 15:54.34 | |
| Kim | Sun-Me | PRK | 12May68 | | 5k | 15:50.91 | |
| King | Michelle | USA | 28Jun64 | 168/57 | 100 | 11.38w | 11.43 11.31w-85 |
| King | Mimi | USA | 7Oct66 | 168/60 | 400h | 57.39 | 57.66-85 |
| King-Jackson | Sue | USA | 9Jun58 | 176/55 | 5k | 16:04.68 | |
| Kingma (Volk) | Gail | USA | 16Dec60 | 170/54 | Mar | 2:35:43 | 2:34:09-84 |
| Kinzel | Gisela | FRG | 17May61 | 172/58 | 400 | 50.83 | 51.68-85 |
| Kirchmann | Sigrid | AUT | 29Mar66 | 180/65 | HJ | 1.90i 1.90 | 1.91-85 |
| | | | | | Hept | 5670 | 5944-85 |
| Kirchner | Sylvia | GDR | 7May63 | 168/54 | 400h | 55.98 | 55.86-85 |
| Kirichenko | Tatyana | SU | 65 | | LJ | 6.66 | 6.51-85 |
| Kirkeberg | Grete | NOR | 3Sep64 | 163/46 | 5k | 15:45.98 | 16:57.9-85 |
| | | | | | 10k | 32:37.99 | 35:13.54-85 |
| Kirpa (Tseshkovskaya) | Viktoria | SU | 7Jan61 | | LJ | 6.54 6.67w | 6.52i-85 |
| | | | | | | | 6.43-85 |
| Kiryukhina | Lyubov | SU | 19May63 | 165/57 | 800 | 1:57.18 | 1:58.87-84 |
| Kitova | Svetlana | SU | 25Jun60 | 168/60 | 800 | 2:01.43i | 1:58.08-84 |
| | | | | | 1k | 2:38.12i | 2:37.93i-85 |
| | | | | | 1500 | 4:01.83 | 4:05.77-85 |
| Klebe | Monika | SWE | 21Sep64 | 178/61 | 400h | 57.18 | 59.26-85 |
| Kley | Kathrin | GDR | 19Jul68 | 161/49 | 10k | 33:23.00 | 0 |
| Klimaszewska | Elżbieta | POL | 3Jan59 | 172/53 | LJ | 6.68w | 6.64-84 |
| Klimova | Yelena | SU | 2Jun66 | 180/66 | 400h | 57.57 | 58.07-85 |
| Klinger | Margrit | FRG | 22Jun60 | 167/54 | 800 | 1:59.98 | 1:57.22-82 |
| Klochko | Lyubov | SU | 25Sep59 | 166/54 | Mar | 2:36:18 | 2:48:10-85 |
| Klüss | Daniela | FRG | 18Apr67 | 177/62 | Hept | 5726 | 5726-85 |
| Knabe | Kerstin | GDR | 7Jul59 | 180/70 | 100h | 12.64 12.54-82 | 12.42w-83 |
| Knetsch | Sabine | FRG | 18Dec66 | | 5k | 15:55.82 | 16:33.4-85 |
| Knighten | Chewuakii | USA | 6Aug67 | 166/50 | 400 | 52.26 | 52.17-85 |
| Knisely | Mary | USA | 29May59 | 162/48 | 1500 | 4:09.35 | 4:05.70-85 |
| | | | | | Mile | 4:31.71 | 4:37.5-84 |
| | | | | | 2k | 5:40.50 | 5:56.39-84 |
| | | | | | 3000 | 8:46.18 | 8:43.82-85 |
| | | | | | 5k | 15:22.33 | 16:17.84-84 |
| Koba | Tamara | SU | 24Feb57 | 164/51 | 800 | 2:01.66 | 2:00.0 -80 |
| | | | | | 1500 | 4:05.46 | 4:01.66-81 |
| Kocembová | Taťána | CS | 2May62 | 170/56 | 100 | 11.40 | 11.31-83 |
| | | | | | 200 | 22.92 | 22.47-84 |
| | | | | | 400 | 49.83 | 48.59-83 |

| Name | | Nat | Yr | Ht/Wt | Event | 1986 Mark | | Pre-1986 best |
|---|---|---|---|---|---|---|---|---|
| Koch | Beate | GDR | 18Aug67 | 180/73 | JT | 58.88 | | 49.38-85 |
| Koch | Marita | GDR | 18Feb57 | 171/62 | 100 | 11.44 | | 10.83-83 |
| | | | | | 200 | 22.20 | | 21.71-79 |
| | | | | | 400 | 48.22 | | 47.60-85 |
| Kochetkova | Viktoria | SU | 18Jun67 | | DT | 57.56 | | 58.58-85 |
| Kochneva | Marina | SU | 11Dec63 | 174/69 | JT | 58.82 | | 58.44-85 |
| Koftunova | Lyubov | SU | 15Sep59 | | SP | 18.54 | | 19.80-85 |
| Kokonova | Yelena | SU | 4Aug63 | 172/64 | LJ | 7.00i | | 7.31-85 |
| Kokowska | Renata | POL | 4Dec58 | 170/57 | 3000 | 9:00.24 | | 9:05.94-85 |
| | | | | | 5k | 15:56.19 | | 16:08.94-85 |
| | | | | | 10k | 33:27.95 | | 34:04.66-84 |
| | | | | | Mar | 2:36:11 | | 0 |
| Kolmakova | Irina | SU | 64 | | 800 | 2:00.8 | | |
| Kolovanova | Natalya | SU | 1Aug64 | 172/60 | 100h | 13.23 | 13.0 | 13.48-85 |
| Kolyadina | Mila | SU | 31Dec60 | 181/78 | Hept | 5736 | | 6541-83 |
| Komsa | Jolanta | POL | 20Dec58 | 183/55 | HJ | 1.88 | | 1.95-84 |
| Kompanyeyets | Irina | SU | 4Jan64 | | LJ | 6.55w | | |
| Konovalenko | Olga | SU | 18Apr62 | 165/58 | Hept | 5860 | | 5689M-85 |
| Konyukhova | Irina | SU | 20Nov59 | | LJ | 6.75 | | 6.60-85 |
| Köpping | Jana | GDR | 12Apr66 | 172/66 | JT | 66.80 | | 64.56-85 |
| Koptyakevich | Lyudmila | SU | 7Apr65 | 177/85 | SP | 17.66 | | 16.24-84 |
| Korablina | Tatyana | SU | 24Jun64 | | JT | 58.84 | | 58.24-85 |
| Korolkova | Svetlana | SU | 23May60 | 175/63 | Hept | 5784M | 5649 | 6150-84 |
| Korotkevich | Larisa | SU | 3Jan67 | | DT | 64.42 | | 59.02-85 |
| Kositsyna | Larisa | SU | 14Dec63 | 182/58 | HJ | 1.98i | 1.94 | 1.98-83 |
| Kostadinova | Stefka | BUL | 25Mar65 | 180/60 | HJ | 2.08 | | 2.06-85 |
| Kostyuchenkova | Irina | SU | 11May61 | 171/75 | JT | 65.56 | | 63.24-85 |
| Kot | Irina | SU | 25Sep67 | 162/57 | 200 | 23.35 | 23.77-85 | 23.6-84 |
| Kotoviene | Elvira | SU | 1Jun58 | 170/63 | 100 | 11.49 | 11.44-83 | 11.2-85 |
| Kotze | Hanlie | RSA | 12Nov60 | 176/64 | HJ | 1.88 | | 1.87-83 |
| Kovacs | Ella | RUM | 11Dec64 | 170/53 | 800 | 1:59.91 | | 1:55.68-85 |
| Kovács | Judit | HUN | 7Jun69 | 166/53 | HJ | 1.89 | | 1.87-85 |
| Kovalyeva | Oksana | SU | 3Sep69 | 172/56 | 200 | 23.36 | | 23.99-85 |
| Kovalyeva | Valentina | SU | 12Apr60 | 179/65 | LJ | 6.56 | | 6.85-85 |
| Kovtun | Natalya | SU | 27May64 | | 100 | 11.51 | 11.51-81 | 11.2-84 |
| Kowina | Grażyna | POL | 6May62 | 163/59 | 800 | 2:01.36 | | 2:03.06-85 |
| Kozoderova | Marina | SU | 1Mar64 | | JT | 58.48 | | 57.28-85 |
| Krabbe | Katrin | GDR | 22Nov69 | 181/63 | 100 | 11.49 | | 11.7-85 |
| | | | | | 200 | 23.31 | 23.25w | 24.63-85 |
| Kraus | Brigitte | FRG | 12Aug56 | 180/58 | 1500 | 4:04.65 | | 4:01.54-78 |
| | | | | | 3000 | 8:47.83 | | 8:35.11-83 |
| Kravchenko | Valentina | SU | 11Nov63 | 168/55 | LJ | 6.82 | | 6.54-85 |
| Kremleva | Lyubov | SU | 21Dec62 | | 800 | 1:59.1 | | 1:58.95-84 |
| | | | | | 1500 | 4:01.57 | | 4:02.04-84 |
| Krieger | Heidi | GDR | 20Jul65 | 187/100 | SP | 21.10 | 20.51i | 20.24-84 |
| Kripli | Márta | HUN | 1Oct60 | 180/108 | SP | 18.16 | | 17.13-85 |
| | | | | | DT | 66.48 | | 65.34-85 |
| Kristiansen | Ingrid | NOR | 21Mar56 | 170/50 | 1500 | 4:05.97 | | 4:10.16-85 |
| | | | | | 3000 | 8:34.10 | | 8:39.56-84 |
| | | | | | 5k | 14:37.33 | | 14:57.43-85 |
| | | | | | 10k | 30:13.74 | | 30:59.42-85 |
| | | | | | Mar | 2:24:55 | | 2:21:06-85 |
| Królkewicz | Monika | POL | 31Jan57 | 177/63 | Hept | 5660 | | 5937-83 |
| Krug | Petra | GDR | 9Nov63 | 181/70 | 400h | 57.72 | | 54.76-83 |
| Kruse | Sabine | FRG | 10Mar66 | 186/80 | SP | 17.34 | | 15.00-85 |
| Kubi | Elju | SU | 25Mar51 | 179/79 | DT | 63.38 | | 64.44-83 |
| Kučeríková | Jana | CS | 30Apr64 | 164/53 | 3000 | 8:56.49 | | 9:02.88-85 |
| | | | | | 5k | 15:55.55 | | 0 |
| Kudryavtseva | Galina | SU | 11Apr61 | 170/85 | DT | 59.40 | | 62.30-85 |
| Kühn | Ute | GDR | 23Jul65 | 182/62 | HJ | 1.91i | 1.88 | 1.91-85 |

| Name | | Nat | Yr | Ht/Wt | Event | 1986 Mark | Pre-1986 best |
|---|---|---|---|---|---|---|---|
| Kukk | Ille | SU | 6May57 | 169/49 | 3000 | 9:00.12 | 8:55.75-84 |
| | | | | | 5k | 15:42.45 | 15:30.84-85 |
| Kumpulainen | Sirkku | FIN | 12Jan56 | 164/53 | Mar | 2:36:05 | 2:38:44-85 |
| Kunkel | Sabine | FRG | 5Sep64 | 184/46 | 3000 | 9:03.77 | 9:10.14-85 |
| Kurochkina | Galina | SU | 2Jan65 | | SP | 18.40 | 18.49-85 |
| Kushenko | Irina | SU | 5Jun65 | 171/63 | Hept | 6202 | 6152-85 |
| Kuzhel | Galina | SU | 4Oct59 | 181/86 | SP | 18.34 | 18.22-83 |
| Kvast | Olga | SU | 27Apr63 | 162/50 | 100 | 11.50 | 11.52 11.2-85 |
| | | | | | | | |
| Laaksalo | Tuula | FIN | 21Apr53 | 171/70 | JT | 63.68 | 67.40-83 |
| Lacambra | Blanca | SPA | 28Aug65 | 163/53 | 100 | 11.49 | 11.62-85 |
| | | | | | 200 | 23.04w | 23.44 23.2-85 |
| | | | | | 400 | 51.53 | 52.19-85 |
| Lagunkova | Natalya | SU | 6May59 | 163/50 | 3000 | 8:48.15 | 8:55.3 -82 |
| | | | | | 10k | 33:18.0 | 32:57.48-82 |
| Laine | Helena | FIN | 30Mar55 | 178/76 | JT | 61.10 | 64.00-83 |
| Lajbnerova | Zuzana | CS | 20May63 | 177/74 | Hept | 5894 5916W | 5895-83 |
| Lammertsma | Ingrid | HOL | 6Sep67 | | JT | 58.86 | 56.32-85 |
| Landry | Kelly | USA | 27Jun63 | 179/82 | DT | 57.68 | 53.58-85 |
| Lange | Andrea | GDR | 3Jun66 | 176/58 | 800 | 2:00.56 | 2:07.7 -85 |
| | | | | | 1k | 2:38.6 | 2:43.97-85 |
| | | | | | 1500 | 4:08.50 | 4:21.67-85 |
| Lange | Malde | SU | 61 | | DT | 58.24 | 54.04-85 |
| Langlacé | Chantal | FRA | 6Jan55 | 155/48 | Mar | 2:33:58 | 2:34:51-84 |
| Lantsova | Maria | SU | 62 | | 3000 | 9:03.96 | |
| | | | | | 5k | 16:04.46 | |
| | | | | | 10k | 33:22.92 | |
| Lapajne | Lidija | YUG | 1Apr59 | 178/60 | HJ | 1.88 | 1.92-85 |
| Lapierre | Odette | CAN | 28Jan55 | 162/50 | 10k | 33:22.71 | 34:20.90-85 |
| | | | | | Mar | 2:31:48 | 2:33:45-85 |
| Larpi | Marja-Leena | FIN | 28Apr59 | 176/82 | DT | 57.60 | 62.00-81 |
| Larrieu-Smith | Francie | USA | 23Nov52 | 163/48 | 5k | 16:01.3 | 15:36.11-83 |
| | | | | | Mar | 2:33:36 | 0 |
| Larsen | Debra | USA | 7Jun64 | 178/65 | Hept | 5827 | 5758-84 |
| Laurendet (Low) | Jenny | AUS | 5Jul62 | 164/50 | 400h | 56.48 | 57.82 57.5&-85 |
| Lawrence | Esmie | CAN | 19Nov61 | 178/ | 100 | 11.43w | 11.42-85 |
| | | | | | 200 | A23.13 | 23.49-85 |
| Laxton | Sonja | RSA | 6Aug48 | 170/50 | Mar | 2:35:43 | 2:36:44-84 |
| Laza | Belsis | CUB | 5Jun67 | | SP | 17.85 | 16.90-85 |
| le Roux | Annie | RSA | 14Mar65 | | 100h | A13.32w | A13.67-84 |
| | | | | | Hept | 5976 | 0 |
| Leal | Ivonne | CUB | 27Feb66 | 164/64 | JT | 69.82 | 71.82-85 |
| Leatherwood | Lillie | USA | 6Jul64 | 168/56 | 200 | 23.16 | 23.66-84 22.84w-85 |
| | | | | | 400 | 50.18 | 50.19-84 |
| Lebedinskaya | Irina | SU | 16Jun61 | 164/52 | 1500 | 4:05.19 | 4:00.18-82 |
| (Nikitina) | | | | | | | |
| Lebonda | Tatyana | SU | 23Mar64 | 161/46 | 1k | 2:37.74i | |
| (Petrova) | | | | | 1500 | 4:07.64i | 4:09.19-82 |
| Ledovskaya | Tatyana | SU | 21May66 | | 400 | 51.87 | |
| Lee | Victoria | UK | 22Jun64 | | 400h | 57.5 | 59.41-85 |
| Leidinger | Petra | FRG | 5Feb66 | 176/75 | SP | 18.87i | 18.32-85 |
| Leist | Sabine | GDR | 20Nov66 | 174/ | 1500 | 4:10.39 | 4:13.81-85 |
| Lelut | Maria | FRA | 29Jan56 | 159/46 | Mar | 2:29:51 | 2:34:02-85 |
| Lengyel | Mariana | RUM | 14Apr53 | 174/86 | SP | 17.78 | 18.22i 17.89-85 |
| | | | | | DT | 69.08 | 66.34-85 |
| Lepping | Claudia | FRG | 2Jul68 | 175/63 | 200 | 23.18 | 24.88-85 |

| Name | | Nat | Yr | Ht/Wt | Event | 1986 Mark | Pre-1986 best |
|---|---|---|---|---|---|---|---|
| Leroux (Philippe) | Françoise | FRA | 4Oct61 | 160/49 | 100 | 11.43 | 11.56 11.43w-84 |
| Leroy | Muriel | FRA | 14Mar68 | 173/62 | 100 | 11.51 | 11.72 11.6-85 |
| Lesnykh | Larisa | SU | 29Jun64 | | 400 | 51.74 | 52.13-85 51.5 -83 |
| Lesovaya | Tatyana | SU | 24Apr56 | 176/93 | DT | 60.60 | 68.18-82 |
| Levecq | Sylvie | FRA | 5Dec62 | 179/59 | Hept | 5849 | 5841-85 |
| Lewis | Carol | USA | 8Aug63 | 178/68 | LJ | 6.90 6.91w | 7.04-85 |
| Li | Baolian | CHN | 8Mar63 | | JT | 64.92 | 60.50-85 |
| Li | Jingmin | CHN | 64 | | 5k | 16:05.56 | 16:44.19-85 |
| Li | Meisu | CHN | 17Apr59 | 176/80 | SP | 18.61 | 18.47-84 |
| Li | Xiaohui | CHN | 12Feb56 | 168/70 | DT | 58.94 | 61.80-80 |
| Li | Xiuxia | CHN | 67 | | 10k | 33:11.17 | |
| Liao | Wenfen | CHN | 30Apr63 | 169/53 | LJ | 6.61 | 6.57-84 |
| Lichagina | Yulia | SU | 7May65 | | JT | 58.06 | 54.38-85 |
| Lillak | Tiina | FIN | 15Apr61 | 181/74 | JT | 72.42 | 74.76-83 |
| Lina | Elena | RUM | 19Feb54 | 171/57 | 400 | 52.29 | 52.01-85 51.3-77 |
| | | | | | 800 | 2:01.19 | 1:59.41-78 |
| Lisovskaya | Natalya | SU | 16Jul62 | 186/100 | SP | 21.70 | 22.53-84 |
| Lisowska | Małgorzata | POL | 18Apr62 | 178/68 | Hept | 5694 | 5641-84 |
| Litvinenko | Irina | SU | 29Jan60 | | HJ | 1.90i | 1.93i-85 1.83-81 |
| Liu | Guohua | CHN | 7Dec63 | | JT | 63.60 | 64.14-85 |
| Lix | Karin | FRG | 3Mar65 | 170/54 | 400 | 51.85 | 52.79-83 |
| Lix | Ute | FRG | 3Mar65 | | 400 | 52.30 | 53.78-85 |
| Loghin | Mihaela | RUM | 1Jun52 | 170/78 | SP | 20.62 | 21.00-84 |
| Loiseau | Christine | FRA | 26Aug60 | 160/45 | 5k | 15:38.09 | 0 |
| | | | | | 10k | 32:25.99 | 0 |
| Lombardo | Patrizia | ITA | 3Sep58 | 175/59 | 100h | 13.19 | 13.39 13.35w-80 |
| López | Aliuska | CUB | 29Aug69 | 164/ | 100h | 13.14 | 13.97 13.5-85 |
| Lorentzon | Susanne | SWE | 11Jun61 | 177/59 | HJ | 1.90i 1.90 | 1.94i 1.94-85 |
| Lorraway | Robyn | AUS | 20Jul61 | 170/57 | LJ | 6.86 | 6.80-85 6.90w-84 |
| Losch | Claudia | FRG | 10Jan60 | 181/84 | SP | 21.46i | 20.59i-85 |
| | | | | | | 20.92 | 20.55-84 |
| | | | | | DT | 62.82 | 63.12-85 |
| Losch | Susanne | GDR | 12Feb66 | 177/60 | 400h | 56.89 | 56.62-85 |
| Luckett | LaVonda | USA | 31Aug65 | 168/52 | 400h | 57.47 | 57.86-85 |
| Lukashevich | Svetlana | SU | 1Aug68 | 176/61 | 400h | 57.2 | 60.03-85 |
| Lukiniv | Nadezhda | SU | 68 | | SP | 17.15 | 14.87-85 |
| Lvova | Olga | SU | 16Aug67 | 182/75 | Hept | 5793 | |
| Lynch | Elizabeth | UK | 24May64 | 168/45 | 3000 | 8:46.53 | 9:03.80-85 |
| | | | | | 5k | 15:41.58# | |
| | | | | | 10k | 31:41.42 | 33:19.14-85 |
| MacDougall | Lynne | UK | 18Feb65 | 160/45 | 1k | 2:38.67 | 0 |
| | | | | | 1500 | 4:10.23 | 4:05.96-84 |
| McCraw | Gervaise | USA | 10Dec64 | 168/54 | 200 | 23.27 | 23.16-83 22.98w-84 |
| | | | | | 400 | 52.24 | 53.42-82 |
| McLean | Megan | AUS | 9Mar64 | 161/50 | LJ | 6.58w | 6.46-85 |
| McMiken | Christine | NZ | 19Jul63 | 165/47 | 3000 | 9:03.32 | 8:58.68i-85 |
| | | | | | 5k | 15:58.05 | 15:45.7-85 |
| | | | | | 10k | 32:51.71 | 33:05.7-84 |
| | | | | | | 32:17.1$ | |
| McPeake | Sharon | UK | 22Jun62 | 183/62 | HJ | 1.90 | 1.85-81 |
| McRoberts | Brit | CAN | 10Feb57 | 178/56 | 800 | 2:00.94 | 2:00.02-83 |
| | | | | | 1k | 2:38.56 | |
| | | | | | 1500 | 4:05.36 | 4:03.36-83 |
| | | | | | Mile | 4:24.69 | 4:29.90-93 |

| Name | | Nat | Yr | Ht/Wt | Event | 1986 Mark | Pre-1986 best |
|---|---|---|---|---|---|---|---|
| Machotková (Votrubová) | Zuzana | CS | 25Mar65 | 174/64 | 400h | 57.87 | 59.00-85 |
| Madetzky | Silvia | GDR | 24Jun62 | 185/95 | SP | 17.83 | 18.28-80 |
| | | | | | DT | 67.08 | 68.24-82 |
| Mai | Christina | FRG | 3Sep61 | 159/49 | 3000 | 9:02.11 | 9:05.36-85 |
| Makarova (Gorbunova) | Galina | SU | 60 | | 100h | 13.17 | 13.80-83 13.2-84 |
| Malešev | Tamara | YUG | 8Jan67 | 182/59 | HJ | 1.91i | 1.92i-84 1.91-85 |
| Maloletnyeva (Polyakova) | Vera | SU | 1Jun66 | | Hept | 6023 | 5910-85 |
| Malone | Maicel | USA | 12Jun69 | 173/59 | 100 | 11.49 | 11.69-85 |
| | | | | | | 11.18w | 11.59w-85 |
| | | | | | 200 | 23.12 | 24.20 23.8-84 |
| | | | | | | | 23.80w-85 |
| | | | | | 400 | 52.42 52.4 | 53.7-85 |
| Malovecz | Zsuzsa | HUN | 21Mar63 | 178/76 | JT | 66.64 | 62.66-85 |
| Maltseva | Olga | SU | 19Sep63 | | LJ | 6.50 | 6.42-85 |
| Malukhina | Marina | SU | 25Sep62 | | 10k | 33:15.00 | 33:41.0-85 |
| Malysheva (Susuyeva) | Tatyana | SU | 64 | | Hept | 5843 | 5666-84 |
| Mamayeva | Tatyana | SU | 15May62 | 165/49 | 800 | 2:01.98 | |
| Marchisio | Rita | ITA | 13Feb50 | 170/53 | Mar | 2:35:41 | 2:32:55-82 |
| Marello | Maria | ITA | 11Mar61 | 173/76 | DT | 57.54 | 54.90-84 |
| Marinova | Yuliana | BUL | 24Jul67 | 168/55 | 400 | 52.05 | 53.28-85 |
| Marot | Veronique | UK | 16Sep55 | 168/52 | Mar | 2:31:33 | 2:28:04-85 |
| Marshall | Janice | USA | | | 100 | 11.51w | 11.69w-85 |
| Marshall | Pam | USA | 16Aug60 | 178/63 | 100 | 11.21 10.9 | 11.15-85 |
| | | | | | | 10.80w | |
| | | | | | 200 | 22.12 | 22.39 21.7$-85 |
| | | | | | 400 | 49.99 | 51.41-85 |
| Marten | Maritza | CUB | 17Aug63 | 177/83 | DT | 66.86 | 70.50-85 |
| Martin | Gael | AUS | 27Aug56 | 173/90 | SP | 19.59 | 19.74-84 |
| | | | | | DT | 62.44 | 63.08-79 |
| Martin | LaVonna | USA | 18Nov66 | 168/59 | 100 | 11.46 | |
| | | | | | 200 | 23.30 | 23.58 22.94w-85 |
| | | | | | 100h | 12.95 | 13.10 13.02w-85 |
| Martin | Lisa | AUS | 12May60 | 167/45 | Mar | 2:26:07 | 2:27:40-84 |
| Martins | Gabriele | GDR | 1Jun62 | 170/52 | Mar | 2:32:38 | 2:32:23-85 |
| Martsenyuk | Yelena | SU | 21Feb61 | | Hept | 6118 | 6071-85 |
| März | Resi | FRG | 15Jan60 | 168/60 | 100 | 11.50 | 11.48 11.33w-85 |
| Maslennikova | Marianna | SU | 17May61 | 173/66 | 100h | 13.41 | 13.37-85 |
| | | | | | HJ | 1.88 | 1.86-84 |
| | | | | | Hept | 6416 | 6374-84 |
| Mason | Philippa | UK | 16Mar69 | 163/44 | 3000 | 9:03.35 | 9:43.9 -85 |
| Massarin | Mary | ITA | 7Nov63 | | 100h | 13.31 | 13.82-85 |
| | | | | | | 13.25w | 13.73w-85 |
| Matava | Patty | USA | 8Oct65 | 160/43 | 5k | 15:56.41 | |
| Matei (Cojocaru) | Cristeana | RUM | 2Jan62 | 172/62 | 400 | 51.44 | 52.11-83 |
| | | | | | 800 | 1:59.45 | 1:59.06-85 |
| | | | | | 400h | 54.55 | 55.10-85 |
| Matei | Monica | RUM | 9Aug63 | 175/56 | HJ | 1.88 | 1.88-85 |
| Matveyeva | Lyudmila | SU | 57 | | 3000 | 9:00.64 | 8:52.49-84 |
| | | | | | 5k | 15:29.36 | 15:16.27-85 |
| | | | | | 10k | 33:06.0 | 32:25.99-84 |
| Maxie | Leslie | USA | 4Jan67 | 178/59 | 400h | 56.72 | 55.20-84 |
| Mednikova (Kuleshina) | Larisa | SU | 4Jan63 | 175/80 | DT | 63.02 | 62.84-84 |
| Medvedyeva | Lyudmila | SU | 18Jan57 | | 10k | 33:27.50 | |
| Medvedyeva | Niole | SU | 20Oct60 | 175/61 | LJ | 6.99 | 7.02-84 |
| Meleshkova | Miglena | BUL | 24May67 | 169/100 | SP | 17.58 | 16.76-85 |

| Name | | Nat | Yr | Ht/Wt | Event | 1986 Mark | Pre-1986 best |
|------|---|-----|-----|-------|-------|-----------|---------------|
| Meleshkova | Svetlana | SU | 13May62 | | 800 | 1:59.50 | 2:03.32-83 |
| | | | | | 1500 | 4:11.52 | 4:10.76-83 |
| Melicherová | Ľudmila | CS | 6Jun64 | 155/44 | 3000 | 9:04.04 | 9:07.26-85 |
| | | | | | 10k | 32:47.24 | 33:55.80-85 |
| Melinte | Doina | RUM | 27Dec56 | 173/60 | 800 | 1:56.2 | 1:55.05-82 |
| | | | | | 1500 | 3:56.7 | 3:58.1 -84 |
| | | | | | Mile | 4:21.88 | 4:29.2i-85 |
| | | | | | 3000 | 8:37.11 | |
| Melnik | Vera | SU | 19Jan63 | 173/69 | Hept | 5691M 5645 | 5566M-85 |
| Menissier | Liliane | FRA | 12Nov60 | 171/63 | Hept | 6165 | 5987-85 |
| Mercurio | Carla | ITA | 26Oct60 | 164/50 | 100 | 11.51 | 11.41-85 |
| Meszynski | Irina | GDR | 24Mar62 | 175/97 | DT | 68.74 | 73.36-84 |
| Michallek | Vera | FRG | 6Nov58 | 168/54 | 1500 | 4:04.29 | 4:06.25-84 |
| | | | | | 3000 | 8:50.99 | 8:52.57-81 |
| | | | | | 5000 | 15:41.68 | 15:52.15-84 |
| Mierzejewska | Grażyna | POL | 28Oct57 | 158/51 | Mar | 2:33:44 | 2:38:56-85 |
| Mikhalchenko | Larisa | SU | 16Feb63 | 179/90 | DT | 64.48 | 64.92-85 |
| Miles | Jearl | USA | 4Oct66 | | 400 | 52.41 | |
| Millar-Cubit | Jocelyn | AUS | 23Mar62 | 167/57 | Hept | 5658 | 5883-85 |
| Mills | Aileen | UK | 13Feb62 | | 400h | 57.76 | 58.28-85 |
| Miromanova (Vinogradova) | Nadezhda | SU | 1May58 | 170/64 | Hept | 5879M | 6552-84 |
| Misaros | Cristina | RUM | 1Jan69 | | 1500 | 4:09.64 | 4:12.3-85 |
| Mitkova | Svetla | BUL | 17Jun64 | 178/96 | SP | 20.05 | 19.11-84 |
| | | | | | DT | 68.90 | 66.80-83 |
| Mitrea | Aurica | RUM | 19Nov59 | 170/60 | 800 | 2:00.28 | 2:00.6-84 |
| Mitrea | Ilinca | RUM | 2Jan64 | 167/52 | 800 | 1:59.71 | |
| | | | | | 1500 | 4:05.07 | 4:17.81-82 |
| Miu | Aurora | RUM | 7Jul63 | 164/54 | 800 | 1:59.79 | 2:02.57-84 |
| Moe | Bente | NOR | 2Dec60 | 168/50 | Mar | 2:33:39 | 2:35:38-84 |
| Moller | Lorraine | NZ | 1Jun55 | 174/58 | 3000 | 9:03.89 | 8:51.78-83 |
| | | | | | 5k | 15:32.90 | 15:35.75-85 |
| | | | | | 10k | 32:40.61$ | |
| | | | | | Mar | 2:28:17 | 2:28:34-84 |
| Molnár | Ilona | HUN | 15Dec65 | 178/76 | DT | 59.58 | 54.50-85 |
| Molokova | Marina | SU | 24Aug62 | 171/61 | 100 | 11.22 | 11.26-84 |
| | | | | | 200 | 22.46 | 22.76-85 |
| Moore | Mary | USA | 8Aug65 | 183/64 | HJ | 1.88 | 1.90i-85 1.88-81 |
| Morgenstern | Heike | GDR | 13Dec62 | 176/58 | 100 | 11.30 | 11.42-84 |
| | | | | | 200 | 22.97 | 23.19 23.06w-84 |
| Morley | Suzanne | UK | 11Oct57 | 161/48 | 1500 | 4:11.49 | 4:11.00-85 |
| Moshicheva | Tamara | SU | 4Aug62 | 170/65 | Hept | 6216M 6017 | 6319M-85 |
| Mosqueda | Sylvia | USA | 8Apr66 | | 5k | 15:52.5 | |
| Mota | Rosa | POR | 29Jun58 | 157/45 | Mar | 2:27:15 | 2:23:29-85 |
| Motuzenko | Svetlana | SU | 25Dec54 | 178/81 | DT | 60.08 | 65.48-85 |
| Mukhomatova | Zukhra | SU | 61 | | 800 | 2:02.0 | |
| Müller | Ines | GDR | 2Jan59 | 182/94 | SP | 21.45 | 21.32-84 |
| | | | | | DT | 64.44 | 66.40-85 |
| Müller | Petra | GDR | 18Jul65 | 180/64 | 400 | 49.79 | 50.14-85 |
| Mulliner | Joanne | UK | 18Aug66 | 175/66 | Hept | 5885 | 5833-85 |
| Murashova | Galina | SU | 22Dec55 | 180/92 | DT | 58.34 | 72.14-84 |
| Murgoci | Elena | RUM | 20May60 | 170/49 | 10k | 32:24.09 | |
| | | | | | Mar | 2:37:01 | 2:41:59-85 |
| Murková | Eva | CS | 29May62 | 168/56 | 100 | 11.38 | 11.43-83 |
| | | | | | LJ | 6.93 | 7.01 7.17w-84 |
| Murray | Patty | USA | | | 5k | 15:48.21 | |
| Murray | Yvonne | UK | 4Oct64 | 172/50 | 1k | 2:37.75 | 2:48.7i-85 |
| | | | | | 1500 | 4:05.76 | 4:09.9-85 |
| | | | | | Mile | 4:23.08 | 4:28.64-85 |
| | | | | | 2k | 5:29.58 | 5:47.75-84 |
| | | | | | 3000 | 8:37.11 | 8:58.54-84 |
| Mylnikova | Irina | SU | 65 | | 100h | 13.08 13.0 | 13.4-83 |

| Name | | Nat | Yr | Ht/Wt | Event | 1986 Mark | Pre-1986 best |
|------|---|-----|-----|-------|-------|-----------|---------------|
| Nagy | Elisabet | SWE | 14Mar60 | 167/63 | JT | 60.66 | 60.26-84 |
| Narozhilenko | Lyudmila | SU | 63 | | 100h | 13.41 | |
| Nasedkina | Natalya | SU | 18Sep63 | 178/70 | JT | 59.18 | 58.38-83 |
| Nastase | Liliana | RUM | 1Aug62 | 169/62 | 100h | 12.85 | 13.03 13.0-85 |
| | | | | | | | 12.8w-84 |
| | | | | | LJ | 6.59 | 6.58 6.78w-85 |
| | | | | | Hept | 6172 | 6200 6310W-85 |
| Nastoburko | Antonina | SU | 20Jan59 | 174/61 | 100 | 11.27 | 11.27-85 10.9-84 |
| Natale | Liz | USA | 11Jun64 | 173/57 | 3000 | 9:01.34 | 9:06.71-84 |
| Naude | Madele | RSA | 2May63 | 174/52 | 200 | A23.10 | A22.98-85 23.99-84 |
| | | | | | 400 | A51.16 | A51.65-85 |
| | | | | | | 51.98 | 52.32-85 |
| | | | | | 400h | A57.1 | 0 |
| Naumkina | Olga | SU | 64 | | 100 | 11.49 | 11.88 11.4-84 |
| Navickaite | Margarita | SU | 10Dec61 | 166/59 | 400h | 55.27 | 55.02-84 |
| Nazarova | Olga | SU | 28Feb62 | 176/60 | 400 | 51.44 | 54.29i 53.8i-84 |
| (Grigoryeva) | | | | | 400h | 55.62 | 56.04-85 |
| Neamţu | Elisabeta | RUM | 16Oct60 | 178/80 | DT | 64.08 | 65.20-85 |
| Nechiporets | Alla | SU | 20Oct64 | 170/62 | LJ | 6.62 | 6.43-85 |
| Neer | Penny | USA | 7Nov60 | 183/75 | DT | 60.42 | 61.36-85 |
| Neimke | Kathrin | GDR | 18Jul66 | 179/85 | SP | 19.68 | 18.09-85 |
| | | | | | DT | 58.82 | 55.52-85 |
| Nekrošaite | Terese | SU | 61 | | JT | 61.40 | 62.96-85 |
| Nelson | Lynn | USA | 8Jan62 | 176/57 | 10k | 32:30.24 | 34:24.9 -84 |
| Nesbit | Joan | USA | 20Jan62 | 152/43 | 5k | 15:52.36 | 15:52.9 -84 |
| Neubauer | Dagmar | GDR | 3Jun62 | 171/56 | 200 | 23.29 | 22.87-84 |
| | | | | | 400 | 50.92 | 49.58-84 |
| Ni | Xiulin | CHN | 23May62 | 173/58 | HJ | 1.91 | 1.90-85 |
| Nicolls | Janet | USA | 9Mar63 | 183/64 | Hept | 5766 | 5521-85 |
| Nikishina | Olga | SU | 29Apr66 | 174/85 | DT | 62.24 | 59.72-85 |
| Nikitina | Larisa | SU | 29Apr65 | | Hept | 6316 | 6276-84 |
| Nikolayeva | Lyudmila | SU | 26Sep64 | 164/50 | 5k | 15:57.44 | |
| Ninova | Lyudmila | BUL | 25Jun60 | 175/54 | LJ | 6.88 | 6.80-84 |
| Nizamova | Almira | SU | 62 | | 100 | 11.1 | 11.5-84 |
| Nordström | Christina | SWE | 3Jul61 | 176/58 | HJ | 1.90 | 1.86-84 |
| Nováková | Vanda | CS | 5Jul58 | 174/67 | Hept | 5689 | 5863W-85 5557-85 |
| Novobáczky | Klára | HUN | 30May58 | 168/60 | LJ | 6.56 | 6.76-84 |
| Nowak | Małgorzata | POL | 9Feb59 | 180/70 | 100h | 13.39 | 13.31 13.27w-85 |
| | | | | | HJ | 1.90 | 1.95-85 |
| | | | | | Hept | 6352 | 6616-85 |
| Nuneva | Anelia | BUL | 30Jun62 | 167/57 | 100 | 11.04 10.9 | 11.07-83 |
| - Vechernikova | | | | | 200 | 22.58 | 22.58-83 |
| Nunn | Glynis | AUS | 4Dec60 | 168/58 | 100h | 13.40 13.31w | 13.02-84 |
| Nurutdinova | Lilia | SU | 15Dec63 | | 400 | 52.47 | 52.5-85 |
| Nybu | Sølvi | NOR | 3Jun66 | 166/58 | JT | 60.86 | 58.12-84 |
| | | | | | | | |
| Oakes | Heather | UK | 14Aug59 | 166/63 | 100 | 11.22 | 11.20-80 |
| | | | | | | 11.20w | 11.01w-80 |
| | | | | | 200 | 22.92 | 23.06 22.9-80 |
| | | | | | | | 23.00w-84 |
| Oakes | Judy | UK | 14Feb58 | 163/81 | SP | 19.00 | 18.35i-84 |
| | | | | | | | 18.28-83 |
| Oanta | Iolanda | RUM | 11Oct65 | 183/63 | 400 | 52.26 | 54.11-85 |
| | | | | | 400h | 57.50 | 0 |

| Name | | Nat | Yr | Ht/Wt | Event | 1986 Mark | Pre-1986 best |
|---|---|---|---|---|---|---|---|
| Obizhayeva | Yelena | SU | 9Oct60 | 180/69 | LJ | 6.62 | 6.79-83 |
| Obukhova | Yelena | SU | 9Jan69 | 181/60 | HJ | 1.88 | 1.83-85 |
| O'Connor | Mary | NZ | 19Apr55 | 153/43 | 10k | 33:20.78 | 33:41.50-85 |
| | | | | | Mar | 2:30:52 | 2:28:20-83 |
| Odintsova | Svetlana | SU | 27Aug62 | 182/72 | HJ | 1.89i 1.89 | 1.88i 1.88-85 |
| Oehme | Heike | GDR | 11Nov63 | 171/55 | 800 | 1:58.16 | 2:04.48-84 |
| (Hadert) | | | | | 1k | 2:34.6 | 0 |
| | | | | | 1500 | 4:02.90 | 0 |
| Ogunde | Lola | NIG | 64 | | 100 | A11.49 | |
| Oqunkoya | Falilat | NIG | 5Dec68 | 168/ | 200 | 23.11 | 23.5-85 |
| Oker | Edith | FRG | 1Feb61 | 168/56 | 100h | 13.29 | 13.09-84 |
| | | | | | | 13.22w | 13.08w-84 |
| Okolo-Kulak | Lidia | SU | 15Jan67 | | 100h | 13.17 | 13.30-85 |
| | | | | | | 12.9 | 13.2-84 |
| Old | Wendy | AUS | 24Jun60 | 162/52 | 800 | 2:00.81 | 2:02.01-85 |
| Olejarz | Genowefa | POL | 17Oct62 | 174/74 | JT | 64.90 | 65.52-84 |
| Olenchenko | Vera | SU | 21Mar59 | | LJ | 6.84 | 6.92-85 |
| Oleynik | Irina | SU | 12Dec63 | 165/58 | Hept | 5969M 5899 | 5788-85 |
| Olijar | Ludmila | SU | 5Feb58 | 169/63 | 100h | 13.03   13.11-84 | 12.9-85 |
| | | | | | | | 12.89w-83 |
| Olijslager | Marjan | HOL | 8Mar62 | 172/58 | 100h | 13.07   13.01 | 12.96w-85 |
| Oliver | Ilrey | JAM | 2Sep62 | 170/57 | 400 | 51.76 | 51.96-85 |
| Olizarenko | Nadezhda | SU | 2%Nov53 | 165/57 | 400 | 51.60 | 50.96-80 |
| | | | | | 800 | 1:57.15 | 1:53.43-80 |
| Oltean | Coculeana | RUM | 23Dec56 | 170/62 | Hept | 5830 | 5845-85 |
| Omagbemi | Lynda | NIG | | | LJ | 6.59w | 5.84-85 |
| Onyali | Mary | NIG | 3Feb68 | 155/52 | 100 | 11.28 | 11.91 11.8-85 |
| | | | | | 200 | 22.90 22.77w | 23.85-85 |
| Oppliger | Martine | SWZ | 19Oct57 | 170/58 | 3000 | 9:00.43 | 9:17.48-85 |
| | | | | | 10k | 32:48.71 | 34:19.21-85 |
| Oreshkina | Irina | SU | 31Dec64 | | LJ | 6.50w | 6.69-84 |
| Orlova | Tatyana | SU | 19Jul55 | | SP | 18.07 | 20.44-83 |
| Ormsby | Kathy | USA | 1Nov64 | 165/49 | 10k | 32:36.2 | |
| Ortina | Yelena | SU | 1Jan61 | | SP | 19.26 | 18.17-85 |
| Oschkenat | Cornelia | GDR | 29Oct61 | 178/68 | 100 | 11.31 | 11.66-82 |
| | | | | | | | 11.1w 11.4-84 |
| | | | | | 200 | 23.36 | 23.15-84 |
| | | | | | 100h | 12.50   12.70 | 12.56w-85 |
| Osipova | Irina | SU | 27May63 | | LJ | 6.66 | 6.71-85 |
| Oswald | Silvia | FRG | 14Jun68 | | HJ | 1.88 | 1.75-85 |
| Ottey-Page | Merlene | JAM | 10May60 | 174/57 | 100 | 11.06 10.7w | 10.92-85 |
| | | | | | 200 | 22.43 | 21.93-85 |
| Ovchinnikova | Svetlana | SU | 31Oct56 | 177/67 | Hept | 594% | 6251-85 |
| Ovsyannikova | Natalya | SU | 64 | | 400h | 57.21 56.4 | 57.98 57.5-85 |
| Öze-Sipka | Ágnes | HUN | 14Aug54 | 170/53 | Mar | 2:28:51 | 2:35:27-85 |
| Ozhenko | Irena | SU | 13Nov62 | 178/64 | LJ | 7.20 | 6.73-82 |
| (Dukhnovich) | | | | | | | |
| | | | | | | | |
| Padurean | Ana | RUM | 5May69 | 173/52 | 1500 | 4:06.02 | 4:10.89-85 |
| Paetz | Sabine | GDR | 16Oct57 | 174/68 | 100h | 12.89   12.54 | 12.51w-84 |
| | | | | | LJ | 6.57i | 7.12-84 |
| | | | | | Hept | 6456 | 6946-85 |
| Page | Pam | USA | 26Apr58 | 166/63 | 100h | 13.01 | 13.00-83 |
| | | | | | | 12.91w | 12.8w-85 |
| Pagel | Ramona | USA | 10Nov61 | 183/86 | SP | 19.03 | 19.13-85 |
| | | | | | DT | 60.04 | 59.14-85 |

| Name | | Nat | Yr | Ht/Wt | Event | 1986 Mark | Pre-1986 best |
|---|---|---|---|---|---|---|---|
| Pain | Angela | UK | 8Feb62 | 162/51 | Mar | 2:37:57 | 2:37:06-85 |
| Painter | Trudy | NZ | 5Sep65 | 174/63 | HJ | 1.89 | 1.87-85 |
| Pakhomchik | Lyubov | SU | 12Mar63 | 184/67 | HJ | 1.89i | 1.92-85 |
| Palacian | Cleopatra | RUM | 3Jan68 | 163/57 | 3000 | 9:01.76 | 9:01.81-85 |
| Palinske | Angela | FRG | 15Nov65 | 184/65 | HJ | 1.89i | 1.85-84 |
| Pallay | Zsuzsa | HUN | 28Sep48 | 173/71 | DT | 59.90 | 62.36-81 |
| Palm | Evy | SWE | 31Jan42 | 166/53 | 10k | 32:47.25 | 33:00.78-85 |
| | | | | | Mar | 2:32:47 | 2:38:59-84 |
| Palombi | Margit | HUN | 5Mar61 | 165/58 | 100h | 13.19 | 13.04 12.9w-85 |
| | | | | | LJ | 6.54 | 6.21-85 |
| | | | | | Hept | 6001 | 5925-85 |
| Panfil | Wanda | POL | 26Jan59 | 166/56 | 3000 | 9:01.71 | 8:58.51-85 |
| | | | | | 5k | 15:42.69 | 15:43.62-85 |
| Papilina | Tatyana | SU | 14Jan67 | 160/54 | 100 | 11.28  11.63-84 | 11.52w-85 |
| Pardaens | Agnes | BEL | 9Oct56 | 165/50 | Mar | 2:37:05 | 2:42:25-85 |
| Parkhuta (Zhukova) | Valentina | SU | 26Oct59 | 168/57 | 800 | 2:00.83 | 1:56.97-84 |
| | | | | | 1500 | 4:06.33 | 4:07.39-84 |
| Parlyuk | Olga | SU | 3May63 | 162/54 | 1500 | 4:03.46 | 4:04.16-84 |
| Parrott | Tina | USA | 10Jan64 | 161/46 | 800 | 2:01.02 | 2:04.88-84 |
| Partridge (Smeeth) | Ruth | UK | 19Jun60 | 162/52 | 3000 | 9:02.78 | 8:51.40-82 |
| Patoka | Antonina | SU | 12Jan64 | 182/95 | DT | 61.58 | 62.52-84 |
| Patzwahl | Kristin | GDR | 16Jul65 | 169/60 | 100h | 13.23 | 13.49-85 |
| Pavlova | Pepa | BUL | 1Jan61 | 162/55 | 100 | 11.30 | 11.31-84 |
| | | | | | 200 | 22.68 | 23.00-84 |
| | | | | | 400 | 51.40 | 0 |
| Pavlova | Tatyana | SU | 12Dec58 | 165/55 | 400h | 56.39 | 54.34-85 |
| Pavlova | Tatyana | SU | 27May60 | | LJ | 6.65 | 6.44-85 |
| Payne | Marita | CAN | 7Oct60 | 173/57 | 200 | 23.12 | 22.62-83 |
| | | | | | 400 | 51.77 | 49.91-84 |
| Pedan | Anna | SU | 1Oct61 | 168/57 | 3000 | 9:03.00 | 8:58.38-84 |
| | | | | | 5k | 15:57.08 | 15:21.92-85 |
| | | | | | 10k | 32:48.80 | 33:07.03-85 |
| Peneva-Dimova | Bonka | BUL | 15Mar56 | 173/60 | 400h | 56.98 | 56.96-80 |
| Peng | Qinyun | CHN | 63 | | SP | 17.50 | 17.98-84 |
| Penkova | Zhanna | SU | 65 | | JT | 58.06 | 57.12-85 |
| Pentukova | Tatyana | SU | 23Jun65 | | 3000 | 9:03.49 | |
| Perez | Cristina | SPA | 30Oct65 | 170/61 | 400h | 57.15 | 57.66-85 |
| Perkins | Jackie | AUS | 29Aug65 | 169/53 | 3000 | 8:52.47 | 9:14.4-84 |
| | | | | | 5k | 15:38.34 | |
| Permyakova | Olga | SU | 4Sep64 | | Hept | 6053 | 6223-85 |
| Perry | Sybil | USA | 9Sep63 | 155/51 | 400h | 57.76 | 57.22-84 |
| Pesnopevtseva | Olga | SU | 17Jan68 | 172/60 | 400 | 51.48 | 53.37-85 |
| Pestretsova | Svetlana | SU | 61 | 173/72 | JT | 62.78 | 61.68-83 |
| Peters | Beate | FRG | 12Oct59 | 178/80 | JT | 69.56 | 66.86-83 |
| Peterson | Inger | USA | 14Apr64 | 172/59 | 100 | 11.47w | 11.41-84 |
| | | | | | | | 11.29w-85 |
| Petkanova – Dragoyeva | Emilia | BUL | 11Jan65 | 170/53 | HJ | 1.93 | 1.84-85 |
| Petkova | Zhivka | BUL | 11Sep67 | 174/61 | 400h | 57.05 | 56.50-85 |
| Petrashkevich | Irina | SU | 9Dec62 | 178/74 | Hept | 5873 | 5468-85 |
| Petrova | Irina | SU | 12Jan62 | | Mar | 2:35:07 | 2:36:51-85 |
| Petrova | Olga | SU | 63 | | 400h | 57.27 | 58.96-85 |
| Petrović (Bojović) | Biljana | YUG | 28Feb61 | 176/60 | HJ | 1.88 | 1.88-83 |
| Petsch | Birgit | FRG | 20Feb63 | 175/78 | SP | 17.33i 17.15 | 17.84-85 |
| Pfeil | Renate | FRG | 4Feb63 | | Hept | 5914 | 5730-85 |
| Pfiefer | Kathy | USA | 4Sep59 | 160/47 | 10k | 33:20.30 | 33:30.68-85 |
| Pfitzinger | Christine | NZ | 24Jan59 | 152/45 | 1500 | 4:11.44 | 4:11.90-85 |
| | | | | | 3000 | 8:58.6 | 8:54.25-84 |
| | | | | | | 8:56.83$ | |

| Name | | Nat | Yr | Ht/Wt | Event | 1986 Mark | Pre-1986 best |
|------|---|-----|-----|-------|-------|-----------|---------------|
| Phipps | Angela | CAN | 17Feb64 | 175/57 | 100 | 11.39 | 11.51-85 |
| | | | | | | | 11.48w-85 |
| | | | | | 200 | 23.26 | 23.39-85 |
| | | | | | | | 23.05w-85 |
| Pinigina | Maria | SU | 9Feb58 | 171/57 | 200 | 23.35 | 22.80-83 |
| | | | | | 400 | 50.29 | 49.19-83 |
| Pintea | Maria | RUM | 10Aug67 | 159/43 | 800 | 1:59.13 | 2:00.90-85 |
| | | | | | 1500 | 4:06.19 | 4:12.69-85 |
| Pippig | Uta | GDR | 7Sep65 | 167/52 | Mar | 2:37:56 | 2:36:45-85 |
| Piquereau | Anne | FRA | 15Jun64 | 172/65 | 100h | 12.95 | 12.89-85 |
| Pishmanova | Snezhana | BUL | 4Mar68 | 170/80 | SP | 17.41 | 16.25-85 |
| Pisiewicz | Ewa | POL | 7May62 | 164/54 | 100 | 11.39 | 11.19 11.0-85 |
| (Rybak) | | | | | 200 | 22.81i | 22.85-85 |
| Platonova | Larisa | SU | 7Mar66 | 180/90 | DT | 59.06 | 61.96-83 |
| Platonova | Lyudmila | SU | 17Aug64 | 186/110 | DT | 60.56 | 61.66-84 |
| Plotzitzka | Iris | FRG | 7Jan66 | 181/80 | SP | 19.76 | 17.82-85 |
| Plumer | PattiSue | USA | 27Apr62 | 162/49 | 3000 | 8:46.24 | 8:53.81-83 |
| | | | | | 5k | 15:20.88 | 15:29.0 -84 |
| Plüss | Caroline | SWZ | 8Jun59 | 165/52 | 400h | 57.15 | 57.36-84 |
| Pluzhnikova | Marina | SU | 25Feb63 | | 1500 | 4:11.3 | 4:11.8-84 |
| | | | | | 3000 | 8:49.91 | 9:02.35-85 |
| | | | | | 10k | 32:31.00 | |
| Podyalovskaya | Irina | SU | 19Oct59 | 168/57 | 800 | 1:57.86 | 1:55.69-84 |
| (Russkikh) | | | | | | | |
| Pogacian | Mihaela | RUM | 27Jan58 | 165/60 | 100h | 12.75 | 12.79-85 |
| Politika | Yelena | SU | 24Aug64 | 172/64 | 100h | 12.71 | 13.10-85 12.8-84 |
| Polledo | Adelina | CUB | 3May66 | 164/56 | LJ | 6.53 | 6.47-83 |
| Pollock | Peggy | USA | 1May60 | 178/82 | SP | 17.58 | 17.56-85 |
| Polovinskaya | Tatyana | SU | 14Mar65 | 164/52 | Mar | 2:36:52 | 2:46:06-85 |
| Poluyko | Valentina | SU | 15Jul55 | 178/66 | HJ | 1.90 | 1.98-83 |
| Pomoshchnikova | Natalya | SU | 9Jul65 | 169/60 | 100 | 11.20 11.0 | 11.27-85 |
| | | | | | 200 | 23.02 23.0 | 23.25 22.6-85 |
| Pressler | Kerstin | FRG | 2Feb62 | 160/49 | 5k | 15:48.25 | |
| | | | | | 10k | 32:46.24 | 33:58.9-85 |
| | | | | | Mar | 2:36:33 | 2:52:35-85 |
| Price | Connie | USA | 3Jun62 | | SP | 17.28 | 15.24i 15.23-85 |
| Prince | Connie | USA | 12Oct57 | | Mar | 2:35:26 | |
| Privalova | Irina | SU | 22Nov68 | 173/63 | 100 | 11.37w | 11.59-85 |
| Prodan | Svetlana | SU | 25Oct62 | 162/47 | 800 | 1:59.41 | 2:02.60-85 |
| Prokhorenko | Taisia | SU | 12Dec67 | | Hept | 5784 | |
| Pronina | Marina | SU | 1Jun63 | | Hept | 5982M 5721 | 5766M-85 |
| Provorova | Yelena | SU | 64 | | 5k | 16:03.68 | |
| Puica | Maricica | RUM | 29Jul50 | 168/54 | 1k | 2:31.5 | 2:35.7 -84 |
| | | | | | 1500 | 3:59.62 | 3:57.22-84 |
| | | | | | Mile | 4:18.25 | 4:17.33-85 |
| | | | | | 2k | 5:28.69 | 5:30.39-85 |
| | | | | | 3000 | 8:35.92 | 8:27.83-85 |
| | | | | | 5k | 15:32.76 | 15:06.04-85 |
| Pujol | Montserrat | SPA | 27Apr61 | 172/56 | 400h | 57.41 | 57.29-82 |
| Purvis | Anne | UK | 5Mar59 | 167/51 | 800 | 2:01.63 | 2:00.20-82 |
| Pushkareva | Inna | SU | 9Mar65 | 170/56 | 5k | 15:59.77 | |
| Qualls | Pam | USA | 28Jul66 | 160/58 | 200 | 23.21w | 23.77-84 |
| Quintavalla | Fausta | ITA | 4May59 | 175/74 | JT | 59.80 | 67.20-83 |
| Quirot | Ana Fidelia | CUB | 23Mar63 | 165/59 | 200 | 23.30 | 23.16 22.9-84 |
| | | | | | 400 | 50.41 | 50.86-85 |
| | | | | | 800 | 1:58.80 | 1:59.45-85 |
| Quisenberry | Mary | USA | 16Jan65 | 170/54 | LJ | 6.63w | 6.33-85 |

| Name | | Nat | Yr | Ht/Wt | Event | 1986 Mark | Pre-1986 best |
|------|------|-----|------|-------|-------|-----------|---------------|
| Racu | Lyubov | SU | 6Feb61 | | Hept | 6383M | 6260-84 |
| | | | | | | 6076 | 6467M-83 |
| Rademeyer | Elinda | RSA | 8Sep65 | 167/54 | 100 | A11.46  A11.51 | A11.40w-85 |
| | | | | | 200 | A22.95  A23.41-84 | 23.53-83 |
| Radtke | Helga | GDR | 16May62 | 171/64 | LJ | 7.17 | 7.21-84 |
| Raduly-Zörgö | Eva | RUM | 23Oct54 | 177/70 | JT | 60.36 | 68.80-80 |
| Rakova | Galina | SU | 7Nov59 | 170/58 | 800 | 2:00.72 | 2:01.48-84 |
| | | | | | 1500 | 4:06.81 | 4:08.25-85 |
| Ramos | Hilda Elisa | CUB | 1Sep64 | 176/80 | DT | 67.92 | 67.56-84 |
| Rasmussen | Dorthe | DEN | 27Jan60 | 181/61 | 5k | 16:02.20 | 15:29.7-83 |
| | | | | | 10k | 32:53.04 | 32:02.89-83 |
| Rata | Lenuta | RUM | 20Nov66 | 169/57 | 1500 | 4:08.54 | 4:11.45-84 |
| Rattray | Cathy | JAM | 19Aug63 | 160/47 | 400 | 52.37  A51.71-82 | 51.82-83 |
| Raunig | Deborah | USA | 29Sep55 | 165/47 | Mar | 2:31:28 | 2:36:24-85 |
| Redetzky | Heike | FRG | 5May64 | 181/64 | HJ | 1.93 | 1.92-85 |
| Regan | Gillian | UK | 28Nov56 | 161 | LJ | 6.51w | 6.52-82 |
| Reidick - Zaczkiewicz | Claudia | FRG | 4Jul62 | 169/56 | 100h | 13.24 | 13.24-85 |
| Reinsch | Gabriele | GDR | 23Sep63 | 186/85 | SP | 17.45 | 17.09-81 |
| | | | | | DT | 65.44 | 65.78-85 |
| Reiter | Anja | GDR | 15Jul69 | 173/67 | JT | 61.70 | 53.74-85 |
| Renders | Marleen | BEL | 24Dec68 | | 5k | 15:49.56 | 0 |
| Renk | Silke | GDR | 30Jun67 | 174/73 | JT | 62.06 | 59.08-85 |
| Renner | Wendy | NZ | 7Jan60 | | 5k | 16:04.32 | |
| Reshetnikova | Tatyana | SU | 14Oct66 | 171/63 | 100h | 13.38 | 13.78 13.5-85 |
| Reynolds | Ellen | USA | 3Apr64 | 161/43 | 10k | 32:40.6 | 33:23.5-85 |
| Richards | Sandie | JAM | 6Nov68 | 165/ | 400 | 52.18 | |
| Richardson | Jill | CAN | 10Mar65 | 172/59 | 200 | A23.25 | A23.61-84 |
| | | | | | 400 | 51.55 | 51.85-84 |
| Richardson | Lorinda | USA | 19Jul65 | 172/56 | LJ | 6.51 | 6.44-85 |
| Richburg | Diana | USA | 2Jul63 | 171/47 | 800 | 1:59.67 | 1:59.61-85 |
| | | | | | 1k | 2:38.16 | 2:37.92-84 |
| | | | | | 1500 | 4:06.47 | 4:04.07-84 |
| | | | | | Mile | 4:28.1 | 4:33.75-85 |
| Ritter | Louise | USA | 18Feb58 | 178/59 | HJ | 1.93 | 2.01-83 |
| Rivera | Xiomara | CUB | 24Dec68 | 177/74 | JT | 64.56 | 56.26-85 |
| Roberts | Kellie | USA | 16Jun69 | 165/56 | 400h | 56.80 | 59.63-85 |
| Rockenbauer | Nóra | HUN | 25Aug66 | 178/78 | JT | 61.82 | 57.58-85 |
| Rochefort | Ellen | CAN | 22Nov54 | | Mar | 2:35:51 | |
| Rocheleau | Julie | CAN | 64 | | 100h | 13.32w | 13.81 13.72w-84 |
| Rodchenkova | Marina | SU | 30Jul61 | | 3000 | 8:49.12 | 8:47.08-84 |
| | | | | | 5k | 15:28.40 | 15:19.26-85 |
| | | | | | 10k | 32:38.96 | 32:32.55-85 |
| Rodgers | Ansie | RSA | 4Sep64 | 181/73 | JT | 58.26 | 61.08-85 |
| Rodionova | Tatyana | SU | 13Jan56 | 174/65 | LJ | 6.85 | 7.04-83 |
| Rodríguez | Marcelina | CUB | 26Apr60 | 170/90 | SP | 18.05 | 17.95-83 |
| Rogachevskaya | Yelena | SU | 22Nov63 | 178/88 | DT | 57.84 | |
| Rohrmann | Heike | GDR | 22Feb69 | 180/80 | SP | 18.58 | 16.59-85 |
| Romanova | Anna | SU | 9Mar68 | 180/87 | SP | 17.50i 17.43 | 17.32-85 |
| Romanova (Malykhina) | Yelena | SU | 20Mar63 | 158/51 | 1500 | 4:04.60 | 4:09.0 -83 |
| | | | | | 3000 | 8:56.34 | 8:56.03-81 |
| | | | | | | 8:47.79i | |
| Rooks | Nancy | CAN | 13Jun59 | 155/40 | 3000 | 9:02.08 | 9:03.9 -83 |
| | | | | | 10k | 32:30.71 | 32:23.04-83 |
| Rosenquist | Kim | USA | 2May58 | 170/53 | Mar | 2:32:31 | 2:35:59-85 |
| Rössler | Susanne | FRG | 21Mar63 | 174/60 | HJ | 1.88i | 1.90-85 |

| Name | | Nat | Yr | Ht/Wt | Event | 1986 Mark | Pre-1986 best |
|---|---|---|---|---|---|---|---|
| Rotar | Tatyana | SU | 18Jul63 | | HJ | 1.88i | 1.86-85 |
| Rougeron | Brigitte | FRA | 14Jun61 | 183/69 | HJ | 1.92 | 1.92-84 |
| Rouillard | Carole | CAN | 60 | | 3000 | 8:59.15 | 9:11.2 -85 |
| | | | | | 10k | 32:30.93 | 0 |
| Royle | Diane | UK | 24Nov59 | 178/72 | JT | 58.72 | 62.22-85 |
| Ruban | Irina | SU | 12Mar62 | | Mar | 2:32:54 | 2:36:37-85 |
| Ruckle | Tani | AUS | 25Jun62 | | Mar | 2:36:06 | 2:48:36-85 |
| Ruškite | Valda | SU | 26Jan62 | 171/66 | 100h | 13.34 | 13.64-85 |
| | | | | | Hept | 6349 | 6054-83 |
| Rust | Sonja | GDR | 21Sep66 | 179/75 | DT | 59.76 | 57.80-85 |
| | | | | | | | |
| Sacheva | Tatyana | SU | 1Jan64 | | 800 | 2:01.0 | 2:00.2-85 |
| Sachse - Gansky | Diana | GDR | 14Dec63 | 183/87 | DT | 73.26 | 69.14-85 |
| Sahli | Luzia | SWZ | 27May56 | 163/50 | Mar | 2:36:13 | 2:44:15-85 |
| Sakorafa | Sofia | GRE | 29Apr57 | 176/65 | JT | 62.50 | 74.20-82 |
| Salo | Galina | SU | 14Jun59 | 170/62 | LJ | 6.88 | 6.84-84 |
| Salyga | Klavdia | SU | 12Mar61 | | 100 | 11.44 | 11.68-85 |
| | | | | | | | 11.60w-84 |
| Samolyenko (Khamitova) | Tatyana | SU | 12Aug61 | 166/57 | 800 | 1:59.21 | 1:58.56-85 |
| | | | | | 1500 | 3:59.45 | 4:02.41-84 |
| | | | | | 3000 | 8:36.00 | 9:20.0i-85 |
| Samy | Marina | UK | 4Sep60 | | 10k | 33:10.94 | 34:22.7-84 |
| Samy | Shireen | UK | 4Sep60 | | 10k | 33:10.25 | 35:00.6-84 |
| Sanderson | Tessa | UK | 14Mar56 | 170/71 | JT | 69.80 | 73.58-83 |
| Satoh | Megumi | JAP | 13Sep66 | 172/53 | HJ | 1.91i 1.89 | 1.92-85 |
| Savchenko | Svetlana | SU | 17Mar65 | | DT | 60.78 | 61.38-85 |
| Savina | Lyudmila | SU | 15Jul55 | 179/94 | SP | 18.50i | 20.21-84 |
| Scaunich | Emma | ITA | 1Mar54 | 163/48 | Mar | 2:37:50 | 2:36:46-85 |
| Schäfer | Monika | FRG | 6Oct59 | 178/56 | 10k | 33:13.23 | 33:15.7-85 |
| | | | | | Mar | 2:34:05 | |
| Schilly-Laetsch | Katy | USA | 19Oct56 | 162/51 | Mar | 2:36:22 | 2:32:40-84 |
| Schima | Christine | GDR | 6Sep62 | 181/68 | LJ | 6.68 | 6.96-84 |
| Schlosser | Doris | FRG | 29Sep44 | | Mar | 2:37:08 | 2:35:43-84 |
| Schmidt | Anke | GDR | 5Feb68 | 176/60 | LJ | 6.48 6.51w | 6.31-85 |
| | | | | | Hept | 5900 6048W | 5613-85 |
| Schmidt | Astrid | FRG | 3Jul63 | | 10k | 33:22.30 | 33:37.1-85 |
| Schmidt | Birgit | FRG | 12Sep63 | 172/57 | 800 | 2:01.63 | 2:02.40-85 |
| | | | | | 1500 | 4:08.19 | 4:10.38-84 |
| Schmidt (Westover) | Carina | USA | 5Jul61 | 181/64 | HJ | 1.88 | 1.88-84 |
| Schmidt | Vera | FRG | 1Mar61 | 180/80 | SP | 18.58 | 18.38-85 |
| Schmuhl | Liane | GDR | 29Jun61 | 184/90 | SP | 18.92 | 21.27-82 |
| Schneider | Corinne | SWZ | 28Jul62 | 177/62 | Hept | 6032 | 6265-85 |
| Schneider | Sue | USA | 3Aug56 | 173/57 | Mar | 2:36:26 | 2:35:59-85 |
| Scholz | Karen | GDR | 16Sep69 | 182/60 | HJ | 1.92 | 1.86-85 |
| Schönleber | Mechthild | FRG | 10Jul63 | 175/82 | SP | 17.24 | 18.61i 18.08-83 |
| Schroeder | Sue | USA | 20Dec63 | 165/46 | 5k | 15:44.27 | 15:42.7-85 |
| Schromm | Elena | RUM | 3Jun60 | 180/60 | HJ | 1.91 | 1.88-85 |
| Schuckmann | Birgit | GDR | 12Sep60 | | Mar | 2:37:23 | 2:46:52-85 |
| Schulz | Ellen | GDR | 13Apr62 | 176/61 | 800 | 1:59.90 | 2:00.29-84 |
| | | | | | 1500 | 4:11.32 | 4:13.45-85 |
| Schulz | Ines | GDR | 10Jul65 | 177/64 | Hept | 6250 | 6011-85 |
| Schulze | Cordula | GDR | 11Sep59 | 189/92 | SP | 19.58 | 21.00-84 |
| Schwarz | Sabine | FRG | 21Feb67 | | Hept | 5670 | 5469-85 |
| Schwass | Julie | AUS | 16Nov57 | 160/52 | 800 | 2:02.07 | 2:03.1-78 |

| Name | | Nat | Yr | Ht/Wt | Event | 1986 Mark | Pre-1986 best |
|------|---|-----|-----|-------|-------|-----------|---------------|
| Schweitzer | Anne | USA | 29Oct65 | 165/48 | 5k | 15:58.90 | 15:51.52-85 |
| Scott-Bowker | Debbie | CAN | 16Dec58 | 163/52 | 800 | 2:01.48 | 2:02.8-79 |
| | | | | | 1k | 2:38.30 | 2:39.76-84 |
| | | | | | 1500 | 4:05.28 | 4:06.89-83 |
| | | | | | 2k | 5:39.90 | |
| | | | | | 3000 | 8:53.28 | 8:48.85-82 |
| Sedacheva | Inesa | SU | 10Jul64 | | SP | 17.36 | 17.38-84 |
| Sedláková | Gabriela | CS | 2Mar68 | 169/51 | 800 | 2:00.61 | 2:03.22-85 |
| Semiraz | Yelena | SU | 21Nov65 | 168/49 | LJ | 6.50 | |
| Sereda | Marina | SU | 12Apr64 | 172/63 | 400h | 54.78 | 55.16-85 |
| (Kotenyeva) | | | | | | | |
| Sergent | Annette | FRA | 17Nov62 | 157/45 | 1500 | 4:11.32 | 4:10.14-85 |
| | | | | | 2k | 5:39.00 | |
| | | | | | 3000 | 8:46.94 | 8:50.56-85 |
| | | | | | 5k | 15:32.92 | 0 |
| Sergiyevich | Natalya | SU | 21Oct65 | 182/64 | HJ | 1.90 | 1.89-82 |
| Seymour | Leslie | USA | 12May60 | | 3000 | 8:53.10 | |
| | | | | | 5k | 16:04.7 | 16:22.14-85 |
| Shabanova | Irina | SU | 64 | | DT | 60.10 | 60.68-84 |
| Sharpilova | Nadezhda | SU | 2Jan59 | 178/66 | HJ | 1.92 | 1.88-83 |
| Shcherbina | Maria | SU | 29Jul68 | 180/65 | Hept | 5953 | 5570-85 |
| Sheffield | Lat.anya | USA | 11Oct63 | 170/50 | 400h | 55.74 | 54.66-85 |
| Shields | Jane | UK | 23Aug60 | 162/45 | 3000 | 8:56.61 | 8:45.69-83 |
| Shikolenko | Natalya | SU | 64 | 179/83 | JT | 63.56 | 64.60-85 |
| Shimanovich | Natalya | SU | 67 | | LJ | 6.51 | 6.49-85 |
| Shlyakhtich | Natalya | SU | 23Jun62 | 180/84 | SP | 18.99 | 19.13-85 |
| Shmonina | Marina | SU | 9Feb65 | | 200 | 22.9w | 23.65-83 |
| Shpak | Tatyana | SU | 17Nov60 | 174/72 | LJ | 6.49 | 6.65-85 |
| | | | | | Hept | 6103 | 6408-85 |
| Shtereva | Nikolina | BUL | 25Jan55 | 172/59 | 800 | 1:59.80 | 1:55.42-76 |
| | | | | | 1k | 2:38.8 | 2:35.64-82 |
| | | | | | 1500 | 4:03.98 | 4:02.33-76 |
| | | | | | 10k | 33:25.7 | 33:44.7-85 |
| Shubenkova | Natalya | SU | 25Sep57 | 172/64 | 100h | 13.23 | 12.93-84 |
| | | | | | LJ | 6.61 | 6.73-84 |
| | | | | | Hept | 6645 | 6859-84 |
| Shulyak | Inessa | SU | 5Oct66 | 172/58 | LJ | 6.61 | 6.45i-85 |
| Sieger | Susann | GDR | 25Jun68 | 178/54 | 400 | 52.02 | 54.77-85 |
| Siepsiak | Ewa | POL | 1Jan57 | 174/79 | DT | 61.06 | 60.82-85 |
| Simeoni | Sara | ITA | 19Apr53 | 178/60 | HJ | 1.94 | 2.01-78 |
| Simon | Livia | RUM | 6Mar65 | 175/82 | SP | 19.61 | 18.75-85 |
| | | | | | DT | 60.46 | 54.64-85 |
| Simon | Nathalie | FRA | 14Apr62 | 170/59 | 400 | 52.18 | 53.34-84 |
| Simova | Stefania | BUL | 5Jun63 | 172/79 | DT | 60.66 | 61.04-85 |
| Simpson | Judy | UK | 14Nov60 | 182/72 | 100h | 13.05 | 13.07-84 |
| | | | | | HJ | 1.92 | 1.92-83 |
| | | | | | LJ | 6.56w | 6.40-84 |
| | | | | | Hept | 6623 | 6347-83 |
| Sipatova | Yelena | SU | 7Jun55 | 163/48 | 3000 | 8:50.82 | 8:33.53-80 |
| | | | | | 5k | 15:30.60 | 15:24.6 -81 |
| | | | | | 10k | 33:14.10 | 32:17.19-81 |
| Siska | Xénia | HUN | 3Nov57 | 174/58 | 100h | 12.77 | 12.76-84 |
| Skibicki | Mila | FRG | 26Dec64 | 178/63 | HJ | 1.90i | 1.87-83 |
| Skeete | Lesley-Ann | UK | 20Feb67 | 166/54 | 100h | 13.24w | 13.51-85 |
| Sklyarenko | Irina | SU | 7Nov64 | 155/49 | Mar | 2:37:06 | 2:42:48-85 |
| Skoglund | Ann-Louise | SWE | 28Jun62 | 174/58 | 200 | 23.32 | 23.27-85 |
| | | | | | 400 | 51.69 | 51.78-83 |
| | | | | | 100h | 13.39 13.24w | 13.25-85 |
| | | | | | 400h | 54.15 | 54.57-82 |
| Skvortsova | Yekaterina | SU | 23Nov61 | 164/50 | 3000 | 9:01.14 | |
| | | | | | 5k | 16:02.19 | |

| Name | | Nat | Yr | Ht/Wt | Event | 1986 Mark | Pre-1986 best |
|---|---|---|---|---|---|---|---|
| Slegers | Lieve | BEL | 6Apr65 | 160/50 | 5k | 15:45.89 | 16:23.7-85 |
| | | | | | 10k | 32:26.90 | 0 |
| Sluzhkina | Marina | SU | 2Aug60 | | 100h | 13.26 | 12.96-85 |
| (Kibakina) | | | | | LJ | 6.55i | 7.01-85 |
| Sly | Wendy | UK | 5Nov59 | 168/52 | 1500 | 4:04.86 | 4:04.14-83 |
| | | | | | Mile | 4:28.18 | 4:28.07-84 |
| | | | | | 3000 | 8:47.00 | 8:37.06-83 |
| Slyadnyeva | Yekaterina | SU | 4Dec64 | | JT | 57.92 | 55.02-85 |
| Slyusar | Irina | SU | 19Mar63 | 165/54 | 100 | 11.09 | 11.11 10.8-85 |
| | | | | | 200 | 22.98 | 22.59-85 |
| Smalls | Odessa | USA | 8Jul64 | 175/61 | 100 | 11.43 | 11.60-85 |
| | | | | | | 11.37w | 11.46w-84 |
| | | | | | 200 | 23.27 | 23.39-85 |
| | | | | | | 23.15w | 23.09w-85 |
| Smeikšte | Ilga | SU | 10Jan66 | 174/73 | DT | 61.70 | 53.98-85 |
| Smekhnova | Raisa | SU | 16Sep50 | 166/52 | Mar | 2:32:46 | 2:29:10-84 |
| Smirnova | Marina | SU | 22Oct60 | 169/61 | 100h | 13.41 | 13.63 13.1-82 |
| Smith | Caryl | USA | 19Apr69 | 165/56 | 100 | 11.46 | A11.70 A11.4-85 |
| | | | | | | 11.28w | 11.66w-85 |
| Smith | Janet | USA | 11Dec65 | | 10k | 33:10.8 | |
| Smith | Maryke | RSA | 15Sep66 | | 100 | A11.43 A11.39w | 11.85-85 |
| | | | | | 200 | 23.27 | 24.38-85 |
| Sokolova | Eva | SU | 25Mar61 | 170/59 | 100h | 13.10 13.0 | 13.34-83 |
| Sokolova | Tatyana | SU | 58 | | 5k | 15:48.10 | 16:04.36-85 |
| Solberg | Trine | NOR | 18Apr66 | 172/65 | JT | 67.80 | 68.94-85 |
| Sorokivskaya | Natalya | SU | 23Jul62 | | 3000 | 8:49.15 | 8:49.28-84 |
| | | | | | 5k | 15:28.55 | |
| | | | | | 10k | 32:06.38 | 35:42.2-84 |
| Sørum | Christin | NOR | 12Jan68 | 169/49 | 3000 | 9:00.13 | 9:07.54-85 |
| | | | | | 5k | 15:51.0 | 0 |
| Sowunmi | Sadia | NIG | 3Nov64 | 163/50 | 400 | 52.43 | 52.77-85 |
| Spence | Vivianne | JAM | | | 200 | 23.23w | |
| Springs | Betty | USA | 12Jun61 | 157/46 | 3000 | 9:01.06 | 8:59.79-83 |
| | | | | | 5k | 15:30.99 | 15:25.24-85 |
| Sripet | Ratjai | THA | 23Dec60 | 160/42 | 100 | 11.51 | 11.65 11.61w-85 |
| Stäheli | Ursula | SWZ | 23Dec57 | 180/79 | SP | 17.78 | 17.58-85 |
| Staicu | Simona | RUM | 5May71 | 164/48 | 1500 | 4:08.85 | 4:21.49-85 |
| Stalmach | Jolanta | POL | 3Aug60 | 168/53 | 400h | 56.79 | 55.89-85 |
| Stamenova | Rositsa | BUL | 6Mar55 | 167/53 | 400 | 51.45 | 50.82-84 |
| Stanciu | Anişoara | RUM | 28Jun62 | 174/65 | LJ | 6.60i 6.58 | 7.43-83 |
| Stanescu | Mariana | RUM | 7Sep64 | 168/51 | 800 | 2:00.49 | 2:02.19-85 |
| | | | | | 1500 | 4:04.69 | 4:07.32-85 |
| | | | | | Mile | 4:25.52 | |
| | | | | | 3000 | 8:38.83 | 8:48.52-85 |
| | | | | | 5k | 15:41.36 | |
| Stanton | Christine | AUS | 12Dec59 | 183/68 | HJ | 1.94 | 1.96-85 |
| Stass | Yelena | SU | 25Jun65 | 170/60 | 400h | 56.55 | 59.16-83 57.9-85 |
| Steely | Shelly | USA | 23Oct62 | 168/52 | 3000 | 9:03.95 | 9:03.86-84 |
| Sterk | Katalin | HUN | 30Sep61 | 178/64 | HJ | 1.98 | 1.99i 1.96-82 |
| Steuk | Martina | GDR | 11Nov59 | 170/63 | 800 | 2:02.04 | 1:56.21-80 |
| Stevens | Rochelle | USA | 8Sep66 | 173/54 | 400 | 51.90 | 53.31-85 |
| Stewart | Sharon | AUS | 17Aug65 | 171/62 | 200 | 23.36 | 23.74-85 |
| | | | | | 400 | 52.27 | 52.92-85 |
| Stolzenburg | Carmen | GDR | 25Mar66 | 167/55 | 400h | 57.70 | 57.88-85 |
| Stolyar | Lyubov | SU | 61 | | 100h | 13.30 | 13.18-84 12.9-85 |
| (Lyakisheva) | | | | | | | |
| Storp | Stephanie | FRG | 28Nov68 | 194/88 | SP | 19.11 | 17.72-85 |
| | | | | | DT | 58.28 | 52.26-85 |
| Stoyanova | Yordanka | BUL | 9May56 | 168/50 | 400 | 52.23 | 52.61-85 |
| (Krumova) | | | | | | | |

| Name | | Nat | Yr | Ht/Wt | Event | 1986 Mark | | Pre-1986 best |
|---|---|---|---|---|---|---|---|---|
| Straschewski | Anke | FRG | 16Apr63 | | Hept | 5694 | | 5409-84 |
| Strejčková | Jarmila | CS | 15Feb53 | 167/57 | LJ | 6.49 | | 6.89-82 |
| Strnadová | Milena | CS | 23May61 | 162/52 | 800 | 1:57.90 | | 1:57.28-83 |
| Strong | Shirley | UK | 18Nov58 | 173/63 | 100h | 13.30 | | 12.87-83 |
| | | | | | | | | 12.78w-82 |
| Struckhoff | Jacque | USA | 6Jul65 | 178/54 | 5k | 15:54.12 | | 15:57.73-85 |
| | | | | | 10k | 33:22.5 | | |
| Styepanova | Marina | SU | 1May50 | 167/60 | 200 | 22.5 | | 23.8-85 |
| | | | | | 400 | 51.69 | 51.6 | 51.25-80 |
| | | | | | 400h | 52.94 | | 53.67-84 |
| Styepanova | Nadezhda | SU | 22Jul59 | 170/60 | 800 | 2:01.0 | | 2:00.1-85 |
| | | | | | 1500 | 4:09.3 | | 4:10.2 -84 |
| | | | | | 3000 | 8:49.71 | | 8:55.8-85 |
| | | | | | 10k | 32:25.19 | | 32:29.28-85 |
| Sui | Xinmei | CHN | 65 | | SP | 18.87 | | 16.24-85 |
| Sukhareva | Marina | SU | 11Apr62 | | 100h | 13.39 | 13.1 | 13.06-83 |
| Sukhareva | Oksana | SU | 63 | | 100h | 13.11 | 13.35-85 | 13.2-84 |
| (Lomot) | | | | | | | | |
| Sukhova | Antonina | SU | 1Jan59 | 178/67 | Hept | 6077M | | 6247M-84 |
| Sulinski | Cathy | USA | 3Apr58 | 175/76 | JT | 60.20 | | 61.10-84 |
| Sun | Xiurong | CHN | 27Mar69 | | JT | 60.74 | | |
| Suter | Esther | SWZ | 25Feb62 | 174/55 | Hept | 5814 | | 5712-84 |
| Svetonosova | Irina | SU | 6Jun58 | 174/62 | 100h | 13.21 | 13.0 | 13.29 13.0-84 |
| | | | | | 400h | 56.51 | 56.3 | |
| Svirskaya | Lyubov | SU | 18Sep60 | 165/52 | Mar | 2:32:21 | | 2:34:53-84 |
| Szabó | Karolina | HUN | 17Nov61 | 149/36 | 5k | 15:34.69 | | 15:32.49-85 |
| | | | | | 10k | 31:55.93 | | 32:38.5 -84 |
| | | | | | Mar | 2:30.31 | | 2:33:43-84 |
| Szélinger | Viktória | HUN | 18Aug56 | 182/87 | SP | 17.32 | | 18.34-84 |
| Szopori | Erika | HUN | 1Dec63 | 172/55 | 400h | 57.56 | | 57.18-84 |
| | | | | | | | | |
| Talbot | Jenny | AUS | 14Jul64 | 178/54 | HJ | 1.88 | | 1.85-85 |
| Tanović | Samra | YUG | 19Jul66 | 178/62 | HJ | 1.89 | | 1.87-85 |
| Tarasova | Alexandra | SU | 6Feb58 | | 3000 | 9:02.50 | | |
| | | | | | 5k | 16:02.35 | | |
| | | | | | 10k | 33:19.5 | | 34:18.6 -84 |
| Tarkalanova | Tanya | BUL | 28Mar65 | 167/57 | 100h | 13.33 | | 14.38-85 |
| | | | | | Hept | 6001 | | 5112-85 |
| Tarolo | Rossella | ITA | 28Dec64 | 174/53 | 100 | 11.45 | 11.42w | 11.64-85 |
| | | | | | 200 | 23.09 | | 23.73-85 |
| Tatichek | Svetlana | SU | 29Jun62 | | SP | 18.29 | | 17.46-84 |
| Ter-Mersobian | Tatyana | SU | 12May68 | 178/59 | LJ | 6.60 | | 6.16-85 |
| Terenchenko | Marina | SU | 18Mar61 | | JT | 59.58 | | 62.12-82 |
| Tesárková | Jitka | CS | 27Oct65 | 163/59 | 100h | 13.39 | 13.38 | 13.21w-85 |
| Teske | Charlotte | FRG | 23Nov49 | 167/55 | Mar | 2:32:10 | | 2:28:32-83 |
| Thacker | Angela | USA | 27Jun64 | 168/60 | 100 | 11.42 | 11.39-84 | 11.20w-83 |
| | | | | | 200 | A23.05w | | 23.15-84 |
| | | | | | | | | 23.07w-83 |
| | | | | | LJ | A6.65 | | 6.81-84 |
| Theele (Terpe) | Heike | GDR | 4Oct64 | 172/63 | 100h | 12.63 | 13.02 | 12.99w-84 |
| Thiele | Sibylle | GDR | 6Mar65 | 177/74 | 100h | 13.14 | | 13.40-85 |
| | | | | | LJ | 6.67i | 6.62 | 6.77-85 |
| | | | | | Hept | 6635 | | 6487-85 |
| Thiémard | Denise | SWZ | 24Mar60 | 168/67 | JT | 62.30 | | 63.96-85 |
| Thieme | Andrea | GDR | 8Jun64 | 185/82 | DT | 65.20 | | 64.36-85 |
| Thimm | Ute | FRG | 10Jul58 | 167/53 | 100 | 11.34 | | 11.31-85 |
| | | | | | 200 | 22.88 | | 22.95-84 |
| | | | | | 400 | 51.15 | | 50.37-84 |

| Name | | Nat | Yr | Ht/Wt | Event | 1986 Mark | Pre-1986 best |
|------|--|-----|-----|-------|-------|-----------|---------------|
| Thomas | Margaret | USA | 21Sep59 | | 5k | 15:58.77 | |
| Thorpe | Helen | UK | 24Oct63 | 169/56 | 800 | 2:02.02 | 2:05.68-85 |
| Thoumas | Nathalie | FRA | 30Apr62 | 165/53 | 800 | 2:00.68 | 2:01.4-85 |
| Thyssen | Ingrid | FRG | 9Jan56 | 171/72 | JT | 67.34 | 68.84-85 |
| Tifrea | Corinna | RUM | 11Feb58 | 169/62 | Hept | 5680 | 6085-82 |
| Tillack | Heike | GDR | 6Jan68 | 171/60 | 100h | 13.10 | 13.24-85 |
| Tkachenko | Lyudmila | SU | 15Jul63 | 175/57 | HJ | 1.88 | 1.85-84 |
| Tochilova | Natalya | SU | 64 | | 100h | 13.28  13.25w | 13.1-85 |
| Tokuyama | Naomi | JAP | 22Oct68 | 163/60 | JT | 58.52 | |
| Tolstoguzova | Yelena | SU | 17Jun62 | | 10k | 33:05.41 | |
| Tomasini | Cristina | ITA | 22Jul58 | 163/53 | 5k | 16:00.49 | 16:04.19-85 |
| | | | | | 10k | 32:40.22 | 33:37.07-83 |
| Tooby | Angela | UK | 24Oct60 | 166/49 | 5k | 15:28.16 | 15:22.50-84 |
| | | | | | 10k | 31:56.59 | 32:58.07-84 |
| Tooby | Susan | UK | 24Oct60 | 165/49 | 5k | 15:41.36 | 15:32.19-85 |
| | | | | | 10k | 32:56.78 | 0 |
| Topchina | Yelena | SU | 28Oct66 | 178/59 | HJ | 1.92 | 1.94-83 |
| Torma | Ibolya | HUN | 22Sep55 | 164/62 | JT | 61.40 | 61.34-81 |
| Torrence | Gwen | USA | 12Jun65 | 170/52 | 100 | 11.30 | 11.40-85 |
| | | | | | | 11.01w | 11.11w-85 |
| | | | | | 200 | 22.53 | 22.96-85 |
| Trojer | Irmgard | ITA | 16Mar64 | 170/57 | 400h | 57.77 | 57.95-85 |
| Trylińska | Elżbieta | POL | 5Oct60 | 177/58 | HJ | 1.94 | 1.94-80 |
| Tsiruk | Natalya | SU | 15Apr55 | 168/58 | 400h | 57.4 | 55.49-81 |
| Tsud | Inna | SU | 17Jan67 | 177/64 | 400h | 57.5 | 59.63-85 |
| Tuffey | Suzie | USA | 15Feb67 | | 5k | 15:51.13 | |
| Turchak | Olga | SU | 5Mar67 | 190/60 | HJ | 2.01 | 1.96-84 |
| Twomey | Cathie | USA | 24Oct56 | 162/50 | 3000 | 9:02.38 | 8:48.55-84 |
| | | | | | Mar | 2:35:42 | 2:39:15-84 |
| Tyukhay | Irina | SU | 14Jan67 | | Hept | 5922 | 5863M 5680-85 |
| Tyurina | Yelena | SU | 3Aug64 | | 1500 | 4:11.08 | |
| Uba | Rufina | NIG | 4Apr59 | 173/63 | 100 | 11.48 | 11.31 11.18w-82 |
| Uebel (Ludwig) | Ronny | GDR | 19Nov63 | 165/54 | 400 | 52.05 | 52.86-85 |
| Uglem | Marit | NOR | 4Apr61 | | 10k | 33:14.07 | 0 |
| Uhliuc | Olga | RUM | 21Mar67 | 182/90 | SP | 17.64 | 15.56 15.41i-85 |
| Uibel | Gloria | GDR | 13Jan64 | 171/54 | 100h | 12.91 | 12.79-84 |
| Ulmasova | Svetlana | SU | 4Feb53 | 163/53 | 1500 | 4:08.17 | 3:58.76-82 |
| | | | | | 3000 | 8.39.19 | 8:26.78-82 |
| | | | | | 5k | 15:05.50 | 0 |
| | | | | | 10k | 32:14.83 | 32:47.81-82 |
| Urish - McLatchie | Carol | USA | 28Oct51 | 173/55 | 10k | 33:23.02 | 33:03.06-84 |
| Usha | Pillavulakandi | IND | 20May64 | 170/57 | 400 | 52.16 | 51.61-85 |
| | | | | | 400h | 56.08  56.0 | 55.42-84 |
| Usifo | Maria | NIG | 1Aug64 | 174/63 | 100 | 11.46w | 12.01-84 11.9-82 |
| | | | | | 200 | 23.22w | 24.83-84 24.6-82 |
| | | | | | 100h | 13.13 | 13.20 13.19w-85 |
| | | | | | 400h | 55.16 | 55.49-85 |
| Usmanova | Nadezhda | SU | 6Dec56 | 160/52 | Mar | 2:37:43 | 2:30:36-84 |
| Ustinova | Valentina | SU | 28Mar57 | 156/46 | Mar | 2:33:02 | 2:34:27-85 |
| Uusitalo | Helena | FIN | 7Nov62 | 167/56 | JT | 60.14 | 61.58-85 |

| Name | | Nat | Yr | Ht/Wt | Event | 1986 Mark | Pre-1986 best |
|------|--|-----|-----|-------|-------|-----------|---------------|
| van der Walt | Nanette | RSA | 22Feb59 | | DT | 58.80 | 57.04-85 |
| van Heerden | Hilsa | RSA | 23Mar61 | 167/46 | Hept | 5678 | 0 |
| (van der Heever) | | | | | | | |
| van Heezik | Edine | HOL | 27Jan61 | 175/53 | LJ | 6.55w | 6.57-80 |
| van Hulst | Elly | HOL | 9Jun59 | 178/58 | 1500 | 4:04.32 | 4:03.78-82 |
| | | | | | Mile | 4:22.40 | 4:28.24-85 |
| | | | | | 2k | 5:39.52 | |
| | | | | | 3000 | 8:48.25 | 8:58.28-85 |
| van Landeghem | Rita | BEL | 19Jul57 | 164/58 | 3000 | 9:01.29 | 9:21.86-85 |
| | | | | | 10k | 32:29.73 | 33:40.30-84 |
| | | | | | Mar | 2:37:27 | 2:34:13-84 |
| van Niekerk | Maryna | RSA | 14May54 | 169/57 | LJ | A6.80  A6.77-80 | A6.82w-82 |
| | | | | | | | 6.64-82 |
| van Rensburg | Ina | RSA | 29Oct56 | 169/56 | 100h | A13.09 | A13.14 13.19-82 |
| | | | | | | | A13.11w-82 |
| Vader | Els | HOL | 24Sep59 | 162/52 | 100 | 11.17 | 11.25 11.0-81 |
| | | | | | 200 | 22.86 22.55w | 22.81-81 |
| | | | | | 400 | 51.92 | 53.10-85 |
| Vahlensieck | Christa | FRG | 27May49 | 160/51 | Mar | 2:34:50 | 2:33:22-83 |
| Vaidean | Petra | RUM | 24Aug65 | 170/66 | Hept | 6217 | 5743-83 |
| (Mihalache) | | | | | | | |
| Valkova | Ivanka | BUL | 2Mar65 | 165/56 | LJ | 6.53 | 6.26-82 |
| | | | | | Hept | 5899 | 5340-85 |
| Vallecilla | Nancy | ECU | 24Nov57 | 172/67 | 100h | 13.25  13.76-80 | 13.2w-85 |
| Valova-Demireva | Valya | BUL | 23Aug61 | 173/60 | 100 | 11.38 | 11.86-79 |
| Valyukevich | Irina | SU | 19Nov59 | 170/60 | LJ | 7.07 7.10w | 7.07-85 |
| Vanatta | Chris | USA | 5Jul64 | 165/ | 5k | 15:55.3 | 16:24.95-85 |
| Vancheva | Ivanka | BUL | 31Oct53 | 170/65 | JT | 61.40 | 65.38-80 |
| Vanyek | Zsuzsa | HUN | 18Jan60 | 168/59 | LJ | 6.72 | 6.81-83 |
| Vašíčková | Soňa | CS | 14Mar62 | 174/78 | SP | 19.70 | 18.61-85 |
| | | | | | DT | 58.24 | 60.16-85 |
| Vasileva | Valya | BUL | 9Apr61 | 166/64 | Hept | 5844 | 5797-85 |
| Vasilyeva | Galina | SU | 17Aug60 | | DT | 59.38 | 60.68-84 |
| Vasilyeva | Lyubov | SU | 14Aug57 | 174/83 | SP | 19.78 | 19.68-83 |
| Vasilyeva | Valentina | SU | 64 | | 5k | 15:40.49 | |
| Vasilyuk | Maria | SU | 26Jan62 | 164/51 | 3000 | 8:57.27 | 9:00.39-82 |
| | | | | | 5k | 15:33.57 | 15:45.70-85 |
| Vasyutina | Irina | SU | 13Jan59 | 184/88 | DT | 57.80 | 63.46-83 |
| Vazhenina | Nadezhda | SU | 18Jul63 | | 800 | 2:00.1 | 2:03.3-85 |
| - Izadyorova | | | | | 1500 | 4:11.63 | 4:09.7-85 |
| | | | | | 3000 | 9:02.36 | 9:04.90-85 |
| Veith | Gabriele | GDR | 24Oct56 | 166/55 | 1500 | 4:11.29 | 4:03.1-78 |
| | | | | | 3000 | 8:50.68 | 8:52.60-78 |
| | | | | | | 8:47.00i | |
| | | | | | 5k | 15:21.90 | 0 |
| | | | | | 10k | 32:17.22 | 32:53.8-83 |
| Veréb | Erika | HUN | 23Oct63 | 160/46 | 5k | 15:23.54 | 15:49.93-85 |
| | | | | | 10k | 32:15.56 | 33:18.10-85 |
| Vereen | Wendy | USA | 24Apr66 | 160/54 | 100 | 11.40  A11.17-83 | 11.32-84 |
| | | | | | 200 | 22.96 | 22.99-83 |
| | | | | | | | 22.75w-84 |
| Verouli | Anna | GRE | 13Nov56 | 165/88 | JT | 64.30 | 72.70-84 |
| Veselinova | Verzhinia | BUL | 18Nov57 | 170/95 | SP | 18.50 | 21.61-82 |
| Vickers | Janeene | USA | 3Dec68 | 170/62 | 400 | 52.25 | 53.83-85 |
| Vidosova | Irina | SU | 8Dec61 | | SP | 18.33i | 17.73-85 |
| Vidotto | Wilma | ITA | 20May65 | 171/72 | JT | 59.12 | 55.26-85 |

| Name | | Nat | Yr | Ht/Wt | Event | 1986 Mark | Pre-1986 best |
|------|---|-----|-----|-------|-------|-----------|----------------|
| Vieira Telles | Soraya | BRA | 16Sep58 | 167/54 | 800 | 2:01.55 | 2:06.18-85 |
| Villeton | Jocelyne | FRA | 17Sep54 | 170/55 | 10k | 32:59.67 | 34:17.13-85 |
| | | | | | Mar | 2:32:22 | 2:35:50-85 |
| Vinogradova | Yelena | SU | 28Mar64 | 170/58 | 200 | 22.81 | 22.87-84 |
| Vitoulová | Alena | CS | 6May60 | 176/89 | SP | 18.78 | 18.56-85 |
| Vizcaino | Natividad | SPA | 27Jan54 | 164/61 | JT | 60.64 | 55.22-84 |
| Vladykina | Olga | SU | 30Jun63 | 170/61 | 200 | 22.58 | 22.44-85 |
| - Bryzgina | | | | | 400 | 49.67 | 48.27-85 |
| Vlasova | Yelena | SU | 1Mar66 | | 800 | 2:00.90 | 2:07.83-85 |
| Vogel | Elmarie | RSA | 7Jun60 | | 400h | A57.24 | A58.17-83 |
| Vörös | Hajnal | HUN | 28Nov59 | 177/86 | SP | 17.50 | 17.63-85 |
| Voyevudskaya | Lyudmila | SU | 22Jun58 | 178/95 | SP | 20.22 | 20.24-84 |
| Wachtel | Christine | GDR | 6Jan65 | 166/56 | 800 | 1:58.59 | 1:56.71-85 |
| Wade | Kirsty | GB | 6Aug62 | 167/56 | 800 | 2:00.01 | 1:57.42-85 |
| (McDermott) | | | | | 1k | 2:35.48 | 2:33.69-85 |
| | | | | | 1500 | 4:03.74 | 4:02.83-85 |
| | | | | | Mile | 4:21.61 | 4:19.41-85 |
| Wagner | Astrid | GDR | 3Nov65 | 184/88 | SP | 18.95 | 19.36-85 |
| Waitz | Grete | NOR | 1Oct53 | 172/52 | Mar | 2:24:54 | 2:25:29-83 |
| Ważendziak | Renata | POL | 18Jan50 | 157/49 | Mar | 2:32:30 | 2:39:27-85 |
| Wall | Gwen | CAN | 16Jan63 | 175/56 | 400h | 56.89 | 56.10-83 |
| Walterová | Ivana | CS | 26May62 | 174/61 | 800 | 2:01.12 | 2:01.36-84 |
| (Kleinová) | | | | | 1500 | 4:01.84 | 4:05.52-84 |
| | | | | | Mile | 4:22.82 | 0 |
| Walton-Floyd | Delisa | USA | 28Jul61 | 173/58 | 400 | 51.44 | 52.34-85 52.0-82 |
| | | | | | 800 | 2:00.00 | 2:00.17-85 |
| Wang | Huabi | CHN | 66 | | 3000 | 9:02.70 | 9:15.64-85 |
| | | | | | 5k | 15:52.19 | 16:41.59-85 |
| Wang | Jing | CHN | 63 | | JT | 59.90 | 64.18-85 |
| Wang | Jinling | CHN | 65 | | JT | 60.58 | |
| Wang | Xiuting | CHN | 11May65 | | 10k | 32:47.77 | |
| Wang | Zhihui | CHN | 65 | | LJ | 6.50 | 6.33-85 |
| Washington | Essie | USA | 12Jan57 | 179/52 | 800 | 2:00.8$ | 2:00.35-84 |
| Washington | Jackie | USA | 17Jul62 | 168/61 | 100 | 11.25 | A11.11-83 |
| | | | | | | 10.94w | 11.33-83 |
| | | | | | 200 | 22.68 | 23.10 22.8w-84 |
| Watkins | Gayle | USA | 5Nov58 | 168/54 | 100h | 13.18w | 13.39-85 |
| | | | | | | | 13.35w-84 |
| Webb | Brenda | USA | 30May54 | 157/41 | 3000 | 8:56.08 | 8:48.09-83 |
| | | | | | 5k | 15:39.44 | 15:22.76-84 |
| | | | | | | 15:37.5i | |
| Weber-Leutner | Carina | AUT | 10Jun60 | 164/42 | Mar | 2:37:09 | 0 |
| Weber | Ursula | AUT | 26Sep60 | 165/66 | DT | 59.04 | 55.86-84 |
| Weidenbach | Lisa | USA | 13Dec61 | 176/57 | Mar | 2:35:42 | 2:31:31-84 |
| (Larsen) | | | | | | | |
| Welch | Lesley | USA | 12Mar63 | 175/56 | 1500 | 4:08.54 | 4:13.58-85 |
| | | | | | 2k | 5:37.86 | 5:54.6i-84 |
| | | | | | 3000 | 8:44.86 | 9:02.92-85 |
| | | | | | | | 9:01.6i-84 |
| | | | | | 5k | 15:19.84i$ | 15:28.33-85 |
| Welch | Lisa | USA | 12Mar63 | 175/54 | 10k | 32:41.9 | |
| Wen | Yanmin | CHN | 19Aug66 | | Mar | 2:36:55 | 2:35:50-84 |
| Wennberg | Christine | SWE | 11May63 | 161/55 | 400h | 56.69 | 57.97-85 |
| Werthmüller | Vroni | SWZ | 5May59 | 170/55 | 100 | 11.39 | 11.50 11.39w-84 |
| Weser | Marion | GDR | 23Dec62 | 174/59 | Hept | 6196 | 6070-81 |

| Name | | Nat | Yr | Ht/Wt | Event | 1986 Mark | Pre-1986 best |
|---|---|---|---|---|---|---|---|
| Wessinghage | Ellen | FRG | 28Jun48 | 159/48 | 10k | 32:52.93 | 33:08.99-85 |
| Whitbread | Fatima | UK | 3Mar61 | 168/68 | JT | 77.44 | 72.98-85 |
| Whittaker | Sandra | UK | 29Jan63 | 168/52 | 100 | 11.50 | 11.63 11.34w-83 |
| Whittingham | Christine | UK | 1Dec56 | 162/49 | 1k | 2:37.05 | 2:37.34-82 |
| (McMeekin) | | | | | 1500 | 4:06.24 | 4:12.43-78 |
| Wiese | Christa | GDR | 25Dec67 | 180/76 | SP | 18.02 | 17.17-85 |
| Wiley | Alison | CAN | 11Oct63 | 165/45 | 3000 | 9:01.2 | 8:51.27-83 |
| | | | | | 5k | 16:04.43 | 15:36.55-84 |
| Wilkenson | Karen | RSA | 7Jan66 | | 400h | A56.77 | 58.93-85 |
| Williams | Diane | USA | 14Dec61 | 163/56 | 100 | 11.18 A11.0 | A10.94-83 |
| | | | | | | 10.92w | 11.00-83 |
| | | | | | 200 | 22.60 | 23.04 22.65w-83 |
| Williams | Lynn | CAN | 11Jul60 | 153/48 | 1500 | 4:07.35 | 4:00.27-85 |
| | | | | | Mile | 4:25.57 | 4:28.03-85 |
| | | | | | 3000 | 8:52.91 | 8:37.38-85 |
| Williams Rodgers | Nedrea | USA | 14Aug65 | 168/56 | 200 | 23.18 | A23.76-85 |
| | | | | | | | 23.58w 23.4-85 |
| Williams | Sabrina | USA | 4Sep63 | 169/59 | LJ | 6.63 6.64w | 6.54 6.55w-85 |
| Williams | Schowonda | USA | 3Dec66 | 160/57 | 100h | 13.32w 13.1 | 13.43-85 |
| | | | | | 400h | 55.38 | 55.65-85 |
| Wilson | Linetta | USA | 11Oct67 | | 400 | A52.38 | 53.10-85 |
| Winkelmann | Antje | FRG | 22May65 | 160/48 | 3000 | 9:00.03 | 9:21.93-85 |
| | | | | | 5k | 15:52.11 | |
| Wittich | Ines | GDR | 14Nov69 | 189/90 | SP | 18.37 | 15.81-85 |
| Włodarczyk | Urzsula | POL | 22Dec65 | 180/69 | Hept | 5721 | 5503-85 |
| Wodars | Sigrun | GDR | 7Nov65 | 166/55 | 400 | 51.95 | 52.96-85 |
| (Ludwigs) | | | | | 800 | 1:57.05 | 1:58.32-85 |
| Wojdecka | Marzena | POL | 3Mar63 | 176/63 | 400 | 51.44 | 53.15-85 |
| Wolf | Gabriele | FRG | 28Oct60 | | Mar | 2:36:34 | 2:35:41-84 |
| Wolska | Małgorzata | POL | 6Sep66 | 177/78 | SP | 17.78 | 16.84-85 |
| Wood | Krishna | AUS | 18May66 | 171/46 | Mile | 4:31.2$ | |
| | | | | | 3000 | 8:53.03 | |
| | | | | | 5k | 15:28.84 | |
| Wray | Yvette | UK | 18Oct58 | 170/63 | 400h | 57.07 | 56.46-81 |
| Wühn | Katrin | GDR | 19Nov65 | 173/57 | 800 | 1:58.80 | 1:57.86-84 |
| | | | | | 1500 | 4:05.96 | 4:10.22-84 |
| Wyludda | Ilke | GDR | 28Mar69 | 184/88 | SP | 19.08 | 18.27-85 |
| | | | | | DT | 65.86 | 62.36-85 |
| Wysocki | Ruth | USA | 8Mar57 | 176/59 | 1500 | 4:10.08 | 4:00.18-84 |
| | | | | | 3000 | 8:53.23 | 8:56.84-85 |
| | | | | | | | 8:49.93i-85 |
| Xia | Yingyi | CHN | 63 | | JT | 59.60 | |
| Xin | Ailan | CHN | 65 | | DT | 57.98 | 57.46-85 |
| Xin | Xiaojian | CHN | 22Sep66 | 165/60 | JT | 60.94 | 58.56-83 |
| Xiao | Hongyan | CHN | 1Jan65 | | 5k | 16:02.61 | 16:16.49-85 |
| | | | | | 10k | 33:11.12 | 34:34.8-85 |
| Xu | Demei | CHN | 67 | | JT | 60.10 | 58.82-85 |
| Yakimova | Elvira | SU | 3May64 | | HJ | 1.94 | 1.85i-81 |
| Yamamoto | Kumi | JAP | 2Oct65 | 163/59 | JT | 58.38 | 57.66-85 |
| Yang | Yanqin | CHN | 28Aug66 | 168/110 | SP | 18.79 | 18.10-85 |

| Name | | Nat | Yr | Ht/Wt | Event | 1986 Mark | Pre-1986 best |
|---|---|---|---|---|---|---|---|
| Yapeyeva | Nina | SU | 3Jan56 | 169/51 | 10k | 32:33.73 | 33:03.5-85 |
| Yatchenko | Irina | SU | 65 | | DT | 57.58 | 60.56-85 |
| Yelagina | Lidia | SU | 1Apr64 | | 100 | 11.34 11.0 | 11.86-82 |
| Yemelyanenko | Larisa | SU | 25Jul64 | | 3000 | 8:57.22 | |
| Yermilova | Svetlana | SU | 12Feb59 | 172/60 | 100h | 13.35 | 13.59-85 |
| Yermakova (Savinkova) | Galina | SU | 15Jul53 | 182/98 | DT | 68.32 | 73.28-84 |
| Yermolovich (Kolenchukova) | Natalya | SU | 29Apr64 | 168/70 | JT | 66.64 | 69.86-85 |
| Yerokhina | Nadezhda | SU | 21Nov56 | | Mar | 2:37:30 | 2:35:56-85 |
| Yeryomina | Alla | SU | 16Nov56 | 168/59 | Hept | 5819 | 6005-83 |
| Yevko | Vera | SU | 28Apr59 | | SP | 18.62i 18.52 | 19.01-85 |
| Yevseyeva | Inna | SU | 14Aug64 | 181/56 | 400 | 50.80 50.6 | 51.88-84 |
| | | | | | 800 | 2:00.6 | 2:02.7-83 |
| | | | | | 400h | 55.85 | 56.93-85 |
| Yevstigneyeva | Marina | SU | 14Apr62 | 180/70 | HJ | 1.94 | 1.88-85 |
| Yokosuka | Hisano | JAP | 7Oct65 | 155/41 | 5k | 16:01.1 | 16:09.0 -84 |
| Young | Candy | USA | 21May62 | 168/58 | 100h | 13.38 | 12.89-82 |
| Young | Dannette | USA | 6Oct64 | 165/57 | 100 | 11.31 | 11.32-85 |
| | | | | | 200 | 23.12 | 22.92-85 |
| | | | | | | 22.84w | 22.85w-85 |
| Younger | Ursula | USA | | 157/52 | 100 | 11.47w | |
| Yu | Hourun | CHN | 63 | | DT | 62.08 | 57.14-85 |
| Yurchenko | Aelita | SU | 1Jan65 | 165/54 | 400 | 51.01 | 52.27-84 51.8-85 |
| Yurchenko | Larisa | SU | 14Apr63 | 176/76 | SP | 17.36 | 17.02-84 |
| Yurchenko | Vera | SU | 9Aug59 | 174/70 | LJ | 6.48 | 6.24-84 |
| | | | | | Hept | 6307 | 6164M-84 |
| Yurlina | Svetlana | SU | 64 | | 800 | 2:00.8 | 2:07.2-83 |
| Yushchenko (Nemkevich) | Lyudmila | SU | 64 | | 400h | 56.48 | 57.28-83 |
| Yushina | Alla | SU | 20Aug58 | 171/60 | 1500 | 4:08.34 | 4:00.26-81 |
| | | | | | 3000 | 8:45.93 | 8:34.02-83 |
| | | | | | 5k | 15:46.99 | |
| Zablotskaya | Liliya | SU | 65 | | HJ | 1.90 | 1.89-83 |
| Zablovskaite | Remigia | SU | 2Jun67 | 169/53 | Hept | 5875 | 5693-85 |
| Zabolotnyeva | Nadezhda | SU | 5Aug61 | | 400 | 52.03 | 52.18-83 51.7-85 |
| | | | | | 800 | 1:57.54 | 0 |
| Zagorcheva | Ginka | BUL | 12Apr58 | 172/53 | 100h | 12.39 12.1w | 12.42-85 |
| Zaituc | Luminita | RUM | 9Oct68 | 163/47 | 1500 | 4:10.63 | 4:12.87-85 |
| Zakharova | Galina | SU | 7Sep56 | 162/50 | 10k | 32:15.00 | 31:15.00-84 |
| Zavadskaya (Skiba) | Yelena | SU | 24Dec64 | 174/56 | 800 | 1:59.74 | 2:03.20-85 |
| Zaytseva | Irina | SU | 28May63 | 168/58 | 400 | 52.32 | 53.16 52.5-85 |
| | | | | | 800 | 1:58.78 | |
| Zheng | Dazhen | CHN | 22Sep59 | 175/61 | HJ | 1.90 | 1.93-82 |
| Zhilichkina | Yelena | SU | 17Aug63 | 179/66 | JT | 59.04 | 58.30-84 |
| Zhirova | Marina | SU | 6Jun63 | 170/60 | 100 | 11.44 | 10.98-85 |
| | | | | | 200 | 22.93 | 22.46-85 |
| Zhitkova | Nadya | SU | 10Mar52 | 168/81 | DT | 58.92 | 61.94-84 |
| Zhizdrikova | Svetlana | SU | 27Aug60 | 164/54 | 200 | 23.04 | 22.69-84 |
| Zhou | Yuanxiang | CHN | 64 | | JT | 62.56 | 58.70-85 |
| Zhupiyeva | Yelena | SU | 18Apr60 | 158/46 | 1500 | 4:05.81 | 4:04.44-84 |
| | | | | | 3000 | 8:40.74 | 8:38.1-85 |
| | | | | | 5k | 15:23.25 | 15:28.30-85 |
| | | | | | 10k | 31:42.99 | 32:25.37-85 |

| Name | | Nat | Yr | Ht/Wt | Event | 1986 Mark | Pre-1986 best |
|------|---|-----|-----|-------|-------|-----------|---------------|
| Ziatdinova | Yelena | SU | 12May64 | 169/56 | 100h | 13.28 | 13.84-83 |
| | | | | | | 13.0 | 13.1-85 |
| Živanov | Danica | YUG | 8Feb67 | 178/78 | JT | 60.58 | 61.98-85 |
| Zöllkau | Antje | GDR | 23Jun63 | 172/70 | JT | 65.18 | 72.16-84 |
| Zolotaryeva | Olga | SU | 1Nov61 | 165/50 | 100 | 11.21 | 11.29-84 |
| | | | | | 200 | 23.21 | 22.80-84 |
| Zorina | Svetlana | SU | 2Feb60 | 173/62 | LJ | 7.01 | 7.04-83 |
| Zubaitite | Vilia | SU | 63 | | DT | 57.62 | 57.82-85 |
| Zubekhina | Natalya | SU | 9Mar51 | 172/95 | SP | 19.48 | 19.94-84 |
| Zuyeva | Tatyana | SU | 17Jun58 | | Mar | 2:35:20 | 2:37:03-85 |
| Zvereva (Kisheyeva) | Ellina | SU | 16Nov60 | 182/90 | DT | 68.96 | 68.56-84 |
| Zverkova | Lyubov | SU | 14Jun55 | 180/101 | DT | 66.84 | 68.58-84 |
| Zwiener | Sabine | FRG | 5Dec67 | 172/58 | 400h | 57.85 | 57.78-85 |

## EUROPEAN INDOOR CHAMPIONSHIPS    At Lievin, France 21/22 February 1987

| MEN | | | WOMEN | | |
|---|---|---|---|---|---|
| 60m: | 1. Marian Woronin (Pol) 6.51 ER | | 60m: | 1. Nellie Fiere-Cooman (Hol) 7.01 | |
| | 2. P.Francesco Pavoni (Ita) 6.58 | | | 2. Anelia Nuneva (Bul) 7.06 | |
| | 3. Antonio Ullo (Ita) 6.61 | | | 3. Marlies Gohr (GDR) 7.12 | |
| 200m: | 1. Bruno Marie-Rose (Fra) 20.36 WR | | 200m: | 1. Kirsten Emmelmann (GDR) 23.10 | |
| | 2. Vladimir Krylov (USSR) 20.53 | | | 2. Blanca Lacambra (Spa) 23.19 | |
| | 3. John Regis (UK) 20.54 | | | 3. Marie-Christine Cazier (Fra) 23.40 | |
| 400m: | 1. Todd Bennett (UK) 46.81 | | 400m: | 1. Maria Pinigina (USSR) 51.27 | |
| | 2. Momchil Kharizanov (Bul) 46.89 | | | 2. Gisela Kinzel (FRG) 52.29 | |
| | 3. Paul Harmsworth (UK) 46.92 | | | 3. Cristina Perez (Spa) 52.63 | |
| 800m: | 1. Rob Druppers (Hol) 1:48.12 | | 800m: | 1. Christine Wachtel (GDR) 1:59.89 | |
| | 2. Vladimir Graudyn (USSR) 1:49.14 | | | 2. Sigrun Wodars (GDR) 2:00.59 | |
| | 3. Ari Suhonen (Fin) 1:49.56 | | | 3. Lyubov Kiryukhina 2:01.85 | |
| 1500m: | 1. Han Kulker (Hol) 3:44.79 | | 1500m: | 1. Sandra Gasser (Swi) 4:08.76 | |
| | 2. Jens-Peter Herold (GDR) 3:45.36 | | | 2. Svetlana Kitova (USSR) 4:09.01 | |
| | 3. Klaus-Peter Nabein (FRG) 3:45.84 | | | 3. Ivana Walterova (Cs) 4:09.99 | |
| 3000m: | 1. Jose-Luis Gonzalez (Spa) 7:52.27 | | 3000m: | 1. Yvonne Murray (UK) 8:46.06 CBP | |
| | 2. Dieter Baumann (FRG) 7:53.93 | | | 2. Elly Van Hulst (Hol) 8:51.40 | |
| | 3. Pascal Thiebault (Fra) 7:54.03 | | | 3. Brigitte Kraus (FRG) 8:53.01 | |
| 60mh: | 1. Arto Bryggare (Fin) 7.59 | | 60mh: | 1. Yordanka Donkova (Bul) 7.79 | |
| | 2. Colin Jackson (UK) 7.63 | | | 2. Gloria Uibel (GDR) 7.89 | |
| | 3. Nigel Walker (UK) 7.65 | | | 3. Ginka Zagorcheva (Bul) 7.92 | |
| HJ: | 1. Patrik Sjoberg (Swe) 2.38 CBP | | HJ: | 1. Stefka Kostadinova (Bul) 1.97 | |
| | 2. Carlo Thranhardt (FRG) 2.36 | | | 2. Tamara Bykova (USSR) 1.94 | |
| | 3. Gennadiy Avdeyenko (USSR) 2.36 | | | 3. Susanne Beyer (GDR) 1.91 | |
| PV: | 1. Thierry Vigneron (Fra) 5.85 =CBP | | LJ: | 1. Heike Drechsler (GDR) 7.12 | |
| | 2. Ferenc Salbert (Fra) 5.85 | | | 2. Galina Chistyakova (USSR) 6.89 | |
| | 3. Marian Kolasa (Pol) 5.80 | | | 3. Yelena Byelevskaya (USSR) 6.76 | |
| LJ: | 1. Robert Emmiyan (USSR) 8.49 ER | | SP: | 1. Natalya Akhrimenko (USSR) 20.84 | |
| | 2. Giovanni Evangelisti (Ita) 8.26 | | | 2. Heidi Krieger (GDR) 20.02 | |
| | 3. Christian Thomas (FRG) 8.12 | | | 3. Heike Hartwig (GDR) 20.00 | |
| TJ: | 1. Serge Helan (Fra) 17.15 | | 3kmW: | 1. Natalya Dmitrochenko (USSR) | |
| | 2. Khristo Markov (Bul) 17.12 | | | 12:57.59 CBP | |
| | 3. Nikolay Musiyenko (USSR) 17.00 | | | 2. Giuliana Salce (Ita) 12:59.11 | |
| SP: | 1. Ulf Timmermann (GDR) 22.19 CBP | | | 3. Monica Gunnarsson (Swe) 13:06.46 | |
| | 2. Werner Gunthor (Swi) 21.53 | | | | |
| | 3. Sergey Smirnov (USSR) 20.97 | | WR- World record, ER- European record, | | |
| 5kmW: | 1. Jozef Pribilinec (Cs) 19:08.44 CBP | | CBP- Championship best performance | | |
| | 2. Ronald Weigel (GDR) 19:08.93 | | | | |
| | 3. Roman Mrazek (Cs) 19:10.77 | | | | |

## AC INDOOR CHAMPIONS    At Madison Square Garden, New York 27 February 1987

MEN
55m: Lee McRae 6.14, 400m: Antonio McKay 48.00, 500m: Ian Morris (Tri) 1:01.55, 800m: Stanley Redwine 1:48.13, 1M: Eamonn Coghlan (Ire) 3:59.25, 3000m: Doug Padilla 7:51.03, 55mh: Greg Foster 6.99, HJ: Igor Paklin (USSR) 2.33, PV: Earl Bell 5.72, LJ: Brian Cooper 8.22, TJ: Mike Conley 17.76 WR, SP: Ulf Timmermann (GDR) 21.63, 351b Wt: Lance Deal 22.68, 5kmW: Tim Lewis 19:30.70.
WR- World indoor record

WOMEN
55m: Anelia Nuneva (Bul) 6.64, 200m: Valerie Brisco 23.58, 400m: Diane Dixon 52.20, 800m: Joetta Clark 2:04.05 (second race won by Christine Wachtel (GDR) 2:03.51), 1M: Doina Melinte 4:30.29, 3000m: Maricica Puica (Rom) 8:43.49, 55mh: Cornelia Oschkenat (GDR) 7.37 WR, HJ: Tamara Bykova (USSR) 1.92, LJ: Heike Drechsler (GDR) 7.32 WR, SP: Ilona Briesenick (GDR) 20.23, 3kmW: Maryanne Torrellas 13:05.41.

WORLD INDOOR CHAMPIONSHIPS   At Hoosier Dome, Indianapolis, USA 6 March 1987

MEN

**60m:**
1. Ben Johnson (Can) 6.41 WR
2. Lee McRae (USA) 6.50
3. Mark Witherspoon (USA) 6.54
4. P.Francesco Pavoni (Ita) 6.59
5. Antonio Ullo (Ita) 6.64

**200m:**
1. Kirk Baptiste (USA) 20.73
2. Bruno Marie-Rose (Fra) 20.89
3. Robson C.Da Silva (Bra) 20.92
4. Gilles Queneherve (Fra) 20.97
5. James Butler (USA) 21.05

**400m:**
1. Antonio McKay (USA) 45.98
2. Roberto Hernandez (Cub) 46.09
3. Michael Franks (USA) 46.19
4. Ian Morris (Tri) 46.57
5. Paul Harmsworth (UK) 46.59

**800m:**
1. Jose Luis Barbosa (Bra) 1:47.49
2. Vladimir Graudyn (USSR) 1:47.68
3. Faouzi Lahbi (Mor) 1:47.79
4. Stanley Redwine (USA) 1:47.81
5. Dieudonne Kwizera (Bur) 1:47.87

**1500m:**
1. Marcus O'Sullivan (Ire) 3:39.04
2. Jose M.Abascal (Spa) 3:39.13
3. Han Kulker (Hol) 3:39.51
4. Jim Spivey (USA) 3:39.63
5. Michael Hillardt (Aus) 3:39.77

**3000m:**
1. Frank O'Mara (Ire) 8:03.32
2. Paul Donovan (Ire) 8:03.89
3. Terry Brahm (USA) 8:03.92
4. Mark Rowland (UK) 8:04.27
5. Doug Padilla (USA) 8:05.55

**60mh:**
1. Tonie Campbell (USA) 7.51
2. Stephane Caristan (Fra) 7.62
3. Nigel Walker (UK) 7.66
4. Colin Jackson (UK) 7.68
5. Arto Bryggare (Fin) 7.68

**HJ:**
1. Igor Paklin (USSR) 2.38
2. Gennadiy Avdeyenko (USSR) 2.38
3. Jan Zvara (Cs) 2.34
4. Javier Sotomayor (Cub) 2.32
5= Roland Dalhauser (Swi) 2.32
5= Sorin Matei (Rom) 2.32

**PV:**
1. Sergey Bubka (USSR) 5.85
2. Earl Bell (USA) 5.80
3. Thierry Vigneron (Fra) 5.80
4. Ferenc Salbert (Fra) 5.80
5. Marian Kolasa (Pol) 5.75

**LJ:**
1. Larry Myricks (USA) 8.23
2. Paul Emordi (Nig) 8.01
3. Giovanni Evangelisti (Ita) 8.01
4. Robert Emmiyan (USSR) 8.00
5. Brian Cooper (USA) 7.91

**TJ:**
1. Mike Conley (USA) 17.54
2. Oleg Protsenko (USSR) 17.26
3. Frank Rutherford (Bah) 17.02
4. Khristo Markov (Bul) 16.96
5. Al Joyner (USA) 16.92

**SP:**
1. Ulf Timmermann (GDR) 22.24
2. Werner Gunthor (Swi) 21.61
3. Sergey Smirnov (USSR) 20.67
4. Gregg Tafralis (USA) 20.26
5. Lars Arvid Nilsen (Nor) 20.09

**5kmW:**
1. Mikhail Shchennikov (USSR) 18:27.79 WR
2. Jozef Pribilinec (Cs) 18:27.80
3. Ernesto Canto (Mex) 18:38.71
4. Roman Mrazek (Cs) 18:47.95
5. David Smith (Aus) 18:52.20

WOMEN

**60m:**
1. Nellie Fiere-Cooman (Hol) 7.08
2. Angella Issajenko (Can) 7.08
3. Anelia Nuneva (Bul) 7.10
4. Angela Bailey (Can) 7.12
5. Merlene Ottey-Page (Jam) 7.13

**200m:**
1. Heike Drechsler (GDR) 22.27 WR
2. Merlene Ottey-Page (Jam) 22.66
3. Grace Jackson (Jam) 23.21
4. Alice Jackson (USA) 23.55
5. Mary Onyali (Nig) 23.56

**400m:**
1. Sabine Busch (GDR) 51.66
2. Lillie Leatherwood (USA) 52.54
3. Judit Forgacs (Hun) 52.68
4. Olga Nazarova (USSR) 52.76
5. Rositzssa Stamenova (Bul) 53.56

**800m:**
1. Christine Wachtel (GDR) 2:01.31
2. Gabriela Sedlakova (GDR) 2:01.85
3. Lyubov Kiryukhina (USSR) 2:01.98
4. Slobodanka Colovic (Yug) 2:02.33
5. Janet Bell (UK) 2:02.96

**1500m:**
1. Doina Melinte (Rom) 4:05.68
2. Tatyana Samolenko (USSR) 4:07.08
3. Svetlana Kitova (USSR) 4:07.59
4. Mitica Junghiatu (Rom) 4:08.49
5. Kirsty Wade (UK) 4:08.91

**3000m:**
1. Tatyana Samolenko (USSR) 8:46.52
2. Olga Bondarenko (USSR) 8:47.08
3. Maricica Puica (Rom) 8:47.92
4. Krishna Wood (Aus) 8:48.38
5. Yvonne Murray (UK) 8:48.43

**60mh:**
1. Cornelia Oschkenat (GDR) 7.82
2. Yordanka Donkova (Bul) 7.85
3. Ginka Zagorcheva (Bul) 7.99
4. Rita Heggli (Swi) 8.11
5. Marjan Olijslager (Hol) 8.12

**HJ:**
1. Stefka Kostadinova (Bul) 2.05 WR
2. Susanne Beyer (GDR) 2.02
3. Emilia Draguieva (Bul) 2.00
4. Tamara Bykova (USSR) 1.94
5. Diana Davies (UK) 1.91

**LJ:**
1. Heike Drechsler (GDR) 7.10
2. Helga Radtke (GDR) 6.94
3. Yelena Byelevskaya (USSR) 6.76
4. Galina Chistyakova (USSR) 6.66
5. Vali Ionescu (Rom) 6.62

**SP:**
1. Natalya Lisovskaya (USSR) 20.52
2. Ilona Briesenick (GDR) 20.28
3. Claudia Losch (FRG) 20.14
4. Heidi Krieger (GDR) 20.00
5. Natalya Akhrimenko (USSR) 19.32

**3kmW:**
1. Olga Krishtop (USSR) 12:05.49 WR
2. Giuliana Salce (Ita) 12:36.76
3. Ann Peel (Can) 12:38.97
4. Dana Vavracova (Cs) 12:47.49
5. Emilia Cano (Spa) 13:02.41

# WORLD INDOOR RECORDS

From 1 January 1987 the IAAF recognize world indoor records. The best performances made before that date have been noted as World Bests, and world records must better these to be officially accepted. Track performances around a turn must be made on a track no larger than 200 metres.

Records as at 1 April 1987:

| Event | Mark | Athlete (Nation) | Venue | Date |
|---|---|---|---|---|
| 50 metres | 5.55 | Ben Johnson (Can) | Ottawa | 31 Jan 1987 |
| 60 metres | 6.41 | Ben Johnson (Can) | Indianapolis | 7 Mar 1987 |
| 200 metres | 20.36 | Bruno Marie-Rose (Fra) | Leivin | 22 Feb 1987 |
| 400 metres | 45.41 | Thomas Schönlebe (GDR) | Vienna | 9 Feb 1986 |
| 800 metres | 1:44.91 | Sebastian Coe (UK) | Cosford | 12 Mar 1983 |
| 1000 metres | 2:18.00 | Igor Lotarev (USSR) | Moscow | 14 Feb 1987 |
| 1500 metres | 3:35.6 | Eamonn Coghlan (Ire) | San Diego | 20 Feb 1981 |
| 1 mile | 3:49.78 | Eamonn Coghlan (Ire) | East Rutherford | 27 Feb 1983 |
| 2000 metres | 4:54.07 | Eamonn Coghlan (Ire) | Inglewood | 21 Feb 1987 |
| 3000 metres | 7:39.2 | Emiel Puttemans (Bel) | Berlin | 18 Feb 1973 |
| 5000 metres | 13:20.4 | Suleiman Nyambui (Tan) | New York | 6 Feb 1981 |
| 50m hurdles | 6.25 | Mark McKoy (Can) | Kobe | 5 Mar 1986 |
| 60m hurdles | 7.46 | Greg Foster (USA) | Indianapolis | 6 Mar 1987 |
| High jump | 2.41 | Patrik Sjöberg (Swe) | Piraeus | 1 Feb 1987 |
| Pole vault | 5.97 | Sergey Bubka (USSR) | Turin | 17 Mar 1987 |
| Long jump | 8.79 | Carl Lewis (USA) | New York | 27 Feb 1984 |
| Triple jump | 17.76 | Mike Conley (USA) | New York | 27 Feb 1987 |
| Shot | 22.26 | Werner Günthör (Swi) | Magglingen | 8 Feb 1987 |
| 4x200m relay | 1:22.32 | Italy | Turin | 11 Feb 1984 |

(P.Francesco Pavoni, Stefano Tilli, Giovanni Bongiorni, Carlo Simionato)

| | | | | |
|---|---|---|---|---|
| 4x400m relay | 3:05.9 | USSR | Vienna | 14 Mar 1970 |

(Yevgeniy Borisenko, Yuriy Zorin, Boris Savchuk, Aleksandr Bratchikov)

| | | | | |
|---|---|---|---|---|
| | 3:06.01 | USA | Cosford | 15 Mar 1987 |

(Walter McCoy, Chip Jenkins, Ken Lowery, Clarence Daniel)

| | | | | |
|---|---|---|---|---|
| 3000m walk | 18:27.79 | Mikhail Shchennikov (USSR) | Indianapolis | 7 Mar 1987 |

## WOMEN

| Event | Mark | Athlete (Nation) | Venue | Date |
|---|---|---|---|---|
| 50 metres | 6.06 | Angella Issajenko (Can) | Ottawa | 31 Jan 1987 |
| 60 metres | 7.00 | Nellie Cooman-Fiere (Hol) | Madrid | 23 Feb 1986 |
| 200 metres | 22.27 | Heike Drechsler (GDR) | Indianapolis | 7 Mar 1987 |
| 400 metres | 49.59 | Jarmila Kratochvilova (Cs) | Milan | 7 Mar 1982 |
| 800 metres | 1:58.42 | Sigrun Wodars (GDR) | Vienna | 10 Jan 1987 |
| | 1:58.4 | Olga Vakhrusheva (USSR) | Moscow | 16 Feb 1987 |
| 1000 metres | 2:34.8 | Brigitte Kraus (FRG) | Dortmund | 19 Feb 1978 |
| 1500 metres | 4:00.8 | Mary Decker-Slaney (USA) | New York | 8 Feb 1980 |
| mile | 4:20.5 | Mary Decker-Slaney (USA) | San Diego | 19 Feb 1982 |
| 3000 metres | 8:39.79 | Zola Budd (UK) | Cosford | 8 Feb 1986 |
| 5000 metres | 15:35.4 | Margaret Groos (USA) | Blacksburg | 20 Feb 1981 |
| 50m hurdles | 6.71 | Cornelia Oschekenat (GDR) | Berlin | 9 Feb 1986 |
| | 6.71 | Cornelia Oschekenat (GDR) | Berlin | 24 Feb 1987 |
| 60m hurdles | 7.74 | Yordanka Donkova (Bul) | Sofia | 14 Feb 1987 |
| High jump | 2.05 | Stefka Kostadinova (Bul) | Indianapolis | 8 Mar 1987 |
| Long jump | 7.32 | Heike Drechsler (GDR) | New York | 27 Feb 1987 |
| Shot | 22.50 | Helena Fibingerova (Cs) | Jablonec | 19 Feb 1977 |
| 3000m walk | 12:05.49 | Olga Krishtop (USSR) | Indianapolis | 6 Mar 1987 |
| 4x200m relay | 1:33.56 | VfL Sindelfingen (FRG) | Sindelfingen | 8 Feb 1986 |

(Andrea Bersch, Ulrike Sarvari, Gabriele Wolf, Heide-Elke Gaugel)

| | | | | |
|---|---|---|---|---|
| 4x400m relay | 3:34.38 | FR Germany | Dortmund | 30 Jan 1981 |

(Heide-Elke Gaugel, Christina Sussiek, Christiane Brinkmann, Gaby Bussmann)

## World bests set during 1986/7 season at other events or superseded by above
### MEN

| | | | | | |
|---|---|---|---|---|---|
| 60 metres | 6.44 | Ben Johnson (Can) | Osaka | 15 Jan 19 |
| | 6.44 | Ben Johnson (Can) | Edmonton | 21 Feb 19 |
| 300 metres | 32.51 | Antonio McKay (USA) | Stuttgart | 1 Feb 19 |
| 500 metres | 1:00.86 | Butch Reynolds (USA) | Saskatoon | 28 Dec 19 |
| | 1:00.17 | Ken Lowery (USA) | Indianapolis | 16 Jan 19 |
| | 59.90 | Roddie Haley (USA) | Oklahoma City | 14 Mar 19 |
| 60m hurdles | 7.47 | Greg Foster (USA) | San Diego | 22 Feb 19 |
| High jump | 2.40 | Carlo Thränhardt (FRG) | Simmerath | 16 Jan 19 |
| Pole vault | 5.96 | Sergey Bubka (USSR) | Osaka | 15 Jan 19 |
| Triple jump | 17.67 | Oleg Protsenko (USSR) | Osaka | 15 Jan 19 |
| 1500m walk | 5:17.17 | Tim Lewis (USA) | East Rutherford | 14 Feb 19 |
| 5000m walk | 18:44.97 | Ronald Weigel (GDR) | Vienna | 1 Feb 19 |

### WOMEN

| | | | | | |
|---|---|---|---|---|---|
| 55 metres | 6.56 | Gwen Torrence (USA) | Oklahoma City | 14 Mar 19 |
| 100 yards | 10.24 | Heike Drechsler (GDR) | Senftenberg | 8 Feb 19 |
| | 10.15 | Heike Drechsler (GDR) | Senftenberg | 8 Feb 19 |
| 55m hurdles | 7.37 | Cornelia Oschekenat (GDR) | New York | 27 Feb 19 |
| High jump | 2.04 | Stefka Kostadinova (Bul) | Genoa | 31 Jan 19 |
| Triple jump | 13.93 | Vali Ionescu (Rom) | Inglewood | 21 Feb 19 |
| 1500m walk | 6:01.16 | Maryanne Torrellas (USA) | East Rutherford | 14 Feb 19 |

## LATE AMENDMENTS TO 1986 LISTS and INDEX

MEN'S All TIME LISTS:
110mh: hand timed 12.8 Nehemiah and 13.0 Foster, Kingston in 1979, wind +1.
WOMEN'S ALL TIME LISTS: Marathon: 2:32:23 Villeton

MEN'S INDEX

| | | | | | | |
|---|---|---|---|---|---|---|
| Ivliyev | b.7 Jan 63 | | Kenworthy | PV, 5.67 | Masunov | b.5 May 62 |
| Rudenik | LJ, 7.90w | | Vanyaykin | b.14 Jan 66 | 181/67 | |

add:

| | | | | | | |
|---|---|---|---|---|---|---|
| Baygush | Viktor | SU | 63 | HT | 72.26 | 75.98 - 83 |
| Popel | Mikhail | SU | 66 | HT | 72.46 | 69.28 - 85 |
| Watson | Dave | USA | 27Jan64 | PV | 5.45 | |

WOMEN'S INDEX

| | | | | | |
|---|---|---|---|---|---|
| Cazier | b.23 Aug 63 | Geffray | Mar, 2:34:40 | Giolitti | 1500m, 4:08. |
| Katona | delete entry | Villeton | Mar, 2:32:23 | | |

add: Evro Pavlina ALB 22 Feb 65 10000m 32:51.0 35:47.3 - 85

## WORLD CROSS-COUNTRY CHAMPIONSHIPS 1987    Warszawa 22 March

### Senior Men at 11950m
1. John Ngugi (Ken) 36:07
2. Paul Kipkoech (Ken) 36:07
3. Paul Arpin (Fra) 36:51
4. Abebe Mekonnen (Eth) 36:53
5. Some Muge (Ken) 36:54
6. Andrew Masai (Ken) 37:01
7. Pat Porter (USA) 37:04
8. Paul McCloy (Can) 37:08
9. Bruno Le Stum (Fra) 37:09
10. David Clarke (Eng) 37:10
11. Steve Moneghetti (Aus) 37:11
12. Ed Eyestone (USA) 37:11
13. Francesco Panetta (Ita) 37:12
14. José Regalo (Por) 37:13
15. Pierre Levise (Fra) 37:13

### Senior Women at 5050m
1. Annette Sergent (Fra) 16:46
2. Elizabeth Lynch (UK) 16:48
3. Ingrid Kristiansen (Nor) 16:51
4. Lynn Jennings (USA) 16:55
5. Lesley Welch (USA) 16:57
6. Mariana Stanescu (Rom) 17:04
7. Cornelia Bürki (Swi) 17:08
8. Krishna Wood (Aus) 17:11
9. Paula Ivan (Rom) 17:12
10. Natalya Sorok vskaya (SU) 17:13
11. Margaret Wairimu (Ken) 17:14
12. Martine Fays (Fra) 17:19
13. Olga Bondarenko (SU) 17:20
14. Mary Knisely (USA) 17:20
15. Lena Romanova (SU) 17:23

### Senior Men's Team
1. Kenya 53
2. England 146
3. Ethiopia 161
4. Italy 223
5. France 245
6. Portugal 309

### Senior Women's Tea
1. USA 46
2. France 50
3. USSR 55
4. Romania 94
5. Kenya 117
6. Norway 143

Junior Men at 7050m: 1. Oanda Kirochi (Ken) 22:18, 2. Demeke Bekele (Eth) 22:18, 3. Debe Demisse (Eth) 22:20, 4. William Kosgei (Ken) 22:27, 5. Mathew Rono (Ken) 22:28, 6. Aligaz Alemayehu (Eth) 22:28. Junior Team: 1. Ethiopia 19, 2. Kenya 20, 3. Japan 73, 4. USA 120.